D0710462

SOUTHERN LITERARY STUDIES

Fred Hobson, Editor

THE
COMPANION
TO
SOUTHERN
LITERATURE

THEMES, GENRES, PLACES, PEOPLE,
MOVEMENTS, AND MOTIFS

EDITED BY
JOSEPH M. FLORA
AND
LUCINDA H. MACKETHAN

ASSOCIATE EDITOR
TODD TAYLOR

LOUISIANA STATE UNIVERSITY PRESS   BATON ROUGE

Copyright © 2002 by Louisiana State University Press
Manufactured in the United States of America

10   09   08   07   06   05   04   03
5   4   3   2

Designer: Barbara Neely Bourgoyne
Typeface: Serlio (display) and Sabon (text)
Typesetter: Coghill Composition Co., Inc.
Printer and binder: Sheridan Books, Inc.

Library of Congress Cataloging-in-Publication Data

    The companion to southern literature : themes, genres, places, people, movements, and
motifs / edited by Joseph M. Flora and Lucinda H. MacKethan ; associate editor, Todd Taylor.
        p.   cm.
    Includes bibliographical references and index.
    ISBN 0-8071-2692-6 (cloth)
    1. American literature—Southern States—Encyclopedias.   2. Southern
States—Intellectual life—Encyclopedias.   3. Southern States—In literature—Encyclopedias.
I. Flora, Joseph M.   II. MacKethan, Lucinda Hardwick.   III. Taylor, Todd W.

    PS261 .C55   2001
    810.9′975—dc21   2001029959

The paper in this book meets the guidelines for permanence and
durability of the Committee on Production Guidelines for Book
Longevity of the Council on Library Resources. ⊗

CONTENTS

CONTENTS ARRANGED BY SUBJECT

6. Historical Entities, Events, and Movements

7. Historical Figures

INTRODUCTION

Beginnings

In 1859 Henry Timrod, Charleston poet and editor, mourned that the southern writer was "the Pariah of modern literature," facing almost insurmountable difficulties within a culture that was indifferent at best, selfish and provincial at worst. Yet he prophesied that "the time must come" when there would be "a demand for Southern poetry and prose which shall call forth the poet and prose writer from the crowds that now conceal them." One hundred fifty years later, that demand has been fed but not sated with dozens of anthologies, hundreds of critical studies, thousands of panels, and millions in book sales. *The Companion to Southern Literature* bears witness to the phenomenon of southern literature—its inventors and re-inventors, its audiences and critics, from Civil War to Culture Wars, enveloping real and imaginary communities and borders marked by William Byrd's Lubberland on one edge and Charles Frazier's Cold Mountain on the other.

Southern literature, which perhaps had its beginnings as early as Shakespeare's ironic imaginings of a "brave new world" in *The Tempest*, has always been, as Michael Kreyling recently reminds us, "an amalgam of literary history, interpretive traditions, and a canon." The canon has expanded dramatically in the last thirty years. New definitions of what constitutes "literature," new cultural imperatives altering perceptions of whose voices must be heard, and new methods for studying, appreciating, and assessing literary productions have greatly enlarged the challenges as well as the rewards that confront today's reader of southern literature. What better time, then, for a *Companion*, defined partly in the old-fashioned sense of a fellow traveler who keeps one "company" on a journey, a companion as someone who offers support, answers questions, keeps the conversation going, blazes a trail, or finds the right direction.

The impetus for this book springs from our experiences teaching southern literature. While grateful for headnotes to the anthologies we used, for the histories of southern literature, for reference books that gave us quick overviews of a particular writer, and for the scholarship in journals and books when we needed to go more deeply into a subject, we came to wish for a one-volume work that would summarize a particular theme or motif of southern literature, or describe how a genre had developed in that literature, or review how an important historical event might be played out in the literature. We wished for something that would do for southern literature what *The Encyclopedia of Southern Culture* (1989) had done for southern culture. We knew such a work could enhance for others the teaching of a subject we ourselves loved teaching.

So *The Companion to Southern Literature* was born. Overriding all of the decisions that would have to be made concerning the *who-what-when-where-and-why* selection of topics was the continuing challenge as to just what *South* and *southern* mean. There is still justice to Flannery O'Connor's observation that "no one has ever made plain just what the Southern school is or which writers belong to it. Sometimes, when it is most respectable, it seems to mean the little group of Agrarians that flourished at Vanderbilt in the twenties; but more often the term conjures up an image of Gothic monstrosities and the idea of a preoccupation with everything deformed and grotesque." We could not settle for the well-defined parameters of a census report, or the borders of the Confederacy, even if we added the slave states that did not secede. We wished to be as inclusive as possible. Although Missouri, for example, was a slave state and parts of Missouri have retained a strong affinity with the southern mind, large parts of Missouri are predominantly midwestern. Independence, Missouri, was the place Americans departed from on their way to becoming westerners. Migrations of large numbers of African Americans from the South to the North resulted from injustices of Jim Crow laws, and eventually the complexity of the southern experience, southern customs, and southern tastes spread widely through most of America. World War II sent many southerners—white and black—to work in the factories of the Midwest and Northeast. One could as easily find a Southern Baptist congregation in Pontiac, Michigan, as in Spartanburg, South Carolina.

In the last quarter of the twentieth century, the migratory patterns were dramatically reversed. Air conditioning transformed the South, bringing to it new industries and the return of blacks and whites with their southern roots. Increasingly, they brought with them other immigrants from nonsouthern states—this time seeking better economic and living conditions in the South, long regarded as the most economically disadvantaged region of the nation. One sometimes hears the Research Triangle area of North Carolina (Raleigh–Durham–Chapel Hill) described by longtime North Carolinians as "occupied territory." Southerners in other areas could easily name pockets altered by massive "Yankee" invasions. With probably a touch of chauvinistic excess, sociologist John Shelton Reed recently declared that no one lives outside the South unless they have to.

Although the South has been transformed in very visible ways as cotton and tobacco give way to "hi-tech" industries, it may also be argued that the South has altered other regions profoundly. In the 1990s, the region has simultaneously provided the nation's president, the Senate majority leader, and the Speaker of the House. In *Dixie Rising* (1996), Peter Applebome has argued that the South is now shaping not only American politics but American culture.

For many reasons, then, we thought it best to be inclusive rather than exclusive in our notion of southern. The boundaries of the South cannot be contained by state borders. Beyond geography, there is a southern mind (as W. J. Cash would have it), and exploring that mind is not only an invigorating challenge but an important one, not only for southerners but for all Americans.

No one is a midwesterner or easterner in quite the same way that a southerner is a southerner. History has set the South apart—a history defined centrally by the tragedy of chattel slavery. Southern apartness does, however, belong to the whole. To learn about the South

is to explore the roots of the racial struggle that remains the nation's continuing conundrum.

Moreover, Southern voices have been eloquent in shaping the idea of America—the voices of Thomas Jefferson, Patrick Henry, Frederick Douglass, Martin Luther King Jr., and a host of others. The paradoxes and complexities of the discourse are many—and they are caught in the literature of the South. Exploring these paradoxes and complexities is surely important for understanding what is happening in other parts of the nation.

We do not, of course, study southern literature only because of its presentation of racial history in intensely dramatic terms, but also because the South has had in abundance what Flannery O'Connor has called "Manners"—speech, traditions, codes, a shared history that gives southern writers a richly concrete world. These manners have impacted the ways in which southerners have related to gender and class issues. Southern writers have explored a range of issues and themes—though race is almost always implied in the configuration. They have confounded the New Critics, ironically a southern-shaped phenomenon (one that tried to emphasize the aesthetic qualities and to downplay the contexts of a work), an exercise that proved more difficult in analyses (even their own) of fiction and drama than for poetry.

O'Connor worried that southern writers and the South were getting more and more like the rest of the country. In 1960 she declared that she hated "to think that in twenty years Southern writers too may be writing about men in gray-flannel suits and may have lost their ability to see that these gentlemen are even greater freaks than what we are writing about now. I hate to think of the day when the Southern writers will satisfy the tired reader." O'Connor did not, however, give up hope: "Southern distinctiveness," she said, "is a slight degree and getting slighter of kind as well as of intensity, and it is enough to feed great literature if our people—whether they be newcomers or have roots here—are enough aware of it to foster its growth in themselves."

How O'Connor might assess the survival of the southern writer's advantage at the beginning of the twenty-first century is uncertain. But we suspect that she would still identify a saving remnant. For our part, we intend that *The Companion to Southern Literature* will foster the growth of understanding that will in turn foster more great literature. The South has, we think, been actively resistant to the surrender of its heritage, though increasingly willing to acknowledge failures in its history. As the twentieth century progressed, with heightened vigor and considerable success, scholars in the South, the nation, and the world have explored southern literature from many perspectives. *The Companion* gives evidence that the legacy is alive and well—and anticipates continuation of that energy in the new century.

Contents, Coverage, Contributors

The contents of the entries that follow—more than five hundred of them—reflects not only the need we felt as teachers but also our anticipation that this book would interest the throng of persons outside the academy who are interested in southern experience as it is depicted in literature. From an initial list of entries collected through brainstorming sessions with colleagues and students, we widened the net on almost a daily basis. After reviewing our prospectus, William Andrews, Minrose Gwinn, Trudier Harris, Bert Hitchcock, Fred Hobson, Daniel Patterson, Peggy Prenshaw, Louis D. Rubin Jr., and Mary Ann Wimsatt encouraged us to proceed and expanded our list of *desiderata* considerably. Anonymous reviewers of our proposal at LSU Press made excellent suggestions that broadened the scope of the book. Then scholars contacted to write entries added more ideas, and when their pieces arrived, we would say, "Shouldn't we include something on ————?," and the hunt would begin for yet another contributor. The process would undoubtedly still be going on if we were not hoping to finish the project before another century passes. Sometimes, it is not a bad thing to run out of time. In some cases, too, no one could be found to tackle an interesting possibility; alas, we have no definitive word on "Motorcycles in Southern Literature." In other cases, an inviting suggestion turned out to be impossibly large, or impossibly precious.

A few basic principles guided our selection process and our directions to contributors:

First, as items in a companion to *literature*, the entries, while defining cultural contexts, should as closely as possible address the question of how their subject has found concrete expression in southern writing. The terms *southern* and *literature* are broadly defined as constituting a cultural territory that has been imaginatively created by all kinds of "makers." We wanted to provide an inclusive map of the terrain, backroads as well as interstates, colorful retreats as well as major tourist attractions. Thus, we sought broad coverage that would assist readers in exploring southern literature from perspectives other than the "author" approach. The writers for whom brief entries appear were selected because their work is uniquely pioneering or they have acted as seminal influences for other writers or whole movements: Faulkner, Poe, Twain, Douglass, Warren, Wright, Hurston, Ellison, Welty, O'Connor. Similar reasoning guided our inclusion of a handful of works—books, essays, poems, etc.—that provide defining moments for the creation of the southern literary mind: "Odes to the Confederate Dead," the Declaration of Independence, *Uncle Tom's Cabin, I'll Take My Stand, The Mind of the South,* "Letter from Birmingham Jail." We have dared to select three major scholarly voices in the field of southern literary study—giants whose decades of engagement have been of supreme benefit to all who have followed: C. Vann Woodward, Louis D. Rubin Jr., and Lewis P. Simpson. Dozens of names might be raised, and we wish there were room to include other distinctive contributions, but we are confident that these three stand above the rest.

As befits a work that emphasizes literature, we have included literary terms, genres (traditional and nontraditional), movements, motifs, types and stereotypes, schools and theories, both old-fashioned and newly minted. Ideologies—political, theoretical, sociological—are, we trust, included as entries and not as an editorial agenda.

The Companion is not a survey of masterpieces or a biographical sourcebook. Nor is it a travelogue. Place entries were chosen with an eye to their centrality in the development of themes, movements, literary landscapes. Historical events and figures—and there are many, for here is a region deeply, if ambivalently, protective of its historical identity—have been chosen for their enactment within and their impact upon the literature. If we have slighted anyone's favorite general, city, town, county, or alma mater, or an indispensable novel or theory, or a religious denomination, we are willing to express regrets and hope that students, teachers, and others will continue to identify other possibilities, and to add to the general store.

Our contributors have been chosen because of their expertise and interest in a particular subject. Many are scholars who have published widely, some are graduate students working on dissertations, some are fiction writers and poets. They come from many disciplines in the academy and many professions beyond it, and they live in many different regions as well. Their geographical and vocational spread indicates how southern literature has taken hold in both academic and nonacademic settings throughout the country. What we asked our contributors to do was no small favor: to provide essential and reliable definitions, background, and contexts for their entries and then to give some key illustrations from literature in order to show how each item has been treated in southern writing, broadly defined. They had to pick and choose, to give up the idea of including every important work or detail and instead select examples that highlighted characteristic aspects or especially colorful treatments of an item. The entries must be well researched, open-minded, readable—and succinct. In other words, the space constraints imposed by the vision of a one-volume reference work had to be respected by all. The diversity in taste, interpretation, critical judgment, and tone that appears in the entries reflects our authors' individual purposes and points of view. As editors, we see the variety inherent in our contributors' unique visions and enthusiasms as the spice of life for the volume.

Finding Your Way with The Companion

The **Entries** in *The Companion to Southern Literature* are arranged alphabetically, from *Abolition* to *Yoknapatawpha*. We have provided an alternate table of contents that groups entries by subject. Authors, historical figures, scholars, southern presidents, and other persons are alphabetized last name first. Unless the word *southern* appears as part of a title or proper name, we have excluded this word from all entry titles (go to

Belle, not *Southern Belle*, for instance). For literary history in overview, consult the belletristic genre listing: *Poetry, Novel, Drama, Short Story*. These entries are divided into separate headings for chronologically defined periods, as are certain other categories such as *Humor, Periodicals, African American Literature*, and *Women Writers*. These last two listings do not segregate African American and women's literature (writers of both categories appear in the genre articles, too) but instead exist to highlight the development of writing by authors long underrepresented in the canon.

In the **Index** we have sought to provide page numbers for all important names, whether the item has an individual entry or not. Titles of the great majority of literary and artistic works mentioned are not included, since that would have made the Index excessively long. The Index also provides alternate headings (for instance, if you look in the Index for *Movies*, you will find "*Movies. See Film*"). In addition, it should be noted that because *The Companion* includes not only an alphabetical table of contents but a second categorical table of contents (entitled "Contents Arranged by Subject"), readers following a theme should consult it as well as the Index.

The "**See also**" section at the end of most entries identifies other entries related to the one under discussion. Following this section is usually a brief **Bibliography** of useful sources. This list is not complete but names instead works, chosen by the contributors, that will provide a useful starting point for more in-depth study of the subject. At the end of this introduction, we provide a list of major reference sources (Encyclopedias, Literary Histories, Bio-bibliographical Sourcebooks) that are primary aids to finding additional information.

Southern Literature: General Reference Works

The following is a listing of general reference sources that contain useful information on many of the literary topics included in *The Companion*. For more specialized sources, see the items listed at the end of the individual entries.

Andrews, William L., Frances Smith Foster, and Trudier Harris, eds. *The Oxford Companion to African American Literature*. New York: Oxford University Press, 1997.

Bain, Robert, and Joseph M. Flora, eds. *Contemporary Fiction Writers of the South: A Bio-bibliographical Sourcebook*. Westport, Conn.: Greenwood Press, 1993.

_____. *Contemporary Poets, Dramatists, Essayists and Novelists of the South: A Bio-bibliographical Sourcebook*. Westport, Conn.: Greenwood Press, 1994.

_____. *Fifty Southern Writers After 1900. A Bio-bibliographical Sourcebook*. Westport, Conn.: Greenwood Press, 1987.

————. *Fifty Southern Writers Before 1900. A Bio-bibliographical Sourcebook.* Westport, Conn.: Greenwood Press, 1987.

Bain, Robert, Joseph M. Flora, and Louis D. Rubin Jr., *Southern Writers: A Biographical Dictionary.* Baton Rouge: Louisiana State University Press, 1979.

Davidson, Cathy N., and Linda Wagner-Martin. *The Oxford Companion to Women's Writing in the United States.* New York: Oxford University Press, 1995.

Hubbell, Jay B. *The South in American Literature, 1607–1900.* Durham, N.C.: Duke University Press, 1954.

Littlefield, Daniel F. *A Bibliography of Native American Writers, 1772–1924.* Metuchen, N.J.: Scarecrow Press, 1981.

Rubin, Louis D., Jr., ed. *A Bibliographical Guide to the Study of Southern Literature.* Baton Rouge: Louisiana State University Press, 1969. [For years following, consult the annual bibliographies on southern literature published in the *Mississippi Quarterly.*]

————, et al., eds. *The History of Southern Literature.* Baton Rouge: Louisiana State University Press, 1985.

Wilson, Charles Reagan, and William Ferris, eds. *The Encyclopedia of Southern Culture.* Chapel Hill: University of North Carolina Press, 1989.

ACKNOWLEDGMENTS

The Companion to Southern Literature has been a huge undertaking and could never have been completed without the help of many persons. Our first thanks go to those who agreed so unselfishly to write entries. Many are teachers or students preparing to teach in a variety of fields related to southern literature. We appreciate the energy and spirit of cooperation they brought to their tasks.

Todd Taylor, our associate editor, brought all the diversity together as he charted the course that would get us through the complexities of disks on different programs, broken disks, and a host of technical problems. He did so with skill and good humor. We don't even want to think about what the editing process would have been without him.

Louisiana State University Press, in keeping with its strong support of southern letters, welcomed our proposal and patiently worked with us through various snags and problems—and provided frequent words of encouragement. Les Phillabaum, director of the Press, and John Easterly, executive editor, are clearly part of the saving remnant. The Press also made helpful suggestions for items to be included and extended the vision of the project beyond the original plan. The scholars who reviewed the proposal and made additional suggestions also have our thanks.

As do William Andrews, Minrose Gwin, Trudier Harris, Bert Hitchcock, Fred Hobson, Daniel Patterson, Peggy Prenshaw, and Mary Ann Wimsatt for their suggestions.

Important support has come from the Department of English at the University of North Carolina at Chapel Hill and the Department of English at North Carolina State University. Professor William Andrews, chair of the department at Chapel Hill, has provided assistantships for graduate students who made the necessary corrections on the computer after we completed our editing and scanned hard copy when disks malfunctioned. Erin Kershner and Miranda Wilson did that hard work. In addition, Bryan Giemza helped resolve textual problems. Susan Marston gave us the benefit of her critical eye. Cindy Peterson coordinated exchanges between the two universities.

Tom Lisk, head of the English department at N.C. State, also found funds for graduate assistants. Ed Hoffman, John Salomone, and Matthew Scialdone kept up with our ever-changing contributor and entry listings. Claire Dannenburg and Karen MacKethan, couriers extraordinaire, braved Interstate 40 carrying our bulging folders back and forth between Raleigh and Chapel Hill.

Our particular thanks go to The Hillsdale Foundation of Greensboro, North Carolina, which gave a generous grant to aid us in many aspects of manuscript preparation.

Near the end of our journey, we were fortunate to have Margaret Fisher Dalrymple as our copy-editor. Her track record with southern texts served us well and saved us from errors and inconsistencies. For any that may remain, the fault would not be hers.

We would be greatly remiss if we did not tip our hats to Christine Flora and John MacKethan. In this project as well as in our daily lives, they have given good advice, put up with our frustrations, and blessed our days.

Finally, we are happy to acknowledge our profound debt to Louis D. Rubin Jr. He immediately became an enthusiastic supporter of this project when we shared our plans with him. He, too, made suggestions for its contents—and pointed us in directions that enabled us to do more. We went to him, of course, because he has been major in each of our lives, fostering our interest in southern literature as no one else has. He taught Lucinda MacKethan as an undergraduate at Hollins College and then directed her Ph.D. dissertation at the University of North Carolina at Chapel Hill. Although he did not formally teach Joseph Flora, he has nevertheless taught him through his works, in professional counsels, and in the corridors of Greenlaw Hall. For many years, he has been to both of us a loyal friend and beloved mentor.

JOSEPH M. FLORA
LUCINDA H. MACKETHAN

THE
COMPANION
TO
SOUTHERN
LITERATURE

A

ABOLITION

In a discussion of Steven Spielberg's 1997 movie *Amistad* on National Public Radio, noted American historian Eric Foner observed that the outpouring of black and white support for Cinque and the other African slaves who staged the shipboard rebellion in 1839 was probably the first major integrated political event in American history. Members of the New England Congregational Church, who had helped found the American Anti-Slavery Society in 1833, marshaled support for the Africans imprisoned in Connecticut, as did black freedmen, a gifted pro-abolition lawyer, Roger Baldwin, and, most famously, former President John Quincy Adams. The *Amistad* case, which gained so much attention as a film at the end of the twentieth century, had broad press coverage in its day, too—all the way to the U.S. Supreme Court. The rebellion focused and dramatized the emotions about slavery that would finally propel the United States into the most destructive war in its history.

As a movement, abolitionism officially started in England in 1790. By 1807, Parliament had abolished the slave trade between England and her colonies. A year later, the slave trade had also been made illegal in the United States, although slavery itself continued in the South, which argued that the national—not just the southern—cotton industry simply could not function without it. In addition to the New England Congregational Church's Anti-Slavery Society, other major supporters of abolition in the middle decades of the nineteenth century included William Lloyd Garrison, who had helped establish the New England Anti-Slavery Society in 1831 and who published his impassioned journal, *The Liberator,* for the next thirty-four years; Abraham Lincoln and the Free Soil movement; and a number of mostly northern orators, writers, and politicians who, like Garrison, kept the issue of the inhu-

manity of slavery a white-hot sociopolitical theme up to and through the Civil War years.

Literary historian James D. Hart notes that among early indictments of slavery were Hector St. John de Crèvecoeur's graphic "Charleston Letter" from his *Letters of an American Farmer* (1782), Bostonian immigrant from England Samuel Sewall's *The Selling of Joseph* (1790), and, the same year, former Bostonian Benjamin Franklin's ironic, Swiftian deathbed essay, "On the Slave Trade." Massachusetts lawyer Richard Hildreth's *The Slave; or, Memories of Archy Moore* (1836) may be America's first antislavery novel; it treats the romantic, episodic, and generally improbable adventures of a runaway octoroon slave who later becomes the commander of a British ship during the War of 1812. Frederick Douglass takes the reader inside the debilitating psychological realities and the grim socioeconomics of slavery in his famous 1845 *Narrative* and in its progressively expanded and revised editions in 1855, 1881, and 1892. Douglass's passionate, at times inflammatory, autobiography is one of an extensive array of abolitionist narratives written by or about former slaves during the nineteenth century. From 1985 to 1993, hundreds of documents about the black abolitionist movement were edited and published by Peter Ripley of Florida State University.

Poet and pro-abolition Massachusetts legislator John Greenleaf Whittier edited Benjamin Lundy's *Pennsylvania Freeman* from 1838–40 and published two volumes of pamphlets and poems opposing slavery in 1838 and 1846; fellow Massachusetts author James Russell Lowell also contributed to Lundy's abolitionist journal and edited the *National Anti-Slavery Standard* from 1848 to 1852. Furthermore, the capture and execution of radical Kansas abolitionist John Brown in 1859 made him a martyr in some circles, inspiring writers to step up their support for the abolitionist cause. Concordian Henry David Thoreau, already active in the antislavery movement (see especially his 1854 lecture "Slavery in Massachusetts"), had met John Brown at Ralph Waldo Emerson's home in 1857. Thoreau wrote three lectures in 1859 and 1860 celebrating John Brown's commitment and ultimate sacrifice to the antislavery cause.

According to family history, the sensational attention, national and international, paid to Connecticut local-colorist Harriet Beecher Stowe's *Uncle Tom's Cabin* (1852) prompted Abraham Lincoln to address the author during her White House visit: "So this is the little lady who made this big war." Technically, Stowe was not an abolitionist, but the unprecedented response to her book prompted her to publish *A Key to Uncle Tom's Cabin* in 1853, in which she documented from numerous public and private sources many of the social and political facts about slavery that she had incorporated fictionally into her text. Her next novel, *Dred: A Tale of the Great Dismal Swamp* (1856), confirmed that she had become a full supporter of abolitionism; her portrait of Dred is loosely based on the slave revolutionary Nat Turner. Turner had led his unsuccessful rebellion in 1831, and a short narrative of the event, published at the time, was Virginia author William Styron's source for his controversial Pulitzer Prize-winning novel, *The Confessions of Nat Turner* (1967).

Predictably, southern politicians opposed abolition, seeing the movement as a threat to the essential way of life and economic structure of the South. Slaveowners defensively rationalized the existence of chattel slavery on paternalistic grounds, too: after all, they maintained, whites protected, nurtured, educated, and provided religious training for the slaves under their jurisdiction, offering them a dramatically higher standard of living than they had enjoyed in darkest Africa—and even a chance for a Christian afterlife thrown into the bargain. Moreover, southern authors with Old South leanings writing before and after the Civil War often portrayed abolitionists as carpetbagging meddlers and as the fomenters of disruption and disorder, if not downright violence and rebellion against all that was southern. Mark Twain's sympathies were with the abolitionist cause, as the irony in Pap's drunken protest early in *Adventures of Huckleberry Finn* (1885) makes plain. "Call this a govment! . . . A man can't get his rights in a govment like this," Pap roars. He curses the injustice of a political system that allows a black freedman from Ohio to buy fancy clothes, vote, and even teach foreign languages at a college, while the same

government only lets Pap "go round in clothes that ain't fitten for a hog. . . . Thinks I, what is the country a-comin' to?"

In "Benito Cereno," his dark and complex 1855 abolitionist narrative that was based on another shipboard slave rebellion off the coast of Chile, Herman Melville terms slavery the "malign evil in man"; his powerful short story reveals how the malignity of slavery progressively infects Africa, Europe, and America. The mulatto Tom (a.k.a. Chambers Driscoll) in Twain's *The Tragedy of Pudd'nhead Wilson and the Comedy of Those Extraordinary Twins* (1894) analyzes his own brutalization and debasement as a slave in a passage Twain subsequently excised from his manuscript. Tom realized that slavery brought out the worst in everyone, sooner or later—master and servant; father and mother; offspring black and white, legitimate and illegitimate; and church and state. The black legacy of slavery, that "moral morass" as Barbara Ladd terms it, doomed the entire Sutpen family in Faulkner's *Absalom, Absalom!* (1936). However, Faulkner also showed the South's animosity toward abolition through his portraits of Joanna Burden and her family in *Light in August* (1932). In real life and in fiction, slaves have often proven themselves to be truly heroic in the face of oppression—such as Cinque of the *Amistad,* or Frederick Douglass, or Margaret Garner, the historical model for Sethe in Toni Morrison's *Beloved* (1987). But proven heroic at what price? Slaves who survived the horrors of the Middle Passage—to invoke Charles Johnson's 1990 novel of that name—or those who survived the inhuman regimen of slavery itself, year after year, were often heroic—or sometimes only physically stronger, or sometimes only luckier. Whatever the reason, they must suffer the survivor's psychology of guilt—guilt not of their own making, of course, but rather guilt ultimately imposed by masters who could not, as former slaveowner John Newton did, find "Amazing Grace" and let their slaves—and themselves, too—go free.

R. Bruce Bickley Jr.

See also Carpetbagger; Chattel Slavery; Civil War; Sectional Reconciliation.

Henrietta Buckmaster, *Let My People Go: The Story of the Underground Railroad and the Growth of the Abolition Movement* (1992); George Fredrickson, *The Black Image in the White Mind: The Debate on Afro-American Character and Destiny, 1817–1914* (1987); Stanley Harrold, *The Abolitionists and the South, 1831–1861 (1995); Barbara Ladd, *Nationalism and the Color Line in George W. Cable, Mark Twain, and William Faulkner* (1996); David Richardson, ed., *Abolition and Its Aftermath* (1985); C. Peter Ripley, ed., *The Black Abolitionist Papers* (1985–1993).

ACADEMY, SOUTHERN LITERATURE AND THE

Southern literature and the academy have enjoyed a prosperous relationship since the late nineteenth century. Beginning in the 1890s, a network of scholars at southern colleges and universities participated in a larger regional cultural movement promoting southern literature. As the new century commenced, they became the most effective agents of the movement as they gave talks, wrote articles, created reading and Chautauqua courses, and produced southern literature anthologies for high-school and college-level use. These activities worked to institutionalize the study of southern literature within universities and to educate a growing audience to appreciate southern authors and literary works. Subsequent generations of southern literary scholars have followed their precedent of active scholarship, each shaping the field and perpetuating its status as a respected academic discipline. The next generation of southern literary scholars produced New Critics such as Allen Tate, Cleanth Brooks, and Robert Penn Warren, whose ideas on southern literature and critical theory had a long-term impact on studies in the field. Tate and Warren also contributed to the body of southern literature, exemplifying the frequently close alliance of southern literature, scholarship, and university teaching.

The study of southern literature received a huge boost at midcentury with Jay Hubbell's extensively researched literary history, *The South and American Literature* (1954), and Thomas Daniel Young, Floyd C. Watkins, and Richmond Croom Beatty's major anthology, *The Literature of the South* (1952). From the 1960s onward, the generation of Louis Rubin, C. Hugh Holman, Lewis P. Simpson, Walter Sullivan, Blyden Jackson, Thomas Daniel Young, and Mary Ann Wimsatt continued to provide important criticism and anthologies that broadened and deepened the serious study of southern literature. This study continues into the twenty-first century with yet a new generation of thinkers and critics who are assessing the recent years of prolific creativity by southern writers as well as providing new ways to look at earlier southern texts. The work

of the academy continues to foster the critical spirit that early scholars of the region's literature deemed essential to the flourishing of a southern literature.

In 1908 Carl Holliday observed of southern literature that "nearly every southern college and university offers a course in the subject." Since that time, many southern colleges and universities have continued to develop curricula in southern literature, offering undergraduate and graduate courses and doctoral minors in the field. Such courses have not been geographically bound; by the 1980s, many colleges and universities throughout the nation and even in some foreign countries were offering classes on the subject. The syllabi of these courses, along with scholarly criticism, have greatly shaped the evolving canon of southern literature.

The academy has also produced and facilitated the publication of anthologies, literary history, and literary criticism that nourishes a lively dialogue in the field. Academic journals, which offer an essential forum and enhance the prestige of the field, appeared early with the *Sewanee Review,* begun at the University of the South in 1892, and the *South Atlantic Quarterly,* launched at Trinity College (later Duke University) in 1902. Subsequent journals specializing in southern literature and culture include *Mississippi Quarterly* (1948–), *Southern Studies* (1961–), *Southern Quarterly* (1962–), and *Southern Literary Journal* (1968–). Presses affiliated with several southern universities, including Louisiana State University, University of North Carolina at Chapel Hill, University of South Carolina, University of Georgia, and University of Virginia, have been instrumental in making both primary and critical texts available. A noteworthy example is Louisiana State University Press's 1979 publication of Louis D. Rubin's much-used classroom anthology, *The Literary South.* At the close of the twentieth century, W. W. Norton, a national academic press, also published a textbook anthology, *The Literature of the American South,* marking another step in the academic nationalization of southern literature.

In 1968 a group of scholars founded the Society for the Study of Southern Literature, an organization that hosts a biennial scholarly conference, as well as panels at the South Atlantic Modern Language Association and the Modern Language Association, and which has supported the publication of bibliographic and reference works furthering the study of southern literature. For example, this group's impetus initiated the 1985 publication of *The History of Southern Literature.*

The academy also undergirds numerous other professional activities, such as regional, national, and international conferences on individual writers, groups of writers, or themes. University-affiliated institutions undertaking research and projects concerning the South include the Institute for Southern Studies at the University of South Carolina, the Center for the Study of Southern Culture at the University of Mississippi, and the Center for the Study of the American South at the University of North Carolina at Chapel Hill. These and other ventures fueled by continuing research and publication in the field are all manifestations of the ongoing symbiotic relationship between southern literature and the academy.

Susan H. Irons

See also Anthologies of Southern Literature; Centers for Southern Studies; Histories of Southern Literature; *Mississippi Quarterly*; *Sewanee Review*; *Southern Literary Journal*, 1968 to Present; University Presses.

ACCENT

Most people can correctly identify a "southern accent," but descriptions of southern writing seldom mention this distinctive feature. The omission is understandable. Oral characteristics of speech are difficult to render on the page. English spelling is at best a treacherous guide to pronunciation and of limited use in suggesting accent. And the South has not one but many accents—geographical, cultural, racial, social. Still, writers past and present manage to depict southern speech on the page. An accent may be an essential character trait. Whereas accents may strengthen the reader's sense of place, some writers use accent to ridicule characters or make them stereotypes.

Deviant spelling and punctuation have limited success in representing accent, although eighteenth-century southern humorists delighted readers with gross distortions of spelling and punctuation. Even edited versions of, for instance, George Washington Harris's Sut Lovingood tales only frustrate modern readers. Some writers alter spelling that has no effect on pronunciation ("sez" for "says"). No spelling can accurately portray variations in vowels (the "ir" in "bird") and diphthongs, or the distinctive consonants in "lily" (light, front). No conventions of transcription record tempo, voice quality, or patterns of intonation—

markers that are often more significant than individual sounds. Finally, for any system of representation, the reader must have some oral image of the dialect to "hear" it in silent reading.

Successful renditions of accent generally use only selective alterations in spelling, such as "dahlin" for "darling," "ev'n" for "even," "rassle" for "wrestle." Writers may also use distinctive words and phrases, especially proper names. Sometimes the storyteller simply announces that a character speaks with an accent. Often the words themselves suggest a slow tempo, as in the following passage from Eudora Welty's "The Wide Net": "And especially Edna Earle, that never did get to be what you'd call a heavy thinker. Edna Earle could sit and ponder all day on how the little tail of the 'C' got through the 'L' in a Coca-Cola sign." And Red Sammy in O'Connor's "A Good Man Is Hard to Find" says "Co'-Colas."

Writers have more success with accents that differ greatly from the general speech of the region. Critics praised Kate Chopin and George Washington Cable for their rendering of Louisiana accents—for instance, Chopin's Pierre Manton in "A No-Account Creole": "W'en a chimbly breck, I take one, two de boy' we patch 'im up bes' we know how. We keep on men' de fence', firs' on place, anudder; an' if it would n' be fer dem mule' of Lacroix—*tonnere!* I don' wan' to talk 'bout dem mul'." The lack of the plural form and the French word clearly indicate the accent.

Zora Neale Hurston's characters have obvious accents, but the accents seem essential to the characters. In Flannery O'Connor's works, however, the characters' accents serve to make them more remote from both storyteller and readers and less sympathetic.

Though writers handle accents today more subtly than their predecessors, neither speakers nor writers have abandoned the southern accent.

Mary Frances HopKins

See also Cajun Literature; Creole Literature; Dialect Literature; Speech and Dialect.

Harold B. Allen and Michael D. Linn, eds., *Dialect and Language Variation* (1986); Walter Blair and Raven I. McDavid Jr., eds., *The Mirth of a Nation* (1983); George Core, ed., *Southern Fiction Today* (1969); Louis D. Rubin Jr., *The Writer in the South* (1972).

ADVICE ON WRITING SOUTHERN FICTION

William Faulkner in *Faulkner in the University* (1959) says that the source of fiction is the writer's experience, observation, and imagination. Fiction writers may use this thought to shake themselves out of writing too close to fantasy or, on the other hand, too close to biography for the good of a story. In the recent past, authors Robert Penn Warren, Eudora Welty, Doris Betts, scholars Cleanth Brooks, Louis Rubin, Blyden Jackson, and many other southern writers and scholars have given fiction writers indirect advice through books and articles about literature, interviews, informal talks—as well as direct advice while teaching courses about writing and literature. Such advice has been passed along, sometimes augmented, by writer-teachers Lee Smith, Randall Kenan, Mary Hood, Louis Rubin, Daphne Athas, and others.

Relatively few "how to write fiction" books seem to come out of the South. Southern writers have apparently learned their craft, by and large, through literary criticism, classroom study, reading and studying their favorite stories and novels, and writing and rewriting.

Caroline Gordon, a teacher and fiction writer, advised Flannery O'Connor through the mail. O'Connor, in her letters, collected by Sally Fitzgerald in *The Habit of Being* (1979), advised other young writers. Some of that advice, paraphrased here, serves as an example of southern advice on writing fiction:

Ignore criticism that doesn't make sense.

Make the reader *see* the characters at every minute, but do this unobtrusively.

An omniscient narrator using the same language as the characters lowers the tone of the work.

Never do writing exercises. Forget plot; start with a character or anything else you can make come alive. Discover, rather than impose meaning. You may discover a good deal more by not being too clear when you start. You sometimes find a story by messing around with this or that. Once you have finished a first draft, see how you can better bring out what it says.

Read *The Craft of Fiction* by Percy Lubbock and *Understanding Fiction* by Robert Penn Warren and Cleanth Brooks.

If there is no possibility for change in a character (i.e., a character is hopelessly insane), then there is little reader interest in that character. If heroes were stable, there wouldn't be any story—all good stories are about a character's changing. Sin is interesting; evil is not. Sin grows out of free choice; evil is something else. Characters need to behave as themselves as people, not as abstract representations of some idea or principle that is dear to the writer. Be careful about a tendency to be too omniscient and not let things come through the characters.

Add a character to make another character "come out."

You can write convincingly about a homesick New Yorker if you have never been to New York but *have* been homesick. A character must behave out of his or her motivations, not the author's. Don't try to be subtle . . . or write for a subtle reader.

Write two hours a day, same time, sitting at the same place, without a view—either write or just sit. Follow your nose. To get a story, you might have to approach a vague notion from one direction and then another, until you get an entrance. Sit at your machine.

In a short story, write for a single effect and end on what is most important. At the end of a story, gain some altitude and get a larger view. You shouldn't appear to be making a point. The meaning of a story must be in its muscle.

Use dialect lightly—suggest. Get the person right.

"A word stands for something else and is used for a purpose and if you play around with them irrespective of what they are supposed to *do,* your writing will become literary in the worse sense."

A novel or short story says something that can be said in no other way. A summary or an abstraction will not give you the same thing.

"The less self-conscious you are about what you are about, the better in a way, that is to say technically. You have to get it in the blood, not in the head."

"My business is to write and not talk about it."

Writers seeking *the secrets* to good writing might keep in mind O'Connor's statement from *Mystery and Manners* (1969): "My own approach to literary problems is very like the one Dr. Johnson's blind housekeeper used when she poured tea—she put her finger inside the cup."

One final—delicate, yet crucial—requirement for writing fiction: "Perhaps you [a correspondent] are able to see things in these stories that I can't see because if I did see I would be too frightened to write them. I have always insisted that there is a fine grain of stupidity required in the fiction writer."

Clyde Edgerton

See also O'Connor, Flannery.

E. M. Forster, *Aspects of the Novel* (1927); Rust Hills, *Writing in General and the Short Story in Particular* (1987); André Maurois, *The Art of Writing* (1962); Louis Rubin, *The Teller in the Tale* (1967); Eudora Welty, *The Eye of the Story* (1978).

AFRICAN AMERICAN COLLEGES AND UNIVERSITIES

From their origins in early-nineteenth-century American society through their present dilemma about their future, historically black colleges and universities (HBCUs) have played a significant role in the preservation and creation of African American culture. The contribution of these institutions to the social, historical, and literary legacy of the American South—as repositories of a rich oral and literary tradition; training grounds for prominent scholars, activists, and artists; and metaphor in African American literature for the generational tensions inherent in the struggle for racial equality—cannot be overemphasized.

The history of African American higher education dates to 1837, when the Institute for Colored Youth was founded in Philadelphia, Pennsylvania. The success of that institution, which began as a secondary school, led to the founding in 1854 of Ashmun, later Lincoln, University, the first college for blacks in the United States. With Ashmun in place, advocates of education for blacks quickly expanded their reach, founding Wilberforce University in 1856. Initially distinguished for its policy of coeducational admissions, Wilberforce was also academic home to noted African American abolitionist poet Frances Ellen Watkins Harper, the author of the first published short story by an African American woman, "The Two Offers" (1859).

From their initial establishment in the Northeast, African American colleges multiplied as numerous public and private institutions for black higher education opened across the South in the late nineteenth and early twentieth centuries, beginning with the Reconstruction era and compounding with the passage of the second Morrill Act, also known as the Land Grant Act of 1890, which mandated that states provide land-grant universities for both black and white students. With the current number of existing HBCUs at 103 (or 117, depending on how one counts), a comprehensive listing of names and dates is not possible in this brief essay. Among the most prominent of the schools founded in that period, however, are Fisk University (Nashville, Tennessee, 1867); Howard University (Washington, D.C., 1867); Morehouse College (Atlanta, Georgia, 1867); Stillman College (Tuscaloosa, Alabama, 1876); Tuskegee Institute (Tuskegee, Alabama, 1881); and Spelman College (Atlanta, Georgia, 1881).

As the new institutions developed educational programming and sought means of fundraising, they became important sources for significant racial and cultural interaction and also participated in the national consideration of the African American's place in society. In 1871, the Fisk Jubilee Singers embarked on a world concert tour to raise necessary operating expenses for Fisk University. Over the next seven years, the Jubilee Singers traversed the globe, performing formalized arrangements of African American spirituals for eager audiences. Their renderings of the former slaves' music caught the ear and the emotions of white listeners worldwide and contributed to the broad misunderstanding of African American culture that prevailed well into the twentieth century, when scholars deromanticized the spirituals by exploring their coded secular political content.

Political content in the educational programs of the more prominent HBCUs also shaped blacks' educational experiences in the late nineteenth and early twentieth centuries, as educators and administrators debated the merits of vocational and classical educational models. Typically associated with Booker T. Washington and W. E. B. Du Bois, respectively, vocational and classical educational models struggled for dominance throughout the early decades of the existence of these institutions. At Tuskegee Institute, Washington taught the principles of economic success over social equality, lessons he had learned at the Hampton Institute in Hampton, Virginia; he recounts his experiences in Up From Slavery (1901), an amalgamation of slave narrative and Horatio Alger–style success story. The typical countertext to Washington's autobiography is Du Bois's landmark work, The Souls of Black Folk (1903), in which the Fisk alumnus discusses the difficulties facing southern African Americans and explains the value of a classical education to the process of racial uplift.

The tensions between classical and vocational models of education extended well into the 1920s, as Washington and his supporters gained the support of white philanthropists, many of whom supported the struggling private black institutions of higher learning. The conservative vocational-educational model even threatened Fisk University in the 1910s and 1920s, when white president Fayette McKenzie instituted a series of control measures so oppressive and regressive that students rebelled against them. Enlisting Du Bois in their cause, the students demanded and got sweeping reforms that abolished McKenzie's insulting attempts to quell the "primitive behavior" he believed was essential to the black students' communal character.

The students' rebellion coincided with the flowering of the Harlem Renaissance. As artists and authors, many of whom were graduates of black colleges, sought new means of expressing their individual and communal identities, the HBCU evolved into a significant symbol in African American literature. That pattern continued long after the end of the Harlem Renaissance and changed as perceptions shifted about the roles played by black educational institutions in the process of social reform. In works such as Atlanta University alumnus James Weldon Johnson's *The Autobiography of an Ex-Coloured Man* (1912, anonymous; republished, 1927), the presentation of the African American college campus is positive and the students are depicted as bursting with promise and potential. More typically, however, portrayals of African American colleges and college students in the literature reflect cynicism about the institutions and a resistance to their conservative racial and educational politics. In *Quicksand* (1928), for instance, Nella Larsen draws on her experiences at Fisk and Tuskegee to create her unflattering portrait of Naxos, a black school clearly modeled on the Tuskegee Institute. At Naxos, the students and faculty care only about conforming and maintaining their established place in the southern racial and cultural hierarchy. Only when protagonist Helga Crane resigns her position at Naxos and relocates to Chicago, then Harlem, can she begin to live more freely and fully. Larsen's portrayal resonates profoundly with Ralph Ellison's representation of Tuskegee in *Invisible Man* (1952), one of the most important and influential novels of the twentieth century. Like Helga Crane, Ellison's Invisible Man must leave the unnamed State College for Negroes and its imperious head, Dr. Bledsoe, behind and strike out on his own to develop a more complete sense of individual and cultural identity.

The pattern that Larsen and Ellison typify changes somewhat in literature from the 1960s and 1970s, as Alice Walker's *Meridian* (1976) suggests. Though she portrays the African American college in her novel as conservative, Walker, a Spelman graduate, shows the increasingly active students protesting against that conservatism and defying school officials as they press for social change. The shift in literary perspective on the HBCU likely reflects the actual increase in social activism that characterizes African American colleges and universities in the late 1950s and 1960s. Indeed, many of the major participants in the Civil Rights movement were HBCU alumni, and both the student sit-in movement of the 1960s and the Student Nonviolent Coordinating Committee (SNCC) were born on black college campuses. Without the efforts of student leaders and HBCU alumni such as Martin Luther King Jr., Whitney Young, Jesse Jackson, and Medgar Evers, the social changes of the 1960s would never have occurred.

For all the benefits those changes brought, however, they also created difficulties for the HBCUs themselves; as barriers to integration have come down, historically black institutions have found themselves competing with white colleges and universities for the most talented African American students entering college. Because of limited resources and facilities, many black schools have suffered in that competition, and some warn that the collapse of the system is imminent. However, with a renewed commitment from alumni and federal funding sources, and with strong, visionary leadership by educators such as Spelman College president Johnnetta Cole, the formerly dire circumstances are reversing somewhat. The HBCUs' legacy of service and leadership in the education of African Americans is the foundation for what will surely be a continued active and important role for African American colleges and universities well into the twenty-first century.

William R. Nash

See also Civil Rights Movement; King, Martin Luther, Jr.; Washington, Booker T.

James D. Anderson, *The Education of Blacks in the South, 1860–1935* (1988); William Edward Burghardt Du Bois, *The Souls of Black Folk* (1903); Ralph Ellison, *Invisible Man* (1952); John Hope Franklin and Alfred A. Moss Jr., *From Slavery to Freedom: A History of African Americans* (7th ed., 1994); *The HBCU Home Page* (http://eric-web.tc.columbia.edu/hbcu, 6/30/98); James Weldon Johnson, *The Autobiography of an Ex-Coloured Man* (1912); Nella Larsen, *Quicksand* (1928); Alice Walker, *Meridian* (1976); Booker Taliaferro Washington, *Up From Slavery* (1901); Raymond Wolters, *The New Negro on Campus: Black College Rebellions of the 1920s* (1975).

AFRICAN AMERICAN FOLK CULTURE

Folk culture encompasses the customs, beliefs, traditions, practices, art, architecture, music, dance, literature, and institutions that reflect and shape the characteristics of a community. The categories of African American folk culture that most directly inform the literature of the American South include West African-derived oral practices, folk literature and song, and spiritual beliefs. Tricksters, conjurers, "haints," and cultural heroes populate southern stories, and idiomatic speech, metaphor, and sermonic rhythms influence their telling. The purposes that African American folk culture serves in southern literature and life are as rich and varied as its characteristic forms. The folktales, proverbs, and legends preserve the collective history of African Americans in the South, keeping alive their legacy of survival. The songs and sermons resonate with folk wisdom, embodying the fundamental beliefs that sustained slaves through bondage, and represent the southern values by which many yet live. The traditional remedies—both medical and magical—reflect the West African foundations of the slaves, tying them to the spiritual beliefs of their ancestral home. Taken together, the varied forms of African American folk culture define the collective character of the African American in the South.

The Oral Tradition

The language patterns and speech-ways of African American slaves evidenced the survival of West African oral practices. Folk cries, field hollers, and work songs are some of the earliest forms of African American folk culture recognized as African-derived. Although stripped of the material vestiges of their homeland, newly arrived slaves brought a bounty of African traditions and beliefs to America and shaped them to respond to their New World existence. Put to work in the cotton, rice, tobacco, indigo, and cane fields of the southern plantations, slaves translated the call and response of their African oral tradition into folk cries and field hollers, as they called to one another for food, water, assistance, or companionship. One worker might call out a phrase or lyric and hear it repeated in the distance by one or more fellow slaves. Work songs, such as "Pick a Bale of Cotton" and "Round 'de Corn, Sally," grew out of these cries and hollers. In addition to providing a sense of camaraderie among the workers, the rhythms of the songs set the work pace, and the lyrics sometimes commented on the inequitable distribution of the results of slave labor. "We Raise de Wheat" observes, "We bake de bread, / Dey gib us de cruss; / We sif de meal, / Dey giv us de huss; / We peel de meat, / Dey gib us de skin / And dat's de way / Dey takes us in."

Like field cries and secular work songs, the religious song recorded slave life and encouraged perseverance. Spirituals, or "sorrow songs" as W. E. B. Du Bois defined them, not only illustrated the difficult conditions of slave life but also served as inspiration, hope, and resistance. In *The Souls of Black Folk* (1903), Du Bois wrote that the songs "tell in word and music of trouble and exile, of strife and hiding; they grope toward some unseen power and sigh for rest in the End." It wasn't until the late 1930s that scholars began to examine the social implications of spirituals, finding that they were more than the lamentations Du Bois considered them to be. John Lovell argues that the songs were expressions of resistance and were not tied to freedom in heaven but on earth. They reflect three central themes: freedom from slavery, the desire for justice, and strategies of resistance. Scholars note the double-voiced nature of the songs and explain the necessity of hiding subversive meanings from the ever-present slave master. Drawing on images from the Bible, specifically references to the bondage of the Israelites, spirituals offered the hope that God would liberate the slaves in the physical realm as well as in a spiritual sense. Songs like "Joshua Fit the Battle of Jericho" demonstrate battle strategies and show God's revenge against the unjust, whereas "Swing Low Sweet Chariot" and "Wade in the Water" illustrate escape on the Underground Railroad. Authors have used spirituals in their works to illustrate both perspectives. Harriet Beecher Stowe includes what she calls the "melancholy dirge" of the slave in *Uncle Tom's Cabin* (1852). Susan and Emmeline sing of "earthly despair after heavenly hope" while they await their turn on the auction block. Contrasting Stowe's sentimental view, and recognizing such songs as tools of resistance, Margaret Walker begins her novel *Jubilee* with the spiritual of the same name, asking "Do you think I'll make a soldier in the year of Jubilee?"

Similar to spirituals in theme, folk sermons are based on Bible stories meant to inspire hope. They venerate cultural heroes like the Hebrew children Shadrack, Meshach, and Abednego, whose faith saved them from death in the fiery furnace, and Moses, who was chosen to lead his people to freedom. Genesis and Exodus were favorite texts that influenced the works of numerous authors, among them Paul Laurence Dunbar, James Weldon Johnson, and Zora Neale Hurston. These authors use dialect, the expressive language of metaphor, and the rhythms of folk oratory to celebrate the black preacher as poet. Dunbar's "An Ante-bellum Sermon" (1896) and Hurston's *Moses, Man of the Mountain* (1939) both recreate the story of the Israelites' escape from bondage. Dunbar's use of the slave's idiom and experience situates the poem, as well as its story, in the antebellum South, despite the narrator's insistence that he is "preachin' ancient, / I ain't talking 'bout today." Nearing the conclusion of the poem, the preacher concedes that he is talking about the slaves' freedom "in a Bibalistic way." An exemplar of the form, Dunbar's "An Ante-bellum Sermon" uses vivid imagery and metaphors, biblical allusions, moral arguments, and repetitious phrases. Hurston's novel depicts Moses as a conjurer and employs black southern dialect as well. Although Johnson eschews dialect in *God's Trombones: Seven Negro Sermons in Verse* (1927), he maintains the metaphors and sermonic form. He contrasts God's gentleness and power, describing the "great God" who created the heavens yet stoops to shape humanity like a mammy cuddling her baby. "The Creation" is an often-cited example of the folk sermon and is said to be the inspiration for William Faulkner's Reverend Shegog in *The Sound and the Fury.*

Animal Tales and Conjure Stories

Folktales are the most easily identifiable form of southern folk culture. Joel Chandler Harris rightfully is credited with popularizing the African American folktale, particularly animal fables; however, the origin of such stories can be traced to West Africa. Whereas dilemma, orphan, and moralizing stories are among the tale types that survived the Middle Passage, the trickster tale proved to be the most enduringly popular. Harris's *Uncle Remus: His Songs and His Sayings* (1880), which first preserved the African American folktale in print, illustrates the conflicts and competitions between Brer (Buh or Br'er) Rabbit and his foes, Brer Bear, Brer Fox, and Brer Wolf. Brer Rabbit, the scion of those classic West African tricksters the Ewe Hare, the Ashanti Spider, and the Yoruba Tortoise, represents the personification of disorder. A West African world view accepts that disorder functions to complement order, creating a complete universe. The trickster injects chaos into order and thus is never fully controlled. He tests social boundaries because he is ruled by his desires and is cunning in achieving his goals. At the center of the tales are themes of escape, resistance, and survival. The characteristic pattern of the West African trickster tale is evident in its African American offspring. The animal protagonists form a false friendship wherein a contract of some sort is entered. The stronger party of the partnership violates the contract, and the weaker

partner escapes exploitation through trickery and deception.

Brer Rabbit's appeal as a cultural hero to slaves becomes apparent as his battle of wits with his physically stronger opponent represents the triumph of the apparently powerless slave over the obviously powerful slave master. Similarly, postbellum animal fables present the economic victory of the sharecropper over the exploitative landowner. John and Old Marster (Marster, Marse, Massa, or Old Boss) tales—human corollaries to the animal fables—became popular during Reconstruction. Not only does John participate in battles of wit with Old Marster, he also attempts to take advantage of him in any way imaginable. Old Marster is the victim of John's thefts and the butt of his jokes. Because John violates numerous southern taboos and traditions, this type of tale was not popular among white audiences. "Old Marster Eats Crow," in which John holds Old Marster at gun point, and "John in Jail," in which John exposes himself to Miss Elizabeth, illustrate the extent to which the form demonstrates contempt for and rebellion against white domination.

Whereas Harris focused primarily, although not exclusively, on animal fables, Charles W. Chesnutt sought to preserve the conjure tale. Recognizing the popularity of the plantation school of literature epitomized by the Uncle Remus tales and characterized by local color and the use of dialect, he viewed such fiction as his entré into the literary world. Rather than replicating plantation literature that romanticized the antebellum South, Chesnutt chose to subvert it in several of his short stories. His first literary success, *The Conjure Woman* (1899), employs the stock characters of the genre. "The Goophered Grapevine" (1887), the first story of the collection, published in the *Atlantic Monthly*, gives us John, the educated northern capitalist, his fragile wife, Annie, and Uncle Julius McAdoo, who regales the two with a conjure tale brimming with mother wit and voiced in black vernacular. However, the story is not a nostalgic re-creation of glorious plantation life. Like Brer Rabbit, Uncle Julius engages in a test of wits with the northern capitalist who goes South to purchase the vineyard on which Julius has made his living. The practice of conjuration or magic, an African survival, serves as Julius's tool of resistance against the superior power of capitalism. Uncle Julius claims that the vineyard has been cursed in the hope of frightening John into abandoning his plans to purchase it.

When the Great Migration shifted black populations from the South to the North, interest in folk culture seemed to wane. During the 1930s, however, Zora Neale Hurston revived interest in black folklore, particularly conjuration and hoodoo (voodoo), with her pioneering works *Mules and Men* (1935) and *Tell My Horse* (1938). She traveled through the South and the West Indies collecting stories, hoodoo rituals, and conjure formulas, as well as folk songs, sermons, and proverbs that resulted in the aforementioned studies.

Spiritual Beliefs

Chesnutt's and Hurston's desire to preserve conjure stories of the African American oral tradition demonstrates their recognition of the importance of the practice in black southern life. A confidence in conjuration, Vodoun, voodoo, or hoodoo is predicated on a system of beliefs that includes animism, ancestor reverence, and the concept of personal and collective immortality. According to a blend of traditional West African cosmologies, the existence of a mystical order—which complements the natural, moral, and religious orders—is necessary for the harmony of the spiritual and the material worlds. This mystical power, which permeates the universe and resides in spiritual places, is available to spirits and to certain human beings who then possess the power to conjure or control others. Conjurers employ spirits, medicinal herbs, rituals, and fetishes in their practice and often were called upon to help slaves transcend the difficulties of their existence.

Scholars suggest that the lack of control over their lives and even their bodies caused slaves to retain West African beliefs in personal and collective immortality and to employ conjuration to exert some measure of control over the slave master. The slaves' belief in ghosts or "haints" (hants, haunts) reflects the notions of immortality and ancestor reverence. John S. Mbiti explains in *African Religion and Philosophy* (1970) that there are two types of human spirits, the recently dead (living dead) and the long dead (ghosts). One is not fully dead until one has passed out of memory. The living dead, those who are remembered, protect their loved ones and intercede in their behalf with other spirits as well as with God and the lesser deities. Ghosts, the forgotten, inhabit places in nature and haunt the living. The slaves, in an effort to control their existence, conjured their masters, causing them to be haunted. Masters, sometimes believing in ghosts themselves, would become afraid to punish slaves for minor infractions. Additionally, slaves employed conjure men and women to alleviate illnesses because they believed

that many ailments were the result of conjuration or ill will. The practice of hoodoo is said to have entered the United States in 1809 in New Orleans and is derived from a system of beliefs originating in Dahomey and emerging in Haiti. Harold Courlander asserts in *The Drum and the Hoe: Life and Lore of the Haitian People* that Vodoun is a "true religion," deeply rooted in the history of African peoples and passed on unbroken to African American believers.

Conjure stories are not the only literary forms influenced by hoodoo practices. Numerous short stories and novels about southern life include or are centered on a belief in ghosts and magic, including Margaret Walker's *Jubilee*, Zora Neale Hurston's "Spunk" and *Moses, Man of the Mountain*, Charles Johnson's *Oxherding Tale* and *The Sorcerer's Apprentice*, and Toni Morrison's *Beloved*.

The folk culture of African Americans in the South reflects the celebration of a history of survival. From the swept yards of Georgia to the bottle trees of Mississippi, folk culture has provided the foundation for the development of African American narratives and enriches the literature of the American South.

Barbara J. Wilcots

See also African American Spirituals; Conjuring; Dialect Literature; Folklore; Novel, 1820 to 1865; Oral History; Trickster; Uncle Remus; Vernacular Voice.

Mary F. Berry and John Blassingame, *Long Black Memory: The Black Experience in America* (1982); J. Mason Brewer, *American Negro Folklore* (1968); Alan Dundes, *Mother Wit from the Laughing Barrel: Readings in the Interpretation of Afro-American Folklore* (1973); Zora Neale Hurston, *Mules and Men* (1935).

AFRICAN AMERICAN LITERATURE, BEGINNINGS TO 1919

The study of literary production by African Americans from the South before 1912 constitutes a field undergoing constant revision and expansion. The radical displacement and political restrictions that racism imposed upon African Americans writing in the antebellum U.S. make the category itself a departure from traditional groupings. African American southern writers—if one interprets that category broadly to include African Americans born as far north as Maryland, as well as born elsewhere but residing in and writing about the South—make up a significant number. Texts in this category constitute a dramatic counterpoint to the traditional body of white, patriarchal, "genteel" literature often associated with nineteenth-century southern culture.

In the late eighteenth and early nineteenth century, the few known African American writers employed multiple genres and world views. In the sparsely populated and fluid society of the colonial era and early Republic, these writers adapted—or appropriated—traditional models. John Marrant's spiritual autobiography/captivity narrative describes his dramatic conversion and providential escapes from death. Marrant (1755–1791)—who left *A Narrative of the Lord's Wonderful Dealings with John Marrant, a Black* (1785), a second autobiography, and several sermons—was born of free parents in New York but moved in childhood to Florida, then Charleston. In the narrative, a stirring sermon by George Whitefield and the family's ridicule of his religious awakening cause Marrant to flee to the wilderness, where he narrowly escapes torture and death at the hands of a Cherokee "king." The narrative portrays Marrant's Franklinesque evolution from trained musician to Methodist minister. The captivity plot reverses racial hierarchies and celebrates the hero's virtue, as Henry Louis Gates indicates in *The Signifying Monkey* (1988), but Marrant's *Narrative* does not directly address slavery or racism.

Maryland-born Benjamin Banneker (1731–1806), free son and grandson of African-born men, was farmer, surveyor, mathematician, musician, and author, from 1792 to 1797, of an almanac. He created the ephemeris, verse, and other material for the almanac, but he is best known for his well-argued letter to Thomas Jefferson, in the 1795 almanac, invoking Jefferson's own revolutionary writings in order to promote the end of slavery and the concept of "one flesh."

George Moses Horton (1797–1883), known as the "slave poet," gained fame in Chapel Hill for his orally rehearsed and dictated poems commissioned by undergraduates at the University of North Carolina. He published three extant volumes of poetry and many individual poems beginning in 1828. The first and most distinguished volume, *The Hope of Liberty* (1829), was sponsored by writer Caroline Lee Hentz to help Horton purchase his freedom and settle in Liberia, a goal never reached. *The Poetical Works of the Colored Bard of North Carolina* (1845) and *Naked Genius* (1865) followed, with two possible later publications not recovered. Periodicals as different as *The Liberator*

and *The Southern Literary Messenger* featured his works. Using conventional forms, often with technical flaws and exuberant language, Horton's unusual range extended from serious lyric to satire and featured subjects from freedom and death to love and historical caricature.

Viewed as the earliest proponent of black nationalism, David Walker (1785–1830) offers a deep contrast to his fellow writers in this category. He voiced his unwavering opposition to the slavery he observed as a freeborn North Carolinian and in travels through the South after relocation to Boston in *David Walker's Appeal in Four Articles; Together with a Preamble, to the Coloured Citizens of the World, but in Particular and Very Expressly, to Those of the United States of America* (1829). The work—ironically patterned on the Constitution, calling for divine retribution on slaveholders, and making an international appeal for racial unity—so alarmed and enraged white southerners that it was suppressed in the South and Walker marked for murder. His death, probably from poisoning, occurred in 1830.

Though this group of early African American texts does not uniformly fit an abolitionist agenda, each writer had support for publication and distribution from white citizens with abolitionist leanings. Horton is most unusual in his combined support from proslavery southerners and antislavery advocates. A clear revolutionary, David Walker in his *Appeal* sounded the clarion call for the three decades that saw the rise of the slave narrative and publication by fugitives in the North. One powerful southern document is *The Confessions of Nat Turner* (1831), Thomas Gray's record of the deadly rebellion that Turner (1800–1831) conducted as the divine agent of retribution against slaveholders. Turner's messianic visions stand in contrast to the recurrent pragmatism of fugitive documents and their claims of authority as witnesses to the wrongs of slavery.

In the proliferation of slave narratives from 1830 to 1865—some of them spurious, others dictated to amanuenses who exercised a distorting editorial privilege, and all addressing a disputed subject—authenticity was a primary concern. Virtually all slave narratives were accompanied by validating apparati to address the pervasive skepticism of white readers. Thus these texts provide sharp portraits of slavery, interpretations of its psychological effects, and rhetorical techniques for presenting experience to a resisting reader. The narratives use the trope of the fugitive's journey, show the struggle for literacy, and assert parity with the reader. Often the narrator is treated as representative.

Some important slave narrators and their dates of initial publication are: Moses Roper (1838), Lunsford Lane (1842), Moses Grandy (1844), Lewis Clarke (and Milton) (1845, 1846), Frederick Douglass (1845), William Wells Brown (1847), Henry Watson (1848), Josiah Henson (1849), Henry Bibb (1849), James W. C. Pennington (1849), Solomon Northup (1853), Noah Davis (1859), William and Ellen Craft (1860), Harriet Jacobs (1861), and her brother, John S. Jacobs (1861).

Whereas the earliest of these works, according to William Andrews in *To Tell a Free Story* (1986), involve "self-declarative autobiographical acts" that suppress the earlier slave self, after 1845 the internal struggles of the slave experience receive primary focus. The inward conflict induced by the slave condition and doubtful moral action involved in self-preservation—as explored by Henson, Brown, Bibb, and Pennington—point to the "psychologizing trend" in these narratives. Similarly, slave narratives become more like novels, with scenes, dialogue, and dramatized events interspersed in the linear narrative and antislavery polemics.

Frederick Douglass (1818–1895) in *Narrative of the Life of an American Slave* (1845) so successfully portrays his struggle with the inverted world of slavery and his practical and spiritual emergence that it sold thirty thousand copies by 1850. Harriet Beecher Stowe's serial publication of *Uncle Tom's Cabin* (1851–52) and the subsequent *Key* (1853) expanded the demand for earlier slave narratives, especially those whose authors she claimed as models. Though Stowe was applauded for her blow against slavery, her novel intensified the claims of African American fugitive slaves for authority to tell their story.

Such claims for authority in the discourse of slavery and conflicting standards attached to class and gender identity influence the major narratives of the 1850s. Douglass's second narrative, *My Bondage and My Freedom* (1855), reveals the dynamics of racial conflict within the abolitionist camp, includes speeches that clarify his stance on such issues as colonization and the Fourth of July, and conveys increased attention to women's issues and portrayals of the slave family. The Crafts, as well, bring a sharper focus on the slavocracy's abuse of women, as does Harriet Jacobs (c. 1813–1897). After almost twenty years of silence about her own experience, Jacobs makes it clear that her writing

is "no fiction." Jean Fagan Yellin's recovery of *Incidents in the Life of a Slave Girl* (1861) as an authentic document ignored for almost a hundred years and, with it, John S. Jacobs's *A True Tale of Slavery* (1861) have provided new ground for examining the genre.

Of some importance also is an early postwar slave narrative by Elizabeth Keckley (1825–1907), *Behind the Scenes: Thirty Years a Slave and Four Years in the White House* (1868). Charting her survival in slavery—and in business—Keckley, like Jacobs, employs the language of the sentimental novel. Keckley's record of slavery and sexual abuse is displaced by the prodigious details about her association with the Lincolns, as modiste and confidante. Suppressed by Robert Lincoln and others who figured in the memoirs, *Behind the Scenes* illustrates a shift in slave narrative to themes of reconciliation and the recurrent Horatio Alger plot.

African American works of fiction, a dominant form after the Civil War, predate that period. Victor Sejour (1817–1874), a French-speaking free Creole from New Orleans, published the first known such work in Paris, *Le Mulâtre* (1837). Although subsequent work by Sejour does not reflect concerns with American slavery, this melodrama, translated as *The Mulatto* and set in Haiti, focuses on the physical and psychic violence constellated around miscegenation. Sejour is the second recorded African American playwright, but the first from the South. In 1844, the Théâtre Français in Paris produced his *Diegarias*, a revenge play addressing the theme of antisemitism, the first of more than twenty plays that Sejour published in France. More French playwright than African American poet or fiction writer, Sejour nevertheless claims a place in early African American writings.

More important, the work of William W. Brown (1814–1884) and Frederick Douglass suggests the close connection between slave narratives and early African American fiction. Like the slave narrative, early fiction focuses on personal or public history and includes actual documents or factual episodes. Brown, traditionally viewed as the major early African American figure to explore the multiple possibilities of belles-lettres, added fiction, poetry, travel writing, history, and drama to his early experiment with slave narrative. In *Clotel; or, The President's Daughter* (1853), a novel revised and reissued at least three times, Brown mingles popular history, abolitionist propaganda, and personal experience with a complexly plotted melodrama exploring the type of the tragic mulatto. In addition, Brown completed his first play in 1856, *Experience; or,*

How to Give a Northern Man a Backbone. Though the play was never published, Brown often gave dramatic readings of it at antislavery meetings. *The Escape; or, A Leap for Freedom,* first read in 1857, was published in 1858.

Douglass—editing and writing for *The North Star,* later named *Frederick Douglass' Paper* and *Frederick Douglass' Monthly* from 1847–1863—published within its pages what is regarded as the first African American novella, "The Heroic Slave" (1853). It gives a fictionalized version of the *Creole* affair in which slaves, under the leadership of Madison Washington, seize the ship taking them from Richmond to the New Orleans market and sail to freedom in Nassau.

Martin R. Delany (1812–1885) published a more overtly revolutionary novel. Lacking style but exploring new substance, *Blake; or, The Huts of America* (1859–1862) argues the necessity of revolution; it is a sweeping melodrama with Cuba on the verge of insurrection and the American South also poised for rebellion. The links Delany makes between Cuba and the South emphasize the international perspective precipitated by African Americans' displacement and disenfranchisement. Delany spent much of his life exploring the possibilities of emigration.

Frances E. W. Harper (1825–1911), one of the best-known abolitionist speakers and writers, receives credit as the first African American woman to publish a short story, "The Two Offers" (1859), in the *Anglo-American Magazine.* This piece focuses on the fulfillment of a woman's life dedicated to social goals and the less-predictable outcome of a decision to marry. However, during the 1850s, Harper was better known as an antislavery speaker and poet, having published *Poems on Miscellaneous Subjects* (1854). Harper's early poems portray a belief that remained consistent in her career, that readers can improve their lives through the inspiration and instruction of art. This first volume included antislavery poems and poems about ordinary people, many of them women, behaving heroically; "Eliza Harris," "A Mother's Heroism," and "The Slave Mother" share these qualities.

In the grim decades following the Civil War, Harper employed both lyric and epic forms to portray the transition from slavery to freedom, highlight themes from the temperance and feminist movements, and explore African American identity. Harper published *Moses: A Story of the Nile* (1869), an epic poem appropriating biblical sources to parallel African American liberation, and *Sketches of Southern Life* (1872), dramatic monologues featuring the folk voice of Aunt Chloe; *The Sparrow's Fall and Other Poems* (1894); *Atlanta Offering: Poems* (1895); *Martyr of Alabama and Other Poems* (1895); and *Poems* (1895).

Frances Foster's striking "rediscovery" of three Harper novels in the *Christian Recorder* has introduced new ways to understand the nature of fiction and readership during the Reconstruction and post-Reconstruction period. *Minnie's Sacrifice* (1867–68), *Sowing and Reaping* (1876–77), and *Trial and Triumph* (1888) join "The Two Offers" (1859) and *Iola Leroy* (1892) to constitute the body of Harper's fiction. These novels use the melodramatic and sentimental modes of popular fiction to introduce the politics of race reform, temperance, and women's issues. Closely allied in theme to her poetry and journalism, these works not only invite reform, both personal and public, but also appropriate biblical themes and elements of plantation fiction to protest the Jim Crow South.

Landmarks in the publication of poetry during the midcentury include a significant volume, *Les Cenelles* (1845), edited by Armand Lanusse and published in French in New Orleans. The work, which contains eighty-five poems by seventeen free Louisiana Creole authors, including Victor Sejour, is the first African American anthology.

Another experimenter with lyric and epic forms, especially with the long narrative poem fashionable during this period, is Albery Allson Whitman (1851–1901). A minister and Rousseauistic romantic about man and nature, Whitman presents the heroic history of both African Americans and Indians in forms and contexts deeply influenced by the English literary tradition. Publishing between 1872 and 1901, Whitman's best-known work is *The Rape of Florida* (1884) in Spenserian stanzas.

Ohio-born Paul Laurence Dunbar (1872–1906) replaced Harper as the most important poet by the end of the century. Often viewed as a social accommodationist in his dialect poetry depicting southern African American folk traditions, Dunbar was greatly influenced by the pre-emancipation tales of his parents and therefore addressed many southern themes. Praised by William Dean Howells, Dunbar developed an extensive white readership for his best-known volumes *Majors and Minors* (1895) and *Lyrics of Lowly Life* (1896). He published eleven volumes of poetry. Whether he uncritically trafficked in stereotypes or brought alive the subversive energy of folk sensibility, he produced poems that almost everyone recognizes, for instance, "We Wear the Mask" (1895) and "Sympathy" (1899). Less known for his fiction, Dunbar published both short stories and novels from 1898 until 1903. Though much of his fiction is discounted as reinscribing racial stereotypes from plantation fiction, his final novel, *The Sport of the Gods* (1903), has gained regard as an unblinking examination of the African American northern migration.

Dunbar's Louisiana-born wife, Alice Moore Dunbar-Nelson (1875–1935), was also a poet, but her prose is far more distinguished. Identified with the local-color tradition that dominated U.S. literature at the end of the century and included white plantation fiction, Dunbar-Nelson evades the color line with racially ambiguous characters in her two early collections of short stories and poetry, *Violets and Other Tales* (1895) and *The Goodness of St. Rocque and Other Stories* (1899). Her romantic themes and poetic language explore the constricted class and gender roles in the Creole culture of her native New Orleans. Her later work as educator, journalist, and diarist conveys far more activist attitudes toward race, women's rights, and sexuality.

Striving to capture a broad African American readership, Sutton E. Griggs (1872–1933) circulated his novels through publishing companies he established in Nashville and Memphis. A Baptist minister by profession, Griggs, on balance, advocated a course of political moderation on race issues; however, he created in his melodramatic and politically speculative novels important characters who advocated a range of solutions, including an aggressive nationalism. His novels include *Imperium in Imperio* (1899), *Overshadowed* (1901), *Unfettered* (1902), *The Hindered Hand; or, The Reign of the Repressionist* (1905), and *Pointing the Way* (1908).

The African American fiction writer who dominates this period is Charles W. Chesnutt (1858–1932). His two volumes of short stories and three published novels make him one of the most influential writers of the period. His career shows a shift from local-color writing to social realism. In "The Goophered Grapevine" (1887), published in the *Atlantic Monthly,* and the collection of his Uncle Julius stories in *The Conjure Woman* (1899), Chesnutt uses a trickster storyteller to reshape his white readers' understanding of the trials of slavery. *The Wife of His Youth and Other Stories* (1899) explores issues of the color line more directly, examining the consequences of miscegenation, displacement, and racial violence. *The House Behind the Cedars* (1900), *The Marrow of Tradition* (1901), and *The Colonel's Dream* (1905) closely examine passing, white supremacist violence, and possible social and political solutions to white racism. Chesnutt's active publishing life ended after the last novel because of his disappointment with its reception and sales, although two more novels have been recently published.

Several women writers working in nonfiction prose also figure prominently into the literary record of race relations and interpret the status of the "New South." Victoria Octavia Rogers Albert (1824–c. 1890)—former slave, teacher, and minister's wife—collected the stories of seven courageous former slaves in *The House of Bondage, or Charlotte Brooks and Other Slaves* (1890). This arrangement of oral histories, made more available to white readers through their treatment as tales presented by a thinly fictionalized narrator, was published posthumously in the *Southwestern Christian Advocate* (1890). In *Reminiscences of My Life in Camp* (1902) Suzie King Taylor (1848–1912) also contributes to the changing representation of women, recording her work as nurse, cook, and teacher to African American troops fighting for the Union in South Carolina. *A Voice from the South by a Black Woman from the South* (1892) by Anna Julia Cooper (1858–1964) addresses the role of African American women in the post-Reconstruction South, in a social document arguing the centrality of women to the culture. Ida B. Wells-Barnett (1862–1931), in the journalistic tradition established by Harper, conducted a newspaper campaign against lynching, resulting in the pamphlet publication of *Southern Horrors: Lynch Law in All Its Phases* (1892), *A Red Record: Tabulated Statistics and Alleged Causes of Lynching in the United States, 1892–1893–1894* (1895), and *Mob Rule in New Orleans* (1900).

The most prominent public African American figure at the close of the century, Booker T. Washington (1856–1915) published more than twenty books between 1896 and 1913. The most famous of these, his postwar slave narrative, *Up From Slavery* (1901), followed a ghost-written autobiography, *The Story of My Life and Work* (1900), far less known. Recording his rise from poverty and slavery in West Virginia and his devotion to the improvement of his race, Washington, in *Up From Slavery,* hoped to reach a wide readership and increase his resources at Tuskegee Institute. White readers enthusiastically received his self-effacing story and most favored the type of vocational training that Washington advocated. The famous Cotton States Exposition speech appears in the volume, a record of Washington's astute ability to exercise political power through a strategy of compromise.

W. E. B. Du Bois (1868–1963) offered the most memorable counterargument to Washington's political strategies in *The Souls of Black Folk* (1903). As champion of liberal arts and civil rights, this ground-breaking scholar of the African American experience created a defining text in the African American tradition. *The Souls of Black Folk* fuses autobiography with social analysis in fourteen memorable essays designed to capture the art and pain of African American life and its "double consciousness." Openly attacking Washington's position on vocational education and political accommodation, Du Bois's work provided new ground for the development of African American artists, intellectuals, and civil activists. He responded to the deep economic and racial crises of the South in two other famous works: his poem, "A Litany of Atlanta" (1906), recording violence against African Americans in the city where he made his home; and a novel, *The Quest of the Silver Fleece* (1911), presenting the exploitative capitalism of the southern cotton industry.

A second figure whose literary career spanned the turn of the century through the Harlem Renaissance, James Weldon Johnson (1871–1938), not only acknowledged the influence of Paul Laurence Dunbar but also created work that looked forward to the themes of the 1920s. Poet, statesman, lawyer, journalist, lyricist, novelist, anthologist, and activist, Johnson is best known as author of the anthem "Lift Every Voice and Sing" (1900). He brought closure to the writing of the Nadir and marked the way for the Harlem Renaissance with the anonymous publication of *The Autobiography of an Ex-Coloured Man* (1912). This work brings past and future together in its artful combining of the slave-narrative tradition with the psychological and social realism of the novel and the aesthetics of ragtime.

Anne Bradford Warner

See also African American Literature, 1919 to Present; Douglass, Frederick; Novel, 1820 to 1865; Plantation Fiction; Slave Narrative; Trickster; Washington, Booker T.

William L. Andrews, Frances Smith Foster, and Trudier Harris, eds., *The Oxford Companion to African American Literature* (1997); William L. Andrews, *To Tell a Free Story* (1986); Benjamin Brawley, ed., *Early Negro American Writers* (1935); Frances Smith Foster, Introduction, *Minnie's Sacrifice, Sowing and Reaping, Trial and Triumph* (1994), and *Written by Herself* (1993); Hugh Gloster, *Negro Voices in American Fiction* (1948); Blyden Jackson, *A History of Afro-American Literature*, Vol. I (1989); Joan Sherman, *Invisible Poets: Afro-Americans of the Nineteenth Century* (1974); Eric J. Sundquist, *To Wake the Nations* (1993).

AFRICAN AMERICAN LITERATURE, 1919 TO PRESENT

The year 1919 is etched in black history because of the ending of World War I and the ensuing mass migration of African Americans from southern farms to northern tenements. It also inaugurated modern African American literature, and specifically the Harlem Renaissance. African American literature may be conveniently charted in four segments: the Harlem Renaissance, 1920–1940; Realism and Naturalism, 1940–1960; the Black Arts Movement and Civil Struggles, 1960–70; and Literature of Redemption and Survival, 1970–present.

The Harlem Renaissance remains a key period in African American literary history, particularly the magnet years of 1920 to 1929. A number of factors led to a sudden influx of blacks into Harlem, marking its subsequent emergence as a segregated "city-within-the-city" of New York. In both Europe and America, the First World War destabilized whole populations. People sought a cohesive sense of self and the means to rediscover or reinvent a national, racial, or ethnic identity. African American soldiers returning from Europe refused to acquiesce to American racism. Race riots across America during 1919 bore out this fact. Believing in the myth of the North as the Promised Land, southern blacks fled the South en masse from 1910 through the 1920s, in what is called the Great Migration. The exodus took the majority to northern urban centers, notably Chicago, Detroit, and New York City.

Harlem, above all, became especially densely populated in the 1920s with black immigrants, including writers, artists, and musicians. They influenced Harlem's development of a glittering, carefree ambiance, attracting a following of both black and white patrons lured by inter- and intracultural activities promoting the "Negro" as the "exotic," "primitive," or "Africanized" Other. Harlem came to represent the dazzling "Jazz Age" to whites, but to blacks it was the center of the "New Negro Movement." Consumers were especially drawn to black culture because of promotion campaigns waged by Manhattan-based radio and record businesses, clubs, restaurants, and Broadway theaters. All of these industries influenced the black labor force, the entertainment offerings, and the black and white clientele who flowed in and out of Harlem.

The South and its images of plantation life also re-emerged in New York because of the presence of African Americans. Some Harlem clubs adopted southern names, such as the Cotton Club and Bamville Club, but Barrons, Connie's Inn, Small's Paradise, and the Savoy were equally popular. All operated under black or white ownerships for their racially specific clientele. Deep South ragtime, blues, and jazz provided by migrant big-band leaders from James Reese Europe to Louis Armstrong, Cab Calloway, and Duke Ellington or records by Ma Rainey and Bessie Smith blared everywhere. Plays with all-black casts, such as *Shuffle Along* and *Chocolate Dandies,* ran on Broadway. Black vaudeville actors performed in theaters, nightclubs, and movie houses both downtown and in Harlem. All of these activities mobilized consumers who released their energies in dances like the "Cakewalk," "Black Bottom," or "Charleston."

Not all migrants, however, arrived in New York or Harlem by accident. Some writers, artists, and musicians answered the call in 1923 of W. E. B. Du Bois, charter member of the National Association for the Advancement of Colored People and founding editor of its magazine, *Crisis,* in which he announced a national campaign to create a new black identity. He was joined in his endeavors by Charles Johnson, founding editor of *Opportunity,* the organ of the National Urban League, and Alain Locke, Johnson's disciple, who became "dean" of the "New Negro" intellectuals. Together, the three writers attracted, groomed, and promoted young talent and published it in their various books, journals, and magazines.

Black writers thrived in this intellectual atmosphere, lending their voices to the recovery and rediscovery of the "Negro" in familiar, "exotic," or newly defined forms. The best-known of these writers were Jean Toomer, Langston Hughes, Zora Neale Hurston, Countee Cullen, and Claude McKay. The list includes Sterling Brown, Wallace Thurman, James Weldon Johnson, Nella Larsen, Gwendolyn Bennett, Arna Bontemps, Eric Walrond, George S. Schuyler, Rudolph Fisher, Jessie Fauset, and Walter White, to name a few. Toomer gained national prominence for his re-envisioning of the slave experience as a redemptive process in *Cane*; Langston Hughes captured the movement by his prolific poetry and prose validating blues and jazz music as integral to black literature.

Du Bois's "Talented Tenth" of African American intellectuals forged a new identity for blacks within American culture. They turned out serious and comedic novels, short stories, poems, plays, biographies, and autobiographies. Most wrote in conventional literary forms; others chose the vernacular language of the masses. Sterling Brown, Langston Hughes, and Zora Neale Hurston validated traditions of the "folk"; Nella Larsen and Jessie Fauset exposed feminist issues and satirized the petite bourgeoisie. Thematically, the authors explored the dilemma of the hybrid African American gifted with a "double consciousness" but conflicted on issues of race, class, and/or gender. Toomer was praised for synthesizing both "low" and "high" art in *Cane* (1923) and for treating unconventional sex tastefully, but Claude McKay was condemned for venerating the "lowly life" habits of the urban black criminal subculture in *Home to Harlem* (1928). Wallace Thurman braved censure as well by portraying homosexuality in his novels. As a group, the writers endorsed the physical or psychological journey back to southern roots in American slavery as necessary for the Negro's redemption. They also reprised slave music, making gospel, ragtime, blues, and jazz integral tropes in literature. Lynching became a common topic because of its frequency in the South, and Europe was perceived as a plausible haven from American racism. Despite the glitter and optimism of the Harlem Renaissance, the 1929 stock market crash signaled the movement's demise. Few black artists and writers were wealthy or became rich from their endeavors, and most depended upon white patrons, such as Carl Van Vechten and Charlotte Mason, to subsidize their art. Moreover, Harlem itself had a tawdry side that contributed to the erosion of the Harlem Renaissance. Illicit booze, drugs, prostitution, and high rents were the norm. Black writers recognized this decadent side of Harlem and continually exposed its corrosive effects through the recursive motif of "disease" in their works.

The Depression cast a sobering shadow over black artists, and their works took a pessimistic turn. Claude McKay's protest poem "If We Must Die," responding to the race riots of 1919, reprised the nineteenth-century militancy of David Walker and set the tone for black protest literature that began in the 1930s. The economic fallout shifted the eyes of America from the elegant lifestyles of the rich to the deplorable lives of the outcast poor. Problems of African Americans remained, but writers of the 1930s took a different approach to resolutions, highlighting black-white racial conflicts. Nevertheless, modernist writing in which Renaissance authors took a passive-aggressive approach to resolving American racism still prevailed. This is exemplified by Hurston in her novel *Their Eyes Were Watching God* (1937).

From 1940 to 1960, realistic and naturalistic writing dominated black creative expressions, inclusive of those writers who claimed not to be disciples of "protest literature." Richard Wright became dominant in black literature and overshadowed those who came after him. Forging a theory of literature in "Blueprint for Negro Writing" (1937), Wright also deliberately quashed the apologetic and servile tone of the Harlem Renaissance writers, espousing instead a candid, aggressive approach to racial issues. It was he who took the predictable plot device of binary oppositions underscoring naturalistic writing to a height never before reached by a black writer. Whereas Claude McKay in the twenties and Langston Hughes in the thirties had only flirted with Russian premises, Wright made Communism avowedly the social salvation for African Americans. At the same time, Wright disparaged Zora Neale Hurston for her apolitical texts. His novel *Native Son* (1940) and autobiography *Black Boy* (1945) cemented Wright's activist aesthetics; his photographic text *12 Million Black Voices* (1941) showed how documentaries served as sociopolitical literature. Complementing leftist and nonleftist writers exposing the plights of the Jew, Indian, or poor white as the outcast American, Wright inserted the African American's voice. At the same time, he erased the comic minstrel face of the blacks peopling the American literary landscape and inserted the image of the new, angry black in its place.

Other black writers were attracted to the sociological approach to literature, and many, unfortunately, became classified as disciples of the "Wrightean School of Naturalism." This ill-placed labeling haunted black feminist writer Ann Petry, whose novel *The Street* (1946) utilized the plot device of a lone black female single parent trapped in a hostile, black-versus-white world. Through the 1960s, other naturalistic novelists included William Attaway, *Blood on the Forge* (1939); Chester Himes, *If He Hollers Let Him Go* (1945); William Demby, *Beetle Creek* (1950); and John A. Williams, *Captain Blackman* (1972). In drama, Lorraine Hansberry's *A Raisin in the Sun* (1959) and Louis Peterson's *Take a Giant Step* (1953) illustrated the bleak racial conditions impeding blacks. In the short story, James Baldwin's "Sonny's Blues" (1957) and Mary

Elizabeth Vroman's "See How They Run" (1953) also painted tragic or grotesque worlds.

James Baldwin and Ralph Ellison rebelled against their literary mentor Wright by publishing essays castigating his "protest literature." At the same time, Baldwin and Ellison proceeded to illustrate their indebtedness to him. Ellison's masterpiece, *Invisible Man* (1952), still invoked the "protest" style, but it also voiced a constrained racio-political temperament and celebrated cultural lore to situate Ellison in the modernist camp. Baldwin, while embracing modernist traditions in his novel *Go Tell It on the Mountain* (1953), also inserted a protest vein into the biblical thematics of his novels and essays.

A third literary era, the Black Arts Movement and Civil Struggles, 1960–1970, lent itself to the religious, political, social, and economic platforms of Martin Luther King Jr., Andrew Young, Malcolm X, Huey Newton, Eldridge Cleaver, and Angela Davis, who shaped the Civil Rights Movement. The 1960s in many ways reprised the aggressive voice asserted by Richard Wright, even though he had fled abroad to Paris in 1946 to escape America's racism (as eventually did James Baldwin and Chester Himes). Larry Neal and Amiri Baraka (formerly Leroi Jones) spearheaded the literary activist side of the struggle for human rights, but it was Baraka in the theater and in poetry who most clearly seized vocal domain. His militant feminist counterpart in poetry came to be Nikki Giovanni. Together, black writers across the country gave their pens and voices in a steady refrain to declare a cultural manifesto of black self-empowerment and self-love not dependant upon white majority approval. They decreed blackness as the way of the new world. Poets who led the cry for freedom included Sonia Sanchez, Mari Evans, Sterling Plumpp, Carolyn Rogers, Alice Walker, Haki Madhubuti, and Pinkie Gordon Lane.

Black writers also developed theoretical premises for art with the corresponding message that literature was to be for and about black people and the vernacular of the masses its medium of expression. Stephen Henderson's *Understanding the New Black Poetry* (1972) set guidelines for poets, and Addison Gayle's collection of essays *The Black Aesthetic* (1971) assembled the theoretical premises of Hoyt Fuller, Houston Baker Jr., and Gayle, Baraka, and Neal on black art. Africa became romanticized as the ancestral home, and African dress, hairstyles, and names reshaped the "New Negro" of the 1920s into the "Afro-American" of the 1960s. Across America, people grappled with the new, militant black voice as writers threw words like daggers and javelins to show America in unflinching terms that they would achieve equality by any means necessary. Originally restrained writers such as Gwendolyn Brooks also adopted a new militancy, while rising poets, novelists, dramatists, and essayists such as Audre Lorde, Ed Bullins, John A. Williams, Ishmael Reed, Adrienne Kennedy, John O. Killens, Paule Marshall, June Jordan, and Ernest Gaines assailed elements of American racism impeding a wholesome black identity.

With all of its efforts, however, the Black Arts Movement, like its counterpart Civil Rights movement, revealed its failings on matters of gender equity by the end of the 1960s. Even though passage of the 1964 Civil Rights Act barred discrimination based upon race, creed, religion, or national origin in public facilities and institutions, women in general and black women in particular were still invisible people. At all levels of religious, sociopolitical, and economic activity, black women remained second-class citizens in the Black Arts Movement and in the organizations of the women's movement. A little-known one-act play by Sonia Sanchez, *The Bronx Is Next* (1968), foreshadowed the revolt of black women against white and black male misogyny and white female subjugation, and predicted their rise to power.

The era of Literature of Redemption and Survival that encapsulates the 1970s to 1990s both begins and concludes on a black feminist note. The era brought publication of Ntozake Shange's choreopoem *four colored girls who have considered suicide when the rainbow is enuf* (1975), Michele Wallace's *Black Macho and The Myth of the Superwoman* (1978), and Alice Walker's *The Color Purple* (1983). The works of these three African American women writers confirmed Sonia Sanchez's prediction of black female supremacy. Their names dominated the 1970s and 1980s as they published works exposing the new enemy, the black male. Black sisterhood, self-validation, and emancipation became the subject matter of black feminist writers and critics. Poet and novelist Alice Walker seized the platform from Nikki Giovanni. She, in turn, was dethroned in the mid-1980s by Toni Morrison. Morrison's *The Bluest Eye* (1970), Maya Angelou's autobiographical *I Know Why the Caged Bird Sings* (1970), Gayl Jones's novel *Corregidora* (1975), and Gloria Naylor's novel *The Women of Brewster Place* (1982) assailed black men for their cruelty to black women, but Morrison refused to abandon hope in a world of

satisfying heterosexual bonding as had Walker and Shange. Walker eventually revised her views on black men in her autobiographical collection of essays entitled *In Search of Our Mothers' Gardens* (1983). In this work, she forged a "womanist theory" of black feminism embracing a shared dialogue between black women and men. She also wrote movingly of her recovery of Zora Neale Hurston's unmarked grave. Walker's research influenced the elevation of Hurston as the foremother of black feminist thought. Black female power was again evident in 1993 when Toni Morrison became the first African American woman to win the Nobel Prize for Literature.

Although black feminist writers contributed ideas to critical theory in the 1970s, black literary critics also helped shape the discourse. Barbara Smith's essay "Towards a Black Feminist Criticism" (1982) proffered embryonic ideas detailing a black female consciousness that would be completed in 1991 with Patricia Hills Collins's *Black Feminist Thought*. Black feminist critics bell hooks, Deborah McDowell, Mae Henderson, and Hortense Spillers became powerful voices, along with black males Henry Louis Gates Jr., Houston Baker Jr., and Robert Stepto. It was Gates's book *The Signifying Monkey* (1988), however, that demolished the 1960s race-based theory of literature promoted in Gayles's *The Black Aesthetic*.

Gates and his followers entered a 1980s debate on what defined "the canon" and/or traditional literature in the academy, which resulted in the production of new anthologies of black literature. Publication in 1971 of *Cavalcade*, an anthology edited by Arthur P. Davis and J. Saunders Redding, had revoiced the Harlem Renaissance methodology of Alain Locke's *The New Negro* (1925). *The New Cavalcade* of 1991 was edited by Davis, Redding, and Joyce Ann Joyce. Gates's ten-year effort, however, stilled arguments in the academy over the nonexistence of a literary canon in African American culture when he oversaw publication of *The Norton Anthology of African American Literature* (1997).

Despite critical theory holding sway in the academy during the past ten years, creative writers have continued to be productive, including several major black male writers. Ishmael Reed and Charles Johnson were 1998 recipients of prestigious MacArthur fellowships. Even though black male writers have not received as much critical attention as black women writers in the last decade, they have continued to produce prize-winning poems, plays, novels, short stories, biographies, and autobiographies: Ishmael Reed, *Mumbo Jumbo* (1972); John Edgar Wideman, *Hurry Home* (1972); August Wilson, *Ma Rainey's Black Bottom* (1982); Ernest Gaines, *A Gathering of Old Men* (1992) and *A Lesson Before Dying* (1997). And while African American women writers still hold a prominent place in American and African American literary discourse, the total cultural voice of the African American remains strong as the new millennium begins. The Literature of Redemption and Survival by both black male and female writers continues to engage the global literary consciousness.

Virginia Whatley Smith

See also African American Literature, Beginnings to 1919; Ellison, Ralph; Harlem Renaissance; Hurston, Zora Neale; Neo-Slave Narrative; Wright, Richard.

Arthur P. Davis, J. Saunders Redding, and Joyce Ann Joyce, eds., *The New Cavalcade: African American Writing from 1760 to the Present*, Vols. I and II (1991); Henry Louis Gates Jr. and Nellie Y. McKay, gen. eds., *The Norton Anthology of African American Literature* (1997); Thomas J. Hennessey, *From Jazz to Swing: African American Jazz Musicians and Their Music, 1890–1935* (1994); Alain Locke, ed., *The New Negro* (1925); Gilbert Osofsky, *Harlem: The Making of a Ghetto—Negro New York, 1890–1930* (2nd ed.; 1996); Steven Watson, *The Harlem Renaissance: Hub of African American Culture, 1920–1930* (1995); Cary D. Wintz, ed., *The Harlem Renaissance 1920–1940* (7 vols.; 1996).

AFRICAN AMERICAN SPIRITUALS

"They that walked in darkness sang songs in the olden days." With these words, W. E. B. Du Bois begins his paean to the "Sorrow Songs" in the concluding chapter of *The Souls of Black Folk* (1903). Du Bois's essay was one of the first full analyses of the spirituals. His study is important for its stress on the songs' roots in the slave experience and on their incorporation of African theology and music creatively blended with Christian musical and doctrinal forms learned in slavery. The African American spiritual reflects the slaves' love of God and identification with biblical lore; their deep desire for freedom; their judgment against those who oppress the weak and powerless; their suffering and mourning because of the loss of home and kin; their covert and overt rebellion against the master (calls to rise up as well as calls to "steal away"). Although anthologies of spirituals began to appear in the immediate post–Civil War period, one school of thought (which includes folklorist Zora Neale Hurston) protests that attempts to transcribe the songs distort their meaning. It is now generally agreed that spirituals were communal compositions involving dance, call and response, and spontaneous extensions and reworkings, and that recording them accurately is therefore difficult, if not impossible. Du Bois himself included notations of the spirituals' melodies, without accompanying words, as chapter headings for *The Souls of Black Folk*.

In 1908 James Weldon Johnson took up the issue of African American ownership of the spirituals in his poem "O Black and Unknown Bards," and his portrait of the song leader "Singing Johnson" in *Autobiography of an Ex-Coloured Man* (1912) is a scholarly as well as dramatic depiction of how the songs were created as they were performed. With his brother, J. Rosamond Johnson, a gifted composer, he published two collections of American Negro spirituals (1925 and 1926), attempting to retain the songs' "primitive swing" in the arrangements. In long introductory prefaces to each volume, he dissects the musicology and the poetry of the texts, emphasizing the biblical roots of the subject matter, the African roots of the rhythms, and the African American development of such elements as harmony and community. He remarks that the singers of the spirituals took a biblical text such as the Crucifixion story and "fused into it their very own pathos." Johnson's most important collection of poetry, *God's Trombones: Seven Negro Sermons in Verse* (1927), found its inspiration in the vernacular language and rhythms of the spirituals, especially the song "Let My People Go."

Spirituals functioned in many different ways for slaves in the American South. The slave narrator Frederick Douglass insisted in his 1845 *Narrative* that "every tone was a testimony against slavery," and many ethnographers have stressed the subversive militancy of the songs. Lyrics such as "Before I'll Be a Slave," "Steal Away," "Go Down, Moses" ("Let My People Go"), and "Didn't My Lord Deliver Daniel" are demands for deliverance and justice and calls to resistance, including escape. Yet the songs also insist upon a sacred world view, as Lawrence Levine has noted. In Levine's study *Black Culture and Black Consciousness* (1977), he insists that "the most persistent single image the slave songs contain is that of the chosen people." Songs such as "Heaven Shall Be My Home," "I Really Do Believe," "I Walk the Heavenly Road," and "Go Tell It on the Mountain" affirm both religious faith and a vision of self-acceptance as children of God. Many lyrics prove Douglass's statement that the slave sings to "represent the sorrows of his heart." "Sometimes I Feel Like a Motherless Child," "All My Troubles, Lord," and "Nobody Knows the Troubles I've Seen" identify the slave's suffering and search, through God, for comfort and release.

The spirituals were first gathered into a collection by white folklorists William Francis Allen, Charles Pickard Ware, and Lucy McKim Garrison, who published *Slave Songs of the United States* in 1867. The spirituals as songs were popularized most effectively by the famous Fisk University choral group, the Jubilee Singers, who began to perform complex arrangements in concerts both in America and abroad in the early 1870s. Spirituals, along with work songs and "shouts," became the basis for the development of later African American musical forms, particularly the gospel tradition that developed in the urban black church beginning in the early twentieth century.

Beyond their religious and musical influence, the spirituals are also an important form of literature. Erskine Peters, analyzing their content in *Lyrics of the Afro-American Spiritual* (1993), enumerates nine categories of themes: sorrow, alienation, and desolation; consolation and faith; resistance and defiance; deliverance; jubilation and triumph; judgment and reckoning; regeneration; spiritual progress; and transcendence.

In southern literature, spirituals have functioned importantly for both white and black writers. Slave narrators like Douglass and early autobiographers like Booker T. Washington, Johnson, and Du Bois reflected upon the meaning of the songs for a distinctive African American culture. In his novel *Blake; or The Huts of America* (1859–62), Martin R. Delany, the child of escaped slaves from Virginia, incorporated spirituals, as have later African American novels of the slave experience, such as Margaret Walker's *Jubilee* (1966), Sherley Anne Williams's *Dessa Rose* (1986), Toni Morrison's *Beloved* (1987), and Arna Bontemps's *Black Thunder* (1938; in 1951 Bontemps published a novel about the Jubilee Singers called *Chariot in the Sky*). Richard Wright calls upon associations with the spirituals in *Uncle Tom's Children* (1938, 1940); one story in the collection, "Down by the Riverside," takes its title from a spiritual, and the story "Long Black Song" makes ironic reference to the hopeful lyrics of "I'll Be There." Ralph Ellison also refers ironically to spirituals in *Invisible Man,* as his protagonist hears the orchestra at his school play Dvořák's *New World* Symphony but

unconsciously translates this Euro-Americanized version of spiritual melodies into "Swing Low, Sweet Chariot." James Baldwin's novel *Go Tell It On the Mountain* (1953) conducts an intense examination of African American religion, using the lyrics and rhythms of the spirituals. Jean Toomer's *Cane* (1923) connects the spirituals to the potential of the African American aesthetic vision in one of the Harlem Renaissance's masterworks, yet he felt that their power was dwindling, part of the "swan song" of black folk life that he, as an artist, must try to capture in a new form.

White southerners in antebellum times often remarked upon the slave songs, mistakenly inferring from them the general happiness of their chattels. William John Grayson, in his poem "The Hireling and the Slave," interpreted the slaves' singing at church ("They love to sing of Jordan's shore, where sorrows cease, and toil is known no more") as evidence of their contentment, as did John Pendleton Kennedy, whose northern white protagonist remarks in *Swallow Barn* (1832) that "the women sing from morning till night," proof of his judgment that the slaves' "gayety of heart is constitutional." In the plantation fiction of the Reconstruction and post-Reconstruction period, writers such as Irwin Russell, Thomas Nelson Page, and Joel Chandler Harris often called attention to slaves' singing in order to argue for happy familial relations between the races in antebellum times. Mark Twain remembered his mother listening to an orphaned boy slave's singing and feeling some relief that the song meant he was not completely unhappy.

Not until William Faulkner used the words of one of the most famous spirituals, "Go Down, Moses," as a title for his collection of stories (*Go Down, Moses,* 1945), did a white southern author fully acknowledge the searing indictment of slavery contained in the spirituals. One interesting note concerning William Styron's portrayal of slavery in *The Confessions of Nat Turner* (1967) is that his character Nat, the revolutionary black slave leader, several times recalls hearing whites singing their hymns (including "Joy to the World"), but never does Styron show Nat as having any awareness of the spiritual tradition. In her novel *Can't Quit You, Baby* (1988), Ellen Douglas offers much more sensitive treatment of the heritage that the spirituals offer to a black character.

The spirituals, from their origins to their reworkings in later literary and musical forms, have powerfully rendered the realities of African American existence. They cover a wide range of complex experiences, and their appearance in southern literature has created many different effects, some ironic, some tragic, some brilliant.

Lucinda H. MacKethan

See also African American Folk Culture; Blues, The; Getting Happy; Gospel Music; Neo-Slave Narrative; Slave Narrative; Whoopin'.

Dean J. Epstein, *Sinful Tunes and Spirituals: Black Folk Music to the Civil War* (1977); Joyce Marie Jackson, "The Changing Nature of Gospel Music: A Southern Case Study," *African American Review* 29.2: 185–200; Lawrence Levine, *Black Culture and Black Consciousness* (1977); John Lovell Jr., *Black Song: The Forge and the Flame* (1972); Erskine Peters, *Lyrics of the Afro-American Spiritual* (1993); John Roberts, *From Trickster to Badman* (1989).

AFRICAN AMERICAN VERNACULAR ENGLISH (AAVE)

Known also by a succession of names from Black English to Black Vernacular English, Afro-American English, and Ebonics, African American Vernacular English (AAVE) refers collectively to the similar varieties of language used by communities of African Americans throughout English-speaking North America. AAVE is a linguistic system, not a collection of haphazard deviations from a standard English norm. AAVE dialects have their own patterns of organization with their own rules of sound combination and verb phrases and their own vocabulary and performance traditions. The description *vernacular* indicates that AAVE is almost always oral, rarely used in writing except in literary or other creative works intended to convey the sounds of speech.

Few, if any, specific linguistic features are heard only in AAVE and not in other varieties of English. For example, the absence of /r/ after a vowel in a word like *here* and monophthongal /a/ in a word like *right* are ordinary pronunciations for all races and classes in parts of the South. Yet in AAVE, features shared with other dialects are used more frequently or consistently and thus become associated with African American usage.

Several features involve consonants. The interdental fricative sounds spelled *th* are often pronounced as /t/ in words like *think* and *thing*, /d/ in words like *the* and *they*, /f/ in words like *three* and *both*, and /v/ in words like *brother*. The liquid sounds /l/ and /r/ tend to disappear or alter, as in words like *help* and *heart* and in the final unstressed syllable spelled *-er* or *-or* but pronounced /ə/, as in *summer* or *doctor*. The tendency in AAVE to avoid clusters of consonants leads to the omission of consonant sounds that are grammatically significant in written English. Thus a word like *cook* requires the creation of the cluster /ks/ for noun plural *cooks*, possessive *cook's*, or third-person singular present tense of the verb *cooks* and requires the creation of the cluster /kt/ for past tense or passive participle *cooked*. AAVE, which systematically eliminates sequences of consonants, often does not signal such grammatical distinctions, and the inflected forms all sound the same as the base *cook*. However, the most noticeable difference in sound between AAVE and other varieties of English is distinctive pitch, intonation, and rhythm—the characteristics of language hardest to isolate and describe.

AAVE diverges from other varieties in use of the verb *be* and in distinctive developments of the verbal category aspect. Neither the main verb *be* nor the auxiliary verb *be* before a verb ending *-ing* need be expressed. For example, *they crazy* and *they dancing* are well-formed AAVE sentences showing present time but not habitual aspect. The use of the invariant form *be* in these sentences—*they be crazy* and *they be dancing*—indicates a habitual or repeated state or action. A stressed occurrence of *been* shows remote time, as in *we been lived in Texas*. Completed action uses auxiliary *done*, as in *she done told me the truth*.

Words and expressions used by AAVE speakers in the 1990s are collected in Geneva Smitherman's *Black Talk* (1994). Many have been adopted into other vernacular dialects. For example, *def* (excellent); *dis* (show disrespect); *go down* (happen); *homey* (person from the neighborhood); and *phat* (excellent) are all used in the casual speech of American adolescents throughout the nation.

No list of the features of the sound system, verbal syntax, or vocabulary can do justice to AAVE. AAVE is the outcome of a long oral heritage of using quick-witted, picturesque, rhythmic language to earn status in the community. Performance style is a crucial component. Some verbal interchanges have become ritualized—for example, rapping, signifying, testifying, playing the dozens, and woofing. Internationally popular rap music is a commercial development of spontaneous rapping practiced in urban African American neighborhoods.

African American performance styles go beyond verbal games to preaching and public speaking. Many

African Americans in national public life use the rhythms and cadences of AAVE combined with the rhetorical structures of African American preaching and the grammar of mainstream varieties. Possibly the two best public speakers in the United States in the second half of the twentieth century have been the Reverend Martin Luther King Jr. and the Reverend Jesse Jackson.

AAVE has been a topic of important and intense linguistic research for the past quarter century, though at times social, political, pedagogical, and legal issues as well as methodological differences among scholars have overshadowed description. A conference in 1981 funded by the National Endowment for the Humanities and organized by Michael Montgomery and Guy Bailey focused on the collection and presentation of data. It gave needed coherence to the scholarly study of AAVE and resulted in the influential collection *Language Variety in the South: Perspectives in Black and White* (1986). The work of scholars such as Montgomery and Bailey, John Baugh, Jeutonne Brewer, Ron Butters, William Labov, Salikoko Mufwene, Patricia Nichols, John Rickford, Edgar Schneider, Walt Wolfram, and others has given the study of AAVE a firm foundation.

However, many questions that scholars raise about AAVE are yet to be answered. Is AAVE a creole language in origin with affinities to other creole languages in the Caribbean area? To what extent and in which features does AAVE preserve traces of African languages? What is the relationship between AAVE and Gullah? Are AAVE features traceable to British-English dialects brought to the American colonies? What was the nature and extent of linguistic contact between slaves and English speakers of European ancestry? What is the relationship between southern dialects of American English and AAVE? Is AAVE becoming less similar to other vernacular varieties of American English? What is the role of AAVE in international youth culture?

Connie Eble

See also Accent; Preaching; Speech and Dialect.

Guy Bailey, Natalie Maynor, and Patricia Cukor-Avila, eds., *The Emergence of Black English* (1991); John Baugh, *Black Street Speech* (1983); J. L. Dillard, *Black English* (1972); Marjorie Goodwin, *He-Said-She-Said: Talk as Social Organization Among Black Children* (1990); James B. McMillan and Michael B. Montgomery, *Annotated Bibliography of Southern American English* (1989); Salikoko Mufwene and Nancy Condon, *Africanisms in Afro-American Language Varieties* (1993); Salikoko Mufwene, John R. Rickford, Guy Bailey, and John Baugh, *African American English* (1998); Edgar Schneider, *American Earlier Black English* (1989); Geneva Smitherman, *Talkin and Testifyin* (1977).

AGRARIANS

When Thomas Jefferson wrote Query Nineteen of his *Notes on Virginia* (1787), entitled "The present state of manufacturers, commerce, interior and exterior trade," he fashioned an idea of the yeoman farmer as the mainstay of an agrarian society. Yet the South's agrarians always faced diminishing returns. John Taylor of Caroline, in his *Arator* essays (1813), was one of the early South's most outspoken agrarians, but he mourned that even in his own time, people viewed farming "with horror" and fled it "with joy." Jefferson hailed the American farmers as "the chosen people of God" because they alone exemplified the ideal of self-sufficiency. In the twentieth century, just as the Depression began to affect America's capitalist economy, southern Agrarianism found its strongest champions. Shortly after the Fugitive poets' literary magazine in Nashville ceased publication in 1925, key Fugitives formed the core of a new endeavor, the Agrarian movement. John Crowe Ransom, Donald Davidson, and Allen Tate began plotting a southern manifesto in the latter 1920s because they saw the South at a crucial decision point: either it would recognize and stand by its traditional values or it would be submerged within the aggressive prevailing culture of America, a culture they came to label urban industrialism. The industrial progress touted by New South boosterism was, they and their allies felt, a Trojan horse—it bore a deracinating and dehumanizing materialism, a culture inimical to the time-honored good features of the southern way of life.

An event that stirred the regional awareness of many of those shortly to become Agrarians was the media spectacle surrounding the Scopes trial in Dayton, Tennessee, in 1925. Ransom, Davidson, and other future Agrarians were not fundamentalists, but they found themselves more in sympathy with the simple piety of southern plain folk than with the condescension of the northern press. The ridicule heaped on the old-fashioned faith of a traditional community ignited their southern affinities and turned poets toward polemics. The South, they felt, must be made aware that it possessed a regional heritage that had much to say for itself, and perhaps much to say to the rest of the nation. The situation, both economic and social, called for a manifesto, an openly partisan defense of the southern inheritance against the incursions of a technocratic and materialist modernity.

I'll Take My Stand: The South and the Agrarian Tradition (1930) was that manifesto, a symposium of essays written, as the title page announced, by "Twelve Southerners." These twelve writers and intellectuals were brought together by a conviction that their birthright compelled them to speak out, and they did so in a fiery indictment of American business civilization. Appropriately enough for a book that was more jeremiad than economic prescription, the authors were predominately literary men, many of them significant or soon to be significant in southern letters. The ringleaders—Ransom, Davidson, and Tate—were poets, principals among the Nashville Fugitives active at Vanderbilt University in the first half of the 1920s. A fourth Fugitive, Robert Penn Warren, was recruited, as was another former Vanderbilt student of Ransom's, the novelist-to-be Andrew Lytle. The two contributors without ties to Vanderbilt—the expatriate Imagist poet John Gould Fletcher and the drama critic and novelist Stark Young—were writers whose established reputations lent extra weight to the project. Other essayists included English professor John Donald Wade, historian Frank Lawrence Owsley, psychologist Lyle Lanier, political scientist Herman Clarence Nixon, and journalist Henry Blue Kline.

The unsigned "Statement of Principles" prefacing the symposium was the work of Ransom. Functioning as a general credo, this introduction sharply described the evils of an urban-industrial system: dehumanizing labor, degrading commercialism, exploitation of nature, loss of spirituality, and other ills. The harmonious and venerable alternative, the statement concluded, was an agrarian order, "one in which agriculture is the leading vocation, whether for wealth, for pleasure, or for prestige—a form of labor that is pursued with intelligence and leisure, and that becomes the model to which the other forms approach as well as they may." Ransom also provided the lead essay, a demonstration of the philosophical pedigree of the South's resistance to American progressivist doctrine. From there, the book ranged widely over many topics, though always cohering as a pastoral critique of what the Agrarians saw as the spiritual confusion of modern culture. Young addressed the significance of manners, Owsley

the meaning of the Civil War, Lanier the idea of progress. Davidson inveighed against what an industrial dispensation would do to the arts. Lytle argued that the difference between agriculture and agribusiness is nothing less than the difference between culture and business. Tate, writing on religion, adjured southerners to regain their tradition by act of will. One of the best contributions was not an essay but a portrait, Wade's story of a kinsman whose honorable life bodied forth the ideals of the Agrarian vision.

Despite the common principles voiced in the symposium's introduction, the twelve authors of *I'll Take My Stand* did not in all respects agree with one another. Tate and Warren, for instance, objected to the volume's title phrase from "Dixie," preferring *Tracts Against Communism* as a title with greater polemical value. There were implicit disagreements as well over just what heritage was being invoked. The yeoman South inspired Lytle's Agrarian ideal; an aristocratic South inspired Young's. Tate was motivated by broadly conceived traditionalism, Davidson by patriotic regionalism. Another example of complications within the ranks was Warren's essay on the black southerner's stake in the southern agrarian community, in which Warren argued the need for legal justice and expanded opportunities for African Americans. Even though the essay supported segregation (a position repudiated by Warren's later work), Davidson found the piece far too progressive in tone and wished to suppress it.

I'll Take My Stand generated considerable comment and controversy when it appeared, modest sales notwithstanding. The movement proceeded through the early 1930s with public debates, letters to editors, and many more essays, over sixty in *American Review* alone. A follow-up symposium of sorts appeared in 1936 entitled *Who Owns America?*, a collaboration with like-minded social commentators from other traditions. Eight of the original Agrarians wrote essays for the book, and a new recruit, the literary critic Cleanth Brooks, contributed a piece as well. This volume was nearly the last expression, however, of the campaign spirit of the Agrarian enterprise; the Agrarians were moving on to new commitments and scattering geographically. Ransom, for instance, retreated from the cause to focus on literary criticism and left Vanderbilt in 1937 for Kenyon College in Ohio. Nashville ceased to provide a center of operations for the movement. When Davidson published *The Attack on Leviathan: Regionalism and Nationalism in the United States* in

1938, it was Agrarianism's parting shot as a group movement.

Despite the relatively short life of the Agrarian episode, *I'll Take My Stand* remains a significant document in the story of southern letters, and the Agrarians' critique of modernism remains a strand in the tapestry of southern thought. Intellectual inheritors of Agrarianism, such as Richard Weaver and M. E. Bradford, explored and extended the principles engaged by *I'll Take My Stand,* and the fiftieth anniversary of the original manifesto was celebrated with a new one, by "Fifteen Southerners," published by the University of Georgia Press in 1981. This new symposium, *Why the South Will Survive,* was an affirmation, in the Agrarian spirit, of southern pride and identity. Its afterword was contributed by veteran campaigner Andrew Lytle, who concluded that the original Agrarians had been "better prophets than they knew."

Mark Lucas

See also Fugitives, The; *I'll Take My Stand*; Nashville, Tennessee; Scopes Trial; Vanderbilt University.

Paul K. Conkin, *The Southern Agrarians* (1988); William C. Havard and Walter Sullivan, eds., *A Band of Prophets: The Vanderbilt Agrarians After Fifty Years* (1982); Mark G. Malvasi, *The Unregenerate South: The Agrarian Thought of John Crowe Ransom, Allen Tate, and Donald Davidson* (1997); Louis D. Rubin Jr., *The Wary Fugitives: Four Poets and the South* (1978); Thomas Daniel Young, *Waking Their Neighbors Up: The Nashville Agrarians Rediscovered* (1982).

ALABAMA, LITERATURE OF

To upstate New Yorker Carl Carmer, the state of Alabama was "a strange country." Even before the unsettling 1833 meteor shower that inspired the title of his best-selling 1934 book, it was, he wrote in *Stars Fell on Alabama,* an "unreal and fated" place, "a land with a spell on it—[and] not a good spell, always." Few if any states have so endured in evoking wide negative image and opinion. H. L. Mencken's scornful "Sahara of the Bozart" label no doubt seemed appropriate for much of the American South in the 1920s, but similarly indicted states like neighboring Georgia and Mississippi have since gained at least literary reprieve. Although the achievements of Alabama literature are not as well known or expressly recognized, the state has a rich literary history and impressive contemporary accomplishment.

Despite one scholar's having discerned a "golden era" prior to 1919, most students of Alabama's cultural history see the major flowerings of literature from the state as occurring after 1920. "Renaissance" is a term used to describe Alabama writing in the closing decades of the twentieth century.

Several important legacies for writers in the state began before official statehood. Sometimes called Alabama's first literary figure, André Penicaut, a chronicler of the early eighteenth-century French presence along the Gulf Coast, was at his best in describing the social life and customs of native inhabitants. Also, if only in a title that wonderfully weds the local and nonlocal, levity and learning, a model of sorts was provided by Lewis Sewall's *The Last Campaign of Sir John Falstaff II, Or, The Hero of the Burnt-Corn Battle. A Serio-Comic Poem* (1815). William Bartram's *Travels* (1791) set a consequential precedent for autobiographical, travel, and nature writing from the state. There came to be a wealth of antebellum travel accounts, many by nonsoutherners journeying the Old Federal Road route (Harriet Martineau, Tyrone Power, Sir Charles Lyell, and Frederick Law Olmsted, for example). Two less-transient sojourners produced books titled *Letters from Alabama.* Anne Newport Royall, whose letters were "On Various Subjects" (1830), later gained notoriety as Washington, D.C.'s original muckraking journalist and the only American ever convicted of being "a common scold." Philip Henry Gosse, the father of Edmund Gosse who worked as a plantation schoolmaster in west Alabama in 1838, proclaimed his epistles to be "Chiefly Relating to Natural History" (1859). A perceptive observer of human society as well, this English naturalist foreshadows two Alabama-born natural scientists and autobiographers, Archie Carr and Edward O. Wilson, who became internationally known more than a century later. Wilson, the winner of two Pulitzer Prizes, begins his memoir *Naturalist* (1994) with a section called "Daybreak in Alabama," its epigraph drawn from Langston Hughes's poem of that title.

Credit for establishing a conventional belles-lettres tradition in the frontier state is usually given to William Russell Smith (1815–1896) and Alexander Beaufort Meek (1814–1865), lifelong friends who were in the first group of students admitted to the University of Alabama in 1831. Smith, called the father of Alabama literature, was a lawyer, judge, and U.S. congressman.

His *College Musings; or, Twigs from Parnassus* (1833) was the first volume of poetry written and published in the state, and his literary magazine *Bachelor's Button* was another first. Despite his devotion to poetry, Smith's most valuable writing today is found in his memoir *Reminiscences of a Long Life* (1889). A. B. Meek became best known for his long poem *The Red Eagle* (1855), a 1,824-line production in varying verse forms about William Weatherford, leader of the Creek Indians during the Alabama wars of 1813. Shorter poems by Meek gained wide notice both regionally and nationally. His "Balaklava" was originally attributed to the English poet Alexander Smith and frequently compared with Tennyson's "Charge of the Light Brigade."

At this time Alabama was also producing a different, more local kind of literature with national and international impact: what now is referred to as Old Southwest humor. Geographically central to this region, Alabama was central, too, to its distinctive writing. Nationally published humorists either born in or with fruitful literary residence in the state were Hardin E. Taliaferro, Kittrell J. Warren, Sol Smith, Joseph M. Field, Thomas Kirkman, John Gorman Barr, Joseph Glover Baldwin, George Washington Harris, and Johnson Jones Hooper. A University of Alabama graduate, Barr (1823–1858) had the fullest biographical and literary association with the state, but the Alabama connections of the better-known Baldwin (1815–1864) and Hooper (1815–1862) were seminal for them. Baldwin gave definition to the whole era with his *The Flush Times of Alabama and Mississippi* (1853). The shifty con man title character of Hooper's *Some Adventures of Captain Simon Suggs* (1845) was immensely popular, the book having at least eleven editions by 1856. This heritage of frolicsome humor and social satire would surface in the stories of some of the state's best writers a century later: William March's "A Memorial to the Slain" and "The Borax Bottle" and Eugene Walter's "The Byzantine Riddle" and "I Love You Batty Sisters."

Hooper and March illustrate that warfare has held perennial attraction for writers in or from Alabama. Hooper utilized certain military campaigns against Native Americans for satire and parody in *Simon Suggs*, and such conflicts before and during the 1830s provided serious literary inspiration for his contemporaries Smith and Meek. Soon the Mexican War would do the same for poets Mirabeau Buonaparte Lamar and Theodore O'Hara, who wrote "The Bivouac of the Dead." The Civil War had perhaps less literary effect than might be expected, or had it in unexpected ways. Confederate veterans Sidney and Clifford Lanier both composed war novels in Montgomery soon after the conflict. Each published in 1867, Clifford's *Thorn-Fruit* is probably superior to his brother's *Tiger-Lilies*. Written before the end of the war but also gaining a northern publisher in 1867 was Mary Anne Cruse's *Cameron Hall: A Story of the Civil War*, which focused on the devastated home front.

So much southern martial and postbellum patriotic verse had a Mobile connection that the city was called the "Capital of Lost Cause Poetry." On the other hand, Union loyalist, former U.S. senator from Alabama, and Mark Twain relative Jeremiah Clemens (1814–1865) authored one of the first Civil War novels to appear in print. Set in North Alabama and published in Philadelphia shortly before his death, the anti-Confederate *Tobias Wilson: A Tale of the Great Rebellion* (1865) was Clemens's fourth novel based on American history and the first in a projected series of novels about life in the South. Alabama was also the setting of actual military duty for two Union soldiers, Ambrose Bierce and George W. Peck, later nationally known writers who made humorous use of that time. Bierce wrote about his U.S. government service in the essays "Four Days in Dixie" and "Way Down in Alabama." Peck's *How Private Geo. W. Peck Put Down the Rebellion* (1887) is a burlesque parody of the exact same kind as J. J. Hooper's Suggs stories—and like Alabama-born Confederate veteran Kittrell J. Warren's *Life and Public Services of an Army Straggler* (1865).

The Civil War continued to be the subject of Alabama fiction in the twentieth century—for example, Andrew Lytle's *The Long Night* (1936) and Perry Lentz's *The Falling Hills* (1967) and *It Must Be Now the Kingdom Coming* (1973). But now there were other wars. *Company K* (1933) by William March is one of the most powerful World War I novels written by an American. Dealing with combat on the Pacific front in World War II are *The Weight of the Cross* (1951) by Robert O. Bowen and *The Right Kind of War* (1992) by John McCormick, both novels, and Eugene B. Sledge's *With the Old Breed at Peleliu and Okinawa* (1981), a memoir. Fiction emerging from the Vietnam War includes Winston Groom's *Better Times Than These* (1978) and Gustav Hasford's *The Short-Timers* (1979). In the late twentieth century, the most prolific, professionally successful writer living in Alabama was Korean War veteran William E. Butterworth, who under such pseudonyms as W. E. B. Griffin wrote war fiction that has sold multi-millions of copies.

Autobiography also has particular 1830s Alabama roots that bore much fruit. Reportedly transcribed by John Greenleaf Whittier, one of the most controversial American slave narratives was *Narrative of James Williams, An American Slave, Who Was for Several Years a Driver on a Cotton Plantation in Alabama* (1838). With transcription assistance, too, but unnoted, *Up From Slavery* (1901) by Tuskegee Institute founder Booker T. Washington became a classic autobiography of the genre. Later in the twentieth century, a striking resurgence of such writing by African Americans occurred. Having modern-day amanuenses for their life stories appearing in the 1970s, 1980s, and 1990s, for example, were Nate Shaw [Ned Cobb], Onnie Lee Logan, Sara Brooks, Sara Rice, J. L. Chesnut, and Rosa Parks—not to mention, then and earlier, such sports greats as Jesse Owens, Leroy "Satchel" Paige, Joe Louis, Willie Mays, Hank Aaron, and Bo Jackson. And, from the 1930s through the 1990s, Angelo Herndon, Hosea Hudson, Angela Davis, James Haskins, Willie Ruff, Ellen Tarry, Deborah McDowell, and Albert Murray did their own autobiographical writing. Not a traditional life story, Murray's *South to a Very Old Place* (1971) is particularly noteworthy.

Another Alabama antebellum literary enterprise does not boast so large a line of descendants. Under professionals such as Noah Ludlow, Solomon Smith, and Joseph M. Field, theater and drama flourished in Alabama communities before the Civil War as it rarely did afterward. Except for Lillian Hellman's use of her mother's relatives from Demopolis as models for characters in *The Little Foxes* (1939) and *Another Part of the Forest* (1946) and Kate Porter Lewis's "Alabama folkplays" produced by the Carolina Playmakers at about the same time, there was little to report regarding Alabama drama or dramatists for a long time. Today, however, the Alabama Shakespeare Festival is one of the nation's finest regional repertory theaters, and its Southern Writers Project has given major playwriting support to state writers Dennis Covington, Randy Hall, Wayne Greenhaw, and Keith Glover.

Most of the chief modes and movements of American fiction during the nineteenth century had Alabama participation. The first novel published in the state, *The Lost Virgin of the South: An Historical Novel, Founded on Facts, Connected With the Indian War in the South, in 1812 to '15* (1833) by "Don Pedro Casender" (actually, either Wiley Connor or Michael

Smith), was a blatant, immoderate imitation of the fiction of such popular northern writers as James Fenimore Cooper, Lydia Maria Child, and Catharine Maria Sedgwick. With Caroline Lee Hentz (1800–1856) and Augusta Jane Evans Wilson (1835–1909) and the so-called domestic sentimental novel, however, Alabama was to play a leading role in the creation of best-selling fiction. Hentz earned popularity with *Aunt Patty's Scrap-Bag* in the 1840s and gained notoriety with *The Planter's Northern Bride* (1854), a transplanted northerner's attempt to picture the South to other parts of the country. Wilson, who published nine novels between 1859 and 1909, had even more phenomenal literary success. Her *Macaria* (1863), like Hentz's *Bride,* was a sectional propagandistic response to Stowe's *Uncle Tom's Cabin,* but her *St. Elmo* (1866) ultimately challenged Stowe's book in a different way. Reaching a million readers in the first four months, influencing the naming of children and commercial products, and later inspiring two movies, *St. Elmo* had sales at the end of the century that were surpassed only by *Uncle Tom's Cabin* and Lew Wallace's *Ben-Hur.* Like Wilson a longtime Mobile resident, another nationally popular novelist at this time was Thomas Cooper De Leon (1839–1914). Considered Alabama's first professional man of letters, De Leon provides an interesting late-century counterpart to William Russell Smith.

A strong legacy of women's writing from Mobile would be realized more widely across the whole state in the twentieth century. Associated with that city also were Octavia Walton LeVert (1835–1909), Mary McNeil Fenollosa (1865–1954), and Amélie Rives (1863–1945). In *The Quick or the Dead?* (1888) and *Truth Dexter* (1901) respectively, Rives (who became the Princess Troubetsky) and Fenollosa (whose pseudonym was Sidney McCall) dealt more explicitly with sex than did most novelists of the times.

Alabama, too, was a donor to the local-color writing that dominated American magazine fiction for several decades after the Civil War. The state's first poet laureate, known to generations of schoolchildren because of his "Grapevine Swing" poem, Samuel Minturn Peck (1854–1938) also wrote stories, eleven of which were collected in *Alabama Sketches* (1902). John Trotwood Moore enjoyed similar success, but the state's preeminent writer of local color was Idora McClellan Plowman Moore (1843–1929), whose "Betsy Hamilton" pieces earned the sponsorship of Joel Chandler Harris. The "Uncle Remus" vogue initiated by Harris had several Alabama devotees. The vernacular tales of Robert Wilton Burton (1848–1917), especially his "Marengo Jake" tall tales, and the African American songs and legends recorded by Martha Young (1862–1941) rise well above the norm. Such literary folklore collecting from the state would be continued in the twentieth century by Ruby Pickens Tartt. The stories of Elizabeth Whitfield Croom Bellamy (1837–1900) appeared in premier national publications, and in its realism, her *Old Man Gilbert* (1888) transcends considerably the standard plantation "dialect" novel of the time. Reminiscent of Old Southwest humor, and deserving to be better known today, are the "Rufus Sanders" sketches of Francis Bartow Lloyd (1861–1897) and the satiric *Down the River; or, Practical Lessons Under the Code Duello* (1874) by George W. Hooper, a nephew of J. J. Hooper.

Also in the Uncle Remus tradition, Louise Clarke Prynelle's *Diddie, Dumps, and Tot* (1882) became an American children's classic. The direct progenitor of racially inspired, nationally marketed books such as *Frawg* (1930), written and illustrated by Annie Vaughan Weaver, it stands at the head of a veritable flood of quite different juvenile, adolescent, or young adult literature by Alabama writers. Early and later, state workers in this field have been numerous, many garnering special honors: Maud McKnight Lindsay, Rose B. Knox, Ellen Tarry, Wyatt Blassingame, Hilary Milton, Lucile Watkins Ellison, Charles Ghigna, Dennis Covington, Stephen Gresham, Faye Gibbons, Ann Waldron, Nancy Van Laan, Julia Fields, Mark Childress, Aileen Kilgore Henderson, Jimmy Buffett, and Han Nolan. The most intriguing publication in this chapter of Alabama's literary history is *The Education of Little Tree* (1976), a tender, acclaimed autobiographical story for young readers. Purportedly written by Native American-blooded Forrest Carter, it was in fact authored by Asa Carter, creator of western novels about the violent outlaw Josey Wales, popularized by Hollywood's Clint Eastwood, and of some of Governor George Wallace's most inflammatory segregationist speeches of the 1960s.

A genuinely autobiographical book from around the turn of the century became one of an Alabama pair inspirationally known to millions of Americans and non-Americans. Helen Keller's *The Story of My Life* (1903) may be seen to have initiated for white men and women, as *Up From Slavery* did for black ones, an impressive line of nationally published twentieth-century autobiographical works from the state. These volumes come from actresses and academics, silversmiths and

orchardists, neurosurgeons and veterinarians, political activists and fly fishermen, clergymen and journalists, literary professionals and graphic artists, even (sometime) snake handlers and garbage collectors. Many, such as Viola Goode Liddell's *With a Southern Accent* (1948) and *A Place of Springs* (1979) about Alabama's Black Belt, have a deep sense of place. The literary achievement and reward of these works rival their variety, and perhaps never so much as in a contemporary burgeoning of the genre. *In My Father's House* (1988) by Nancy Huddleston Packer; *A Serigamy of Stories* (1988), *Odd-Egg Editor* (1990), and *Twice Blessed* (1996) by Kathryn Tucker Windham; *Sweet Mystery* (1996) by Judith Hillman Paterson; *Confederate Jasmine and the Fat Tuesday Tree* (1997) by Ann Lewis; and *All Over But the Shoutin'* (1997) by Rick Bragg are but a small sampling.

Although Alabama's literary flowering in the twentieth century was not just in fiction, in fiction it was to be especially profuse and significant. As the century progressed, two historical explanations for Alabama's not having a literary culture commensurate with that of other states came to be effectively addressed. One was that there was no major literary figure associated with the state, and the second was that there were no literary centers located there.

By the mid-1960s, Harper Lee would be an internationally honored writer immediately identified with her home state. From twentieth-century Alabama, however, increasingly came serious writers familiar to serious readers and critics nationwide. Zelda Sayre Fitzgerald and Sara Haardt Mencken, both from Montgomery, remain overshadowed by their more famous husbands despite impressive literary achievement of their own. Also with an important Montgomery connection is Shirley Ann Grau, whose *Keepers of the House* won the Pulitzer Prize for fiction in 1965. The 1933 Pulitzer went to Alabamian T. S. Stribling for *The Store*, part of an Alabama family-saga trilogy that includes *The Forge* (1931) and *The Unfinished Cathedral* (1934). Lella Warren published only two volumes of her projected Alabama trilogy, but the first, *Foundation Stone* (1940), was nominated for the Pulitzer, was for a time the best-selling American novel in the world, and attracted serious but unfulfilled Hollywood film attention. Other Alabama writers would later secure celebrated film versions of their fiction: Joe David Brown's *Addie Pray* [*Paper Moon*] (1971), William Bradford Huie's *The Americanization of Emily* (1959), Fannie Flagg's *Fried Green Tomatoes at the Whistle-*

Stop Café (1987), Winston Groom's *Forrest Gump* (1986)—and, of course, Lee's *To Kill a Mockingbird* (1960).

Publishing their first novels three decades before Harper Lee's first and only one, William March [William Edward Campbell] (1893–1954) and Zora Neale Hurston (1891–1960) are important Alabama-born writers whose careers mirror the ebbs and flows of critical reputation. March was thought by one British reviewer to be infinitely superior to Faulkner. Although his prose style affords striking contrast, he does have impressive parallels with Faulkner, including creation of his own imaginary "postage stamp" of Alabama land, Reedyville and Pearl County, in which he sets multiple works of fiction. His best-known books, the World War I novel *Company K* and the best-selling *The Bad Seed* (1954), are not set there, but the work considered his finest literary achievement, *The Looking Glass* (1943), is. *Trial Balance* (1945) is a collection of March's short stories. Zora Neale Hurston lived in her native Notasulga, Alabama, for only about two years before moving to Florida, but this little community vividly appears in her first novel, *Jonah's Gourd Vine* (1934). Rediscovered as part of later-twentieth-century interest in African American and women's writing, Hurston is now approaching major writer status based primarily, and properly, on the basis of her 1937 novel *Their Eyes Were Watching God*.

An acknowledged if hard-to-classify work of art, James Agee's *Let Us Now Praise Famous Men* (1941) is a highly personal account of the time he spent with poor white tenant farmers in West Alabama. Precisely where Agee was a visitor is the home territory of Mary Ward Brown, whose short stories set here and collected in *Tongues of Flame* (1986) won their sixty-nine-year-old author the Hemingway Award for Best First Fiction.

Harper Lee's chief state rival for wide literary fame may be her childhood playmate Truman Capote, whose youthful periodic residences with relatives in Monroeville made him as indebted to that place as she was. "A Christmas Memory," "The Thanksgiving Visitor," "Children on Their Birthdays," and *The Grass Harp* (1951) are among the best of Capote's works rooted here. Monroeville, designated the "Literary Capital of Alabama" by the state legislature, is also the birthplace of Mark Childress, whose novels include *A World Made of Fire* (1984) and *Crazy in Alabama* (1993).

Finally, however, at the end of the twentieth cen-

tury, it is Harper Lee who is Alabama's preeminent literary presence for the wider world. Lee's description of an 1851 Alabama history book as being composed of small dramas within a huge drama, much of it drawn from the memories of those who were there, is also a revealing description of her famous 1961 novel. Selling over eleven million copies in the first fifteen years, translated into over thirty languages, and showing no signs of ever going out of print, *To Kill a Mockingbird* is one of the most influential works of American literature, a book that has changed the lives of countless individuals and affected whole cultures. Its enduring impact demands greater serious critical attention, and in the future the artful realism-romanticism amalgam and catalyst of wit and humor that are among Lee's extraordinary achievements may be better understood.

If Monroeville may be considered a literary center of sorts, two institutions of higher education in the state are more clearly, traditionally that. Tuskegee Institute, later Tuskegee University, has been a seat of education and literary inspiration for a number of African American writers from Alabama and beyond. Ralph Ellison's experience here is reflected memorably in *Invisible Man* (1952), and Albert Murray, a native Alabamian, has distinguished himself in several artistic fields. Murray's *Train Whistle Guitar* (1974) initiated a series of autobiographical novels, as did his *The Hero and the Blues* (1973) for important collections of essays on the blues. An earlier Tuskegee student who became a Harlem Renaissance participant was George Wylie Henderson, who set his lyrical novel *Ollie Miss* (1935) in his native rural East Alabama. Onetime Tuskegee faculty members whose experiences here imprinted their literary work include Nella Larsen, Melvin Tolson, Samuel Allen, and Rita Dove.

Tuscaloosa, home of the University of Alabama, became a fabled center of literary activity. In only about a dozen years, beginning in the mid-1930s, Professor Hudson Strode established a creative writing program that was considered one of the best in the country. In its heyday, from one to four novels a year were being published by Strode students, who were also winning prestigious national short-story contests and having their *Atlantic Monthly* and *Saturday Evening Post* stories reprinted in the short-story award annuals. Strode is estimated to have "influenced into print" by major publishers close to a hundred novels by his students, including Harriet Hassell's *Rachel's Children* (1938), Robert Gibbons's *Bright Is the Morning* (1943), Douglas Fields Bailey's *Devil Make a Third* (1948), Catherine Rodgers's *The Towers Inheritance* (1958), and Lonnie Coleman's *Beulah Land* trilogy (1973, 1977, 1980)—just to mention a few by longtime state residents. *Spring Harvest: A Collection of Stories from Alabama,* published by Knopf in 1944, showcased the short fiction of the Strode program.

Babs and Borden Deal became probably the most prolific and professional creative writers from Strode's classes. With such novels as *It's Always Three O'Clock* (1961) and *The Walls Came Tumbling Down* (1968), Babs Deal secured popular notice as well as critical praise. Borden Deal claimed that the body of his serious work, most impressive in the novels he called the "Olden Times" books and "The New South Saga" trilogy, constituted a panoramic history of the twentieth-century American South. Elise Sanguinetti and Helen Norris, both of whom remained in their native Alabama, are other noteworthy Strode protégées. Sanguinetti's first, and best, novel, *The Last of the Whitfields,* appeared in 1962; her fourth and most recent, *McBee's Station,* in 1971. Norris's first novel, *Something More Than Earth,* was published in 1940, but she published only one other book before her fine short stories began to be collected in *The Christmas Wife* (1985), *Water into Wine* (1988), and *The Burning Glass* (1992).

A strong creative-writing faculty has been maintained at the University of Alabama-Tuscaloosa, and impressive literary enclaves have emerged at a number of other colleges and universities in the state. Poet R. T. Smith and novelists Madison Jones and Oxford Stroud taught at Auburn University, for instance. Jones, like Stroud a faculty member there for thirty years, has authored nine highly regarded books of fiction, the best of which is the classically tragic *A Cry of Absence* (1971). Stroud, the son of Viola Goode Liddell, published his autobiographical novel *Marbles* (1991) eight years after his retirement from teaching. Other writer-professors with strong, extended ties to the state include William Cobb at the University of Montevallo; John Craig Stewart, Thomas J. Rountree, and Sue Walker at the University of South Alabama; H. E. Francis at the University of Alabama-Huntsville; and Hilary Milton at Samford University. The inspiration of James Saxon Childers and Richebourg McWilliams at Birmingham-Southern College is evidenced by such former students as Charles Gaines, Howell Raines, and Nancy Huddleston Packer. A teacher of creative writing at Stanford University for many years, Packer has

a deeply knowledgeable Alabama setting for her short-story cycle *Jealous-Hearted Me* (1997).

In the fluid society of the last half of the twentieth century, Alabama was an influential place for the creators of literature to remain, to move to, and to return to. Some, like novelists Caroline Ivey (1912–1972) and Jack Bethea (1892–1928), stayed in their home state. *The Family* (1952) reflects Ivey's lifelong residence on a farm near Smith's Station. Bethea, a Birmingham newspaperman, called for economic and political reform in such novels as *Honor Bound* (1927). Vicki Covington, Dennis Covington, and Robert R. McCammon are among later, contemporary natives who have remained bound to that city.

Of writers with important earlier ties to the state but extensive later residence elsewhere, the most acclaimed is Walker Percy, whose intimate knowledge of Birmingham is seen in *The Last Gentleman* (1966). Birmingham has also been a formative influence in the literature of poets Margaret Walker (best known for her 1966 novel *Jubilee*) and the Whitmanesque John Beecher (*Collected Poems, 1924–1974*). Robert Inman's youth in Elba and later television and political news career in Montgomery are manifest in his novels *Old Dogs and Children* (1991) and *Dairy Queen Days* (1997). Although later identified with Kentucky, James Still did not forget his East Alabama roots, nor did Jesse Hill Ford, who became a Tennessee resident. Like Shirley Ann Grau, Ellen Gilchrist employs the state as a setting for certain of her literary works, choices rooted in personal biographical fact. The same is true even more consequentially in the poetry of Gerald Barrax, Rodney Jones, and Andrew Hudgins. Hudgins's collection *The Glass Hammer* (1994) is subtitled *A Southern Childhood.* Also in this category of writers, with varying indebtednesses to the state, could be enumerated Cecil Dawkins, John Henrik Clarke, Thomas McAfee, Andrew Glaze, Ann Deagon, Sara Henderson Hay, Sonia Sanchez, Patricia Storace, Robert Bell, Julia Fields, Charles McNair, C. Eric Lincoln, Susan Monsky, Nanci Kincaid, and Patricia Foster.

Immigrants from nearby states and beyond have added much to the literature of Alabama—Charles Ghigna, Sam Hodges, Carolyn Haines, Harry Middleton, and Faye Gibbons, for example. In one instance, that of Octavus Roy Cohen, a prolific creator and immensely popular purveyor of African American stereotypes in the 1920s and 1930s, the contribution came to be a notoriously negative one.

Of particular interest are native Alabama writers

who moved away but returned to the state to complete their careers. Poet John Finlay (1941–1991) is yet another important southern writer who was Roman Catholic. Howell Vines's novel titles *A River Goes with Heaven* (1930) and *This Green Thicket World* (1934) reflect his concern with natural Alabama landscape. The concern or "business" of William Bradford Huie (1910–1986) was "truth," he said, and Huie carried on his business in books ranging from *The Revolt of Mamie Stover* (1951) and *The Execution of Private Slovik* (1954) to *Three Lives for Mississippi* (1965) and *The Klansman* (1967). Eugene Walter (1921–1998), who lived for more than twenty-five years in Paris and Rome, sandwiched a multifaceted artistic career between residences in his native Mobile. His novel *The Untidy Pilgrim,* which won the 1954 Lippincott Prize, and short-story collection *The Byzantine Riddle* (1985) brought the charm of the Alabama Gulf Coast to an international audience.

Over the years, Alabama's writers have dealt both expectedly and unexpectedly with perceived typical conditions or concerns of this Deep South state. One recent outline of such essences included race relations, politics, and enthusiasm for hunting, automobile racing, and football. State writers have made large quantitative contributions to creative literature about the Civil Rights Movement and, with works by Harper Lee, Madison Jones, Howell Raines, and others, a widely recognized qualitative contribution as well. A series of novels—including Huie's *Mud on the Stars* (1942) and Borden Deal's *Dunbar's Cove* (1957)—that dramatize local consequences of the ideology and activity of the Tennessee Valley Authority brings issues of political philosophy and pragmatic politics into elemental focus. And while there are specific literary works exemplifying the multi-sports culture of Alabama, one can wonder more deeply, since it was true for Stephen Crane's *The Red Badge of Courage,* whether football fanaticism does indeed offer any explanation for all the war writing emanating from the state.

Like serious artists everywhere, Alabama's creators of literature have written best out of what they personally know and feel. In *A Walk Across America,* recounting a 1970s journey through the South, Peter Jenkins reports a coded message he wrote to himself: "TAA-Totally Amazed by Alabama." Just as what this Connecticut Yankee actually experienced was not the Alabama he had preconceived, neither does the state's actual literature accord with the perception of a literary vacuum in the heart of Dixie. *Alabama* is a Choctaw Indian word that for many years was rendered as the phrase "Here we rest." Only recently has more accurate translation as the noun "thicket-clearers" been recognized. Such meaning is much more fitting for the early Native Americans who, physically and culturally, toiled in this place, as well as for its later literary laborers, who worked here spiritually and artistically. In Alabama, as elsewhere, the creation of literature has been hot earthly work, but here, too, it has had inspiration and insight, and has risen to create its own artistic spells.

Bert Hitchcock

See also Alabama, University of; Birmingham, Alabama; Mobile, Alabama; Tuskegee Institute.

Alabama English (Special Issue Featuring Alabama Authors) 2.1 (Spring 1990); Jerri Beck and Anne George, eds., *A Baker's Dozen: Contemporary Women Poets of Alabama* (1988); Philip D. Beidler, ed., *The Art of Fiction in the Heart of Dixie: An Anthology of Alabama Writers* (1986) and *Many Voices, Many Rooms: A New Anthology of Alabama Writers* (1998); Rosemary Canfield, ed., *Perspectives: The Alabama Heritage* (1978); Bill Caton, *Fighting Words: Words on Writing from 21 of the Heart of Dixie's Best Contemporary Authors* (1995); James E. Colquitt, ed., *Alabama Bound: Contemporary Stories of a State* (1995); O. B. Emerson, ed., *Alabama Prize Stories 1970* (1970); William T. Going, *Essays on Alabama Literature* (1975); Ralph Hammond, ed., *Alabama Poets: A Contemporary Anthology* (1990); *The Library of Alabama Classics* [Reprint Series], University of Alabama Press; Jean P. McIver and James P. White, eds., *Black Alabama* (1997); William Warren Rogers, Robert David Ward, Leah Rawls Atkins, and Wayne Flynt, *Alabama: The History of a Deep South State* (1994).

ALABAMA, UNIVERSITY OF

Opening officially in 1831, the University of Alabama at Tuscaloosa had its beginnings thirteen years earlier, before Alabama even became a state. The school's original charge was simply "promotion of the arts, literature, and sciences." As a functioning institution, it began early and has continued impressively to fulfill that obligation in the literary realm.

Included in the University's very first class of students—and particularly influenced by a gifted young faculty member named Henry Washington Hillard—Jeremiah Clemens, William Russell Smith, and Alexander Beaufort Meek all gained national publication and became political as well as literary leaders in their home state. Two later-nineteenth-century graduates of the University who followed this creative precedent were John Gorman Barr, a talented writer of Old Southwest humor, and Samuel Minturn Peck, Alabama's first poet laureate.

Distinguished men and women of letters as students and graduates increased greatly in number in the twentieth century, both before and after, both inside and outside the flowering of what became one of the nation's premier creative-writing programs at the University by midcentury. Hudson Strode (1892–1976), an Alabama faculty member from 1916 to 1963, doubted at first that creative writing could be taught, but the literary output and publication achievements of his students beginning in the late 1930s were phenomenal and provided a solid base for establishment of the strong M.F.A. program that continues in Tuscaloosa today. Among Strode's many protégés may be numbered Harriet Hassell, Robert Gibbons, Lonnie Coleman, Cecil Dawkins, John Craig Stewart, Borden Deal, Babs Deal, Elise Sanguinetti, and Helen Norris. Pre-Strode University students who earned a wide literary reputation were William March, T. S. Stribling, and William Bradford Huie. Later graduates include Howell Raines, Charles Gaines, Robert McCammon, Rodney Jones, Andrew Hudgins, Mark Childress, Winston Groom, Brad Watson, Nanci Kincaid, Vicki Covington, and Harper Lee.

Bert Hitchcock

See also Alabama, Literature of.

Alabama English (Special Issue Featuring Alabama Authors) 2.1 (Spring 1990); Hudson Strode, ed., *Spring Harvest: A Collection of Stories from Alabama* (1944); Allen Wier, ed., *Walking on Water and Other Stories* (1996).

ALGONQUIN BOOKS

In the late 1970s, mergers, conglomerate takeovers, increasing costs, and trends in the marketplace constrained the established publishing houses of the Northeast, limiting their willingness to take risks with new writers or experiments with form and subject matter. In response to New York's conservatism, Louis D. Rubin Jr., one of the nation's leading literary scholars and a promoter of southern literature, decided to create a publishing house of his own. His purpose was to offer support to young, talented, but unproven writers.

Rubin reasoned that even though the first books of such writers would undoubtedly lose money initially, they would eventually win critical acclaim for themselves and financial success for their publisher. He rejected the idea of a small regional press in favor of a full-fledged independent trade publishing house, because his objective was to do more than publish new authors' works. Launching careers, which involved getting books reviewed and stocked in good bookstores, was the ultimate goal. In an early statement about Algonquin Books, Rubin wrote, "What was needed was a small but good publishing house which wasn't located in the metropolitan Northeast, and whose books would be so good that bookstores everywhere would stock them, and newspapers and magazines everywhere would review them. It would have the highest standards—but they wouldn't necessarily be the standards currently fashionable in the Big City."

In 1982 Rubin—a writer, critic, and at that time literature professor at UNC–Chapel Hill—wrote to good friends and former students who invested in his vision, named Algonquin Books. In collaboration with one of his former students at Hollins College, Shannon Ravenel, Rubin began work on his first list. Ravenel became senior editor, even while living in St. Louis, Missouri, and working without a paycheck. Algonquin's first five books appeared in the fall of 1983. Over the next several years, Algonquin proved itself with the publication of unknown writers who have become major national talents. Many, but not all, are southerners.

Along the way, Rubin and Ravenel took some interesting risks, among them bringing out, in 1984, two "first" works by the same author—*The Cheer Leader* and *July 7th*, written by the very young (twenty-four-year-old) Jill McCorkle of Lumberton, North Carolina. In 1990 Algonquin took a chance on the first novel of a fifty-six-year-old African American peach farmer from South Carolina, publishing Dori Sanders's *Clover*, about an interracial marriage and the attempt by a white widow to raise her black stepdaughter within an African American community. These and other gambles paid off in making Algonquin a well-established and respected press by the end of the decade. In 1992 Algonquin went far beyond the South to pick up the novel *How the Garcia Girls Lost Their Accents* by Julia Alvarez, a native of the Dominican Republic raised in New York and living in Vermont. It was an immediate hit.

In 1989 the difficulty of making ends meet brought

Rubin and his backers to a critical decision. Algonquin was acquired by Workman Publishing of New York, a move that was designed to move the company's finances out of the deficit column without sacrificing the editorial freedom that the house enjoyed. The arrangement, which involved Elisabeth Sherlatt's appointment to handle subsidiary rights with Workman, has worked well. Workman provided financial support, marketing strengths, and a large sales force, which carried Algonquin successfully through the 1990s.

Rubin retired in 1992 after Shannon Ravenel moved to Chapel Hill to become the hands-on literary director. The names of writers whose works have been brought out to high acclaim include (in addition to Sanders, Alvarez, and McCorkle) Leon Driskell, Robert Love Taylor, Larry Brown, Clyde Edgerton, Lewis Nordan, Jim Grimsley, Robert Morgan, and Kaye Gibbons. Gibbons's first novel, *Ellen Foster* (1987), and Morgan's *Gap Creek* (1999) were selected for Oprah Winfrey's television book club series. The untiring energy of Louis Rubin and the editorial gifts of both Rubin and Ravenel have sustained his vision in ways no one could have predicted. Algonquin's books are routinely reviewed in the *New York Times,* while a generation of young writers find themselves respected throughout the country thanks to big beginnings in a small southern college town.

Darnell Arnoult

See also Publishers; Rubin, Louis D., Jr.; University Presses.

AMERICAN MERCURY

In 1924 H. L. Mencken and his partner, George Jean Nathan, abandoned the *Smart Set,* a monthly magazine that they had edited for ten years, for a new vehicle, the *American Mercury.* Mencken and Nathan could not agree on the scope and focus of the new magazine, and after one year, Mencken assumed complete editorial control. Already famous as a satirist and critic, Mencken was anxious to abandon the largely literary cast of the *Smart Set* for a more journalistic approach that would concentrate on the broad diversity of American society.

Although the *Mercury* covered virtually every region of the country, the attention given to the South reflected the editor's already well-established interest in the area he had once likened to a cultural Sahara desert, a waste land dominated by corrupt politics, intolerant fundamentalists, and the Ku Klux Klan. Mencken believed that only satiric ridicule and merciless exposure of irrational bigotry would free the South from the post–Civil War triumph of poor whites and rapacious business interests.

During his years with the *Smart Set,* Mencken had put together a network of southern writers and editors, all of whom were dedicated to "liberating" the South. As he prepared to launch the *Mercury,* he drew upon his southern contacts for ideas and contributions. Throughout the ten years of his editorship of the magazine, Mencken encouraged and published a group of young southern writers who were willing to take on the region's sacred cows. During the magazine's first eighteen months, the *Mercury* published fifty-five contributions from twenty-three southerners.

Unlike the *Smart Set,* the mainstay of which had been fiction, the *American Mercury* was a magazine of satiric social commentary. Although Mencken published short-story writers such as Emily Clark, Julia Peterkin, and Sara Haardt (whom he eventually married), he was more interested in journalists and even scholars who could report on the changing South. Howard W. Odum of the University of North Carolina and founder of the *Journal of Social Forces* supplied advice and articles to the *Mercury.* W. J. Cash had eight pieces published in the magazine, one of which formed the basis of his famous *The Mind of the South* (1941). Among southern journalists published in the *American Mercury* were Nell Battle Lewis and Gerald W. Johnson. Mencken eventually enticed Johnson to Baltimore to join the staff of the city's Sunpapers chain, with which Mencken himself was closely associated.

White southern writers sometimes found themselves sharing the *Mercury*'s pages with black writers, such as James Weldon Johnson, W. E. B. Du Bois, Walter White, E. Franklin Frazier, George S. Schuyler (the *Mercury*'s most frequent contributor), and Langston Hughes. Although most of the black writers whom Mencken published were associated with the Harlem Renaissance, some of them were from the South. More important, their very presence in the magazine, not to mention their discussions of race relations and especially lynching, gave a special edge to the *Mercury*'s commentary on the South.

Mencken's style and satiric point of view dominated the *Mercury* and was often reflected in the pieces he printed. During the 1920s, many of the magazine's southern writers, white and black, seemed to accept

Mencken's assumption that in order to achieve a vibrant modern culture, the South would have to reject its traditions. It was this attitude that the "Fugitives" attacked in *I'll Take My Stand: The South and the Agrarian Tradition,* published in 1930. In his *Mercury* review of the book, Mencken dismissed the Fugitives' stand as "utopian," without realizing how much of their distaste for the values of industrial America he shared with them.

Mencken gave up the *American Mercury* in early 1934. By that time, his involvement in the cultural debates over the South had come to an end. Yet Mencken and his magazines had played an important role in those debates. However negative Mencken's satire may have seemed, what had begun as a war on the South had become a war for the South.

William H. A. Williams

See also Baltimore Sunpapers; Harlem Renaissance; *Mind of the South, The;* "Sahara of the Bozart"; *Smart Set.*

Fred C. Hobson Jr., *Serpent in Eden: H. L. Mencken and the South* (1974); Charles Scruggs, *The Sage of Harlem: H. L. Mencken and the Black Writers of the 1920s* (1984); M. K. Singleton, *H. L. Mencken and the "American Mercury" Adventure* (1962).

AMERICAN RENAISSANCE

The term *American Renaissance* refers usually to the literature of 1830 to 1860, a period dominated, in letters, by the Transcendentalists and the novels of Melville and Hawthorne. F. O. Matthiessen's *American Renaissance: Art and Expression in the Age of Emerson and Whitman* (1941) makes no mention of Henry Timrod or William Gilmore Simms, and only passing reference to Edgar Allan Poe. Needless to say, Frederick Douglass is also excluded. However, more-recent criticism pertaining to the American Renaissance expands to include some southern writers. Simms is the subject of an essay by Miriam J. Shillingsburg published in the annual *Studies in the American Renaissance* (1977–96). Poe as a major contributor to the literary richness of this period is given ample treatment in the annual as well as in books such as *The American Renaissance: New Dimensions* (1983), ed. Harry R. Gawin; *Beneath the American Renaissance* (1989) by David Reynolds; and *Poetry of the American Renaissance: A Diverse Anthology from the Romantic Period*

(1998), ed. Paul Kane. Kane also includes selections by George Moses Horton and Henry Timrod.

Yet given the authors typically examined, the American Renaissance more properly ought to be called, to cite a title by Joel Myerson, *The American Renaissance in New England* (1978). Antebellum southern writers too often have been slighted. Jay Hubbell, in *The South in American Literature, 1607–1900* (1954), considers William Gilmore Simms rather than Poe to be "the central figure in the literature of the Old South," but points to the suppression of the South during that period. Lewis P. Simpson, in *Mind and the American Civil War: A Meditation on Lost Causes* (1989), cites Ralph Waldo Emerson's "attacks on the South as a mindless slave society." Yet Simms himself, in 1830, lamented a "general dearth of letters prevailing among us." Too, a narrowing of interests and greater involvement with the region's peculiarities kept southern writers from full prominence during the American Renaissance.

Richard D. Rust

See also Southern Renascence.

Leon Chai, *The Romantic Foundations of the American Renaissance* (1987); Stephen Railton, *Authorship and Audience: Literary Performance in the American Renaissance* (1991).

ANCESTOR WORSHIP

Ancestor worship in the South derives largely from the myth of southern aristocracy, of superior merit inherited through blood and genteel culture. Its depiction in southern literary works, both fictional and nonfictional, has been treated sometimes with high seriousness, sometimes with irony. The yearning for aristocratic forebears can be found in southern writings before the Civil War and even more since. In *Social Relations in Our Southern States* (1860), Alabaman Daniel Hundley praised the earlier Virginia gentry as true models in contrast with the nouveau-riche Deep South "Cotton Snobs" of his own time. By the time of his *The Mind of the South* (1941), W. J. Cash thought that having noble or aristocratic ancestors was one of the favorite illusions of southerners. It was, he said, their way of romancing about themselves.

Cash also identified two basic motives for claiming aristocratic ancestors. One was to enhance claims to social position by those who had only recently made their fortunes—bankers and brokers were his examples. The other was to justify claims of worth by exalting impoverished gentility.

Well before the Civil War, William Alexander Caruthers began showing Virginians of his time serious claims of descent from the original seventeenth-century cavaliers in his historical novel, *The Cavaliers of Virginia, or The Recluse of Jamestown* (1834). By the 1930s, T. S. Stribling, in *Unfinished Cathedral* (1934), could satirize the claims of the newly enriched Vaiden family of Alabama to aristocratic ancestry in genealogies prepared for recognition by the Daughters of the American Revolution. Both inside and outside fiction, among southerners claiming ancestral distinction were members of the Jamestown Society and the Society of Cincinnati, descendants of Revolutionary War officers who hoped to become the landed aristocracy of the new Republic on the basis of land given them in payment for war service.

Claims of prestigious ancestry by the impoverished genteel carried with them in most literary fictions the motif of decline in later generations. They looked back to nobler, stronger ancestors who lived before the deluge of the Civil War and saw themselves living in less heroic times with diminished opportunities. Caroline Gordon saw her Kentucky ancestors cast in heroic mold, pitting their virtue in the desperate odds of "the War." In Eudora Welty's *Losing Battles* (1970), the Depression-poor Renfros, Beechams, and Vaughns in hill-country Mississippi tell each other stories of a heroic past for their clan that belies their present poverty.

In other novels, families of a less-heroic, perhaps weaker, present find other reasons for honoring the ancestors. When Penhally Plantation is sold to become a modern Virginia-style hunt club in Caroline Gordon's *Penhally* (1931), Chance Llewellyn, twentieth-century descendant of the builder of the early-nineteenth-century great house, shows the new owner the grave marker of the first Kentucky Llewellyn and thinks how, as a younger son unable to inherit, his ancestor had followed the Wilderness Trail through the mountains from Virginia to begin a new dynasty in Kentucky. In Faulkner's *Absalom, Absalom!* (1936), however, Mr. Compson knows he is the lesser son of a greater father and explains his weakness by his diminished place in history, when the time for heroic deaths is over and all that is left is to die by inches. In *The Keepers of the House* (1964), Shirley Ann Grau has her heroine Abigail find strength in the ghosts of her ancestors as she defends the Howland place against night raiders.

A further development in the veneration of ancestors is the tendency to see them as legendary, living beyond the limits of history. In *The Keepers of the House*, Abigail learns to see her black surrogate mother, Margaret, as an extension of the legendary Alberta, known in folktales as consort of the "Black Prince" Stanley. In *Roots* (1976), Alex Haley presents his ancestor Kunta Kinte living in the timeless Mandinka village of Juffure before he is captured and made a slave. Although Haley's family chronicle concerns seven generations and in the later generations includes persons of increasing importance in the world, two-thirds of the narrative is devoted to "the African," and it is the noble but humiliated first generation whose memory is celebrated. In Toni Morrison's *Song of Solomon* (1977), modern city man Milkman Dead has to find the memory of his ancestor Solomon, the flying African, in legendary Shalimar, which is not located on any maps.

When honoring ancestors involves searching into their lives through family and public records, later descendants have often begun to think of their forebears as spirits still lingering over them. The later descendants also begin to think the ancestors dislike being disturbed. As she worked into the past to find her ancestral voices to tell of them in *Somerset Homecoming: Recovering a Lost Heritage* (1988), Dorothy Spruill Redford felt the need to apologize to them for robbing them of their magic and mystery: "the less we know about the lives they led, the more we make them myths when they are gone." In *Wake for the Living* (1975), Andrew Lytle similarly asked forgiveness of his ancestral ghosts for trying to understand them but insisted that knowledge is necessary for communion with them.

In practical terms, reverence for ancestors comes down to rituals such as visiting the graves and monuments of the glorious departed, holding family reunions to celebrate the results of the ancestors' lives and spreading word about them to the uninitiated, and constructing genealogies, now with the help of computer programs and searches as well as with old Bibles and letters. After her researches into the descendants of the original eighty African slaves of Somerset Plantation, Dorothy Redford called together nearly a thousand of those descendants for a reunion on the two-hundredth anniversary of their ancestors' arrival so that they could lay claim to the ancestors' contribution to the plantation, this time as honored guests rather than as slaves. In Welty's *Losing Battles*, the gathered Renfros, Beechams, and Vaughns reaffirm not only their past but their hope for a future together. And like others, they imagine that future generations may see them as honored ancestors.

Robert O. Stephens

See also Cemeteries and Graveyards; Family; Family Feuding.

W. J. Cash, *The Mind of the South* (1941); Fred Hobson, *Tell About the South: The Southern Rage to Explain* (1983); Andrew Lytle, *The Hero with the Private Parts* (1966); Robert O. Stephens, *The Family Saga in the South: Generations and Destinies* (1995).

ANTHOLOGIES OF SOUTHERN LITERATURE

Southern literary anthologies have played an influential role in defining, promoting, and perpetuating the collective identity of a southern literature. Such texts have served as powerful tools in the creation and dissemination of the concept of southern literature and in fashioning the canon of southern writers and works. Since the 1860s, southern literary anthologies have prospered, each embodying the cultural, literary, and political agendas of its editors. Through the selections chosen for inclusion and through the attitudes and critical perspectives of their prefaces, introductions, and headnotes, these anthologies both reflect and shape southern literary identity.

Southern literary anthologies share many common characteristics. The vast majority of them, especially after 1910, were compiled by scholars in southern universities, most often for a classroom audience. Each generation of anthologists has self-consciously negotiated some central points: the tension between regionalism and nationalism, defining *southern* and *the South*, establishing criteria for inclusion of authors and works, and informing the reader of the intent and critical perspective of the collection. The most frequently stated goals of these anthologies of a historically marginalized literature are to make texts available that have not been readily so and to encourage the appreciation and study of southern literature. Issues germane to all anthologies, which each has navigated according to its cultural moment and its editor's ideology, are representations of gender, race, and class.

Although calls for a uniquely southern literature began earlier in the nineteenth century, no exclusively southern literary anthologies appeared before 1860. Perhaps surprisingly, the first anthology emphasizes women; Mary Forrest's (also known as Mrs. Julia Freeman) *Women of the South Distinguished in Literature* (1860), focusing more upon gender than region, contains admiring biographical sketches of thirty-four women authors and brief selections from their works. With the Civil War and the assumption of a national Confederate identity came the publication of the earliest patriotic southern poetry collections: *War Songs of the South* (1862), by "Bohemian," later identified as W. G. Shepperson, and *Lays of the South: Verses Relative to the War Between the Two Sections of the American States* (1864), no editor given, published in England for the aid of the Southern Prisoners' Relief Fund. Immediately following the war's conclusion, several editors responded to fervid regional patriotic emotionalism with further collections of poetry: *War Lyrics of the South* (1866), no editor given; *War Poetry of the South* (1866), William Gilmore Simms; *Songs of the South: Lays of Later Days* (1866), T. C. De Leon; *The Southern Poems of the War* (1867), Emily V. Mason; and *The Southern Amaranth* (1869), Miss Sallie A. Brock.

In addition to the poetry, three other postwar volumes are noteworthy. In *The Living Writers of the South* (1869), James Wood Davidson compiled a list of 241 living southern writers from multiple disciplines, offering brief biographical information on each and very short selections from the works of some. Mary T. Tardy (Ida Raymond) compiled *Southland Writers: Biographical and Critical Sketches of the Living Female Writers of the South* (1870) in two volumes (a one-volume edition was published in 1872 as *The Living Female Writers of the South*). In contrast to Forrest's work ten years earlier, Tardy's work is aggressively sectional, with a partisan introduction defending southern literature and a format organizing the included authors by state. Heralding a later southern textbook movement, John G. James edited *The Southern Student's Hand-Book of Selections for Reading and Oratory* (1879), a work focusing on recent southern literature intended to rectify the omission of southern material in northern-edited classroom textbooks.

The 1890s brought a confluence of cultural movements that fostered a proliferation of southern literary anthologies in the late nineteenth and early twentieth centuries. Factors interacting to set the stage for these collections included southern resistance to the northern-generated American literary narrative, a new demand for southern textbooks, a resurgence of nostalgic Confederate sentiment, and the New South movement. Through generating prosouthern literary narratives, southern literary anthologists sought to challenge the national literary narrative dictated by the New England literary culture and evident in the publication of American literary anthologies that neglected or dismissed southern literature. The southern literary anthology offered a vehicle for assuming control of the South's literary identity by simultaneously proving and promoting the existence of a body of southern literature, all while engendering regional pride. Many of these anthologies catered to the market created for southern-written textbooks to replace the northern-originated ones deemed unfair to the southern perspective.

All of the anthologists of this period speak in the dominant white voice and present a monolithic South in their collections. But within that white South, two concurrent cultural movements shaped the anthologies: the resurgence of strong Confederate sentiment and the New South movement. The celebration of the South's Confederate history that spawned numerous monuments and memorials also produced often effusive and sentimental anthologies that endeavored, without critical standards, to preserve past southern literature. While accepting nationalism, these anthologists are vocal boosters for southern literature, and their texts reflect varying degrees of sectional bias. Their work created an inclusive and extensive canon. Influenced by a different agenda, many anthologies reflect the dogma of the New South movement that sought to present an edited progressive view of the South attractive to the rest of the nation. Composed primarily by a network of scholars in southern universities who sought to apply current critical standards to their selection of southern literature, their works present a controlled image of southern literature that is, while regionally patriotic, less sectionally rabid. Their criteria shaped a smaller canon and included far fewer women. This group of anthologists, working within the universities and producing the college-level texts, was the group initially responsible for institutionalizing the study of southern literature.

Poetry collections claimed a major share of the anthology market from 1890 to World War I. Consistently their editors deplore the lack of knowledge and appreciation of southern poets and want to encourage further study. The two most influential poetry anthologies of these times were Jennie Thornley Clarke's well-respected collection, *Songs of the South: Choice Selections from Southern Poets from Colonial Times to the Present Day* (1896), with an introduction by Joel

Chandler Harris, and Carl Holliday's *Three Centuries of Southern Poetry, 1607–1907* (1908). Motivated to address the slighting of southern literature in northern anthologies, Clarke targets a general audience with the first extensive anthology including poems on a range of topics. Holliday's ambitious work is a chronologically arranged collection he hoped would fuel the rising interest in southern literature. An established academic and author of *A History of Southern Literature* (1906), Holliday makes one of the few gestures toward African American literature of his generation by including five pages of "plantation melodies"; he includes, however, far fewer women writers than does Clarke.

Several other poetry anthologies also made contributions to southern literary culture. Charles W. Hubner, a poet himself, published *War Poets of the South and Other Confederate Campfire Songs* (1892), a work honoring surviving Confederate veterans, and *Representative Southern Poets* (1906), which offers biographical sketches and excerpts from the work of eight southern poets. William Lander Weber's *Selections from the Southern Poets,* a small popular collection, went through several printings, following the first in 1901; F. V. N. Painter's *Poets of the South* (1903) offers biographical sketches and selections highlighting five major southern poets; and Henry Jerome Stockard's *A Study in Southern Poetry: For Use in Schools, Colleges and the Library* (1911) provides a well-designed student text. Charles W. Kent, a regionally well-known scholar and a leader in southern studies for his generation, published *Southern Poems* (1913) as part of the Riverside Literature Series. His organization is chronological, and he chose poems that "portray southern life and sentiment" and have literary merit.

The success of southern fiction in the national local-color movement and a growing group of contemporary writers encouraged the appearance of an increasing amount of prose in the anthologies between 1890 and World War I. The earliest successful attempt at a comprehensive anthology of southern literature was Louise Manly's *Southern Literature from 1579–1895* (1895). Manly's work was consistently cited by subsequent anthologists for years, and those who followed her had to react to the initial canon of writers her work suggested, a list that has had surprising durability, with the exception of many of the women writers. Designed as a textbook to urge the concurrent study of history and literature, the chronologically arranged collection is comprised of brief biographical and critical comments followed by selections from the author's work. The anthology is well indexed and equipped with study questions and a list of additional authors and works at the end of the book.

Ten years later, W. P. Trent, a scholar who left the South to take a position at Columbia University and achieved national recognition for his involvement with *A History of American Literature, 1607–1865* (1903), published an important classroom anthology, *Southern Writers: Selections in Prose and Verse* (1905). Scholarly care, careful selection, and objectivity characterize Trent's volume, and his editorship of a southern anthology lent increased credibility to the genre and to the field of study.

In contrast to Trent's scholarly objectivity, Mildred Lewis Rutherford's *The South in History and Literature* (1906) embodies the views of the Confederate celebration continuing into the twentieth century. Rutherford's historically oriented classroom anthology is defensive of southern literature, zealously patriotic, and eager to assert the existence of a large body of southern writing. An extensive index of hundreds of southern writers whom she was unable to include in her volume precedes the chronologically arranged text. Representative of a prominent school of thought in her time, the volume is an excellent resource of names of neglected southern writers.

Other editors also made significant contributions in this time period: Kate Pleasants Minor edited *From Dixie* (1893), a compilation to raise money for a Confederate monument and museum; and Kate Orgain produced *Southern Authors in Poetry and Prose* (1908), a collection with extensive headnotes and brief selections from twenty-six authors after 1850. Four southern professors added to the list of textbooks for the southern classroom: Edwin Mims and Bruce R. Payne, *Southern Prose and Poetry for Schools* (1910); Leonidas Warren Payne Jr., *Southern Literary Readings* (1913); and Maurice Garland Fulton, *Southern Life in Southern Literature* (1917). The anthology selections in Volume VIII of the multivolume *The South in the Building of the Nation* (copyrighted in 1909)—*History of Southern Fiction*, edited by Edwin Mims—reflect the New South attitude and scholarly critical perspective of its editor.

The consummate anthology of the period was the *Library of Southern Literature*, a seventeen-volume southern literature anthology (copyrighted in 1907 and published between 1909 and 1923). Editors-in-chief of the venture were both well-known and highly respected southern figures: Joel Chandler Harris, who

died in 1908 and was never directly involved in the project, and Edwin A. Alderman, president of the University of Virginia. Much of the actual editing work was done by the literary editor Charles W. Kent and the associate literary editor C. Alphonso Smith. Many professional and amateur scholars wrote the individual entries, which contain a biographical and critical essay followed by selections from the author's works. Although the editors profess to avoid "vainglorious or sinister sectionalism," the overall tone of the work is eulogistic of southern writers and intensely patriotic of southern history and traditions. A revised edition of the work appeared in 1929.

Anthologies published after World War I until midcentury were written by male scholars who created a canon including few women and excluding African Americans, though sometimes self-consciously noting the omission. In an era of increasing academic specialization that emphasized standards of scholarship and careful criticism, the few regional collections published were crucial in holding an academic niche for southern literature. Claiming to judge poems by their merit and to avoid sectionalism, Addison Hibbard declared his *The Lyric South: An Anthology of Recent Poetry from the South* (1928) to be the first representative collection of southern verse in years. He announced his willingness to include selections by African American poets but found none to meet his criterion of living in the South while writing; "Negro writers of the new day simply do not remain in the South," he concluded. In *Southern Literature: Selections and Biographies* (1932), William T. Wynn has a section titled "The Negro"; however, African Americans prove to be the topic, not the authors. Edd Winfield Parks and Gregory Paine, conservative scholars both active in the formative years of the American Literature Group of MLA, each contributed a volume to the American Writers Series edited by Harry Clark. In *Southern Poets* (1936), Parks was intent upon presenting the "best" southern poems, denouncing Hibbard's earlier collection as "uncritical." He included a section on Negro songs and spirituals but demeaned them as poor poetry and derivative of white camp-meeting songs. Paine's *Southern Prose Writers* (1947), confined to nineteenth-century works, included three women authors. Both volumes reflect careful scholarship and contain worthy introductions and excellent bibliographies.

During this period, three Agrarians published minor anthologies: *A Southern Harvest: Short Stories by Southern Writers* (1937), Robert Penn Warren; *South-*

ern Treasury of Life and Literature (1937), Stark Young; and *A Southern Vanguard* (1947), Allen Tate. Richmond Croom Beatty and William Perry Fidler saw their *Contemporary Southern Prose* (1940) as a corrective to the neglect of contemporary literature by anthologists. The editors anthologize Agrarian essayists and Renascence writers, particularly calling attention to the inclusion of several narratives about "po whites," who represented, for them, a social phenomenon.

The 1952 publication of *The Literature of the South* (revised in 1968) is a watershed mark in the study of southern literature. Editors Thomas Daniel Young, Floyd C. Watkins, and Richmond Croom Beatty compiled an influential anthology that became a major classroom text for many years and gave momentum to the study of southern literature for the second half of the century. Capitalizing upon the impressive productivity of the Southern Renascence, the preface declares that "the South's leadership during the last twenty-five or thirty years is now generally recognized," and the editors devote 40 percent of the contents to those works. With an ideology infused with Agrarian ideas, the book provides historical context and stresses the continuity of southern literature, making connections between its past and present. After ninety years of anthologies presenting a monolithic white South, this anthology begins to change the dynamic with the inclusion of African American writers Booker T. Washington and Richard Wright.

Amidst the other midcentury anthologies, Willard Thorp's *A Southern Reader* (1955) is a maverick in attitude and approach. Technically, it is not a southern anthology because it contains a few selections from nonsouthern writers who wrote about the South. A careful scholar, Thorp himself was a lifelong northerner who taught at Princeton University. Among the interesting aspects of his collection was his effort to encourage dialogue about race issues: he included nine African American writers speaking directly upon race issues and juxtaposed them against the voices of white men addressing race issues.

During the social upheaval of the Civil Rights Movement in the 1960s, the anthologizing emphasis was on contemporary literature, and current African American writers were finding a spot in some of the works. The 1960s anthologies include *Southern Stories* (1960), Arlin Turner; *Southern Poetry Today* (1961), Guy Owen and William Taylor; *The Fugitive Poets* (1965), William Pratt; *Southern Writing in the Sixties:*

Fiction (1966) and *Southern Writing in the Sixties: Poetry* (1967), John William Corrington and Miller Williams; and *Poetry Southeast 1950–1970* (1968), Frank Steele.

With the 1970s and 1980s came an intensified countrywide focus on regionalism, and anthologies of that time displayed the impact of the South's social changes. Many scholars began to insist upon the existence of multiple southern perspectives. By the 1980s, women again began to appear as editors of collections and as entries in the tables of contents. The 1970s opened with *Southern Writing 1585–1920* (1970), edited by respected scholars Richard Beale Davis, C. Hugh Holman, and Louis D. Rubin Jr., which focuses on the years of southern literature before the Renascence, expanding that early canon considerably by appropriating a wide variety of literature, including prefaces from plays, travel writing, diaries, speeches, etc. The work exhibits a resounding historical orientation in its introductions but presents individual selections free of editorial comment. This collection was the first major anthology to include several African American writers as equals to white writers; overall, however, the work was not generous to women writers.

In 1979 Louis D. Rubin Jr., one of the editors of *Southern Writing 1580–1920*, published his influential anthology *The Literary South*. After years of teaching and writing about southern literature, Rubin wanted this anthology to represent the full spectrum of southern literature. In contrast to the larger *Southern Writing 1580–1920*, Rubin chose to omit historical documents and concentrated on imaginative literature, reflecting a New Critical approach de-emphasizing history. He commented on the importance of African American writers and included more of them than any previous southern anthologist; women writers overall did not fare quite as well. Many professors found *The Literary South* an accessible text for the numerous southern literature courses continuing to grow throughout the South and beyond.

Various other anthologies appeared during the 1970s: *Nineteenth Century Southern Fiction* (1970), John C. Guilds; *The Southern Experience in Short Fiction* (1971), Allen F. Stein and Thomas N. Walters; *New Southern Poets* (1974), Guy Owen and Mary C. Williams; *America in Literature: The South* (1979), Sara Marshall (textbook for secondary level); and *Contemporary Southern Poetry: An Anthology* (1979), Guy Owen and Mary C. Williams.

The first of several anthologies compiled by scholars

Benjamin Forkner and Patrick Samway, S.J., appeared in 1977—*Stories of the Modern South*. Others following are *A Modern Southern Reader: Major Stories, Drama, Poetry, Essays, Interviews and Reminiscences from the Twentieth-Century South* (1986), *Stories of the Old South* (1989), and *A New Reader of the Old South: Major Stories, Tales, Slave Narratives, Diaries, Essays, Travelogues, Poetry and Songs, 1820–1920* (1991). Forkner and Samway's anthologies have been important in making a wealth of material easily available and in expanding the canon to include more women and African American writers.

The last twenty years of the twentieth century saw continued productivity among southern writers and a growing demand from consumers of that literature. Responding to both of those situations, many anthologies of contemporary southern literature appeared, both for general readers and students. Examples of these anthologies include *New Stories from the South*, an annual publication of the editor's choice of the best of the year's newly published southern short stories, initiated in 1986 by Shannon Ravenel; *The Made Thing: An Anthology of Contemporary Southern Poetry* (1987), Leon Stokesbury; *New Writers from the South: A Fiction Anthology* (1987), Charles East; *Stories: Contemporary Southern Short Fiction* (1989), Donald Hays; *Growing Up in the South* (1991), Suzanne Jones; and *Best of the South* (1996), Anne Tyler. In addition, encouraged by the women's movement, anthologies of southern women's literature are appearing again, over one hundred and twenty years after Forrest's and Tardy's early collections. Such anthologies include *New Stories by Southern Women* (1989), Mary Ellis Gibson; and *Southern Women's Writing: Colonial to Contemporary* (1995), Mary Louise Weaks and Carolyn Perry.

Echoing the early anthologists who advocated the joint study of literature and history, two historians published a literary anthology of writings by southerners about the South for compatible use with historical studies: *The Oxford Book of the American South: Testimony, Memory, and Fiction* (1997) by Edward L. Ayers and Bradley C. Mittendorf.

A century after a group of scholars in southern universities began their work to institutionalize the study of southern literature, four contemporary scholars of southern literature have edited *The Literature of the American South: A Norton Anthology* (1998). Reflecting the multicultural politics of their time, William L. Andrews (general editor), Minrose C. Gwin, Trudier Harris, and Fred Hobson produced an anthology that delivers a resounding death blow to past images of a monolithic South, describing southern writing as "a multi-ethnic, polyglot phenomenon existing in a perpetually creative tension with a southern polity whose official myths and ideology have long resisted, if not repressed, the diversity and significance of much of the South's cultural heritage." The largest portion of the anthology is devoted to post–World War II writers, and the volume's contents reflect significant diversity of gender, race, and class. Once again, an anthology is informed by the agenda of its editors and their culture; and once again, the anthology is a vehicle for the next generation to discuss, judge, and respond to those perspectives and the southern literary canon that they create.

Susan H. Irons

See also Academy, Southern Literature and the; Histories of Southern Literature; *Library of Southern Literature; South in the Building of the Nation, The*; Southern Literature, Idea of.

APPALACHIA

Appalachia is a cultural region associated with the Southern Highlands, the Upland South, and during colonial history the Back (as opposed to the Low) Country. The region takes its Indian name from the Appalachian Mountains, mapped by the De Soto expedition (1539–41). The range extends from Alabama to the highest point at Mount Mitchell, North Carolina, and on even to Newfoundland. Embracing the Allegheny, Blue Ridge, and Smoky Mountains and parts of nineteen eastern and southern states, the range includes parts of Maryland, Virginia, West Virginia, Kentucky, Tennessee, North Carolina, South Carolina, Georgia, Alabama, and Mississippi. By extension, the cultural region also includes the Ozark and Ouachita ranges and parts of Arkansas, Missouri, Oklahoma, and northeast Texas. Appalachian people are typically identified as those who grew up in the Southern Highlands (and sometimes those initiated and experienced in the history, ways, and concerns of the region, whatever their birthplace). Geologists and geographers have emphasized the influence of the land upon the people. The mountain terrain is suitable for forest harvesting and grazing and for subsistence farming even where the growing season is short; it possesses abundant natural resources attractive despite limited access (wagon roads, railroads, and finally paved highways). As early as 1901, a geographer argued that the topography showed the country "devoted by nature to isolation and poverty."

But, as W. K. McNeil demonstrates in *Appalachian Folklore and Popular Culture* (1989), outsiders have repeatedly generated distortions about the region and its people. Many have defined Appalachia, more so even than the broader region of the South, exclusively in terms of poverty. President Lyndon Johnson's Commission launched a national War on Poverty in Appalachia in 1964, just as in a fireside chat, President Franklin D. Roosevelt had three decades earlier proclaimed the South the "nation's number one" economic problem. In spite of misconceptions, economic problems, and a tragic history, the South and especially Appalachia have remained distinctive for their cultural resources and natural beauty.

New and diverse anthropological, historical, and ethnographic evidence clarifies the contradiction between the material poverty and the creative spiritual resources of the region; the paradox is in part a result of the contrasting world views of English colonizers and tribal Celts. Among the diverse early European settlers who sought a home in the New World, the English dominated the coastal ports and plains, whereas during the late eighteenth century the Ulster Scots and other English-speaking Celts provided the largest population (65 percent) settling the Back Country. The Celts left a formative cultural imprint, especially through their keen stories and eloquent talk. The cultural differences between the English and the Celts, exacerbated by class differences, emerged in numerous tensions between planters and frontiersmen. The values of hierarchy, order, writing, materialism, efficiency, expediency, territorialism, and capitalism conflicted with the Celtic values of confederation, creativity, eloquent oral arts, impassioned spiritedness, craftsmanship, individualism, generosity, and egalitarianism. These latter characteristics were typically maligned, especially by economic developers, as disorganization, illiteracy, impetuousness, and laziness, assumptions that precipitated the typing of the "redneck" and "hillbilly."

Appalachian literature eschews the story of the planters, whose aspiration to the cavalier ideal absorbed much of William Faulkner's creative energies. The imaginative work of Appalachia documents the tales of "just plain folks," the white rural people of the hills and mountain country. Often these folk have been stereotyped as "wonderful Waltons" or "Deliverance deviants." Avoiding these extremes, Faulkner did write

some stories that reveal the fabric of the nonplantation rural South and even mountain culture. The story of the Scots-Irish settlers who took the Great Wagon Road into the Piedmont and then the hill country, finally ending up in Mississippi, appears in the depictions of Thomas Sutpen of *Absalom, Absalom!*, the Snopeses and Ratliff in *The Hamlet*, the McCallums of "The Tall Men," and other works. These plain folks inherit some of the mythic qualities of the Celts through their rugged individualism and eloquent storytelling arts.

Even more than the settlers of the Piedmont, many of whom were African American, those who moved into the mountains tended to be descendants of the pre-written-history Celts who had consolidated European regional traditions before the Mediterranean peoples overtook Europe. The Celts (Broad Axe and Beeker pottery people) invented the iron sword and plow that helped them to settle Europe and later to clear new ground in the frontiers of the British Isles and, finally, the Appalachian Mountains.

The Celtic patterns that helped to establish a vibrant culture across much of the nonplantation South have been more slowly besieged in the mountains—perhaps because of remoteness—than in the Piedmont. Old-World Celtic patterns still identifiable in contemporary Appalachia include a preference for forest grazing (cattle and pigs) and subsistence farming over plantation or industrial economy; a tradition of gathering at the crossroads for church suppers, reunions, house parties, country-store get-togethers, or fiddlers' conventions; a strong commitment to kith and kin; a passion for freedom and the land to sustain it; a justice system involving settling conflicts as a matter of personal right and duty. Appalachian fine crafts growing out of Celtic practice include metalworking and the verbal arts of ballads, Jack tales, and love songs.

The Scots-Irish settlers were mostly Presbyterians. In search of religious freedom, "Old Side" Presbyterians became Primitive Baptists, or Calvinists, or they drifted away from organized religion altogether, sometimes returning to a pre-Christian, often Celtic-inspired spirituality. Diverse and distinctive independent churches and sects are derived from "New Side" Presbyterians drawn to the Methodist and Baptist revivals of the Great Awakening. All these denominations, especially the Baptists, still form associations or "split off," and thus stylistically resemble the old Celtic tribes that were organized in loose confederations.

Folklore, especially instrumental music, song, and narrative, provided the first American literature by embodying both native content and style. Folklorist Richard M. Dorson considered southern Appalachia "folklore's natural habitat" and the region of the United States "most customarily linked with folklore." Cratis Williams, a longtime scholar of the region, has identified three periods of Appalachian literary history: pioneer literature dating from the earliest journal and travel accounts through settlement up to 1880; the period 1880–1930; and the 1930s through the 1960s. Now we can begin to see a new period encompassing the 1960s to the end of the twentieth century.

During the pioneer period, trappers and traders, predominantly the Scots-Irish descendants of the Celts, made early explorations of the mountains, befriended or fought Indians, and began to establish a diverse frontier culture and to document their adventures. During the colonial era, the settlers with Celtic backgrounds encountered new influences (e.g., tobacco, corn, herbs, and woodcrafts) from the Indians who had long lived upon the land and intermarried with settlers. As game vanished during the eighteenth century, more Scots, Irish, Welsh, and other settlers began to practice subsistence farm and forest agriculture; most wanted large family gardens and range-lands, not plantations or huge cash crops. Corn provided abundant food and could be converted to liquor, easily transportable, to bring in cash for staples such as salt and coffee. The early Scots-Irish settlers were joined by Germans, who maintained their language and religion, made hewn log cabins, practiced more settled farming, used home-dyed and homemade plain fabrics of solid colors in their quilts, and carved designs front and back on their gravestones. In the Shenandoah and the Piedmont, German settlers established centers in Staunton, Virginia, and Winston-Salem, North Carolina. Small numbers of African Americans brought singing traditions, the "banjars," Brer Rabbit, and basketmaking, among other traditions. While plantation and frontier peoples had conflicting political interests before the Civil War, Celtic, African, and other musicians crossed social, class, and racial borders to create a music that joined the Scots-Irish fiddle with the African American banjo to produce the old-time string band. As generations passed and this cultural exchange continued, rootedness to the land emphasized ethnicity less than community.

Authors such as George Washington Harris and Mark Twain, as well as numerous journalists, helped document the local color and the humor tales of tricksters, "ring-tailed roarers," and legendary heroes, including Daniel Boone and Davy Crockett. *Sketches and Eccentricities of Colonel David Crockett of West Tennessee* (1833) produced a folk hero who could "run faster, jump higher, squat lower, stay under longer, and come out drier than any man in the whole country." Known as a "straight shooter," the real Crockett felt compelled to respond with a corrective autobiography, *A Narrative of the Life of David Crockett* (1834), which also served as publicity for his presidential campaign. After his defeat in this effort, Crockett declared, "You may all go to hell and I will go to Texas." He lost his life at the Alamo.

The early literary accounts of Appalachia, frequently either naïve or condescending, sometimes documented folklore and often emphasized the heroic, but they seldom told the real stories of conflicts that tore apart mountain communities. The ballads ("Gypsy Laddie," "Jack Went A-Sailing," "Butcher Boy"), tales ("Jack and the Heifer Hide"), work songs ("Run [Slave] Run"), and banjo songs ("Roustabout," "Sugar Hill") of the era were actually more revealing of the hearts, minds, and challenges of the region. Eventually, despite little investment in slavery or plantations, many mountain folk were drawn into the Civil War on one side or the other—often by the mountain elite with political ties to the lowlands.

From 1880 to 1930, native Appalachian authors such as Mary Murfree (a.k.a. Charles Egbert Craddock), John Fox Jr., and Elizabeth Madox Roberts wrote historical romances about the Civil War, moonshining, or family feuds. Four early-twentieth-century books by educators emphasized Appalachian culture, providing data used by environmental determinists as well as contexts for folklorists and ethnographers studying the region. In *The Spirit of the Mountains* (1905), Emma Bell Miles stressed the role of women as "repositories of tribal lore—tradition and song, medical and religious learning." Horace Kephart's *Our Southern Highlands* (1913) balanced the stereotypes of moonshiners and mountain feuders with men who acted responsibly as bearers of farming, hunting, woodcraft, and other outdoor traditions. These authors made useful distinctions between well-to-do "valley people," "average hillmen," and scrabbling "branchwater folks." While editing the work of her husband after his death, Olive Dame Campbell included her research on folk songs, which helped collectors Cecil Sharp and Maud Karpeles to gather 1,600 songs from 1916 to 1918, documenting a "golden age" of balladry. In *The Southern Highlander and His Homeland* (1921), John C. Campbell, founder of the

Campbell Folk School, surveyed the geography, history, and culture of Appalachia.

Many northern educators and missionaries sought to change the "peculiar" otherness of mountain people, but Cecil Sharp advised in a 1916 letter, "I should leave them as they are and not meddle. They are happy, contented, and live simply and healthily, and I am not at all sure that any of us can introduce them to anything better than this." During these years, professional ballad collectors and other folklore scholars helped to expand, contextualize, and deepen the portrait of mountain folk by letting them present their own culture in their own words.

Henry Ford and other conservative entrepreneurs supported fiddlers' conventions and recorded mountain folk music, often in resistance to cultural expression emerging from African Americans and white women. The African American steam-drill worker John Henry had become a subject for black as well as white old-time mountain banjo and later guitar and bluegrass musicians; he was the hero who stood against the threat of industrial exploitation for all mountain folk.

After 1930, Appalachian artists developed a high-lonesome, intense regional style and increasingly acquired national stature. The period 1930 to 1960 includes Appalachian-born writers such as Jesse Stuart, Thomas Wolfe, James Agee, James Still, Harriette Simpson Arnow, and Wilma Dykeman. These writers transformed folklore and regional materials from stereotype into art and set their local values against overzealous modernity and progress.

Unlike Faulkner's symbolic romances anchored in local communities of the Deep South, Southern Appalachian fiction tends to record the lyrical, open-ended autobiographical journeys of ordinary people. Thomas Wolfe heralded the period with *Look Homeward, Angel* (1929), his highly personal novel of growing up in the North Carolina mountain resort town Asheville (renamed Altamont) at the turn of the century. Wolfe characterized his resistance to commercialism and urban ugliness when he wrote to his mother to complain about the "village virus" of "those people who shout 'Progress, Progress, Progress'—when what they mean is more Ford automobiles, more Rotary Clubs, more Baptist Ladies Social Unions."

The classic era (1930–1960) of Appalachian art emerged after the region became tangled in mining wars. Several novels documented these and other economic struggles. In addition to tracing resistance to the timber cutting and mining that followed the railroads into the mountains, the literature of this period follows the out-migration of laborers seeking work in Piedmont furniture factories, textile mills, and later in midwestern auto factories. Other Appalachian authors depict the endangered farm and forest life-styles and the related mountain culture.

During this period, liberals and radicals found folk songs a useful tool for labor organizing, and the Works Progress Administration (WPA) supported the collecting of such mountain folk materials. In the 1930s, Robert Winslow Gordon established the Archives of American Folk Song at the Library of Congress and claimed that the government "recognizes the hill-billy and the American Negro as the basis of American folk-song and music."

After World War II, mountain music was refashioned to express concerns over civil rights and then the Vietnam War. In the 1960s, folk revivalists experienced closer contact with Appalachian musicians to learn the style as well as the content of their music.

Appalachian folk arts have been enriched by Celtic, Indian, African, and now Latino and other cultural exchange. Many mountaineers have refused to sacrifice culture for wealth and, like the frontiersman Davy Crockett, steel-driver John Henry, mill worker and labor organizer Ella May Wiggins, and Cherokee warrior Tsali, have been willing to fight or die for home, land, and honor. But forced to choose between family and land, as poet Jim Wayne Miller documented in his collection *Brier, His Book,* some have moved on to Detroit or to death.

The fourth period, self-analytic and revisionist, of Appalachian literary history has emerged since the 1960s primarily through academic studies. In part, the economic policies of the 1960s War on Poverty and the desire, yet again, to protect the Appalachian heartland produced these works: Harry Caudill's *Night Comes to the Cumberlands* (1962); Archie Green's *Only a Miner: Studies in Recorded Coal-Mining Songs* (1972); Henry David Shapiro's *Appalachia on Our Mind* (1978); Helen Lewis et al., eds., *Colonialism in Modern America* (1978); and Ron Eller's *Miners, Mill Hands, and Mountaineers* (1981). Some scholars have analyzed individual artists, while others have written community studies: Jack Weller's *Yesterday's People* (1965); Phillip Paludan's *Victims: A True Study of the Civil War* (1981); John Gaventa's *Power and Powerlessness* (1980), which offers theory and history about the 1930s mine wars; David Whisnant's *All That Is Native and Fine: The Politics of Culture in an Ameri-*

can Region (1983), concerning outsider cultural intervention; Pat Beaver's *Rural Community in the Appalachian South* (1986); Thomas P. Slaughter's *The Whiskey Rebellion Frontier* (1986); William Turner and Edward S. Cabbell, eds., *Blacks in Appalachia* (1985); Altina Waller's *Feud: Hatfields, McCoys, and Social Change in Appalachia 1860–1990* (1988); Michael Owen Jones's *Craftsman of the Cumberlands: Tradition and Creativity* (1989); John Inscoe's *Mountain Masters, Slavery, and the Sectional Crisis in Western North Carolina;* and J. W. Williamson's *Hillbillyland: What the Movies Did to the Mountains and What the Mountains Did to the Movies* (1995).

Folklore helped community organizers in the 1970s by contributing to broad educational ventures, such as the collecting and publishing projects of *Foxfire.* Oral history and folklore have also provided an ethnographic rather than reductive approach to religious studies, resulting in such works as Brett Sutton and Peter Hartman's *Primitive Baptist Hymns of the Blue Ridge* (1982); Jeff Todd Titon's *Powerhouse for God* (1988); James L. Peacock and Ruel W. Tyson's *Pilgrims of Paradox: Calvinism and Experience Among the Primitive Baptists* (1989); Beverly Patterson's *The Sound of the Dove* (1995); Howard Dorgan's *In the Hands of a Happy God* (1997); Loyal Jones's *Faith and Meaning in the Southern Uplands* (1999); and Deborah McCauley's *Appalachian Mountain Religion* (1995). Some scholars, belatedly following in the footsteps of Lynwood Mitchell's *Saga of Coe Ridge* (1970), are merging folklife study and oral history. Recent integrative cultural histories include Rodger Cunningham's *Apples on the Flood* (1987); David Hackett Fischer's *Albion's Seed: Four British Folkways in America* (1989); and Cecelia Conway's *African Banjo Echoes in Appalachia* (1995).

Although used by others in diverse ways, Appalachian folklife and literature present the heart, identity, and history that mountain folk have attempted to preserve from the American Revolution, through mining wars, and on to the community organizing of the 1960s. In the twentieth century, the region's folklore and literature have received national recognition, while its natural resources have continued to be exploited. Today, Appalachia has received an exceptional number of National Endowment for the Arts Heritage Awards. The mountain authors of the 1930s had an important influence on the generation of late-twentieth-century writers now achieving success, including, among others, Fred Chappell, Robert Morgan, Jim Wayne Miller,

George Ella Lyon, Gurney Norman, Lee Smith, Cormac McCarthy, Marilou Awiakta, Denise Giardina, and Donald Harington. Appalachian folk singers, musicians, and tale-tellers such as Jean Ritchie, Tommy Jarrell, Etta Baker, Ray Hicks, Orville Hicks, and Walker Calhoun are securing a place of honor. On the threshold now are Sheila Kay Adams, a seventh-generation banjo player and author (*Come Go Home With Me,* 1995), and the University of Kentucky Affrilachian Poets, including notably Nikky Finny (*Rice,* 1995). Appalachia continues to generate novels that dramatize resistance to exploitative industrial, environmental, or tourist practices in the southern mountains. The indomitable spirit of a distinctive people, united by the mountains that form the South's heartland, still prevails.

Cecelia Conway

See also Appalachian Literature; Folklore; Folk Music; Highland Scots; Minstrelsy; Scots-Irish.

George Brosi, *The Literature of the Appalachian South* (1993); Robert J. Higgs, Ambrose Manning, and Jim Wayne Miller, eds., *Appalachia Inside Out: A Sequel to "Voices from the Hills,"* Vols. 1–2 (1995); C. Hugh Holman, *Three Modes of Modern Southern Fiction* (1966); Helen Lewis, et al., eds., *Colonialism in Modern America* (1978); W. K. McNeil, ed., *Appalachian Images in Folklore and Popular Culture* (1989); Cratis Williams, *The Southern Mountaineer in Fact and Fiction* (1961); J. W. Williamson and Chip Arnold, *Interviewing Appalachia* (1994).

APPALACHIAN LITERATURE

A historic division exists between the Upland South and the Lowland South. This division is first and foremost topographical, because the Upland South, commonly known as the Appalachian South, is the mountainous and hilly part of the region. This region includes all or almost all of West Virginia, Western Virginia, Eastern Kentucky, Western North Carolina, East Tennessee, and North Georgia. The hills of northeastern Alabama, northwestern South Carolina, and Western Maryland are often included as well. The U.S. government's Appalachian Regional Commission's jurisdiction stretches from New York State to Mississippi, but this political definition of Appalachia—adopted because its advocates needed extra congressional districts to attract votes—defies geological or cultural reasons. A hilly hinterland does stretch west from the foothills of the Appalachians all the way to the Great Plains, including the Ozarks, making the western boundary of the Appalachian Region especially ambiguous, but this entire area could not readily be identified as "Appalachian." Furthermore, the Great Valley, which stretches from the Shenandoah Watershed to the Tennessee Watershed, cuts the region in two with the Blue Ridge to the east and the Cumberlands to the west. This valley, and other, smaller valleys, share much with the Lowland South and further complicates any urge to make definitive boundaries. Nevertheless, the land and the people of Appalachia are distinctive.

Appalachian literature attracted little attention except for a few master's theses until 1960, when Cratis Williams (1911–1985), a native of Eastern Kentucky who served as a top administrator of North Carolina's Appalachian State University, published a Ph.D. dissertation written for Columbia University. "The Southern Mountaineer in Fact and Fiction" runs over 1,500 pages and transcends anything written about regional literature before or since. The charismatic Williams also promoted regional literature ardently in lectures and talks to a wide variety of groups. The Tennessee state historian, novelist Wilma Dykeman (1920–), a native of Asheville, North Carolina, who lived most of her adult life in Newport, Tennessee, has also been a leading promoter of regional literature on the lecture circuit. The summer classes she taught at Berea College in Berea, Kentucky, from the mid-1970s to the mid-1990s also trained a large body of enthusiasts. Jim Wayne Miller (1935–1996), a western North Carolinian who taught German at Western Kentucky University throughout his career, was another strong promoter of Appalachian literature. One of Williams's students, Grace Edwards of the English Department at Radford University in Radford, Virginia, was instrumental in the establishment of an official interest group in the National Council of Teachers of English and has directed a summer course that emphasizes regional literature for over twenty years. In the 1990s, at least a dozen colleges and universities offered Appalachian literature courses regularly, and courses were also taught at places as distant as the University of Alaska and the University of Rome in Italy.

Appalachian literature may be considered any literature, fiction or nonfiction, that is set in the southern mountains and hills. It could also be considered more narrowly to include only the fiction of natives of the region writing about their own homeland. A cultural definition would include only those writers from traditional rural locales who epitomize the mountain folkways associated with the region. However, even this definition would embrace considerable diversity, despite the category "Mountain Whites," which still exists in some academic databases. Certainly some black and Cherokee families live in a way as quintessentially Appalachian as any whites. Some recent Asian and Chicano immigrants have also adapted traditional mountain ways.

This article will emphasize the fiction of natives of the Appalachian South who focused throughout their literary work on the region. Thus it will exclude such important works by outsiders as *Christy* (1967) by Catherine Marshall and *Deliverance* (1970) by James Dickey. It will also exclude the work of natives of the region, such as Lisa Alther, Cormac McCarthy, and Barbara Kingsolver, whose books are usually set in other parts of the country. Also excluded will be children's and youth fiction and the work of writers best known for their nonfiction, such as Harry Caudill, the author of a biography, *Night Comes to the Cumberlands* (1963), as well as three novels.

Members of Hernando De Soto's 1540 expedition became the first to write about the southern Appalachian region. They found the dominant civilization to be the Cherokee, who enjoyed a rich oral tradition of storytelling, a tradition transcribed most completely by James Mooney (1861–1921) from Swimmer, a Cherokee elder, at the end of the nineteenth century and published in book form as *Myths of the Cherokee and Sacred Formulas of the Cherokee* (1972). In the 1700s, the Scots-Irish became the dominant group of Europeans, sometimes accompanied by slaves of African descent. They brought with them traditional stories quickly given local embellishments, first collected by Hardin Taliaferro (1811–1875) in *Fisher's River Scenes and Characters* (1859). The best-known contemporary source of these folk tales is *Jack Tales* (1946), collected by Richard Chase.

As the frontier era of the Lowland South evolved primarily into a plantation economy during the early nineteenth century, the mountain South remained dominated by subsistence farms, widening the gap created by the contrast between the English origins of those who populated the Lowland South and the Scots-Irish roots of the southern uplanders. *Georgia Scenes* (1835), by Augustus Longstreet (1790–1870), was the first work of fiction that found a popular audience for writing that exploited the dialect and folkways of the highland whites of the South. The book also caricatured plantation blacks. "The Humor of the Old Southwest" is a common category in American literature, referring to the area southwest of the Ohio River when European settlers had not yet crossed the Mississippi. The leading practitioner from the Appalachian South was George Washington Harris (1814–1869) of Knoxville, Tennessee. He published *Sut Lovingood's Yarns* (1858), a work that established an antiauthoritarian, slapstick literary tradition that has remained a vital thread in regional literature ever since.

When the Civil War erupted, the Appalachian area, on the whole, was more sympathetic to the Union, while the Lowlands were mostly united on the side of the Confederacy. This reinforced the division between Appalachia and the rest of the South. Immediately following the Civil War, a number of articles in periodicals and books appeared calling attention to the southern Appalachians as a culturally distinct region. Commentators described the rich folk music and folklore of the region, the isolation of its inhabitants, and their fierce independence tempered by an unyielding patriotism.

After the Civil War, local-color writing thrived throughout the nation, and Appalachia produced one of its most respected and prolific practitioners, Mary Murfree (1850–1922), writing under the pen name Charles Egbert Craddock. She grew up in Middle Tennessee near the mountain region and created many of the archetypal mountain characters that have been featured in regional literature ever since, including the old crone, the preacher, and the fiddler. She also established some lead motifs, including romance between locals and outlanders. Her first collection of short stories was *In the Tennessee Mountains* (1888), and her *The Prophet of the Great Smoky Mountains* (1885) was the first novel set in the mountain region and peopled entirely by characters native to the region. John Fox Jr. (1862–1919), a native of the Kentucky Bluegrass, kept the region in the national literary spotlight after the local-color movement began to fade. He wrote two best-selling romantic novels, *Little Shepherd of Kingdom Come* (1903), a Civil War novel, and *The Trail of the Lonesome Pine* (1908), which dealt with the disruption caused by the arrival of the coal industry.

Because only a very few native mountain writers were active earlier, a totally continuous tradition of mountain writing by natives emerged only in the 1920s. The first generation of mountain writers was born primarily in the very first decade of the century. Thus they experienced the social activism of both the

teens and the 1930s, as well as the relative prosperity of the 1920s, at formative times of their lives. The spirit of the 1930s that greeted them in their early maturity not only encouraged them to write and publish but also helped create a readership receptive to stories about the humble folk that these regional writers knew best. Thomas Wolfe (1900–1939), a native of Asheville, North Carolina, a small valley city surrounded by some of the highest mountains in the South, was raised by a mother who had come to Asheville from even deeper in the North Carolina mountains and a father who was a native of Pennsylvania. Although European writers, including D. H. Lawrence and James Joyce, had pioneered autobiographical fiction, Wolfe was an early southern practitioner of this craft. *Look Homeward, Angel* (1929), set in the Asheville of Wolfe's boyhood, is still widely regarded as an American classic.

The writing of Harriette Arnow (1908–1986) is marked by strong female protagonists who fight their oppression by men and by a mechanistic industrial system. She served as a schoolteacher in remote mountain communities near her Kentucky home and thus become familiar with the most primitive conditions in the mountain region of her time. Arnow graduated from the University of Louisville but lived most of her life in Ann Arbor, Michigan. Arnow's best-known work, *The Dollmaker* (1954), remains in print as an Avon paperback with an introduction by Joyce Carol Oates. It is the quintessential work on the migration of mountain folk to the industrial North and won Jane Fonda an Emmy Award in 1984 when she produced and starred in it as a television drama.

Like Harriette Arnow, Hubert Skidmore (1909–1946) had his beginnings in an isolated Appalachian home, and like Arnow, Skidmore gravitated to the cultural oasis of Ann Arbor, Michigan, where he attended the University of Michigan. Skidmore is best known for his novel *Hawk's Nest* (1941), which speaks starkly to the horrors that accompanied the building of the Hawks Nest tunnel in West Virginia during the Great Depression.

Like Thomas Wolfe, James Agee (1909–1955) had one parent from the mountains and one with roots in the North. His autobiographical novel, *A Death in the Family* (1957), which takes place in Knoxville, his hometown, is the only novel set entirely in the Appalachian South to have been awarded a Pulitzer Prize.

This first generation of mountain writers has at its core three men who graduated from Lincoln Memorial University in 1929. LMU is the school founded by northern Civil War generals at Cumberland Gap in appreciation for the service of mountain folk in the cause of the North. Not only did Jesse Stuart (1907–1984), Don West (1906–1972), and James Still (1906–) graduate from LMU at the same time, they all went on to Vanderbilt University for graduate school. There, they were all exposed to Vanderbilt's Agrarians. All three came from rural backgrounds—Stuart from northeastern Kentucky, West from North Georgia, and Still from the foothills of the Appalachians in eastern Alabama. All three shared a kind of Jeffersonian vision that called for society to encourage respect for the land and people and viewed small landowners working closely with nature as the core of society. These three men each had a different way to express this common vision politically. Jesse Stuart, the most prolific and best known of the three, was a conservative Republican; Don West, the poet and labor organizer, was on the left, and James Still is a liberal intellectual. Although Stuart published over sixty books, he is best known for *The Thread That Runs So True* (1949), an autobiographical novel of teaching in a one-room school. West is best known for his militant poetry collection, *Clods of Southern Earth* (1946). Still's novel, *River of Earth* (1940), is one of the classics in Appalachian literature. Stylistically, this novel excels in dialect made compelling by rich extended metaphors and similes.

Mildred Haun (1911–1966) grew up as close to the old-fashioned mountain ways as any writer ever will. In contrast to Wolfe's small-city roots and Arnow's small-town origins, Haun was raised in Hoot Owl Haller during the time when the U.S. government was purchasing land less than fifty miles away to create the Great Smoky Mountains National Park. As a student at Vanderbilt University and later as an employee of the *Sewanee Review,* Haun was thoroughly exposed to Agrarian writing traditions. Her only book, *The Hawk's Done Gone,* was published by Bobbs Merrill in 1940, when Haun was a graduate student at the prestigious University of Iowa Writing Program.

A dramatic difference exists between the contexts in which the first and second generations of mountain writers were raised. Whereas the first generation enjoyed childhood at a time of relative prosperity and became adults at a time of great social controversy, the second generation lived through the Great Depression and then became adults at a time when the Fascist threat from overseas produced perhaps the most complete political consensus in American history. Perhaps partly because the 1940s and 1950s were widely viewed as uneventful decades on the domestic front, this generation distinguished itself primarily in the field of historical fiction. In this generation, Appalachian writers who had gone to some of the country's finest universities were joined by equally compelling writers who had not benefited from educations received away from the mountains. Arguably, this development was at least in part due to improvements in mountain schools after World War I had opened up the region and the Progressive Era had affected the country's political priorities.

The background of Byron Herbert Reece (1917–1958) was similar to that of many in the previous generation. He lived almost his entire life on a very small mountain farm in North Georgia that had been in his family for generations. Although Reece did attend nearby Young Harris College intermittently and enjoyed short-term residencies there and at UCLA and Emory University, he was more influenced by the Bible and the classic English poetry books in his home than by mainstream literary study. *Ballad of the Bones and Other Poems* (1945) is his best-known collection.

Asa Carter (1927–1979), who used the pen-name Forrest Carter, was an even more unlikely literary figure. He grew up in Calhoun County, Alabama, near the southern end of Lookout Mountain. He became deeply involved in "massive resistance" to integration and wrote Governor George Wallace's famous "Segregation Forever" speech. When a 1991 reprint of his book *The Education of Little Tree* (1976) won the very first Abbey Award as the book that booksellers loved most to sell, few knew that this book, which extolls the Cherokee way of life, was written by a former leader of the White Citizens Council whose claim to Indian blood was remote and undocumented and whose book was fiction, not autobiography.

Two of the very best writers of this generation have careers that contrast dramatically with Asa Carter's racism. Both Wilma Dykeman and John Ehle were born in Asheville, North Carolina, in the 1920s. Ehle went to the University of North Carolina after he returned from service in World War II; Dykeman got a degree from Northwestern University near Chicago. In the 1950s and 1960s, both took strong stands for racial integration, providing important leadership among white southerners. Both writers have reputations as the outstanding contemporary historical novelist of their respective states. Wilma Dykeman is best known as the author of *The Tall Woman* (1962), a novel set in East Tennessee after the Civil War, and John Ehle is best known for *The Land Breakers* (1965), a novel of pioneer settlers in the North Carolina mountains.

Mary Lee Settle (1918–) holds the title of outstanding historical novelist for West Virginia. Her *Beulah Quintet* consists of five novels that together encompass the entire history of her home state. *Scapegoat* (1980), a mine-war novel, is perhaps the best known of these, although it was *Blood Tie*, set in an expatriate community in Turkey, that won Settle the National Book Award in 1977.

The writers who began their careers in the 1960s sometimes resemble the writers born in the first decade of the twentieth century who became adults in the 1930s. In both cases, these generations experienced childhood in an era of relative prosperity and came of age at a time of questioning, conflict, and tolerence of diversity. Many of the best Appalachian writers of the current generation benefited from close relationships with grandparents and others from earlier generations. The conservative values of their parents' generation produced a family context that allowed them to receive excellent mainstream educations, while at the same time they were exposed to their grandparents' old-fashioned way of life. The result has been an impressive blend of sophisticated talent and dedication to time-honored values.

Wendell Berry (1934–) exemplifies this phenomenon. His father was a lawyer, a lobbyist for the tobacco industry, and a bank director. After graduating from the University of Kentucky, Berry taught briefly at New York University and Stanford. Yet he and his wife, Tanya, yearned for something more. Early in the 1960s, they bought the farm of one of Berry's uncles. During his youth, the farm had provided young Berry with a kind of sanctuary from his intensely upwardly mobile family. Since that time, Wendell and Tanya Berry have farmed this land organically, using draft animals rather than gasoline-powered implements. All of Berry's short fiction and novels are set in "Port William, Kentucky," and their characters remain consistent in each book where they appear. In addition to adding a memorable place to the landscape of American literature, Wendell Berry has informed his work with an underlying philosophy that attests to its true sophistication. Berry sees civilization and community as resting upon the relationship of people to the land and feels that as people become alienated from their roots they lose meaningful connection with each other. Berry's *Collected Poems* (1982) are especially well loved, as is his novel *The Memory of Old Jack* (1974).

Gurney Norman was born in Grundy, Virginia, in 1937 and spent most of his childhood living in different southwestern Virginia and eastern Kentucky communities with various relatives, particularly his grandfather who ran the company store in a Perry County, Kentucky, coal camp. After graduating from the University of Kentucky, Norman joined many of the best and brightest of his generation in California, where his talents were recognized and his first novel was printed in the margins of *The Last Whole Earth Catalog*. Like the characters in that novel, *Divine Rights Trip* (1972), one of the classics of the 1960s counterculture, Norman returned to Eastern Kentucky to teach at the University of Kentucky.

Lee Smith (1944–) was also born in Grundy, Virginia, in the heart of the Virginia coalfields. Her novels feature down-to-earth female characters and mountain people who live by storytelling. *Fair and Tender Ladies* (1988), her sixth novel, was written in the epistolary mode and tells the story of Ivy Rowe, a mountain woman, from her birth in 1900 to her last years in her eighties. Smith, in eight novels and four story collections, concentrates on the speech and the resilience of Appalachian folk throughout the twentieth century, emphasizing their love of story and loyalty to family and place.

A leading literary bookseller in New York City, Cahill and Company, recently called Fred Chappell (1936–) "America's most variously-talented living writer." He was born and raised in Canton, North Carolina, a paper-mill town in the mountains west of Asheville, and has taught for many years at the University of North Carolina at Greensboro. He is most appreciated in the mountains for his collection of interrelated short stories, *I Am One of You Forever* (1985), which incorporates magical realism among its stylistic techniques.

Jim Wayne Miller (1936–1996) was born and raised in rural Leicester, North Carolina. He completed a degree at Berea College, received his Ph.D. from Vanderbilt University, and taught German literature and language throughout his career at Western Kentucky University. He is best known for his poetry collection *Brier, His Book* (1996).

Robert Morgan (1944–) was born and raised in Zirconia, North Carolina, very near the South Carolina border. Like Miller, Morgan has a working-class background. Morgan's father was actually employed to paint the house that Carl Sandburg occupied during his last years. A superior student and an exemplary teacher, Morgan has taught since 1977 at Cornell University in Ithaca, New York. Morgan's ninth poetry collection, *Green River* (1991), offers primarily a compilation of his best work.

Any consideration of the youngest generation of regional writers has to begin with Breece Pancake (1952–1979), the native of Milton, West Virginia, who ended his own life in 1979 at the age of twenty-six. He belonged, with Thomas Wolfe and James Agee, in that special category of mountain men—looked up to by many, but close to very few. Intense, hard-drinking, hard-working, introspective, and close observers of the world around them, they wanted to live life at a deep level and had a desperate need to share what they had learned. Breece Pancake was a rural counterpart to Wolfe and Agee. He loved to hunt, fish, hike, and wander the backroads in his Volkswagen, often ending up at a low-class dive or pool hall, hanging out, playing pinball, and drinking beer. When Pancake's first story was accepted by the *Atlantic Monthly,* a typographical error resulted in the unusual middle initial "D'J," which he adopted. His posthumous collection of stories is entitled *The Stories of Breece D'J Pancake* (1983).

Denise Giardina (1951–) was at West Virginia Wesleyan College during the same time as Breece Pancake. Giardina's father, one of many Sicilians drawn to the coalfields, was a bookkeeper at Pageton Coal until they mined out their holdings and bulldozed Black Hawk, the McDowell County coal camp where Denise had lived all her life. A progressive activist who was a third-party candidate for governor of West Virginia in 2000, Giardina currently teaches at West Virginia State College. Her historical novels of coalfield struggles are *Storming Heaven* (1987) and *The Unquiet Earth* (1992).

Four promising contemporary regional writers who were born in the late 1950s and early 1960s all attended the University of Iowa's graduate program in fiction writing. Pinckney Benedict (1964–) was raised on a seven-hundred-acre gentleman's farm in Greenbrier County, West Virginia. He went to a Pennsylvania boarding school and graduated from Princeton. After publishing two short-story collections, *Town Smokes* and *The Wrecking Yard and Other Stories* (1987), Benedict brought out his first novel, *The Dogs of God,* in 1994. Chris Offutt (1958–), a native of Rowen County, Kentucky, also depicts lower-class characters. He has published two short-story collections, *Kentucky Straight* (1992) and *Out of the Woods*

(1999). Lisa Koger (1953–) is a West Virginia native who lives in Somerset, Kentucky. Her *Farlinburg Stories* was published by Bobbs Merrill in 1990. Chris Holbrook (1961–) is a lifelong resident of Knott County, Kentucky. His *Hell and Ohio: Stories of Southern Appalachia* (1995) is a short-story collection published by Gnomon Press of Frankfort, Kentucky.

The unpredictability of Appalachian literature was underscored when novels set in the region and written by natives made the *New York Times* fiction best-seller lists five years in a row around the turn of the twenty-first century: *Cold Mountain* by Charles Frazier (1950–), a Civil War novel by a previously unpublished native of the North Carolina mountains, in 1997 and 1998; *Gap Creek* by Robert Morgan in 1999; and *Prodigal Summer* by Barbara Kingsolver in 2000 and 2001.

Some argue that Appalachian literature is exclusively a twentieth-century phenomenon because the region was too backward to support literary careers in the nineteenth century and will be too mainstream to be unique in the twenty-first century. Time will tell.

George Brosi

See also Appalachia; Folklore; Folk Music.

George Brosi, *Appalachian Literature and Music: A Comprehensive Catalogue* (1981); Cratis Williams, *The Southern Mountaineer in Fact and Fiction* (1961).

ARCHITECTURE

The great icon of southern architecture is the "Big House," traditionally a rectangular, gabled façade with the porticos, pilasters, and capitals of a Greek temple. The origins of this familiar symbol of southern aristocracy lie in the pattern books of the Italian sculptor, stonemason, and architect Andrea Palladio (1508–1581), whose drawings of piazzas, basilicas, temples, and villas profoundly influenced the shape of European architecture in the seventeenth and eighteenth centuries. Drawn largely from the works of the Roman architect Vitruvius, Palladio's masterpiece, *The Four Books of Architecture* (1570), was first published in English in 1715 by the Venetian architect Giacomo Leoni. By the mid-eighteenth century, elements of the Palladian style could already be seen in American houses, though not until around the time of the American Revolution did the classic three-part Palladian form—a triangular gable supported by four columns—become the fashion. Before then, American architects relied almost entirely on English models, though increasingly they looked to antiquity for inspiration, finding in Palladio's classical forms the order and harmony they sought to establish in their new nation.

In the South, the classical revival was officially inaugurated with Thomas Jefferson's construction of the Virginia State Capitol (1786–1789), patterned after his own sketches of a ruined Roman temple in the south of France. By adapting this temple form for his state's new democratic hall of government, the amateur architect from Virginia was signaling America's architectural independence from England. Jefferson's subsequent design of the University of Virginia, with its parallel rows of Palladian villas and Pantheon-inspired Rotunda, as well as his own eclectic variation on Palladio's domed three-part Villa Capra at Monticello, firmly established the classical tradition in the South. His *Letters on the State of Virginia* (1787), which dismiss the "rude mis-shapen piles" of his own alma mater, the College of William and Mary, and the scantling-and-board houses that were then spread like so many "maledictions" across Virginia, reveal as much about Jefferson's Old-World prejudices as they do about the state's native architecture.

The white columns of the classical revival rose with King Cotton's ascendancy in the antebellum South, as new settlements with names such as Sparta, Athens, Rome, and Troy sprang up from the mountains to the Mississippi. Heeding Jefferson's lesson, southern architects wrote into their temple-fronted statehouses, churches, and plantation manors a language of classical form and beauty, of democracy and the heroic ideal, newly translated and appended with a justification of the "peculiar institution" that between the South and antiquity was a shared tradition. The same slave labor that had built Greece and Rome now built the new temples of the South, though many more generations of southerners would live and work and die in those same proud but defeated structures before their children would begin at last to reexamine the foundations left exposed by war and reconstruction.

Even before war reduced many of the South's great mansions to ruins, southern writers were already lamenting their passing, much as their English cousins had a generation before indulged in a precious nostalgia for the English country house and old John Bull. Everywhere one turns in George Tucker's *The Valley of*

Shenandoah (1824), the story is the same: the old houses are falling into decay as the first families leave their plantations for new accommodations in the city. Inquiring after old friends, Mrs. Grayson, the family matriarch, learns that the old mansion where she had passed some of the happiest days of her youth has been abandoned; "The portico is rotting down," her son tells her, "and the whole building begins to look like a ruin." By the novel's end, the Grayson house itself, once the seat of "fertility, abundance, and comfort," is sold at auction, its "bare floors . . . defiled," says Tucker, "with the stain which the chewers of tobacco had left on it." The Grayson family collapses soon thereafter, following the tragic death of its noble scion, Edward, who falls in a duel with the Yankee scoundrel, James Gildon. Though melodramatic and stylistically amateurish, Tucker's chronicle of the decline of the Virginia aristocracy nevertheless remains vital for its early portrait of the intimate relation between house and master in the South.

The plantation house assumes even greater significance in *Swallow Barn* (1832), John Pendleton Kennedy's episodic sketchbook of tidewater life. Part travelogue, folk narrative, and novel of manners, *Swallow Barn*, like the irregular mansion that is its namesake, seems to have been built "in defiance of all laws of congruity." Kennedy was in fact following Washington Irving's blueprint for *Bracebridge Hall* (1822), and though he largely succeeds in painting a faithful picture of plantation life in Virginia, his sketches frequently betray the influence of his Knickerbocker predecessor. When Kennedy's narrator, the Baltimore lawyer Mark Littleton (whom readers would have recognized as a southern cousin to Geoffrey Crayon), returns to his ancestral home, he seems momentarily to have stumbled upon Bracebridge Hall itself in the heart of tidewater Virginia; arriving at dusk, he beholds a castlelike eminence bathed in "the last blush of twilight." Daylight and sober reflection reveal a more modest scene—a one-story, hipped-roof house that looks more like a "ship bottom upturned" than a Yorkshire manor.

Though it stands at the center of Littleton's "agreeable picture" of tidewater life, Swallow Barn, like the ruined mill and the old schoolhouse behind it, is but one sketch in the picturesque traveler's "little gallery of landscapes and portraits," a painted backdrop to Kennedy's Negro burlesque and winsome tableau. For all the jests at his subjects' expense, Kennedy's portrait of Swallow Barn, sitting "like a brooding hen, on the southern bank of the James River," remains an image of pastoral permanence, the seat of feminine grace, gentlemanly virtue, and southern hospitality. By the time he wrote the preface to the book's second edition in 1851, Kennedy had begun to grasp the significance of his "faithful picture" and revised his work accordingly, granting, as Lucinda MacKethan has noted, "increasing grace and dignity to the home itself." Though aware that his "series of detached sketches" was already a "relic of the past," Kennedy could appreciate *Swallow Barn*'s "accuracy of delineation" in an age when an increasing "uniformity" of style and manner was "visibly effacing all local differences." Whatever their "want of skill or defect of finish," Kennedy viewed his imaginative reconstructions of Swallow Barn and its people as a necessary means of preservation.

In the work of Kennedy's contemporary Edgar Allan Poe, the plantation house *is* the past, the "old time entombed," the concretion of a "mystery all insoluble." Set in a dominion far older than Virginia, Poe's "The Fall of the House of Usher" (1839) is less concerned with the preservation of the past than with its disintegration. Looking at the house, at its "vacant and eye-like windows" and the "barely perceptible fissure" down its front, one sees Roderick Usher himself, crumbling under the strain of his own riven psyche. Beyond these prominent features, however, and the "gray walls and turrets" that might be found in any gothic tale, the House of Usher is largely indistinguishable from the "pestilent and mystic vapor" that enshrouds it. Like the haunted palace that Roderick Usher constructs in verse, the House of Usher is built upon ambiguities; its terror derives not from its bleak walls or rank sedges but from their particular arrangement, the peculiar combination by which the observer is infected with the "insufferable gloom" that suffuses the house and its environs. Poe's house is not so much seen as felt, and as such it occupies a solitary space among the fictive architecture of the South. Here the old plantation myth so familiar in the works of Tucker and Kennedy is but a "dim-remembered story." The *house* is master, is *alive,* so Roderick Usher insists, its gray stones exerting a "silent, yet importunate and terrible influence" on his family's destiny.

In Poe's gothic inversion of the plantation manor, one finds little that is identifiably southern—no slaves, no crop, no sentimental tableau, only the house itself and its inhabitants, shut up *"living in the tomb."* The last blush of twilight that hung so dreamily over Swallow Barn here burns with a lurid intensity in the House of Usher's "red-litten windows," whose infernal glow expires with the "full, setting, blood red moon" that follows the house's descent. Whether Poe's tale is simply another chapter on the decline of the southern aristocracy or, as Lewis Simpson has suggested, a dark fable about the alienation of the southern literary mind, the House of Usher, like the past itself, will continue to stand on the edge of memory and history, shrouded in ambiguity in the "monarch Thought's dominion."

In the House of Usher, one sees the foundations for the symbolic architecture of another southern writer, George Washington Cable, whose Creole tale "Belles Demoiselles Plantation" (1879) reinterprets Poe's work in terms that are as explicitly southern as Poe's are intentionally ambiguous. From the "tall, branchless" family tree of the tale's old patriarch, Colonel De Charleu, and the "long crevice just discernible" running between the Mississippi River and the family mansion, to the final fall of the Belles Demoiselles mansion itself, which sinks "with one short, wild wail of terror" into the Mississippi, Cable's tale draws its most evocative images from Poe's apocalyptic vision of the plantation South. And yet the collapse of the De Charleu mansion is perhaps more shocking because here, unlike Poe's tale, there is no ancestral curse, no impending gloom hanging over the colonel's estate, save for the caving bank that threatens to dissolve the plantation's edge. For all his vices, De Charleu has no guilty conscience and, like any respectable Creole, is "never ashamed of his father's sins" (124). Indeed, the last impression Cable gives of this, the "realm of maiden beauty" and "the home of merriment" before its violent seizure, is one of idyllic splendor—"the sparkling foliage of magnolia and bay," the swaying of colored lanterns on "spacious verandas," the "sound of revel," and the "music of harps." The irony, of course, is that De Charleu is eager to abandon the plantation and was, in fact, about to hand the property over to his Choctaw relative, old De Carlos, moments before its collapse. This exchange between De Charleu, the "high up *noblesse,*" and the "low-down" half-breed, Injin Charlie, is the true heart of the story, which turns not so much on the story's cataclysmic conclusion but on the confrontations between class and caste that precede it. That the land later collapses beneath De Charleu is, in a sense, ironic compensation for his agrarian dream of plowing the foundations of commerce under to raise a new plantation in the city.

Cable clarifies the source of the Belles Demoiselles's

downfall in another tale, "Jean-Ah Poquelin," where the Mississippi becomes a metaphor for that "Anglo-American flood" that "made the Creole tremble for his footing" at the turn of the century. Again one sees traces of Poe's "Usher" in Cable's tale of the title character, a former smuggler and slave trader who is the "last of his line" and lives "aloof from civilization" in a haunted mansion on the edge of town. As in "Usher," both "man and house [are] alike shunned" as the "omen and embodiment of public and private ill-fortune," though rather than being destroyed by an ancestral curse, Poquelin's house is dismantled by public opinion; the swampy morass surrounding it (an allusion to the House of Usher's "rank miasma") is drained, its noxious exhalations replaced with the "sweet, dry smell of salubrity," suggesting that in this new South even the House of Usher's formidable presence would be no match for the efforts of a determined civil engineer. The plantation mansion still stands as a symbol of the Old South, not as the inscrutable, ineffable embodiment of evil that one sees in Poe's House of Usher but as the perceived object of evil in the community, the "object of a thousand superstitions" and that worst kind of evil in an industrious society—a wasted resource, a health hazard, an obstruction on the road to progress, ground that would better serve as a "capital site for a market-house." Poquelin's house is seen as anything but what it really is—a sanctuary for the old man's leper brother, the reputed "white ghost" of the estate, who finds refuge within the estate's shadowy interiors.

Cable's satire on progress and its consequences for the houses of southern fiction contrasts sharply with the observations made by his friend and contemporary Mark Twain on the Louisiana State Capitol building in *Life on the Mississippi* (1882). As one who dated the beginning of American architecture with the end of the Civil War, Twain deplored Baton Rouge's "little sham castle," seeing in its "architectural falsehoods" a "symbol and breeder and sustainer of [the] maudlin Middle-Age romanticism" that originated in the "romantic juvenilities" of Sir Walter Scott. A progressive in taste and politics, Twain prized the practical, the "old brick salt-warehouse," the "plank wharves," the "austerely plain commercial houses" of New Orleans' "sugar and bacon region," all of which constituted, in his estimation, a "radical improvement over the old forms," the whitewashed slave cabins now faded, and the "big, square, two-story" mansions whose "imposing fluted

columns and Corinthian capitals [are] a pathetic sham."

The problem with southern architecture, Twain thought, was that it lacked vision, "a model to build toward; something to educate eye and taste, a *suggester*, so to speak." Twain extended this model to southern literature, seeing himself and a few choice southerners (namely Cable and Joel Chandler Harris) as "suggesters" distinct from those southern writers who construct falsehoods from "obsolete forms" by writing in a "dead language," the "inflated language" of the romance, the same "wordy, windy, flowery 'eloquence'" he saw in the empty towers and turrets of the South's whitewashed castles. In his tales, and in the "Steamboat Gothic" mansion he called home, Twain favored native materials over those "materials all ungenuine within and without, pretending to be what they are not." Writing almost a century after Twain, Andrew Lytle would view the sentimental medieval architecture of the South from a different angle in his memoir *A Wake for the Living* (1975), finding in his grandfather's own medieval monstrosity a protest of the inherited architecture of the South.

In *The Old Dominion* (1908), Thomas Nelson Page recalls an anecdote about a Virginia gentleman who found one of his old haunts—a southern mansion that was once the "home of culture, elegance, and princely hospitality"—occupied by commoners who had hung a dinner pot "on a spike driven into a crack in a fine old marble mantel." Whether the spike was driven into the mantel out of spite or out of ignorance, the gesture shows the poor white's disregard for the wealth and privilege that built the house. For Page, this desecration of house and hearth signals the spiritual death of the plantation house. The house "dies" when it ceases to mean anything, when its inheritors are replaced by mere inhabitants, the dirty children and barefooted women to whom one house is as good as the next.

Perspectives on the South's architectural icons changed significantly during the literary renaissance in the first half of the twentieth century. In John Crowe Ransom's poem "Old Mansion," the poet's lament is not so much for the old mansion he passes on the street, or for the fading beauty and tradition the house represents, as for his own inability to depict with any accuracy of description the old iconic truth. As such, his poem becomes an elegy for the elegist—for the poet who self-consciously avoids the "old vulgarian/Reiterations" of his romantic predecessors yet finds himself frustrated in his attempts to penetrate his subject's dark interior. Ransom's theme is the inaccessibility of the past as poetic subject; the poet is here an intruder, a "tired historian" feeding on the "crumbs of history," an "antiquary . . . finger[ing] the bits of shard." At the poem's end, the poet concedes defeat and seeks a new subject in the "unseemlier world" of the present.

That unseemlier world is the focus of a work by Ransom's fellow Fugitive Donald Davidson, whose poem "On a Replica of the Parthenon" addresses the New South's misguided reverence for old forms. Davidson sees his subject—a full-size replica of the Parthenon in Nashville's Centennial Park—as less an homage to the South's architectural foundations than "a bribe against fate" constructed by those who have "[slain] their past." The emphasis here, as in Ransom's poem, is not so much on the structure itself but on the perceptions of the observer, on the "plaster thoughts" of those "who build but never read their Greek," like the shop girls who lunch on the temple steps, "eye[ing] Poseidon's loins ungirt" but "never heed[ing] the brandished spear." As an emblem of the Old South, the replica fails, not because the form itself is flawed but because the New South has failed to preserve the foundations on which it rests, the "wisdom [and] virtue" of the classical world and the Old South now forgotten.

In *Killers of the Dream* (1949), Lillian Smith exposes the foundations obscured by magnolia and moonlight, finding in the icons of the Old South the patterns of racism that shaped her childhood. Here, architecture functions as a complex cultural metaphor, a concretization of the color line between the "big white church on Main Street" and the "little unpainted church on the rim of town." Standing in the shadows of a tradition that looms like a "Big House" over the South, Smith shows her readers the house that Jim Crow built and the white columns behind which her people rested their prejudices.

Andrew Lytle's psychological novel *A Name for Evil* (1947) relies heavily on architectural metaphor in its deconstruction of the plantation myth. Henry Brent's attempted restoration of his ancestral home becomes an effort to regenerate his family's legacy and assume his own place in the family history. Despite his attempts to establish his own family on this haunted ground and thus "make up for the failure . . . of those who had gone before," Brent learns that "one does not make a house. A house grows and as it grows binds together the continuous past." Throughout his novel, Lytle draws upon images of foundations, doors, win-

dows, and walls to describe his characters' exits and entrances through the halls of memory and history.

In James Agee's *Let Us Now Praise Famous Men* (1941), the past is a forgotten abstraction in the presence of the very new and very humble dwellings of Alabama sharecroppers. Heeding the words of Ransom's "tired historian," Agee avoids the "vulgar/Reiterations" of the past and embarks on "a new quest" in the present, finding in these "timelessly ancient" structures a "bareness, cleanness, and sobriety" "more naked and noble than sternest Doric." Though Agee titles his chapter on the Gudger house "Shelter," he admittedly "neglect[s] function in favor of esthetics," juxtaposing his appreciation of the "plain essences of structure" with poetic rhapsodies on the "patternings and constellations" seen in nailheads. Agee may have intended, as he claims, to describe an ordinary house in "ordinary terms," but the house he reconstructs here is built largely of metaphor and simile, transforming the home's "mute furnishings" into objects of "beauty and . . . deep wonder" and the "partition wall . . . [into] a great tragic poem"; this "human shelter," says Agee, is "a strangely lined nest, a creature of killed pine, stitched together with nails into about as rude a garment against the hostilities of heaven as a family may wear." Evoking his subject through free association, Agee becomes a "bodyless eye," opening the house's "hidden places" to see "[w]hat is taking place here . . . in this silence," the transactions "between this house and external space." Thus the Gudger house takes its place in the cosmos as the "hollow center" upon which "the whole of heaven is drawn into one lens." Unique among the architectural writings of this period (and of any period, any region, really), Agee's observations in "Shelter" echo the concerns of his southern contemporaries who struggled to express ineffable truths through architectural metaphors.

From Major de Spain's porticoed mansion in "Barn Burning" (1939) to Wash Jones's pine-plank shack in *Absalom, Absalom!* (1936), to the coquettish scrolls and spires of the Grierson's Victorian eyesore in "A Rose for Emily" (1930), the fiction of William Faulkner forms a comprehensive chronicle of southern architecture. Faulkner traces the evolution of architecture itself in "The Courthouse" (1951), where "fifteen pounds of useless iron" transform the back room of the local trading post into Jefferson's first jail, which in turn becomes the site of the local courthouse, "the sum of all . . . their hopes and aspirations." The captive Parisian architect who stands in the "trackless wilderness" of early Jefferson "dreaming colonnades and porticoes and fountains and promenades in the style of David" is as much responsible for the town's identity as any of its founding fathers. His molds and kilns lay the foundations for the local churches, the female academy, the courthouse, and the town square, though it is the design for the colossal mansion at "Sutpen's Hundred," a monstrosity comparable to "a wing of Versailles glimpsed in a Lilliput's gothic nightmare," that looms in the imaginations of those like Quentin Compson, whose "very body," says Faulkner, is "an empty hall echoing with sonorous defeated names . . . a barracks filled with stubborn backward-looking ghosts."

In the works of Tennessee native Peter Taylor, whose devotion to fiction was matched only by his passion for restoring old houses, architecture evokes the intense psychological and social complexities that his characters encounter in a changing South. The dark dungeonlike basement that haunts Old Ben in "Porte-Cochere"; the ill-furnished bedroom intended as a nursery but now home to the family's old African American servant in "Bad Dreams"; the three-storied mansion a father lavishes on his only daughter in *A Woman of Means* (1950); and "the little clapboard Gothic citadel" where Cousins Johnny and Annie Kincaid stand "rigid as two pieces of graveyard statuary" in "Guests," are but a few of Taylor's many architectural ambiguities. In "The Decline and Fall of the Episcopal Church," Taylor unravels the controversy over the proposed demolition of an old Episcopal church in a small Tennessee town. Whether the church should be saved concerns Taylor less than the anxiety one feels at its passing: is it, in the case of the church, the stirring of one's own inner piety, or merely a "romantic fondness for ruins"? The answer becomes clearer when a member of the salvage crew turns the baptismal font into a birdbath. Though Taylor's architectural images continue the theme of transition so common in the southern literary renascence, his ironic juxtapositions anticipate the disassociated symbols of Walker Percy's suburban landscapes.

Percy's *The Moviegoer* (1961) is a primer in New South architecture, an existential tour through the anonymous shopping centers and duplexes of Elysian Fields and the shotgun cottages turned California-style bungalows that Binx Bolling's cousin sells to young professionals. In Percy's fictional Feliciana Parish, one finds the strange hybrid of old and new in the "curlicues of iron on the Walgreen drugstore" and the brand-new school building that starts Binx ruminating about

the spick-and-span sublimities of aluminum, brick, and glass. For someone who thinks of himself as an existential exile, an "Anyone Living Anywhere," Binx demonstrates an acute awareness of his surroundings; it is he, after all, who designs his brokerage to look like a "miniature bank with its Corinthian pilasters, portico, and iron scrolls over the windows," who notices that the Catholic church in Biloxi looks more like a post office than a place of worship, and who plans to convert the little strip of land his father left him into a service station, a modernist cube of styrene and "silky concrete."

In Percy's novels, even the Old South is new again, restored by the wives and decorators of the nouveaux riches to a splendor it never knew and a grandeur that never was. Once his West Texas wife finishes restoring their Belle Isle mansion, Lancelot Lamar finds himself remade as "a proper Louisiana gent," a composite of Ashley Wilkes, Jefferson Davis, Gregory Peck, and Clark Gable. Percy's gentlemen are planters without plantations, living by the golf course in brick and marble mansions modeled after "fat Norman towers" and the set designs for *Gone With the Wind*.

This mistrust of so-called traditional southern icons can also be seen in Bobbie Ann Mason's story "Shiloh," where Leroy Moffitt tries to rebuild his marriage by building "a real home" for his wife, Norma Jean. Leroy's dream of building a log cabin fails when he realizes that there is no place for it—neither in the new subdivisions where "[a]ll the houses look grand and complicated" nor in his own life or Norma Jean's. After a visit to a bullet-riddled cabin at the Shiloh Civil War cemetery, where the endless rows of tombstones remind him of a subdivision site, Leroy sees how the old icon of self-reliance offers no refuge for those who have yet to understand the "insides of history" or, in his case, the "real inner workings of a marriage."

In Allan Gurganus's novella "Preservation News" (which first appeared in the journal of the same name), the labors of the preservationist Tad Worth become a "love poem" to the properties he restores, be they old North Carolina mansions or that other "rickety old structure," his friend and confidante Mary Ellen Broadfield, whose "structural integrity" Worth comes to depend on. Worth's "missionary fervor," his "glorying enslavement to the work of 'binding up again,'" and his good and faithful service for the "salvation of noble houses," all suggest that his is a "higher calling"; he is a priestly (if not saintly) medium, a "sort of go-between for occupants living and dead," whose devotion to the "rejuvenation of fallen temples" is a "mission doubly religious." Ironically, it is the preservationist's own self-sacrificing nature, that particular quality that allows one to see through him the house, its history, and all the revelations of the past, that makes him, like some "anonymous cathedral craftsman," "oddly apt to disappear." By showing how houses give life to stories and how those same stories are sometimes all that sustain them, Gurganus reveals the way architecture and literature combine to form the freestanding poetry of the South.

Brian Carpenter

See also Architecture, Domestic; Cotton; Domesticity; Domestic Novel; Family; Gardens; Plantation; Plantation Fiction.

Guy Cardwell, "The Plantation House: An Analogical Image," *Southern Literary Journal* (Fall 1969); Jay Cohn, *The Palace or the Poorhouse* (1979); Richard Beale Davis, *Literature and Society in Early Virginia* (1973); Dorothy Griffin, "The House as Container: Architecture and Myth in *Delta Wedding*," in *Welty: A Life in Literature* (1987); Allan Gurganus, "Preservation News," *Preservation News* (July/August 1997); Talbot Hamlin, *Greek Revival Architecture in America* (1944); Thomas Hines, *William Faulkner and the Tangible Past* (1996); Lucinda MacKethan, *The Dream of Arcady: Place and Time in Southern Literature* (1980); Lewis Mumford, *The South in Architecture* (1941); William Ruzicka, *Faulkner's Fictive Architecture* (1987); Kenneth Severens, *Southern Architecture* (1981); Lewis Simpson, *The Dispossessed Garden* (1975); Alexander Stille, "Who Burned Atlanta?" *New Yorker* (July 29, 1996); Dell Upton, *Common Places* (1986); John Vlach, *Back of the Big House: The Architecture of Plantation Slavery* (1993).

ARCHITECTURE, DOMESTIC (BARNS AND CABINS)

Artifacts of vernacular architecture such as cabins and barns are as potent images in southern literature as is the plantation house. Lying at an opposite end of the social spectrum from the "big house," they are reminders of the sharply divergent class composition of southern society.

The necessary choice of the frontier house-builder, cabins remained an important type of low-cost southern housing until the advent of the mobile home. Although in the popular imagination cabins were built of logs, in actuality the form, not the building materials, defines the cabin (large homes could also be built from logs, as Mark Twain illustrates in *Adventures of Huck-*

leberry Finn [1884]). Constructed according to a traditional floor plan, composed of one or two rooms, and standing less than two stories high, southern cabins were of two separate designs; the regional prevalence of a type indicates the ethnic origin of the area's original settlers. Square cabins, built from the eastern seaboard westward to the eastern slopes of the Blue Ridge Mountains, took their pattern from the traditional cabin of early English settlers. In contrast, the Scots-Irish brought a rectangular cabin plan with them as they moved southward through the Shenandoah Valley and then fanned out into the Virginia-Carolinas Piedmont, western Kentucky, Tennessee, and other areas in which this rectangular form came to predominate. Although cabins in the tidewater region typically had board siding, throughout the rest of the region log construction became the favored technique after its introduction by German and Scots-Irish settlers (who had themselves learned the technique from Finns in the Delaware Valley). Improvements in framing techniques and sawmilling in the late nineteenth century led to a wider regional adoption of board siding.

The treatment of cabins in southern literature reflects the opposing signification of cabins nationally. As early as William Byrd's descriptions of North Carolinians' mean hovels (*History of the Dividing Line* and *Secret History of the Dividing Line*, written c. 1728), cabins have signified poverty's squalor. Shack residence in such novels as *Adventures of Huckleberry Finn* or Erskine Caldwell's *Tobacco Road* (1932) functions as a symbol of characters' shiftlessness or moral depravity.

In contrast, the cabin also conveys the highly positive idea of pioneer self-sufficiency and regional rootedness, particularly in the literature of the Appalachian South. In this literature, raising the cabin is emblematic of the heroic act of establishing oneself on the land; descriptions of cabin interiors emphasize their coziness and represent family closeness and the importance of women's work. Examples of this positive treatment include Wilma Dykeman's *The Tall Woman* (1962) and John Ehle's *The Land Breakers* (1964). But even Appalachian writers have mixed attitudes toward cabins; in Jesse Stuart's *Taps for Private Tussey* (1943), shacks suggest the difficulty of breaking free from the cycle of poverty.

In southern literature by and about African Americans, the cabin has a similarly dual signification, although with a different political motivation. Attempting to defend slavery, plantation fiction such as John Pendleton Kennedy's *Swallow Barn* (1832) presents the slave quarters as the nexus of slave contentedness. In contrast, accounts by former slaves themselves, such as *The Narrative of the Life of Frederick Douglass* (1845) and Booker T. Washington's *Up From Slavery* (1901), insist on the hardships of life in a slave cabin. Despite their primitive conditions, slave quarters did fulfill an important community function, since in them slaves could exercise some control over their own space, an idea that Harriet Beecher Stowe explores in *Uncle Tom's Cabin* (1852).

Barns, vital in an agricultural society, are prevalent in southern literature; like cabins, they possess a complex signification. On the one hand, they (and other farm buildings) represent domestic prosperity and call up a nostalgic view of the agrarian past, as in the Appalachian poetry of Jeff Daniel Marion and Robert Knox. Their destruction is horrific (Faulkner's *As I Lay Dying* [1930]), even though it can also be a covert means of striking out against the social order (Faulkner's "Barn Burning" [1938]). On the other hand, as outbuildings, barns occupy a liminal space, a site for non-socially-sanctioned behavior ranging from sexual experimentation (Flannery O'Connor's "Good Country People" [1955] and Lee Smith's *Saving Grace* [1995]) to rape and murder (Faulkner's *Sanctuary* [1931]).

Theresa Lloyd

See also Appalachia; Cracker; Folk Art; Poor White.

Mac E. Barrick, "The Log House as Cultural Symbol," *Material Culture* (1986); Henry Glassie, "Types of the Southern Mountain Cabin," *The Study of American Folklore* (3rd ed.; 1968); William Lynwood Montell and Michael Lynn Morse, *Kentucky Folk Architecture* (1976); Parks Lanier, *The Poetics of Appalachian Space* (1991); Michael Ann Williams, *Homeplace: The Social Use and Meaning of the Folk Dwelling in Southwestern North Carolina* (1991); John Michael Vlach, *Back of the Big House: The Architecture of Plantation Slavery* (1993).

ARISTOCRACY

Aristocracy in America has been the subject of ongoing debate since early in the colonial era. The argument has centered on such questions as: Does aristocracy have any place in a new and evolving society, established largely by Europeans sharing a common enterprise free from the strictures of entrenched rank and privilege? If superior social rank and influence were acknowledged (as they were by many), then what constituted the basis for such exclusivity? Was it lineage, wealth, natural ability, or superior intellect? Would a de facto aristocracy govern the newly constituted Republic, recently freed from British rule? Would—should—an aristocratic element be tolerated within a resulting democratic social order?

Although history records how many of the above questions were resolved, the tensions between elite minorities and the democratic mainstream continue to be felt in varying ways and degrees. In the South, however, an aristocracy had begun to form by the late seventeenth century, and over time its existence has been widely accepted as part of the established order. Perhaps this is owing to several underlying principles upon which the southern aristocracy was built. Arguably the most basic is that southern aristocracy was, and is, largely a homegrown rather than a transplanted entity. Although it is sometimes assumed that blue European blood coursed through the veins of the early southern aristocrat, the facts presented by modern historians tell a different story. The southern aristocrat was characteristically a self-made person. Seizing upon ready-made advantages, such as the vast supply of arable land, the availability of cheap (often slave) labor, and European markets eager for the products of colonial soil, the early aristocrat arrived at social and political prominence by following the path of entrepreneurial wealth. This was as true for the Tidewater, or "Chesapeake" aristocrats (from eastern Virginia or Maryland), whose chief money crop was tobacco, as for their counterparts in the South Carolina Low Country, whose agricultural mainstays were rice and indigo.

As a class, the southern aristocrats were not usually scions of the European nobility, although the "second sons" of some prominent families did seek their fortunes in the colonies. Many came from the trade or merchant classes, but the origins of most are simply not known. Though typically possessing little education, they demonstrated extraordinary natural ability and an eagerness to work and take chances. The emerging aristocracy proved itself not only adept at husbandry but was also skillful at management—carefully supervising their agricultural enterprises and dealing with merchants in colonial ports and in London.

Without having a specific name for it, they profited from what we would today call "upward mobility"—a privilege open to many in America that was not available in England. Many came with adequate financial backing, and it was not uncommon for those who began small-scale tobacco operations to increase their acres gradually, perhaps even to the point of becoming major "planters" of hundreds or even thousands of acres. It is true that many attempted this upward climb with a burden of debt. It is also true that some who displayed the outward accoutrements of wealth landed in bankruptcy court. However, this should not diminish the fact that wealth and its attendant aristocratic trappings were not only attainable goals but goals reached by many families in the colonial South.

All aristocracies build upon themselves. Expansion of one's landholdings was the standard pattern for the aspiring planter/aristocrat. Also, many made advantageous marriages, often to widows (a commonplace circumstance in colonial Virginia) who might bring land, handsome incomes, or important family connections to the union.

In fact and in fiction, the prevailing image of the southern aristocracy has been the mansionlike dwellings of the most successful planters. Here, material success was embodied in an architecture of grandeur and elegance that asserted a confident authority to the lesser colonial world. That these edifices and the families who created them represent a tiny percentage of the colonial population is indisputable. And that the few could live so well obscures the troubling fact that by the second quarter of the eighteenth century, approximately half of the Chesapeake population consisted of African slaves and their descendants. However, to view the surviving mansions on the north bank of the James and other eastern Virginia rivers, as well as in the Carolina low country, is to see at first hand physical evidence of the scale on which the southern aristocracy thought and lived. It was a scale worthy of the rural English squirearchy that it emulated.

William Byrd II's Westover is a primary example. The mansion itself has been called the finest Georgian structure in America, its builder (1674–1744) an emblem of the cultured colonial aristocracy. The latter assumption is erroneous in several respects. Although Byrd was educated in London, possessed a library of some four thousand volumes, wrote poetry, and felt as comfortable in London as in Williamsburg, the average aristocrat placed scant emphasis upon purely intellectual pursuits and possessed few books. Chesapeake society was rural; large agricultural operations required constant hands-on management. In the absence of cities like Charleston, where a seasonal urban society gathered for social and cultural stimulation, the Chesapeake culture socialized in less communal ways. In the

absence of music or dance, there were hunting, gaming, and racing for recreation. The Chesapeake aristocrat seldom traveled beyond the precincts of the local community.

Southern aristocracy is often characterized as a power elite. Politics generally did take precedence over things cultural; however, it was ultimately in the political realm that the Virginia aristocracy shone most brilliantly. When we consider the aristocratic Virginia names Braxton, Harrison, Lee, Jefferson, Nelson, and Wythe affixed to the Declaration of Independence, it becomes obvious that they represented politics in the very highest sense of the word. Still, formal education was a rare commodity. Philip Vickers Fithian (1747–1776), the Princeton-trained tutor to the children of Robert Carter at Nomini Hall in 1773, was treated with great respect and was considered an ideal "catch" for an aristocrat's daughter.

While the true southern aristocrats differ in important particulars from their counterparts in historical romance, their way of life and their influence on American history constitutes a story every bit as captivating as any ever told by a writer of fiction.

Welford Dunaway Taylor

See also Ancestor Worship; Caste; Class; Declaration of Independence; Gentleman; Gilded Age; Hunting; Lady; Plantation; Plantation Fiction; Tidewater.

Carl Bridenbaugh, *Myths and Realities: Societies of the Colonial South* (1952); Nathaniel Burt, *First Families: The Making of an American Aristocracy* (1970); Edwin H. Cady, *The Gentleman in America* (1949); Francis Pendleton Gaines, *The Southern Plantation: A Study in the Development and Accuracy of a Tradition* (1925); Lucinda MacKethan, *The Dream of Arcady: Place and Time in Southern Literature* (1980); Henry Dwight Sedgwick, *In Praise of Gentlemen* (1935); Ritchie Devon Watson Jr., *The Cavalier in Virginia Fiction* (1985); Louis B. Wright, *The First Gentlemen of Virginia* (1940).

ARKANSAS, LITERATURE OF

Arkansas's place in southern American literature is partly a result of its place on the map. Its eastern border, the Mississippi River, isolated Arkansas from the rest of the South, and on the other side the Indian Territory pulled it toward the western frontier. Not only is Arkansas separated from its sister states, it is divided within itself. The Arkansas River, slicing diagonally from northwest to southeast, further divides the state culturally and economically. To the north lie the Ozark Mountains, settled mostly by white immigrants from the southeastern United States, living on small farms separated from rather than joined by winding, difficult roads. South of the Arkansas River lies the flat and fertile Delta, the Southland of myth and movies, of planters, belles, sharecroppers, and the descendants of the slaves who once made the crops that supported the myth.

The geography of Arkansas determined its economy. The first settlers were loggers and trappers attracted by the forests and swamp of "the Creation state," as Thomas Bangs Thorpe called it in "The Big Bear of Arkansas." Once the swamps had been drained and the forests cleared, agriculture became the overwhelming source of economic development, "the Land of Opportunity," as the license plates declared. Industry until recently was mainly the exploitation of natural resources like minerals and timber. There were few towns. In fact, as recently as 1990 nearly half the population of Arkansas still lived in communities with a population less than 2,500.

Today, the Ozarks are among the most rapidly developing areas in the country. Roads are improving to accommodate tourists and the gigantic trucking fleets that supply the nation's Wal-Marts from corporate headquarters in Bentonville. Pickup trucks carry Ozark farm wives to town to work in a factory or a hospital for cash to keep the farm going. A surprising number of Mexican workers have joined the construction and poultry industries, and cattle and chicken houses dot hillsides long since denuded of their hardwood forests. In the Arkansas Delta, however, the economy is stagnant. King Cotton now shares the realm with rice and soybeans, but large-scale agribusiness has left a pool of unskilled and poorly educated laborers with no other opportunities. The plantation culture has given way to bankers, paper mills, unemployed agricultural and garment-factory workers, and real-estate developers.

The lack of an urban base has affected intellectual and creative life in Arkansas from the beginning. The population could not easily support public education or other humanistic endeavors, and the old-time religion often regarded aesthetic expression with suspicion or hostility. Traditional language arts, however, flourished, including folk songs, storytelling, and preaching, and the state's isolation from the mainstream probably helped to strengthen the influence of these genres on Arkansas writing well into the second half of the twentieth century.

The earliest writings in and about Arkansas were by outsiders from as far away as Spain and France, recording the explorations of the sixteenth and seventeenth centuries. In the nineteenth century, another spate of travel writing appeared, including the naturalist Thomas Nuttall's journal of his travels in the Arkansas River Valley (1819); Henry Rowe Schoolcraft's description (1816–1819) of Indians, early settlements, and the Ozarks; *Excursions Through the Slave States* (1837) by the English geologist George William Featherstonhaugh, who nearly 150 years later turns up in a novel by Donald Harington. Friederich Gerstaecker wrote *Wild Sports in the Far West* about his experiences in Arkansas soon after statehood. Washington Irving wrote, in 1832, of a visit to Fort Smith. These writers were published by and for people outside of Arkansas, and the stereotypes they created of an Arkansas populated with indolent farmers and shiftless woodsmen; barefoot, snuff-dipping women; riverboat gamblers and desperados—and the resentment and defensiveness they aroused—have scarred the collective soul of Arkansas ever since.

A further development line immortalized Arkansas in the Southwest humor tradition, which includes some of the most influential writing in and about Arkansas. James R. Masterson, in his book *Tall Tales of Arkansas* (1943), defines Arkansas humor as largely oral in origin and transmission. Printed forms of Arkansas humor have been mostly ephemeral—newspapers, magazines, and pulp books. The genre uses exaggeration rather than understatement, explicitness rather than implication, efforts to penetrate the understanding rather than hints to challenge it. Arkansas humor is characterized by boisterous wit, heavy satire, or the improbable. These observations might be applied to much Arkansas writing for the past century and a half, even that of Arkansas's most literary and academic authors.

But Charles Fenton Mercer Noland was neither literary nor academic when he moved to Batesville, Arkansas, in 1826 and became the editor of the *Batesville Eagle*. He fled after fighting a duel but returned in time to carry the first Arkansas constitution to Washington in 1836. He wrote for the *Spirit of the Times,* a New York weekly subtitled *A Chronicle of the Turf, Agriculture, Field Sports, Literature and the Stage.* His chief contributions were forty-five letters published over the signature of "Col. Pete Whetstone." Like his literary descendants all over the South, he created a family, an entire neighborhood—the Devil's Fork—and a culture that became the background of his stories. Hunting and sporting, especially horse racing, are his two main themes. The Arkansas stories of the transplanted New Englander Thomas Bangs Thorpe (1815–1870) were nationally popular and were translated into several European languages. They were collected in two volumes, *The Big Bear of Arkansas* (1845) and *Colonel Thorpe's Scenes in Arkansaw* (1858). Thorpe's characters have the crudeness of their type as well as boundless enthusiasm for the glories of the Arkansas swamps and the wildlife they found there.

The natural evolution from Noland, Thorpe, and their ilk was publication for readers within the state. The scattered and sparse population could not support a book-publishing culture, but those very circumstances encouraged the development of newspapers, whose importance in the history of the state cannot be overestimated. The *Arkansas Gazette* was first published at Arkansas Post, the territorial capital, on November 20, 1819, the same day as the first election in the territory. The *Gazette*'s founder, William Woodruff, is one of Arkansas's icons, and the picture of his entrance into the territory, poling two pirogues lashed together bearing his printing press, is impressed on the imagination of every schoolchild. Within the first month of its history, the *Gazette*'s pages contained the spirited and opinionated letters that were so much a part of its influence and popularity in the state. When Little Rock became the capital, it had a population of six hundred—and three newspapers, including the *Gazette*, which continued to be a statewide influence until its takeover in 1991 by the *Arkansas Democrat*. Between 1819 and 1993, more than 2,500 papers were published in Arkansas, and in the beginning they were frequently the only reading matter, beyond perhaps the Bible, available. They were often the only outlet for writers not only of the news and opinion of the day (or week), but for columnists, poets, and anybody else with something to put before the public.

The defensive posture of Arkansas's people is a reaction against so many jokes in newspapers and pulp jokebooks. William Quesenbury, writer and cartoonist for the Fayetteville *Southwest Independent*, read his poem entitled "Arkansas" at a meeting of editors in Hot Springs in 1878, in which he asks

What stigma rests on Arkansas?
What crime or foul disgrace upon her?
Where is the hand would dare to draw
     a black line on her shield of honor?

His answers to these questions are much the same today, when the questions are still being asked, though not in tetrameter stanzas: the Mississippi River and the Ozark Mountains made Arkansas much less accessible to immigration than other parts of the continent. And when immigrants *did* begin to settle in Arkansas, they were not from the best society but included many who had already failed elsewhere. They did not develop any loyalty to the state but were always claiming their old home. "No, me and Jack was born out here, / But daddy come from Indianer." The author maintains that textbooks don't teach the real Arkansas and that men who go to Arkansas to make their living are all too willing to slander the state to their friends when they return home. These complaints are still alive in the state, where regular attempts are made with varying degrees of success to promote teaching Arkansas history to counteract what is felt to be the state's inferiority complex.

Opie Read was a reporter for the *Prairie Flower* of Carlisle, the *Gazette*, and other papers, but his reputation is due to *The Arkansas Traveler*, which first appeared in 1882, purporting to expose the hicks of the backwoods for the amusement of citified Little Rock readers. It quickly achieved a circulation of 85,000. His description of Arkansas "characters" drew much local resentment, but even after he moved to Chicago, his paper was a national institution. Read also wrote several loosely autobiographical novels and a memoir, *I Remember* (1930).

Many twentieth-century Arkansas writers have honed their skills and acquired their readership in the *Gazette*, the *Democrat*, and other papers in the state. Their columns, stories, humor, and verses have frequently been reprinted as books. The "Arkansas Traveler" column in the *Gazette* has had excellent writing from Ernie Deane, Charles Allbright, Bob Lancaster, and Mike Trimble. Paul Greenberg, Gene Lyons, and others have practiced a very literate craft in investigative pieces and commentary, some of it later published separately as books. Some of Lancaster's pieces for the *Arkansas Times*, now a monthly magazine, evolved into *The Jungles of Arkansas: A Personal History of the Wonder State* (1989). Writers of this generation are generally very far from Arkansas boosterism, but their criticism is more acceptable because they are perceived as local.

Other writers have used state magazines and newspapers as their creative outlet: Robert Wynn for his historical pieces and memoirs of the Boston Mountains;

Rosa Zagnoni Marinoni, Marie Rushing, and many others for their verses. Otto Ernest Rayburn published several magazines extolling the "Anglo-Saxon seed-bed," which led to his *Ozark Country* (1941).

Bearing out the contention that Arkansans like stories better than any other writing, memoir and autobiographical writing comprise perhaps the most impressive body of Arkansas literature. Their authors are black and white, male and female, rich and poor, celebrated and obscure. Wayman Hogue, in *Back Yonder* (1932), combines his personal reminiscence with a systematic treatment of the hill culture. Hogue's daughter Charlie May Simon, a writer of biographies for younger readers, wrote two memoirs, *Straw in the Sun* (1945), recounting her return to backwoods Arkansas to become a writer, and *Johnswood* (1953), the story of her life with the poet John Gould Fletcher, himself the author of *Life Is My Song* (1937). Otto Rayburn's *Forty Years in the Ozarks* (1957) celebrates a life of writing and publishing. Maya Angelou's *I Know Why the Caged Bird Sings* (1969), the most Arkansas-connected of her books, recounts her childhood years with her grandmother in Stamps. Brooks Hays's memoir *A Hotbed of Tranquility* (1968) describes his careers in the Southern Baptist Convention and the Arkansas Democratic Party. Shirley Abbott wrote two volumes about her family in Hot Springs, *Womenfolks* (1983) and *The Bookmaker's Daughter* (1991). Margaret Jones Bolsterli, a professor at the University of Arkansas, wrote *Born in the Delta: Reflections on the Making of a Southern White Sensibility* (1991). *Looking for Hogeye* (1986) recounts the return of *New York Times* reporter Roy Reed to his home state.

Hogeye is the setting of a novel, *Acres of Sky* (1930), by Charles Morrow Wilson. After he left Fayetteville, he wrote chiefly nonfiction about the tropics, but he produced a collection of tales, *The Bodacious Ozarks* (1959). He also edited *Ozark Fantasia* (1927) by Charles J. Finger, a transplanted English globetrotter who operated a magazine, *All's Well*, from a farm outside of Fayetteville, and worked on the WPA Writers Project that produced the *Guide to the State* (1941).

Arkansas had at least two successful practitioners in the nineteenth-century heyday of American short fiction. Ruth McEnery Stuart (1852–1934), a New Orleans lady who married a farmer from Washington, Arkansas, wrote stories for *Harper's* and other national magazines. Washington became her fictional village of Simpkinsville, whose residents spoke the dialect of the Arkansas plain folk, dipped snuff, and espoused the gentle and genteel beliefs of mid-South Protestantism. Alice French (1850–1934) wintered in northeastern Arkansas, where she wrote, under the name Octave Thanet, stories of a grittier Arkansas life of trappers and squatters along the cypress swamps, as well as of cavalier planters and their family secrets. French made a serious effort to reproduce the language of her region. She also wrote a series of nonfiction pieces about several Arkansas towns, including Hot Springs and Pine Bluff.

Bernie Babcock (1868–1962) was one of the first Arkansas women to support herself, as well as her children, by writing. She published more than forty novels, many of them sentimental treatments of the Lincoln and Lee myths of the Civil War era, as well as *When Love Was Bold* (1928), which depicts the Osage and the Cherokee, several children's books, and *The Man Who Lied on Arkansas and What It Got Him* (1909). Babcock also participated in the WPA Writers Project, supervising the collection and transcription of the slave narratives.

Historical fiction continues to engage some Arkansas writers. Douglas Jones and Dee Brown both returned to Arkansas in middle age. Jones has written a notable body of work about the American West and Native American history. Some of his work is set in northwest Arkansas and the adjacent Indian Territory, including *Elkhorn Tavern* and *Weedy Rough*. Dee Brown has written historical nonfiction, including *Bury My Heart at Wounded Knee,* as well as the novels *Creek Mary's Blood* and *They Went Thataway.* Charles Portis's *True Grit* (1968) is set athwart the Arkansas boundary with what was then Indian Territory and makes splendid comic use of the Wild West material usually devoted to the casualties of Fort Smith's Hanging Judge Parker. The western writer Cynthia Haseloff mines this material for the genre market, as does the romance writer Velda Brotherton.

For much of the twentieth century, Arkansas writers left home to make their reputations, at first in New York or Europe and later in graduate school as well. Although their detachment from Arkansas led eventually out of regionalism into a generic American fiction, their work often used elements of southern and Arkansas life. Thyra Samter Winslow (1885–1961) left Fort Smith for New York, where she published more than a hundred pieces in the *Smart Set* between 1915 and 1923, as well as stories in *Redbook, Cosmopolitan,* and the *New Yorker.* Her depiction of small-town life, with mean-spirited, conventional characters in run-down neighborhoods or stuffy country clubs, contains many details drawn from her early experience in Arkansas. Some of these were collected in 1935 in *My Own My Native Land.*

Another Arkansas exile to New York, David Thibault (1892–1934) of Little Rock, published stories in *Collier's Magazine* between 1928 and 1931. He had also virtually completed a novel, *Salt for Mule,* set on a Delta plantation, when he died, and it was never published, though several chapters appeared in *Harper's Monthly Magazine* in 1937.

Arkansas writers in the last decades of the twentieth century made use of an Arkansas where mobile homes and shopping malls stand among or instead of fields and forests. The sense of place includes attention to local language, customs, and especially characters, and often these elements are links to or evolutions from the past. Mary Elsie Robertson's first collection of stories, *Jordan's Stormy Banks* (1961), draws on her roots in Charleston, hometown of several celebrated Arkansans, including the novelist Francis Gwaltney, author of *A Step in the River* (1960) and other novels portraying the New Southerner struggling to understand the changes in his way of life. Henry Dumas (1958–1987), an African American writer born in Sweetwater, became something of a cult figure after he was killed by a New York policeman. Some aspects of his work resemble science fiction, parable, and sermon, but the elegiac "Goodbye, Sweetwater" (1988) is a beautiful Arkansas story.

Some writers have remained physically in Arkansas but work in mainstream American modes with more or less reference to their homeplace. *Living in Little Rock with Miss Little Rock* (1993) by Jack Butler (who now lives in New Mexico) is an American blockbuster, although it is narrated by the Holy Spirit, centers on a millionaire lawyer and his wife, and obliquely includes the Creation Science trial. Joan Hess and Grif Stockley, on the other hand, have created Arkansas characters in crime fiction. Ellen Gilchrist and William Harrison, skilled fiction writers with national reputations, live and write in Arkansas, but they are not otherwise Arkansas authors.

Some of Donald Harington's work bears the sentimental or romantic stamp of his artistic forebears, but at his best, he represents a high point in working as a contemporary novelist with the traditional Ozark materials. He has created his own place, Stay More, home of the Stay Morons, who recur throughout his fiction. His novels, particularly *The Architecture of the Arkan-*sas Ozarks* (1975), use elements of the tall tale, the travel narrative, and the bawdy joke with a modern sensibility. Harington's nonfiction work *Let Us Build Us a City: Eleven Lost Towns* (1986) combines personal reminiscence with local history, a blend that is particularly appealing to Arkansans, or as he would say, Arkansawyers.

As throughout the South, nineteenth-century poetry in Arkansas was largely in the Romantic Victorian vein. Boston-born Confederate general Albert Pike wrote technically competent verses from his vast knowledge of the arcane mythology of Freemasonry. His *Prose Sketches and Poems, Written in the Western Country* (1834) preceded the obligatory "Letters from Arkansas," published in the *American Monthly Magazine* in 1836. Until well into the twentieth century, the list of published poets runs heavily to Civil War veterans and pious ladies, many of whom met for meetings of the Poets' Roundtable, the Arkansas Writers' Associations, the Ozark Writers and Artists Guilds, and other groups. Their works were published privately or in newspapers and popular magazines of the time, though generally their reputations were local or regional. A few small presses turned out books of verses, notably the Bar D Press of Siloam Springs in the 1930s, which published three members of the Davis family, as well as other poets and Otto Rayburn's various Ozarks publications.

Governor Ben Laney proclaimed an Arkansas Poetry Day in 1948, but it lapsed afterward. In 1963 the General Assembly enacted Poetry Day legislation, ordering it to be observed annually on October 15. The poets laureate of the state have generally been from the popular and confessional rather than the high-culture end of the literary spectrum. The first was Charles Davis of the *Gazette* staff, followed by Rosa Zagnoni Marinoni of Fayetteville, author of many volumes of verse and tireless promoter of poetry clubs and magazines. Next came Lily Peter of Marvel, another of Arkansas's great women personalities—farmer, teacher, environmentalist, and poet. The present poet laureate is Verna Lee Hinegardner.

John Gould Fletcher is arguably the only Arkansas writer until late in the twentieth century whose life and work show any connection with the wider literary world. Although he was proud of his southern heritage, he lived for more than twenty years in England and Europe, where he participated in various modernist movements, especially Imagism, before he returned to Little Rock to take up regionalism and folklore.

Fletcher's *Breakers and Granite* (1921) includes "Songs of the Arkansas." He also wrote an impressionistic history of the state, *Arkansas* (1947), as well as a memoir, *Life Is My Song* (1937). He received the only Pulitzer Prize yet to have been awarded an Arkansas writer for his *Selected Poems* (1938).

Toward midcentury, instances of poetry as a craft and an art, rather than an effusion of sentiment, began to occur more frequently. One reason for this, aside from the changes in taste and education in the country as a whole, is the creative-writing program at the University of Arkansas, founded in 1965 by James Whitehead and William Harrison. Faculty have included Miller Williams, Heather Ross Miller, and Joanne Meschery. While a number of the students and faculty, as well as other poets in the state, have achieved significant recognition, it is not for any particular regional character in their work, which has tended to follow the currents of American literature generally. Nevertheless, both older and younger poets often use the material of Arkansas traditional culture, especially the vernacular language (not to be confused with the dialect verse of an earlier age), and imagery, characters, and incidents of rural life.

Miller Williams is probably the best-known living Arkansas poet, especially since his performance at the second inauguration of President Clinton. Both he and his predecessor at the first Clinton inauguration, Maya Angelou, have used the imagery and language of rural Arkansas with considerable success. Both have traveled extensively, but unlike Angelou, Williams remains a rooted Arkansan, although the forms of his poetry come from many other traditions and languages.

Other poets have emerged late in the century, sometimes alumni of MFA programs in Fayetteville or elsewhere. C. D. Wright teaches writing at Brown, but she still often writes from her Arkansas sensibility. In 1994 she compiled an anthology and traveling exhibition celebrating Arkansas writing, *The Lost Roads Project*. The title is a reminder of Frank Stanford, Wright's collaborator in the Lost Roads Publishers. Before his suicide in 1978, shortly before he was thirty, Stanford had published seven books of poetry full of knives, hogs, privies, and death. A remarkable poet presented in the Project, virtually unknown to Arkansas and the world, is besmilr brigham of Horatio, whose lower-case signature disguises a commanding if obscure gift.

Jo McDougal teaches writing, but her poetry draws on her life on a farm in the Arkansas Delta. Andrea Hollander Budy teaches writing and operates a country

inn. Trombonist Gerald Sloan writes finely crafted and gently ironic poems while teaching at the University of Arkansas.

These poets generally share the inclination of other Arkansas writers to commemorate the past. It is not the "Natural State" of Pete Whetstone, and not the magnolia and hill-farm past, but a less-distant time populated by rock-and-roll and country singers, beauty queens, preachers, and grandparents in bus stations, house trailers, and small-town cafés, telling stories for all they are worth.

Ethel C. Simpson

See also Indians; Old Southwest; Southwestern Humor.

Fred Allsopp, *History of the Arkansas Press for a Hundred Years and More* (1922); William M. Baker and Ethel C. Simpson, *Arkansas in Short Fiction* (1986); Cassie M. Campbell Brothers, "Bibliography of Arkansas and Arkansas Authors' Materials" (M.L.S. thesis, University of Arkansas, 1962); Tom Dillard and Michael Dougan, *Arkansas History: A Selected Research Bibliography* (1984); John Gould Fletcher, *Arkansas* (1946); Sarah Fountain, *Arkansas Voices* (1941; 2nd ed., 1989); Bob Razer, *Contemporary Arkansas Authors: A Selective Bibliography* (1982); C. D. Wright, *The Lost Roads Project: A Walk-In Book of Arkansas* (1994).

ARKANSAS, UNIVERSITY OF

The University of Arkansas enrolled its first class in January 1872 in Fayetteville, Washington County. Although the University was and is considered a cultural and economic asset, the Arkansas General Assembly and rural interests wanted to expand its agricultural and technical curricula, so for many years literary study was not a preeminent concern. The limitations of the University library hampered close study of literary works. American literature was not permanently added to the curriculum until 1906, and the *production* of literature was entirely outside the University's sphere.

"Literary societies" like the Euphradian and the Cleosophic were actually debating clubs and by 1923 had ceased to exist. Student publications began with the *Arkansas University Magazine* in 1893. The *University Weekly* appeared in 1906; in 1920 it became the *Arkansas Traveler* and continues today as the campus newspaper. The yearbook began in 1897 as *The Cardinal*, but in 1916, after University athletes adopted a more ferocious mascot, it became *The Razorback*. *Preview*, begun in 1947 as an outlet for the undergraduate creative writing course, survives at the present time. The first humor magazine was *The White Mule* (1923–24). "Arkansas's Sharpest Magazine," *The Razor Blade,* appeared in 1954.

Unofficial or underground newspapers have appeared at least since *The X-Ray* precipitated a student strike in 1912. *Scuse Me,* an antiwar sheet, appeared sporadically from 1963 to 1967. *The Grapevine,* begun as an "alternate newspaper" in 1970, evolved into an independent weekly and continued until 1993.

The scholarly output of the English department reflects the status of literature in the University's earliest history. Before the 1960s, teaching occupied the faculty far more than research, although at least a few professors published scholarly projects. John Clark Jordan published *A Grammar for Heretics* in 1949. Robert L. Morris wrote a study of journalist Opie Read. H. Blair Rouse edited the writings of Ellen Glasgow. Duncan Eaves edited William Gilmore Simms's correspondence and, with Ben Kimpel, published extensively on Samuel Richardson. James C. Cowan founded the *D. H. Lawrence Review* in the 1960s, and J. R. Bennett edited *Style* and compiled bibliographies on political issues. During the last twenty-five years, the English department has included such scholars as John C. Guilds, Keneth Kinnamon, Brian Wilkie, Robert Cochran, the poet Sidney Burris, and more recently, Keith Booker and Sandra Sherman.

In 1965 the Program in Creative Writing was founded by James Whitehead and William Harrison. Faculty have included Miller Williams, Michael Heffernan, Joanne Meschery, and the translator John DuVal. Their students have been published in *Harper's,* the *Atlantic Monthly, American Poetry Review, Cimarron Review, Southern Poetry Review, Shenandoah, Esquire,* and *Aethlon: The Journal of Sport Literature,* and by Penguin, Ticknor and Fields, Viking, and Johns Hopkins. Their honors and prizes include Ellen Gilchrist's American Book Award and grants from the National Endowment for the Humanities to C. D. Wright and Frank Soos. Former MFA students now teaching writing include Wright at Brown, Lewis Nordan at Pittsburgh, and Lee K. Abbott at Ohio State.

The English department is not the only University division with writers among its students and faculty. Librarian Otto Salassi wrote young adult novels. Gerald Sloan, who teaches trombone, is an accomplished poet. Donald Harington, who teaches art history, has published novels, including *Cockroaches of Stay More.*

The University has not been the subject of a noticeable body of literature. In 1927, shortly before leaving the University, Murray Sheehan published *Half Gods,* satirizing both town and gown as provincial and narrow-minded. Poets from Rosa Zagnoni Marinoni to R. S. Gwynn have alluded to the University, as Ellen Gilchrist did in *The Annunciation* and Joan Hess in detective fiction set in Fayetteville. Grif Stockley's *Illegal Motion* is based on a scandal among the University's athletes.

Ethel C. Simpson

See also Arkansas, Literature of.

J. H. Reynolds and D. Y. Young, *History of the University of Arkansas* (1910); Ethel C. Simpson, *Image and Reflection: A Pictorial History of the University of Arkansas* (1990).

ART AND ARTISTS

The fine arts flourish where there are cities with complex economies and sophisticated audiences. The South was, for most of its history, the American region with a distinct lack of cosmopolitan centers. Art in the United States has flourished successively in the small but opulent colonial seaports of the eighteenth century both north *and* south, and then, after 1789, in the Northeast (Philadelphia, Boston, and New York City), the Midwest (Cincinnati, St. Louis, and Chicago), and then the Far West (San Francisco). These were the places most intensively urbanized before 1900 and thus the most productive historically. New York City, the most densely urban of all American cities and the one most intimately linked with all of Europe, has dominated American art since the 1840s, the decade it emerged as economically preeminent nationally. As the Northeast came to dominate the nation, American art came to mean northeastern art; everything else was relegated to the status of merely regional art. Margaret J. Preston of Louisville, Kentucky, lamented in the *Southern Review* in July, 1879, that "it is somewhat remarkable that our Southern States have never produced an artist of world-wide, or, indeed, of universally acknowledged national reputation, if we except Washington Allston (1779–1843) [who was born on a family plantation near Georgetown, South Carolina, but who moved north to Harvard, then London, then back to Boston]. . . . This sectionality of the art-spirit in our country is something unaccountable."

The South's social, economic, political, and religious patterns have deviated in significant ways from those of the rest of the United States. American historians have long debated whether the South's history has been marked more by continuity or discontinuity. Among the pivotal "breaks" that historians identify in the southern experience are the long duration of plantation agriculture and chattel slavery, the lack of cities, the inability to attract fresh European migration, a destructive and bitter military defeat in the Civil War, the social and political failure of biracial Reconstruction in the 1870s, almost a century of subsequent de jure racial segregation, the deep changes wrought by the Civil Rights Movement after 1950, and the region's recent unprecedented widespread prosperity. (The South, for the first time in its history, is no longer poor.) A crucial side effect of the South's contentious history was the engendering of antisouthern prejudices among many other Americans, especially among the critics and tastemakers of the victorious North. In the art world, this animosity exacerbated the neglect of what visual art the peripheral South did produce. The great migration of African Americans during and after the two world wars—as well as the lesser-known but similarly important exodus of Appalachian whites at the same time—carried aspects of popular southern culture into the heart of the great cities of the Northeast, Midwest, and Far West in the twentieth century. In the visual arts, these migrations are most dramatically manifested in folk, or self-taught, art after about 1940.

The South, for so long an agrarian society with only a few commercial seaports and only tax-starved, seasonal political seats inland, did not develop a wide social base for artistic patronage. Portraits of planters made by itinerant limners were not the strong art market that commissions from church vestries, merchants, lawyers, and civic institutions in the Northeast were so early in the nation's history. Another result of the South's lack of urbanization was that relatively few European immigrants came to the region after about 1850, and it was European master craftsmen, musicians, artists, and art teachers who advanced the fine arts across expanding nineteenth-century North America.

As inhibiting as the absence of major cities was the South's lack of heavy industry. Artist and influential Tulane University teacher Ellsworth Woodward wrote in the *Art Bulletin* of September, 1923, that because the South was agrarian rather than industrial, the region did not develop an appreciation for the commercial value of art. "The appreciation of spiritual values in art," he added, "the support of art education, the building of art galleries, and the patronage of artists are not likely to be conspicuous in countries or sections of countries that sell raw material and buy back all their finished products." The efflorescence of the visual arts in the South since World War II parallels the region's urbanization and industrialization, its rapid ascent out of rural poverty, and its convergence with national patterns in everything from educational attainment to suburbanization.

Religiously, southern culture was a layering of a white Episcopalian and Presbyterian upper class over a much larger mass of working-class evangelicals, mostly Baptists and Methodists, both white and black. This militantly religious society only crystalized as late as the 1830s, and it fostered a culture of "the Word," of emotional preaching and spirited hymn-singing. In the visual realm, southern denominations tended toward a dour Calvinism that was distrustful, if not virtually iconoclastic, in its attitudes toward image-making. Painting and sculpture were not integrated into religious architecture in most of the South, and "luxuries" like painting and statuary were—and still are—rare in the region's many Baptist churches, which often have unadorned, almost bleak, interiors. No tradition of religious art developed in the South to foster a love of visual symbolism as a means to express ultimate concerns. The sad childhood history of homosexual Kentucky-born artist Henry Lawrence Faulkner (1924–1981), whose parents and foster parents thought art ungodly, provides a painful example of how evangelical southern Protestantism discouraged aspiring artists. The sexual prudery that developed in the Bible-Belt South precluded the drawing and painting of nudes, one of the fountainheads of art in Western, African, and many other cultures. Conversely, a long heritage of Sunday-school sessions and Wednesday-night prayer meetings continues in the contemporary South among both white and black congregations and manifests itself in a knowledge of biblical allusions lost almost everywhere else. (Do *you* know where Mount Moriah is and what was atop it? Southerners, no matter what their class or color, usually do.) Bible stories and ballads help account for the continuing regional interest in narrative, as opposed to abstract, intellectualized, visual art.

In the United States, a country long without established churches, princes, aristocrats, or serious and continuous state support for the arts, most art patronage has come from wealthy city-dwellers emulating European elites. Despite the romantic image of the unappreciated artist painting in a garret, important visual art is only rarely created in isolation; significant bodies of work need continuing economic support. In *all* of the United States, the sustenance of artists has depended on prospering urban elites with the means and motivation to collect and commission art. The fertile Chesapeake Bay region of Virginia and Maryland had such easy direct water communication with England that its scattered tobacco plantations did not develop a truly dominant seaport city. Tidewater planters looked directly to London as the seat of fashion and touchstone of artistic styles, as did residents of Charleston and Savannah. Charleston's cultural life was leavened by French Huguenot settlers. Baltimore developed strong commercial links with German ports in northern Europe, while New Orleans had many connections with Bordeaux, France. After 1840, New Orleans blossomed as the largest and only truly cosmopolitan city in the Cotton Kingdom, with many northern and European immigrants and a precocious art and auction market. (Roman Catholic New Orleans with its painted church interiors and devotional images in virtually every Creole home was peculiar in the iconoclastic Calvinist Protestant South.)

The southern cities that did nurture the fine arts—New Orleans, Baltimore, Charleston, and Savannah—were worldly seaports with more sophisticated populations than their agrarian hinterlands. They were the urban centers that patronized artists in the eighteenth century and that later established art museums in the nineteenth century. George Cooke opened his National Gallery of Paintings in New Orleans in 1844, but it did not survive his early death in 1849. The Gibbes Museum of Art in Charleston was founded in 1858. The Telfair Academy opened in Savannah in 1875. The only other nineteenth-century foundation in the South was the Valentine Museum of Art in Richmond, Virginia, organized in 1892. The role of Jewish art collectors has been of marked importance in the modern period, but with the notable exception of New Orleans, important Jewish communities were not a feature of southern urban life before perhaps the 1950s. Today there are African American collectors across the region, often, though not always, collecting the work of self-taught black artists. As the South has flourished, the number and diversity of serious art collectors in the region has grown accordingly.

There are very few surviving drawings or paintings from the first generations of European settlement in the South, and most of these rarities are in European museums. Among the earliest were the watercolors of aboriginal life in Virginia executed by John White in 1585–86 and published in London in copper engravings by Theodore de Bry in 1590. In the eighteenth century, the scientific urge to record the New World resulted in an outpouring of botanical and animal art. Among the earliest extant works of southern art are those created to catalogue the region's extravagant flora and fauna. The self-taught English artist Mark Catesby (1679?–1749) first visited Virginia in 1712, staying for seven years, and then made a second trip to South Carolina from 1722 to 1725. His two-volume *Natural History of Carolina, Florida, and the Bahama Islands,* published in London, depicted southeastern animals and birds in their natural habitats. In the 1830s, Haitian-born and French-educated John James Audubon's (1785–1851) monumental *Birds of America* depicted many magnificent examples of southern bird life in the Lower Mississippi Valley flyway. During the next half-century, pictures of game became popular among art buyers. Hunting and fishing became key experiences in southern life among both rich and poor, and they have fostered a strong taste for art about animals. Today, duck-hunting prints continue to be popular, as are nostalgic English fox-hunting scenes. New Orleans's Achille Perelli (1822–1891) and George Louis Viavant (1872–1925) deftly depicted the trophies of the hunt and other wildlife from fish to dragonflies. These pictures were often hung in dimly lit dining rooms as backdrops to elaborate dinners. A specialized kind of animal painting that became popular in the nineteenth-century South was the horse portraiture that gentlemen hung in their libraries and offices. Owning strings of prize thoroughbreds was a prestigious kind of conspicuous consumption in the South, analogous to the private railroad cars, yachts, and art galleries attached to the mansions of northern cities. Swiss-born Edward Troye (1808–1874) worked in Kentucky and the Gulf South and became the most important horse painter in the horse racing–mad antebellum South.

Visual art in the South, from the earliest explorers' sketches to later planter portraits by itinerant painters to the latest conceptualist movements, has developed at the periphery of national and seminal European artistic developments. In the early nineteenth century, painters came from the North or from Europe on expeditions during the fever-free winter and spring months to make portraits of rich seaboard merchants and opulent inland planters. These portraits were rather flat in the eighteenth and early nineteenth centuries but became more modeled over time. The first known professional portrait painter to settle in tidewater Virginia was Charles Bridges (1670–1747), who arrived in Williamsburg in 1734. Swiss-born Jeremiah Theus (1716–1774), a Protestant refugee who settled in Charleston in 1735, looked to English engravings for the poses in his rigidly formal portraits of elite South Carolinians. Yucatan-born Antonio Salazar (c. 1700s–1802), the first portrait painter resident in New Orleans, arrived during the Spanish era in about 1782. Simply documentary at first, portraiture in the South increasingly became a psychological study of the sitter, following European Romantic sentiments.

At the close of the eighteenth century, colonial portraiture gave way to the classicist influence of Benjamin West (1738–1820), whose school in London trained many American artists. Among West's best-known students were Charles Willson Peale (1741–1827) and Thomas Sully (1783–1872). Between 1803 and 1805, Gilbert Stuart (1755–1828) was active in the new capital in Washington painting iconic portraits of national leaders, many of them southerners. There were a few African American painters in the late nineteenth-century South, such as free man of color Joshua Johnson (active 1795–1825) in bustling Baltimore. Jules Lion (c. 1809–1866), a French-born free man of color, was active as a lithographer and later exhibited the first daguerrotypes in New Orleans. Louisianian Eugene Warburg (1826–1859), born a slave, was a tomb-sculptor who became a sculptor of marble busts, though very few of his works survive. He eventually settled in Italy, where so many other American sculptors worked. These earliest African American artists worked within mainstream American and Western art and sought universal acceptance; they did not generally create specifically black art.

The vast American land itself is perhaps the greatest theme in American painting and photography, arguably more important than depictions of people. A demand for landscape paintings emerged in the South only after about 1850, twenty years after the flowering of what is now called the Hudson River School. These tended to be moderate-sized canvases that were hung in gilded frames on the walls of parlors and sitting rooms. Most often these Luminist works were of primeval scenes, such as the mysterious cypress swamps of southern Louisiana. Looking at these pictures, one

might think that the nineteenth-century South was a virgin wilderness. It was not; it was, by and large, an unkempt, export-oriented agricultural landscape. In Natchez, Mississippi, site of one of the greatest concentrations of grand 1850s houses in the South, nearly all the nineteenth-century pictures hung in the formal rooms there are European scenes painted by European artists and bought by Natchez planters on sojourns abroad. There is not one painting of the fertile cotton fields that produced the wealth that built these palatial antebellum villas.

Heroically scaled historical paintings fit for state buildings were rare in the Old South. Huge works that take years to paint generally require state or institutional patronage, and this the South did not have. Southern state capitols were rare exceptions, but most of their art consisted of nothing more ambitious than head portraits, not grand didactic historical tableaux. Public statuary was also scarce in the antebellum South, and where it existed, as in Washington, D.C., and Richmond, Virginia, it was likely to have been commissioned from the Italian Neo-Classical sculptor Antonio Canova (1757–1822). After the war, in the once-sovereign Republic of Texas, history painting became an important vehicle of Anglo-Texan identity in the large-scale history paintings that Henry Arthur McArdle (1836–1908) and William Huddle (1847–1892) executed for the state capitol in Austin.

During the Civil War, little fine art was produced in the South. For one thing, artists' supplies were imported and blockade-runners had other priorities. The one place where artists did gather was at Richmond, Virginia, the Confederate capital. Painters including William James Hubbard (1807–1862), William D. Washington (1833–1870), and William Ludwell Sheppard (1833–1912) were active painting portraits and contemporary military scenes. But the chief art of that protomodern war was photography, and it was most tellingly practiced by photographers from the industrial North, including Mathew Brady (1823–1896) and George N. Bernard (1819–1902), among others. Confederate prisoners of war sometimes whiled away their confinement in northern camps doing whittling and scrimshaw, but this, of course, was more craft than fine art.

Not until the wave of statuary commemorating the Lost Cause—an enthusiasm that took off in the mid-1880s and that lasted into the late 1920s—did southern cities have much in the way of public sculpture. Richmond, Virginia, the capital of the defeated Confederacy, attracted the most commemorative statuary. The Confederate Memorial at the University of North Carolina at Chapel Hill by John Wilson (a Canadian), and the monument to the Women of the Confederacy on the capitol grounds at Raleigh by Augustus Lukeman (1872–1935) are fine pieces of Beaux-Arts bronze statuary commemorating an idealized secessionist South. In 1884, New York sculptor Alexander Doyle's (1857–1922) statue of Robert E. Lee atop a Doric column was unveiled at Lee Circle in New Orleans. The stock gray-granite statues of Confederate soldiers so often encountered in courthouse squares throughout the post-1877 "Redeemed" South were usually carved in New England quarries and shipped south on the railroad. In 1915 the United Daughters of the Confederacy commissioned Gutzon Borglum to begin carving a relief of Robert E. Lee, Jefferson Davis, and Thomas J. "Stonewall" Jackson across the face of Stone Mountain, a granite outcropping just outside Atlanta, Georgia. This gargantuan project, considered by some the world's largest sculpture, was not completed until 1970.

From the mid-nineteenth century until after World War II, many if not most southerners with artistic aspirations traveled outside the region to the Art Students League in New York City, the Pennsylvania Academy of the Fine Arts in Philadelphia, the School of the Art Institute of Chicago, or to the Académie Julian in Paris. The Académie Julian was especially popular with Americans because it did not demand French-language entrance exams, had no age restrictions, and kept its studios open later than the École des Beaux Arts. In Paris, New York City, Philadelphia, and Chicago, southern students were exposed to a stimulating array of art in museums and galleries and came under many influences that they brought back when—and if—they returned to the South, which many did not.

Like other Americans in the burgeoning professions during the nineteenth century, artists were highly mobile and went where training, and later professional opportunity, beckoned. The more ambitious the student, the more likely he or she was to range far from home. Not only did artists travel outside the region to study, they often later made several moves in their professional lifetimes. Artists in the South were probably less marked by provincialism than the members of any other profession. They put the region's art in touch with national and international changes in perceptions, though artistic styles tended to come late and stay longer in the peripheral South. Abstract art was espe-

cially late in coming to the South, and it was not widely embraced by artists or collectors. There were exceedingly few art galleries in the South outside antique shops before about 1970. Wealthy southerners bought art in Chicago, New York City, or Europe, but rarely in their own region.

Economics influenced visual culture in the South in another negative way in the post–Civil War era. Whereas the antebellum South was a mercantile colony of England, which bought southern cotton for its textile mills, after the war the conquered ex-Confederacy became an economic colony of the industrial North. Southern railroads, and then southern coal and iron deposits, were bought by northern investors, who amalgamated them into national corporations that drained wealth out of the region. The one colossal fortune amassed by a southerner after the Civil War was Washington Duke's tobacco empire. But in 1884 Duke moved the American Tobacco Company from North Carolina to New York City, where his heir, James Buchanan Duke, built an imposing limestone mansion off Fifth Avenue in 1912; today, emblematically, it is the home of New York University's Institute of Fine Arts. Economic colonization by the victors deprived the South of any of the untaxed fortunes of the Gilded Age, the massive wealth that assembled the great private collections of European, Asian, African, and Oceanic art and that later endowed the encyclopedic art museums of the Northeast and Midwest. These museums, in turn, were often the sponsors of the nation's first serious art schools.

Despite all these inhibiting factors, during the 1870s and 1880s an important school of landscape painting emerged in the Deep South. Often horizontal in composition, precisely drawn, and radiating a sense of expansiveness and solitude, these pictures are an afterglow of American Luminist painting. Many of them capture the transforming power of a moment, especially dawn, sunset, or the passing of dramatic cloud formations. The coastal swamps along the Gulf of Mexico, with their dense vegetation, still waters, peculiar light, and atmospheric effects, attracted both painters and their patrons. New Orleanians Richard Clague (1821–1873), William Henry Buck (1840–1888), and Marshall Joseph Smith Jr. (1854–1923) painted many swamp scenes, as did St. Louis-based Joseph Rusling Meeker (1827–1887). This strange, watery world was not the only primeval southern landscape recorded and celebrated during the period; Carl Christian Brenner

(1838–1888) painted the surviving virgin beech forests of Kentucky with similar awe.

Genre painting—art depicting ordinary people involved in everyday activities—also flourished in the South. A master of recording the domestic and political life on the frontier was George Caleb Bingham (1811–1879), who was born in Virginia but worked in the Missouri borderland and on the Mississippi River. Toward the close of the nineteenth century, when slavery had been abolished for a generation but cotton plantations still existed, some artists were drawn to depicting the life of hard-pressed black tenant farmers and sharecroppers. White artists such as Louisiana-reared George Henry Clements (1854–1935) painted genre scenes of African Americans engaged in their tasks in the 1880s. South Carolinian William Aiken Walker (1838–1921) found a profitable niche painting pictures of black field hands dressed in rags, works that confirmed northern views of the backward South and that sold well to tourists in the postwar era. The stereotyping of blacks (later continued by the movies) pervades many of Walker's works. King Cotton had long been both the South's chief source of concentrated wealth and, because of the wild unpredictability of cotton prices on the world market and the relentlessly downward trend in cotton prices, its greatest obstacle to progress.

There were few paintings of urban scenes in the nineteenth-century South. A body of city scenes only began in the early twentieth century in Charleston and New Orleans as artists turned their gaze on the old landmarks of their historic towns, which by then were usually sadly, if picturesquely, decayed. Rhode Island–born Tulane University artist and professor William Woodward (1859–1939) and Charleston-born Elizabeth O'Neill Verner (1883–1979) changed the awareness of their cities through their art. These and other artists' views of the melancholy condition of the region's few historic cores made cultivated southerners aware of their endangered landmarks and helped spur the South into becoming the national leader in architectural preservation. New Orleans's French Quarter, Charleston, Savannah, and Natchez became pioneers in architectural preservation in the United States in the 1920s and 1930s.

All the way into the 1920s, Impressionism was a major influence on many southern artists. It is a good example of the way artistic movements tended to come late and stay longer in the peripheral and conservative South. Sunlit and cheerful, most Impressionist-influ-

enced works employed everyday subject matter, a light palette of colors laid down side by side, and broken brushstrokes. Impressionists liked to paint *en plein air,* outdoors in natural light. In New Orleans, Ellsworth Woodward (1861–1939) and his brother William both employed Impressionist techniques and taught them to their students. Savannah-born William Posey Silva (1859–1948) painted Impressionist scenes in Tennessee, Georgia, and the Carolinas.

Tonalism was another important stylistic movement in early twentieth-century southern painting. Employing a deliberately restricted palette and usually one dominant color, tonalist art was evocative and dreamlike. The prolific Louisiana landscape painter Alexander John Drysdale (1870–1934) invented his own fluid technique using pigments diluted with kerosene to produce tonalist landscapes that had the soft look of watercolors or pastels.

As in the rest of the United States, there was a burst of artistic activity in the South during the prosperous years between World War I and the stock market crash of 1929. From about 1915 into the 1930s, New Orleans's French Quarter harbored an active bohemia that attracted both artists and writers. Small proprietary art schools sprang up in the picturesque and then-low-rent Quarter. Accomplished artists from northern cities came to the Crescent City to paint during its mild winters, among them Chicagoan Robert Wadsworth Grafton (1876–1936). In 1921 the Southern States Art League was founded as a regional advocate for local artists and art clubs. It organized the first traveling exhibitions of art created in the South, and its yearly conferences, exhibitions, and prizes encouraged specifically southern works. Two years after its founding, the League moved from Charleston to New Orleans, where it remained until it surrendered its charter in 1950.

The call for art that embodied a specifically African American aesthetic was led by Massachusetts-born W. E. B. Du Bois (1868–1963) and Howard University philosopher Alain Locke (1885–1954). They helped stimulate what came to be called the New Negro Movement, which flourished not in the then-segregated South, where most blacks lived, but in the freer air of the North. It was not until the twentieth century that many pictures of blacks *by* blacks were made in the South. Until a generation or two ago, African American southerners had to move north to pursue careers as recognized visual artists. In the 1920s and 1930s, a great flowering of African American art took place in

New York City's Harlem especially, but also in Chicago's Bronzeville. Many of its key figures were born in the South or in border states. Kansas City art teacher Aaron Douglas (1898–1979) moved to New York City in 1924. There, his art moved from conventional realism to patterned designs that fused Art Deco with black subject matter. Many of Douglas's works served as illustrations for the burst of literary activity known as the Harlem Renaissance. Louisiana-born Archibald J. Motley Jr. (1891–1981) studied art in Chicago, where he painted portraits of the new, educated African American middle class.

Women achieved recognition in visual art in the South only in the early twentieth century. The earliest known professional woman portraitist in the South was Henrietta Johnson (active 1703–1729), who made pastel portraits of fashionable Charlestonians in the 1720s. In the very late nineteenth and early twentieth centuries, some genteel white women, excluded from business, government, and college teaching, and confined to the realms of domesticity and culture, became watercolorists and oil painters. Among them were Anne Goldthwaite, Nell Choate Jones, Alice Ravenel Huger Smith, and Helen M. Turner. Anne Goldthwaite (1869–1944) was born in Montgomery, Alabama. In the early 1890s, she moved to New York City to study art and later continued her studies in Paris. In 1921 she became an instructor at the Art Students League in New York City, where she taught until her death. Portraits and floral still lifes boldly outlined in black were among her best-known works. Though far from her native region, she always considered herself a southerner. Nell Choate Jones (1879–1981), a native of Hawkinsville, Georgia, moved to Brooklyn at an early age. Married to painter and etcher Eugene H. Jones, she summered among other artists in Woodstock, New York, and also studied in France. She painted in Brooklyn, Italy, and the South. Though a white woman, her southern subjects were often black folk at work. Alice Ravenel Huger Smith (1876–1958) was born into a prominent family in Charleston, South Carolina, and spent her entire life there. Essentially self-taught, she worked successively in oil, etching, wood-block prints, and then watercolor. Smith's Carolina Low Country watercolors are especially evocative and reflect a Japanesque sensitivity to the coastal lowland and its flora. Elizabeth O'Neill Verner (1883–1979) was another Charlestonian artist active in the early twentieth century. Unlike Smith, Verner was drawn especially to urban scenes and painted the black flower vendors of

Charleston as well as views of the old city. Both artists were important in spurring an appreciation of their venerable city that resulted in early and successful efforts at historic preservation.

The first three decades of the twentieth century also saw the emergence of many gifted women ceramacists. The best-known art potters of the period were educated at the Sophie Newcomb College for Women in New Orleans (Tulane University). Joseph F. Meyer (1845–1931) and George E. Ohr (1857–1918) threw the pots, which were then carved and glazed by Newcomb students. Henrietta Bailey (1874–1950), Sadie A. E. Irvine (1887–1970), Corinne Marie Chalaron (c. 1900–1977), and Jane Randolph Whipple (1910–) were among the Newcomb artists who brought Art-Nouveau ceramics to the highest level of achievement. Many of their best works used southern flora as their motif and captured the effects of moonlight glimpsed through palms, pines, oaks, and cypresses.

The nostalgic "return to the land" evident among the famed, if mistaken, Vanderbilt Agrarians was also evident in painting. The regionalist movement espoused by Missouri-born Thomas Hart Benton (1889–1975) had a profound influence on Mississippi-born John McCrady (1911–1968), who briefly studied under him. Much regionalist art looked back to an earlier agrarian America, and the South was still predominantly agricultural in the 1930s, still wed to fickle, ever-less-profitable cotton. McCrady created an urban regionalism in his studies of the buildings and customs of New Orleans and established his own art school in the French Quarter. In Georgia, Lamar Dodd (1909–) painted raw and powerful pictures of an exploited South of open copper mines, wasted farms, and Birmingham, Alabama, coke furnaces and steel mills. In Alabama, John Kelly Fitzpatrick (1888–1953) painted rural scenes tinged with humor.

As part of its economic recovery program, the New Deal created the Federal Arts Project of the Works Projects Administration, which employed many artists between 1934 and 1939. Artists' workshops, easel-painting projects, and especially the decoration of public buildings with murals sprang up across the nation, including the South. Every state had its active federal arts programs. This federal patronage was so widespread that it even included African American artists. Hale Woodruff (1900–1980), a northern-born, Paris-educated sometime teacher at the Atlanta University complex, painted a three-part mural on the *Amistad* mutiny at the Talladega College library in Alabama for the Federal Arts Project in 1939. Self-taught Tennessee stonecarver William Edmondson (1863–1951), who began carving figures from abandoned limestone curbing, was also employed in a New Deal art project. His primitive figures, often of biblical subjects, appealed to art lovers accustomed to abstract modernist works, and Edmondson went on to a solo exhibit at the Museum of Modern Art in 1937, the first African American artist so recognized.

One of the paradoxes of visual art in the South is that the wrenching Depression of the 1930s resulted in the creation of great work—the black-and-white documentary photographs of the suffering of southerners, many of them commissioned by the New Deal's Farm Security Administration. These photos were—and this is unusual in the United States—art with a reforming social purpose. To President Franklin D. Roosevelt, the South's endemic poverty was "the nation's number one economic problem." Photographers from both the North and South combed the recesses of the rural and urban slum South to record the plight of its people both black and white. Photographers such as New Jersey-born Marion Post Wolcott (1910–1990) and young Mississippian Eudora Welty (1909–2001) created profoundly humane portraits of life in the hard-pressed South. They did for the poor southerners of the Great Depression what the itinerant portrait painters had done for the opulent planters of the Old South—remember their faces for posterity. A portraitist who turned to similar themes was Mississippian Marie Atchinson Hull (1890–1980), who conveyed the anguish of tenant farmers and sharecroppers about to be pushed off the land by falling cotton prices.

A singular southern photographer was Clarence John Laughlin (1905–1985), whose significant work began when the U.S. Army Corps of Engineers commissioned him to document the construction of new levees along the lower Mississippi River in 1940. His great book, *Ghosts Along the Mississippi* (1948), wed French surrealism with a melancholy nostalgia for an imagined Old South. His haunting, staged photographs seem a visual parallel to William Faulkner's mythic southern novels. Both artists created powerful interpretations of an intricately imagined Old South just as the region was breaking with its confining past and entering the modern age.

The most important link between the South and modernism occurred at Black Mountain College between 1933 and 1949 when German-born Joseph Albers (1888–1976) was dominant there. Tellingly, this was not a colony of artists from the South but rather an encampment in the North Carolina mountains of urban artists from Europe and the Northeast. Robert Rauschenberg (1925–), noted for his "combines" of painting and collage and for his use of silk screen and photographic processes, was Black Mountain's most famous visual artist.

World War II slowed the production of art throughout the United States, except for the military services, which engaged many artists to record American forces around the world. The 1940s were a turning point in southern history, and eventually for musical, visual, and theatrical art in the South. Massive federal wartime investment in the region, the stimulation of industry, induced urbanization, accelerated migrations among southerners within and beyond the region, and migrations of northerners to the South laid the groundwork for the booming, air-conditioned, auto-oriented Sunbelt South of today.

The life and art of Will Henry Stevens (1881–1949) are a key example of the artistic changes that took place in the South in the late 1940s. This southern Indiana-born painter, who visited New York City's galleries almost every summer, moved to New Orleans to teach at Tulane University's Newcomb College in 1921 and stayed at the college until 1948. He became a pioneer modernist and helped introduce abstract art to the South. The act of painting became more important than the representation of the thing being painted. Strong colors, abstract patterns, and nonrepresentational designs characterized this new and challenging kind of art. (Stevens' interest in Chinese Taoist philosophy was another way he broke with conventional thinking.) Another artist who explored nonobjective painting, among other modes, was Paul Ninas (1903–1964), some of whose works convey a surreal quality. Nonrepresentational art came relatively late to the South, and unlike Impressionism, abstract expressionism never became widespread in the region. Representational and narrative art, on the other hand, endured in the South, and they continue to thrive today, finding new interpreters and interpretations even when the means appear deliberately modern or postmodern.

In the 1940s and 1950s, with racial prejudice still virulent in the United States, many black artists were drawn to Paris for both its artistic and its social freedom. In the wake of the Civil Rights Movement of the 1950s and 1960s, southern-born and -based African American artists began to achieve critical recognition in their own country. New Orleans artist John Scott

(1940–) creates sculpture that is self-consciously West African and African American in inspiration. New Orleanian Willie Birch (1942–), who worked for many years in Bedford-Stuyvesant in New York City, makes life-sized papier-mâché sculptures of African American life. Louisiana-born Michael Ray Charles (1967–) paints confrontational circus-posterlike paintings with a searing view of African Americans (and whites) in a contemporary America he calls the "Liberty Bros. Permanent-Daily Circus." But not all black artists can be identified so directly with one community. Washington-based color-field painter Sam Gilliam's (1933–) work, for example, is distinctly universalist in spirit; his work makes no particular reference to Africa.

The South's rich strain of indigenous folk art began to attract the attention of critics and collectors in the postwar 1940s as northerners moved south. Often, though not always, from rural areas, these untutored "outsider" artists felt driven to create painted or carved images. Their work is often autobiographical, patriotic, deeply religious, or visionary, and many began their creative careers after experiencing what they believed to be a divine call. A few curators and pioneer collectors discovered this wonderland of vital "primitive art" and brought it to public attention. Among the earliest to come to national attention was Clementine Hunter (1886–1988), who painted scenes from African American communities on Louisiana plantations. Black New Orleanian Sister Gertrude Morgan (1901–1980) painted small pictures of her religious visions and sold them on the streets to care for the orphans she took in. North Carolina-born Minnie Evans (1892–1987), another African American woman, created intricate, untitled anthropomorphic drawings. White Mississippian Theora Hamblett (1895–1977) developed her own pointalist technique and employed naïve perspectives. Black Georgia-born Bessie Harvey (1929–1994) came to art late in life and fashioned sculptures out of tree branches and roots rejected by sawmills. Black Louisianian David Butler (1898–) was discovered by a museum curator who came across his yard alive with moving, painted metal whirligigs. Purvis Young (1943–), a sometime homeless African American man in Miami, Florida, makes vibrant art out of found materials and house paint recording life in the violent inner-city ghetto. White Alabamian Reverend Howard Finster (1916–) makes painted constructions of wood and plastic that manifest his heavenly visions. These works of indigenous art are appreciated by a sophisticated public prepared by the revolutionary visual innovations of modern Western art to seek highly individualized ways of seeing. The emergence of this often religiously inspired folk art makes what Donald Davidson wrote in the *Saturday Review* of May 15, 1926, seem prophetic: "Fundamentalism, in one aspect, is blind and belligerent ignorance; in another, it represents a fierce clinging to poetic supernaturalism against the encroachments of cold logic; it stands for moral seriousness."

Utilitarian needs resulted in the making of pottery vessels in the early South. The most proficient early potters were the German-speaking Moravians, members of an industrious and communal-minded Protestant sect who filtered through Pennsylvania into the Piedmont of North Carolina to what is now Old Salem. They produced locally sought-after lead-glazed earthenware made from local red clays with white, green, or brown decorative flourishes. Fragile earthenware, with its toxic lead glaze, was superseded by more rugged salt-glazed stoneware in the second quarter of the nineteenth century; alkaline glazes evolved later. Early southern potteries clustered near clay beds and ample timber supplies (to fuel the kilns) and flourished in the Piedmont of North Carolina; they produced jars, jugs, milk crocks, and butter churns along with pitchers and dishes. Many of the potteries were family enterprises that passed down the generations. Sturdy and utilitarian, their output was not considered art, though modern collectors prize the simplicity and purity of their elegant forms and dark glazes. The Edgefield District in central west South Carolina was a secondary center of southern pottery production from about 1810 to 1865. Among the more fanciful occasional works produced there by both slave and free potters were whimsical face jugs with grimacing visages. Georgia also became a center of utilitarian southern pottery-making in the antebellum period. The glass Mason jar, patented in 1858, and later metal cans eventually displaced handmade pottery across the region. In the early twentieth century, art potteries appeared in the North Carolina Piedmont, especially in the Seagrove area in Moore County. Beginning with colorful domestic and touristic wares in the 1920s and 1930s, some North Carolina potters began making more self-consciously artistic pieces in the mid-twentieth century. Pottery-making was reborn as an acknowledged southern art practiced by old families such as the Aumans, Browns, Coles, Owens, and Teagues. Masters of the craft today include Ben Owen III (1968–), a student of Asian ceramics who has taken his long family heritage and fused it with both ancient and contemporary forms and glazes.

Color photography emerged as an important art in the South in the 1970s and 1980s. Alabamian William Christenberry (1936-) began as a painter, achieved renown as a color photographer, and then moved on to collages and sculpture. Although he lives in Washington, D.C., he returns to photograph the disappearing vernacular dogtrot houses of Alabama's Black Belt, sometimes making sculptures of the same structures. He even incorporates red Alabama dirt in some of his pieces. William Eggleston (1939–) of Memphis, Tennessee, is another important contemporary color photographer. Although his subjects are often mundane, even banal, his unusual point of view makes his images extraordinary. Mississippian Birney Imes (1951–) studied art in Knoxville, Tennessee, and then went to work as staff photographer for his father's small-town newspaper. He opened a studio in Columbus, Mississippi, and continues to photograph the life of the people in his home county and in the Mississippi Delta. He has made memorable color-saturated photographs of the black juke joints of the rural South.

The deep changes that reshaped the South after World War II drew white and black southerners away from the land, attracted them to cities, and after 1970 to rapidly expanding suburbs. Americans from other sections were also induced to move to the low-living-cost South. What had been a thin patchwork of art museums increased greatly in number and improved vastly in quality after about 1970, becoming by the mid-1980s a formidable network of active institutions. The link between nineteenth-century heavy industry and late-twentieth-century support of the fine arts is evidenced by the founding of the Birmingham Museum of Art in 1951, which has become a leading art institution in the South. Every metropolitan area built an art museum and also publicly financed performing-arts facilities that made the arts accessible to a much wider public than before. Southern universities grew and matured, adding fine-arts programs. The South began to draw some out-of-region students and many out-of-region art teachers. Though many aspiring artists continue to study in New York City or Chicago, the region now had its own university-affiliated studio programs, not just the small private art schools that had previously been available. Arts education and exposure to old and new works stimulated both the appreciation and making of art in the region. And since the appreciation and the purchase of fine art are closely linked to educational and economic achievement, the marked elevation of living standards and educational levels in the post–World War II Sunbelt has been a great boost to the visual and performing arts across the South. Explosively growing Florida and Texas have seen the most ambitious art activity, worthy of more attention than this brief notice can give.

Colonial Williamsburg in Virginia, whose restoration and reconstruction began in 1926 with funding from John D. Rockefeller Jr., can be considered the first important museum of southern culture. But significant scholarly attention to southern visual art only began in 1960, when the Corcoran Gallery of Art in Washington, D.C., organized an exhibition entitled *American Painters of the South*. It featured mostly works from Maryland, the District of Columbia, Virginia, and South Carolina from the 1710s to the 1860s. In 1965 the Museum of Early Southern Decorative Arts opened in Winston-Salem, North Carolina, with the furniture, architectural interiors, and paintings collected by Frank L. Horton and his mother, Theo L. Taliaferro. In 1983 the Virginia Museum of Fine Arts in Richmond mounted an exhibition that traveled to six major southern museums and that was accompanied by an important catalogue. Between 1984 and 1986, an exhibition of southern art collected by Dr. Robert Coggins of Marietta, Georgia, traveled to eleven museums and was accompanied by a seminal book. Estill Curtis Pennington curated an important show of Louisiana works at the New Orleans Museum of Art in 1990. In 1992 the Morris Museum of Art opened in Augusta, Georgia, the first museum devoted exclusively to southern fine art; Estill Curtis Pennington wrote its catalogue. Previously, museums in the South that in the early twentieth century had acquired or inherited regional works had consigned most of them to storage or even de-accessioned them in an effort to present "national" art. It was left to state and local historical societies to collect and exhibit southern art, an enterprise they pursued and continue to pursue with real imagination and consistent dedication. Recently, many of the major museums in the region have opened galleries dedicated to southern art, often specifically local art. In 1985 the Greenville County Museum of Art in South Carolina decided to focus its holdings on the South, and within a decade it had amassed an outstanding regional collection. Today, there is an increasing number of exploratory temporary museum exhibitions and ever-better monographs on individual southern artists.

In 2001 the University of New Orleans opened the Ogden Museum of Southern Art.

The booming contemporary South, with its interstate highways, international airports, high-rises, office parks, new suburbs, and shopping centers drew new people (especially from the Northeast and Midwest) and broke the early-twentieth-century isolation of life in the region. Southern culture blossomed with a new self-confidence particularly evident in music: rhythm-and-blues, gospel, soul, country, and rock attracted national, even international, audiences. Though the South's visual arts have not achieved the wide popularity of its music, they, too, have flourished prodigiously over the last two generations. The South is also now attracting Latino and Asian immigration, which is making its impact on the region, especially in Texas and South Florida. Anglo and Mexican American artists are flourishing in Texas, and Anglo and Cuban (and other Latino) American artists are active in South Florida. Among the most noted artists working in the South today or associated with the region are Washington color-field painter Kenneth Noland (1924–), Cy Twombly (1929–) in Virginia and Italy, Jasper Johns (1930–), James Rosenquist (1933–), and assemblage sculptor John Chamberlain (1927–) in Florida. Northern artists such as Robert Rauschenberg (1925–) have established studios in Captiva Island, Florida. Sculptor Donald Judd (1928–1994) occupied a former military base in Marva, Texas, with a vast minimalist installation open to the public.

The prosperity and cultural self-confidence of today's South have encouraged the region's artists to develop highly individual and disparate styles. The influences available to the open-minded late-modern southern artist are eclectic and unpredictable. Europe and New York City are still important to many, but so are California, Asia, Latin America, and for many black artists, West Africa. Young artists are as likely to be aesthetically fed by looking at reproductions of ancient Anatolian art as by examples of contemporary European works. Louisianian Clyde Connell (1901–1998) made monumental and enigmatic sculptures that look equally back to "primitive" tribal art and forward to cutting-edge sculpture. Louisianian John Geldersma (1942–) fashions masks and "spirit poles" that look to New Guinea while being wholly of our time and made of a specifically southern material, cypress driftwood. Other artists take the opposite tack and seek to establish abstract, personal aesthetics seemingly unconnected with anything that went before. The work of Ida

Kohlmeyer (1912–1997), an abstract artist long active in New Orleans, epitomizes the postmodern fascination with signs and symbols and seeks to move beyond any particular culture to imagine its own visual universe, its own system of meaning.

As the South has become more self-confident, some artists have chosen to probe evolving southern culture itself. Mississippi-born William Dunlap (1944–) paints panoramic and sometimes troubling or melancholic landscapes. Nor is ironic humor absent in southern art today. Alabama-born Clyde Broadway (1944–) juxtaposes religion, politics, and popular culture in witty reconsiderations of regional icons.

The South has emerged as a battleground in the politicization of the public funding of writing, history, theater, and visual art in the 1990s. Jesse Helms, the senior senator from North Carolina, among others, has spearheaded a campaign to eliminate *all* federal support for the arts in order to prevent the possible dissemination of any of what he considers obscene, homoerotic, or blasphemous works with tax monies. This crusade has sought to create a division between purportedly "amoral" art elites and a presumedly monolithic, moralistic South. The paradoxical result of this campaign has been to reveal how widespread and democratic federal funding for the arts and humanities has been since the establishment of the National Endowment for the Arts and the National Endowment for the Humanities in 1965, and how much local public acceptance the visual and performing arts have achieved in the contemporary South. Nonetheless, the "culture war" has cut federal funding for the arts from $162 million in 1995 to $99 million in 1996 and has resulted in the complete elimination of all individual artists' grants. (Institutions feed on art; only individual artists create important art.) There has also been a shift in public arts funding to the state level through block grants (40 percent), while simultaneously diminishing the role of federal arts and humanities agencies. Thus the crusade against "elitism" has shrunk the public sector and put even more emphasis on the role of the rich, both individuals and corporations, in American art in the now-prosperous South.

Randolph Delehanty

See also Architecture; Photography; "Sahara of the Bozart."

Bruce W. Chambers, *Art and Artists of the South: The Robert W. Coggins Collection* (1984); Randolph Delehanty, *Art in the*

American South: Works from the Ogden Collection (1996); Jessie Poesch, *The Art of the Old South: Painting, Sculpture, Architecture, and the Products of Craftsmen, 1560–1860* (1983); Thomas W. Styron, *Impressionism and the South* (1968); Alice Rae Yelen, *Passionate Visions of the American South: Self-Taught Artists from 1940 to the Present* (1994).

ASHEVILLE, NORTH CAROLINA

The secretary of the Altamont Board of Trade, as a character in Thomas Wolfe's 1923 play, *Welcome To Our City,* promotes Altamont to a real-estate client as "a city of 30,000 souls, situated on the crest of a plateau 2,300 feet above the level of the ocean." He goes on to describe the mountain ranges, crystal streams, and virgin forests surrounding this small city. Secretary Bailey also brags of the schools, roads, banks, hotels, inns, boardinghouses, churches, paved streets, and the air that works wonders for all who come to stay in Altamont. In this satirical play, the young Thomas Wolfe, Asheville's most famous writer, established his literary venue, using his hometown as the setting of much of his work.

Asheville as Altamont (and in later Wolfe novels, Libya Hill) would be used again as the setting for Wolfe's 1929 novel, *Look Homeward, Angel.* Eugene Gant, the young protagonist, wanders the streets of an Altamont graphically modeled on the Asheville where Wolfe had grown up with remarkably similar experiences. Wolfe depicts the small mountain city as contradictory in its beauty and cultural barrenness. Its native Scots-Irish settlers, prosperous Charlestonians, descendants of slaves, tourists, northern investors, and "lungers" who come hoping for a reprieve from the deadly pestilence of tuberculosis meet in this complex urban setting amid the rural surroundings of western North Carolina. In *Look Homeward, Angel,* as well as in other Wolfe novels and stories such as "The Lost Boy," the square with its obelisk monument is a distinctive, still-recognizable setting in the center of town.

Wolfe, though Asheville's best-known writer, is certainly not the first or only one to write of the city. The completion of the railroads connecting Asheville to Tennessee and South Carolina in the 1880s sparked Asheville's metamorphosis from a small rural town to a thriving cosmopolitan resort that advertised its varied accommodations for travelers and its ideal climate for the "debilitated and the consumptive." Trains provided transportation for authors and journalists who came to visit and for their characters who enjoyed the

geographical wonders of Asheville and the Appalachian region. Christian Reid (pseudonym for Frances Tiernan of Salisbury, North Carolina) in her tenth novel, *In the Land of the Sky* (1876), wrote of young people who travel to Asheville by train to experience the beauty of the mountains. While residing at the Eagle Hotel, Reid's characters hike to Beaucatcher Mountain, gaze at the peaks of Pisgah and Cold Mountain, and admire the Swannanoa and French Broad Rivers. These travelers comment on Asheville's elevation of 2,250 feet and note that it is less a town than a "collection of county seats scattered irregularly and picturesquely over the innumerable hills." Reid's title, *In the Land of the Sky,* popularized a phrase still used in promoting Asheville and western North Carolina.

Other local-color writers of the 1800s, such as Constance Fenimore Woolson, visited Asheville in the 1870s; Woolson used it as the setting of her 1894 novel, *Horace Chase.* A character in the novel remarks on the rivers that run to the east and west of Asheville, "it would have been difficult to say which river danced more gayly along its course, the foam-flecked French Broad, its clear water open to the sunshine, or the little Swannanoa, frolicking through the forest in the shade." Maria Louise Pool was less effusive about the area in her novel *In Buncombe County* (1896). Pool depicts the simple mountain people in contrast to the sophisticated, impatient travelers waiting in a grocery store at Asheville Junction, who remark on the nearby river, "We knew it must be the Swannanoa which was brawling along just the other side of the dismal structure said to be a boarding-house."

Edgar W. "Bill" Nye, a popular nineteenth-century humorist, came to Asheville during the winter of 1886 in hopes of improving his health. He wrote to Joseph Pulitzer, editor of the *New York World,* describing his experience in a place where he thought he would find birds flitting through boughs of southern magnolia and instead encountered a two-foot fall of snow that he dug through in his seersucker suit in order to get to a grocery store. The humorous letter led to a syndicated column in which Nye often wrote fondly of the area: "The sun never lit up a cuter little city than Asheville." Nye died in 1896 at the age of forty-five and was buried south of Asheville.

The twentieth century brought other notable writers to the area, including William Sydney Porter—O. Henry—who lived in Asheville shortly before his death in June 5, 1910; his grave is in Riverside Cemetery near the Wolfe family plot where Thomas Wolfe was buried in 1939. "Let Me Feel Your Pulse," in *Sixes and Sevens* (1910), is a humorous autobiographical story of Porter's seeking a cure in the mountains. Olive Tilford Dargan moved to Asheville from her rural home in Swain County in 1925. That year, she published a collection of prose pieces, *Highland Annals,* about her neighbors in the southern mountains. Inspired by the textile strikes in the Piedmont and coal-mine strikes in Appalachia, Dargan, under the pseudonym of Fielding Burke, moved from the genres of essays and poetry to write three feminist-proletarian novels, including *Call Home the Heart* in 1932. Dargan died in Asheville in 1968 at ninety-nine.

F. Scott Fitzgerald spent considerable time in Asheville between 1935 and 1938 after his wife, Zelda, became a patient at Highlands Hospital. Fitzgerald's use of the fictional return address, "Gant's Tomb, Asheville," while staying at the Grove Park Inn, indicates a less-than-favorable view of his residence. Zelda Fitzgerald died in a fire at Highlands Hospital in 1948.

The works of four contemporary authors—Wilma Dykeman, John Ehle, Gail Godwin, and Fred Chappell from nearby Canton—continue to enhance Asheville's literary identity. Wilma Dykeman's works include a nonfiction book, *The French Broad* (1955), which recounts the history of the area and the importance of the river. In Chapter 11, entitled "The Chateau and the Boarding House," Dykeman describes Asheville's two most famous residents and their residences—the Biltmore House, George Vanderbilt's mansion, and the Old Kentucky Home, Julia Wolfe's boardinghouse and the childhood home of Thomas Wolfe. Two Dykeman novels contrast the rural roots of the area and the changes brought about by urbanization. *The Far Family* (1966) has descendants of Lydia, the protagonist of *The Tall Woman* (1962), flying into Asheville's airport. John Ehle, born in Asheville in 1925, writes of Asheville in *Last One Home* (1984), his tenth novel: "The town . . . flowed along its own valleys, like a broad living river, shaped by the mountains all around." Pink Wright, the protagonist who moves from the rural mountains to Asheville in 1904, watches the building of the Battery Park Hotel and rides the trolleys on still-familiar streets. Fred Chappell's *The Gaudy Place* (1973) has Arkie, a young street hustler, living on Lexington Avenue. Gail Godwin's novel *A Mother and Two Daughters* (1982), set in Asheville, begins with the father's death as he drives through the Beaucatcher Cut, a dramatic entry to Asheville from the east. *A Southern Family* (1987) further explores this change in

social relationships and families as well as concern for environmental destruction threatening the beauty of the area. It is this beauty, high elevation, nearby mountains, mild climate, and wonderful air, as well as the colleges, bookstores, small presses, publications, and appreciative literary community, that continue to draw gifted writers and nurture their creativity in a city now of 68,000 souls.

Gwen McNeill Ashburn

See also North Carolina, Literature of.

Thomas Rain Crowe, "Tracking the Asheville Literary Renaissance," *North Carolina Literary Review* (1995); David Herbert Donald, *Look Homeward: A Life of Thomas Wolfe* (1987); Richard Walser, *Literary North Carolina* (1986).

ATLANTA, GEORGIA

From its beginnings, the city of Atlanta built its fortunes on the forces of industry and commerce, and on transportation, distinguishing itself from the rest of the predominantly agricultural South. The city's genesis was made possible by two separate but related events: the decision of railroad engineers, ratified by the state legislature in 1836, to build the Western & Atlantic rail line from the Chattahoochee River in North Georgia to the Tennessee River, and the expulsion in 1838 of the Cherokee Indians from their territories in northern portions of the state. The southern terminus of the rail line, aptly named Terminus, was located near an old Indian settlement, Standing Peachtree. When building of the rail line began, Terminus was the home of one family of permanent residents. Other residents soon joined them, however, and the town was renamed Marthasville, after the daughter of Governor Wilson Lumpkin, who had pushed for the new railroad. Finally, in 1845, for reasons that are not entirely clear, the town was renamed Atlanta. It soon became the center of a network of rail systems connecting many points in Georgia with the rest of the Southeast.

With completion of the rail line to Chattanooga, and of other lines to Augusta, Macon, and Savannah, the fortunes of Atlanta quickly began to rise. In 1850 the city census listed 2,600 inhabitants. By 1860 the number had grown to nearly 10,000. Throughout the Civil War, the city served as an important center of industry, commerce, and transportation and as a military depot for the Confederate South. The Northern army and General William Tecumseh Sherman viewed the conquest of Atlanta as a goal that would be in symbolic and practical terms devastating to the Confederacy. In September, 1864, after a horrendous campaign, pitched battles near Kennesaw Mountain and on the banks of the Chattahoochee River, and a month-long siege, Sherman and his forces occupied the city. Two months later, ready to move further south, he ordered his troops to set it afire, and they obeyed; only four hundred structures were left standing. The devastation can be measured by the fact that a few days after the fire, the city treasury counted $1.64 in its coffers.

Atlanta immediately began to rebuild. In 1868 it became the state capital. By 1870 it was reaping the benefits of a post–Civil War boom, and its fortunes grew rapidly. During the last three decades of the nineteenth century, Atlanta and the so-called New South were almost synonymous. The city built hospitals, banks, and institutions of higher learning, sewer systems, paved roadways and sidewalks, electric streetlights, and streetcar lines. In 1872 a public-school system of two high schools and seven elementary schools was organized. In 1881 and 1895, major cotton expositions attracted national attention and business interests. In 1886 a tonic later to be known as Coca-Cola was developed. In 1887 the Georgia Institute of Technology began admitting students for the first time. Exploiting the railroad lines and later the highway systems that connected it to the rest of the South and the nation, Atlanta built itself into a regional center of commerce, industry, banking, and finance.

During the 1880s and 1890s, and throughout the next century, Atlanta played a major role in the growth of African American culture. At the Atlanta Cotton Exposition in 1895, Booker T. Washington advocated moderation and economic independence for southern blacks, a position later named the Atlanta Compromise. Ironically, a period of inflamed racial tensions in the city followed, culminating in a horrible race riot in 1906, during which a mob of several thousand whites murdered twelve blacks. W. E. B. Du Bois, who moved to the city in 1897 to teach sociology at Atlanta University, disagreed with Washington; he urged activism, social equality, and education. Du Bois wrote some of his most influential works, including his monumental *The Souls of Black Folk* (1903), while he lived and worked in Atlanta. As a professor and later as president of Atlanta University, he played a major role in the development of this complex of schools and universities, one of the leading traditionally black institutions

of higher learning in the nation. Georgia Douglas Johnson was a graduate of Spelman College and became a significant black poet and a figure in the Harlem Renaissance centered further to the North.

During the 1950s and 1960s Atlanta proudly boasted that it was a "city too busy to hate," though the atmosphere of racial moderation was carefully orchestrated by white businessmen and moderate black leaders who feared that violence and confrontation would threaten the city's prosperity. The fact that the nonviolent Civil Rights Movement was largely centered in Atlanta, and that many of its leaders lived there—Martin Luther King, Ralph David Abernathy, and Julian Bond, for instance—also contributed to the atmosphere of moderation. In the 1990s, the illusion of racial harmony gave way to an uneasy racial accommodation, with African Americans commanding the political power structure at the city's center and white citizens controlling much of the economic wealth from the comfort of northern suburbs.

Atlanta at the end of the twentieth century became more an international city than a regional one. Like many large cities, it suffers from overpopulation and crowding, crime, racial divisions, and political corruption. Nonetheless, with a metropolitan population of several million, three professional sports teams, an internationally known symphony, a still-growing economy, and some of the most striking skyscrapers in urban America, its cultural and economic achievements are remarkable.

Atlanta is also known worldwide as the city at the heart of Margaret Mitchell's famous novel, *Gone With the Wind* (1936). Mitchell was a reporter for the *Atlanta Constitution,* a newspaper closely aligned with the fortunes of the city since its founding in 1868. Its early editor, Henry Grady, was a major proponent of the New South, and Joel Chandler Harris, a reporter and editor, published many of his writings, including the famous Brer Rabbit stories, in its pages. In the twentieth century, Ralph McGill, a Pulitzer Prize–winning editor of the *Constitution,* was widely known and admired for his editorials counseling racial moderation. Atlanta has been the home, or the subject, of writings by such distinctive writers as Frances Newman (*The Hardboiled Virgin*), Pat Conroy (*Prince of Tides*), Donald Windham (*Emblems of Conduct, The Warm Country*), James Dickey (*Poems 1957–1967, Deliverance*), Melissa Fay Greene (*The Temple Bombing, Praying for Sheetrock*), David Bottoms (*In a U-Haul North of Damascus, Shooting Rats at the Bibb*

County Dump), and many others. Since 1998, Atlantans have been divided about the merits of Tom Wolfe's *A Man In Full* as an accurate depiction of the city in the late twentieth century.

Hugh Ruppersburg

See also *Atlanta Constitution*; Cities.

Kenneth Coleman et al., *A History of Georgia* (2nd ed.; 1991); Franklin M. Garrett, *Atlanta and Environs: A Chronicle of Its People and Events* (1954).

ATLANTA CONSTITUTION

In continuous publication since 1868, the *Atlanta Constitution* is one of the oldest and most influential of southern newspapers. Under Henry Grady, the first of its two most influential editors, it was linked with moderate editorial stands, energetic coverage of local and regional events (such as the Charleston earthquake of 1885), and the ascendancy of the New South after the Civil War. Grady bought one-fourth interest in the paper in 1880 and became its managing editor. As the spokesman most closely identified with the concept of the New South, he brought national attention to the *Constitution* as well as to Atlanta itself. After his death in 1889, he was succeeded as editor by Clark Howell, who edited the paper until his death in 1938. Early in the 1880s, the newspaper found itself in fierce and long-lived competition with the more conservative *Atlanta Evening Journal*, later simply the *Atlanta Journal*. In 1906, the rivalry reached such a pitch that *Constitution* editor and publisher Clark Howell ran and lost a gubernatorial campaign against Hoke Smith, a former *Journal* owner. The rivalry continued until 1950, when *Journal* owner James M. Cox purchased the *Constitution*. Since then, the two papers have essentially merged, though they maintain separate editorial staffs.

Under the leadership of Ralph E. McGill, who became editor of the *Constitution* in 1938 and who later became the publisher, the *Constitution* gained a reputation for its moderate stands on racial integration and its opposition to regional and national extremism. McGill was a particularly effective spokesman for these interests, and for the South as a whole, and his editorials on civil rights, Governor Eugene Talmadge, the bombing of the Atlanta Jewish Temple in 1961, and the assassination of Martin Luther King gained him a wide following. One of his best-known editorials extolled the virtues of mules. In 1959 he won the Pulitzer Prize. His death in 1970 marked the end of the newspaper's most significant period.

Despite its relative liberalism in a conservative region, the *Constitution* has taken pride in its role as a leading southern newspaper. Early in its history, such staff members as Grady, Harris, "Bill Arp," and Frank Stanton were recognized as leading writers in the state. In the twentieth-century, McGill earned respect for his own writing and championed such local authors as Byron Herbert Reece, a North Georgia poet and novelist. A number of well-known Georgia writers have also been associated with the newspaper, including Frances Newman, Terry Kay, Lewis Grizzard, Celestine Sibley, and especially Margaret Mitchell, who wrote *Gone With the Wind* while she worked as a reporter during the 1920s. For a number of decades, the Sunday paper included a magazine section with articles about the state and its people, and a book-review section that focused on local writers. In recent decades, the *Constitution* has turned its compass more toward national and international coverage.

Hugh Ruppersburg

See also Atlanta, Georgia

Kenneth Coleman et al., *A History of Georgia* (2nd ed.; 1991).

AUDUBON, JOHN J.

John James Audubon, famed naturalist and artist, not only brought the wildlife of the South to the attention of an international audience with his *Birds of America* (1827–1838), *Ornithological Biography* (1831–1839), and *Viviparous Quadrupeds of North America* (1842–1854), he also captured the spirit of the Old Southwest in these works—and in his many journals—to such an extent that his association with the region still endures in the twenty-first-century southern literary imagination.

Though at the height of his popularity, rumors abounded that Audubon was the lost Dauphin—son of Louis XVI and heir to the French throne—he was in fact the illegitimate son of an adventurous French merchant and a mistress. Born Jean Jacques on Santo Domingo (now Haiti) in the West Indies in 1785, he—along with a part-African half-sister—was taken by his father to Nantes in France, where they were kindly adopted by his father's legal wife. In the aftermath of the French Revolution, Audubon received a solid bourgeois education and showed early interest in natural history and art; his supportive father enabled him to study briefly under painter Jacques-Louis David in Paris during 1802 and 1803. In the latter year, Audubon left Europe for an estate his father had purchased in Pennsylvania, and there he began the immersion in the American outdoors—he was a passionate hunter— that would shape his future.

Marrying in 1808, Audubon decided to try his hand at business in the West. He would spend the next decade in Kentucky, failing at entrepreneurial ventures but increasing his knowledge of the wildlife—and frontier culture—along the Ohio River. He was jailed for debt in 1819 and only then hit upon the idea of supporting his family by use of his artistic skills. In autumn of 1820, he set off alone down the Ohio and the Mississippi, making his living by hunting and painting portraits—but ultimately intending to draw as many birds as possible for a future book. Settling his family in Louisiana, which he used as a base of operations over the next several years, Audubon was by the middle of the decade ready to seek a publisher for his work. In 1826 he traveled to Europe, and—after being warmly received in Edinburgh and London—in 1827 saw the first volume of *The Birds of America* printed by a London engraver. Its success was immediate.

This collection of vivid engravings has been the mainstay of Audubon's reputation, while his literary accomplishments have generally been overlooked. Audubon in fact devoted considerable time to his *Ornithological Biography*, which he initially conceived as a simple descriptive text to accompany his engravings. The five-volume set that he produced, however, contained not only lengthy "bird biographies"—elaborate accounts of avian habits and habitats—but also what Audubon called "episodes," short sketches and memoirs interspersed among the more objective essays (which themselves contained incongruous personal anecdotes). These "Delineations of American Scenery and Character"—bearing titles such as "Colonel Boone," "Kentucky Sports," "Squatters of the Mississippi," and "Natchez in 1820"—resembled the frontier sketches of Longstreet, Hooper, and Thorpe. Other episodes—such as "The Hurricane" and "The Earthquake"—present Audubon himself as a solitary figure in the wilderness, an appropriately Romantic child of the early nineteenth century. These pieces, as well as his *Mississippi River Journal* (1820–1821, published in

1929) and *Missouri River Journal* (1843, published in 1897), mark his place in American letters as well as art and science.

After his success publishing *Birds of America*, Audubon spent the 1830s traveling between Europe, the United States, and Canada. He maintained his connections to the South—he explored extensively in Florida and the Florida Keys in 1832 and along the coast of the Gulf of Mexico in 1837. In the 1840s, however, he purchased an estate on the Hudson in New York; he would travel through the South again only en route to St. Louis, where he began his last great journey—up the Missouri River—in 1843. After this trip, he devoted himself to beginning his engravings for *Viviparous Quadrupeds,* but a stroke in 1847 cut his work short; it passed on to his sons at his death in 1851.

Twentieth-century southern writers exploring the legacy of the Old Southwest found in Audubon an archetype of the lone visionary on the cusp of the civilized world. In Eudora Welty's *The Wide Net* (1943)—a collection of stories largely concerned with the Natchez Trace—Audubon is one of three main characters in "A Still Moment," one who yearns "to see all and to record all life that filled this world—all, all." Nonetheless, he must take life in order to record it, and he does so in the central act of the story—the shooting of a white heron. Robert Penn Warren's *Audubon: A Vision* (1969) describes the artist as American pioneer, a man who "Was not the lost dauphin, though handsome was only / Base-born and not even able / To make a decent living, was only / Himself, Jean Jacques, and his passion—what / Is man but his passion?" Such passion, finally, marked not only Audubon's art but also the character of the frontier he traversed and captured in his writings.

Farrell O'Gorman

See also Natchez Trace; Nature; Southwestern Humor; Travel Literature.

John James Audubon, *Selected Journals and Other Writings,* ed. Ben Forkner (1996); Alice Ford, *John James Audubon* (1964); Frances Hobart Herrick, *Audubon the Naturalist* (1917).

AUTOBIOGRAPHICAL IMPULSE

The questions are simple. Is there a southern autobiographical impulse, and if so, what are its sources? How does it express itself, and how does it differ from other American autobiographical impulses? Have the impulse and its expression changed over time, and if so, why? Is there a territory ahead, and what does it look like?

Of the existence of an impulse there can be little doubt. It helps explain the meandering, anecdotal style of southern conversation. It's central to the southern habit of storytelling. Even when the stories are not explicitly autobiographical, they come down to the self of the teller—his identification with or repudiation of the neighbor, relative, or outsider who is the focus of the story. Down to the self, too, in terms of the teller's ability to grip listeners and work his way on them. Style is the man—vividly individual but simultaneously connected to the audience. He speaks my language, listeners inwardly affirm. Story calls to story in a game of conversational chairs. Each becomes teller and listener in turn. Not only content and style but the process itself assumes and promotes a sense of community, wide or narrow—our family; fellow Methodists and others of the better sort; our race; this beloved state; the South; this country, beloved, too, right or wrong. Especially, for southerners, when wrong. All kinds of people can be loyal to the right. It's loyalty to the wrong that's considered the true test of character.

This could lead to many a story in which the fates of individual and community become one and inseparable, for better and worse. Almost no autobiography (except nature writing) treats the individual totally in isolation from others, but the degree of embeddedness differs radically. Consider an axis with the individual at one pole and community at the other. American autobiography has exalted the individual as the end, measure, and symbol of the country, constitutive of community rather than the other way around. The myth of America has transported the individual out of community, out of history itself, and into a present, endlessly rocking. American loneliness begins in American ideology. The southern myth is one of community with a torn and tragic past. For southern autobiographers, the axis has been short—no community without the individuals it exists to nurture and protect; no individuals without the community, which shapes, confers purpose and meaning, and carries the memory of its members.

So why (prior to the post–World War II period) was there so little formal autobiography from the white South? All talked out? To be sure, the South, from its colonial origins, had participated in autobiographical writing in the form of letters and diaries. The National

Book Award–winning *The Children of Pride,* a collection of letters written in the 1850s and 1860s by the family of a wealthy Georgia slaveholder and minister, illustrated how revealing a portrait of self and the South personal correspondence could paint. For diaries, one thinks first of that of William Byrd of Westover, although Byrd, who died in 1744, wrote before there was a United States, let alone a South. Unquestionably southern and fine is the Civil War journal of Mary Boykin Chesnut, revised and added to by Mrs. Chesnut and the whole so artfully crafted that it reads like an epistolary novel addressed to the self. Yet letters and diaries do not constitute autobiography, nor, judging from what has survived, did the South produce so much of this material as did other regions.

Only once prior to the 1950s did the white South contribute much autobiography. After the Civil War, Confederate generals and others rivaled their northern counterparts in the furious fire that was military memoir. A number of the memoirs make good reading. H. K. Douglass's *I Rode with Stonewall* (1940), for example, is full of vivid characterization and colorful stories—the sheer dash and tumble of military action. In its depiction of the war's last months, it haunts, with its dance macabre from ball to battlefield, and anticipates the hallucinatory weariness of certain World War I memoirs, poetry, and fiction. Yet none of the Confederate works is so distinguished as those of Grant and Sherman, whose widely read, hit-and-keep-moving-on narratives arguably helped create American prose style. Allow for the brute, inescapable fact of defeat, and many Confederate memoirs have more in common with Caesar's than with anything else in American autobiography.

By contrast, autobiography may be the preeminent form of American literary expression. The very word dates from just after the American Revolution, which helped establish the worth of the individual, without which there would not have been the post-Revolutionary outpouring of autobiography. Perhaps no other people has written so many—10,000 by one outdated count that did not include captivity narratives or volumes of personal essays. Thoreau's *Walden* (1854) and Adams's *The Education of Henry Adams* (1907) rank among the classics of our literature. James M. Cox would add Franklin's *Autobiography* (1793) to his list of the ten major American prose works. Franklin remains the archetypal American autobiographer, and his book, the first great American success story, defines what is American in American autobiography. Franklin answered Crèvecoeur's question, "What is this new man, this American?" He did so for the instruction of future generations, whose choired answers would form the new American community. Since Franklin, American writers have tended to identify with Franklin or some idea, such as freedom, that is held to be fundamentally American. Thoreau, Whitman, Adams (or, to descend from these mountains, P. T. Barnum and Norman Podhoretz) have commented on themes—honesty, the success myth, the ideal of the self-made man, the belief in social progress—classically set forward by Franklin. The memoir embodies what Americans have liked to think of themselves as individuals and as a unique people. That is why D. H. Lawrence called Franklin "the pattern American" and why Robert Sayre called the autobiography "a version of the national epic."

Antebellum white southerners had their own versions of social progress, their own examples of the success myth. Plantation slavery produced many a self-made aristocrat, as Faulkner would recognize. Further, stereotypes and popular history obscure how early gentility began to mean adherence to a code of conduct rather than wealth or lineage. Even so, Franklin's emphasis on the individual ran against the notion of an organic community on which any philosophical justification of slavery had to rest. His pattern ill-suited what southerners wanted to believe of themselves. A celebration of the self-made man would have challenged the idea of aristocracy. Franklin dedicated his autobiography to generations of American sons yet unborn—a metaphor—and gave readers little of his actual family. Their absence made him all the more self-made. By contrast, family is of the essence to the aristocratic ideal. One can scarcely imagine a southern autobiography that did not emphasize family, yet a Franklinesque dedication to southern sons, taken literally, would all too often have included some of sable hue. Just as well that it would have shown a lack of breeding to accept autobiography's invitation to write of oneself baldly, at length, to unborn generations.

Franklin had cornered the market in American autobiography, and it was nearly impossible for southerners to buy in. One of genius, of course, might have invented an alternative pattern, particularly after the old order cracked wide open with the Civil War and the overthrow of slavery. Mark Twain would try, and the effort stood Franklin on his head. Twain's narrative drifts and circles, spurred on or driven back by a thousand accidents of time and place. It denies by its very form Franklin's idea of linear progress—for the self, the nation, the human race. Franklin uses guilt and learns tidy little lessons from it. Twain's guilt torments, doesn't go away, and cannot be converted to the cash of self-improvement. Franklin thanks his wife and pats his mother and father, also, before swallowing them into his past. Twain's pages swell with family—daughters and wife and mother and various kindly and eccentric relations, and are haunted by the brother for whose death Twain blamed himself. Twain sacrifices simplicity to be faithful to the tone of conversation. So committed to spontaneous memory and conversation's natural flow is he that he dictates large portions of the narrative to his daughter. At one period, he swaps with her—she tells his and the family's story. The result is that not even the autobiography is fully self-made.

Since Twain, southern autobiographers have identified with the idea of the country, but they have at the same time identified with southern places that have often been in conflict with the larger nation. They have defined themselves in the context of families and communities. The self has been a social one, rather than an individual essence confronting the forest or a symbol of American ideal. Southern writers have paralleled a distinction, drawn by some feminist critics, between the autobiographies of American women and American men, one more way in which the South has been more female-centered than most of the country. Southern autobiographers have operated in the territory between southern place and American idea. In so doing, they have reflected the dualities of the communities of which they have been the self-conscious fruit and product. This is in part a southern version of a national story. Most, perhaps all, Americans are members of multiple communities, and they suffer and benefit from some sort of double consciousness. This is a key to what it means to be an American and one of several ways the country has anticipated the dilemmas of the modern self. But it may be that only nonwhites and recent immigrants have experienced the division so keenly as southerners. William Alexander Percy, Ellen Glasgow, B. L. Reid, George Garrett, Pat Hoy—the emphases shift, but southern personal narrative is a conversation, often heated, within the self, between the self and the community, between the South and the country, and with those outsiders within, the other race. Literary southerners, called by American opportunities for self-making, have left the South often enough. The South, nonetheless, abides in them, as it did in Twain. Love, leave, or love it and leave it, the writers' lives have been located. That is the point of Harry Crews's apt title *A Childhood: The Biography of a Place* (1978).

Aberrational in some respects, the post–Civil War outbreak of personal narrative points to an essential continuity—southern autobiography, pretty much from the beginning, has been an art of self-defense. Central to southern identity is the ideal of loyalty. Without it, no South, no southerner. Much united white southerners: dependence on soil and weather and the rhythms of the seasons; dependence, too, whether direct or indirect, on another race, familiar as closest neighbors, yet strange, too, and ultimately unknown and maybe unknowable. The southern states did not become the South until they were under attack as backward and undemocratic, the practitioners of slavery in freedom's land. The sense of being under attack "placed" individual identity to a degree that did not occur in other regions. The autobiographer from Ohio or Wisconsin is unlikely to toil over-much with the idea of the Midwest, seen as the nation's heartland and whole-grain quintessence of the idea of America. Likewise other regions have always reflected some extension of the idea of America, from New England's moral bedrock on which the quintessence rests to the West's wild American spaciousness. But the South is the other, or at best the apostate brother who stains the sheets of our *e pluribus unum* bed. From Virginia to Arkansas (and sometimes Missouri, Texas, and Oklahoma), autobiographers must deal with the idea of the South. Nor is the idea abstract, not in the way the idea of America, representing democratic principles, is abstract. Franklin's community was one of ideals. It moved away from the local and concrete to universal principle. In theory, it was open to all and transportable. Whitman took it to the open road and loved right well the Americans he met in passing. Thoreau took it to the wilderness, riotous fact and perfect metaphor for unbounded freedom. He found himself in Walden's world of mirroring symbol. The idea of the South is weathered and sweating, vegetative, and manifestly existing in time and place. It's localized and made real and corporeal by the flaws and contradictions of its divided and inevitably tied and cross-tied community. The other regions by definition have their differentiating features, but their differences have not set them against the rest of the country. Sectionalism has not inscribed them in blood. For most of our history, the South has been the stage for the nation's major moral drama.

When the first Civil War memoirs appeared, the tradition of the slave narrative was already more than a century old. That tradition began with Briton Hammon; achieved its prewar apotheosis with Frederick Douglass; continued into the postwar era with Booker T. Washington and many others; flowered again, surprisingly, during the 1930s with the interviews of former slaves by WPA workers; and became the model not only for later black autobiography but also for much of black fiction down to the present. Witness the several volumes of W. E. B. Du Bois and of Maya Angelou and, in fiction, *The Autobiography of an Ex-Coloured Man* (1912), *Invisible Man* (1952), and *The Autobiography of Miss Jane Pittman* (1971)—the last three, novels in the guise of autobiographies.

Some scholars have argued that European and American examples of autobiography were inaccessible to black writers, but escaped or manumitted slaves (or their amanuenses) and later authors found wonderfully useful Franklin's self-identification with the country and the ideal of freedom. Consider how densely packed and explosive was Douglass's subtitle, *An American Slave,* how convulsively contradictory to the idea of the self-made man was Richard Wright's *Black Boy* (1945). Booker T. Washington rose from slavery and renamed himself (fathered himself) in an exercise in self-making that not even Franklin could equal. Black autobiographers have at the same time paralleled white southerners in that the axis of community and individual has been short. Black autobiographers have written both American and southern traditions upside down in an intensification of each.

American autobiographers in general have attempted both to testify to common American experience and to fashion memorably individual voices. This tension, which is fundamental to the tradition of American autobiography, springs from the often-conflicting emphases on democracy and equality, on the one hand, and individuality and self-fulfillment, on the other. It has gripped black writers with special power.

Over and over, black authors have found it urgently necessary to utter themselves directly without resort to fiction, to force upon Franklin's sons and daughters a recognition of what it means to be black in white America, and to assert their own claims as heirs and joint heirs to Franklin's legacy. They have seized possession of themselves from stereotypes that would teach them to hate themselves. For some, the struggle against fictive or stereotypical versions of the self has imparted a novelistic concentration and focus, has made lives an imitation or a resistance to an imitation that in itself structures and has the quality of art. Black writers have at the same time and with great inner conflict struggled to establish themselves within a black community that, however understandably, has closed ranks in ways that some have found as likely to smother as to strengthen. Layered and complicated tensions, the stuff and crux of fiction, are inherent in the life. The drama is there, ready and inevitable: the life is a page-turner.

For the generation of white southern writers who emerged in the 1920s and 1930s, it was the history or myth of the South that was the page-turner. The Southern Renascence depended in part on what Allen Tate described as a shift from rhetoric to dialectic, an opening of an "internal dialogue, a conflict within the self," through which writers examined "the Southern legend of defeat and heroic frustration." George Core has argued persuasively that the legend so engrossed writers that it, along with a genteel stress on privacy, largely explains why the Agrarians, Faulkner, and others were not attracted to autobiography. The Agrarians in particular saw the antebellum South as the last genuine community in the Western world and, as such, a bulwark against the corrosive individualism represented by the rest of the country. Classic American autobiography, if the question had been posed to them, might well have epitomized such individualism. Yet the point should not obscure the degree to which personal and regional history had merged. The myth of the South and of family and, by extension, of self had become one and the same. Faulkner was not so directly autobiographical as were, say, Thomas Wolfe or James Agee. Even so, the merging of self with the South is a source of his violent lyricism. It is a key to how he could condense so much of southern history in one family (not unlike his own), the Compsons. The myth had become a kind of alter ego that Faulkner may have known better than he knew himself, one into which he poured himself, the creature of what was in part his own creation. His self-written epitaph, then, is a fuller autobiography than many have recognized: "He wrote the books, and he died."

Individual in his genius, Faulkner was representative of his and proximate generations in that for them, too, history deeply implicated individual identity. He defined a common intuition when one of his characters declares that the past wasn't dead, it wasn't even past. This perception contributed to the appearance of an especially talented set of southern historians. The auto-

biographical spring helps explain the relative liveliness of southern historical writing—one thinks of C. Vann Woodward's very personal *Burden of Southern History* (1960). Far less scholarly and far more self-revealing is the sweet, canorous drunkenness of W. J. Cash's *The Mind of the South* (1941). If one will accept a broad definition, the mind of Jack Cash deserves to be recognized with Wright's *Black Boy* as one of the two most important southern autobiographies of the first half of the twentieth century. Both are also landmarks of American autobiography.

By the post–World War II period, the legend of the South held lessening appeal as a source of fiction. Its charge was spent, although the wire could still spark and raffle alarmingly in the dark southern night. Since the 1950s, the southern world has turned over, and of making many autobiographies there has been no end. The South has prospered, and a wider middle class, black and white and increasingly educated, has developed. A greater number of southerners can tell whatever stories they have to tell and do so for a broader public. World War II itself made Americans more conscious of racism, and the Cold War heightened national embarrassment and ensured that racial sins had international consequences. The Civil Rights Movement would make the 1950s and 1960s a time for bearing witness. Autobiography had perhaps always been the most profoundly American form of social criticism, and in the 1950s and 1960s it became a form of political action, with autobiographies such as those of Eldridge Cleaver and Anne Moody and of crusading journalists such as Ralph McGill and Harry Ashmore.

The multiplying of autobiographies has not come easily. White southerners born before the 1970s have generally felt that they have a lot of explaining to do. That's one reason why so many of the finest southern autobiographies focus on childhood, the site of learning who and what you are and come from. This strategy limits self-incrimination and allows writers to reconcile liberal principles with southern loyalties by showing the humanity of family and neighbors—good people, accidental racists, it may seem, made so by the deep circumstances of time and place. One thinks of Harry Crews, of William Humphrey's *Farther Off from Heaven* (1977), and of Melton A. McLaurin's *Separate Pasts* (1987). One returns also to what is arguably the finest autobiography of an American childhood, *The Autobiography of Huckleberry Finn*, to use Twain's original title. That work also contains a hilarious and, to this day, misunderstood satire of abolitionist autobiography in its portrayal of Huck and Tom Sawyer as conductors on the Underground Railroad. That is the key to understanding the alleged flaw in the conclusion of the work.

Economic, educational, and racial progress, and an increasingly national popular culture (of which the South has been one source) would by the 1970s allow the South to merge in the common traffic of American life. Diminishment of guilt can feel like innocence. It is now possible for southerners to be more full-throatedly the children of Franklin than ever before. One irony is that the South may become the last home of classic American autobiography. Willie Morris's *North Toward Home* (1967), for example, is richly in the tradition of American success stories, although one need only to read Podhoretz's parallel memoir, *Making It* (1967), to realize how thoroughly southern Morris remains.

That's the question: Is there any longer a South, one sufficiently different to produce something called southerners? The answer must be a qualified yes. The territory seems to be shrinking, and the portion of the population (and of the individual self) that is distinctively southern seems to be diminishing as well. Those to the territory born can still put the old boy or girl (this self-consciousness itself illustrates the shrinkage) through the paces. But the old boy may be just one more voice in the multiplicity of voices learned from travel, radio, television, the movies. The southerner becomes an image of himself, a relic or a fiction, whose story is unlikely to be a page-turner. In an age of hyphenates, maybe the time for Southern-American is at hand.

A southern identity could always be as bogus as any other, but being on the defensive produces the assumption that one has something to defend, something in this case that had all the blood of southern history behind it. Southerners are relatively late to face postmodernism's need to establish the authenticity of the self. To the extent that the need arises, the southern conversation becomes more internal and less dialectical—a colloquy among one's possibilities. Franklin wrote to record a self that he believed he had, through rigorous self-discipline, made. Others have written to discover and free a self from social constraint and the very self-discipline Franklin so commended. In a postmodern age, autobiographers may write to make a self, autobiography being perceived as the only self there is. If the communal pole of the axis wishes to exist, let it write

itself. Southerners are gaining the right to be as lonely as anyone else.

In some sense, the southern storyteller always created himself in conversation. Certainly, he was conscious of performance, but this self-consciousness assumed a relatedness to community and responsibilities that went on after the curtain came down. Whatever the theatricality, the role was fundamentally a social one. The reviews were friendships, blood ties, and lasting loyalties. The best gift that the American ideal has given to the South is that the ties and loyalties increasingly include all southerners. A paradox: to deserve this gift, the South must remain apostate in the cult of individualism and the culture of consumerism. It won't be the South unless it rejects the impersonalization that ultimately results from each. A hard act, but the best southern autobiographies continue to pull it off.

J. William Berry

See also Autobiography; Diaries, Men's; Diaries, Women's; Letters.

J. Bill Berry, ed., *Located Lives: Place and Idea in Southern Autobiography* (1990); J. Bill Berry, ed., *Home Ground: Southern Autobiography* (1991).

AUTOBIOGRAPHY

Arriving at a clear-cut definition for the genre of autobiography is as difficult a task (and almost as common) as defining what's especially southern about southern literature. Although autobiography would at first seem clearly enough defined as the story of a person's life written by the person who lived it, in fact that standard definition has been called into question by numerous theorists who argue that the inherent referentiality of the story—its pull between fictional and nonfictional poles—is difficult or impossible to decide. Furthermore, the line that seems to separate autobiography from such closely related genres as memoir, diary, journal, slave narrative, or oral history is often hard to draw, a parallel to the recurring problem of deciding exactly which states are southern and which are not. We have no generic Mason-Dixon Line separating autobiographical novels such as Thomas Wolfe's *Look Homeward, Angel* (1929) or such fictional autobiographies as Ernest Gaines's *The Autobiography of Miss Jane Pittman* (1971) and William Styron's *Confessions of Nat Turner* (1968) from texts that seem unambiguously southern autobiography, such as Reynolds Price's evocative and lyrical *Clear Pictures* (1989).

In the case of southern autobiography, questions about geography and genre are especially difficult to determine. Not only do we need to contend with the fact that the person who lived the life might be significantly different from the person who is constructed by the act of writing about it, as is the case with all autobiography, but we also need to consider that the writer may have grown up in the South but lived a majority of his or her life in other regions, or moved to the South after a lifetime lived elsewhere. Although Conrad Aiken was born in Savannah and lived the last years of his life there, his *Ushant* (1952) is not about the South. Would one count as southern autobiography a book such as *Imaginary Parents: A Family Autobiography* (1996), writer Sheila Ortiz Taylor's fascinating collaboration with her artist sister, Sandra Ortiz Taylor, because Sheila has lived in Tallahassee for decades, despite the fact that the book is set in Mexico and California, where Sandra still lives? Is Lillian Hellman's *An Unfinished Woman* (1969) a southern autobiography when it describes the author's childhood in New Orleans but not when she talks about her adult life in Hollywood, New York, or Spain? Is Styron's *Darkness Visible: A Memoir of Madness* (1992) southern despite the fact that it has nothing to do with southern experience?

Using these two defining aspects of the genre—congruence between author and protagonist and geographical setting—to isolate examples of southern autobiography becomes especially difficult in the case of African American autobiography, which has its roots in the slave narrative and which often calls into question the congruence between actual author and life experiences and makes the insistence on a southern place especially problematic because the major movement of those narratives is toward the North. In that light, Willie Morris's classic *North Toward Home* (1967) might serve as an appropriately ironic title, not only for slave narratives but also for numerous autobiographies by African American authors.

The standard definition's requirement that the text be *written* also makes problematic the many forms of southern autobiography that tell a life story through photography, examples of which include James Agee and Walker Evans's *Let Us Now Praise Famous Men* (1941), *"Deaf Maggie Lee Sayre": Photographs of a River Life* (1995), and the individual autobiographical entries by Josephine Humphreys, Bobbie Ann Mason,

Al Young, T. R. Pearson, Padgett Powell, and others keyed to photographs in Alex Harris's *A World Unsuspected: Portraits of Southern Childhood* (1987). Equally interesting, though unwritten, examples of autobiographical narrative occur in such crafts as quilting and embroidering, the oral tradition in general, or in the numerous blues, folk, and country songs that tell life stories. All of these factors make the topic of southern autobiography both complicated and compelling.

Considering the fact that a concern with memory and the past are such essential themes in southern literature, it is surprising that so important a critic of autobiography as James Olney, editor of the *Southern Review* and author of major books on autobiography, should argue, in an essay that appeared in Bill Berry's *Located Lives,* that there is no southern autobiographical tradition. Olney modified this claim by positing that, although there is no clear tradition of southern autobiographical writing for white writers, black authors have a traceable tradition that begins with the slave narrative and is continuous from the various versions of Frederick Douglass's narratives to Maya Angelou's series of autobiographies that began with *I Know Why the Caged Bird Sings* (1970).

Using Richard Wright's *Black Boy* (1945) as his touchstone, Olney compares that book with another Mississippi autobiography, Eudora Welty's *One Writer's Beginnings* (1984), to demonstrate his major point. However, the fact that *Black Boy* has now been republished in The Library of America series in a restored version that pairs the original text, now called by its original title, "Southern Night," with a second part, called "The Horror and the Glory," a section that details Wright's life, not in the South, but in Chicago, might be said to undercut the claim that *Black Boy* is an exemplar of southern autobiography. And while the standard trajectory of many autobiographies by southern African Americans traces a northward path, recently a number of autobiographies by southern blacks have celebrated a movement in the opposite direction, as can be seen in Henry Louis Gates's *Colored People* (1994) and Deborah E. McDowell's *Leaving Pipe Shop* (1996). If southern African American autobiography has a long-standing tradition, how do we fit into that tradition books from a growing genre that tell about families of mixed racial heritage, such as Gregory Howard Williams's *Life on the Color Line* (1995), subtitled *The True Story of a White Boy Who Discovered He Was Black,* or James McBride's *The Color of Water: A Black Man's Tribute to His White Mother*

(1996), a combination of biography of a Jewish woman who grew up in Virginia and autobiography of her son?

Separating the southern autobiographical tradition into white and black is also complicated by the fact that even in the world of white autobiographers, race is often a major consideration, the writer's experiences with black people being at the center of the narrative. Fred Hobson's *But Now I See: The White Southern Racial Conversion Narrative* (1999) studies autobiographies and memoirs of the mid-twentieth century in which authors write of growing up racist or segregationist and then coming to see the error of their ways. The language is often that of sin and repentance. Examples in this category include Lillian Smith's *Killers of the Dream* (1949), Katharine Du Pre Lumpkin's *The Making of a Southerner* (1946), and Larry L. King's *Confessions of a White Racist* (1971).

James Olney may be right in suggesting that there is no southern white autobiographical tradition in the sense that there are no major autobiographies from which all others are derived, no major texts that all southern autobiographers must take into account—in short, no autobiographical equivalent for Faulkner. The list of major southern novelists who have not chosen to write autobiography is extensive. Of writers discussed in Joseph Flora and Robert Bain's *Fifty Southern Writers After 1950,* only nine have written autobiographies: James Agee's *Let Us Now Praise Famous Men* (1941), a text that many would not consider autobiography; Harry Crews's *Childhood: The Biography of a Place* (1978); Ellen Glasgow's *The Woman Within* (1954); Lillian Hellman's *An Unfinished Woman* (1969), *Pentimento* (1973), *Scoundrel Time* (1976), and *Maybe* (1980); James Weldon Johnson's *Along This Way* (1933), an actual autobiography to counter his autobiographical novel, *The Autobiography of an Ex-Coloured Man* (1912); Reynolds Price's *Clear Pictures* (1989) and *A Whole New Life* (1994); Elizabeth Spencer's *Landscapes of the Heart: A Memoir* (1998); Eudora Welty's *One Writer's Beginnings* (1984); and Richard Wright's *Black Boy* (1945), published in a restored edition as *Black Boy (American Hunger)* in 1991. In a long list of topics in need of critical work that they include in *Southern Literary Study: Problems and Possibilities* (1975), Louis Rubin and C. Hugh Holman recommend that a study is needed of not just southern autobiography, but also other forms of life-writing from the South, including diaries, journals, and memoirs. However, by the end of the twenti-

eth century, only Will Brantley had taken up this task, and he limited his field to six women memoirists, although his use of that term is quite broad. In addition to writing about the autobiographies of Glasgow, Hellman, Lillian Smith, and Welty already mentioned above, Brantley covers Katherine Anne Porter's *The Never-Ending-Wrong* (1977) and Zora Neale Hurston's *Dust Tracks on a Road* (1942).

Rather than separating out white and black autobiographical traditions, William L. Andrews, in his essay "In Search of a Common Identity: The Self and the South in Four Mississippi Autobiographers," comes to see that for both blacks and whites, coming to terms with the southern self involves some form of dealing with racism. And it is for that reason that autobiography continues to flourish in the region, for one of autobiography's most salient characteristics is its simultaneous and contradictory need to conceal as it reveals, to disclose as well as enclose.

One of the reasons that so much personal narrative can be characterized by deliberately ambiguous combinations of the fictive and the factual is that autobiographers, not just in the South but everywhere, are often trying to tell about their lives with enough honesty and directness that their struggles with the truth of their lives will be meaningful but with a sufficient degree of disguise that the constructed self will help them in coming to terms with the contradictions between self and life. In short, autobiography is often an attempt to reconcile one's sense of self and one's life, and for southerners, often conflicted over racial matters, the genre is therefore especially apt. In an essay in Berry's *Located Lives* called "Between Defiance and Defense," James M. Cox describes that familiar conflicted sense of pride and pain about the South's history that is present in almost every autobiography that comes from the region, a recurring echo of Quentin Compson's celebrated declaration to Shreve at the end of *The Sound and the Fury.*

Although Robert Southey has usually been credited with introducing the term *autobiography* into English in 1809, credit for coining the word should probably go to the English poet Ann Yearsley, who prefaced her 1786 *Poems* with the term *autobiographical narrative.* The very first entries in Robert Sayre's *American Lives: An Anthology of Autobiographical Writing* come from a southern author, John Smith's *A True Relation* (1608) and *The General Historie of Virginia* (1624). Several other examples of travel writing, journal, or diary are excerpted in the early sections of Sayre's collection, including selections from William Byrd's post-humously published *History of the Dividing Line* (1841) and *Secret History of the Line* (1928), and entries from the journals of South Carolinian Charles Woodson (c. 1720). However, little of what we might recognize as southern autobiography was written until the posthumously published *Autobiography of Thomas Jefferson* (1830). Other early examples of southern autobiography include Harriet Jacobs's *Incidents in the Life of a Slave Girl* (1861); *Mary Chesnut's Civil War* (1981), her combination of diary, autobiography, and novel; Booker T. Washington's *Up From Slavery* (1901); and *A Narrative of the Life of David Crockett of the State of Tennessee, Written by Himself* (1835), which might not be an autobiography because, despite the subtitle, it is generally credited to Richard Penn Smith.

Valuable examples of the genre in recent years include a number of books that carry somewhat misleading labels, such as "diary" or the currently popular "memoir," although in fact they are actually autobiography, focusing as much inwardly on authors' lives as outwardly on others. Especially worthwhile are Florida Scott-Maxwell's *The Measure of My Days* (1968), Harriette Arnow's *Old Burnside* (1977), Verna Mae Sloan's *What My Heart Wants to Tell* (1981), Rodger Kamenetz's *Terra Infirma* (1985), C. Vann Woodward's *Thinking Back: The Perils of Writing History* (1986), Florence King's *Confessions of a Failed Southern Lady* (1990), Shirley Abbott's *The Bookmaker's Daughter: A Memory Unbound* (1992), Cecil Brown's *Coming Up Down Home: A Memoir of a Southern Childhood* (1995), Noel Polk's *Outside the Southern Myth* (1997), and Tom Andrews's *Codeine Diary* (1998).

Timothy Dow Adams

See also Autobiographical Impulse; Biography; Blues, The; Diaries, Civil War; Diaries, Men's; Diaries, Women's; Letters; Past, The; Photography; Quilting; *Southern Review;* Travel Literature.

J. Bill Berry, ed. *Located Lives: Place and Idea in Southern Autobiography* (1990); J. Bill Berry, ed., *Home Ground: Southern Autobiography* (1991); Will Brantley, *Feminine Sense in Southern Memoir* (1993); Robert F. Sayre, *American Lives: An Anthology of Autobiographical Writing* (1994).

AUTOMOBILE

In 1895 the entire United States contained only four American passenger cars, but by 1905, two cars existed in William Faulkner's largely rural Yoknapatawpha County. After World War II, southerners bought more automobiles than did residents of any other section of the country.

Lucius (Boss) Priest, a bank president in Faulkner's *The Reivers* (1962), bought an automobile only because Colonel Sartoris, president of the rival bank in Jefferson, had enacted an ordinance prohibiting the use of mechanically propelled vehicles. Although the Winton Flyer had to be hand-cranked at great risk to limbs, Boss Priest simply could not be dictated to by the president of a junior bank. Jefferson's first car had come from Memphis, but the owner, convinced by Mr. Buffaloe that the muddy roads were impassable, went home on the train, leaving his automobile behind. Buffaloe disassembled and studied the vehicle and eventually constructed his own. Both banks refused to lend money for the purchase of automobiles. The Flyer is the vehicle that initiates the grandson Lucius into manhood, as he confronts in a Memphis brothel the conflict between good and evil. After a heroic journey through Hell Creek Bottom, he learns at the horse race about bargaining and what constitutes gentlemanliness. Contrasts between the mule, Priest's preferred mode of transportation, and the Flyer enhance the comedy.

Robert Penn Warren saw literature as questioning how machines can serve human needs. In *All the King's Men* (1946), Adam Stanton looks on his car only as a utilitarian necessity; Jack's car takes him to the West on a quest; and Willie Stark's automobiles increase in size, cost, and beauty, emblematic of power as he moves up the political ladder. Warren has long been associated with the American dream of an agrarian, individualistic society, and machines are part of his nightmare because of their destruction of nature and the individual.

Flannery O'Connor's mouse-colored cars are not completely evil because they represent action. Often, however, the automobile is associated with human pride and materialism. Hazel Motes, in *Wise Blood*, puts mistaken faith in his junk-heap car. In "A Good Man Is Hard to Find" (1953) the grandmother and her son's family set out for Florida, but their car overturns when the cat Pitty Sing jumps on the driver. The story's comic tone ends with the accident and the appearance of The Misfit, who is driving a black, hearselike automobile. In "The Life You Save May Be Your Own," Mr. Shiflett marries Mrs. Crater's idiot daughter to get her automobile, saying, "The spirit, lady, is like an automobile."

R. J. Bowman (Cupid), in Eudora Welty's "Death of a Traveling Salesman" (1936), is on his way to Beulah (Beulah Land of the old hymn) when he becomes lost and drives his Ford into a cow trail and a ravine. In Welty's novel *Losing Battles,* the Judge's car hangs precariously above a precipice, its wheels spinning helplessly.

Another automobile representing a quest and the contrast between good and evil is that of Dwight Anderson in Doris Betts's *Heading West* (1981). Dwight kidnaps North Carolina librarian Nancy Finch and forces her to accompany him in his black car, which has a bobbing black cat in the rear window. Their journey ends with Nancy's rescue in the Grand Canyon.

Harry Crews, in *Car* (1983), expresses his hatred of cars and of the proliferation of filling stations. In this comic novel, Herman, whose family business is crushing wrecked cars into suitcase-sized bundles, wants more from life. He sells his soul to Mr. Edge, who exploits Herman's willingness to eat an entire red Ford Maverick. Herman's twin, Mister, buys a Cadillac with a percentage of the television rights to the bizarre enterprise. The novel, a parody of our secular life, suggests that the ultimate dream of a southerner is to own a gadget-loaded Cadillac. The dream is flawed, however, because the Cadillac has an irreparable squeak.

The poet James Dickey associated the automobile with the desire and follies of youth, in perhaps the most important poetic evocation of automobile culture, "Cherrylog Road" (1964). His young protagonist, "Wild to be wreckage forever," shows how the automobile, in the rural South, houses a young man's dreams of sexual conquest and freedom.

Sue Laslie Kimball

See also Faulkner, William.

John Jerome, *The Death of the Automobile* (1972).

B

BACON'S REBELLION

Although there were no lasting consequences resulting from Nathaniel Bacon's rebellion (1676) against the authority of Governor William Berkeley and the royal government of Virginia, the event foreshadows later rebellions. If Virginia, in the wake of Nat Turner's slave insurrection in 1831, would come to fear the very notion of "rebellion," it is also the state that gave the nation Thomas Jefferson, who argued that revolutions (revolt, rebellion) were healthy for the progress of humankind. Historians have sometimes credited Bacon's Rebellion as the first resistance to the Crown in the colonies. The event is also important as an early manifestation of populist sympathies in the South.

As a result of the recent Navigation Acts and large grants of land that the king had made to friends, the divide between rich and poor was widening in late-eighteenth-century Virginia. Governor Berkeley was not responsive to the wishes of an increasingly diverse population for some representation in his political organization. He also failed to provide a clear policy regarding increasingly hostile Indians. In challenge to Berkeley's authority, in May 1676 the disgruntled young planter Nathaniel Bacon led unauthorized expeditions against the Indians. When Berkeley countered, Bacon's troops were able to force the governor from Jamestown to the Eastern Shore, and then re-engaged the Indians. When Berkeley's forces attempted to return, Bacon burned Jamestown. The majority of the colonists remained neutral in the struggle, which ended abruptly in October with Bacon's sudden death from dysentery and exhaustion. A warship and troops arrived to put down a rebellion that had already died with its leader. Berkeley quickly executed many of Bacon's followers, action that caused King Charles to recall Berkeley to England, where he soon died. Observed the king, "That old fool has hanged more men in that naked country than I have done for the murder of my father."

Although the political effects of the rebellion were negligible, it produced a poem by John Cotton of Queen's Creek that Louis Rubin has called "the best poem written in America in the seventeenth century—and quite possibly the best during the colonial era." Cotton's plantation adjoined that of the elder Colonel Nathaniel Bacon, where the nephew headquartered at the time of the rebellion. Following the rebellion, Cotton quickly wrote "A History of Bacon's and Ingram's Rebellions" (1676). It includes two poems in rhymed iambic couplets, the remarkable (44 lines) "Bacons Epitaph, Made by His Man" and a contrapuntal poem, "Upon the Death of G.B. [General Bacon]" (48 lines) from the perspective of the Loyalists, who have only blame for Bacon. Cotton's own position—whether for governor or rebel—is ambiguous. The companion poems foreshadow a tension between populist and conservative instincts that still characterizes the South in the twenty-first century.

In 1834–1835 William Alexander Caruthers published *The Cavaliers of Virginia, or the Recluse of Jamestown* (two volumes), a historical romance using Bacon's Rebellion as its backdrop that helped establish the cavalier myth.

Joseph M. Flora

See also Cavalier; Class; Conservatism; Liberalism; Slave Revolts.

Wesley Frank Craven, *Southern Colonies* (1949); W. E. Washburn, *Bacon's Rebellion* (1957); T. J. Wertenbaker, *Bacon's Rebellion* (1964).

BALTIMORE, MARYLAND

According to the 1990 census, Baltimore, Maryland, has a population of over 700,000, making it ten times larger than any other Maryland city, yet much diminished from its status as the largest American city in the 1820s. Maryland was one of the thirteen original colonies; Baltimore, Maryland's major city, was settled in 1661 and chartered in 1729. Since the end of the eighteenth century, Baltimore has been the cultural and literary capital of the state. Formerly referred to as "the old capital of the Upper South," Baltimore is now commonly called "Charm City," with most observers citing Baltimore's southern flavor as the key to its identity.

In the national literary consciousness, Baltimore is identified with three important writers—Francis Scott Key, Edgar Allan Poe, and H. L. Mencken. Key, a local lawyer and poet, wrote the words to America's national anthem, "The Star-Spangled Banner," as he watched the flag fly over Fort McHenry in the Baltimore harbor, where American troops repulsed the British in 1814. The mysterious circumstances surrounding Poe's death—he was found incoherent on a Baltimore street in the autumn of 1849 and died in a local hospital some days later—still provide a basis for assorted theories about his macabre poems and stories and his enigmatic character. Mencken, referred to as the "Sage of Baltimore," was a lifelong Baltimorean (1880–1956), associated for most of his career with the Baltimore Sunpapers. In fact, his work as a columnist for the *Baltimore Evening Sun* during the 1920s and 1930s accounts for that newspaper's reputation; his special genius was to convert local issues into national concerns in his weekly columns.

As a city noted for commerce and industry, Baltimore is nonetheless responsible for major contributions to literature and communications. The Enoch Pratt Free Library was the first public library in America; the first telegraph message was sent between Baltimore and Washington; and the Linotype machine, which revolutionized printing, was designed and patented in Baltimore. Since 1816, when the Delphian Literary Club was founded, Baltimore has maintained its reputation for active literary societies, and any number of major critics and writers have been associated with the Johns Hopkins University.

A complete literary history of Baltimore is complicated by the fact that many Baltimore writers are Maryland writers as well. Additionally, in the nineteenth century, many authors owed dual allegiance to both Virginia and Maryland; in the twentieth century, Baltimore and Washington, D.C., have all but blended into a single metropolitan region. A review of anthologies and literary histories documents that often no mention of Baltimore appears for many major American authors whose careers or styles were inflected by some formative Baltimore experience. Gertrude Stein, for example, the matriarch of the Lost Generation, listed Baltimore as her place of residence for her entire life; John Dos Passos, who had family connections in tidewater Maryland, lived and wrote in Baltimore for almost twenty years; Thorstein Veblen's seminal socioeconomic study, *The Theory of the Leisure Class* (1899), was based upon Baltimore research conducted during his graduate studies at Johns Hopkins. Thanks to Poe, Baltimore is also the birthplace of the detective story form. Eighty years later, Dashiell Hammett, a former Pinkerton detective in Baltimore, created the tough-guy detective story in the pages of *Black Mask* magazine, owned and edited by H. L. Mencken, while *Sun* reporter James M. Cain was a pioneer in writing some of America's earliest and best noir thrillers. Baltimore also participates in the history of African American literature, not only for the city's role in the life and autobiography of Frederick Douglass and as the birthplace of Frances Harper, but as well for the *Baltimore Afro-American,* the oldest continuously published black weekly in America.

Contemporary writers with meaningful Baltimore connections include fictionist John Barth, autobiographer and journalist Russell Baker, and poets Lucille Clifton, Josephine Jacobsen, and Adrienne Rich. In the last analysis, Baltimore's lack of identification with a single author, style, or movement is perhaps testimony to the richness and variety of the city's influence on such a panorama of major American authors.

K. Huntress Baldwin

See also Autobiography; Baltimore Sunpapers; Clubs; Grotesque, The; Maryland, Literature of; Mystery and Detective Fiction; Newspapers; Women Writers, World War II to Present.

Clarinda Harriss Lott, "Poetry and Literature," *Baltimore: A Living Renaissance* (1982); Harold A. McDougall, *Black Baltimore* (1993); Sherry H. Olson, *Baltimore: The Building of an American City* (1997); Frank R. Shivers Jr., *Maryland Wits & Baltimore Bards* (1985).

BALTIMORE SUNPAPERS

The Baltimore *Sun,* founded by Arunah S. Abell, first appeared in 1837, two years before the Annapolis-based *Maryland Gazette,* the first newspaper in the

South, ceased publication. The *Sun* promised "Light for All" in its masthead and announced itself as an advocate of states' rights. The *Sunday Sun* was added in 1901 and the less-conservative and more politically oriented *Evening Sun* in 1910; today, the various editions of the Sunpapers constitute Baltimore's only major newspaper. In their long and distinguished history, the Sunpapers have had many significant literary connections: the *Sun* was the only local paper to note the death of Edgar Allan Poe (8 October 1849), highlighting his achievements as poet, scholar, and critic; H. G. Wells covered the 1921 Naval Disarmaments Conference for the *Evening Sun*; James M. Cain, author of *The Postman Always Rings Twice* (1943) and other tough-guy detective novels, was a Sunpaper reporter; and *Sun* columnist Russell Baker received one of his two Pulitzer Prizes for his autobiographical *Growing Up* (1982), in which he recounts the events of his Baltimore childhood.

The most famous literary figure associated with the Sunpapers is H. L. Mencken (1880–1956), the Sage of Baltimore, who joined the paper in 1906 as editor of the *Sunday Sun* and remained with the Sunpapers in varying capacities for the rest of his life. An iconoclastic columnist whose satire spared few aspects of American economics, politics, and culture, he had special disdain for Roosevelt's New Deal and Prohibition. Mencken was the voice of the people during the 1920s and 1930s, and the Sunpapers provided the outlet for his social commentary and literary criticism; his general popularity is partially attested to by his "Monday column," begun in 1920 and appearing some eight hundred times.

K. Huntress Baldwin

See also Baltimore, Maryland; Maryland, Literature of; Newspapers; Scopes Trial.

Gerald W. Johnson et al., *The Sunpapers of Baltimore* (1937); Harold A. Williams, *The Baltimore Sun 1837–1987* (1987).

BAPTISTS

The Baptist denomination of Protestant Christianity was emerging just as some Puritan Anglicans were settling in tidewater Virginia. In the years around 1610, small bands of English dissenters were, by their intentions, taking the Protestant Reformation to its logical conclusion. These third-generation heralds of the movement to reclaim the message of the Bible without addenda or compromise were forming a rather radical sect that was destined to be a continuous presence in Britain and a dominant force in North America, most especially in its southern region.

Significantly, this upstart company shared with the rejected tradition, Roman Catholicism (and to a smaller degree the Church of England), a preoccupation with church as the community of believers. Yet it would be hard to imagine two more divergent views on a central teaching. What impelled the early Baptists was the conviction that only regenerated people are qualified to be members in a local congregation of the faithful. One does not inherit faith and one does not have Christian identity imputed by rites of institutional conferral; rather, one confesses personal faith and testifies to its reality in the heart. Accordingly, the symbol of entry into the congregation assumed defining proportions. These who believed in "believers' baptism" were called Baptists.

It did not follow that they rejected the notion of the universal church as they concentrated on the gathered community in a place; instead, they interpreted that the whole church was present in each local manifestation. But they insisted that each congregation was self-governing, not subject to any ecclesiastical or other earthly authority.

Elements of the democratic vision were implicit in this conception. They thus proved to be quite modern, just as they were dedicated to the ancient, the primitive—that is, to the recovery of authentic New Testament practices. By the nineteenth century in the New World, they rode the crest of the tide—indeed, helped to generate it—that favored individual and local units over centralized and received forms of authority.

Displaying a progressive outlook was hardly the reputation of the Baptists in their early history. Indeed, they were viewed askance in the country of founding and were often treated intolerantly in the American colonies. But history lay on their side; some of their courageous followers were stalwarts in the long experiment toward religious liberty. Their association with forward-looking public policy helped endear them to the common people, among whom they gained many converts once American patterns had displaced customary European ways in church and society.

American Baptist beginnings occurred in New England. From that time on, the denomination has been a notable presence in those states and across America, where it is more often "mainstream" than sectarian or radical. But the South was to become the locus of greatest Baptist influence. Some of the brothers and sisters removed from Maine and New Hampshire to coastal southern Carolina around 1690, to be followed by a band who settled in tidewater Virginia. These were a rather quiet, mind-the-congregation's-business species of Baptists, very much along the lines of their English forebears. They were joined by a different strain of Baptists when some "Separates" (Congregationalists turned Baptists) migrated in the 1750s from rural Connecticut to northern Virginia, thence quickly to piedmont North Carolina.

The primary denominational dynamic and reputation was to lie with that less-conventional cluster. From small and rather rustic beginnings, they evangelized far and near, becoming a popular force in the countryside and the towns. Along with spirited Methodist (still officially Anglican) and zealous Presbyterian people, they brought the "Great Awakening" to the South. The dual impact of this social movement and the "Great Revival" that erupted on the Kentucky-Tennessee frontier around 1800 shaped the South as evangelical Protestant territory. Of course they were bearers of orthodox doctrine, but what distinguished them was their passion for "converting lost souls" to Christ through a one-time experience in the heart that was often dramatic.

As mentioned, this strain of Baptists has been the largest and most-recognizable company within the movement. Yet the earlier, less-aggressive form has persisted, with special strength in the upper seaboard South. And other genera were to appear—the institutional-growth and organization-minded people, and around 1860 the most-radical sect, the Landmarkists, who both opposed institutionalization and asserted that Baptists stood in an unbroken succession from the era of the early church and thus were the true Christians.

Baptists were numerous and growing by the 1830s; indeed, they were on their way to becoming the de facto established church of the society—that is, in league with many Methodists and, later, the Pentecostal and Holiness people.

This extensive network of Protestants has constituted the "southern evangelical" tradition; when thinking comparatively, we may say that Baptist and Baptist-like forms have comprised the heart of popular regional church life. Statistically, and in point of influence, their ways and means have been normative for the career of Protestantism in the South. For this rea-

son, it has not always been easy for other, more traditional denominations to inculcate in their members a sense of their distinct identity. So, when William Faulkner refers to the religious culture of his upbringing, he writes of it as "just there," an inescapable element of his cultural legacy, so ingredient as to be taken for granted. Regional culture was "suffused" with evangelical faith, much of it Baptist and Baptist-like.

The Southern Baptist Convention was formed in 1845, as if to acknowledge a distinctive regional direction. Sectionalism fueled this creation; southern sovereignty in such matters as racial practices and states' rights were primary determinants of this new formation. But already the regional Baptist tradition had developed its own theological patterns, "patterns" more than specific doctrines. The implications of a "revivalist" approach to preaching and understanding highlighted its peculiar character. The tendency was to make every gathering less an opportunity for worship than a means for converting any unconverted person in attendance to personal faith. In some sense, most services were evangelistic. Relegated to secondary position were concerns long considered as elemental to the full complex of church life—worship itself, thoughtful attention to biblical and theological teaching, and ethical sensitivity. The assumption, and often the stated claim, was that conversion set everything right and could be expected to accomplish the ends of commitment to God. The ethical instruction that was most common was the call to personal righteousness, and less emphasis was given to participation in social ethics.

In the hands of most preachers, conversion was equated with the "conversion experience," a one-time, datable, memorable event of the heart, signifying that one has "passed from death unto life." Sometimes dramatic, perhaps even accompanied by great emotional release, this experience was presented as the individualization of history—that is, the shift from a personal B.C. to a personal A.D. One was lost and now is saved. Of course, the churches urged the convert on to personal righteousness and Bible study, but the one essential requirement had been met.

Significantly, the faithful have taken this singular preoccupation of many clergymen rather lightly in carrying out their Christian life. They have seemed to hear both more and less than their preachers have communicated in the content and the passion of sermons. That is to say, they have not typically looked on neighbors and friends as either lost or saved, infrequently treating their mission in life as "witnessing" to others with the goal of converting them. But this urgent call to conversion has been the dominant platform in the ministry of the professional clergy and the organized life of the denomination.

Viewed historically, these Baptists stood in the Calvinist line of theological thinking, but, as implicit in the discussion above, they came to exchange Calvinist strictures for those they developed in the course of their career in the American South. The classic doctrine of election, whereby each person's eternal destiny was determined by the Almighty "from the foundation of the world," gave way to a thoroughgoing doctrine of free will: each person may and must decide whether to accept or reject God's gracious proffer of forgiveness and eternal life in heaven. A tiny minority of Baptists in the South retained this Calvinist affirmation of the sovereignty of God in the matter of personal destiny. From the eighteenth century, there have been so-called Primitive Baptists upholding an older hard-line Calvinism. Their distinctive nature showed up most popularly in opposition to missions and to Sunday schools. In this century, their ranks have been confined largely to the Appalachian highlands. Before the Civil War, they were more numerous, often contending with the newer-style Baptists in debates and tracts.

Nevertheless, some continuities link the Calvinist heritage with Baptist practices. Most notably, they live with a strong sense of duty. God's call to obedience and service persists as characteristic, and there is nothing casual about their response. They are to be self-conscious with their discipleship, clear on their identity and calling, busy about the work of doing the business of their God. The Calvinist sense of trusting God's sovereignty while acting as if everything depended on their own activity survives almost everywhere, except in the matter of personal salvation, one's own and that of every other person. They have embodied much of the Calvinist legacy while modifying it with a strong strain of Arminianism.

In the process of attending to the impact that their teachings and practices have had on the regional culture, we learn just how influential they have been. First, they have rendered the ordinance (sacrament) of the Lord's Supper secondary. In the interest of acquainting people with the message of the Bible, they have placed heavy emphasis on preaching, especially on the theme of human sinfulness and the sacrificial death of Jesus to atone for that universal hopeless condition. In the process of doing that, they have largely dispensed with any sense of mystery about what God is and requires, and what human beings must do. Words as the medium of revelation virtually exhaust what the Christian faith is and means. The operative sensibilities are speaking and hearing, not the other senses, not even sight. Mystery is dispelled by certainty, by definitions and truth claims expressed usually in propositions. That is particularly true of the Baptists who are fundamentalist, most of them "independent Baptists," and in recent decades the militant conservatives who have realized success in their campaign to gain almost total institutional control over the sixteen-million-member Southern Baptist Convention.

The southern African American population, too, has been dominated by the Baptist version of the Christian faith. Largely outside the Christian fold until the 1790s or so, these people have responded to Baptist and Methodist evangelistic overtures, coming to conversion and developing distinctive forms of worship, music, piety, and preaching. Participation in, thus familiarity with, Baptist (and here too Methodist) church life positioned African Americans to form their own congregations and denominations once Emancipation took effect at the end of the Civil War. Church has been the primary institutional form created by southern African Americans, also a primary source of identification and participation in society. Although that is less generally the case in the late twentieth century, the churches persist as central for that large sector of the regional population. Despite many efforts to bring together black and white Baptists, separation and distinctiveness remain typical. Faith, doctrine, and worship seem to come in two Baptist flavors, one reflecting the history of the African American culture, the other the Anglo-American culture.

On historic grounds, the argument is strong that Baptistism was meant to be a minority, countercultural, sectarian expression of Protestantism. Precisely the opposite describes the Baptist career in the South. Its numbers are huge, its influence powerful. Although this condition was more prevalent from the second quarter of the nineteenth century to the 1960s, the Baptist presence remains formidable. The Baptist affiliation of major public figures such as Jimmy Carter, Martin Luther King Jr., Newt Gingrich, Trent Lott, Jesse Helms, Bill Clinton, and Al Gore only dramatizes a standard feature of southern religious life.

Baptist mentality (Faulkner's Tulls fit the pattern) informs much southern fiction, but few classic texts have highlighted Baptists. Eudora Welty's Uncle Daniel, in *The Ponder Heart* (1954), "crosses the street" from the "good Presbyterian" church to find his first wife, Miss Teacake Magee, singing in the Baptist choir—she's a Sistrunk, and all the Sistrunks are Baptists. In Welty's *Losing Battles* (1970), Grandpa Vaughn is a staunch Baptist preacher, the family all belongs to Damascus Church in the heart of Banner, Mississippi, and the clan looks down upon the Methodists across the street. Clyde Edgerton's *Raney* (1985) gains much of its force by juxtaposing the mind-set of an Episcopalian male and his Primitive Baptist wife. Will Campbell (1924–   ) exemplifies the Baptists' spirit of strong independence and conscience. After pastoring a Baptist church in Taylor, Louisiana, he became a consultant on race relations for the National Council of Churches, an experience that led to his writing a memoir about his work in the Civil Rights Movement, *Forty Acres and a Goat* (1986), and *And Also With Thee: Duncan Gray and the American Dilemma* (1997), which intertwines the crisis over integration at the University of Mississippi with the story of the Ole Miss Greys, who all perished at Gettysburg. Campbell's many books include the novella *Cecelia's Sin* (1983), whose context is the Anabaptist movement in northeast Europe in the seventeenth and eighteenth centuries. His other fiction includes *The Glad River* (1982) and *The Convention* (1990).

Samuel S. Hill

See also African American Spirituals; Bible Belt; Black Methodists; Carter, Jimmy; Evangelical Christianity; Preaching.

John L. Eighmy, *Churches in Cultural Captivity* (1987); Paul M. Harvey, *Redeeming the South: Religious Cultures and Racial Identities Among Southern Baptists, 1865–1925* (1997); H. L. McBeth, *The Baptist Heritage* (1986); J. M. Washington, *Frustrated Fellowship: The Black Baptist Quest for Social Power* (1986).

BARTRAM, WILLIAM

William Bartram was a Pennsylvania Quaker and naturalist whose *Travels Through North and South Carolina, Georgia, East and West Florida, the Cherokee Country, the Extensive Territories of the Muscogulges, or Creek Confederacy, and the Country of the Chactaws* (1791)—along with his engravings of the flora and fauna of those regions—first brought the lush natural beauty of the South to the attention of an international literary audience.

Born at Kingsessing (now a part of Philadelphia) to the famed botanist John Bartram in 1739, William displayed talent at drawing realistic likenesses of plants and animals as a young boy. But after attending what would become the University of Pennsylvania, where he gained a grounding in the Classics, and being offered work as an engraver by Benjamin Franklin, Bartram was steered toward business pursuits by his father, who thought him too unsystematic of mind for science. Finding his way south, he spent several years working unsuccessfully as a trader at Cape Fear, North Carolina. In 1765–1766, he joined his father on an expedition up the St. John's River in newly acquired British Florida. William Bartram was so taken with the region that he attempted a living there as a planter of indigo and rice, at which he also failed; but artwork inspired by his river expedition would lead to his greatest success.

Bartram's exceptionally detailed drawings of mollusks and turtles came to the attention of a wealthy British botanist, Dr. John Fothergill, who in 1772 commissioned him to undertake an ongoing exploration of Florida. He was not only to keep a journal and illustrations but also to collect seeds and plant specimens. These instructions Bartram followed, but in the pattern of his travels—and in maintaining communication with his employer—he was wildly erratic. Setting forth from Charleston, South Carolina, in March, 1773, Bartram would spend the next four years wandering, usually alone and without apparent plan, through not only Florida but also the Carolinas and Georgia—mainly along the coastline and the Savannah River—and finally into parts of Alabama and Louisiana. Even when the Revolution broke out and thoroughly severed his connection with his English employer, Bartram continued on his solitary quest through the southern wilds, living among Native Americans far from the front lines of the conflict.

Though Bartram returned to Philadelphia in January 1777, the book that resulted from this journey—no crude field journal but rather a mammoth, carefully crafted tome—would not see print for another fourteen years.

Bartram's *Travels* would prove to be one of the most distinctive and influential books to come out of the early Republic. The Quaker's account of the southern wilderness was accurate in most details, but nonetheless was no dry, objective report; following his creed's conviction that the natural world bore witness to the divine, Bartram approached a mystical ecstasy in proclaiming that "this world" was "a glorious apartment of the boundless palace of the sovereign Creator." Balancing his Christian vision with occasional Classical allusions, Bartram was unfailingly enthusiastic in describing even seemingly mundane technical subjects, as when he exclaims: "But admirable are the properties of the extraordinary Dionea muscipula!"

Bartram's vivid rendering of the alien natural world he found in the South caught the attention of Europe before it did the United States. British Romantics such as Wordsworth and Coleridge eagerly welcomed his account of an exotic paradise, which influenced their poetry both in its general account of nature and sometimes even in specific lyrics; Coleridge, for example, directly borrowed from Bartram in descriptive passages in *Kubla Khan* (1797)—so that one might claim that at least parts of Xanadu lie south of the Potomac. *Travels* saw multiple editions in French, German, and Dutch, and France's Chateaubriand drew heavily on Bartram in writing *Atala* (1801), his novel of North America that has been frequently cited as beginning the Romantic movement in French literature. Thomas Carlyle attempted to remedy the book's relative neglect in America when he recommended the book to Emerson, advising him that his young nation had fostered a classic.

Bartram himself slowly sank into relative obscurity after the journey (though he maintained a long correspondence with Thomas Jefferson, who unsuccessfully urged him to join the Lewis and Clark expedition) and died in 1823. His position as a literary naturalist and illustrator has long been overshadowed by such figures as Thoreau and Audubon, but his reputation saw a revival in the 1930s when the Romantics' debt to him was first explored. Charles Frazier's novel *Cold Mountain* (1997) contains a fitting tribute to Bartram from a southern writer who seems to have Romantic inclinations of his own: as the protagonist walks alone through the wilds of North Carolina and away from the Civil War, he reads the *Travels*—much as the naturalist himself wrote it while walking blithely away from the Revolution.

Farrell O'Gorman

See also Diaries, Men's; Nature; Romanticism; Travel Literature.

Helen Gere Cruikshank, ed., *John and William Bartram's America* (1956); Pamela Regis, *Describing Early America: Bartram, Jefferson, Crèvecoeur, and the Rhetoric of Natural History* (1992); Thomas P. Slaughter, *The Natures of John and William Bartram* (1996).

BATON ROUGE, LOUISIANA

Although Baton Rouge was founded in 1719, replaced New Orleans as the capital city of Louisiana in 1850, and has been the scene of rich and varied historical events in the complex and often exotic history of the state, its literary history is comparatively insignificant in contrast to that of New Orleans. In fact, no notable mention of Baton Rouge in American literature occurs earlier than Mark Twain's vitriolic reference to the city in *Life on the Mississippi* (1883) as the site of a state capitol building that symbolizes perfectly the "pathetic" brand of Sir Walter Scott romanticism that drove the southern people "mad a couple of generations ago." Thomas Bangs Thorpe, the only notable pre–Civil War writer who lived in Baton Rouge, however, was a New Yorker. A resident of Baton Rouge for varying periods in the 1830s, 1840s, and 1850s, Thorpe was a painter and a journalist who became a practitioner of the art of the "tall tale" and is best known as the author "The Big Bear of Arkansas" (*Spirit of the Times,* 1841), which has been called the best single story in the tradition of Southwestern humor. The only other notable nineteenth-century writer associated with Baton Rouge is the Civil War diarist Sarah Morgan. Born in New Orleans but brought up in Baton Rouge, her remarkable diary detailing life and emotion in the occupied cities of Baton Rouge and New Orleans during the war (first published in 1911, but not in complete form until 1991) has been praised both by historians and literary scholars as one of the two or three best Civil War diaries.

Two writers of distinctive, though minor, note were reared in twentieth-century Baton Rouge. One, Lyle Saxon, although he always maintained his connection with his native city, lived most of his adult life in the city he celebrated in *Fabulous New Orleans* (1928); the other, Harris Downey, though never a commercial success, was devoted to the art of fiction and made effective use of Baton Rouge settings in carefully crafted stories and novels. By far the two best-known authors associated with the literary history of Baton Rouge are Huey Pierce Long, author of *Every Man a King* (1933) and *My First Days in the White House* (1935); and Robert Penn Warren (1905–1979), author of *All the King's Men* (1946). During his years as a member of the Louisiana State University English faculty and a coeditor, with Cleanth Brooks, of the original series of the *Southern Review*, Warren wrote a play about a fictional dictator and later transformed this into his classic novel, in which Jack Burden, formerly a graduate student of southern history at a school very much like Louisiana State University, tells the story of giving up an academic career to work for a charismatic politician very much like Huey Long, who becomes the dictatorial governor of a southern state very much like Louisiana and is eventually assassinated by a young physician who is very much like the young Baton Rouge doctor who actually did kill Long. During the 1930s and 1940s, publication of the *Southern Review* at LSU and the creative and critical work of its editors drew several young writers to Baton Rouge, including Robert Lowell, Peter Taylor, and Jean Stafford. Katherine Anne Porter, who was briefly married to Albert Erskine, a member of the *Southern Review* staff, also resided in Baton Rouge for a time. In more recent years, a number of writers have resided in Baton Rouge as members of the faculty of the Writing Program of the LSU English Department, including three southerners, David Madden, Moira Crone, and Dave Smith, who also serves, with James Olney, as coeditor of the new series of the *Southern Review*.

Lewis P. Simpson

See also *Southern Review*.

Thomas W. Cutrer, *Parnassus on the Mississippi: The "Southern Review" and the Baton Rouge Literary Community, 1935–1942* (1984); Milton Rickels, *Thomas Bangs Thorpe: Humorist of the Old Southwest* (1962); Charles East, ed., *The Civil War Diary of Sarah Morgan* (1991); James A. Grimshaw Jr., ed., *Cleanth Brooks and Robert Penn Warren: A Literary Correspondence* (1998); Lewis P. Simpson, Donald E. Stanford, James Olney, and Jo Gulledge, eds., *Selected Stories from the "Southern Review"* (1988); Lewis P. Simpson, James Olney, and Jo Gulledge, eds., *The "Southern Review" and Modern Literature, 1935–1985* (1988); Cleanth Brooks and Robert Penn Warren, eds., *Stories from the "Southern Review"* (1953).

BEACHES

As setting, beaches in southern fiction put characters at the edge of their landscape, outside the familiar patterns of their lives, sometimes permanently, sometimes just long enough to re-evaluate a dilemma or their whole lives, for that matter. The coastal formation of the South leaves much room for such wanderings, as there are few landlocked southern states. In general, though, fiction from and about the coast has been less prolific than piedmont or mountain writings, though nonfiction is well represented, the coastal areas being rich with history still perceivable in the coastline and interior flatlands.

In fiction, the following themes predominate. Among southern writers, Kate Chopin first discovered the dramatic possibilities of a beach setting. In several short stories and, most famously, in *The Awakening* (1899), she takes her characters to the seaside, where her women find liberation from stifling convention. Things get tangled at the beach, as unlikely lives cross and uncross lines of class, taste, and values. Padgett Powell's *Edisto* (1984) and the more recent *Edisto Revisited* (1996) give us a good, if one-sided, look at the displaced communities of whites who try to inhabit territory wilder and older than they can handle. Elizabeth Spencer's *The Salt Line* (1984) opens up the displacement theme to issues of middle-age conflict and environmental battles over control, as does Doris Betts's earlier *The River to Pickle Beach* (1972). But characters find their lives untangling on the coast as well. Lee Smith's story "Gulfport," from *Cakewalk* (1983), opens up its heroine to possibilities she could not imagine inland; the slow unwinding of the heroine in Smith's "Bob, a Dog" (*Me and My Baby View the Eclipse*, 1990) reaches an important turn at the beach; and the crisis between the young married couple in Clyde Edgerton's *Raney* (1985) best illuminates itself during the family's vacation by the sea. The sea is also symbolic of magic, the drawing up and resolution of unseen disturbances. Several of Smith's stories from *Cakewalk* ("Georgia Rose," "Mrs. Darcy Meets the Blue-Eyed Stranger at the Beach," etc.) revolve around explicit images of the occult. Betts's character Jack, from *The River to Pickle Beach*, explains why the coast is so open to such fancies: he thinks of the ocean as just another word for chance, something he doesn't trust because he can't control it. But the need for chance—for something you shouldn't count on but are willing to bet on, something that might bring you magic—is the reason these characters head for the beach to begin with, to be where their horizons are instantly and infinitely expanded. Therefore the beach is also symbolic of romance, looseness, openness to love. Among others, William Faulkner's *The Wild Palms* (1939) tries to make a story of these symbols. Though not his most acclaimed novel, it is most representative of the role that the coastal landscape—wind, water, tropical vegetation, tourists on the loose from their everyday routines and morals—plays in the fictional imagination of the South.

Rachel V. Mills

Robert Ruark, *The Old Man and the Boy* (1957); Bland and Ann Cary Simpson, *Into the Sound Country* (1997).

BELLE

During the early decades of the nineteenth century, influenced in part by the historical romances of Sir Walter Scott, writers began to represent the plantation society of the South as an aristocracy modeled on the feudal system of lords, knights, and ladies with attending servants. Following the Civil War, this vision of a plantation South took on mythic proportions as southerners grew defensive and nostalgic about the Old South. In particular, the southern woman of the Old South was presented, through the image of the southern lady, as the ideal of nineteenth-century womanhood.

But being a totally admirable character, the southern lady was not a very enticing subject for storytelling. A marble figure on a pedestal, she was static. A more appealing character, in this idealized vision of the South, was the southern belle, the younger, unmarried, and hence incomplete version of the southern lady. The lady was what the belle was supposed to grow up to be, and it was the getting-there that created action, tension, and story.

If trained right, the belle had, by her early teen years, already acquired most of the makings of the southern lady: she was beautiful or potentially beautiful, graceful, charming, virtuous, loyal to family, submissive to father, in need of men's protection, yet resourceful and brave when unusual circumstances called on her to be. But even into her late teens, she might not yet have perfected self-sacrifice and calm self-possession. These characteristics would come, or must come, once she married—and marrying was supposed to be her goal in life. That being so, the belle was allowed a few additional characteristics that might aid her in pursuit of a good husband but that she would have to abandon once she got him: she could be innocently flirtatious, winsome, spirited, haughty, spunky, mischievous, impulsive. It was chiefly these little liberties, and the lack of a husband to serve and a household to manage, that separated the belle from the lady.

Anne, the major female character in Thomas Nelson Page's short story "Marse Chan" (1884; collected in *In Ole Virginia,* 1887), epitomizes the southern belle. Young, feminine, beautiful, aristocratic, virtuous, charming, she captures Marse Chan's heart when, as only a child, she needs his protection from the teasing of bullies. Growing up on neighboring plantations, the two fall in love, but Anne subsequently rejects Channing out of loyalty to her father when political differences between the two families lead, she thinks, to Channing's insulting her father. Popular and beautiful, she flirts with her other suitors and snubs Channing or reacts haughtily when she meets him—behavior that heightens rather than deters his passion. She later relents, however—with her father's blessing—after learning that Channing, now a Confederate soldier, had defended her father's reputation when another rejected suitor, also a soldier, had gossiped unscrupulously about him. But Channing dies heroically in battle before the two young lovers can be reunited. With his death, Anne graduates to the status of southern lady: though they never married, she grieves as though she is his widow. Fulfilling the idealized role expected of her, she remains faithful to Channing through the remaining days of her short life, sacrificing any possible happiness or future for herself in staying with and serving Channing's bereaved parents until they die and subsequently in devoting her life to helping the sick. When she dies, she is buried at Channing's side.

The most famous literary portraits of southern belles appear in that most famous of plantation and Civil War novels, Margaret Mitchell's *Gone With the Wind* (1936). Mitchell presents two deliberately contrasting images of the belle. Melanie is a sweet, proper, virtuous, passive belle and Scarlett a daring, resourceful, sometimes self-centered one. But both are faithful and loyal to family and home. Scarlett, of course, is passionate about Tara. With spiritedness bordering on naughtiness and, in difficult circumstances, on harshness, Scarlett is also, of course, the more interesting character. She stretches the freedom allowed the southern belle to its limits. As her foil, Melanie cultivates none of the freedom that the belle is allowed and that Scarlett relishes. Rather, even before she marries Ashley, she is already the southern lady, selfless, good, accepting, and essentially static. She skips belledom, passing from childhood to ladyhood without going through the excitement of becoming. Seeing Melanie and Scarlett side by side makes clearer the essential distinction between the lady and the belle.

Whereas Mitchell uses and bends the mythology about southern women, many other writers of the twentieth century have undertaken to undermine the mythology more directly. They are realists aware not only that the Old South has been glamorized but also that the glamorized view can be harmful. In particular, many women writers suggest that the idealized vision of southern womanhood misleads and harms young girls and women who seek to live up to that image. Their stories are critiques of the southern belle and lady concepts.

Kate Chopin, for one, was writing such critiques even before the turn of the century. Suggesting the pervasiveness of the southern mythology, she locates its effects in a Louisiana Cajun society rather than in the more familiar Caucasian plantation families. In her story "Athénaïse: A Story of a Temperament" (1896), the major character is a pretty, young wife who has not been able to settle into her expected role as southern lady. Athénaïse finds wifehood boring; she feels isolated and buried out on her husband's plantation with nothing to do but to carry around a bunch of household keys and no one to talk to but the servants. She much preferred her life as southern belle, when there were always dances or parties to go to, boys to flirt with, and the certainty that life was meant to be gay and exciting. Young and innocent, swept off her feet by the attentions of an older man, she had married with little knowledge of the mundane life that was to follow. She tells her brother that she despises being married: "I hate being Mrs. Cazeau, an' would want to be Athénaïse Miché again. I can't stan' to live with a man: to have him always there; his coats an' pantaloons hanging in my room; his ugly bare feet—washing them in my tub, befo' my very eyes, ugh!" To escape the mundane and to try to recapture the romance and excitement of belledom—the romance of being pursued, the excitement of being the center of attention—she returns to her parents' home to the dances there and later runs away to New Orleans, in both cases silently hoping her husband will become the courtier and will pursue her again. While mocking Athénaïse as an immature, temperamental young woman, Chopin also implies that the southern-belle role does not prepare women for the reality of life as wife and lady.

Ellen Glasgow and Katherine Anne Porter offer more expansive critiques of the mythology of southern womanhood. In The Sheltered Life (1932), Glasgow shows that the southern code of behavior is detrimental to males as well as females, but she points most often to the harms visited on women through the society's infatuation with the southern-belle image. Handsome, dashing Isabella Archbald is a much-courted and admired belle until her innocent and acceptable flirtation with a man other than her fiancé appears to go too far—and appearances are everything. Jilted by her fiancé, she is considered ruined. Eva Birdsong's case is more dire. Though married and approaching middle age, she feels compelled to be still the beautiful, vivacious belle she had been in her youth. She cannot settle comfortably into ladyhood for several reasons: she is constantly reminded of the famous beauty she once was and should still be by an adoring, unforgetting society; she fears losing her handsome husband, who has a roving eye; and she has no children, who would give her a new focus and confirm her identity as the lady rather than the belle. Etta Archbald's case is different, yet she suffers as well from her society's infatuation with the image of the belle: as homely as Isabella and Eva are beautiful, Etta is painfully aware that she can never be a belle, will likely never be loved by a man or marry. She knows she is a failure as a woman.

Katherine Anne Porter criticizes the idealization of the belle role just as sharply in "Old Mortality" (1939) and also, like Glasgow, through its effects on several characters; Aunt Amy is remembered by her family as a beautiful, spirited, reckless belle who had been much loved yet unhappy and who had died young. Though separating fact from legend in this novella is difficult, the reader surmises that what had made Amy unhappy was her awareness that her life as a southern belle had to end. Like Athénaïse, Amy finds belledom exciting and glamorous, even liberating, yet unlike the immature Athénaïse, Amy is acutely aware that belledom is only a stage, only a role, and that its object—its end—is marriage and ladydom, which she does not find enticing at all. Her mother recalls, "Amy insisted that she could not imagine wanting to marry anybody," and that when she finally did marry, she insisted on wearing gray: "I shall wear mourning if I like," she said, "it is my funeral, you know." That is, the belle must die and, if she can bear it, be resurrected as a lady. Just as Amy recognizes belledom as only a role, and a brief one at that, so does she recognize the idealized southern lady that she is expected to become as a role, but a long-lasting one. Further, she realizes that the role *is* idealized, and the reality of life as a lady and wife does not appeal to her. So Amy dies soon after marrying—perhaps of suicide.

Southern fiction after the mid-twentieth century is generally less concerned with the belle and lady concepts. As the Old South mythology itself has faded, its effect on southern literature has diminished—but by no means ended.

Carol S. Manning

See also *Gone With the Wind*; Lady; Plantation Fiction.

Peggy Whitman Prenshaw, "Southern Ladies and the Southern Literary Renaissance," in *The Female Tradition in Southern Literature*, ed. Carol S. Manning (1993); Anne Firor Scott, *The Southern Lady: From Pedestal to Politics 1830–1930* (1970); Kathryn Lee Seidel, *The Southern Belle in the American Novel* (1985).

BIBLE

The United States is a nation identified with a strong Puritan heritage that still plays an important role in setting national agendas and confirming national mores. The importance of the Bible in the national culture has, accordingly, been strong. In colonial times, New England was strikingly characterized by Bible-dominated discourse. But as a strong sense of southern identity emerged and the South became overwhelmingly Baptist and Methodist in the wake of the first Great Awakening (c. 1725–1750) and the second Great Awakening (1795–1835), the region increasingly made the King James Bible its text. In the early twentieth century, H. L. Mencken coined the phrase "Bible Belt" to mock fundamentalist fervor chiefly in the South and Midwest and what he saw as narrow, unreflective thinking, but many southerners continued to take pride in the centrality of the Bible in their region. In *Dixie Rising: How the South Is Shaping American Values, Politics, and Culture* (1996), Peter Applebome reports on his talk with Michael Hill, a neo-conservative and founder of the Southern League. Defending the actions of the South before the Civil War, Hill said, "The South was not the evil society it was portrayed as by the abolitionists. . . . It was the most Bible-believing Christian part of the country."

The extent of the believing (as well as the selectivity of the believing) is a matter that can be challenged, but

about the importance of the Bible as southern text there is little doubt. Several decades after Mencken coined "Bible Belt," Flannery O'Connor declared, "While the South is hardly Christ-centered, it is most certainly Christ haunted." In the May, 1990, issue of *Southern Living*, Isie Peat and Diane Young reported on a poll of southern novelists, poets, journalists, critics, and scholars on their ten favorite works of southern literature. In his response, the poet Andrew Hudgins identified the King James Bible as *the* most important work in southern literature: "Every Southern writer knows it and has been influenced by it, and almost all Southern writing can be read as commentary, positive or negative, on it. . . . The biblical sense of each human life being an ongoing dialogue with God is a bone-deep reality of Southern life and Southern writing."

Hudgins's point carries more than a modicum of truth, but the paradigm is shifting as southern writing becomes increasingly postmodern. As Hudgins notes, the King James Bible has had a powerful influence on southern writing—it has been the text that most southerners grew up with, learned to memorize, and later echoed its rhythm and its diction. Although the King James version continues to exert a powerful influence in fundamentalist circles, in mainstream churches in the South and throughout the nation, parishioners will likely confront more recent, more "readable" translations—older worshipers may miss the poetry of the King James, but younger listeners will not. On confirmation Sunday, confirmands may be given a Bible, but likely not the King James. Competing translations include the New Revised Standard Version, the New International Version, the New American Standard Bible, and the New Jerusalem Bible. The ultimate insult to the King James version came with the Living Bible, which paraphrases the ancient text rather than translates it. Although one aim of these newer translations has been to make the Scriptures more accessible, the postmodern generation has not become as familiar with the Bible as earlier generations were. Sunday schools and youth groups, no longer well attended, are no longer centered on Bible reading, "sword drills," or memorization as they once were. The King James Bible must compete not only with other translations but with multiple leisure possibilities unknown to earlier generations. Early-twenty-first-century southerners typically are much less familiar with the Bible stories than were their ancestors.

The slide of the King James Bible began with the

publication of the Revised Standard Version in 1952 by the National Council of Churches. Fundamentalist reaction in the South was strong: the cry was that the translation undermined the historic faith. Bob Jones Sr., founder of Bob Jones University in Greenville, South Carolina, and an old-fashioned Methodist, raged and challenged the translators to come to his school at University expense to debate with his scholars on the correct translation of Isaiah 7:14, which in the Revised Standard Version has "a young woman" rather than a virgin giving birth to Immanuel. There were no takers.

In the twentieth century, the South produced a number of evangelical schools to counteract the liberal influences of the mainstream denominations and to promote a literal interpretation of the Bible. They include Bryan College (named for William Jennings Bryan, who had argued in the Scopes trial against the Darwinian theory of evolution and for a literal understanding of the account of Creation in Genesis) and, most visibly near the end of the century, Liberty University of the Reverend Jerry Falwell, located in Lynchburg, Virginia. The founders of these schools usually play the dominant roles in their direction. In the case of BJU, the leadership mantel has been hereditary, Bob Jones Jr. succeeding his father as president, to be followed eventually by Bob Jones III. Numerous small Bible colleges mark the southern landscape as well, though it should be emphasized that the evangelical college and Bible school are in no way uniquely southern (though they have sometimes been more flamboyantly defiant in the South). The model of the Bible college is the Moody Bible Institute of Chicago. When Billy Graham from Charlotte, North Carolina, left Bob Jones College (then in Cleveland, Tennessee) after a semester, he transferred to the Florida Bible Institute in Tampa. After graduation from the institute, he was advised to enroll in Wheaton College in Illinois; he soon become its most famous alumnus and the most famous evangelist of the twentieth century. From the South, Bob Jones Sr. and Bob Jones Jr. vehemently attacked Graham's ecumenical emphasis and branded him as too liberal and a danger to Christianity. In reaction to religious liberalism following World War II, the Bible Church began to emerge in the South and elsewhere, an easy step for the independent Baptist churches to take.

Although fundamentalist theologians judged no translation infallible, the King James continues to be the preferred text, in many circles the exclusive text. Other southern Christians welcomed the new transla-

tions and embraced the more demanding, to their minds, challenge of the higher criticism. In this view, the evangelicals tended to make an idol or icon of the Bible, tended to worship it rather than to search its meanings. The liberal view emphasizes that the Bible is a library of several texts, each needing to be read with prayer and humility, but in the understanding that each comes from a time and place and reflects those times and conditions. In poet Andrew Hudgins's words, the reader engages in "an ongoing dialogue with God." If the South counts many conservative seminaries and colleges within its states, it has major seminaries as well that have not been frightened by the higher criticism. These include Union P.S.C.E. Theological Seminary (Presbyterian) in Richmond; Duke University Divinity School (United Methodist) in Durham; the University of the South (Episcopal); Candler School of Divinity at Emory; Perkins School of Theology at Southern Methodist; and the School of Divinity at Vanderbilt.

Roman Catholics in the South have not approached the King James Bible with the same awe that their Protestant neighbors did. Their church traditionally uses the Douai version (the 1963 Confraternity version is based on it). The Bible of Roman Catholics includes eleven books considered uncanonical by Protestants because they are not in the Hebrew Scriptures, but Catholic tradition places much less emphasis on the text in the reader's hands. Catholics learned the Bible stories through art, sermon, and ritual. Whereas the Baptist child in Sunday school would likely be holding the text, the Roman Catholic child would be learning about the lives of the saints. In a South still largely rural, most people had little understanding or acquaintance with Roman Catholics. That would change in a more urbanized South in the later twentieth century. Many southerners would also become acquainted with a growing Mormon population, who brought with them the Book of Mormon, a further challenge to the mainstream Scriptural heritage.

The Bible became an important text for African Americans in the South, although the right to own, hold, or read it was often denied to slaves—literacy being actively discouraged or even illegal. For slaves who learned to read, the Bible was often the primary goal and primary text. The importance of the Bible to the emerging community of literate slaves and ex-slaves is made clear in the slave narratives and other writings of Frederick Douglass, whose sentences frequently echo it. Douglass recognized that his assimilation of scripture was a powerful tool for emphasizing the error of his Christian readers, who held that the Bible was the primary guide not only for salvation in the next life but as guide for this life. How could a Bible-believing people deny this text to a quarter of its population? And was it not clear that the Bible revealed that a slave-holding society was violating the very message of those scriptures? The King James version also informed the poetic sensibility of George Moses Horton, the first black poet in the South to publish a volume of poetry; he learned his prosody from the Wesley hymnal.

In Reconstruction and beyond, educational opportunities for African Americans were limited, but the importance of the Bible in their culture and worship is strong. Even when the preacher could not read, Bible stories were at the core of the sermons, told and retold and made relevant to African American life. James Weldon Johnson pays tribute to that heritage of Bible preaching in *God's Trombones* (1927) and in "O Black and Unknown Bards," his moving paean to the line of unlettered singers who "sang a race from wood and stone to Christ." Near the end of *The Sound and the Fury* (1929), William Faulkner recognizes the same tradition of black preaching in the sermon of the Reverend Sheegog. The reader finds a Christianity in the black worshippers that is not to be found in the dominant white society.

Biblical cadence, diction, allusion, and theme have also been strong in much southern discourse from the colonial period to the present. William Wirt echoed the biblical rhetorical flare of the southern platform in his 1817 rendition of Patrick Henry's 1775 oration at St. John's Church in Richmond. More than a century later, when Governor Frank Clement of Tennessee gave the keynote address at the Democratic National Convention of 1956 nominating Adlai E. Stevenson, his style and content were decidedly in the same tradition of heightened rhetoric; the speech could scarcely have come from another section of the country.

Belles-lettrists were more subtle, but the fact remains that many of the great southern writers grew up learning about and reading the Bible—as did many of the characters they depict. Faulkner's case is primary. Biblical analogue is central to his masterpiece, *Absalom, Absalom!* (1936). *Go Down, Moses* (1942) also looks at race relations in the South in a context of biblical image and judges the South against a Christian ideal. Faulkner recast the Christ story as *A Fable* (1952), set in 1918. Critics have identified several

Christ figures in Faulkner's work, including Joe Christmas, the protagonist of *Light in August* (1932). Faulkner told of his grandfather's habit of demanding a verse from the King James Bible each morning at breakfast.

If biblical analogues are less insistent in other writers of the Renascence, the tradition remains highly visible in several contemporary writers: for example, Doris Betts, Lee Smith, and Clyde Edgerton. But no contemporary writer would better illustrate the importance of the Bible as southern text than Reynolds Price, who has frequently taught the Bible as literature at Duke University. So important is the New Testament to his own thinking that he learned Greek so that he could read the Gospels in the original. In *A Palpable God* (1978), Price recounted his need, as a person and as an artist, to come to terms with the Bible. The work provides his translation from Hebrew and Christian texts. In 1998 Price published *Three Gospels,* providing readers with his translations of the "Good News" according to Mark and according to John, followed by his own "A Modern Apocryphal Gospel: A Preface to an Honest Account of a Memorable Life." In his fiction, Price has pursued themes of original sin, free will, and "permanent errors." Price's account of his struggle with cancer, published as *A Whole New Life: An Illness and a Healing* (1994), makes immediate the centrality of the Bible for Price the person.

But for many contemporary southern writers, the Bible seems a distant influence (e.g., Bobbie Ann Mason), or one not central to contemporary realities (e.g., Ellen Gilchrist, Barry Hannah). Given, however, Flannery O'Connor's contention that the South remains Christ-haunted, responses to the Bible will continue to play a part in its literature, though increasingly younger writers—and readers—are less likely to know it well.

Joseph M. Flora

See also Bible Belt; Preaching.

Robert Alter and Frank Kermode, eds., *The Literary Guide to the Bible* (1987); John Boyles, *The Great Revival, 1787–1805: The Origins of the Southern Evangelical Mind* (1972); Peter J. Gomes, *The Good Book* (1996); Samuel Hill, *Southern Churches in Crisis* (1967); Charles R. Wilson, ed., *Religion in the South* (1985).

BIBLE BELT

The term *Bible Belt* is a metaphor that H. L. Mencken gave to the nation in the 1920s. Although Mencken first used the term to deride the prevalence of religious fundamentalism in the South and the Midwest, the metaphor has been especially useful to political and social commentators looking at the American South. The *American Heritage Dictionary* (3rd edition) defines the term as "those sections of the United States, especially in the South and Midwest, where Protestantism is widely practiced." Emphasizing the pejorative meaning he intended, Mencken linked the Bible Belt with other belts, *hookworm* and *lynch*, extensions that produced a strongly southern association for *Bible Belt* in the national mind. Midwesterners did not typically think of themselves as living in "the Bible Belt"—though it should be recalled that Billy Graham migrated that way, to Wheaton College in Illinois, then to presidency of Northwestern Schools in Minneapolis, where the Billy Graham Evangelistic Association is headquartered. In time, Mencken's belt metaphor would find numerous companions—"sun belt" and, in the Midwest, "rust belt," especially. But the reminders of realities that caused Mencken to coin the phrase *Bible Belt* are frequent. A recent example: in the late 1990s Governor Fob James of Alabama threatened to call in the National Guard to keep the Ten Commandments on a courtroom wall. James also appealed a ban on school prayer, claiming that state officials do not have to follow rulings they consider "unconstitutional."

Bible Belt never described the South monolithically, certainly in any strict geographic sense, as the state of Louisiana exemplifies. Southern Louisiana, predominantly Catholic, may be described as outside the Bible Belt; northern Louisiana is in the Bible Belt. As the South continues to become urbanized, geographic lines attempting to identify the Bible Belt must constantly shift. As much as a geographic reality, the concept is a state of mind, and it refers as much to attitudes as to examination of any text. In Mary Ward Brown's "A New Life," the protagonist, beleaguered by Christians who hope to "save" her, thinks: "This is the southern Bible Belt where people talk about God the way they talk about the weather, about His will, and His blessings, about why He lets things happen." Brown's characters, in contrast to Flannery O'Connor's Bible-believing people or Faulkner's Cora Tull, are not poor whites with minimal formal education. They can be found throughout the South and throughout the nation; increasingly, they have become politically active. Mencken had used the term *Bible Belt*, especially as he compounded it with other "belts," to underscore ignorance and class origins. The term has come to be

viewed more neutrally, even as an identification to be welcomed. In *A Turn in the South* (1989), V. S. Naipaul comments on the sensibility of the region: "Religion was like something in the air, a store of emotion on which people could draw according to their need. . . . In no other part of the world had I found the people so driven by the idea of good behavior and the good religious life. And that was true for black and white." Naipaul sensed that he had entered the Bible Belt.

Joseph M. Flora

See also Bible.

Randall Balmer, *Mine Eyes Have Seen the Glory* (1984); Michael Chitwood, *Hitting Below the Bible Belt* (1998); Susan Ketchin, *The Christ-Haunted Landscape: Faith and Doubt in Southern Fiction* (1994); H. L. Mencken, *Prejudices: Sixth Series* (1927); Noel Polk, *Outside the Southern Myth* (1997).

BIOGRAPHY

Writing the lives of southerners has been a significant undertaking since the time before there were southerners. Mason Locke "Parson" Weems's life of Virginian George Washington (1809) introduced its American audience to the southern hero as warrior-statesman before sectional rivalry seriously polarized the nation. Bits of this mythology eventually trickled into James Fenimore Cooper's Leatherstocking saga. By 1859, well past the point of no return for sectional fever, Washington Irving used his life of Washington to plead the unionist cause. The Confederate States of America answered by making George Washington into a partisan symbol of the South when it adopted his image for its official seal. War by biography preceded the shooting war.

The character of the South as a civilization was formed in the biographies of its representative men (and much later, of its women) before there was a clearly defined tradition of doing so. South Carolinian William Gilmore Simms (1806–1870), one of the antebellum South's most industrious writers, produced "lives" of Captain John Smith (1846) and the Chevalier Bayard (1847), in addition to lives of southern Revolutionary heroes, as a way of establishing the aristocratic, cavalier roots of southern civilization. William Wirt (1772–1834) wrote a biography of Patrick Henry (1818) in which he reconstructed the famous "Liberty or Death" speech. John Pendleton Kennedy (1795–

1870), probably best known for his early plantation novel, *Swallow Barn* (1832), returned Wirt the favor by writing the biographer's life as a gentleman and public servant (1850). Each generation of southerners, responding consciously and unconsciously to the circumstances of southern identity, has used biography to clarify the heritage of the past and the meaning for which they are responsible in the present.

After the Civil War, memoir and autobiography supplied the demand for southern lives. Surviving Confederate generals wrote their memoirs of the late unpleasantness in order to generate income that a loser's pension could not. Perhaps the most famous of these was ex-President Jefferson Davis's memoir of the rise and fall of the Confederacy. The most famous unwritten memoir was that of Robert E. Lee, of which Donald Davidson makes much in his poem "Lee in the Mountains" (1938).

The Fugitive poets, as they were transforming themselves into social theorists in *I'll Take My Stand* (1930), undertook biographies of significant Civil War–era heroes. Their choices say as much about the biographers as about the historical figures. Andrew Lytle chose Nathan Bedford Forrest, still a lightning rod of cultural controversy, in *Nathan Bedford Forrest and His Critter Company* (1931). Lytle emphasized the yeoman-class origins of Forrest, his lack of formal education, his frequent clashes with military dolts educated at West Point, and his attachment to clan both in the sense of Forrest's blood kin and in the sense of the first incarnation of the Ku Klux Klan, which Lytle argues was formed as a response to civil disorder rather than as a vehicle for Reconstruction racism. All of these issues are still evocative, and Lytle's biography of Forrest, reissued in 1984 with a new introduction by the author, reminds us of that residual cultural power.

Allen Tate used his early biographies similarly. He wrote two and began a third, on Robert E. Lee, which he eventually abandoned. Tate's two completed biographies tell the lives of Stonewall Jackson (1928) and Jefferson Davis (1929). In both cases, the subject of the biography mirrors the demons and obsessions of the biographer. Jackson, for Tate, is the consecrated warrior for whom killing in a righteous cause was a transcendental action. In his biography of the Confederate hero, Tate continually stresses the near-mystical rapture of Jackson in the long marches and the heat of battle. Tate's Jackson is the southern warrior who answers in substance all the questions that Tate asks but never answers in his poem "Ode to the Confederate Dead."

If, in the poem, the modern Tate cannot concretize the emotion that sent waves of southern soldiers to certain death for a cause, in the biography Tate can locate all of the affirmation in the character of Jackson. In choosing Davis, one of the most maligned "heroes" of the Lost Cause, Tate matched his own intellectual capabilities (by no means insignificant) with those of Davis. He found in Davis an intellectual alienated in a culture of macho men of action. Tate, himself a southern intellectual for whom the idea of the South was always more intriguing than its nuts and bolts, found a cognate in Davis. When Tate tried to continue the momentum from Davis to that southern cultural god, Robert E. Lee, he found just the opposite: a man so embedded in the daily enacting of southern identity as to be almost free of thinking about it. When Tate could find no gaps between Lee's seamless actions and his scant statements (in letters and other forms of communication), he gave up on the life of Lee.

One very material reason that prompted Tate to shelve his life of Lee was the publication of Douglas Southall Freeman's three-volume life in 1936. In the 1930s, when William Faulkner's and Erskine Caldwell's depictions of depraved and grotesque southerners were popular in books and on the New York stage, and when the Depression was rapidly making the South into the nation's number-one economic problem (as FDR declared in 1938), Freeman's *Lee* was a magisterial counterattack. For Freeman, Robert E. Lee was not the low road to southern confessions of depletion as a culture; rather, he was the occasion for a restatement of the high road to disinterested self-sacrifice, duty, loyalty, and virtue. Lee was everything that Americans, not only southerners, needed as a beacon in the confusing days of economic depression and the seeming failure of the triumphant national economic forces that had prevailed since Appomattox.

Robert Penn Warren, perhaps the most viscerally southern of the Agrarian group, stepped outside the predictable grooves of southern biography by writing a life of abolitionist John Brown (1929). Whereas for Lytle southern biography was an opportunity to strike a blow for the yeoman origins of southern culture, and for Tate a chance to explore the muddled territory between South-as-historical-artifact and South-as-cultural-ideal, for Warren biography was a chance to put himself, body and soul, at risk in the charged territory of conscience and conviction. Readers of his later works will recognize that territory as the condition in which Cass Mastern lives in *All the King's Men* (1946), the territory that puzzles the will of that novel's narrator, Jack Burden.

The southern literary renascence, variously dated in the middle decades of the twentieth century from 1930 into the 1950s or 1960s, produced more literature than biography. While the fixtures of that Renascence were still alive and producing work, their "lives" were on hold.

Joseph Blotner's two-volume *William Faulkner* (1974) did less to ignite discussion about southern identity than it did to initiate discussion about literary "greatness." Nevertheless, Blotner's massive work was important in the way it irritated several other biographers to complete lives of Faulkner that the secretarial life by Blotner had omitted. Michael Millgate, David Minter, Frederick Karl, Susan Bryant Wittenberg, and more recently literary historian Richard Gray, southern historian Joel Williamson, and intellectual historian Daniel Singal have published biographies of Faulkner. More than any single southern figure, writer or whatever, Faulkner has functioned as the ritual vessel into which the content of southern identity has been poured.

The lives of white southern women writers are increasingly represented. Ellen Glasgow's long and significant life has generated Susan Goodman's recent biography (1998). Caroline Gordon, in her own right, is the subject of a biography by Nancylee Novell Jonza (1995). As the wife of a southern writer (once divorced from and twice married to Allen Tate), Gordon is the focus of a biography by Ann Waldron (1987). Darden Asbury Pyron's *Southern Daughter: The Life of Margaret Mitchell* (1991) goes well beyond the years of *Gone With the Wind*'s popularity and centers Mitchell in a constricting web of southern female identities. Bertram Wyatt-Brown's *The House of Percy: Honor, Melancholy, and Imagination in a Southern Family* (1994), although it concentrates on the male writers of the family—William Alexander Percy and Walker Percy—also gives valuable attention to the modern Percy males' female ancestors, notably Sarah Anne Ellis Dorsey (1829–1879), author of several Lost Cause novels and benefactress of Jefferson Davis. It was Ellis's bequest that financially enabled Davis to complete his memoirs.

As the writers of the Renascence have died, they have in turn become the subjects of biography in which the meaning of the South in its literary heyday is defined and redefined. Thomas Daniel Young's biography of John Crowe Ransom (1976), the mentor of the Fugi-

tive-Agrarians as students and the grand vizier of the New Criticism, capped Ransom's literary career by asserting the absolute victory of formalist literary study just about at the moment when it was being displaced by various strains of structuralism, deconstruction, and historicism. The literary-critical battle was continued several years later by one of Young's Vanderbilt Ph.D. students, Mark Royden Winchell, in the latter's *Cleanth Brooks and the Rise of Modern Criticism* (1996). Winchell sees Brooks, who took his B.A. at Vanderbilt a few years after the heyday of the Fugitives, as a founding father of "modern," as opposed to "contemporary," literary criticism. Joseph Blotner's *Robert Penn Warren: A Biography* (1997) eschews the ideological crusade of Winchell's *Brooks* and substitutes an exhaustive and exhausting chronology of Warren's peregrinations and publications. Like his earlier *William Faulkner,* Blotner's *Warren* is a narrated chronology that summarizes the plots of novels, reviews, and some poems (although the latter often frustrate paraphrase) and attempts to knit them to Warren's life rather than analyzing them with any consistent method of literary criticism.

Patrick Samway, S.J., who has co-edited two volumes of southern short fiction and a classroom anthology, uses his biography of Walker Percy (1997) to advance his view of southern writing as preserving the last vestiges of a religious communitarianism on mortal earth. Samway's Percy is more Catholic intellectual and philosopher than southern writer—a critical view that in many respects fits Percy's self-perception. Jay Tolson's earlier biography of Percy, *Pilgrim in the Ruins* (1992), takes a cue from the imagery of Percy's novels—the existential and wry anti-hero trying to see something steadily and whole while everything around him is dissolving.

Lyle Leverich's excellent *Tom: The Unknown Tennessee Williams* (1995) is refreshingly free from the literary turf battles of the biographies of the Agrarian critics. Although for Leverich issues of creativity and sexuality are paramount, Williams's quarrel with his southern identities—both publicly as a playwright and privately as a gay southern son—readjusts the frame in which southern biography defines the terms of southern identity. What Wyatt-Brown was barred from saying in *The House of Percy*—that William Alexander Percy was gay and that his sexuality significantly shaped his life and versions of southern identity derived from it—Leverich has dealt with frankly and sensibly.

An authorized biography of Allen Tate is under revision at present and could be published at any time. Tate was so crucial to the ideological configuration of the South in the cultural and literary debates of his lifetime and since his death that this biography promises to be just as crucial. An unauthorized biography of Eudora Welty has just appeared. Sally Fitzgerald has been at work on a biography of Flannery O'Connor for several years, editing collections of letters along the way. Since Flannery O'Connor, next to Faulkner, is the source of most of the literary criticism written on southern writers, and since she ranks as probably the most widely read southern writer after Faulkner, a biography of O'Connor is sure to jump-start a reevaluation of her work and of the southern writing of which it was a part. Formerly underappreciated southern women writers, such as Evelyn Scott, Julia Peterkin, and Frances Newman, have recently received biographical notice.

Literary biography is not the only genre in which the identity of the South is forged. Peter Guralnick's biography of Elvis Presley, *Last Train to Memphis: The Rise of Elvis Presley* (1994), not only tracks the life of the singer from his Tupelo origins to his first crest of popularity in the 1950s; it is also by the way a portrait of race and class in the South during the crucible years after World War II and through the beginnings of desegregation. Marshall Frady's biography of Billy Graham (1979) illuminates a nonliterary South of public piety so familiar as to be stereotypical. And Taylor Branch's two volumes (of three projected) on Martin Luther King (1988 and 1998) offset Freeman's three-volume life of Lee, the other southern hero with a contested holiday in January.

Biographies of African American southern writers have not been scarce, although the emphasis in many of these works is understandably *not* on the South as a nurturing cultural system. Robert E. Hemenway's *Zora Neale Hurston: A Biography* (1977) deserves much of the credit for resurrecting that writer's reputation, and for triggering a wave of reconsiderations and recoveries of African American women's writing. Hemenway takes Hurston basically as she saw herself: as a woman, an African American, an artist, a folklorist. If any of those phases of her identity overlapped with southernness, so be it. The same can be said (and illustrated in richer detail) with the biographies of Hurston's antagonist, Richard Wright. Wright's own autobiographical writing leaves the South with no shining halo; his biographers tend to follow that lead. Constance Webb's *Richard Wright: A Biography* (1968) bears the stamp of the 1960s in its portrait of Wright as a protester. Webb also hews closely to the chronicle of Wright's life that is available in his own writing. Michel Fabre, perhaps true to his Gallic roots, sees Wright as the existential wayfarer in his *The Unfinished Quest of Richard Wright* (1973). And Margaret Walker, who knew Wright in Chicago in the 1930s, presents a sui generis Wright aptly summed up in her title, *Richard Wright: Daemonic Genius* (1988). The pivotal importance of the African American writer to the character of southern writing, and to the image of the South promulgated by it, is clear in the jockeying of these biographies. Much will be clarified, it is to be hoped, if and when a biography of Ralph Ellison is published.

Michael Kreyling

See also Agrarians; Autobiographical Impulse; Autobiography.

BIRMINGHAM, ALABAMA

"Birmingham," contemptuously thinks "Miss Kate" McCowan in Andrew Lytle's short story "Jericho, Jericho, Jericho" (1936), "I've got a mule older'n Birmingham." Named for England's iron and steel center in Warwickshire, Alabama's Birmingham is a commercially created city that was not incorporated until 1871. Later, it would become home to the powerful industrial and financial entrepreneurs whom Alabama governors referred to as the "Big Mules." Whether the city has dominated the state's literature the way it did its economy and politics is more open to question, but there is ample evidence of serious literary activity and accomplishment in its relatively short existence.

Birmingham's sobriquets of "The Magic City" and "Pittsburgh of the South" testify respectively to the city's rapid growth and the reason for it. Less positive is the appellation "Bad Birmingham," an early characterization that surged back into application with the Civil Rights Movement of the 1950s and 1960s. All point to central elements of Birmingham's history, culture, and literature that entail distinctive issues of ethnicity, race, and social class.

Pointedly depicting the mining industry and, relatedly, labor relations and political corruption are novels *Bed Rock* (1924), *The Deep Seam* (1926), and *Honor Bound* (1927) by Jack Bethea, lifelong Birmingham resident and newspaperman (historically a significant profession for the city's literati); Thomas Rowan's *Black Earth* (1935), more realistic than many of the genre; and *Mountain* (1920) by Clement Wood, an immensely prolific writer who moved away from his native state to write. Wood's *Nigger* (1922), which carried the third generation of an Alabama African American family to steel-mill employment, also drew upon the distinctive local element of race relations. More recently, dealing also with mining, race, and politics are *Night Ride Home* (1992) and *Gathering Home* (1988) by Vicki Covington. No poet has dealt more memorably with industrial and other conditions of oppression than did John Beecher (*Collected Poems, 1924–1974*), who knew Birmingham steel mills from early personal experience.

Diametrical opposites in reflecting black-white relations in the city are the works of Octavus Roy Cohen and Martin Luther King Jr.'s "Letter from Birmingham Jail." A member (along with O. Henry Prize–winning short-story writer Edgar Valentine Smith) of the white literary "Loafers' Club" and the creator of such "Darktown" denizens as Florian Slappey, Cohen was a major purveyor of African American stereotypes of the Amos 'n' Andy variety. His sketches were published regularly in the *Saturday Evening Post* and collected into more than a dozen popular books in the 1920s and 1930s. Addressed to his "dear fellow [white] Clergymen," King's masterful epistle was the historic consequence of his arrest in Birmingham in April 1963.

King's chief antagonist, Commissioner of Public Safety Bull Connor, is a featured character in a novel set at this tumultuous time, Vicki Covington's *The Last Hotel for Women* (1996). An earlier fictional account of a different response in a racist society is James Saxon Childers's *A Novel About a White Man and a Black Man in the Deep South* (1936). Iron City College in Childers's *Hilltop in the Rain* (1928) is based on Birmingham-Southern, a Methodist-affiliated school that would figure importantly in local civil rights history.

An extraordinary number of African American women have written personally and memorably about their individual Birmingham-area experience, including Margaret Walker, Sonia Sanchez, Julia Fields, Angela Davis, Ellen Tarry, and Deborah E. McDowell. Specific volumes of autobiography include *Angela Davis: An Autobiography* (1974), Tarry's *The Third Door* (1955), and McDowell's *Leaving Pipe Shop* (1996). Other honored, nationally published memorialists of the city include Howell Raines, Virginia Van der Veer Hamilton, Dennis Covington, Nancy Hud-

dleston Packer, Harry Middleton, and Paul Hemphill. Hemphill's *Leaving Birmingham: Notes of a Native Son* appeared in 1993. In poetry, early and later personal connections with the city may be seen in the work of Margaret Walker, Ann Deagon, and Andrew Glaze.

Perhaps a strange manifestation of Birmingham's reputation for violence (historically involving religious as well as racial strife), the city has produced such mystery/crime writers as Sara Elizabeth Mason, Octavus Roy Cohen, John Logue, and Anne George, and horror/supernatural-fiction writer Robert R. McCammon.

Most critically acclaimed of native Birmingham novelists is Walker Percy, whose familiarity with his birthplace is evidenced in *The Last Gentlemen* (1966). Fannie Flagg's *Fried Green Tomatoes at the Whistle-Stop Café* (1987), which was made into a major Hollywood film, is in several respects importantly rooted in Birmingham. The all-time best-selling historical novel about the city remains, no doubt, *The Calico Ball* (1934) by Emma Gelders Sterne. Noteworthy books of fiction not so tied to historical fact but making marked, particular use of Birmingham locale and atmosphere are Charles Gaines's *Stay Hungry* (1972), Howard Lewis Russell's *Iced Tea and Ignorance* (1989), and Sam Hodges's delightful *B-Four* (1992).

Bert Hitchcock

See also Alabama, Literature of; Civil Rights Movement.

Steven Ford Brown, ed., *Contemporary Literature in Birmingham: An Anthology* (1983); Patrick Cather, *Birmingham Bound: Opinionated and Often Irreverent Essays on the Fifty Most Important Books About Alabama's Largest City* (1993); Ruth S. Spence, *Bibliography of Birmingham, Alabama, 1872–1972* (1973).

BIRTH OF A NATION, THE

David Wark Griffith's career as a filmmaker is marked by the landmark film *The Birth of a Nation* (1915). Based on Thomas Dixon's two novels, *The Leopard's Spots* (1902) and *The Clansman* (1905), and his play *The Clansman,* the film was first screened under the title *The Clansman* at Clunes Auditorium in Los Angeles, California, on February 8, 1915. By the time the film premiered at the Liberty Theatre in New York City on March 3, 1915, Griffith had revised it and renamed it *The Birth of a Nation* (reportedly, at Dixon's prompting). Indeed, the February 8, 1915, version of the film is no longer available. Reissued with sound in 1930, the version that audiences typically view runs approximately 159 minutes.

The film is divided into two parts. In Part One, members of the northern Stoneman family meet their southern cousins, the Camerons, just prior to the onset of war. The Civil War literally and figuratively disrupts the opportunity for romance between Ben Cameron and Elsie Stoneman. In Part Two, the romance resumes following the war, symbolizing the renewed union of northern and southern whites. The underlying premise of the film and Dixon's book is that the black presence in America caused a rift between white northerners and southerners. Southerners, outraged by the war and its aftermath, Reconstruction, must suppress the "enemy" (now free blacks) in order to heal the rift. Thus, Dixon and Griffith posit that the birth of the Ku Klux Klan is necessary to rid the emerging nation of the threat represented by the menacing, power-hungry, lust-filled demon—the Negro. Griffith's film suggests that this be accomplished through disenfranchisement and lynching.

The film gave birth to the stock "Mammy" character, played in this case by actress Jennie Lee. Other cast members include Walter Long as the lust-filled Gus; Henry B. Walthall as Ben Cameron; Maxfield Stanley as Wade Cameron; Lillian Gish as Elsie Stoneman; Mae Marsh as Flora; Spottiswoode Aitken as Dr. Cameron; Mary Alden as Lydia Brown; Joseph Henabery as Abraham Lincoln; Howard Gaye as Robert E. Lee; Donald Crisp as Ulysses S. Grant; and a host of other actors and actresses.

Presented in epic-like fashion, the film was the first to use a fully developed story line; previously, films featured fragmented story lines and ran for only a fraction of the three hours Griffith allowed for *The Birth of a Nation*. The score, along with Griffith's innovative use of the montage, the dissolve, the close-up, and wide panoramic camera angles, set the film apart from what had been done in the medium up to that point. Before the film was reissued with sound, orchestras performed the film's musical score, which included selections from black folk songs, Wagner, Bellini, and Reinzi.

As one might expect, the film was both praised and protested. President Woodrow Wilson lauded it, while others denounced it as yellow journalism. Noted educator Jane Addams came out against the film's obvious racism. Francis Hackett wrote in a March 20, 1915, re-

view in the *New Republic* that Dixon had displaced his own malignity onto the Negro. A *New York Globe* editorial asserted that the name of the film was an insult to George Washington because the film was such a distortion of history, reducing freed blacks to lust-filled fiends who chase after fair white maidens. Despite ongoing protest, the film was immensely popular with audiences, and its attendance records would only be surpassed with the release of *Gone With the Wind* (1939). Today, the film is a staple of introductory film classes, solidifying D. W. Griffith's legacy as a major figure in the history of the film industry.

Lovalerie King

See also Film; Race Relations.

Donald Bogle, *Blacks in American Film and Television* (1989); Robert Lang, ed., *The Birth of a Nation: D. W. Griffith, Director* (1994); James Snead, *White Screen/Black Images* (1994).

BLACK METHODISTS

Black southerners belonged to several branches of the Methodist family. Methodist denominations were political and apolitical, conservative and radical. They were founded by slaveholders and abolitionists, blacks and whites, northerners and southerners.

As pioneer preachers established Methodism in the South, they sought out black worshippers. When Reverend William Meredith began preaching in Wilmington, North Carolina, in 1784, his largest and most receptive congregations were black. During a visit to Charleston, South Carolina, in 1786, Bishop Francis Asbury wrote, "I had nearly two hundred fifty of the African Society at the love feast held for them this evening." The founding bishop of American Methodism also observed, "Religion is reviving here among the Africans. These are poor. These are the people we are more immediately called to preach to." One of the most influential early preachers was a free black named Henry Evans, who established Methodism in Fayetteville, North Carolina. Intense religious revivals swept through the South in the 1770s and 1790s, affecting blacks as well as whites, and motivating many to seek a safe harbor for their souls in Methodism.

By 1816, there were about 42,000 black Methodists in the United States, and over 70 percent of them were in the South. In 1826, 40 percent of the Methodists in Georgia and South Carolina were black. After southern Methodist preachers distanced themselves from the antislavery views of some of their northern and British coreligionists, they were allowed and even encouraged to carry their faith into the slave quarters on large plantations. Reverend William Capers launched the denomination's mission to plantation slaves in 1829. In fifteen years, the project grew from two missionaries with little financial support, working with 417 slaves on three plantations, to seventy-one missionaries with a budget of $22,377, serving sixty-eight missions and a total of over 21,000 slaves. The mission continued to grow until the outbreak of the Civil War.

In addition to the slaves on plantations, urban slaves and free blacks comprised substantial parts of the membership of Methodist churches in cities such as Baltimore, Charleston, Louisville, Nashville, and Norfolk. It was a common practice for slaves to worship in the galleries of white churches, but there were also some urban Methodist churches just for black worshippers, although they were always under the supervision of white pastors.

In 1844 a distinctively southern Methodist denomination came into being. The Methodist Episcopal Church, South (M.E.S.), began as a protest against some specific antislavery policies adopted by the "mother" denomination, the Methodist Episcopal (M.E.) Church. After the split, the M.E. Church became inoperative and unwelcome in the South, until the Civil War and Union troops made it possible for northern Methodists to reestablish themselves in the region. In addition, the missionaries of two independent, northern-based black Methodist denominations entered the South during the war seeking the membership of newly freed slaves. Both the African Methodist Episcopal Church (A.M.E.) and the African Methodist Episcopal Zion Church (A.M.E. Zion) denominations had separated from the M.E. Church during the early nineteenth century in order to escape racial discrimination. Yet another Methodist denomination, the Colored Methodist Episcopal Church (C.M.E.), was founded in 1870, and it competed vigorously with the others. During the years after the Civil War, black southerners were confronted with a bewildering number of Methodist options.

All Methodist denominations believed in conversion, redemption, and salvation, but they had very different positions concerning race, freedom, and equality. The popular African Methodist denominations emphasized black pride and independence. A radical minority within the M.E. Church courageously attempted to achieve racial integration, although their efforts had no lasting effect. Colored Methodism stressed the importance of maintaining good relationships with southern whites while cautiously pursuing new opportunities. Finally, the M.E. Church, South tried to preserve the antebellum racial order, a position that cost that denomination almost all its black members.

During the years following Emancipation, Methodists attempted to provide the freed people with everything from basic literacy through medical training. Educational institutions are among the most enduring manifestations of the Methodist impact on the black South. Prominent among the schools founded during this period are the following southern colleges and universities: Allen (A.M.E.), Bennett (M.E.), Claflin (M.E.), Clark (M.E.), Lane (C.M.E.), Livingstone (A.M.E. Zion), Morris Brown (A.M.E.), Paine (C.M.E.), and Meharry Medical School (M.E.). Although the M.E. Church, South did not establish schools for the freed people, it did help support and administer Colored Methodist institutions. Linda Beatrice Brown, now distinguished professor at Bennett College in Greensboro, North Carolina, wrote of academic and religious life for blacks there in her 1989 novel, *Rainbow Roun' Mah Shoulder*.

In 1939 the M.E. Church and the M.E. Church, South came together to form the United Methodist Church, healing the breach that had existed between the North and South since 1844. One of the conditions for reunion was that black churches and ministers be set apart in a separate administrative unit, benignly called the Central Jurisdiction. The Central Jurisdiction was formed over the objections of a majority of the black Methodists who were consigned to it. United Methodism remained segregated until the impact of the Civil Rights Movement of the 1960s caused the denomination to dismantle official barriers to integration. The Central Jurisdiction ceased to exist in 1972.

The three major black Methodist denominations continue to exist as separate organizations. Perennial plans for union have come to naught, even though the differences between black Methodisms are now inconsequential. In 1954 the Colored Methodist Episcopal Church dropped its racial appellation and became the Christian Methodist Episcopal Church in accord with the spirit of the times. It should be noted that a small number of southern black people belonged to the Methodist Protestant Church before that denomination became a part of United Methodism. In addition, a few blacks in Maryland belong to a small regional denomination called the African Union Methodist Protestant Church.

Intra-Methodist competition is interesting, but the great divide in black religion was between Methodists, of all kinds, and their more numerous Baptist rivals. That friendly, but serious, rivalry was a prominent aspect of southern black religious culture during most of the nineteenth and twentieth centuries.

Reginald F. Hildebrand

See also Methodists.

Mason Crum, *The Negro in the Methodist Church* (1951); Reginald F. Hildebrand, *The Times Were Strange and Stirring: Methodist Preachers and the Crisis of Emancipation* (1995); Harry V. Richardson, *Dark Salvation: The Story of Methodism as It Developed Among Blacks in America* (1976); J. Beverly F. Shaw, *The Negro in the History of Methodism* (1954).

BLACK MIGRATIONS

A major theme in both African American history and literature is migration. From the grueling journey of the Middle Passage to the more recent sojourns of reverse migration, movement has been a staple in African American life. For cultural critic Cornel West, this mobilization reflects a need for escaping oppression, a major thrust in African American life. As well, movement signals African American modernity. As blacks have had to recast, revise, and recreate themselves (often in the throes of transience), they have emerged, says West, as the most modern of people.

African American literature has traced this movement from its inception. The slave narrative is significant for punctuating key moments in black migration, beginning with one of the earliest examples of the form, *The Interesting Narrative of the Life of Olaudah Equiano, or Gustavus Vassa, the African* (1789). This work provides a rare glimpse into the horrors of the Middle Passage and an insider's view of tribal life in eighteenth-century Africa. Foremost among nineteenth-century narratives reflecting migration are *Narrative of the Life of Frederick Douglass, An American Slave* (1845) and *Incidents in the Life of a Slave Girl* (1861) by Harriet Jacobs. These texts introduce a significant migration motif, the northern ascent, whereby slaves, in an effort to achieve freedom, seek access to northern states. This particular movement, according to Robert Stepto, marks an ascent not only geographi-

cally but also socially, as these migrants transfer themselves from South to North and from slave to free person. This perceived improvement in status would shape two major migratory patterns in the twentieth century.

After World War I and again after World War II, hundreds of blacks left southern agrarian environs in search of better lives in northern urban centers, as Jim Crow segregation and rampant incidents of lynching were daily realities of black life in the South. Chicago, Detroit, New York, and other large cities became the centers of black urban activity. The 1920s saw the inception of the Harlem Renaissance, an artistic movement that fostered black creativity and enticed black southerners to venture north. Although these migrants hoped for improved circumstances, they often found themselves living in conditions more squalid than those they had left behind, and they also suffered social and political limitations similar to those in the South. Several texts that addressed such migration at the beginning of the twentieth century are Paul Laurence Dunbar's *The Sport of the Gods* (1902) and James Weldon Johnson's *The Autobiography of an Ex-Coloured Man* (1912). Jean Toomer's *Cane* (1923) and Nella Larsen's *Quicksand* (1928) chart south-to-north and north-to-south migration in important works of the Harlem Renaissance. Later, the autobiographies of Richard Wright (1945) and Zora Neale Hurston (1942) show how black writers found important empowerment when they left southern birthplaces for northern cities. Hurston's return south was a journey of recovery resulting in her Negro folklore collection, *Mules and Men* (1935).

While the south-to-north journey has been dominant, black migration has witnessed reversals, especially in the post–Civil Rights era, as northern blacks returned to the New South (to thriving cities such as Atlanta, Raleigh, Charlotte, and others). Stepto defines this process in literature as a journey of immersion, whereby the protagonist yearns for a feeling of connectedness with his/her southern roots. In immersion narratives, feelings of dislocation and isolation have so overwhelmed the figure that she or he requires the nurturance of the southern home. Texts that address this issue, at least moderately, include John Oliver Killens's *Youngblood* (1954), Bebe Moore Campbell's *Your Blues Ain't Like Mine* (1992), and Ernest J. Gaines's *A Lesson Before Dying* (1993).

Charles E. Wilson Jr.

See also Harlem Renaissance; Slave Narrative.

Melvin Dixon, *Ride Out the Wilderness: Geography and Identity in Afro-American Literature* (1987); Farah Jasmine Griffin, *Who Set You Flowin'?: The African American Migration Narrative* (1995); Lawrence R. Rodgers, "Paul Laurence Dunbar's *The Sport of the Gods*: The Doubly Conscious World of Plantation Fiction, Migration, and Ascent," *American Literary Realism* 24.3 (1992); Charles Scruggs, *Sweet Home: Invisible Cities in the Afro-American Novel* (1993); Robert Stepto, *From Behind the Veil: A Study of Afro-American Narrative* (1979); Cornel West, *Keeping Faith: Philosophy and Race in America* (1994).

BLUE-COLLAR LITERATURE

The history of working-class authorship in the South is a short one. Although women and African American authors had made significant strides toward claiming a place for themselves in southern literature by the midpoint of the twentieth century, blue-collar whites had not yet joined the southern literary consciousness. The poor rural white had long occupied a persistent if limited place in southern letters (notably in the works of the Southwestern humorists, Erskine Caldwell, T. S. Stribling, and Faulkner), but whites of modest means, or with backgrounds in manual labor, had yet to speak for themselves in the region's literature.

By the latter half of the century, however, the cultural landscape of the South had changed. The Renascence that Allen Tate aptly described as a momentary backward glance from the juncture of a cultural "crossing of the ways" was over. The Old South was giving way (for better or worse) to something more urban and inclusive, and a new generation of southern writers emerged to chronicle the postagrarian, Sunbelt South. With the help of the G.I. Bill, a sharecropper's son named Harry Crews entered the University of Florida, the first in his family to graduate from high school, much less harbor aspirations of a literary career. When Crews began to publish his fiction and memoirs, the literary status of the poor white—and indeed the image of the southern writer—entered a new phase. The blue-collar perspective began to challenge and augment prevailing literary representations of the South.

Because of his background, Crews depicts a very different South from that of his predecessors. As his memoir *A Childhood: The Biography of a Place* (1978) attests, the rural life was for Crews a harrowing experience fraught with poverty, debilitating

farm work, and the perennial threat of hunger. The characters of Crews's fiction, reflecting this experience, often flee the rural sphere for the city. In contrast to the poor whites of tradition, Crews's rural emigrants thrive on mobility; too impoverished to savor their place in rural culture, they find an attenuated sort of deliverance in the relative prosperity of blue-collar labor in the cities of northern Florida. The persistence of this character type, in *The Hawk Is Dying* (1973), *The Knockout Artist* (1988), *Body* (1990), and *Scar Lover* (1992), has allowed Crews to explore another crossing of the ways: the interstice between a benighted rural past and the uncertain future of the blue-collar individual in an urban, postmodern South.

Bobbie Ann Mason charts a similar sociological terrain in her fiction. The truck drivers, housewives, and disillusioned Vietnam veterans of her work occupy an intermediary moment in cultural consciousness in which tradition and a sense of place appear less real than the myriad products and messages of popular culture. Although her fiction is often set in semirural Kentucky, Mason's characters seem more enamored of consumer culture than they do of anything local or indigenous—they are not "southern" in the manner of traditional Renascence characters. Despite the presence of tradition and cultural monuments to the past, Mason's common people find history mostly beyond their reach—beyond their postmodern frame of reference, as in the title story of *Shiloh and Other Stories* (1982). Blue-collar pop icons such as Bruce Springsteen loom larger than historical figures or local tradition. When a quest for historical connection is undertaken, as it is for Sam Hughes of *In Country* (1985), the past must be recovered from its ephemeral status through a welter of radio airwaves and television images.

Many contemporary blue-collar writers carry Mason's themes a step further, questioning the validity of heritage and rendering ambiguous the once nearly perennial southern theme of the past. As the protagonist of Kaye Gibbons's *Ellen Foster* (1987) might argue, for those of southern backgrounds fraught with poverty, the past is best left where it lies. Others take a more polemical stance against the South of tradition. In *Bastard Out of Carolina* (1992) and *Cavedweller* (1998), Dorothy Allison depicts a region obsessed with aristocracy and class distinctions by using the vantage point of the "white trash" to deconstruct the southern social hierarchy. Larry Brown's *Joe* (1991) and *Dirty Work* (1989) explore the tribulations of the bottom social strata of the South in a manner reminiscent of the proletarian literature of the 1930s. Both Allison and Brown accentuate the importance of labor for their characters in professions that often comprise the "dirty work" shunned by others with the means to avoid them. At times, their vision resembles that of naturalistic authors: economic determinism and restrictive class structures pervade their fiction. Like Caldwell, they use the conventions of naturalism to chronicle a segment of southern culture seldom accorded full representation. Yet their extensive first-hand experience with urban poverty (Allison) and manual labor (Brown) lends their work an authority on these issues not to be found even in sympathetic outside observers such as Caldwell.

If the deterministic conventions of naturalism may be discerned in contemporary blue-collar works, so too may be violence. David Bottoms's *Easter Weekend* (1990) sets up a kidnapping and ransom attempt as the crucible for a bloody clash between rich and poor in Macon, Georgia. Tim McLaurin's *The Acorn Plan* (1988) and Chris Offutt's *The Good Brother* (1997) also deal with violent events in a North Carolina mill town and the Kentucky hill country, respectively. These works reflect the tensions of characters caught between cultures and without many options; often a violent denouement provides the only resolution to their precarious existence. Violence here is something rather different from traditional expressions of the southern code of honor: often it is the final, blunt assertion of frustrated and otherwise inarticulate lives.

In addition to this strong fictional output, the recent proliferation of memoirs by blue-collar southerners indicates that the terrain of the working-class South may be one of the most promising areas left for southern letters. Crews, Allison, Brown, McLaurin, and Offutt have published autobiographical books rife with urgent prose that indicates their stories have been too long delayed in entering the South's cultural record. A sense of historical exclusion prevails in these works. Rick Bragg's nationally successful memoir *All Over But the Shoutin'* (1997) begins with the declaration that "poor people in the South do not make the historical registers unless we knock some rich man off his horse." Likewise, Dennis Covington's *Salvation on Sand Mountain* (1994), with its recollections of growing up in working-class Birmingham, describes poor southern whites as "the only ethnic group in America not permitted to have a history." Yet if this rhetoric of protest indicts the South of tradition, it also indicates great opportunity, for as blue-collar southerners continue to publish fiction and memoir—and thus to claim their history in the South—southern literature finds itself at yet another prolific crossing of the ways, at a point where an emergent class of very different writers contemplates not the past, but the future.

Matthew Guinn

See also K Mart Fiction; Poor White; Proletarian Novel.

Fred Hobson, *The Southern Writer in the Postmodern World* (1991); Frank Shelton, "The Poor-White's Perspective: Harry Crews Among Georgia Writers," *Journal of American Culture* 11.3 (Spring 1979).

BLUEGRASS MUSIC

Bluegrass music is a concert form of traditional southeastern mountain string-band music marked by a distinctive rhythmic division of labor that allows for improvised solo choruses on the model of New Orleans or Dixieland jazz, as well as for responsorial interplay among instruments, or between vocalist and instrumental accompaniment, derived from the call-and-response patterns characteristic of early jazz and other forms of African American social music. Although the term *bluegrass* has come generally to refer to the entire folk tradition of string-band and self-accompanied solo music of the southeastern Appalachian mountains, with its Scots-Irish and Anglo-American roots, in fact bluegrass music belongs to the broader family of African American music that includes jazz and blues. Bluegrass emerges quite audibly in 1946 on a well-known radio barn dance, *The Grand Ole Opry*, in a by-then well-established "hillbilly" string band, "Bill Monroe and the Bluegrass Boys."

Mandolinist and singer Bill Monroe (1911–1997), now generally acknowledged as "the father of bluegrass music," having migrated as a teenager to the Chicago area from rural central Kentucky, began his career in 1928 with his brother Charlie as part of a hillbilly duet traveling through the Southeast and Midwest under the sponsorship of a patent medicine, "Crazy Water Crystals." After breaking with Charlie in 1938, Monroe hired to his band in 1946 three new musicians whose special contributions were to define the form: Robert Russell "Chubby" Wise, a western-swing fiddler from Jacksonville, Florida; Lester Flatt, a singer-guitarist from Sparta, Tennessee; and nineteen-year-old Earl Scruggs, a banjoist from Shelby, North Carolina.

Wise brought western-swing's elastic note values and blues inflections; Flatt introduced a resonant open-chord guitar style punctuated with stout bass runs. Most significant for the emergence of bluegrass, however, was Scruggs's banjo style, a continuous three-finger "roll" whose three-against-two accentual pattern, played in double time, reflected the influence of ragtime, which with other turn-of-the-century popular elements had established itself in the cotton-mill region of piedmont North Carolina to reshape the more conservative styles that had migrated there from the mountains farther west.

This technique, brought under the steadying influence of Monroe's marked preference for off-beat accentuation, transformed the band's then-popular peppy two-step western-swing rhythm to the more spacious four-beat measure typical of early jazz and blues. A redistribution of accents followed, yielding what remains the rule in bluegrass instrumentation, where behind vocal and instrumental leads, an acoustic guitar strongly enunciates the rhythmic pulse in the form of bass runs and open chords; a backup instrument, typically banjo or mandolin, carries the off-accent or "backbeat" in the form of closed or "chop" chords; while a string bass unrolls the meter. Crucially important in the success of this arrangement was the microphone itself, which brought the lead instrument audibly into the foreground.

This tight orchestration, supplemented by Monroe's emotionally fraught high-pitched vocal solos, close parallel trio or quartet harmonies, a repertoire both traditional and original of ballads, sentimental "heartsongs," gospel hymns, instrumental breakdowns, and blues, created a sensation on the *Opry* and forced Monroe, already revered for his vocal intensity and instrumental virtuosity, to share the spotlight with the young Earl Scruggs, whose banjo style quickly became emblematic of the new music. Monroe's dignified demeanor and poker-faced delivery, coupled with the grave deportment of his band—in the 1940s, the group appeared in the uniforms of Smoky Mountain Park Rangers, hats and all—offered resistance to the comedic mood of the *Opry,* which from its beginning in 1928 had presented traditional musicians in a satirical context reminiscent of the blackface minstrel show. This context permitted appreciation in the guise of ridicule of a traditional music supplanted in the marketplace by western swing bands such as Bob Wills's and honky-tonk singers such as Hank Williams, whose music in different ways spoke to new urban conditions

and to the new liberties and new confusions associated with them.

Although the *Opry* remained the principal site of the dissemination of Monroe's music, critically important as well was the aural imitation of the bluegrass sound by diverse musicians with distinctive individual and traditional approaches out of several genres and regions. Phonographs and especially battery-operated radios had been aggressively distributed by Emerson, RCA, and other manufacturers in mountain regions during the 1930s, so that few areas were so remote as to be out of reach of WSM's radio signal. A handful of mountain musicians in the late 1940s and early 1950s, already steeped in regional musical traditions or performing professionally or semiprofessionally on local radio, emulated the impressively high-powered string-band style called "bluegrass" that they had heard at Monroe's traveling shows, on recordings, or on the radio. One of the earliest and most important of the bands to model themselves on the Monroe sound was a duet from the Clinch Mountain region of Virginia, Ralph and Carter Stanley, the Stanley Brothers, whose deeply traditional repertoire, Baptist-inspired hymn and harmony singing, and husky vocal tone re-embedded the practice in earlier and more parochial musical sources, tying bluegrass for new practitioners more closely to the Appalachian cultural milieu and associating it with the idea of cultural preservation.

Within ten years, bluegrass bands were spread widely throughout the rural Southeast, supported by several emergent independent regional record labels. More important, however, for the cultural visibility the music would later acquire was the postwar outmigration from rural Appalachia to the industrial border cities of Baltimore, Washington, D.C., Cincinnati, Pittsburgh, Columbus, and, farther north, Detroit and Chicago, where in nightclubs, on radio stations, and in country-music parks catering to the migrant population, bluegrass would attract the attention of the nascent "folk revival" of the early 1960s.

While resisting any fundamental alteration of its basic musical conventions and cultural affinities, revivalist players in the 1960s and 1970s absorbed influences from every quarter of popular music, touched by the revolutionary spirit of the epoch. Second-generation folk-revival bands, such as "The Country Gentlemen," and younger musicians, such as mandolinist Sam Bush and guitarist Tony Rice, embraced folk, folk-rock, and ultimately rock-and-roll into bluegrass, even while retaining its basic instrumentation; more tradition-minded musicians, such as Ricky Skaggs, who as a teenager had played in Ralph Stanley's band, and country-folk singer Emmylou Harris, attempted with middling success to introduce the bluegrass repertoire, vocality, and instrumentation into mainstream commercial country music.

Bluegrass is a syncretic music whose double nature—an Appalachian traditional music with origins in the British Isles internally charged with African American counter-rhythms and improvisatory schemes—has made it a rich and sometimes paradoxical bearer of symbolic meaning. The transformations of bluegrass music in the half-century since its inception in 1946 betoken its metamorphosis from a rural form, invested with ideas arising from the economy of scarcity—such as self-sufficiency, hard work, and mechanical skill—into a kind of symbolic enactment of conservative rural values in an irreversibly urban, technological, and deracinated postindustrial world. In its first generation arguably an informal oral/aural folk-musical practice associated with people of mountain culture and affiliation, bluegrass music, a practical touchstone of identity and community, helped to sustain for Appalachian migrants a sense of the cultural past. In succeeding years, bluegrass has been enlisted both as a sectional and a national music; as an antimodernist icon and as a badge of cultural modernization; as handmaiden of progressive as well as of conservative or even reactionary political ideologies; as an embodiment of frontier individualism and independent artisanship as well as of industry, technocracy, efficiency, and speed; as a ritual of pastoralism as well as a hip urban trend. In the 1990s, it became a minor industry of global proportions, in which a lively commerce in tape and video teaching regimes, song and tabulature books, hands-on instrumental instruction, annual festivals, and summer camps sustained the art for enthusiasts and practitioners ranging from farmers and tradesmen to technicians, service workers, and corporate executives.

For acoustic musicians, bluegrass remains the arena in which technical virtuosity and musical experimentation, in the context of "respect for tradition," remain foremost. Dedicated vanguardists of the genre, such as banjoist Bela Fleck, annexing techniques and ideas from jazz, rock, and world music, have thoroughly professionalized the form, raising it to a level of complexity well beyond what a purely aural tradition could plausibly transmit and bringing it decisively into the musical avant-garde. A self-consciously retrospective "classical" form of the music has emerged in response

to this trend, in which bands constituted expressly for the purpose, such as "The Bluegrass Album Band," the "Nashville Bluegrass Band," and the "Johnson Mountain Boys," recapture the recordings of the first generation of musicians, often with great fidelity to the original musical "texts," at the same time creating or adopting original music along the lines of "classic" or "first-generation" bluegrass.

Once male-dominated, competitive, technically aggressive, and emotionally raw, bluegrass music has acquired in some quarters the nuance and subtlety of a kind of folk-based chamber music, in which a sensitive and introspective young female vocalist such as Allison Krauss, also a prodigiously talented fiddler and veteran of the youth-contest circuit, can win fame in mainstream country music as the leader of an all-male bluegrass consort who handle their instruments as delicately as any conservatory-trained musicians. Women singer-musicians such as Kathy Kallick and Laurie Lewis have lent to bluegrass a distinctively feminist coloring, leading mixed-gender bands with outspoken songs addressed to women's issues and personal lives.

Having followed its audience from the coalfields and hillside farms of eastern Kentucky and western Virginia to the poor-white enclaves of northern cities to the new mall-centered suburbs, bluegrass music, like commercial country music itself, represents the successful conversion of one of the arts of poverty into one of the perks of prosperity, an expression of life into a fetish of life-style. Treatments of bluegrass music are rare; but for recent sympathetic narrative accounts of the traditions of mountain music and musicians, see Charles Frazier, *Cold Mountain* (1997); Bland Simpson, *Heart of the Country: A Novel of Southern Music* (1996); and Lee Smith, *Devil's Dream* (1992).

Robert Cantwell

See also Country Music; Minstrelsy.

Robert Cantwell, *Bluegrass Breakdown: The Making of the Old Southern Sound* (1984); Rachel Liebling, *The High Lonesome Sound: The Story of Bluegrass Music* (film; Tara Releasing, 124 Belvedere St. #6, San Rafael, CA 94901); Bill Malone, *Country Music, U.S.A.* (1968); Philip Nusbaum, "Bluegrass and the Folk Revival: Structural Similarities and Experienced Differences," in *Transforming Tradition: Folk Music Revivals Examined,* ed. Neil V. Rosenberg (1993); Richard A. Peterson, *Creating Country Music: Fabricating Authenticity* (1997); Neil Rosenberg, *Bluegrass: A History* (1985); Neil Rosenberg,

"Starvation, Serendipity, and the Ambivalence of Bluegrass Revivalism," in *Transforming Tradition: Folk Music Revivals Examined,* ed. Neil V. Rosenberg (1993); John Wright, *Traveling the Highway Home: Ralph Stanley and the World of Traditional Bluegrass Music* (1993).

BLUES, THE

The blues, as proliferated in southern literature, refers to three separate but related concepts—blues, blues music, and the blues aesthetic. Blues is a feeling of dread, disappointment, and sadness that hovers around all people of all circumstances at some time. The term *blues* is derived from a Middle-English word that connotes an emotional state that causes a person to look blue as a result of anxiety, fear, discomfort, and low spirits. The term's figurative use in the United States can be traced back to the early seventeenth century.

Around the turn of the twentieth century, African Americans in the American South, in an effort to keep at bay the blue feeling, crafted the unique art form known as blues music. Although the lyrics of blues music are preoccupied with hardships, misfortunes, and low spirits, the high-spirited music counters the lyrics with an infectious, good-time rhythm that induces dance and movement. If blues is an affliction, blues music is the antidote.

Blues music is by no means a sad music. Instead, it is a music that confronts harsh actualities. The lyrics are sometimes shaped into stanzas in which the first line is repeated twice, and a third rhyming line often completes the confrontation with the blue feeling: "Good mornin', blues, Blues, how do you do? / Good mornin', blues, Blues, how do you do? / Good morning, how are you?" The blues musician acknowledges the harshness of life and improvises on the possibilities for reaffirmation.

If the lyric itself does not counter the blue feeling, the accompaniment does. A single voice sings the lyrics over a I-IV-V chord progression, which is played with a compellingly rhythmic inflection on guitar, piano, and/or harmonica. Blues music often relies on a call-and-response pattern between instrumentation and vocals, and this pattern is reminiscent of the communal artistic strategies of the African diaspora. However, the United States is the only African-influenced area in the world where blues music emerged. It is an African American art form.

Blues music is an accretion of African and European musical and vernacular forms. Its musical sources include hymns, ballads, spirituals, slave songs, folk songs, work songs, and field hollers. Its vernacular sources include sermons, folktales, tall tales, games, jokes, and the dozens. As such, the flavor of blues music can be found in examples from southern literature that include these forms. A good example is "We Raise de Wheat" from Frederick Douglass's autobiographies.

Because blues music is part of the African American vernacular tradition, its influence also can be seen in the literary works of writers who emulate African American oral expression, such as Richard Wright, Mark Twain, William Faulkner, Sterling A. Brown, Jean Toomer, Langston Hughes, and Zora Neale Hurston. For instance, in *Their Eyes Were Watching God* (1937), Janie Crawford speaks an actual blues lyric: "Some of dese mornin's and it won't be long, You goin tuh wake up callin' me and Ah'll be gone." In this novel, as in several other southern works, blues music specifically is referred to, and it plays a role in the narrative development of the novel.

Other southern writers, such as Eudora Welty, Tennessee Williams, Alice Walker, and Lewis Nordan, for example, have represented blues music in their works through depictions of blues musicians and the juke joints in which they perform. Bessie Smith, Ma Rainey, Leadbelly, and Fats Waller are just a few of the performers of traditional blues music who are alluded to by southern authors.

More often the blues is manifested in southern literature through use of the blues aesthetic. The blues as a set of uniquely American aesthetic principles and values was formulated and articulated primarily by Ralph Ellison and Albert Murray. Ellison's description of the blues in "Richard Wright's Blues" has been cited in numerous critical readings of southern literature as perhaps the definitive statement on the blues: Ellison claims that the blues "fingers the jagged grain" of a painful existence in order to transcend it through an artistic expression that is both tragic and comic (*Shadow and Act*). The tragic/comic nature of the blues as an aesthetic strategy is expressed in the classic blues line from "Trouble in Mind": "I'm laughin' just to keep from cryin'."

Laughing at pain, specifically at the hardships endured by African Americans, is a strategy of resilience that entered American humor through the minstrel tradition. Use of the minstrel mask prefigures the blues aesthetic because minstrelsy established the platform on which authentic African American art forms like the blues could flourish. As such, plantation fiction and Old Southwest humor, which draw on minstrel stereotypes, can be read as a foregrounding to the literature of the blues. According to Ralph Ellison, the blues reverses the joke of minstrelsy, which often built its humor on the tragedies of African American experience, because the blues is emblematic of African American resilience, and because it speaks to the fact that African American experience underlies the construction of the American identity.

For Ellison and Murray, the blues is a key metaphor for American culture and art, throughout which African American experience is diffused. Ellison's suggestion in *Invisible Man* (1952), that the whitest white is made by adding a drop of black, is representative of this diffusion. *Invisible Man* is considered the definitive blues novel. Other literary works that explore the American cultural configuration as a confluence of African American and European American ways of knowing and interpreting the world, such as works by Charles Chesnutt, William Faulkner, and Toni Morrison, can also be read as embodiments of the blues aesthetic.

Both Ellison and Murray have written about the blues as an integral part of the continuity of African American expression. For them, the finest artistic achievement results from shaping the raw materials of experience into universal statements that speak beyond the vernacular and beyond the particulars of a specific experience. Blues music itself is an example of fine art because it orders the chaos of life through an aesthetic strategy of confrontation, improvisation, affirmation, and continuity. The blues aesthetic can be read in the works of many southern writers, some of whom are mentioned above. Murray's novels, especially *Train Whistle Guitar* (1974), are representative of the blues aesthetic not only because the hero engages the blues strategy but because the language of the novel illustrates continuity with the African American vernacular tradition and because Murray draws an accurate portrayal of the blues musician (Luzana Cholly) and his life.

The blues and blues-derived jazz music are among the United States' most significant artistic contributions to the world, and the blues aesthetic reaches far beyond the American South. A full study of the sources and implications of the art form known as the blues would reach back as far as the first days of contact between Africans and Europeans in the United States, and as far forward as today's blues-inspired jazz, rock, and rap music.

Barbara A. Baker

See also African American Folk Culture; African American Spirituals; Folk Music; Gospel Music; Jazz; Minstrelsy; Vernacular Voice.

Ralph Ellison, *Shadow and Act* (1953); Albert Murray, *The Blue Devils of Nada: A Contemporary American Approach to Aesthetic Statement* (1996), and *Stomping the Blues* (1976).

BOONE, DANIEL

Among the Long Hunters—explorers and pioneers of America's first frontier west of the Appalachian Mountain chain—Daniel Boone (1734–1820) is perhaps the most famous, having achieved mythic and symbolic status based as much on folklore as on truth. Boone's transformation from backwoodsman/pioneer into national and international mythic icon of the American frontier experience is largely due to others. In 1784 John Filson, a schoolteacher from Chester County, Pennsylvania, hoping to improve his own land investments in Kentucky by attracting other settlers to the region, interviewed many of Kentucky's early settlers, including Boone, for a book about the region. His interview with Boone aroused Filson's literary imagination to the degree that the resultant book contained an "appendix," purportedly a memoir in Boone's own words but actually written in Filson's own voice. Filson's *The Discovery, Settlement and Present State of Kentucke . . . To Which Is Added An Appendix Containing the Adventures of Col. Daniel Boon* depicted Boone the pioneer as an epic hero of the American frontier, a philosopher as much as an Indian fighter.

Though not an immediate success in America, Filson's book was immediately popular in Europe, translated into French and German and reprinted in England and Ireland. Boone was seen as an exemplar of the "natural man" expounded upon by the European intellectuals. Lord Byron further strengthened this image (which was also indebted to Henry Marie Brackenridge's accounts of his travels in America published in 1614) when he devoted several stanzas of his poem *Don Juan* to a description of Boone in which he called Boone "An active hermit, even in age the child / Of Nature." Byron was also surely familiar with the work of

Gilbert Imlay, who had engaged with Boone in a property deal in Kentucky and who praised Boone as a "natural man" in his *Topographical Description of the Western Territory of North America,* to which he added Filson's narrative as an appendix in the second edition in 1793. Imlay was the lover of Mary Wollstonecraft, whose daughter Mary Godwin married Percy Bysshe Shelley, all members of Byron's circle of friends.

At the same time, Boone's status as a national hero was strengthened in America by the issuance of an abridged version of Filson's narrative by the printer John Trumbull. In 1813, two years before Boone's death, a distant cousin of his wife, Rebecca Bryan Boone, Daniel Bryan, wrote *The Mountain Muse,* an epic poem that contributed to Boone's emerging mythic image, although it was poorly received and Boone himself was offended by the inaccuracies of the poem. James Fenimore Cooper's hero in his Leatherstocking series, Natty Bumppo (beginning with *The Pioneers* in 1823 and ending with *The Deerslayer* in 1841), was obviously based on Boone, as noted by the first reviewers of *The Pioneers,* and a major episode of *The Last of the Mohicans* (1826) was based on the capture by Indians and later rescue of Boone's daughter Jemima and Betsy and Fanny Callaway. Cooper's works helped to further the emerging image of Boone as frontier philosopher and even friend of the Indians. Other semifictional representations of Boone, however, depicted a contrasting figure who was an Indian-hater, as in Robert Montgomery Bird's *Nick of the Woods* (1837), William Gilmore Simms's *The Yemassee* (1833), and Emerson Bennett's dime novel *Ella Barnwell* (1853). Modern historical novels based on Boone's life include Winston Churchill's *The Crossing* (1904), Stewart Edward White's *The Long Rifle* (1932), Elizabeth Madox Roberts's *The Great Meadow* (1930), Caroline Gordon's *Green Centuries* (1941), Janice Holt Giles's *The Kentuckians* (1953), and Shirley Seifert's *Never No More* (1964). Boone has likewise been written about as symbolic American icon by D. H. Lawrence (in an essay on Leatherstocking) and by William Carlos Williams. Boone is the subject of the outdoor drama, *Home Is the Hunter,* by Robert Emmett McDowell, first performed in 1965 at Fort Harrod State Park. Several important children's books have also been written about Boone, including James Daugherty's *Daniel Boone* (1939), John Mason Brown's *Daniel Boone* (1952), and Lillian Moore's

Daniel Boone: Hunter, Trapper and Indian Fighter (1955).

Danny Miller

See also Kentucky, Literature of.

Lawrence Elliott, *The Long Hunter: A New Life of Daniel Boone* (1976); John Mack Faragher, *Daniel Boone: The Life and Legend of an American Pioneer* (1992); William S. Ward, *A Literary History of Kentucky* (1988).

BORDER STATES

For a region established so clearly in the American imagination and named so definitely for a point of the compass, the South actually has quite indeterminate borders. The region has traditionally been considered to extend from the Gulf of Mexico north to the Potomac and Ohio rivers, and from the Atlantic Ocean west to the dry plains of mid-Texas; conservative descriptions of the South have included not only the eleven states of the Confederacy but also those slave states that remained Union-loyal—or at least "neutral"—during the Civil War: Maryland, Delaware, Kentucky, and Missouri. These last four—along with Oklahoma and West Virginia—have most frequently been designated southern "border states." A truly comprehensive consideration of southern border regions might also include those far-flung "Little Dixies," settled by southerners and maintaining elements of traditional southern culture, which have been located not only in northern Missouri (in the region encircling Mark Twain's childhood home) but also in southern Illinois and Indiana, Utah, and Wyoming; in addition, there are enduring pockets of southern culture in the urban North and Midwest—to say nothing of Liberia or Manaus, Brazil.

Borders themselves have been of central concern to the southern consciousness from colonial times to the present, as suggested by literature ranging from William Byrd's *History* (composed c. 1728) of the "Dividing Line" between Virginia and North Carolina to Allen Tate's "The Profession of Letters in the South" (1935). Certainly the single most crucial factor in defining the South was the besieged practice of slavery and the rise of a defensive southern nationalism in the decades preceding the Civil War; political boundaries such as the Mason-Dixon Line and its 1820 extension under the Missouri Compromise marked the division of America into two parts—slave and free. For this reason, the border itself becomes theme in such primary works of southern literature as Mark Twain's *Adventures of Huckleberry Finn* (1885) and Toni Morrison's *Beloved* (1988). In both works, the significance of the border is heightened by its existence as a physical entity, the river: in Twain's novel, the Mississippi initially divides slave Missouri from free Illinois and ultimately carries Huck and Jim through a liminal zone of liberty in the heart of the Deep South; in Morrison's, the Ohio marks the final tormenting obstacle between the horrors of Kentucky's ironically named "Sweet Home" plantation and a new life outside of Cincinnati (though Ohio itself, as it turns out, is at best a border state for escaped slaves).

The border is a particularly important presence, of course, in Delaware, Maryland, Kentucky, and Missouri—all along the northernmost frontiers of slaveholding America. Slavery had existed in Maryland since at least 1644 and was important enough to be deemed legal in 1664; the state was therefore long a final barrier for fugitive slaves—and an appropriate starting point for Frederick Douglass's escape in *Narrative of the Life of an American Slave* (1845). During the Civil War, Maryland was under martial law to protect the Union's capital, so secession was not an issue. The proximity of the free states, of course, adds a realistic element of suspense to literature concerned with slaves escaping from any of the traditional border states. The Bluegrass State is particularly prominent in such literature, featured not only in *Beloved* but also in Charles Chesnutt's "The Passing of Grandison" (1899), where an elderly Kentucky slave on a trip with his master foregoes opportunities to escape alone in New York and Boston only so that he might return home and slip through Ohio and into Canada with his entire family; similarly, in Harriet Beecher Stowe's *Uncle Tom's Cabin* (1852), Eliza is able to flee the Shelby plantation by hopping across ice cakes in the Ohio River, thereby avoiding Uncle Tom's fate of being sold down the Mississippi to the Deep South and true brutality. Delaware, Maryland, Kentucky, and Missouri would all remain officially in the Union during the Civil War, though each—especially the western states—also held contingents of Confederate sympathizers and experienced internal conflicts of their own in the midst of the larger war. Ironically, Kentucky's and Delaware's loyalty to the Union would make them the last states to hold slavery legal; when the Thirteenth Amendment passed in December, 1865, all the

other slave states had already abolished the "peculiar institution" under Reconstruction legislation (or, in the cases of Maryland and Missouri, by slim votes in established state legislatures).

Several historical novels about the war written in the wake of Reconstruction would not focus on slavery but instead use the border states as appropriate settings for white characters with divided loyalties, whose "reconciliation romances" suggested a desirable pattern for the nation at large; Churchill's *The Crisis* (1901), set in St. Louis, Missouri, and Fox's *The Little Shepherd of Kingdom Come* (1903), set in central Kentucky, exemplify the genre. Later, Allen Tate's *The Fathers* (1938), set in and around the nation's capital, would rely upon the Buchans of northern Virginia and the Poseys of Maryland to heighten the tension between not only North and South but also the old social order and the new (ironically, the classically minded Major Buchan of Virginia remains loyal to the Union while the romantic modern man George Posey fights for the South).

Contemporary literary debates about southern border states have less to do with the legacy of slavery and the Civil War than with shifting notions of the South itself. The very definition of southern literature depends upon some agreement about what is the South and what is not, about what criteria define the southern writer and southern writing. All of these questions are to some extent questions of borders and might most simply be broken down into enduring questions about the northern and western limits of the South.

In one sense, the South has steadily been losing ground along its northern border on the Atlantic coast. Early Maryland writers John Pendleton Kennedy, whose *Swallow Barn* (1832) set the mold for plantation literature, and Douglass are clearly southern writers in a way that John Barth is not (though some critics have placed both him and—more convincingly—Baltimore's Anne Tyler in the southern tradition). In addition, it seems unlikely that twenty-first-century Washington, D.C., will produce the likes of Jean Toomer or Marjorie Kinnan Rawlings, both of whom even in their own day moved down the coast to write of the South. And northern Virginia, now largely a suburb for transients working in the nation's capital, will not likely be the setting for future novels such as *The Fathers*, at least not without a great sense of irony. Even at the southern end of the Atlantic coastline, Florida—with its influx of northeastern retirees and Hispanic immigrants—might now be designated a border state.

On the other hand, southern literature increasingly gained a foothold in northern and midwestern locales in the twentieth century, and not only in the transition zones that have always existed in the southern Midwest. Of course, many individual writers raised in the South have chosen to work in the North, from members of the Nashville Agrarians to Carson McCullers, Tom Wolfe, and Andre Dubus, to name just a few. But perhaps most significantly, African Americans have expanded the borders of southern literature into the urban North. Slaves and their descendants had been migrating northward since the days of the Underground Railroad but began to do so increasingly in World War I and its wake; regular connections were established between one region and another, such as Mississippi and Chicago or the Carolinas and New York (the 1940s and 1950s saw many southern whites, drawn by jobs in industry, following the same paths). The result was that James Baldwin could call Harlem in the 1920s "a southern community displaced on the streets of New York," an observation confirmed by the literature of the Harlem Renaissance—and by the juxtaposition of South and North in his own *Go Tell It on the Mountain* (1953). In the closing paragraphs of *Black Boy* (1945), Richard Wright moves toward Chicago, claiming that "in leaving, I was taking a part of the South to transplant in alien soil"; similarly, the narrator of Ralph Ellison's *Invisible Man* (1952) ends in New York but voices his desire "to return across that Mason-Dixon line . . . to affirm all of it, the whole unhappy territory . . . for all of it is a part of me." New York–born Gloria Naylor's *The Women of Brewster Place* (1982), which traces the movement of African American women from rural South to urban North, is just one example of the trend's continuation in contemporary literature.

Ellison himself was originally from Oklahoma, which is itself only problematically a southern state and therefore raises another question. The southern border with the "Southwest"—which in the early nineteenth century included Alabama, Mississippi, Kentucky, Arkansas, and Louisiana (North Carolina was the unlikely first target of "Southwestern Humor" in Byrd's *History*)—has steadily moved west and finally come to a standstill somewhere in Texas. The eastern halves of Oklahoma and Texas are generally considered part of the South, and these states were both politically established and settled by white southerners—as well as by those African Americans and Native Americans whom they had forced west. Such works as George Sessions Perry's *Hold Autumn in Your Hand*

(1941), a novel about sharecropping life in north and east Texas, depict a very southern state, and such Texans as Katherine Anne Porter and Horton Foote have been traditionally designated as southern writers.

But somewhere in mid-Texas the South ends and becomes the West (Willie Morris has written of a Texan who drew the line at the town of Conroe, using a unique criteria: east of Conroe, barroom brawls are decorously taken outside, whereas west of the town they continue in the bar itself), a region that claims writers such as Larry McMurtry. Actually, even western literature has been considered derivative of southern literature; popular novelist Owen Wister's hero in *The Virginian* (1902) was a romantic southern horseman—almost a cavalier—who in the West metamorphosed into the more rugged cowboy. But generally western literature has been characterized as less marked by a tragic sense of history and of community, as more optimistic and individualistic— more American?—than southern literature. There are, of course, writers born in the South who have spent significant time in the West (e.g., Mark Twain, Ernest Gaines, and Maya Angelou) and southerners who write imaginatively of the West, as Doris Betts does in *Heading West* (1981) and *The Sharp Teeth of Love* (1997) and Clyde Edgerton in *Redeye: A Western* (1995). And what to make of Cormac McCarthy, born in Rhode Island but reared in Knoxville, who early wrote of Tennessee in such works as *The Orchard Keeper* (1965) but has since moved to El Paso and taken to writing of Mexico? Or Richard Ford, raised in Mississippi but schooled in Michigan, best known for writing of New Jersey but now resident in Montana? The borders of the South—and therefore of southern literature—are finally perhaps only those of the imagination of southern writers and readers alike.

Farrell O'Gorman

See also Mason-Dixon Line; Regionalism; Southwestern Humor; Travel Literature.

Philip Castille and William Osborne, eds., *Southern Literature in Transition* (1983); Jefferson Humphries and John Lowe, *The Future of Southern Letters* (1996).

BOURBON

If civilization began with distillation, as William Faulkner once observed, it achieved a genial and ruddy perfection in the South with the creation of that velvety smooth distillate of sour mash and sparkling limestone water known as bourbon. The traditional formula for bourbon—a delicate fusion of barley, rye, and at least 51 percent corn malt, mellowed in new, charred oaken barrels—is believed to have originated with either of two Baptist preachers, the Reverend Elijah Craig or the Reverend James Garrard, both of whom history records as being distillers of spirits to the residents of central Kentucky in the late 1780s. Bourbon takes its name from Bourbon County, Kentucky, though no bourbon is produced there (legally) today, and most historians contend that it was first developed at Georgetown, in neighboring Scott County.

Though Kentuckians are thought to have called their whiskey "bourbon" as early as the 1830s, the first known appearance in print of the word *bourbon* did not come until 1846, in the humorous sketch "A Tight Race Considerin'," by Louisiana doctor Henry Clay Lewis (writing as Madison Tensas). Kentucky humorist Irvin S. Cobb (1876–1944), whose newspaper column "Sourmash" made him a favorite in the Louisville press, drew upon his intimate acquaintance with John Barleycorn's genteel cousin to write *Red Likker* (1929), the only American novel to chronicle the rise and fall of Kentucky's "bourbon aristocracy." Mississippi poet William Alexander Percy associated bourbon with the defenses of honor and *noblesse oblige* that he heard as a boy while waiting on the family porch to drain the sweet nectar from the bottom of his father's silver julep cup. His elegiac memoir, *Lanterns on the Levee* (1941), includes a detailed prescription for mint juleps guaranteed to bring about "half an hour of sedate cumulative bliss." Percy's cousin, the novelist Walker Percy, preferred to knock his bourbon back "neat," much like the title character of his novel *Lancelot* (1977), who drinks toddies and juleps only because his West Texas wife thinks he should. Percy's essay "Bourbon" (1975), an anecdotal reflection on the aesthetic of bourbon drinking in the South, comes as close as any attempt to decipher the message in the bottle. William Faulkner, it should be noted, preferred Tennessee whiskey to bourbon, and by his own account kept a fifth of Jack Daniel's within reach when he wrote. The half-empty liquor bottles routinely left at his gravesite attest to bourbon's enduring reputation as the South's thirsty muse.

Brian Carpenter

See also Gentleman; Kentucky, Literature of.

Brian Carpenter, "The South's Thirsty Muse," *Southern Cultures* (2000); Gerald Carson, "How Old Is Bourbon?" *American Speech* (1963); Gerald Carson, *The Social History of Bourbon* (1963); Tom Dardis, *The Thirsty Muse* (1989); Walker Percy, *Signposts in a Strange Land* (1991).

BRITISH-AMERICAN CULTURE

For much of the seventeenth century, the literature from the southern mainland of America and the West Indies was more English than American. Exploration narratives, settlement tracts, histories, and reports addressed a metropolitan audience in order to move Englishmen and sometimes women to action in behalf of various colonial enterprises. There is very little material concerned with what in the eighteenth century would be termed "Creolian" identity—that is, writing intended to give shape to a colonial *sensus communis*. Rather, various discourses enticed English readers with representations of desirable lands filled with commodity, exploitable land, and benign inhabitants (if inhabitants were mentioned at all). In the most provocative of the seventeeth-century settlement tracts, one gets something more—a dream of establishing in the New World a civil order with greater wealth, virtue, and efficiency than that managed in the Old. In Captain John Smith's writings about Virginia or George Alsop's about Maryland, one glimpses the potentialities of these unformed settlements.

An adherent of the commonwealth ideals of Sir Nicholas Cotton, Captain John Smith dramatized the virtues of the yeomanry, presenting able soldiers like Anas Todkill as the heroes of his histories of Virginia and various aristocratic reprobates as Virginia's bane. The allure for Smith of colonial adventure did not differ greatly from that animating the Spanish conquistadors—the desire for reputation, wealth, and personal autonomy fired his imagination. Yet Smith extended the promise of personal transformation in the New World to the commonality, and he announced unambiguously that fortune would arise from agricultural labor and trade, not by conquest or mines of precious metal. Smith's recognition that labor would be the crucial issue determining the shape of New World culture was prescient. He, not the advertisers of zero-labor Edens, glimpsed the problems that lay ahead. In particular, he saw how the fantasies of aristocratic projectors who envisioned America as a place to rehabilitate the landed classes would give rise to a labor crisis. After the English Restoration, this vision became imperial policy, inscribed in the charter and governmental articles of Carolina and in the renovated administrative scheme for the West Indies. Whitehall's ambition to create in America a countryside of baronies was thwarted by the problem of securing the labor to service large estates. Few able persons felt moved to come to America to enrich others. After reports of the arduousness and sickliness of settler life began filtering back to England, out-migration to the colonies dwindled and grants of land (head-right property) had to be used to lure capable colonists. The head-right system (envisioned by John Smith) tended to undermine North America's transformation into a restored aristocratic preserve. Why labor for another if one has one's own plot? In the end, what could not be obtained by temptation was secured by compulsion as transported felons were brought over to supply a labor force. The circumstances of captive labor were given force in a memorable pamphlet of the Restoration, *The Poor Unhappy Transported Felon,* the story of a young man who fell in with bad company and opted for fourteen years hard labor on the Northern Neck of Virginia rather than face the gallows. This portrait of toil side-by-side with enslaved Africans under the control of rapacious planters and overseers conveys, as do other first-person accounts, the emotional forces driving the economic transformation to dependency on chattel enslavement of Africans. Planters desired a work force that could not disappear into the resident population by running away and shamming free status. They desired workers who would not, upon release from a term of service, set up as competitors in the local markets. These frequent results of convict transportation led to an increasing use of African chattel slavery.

The economic and cultural rationales driving African slavery conflicted with the religious and moral objections of those who found the enslavement of human beings repulsive. With the beginning of the eighteenth century, the contest over African slavery became clearly defined, and the debate would come to dominate discussions of the colonial system over the course of the century.

Metropolitan belle-lettrists across the political spectrum, from Tories like Pope and Johnson to Whigs like James Thomson and William Cowper, joined in a literary critique on the imperial system's resort to African slavery. The most pointed attacks—those contained in Thomson's "Liberty" or in the abolitionist literature of Cowper and Hannah More at the end of the century—combined a philanthropic idealism focused upon the concept of humanity and a sentimental appeal to the reader to feel the sufferings of the African victims of slavery's oppressions. While conditions on the sugar islands most seized the metropolitans' attentions because of the economic prominence of the West Indies in the imperial scheme, no distinction was made in their attacks between the practice on the islands and that on the mainland. Wherever staples were cultivated, and particularly those staples enumerated in the Acts of Trade and Navigation, African slavery was established.

When American writers sought to legitimate their activities in the eyes of the empire, they displaced the question of labor from the center of their representations and spoke of the staples themselves. Using Virgil's *Georgics* as a model, numbers of would-be laureates of British-American civilization claimed the importance of the staples and the colonies founded upon them to the world system. James Grainger's four-book *The Sugar Cane* (1764) was the most renowned work in this literature, earning Samuel Johnson's commendation of the poem as the first significant poem to have been written in America. Charles Woodmason's "Indico" and George Ogilvie's *Carolina; or, The Planter* (1776), about rice culture, followed Grainger's lead. One advantage of the georgic form was its representation of the planter as a figure strengthened by conflict. The American staple laureates made the moral war about slavery part of the conflict. They asserted the essential humanity of the planter discovered in his paternal care for his bondsmen and -women. This humanity was consciously cultivated as an alternative to the cruelty and despotism that arises when one has absolute power over the many. There were dual audiences for this message: in the metropolis, the staple poets countered the critics of the imperial scheme while avowing a shared humanist ethic; in the staple colonies, the poets waged a war for the hearts and minds of the plantocracy. The context of this battle is revealed in Samuel Martin's famous *An Essay on Plantership,* where the Antiguan author describes the brutally instrumental mind-set of most planters and their blindness to the potentially violent consequences of a program of inhumane repression. The staple laureates hoped to inculcate philanthropy to give slavery a moral foundation in a humane paternalism. Curiously, these most-eloquent defenders of the staple system proved to be the most prescient prophets of Haiti and the massacre at Santo Domingo at century's end, for they repeatedly warned of the terror that would fall upon the heads of those who did not rule the plantation humanely.

While the staple georgics projected a cultural ideal peculiar to the tobacco, sugar, rice, and indigo colonies, centered on the productions of the plantation and concerned with the duties of a planter, other writings took up more general themes of imperial life. One important promise extended by the British "empire of the seas" to its colonists was that they would participate in a great global project of civility. All of the graces and manners of the metropolis would be available by trade to those provincials and colonists who wished them. A never-ending enrichment of life and culture would recompense colonists for their removal from the seat of power. The fashionable equipment of London life—tea, card tables, whalebone corsets, wigs, wine, silk clothing—would all be made available to the colonies in exchange for local commodities. Books and periodicals, too, played an important role in making Norfolk, Alexandria, Edenton, Wilmington, Charleston, Savannah, and Annapolis mock metropoli. In places where the welter of nationalities, backgrounds, and wealth led to confusion about one's place in the hierarchy, a civil tongue and a stylish outfit could secure precedence. Given the relative lack of a governmental presence—the paucity of placemen, the quick transits of governors and military officers, the short sittings of the legislatures—civil society rather than gubernatorial courts became the place of public contestation over status. Ethnic societies (the St. Andrews, the St. Davids, the St. Georges, the Saint Patricks) took over much of the task of patronage, easing the incorporation of immigrants and likely strangers into local life. These societies embraced the methods of sociability, promoting good fellowship by song, liquid refreshment, and wit. An ample literature of their songs and society records survives.

One way that governors could project themselves in a colony was by promoting a court culture. This entailed setting up a laureate, sponsoring state balls, inaugurating civic ceremony, and vesting public actions with an aesthetic element. Laureates proved particularly useful as a means of publicizing and mythologizing an executive's actions. The Calverts were particularly lucky in having Richard Lewis, the Latin master of Annapolis and an accomplished neoclassical poet, as their panegyrist. Indeed, Speaker Dulany, the principal opponent of the Maryland proprietor, commissioned Ebenezer Cooke to be the laureate of the legislature to provide a literary counterweight to the governor's oracle. Governor Gooch of Virginia was nearly as fortunate with the verse of John Markland. Poetry lent a

mystique to civic action, taking it away from the plain exercise of interest and power, supplying it with resonance and charm. Ceremony accomplished a similar end of aestheticizing civic action. Sometimes the two were combined in quite fanciful public expressions, such as Governor Spottswood's "expeditio ultramontana," a journey of Virginia gentlemen who styled themselves "the Knights of the Golden Horseshoe" into the western territory to picnic and claim more territory for the empire. This expedition was celebrated in Latin verse by Arthur Blackamore and later translated into English by the Reverend George Seagood and published in the June 24, 1729, *Maryland Gazette*. The two versions of the poem speak to one of the characteristic literary developments of the provincial period, the vernacularization of learning.

Learned culture, the university-based cultivation of the ancient literatures and arts, was exclusive. The value placed on classical learning was attested in the unusual annual rent that the College of William and Mary owed to the Crown—two Latin poems composed by the young scholars. Yet the numbers of colonists who attended the College of William and Mary or the British universities were few, while the number of planters, merchants, and officials who wished to enjoy the "beauties of the ancients" grew as they improved their material circumstances in light of a metropolitan model. The yearning of the aspiring classes for some sense of the ancient arts pervaded the Western world. Southern colonists participated in that burgeoning audience for the floodtide of printed translations that followed in the wake of the success of Pope's *Iliad*. Among the literati, many manuscripts circulated, such as Thomas Cradock's "Maryland Eclogues" or James Sterling's Horatian ode to Samuel Ogle (1747). With Pope's example in mind, certain authors, aspiring to public notice, sought to capture the world of polite learning in print. Richard Lewis's translation of Holdsworth's neo-Latin mock epic, *Muscipula,* as *The Mouse-Trap, or the Battle of the Cambrians and Mice* (Annapolis, 1728) proclaimed that it was the "First Essay of Latin Poetry, in English Dress, which Maryland hath publish'd from the Press." A subscriber sheet identified those who participated in the genteel world. While the imprint's locality mattered, it did so as a mark of the colony's achievement of a threshold of civility, not as an expression of native genius. Belles-lettres and polite learning indicated that its creators and admirers belonged to a larger world. Cosmopolitanism, not parochialism, was the ideal of the provincial gentry and the aspiring professional classes. Classical learning supplied a body of sentiments and a trove of philosophical ideas that, like Christian scripture, could provide a means of communicating with persons from other European cultures. The colonial port cities were filled with merchants and settlers from a host of European cultures, and the colonial frontiers were zones of conflict between competing European imperial powers. Legitimizing one's status as a person of consequence required presenting the proper markers of class, education, breeding, and wealth. We should recall that the young George Washington was selected by Virginia's governor to treat with the French in the wilderness precisely because he has embodied so well the "Rules of Civility" he had drawn up as a boy. He was an adequate representative of British-American culture and gubernatorial authority. Civility, neoclassicism, and worldliness would all be traits that would remain central to the style of southern gentility long after the end of the colonial era.

David S. Shields

See also Virginia, Literature of; William and Mary, College of.

Richard Beale Davis, *Intellectual Life in the Colonial South, 1585–1763* (1978); J. A. Leo Lemay, *Men of Letters in Colonial Maryland* (1972), and *The American Dream of Captain John Smith* (1991); David S. Shields, *Oracles of Empires: Poetry, Politics, and Commerce in British America* (1990); Louis B. Wright, *The First Gentlemen of Virginia: Intellectual Qualities of the Early Colonial Ruling Class* (1940).

BROWN V. BOARD OF EDUCATION

Racial segregation in "separate but equal" facilities had been legal in the United States since the Supreme Court handed down its decision in *Plessy v. Ferguson* in 1896, but the segregated schools of the 1950s were hardly equal for black and white students. White students in Linda Brown's neighborhood in Topeka, Kansas, only needed to walk seven blocks to reach their school. On the other hand, Brown, an African American, needed to walk six blocks across a dangerous railroad yard to get to her bus stop. Her bus then dropped her off at a school twenty-one blocks from her home and a half-hour before it opened. Her father, Reverend Oliver Brown, sued the Topeka school system in her behalf with the help of the National Association for the Advancement of Colored People (NAACP). The U.S. District Court for the District of Kansas heard the case

in June 1951; although sympathetic to the plaintiff's case, the court sided for the defendant, citing the precedence of *Plessy v. Ferguson*. Brown and the NAACP appealed to the Supreme Court in October 1951. Their case was combined with other cases from South Carolina, Virginia, Delaware, and the District of Columbia that challenged school segregation.

The Supreme Court failed to reach a decision when it first heard the case in December 1952. At the Court's request, the re-argument, heard one year later, focused on how the cases related to the Fourteenth Amendment. This discussion was deemed "inconclusive," partly because public education was not well established in the South when the amendment was ratified in 1868. The Court determined that it must "consider public education in the light of its full development and its present place in American life throughout the Nation." It concluded that education is a right that must be made equally available to all and that segregated schools deprived minority children of equal educational opportunities. Segregation, Chief Justice Earl Warren wrote in behalf of a unanimous Court, was detrimental to children of color because it implied their inferiority. This sense of inferiority threatened the children's motivation to learn and their educational and mental development. Warren concluded, "Separate educational facilities are inherently unequal" and therefore violate the Fourteenth Amendment, which guarantees equal protection under the law.

The decision in *Brown v. Board of Education,* handed down in 1954, did not technically overturn *Plessy v. Ferguson,* and segregation still existed in other public areas, such as rest rooms and restaurants, for several years to come. Neither did it lead to the immediate desegregation of public schools, even after a case known as *Brown II* ordered in 1955 that its ruling be executed with "all deliberate speed." *Brown* was a landmark case in United States constitutional history, however, and it became the legal foundation for the Civil Rights Movement of the 1950s and 1960s.

Southern literature has not overtly addressed the case of *Brown v. Board of Education,* but issues of segregation and integration permeate southern literature. Autobiographies by white writers, such as Lillian Smith's *Killers of the Dream* (1949) and Willie Morris's *North Toward Home* (1967), as well as autobiographies by African American writers, such as Anne Moody's *Coming of Age in Mississippi* (1968), address growing up in a time of segregation and integration. Many black writers since the 1950s have dealt with the issue of desegregation in the broader scheme of the civil rights struggle; such works include Lorraine Hansberry's *A Raisin in the Sun* (1959); Gwendolyn Brooks's poem "The Chicago Defender Sends a Man to Little Rock/Fall, 1957," published in *The Bean Eaters* (1960); Alice Walker's *Meridian* (1976); and Ted Shine's *Contribution* (1969).

Brigette Wilds Craft

See also Civil Rights Movement; Jim Crow; NAACP; *Plessy v. Ferguson.*

Richard Kluger, *Simple Justice: The History of Brown vs. Board of Education and Black America's Struggle for Equality* (1976); Mark Whitman, ed., *Removing the Badge of Slavery: The Record of Brown vs. Board of Education* (1993); Paul E. Wilson, *A Time to Lose: Representing Kansas in Brown vs. Board of Education* (1995).

C

CAJUN

The term *Cajun* identifies French descendants native to South Louisiana who have consciously maintained cultural ties with their history. Eighteenth-century French immigrants, who originally called themselves Acadians, settled in South Louisiana after being driven from Acadia (currently Nova Scotia) by the British government. A French colony consisting mainly of peasants had established itself in Acadia early in the seventeenth century until the British ordered them to leave in 1755.

Several decades of exile brought Acadians to South Louisiana, where there was an established francophone community. The Creoles in New Orleans had descended from French aristocracy, however, and although generations had been born locally and intermarried with the Spanish, Haitian, Anglo, and African American populations, Creoles considered Acadians socially inferior. The poorer Acadians chose to settle in land southwest and west of the city where they could maintain a group identity. The earliest Acadian settlements appeared along the banks of the Mississippi River and along Bayous Teche and Lafourche. Today, some distinguish between those who inhabit the grassland areas near Bayou Teche, the Vermilion River, and westward as prairie Cajuns and those who live further east, along Bayous Lafourche and Terrebonne, as bayou Cajuns.

Regardless of this distinction, both groups intermarried with Spanish, German, Native Americans, Irish, Scottish, and Anglo Americans after they settled in Louisiana. There, the Acadians came to be identified by the shortened term *Cadiens,* which then became *Cajuns.* Their traditions, Roman Catholic faith, and language made them a recognizably distinct group until the early twentieth century, when speaking French at schools was banned. While early- to mid-twentieth-

century innovations encouraged assimilation, the late twentieth century has seen a resurgence of the culture. With an institutionalized revival of Cajun French, efforts are ongoing to preserve the traditional music, cuisine, traditions, and voice of the Cajun people.

Tiffany Duet

See also Cajun Literature.

Barry Jean Ancelet, Jay D. Edwards, and Glen Pitre, *Cajun Country* (1991); Carl A. Brasseaux, *The Founding of New Acadia: The Beginnings of Acadian Life in Louisiana, 1765–1803* (1987); Carl A. Brasseaux, *Acadian to Cajun: Transformation of a People, 1803–1877* (1992).

CAJUN LITERATURE

Cajun literature shares a relationship to southern literature in that it can be characterized by its regional flavor. Most Cajun literature depicts a kinship between residents and their native terrain, and setting serves a more crucial role than simple backdrop against which plots develop independently. Rather, characters survive on and define themselves by the land they inhabit, as well as by the distinctive dialect they speak. Still, writers of Cajun literature do not idealize the region. Authors use realistic detail to investigate difficulties resulting from cultural stigmas, racism, economic hardship, and modern industrialization. Generally speaking, tradition, both religious and secular, and family and community ties help characters prevail in an often threatening world.

Before the turn of the century, George Washington Cable began writing about Louisiana's southern residents both historically and fictionally. Although he devoted much of his fiction to writing about the Creoles of New Orleans, his native city, he did write about Cajuns in *Bonaventure: A Prose Pastoral of Acadian Louisiana* (1888). He is among the first in fiction to have distinguished between the French backgrounds of Creoles, who descended from nobility, and Cajuns, who descended from exiled peasants. The book shows admiration for the industrious but simple Cajuns through three sketches, all of which are set in rural southern Louisiana. In "Carancro," the narrator informs the reader that his characters are speaking Cajun French, although Cable writes dialogue in standard English. However, in "Grand Pointe," Cable manipulates English syntax and phonetics to reflect the Cajun dialect. The author characterizes Cajuns as easygoing folk who work hard and allow themselves to enjoy leisure activities. In fact, Cable describes several pastimes that continue to be part of the Cajun tradition in literature. A large wedding celebration occurs in "Carancro," and although the women do not participate in all activities, men enjoy fiddling, dancing, pony racing, shooting matches, and poker playing. "Au Large," the last story in *Bonaventure,* accurately portrays Cajun men earning money through rice harvesting, game hunting, cotton farming, trapping, and fishing. Although criticized as melodrama, the book does succeed in depicting a time and place rarely represented until its publication.

Kate Chopin, also writing at the turn of the century, makes some literary space for Cajuns, though not exclusively, in her first volume of collected short stories entitled *Bayou Folk* (1894). Chopin defines her Cajun characters according to their work and social ethics. Juxtaposed against wealthy Creole planters, Cajun farmers barely earn enough to clothe themselves, and when the men cannot or will not work, Cajun women are just as likely to pick cotton or drive a mule team. Female characters in "Loka," "A Rude Awakening," and "In Sabine" work harder than their husbands or fathers when they must to survive. In a style similar to Cable's, Chopin differentiates between African American, Creole, and Cajun characters' dialects through phonetic and syntactic strategies. While Cajuns speak nonstandard English, they maintain a sense of dignity, as Evariste, in "A Gentleman of Bayou Teche," shows when he refuses to pose for a magazine artist unless he can title himself a gentleman.

Although Grace King also sets her stories in south Louisiana, she incorporates few Cajun characters or traditions. Most of her characters are Creole, even those who must temporarily live in the bayou region. In *The Pleasant Ways of St. Médard* (1916) and "Bayou L'Ombre" (1892), the Civil War drives Creole characters to live on plantations outside of New Orleans. Accustomed to an aristocratic socialization, these Creoles' life-styles are far removed from Cajun ones. One short story entitled "The Story of a Day," which was published in *Balcony Stories* (1893), contributes to Cajun literature. Adorine Mérionaux resides in a simple cottage along the bank of a serene bayou. On the night before her wedding day, Adorine experiences what the narrator calls a miracle when she hears the voices of saints, her last earthly contact with her fiancé, Zepherin, who dies on his journey home through the swamp.

This story reflects the spirituality of many Cajun characters in literature. Often authors of the fiction incorporate religious traditions of the Roman Catholic faith into their stories. At the same time, Cajun literature also contains some arcane traditions, which seem historically apropos. Before the turn of the century, when professional doctors were scarce in rural areas, some south Louisianians relied on herbal healers or on the intercession of saints for curing ailments. Despite their religious devotion, some Cajuns also visited seers or *traiteurs* and conjurers, who dispensed potions of gris-gris, for help.

Characters tolerant of both religious and occult traditions often appear in the fiction. For example, in Thad St. Martin's all-but-forgotten novel *Madame Toussaint's Wedding Day* (1937), characters believe in the saints' protection of children, and they say rosaries or beads for those ill or recently deceased. Furthermore, Madame Toussaint refuses to be married by the only available, and Protestant, preacher because she is too devoted to her Catholic faith. Instead, by burning candles on her wedding day, she appeals to the Virgin Mary to bless her second marriage. Yet in the same small island community lives a *traiteuse,* Polissonne. Although known to perform abortions, proscribe dark remedies, and cast spells, she is tolerated by the community.

Less disturbing than Polissonne with her preternatural associations are those characters who squander possessions and who refuse to work. The fishing community depends so much on the erratic sea for sustenance and survival that when fish are plentiful, all capable persons on the island join hands to haul in the largest possible catch. Afterward, they split the profits. Madame Toussaint feels this drive to work so strongly that she cannot idly watch the activity, even though she has been excused from working because it is her wedding day. Clad in her simple wedding dress, she takes her six children aboard her boat to catch shrimp, which she will be able to sell for eighteen cents per pound. This detail befits one of the most common characterizations of Cajuns in literature—their dedication to earning a livelihood from the bounty of the land.

Ernest Gaines began publishing in 1956, and while the majority of his characters are African Americans of the bayou region, he does include Cajun characters in *Catherine Carmier* (1964), *Of Love and Dust* (1967), and other novels. Gaines uses Cajun characters primarily to show the complicated race relations in south Louisiana. Both novels explore the relationships between African American and Cajun sharecroppers working on the same plantation. Though both are poor, the racially divided groups show antagonism toward one another. African American narrators in both of these novels resent Cajuns, who have been able to take over the most productive land mainly because of their skin color. As a result of having better land, Cajun sharecroppers raise more money from their crops, thus enabling them to purchase more efficient mechanical harvesters. Despite the negative portrayal of Cajuns in these novels, their fierce dedication to working the land cannot be denied. Furthermore, Gaines turns an experienced ear to capturing the dialect of both African Americans and Cajuns of South Louisiana as well as the nuances of their oral culture.

In the nineteenth and early twentieth century, when many Cajuns spoke French, the oral tradition was perhaps the most prevalent type of Cajun storytelling. That the educational system mandated the use of English early in the twentieth century accounts for the weakening of this custom. Older Cajun generations had not received much, if any, formal education; thus, they continued to speak the French that they had been taught to speak but never learned to write. Without schooling, few learned to speak, write, or read English. This situation is probably the most significant reason that only traces of Cajun literature exist before the twentieth century. Those who intimately knew the Cajun culture were unable to write about it.

Yet oral storytelling is a sustained tradition. Barry Jean Ancelet's collection entitled *Cajun and Creole Folktales* (1994) includes a variety of folktales such as animal tales, magic tales, legendary tales, historical tales, and tall tales that he began collecting in 1974. The collection includes tales in Cajun French along with English translations and critical commentary. An interesting detail about these folktales, indicative of Cajun literature, is that the stories, no matter what their origins, have been adapted to reveal aspects about Cajun culture. Many of the plots revolve around rural settings with characters who participate in specific forms of Cajun traditions. For example, a typical tall tale involving a lying contest has a Cajun variation, "Une Plus Fort," depicting characters who speak Cajun French and lie about hunting deer, a popular sport and livelihood.

Among the newest and most successful group of contemporary writers who show a continued interest in fictionalizing the Cajun experience are Cajun by birth. Absorbed by some of the same thematic issues as their predecessors, contemporary writers explore the relationships between Cajuns and spirituality, oral tradition, and the land. Generally speaking, these authors write in a realistic tradition, while some experiment with narrative structure.

Albert Belisle Davis's first novel, *Leechtime* (1986), for example, is told through several voices while the action unfolds in a single day in October, 1976. Events and voices from the past blur in a story initially begun by an old Cajun bard, who weaves his oral tales as intricately as he does his fishing nets. The central character, Adrian, who journeys through swamps, rivers, and bayous, seeks to escape his great aunt's curse as he uncovers the full story of his wife's departure. Although his sometimes humorous behavior helps earn him jail time, his sentence as bridgetender seems most fitting for him to begin to know himself and his place in Chinese Bayou. Other Cajun speakers voice their philosophies about living and loving in Chinese Bayou in Davis's book of poetry entitled *What They Wrote on the Bathhouse Walls* (1988).

Like Davis, Chris Segura depends upon setting for characterization and plot development in his most recent collection of short stories, *Marshland Trinity* (1997). Instead of using phonetic misspellings, Segura, Davis, and Tim Gautreaux reveal the nuances of the dialect through nonstandard syntactical structures and Cajun French words and phrases. The use of dialect helps Segura render realistic portraits of trappers in "Tranasse" and "Les Perdues," the first two stories in his collection. Set in a swampy marshland, "Les Perdues" describes a teenager who learns to balance two worlds. One requires his becoming intimate with the marsh of Chenière au Tigre in order to learn how to earn a living through trapping, and the other initiates him into a world of books and schooling in the nearby town of Abbeville. Set in the 1950s, this story resonates with conflicting attitudes about the values of parochial education.

The Next Step in the Dance (1998), Tim Gautreaux's latest novel, argues that traditional schooling does not ensure a prosperous future for residents of Tiger Island. Set in the 1980s, the novel illustrates the plight of South Louisianians during and after the oil industry collapse of that decade. Like other characters in Gautreaux's short-story collection *Same Place, Same Things* (1996), his main characters, the Thibodeauxs, decide resolutely to preserve their culture and survive in a place that challenges and soothes their spirits, thus making *The Next Step in the Dance* a fine representative of Cajun literature.

Tiffany Duet

See also Cajun; Creole Literature; Louisiana, Literature of.

Barry Jean Ancelet, *Cajun and Creole Folktales: The French Oral Tradition of South Louisiana* (1994); Valerie Melissa Babb, *Ernest Gaines* (1991); John Cleman, *George Washington Cable Revisited* (1996); David Kirby, *Grace King* (1980); Peggy Skaggs, *Kate Chopin* (1985).

CALVINISM

A theological perspective and system, as well as a way of thinking about the meaning of Protestant Christianity, Calvinism derives from the middle third of the sixteenth century. It takes its character as well as its name from John Calvin (Jean Cauvin), a Frenchman who lived from 1509 until 1564, with Geneva as the place with which he is most significantly associated.

Calvin was one of the two first-generation Reformers—that is, progenitors of the Protestant Reformation—along with Martin Luther. Indeed, they stood and still stand as the great figures of the movement, not only in Continental Europe, but in the British Isles as well (where Lutheranism has always been weak). Among other individuals who took important places in the formation of the Protestant tradition in theology, the majority belonged to the Calvinist school and numbered the leading Puritan divines.

No sixteenth-century stalwart in this tradition surpasses John Knox of Scotland, who wielded heavy influence on that land's culture and people, especially the Church of Scotland and sequentially the Scots-Irish people (Scots who moved to the north of Ireland between 1690 and 1750). Many of them eventually migrated to America and contributed ideas and energy to the religious and social life of the American colonies.

While the Scots-Irish comprised the largest sector of early southern Calvinists, there were others: Huguenots, Welsh Baptists—indeed, theologically, all Baptists. Wherever these people settled, they established institutions of learning, making concrete their respect for the life of the mind and their belief in humane civilization. As striking an example as any was their founding, over a period of several decades, seven colleges within a hundred or so miles of Asheville, North Carolina.

Most Scots-Irish Presbyterians who settled in the South in the late colonial period made their way from Middle Colony ports to or through the upper Valley of Virginia; the western piedmont and highland areas attracted many. Migrating Highland Scots entered through southern ports and established their communities in the Sandhills region of North Carolina. A reflection of the larger Scotland-derived concentration persists; in the 1990s, the heaviest urban assemblage of Presbyterians in the United States was found in Charlotte, North Carolina.

The growing southern population was there for the Presbyterians' taking, or so their prominence would have seemed to augur. But that is not what happened. Instead, the less "ethnic" and more informal and experience-attuned Baptists and Methodists won over the people, in principle by 1800, and in fact by the 1830s. While the failure of the Calvinist heritage to attract large numbers is significant, the disproportionate impact that this minority movement made on the culture is more so. The leadership places that these churchmen assumed (owing to their educational and political experience and resources) were impressive, but in no small part, their ascendancy derived from the comprehensiveness of Calvinism's theological agenda.

The scope of Calvinism's addressing of life-in-the-world is vast. It concerns itself with so-called secular matters as well as sacred; indeed, the distinction is not theologically valid. Besides education—in general, the life of the mind—it attends to the organization of living in society, through a theological category called "the orders of creation." Human involvement in political, economic, and familial spheres is not accidental or of social construction; rather, it belongs to the divine plan in creation. By implication, the scientific and ecological spheres are also part of the divine plan. Even the psychological dimension of human existence figures in the Calvinist design. It takes shape in the (controversial) Weberian formulation concerning the "spirit of Calvinism" that contributed to the rise of capitalist economic theory. That is to say, a theological ethic of responsibility—duty is a central feature, whether or not to give evidence to one's "election" to positive destiny under God—roots deeply in the inner soul of his human creatures. The whole person and the whole world fall under the sovereignty of God.

The aspect of Calvinist teaching most frequently associated with it is predestination. On that view, the Christian God's primary concern and provision is with the relation of each individual to himself. Being justified by him and brought into line with his requirements thus is treated as the defining subject of the divine activity in the world, and the central element in human existence. But, as implied in the previous discussion, that is misleading, inasmuch as the divine concern ranges very broadly. Moreover, we must note that realization of justification is not possible for humankind, since people are the problem. Both the demand and the gift are God's to define and to provide. It is popularly taken to follow that each human creature is "predestined" by the eternal God to be one of those forgiven and granted eternal life, or one of those alienated from him and imprisoned forever in that alienation.

Much about this line of reasoning does reflect Calvinist teaching. Human beings are creatures, God's human creation; they are fallen, and the righteous Lord stands over them. Being fallen, they lack any capacity at all, even for choosing to serve God. Not only is their moral nature incapacitated, so also is the volitional. At great remove from American "common sense," this theology asserts that human beings are totally "at God's mercy." A very good thing, according to Calvinism. Infinitely better that we should be in the hands of the creator who is just and cares more about us than we care about ourselves, than responsible for our own destiny. Thus what popularly is regarded as heartless and fatalistic turns out to be the very ground of confidence, the ultimate solace—best of all, the truth.

"Fatalistic" and "responsible" are elemental concepts. While this high doctrine of divine election can be thought to shade into fatalism, the two differ profoundly. The agent of fatalism is unknown, or does not exist; in truth, agency is irrelevant. The agent of election, of sovereignty more broadly, is the eternal, personal, purposive God of the Bible. He demands all and gives all. Shrugging the shoulders as if in resignation is the opposite of the appropriate human response. Instead, the discerning believer responds in obedience

and with gratitude by comporting life around the will of the Lord in responsible living.

No brand of Christianity has been more active than Calvinistic Protestantism. Christians of this persuasion have sought to evangelize the world since, although no one can fathom the divine mystery, anyone may be the instrument through which the divine election is made actual. Beyond the question of eternal destiny, Calvinists have, as noted, been busy about educating and building civilization. "Order" is endemic to this understanding. The Calvinistic Puritans who settled in New England were a busy lot, committed as much to aligning civil society with the divine plan as to building a church. In the South, their concerns were similar, even though their influence was smaller and the pre-organic society less malleable to their vision. Everywhere in the new land, Calvinism contributed formative ideas and vigorous activity to the generation of republican government.

Regarding obedience as their duty, Christians of this school have been deeply moral, sometimes moralistic. They have set high standards for personal, family, and social behavior. Their spirit has contributed to southern crusades against alcoholic beverages and other vices, and has instilled a sensitive conscience. Some have been social activists in support of racial justice, amelioration of the ravages of poverty, and improvement of working conditions, for example. Another sector has promoted "the spirituality of the church," believing that Christians should concentrate on edifying church life and personal piety and purity, abstaining from participation in efforts to redeem the structures of public life. Although the strictest forms of Calvinist propriety in doctrine and ethics have not dominated this heritage's career in the South, its upholding the particularity of Christian understanding has long been a major presence in regional culture. Thus, although William Faulkner came from Methodist roots, he studied the Calvinist consciousness, notably embodied in the Reverend Gail Hightower in *Light in August* (1932) and Mr. Goodhue Coldfield in *Absalom, Absalom!* (1936). Among contemporary writers, Doris Betts has been shaped by the Calvinist mind-set.

Samuel S. Hill

See also Appalachia; Clergy; Highland Scots; Preaching; Presbyterians; Puritanism; Puritan Writers; Sermons; Valley of Virginia.

John H. Leith, *Introduction to the Reformed Tradition* (1981); John T. McNeill, *The History and Character of Calvinism* (1967); E. T. Thompson, *Presbyterians in the South* (3 vols.; 1963–1973).

CARPETBAGGER

One can easily envision Washington Irving's Geoffrey Crayon touring England and the Continent with his sketchbook in one hand and a bulky, brocaded valise in the other. But the first significant American literary allusion to the carpetbag was probably Herman Melville's, in chapter 2 of *Moby-Dick* (1851), "The Carpet-Bag." Ishmael stuffs "a shirt or two" into his old portmanteau before beginning his epic voyage out of New Bedford and Nantucket. Coincidentally, the same year *Moby-Dick* was published, B. P. Shillaber's short-lived weekly humor magazine, *The Carpet-Bag,* began a two-year run of publication in nearby Boston. Both Mark Twain, then only sixteen years old, and Artemus Ward, seventeen, would publish short pieces in the May, 1852, issue of Shillaber's fledgling journal; thirty-two years later, two characters in Twain's most famous novel would literally pick up their carpetbags and run with them.

Since the mid-1860s, and particularly in southern literature and popular culture, "carpetbagger" has moved from the literal description of a traveler's valise to both stereotype and metaphor. Carpetbaggers were originally northern, or occasionally European, government political appointees, teachers, entrepreneurs, and self-serving opportunists and con-artists who moved into a defeated and dysfunctional South immediately after the Civil War. Richard N. Current describes one of the dominant popular images of the carpetbaggers, that of the cowardly scavenger: "Having waited for the real soldiers to subdue the South, these soldiers of fortune followed at a safe distance, like jackals in the track of a lion." The carpetbaggers, who were both black and white, had no roots in the South, and many of them lived quite literally out of their suitcases when they first moved into a community. These carpetbaggers opened small businesses and large ones, bought up discounted or foreclosed property, found political positions, and forged deals both shady and legitimate in the debilitated, yet-to-be-reconstructed South. Many carpetbaggers hoped to turn a quick profit, get in on the ground floor of a longer-term investment opportunity, or establish a permanent political power-base. At the same time, as Current and John Hope Franklin observe, carpetbaggers also came south for official governmental and humanitarian purposes, to help restore order, rebuild the southern political, social, and economic infrastructure, and found schools and colleges.

Southerners typically were suspicious of carpetbaggers—who reminded them of an earlier group of carpetbagging, disruptive outsiders, the abolitionists—and citizens were often openly hostile and even violent in their response to these "furriners." Southerners saw the carpetbaggers, and their traitorous, pro-North although southern-resident black and white "scalawag" co-conspirators, as meddlers actively soliciting black Republican voters' support, dangerous to have around and clearly bent on personal gain—even when they had moved to the South in order to help the South. Carpetbagger money and false promises, on one end of the moral spectrum, often proved irresistible to down-and-out southerners. On the other end of the spectrum, these outsiders often helped bring desperately needed capital and know-how to the South. In fact, by 1886, when Henry Grady gave his famous "New South" speech at New York City's Delmonico's Restaurant—a reconciliatory sales-pitch that, in effect, openly invited the right kind of carpetbaggers into the region—the South had begun to realize that it could indeed benefit by using northern capital and enterprise to help stabilize and rejuvenate the region. Many northern carpetbaggers came to stay, acquired wealth and legitimate political power, married into higher-class southern society, and went on to become accepted and important state government, industrial, civic, educational, and philanthropic leaders in the South.

But even if individual carpetbaggers successfully entered mainstream southern society, or returned to the North again, or simply vanished from sight, the stereotype lingered on for decades. Daniel E. Sutherland has also done a full-length study of the phenomenon of the "Confederate carpetbagger," a mirror-image group of southern opportunists who left the South before or during Reconstruction to seek their political, social, or economic fortune in the North. The dastardly interloper who exploited his southern hosts was a stock character in popular melodramas, and several novels of the period, such as Opie Read's *Carpetbagger* (1899) and Joel Chandler Harris's *Gabriel Tolliver: A Story of Reconstruction* (1902), worked variations on this motif. Two of the most celebrated carpetbaggers in American literary realism are, of course, the endlessly inventive but unethical, immoral, and finally pitiable

Duke and King in Twain's *Huckleberry Finn* (1884). The King and Duke lug their "big fat ratty-looking carpet-bags" and ply their con games down the Mississippi River during the 1840s, according to the internal setting of the novel; but they effectively represent the stereotypical, small-time carpetbagger of the Reconstruction and post-Reconstruction period in which Twain actually composed his narrative. Twain's con men are also partly reminiscent of Melville's shape-shifting, multi-incarnation confidence man on the Mississippi River steamboat, *Fidele,* in the complex postmodern allegory, *The Confidence-Man* (1857).

Twentieth-century avatars of the carpetbagger include the rodent pack of Snopeses that arrives out of nowhere, Flem Snopes in the lead, sniffing out all opportunities to bore deep into the southern social, economic, and political woodwork, made even more rotten by Reconstruction politics. But assorted wheeler-dealers, con-artists, and drifters from outside the region continue to infiltrate southern writing on into the later twentieth century, as if to remind the reader that no region—especially one still trying to recover from the devastation of the Civil War—is free from the effects of manipulation, exploitation, and outright moral brigandage. And thus the sullen, knife-wielding mysterious stranger who suddenly turns up, dressed all wrong, on the small Tennessee farm in Robert Penn Warren's 1947 short story "Blackberry Winter" belongs to the carpetbagger tradition, as do several characters from Flannery O'Connor's southern stories of the 1950s. The opportunistic Tom T. Shiftlet, the one-armed bandit in "The Life You Save May Be Your Own," prides himself on his "moral intelligence," but in order to steal the family automobile and hit the big road to Mobile he agrees to marry, and then promptly abandons, Mrs. Crater's retarded daughter, Lucynell. Or consider the hypocritical, carpetbagging Bible salesman in "Good Country People," whose customized valise contains a symbolically hollow Bible that conceals a whiskey flask, a packet of prophylactics, and some obscene playing cards; after he seduces her, he also adds Hulga's artificial leg to his suitcase. In "The Displaced Person," Mr. Guizac is, in southern eyes at least, something of a carpetbagger, too. An industrious tenant farmer displaced by World War II from Poland, Guizac's resourcefulness, no-nonsense work-ethic, and foreign ways make Mrs. McIntyre and her other tenants uncomfortable and resentful; finally, the whole southern farming community participates in his death. Carpetbagging has, moreover, transcended the South

to become an internationally recognized cliché. For example, a popular-culture monument to the enduring metaphoric power of the stereotype, here in the context of corporate and governmental power-broking, is Harold Robbins's *The Carpetbaggers* (1961), which was loosely based on the career of Howard Hughes and was later made into a movie starring George Peppard and Carroll Baker (1964).

R. Bruce Bickley Jr.

See also Abolition; Civil War; New South; Reconstruction; Sectional Reconciliation.

Richard Nelson Current, *Those Terrible Carpetbaggers* (1988); Eric Foner, *Reconstruction: America's Unfinished Revolution, 1863–1877* (1988); John Hope Franklin, *Reconstruction After the Civil War* (1994); William F. Lenz, *Fast Talk & Flush Times: The Confidence-Man as a Literary Convention* (1985); Otto H. Olsen, *Carpetbagger's Crusade: The Life of Albion W. Tourgée* (1975); Otto H. Olsen, ed., *Reconstruction and Redemption in the South* (1980); Daniel E. Sutherland, *The Confederate Carpetbaggers* (1988).

CARTER, JIMMY

Thirty-ninth President of the United States (1977–1981), Georgian James Earl Carter Jr. confirmed the electability of a southerner to the nation's highest office. He was able to carry much of the South, but the region (once solidly Democratic) would turn from him when he sought reelection. When Bill Clinton from Arkansas recaptured the White House for the Democratic Party twelve years later, the South would not provide the base of his victories.

Even while he was president, Carter remained pointedly a citizen of Plains, Georgia. Concurrently citizen of the world, Carter has maintained his identity with his native town and state as no president since Truman has. Carter took to the White House not only many associates from Georgia but a distinctive southern flavor, for which he paid some political price. His brother, Billy, who exuded the aura of the good old country boy, was frequently in the news, and the nation got to know Miss Lillian, Carter's mother, as well. Carter made no apologies for the authenticity of his Baptist faith: he was not ashamed to identify himself as a born-again Christian. For many years—before the presidency, during, and afterward—he taught an adult Sunday school class. Born and raised in rural Plains,

Carter brought to the presidency a keen intelligence and trained mind. In his memoir, *A Reporter's Life* (1996), Walter Cronkite credits Carter with possessing the best brain of presidents he has known from Hoover on.

Carter brought to Washington a populist vision. He had been able to secure his party's nomination because George McGovern's forces had altered the party's rules to enable the likes of an outsider like Carter (who had been a populist governor in Georgia) to win on his own in the state conventions and primaries. In a populist spirit, Carter and his family departed from the traditional drive to his swearing-in and walked the inaugural route, though the cold was bitter. He had campaigned and won election as an outsider, which presented him with problems once in office. Working outside the established bureaucracies proved difficult. He was, however, able to achieve some of his goals. Looking at a century of conservation efforts, *Audubon* magazine places him among the champions of conservation, declaring that "no U.S. president since Teddy Roosevelt has done more for the protection of public land than Jimmy Carter." Carter convinced Congress to pass the Alaska National Interest Lands Conservation Act of 1980, protecting 104 million acres (the largest conservation initiative in the nation's history); he signed the law preventing strip-mining of public lands and the Superfund law for cleanup of hazardous-waste sites. But the economy (inflation and high unemployment) and the holding of American hostages by the Iranians for 444 days would force him from office after one term. Bobbie Ann Mason's story "The Ocean" suggests the view of the common (albeit poorly informed) southerner as criticisms of Carter mounted. In *Crackers: This Whole Many-Angled Thing of Jimmy, More Carters, Ominous Little Animals, Sad-Singing Women, My Daddy and Me* (1980), humorist and fellow-Georgian Roy Blount Jr. used the Carter image and legacy to comment on his own southernness, perceptions of the South, and the state of the national culture.

Only fifty-six when he left office, Carter was determined to continue to lead a productive life, furthering the goals that led him into politics. His partner in the new life remained his wife, Rosalynn, who had been an active (consequently controversial) first lady. Carter proceeded to make a new career, becoming the most energetic and productive past-president of modern times; Rosalynn Carter has concurrently been the most active and productive of former first ladies. Their la-

bors have continued to exemplify a populist flavor. They have worked unceasingly for Habitat for Humanity, seeking funds for its global activity and setting an example by working with construction crews. Carter has been an unofficial ambassador for peace in troubled spots. In Atlanta, the Carters have established the Carter Center, which not only houses his papers but is a nonpartisan, nonpolitical organization aimed at alleviation of human suffering and the advancement of peace and freedom, especially in developing nations. Carter regularly teaches political science at Emory University and lectures widely.

Always a good reader and word craftsman, Carter has enjoyed the challenge of writing. His works include *A Government as Good as Its People* (1977); *Keeping Faith: Memoirs of a President* (1982); *An Outdoor Journal: Adventures and Reflections* (1994); *Living Faith* (1996); *Why Not the Best? The First Fifty Years* (1996); *Sources of Strength: Meditations on Scripture* (1997); *The Virtues of Aging* (1998); and a book of poems, *Always a Reckoning and Other Poems* (1995). Rosalynn Carter wrote her own memoirs, *First Lady from Plains* (1984). Jointly she and her husband wrote *Everything to Gain: Making the Most of the Rest of Your Life* (1987), which recounts their dilemma when they left Washington and their determination to chart a constructive course—and reflects their need to share and to inspire.

Joseph M. Flora

Peter G. Bourne, *Jimmy Carter: A Comprehensive Biography* (1997); Douglas Brinkley, *The Unfinished Presidency* (1998).

CASTE

Caste, a system of social hierarchy more rigid than class and governed by law, custom, and/or religion, is a prominent part of the South's history. The South's variety of caste was influenced most significantly by its peculiar institution—chattel slavery of African Americans. Because the system of chattel slavery was justified based on racial difference, race played a major role in determining caste status. Slavery also affected other issues related to caste, such as economics and heredity, since most of the South's landed gentry were slave owners and their wealth, power, and social status were passed down to their legitimate white heirs. Consequently, the white slave-owning aristocracy was at the top of the social hierarchy, followed by white middle-class business owners and farmers, with poor whites holding the lowest caste-ranking among European Americans. African Americans occupied the bottom rung of the caste ladder in the South and in the United States at large. With few exceptions, social custom and law continued to support the early caste system in the South throughout the antebellum period. After the abolition of slavery, a relaxed version of the same caste system existed throughout the post-Reconstruction period with the advent of sharecropping. Many remnants of the discrimination that this caste system engendered still exist in the modern South.

The southern caste system's prevalence throughout the region's history is prolifically evinced in southern literature. It is particularly prominent in the work of one of the South's finest writers, William Faulkner. In works such as *Absalom, Absalom!* (1936), *Go Down Moses* (1942), and *Light in August* (1932), Faulkner brilliantly illustrates the intricacies of southern caste and its ramifications for generations of southerners. Faulkner is especially adept at portraying the destructive effects that caste has on southern society where race and class are concerned. Characters such as the deteriorating aristocratic Compsons, the poor-white-turned-land-baron Thomas Sutpen, and the "poor white trash" Bundrens and Snopeses are enduring portraits of white southern society. African American characters, though less prominent in his work, often serve to emphasize the dehumanizing effects of caste prejudice on whites in the South. In the case of Dilsey and her family in *The Sound and the Fury* (1929), the African American family serves as a positive contrast to the dysfunction of the deteriorating southern aristocracy.

Many other southern writers have addressed white caste distinctions. Peter Taylor's stories treat both black-white divisions ("The Long Fourth") and strict economic and social barriers between whites ("There" and "Guests"). Other writers concentrate on "poor white trash," a character type that has served as a "lynch" pin in southern literature because of the compelling position that lower-class whites in the South occupy between the white upper class and people of color in the hierarchy of the traditional southern caste system. These characters are a longstanding element in the literature, beginning in the antebellum period with comedic portrayals by Augustus Baldwin Longstreet and George Washington Harris, satirically captured by Mark Twain with his "First Families of Virginia" in

Pudd'nhead Wilson (1894), and continued by twentieth-century writers like Eudora Welty and Flannery O'Connor. Southern writers have also done serious, sympathetic or satirical portrayals of working-class whites. Examples of these include James Agee and Walker Evans's *Let Us Now Praise Famous Men* (1941); Erskine Caldwell's satirical, grotesque novel *Tobacco Road* (1932); and Linda Flowers's moving memoir *Throwed Away* (1990).

Because of the racial dynamics involved in making caste distinctions in the South, southern African American writers have also participated in treating caste in their fiction. This tradition begins with the classic slave narratives by William Wells Brown, Frederick Douglass, and Harriet Jacobs and continues with works such as Charles Chesnutt's *The Wife of His Youth and Other Stories of the Color Line* (1899), Jean Toomer's *Cane* (1923), Richard Wright's *Black Boy* (1945), Ernest Gaines's *Catherine Carmier* (1964), Alice Walker's *The Third Life of Grange Copeland* (1970), and Bebe Moore Campbell's *Your Blues Ain't Like Mine* (1992). Because of a proliferation of racial mixing in the South beginning in the antebellum period, color caste is an especially complex component of the southern caste system and has been particularly divisive in families and communities. Many African American writers from the South have paid close attention to the hypocrisy in a system of discrimination based on socially constructed definitions of "race" and "color."

In recent decades, writers have begun to expand their portrayals of caste in southern literature as the list of "isms" that pervades the whole of American culture grows. Randall Kenan, E. Lynn Harris, Rita Mae Brown, and Anne Allen Shockley treat heterosexism in their novels as a particularly pernicious problem in the South. Randall Kenan treats a variety of "isms" in his collection of stories *Let the Dead Bury Their Dead* (1992), and skillfully illustrates how the rigidity of southern caste provides little space for both black and white homosexuals and their families to function in a healthy manner in small southern towns.

Valerie N. Matthews

See also Class; Mulatto; Poor White; Racism.

John Dollar, *Caste and Class in a Southern Town* (1957); Willard Gatewood, *Aristocrats of Color: The Black Elite, 1880–1920* (1990); Fon Louise Gordon, *Caste and Class: The Black Experience in Arkansas, 1880–1920* (1995).

CAVALIER

Although it has enjoyed widespread currency throughout the South, the cavalier ideal is more closely associated with Virginia than with any other southern state. This close association is explained in part by the fact that the mid-seventeenth-century Old Dominion was the first colony to develop a plantation system founded on the extensive cultivation of a staple tobacco crop by slave labor, a system for which the notion of nobly descended cavalier landowners was a useful complement. More specifically, the cavalier myth is linked to the widely accepted idea that the substantial immigration from England to Virginia between 1645 and 1675, a migration that included the founders of many of the colony's most prominent families, was composed overwhelmingly of noble and titled cavalier supporters of Charles I fleeing the repression following the victory of Oliver Cromwell's Puritan forces in the English Civil War (1642–1649).

In spite of popular acceptance, there has never been strong historical support for the proposition that Virginia was settled by large numbers of cavaliers. Contemporary historical accounts, such as John Hammond's *Leah and Rachel* (1656) and Robert Beverley's *The History and Present State of Virginia* (1705), emphasized the modest origins of Virginia's first families. Twentieth-century historical accounts of the Old Dominion's settlement, from Thomas Jefferson Wertenbaker's *Patrician and Plebeian in Virginia* (1910) to Wesley Frank Craven's *White, Red, and Black: The Seventeenth Century Virginian* (1971), have reaffirmed the socially middling, politically and religiously unaffiliated complexion of the state's settlement. Virginians, however, have always been loath to surrender their cavalier myth. As late as 1883, romance writer John Esten Cooke published *Virginia: A History of the People.* In this popular work, he asserted that the state owed its unique character to its equally unique settlement, which had consisted of a "great tide of fugitive Cavalierdom." Such historically suspect but romantically potent notions continued to exert a lingering appeal in the twentieth century to the imaginations of Virginians, southerners, and all Americans.

The rules of conduct to which the mythical Virginia cavalier subscribed were copied from an Old-World Elizabethan pattern. From the sixteenth to the eighteenth century, a loosely defined and flexible social code developed to mold the manners of the newly evolving class of English gentry, a code articulated in courtesy books like Thomas Elyot's *The Book Named the Governor* (1531). This code of gentility strongly influenced the social attitudes of the plantation owners of colonial Virginia. Whether or not he embraced the idea of his cavalier blood, by the eighteenth century the Virginia planter clearly embraced the ideal of the gentleman, and he considered himself the preeminent example of the type. This polished and cultivated self-image is clearly on display in colonial Virginia writing, from the poems and essays decorating the pages of the *Virginia Gazette,* published in Williamsburg from 1736 to 1778, to the supercilious descriptions of uncouth backwoods North Carolinians by William Byrd, the consummate eighteenth-century Virginia cavalier, in his *History of the Dividing Line* (written c. 1728, published 1841).

The plantation system, which nourished the aristocratic cavalier ideal and the code of the gentleman and which flourished in Virginia from 1725 to 1775, was severely damaged by the coming of the Revolution. The gradual effects of declining soil fertility and tobacco yields were exacerbated by the economic disruptions of war and, even more significantly, by the loss of the English tobacco market. Virginia, which provided the greatest leaders of the Revolution, ironically suffered a prolonged economic and cultural decline in the decades following independence. But the cavalier ideal that had nourished the state's leaders did not experience a corresponding diminishment.

There are two primary reasons for the survival of the cavalier myth in the new nation. First, it was an ideal complement to and justification for a plantation system dependent on slave labor. Southern Americans came ever more widely to accept the notion that slavery made possible the most exquisite flowerings of their social order, the noble and highly bred planter and his refined and pure lady. Wherever the plantation system spread into the cotton- and sugar-producing areas of the middle and lower South, so too did the cavalier ideal. Second, severe economic decline produced a Virginia diaspora that lasted roughly from 1780 to 1830. Residents fled the Old Dominion by the thousands for more promising economic prospects in the newly developing states to the south and west. Joseph Glover Baldwin's *The Flush Times of Alabama and Mississippi* (1833) vividly describes the rough-hewn, primitive nature of the society that Virginians encountered in the Old Southwest, but it also clearly shows that wherever they went, these emigrants from the Old Dominion carried with them their household gods—their cavalier heritage and their reverence for their state's glorious past.

By the early decades of the nineteenth century, the mythic cavalier had spread from its tidewater Virginia birthplace all over the South, and southern writers were at work creating for their region a magnificent fictional aristocracy. Not surprisingly, the Old Dominion's writers contributed some of the most effective and idealized portraits of southern cavaliers. George Tucker's *The Valley of Shenandoah* (1824) and John Pendleton Kennedy's *Swallow Barn* (1832) were among the earliest fictional portraits of Virginia plantations presided over by high-minded country squires. In these works, defects in the cavalier character type could be detected within the admiring and sympathetic treatment, but the relatively tempered tone of early Virginia fiction quickly vanished. By 1836, Nathaniel Beverley Tucker in *The Partisan Leader* had created a cavalier hero who led his state in open rebellion to the federal government. William Alexander Caruthers, in *The Cavaliers of Virginia* (1834) and *The Knights of the Golden Horse-shoe* (1845), fashioned completely idealized portrayals of colonial Virginia aristocrats. And John Esten Cooke's *The Virginia Comedians* (1854) and *Henry St. John, Gentleman* (1859) likewise retreated on the eve of the Civil War into the golden age of the state's colonial and Revolutionary past, ignoring the issue of the obsolescence of its idealized heroes.

Writers in the newer southern states followed the lead of Virginia's authors and glorified the cavalier character ideal in their antebellum works. In Charles Gayarré's *The School for Politics* (1854), a Virginia-born aristocrat stood loftily above the rampant corruption of contemporary Louisiana politics. Virginius Dabney, though he had immigrated from the Old Dominion to Mississippi when he was a baby, returned fictionally to his birthplace in *The Story of Don Miff* (1886) to describe the Edenic life of an antebellum Tidewater plantation.

As the South moved toward civil war, its cavalier heroes became more and more warped by sectional paranoia and by the need to make them purely expressive of southern ideology. In *The Sunny South* (1860), Joseph Holt Ingraham invested his Tennessee plantation with a feudal ambiance, linking southern society, like many of his antebellum contemporaries, to the magnificence of the Middle Ages as depicted in the wildly popular romances of Walter Scott. Southern women writers were, if possible, even more defensive of the South and even more extravagantly romantic in depicting its cavalier heroes. Caroline Lee Hentz wrote a number of popular plantation novels, most notable among them *The Planter's Northern Bride* (1854), a paean to the chivalric and spiritually elevated qualities of the South's aristocracy and a vigorous defense of the institution of slavery on which the power of that aristocracy rested. The female protagonists of Augusta Jane Evans's Civil War novel, *Macaria* (1864), devote themselves body and soul to the holy cause for which their cavalier warriors were fighting, even though that cause was doomed.

Through the fictional glorification of its cavalier heroes, southern writers sought to assert the superiority of the region's way of life in the face of the increasingly malignant censure of the North. They also supported the idea of a distinct race, descended from the English Norman aristocracy and manifesting that culture's generous, honorable, brave, and gallant nature. Such a "southron" race, they believed, was clearly distinct from a less-favored northern race, which unhappily combined "Saxon" intellect and drive with Puritan avariciousness and moral fanaticism. Buoyed by its romantic fiction, Dixie carried the cavalier ideal into battle like an icon, convinced that it justified the righteousness of its cause and that it vouchsafed victory and vindication.

The Civil War destroyed slavery and the plantation system, but it did not destroy the appeal of the cavalier myth. Southerners convinced themselves that the cause for which they had fought had not been cast into disrepute by defeat. Indeed, it had been sanctified by that defeat and transformed into a holy Lost Cause. Inevitably, the central figure of the Lost Cause myth was the gallant and chivalrous cavalier. In the years following the war, southerners turned worshipfully toward the great military leader who represented the epitome of their culture's chivalric aristocracy—Robert E. Lee. And the South's writers willingly created military heroes along the lines of the revered general. Thomas Nelson Page's *In Ole Virginia* (1887) was a rose-colored description of antebellum plantation life in the Old Dominion and a celebration of the honorable and high-principled cavaliers who inevitably sacrificed themselves at the altar of war. In *Tiger-Lilies* (1867), Sidney Lanier eulogized a benevolent plantation patriarchy swept away by the barbaric armies of chaos unleashed by the Civil War.

Southern writers were aided and abetted in their postbellum resurrection of the cavalier by northern readers willing to let bygones be bygones and eager for stories of a glorious though vanquished Old South. Even into the twentieth century a highly wrought nostalgia dominated most southern writing. More than twenty years after his critically acclaimed and realistic *The Grandissimes* (1880), George Washington Cable published *The Cavalier* (1901), a blatantly romantic and clichéd treatment of the Civil War. In Henry Selden's *A Gentleman of the South* (1903), the death of the novel's chivalric hero symbolically prefigured the fall of the Old South, much as it did in the fiction of Thomas Nelson Page.

With the coming of the twentieth century, younger southern writers removed from the memories of the Civil War began to disentangle themselves from the idealization and the ideology surrounding the cavalier figure and to treat the character type with more irony and complexity. This process was first evident in Virginia. Here, Ellen Glasgow in her Queenborough novels—*The Romantic Comedians* (1926), *They Stooped to Folly* (1929), and *The Sheltered Life* (1932)—strove determinedly to bring realism, "blood and irony" she called it, to her treatment of upper-middle-class Virginia gentlemen. Though most of James Branch Cabell's novels were set in the imaginary medieval land of Poictesme, works such as *Jurgen* (1919) and *The Silver Stallion* (1926) addressed with seriousness and wit the power and necessity of myth and cast oblique light on the way the survivors of the Confederacy had created their own pantheon of cavalier demigods. The most powerful and penetrating fictional meditation on the cavalier ideal in the twentieth century was William Faulkner's *Absalom, Absalom!* (1936), which dramatized in the character of Thomas Sutpen the translation of the myth from tidewater Virginia to the Deep South and detailed in the lives of Sutpen's family the tragic consequences of the region's complex mythic inheritance.

In spite of the efforts of such writers as Glasgow and Faulkner to achieve distance and irony in southern fiction, the attraction of the cavalier myth has remained irresistible for many twentieth-century writers. In Stark Young's *So Red the Rose* (1934), the plantation is depicted as a paradisiacal social order destroyed by rapacious Yankees like William T. Sherman. Margaret Mitchell's *Gone With the Wind* (1936) detects few snakes in the Edenic garden of Tara and presents in its cavalier hero, Ashley Wilkes, the finest likeness of the nineteenth-century romantic prototype. The phenomenal and enduring popularity of Mitchell's novel suggests the equally enduring appeal of the cavalier myth, which has transcended puny historical fact and remains today a significant part of the region's and the nation's mythic fabric.

Ritchie D. Watson

See also Aristocracy; Gentleman; Lost Cause; Novel, 1820 to 1865; Plantation; Plantation Fiction; Tidewater; Virginia, Literature of; Yankee.

Carl Bridenbaugh, *Myths and Realities: Societies of the Colonial South* (1952); Rhys Isaac, *The Transformation of Virginia, 1740–1790* (1982); Ritchie D. Watson, *The Cavalier in Virginia Fiction* (1985); Ritchie D. Watson, *Yeoman Versus Cavalier: The Old Southwest's Fictional Road to Rebellion* (1993); Louis B. Wright, *The First Gentlemen of Virginia: Intellectual Qualities of the Early Colonial Ruling Class* (1940).

CAVES

Caves appear in southern writing with the full range of their associations in Western thought: with death and resurrection, the Platonic realm of illusions and shadows, the primal origins of humankind, and the womb of earth. Bound up with the cave as symbol are questions of the relation of spirit and matter, life and death, the limitations of knowledge and its possibility. From Edgar Allan Poe to Dorothy Allison, southern writers have continued to explore caves for paths to the deeper reaches of our identity.

Caves, as a region separated from our daily experience, suggest a realm of the fantastic, a region outside the bounds of society. Mark Twain (Samuel Clemens, 1835–1910) created the most famous cave episode in American literature by exploiting this potential in *Tom Sawyer* (1876). The two children, Tom and Becky, become lost in McDougal's Cave and narrowly escape death, and Tom is able to fulfill the childhood dream of finding stolen treasure when he discovers the lair of Injun Joe, who gets sealed in the cave and dies. Stolen treasure in caves has reappeared more recently in *Cold Mountain* (1997) by Charles Frazier (1950–), which has a band of vigilantes during the Civil War depositing their loot in an Appalachian cave. Working with another aspect of popular tradition, Lee Smith (1944–) has one of the many narrators of her novel *Oral History* (1983) tell of a man encountering a young, beautiful girl emerging from a cave who later proves to be an ancient witch. Suggestive though the popular traditions concerning caves might be, other writers have mined their symbolic potential more deeply.

Caves, as passages to a dark, labyrinthine realm, present a challenge to the rational mind and to the very identity we possess in the upper world of daylight. Thomas Jefferson (1743–1826) devoted Query V of his *Notes on the State of Virginia* (1785) to a scientific account of the caverns of Virginia, and his account, complete with a map, measurements, and hypotheses to account for various phenomena, represents an extension of the rational mind (as the Enlightenment conceived it) into an unexplored region. Whereas Jefferson remained secure in his faith in reason and the stability of identity, Edgar Allan Poe (1809–1849) found in caves the threat of entrapment of consciousness. In *The Narrative of Arthur Gordon Pym* (1838), the protagonist becomes trapped in a cave on the island of Tslal (inhabited by a savage black tribe) with his beastlike companion, Dirk Peters. This episode takes its place with the many other instances of imprisonment and premature burial in Poe's works (and elsewhere in this novel) that suggest the forces impinging on the rational mind, and the ultimate threat of annihilation.

Because of the pervasive influence of Plato's Allegory of the Cave on Western thought, writers frequently use caves to explore a problem of knowledge: how do we know truth in a realm of shadows? James Branch Cabell (1879–1958) structures *Jurgen* (1919) around Jurgen's three encounters in caves with figures from mythology as he seeks his destiny. Robert Penn Warren's (1905–1989) *The Cave* (1959) provides an extensive exploration of the Platonic dilemma. Warren, writing long after the fading of the Romantic possibility of transcendent knowledge, concentrates on the problem of identity, of knowledge of the self. When a young man, Jasper Harrick, becomes trapped in a cave, the entire community focuses on his rescue. Warren portrays the experience of the cave as an awful concentration of self in isolation, and all of the primary characters, even if never actually entering the cave, are spurred to attempt a more adequate self-definition (with varying degrees of success). All, within themselves and in the larger community, are confronted by a variety of false identities and complex mirrorings, and the cave functions as the anchoring symbol for the drama of their struggle. Those who are successful in their effort emerge to find the possibility of communion with others in the upper world. The speaker in Robert Morgan's (1944–) poem "The Way Back" (1990) also faces the threat of entrapment, isolation,

and death before finding his way out of the cave by means of a clue given him by another.

For African Americans, the problem of identity is further complicated by racial images that distort perception. Ralph Ellison (1914–1994) places his narrator below ground to explore the problem in *Invisible Man* (1952). Taking a cue from "The Man Who Lived Underground" (1942) by his contemporary Richard Wright (1908–1960), Ellison situates his narrator underground in a position of existential strength, freed from all of the false conceptions of his identity that society would foist upon him. The narrator, having assumed various roles in the eyes of others, realizes that he is invisible to everyone, black and white alike, and begins to forge a new dynamic identity after dropping into the caverns of the metropolitan sewer system. His narrative attests to his mastery of the realm of shadows.

Much of the underlying threat of the cave is found in its archetypal connection to female sexuality—the giver of life is also a threat to discrete identity—perhaps explaining the prevalence of male writers in our survey here. This tension is present in almost all of these works, to varying degrees, but Cormac McCarthy (1933–) provides the most explicit treatment in his *Child of God* (1973). The novel deals with a poor white in the Tennessee mountains, Lester Ballard, who is dispossessed at the novel's opening by the auction of his farm and falsely accused of rape. Descending into a complete alienation from the larger community, Lester stumbles into a desperate course of murder and necrophilia and retreats to the caves. He begins wearing the clothes and even the hair of his female victims, finding his route to identity in a savage travesty of human sexuality. Dorothy Allison (1949–), in her novel *Cavedweller* (1998), presents a radically different vision, in which caves become a symbol of the feminine wellsprings of life and communion. The main character, Delia, returns to the small Georgia town of Cayro after the death of her second husband, bringing her daughter Cissy with her in search of two lost daughters from her violent first marriage. Her success in finding reconciliation and redemption, and Cissy's discovery of her lesbian sexual identity, are tied symbolically to the exploration of the network of caves beneath Cayro.

Other writers have used caves in their work as a path to regeneration as well. Reynolds Price (1933–), in his poem "Two Caves, a House, a Garden, a Tomb (Memories of Israel and the West Bank with J. C. A., 1980)," uses the speaker's encounter with sites associated with the life and death of Jesus (the cave of his birth and the cave of his tomb) as the occasion for meditations on the meaning of the Incarnation and Resurrection in the speaker's own struggle with life and mortality. The poem ends not with a religious epiphany but with an affirmation of his communion with his companion. Similarly, in *The Second Coming* (1980) by Walker Percy (1916–1990), Will Barrett emerges from an encounter with death in a cave to find the possibility of communion with another. Barrett suffers, as Percy sees it, from the modern condition of the alienation of the self from itself, and the extremity of his alienation leads him to attempt suicide by drugging himself in a cave. Escaping from the cave, he falls (literally) into a greenhouse occupied by Allie, an escaped mental-asylum patient, and their discovery of love and inter-subjectivity allows the possibility of a new life.

Other writers have found the possibility of recovery from alienation in a return to the primal origins of humanity, allowing a recovery of language and meaning. James Dickey (1923–1997) in "The Eye-Beaters" presents a speaker who visits a hospital for blind children and struggles to understand the fact that many of the children strike and bruise their eyes. Refusing to accept the physician's explanation, he sees the act as an attempt to gain vision, a violent groping toward the light, and a repetition of the origins of the vision of mankind as it made the leap to symbol in the dark of caves. Resisting the closure of vision in his own age, the work of the poet is to reinvent the vision of his race by imaginative violence, to return to the cave and beat his eyes. James Seay (1939–   ) seeks a similar encounter in his poem "Deep in Dordogne" (1997). The speaker sits in a cave inhabited by his primitive ancestors and projects himself into a time when humans were barely lingual and groped in their need toward word and song; again, the poet attempts to recover the power of language through a recovery of the need that produced it.

Douglas L. Mitchell

James H. Justus, *The Achievement of Robert Penn Warren* (1981); Clark Griffith, "Caves and Cave Dwellers: The Study of a Romantic Image," *Journal of English and Germanic Philology* 62 (1963); Gordon Wilson Sr., *Folklore of the Mammoth Cave Region* (1968); Margaret Homans, "The Woman in the Cave: Recent Feminist Fictions and the Classical Underworld," *Contemporary Literature* 29 (Fall 1988).

CEMETERIES AND GRAVEYARDS

Even now, graveyards are the focus of the Old South. The shady iron-fenced plots curled around the edges of churches provide a town with its first source of historical affluence: visitors lingering among the flat, moss-edged ellipses and crypts squint to see what famous men are buried there, how early their dates, what wars they represented. In the cities, where civic groups marshal gravesites like old political machines, cemeteries have become monuments, not only to war heroes and founders but to social inheritance and pretension alike; their huge locked and decorated gates seem tombs in themselves. In suburbia, the increasing plots where the homogenous memorials grow hideous plastic-flower heads are only of passing significance. Out in the country, however, the most forgotten, weed-crusted family burial ground shows more dignity and interest than those outliers.

It is not only the indigenous who concern themselves thus. Local cemeteries are the drawing place of tour buses and interstate travelers, too. Counting on the tourist trade, chambers of commerce petition for brown highway markers and include their old cemeteries on historical maps; the gravesites are marked that hold some entertainment beyond the dead's rest and beg attention to the certifying historicity they supply the place. In Savannah and Richmond, one comes looking for justification—for colonial revolution, for agrarian resistance, for civil disobedience. In Charleston and Beaufort (either one), one revels in the thorny vines of first-family connection; at Chapel Hill and Asheville (it must be this way at Vanderbilt, too) in literary and political name-dropping.

But even the tiny family plots one finds along the country roads reflect the way cemeteries fit into the southern landscape. Nearly out of view between drooping road foliage might be a small rusting sign, raised tin, once painted with ornamental leaves, which reads "Simmons." The sign hangs on a sturdy knotted wire across a narrow sandy drive that must be flooded every time it rains. Although clearly the road is used often, the graveyard itself is entirely hidden from view. Nearby, less than two miles up the same road, neat rows of cleaned graves, old and recent, are cordoned off with new posts and wire in the high middle of a rich hayfield, and both passersby and field workers are aware at any moment of its central position. Not so the Kerr cemetery, at the end of a road that winds around to the back of a farm field; Do Not Enter is the clear and somewhat ironic injunction there. Sometimes only a single grave in the woods, barely marked by a worn stone, marks the place where there was once civilization enough to bury the dead. Where once might have been a church and yard, now only the crusted, arrow-headed wrought-iron fence encloses a small plot next to the encroaching highway, its graves still shaded by an enormous magnolia, in full bloom by late spring.

These signs to the cemetery are clearly marked in southern literature as well. "Row after row with strict impunity / the headstones yield their names to the element," begins Allen Tate's "Ode to the Confederate Dead" (1932), and continues, "The brute curiosity of an angel's stare / Turns you, like them, to stone." So echoes the next foremost image of the southern graveyard: Thomas Wolfe's *Look Homeward, Angel* (1929), whose elegant Italian wings became a mythic figure for a generation of lost-home writers and helped define what many would say is the strongest element of southern writing—the yearning to hold on to the thick, entangling cultural and emotional roots its writer inevitably tries to escape. Eudora Welty, on the other hand, succinctly enjoins the cemetery of Mount Salus, Mississippi, as metaphor of the changing nature of the South. In *The Optimist's Daughter* (1972), Laurel McKelva Hand, the title character, rides up to her family's old camellia-scented gravesite before she is told firmly that her father will be buried not here, with his first wife and with his venerable McKelva ancestors, but in the "new part," on "the very shore of the new interstate highway," where his new wife, Fay, not from there, has chosen his plot.

Faulkner draws a whole myth out of the comic-tragic journey to the final resting place of Addie Bundren (*As I Lay Dying,* 1930), during which journey all the eccentricities, meanness, craziness, and poignancies of her family come glaringly to light. For all of her husband's talk about "the way she would want it," her grave is literally a quick site (dug with borrowed tools, like their borrowed values) on which to reconstruct a new life without her.

This same theme is echoed years later in Bobbie Ann Mason's "Shiloh" (1982), where the famous Civil War shrine becomes for Leroy and Norma Jean Moffit the site of their marital undoing in another way. At the cemetery for the Union dead, where general victory joins individual defeat, she tells him she wants to leave him. Surrounding them are campers, "bumper to bumper," and families on noisy outings to visit "history." Another story from Mason's *Shiloh* collection, "Graveyard Day," looks at broken families as they reset themselves after divorce, but also examines the importance of the ancestral stones as stability in a family's life, even for those not yet—but perhaps soon to be—part of that family. On the other hand, the family graveyard in Reynolds Price's *Blue Calhoun* (1992) becomes the undoing of a man's family, not once but twice.

There are cemeteries of the mind, too, for example in Toni Morrison's *Song of Solomon,* which centers its multigenerational revelation around a bag of mistaken bones carried out of its grave and into a fantastic legend come alive before those bones are settled once more. There is the strange cemetery, firmly fixed in place though untitled, of Cormac McCarthy's *The Orchard Keeper* (1965), where its main characters find rest of one sort or the other, after the tortured ironies of misidentification outside. There is the quiet one-woman grave kept so carefully by the grandmother of Mary Hood's title story in *How Far She Went* (1984); that grave serves as the keeper of her life sorrows, which, to save her reluctant granddaughter, she must reconsider in a new light.

As these and other works in southern literature exemplify, cemeteries remain the home ground of southern roots, both in monumental and in personal ways. In those graves, they suggest, lie not only the remains of those who came before, but also the forecasts of those who have wandered too far afield to remember and those who are yet to come.

Rachel V. Mills

See also Ancestor Worship.

Mary H. Mitchell, *Hollywood Cemetery: The History of a Southern Shrine* (1985); Louis D. Rubin Jr., "Fugitives as Agrarians" (1972) and "Thomas Wolfe Once Again" (1973) in *William Elliott Shoots a Bear: Essays on the Southern Literary Imagination* (1975).

CENTERS FOR SOUTHERN STUDIES

As the distinctive character of the South as a uniquely rich and identifiable culture has matured in the twentieth century, so has the realization among scholars and other interested folks that this culture is deserving of preservation, investigation, and dialogue. Whether the roots of this realization were planted in the soil of the Reconstruction, the northward migrations of the early 1900s, the Agrarians, the rhythm-and-blues and rock-'n'-roll explosion, or the Civil Rights Movement remains a point of debate. In any case, it was clear by the 1970s that the South was generating a vast amount of information, and that the evolution (and revolution) that had taken place there would be forever lost to posterity if it weren't seized upon quickly. As an almost inevitable development within a culture obsessed with its own history, centers for study of the South and things southern began to sprout in the last two decades of the twentieth century like kudzu in a Georgia pine.

In 1977 the University of Mississippi created the Center for the Study of Southern Culture, the first and perhaps still most prominent among the major centers. The Universities of North Carolina and South Carolina followed suit over the next fifteen years with the Center for the Study of the American South and the Institute for Southern Studies, respectively. Likewise, but with slightly more focused content, East Tennessee State University began the Center for Appalachian Studies and Services and Louisiana State University created the United States Civil War Center.

These five major centers share several common goals and execute them by similar means. The centers each maintain as central to their purpose the preservation of the culture of the South, the study of that unique culture, interdisciplinary dialogue on both the history and future of the South, and a variety of services to the public. These goals are accomplished by documenting, preserving, and cataloguing primary documents and source material from the South, making these materials available to a wide range of scholars in all fields, and creating forums where people discuss, analyze, and compare ideas across disciplines in pursuit of a better understanding of the South's continuing development. Because each center is affiliated with a university, undergraduate, graduate, and postgraduate education as well as advanced research are priorities. By linking undergraduate and graduate curricula to the materials and expertise represented by their centers, and by providing scholarship and fellowship opportunities for students, the respective universities encourage forward-looking learning at all academic levels.

Publishing is inherently connected to the scholarship at these centers, with scholarly journals published by each and books on topics of both scholarly and general interest published by most. The University of Mississippi's Center for the Study of Southern Culture produced in 1989 the major scholarly work in the field, the *Encyclopedia of Southern Culture*. It additionally reaches a wide general readership with its trio of musical magazines *Living Blues, Rejoice!,* and *Old Time Country.* UNC–Chapel Hill's Center for the Study of the American South likewise satisfies both the scholar

and the general enthusiast with its *Southern Research Report,* focusing on archival and research issues, and *Southern Cultures,* "exploring Southernism from Faulkner to funk."

In addition to their physical research facilities, each of the centers maintains a virtual presence on the World Wide Web as a crucial component of their research mission. These web sites offer fairly extensive research possibilities through digitized documents and on-line publishing, as well as providing extensive links to an incredible array of all things southern.

John Salomone

See also Manuscript Collections.

University of Mississippi's Center for the Study of Southern Culture, http://www.olemiss.edu/depts/south/; University of North Carolina's Center for the Study of the American South, http://www.unc.edu/depts/csas/; University of South Carolina's Institute for Southern Studies, http://www.cla.sc.edu/ISS/; East Tennessee State University's Center for Appalachian Studies and Services, http://cass.etsu.edu/; Louisiana State University's United States Civil War Center, http://www.cwc.lsu.edu/.

CHAPEL HILL, NORTH CAROLINA

Chapel Hill, the seat of the University of North Carolina, had its origin at some unrecorded time about the middle of the eighteenth century when a Church of England chapel was established on a high point of ground with a sweeping view toward the broad coastal plain. Called New Hope Chapel Hill, this undeveloped site was chosen in 1789 as the location for America's first state center of higher education. A new town was envisioned and its main street was named for Benjamin Franklin.

Hardly more than a small dot on the map, it was not really considered a town until the General Assembly chartered it thirty years later. Drawn to the site were builders, keepers of boardinghouses, merchants, and teachers, some of whom moved there from the eastern part of the state; others came from New England or even abroad. From its earliest days, Chapel Hill attracted people with broad interests and talents. As it slowly grew, it was recognized as a place with mixed attractions. It developed at the crossing of east-west and north-south roads, marked at first by deep ruts or puddles, dusty or muddy as the seasons passed. Nevertheless, during its first century and a half, the slow-growing town was at least accessible to those determined to go there. In letters home, students for more than two centuries progressed from quill pen to fountain pen to typewriter and ultimately to word processor to recount their delight (and occasional disgust) with what they discovered in Chapel Hill.

Although the setting was small, remote, and for the early years unattractive, the academic atmosphere, rare elsewhere in the region, was appealing to some students but even more so to adults. Members of the faculty and their families residing in Chapel Hill led the list of writers who added distinction to the village. The scarcity of textbooks in the early nineteenth century obliged them to become authors. Geologist Elisha Mitchell contributed articles to the *American Journal of Science and Arts* and prepared a geology textbook for his classes. The state employed him to compile geological surveys.

Mitchell's contemporary, Nicholas Marcellus Hentz, was professor of modern languages and belles-lettres. A Paris-trained miniaturist and entomologist, he wrote a textbook in his field and was America's first arachnologist; his masterwork in that field was *The Spiders of the United States*.

Professor Hentz's wife, Caroline Lee Whiting, like many Chapel Hill faculty wives who came after her, engaged in public work by teaching and writing to help support their family. Her short stories and novels were well received, and *Lovell's Folly*, published in 1833, is believed to have been the first novel to include North Carolinians as characters. Her writing also emphasized the role of women in molding the character of children and maintaining the stability of family life. Caroline Hentz also encouraged and taught the very gifted young slave George Moses Horton, whose poems were popular then and since.

Chapel Hill saw the birth and death of numerous newspapers, some of which were unique. *The Harbinger* in the 1830s proclaimed itself devoted to literature, science, and general intelligence. After it came a proposal to establish a literary paper called the *Columbian Repository*. Women as newspaper editors were not unknown, but they were rare enough to be noteworthy; Cornelia Phillips Spencer, whose advice was sought by politicians of the day, became editor of the *Chapel Hill Ledger* in 1879. In the twentieth century, the *Chapel Hill Weekly* was noted as much for its literary standards as for its news.

Individuals who added to the character of Chapel Hill have constantly appeared on the scene, generation

after generation. Edwin Wiley Fuller's *Sea-Gift,* the first novel set in part in Chapel Hill, appeared in 1873 and was long acclaimed by students at the university. Thomas Wolfe's Pulpit Hill, nearly a century later, was a thinly veiled version of Chapel Hill, recreated for the town's most famous treatment in *Look Homeward, Angel* (1929).

Chapel Hill, in the memory and the imagination of thousands of students, has woven a spell making them feel forever young. It remains in their mind just as it was when they first knew the place. This was true of those who were there even briefly. University archives, alumni records, and something in almost each issue of some newspaper in the state will bear witness to this lasting illusion.

William S. Powell

See also North Carolina, Literature of.

Raymond Staples, "The Town Remains, Seven Angels Look Homeward," *Carolina Magazine* (February 1940); Raymond Staples, "Chapel Hill Is 'Our Town' in Novels," *University of North Carolina Alumni Review* (March 1940); Jeaneane Williams, "Authors Write About Chapel Hill, The Fabric of Their Lives," and "More Authors Write About Chapel Hill, Even When They 'Change Their Skies,' " *University of North Carolina Alumni Review* (December 1980), (February 1981).

CHARLESTON, SOUTH CAROLINA

In southern literature, Charleston is perhaps best known as the city that produced Rhett Butler, an aristocratic city of grace and charm. Enormous wealth from the shipping trade (rice, indigo, cotton) and from slavery built a small but powerful economy during the colonial period. Planter and merchant families of good breeding and education, as well as an aesthetically beautiful landscape, created a hedonistic and sociable way of life and in turn made the city a cultural center. Charleston established the first public library in America, for example, in 1743, and as early as 1735 boasted a theater. By the late colonial period, in fact, Charleston was the undisputed theatrical center in the colonies, an important venue for scores of traveling actor troupes.

In the antebellum era, Charleston became the literary capital of the South. In addition to two newspapers, there were at least six successful magazines of regional and national repute, among them the *Southern*

Review, DeBow's Review, Russell's Magazine, and William Gilmore Simms's *Southern Quarterly Review* and *Magnolia.* Simms's twenty-five novels, or "romances," depict the South Carolina past and forecast the disorder and instability that were to come with the Civil War. Edgar Allan Poe was also acquainted with Charleston, having been stationed at Fort Moultrie on nearby Sullivan's Island for a brief time in 1827; three of his stories, "The Gold-Bug" (1843), "The Oblong Box" (1844), and "The Balloon Hoax" (1844) are set there.

The prominence of Charleston during the Civil War produced several important literary documents, such as Mary Boykin Chesnut's diary, a remarkable first-hand account of the Confederacy. The verse of Henry Timrod, poet laureate of the Confederacy, evokes the pathos of war and the tragic dignity of the common soldier. In the poetry of Paul Hamilton Hayne, southern nationalism likewise looms large. In the fallow period of Reconstruction, intellectual life in Charleston was virtually dormant, but in the early twentieth century, after enduring the agonies of war and defeat, Charlestonians began to turn inward and represent their lives imaginatively. Thus began a remarkably fertile period of painting, sculpting, etching, singing, and writing that in part helped spark the southern literary renascence.

In 1920 the Poetry Society of South Carolina was founded by John Bennett, Hervey Allen, and native son DuBose Heyward. It nurtured poetry writing and brought to the city a talented array of national poets, among them Robert Frost, Carl Sandburg, and others, and stimulated activity in the sister arts: a number of prominent white Charlestonians founded the Society for the Preservation of Spirituals; the Gibbes Art Gallery exhibited the work of resident etcher Alfred Hutty and watercolorist Alice Smith; and the city attracted the likes of Edward Hopper, Henry Botkin, and George Biddle, who painted scenes of low-country life.

But it was in literature that the city made its biggest strides: Bennett and Allen each produced fiction (*Madame Margot,* 1921; *Anthony Adverse,* 1933), as did many women writers, some of whom, such as the novelist Josephine Pinckney (*Three O'Clock Dinner,* 1945) and the poet Beatrice Witte Ravenel (*The Yemassee Lands,* 1969) went on to illustrious careers. Other writers included Ambrose Gonzales, Archibald Rutledge, Herbert Ravenel Sass, and DuBose Heyward's mother, Janie Screven Heyward, famous for her sketches and dialect poems celebrating the life of the sea-coast Negroes, the Gullahs.

Oddly for so elite a white culture, the city's greatest literary enterprise was the representation of African American life, and its most famous interpreter was Du-Bose Heyward: first in *Porgy* (1925), then in *Mamba's Daughters* (1929), and later in the folk opera *Porgy and Bess* (1935), all set in Charleston. Heyward presented an "exotic," primitive culture whose rich array of story and song—transmitted primarily through folk-tale and metaphor—captured the imagination of numerous writers, musicians, and painters and disseminated the imagery of the Carolina low country to a nation of readers and theater-goers.

Today the home of the arts festival Spoleto U.S.A., Charleston continues to attract artists of great renown and to produce talented writers, among them Josephine Humphrey, Brett Lott, and such near-neighbors as Dori Sanders, Ruthie Bolton, and Pat Conroy, all of whom have featured Charleston in their fiction.

James M. Hutchisson

See also African American Spirituals; *De Bow's Review*; Folk Art; Folklore; Folk Music; *Gone With the Wind*; *Porgy and Bess*; Race, Idea of; *Russell's Magazine*.

Walter J. Fraser, *Charleston! Charleston! The History of a Southern City* (1989); David Moltke-Hansen and Michael O'Brien, eds., *Intellectual Life in Antebellum Charleston* (1986); Curtis Worthington, ed., *Literary Charleston: A Lowcountry Reader* (1996).

CHARLOTTESVILLE, VIRGINIA

Founded in 1762, Charlottesville, Virginia, has long been one of the most important intellectual centers in the South. Its most famous resident, Thomas Jefferson, was an active, eloquent contributor to the country's revolutionary efforts and later its third president. The principal author of the Declaration of Independence, Jefferson was also a chronicler of his state. His sole book, *Notes on the State of Virginia,* testifies to his polyglot intellectual interests with observations touching, but by no means limited to, the natural sciences, religion, political science, and philosophy. Written throughout the 1780s at his home, Monticello, which is just south of the city's center, Jefferson's book continues to evoke intrigue and controversy.

Even more than his writings, however, another of

Thomas Jefferson's achievements links Charlottesville to the world of southern letters: his creation of the University of Virginia. Chartered in 1819, the university was intended to capture at once Jefferson's zest for learning and his own ideas of democratic opportunity. The state school was constructed in the underdeveloped western portion of Charlottesville, with Jefferson's Academical Village at its center. Edgar Allan Poe was a member of one of the first classes to attend the university.

Charlottesville's fate has mirrored that of its home institution. Throughout the nineteenth century, the university's reputation and regional importance grew, particularly during the period of sectional tensions preceding the Civil War. As the school came increasingly to be the educational site for the South's elite, Charlottesville, too, came to be regarded as a place of distinction, giving the school and the town a semblance of gentility once reserved solely for the Tidewater region.

Having received minimal damage during the Civil War, the town and its university continued to be a culturally influential site approaching the turn of the century. The fate of the two entities has grown even closer during the twentieth century. The expansions of both city and university brought the eastern and western portions of Charlottesville closer together until they finally ceased to possess identifiable borders. This union has spawned a raft of bookstores and film and literary festivals that have enhanced Charlottesville's cultural importance.

The reputation of the university and the beauty of the town have attracted the attention of writers and scholars alike. Whether for faculty appointments, conferences, speaking engagements, or to establish their homes, important figures in the field of southern letters have been drawn to Charlottesville. Some have come for one reason and remained for another. William Faulkner, who had visited Charlottesville in the 1930s, accepted a position as writer-in-residence at the university in 1956, in part to be near his daughter, Jill. It did not take long for Faulkner to decide to make Charlottesville his permanent residence—not because of his ties to the university so much as his love of the horse country and the people who inhabited it. Peter Taylor was another writer to come to Charlottesville and stay. Taylor joined the English department as a creative writing instructor in 1967.

Christopher Goodson

See also Jefferson, Thomas.

Philip Alexander Bruce, *History of the University of Virginia 1819–1919* (5 vols.; 1920); Virginius Dabney, *Mr. Jefferson's University: A History* (1981); Joel Williamson, *William Faulkner and Southern History* (1993).

CHATTEL SLAVERY

Chattel slavery developed in the British North American colonies and later in the United States as a unique form of bondage in which, by law, the master had absolute rights over the person and labor of the slave, who was "chattel," or personal property, to be used and moved as suited the master's interest. Although not exclusive to the plantation system that emerged in the staple-producing colonies and later came to dominate the antebellum South (small farmers, manufacturers, and others owned slaves, too), chattel slavery was almost synonymous with plantations in practice and in the public mind—so much so that the "peculiar institution," as slavery became known when it was the domain of southern states alone by the early nineteenth century, invariably conjured up images of broad acres and big house in print, song, and picture.

Early American (and southern) depictions of slavery were vague and incomplete, for chattel slavery was rarely the focus of poetry, drama, or story and more often served as a backdrop. Blacks as slaves, however, appeared as literary tropes and images in forms that would persist thereafter. The slave as savage, whether bestial, buffoonish, or noble, dotted the pages of early American accounts of "new world" life and became a fixture in southern writings by the late eighteenth century. In their own efforts to describe, and attain, an orderly society, colonial southern writers such as William Byrd II invariably contrasted their "English" manners and morals with those of the "savages" around them, who needed to be tamed or tempered and who could never be English. As these writers celebrated the plantation ideal, they also emphasized that the planters' "independency" hinged on the careful management of both their slaves and their crops.

Colonial American writers borrowed much from British literary forms and morality in assessing their new world. So it was in considering slavery as a subject. Most influential in that regard was Mrs. Aphra Behn's *Oroonoko: Or, The Royal Slave* (1688), about the sufferings of a kidnapped African prince in Surinam, which cast the royal slave as a noble savage and appealed to readers' sentimentality in condemning the psychological effects of enslavement. American authors echoed such themes in several works, such as Thomas Branagan's *Avenia* (1805), which depicted Africans, like American Indians, noble in their natural environment but defeated and wretched in servitude and incapable of living an ordered life. In contrast to white characters fortified by faith and freedom, the black slave became, in the words of one eighteenth-century poet, "a Man almost unman'd." And in early drama and blackface musical theater, the black slave as "Sambo" was often a fool.

Chattel slavery crippled progress and the soul as well as the slave. Eighteenth-century Enlightenment ideas about natural rights informed the work of several writers who essayed slavery's character. Most important was Thomas Jefferson's *Notes on the State of Virginia* (1787), in which Jefferson condemned the tyranny of slavery. But for Jefferson, as for other southern writers, the concern was more slavery's blight on whites than its effects on blacks. Chattel slavery degraded work, corrupted the master with too much power, and invited social chaos. Antislavery writers later grafted such indictments onto their own attacks on chattel slavery.

Jefferson and other writers also perpetuated stereotypes from earlier European travel accounts of supposed black mental inferiority and sexual prowess. As such, Jefferson warned, blacks could never be assimilated "without staining the blood" of whites and disrupting republican order. Therein lay the seeds of what grew into the proslavery apology in the nineteenth century, once shorn of suggestions that chattel slavery had made masters greedy and cruel. By emphasizing the differences between black and white, even when condemning chattel slavery as an institution, such writings as Jefferson's *Notes* fed fantasies and fears of miscegenation and portended racial conflict. In the popular imagination, chattel slavery became a world of shadows and secrets, a dark psychological, sexual, and social terrain that countless southern writers explored and exploited over the next two centuries.

Virginia writer George Tucker's *The Valley of Shenandoah* (1824), the first American novel to center its narrative on the plantation, introduced what became another staple in southern depictions of chattel slavery when he countered descriptions of a slave sale, slave resistance, and wasteful management with the story of the Virginia master as paternalistic and opposed to dividing slave families and his slaves as loving and respectful. Akin to renderings of black characters in James Fenimore Cooper's works, Tucker also presented the slave as comic relief. Also significant was John Pendleton Kennedy's *Swallow Barn* (1832), set on a James River, Virginia, plantation where faithful slaves served a genteel master amid a round of balls, jousting matches, and other romantic expressions of chivalry. Chattel slavery promised to make masters knights and women ladies.

But Tucker's suggestion that chattel slavery weighed heavily on the morality and economy of Virginia did not sit so well with southern readers by the 1830s. By then, northern abolitionists were blasting away at the hypocrisy of southern slaveholders who preached Christian duty and family unity while breaking up slave families, abusing their power, and corrupting every political and social institution with slavery's "hateful embrace." Politics ruled cultural expression during the antebellum era. Southern poets, short-story writers, and novelists abandoned even tentative criticisms of slavery and enlisted in the proslavery cause. In idealizing the southern social order, writers used novel, poem, song, stage, and history to present the plantation as the embodiment of a stable, moral society, with the loyal slave as footman to the paternalistic master. William A. Caruthers, John Pendleton Kennedy, William Gilmore Simms, and Nathaniel Beverley Tucker sacrificed narrative complexity to prove to the world that patriarchy and slavery undergirded the best possible social order. Indicative of the movement, poet William Grayson, in his "The Hireling and the Slave" (1851), contrasted the benign plantation where master and slave lived in reciprocal kindness and duty with the impersonal northern factory where hard-driving, grasping mill owners crushed their workers. Chattel slavery stood against modernizing, industrial capitalism as the bastion of republicanism and the realization of God's Edenic design, only now with a master's mansion over all.

Such images were galvanized in the southern response to Harriet Beecher Stowe's *Uncle Tom's Cabin* (1852), which portrayed chattel slavery as evil incarnate. In more than thirty "anti-Tom" novels and numerous similar short stories and poems published between 1852 and 1861, southern authors such as William Alexander Caruthers and Caroline Lee Hentz relied on "personal observation and recollection" to cast chattel slavery and plantation life in the mold of aristocratic chivalry made popular by Sir Walter Scott.

Black writers told a different tale. Until the nineteenth century, black southern voices on chattel slavery were heard in cries of protest such as freedom-seeking letters and petitions to legislatures during the Revolutionary era, song, and acts of rebellion. No published poetical or literary works came from black southern hands. The writings of slaves from New England and New York, especially Briton Hammon's *A Narrative of the Uncommon Sufferings* (1760), initiated the slave narrative form, and the slave Phillis Wheatley's poems mixed calls for obedience with ones for Christian redemption in questioning slavery, especially the African slave trade. But not until Olaudah Equiano's influential *The Interesting Narrative of the Life of Olaudah Equiano, or Gustavas Vassa, the African, written by Himself* (1789), an account of his capture and enslavement in Africa and subsequent life as a slave in Virginia and then a freeman in England and elsewhere, was southern chattel slavery observed from an African perspective.

Ex-slaves wrote or narrated over two hundred published slave narratives before the Civil War. The most important of these was Frederick Douglass's *Narrative of the Life of Frederick Douglass, an American Slave, Written by Himself* (1845), an immediate best-seller that went through numerous editions and was translated into several languages. In relating how chattel slavery dulled the human spirit, morality, and political economy of southerners, he also showed how "a slave became a man" by an act of will and by acquiring his own literary voice. In time, the fugitive-slave narratives became somewhat predictable and stylized, with the focus on the physical brutality of bondage and on the fugitive's escape, but they formed the marrow of African American literature with their emphasis on the slave's redemption through self-willed action. Self-pride and rebellion became the watchwords, as did the slaves' ability to "put on ole Massa" while taking the measure of their oppressors. African American novelists William Wells Brown, in *Clotel; or, The President's Daughter* (1853), and Martin Delany, in *Blake; or, The Huts of America* (1859), cast their first literary slave characters with such traits, while also introducing the figure of the "tragic octoroon" in tallying the costs of miscegenation, and poets such as Frances Ellen Watkins and James Whitfield found their heroes in Nat Turner and Joseph Cinque (of *Amistad* fame) and in the fugitive slave.

Southern wartime accounts of chattel slavery followed paths already charted by earlier writers. White southern writers served up romanticized clichés of gen-

teel planters and loyal slaves, often with special intensity as the real war tore old Dixie down. Augusta Jane Evans's paean to the Confederacy, *Macaria, or Altars of Sacrifice* (1864), enjoyed enormous success in part because it traded on that theme. Confederate popular literature and song turned to fictional slave characters to repudiate emancipation and speak for a return to the old ways. In reality, the slaves sang songs of crossing Jordan's River and joined the Union army. Chattel slavery was dead except in memory and fiction.

The moves toward sectional reconciliation during the late nineteenth century brought forth thousands of memoirs, histories, and stories in which the "plantation legend" held sway. National magazines such as *Scribner's* and *Lippincott's* capitalized on a mania for southern local-color writing by publishing supposed folktales from white-haired ex-slaves, speaking in dialect, who longed to be back in old Virginia and to sit at their master's knee. Joel Chandler Harris's Uncle Remus tales were the best known of the type. Even black writer Paul Laurence Dunbar, eager to hold a white audience, peopled his prose and poetry with faithful tale-telling retainers. Likewise, in numerous memoirs and potboilers recalling the Old South, chattel slavery lost any hint of brutality and chivalry ruled. "Happy darkies" abounded, with only outsiders providing the source of any unhappiness. John Esten Cooke, Thomas Nelson Page, and others glorified white southern manhood, the plantation system from which it sprang, and the Confederate soldier who fought and died for a noble cause.

Less benign were the works of white supremacists. Especially influential was Thomas Dixon, whose crude, but widely read, novels of the Old South, the war, and Reconstruction depicted blacks as beasts, or at least dupes, and warned of racial apocalypse. The romantic views of the Old South combined with Dixon's picture of impending doom to shape filmmaker D. W. Griffith's monumental *The Birth of a Nation* (1915), which fixed the image of blacks as happy slaves (and unhappy freedpeople) and whites as paternalistic masters for half a century. In the race-conscious America of the early twentieth century, chattel slavery had become a "civilizing" influence in much popular literature and film, while on the stage, the banjo-plucking, high-stepping happy slave survived as a stock figure.

Blacks demurred. Novelist Charles W. Chesnutt, in *The Conjure Woman* (1899) and several stories, subverted racial stereotypes and undercut the proslavery local-color fiction by creating his own plantation storyteller, Uncle Julius, who related tales of cruel masters and sly slaves capable of outwitting whites with spells and folk wisdom. By the 1920s, though, some black writers, such as Countee Cullen, Langston Hughes, Sterling Brown, and others in the "New Negro Movement," rejected the use of slave dialect, which they considered demeaning and false. They approached the slave experience straight on, using slaves' remembrances and family histories to instruct their own generation on the slaves' strength in enduring hardship, and they saw in the epic struggle against chattel slavery the inspiration to fight poverty and injustice in their own day. As the character Mingo in Arna Bontemps's novel *Black Thunder* (1936) declared, "You ain't free for true till all yo' kin people is free with you."

Other black writers turned to the slave-based oral tradition as vital to black culture. Among southern-born writers of the Harlem Renaissance, for example, Jean Toomer, in *Cane* (1923), drew on slave folktales, dialect, and music to reclaim for the children of slavery not only their own identities but also the South as "their place." Their "new Negro" was not to be the slave of white attitudes and literary uses. Thus, as in *Cane,* ordinary people rooted in the soil and soul of their own poetic rhythms of speech and song offer the promise of emotional release and freedom for blacks. Likewise, Zora Neale Hurston unabashedly employed dialect to let her black characters tell their stories their own way. The Federal Writers' Project collection of over two thousand ex-slave narratives during the 1930s added immeasurably to the stock of African American stories about bondage and, by the 1970s when many such narratives were published, made more credible and available in the academic world, and then among fiction writers, the slaves' side of chattel slavery.

Until recently, southern white writers were not much impressed by blacks' writings on slavery or anything, if they read them at all, and chattel slavery as literary subject found few takers in the early twentieth century. The Fugitives, for example, shunted chattel slavery to the margins of their consciousness as they unearthed a yeoman antebellum South. In much popular writing, the plantation legend prevailed into the 1950s, with chattel slavery implied rather than presented. The legend reached its apotheosis in Margaret Mitchell's enormously successful, Pulitzer Prize–winning *Gone With the Wind* (1936), which, recast in movie form, won an Academy Award for best picture in Hollywood and millions of fans worldwide. Mitch-

ell's vivid prose burned the plantation legend into the public mind. For her, chattel slavery was a mix of inept but jolly slaves and indulgent masters who somehow managed to provide for a liveried life of grand porticoes and grander balls. Still, Mitchell did not subscribe fully to proslavery notions of chattel slavery breeding the best people, for selfishness and impotence reigned along with nobility in her white characters, and, among her slave characters, Mammy was nobody's fool. The magical world of Tara all came crashing down with the war, though the ex-slaves stayed on to try to save their former masters amid Yankee perfidy and Republican misrule.

Virtually every plantation novel thereafter stood in the shadow of *Gone With the Wind,* though with sometimes very different social relations in the big house and slave quarters. Many pulp-fiction accounts perpetuated the stereotype of the slave as primitive, comical, and dependent and of the master class as made of finer stuff, if now eager to bed down with likely slaves. The Falconhurst series (1957–1983), which began with Kyle Onstott's *Mandingo* (1957), throbbed with interracial sex. Even a black writer, Georgia-born Frank Yerby, in his early popular fiction such as the best-selling *The Foxes of Harrow* (1946), adapted the form, if in part to mock it, filling his pages with uncouth, hot-blooded masters who lived in quarters "one cut above a dogtrot cabin" and with unassuming slaves who loved their masters and betrayed slave rebels.

But Mitchell hardly had the last word. As historians and photojournalists of the 1930s and 1940s emphasized a new realism and even acknowledged the perspectives of some black writers, so too white southern "realists" dropped the use of dialect and local-color stories and sought accurate renderings of the southern psyche, spirit, and social condition. Regarding chattel slavery, they emphasized the greed of planters rather than any noble cause. Money, not manners, made their men, who, like William Faulkner's rough-hewn Thomas Sutpen in *Absalom, Absalom!* (1936), bullied their way to power but "always smelled of his own dogs." Masters in such accounts were sometimes as brutish as the slaves, and the slaves sometimes smarter than their masters. And hints of miscegenation scented many stories. Echoes of Chesnutt's Uncle Julius were heard in Katherine Anne Porter's *The Leaning Tower and Other Stories* (1944), wherein her ex-slave storyteller terrified white listeners with grisly tales of bondage. Slave resistance appeared as understandable and even inevitable in several novels. In Robert Penn Warren's *Band of Angels* (1955), contrasting images of slaveholders as both ogres and decent folk and slaves as surly and savvy promised new readings of chattel slavery and a willingness to experiment with complexity of motive and character in the well-traveled plantation genre.

The most controversial southern white treatment of chattel slavery was William Styron's Pulitzer Prize–winning *The Confessions of Nat Turner* (1967), which came at a time of heightened racial tension and militant black pride. Styron's Turner was a masturbating rebel ambivalent about his own identity and disdainful of his fellow slaves, who were, in Turner's words, "snivelin' black toadeatin' white man's bootlickin' scum." On a lower scale of literary merit, Lonnie Coleman's potboiler *Beulah Land* (1973) created a sensation less for its ribaldry than for reverting to older racial stereotypes in depicting slaves as coarse and ignorant. Among black critics, a hue and cry went up against Styron's emasculation of their hero and the exploitation of racial stereotypes in popular fiction and film. To liberate slave characters from white authors, black writers drew on folklore, slave narratives, and contemporary Black Power ideas to discover slave characters who fought every indignity, took pride in their blackness, and showed the masters for the devils they were.

Resentful of white racism she experienced, Margaret Walker turned to oral history to suggest how the slaves' spirit and endurance foreshadowed black pride in the Civil Rights era. In *Jubilee* (1966), Walker used her grandmother's "harrowing tales" of Georgia slave life to present Vyry, a mulatto child of her master who never yielded to him in any way and found freedom in education and group solidarity. Ernest Gaines, in *The Autobiography of Miss Jane Pittman* (1971), further linked literature to personal history. And Alex Haley's *Roots* (1976), grounded in his family's oral tradition, as novel and then as television series provided the counterweight to Mitchell's and others' plantations of moonlight and magnolias by relating the horrors of the Atlantic slave trade, the brutality of the masters, and the many wrongs of bondage. The slaves became the keepers of their own history and identity and of America's moral compass. The focus shifted from the big house to the slave quarters and even to Africa, where Haley, and others, found the roots of black courage and the antidote to chattel slavery.

By the 1990s, southern writers had stripped any romantic gloss from the plantation legend and revealed the base metal of chattel slavery below. The reliance on African American oral traditions, and even a return to dialect, ensured a black voice in the literature, and stories of the physical flight from bondage while remaining trapped by the possibility of betrayal, as in Toni Morrison's *Beloved* (1987), reiterated African American themes dating back to the days of chattel slavery. Nobility was inverted from the old days, too, with black heroines and heroes leading the way to freedom and truth and white masters crippled by racism and their own past. In serious literary representations anyway, chattel slavery had been turned upside down.

Randall M. Miller

See also African American Folk Culture; African American Literature, Beginnings to 1919; African American Literature, 1919 to Present; Confederacy, Literature of the; Dialect Literature; Faithful Retainer; *Gone With the Wind*; Happy Darky; Harlem Renaissance; Miscegenation; Plantation; Plantation Fiction; Race, Idea of; Reconstruction; Slave Narrative.

Charles Davis and Henry Louis Gates Jr., eds., *The Slave's Narrative* (1985); Lucinda MacKethan, *The Dream of Arcady: Place and Time in Southern Literature* (1980); Rollin G. Osterweis, *Romanticism and Nationalism in the Old South* (1949); Werner Sollors, *Neither Black nor White Yet Both: Thematic Explorations of Interracial Literature* (1997); William R. Taylor, *Cavalier and Yankee: The Old South and American National Character* (1961); Susan J. Tracy, *In the Master's Eye: Representations of Women, Blacks, and Poor Whites in Antebellum Southern Literature* (1995); William L. Van Deburg, *Slavery & Race in American Popular Culture* (1984); Jean Fagan Yellin, *The Intricate Knot: Black Figures in American Literature, 1776–1863* (1972).

CHILDHOOD

Childhood, for southern writers, is the deep, dank, root-bound well of literary experience. Not only have they drawn on their southern infancies for fictional purposes; they have often drawn it into autobiography, casting early years into a good story for their audiences and also drawing for themselves a version of childhood artistically and personally comfortable. Eudora Welty's *One Writer's Beginnings* seems one high example of that carefully crafted early history, in which we see, and not quite see, how childhood creates her stories. Harry Crews's *A Childhood: The Biography of a Place* (1978) is another example of the connection between childhood and creativity.

Whether the theme comes in autobiographical or in

fictional form (and all the blurrings between), childhood as portrayed by southern writers comes in several significant versions. First, it is a rite of passage. Classic stories such as Faulkner's "The Bear" (1940) and "Barn Burning"(1950), Carson McCullers's *The Member of the Wedding* (1946), and Ralph Ellison's *Invisible Man* (1948) more or less violently bring characters to and through an event in order to bridge childhood innocence and the ruination of adolescent enlightenment. The standards of maturity offered to the young protagonists are designed by the community to ensure their social place in it; they can rise to the occasion and/or rise to much higher personal standards they find in themselves. The boy in "The Bear" idolizes his mentors and the power of nature they bring him to; the boy in "Barn Burning" chooses to deny his father's inheritance of meanness and spite. But Ellison's boy learns not only the despicable nature of the slavish fraternity into which he is expected so cruelly to be inducted but also his own ironic commission in it. He cannot run away; he will, in his own time, and in his own way, have to walk, very slowly and very deliberately, away.

The next grouping of childhood stories can be seen as revelation. Leading these is Welty's *Delta Wedding* (1946), a poignant vision of the necessary alienation of Laura McRaven, whose mother has died and who, because of that, knows many things, "the most intimate" being "that her age was nine." A child, finally, of great tolerance, she opens her arms wide to encompass all the idiosyncrasies of her southern place, time, and inheritance, learning earlier than most what it takes to accept where one comes from. Alice Walker's essay "Beauty: When the Other Dancer is the Self," from *In Search of Our Mothers' Gardens* (1983), is a good example of the extent to which an early childhood betrayal can cloud vision—literally as well as figuratively—for many years, until an experience with her own child vindicates it. Ernest Gaines in "The Sky Is Gray" (*Bloodline*, 1963) has his character James, the boy who must be a man before his time, come to see, through the dire circumstances of the immense poverty of his youth and the violence of family loyalty, where the lines we draw between each other blur into opportunities for understanding.

There are also comical obfuscations of the necessary traumas of growing up: Lewis Nordan's "A Hank of Hair, A Piece of Bone" (1988) rescues the traumatic discovery to a young boy of romance and sexual politics and remakes it into a fantasy of mystery, though it ceases to be amusing to him when it overlaps with the reality of his own parents' lives. Like Nordan's fictional anecdote, Russell Baker's autobiography *Growing Up* (1982) depicts the sometimes terrible tensions of his family, from historical, social, and personal strife to actual war, with the playfulness of the resigned naïf. Thus he manages to tame the ties that bind him to his past enough, at least, to see that past as a closable book we can read and re-read however far we have come from it and no matter how much it still threatens to haunt us.

There are also depictions, not at all comical but enduring, of the travesties of childhood. Alice Adams's title story in *Beautiful Girl* (1971) re-invents through the perspective of both mother and daughter the spoiled, charmed life of a southern belle and its unraveling. Ellen Gilchrist, in her title story from *Victory Over Japan* (1983), portrays the effect on a young girl of man's betrayal of childhood virtue. Some travesties, pictures of terrible childhood neglect and abuse, however, bring their young sufferers to self-sufficiency and independence, showing the resilience of not only childhood but memories of childhood: Walker's *The Color Purple* (1982), Kaye Gibbons's *Ellen Foster* (1987), and Dorothy Allison's *Bastard Out of Carolina* (1992).

To the southern writer, childhood—tortured, tamed, blessed or blasted—seems to be best defined by James Agee in what became the prologue to *A Death in the Family* (1957): "the time that I lived . . . so successfully disguised to myself as a child."

Rachel V. Mills

See also Family

CHILDREN'S LITERATURE

Literature for southern children begins with Bible stories. Southern children hear about Baby Moses in his basket of bullrushes long before they know what bullrushes are. They hear the story at the same age they are sung "Rockabye baby in the tree tops, when the wind blows the cradle will rock." Later, they memorize Bible verses and Psalms along with "The Swing" and "My Shadow" by Robert Louis Stevenson. "Little Orphan Annie" by James Whitcomb Riley, from the anthology *Poems Worth Knowing* (1909), standard stock in many households, was widely memorized.

In the rural South, *The Progressive Farmer,* a magazine started in 1886 by Colonel Leonidas L. Polk, a former Confederate officer and a farmer in Anson County, North Carolina, had a popular children's page. Most homes bought, or borrowed yearly, an *Old Farmer's Almanac* to check the signs before planting, harvesting crops, or canning. For fillers, the *Almanac* used jokes and vignettes, which were read and repeated, though not always appropriately, by all ages. And until about age ten, children came home every Sunday with printed cards of Bible stories, which were called "Sunday School papers."

Someone in the family, father, mother, or grandmother, usually read aloud books by Charles Dickens, Johann Wyss's *Swiss Family Robinson,* Lewis Carroll, or Mary Mapes Dodge's *Hans Brinker and the Silver Skates*. A favorite adventure book that rivaled these works was written by a minister from Liberty County, Georgia. *The Young Marooners* (1852) and its sequel, *The Marooners' Island,* were enormously popular in the United States and Europe, rivaling *Robinson Crusoe* as a sea-island adventure. Books about plantation life, such as *Diddie, Dumps and Tot* (1930) by Louise Clarke Pyknelle, a southern answer to Little Goody Two Shoes, were also widely read. Another favorite was *Two Little Confederates* (1931) by Thomas Nelson Page, a tale of two Virginia boys and their part in the Civil War.

Southern children read *Grimm's Fairy Tales* along with the stories of Moses and the burning bush, David defeating Goliath, and Noah building his ark. After Louisa May Alcott's *Little Women* was published in 1868, it became a national best-seller and one of the first books to feature a family of girls with an unconventional father who believed in educating daughters. Though the author was a New Englander, Alcott's books were as popular in the South as elsewhere.

Mark Twain's *Tom Sawyer* (1876) and *Huckleberry Finn* (1885) were favorites in the South, along with Joel Chandler Harris's *Uncle Remus: His Songs and Sayings* (1908). Harris's stories were read and retold around southern hearths from the big house to the tenant cabins. There, too, children heard ghost stories of the region, Indian lore, pirate stories, and tales of the lives of southern American heroes such as Daniel Boone and Davy Crockett, George Washington, Thomas Jefferson, Andrew Jackson, Robert E. Lee, and Jefferson Davis. Folk tales of simpletons and fools told through the generations in the Appalachians were later collected by author Richard Chase in several books called *The Jack Tales* (1943).

One of the late nineteenth century's most popular children's books on both sides of the Atlantic was Francis Hodgson Burnett's *Little Lord Fauntleroy* (1886), later dramatized and still later made into a highly admired film. Burnett was born in Manchester, England, but began her writing career after her family moved to Knoxville, Tennessee. Burnett became editor of *The Children's Magazine,* published in New York City, in 1907.

Mrs. Wiggs of the Cabbage Patch by Alice Hegan Rice was published in 1901 and quickly became a favorite. *Mrs. Wiggs* and its many sequels continued to be popular throughout the first half of the twentieth century. The stories deal humorously with plain southern folk but also perpetuate racist stereotypes of African Americans. Nonsouthern books such as those by A. A. Milne were read, along with Carl Sandburg's Abe Lincoln books, Rachel Field's *Hitty, Her First Hundred Years* (1929), and Laura Ingalls Wilder's *Little House on the Prairie* books throughout this period.

Laura Lee Hope set one of her popular syndicated series in the South. *The Bobsey Twins in the Land of Cotton* was published in 1942. Lois Lenski wrote and illustrated *Strawberry Girl* (1945), set in Florida, for her series of American books. James Boyd's historical novel *Drums,* illustrated by N. C. Wyeth, was published in 1928 and quickly became a classic.

A prized possession in southern households where printed material was scarce and treasured was the Sears, Roebuck catalogue, affectionately called "The Wish Book." "The Wish Book" was swapped with neighbors who had mail-order catalogues from Montgomery Ward or Spiegel. For many years, "The Wish Book" was printed in black and white with only a color cover. Outdated catalogues, when they were finally turned over to children, made coloring books or were cut up to make flimsy paper dolls that became, when acted out with dialogue and plot, whole families, communities, and congregations in various states of dress and undress.

James Street's dog stories, *The Biscuit Eater* (1941) and *Goodbye My Lady* (1954), were popular in the South, as elsewhere. And Marjorie Kinnan Rawlings's *The Yearling* (1938), set in Florida, about a foundling deer, was, and still is, widely read and loved.

Manly Wade Wellman in North Carolina published over eighty books for young people, some historical, such as *Rifles at Ramsour's Mill* (1961), some science fiction or folklore, such as *The Haunts of Drowning Creek* (1951). Nell Wise Wechter's *Taffy of Torpedo Junction,* about a Civil War heroine, published in

1957, was recently reprinted after only a short period out of print. Vera and Bill Clever authored many children's books, and their best-known work, *Where the Lilies Bloom* (1969), was made into a popular movie. Betsy Byers, who was born in Charlotte, North Carolina, has made a career of creating books for young readers. Her best-known book, *Summer of the Swans* (1970), won the Newberry Award. Gail Haley, also of Charlotte, has written and illustrated many children's books. *A Story, A Story* (1970), an African folktale, which Haley wrote and illustrated with woodcuts, won a Caldecott, the highest award in children's literature for art.

William Hooks, who was born in Bladen County, North Carolina, published over fifty books for children that range from retold and localized fairy tales, such as *Moss Gown* (1987) and *Snowbear Whittington* (1994), to picture books and easy readers. Set in Spruce Pine, North Carolina, where she was born, Gloria Houston's *The Year of the Perfect Christmas Tree* (1988) received a Caldecott Honor medal.

Wiley Folk St. John in Georgia wrote many mysteries for young readers. Doris Buchanan Smith's *The Taste of Blackberries* (1973) and Katherine Paterson's *Bridge to Terebithia* (1977) introduced death as a theme in books for children. Glen Rounds of Southern Pines, North Carolina, who was born in 1906, wrote and illustrated more than thirty-five books for children, including *Once We Had a Horse* (1996).

Belinda Hurmence, a New York editor who retired to Statesville, North Carolina, published several young-adult books, including *A Girl Called Boy* (1982). Mildred Taylor's *Roll of Thunder, Hear My Cry* (1976) won a Newberry Medal for its portrayal of a family facing race prejudice, reflecting her own family's trials in Jackson, Mississippi. Virginia Hamilton, an Ohio writer whose great-great-grandmother escaped from slavery in Virginia, was the first African American to win the Newberry Award (1974) and the first children's writer to receive a MacArthur fellowship. One of her best books, *The House of Dies Drear* (1970), is based on slave history, and another, *The People Could Fly* (1985), is a collection of African American folklore.

Two award-winning North Carolina writers of young-adult books are Suzanne Newton of Raleigh and Sue Ellen Bridgers of Sylva. Newton's prize-winning works include *An End to Perfect* (1986), *I Will Call It Georgie's Blues* (1983), and *M. V. Sexton Speaking* (1990). Bridger's works, often dark, include

All We Know of Heaven (1996) and *Home Before Dark* (1998). The Kentucky writer George Ella Lyon has captivated young children with *Ada's Pal* (1996), *Book* (1999), and *Cecil's Story* (1991), a Civil War tale.

Southern children may cut their teeth on the Bible, but they widen their taste for stories and reading with whatever their heights can reach in local libraries—libraries that are scattered and small and still struggling to catch up and keep up.

Ruth Moose

See also Sears Catalog.

Southern Life and Literature Culture Series No. 3, directed by Susan B. Riley for the George Peabody College for Teachers in Nashville, Tenn. (1946).

CITIES

The great southern urban novel has yet to be written, although most southerners now live in metropolitan areas. Writers often use the small-town and rural South as background for their stories. Part of the reason for this tendency is that readers have come to expect southerners to work in mills, live in trailers, hunt with their dogs, fish with their pals, and sport wardrobes contrived from flour sacks. The writers themselves often hail from these environments or are only a generation or so removed from them. In this sense, the South has changed more than southern literature has changed.

The persistent popularity of John Berendt's saga of Savannah society, *Midnight in the Garden of Good and Evil* (1994), is proof that urban hijinks and southern culture can coexist with both commercial and artistic success. Berendt's opus is nonfiction, or at least not a southern novel per se, although in the South the distinction between fiction and nonfiction is often indistinct.

Margaret Mitchell's classic *Gone With the Wind* (1936) is in part an urban novel. Generations of southerners have taken Mitchell's portrayal of Reconstruction as the gospel truth. In her defense, she avidly read what professional historians wrote about the period and their almost unanimous conclusion that Reconstruction was a horrible time of struggle and pain inflicted upon the white South by an overbearing and cruel North and uppity blacks. But what is often lost in the novel's enduring fame is the fact that although the war ruined Tara and doomed the plantation system and the institution of slavery that supported it, the fortunes of both Scarlett and the South were resurrected in Atlanta. Few writers have grasped the dynamism and pluck of that city and its residents in the years after the Civil War better than Mitchell.

When southern writers have deigned to comment about cities, their depictions often stress the rural or secluded parts of those places that serve as buffers from the harsh urban environment. This is not surprising, considering the rural origins of many southern urban inhabitants who often apply the habits and the culture of the countryside to cityscapes. The cultural boundaries between city and countryside in the South have always been indistinct. The characteristic southern urban settlement has been the small town, and as late as the 1940s, a majority of the region's urban residents lived in places of fewer than twenty thousand inhabitants.

Even in larger cities, citizens take great pains to soften the urban landscape; they also recreate rural institutions, including religion, music, food, and family visiting patterns, as much as geography will allow. While it may be difficult to distinguish Charlotte visually from, say, Indianapolis today, surface appearances deceive. Southern novelists often describe their cities in ways that chroniclers of a New York or Chicago would rarely consider. William Faulkner's early novel *Mosquitoes* (1927), for example, contains delightful passages on the lush flora of semitropical New Orleans. Even Atlanta in both Pat Conroy's *Prince of Tides* (1986) and Anne Rivers Siddons's *Peachtree Road* (1988) possesses islands of refuge to soften the hard edges of the city.

John Kennedy Toole in *A Confederacy of Dunces* (1980) casts a cynical eye toward these pastoral pretensions. Toole disengages New Orleans from natural romanticism, especially from the river: "Actually, the Mississippi River is a treacherous and sinister body of water whose eddies and currents yearly claim many lives. I have never known anyone who would even venture to stick his toe in its polluted brown waters, which seethe with sewage, industrial waste, and deadly insecticides." As for the other purported rural connections of New Orleans, Toole writes, "I have never seen cotton growing and have no desire to do so."

But Toole's candor is rarely repeated in southern literature. More likely are denunciations of encroaching urbanism. Thomas Wolfe's apoplectic comments on Asheville's willy-nilly urban renewal of the 1920s dem-

onstrate both that writer's proclivity toward excess and his distaste for the nouveau-riche newcomers who plotted the city's transformation from a sleepy mountain community to the hub of a resort region. In *You Can't Go Home Again* (1934), the protagonist, George Webber, returns to a fictional replica of Asheville for his aunt's funeral, only to plunge into deeper mourning at the death of his hometown. "A spirit of drunken waste and wild destructiveness was everywhere apparent," he observed. "The fairest places in the town were being mutilated at untold cost. In the center of town there had been a beautiful green hill, opulent with rich lawns and lordly trees, with beds of flowers and banks of honeysuckle, and on top of it there had been an immense, rambling, old wooden hotel. From its windows one could look out upon the vast panorama of mountain ranges in the smoky distance. It had been one of the pleasantest places in the town, but now it was gone. An army of men and shovels had advanced upon this beautiful green hill and had leveled it down to an ugly flat of clay, and had paved it with a desolate horror of white concrete." Parts of the town "looked like a battlefield, cratered and shell-torn with savage explosions of brick, cement, and harsh new stucco."

Anne Rivers Siddons similarly laments the destruction of her beloved Buckhead, an erstwhile Atlanta suburb annexed by the city in 1952 and engulfed by a wave of development in the 1960s. As the George Webber of a later generation, Sheppard Gibbs Bondurant has returned to Atlanta only to find his neighborhood besieged by a "river of automobile lights and the glare of neon." He concludes his eulogy, "While I was not looking, the city had beaten Buckhead."

Similar laments are featured in Peter LaSalle's book about boom and bust in Austin, Texas, *Strange Sunlight* (1984), and in William Faulkner's *Intruder in the Dust* (1948), where the Yoknapatawpha master regrets the raw, ugly suburban landscape that has reared up outside of Jefferson.

The sorrow reflects how characters experience changes in their environment as a personal loss, as the natural landscape succumbs to urban desecration. It's an old southern literary theme; one can almost see the Snopes family eagerly wiping out vestiges of Asheville's past or paving Buckhead. A newer materialistic South, while perhaps more egalitarian than the older version, has lost whatever virtues the ancien régime possessed and has not replaced them with anything virtuous. Anne Rivers Siddons's *Downtown* (1994), a novel set in dynamic Atlanta of the late 1960s and early 1970s, a time of tremendous growth and optimism in the city, underscores the moral decay and human vulnerability that the urban environment has encouraged. Siddons's novel harks back to the realist work of Theodore Dreiser, whose *Sister Carrie* (1900) depicted the urban environment as a morally destructive force. At least some of Siddons's characters transcend the urban mess, albeit not without a great deal of struggle and debris.

The southern city not only destroys traditional spaces and values, writers have noted, but civic leaders have erected an ersatz South in its place. What is worse than a vanishing region is an artificial re-creation. Amid contemporary Atlanta's sprawling metropolitan domain, the magic name of "Tara" affixes itself to dry cleaners, car washes, and a shopping center. Flannery O'Connor's story "The Artificial Nigger," about an elderly man and his grandson visiting Atlanta for the first time and their encounter with a lawn ornament popular in the 1950s, captures the artificiality of Atlanta's Old South re-creations. As the grandfather marvels, "They ain't got enough real ones here. They got to have an artificial one." Had O'Connor's characters stayed around a decade or so, they would have seen an equally incomprehensible site as John Portman attempted to re-create the great outdoors with the prototype Hyatt Regency Hotel in the 1960s. O'Connor summed up her attitude toward Atlanta by saying, "Get in, get it over with, and get out before dark."

Most writers have not seen the southern city as a complement to the larger southern culture but, rather, as antithetical to rural and small-town values. They have mistaken the southern city for an alien landscape when, in fact, whatever its physical and economic attributes, it has demonstrated a great ability to serve as a resilient repository for southern culture. But if city-bashing is a traditional southern literary device, it is also true that a handful of writers have dealt more positively with the urban environment. For all its mindless boosterism, the urban South represents a degree of liberation from the strictures of family, religion, and traditions while not necessarily casting aside those traditions entirely. Sometimes this liberation could be disorienting, but at other times it proved salutary.

The southern city represented a measure of freedom for southern women. Kate Chopin writes of the freedom of Edna Pontellier in New Orleans to choose to live apart from her husband and children and pursue her own desires, even to the point of suicide, in *The Awakening* (1899), and Margaret Mitchell, in *Gone With the Wind* (1936), gives Scarlett O'Hara the free-

dom to shed the restraints of plantation society on her gender and become a prosperous businesswoman in post–Civil War Atlanta. As Mitchell writes, "Scarlett had always liked Atlanta. . . . Like herself, the town was a mixture of the old and new in Georgia, in which the old often came off second best in its conflicts with the self-willed and vigorous new." Scarlett drew strength and determination from the city's rise from the ashes of defeat. Surrounded by the clamor of rebuilding on Peachtree Street, Scarlett silently roared encouragement to her adopted city and to herself as well: "They burned you and laid you flat. But they didn't lick you. They couldn't lick you. You'll grow back just as big and sassy as you used to be!"

Another woman character deriving inspiration from the city, instead of despair and anomie, is Lee Ann Deehart, who achieves liberation in Peter Taylor's story "The Old Forest." Taylor was one of the most sensitive portraitists of the urban South. Set in Memphis in the 1930s, his story turns on a minor automobile accident in Overton Park. Nat Ramsay, son of a prominent Memphis family, is driving his car on an icy day with Lee Ann seated next to him. Ramsay is betrothed to the equally well-connected Carolina Braxley. Unlike Lee Ann, both Nat and Caroline are bound by southern traditions of gender. Lee Ann and her single girlfriends have all come to Memphis from someplace else, from small towns and farms in Arkansas, Mississippi, and Tennessee. But in Memphis they have found jobs and a freedom from traditional southern society, especially from place and status. Taylor celebrates the rootlessness of southern urban life that so disturbed Faulkner and Wolfe.

Ironically, Lee Ann cannot totally free herself from southern expectations. The southern city is not yet unbound from the region, if it ever will be. She flees the scene of the accident through the old forest, itself a metaphor for freedom. The city that has helped Lee Ann become a more natural person (an irony in itself) enables her to survive the old forest and seclude herself with friends. It is Caroline who insists on finding Lee Ann. Caroline's reputation as a southern woman is at stake: a broken engagement and the potential rumor of her fiancé in the arms of another on the eve of their wedding would stain her reputation in the traditional society in which she resides. Caroline eventually finds Lee Ann living with her grandmother, the owner of a disreputable roadhouse across the river in Arkansas. Saving Nat from scandal had not, after all, compelled Lee Ann into flight; rather, the public discovery of her connection to a woman of dubious repute—her own grandmother—could damage her reputation, even in liberated Memphis. The city provided a cover for unconventional behavior, but in a crisis like Lee Ann's, southern conventions could resurface in force. Scarlett O'Hara's bittersweet career in Atlanta underscores this point as well. The city might defy regional traditions, but its more traditional residents, well schooled in those traditions, understand the limits of their freedom.

Taylor's writing on Memphis from the Great Depression to the 1980s reflects a change in southern urban literature that, in turn, indicates a maturation of urban life in the South. When Ellen Glasgow wrote *The Sheltered Life* (1932) and other novels about the faded aristocracy of Richmond, she portrayed that city as more of a decaying relic of Old South culture than as an environment that inspired change. Glasgow's turn-of-the-century Richmond, though infused with modern technology, seemed impervious to the new urban age. As the living shrine of the dead Confederacy, Richmond played a role as conservator of the past. By the 1930s and 1940s, the era of Taylor's "The Old Forest," the urban South had begun the process of transforming southerners and the South.

Memphis also plays a significant role in Richard Wright's *Black Boy* (1937), highlighting how the urban environment provided more options not only for women but for southern blacks as well, even in the confines of a segregated society. And just as southern cities proffered those options to women only up to a point, so too the liberation of blacks in the southern urban milieu was limited. If Memphis had shaken off the Old South ethos of Glasgow's Richmond, it had not yet assumed the culture of a newer South less encumbered by its past, nor would it until after the Civil Rights Movement a generation later. Wright recounted his move from Mississippi to Memphis and how he devoured the city's diversity and educational opportunities. At the same time, the city also reminded him of the humiliation of second-class citizenship. Lillian Smith, in *Killers of the Dream* (1949), noted the contrasts in city neighborhoods, churches, and schools that reminded blacks and whites of their respective positions in all aspects of southern society.

The urban South is perhaps the epitome of the changes that have occurred throughout the region since World War II. Perhaps the dearth of southern urban novels reflects the fact that the battle is already won (or lost), that modernism has triumphed over tradition, or

at least that what passes for southern is operational only in nostalgia.

When James Dickey's city boys venture into the wild in *Deliverance* (1970), the results are disastrous. The city becomes a refuge of numbing safety. Still, a distinctively southern soil may yet persist beneath the concrete; perhaps southern writers have yet to dig deep enough. Sociologist John Shelton Reed maintains that it is precisely metropolitan southerners who travel and read widely, who recognize the differences between North and South and who seek to accommodate regional traditions to a modern, postindustrial region without sacrificing either, who are the most faithful carriers of the southern cultural gene and more likely to mold a new South to their own image rather than that of others. In the 1920s and 1930s, when the Nashville Agrarians cast back to a halcyon southern era of rural landscapes and values, one of their number, Stark Young, expressed a less pessimistic view of impending urban and economic development in *I'll Take My Stand* (1930) that prefigured Reed's assertion: "We can accept the machine, but create our own attitude toward it." It is this struggle that is worthy of novelistic treatment, for it is the most common and most southern battle of the day.

Earlier twentieth-century southern writers have generally provided views of a region and a people in conflict with themselves, their past, and outsiders. They have explored the rural South, the small-town South, and even a bit about the big cities. In the last two decades of the century, contemporary southern writers have given readers more visions of the modern city and urban life. Cormac McCarthy's Knoxville in *Suttree* (1979), Ellen Gilchrist's and Walker Percy's New Orleans, Anne Tyler's Baltimore, Harry Crews's Jacksonville, and Josephine Humphreys's Charleston provide diverse and divergent views of the quality of metropolitan experience, southern-style. In 1998 Tom Wolfe took on modern Atlanta in the best-selling *A Man in Full*. But there is even more going on in the loose egg yolk that is the metropolitan South. Historians can cite statistics, quote anecdotes, and chronicle change. More southern literature needs to interpret what these findings mean for southerners and the South. The novels that probe this newest South remain largely unwritten.

David Goldfield

See also African American Literature, 1919 to Present; Asheville, North Carolina; Atlanta, Georgia; Birmingham, Alabama; Charleston, South Carolina; *Gone With the Wind*; Memphis, Tennessee; Mobile, Alabama; Nashville, Tennessee; New Orleans, Louisiana; Richmond, Virginia; Savannah, Georgia; Sunbelt; Town and Country.

Peter Applebome, *Dixie Rising* (1996); Blaine A. Brownell, *The Urban Ethos* (1975); Onita Estes-Hicks, "The Way We Were: Precious Memories of the Black Segregated South," *African American Review* 27 (Spring 1993); Leslie A. Field, ed., *Thomas Wolfe: Three Decades of Criticism* (1968); Sally and Robert Fitzgerald, eds., *Flannery O'Connor: Mystery and Manners* (1979); David Goldfield, *Cotton Fields and Skyscrapers: Southern City and Region, 1607–1980* (1989); David Goldfield, *Region, Race, and Cities: Interpreting the Urban South* (1997); Suzanne W. Jones, ed., *Growing Up in the South: An Anthology of Modern Southern Literature* (1991); Victor Kramer, ed., "Cultural Conflict in Contemporary Southern Fiction," *Studies in the Literary Imagination* 22.2 (Fall 1994); John Shelton Reed, *One South: An Ethnic Approach to Regional Culture* (1982); Christopher Silver and John V. Moeser, *The Separate City: Black Communities in the Urban South, 1940–1968* (1995); Stephen A. Smith, *Myth, Media, and the Southern Mind* (1985).

CIVIL RIGHTS MOVEMENT

After the federal government's mandated desegregation in the Reconstruction South ended in 1895 with the *Plessy v. Ferguson* case, the South quickly reverted to a racially divided, caste-based society. In 1910 the National Association for the Advancement of Colored People began to challenge Jim Crow laws through litigation. This organization's successes culminated in the 1954 *Brown v. Board of Education* decision, which deemed "separate but equal" racially segregated schools unconstitutional and set the stage for the civil rights movement.

The *Brown* decision antagonized whites determined to perpetuate the status quo. Congressmen from southern states presented their Southern Manifesto to Washington; Ku Klux Klan membership swelled; the (white) Citizens' Council was organized in Mississippi. In response to white intransigence, the NAACP rolls grew, Dr. Martin Luther King Jr. founded the Southern Christian Leadership Conference in 1957, and in 1960 Ella Baker helped organize students from southern colleges into the Student Nonviolent Coordinating Committee. Whereas the NAACP was dedicated to improving the lives of African Americans through legislation, the SCLC, SNCC, and similar organizations pledged themselves to public protest and nonviolent direct action.

For every mountaintop victory of the Civil Rights Movement there was a valley of backlash and violence. The initial triumph of the *Brown* decision triggered years of protest and mob violence at southern schools and universities; the court's "Black Monday" decision was also blamed for the murder of Emmett Till. The victory of the Montgomery bus boycott in 1956 was followed by the bombings of the homes of movement leaders. The sit-ins organized by SNCC in the early 1960s put demonstrators at the mercy of hecklers and police. The Freedom Riders were ambushed several times along their southern route, and their bus was firebombed. The landmark March on Washington in 1963 was both a reaction to attacks on activists and a spark igniting even more hostility. In the months preceding the march, a member of the Citizens' Council killed Medgar Evers, a NAACP leader in Mississippi, and Eugene "Bull" Connor, the Birmingham Public Safety Commissioner, turned attack dogs and fire hoses on demonstrators. A month after Dr. King's triumph in Washington, the Klan destroyed the Sixteenth Street Baptist Church in "Bombingham" with an explosion that killed four girls.

The 1964 Mississippi Summer Project, in which hundreds of college students from northern schools converged on Mississippi to participate in voter-registration drives, was steeped in violence. Activists Andrew Goodman, Michael Schwerner, and James Chaney were murdered at the beginning of the summer. The 1965 Voting Rights Act owed its passage in part to violence in Selma, Alabama. In March of that year, voting-rights demonstrators were attacked by state troopers on "Bloody Sunday" at the Edmund Pettus Bridge. Two weeks later, the demonstrators, led by Dr. King, were allowed to make their symbolic march to the state capital, but this victory was tarnished by the fatal Klan shooting of Viola Liuzzo, a volunteer who was driving march participants back to Selma.

Despite the South's massive resistance, civil rights activists had by 1965 achieved many of their goals. The federal government was supporting school desegregation, the Civil Rights Act of 1964 guaranteed equal employment opportunities, and the Twenty-fourth Amendment and the 1965 Voting Rights Act abolished poll taxes and other barriers preventing African Americans from registering to vote. Still, true equality was elusive, and civil rights leaders began advocating racial separatism and black power. The fury of the last years of the Civil Rights Movement—the assassinations of President Kennedy, Malcolm X, and Dr. King, and the riots in New York, New Jersey, Chicago, and in Watts—set the tone for the next phase of the struggle.

The Civil Rights Movement proper, dating from 1954 to 1965, is distinguished from the activism that preceded and followed it by its primarily southern setting, by the national support and sympathy given to King and other leaders, by the legislative gains made, and by the nonviolent philosophy guiding the protest. These ten years of intense media coverage disgraced the South and forced a reconfiguration of the region's social, legal, and economic systems not seen since the Civil War and Reconstruction.

Well-known southern voices such as William Faulkner, Katherine Anne Porter, and Eudora Welty were looked to for commentary on the outrages occurring in their region, but these writers and others of their generation persevered in exploring "the affairs of the human heart" rather than transcribing news events into fiction. In "Must the Novelist Crusade?" (*Atlantic*, 1965), Welty distinguished between the "novelist and the crusader who writes." The first creates works that are "as true at one time as at another," whereas the second writes stories that are only "the voice of the crowd . . . ephemeral." As if in evidence of this claim, Welty's topical stories "Where's the Voice Coming From?" and "The Demonstrators" have received little attention.

Flannery O'Connor, Carson McCullers, and Walker Percy incorporated Civil Rights Movement material into their later work, but the inclusion, as Percy once remarked, was "hardly essential." In "Everything That Rises Must Converge" (1965), O'Connor neither condemns outmoded race relations nor commends the new etiquette. The effects of the *Brown* decision are the foundation of the plot in McCullers's *Clock Without Hands* (1961), but the ensuing confusion merely provides a setting for her familiar themes of isolation and loneliness. In much the same way, the 1963 riots at Ole Miss provide a new context for Percy's absorption with modern existential crisis in *The Last Gentleman* (1966).

The movement more clearly influenced the younger generation of southern writers. It opened doors for new writers as publishers met the demand for novels about the South and the revolution taking place there. By the mid-1960s, the market abounded with stories of interracial love, racism, guilt, lynching, and corrupt politics in Dixie. A few novels—for example, Harper Lee's *To Kill a Mockingbird* (1961)—addressed the complexity of the region's race issues, but many others exploited social injustice in the South to create sensational and "ephemeral" stories.

The resistance to federal legislation by southern congressmen and governors aroused national public interest, and shady politics and interracial sex became common themes in novels set in the South after 1954. Borden Deal's trilogy *The Loser* (1964), *The Winner* (1964), and *The Advocate* (1968), Ben Haas's *Look Away, Look Away* (1964), and Larry King's *The One-Eyed Man* (1966) recreate the machinations of politicians ensnared by the issue of desegregation. Southern candidates often exploited their constituents' deep aversion to interracial relationships, and the politicization of miscegenation made this one of the South's most notorious issues. Though representations of interracial sexual intimacy had been previously limited to lurid works (such as Kyle Onstott's *Mandingo* and its paperback spin-offs), the Civil Rights Movement made the keystone of the caste system, the legal and social condemnation of interracial sexual relationships, a recurrent theme in southern literature. Lillian Smith's 1944 *Strange Fruit,* the story of a doomed love between an African American woman and a white man, was exceptional in sympathetically exploring cross-caste passion. Novels published in the 1950s and later freely probed such relationships. *The Voice at the Back Door* (1956) by Elizabeth Spencer, *Tiger in the Honeysuckle* (1965) by Elliot Chaze, *Of Love and Dust* (1967) by Ernest Gaines, *The Liberation of Lord Byron Jones* (1965) by Jesse Hill Ford, *Keepers of the House* (1964) by Shirley Ann Grau, *'Sippi* (1967) by John Oliver Killens, *Meridian* (1976) by Alice Walker, *The Rock Cried Out* (1979) by Ellen Douglas, and *And All Our Wounds Forgiven* (1994) by Julius Lester examine this strong taboo. The 1967 movie *Guess Who's Coming to Dinner?* reflects the fascination with the subject, but, in contrast to the movie's happy resolution, interracial relationships in most southern fiction end disastrously.

Literature by many white southerners has qualities of a confession; it tends to be critical of the South, sympathetic to the Civil Rights Movement, and often vexed by feelings of shame. In *Requiem for the Renascence: Black and White in Recent Southern Fiction* (1976), Walter Sullivan denounced the frequent characterization of African Americans as noble and whites as villains, a trend he attributed to an exorcism of white guilt and "a desire to do something for the Negro."

Sullivan limited his study to works of fiction, but

nonfiction by white southerners was also often accusatory and guilt-ridden. Journalists witnessed the violence of the movement, and some wrote emotional, confessional memoirs about their experiences. Ralph McGill's *The South and the Southerner* (1963), Willie Morris's *North Toward Home* (1967), Pat Watters's *Down to Now: Reflections on the Southern Civil Rights Movement* (1971), and Larry King's *Confessions of a White Racist* (1971) represent the emotional struggle of many southerners in the years of the movement. Southern journalists were also among the South's well-known critics: John Howard Griffin described his experiences on both sides of the color line in *Black Like Me* (1961), and Howell Raines recorded numerous interviews with civil rights activists in *My Soul Is Rested* (1977). William Bradford Huie's support for the movement is evident in his work, including his documentaries *Wolf Whistle and Other Stories* (1959), *Three Lives for Mississippi* (1965), and *He Slew the Dreamer: My Search with James Earl Ray for the Truth About the Murder of Martin Luther King* (1970). Following the Emmett Till murder trial, Huie tried to report the story objectively in "Wolf Whistle." In his novel *The Klansman* (1967), Huie dismantles the South's centuries-old stereotypes of the pure, frail white lady and the libidinous African American woman in a direct repudiation of Thomas Dixon's *The Clansman* (1905).

The South also had loyal native sons. In *A Cry of Absence* (1971), Madison Jones countered what he felt were simplifications and distortions of the South's problems by offering a sympathetic portrait of white southerners. The novel contends that the admirable values of the Old South should be allowed to temper the inimical qualities of the post-movement South.

While white writers were defending themselves and the South or resolving their guilt and disorientation (or merely catering to popular taste), African American writers were emerging jubilant and increasingly confident. Alex Haley's *Roots* (1976) made African American history, including slavery, a source of pride; Albert Murray celebrates the culture and music in *Train Whistle Guitar* (1974) and other novels. This regard for African American culture and increasing self-respect and self-assertion are also important in the nonfiction of civil rights activists. Eldridge Cleaver's angry *Soul on Ice* (1967), Anne Moody's *Coming of Age in Mississippi* (1968), Martin Luther King's "Letter from Birmingham Jail," and Maya Angelou's *Heart of a*

Woman (1981) are personal narratives of the fear, outrage, defeats, and victories in the civil rights era.

African American novels published in the wake of the movement generally trace the success of characters motivated by hope for a better future. John Oliver Killens's *'Sippi* (1967) opens with an elderly sharecropper renouncing his subservience to the white landowner, and it concludes with the same sharecropper's college-educated son taking an active role in civil rights work. Ernest Gaines incorporates this second emancipation in *The Autobiography of Miss Jane Pittman* (1971), which begins in slavery and ends with Miss Jane leading a group of protesters to a "whites only" water fountain. Two of Gaines's later novels, *In My Father's House* (1978) and *A Gathering of Old Men* (1983), explore changed relationships between members of the African American community and between the races in the post-movement South.

The best-known Civil Rights Movement play, which is based on the murder of Emmett Till and inspired by the murder of Medgar Evers, may be *Blues for Mr. Charlie* (1964) by northerner James Baldwin. *Blues* is representative of the anger of northern dramatists; although African Americans in the South also wrote in a civil rights genre, their plays usually support the nonviolence of Dr. King's protests. The protagonists of many plays are preachers similar in character to Dr. King, as in Randolph Edmonds's *Earth and Stars* (1946, revised 1961), Lofton Mitchell's *Land Beyond the River* (1952), and Ossie Davis's *Purlie Victorious* (1961). In *Contribution* (1969), Ted Shine reveals the teeth behind the nonviolent movement when an old woman describes how she has manipulated her invisibility as a domestic to strike a blow for civil rights by poisoning her white employers. African American theater has a long association with southern colleges. Edmonds, Mitchell, Davis, and Shine have all been strong promoters of drama programs at African American schools. The Free Southern Theater, established by SNCC in 1963, also owes its origins to African American colleges in the South.

Poetry inspired by the Civil Rights Movement was initially a genre of lamentation and outrage. Poetry by white writers Stephen Mooney (*News From the South*, 1966) and Andrew Hudgins continues in the vein of confession. Mooney denounces the violence in Birmingham and Selma and concludes in wonder that "still we call this foreign country home." Hudgins's poems "The Social Order" and "The Unpromised

Land: Montgomery, Alabama" recall the shame of witnessed racist incidents.

The most significant influences of the Civil Rights Movement on southern poetry, however, are again in African American literature. Margaret Walker, Gerald W. Barrax, and Julia Fields combined Western literary tradition with African American culture. In *Prophets for a New Day* (1970) and *This Is My Century* (1989), Margaret Walker expresses the hope and triumph engendered by the movement. Many African American southern poets dedicated creative effort to interpreting the violence in Birmingham, Selma, Mississippi, and elsewhere. In poems entitled "Birmingham," Walker and Fields create wasteland images of the South's most segregated city even as they express an affection for the South. African American poetry of the late 1960s gives voice to the militant Black Power movement. Etheridge Knight's *Poems from Prison* (1968) echoes the outrage of Cleaver's prison journey in *Soul on Ice*. Nikki Giovanni and Sonia Sanchez wrote in the vernacular of the inner city to express African American pride and anger, emotions represented in the titles of Giovanni's *Black Feeling, Black Talk* (1968) and *Black Judgement* (1969), and of Sanchez's *Homecoming* (1969) and *We a BaddDDD People* (1970).

Later in their careers, Giovanni, Sanchez, Walker, and other African American women from the South began writing more woman-centered social critiques, a shift that reflects the growing women's liberation movement of the 1970s. Giovanni published *My House: Poems* (1972); Sanchez's poems *Homegirls and Handgrenades* (1984) won the National Book Award. Among Maya Angelou's celebrations of African American womanhood are the well-known poems "Still I Rise" and "Phenomenal Woman." Novels like *Betsey Brown* (1985) by Ntozake Shange and *1959* (1991) by Thulani Davis incorporate events from the Civil Rights Movement to write coming-of-age stories about African American girls. Both novels describe the experiences of adolescent girls selected to attend all-white schools in the early days of school desegregation.

In her fiction and nonfiction, Alice Walker is Welty's "crusader," but Walker, who has struggled to understand the role of the revolutionary artist, finds that it is important for a writer to be the voice of the people. Her collection *Revolutionary Petunias and Other Poems* (1973, winner of the Lillian Smith Award in 1974 and nominated for the National Book Award), and her 1966 essay "The Civil Rights Movement: What Good Was It?" (winner of *The American Scholar*

essay contest) demonstrate Walker's belief in the power of activism to transform society and people. Her first novel, *The Third Life of Grange Copeland* (1970), ends with protest marches promising improvement in the African American community. Walker's partly autobiographical second novel, *Meridian* (1976), concerns the role of the artist and of women in revolution; it is as much a feminist ("womanist" is Walker's term) novel as a civil rights novel.

The role of women in southern society is a common theme in southern literature, but the confluence of the Civil Rights Movement and women's lib initiated a reexamination of the lives of southern women. Held to nearly Victorian standards of conduct, southern women began to feel their own oppression about the time African Americans were finally shedding theirs. (One of the obstacles to Meridian's self-knowledge is the curriculum of ladyhood forced on her at Saxon College.) Virginia Durr, in her autobiography *Outside the Magic Circle* (1985), comments that, after watching the civil rights struggle, women "began to realize that they weren't very well emancipated either."

In the 1970s and 1980s, southern women comprised the majority of novelists writing about the civil rights era, and they challenged the strictures of life in the South. Ellen Douglas's *The Rock Cried Out* (1979) undermines the rape complex by writing about the love of an African American man and a white woman, and Shirley Ann Grau's Pulitzer-winning *Keepers of the House* (1964) describes a white woman's dangerous defense of her father's marriage to an African American woman. Joan Williams's heroine in *County Woman* (1982), inspired by James Meredith's matriculation at Ole Miss, runs for elected office. Novels by women emphasize the changes that the Civil Rights Movement made in the domestic, rather than public, sphere. In *Can't Quit You, Baby* (1988), Douglas plumbs the intricate companionship of a sheltered white housewife and her black domestic. Altered relationships between African American domestics and their white employers during and after the civil rights era has been the subject of many stories, among them Anne Tyler's "The Geologist's Maid" and Mary Ward Brown's "Beyond New Forks."

Far from diminishing in interest, the Civil Rights Movement is a recurrent theme in contemporary southern fiction. In 1993, Lewis Nordan published *Wolf Whistle*, a novel based on the murder of Emmett Till. Popular novelist Anne Rivers Siddons reflects on the role of the movement in liberating southern belles in *Heartbreak Hotel* (1976), *Peachtree Road* (1988), and *Homeplace* (1987). John Grisham's *The Chamber* (1994) follows the death-row appeals of a white man convicted of a hate crime he committed thirty years before in Mississippi. Novelists Mark Childress (*Crazy in Alabama*, 1993), Bob Inman (*Old Dogs and Children*, 1991), and William Cobb (*A Walk Through Fire*, 1992) also return to the civil rights era in their stories.

Movies about the movement include *The Long Walk Home* (1991) about the Montgomery bus boycott; *Mississippi Burning* (1989) about the murder of Chaney, Schwerner, and Goodman; and Spike Lee's recent documentary on the Sixteenth Street Baptist Church bombing, *Four Little Girls* (1997). The movie version of Alfred Uhry's play *Driving Miss Daisy* (1988), which concerns the twin legacy of southern prejudice against African Americans and Jews, won the Oscar for Best Picture in 1989. Willie Morris produced *Ghosts of Mississippi* (1996), the story of the murder of Medgar Evers, and later published *The Ghosts of Medgar Evers* (1988) about making the movie.

Regina Dragoin

See also *Brown v. Board of Education;* Free Southern Theater; King, Martin Luther, Jr.; Ku Klux Klan; Miscegenation; NAACP; Race Relations; Segregation; Till, Emmett; Women's Movement.

James McBride Dabbs, *Civil Rights in Recent Southern Fiction* (1969); Melissa Walker, *Down from the Mountaintop: Black Women's Novels in the Wake of the Civil Rights Movement, 1966–1989* (1991).

CIVIL WAR

"The Civil War defined us as what we are," said southern historian and novelist Shelby Foote in Ken Burns's film series *The Civil War,* "and it opened us to being what we became—good and bad things. . . . It was the crossroads of our being." For the southern person of letters, especially, the Civil War was crucial. It was significant as a defeat, as "the lost cause"; it enforced the southerners' love of place; and it, together with the circumstances that caused it as well as the war's aftermath, formed the core of the "burden of the past in the present," in William Faulkner's words, that authors such as Faulkner and Robert Penn Warren developed so poignantly in their writings. Warren's Jack Burden in *All the King's Men* understands from reading the

journal of Civil War soldier Cass Mastern that "if you could not accept the past and its burden there was no future, for without one there cannot be the other." And as Warren says in *The Legacy of the Civil War: Meditations on the Centennial* (1961), "The Civil War is, for the American imagination, the great single event of our history. . . . It is an overwhelming and vital image of human, and national, experience. . . . It is the story of a crime of monstrous inhumanity, into which almost innocently men stumbled; . . . of a climax drenched with blood but with nobility gleaming ironically, and redeemingly, through the murk."

When asked why the South has produced so many good writers, Walker Percy replied simply, "Because we lost the war." From Mark Twain's perspective in *Life on the Mississippi* (1883), the war became "the great chief topic of conversation. . . . In the South, the war is what A.D. is elsewhere: they date from it." And they were as likely to call it the War of Northern Aggression or the War Between the States as the Civil War. Although Walt Whitman was no doubt correct in saying "the real war will never get in the books," there is connected in some degree or another with it a rich body of belles-lettres: fiction, poetry, and drama as well as nonfictional literary forms.

Southern fiction published during the war is generally sentimental in character and polemic in tone. Representative works are James Dabney McCabe's *The Aide-de-Camp; a Romance of the War* (1863), Alexander St. Clair Abrams's *The Trials of the Soldier's Wife: A Tale of the Second American Revolution* (1864), and Reverend Ebenezer Warren's *Nellie Norton; or Southern Slavery & The Bible—A Scriptural Refutation of the Principal Arguments Upon Which the Abolitionists Rely* (1864). The best of the Confederate novels is Augusta Jane Evans Wilson's *Macaria, or Altars of Sacrifice* (1864). Wilson drew on General P. G. T. Beauregard's account of the first Battle of Manassas to give a context to her story of a romance between a rich girl and a poor boy. Both battle and romance figure as well in Sallie Rochester Ford's *Raids and Romance of Morgan and His Men* (1864). According to his preface, "the wrongs, indignities, and outrages to which the Southern Union men have been subject" are fictionalized by Jeremiah Clemens, former U.S. senator from Alabama, in *Tobias Wilson, A Tale of the Great Rebellion* (1865).

There are also humorous responses to the war and events leading up to it. The most popular southern humorist was Charles H. Smith, who through his persona of a Georgia cracker named Bill Arp wrote a series of anecdotes bragging about the South and satirizing the North. In one sketch, he advises Mr. Lincoln not to cross Virginia rivers since the "Lee side of any shore is unhealthy to your population." Smith's wartime letters and sketches were collected and published in New York after the war in *Bill Arp, So Called: A Side Show of the Southern Side of the War* (1866). The comic figure Sut Lovingood, created by George Washington Harris, was a secessionist who also had advice for Mr. Lincoln to act as though "you haint sponsibil while onder a skeer." Mozis Addums, another fictive rednecked lout who reacted to the times, was created by George William Bagby.

The most important southern novels to appear soon after the war are *Surry of Eagle's-Nest: Or, The Memoirs of a Staff-Officer Serving in Virginia* (1866) and its sequel, *Mohun; Or, the Last Days of Lee and His Paladins* (1869), by John Esten Cooke. A lieutenant in Jeb Stuart's cavalry, Cooke was also a close companion of Stonewall Jackson and knew the war first-hand. Although Cooke exalted chivalry and emphasized romantic elements, he was aware that "battle is a stern, not a poetical affair." Also of note are *Cameron Hall, A Story of the Civil War* (1867) by Mary Ann Cruse, a Virginia-born schoolteacher of Huntsville, Alabama, and *Tiger-Lilies* (1867) by Sidney Lanier. Known more for his poetry, Lanier wrote this novel out of personal experience in battle and as a prisoner of war. Romantic in tone and reflecting Lanier's chivalric views, the novel nevertheless acknowledges that "the blood-red flower" of war was enormous and terrible.

Maria I. Johnston treated fictionally *The Siege of Vicksburg* (1869). Mary Noailles Murfree responded to the Civil War in her area of Murfreesboro, Tennessee, in *Where the Battle Was Fought* (1884). Presented hauntingly, the battle was fought at Fort Rosecrans, also named Fort Despair. This was followed by her second Civil War novel, *The Storm Centre* (1905), and three stories that connect with the war, "The Bushwhackers" (1899), "The Raid of the Guerrilla" (1909), and "The Lost Guidon" (1911). Eugene Jones Bacon's *Lyddy: A Tale of the Old South* (1898) shows the devastation that came to Liberty County, Georgia, during Sherman's march to the sea.

George Washington Cable brought to his first Civil War novel, *Dr. Sevier* (1885), knowledge from his experiences as a soldier of the Confederacy as well as his great familiarity with New Orleans, where the majority of the novel takes place. Writing with some detachment and with a desire to improve the South, Cable considers the Union cause to be just. Cable's subsequent Civil War novels were more romantic in mode: *The Cavalier* (1901) and *Kincaid's Battery* (1908). Joel Chandler Harris, also a widely read author of the time, wrote fictionally of the war in *A Little Union Scout* (1904) and *The Shadow Between His Shoulder-Blades* (1909), and produced five tales about the Confederate secret service in *On the Wing of Occasions: Being the Authorised Version of Certain Curious Episodes of the Late Civil War, Including the Hitherto Suppressed Narrative of the Kidnapping of President Lincoln* (1900).

Other perspectives by southerners not sympathetic with the Confederate cause are offered by African American writer Frances Ellen Watkins Harper and by Thomas Cooper De Leon, a white Unionist. Harper's *Iola Leroy; or, Shadows Uplifted* (1892) begins during the Civil War and affirms black heroism and nursing skills. De Leon, in *John Holden, Unionist: A Romance of the Days of Destruction and Reconstruction* (1893), fictionally presents the career of an Alabama mountain man, Unionist, and later scalawag. The novel's Confederate heroine, Jem Freeman, is the barely disguised fictional Emma Sansom, who rode for Nathan Bedford Forrest. De Leon portrays the pressures and animosities forcing the southern Unionist to become isolated.

Thomas Nelson Page nostalgically celebrated the Lost Cause in *Meh Lady: A Story of the War* (1893) and *Two Little Confederates* (1888), a story for children. In a typical mode of reconciling North and South, Page has a northern man marry a southern woman. Page also edited *The Old Virginia Gentleman, and Other Sketches* (1910) by George William Bagby, with stories pertaining to the war including, besides the title story, "John M. Daniel's Latch-Key" and "The Virginia Negro." Bagby's perspective on the Old South is similar to Page's.

Paul Laurence Dunbar, who was under Page's influence, wrote a story of war divisions in an Indiana town in *The Fanatics* (1901). Not technically a southerner (he was an Ohioan by birth), Dunbar brought to his writing the knowledge of his parents' experience as Kentucky slaves. This border state is the location of John Uri Lloyd's Civil War novel, *Warwick of the Knobs: A Story of Stringtown County, Kentucky* (1901).

Some of the prominent concerns of southern Civil War fiction into the twentieth century are admiration for the chivalric capacities and courage of southern soldiers; a strong sense of place, with affection for the southern community; disruption of stable family and social structures; loss of status; causes of the war; opposition to what was considered Puritan fanaticism in New England; the suppression of the South; defense of one's homeland, of liberty, and of states' rights; lament for the unrealized promises of what southerners considered their superior civilization; economic conflicts; antagonism of family members with contrary sympathies and involvement; military history; desolation and defeat; and reconciliation.

Reacting against the false and sentimental in southern writing, Ellen Glasgow writes out of a sense of blood and irony in *The Battle-ground* (1902). Molly Elliot Seawell writes realistically in *The Victory* (1906), as does Mary Johnston in *The Long Roll* (1911) and its sequel, *Cease Firing* (1912). The author of a couple of dozen popular historical romances, Johnston treats both battle action and a love affair in *The Long Roll*, featuring Stonewall Jackson and climaxing at the Battle of Chancellorsville. In *Cease Firing*, Johnston continues from the Siege of Vicksburg to the end of the war.

The Little Shepherd of Kingdom Come (1903) by John William Fox Jr. poignantly relates the tragic losses of the war as well as the reconciliation of divided kinsmen. Fox sets forth the view that "every man, on both sides, was right—who did his duty." James Lane Allen's *The Sword of Youth* (1915) is also set in Kentucky, with the hero, Joe Sumner, leaving the bluegrass area near the end of the war to fight for a cause given him by his elders, and after the war striving for unity and peace.

Known for his collaboration with D. W. Griffith to produce the film *The Birth of a Nation* (1915), which includes the Civil War, Thomas Dixon also wrote three novels featuring leaders central in the nation's conflict. *The Southerner* (1913) is a sympathetic novel about Abraham Lincoln, whom Dixon considered to be a southerner by upbringing and character. The novel includes detailed relationships of Lincoln with his generals and secretary of war. *The Victim* (1914) is a fictional life of Jefferson Davis and includes dealings of Davis with his generals. Finally, *The Man in Gray, A Romance of North and South* (1921) portrays Robert E. Lee during the war. In it, Dixon castigates the northern Puritan who "early learned to love the pleasure of hating."

The modern Civil War novel, according to Robert A. Lively in *Fiction Fights the Civil War* (1957), was born in the mid-1920s. A premier example of this kind of novel, which is historically realistic, psychologically valid, and devoid of glamour, is James Boyd's *Marching On* (1927). Boyd gives us inside views of the battles of Antietam and Chancellorsville and of a Federal prisoner-of-war compound. Boyd's poor-white hero, James Fraser, fights in Stonewall Jackson's Shenandoah Valley campaign and is taken prisoner. Although a North Carolinian, Boyd shows no strong allegiance for either side of the conflict but rather focuses on economic causes of the war. Another notable modern novel is Evelyn Scott's *The Wave* (1929). She brings together pieces such as letters and stream-of-consciousness fragments that "together form the history of the war like an overwhelming wave."

More often, novels from the late 1920s until today center on an individual or a family, with the war sometimes being peripheral to the action. For example, Thomas S. Stribling wrote a trilogy on the Vaiden family of Alabama, with the first entitled *The Forge* (1931), referring to the blacksmith's forge used by Jimmie Vaiden, the patriarch of the family. *Peter Ashley* (1932), the title of DuBose Heyward's story of Charleston during the Civil War, also emphasizes the person at the center of the story—a Harvard- and Oxford-educated young man with a poetic temperament who resists joining the Confederate forces.

Many important works about the Civil War came out during the 1930s. John Peale Bishop in *Many Thousands Gone* (1931) published short stories about the effects of the war in Virginia. Stark Young's *So Red the Rose* (1934) is a notable novel of life in Mississippi during the Civil War. (Also pertaining to the Civil War are his *Heaven Trees* [1926], *The Three Fountains* [1924], and *The Torches Flare* [1928].) Andrew Lytle, a fellow Agrarian, published *The Long Night* (1936), a dark tale of ongoing revenge by Pleasant McIvor for the death of his father, finally quenched through Pleasant's experiences in Confederate service. Hamilton Basso brought out *Beauregard: The Great Creole* (1933) and, later, *The Light Infantry Ball* (1959). The blockbuster novel of the 1930s, best known from the motion picture made from it, is *Gone With the Wind* (1936) by Margaret Mitchell. Everyone, it seems, knows about Scarlett O'Hara and her beloved Georgia plantation, Tara. Clifford Dowdey's *Bugles Blow No More* (1937), set mainly in Richmond, is praised by Lively as one of the best Civil War novels, as is Caroline Gordon's *None Shall Look Back* (1937). Set in the Kentucky-Tennessee area around Clarksville, Tennessee, Gordon's novel movingly and realistically portrays the tragedies of the war. The novelistically connected stories by William Faulkner in *The Unvanquished* (1938) are based in part on stories of his own family, replicating, for instance, his great-grandfather, William Clark Falkner, in the character of Colonel John Sartoris. Allen Tate not only wrote biographies of Stonewall Jackson and Jefferson Davis but fictionally treated the Civil War in *The Fathers* (1938), a story of guilt connected with divided kinsmen, the Buchans and Poseys.

William Faulkner is undoubtedly the foremost person who comes to mind in respect to the Civil War in the southern imagination. While *The Unvanquished* is his fullest novelistic treatment of the war, that conflict is connected with much that he wrote. In his semiautobiographical essay "Mississippi," Faulkner identifies with "the boy" whose imagination kept alive "the descendants of the Sartorises and De Spains and Compsons who had commanded the Manassas and Sharpsburg and Shiloh and Chickamauga regiments, and the McCaslins and Ewells and Holstons and Hogganbecks whose fathers and grandfathers had manned them." In *Go Down, Moses* (1942), Faulkner has Ike McCaslin lament that the proud and courageous southerners apparently "*can learn nothing save through suffering, remember nothing save when underlined in blood.*" Through Ike, Faulkner also marvels, "Who else could have declared a war against a power with ten times the area and a hundred times the men and a thousand times the resources, except men who could believe that all necessary to conduct a successful war was not acumen nor shrewdness nor politics nor diplomacy nor money nor even integrity and simple arithmetic but just love of land and courage." Yet carried to an extreme, the romantic views of the war reach the level of Gail Hightower's imaginings in *Light in August* (1932): "They rush past, forwardleaning in the saddles, with brandished arms, beneath whipping ribbons from slanted and eager lances; with tumult and soundless yelling they sweep past like a tide whose crest is jagged with the wild heads of horses and the brandished arms of men like the crater of the world in explosion. . . . It seems to him that he still hears them: the wild bugles and the clashing sabres and the dying thunder of hooves." Similarly bound to the past, Quentin in *Absalom, Absalom!* (1936) imagines that "he could actually see them: the ragged and starving troops without shoes, the gaunt powder-blackened faces looking back-

ward over tattered shoulders, the glaring eyes in which burned some indomitable desperation of undefeat."

Shelby Foote is another southerner whose name is intimately associated with the Civil War, most recently from his prominent role as commentator in Ken Burns's television series on the Civil War, and before that from his three-volume *The Civil War: A Narrative History* (1958, 1963, 1974) and his novels *Shiloh* (1952) and *Jordan County* (1954). In *Shiloh,* he provides perspectives of the battle from both the Union and Confederate sides. Frank Yerby is also a well-known southern writer whose many novels include *Captain Rebel* (1956), which deals with a New Orleans gambler who fights the Union blockade by running arms and supplies from England, and *Griffin's Way* (1962). And Robert Penn Warren, who is often associated with Faulkner in having a passionate interest in the war, wrote two novels dealing with the Civil War: *Band of Angels* (1955) and *Wilderness, A Tale of the Civil War* (1961). The latter, as its title suggests, treats battles in the wilderness of northeast Virginia in 1864.

Writing about the war continues up to the present. More recent novels by southerners include John William Corrington's *And Wait For Night* (1964); John Ehle Jr.'s *Time of Drums* (1970); Ernest J. Gaines's *The Autobiography of Miss Jane Pittman* (1971), which was also made into a well-received film; Jesse Hill Ford's *The Raider* (1975); Tom Wicker's *Unto This Hour* (1984), about Jackson's brigade; Rita Mae Brown's *High Hearts* (1986), about a woman who disguised herself as a man so she could join her soldier husband; David Madden's *Sharpshooter: A Novel of the Civil War* (1996); Donald McCaig's well-researched *Jacob's Ladder: A Story of Virginia During the War* (1998); and Charles Frazier's *Cold Mountain* (1997), about a soldier's return to the mountains of western North Carolina at the end of the Civil War.

Southern poetry written about the war was prolific, particularly in the 1860s. William Gilmore Simms collected some of the best poems in his *War Poetry of the South* (1866). He inscribed this work "to the women of the South," saying, "They have lost a cause, but they have made a triumph!" He affirms in his preface, "The mere facts in a history do not always, or often, indicate the true *animus* of the action. But, in poetry and song, the emotional nature is apt to declare itself without reserve." His collection begins with "Ethnogenesis" by Henry Timrod, one of the southern Civil War poems worthy to be preserved for its aesthetic qualities, and ends with A. J. Requier's "Ashes of Glory," following roughly the progress of the war. In addition to Timrod and Requier, the poets most represented are Paul Hamilton Hayne, James R. Randall, John R. Thompson, and Simms himself.

These southern poets continue to be considered the best of that era. Colonel Henry T. Thompson called Timrod the poet laureate of the Confederacy, and Hayne also has been called "the poet laureate of the South." Timrod's best poems are related to the war, including "A Cry to Arms," "The Unknown Dead," "Spring," "Charleston," and the "Ode" sung at the memorial exercises at Magnolia Cemetery on June 16, 1866. The "Ode" is especially noteworthy for its simple eloquence in memorializing the valor of the defeated Confederates. Representative poems by Hayne are "My Motherland," "Charleston at the Close of 1863," "Sesqui-Centennial Ode," "Charleston Centennial Poem," and "Bombardment of Vicksburg."

Randall's "Maryland, My Maryland," designed to rouse Maryland to the Confederate cause, gained great popularity as originally sung to "O Tannenbaum." Thompson, editor of the *Southern Literary Messenger,* wrote, among others, "Lee to the Rear" and "Music in Camp"—which relates an emotional response on both sides of the Rappahannock River to the playing of "Home, Sweet Home." Simms, an enthusiastic supporter of secession, wrote poems such as "Fort Wagner" and "Ode—'Do Ye Quail?'" The latter poem challenges: "To the breach, Carolinians!— / To the death for your sacred dominions!"

Father Abram Joseph Ryan, with his poem "The Conquered Banner," was known as the spokesman of the Lost Cause. The furthest-reaching poetry, however, was that put to music. Ironically, what might be considered the Confederate's national song, "Dixie," was written by northerner Daniel Decatur Emmett and was put to a minstrel tune attributed to Thomas and Ellen Snowden. Albert Pike, a product of Massachusetts who settled in Arkansas, adapted it for his "Dixie"—which includes the line, "For Dixie's land we take our stand." And Harry McCarthy's words were sung as "The Bonnie Blue Flag," concluding: "Hurrah! Hurrah! for Southern Rights hurrah! / Hurrah! for the Bonnie Blue Flag that bears a Single Star."

Other patriotic verse suggests its character by the titles: "'We Conquer or Die,'" by James Pierpont; "The Right Above the Wrong," by John W. Overall; "Melt the Bells," by F. Y. Rockett; "Virginia—Late but Sure!," by W. H. Holcombe; "The Battlefield of Manassas," by M. F. Bigney; "The Southron Mother's

Charge," by Thomas B. Hood; "The Cavaliers of Dixie," by Benjamin F. Porter; "The Strife of Brothers," by Joseph Tyrone Derry; and "The Dying Soldier," by James A. Mecklin. "The High Tide at Gettysburg" by Will Henry Thompson laments the failure of Pickett's charge ("The tattered standards of the South / Were shriveled at the cannon's mouth, / And all her hope were desolate") yet considers the outcome of the war as being determined by God. "The Bivouac of the Dead" by Theodore O'Hara, considered the elegy of the Civil War dead, initially was written to honor Kentuckians killed in the war with Mexico. Mary Ashley Townsend's poem, "A Georgia Volunteer," memorializes the "Unknown, unnamed, forgotten" volunteer. And Paul Laurence Dunbar reminds northern whites in "The Colored Soldiers" that these soldiers' "blood with yours commingling / Has made rich the Southern soil."

The Civil War continued to engage a number of twentieth-century southern poets. Robert Penn Warren in "Two Studies in Idealism: Short Survey of American and Human History" relates perspectives of two soldiers, Confederate and Federal, who kill and then are killed. Fellow Fugitive Donald Davidson in "Lee in the Mountains" wrote a long meditation on the Confederate leader's review of his life and ancestry. Another Fugitive, Allen Tate, wrote one of the best-known Civil War poems of this century, "Ode to the Confederate Dead," with its haunting reflection on loss in which the soldiers, like the leaves, "Flying, plunge and expire." Tennessee-born Randall Jarrell in "A Description of Some Confederate Soldiers" reflects on the ironies of once-vital soldiers now dead on a torn hillside. And James Dickey in "Hunting Civil War Relics at Nimblewill Creek" imagines that "The dead regroup, / The burst metals all in place, / The battle lines be drawn / Anew to include us / In Nimblewill."

The first original dramas produced in the southern Confederacy were *The Guerrillas; an Original Domestic Drama* (1862) by James D. McCabe Jr., and *The Confederate Vivandiere; or, The Battle of Leesburg, a Military Drama in Three Acts* (1862) by Joseph Hodgson. Two other representative dramas of the period are J. J. Delchamps's *Love's Ambuscade; or, The Sergeant's Stratagem, a War Drama* and W. D. Herrington's *The Captain's Bride, A Tale of the War* (1864). Joel Chandler Harris wrote a play he never finished entitled *Butler the Beast.* Other plays that might be mentioned are *The Tyrant of New Orleans* by Charles Smith Cheltnam, who was billed as "an ex-Confederate officer," and *Under the Southern Cross* by Christian Reid (Frances Christine Fisher Tiernan).

Three twentieth-century Civil War dramas of note are John Fox's *The Little Shepherd of Kingdom Come*, as dramatized by Eugene Walter (1912), and Paul Green's *Wilderness Road: A Symphonic Outdoor Drama* (1956) and *The Confederacy: A Symphonic Outdoor Drama Based on the Life of General Robert E. Lee* (1959).

There are several nonfictional narratives that have been praised for their literary merit. In this respect, Edmund Wilson in *Patriotic Gore: Studies in the Literature of the American Civil War* (1962) singles out the diaries of Kate Stone, Sarah Morgan, and Mary Chesnut. Stone's observations have been published as *Brokenburn: The Journal of Kate Stone* (1955), describing life during the war on a northern Louisiana plantation and in East Texas. Sarah Morgan Dawson's *A Confederate Girl's Diary* (1913) is an account of war years in Baton Rouge and New Orleans. Chesnut's literary portrait of the Confederacy is published as *Mary Chesnut's Civil War* (1981); an earlier version is entitled *A Diary from Dixie* (1905). Daniel Aaron in *The Unwritten War: American Writers and the Civil War* (1973) defines the literary character of Chesnut's diary. It abounds, he says, with "evocative description, turns of phrase, comic episodes, anecdotes, dramatic situations, conversational exchanges, trenchant comment, and down-to-earth realities conspicuously absent in the sappy fiction of her day and later, and it is filled with nostalgic sad, bitter, and funny Confederate scenes."

Also of literary merit are General Richard Taylor's vivid and engaging *Destruction and Reconstruction: Personal Experiences of the Late War* (1879); John Singleton Mosby's *War Reminiscences and Stuart Cavalry Campaigns* (1887); Mark Twain's "The Private History of a Campaign That Failed," published in *Century Magazine* in 1885 as a mainly humorous contribution to a series of reminiscences on "Battles and Leaders of the Civil War"; George Cary Eggleston's *A Rebel's Recollections* (1875); the letters of John Hampden Chamberlayne, *Ham Chamberlayne: Virginian*, ed. C. G. Chamberlayne (1932); John B. Jones's *A Rebel War Clerk's Diary* (1866); a two-volume biography of Jefferson Davis by his second wife, Varina Howell Davis, *Jefferson Davis, Ex-President of the Confederate States of America: A Memoir* (1890); Cornelia Phillips Spencer's *The Last Ninety Days of the War in North Carolina* (1866); Mary Ann Loughborough's *My Cave Life in Vicksburg, with Letters of Trial and Travel* (1864); Confederate spy Belle Boyd's memoirs, *Belle Boyd in Camp and Prison, Written by Herself* (1865); John Esten Cooke's *Wearing of the Gray; Being Personal Portraits, Scenes and Adventures of the War* (1867); Sam R. Watkins's *Co. Aytch* (1882), a vigorous and readable account with irrepressible humor; and Eliza Frances Andrews's *The War-time Journal of a Georgia Girl* (1908), which describes the devastation Sherman's army made in Georgia, as does Cornelia Jones Pond's *Recollections of a Southern Daughter* (1998).

Poet William Gilmore Simms employed literary talents in his account of the *Sack and Destruction of the City of Columbia, S.C.* (1865). He writes, "The schools of learning, the shops of art and trade, of invention and manufacture; shrines equally of religion, benevolence and industry; are all buried together in one congregated ruin. Humiliation spreads her ashes over our homes and garments, and the universal wreck exhibits only one common aspect of despair." Grace King in *Memories of a Southern Woman of Letters* (1932) writes about the war and claims "the past as our only possession."

The African American author of *Clotel* (1853), William Wells Brown, wrote a historical analysis entitled *The Negro in the American Rebellion: His Heroism and His Fidelity* (1867). Frederick Douglass in "Men of Color, To Arms!" which appeared in *Douglass' Monthly* in March, 1863, wrote a stirring call to arms: "to unchain against her foes her powerful black hand." And Alex Haley in *Roots: The Saga of an American Family* (1976) discusses the Civil War as seen through the eyes of black Americans brought to the New World in bondage.

Mark Twain in his reflections on southern responses to the Civil War, recorded in *Life on the Mississippi* (1876), noted "how intimately every individual was visited, in his own person, by that tremendous episode." Through the vast body of literary treatments of the war, we all continue to be visited by "that tremendous episode."

Richard D. Rust

See also Confederacy, Literature of the; Confederate Flag; Diaries, Civil War; Forrest, Nathan Bedford; Jackson, Stonewall; Lee, Robert E.; Lost Cause; Military Tradition; Odes to the Confederate Dead; Rebel; Rebel Yell; Sherman, William T.

Daniel Aaron, *The Unwritten War: American Writers and the Civil War* (1973); Esther Parker Ellinger, *The Southern War

Poetry of the Civil War (1918); Richard Barksdale Harwell, *Confederate Belles-Lettres: A Bibliography and a Finding List of the Fiction, Poetry, Drama, Songsters, and Miscellaneous Literature Published in the Confederate States of America* (1941); Richard Barksdale Harwell, *Songs of the Confederacy* (1951); Lois Hill, ed., *Poems and Songs of the Civil War* (1990); Robert A. Lively, *Fiction Fights the Civil War* (1957); David Madden and Peggy Bach, eds., *Classics of Civil War Fiction* (1991); Richard Marius, *The Columbia Book of Civil War Poetry* (1994); Albert J. Menendez, *Civil War Novels: An Annotated Bibliography* (1986); Frank Moore, *Songs and Ballads of the Southern People, 1861–1865* (1886); Ralph C. Most, *Civil War Fiction, 1890–1920* (1951); Richard Dilworth Rust, ed., *Glory and Pathos: Responses of Nineteenth-Century American Authors to the Civil War* (1970); Richard Schuster, *American Civil War Novels to 1880* (1978); Lewis P. Simpson, *Mind and the American Civil War: A Meditation on Lost Causes* (1989); J. Sherwood Weber, *The American War Novel Dealing with the Revolutionary and Civil Wars* (1947); Edmund Wilson, *Patriotic Gore: Studies in the Literature of the American Civil War* (1962); Steven E. Woodworth, ed., *The American Civil War: A Handbook of Literature and Research* (1996). The Wilmer Collection of Civil War Novels in the University of North Carolina's Rare Book Collection is the single most comprehensive source on this subject.

CIVIL WAR WEAPONRY

The Civil War was the first large-scale conflict fought with modern weapons of mass destruction. Commanders on both sides tragically underestimated the revolution in warfare wrought by the new rifled firearms.

Shock tactics could succeed before the Civil War because of the inaccuracy of smoothbore muskets, the standard arm of the infantry. Civil War armies, however, were equipped with rifled muzzleloaders fitted with a percussion cap, a technological advance that exploded a powder charge with greater reliability than the old flintlock system. The standard arm for Union soldiers was the .58-caliber Springfield and for most Confederates the .577-caliber Enfield rifle. What made these rifles both practical and devastating was the introduction in the 1850s of the minié ball, an elongated bullet with a soft, hollow base that expanded upon firing into the rifle's grooved barrel, thereby greatly increasing its range and accuracy. Rifles were deadly at the range of four hundred yards, some five times the killing field of smoothbores. Such a withering fire could be laid down that artillery gunners, although often equipped with new rifled cannon, could no longer close in for effective support of the advancing infantry.

The new rifles gave the defense an inherent advantage of three to one over attackers, and five to one if the defense was entrenched behind breastworks or supported by artillery. As a result, most battles produced mass slaughter with casualty rates of 20 percent and higher. Only one of eight frontal assaults succeeded in the Civil War. Still, most generals persisted in their outmoded tactics, formations, and battle plans.

In naval warfare, the technological revolution in warfare tended to favor the offense. Steam-driven and iron-clad gunboats provided Federal forces with the firepower and maneuverability needed to control the western rivers of the Confederacy, and those rivers in turn became avenues of invasion that turned the tide of the war in favor of the Union. New, heavier rifled guns enabled attacking Union fleets to batter the Confederacy's coastal defenses and seize its major ports. The Confederate navy responded with such technological innovations as the first operational submarine, underwater mines, and torpedo boats, but it could not match the vastly greater industrial resources that sustained and expanded the Union navy.

In addition to new weaponry, the Industrial Revolution also introduced the railroad and the telegraph to military operations in the Civil War, the first war of the industrial age. War now had become an increasingly mechanized struggle fought between huge armies supplied and coordinated by rail and telegraph lines. Before the Union ground its way to victory, some 650,000 war dead had piled up.

The best of war fiction recognized, as John Esten Cooke conceded in 1867, that "in modern war, when men are organized in masses and converted into insensate machines, there is really nothing heroic or romantic." Yet no classic of southern literature emerged from the war. Despite some fine poetry by Henry Timrod and glimpses of the war's horrors captured in Sidney Lanier's *Tiger-Lilies* (1867), much popular southern literature during and after the war consisted of diatribes against materialistic Yankees or the deification of gallant Confederate heroes. The novels of two southern women, Mary Johnston's *The Long Roll* (1911) and *Cease Firing* (1912) and Evelyn Scott's *The Wave* (1929), represent the wholesale slaughter attendant upon mechanized warfare with remarkable and vivid accuracy.

William L. Barney

See also Civil War.

Daniel Aaron, *The Unwritten War: American Writers and the Civil War* (1973); Edward Hagerman, *The American Civil War and the Origins of Modern Warfare* (1988).

CLASS

If one version of the American Dream is that of a class-less society, then southern literature from the antebellum period to the present has countered this egalitarian impulse with its exaggerated representations of class differences among southern whites. As a result of the stereotypes created in the plantation fiction and southwestern frontier humor of the antebellum period then perpetuated in later literature, the image of the South that exists in the popular imagination today is bifurcated along class lines into such familiar figures of contrast as the planter aristocrat and the poor white, the southern belle and the white-trash slattern, the dignified house slave or servant and the smiling Sambo, the patrician liberal lawyer and the pugilistic redneck. Even twentieth-century attempts to humanize the image of the poor white, for example, have in many cases left the stereotypes intact while merely asking readers to view members of this class of southerners as either victims of larger social forces beyond their control, on the one hand, or as comic bumpkins lacking any semblance of restraint, on the other. One of the many ironies at play in the development of southern fiction has been the conspicuously minor role played in that literature by the yeomanry and middle class, by far the largest class of southerners.

Considering the economic, political, and intellectual dominance of the planter aristocracy in the Old South, it is not surprising that members of this particular class would figure prominently and favorably in the literature of the period, nor is it surprising that the lowest class of southerners would be used as foils against which the natural ascendency of the planter elite would become manifest. The existence of slavery in the Old South complicated class relationships, allowing poor whites to enjoy a full degree of racial privilege that likely served to diffuse—or at least postpone—political friction between upper- and lower-class whites. In addition, criticism from northern abolitionists motivated privileged southern writers to represent the South as a squirearchy in which each class possessed attributes that made existing disparities of wealth and prestige among whites to appear natural, inevitable, and desirable. As early as 1728, in his *History of the Dividing Line* (published in 1841), the decidedly aristocratic William Byrd of Westover describes the "lubberlanders" whom his party encounters in the North Carolina backwoods as an indolent, ignorant, and dishonest class of settlers whose proximity to the wilderness has resulted in a degeneration into savagery. In the plantation-novel tradition that arose in the 1820s and 1830s, John Pendleton Kennedy, George Tucker, and other writers depicted the southern planter as essentially paternalistic in his concern for his social inferiors, while in general continuing to represent the poor white as an object of pity or ridicule. At around the same time, southwestern frontier humorists such as Augustus Baldwin Longstreet, George Washington Harris, and Johnson Jones Hooper observed from the perspective of the amused aristocrat the colorful misbehavior and propensity toward violence and chicanery of lower-class figures. Meanwhile, runaway slaves began to publish their accounts of bondage in the South in which class relations were often examined. One former slave, Harriet Jacobs, observed astutely in *Incidents in the Life of a Slave Girl* (1861) that the poor white vigilantes who had ransacked her grandmother's home in search of evidence of slave-revolt conspiracies "exulted in such a chance to exercise a little brief authority . . . not reflecting that the power which trampled on the colored people also kept themselves in poverty, ignorance, and moral degradation."

In the later decades of the nineteenth century, local-colorists such as Thomas Nelson Page, Joel Chandler Harris, George Washington Cable, Charles W. Chesnutt, and Kate Chopin would continue to draw on the stock images of lower- and higher-class southerners that had been established in the plantation fiction and southwestern humor of the antebellum years, though Cable and Chesnutt, especially, introduced a degree of criticism in their depictions of the planter. Drawing upon the southwestern humorists in his negative depiction of Pap Finn and other poor whites, Mark Twain also subjected the upper-class southerner to his scorn, as in his depiction of the feuding Shepherdsons and Grangerfords in *Adventures of Huckleberry Finn* (1885). Nevertheless, it would not be until the Southern Renascence that southern writers would explore in great detail the relations between the classes in the South.

During the Renascence, southern class relations came to be examined in increasingly realistic and complex ways, even as some writers, notably Margaret Mitchell and Erskine Caldwell, produced best-sellers that perpetuated romanticized notions of a genteel Old South aristocracy, on the one hand, or lurid stereotypes of morally lax, imbecilic poor whites, on the other. In Faulkner's literary cosmos, the families that had held large numbers of slaves (e.g., the Compsons, Sartorises, and McCaslins) seemed to be doomed in the twentieth century to genteel poverty, ineffectuality, and madness, while families such as the Snopeses, who had once been a part of the poor-white class, are in ascendency. Thomas Sutpen, trying to buy his way to gentility, receives the scornful judgment of Rosa Coldfield: "He wasn't even a gentleman." Yet Faulkner also took care to populate his fiction with yeoman farmers like the McCallums and Armstids, who lived their lives close to nature in simplicity and humility.

As labor unrest among textile workers and tenant farmers became common across the South, writers such as Olive Dargan, James Agee, Erskine Caldwell, and Elizabeth Roberts turned their attention to the plight of the working poor and the yeoman farmer. For instance, portions of Dargan's *Call Home the Heart* (1932), written under the pseudonym of Fielding Burke, are set during the bloody strikes in Gastonia, North Carolina, and Agee and photographer Walker Evans exposed in *Let Us Now Praise Famous Men* (1941) the hardships endured by tenant farmers in Alabama. In recent years, writers from lower-class backgrounds, such as Harry Crews, Will D. Campbell, Kaye Gibbons, Larry Brown, Dorothy Allison, and Tim McLaurin, have begun to tell about the South from their own perspectives, thus adding a degree of realism to the collective literary portrait of class relations in the region.

James H. Watkins

See also Aristocracy; Belle; Caste; Cavalier; Gentleman; Lady; Poor White; Proletarian Novel; Yeoman.

Duane Carr, *A Question of Class: The Redneck Stereotype in Southern Fiction* (1996); J. Wayne Flynt, *Dixie's Forgotten People: The South's Poor Whites* (1979); Shields McIlwaine, *The Southern Poor White from Lubberland to Tobacco Road* (1939); John Shelton Reed, *Southern Folk, Plain and Fancy: Native White Social Types* (1986); William R. Taylor, *Cavalier and Yankee: The Old South and American National Character* (1961).

CLERGY

In southern life and literature, a clergyman is a person, black or white, who leads a formal Protestant denomination or an Episcopal or Roman Catholic parish. Considered an obsolescent term today, *clergyman* is slowly being replaced by *clergy, pastor,* and *minister.*

In the Episcopal Church, a woman priest may use the term *mother,* but the terms *clergywoman* and *clergyperson,* while used occasionally, have not found much acceptance among the general population. In the literature of the South, a clergyman clearly differs from a preacher in level of education, in the use of church ritual, and in the type of sermon he is likely to deliver. The sermon of a clergyman is generally reserved, formal, and literate, in contrast to a preacher's spontaneous emotional outpouring. Southern writers portray the clergyman as an intellectual given to philosophical speculations, whereas the preacher is seen as a person more in touch with the emotional side of the human experience.

While the South is sometimes considered synonymous with the Bible Belt, such was not the case when the South was formed during the colonial period and the early days of the Republic. Before the American Revolution, most white southerners who held church affiliation belonged to the Church of England, and after the break with the mother country, white southerners remained Anglican in the American Episcopal Church at least until the Second Great Awakening (or the Great Revival, 1798–1805), when a wave of religious fervor made Protestant fundamentalism with its energetic preachers and emotional sermons the dominant religion in the region. Initially in the literature of the South, the distinction between the Episcopal churches (plus a few Roman Catholic ones) and the fundamentalist churches was a matter of class based on wealth and education. Since the wealthy planters were influenced by the Church of England and its Episcopal successor, poor whites and African American slaves found the informal sectarian religion attractive. Later, as sectarian churches became more denominational, the distinction between the Episcopalian/Catholics and the High-Church Protestants became blurred as the race and class differences tended to fade with the passage of time.

As a result of this broad development in the churches in the South, the Anglican/Episcopalian denomination has exerted an influence over southern culture greater than its size might suggest. Thus, southern writers chose the Anglican/Episcopalian priest as the clergyman most likely to move comfortably among the aristocratic planters. In the novel with the earliest example of an Episcopalian clergyman, George Tucker's *The Valley of Shenandoah; or Memories of the Graysons* (1824), the minister is greatly admired by the cream of Old Virginia society. Parson Chub, an ineffective man of God but a charmer nonetheless, attends to the whims of an aristocratic family in John Pendleton Kennedy's *Swallow Barn, or A Sojourn in the Old Dominion* (1832), considered the first plantation romance. In 1855 Caroline Lee Hentz developed in her romance *Robert Graham* a central character as a plantation owner who responds to a call from God to become an Episcopalian missionary. Thomas Nelson Page, in *Red Rock* (1898), includes an Episcopalian, the Reverend Mr. Langstaff, to serve the gentry of a Virginia parish. After the turn of the century, George Cary Eggleston's romance *Dorothy South* (1902) pays tribute to an Episcopalian clergyman who serves the ladies and gentlemen in the plantation society of the Old South.

Although southern writers of the twentieth century are more likely to prefer the dramatic gestures of the pulpit-pounding preachers to the more sedate meditations of the clergymen, several authors have found continued literary possibilities among the priesthood of the Roman Catholic and Episcopal churches. Thomas Wolfe's "In the Park" (1935) finds two quaint but cheerful Catholic priests full of lively wit and fun-loving manners, Father Dolan and Father Chris O'Rourke, joining the narrator and her father on their late-night rambles through New York City. Flannery O'Connor, a Catholic writer well known for her many comic and gothic portrayals of fundamentalist preachers, on rare occasion introduces a clergyman, usually a Catholic priest such as Father Flynn in "The Displaced Person" (1954), who admires peacocks as the promise of the return of Christ and ministers to the Guizacs, the war-refugee Polish family on Mrs. McIntyre's Georgia farm.

Other writers, however, have chosen the failed or troubled priest as the clergyman best suited to explore the aridity and spiritual wasteland they discover in twentieth-century society. William Styron's *Lie Down in Darkness* (1952) gives us the Reverend Carey Carr as Helen Loftis's ineffectual minister who is unable to prevent her slide into despair after the death of her handicapped daughter. In Tennessee Williams's *The Night of the Iguana* (1961), T. Lawrence Shannon is a near-classic example of the whiskey priest, an ordained Episcopal cleric who has been defrocked for heresy and fornication and whose struggle for control over his addictions is the center of the whole play.

The southern writer who has found the greatest possibilities for the character of the clergyman is the Catholic novelist Walker Percy. A broad spectrum of Catholic priests, both good and bad, inhabit his novels, which explore the seductive power of science with the attending loss of faith in the modern world. A dissident Catholic priest works as an absurdist clinician at the Love Clinic in *Love in the Ruins* (1971). In *The Second Coming* (1980), Father Weatherbee and the nursing-home chaplain, Jack Curl, participate in meaningful ways in the plot. In two novels, *Lancelot* (1977) and *The Thanatos Syndrome* (1987), priests are major characters central to the understanding of the basic spiritual issues under investigation. In *Lancelot*, the failed priest Percival, acting initially as Lancelot's father confessor, discovers that he must struggle for his own redemption. Through an ironic reversal, the troubled Lancelot helps Percival save himself by accepting a small pastorate in a rural community. At the heart of Percy's attack on twentieth-century genocide in *The Thanatos Syndrome* is Father Rinaldo Smith's inset narrative called "Father Smith's Confession," which stands as the most provocative section in the novel by equating abortion with the Nazi programs for killing massive numbers of human beings. The most highly developed clergyman in Percy's novels, Father Smith leads the Christian forces against modern science with its misdirected designs to create a Brave New World, one in which human beings would be denied free will. Thus, clergymen, in these and other modern novels, are frequently employed by the modern southern writer who wishes to explore the abiding philosophical concerns that engage the human spirit.

Harold Woodell

See also Aristocracy; Bible Belt; British-American Culture; Class; Episcopalians; Novel, 1820 to 1865; Plantation Fiction; Preaching; Roman Catholics; Sermons.

Samuel Hill, *Southern Churches in Crisis* (1967); E. Brooks Holifield, *The Gentlemen Theologians: American Theology in Southern Culture, 1795–1860* (1978); Charles H. Lippy and Peter Williams, eds., *Encyclopedia of the American Religious Experience* (1988); Charles D. Rota, "Rhetorical Irony and Modern American Fiction: The Clergy in the Novels of William Faulkner, Flannery O'Connor, and John Updike" (Ph.D. Diss., Southern Illinois University, 1993); Charles R. Wilson, ed., *Religion in the South* (1985); Charles H. Woodell, "The Preacher in Nineteenth Century Southern Fiction" (Ph.D. Diss., University of North Carolina–Chapel Hill, 1974).

CLINTON, WILLIAM JEFFERSON

When in 1993 Bill Clinton (1946–) invited the African American poet Maya Angelou to read at his first inauguration, he consciously mimicked his hero, John F. Kennedy, who had invited Robert Frost to read on such an occasion thirty-two years before. In Angelou were met many of the themes of Clinton's own life: a troubled youth spent in Arkansas, enormous intellectual and professional accomplishment, and deep commitment to civil rights. "On the Pulse of Morning," a long poem tracing America's history from the age of the mastodons to the very day of Clinton's inauguration, generated excitement among listeners, some of whom took it as a sign of a cultural, as well as a political, renaissance in the country. By 1997, when Miller Williams, a white professor from the University of Arkansas, read his poem "Of History and Hope" at Clinton's second inauguration, that excitement had largely died down. And in 1998, the association that would most readily be made between the president and poetry was keyed to *Leaves of Grass,* a book Clinton was said to have given Monica Lewinsky, the central figure in a sex scandal that led to his impeachment.

It is probably fair to say that the poems by Angelou and Williams show, on paper, varying strains of the typical requirements of the occasional poem; and that they depended upon the context of their first live readings for their best effects. Similarly, much of what might qualify as Clinton's literary output was trimmed, by staffers and ghostwriters, to fit political circumstance. Clinton produced two books—*Putting People First: How We Can All Change America* (1992), coauthored with vice-presidential candidate Al Gore, and *Between Hope and History: Meeting America's Challenges for the 21st Century* (1996)—timed for his presidential campaigns. These statements of economic and social policy address Clinton's consistent and popular themes—opportunity, responsibility, community—but they are filled with the bland platitudes ("If we are driven by our vision of a better future, we will achieve it," "We know that when we stay true to our values and work together, America always wins") that require the expert campaigner's performance to spark them. Clinton's oratory, whether in the style of a stump speech, formal address, or Baptist sermon, usually succeeded because of his ability to connect with each audience in the way that met its expectations best. This was seen by some as a mark of Clinton's capacity—perhaps born of a childhood spent in the company of an alcoholic and abusive stepfather—to empathize and to please; by others, as a sign of his mendacity, his "slickness."

The mystery of Clinton's wide appeal was explored in *Primary Colors: A Novel of Politics* (1996), a *roman à clef* about the presidential campaign in 1992. A candidate named Jack Stanton—like Clinton, the governor of a small southern state—is seen through the eyes of an aide, Henry Burton, to be an admixture of idealist, opportunist, and libertine. At the time of its publication, there was much speculation as to which character in *Primary Colors* matched which person in the campaign, and which scandal matched which rumor of Clinton's political or personal misbehavior. Before Joe Klein, a journalist on the campaign trail, was revealed to be the responsible party, intense curiosity was also generated by the initial anonymity of the novel's author. One of those thought to have written *Primary Colors* was Erik Tarloff, husband of Clinton's chief economic adviser, and a speech-writer for Clinton. In the second term, Tarloff did write *Face-Time: A Novel* (1998), about a president's affair with a White House staffer. It became clear, however, that no fictionalized account equaled, in detail or interest, what reality—and the Office of the Independent Counsel—could provide to a rapt electorate of readers.

The findings of independent counsel Kenneth W. Starr (1946–) were first published on the Internet (September 11, 1998). The voluminous document, which was quickly dubbed *The Starr Report,* describes the relationship between Clinton and Lewinsky, their numerous assignations in the White House, and their alleged attempts to hide all this from Paula Jones, a woman from Arkansas who was suing Clinton for sexual harassment. Some observers made comparisons between Clinton and the polite but dour Texan Starr, exact contemporaries born and raised in the South, steeped in the South's Baptist traditions, but seemingly opposite in philosophy and manner. Other responses to the report and to the subsequent impeachment hearings and trial ranged from the sensational to the scholarly. *And the Horse He Rode in On: The People v. Kenneth Starr* (1998) was a diatribe by James Carville, who had come from the hotbed of Louisiana politics to guide Clinton's first presidential campaign and had been anointed a celebrity in the process. At the same time, "Historians in Defense of the Constitution" (October 30, 1998), a statement signed by more than four hundred scholars, was published in the *New York Times.* Among the three co-sponsors of this statement setting out the appropriate uses of impeachment—in opposition to the Republican majority's stance—was C. Vann Woodward, well-known historian of the New South. It was fitting that Woodward should have lent his support to the president's successful defense against the impeachment charges, for Clinton had been the New South's most effective representative so far. Throughout the trial, public support for Clinton, particularly among African Americans, remained firm. But fairly or unfairly, a distinct and unflattering image of the president was being traced by commentators and editorialists. Though his education at Georgetown and Oxford and Yale might have lent him some polish, Clinton seemed to them, at base, a provincial interloper unsuited to the national stage, a charlatan who had finally been found out. Not only the passage of time, but an historian of Woodward's caliber or a novelist as adept as Woodward's friend Robert Penn Warren may be required to produce the full and complex assessment that will satisfy more of this president's puzzled constituents.

Amber Vogel

See also Caste; Class.

David Maraniss, *First in His Class: The Biography of Bill Clinton* (1995); James B. Stewart, *Blood Sport: The President and His Adversaries* (1997).

CLUBS

Clubs became the central institution of southern literary culture during the second quarter of the eighteenth century, forming in taverns and coffeehouses from Maryland to Barbados. Designed to promote sociability, conversation, learning, and the refinement of manners, these groups mixed amusement with the project of instilling life in the colonies with civility. Every urban center in the colonial South hosted a multitude of clubs, and most country taverns of any pretension housed a regular company of local men who considered themselves a club. During the eighteenth century, the membership of these groups was all male. (Mixed-sex society met under the auspices of two female-superintended institutions, the drawing room and the salon; women's sociability organized about the tea table.) Literature was one of several sorts of discursive performances taking place in the clubs and was usually subordinated to the primary sociable art, conversation. The earliest surviving literature of the clubs is dominated by two sorts of writing: belles-lettres and formal written records of club activities.

Belles-lettres projected the pleasurability of artful

communication and ranged in form from witty jests to *vers de société* and mock history. The majority of the earliest literature circulated in manuscript. Certain of the club archives include texts that were performed as part of club proceedings—the papers of the Homony Club of Maryland (at the Maryland Historical Society) contain odes, letters, and mock legal depositions declaimed as part of a night's amusement. The records of the Tuesday Club of Annapolis contain copies of the choicest conundrums and jests spoken at the club's sittings. These records are notable too for their archive of music composed by Thomas Bacon for performance at club anniversaries. A rather substantial literature of song lyrics survives for performance at Masonic lodges, including items from Savannah, Charleston, Wilmington, Williamsburg, Annapolis, and Richmond. Much of the eighteenth-century manuscript literature of the clubs remains unpublished, but the most substantial archive, the "Records," "History," and music of the Tuesday Club, has been made available in several volumes since 1988. *The History of the Ancient and Honourable Tuesday Club,* composed by secretary Alexander Hamilton, is the masterwork of Anglo-American club literature—a work on the par with the club writings of the Scriblerians or the Kit Kats in London for artistry and extravagance. It reveals a singular aesthetic perspective and a profound sensitivity to the history and importance of clubs as an institution in the West. Yet its signal characteristic is its tone of mockery, the distinctive witty cast that colors all its pronouncements.

The importance of this club wit—or raillery—to enlightened conversation and the formation of a public opinion in the English-speaking world was asserted by the Third Earl of Shaftesbury in *Sensus Communis.* Shaftesbury advanced the thesis that the club, because it was predicated on friendship, possessed the requisite precondition for honesty of communication. Shaftesbury connected the notions of absolute liberty of conversation, individual improvement, and social health with the club. In effect, Shaftesbury proposed a politics of private society based on aesthetics rather than interest or social contract. The role of wit, humor, and raillery in policing the conversation rather than the coercive administration of rules by an executive made the club a singularly democratic institution. There, opinions were formed in security and polished to a strength that could withstand public exposure. One sees from the eighteenth-century South examples of the projection of club wit into the public sphere to mold opinion on men and affairs of state. The Hickory Hill Club of Virginia (an affiliate of the Tuesday Club) floated a manuscript satire, "Dinwiddiana," to ridicule the policies of Governor Dinwiddie. The St. George's Society composed and dispersed many of the satires that flooded Charleston during evangelist George Whitefield's first tour. The Scots Club—the "clamorous malcontents" that troubled the administration of Georgia during its first decade—composed pasquinades, parodies, and mock letters excoriating the publicity of the "philanthropic colony" until the members were hounded into South Carolina.

The liberties of conversation arrogated by clubs and the security they offered as havens of social pleasure were so potent that political opponents would at times belong to the same club in order to interact familiarly in ways that public roles did not permit. The Homony Club of Maryland included the chief loyalists and several patriots on the eve of the Revolution and amused itself by trying members on patently trumped-up charges of treason against the club. So long as the club was designed for innocent amusement (eating hominy, hunting, playing cards, toping) and did not organize around a specific public project, it might prove a place where public masks were taken off and a more honest and flexible interaction was attempted. It was this quality that distinguished clubs from that other form of voluntary association ubiquitous in the South, the gentlemen's society.

The society and the club differed in social aesthetics yet abided by the same vision of associational polity. Both institutions were organized as self-governing corporations, with officers, covenants, laws, and civil ceremonies. Because these were societies or polities in miniature, they became laboratories of self-rule in an empire notoriously lax in its forms of colonial administration. They provided experience in institutional politics and rule. It is worth noting that every Founding Father from the South was an actor in the world of associations, from Freemason George Washington to James Madison, member of the American Whig Society at Princeton. When we turn to the vast literature (manuscript and printed) of club regulations, charters, and proceedings, we should understand it as an index of the seriousness with which eighteenth-century southerners (and Americans generally) took the business of social order. For there to be liberty of conversation and action, there must be something more than fellow-feeling and general good will; there must be a clearly articulated code of law—*leges convivales*—

clarifying who can be a member, what membership entails, and the conditions of expulsion. Frequently, the only surviving artifacts of clubs and societies are the codes of regulation they instituted. Sometimes historical consciousness moved a body to keep a record of proceedings or minutes of club meetings. This was particularly the case with learned societies engaged in the consolidation of knowledge.

Historically, the college has been recognized as a model for the private associations that sprang into being in the West during the early modern period. Yet the spirit of sociability that gentlemen's private societies cultivated, linked to their aesthetic interests, quickly caused them to conduct affairs in manners markedly different from learned foundations. In the eighteenth century, young men sought to invigorate life within the colleges by importing into them the forms and practices of clubs and private societies. At the College of William and Mary, the F.H.C. Society (to which Thomas Jefferson belonged) pioneered this endeavor. Yet the lasting contribution that the South made to the history of clubbing would be made by the F.H.C.'s successor, Phi Beta Kappa, the first collegiate fraternity. In PBK the ideal of learning was bonded with sociability. Under the aegis of classical ideals and protected by an oath of secrecy, its members composed literary works, debated current affairs, practiced elaborate rites of initiation and installation, and held periodic social festivities. Its forms and practices reveal it to have been the synthesis of those three informing institutions of masculine sociability, the college, club, and gentlemen's society.

David S. Shields

See also Class; Gentleman.

David D. Hall and Hugh Amory, *The History of the Book in America*, Vol. 1 (1999); J. A. Leo Lemay, *Men of Letters in Colonial Maryland* (1972); David S. Shields, *Civil Tongues & Polite Letters in British America* (1997).

COCKFIGHTING

Shakespeare's reference to the Globe Theater as a "cockpit" in the prologue to *Henry V* (1599) acknowledges a floor plan indebted to a sport begun in Asia thousands of years before and popular in England at least since around 1500, when Henry VIII installed a cockfighting arena at Whitehall Palace. Henry's interest in gamecocking led to its denomination as a "royal" sport. Before its prohibition in 1849, cockfighting was widespread among both nobles and commoners in England, passing to America during colonial times to engage such distinguished followers as Washington, Jefferson, and Hamilton. Though banned in much of New England by 1850 and later throughout most of the other states, the practice survives into the present across the country, centered in the rural South and numbering in enthusiasts, according to one well-informed estimate, possibly upward of a hundred thousand people. A United Gamefowl Breeders Association promotes the sport, and several periodicals cover it, notably one called *Grit and Steel.*

Cockfighting involves chickens of many breeds descended from and still genetically close to the red jungle fowl of ancient India. Appearing today in many colors, the basic fighting cock is a muscular, compact bird of five or six pounds, broad of back and small of belly, with a long, lithe neck and thick, wide-spaced legs. Its wings are clipped to limit flight and its comb is trimmed to minimize injury. Equipped for combat, its natural spurs are replaced with razor-sharp curved steel gaffs some two inches or slightly more in length.

Chapters relating to the career of "Chicken George" as a cockfighter in Alex Haley's novel *Roots* (1976) provide a detailed and well-researched view of southern cockfighting during the half-century before the Civil War. Practices remain essentially the same today, with concessions made necessary by the generally illegal nature of the sport. In Ellen Gilchrist's *Net of Jewels* (1992), Rhoda Manning's free-spirited friend Charles William takes her to a cockfight; she is repulsed and flees the "poor-white" culture it represents.

Cocks are ready for competition around the age of two years. Before that, they will have been watched closely for evidence of inherited traits of aggressiveness, valor, agility, and resilience, deficient individuals being relentlessly culled to avoid transmission of any strains that might weaken the breed. Cocks are exercised to increase stamina and wing strength, while receiving special diets of various concoction, often a trainer's personal, secret recipe.

The fights themselves may be part of a "main," or tournament involving escalating levels of competition among survivors, or of "hackfights," less formal affairs involving lesser birds and a more modest volume of betting. Events occur in circular rings called "pits," often in barns or clearings in the woods but in more elaborate settings when local authority permits. The

pits have walls two or three feet high and sometimes padded. Packed clay or sand provides a floor. In the middle of the ring is a smaller circle, to focus the point of initial contact, with straight lines equidistant on either side to indicate where birds are to be held by the trainers when they "pit" them—i.e., release them toward each other as the referee or judge commands. Before the release, owners and spectators alike—crowded in for the spectacle, the gambling, and the (frequently alcohol-fueled) social experience—call out bets of often very substantial sums.

Roosters fight with beak, wings, and gaff-covered spurs, but the killing and disabling blows are struck with the latter, as each bird attempts to jump or fly above the other and inflict a downward stroke to the head or neck. When a cock is wounded, combat may be halted briefly while a trainer attempts to reinvigorate it with any of a traditional set of techniques that include licking the chicken's head and eyes, sucking clotted blood from nasal passages, blowing vigorously on certain body parts, or ministering to serious cuts with antiseptics—in years past, with swabs dipped in urine. Then the cocks are re-pitted to fight, either to the death or until a trainer withdraws a bird that is unable or no longer willing to continue. The style, violence, and visual spectacle of the event have inspired many representations in art, not least among them the label illustration for Fighting Cock bourbon, bottled and marketed, appropriately, at 103 proof.

Jerry Leath Mills

See also Sports Literature.

"Cockfighting," *Encyclopaedia Britannica,* Vol. 6 (1968); Alex Haley, *Roots* (1976).

COLLEGE LANGUAGE ASSOCIATION

In April, 1937, Hugh M. Gloster, an instructor of English at LeMoyne College in Memphis, Tennessee, founded the Association of Teachers of English in Negro Colleges. Eager to address professional issues but barred from participation in the segregated southern regional meetings of national organizations such as the Modern Language Association, Gloster and nine other participants, meeting at LeMoyne, dedicated themselves to establishing a forum for exchanging ideas and promoting professional concerns. In 1940 this group opened its membership to include teachers of modern foreign languages and became the Association of Teachers of Languages in Negro Colleges. Further expanding in 1949, the organization dropped "Negro" from its name, becoming the College Language Association (CLA).

Except for three years during World War II, when travel was restricted, CLA has held annual conventions featuring the presentation of scholarly papers; the CLA Award for members whose creative work, research, and service during the preceding year are judged most outstanding; and the Margaret Walker Creative Writing Awards for distinguished student writers. Since 1957, the CLA has published the *College Language Association Journal* (*CLAJ*), a quarterly collection of scholarly essays and book reviews. Also, the organization has produced *A Twenty-Five-Year Author-Title Cumulative Index to the CLA Journal* (1985) and three volumes of essays—*Langston Hughes: Black Genius* (1971); *James Baldwin: A Critical Evaluation* (1977); and *Jean Toomer: A Critical Evaluation* (1988)—all edited by Therman B. O'Daniel, founding editor of *CLAJ*.

While broadly humanistic and racially integrated since its founding, first and foremost, the CLA has remained resolute in defining and promoting issues important to African American language professors, creative writers, and scholars, thereby earning its position as *most prominent* among African American literary associations.

Patsy B. Perry

See also *College Language Association Journal.*

Marie H. Buncombe, "Legacy from the Past, Agenda for the Future: The College Language Association, 1937–87," *CLAJ* 31 (September 1987); Carolyn Fowler, *The College Language Association* (1988); Dolan Hubbard, "Slipping into Darkness: CLA and Black Intellectual Formation," *CLAJ* 40 (September 1996).

COLLEGE LANGUAGE ASSOCIATION JOURNAL

The College Language Association Journal (*CLAJ*), official publication of the College Language Association (CLA), was founded in April, 1957, during the Association's annual meeting at Arkansas A.M. and N. College in Pine Bluff. Therman B. O'Daniel, the newly elected *CLA Bulletin* editor, proposed to the associa-

tion's president, Blyden Jackson, and to the vice president, Charles A. Ray, that the organization publish a scholarly journal instead of a bulletin. With approval, encouragement, and the promise of financial assistance if needed, Jackson and Ray joined O'Daniel in launching *CLAJ*, successor to the organization's *News Bulletin* and the *CLA Bulletin*.

The first volume of *CLAJ* consisted of two issues (November, 1957, and March, 1958), while volumes 2 through 9 carried three issues each, published in September, December, and March. The 1966 Tenth Anniversary volume marked the beginning of quarterly publication, with September, December, March, and June issues.

In a statement of purpose, O'Daniel announced in the *Journal*'s first issue that it was established to provide another medium for the publication of scholarly essays by CLA members and others with similar scholarly interests. Thus he presented two principles that have characterized *CLAJ* throughout its existence: broad access to writers and high scholarship standards. During its first decade, following the 1954 U.S. Supreme Court's decision outlawing public-school segregation, the *Journal*'s content was wide-ranging, with emphasis on integration. By the late 1960s, however, the goal of a fully integrated educational system was still unrealized, and *CLAJ*, a barometer of the values, mood, and outlook of numerous African American scholars, began to reflect disillusionment. Indeed, during its second period, 1969 to the mid-1970s, *CLAJ* recorded its contributors' deep frustration and disappointment in their continuing isolation from mainstream language and literature associations. It was during this period, also, that these scholars demonstrated a renewed appreciation for and promotion of their own racial heritage and creative productions, as well as their sense of oneness with other blacks throughout the world. Since the late 1970s, again reflecting intellectual and cultural interests, *CLAJ* has included essays on women's studies and Francophone and Afro-Hispanic subjects. In its entire history, *CLAJ* has had only three editors—the founding editor, Therman B. O'Daniel (November, 1957–December, 1977); Edward A. Jones (March, 1978–June, 1979); and Cason L. Hill (September, 1979–present). Their meticulous editing and careful financial management resulted in a sterling record of uninterrupted publication, with a current national and international distribution to approximately 1,700 subscribers.

On October 8, 1972, in its fifteenth year of publication, *CLAJ* was honored by the Black Academy of Arts and Letters with its Alice E. Johnson Memorial Fund Award. In his presentation of this award, "Citation for the CLA Journal" (*CLAJ* 16 [December 1972]), Benjamin A. Quarles likens the *Journal* to Alice Johnson, the award's namesake, characterizing both as having a wide outlook; being reflective, humanistic, ever-growing; and valuing writers among the greatest teachers. Subsequently, in 1974, 1977, 1986, and 1996, CLA Awards have honored *Journal* editors, extending well-deserved recognition for maintaining and enhancing in *CLAJ* those sterling attributes that Quarles enumerated and for achieving the ambitious plans and great hopes for the success that O'Daniel projected in the inaugural issue.

Patsy B. Perry

See also College Language Association.

A. Russell Brooks, "The *CLA Journal* as a Mirror of Changing Ethnic and Academic Perspectives," *CLAJ* 26 (March 1983); Carolyn Fowler, *The College Language Association* (1988); Therman B. O'Daniel, "*CLA Journal* Receives One of Five Awards . . . ," *CLAJ* 16 (December 1972); Therman B. O'Daniel, comp., *A Twenty-Five-Year Author-Title Cumulative Index to the "CLA Journal," 1957–1982* (1985).

COLONIAL LITERATURE

The South before 1789 had a rich and varied intellectual and literary tradition that both stoops to and surpasses the limitations of time, place, and mores. Peopled by numerous native tribes, traversed or colonized by Spanish, Italian, Portuguese, French, and English rovers, explorers, and exploiters, and worked under duress by African slaves, the South developed a set of literary types and styles that well before the nineteenth century was becoming distinctive in American letters. Southern writers of the colonial era were usually employed in something other than authoring when they put quill to paper. Soldiers, sailors, and servants at first, those who touched southern soil became also recorders of events, authors of verse, satirists, historians, travel narrators, and propagandists for development. Politicians, preachers, and planters as well, southern authors often wrote for local rather than national or global audiences. By 1789, in the era of the new republic, colonial writers had bequeathed to their descendants a love of language and its expression that continues to inform southern literature to this day.

Although many aspects of colonial writing have been well examined, comparatively little has been done to integrate the oral narratives and poetry of the many Native American peoples into cultural histories of the region. Captain John Smith and William Byrd II, among others, recorded the stories and speeches of natives they encountered, and ethnographic observers, writing in the national period, preserved oral narratives that have their origins in the colonial and precolonial eras. A Koasati story, "The Still Crawling Sister," contains incest, violence, mysterious births, descriptions of genitalia, and interactions between animals and human beings in a mixture of what in Western literature would be considered Gothic, fantastic, and comic elements. "The Dead Wife," an Alabama tale, depicts love, death, and resurrection in a way that suggests the mysteries of all elements of the life process. Byrd's version of the Indian afterlife, in the narrative of his companion, Bearskin, is one of the high points of the Virginian's *Secret History of the Dividing Line* (written c. 1728). Meanwhile, some native speakers responded to the colonizing of their homeland. Smith's transcription in *The Generall Historie of Virginia* (1624) of the speeches of his rival, the supreme chieftain Powhatan, gives glimpses of an elegant oratory in opposition to untrammeled white settlement. In a different vein, the Yuchi tale, "The Creation of the Whites," portrays in natural allegories the arrival of explorers and settlers to the continent's coastal lands. Although many white colonial writers purport to scorn native stories and religion, some may have been influenced beyond their own knowledge by the speaking of the people who lived in the South before them.

In fact, the arrival of Africans in 1619 and thereafter brought to America another group of peoples with a deep oral tradition. To be sure, Olaudah Equiano in his *Interesting Narrative* (1789) provides a rare first-hand written account by a native African of slave conditions in Virginia and Georgia, but oral tradition would dominate African American expression in the colonial period. Early versions of Joel Chandler Harris's Uncle Remus stories were no doubt told by slaves and free blacks in southern communities. Many African stories also got mixed with native tales, to the point that recorders of Indian narratives in the early twentieth century took down versions of animal fables that sound very like well-known African types and situations. Thus European settlers, bringing their expressive traditions with them, encountered one or both of these oral literatures, while natives and Africans heard each other, as well as whites, producing textual influences in several directions.

Before the English arrived at Roanoke in 1584, European explorers and military men had sailed along or settled various spots in the South and left accounts. Among many who wrote, the Spanish Gentleman of Elvas in Florida, the French Jean Ribault in Florida and South Carolina, and René de Laudonnière in Florida prepared texts, some of which may have been known by English adventurers coming after them. The collections of translated travel accounts assembled by the Hakluyts and Samuel Purchas provided English navigators with firsthand versions from their maritime and economic rivals of the viability of the American South for habitation; they also gave much-needed information—and often fanciful stories—about the native peoples with whom they would have to contest for the land.

The colony sponsored by Walter Raleigh on Roanoke Island, North Carolina, offered English colonizers their first opportunity to write in detail about a southern landscape and experience. Participants in several voyages there, including Arthur Barlowe, Ralph Lane, and John White, left accounts, while letter writers, including those Spanish figures concerned about the colony, exposed political and economic motives. The best-known work is Thomas Hariott's *A Brief and True Report of the New Found Land of Virginia* (1588). Not only is this one of the most complete English accounts of the land and people in the Roanoke region, but it also shows the influence of the contact between natives and whites by including many Indian words for plants and animals, such as *mangummenauk* for acorns. Hariott justifies the settlement process, takes a providential view, yet recognizes that the Indians have a religious life, albeit not Christian.

The building of Jamestown in 1607 produced another set of texts about a southern setting. John Smith wrote the first published account by a participant, *A True Relation* (1608), which chronicled the voyage and first year of the settlers. Whereas Smith describes struggles for power among the colonists and natives, another Jamestown voyager, George Percy, wrote in his 1607 *Observations* (1625) a list of the sufferings and deaths that the men experienced in the first months. In that same vein, the letters of Richard Frethorne (or Trethorne) provide an indentured servant's views of the starvation and brutal conditions experienced by colonists in the aftermath of the 1622 massacre. Other reports by early Jamestown residents, such as deposed president Edward Maria Wingfield's *A Discourse of Virginia* (1608), or William Strachey's *The Historie of Travaile into Virginia Britannia* (1849), give differing perspectives on politics and dealings with the Indians. But it was Smith who strove for fame with his series of writings on Virginia, culminating in the *Generall Historie*. The sometime president of the colony enlarges the enterprise to near-mythic status while retaining a realist's sense of resources and possibilities. The combination of an enhanced vision of the region's history coupled with well-aimed critiques of opponents would serve as a pattern for later southern narrative.

The settling of Maryland, a proprietary colony under the leadership of the Catholic Lord Baltimore, inspired its own founding and early historical literature. Father Andrew White's *A Briefe Relation of the Voyage unto Maryland* (1634) follows the usual ocean crossing and native contact pattern of many other accounts but has value for the specifics of the particular Indians he meets. White's *A Relation of Maryland* (1635) offers the view of a benign colonial situation with friendly natives and mild climate. With the coming of Puritans to Maryland, however, conflict between the proprietary government and Protestant contenders led to the publication of several pamphlets on both sides of the issue. Puritan Leonard Strong's *Babylon's Fall* and Catholic John Langford's *A Refutation of Babylon's Fall* (both 1655) reflect the ideological and political hostility of the period, while the best-known work to arise from the conflict, John Hammond's proproprietary *Leah and Rachel, or, the Two Fruitfull Sisters Virginia and Mary-land* (1656), has some lively writing, as in his attack on abusers of the colonies for being "blackmouthed babblers." A more complete, and more arch, depiction of early Maryland appears in George Alsop's *A Character of the Province of Maryland* (1666). Using the persona of a servant and seeming to tout Maryland as an ideal place for the lower classes to go, Alsop through his style leaves one uncertain of his true motives.

The economic possibilities of the lands farther to the south provoke several more writers to describe incipient colonies. William Hilton's *A Relation of a Discovery, Lately Made on the Coast of Florida* (1664), John Lawson's *A New Voyage to Carolina* (1709), and James Oglethorpe's *A New and Accurate Account of the Provinces of South Carolina and Georgia* (1732) describe the beginnings of English settlement below

Virginia. Thomas Ashe's *Carolina, or a Description of the Present State of That Country* (1682) and Samuel Wilson's *An Account of the Province of Carolina* (1682) pay special attention to natural history, painting South Carolina in particular as a land of extraordinary abundance. The romance of the southern landscape begins with these early reports, suggesting the sort of super fertility that would become endemic to fiction as well as nonfiction in the South. At the same time, Robert Witherspoon's narrative of his migration from northern Ireland to South Carolina in 1734 and the years following is a more sober reminder of the harshness of conditions for those without wealth.

With settlement came another kind of travel narrative, that of the resident to differing parts of what was now his or her own country. Most famous of southern travelers is William Byrd II, whose *History of the Dividing Line* (written c. 1728) and *Secret History* feature barbed as well as light-hearted and gently satiric views of the Virginia-North Carolina backcountry. His *A Progress to the Mines in the Year 1732* and *A Journey to the Land of Eden Anno 1733* chronicle descriptions of visits to lands he had acquired mixed with keen observations on people he encounters. Dr. Alexander Hamilton, a Scottish physician who settled in Maryland, wrote one of the best colonial travel narratives, the *Itinerarium* (written 1744). His chronicle of a journey to New York and New England allows him opportunity to lampoon New Light enthusiasts and the poor state of medical education in the country as well as to describe the social and intellectual life of many colonial cities.

If satire is one of the chief southern colonial modes, then history is another. John Smith's conversion of less than twenty years of settlement in a "historie" is only the first of many attempts by residents in the South to shape the colonial enterprise into historical narrative. Sometimes those histories can mock their own subjects, as John Cotton does Nathaniel Bacon in his "History of Bacon's and Ingram's Rebellion" (c. 1676) and Patrick Tailfer, Hugh Anderson, and David Douglas do Governor Oglethorpe in *A True and Historical Narrative of the Colony of Georgia* (1741). Others, however, have more straightforward intent, as in Robert Beverley's *History and Present State of Virginia* (1705) and William Stith's *History and First Discovery of . . . Virginia* (1747). Beverley, perhaps influencing Byrd, argues for mixed-race marriage with the Indians and shows himself a keen observer of native ways. Stith sees history allied to an incipient American nationalism, with the early colonial period a golden age of freedom and the current situation one of increasing British tyranny. This consciousness of a particular history would persist well past Stith's midcentury view.

Connected, perhaps, to this emerging historical consciousness in the South was a lively interest in politics and political discourse. Many of the works previously or subsequently mentioned include political commentary, often satiric. During the Stamp Act crisis, however, writers such as Daniel Dulany (the younger) of Maryland, Maurice Moore of North Carolina, and Richard Bland and Landon Carter of Virginia broached issues of parliamentary authority over the colonies. James Madison and Thomas Jefferson contributed to the serious discourse of the Revolution, the former in essays for *The Federalist* and *Views of the Political System of the United States* (both 1787), the latter in the Declaration of Independence and the Virginia Statute of Religious Liberty (1786). Orations by South Carolinians David Ramsay and William Tennent III, by Virginian Patrick Henry, and others, not to mention hundreds of politically inscribed letters by George Washington and his contemporaries, indicate a keen interest in theories of government, relations between church and state, and the practicalities of shaping a newly independent republic.

Although less well known for its religious life than New England, the South was a place where ministers wrestled with impious congregations, sectarian contention, and the increasing moral dilemma posed by slavery. Anglicans settled first and remained the dominant church group in the South through the colonial period. From Alexander Whitaker in Virginia to Alexander Garden in South Carolina more than a century later, Anglican clerics supported an established church that generally limited dissenting faiths from gaining converts. Occasionally, an unusual voice asserts itself. The Anglican Morgan Godwyn, after preaching in Virginia, published *The Negro's and Indian[']s Advocate* (1680) for the purpose of encouraging conversions among marginalized races, but for the most part the settled clergy, exemplified by the polished speaker Thomas Cradock in Maryland, preached a doctrine of rational moderation and support for the status quo. At the same time, however, British itinerant George Whitefield stirred up an evangelical desire for an intense, immediate faith that would be more permanently addressed by Methodists and Baptists late in the century. From the Quaker George Fox to the Presbyterian Francis Makemie, Methodists John and Charles Wesley, and Swiss Calvinist John Zubly, European-born clerics visited or stayed and wrote about their experiences. Some eighteenth-century ministerial writers, like the Congregationalist Josiah Smith in South Carolina or the Presbyterian Samuel Davies in Virginia, brought an intellectual rigor to southern preaching that was notably absent, as Anglican Charles Woodmason so scornfully observed, in the backcountry. Smith and Davies are relatively rare among southern clergy for publishing their sermons during the colonial period, but the manuscripts of a few, like Cradock, have been preserved.

In belles-lettres, however, a number of writers found their way into print, sometimes in the North or in Great Britain, if not at home. George Sandys translated ten of fifteen books from Ovid for his influential edition of *Metamorphoses* (1626) during his voyage to and residence in Virginia. Ebenezer Cooke's notable satiric poem, *The Sot-Weed Factor* (1708), seems both to skewer Maryland tobacco culture and the foreign observer of it at the same time. The Land of Cockaigne model was a popular one for southern satirists, but not every poet found satire to his liking. Samuel Davies wrote a collection of poems, *Miscellaneous Poems, Chiefly on Divine Subjects* (1752), that, while religious, shows his own knowledge of eighteenth-century British forms and poets. Marylander Richard Lewis in his short life penned a few very fine poems, including the meditative travel piece "A Journey from Patapsko to Annapolis, April 4, 1730" (1732), and others were published in London and gained him some reputation there. Transplanted Philadelphian Thomas Godfrey Jr. published his *Court of Fancy* (1762) while trying to encourage literary culture in Wilmington. One of the most notable productions is Alexander Hamilton's *The History of the Ancient and Honorable Tuesday Club* (written in 1754). Both a history and a genial satire of the men who met in Annapolis for conversation and literary production, Hamilton's work reflects, at least among an urban elite, a witty engagement with a literary culture something like the one he might have found in London or Edinburgh. From the Tidewater blacksmith poet Charles Hansford, the classically influenced Robert Bolling of Virginia, the broad-ranging Joseph Dumbleton of Virginia and South Carolina, and the South Carolina poet Dr. James Kirkpatrick, to the satiric author of the "Dinwiddianae" poems and the religious poet and prose satirist James Reid, southern letters flourished in both cities and rural retreats.

In drama, one might start with George Chapman,

Ben Jonson, and John Marston's *Eastward Ho!* (1605), where the character Seagull spins fables of the wealth to be found in Virginia, and William Shakespeare's *The Tempest* (written c. 1611), possibly inspired by the wrecked Virginia supply voyage of Thomas Gates, as well as several plays that mock Captain Smith on the seventeenth-century London stage. Aside from the court record in Accomack county of the first English play known to have been performed in America, *The Bear and the Cub* (1665), and the posthumous publication of Thomas Godfrey's verse tragedy *The Prince of Parthia* (1765), the only plays of note to have been written by a southerner in the colonial period are the two by Robert Munford, *The Candidates* and *The Patriots* (1798), both written in the 1770s. They expose the political culture and pretensions of Virginians first during local elections, where alcohol threatens to determine the outcome, and then in the growing conflict with England, just before the Revolution. Although not known to have been acted, Munford's plays present further evidence of the prevalence of satire among southern writers.

Many planters and other individuals with time to do so left letters, diaries, and journals that reveal private thoughts and domestic interactions. The letters (written 1679–1699) of William Fitzhugh of Stafford County, Virginia, describe the often mundane details of buying slaves and transporting agricultural goods, but behind the business is an evolving consciousness that increasingly accepts slaves as objects, not persons or souls to be converted. Among the next generation, William Byrd's diaries, from both London and Westover in Virginia, offer an often bawdy, then temporarily contrite man whose comments on the social world of the elite slavocracy of the early eighteenth century illuminate only partially the extremes of southern society. Later in the century, the diary of Philip Fithian gives the perspective of a visiting Princeton graduate on plantation life, with an often withering eye, while Landon Carter writes frequently of his extensive reading from his well-stocked library and his political quarrels with his fellow Virginians.

With relatively few printing presses in the South during the colonial period, the publication record does not accurately reflect the extent of literary activity in the region. Increased examination of diaries and letters will allow fuller understanding of southern writing habits and culture. Using new ways of reading, scholars may be better able to document the contribution of black and native speakers to the discourse of the early

South. Writings by southern women of the period remain largely unexplored, while the contributions of Puritans are only beginning to be recognized. Despite the fame of a few writers of the period, such as Smith and Byrd, the textual riches of the colonial South have yet to yield all their secrets.

Jeffrey H. Richards

See also African American Literature, Beginnings to 1919; Bacon's Rebellion; Calvinism; Declaration of Independence; Drama, Beginnings to 1800; Humor, Beginnings to 1900; Jefferson, Thomas; *Lost Colony, The*; Native American Literature; Periodicals, 1800 to 1860; Periodicals, 1860 to 1900; Poetry, Beginnings to 1820; Puritan Writers; Revolutionary War (American); Smith, Captain John; Travel Literature; Virginia, Literature of; Washington, George; Women Writers, Beginnings to 1820.

Wesley Frank Craven, *The Southern Colonies in the Seventeenth Century, 1607–1689* (1949); Richard Beale Davis, *Intellectual Life in the Colonial South, 1585–1763* (1978); J. A. Leo Lemay, *Men of Letters in Colonial Maryland* (1972); David S. Shields, *Oracles of Empire: Poetry, Politics, and Commerce in British America, 1690–1750* (1990).

COLONIAL NEWSPAPERS

Like early colonial northern printers, those in the South were usually appointed by the Crown to print laws. Most of them also published pamphlets and even books, as well as newspapers. Printers served as publishers and editors. Early publishers often feared the monarch, the Crown-appointed local governor, and the public; thus, they often printed European news, locally written poems and essays, and advertisements (including those for runaway slaves), but little local news or commentary. Colonial papers generally lacked spice, except for the advertisements, until the 1770s.

Most colonial newspapers were weeklies, and local ads comprised almost half the copy in two or four pages, often as small as loose-leaf paper. Hand-operated wooden presses were slow, as a visit to the printer's shop in restored Colonial Williamsburg shows, but few papers had over 350 subscribers.

In 1682 William Nuthead established the first press in the South in Jamestown. By 1683 Britain closed it at the request of the local government, and a new royal governor came to Virginia with an order forbidding all printing, an edict that stood until 1730, when William Parks opened a press in Williamsburg and later became the state's public printer. He published the *Virginia Gazette* in Williamsburg from 1736 until his death in 1750. A year later, his apprentice, William Hunter, started the *Gazette* again and ran it until 1760, when his brother-in-law, Joseph Royle, took over.

In 1766 William Rind opened Williamsburg's second press. *Rind's Virginia Gazette* operated without the government influence its predecessor had experienced. Rind's widow, Clementina, ran the paper from 1773 to 1775; she was succeeded by John Pinkney. Virginia's third paper, the *Virginia Gazette or, Norfolk Intelligencer,* appeared in Norfolk in 1774 and was run by William Duncan, John Hunter Holt, and Robert Gilmour before the printing shop was attacked by the British in 1775.

Although Virginia had the first press in the South, South Carolina had the first newspaper. In January, 1732, both Eleazer Phillips Jr. and Thomas Whitmarsh established papers in Charleston, lured there by the offer of £1000 for a royal printer. Six months after beginning the *South-Carolina Weekly Journal,* Phillips died. Whitmarsh succeeded him as government printer but died less than two years after starting the *South-Carolina Gazette.* Sent to Charleston by Benjamin Franklin, as was Whitmarsh, Louis Timothée (later Lewis Timothy) revived the paper in 1734; his widow, Elizabeth, took over the *Gazette* in 1738 until their son Peter became old enough to run it, which he did until his arrest during the Revolution. Other colonial Charleston papers were the *South-Carolina Gazette; And Country Journal,* run by Charles Crouch from 1765 to 1775 and by his widow, Mary, from 1778 to 1780; and the *South-Carolina Weekly Gazette* (later the *South Carolina and American Gazette* and the *Royal Gazette*), which lasted from 1758 to 1782, run by Robert Wells and then John Wells Jr.

North Carolina's first newspaper was the *North Carolina Gazette,* published from 1751 to 1759 by James Davis in New Bern. In 1764 he began the *North Carolina Magazine* but reverted in 1768 to the name *Gazette.* The colony's second paper, the *North Carolina Gazette and Weekly Post-Boy,* was established in Wilmington in 1764 by Andrew Steuart, Printer to the Government until he published a letter criticizing it in 1766. Adam Boyd ran North Carolina's third paper, the *Cape Fear Mercury,* in Wilmington from 1769 to 1775.

James Johnston, Georgia's first printer, established the *Georgia Gazette* in Savannah in 1763. In 1779

John Daniel Hammerer began the *Royal Georgia Gazette,* which Johnston bought.

Louisiana and Florida remained colonies longer than most other states. Although New Orleans had a press as early as 1764, its first paper was the *Moniteur de la Louisiane,* published by Louis Duclot from 1794 to 1814. Beleurgey et Renard began *Le Telegraphe, et le Commercial Advertiser* in 1803, the year Louisiana became part of the United States. Florida's first newspaper, the *East-Florida Gazette,* was established in St. Augustine by William Charles Wells in 1783.

Besides news, many colonial papers published early literature. For example, the *Virginia Gazette* published the "Monitor" essays, probably by William and Mary students and faculty. Though modeled stylistically on Addison and Steele, the essays were obviously written on this side of the Atlantic. Local readers wanted local writers and tolerated England's news better than its literature.

Although colonial newspapers in the South had neither the influence nor the proliferation of those in the North, they were important both in publishing the work of local writers and later in stirring the patriotic or loyalist blood of their readers.

M. Katherine Grimes

See also Colonial Literature.

Douglas C. McMurtrie, *The Beginnings of Printing in Virginia* (1935), and *The Book: The Story of Printing and Bookmaking* (1943); John Clyde Oswald, *Printing in the Americas,* Vols. 1 and 2 (1937, 1965); Parke Rouse Jr. and Thomas K. Ford, *The Printer in Eighteenth-Century Williamsburg* (1974); Isaiah Thomas, *The History of Printing in America* (1810, 1970); Lawrence C. Wroth, *The Colonial Printer* (1938).

COMMUNITY

Anyone looking to create an image of community in the South could, with intuitive insight, turn to a haphazardly spun, tangled web for inspiration. From its earliest moments until the present, the South had no master spinner of social design, of cultural cohesiveness, of political uniformity. The filaments that constitute southern society are many, change from time to time, react to external forces, and join together to preserve something that likes to be called southern ways. One filament, one celebrated for its hold upon the imagination of people living within or outside the re-gion, could be labeled "The Mythic South." At the heart of this myth is a plantation society, an oligarchy patently patriarchal, slaveholding, looking to the British aristocracy for its model. It is given human embodiment in southern gentlemen, devotees of honor and courage; in southern belles, graceful, syrupy, concealing steel hands beneath velvet gloves; in loyal servants, particularly family cooks and wet nurses who don't mind being enslaved. It is the world of popular fiction, of Hollywood, of television specials.

As myth it is, of course, Arcadian and utopian, for it fosters an image, an ideal, of a society that never really existed in the South, at least in any significant way. For every Swallow Barn there are many Tobacco Roads. From the beginning, the South had a mixture of would-be aristocrats and Lubberlanders, as William Byrd sneeringly called the laid-back inhabitants of northeastern North Carolina. If dwellers along the James River would be American counterparts of British landed gentry, they would find themselves neighbors to people who would one day be tagged "good ol' boys, crackers, rednecks, and hillbillies." If the aristocratically minded bent their knees in an Episcopalian church, their neighbors were piling their wagons with provisions and heading out for a camp meeting.

Yet the James River model was potent. As southern planters sought new ground for their crops, principally cotton, they envisioned themselves as landed gentry, biblically authorized to own slaves, whom they took with them as they displaced Native Americans in Georgia, Alabama, Mississippi, and Arkansas. They could view themselves as workers in God's vineyard because they were Christianizing their bondservants. Although powerful because of their wealth and social status, these planters were a minority group, with more than 60 percent of their neighbors owning no slaves, many of them engaged in running farms that provided subsistence or less. Yet a bond was forged between planters and yeoman, since both groups sought to keep control over slaves through upholding the South's "peculiar institution." They were joined in this effort by crackers and rednecks because freeing slaves would put poor whites in competition with a cheaper labor force.

Up through the Civil War and beyond, the South still functioned in many ways as a frontier society, there being few sizable urban areas and frequent migrations west and southwest as both established planters and would-be planters, many of them restless younger sons looking for ways to emulate their fathers and older brothers, sought fertile soil. In both historical accounts and in fiction, this westward push left a legacy of frontier brawling, fighting, squabbling, and high jinks, as can be seen in the works of William Gilmore Simms, Augustus Longstreet, Joseph Baldwin, Mark Twain, and others. This mix of the well-bred and the ill-bred often created strained political and cultural relations but worked to the advantage of both in that neither wanted to see an end to slavery. The Nat Turners of the South had to be suppressed, else more than gentlemen farmers would suffer.

Thus an uneasy economic bond fostered a kind of community and allowed planters, who controlled much of the region's wealth and acted as commercial agents in the absence of banks or other lending institutions, to exert considerable fiscal muscle in all levels of society. That muscle was felt before and after the Civil War. Yeoman antebellum farmers seeking to better their lot could raise little cash unless it came from the planter class, and former slaves were often reduced to peonage as they turned to sharecropping to support themselves and their families. Yet many stayed put, hoping for better days and treatment ahead, while others began migrating to northern and midwestern towns and cities, bringing with them few if any skills to ensure anything beyond menial employment.

Although the cash-nexus produced conflicting and conflicted conditions in social bonds, a few relationships engendered a strong sense of community, the most powerful among them being kinship, the courthouse, the county government, and the church. These are strong, tangible filaments in the web of southern society. Kinship fostered a network of interdependence economically and socially, fathers launching sons, cousins marrying cousins, kinfolk gathering at weddings, burials, reunions, family members exchanging letters as they sought to keep their circle unbroken. The concept of an unbroken circle found its way into the religious beliefs and hopes of many, especially persons of evangelical faith, since true believers lived with the expectation of seeing their loved ones again in paradise. The ties that bind naturally came to be a central theme in southern literature, receiving treatment from Simms, Mark Twain, Ellen Glasgow, William Faulkner, Thomas Wolfe, Erskine Caldwell, Richard Wright, Eudora Welty, Alice Walker, Pat Conroy, among others. The bonds of kinship also led, in time, to one of the best-attended of all events in African American culture, the family reunion.

Courthouses were not simply places to attend to legal affairs or to witness the justice system in action;

they have been, and in some areas of the South remain, gathering places for swapping news and gossip, making deals, renewing acquaintance, discussing the weather and politics and politicians, and passing the time pleasantly away from the chores of farm and home. In horse-and-buggy days, the courthouse square often resembled a campground, as families from distant farms and hamlets came and stayed for days when court was in session. Southern writers were quick to recognize the role of courthouses in the lives of both fancy and plain folk. Perhaps the quintessential treatment of a southern courthouse occurs in Harper Lee's *To Kill a Mockingbird* (1960).

If county government was not centered in the courthouse, many who constituted a county's governing body lived within its shadow. Until fairly recent times, southern courthouses provided quarters not only for judges but for clerks of court, registrars of deeds, sheriffs, and magistrates. For the average white citizen, the courthouse and county government represented democracy in action or perhaps a tolerable oligarchy. For persons of African origin, courthouses and county governments long remained symbols and agencies of suppression and injustice. County government, for Anglo-Americans, was supposed to protect property, punish criminals who came from outside the family circle, and facilitate deals that stood to fatten the coffers of the landed gentry or socially acceptable professional men. Most important, however, county governments were to be watchdogs of the status quo, for, at heart, most white southerners were conservative. That fact appears in the essays making up *I'll Take My Stand* (1930) and in the analysis of southern thought presented in W. J. Cash's *The Mind of the South* (1941).

The evangelical church, yet another conservative force in southern life, claims the largest congregations, the Southern Baptists far outnumbering Methodists, Pentecostalists, and other denominations. Since the late colonial period, when the Anglican Church allowed much of the frontier to remain spiritually fallow, evangelical preachers discovered eager ears and willing hearts among backwoods folk. In bringing God to the wilderness, they encouraged the building of churches and later provided the spiritual firepower that made camp meetings a dynamic event in the lives of countless southerners who flocked to hear the gospel preached, to lift their voices in song, to bend their knees in prayer, to get right with God, and to enjoy the company of others whose spiritual cravings became confused by, or mingled with, fleshly desires.

Within churches situated on firm spiritual ground, both among white and black congregations, women enjoyed influence and power beyond anything that most of them experienced at home or in the few secular institutions open to them. They organized drives to build or restore churches, to provide aid to the needy, to raise funds for missionary work, and to undertake, when custom freed them from the Cult of Domesticity, missionary work themselves. The sisterhood of church-going women accommodated all of the social types associated with the South—southern belles, good ol' girls, redneck women, and reformed honky-tonk angels. Ultimately, the ties binding them spiritually were almost as strong as kinship bonds, and for some of them, stronger. Perhaps the keenest observer of the ways and values of evangelical women was a Catholic writer, Flannery O'Connor, but then she was no slouch when it came to recording the ways of evangelical men, as proved by *Wise Blood* (1952).

Had the South somehow managed to avoid the challenge of external forces, enough internal divergence from the mythic norm could keep crews of analysts busy sorting out how families from southern Appalachia found common ground with families from the Piedmont and Tidewater areas. Beyond the bonds of kinship and cohesion resulting from shared emotional, political, and spiritual interests in courthouse, county government, and church, mountaineers joined lowlanders in appreciating more than a modicum of independence and relative freedom to determine among themselves who should escape or endure the penalties of the law. Speedier methods than the slow-grinding wheels of justice gained favor, a circumstance leading to lynchings, vigilantism, and uninhibited revenge. The victims of this extralegal system were chiefly persons of African origin. Another factor bonding uplanders and lowlanders was pride, something stemming from the belief that life in the South, for all its hardships occasioned by searing summers, malaria, large tracts of exhausted land, backwardness in industrial development, late-starting and inadequately funded schools, and lack of capital, afforded unmatchable opportunities to find fulfillment in nature and with family and friends. While New Englanders fretted over their failure to raise a New Zion, many southerners were sure that they had discovered a lost corner of Eden. And in what better place could one pursue happiness? That pursuit sometimes came at the expense of races that had to endure an Egyptian bondage or pile their belongings on their backs and straggle along a Trail of Tears.

External forces could not be repelled forever. As confederacy fell to the concept of union, the South would gradually at first and then speedily seek to become a part of the Industrial Age. It would fashion its own form of the Cult of Domesticity, a development that further disadvantaged the southern belle by hoisting her upon a pedestal. Eventually, however, with modernization of the workplace and increasing demands by both family and commerce that households should have two wage-earners, the southern belle packed her bags for college and joined good ol' girls and aspiring rednecks in preparing to be partners with their spouses in keeping up with the Joneses, whether they lived next door or in Seattle. And, except for a lingering drawl in their speech and patterns of behavior best described as southern manners, they would not betray their achievement of yuppiedom as products of southern educational and commercial institutions. In moments of boastfulness, they could brag about helping to build BMWs in South Carolina and designing hi-tech equipment in Atlanta or the Research Triangle Park. In a reflective moment, they could agree that the community that produced them had changed greatly from the one molding their forebears, that they were products of a homogenization beginning with the goals sought by leaders of the New South movement, that they had little or no indignation for descendants of persons responsible for the hardships and indignities suffered by their great-great-grandparents during Reconstruction, that they saw, in the main, no reason to vote for someone running for office as a Democrat, that they agreed with their college presidents and with bumper stickers about thinking globally, that they understood perfectly well why some among them took classes promising to rid them of a southern accent, since the presence of one could be a professional handicap, and that they would have to confront and educate the Snopeses among them if any vestiges of southern manners were to survive.

If, in the midst of their reflection, they paused to select a symbol for the postindustrial South, they might well choose the Moreland interchange near Atlanta, a weblike marvel of engineering popularly called "Spaghetti Junction." Here swiftness, efficiency, and pleasing design work together to speed suburbanites to their jobs and back. Here is no haphazardness, that element in southern life that gave it color, flavor, interest, and unpredictability, that gave it the Heywoods, the Peterkins, the Williamses, the Dickeys, the Percys, the Prices, the McCullerses, the Haleys, the Dillards, the

Smiths, the Hurstons, the Edgertons, the Hannahs, and that grand procession of writers from William Byrd's time to the present that have, with the ones named in this essay, created a literature that best explains and illustrates what we are trying to say when we speak of the southern community.

John L. Idol Jr.

See also Belle; Caste; Class.

Orville Vernon Burton and Robert C. McMath Jr., eds., *Class, Conflict, and Consensus: Antebellum Southern Community Studies* (1982); Bruce Collins, *White Society in the Antebellum South* (1985); Jean E. Friedman, *The Enclosed Garden: Women and Community in the Evangelical South, 1830–1900* (1985); Eugene D. Genovese, *The Southern Front: History and Politics in the Cultural War* (1995); Jack Temple Kirby, *The Countercultural South* (1995); Sharon McKern, *Redneck Mothers, Good Ol' Girls and Other Southern Belles: A Celebration of the Women of Dixie* (1979); Frank L. Owsley, *Plain Folk of the Old South* (1949); John Shelton Reed, *One South: An Ethnic Approach to Regional Culture* (1982); John Shelton Reed, *Southern Folk, Plain and Fancy: Native White and Social Types* (1986).

CONFEDERACY, LITERATURE OF THE

Writing in the Confederate states during the struggle for independence dealt mainly with the war and all that related to it. The central topic provided opportunities for established authors such as William Gilmore Simms, John Esten Cooke, Paul Hamilton Hayne, Augusta Jane Evans (later Wilson), and Henry Timrod to treat and develop themes, methods, and subject matter in verse, essays, lectures, biography, and fiction published mainly in southern magazines and newspapers and more rarely in book form (collections of poems by Hayne, Thompson, Timrod were lost in the blockade, but Evans's *Macaria* and Cooke's *Stonewall Jackson* were brought out in editions in both the North and the South). Concurrently, relatively new names, among them James Ryder Randall, Francis Orray Ticknor, Margaret Junkin Preston, and Abram Joseph Ryan began to publish in their own names or pseudonymously. During the life span of the Confederacy, a modest body of literature made its way to the public.

In the beginning, appearing in print was not too difficult. The call for a literature to explain, justify, defend, and celebrate the new nation followed closely after the demand for troops to fight its battles. More-

over, there had been appeals for a southern literature since the 1840s, but the organization of the Confederate government in 1861 led directly to the acute awareness that the new country must have its own literature as quickly as possible. And nowhere was the requirement more eloquently expressed than in Timrod's laureate-like odes, "Ethnogenesis" (February 13, 1861) and "The Cotton Boll" (September 3, 1861). In each poem, a narrator celebrates the nation's past and present ("No fairer land both fired a poet's lays / or given a home to man") and prophesies a future for it in which its mission is not merely to praise and promote itself but "to bless" "distant peoples" the "whole sad planet o'er" by sharing its "mighty commerce" with "mankind" and reviving "the half-dead dream of universal peace."

The new nation's purpose having been characterized, Simms, Hayne, Cooke, John R. Thompson, and other established writers commemorated battles and leaders in verse on Fort Sumter, Manassas, Charleston, Shiloh, Vicksburg, Gettysburg, Petersburg, and Richmond, and on P. G. T. Beauregard, J. E. B. Stuart, Albert Sidney Johnston, John Pelham, Turner Ashby, Stonewall Jackson, Joseph E. Johnston, Robert E. Lee, and Jefferson Davis. Relative newcomers like Randall, Ticknor, Mrs. Preston, John Williamson Palmer, and Ryan sometimes published anonymously or pseudonymously, and on occasion their best work came out after the war. Palmer's "Stonewall Jackson's Way" (1862) appeared without his name, and Ryan's "The Conquered Banner" (1866) was brought out under the pseudonym of Moina. Ticknor's "Little Giffin" was printed in 1867, whereas Randall's "Maryland, My Maryland" (1861) and Preston's "Stonewall Jackson's Gravel" (1864) and *Beechenbrook* (1865) were printed during the war under their own names. None of the above verse, save *Beechenbrook*, was collected until after the cessation of hostilities, and in the case of "Maryland" not until 1908.

In the early days of the conflict, patriotic verse could readily be printed in newspapers and magazines, but by 1864, after paper, personnel, and equipment shortages and the failure of publishers to pay for contributions or of subscribers to pay their bills, the number of periodicals diminished substantially. Even when materials were available, few volumes of verse, as already has been suggested, were published, although there were some exceptions, among them John H. Hewitt's *War: A Poem, Founded on the Revolution of 1861–1862* (1862) and Preston's aforementioned *Beechenbrook*.

Aside from the latter volume, little of this verse has been reprinted or remembered.

Prose, especially extended narrative, could not normally be accommodated in newspapers nor be so readily exchanged among newspapers as verse. Consequently, fiction, more particularly novels, usually appeared in book form. Serial fiction and short tales, their natural popularity notwithstanding, were generally in short supply. A few publishing houses brought out an occasional novelette, but over the life-span of the Confederacy, fewer than thirty novels were printed or reprinted, including Augustus Baldwin Longstreet's *William Mitten* (1864); Mrs. Sue Bowen's (Susan Petigru King) *Gerald Gray's Wife* (1864); various novels by M. E. Braddon (later Maxwell), such as *Lady Audley's Secret* (1864); James Dabney McCabe Jr.'s *Aide-de-Camp, A Romance of the War* (1863); and Augusta Jane Evans's *Macaria* (1864), by far the most popular of all Confederate novels and one that was written specifically to promote the cause. Several novels were republished—Nathaniel Beverley Tucker's *Partisan Leader* (1862) and Francis R. Goulding's *Robert and Harold; or the Young Marooners on the Florida Coast* (1863), to mention only two. Some reprints of English novels by others appeared, such as Dickens and Thackeray, and translations from German and French fiction. Victor Hugo's *Les Miserables* (1863–1864) was an overwhelming favorite among Confederate soldiers and was wittily transliterated by them into "Lee's Miserables." Moreover, books of humorous tales and sketches were available, including George W. Bagby's *The Letters of Mozis Addums to Billy Ivvins* (1862) and Richard Malcolm Johnston's *Georgia Sketches* (1864). Some drama also was published, namely J. J. Delchamps's *Love's Ambuscade* (1863), McCabe's *The Guerrillas* (1863), and William Russell Smith's *The Royal Ape* (1863).

Ironically, few of the more significant southern writers published books during the Confederacy. Hayne, Timrod, and Thompson, as noted earlier, collected their pieces and sought to send them to England for publication, but the manuscripts were lost in the blockade. Simms managed to complete a novel in 1863, *Paddy McGann*, and to contribute it to the *Southern Illustrated News*, but it did not appear as a book for well over a century. Cooke's life of *Stonewall Jackson* was brought out in Richmond in 1863 and New York in 1864, but his newspaper sketches of his experiences in the Army of Northern Virginia were not published until 1867 and his novels on the war did not begin to

appear until it was over. As a matter of fact, a fair amount of writing during the period—including both poetry and prose—was not put between covers until later—much later, as remarked in the case of *Paddy McGann* (1972). Mary Boykin Chesnut's *Diary* (1905) and William J. Grayson's *Autobiography* (1990) may also be added here.

The literature of the Confederacy, in the final analysis, is characteristic of its period and place. Limited by time, the pressure of events, and the deprivations incidental to the ravages of war, writers found it difficult if not impossible to sustain works of any kind or length or to publish them by mid-1864 even if they had been successfully completed. Simms's *Paddy McGann*, Longstreet's *William Mitten*, and Evans's *Macaria* are not novels of much consequence either in a high literary or an aesthetic sense, and the short fiction and drama by Bagby, Johnston, McCabe, and others was even less significant. The best southern prose on the war appeared later in novels and tales published mainly in the North by Cooke, George Washington Cable, Mary Murfree, Sherwood Bonner, Joel Chandler Harris, Grace King, and Thomas Nelson Page, among others, and in history, biographies, and diaries by Simms, Chesnut, Cooke, King, and Page. The greatest literary achievement in the Confederacy was the short poetry the war inspired. Randall's "Maryland, My Maryland," Hayne's "Vicksburg," Cooke's "The Band in the Pines," Thompson's "Lee to the Rear," Palmer's "Stonewall Jackson's Way," and Ticknor's "Little Giffin" express patriotic passion within artistic control. In the end, however, Timrod's lyrics are assuredly the ultimate attainment of Confederate literature. His "Ethnogenesis," "The Cotton Boll," "A Cry to Arms," "Carolina," "Christmas," "Spring," "The Unknown Dead," "Carmen Triumphale," and the memorial "Odell" (1866) embody a contribution to war verse comparable in quality though not in mass to Whitman's *Drum-Taps* (1865) or Melville's *Battle-Pieces* (1866). Not a literary accomplishment of great magnitude, to be sure, but one not unworthy of the Lost Cause.

Rayburn S. Moore

See also Confederate States of America; Lost Cause; Odes to the Confederate Dead.

James E. Kibler Jr., ed., *Selected Poems of William Gilmore Simms* (1990); Daniel M. McKeithan, ed., *A Collection of Hayne Letters* (1944); Rayburn S. Moore, ed., *A Man of Let-*

ters in the Nineteenth-Century South: Selected Letters of Paul Hamilton Hayne (1982); Mary C. Simms Oliphant et al., eds., The Letters of William Gilmore Simms (6 vols.; 1952–1982); Edd W. and Aileen W. Parks, eds., The Collected Poems of Henry Timrod (1965); T. Michael Parrish and Robert M. Willingham Jr., comps., Confederate Imprints: A Bibliography of Southern Publications from Secession to Surrender (1987); William Gilmore Simms, ed., War Poetry of the South (1867).

CONFEDERATE FLAG

Although one of the most visible, recognizable, and divisive symbols in modern American culture, the Confederate flag has not been a similarly visible and diverse motif in modern southern literature. Instead, most literary representations of the flag pertain to its historical role as a battle flag of the Confederate armies.

The star-studded blue St. Andrew's cross emblazoned on a field of red has, since the Civil War, become the most familiar flag associated with the Confederate States of America. Contrary to modern misconceptions, this pattern was not the Confederate national flag, and it was not called the "stars and bars." In late 1861, it was introduced as a battle flag to be used in place of the first Confederate national flag (which was called the stars and bars) because the latter was easily confused with the U.S. stars and stripes. By the end of the war in 1865, the pattern had become the most universal (though not entirely uniform) flag used in the field by Confederate military units. "Sanctified" by the blood of Confederate soldiers, the St. Andrew's cross by 1863 was clearly the symbol that embodied Confederate nationalism and was, for this reason, incorporated into new national flag patterns.

The battle flag became an object of reverence among Confederate soldiers, their families, and their descendants. This reverence was reflected in literature during the postwar "Lost Cause" era of southern history, especially soldiers' memoirs and reminiscences. Carlton McCarthy, a veteran of the Richmond Howitzers artillery unit, concluded his Detailed Minutiae of Soldier Life in the Army of Northern Virginia (1884) with a paean to the flag and its importance as a nonideological (and thus sectionally inoffensive) symbol for the common Confederate soldier, whose valor all could respect.

Southern novelists echoed McCarthy's viewpoint. Thomas Dixon's The Southerner (1913) included an unembellished historical description of the battle flag on the ramparts during "Pickett's Charge" at Gettys-

burg; Margaret Mitchell's Gone With the Wind (1936) used the flag as a metaphor for support of the Cause and the "Spirit of the Confederacy." In Thomas Nelson Page's Negro dialect stories, In Ole Virginia (1892), "Marse Chan" was killed in action holding the regimental colors; his loyal black body servant bore him from the field and wrapped him in the flag. Acting out other stereotypical episodes, Dan Lightfoot, the hero in Ellen Glasgow's The Battleground (1902), picked up the battle flag from the hands of a fallen flag bearer then bore it "impetuously" until forced to retreat. Three days later, Dan and his comrades subsequently cut up the flag and divided it into pieces rather than surrender it to the enemy.

Southern poets emphasized not only the emotional link between soldiers and their flag but also used the flag as a motif for the honorable surrender of the Confederacy. The most ubiquitous Lost Cause poem, "The Conquered Banner" by Father Abram Ryan (1865), counseled southerners to "furl that Banner / it is holy." Poets John R. Thompson and Henry Mazyck Clarkson similarly used the imagery of a proud flag "furled forever" to assure a reunited nation that it had nothing to fear from southerners intent on honoring their dead.

As the most recognizable symbol of the Confederacy and a veritable logo for the white South, the flag has assumed a diversity of meanings in post–World War II American life. It is most notably associated with "redneck" culture and the racist backlash against the Civil Rights movement. Though novelist Walker Percy, novelist/historian Shelby Foote, and such notable southern columnists as Hodding Carter, Ralph McGill, Virginius Dabney, Jonathan Daniels, John Temple Graves, and William D. Workman commented on the flag's transformation from a sacred to a profaned symbol, literary representations of rednecks and of Civil Rights themes have not followed suit. Perhaps events in South Carolina's capital, Columbia, in the spring of 1999 will stimulate some literary representations. An important Republican presidential primary and an aggressive NAACP call for a tourism boycott showed the nation the old symbol flying above the statehouse of the first state to secede from the Union 140 years earlier.

John M. Coski

See also Confederate States of America; Lost Cause; United Daughters of the Confederacy.

Devereaux D. Cannon, *The Flags of the Confederacy* (1988); John M. Coski, "The Confederate Battle Flag in American History and Culture," *Southern Culture* 2 (Winter 1996); Peleg Harrison, *The Stars and Stripes and Other American Flags* (1906); Chris Springer, "The Troubled Resurgence of the Confederate Flag," *History Today* 43 (June 1993); Kevin Thornton, "The Confederate Flag and the Meaning of Southern History," *Southern Culture* 2 (Winter 1996).

CONFEDERATE STATES OF AMERICA

Existing as a de facto independent state from February, 1861, to May, 1865, the creation of the Confederate States of America was the most important watershed in southern history. It embodied the South's schizophrenic sense of separateness from the rest of the nation, and its demise brought the end of African American slavery, a sharp break with the Old South, and the beginning of the South's early-twentieth-century identity as the nation's "number one economic problem."

The Confederate States of America consisted initially of seven states—South Carolina, Mississippi, Louisiana, Florida, Georgia, Alabama, and Texas—that seceded from the federal Union between late December 1860 and February 1861. Delegates from those states met in Montgomery, Alabama, drafted a provisional constitution, appointed a provisional president and vice president (Jefferson Davis and Alexander H. Stephens, respectively) and created a government modeled closely on that of the old Union. Four other states (Arkansas, Virginia, Tennessee, and North Carolina) that at first had voted against secession decided to join the Confederacy after the showdown between the Confederate and Federal governments led to conflict at Fort Sumter, Charleston, South Carolina, in April 1861. The Confederacy later recognized the secessionist factions of Missouri and Kentucky as Confederate states.

While the founders of the Confederacy were committed philosophically to a states' rights interpretation of the U.S. Constitution, their own words leave no doubt that fear of Federal interference with slavery was the proximate motive for secession. Secession led to war when the Federal government refused to recognize the right of secession. Though the Confederacy never commanded the loyalty of all southerners (white and, especially, black), the majority of white citizens rallied behind the cause out of patriotism or ideology. Approximately two-thirds of southern white men eventually fought for the Confederacy, though an estimated 90 percent of soldiers did not own slaves.

Historians debate not only the Confederacy's origins but also the causes of its collapse. Never recognized as an independent nation in the world community, the Confederacy managed to create a functioning government and exist for more than four years, thanks in large part to its armies' success on the battlefield. Many recent historians have emphasized the failure of a Confederate nationalism, a failure of popular will, and the enervating effects of internal social and political divisions; others argue that enduring for four years was a remarkable social as well as military achievement.

The Confederate States of America looms large in southern literature as it does in southern history, but most literary representations use it as a backdrop, not a primary subject. Lost Cause–era novelists and poets such as Thomas Nelson Page, John Esten Cooke, and Abram Ryan dwelled on the Confederacy as a setting for their works. Southern Agrarian authors similarly dwelled on the Confederacy: Allen Tate wrote an ironic ode to Confederate dead and biographies of Confederate leaders Jefferson Davis and Thomas J. "Stonewall" Jackson, and Robert Penn Warren wrote extended philosophical essays, *Jefferson Davis Gets His Citizenship Back* (1980) and *The Legacies of the Civil War* (1961).

Twentieth-century writers as different as Ellen Glasgow, Clifford Dowdey, George Washington Cable, Caroline Gordon, Ellen Glasgow, and William Faulkner wrote novels set in the Confederacy, though their works did not achieve the status of Confederate epics that Margaret Mitchell's *Gone With the Wind* (1936) and Stark Young's *So Red the Rose* (1934) achieved (with the help of Hollywood). Though generalization is dangerous, southern novels of the Confederacy tended to romanticize the nobility of the Confederate soldier and the plain people of the South and to emphasize causes and motives other than slavery without conversely romanticizing slavery or entirely dismissing slavery as a cause of war. Explicit and critical depiction of slavery and slaveholders have come with later-twentieth-century works such as Alex Haley's *Roots* (1976) and Alan Gurganus's *Oldest Living Confederate Widow Tells All* (1984); Charles Frazier's *Cold Mountain* (1997) portrayed wartime southern civilization degenerating into barbarism.

In the late 1930s, Douglas Southall Freeman, the Pulitzer Prize–winning biographer of Robert E. Lee and the most influential historian of the Confederacy, surveyed the memoirs, articles, histories, and novels about the Confederacy written since 1865. Having labored hard in his own works to vindicate the principles of the Confederacy and the men who fought for it, Freeman wondered aloud—with approval—"if the children of the Confederates who lost the war in the field were, in the realm of letters, winning the peace." The Confederate chic that Freeman noted in 1939 has persisted in the subsequent sixty years as southern and nonsouthern writers alike find themselves attracted to the romance of defeat and failure.

John M. Coski

See also Civil War; Confederacy, Literature of the; Lost Cause.

Douglas Southall Freeman, *The South to Posterity: An Introduction to the Writing of Confederate History* (1939); Richard Barksdale Harwell, *In Tall Cotton: The 200 Most Important Confederate Books for the Reader, Researcher and Collector* (1978); Robert A. Lively, *Fiction Fights the Civil War* (1957); Edmund Wilson, *Patriotic Gore: Studies in the Literature of the Civil War* (1962). The recent historical debate over the Confederacy's life and death is summarized in Gary W. Gallagher, *The Confederate War* (1997), and Drew Gilpin Faust, *The Creation of Confederate Nationalism* (1988).

CONJURING

Conjuring is the process of influencing human behavior through means of sympathetic magic or through the use of herbs, roots, or commercial paraphernalia. Frequently, conjurers take bodily waste (urine, feces), clothing, or other materials (hair, fingernails) from the body of the person to be affected and, through the addition of various powders, herbs, and roots, attempt to bring about a specific result. For example, in Charles W. Chesnutt's *The Conjure Woman* (1899), Aun' Peggy creates a sympathetic relationship between Henry and the grapevines in "The Goophered Grapevine." Whatever happens to the grapes will happen to Henry, since their fates have been magically linked. When the grapes are green and then ripen in the spring, Henry is lively and spry; conversely, when they droop and die in the fall, Henry gets arthritic until finally, after a period of years, he also dies. All of the stories in *The Conjure Woman* rely on some extranatural occurrence, and they feature male and female conjurers. Conjuring, as John W. Roberts and other scholars have noted, was—and is—a way for persons of lesser power, by way of a strong advocate (the conjurer, who can be

either male or female and who can work for good or for evil), to gain power over a loved one, a judicial system, or any other arena in which they want to influence behavior or outcomes.

Conjurers acquire their power as much from their relationships to the communities they serve as from actual supernatural or otherwise gifted ability. Since the primary ingredient for conjuration is belief, any series of patterns that tends to foster belief will enhance the reputation of the conjurer. If, for example, a conjurer intimates that someone is going to die, and the person actually does, then belief in the conjurer's power grows. As Alice Walker's narrator indicates in "The Revenge of Hannah Kemhuff" (1973), the clientele for such services is already pretty much persuaded; all the conjure woman, Tante Rosie, has to do, therefore, is go through the motions of affecting an outcome. More likely than not, if the outcome indeed occurs, people will believe that it is *because* of the conjurer.

Conjurers also succeed in intensifying beliefs in their abilities by their physical appearance and their geographical relationships to the communities they serve. As Newbill Niles Puckett points out, many conjurers had distinctive physical features, such as one black and one blue eye, a pronounced hump, or an unusual skin coloring. They frequently, as Aun' Peggy does, live apart from the community. That is the case with Toni Morrison's M'Dear, who appears in the southern remembrance section of *The Bluest Eye* (1970) and who is considered a powerful conjurer/healer. A mysterious air thus surrounds conjurers, which enables clients to speculate even more about the secrecy of their work and the power they presumably possess. Whereas some conjurers, such as the Swamp Woman in Charles Johnson's *Faith and the Good Thing* (1974), actually possess powers because they have, like preachers, been "called" to such work, others, such as Walker's Tante Rosie, clearly take a more practical approach. Tante Rosie is able to effect being powerful because she has extensive files on everybody who lives in the county; the narrator, who is her assistant, conveys this information to readers and participates in keeping the sham going.

Conjurers are also presumed to gain power through the process of being initiated by a conjurer who is believed to hold such power. Zora Neale Hurston documents in *Mules and Men* (1935) her studying with several conjurers in New Orleans and being initiated into the art. Reputedly, the most powerful person who initiates her is Luke Turner, who claims to be a descendant of Marie Laveau, the most powerful conjurer ever to appear on American soil. Such power enables strong conjurers (and some are indeed stronger than others) to effect spells that medical doctors cannot reverse. In fact, it is commonly believed that once someone is conjured, only another conjurer can remove the spell. If the spell is too powerful to be removed, then the victim will surely die.

As in many African American cultural forms, the secular and the sacred sometimes come together in conjuring. Hurston lights candles and intones prayers on many occasions when she is seeking the spirit—that is, the power of one of the African *orisha* or *loa*. It is not unusual for African Americans to solicit the counsel of a conjurer on Saturday and pray and shout in church on Sunday. Mim, a transplanted southern woman and one of the characters in Ann Petry's *The Street* (1946), seeks conjuring help from a man who refers to himself as a "prophet" and who gives her a cross to effect the outcome she desires with the man with whom she lives.

Potential conjuring as the site for the creation of new African American myths engages Henry Dumas's creative imagination, and it influences Randall Kenan as well. In stories such as "Ark of Bones," "Fon," and "Will the Circle Be Unbroken?"—all from *Ark of Bones and Other Stories* (1974)—Dumas bridges the gap between the natural and the supernatural and suggests that a greater understanding of the spirit world and the place of humans in it will enable African Americans to have a clearer sense of their destiny in the world. In *Let the Dead Bury Their Dead* (1992), Kenan uses the title story to explore the relationship between slavery and conjuration. A well-known conjurer is able to sustain a maroon colony for years; during that time, the people come to a new understanding of who they are and how they can be in the world. Kenan also incorporates hints of supernaturalism or conjuration into other stories in the volume.

It is also noteworthy that, in southern territory, Louisiana, particularly New Orleans, and North Carolina are rumored to be sites where the conjuring tradition is especially strong. Hurston clearly documents that with New Orleans, and the *Frank C. Brown Collection of North Carolina Folklore* (7 vols.; 1952–64) makes clear the prevalence of the tradition there. Writers such as Chesnutt and Ernest J. Gaines have also made that clear. Frank Yerby, in *The Foxes of Harrow* (1946), which is set in New Orleans and on a plantation just outside the city in the mid-nineteenth century, features a black woman believed to be a *mamaloi* (hav-

ing special powers because of her Haitian background). Believing that she has saved him once during an illness, her employer refuses to allow anyone to cook for him but her. In contemporary times, Brenda Marie Osbey has made New Orleans her entire fictional territory. In works such as *Ceremony for Minneconjoux* (1983), she draws upon the intersections of West Indian and African American backgrounds to give her conjure women their special powers. The New Orleans area, as John W. Roberts points out, is also the site where Bras Coupé, a legendary runaway believed to have magical powers, earned his place in African American folk tradition.

Of the requests that clients make of conjurers, love relationships can safely be judged to consume the majority. Conjurers may give the requester a powder to sprinkle in the loved one's food or on his or her clothing, a prayer to say, some fetishistic piece of material to use, or simple advice. Indeed, carrying High John the Conqueror root, burying something under a step or placing it under a bed, or carrying a "mojo hand" (a conjuring bag) are common features of conjuring. In Ernest J. Gaines's "A Long Day in November" (1963), however, advice dominates; a husband estranged from his wife seeks the advice of the local conjure woman, Madame Toussaint, on how best to be restored to his wife's good graces. Margaret Walker, in several of her poems, but especially in "Molly Means," also documents conjuring that focuses on romantic relationships. When a conjure woman places a spell on the wife, the husband resolves to "turn it back" on the conjurer and thereby save his wife.

African American writers whose ancestral roots are in the South, such as Gloria Naylor, also incorporate conjuring into their work—as Toni Morrison does. Naylor's *Mama Day* (1988) depicts one of the most powerful conjure women in African American literature. Reputed to be able to heal anything that walks on two feet or four, Mama Day can also induce pregnancy in infertile woman, blow up houses by striking her cane against their doors, and call forth hurricanes. Her reputation is said to be comparable to that of the real-life, infamous Dr. Buzzard of South Carolina (who inspires a minor, less powerful conjurer in the novel). Julie Dash's Mama Peazant, the matriarch of *Daughters of the Dust* (screenplay and film, 1992), is a similar figure to Mama Day.

In character development, especially, but also in moving their various plots along, African American writers have given conjurers and conjuring noteworthy space. By incorporating these traditions, they illustrate the development of African American literature from the oral traditions with which African Americans kept their culture alive. The place where folklore intersects literature is therefore one of the richest sites for scholarly inquiry into African American literature, especially that developed in the South or by transplanted southerners.

Trudier Harris

See also Voodoo.

Daryl C. Dance, *Shuckin' and Jivin': Folklore from Contemporary Black Americans* (1978); Alan Dundes, ed., *Mother Wit from the Laughing Barrel: Readings in the Interpretation of Afro-American Folklore* (1973); Langston Hughes and Arna Bontemps, *The Book of Negro Folklore* (1958); Zora Neale Hurston, *Mules and Men* (1935); Harry M. Hyatt, *Hoodoo, Conjuration, Witchcraft, Rootwork* (1970); Newbill Niles Puckett, *Folk Beliefs of the Southern Negro* (1926); John W. Roberts, *From Trickster to Badman: The Black Folk Hero in Slavery and Freedom* (1989).

CONSERVATISM

Conservatism is that complex of ideas that a conservative might be said to support. In general terms, it stresses preservation, tradition, and order. Conservatism may also describe a conservative's way of life, including standards of conduct, behavior, tastes, attitudes, and manner of judging. Whereas the term is often and narrowly applied to politics, it aptly refers to the comprehensive philosophy and/or cultural heritage one might wish to "conserve" in any given socio-political, economic, historical, or religious context. The word *conservative* was coined from the French *conservateur,* a name given to certain French literati who preferred conditions as they had existed prior to the French Revolution or the rise of Napoleon. The word was passed into its present English sense by the British statesman, later prime minister, George Canning in 1820. In the 1830s, *conservative* and *conservatism* were applied to and by Whigs in America. Following the Civil War, Old Whigs in the South started to call themselves "Conservatives" to distinguish themselves from Democrats, before Radical Reconstruction forged the Solid (Democratic) South.

Conservatism is referential to something, but it is also contextual to something else. American conserva-

tives, for instance, take the United States Constitution and the Founders' original intent as their reference for what is legitimate in government. Depending on present political context and what they think of it, conservatives might work to conserve and maintain or fight to restore. Further, conservatives will apply the old to the new so far as possible. American conservatives take Judeo-Christian principles and values, as well as selective heritage from Western democracies, as their reference for what is good. But they also tend to affix innovations, if such are consistent or extrapolated, or if events alter de facto the traditionally received inheritances. The Civil War ushered in a new constitutional regime in the United States, albeit with much of the antebellum inheritance intact. The South's defeat, however, removed the institution of slavery from received inheritance, as well as the intellectual defense of it in postbellum political context. Tensions continue to exist in conservatism over matters of historical or theological interpretation, which ebb and flow, and American conservatism has never been a stagnant quantity. Moreover, within their ranks, conservatives constantly argue over what is most worthy to conserve.

The dynamic nature of conservatism's content means that, strictly speaking, there are no status-quo parties in American political tradition and American intellectual tradition is one of constant dialogue with very few resolutions. At root, however, a few classical liberal propositions (self-government, ordered liberty, public happiness, and the like) mostly guide the American conservative project. Enlightenment liberal Thomas Jefferson, who drafted the Declaration of Independence at thirty-three, became an elder conservative statesman to sustain his liberal achievements. At the same time, his characteristically *southern,* conservative love of agriculture, his advocacy of state and local rights, and his strong distaste for manufactures, cities, and mobs stayed the same. In the twentieth century, American conservatism has continued to develop in reaction to the influence of Darwin, Marx, and Freud, and to specific challenges posed by the New Deal, communism, and the counterculture.

Southern conservatism has been and remains a particularly important supporting and variant strain of American conservatism, with a regional base and a unique history. It finds antebellum expression in the work of John Taylor of Caroline (i.e., *Arator*), in the fiery Burkean rhetoric of John Randolph of Roanoke, in the treatises of John C. Calhoun—all examples with considerable literary artistry. Conservatism also infuses early southern historical literature, including work by Robert Beverley (*The History and Present State of Virginia*) and that pre-eminent man of letters of the Old South, William Gilmore Simms (*The Life of Captain John Smith,* and many others). In politics and Protestant religion, the South is the most conservative region of the country and has been since the antebellum period. The conjunction between history, literature, and politics has likewise remained strong. The integrated perspective is such that aspects of southern conservatism spill easily into the humanities, and southern novelists, essayists, and poets are as likely to be southern historians.

Besides a certain ambivalence exhibited by politically dominant, contemporary neoconservatives, the southern ideational and geographical component to national conservative coalitions has been a key to political success of the GOP since the 1960s, including the Reagan Revolution in 1980 and the Republican sweep of Congress in 1994. The irony of white Southerners embracing the party of Lincoln is obvious, but pales if one traces the South and Lincoln to Whiggish American conservatism and omits positions on race and secession from the necessary panoply belonging to it. Notwithstanding historic racial segregation, violence, and mutual distrust between races in the South, Anglo and African Americans in the South share much in the way of values, religion, and culture that is conservative, but race so far has trumped the natural political and philosophic proclivities.

Lincoln referred to conservatism as "adherence to the old and tried against the new and untried." The driving if reflexive sentiment, however, is not for stasis, nor does conservatism follow a master plan. To "conserve" in one sense virtually assures a gradual concession, but conservatism adheres to the old with an active process-orientation that emphasizes social and political stability and continuity to the past. Forces of change are channelled through existing institutions, in accordance with custom and traditions. Indeed, Edmund Burke viewed change as a means toward conservation, but change itself must be carefully weighed and weighed with suspicion, then gradually and deliberately integrated. The fundamental institutions in southern conservatism through which changes run are family, church, private property, individual prerogative, local autonomy, and state sovereignty. Conservatism would presume that changes ought to conserve society's foundations and that the future regard the past with respect. In the South, this means the primacy of

liberty over egalitarianism, even sanctity over well-being. Paternalism, natural privilege, and disparities are not derided per se.

Presumption in favor of the past rests on assumptions concerning human nature and nature itself. American and southern conservatism eschew human reason unchecked by tradition, because man is neither altogether good nor capable necessarily of self-perfection. If man is a flawed being or a sinner, then his knowledge is limited, which makes history the surest and most concrete guide to the future. Of course, disputations occur over concretes as well, and even consciously conservative African Americans may find empirical evidence in history to doubt the efficacy of southern institutions, at least when it comes to the protection and guarantee of minority rights. History may also be instructive because it reveals divine will, and is directional according to providence. Therefore, say conservatives, it behooves man to approach life with humility and attentiveness to the transcendent order of things and to the efforts required for personal redemption, as well as voluntary social improvement. Mystery and a skeptical regard for the works of man, antimaterialism and a measure of creative imagination, these displace the cult of scientism, unfettered rationalism, or utopian abstractions. Conservatism thus evinces rational pragmatism and anti-intellectualism and is mostly antithetic to assumptions of modernity embraced by Progressive-Era reformers, though conservatives did not oppose all of their reforms. The complex nature of the southern conservative critique is exacerbated by the urban and middle-class origins of progressivism. The most thoroughgoing exposition against progressivism in favor of the traditions and values of rural and small-town America came from the self-styled southern "Fugitives" and "Agrarians," among them Allen Tate, Robert Penn Warren, John Crowe Ransom, and a coterie at Vanderbilt University in the 1910s and 1920s. The Fugitives and Agrarians were distinct but connected by key persons and some common interests. The Fugitives, it might be said, were more interested in literary affairs. They even struck a chord of independence from so-called high-caste Brahmins of the Old South. By contrast, the Agrarians were mostly interested in social affairs and looked to the Old South, in particular to its yeomanry, for inspiration. The Agrarians' manifesto was *I'll Take My Stand: The South and the Agrarian Tradition* (1930), written by "Twelve Southerners," including Tate, Warren, Ransom, Andrew Nelson Lytle, and Donald Davidson.

Lytle and Tate were first-rate biographers of Confederate war heroes. Davidson, perhaps the most stalwart conservative of the group, wrote history also. In *The Attack on Leviathan: Regionalism and Nationalism in the United States* (1938), Davidson scathingly attacks modern centralizing tendencies.

In the field of literary criticism, Ransom, Tate, and Warren had national and even worldwide influence by contributing substantially to the movement of the New Criticism. Southerner Cleanth Brooks probably did more than any other to steer literary study in a direction that emphasized primacy of the text over historical, philological, or biographical considerations. Indeed, he applied the methods of the New Criticism to the entire canon of English poetry, not just to modernist works. He also contributed an important essay to the Agrarians' second published symposium, *Who Owns America?: A New Declaration of Independence* (1936), intended to pick up where *I'll Take My Stand* left off and to roll back the New Deal. Universalist application of southern conservatism, however, was worked out by Richard M. Weaver, spiritual heir to the Agrarians, in the late 1940s, 1950s, and early 1960s, while he taught at the University of Chicago.

Although explicit southern conservatism developed largely outside the American intellectual mainstream and its influence has been eclipsed during this century in terms of policy, it has nonetheless remained pervasive in literature. Southern literature bears unmistakably its ethos, whether for—or against, as in cases drawn from negative reference. For the first century and a half of the country's history, southern imaginative energies were primarily focused on politics and statesmanship. Edgar Allan Poe represents a notable exception, but it was military defeat in the Civil War and related economic and psychic devastation that established conditions for literary renascence. Powerful archetypal ingredients of the Old South were manifested in postbellum writing steeped in nostalgia (in stories by Thomas Nelson Page, for example). The 1870s, 1880s, and 1890s produced a flowering of excellent local-color literature that received national recognition (works by Samuel Langhorne Clemens, George Washington Cable, Joel Chandler Harris; and the first important fiction by the African American writers Charles Chesnutt and James Weldon Johnson).

Since the 1920s, southern literature has come to dominate the American scene. The Harlem Renaissance was largely the product of African American expatriates from the South, whose work often stands as critique of past experience. In the 1930s, William Faulkner transformed Anglo-conservative myth into parables representative of existence and human potential, good and bad. Cleanth Brooks and historian M. E. Bradford both find a recognizably conservative and traditional voice in much of Faulkner's work. Indeed, the South's institutions and attachments to them have remained characteristic of twentieth-century southern literature. Southern writers are either personally attached to the past, to family, community, place, and religion, or they are keenly aware of the importance of these values. This is true for literally dozens of outstanding southern writers, who have made names for themselves in the United States and attained international repute since 1920, among them Elizabeth Madox Roberts, Caroline Gordon, Flannery O'Connor, and Walker Percy, as well as Wendell Berry, Marion Montgomery, George Garrett, Fred Chappell, and Ferrol Sams. In *The Burden of Southern History* (1960), C. Vann Woodward contrasts this definitively conservative aspect with the rootlessness inherent in the works of many modern writers from other regions. Southern writers might depict distortions associated with their history or local institutions, but "a Hemingway hero with a grandfather is inconceivable." Southern literature also continues to emphasize the concrete, the particular, the actual over the abstract or perfect, even when it is ugly. It portrays local themes and settings, even if the *oeuvres* are American or universal in their portent. The relationship between conservatism and literature in the South is truly direct if, as Louis Rubin says, "the impulse to write is the impulse to give order and definition to one's world."

Wesley Allen Riddle

See also Agrarians; Fugitives, The; History, Idea of; New Criticism; Politician; Religion in Nineteenth-Century Literature; Vanderbilt University.

George M. Curtis III and James J. Thompson Jr., eds., *The Southern Essays of Richard M. Weaver* (1987); Donald Davidson, *The Attack on Leviathan: Regionalism and Nationalism in the United States* (1938); Charles W. Dunn and J. David Woodard, *American Conservatism from Burke to Bush: An Introduction* (1991); Eugene D. Genovese, *The Southern Tradition: The Achievement and Limitations of an American Conservatism* (1994); Russell Kirk, *The Conservative Mind: From Burke to Eliot* (1953); Jerry Z. Muller, ed., *Conservatism: An Anthology of Social and Political Thought from David Hume to the Present* (1997); George H. Nash, *The Conservative Intellectual Movement in America Since 1945* (1996); Clinton Rossiter,

Conservatism in America (1962); Joseph Scotchie, ed., *The Vision of Richard Weaver* (1996); Richard M. Weaver, *Ideas Have Consequences* (1948); Richard M. Weaver, *The Southern Tradition at Bay: A History of Postbellum Thought* (1968).

COTTON

Cotton has figured prominently in shaping southern life and literature. After Eli Whitney's invention of the cotton gin in 1793, cotton quickly replaced tobacco as the mainstay of the region's plantation economy. By the time of the Civil War, the American South was the world's leading producer of cotton fiber. Cotton culture survived both the South's defeat and Emancipation. In the decades immediately following the war, the old plantation system gave way to sharecropping and tenantry, which ensnared former slaves and white yeomen alike. Under that new system, cotton production continued to climb, until it peaked in 1926 at eighteen million bales.

Sharecroppers began the agricultural year in December, when they visited a furnishing merchant to take out a loan in the form of the seeds, tools, and supplies they needed to get a crop in the ground and to survive until harvest time. Throughout the spring and summer, they chopped and hoed to protect their crop from the competition of weeds, and then in the fall, entire families entered the fields to pick the ripe cotton bolls. When the cotton was ginned and sold, most sharecroppers found that they had earned less than enough to settle up their accounts—plus interest payments that sometimes ran as high as 50 percent. Beginning in the early twentieth century, cotton farmers also struggled with the Mexican boll weevil, which moved northeastward and severely reduced yields. For many farmers, these challenges proved insurmountable. They fell into a form of debt peonage that bound them to the land and a life of poverty, illiteracy, and ill health.

During the Great Depression, the New Deal's Agricultural Adjustment Administration paid southern growers to take cotton acreage out of production, and many large landowners used the fees that they received to mechanize their operations. The result was what one historian has described as a "mechanical enclosure movement" that dramatically reduced the need for farm workers and turned tens of thousands of sharecroppers and tenants off the land. By the 1970s, new crops such as soybeans had taken command of the old

cotton belt, and all but a small fraction of the cotton that remained was harvested by machine.

Cotton provides the backdrop to tales of the South written throughout the late nineteenth and early twentieth centuries, but it was the plight of sharecroppers that made cotton culture itself the focus of literary concern. Ellen Glasgow published *The Voice of the People* in 1900, partly in response to the Populist revolt of the 1890s, and then, during the crisis years of the 1920s and 1930s, a flood of similar novels followed, including Dorothy Scarborough's *In the Land of Cotton* (1923) and *Can't Get a Red Bird* (1929); Jack Bethea's *Cotton* (1928); T. S. (Thomas Sigismund) Stribling's *The Store*, winner of the Pulitzer Prize in 1932; Welbourn Kelley's *Inchin' Along* (1932); and Robert Rylee's *Deep Dark River* (1935).

James L. Leloudis

See also Great Depression; New Deal; Plantation; Sharecropping.

Pete Daniel, *Breaking the Land: The Transformation of Cotton, Tobacco, and Rice Cultures Since 1880* (1985); Theodore Rosengarten, *All God's Dangers: The Life of Nate Shaw* (1974); Harold D. Woodman, *King Cotton and His Retainers: Financing and Marketing the Cotton Crop of the South, 1800–1925* (1968).

COUNTRY MUSIC

For most of the twentieth century, one of the most popular, directly accessible, and easily recognizable American musical forms has been country music. Its lyric lamentations range from the earnestly heartfelt to the dolorously maudlin, and its enthusiasms tend to be straightforward and frequently rip-roaring. Country singers, likewise, cover the vocal map, from stratospheric bluegrass tenors like Bill Monroe to downhome baritones like Don Williams to simultaneously earthy and stylish barroom chanteuses like Patsy Cline. The instrumental sound of most country bands is typified by some ensemble mixture of guitar, fiddle, banjo, mandolin, dobro, lap or pedal steel guitar, piano, percussion, and occasionally harmonica and accordion.

Really an amalgam, country music is the commercial outgrowth of several strands of folk and regional music; its constituent parts have been known over country music's eighty-year commercial history by such names as hillbilly, mountain, old-time, string-band, bluegrass, western, cowboy, western swing, white gospel, country-and-western (or C&W), and, simply, country. This music began to take identifiable commercial form in the 1920s; during that decade, an informal radio picking session in Nashville acquired the nickname *Grand Ole Opry,* and this still-extant and more-successful-than-ever radio variety-showcase, along with others like it (such as Shreveport's *Louisiana Hayride,* the *Chicago Barn Dance,* and the *Capital City Music Hall* in Charleston, West Virginia), presented country music to the South and to the world at large. When an RCA Victor producer named Ralph Peer signed Jimmie Rodgers ("the Yodeling Brakeman") and the Carter Family in Bristol, Virginia, on the same day in 1927, country music had found its first national recording and radio stars.

Country music has many debts, owing much to old English and Scottish folk ballads; to nineteenth-century religious music and sacred-harp, shape-note songs; to the minstrel-show music that first put the European fiddle with the African banjo; to medicine shows, jug bands, vaudeville; and to Hollywood's many singing cowboys. Black gospel and country blues inform the admixture, and Cajun influences, too, have come into country music over the years (as illustrated by songs such as Hank Williams's "Jambalaya" and Doug Kershaw's "Louisiana Man"). So have strains of border music from the Rio Grande (Freddie Fender's Tex-Mex "Till the Last Teardrop Falls").

Over its eight decades, country music has produced legions of accomplished and distinctive instrumentalists, such as fiddlers Curly Ray Cline, Vassar Clements, Kenny Baker, and Laurie Lewis; banjoists Uncle Dave Macon, Earl Scruggs (who developed the three-finger bluegrass style), Bill Keith, Tommy Thompson, and Bela Fleck; pianists Floyd Cramer and Hargus "Pig" Robbins; dobroist Jerry Douglas; and the extraordinary multi-instrumentalists Doc Watson, Ricky Skaggs, and Mark O'Connor.

Pop record-production styles and the sheer force and ubiquity of rock-and-roll—as well as the American population's rapid divorce from the land—have taken a toll on the regional particularities and peculiarities of the country music of prior generations. There are few, if any, contemporary analogues to Uncle Dave Macon's decades-ago noting of a "Rabbit in the Pea Patch," and the vein that produced Merle Travis's classic, fatalistic miner's song "Sixteen Tons" (a hit for hymn-singing Tennessee Ernie Ford forty years ago) and Loretta Lynn's autobiographical "Coal Miner's

Daughter" (the inspiration for a popular 1970s film of the same name) now seems about played out. In the 1990s, one "country" radio format has called itself "Real Country," though its playlist sounded more like countryfied rock-and-roll aimed at suburban line-dancers than anything Hank Williams (the author of "Cold, Cold Heart," "Hey, Good Lookin'," and "I'm So Lonesome I Could Cry," not Hank Junior) ever penned or performed. Still, a certain irrepressible, earthy spirit remains: Roseann ("Seven-Year Ache") Cash, a spunky performer with a foot in both country and rock, once shocked her famous veteran-performer parents June Carter and Johnny ("I Walk the Line") Cash, who were in the New York audience the night the younger Ms. Cash introduced one song by saying, "Here's a song that'll really put the c—t back in country!"

Many observers have suggested that one of the major signifiers of country music has always been that its lyric content was about and intended for adults, with songs of ardent love and lust, betrayal and loss, sin and guilt, and also was imbued with an aching nostalgia for home, farm, and small-town life. Indeed, in country music there is an affection for the American land—and living on it—almost without compare in any other form of our popular music ("Hickory Wind," "Blue Bayou," and "You're the Reason God Made Oklahoma"). The desire to ramble (Hank Williams's "Rambling Man") is countered by the desire to stop rambling and return home ("Blue Ridge Mountain Blues"), and there is a readily apparent yearning to leave postagrarian industrial city life and return to the land ("Detroit City").

Though country music has occasionally foundered on self-parody ("All my Ex's Live in Texas"), the form has regularly given voice to an honest depiction of class consciousness ("I'm a Common Man, I Drive a Common Van") and the forthright frustrations of men and women overworked, underpaid, and stretched to the limit in their personal lives (Merle Haggard's "Workingman's Blues" and "If We Make It Through December," and Johnny Paycheck's "You Can Take This Job and Shove It"). Country songwriting also comprises the narrative (Jimmy Driftwood's setting of "The Battle of New Orleans" to the old fiddle tune "The Eighth of January," Tom T. Hall's "I Remember the Year Clayton Delany Died"); the sentimental and maudlin ("Mama, Put My Little Shoes Away," "He Stopped Loving Her Today"); the religious ("Great Speckled Bird," "I Saw the Light," "Will the Circle Be Unbroken?"); the guilt-ridden ("Lyin' Here with Linda on

My Mind") and sin-obsessed ("I Started Hatin' Cheat-in' Songs Today"); the ridiculous ("Mama Was a Con-vict"); and the jingoistic (the Vietnam-era "Okie from Muskogee" and "Fightin' Side of Me"). It is worthy of note that the author of this last pair, Merle "the Hag" Haggard, has had one of the longest and most prolific writing, performing, and recording careers in country music, and that he also once penned a critical post-Watergate song nostalgically wishing for a time "back before Nixon lied to us all on TV."

Because of the outsized (and more than occasionally outlandish) lives of many of country music's best-known practitioners, feature writers, star biographers, and serious journalists alike have never wanted for ma-terial here.

Literary works concerning country music include North Carolinian Bland Simpson's *Heart of the Coun-try: A Novel of Southern Music* (1983); Virginian Lee Smith's *The Devil's Dream* (1992), which was success-fully adapted to the musical stage; and Kentuckian Jean Ritchie's memoir, *Singing Family of the Cumber-lands* (1955). Cinematic treatments include Robert Alt-man's *Nashville,* Bruce Beresford's *Tender Mercies,* as well as *Coal Miner's Daughter* and *W.W. & the Dixie Dance Kings.*

Significant archives are those of the Country Music Association (Nashville, Tennessee); the Library of Con-gress American Folklife Collection (Washington, D.C.); and the Southern Folklife Collection (University of North Carolina at Chapel Hill).

With countrymen like the career muleskinner Uncle Dave Macon ("Whoa, Mule, Whoa," "Keep My Skil-let Good and Greasy All the Time") and his successor Grandpa Jones ("Old Rattler"), hilarious parodists like Homer and Jethro ("We're the Boys from Camp Koo-kamonga," "Pal-ya-chee"), and powerful American-treasury vocalists such as Doc Watson (now Doctor Doc, with a 1997 honorary degree from the University of North Carolina at Chapel Hill), Willie Nelson, Patsy Cline, Dolly Parton, Loretta Lynn, Emmylou Harris, Mary Chapin Carpenter, and Iris Dement, country music is clearly one of our richest, most varied, and vital popular arts—standing alongside jazz, the Broad-way musical, and rock-and-roll as a distinctly Ameri-can twentieth-century form. Country's roots may well be the deepest.

Bland Simpson

See also Fiddlers' Conventions; *Grand Ole Opry.*

Cece Conway, *African Banjo Echoes in Appalachia: A Study of Folk Traditions* (1995); Nick Dawidoff, *In the Country of Country: People and Places in American Music* (1997); Frye Gaillard, *Watermelon Wine: The Spirit of Country Music* (1978); Douglas B. Green, *Country Roots: The Origins of Country Music* (1976); Paul Hemphill, *The Nashville Sound: Bright Lights and Country Music* (1970); Bill C. Malone, *Country Music, U.S.A.* (1968, rev. ed. 1985); Bill Malone, *Stars of Country Music: Uncle Dave Macon to Johnny Rodri-guez* (1975); Bill Malone, *Singing Cowboys and Musical Mountaineers: Southern Culture and the Roots of Country Music* (1993); David Whisnant, *All That Is Native & Fine: The Politics of Culture in an American Region* (1983); Charles K. Wolfe, *Tennessee Strings: The Story of Country Music in Ten-nessee* (1977); Charles K. Wolfe, *In Close Harmony: The Story of the Louvin Brothers* (1996); Charles K. Wolfe, *The Devil's Box: Masters of Southern Fiddling* (1997).

CRACKER

The origin of the term *cracker* is hard to determine. It seems to have risen out of two contexts. There were "corn crackers"—poor white farmers who pounded, or cracked, corn for food—and "whip crackers," more affluent folk who managed their livestock with a long whip whose tip was called a cracker. Originally, in the early and middle nineteenth century, both kinds were concentrated in the piney woods of south Georgia and north Florida. Eventually, the term *cracker* came to be associated almost exclusively with the state of Georgia. *Cracker* differs from other terms that are roughly syn-onymous, such as *redneck* and *poor white,* by having a more restricted geographical application. Fittingly, Georgia writers have been the principal chroniclers of crackers.

In southern literature, the cracker has usually been portrayed as a poor white—the corn cracker instead of the whip cracker. Early representations of the cracker were included in sketches in Augustus Baldwin Long-street's *Georgia Scenes* (1835) and William Tappan Thompson's *Chronicles of Pineville* (1845). After the Civil War, Sidney Lanier composed a number of poems in what might be called cracker dialect. Told in the lan-guage of Middle Georgia farmers and published in newspapers and magazines, the poems—"Thar's More in the Man Than Thar Is in the Land" (1871), "Jones's Private Argument" (1871), and "9 from 8" (1884)—criticize cotton culture and make an urgent plea for ag-ricultural diversification. Joel Chandler Harris portrayed crackers with great sensitivity in stories contained in *Mingo and Other Sketches in Black and White* (1884), *Free Joe and Other Georgian Sketches* (1887), and *Balaam and His Master and Other Sketches and Stories* (1891).

Early in the twentieth century, Erskine Caldwell emerged as the preeminent delineator of crackers. His first published work, an essay that appeared in 1926, bore the title "The Georgia Cracker." In the piece, which contains many of the themes that Caldwell would later develop in fiction, *cracker* referred to white Georgians, not only the poor but also the rich, who embraced the savage ideal of intolerance. Caldwell depicted poor white Georgians much more sympathetically in his fiction, notably the short-story collections *American Earth* (1931), *We Are the Living* (1933), *Kneel to the Rising Sun and Other Stories* (1935), and *Southways* (1938) and the novels *Tobacco Road* (1932) and *God's Little Acre* (1933). Later in the twentieth century, Flannery O'Connor portrayed such people less sympathetically in the novels *Wise Blood* (1952) and *The Violent Bear It Away* (1960) and in the short-story collections *A Good Man Is Hard to Find* (1955) and *Everything That Rises Must Converge* (1965). Later still, Harry Crews, the son of a south Georgia sharecropper, presented crackers in novels such as *The Gospel Singer* (1968) and *A Feast of Snakes* (1976) and in the memoir *A Childhood: The Biography of a Place* (1978). The election in 1976 of the Georgian Jimmy Carter as president of the United States brought a brief interest throughout the nation in what was called cracker chic, a phenomenon portrayed in the humorous sketches in *Crackers* (1980) by Roy Blount Jr.

Wayne Mixon

See also Caste; Class; Georgia, Literature of; Poor White; Redneck; Savage Ideal; Sharecropping.

Duane Carr, *A Question of Class: The Redneck Stereotype in Southern Fiction* (1996); Sylvia Jenkins Cook, *From Tobacco Road to Route 66: The Southern Poor White in Fiction* (1976); Shields McIlwaine, *The Southern Poor White from Lubberland to Tobacco Road* (1939); Wayne Mixon, *The People's Writer: Erskine Caldwell and the South* (1995); Merrill Maguire Skaggs, *The Folk of Southern Fiction* (1972).

CREOLE

There have been many meanings of the word *creole* over time. According to Gwendolyn Midlo Hall, the Portuguese word *crioulo* first meant a slave of African descent born in the New World. Eighteenth-century Louisiana, as well as other Spanish and French colonies of the Americas, used the term *creole* to distinguish American-born slaves from African-born slaves. Midlo Hall writes, in *Creole New Orleans,* that "all first-generation slaves born in America and their descendants were designated creoles." Louisiana Creole slaves were united by their common identity and even more by the Louisiana Creole language, which was created by early slaves of Louisiana.

Another account of the origin of the term *creole* is that it derives from the word *criollo* and was used by Spanish conquistadors to distinguish European whites born in the New World from natives of Spanish colonies and from those that were European-born. The story is that the Spanish brought the term to Louisiana when the territory was taken over by the Spanish in 1763. However, the French colony of Saint Domingue, for instance, used the term *creole* in the seventeenth and eighteenth centuries to mean simply native-born. It was this tradition that was adopted in colonial Louisiana at its very beginnings, before the transfer to Spain, as can be seen in church records and communication between Louisiana and royal officials.

The term became important in Louisiana, however, only when Louisiana was ceded to the United States in 1803 and the original Louisianians called themselves *creole* to distinguish themselves from the newcomers, the Americans, and the Latin versus Anglo-Saxon struggle for dominance in the city began. In 1836 the city was divided into three municipalities because of the animosity between the two groups. Even then, New Orleanians continued to consider the word *creole* to be without racial connotation and the term continued to be used by both blacks and whites.

After the Civil War, the Creole struggle against the Americans took another turn. The possibility of the ascendancy of people of color in politics and business led to a fury over the matter of race. After George Washington Cable's publication of *The Grandissimes* in 1880, the well-respected Creole historian Charles Gayarré and others took on the challenge of righting the false conception of Creoles they felt Cable had fostered intentionally—the conception that Creoles were a mixed race. In his address at Tulane University in 1885, "The Creoles of History and the Creoles of Romance," Gayarré defined Creoles as a "pure white" race. His ideas were so quickly accepted by Creoles that by 1938, when the WPA wrote and published the

New Orleans City Guide, the definition of *creole* as "a white descendant of the French and Spanish settlers in Louisiana during the Colonial period (1699–1803)," had been almost universally accepted as truth by white Louisianians for at least fifty years.

Yet in the 1990s, the Creole poet Sybil Kein defined the term *creole* as "a Louisiana native of mixed heritage usually including African, French, Spanish and Native American," and today that definition of the term prevails in most societies.

Kein's definition reflects the circumstances of Louisiana's Creoles of color, or *gens de couleur libres,* whose lives have been a part of New Orleans's history since its beginnings. They were, and are, a group of men and women joined by their Creole culture but separated from white Creoles by distinction of race. They were largely Catholic and were bound by a love of family and duty to their country. Creoles of color fought in every major battle of the Louisianians, including the Battle of New Orleans in the War of 1812 and the Civil War. In 1724 their legal status as quasi-citizens was defined by the French Code Noir: they could own slaves and real estate and be recognized in the courts, but they could not vote or marry white persons. They owned over two million dollars of real property by 1830; much of it was in the center of New Orleans. De Tocqueville described the group as a "third race" in New Orleans. They had much to suffer in the decision of white Creoles following the Civil War and Reconstruction to ignore them and their relationship in culture, language, and often family. The Comité des Citoyens, a group of prominent Creoles, was organized to fight the continuing ascendancy of Jim Crow laws in the South, in terms of education, the law, and public accommodations. They handled the case for Homer Plessy in his famous suit to prevent segregation on trains, which went to the Supreme Court as the *Plessy v. Ferguson* case. But the mood of Louisiana, as well as the country, was to move toward reconciliation between the North and the South at all costs. The Comité lost the *Plessy v. Ferguson* case.

By the late 1990s, the word *creole* was seldom used by whites because of the loss of interest in the old dispute between Creole and American, and the prevailing concern about the word being taken to mean a "mixed" race. Primarily blacks use the word. The term has heavy social and political connotations and is an inclusive term rather than an exclusive one. It is a positive term socially in the black and white worlds, but is critiqued negatively by most of the world that is excluded by the term. The differences between Creoles (who live downtown, in the old Second Municipality) and Negroes, or blacks (who live primarily uptown, or in the Third Municipality) continued to affect politics in New Orleans well into the beginning of the twenty-first century.

The Creole is generally thought to be a Louisiana native who is of French or Spanish and African, sometimes Native American ancestry, although it is still considered to be only French and Spanish among white Creoles. Those who have Native American ancestry do not consider themselves Creole unless they also have colonial French or Spanish ancestry. Creoles have their origin in several parts of Louisiana: primarily in New Orleans, southwest Louisiana (where Cajuns are also dominant), and in the Cane River, or Natchitoches, area.

Violet Harrington Bryan

See also Creole Literature; Louisiana, Literature of.

Arnold Hirsch and Joseph Logsdon, eds., *Creole New Orleans: Race and Americanization* (1992); Sybil Kein, *The American South* (1996), and Kein, ed., *Creole: The History and Legacy of Louisiana's Free People of Color* (2000).

CREOLE LITERATURE

The Creole character in southern literature functions as a specialized "other" within a culture that itself represents something different from the American norm. The term originally referred to individuals born in America of European parents, but in Louisiana, the only territory where the distinction remained significant after colonial immigration stopped, it came to represent whites, blacks, Indians, and various mixtures of these racial groups complicated by the addition of French or Spanish ancestry. Creole folklore, containing colorful figures such as the pirate Jean LaFitte and the exotic traditions of Mardi Gras, provided fascinating material. White Creole characters became most popular in the era of local color, a time when they helped to satisfy the national public's hunger for quaint and unusual figures, speaking a native dialect, and illustrating regional differences for audiences increasingly homogenized in northern cities. George W. Cable's *Old Creole Days* (1879) and *The Grandissimes* (1880), Grace King's many stories, such as "Monsieur Motte" (1885), and later Kate Chopin's *Bayou Folk* (1894), *A*

Night in Acadie (1897), and *The Awakening* (1899) all contain memorable portraits of the white Creoles of southern Louisiana. Cable, King, and Chopin were not themselves Creoles but captured the distinctiveness of a fiercely proud people who saw themselves as an embattled culture within a culture. Creole characters, such as the white and black Grandissime brothers of Cable's novel, represent the troubling racial dichotomies and mixtures of New Orleans. Cable was sympathetic to the New Orleans white Creole's sense of disfranchisement, but he also saw their culture as a way to explore a racist mentality built on fear of change and a willful arrogance built on ideas of "blood."

Charles Gayarré, a Creole historian and loyal Confederate, wrote to defend his heritage after the Civil War, particularly from what he felt were the cruel falsehoods of Cable's work (see especially his *The Creoles of History and the Creoles of Romance,* 1885). In all of the local-color representations of the Creole, dialect plays a central part. Language promotes not only a sense of difference but the pervasive charm and innocence, if not blindness, to mainstream realities. Gender also figures importantly in portrayals of Creole character. Chopin's *The Awakening* best illustrates the ideal of the Creole woman, who is sensuous but also motherly, openly tolerant of sexual innuendo but also obedient and family-oriented.

In the twentieth century, the white Creole's outsider status and exoticism were stressed. Lafcadio Hearn lived in New Orleans only for one decade in his twenties (1877–1887), but his time there was enough to heighten his interest in Creoles and to result in several important works reflecting their culture, including *Creole Sketches,* collected in 1924. In Faulkner's *Absalom, Absalom!* (1936), the dark, rejected son of Thomas Sutpen, Charles Bon, is consistently associated with the New Orleans Creole culture of his unacceptable (because part-black) mother. The black Creole in white fiction, as exemplified by Charles Bon and the f.m.c. (free man of color) Honoré Grandissime in Cable, easily became an example of the "tragic mulatto," intelligent, gifted, but always rejected within cultures defined by purity of "blood."

In African American southern literature, Creole writing has an important place. The first poetry anthology of African Americans, *Les Cenelles,* was published by Creole "free men of color" in New Orleans in 1845. Louisiana-born Alice Dunbar-Nelson (1875–1935), wife (later divorced) of Paul Laurence Dunbar, benefitted from the public's local-color appetite as she published stories of New Orleans mixed-blood Creoles like herself in her collection *The Goodness of St. Rocque and Other Stories* (1899). Ernest J. Gaines (1933–) grew up among white and black Creoles in Oscar, Louisiana. His first novel, *Catherine Carmier* (1964), dealt with black Creoles who practiced their own forms of discrimination based on color, and *A Gathering of Old Men* (1983) returns to the Louisiana plantation of more modern times to study the relations between white and black Creoles. Brenda Marie Osbey, a New Orleans poet, explores the rich folklore of Creole African Americans of her native city in several volumes, including her recent *All Saints* (1997). In the 1990s, Osbey tells us, Creole heritage became an exhilarating factor; now, she says, "people cling to their ethnicity, and even flaunt it." A culture of change, of difference, then, is helping to redefine the South in ways that use the past instead of discarding it.

Lucinda H. MacKethan

See also Creole; Louisiana, Literature of; New Orleans, Louisiana; Quadroon Balls.

John Lowe, "An Interview with Brenda Marie Osbey," in *The Future of Southern Letters* (1996).

CRIMES AND CRIMINALS

Anecdotes and statistics both attest that throughout its history, the South has been a violent place. Modern scholars frequently begin with the quantitative study of H. V. Redfield, written in 1880. Using newspaper accounts of killings in three southern states—a method destined to produce an undercount—Redfield estimated a murder rate in those states at least ten times that of the rates in New England or the Midwest. Statistics published by the federal government and the FBI throughout the twentieth century show that the eleven states of the Confederacy plus Kentucky regularly appear among states with the highest murder rates. In the late 1900s, southern cities usually placed high on lists of the most dangerous urban areas. This history of statistically excessive violence coexists with a southern affection for extralegal remedies to crimes, remedies which themselves often bleed into the realm of criminal behavior. Many theories exist to explain this violence: among the most often cited are the continuation of the rough ethos of the frontier (a view developed by W. J. Cash), the effort to control the African American population both slave and free (a view favored by historian Roger Lane), and a tradition of personal honor by which redress for wrongs occurs outside of law (offered by Edward L. Ayers and Fox Butterfield).

Iconic southerners as diverse as William Faulkner and Senator Strom Thurmond had fathers who were involved in shootings that sprang from personal disputes. Neither father suffered at the hands of the law courts after the incidents. Indeed, Faulkner's great-grandfather was shot in the face on the town square, yet in court his killer was acquitted of murder. Such events illustrate the southern disregard for established legal codes. The antebellum southern practice of dueling—and its less-refined manifestations in the brawl and the feud—derives from notions of personal honor, the belief that matters are best handled individually, according to individual codes, without appeal to the governmental authorities, whom southerners have always seemed to view with suspicion and even contempt. Dueling did not survive the Civil War, but personal codes did. Faulkner's story "Tomorrow" (1940) depicts a trial in which extralegal justice almost wins official approval. The defendant shot a scoundrel who intended to run off with the man's daughter. The defendant expects his jury to set him free; the one juryman who insists on a guilty verdict is seen by his fellows as perverse and obtuse. John Grisham's *A Time to Kill* (1989) features a murder trial in which a defense attorney righteously argues that the jury should sanction vigilante justice across racial boundaries: if they would acquit a white father who kills African Americans who raped his daughter, they should do likewise when the races are reversed. While these stories may reflect popular sentiments, the authors build into their plots an unease, a question of where justice really lies if it exists outside of established legalities. Yet such tolerance for violence and law-breaking among southern characters appears across the literature. In her novel *South Moon Under* (1933), Marjorie Kinnan Rawlings sympathetically describes the lives of men who ran illegal stills and defended them with violence against government agents. Even African American folk and blues songs reflected admiration for the legendary Stagolee, a remorseless murderer who refused to obey any social standards.

Personal redress easily becomes vigilantism (as in *A Time to Kill*); in the South, the most infamous form of vigilantism was lynching. By its broadest definition, lynching was a communally sanctioned attack on an alleged lawbreaker. Because of the disrespect for law and

the sadism implicit in lynchings, such attacks, when widely reported across the United States during the late 1800s and first decades of the 1900s, came to represent the savage, benighted South. To assure their readers that all southerners were not brutes, writers as diverse (or as similar) as Mark Twain, Charles Chesnutt, Irvin S. Cobb, and Harper Lee presented tales in which a noble figure somehow repels an angry lynch mob. Other writers probed how lynchings revealed the rage that existed below the surface of rural southern society, a rage usually directed at African Americans, a rage that emerged on the slightest pretexts. Faulkner portrays lynchings in *Sanctuary* (1931), *Light in August* (1932), and "Dry September" (1931) as in part reactions by outraged men to reports of horrid crimes, yet principally as exercises of power and control over African Americans and other outsiders. Richard Wright's stories in *Uncle Tom's Children* (1940) reveal how seemingly benign encounters between the races (such as African American boys swimming in a white man's pond or a white salesman visiting an African American woman) quickly escalate to violence because the whites know they can persecute the African Americans with impunity. Other writers who have sensitively handled racially motivated crime include Lillian Smith (*Strange Fruit*, 1944) and Ernest J. Gaines (*A Gathering of Old Men*, 1983, and *A Lesson Before Dying*, 1993).

Many writers have found in re-creating real-life southern crimes the opportunity to deal critically with the region's violent habits. The trial in Harper Lee's *To Kill a Mockingbird* (1960) recalls the Scottsboro case from the 1930s, in which nine African American youths were repeatedly convicted of rape despite plain evidence to the contrary. In *World Enough and Time* (1950), a fictionalization of an early-1800s Kentucky tragedy, Robert Penn Warren portrays how the murderer acted from youthful idealism and idolization of women. The killer finds himself at the mercy of a corrupt court system, and when he flees, he enters the realm of lawless frontier gangs. Warren crafts his novel as an epic of Kentucky's early, bloody history, a time without absolute standards of morality. In *Carolina Skeletons* (1988), David Stout describes the racism that led to the death in 1944 of the youngest African American ever executed for murder, a fourteen-year-old in South Carolina. John Grisham's *The Chamber* (1994) uses elements from the case of Byron de la Beckwith, who after three trials was convicted of murdering Medgar Evers, to explore both how the South remembers the reactionary violence of the Civil Rights era and how the South embraces capital punishment. Eudora Welty's story "Where Is the Voice Coming From" also deals fictionally with Medgar Evers's murderer. In these and other books, most characters too easily accept the violence and injustice around them and do little to bring about reform.

Crime as literary entertainment enjoyed its own renaissance in the 1980s and 1990s, when nearly one hundred mystery and detective novels with southern settings appeared each year. The local-colorists of the late 1800s sought to depict the sentimental quaintness of southern locales; in the late 1900s, many popular southern crime writers similarly portrayed the cliché of the happy southern town and updated it by showing how southern society has sloughed off its old benighted ways. These writers, such as Joan Hess, Rita Mae Brown, Margaret Maron, and Sharyn McCrumb, employed southern trappings—old family houses, Civil War monuments, dirt roads—to appeal to the South of the popular imagination. The books likewise show how the South has progressed mightily in race relations, the status of women, standard of living, and other social conditions. These authors link an awareness of past sins with an optimism for the future. The crimes in the books are temporary disturbances, vestiges of an embarrassing past in the otherwise peaceful and socially progressive modern South.

The alternate current that runs through southern crime writing of the late 1900s sees crime not as an aberration but as a signal of a sick society. Such writers apply the ethos of the hard-boiled detective novel, usually associated with bleak urban settings, to the rural South to expose the region's inherent evils. *Chiefs* (1981) by Stuart Woods intertwines the hunt for a serial killer with the changes in race relations in a Georgia town across five decades. *In the Electric Mist with Confederate Dead* (1993) by James Lee Burke describes how the detective hero finds continuities between a lynching from the 1950s and organized crime of the 1990s. Writers such as Woods and Burke, along with Patricia Cornwell, Michael Malone, and James Sallis, conjoin detective fiction with the respected tradition of southern literature as social critique, inheriting the vision of Faulkner, Robert Penn Warren, and Harper Lee.

John F. Jebb

See also Family Feuding; Honor; Kentucky Tragedy; Law Before 1900; Law, 1900 to Present; Lawyer; Lynching; Mystery and Detective Fiction; Scottsboro Trial; Till, Emmett; Tobacco Wars; Violence.

Edward L. Ayers, *Vengeance and Justice: Crime and Punishment in the 19th Century American South* (1984); Fox Butterfield, *All God's Children: The Bosket Family and the American Tradition of Violence* (1995); W. J. Cash, *The Mind of the South* (1941); Roger Lane, *Murder in America: A History* (1997); David M. Oshinsky, *"Worse Than Slavery": Parchman Farm and the Ordeal of Jim Crow Justice* (1996); J. K. Van Dover and John F. Jebb, *Isn't Justice Always Unfair? The Detective in Southern Literature* (1996).

CRISIS

Crisis magazine was founded in 1910 as the official publication of the National Association for the Advancement of Colored People (NAACP). Its influential inaugural editor, W. E. B. Du Bois, would set the tone for this significant magazine whose goal was to assert and prove African American equality in a postwar American society that continuously demonstrated its belief that African Americans were inferior to their European American counterparts.

In literary circles, the magazine is best known as a vehicle for helping to begin and sustain the Harlem Renaissance. It was in *The Crisis* that W. E. B. Du Bois called for a "Negro Renaissance" that would affirm African American social, political, and intellectual viability in a hostile American milieu. Because of Du Bois's editorial goal to put the African American community's "best foot forward," the magazine primarily featured articles, literature, and visual art that treated issues concerning the black bourgeoisie, such as cultural atavism, miscegenation, northern discrimination, and racial equality; however, these concerns inevitably encompassed issues that were particularly pertinent to African Americans in the South who were not part of the Great Migration. Articles and literature that discussed rapes, lynchings, racial injustice, and the legacy of slavery often concentrated on southern locales. Furthermore, fiction and poetry by some of the most prominent African American southern writers of the 1920s and 1930s, such as Charles Chesnutt, Jean Toomer, and James Weldon Johnson, were published in *Crisis.*

Crisis remains in circulation currently and continues to address political, social, and economic issues that affect the African American community.

Valerie N. Matthews

See also African American Literature, 1919 to Present; Harlem Renaissance.

Roseann Pope Bell, *The Crisis and Opportunity Magazines: Reflections of a Black Culture, 1920–1930* (1973).

CROCKETT, DAVY

This frontiersman, Tennessee and U.S. congressman, and folk hero was born in Green County, Tennessee, the son of John and Rebecca Hawkins Crockett. Although he was elected a lieutenant in the 32nd Militia, served as a justice of the peace, town commissioner of Lawrenceburg, Tennessee, and colonel of the 57th Militia Regiment of Lawrence County by 1818, David Crockett was still a relatively unknown backwoods hunter with a talent for storytelling until his election to the Tennessee legislature in 1821 and then to the U.S. House of Representatives in 1827. Reelected to a second term in 1829, he split with President Andrew Jackson on land-reform issues and the Indian removal bill. Crockett was defeated in a bid for a third term when he openly and vehemently opposed Jackson's policies, but he was reelected in 1833.

Political notoriety gave his image a life of its own. By 1831 Crockett had become the model for Nimrod Wildfire, the hero of James Kirke Paulding's play *The Lion of the West,* as well as the subject of articles and books. Crockett said he was compelled to publish his autobiography, *A Narrative of the Life of David Crockett of the State of Tennessee* (1834), which was written with the help of Thomas Chilton, to counteract the outlandish stories printed under Crockett's name as the *Sketches and Eccentricities of Colonel David Crockett of West Tennessee* in 1833. A good deal of the information in *Sketches and Eccentricities,* a work that helped to initiate the humor of the Old Southwest, was, however, likely supplied by Crockett. The more outrageous stories were expanded by anonymous eastern hack writers who spun out tall-tale yarns for the

Crockett *Almanacs* (1835–1856). In their hands, the fictional Davy became a backwoods screamer and, with the death of the historical Crockett at the Alamo in 1836, the floodgates of fiction were loosed. He could not only "run faster, jump higher, squat lower, dive deeper, stay under longer, and come out drier, than any man in the whole country," but could save the world by unfreezing the sun and the earth from their axes and ride his pet alligator up Niagara Falls.

Subsequent works published under Crockett's name included *An Account of Col. Crockett's Tour to the North and Down East* (1835), *The Life of Martin Van Buren* (1835), and *Col. Crockett's Exploits and Adventures in Texas* (1836). All these works, together with his heroic death, completed an enduring union of history and legend. Clearly the present image of Crockett in American culture was continued and modified by scores of nineteenth- and twentieth-century biographies and "autobiographies" that merged fact and fantasy and most recently resulted in the 1990s fiction of Cameron Judd and David Thompson. This image, however, was also the descendant of the tradition of Davy as the hero of romantic melodrama. From his characterization by Paulding as Nimrod Wildfire to Frank Mayo serving as the coauthor and lead in the long-running play *Davy Crockett; Or, Be Sure You're Right Then Go Ahead,* the heritage was passed on through a series of silent and modern films that culminated in the Davys played by Fess Parker and John Wayne, both in theaters and on television, and in the Crockett craze of the mid-1950s. These traditions firmly established Crockett as a hero and preeminent representative of freedom and frontier individualism in the American mind.

Michael A. Lofaro

Michael A. Lofaro and Joe Cummings, eds., *Crockett at Two Hundred: New Perspectives on the Man and the Myth* (1989); James Adkins Shackford, *David Crockett: The Man and the Legend* (1956).

D

DAVIS, JEFFERSON

Born in Christian County (now Todd County), Kentucky, on June 3, 1808, Jefferson Davis was the first and only president of the Confederate States of America. Davis's family moved to Louisiana and later to Mississippi during his youth. In his precollege years, he attended various schools, including a Catholic school in Kentucky, Jefferson College near Natchez, and rural public schools in Mississippi. When it was time for college, he returned to Kentucky to study law at Transylvania University in Lexington. As he reached his senior year, he was appointed to West Point and so forsook graduation at Transylvania for the promise of a military career. He graduated from West Point in 1828. His West Point record was relatively lackluster, but Davis's formal education left him with a lifelong love for history and classical literature. He spent only seven years as an army lieutenant on the western frontier before returning to his home state of Mississippi to become master of a plantation carved from his brother's larger one. He was a slaveholder, but records indicate that he treated his slaves with more respect than was normally given slaves at the time.

In 1835, Davis married Sarah Knox Taylor, much to the consternation of her father, Zachary Taylor, military hero of the Mexican War and twelfth president of the United States. After three months of marriage, both Davis and his new bride contracted malaria; Sarah did not survive. Ten years later, he married Varina Howell, who supported Davis in good times and bad for the rest of his life. Both relationships have been romanticized in fiction. The relationship with Sarah is the centerpiece for Theodore Olsen's *There Was a Season* (1972), and Varina and Jefferson's courtship and marriage are fictionally examined in Shirley Seifert's *Proud Way* (1948). Since Davis is one of the principal characters in each of these novels, it appears as if his court-

ships have been more inviting to novelists than the remainder of his life, since novels with Davis as the main character are scarce to nonexistent.

Even though fictional center stage may have escaped this major historical figure, the political career that began in 1845 with Davis's election to Congress has formed the background for most fictional literature that uses the Civil War era as its setting. Shortly after his election to Congress, Davis felt that the Mexican War compelled him to again use his military training, so he resigned to become a colonel of the First Mississippi Rifles. His performance in the Mexican War was exemplary, particularly at the Battle of Buena Vista. Because of a wound he received in that battle, he returned to Mississippi to resume his career in agriculture, but he was shortly thereafter appointed to serve as a U.S. senator. He resigned to run unsuccessfully for the governorship of Mississippi in 1851. His absence from public life was brief; Franklin Pierce appointed him to be his secretary of war, a post that he retained throughout Pierce's presidency. In 1857, he returned to the Senate, where he remained until Mississippi seceded from the Union, which precipitated another resignation.

Davis was inaugurated in Montgomery, Alabama, as the president of the Provisional Government of the Confederate States of America on February 18, 1861, and in Richmond, Virginia, as the president of the Permanent Government of the Confederate States of America on February 22, 1862. His tenure as president came to a final end when he was captured in Irwinville, Georgia, as he fled with the remnants of the militarily defeated Confederate government on May 10, 1865. He was charged with treason and incarcerated at Fort Monroe, Virginia, only to be released on bail two years later, after Varina's long public campaign for his release. He had wanted to be tried publicly so that he could prove his innocence, but he was never given that opportunity because the Federal government eventually dropped the charges. During his tenure as president of the C.S.A., Davis had proven to be a determined individual who did not cooperate well with other politicians. His interests lay more in the military aspects of the job, so he often intervened in military matters, somewhat to the determent and fury of his generals. Davis was a very loyal friend to those he liked, often to a fault, and very much the enemy of those he did not. He was always single-mindedly dedicated to the best interests of the Confederacy, based upon his own view of each situation. As the Confederacy went into decline, he was sorely criticized for his failures as president, and he eventually became the scapegoat for the fall of his government. When both the North and the South began to realize the mistreatment that he was enduring at Fort Monroe, they became more sympathetic to Davis and his role in history. Again, he was viewed as a man who had honestly lived his beliefs and had steadfastly maintained his loyalty in the face of great adversity. After his release, Davis wrote a two-volume history of the Confederacy, *The Rise and Fall of the Confederate Government* (1881), in which he was intent particularly upon justifying his own actions as Confederate president. Davis died on December 9, 1889, still believing that his life as a politician had been completely justified and honorable.

Literature has been fairly kind to Davis, when he is considered at all. In her experimental, fictional, multi-voiced account of the Civil War, *The Wave* (1929), Evelyn Scott portrayed Davis as a highly intelligent victim of his times, much to be pitied as he tried to avert his inevitable arrest for being the president of the fallen government. But in most fiction about the period, Davis is mentioned in passing or is treated only as part of the scenery. Nonfiction explorations of his life by southern authors of fiction are a different matter. Two famous Fugitives have used Davis's life as a vehicle for an investigation of what it means to be "southern." Allan Tate wrote two biographies of southern heroes, *Stonewall Jackson* (1928) and *Jefferson Davis* (1929). He had planned to write a trilogy of biographies as an exploration of southern heroism, but he failed to complete his work on Robert E. Lee because of his growing disillusionment with his subject. Tate completed the work about Davis without reservation, finding him to be true to his cause in all circumstances.

In contrast to Tate's early-life exploration, another Fugitive, Robert Penn Warren, explored Davis's life late in his own career—*Jefferson Davis Gets His Citizenship Back* (1980)—on the occasion of the reinstatement of Jefferson's U.S. citizenship by Congress in 1979. He found Davis a man with unwavering integrity to his own beliefs and to his region, a man who would not have believed that any congressional action was necessary for his pardon, since he always felt justified in his actions as they related to his citizenship. This integrity and a no-nonsense approach to duty is highly valued by southern authors who consider Davis. Well-known historical figures continue to be closely scrutinized on these points; Jefferson Davis generally comes away from such scrutiny with a very positive report, as long as the investigation is restricted to historical southern values. After exhaustive examination by his fellow southerners, he remains an icon of southern honesty, single-minded dedication to duty, and steadfastness. Even when analysis proves that he made some political and military decisions that were less than perfect, his abiding qualities are claimed as a vital part of "southernness."

D. Michael Snider

See also Confederate States of America.

William C. Davis, *Jefferson Davis: The Man and His Hour* (1991); Clement Eaton, *Jefferson Davis* (1977); Michael Kreyling, *Figures of the Hero in Southern Narrative* (1987); Lewis P. Simpson, *The Fable of the Southern Writer* (1994).

DE BOW'S REVIEW

Begun in New Orleans in 1846 under the editorship of James Dunwoody Brownson De Bow, this publication was the premier magazine of commerce and politics in the South in the fifteen years before the Civil War. De Bow, a self-taught lawyer born in Charleston in 1820, began his literary career with essays in the *Southern Quarterly Review* of Charleston in 1844. Sensing a need to develop a national awareness of economic opportunities in the South and West, De Bow envisioned his *Review* as a vehicle for dispensing vital economic statistics of the region and for presenting southern opinion on the controversial political issues then developing in the nation.

In its early issues, *De Bow's Review* advocated the development of a transcontinental railroad along a southern route, encouraged the establishment of public schools and libraries, and provided statistics on production of major southern crops: sugar, cotton, rice, and tobacco. "The Editor's Armchair" each month included reviews of literary works for a general audience and focused primarily on books by southern authors.

During the 1850s, through contributions by George Fitzhugh, Edmund Ruffin, and William Gilmore Simms, the *Review* was extremely vocal in its defense of slavery and the concept of secession. Through his endorsement in the late 1850s of the Southern Commercial Convention Movement, De Bow encouraged southerners to regard regional loyalty as a solution to their economic problems.

From April 1862 to December 1865, publication of the *Review* ceased with only one issue in 1864. Publication resumed after the war with De Bow's more conciliatory editorials in favor of the Union and his rejections of the need for Federal troops to remain in the South during Reconstruction. With the deaths in 1867 of De Bow and his brother Benjamin Franklin De Bow, who served as managing editor, *De Bow's Review* continued publication by the estate until 1870. Then it was sold to northern publishers and ceased publication in 1884.

Alan T. Belsches

See also Old South; Periodicals, 1800 to 1860.

Paul F. Paskoff and Daniel J. Wilson, *The Cause of the South: Selections from "De Bow's Review," 1846–1867* (1982); Ottis Clark Skipper, *J. D. B. De Bow: Magazinist of the Old South* (1958).

DEBUTANTE

The debutante tradition, as it began in late-sixteenth-century England, was a rite of passage whereby an aristocratic young girl of marriageable age, about fourteen or fifteen, was presented to society with the expectation that a suitor and, with luck, a husband, would manifest himself shortly thereafter. Queen Elizabeth I's presentation of eligible young women at court is said to be the progenitor of the presentation ball. The word *debutante* comes from the French word *debuter,* which means "to lead off," reflecting how the debut marks a girl's passage into womanhood as well as her family's status in high society. Colonial America adopted the model of the presentation as early as 1748, when fifty-nine Philadelphia families held "Dancing Assemblies." Participation nationwide increased with

the economic success of the nineteenth-century Gilded Age.

The seed of English tradition flourished in southern soil, where veneration of womanhood, belief in social strata, and a tradition of male chivalry nourished the custom. The debutante ball was an opportunity to present young ladies to friends of the family and to young men of similar background and of marriageable age. The exclusive St. Cecilia Society of Charleston, South Carolina, was founded in 1737 to bring concert music to the South, but it later became solely a social organization. Debutantes are still presented at the annual St. Cecilia Ball. Caroline Gilman's heroine Cornelia Wilton, in *Recollections of a Southern Matron* (1838), goes to the St. Cecilia Ball. Although most of the young southern women in the novel yearned to attend the ball, Wilton dislikes it, and Gilman uses her heroine's experience at this paragon of debutante balls to establish Wilton as a kind of anti-belle who prefers plantation life to high society.

Today, young women are invited to make their debut according to their family's social standing and the members' perception of the girl's worthiness to be presented. The debutante season usually includes a series of parties given by the girls' families, culminating in the presentation. At the presentation, the young ladies, usually around eighteen years old, are presented one by one in white gowns before a crowd of society members, friends, and family. The presentation sometimes includes a curtsy, and the debutante is usually escorted by her father and one or two marshalls (a brother, friend, or boyfriend elected by the girl). Many larger southern towns have more than one debutante club or society—generally one club whose members are considered "old money" and others whose members are considered "new money." The newer clubs often have a volunteer-service requirement for entry into the society, whereas the older clubs base the decision for membership solely on the social status of the family and the reputation of the girl. Southern debutante clubs today are often all-male societies, such as the Redstone Club in Birmingham, Alabama, which sponsors the Redstone Ball at the Birmingham Country Club, and the Terpsichorean Club of Raleigh, North Carolina, which hosts the North Carolina Debutante Ball. Every major southern city has its debutante ball and society. Other examples include the Halloween Ball at the Piedmont Driving Club in Atlanta and the German at the Commonwealth Club of Virginia in Richmond.

Black debutante balls also include the presentation of debutantes wearing white gowns and the exclusive selection of the girls invited to debut. For example, in Savannah, Georgia, the Beta Phi Lambda chapter of the Alpha Phi Alpha Fraternity, Inc., sponsors the second-oldest black debutante ball in the South, the Debutante's Cotillion Ball, which began in 1944. The narrator-journalist in John Berendt's *Midnight in the Garden of Good and Evil* (1994) attends this ball and describes in detail the elegance of the event, noting especially its formality and the seriousness with which the participants regard it.

The southern debutante in literature is inextricably linked to the mythology of the southern belle. Since the southern belle is presumed to be physically beautiful and sexually pure, the debutante wears a white gown and long gloves; since the belle is sheltered by her father, the debutante is presented at the ball by her father, who, after her curtsy, escorts her around the perimeter of the crowd of friends and family in the audience. Ellen Glasgow's character Juliet, a southern aristocrat in *The Voice of the People* (1900), presumes that her daughter Julie will "come out." In this way, Glasgow marks the family as wealthy and elite and hints to the perpetuation of the family's class through the tradition of the debut. Belle Kearney, in her book *A Slaveholder's Daughter,* also written in 1900, states that a young lady would have to learn to dance after she made her debut or she would become a "wall-flower" in society. Kaye Gibbons's *On the Occasion of My Last Afternoon* (1998) is the story of a Civil War–era southern belle who refers to her coming out as an expected event of her life. The heroine's sister also debuted, but because her father did not approve of a single man who courted her thereafter, she never married.

Because the southern belle is synonymous with high society, writers today often refer to debutante balls or to a girl's coming out to demonstrate a character's social status. Peter Taylor in *The Old Forest* (1941) tells the story of Nat Ramsey, a "well-brought-up" young Memphis man who is torn between two young women. Taylor describes Caroline Braxley, Ramsey's fiancée, as a "society girl," whereas he describes Lee Ann Deehart as "a girl who was not in the Memphis debutante set." Taylor uses the debutante tradition to contrast the two girls' backgrounds. Lee Smith's "The Happy Memories Club" (1997) tells of a group of senior citizens who form a writing club. One of the writers creates a wealthy, beautiful, and sought-after character whom she describes as a "voluptuous debutante."

Whereas some southern writers innocuously describe a character as a debutante to evoke the image of a southern belle, others parody the archaic quality of debutante societies. *Southern Ladies and Gentlemen* (1975) by Florence King is a ribald parody of the debutante season seen through the perspective of a society columnist. King reveals the hypocrisy of the season's social affairs with wit and humor. Frances Newman in *The Hardboiled Virgin* (1926) also parodies the debutante tradition.

Although the debutante tradition's original purpose of finding a husband for a young girl at the completion of the debutante season is anachronistic, debutante societies continue to thrive in the South for reasons connected both to class consciousness and to nostalgia.

Mary Michaels O. Estrada

See also Aristocracy; Belle; Lady.

Kathryn Lee Seidel, *The Southern Belle in the American Novel* (1985); Dixon Wecter, *The Saga of American Society: A Record of Social Aspiration 1607–1937* (1937).

DECLARATION OF INDEPENDENCE

The Declaration of Independence (1776) stands as the originary document of the United States. Although the Constitution provided the actual foundation of government and laws for the country, the words of the Declaration have remained its animating spirit, and they have not lost their power to move people in the hope of freedom and democracy worldwide over the course of the ensuing two centuries. Much as Americans might make the Puritans the national forebears, these words were penned largely by a Virginian, Thomas Jefferson (1743–1826), plantation master and American *philosophe.*

Jefferson himself was only too keenly aware of the contradictions underlying the visionary hopes he held and expressed in the Declaration: between inalienable human rights and chattel slavery; between the sovereign claims of the individual and the needs of the modern nation-state. Put another way, the contradiction is between a nation that proclaims its own emancipation *from* history and the burden of an all-too-present past, and the nation's need to act *within* history. The problem is an American one, but the South has had to respond to the legacy of the Declaration from its own vantage point. Many of the recurring concerns of southern literature—the burden of the past, the relation between the individual and the community, the limits of human freedom—stem in part from the words of Jefferson the Virginian.

Jefferson wrote the Declaration in June 1776. He was part of a committee assigned the task of drafting it for the Continental Congress, a committee made up of Jefferson, Benjamin Franklin, John Adams, Robert Livingston, and Roger Sherman. The only definite factor in Jefferson's being assigned the task of drafting the document was his proven talent for writing, as demonstrated by his *A Summary View of the Rights of British America* (1774). But perhaps equally important were Jefferson's role as a delegate of Virginia, the largest and most populous of the British holdings in North America, and his role as champion of the rational, lettered mind. He was steeped in the most advanced thought of the European Enlightenment: the ideas of Locke, Rousseau, and the Scottish Common-Sense philosophers. At the time, Virginia was at the high-water mark in its intellectual history, producing such figures as James Madison (1751–1836) and George Mason (1725–1792) before the closure of the southern mind in defense of its peculiar institution, chattel slavery.

Jefferson's Declaration has caused a great deal of discomfort for southern traditionalists over the years. While those like the Jacksonians and the populists were able to embrace the radical democracy implicit in Jefferson's words, many in the antebellum establishment had a much more difficult time with what they saw as the dangerous abstractions in this vein of Jeffersonian thought. All men were not created equal in their eyes—not by birth, wealth, virtue, knowledge, or any other standard—and to claim such struck at the foundations of a well-ordered society. In the twentieth century, the southern Agrarians found the radical implications of Jefferson's thought at odds with their claims for the South as a traditional society, and they set the claims of kin and land over those of the individual considered in isolation. The Declaration's hope has retained its power nonetheless. Robert Penn Warren (1905–1989), himself an Agrarian in his early years, finally came to terms with Jefferson's legacy in a book-length poem, *Brother to Dragons: A Tale in Verse and Voices* (1953; new version, 1979), an attempt to reconcile Jefferson's vision of man with the realities of corruption and the forces of history.

The most powerful response to Jefferson's words in the Declaration has come from dissenters from any vision of southern orthodoxy, especially in regard to its central problem, race. African Americans, and whites in agreement with them, have long challenged the nation with its failure to realize the ideals of the Declaration, whether in the age of slavery, Jim Crow, or continuing inequality. Frederick Douglass (1818–1895), one of the great orators of the nineteenth century and an escaped Maryland slave, seized the nation's founding words to assert the rights of the slave as a human being; both in his autobiography and such addresses as "What to a Slave is the Fourth of July?" (1852), he used the rhetoric of the Declaration to convey the nation's distance from its founding ideals. This challenge was repeated by generations of African Americans through the time of the Civil Rights Movement, in which it found its greatest expression since the time of Douglass in the words of the Reverend Martin Luther King Jr. (1929–1968).

Douglas L. Mitchell

See also Civil Rights Movement; Douglass, Frederick; Jefferson, Thomas.

Joseph J. Ellis, *American Sphinx: The Character of Thomas Jefferson* (1997); Lewis P. Simpson, *The Brazen Face of History: Studies in the Literary Consciousness of America* (1980); Garry Wills, *Inventing America: Jefferson's Declaration of Independence* (1978).

DEEP SOUTH

As has been said about the porch, a traditional icon of the area, "Deep South" is a concept as well as a place. Most commonly considered to include the states of South Carolina, Georgia, Alabama, Mississippi, and Louisiana, this geographical regional designation is complexly relative. Just as *south* exists in relation to other compass points, *deep* is defined in terms of something upper, higher, or nondeep. All of these, from a national map down, involve imaginative constructs, but few other such designations in or for the United States are so imaginatively loaded or vividly constructed.

In land area, the Deep South corresponds roughly to the Old Cotton Kingdom, where annual rainfall and the number of warm, frost-free days were sufficient for cultivation of this cash crop. Required also, it was thought, was sufficient slave labor, and the extensive enmeshed lives of blacks and whites remains a chief defining characteristic of the conceptual Deep South.

Such interrelationships may, too, have influenced certain elements of definitive speech. In contour a long arc extending from eastern North Carolina to east Texas, the South's middle, centered in Mississippi and Alabama, is sometimes referred to as the Southern Trough. The term is connotative as well as denotative, for much of what is popularly thought of as "southern," especially in extreme and negative manifestation, is thought of as flourishing here. "Deeply southern," for example, are alligators, possums, swamps, Spanish moss, racial oppression, redneck sheriffs, lynchings, sultry days and sultry nights, steamy women, frigid belles, good old boys, voting irregularities, fundamentalist religious fanatics, political reactionaries, gentility, degeneracy, illiteracy, cigar-mouthing demagogues, magnolia trees, mockingbirds, chain gangs, drawls, poverty, cultural backwardness, and picturesque abnormality generally.

The literature of and from this area has contributed to, fought against, artistically used, and ignored such mythic stereotyping. William Faulkner, Margaret Mitchell, Erskine Caldwell, and Richard Wright are the writers of the 1930s, from Mississippi and Georgia, most responsible for forming the American reading public's basic picture of the Deep South in the twentieth century. In tone, cast of characters, outlook, and public receptivity, however, much of their literary base was set a hundred years before in the writings now referred to as Old Southwest humor.

The 1820s, 1830s, and 1840s saw significant migration from the middle Atlantic seaboard, much of its natural agricultural richness now depleted, to what was then the frontier Southwest, later the Deep South (east). The society that took shape here, including its violence and raucousness, its pretensions and its perversities, became raw material for nationally popular tales and sketches. Among the best purveyors of Old Southwest humor were Augustus Baldwin Longstreet of Georgia, George Washington Harris of Tennessee and Alabama, Johnson Jones Hooper and Joseph Glover Baldwin of Alabama, and Henry Clay Lewis of Louisiana. These men, and a number of others, as Hooper recognized, were indeed writing about "a new country." Here the earlier wilderness-conquering American experience was reproduced and extended, but with significant exotic differences rooted in a new and different climate and topography.

The local-color movement in American literature during the later nineteenth century crystallized regional and subregional identities. Ultimately less formative and influential for the "Deep South" than the fiction of the 1830s and the 1930s, local-color works clearly had historical impact. Tennessee's Mary Noailles Murfree and others wrote about life in the southern mountains, a subregion that does not figure as centrally or commonly in the concept of the Deep South as do other kinds of geographies. Richard Malcolm Johnston, however, portrayed the yeoman cracker society of middle Georgia in a host of short stories and sketches, while other writers, including George Washington Cable, Grace King, Lafcadio Hearn, Alice Dunbar-Nelson, and Kate Chopin, gave hot literary popularity to climatically warm, racially exotic Louisiana. Although Thomas Nelson Page from Virginia, Charles W. Chesnutt from North Carolina, and Ruth McEnery Stuart of Arkansas all affectingly reached national audiences with their varying portraits of southern African Americans, they did not have the same immediate and residual impact of Mississippi's Irwin Russell or Georgia's Joel Chandler Harris. Russell's "Christmas Night in the Quarters" (1878) long remained a very widely known black "dialect" poem. Harris, through his Uncle Remus books, the first of which appeared in 1880, contributed a distinctive context and at least two characters, Uncle Remus and Brer Rabbit, not only to national but to world literature. In the mind of a later public, the Walt Disney animated feature film based on Harris's creations was Song of the "Deep" South.

In the 1920s, from the same central Georgia that was the birthplace of Johnston and Harris, there emerged a contrasting but deeply localized and impressive book, this time from an African American—Jean Toomer's Cane (1923). Although Toomer actually lived for only a few months in Georgia, Cane's sensuous lyricism and lush imagery as well as its explicit contrast of northern and southern black life made it regionally defining as well as artistically groundbreaking.

Literary pictures of the old and new Deep South that were culturally operative before the late 1920s were given vital new life by writers of the Southern Renascence. Historical and contemporaneous elements each received extensive separate treatment, but the two now were also intertwined and related in profound and unprecedented ways. So also were, particularly and consequently, the lives of the two chief racial groups of the region.

Two Georgia writers who depicted contrasting times and social classes in their fiction produced comparably enduring images. The quintessential Old South novel, Margaret Mitchell's Gone With the Wind (1936), may prove to be the most popular U.S. book of the twentieth century. Not as many persons today can name Erskine Caldwell's *Tobacco Road* (1932) or *God's Little Acre* (1933), but members of the general public are just as indebted to Caldwell for their operative images of Deep South poor-white trash as they are to Mitchell for other conceptions.

Mississippians Richard Wright and William Faulkner wrote out of their different racial backgrounds to secure international attention. Wright's *Uncle Tom's Children* (1938) seared the tribulations of African Americans in the Deep South into national and world consciousness. Faulkner, in an astounding sequence of books in just a little over a dozen years—*The Sound and the Fury* (1929), *As I Lay Dying* (1930), *Sanctuary* (1931), *Light in August* (1932), *Absalom, Absalom!* (1936), *The Unvanquished* (1938), *The Hamlet* (1940), and *Go Down, Moses* (1942)—created a physical and spiritual world. He endowed his fictional Yoknapatawpha County, Mississippi, with an individualized population, social structure, history, economy, geography, climate, daily travail, and peculiar torment. Almost everything that is identified with the American Deep South was memorably realized in the art of Faulkner.

All subsequent southern writers, and especially those writing about the Deep South, have had to function in Faulkner's literary world. Two who were able to make their own unique literary way and achieve major public impact with a specific work are Robert Penn Warren and Tennessee Williams. Emerging out of Warren's firsthand knowledge of Louisiana in the 1930s, *All the King's Men* (1946) may be the essential American political novel, but in the minds of most readers, and for good reasons, it is first of all a picture of the epitome of *southern* politics. Tennessee Williams, a native of Mississippi, created several dramatic masterpieces but perhaps contributed best and most artfully to the conceptual Deep South with his *Cat on a Hot Tin Roof* (1955). It would be difficult to surpass Williams's title alone in suggesting substance, atmosphere, and state of mind.

In their respective bodies of work rather than in any single work, Eudora Welty of Mississippi and Flannery O'Connor of Georgia are worthy peers of Warren and Williams. Their moving, often humorous portrayals of small-town and rural country life in the Deep South are best realized in their short fiction. Among Welty's story collections are *A Curtain of Green and Other Stories* (1941) and *The Wide Net and Other Stories* (1943); in *A Good Man Is Hard to Find* (1955) and *The Violent Bear It Away* (1965), O'Connor, a Roman Catholic, drew striking portraits of devout Protestant Bible-Belt believers.

Asked why southern writers wrote so often about freaks, O'Connor said that it was because southerners were still able to recognize one. Another Georgia writer, one often associated with Tennessee Williams and considered, with him and O'Connor, to be a major purveyor of grotesque characters, was Carson McCullers. If *The Ballad of the Sad Café* (1951) may be thought to contain her most grotesque figures, it would also be considered her most deeply southern work. Truman Capote, born in Louisiana but drawing tellingly on youthful residences in Alabama, is also commonly put in the gothic and grotesque grouping. Like McCullers's fiction, Capote's work, such as *Other Voices, Other Rooms* (1948) and *The Grass Harp* (1951), was seen to be more personally psychological and symbolic than earlier Deep South novels with mainly realistic and sociological concerns. Both of these writers produced sensuous physical descriptions of the actual worlds they knew, however, and the internal worlds they reflected became an integral part of the conception of Deep South life and literature.

There is some justification in claiming for the Deep South what has been suggested about one particular constituent state. Just as the exotic was a persistent association with Louisiana until well after World War II, the chief commonality of contemporary writers from that state may be the negation of that image. Creators of literature write out of their personal experiences in time and place, and human lives and the culture of a place change over time. They also write within and against a literary culture, the accumulation of past treatments of what they wish to make use of in their own writing efforts. Because the Deep South has had such major accumulation, conscious reaction to, ignoring of, or attempted negation of it by serious writers should not be surprising. Its nondeliberate or unintended continuation—for a while longer at least—should also not be surprising. Among contemporary writers thought of as portraying Deep South experiences might be numbered Ernest J. Gaines, Larry Brown, Beth Henley, Mary Ward Brown, Mary Hood, Bailey White, Harry Crews, Josephine Humphreys, and Lewis Nordan. Because there have been so many gifted writers from this area, its concept in some form seems likely to exist for as long as talented creators from here continue, in either old or new ways, to captivate both American and overseas readers.

Bert Hitchcock

See also Accent; Alabama, Literature of; Bible Belt; Cracker; Georgia, Literature of; Grit Lit; Louisiana, Literature of; Mississippi, Literature of; Old Southwest; Race Relations; Regionalism; South Carolina, Literature of; Sunbelt.

Allison Davis, Burleigh B. Gardner, and Mary R. Gardner, *Deep South* (1941); Robert B. Highsaw, ed., *The Deep South in Transformation* (1964); Michael O'Brien, *The Idea of the American South 1920–1941* (1979); John Shelton Reed, *The Enduring South* (1972), and *Southern Folk, Plain & Fancy* (1986); Louis D. Rubin Jr., ed., *The American South: Portrait of a Culture* (1980); Frank E. Vandiver, ed., *The Idea of the South* (1964).

DELAWARE, LITERATURE OF

Situated to the south of Philadelphia, New York, and Boston, and to the north of Baltimore, Delaware was in a precarious position at the beginning of the nineteenth century, when literati were scrambling for the cultural centers of the East. Many writers who were born in Delaware and eventually wrote of Delaware, the Delmarva Peninsula, or the Brandywine River Valley were drawn to Philadelphia. With Benjamin Franklin's Library Company (1731) and the first American Philosophical Society (1741), Philadelphia was a true literary center. But Delaware's proximity to Philadelphia also allowed for its exposure in literature. The first state has been remembered and commemorated in the literature of well-known artists such as Benjamin Franklin, Bayard Taylor, Howard Pyle (who also illustrated children's books with Delaware settings), and more recently, John Dos Passos. Perhaps Delaware's most enduring and commonly known claim to fame is the depiction of Wilmington in a story by F. Scott Fitzgerald from *Flappers and Philosophers* (1922).

Delaware writers of the nineteenth and early twentieth century were conscious of the influence of history on a place, of the Civil War and slavery, of movements such as Romanticism and Realism, and of universal themes and motifs. Most of them failed to secure a lasting audience. A few, however, have endured the test of time.

Historical fiction was popular with Delawarean authors throughout the late nineteenth century. George Morgan and George Brydges Rodney produced two novels in 1897 that take the Revolutionary War as their subject: *Little John of J,* set at Valley Forge in 1778, and *In Buff and Blue,* which depicted the battle at Brandywine. George Lippard's *Blanche of Brandy-wine* (1856), though less well known, has a comical strain. It too depicts the Battle of the Brandywine and figures George Washington as its hero. These novels are notable because they have an epic quality coupled with great historical detail, and they have endured even though the Revolution was not a popular theme.

The Swedish-Dutch settlements in the Delaware valley provided a subject for James Kirke Paulding's *Konigsmarke, or the Long Finne* (1823) and Emily Read's *Two Hundred Years Ago, or Life in New Sweden* (1876). Pirate stories were popular with authors such as Howard Pyle (1853–1911) and Rupert S. Holland (*Pirates of the Delaware,* 1925), the latter having written about the coastal towns of Lewes, Milford, Dover, and New Castle. Slavery offered itself as a subject for many writers, one of whom, George Alfred Townsend (1841–1914), wrote mostly about the Chesapeake Bay area in his 1880 novel, *Tales of the Chesapeake,* and his 1881 *The Bohemians.* A few female authors who wrote historical fiction of the Brandywine have also endured. Gertrude Crownfield was a prolific novelist, choosing for her subjects the Revolutionary War (*Where Glory Waits,* 1934), pirates at Henlopen, Lewes, and New Castle (*King's Pardon,* 1937), and Swedish settlements in Wilmington (*Proud Lady,* 1943). Katherine Virden wrote a memorable detective story about pirates at New Castle and Sussex in *Crooked Eye* (1930).

Wilmington provides a locus for many fictions of Delaware. John Lofland (1798?–1849), also known as the "Milford Bard," briefly edited *The Blue Hen's Chicken* (1848–1854), a Wilmington weekly newspaper, and wrote several stories based in Wilmington. He followed in the Romantic style made popular at the time by Edgar Allan Poe and James Fenimore Cooper; and Robert Montgomery Bird (1806–1854), a playwright and novelist who owes his debt to Charles Brockden Brown, wrote of the Brandywine River Valley in his 1835 *The Hawks of Hawk Hollow.* Didactic, sentimental, and romantic tales were also popular among writers in Delaware. Novelists such as Mary Jane Windle, Rebecca Gibbons Beach, Caleb Harlan, Harriet Pennawell Belt, Eleanor G. Walton, Algernon S. Logan, and Martin W. Barr contributed to these genres with local-color or regionalist stories and coming-of-age novels. These authors selected composites of Delaware towns or cities, Wilmington or the Chesapeake Bay area, or the shores of the Delaware beaches for their settings.

Many realistic writers throughout the nineteenth

and early twentieth century also chose Wilmington or the Brandywine for the settings of their novels and biographical writings. Elizabeth Montgomery's *Reminiscences of Wilmington* (1851), Mary Jane Windle's *Life in Washington and Elsewhere* (1859), and Elizabeth Booth's *Reminiscences of New Castle, Delaware* (1884) can be described as local lore or local-color stories. Similarly, A. S. Logan portrays Kent County in his 1934 *Vistas from the Stream.* Two writers told of their experiences growing up black in Wilmington and the surrounding regions of Delaware, which was unusual for the time: J. Saunders Redding (1906–   ) published *No Day of Triumph* in 1934, and Paul Laurence Dunbar also wrote about black life. Other "Wilmington books" include *One Little Man* by Christopher Ward (1868–1943) and Anne Parish's *Perennial Bachelor,* both published in 1925.

Perhaps the most famous writer to come out of Delaware, Henry Seidel Canby, a literary critic, fiction and prose writer, and instructor of literature at Yale University, also wrote of his birthplace, Wilmington. A prolific novelist throughout the 1930s, 1940s, and 1950s, Canby wrote frequently with true appreciation for the Brandywine Valley. His 1941 *Brandywine* is still considered a must-read by students of the region. He also wrote critical studies of American authors and genres and was the founding editor of the *Saturday Review of Literature* (1924), as well as sometime editor of the *Yale Review.*

Delaware has produced few well-known poets. Robert M. Bird, a Romantic writer, also wrote memorable verse drama: "Pelopidas," "The Gladiator," "Oralloosa," and "The Broker of Bogota," published respectively in 1830, 1831, 1832, and 1834. John Lofland, "the Bard," also wrote poetry, as did G. A. Townsend, who published a collection entitled *Poems* in 1870. These poets continued to write of the surrounding regions of Delaware, showing mostly their appreciation for the beauty of the land. George B. Hynson, best known as the author of the state hymn, "Our Delaware," also wrote of Kent and Sussex Counties. Christopher Ward published *The Saga of Captain John Smith* (1928) and *Sir Galahad and Other Rhymes* (1936), as well as longer prose works throughout the 1920s, 1930s, and 1940s, an example of which is his *Delaware Tercentenary Almanack* (1937). Jerome B. Bell (*A Harvest of the Years,* 1913, and *Moods and Other Poems,* 1919) and Carrie Hoffecker (*Memories, Melodies,* 1945) are notable, perhaps even better known than John Lofland. But the best-known post–

World War II poet from Delaware is David Hudson, who was affiliated with the Delaware Poetry Center and who served several terms as Delaware's poet laureate (1956–1960 and 1975–1976). Other celebrated poet laureates include Jeannette S. Edwards (1950–1953) and Henry O. Eisenberg (1971–1974). Hudson, with the annual series *Delaware Poets,* commemorated some of the artists whose names have been lost to contemporary audiences. Just a few of the poets he includes in his bicentennial edition of the series (1976) are Lysbeth Byrd Borie, Katherine Garrison Chapin, Carrie Hoffecker, Ulrich Troubetzkoy, and Florida Watts Smyth, all of whom have national reputations. Finally, there are some writers who are affiliated with Delaware, regardless of whether or not they were born or reside there. Jeanne Murray Walker is one of those. She is a poet and playwright, the 1998 recipient of the prestigious Pew Fellowship in poetry, and she teaches English at the University of Delaware.

There is currently no single source indexing literary works produced in or concerned with Delaware. *Delaware History,* however, is a journal devoted to historical research, and it offers a useful bibliography of works published on the history of Delaware in every fourth issue.

Amy R. Moreno

See also Civil War; Local Color; Regionalism; Revolutionary War (American); Sentimental Novel.

Augustus Able, "Delaware Literature," in *Delaware: A History of the First State,* ed. H. Clay Reed (1947); *Delaware History* (serial); Carol Hoffecker, *Delaware: A Bicentennial History* (1977); David Hudson, *Delaware Poets, 1940–1976* (serial, 1940–63; 1976); John A. Munroe, *History of Delaware* (3rd ed.; 1993); H. Clay Reed, *A Bibliography of Delaware Through 1960* (1966).

DEMAGOGUE

The term *demagogue* comes from the ancient Greek word meaning "leader of the people," particularly the common people. Typically a person with a colorful and charismatic personality and skilled in inspirational oratory, the demagogue attempts to appeal to the emotions, fears, and prejudices of a disenchanted and underprivileged electorate through impassioned rhetoric, the principal intent being to gain power. Other trademarks of the demagogue include the showman's ability to entertain and to pander to the masses' fascination for fanfare; speeches characterized by homely jokes, anecdotes, and personal invective; flamboyant political campaigns featuring parades, music, and catchy slogans and songs; the exploitation of race (as reflected in hostility to black civil rights) or other controversial public issues dear to the hearts of the common people; and the projection of an image as a protector of the rights of the impoverished and disadvantaged and as an enemy of the prosperous, the traditional political leadership, and mercantile and corporate interests.

In the United States, where democracy has encouraged freedom of speech and the broadening of franchise, demagoguery has thrived from virtually the earliest days of the Republic. Although historical evidence has shown the emergence of a few politicians of a demagogic persuasion in late-eighteenth-century America, and although demagogues became an even more recognizable presence during the Jacksonian era of the 1830s, it was not until the Populist era of the 1890s, especially in the South where social, political, and economic discontent was widespread among the rural poor, that demagoguery flourished. Moreover, demagoguery has continued to have a significant political impact in many southern states throughout much of the twentieth century.

Among the best known of the southern demagogues—all of whom became governors of their respective states and some of whom likewise won seats in the U.S. Senate—are Benjamin R. Tillman of South Carolina, Robert L. Taylor and Alfred Taylor of Tennessee, Thomas E. Watson of Georgia, James S. Hogg of Texas, Jeff Davis of Arkansas, James K. Vardaman of Mississippi, J. Thomas Heflin of Alabama, Ellison D. Smith of South Carolina, James Edward and Miriam Amanda Ferguson of Texas, Coleman L. Blease of South Carolina, Theodore G. Bilbo of Mississippi, Eugene Talmadge of Georgia, Huey P. Long and Earl K. Long of Louisiana, W. Lee O'Daniel of Texas, Orville Faubus of Arkansas, George Wallace of Alabama, Ross Barnett of Mississippi, and Lester Maddox of Georgia. All were obsessed with power, and most adopted shrewd, unscrupulous, often scandalous methods of operation, sometimes even resorting to militia force, to carry out their political designs. Few lived up to their political promises to their constituents.

Of these figures, Huey Long, governor and subsequently U.S. senator from Louisiana until his assassination in 1935, was the most notable and the only southern demagogue to generate significant literary in-

terest. Long, in fact, provided the inspiration for several novels of varying artistic merit—Hamilton Basso's *Sun in Capricorn* (1942), Sinclair Lewis's *It Can't Happen Here* (1935), John Dos Passos's *Number One* (1943), Adria Locke Langley's *A Lion Is in the Streets* (1945), and Robert Penn Warren's *All the King's Men* (1946). Of these, only *Sun in Capricorn* and *All the King's Men* were authored by southerners. *Sun in Capricorn,* a popular book whose plot centers on a slanderous attack to discredit a political opponent in a gubernatorial race, was a blatant reflection of Basso's own anti-Long bias. It features a poorly developed and despicable fascist-like character named Gilgo Slade, a governor modeled on Huey Long, who, like Long, is ultimately assassinated by one of his political enemies.

A far better representation of the Huey Long analogy in southern fiction, a novel of the highest artistry, and a veritable masterwork of twentieth-century American literature is *All the King's Men*. Warren portrays the central character, Willie Stark, as an aggressive, sometimes unethical demagogue who manipulates power and becomes fascinated with its uses, and who exhibits many resemblances to Long. Parallels between Long and Stark include an unsuccessful first attempt to be elected governor, subsequent election to that office, the compromise of personal integrity by succumbing to political graft, an impeachment attempt for power abuse, and a successful assassination by a person whose humanity the demagogue has violated. Also like Long, Stark is somewhat of an enigma. On the one hand, he has a social consciousness and seems determined to promote reforms to help the poor rural people of his state to find a better life and some semblance of financial security. On the other, Stark displays an unyielding obsession to gain and assert power and, when necessary, to resort to corrupt tactics to accomplish his goals. Of the southern literary demagogues, only Warren's Willie Stark approaches the magnitude of a modern tragic hero.

Yet the social, economic, and political structure of the South has changed dramatically since the end of World War II. Agriculture and the population of rural areas have declined; industry and service-related businesses have proliferated; segregation and the violent protests and social upheaval resulting from the Civil Rights Movement have ended; and cultural diversity resulting from the in-migration of many people from other sections of the country as well as from other parts of the world has left its mark. And the South will continue to undergo further alterations. For these reasons, it seems certain that the kind of climate favorable to the re-emergence of demagoguery as a viable subject for southern literature will cease to exist.

Ed Piacentino

See also Long, Huey; Politician; Populism.

Reinhart H. Luthin, *American Demagogues: Twentieth Century* (1954); Reinhart H. Luthin, "Flowering of the Southern Demagogue," *American Scholar* (Winter 1950–51); Louis D. Rubin Jr., "All the King's Meanings," *Georgia Review* (Winter 1954); T. Harry Williams, "The Gentleman from Louisiana: Demagogue or Democrat," *Journal of Southern History* (1960).

DIALECT LITERATURE

Dialect literature was a phenomenon of the post–Civil War decades, when southern authors vied with each other to publish highly inflected local-color works in *Atlantic Monthly, Lippincott's, Century,* and other major magazines. Promoted by William Dean Howells, Charles Dudley Warner, and other northern editors, regionalist writing became an agent of national reunion, and much dialect literature contributed to the comforting mythology of the plantation South as a lost Eden whose kind and well-spoken masters and illiterate but loyal slaves nurtured each other in a pastoral landscape.

Southern local-colorists had a particular interest in representing African American speech, with Irwin Russell and Sherwood Bonner (Katharine McDowell) among the earliest practitioners. But dialect literature was inventive and diverse, ranging from Kate Chopin's Creole stories and Mary Murfree's Appalachian fiction to Ruth McEnery Stuart's comic narratives about Irish, German, and Italian immigrants in New Orleans. In an era of much scholarly activity by folklorists and anthropologists, many poets and fiction writers emphasized the cultural role of their own work in preserving the ways and the very voices of the rapidly changing South.

Antecedents of the postbellum dialect authors included Augustus Baldwin Longstreet, Johnson Jones Hooper, and other Southwest humorists whose extensive use of the frontier vernacular distinguished their stories from earlier American comedy. In the earthy Sut Lovingood tales, George Washington Harris's syntax, misspellings, word coinages, and other elements of vig-

orous backwoods East Tennessee speech presented such a challenge to readers that a modern editor actually translated the pieces into recognizable English. Sometimes identified as the last and best of the Southwest humor school, Mark Twain is rarely viewed in the context of postbellum dialect writing, yet he prefaced *Adventures of Huckleberry Finn* (1885) with the observation that his characters speak numerous dialects, distinctive "shadings" of language that he "painstakingly" recorded.

Twain's friend George Washington Cable is considered the first major southern local-colorist. Early in the 1870s, he began to write sympathetic stories, such as "Belles Demoiselles Plantation," about mixed-blood Creoles whose speech is often very similar to that of their white Creole kin. Cable's popularity was enhanced when he and Twain went on the road together for a lengthy reading tour that literally gave voice to several of their vernacular works. Many of Cable's stories seem romantic, even nostalgic, because of their antebellum plantation settings, but his progressive attitudes on race antagonized a large segment of the southern elite. Grace King's resentment of Cable's treatment of Louisiana society was the impetus for her career as a chronicler of Louisiana culture in fiction and in history, and she developed a literary equivalent of white Creole speech that sounded much more refined than Cable's broken representations. Of the several Louisiana authors who earned national fame by the end of the nineteenth century, Kate Chopin is the only one who has a large readership today—and her current audience is more attracted by Chopin's rebellious female characters than by the dialect of her Acadians, French and Spanish Creoles, and African Americans. In Chopin's bayou stories, "Americans" are foreigners with a dialect of their own.

Ruth McEnery Stuart's fiction and poetry reflect an even greater variety of speech, from the awkward English of new immigrants to the rhythmic work songs of plantation slaves. Joel Chandler Harris, who strove for linguistic accuracy in relating Uncle Remus's folktales, praised Stuart's portrayals of "the Negro." Half of her work incorporates African American dialect, but the most popular of Stuart's twenty books was *Sonny: A Christmas Guest* (1896), a group of humorous monologues by Deuteronomy Jones, a middle-aged farmer who boasts in Arkansas idiom about his precocious young son. Stuart also wrote several Arkansas dialect stories about resourceful women in the fictitious town of Simpkinsville. One of the few female writers who traveled throughout the country during the 1890s to read from her own works, Stuart was applauded for the effective combination of "humor and pathos" in her dialect pieces.

Not all dialect literature was comic, but when it was it differed greatly from the male-generated and vulgar humor of the Southwest. Besides extending authorship to many capable women, the new genre accommodated sentimentality as well as satire. And, for the first time in American history, a number of African Americans joined the literary mainstream. A leading poet of the 1890s was Paul Laurence Dunbar, whose dialect verse was so enthusiastically reviewed by William Dean Howells that readers generally ignored his poems in standard English. Alice Dunbar-Nelson, Dunbar's wife, incorporated the Creole patois of whites and mixed-blood New Orleanians into the tragic "The Stones of the Village" and other short stories.

The most famous African American writer at the end of the nineteenth century was Charles Chesnutt, who—like Dunbar—became so closely identified with his dialect pieces that he had little luck in developing a white audience for his more overtly serious work. Recently, however, scholars have explored the racially subversive features of *The Conjure Woman* (1899), a collection that assimilates many African folkways. In contrast to the nostalgia for the antebellum past that Thomas Nelson Page puts into the mouth of the former slave Sam in "Marse Chan," the vernacular tales of Chesnutt's Uncle Julius evoke a much less sunny South.

Tennessee mountain dialect and folklore were the territory of Sarah Barnwell Elliott and of Mary Murfree, who wrote under the pseudonym Charles Egbert Craddock. Like Ruth McEnery Stuart and several other southern writers, Elliott lived in the North for several years to be close to her publishers. *Jerry* (1891), a coming-of-age story about a poor white boy from a mining town, was a popular novel, but, unlike Murfree, Elliott has not benefited from critics' recent attention to female regionalists. The daughter of a linguist, Murfree spent her summers at Beersheba Springs in the Cumberlands, and she aimed at a faithful documentation of local speech in such stories as "The 'Harnt' That Walks Chilhowee" and "The Dancin' Party at Harrison's Cove."

By the turn of the century, readers' tastes had changed and editors complained about a glut of dialect literature. Consequently, writers who had built national reputations on their facility with the southern vernacular experimented with other genres. Sarah

Barnwell Elliott set a 1904 play in seventeenth-century England; Ruth McEnery Stuart wrote a rest-cure novel about an affluent twentieth-century New Yorker; and Mary Murfree and George Washington Cable turned to historical romance. When Stuart died in 1917, the *New York Times* described her as the last of the writers of African American dialect. With the advent of literary modernism, local-color writing—especially dialect works—seemed parochial and old-fashioned, but southern speech forms gained new life during the 1920s and 1930s in Julia Peterkin's Gullah stories and in novels and plays about African American life by Zora Neale Hurston, Paul Green, and DuBose Heyward.

Joan Wylie Hall

See also African American Folk Culture; African American Literature, Beginnings to 1919; Appalachian Literature; Cajun Literature; Creole Literature; Humor, Beginnings to 1900; Local Color; Northern Audiences; Oral History; Speech and Dialect; Twain, Mark; Uncle Remus; Vernacular Voice.

Elizabeth Ammons and Valerie Rohy, eds., *American Local Color Writing, 1880–1920* (1998); Dickson D. Bruce Jr., *Black American Writing from the Nadir* (1989); Alan Dundes, *Mother Wit from the Laughing Barrel: Readings in the Interpretation of Afro-American Folklore* (1973); Shelley Fisher Fishkin, *Was Huck Black?: Mark Twain and African-American Voices* (1993); George M. Fredrickson, *The Black Image in the White Mind* (1987); Henry Louis Gates Jr., *Figures in Black: Words, Signs, and the "Racial" Self* (1987); Michael North, *The Dialect of Modernism: Race, Language, and Twentieth-Century Literature* (1994); Merrill Maguire Skaggs, *The Folk of Southern Fiction* (1972); Helen Taylor, *Gender, Race, and Region in the Writings of Grace King, Ruth McEnery Stuart, and Kate Chopin* (1989).

DIARIES, CIVIL WAR

The diary flowered as a literary form in the nineteenth-century United States, and its densest blooms clustered in the Civil War South. Literate whites of every stripe kept war diaries: soldiers, civilians, travelers, plantation mistresses, teenage belles, government clerks, and relief workers. Many southerners knew by 1861 that they were living through history-in-the-making and wished to record their daily impressions for posterity. A number became so habituated that they kept diaries long after the war, chronicling the demise of the plantation system and the vagaries of Reconstruction politics. Some diarists wrote with a view toward postwar publication; others, like nineteen-year-old Lucy Breckin-ridge of Grove Hill, Virginia, hoped to pass the time hanging heavy on their hands because most of the men were at war. The regulating impulse at the heart of diary-writing helped southerners—whether soldiers or civilians—make sense of the upheavals and disloca-tions brought about by war.

In its purest form, the Confederate diary or "jour-nal," as southerners were fond of calling them, was a periodic record preserved without revision. Although generically distinct from memoirs, published diaries have also been subject to revision: authors have deleted sensitive material or embellished their predictions based on 20–20 hindsight; editors in pursuit of candor, orthographic standardization, or an economy of words have altered original texts at the behest of readers or publishers.

The most prolific and dedicated keepers of wartime diaries were white women of privilege. Their social and economic advantages created conditions favorable to writing that were not shared by slaves or women of more modest means. Elite women recorded plantation, community, and family business, whereas unmarried daughters wrote about the social consequences of beaux and brothers leaving for the front. Eighteen-year-old Kate Stone watched her thirty-seven-year-old mother manage 150 slaves on their Louisiana cotton plantation while she retreated to her bedroom to read. Like Stone, many female diarists were avid readers. Their literary tastes ran the gamut from Sir Walter Scott and Dickens to the homegrown Marion Harland (Mary Hawes Terhune) and Augusta Evans, whose *Macaria* swept the Confederacy in 1864. The center-piece of Stone's diary (*Brokenburn*, 1955) was the fam-ily's 1863 flight to elude U. S. Grant's siege of Vicks-burg. Away from home for more than two and a half years, Stone likened refugee life in Lamar County and Tyler, Texas, to a social prison sentence. When her family's Baton Rouge home was invaded by Union forces occupying New Orleans in 1862, twenty-year-old Sarah Morgan also became a refugee. Despite little formal education, Morgan's intellect and humor jump off the pages of *A Confederate Girl's Diary* (1913) ("Arkansas troops," she observed, "have acquired a reputation for roughness and ignorance which they seem to cultivate as assiduously as most people would their virtue.") More than other youthful diarists, Mor-gan looked beyond the concerns of her immediate fam-ily, several of whom supported the Union cause, to the larger world around her.

Too often overlooked is the *Journal of Julia Le Grand* (1911), also written during the Union occupa-tion of New Orleans. Le Grand's father, the scion of an immense cotton plantation, lost his fortune in the 1850s. By the time the war began, Le Grand and a sis-ter, both in their thirties, were running a girls' school in the Crescent City. Her privileged background height-ened Le Grand's sympathy for the misfortunes of oth-ers, which led to insightful entries about race relations and the human condition. Keenly aware of the costs of war, Le Grand was a humanitarian first and a rebel sec-ond: "Even a great victory to one's own side is a sad thing to a lover of humanity," she wrote. "I accept a bloody triumph only as the least of two evils."

The diaries of Anna Green (*Diary of a Milledgeville Girl*, 1964), Eliza Frances Andrews (*The War-time Journal of a Georgia Girl*, 1908), and Lucy Buck (*Sad Earth, Sweet Heaven*, 1973) are less introspective. Caught up in the drama of her romantic life, the six-teen-year-old Green said little about Sherman's inva-sion of her Georgia town in 1864. Andrews said more about the March to the Sea but maintained a provincial outlook. Before publishing the diary, she deleted mate-rial condemning her father's Unionist views and the family's compromised social position. There is little self-censorship in eighteen-year-old Lucy Buck's diary of the turbulent life around Front Royal, Virginia. More self-absorbed than other teenage diarists, Buck fretted about her two soldier brothers (both of whom survived the war, unlike two of Kate Stone's, two of Sarah Morgan's, and three of Lucy Breckinridge's), Yankee invaders, and her awkward entrance to wom-anhood.

Mary Boykin Chesnut's diary may well be the rich-est personal account penned by southerner or north-erner. Making the diary her life's work, Chesnut metic-ulously wrote and rewrote entries, compiling more than 400,000 words in all. The wife of a well-con-nected senator from South Carolina and the daughter and daughter-in-law of a governor and a planter patri-arch, Chesnut spent the war years in Richmond at the center of an elite circle of generals, politicians, cultural celebrities, and women admired for their intimacy with powerful men. Brutally frank about the personal costs of slavery ("Ours is a *monstrous* system"), Chesnut ex-posed the sexual profligacy of white men and the collu-sion of their wives and daughters but expressed little sympathy for slave women trapped in concubinage. Endlessly fascinated by human frailty, Chesnut was an ironist of the first order. She was light-hearted enough to render a mock-heroic portrait of John Bell Hood's courtship of her ally, Buck Preston, but grieved with Varina and Jeff Davis over the loss of a young son and lamented the future prospects of young Confederates hurrying to the altar amid the slaughter. The publication history of Chesnut's diary is nearly as complex as the text itself. First published in 1905 by Chesnut's friend and crony, Myrta Lockett Avary, this version excluded half of the original, reflecting Chesnut's desire to correct the past and avoid giving offense. The 1949 "unabridged" edition claimed to retrieve the material expunged from the first published version. Not until C. Vann Woodward published *Mary Chesnut's Civil War* in 1981 was the extent of the author's emendations revealed. A 1984 edition restored what are now believed to be the original journals, which differ from the 1905 version more in language than critical intent.

A diary that rivals Chesnut's in length and in the contradictions it betrays about the lives of the landed gentry is *The Journal of Ella Gertrude Clanton Thomas* (1990). Covering the years from 1848 to 1889, the diary takes Thomas from the lap of privilege—complete with advantageous marriage and the gift of a plantation and slaves near Augusta—to impoverished living on credit. As family fortunes fell with the Confederacy, the thirty-one-year-old Thomas supplemented her husband's meager income by teaching school for thirty dollars a week. Poignant in its rehearsals of her seven children's loss of status and shrewd in its understanding of racial and sexual politics in the plantation household, Thomas's journal is to date the most complete personal record of aristocratic decline to come out of Georgia.

Many other elite women produced diaries of note. Virginia's Judith Brockenbrough McGuire published *The Diary of a Southern Refugee* in 1867. Like Thomas, McGuire was forced to seek work outside the home and landed a Commissary Department clerkship along with women of less-prestigious pedigrees. One of nine in a prominent Charleston family, Emma Holmes went to work as a teacher and governess to help her widowed mother meet expenses. Her *Diary* (1979) sheds light on civil and military matters but misreads some of the war's most crucial outcomes—for instance, the belief that Lee took Gettysburg for the Confederacy. Rabidly antinorthern, Holmes was inconsolable when Lee surrendered and predicted with haunting accuracy that "peace on such terms is war for the rising generation." Catherine Devereux Edmondston's *Journal of a Secesh Lady* (1979) is a mammoth work de-

scribing plantation life in and around wartime Raleigh. Mistress of a large estate with nearly a hundred slaves but none of her own children, Edmondston painstakingly chronicled domestic news from 1860 to 1866. Articulate in their portraits of domestic tribulation are Cornelia Peake McDonald's *Diary with Reminiscences of the War* (1935), which related depredations on her Winchester, Virginia, home; and *The Confederate Diary of Betty Herndon Maury* (1938), which detailed similar events in Fredericksburg and Richmond. Laetitia Nutt's *Courageous Journey* (1975) recorded daily life with her husband's cavalry unit in Kentucky and Louisiana, whereas *The Private War of Lizzie Hardin* (1963) tells of the arrest, imprisonment, and exile of a Kentucky family for its Confederate sympathies. The recently published diary of Ellen Renshaw House, *A Very Violent Rebel* (1996), similarly records the extradition of Kentuckians in Unionist territory.

Among the numerous accounts compiled by civilian men, *The Diary of Edmund Ruffin* (1972) is notable for its proslavery rhetoric and anatomy of Confederate values. Too old to enlist as a soldier, the sixty-seven-year-old Virginian became the Confederacy's first citizen, buoyed by the rebel rout of Union forces at Manassas, which he described in detail, and driven to suicide only two months after Appomattox. Daily entries show a keen understanding of political and military strategy, as well as personal disappointment. The diary thus presents the parallel collapse of the dream of southern independence with Ruffin's own psychological collapse. Accounts written by wartime travelers to the South constitute a unique branch of civilian diaries. The two most interesting are William Russell's *My Diary North and South* (1863) and Arthur Fremantle's *Diary* (1864). Russell was a correspondent with the *London Times* and Fremantle a British career army officer. Russell, who had covered the Crimea, went to Norfolk, Charleston, Savannah, Montgomery, Mobile, and New Orleans all before the First Battle of Manassas. Known for his prediction that the South would win the war, Russell was pugnacious in his judgments of people and places. Unlike Russell's eyewitness account of the war's first months, the Fremantle diary offers a droll index of southern manners on the eve of Gettysburg. A visitor to all the southern states except Arkansas and Florida and an unofficial guest of Lee's army, the twenty-eight-year-old looked with humor at frontier conditions, describing travel by stagecoach as a greater hardship than military life. Fremantle's assessments of Confederate officers are delightful, like this

one of General Hardee: "He was in the habit of avail-
ing himself of the privilege of his rank and years and
insisted on kissing the wives and daughters of all the
Kentuckian farmers. And although he is supposed to
have converted many of the ladies to the Southern
cause, yet in many instances their male relatives remained either neutral or undecided."

Thousands of Confederate soldiers in the ranks kept
diaries, hundreds of which have been published. But
virtually none of the highest-ranking officers published
diaries, preferring to write postwar memoirs. An exception is Josiah Gorgas, whose *Journals* (1995) from
1857 to 1878 cover his service as chief of ordnance. A
Pennsylvanian who adopted the South and a large extended family when he married the daughter of Alabama governor John Gayle, Gorgas's diary is as interesting for its commentary on parental duties as for its
military news. Major Edward Manigault, son of a well-
to-do Charleston family, was artillerist in charge of
that city's defense in 1863. *Siege Train* (1986) is the official diary of his unsuccessful campaign. Manigault's
younger brother Arthur, who rose to the rank of brigadier, is also known for his war journals (*A Carolinian
Goes to War*, 1983).

Literate men in the ranks were more likely than officers to find time for diaries. John Jackman's *Diary of
a Confederate Soldier* (1990) records events in the
Army of Tennessee from Shiloh forward, complete
with hand-drawn maps of entrenchments. A member
of the First Kentucky, also called the Orphan Brigade,
Jackman participated in five major campaigns interrupted only by illness and a head wound sustained at
Pine Mountain, Georgia, in June 1864. His diary provides a soldier's perspective on field hospitals and relief
in private homes. John Dooley of the First Virginia also
comments on hospital and medical matters, but *John
Dooley, Confederate Soldier: His War Journal* (1945)
is best known for its description of first combat at Antietam. Alfred Peticolas's *Rebels on the Rio Grande*
(1984) presents a soldier's view of the war in the
Southwest and, like Jackman's diary, includes sketches
of people and terrain.

Straddling the military and civilian worlds, non-
combatant workers offered glimpses of daily operations in the Confederate government. John Beauchamp
Jones found sanctuary for his proslavery sympathies in
the War Department as soon as a mob threatened to
hang him in his New Jersey newspaper office. His
Rebel War Clerk's Diary (1866) provides good accounts of the Richmond bread riots in 1863 and infla-

tion in the Confederate capital. Not as well known but
more nuanced than Jones's diary is *Inside the Confederate Government* (1957) by Robert Garlick Kean,
who was chief of the Bureau of War. Kean's observations of domestic life are not as extensive as Jones's,
but his intimate knowledge of Confederate powerbro-
kers makes his account more reliable. Robert Patrick's
Reluctant Rebel (1959) records the trials of a Confederate supply officer working in the western Commissary and Quartermaster's Departments. Unlike his
peers, Patrick was content to serve behind a desk instead of a gun.

Surprisingly few diaries were left by Confederate relief workers. The best of these is Kate Cumming's *A
Journal of Hospital Life in the Confederate Army of
Tennessee* (1866), which provides detailed information
about the "flying" field hospital system established by
surgeon Samuel Stout. Born in Scotland and raised in
Montreal and Mobile, Cumming was twenty-six when
she arrived at Tishomingo Hotel in Corinth, Mississippi, to care for soldiers wounded at Shiloh. Not one
to mince words, Cumming was critical of genteel
women for their reluctance to serve in hospitals, of
slaves for what she deemed disloyalty and indolence,
and of Abraham Lincoln, whom she held responsible
for the carnage. Cumming's diary documents scarcity
and provides a valuable portrait of the nurse/patient
bond. A less-extensive account of hospital life can be
found in Ada Bacot's diary, *A Confederate Nurse*
(1994). Mistress of a small plantation in South Carolina, Bacot joined the staff of a Charlottesville hospital
in 1861, happy for the respite from family trials. But
new trials awaited her: she was squeamish, disliked her
coworkers, and was endlessly teased by them. Although Confederate surgeons published their letters
and wrote reminiscences, there are no extant diaries.
Surgeon Herbert Nash of Norfolk lamented that his
three-year daily record was lost in a fire the day before
the war ended. Readers must content themselves with
the account of Texas chaplain Nicholas Davis, *The
Campaign from Texas to Maryland* (1863); with soldier diaries like John Dooley's; or government diaries
like John Beauchamp Jones's (1866)—all of which are
relevant to the medical war.

A number of Civil War diaries highlight specific
events, like Sherman's March to the Sea or Pickett's
charge at Gettysburg. The most poetic of the diaries
chronicling the Yankee invaders is seventeen-year-old
Emma LeConte's *When the World Ended* (1957),
which recounts the burning of Columbia in 1865. Elea-

nor Cohen Seixas's diary of this event can be accessed on the World Wide Web. The *Diary of Dolly Lunt Burge* (1962) gives a stunning account of Union depredations in the Georgia countryside. Mary Loughborough's *My Cave Life in Vicksburg* (1864) details the siege of that city in an eyewitness narrative, which reads more like a diary than a reminiscence. A brief but fascinating account of the relationship between gender and military power is Eugenia Levy Phillips's diary of incarceration on desertlike Ship Island during 1862. The sister of Confederate matron Phoebe Pember, Phillips was arrested for allegedly insulting Union officers in a funeral cortege passing by her New Orleans residence.

Despite the scores of Civil War diaries published annually, hundreds remain in southern repositories. The largest collections of southern diaries may be found in the Library of Congress, the Southern Historical Collection in Chapel Hill, the Perkins Library at Duke, the South Carolina Library in Columbia, and Louisiana State University's Louisiana and Lower Mississippi Valley Collection. Smaller collections also boast gems, such as Emma Balfour's diary of the 1863 siege of Vicksburg at the Mississippi Department of Archives and History (Jackson) and Captain James McMichael's late-war diary of incarceration in a Union prison at the Atlanta Historical Society.

Jane E. Schultz

See also Civil War; Confederate States of America; Diaries, Men's; Diaries, Women's; Manuscript Collections.

Daniel Aaron, *The Unwritten War* (1973); Drew Gilpin Faust, *Mothers of Invention* (1996); Elizabeth Fox-Genovese, *Within the Plantation Household* (1988); Judith Lee Hallock, "Memoirs, Diaries, and Letters," in *Guide to Civil War Sources*, ed. Steven Woodworth (1998); Katharine M. Jones, *Heroines of Dixie* (1955); Thomas Mallon, *A Book of One's Own* (1984); George Rable, *Civil Wars* (1989); Bell Wiley, *The Life of Johnny Reb* (1962); Edmund Wilson, *Patriotic Gore* (1962).

DIARIES, MEN'S

During the first two centuries of European presence in what is now the American South, men's journal and diary writing held a dominant if not preeminent position in the region's list of literary accomplishments. The first published account of life in the British colonies of North America, Captain John Smith's *A True Relation* *of Such Occurences and Accidents of Noate as Hath Hapned in Virginia* (1608), was begun as a journal, and the travel journals of naturalists William Bartram and John James Audubon were read widely in the North and in Europe. But compared to the rich tradition of journal and diary writing in New England by Cotton Mather, John Winthrop, and Jonathan Edwards, the southern counterpart to that tradition may strike modern readers as lacking in psychological depth and complexity. Whereas New England male writers were drawn to such activities primarily out of a desire for inward reflection and spiritual self-examination, male diarists and journal writers in the South seem to have been motivated almost exclusively by the urge to describe the external world and their actions within that sphere.

The one eighteenth-century southern male writer whose journal and diary writings alone have earned him a secure place in the southern and national literary canon is William Byrd of Westover (1674–1744), arguably the leading intellectual of his day in the southern colonies. In his most famous works, *The History of the Dividing Line* (written c. 1728 but not published until 1841) and *The Secret History of the Dividing Line* (published in 1929), Byrd recounts the picaresque exploits of the surveying team that ran the boundary between Virginia and North Carolina in 1728. A master of satire and irony, Byrd (who assumes the fictional persona Steddy) carefully straddles an imaginary dividing line between participant and observer, describing with thinly veiled amusement the more pious team members' degeneration into savagery and debauchery as they leave behind the civilizing influences of colonial society and venture farther into the western wilderness. If Byrd takes some pains in his *Dividing Line* histories to mask his true feelings behind his fictional persona, *The Secret Diary of William Byrd of Westover* (1941) reveals an even more guarded author. Composed in a secret code of his own devising, *The Secret Diary* is obsessively formulaic, indiscriminately combining mundane minutiae, such as details of plantation management, daily diet, and exercise regimens, with startlingly matter-of-fact references to slave whippings and sexual relations with his wife, his slaves, and others. For all its eccentricities, Byrd's diaries remain an invaluable source of knowledge about the workings of the southern colonial plantation and, less directly, the mind of the privileged southern male.

The written records of men born outside the South who traveled through the southern colonies or states constitute an important branch of journal and diary in the region. Bartram's *Travels* (published in 1791 and soon translated into several languages) is considered the most important—and stirring—description of the southern colonies written in the eighteenth century. In the 1850s, New Englander Frederick Law Olmsted traveled through the South and drew from his journals to publish a series of authoritative accounts that called attention to the social diversity of the region. His *Journeys and Explorations in the Cotton Kingdom* (1861), comprised of material from the three books based on his southern travels published in the 1850s, was read with considerable interest by northerners curious to learn about their rebellious neighbors to the South.

The Civil War served as a fruitful if costly occasion for southern men's journal and diary writing. From leading officials in the Confederate government and generals in the army to common foot-soldiers, thousands of southern men kept diaries in which they recorded the details of life during wartime. Among the most famous of these are *The Recollections of Alexander H. Stephens* (1910), written by the former vice president of the Confederacy during his imprisonment in 1865, and John B. Jones's *A Rebel War Clerk's Diary* (1866). Many memoirs based on southern men's wartime journals and diaries were published later in the nineteenth century, including George Cary Eggleston's *A Rebel's Recollections* (1874), William R. Taylor's *Destruction and Reconstruction* (1877), and Sam R. Watkins's *"Co. Aytch"* (1882). Joseph LeConte's diary of Civil War activities became *'Ware Sherman* when published in 1937.

As the more retrospective and publication-oriented genre of autobiography flowered in the nineteenth century, public interest in diaries and journals dwindled. In recent years, however, scholars wishing to learn more about the Old South have turned increasingly to the vast body of unpublished journals and diaries held in historical archives across the region. Although this collective record of southern life gives voice only to the more privileged members of that society (illiterate southerners—and literate slaves who out of necessity concealed their writing abilities—left no such records), it nevertheless remains the most valuable untapped source for understanding the complex fabric of social life in the Old South.

James H. Watkins

See also Autobiography; Bartram, William; Diaries, Civil War; Diaries, Women's; Letters; Smith, Captain John; Travel Literature.

Alan Gallay, ed., *Voices of the Old South: Eyewitness Accounts, 1528–1861* (1994).

DIARIES, WOMEN'S

Through the act of writing a diary, the author composes her own character as she constructs an autobiographical persona, and she moves that character to center stage. Thereby she becomes the principal actor in the drama of her own story, irrespective of her actual roles in real life. Indeed, to be interesting, a diary has to convey a sense of drama. The drama may take place in the events being recounted in the diary: will Lewis and Clark complete their transcontinental journey despite the hostilities of weather, terrain, and enemies animal and human? Or the large-scale drama may take place offstage, viewed through the diarist's window on the world reminiscent of the Flemish painters' outward vistas glimpsed from cosy interior rooms. Yet in the most engaging diaries, the external drama is juxtaposed with the day-by-day drama of the events, characters, relationships unfolding in the interior—whether literal or metaphorical.

The steady drumbeat of the Civil War in Manassas, Richmond, Petersburg, Vicksburg, or Atlanta reverberates like a heartbeat through the accounts of plantation life—intrigues and alliances, business and boredom, hard work and harder times—that are the staple of southern women's Civil War diaries. The war itself provides a naturally dramatic context, but the central question raised by the accounts of such diarists as Mary Boykin Miller Chesnut and Ella Gertrude Clanton Thomas is not who will win, but what will the effects of the war and its aftermath be on the people of the South, white and black, and on the state of the Union? As the consciousness through which that story is filtered, the diarist gains control over her experience in the course of interpreting it, even if she is unable to control all but a minuscule corner of the universe that in antebellum times had seemed limitless.

This process operates with particular effectiveness when and if she revises her original material for publication, as did Mary Chesnut, and in so doing transforms the central character from a private person, talking to herself in *The Private Mary Chesnut* (1984), to a public character speaking to an external audience through the printed *Diary* in three dramatically revised editions (1905, 1945, 1981). Thanks to C. Vann

Woodward's meticulous research on the 1981 edition, *Mary Chesnut's Civil War*, it is now well known that the magnificent, mammoth volume that makes Chesnut the Shakespeare among American women diarists was not the actual diary that the private Mary Chesnut wrote between 1861 and 1865. Instead, it is a 2,500-manuscript-page expansion—of character, context, and significance—that looks and sounds like a diary. As such, it adheres to the diary's day-by-day format and the convention that the author never knows what the as-yet-unexperienced future will bring. Contemporary in its feminist, abolitionist sensibility and in its unsentimentality, *Mary Chesnut's Civil War* is the great American Civil War novel, replete with characters, dialogue, scenes, plots, subplots, intrigues, gossip, and intellectual treatises. And it rings utterly true. In it, Chesnut provides comprehensive coverage of themes common to many southern women's diaries of any era—family, friendship, community; reading and recreation; work; political and domestic economy; race relations and slavery; secession; and always, the war, its causes, conduct, and aftermath.

For most southern women diarists of the nineteenth century, when this form flourished, writing the diary provided a way into their own self-understanding, and a way out—a window on the world beyond their restricted purview. These diarists were educated women, nearly all married and living on plantations where much of the daily work was done by slaves. They had sufficient education to encourage a sensibility as readers, fluency as writers, and the leisure to write—often copious—diaries. After the war, a sense of family and significance that might never be recaptured led them to preserve these volumes, paper bulwarks against an uncertain future. For most diarists, schooled in the Cult of True Womanhood, publication was not an option until near the century's end. Had she survived her untimely heart attack in 1886, Mary Chesnut might have accomplished this.

All the best Civil War diaries were published by twentieth-century editors, except for Eliza Frances Andrews's *The War-Time Journal of a Georgia Girl 1864–1865*, which the author edited herself "after the lapse of nearly half a century" and published with historical commentary in 1908. Some of the diarists wrote exclusively as young girls: Elizabeth Ruffin (1993), Jane Caroline North (Pettigrew) (1993) (both antebellum), Eliza Francis Andrews (1908, 1997), Harriet Bailey Bullock (Daniels) (1993), Sarah Morgan (Dawson)

(1991). Indeed, the private writings of many women, southern and northern alike, stopped with marriage. Others wrote into their mature years, as did Mary Chesnut, Gertrude Clanton Thomas (1990), and Ann Lewis Hardeman (1993)—whose bare-bones entries are devoid of the scenes, robust characters, and realistic dialogue that enliven the other works. Cornelia Jones Pond dictated her memoir to her daughter in 1898; it covers the years 1834 to 1875 experienced by a belle in Liberty County, Georgia.

The published twentieth-century southern women's diaries in the main seem pale in comparison with those of their forebears, subdued, self-conscious, restricted in scope—perhaps a consequence of the aftermath of the war. In the twentieth century, the great works of women's self-reflective literature are autobiographies rather than the diaries that authors of comparable talent might have written a hundred years earlier. These include works by such professional writers as Zora Neale Hurston, Ellen Glasgow, Lillian Hellman, Maya Angelou, Eudora Welty, Mary Mebane, Pauli Murray, and Rita Mae Brown, published to considerable critical and popular acclaim. (The nineteenth-century exception is ex-slave autobiographer Harriet Jacobs, who escaped to the north and published *Incidents in the Life of a Slave Girl* under the pseudonym of Linda Brent.)

In combination, southern women's nineteenth-century diaries and twentieth-century autobiographies present the first and second acts in the continuing, compelling drama of significant selves and southern society.

Lynn Z. Bloom

See also Autobiography; Diaries, Civil War.

Eliza Frances Andrews, *The War-Time Journal of a Georgia Girl 1864–1865* (1997); Suzanne L. Bunkers and Cynthia A. Huff, *Inscribing the Daily: Critical Essays on Women's Diaries* (1996); Virginia Ingraham Burr, ed., *The Secret Eye: The Journal of Ella Gertrude Clanton Thomas 1848–1889* (1990); Charles East, ed., *The Civil War Diary of Sarah Morgan* (1991); Lucinda H. MacKethan, ed., *Recollections of a Southern Daughter: The Memoir of Cornelia Jones Pond* (1998); Michael O'Brien, ed., *An Evening When Alone: Four Journals of Single Women in the South, 1827–67* (1993); Carroll Smith-Rosenberg, *Disorderly Conduct: Visions of Gender in Victorian America* (1985); C. Vann Woodward, ed., *Mary Chesnut's Civil War* (1981); C. Vann Woodward, ed., *The Private Mary Chesnut: The Unpublished Civil War Diaries* (1984).

"DIXIE"

"Dixie" is the familiar title of a song that was heard for the first time in a program by Bryant's Minstrels at Mechanics' Hall in New York on April 4, 1859. It was listed as "Mr. Dan Emmett's new and original Plantation Song and Dance 'Dixie's Land.' " According to the playbill, the song would be presented "introducing the whole troupe in the festival dance." Closing the evening's entertainment was " 'Our American Cousin' Bill" [sic], according to the playbill "brought from 'Laura Keene's Theatre' . . . without any alterations." Firth, Pond, and Company issued the first authorized edition of the song in 1860, with the title "Dixie's Land," but on the cover the words "I wish I was in" appear in smaller print, these arranged in an arch above the main title.

As part of a minstrel show, the song was conceived as a "walk-around," with the entire minstrel company participating. Various members stepped forward from the group to sing the verses of the song, the rest of the company responding at various points. That the words "Look away" are repeated in each verse suggest that these were responses by the chorus, the rest of the verse sung by a soloist. The entire company probably sang the chorus at the end of each verse, perhaps with the audience joining in. A musical interlude at the end of the published version suggests that dancing might separate the singing of the verses. Dancing would likely feature movements such as lifting the knees high, waving the hands, and turning the body around. Dancing might involve either soloists one at a time or the entire company.

"Dixie's Land" was reputedly the creation of Daniel Decatur Emmett, who was born in Mount Vernon, Ohio, in 1815. After a brief stint in the army, in his early twenties he was found in Cincinnati as member of a circus. Very early in his career, he became known as a black impersonator and as a banjo player, both talents making him apt as member of a minstrel troupe. As a member of the Virginia Minstrels, he toured in England; then he joined Bryant's Minstrels in 1859 just about the time he composed the song that made him famous.

In his *Dan Emmett and the Rise of Early Negro Minstrelsy* (1962), Hans Nathan advances several theories concerning the origin of the word *Dixie*. It could refer directly to the Mason and Dixon Line. A New York play of 1850 entitled "United States Mail and Dixie in Difficulties," featured a black postboy named Dixie. The expression "Dixie's Land" implies a land of paradise. Nathan suggests that it was Emmett's song that actually gave the word its identity and fame. The *American Heritage Dictionary* defines *Dixie* in three ways: as the South; as a nickname for New Orleans; and as a ten-dollar bill, a dix, issued before the Civil War in New Orleans. The *Oxford English Dictionary* and *Webster's* also maintain the chief definition as a geographical region, the former mentioning Emmett's song.

During the Civil War, Albert Pike—poet, editor, publisher, Confederate brigadier general in command of the Indian Territory—made "Dixie" a war hymn with several stanzas. Pike's chorus runs: "Advance the flag of Dixie! / Hurrah! Hurrah! / For Dixie's land we'll take our stand, / To live and die for Dixie!"

There are many variations of "Dixie," but Emmett's version is the most popular, and from the Civil War to the present, the song represented southern identity more than any other. It is as familiar as the Confederate flag as a symbol of the South but does not carry the same racist weight as the flag. More than any song, it evokes the Confederate legacy.

Thomas Warburton

See also Confederate Flag.

DOMESTICITY

It is mistake to generalize too broadly about domesticity in southern literature, because both the ideals and the social practices associated with the domestic have varied widely with class, region, period, and a person's status as slave or free. Customs and beliefs about proper domestic roles inevitably became entangled in questions of slavery and race. Despite these complexities, regional cookery, domestic customs, and notions of hospitality have long been markers of southern identity, and southerners have become increasingly worried that the distinctiveness of the South is being lost in the cultural homogenization of global capitalism. In literature and popular culture, domestic stereotypes persisted in the nineteenth and twentieth centuries and included the benevolent planter, the steel magnolia who was his lady, the sturdy yeoman, the mammy, faithful and treacherous slaves, and the undomesticated frontiersman.

In the antebellum period, domesticity was first defined in southern writing as practical skill—with early European settlers learning to produce local agricultural products for trade and domestic consumption and importing many household goods along with slaves, apprentices, and African agricultural practices, such as wet-land rice production. Colonists produced manuals of practical living, as in Thomas Johnson's *Every Man His Own Doctor* (1784), and many manuscript receipt (recipe) books, including those of Harriott Pinckney Horry and Eliza Lucas Pinckney; early published advice books included Mary Randolph's *The Virginia House-wife* (1824). The single-crop system, whether the crop was tobacco, indigo, rice, or cotton, had significant shaping force on southern agriculture and domestic life, making prosperity vulnerable both to weather and to fluctuations in world markets. The letters of William Byrd of Westover (1652–1704) provide an early and detailed picture of plantation culture, the interdependence of agriculture and international trade, the lack of good local education even for the middle and upper classes, the threats of disease and natural disaster that were facts of life even for the relatively wealthy. The letters provide glimpses of Byrd's wife, Mary, constantly pregnant and apprehensive about the lives and education of their children. Despite their difficulties, Byrd claimed, in an early instance of southern hospitality and frontier necessity, that he always kept an open house. Plantation life was later idealized in John Pendleton Kennedy's *Swallow Barn* (1832), where the back-breaking work of early agriculture was obscured in the idyllic picture of southern leisure among the planter class. Caroline Lee Hentz's *The Planter's Northern Bride* (1854) was an even more thorough apology for slavery; though Hentz obliquely drew the connection between masters who beat their wives and those who beat their slaves, her central characters exemplified southern domestic stereotypes.

A very different and much more powerful description of antebellum domesticity came in Harriet Jacobs's *Incidents in the Life of a Slave Girl,* published under the pseudonym Linda Brent in 1861. Jacobs's story was vivid testimony to slave labor's importance in the southern domestic economy and to the ways the slave system put domestic ideals and family relationships under pressure at every turn.

Given the ideological complicity of slavery and domesticity in the antebellum South, it is not surprising that Mark Twain's *Huckleberry Finn* (1884) portrayed escape from slavery and from domesticity as essentially coeval. Twain's novel also represented a different nine-

teenth-century response to domesticity—the tradition of Southwestern humor. Southwestern humor and its heirs relied in part on a contrast between the domestic "civilization" of the urban and seaboard South and a frontier ethos; regional and dialect differences allowed storytellers to ridicule the pretensions often associated with domestic ideals.

Regional as well as class differences, of course, shaped the definition of the domestic both in humorous and in serious writing. Beginning with the local-colorists at the turn of the twentieth century, many southern writers redefined domesticity in light of regional and class differences within the South. Like George Washington Cable's fiction, Kate Chopin's work often relied on the contrast between the domestic mores of the Upper South and a different Creole society. Appalachian writers also examined domestic customs that differed from the lowland South. Interesting among these in the twentieth century was Olive Tilford Dargan's *Call Home the Heart* (1932; published under the pseudonym Fielding Burke), examining the material hardships of making a living on mountain farms and the different hardships of migration to Piedmont textile mills. Harriette Arnow's *The Dollmaker* (1954) recounted the pull of home among economic migrants from the Appalachians to the upper Midwest. Fred Chappell drew on the traditions of Southwest humor and mountain tales in his send-up of domesticity beginning with *I Am One of You Forever* (1985), whereas Lee Smith's *Oral History* (1983) traced the impact of modernization on the music, mores, and family history of the southern Appalachians.

Oral History also exemplified an important trend in the representation of southern domesticity, the family saga, which traces the vicissitudes of domesticity across generations. Robert O. Stephens's *The Family Saga in the South* (1995) argued that the southern family, like the ethnic family, functioned as a source of group identification and cultural continuity; he traced the genre from Cable through Faulkner, Caroline Gordon, Reynolds Price, Allen Tate, Margaret Walker, and Eudora Welty, among others.

Southern writers in the twentieth century have as often as not represented the family as though under the burden of Tolstoy's famous dictum that all happy families are alike; by this measure, most southern families as represented in literature are anything but happy and anything but alike. If the group identification suggested by family in the saga is essential to southern manners, in much southern fiction family is smothering or downright peculiar. The gothic and grotesque elements in southern fiction often have had as much to do with families gone awry as with religion or race—though indeed the three elements often make a heady mix. Rather than the stereotypes of plantation fiction or the details of local color, fiction by Flannery O'Connor, Truman Capote, Carson McCullers, Gayl Jones, Gail Godwin, Harry Crews, Anne Tyler, and McCullers's plays, along with those of Tennessee Williams and Beth Henley, all suggest the family as a scene of alienation.

At the end of the twentieth century, southern writers are coming to grips with changes in domestic life caused by the final demise of the family farm along with rapid urbanization and suburbanization. Ellen Gilchrist and Josephine Humphreys have been particularly acute observers of urban and suburban domesticity. In *Rich in Love* (1988), Humphreys captured the way the old domesticity of Charleston, in all its racist violence and physical beauty, became the virtual reality of tourism. As Humphreys's work and those of her contemporaries demonstrate, the domesticity of the twenty-first century may scarcely resemble the persistent stereotypes that have long haunted southern writers.

Mary Ellis Gibson

See also Appalachian Literature; Creole; Domestic Novel; Family; Patriarchy; Plantation Fiction; Slave Narrative; Southwestern Humor.

John W. Blassingame, ed., *Slave Testimony* (1977); Catherine Clinton, *The Plantation Mistress* (1982); Elizabeth Fox-Genovese, *Within the Plantation Household: Black and White Women of the Old South* (1988); Mary Ellis Gibson, *Homeplaces: Stories of the South by Women Writers* (1991); Minrose Gwin, *Black and White Women of the Old South* (1985); Lucinda H. MacKethan, *Daughters of Time: Creating Woman's Voice in Southern Story* (1990); Bill Neal, *Biscuits, Spoonbread, and Sweet Potato Pie* (1990); Anne Firor Scott, *The Southern Lady: From Pedestal to Politics* (1970); Robert O. Stephens, *The Family Saga in the South* (1995); Claudia Tate, *Domestic Allegories of Political Desire: The Black Heroine's Text at the Turn of the Century* (1992); Linda Tate, *A Southern Weave of Women* (1994); Ritchie Devon Watson Jr., *Yeoman Versus Cavalier* (1993); Deborah Gray White, *Ar'n't I a Woman? Female Slaves in the Plantation South* (1985); Bertram Wyatt-Brown, *Southern Honor: Ethics and Behavior in the Old South* (1982).

DOMESTIC NOVEL

Domestic novels, moralistic and prescriptive works of fiction focusing on women's lives and experiences,

were the best-sellers of mid-nineteenth-century America, penned largely by the "damned mob of scribbling women" against whom Nathaniel Hawthorne railed in a now-infamous letter to his publisher in 1854. During this period, women writers were being published in unprecedented numbers; while women wrote about one-third of the fiction published in the United States before 1830, by 1872 nearly three-fourths of the novels published in America were written by women. The domestic novel also targeted women as readers, benefiting from the rising middle class of women who had leisure time for reading and increased access to printed materials. Domestic novels were often serialized in women's magazines—and later, because of their tremendous popularity, in such "serious" literary magazines as *Atlantic Monthly* and *McClure's*—before appearing in book form. Lending libraries also made novels widely available, and reading for women was often a group activity, one woman reading aloud while others listened and quilted, mended, or performed other household chores.

The domestic novel is largely an outgrowth of the ideology of the separate spheres that dominated American society in the nineteenth century. The rise of industrialism brought about the move of production from the home, where it was shared by women, men, and frequently children, to the marketplace, a male domain. Home then became the primary province of women, with its attendant responsibilities of housekeeping, child rearing, and preserving religion and morality within the family. Although this ideology grew out of political and economic arrangements that served the growth of industrialism and a capitalist economy, its persuasive power came largely from the moral ideology used to promote it: women and men were created by God for different roles, and to chafe against one's responsibilities within these roles was not merely to threaten the stability of home life but to challenge the natural and Godly ordering of the universe. Most domestic novels mirrored and reinforced this conservative social and cultural milieu. Their aims were didactic and reformist, promoting home as an ideal realm where love and virtue ruled. Using melodramatic plot lines and emotional scenarios, domestic fiction sought to warn against the corrupting values of the marketplace—individuality, materialism, competition—and to promote the redeeming values of love, purity, and community associated with the home.

Domestic novels have, for most of American literary history, been disregarded as serious literature, subject to charges of sentimentality, idealizing, and triviality. Despite enormous popularity in their day, most writers of domestic fiction are now unfamiliar names whose works, once widely available, are now long out of print. During the past two decades, however, feminist scholars have challenged both the marginal status of domestic novels and the presumption that they simply reinforced a social order that limited women to a domestic sphere. Although domestic fiction is often dismissed as sentimental, most of these novels seem, in retrospect, to offer a combination of idealism and realism that often portrays more graphically and realistically than their canonical male counterparts the hardships of women's lives. The heroine of the domestic novel frequently loses the protective parent or guardian of her childhood, only to be faced with making her way alone in a hostile world. All around her, the lives of other women serve as cautionary tales. Women who are seduced by unscrupulous men inevitably face lives of shame and poverty, usually culminating in premature death. Just as unsavory, however, are the lives of women who marry honorably, but marry the wrong men. Many domestic novels offer gruesome accounts of unwise parents ushering their hapless daughters into undesirable marriages, of lives with men who are controlling, unfaithful, or cruel, of the hardship of frequent pregnancies and endless childrearing. Thus, while the unhappy specter of spinsterhood looms large for the heroine of the domestic novel, she also needs to be educated in making wise choices about marriage. More often than not, the domestic novel seems to criticize not the individual woman who makes unwise choices but a society that provides women so few choices and so little education for making their way in the world. Rather than portraying home as an escape for women from the harsher world of the marketplace, the domestic novel promoted home as an ideal world for both women and men, and depicted the world of the marketplace as essentially corrupt. Like the ideology of separate spheres itself, the domestic novel granted a measure of power—gained through love, superior virtue, and gentle influence—to women who, in political and economic terms, had no power.

Although the bulk of domestic novel writers lived in and wrote about New England, several native or transplanted southerners were among the most prolific contributors to the genre. Like their northern counterparts, southern domestic novelists exposed women's victimization within a patriarchal society and their efforts to transcend victimhood through struggle, escape,

and a new life in a female-centered household. The southern domestic novel provides an interesting departure from another enormously popular genre of its day, the plantation novel, which largely celebrates the planter's life of ease, gentility, and power. In contrast to the plantation novel, southern women's fiction of the antebellum period often emphasizes the rural plantation's isolation and its life of hard work for the planter's wife and daughters. In their depiction of slavery, however, southern domestic novelists have more in common with their male counterparts in the South than with northern women writing during the same period. Southern domestic novelists often defended the "peculiar institution" through their portrayal of a domestic bliss that extended to happy, docile slaves and beneficent slaveholders alike.

Caroline Gilman, born in Boston, Massachusetts, in 1794, became a transplanted southerner after moving with her new husband to Charleston, South Carolina, in 1819. Despite her northern origins, Gilman's loyalties gradually shifted toward the South, and she became known as an important southern woman writer during the 1830s and 1840s. Gilman's books promoted domestic tranquillity as a solution not only for her heroines' ills but for those of the nation. Writing in the pre–Civil War South, Gilman believed that she understood the tensions between her native North and adopted southern homeland and attempted to effect reconciliation between the two regions in her fiction. Her depictions of a mutually devoted relationship between loyal house slaves and their grateful masters and mistresses seem less an angry retort to reformist northern fiction than an effort to facilitate reconciliation between North and South by promoting a shared vision of domestic tranquillity.

Another transplanted northerner, Caroline Hentz, was born in 1800 in Massachusetts but lived in a number of southern states after her marriage. She is best remembered for her 1854 novel *The Planter's Northern Bride*, largely because it was written as a southern response to *Uncle Tom's Cabin*. In *Uncle Tom's Cabin*, Harriet Beecher Stowe uses the form of the domestic novel to attack slavery as an institution threatening home and family. Hentz uses the domestic novel to make the opposite argument, writing in her preface that she has "never witnessed one scene of cruelty or oppression, never beheld a chain or a manacle, or the infliction of a punishment more severe than parental authority would be justified in applying to filial disobedience or transgression"; she claims, rather, to have been "touched and gratified by the exhibition of affectionate kindness and care on one side, and loyal and devoted attachment on the other." Hentz replaces Stowe's stock characters with her own; most notably, the cruel slaveholder is replaced by a crafty and hypocritical abolitionist. Although Hentz's defense of slavery is familiar, her status as a transplanted northerner gave her argument added weight and interest; like Gilman, Hentz was praised by reviewers and the public for her antisectionalism and her peacemaking efforts.

E. D. E. N. Southworth, born in Washington, D.C., in 1819, was one of the few southern domestic novelists who spoke out against slavery both personally and in her fiction. Her fiction, like that of Gilman and Hentz, was reformist, and the most exemplary of her white characters always free their slaves by the novel's close. Southworth's fiction is marked by fearless heroines, melodramatic plot lines, and extravagant prose that Sarah Hale, editor of *Godey's Lady's Book*, criticized as "beyond the limits prescribed by correct taste or good judgment." Nearly all of her diverse and colorful heroines are beset by cruel and self-centered men: greedy fathers, opportunistic suitors, and selfish husbands. Thus, the female ideal of home is corrupted by male influence and must be reclaimed as woman's proper sphere—a place of virtue, comfort, and love. On one level, this plot line is indeed a conservative one, reinforcing the idea of separate spheres as the ideal social arrangement for women and men. On another level, however, Southworth's novels are deeply critical of male culture, exposing it as a corrupting influence for both men and women. Southworth insists on reform, and in novel after novel, that reform is shaped by a woman's image of an ideal man who recognizes, appreciates, and respects her superior virtue and values and takes his rightful place in a domestic realm dominated by her. Southworth was among the most popular and prolific of the domestic novelists. Although her publishing strategies make an exact count of her novels difficult—a genius at marketing and self-promotion, she serialized all of her novels but retained the copyrights and later published them in book form under new titles—she is generally thought to have written from fifty to sixty novels between 1849 and 1886.

Augusta Jane Evans Wilson, born in Georgia in 1835, was a staunch Confederate supporter whose third novel, *Macaria; or, Altars of Sacrifice* (1863), was dedicated "To the Brave Soldiers of the Southern Army." Wilson is best remembered for her novel *St. Elmo,* published in 1867; she wrote eight other novels

during her lengthy career, publishing her last book in 1907. Like Gilman and Hentz, Wilson presented an idealized portrait of the South while criticizing northern abolitionism. She was equally conservative on matters of women's rights, and her novels are passionately antisuffrage. Despite her conservative politics, however, Wilson created fiery, intelligent, and accomplished heroines who consistently refuse tempting offers of romance, wealth, and protection in favor of thoughtful self-determination and the examined life. Indeed, Wilson's extravagant vocabulary and relentless use of literary and cultural references in her writing, which sometimes create an unintentionally comic effect and invited parody from literary critics, seem intended to show off both her own education and that of her heroines. As in the case of many other domestic novelists, Wilson's fans cared little for her critics; *St. Elmo* is believed to have sold more copies than any other work of domestic fiction and was one of the most commercially successful works of the nineteenth century.

Although domestic fiction was clearly the province of middle-class white women, its wide influence may be seen among the earliest African American women writers as well. Harriet Jacobs's slave narrative *Incidents in the Life of a Slave Girl* (1861) responds clearly and startlingly to the ethics of virtue and domestic tranquillity promoted by domestic fiction. Jacobs, born into slavery in North Carolina around 1813, uses the story of her own victimization as a vehicle for telling the larger story of the sexual exploitation of slave women. In many ways, Jacobs's story parallels that of the heroine of the domestic novel: as a young girl, she passes from her grandmother's protection to the vulnerable condition of being seduced by an unscrupulous man—in this case, her master. Jacobs borrows the language of the domestic novel's virtuous heroine, including florid prose and direct address to the reader, to describe her plight. After begging the reader's forgiveness for her lost virtue, however, Jacobs makes an abrupt turn, refuting the rhetoric of the romantic novel by claiming that slave women should not be held to the same standards of virtue as other women. Thus Jacobs, while acknowledging a code of morality that she would like to adhere to, condemns the institution that makes female virtue an impossible practice. Further, Jacobs identifies slavery as the enemy of the family and domestic life at every turn: the domestic bliss of a southern bride is destroyed when she discovers that her new husband is fathering slave children; children gain inappropriate knowledge of sexual matters because of the mistress's jealousy; and Jacobs's own home life is destroyed when she must go into hiding in order to ensure her children's escape from slavery.

Harriet Wilson's 1859 novel *Our Nig,* thought to be the first novel published by an African American writer, also shows the influence of the domestic novel. Wilson, believed to be born in Virginia in 1807 or 1808, recounts in her largely autobiographical text her experience of racism as an indentured servant in antebellum New England. Like Harriet Jacobs, Wilson uses both the elaborate language and the melodramatic devices of the domestic novel; her story includes accounts of abusive treatment, betrayal, and suffering at the hands of those who should protect and care for her. Like Jacobs, too, Wilson uses the form of the domestic novel for political ends, indicting both racial and class oppression in her depiction of Mrs. Bellmont, the heroine's cruel employer. Both Jacobs and Wilson also question traditional Christian beliefs and practices to a larger degree than do most of the domestic novelists. In *Incidents in the Life of a Slave Girl,* Jacobs indicts the white slaveholders who piously profess their faith while heaping abuse on their slaves; she also rejects her grandmother's faith, which preaches submission and suffering in this world in order to gain rewards in the next. Jacobs recognizes the way that this Christian tradition has been used to maintain the subservience of slaves and boldly rejects it, claiming for herself and her children the right to freedom while they are yet alive. Harriet Wilson's heroine also rejects traditional notions of heaven when she learns that her cruel mistress professes religion; she is comforted not by traditional Christian platitudes about grace and forgiveness but by her own hope of a justice that would punish those who are cruel to her and reward those who are kind.

Although domestic fiction is generally recognized as a nineteenth-century phenomenon, its influence is found in many texts by twentieth-century southern women writers. Like their nineteenth-century counterparts, many of these texts seem to counter literary traditions that treat domesticity as the marginal or invisible backdrop for male activity. They question values associated with individual quests in the public world, privileging instead values associated with community and home. Willa Cather's *O Pioneers!* (1913), for example, which has been variously interpreted as the triumph of female over male, nurture over conquering, and intellect over physical strength, may also be read as the triumph of the woman gardener over the male farmer. Harriette Arnow's *The Dollmaker* (1954) pos-

its the domestic values of child rearing, housekeeping, and gardening against the canonical male story of quest and war. Her novel emphasizes not the individual adventure often associated with war as it is depicted in the American novel but the destructive effect of war on family and community. In Kaye Gibbons's 1987 novel *Ellen Foster,* Gibbons revises the male quest story by depicting not the canonical hero's flight *from* home and the restrictions it imposes, but a flight *to* home and its promise of physical and spiritual nurturance. Other twentieth-century texts by southern women writers, including Ellen Glasgow, Katherine Anne Porter, Eudora Welty, Alice Walker, and Gloria Naylor, are similarly shaped by domestic spaces, rituals, and relationships. Domestic novels thus continue to function as subversive texts which, although apparently reinforcing a social order that assigns women to domestic spaces, nonetheless depict home as a source of not only comfort but also power.

Kristina K. Groover

See also Domesticity; Novel, 1820 to 1865; Sentimental Novel.

Nina Baym, *Woman's Fiction: A Guide to Novels By and About Women in America, 1820–1870* (1978); Gillian Brown, *Domestic Individualism* (1990); Susan Coultrap-McQuin, *Doing Literary Business: American Women Writers in the Nineteenth Century* (1990); Cathy N. Davidson, *Revolution and the Word: The Rise of the Novel in America* (1986); Ann Romines, *The Home Plot* (1992).

DOUBLE DEALER, THE

In January 1921, several New Orleans poets and newspapermen established a new literary journal, *The Double Dealer,* which they published for five and a half years. Motivated by H. L. Mencken's infamous denigration of the South as "the Sahara of the Bozart," they subtitled their review *A National Magazine from the South.* The group included John McClure, Harold Levy, Albert Goldstein, Julius Friend, and Lillian Friend Marcus. Although they did not limit themselves to southern authors, one of their intentions was to end the antebellum romanticism that had long dominated the region's literature. They attracted and published established authors—Sherwood Anderson, Ezra Pound, and Thornton Wilder—and newcomers such as William Faulkner, Ernest Hemingway, Hart Crane, and several of the Agrarians, to produce a journal that was widely read and that Mencken himself praised.

Faulkner's first appearance in *The Double Dealer* was in June, 1922, with a poem entitled "Portrait." He became friends with the editors in 1925 while residing in New Orleans, and subsequently they published several of his essays, reviews, and other poetry, as well as a series of sketches under the title "New Orleans."

Although the journal did not have a long life, *The Double Dealer* achieved a national reputation, influenced the Southern Renascence, and brought several important new authors to the attention of the public. The journal was one of the influences in New Orleans that turned Faulkner, a minor poet when he arrived in the city, into a budding major novelist.

W. Kenneth Holditch

See also Literary Magazines to 1960; Periodicals, 1900–1960; *Reviewer.*

Charles L. Dufour, *Ten Flags in the Wind* (1967); Richard S. Kennedy, *Literary New Orleans* (1992); Lyle Saxon, *The New Orleans City Guide* (1938).

DOUGLASS, FREDERICK

Autobiographer, orator, editor, journalist, and political activist, Frederick Douglass is best known for *Narrative of the Life of Frederick Douglass, an American Slave, Written by Himself* (1845), a prototype of the antebellum slave narrative.

Born Frederick Augustus Bailey in 1818 near Tuckahoe, Maryland, to Harriet Bailey, a slave, and an unknown white man, Douglass spent his early childhood on the rural Eastern Shore. In 1826 he went to Baltimore as house servant to Hugh Auld. Introduced to city life and instructed in reading by Sophia Auld before her husband forbade it, Douglass recognized the liberating power of literacy and determined to seek freedom. His return to St. Michaels in 1833 precipitated a defining event: because he was rebellious, Douglass was sent to Edward Covey, a notorious slave-breaker charged with transforming the young man into a productive, manageable slave. Douglass describes his encounter with Covey as the "turning point" in his life, and his scene of self-defense became a reference point in autobiographical writings of the African American tradition.

After a foiled escape from the Freeland farm in 1836, Douglass was returned to Baltimore, where he apprenticed as caulker at local shipyards and met Anna Murray. On September 3, 1838, disguised as a sailor, Douglass escaped to New York, rejoined and married Anna Murray there, and relocated to New Bedford, Massachusetts. At the suggestion of his host, Frederick adopted the name Douglass, from Walter Scott's *Lady of the Lake.* Douglass became active in the community, subscribing to William Lloyd Garrison's abolitionist newspaper, the *Liberator.* Just three years out of slavery, Douglass spoke so brilliantly at a Nantucket anti-slavery meeting that he received the recognition of Garrison and an invitation to join the antislavery circuit. His dramatic characterization and charged rhetoric launched his career as orator and agent for the American Anti-Slavery Society.

To authenticate his slave experiences, Douglass wrote his *Narrative* (1845), selling over thirty thousand copies in five years. Unlike earlier, more picaresque slave narratives, Douglass's shows his Franklinesque rise from obscure poverty to public stature, charting his moral and psychological development toward manhood. Its success jeopardized Douglass's freedom, forcing his escape to the British Isles, where supporters negotiated his freedom in 1846 and raised money to help him establish a newspaper.

Douglass started his African American-owned and -edited newspaper in 1847 in Rochester, New York; for sixteen years, he edited the *North Star,* later *Frederick Douglass' Paper* and *Frederick Douglass' Monthly.* Douglass attacked slavery, exposed northern racism, and espoused women's rights. Although he played a key role in the women's movement, beginning with the Seneca Falls Convention in 1848, he perceived the political expediency of keeping the movements separate and making antislavery politics a priority.

Douglass's changing political loyalties and insistence on editorial independence in the early 1850s meant a break with Garrison. His writing reflected the energy of experiment and revision. In 1853 he published a novella describing the 1841 *Creole* slave ship mutiny, *The Heroic Slave,* which appeared first in the *North Star* and later in *Autographs for Freedom,* edited by Julia Griffiths, to raise money for the newspaper. *My Bondage and My Freedom* (1855), Douglass's second autobiography, chronicles his political metamorphosis and self-conscious literary construction of the self-made man.

A staunch supporter of the Republican Party, Douglass served Lincoln as advisor during the Civil War and, with his moving speech "Men of Color to Arms" (1863), recruited over one hundred African American men for the 54th Regiment. He received appointments as Emissary to the Dominican Republic (1871), Marshall of the District of Columbia (1877–1881), Recorder of Deeds for the District of Columbia (1881–1886), and U.S. Minister to Haiti.

At the vanguard for African American suffrage, Douglass campaigned relentlessly from 1857 until 1867 to dispel myths that fed opposition. He joined activists Ida B. Wells-Barnett to protest lynchings in the South and delivered an indictment of lynching at the World Columbian Exposition in Chicago in 1893.

The noted statesman retired briefly from the political arena in 1880, once more reshaping his own story in the *Life and Times of Frederick Douglass, Written by Himself* (1881). The last years of his life, like the early ones, were spent on the lecture circuit, and Douglass died shortly after delivering a speech before the National Council of Women on February 20, 1895.

Geneva H. Baxter

See also African American Literature, Beginnings to 1919; Slave Narrative.

William L. Andrews, ed., *Critical Essays on Frederick Douglass* (1991); John W. Blassingame, ed., *The Frederick Douglass Papers* (1979–); Frederick Douglass, *Autobiographies* (1994); Waldo E. Martin, *The Mind of Frederick Douglass* (1984); William S. McFeely, *Frederick Douglass* (1990); Benjamin Quarles, *Frederick Douglass* (1948); Eric J. Sundquist, ed., *Frederick Douglass: New Literary and Historical Essays* (1990).

DRAMA, BEGINNINGS TO 1800

Conditions in the colonial South were more amenable to the drama than those of the puritanical northern settlements. Although puritan attitudes drove actors out of both England and the northern colonies, the theater was enjoyed in Williamsburg, Annapolis, Baltimore, and Charleston, where it was viewed as acceptable entertainment. The first play in English to be staged in the American colonies, *Ye Bar and Ye Cubb* (1665), was presented on Virginia's Eastern Shore in Accomac County. Northern colonists were wary of the drama, but southern life was more conducive to its enjoyment. The landed gentry could afford to take time for enter-

tainment and were largely free of puritan objections to the theater.

The theater needs a central audience to survive, so early performances took place in urban centers. Williamsburg, the first town to plan a theater (1716), hosted companies such as the Walter Murray and Thomas Kean acting company, which helped to create interest in the theater. Lewis Hallam and David Douglass (who married Hallam's widow) led famous acting troupes. Charleston was another important theatrical center, with seasons running from 1735 on, both in the theater on Dock Street (opened in 1736) and the Charleston Theatre (1793). Throughout the South, newspapers served as forums for debate about the theater and the virtues of various plays; George Washington was a frequent playgoer in Annapolis.

But there were very few southern playwrights. Most of the plays staged in colonial times were British works, Shakespearean drama, or versions of Continental successes. What was written in the South seems to have been of inferior quality. Toward the end of the eighteenth century, political plays by American playwrights appeared. In the North, Mercy Otis Warren and others wrote patriotic plays; a few Loyalist plays emerged as well, mostly as propaganda. The most famous southern playwright of the new country was Colonel Robert Munford (ca. 1737–1783).

Munford, a native Southside Virginian, wrote political plays that captured the spirit of the new American while being firmly nonpartisan. Both his plays deal with Virginia politics in broad, farcical, or comic strokes, and both advocate a moderate, measured approach toward government in the face of human passions and vicissitudes. Published by his son, William Munford, in 1798, neither was produced, it seems, until their rediscovery in the 1940s, when they were both published in the *William and Mary Quarterly* (April 1948; July 1949) and the three-act *Candidates* was staged at the William and Mary Theatre in Williamsburg in 1949.

The Candidates; or, the Humors of a Virginia Election is set during an election for the House of Burgesses in 1770 and was probably written soon thereafter. The candidates are various types, with names to match: the drunken Sir John Toddy and the minor candidates Strutabout and Smallhopes oppose Mr. Wou'dbe, our hero, whose name is slandered. His reputation and the election are secured when he receives the backing of Mr. Worthy, a former delegate who emerges from retirement to be Wou'dbe's running mate. The Freeholders, as the electorate, are easily swayed to one candidate's camp or the other. Their wives seem better judges of character. There is plenty of local criticism both here and in *The Patriots*; Munford is making fun of various Southside Virginia figures.

The Patriots (ca. 1777–1780) takes full five-act comic form, focusing on three romances. The serious one is between Trueman and Mira, and its obstacle is his supposed Tory sympathies. Trueman's reputation, and that of his friend Meanwell, have been sullied by Mr. Tackabout, himself a Tory. True loyalties come to light at the play's end, and the comic romance between Pickle, a gentleman in disguise, and Melinda, the hidden niece of Meanwell, is to be resolved in marriage. A third, satirical romance between Colonel Strut and the ambitious Isabella, "a female politician," ends when he will not force a duel to suit her overzealous patriotism. The play contains pointed satire of Mecklenburg County figures, but its sentimental comic nature makes it accessible for modern audiences as well.

Although Royall Tyler, author of *The Contrast* (1787), is called the first American comic playwright, Munford wrote earlier, but his plays were published posthumously and not performed until this century.

Sage Hamilton Rountree

See also Colonial Literature.

Rodney M. Baine, *Robert Munford: America's First Comic Dramatist* (1967); Walter Meserve, *An Outline History of American Drama, Second Edition* (1994), and *An Emerging Entertainment* (1977); Anthony Hobson Quinn, *A History of the Drama from the Beginning to the Civil War* (1943); Charles S. Watson, *The History of Southern Drama* (1997).

DRAMA, 1800 TO 1900

After numerous theatrical seasons and attempts at playwriting in the eighteenth century, drama in the South made important strides in the nineteenth century. Charleston, South Carolina, became the first theatrical center of the South. With the indispensable support of active companies, managers, and newspaper critics of the city, the first group of native dramatists wrote a substantial series of plays in the first quarter of the nineteenth century. These dramatists inaugurated the true beginning of southern drama.

After the Charleston Theatre was built by the English manager Thomas Wade West in 1793, he was suc-

ceeded by the native Frenchman, Alexander Placide, a partisan of the American and French Revolutions, who sided with the Jeffersonian Republicans in the Federalist-Republican controversy of the day. A first-rate impresario, Placide welcomed plays by local dramatists to enliven theatrical seasons at the Charleston Theatre from 1800 to 1812. Charles Gilfert, from New York City, successfully managed the Charleston Theatre and directed the Southern Circuit from 1817 to 1825.

William Ioor (1780–1850), a physician and legislator born in Dorchester, not far from Charleston, was the first South Carolinian to author a produced play. A Jeffersonian Republican, Ioor first composed *Independence; or, Which Do You Like Best, the Peer, or the Farmer?* (1805). This adaptation of an English novel, set in Britain, indirectly extols the independent farmer of America, the mainstay of the Republican Party. Praising country life and ridiculing a pompous noble woman's hatred of the country, this comedy is an early expression of Agrarianism in southern literature.

Ioor's second play, *The Battle of Eutaw Springs* (1807), celebrates the last Revolutionary battle in the state, after which the British occupiers departed. It contains a prototype of the hospitable old gentleman. Jonathan Slyboots befriends an English soldier forced into His Majesty's service who decides to become an American citizen. He proclaims that every "child of sorrow" should be treated "by a native of the hospitable, and charitable state of South Carolina" as his brother. This play also preserves southern legend by dramatizing the civil strife of Tory and Whig in South Carolina. The heroine describes graphically how Tory plunderers tortured her father to find where the family treasure was hidden and set fire to their "elegant" mansion while inveigling the slaves to escape—a foreshadowing of such episodes during the Civil War, which was often compared to the Revolution by southerners during that conflict.

Reflecting Federalist-Republican strife, Stephen Cullen Carpenter, drama critic of the Federalist *Courier,* censured this play for its poor craftsmanship, but the Republican *City Gazette* praised the anti-British work as a true account of the Revolutionary battle.

John Blake White (1781–1859), Charleston artist and author of five plays, stands out for his works advocating moral reform. He anticipates dramatists of social protest in the twentieth century, for example Paul Green. *Modern Honor* (1812), produced by Placide, condemns dueling, a custom that ran rife in the South and especially in Charleston. Woodville, influenced by a voyage to Europe, challenges Forsythe, his rival for Maria, to a duel. Though the hero's second pleads with him to replace so-called modern honor with true honor, Woodville proceeds to the dueling ground, where he is killed on stage, thus forcing the audience to face the stark consequence of this violent practice. The other evil that most aroused southerners was intemperance, the effects of which were described luridly in White's *The Forgers,* an unperformed piece published in the *Southern Literary Journal* (1837).

Isaac Harby (1788–1828), a proponent of the Jewish Reform Movement, composed two plays with foreign settings that were performed in Charleston: *The Gordian Knot* (1810) and *Alberti* (1819), both set in fifteenth-century Florence. He did his most interesting work, however, as a drama critic. Opposed to the gothic play, Harby objected to divergences from nature in White's *The Mysteries of the Castle* (1806). Under the pseudonym "Stefanolf," he doubted the truthfulness of the villain, whose high-pitched emotion was abnormally different. Disagreeing with Harby, a journalistic defender of the Gothic declared that anyone acquainted with the human heart would have no trouble believing in such a character. This debate over alleged gothic excesses could be transferred *mutatis mutandis* to those over Tennessee Williams's plays in the next century.

Similar to the plays of Charleston were those being composed in Virginia during the same period. Here we also find nationalistic plays by Jeffersonian Republicans John Daly Burk and St. George Tucker. The most successful of Virginia playwrights was George Washington Parke Custis (1781–1857), step-grandson of George Washington, who resided at Arlington mansion near Washington, D.C. The author of seven plays, Custis reveals the Romantic influence of Sir Walter Scott by his fondness for colorful history. His best play is *Pocahontas, or, The Settlers of Virginia, A National Drama* (1830), first presented in Philadelphia and later in Charleston. Dramatizing the Indian maiden's famous rescue of Captain John Smith, this piece calls on Virginians never to forget the birth of Virginia. John Rolfe, an early cavalier of Virginia, courteously addresses the Indian damsel and joins in the conquest of Virginia. Custis, like Ioor in Charleston, combined state pride and nationalism in his plays before sectionalism prevailed in the South.

Dramatic activity next shifted from the Atlantic to the Gulf South, with New Orleans as its center. Three managers exploited the potential for theatrical performance in the Southwest. James H. Caldwell, an Englishman, arrived from Charleston. Noah H. Ludlow and Solomon ("Old Sol") Smith, both native-born Americans, competed with him in New Orleans. They organized a theatrical company in the 1830s that crisscrossed the Mississippi Valley and contiguous areas of Alabama, Mississippi, Tennessee, and Missouri for the next twenty years.

The writing of frontier plays, following fiction, invigorated the stages of New Orleans with the exciting adventures of outlaws and western emigrants. Nathaniel Bannister from Baltimore dramatized the legends and exploits of a famous criminal in *Murrell: The Great Western Land Pirate* (1837). This play included among its characters Bob Steelborn, a Kentuckian, who was half-horse, half-alligator. Showing the closeness of drama and fiction at this time, William Gilmore Simms wrote two novels based on John A. Murrell's gang of robbers in Alabama and Mississippi. Mark Twain remembered stories told about the outlaw in *Life on the Mississippi* (1883).

The most talented dramatist fostered by the southwestern theater was Joseph M. Field. This actor-journalist emigrated from the East when young and traveled with Ludlow and Smith's company from 1835 to 1844. An extremely versatile man, Field, as a frontier humorist, published *The Drama in Pokerville* (1847), a number of the famous Library of Humorous American Works. This fictional narrative recounts the visits to backwater villages based on the tours Field joined. It caricatures Ludlow as a pompous manager who proposes to establish "the temple of the Drama" on the crude frontier. Field also edited the *St. Louis Reveille,* a weekly devoted to humorous yarns, from 1844 to 1850. He ended his career as the impecunious manager of a theater in Mobile.

Field wrote many farces for the New St. Charles Theatre in New Orleans during the 1840s, the heyday of humorous writing in the Southwest. Field, like Mark Twain, considered con men to be most deserving of satirical chastisement. He targeted the exponents of spiritual movements, believing that Americans were especially vulnerable to them. On April 20, 1843, in *The Twenty-Third of April; or, Are You Ready?* he satirized the Millerites, who predicted the Second Coming on that date. According to the *New Orleans Picayune* notice, Sol Smith would enact Judge Lynch on Judgment Day. Lampooning pseudoscientific charlatans, Field offered *Dr. Heavy Bevy* during the same month. The title character, based on the actual Dr. Dionysius Lardner, would deliver lectures on nebular and stellar clusters with "speculation upon cometary influence." In 1845, Field presented *Foreign and Native* in St. Louis, ridiculing, like Twain, the deception of American families by bogus noblemen.

In the decade before the Civil War, politics dominated southern plays. Rebuttals to *Uncle Tom's Cabin* (1852) flourished in New Orleans. Four known plays of this type, including Joseph M. Field's *Uncle Tom's Cabin, or, Life in the South As It Is* (1854), regaled large crowds with music and such engaging characters as Little Eva. For the first time, the Negro took center stage, suggesting more complex treatments of the race question in southern drama stemming from this problematic debut. William Wells Brown (1816–1884), who grew up in Missouri, was the sole African American to join the stage debate over slavery. He wrote a play about one slave's escape entitled *The Escape; or, A Leap for Freedom* (1858), which he delivered widely as a dramatic reading.

Sectional arguments provided the themes of southern plays in the decade preceding the war. Applying the past-present parallel used by Simms to support secession in his Revolutionary novels, dramatists presented previous historical events to argue current issues indirectly. Simms himself advocated admission of Texas by his melodrama of the previous battle between Texans and Mexicans at the Alamo in *Michael Bonham; or, The Fall of Bexar* (composed in 1844; published in the *Southern Literary Messenger* in 1852). L. Placide Canonge, a New Orleanian, composed for the French theater *France et Espagne* (1850), depicting the colonials' revolt against Spanish tyranny in 1768 to champion southern secession at the time of the Compromise of 1850; Clifton W. Tayleure of Baltimore dramatized John Pendleton Kennedy's Revolutionary romance *Horse-Shoe Robinson* (1835) for the stage in 1856; in topical allusions, southerners are called "rebels" and a slave defends slavery.

Differing from American drama in general, southern drama's defining event is the Civil War. Early plays had glorified the states, such as *The Battle of Eutaw Springs* in South Carolina. Unlike Simms's novels, which conceive of the South as an entity, the early plays do not encompass a whole region. During the war, however, Confederate plays envision the South as a distinct section, culture, and independent nation. Significantly, a prize of $300 was offered in Augusta, Georgia, for the best play on a southern theme during the war.

The central and most vital figure in the Confederate plays is none other than a female soldier. Although women had filled such roles previously in northern plays, they had not in the South until the Civil War. It is the woman, not the man, who champions the southern cause most strongly on the stage of Richmond theaters.

John Hill Hewitt (1801–1890) featured female soldiers in his plays. He became the leading composer of plays in the Confederacy. After writing *The Scout* (performed in 1861), in which Kate Ashwood leads a band of women in capturing a Federal picket, he transferred from Richmond to the safer venue of Augusta, Georgia. Here, Hewitt created his best female role in 1863 for the Queen Sisters Company. In *The Vivandiere* (the popular term for a female soldier), Louise of Louisiana (played by Laura Waldron) has such zeal that she joins the soldiers near Manassas, Virginia, singing, "At my country's call, I come / With cheerful lips and eyes." She discovers her long-lost brother from New York and converts him to Southern Rights. Hewitt's plays have survived only in prompt books held at Emory University.

The Guerrillas (1863), by the Virginian journalist James Dabney McCabe, was first performed in Richmond in 1862 and became the most widely produced Confederate play because of its availability in print. The brave heroine is Rose Maylie, who defies the Union general John C. Frémont in the Valley of Virginia; she informs him that after killing all the men "you will then have to meet the women."

The imaginary heroines of Dixie, based on real ones like Augusta Evans Wilson, militant novelist of the Confederacy, stand out as predecessors of later women in southern fiction and drama. Drusilla Sartoris of Faulkner's *The Unvanquished* (1938) is literally a female soldier riding from one battlefield to another. The female soldiers are the direct predecessors of women who combine steely tenacity with feminine grace in modern plays, such as the spunky Amanda Wingfield of *The Glass Menagerie* (1945) and the determined Carrie Watts of *The Trip to Bountiful* (1953) by Horton Foote.

Without Espy Williams (1852–1908), a chasm would gape in southern drama from the Civil War to World War I. This New Orleanian, the composer of plays in the school of Ibsen, enjoyed success on the commercial stage but also held serious aims as a self-conscious modern dramatist. In a lecture entitled "Modern Drama: Its Moral and Literary Value" (ca.

1906), Williams lauded "the late Henrik Ibsen" as the greatest of modern dramatists.

Choosing the theme of marital infidelity, as had James A. Herne in *Margaret Fleming* (1890), Williams in *The Husband: A Society Play* (1895) shows how the husband suffers from a wife's infidelity. Like Ibsen and Shaw, Williams attacks religious intolerance in *The Atheist* (1892). He showed his adoption of the New South creed, another aspect of his modernism, by supporting reconciliation between North and South. In a poem about Jefferson Davis, he called for cessation of attacks by his tormentors, while in another he praised General Grant's work for peace, "his crown of fame."

Williams's most interesting and southern play is *The Clairvoyant: A Living Lie* (1899), an unperformed piece set in contemporary New Orleans, complete with ambience and Creole dialect. Here we have a distinct southern type, the putative mulatto, seen in "Désirée's Baby" (1893) by Kate Chopin. On the testimony of her foster mother, the heroine believes that she is part Negro. This fear causes her to take the name of Estelle Ruchard and sometimes the disguise of a clairvoyant, that is, a fortune teller, by the name of Zenobia. The best part of this highly melodramatic play is Estelle's agonizing that her Negro blood will be discovered. When Ziz, her "before the war" mammy, states that purple spots beneath the fingernails signify Negro blood, she vows to wear gloves for the rest of her life. In the sensational denouement, the villainous Paul Foscari informs the clairvoyant that he will expose the ancestry of Estelle; Arthur Steadman, her true lover, proves that she is pure white; and Estelle, throwing off her disguise as Zenobia, stabs Foscari with a stiletto.

Espy Williams, a dramatist, adds to the roster of New South writers who boldly depicted sensitive subjects, thus strengthening the new critical temper exemplified by Ellen Glasgow. From William Ioor to Espy Williams, southern dramatists prepared the way for superior works with plays focusing on nationalism, state pride, humor, Confederate heroines, and the ideas of Ibsen.

Charles S. Watson

Charles S. Watson, *The History of Southern Drama* (1997); Walter Meserve, *An Emerging Entertainment: The Drama of the American People to 1828* (1977), and *Heralds of Promise: The Drama of the American People During the Age of Jackson, 1829–1849* (1986).

DRAMA, 1900 TO PRESENT

Most analysts of southern literature consider Tennessee Williams to be the region's leading playwright, followed by Lillian Hellman, Paul Green, and Horton Foote.

Paul Green is the South's first truly significant twentieth-century playwright. Making his start as a dramatist with folk plays, Green nevertheless became closely identified with the Group Theater movement in New York City. In fact, *The House of Connelly,* the last of Green's early folk plays, launched the Group Theater. Green concentrates on the theme of racial guilt, and the play's protagonist, Will Connelly, is at first incapacitated by his sense of his family's complicity in slavery. Will is the last master of a decaying plantation, the scion of a family once but no longer wealthy and powerful. The themes of dynastic disintegration, guilt, and the inability to assume leadership anticipate Tennessee Williams's characters. As with some of Williams's texts, alternate texts (*Cat on a Hot Tin Roof,* for example) provide both optimistic and pessimistic outcomes. In one version, Will's family is redeemed by his marriage to the energetic daughter of a white tenant farmer, Patsy Tate; in another, Patsy is murdered by Connelly servants who resent her movement up the social ladder. In its emphasis on antebellum prosperity versus postbellum deprivation and decay and the gradual decline of a once-great family, *The House of Connelly* fulfills many expectations of contemporary southern mythology. Green's greatest success with the Group Theater came with *Johnny Johnson* (1937), an antiwar musical in collaboration with Kurt Weill.

Green captured national attention in 1927 with *In Abraham's Bosom: The Biography of a Negro,* winning the Pulitzer Prize in drama for that year. Green's sympathetic treatment of African American experience is a constant in his work. In 1926 Green published *Lonesome Road: Six Plays for Negro Theatre. Potter's Field: A Symphonic Play of the Negro People* (1931) gives a realistic overview of life in shantytown, revealing the strength of the black community as well as its impotence in the white power structure. In 1940–1941 Green dramatized Richard Wright's *Native Son,* meeting with Wright as he planned this work.

Green's most enduring legacy is in the folk play. *The Lost Colony* (1937) builds on Green's experiments with Group Theater and symphonic drama. The success of this outdoor drama led Green and his followers to establish a "theater of the people" away from

Broadway depicting significant events in American history.

Lillian Hellman achieved national distinction that has proven more lasting than Green's. It is especially remarkable that a woman should have been able to command such respect in the male-dominated world of theater producers and directors. Hellman experiments with many themes, from possible lesbianism in *The Children's Hour* (1934)—ironically bearing the title of Longfellow's famous poem about domestic bliss—to the rise of Nazism in *Watch on the Rhine* (1941). But it is *The Little Foxes* (1939), first a play and then a movie, and its companion, *Another Part of the Forest* (1946), which, in the mode of Faulkner's novels *The Sound and the Fury* (1929) and *Absalom, Absalom!* (1936), reverse the chronological order of events in the two works, that established Hellman's southernness. Exploitation by the upstart white Hubbard family of blacks is a theme in both plays, but industrial challenges to the agrarianism of the Old South, the decline of personal and family honor, and the ineffectuality of aristocratic relics of the southern past, such as Oscar Hubbard's lovable, fragile and dypsomaniacal wife, Birdie, create an atmosphere of irreversible decadence and corruption. Regina Hubbard anticipates to a degree the complex and powerful women of Williams's plays. Her weakness is greed and cold-heartedness, but unlike so many of Williams's female characters, she is capable of controlling her sexual impulses—although apparently willing to seduce a Chicago business partner should such a relationship provide her with social or financial advantages.

Alongside the white playwrights Green and Hellman, there emerged an impressive roster of southern black dramatists. One of the first African Americans to be produced on Broadway was Willis Richardson (1889–1977), whose one-act play *The Chip Woman's Fortune* was produced there in 1923. Writing in the same period was Georgia Johnson, whose antilynching play, *A Sunday Morning in the South,* was written in 1925. Langston Hughes, better known for his poetry, was also the author of *Mulatto* (1925), which drew New York audiences for more than a year. The fiction writer Zora Neale Hurston coauthored a play with Hughes (*Mule Bone* in 1930) and wrote several other theater pieces. Louisiana-born Theodore Ward organized a Harlem theater company with Hughes and Richard Wright and authored a powerful historical drama, *Our Lan',* which was produced on Broadway in 1947. Randolph Edmonds (1920–1982) wrote many plays to be performed in black colleges across the country. Black actor-turned-playwright Ossie Davis (1917–   ) wrote *Purlie Victorious* in 1961, starring Davis's wife, Ruby Dee. None of these plays by southern blacks is thought to have been an influence on Williams's dramaturgy, and certainly none enjoyed Williams's commercial success. What is interesting about black southerners' depictions of their region on stage is their constant focus on the dilemma of black individuals, caused for the most part by unjust social institutions and corrupt white men. The belief that the South had produced a complex civilization brought low both by its own flaws and a harsh enemy is not part of a black aesthetic or historical tradition.

Tennessee Williams (1911–1983) belongs to the first group of southern writers in the twentieth century who gained international recognition. He is more frequently compared to novelist William Faulkner than to his contemporaries in the theater world. Like every other twentieth-century American playwright, he owes a debt to Eugene O'Neill, whose dramatic achievements elevated the status of all American theater. Williams deftly employs expressionistic devices that had been the forte of the early O'Neill.

Williams's lyrical dialogue, his sympathetic and expansive roles for female actors, and his imaginative embellishment of naturalistic situations and dialogue with expressionistic staging techniques are deservedly admired contributions of the Mississippi-born playwright, fiction writer, and poet. Because Margaret Mitchell's novel *Gone With the Wind,* and more significantly the movie made from that novel, preceded Williams's first great stage plays and established certain enduring international assumptions and myths about southern culture, Williams had to choose between perpetuating Mitchell's stereotypes or shattering them. In Mitchell's pages, plantation life is perceived to have been lavish, almost regal. Slaves are seldom mistreated and, consequently, are loyal to their owners; northerners are mainly predators who ruthlessly destroy a genteel civilization.

In Williams's plays, however, the evils of racism are explored in *Battle of Angels/Orpheus Descending* (1940) and *Sweet Bird of Youth* (1956) in particular. A patriarchal society, dedicated to worshipping a deceased elite, joins with a more updated money-hungry, pleasure-seeking culture to create a symbolic torture chamber for the sensitive or idealistic individual. Still, one might conclude that the penchant of Blanche DuBois for "magic" over realism mirrors her creator's preferences. What Williams succeeds in doing is to convey the magnetic appeal of southern cultural myths as he deconstructs them in play after play. The tension between a southerner's dream of an idyllic life and the reality of living it breathes energy into all of Williams's art.

Many perversions and distortions of human behavior are attributed by Williams to the rigid gender stereotypes he uncovers in the southern landscape. The nearly schizophrenic division between the strong sexual needs and chaste public image that both Lucretia Collins and Blanche DuBois try to maintain is not a conflict shared by male characters, who are free to boast of their sexuality (Val in *Orpheus Descending,* Stanley in *Streetcar Named Desire,* Big Daddy in *Cat on a Hot Tin Roof,* etc.). In fact, the veneration of the male as "stud" and progenitor and the codification of physical bravery and strength, leadership, decisiveness, and aggressiveness are carried to such an extreme that certain male characters seem to surrender their masculinity rather than compete with the macho prototypes they have witnessed at close hand. The puerile, alcoholic, and possibly homosexual Brick as well as Blanche's suicidal young husband and Sebastian Venable are prepared to reject life itself if it necessitates the assumption of a dominating sexuality. The hypocrisy of a society that denies a woman's sexuality is also anathema to Williams. Lucretia, Blanche, Carol in *Orpheus Descending* and Catherine in *Suddenly Last Summer* (1958), as well as Maggie the Cat, Alma in *Summer and Smoke* (1947), and Hannah in *Night of the Iguana* (1962) are misled by the discriminatory double standard into hating themselves for showing the libidinal urges considered healthy in men.

Between the years from 1944 to 1961, Williams wrote what are arguably his most famous plays, all of which were made into films that increased their influence on American popular culture: *The Glass Menagerie* (1944), *A Streetcar Named Desire* (1947), *Summer and Smoke* (1948), *The Rose Tattoo* (1951), *Cat on a Hot Tin Roof* (1955), *Suddenly Last Summer* (1958), *Sweet Bird of Youth* (1959), and *The Night of the Iguana* (1964).

Toward the end of the playwright's life, Williams continued to experiment with new dramatic forms, as in *Clothes for a Summer Hotel* (1980), his last play, which is postmodernist in its self-conscious challenge to traditional narrative assumptions and stage conventions. Fictitious versions of writers Scott Fitzgerald and Ernest Hemingway anachronistically converge in Asheville for a series of discussions with Zelda, a patient at a mental hospital euphemistically referred to as "a summer hotel." Even the play's title, which included a homonymic pun—"clothes" for "close"—self-consciously draws attention to the distinctive literary styles and precise word usage for which Fitzgerald and Hemingway are famous. Does Williams question the mutability of word definitions or subtly suggest that the two novelists mask, rather than reveal, their secrets by manipulating words? Blatant meddling with historical facts in *Clothes for a Summer Hotel* disrupts the suspension of disbelief, as does the playwright's introduction to the play, which suggests that the actors who appear to be playing Scott, Zelda, and Hemingway are possibly depicting the author's own internal conflicts. Both Hellman and Williams transcended their regional subject matter and became internationally important twentieth-century dramatists, particularly Williams.

The power of Williams's dramaturgy is a daunting legacy for his successors. Preston Jones (1936–1979), Marsha Norman (1947–), and Beth Henley (1952–) all appear to owe a debt to Tennessee Williams, and they continue his exploration of southern value systems and conflicts. Jones, a Texan, and Norman, a Kentuckian, belong to border states, ones not always associated with the antebellum South but which nonetheless shared certain cultural assumptions with Williams's South. Henley is a Mississippian and hence unquestionably belongs to the group of literary stalwarts produced by that state in the twentieth century.

In all of Preston Jones's work, especially his best-known Texas trilogy, sexist attitudes, racism, the loss of religious conviction, and the ravages of time are major themes. Each generation seems more shallow and greedy than its predecessor. The new Texan has no respect for tradition, and he dreams only of developing for profit the last unspoiled wilderness in his hometown. Jones's personal dream of a small rural paradise is similar to Lady Torrence's recollection of her father's wine-garden restaurant in Williams's *Orpheus Descending,* which was burned down by local racists because her Italian father had sold whiskey to blacks. It was also the setting of her first love affair. Jones lacks Williams's lyrical gifts, however, and neither the romance of the past nor the evil of the present is wholly convincing. Jones's artistic strength depends upon his recognition that the feudal hierarchy of white male dominance celebrated in the tales of a glorious past are the roots of contemporary dissatisfaction and decay. His plays lack either a compelling plot or suffer from obvious contrivances. He is often depressing without being "affecting." The reappearance of characters and allusions to mythic or historical events in his seven plays may recall William Faulkner's or Thomas Wolfe's pageantry but does not create a metaphorical universe similar to theirs.

If one compares Jones to other American writers, the influence of Williams is apparent, especially in Jones's sympathy toward exploited, neurotic women and his revulsion at male chauvinists. Yet his male characters generally lack the electrifying meanness that makes Williams's so threatening, and the women are incapable of delivering the lyrical, memorable soliloquies of a Blanche DuBois or Maggie the Cat.

Marsha Norman and Beth Henley are also contemporary southern playwrights. Norman's best-known play, 'Night, Mother (1983), depicts a mother-daughter relationship similar to Amanda's and Laura's in The Glass Menagerie. Jesse has epilepsy rather than a clubfoot, but her disability is an embarrassment as well as a concern for her mother, who while not literally abandoned by her late husband as Amanda had been, was emotionally rejected by him years before his death. A son/brother who tries to be helpful but maintains his own emotional distance as a means of survival completes the similarities between the Norman and the Williams plays. Following 'Night, Mother, Norman wrote the less commercially successful Traveler in the Dark (1984). The theme of a physician estranged from his father as a result of the latter's fundamentalist religious beliefs is reminiscent of the spiritual ambiguities of Summer and Smoke.

The small-town southern characters of Beth Henley's work are thought to owe much to the fictional creations of Faulkner, Welty, and O'Connor. Nevertheless, the witty, gossipy conversations of her characters, the mixture of the comic and tragic in the tradition of the grotesque (Mrs. Magrath's suicide by hanging is accompanied by her simultaneous lynching of her favorite cat, and Babe's shooting of her husband prompts her comment that she "just didn't like his looks") connects Henley to southerners from Poe to Faulkner. Racial exploitation, discrimination against women, and recalcitrant macho males as well as a strong reliance on music and dancing for theatrical mood reflect the benefits of Williams's stage triumphs. Even two of her later plays, The Miss Firecracker Contest (1985) and The Debutante Ball (1992), have at their center stereotypical southern rituals, such as the beauty pageant (referred to in Williams's Cat on a Hot Tin Roof) and

the coming-out party in Williams's Suddenly Last Summer).

Unlike Jones, Henley, and Norman, Horton Foote was not directly influenced by Tennessee Williams. Born only five years after Williams, Foote first produced a play on Broadway in 1944. During this same year, Williams wrote The Glass Menagerie, which occupies a more permanent place in the modern theater than any of Foote's many plays. Furthermore, Foote's first truly memorable play was The Trip to Bountiful in 1953, by which time Williams had already written five major dramas. Although the two playwrights share themes of individuals seeking their own identity in the presence of a monolithic, patriarchal southern culture, Foote is more optimistic than Williams, and his characters often have a stoicism and toughness that separate them from the vulnerable, martyred characters of Williams's universe.

In all of Foote's works, there is a blending of naturalistic surfaces with religious or mystical overtones. Dramatic events are created out of everyday occurrences, yet the playwright manages to reveal the uniqueness of each character and the intensity of painful or pleasurable moments in his or her life.

Foote is sensitive to issues of racial justice, and it is not surprising that he was chosen to write the famous screenplay for Harper Lee's novel To Kill a Mockingbird. In The Death of Papa (1997), Elizabeth, deeply moved by the poverty of black families in her community when she attends a servant's funeral, cannot account to her young son for social injustices perpetrated in the name of race. She can only comment, "I don't know why; that's just the way it is." Not only society's flawed sociological structures but the land itself can destroy a generation of hard workers, both blacks and whites. The failure of the cotton crop is slowly bringing down Harrison, Texas, in 1928, a full year before the stock-market crash added to national woes. Yet, returning to manage the land, as Horace Robedaux does when his father-in-law dies, suggests that the traces of an agrarian ideal can occasion a spiritual or emotional rebirth.

Foote will be remembered primarily for his "Orphans' Home" cycle of nine plays, which began with Boots in a Parched Ground (1994) and ended with The Death of Papa (1997), developing a portrait of Horace Robedaux Sr., the "orphan" of the series and the fictitious counterpart of Foote's own father. Foote continually strives to understand himself and the southern community that shaped him.

A respect for dramatic literature has existed in the South since colonial days. Many southern playwrights were minor writers and partisan supporters of outmoded ways. Nevertheless, the South has produced one of the twentieth-century's leading dramatists, Tennessee Williams; Lillian Hellman became the first internationally known female American playwright; and Paul Green, Horton Foote, Preston Jones, and Marsha Norman made a lasting impact on the modern stage. Any survey of twentieth-century American drama must include notice of the South's contribution.

Kimball King

See also Williams, Tennessee.

DUKE UNIVERSITY

Tracing its origins to Union Institute Academy in Randolph County, North Carolina, in 1839, changing its name to Trinity College in 1859, and relocating in Durham in 1892, largely through the generosity of Washington Duke and Julian Carr, Trinity, with the abundant support of James B. Duke, became a central part of Duke University after the establishment of the Duke Endowment in December 1924. Under the direction of Trinity president William Preston Few, the new institution promptly assumed a prominent place among southern universities by recruiting well-known scholars such as William McDougall (psychology), J. Fred Rippy (history), and Jay B. Hubbell (American literature). Also, young scholars were brought in and encouraged, including Joseph B. Rhine (parapsychology), Harvie Branscomb (religion), and Clarence Gohdes (American literature). In addition, the Trinity Library under the leadership of William K. Boyd (history) was turned into a research library that by 1941 ranked fifteenth in holdings in the nation. Finally, a university press was formed that published among its other titles two influential magazines, the *South Atlantic Quarterly*, founded by John Spencer Bassett and Edwin Mims at Trinity in 1902, and the source of a famous defense of academic freedom in 1903, and *American Literature*, established by Hubbell and others in 1929 as the first professional journal devoted entirely to scholarship on American writing. In 1938, slightly more than a decade after changing its status, Duke, still under Few's guidance, became a member of the Association of American Universities, a sign of recognition from institutional peers. Writers of note who studied at Duke include William Styron, Mac Hyman, Fred Chappell, James Applewhite, Reynolds Price, Guy Davenport, Anne Tyler, and Josephine Humphreys.

Rayburn S. Moore

Nora C. Chaffin, *Trinity College, 1839–1892: The Beginnings of Duke University* (1950); Robert F. Durden, *The Launching of Duke University, 1924–1949* (1993); Earl W. Porter, *Trinity and Duke, 1892–1924: Foundations of Duke University* (1964).

E

ELLISON, RALPH WALDO

The place of Ralph Ellison (1914–1994) was fixed in American literary history with the appearance of his first novel, *Invisible Man* (1952). This is the first-person narrative of a southern black man who—secluded in a New York basement lit by 1,369 bulbs kept burning with electricity siphoned from the power company—is in the process of integrating his experiences into a definition of his identity as Invisible Man. At each stage of his life, he has had to endure absurd and violent events to which he was subjected by his wish, his poignant need, to be valued and thus defined by people who could not actually see him. This pattern, each time beginning with the unnamed narrator's trust in other people's intentions and authority, was played out again and again—when he was a student at a black college in the South, a worker in a paint factory in New York, an operative of a leftist political organization in Harlem—until his withdrawal to the basement in which he is telling his story, and from which he is planning to re-emerge, an enlightened man.

Two books, *Shadow and Act* (1964) and *Going to the Territory* (1986), gather a number of Ellison's interviews, addresses, and occasional essays. These often refer to two defining phases in Ellison's life. In the 1930s, in the three years he spent as a music student at Tuskegee Institute in Alabama, he was discovering profound affinities between T. S. Eliot and Louis Armstrong and, through that discovery, a pathway from music to literature. He had ridden the rails to Tuskegee while the Scottsboro Case was being tried, an experience that honed his awareness of the precarious position of the black man in America. In the years after he arrived in New York, in the late 1930s and early 1940s, he met Richard Wright and, through him, became involved in the worlds of leftist politics and of professional letters. The latter involvement inspired the

longer-lasting sympathy and allegiance, as Ellison defined himself and his art in personal rather than ideological terms, with reference to his own encounters since childhood with the diversity of American culture. This changing, or sharpening, self-definition strained Ellison's relationship with Wright, as it would have done with any mentor. But he honors Wright, who had further nurtured Ellison in the tradition of the nineteenth-century novel, which he had discovered at Tuskegee, and who had shown him that a black man in twentieth-century America could join and enrich that tradition. Their relationship and the tension between their views of what a black author in America was, by the interconnected facts of his race and his nationality and his talent, obligated to do within that tradition is explored in several of these pieces, including "Richard Wright's Blues" (1945), "The World and the Jug" (1963–1964), and "Remembering Richard Wright" (1971).

A number of the pieces deal with Ellison's continuing interest in music, particularly jazz and the blues, and a number treat politics, sociology, and law. But almost always, his terms of reference tend to be autobiographical and literary. "Going to the Territory" (1979) recounts Ellison's introduction to America's diverse cultural offerings while he was a student in Oklahoma City's segregated schools. "An Extravagance of Laughter" (1985) describes his own fit of hysterical laughter during a Broadway performance of Erskine Caldwell's *Tobacco Road* that Ellison, having just come from Alabama and recently adopted what he thought might be a cool New York mask, was attending with his hero, Langston Hughes. William Faulkner's name recurs. "The Shadow and the Act" (1949) analyzes Hollywood's treatment of Faulkner's *Intruder in the Dust* in view of the history of African Americans in film since D. W. Griffith's notorious *The Birth of a Nation*. The pieces after the publication of *Invisible Man* tend to comprise a complex, personal, and sometimes oblique response to interviewers and critics who had questioned how well, or even if, Ellison had framed *Invisible Man* as a political argument to benefit his race. The complexity of Ellison's answer, which seeks to embrace the whole of human consciousness, all the pathways we have to understanding and self-definition and survival, is suggested by his appreciation of writers like Caldwell, Faulkner, and Twain, who include the comic in their rhetorical arsenals; and also by a somewhat exasperated answer given to the two very earnest interviewers from the *Paris Review* in 1955. They were probing for a more definite laying of blame in *Invisible Man,* a more precise indictment of American society. "Look," Ellison asked, "didn't you find the book at all *funny?*"

Since Ellison's death, his literary executor, John F. Callahan, has been culling through the relics and begun to add to the previously slim Ellison canon. *Flying Home and Other Stories* (1996) gathers thirteen previously published and unpublished short stories. One that has been singled out for praise is "King of the Bingo Game" (1944), which concerns a narrator—a man from "Rock' Mont, North Car'lina"—who has come north, where he and his wife have fallen on hard times. Winning a turn at a bingo wheel in a movie house, he becomes so mesmerized by the possibility of good fortune, now literally within his grasp, that he cannot take his thumb off the button that keeps the wheel spinning. This collection also includes Ellison's first story, "Hymie's Bull," about a murder witnessed by a black youth riding the rails back to Alabama in 1934. *Juneteenth: A Novel* (1999) is what Callahan has made from an enormous quantity of material that comprises Ellison's long-awaited and unfinished second novel, or cycle of novels. *Juneteenth* begins at some point in the 1950s, when Adam Sunraider, a senator and a racist, is mortally wounded by an assassin. Sunraider calls to his bedside an old black preacher named Daddy Hickman, who had come to Washington to warn him. Talking and remembering, these two men—the jazz musician turned preacher, the child preacher turned moviemaker turned politician—spin out again the two threads of their lives, which were interwoven from the time a fatherless child was forced into Hickman's care. In part because the child's racial identity was unknown, Hickman named him Bliss, as in "ignorance is bliss." The novel takes its title from the date—June 19, 1865—on which slaves in Texas learned that they had been freed. That we must know

and own the central facts of our existence seems to be a lesson toward which Ellison was always leading us.

Amber Vogel

See also African American Folk Culture; African American Literature, 1919 to Present; Alabama, Literature of; Clergy; Faulkner, William; Folklore; Miscegenation; Modernism; Novel, 1900 to World War II; Novel, World War II to Present; Oratory; Preaching; Proletarian Novel; Race Relations; Racism; Scottsboro Case.

Bernard W. Bell, *The Afro-American Novel and Its Tradition* (1987); Ralph W. Ellison, *The Collected Essays of Ralph Ellison* (1995); Maryemma Graham and Amrjit Singh, eds., *Conversations with Ralph Ellison* (1995); John Hersey, ed., *Ralph Ellison: A Collection of Critical Essays* (1974).

ELVIS

He was as southern as the hound dog he sang about, the cornbread soaked in buttermilk that was one of his favorite delicacies, and the home he bought for his Mama—a mansion, by the time he got through adding onto it, worthy of a Thomas Sutpen but certainly not designed with the same dynastic impulse. Elvis, like Faulkner's Sutpen, came from poor, hardscrabble stock, but unlike the doomed character of *Absalom, Absalom!* (1936), he never tried to forget or to hide who his people were or where he had come from. Where he came from was Tupelo, Mississippi, a town full of Presley kin. Born in 1935 to Vernon and Gladys Presley, he came into the world thirty-five minutes after his twin brother had arrived, stillborn, a feature of Elvis Aron Presley's birth that haunted him all his life. At age eleven, he got his first guitar—like every good southern boy, he had wanted a .22 rifle (some versions say bicycle instead), and the guitar was his mother's way of trying to appease him. His daddy had been in trouble, had been sent years earlier to the famous Parchman Prison; in 1948 he was, according to some sources, in trouble with the law again, perhaps for selling moonshine, perhaps for getting caught with a stolen pig, depending on the version you buy. The family, at any rate, left Tupelo in a hurry and made their way to Memphis.

Elvis went to work as a truck driver after he graduated from high school, but he could sing and play his guitar, and he hustled to be noticed by Sam Phillips, owner of a local record company. At his first recording session, in 1954, he began playing around with a blues song written by Arthur (Big Boy) Crudup, "That's All Right, Mama." Listening in, Phillips heard the sound he had been trying to find for years, the sound of a white singer who could belt out the blues and other African American sounds the right way, an "exciting, alive way," he was to say. He wondered, "where you going to go with this, it's not black, it's not white, it's not pop, it's not country." What it was, was Elvis. As John Shelton Reed has noted, in the same year that *Brown v. Board of Education* came down, Elvis integrated the South in his voice, his swing, his internal rhythms, and he also started down the road that would make him, simply, "the King."

Twenty-three years later, he was dead, at age forty-two. He began and ended his life as a southern performer, playing southern audiences who, whether they could admit it or not, understood his crossover sound and the racial gulf it spanned. In 1955 he transformed the *Louisiana Hayride*. Then, in a year of mostly southern tours, he transformed a generation of budding belles into the world's first screaming groupies. Then came the *Ed Sullivan Show*, three appearances in late 1956–early 1957, that burned up the northern air waves faster than Sherman had burned up southern railroad ties. There was a new national youth anthem—any song by Elvis—in the late fifties, changing almost weekly from "You Ain't Nothin' But a Hound Dog" to "Blue Suede Shoes" to "Heartbreak Hotel" to "Lawdy Miss Clawdy" to "Don't Be Cruel" to "Love Me Tender" (also the title of his first movie) to "Are You Lonesome Tonight." The South had risen again, and throughout the 1960s there were two Mississippi-made media images to follow on an almost daily basis—the sad, worn-out faces of blacks and whites both in front of desegregating schools, in streets wetted down with water hoses, in front of bombed churches, and then the face of Elvis, as he dutifully accepted his army service and went off to Germany, as he returned triumphant to begin a movie tour that showed off the blue eyes and the undulating hips from *Viva, Las Vegas* to *Blue Hawaii* to *Fun in Acapulco*, singing all the while ("Return to Sender," "It's Now or Never," "Suspicion").

The sad death of his much-beloved mother in 1958, the building of Graceland, the managing by Colonel Tom Parker (a literary type himself, P. T. Barnum his progenitor), the marriage to Priscilla, the birth of Lisa Marie, the parade of Cadillacs, and then the parade of pills—all these became personal accouterments belonging not so much to Elvis as to his fans. In the 1970s,

while some of the great songs still hit the charts ("Separate Ways," "Steamroller Blues," "The Fool"), his fame went up and down faster than his hips. In the last two years of his life, it was, as it had been in the beginning, southern tours that sustained him when he could no longer record, or remember his lines. He died at Graceland on August 16, 1977, almost certainly as the result of a drug overdose. He was buried next to the grave of his mother in a Memphis cemetery, but both were reinterred at Graceland on October 2. Along the way, he collected fourteen gold singles, starred in thirty-one films.

In his book *Elvis After Elvis* (1996), a scholarly work documenting the rise of the culture of the "King" that came into being and still thrives long after Elvis's death, Gilbert B. Rodman begins with this sentence: "For a dead man, Elvis is awfully noisy." It is safe to say that Elvis himself is now text as well as food for text. We can study the literature of his lyrics, those he appropriated or those that were written just for him. We can study the literature of his films, the heroes and antiheroes he played: from *King Creole* (1958) to *Kid Galahad* (1962), through all the Hawaiian types, to the jailhouse rebel, and always, the lover-in-spite-of-himself. We have the literary mythology of his personhood—he was trickster, outlaw, mama's boy, dream lover, sexual predator, the last best example of the Horatio Alger success, and in terms of southern types and stereotypes, he was redneck, hillbilly, good old boy, white trash, good country people, just folks. We have the iconized details of his physical features—the ducktails, the gyrating hips, the pout, the athleticism of the young man, the puffiness of the prematurely aged one—and of his clothes—from black shirt to pink one and jeans, to white suit with sequins, to gold lamé tuxedo.

We also have all the books, nonfiction and fiction, far too many to begin sorting out, except to highlight a few standouts. The two-volume biography by Peter Guralnick (*Last Train to Memphis*, 1994, and *Careless Love*, 1998) offers as compelling a portrait of a life in rise and fall as could be conceived and is itself a work of art. The collection of essays and oral performances from the first International Conference on Elvis, held at the University of Mississippi in 1995, has literary importance for several reasons. Organized and promoted by Elvis scholar extraordinaire Vernon Chadwick, this event became, as Chadwick at least calls it, "one of the most publicized and controversial academic conferences on record." Headlines from the *Bos-*

ton Globe, which covered the controversy, show what literary link immediately suggested itself through the location of the conference: "Sound and Fury Arising Over Elvis at Ole Miss." Faulkner's Rowan Oak and Elvis's Graceland might both be graced with pillars, but the ground between them, in the minds of many Oxford, Mississippi, academics, was more than the distance from their famous town square to the Memphis airport. As participating scholars read papers on Elvis's relation to Bahktin, Forrest Gump, Jesus, and Bill Clinton, university officials met to make sure that the first conference would be the last hosted in Oxford (subsequent meetings have moved on, like Chadwick, to Memphis). Beyond the squeamishness of older-fashioned academics, most cultural scholars now accept the idea that Faulkner and Elvis need to share the same stage in any assessments of southern or national culture. As Chadwick notes, "Elvis names a fateful intersection of the regional and global in American culture," as well as naming "the art and education of self-taught peoples outside the boundaries of mainstream culture."

Beyond the literatures of Elvis, there is the literature of Elvis impersonators. Here, literarily speaking, William McCranor Henderson has held court through two significant works. In an eerie example of how life comes to imitate art, Henderson, in 1984, wrote a novel about an Elvis impersonator, catching, before the fact, the separate mystique, the "twinning" of Elvis that the phenomenon of his imitators would become. *Stark Raving Elvis* imagined the major contests, and even the Las Vegas convention, that had not yet happened in his story of an obsessed fan who "would be King." Then Henderson took on, in the 1990s, the challenge of becoming an Elvis impersonator himself in order to experience, as well as observe, as closely as possible, what happened within the cult of impersonation. The result, in *I, Elvis: Confessions of a Counterfeit King,* is more than a study, more than an autobiography, and more than an exposé. With humor, respect, and engrossing detail, Henderson charts his own metamorphosis and reveals the protean shapes of Elvis through his pantheon of resurrectors. A recent novel that fictionally draws on the life and times of Elvis is Mark Childress's *Tender: A Novel* (1998). Childress closely follows the life story of Elvis with his character Leroy Kirby, whose rock-star rise is poignantly, poetically charted. In Doris Betts's *The Sharp Teeth of Love* (1997), it is the phenomenon of the Graceland/Memphis pilgrimage that is invoked, as Betts's main charac-

ter, with her fiancé, stops there on the couple's way to a Reno wedding that never occurs. The tension over this odd stopover foreshadows the young woman's doubts about her relationship and the ideal of love beyond it. The novel *Forrest Gump* contains a brief but memorable Elvis appearance, captured perfectly in the film (1995), as Forrest, who wears leg braces at the time, shows one of the young male guests at his mother's bed-and-breakfast a new way to move; the guest, Elvis of course, accompanies Forrest's jerky rhythmic gyrations with a song he is picking out, a song about a hound dog. Marianne Gingher taps into the "King's" mystique with a novel, *Bobby Rex's Greatest Hit* (1987), about a young woman who was the inspiration for a rock-and-roll star's most popular song. The novel evokes what might have been Elvis's own beginnings, and what was certainly the aura of hot southern nights in the late 1950s that stirred the girls who fell in love with the boy who, with one look, and one move, could get them so "all shook up." In Don DeLillo's acclaimed *White Noise* (1985), the Elvis-scholar character envies what a colleague has done with his Hitler studies: "You've evolved an entire system around this figure," and he announces his intention to do the same with Elvis. Through Elvis studies, Elvis literature, Elvis impersonations, and Elvis publishing, an entire system expands year by year, yet somehow the man remains, the Hillbilly Cat from Tupelo who never forgot where he came from.

Lucinda H. MacKethan

See also Sixties, The.

Kevin Quain, ed., *The Elvis Reader* (1992); Fred Worth and Steve D. Tamerus, *Elvis: His Life from A to Z* (1992).

EPISCOPALIANS

The Episcopal Church came to the South with the first settlers as the Church of England. Both the Lost Colony and Jamestown had Anglican chaplains; the first formal Christian worship services in English in North America were conducted according to the Elizabethan Book of Common Prayer. The Church of England was officially established in the southern colonies, although even in Virginia it never had the political or social power that it maintained in Britain. As the colonies needed people, they welcomed representatives of various denominations and nationalities. Some of these, such as the Huguenots in South Carolina, ultimately merged into the Anglican tradition; others, such as the Moravians, Lutherans, and Quakers, maintained their religious identity. But so long as Britain ruled the colonies, Anglican parishes were supported by grants of land and the clergy by official status. Anglicanism in the southern colonies was the denomination of the planter and urban elite; most of the southern Founding Fathers were at least nominally Anglican. In major colonial towns such as Charleston, Williamsburg, Savannah, Wilmington, Alexandria, and Norfolk, the spires of the Anglican churches are a feature of the skyline.

In the last quarter of the eighteenth century, the Anglican Church in the South faced two challenges that in some areas nearly ended its existence. Most Church of England clergy in the South were not American-born. Many did not sympathize with independence; during and immediately after the Revolution, they left the United States. A number of Anglican parishes ceased to function for some years owing to the shortage of clergy. The state-supported position of the Anglican Church also ended with the Revolution, so that it was necessary for the laity to find funds to pay the clergy. In the latter 1780s, a convention of American clergy and laity organized the Episcopal Church in the United States. An American Prayer Book was approved in 1789; American bishops were elected by conventions and consecrated in the apostolic succession. Both southern clergy and leading southern laymen were active in this process.

The other challenge to the Anglican Church was the growth of Methodism. Begun as a movement within the Church of England, by the latter part of the eighteenth century, Methodists were breaking away from their original institution. The ordination of lay preachers by Methodist leaders was the final cause of separation. Methodism's emphasis on lay leadership and evangelical preaching and teaching was especially popular in the South, where it appealed to those not served and often ignored by Episcopalians.

In the years between the Revolution and the Civil War, the Episcopal Church in the South continued to be the denomination of the planter and urban elite. Its strength among these groups in Virginia and South Carolina was largely untouched; by about 1820, the church was experiencing a revival in North Carolina and Georgia. As new states were admitted to the union, the Episcopal Church was carried into the frontier areas by planters moving from the older southern

states; its numbers, however, always remained less than those of the Methodists and the Baptists. In the 1830s, 1840s, and 1850s, dioceses were organized in the newer southern states as the population and economic resources were sufficient to support them. Episcopalians were often prominent in politics disproportionately to their number in the population. They were also often active in educational ventures. The College of William and Mary was closely identified with the church, and in Virginia a number of Episcopal schools for boys and girls were established. North Carolina Episcopalians started schools for both sexes. There is also considerable evidence that laywomen conducted Sunday schools or other classes for the education of their own and other children, including slaves.

The first half of the nineteenth century saw the division of the church into High and Low Church factions. The High Church group looked to historic traditions of liturgy, stressing the church's Catholic and medieval roots and the importance of the sacraments, especially Communion. Though the Prayer Book was the essential element in worship for both groups, Low Churchmen put more emphasis on Morning Prayer and preaching. The South was almost uniformly Low Church, and the Virginia Episcopal Seminary was established to balance the perceived High Church position of the General Seminary in New York. When Bishop Ives of North Carolina, who was closely tied to northern High Church leaders, defected to Rome, the victory of Low Churchmanship in the South was sealed for a century or more. The most important legacy of the High Church movement in the South was the popularization of Gothic as the proper architectural style for churches. Even in the Low Church South, most Episcopal churches built since the 1840s have been Gothic in their inspiration.

The denominational divisions were also a part of increasing southern sectionalism. The Virginia Seminary educated southern clergy. Just before the Civil War, the southern Episcopal dioceses established their own University of the South on a vast domain at Sewanee, Tennessee, to provide proper education for their young men. The Episcopal Church never took an official stand on slavery; in the South, most churchmen supported the peculiar institution. When the southern states seceded, the southern dioceses withdrew from the national body and formed a Confederate Episcopal Church. After the war, unlike their Protestant brethren whose sectional divisions continued for some years, the southern dioceses quickly rejoined the national church.

In the century and a half since the Civil War, the Episcopal Church in the South has continued to be primarily an urban institution whose members are generally affluent and well educated. It appeals to those who want a fixed and regulated liturgy. For those who grow up in the church, the Prayer Book establishes language patterns and phrases that unconsciously appear in their speech and writing. The liturgical movement of the second half of the twentieth century has ensured the victory of the old High Church party. The Episcopal Church generally accepted the social gospel of the late nineteenth century. Parishes and dioceses established hospitals and orphanages, missions to Appalachia and to indigent rural workers. In more recent years, Episcopal parishes have been active in various ministries to the urban poor and underprivileged.

After the Civil War, the church established a ministry to African Americans somewhat detached from the regular diocesan structure. In each southern diocese, there were a few black parishes whose priests were never full members of the diocesan hierarchy. Episcopal schools and colleges for African Americans were also established. The integration of the church at all levels was a sometimes painful process in the second half of the twentieth century. The church was visible on both sides of the Civil Rights Movement. Sarah Patton Boyle and other Episcopalians were among the early challengers of segregation; one of the addressees of Martin Luther King's "Letter from Birmingham Jail" was Bishop Carpenter of Alabama. Some white Episcopalians opened their churches to marchers and marched themselves; other moved to the suburbs and opened church schools to escape integration.

In the twentieth century, the Episcopal Church in the South lost much of its political and economic power, although it still carries a certain social prestige. The colonial spires or Gothic towers of Episcopal churches continue to be a feature of the urban skyline. Given its long history in the South, the church seems strangely absent from much of southern literature. Colonial and early Republic authors took its presence and prestige for granted but generally wrote little specific about the church. Mason Locke Weems, an Episcopal cleric, wrote biographies stressing the moral but not denominational values of revolutionary heroes. Novelists usually found the emphasis on personal conversion and biblical fundamentalism of the evangelical Protestant denominations more useful for plots than the ritualistic and liturgical squabbles of Episcopalians. In recent years, a few writers such as Gail Godwin have

begun to explore the novelistic possibilities of the American Episcopal Church.

Barbara Brandon Schnorrenberg

See also Baptists; Bible Belt; Evangelical Christianity; Fundamentalism; Methodists; Preaching; Roman Catholics; Scots-Irish.

Raymond W. Albright, *A History of the Protestant Episcopal Church* (1964); E. Brooks Holifield, *The Gentlemen Theologians: American Theology in Southern Culture, 1795–1860* (1978); Lawrence Foushee London and Sarah McCulloh Lemmon, eds., *The Episcopal Church in North Carolina, 1701–1959* (1987); Henry Thompson Malone, *The Episcopal Church in Georgia, 1733–1957* (1960); Robert Prichard, *A History of the Episcopal Church* (1991); Albert Sidney Thomas, *Historical Account of the Protestant Episcopal Church in South Carolina 1820–1957* (1957).

EPISTOLARY FICTION

The use of letters to tell stories is an honored tradition in English fiction. With ample antecedents in the sixteenth and seventeenth centuries, it was most extensively used in the eighteenth century, which produced several classics in England: Samuel Richardson's *Pamela* (1740) and *Clarissa Harlowe* (1748), Tobias Smollett's *Humphrey Clinker* (1771), and Fanny Burney's *Evelina* (1778). The epistolary method provided immediacy and gave authors an opportunity for multiple points of view on an event. Although nineteenth- and twentieth-century writers have used them less, fiction writers have continued to use letters within novels. In the American South, the epistolary technique, though not dominant, has proven attractive to several writers and has had some notable successes.

Although John Pendleton Kennedy's *Swallow Barn* (1832) is rightly acclaimed the prototypical plantation novel, it must also be counted important in the history of the southern epistolary novel. The 1832 edition begins with a letter from the fictive Mark Littleton (who derives from Washington Irving's Geoffrey Crayon), dedicating the novel to William Wirt, most famous for his *Sketches of the Life and Character of Patrick Henry* (1817). Wirt, who had worked in the tradition of the letter in his *The Letters of a British Spy* (1803), kept the joke going with a letter to Kennedy in regard to Mark Littleton's dedication. *Swallow Barn* then begins with a letter to Zachary Huddleston, explaining the reasons for Littleton's sojourn to Swallow Barn and describing the journey there up the James River and his ensuing welcome. The novel that follows becomes a long letter to Huddleston describing the events that Littleton encountered on the Meriwether plantation. The reader may forget that fiction as the story progresses, though a "postscript" reminds the reader of the epistolary tradition important to the lives of these characters and to the narrative device that got the novel going.

The epistolary format also proved useful to the development of Southwestern humor. In the late 1830s, C. F. Noland was contributing letters to the *Spirit of the Times* as N. of Arkansas and Pete Whetstone, juxtaposing a gentlemanly persona and a backwoods Arkansan. The spirited letters continued until 1856 but were not collected until 1957. Concurrently with Noland's work, William Tappan Thompson wrote letters as Major Jones, who found a large public responsive to the depiction of the light-hearted middle-class southern farmer and townsman, collected as *Major Jones's Courtship* (1843, 1844, 1847), *Major Jones's Chronicles of Pineville* (1845), and *Major Jones's Sketches of Travel* (1848). Charles Henry Smith won the hearts of throngs of southerners through the creation of Bill Arp by means of Arp letters and lectures. These were written over a period of some forty years, during which Arp evolved from a semiliterate Georgia cracker to an educated gentleman, portraying the history of his region through the Civil War and Reconstruction. Arp's letters were printed in over seven hundred newspapers and were collected in several volumes from *Bill Arp So Called* (1866) to *Bill Arp: From Uncivil War to Date* (1903).

Letter-writing was important to the private and the public life of Mark Twain, and his letters (whether written for the public or to individuals) carry the hallmark of his bite and vigor. He made his early reputation on the West Coast from the twenty-five letters he wrote for the *Sacramento Union* to report his experiences on the Sandwich Islands, as Hawaii was then called; the letters were eventually incorporated into his *Roughing It* (1872). He liked to embed letters into his fiction. Eventually, the epistolary form provided him with a persona and a vehicle to address posterity posthumously about his views on humankind. In 1962 *Letters from the Earth* appeared. Written over several decades, the letters from Satan, exiled to earth, to the archangels Michael and Gabriel delineate Twain's amusement with and scorn for human absurdity.

Among early-twentieth-century authors, James Branch Cabell was especially drawn to the possibilities

of the letter, through which he created fiction and affirmed the power of the fictive. He prefaced his two early story collections—*The Line of Love* (1905) and *Gallantry* (1907)—with letters to Mrs. Grundy. That much-ridiculed mythological recipient allowed Cabell to further his preferred vein of whimsy and irony. Much later in his career—the high tide of his popularity now gone—he gave the epistolary mode sustained attention. In *Special Delivery: A Packet of Replies* (1933), he provided the letters he would have liked to have sent to correspondents about his writing as well as the proper letters he actually sent. *Ladies and Gentlemen: A Parcel of Reconsiderations* (1934) is composed of letters to dead persons, some real and some figures from literature and legend. The recipients range from Penelope and Dr. Faustus to George Washington, Poe (a fellow Richmonder), and John Wilkes Booth to Hamlet and his own Jurgen. He credits Booth for being largely responsible for the Lincoln myth and finds Poe's judgment that "as a literary people we are one vast perambulating humbug" still essentially true. In *Let Me Lie: Being in the Main an Ethnological Account of the Remarkable Commonwealth of Virginia and the Making of Its History* (1947), he probed Virginia's past in part by writing a letter to General Robert E. Lee, whom he regarded as alive and "real," as he does Thackeray's Colonel Esmond, to whom he also addresses a letter.

In 1979 John Barth reincarnated the epistolary novel as a quintessential postmodern text. His *LETTERS* has been compared to Joyce's *Finnegans Wake* for its daring and ambition (Barth's novel describes itself as a "work in progress"—the title by which Joyce's *Finnegans Wake* was widely known before its publication). *LETTERS* may be considered an epic metafiction, for it is a fiction about fiction (certainly Barth's) and has the history of the novel as one of its concerns. Hence the revival of the epistolary method is natural. His seventh novel, *LETTERS* is composed by seven letter writers—five familiar to readers of Barth's earlier novels (Todd Andrews, Jacob Horner, Bray, Ambrose Mensch, "The Author"), another a composite from earlier Barth creations (A. B. Cook), and the seventh (Lady Ambrose), a new creation. The title of Barth's novel refers not only to the epistolary method but to the acrostic structure of the novel (individual letters of the alphabet), and to letters in the sense of literature. As with Joyce, playfulness abounds. If there is no verifiable meaning in life or letters, the writer can play games with language and meanings and create grand fictions. Though the verdict is not unanimous, some count *LETTERS* as Barth's greatest novel. It is likely his most complex novel; understandably its audience is somewhat specialized.

Two years after the publication of *LETTERS*, Alice Walker used the epistolary form in a way that caught both popular and critical acclaim. Her phenomenally successful *The Color Purple* (1982) became a bestseller and winner of the Pulitzer Prize as well as the basis of a popular motion picture. The novel, told exclusively through letters, hearkened back to Samuel Richardson, who realized that the letter was an especially appropriate vehicle for a woman repressed by her gender—and an especially dramatic device for a desperate woman in need of some sympathetic reader, in need of some helping presence. The sexually victimized black girl Celie is only fourteen when she seeks for some voice—some articulation of her plight. Unlike Clarissa Harlowe, Celie has no friend who can respond and advise. Instead, she addresses her letters to God, turning to grasp for help where the desperate, the helpless often turn when no human help can be found. Almost half-way through the novel, Celie at last gets a letter—from her sister Nettie. Thereafter, letters between the sisters carry the story. Like Clarissa, Celie finds help from another woman. Walker's novel became one of the major statements about the plight of black women—and received some criticism for its depiction of black men. Whereas *Clarissa Harlowe* ends with Clarissa's death, Walker ends her novel with woman triumphant. The final letter of the book is again to God—and it is a statement of victory, celebration, joy.

A few years later, Lee Smith also turned to the epistolary form to give a woman voice. The epistolary method seems a natural for Smith, who is fond of first-person narrative and acclaimed for her capturing of voice. *Fair and Tender Ladies* (1989) uses letters by Ivy Rowe to recount the events of her life from age twelve into her seventies. Through letters to friends and relatives, Ivy shares her dream to become a writer, a dream a girl born in the mountains of Virginia at the turn of the century would have small chance to realize. The intervening circumstances of Ivy's life make her a wife and mother instead—though, like Walker's Celie, through her letters she has become a "writer." Ivy Rowe is counted among Smith's most memorable (and inspiring) characters, and *Fair and Tender Ladies* has proven to be one of Smith's most successful works.

Having found the epistolary novel congenial once, Smith returned to the form a few years later, bringing to fiction the subgenre of the Christmas letter—a form that came into being with the advent of inexpensive copy techniques after World War II. Though the Christmas letter is often maligned, Christmas letters do tell stories of families. Smith's *Christmas Letters* (1996) is a novella that portrays the drama of a family into the third generation, with letters dating from December 24, 1944, to Christmas, 1996. As with *The Color Purple* and *Fair and Tender Ladies*, the letters are all written by women and portray experience of the woman's world. Christmas letters are supposed to be cheerful, and the letters of Birdie Pickett (section I) and her daughter Mary (section II) abound with cheer and good humor—and both are given to ending their Christmas letters with a recipe (food and its preparation and its meaning in family legacies is a recurring theme). At the end of the novel, Mary (her marriage ended by divorce after many years) reviews all of her Christmas letters—and with her the reader probes realities that Christmas letters usually glide over or do not mention. Even in the brief space of the novella, Smith creates the inner drama of her characters' lives. Like *Fair and Tender Ladies*, *Christmas Letters* is also about a woman's finding a voice. In the brief third section, Mary's daughter Melanie is becoming a serious writer—a development that owes much to her own mother's journey of self-discovery.

Joseph M. Flora

See also Postmodernism.

Lucinda H. MacKethan, "Postscript: Writing Letters Home," in *Daughters of Time: Creating Woman's Voice in the Southern Story* (1990).

EVANGELICAL CHRISTIANITY

A family of Protestant Christianity, evangelicalism ranges across several denominations and includes groups that are lightly or not at all identified with any particular historic tradition. Most Baptist groups qualify as members of this family, as do some Methodist and Reformed (Calvinist) communions and a number of individuals from other "mainline" denominations.

Some efforts at classifying this huge Protestant company incline to label all branches as evangelical that do not fit neatly anywhere else. That is especially true if they are not large, have a brief history, and/or manifest consistent conservative leanings. Although evangelical-ism does take many forms, it is subject to description and delineation.

Yet it is true that among smaller, younger, and decidedly conservative bodies, the evangelical outlook is dominant. Families rightly deserving of this classification include the Adventists, the Holiness people, the charismatic fellowships, and rationalist-oriented groups that are truly fundamentalist. Representative bodies include the Christian and Missionary Alliance, the Wesleyan Church, the Evangelical Free Church, Campus Crusade for Christ, the Church of the Nazarene, the Baptist Bible Fellowship, and the Presbyterian Church in America; the full list is much longer. Some fellowships that are often thought of as evangelical in actuality are not—for example, the Mormons and the Churches of Christ. The churches of African Americans are sufficiently distinct from those founded by whites that it is at best tendentious so to think of them. Yet common characteristics bind many in these two camps, making it defensible to associate them in spirit.

Perhaps there is no better way to characterize evangelicalism than to make clear its profound commitment to the supernatural essence of authentic Christian doctrine. Its understanding of the reality of the triune God posits his radical transcendence, his irreducibility to any "natural" description, and his inaccessibility to human comprehension and experience except on his own terms and by his own choosing. Thus miracle, revelation, and governing providence are central categories. It follows that human beings can know nothing about the Almighty God apart from the revelation he deigns to offer through the Bible, which records infallibly, and to many inerrantly, his saving action through Jesus Christ, the divine Son of God. The Old Testament is integral to this revelation of the Truth, but its effectual significance has to do with preparation for and pointing to the Christ event. The Bible is indeed Holy Scripture; it alone and it completely discloses the one God and total truth to the world.

In practice, American evangelicalism falls into two camps, those who build their message around correct belief and those who build it around the personal experience of conversion. The former makes much of adhering to "confessions of faith," subscription to sound doctrine. The latter, the conversionist school of thought, makes central an experience by which one is and knows self to be transformed from guilty to forgiven, from being lost to being saved, from living in a natural state to being one of the Lord's redeemed. The conver-

sionist approach has predominated in the South. Yet this must not be taken to imply that Scripture and doctrine are other than rigorously held and elaborated.

In the American South, as nowhere else in Christendom, the evangelical family of the Protestant sector of Christianity is predominant. Historically in Europe and Latin America, one institution has been normative, all others minor or even marginal. For centuries, a nation's established church—Roman Catholic, Lutheran, Anglican, or Presbyterian—enjoyed favored status. In the northern states of this country, usually there has been shared standing in size and influence, often among several Christian groups. In the South, the evangelical family has been the principal form of faith without challenge from the 1830s to the present. Accordingly, Baptist, Methodist, and Presbyterian strength has been substantial, the religious and social standing of these people and institutions a major social force in the region.

It would be difficult to overstate the impact that this religious-cultural phenomenon has made upon the South. And the fact that it is the evangelical variant that has imbued this force with its character has made this regional culture distinctive in Christendom. In other words, an understanding of Christian meaning and responsibility that focuses on personal and congregational issues has acquired standing that has resulted in its assuming almost "state church" proportions. The complex social-cultural-religious arrangement produced by these developments is one of the peculiar features of the historic southern region. Even people in other parts of America find the southern religious situation difficult to grasp. Expressions they sometimes use are: in the southern churches there are more chiefs than Indians; those people wear their religion on their sleeves; why are they so intense and outspoken?; why does every town have so many churches? Furthermore, other Americans moving into the region are charmed, puzzled, and irritated, variously, by the readiness with which they as new neighbors are queried, where do you go to church?; or even, have you been saved?

Not that evangelicalism is unknown in the Middle West or the western coastal states. From New England to southern California, evangelical people, churches, and institutions are present and often quite visible, much more so within the past quarter century. Yet there are differences in the relation of those Christian entities to the surrounding culture. There, they are visible precisely because they depart from what has been the norm of religious convention. There is no confusing them with the older, established, "mainline" churches—Roman Catholic, Lutheran, Episcopal, Presbyterian, Reformed, Methodist (in most cases), and Disciples of Christ. Evangelical churches are not "at home" in the culture, or at least are not meant to be. Membership in them is intentional, not a function of heredity. It costs something to be evangelical; identity is chosen and is worn as if a badge. Some Christians of this description are contentious and judgmental, and may give the movement a displeasing aroma. Most, however, are so convinced, dedicated, and busy being, speaking, and doing that they have little disposition to challenge others' authenticity. When neighbors and friends know evangelicals, they know them to be Christians, convinced and consecrated, clear on who they are and quite willing to own up to their identity, often quite gently. Of course, perfection is as rare in their company as it is in all human groups.

By rather sharp contrast, southern evangelical people and churches blend in with their surroundings; at least that is true of the traditional groups, which are often culturally dominant. Traditional Baptists and (many) Methodists are evangelical without "making a fuss" about it. They too are earnest, sometimes possessed with the "burden" of "bringing people to Christ." But generally they have been able to assume that the people they see are already "in the fold." Perhaps the greatest single difference between the South and the rest of American society in this regard is that in Dixie there are few moribund, "has-been" churches, cool to dead, that have served the function of carriers of the Christian tradition for the region. Its "carriers" have been the evangelicals, who are characteristically "world changers." Their success may have made them susceptible to "cultural captivity," as implied, but they are forever "stirring things up." Still, nothing in the South's life compares with the casual fit of, say, Catholicism in New England or Lutheranism in the states of the upper Middle West. In those cases, family affiliation and community tradition make it inviting to treat religion as something you take for granted. No well-meaning evangelical can look on faith and commitment as something to be taken for granted (although that sometimes happens).

Such an outlook is transparent to the nature of evangelical Christianity. There, identity is sharp and clear. Commitment is required and must be expressed in conduct and spoken testimony. The courage of one's convictions typifies faithfulness. Being steeped in and clear on biblical and doctrinal teaching puts one in po-

sition to reflect on what is an obedient course of action, also to speak a word of testimony to one who has not yet come to faith. No "taking for granted" here; instead, a conscious, intentional, and formulated world view for both behavior and conversation. One of the temptations always facing southern evangelicals is forging an unhealthy alliance between church and culture. The truth is not much exaggerated by the observation that evangelical forms of Protestantism long ago attained a quasi-established status, an ecology not challenged until quite recently.

That challenge is curious: it has come from newer denominations and families who are more evangelical, at least in their understanding. They are charismatics, pentecostalists, and fundamentalists. The first company comprises Christians who feel the Lord's reality with great intensity and who are granted intimate knowledge of what is true and what is the purpose of events in the world, natural and historical. The mystery of divine activity is replaced by a link of knowledge attained through prayer and Scripture study. Thus the present is interpretable and the future predictable. Public events may be as subject to deciphering as the private stirrings of the Spirit. More elemental in charismatic behavior, though, is the intimacy of the spiritual connection that the Holy Spirit provides to the open Christian's heart. God is not a force to be affirmed but a nearer-than-breathing presence to be experienced—"how sweet it is." The loving Savior is one's own to know, cherish, be joyful over. Radiance results. So does knowledge about, yes, but better, knowledge *of* through direct union, spirit to Spirit.

Pentecostalists are kin to charismatics in confidence that the Almighty Lord is near and precious. In this instance, though, specified forms of that direct experience are characteristic. There is the experience of forgiveness, followed by the experience of being equipped to "speak in tongues," in turn followed by the gift of moral empowerment toward sanctification. In this way, a "second blessing" and a "third blessing" may be claimed as completing the work of the Spirit in one's heart. Disagreement exists in this community on the details of such spiritual events, but there is a kind of scheduled, formulaic pattern of the divine spirit's intervention in human life that is absent from the charismatic perspective.

Whereas both of these clusters of more conservative Christians focus on spiritual experience (without, of course, denying the direct access of the faithful to certain knowledge of absolute truth), fundamentalists rest their case on rational claims. Theirs is head knowledge. They know for certain what the truths of God are. More than biblical literalists, they are absolutists concerning what God is, what sound doctrine is, and what people are required to believe. Because their governing category is the rational, they are in position to distinguish truth from falsehood, the true believers and churches from the heretical. By their nature, they are judges of authenticity in belief, and are exclusivists. Holding the line against error, regarding compromise as the ultimate besmirchment of purity of mind, they occupy a nonnegotiable stance. By rights, they are not given to "working things out" with those fellow believers who differ. Intractability is their nature—in a sense, their obligation.

As with all forms of faith, this community of believers generates its own styles and products. Its music is expressive, usually simple and joyous to sing. Its sermons are spirited, often hortatory, dogmatic (in the original meaning of that term), passionate, urgent, and always Bible-referential. In the setting of the South's conversionist emphasis, the preacher may virtually limit his concerns to convincing people that they are sinners, persons in desperate need of salvation. The end being so clear and imperative, he may resort to strong rhetorical measures toward bringing the unsaved to their senses in the accomplishment of redemption in Christ. Its prayers are personal, indeed they reflect the intimacy of a personal relationship, the redeeming Lord to the grateful and obedient person. The visual arts play at most a small part in the sensibilities of this community. Evangelical epistemology relies on speaking and hearing. Irony—indeed, all forms of indirect expression—is largely foreign to this way of understanding truth and reality.

Samuel S. Hill

See also Baptists; Bible; Gospel Music; Preaching; Sermons; Televangelist.

David Edwin Harrell Jr., ed., *Varieties of Southern Evangelicalism* (1981); Samuel S. Hill, *Southern Churches in Crisis* (1967); George M. Marsden, ed., *Evangelicalism and Modern America* (1984); Leonard I. Sweet, ed., *The Evangelical Tradition in America* (1984).

EXPATRIATION

The American South has been considered almost a nation within a nation since several decades before the Civil War, and so the expatriation of southerners connotes not only extended stays outside the United States but also and even primarily residence outside the region. Expatriated natives of the South (like other displaced persons) may have fled social injustice or personal danger; they may have sought to free themselves from restrictive families and oppressive communities. The southern community could cruelly destroy, torment, or expel those who could not or would not conform; in its benevolent form, it could stifle as well as nurture. Consequently, many of the region's more creative children sought refuge or liberation in places where their identity and their history were not common knowledge. Few southerners have been able, however, to forget that identity and that history, and many have experienced ambivalent mixtures of love and hate for the region from which they yearned to escape and to which they longed to return. The paradoxical repulsion and attraction of the homeland have informed the character of southerners and of the literature they have created for almost two centuries.

As American and southern consciousness was forged, the descendants of displaced Europeans and Africans developed ties to territories in which their ancestors had been adventurers, settlers, refugees, or slaves. William Byrd of Westover, son of a London-born father, was educated in England and admitted to the English bar. Byrd illustrates in his life and writings the creation of a Virginian identity that would lead to broader regional affiliation. By 1834, when William A. Caruthers's novel *The Kentuckian in New York* was published, that southern identity was established: distinctions were being drawn between the culture of the agrarian South and that of a North incipiently urban and industrial. Hoping to alleviate emerging sectional antagonism, Caruthers condemned slavery from a southern perspective and urged northern appreciation of the virtues of compatriots in the South. His comparisons of regional customs and values may be seen to initiate the expatriate theme in fiction of the South.

Southern literature was, however, increasingly to be shaped by a perceived need to justify the peculiar institution and the society it supported. As literature by white southerners retreated into romantic escapism and defensiveness, accounts of escape from slavery constituted the antebellum South's major narratives of expatriation. Although the *Narrative of the Life of Frederick Douglass, an American Slave, Written by Himself* (1845) details experiences of chattel slavery in Maryland and the jubilation of escape, it records also the author's ironic realization that in leaving Baltimore he leaves not only bondage but also friends. The *Narrative of William Wells Brown, a Fugitive Slave, Written by Himself* (1847) constitutes another outstanding example of the genre, and Brown's novel *Clotel* (published in successive versions in 1853, 1860–61, 1864, and 1867) uses the arts of fiction to shape a story of escape from slavery into a "romance." As Douglass and Brown attest in later works, Europe received people of color more hospitably than the northern United States. The prejudice encountered in the North makes all the more poignant Brown's sentiments on boarding ship for Liverpool and leaving his "native land" (*The American Fugitive in Europe*, 1855).

Only after sectional antagonism erupted into warfare that ended in the defeat of the Confederacy could southern writers, like their less-literary compatriots, turn back to what was left of normal pursuits. Some writers like Mark Twain (by way of the West), Sherwood Bonner, George Washington Cable, Charles Waddell Chesnutt, Opie Read, and Walter Hines Page would sooner or later move north; others (like William Gilmore Simms and Paul Hamilton Hayne) resumed contacts with literary friends and acquaintances in other parts of the reunited nation. For northern readers in the second half of the nineteenth century, the South began to figure as a locale of exoticism. Countering the popular romanticized evocations of antebellum life were critics Cable and W. H. Page, whose pseudonymously published novel, *The Southerner: . . . Being the Autobiography of Nicholas Worth* (1909), traces the protagonist's Civil War childhood, his education in the North, and his repatriated life of service to a native state afflicted by the legacies of slavery.

Virginian Ellen Glasgow's criticism of southern society encompassed issues of religion, caste, and class; she also exposed the evasions of a social ideology that imprisoned women. Three of her distinguished works of fiction feature southern women who go to New York in search of artistic fulfillment: *The Descendant* (1897), *Phases of an Inferior Planet* (1898), and *Life and Gabriella* (1916). Evelyn Scott's 1923 memoir, *Escapade*, tells the story of her defiance of convention and six-year sojourn in Brazil; her novel *Eva Gay* (1933) portrays a rebellious woman who escapes the South. Katherine Anne Porter of Texas lived all over the world during her long and adventurous life, contributing notably to the literature of expatriation in her short stories set in Mexico and, more allegorically, in *Ship of Fools* (1962).

In the years following World War I, young African American intellectuals began to gather in Harlem, a district of New York City that soon became the center of a renaissance of black arts and letters. Many important figures of the New Negro Movement came from the South, among them Georgia Douglas Johnson, Zora Neale Hurston, Arna Bontemps, Joshua Henry Jones Jr., and Walter White. The complex relationship of southern landscape and experience to the construction of African American culture is specifically explored in Jean Toomer's *Cane* (1923). The poems, sketches, and stories of the first part of *Cane* locate defining meaning in the folk life of rural Georgia. The second section presents displaced black southerners alienated by the realities of the northern city, and the third dramatizes the complexities of return to the South. Expatriation in response to the threat of interracial violence organizes several African American novels of the 1930s and 1940s, but black refugees from lynching faced other threats to their identity and dignity in the cities of the North, as shown in Waters Turpin's *O Canaan!* (1939), William Attaway's *Blood on the Forge* (1941), and George Wylie Henderson's *Jule* (1946).

Among the greatest escape-from-the South narratives are the works of Richard Wright, who left Mississippi for Chicago, New York, and finally Paris. Wright's memoir *Black Boy* (1945), his stories, and his novels, including *Native Son* (1940), paint powerful portraits of southern black protagonists in the supposedly free North. As unforgettable as Wright's Bigger Thomas, if less irrevocably doomed, is the unnamed protagonist of Ralph Ellison's *Invisible Man* (1952). Expelled from the false Eden of his Deep-South college, the invisible man is inspired by the smell and taste of yams roasted on a Harlem street to consider his identity. By novel's end, he is sometimes "overcome with a passion to return into that 'heart of darkness' across the Mason-Dixon line."

The years after World War I witnessed a flowering of literature among writers of the American South, white as well as black. By the end of the 1920s, a book of poems by Allen Tate and first novels by William Faulkner and Thomas Wolfe had been published; a renascence was underway. As Robert Penn Warren observed, almost all the writers of the 1920–1950 period "had some important experience outside the South." In 1920 Thomas Wolfe took the train northward, never again to live in his native state. Wolfe, perhaps above all others, lived and wrote the expatriate story. Far from North Carolina, he could contemplate his youthful experiences and create from them the book we know as *Look Homeward, Angel* (1929). *Of Time and the River* (1935) and the textual compilations published posthumously as *The Web and the Rock* (1939) and *You Can't Go Home Again* (1940) powerfully evoke the expatriate's ambivalent relationships to both the lost homeland and the great city of his exile.

William Faulkner lived close to home for much of his life and set most of his works in the Mississippi county he claimed as his own. He did, however, send his fictional Quentin Compson northeast to Massachusetts; in memorable scenes from two of Faulkner's major novels, Quentin experiences the expatriate dilemma. In *The Sound and the Fury* (1929), Quentin's homeward-bound train crosses the border into Virginia, where he catches sight of the iconic Negro on the mule. In *Absalom, Absalom!* (1936), Quentin tries to explain the complexities of home to a perplexed Canadian roommate. To Shreve's logical inquiry as to why he hates his native place, he can offer only unconvincing denial: "I don't hate it. . . . *I don't hate it.*"

In the fiction of Faulkner, Wolfe, Ellison, and other Southern Renascence modernists, memory serves as both technique and theme. For those writers of the period who lived outside their native South, recollection of times past was often paralleled by recollection of faraway places. Georgia-born Carson McCullers moved to New York in 1940, determined to escape the "horror" of southern society, although that society continued to serve her for subject. Dramatist Lillian Hellmann, living in Hollywood and New York, drew on her southern memories for several plays, notably *The Little Foxes* (1939). Tennessee Williams included southern characters, language, and themes in many of his most famous plays: *The Glass Menagerie* (1945), *A Streetcar Named Desire* (1947), *Camino Real* (1953), and *Cat on a Hot Tin Roof* (1955).

Journalist-novelists James Agee of Tennessee and Hamilton Basso of Louisiana lived in the Northeast and made occasional southward forays. Struggling to write the text of *Let Us Now Praise Famous Men* (1941), Agee came to recognize his southern and agrarian roots—and to realize that they could never be reclaimed. Expatriated southerners fail to go home again in several Basso novels, notably *Courthouse Square* (1936) and *The View from Pompey's Head* (1954). A less-autonomous expatriate figures in Harriette Simpson Arnow's 1954 novel, *The Dollmaker*. Gertie Revels, a Kentucky mountain woman, is displaced by war

and economic necessity to a slum in industrial Flint, Michigan, where she struggles to hold on to a connection with nature, family, and creative work.

Fictional works by Eudora Welty, Robert Penn Warren, Julian Green, and William Styron associate the southern homeland with personal and regional legacies not easily evaded even in exile. "Music from Spain," the penultimate story in Welty's *The Golden Apples* (1949), recounts Mississippian Eugene MacClain's experiences of expatriation, not over the North-South border but rather on the distant coastal margin of the American West. In *All the King's Men* (1947), Warren illustrates Jack Burden's vain attempt to escape the past with a desperate road trip beyond history and into the West. Not until his 1977 novel, *A Place to Come To*, however, does Warren recount the repatriation of an exiled southern protagonist; after years away, Jed Tewksbury comes back home and makes his peace not only with Nashville but also with Dugton, Alabama. Julian Green, born in Paris to southern parents, spent relatively few years in America and became an acclaimed writer in his adopted France. His tragedy *South* (1953) and his novel *The Distant Lands* (1987) focus on the experiences of exiled Europeans in an ironically rendered antebellum South. Among Green's many impressive works, these two particularly reveal the legacy of his family's expatriation and his mother's bitter preoccupation with the destruction of the Old South.

William Styron, himself an expatriate, created major characters who are displaced southerners: Peyton Loftis of *Lie Down in Darkness* (1952), who commits suicide in New York, and the narrator of *Sophie's Choice* (1979). In *Set This House on Fire* (1960), Styron fully explores themes of expatriation. Cass Kinsolving flees a southern sense of sin, first to New York and then to Europe. In the south of Italy, Cass kills and repents, learning finally that to love himself he must love his country and go home. The displaced southern protagonist of Walker Percy's *The Last Gentleman* (1966) leaves his New York refuge in search of home and father, only to discover that he feels estranged both South and North. Doubly if perversely alienated in the newly happy South to which he returns, Percy's young Will Barrett once more flees—this time into a southwestern "locus of pure possibility."

During the post–World War II period, Warren and Styron resided in Connecticut, Georgia-native Frank Yerby in Paris, Truman Capote in New York, and Ernest Gaines in San Francisco. Although Gaines's native Louisiana serves as locale for most of his fiction, *Catherine Carmier* (1964) treats the expatriate experience of a young black man alienated in both California and his native South. Yerby's uncharacteristically political *Speak Now* (1969) features an African American Vietnam veteran living in 1968 Paris: painfully ambivalent toward the country and region that denies him full citizenship, Harrison Forbes reluctantly becomes involved with and marries a white southerner.

As the social changes of the 1960s began to take effect, not only black southerners but also a new generation of southern women sought freedom by leaving home. North Carolinian Gail Godwin has lived outside the South since the early 1960s. In addition to distinguished novels with southern settings, Godwin has written several that feature as protagonists southerners outside the South: *Glass People* (1972), *The Odd Woman* (1974), *Violet Clay* (1978), and *The Finishing School* (1985). Rita Mae Brown fled the University of Florida accused of racial and sexual transgressions; her novels *Rubyfruit Jungle* (1973) and *In Her Day* (1976) feature southern protagonists traveling between North and South in search of identity. Lisa Alther left Tennessee to study at Wellesley and settled in Vermont: her *Kinflicks* (1976) juxtaposes accounts of a young southerner's quest for sexual freedom and her return home to care for her dying mother. Although Ellen Gilchrist has lived mostly in the South, some of her short fiction is set elsewhere, and *The Anna Papers* (1988) tells the story of a self-exiled southern writer who comes home to die.

In a 1985 report on the state of southern literature, *Newsweek* names as "expatriates," in addition to Warren, Styron, and Gail Godwin, Andre Dubus, William Humphrey, Bobbie Ann Mason, Jayne Anne Phillips, Alice Walker, James Wilcox, and John Yount. *Newsweek*'s Gene Lyons could have mentioned also Alther, Brown, Calder Willingham Jr., Elizabeth Spencer, and playwright Beth Henley (he had no way of knowing that North Carolinian Allan Gurganus was installed in a Manhattan apartment working on *Oldest Living Confederate Widow Tells All* [1989]).

From the time that southern identity was established, important writers have lived outside the region for some part of their lives and careers. Some have come back periodically to replenish the raw materials of their artistic inspiration. Others have stayed away, visiting primarily through the exercise of memory. Still others have returned once again to live in the South. By the close of the twentieth century, expatriate southern artists were less likely than their predecessors to be on the run from racism, religious fanaticism, and other strains of bigotry, although, unfortunately, intolerance and philistinism persist in the South as elsewhere. Perhaps southerners can now less self-consciously live—as "accidental expatriates"—wherever they choose, or just wind up, in their country or indeed the world. Nevertheless, the American South still exerts particularly strong forces of attraction and repulsion on its sons and daughters, and the homeland's powerful influence continues to inform a rich literature by and about southerners at home and outside the South.

Anne Ricketson Zahlan

See also Black Migrations; Harlem Renaissance.

F

FAITHFUL RETAINER

The faithful retainer as literary device and theme has played an important part in fiction by white southerners, especially following the Civil War. The African American, while technically free, casts his or her lot with the white master or mistress, presumably finding identity and fulfillment with the master or mistress, who continues to provide security for the retainer throughout life. The relationship was meant to mirror the patterns of life on humane plantations under slavery. In the immensely popular work of Thomas Nelson Page, the image helped make the Old South sympathetic and romantic to northern readers.

The boundaries of proper behavior between black and white have always been complex in the South. During slavery and Reconstruction and in the era of Jim Crow, the boundaries were defined chiefly by the whites. Usually the boundaries were rigid, but they could be crossed. House slaves were in a favored position to develop lasting personal relationships with masters and mistresses. Sometimes the slaves carried some of the blood of their white families. There was, however, little choosing on the African American side.

Possibilities for close friendships between blacks and whites in the South were not only few but discouraged, save in the retainer relationship and its mutations, especially in the mammy figure. With the mammy, the bonds could be very close. James Branch Cabell dedicated *The Cream of the Jest* (1919) to Louisa Nelson, the "mammy" who ruled over the Cabell household for a quarter century, whom Joe Lee Davis describes as "one of the begetters of Cabell's aristocratic egoism." William Faulkner dedicated *Go Down, Moses* (1942) to Caroline Barr, "who was born in slavery and who gave to my family a fidelity without stint or calculation of recompense and to my childhood an immeasurable devotion and love." About Barr, Faulk-

ner's mother said, "We all loved her. But I'll tell you one thing, she always wanted you to know that she was a 'nigrah.'" Louisa Nelson and Caroline Barr reflect, however, a fraction of the realities between the races. Richard Wright's autobiography *Black Boy* (1945) makes clear how separate the two races were, how much distrust could exist between black and white. In Wright's work, the more urban the setting, the greater the distance between the races. In *Landscapes of the Heart: A Memoir* (1998), Elizabeth Spencer depicts the separation in her aptly titled chapter about blacks, employed by the family or not: "Them." Walter Cronkite, in his memoir *A Reporter's Life* (1996), recounts the active, hateful discouragement of not only friendship but respectful relationships between black and white in the Texas of his young manhood. As Cronkite notes, the Civil Rights Movement received an unexpected ally when President Lyndon Johnson, a Texan, pushed through the Civil Rights Act of 1964.

In literature, the tradition of the faithful retainer provided a gentler, kinder view of black-white relations in the South than was evident in the century following the Civil War or in the turmoils of the struggle for civil rights. It is a long tradition, its roots antebellum. In "The Gold-Bug" (1843), Poe's Jupiter provides an early example of the type, some would say stereotype. Jupiter is an old black man "who had been manumitted before the reverses of the family, but who could be induced, neither by threats or promises, to abandon what he considered his right of attendance upon the footsteps of his young 'Massa Will.'" Stay with William Legrand he does, providing humor to the story and much of the necessary labor for Legrand to show his skill at ratiocination. But Jupiter's choices as a manumitted black were limited, perhaps illusory. In "Free Joe and the Rest of the World" (1884), Joel Chandler Harris portrays the tragic consequences to a slave who is freed by a master unable to meet a gambling debt who then commits suicide. Joe has nowhere to go—is perceived as a threat to the social order, denied the company of his wife (still a slave), suffers harsh treatment from poor whites. An independent black male would not do in the antebellum South.

It was, however, in stories that portray the South after the war that the faithful retainer became a major figure. Joel Chandler Harris made the retainer a favorite character in all sections of the country through his Uncle Remus stories; after the popular success of *Uncle Remus: His Songs and Sayings* (1880), Harris built on that success with other Remus books published in 1883, 1892, 1905, and 1906. Although Remus preferred life before the war, Harris made Remus's intelligence central in his portrait and gave him a convincing sense of self and purpose. Charles Wadell Chesnutt, the first major African American writer of fiction, sensed the complexity of Remus and created his own memorable retainer in Uncle Julius, who narrates the folk stories of *The Conjure Woman* (1899), exposing pointedly the evils of slavery and cleverly manipulating his listeners. In his short story "The Passing of Grandison," from *The Wife of His Youth, and Other Stories of the Color Line,* also published in 1899, Chesnutt turns the image of the faithful retainer on its head and mocks the deluded master who takes pride in the loyalty of his slave.

In "Two Gentlemen of Kentucky" (1888), James Lane Allen makes the relationship between former master and former slave the center of his story. In a culture that denied the appellation "Mister" to a black man, the black male is honored as a "gentleman," coequal with a white. Set in a slave state that did not secede, Allen's story deals with several boundaries, certainly the boundary between the South before the war and the South after the war and the boundaries within Kentucky. He portrays a society in disruption: "The war had divided the people of Kentucky as the false mother would have severed the child." An aging representative of the old social order, Colonel Romulus Fields must give up his depleted estate and move to Lexington. Accompanying him is Peter Cotton, who as a freed slave chooses to stay with the colonel, who has never married. Because Peter's wife, Phyllis, dies before the move, Allen's focus is on two elderly males and their effort to make a new life. Neither finds a comfortable place in the postwar South, but they find their chief rewards in each other: "the colonel and Peter were never so happy as when ruminating side by side." Unusual in such portrayals of retainer relationships,

there is an essential equality of commitment and reward. In the extended death scene of the colonel, Allen makes clear that each is the great love of the other's life. Although the scene meets every standard of nineteenth-century decorum and Allen reports that the colonel has lived a chaste life, the farewell scene is markedly physical: " 'Come up here—closer'; and putting one arm around Peter's neck, he laid the other hand softly on his head and looked tenderly in his eyes." Fields thanks Peter for his devotion and asks that when Peter's time comes, they "take the long sleep together." And the two are eventually laid side by side. If the story is idealized, sentimentalized, it was also nudging southerners—and northerners—to acknowledge the humanity of blacks and to grant the possibility of profound love across the boundaries of race and gender.

When Thomas Nelson Page wrote his stories to honor the ideals of the Old South and to further the goal of reconciliation between North and South, the faithful retainer proved essential to his purpose. The chief voice articulating the tales found in *In Ole Virginia* (1887) is the voice of the retainer, a black voice. The issue of slavery had led the nation to war. Although Page did not favor slavery and was well aware of its more sinister manifestations, he would show North and South that there were southerners of honor and courage—like his Marse Chan—who were moving toward a southern solution. The loyalty of Page's retainers to their former masters was manifest in the very telling of the stories. These dialect stories also provided local color and the charm of the exotic. The image of the kind, gentle, unthreatening black male narrator provided white readers (as Page's readers were) not only with humor but also reassurance. (The type would endure into the twentieth century in popular media such as the *Amos and Andy* radio shows. H. L. Mencken would warn that if the nation lost that dimension, the black would become "a menacing stranger.")

Later readers of Page find the depiction of race and the faithful retainer much more complicated and problematic than did Page's contemporary audiences. The contrasts between black and white life are telling. In "Marse Chan," the birth of the young master is an event of the greatest magnitude—unlike the births that might occur in the quarter. Sam's whole purpose is to serve. He is even serving the Channings after all their deaths. Old before his time, he has only a past (though he is married, Judy seems no rival for the bonding with the Marse Chan).

In "Meh Lady: A Story of the War," another retainer, Billy, tells the story of the courage of his white people as the war ravages the area. Their losses are also his losses. Like Sam, he is a talker. Like Sam, "Uncle" does not consider moving away after the war. Not only would he have nowhere to go, he has no desire to go. A high moment in his life comes after the war when "Meh lady" (unnamed to emphasize the chivalric aura) marries a Union veteran, albeit one with Virginian ancestors, one about to resume life as a Virginian. In this symbolic union between North and South, when the minister asks who is giving the bride away, the retainer steps forward to declare " 'Ole Billy.' " Thus the union between North and South is also a fulfilling moment for the black. But the retainer knows his place in the new order. When the narrator of the framed story asks if the child named Billy is named for him, "Ole Billy" replies deprecatingly, "Go 'way, Marster, who gwine name gent'man after a ole nigger?" The last line to the story may be meant as a sentimental moment, but the contemporary reader will likely find it a painful one. The postbellum mentality seems not very different from that prevailing before the war. Page was revealing more than he fully realized.

Depictions of the faithful retainer abound in Faulkner's fiction, though the dynamics are much different from those in Page. Against the relationship between Marse Chan and Sam, the depictions of the interaction between white and black males in *Go Down, Moses* are infinitely more probing and complex. Sam has evolved into a Lucas Beauchamp, part of the McCaslin family—by blood and history—and a severe judge of it. Faulkner's treatment of "retainer" relationships is gentler in *The Unvanquished* (1938) but equally important. Bayard Sartoris is too young to fight in the Civil War, though emotionally he (read, Marse Chan) and Ringo (read, Sam) fight it together. The realities of postwar life ensure that in adult life the close bonds of childhood do not hold, and Faulkner highlights the sad distance. *Absalom, Absalom!* (1936) concludes with several images of retainers. With Sutpen's Hundred now in ruins, Judith Sutpen and Clytie work together without the avowed affection highlighted in Allen and Page; they work together because they must, because they can, because they are also sisters. Because Sutpen himself had been so driven by an abstraction, he has made no emotional commitment to another human being—white or black. In his short story "Wash," Faulkner provides Sutpen with another kind of retainer, the white Wash Jones, who has given the failed Colonel the devotion so frequently portrayed between master and former slave. At story's end, Wash realizes how deceived he has been and murders Sutpen. The last retainer—"heir" and only inhabitant—in the ruins of Sutpen's Hundred is the demented grandson of Charles Bon, to whom Sutpen would not say "my son" because he carried some Negro blood.

Faulkner's gallery of masters and retainers is, as one would expect, diverse. In "Mountain Victory" (1932), the master, Major Wedell, decidedly embodies the responsibility found in Page's Channings. But, Appomattox now reality, Jubal, who accompanies "Master Major Soshay Wedell" on his way back to Mississippi, embodies a foolish pride in his own status: he is not a "field nigger." Because Jubal acts irresponsibly and gets drunk when the two need to escape from a section in Tennessee where Rebels are hated, both lose their lives. Wedell, however, never flinches from his duty to Jubal. In "A Rose for Emily" (1931), Faulkner provides a memorable image of a retainer crossing gender lines. Although Emily Grierson has had the corpse of Homer Barron in her bed for many years, she has been abetted and loyally served all that time by a black man: "He talked to no one, probably not even to her, for his voice had grown harsh and rusty, as if from disuse." After Emily dies, the faithful retainer admits the town officials into the previously off-limits house, then "walked right through the house and out the back and was not seen again."

Women writers have also found the retainer important to their fiction. In 1898, former slaveholder Eugenia Bacon Jones published *Lyddy: A Tale of the Old South*, intending to provide a realistic portrayal of life in the Deep South before, during, and after the war—especially the place of blacks on the plantation. Jones's novel is based on her own family. Late in the novel, the South reeling and the Emancipation Proclamation a reality, the master explains to the assembled blacks formerly his slaves: "This changes all of you from slaves into free men and women. Many of you were born slaves to our parents. God knows we, their children, have tried to do our duty to you. Your young mistress has nursed you on cold winter nights when death seemed hovering over you." His listeners voice assent and accept the justice of his proposal. The former master is able to proceed under the new realities with loyal blacks. Jones presents her reader with multiple faithful retainers.

In her sentimental novel *The Comings of Cousin Ann* (1923), Emma Speed Sampson foregrounds the convention of the faithful retainer to emphasize the loyalty across the color line that could also cross the gender line. Unmarried, elderly Cousin Ann Peyton has no real place, so she is repeatedly making the rounds of her relatives for varying durations, hoping not to stay too long anywhere. She is escorted each time by her loyal black servant, elderly Uncle Billy. At novel's end, Sampson brings the comedy to a happy solution, primarily because Uncle Billy has been able to maneuver events so that Miss Ann has a stable and secure family home—her pride secure. At this point, happy for Ann, he is also free, at last, to make a marriage for himself, and does.

Katherine Anne Porter made especially trenchant use of the faithful retainer, probing where male writers had often only intimated. In the stories that make up *The Old Order,* Sophia Jane Gay is the "source" of her family, outworking the males, dominating them, outliving them. Her confidante, especially in her later years, is Nannie. Born in slavery, from childhood Nannie has lived life with a bossy but loyal mistress, Sophia Jane. Both women marry, but each finds her best listener in the other. Nannie's husband, Uncle Jimbilly, is also a retainer, living on the land but not in the intimacy that Faulkner's Dilsey lived with Roskus. Now old, Jimbilly stays on the land, primarily to tell the stories of slavery, which he cannot shake. Nannie has long since left his bed and abode for Sophie Jane's house. There they tell their stories to each other, reliving their pasts. For each, the other has been a ballast in the life of the old order.

Beyond the Renascence, the faithful retainer has continued to play a part in southern fiction in its depiction of changing social patterns. In "What You Hear From 'Em," Peter Taylor depicts the association of the Tolliver family with "Aunt Munsie," who keeps asking when her favorites among the children—Mr. Thad and Mr. Will, now grown and citizens of the New South—will return from Memphis and Nashville to live in Thornton. Munsie thinks, "No matter how rich they were, what difference did it make; they didn't own land, did they?" How, then, could they be rich in Cameron County? Munsie has become a figure of amusement for whites who pass her and her slop wagon on the increasingly dangerous streets of Thornton. Munsie's hearing and sight now dim, the community eventually makes keeping pigs in town illegal, thus keeping Munsie off the streets. The Tolliver children and grandchildren make dutiful visits until Munsie dies, many years later. Born in slavery, Munsie had lived a century.

Depictions of loyal black servants whose identity is tied up with the family they serve are numerous—in the Renascence and beyond. Contemporary writers emphasize that these "retainers" also have lives beyond those of their white families, as Ellen Gilchrist does in her depictions of Traceleen, black maid to wealthy Crystal Ann Manning, in *Victory Over Japan* (1982). In the Traceleen stories of that collection, Gilchrist takes the same risk Page took: Traceleen tells the stories. She emerges as bemused, compassionate, and more wholesome than her employers. In *Can't Quit You, Baby* (1988), Ellen Douglas (Josephine Ayres Haxton) portrays the relationship between a middle-aged white woman and her black maid during the 1950s and 1960s, their growing sense of each other and themselves. When African American writers utilize the tradition, the effect is more stringent. In *The Color Purple* (1982), Alice Walker puts a harsh slant on the whole tradition of the faithful retainer in her depiction of Sofia, forced into the servitude of the mayor's wife and family, denied a meaningful life with her own children. In Ishmael Reed's fantasy-satire *Flight to Canada* (1976), the relationship between the "faithful" Uncle Robin, who did not flee to Canada, and his decadent master is pivotal. When the master asks Uncle Robin if he's heard of Canada, the slave replies, "I do admit I've heart about the place from time to time, Mr. Swille, but I loves it here so much that I would never think of leaving here." Eventually Uncle Robin is able to rewrite Swille's will and inherit his Virginia plantation.

Joseph M. Flora

See also Happy Darky; Mammy; Plantation; Uncle Remus.

R. Bruce Bickley, *Joel Chandler Harris* (1987); Elizabeth Fox-Genovese, *Within the Plantation Household: Black and White Women of the Old South* (1988); Theodore L. Gross, *Thomas Nelson Page* (1967); Trudier Harris, *From Mammies to Militants: Domesticity in Black American Literature* (1982); Clarence Mohr, *On the Threshold of Freedom: Masters and Slaves in Civil War Georgia* (1986).

FAMILY

When southern writers refer to "family," they almost always mean the extended, consanguine family, not the conjugal family of husband, wife, and children. "The connection," as it is sometimes called, includes uncles, aunts, and cousins to the third and fourth degree of kinship as well as great-grandparents, grandparents,

parents, brothers, and sisters. The kinship family extends to the collateral as well as direct line of descent, and the conjugal family counts as only a small unit in the larger web of relationships, whether in matters of authority, loyalty, sense of identity, or economic and political fortunes. Further, the southern family participates in an awareness of generations who lived earlier than the family described in a particular time or circumstance. That is, the family lives through history as well as in the present and has genealogies and listings in family Bibles as ways of recording the lives and memories of those who have gone before as well as ways of reckoning their degrees of kinship.

Such families show an inherited and taught sense of identity that sets them apart from other families in the community. They tell each other about the particular, sometimes peculiar, forms of behavior that become known as family traits, of behavior "come by honestly" through inheritance. Beyond traits, families often share knowledge of a special attribute learned from earlier generations—a pride in social preeminence, descent from a famous ancestor, the lingering curse of an old family crime, the recognition of suicide or suicidal behavior as a family option, readiness to fight duels in the name of family honor, the need to hold to the land with which the family has been identified. In Shirley Ann Grau's *The Keepers of the House* (1964), the code of the Howland family, through the generations, is to exact vengeance on those who betray or injure the family. In Alex Haley's *Roots* (1976), the descendants of Kunta Kinte keep alive the story of "the African" and think of themselves as different from families who lack such a memory.

One effect of holding the vision of a special family attribute, however, is to exclude from true membership those in the family who do not share loyalty to the vision. In William Faulkner's *Go Down, Moses* (1942), Isaac McCaslin shows how, because he shuns and renounces the McCaslin legacy, he becomes the object of pity and perhaps contempt by both collateral family and community. And those who would marry into a family of cohesive vision realize they must accept the family legend in order to belong. This happens to Will Palmer, successful lumberman, in *Roots*. Because of Cynthia's family loyalty to memory of "the African," he is seen as marrying into her family rather than she into his. When he does so, the marriage demonstrates the family practice of choosing spouses who accept the order of authority within the family.

Identity of the extended and multigenerational fam-

ily typically begins with removal of the family or progenitor from the old homeland to the new place where the family will live through history and into memory. For families in southern writing, this removal most often comes by migration from an older colony or state to a newer one, from Virginia, Maryland, or one of the Carolinas to Kentucky, Tennessee, Alabama, or Mississippi. In some cases, the removal may feature the first arrival on New World land from Europe or Africa. In most cases, almost nothing is known of the families' lives in the old homeland. In *Roots*, however, a third of the story of Kunta Kinte's family concerns his life in a Mandinka village and his capture before he lands as a slave in Maryland—a necessity so that his seventh-generation descendant can return to the place of origin. The Vaidens in T. S. Stribling's *The Forge* (1931) begin their history in Alabama after removal from Carolina. The most frequently given reason for removal is to find more fertile land after the old land has been exhausted by profligate tobacco culture, but reasons may vary. In Caroline Gordon's *Penhally* (1931), for example, Frances Llewellyn moves from Virginia to Kentucky to escape Thomas Jefferson's abolition of entailment.

In southern history and culture, the family has served not as one among several supporting institutions but, in Andrew Lytle's now-classic recognition, as *the* institution of southern life. Because southern life until well into the twentieth century was predominantly agrarian and rural, the family stayed in place over the years and combined social and economic activities in one unit. In "What Is a Traditional Society?" (1936), Allen Tate saw that such unity of economic and moral functions was necessary for the transmission of values through generations, that "to make a livelihood men do not have to put aside their moral natures." Family then became an expression of the culture, often having to do more than it realistically could as one institution.

More than in other parts of the nation, but perhaps not more than in many non-American parts of the world, the family in the South became the institution to fall back on when the public world changed, was convulsed by wars and depressions and poverty, when national policy brought about fundamental changes in public life. The family functioned as the individual's link with the past, so that what the family member knew of the past was what had shaped or affected the family. It became an extension of, often a replacement for, church and school. The family religion became the only religion one knew, and the level of education in the family became one's expectation of the need for education in the world beyond the family. Until the rise of scientific agriculture, farming was a repetition of the practices of the parents and grandparents. The family served as the model for manners, and the individual learned his or her prayers and manners at the mother's knee.

The family also served as the matrix for models of citizenship and leadership, of how one was expected to relate to the public world. The organization of family mirrored the organization of the region, with authority vested in hierarchies and ranks of patriarchs and matriarchs, and getting necessary business done was a matter of speaking with the right person of authority rather than of persuading a public assembly. The legends of the family reflected the larger legend of the region. The losses of the family as a result of the Civil War or one of the great floods, for example, explained those of the region. Or the family legend might take on biblical resonance where the family's arrival at the new homeland became arrival at "the promised land."

As John Shelton Reed has shown in *The Enduring South: Subcultural Persistence in Mass Society* (1974), the southern family has functioned as families do in ethnic groups, by serving as a source for identification of the group, by allowing the family member to confine social relationships to his or her own ethnic group during all stages of life, and by adapting national patterns of behavior to the group's cultural system. Further, through their cultural orientation, families can instruct members about what is comic or tragic and sometimes provide a sense of destiny or purpose.

For many in the South, the sense of family depends on a sense of place, the family home especially, but also the community. Place in this sense becomes not a geographical point but a historical continuum, a locale having been lived in and modified through time. The homeplace, the farmhouse and its surroundings in the country or the house in town to which the family has moved and kept its country ways, becomes a virtual member of the family. Paintings or photographs of it may hang on the wall next to family faces, and its loss is grieved like loss of a family member. The architecture of the family home, with its additions and wings, reflects the growth of the family over time and, in effect, becomes a family trait. Within or around the homeplace, architectural or decorative features may hold talismanic meaning for the family. In *The Keepers of the House,* for example, the charred handrail,

burned when bandits attacked the Howland place, was kept "to remember by" through the generations.

Older southern families in literature, if not in official records kept by families, have a black line of descendants running parallel with the white line. Sometimes the family past may include a strain of Indian blood. This feature is almost unique to southern families as a carryover from slaveholding times. For the most part, this other line of the family is known and lived with but seldom acknowledged. But the shape and fortunes of families in southern literary works are often determined by the family's response to that knowledge. In his short stories of *Old Creole Days* (1879) and in *The Grandissimes* (1880), George Washington Cable was among the first to use this knowledge for narrative purposes. Since his time, it has been almost a standard motif. In *The Grandissimes,* the family fortune of the whites is saved by Honoré's acknowledgment of his dark half-brother, also named Honoré. In Faulkner's *Absalom, Absalom!* the destruction of the white Sutpens comes finally from their denial of the claims of the black descendants. In Ernest Gaines's *The Autobiography of Miss Jane Pittman* (1971), Robert Samson treats his half-black son Timmy as black man, not son, and sends him away. His white son Tee Bob later commits suicide in guilt because he knows how white men have treated black women in the family.

Naming within families serves as a means of recognizing or denying family membership. Those with baronial pretensions may give member after member the same name, giving the newborn the name of one who has died, as if members were interchangeable units in an army. In Grau's *The Keepers of the House,* each generation names a son William Howland, and when sons fail to appear, generations of daughters are named Abigail. In Eudora Welty's *Delta Wedding* (1946), the Fairchilds are ready to name the next child Denis to replace the Denis lost in the World War. Names also reflect the cultural matrix in which the family sees itself. Families in the Bible Belt may give biblical names. The Creoles in Cable's *The Grandissimes* give classical or French neo-classical names. After the Civil War, sons were often named after Confederate heroes, though as Atticus Finch observes about Braxton Bragg Underwood in Harper Lee's *To Kill a Mockingbird* (1960), "naming people after Confederate generals made slow steady drinkers." Heroes' names could also be corrupted. Redneck Bob Ewell in *To Kill a Mockingbird* and the Misfit's crony Bobby Lee in Flannery O'Connor's "A Good Man Is Hard to Find" (1953) are named after Robert E. Lee.

Slavery and postslavery times posed the problem of naming for former slaves, whether to take the former master's name or find a new one without echoes of slavery. Macon Dead in Toni Morrison's *Song of Solomon* (1977) accepts his curious misnomer "because it was new and would wipe out the past." Ticey is renamed Jane by the Yankee soldier Brown in *The Autobiography of Miss Jane Pittman* because he sees Ticey as a slave name. In *Go Down, Moses*, Lucas Beauchamp changes his ancestral name from Lucius to Lucas when he re-creates himself as a free man.

Depictions of families in southern fiction often have a tacit background of family stories told and retold around the fireside or dinner table or on the porch. The stories tell the family's sense of itself, its past, its status, its destiny. They provide a version of the past needed by the family in the present. They may be tales of endurance through hard times, explanations of how key traits came into the family, warnings to the young to marry for money instead of romantic infatuation, ways of accounting for the present status of the family with accounts of old catastrophes or moments of luck or vision by an ancestor, stories about "How The Family Began" with accounts of fateful meetings of the matriarchs and patriarchs, or tales that link the family with events in public history. Their interest is not in the story itself but in what it means to the family. They also suggest the work of a family bard, a member who, because of his or her connection with events or persons or because of a talent for making behavior meaningful through narration, is able to collect and integrate anecdotes into a coherent story. Andrew Lytle sees that "by hovering above the action to see it all," the bard "collects the segments. In the end, in the way he fits the parts together, the one story will finally get told." Faulkner uses this device in *Go Down, Moses* to interpret actions even while he narrates them.

But as the South, particularly since World War II, has become urban and suburban, commercial and industrial, the agrarian basis of southern family life has receded into the background, remembered but not lived. The nuclear unit of parents, often single parents, and children is the family in the social, statistical, tax, and legal sense. Family reunions of siblings, parents, grandparents, uncles, aunts, and cousins are the modern version of extended family after its dispersal into small units.

Robert O. Stephens

See also Ancestor Worship; Diaries, Men's; Diaries, Women's; Family Feuding.

Fred Hobson, *Tell About the South: The Southern Rage to Explain* (1983); Andrew Lytle, *The Hero with the Private Parts* (1966); Michael Ragussis, *Acts of Naming: The Family Plot in Fiction* (1987); John Shelton Reed, *The Enduring South: Subcultural Persistence in Mass Society* (1972); Robert O. Stephens, *The Family Saga in the South: Generations and Destinies* (1995); Elizabeth Stone, *Black Sheep and Kissing Cousins: How Our Family Stories Shape Us* (1988).

FAMILY FEUDING

In southern literature, family feuding generally consists of one or both of two kinds: long-running conflicts *between* families and those *within* families. Both kinds imply extended consanguine families with numerous degrees of kinship involved, rather than conjugal families of parents and children. When feuding involves violence, as it often does in conflicts between families, it typically acts as an extension of the dueling code, where satisfactions from law fail to meet the demands of family honor or pride, and rational interests are sacrificed in the cause of revenge or retaliation. Family feuding in southern culture tends to follow the pattern in earlier examples of feuds, such as that of the Montagues and Capulets in Shakespeare's *Romeo and Juliet*. Only the causes and occasions found in southern life are different. Some feuds, like that of the Hatfields and McCoys in the southern mountains, achieve lasting repute in folklore.

Mark Twain's depiction of the Grangerford-Shepherdson feud in *Adventures of Huckleberry Finn* (1885) shows the classic features of feuds between families. The feud occurs in Kentucky before the Civil War, but its pattern is that of such feuds in other times and places: (1) the feud began long before, and Buck Grangerford cannot tell Huck Finn exactly how or when it began; (2) a lawsuit, the issue now forgotten, failed to resolve the dispute between parties; (3) the loser of the lawsuit shot the winner; (4) the winner's kin shot the assassin, the loser's kin killed in revenge, and a succession of reciprocal killings for revenge spread to include the extended families, and Buck tells Huck how boy cousins were hunted down and shot; (5) the opposing feudists respect the courage and cunning of their enemies—no cowards among the Shepherdsons, Buck says; (6) the feuding families have no idea how the feud will ever end, its burden being passed from generation to generation; and (7) the feud is brought to crisis when lovers from opposing families elope as do Sophia Grangerford and Harney Shepherdson in Twain's story. Sometimes the elopement results in reconciliation, sometimes in the massacre of one family by the other.

Variations on the pattern reflect different degrees of intense feeling, extent of violence, the success of lovers, differences in region—mountain, piedmont, or tidewater—and placement in the social hierarchy. Typically, women are exempt from violence, though they may encourage it, and in some cases they are thought to be causes of the feud or sharers in guilt, as was Rosanna McCoy with Jonce Hatfield. Some mountain folklore suggests that the practice of violent pursuit, ambush, and killing developed during the Civil War when loyalties between or within families were divided.

As early as John Pendleton Kennedy's *Swallow Barn* (1832), the conflict between the aristocratic Hazard-Meriwether and Tracy families in the Virginia tidewater over disputed land between their plantations stayed in the law courts while the families met in cautious courtesy and became so much a part of old Isaac Tracy's purpose for living that he could not let it rest when the suit was settled in his favor and his daughter Bel married Ned Hazard. In Thomas Nelson Page's "Marse Chan" (1884), another story of Virginia tidewater plantations, the Chamberlain and Channing families and lovers are separated by pre–Civil War politics and disputes over sales of slave families, and the lovers Marse Chan and Ann Chamberlain are united finally in the grave. In George Washington Cable's *The Grandissimes* (1880), a showpiece of feuds between and within Creole families of early Louisiana, the long-standing rivalry among the De Grapion-Nancanou, Fusilier, and Grandissime families dates from colonial times; it is marked by early deaths of De Grapion and Nancanou men in duels and by occasional truces brought about by marriages. In the climactic years of 1803–1804, the possible marriage of Honoré Grandissime and Aurora Nancanou is seen in the context of Montagues and Capulets. In Lee Smith's *Oral History* (1983), the old Virginia mountain families of Cantrells and Blankenships kill each other over disputed whisky money until the Cantrell sons go into exile in Ohio and Parrot Blankenship and Ora Mae Cantrell produce a son destined to be shot by a deranged and jealous modern teenager.

Within families, the feuds tend to reflect divided family loyalties. In Caroline Gordon's *Penhally* (1931),

the Llewellyn family of Kentucky are in dispute over their divided allegiance to the old practice of entailment, of keeping the family estate undivided and passed to the eldest male heir. In Shirley Ann Grau's *The Keepers of the House* (1964), the Howland family, probably of Alabama, is outraged and split when, after the Civil War, William Howland marries a woman from New Orleans and brings her French Catholicism and her father's war profits into the Protestant and Confederate family. In the later generation, Abigail Howland exacts vengeance against a half-black member, not because he is black but because he betrayed the family to their political enemies.

In modern southern nuclear families, feuds or alienations tend to occur within, often over disputed oral bequests of heirlooms, sometimes over property distributed in wills showing favoritism or distaste for members, sometimes over expected rewards for keeping the elderly or disabled kin, where daughters are expected to be kin-keepers or caretakers and sons left to follow their fortunes in faraway places, as in Peter Taylor's *A Summons to Memphis* (1986).

Robert O. Stephens

See also Ancestor Worship; Appalachian Literature; Family; Folklore.

B. A. Botkin, ed., *A Treasury of Southern Folklore* (1949); Samuel L. Clemens (Mark Twain), *Adventures of Huckleberry Finn* (1885); Robert O. Stephens, *The Family Saga in the South* (1995).

FAMILY REUNION

For most southerners, the phrase "family reunion" conjures the image of a long table covered with checkered cloth and overfilled with treasured southern delicacies such as fried chicken, potato salad, watermelon, and iced tea. They think of a hot Saturday afternoon in July at the family homestead or church, and remember stout aunts in large, flowered dresses fanning themselves with paper plates and second cousins from "up north" or "down the way." For black and white southern families, reunions are a celebration of traditional southern food, a means of passing down family lore and history to younger generations, and a chance simply to talk and make memories together.

The southern family reunion follows a general pattern of ritual in terms of where it is held, when it takes place, who attends, and what happens. Beyond a framework common to most southern reunions, families adapt their own customs and rituals. Not unique to the South, family reunions reflect the unique importance of family, place, and ritual to southerners.

Food is a major part of the ritual of the family reunion, and a long lunch is usually the focal point of an afternoon gathering. Typically, each family brings one dish and the food is served buffet-style on long tables outdoors. Food is bountiful. Corn pudding, ham biscuits, deviled eggs, fried okra, banana pudding, and blackberry pie comprise part of the surfeit of food at the family's table in Doris Betts's novel *Souls Raised from the Dead* (1994). In Alice Walker's *The Color Purple* (1982), the family enjoys lemonade, potato salad, and barbecue. The ritual of preparing, displaying, and then consuming (buffet-style) typical "southern" food is central to the reunion.

Most family reunions are held during the summer, often on the Fourth of July weekend. The Thompson family reunion in *Souls Raised from the Dead* and the reunion of Celie's family in *The Color Purple* are both held on the Fourth of July. Those attending southern family reunions may include the descendants of a given couple, but friends who are considered family sometimes are invited. Some southerners might attend two family reunions in one year. In her *Somerset Homecoming* (1988), Dorothy Spruill Redford recalls that the Cabarruses would have their reunion one weekend and the Baums the next, and that many would attend both reunions because members of both families were related. In *Souls Raised from the Dead*, Frank Thompson and his ex-wife were second cousins. When they married, the two families combined their reunions. When the couple divorced, the reunions continued jointly. In addition, many of the guests at their reunion were friends who were considered family. The important factor in the ritual of southern family reunions is for family to gather together; the issue of who is considered family is left largely to the discretion of the reunion organizers.

Although families may invite nonblood relatives to attend their reunions, the events are almost never biracial. Even though both white and black families have reunions, it is almost unheard-of that they have them together. A remarkable exception to this rule is Redford's autobiographical *Somerset Homecoming*. Redford organizes an all-day family reunion held on the grounds of Somerset Plantation, formerly a 4,000-acre corn and rice plantation south of Edenton, North Carolina, so that descendants of the plantation's slaves could recognize the accomplishments of their ancestors and celebrate their past. Most remarkable about this reunion is that, although Redford organized the event to celebrate the black descendants of the slaves, descendants of the white plantation owners were invited as well. Hundreds attended the event, which was covered by national newspapers and news magazines. The cathartic but joyful day enabled the black and white attendees to, as Redford writes, "put all the negative baggage behind us and move forward in love."

Traditionally, southern family reunions occur annually, biannually, "every once in a while," or on a special occasion, such as an older member of the family's decade birthday. In Eudora Welty's *Losing Battles* (1970), which is set in the 1930s, three generations of Granny Vaughn's descendants gather at her Mississippi home to celebrate her ninetieth birthday. Caroline Gordon, in *None Shall Look Back* (1937), opens her novel with the departure of two sons for the Civil War. The family gathers together before the boys' departure to celebrate the birthday of the family patriarch. In Clyde Edgerton's *The Floatplane Notebooks* (1988), the Copeland family of Listre, North Carolina, comes together annually in May for a grave-cleaning. In another example, Harpo, in *The Color Purple*, says the family gets together annually on the Fourth of July because white families are busy celebrating their own holiday so "us can spend the day celebrating each other."

While the family reunion in southern literature generally is depicted as a celebratory gathering of young and old, the writer can also use the reunion as a theater in which complicated family tensions are acted out. This device is best exemplified in Tennessee Williams's *Cat on a Hot Tin Roof* (1955). In this play, Big Daddy and Brick's father-son animosities are among the many family conflicts played out as the family reunites for Big Daddy's birthday at the family plantation-home in the Mississippi Delta. In Julie Dash's film (and later, novel) *Daughters of the Dust* (1991), the Pezant clan gathers with matriarch Nana on their South Carolina barrier island home for one last reunion, replete with food and stories, before many of the family leave permanently for a northern city. Children of slaves, this family celebrates its strengths and resolves tensions during their gathering.

As "place" holds unique importance to southerners, reunions are most often held at the family homeplace, church, or any location traditionally special to the family. In *Souls Raised from the Dead*, the Thompsons hold their reunion at their family homeplace, bought in the 1700s for fifty shillings by the earliest Thompsons. The Copeland family in *The Floatplane Notebooks* gathers at the family's graveyard that predates the Civil War.

Storytelling and reminiscence are essential components of southern family reunions. The reunion is an occasion for older generations to pass stories and family lore to younger family members. In Welty's *Losing Battles,* stories are told throughout the afternoon. In *Souls Raised from the Dead,* Frank Thompson visits the family graveyard; books on family history are set up on a table near the food. The Copeland family elders in *The Floatplane Notebooks* tell stories about the family's ancestors while the group cleans the graveyard and talks. They work near an enormous, overgrown wisteria vine, planted as a seedling by one of the early Copelands, which symbolizes the sweetness and beauty of the family gathering, as well as the family's interconnectedness and promise of continued proliferation.

Mary Michaels O. Estrada

See also Community; Family.

John Shelton Reed, *One South: An Ethnic Approach to Regional Culture* (1982).

FAULKNER, WILLIAM

We are only beginning to gauge the magnitude of William Faulkner's literary achievement. Faulkner, who won the 1949 Nobel Prize for Literature, produced nineteen novels between 1926 and 1962, and at least six of these—*The Sound and the Fury* (1929), *As I Lay Dying* (1930), *Light in August* (1932), *Absalom, Absalom!* (1936), *The Hamlet* (1940), and *Go Down, Moses* (1942)—are widely regarded as masterpieces of world literature. Incredibly, this writer, who avoided metropolitan literary centers and isolated himself in the small Mississippi town of Oxford, appears to be exerting an influence on world literature and culture comparable only to Shakespeare's. As early as 1975, a survey taken by the Modern Language Association revealed that more criticism had been written about Faulkner than any other modern writer; that the only authors who had received more critical attention than Faulkner were Shakespeare and Chaucer. And since 1975, as any beleaguered Faulkner scholar can attest, Faulkner

scholarship has increased dramatically. According to recent surveys, over five hundred books have been published about him or his work, and over seven hundred doctoral dissertations on him have been completed. Faulkner's novels apparently can be discussed endlessly, perhaps because they answer some unchanging psychological need, perhaps because they reflect what one Faulkner scholar has called "a continuous, turgid thickness of meaning, the significant indefiniteness of life itself." Not only southern or American writers but writers from all over the world have expressed a profound indebtedness to Faulkner. The nature of this indebtedness may have been articulated most clearly by French novelist Claude Simon, who, in a review in *Nouvelles littéraires* (1971), explained that *The Sound and the Fury* "truly revealed to me what writing could be." But if Faulkner's novels teach writers to write, they also teach readers to read. For example, when we read Benjy's interior monologue in *The Sound and the Fury,* we inhabit the consciousness of a helpless, uncomprehending man-child; we have no cultural markers to interpret experience; and we are forced to make sense of a world of pure sensation, of sound and fury.

While it is impossible to identify the source of Faulkner's greatness, we can note at least that Faulkner's novels are subversive in the sense that they ceaselessly question the assumptions on which our cultural meanings rest. His works investigate the way we make our meanings and the way we make ourselves in culture. Arguably, identity is Faulkner's central subject, particularly gender identity and racial identity. With regard to gender, in novel after novel—perhaps most notably in *The Sound and the Fury, Light in August,* and *Absalom, Absalom!*—Faulkner examines the slippage between male and female; that is, he examines the way male inheres within female and female within male. As for race—a subject conspicuously missing from the work of most white American writers—in novels published in 1932 and thereafter, Faulkner explodes racial stereotypes. In *Light in August,* for example, Faulkner creates a character who resists all categorizations, Joe Christmas, who may be white or African American, and thus is neither, something we cannot name. In the work that some call the greatest American novel, *Absalom, Absalom!,* Faulkner turns the narration over to four character-narrators, and his subject becomes their construction of racial meanings—in particular, their erasure of blurred racial distinctions. In discussing race, it perhaps also should be mentioned that, after winning the Nobel Prize, Faulkner, an intensely private man, used his celebrity to speak out against racial injustice in America, and that he used the Nobel Prize award money as the basis for a foundation that he charged with the aims of encouraging writers in Latin America and of awarding university scholarships to African American Mississippians.

Doreen Fowler

See also *Double Dealer, The;* Gothicism; Mississippi, Literature of; Mississippi, University of; New Orleans, Louisiana; Oxford, Mississippi; Short-Story Cycles; Southern Renascence; Virginia, University of.

André Bleikasten, *The Ink of Melancholy: Faulkner's Novels from "The Sound and the Fury" to "Light in August"* (1990); Joseph Blotner, *Faulkner: A Biography* (1984); Doreen Fowler, *Faulkner: The Return of the Repressed* (1997); John T. Irwin, *Doubling and Incest/Repetition and Revenge: A Speculative Reading of Faulkner* (1975); Thomas L. McHaney, "Watching for the Dixie Limited: Faulkner's Impact upon the Creative Writer," in *Fifty Years of Yoknapatawpha,* ed. Doreen Fowler and Ann J. Abadie (1980); Eric J. Sundquist, *Faulkner: The House Divided* (1983); Joel Williamson, *William Faulkner and Southern History* (1993).

FEDERAL WRITERS' PROJECT

A division of the Works Project Administration (WPA), the Federal Writers' Project (FWP) was part of Franklin Roosevelt's New Deal, providing wages and socially beneficial work to thousands of otherwise unemployed writers and researchers across the nation. Although the agency was in existence from 1935 to 1943, its most productive years were from 1935 to 1939, when it was under the leadership of its first director, Henry G. Alston.

Aside from giving relief to victims of the Great Depression, the FWP's primary objective was the publication of the American Guide series of auto-touring guidebooks containing historical, cultural, and geographical items of interest for each state of the union. Almost as an afterthought and at the insistence of Sterling Brown and other African American writers associated with the FWP, its workers undertook from 1936 through 1938 the most ambitious collection and transcription of slave narratives ever, interviewing more than 2,200 former slaves and producing some ten thousand pages of manuscript, which eventually resulted in the publication of the sixteen-volume series, *The American Slave: A Composite Autobiography*

(1972). Although its methods have been criticized—most interviewers were southern whites, many of whom displayed patronizing attitudes toward their subjects that likely encouraged reticence or dissimulation on the part of the former slaves—the FWP documented valuable eyewitness accounts that have been used by later scholars to reconstruct a more complex, balanced understanding of the mechanisms of oppression within the institution of human bondage.

At the urging of W. T. Couch, southern regional director of the FWP as well as head of the progressive University of North Carolina Press, field workers in Tennessee, Georgia, and North Carolina expanded their scope beyond the accounts of former slaves to include the life histories of working-class southerners from all walks of life. A sampling of these narratives was published as *These Are Our Lives* in 1939, and in 1978 the University of North Carolina Press issued a sequel of sorts titled *Such As Us,* which draws from the body of work produced by the FWP.

A number of southern-born authors of note contributed their talents to the FWP. Zora Neale Hurston, one of the few of these to conduct fieldwork in the southern states, collected folklore in African American communities in Florida and contributed to the Florida guidebook as well as to an unpublished manuscript, *The Florida Negro.* In Chicago, Richard Wright composed four of the stories collected in *Uncle Tom's Children* (1938) and began work on his Pulitzer Prize–winning novel, *Native Son* (1940), while on the FWP payroll. Sterling Brown, Arna Bontemps, and Margaret Walker are among other African American natives of the South who worked for the FWP in the Chicago area. Although Eudora Welty had some peripheral association with the FWP in her native state of Missisippi, she was actually employed as a publicist for the WPA; her photographs of Depression-era Mississippi were later published in *One Time, One Place* (1971).

Under attack from congressional opponents of the New Deal, the FWP was accused of boondoggling and, more seriously, labeled as a hotbed of Communist activity. Though some of its employees were found to be or have been members of the Communist Party, investigators found no evidence of widespread "infiltration"; nevertheless, the damage had been done and congressional support for the FWP dwindled after hearings by the House Committee on Un-American Activities in 1938. Shortly thereafter, its funding was severely curtailed, Alston was replaced, and little fieldwork was conducted in the last four years of its existence. The

FWP left as its legacy a rich body of oral history, folk-lore, and social documentary that helped initiate popular interest in Americana and provided scholars with a wealth of information on the cultural history of the South.

James H. Watkins

See also Great Depression; Hurston, Zora Neale; New Deal; Slave Narrative; Wright, Richard.

Richard D. McKinzie, *The New Deal for Artists* (1973); Jerry Mangione, *The Dream and the Deal: The Federal Writers' Project, 1935–1943* (1972); Monty Norm Penkower, *The Federal Writers' Project: A Study in Government Patronage of the Arts* (1977).

FELLOWSHIP OF SOUTHERN WRITERS

In 1987, after discussions with George Core (editor of the *Sewanee Review*) and Louis D. Rubin Jr. (professor of English at the University of North Carolina–Chapel Hill), Cleanth Brooks wrote to eighteen writers calling a meeting on October 30–31 in Chattanooga, Tennessee, to discuss the founding of "a society or fellowship of southern writers." Its purpose would be to encourage excellence and recognize distinction in southern writing.

Though the three leaders knew that Vanderbilt and Chapel Hill might seem the obvious campus homes for such an organization, they had already been impressed by the successful biennial Conference on Southern Literature spearheaded by Chattanooga's Arts and Education Council. A headquarters there could build on an existing conference, associate with an academic institution, but at the same time avoid any implication of favoring academic or coterie writers.

The Arts and Education Council's director, Sally Robinson, obtained an organizational grant from the Lyndhurst Foundation to host the first meeting, which was attended by Brooks, Core, Rubin, Fred Chappell, Shelby Foote, George Garrett, Blyden Jackson, Andrew Lytle, Lewis P. Simpson, Elizabeth Spencer, Walter Sullivan, and C. Vann Woodward. Not present but expressing support were John Hope Franklin, Ernest Gaines, Walker Percy, Peter Taylor, Robert Penn Warren, and Eudora Welty. Brooks was chosen as the Fellowship's first chancellor, George Garrett as vice-chancellor, George Core as secretary-treasurer, and Louis Rubin as chair of the Executive Committee.

Completing the list of founding members were James Dickey, Ralph Ellison, Reynolds Price, and William Styron.

The first biennial awards convocation was held in Chattanooga in April 1989, with medals and prizes presented in fiction, poetry, drama, and nonfiction; eight awards, for example, were presented in 1996. Meanwhile, the conference ran concurrently, with FSW members participating in panels and prize-winners doing outreach presentations in the local schools.

After two terms, Brooks was succeeded by Rubin as chancellor, then by George Garrett—with Elizabeth Spencer as vice chancellor; and Doris Betts was elected chancellor in 1996. Under a membership cap, with membership by invitation only, the Fellowship has added a number of other writers, including A. R. Ammons, James Applewhite, Richard Bausch, Wendell Berry, Ellen Douglas, Clyde Edgerton, Horton Foote, Gail Godwin, William Hoffman, Madison Jones, Donald Justice, Eric Lincoln, Dave Smith, Romulus Linney, Marsha Norman, Mary Lee Settle, Lee Smith, Monroe K. Spears, and Charles Wright. Its archives are housed in the Lupton Library at the University of Tennessee, Chattanooga.

Doris Betts

FEMINISM

Although feminism grew out of the women's movement of the nineteenth century, it is a distinctly twentieth-century creation. Feminism differs from the women's movement in that it moves beyond the political and economic issues at the heart of the women's movement—gaining the vote and political rights for women—to deeper social and personal issues, such as tearing down the hierarchical structure of sex and gender roles and changing the way people view men, women, and gender. It has challenged all people to rethink preconceived notions of a woman's "place" and so includes discussions of sexuality, marriage, and childbirth; in doing so, it asserts that "the personal is the political," for wherever power structures exist, even in personal relationships, politics are involved. The women's movement of the nineteenth and early twentieth centuries is sometimes referred to as the "first wave" of feminism; the "second wave" grew out of the political unrest of the 1960s and the women's liberation movement in particular. It has resulted in the evolution of many branches of feminism, but all come together to uphold the value and the rights of women and to fight gender-based oppression.

A significant outgrowth of the feminist movement, feminist literary criticism has influenced the teaching of literature on practically every college campus in this country. Although it is a political movement at its core, in that it seeks to ensure the status of women writers in the academy, feminist criticism has far-reaching implications for the study of literature. The first organized effort to practice and promote feminist criticism began with the formation in 1970 of the Modern Language Association Commission on the Status of Women. Since then, a number of publications have emerged that focus on women's studies from several disciplinary perspectives, including the *Women's Studies Quarterly, Feminist Studies, Signs,* and *Belles Lettres: A Review of Books by Women.* In an attempt to transform the view of literature as a masculine institution and therefore woman as "other," feminist criticism seeks to uncover texts by women not previously considered part of the canon and to move them from their marginalized position to the center of literary study; at the same time, feminist criticism seeks to interpret or reinterpret the portrayal of women in texts by both men and women and to examine differences in the nature of "voice" in works by men and women.

Defining feminism is particularly complex in relation to the contemporary South. Although some issues are openly questioned by southerners, such as male supremacy, others are more subtly handled, such as the economic disadvantages that women continue to face, societal expectations concerning marriage and primary care of children, and the prevalence of women being defined largely in relation to men and male desires. Yet feminism and feminist literary criticism has made a significant impact on the study of southern literature, which in turn is shaping notions of womanhood in southern culture. Before the rise of feminism in the 1970s, the southern literary canon included few women and scarcely any minorities; since then, the entire study of southern literature has faced radical changes. Until recently, the Southern Renascence has been defined by literary groups such as the Fugitives and the Agrarians, which were almost exclusively male; now, the borders of the Renascence are being seriously reconsidered to take into account the work of Ellen Glasgow, Mary Johnston, and others. Works by southern women writers Kate Chopin, Zora Neale Hurston, and Lillian Smith have all experienced revival since the 1970s, and definitions of southern woman-hood have been radically revised to include the perspectives of African American, Native American, and lesbian writers. Recently, Marilou Awiakta has been recognized for her poetry and prose, which encompasses an ecofeminist perspective within the Cherokee tradition; in a recent review, lesbian writer Dorothy Allison, known best for her novel *Bastard Out of Carolina* (1992), was referred to as a "rebel belle."

Through the lens of feminist criticism, Adrienne Rich's classic essay "Compulsory Heterosexuality and Lesbian Existence" (1980) offers much to an analysis of southern culture, for in the essay Rich claims that in upholding a patriarchal social structure, women have destroyed bonds between themselves. Through acceptance of what she describes as a "lesbian continuum," Rich calls for love and loyalty among all women that is not necessarily connected to sexuality but that seeks to empower and strengthen all women. Recent studies of plantation culture support Rich's notion of how southern white women's loyalty to men hurt other women, in particular Minrose Gwin's *Black and White Women of the Old South: The Peculiar Sisterhood* (1985) and Elizabeth Fox-Genovese's *Within the Plantation Household: Black and White Women of the Old South* (1988). Yet contemporary southern literature is marked by the creation of community among women. In *Meridian* (1976) as well as in many of her essays, Alice Walker promotes women supporting women through a wide range of relationships. Likewise, in an essay from *My Mama's Dead Squirrel: Lesbian Essays on Southern Culture* (1985), Mab Segrest calls for a "women's literature of wholeness" that challenges southern women to work together through literature to combat both sexism and racism. Finally, from the prominence of women writers in southern literature published today and using the perspective of works such as Rosemary Magee's *Friendship and Sympathy: Communities of Southern Women Writers* (1992), it is clear that communities of women writers have added range and vitality to southern literature.

Feminism has left a distinct mark on the study of southern literature by opening up new ways of writing, reading, and interpreting literature. In an article for *Women's Studies Quarterly,* Sara Smith claims that until she understood Eudora Welty as "mainstream," she had no idea how incomplete her picture of southern womanhood, gained almost entirely through Faulkner, had been. Feminism is a dynamic force in the South today because it not only offers new perspectives on literature but also hope for social and cultural change.

Carolyn Perry

See also Belle; Lady; Women's Movement; Women's Studies; Women Writers, World War II to Present.

Nancy Cott, *The Grounding of Modern Feminism* (1987); bell hooks, *Feminist Theory: From Margin to Center* (1984); Kate Millett, *Sexual Politics* (1970); Sara W. Smith, "Rethinking the 'Southern Lady,' " *Women's Studies Quarterly* (Fall 1996); Donna C. Stanton and Abigail J. Stewart, eds., *Feminisms in the Academy* (1995).

FIDDLERS' CONVENTIONS

In 1925 the community of Mountain City in East Tennessee held a large fiddlers' convention, a gathering of rural and small-town instrumentalists featuring but not limited to the country fiddle—i.e., the violin played country-style, with an edge of attack and lustiness of execution easily distinguishable from the classical violin. Such string-band convocations and their attendant contests went on regularly all over the South for most of the twentieth century. Many of these musical meetings were known as fiddlers' conventions and, by midcentury, as "old-time" fiddlers' conventions—the widespread popularity of bluegrass music (with its smooth, long-bow fiddle style and the three-finger Scruggs-style crawl of the accompanying banjo) having prompted use of the modifier "old-time" to signify both a playing style and a repertoire that predated and, to the initiated, stood well apart from bluegrass music.

In addition to Mountain City, Tennessee, other well-known fiddlers' conventions have been held at such spots as Galax, Virginia; Mount Airy, North Carolina; West Jefferson in Ashe County, North Carolina; Star, North Carolina; and Hillsville in Carroll County, Virginia. Legendary old-time fiddlers such as West Virginia's Clark Kessinger and North Carolina's Tommy Jarrell frequented these events, but younger players did, too, and not infrequently came out well—Red Clay Rambler fiddler Clay Buckner, for example, won at both Star and Hillsville.

Even in so-called folk festivals—events that, though similar, were not specifically dedicated to fiddle music—the presentation of accomplished fiddlers and contests between them have still been important elements. In the six-year period between 1928 and 1934, four large

festivals celebrating traditional music were begun, including banjoist Bascom Lamar Lunsford's Mountain Dance and Folk Festival in Asheville, North Carolina (started in 1928) and the Interstate Musical Festival, popularly called the White Top Festival because it was staged on White Top Mountain in southwestern Virginia (1931 to 1939), featuring fiddle, banjo, and group instrumental contests. When Eleanor Roosevelt came to White Top in 1933, a crowd of twenty thousand came to see the shows and the First Lady as well.

The fiddlers' convention at Union Grove, North Carolina—like the one at Galax, Virginia, quite popular, well thought of and well attended—grew from being a community event held at a school in the 1960s, with visitors and participants numbering several thousand, into a post-Woodstock tourist destination that in the early 1970s drew an estimated 100,000 people to its relocated venue, the VanHoy farm in Union County. So overpowering was this Easter Weekend population explosion to many of the older traditional musicians that an offshoot convention—called Fiddlers' Grove—formed to accommodate those who had gotten Union Grove going to begin with.

As important as the all-day, all-evening onstage presentations at such conventions have always been the on-the-margins, tailgate, and fireside pickup sessions that typically occur before, during, and after the formal shows of the day. Fiddlers, banjoists, dobroists, mandolinists, and guitarists wander the festival grounds, going from group to group, joining in, playing a few numbers, then moving on. Many encounters, though, are even more personal, as exemplified by the Galax parking-lot meeting of the late North Carolina Folk Heritage Award-winner Tommy Jarrell, of Toast, North Carolina, and the energetic, bow-twirling fiddler A. C. Bushnell of Chapel Hill. It was about midnight, but Jarrell, who was leaving the festival grounds, gladly stopped and honored the younger man's request, got out his fiddle, and played and sang for Bushnell "When Sorrows Encompass Me Round."

Since the 1970s, the steadily increasing popularity of southern string-band music—indeed, of acoustic "roots" music of all sorts—has sent the old-time repertoire, the meat of the fiddlers' conventions, out of the region and into the larger world of American folk music. One commonly hears strains of Union Grove and Galax at such nonsouthern venues as the Wheatlands Festival in Remus, Michigan, and the Champlain Valley Festival around Burlington, Vermont, and a favorite of string-band musicians in the late 1990s could hardly have been farther west—the Festival of American Fiddle Tunes held in Port Townsend, Washington, on Puget Sound.

Bland Simpson

See also Country Music.

Les Blanc, Cece Conway, and Alice Gerrard, *Sprout Wings and Fly,* a film about Tommy Jarrell (1983); David Whisnant, *All That Is Native & Fine: The Politics of Culture in an American Region* (1983); Charles K. Wolfe, *The Devil's Box: Masters of Southern Fiddling* (1997).

FIGHT, THE

The prevalence of fistfights in southern literature reflects the violence of southern culture, which has been variously attributed to the effects of temperature, poverty, and slavery. The eagerness of southerners to fight has also been traced to the centrality of herding as an early southern occupation. Farmers can feel confident that their farmland will not disappear while their backs are turned; herders, on the other hand, can never be sure that their cattle are safe. A herder, therefore, must not show any sign of weakness that might tempt another to snatch away his livelihood. Thus herders are quick to respond when their honor is challenged, and they benefit from having reputations as fighters who will do anything necessary to protect what is theirs. In addition, herding requires less work than farming. While a farmer labors in his fields, a herder may let his cattle roam and bide his time, perhaps by fighting just for the sake of fighting.

The style of fighting described in much early southern literature is so violent that readers may doubt its realism. There is ample evidence, however, that historical "rough-and-tumble" fights were brutal indeed. In the eighteenth century, for example, at least two colonies and one state passed laws in efforts to temper these fights. In 1746, it became a felony in North Carolina to cut out another man's tongue or to gouge out one of his eyes. When this proved insufficient, the colony also passed legislation that protected noses. Virginia's anti-fighting law, originally passed in 1748, proved inadequate as well, because it had to be revised in 1772 to include gouging out eyes and "stomping" on people. In 1786, South Carolina made it a capital crime to gouge out an eye or bite off a finger. Naturally, such brutality is reflected in the era's travel literature. While some

travelers reported witnessing rough-and-tumble fights, others reported meeting veteran fighters. An Englishman passing through Virginia escaped from a "cyclops" whose empty eye socket offered silent testimony to his fighting experience, and a Presbyterian missionary en route to Louisiana encountered numerous one-eyed men.

Augustus Baldwin Longstreet's "The Fight" (1833) may be the archetypal literary treatment of rough-and-tumble fighting. The story, which Longstreet set in the "younger days of the Republic," centers on the strong Billy Stallings and the quick Bob Durham. Stallings and Durham are acknowledged the "*best men*"—that is to say, the best *fighters*—in their county, but they have never fought each other. Thus the top of the county's social hierarchy remains unsettled. Enter Ransy Sniffle, whose life centers on fomenting, watching, and talking about fights. Ransy, of course, wants nothing more than to see the men fight, and he tries to convince each that the other has insulted his honor. Neither, however, feels threatened by the meddling of a ninety-five-pound clay-eater. But when most everyone in the county gathers for a regimental parade, Mrs. Stallings and Mrs. Durham, who know neither each other nor each other's husbands, argue and trade insults. Billy, finding his honor seriously threatened, insults Mrs. Durham as well and tells her that he will whip her husband, whoever he might be. Ransy Sniffle cannot believe his luck. He races to Bob with the good news. When Bob confronts Billy, the men have no choice but to fight.

Billy and Bob agree to a "fair fight" that is "rough and tumble." According to the research of Elliott J. Gorn, however, these terms are contradictory. "Fair fights" followed "Broughton's Rules," which dictated that fighting stopped whenever either fighter fell. In rough-and-tumble fighting, as the name suggests, most of the battle took place while combatants were on the ground. This manner of fighting had but one or two rules. Eye-gouging and scrotum-ripping were allowed, but weapons were not. In Longstreet's story, "fair fight" may emphasize another rule as well: no man is allowed to interfere with the fighters until one of them quits.

Billy's and Bob's friends form a human ring for the contest. In the course of the fight, Bob loses an ear, a finger, and a chunk from one cheek. Billy loses part of his nose, and his face becomes so swollen and bruised that he no longer looks human. Billy ends the fight when he is helpless to stop Bob from grinding sand and dirt into his eyes. Both men require weeks in bed to recover. When next they meet, Billy acknowledges that he lost a "fair fight," but he will not admit that Bob is the better fighter. His loss, Billy explains, was a matter of honor: knowing that he should never have insulted Bob's wife, he felt "cowed" while in the ring and could not fight his best.

Longstreet and later writers of the Old Southwest wrote of an era when rough-and-tumble fights occurred among only lower-class men. This, however, had not always been the case. In the early eighteenth century, both the lower and upper classes engaged in brutal fighting. As the century progressed, however, gentlemen increasingly tried to distance themselves from crackers, and among the upper classes rough-and-tumble fighting gave way to dueling. Over the course of the nineteenth century, the violence of rough-and-tumble fighting became less common among the lower classes as well, but the importance of fighting faded hardly at all, even in the twentieth century.

Perhaps no author better illustrates the importance of fighting to twentieth-century southern culture than William Faulkner. In "Faulkner's Fist-Fights," Calvin S. Brown identifies five "major" fights that are crucial to understanding Faulkner's protagonists: Quentin Compson's fights with Dalton Ames and Gerald Bland in *The Sound and the Fury* (1929); Byron Bunch's fight with Lucas Burch in *Light in August* (1932); and Gavin Stevens's fights with Manfred de Spain and Matt Levitt in *The Town* (1957). In four of these five fights, Brown notes, Faulkner's protagonist is the aggressor, and in each case he knows that he will probably lose. Compson attacks Ames, who has a gun, and Bland, who has been learning to box. Bunch challenges the bigger, stronger Burch to fight, just as Stevens challenges the formidable de Spain. Brown finds this pattern repeated in "minor" fights as well: the boy in "Barn Burning" (1939), for example, attacks a much bigger boy. In all of these fights, honor is at stake. These characters will not see women insulted, nor will they tolerate insult to themselves. Compson defends his sister; Bunch defends Lena Grove; Stevens defends Eula Snopes; the boy reacts when called a "barn burner." In every fight, the aggressor gets whipped, yet in every fight the aggressor claims a moral victory. Here, winning the fight is less important than the willingness to fight in the first place. Honor survives if someone will fight for it, no matter the result.

In much southern literature, fighting is the domain not just of lower-class men but of lower-class *white* men. Just as eighteenth-century gentlemen used dueling

to distinguish themselves from crackers, crackers used fighting to distance themselves from slaves. Given that slaves were obsequious and thus had no honor, the greater a cracker's sense of honor and the greater his skill as a fighter, the higher he rose above them. If a black man ever fought a white man on equal terms, this would jumble the social hierarchy—which is exactly what happens when Frederick Douglass fights slave-breaker Edward Covey in *Narrative of the Life of an American Slave* (1845). Douglass writes that over the course of their long brawl, he became a man. But then there is a famous fictional fight that pits young black males against one another with no hope for social advancement. In Ralph Ellison's "Battle Royal" (1947), the ten blindfolded combatants merely entertain the white male audience; in return, they get five dollars apiece, ten for the "winner."

Given that fighting is primarily a male sport, it is primarily the domain of male writers as well. This is not to say, however, that fighting never figures in the writings of southern women. When the combatants are men, these fights operate much as they do in Longstreet and Faulkner. In Kate Chopin's "A Night in Acadie" (1896), for example, Telèsphore Baquette fights André Pascal to defend the honor of Zaïda Trodon. To ensure "fair play," Zaïda removes André's pistol from the scene; otherwise, the woman watches passively as the men fight. But in Carson McCullers's *The Ballad of the Sad Café* (1943), Miss Amelia Evans is anything but passive. Amelia survives an abusive ten-day marriage to Marvin Macy—in which she is the abuser. After a stretch in the penitentiary, Marvin returns and Amelia must deal with him again. Amelia appears to win their hand-to-hand, weapon-free combat, but at the last moment, hunchback Cousin Lymon Willis—who is loved by Amelia but who worships Marvin, and who foments fights in somewhat the same vein as Ransy Sniffle—interferes. Of course, the physically powerful Amelia is not the southern literary norm. More common are characters such as Celie in Alice Walker's *The Color Purple* (1982) and Bone in Dorothy Allison's *Bastard Out of Carolina* (1992), who receive blows rather than trade them.

The modern South continues to be more violent than the North. In his essay "In the Face" (1996), Richard Ford describes his many fights while growing up in Mississippi in the 1950s. Ford's grandfather was largely responsible for teaching him the importance of fighting. A recent study indicates that southern boys are continuing to learn this lesson. In *Culture of*

Honor: The Psychology of Violence in the South (1996), psychologists Richard E. Nisbett and Dov Cohen argue that today's southern men are still more likely than northerners to feel insult and thus are still more likely to fight. One possible weakness of Nisbett and Cohen's experiments is that their subjects were all students at the University of Michigan—hardly the place to round up a representative cross-section of southern men. That said, it seems fairly certain that fighters will continue to populate the southern literary landscape.

David Rachels

See also Family Feuding; Honor; Violence.

Calvin S. Brown, "Faulkner's Fist-Fights," *Materials, Studies, and Criticism* (Japan) (1979); Elliott J. Gorn, "'Gouge and Bite, Pull Hair and Scratch': The Social Significance of Fighting in the Southern Backcountry," *American Historical Review* (1985); Richard E. Nisbett and Dov Cohen, *Culture of Honor: The Psychology of Violence in the South* (1996).

FILM

American movies often allude to the South. War films, disaster movies, and other genres with cross sections of American culture usually include southerners whose origins and even names (Bubba, Norma Rae) may imply certain traits. Allusions to the South may be subtler: in John Ford's *Stagecoach* (1939), an itinerant gambler recognizes "a lady" and boards the stage to give her his "protection." When he mentions "the war for southern independence" (the drunken doctor calls it "the war of the southern rebellion"), his chivalry begins to make sense. It costs him his life, and his last words reveal him as the son of a judge in the Old South.

Some genres and subgenres aim at audiences inherently interested in bootlegging, stock-car racing, racism, chain gangs, revivalism, violence, rednecks, hillbillies, and other subjects stereotypically "southern." All works of art and entertainment, of course, must emerge against a background of stereotypes and audience expectations. The present overview of nine decades of movies will be limited to the "best" (according to film historians, critics, and reviewers) American feature films *set in* the South, whatever their subject matter.

The earliest American movies shared the racism of popular minstrel shows, fiction, and music. In the silent era, at least ten *Uncle Tom's Cabin*s either cut out the novel's cruelties or reduced them to mere aberrations from the supposedly happy norms of plantation life. D. W. Griffith's *The Birth of a Nation* (1915), the first and most influential American epic film, led the way for later movies and a huge industry that would not only reflect, but shape, American ideology. Silent, but with orchestral accompaniment, it dramatizes the "Southland" in the Civil War era. Less crudely than its source, Thomas Dixon's *The Clansman*, it exalts the Ku Klux Klan for fighting interracial marriage and restoring order. Its operatic style has power, even grandeur. James Agee called its images "as impossible to forget . . . as some of the grandest and simplest passages in music or poetry." Seldom seen now at the original speed (16 frames per second rather than today's 24), some scenes (the final attack, Lee's surrender, Lincoln's assassination) still have power even with the wrong speed and added sound. At the end, a double wedding reunites South and North. The newlyweds imagine an idyllic future: "Bestial War" gives way to the "Prince of Peace," and the couples' musical motifs blend into "The Star Spangled Banner."

The first audiences rose, cheering. President Wilson called it "like writing history with lightning. . . . My only regret is that it is all so terribly true." But there were also protests, demonstrations, and lawsuits. Born in Kentucky, Griffith absorbed the views of his father, a Confederate officer, and was surprised to be attacked for showing what he regarded as self-evident: childlike blacks and lustful mulattos. Provocative but profitable, the film played in the largest theaters at two dollars (not the usual fifteen cents), and its visual power masked its racism. So the 1920s saw the South, apart from glimpses of Twain's Tom Sawyer and Huck Finn, mostly in happy plantation scenes. The era's best movie, Keaton's *The General*, avoids race and turns the Civil War into slapstick. But an early talkie with an all-black cast, Vidor's *Hallelujah* (1929), shows African American life, music, and religion much more fully.

In the 1930s, soundtracks, movie palaces, the Depression, the exodus from farms—all drew people to movies. To entertain them, Hollywood looked "down South," where the population was shrinking, scattered, and poor. In the studios, black actors found stereotypical roles in comedies and musicals. Among the best films of 1935 were *The Little Colonel, The Littlest Rebel, Mississippi,* and *Steamboat 'Round the Bend*; in the first two, little Shirley Temple dances with "Bojangles" Robinson; in the last, folksy philosopher Will Rogers and masterfully subservient Stepin Fetchit provide entertaining stereotypes. But such films can also rise above formulas. *Steamboat* was made by John Ford, as were *Judge Priest* and *The Prisoner of Shark Island* (about Dr. Mudd, who treated Lincoln's assassin). With an all-black cast, *The Green Pastures* filmed Marc Connelly's drama of life in heaven. Mervyn LeRoy's *I Am a Fugitive from a Chain Gang* and his *They Won't Forget* exploited new interests in crime and southern justice. Anticipating the upcoming epic *Gone With the Wind* (1939, honored with a separate entry here), *Jezebel* introduced the archetypal southern belle.

In 1941 films of the play *The Little Foxes* and the story of Sergeant York appeared. In World War II, Hollywood aimed to inspire audiences. *The Southerner,* about a farm family, does that effectively. After the war, *The Song of the South* (Disney's animation of Uncle Remus) and *The Yearling* won critical praise. But in the later 1940s the best movies turned darker: films of Robert Penn Warren's *All the King's Men* and William Faulkner's *Intruder in the Dust,* as well as Elia Kazan's *Pinky,* where a black girl passes for white, revealed political and racial ambiguities. In the *noir* classic *They Live by Night* and in *Panic in the Streets,* poor whites drift into crime.

In the 1950s, the locks of the studios on their theater chains were broken by the Supreme Court and competition from an addictive new medium forced movies into areas too difficult for television. This led to the best adaptation of Tennessee Williams, *A Streetcar Named Desire* (with Vivien Leigh and Marlon Brando), and to other good ones: *The Glass Menagerie, The Rose Tattoo, Baby Doll, Cat on a Hot Tin Roof,* and *Suddenly Last Summer.* There were also good adaptations of Carson McCullers's *The Member of the Wedding* and Ross Lockridge's *Raintree County*; and, based on works by Faulkner, *The Long Hot Summer* and *The Tarnished Angels.* These films portrayed the South more from the inside, through the views of southern authors. But fine original scripts were also filmed: *A Face in the Crowd,* turning a nobody into a TV star; *The Three Faces of Eve,* revealing a character with multiple personalities; *The Defiant Ones,* forcing integration of two escaping convicts. *The Red Badge of Courage* complicated earlier views of the Civil War. Southernness is more important in some of these than in others, but all have more psychological depth and subtlety than earlier movies with southern settings.

In the 1960s, censorship dissolved throughout the arts, and so did the movies' Production Code. The gates opened for charismatic preaching in *Elmer Gantry* and for defending a black man in a white town in *To Kill a Mockingbird*; for plays on the "monkey trial" (*Inherit the Wind*), Helen Keller (*The Miracle Worker*), and James Agee's *A Death in the Family* (*All the Way Home*); more Williams (*Summer and Smoke, Sweet Bird of Youth*) and Faulkner (*The Reivers*). *Wild River* portrayed Tennessee in the 1930s, and *The Hustler* looked into dark pool halls. Two good films about black life were underattended: *Nothing But a Man,* on tensions within black subcultures, and *Once Upon a Time . . . When We Were Colored,* on coming of age in Mississippi after World War II.

In the mid-1960s, under European influences (neorealism, existentialism, and the *auteur* idea), more taboos fell and viewers learned to like movies that reward thought, analysis, and a sense of irony. American troubles found expression, too. In *Bonnie and Clyde,* the beautiful young lovers meet death in Louisiana, ambushed by "laws"; the back of Clyde's skull explodes (alluding to Zapruder's film of the Kennedy assassination). *Easy Rider* ends with rednecks killing the bikers whose pilgrimage led (like many dark quests) to New Orleans. Seeing violence at home and atrocities in Vietnam, movies in the late 1960s mock "justice" in such anti-establishment films as *Cool Hand Luke* and *In the Heat of the Night.*

In the 1970s, the range of subjects continued to grow. Male Atlantans seeking bonding in the wilderness find more than they wished for in *Deliverance. Payday* sees the darkness of country music. Robert Altman's *Nashville* goes to its Parthenon for a view of the ruins: not just music but politics, sex, and show business degenerating. His *Thieves Like Us* retells a tale (first filmed as *They Live By Night*) of the Depression: young lovers caught in poverty and addictions to Coca Cola, cigarettes, radio, and crime. But *Sounder* and its sequel tell a more inspiring saga about black sharecroppers, and the TV movie *The Autobiography of Miss Jane Pittman* takes an indomitable woman from the Civil War to civil rights. The TV series *Roots* (1977 and 1979) proved that large white audiences could be moved by black experience. *Leadbelly* warmly affirms that folk singer's life. *Pretty Baby* portrays a child prostitute and her mother in 1917; the film's beauty makes it all the more disturbing. The adaptations of *Gal Young 'Un* and *Wise Blood* are also beautiful and disturbing. Two other powerful movies show slightly fictionalized versions of real lives: a Marine aviator in

The Great Santini and a reluctantly militant textile worker in *Norma Rae.*

In the 1980s, this genre included *Coal Miner's Daughter* and *Cross Creek.* Nostalgia for the idealistic 1960s haunts the TV movie *Crisis at Central High* (in Little Rock) and *The Big Chill.* The New Orleans remake of *Cat People* may be nostalgic, too—compared to the more confined horror of 1942, it now seemed either excessively sick or too symbolic of the heart of the Reagan era. That could also be said of *Swamp Thing,* its sequels, and their locale. In *Southern Comfort,* National Guardsmen, after dodging Vietnam, find defeat in the Louisiana swamps. Hollywood's interest in African Americans produced more feature films. In *The Color Purple,* Steven Spielberg softens the book's view of black males and adds to the gallery of admirable women. *A Soldier's Story* shows a courageous black officer investigating a murder in an army camp in World War II.

The South darkened in the later 1980s. The TV docudrama *The Atlanta Child Murders* exposes secrets in the New South's largest city. *Blue Velvet* finds horrors beneath the lawns of Lumberton, North Carolina. *Crimes of the Heart* explores the inner realities of three respectable sisters. *Crossroads* sends an old man and a boy southward toward a spiritual—or satanic—rendezvous. *Down By Law* tours the South through the eyes of the independent, idiosyncratic director Jim Jarmusch. With similar material, *Hard Choices* achieves more depth. *The Big Easy* basks in the corrupt ambiance of New Orleans. Andrei Konchalovsky's *Shy People* takes an artful foreign view of the mysteries of the bayous and women, and Percy Adlon satirizes southern culture in *Rosalie Goes Shopping.* But the most fascinating descent into darkness came in Steven Soderbergh's first film, *sex, lies, and videotape.*

Other movies showed southern life in a more positive light. *Bull Durham* elegizes the beauty of baseball. *School Daze* turns conflict in an all-black college into comedy. In *Blaze,* Louisiana governor Earl Long's connection with a stripper becomes a warm affirmation of their humanity. *Polly,* an all-black TV musical, restages Disney's *Pollyanna* (1960). *Miss Firecracker* makes a beauty pageant interesting. A deepening interracial friendship fuels *Driving Miss Daisy.* And *Steel Magnolias* aims for the ultimate tribute to southern women.

In the 1990s, film technology (particularly special effects) and commercialism grew explosively, but serious examinations of the South continued. *Gettysburg* recreates in detail the decisions and the battle that doomed the Confederacy. Other films looked back at racial and civil-rights violence: *The Long Walk Home,* on the roles of a housewife and her maid during the bus boycott; *Murder in Mississippi,* on the 1964 murder of three civil-rights workers; *Mississippi Burning,* a looser, even distorted, dramatization of that investigation; *Paris Trout,* on a racist who kills a black girl; *The Vernon Johns Story,* the TV movie on the pastor who gave Martin Luther King his start; *Ghosts of Mississippi,* on the reopening of the Medgar Evers murder case. *Mississippi Masala* tells an unusual interracial love story about a young black man and a young woman from India via Uganda. And *Daughters of the Dust* is a beautiful elegy for the Gullahs of Georgia's Sea Islands.

Several movies find inspiration in the lives of disadvantaged whites. *Rambling Rose* shows a family, especially a teenaged boy, responding to a new, beautiful, dim girl who enjoys sex; *Passion Fish* sees a paraplegic actress, helped by a nurse from Chicago, fighting toward peace in the bayous; *Forrest Gump* guides a tour of simple truths in recent American history; *Sling Blade* cuts to the heart of familial love; so does *Ulee's Gold,* about multiple redemptions in the Florida Panhandle. Redemption also haunts *Dead Man Walking,* in Sister Helen Prejean's caring for a man on death row, and *The Apostle,* a searching look at a pentecostal preacher and the paradoxes of his narrow dogma and astonishing compassion.

Secular quests for salvation, always prominent in southern literature, continue in recent movies. *Fried Green Tomatoes* seeks shelter for its battered women in feminism; *The Prince of Tides* for its impotent male in psychiatric and sexual insights; and *Ruby in Paradise* for its young Tennessean in finding her own authenticity in the strange new environment of Panama City. Political quests end less convincingly. Oliver Stone's *JFK* twists the meanings of the Kennedy assassination to fit New Orleans district attorney Jim Garrison's obsessions and Stone's own, and *Storyville* gets lost in its own delicious darkness. Cities have become favorite southern settings: New Orleans, Charleston, Savannah. Clint Eastwood's *Midnight in the Garden of Good and Evil* sees Savannah through the eyes of a tourist (unfortunately straighter than those of the book). Deeper, darker visual truths in Savannah are sought in Altman's *The Gingerbread Man.*

New technology and lower costs have drawn more films to such locations, where even now the South still appears as Other, in some ways foreign to the realities, values, and experiences of mainstream audiences. But Hollywood has always shown human experience magnified and essentialized. Its South has always been a mindscape, more proud, courageous, religious, angry, bigoted, violent, sensual, suspicious, unpredictable, and interesting than the minds of its audience. From the first century of the cinematic South, countless icons have emerged: Ben Cameron and his Yankee bride, Scarlett, Rhett, and Melanie, Alvin York, Atticus Finch, Miss Jane Pittman, Miss Daisy and Hoke Colburn, Sister Helen, and many others—each facing heightened forms of the audiences' own troubles. As Old Souths dissolve into the mainstream, that Other South will live on in filmic Savannahs, Storyvilles, towns, farms—but ultimately, in the imaginations of filmmakers and audiences, where everyone will always need the Other.

Howard Harper

See also *Birth of a Nation, The*; *Gone With the Wind*.

Edward D. C. Campbell, *The Celluloid South* (1981).

FISHING

Because of its extensive Atlantic coastline and an interior terrain varying from swamp and bayou to the highest mountain east of the Rockies, the South possesses an immense range of sport and recreational fishing and associated culture.

As in most other parts of the country, common angling—the seeking of bream, crappies, perch, and catfish with both natural baits and artificial lures—remains popular with a very large cross section of the populace, and the good-weather days of spring, summer, and fall draw anglers of every age and status to farm ponds, streams, and municipal reservoirs. In the coastal regions, the bridges and creek banks take on seekers of the anadromous species as well, fishes such as shad, herring, and striped bass on their annual runs upriver to spawn; and on the ocean piers, the big runs of spot, whiting, Spanish mackerel, bluefish, sea trout, spadefish and the like, along with the rarer pompano and sheepshead, keep anglers' enthusiasm alive. In the sounds and in the salt and brackish bays, flounder, croakers, and white perch alternate with freshwater species according to season and tide. Many of these set-

tings contain the majestic tarpon that Charles Gaines depicts in the novel *Stay Hungry* (1978).

Offshore anglers, both on private craft and charter boats, troll for the big billfish (blue marlin, white marlin, sailfish), king mackerel, tuna, albacore, and bonita, and over the many reefs and shipwrecks bottom-fishermen catch such varieties as black sea bass and the numerous members of the snapper and grouper clans.

In the high-elevation streams of the Appalachians and Ozarks, native brook trout share waters with transplanted brown and rainbow trout, regularly stocked in many areas from the hatcheries of the several states. Trout fishermen include both flyrod anglers with their extensive and often expensive gear (some streams are designated for flyfishing only) and the less-fussy users of spinning tackle with baits ranging from flashy metal blades to live grasshoppers and kernels of canned yellow corn.

Methods and opinions vary somewhat within these kinds of angling from region to region, as do the ways of cooking their results; but a trout fisherman from Montana or a mar enthusiast from the California coast rarely feels any significant cultural jolt when he or she pursues the chosen sport in southern waters. Ernest Hemingway has written at least as feelingly and proficiently about both trout streams and saltwater big game as any southern writer, and his fishing tales are read as widely throughout the South as anywhere else. When it comes to a distinctively southern angling style and sporting culture, however, it is the pursuit of the largemouth bass that comes immediately and most vividly to mind.

Bass fishing, in the contemporary southern style, has little to do with relaxation and everything to do with technology. In its tournament form, it bears to common angling the same relationship that stock-car racing bears to motoring around the countryside, or that military invasion bears to foreign travel. Having now spread—mainly through the promotion of B.A.S.S. (Bass Anglers Sportsman Society)—to enclaves in most parts of the nation, southern bass fishing is to many an object of envy and to many others an object of satire—the latter most successfully wrought in Florida author Carl Hiaasen's bass-fishing mystery novel, *Double Whammy* (1987).

What generates envy among anglers from colder climes is the size, power, willingness to strike artificial bait, and relatively wide availability of the largemouth bass in the South. Though found over much of the nation, the species achieves its greatest natural growth in the Deep South, especially Florida. Back in 1932, George Perry, a teenager fishing at Montgomery Lake in South Georgia with a wood-and-metal lure called a Creek Chub Wiggle-fish, caught what has remained the world's record largemouth at twenty-two pounds, four ounces; and that record has been the target of southern bass fishing ever since. Though Florida bass transplanted to California reservoirs have achieved great size, no one has come within two pounds of Perry's prize. An enormously prosperous financial empire has been built on its pursuit.

Not all bass fishermen enter tournaments, of course; but a great many noncontestants follow the careers of the professionals with the same avidity as other sports fans. Like golfers and tennis players, the bass pros are rated by cumulative season's winnings, and many of the amounts are in six figures, not to mention promotional fees and free equipment from the manufacturers. Like rodeos, auto races, and football games, the events appeal through noise, spectacle, suspense, and ceremony, the latter being concentrated on two phases of pageantry, the blast-off and the weigh-in.

At blast-off time in the predawn mist, as many as forty or so boats sit poised for take-off while a minister blesses the fleet and prays for a safe, fair contest. Then a starter calls out for engines to be cranked, and in the steady rumble of the big outboards a pistol cracks to signal what Hiaasen describes in *Double Whammy* as a moment "almost military in its high-tech absurdity: forty boats rocketing the same direction at sixty miles per hour. In darkness."

At day's end, as the boats return and the fans regather, each angler's catch is quickly weighed and then liberated back into the lake or into a holding tank for later release. Winning ranks are determined by total pounds of fish within the current legal limit, with a special "lunker prize" for the biggest fish. As a judging crew weighs each limit, anticipation grows with the cheers and sighs until the proud winner gets the big trophy, the big check, and the big kiss.

Jerry Leath Mills

Jim Dean et al., *Wildlife in North Carolina* (1987); William Elliott, *Carolina Sports by Land and Water* (1846); Jim Gasque, *Hunting and Fishing in the Great Smokies* (1946); Grits Gresham, *Bass Fishing* (1971); Larry Koller, *The Treasury of Angling* (1963); Buck Paysour, *Bass Fishing in North Carolina* (1977); Louis D. Rubin Jr., *The Even-Tempered Angler* (1983).

FLORIDA, LITERATURE OF

In *Up for Grabs: A Trip Through Time and Space in the Sunshine State* (1985), John Rothchild concludes that there are significant writers in Florida but questions whether they are Florida writers: "Marjorie Kinnan Rawlings had her palmetto scrub culture; Hemingway had his Key West bar; Frank Conroy had his yoyo; Tennessee Williams did lesser work here . . . Harry Crews is in Gainesville putting snakes in discarded Deep South washing machines. . . . Certainly, there is no Yoknapatawpha County under here, dig two feet and you hit water." In his article "Florida's Fudged Identity," Stephen Whitfield also argues that Florida has lacked writers of the magnitude of Jack London or John Steinbeck, who depicted the imaginative allure of California.

Rothchild raises an interesting question—one that invites another. Is there a literature written by Floridians or is the more compelling topic that of the literature *about* Florida, whether written by Floridians or others? Certainly Florida has inspired a good deal of writing, and many have described the place in similar terms to Mark Derr, who in *Some Kind of Paradise: A Chronicle of Man and Land in Florida* (1989) asserts that this state "is as much a state of mind as of being," a place "where fantasies come true, although the nature of the dreams, like the land itself, has changed with shifting social fashions."

Florida's place in the literary imagination can best be understood by viewing its historical past. Its recorded history by European explorers is generally traced to the landing of Ponce de Leon on the coast of Florida in 1513. In "Ponce de Leon's Fountain of Youth: History of a Geographical Myth," one early historian of Florida, Leonardo Olschki, notes that the Spanish explorer and others were certain that this land was part of territory "spread out before that part of fabulous Asia which was principally known as a land of wonder and marvels," including the Fountain of Youth. The fact that Florida failed to yield up the gold, silver, and fountain of eternal youth did not seem to deter the many who would follow. Historian J. E. Dovell has remarked about the persistence with which the Spanish held on to what they thought was a land of promise: "That Spain held Florida for two centuries, despite enemy attacks, with but a few hundred men in the first century, and a few thousand men in the second century is evidence of strength of purpose, if little else."

In the eighteenth century, the lure of Florida was

still clearly evident. One of the best-known and most articulate writers about Florida was William Bartram, whose *Travels, an Account of His Expeditions to Florida in 1773* shows the strong imaginative allure of Florida. Bartram visited Florida to observe and to gather specimens of its many varieties of plants. Commenting on its paradisial aspects, Bartram called it a "blessed unviolated spot of earth" and a "blissful garden."

Nineteenth-century writing about Florida continued to respond to its imaginative pull. Although the reasons for writing about Florida are many, they have in common the premise that Florida promises escape from ordinary, everyday life, the chance for wealth, and if not the fountain of youth, at least increased health and vigor. One of the most unlikely recorders of the imaginative appeal of Florida was Ralph Waldo Emerson who, arriving in St. Augustine in the winter of 1827 in hopes of recovering from a severe lung ailment, recoiled from the sloth and indolence he saw there. In *Emerson, The Wisest American* (1929), Phillips Russell describes Emerson's response as he delighted in the temperate climate: "his New England soul, nourished firmly on the belief in Purpose and the preciousness of Time, contracted like the sepals of a Calvinistic anemone at the sight of Southern laziness and slackness, accompanied by not a little dinginess and dirt." Although Emerson later lauded the restorative powers of the Florida climate and even wrote a poem praising Florida, his initial response is typical of a kind of love-hate relationship that a number of writers would have with Florida as they admired its climate but were wary of its beckoning toward indolence.

A few years later, Sidney Lanier, hired by the Great Atlantic Coastline Railroad Company to write a guidebook based on his tour of the state, also noted the restorative powers of the climate. In *Florida: Its Scenery, Climate, and History* (1875), he asserted that consumptives quickly underwent full recoveries, turning from "cadaverous persons" to "successful huntsman and fishermen, of ruddy face and portentous appetite." Similar to Bartram's descriptions are Lanier's accounts of the Oklawaha River, which he called "the sweetest water-lane in the world." Of the climate, Lanier concluded that it was "just cool enough to save a man from degenerating into a luxurious vegetable of laziness, and just warm enough to be nerve-quieting and tranquilizing."

Another writer who chronicled her life in Florida after the Civil War was Harriet Beecher Stowe, who wintered from 1868 to 1884 in a cottage situated in an orange grove at Mandarin on the St. John's River. In contrast to the moral outrage about the South that she expressed in *Uncle Tom's Cabin*, Stowe wrote of the pleasant climate and the enjoyable life-style afforded in Florida, and in a letter home she remarked that Florida allowed her the opportunity to be indolent: "I sit and dream and am happy and never want to go back north."

In contrast to Stowe's praise of Florida were the writings of Albery Whitman, who was born a slave in Hart County, Kentucky, in 1851 and after the Civil War wrote several books of verse, including *Twasinta's Seminoles, or The Rape of Florida* (1884). Whitman refuted the glowing descriptions of Lanier and Stowe, describing instead the oppressed people of the state, including former slaves and Indians dispossessed of their land. Florida is compared in his poem to the Garden of Eden, but is depicted as being despoiled by those who rape the land and displace the Indians who inhabit it. Whitman's verse reflects an imaginative use of Florida not only in terms of its idyllic or Edenic aspects but also in its foreshadowing of what would become an increasing concern for writers of the twentieth century: the likelihood that those things that made Florida so attractive might also lead to its undoing.

Much has been written of the profound impact in the latter part of the nineteenth century that Henry Flagler and other developers had upon Florida. Fifty-three-year-old multimillionaire Flagler came to the state in 1883 to relax, but as John Rothchild notes, "Florida turns the most confirmed seekers of peace and quiet into reborn speculators in shell shops, motels, restaurants, condominiums, and in Flagler's case, the entire Atlantic coast." Flagler spent only one winter of indolence before he began an unwavering march toward Key West as he developed resorts and helped found cities. Rothchild notes, "He transported settlers with him, and the first settler's outpost in each successive instance was neither a trading post nor a fort, but a Flagler hotel."

The effects of Flagler and other developers were not lost upon Henry James when he visited Florida in 1904. Writing in *The American Scene* (1907), James eloquently described the allure of and the problems with Florida. He was charmed by the temperate weather as well as the tropical foliage: "the velvet air, the extravagant plants, the palms, the oranges, the cacti, the architectural fountain, the florid local monument, the cheap and easy exoticism." In contrast to his reaction to the setting, however, James was hostile to what he called the "boarders," the hordes of pleasure-seekers now pushing into Florida to fill the great hotels, of which he wrote, "There, as nowhere else, in America, one would find Vanity Fair in full blast."

James clearly articulated one of the greatest concerns about Florida—that as more people came to the state, the very qualities that caused it to be seen as an escapist paradise were in danger of being destroyed. In fact, this turned out to be the case for Ernest Hemingway, who moved to Key West in 1928. He liked this remote part of Florida not only for its laid-back life style and excellent fishing, but also because he found it conducive to his writing. Key West was the setting for his novel *To Have and Have Not* (1937), in which he seized upon the remoteness and primitiveness of the place. Hemingway described Key West and the Gulf Stream as "the last wild country there is left." Only in the 1940s, after Key West had been linked to Florida by the overseas highway, allowing easy access for a multitude of tourists, did Hemingway make a final break with Key West and escape farther south to Cuba.

Marjorie Rawlings's arrival in Cross Creek in the same year that Hemingway moved to Key West also evoked a response to Florida as a remote and faraway place. Coming from Rochester, New York, Rawlings, aside from newspaper work, had achieved little success with her writing. Florida fired her imagination. Although *The Yearling* (1938) is probably her best-known Florida work, *Cross Creek* (1942) is her fullest account of her own imaginative response to Florida. She wrote of the orange grove near her house that it was a place of enchantment that brought back to her "the mystic loveliness of childhood."

About the same time that Hemingway and Rawlings settled in Florida, James Branch Cabell began to winter in St. Augustine for health reasons. There, the aging author of mythic realms found new material to stimulate his imagination, leading to his final trilogy, known collectively as *It Happened in Florida. The St. Johns: A Parade in Diversities* (1943), written in collaboration with historian A. J. Hanna as part of the Rivers of America Series, provides a panorama of lives and events associated with the river. *There Were Two Pirates* (1946) and *The Devil's Own Dear Son* (1949) explore the legend and early history of St. Augustine in the high spirit that marks Cabell's comedic vision.

Key West, Tampa, and other Florida towns have also been the setting for the important but often overlooked writing of Cubans in Florida. In *A Century of Cuban Writers: Selected Prose and Poetry* (1996), Carolina Hospital and Jorge Cantera have collected representative works from thirty-seven writers. For example, as the cigar industry developed, workers would pay *lectores* to read to them as they labored. The poet José Martí, who led Cuba's movement of independence, spent a great deal of time in Florida. The contributions of Cuban writers continues today with the work of Virgil Suarez, Roberto Fernandez, Carolina Hospital, and others.

Although, as Rothchild and Whitfield have argued, many of the imaginative portrayals of Florida were written by those who came from other places, one of the most engaging depictions was by a native Floridian. Zora Neale Hurston, born in Eatonville, near Orlando, one of the first all-black towns to be incorporated in this country after the Civil War, described her experiences growing up in *Dust Tracks on a Road* (1942). Eatonville she describes in *Mules and Men* (1935) as "a city of five lakes, three croquet courts, three hundred brown skins, three hundred good swimmers, plenty [of] guavas, two schools and no jail house." In her novel *Their Eyes Were Watching God* (1937), the story of Janie, a black woman who suffers through two conventional, stifling marriages until she achieves happiness with a man with whom she shares equality, Hurston skillfully uses the Florida setting as a backdrop and catalyst to Janie's achieving of independence. In the novel, Eatonville and its unique all-black, autonomous status, as well as the almost classless life in the Everglades (which Hurston terms "the muck"), serve as places where one can achieve one's dreams. Florida is not an Eden here, perhaps, but is certainly presented as a land of opportunity.

Another important literary figure in Florida at this time was Wallace Stevens, who as representative of the Hartford Accident and Indemnity Company traveled frequently to Florida beginning in 1916. Like other writers, Stevens immediately recognized the literary possibilities of Florida. Looking back over the time he spent there, Stevens wrote in a letter in 1943: "My particular Florida shrinks from anything like Miami Beach. In any case, unless your mind is made up, you may find that you have picked up an individual Florida of your own which will keep coming back to you long after you are back home."

Stevens wrote more than thirty poems about Florida, which are collected in *Harmonium* (1923) and *Ideas of Order* (1936). In "Nomad Exquisite," he depicted the lushness of the landscape that so attracted

him, "the immense dew of Florida" that "brings forth
. . . [the] green vine angering for life." Stevens eventually rejected Florida as a place too lush and languid for
a person of his austere New England background, but
his Florida experience was a catalyst for his expression
in poetry of the relationship between reality and the
imagination. He articulated clearly how Florida was
not only a place but a state of mind. In one of his best-
known poems, "The Idea of Order at Key West," as he
depicts the singer of the song in the poem, the one he
calls "the single artificer of the world," he shows how
the poet transforms the setting into art, what Stevens
calls "the reality of the imagination."

By the mid-twentieth century, the number of Florida
writers began (like the population of the state) to increase in geometric proportions. *The Booklover's
Guide to Florida* (1992) includes 2,200 writers and
5,000 books. Stetson Kennedy, in an essay in this book,
asks whether in the future there will remain "a natural
and cultural Florida worth writing about."

A writer who shared his concern was Marjory
Stoneman Douglas. In *The Everglades: River of Grass*
(1947), Douglas wrote that her study of the Everglades
led her to conclude that the Everglades were not a
swamp but, as her title indicates, a river of grass, a misunderstood part of Florida's delicate ecological system.
Until her death in 1998, Douglas continued to be a tireless advocate for the protection of the fragile ecology in
Florida, and her work continues to influence contemporary Florida writers such as Connie May Fowler,
whose novel *River of Hidden Dreams* (1994) is also
concerned with the despoiling of the environment.

That concern continues to be an issue for contemporary Florida writers. T. D. Allman, in *Miami: City of
the Future* (1987), argues that Miami may be a harbinger for what lies ahead. Allman writes, "You see what
Wallace Stevens once described in his poem 'Nomad
Exquisite,' because right at you 'come flinging / Forms,
flames and the flakes of flames.' New York is granite;
New York is about cold. Miami is very different because Miami is vegetal and Miami is about fire, and
that is the first paradox of Miami, photosynthesis and
fire together." Allman says that Miami "was built on
the bedrock of illusion—the dream that if only people
pushed far enough, fast enough, into the uncharted
vastness, they could escape the cold and corruption of
the past, and build for themselves a sunny and virtuous
New World." In contrast to other cities begun "as forts
or foundries, trading centers or ports, Miami is surely

the only city of its size that started out as a place to get
away from it all."

A recent novel by Joy Williams, *Breaking and Entering* (1988), also describes a Florida where the desire
to build an idyllic New World has had disastrous results. In Williams's novel, the houses are fortresses
with artificial landscapes where even the beaches have
been rigidly categorized into "the nude homosexual
beach, the nude heterosexual beach, the surfing beach,
and the shelling beach, as well as the beaches that belonged to the condos and the beaches that belonged to
the rich. It was all the same thin, sparking ribbon, but
mind and predilection had divided the areas as effectively as shark-infested inlets."

Harry Crews's fiction set in Florida in the past decade also pictures a place no longer idyllic. His *Scar
Lover* (1992), set in Jacksonville, depicts both people
and places horribly maimed. Unlike William Bartram's
description of the St. John's River as a paradise,
Crews's main character calls it "the dirtiest river in the
country. The thick hot wind blowing off of it smelled
of garbage, gasoline, and raw human waste [that
would] burst into flame if you set a match to it."
Crews's work is far different from the idyllic visions of
earlier writers about Florida. In his world, the St.
John's is no longer pristine; the lush foliage described
by Wallace Stevens has become the fetid swamp. As
Stephen Whitfield comments, "Promise and closure,
inauguration and fulfillment, beginning and end—such
combinations make the image of Florida paradoxical.
Fresh starts are much of its appeal; among states with
the highest proportion of plastic surgeons, Florida is
second only to California. But Florida is also the finish
line—the Fountain of Youth crumbling under the pressure of an inexorable mortality." As the beauty of Florida is threatened and diminished, it may eventually become "the tip of a wounded civilization."

It seems clear that Florida will continue to evoke an
imaginative response—as an escapist place in some
ways different from the rest of the nation and, at the
same time, in its susceptibility to the despoiling of the
environment, a harbinger for the rest of the nation. It
is likely that the literature of Florida will continue to
serve as a chronicle for these changes.

Anne E. Rowe

See also Hispanic Literature; Lazy South.

T. D. Allman, *Miami: City of the Future* (1987); Mark Derr,
Some Kind of Paradise: A Chronicle of Man and Land in Flor-

ida (1989); J. E. Dovell, *Florida: Historic, Dramatic, Contemporary, I* (1952); Kevin M. McCarthy, ed., *The Book Lover's Guide to Florida* (1992); Leonardo Olschki, "Ponce de Leon's Fountain of Youth: History of a Geographical Myth," *Hispanic American Historical Review* 21 (August 1941); John Rothchild, *Up for Grabs: A Trip Through Time and Space in the Sunshine State* (1985); Wallace Stevens, *The Collected Poems of Wallace Stevens* (1955) and *Letters of Wallace Stevens* (1966); William White, ed., *By-Line: Ernest Hemingway: Selected Articles and Dispatches of Four Decades* (1967); Stephen J. Whitfield, "Florida's Fudged Identity," *Florida Historical Quarterly* 71 (1993).

FOLK ART

Folk art is the aesthetic dimension of everyday life. It is not embodied in formal works of sculpture or painting, enshrined in museums under vitrines or track lights. Rather, folk art is embodied in a wide range of utilitarian objects, from the landscape itself to buildings, textiles, and tools. Through the maker's self-conscious attention to matters of form, texture, color, or decoration, a patently useful artifact such as a dogtrot house, a slatback chair, an alkaline-glazed churn, or a log-cabin quilt may also enliven the senses and impart beauty to daily tasks.

Folk art is also a shared, communal art. It is learned informally—through oral tradition, observation, and imitation—and is engendered in face-to-face exchanges in small groups based on unifying factors such as age, gender, family, region, class, occupation, ethnicity, and religion. Southern folk art reflects many themes important to southern literature: an agrarian way of life, a closeness to the land and nature, a sharply defined social hierarchy, a complex mix of cultures, and a relatively stable population.

During the formative years of the seventeenth century, English settlers in the lowland South focused their energies on raising labor-intensive crops: tobacco, indigo, and rice. They were content to live in relatively impermanent one- and two-room houses, surrounded by irregular clusters of small outbuildings, scattered fields, and free-roaming livestock. By the end of the century, however, wealthier planters had begun to apply a new aesthetic to their holdings. Working within the Georgian architectural mode, they developed carefully ordered estates with fields, gardens, outbuildings, and roads all precisely laid out and a large, highly visible, symmetrical house at its core. With its tight geometry, the plantation model suggested control over nature and society, and openly embodied a hierarchical relationship among people.

While only a few southerners achieved plantation status (that is, owned twenty slaves or more), their creations strongly influenced others. By the late eighteenth century, vernacular architecture in both the lowland and upland regions had begun to change in subtle ways. The façades of such familiar forms as the hall-parlor or I-house became rigidly symmetrical, with balanced fenestration, matching chimneys, and additions to the rear where they could not be seen. Inside, a new central hallway divided rooms of equal size; visitors now had to pass through two doors to reach the internal living space. In his more modest way, then, the yeoman farmer was employing the new aesthetic to signal his own desire for greater control and privacy in his life.

Not all ethnic groups subscribed to these principles of balance and order. During the second quarter of the eighteenth century, many Germans entered the upland South, bringing with them their very asymmetrical three-room German house form, with its off-center chimney and door, and direct entry into the *Küche* or kitchen. They also persisted in building with natural materials such as log and stone, or left the frame of the building exposed in their half-timber structures (*Fachwerk*). While the Germans thus appeared more accepting of natural forms, Anglo-Americans consistently built in frame construction. In laboriously hewing and sawing their posts, beams, and clapboards and molding their bricks, they demonstrated their desire to dominate nature through the very means of construction. However, by the early nineteenth century, the Germans, too, had begun to adapt to the dominant aesthetic. While often retaining the unbalanced, three-room interior, they devised more symmetrical façades for their homes and gradually shifted to frame construction.

African Americans also contributed alternative aesthetic patterns to the dominant Anglo culture. The well-known shotgun house, which entered New Orleans from Haiti at the beginning of the nineteenth century, differs from other vernacular forms because its narrow gable end faces the road. With three rooms from front to back, the occupants must pass through one room to get to the next. Thus, the house is very open and egalitarian in nature.

Quilting provides a more dramatic example of African American creativity—specifically, the essential quality of improvisation. Anglo-American quilters tend

Folklife Documentary / 269

to start with a clear pattern in mind—the Texas star or the North Carolina lily—and then follow it closely, assuring that design and colors are precisely balanced and symmetrical. African American quilters also begin with a general concept of what they might make, but as they work, they play freely with the design elements and colors, sacrificing balance and control to explore new forms and textures. With their bright contrasting colors and unstable patterns, these quilts exhibit a remarkable energy and spontaneity that often shocks viewers unaccustomed to them. Much like the blues or jazz, African American quilts emerge in performance; immersed in the act of creativity, the quilter is sometimes surprised by the result. The aesthetic mode here is almost existential; each quilt is an act of discovery, an assertion of self.

To many, art implies overt decoration: lively surfaces covered with designs and colors that signify the maker's intent to move beyond necessity. Much of southern folk art, however, is not decorated in any explicit sense. Characteristic southern furniture forms, such as the slab (huntboard), sugar chest, pie safe, or slatback chair, often seem almost Shaker-like in their starkness. Generally, their lines are spare and rectilinear, and they exhibit little embellishment through carving, inlay, or painting. Likewise, the life-preserving food containers—alkaline-glazed storage jars, molasses jugs, and buttermilk pitchers—lack the cobalt-blue flora and fauna so common on northern ceramics. But surface decoration is not the *sine qua non* of art. With their bold forms and rich, earthy textures and colors, these everyday objects please the hand and the eye, and manifest a common aesthetic of simplicity and restraint, reflecting a practical world in which usefulness is primary.

Religion has also exerted a powerful shaping force on southern folk arts. Nowhere is this better seen than in the numerous family and church cemeteries that dot the landscape. Southern grave markers are extremely diverse. Because the Tidewater contains little stone, wealthy families there imported their gravestones from New England, New York, and even England. However, African Americans covered their burials with white seashells and broken household items, all reflecting African beliefs about the land of the dead and the power of the ancestors. By contrast, the rocky upland region holds abundant materials for the carver. In Virginia and North Carolina, the Germans employed a rich body of natural symbols: the tree of life, swastikas, stars, moons, and flowers. Scots-Irish carvers, on the other hand, initially cut thistles, doves, and coats of arms into their stones, but by the Revolution, they had begun to integrate the American eagle, the flag, and other popular patriotic emblems into their repertory. Ethnic groups also borrowed motifs from one another, most likely for aesthetic rather than religious reasons. The Scots-Irish adopted the German swastika on their stones, and Anglos placed shells on their burial mounds.

Many forms of southern folk art have persisted well into the twentieth century, sustained by the late arrival of industry and the rural emphasis of southern life. Large, stable families have nurtured the knowledge of local materials and the time-tested technologies that keep traditions alive. Some of the great southern pottery families are approaching the tenth consecutive generation at the wheel. And, since the late nineteenth century, southern folk arts have attracted attention outside the region. Notably in Appalachia and the Sea Islands, well-meaning if culturally biased outsiders have encouraged the arts of weaving, chairmaking, and basketry through schools and guilds to promote economic and social improvement. Finally, over the last three decades, Americans from all quarters have actively sought out southern folk arts—walking sticks, carved animals, face jugs, sweetgrass baskets, and memory paintings—to fulfill their needs for authenticity, nostalgia, and sense of place.

Charles G. Zug III

See also African American Folk Culture; Architecture, Domestic (Barns and Cabins); Gardens; Quilting; Textiles.

Allen H. Eaton, *Handicrafts of the Southern Highlands* (1937); William Ferris, *Local Color: A Sense of Place in Folk Art* (1982); Henry Glassie, *Folk Housing in Middle Virginia: A Structural Analysis of Historic Artifacts* (1975); John Michael Vlach, *The Afro-American Tradition in Decorative Arts* (1978) and *Back of the Big House: The Architecture of Plantation Slavery* (1993).

FOLKLIFE DOCUMENTARY

Films making a serious effort to document and present American folklife first appeared in the early 1960s, encouraged by a number of influences: the development of portable cameras and recording equipment; interest stirred up by academic folklife programs, by the folk-music revival, and by the Civil Rights Movement; the example of ethnographic and anthropological documentaries; shifts of focus in anthropological and folklore theory; and eventually the availability of modest funding from the National Endowment for the Arts. The South has from the first led other regions as a subject of these folklife documentaries.

The approach in some of the films has reflected folklorists' earlier preoccupation with song or tale as text. *Music Makers of the Blue Ridge* (1966), for example, featured singer/collector/festival-organizer Bascom Lamar Lunsford traveling from spot to spot in western North Carolina eliciting short performances from musicians of his acquaintance. Other films have continued a useful but old-fashioned exposition of the history of a genre or ethnic or regional tradition, using historical sound recordings and still photographs, filmed performances, and a narrator and script. Les Blank's overview of Cajun music, *J'ai été au bal* (1989), is one of the better examples of this style. The approach is probably most successful when employing the authoritative voice of a member of the subject community, as when B. B. King narrates *Good Mornin' Blues* (1979). Folklife documentaries have more commonly shifted away from the "voice of God" narrator, however, toward performances and interviews interspersed with occasional "talking heads" of experts who interpret the material. One film that illustrates this mode is the Appalshop film *Dreadful Memories* (1988), which explores the life of Kentucky mining-town singer and songwriter Sarah Ogun Gunning, using commentary by folklorists Archie Green and Ellen Stekert, labor organizer Tillman Cadle, and many others. Another strong example is Pat Mire's *Dance for a Chicken: The Cajun Mardi Gras* (1993), which scatters commentary from folklorists Barry Ancelet and Carl Lindahl, historian Carl Brasseaux, and a Roman Catholic priest intermittently through its lively footage of rural Mardi Gras "runs" from a number of Cajun communities in southwestern Louisiana.

But the strength of documentaries is not the information or the historical, political, or aesthetic interpretation they deliver. Such material is sometimes better presented in publications that come from the same project—for example, books, such as Alan Lomax's *The Land Where the Blues Began* (1993) and Jeff Titon's *Powerhouse for God* (1988), that parallel respectively their films of the same name, or the background booklet written by Allen Tullos and others for *A Singing Stream* (1983). The film, on the other hand, gives viewers a glimpse of traditional practices in their nor-mal contexts of family life, work, recreation, and worship. Through them, viewers may to some degree have a personal experience of unfamiliar places, activities, and lives.

The documentaries provide this most successfully when they are the product of a sensitive collaboration between a skilled filmmaker, folklorists, and the community. In these cases, the documentarians recognize the community members as the experts on their own traditions and facilitate their self-presentation. They make the films because of their belief in the importance of these communities and their traditions, but they often discover the form or story of the film in the process of making it. Three examples of this kind of film are *A Singing Stream,* made by Tom Davenport in collaboration with the University of North Carolina Curriculum in Folklore, about a black family's purposive use of its musical heritage; Judy Peiser and Bill Ferris's Center for Southern Folklore film *Fannie Bell Chapman* (1978), on an African American gospel singer, song maker, and healer in Mississippi; and Les Blank and Cece Conway's film *Sprout Wings and Fly* (1985), about North Carolina fiddler Tommy Jarrell. Some southern documentary filmmakers quite self-consciously seek to speak in behalf of the subcultures from which they come. Cajun filmmaker Pat Mire, for example, not only produced but also took part in the filmed action of his *"Anything I Catch": The Handfishing Story* (1992), which explores the impact of environmental degradation upon a Cajun cultural practice. Appalshop, Inc., an activist organization in Whitesburg, Kentucky, has an extensive catalogue of films about not only the folklife but also the political and social problems of the Appalachian region.

Folklife films have several values for students of southern literature and culture. They document and show the context of many traditional forms that have intrinsic value as literature—the ballad in John Cohen's *The End of an Old Song* (1970); the blues in Alan Lomax's *The Land Where the Blues Began* (1990); wood-chopping and hoeing songs in Pete, Toshi, and Daniel Seeger's *Afro-American Worksongs in a Texas Prison* (1966); wonder tales in the Appalshop film on storyteller Ray Hicks, *Fixin' to Tell About Jack* (1974); tall tales, comic anecdotes, war stories, and religious narratives in Tom Davenport's *Being a Joines* (1980); historical legends in Davenport's *The Ballad of Frankie Silver* (1998); spirituals in his *A Singing Stream* (1983); African American harmonica songs, tales, and a sermon parody in his *Born for Hard Luck* (1975); improvised chanted sermons of the Kentucky Old Regular Baptists in Appalshop's *In the Good Old Fashioned Way* (1973) and in Kevin Balling's *While the Ages Roll On: A Memorial* (1990); Virginia Independent Freewill Baptists in Jeff Titon, Barry Dornfeld, and Tom Rankin's *Powerhouse for God* (1988); and African Americans in Gerald Davis's *The Performed Word* (1982) and also in Alan Lomax's *The Land Where the Blues Began*.

All of these traditional forms were known to and drawn upon by southern writers. Familiarity with the traditional models is essential to an assessment of the writers' knowledge, skill, and intentions. But these films also serve students of the South by reminding them of the incompleteness of the literary presentation of the region. It is Andrew Kolker's film *Mosquitos and High Water* (1983), for example, not literature, that records the experience of the Isleños, descendants of eighteenth-century Spanish Canary Islands immigrants to Louisiana. In addition, films like *A Singing Stream* and *Being a Joines* give corrective pictures of southern African American or white working-class life. Where writers often show these groups' ignorance of "the best that has been known and thought in the world," the filmmaker offers a different measure of their worth and culture, showing their members' command of work and life skills and mastery of the expressive arts of their own communities.

Daniel W. Patterson

See also Blues, The; Country Music.

Daniel W. Patterson, "A Case for the Folklife Documentary," in *Documenting Cultural Diversity in the Resurgent American South: Collectors, Collecting, and Collections,* ed. Margaret R. Dittemore and Fred J. Hay (1997); Sharon R. Sherman, *Documenting Ourselves: Film, Video, and Culture* (1998); Allen E. Tullos, Daniel W. Patterson, and Tom Davenport, *"A Singing Stream": A Black Family Chronicle*: Background and Commentary," *North Carolina Folklore Journal* 36 (Special Issue, 1989).

FOLKLORE

The term *folklore* was coined in 1846 by the English writer William Thoms to replace the phrase "popular antiquities." His model was the German word *Volkskunde.* Because of this history, *folklore* from the first rang with overtones of both romantic nationalism and antiquarianism. Over the next century and a half, the term continued to gather additional associations from successive intellectual movements in evolutionary, economic, political, linguistic, or anthropological theory and also from scholars' attempts to understand the actual nature of the materials they encountered and studied. Increasingly aware of the importance of tracing the connections between a folkloric item and the culture that employs it, folklorists have also moved toward use of a more encompassing word—*folklife*—and embraced a holistic approach. The chief value of the term *folklore* is in fact heuristic. The effort to analyze the degree to which something is folkloric in its origins, content, transmission history, performance style and context, and uses can teach much about the material.

Two central issues emerge in attempts to define and analyze folklore, each condensed in one half of the word. *Lore* implies oral transmission, which affects both the form and the content of the material. Its processes are genuine and significant, but have a long and complex history of interaction with the written word. *Folk,* the other half of the term, implies a community of bearers of oral traditions. Early writers identified the tradition-bearers as an illiterate rural peasantry living in small, homogeneous, face-to-face communities. Recognition that every human being participates in numerous ways in oral culture has, however, led recent theorists such as Alan Dundes to define the folk as any group sharing a body of oral lore and to recognize the omnipresence of "code switching," as people move between the literate and the oral parts of their lives or between the various oral traditions in which they participate—those of their family, their gender, their generation, their work, their religion, their region, and their ethnicity. Some communities, however, have less access to literacy than others, and some literate groups hold fast to particular oral traditions they regard as crucial to their beliefs, identity, or survival. The study of folklore addresses the entire range of oral traditions, but focuses most on those groups having the richest and most serious development of traditional oral culture.

Folklore and southern literature interact on many levels. Although folklore may have features not shared by most literature (such as a variable text, community rules governing its appropriate use, and musical dimensions that include both melody and a traditional performance style), some oral forms like ballads, blues, animal and wonder tales, and chanted sermons have long been respected for their narrative and verbal artistry. They may be studied as literature, and their interpretation presents problems at least as difficult as those posed by the work of a writer. An item of folklore has multiple levels of meaning—some discoverable in its origin, some in its form, some in its performance style, some in the aesthetic standards that govern it, some in changes it has undergone in many of these areas while passing through time and across cultural boundaries, some in the performer's personality and immediate rhetorical strategies, some in the group's varying responses to it.

Folklorists may also quarry from literature much information about southern folksongs, tales, beliefs, and customs. They can partially reconstruct the history, for example, of a still-current tall tale about the hoop snake, finding evidence of its nineteenth-century currency in Hardin Taliaferro's *Fisher's River (North Carolina) Scenes and Characters* (1859) and of its circulation in the early eighteenth century in John Lawson's *The History of Carolina* (1714). The exploration may offer insights into when and why the tall tale exploded into a form far more important in the southern backwoods than it had been in the British Isles. Many writings as early as Lawson's, as lively as "the humor of the old Southwest," as patronizing as local-color writing, as knowledgeable about traditional expression as Zora Neale Hurston's *Their Eyes Were Watching God* (1937), as reflective as Ralph Ellison's *Invisible Man* (1952), as profound as Faulkner's *As I Lay Dying* (1930), or as recent as Harry Crews's *A Childhood: The Biography of a Place* (1978) and Lee Smith's *The Devil's Dream* (1992) depict one of the traditional cultures in the South. The reader needs to remember, however, that these are not works of reportage but imaginative creations. They are rooted in southern traditional life but mostly disclose the authors' sensibility, limitations, and distinctive gifts.

Daniel W. Patterson

See also Appalachia; Folk Art; Folk Narrative; *Foxfire.*

Dan Ben-Amos, "The Name Is the Thing," *Journal of American Folklore* 111 (1988), and "Toward a Definition of Folklore in Context" in *Toward New Perspectives in Folklore,* ed. Américo Paredes and Richard Bauman (1972); Richard M. Dorson, "A Foreword on Folklore" *American Folklore* (1959); Alan Dundes, "Who Are the Folk?" *Interpreting Folklore* (1980); George M. Foster, "What Is Folk Culture?" *American Anthropologist* 55 (1953).

FOLK MUSIC

Folk music—transmitted by means of traditional patterns, learned usually by ear and imitation, and performed for friends, neighbors, and others—expresses the deepest values and fears of its community. Rural southern folk communities often distinguish between tunes (melodies) and songs (sung words). Instruments, including the solo voice, also express the creative variations or improvisations of individual performers. Scholars classify folk music and song in various ways, including by topic (love, work, or war), genre (ballads and blues), occupational group (field hollers, cowboy, railroad, or coal-mining songs), cultural group (Cherokee), region (southern, Delta), dimension (sacred or secular, often stylistically similar). Three major stylistic song categories include the catalogue, the oldest, often linked with action and characterized by repetition and inventories of the component parts of the subject; the lyric, characterized by images linked to the emotional response of the usually first-person speaker; and the ballad, a sung tale in which the chronological, "leaping-and-lingering" narrative links the stanza-images.

Folk music, song, lore, and customs provided the first genuinely American expressions of native content and style. European, African, and other folk traditions remain especially strong in the cultural diversity of the South where eloquent talk and song have been cherished even more than writing. Consequently, when the American Folklore Society was founded in 1888, scholars focused upon collecting the British American, African American, Native American, French American (e.g., Cajun), and Mexican American traditions that were especially vital in the South. In the Old World, Celtic ways had consolidated to create a European tradition before they were overcome by the Mediterranean tradition. The Celtic fringe of the British Isles and Brittany, which escaped the colonization of Rome and the Anglo-Saxons, populated probably more than 70 percent of the South and set a formidable English-speaking Celtic imprint upon its folk music.

In the South, tracing the instrumental preferences of influential early ethnic settlements proves useful. Cherokee and other Southeast Indians were the first musicians along the Blue Ridge and Smoky Mountains and throughout the South. The rattle, drum, and simple cane or bone flute were their instruments. Their music, dancing, and ritual intertwined to mark the significance of hunting, harvests, war, healing, and funerals, and were believed to contribute to health and happiness. Made of different sized gourds attached to stick handles, rattles were filled with corn, dried beans, or small stones. The Cherokee sometimes decorated these gourds with rattlesnake rattles or hawk feathers. Women danced with terrapin-shell rattles attached to their legs with heavy leather straps. Many ceremonial dances were named after the animals hunted and honored. In *New Voyage to Carolina* (1709), John Lawson described with gusto Indian deer hunters disguised with skins and antlers. His travel account recorded the words to a "Peace Dance" that suggests a desire for a shift from racism to regionalism: "The bad spirit made them go to War and destroy one another . . . but their Sons and Daughters shall marry together, and the two Nations love one another, and become as one People." Drums were made from deerskin stretched over wood, gourds, or earthenware pots. The favorite earthenware drum was filled with water that affected the sound and could be used to moisten the drumhead. Drums were sometimes made from hollow sections of black gum trees covered with a skin head and attached by easily tightened hoops. (Such a drum is indigenous to West Africa, and early in this century near the Peaks of Otter in Virginia, African American banjo player Rufus Kasey learned to make a gum tree banjo from his father.)

Flute players accompanied chiefs in procession and welcomed early European explorers. In colonial times, Tidewater explorers found Powatan cane and reed flutes in the general region where contemporary African American blues player John Jackson learned to make flutes from his father. Choctaw conjurers in Mississippi sometimes played flutes before and during ball games. Drum and fife music, characteristic of West Africa, appears in a few places in this country. Nonetheless, around Como, Mississippi, African Americans Ed Young and Napoleon Strickland have made and played cane fifes for Labor Day picnics and other events. Othar Turner, who played drum for Strickland, still plays fife today. The vocal, much like a field holler, uses a tonic a full tone higher than the fife; both the vocal and fife use a pentatonic scale. Fife and drum bands, also with European antecedents, had become widespread among whites and blacks during the Civil War.

Songs of variable lengths are the fundamental unit of Southeast Indian music. Most consist of short sections repeated and combined in various ways. The Cherokee characteristically use four- or five-note scales and combine phrases in fours or sevens (e.g., seven phrases repeated four times). Sung with moderate vocal tension, the Southeast Indian melodies are throbbing, undulatory, and gradually descend.

Although there are few Native American commonalities with the music of black or white settlers, some exchange did occur. In an 1801 report from Wheeling, West Virginia, a Native American "lute" player accompanied a black musician. Cherokee fiddler Manco Snead and singer, dancer, flute and banjo player Walker Calhoun remain well respected among musicians today. The unusual way that Southeast Indians begin and end their songs with yells or shouts, and the use of call-and-response techniques, in which a group of singers repeats the phrase sung by a group leader, may result from black influence.

During the eighteenth century, English-speaking Celts (mostly Ulster Scots) and others traveled down the Great Wagon Road into the Piedmont to form, for example, the Irish settlement on the Yadkin River. Some took the Shenandoah Valley into the back country, including the southern Appalachian mountains after the Trail of Tears. The Scots-Irish brought their ballads, lyric songs, fiddles, and other traditions with them during this pioneer era that lasted until after the Civil War. Trappers and traders explored the Piedmont and mountain back country, befriended or fought Indians, and established a diverse frontier culture with their lively talk, songs, and music. During this colonial era, Celtic and other patterns mingled with new influences from the Indians in the South (e.g., woodcrafts and planting, as well as possibly instrument-making) to address the changing experiences and adventures in the New World.

The medieval or Child ballads (named for collector Sir Francis James Child) were fully established in Europe by the late fifteenth century and flourished in Scotland in the late 1600s. Their topics include: (1) the magical and marvelous (Christian and pre-Christian); (2) romantic and tragic loves (especially widespread); (3) history and legends (e.g., border ballads, crimes, Robin Hood); and (4) comedy ("Three Nights Drunk"). Settlers brought more than one hundred ballads to this country, and many retain kings, queens, castles, steeds, and other indications of the time of their departure from the British Isles, as well as references to American places and experiences. Traditionally sung solo without vibrato in an intense, understated manner, these ballads are noted for their accentual, often parallel, and exactly or incrementally repeating lines that convey a sparse yet compelling drama, propelled by dialogue and vibrant, often conventional images.

Broadside ballads, printed and sold on the street and at markets in eighteenth-century Britain, provided concrete journalistic details about actual disasters or sensational crimes in a more predictable (usually rhymed, four-line stanza) structure than the Child ballads. Although later honed by tradition into sparser, more intense forms, broadside ballads such as "The Butcher Boy" were closely related to lyric song. They tend to concern a first-person participant and commemorate or moralize about the situation. The broadside form remained popular until the end of the nineteenth century and focused upon the emergence of middle-class and working-class protagonists. G. Malcomb Laws distinguished between British Isle broadsides (often songs about how lovers respond to disapproving parents or become embroiled in disguises while displaying intense loyalty) and those that address the American settlers' work experiences, as well as murder or disaster (e.g., "The Titanic") ballads. African American blues ballads and Mexican American *corridos* offer interesting parallels to ballads.

By 1650, the baroque fiddle had arrived in Scotland and then Ireland and began to replace the Highland bagpipes as the favorite instrument for dancing. The Highland pipes strongly influenced the old angular classical performances that became the formative staccato short-bow styles of Scotland and Ireland. Immigrants soon carried these vigorous, "all in the wrist" (rather than fingering), short-bow styles to America.

Scots-Irish singers and fiddlers eventually began to have contact with the African American songster traditions. The complex rhythms of the banjo, considered the emblem of the southern mountaineer and documented on "hillbilly" 78-rpm recordings of the 1920s, actually echo the music of the griots of West Africa. For almost one hundred years, African Americans were the only ones who improvised lyric songs on a three- or four-string gourd "banjar" covered with a bladder or skin head, and strung with horsehair, hemp, or catgut. They played the short, thumb string banjar in a "thumping" style. In Virginia in 1838, a "'banjor-man' decorated himself by wearing a 'long white cowtail, queued with red ribbon' and a hat 'decorated with peacock feathers' and 'pods of red pepper' when he played for a persimmon beer dance." In appreciation for his music, he was the first to receive a "huge loaf of larded persimmon bread with a gourd of beer."

The subtle face-to-face, call-and-response musical exchanges of shanties, field hollers, group corn-shucking songs, spirituals, and banjo songs and dance music flourished with the mixing of diverse African groups and the longing for home. Animal tales were crucial to blacks during slavery times, and talking animals often appear in their songs. The African spider Anansi metamorphosed into Brer Rabbit and other trickster figures and allowed blacks to signify about their social conditions with less fear for their lives. Brer Rabbit's antics and escapades have been popularized by Walt Disney, relying on Joel Chandler Harris, who dramatized the influence of a black storytelling mentor upon a young white boy through the characters of Uncle Remus. Today, folklorists prefer folktales recorded directly from black storytellers.

Some twentieth-century black banjo songs come from the early period. John Snipes's "Old Rattler" is primarily an affectionate praise song of respect for his hunting dog who runs the fox. The lyrics are conversational; they include conversation between the father and son, the singer and listener, and with the dog! The magic of a speaking dog becomes even more evident in the gleeful irony of Dink Roberts's "Fox Chase": after running all night, the "fox looked back in the East" at the rising sun and said, " 'God bless my red-eyed time, I've done set the world on fire.' "

Black songster and banjo traditions were strongly influenced by sea shanties, rowing, longshore, and river roustabout songs, where blacks often worked side by side with Irish and Germans. Washington Irving and Charles Dickens documented exceptional black dancers and musicians. But like the African American banjo player in the *Sketches and Eccentricities of Col. David Crockett in West Tennessee* (1833), the names of most early black musicians were unrecorded, as in this description: "When the Negro banjoist at this dance called out, 'Now weed korn, kiver taters, an' double shuffle,' the following scene ensued: 'They spin round—they set to—they heel and toe—they double-shuffle—they weed korn—they kiver taters—they whoop and stop.' "

By the 1830s, many Irish and some other whites began to take up the banjo. Joel Sweeney of Virginia popularized or invented a new banjo in the 1840s that added a fifth string in fourth (bass) string position and replaced the gourd body with the open-back wooden rim of a cheese hoop. These changes led folklorists John and Alan Lomax to declare that the five-string banjo is "America's only original folk instrument."

Banjo music shows the significance of the instrument to the working and singing of black rounders and roustabouts on boats, in the fields, on the railroad, around the mines, and elsewhere. While plantation and frontier leaders struggled over conflicting interests before the Civil War, Celtic, African American, and other musicians crossed social, class, and racial borders to create a music symbolized by the joining of the Scots-Irish fiddle with the African American banjar in the old-time traditional, as well as emerging and popular minstrel, string band.

German settlers were especially gifted in material culture crafts (e.g., building the Scandinavian log cabin) and the collecting and publishing of song collections, but they also had prominent roles as instrument makers and sometimes played the fiddle as well as the dulcimer. The dulcimer, a northern European zither called a *sheitholt* and similar to a "strung fence post," appeared along the Shenandoah Valley and in Kentucky before 1800. After 1800, boat-shaped dulcimers appeared in southwest Virginia, east Tennessee, and northwest North Carolina. The damsel-shaped dulcimer appeared after 1850. In the southern mountain region, instrument-makers like Leonard and Clifford Glenn continue to this day to make dulcimers and fretless, open-back banjos that permit the sliding and bending of notes so influenced by blacks and enjoyed by mountain whites. Alfred Michaels, who emigrated from Germany, makes fiddles.

After musical exchange intensified during the Civil War, George Washington Harris, Joel Chandler Harris, and Mark Twain helped create the legendary frontiersmen by documenting the local-color and humor tales of the South and its music. In *Life on the Mississippi*, Mark Twain described rafts "manned with joyous and reckless crews of lumber raftsmen—the worthy descendants of the earlier black and white roustabouts who were fiddling, song-singing, whiskey drinking, breakdown-dancing rapscallions." As generations passed and this cultural exchange continued, rootedness to the land emphasized ethnicity less than community with markers such as "this country," "homeplace," "homecoming," "Southern," and "Mountain."

Black banjo tradition led to the emergence of a distinct and complex new but little recognized genre—the banjo song—and of the string band built around the interaction of the fiddle and banjo. But soon after the turn of the twentieth century, many black banjo players put down their banjos, set their songs with increasingly assertive commentary to the now readily available guitar, and created the blues. Thus, banjo tra-

dition charts a pathway from unaccompanied field hollers and group work songs to guitar-accompanied solo blues songs that express the shift from enslaved Africans to American citizens.

After the fieldwork of Cecil Sharp and Maud Karpeles, scholars began to collect tunes and sometimes contextual materials as well as the texts for songs. The seven-volume *Frank C. Brown Collection for North Carolina* is the most complete of these state efforts. Recording technology soon enhanced fieldwork by documenting performance styles. Commercial mass media during the early days of 78-rpm recordings in the 1920s documented fiddlers and blues musicians until singing to the (Spanish) guitar, recently and inexpensively available through mail-order for rural communities, moved center stage with early country music (e.g., Jimmie Rodgers and the Carter Family). These developments set the scene, with the increase of industrialism in the South, for the (Italian) mandolin to join the string band and contribute to the emergence of the high lonesome sound of fast-paced bluegrass. The radio broadcasts of the Carter Family from Del Rio and later the *Grand Ole Opry* in Nashville sent country music and bluegrass across the nation. Mass-media marketing strategies eventually encouraged the descendants of home music makers and other audiences to become passive consumers of professional singers and musicians.

Nonetheless, the banjo still echoes at the crossroads between West African griots, traveling country bluesmen, and the mountain and minstrel banjo songsters who played for dancing and eventually formed old-time bluegrass bands and banjo orchestras, and also contributed to ragtime, jazz, and modern country music. All of these musics moved to the sidelines with the emergence of rock-and-roll and amplified music. Yet mountain fiddlers, black banjo players, and other traditional players and sometimes unlikely revivalists continue to make music, and the old-time stringband symbolizes the heartbeat of the best of America's democratic ideals.

Cecelia Conway

See also African American Folk Culture; African American Spirituals; Appalachia; Bluegrass Music; Blues, The; Country Music; Folklore; Folk Songs, Religious; Scots-Irish.

Roger D. Abrahams and George Foss, *Anglo-American Folksong Style* (1968); Bertrand Harris Bronson, *Traditional Tunes of the Child Ballads* (4 vols., 1959–72); Cecelia Conway, *Afri-*

can *Banjo Echoes in Appalachia* (1995); Cecelia Conway and Scott Odell, Booklet for *Black Banjo Songsters of North Carolina and Virginia* (CD, 1998); Dean J. Epstein, *Sinful Tunes and Spirituals: Black Folk Music to the Civil War* (1977); Charles Hudson, *The Southeastern Indians* (1976); Tommy [Jarrell] and Fred [Cockerham], *Best Fiddle-Banjo Duets* (1992); Malcolm G. Laws, *Native American Balladry* (1964); Gerald Milnes, *Play of a Fiddle* (1999); Roddy Moore, Bethany Worley, and Vaughn Webb, *Blue Ridge Folk Instruments and Their Makers* (exhibit catalogue, 1993); Betty Smith, *Jane Hicks Gentry: A Singer Among Singers* (1998); Robert Lloyd Webb, *Ring the Banjar! The Banjo in America from Folklore to Factory* (1984); Ruth Y. Wetmore, *First on the Land: The North Carolina Indians* (1975).

FOLK NARRATIVE

Southerners love a good story. In settings as varied as hunting camps, quilting bees, general stores, front porches, church suppers, and courthouses, they spin yarns about trickster rabbits, libidinous preachers, giant mosquitoes, violent murders, malevolent ghosts, buried treasures, and even giants and princesses. Using a variety of narrative styles ranging from the dramatic to the laconic and offhand, southern storytellers play skillfully to their audiences. They weave their tales to entertain, instruct, persuade, ridicule, express anger, or resolve uncertainty. Southerners enjoy all types of folk narratives, but four genres are quintessentially southern: the tall tale, the Jack tale, the conversion experience, and the animal tale. For varied reasons, each has flourished in the region for centuries and remains active today.

Performing tall tales (also known as lying or talking trash) is a male pastime, one that is rooted in a close relationship with the natural world. Fantasy and hyperbole are the key elements here in oft-told stories of horn snakes whose venom can fell trees, epic horse trades or fights, hot weather that makes hens lay hard-boiled eggs, or incredible hunts in which a single shot fells a year's supply of game. Essentially a lie told with a straight face, the tall tale is a verbal ruse or practical joke. By piling up realistic if increasingly exaggerated details and then springing an outrageous conclusion, a skilled narrator can manipulate the genre to embarrass his audience and thus assert his superiority over both man and nature.

During the settlement of the South, exaggerated accounts of flora and fauna appeared in the writings of travelers and explorers like John Lawson and John Brickell. For example, in his *History of the Dividing Line Betwixt Virginia and North Carolina* (ed. Ed-

mund Ruffin, 1841), William Byrd describes the Native American practice of lassoing huge river sturgeons and riding them underwater until they suffocate. The gullible audience for these early tall tales was Europe, which unquestioningly accepted them along with other descriptions of the vastness and diversity of the New World. However, the heyday of the tall tale was the nineteenth century, when the antebellum humorists—David Crockett, Augustus Baldwin Longstreet, Johnson Jones Hooper, Thomas Bangs Thorpe, and George Washington Harris—raised the form to a literary art. While most of these authors felt superior to their characters, they also admired their raw energy and their ability to offend sophisticated and critical outsiders (e.g., northerners). Appropriately, Samuel Clemens (Mark Twain) cut his literary teeth on this type of humor with newspaper sketches such as "The Dandy Frightening the Squatter" (1852). In the twentieth century, tall tales remain a lively part of southern oral tradition, perhaps because they embody the older rhythms of the natural world as opposed to the five-day work week of contemporary middle-class life. William Faulkner greatly admired this genre. In *The Hamlet* (1940), *Go Down, Moses* (1942), and *The Reivers* (1962), he weaves common motifs, comic vitality, and the spirit of excess of the tall tale into much richer, more extended fictions.

Deep within the Appalachian Mountains, another venerable narrative tradition survives, the fairy tale, or Jack tale as it is locally known. English, German, and Scots-Irish settlers carried it into the region; it has been extensively collected in Arkansas, Kentucky, North Carolina, Virginia, and West Virginia. The protagonist is an everyman figure named Jack who, true to the melodramatic nature of the form, always triumphs over his adversaries. However, he is a much richer character than his European counterparts; he is variously cunning and boastful, self-reliant and frightened, generous and cruel, but always very practical and quick to take advantage of a situation. The stories are also well localized in mountain culture. The king usually hangs out at the courthouse; the action takes place in hollows, log cabins, and new grounds; and Jack is frequently less interested in princesses than in collecting a cash reward and returning home. Although the fairy tale has survived only in the southern United States, writers do not appear to have used local tradition for inspiration. Instead, authors such as Eudora Welty have turned to literary sources; for example, *The*

Robber Bridegroom (1942), set in the Natchez Trace, is an adaption of a fairy tale from the Brothers Grimm.

Religious revivalism in the form of the camp meeting reached the southern frontier about 1800, bringing an emotionally charged Protestantism. Essential to this experience was the conversion ritual, in which individuals moved from a state of sin and guilt to the acceptance of God's grace. A key part of this process is the conversion narrative, a powerful personal testimony featuring supernatural beings, stern voices and divine music, transportation to distant regions, and a wide range of signs and revelations. These personal experience narratives are told over and over in public settings, both to validate the faith of believers and to offer a way of salvation for potential converts. Although central to evangelical Protestantism, the conversion experience has largely served as a target for satire among southern writers. Johnson Jones Hooper ridicules the camp meeting in *Some Adventures of Captain Simon Suggs* (1845), but the classic treatment of the born-again syndrome appears in *Huckleberry Finn* (1885), in which the king easily dupes the crowd at a revival by declaring himself to be a reformed pirate from the Indian Ocean. In many respects, Flannery O'Connor has best depicted the terrible need for grace and redemption in her stories, but few of her anguished characters find salvation.

Among the many contributions made by enslaved Africans to southern culture, the animal tale was one of the first to be recognized, through the late-nineteenth-century Uncle Remus tales of Joel Chandler Harris. As a sort of literary ethnologist, Harris unearthed a rich vein of oral tradition, which quickly appealed to the entire nation. Stories of trickster animals (spider, hyena, rabbit) are common in West Africa and quickly spread throughout the Caribbean and the South. In recounting stories in which the weak but cunning rabbit repeatedly overwhelms large, predatory animals (fox, bear, wolf, alligator), African Americans achieved at least vicarious relief by seeming to triumph over their masters. Very likely, their pleasure was doubled when they told such tales directly to whites and laughed with them at the rabbit's all-consuming power. At a deeper level, the tales posed ways to undermine the social system by offering an alternative morality for dealing with the dominant culture: the rapacity of the trickster. Closely related to the animal tales is a cycle of stories about a clever slave named John and his Old Marster. These tales are much more realistic in their portrayal of plantation life; they depict starvation, beatings, and even the death of slaves. Sometimes John deceives his master, but just as often the master prevails, or the two work together.

Southern writers have made varied use of these African American trickster tales. Joel Chandler Harris defused the subversive power of the animal tale by embedding it in a benign plantation framework. Like Thomas Nelson Page's Sam in "Marse Chan" (*In Ole Virginia*, 1887), Uncle Remus is content with the ordered world of master and servant; he tells his stories for entertainment. Charles W. Chesnutt uses a similar setting in *The Conjure Woman* (1899), but his wily Uncle Julius is another matter. Although comical and deferrential on the surface, Uncle Julius is much more self-serving and independent, competes with his masters (John and Annie), and uses his wisdom to educate them in the ways of a changing world. In the twentieth century, African Americans have increasingly spurned the trickster for a strategy of direct confrontation (reflected in such heroes as John Henry and Stagolee). In *Invisible Man* (1952), Ralph Ellison discards the earlier framework structure containing a series of tales and instead integrates the trickster's qualities into his narrative. Here Brer Rabbit symbolizes the Invisible Man's ability to survive and maintain his sense of identity in the face of the dehumanizing forces of contemporary society.

Charles G. Zug III

See also African American Folk Culture; Folklore; Local Color; Oral History; Sermons; Storytelling; Tall Tale.

Carolyn S. Brown, *The Tall Tale in American Folklore and Literature* (1987); John A. Burrison, ed., *Storytellers: Folktales & Legends from the South* (1989); Hennig Cohen and William B. Dillingham, eds., *Humor of the Old Southwest* (1964); Richard M. Dorson, ed., *American Negro Folktales* (1967); Lawrence W. Levine, *Black Culture and Black Consciousness: Afro-American Folk Thought from Slavery to Freedom* (1977); William Bernard McCarthy, ed., *Jack in Two Worlds: Contemporary North American Tales and Their Tellers* (1994); Patrick B. Mullen, *I Heard the Old Fishermen Say: Folklore of the Texas Gulf Coast* (1978).

FOLK SONGS, RELIGIOUS

In the American South, religious folk song has been predominantly the congregational song of Protestant worship. It arose toward the end of the eighteenth century in denominations within which congregations were free to determine their own forms of worship. Across the decades and from one denomination, region, and ethnic group to another, southern religious folk songs show astonishing diversity in verse forms, musical structures, themes, styles of performance, uses, and degrees of traditionality. Collectively, they form one of the most important branches of southern folklore. Many of them are among the most beautiful of our indigenous folk songs.

The song of worship among colonial Presbyterians and Congregationalists was psalmody, in which the text was a metrical version of a psalm, normally "lined out" by a precentor to facilitate singing by congregations that were illiterate or lacked books. The tune was a composed one, and the only folk element was a slow, embellished performance style sung without accompaniment or harmonizing. Before the end of the eighteenth century, many Presbyterian and Baptist congregations began to use hymn texts (songs of prayer and praise by English and American versifiers) and to put them to traditional ballad and song melodies, sung unaccompanied and unharmonized and often "lined out" in congregations that were illiterate or lacked books. Primitive Baptists across the South and Old Regular Baptists centered in Kentucky continue these practices, although the congregations show marked individuality in their ways of treating them.

Early-nineteenth-century camp meetings and revivals brought another song form into popularity, one even more completely oral. This was the camp-meeting spiritual or chorus. These songs drew many of their melodies from fiddle tunes, performed unaccompanied and without harmony. Their stanza structures used repeated lines and set refrains and choruses. Crowds could easily learn them by ear or even spontaneously improvise new stanzas. Not surprisingly, their texts used plain language and syntax and powerful imagery. They were songs of religious experience, exhortation, and testimony, and were frequently apocalyptic. They were intended to convert the sinner. The repertory was to some degree interdenominational, although most favored by Methodists. Methodist leaders eventually led their congregations to give up this oral repertory in favor of hymnals holding composed songs of worship reflecting urban and genteel tastes.

For this reason, much of our knowledge of the camp-meeting spirituals comes to us from nineteenth-century tune books compiled before the Civil War and printed, along with hymns and songs of other denominations, in standard notation for use in the northern states and in shape-note notation for use in the South. The traditional songs they held were recorded by members of the singing community a century before folklorists began to try to collect such songs.

The tune books appear to have had some use in southern congregations but to have been fostered chiefly by singing schools that began to spread south down the Valley of Virginia by 1815, at later dates reaching Tennessee, Kentucky, North and South Carolina, Georgia, Alabama, Mississippi, Florida, Texas, and Arkansas. In Georgia and Alabama, the tune books have survived strongly into the late twentieth century under the sponsorship of a third institution, the singing convention. They have even spread out to other regions through a "Sacred Harp revival" movement, centered on the use of B. F. White's *The Sacred Harp* (1844, 1993). The pieces in this book draw upon a variety of sources: tune books from both Britain and New England, the oral traditions of Old Baptist groups and the camp meetings, popular compositions from late-nineteenth-century gospel composers, and compositions by shape-note singing masters and convention participants. The hallmark of this tradition is the shape-note notational system. The most traditional elements in the tune books are the camp-meeting song texts, the folk tunes, their two-, three-, and four-voice settings in a nonstandard harmonic system, a markedly traditional vocal production and performance style, and rituals that govern and accompany the performances.

Two subsequent developments have produced additional changes in style and repertory. One was the late-nineteenth-century Holiness movement that gave rise to an enormous number of denominations that encourage vernacular congregational song, frequently with instrumental accompaniment and solo or small-group performances. The other was the emergence of professional and semiprofessional performing groups in fields such as country music and gospel, whose careers and creativity have been fostered by sound recordings, radio performances, tours, and television.

The richest branch of southern religious folk song has been that of African Americans. Although participating with whites in antebellum Baptist churches and Methodist camp meetings, they combined what they heard there with a complex heritage of forms and stylistic elements synthesized from the musical traditions of many African peoples. With less access to literacy than even contemporaneous rural white congregations, they perpetuated their oldest traditions into the mid-twentieth century, along with many subsequent layers of song. Because the singers viewed Christianity through the lens of an African world view darkened by the harsh conditions of their lives here during and after slavery, the African American spirituals show a distinctiveness, depth of feeling, and humanity that have justly won them universal appeal and respect.

Southern literature, however, has mostly not offered an admiring impression of religious folk song and its accompanying institutions and practices. The reader may chuckle at Johnson J. Hooper's depiction of the sisters at Simon Suggs's camp meeting shrilly piping forth nonsense like "I rode on the sky, / Quite ondestified I, / And the moon it was under my feet." But when Fannie Bell Chapman in a documentary film sings "God Spoke" and tells of the gift of inspiration in which she received this song, the viewer grasps their high order of seriousness. For Chapman and other singers, these songs are a means for achieving, in the face of "troubles of the world," a respected role in their community, an opportunity for service, and a joyous affirmation of life. Lee Smith's *The Devil's Dream* (1992) captures this spirit in the story of an Appalachian country singer.

Daniel W. Patterson

See also African American Spirituals.

Dickson D. Bruce Jr., *And They All Sang Hallelujah: Plain-Folk Camp-Meeting Religion, 1800–1845* (1974); Buell E. Cobb, *The Sacred Harp: A Tradition and Its Music* (1978); Bill Ferris and Judy Peiser, prods., *Fannie Bell Chapman* (1978); Lawrence W. Levine, *Black Culture and Black Consciousness: Afro-American Folk Thought from Slavery to Freedom* (1977); John Lovell, *Black Song: The Forge and the Flame; The Story of How the Afro-American Spiritual Was Hammered Out* (1972); Beverly B. Patterson, *The Sound of the Dove: Singing in Appalachian Primitive Baptist Churches* (1995).

FOOD

In her 1824 cookbook, *The Virginia Housewife or Methodical Cook,* Mary Randolph provides a beaten-biscuit recipe called Apoquinimic Cakes. The Native American name, English ingredients, and, perhaps, African mode of preparation evidence the rich cultural mix that gives rise to southern cuisine. In southern foodways—the foods themselves, the methods of preparation, the rituals governing eating, the meanings as-

signed to each and every dish—can be found the unfolding story of the region. Food provides a rich resource for southern cultural expression, one deeply tapped and endlessly enriched by generations of southern writers.

In colonial narratives of the region, whether accounts of abundance and feasting, or of starving settlers, or of the strange diets of native inhabitants, foodways articulate particular world views. In Captain John Smith's *The Generall Historie of Virginia, New-England, and the Summer Isles* (1624), for example, corn serves as the medium for expressing social order and power. Native Americans map their world with grains on the ground and barter corn for swords and copper kettles. William Byrd's *Secret History of the Line* (published 1929) draws lines of social class by commenting on the diet of Virginia's porcine settlers.

From these earliest accounts onward, corn and pork dominate southern cuisine, and their innumerable variations from soufflés to pones, smoked hams to chitterlings, offer bottomless resources for culinary metaphor. Through the infinite individuality of recipes or the consumption of special subregional foods, ethnic, regional, and familial groups express identity. Cookbooks form a strong thread in southern literature, binding region to foodstuff: crawfish to the Cajun country, crabcake to the Maryland shore. Many southern cookbook writers combine recipe and commentary, some like Bill Neal framing their collections with informative essays, others moving further toward a rich hybrid genre. Martha McCulloch-Williams's *Dishes and Beverages of the Old South* (1913) or Marjorie Kinnan Rawlings's *Cross Creek Cookery* (1942) are, for example, equally cookbook and cultural record, mixing family memoir or regional anecdote with recipes.

Southern cuisine remains immeasurably indebted to the knowledge and artistry of generations of African American cooks. African American writers, seeking to preserve heritage and affirm cultural identity, have notably contributed to the South's interwoven record of culture and cuisine, as is evidenced by the rich array of soul-food cookbooks in the late 1960s or Norma Jean and Carole Darden's noteworthy *Spoonbread and Strawberry Wine* (1978), where recipes form part of family narrative, or the "recipes and food memories" that make up the National Council of Negro Women's recent *Black Family Reunion Cookbook* (1991).

Southern culture celebrates food and sustains a tradition of big eating. In backwoods legends, Davy Crockett's hearty consumption of bear testifies to his physical power and sheer zest for life; from him descend such prodigious feeders as the Gants in Thomas Wolfe's *Look Homeward, Angel* (1929). Images of laden tables recur in southern texts, the catalogues of meats, vegetables, sauces, and desserts, luxuriantly detailed, celebrating regional plenty while confirming the provider's social status. Writers in the agrarian tradition, such as Andrew Lytle in his contribution to *I'll Take My Stand* (1930), delineate the home-grown, home-cooked foods on the tables of southern rural homes to evidence meaningful, orderly lives rooted in family and land. Throughout the literature devoted to the myth of plantation aristocracy from John Pendleton Kennedy's *Swallow Barn* (1832) to Susan Dabney Smedes's *Memorials of a Southern Planter* (1887), enormous meals served ceremoniously in elegant dining rooms endorse the caste and class system of the antebellum South.

African American writers, vigorously disputing the plantation myth, subvert the implications of the laden table. In *My Bondage and My Freedom* (1855), Frederick Douglass describes the heaped foods as "heavy and blood-bought luxuries" that signify not civilization and plenty but slavery's greedy and inhumane consumption of human beings. In her *Incidents in the Life of a Slave Girl* (1861), Harriet Jacobs depicts a white mistress spitting in food, thereby attacking popular images of refined white southern womanhood. Against the slaveholding household's degradation, Jacobs sets her grandmother's orderly home, where delicious crackers and preserves nourish family and community. Hunger too can become a metaphor in texts formally descending from the slave narrative, powerfully expressing both deprivation and yearning in, for example, Richard Wright's *Black Boy* (1945).

Under slavery and subsequent domestic labor practices, African American women often managed kitchens in white homes. As a result, the divided landscapes of food preparation and consumption are deeply overwritten with racial and gender ideologies in southern literature; kitchens, dining rooms, and the thresholds dividing them function as symbolic landscapes in texts ranging from the physical layout of Jefferson's Monticello to Peter Taylor's finely drawn tales of private life. From antebellum records, readers can discern how African American women consolidated enough power in the kitchen to contest a white mistress. The apron-bound figure of the mammy, a popular stereotype in white-authored texts endorsing the plantation myth, rises from such tensions, romanticizing the actual Afri-

can American women laboring in white homes by covering over their complex individuality with a one-dimensional myth of devotion. Postbellum writers portray African American cooks, such as Dilsey in Faulkner's *The Sound and the Fury* (1929) or Berenice in Carson McCullers's *The Member of the Wedding* (1946), to explore the complex and evolving interrelations of race and family roles in southern homes. Some, by reversing traditional nurturing relations, express social change, as when Sophia Jane nurses Nannie's baby in Katherine Anne Porter's *The Old Order* (1944), or Eleanor Jane hides yams in a tuna casserole in Alice Walker's *The Color Purple* (1982).

The dining room provides a symbolic landscape for delineations of class as well as race. The room's physical contents, from elegant sideboards to expensive silver, the dishes served and modes of serving, the fine class demarcations inscribed in table manners—all codify and articulate social relations. Guest lists script boundaries as well, from exclusive dinners, to family reunions, to fire-department barbecues. Eating together signifies community and social equality; hence battles for civil rights were staged on restaurant tables. In *Killers of the Dream* (1949), Lillian Smith describes the resolve of white church women forming the Association of Southern Women for the Prevention of Lynching in the 1930s to sit and dine with African American women; though modest, these meals were momentous.

For southern women writers, foodways also provide a language for expressing gender identity. Recipes and kitchen rites express feminine powers of fertility and healing in Eudora Welty's fiction, most notably in *Delta Wedding* (1946). As female-dominated space, kitchens can nourish female creativity and conversation; however, in the work of many contemporary southern women, they as often become stages for rebellion against oppressive female roles. Hulga's comic failure to bring a picnic in Flannery O'Connor's "Good Country People" (1955) underlines her rejection of traditional femininity. Southern playwrights—notably Beth Henley in *Crimes of the Heart* (1982) and Marsha Norman in *'Night Mother* (1983)—ably employ food in kitchen settings to depict generational conflict, as daughters long for a mother's nourishing love yet struggle to define and determine their own lives. Women writers also expose patriarchal power by staging violence in kitchens, as when, for example, Bone is raped by her stepfather on the kitchen floor in Dorothy Allison's *Bastard Out of Carolina* (1992).

Considering the import of foodways to the region

and its writers, it is no surprise that restaurants, too, carry meaning in southern literature. The traditional association of home cooking with nurturing women and restaurant cuisine with male chefs provides a backdrop for critical or revisionary views of gender identity. In Anne Tyler's *Dinner at the Homesick Restaurant* (1982), a son serves his customers the comfort food that he longed for in his own unnourished childhood. Both Carson McCullers in *The Ballad of the Sad Café* (1943) and Fanny Flagg in *Fried Green Tomatoes at the Whistle Stop Café* (1987) find in the café's indeterminate space a free zone for addressing the ties between heterosexuality and patriarchal power that they identify in southern culture. And contemporary writers such as Bobbie Ann Mason employ ubiquitous processed, store-bought, and fast foods to express a vision of individual and regional loss of identity.

Past and present, southern writers have attended to the implications of foodways, offering their readers endless opportunities to sample the rich intermingling of culture and cuisine that runs through southern literature.

Mary Titus

See also Grits; Weddings.

John Egerton, *Southern Food: At Home, on the Road, in History* (1987); Peggy Prenshaw, ed., "The Texts of Southern Food," *Southern Quarterly* 30. 2–3 (1992).

FORREST, NATHAN BEDFORD

Nathan Bedford Forrest is esteemed in the southern imagination as the epitome of a brilliant and resourceful cavalry leader. His intelligence, hard work, and resourcefulness were tested early when, as a sixteen-year-old in Mississippi, he assumed responsibility for a fatherless family. A wealthy man at the outbreak of the Civil War, he enlisted as a private but soon became a lieutenant-colonel over a mounted battalion he had raised, and ultimately he was promoted to lieutenant general. He saw notable action at Fort Donelson, where he led his command to safety; at Shiloh; outside Vicksburg, where he temporarily halted General Grant's forces; at Rome, Georgia, where he captured a large force of Federal soldiers; at Chickamauga, where he contested General Bragg's leadership; and at the Battle of Brice's Cross Roads, where he accomplished one of his most notable victories.

Joel Chandler Harris in *A Little Union Scout* (1904) describes how this man who was noted for being mild-mannered could change, in a melée, his face, "which was almost as dark as an Indian's when in perfect repose," becoming "inflamed with passion and almost purple." In Caroline Gordon's *None Shall Look Back* (1937), Forrest heroically exemplifies selfless devotion to duty. The general and his "critter company" figure prominently in *A Mockingbird Sang at Chickamauga: A Tale of Embattled Chattanooga* (1949) by Alfred Leland Crabb. One humorous scene has Forrest eating a critter specialty—opossum stew. And Forrest is an important actor in Perry Lentz's *The Falling Hills* (1967), which climaxes in the massacre of African American troops at Fort Pillow. Appropriately, one of the soldiers exonerates Forrest.

Richard D. Rust

See also Civil War.

Andrew Nelson Lytle, *Bedford Forrest and His Critter Company* (1931).

FOXFIRE

In 1967, *Foxfire* magazine was begun by high-school English teacher B. Eliot Wigginton and his ninth- and tenth-grade students in rural Ruben County, Georgia. Responding to community demand after its first issue, the magazine, written and edited entirely by Wigginton's students under his tutelage, soon found its focus in the reporting of local history and culture. Within a few years of its inception, *Foxfire* began to attract national attention both as a successful experiment in experiential education and as a highly regarded vehicle for the publication of southern Appalachian traditions and folk wisdom.

The collection and publication of localized customs and history, called "cultural journalism," has remained for more than thirty years the mainstay of *Foxfire* magazine. Articles, which continue to be written by Ruben County High School students, generally originate from student interviews with elders of the Appalachian community, the most famous of whom has been "Aunt" Arie Carpenter. These interviews often serve as source material for essays on traditional customs, such as hunting and snakelore, or "how-to-do-it" essays on varied topics, such as log-cabin building and hog slaughtering. In preserving and disseminating the cultural uniqueness of the region, *Foxfire* has helped to battle the "hillbilly" stereotype commonly attributed to the southern Appalachians.

As a result of the success of the magazine, a popular series of nine *Foxfire* books was published by Doubleday between 1972 and 1986. Most of the books have been collections of favorite articles from past issues of the magazine, although some have been dedicated to particular topics. The Foxfire project inspired a 1982 Broadway hit play, as well as hundreds of similar community-based, progressive educational projects throughout the world.

Edward Hoffman

See also Hillbilly.

John L. Puckett, *Foxfire Reconsidered: A Twenty-Year Experiment in Progressive Education* (1989); Eliot Wigginton, *Sometimes a Shining Moment: The Foxfire Experience* (1985); Eliot Wigginton, ed., *Foxfire: 25 Years* (1991).

FRAME NARRATIVE

A frame narrative, a story that encloses a central narrative or a speaker who tells the story and who may comment on the action, can take a number of forms and may serve various purposes. A story may have a frame within a frame. Some frame narratives have their own plot. Quite frequently, the narrator plays a minor role in the action of the core story. The frame's primary purpose is to vouch for the veracity of the events or narrator of the inner story. The "authenticating documents" that accompanied antebellum slave narratives served this purpose. More complex and subtle is the use of a narrator or frame character who in some way needs to learn from the story told. Presumably, the narrator's audience within the narrative frame possesses a similar need to understand the story's meaning. By implication, the reader needs to learn the same lesson. Of course, the narrators and their audiences may not achieve the same understanding. In addition, a frame narrative further distances the actual author from the core story. Theoretically, it is the speaker who tells the frame narrative and to whose voice readers listen. For an author anxious about readers' reactions, this distance may provide a partial defense against criticism.

The frequency with which southern writers have used a narrative frame might be related to the strong oral tradition in southern literature. In oral literature, the narrator contributes more than a narrative voice. In the oral tradition, narrators are physically present to their audiences. The narrative situation usually involves an intimate gathering where narrators act out and comment on the story's action as well as draw their listeners into the story. The oral tradition assumes a story's strong significance for both the speaker and the audience.

Thus, with perhaps a nod toward oral tradition, Charles Chesnutt's *The Conjure Woman* utilizes a double frame. In *The Conjure Woman*, a transplanted northerner relates tales he has heard from Uncle Julius, an untutored former slave. Yet the Yankee narrator, presumably an intelligent, educated man with antislavery sentiments, is blinkered by preconceptions that keep him from understanding central truths in the tales he hears. While the Yankee narrator, John (perhaps a sly reference on Chesnutt's part to Mars' John of African American oral tales), prides himself on seeing through Uncle Julius's minor scams, he misses the far more subversive qualities inherent in Julius's stories. For instance, in "Sandy," the second story in the collection, Sandy's master—with the assurance that Sandy is, after all, his legal chattel—utilizes the hard-working slave's body and talents by lending him out to almost anyone who asks. By turning Sandy into a pine tree, Sandy's second wife, who is a conjure woman, attempts to hide Sandy from his master's incessant demands. Despite her best efforts, however, in her forced absence the tree is cut down and sawed into boards. The complexity of "Sandy" depends on the vicious reality of slavery—metaphorically portrayed by the fate of Sandy and his wife, the trickster qualities of Uncle Julius, the emotional insight of the Yankee narrator's wife who intuits the story's sense, and finally the obtuseness of the Yankee narrator who thinks he understands but does not. Chesnutt's readers who enjoyed this and the other stories when they were published in 1899 may have identified with any of these levels, while the double frame also allowed Chesnutt to speak unpalatable truths to his mostly white audience.

Popular during the nineteenth century in, for example, the Southwest humor tales and plantation novels such as John Pendleton Kennedy's *Swallow Barn*, the frame narrative reached a peak of popularity around the turn of the nineteenth century in the work of Chesnutt, in Joel Chandler Harris's Uncle Remus tales, and in Thomas Nelson Page's sentimental tales. The use of a frame story has never ceased, however. One of the most prominent novels of the twentieth century, Robert Penn Warren's *All the King's Men,* frames the story of Willie Stark in the perception of his youthful aide and critic, Jack Burden. Upon occasion, both William Styron and John Barth have utilized frame narratives in their fiction.

Winifred Morgan

See also Oral History; Plantation Fiction; Slave Narrative; Southwestern Humor.

FRANK, LEO

The Leo Frank case is perhaps one of the best known and most often written about in southern and American history. On Confederate Memorial Day in 1913, thirteen-year-old Mary Phagan came to the pencil factory in Atlanta where she worked to receive her weekly pay. She was later found brutally murdered in the factory basement. Leo Frank, the factory manager, was accused and convicted of the crime. Awaiting execution at the penitentiary in Milledgeville, Frank survived having his throat slashed by another prisoner only to be taken from the jail, transported to Marietta, Phagan's home, and lynched. In 1982 Alonzo Mann, a factory office boy at the time of the murder, issued statements exonerating Frank and implicating James Conley, the janitor. Subsequently, in 1986, the State of Georgia posthumously pardoned Frank.

The details provide the continued fascination. Despite discrepancies in various re-tellings, the critical evidence was the testimony of James Conley. This was one of the few times that an African American's word was accepted against a white man in a Jim Crow–era court. Frank was also one of the few whites lynched in the South, and his lynching followed rituals associated with the lynching of black men.

Leo Frank symbolized dramatic change, and the Frank case highlighted fears and cleavages in society. Although born in Texas, Frank was raised and educated in New York. He was Jewish and ran a Jewish-owned factory in the New South. Mary Phagan symbolized the young, innocent white girls forced from their rural roots into the maelstrom of the big cities and exploited by industry. Although there were no charges or evidence of rape, rumors spread wildly about Frank's supposed sexual perversion. During Frank's trial, people yelled through the courthouse windows,

"Kill the Jew." Former Populist leader Thomas Watson resurrected his flagging political career by scurrilously attacking Frank in the pages of his *Jeffersonian,* and prosecutor Hugh Dorsey rode the wave of his popularity into the governorship. An organization that called itself the Knights of Mary Phagan served as the forerunner of the modern Ku Klux Klan.

The case became a cause célèbre as lawyers including Louis Marshall took the appeals concerning the fairness of a trial in such an environment to the U.S. Supreme Court and as northerners denounced what they perceived as the immoral South. After reviewing the evidence, Governor John M. Slaton, flooded with petitions for clemency and simultaneously threatened, commuted the sentence from execution to life in prison and fled the state as an angry mob marched on the Governor's Mansion. Although Slaton returned to a successful legal practice and eventually served as the president of the state bar, his once-promising political career was ended.

The Leo Frank episode is a watershed in southern and American Jewish history. Frank, president of the local B'nai B'rith, had been a successful representative of the German Jewish Reform community, which had believed itself to be highly accepted. What happened to him shattered that perception and contributed to the establishment of the Anti-Defamation League of B'nai B'rith. Historians now trace the episode to the Atlanta race riot of 1906, black/Jewish interaction, factionalism in politics, labor/management conflict at Jewish-owned Fulton Bag and Cotton Company, and issues of gender and identity. Rather than an aberration, it reflected the racist environment and the precarious position of a minority group struggling for acceptance.

Accounts of the episode have run the gamut from the journalistic account of Harry Golden (1965) to the Camille Baum novel *Member of the Tribe* (1971) to a musical drama, *Parade* (1998), by Alfred Uhry. "The Ballad of Mary Phagan," sung for decades in the rural South, has been studied by Saundra Keyes (*Journal of Country Music,* 1972).

Mark K. Bauman

See also Jewish Tradition; Judaism; Ku Klux Klan.

C. P. Connolly, *The Truth About the Frank Case* (1915); Leonard Dinnerstein, *The Leo Frank Case* (1968); Eugene Levy, " 'Is the Jew a White Man?': Press Reactions to the Leo Frank Case, 1913–1915," *Phylon* (1974).

FREE SOUTHERN THEATER

Created to provide southern African Americans with representation of African American life through, in the words of its founders, "myth, allegory, public performance," the Free Southern Theater worked to provide theater relevant to the lives of its audience. When writer Gilbert Moses and Student Nonviolent Coordinating Committee field director John O'Neal joined with Richard Schechner, editor of the *Tulane Drama Review,* the theater moved from Tougaloo College, where it began in 1963, to New Orleans. There it became closely linked with the Civil Rights Movement. Free both in ideology and admission, the FST staged plays and held postproduction discussions in churches, schools, and theaters throughout the rural Deep South, funded both locally and by the New York literati. Productions included works by Samuel Beckett, Ossie Davis, Theodore Ward, and Langston Hughes, as well as more experimental works written expressly for the FST. Although Moses left the FST in 1966 after an ideological split, it continued functioning under O'Neal until 1982.

Sage Hamilton Rountree

See also Civil Rights Movement; New Orleans, Louisiana.

Thomas C. Dent, Richard Schechner, and Gilbert Moses, *The Free Southern Theater by the Free Southern Theater* (1969); Geneviève Fabre, *Drumbeats, Masks and Metaphor: Contemporary Afro-American Theatre* (1983); Mance Williams, *Black Theatre in the 1960s and 1970s: A Historical-Critical Analysis of the Movement* (1985).

FUGITIVES, THE

The history of the Fugitive poets begins with a Jewish mystic and adventurer named Sidney Mttron (pronounced ma-*ta*-tron) Hirsch. As a young man, he ran away from his home in Nashville to join the navy. He eventually became boxing champion of the Pacific Fleet. More important for the Fugitives, he also began to study Taoism and Buddhism. From there, he began to study mysticism of all sorts, from Rosicrucianism to numerology. After leaving the navy, he moved to Paris, where he met Gertrude Stein and Irish playwright A. E. (George Russell) and served as model for several of Rodin's sculptures. He also continued his study of mysticism and developed an interest in etymology and an-

cient languages. He returned to Nashville in the years just before World War I.

One afternoon in the summer of 1915, a Vanderbilt University student named Stanley Johnson invited a friend, aspiring poet Donald Davidson, to call on Hirsch's younger half-sister Goldie. Hirsch argued philosophy with Johnson and read Davidson's work and encouraged him. The visits became regular. Davidson and Johnson later invited their Shakespeare professor John Crowe Ransom, an Oxford-trained classicist and philosopher, to accompany them to the Hirsches'. Ransom's logical mind and rationalist outlook provided a perfect counterpoint to Hirsch's flights of mysticism. The group was later joined by William Yandell Elliot, a friend of Hirsch's brother Nat, and Alec Brock Stevenson, son of a Vanderbilt faculty member. Another member of the Vanderbilt English faculty named Walter Clyde Curry was the last to join before World War I.

When America entered the war, the group temporarily broke up, as many of them joined the military. Before leaving for France, Ransom left a collection of poems with his friend Christopher Morley, who submitted them to Henry Holt and Company publishers. On the recommendation of Robert Frost, the collection, *Poems About God,* was published in 1919.

By the early 1920s, most of the group was back in Nashville. Davidson joined and Ransom rejoined the Vanderbilt English department. William Frierson joined the group. Because of an obscure injury, Hirsch had moved in with his sister and brother-in-law, Rose and James Frank. The future Fugitives resumed their meetings at the Franks'. Their prewar discussions had centered on philosophical issues, though they had occasionally touched on literary topics. Now, they concentrated mainly on matters of literature and aesthetics. Hirsch still presided over the meetings, but Ransom had become the primary influence on most of the group.

In 1921 Allen Tate joined the group. Although Ransom was skeptical of the poetic experimentation of the early twentieth century, Tate was deeply influenced by the French symbolist poets and by such modernists as Ezra Pound and, later, T. S. Eliot. Despite several temporary rifts caused by their poetic disagreements, Tate and Ransom became and remained friends. And their debates enlivened the Fugitives' meetings. Those meetings were increasingly devoted to members' discussions and critiques of each other's poems.

Hirsch suggested in 1922 that the group publish a

poetry magazine. Stevenson suggested entitling the magazine *The Fugitive* from a line in one of Hirsch's poems. The name had different meanings for different members of the group. For Tate, the fugitive was the poet, "the man who carries the secret wisdom of the world." Davidson thought of the fugitive as fleeing the stale conventions of nineteenth-century poetry. The foreword of the inaugural issue, written by Ransom, claims that "the fugitive flees from nothing faster than from the high-caste Brahmins of the Old South." Whatever their interpretation of the title, all the members of the group enthusiastically supported the idea of publishing a magazine. The Vanderbilt English department did not. When informed of the project, the chair of the department, Edwin Mims, invited members of the group to a luncheon and attempted to dissuade them from going ahead with their plan.

Despite Mims's opposition, the Fugitives published the first edition of the magazine in April 1922. In the first two issues, the poets published their work under pseudonyms: Roger Prim (Ransom), Henry Feathertop (Tate), Robin Gallivant (Davidson), Marpha (Curry), Jonathan David (Johnson), Drimlonigher and King Badger (Stevenson), Dendric (Merrill Moore, who joined the group after he read the first issue), Philora (Frank), and L. Oafer (Hirsch). Tate later claimed the pseudonyms were used more for romance than anonymity. They were abandoned when some critics maintained that the poems were all by Ransom writing under multiple names.

By October 1922, the magazine was getting positive reviews in such literary periodicals as *The Literary Digest* and the London *Poetry Review*. In the December issue of that year, along with poems by regular members, *The Fugitive* published poetry by internationally known poets William Alexander Percy, Witter Bynner, and Robert Graves. Despite the critical praise and publication of famous poets, the magazine faced financial difficulty by early 1923. The problem was temporarily relieved by exchanging advertising with three other poetry magazines, *The Nomad, The Modern Review,* and *The Double Dealer.* Later that year, a Nashville businessman, Jacques Back, agreed to finance the magazine.

In the spring of 1923, a shy young Vanderbilt sophomore wandered into the room Tate shared with Curry. Tate was working on a poem. The young man hesitantly walked up to Tate, read the poem, and handed him one of his own. That was Tate's introduction to "Red," Robert Penn Warren, whom Tate later described as the most gifted person he knew. Warren moved in with Tate and Curry and joined the Fugitive group.

In an attempt to boost circulation in mid-1923, the Fugitives convinced a group of Nashville businessmen to contribute $100 as first prize in a poetry contest sponsored by the magazine. The judges of the contest were William Alexander Percy, Gorham Munson, and Jessie Rittenhouse. Over four hundred poets entered the contest, including Warren and Hart Crane. The three judges had vastly different views on poetry, and none ranked any poem the same. When the results were averaged out, the prize went to Louise Patterson Guyol. Guyol has not been remembered, but the contest introduced the Fugitives to the poetry of a northern housewife named Laura Riding Gottschalk. Gottschalk's poetry was published in *The Fugitive,* and she became an honorary member of the group, the only female member.

With the February 1924 issue, *The Fugitive* began to publish criticism as well as poetry. The first critical essay was Ransom's "The Future of Poetry," a criticism of modernist poetry's abandonment of traditional forms. Tate published a defense of modernist poetry in the April issue. The group members' poetry was improving. Despite these changes, however, the magazine was losing money, and Back withdrew support for it. At the same time, the group was showing signs of strain. Only Davidson, Tate, Warren, and Ransom were dedicated to poetry as a profession, and the quality of their poetry was beginning to far outstrip that of the others. Differences over poetics were also starting to take a toll. The Fugitives considered discontinuing publication of the magazine, but decided to stick with it.

At the beginning of 1925, *The Fugitive* received enough contributions from patrons to relieve its financial difficulty, at least temporarily. But the group continued to deteriorate. In February, Tate, who had moved to New York to make a living as a man of letters, resigned from the editorial board. He believed the magazine had outlived its purpose—the introduction of a group of new poets. The other members of the Fugitives were becoming more involved in other projects. Ransom was engaged in writing a book of criticism. Davidson was editing a literary page for a local newspaper. Warren had graduated from Vanderbilt and was preparing for graduate school. Curry was concentrating on a scholarly study of Chaucer. Ransom, Warren, and Davidson assumed the primary editorial responsibility in 1925. When Warren left for graduate studies in California, Ransom and Davidson decided to resign. The December issue was the final one. *The Fugitive* was dead, but the Fugitives continued to meet until most of them had left Nashville.

Ironically for a group that fled from nothing faster than the high-caste Brahmins of the Old South, several of the Fugitives became involved in the Agrarian movement. Spurred first by the Scopes trial in 1925 and then by the Depression, the Agrarians maintained that a return to Old South values and traditions could save the South from the chaos of the modern world. Tate, Ransom, Davidson, and Warren contributed essays to the Agrarian manifesto *I'll Take My Stand* in 1930. In 1936 Tate discovered the British Distributists, a group with an outlook and politics similar to that of the Agrarians. When he and Distributist Herbert Agar edited a collection of essays called *Who Owns America? A New Declaration of Independence,* Ransom, Warren, and Davidson contributed. By the end of the 1930s, however, all but Davidson had abandoned Agrarianism. Davidson remained committed to Agrarianism until his death in 1968.

Another important movement arising from the Fugitive group was southern New Criticism. Although Davidson wrote some criticism, he is not primarily remembered as a critic. The major Fugitive New Critics were Ransom, Tate, and Warren. In addition to those movements, the Fugitive group produced some of the best poetry ever to emerge from the South.

Fred R. Thiemann

See also Agrarians; *I'll Take My Stand*; New Criticism.

John M. Bradbury, *The Fugitives: A Critical Account* (1958); Louise Cowan, *The Fugitive Group: A Literary History* (1959); Louis D. Rubin Jr., *The Wary Fugitives: Four Poets and the South* (1978).

FUNDAMENTALISM

A variant of one Protestant family, the evangelical, Fundamentalism is certainly present in the South, although the scope of its following and its influence are often exaggerated. This reckoning is due to the confusion between generic Evangelicalism and specific Fundamentalism. It is accurate to say that all Fundamentalists are evangelical but most Evangelicals are not fundamentalist.

The commitment of such Protestants to biblical literalism is consistent and profound. The biblical text is affirmed to be both infallible—the question of authority—and inerrant—the issue of veridicality. In the Fundamentalist understanding, the doctrines that the Bible propounds tend to be ranked by importance, even though no possibility of error exists for any in that corpus of teachings. Commonly, some doctrines are regarded as test cases for a person's or group's authenticity. Serial thinking obtains, rather than systematic, correlative, or dialectical.

Just as characteristic as absolute biblical and doctrinal reliability is the attitude toward life in the world and all social institutions. This attitude is generally negative, since all human constructions are only human, therefore fallible and inevitably perverted. Historically, Fundamentalism has been hostile to or alienated from culture, requiring its adherents to be at least suspicious of worldly allegiances and involvements.

In what amounts to a significant shift, American Fundamentalism in recent decades has been given to working aggressively to transform society and culture through political and public morality crusades. The South's versions were culture-hostile from the 1920s into the 1970s. Lately, sectors of the standard denominations, dominant in the culture, have invested their efforts in Fundamentalist-style culture transformation. (Accordingly, the term takes on particular time and place applications.) Only minority expressions, generally extremist, now manifest a spirit of world-rejection. Thus, a movement that was long marginal has in some of its forms become part of "mainstream" regional religious life.

This new southern Fundamentalism is epistemically rationalist, as the movement characteristically is. Divine revelation is primarily propositional. What the faithful are given and what they can place their confidence in are scriptural facts and doctrinal dogma. Such teachings are truth-assertions, on which there is to be no compromise, and no human tampering; many forms of interpretation are disallowed. Indeed, compromise is the ultimate besmirchment of truth, and purity is the precise character of revelation. Even so, southern forms are usually less exclusively rational than earlier forms that arose, mostly in "the North" in reaction to modern ("modernist") theories in the sciences, natural and social. This distinctiveness owes also to southern Evangelicalism's placing so much stock in the experience of conversion. Experienced-based faith, after all, is of a different sort from faith defined as truth grounded in propositions.

Thus, Fundamentalism is more popular in the South now than it has been, but in forms that reflect regional history and culture. Lee Smith captures Fundamentalist fervor in "Tongues of Fire" (1990) and in the novel *Saving Grace* (1995). Before her, Flannery O'Connor depicted it throughout her work as the defining southern religious view.

Samuel S. Hill

See also Bible; Bible Belt; Evangelical Christianity; Modernism; Scopes Trial; Snake Handling; Televangelist.

George Dollar, *A History of Fundamentalism in America* (1973); Barry Hankins, *God's Rascal: J. Frank Norris and the Beginnings of Southern Fundamentalism* (1996); George M. Marsden, *Fundamentalism and American Culture* (1980).

GARDENS

Writers have portrayed the agrarian landscape of the South as a metaphoric Garden of Eden since the first European colonists arrived at Jamestown, Virginia. In contrast to William Bradford's description of New England as a howling wilderness full of "savages," many explorers who visited and eventually settled in the southern colonies discovered a beneficent land that provided them with the opportunity to make money and become prosperous. In his *Letters from an American Farmer,* a Frenchman, J. Hector St. Jean de Crèvecoeur, sent an image of America back to Europe that confirmed this ideal. For Crèvecoeur, America was a country of profitable small farms that provided inhabitants with a peaceful, independent way of life. The image of the cultivated Garden of Eden allowed colonists to view the land as provided by God for their use—to subdue and possess, as God tells Adam in Genesis.

The metaphor of the Garden of Eden suggests a taming of the wilderness, the creation of a cultivated garden out of chaos, but settlers achieved this order only through violence and domination. As Louise Westling has pointed out, Native Americans had managed the landscape even before the settlers began to arrive, with seasonal burning and the creation of small farms. However, they were pushed farther back into the wilderness as settlers began to establish large plantations and more and more people arrived in the southern colonies. Decimated by sickness and disease brought by the newcomers, the Native Americans were banished from the Garden. In addition, landowners soon began to import slaves to perform the heavy labor needed to achieve profit from the land. Gradually, the plantation replaced the small farm as the symbol of a cultivated, agrarian Garden of Eden.

Slavery turned out to be the snake in the garden, and the Civil War effectively destroyed the ideal of the plantation. Writers in the twentieth century, however, have continued to employ the metaphor of the garden in a variety of ways. In *Absalom, Absalom!* and other works, William Faulkner portrays gardens hewn by men from the wilderness only to be destroyed by their own sins. Other writers as disparate as the Agrarians and James Dickey have depicted the invasion of the garden by the modern world of advertising, technology, and the machine. Since the 1960s, the prosperity of the New South has caused many writers such as Bobbie Ann Mason and Walker Percy to explore the loss of rural traditions in a world increasingly overrun by golf courses and shopping malls.

Other southern writers have described gardens as sources of art and community. In her essay "In Search of Our Mothers' Gardens," Alice Walker explains that in times when women, especially African American women, were not free to pursue other artistic forms, gardens were a means of creative expression. They are often associated with a strong sense of place, with identity and community. In Eudora Welty's *The Optimist's Daughter,* the main character experiences an emotional rebirth while working in her mother's garden. Gardening, like sewing, cooking, and other domestic arts associated with women, signifies connection with the land, the community, and the family, and also becomes a metaphor for writing. After the Civil War and throughout the twentieth century, women joined organizations devoted to the cultivation of gardens, providing a social outlet for women, and encouraged gardening as an art form.

Clearly, gardens have long been an important part of the tradition of southern literature. Even before America separated from England to form an independent nation, writers such as Thomas Jefferson and Virginia plantation owner William Byrd discussed the southern garden in their works. Domestic novelists such as Augusta Jane Evans Wilson and Caroline Gilman made gardens into feminine settings with sentimental associations. Today, writers Tina McElroy Ansa and Kathryn Stripling Byer depict the cultivation of gardens as a woman's art. All of these writings reflect a long history of close association with a continually changing landscape. The cultivated garden symbolizes change, creativity, community, and rebirth, themes that southern writers will continue to explore in their works as they attempt to reconnect with the past and create their own gardens.

Mae Miller Claxton

See also Agrarians; Pastoral; Plantation.

Annette Kolodny, *The Lay of the Land* (1975); R. W. B. Lewis, *The American Adam* (1955); Lucinda MacKethan, *Daughters of Time* (1990); Henry Nash Smith, *Virgin Land* (1950); Louise H. Westling, *The Green Breast of the New World* (1996), and *Sacred Groves and Ravaged Gardens* (1985).

GAY LITERATURE

To examine the intersections of gay male literature and southern literature is to stumble immediately upon questions of definition. Though Truman Capote and Tennessee Williams mark a central strain of such writing, social constraints on gay life in the South have inhibited the development of a fully realized literary tradition. Comprehending the full range of literary expression of same-sex desire between men by southern authors requires careful analysis of both sexual and regional identity.

What, for example, is the place of writers who do not publicly acknowledge their sexual orientation? William Alexander Percy's importance as an exemplar of white southern aristocratic tradition is unchallenged; recent scholarship examining his homosexual identity and same-sex relationships offers new perspectives on how his writing reveals and conceals a more complex relation with this tradition. Reynolds Price thoughtfully explores homoerotic and homosocial relationships throughout his fiction and poetry, though he is less concerned with gayness as a defining social characteristic or political issue; for Price, these friendships are important as figures in a larger pattern of love and loyalty, betrayal and forgiveness. An account of gay southern literature must acknowledge not only writers who have chosen such a genteel silence, but

also those for whom the strictures of silence were so unbearably oppressive that they committed suicide before their full contributions were made.

The definition of "southern" is of equal import, since homophobic social and religious attitudes encouraged the emigration of such southern-born writers as Donald Windham, Mart Crowley, John Rechy, and Armistead Maupin. One strain of gay southern literature focuses on this expatriate experience. In *Plays Well with Others* (1997), Allan Gurganus writes of the experiences of a gay southerner in New York City. Andrew Holleran, in *Nights in Aruba* (1983), traces the distances, both geographical and social, between that city and the Florida landscape where his protagonist's parents live. David Sedaris's satiric essays in *Barrel Fever* (1994) and *Naked* (1997) often focus on his upbringing in suburban Raleigh, North Carolina. Even Mart Crowley's *The Boys in the Band* (1968), a play that seems the quintessential depiction of Manhattan gay life, includes a Mississippi native among its cast. When San Francisco resident Michael Tolliver—a central character in Armistead Maupin's *Tales of the City* (1978) and its sequels—writes a letter to his parents in Florida, explaining why he cannot support Anita Bryant's antigay campaign, he engages the very issues of family, community, and religion that made it impossible for him to stay in the South. Playwright Tony Kushner has spoken of the deep influence of his southern upbringing in Lake Charles, Louisiana, even though his best-known works have not yet dealt with southern characters or settings.

Donald Windham holds a particular place in the gay southern literary tradition as the long-time friend (despite occasional strains) of Tennessee Williams and Truman Capote. Though both Williams and Capote lived outside the South for much of their lives, each maintained ties to the region. Williams wrote of southern people and places even while living in New York, and he kept homes in New Orleans and Key West. New Orleans native Truman Capote retained similar emotional attachments to his southern upbringing, returning to the French Quarter to write his first novel, *Other Voices, Other Rooms* (1948), and writing about the South as late as *Music for Chameleons* (1980). By leaving the South, Williams and Capote were able to live more openly and with a higher profile as gay authors, thus offering inspiration to younger writers.

One strain of gay southern writing (for example, Edward Swift and Harlan Greene) builds on the public personae of Williams and Capote, producing a comic literature marked by camp extravagance and a glittering surface. Capote and Williams have often used female characters to express facets of their identity, as in Holly Golightly's embrace of the freedom of city life (*Breakfast at Tiffany's,* 1958) or Blanche DuBois's embodiment of a transgressive sensitivity at odds with the dominant public discourse of Stanley Kowalski and his New Orleans cronies (*A Streetcar Named Desire,* 1947). The urban encounters of Holly and Blanche mark another feature of gay culture—that it flourishes most in cities; Lyle Saxon's French Quarter salon in the 1930s and Atlanta's flourishing gay literary scene in the 1980s are but two examples: many of the gay literary communities in such cities as Richmond, Charleston, Savannah, and Mobile have yet to be fully documented.

In *Southern Ladies and Gentlemen* (1975), Florence King describes the unique place of gay men in southern society in the chapter "He's a Little Funny, But He's Nice." While asserting that most gay men either leave the South (or at least settle in New Orleans or Atlanta), King notes the uniquely flamboyant profile of a gay man who chooses to remain in his hometown. His eccentricities (whether an effeminate personality or an odd devotion to classical art) are acceptable because they mark his difference clearly and unambiguously to the larger community.

King's satiric description captures much of the paradoxical place of gay men in southern society and in southern literature, with its well-attested concern with the values that bind a community together and define its boundaries. Despite the inhibiting influence of traditional Christian precepts against homosexual behavior, there has often been a place for gay people on the community's edge, their liminal status marked for all by the distinctive features that King describes.

In its most extreme manifestation, the exotic appearance of the markedly gay man signals an inner depravity, as in Flannery O'Connor's *The Violent Bear It Away* (1960); the lavender car and lavender shirt of the stranger who encounters would-be prophet Francis Tarwater prefigure the lavender handkerchief with which he will bind the drugged young man as part of an apparent sexual assault. Such a portrait demonstrates the extreme fear and loathing of gay men imaged as threat not only to vulnerable young men but also to the larger community.

Only slightly less threatening on first encounter is Cousin Randolph in Capote's *Other Voices, Other Rooms.* A virtual archetype of the "classic queer,"

Randolph's cultured voice and the kimono-clad elegance of his sexless body clearly mark him as different, a difference that both attracts and repels young Joel Knox, the novel's central figure. To Randolph, Capote gives a speech that serves as a credo for the gay person struggling for truth against the constraints of a traditional southern community: "The brain may take advice, but not the heart, and love, having no geography, knows no boundaries: weight and sink it deep, no matter, it will rise and find the surface: and why not? any love is natural and beautiful that lies within a person's nature: only hypocrites would hold a man responsible for what he loves, emotional illiterates and those of righteous envy, who, in their agitated concern, mistake so frequently the arrow pointing to heaven for the one that leads to hell" (147). Although Joel sets his course away from Randolph's house (and by extension away from his life choices), his cousin's extreme example allows Joel to accept his own difference and move into a confident maturity free of the constraints of his upbringing.

In *Reflections in a Golden Eye* (1941), Carson McCullers depicts the lonely and often desperate lives of characters whose sexuality is atypical or ambiguous; her representations of gay men were enormously influential on both Capote and Williams. Texas-born novelist John Rechy makes the outsider's marginality a positive theme in *City of Night* (1963), in which a young loner travels the country on a sexual quest that brings him in contact with the gay underworld in several large cities, including New Orleans. Williams wrote of this gay subculture in his short stories and poems, portraying gay men uniting with other outcasts in a new community. Jim Grimsley's play *Mr. Universe* (1998) follows Williams into this world of drag queens, prostitutes, and body builders, brought together in a New Orleans jail cell. Grimsley's novel *Dream Boy* (1995) and play *Mr. Universe* offer striking new interpretations of pastoral romance and urban farce. For Rechy, Williams, and Grimsley, the bonds formed among those separated from their communities of birth are more intense and passionate, despite their transience. Less positively portrayed are the raucous party boys in John Kennedy Toole's *A Confederacy of Dunces* (1980), representing a segment of the larger society from which Ignatius Reilly (and perhaps his creator) felt estranged. Anne Rice's *Feast of All Saints* (1979) deals sympathetically with the homosexuality of a *gen de coleur libre* in antebellum New Orleans, although the end of the novel leaves him an outsider to the family-centered life of Creole society. For Lestat and Louis, the vampires introduced by Rice in *Interview with the Vampire* (1976), their supernatural exclusion from the mortal world of the French Quarter is marked by the homosocial and homoerotic relationship they form.

A more realistic portrayal of such a community linked by thirsting physical desire is found in Andrew Holleran's *The Beauty of Men* (1996); the men Lark encounters in arenas of public sex constitute a community defined purely by carnality, in contrast to the more positive family relationships from which their homosexuality excludes them. For others, the extravagance of Cousin Randolph can be the defining feature of a new community, as in Harlan Greene's glamorously and scandalously elegiac Charleston novels *Why We Never Danced the Charleston* (1984) and *What the Dead Remember* (1991). In Edward Swift's *Splendora* (1978), the self-made woman Miss Jessie Gatewood (who left her alter ego Timothy John Coldridge behind in New Orleans) plants this transgressive community at the heart of an East Texas town; in the truest comic tradition, Timothy re-emerges at novel's end to live happily ever after (one presumes) with the town preacher.

Yet the gay presence in a text need not be marked by such flamboyance; in fact, same-sex desire is often forced underground by social opprobrium, to be discerned only by hints and indirection. Critics have found in *Absalom, Absalom!* (1932) an unspoken homoerotic attraction binding Henry Sutpen and Charles Bon. Absent a supportive community, no matter how fragile or untraditional it might be, same-sex desire becomes the stuff of tragic plots and hidden identities. The most notable examples of these "normal" boys gone bad are Tennessee Williams's early plays: injured athlete Brick Pollitt tortured by conflicted feelings for his dead friend Skipper in *Cat on a Hot Tin Roof* (1955); the doomed poet Sebastian Venable in *Suddenly Last Summer* (1958), consumed by his passion; Blanche DuBois's young husband Allan Grey in *A Streetcar Named Desire,* who shoots himself after Blanche discovers him with an older man. In his later plays, such as *Vieux Carré* (1979), Williams offers an autobiographical and more sympathetic portrait of a young man coming to understand and accept his sexual identity.

Randall Kenan's *A Visitation of Spirits* (1989) makes this tragic figure the center of his novel, dramatizing the forces of community, religion, and family as demons that drive young Horace Cross to suicide. Kenan's critical depiction of these societal forces marks the novel's advance over the traditional plot of the doomed gay man; his evocation of the community of Tims Creek is also notable as an examination of homophobia in an African American community. The short stories of Kenan's *Let the Dead Bury Their Dead* (1992) present several gay male characters, both white and black, among the tapestry of inhabitants of the fictional town of Tims Creek, North Carolina.

More-affirmative portraits of gay men focus not on the separation from the community impelled by same-sex desire, but on the relationships that such desire enables or complicates. Reynolds Price offers a full and complex account of men relating to other men as friends, lovers, and comrades. In his trilogy *A Great Circle,* a youthful sexual relationship in *The Source of Light* (1981) ripens into a lifelong friendship between these two predominantly heterosexual men; in *The Promise of Rest,* Hutch Mayfield must reconcile himself to the more openly expressed sexual identities of a younger generation when his son Wade, dying of AIDS, returns home. In *Good Hearts* (1988), Price depicts another facet of male friendship in Wesley Beavers and Stanley, a gay man who offers, through their nonsexual interaction, a safe masculine haven that shepherds Wesley through a difficult point in his life. The tremendous shaping force of passion courses through Price's *The Tongues of Angels* (1990), the account of a camp counselor's friendship with a troubled camper; the bond between the two, a friendship allowed to flourish only because of the separation of summer camp from the everyday community, is characterized by erotic tension no less potent for being unrealized and unexpressed.

This yearning for connection and relationship despite the weight of community disapproval finds a remarkable fruition in Jim Grimsley's novel *Dream Boy* (1995), where Nathan's growing affection for Roy (literally "the boy next door") unfolds with a gentle sweetness. In their love for each other, Nathan and Roy create their own community of two (which Grimsley roots in that most southern-gothic of settings, the ghost-haunted plantation house), a union that transcends small-town hate, reaching beyond even death itself to rescue the young men and lead them away from those who would harm them. Although their future is unknown, they travel, unlike Joel Knox, together.

J. Randal Woodland

See also Lesbian Literature; Sex and Sexuality.

John Howard, ed., *Carryin' On in the Lesbian and Gay South* (1997), and *Men Like That: A Southern Queer History* (1999); Gary Neal Richards, "Another Southern Renaissance: Sexual Otherness in Mid-Twentieth-Century Southern Fiction" (Ph.D. Dissertation, Vanderbilt University, 1996); James Sears, *Lonely Hunters: An Oral History of Lesbian and Gay Southern Life* (1997).

GENTLEMAN

The concept of the southern gentleman is inextricably mingled with that of the southern cavalier. The major distinction between these two terms is that the cavalier ideal carries more specific geographical and genealogical associations, reflecting the widely accepted myth that the seventeenth-century settlement of the colony of Virginia was composed overwhelmingly of aristocratic Cavalier followers of Charles I fleeing the Puritan repression of Commonwealth England. The southern gentleman is a character type with broader social and geographical applications. He is intimately associated with the southern plantation system and is defined by a code of gentility that expresses the ethos of the planter class throughout the South. Because the plantation system was first established in Virginia, the colony served as the incubator for both the cavalier ideal and the concept of the southern gentleman; here, the concepts were virtually interchangeable. In defining himself as a nobly descended cavalier, the colonial Virginian also defined himself as a gentleman, and he embraced a fully articulated code of conduct and manner of living. The seventeenth-century Virginian's ambition was to recreate in the new colony the country life of the English gentry as well as its conception of gentility and refinement. The code of the New World Virginia gentleman was thus copied from an Old World Elizabethan pattern, and it subsequently spread throughout the South along with the plantation system that nourished it.

The first commandment of the code of the gentleman—expressed in treatises on manners and conduct such as Sir Thomas Elyot's *The Book Named the Governor* (1531), Henry Peacham's *Complete Gentleman* (1622), and Richard Brathwaite's *The English Gentleman* (1630)—dictated a recognition of the inherent inequality of man and the acceptance of the idea that certain men were born to lead and that others, the great majority, were born to follow and serve. Assured of his

own superiority, a gentleman was expected at all times to be graceful and dignified in his deportment, as well as courteous and thoughtful toward all men, regardless of their social status. In designing a moral code to complement their dignified bearing, Virginia gentlemen, like their English counterparts, sought to attain qualities of fortitude, temperance, prudence, justice, liberality, and courtesy. Not surprisingly, these Aristotelian virtues tended to supersede strict adherence to the Ten Commandments. Sins of the flesh, for example, might be forgiven if they were not blatant, excessive, or destructive of a gentleman's essential integrity.

Observers of manners and conduct agreed that learning was an essential quality for a gentleman. However, the well-educated social leader scorned crabbed pedantry that delved into esoteric subject matter. He believed the best and most useful knowledge was broad rather than deep. Learning was an adornment, worn lightly and gracefully, which—along with dancing, fencing, hunting, riding, and occasionally the playing of a musical instrument—combined to produce a complete and smoothly functioning social creature.

Writers of courtesy books were rather vague about the source of a gentleman's honor. Honor was variously identified with virtue and with reputation. But though there was disagreement concerning its precise definition, there was widespread agreement that the gentleman's primary purpose in following his code was to possess and maintain a personal honor that commanded the respect of all his peers as well as of all those of lower social order. Colonial southern gentlemen thus placed great importance on the preservation of individual honor. Unlike their nineteenth-century successors, however, they did not generally approve of dueling as an effective means of defending it.

The gentlemanly code expressed an ideal of character, an ideal roughly translated from the English rural gentry to southern planters who presided over moderate-to-large landholdings cultivated by slave labor. In the eighteenth and early nineteenth centuries, wherever the plantation system spread from Virginia into the middle and lower South, so too did the myth of the South's cavalier inheritance and the allied code of the southern gentleman. Indeed, as the institution of slavery came to be viewed by northerners with increasing moral opprobrium in the decades preceding the Civil War, it became more essential for southern planters to view themselves as refined individuals practicing a humane and noble code of conduct. Slavery could thus be justified as a paternalistic system that produced twin social paragons—the patriarchal planter aristocrat and his consort, the exquisitely pure and submissive southern lady.

Abetted by the enormous influence of the romantic historical novels of Walter Scott and the nineteenth-century medieval revival, the South's increasingly exalted interpretation of the gentlemanly ideal was lavishly articulated by the region's antebellum writers. Virginia novelists George Tucker, John Pendleton Kennedy, Nathaniel Beverley Tucker, William Alexander Caruthers, and John Esten Cooke were joined by novelists of the interior and lower South—Joseph Holt Ingraham, Charles Gayarré, Caroline Lee Hentz, and Augusta Jane Evans. Together, these writers produced plantation novels that apotheosized their southern heroes.

In their romantic inflations, the South's writers added two significant appendages to the eighteenth-century concept of the gentleman. The first of these was the *code duello*. During the period from 1830 to 1860, a dramatic confrontation on the oak-shadowed dueling ground became a part of the conventional background of the plantation novel. Antebellum southern fiction utterly ignored the disturbing implications of the revival of this supposedly aristocratic custom, and it turned a blind eye to the coercive societal spirit, the summary justice, and the primitive notion of honor that the duel emblematized.

The second fictional appendage was the southern gentleman's reverential love for his chaste and refined lady. By having their heroes worship the southern lady, writers were able to associate them with qualities of sensitivity, sentiment, morality, and benevolence without depriving them of their manliness. This combination of martial vigor and chivalric love was an antidote to the poisonous abolitionist image of the southern planter as a cruel and heartless monster presiding over a barbarous social system.

In embellishing and exalting the southern gentleman, antebellum novelists, like most other southerners, refused to acknowledge the tensions and contradictions implicit in the code that defined their heroes. They ignored the basic incompatibility of that code with the sustaining myths of the new nation. How, for example, was the key doctrine of the inherent inequality of man to be squared with the Declaration of Independence, the Constitution, and the Bill of Rights? Was there not a deep and perhaps disturbing irony in the fact that these documents, expressive of the nation's most cherished democratic principles, had been sub-

stantially the work of Virginians, men like Thomas Jefferson, who were slaveholders molded by the gentlemanly code? How could the code be meaningfully applied to the great majority of southerners? What relevance could notions of noblesse oblige, broad learning gracefully worn, and dueling have for the mass of southern yeomen who laboriously farmed their own acres and sustained a modest, if not Spartan, standard of living?

The South and its romance writers refused to examine critically the relevance of the southern gentleman ideal to their nation and their region. Instead, they concocted a fictional landscape completely dominated by highborn plantation aristocrats in which yeoman farmers and middle-class southerners were virtually absent. The southern gentleman became a crucial element in the defense of the plantation system and of slavery, institutions that most southerners came to believe were essential to the survival of their way of life. When the South's warriors marched to battle in 1861, they saw themselves not as products of a backward, benighted, anachronistic culture, but as a nation of highly bred and refined gentlemen bravely defending their ladies, their honor, and their civilization against hordes of low-bred, fanatical Yankee invaders.

The Civil War resulted in the defeat of the South, the devastation of its plantation economy, and the abolition of its peculiar institution. But the southern gentleman did not vanish. Instead, he was resurrected and refurbished for literary consumption. Thomas Nelson Page, Sidney Lanier, George Washington Cable, and Henry Selden made their heroes part of an implicit justification of the antebellum way of life. The Old South might be gone; but there was much to be lamented in its passing, a graciousness of living and a nobility of character epitomized by the old-style southern gentleman. Flush with victory, eager to let bygones be bygones, uneasy about the excesses and corruption of the Gilded Age, most northerners enthusiastically welcomed these southern literary apologias. They embraced the South's romanticized fictional gentlemen and wept over their defeat.

By the early decades of the twentieth century, southern writers were able to approach the heroic figure of the southern gentleman with more irony and complexity. Ellen Glasgow produced a number of realistic novels of Virginia life. In one of her best, *The Sheltered Life* (1932), she examined the passing away of the old social order in the character of General Archbald, a man who sacrifices his happiness to a code that mandates, above all, the preservation of propriety and the saving of appearances. In James Branch Cabell's *The Rivet in Grandfather's Neck* (1915), Rudolph Musgrave's life is shaped by a series of gentlemanly sacrifices at the altar of the southern lady and by gestures that are noble, if not notably successful or useful. Both Virginia writers modified the ironic distance from their southern gentlemen by their underlying sympathy for a code that, if not effective, at least offered a point of order in a morally chaotic modern world.

A similarly complex and nuanced tone characterizes William Faulkner's *The Unvanquished* (1938). Civil War hero John Sartoris is depicted as embodying the high courage and unassailable honor of the conventional southern gentleman, but Faulkner also shows the moral abstraction and the obsession with power that mar his character in his later years. His son Bayard does not so much reject the conventional dictates of his father's code as transcend that code to achieve a higher moral understanding without sacrificing his traditional understanding of personal honor.

Twentieth-century southern writing frequently conveys a nostalgia for the gentlemanly ideal. William Alexander Percy's *Lanterns on the Levee* (1941) is a restrained elegy for a vanishing way of life that, in Percy's view, made the southern gentleman possible. But even the most romantic of modern southern novels often acknowledge complexities that nineteenth-century writers denied. In Margaret Mitchell's *Gone With the Wind* (1936), Ashley Wilkes, a paragon of gentlemanly virtue, is a foil to the magnetic and apostate Rhett Butler. Rhett goes to war for profit, not honor; and his successful adaptation to the demands of change and progress in the postbellum South stands in stark contrast to Ashley's obsession with the past and his ineffectuality.

More-recent southern fiction has continued to engage provocatively with the idea of the southern gentleman. In *Lie Down in Darkness* (1951), William Styron describes with a knowing eye modern tidewater Virginia society. His alcoholic and morally repugnant Milton Loftus goes beyond the spiritual lassitude of Cabell's and Glasgow's characters. Indeed, he represents a daring inversion of all the qualities of character that the ideal of the southern gentleman has traditionally implied. The hero of Walker Percy's *The Last Gentleman* (1967) commands the restrained intelligence, self-modesty, and politeness of the traditional code; but Percy seems well aware that these qualities are of little relevance in the contemporary South. In *To Kill a Mock-ingbird* (1960), Harper Lee strives through her characterization of Atticus Finch to find a modern idiom for the southern gentleman, to adapt the traditional gentlemanly code in ways that will make it meaningful to the present. Such novels suggest that the region has not altogether abandoned the idea of the southern gentleman and that some of its most thoughtful writers will continue to seek in the gentlemanly code keys for addressing the social problems of the present-day South.

Ritchie D. Watson

See also Aristocracy; Cavalier; Lost Cause; Novel, 1820 to 1865; Plantation; Plantation Fiction; Tidewater; Virginia, Literature of; Yankee.

William R. Taylor, *Cavalier and Yankee: The Old South and American National Character* (1961); Ritchie D. Watson, *Yeoman Versus Cavalier: The Old Southwest's Fictional Road to Rebellion* (1993), and *The Cavalier in Virginia Fiction* (1985); Louis B. Wright, *The First Gentlemen of Virginia: The Intellectual Qualities of the Early Colonial Ruling Class* (1940); Bertram Wyatt-Brown, *Southern Honor: Ethics and Behavior in the Old South* (1982).

GEORGIA, LITERATURE OF

The founder of the Georgia colony, James Edward Oglethorpe (1696–1785), was also its first writer, being largely responsible for the chief legislation by which the colony was governed. But Oglethorpe and his contemporaries and their successors were too busy establishing and defending Georgia and taking part in the American Revolution and its aftermath to contribute anything significant to belles-lettres. Indeed, it was not until the early nineteenth century, the 1830s to be precise, that prose fiction in Georgia (and not in one of the genres of prestige) began to appear and be noticed elsewhere.

In 1832 Augustus Baldwin Longstreet (1790–1870), an Augusta lawyer and journalist and later president of four southern colleges, started printing in newspapers in Milledgeville and Augusta his sketches and tales dealing with local scenes, characters, language, and manners that were collected as *Georgia Scenes, Characters, Incidents etc. in the First Half Century of the Republic* in 1835, the first book of Southwestern and/or frontier humor that subsequently influenced writing in the South from Mark Twain to Faulkner to Lewis Grizzard. Such pieces as "Georgia

Theatrics," "The Horse-Swap," "The Fight," and "The Character of a Native Georgian" not only reflect life on the Georgia frontier in the late eighteenth and turn of the nineteenth centuries, but they demonstrate characteristics such as the "envelope structure" in which an educated narrator sets up an uneducated one who tells the tale in a dialect and usually returns the narration to the first narrator. This technique was later employed by George Washington Harris in the *Sut Lovingood Yarns* (1867) and by Mark Twain in "The Notorious Jumping Frog of Calaveras County" (1865), "Jim Wolf and the Tom-cats" (1867), "Baker's Blue-jay Yarn" (1880), and various other pieces.

One of Longstreet's near contemporaries and friends, William Tappan Thompson (1812–1882), another journalist and lawyer and an adopted Georgian, tried his hand with his fictional Middle Georgia farmer, Major Jones of Pineville, who in a series of letters to the author ("Mr. Thompson") describes his activities in dialect based mostly on spelling. The letters appear in *Major Jones's Courtship* (1843) and in *Major Jones's Sketches of Travel* (1848). The humor in these books is based upon the Major's efforts to court and marry Miss Mary Stallings, to tell about the affairs of the folks in his vicinity, and to characterize in his own limited vocabulary a performance of *The Bohemian Girl* in "Filladeffy," among other interesting entertainments of his travels. Though much of Thompson's best work is in the epistolary form he used for the Major Jones series, he also managed other kinds of narration in *The Chronicles of Pineville: Embracing Sketches of Georgia Scenes, Incidents, and Characters* (1845), the very title of which suggests his debt to his old friend Longstreet and in which he demonstrates his skill with double narration in such tales as "The Fire-Hunt." An even better example of his technique appeared later in the much-anthologized "A Coon-Hunt; or, a Fency Country" (1851). Both Thompson and Longstreet vigorously defended the South before, during, and after the Civil War. But it's not just humor, satire, or irony the reader gleans from Longstreet's or Thompson's prose, for, as the former indicates in the preface to the first edition of *Georgia Scenes*, he is as much interested in recording the social history of his time and place as in anything else.

Over a generation younger than Longstreet and half a generation younger than Thompson, Richard Malcolm Johnston (1822–1898) did not collect his sketches of Middle Georgia until 1864, and his *Dukesborough Tales* did not appear in book form out-

side his native state until it was published, still under the pseudonym of Philemon Perch, in Baltimore in 1871 and subsequently in New York in 1883; the chief piece in it, eventually called "The Goosepond School," had appeared first in the *Spirit of the Times* in 1857. Written for the author's "own entertainment," as he acknowledged in a preface to an edition of 1892, and drawn partly from memories of "incidents of old times" ("the grim and rude but hearty old times"), these pieces describe the religion, customs and manners, speech, and relations between the sexes in the rural area of Powelton. Tales dealing with the lives and foibles of country people appear in various editions of *Dukesborough Tales,* six other collections published from 1888 to 1897, and four novels: *Old Mark Langston* (1884), *Ogeechee Cross-Firings* (1889), *Widow Guthrie* (1890), and *Pearce Amerson's Will* (1898). Mining the vein opened by Longstreet and Thompson and writing mostly in the heyday of local color, Johnston, as many have pointed out, was a transitional figure between the backwoods humor of the antebellum period and the local color of the 1880s. Friendship with Alexander H. and Linton Stephens, Sidney Lanier, and other Georgians, pleasure in the work of Longstreet, Thompson, and Lanier, and his deep roots in Middle Georgia kept Johnston writing about his experience of the "old times" in Georgia long after he had moved to Baltimore in 1867, as his account of the old-field schools of his youth demonstrates in "Early Educational Life in Middle Georgia" (1896, 1897).

Connections also played their part in the career of Joel Chandler Harris (1848–1908), the well-known creator of Uncle Remus and many other Georgia characters black and white. Brought up near Eatonton as a printer's devil and eventually as a writer for Joseph Addison Turner's *The Countryman*, Harris later became associated with William Tappan Thompson on the *Savannah Morning News* for six years (1870–1876) and then moved to Atlanta to work with Henry Grady and others on the *Constitution* from 1876 to 1900. There, in his first year on the staff, he introduced Uncle Remus to its readers, collected the early tales in *Uncle Remus: His Songs and His Sayings* (published in 1880, dated 1881), and gradually became an unwilling celebrity with the publication of four more books on Uncle Remus and numerous collections of other sketches and tales, among them *Mingo and Other Sketches in Black and White* (1884), *Free Joe and Other Georgia Sketches* (1887), *Balaam and His Master and Other Sketches and Stories* (1891), *The Chron-*

icles of Aunt Minervy Ann (1899), and several novels, including *Sister Jane* (1896) and *Gabriel Tolliver* (1902). Harris focused on the favorable aspects of plantation life before the war, especially the warm, easy relations between household servants and masters, yet he recognized the plight of the slave in the situation of the rabbit who survives by wit and shrewdness and clever manipulation of the more powerful animals. Thus Harris provides a picture of antebellum life in Middle Georgia that differs from Thompson's and Johnston's portraits of chiefly white common folk in villages and on small farms, though the treatment of dialect and language, customs and manners, setting, and locale in the work of all these writers is similar and lends an air of reality and authenticity. In Harris's case, his effort to show the local and regional as important aspects of national life, his awareness of and willingness to deal with both the virtues and the faults of the old regime in the South, and his creation of such memorable characters as Uncle Remus, the little boy, Brer Rabbit, Mingo, Free Joe, Minervy Ann, Billy Sanders, and others reflects a view of Georgia life that in some ways anticipates the work of Erskine Caldwell and Flannery O'Connor, especially as regards authorial sympathy for poor white and black characters. A part of Harris's canon also suggests a literary connection with Will Harben (1858–1919), merchant, editor, and proponent of the New South, and his fiction on north Georgia in such works as *Northern Georgia Sketches* (1900) and *The Georgians* (1904). Harris can also be connected with Harry Stillwell Edwards (1855–1938), Macon lawyer, newspaper editor, and columnist, and his conception of rural and small-town life in middle and north Georgia in such collections of dialect stories as *Two Runaways and Other Stories* (1889) and *Defense and Other Stories* (1899) and in his best-known work, *Eneas Africanus* (1919), a long tale in the black dialect of its central character that has demonstrated its popularity over the past seventy-five years by selling well over two million copies.

The last writers of prose of the nineteenth century who merit attention—Henry Grady, Charles Henry Smith, and Augusta Jane Evans Wilson—are different in various ways from those previously discussed. Grady and Smith were both journalists, and in that way not unlike Longstreet, Thompson, or Harris, but both men devoted themselves to newspaper work without turning their prose into fiction. Grady (1850–1889), for example, a native of Athens and involved with newspapers in Rome, Augusta, and chiefly At-

lanta, devoted his energies to the editorial page and speeches advocating the so-called New South policies he became identified with in the 1880s. Smith (1826–1903), on the other hand, practiced law in Rome before the war, served on special judicial duty in Macon during the conflict after his service in the army ended in 1862 because of ill health, and returned to legal practice in Rome after the war. A good friend of Grady and of J. C. Harris, he made his contributions to literature in the form of letters from "Bill Arp" to various newspapers, beginning in 1861–1862 with his satiric epistles to Mr. Linkhorn in the Rome *Southern Confederacy* and continuing on various topics until over two thousand had been printed by his death in 1903. These were collected in books from *Bill Arp, So Called* (1866) to *Bill Arp, From the Uncivil War to Date* (1903). Aside from her birth in Columbus, Augusta Jane Evans Wilson's (1835–1909) literary experience was unlike that of Grady and Smith. Not only did Evans spend most of her life in Alabama, but she also devoted her energies to popular novels, such as *Macaria* (1863), a work written to support the Confederate cause and one that was successful throughout the country, despite prohibitions placed upon its sale by officials in the North. Evans's novels embrace Victorian standards and usually include her opposition to women's suffrage, populism, and prohibition, yet *Beulah* (1859) and *St. Elmo* (1866) were best sellers, and, along with *Macaria*, are still in print today. Her style may be flowery and wordy, and her characters affected and stilted, but her narratives move in a lively way and her main female characters usually make an effective case for whatever cause they espouse.

Of the poets of the period, Richard Henry Wilde (1789–1847), Thomas Holley Chivers (1809–1858), Paul Hamilton Hayne (1830–1886), and Sidney Lanier (1842–1881) merit consideration, a group of bards near in quality and achievement to their contemporaries in Virginia and South Carolina, states associated with Poe and Simms, respectively.

Wilde (1789–1847) was born in Ireland, but his parents moved to Maryland in 1797 and his widowed mother to Augusta in 1803. There he studied and practiced law, became attorney general of Georgia at twenty-two, and eventually served six times in the U.S. Congress before being defeated in 1835, at which point he went to Italy to study Italian literature and write poetry. Returning to Georgia in 1841 and resuming his legal practice, he removed to New Orleans in 1844 and died in 1847 during a yellow-fever epidemic. Wilde's poems, then, were an avocation, though he would have been happy to devote himself to poetry had he been financially able to do so. As it was, he managed to publish a number of fugitive poems, of which the best known is "The Lament of the Captive" (1815?, 1819); an incomplete long narrative, *Hesperia: A Fragment* (1867); and translations from Tasso and other Italian poets. "The Lament" might have helped to make his literary reputation, but it was involved in a plagiarism controversy for over fifty years that was not settled until Wilde had been dead for more than twenty years. Some of his poems were known to Irving, Paulding, Poe, Simms, and Longfellow, but they were not collected until 1966 and even then only as parts of a selected edition.

A much more thoroughly romantic, transcendental poet than Wilde was his young contemporary, Thomas Holley Chivers (1809–1858) of Washington, Georgia. A man of medicine who soon ceased to practice it, Chivers turned to poetry and managed to see that his poems were gathered and printed, usually at his own expense, in ten books of verse and drama from *The Path of Sorrow* (1832) to *The Sons of Usna* (1858). A follower, to some extent, of Swedenborg, Chateaubriand, Emerson, and Poe, Chivers nevertheless put together his own thoughts on aesthetics and prosody, and despite some imitation and borrowing from others— the cross currents of influence between Chivers and Poe are still a matter of difficulty to decide—Chivers's work as a whole demonstrates an originality and individuality that make it almost unique in concept and development, if not in achievement. His interest in word color, music, and verbal magic, not unlike that in general of Poe, Hayne, and Lanier, led him to attempt to express the rhythms and harmonies of black speech and music in such a piece as the "Corn Shucking Song" (1855) and at the same time to suggest his awareness of his own Georgia background.

Paul Hamilton Hayne (1830–1886) was a native of Charleston who sought exile near Augusta after the Civil War and there spent the last twenty years of his life as the representative poet of Georgia (of the South, too, for that matter), as his authorship of the official poems on the occasions of the International Cotton Exposition in Atlanta in 1881, "The Return of Peace," and the 1883 "Sesqui-Centennial Ode" on the founding of Georgia readily affirms. Hayne's debt to his adopted state is reflected in his use of his natural surroundings in the Copse-Hill nature poems of the 1870s—"Aspects of the Pines" (1872) and "The Voice

of the Pines" (1873) among them—mostly published in the *Atlantic Monthly* and collected in *Poems: Complete Edition* (1882), and in the lyrics celebrating the rural and agricultural virtues of the area—"In the Wheat Field" (1882), "Midsummer (On the Farm)" (1884), and "The Last Patch (of Cotton)" (1883), to select only three—chiefly printed in *Home and Farm* and never collected since many of them appeared after the so-called Complete Edition. Hayne's employment of Columbia County materials was fundamental to his postwar poetry and to his fiction and essays as well. In the apostrophe to Georgia at the end of the "Sesqui-Centennial Ode," he acknowledges this debt to his adopted home for a beneficent nature to write about, for bringing peace to his restless spirit, and for "bread and balm and wine."

Hayne's young colleague and friend Sidney Lanier (1842–1881), a native of Macon, was, like Hayne, a victim of consumption. Preparing for a legal career before the war and practicing with his father from time to time after it, Lanier devoted himself to music and poetry when his health and poverty allowed him. He began publishing dialect verse and other poems after the war, using his Georgia surroundings especially in such pieces as "Thar's More in the Man Than Thar Is in the Land" (1869?), which features rural dialect and deals with the predicaments of the small Middle Georgia farmer. Eventually in major poems "Corn" (1875) and "The Marshes of Glynn" (1878), Lanier stresses the plight of the farmer and improperly used land and sings of the live oaks, marshes, and water caught in an instant of time and place. In his best poems, a union of natural forces occurs, and the narrator-observer intuitively and momentarily feels at one with these forces. What with ill health and the difficulty of choosing between music and literature as a career, to say nothing of the constant struggle to make a living (including the writing of a travel book on Florida, 1876, and the editing of four boys' books for Scribner), Lanier never succeeded in fulfilling his promise as a poet. He had some innovative ideas, some knowledge of prosody (he published *The Science of English Verse* in 1880), a keen ear for verbal melody and the relation between music and poetry, an awareness of the natural world around him, and some useful interest in dialect and occasional success with spare language in such lyrics as "The Raven Days" (1868), "The Stirrup-Cup" (1877), and "A Ballad of Trees and the Master" (1880); however, Lanier could not avoid overusing the trappings of romantic poetic diction in his most ambitious poems, including

"The Symphony" (1875), "The Marshes of Glynn" (1878), and "Sunrise" (1882).

Prose fiction in twentieth-century Georgia developed in various ways that would probably have seemed strange to authors in the nineteenth, despite the fact that the germs of some of the differences may be found in work of the earlier period. The locales and some of the characters and dialect in the fiction of Erskine Caldwell, Carson McCullers, and Flannery O'Connor may not have seemed especially peculiar to Longstreet or Harris, but some of the subject matter, language, and authorial attitude toward this material might have appeared strange indeed to them, changes that have been intensified in the work of such later writers as Harry Crews, Alice Walker, and Pat Conroy. The fiction of Ferrol Sams (1922–   ), a Fayetteville physician, is a modest exception to this view, since his depictions of rural and small-town life are rooted in an earlier Georgia that Johnson, Harris, and Harben might recognize. The adventures of Porter Osborn in *Run With the Horseman* (1982) and *The Whisper of the River* (1984) differ from earlier Georgia scenes mainly in the treatment of sex and in the use of other postwar innovations.

Margaret Mitchell (1900–1949) and Lewis Grizzard (1946–1994) have predecessors including Augusta Jane Evans Wilson and Harris, Smith, and Edwards, respectively. Mitchell's *Gone With the Wind* (1936) is far more than an update of one of Wilson's sentimental novels, but it transcends the mode of conventional historical fiction in part by offering such unforgettable characters as Scarlett O'Hara and Rhett Butler and characterizing the New South ways of Atlanta so presciently as to anticipate the city's late-twentieth-century progressive state. On the other hand, Grizzard, a long-time columnist for the *Atlanta Journal-Constitution* (under another title, Harris's old paper), has created a Georgia world slightly reminiscent of the newspaper characters of Bill Arp and Harry Stillwell Edwards, and definitely in the tradition of southern humor back to Longstreet. Grizzard's scene unabashedly honors the southern way of life and happily satirizes the so-called sophistication of urban civilization outside Georgia and the South in a series of very popular collections of his columns beginning with *Won't You Come Home, Billy Bob Bailey* (1980) and ending with *The Last Bus to Albuquerque* (1994).

Georgia has produced many nationally recognized writers of fiction in the twentieth century. Erskine Caldwell (1902–1988), a preacher's son, grew up in Wrens and became a journalist, a scriptwriter in Hollywood, and a novelist. His early books—*Tobacco Road* (1932), *God's Little Acre* (1933), and *Georgia Boy* (1943), the first of which became a long-running Broadway play and the second of which sold over four million copies by 1946—created a sensation with their earthy treatments of the lives of rural poor-whites in Georgia, especially their sexual antics. Jeter Lester, the central character of *Tobacco Road,* the father of a large brood of shiftless children and a symbol of the predicament of the poverty-stricken farmer in the South, became one of the best-known literary characters of the 1930s, a source of humor and pity at the same time. Jeter is the ultimate extension of Longstreet's Ransy Sniffle, the first poor-white depicted in Georgia fiction, and yet Lester's plight represents the situation of his class in Depression-driven Georgia. Caldwell was interested, too, in the condition of the black man, as is clear from a collection of his stories, culled from throughout his career, called *Black and White* (1984). In the foreword, he maintains that the short story "is the ideal form of fiction to . . . reveal the inner spirit of the individual," an opinion well demonstrated in this collection and in others such as *Stories of Life: North and South* (1937, 1938).

Like Sidney Lanier, Carson Smith McCullers (1917–1967) was interested in both literature and music and at one time intended to study at Juilliard in New York, but, unlike Lanier, McCullers, by selling her first novel at the age of twenty-two, focused early on a literary career. A native of Columbus, Carson Smith moved north in 1934, married, and spent much of the rest of her life there, though most of her fiction deals with Georgia and the South. Her major works, three novels and a book of short fiction—*The Heart Is a Lonely Hunter* (1940), *Reflections in a Golden Eye* (1941), *The Member of the Wedding* (1946), and *The Ballad of the Sad Café* (1951), which consists of a novella and six stories—were published in slightly over a decade, for McCullers spent much of the 1950s and 1960s struggling with ill health. Her books deal frequently with adolescence, grotesques, loneliness and heartache, and the shadowland between fantasy and reality, all grounded nevertheless in settings palpably authentic. *The Heart Is a Lonely Hunter,* a narrative concerning the strange interconnected existences of a deaf mute, a twelve-year-old girl, a drunk, and other rejected and lonely characters in a small southern town, remains a haunting novel. *The Member of the Wedding,* a story centered on the dual lives of another twelve-year-old girl that McCullers turned into a prize-winning Broadway play in 1949–1950, is probably her best-known work. Both novels were later made into successful films in 1953 and 1968, respectively. In the final analysis, her long fiction and such shorter pieces as "The Ballad of the Sad Café," a novella, and "A Tree. A Rock. A Cloud," among other short stories, entitle her to high rank among writers of fiction in Georgia.

Eight years younger than McCullers but no less interested in strangeness and eccentricity, Flannery O'Connor (1925–1964) grew up in Milledgeville and took degrees from the Georgia State College for Women and the University of Iowa, where she offered a collection of stories to the Writer's Workshop for the M.A. Subsequently she lived and worked on her fiction for several years in New York City and Connecticut until the first major attack of lupus forced her to return to her mother's farm near Milledgeville, where she wrote and published novels and stories for the rest of her brief life, beginning with *Wise Blood* (1950), her first novel; continuing with *A Good Man Is Hard to Find* (1955), a gathering of short fiction that brought her national recognition; and concluding with another novel, *The Violent Bear It Away* (1960). A final volume of stories, *Everything That Rises Must Converge* (1965), appeared posthumously, as did *The Complete Stories* (1971), *Mystery and Manners* (1969), a book of uncollected essays, and *The Habit of Being: Letters* (1979). This is a small body of work perhaps, but it has antecedents in Georgia humor going back to Longstreet, sharpened by a strong Roman Catholic angle of vision on Protestant backgrounds and characters, and enlivened by a pungent commentary on the times. Her novels give O'Connor a chance to elaborate on her moral and theological concerns, but it is in her stories that, like Katherine Anne Porter and Eudora Welty before her, she achieves mastery of form and content. "A Good Man Is Hard to Find" (1953), "The Life You Save May Be Your Own" (1953), "The Artificial Nigger" (1955), "Greenleaf" (1956), "Everything That Rises Must Converge" (1961), and "Revelation" (1964), to mention only a few, are among the best stories of the period. Some of the characters and situations might not be out of place in the grotesque and macabre Georgia world of McCullers except for the theological context and slightly more rural background of O'Connor's world. But the theological situation of O'Connor's characters make for a considerable difference. The implications are serious to the last degree for the

Grandmother and the Misfit in "A Good Man," for Mr. Shiftet and Mrs. Crater in "The Life You Save," and for Mrs. Turpin in "Revelation," to select only a few of the weak and sinful characters whose souls are in jeopardy of hellfire and damnation. At the same time, O'Connor's stories can be read without full awareness of their theological overtones, and their comic context and realization of the appropriate Georgia scene in terms of locale, language, and manners are also worthy of full appreciation. In brief, her short fiction ranks with the best in Georgia, in the South, and in the nation as well.

More recent writers of prose fiction—Harry Crews, Alice Walker, and Pat Conroy—extend the range of possibilities of technique and subject matter. Harry Crews (1935–), a son of a poor farmer in Bacon County, grew up there, served in the Marines, and earned two degrees from the University of Florida, where he eventually joined the faculty in 1968 as a teacher of creative writing. In the same year, he published his first novel, *The Gospel Singer,* which was followed by fifteen other novels by 1993. In addition to those, Crews wrote *A Childhood: The Biography of a Place* (1978), an autobiography; *Florida Frenzy* (1982), essays and stories; and *Classic Crews: A Harry Crews Reader* (1993), an anthology composed of the aforementioned *Childhood,* two novels—*The Gypsy's Curse* (1974) and *Car* (1972)—and three essays. Much of Crews's work has a Florida setting, but the action in *The Gospel Singer* takes place in Enigma, Georgia, not far from Tifton, and *Childhood* is an account of Crews's boyhood in Bacon County. Both books describe the hard lives of sharecroppers in the area, though the novel focuses on a village of six hundred in scrub farming country. There, the Gospel Singer, a local boy who has made good on TV all the way from Albany, Georgia, to New York City, is scheduled to sing at a revival in the Reverend Woody Peals's tent, but all goes wrong when he tells the assembled audience of locals that as a sinner himself he cannot heal anyone, teach anyone about sin, or save anyone. At that point, the people of Enigma strip him, put him on a mule, and hang him from a nearby tree. At his death, his two young talentless siblings promise a reporter sent to cover the revival that they will take their brother's place on TV. The Gospel Singer is no Elmer Gantry, but he does point toward the coming escapades of Jim Bakker and Jimmy Swaggart, and Crews depicts the Singer, his manager, his poor-white family, and the townspeople of Enigma with authority and gusto. In later work, he treats the world of freaks and the car-crushing business, usually with Florida settings, a fair amount of violence, and casts of dispossessed and cursed characters for whom there is precious little hope in an uncaring world. Crews's Georgia is closer to Caldwell's than to that of McCullers or O'Connor.

Like Crews, Alice Walker (1944–) also came from a sharecropping background, though in her case her family lived in Eatonton in northeast Georgia and her mother served as a maid to white families in town. Despite this background, she attended Spelman College and then received a B.A. from Sarah Lawrence College in 1965. Her first book, *Once,* a collection of poems, appeared in 1968 and her first novel, *The Third Life of George Copeland,* in 1970. By 1992 she had published four more novels, including *The Color Purple* (1982), winner of a Pulitzer Prize; two volumes of short stories, *In Love and Trouble: Stories of Black Women* (1973) and *You Can't Keep a Good Woman Down* (1981); a book of essays, *In Search of Our Mothers' Gardens: Womanist Prose* (1983); and four more collections of verse, including *Her Blue Body Everything We Know: Earthling Poems, 1965–1990 Complete* (1991). As she has indicated on numerous occasions, Walker identifies with the lives of black women because of her own experience of oppression in Georgia and elsewhere. This is a topic of significance in *The Color Purple,* where sex is viewed as a tool of male dominance, mainly of black males, and must be dealt with accordingly by black females. The treatment of sex is graphic and forthright, beyond anything in Caldwell or Crews. An epistolary novel, conceived of as historical fiction, *The Color Purple* uses history as a referent that lends credibility to what may seem improbable or fantastic. An air of reality and specificity is achieved, for example, by the use of the central character's voice in her letters to a genderless God. Celie writes as she speaks in a dialect appropriate to her limited knowledge and experience, and her account of what happens seems possible in the society and setting (the Macon area) where the action takes place. Oral transmission, then, is vital to Celie's identity and to her development and maturation. These qualities, among others, contributed to the book's popular reception and to the award of the Pulitzer Prize the following year. A film adaptation came two years later, and though criticized by some reviewers and moviegoers for its treatment of black men, it generally extended the work's appeal to another audience. A sequel, *Possessing the Secret of Joy* (1992), treats female genital mutilation.

A year younger than Walker, Pat Conroy (1945–) was born in Atlanta, grew up on military bases where his father, a Marine Corps pilot, served, and idolized his mother, a native of Rome, Georgia. He spent much time with his grandparents in Atlanta, attended the Citadel, and subsequently lived in Atlanta, Charleston, and San Francisco. In the meantime, he wrote six books: *The Boo* (1970); *The Water Is Wide* (1972); *The Great Santini* (1976); *The Lords of Discipline* (1980); *The Prince of Tides* (1986); and *Beach Music* (1995). Much of this fiction is autobiographical and deals with his family (*The Great Santini* and *The Prince of Tides*), his college experience (*The Lords of Discipline*), or his teaching experience with black children on an island off the South Carolina coast (*The Water Is Wide*). All these books were turned into movies, and Conroy himself co-authored the script for *The Prince of Tides,* a work nominated for an Academy Award in 1991. Conroy's novels are frequently set in the South, and his narrators or central characters are usually southerners. He favors South Carolina for his backgrounds, although Atlanta is the scene of a memorable episode in *The Prince of Tides.* He is critical of the South for its racial discrimination, its devotion to class, and its violence, but he at the same time celebrates its rich land, memorable food, and appealing, fascinating women. Even in *Beach Music,* Jack McCall, the narrator, has left Charleston and South Carolina for Rome in order to get away from what has led to his wife's suicide and to save his daughter Leah from her native culture; even so, he repeats nightly the stories of his Carolina past, purged and purified, in response to Leah's "lust" for the "fierce, rarefied beauty of her birthplace," and in the end he marries his old Waterford sweetheart in Rome with "Carolina beach music" in the background at the wedding reception. As Jack acknowledges (and he may well speak for Conroy and many others as well), "the South was carry-on baggage I could not shed no matter how many borders I crossed."

As for poetry in twentieth-century Georgia, three names come immediately to mind—Conrad Aiken, Byron Herbert Reece, and James Dickey. There are other writers of verse, of course—Alice Walker, also a poet of standing; Bettie Sellers, the present poet laureate of the state; and David Bottoms, the prize-winning bard from Canton, to mention only three of the better-known authors.

Conrad Aiken (1889–1973), a native of Savannah who moved to New England in 1901 and returned to his birthplace late in life to spend his winters there, is one of the most important writers in the history of literature in Georgia, though ironically he seldom wrote about his state or used it in his work. After graduation from Harvard in 1912, he published in a career of almost sixty years more than fifty books of fiction, poetry, criticism, drama, and autobiography, including *Selected Poems* (1929), for which he won a Pulitzer Prize in 1930, and *Collected Poems* (1953), which earned him a National Book Award in 1954. He was consultant in poetry for the Library of Congress in 1950–1951 (a post whose title has been changed to Poet Laureate of the United States) and the recipient of many major prizes and awards for poetry. A member of the modernist movement in literature from his time at Harvard (T. S. Eliot read and criticized his poems there), Aiken's verse never appealed to a large audience. A further difficulty for his readers was his effort to relate the structure of music to poetry in such works as *The Jig of Forslin: A Symphony* (1916) and *The House of Dust: A Symphony* (1920). In expressing this interest, Aiken reminds one of Lanier, but his verse is much more obscure and complicated than Lanier's. Related by extension to these books are what many critics consider Aiken's greatest works: *Preludes for Memnon* (1931) and *Time in the Rock: Preludes to Definition* (1936), efforts, as he pointed out, "at a probing of the self-in-relation-to-the-world." Although there is little of Georgia in any of this work, his connection with Savannah and his distinction as a poet led Governor Jimmy Carter to appoint Aiken poet laureate of Georgia in 1973.

A poet much more concerned with Georgia in his work than Aiken is Byron Herbert Reece (1917–1958), who was born in Blairsville and grew up in the North Georgia mountains near Dahlonega. He attended Young Harris College, returned to his father's farm in 1940, and after tours as poet-in-residence at UCLA and Emory, he served on the faculty at Young Harris off and on from 1953 until his death by suicide in 1958. During this period, he managed to publish two novels—*Better a Dinner of Herbs* (1950) and *The Hawk and the Sun* (1955)—and five books of verse: *Ballad of the Bones* (1948); *Remembrance of Moab* (1949); *Bow Down in Jerico* (1950); *A Song of Joy* (1952); and *The Season of Flesh* (1955). Reece knows and uses the Bible, *Pilgrim's Progress,* and both folklore and literary tradition. He is a keen observer of the natural world and manages to get the people, the scene, and the language of his area into his spare mountain

ballads and to wed content and form so that the result seems inimitable and representative at the same time.

Another Atlantan, James Dickey (1923–1997), served in the air force in World War II and in the Korean "police action," studied at Clemson and later was awarded the B.A. and M.A. by Vanderbilt, where he found the teaching of Donald Davidson congenial to his interest in writing. He subsequently taught at Rice and the University of Florida, worked as an advertising writer in New York and Atlanta, and began composing poetry seriously in the 1950s. He gradually earned a reputation with *Into the Stone* (1960); *Drowning With Others* (1962); *Helmets* (1964); *Buckdancer's Choice* (1966, National Book Award), and *Poems, 1957–1967* (1968). Later titles include *The Eye-Beaters, Blood, Victory, Madness, Buckhead and Mercy* (1970); *The Zodiac* (1976); *The Strength of Fields* (1979); *Puella* (1982); and *The Eagle's Mile* (1990). He was consultant in poetry to the Library of Congress from 1966 to 1968. He also published two novels—*Deliverance* (1970), made into a movie for which he wrote the script, and *Alnilam* (1988)—and four books of criticism. He was poet-in-residence at the University of South Carolina from 1969 until his death in 1997. Georgia was available to Dickey for some of his poems as well as for *Deliverance,* but he uses it far more generally in his poetry than in his fiction. In "Cherrylog Road" (1963), for example, the speaker is in a junkyard of old cars off Highway 106, a Georgia road, but it could be another lot in another southern state and not much would be changed. The same point might be made about "Kudzu" (1963), referring to a groundcover brought into the South at large from Japan in the 1920s to halt erosion on hills and valleys, though there is now enough kudzu in Georgia to blanket most abandoned houses, barns, and pine trees in the state. And "The Shark's Parlor" (1965), a narrative of a struggle between men and a hammerhead shark on Cumberland Island, might easily have its scene moved to another part of the coast without damaging its integrity. Still, in each poem, place is established and necessary for what follows, a context for the artist to insert such disparate examples of life as junkyards, kudzu, and sharks. Content, technique, and form matter; language is revelation and control—through form, cadence, and metrically intricate and compressed statement.

It's a long way from Longstreet and Wilde to Conroy and Dickey in terms of time, subject matter, language, and authorial point of view, but there are common denominators in Georgia's history—its natural environment and its Christian view of the human condition from Tidewater to Piedmont to mountains. These factors and a distinctive sense of humor are all reflected in Georgia's literature and provide an abundant and varied anthology of writing for the state, the region, and the nation.

Rayburn S. Moore

See also Atlanta, Georgia; Macon, Georgia.

Hennig Cohen and William B. Dillingham, eds., *Humor of the Old Southwest* (1964); Kenneth Coleman and Charles S. Gurr, eds., *Dictionary of Georgia Biography* (2 vols.; 1983); Henry Louis Gates Jr. and K. A. Appiah, eds., *Alice Walker: Critical Perspectives Past and Present* (1993); Rayburn S. Moore, "Southern Writers and Northern Literary Magazines, 1865–1890" (Ph.D. diss., Duke University, 1956); Hugh Ruppersburg, ed., *Georgia Voices* (2 vols.; 1992, 1994).

GEORGIA, UNIVERSITY OF

The University of Georgia was chartered in 1787 as the nation's first state-sponsored institution of higher learning. Classes began on a 633-acre tract of land near the Oconee River in Athens, Georgia, in 1801, and except for a brief hiatus during the Civil War, the University has been open ever since. During most of its first century, the University offered a traditional liberal-arts curriculum to a student body numbering fewer than one hundred students. Financial support from the state was negligible, though the University's financial status improved when it became a land-grant institution in 1871. Courses in law were added in 1843, and in agriculture in 1872. As the University diversified its curriculum, state support grew, along with the number of students. By the early 1950s, more than 4,000 students attended the University, and by 1970 enrollment had risen to 21,000. The two most tumultuous events in the University's history (other than the interruption by the Civil War) came in 1940 when interference in University affairs by Governor Eugene Talmadge threatened accreditation, and in 1961 when the University admitted its first African American students. Presently, the University of Georgia enrolls more than 30,000 students per year and consists of thirteen schools and colleges, including Arts and Science, Agriculture, Journalism, Education, Business, and others. In the last two decades, the University has gained recognition as a leading public research university.

The University of Georgia is occasionally mentioned as the Franklin College in nineteenth-century southern writings. Henry Timrod, poet of the Confederacy, and Henry Grady, author of the famous "The New South" address (1886) and editor of the *Atlanta Constitution,* were among its graduates. In the twentieth century, its most prominent literary appearance came in the novel *A Song of Daniel* by Georgia writer Phillip Lee Williams. Set on the University campus, the novel's main character is an English professor obsessed with a fictional version of the North Georgia poet Byron Herbert Reece. Williams is a public-relations writer for the University. The University has had a significant secondary role in the support of southern culture and writing. In 1947 the *Georgia Review* was founded by southern literary scholar John Donald Wade, one of the Vanderbilt Agrarians. Under the editorship of Stanley W. Lindberg, the *Review* achieved prominence in the 1980s and 1990s as one of the nation's leading literary reviews. An active creative-writing program has counted among its faculty such contemporary southern writers as Marion Montgomery (*Darrel, Fugitive*), Coleman Barks (*The Juice, The Essential Rumi*), James Kilgo (*Deep Enough for Ivory Bills, An Inheritance of Horses, Daughter of My People)*, Warren Leamon (*Unheard Melodies*), and Judith Ortiz Cofer (*The Line of the Sun, Silent Dancing, The Latin Deli*).

Hugh Ruppersburg

See also Georgia, Literature of.

F. N. Boney, *A Pictorial History of the University of Georgia* (1984); Thomas G. Dyer, *The University of Georgia: A Bicentennial History, 1785–1985* (1985).

GERMANS

German-speaking immigrants from Central Europe constitute the largest ethnic group to settle in the United States. Germans appeared as early as 1608 in company with Captain John Smith in Jamestown, but their first settlement in the New World was Germantown, Pennsylvania, established near Philadelphia in 1683. Large-scale migration commenced in the early eighteenth century and continued until the American Revolution. Tens of thousands left Europe seeking religious freedom and better economic opportunity; most entered through the port of Philadelphia and then headed west and south.

Like the Scots-Irish, the Germans streamed down the Valley of Virginia and then fanned out across the Piedmont and mountains of the Carolinas and Georgia. Some settled in the cities—Baltimore, Richmond, Charleston, and New Orleans—where they were craftsmen or merchants, but the vast majority in the South worked the land. Contemporary writings suggest that the Germans were exemplary farmers. In contrast to the English and Scots-Irish, who frequently exhausted the soil with crops like tobacco and then moved on, the Germans were more stable and farmed intensively, rotating their crops and achieving superior production. They were also quick to adapt to prevailing southern settlement patterns, crops, and livestock. However, they left their mark on the land with their asymmetrical, three-room house form and their preference for construction in log, stone, and half-timbering (*Fachwerk*).

The Germans were also characterized as somewhat clannish. They showed less interest in commerce, cash crops, and politics than their neighbors and tended to be more self-sufficient and family oriented. Most were members of the Lutheran and Reformed churches, with a scattering of Moravians in North Carolina and sectarian groups such as the Mennonites, Dunkers, and United Brethren in Virginia. Language also proved an isolating factor, but by 1830 English was in common use, and most Germans were well acculturated into southern life. At this time, a second wave of German immigration from Europe began, spurred by social and political unrest and the impact of the Industrial Revolution. However, most of these new Germans chose cities in the mid-Atlantic and midwestern regions over the agrarian South. A substantial number did settle in central Texas, while others moved up the Mississippi into Memphis, St. Louis, and Louisville.

Despite their numbers, long history of settlement, and wide distribution, the Germans did not have a significant impact on southern literature, nor were they stereotyped as were Creoles, mountaineers, or crackers. Perhaps this was due to their agrarian orientation or their lack of involvement in public life. In the cities, there was an active German-language press, which produced an extensive body of religious writings, travel literature, political tracts, fiction, and poetry. Much of it was written by German-born authors; for example, Charles Sealsfield (Karl Anton Postl), who landed in New Orleans in 1823 and traveled extensively in the U.S. and Mexico. His sketches of southern frontier life and historical romances—*Tokeah, or the White Rose* (1829) and *Das Kajutenbuch* (1841)—were widely read on both sides of the Atlantic and influenced several writers, including Simms and Longfellow. However, the bulk of German-American literature reached only a limited audience and focused quite narrowly on issues of German-American identity.

Charles G. Zug III

See also Boone, Daniel; Folk Art; Valley of Virginia.

Terry G. Jordan, *German Seed in Texas Soil: Immigrant Farmers in Nineteenth-Century Texas* (1966); Don Heinrich Tolzmann, ed., *German-American Literature* (1977); Klaus Wust, *The Virginia Germans* (1969).

GETTING HAPPY

Getting Happy is a Christian religious phenomenon that involves spontaneous reactions to the "movement" of the Holy Ghost in the worshipper. For this reason, it is often called "getting the holy ghost." Getting Happy includes a wide range of physical manifestations, such as shouting, dancing, running, jumping, speaking in tongues, fainting or "falling out," waving the arms, clapping, and other involuntary ecstatic movements performed by a worshipper either inside or outside of an organized church service. In its broadest terms, getting happy can be simply a matter of expressing religious joy and exuberance.

This phenomenon is most often associated with evangelical church traditions such as Pentecostal, Holiness, and Church of God in Christ (C.O.G.I.C.); however, it can be found throughout other denominations as well, to varying degrees, especially where African American churches are concerned. In the C.O.G.I.C. church, for example, church doctrine states that those who are saved receive a "holy ghost experience" evidenced by various forms of getting happy, especially speaking in tongues, and further mandates that a holy ghost experience is a necessity for everyone. Because of this belief, and their highly emotional worship services, people belonging to C.O.G.I.C., Holiness, and Pentecostal congregations are often perjoratively called "holy rollers" by outsiders. In several other denominations, such as the Baptist and Methodist, the church covenant does not address religious ecstasy or indicate that getting happy is a necessity for salvation or proper worship, but congregants may exhibit different types of ecstatic behavior in church such as shouting or clapping. This is especially true of African American congregations.

Some scholars have explained the tendency of African American churches to have spirited, physically engaged worship services as a carryover from African ceremonial worship that enslaved persons syncretized with Christianity. Practices in slave religion, such as the "ring shout," a kind of holy dance observed in the Georgia Sea Islands during the antebellum period, seem to support this theory. Other scholars contend that the enthusiasm of European American Protestant camp meetings and church services during the religious Great Awakenings influenced African Americans to embrace ecstatic worship. Evangelists at these meetings also encouraged ecstatic conversion, but their services were markedly different from what developed as African American ecstatic religious expression.

Much of the literature that illustrates people getting happy refers to African American religious experience. *God Struck Me Dead: Religious Conversion Experiences and Autobiographies of Ex-Slaves* (1969) provides numerous examples from African Americans in the South from the antebellum period to the early 1900s. Anne Moody's *Coming of Age in Mississippi* (1968) gives a more contemporary example. William Faulkner's *The Sound and the Fury* (1929) and Jean Toomer's *Cane* (1923) are other southern texts that portray religious ecstasy in a southern African American context. One of the best literary examples of religious ecstasy in the African American church tradition, regardless of region, is James Baldwin's autobiographical novel *Go Tell It on the Mountain* (1953).

Valerie N. Matthews

See also Black Methodists; Evangelical Christianity; Whoopin'.

Peter D. Goldsmith, *When I Rise Cryin' Holy: African American Denominationalism on the Georgia Coast* (1989); Ruel W. Tyson Jr., James L. Peacock, and Daniel W. Patterson, eds., *Diversities of Gifts: Field Studies in Southern Religion* (1988).

GHOST STORIES

Ghosts have haunted southern literature from early in its tradition. In his *History of North Carolina* (1714), John Lawson presents colonist testimony that "the ship that brought the first colonies does often appear among them, in a gallant posture." Dubbed "Sir Walter Raleigh's ship" by the community, the spectral craft prowls the North Carolina coast, searching in vain for Virginia Dare and the ill-fated Lost Colony. Even as early as the beginning of the eighteenth century, ghost stories served to remind southerners of the tragic beginnings of their communities. Ghosts are visible and recurring manifestations of the past, history constantly present and influential. Unquiet spirits relive the moments of their demise, a death caused by another's evil or brought on by their own bad behavior. Their appearances serve as reminders to those they visit. Ghosts, their hauntings limited to tragic action and bound to the scene of their demise, also epitomize the intimate connection between history and place in southern culture.

An important part of oral tradition, ghost stories help bind together southern communities. Alternately called harnts, haints, or hants, ghosts often become the focus of stories told at family and community gatherings. Adults tell and retell stories of the headless apparitions of murdered men, the sounds of phantom riders on the road or crying babies killed by young mothers, and troubled souls with unfinished business or on a mission to correct an injustice. The storytellers offer the tales as entertainment, yet the ghosts carry the troubled history of the community and the ever-present threat of tragedy and sudden death. When told to children, ghost stories can serve as a tool for moral instruction, the ghosts themselves object lessons of misbehavior and ignored warnings.

The oral tradition of the haint tale has directly influenced the literary ghost story. Demonstrating the primacy of ghost stories in southern culture, Mark Twain uses a traditional African American ghost story, "The Golden Arm," to illustrate the importance of performance in storytelling in his essay "How to Tell a Story" (1895). In the tale, a ghost searches for the thief of its golden arm. The storyteller, taking on the persona of the ghost, eventually points a sudden accusing finger at a young listener, much to the frightened delight of the audience. Joel Chandler Harris tells another version of the same tale in "A Ghost Story," from his collection *Nights with Uncle Remus* (1883). Other writers such as Charles Chesnutt, Zora Neale Hurston, and Mary Noailles Murfree reproduce in their fiction the important, sometimes complex, relationship between the spinner of the ghost yarn and the yarnspinner's audience.

Like the British literary ghost story, though, the

southern literary ghost story largely generates from English gothic fiction and its gloomy castles, haunted landscapes, obsessed villains, shadowy figures, and impinging madness. Edgar Allan Poe was the first to adapt this tradition to southern literature. Although he never wrote what may today be called a traditional ghost story, he explored the hazy borderland between the living and the dead. Often his characters cross over into that nether territory, physically transformed into the image of a husband's first wife, like Rowena in "Ligeia" (1838), or held for months in a hypnotic trance to stay the bodily decay of death, like the title character in "The Facts of the Case of M. Valdemar" (1845). Presences and apparitions, both dead and living, haunt Poe's characters, such as the narrator of "The Tell-Tale Heart" (1843), who murders a man and buries his dismembered body beneath the floorboards, only to hear the heart insistently beat as officers question him. The narrator of "William Wilson" (1839) finds his physical double in the title character, a constant and unavoidable attendance that slowly drives the narrator to insanity and death. The idea of the persistent and vexing presence surfaces again in Truman Capote's ghost story "Miriam" (1945): a precocious ghost-child moves in with an aging spinster and refuses to leave. Only rarely do Poe's characters come face to face with an apparition. In "Ms. Found in a Bottle" (1833), a survivor of a shipwreck discovers himself aboard an immense spectral ship as it heads inexplicably toward its own doom.

In one of his most significant contributions to the southern ghost story, Poe adapted the ruinous castle of English gothic fiction to the southern landscape. His story "The Fall of the House of Usher" (1839) serves as a prototype for the southern haunted-house story. The decaying, decrepit manor house verges on collapse under the weight of its own profane history. The ruinous plantation house will later find its way into Thomas Nelson Page's ghost story "No Haid Pawn" (1887), Andrew Lytle's short novel *A Name for Evil* (1947), and William Faulkner's *Absalom, Absalom!* (1936), among other works. Local-color writers use ghost stories as an example of quaint superstition, easily explained. To the eye of the reader, the ghosts often turn out to be men on the run from the authorities, even though the mountain community embraces the tales that arise from their lurking. The ghost in George Washington Cable's "Jean-Ah Poquelin" (1879) turns out to be a man suffering from leprosy. Mary Noailles Murfree, who wrote under the name Charles Egbert

Craddock, placed her ghost stories in the context of the local superstition of a mountain community. In "The 'Harnt' That Walked Chilhowee" (1884), young Clarsie, influenced by the tales of her parents, continues to see a fugitive as a ghost even after she has fed him.

The South's history of racial violence appears often in ghost stories by writers of local color. Although Cable describes mysteriously closing doors and ghostly moans in "The 'Haunted House' on Royal Street," a chapter in his nonfiction work *Strange True Stories of Louisiana* (1888), the house is more haunted by the brutality that Madame Lalaurie visited upon her slaves within its walls. In Thomas Nelson Page's "The Spectre in the Cart" (1899), a young district attorney witnesses the apparition of a lynching he could not prevent, the black man swinging limply from the limb, the victim's father riding mournfully in a cart. The ghosts, though, do not frighten the attorney as much as the violence that caused it. "Yes, I have seen apparitions," he says, "but I have seen what was worse." An African American writer influenced by local color, Randall Kenan also probes the ghostly result of vigilante violence and the relationship of that violence to official law in "Tell Me, Tell Me" (1992). In the story, the spirit of an African American boy haunts a woman who, in her youth, witnessed his murder at the hands of her brutish husband-to-be, a future respected judge.

The ghost story is central to African American oral and written tradition, a presence that is not accidental. In an attempt to limit slave movements and discourage runaways, slavemasters used ghost stories. Overseers endowed places along possible escape routes with violent ghosts, believing that the fear of ghosts would keep slaves safely indoors during the night. According to Gladys-Marie Fry in her book *Night Riders in Black Folk History*, the masters even went as far as impersonating ghosts in order to convince dubious slaves. Fry also claims that the costume of the Ku Klux Klan—the white sheet and hood—derives from these masquerades. Elements of these efforts to control African American behavior can be found in mid-nineteenth-century Southwestern humor. In "Frustratin' a Funeral" (1867), George Washington Harris's character Sut Lovingood paints and dresses up as devilish haint-figures an African American corpse and its sleeping attendant in order to put fear in the African American community.

In the works of African American writers, though, slaves use ghost stories to undermine white authority.

Uncle Julius, from Charles Chesnutt's collection *The Conjure Woman* (1899), tells the plantation owners of "The Gray Wolf's Ha'nt" in order to protect his favorite source of honey from demolition. In a tale that Zora Neale Hurston collected in her book *Mules and Men* (1935), John the slave uses his fear of ghosts to turn the tables on his master. Under orders, John tries to fetch water for his master, but a bullfrog frightens him. He tells a story of a hopping haint to his master, who must accept the explanation to encourage further superstition in his slave. By embracing superstition, John forces his master to get his own water. In the hands of the African American storyteller, the ghost story becomes a subversive weapon against the power of the master.

Ghosts serve as a metaphor for those characters burdened with history, the South's or their own. Those who succumb to the repetitive re-creation of the past become ghosts. William Faulkner describes those who cannot disentangle themselves from the memory of the Civil War as ghosts. In *Absalom, Absalom!*, Quentin Compson, preparing to leave for college in the North, sits in Miss Rosa Coldfield's house listening to tales of a South "dead since 1865 and peopled with garrulous outraged baffled ghosts, listening, having to listen, to one of the ghosts which had refused to lie still even longer than most had, telling him about old ghost times." In her story "First Dark" (1960), Elizabeth Spencer's ghosts are both literal and figurative. The ghost of an African American man in a wagon repeats his journey to search for a doctor to help his sick little girl. Finding herself likewise repeating history, trapped in the stifling atmosphere of the small Mississippi town and a family house haunted by the possessions that generations have collected, Frances Hardy, the story's protagonist, refers to herself and other townspeople as ghosts.

Although usually depicted as a potentially malevolent force, ghosts in the hands of southern women writers also have the capacity to soothe and release. Spencer's ghost eventually helps to release Frances from the town's hold on her. The ghosts in Ellen Glasgow's "Whispering Leaves" and "The Shadowy Third" (1923) are nurturing figures who protect the people they haunt. In Doris Betts's *The Sharp Teeth of Love* (1997), Tamsen Donner of the ill-fated Donner Party haunts Luna Stone. The ghost's presence helps Luna heal the physical and emotional starvation in her life.

Tales of ghosts still haunt southern literature. Along with Kenan and Betts, contemporary writers Padgett Powell, in his short story "Letter from a Dogfighter's Aunt, Deceased" (1991), and Lee Smith, in her novel *Oral History* (1983), attempt to preserve and reinvent the tradition of the southern literary ghost story. For her novel, Smith harkens back to the mountain people of Murfree's fiction. In the frame of the novel, Jennifer, a college student with an oral-history assignment, records the superstitions of the relatives from Hoot Owl Holler, a place they claim is haunted. She finds them quaint in their beliefs and even tries to record the ghostly sounds of the haunted cabin. The cabin will become, Smith tells us, the centerpiece of a garish theme park called Ghostland, reduced to an artifact of discarded superstition in the midst of contemporary commercialism. Ghosts and ghost stories, though, do not easily fade away. People still gather to see "when that rocking chair starts rocking," as they will always gather, Smith implies, to hear and read tales of haints.

Charles D. Martin

See also African American Folk Culture; Folklore; Gothicism; Local Color; Oral History.

Ray B. Browne, *"A Night with the Hants" and Other Alabama Folk Experiences* (1976); Gladys-Marie Fry, *Night Riders in Black Folk History* (1975); W. K. McNeil, ed., *Ghost Stories from the American South* (1985).

GILDED AGE

In 1873 Charles Dudley Warner and Mark Twain published a "partnership" novel, *The Gilded Age: A Tale of To-day*. It focuses on the interrelationship of speculators, lobbyists, and politicians. Though unsatisfactory as a work of art, the book provides an effective portrait of the post–Civil War era, with its get-rich-quick mentality and political corruption in Washington, especially in the United States Senate. It quotes a speculator in lands: "I wasn't worth a cent two years ago, and now I owe two million dollars," and asks "Who shall say that this is not the golden age of mutual trust, of unlimited reliance upon human promises?" The book gave a name to the era.

Political corruption is especially identified with the administration of President Ulysses S. Grant (1869–1877), who was supportive of the demands of business, such as high tariffs. Low public morality flourished. Even the president's private secretary was indicted—he had helped protect corrupt internal revenue agents who made deals with whiskey distillers. Brought to trial, he was defended by Grant himself. Everywhere, politicians successfully won places of power through patronage. Especially notable was the power of "Boss" William Tweed in New York City. What was happening was soon in the headlines. Newspaper editors, notably those of the *New York Times* and the *Baltimore Sun,* were publishing exposés that attracted the attention of the nation. One major result was that the North focused on its own problems, not those of the South and the freedmen, who were nearly powerless without outside help. Thus as early as 1867, the *Nation* proclaimed, "The diminution of political corruption is the great question of our time. It is greater than [Negro] suffrage, greater than reconstruction."

The South was too poor to have a "gilded" age, but it too suffered from corrupt politics. Many of those identified with the Freedmen's Bureau were active supporters of the Republican Party and did what they could to bring the former slaves into it. Indeed, as the party of Lincoln, the Republican Party was attractive to African Americans, who were told that the Democrats favored a return to slavery. But, in fact, in the South as in the North, both political parties were largely controlled by the railroads and other businesses that had the money to win special privileges. As the party out of power in the South, the Democrats—more properly called Conservatives—were in a better position to point to corruption than those in the other party. It was easy for racist southerners to identify political corruption with carpetbaggers and blacks. Even honest Republicans were casualties of what became a preoccupation with corruption. The Ku Klux Klan and the White League, which sought to return blacks to a position not much better than slavery, could pretend to take the high moral ground, though as Mark Summers asserts, "blacks neither did most of the stealing nor took most of the profits . . . because they held fewer offices and fewer of the important ones." Nonetheless, blacks suffered most from the political climate. Reconstruction was the victim of corrupt politics, but there were other powerful forces at work, the foremost being racism. In the North, there was both disapproval of blacks' having political power and a diminishing interest in what was going on in the South.

For example, a *New York Tribune* reporter, a Republican and a racist who was sent to the South, interviewed white conservatives in South Carolina and reported that "Reconstruction" had utterly failed. The book that resulted, James Pike's *The Prostrate State: South Carolina Under Negro Government,* has been called "the *Uncle's Tom Cabin* of the redemption of the South."

A turning point occurred in the election of 1876. Democrats thought that they had won the election and had elected Samuel Tilden president, but the Republicans, who still ruled South Carolina, Louisiana, and Florida, swung the election to Rutherford B. Hayes. It was a "stolen election." To make peace, the Republicans agreed to withdraw troops from the South, in effect ending Reconstruction.

Everett Emerson

See also Twain, Mark.

Bernard Bailyn et al., *The Great Republic: A History of the American People* (1977); Mark W. Summers, *The Era of Good Stealings* (1993).

GONE WITH THE WIND

Margaret Mitchell, born in 1900, liked to say that she was ten before she knew that the South lost the Civil War. "I heard so much when I was little about the fighting and the hard times after the war that I firmly believed Mother and Father had been through it all." As a girl, she dramatized Thomas Dixon's novel *The Traitor* and saved photographs of herself in costume as its leading man. A childhood playmate told of their enacting scenes from the movie *The Birth of a Nation* (adapted from Dixon's *The Clansman*), in which Mitchell also played the male lead. Many years later, Dixon wrote to congratulate her on *Gone With the Wind.*

After a year in New England at Smith College, where she protested being assigned to a history class with a Negro student, her mother's death called her home to Atlanta to be with her ailing father, a prominent attorney. As a debutante with six suitors, she chose the one who drank, and then, to escape the failing marriage, she went to work at the *Atlanta Journal* as a reporter and feature writer. Hard work and style brought her success and confidence. Two months after her divorce, she married the safest suitor, John Marsh, her ex-husband's roommate, a copy editor and proofreader who aided her literary efforts. His shyness and psychosomatic illnesses matched hers, and their marriage became a mutual dependency.

When a rheumatic ankle made reporting difficult, she stayed home, and to pass the time, began writing a novel about the Civil War. (She was also reading Wilhelm Stekel's *Frigidity in Woman in Relation to Her Love Life*.) Doubtful about her novel, she told herself (and a few friends) that she was writing merely for her own amusement. Harold Latham, an editor seeking new fiction, persuaded her to let him read it and saw that it could become a best-seller. His view was confirmed by Charles W. Everett, a professor at Columbia, who urged Macmillan to "take the book at once." As Mitchell and Marsh edited the final version, she read Civil War history intensively and found it far more complex than she had imagined. With Everett's comments in mind, she muted some of her inadvertent racism. The book's theme, for her, was survival—what factors allow some people to survive while others do not.

Mitchell saw women as crucial in shaping those outcomes. In her own life, her mother, Maybelle, strong, good, compassionate, realistic, and courageous, had been the ideal woman. In the book, Ellen O'Hara holds Tara together until her death (like Maybelle's, from an illness contracted in caring for others), when Scarlett takes over. But at the very end, Scarlett turns to the black *magna mater* for comfort. The critic Leslie Fiedler sees Mammy as dominant at the end. The book's final moment of terrible loss was its point of origin for Mitchell herself: it was the first scene she wrote, and she then imagined the rest of the events to lead up to it. And she claimed not to be able to see beyond it: "I left them to their ultimate fate."

Many advance copies and some reviews built nationwide excitement before official publication on June 30, 1936. The *New York Times* national reviewer liked its narrative force and details, but not its lack of depth and literary quality. Other New York reviewers were more enthusiastic: they loved its epic sweep, power, and vitality, a welcome relief from the pessimism of the era's more "literary" authors. By the time reviews began to appear in national magazines, the book was already a runaway best-seller. Although the skepticism of prestigious journals like *New Republic* and *Saturday Review* may have kept it out of college classrooms, it sold 1.7 million copies in the first year (by today, 28 million plus). Fascination for *GWTW* remains so high that Alexandra Ripley's authorized (by Mitchell's heirs) "sequel," *Scarlett* (1991), sold over 20 million and spawned the most expensive TV miniseries ever.

Producer David Selznick paid $50,000, then a new record, for movie rights. He designed the production to appeal to the millions who had already read—and loved—the book. He wanted to remain faithful to it in every important way, though the movies' Production Code was more restrictive than publishers' standards. Still, the movie was "pre-sold," and public interest in making it remained high. Selznick's search for the perfect Scarlett, the longest-running drama in Hollywood, ended suddenly when he recognized her in the lovely, troubled young English actress Vivien Leigh. From the first, most Americans who cared saw Clark Gable as Rhett Butler; Gable was reluctant, because expectations for the movie were so high.

Selznick's faith in the book led him to insist that his screenwriters use its exact words. That was a daunting task: its dialogue, unlike that of Scott Fitzgerald (who also worked on the film for a while), didn't always ring true. It also had to be cut drastically: as Sydney Howard, the main screenwriter, noted, Mitchell said everything at least twice. Digressions, characters, and subplots were eliminated or streamlined. In that process, valuable aspects were also cut. The movie has little room for the nuances of social status that preoccupy, indeed define, the families in whom Mitchell and Scarlett were most interested, the aristocracies of Virginia (the exquisitely exhausted Wilkeses) and Charleston (the darkly passionate Butlers). Scarlett loves and longs for both but can really reach neither, and she never overcomes her social inferiority.

GWTW had to be cleaned up politically too. Its minstrel-show view of blacks was a problem. In the book, Ashley Wilkes joins the Klan during Reconstruction; in the movie, he wants Scarlett to hire black freedmen instead of convicts in her lumber business. The movie doesn't mention Rhett's killing a black man who tried to rape a white woman. Big Sam, who becomes foreman after Ellen O'Hara fires Jonas Wilkerson, is more prominent in the movie, which emphasizes his saving Scarlett from attempted rape in Shantytown. And since most viewers would be in the nation's cities, the book's contempt for Yankees had to fade.

Like *The Birth of a Nation*, *GWTW* played to its audience's high expectations for a new cultural experience. Technicolor was new to them, and the film was gorgeous. Although the acting style is somewhat exaggerated, that too is faithful to the book: operatic and extravagant. The film's form, style, ostentation, and politics are also reminiscent of *The Birth of a Nation*. A musical overture allows viewers to be seated and to get serious. Ben Hecht, called in repeatedly as a script doctor, wrote—or overwrote—the pompous introductory lines:

> There was a land of Cavaliers and
> cotton fields called the Old South. . . .
> Here in this patrician world
> the age of Chivalry took its last bow. . . .
> Here was the last ever seen
> of Knights and their Ladies Fair,
> of Master and of Slave. . . .
> Look for it only in books, for it
> is no more than a dream remembered,
> a Civilization gone with the wind.

Slightly past midpoint, an intermission sustained by music just after Scarlett's famous line, "I'll never be hungry again!," invites viewers to the refreshment counters. Again, music beyond the final credits links her final words, "Tomorrow is another day," to the Depression outside the theater: if Scarlett could still be hopeful, after all this, perhaps the audience could too.

Most reviewers responded enthusiastically. In Hollywood, ecstatic strings of superlatives emphasized that *GWTW* was unprecedented in every way. Some critics attacked its condescension toward Negroes and glorification of the myth of the Old South. Mitchell, who saw herself as an enlightened friend of Negroes, dismissed such complaints as "twisted and erroneous and insulting"—and inspired by radicals and Communists. And the box office was indisputable: this was (and still is, adjusted for inflation) the most profitable movie ever made.

Today, its views of history, race, and character seem simplistic, but it still deals vividly, powerfully, and memorably with appearances, talk, feelings, and actions. Its superb color, music, acting, and production values invite viewers to empathize with Scarlett, Melanie, Rhett, and Ashley, and to suspend disbelief in its nostalgic view of the Old South, the Civil War, and Reconstruction. Even a healthy skepticism cannot negate its deeper, terrible truths about the human, and especially the feminine (its most responsive audience) condition. Both book and film create a haunting primal scene. There, the most terrible convulsion in American history, a nightmare of selfishness, cruelty, injustice, violation, and mass slaughter driven by "pure" patriarchal obsession and desire, is relived primarily through the mind of a child traumatized by what she has overheard—and can't help imagining over and over again. Scarlett, despite her glorious physical maturation, can't find her way emotionally, morally, or spiritually, and

still resists the path taken by her mother and Melanie, of total commitment to a man who doesn't measure up. Her story ends suspended in a recognition of total loss (of Bonnie, Melanie, Ashley, and Rhett); perhaps even the meaning of her own life is now in question. She wants it all, consuming love (even rough sex), motherhood, success in business and society. She can't settle for less, and her audience loves her for that—not only her "female fans," but also her Ashleys and Rhetts, whether they admit it or not.

Howard Harper

See also Old South; Patriarchy; Plantations.

Aljean Harmetz, *On the Road to Tara: The Making of "Gone With the Wind"* (1996); Richard Harwell, ed., *"Gone with the Wind" as Book and Film* (1983); Cynthia Marylee Molt, *"Gone With the Wind" on Film: A Complete Reference* (1990); Darden Asbury Pyron, *Southern Daughter: The Life of Margaret Mitchell* (1991); Helen Taylor, *Scarlett's Women: "Gone With the Wind" and Its Female Fans* (1989).

GOOD OLD BOY

The term *good old boy* has been so widely misapplied, misinterpreted, and even mispronounced in recent years that it is now useful as a kind of shibboleth to distinguish people with experiential knowledge of southern culture and speech from those who derive their impressions from the national media. Inappropriate usage dates from the 1960s, among northern reporters covering civil rights in the South, compounded by stories on Jimmy Carter's Georgia origins during his presidential term (1977–1981). This coverage perpetuated certain misconceptions: that *good old boy* was synonymous with *redneck;* that it could be used to describe a particular social class; and that it was properly pronounced as though it were a single word with the emphasis on the first syllable.

In correct southern form, the phrase is pronounced as three distinct and equally accented words. It is always an *individual* distinction: a good old boy may be of any age, hold any job or profession, and belong to any economic class. And it is an honorable term, one that conveys approval and respect. West Virginia author Breece D'J Pancake, in a letter to his mother, wrote of his recently deceased father that "he was a good old boy and to imitate him wouldn't be a mistake," in the same spirit with which Willie Morris entitled his autobiographical account of a cherished Mississippi childhood *Good Old Boy* (1971).

The qualities of a good old boy are more or less formally defined by the journalist Tom Wolfe, a Virginian, in a famous essay on racecar driver Junior Johnson. Wolfe declares that such a person is "one who fits in with the status system of the region," displaying a good sense of humor, an acceptable amount of physical courage, and a tolerant and easygoing manner. John Shelton Reed elaborates on this description, producing a convincing figure who is "positive, independent, competent, and strong."

None of this is to say, of course, that a good old boy shuns all breaches of decorum, especially in areas of conviviality and fellowship and of nonpassive response to what he regards as affronts to institutions he holds in reverence. A notable example of a working-class good old boy is the title character of Larry Brown's novel *Joe* (1991). One from the professional classes is the judge of Ozona, Texas, in Cormac McCarthy's *All the Pretty Horses* (1992).

Jerry Leath Mills

F. G. Cassidy, ed., *Dictionary of Regional English*, Vol. 2 (1991); John Shelton Reed, *Southern Folk, Plain and Fancy* (1986); Tom Wolfe, *The Kandy-Kolored Tangerine-Flake Streamline Baby* (1966).

GOSPEL MUSIC

Rising from churches, household kitchens, brush arbors, and bluegrass festivals, gospel easily ranks as one of the defining musics of the working-class South. The singing takes myriad forms, with Euro-American, African American, Hispanic, and Native American communities all claiming distinctive styles, and denominational differences further enriching the musical range. The hallmark of this song spectrum is harmony, while its foundation is faith. In a region where evangelical Protestantism maintains the ascendancy it achieved in the fiery revivals of the early nineteenth century, gospel stands as the South's most passionate vehicle of praise, personal witness, and evangelical outreach.

Gospel emerged as a distinct form in the latter decades of the 1800s, when the holiness revival brought a new sense of evangelical urgency to the South, and a new wave of songs supplemented the hymns and spirituals that heretofore had been congregational staples.

For many African American congregations, the revival signaled a new acceptance of musical instruments (including drums, horns, and guitars) in the church and a renewed commitment to reclaiming "worldly" music for the purposes of praise. At the same time, it foregrounded the importance of fully engaged, passionate performance, urging singers to "let go and let God," using song as a vehicle for inviting the Holy Spirit's ecstatic "touch." Among white southerners, the revival's most enduring contribution was probably the shape-note "singing school," thousands of which sprang up across the region and popularized a vast body of recently composed gospel songs. By the early 1900s, southern songbook publishers (most notably James D. Vaughan of Tennessee and Stamps-Baxter of Texas) were sending piano-accompanied male quartets to these schools to promote their songbooks. Within a few decades, many of these quartets had broken away from their music-house sponsors and had set out on their own, traveling a professional circuit and honing a harmony style that came to define what is now called—among whites—"southern gospel."

Early African American gospel relied less on formal texts and more on the improvisatory lyric frames that found voice in congregational singing, solo and quartet performance, and the singing of street evangelists. Although many songs circulated by means of privately printed songsheets, most found their way into tradition by oral transmission and the commercially recorded performances of congregations and quartets. The first African American songwriter to exploit fully the potential of gospel publishing was Georgia-born Thomas Dorsey, who in the early 1930s sent song teams across the Midwest and Upper South to introduce his spirited compositions and to organize church-based "gospel choruses." Taking the lead in these song teams were singers from holiness and Pentecostal churches, who lent a distinctly sanctified edge to the music. In the ensuing decades, this sanctified spirit—with its emphasis on performative intensity, its openness to the Spirit's guidance, and its endorsement of such Spirit-induced behaviors as "shouting" and holy dancing—has become a defining feature of African American gospel.

"Southern gospel," meanwhile, charted a somewhat different path. Loosely grafting quartet-based harmonies onto a country-music base, southern gospel placed less stress on sanctified stylings and more on smoothly blended voices and carefully crafted lyrics. The 1950s and 1960s saw a dramatic upswing in southern gospel's popularity, yielding scores of independent record companies, hundreds of gospel radio stations, long rosters of professional and semiprofessional gospel groups, and a growing presence on television. Despite its commercial face, however, southern gospel remains at heart a vernacular form whose creative wellsprings still lie at the local level.

Gospel's premier contribution to southern literature undoubtedly lies in its lyrics; gospel *does,* after all, constitute a vibrant genre of vernacular poetry. One need only look to the enduring popularity of songs by such composers as Memphis's Reverend William Herbert Brewster (e.g., "Move On Up a Little Higher" and "Our God Is Able") and Thomas Dorsey (e.g., "Precious Lord" and "Peace in the Valley," gospel's first million-seller) to recognize the deep meanings accorded to these lyrics.

Constituting an attendant literary genre—one that has blossomed in the late twentieth century—are gospel singers' autobiographies, extended testimonies that typically chronicle the spiritual and musical journeys of their authors. Among the more notable of these are Mahalia Jackson's *Movin' On Up* (1966), James Blackwood's *The James Blackwood Story* (1975), Kenneth Johnson's *The Johnson Family Singers* (1997), and Shirley Caesar's *The Lady, the Melody and the Word* (1998).

Gospel singing has not fared as well as a theme in southern fiction. Although references abound, most portrayals—and particularly those by white authors presenting southern gospel—suffer from stereotypes that caricature believers' passion and subtly belittle their beliefs. The most common depictions present gospel in a frame of "frenzied" Pentecostalism, where singing adds to an atmosphere of exoticism and eccentricity (see, for example, the portraits of snake-handling worship in Lee Smith's *Saving Grace* [1995] and Dennis Covington's 1995 memoir *Salvation on Sand Mountain*). Gospel also often appears as a vehicle of spiritual deceit, a hallowed mask hiding a hell-bound soul. This theme is perhaps most fully realized in Harry Crews's *The Gospel Singer* (1968), a lurid tale of a traveling singer's duplicity and ultimate destruction. These and related tellings treat gospel as a key component in a broader—and essentially pathological—religious complex among working-class whites. Lee Smith's *The Devil's Dream* (1992) is a more sympathetic portrayal of the religious impulse involved in gospel singing.

Portrayals in African American fiction tend to be more sympathetic to believers' perspectives. The tent-

revival singing in Maya Angelou's *I Know Why the Caged Bird Sings* (1970), for example, conveys a spirit of joyous exaltation, whereas the funeral singing in C. Eric Lincoln's *The Avenue, Clayton City* (1988) unfolds as a sublime whisper of impassioned quietude. Both accounts present gospel as a mode of spiritual and emotional elevation that leads to congregational "shouting"; neither, however, treats this "shouting" as in any way bizarre or frenzied. Perhaps the most sensitive portrayal of this essential song/transcendence link is Sandra Hollin Flowers's short story "Hope of Zion" (1980), which closes as the narrator, caught up in the power of a choir-led song, begins to feel the touch of the Spirit.

Glenn D. Hinson

See also African American Spirituals; Bluegrass Music; Blues, The; Country Music; Pentecostals.

Lois S. Blackwell, *The Wings of the Dove: The Story of Gospel Music in America* (1978); Horace Clarence Boyer, *How Sweet the Sound: The Golden Age of Gospel* (1995); Don Cusic, *The Sound of Light: A History of Gospel Music* (1990); Anthony Heilbut, *The Gospel Sound* (1985); Glenn Hinson, *Fire in My Bones: Transcendence and the Holy Spirit in African American Gospel* (1999); William Lynwood Montell, *Singing the Glory Down: Amateur Gospel Music in South Central Kentucky, 1900–1990* (1991); Bernice Johnson Reagon, ed., *We'll Understand It Better By and By: Pioneering African American Gospel Composers* (1992).

GOTHICISM

Gothicism can be defined as a mode of fiction utilized by critically acclaimed modernist writers of the Southern Renascence, characterized by grotesque characters and scenes, explorations of abnormal psychological states, dark humor, violence, and a sense of alienation or futility. Many southern gothic tales utilize similar myths of southern society: an inbred, patriarchal plantation aristocracy, built upon and haunted by a racist ethic, besieged by civilization and democracy, and, ultimately, defeated—as much by its own intransigence as by external forces; and an inbred lower class living in extreme isolation in closed communities, which are plagued by economic impoverishment, educational ignorance, religious fundamentalism, racial intolerance, genetic deformities, perverted sexuality, and unrequited violence. A sense of horror is often evoked in the reader's perception that these characters not only accept their limitations but also sometimes promote these social ills as their best characteristics.

The traditional gothic novel was established in Britain circa 1764–1820. Though the Goths were a single Germanic tribe of ancient and early medieval times, the meaning of *gothic* was broadened to signify *medieval* in general. The term was used by eighteenth-century neoclassicists as synonymous with *barbaric* to indicate anything that offended their classical tastes by its lack of verisimilitude, improbability, and wild flights of fancy and imagination. The classic gothic novel is characterized by elements of magic, mystery, and chivalry and by supernatural occurrences and horrific settings that impart an uncanny atmosphere of terror. Horace Walpole's *Castle of Otranto* is generally referred to as the first of a group including Anne Radcliffe's five romances (1789–1797), Matthew Lewis's *The Monk* (1796), William Godwin's *Caleb Williams* (1794), Mary Wollstonecraft Shelley's *Frankenstein* (1818), and Charles Robert Maturin's *Melmoth the Wanderer* (1820).

Walpole's novel set the thematic pattern for later gothic novels: a delicate female sensibility is subjected to the onslaught of elemental forces of good and evil within a plot designed for suspense in which sanity and chastity are constantly threatened and over which looms the suggestion that evil and irrationality will destroy civilization. Horror is aroused by the creation of a gothic world in which the heroine—the virtuous, weak, cultural ideal traditionally entitled to protection—receives neither the reward that her society has taught her must follow virtue nor the respect and honor she has received in her own ordered world. The second wave of British gothics, or the writers of the Gothic Revival, take on more complexity and technical skill and include the novels of Charlotte Brontë, Charles Dickens, Robert Louis Stevenson, H. G. Wells, and Bram Stoker. These novelists present a world of mysterious inhuman forces that cannot be adequately explained by the metaphors of psychology, sociology, or well-meaning humanism. Although these novels may seem to contain many more differences than similarities, Linda Bayer-Berenbaum identifies in them three important elements in common: "an intensification of consciousness, an expansion of reality, and a confrontation with evil"—three important qualities that carry over to the twentieth-century southern gothic. For instance, Flannery O'Connor identifies her southern gothic as fiction that is always "pushing its own limits outward toward the limits of mystery" and

features "characters who are forced out to meet evil and grace and who act on a trust beyond themselves."

David Punter identifies three potentially disturbing themes of the gothic. The first, *paranoia,* is fiction in which doubt and uncertainties abound, the pervading sense of fear is ambiguous, and the attribution of persecution remains uncertain. Tennessee Williams defines this "true sense of dread" as "not a reaction to anything sensible or visible or even, strictly, materially, *knowable.* But rather it's a kind of spiritual intuition of something almost too incredible and shocking to talk about," the "incommunicable something that we shall have to call *mystery.*" Most fictions of the beleaguered heroine based on the prototype of Ann Radcliffe are of this type. Writers in this vein tend to continually throw the supernatural into doubt, and by doing so they also remove the illusory halo of certainty from the so-called "natural" world.

The second theme is the *barbaric,* or fiction that brings us up against the boundaries of the civilized, demonstrates the relative nature of ethical and behavioral codes, and contrasts the conventional world with a different sphere in which these codes do not operate, or operate only in distorted forms. The majority of the social-protest novels of the gothic fall under this category, including *The Scarlet Letter, Moby-Dick, The Strange Case of Dr. Jekyll and Mr. Hyde,* and *Dracula;* and in the South, *Absalom, Absalom!, Tobacco Road, The Heart Is a Lonely Hunter, Invisible Man, Native Son,* and the novels of Alice Walker.

Finally, there is the *taboo,* or fiction that constantly approaches areas of socio-psychological life that offend, are suppressed, or are generally swept under the carpet in the interests of social and psychological equilibrium. Novels of this form stretch from the lurid details of *The Monk* to the graphic horror of *American Psycho,* and in between include many southern and African American gothic fictions, such as Tennessee Williams's *Suddenly Last Summer,* William Faulkner's *Sanctuary,* and Truman Capote's *Other Voices, Other Rooms.*

Gothic fiction is a gradually evolving art form that mirrors the concerns of a given era or society. In *The Secular Scripture,* Northrop Frye makes the case that members of a society reveal the "primary concerns," or what Frye terms the "myths," of their society, which are features of that society's "religion, laws, social structure, environment, history, or cosmology," through romance or popular fiction. Through these means, Frye asserts, popular fiction helps to indoctrinate new members with the accepted mores and customs of a particular society. Gothic novels, on the other hand, as the dark side of romanticism, highlight or criticize the failures or distortions in the mores and customs of society. Punter states that gothic novels exhibit a "process of cultural self-analysis" and their images become the "dream-figures of a troubled social group," which demonstrate "the *potential* of revolution by daring to speak the socially unspeakable." Thompson asserts that the Romantic mind is thus "divided against itself": its optimistic phase, romanticism, "affirms a world order," but its pessimistic phase, gothicism, "agonizes over the inevitable dissociation both between man and the universe he inhabits and between the various aspects of his own psyche." Some gothic novels satirically expose failed or flawed social structures, whereas others address some sickness in the permanent nature of humankind, some innate spring of cruelty and unease that goes deeper than perverted religion or mere insanity. William Van O'Connor simply states, "Our writers believe that man carries in his unconscious mind not merely willfulness or the need to indulge himself, but a deep bestiality and dark irrationality."

Beginning with the novels of Charles Brockden Brown (1798–1801), American gothics took a more indepth look at psychological extremes and the effect on an individual's mental state of the supernatural, the pseudo-supernatural, or extremes of common existence. During the antebellum era of southern writing, the fictional individual's needs are often sacrificed to larger societal concerns—indeed, a "primary concern" of antebellum politicians and rhetoricians, which seems to preclude the standard gothic conventions of subversion and societal criticism. Typically, writers of the antebellum white southern society, such as William Caruthers, Robert Montgomery Bird, Washington Allston, William Gilmore Simms, and Joseph Holt Ingraham, who forayed however briefly into the realm of gothic fiction, express philosophies similar to the early gothics in England, those whom Donald Ringe terms Rationalistic gothics, or "firm believers in the providential doctrine" who "saw the hand of a just and benevolent God at work in the affairs of men." Ringe explains that although these writers "go to great lengths to suggest the supernatural, they are all fundamentally rationalists who always anchor the main events of their books in the world of material reality," often by depicting a fictive world in which apparently supernatural phenomena are all revealed as merely delusive appear-

ances. In these fictions, "the world is rationally ordered and operates by natural law," and the supernatural events and agents "who invade their dreams and lead them to important discoveries" function as "instruments of good divinely sent to restore the disrupted order of society," and thus "the Divine Will validates both the supernatural messenger and his message."

Lewis P. Simpson writes that these antebellum southern authors were repressed "by the compelling, though anachronistic, historical effort of the South to establish itself as a great modern slave state"; however, Simpson suggests that subconsciously, writers of the South allowed fears, doubts, and societal criticisms to emerge in their writings. As one might expect, some antebellum writings expressive of the "Other"—such as the works of Southwest humorists like Johnson Jones Hooper and Thomas Bangs Thorpe, fictions from African American writers such as Delany's *Blake,* and slave narratives such as Harriet Jacobs's *Incidents in the Life of a Slave Girl* (1861), all of which portray some gothic or grotesque elements—do not portray the "Golden Era" myth of society. Protests against the status quo are expected from such groups with outsider voices. More surprising are the elements of subversion that Simpson detects in the writing of prominent southern literary advocates such as Thomas Jefferson and Edgar Allan Poe. As the early British gothic novels of Walpole, Radcliffe, and Lewis might be taken as an "expression of dissatisfaction with eighteenth-century rationalism," so might the "pastoral gothic" of the antebellum South be taken as "an inversion of the motives of the western pastoral mode." While antebellum rhetoricians prophesied a glorious utopia founded by the plantation/slavery system, Simpson asserts that pastoral gothics such as Thomas Jefferson in the enigmatic nineteenth query of his *Notes on the State of Virginia* (1785) and Edgar Allan Poe in works such as "The Fall of the House of Usher" (1839) depict "a southern landscape of nightmare, homeland of a decadent aristocracy of slave holders and of their descendants, prone to neurotic terrors and violence." Poe, in particular, fashioned ironic gothic images of nineteenth-century man's anxiety and distress resulting from his search for values that forecast the twentieth-century wasteland as a theme for literature. Simpson concludes that the antebellum southern gothic, intentionally on the part of the humorists, offered an ironic comment on the American vision of a people for the first time in history forming and conducting a national order on the basis of the human capacity for "reflection and choice," or democracy.

A fascinating example of antebellum authors' subconscious societal criticism is the grotesque characterization of the stereotypical deformed dwarf Negro slave, which if read as symbolic, raises the interesting possibility of antebellum southern writers' unstated acknowledgment of the stultifying effects of slavery and its potential threat to whites. In his short story "A Struggle for Life" (1843), Henry Clay Lewis describes this stereotypical figure: "He was a Negro dwarf of the most frightful appearance; his diminutive body was garnished with legs and arms of enormously disproportionate length; his face was hideous: a pair of tushes projected from either side of a double hair-lip; and taking him altogether, he was the nearest resemblance to the ourang-outang mixed with the devil that human eyes ever dwelt upon." Similarly, in his first novel, *Lafitte* (1836), Joseph Holt Ingraham describes two such dwarves: Cudjoe, whose facial features are described as exaggerated and distorted, including the two obligatory projecting "tusks," "wall-eyes," and a "very high and round" forehead that was "the mere mockery of that intellect it indicated" (suggesting the potential for intellectual development that was denied to slaves), and whose arms are described as long "like those of the ourang-outang"; and Quacha, a "little deformed Negro" who had "the head of an adult, placed upon the shriveled body of a sickly child" (suggesting the emotional development and economic independence denied to slaves). Both Cudjoe and the unnamed slave of Lewis's narrative display subservient demeanors and servile acquiescence until "unmasked," Lewis's slave by liquor and Ingraham's slave by being tricked by a hoodoo woman. Both at the moment of their unmasking suddenly and savagely murder or attempt to murder others, and die horrible deaths themselves. Symbolically, then, slavery both stunts and distorts the potential of African Americans, who appear submissive on the surface but who surprise those around them with sudden, unpremeditated uprisings that result in death or pseudodeath (Lewis's narrator regains consciousness from his "murder" by the slave) for both parties.

Similarly, in each successive phase of the southern gothic, Simpson finds an inversion of a contemporary vision of an idealized utopia or "the attempt to redeem the world from unreason." After the massive destruction and horrible defeats of the Civil War, postbellum literary endeavors were subverted by the victorious

northern industrial culture, just as Frye describes when he writes that a mythology "may itself cease to carry the sense of superior importance or authority . . . whenever one culture supersedes another." Postbellum authors began to weave their romances around the myth of "The Lost Cause" and nostalgia for an idealized view of antebellum society—another type of "enslavement of the mind" that centered on writing the southern apologia. In this postbellum era of reconstructing and reviewing their world, a few southern writers chose gothic forms to reveal a different view of both contemporary and past southern societies. Authors such as George Washington Harris, Mark Twain (Samuel Clemens), George W. Cable, Thomas Nelson Page, and Charles W. Chesnutt paint a gothic portrait of southern society, even in some cases unwittingly, revealing a less-idealized myth. For instance, in *The Conjure Woman,* Chesnutt creates a gothic underworld of nightmare, not in the animistic "conjure" tales narrated by Uncle Julius but in the rationalistic, arrogant, dehumanizing world of the slave masters (also represented by John), which forces desperate slaves to resort to conjuring, or hoodoo, for relief from and redress for slavery's horrors. Likewise, alongside the plantation-glorification myths of "Marse Chan" and "Meh Lady" in Page's *In Old Virginia,* the gothic ghost story "No Haid Pawn" reveals the realistic terrors of brutal slave mutilations, the threat of slave insurrections and massacres, and fearful epidemics spawned by the unsanitary and pestilent swamps that the slaves were forced to clear. Simpson writes that Twain "penetrated the darker aspects of the Antebellum slave society," but the pressures of "kidnapped romances" prohibited the southern literary imagination from making "a general exploration of the dark unreason of the Civil War—and of the years leading up to and following the catastrophe."

These nineteenth-century writers provided the springboard from which the gothic works of the Southern Renascence were launched. The modern and contemporary southern gothics adapt the repudiation or inversion of social ideals that they learned from their nineteenth-century gothic predecessors to their twentieth-century "awareness of cultural displacement" and create a unique version of literary gothicism. In 1985 Lewis Simpson could declare in the introductory essay to the anthology *3 by 3: Masterworks of the Southern Gothic* that "the present-day southern gothic defines itself in examples as a vision of life that blends realism and grotesquery in a manner that we readily grasp as typical of the southern literary imagination." Not only is this mode "typical," but it is also distinctive to the South; Simpson claims to recognize "early on in American literary history the development in the South of a unique version of literary gothicism." Flannery O'Connor identifies three literary predecessors to the modern southern gothic: the "dark and divisive romance novels" of traditional gothics (especially the antebellum plantation gothic, which deals with failures of the southern honor code, distorted family relationships and obligations, and community expectations and pressures); the comic-grotesque tradition (especially the graphic absurdities of the humor of the Old Southwest, utilizing the ambivalent clash between violence and humor characteristic of the grotesque); and finally, the "lessons all writers have learned from the naturalists" (especially the frank and clinically direct presentation of the fundamental urges and violent actions of primitive characters who respond to but do not understand the environmental forces, internal conflicts, and biological drives that motivate their brutal struggle for survival and over which they have no control).

The melding of these three strands—the gothic, the grotesque, and naturalism—produces elements of fiction recognizable in a succession of modern southern writers: the nightmare pastoral plantation setting of the antebellum gothic becomes the warped rural communities and small towns of the modern South; the comic antics of the characters in Southwestern humor become the often-farcical attempts of lost individuals to find redemption in self-actualization; the flat indifference of the naturalistic world gives way to a perceived element of mystery invoking a haunting suspicion of some entity just beyond our verifiable perception; and the outrageous and graphic tall tales and "stretchers" of Southwestern humor become the grotesque characters, scenes, and situations of the modern southern gothic. Writers of the modernist and postmodernist era of southern gothics include William Faulkner, Robert Penn Warren, Erskine Caldwell, Eudora Welty, Allen Tate, Flannery O'Connor, Tennessee Williams, Carson McCullers, and Truman Capote.

In the fiction of the Southern Renascence, Simpson describes a return of the southern author to the world community of writers, participating at last in the sense of modern alienation that had claimed the focus of great writers throughout Western civilization for the past century. Bayer-Berenbaum writes that the modern gothic revival "is an expression of some of the most exciting and most disturbing aspects of modern exis-

tence," such as "the greater sophistication of our technology, its greater scope and power" that pushes us "closer than ever before to a fulfillment of the gothic fear of monstrous devastation, of the violation of nature, or of an altered, maimed existence." Simpson concurs that modern southern gothics "associate contemporary southern life with the 'absurdity' of human existence in the twentieth century" and therefore take up the same "underlying subject of modern literature" as other writers: the "drama of the estrangement of the soul from the tradition of faith" and "the soul's transformation into the alien entity of the 'self,' isolated in the modern society of science and history."

Tennessee Williams also felt that the theme of modern alienation was the driving force of southern writers, and he likewise associated this theme with the literary form of southern gothic. He writes in the introductory essay to Carson McCullers's *Reflections in a Golden Eye* (1950) that "a sense, an intuition, of an underlying dreadfulness in modern experience" is the particular "something in the region, something in the blood and culture, of the southern state[s] that has somehow made them the center of the gothic school of writers." In another essay titled "The World I Live In" (1957), Williams states that the "basic, allegorical theme" of his plays is the "crying, almost screaming, need of a great world-wide human effort to know ourselves and each other a great deal better" to avoid the corruption caused by mankind's ignorance of a "self-manifest truth": "that no man has a monopoly on right or virtue any more than any man has a corner on duplicity and evil." Williams declares that the incomprehensible result of this ignorance is that "our propaganda machines are always trying to teach us, to persuade us, to hate and fear other people on the same little world that we live in." "To know oneself," Flannery O'Connor adds in warning, "is, above all, to know what one lacks." The modern southern writer, Simpson claims, utilizes gothic forms to create a "vision of the south illustrative of the bizarre terrors of existence under the conditions of modern history" by focusing on "the terror and pathos of the self's difficult, maybe impossible, attempt to achieve a meaningful identity."

The attempt by the Faulkner generation of writers "to discover the meaning of the South as integral with modern history" is an effort "directed by a complex mingling of piety and irony" resulting in "a harsh but an ambivalent interpretation of southern life by its own storytellers," writes Simpson. In this interpretation of its society, southern gothic novelists "tended to render the image of the South as a symbol of the disorder and depravity of the modern age at its worst, filling their stories with a complete catalogue of the bizarre and the horrible: rape and incest, murder and suicide, lynching (by fire or rope), castration, miscegenation, idiocy and insanity." In this depiction of life in the South as a horror story, Punter writes that "feelings of degeneracy abound," society is "infested with psychic and social decay, and coloured with the heightened hues of putrescence," key motifs are "violence, rape and breakdown," and "the crucial tone is one of desensitized acquiescence in the horror of obsession and prevalent insanity." Such depictions of the South are given "unique authority through the language of the Negro author," according to Theodore L. Gross in *The Heroic Ideal in American Literature* (1971), who observes that modern African American writers "instinctively adopted the gothic tradition of American literature" and gave "its more supernatural and surrealistic characteristics a realistic basis, founded on actual lives lived in the gothic manner, that is indeed terrifying," in which "the nightmare world of Poe or Hawthorne has become the morning of the Negro author." A list of such authors might include Jean Toomer, Zora Neale Hurston, Ralph Ellison, and Toni Morrison, and one cannot forget the lynching of Richard Wright's uncle Silas Hoskins by a white mob and his mother's and aunt's subsequent flight of terror from Elaine, Arkansas.

It is no wonder then that contemporary criticisms of modern southern gothics were numerous and scathing, much like criticisms of gothic literature in times past. In a recent essay, Fred Hobson quotes Gerald Johnson's bitter characterization of the southern novelists of the 1930s as "merchants of death, hell and the grave," altogether "horror-mongers in chief." In 1950, Tennessee Williams, like Flannery O'Connor in her essay "Some Aspects of the Grotesque in Southern Fiction," expressed frustration that the label "southern gothic" was a derogatory designation "used as a major line of attack" by "critics, publishers, distributors, not to mention the reading public" to denigrate that southern mode of expression as unhealthy and unsavory. But Simpson claims that "at least in moments," the southern gothic vision "intimates the equally bizarre hope of redemption," because "the imagination of damnation in the south" is still "inextricably linked to the imagination of salvation." The hope of redemption involves "the recovery of the self as the soul open to transcen-dence or the assertion of the self's identity even in the face of its immutable enclosure in time," representing that the "consciousness of individual being—of the self as a spiritual entity in the universe—has remained for the southern writer a mystery beyond scientific analysis."

In the wake of the Southern Renascence, contemporary southern writers adapt the southern gothic mode to their own uses. Walker Percy, Shirley Ann Grau, William Styron, Doris Betts, Cormac McCarthy, James Dickey, and Mark Steadman create a new myth of the South through their fictions. In the widespread societal criticism that precipitated and followed the Civil Rights Movement, some of these authors' works are dark and judgmental. Others continue to celebrate the South. Still others address the agony of alienation that so occupied their immediate literary predecessors. Jerry Elijah Brown notes in a review of Steadman that "instead of condemning or scolding, the humor celebrates and preserves. The human spirit in its commonest, randiest forms triumphs, somehow, over the awfulest of circumstances and survives." Another reviewer, Kathy Hill, further explains, "Regional peculiarities are the focus of humorous and often ironical treatment, but the humor is not belittling. Steadman's characters rise above the absurd stereotype of the rural, uneducated populace; they maintain an essential dignity of spirit in spite of their most undignified antics." As these reviewers perceived, the indomitable human spirit proves the counterbalance in Steadman's fiction, and in much of southern gothic literature, to the cultural malaise of modern alienation.

Molly Boyd

See also Grotesque, The; Naturalism; Novel, 1820 to 1865; Old Southwest; Plantation Fiction; Protest, Novel of; Romanticism; Slave Narrative; Southern Renascence; Violence.

Linda Bayer-Berenbaum, *The Gothic Imagination* (1982); Northrop Frye, *The Secular Scripture* (1976); Louis S. Gross, *Redefining the American Gothic* (1989); Elizabeth MacAndrew, *The Gothic Tradition in Fiction* (1979); Flannery O'Connor, *Mysteries and Manners* (1969); William Van O'Connor, *The Grotesque: An American Genre and Other Essays* (1962); David Punter, *The Literature of Terror* (1980); Donald Ringe, *American Gothic* (1982); *3 By 3: Masterworks of the Southern Gothic* (1985); Tennessee Williams, *Where I Live* (1978).

GRAND OLE OPRY

"Barn dance" radio programs aiming country music at rural and small-town audiences began at WBAP, Fort

Worth, Texas, in 1923; at WLS in Chicago in 1924; and at WSM in Nashville, Tennessee, in 1925. A musician's quip about the Nashville radio picking-session, which followed a more formal program of grand opera, gave the name to the show that became early country music's most important regular broadcast: "Well, this here ain't opera," he said, "but it is grand ole opry!"

Commercial country music's earliest years were focused on Nashville because of the *Grand Ole Opry,* with its large cast of singers, players, and performers that high-powered WSM broadcast across the South. Millions of people listened to these weekly shows on small battery-powered Philco sets that only offered the listener an earphone, and on big living-room plug-in Motorolas that whole families, if not entire neighborhoods, would gather around. Because of its sponsorship of the *Opry,* Martha White Flour was the best-known cooking material from the Atlantic to the Mississippi. Before Nashville's interrelated Music Row booking, management, and publishing businesses flowered, *Opry* entertainers and bands were booked for live shows in performance halls away from Nashville by callers who sought these performers directly through the *Opry* telephone switchboard.

From the 1930s till mid-March, 1974, the *Grand Ole Opry* was virtually synonymous with its venue, downtown Nashville's Ryman Auditorium, a great red-brick tabernacle built by reformed rakehell riverboat captain Tom Ryman in the 1890s. Its bricks were the color of oxblood and its window frames and buttresses stark and bright like chalk, and the hall could seat upwards of three thousand for the *Opry*'s performances. When she was a child growing up in Grundy, Virginia, novelist Lee Smith made the trek to Nashville with her family to attend an *Opry* show. Years later, she recalled the scores of people who couldn't get tickets but who stuck around anyway, all of them pressed up to the Ryman Auditorium's rear windows, faces to the glass, children on their shoulders, all yearning to be a part of the evening's service at the Mother Church of country music.

The best-known single evening in the *Opry*'s long and colorful history at the Ryman is probably the legendary night in June 1949, when Hank Williams—already a favorite on Shreveport's *Louisiana Hayride* radio show—took the stage and sang "I got the lo-o-onesome/I got the Lovesick Blues!" Six encores later, Red Foley had to plead with the crowd to let the *Opry*'s show go on.

Since 1974, the *Grand Ole Opry* has been performed, headquartered, and operated out of a television studio, hotel, and entertainment complex called Opryland on the eastern edge of Nashville, miles from downtown. Highly successful in its modern incarnation, the *Grand Ole Opry* has nonetheless receded in importance from its once-central, almost make-or-break position in American country music, and its broadcast is no longer the major weekly southern cultural event and regional signifier it was during the *Opry*'s Ryman days.

Bland Simpson

See also Country Music.

Paul Hemphill, *The Nashville Sound: Bright Lights and Country Music* (1970); Bill C. Malone, *Country Music, U.S.A.* (1968, rev. ed. 1985), and *Stars of Country Music: Uncle Dave Macon to Johnny Rodriguez* (1975); Bland Simpson, *Heart of the Country: A Novel of Southern Music* (1983); and Charles K. Wolfe, *Tennessee Strings: The Story of Country Music in Tennessee* (1977).

GREAT DEPRESSION

For many southerners, the Great Depression commenced at the beginning of the 1920s, not at the end of that decade. Still primarily a farming region despite the efforts of many people to make it an industrial region, the South was hard-hit by the depression that struck agriculture shortly after World War I ended. The agricultural depression of the 1920s increased the level of farm tenancy, which had been growing since the end of the Civil War, so that by 1930 three of every five farms in the South were operated by tenants. The plight of southerners caught in the snare of tenancy provided the theme of novels by the sharecropper realists Edith Summers Kelley (*Weeds,* 1923), Dorothy Scarborough (*In the Land of Cotton,* 1923), and Harry Harrison Kroll (*The Cabin in the Cotton,* 1931). The stock-market crash of 1929 that ushered in the Great Depression signaled a difference in hardship only in degree, not in kind, for many southerners.

The South, President Franklin D. Roosevelt rightly noted in 1937, was America's worst economic problem. Thousands of southerners had been forced off the land to look for work in factories. If the displaced farmers were fortunate enough to find factory jobs, they were usually working under deplorable conditions that featured low wages and long hours. For example, in a South Carolina cotton mill in 1933, workers labored fifty-five hours a week for $9.50. Despite—and occasionally because of—New Deal programs, there was unspeakable destitution throughout the South. Seeking nourishment, children in Harlan County, Kentucky, gnawed their hands, and a baby in Jefferson County, Georgia, nursed at a dog.

Some southern writers were deeply concerned with the plight of the Depression's victims. A few of those writers embraced the proletarian ethos, notably Olive Tilford Dargan (*Call Home the Heart*, 1932, and *A Stone Came Rolling*, 1935); Grace Lumpkin (*To Make My Bread*, 1932, and *A Sign for Cain*, 1935); and Myra Page (*Gathering Storm*, 1932).

Given the urgency of the situation, some creative writers believed that fiction was inadequate to portray the travail that real people were suffering. Working in the genre of the photodocumentary, those writers and the photographers who accompanied them attempted to depict in word and in picture the enormity of the Depression. Among other productions, there were two masterpieces: *You Have Seen Their Faces* (1937) and *Let Us Now Praise Famous Men* (1941).

In *Let Us Now Praise Famous Men*, writer James Agee, a Tennessean, and photographer Walker Evans presented their impressions of three tenant-farmer families in Alabama. Agee's words and Evans's pictures provided powerful commentaries on the lives of people with whom Agee and Evans had resided for six weeks in the summer of 1936. *You Have Seen Their Faces* was a collaboration involving writer Erskine Caldwell, a Georgian, and photographer Margaret Bourke-White. In the summer of 1936 and again early in 1937, Caldwell and Bourke-White traveled throughout the Deep South gathering information about, and taking pictures of, the rural poor. The book that resulted from the trips featured seventy-five photographs—many of them striking—and some profoundly moving writing.

Caldwell was the preeminent commentator on the Great Depression among southern writers. One reason for his undertaking the project that produced *You Have Seen Their Faces* was to demonstrate to skeptics that his earlier fiction was based in reality. A master of the plain style of writing who possessed a strong social conscience, Caldwell wrote novels and short stories that were at once accessible to the general reader and deeply moving. In the novel *Tobacco Road* (1932), he combined black humor and pathos to present an unforgettable picture of the desperate conditions that could

occur among sharecroppers, the poorest people in the poorest part of the country. The year following the publication of *Tobacco Road* saw the issuance of *God's Little Acre,* a novel in which Caldwell compellingly portrayed the hard times confronting southern industrial workers.

In addition to the nonfictional *You Have Seen Their Faces* and the novels *Tobacco Road* and *God's Little Acre,* Caldwell published four collections of short stories in the 1930s: *American Earth* (1931), *We Are the Living* (1933), *Kneel to the Rising Sun and Other Stories* (1935), and *Southways* (1938). Many of the stories in those volumes portray the impact of the Great Depression on southerners, white and black. As they depict the poverty of the times, some of the stories also present powerful indictments of white racism. Although other southern writers of the 1930s treated the Great Depression, only Caldwell dealt with it to such an extended degree.

Wayne Mixon

See also Federal Writers' Project; Long, Huey; New Deal; Proletarian Novel; Protest, Novel of; Sharecropping; Tennessee Valley Authority (TVA).

Sylvia Jenkins Cook, *Erskine Caldwell and the Fiction of Poverty: The Flesh and the Spirit* (1991); Sylvia Jenkins Cook, *From Tobacco Road to Route 66: The Southern Poor White in Fiction* (1976); Shields McIlwaine, *The Southern Poor-White from Lubberland to Tobacco Road* (1939); Wayne Mixon, *The People's Writer: Erskine Caldwell and the South* (1995); William Stott, *Documentary Expression and Thirties America* (1973).

GREENVILLE, MISSISSIPPI

Greenville is in the heart of the Yazoo-Mississippi Delta in the northwestern part of Mississippi and is the largest still-water port between St. Louis and New Orleans on the Mississippi River. On the highest ground between Memphis and New Orleans, Greenville was rebuilt after being burned to the ground during the Civil War. As the county seat of Washington County, Greenville was named in 1827 for the Revolutionary War hero Nathaniel Greene. Historical attractions include Cotton Row, the trading district on Main Street; the Flood Museum, picturing the devastation of the great 1927 flood; the Levee Board Complex and the levee system; the restored Wetherbee House; and the old office of the *Delta Democrat-Times,* Hodding Carter's well-known newspaper. Surrounding attractions include Rattlesnake Bayou, a slave-built levee from the 1840s; Belmont, Mount Holly, Linden, and Hampton plantations; the Native American mounds at Winterville; and muppet creator Jim Henson's museum. Old Highway 61, the original "blues highway," defines the chitlin' circuit for B. B. King, Little Richard, Muddy Waters, Son Thomas, and Robert Johnson. The Mississippi Delta Blues Festival is an annual event.

Greenville has had a surprising number of significant writers throughout its history, in large part because of the influence of William Alexander Percy, whose autobiography *Lanterns on the Levee* appeared in 1941. W. A. Percy influenced not only his younger relative Walker Percy, who came to live with him, but Walker's peers Charles Bell and Shelby Foote. Hodding Carter was attracted to Greenville by Percy, and his editorship of the *Delta Democrat* during the civil rights era attracted national attention. Other writers of significance in Greenville's history include William Attaway, whose *Blood on the Forge* (1941) chronicles the Great Migration; the contemporary poet D. C. Berry; and Beverly Lowry. Lowry says, "Growing up in Greenville meant growing up in a town the patron saint of which was a poet/scholar as well as a soldier. William Alexander Percy was our greatest hero. From the time I was in elementary school I always knew it was not only respectable to be a writer but honorable; desirable." Shelby Foote says, "There were literally thousands of books in the Percy house; it's probable that if those Percy boys hadn't moved to Greenville, I might never have become interested in literary things." David Cohn, born in Greenville, says in *Where I Was Born and Raised* (1948) that "the Mississippi Delta begins in the lobby of the Peabody Hotel in Memphis and ends on Catfish Row in Vicksburg." In between, of course, is Greenville, in the middle of what James Cobb has called the most southern place on earth.

Thomas J. Richardson

See also Mississippi, Literature of.

James Cobb, *The Most Southern Place on Earth* (1992); Jay Tolson, *Pilgrim in the Ruins* (1992); Bertram Wyatt-Brown, *The House of Percy: Honor, Melancholy and Imagination in a Southern Family* (1994).

GRIT LIT

"Grit lit" is a facetious shorthand for fiction devoted to the rough edges ("grit") of life, or to the regionally commonplace or comic ("grits"), or to both. Such homespun stories grounded in the grime or "grit" of reality typically deploy stark, sometimes violent narratives of poor white southerners. These works are as various as Dorothy Allison's *Bastard Out of Carolina* (1996); Doris Betts's "This Is the Only Time I'll Tell It" (1977); Larry Brown's *Big Bad Love* (1990); Harry Crews's *Scar Lover* (1993); Charles Frazier's *Cold Mountain* (1997); Cormac McCarthy's *Suttree* (1979); Tim McLaurin's "Below the Last Lock" (1992) and *Cured By Fire* (1997); and Elizabeth Spencer's powerful, spare "The Fishing Lake" (1964). Grit lit often mixes violence and humor, as in the fiction of Brown, Faulkner, O'Connor, and the sometimes violently funny novels by both Lewis Nordan (*The Sharpshooter Blues*, 1996) and Don Secreast (*White Trash, Red Velvet*, 1993). These writers exploit the full power of the gritty, mundane particular, their voices and visions finely attuned to the extent that humankind resists or re-invents what-is in order to survive.

Regardless of whether humorous grit lit avoids harsh conditions, brutal language, or potentially violent situations, it typically weights its matter with regional, often self-mocking humor, southern manners, pop-culture details and brand names (grits, Moon Pie, Nehi, Cheerwine, gas stations, quickie marts, Bruce Springsteen, and theme parks). This variety of southern literature is often proudly insistent on its own cultural distinctiveness. Examples run the range of Erskine Caldwell's *Tobacco Road* (1932), Clyde Edgerton's *Walking Across Egypt* (1987), Faulkner's Snopes novels, William Price Fox's *Ruby Red* (1971), Bobbie Ann Mason's *Shiloh and Other Stories* (1982), Jill McCorkle's *Final Vinyl Days* (1998), Lee Smith's *Oral History* (1983), or even the satirical essays of Roy Blount Jr. and Florence King. Some readers see this species of grit lit as a kind of preemptive, comical strike against the invidious regional generalizations that emanate from the North. The landscape of "grit literature" may be so charged with a sense of ordinary manners that unusual events take on new meaning, sometimes with wildly humorous results. The comic nature of this genre is similar to that of the so-called local-color movement, one gleaned from closely listening to stories, small-town folkways, and irresistible, grit-real affronts to abstract thinking.

In the hands of Larry Brown and Flannery O'Connor, writers with religious intent, grit-poor poverty is a useful theme. The poor lower-class figures of grit lit are frequently up to no good, but their condition is less important as a sociological or economic feature than as a metaphor for common spiritual poverty. Since fiction points toward human aspiration and limitation, the poor make ideal representatives before "the raw forces of life." The disenfranchised down-and-outers haunting grit lit serve a useful purpose here. Because elemental "grit" overwhelms a character's habitual distractions and ritual camouflage, it heightens the reader's sense of the essential spiritual poverty of humankind. In this way the gritty conditions of human struggle and defeat are an indispensable medium for southern visionaries writing in what O'Connor called the "Christ-haunted South." Against such a landscape, human charity or the lack thereof stands out starkly, and the characters reveal in large scale what they will take with them into eternity.

The sense of gloom and indifferent causality may at first seem a southern answer to the turn-of-the-century naturalistic movement. But in the fiction of Larry Brown, for example, there is an element of hope amidst the stacked odds of calamity. In this way, grit lit, with its roots in realism, offers a more optimistic outlook than nineteenth-century biological and economic determinism would have allowed. Where the naturalism of Crane, Norris, London, and later Dreiser, Dos Passos, and Farrell paints an indifferent world of chance, writers of grit lit tend, like John Keats, to view suffering as the soul's school and any lesson of value in precise proportion to its difficulty of achievement. Grit lit writers find such stark, often violent conditions as necessary for reaching an essentially hostile audience as for startling constitutionally hard-headed characters (and, by extension, readers) into some shocking new valuation of their true position on earth. Violence, as a useful feature of the "grit lit" school, is often crucial as a prelude to grace or some fundamental transformation in character.

Robert Gingher

See also Grotesque, The; Magic Realism; Naturalism; O'Connor, Flannery; Realism; Violence.

GRITS

It is no accident that "grit lit" is the moniker of choice employed by those literary snobs and scalawags who disparage (or perhaps secretly envy) the utter abundance and versatility of southern writing, much as sim-ilarly motivated carpers in 1976 belittled the administration of the first southern president in a century as "Grits and Fritz."

Indeed, grits are (Webster recommends: "noun, plural, but singular or plural in construction") so closely identified with the southern ethos that it is difficult to imagine anything that is, or ever has been, more representative of the region, in both the eyes of its inhabitants and of those who live elsewhere.

According to many accounts, admittedly including some apocryphal or romanticized ones, those fabled settlers of the London Company who came ashore at Jamestown in the spring of 1607 may have had grits for their literal first taste of the New World.

The late Turner Catledge, a Mississippian and a longtime editor of the *New York Times,* wrote in that journal in January, 1982, that those early English, er, carpetbaggers "were greeted by a band of friendly Indians offering bowls of a steaming hot substance consisting of softened maize seasoned with salt and some kind of animal fat, probably bear grease. The welcomers called it 'rockahominie.' The settlers liked it so much they adopted it as a part of their diet."

That purported Indian name *rockahominie* opens the discussion of terminology, which for grits is more complex than it is for, say, the Moon Pie. By most definitions, grits are what you get when you take dried, usually white corn kernels and soak or boil them (traditionally but no longer) in lye to loosen the hulls. The resulting "hominy" is then dried before being ground into grits. The word *grits* comes from the Old English *grytt,* which basically means "coarsely ground grain," although most grits nowadays are made from simple dried corn rather than from hominy.

There's more: Charlestonians, idiosyncratically and therefore typically, call the uncooked granules "grist" and the dish itself "hominy." But maybe they have a right to, since Charlestonians eat more of the stuff per capita than anyone else, according to food-industry figures.

Direct literary references to grits, or the use of grits per se as a theme or motif, are difficult to nail down. A Faulkner scholar at North Carolina State University says he has been reading and writing about the Bard of Oxford for twenty years, but he doesn't recall ever having seen the word *grits.* "But I'll bet Benjy had grits for breakfast before he went to church with Dilsey in 'The Sound and the Fury'," he says.

North Carolina writer and teacher Tim McLaurin has a Yuppie-Yankee transplant disparage the Southern National Dish in his 1993 novel *Woodrow's Trumpet.* "Mary chuckled. This culture was strange. . . . The university's basketball team was idolized to the point of absurdity. Grits came on your breakfast plate in most restaurants even if you didn't order them. Grits— ugh!"

And from a somewhat less-literary source, comedian/author Fannie Flagg notes in *The Original Whistle Stop Cafe Cookbook* (1993), spun off from her best-selling novel *Fried Green Tomatoes,* that she "personally has used uncooked grits to put out kitchen fires, as emergency kitty litter [for a southern cat], to kill the ants . . . and as mounds of fake snow in a Christmas manger."

Still, even casual readers of all types of southern writing know that grits are profoundly, if only most often implicitly, there in the region's writing—in Benjy's bowl, in a pot on Phoenix Jackson's wood stove before her homespun odyssey, on Scarlett O'Hara's polished Sheraton sideboard at Tara before, during, and after the Late Unpleasantness.

Indeed, grits are a unifier of southern folk and food so pervasive and soul-deep in the culture that any concordance-style cataloguing of the word itself would be as pointless as it would be unnecessary.

Rod Cockshutt

See also Carter, Jimmy.

GROTESQUE, THE

Grotesque is a term applied to a decorative style in sculpture, painting, and architecture characterized by fantastic representations of intricately woven human, animal, and vegetable forms creating distortions of the natural to the point of comic absurdity, ridiculous ugliness, or ludicrous caricature. It was so named after the ancient paintings and decorations in the underground chambers (*grotte*) of Nero's first-century Domus Aurea, or Golden House, which were first excavated in the fifteenth century. In literature, the term *grotesque* is applied to anything deviating from an explicit or implicit norm: bizarre, incongruous, ugly, unnatural, fantastic, abnormal. Literary grotesques appear in many recognizable forms: as figures, or human beings who appear dehumanized because of physical deformity, the discordance of body and soul (or mind), incoherent behavior, or the assumption of traits from the animal,

vegetable, mineral, or mechanical kingdoms; as objects, or nonhuman things that appear to have become animated, to possess an unusual amount of energy or even something akin to human will, or to be the instrument of an ominous force; and as situations, or violations of static laws, disturbances of space-time perceptions, contrasts between expectation and fulfillment, disruptions of cause and effect, or juxtapositions of incompatible actions, elements of setting, or tones that evoke concrete images of an estranged world. In addition, grotesque fictions are often marked by literalization or the drive toward the concrete: paradoxical ideas, fabulous speculation, figurative imagery, stereotypes, and dead metaphors materialize, take shape, become literal, and assume autonomous lives, such as when O. E. Parker in the Flannery O'Connor short story "Parker's Back" literally "faces" his own back with a giant tattoo of Jesus, and thus brings alive the somber maxim "God's eyes are always upon you."

The crucial element in defining the grotesque, however, is the juxtaposition or fusion of contrasting, paradoxical, and incompatible elements, such as an impossible or horrific event narrated matter-of-factly and with great detail, often provoking a humorous response. The intrusion of the comic element, totally out of place and inappropriate, creates a strong tension in readers who vacillate between incompatible reactions—between laughter and horror or disgust, for instance. This violent and ambivalent clash of opposites in the grotesque evokes a powerfully emotional response in readers, who often attempt to escape their discomfort through rationalization and other psychological defense mechanisms to avoid the discomforting notion that alongside their civilized response, hidden but very much alive sadistic impulses deep within some area of the unconscious make them react to the grotesque with unholy glee and barbaric delight. A significant key to this effect is the unresolved nature of the tension produced in the reader, unresolved by authors who refuse to explain away, rationalize, define, or otherwise alleviate the reader's distress. The use of the grotesque may either be the expression of the artist's profound sense of dislocation or alienation, or it may be employed as an aggressive device in the service of satire, to alienate, to bewilder and disorient, to shock out of accustomed ways of perceiving the world, and to confront readers with a radically different, disturbing perspective.

The grotesque exhibits a strong affinity with the physically abnormal in complex representations. The

Hebrew term *mum* ("deformity" or "blemish") occurs primarily in Leviticus, where it is used to describe not only the types of growths and malformations usually associated with the English terms, but also such infirmities as blindness, lameness, "a flat nose, or any thing superfluous," a man that is "broken-footed, or broken-handed, or crookbacked," or one who has "a blemish in his eye" or is "scurvy, or scabbed, or hath his stones broken" (castrated), or who is a dwarf (Leviticus 21:18–23). These ordinances emphasize the purity and holiness of God, whose sanctuaries are not to be profaned, and also provide for an expression of the wholeness or holiness to which humanity aspires. St. Augustine, in his *De Civitate Dei,* uses the concept of deformity in order to discuss the problem of humanity's limited perspective, and in the late middle ages, the *Glossa Ordinaria* gives deformity its fullest tropic expression through both typology and allegory. The glosses on Leviticus 21:18–23 give a moral figurative value to each of the enumerated deformities, thus associating physical deformities with moral and mental deficiencies. For instance, blindness is interpreted as the exterior sign for one who is suppressed by the darkness of this present life, ignorant of the light of contemplation; lameness is seen as an inability to follow God; and a deformed nose is said to signify a lack of discretion or discernment. In Leviticus, the "deformed" are forbidden to perform sacrificial rites but are not excluded from the saving justice of God, a distinction that fuels the two opposing presentations of deformity in literature—a focus on their exclusion from traditional social functions and their inherent depravity, or an opposing focus on their innate goodness and the promise of their redemption as expressed in Isaiah 35:3–10. Flannery O'Connor uses grotesque images of deformity to indicate the moral and spiritual incompleteness of characters and the essentially fallen or corrupt nature of all men, whereas Carson McCullers's grotesque figures make physically manifest the interior barriers to communication that plague modern southerners.

John Ruskin asserts in *The Stones of Venice* (1851–1853) that as a literary genre the grotesque can assume one of two forms: "high" grotesque that reveals man's tragic and imperfect nature, causing a reaction of horror, anger, or awe at the human condition; and "low" grotesque, an expression of physical exuberance and abandonment employed merely for comic diversion and willful frivolity, revealing a primitive delight in obscene, cruel, and barbaric behaviors, what Bakhtin terms the "carnival grotesque." The former is ably rep-resented in the nineteenth-century works of Edgar Allan Poe and Mark Twain; the latter is the type seen in Southwestern humor, most notably in Augustus Baldwin Longstreet's *Georgia Scenes* (1835), Madison Tensas's (Dr. Henry Clay Lewis's) *Odd Leaves from the Life of a Louisiana Swamp Doctor* (1843), and George Washington Harris's *Sut Lovingood* (1867), all of which, at least in particular scenes, evoke the ambivalent tension created by horrific situations narrated comically. For instance, Lewis's "Stealing a Baby" narrates the disastrous conclusion to his courting of a young maiden by her discovery of his attempt to smuggle home the corpse of a dead baby for dissection purposes, and "The Judgment Day" describes the disruption of a particularly intense camp meeting by a group of drunk men who set a live mule on fire and drive it through the congregation to terrify the spectators with the appearance of the apocalypse.

In the twentieth century, southern writers primarily utilize elements of the "high" grotesque to suggest a wholly inscrutable universe with which twentieth-century man no longer feels any intimate moral kinship and to suggest that man himself is an inextricable tangle of rationality and irrationality, love and hatred, self-improvement and self-destruction. Modern grotesque narratives are preoccupied with the irrational, the unpredictable, the bizarre, and with the frustrations that turn trusting, aspiring, decent people into grotesques. Sherwood Anderson subtitled his *Winesburg, Ohio* "The Book of the Grotesque," and defined a grotesque character as a person who "took one of the [many] truths to himself, called it his truth, and tried to live by it." Such a person, Anderson asserted, "became a grotesque and the truth he embraced a falsehood." Grotesque protagonists suffer from an inability to communicate, to express their affections and to be loved in return, or to fulfill themselves creatively because their minds are twisted or they simply lack intelligence. William Van O'Connor explains that the South "has produced more than its share of the grotesque," possibly because "the old agricultural system depleted the land and poverty breeds abnormality," or because "in many cases people were living with a code that was no longer applicable, and this meant a detachment from reality and loss of vitality." Tennessee Williams thought that southern authors emphasized the grotesque and the violent because "a book is short and a man's life is long" and the "awfulness has to be compressed."

Many twentieth-century southern creators of literary grotesques, including William Faulkner, Flannery O'Connor, Cormac McCarthy, Erskine Caldwell, Walker Percy, John Kennedy Toole, and Mark Steadman, have incorporated into their fiction elements of grotesque humor. C. Hugh Holman defines the use of the comic mode as the most typical method of the writers of humor in the South to permit the realistic portrayal of characters and actions that might otherwise overwhelm readers with their crudeness or their horror, as a means of achieving "distance, perspective, and the redemption of detachment." Holman makes clear the advantages of choosing this mode of humor for the authors who, as Flannery O'Connor writes in her essay "The Fiction Writer and His Country," "find in modern life distortions which are repugnant" and whose difficulty is in making these distortions "appear as distortions to an audience which is used to seeing them as natural."

Modern authors utilize the grotesque for a variety of purposes. Eudora Welty uses comic grotesques to relieve the intense spiritual questionings of her touchstone characters in a sometimes eerie and incongruous land of memory and dreams. In Welty's novels, sentiment and sympathy prevail as guiding principles over morality and righteousness. Truman Capote portrays a gothic world of decay, chaos, and psychological horror in a world so broken that the choices it offers are between several kinds of horror and defeat. The "normal" world in Capote's fiction is monstrous: the "nice" people are sexually abnormal, demented, or at best eccentric, and the young frequently have the appearance of wizened midgets. Carson McCullers uses grotesques to reflect internal, psychological horrors and to characterize a no-exit, nightmare world unrelieved by a didactic social message or the promise of redemption. McCullers says her fiction focuses on the "love of a person who is incapable of returning or receiving it," a condition engendering enforced solitude and spiritual isolation for her characters. However, McCullers's characters are grotesque in form only; they are not inwardly evil but often suffer internally from abnormal or perverse psychological motivations. Faulkner, on the other hand, uses the grotesque to present spiritual matters of deep moral seriousness; grotesque images objectify depths of meaning and highlight the enduring qualities that define man at his worst and his best. Even though Faulkner's fictional world is filled with depravity, decay, and frustration, there is nevertheless something more important, an intangible and often mysterious exponent of all such features, that redeems them.

Flannery O'Connor is perhaps the most frequently cited southern author who utilizes the grotesque in her fiction, in part because her stories universally produce the strong, unresolved tension and dualities characteristic of the grotesque. O'Connor notes that her fiction "almost of a necessity is going to be violent and comic because of the discrepancies it seeks to combine." The violent and ambivalent clash of opposites provokes incompatible reactions in readers whose discomfort O'Connor often refuses to relieve by asserting the "intellectual and moral judgment" she claims is implicit in all her fiction—the fallen nature of man and the corresponding saving grace of God. The fusion of incompatible elements is especially effective in O'Connor's writing, in part due to her rich irony, a literary device that itself depends upon duality or the incongruity between reader expectations and the actual result. The duality in O'Connor's fiction is also evident in her dramatic weaving of images and metaphors into an intricate pattern functioning both at the level of naturalistic details and at the symbolic level of her spiritual theme. O'Connor writes that she uses "one image that will connect or combine or embody two points; one in the concrete, and the other in a point not visible to the naked eye."

O'Connor's surreal similes transform what might otherwise be a fairly innocent scene into one of humorous grotesquerie and impending violence, such as when she describes the car horn of Hazel Motes's Essex in *Wise Blood* as sounding "like a goat's laugh cut off with a buzz saw," or the sound of its windshield wipers as "a great clatter like two idiots clapping in church." O'Connor's displaced narrative voices produce a strange, unsettling tone in which the most gruesome or grotesque episodes are depicted with an almost total absence of emotion, an undemonstrative narrative reserve in moments of dramatic intensity and pain that denies a behavioral norm that might provide a respite from the sudden outbursts of grotesque nihilism, thereby increasing the reader's discomfort.

The tension thus created in the reader is often unrelieved by the dualistic epiphanies experienced by the protagonists. O'Connor's fiction produces what might be called grotesque epiphanies, *epiphany* itself a word that has dual meanings applicable to O'Connor's fiction: "an appearance or manifestation of a divine being," or "a sudden manifestation or intuitive grasp of the essential nature or meaning of reality through something usually simple and striking." While fully articulated in "The Lame Shall Enter First" and "The Artificial Nigger," the protagonists' epiphanies in "Good Country People" and "A Good Man Is Hard to Find" are unexplained and unresolved; they function more like a dousing of corrosive battery acid that will gradually eat away the protective layers of moralism and rationalization, revealing the spiritual malaise and corruption infesting the unconscious of the protagonists. In most of her stories, the impact on the life of the protagonist, the result of the epiphany, is left ambiguous, provoking a nagging doubt and sense of futility in the reader.

Paradoxically, O'Connor presents the traumatic collapse of her characters' illusions of self-righteousness and self-sufficiency as in actuality their saving moment of grace. Adding to the sense of grotesquerie is the realization that these epiphanies are not precipitated by love but by violence. O'Connor accounts for the paradoxical fusion of violence and an implied saving grace in her fiction, explaining that "violence is strangely capable of returning my characters to reality and preparing them for their moment of grace. Their heads are so hard that almost nothing else will do the work." The wealth of these dualities and paradoxes in O'Connor's fiction—the irony, the symbolic images, narrative displacement, and grotesque epiphanies—amplify the confusion and discomfort of the reader and render her fiction perhaps the most technically complex representation of the modern use of the grotesque.

Molly Boyd

See also Gothicism; Humor, Beginnings to 1900; Humor, 1900 to Present; Violence.

Arthur Clayborough, *The Grotesque in English Literature* (1965); C. Hugh Holman, "Detached Laughter in the South," *Comic Relief* (1981); Wolfgang Kayser, *The Grotesque in Art and Literature* (1963); Flannery O'Connor, *Mysteries and Manners* (1969); William Van O'Connor, *The Grotesque: An American Genre and Other Essays* (1962); David Punter, *The Literature of Terror* (1980); Philip Thomson, *The Grotesque* (1972); Tennessee Williams, *Where I Live* (1978).

GUILT

Before the southern literary renaissance, guilt in southern literature—especially guilt related to slavery and the South's racial sins—is most present by virtue of its absence. In the antebellum period, few southerners publicly expressed any guilt or regret about slavery.

Thomas Jefferson, in his *Notes on the State of Virginia* (1787), trembled at the thought of God's justice and retribution for the inhumanity of slavery, but by and large his troubled southern conscience was an aberration. In *Who Speaks for the South?* (1964), South Carolinian James McBride Dabbs observes that nineteenth-century southerners, especially those of Scots-Irish Calvinistic persuasion, were actually predisposed to a strong sense of guilt, but any self-conscious expression thereof was limited almost exclusively to matters of personal, as opposed to social, morality. Thus, says Dabbs, while the southern conscience could easily be burdened by sins like adultery, drunkenness, and gambling, it is likely that this sensitivity of conscience "stemmed from the backlog of unrecognized guilt resulting from the unjust treatment of the Negro."

As he himself writes in a largely confessional and apologetic spirit, Dabbs aptly describes the lineaments through which guilt is made manifest in southern literature. Late-twentieth-century readers have at times forcefully argued for the presence of repressed guilt in antebellum southern literature. For example, Lewis Simpson makes a persuasive case for reading Edgar Allan Poe's "Fall of the House of Usher" as an allegory of southern fear and guilt about slavery. However, no self-conscious, self-critical spirit in the South emerges prior to Mark Twain and George Washington Cable. In Twain's *Adventures of Huckleberry Finn* (1885), Huck is burdened by what Henry Nash Smith has termed a "sound heart and deformed conscience," through which he intuits but cannot give conscious voice to the evil of slavery. Unable to recognize the guilt of his community, Huck is instead convinced that he will go to hell for helping Jim gain his freedom. A somewhat more guarded expression of the South's societal guilt is Cable's autobiographical novel *The Grandissimes* (1880), in which he tentatively reveals his ambivalence and misgivings about southern social and racial arrangements, specifically in Louisiana.

In the twentieth century, racial guilt emerges as a major theme in both southern literature and autobiography. A number of William Faulkner's characters are overwhelmed by the South's racial transgressions. In *Go Down, Moses* (1942), Isaac McCaslin is so ashamed of his grandfather's sins of incest and miscegenation that he repudiates his inherited claim to the McCaslin plantation. If Ike considers this disavowal as noble and courageous, Faulkner ultimately characterizes it as sterile and even cowardly. By the end of *Go Down, Moses,* it is clear that Ike's failure to confront affirmatively his family's guilt has robbed him of any moral authority. Quentin Compson's guilt in *Absalom, Absalom!* (1936) is arguably more communal than familial. Nevertheless, he is dismayed and ultimately undone by the South's and Yoknapatawpha's legacy of slavery and racial sin as it is embodied in the story of Thomas Sutpen, who rejects his own son because he is presumably part black. As the negative examples of Ike and Quentin demonstrate, for Faulkner it seems that the only way to face and finally vanquish the South's guilt is to engage its origins and history directly and affirmatively, although he seldom if ever dramatizes such a courageous and honest act. Through the very failure of his characters, however, Faulkner perhaps partially absolved himself of his own sense of guilt as a southerner.

Beyond the field of fiction, a number of twentieth-century southern memoirs focus extensively on the problem of personal and communal racial guilt. Among the most important of these are Lillian Smith's *Killers of the Dream* (1949) and Willie Morris's *North Toward Home* (1967). In a mode that Fred Hobson has recently compared to the New England Puritan confession narrative, both Smith and Morris first recount their realization of their own racial guilt, and then go on to offer searching indictments of their southern homeland.

Finally, if Dabbs is correct in arguing that the nineteenth-century southerner's strong sense of religious personal guilt was often an outward manifestation of racial guilt, this same tendency remains strong in the generation of writers who follow Faulkner. In *All the King's Men* (1946), Robert Penn Warren uses the Cass Mastern episode to demonstrate the confluence of racial and religious guilt. In his letters and journals, Cass is haunted not only by his adulterous relationship with Annabelle Trice but also by the fate of the female slave who discovered their secret and was consequently sold south. By linking the two, Warren powerfully affirms the contention of Dabbs, Lillian Smith, and others that, in the white southern mind, blackness is a troubling and inescapable provocateur of intense white racial guilt. At last, the religious aspects of this dilemma are most extensively explored by Flannery O'Connor. Although she writes about the problem of race only obliquely in her short stories and novels *Wise Blood* (1952) and *The Violent Bear It Away* (1960), O'Connor dramatizes the complexities of individual guilt and redemption with a spiritual seriousness and intensity that are unmatched by most of her peers.

Collin Messer

See also Calvinism; Chattel Slavery; Faulkner, William; Fundamentalism; O'Connor, Flannery; Puritanism.

W. J. Cash, *The Mind of the South* (1941); James McBride Dabbs, *Haunted By God* (1972); Fred Hobson, *But Now I See: The White Southern Racial Conversion Narrative* (1999); Louis D. Rubin Jr., *The Writer in the South* (1972); Lewis P. Simpson, *The Dispossessed Garden: Pastoral and History in Southern Literature* (1975).

GUNS

One respect in which the South is more American than most of the rest of the country is the special emphasis that the region adds to the general American fascination with firearms. Lewis Nordan has devoted a novel to the subject, *The Sharpshooter Blues* (1995), in which a boy's reaction to a watermelon-shooting exhibition displays a cultural as well as personal reflex: "You couldn't watch anything as beautiful as two melons busting open and slick seeds blowing out into a sugarcane field without falling in love." Guns figure so prominently in southern literature that some of them seem almost to take on the status of characters themselves: the sinister string-triggered shotgun in James Dickey's *Deliverance* (1970); Boon's frustratingly malfunctioning squirrel gun at the end of Faulkner's "The Bear" (1940); the mule-slaying two-dollar pistol in Richard Wright's "The Man Who Was Almost a Man" (1940); Mattie Ross's Colt dragoon revolver in Charles Portis's *True Grit* (1968); the big LeMat handgun that Inman carries through most of Charles Frazier's *Cold Mountain* (1997).

Reasons for the South's enduring affection for guns would seem to fall into two large groups. One contains the practical uses associated with a once primarily agricultural region strong on wild spaces, abundant game, and a flourishing tradition of hunting and outdoor life. The other, less easily definable set of reasons has to do with values placed on individual responsibility for defense of self, home, and honor; with a tradition of wariness toward social regulation; and with a sense of ease and familiarity around weapons perhaps engendered by the disproportionate participation of southern men in the military services. Walker Percy's narrator in *The Moviegoer* (1961) reveals a very southern identity in the itemization of his personal papers: "my birth certificate, college diploma, honorable discharge, G.I. insurance, and my inheritance: a deed to ten acres of a defunct duck club down in St. Bernard Parish."

The types of firearms employed historically and currently in the South are far too numerous for description here, except in terms of a few generalizations. In the eighteenth and nineteenth centuries, hunting arms reflected both regional conditions and the parameters of prevailing technology. In the upland, heavily forested regions, the rifle held sway, because much of the hunting involved shooting at stationary targets such as squirrels, game treed by hounds (bear, raccoons, opossums), and deer taken by ambush; but also because of the need to have weapons able to do duty in local militia as well as in the field. In coastal plain and other regions where the land was flat and more extensively cleared for plantation farming, the shotgun was usually the weapon of choice, because most deer hunting involved moving targets pursued by dogs in the ancient English fashion, and winged game such as quail, ducks, and geese flourished in the agricultural regions.

For modern hunting, conditions have altered such patterns. Increased human settlement of the countryside and the concomitant immense growth in numbers of whitetail deer have curtailed deer hunting with hounds and offered increased opportunities for riflemen hunting from tree stands over fields and clear-cut areas far larger than shotgun range. Interest in rifles has increased markedly in the South during recent decades, although shotguns remain, of course, the only weapons applicable among hunters of doves, quail, waterfowl, and wild turkeys.

In noncriminal contexts, the handgun is always a defensive weapon, since for purposes of war and open aggression both rifles and shotguns are vastly more effective. Pistols and revolvers, therefore, have always tended to reflect in size and degree of concealability whether their intended use is for personal defense or enforcement of public justice.

For the former employment, the standard concealable arm in the South in the years from about 1825 until well past the Civil War was the pocket pistol invented by Henry Deringer and customarily known by some variation of his name—usually "derringer." This was a handgun around three inches in overall length, most commonly in .41 caliber, in single- or doublebarreled (over/under) models. Its very short range limited its use to close combat. Though seldom chosen for criminal purposes, it was the weapon used in the assassinations of both Lincoln and McKinley. Contemporary with the derringer was the "pepper-box" revolver, a small defensive arm in which three to six fused barrels rotated in the manner that the cylinder rotates in modern revolvers. The pepper-box (which also appears in Portis's *True Grit*) was usually in .31 caliber.

For law enforcement and for personal defense not requiring concealability, early southerners favored a variety of sidearms such as the Walker and the .36 Colt navy revolver designed in 1850 and known as the "hogleg" because of its size and shape. Invention of the more powerful smokeless powder in 1884 made smaller handguns feasible and led to development of a wide selection of revolvers, including the Iver Johnson "owlhead" model, a turn-of-the-century model of today's "Saturday night special." In 1911 the Colt semiautomatic pistol was adopted by the U.S. military and led to today's taste for semiautomatic (often erroneously called "automatic") handguns for law enforcement and home defense.

Jerry Leath Mills

See also Civil War Weaponry; Hunting.

Robert Abels, *Early American Firearms* (1950); Raymond Camp et al., *The New Hunter's Encyclopedia* (1972); Jerry Leath Mills, "Firearms of History," in *A Writer's Companion,* ed. L. D. Rubin and J. L. Mills (1995).

H

HAPPY DARKY

In George Washington Cable's *The Grandissimes* (1880), the old slave Clemence gives definitive expression to the meaning behind the stereotype of the Happy Darky. In heavily represented dialect, she says, "White folks is werry kine. Dey wants us to b'leib we happy— dey *wants to be'leib* we is. W'y, you know, dey 'bleeged to b'leib it—fo' dey own cyumfut." The comforting (to whites) image of singing, carefree slaves was a political necessity for works portraying the plantation before the Civil War. Thus in novels such as *Swallow Barn* (1832) by John Pendleton Kennedy and *Woodcraft* (1855) by William Gilmore Simms, black "servants" are uniformly contented and therefore loyal, and therefore proof positive that slavery was a benign institution. In the North, the minstrel shows developing from blackface Jim Crow routines entertained white audiences with musical happy darkies and demonstrated pervasive racism above the Mason-Dixon Line. Even northern abolitionist writers, Harriet Beecher Stowe chief among them, resorted to figures such as her Topsy, who catered to whites' preference for ignorant and blissful black characters. Cable left the South during post-Reconstruction times, in part because his criticism of southern racism made him unpopular in his home state of Louisiana. In his most stinging attack on the Happy Darky syndrome in *The Grandissimes,* he states bluntly, "It is not a laughable sight to see the comfortable fractions of the Christian communities everywhere striving, with sincere, pious, well-meant, criminal benevolence, to make their poor brethren contented with the ditch." A few years later, Mark Twain, in *Adventures of Huckleberry Finn* (1885), created in the figure of Jim a black man who shifts from Happy Darky to tragic slave father—and back again, a portrayal that has confused readers for over a century.

Cable wrote *The Grandissimes* as Reconstruction was ending and as plantation literature depicting the singing, dancing, laughing Jim Crow was poised to make a comeback. Northern editors and readers, after the Civil War had settled the slavery question, were eager to accept nostalgic portrayals of the "good old times" of the Old South served up by white southerners who could win political leverage with such portraits. A phalanx of southern writers courted by northern magazines such as *Scribner's* and the *Atlantic Monthly* made the Happy Darky the centerpiece, and often the mouthpiece, of their vision of slave times as a Golden Age. Thus Uncle Sam, Thomas Nelson Page's narrator in the story "Marse Chan" (1885), tells a post–Civil War northern visitor, "Dem wuz good ole times, marster, de bes' Sam ever see!" It can be noted that almost never does the Happy Darky speak standard English in these plantation paeans. Joel Chandler Harris, with Uncle Remus, created the most popular version of the laughing former slave looking back nostalgically to the times when he was cared for by the good master and "mistis'." The "wooly-headed" teller of five volumes of Brer Rabbit folktales is an ironic figure. He clearly understands that the animal tales gave slaves a way to address the imbalance of power between whites and blacks; at the same time, chatting with his little boy listener, he announces his preference for the times "befo' dah war." Another of Harris's good-humored storytellers, Aunt Minervy Ann, also upholds her whitefolks at every opportunity. She is the comic prototype of the Mammy figure who resurfaces in Margaret Mitchell's *Gone With the Wind* (1936).

By the end of the nineteenth century, the image of the Happy Darky was beginning to be supplanted by even more unflattering figures, the ignorant buffoon Sambo or the clearly threatening black beast of Thomas Dixon's white racist fictions, notably *The Clansman* (1905) and *The Leopard's Spots* (1902). African American writers Charles Chesnutt in fiction and

Paul Laurence Dunbar in poetry, at the beginning of the twentieth century, demonstrated great ambivalence concerning how to portray plantation blacks, Chesnutt experimenting with a subversive "Uncle" storyteller in *The Conjure Woman* (1899) and Dunbar countering the Happy Darky image with his lines, "We wear the mask that grins and lies." As the twentieth century progressed, black writers Langston Hughes, in his Semple tales, and Zora Neale Hurston, in fiction rooted in black folkways, used the seemingly carefree black comic in subversive ways. Ralph Ellison began his young protagonist's saga in *Invisible Man* with the grandfather's enigmatic advice, "Agree 'em to death and destruction." In Ishmael Reed's *Flight to Canada,* we meet probably the most outrageously successful Happy Darky of all, Robin, who "yassuhs" his master so effectively that he ends up inheriting all of "Massa" Swille's property. While Happy Darkies attest to white Americans' need to dehumanize and also to disarm African Americans, black writers, from slave narrators to the present, have recognized ways to use the grinning mask for their own ends.

Lucinda H. MacKethan

See also Faithful Retainer; Plantation Fiction; Sambo; Trickster.

R. Bruce Bickley, ed., *Critical Essays on Joel Chandler Harris* (1981); Joseph Boskin, *Sambo: The Rise and Demise of an American Jester* (1986); Lucinda H. MacKethan, *The Dream of Arcady: Place and Time in Southern Literature* (1980).

HARLEM RENAISSANCE

The "Harlem Renaissance" (1920–1940), also known as the "New Negro Renaissance" or "New Negro Movement," enveloped the American consciousness for twenty years, especially during its magnet years of 1920 to 1929, and it still remains influential. Current literary critics have even realigned the dates of the literary upsurge, readjusting the earliest date to 1912 to embrace *The Autobiography of an Ex-Coloured Man* by James Weldon Johnson and extending it to the late 1930s in order to incorporate *Their Eyes Were Watching God* (1937) by Zora Neale Hurston. These revised dates for the Harlem Renaissance recognize social forces that led to an influx of blacks into New York and other urban areas, resulting in an intellectual and artistic flowering of expression.

World War I (1914–1918), with all of its gore and horror, also introduced a critique of nationalism. In Western literature, a sense of uncertainty and indeterminacy beginning with pre–World War I upheavals and extending through the end of World War II (1945) was called "modernism." In Europe and America particularly, individuals responded to the post–World War I severance of traditions and loss of identity by becoming mobilized. African Americans also reacted to this postwar trauma by seizing the opportunity to forge a new sense of self. Negro soldiers returning from fighting abroad in Europe became direct agents of change in 1919 when they resisted ongoing American racism. Their involvement in race riots across the nation marked a new will to fight for rights due all Americans. These resistant soldiers in essence expedited another social force already in the process. Southern Negroes began to flee the South in increasing numbers. Their mass exodus throughout the decade 1910 to 1920 became known as the "Great Migration."

Southern blacks poured into northern cities, and those who settled in New York City profoundly influenced the literary movement that became the "Harlem Renaissance." The "Negro" became a rediscovered enterprise and cultural icon as Manhattan-based theaters, nightclubs, and restaurants joined the new radio and recording industries during the 1920s in promoting the Negro as the "exoticized" Other. In Harlem, on Broadway, outside New York, and in Europe, the Negro was "in vogue." Harlem clubs, theaters, movie houses, and restaurants became consortiums for both mixed and racially specific clientele imbibing Prohibition gin, blues, ragtime, jazz, and dance: the "Turkey Trot," "Charleston," or "Boogie Woogie." Black writers thrived in this intellectually charged atmosphere by becoming interpreters of the dynamic new scene. Perceiving the significance of the literary awakening taking place, Alain Locke dubbed this intellectual activation the "New Negro Movement."

African American writers responded to Harlem's evolution into a mecca for black intellectuals. W. E. B. Du Bois, esteemed Harvard graduate, author of *The Souls of Black Folk* (1903), and a founding member of the National Association for the Advancement of Colored People (NAACP), in 1923 used the organization's magazine *Crisis* to launch a national campaign announcing a black identity that overturned prevailing plantation stereotypes. He was joined in his endeavors by Charles Johnson of the National Urban League and editor of *Opportunity,* and by Johnson's disciple Alain

Locke, on leave from Howard University, who became "dean of the Negro intellectuals." And the literati responded to the call to Harlem orchestrated by Du Bois, Johnson, and Locke.

Some Renaissance writers wrote from Harlem-based domiciles, while others merely passed through or corresponded with denizens of what James Weldon Johnson dubbed the "Culture Capital." Jean Toomer spent only a short sojourn in Harlem. Jamaican-born Claude McKay passed through Harlem and wrote the first of his novels, *Home to Harlem,* from Marseilles, France. For some Renaissance participants, Harlem was an idea more than a geography, and they identified with the Renaissance even while remaining in their respective state home sites. But others, such as Zora Neale Hurston and Langston Hughes, sensing the urgency of the times or responding to Du Bois's appeal, relocated to Harlem in order to be part of history. They witnessed the emergence of the elite black neighborhoods of "Strivers Row" on West 139th and "Sugar Hill" on West 143rd and participated in the gentrifying process themselves. Hurston would later dub the artist colony for blacks on West 136th as "Niggerati Manor." For all, however, 135th Street at 7th Avenue became "the campus" for meeting and 7th Avenue the "promenade" for strolling.

Alain Locke captured the optimism of this new African American collective in his benchmark anthology *The New Negro* (1925). This body of work by young talent bore out Du Bois's prophecy in *Souls* of a "Talented Tenth" of black intellectuals—writers, artists, and musicians—who would forge a solution to the continuing "Negro Problem" in America by elevating a distinctive African American culture. By 1924 Du Bois and Locke were already lauding Jean Toomer for *Cane* (1923) and Jessie Fauset for *There Is Confusion* (1924) and heralding Langston Hughes, Countee Cullen, Gwendolyn Bennett, Georgia Johnson, and Claude McKay as the rising young poets of the movement. They would be joined in their endeavors by Zora Neale Hurston, Sterling Brown, Wallace Thurman, NAACP Secretary James Weldon Johnson, Nella Larsen, Arna Bontemps, Eric Walrond, George S. Schuyler, Rudolph Fisher, Walter White, and Dorothy West.

In their singular ways, these writers formed a collective consciousness that forged a "New Negro" identity by turning inward to self, thereby redeeming and recovering diverse roots of culture that had enabled blacks to survive in racist America for three hundred years. The result during the Renaissance was a new-

found pride in those things previously profaned as shameful. Thus, the pastoral, the simple, and the natural were lauded, inclusive of African heritage and dark skin color, while the urbane, sophisticated, impure, and contrived were condemned as unnatural. And the New Negroes lent their voices, although not necessarily in harmony, to aesthetic discourses on what constituted "high" versus "low" art, or verisimilitude versus propaganda.

Toomer injected such an inspiriting influence and pride of racial heritage in *Cane* that it led Du Bois to declare that a literary epoch was taking place. *Cane* became the precursor text for other writers to converse with or contend against in form and content. Toomer assembled a three-part, enigmatic text comprised of poetry, prose, and drama. His design was represented by partial arcs at chapter divisions and symbols fragmented in Part III but integrated throughout Parts I and II. Toomer's techniques and language clearly denominated the work as an experimental, modernist novel. He ultimately encapsulated in *Cane* what other writers would explore more partially. He expressed the racial quandary of the black poet gifted in song but handicapped by race, which Countee Cullen would invest in his poem "Yet Do I Marvel" (1925). Toomer also explored biracial heritage, racial shame, and the confusion of the tragic mulatto that Fauset (*There Is Confusion,* 1924), Larsen (*Quicksand,* 1928), and Johnson (*The Autobiography of an Ex-Coloured Man,* 1912, 1927) would corroborate, redefine, and even repudiate.

Before Toomer, Johnson demolished cultural perceptions of the superior Anglo blood lineage of the "tragic mulatto" to expose it as a weak racial link in *Ex-Coloured Man.* Later, Claude McKay represented it in its most grotesque form in *Home to Harlem* (1932). Fauset and Larsen also concentrated on middle-class issues, exposing women's problems with the black bourgeoisie that Toomer had expressed as the turmoil of his male hero. Claude McKay, however, went to the extreme on the class issue. He extolled the "lowly life"— the immoral habits of the black urban criminal subculture that Toomer had presented tastefully as "natural" or the socially denatured activities of the lower or middle classes in the rural and urban worlds.

Redemption of the "folk" culture of the masses, one of Toomer's considerations, was also a primary concern of Zora Neale Hurston, Langston Hughes, and Sterling Brown. Whereas some writers such as William Stanley Braithewaite chose to follow conventional forms, Hurston, Hughes, and Brown turned to the black vernacular language and habits of the lower class. In her short story "Sweat" (1926), Hurston preceded Georgia Johnson, author of the folk play "Plumes—A Folk Tragedy" (1927), in exploring the hardships of a poor washerwoman. Langston Hughes recovered and integrated secular blues and jazz music from the Mississippi Delta into his poetry and prose. However, James Weldon Johnson's recovery and invention of Negro spirituals and sermons preceded both Toomer's and Hughes's excavation of African American music. Nonetheless, Hughes's poems "The Cat and the Saxophone—2 A.M." (1926) and "Bound No'th Blues" (1927) illustrated his brilliant incorporation of blues-jazz music as a literary trope; his stories of his folk hero Jesse Semple also demonstrated why Hughes would become the foremost writer of the Renaissance through his prolific productions in varied genres. New Negroes sang, quarreled, and produced in many arenas. Toomer rose like a meteor and disappeared from the scene just as quickly because of his own personal agony over how racial heritage defined artistic ability. The others carried on. Some Renaissance members started magazines, such as Wallace Thurman's one volume of *Fire!!* (1926). Dorothy West was more successful in her editorial endeavors with *Challenge,* a magazine that ran from 1934 to 1937, and one edition of *New Challenge* (1937). Both editors also produced novels of stature as Renaissance participants. Thurman exceeded Toomer's exploration of repressed or dysfunctional sex by openly discussing homosexuality in *The Blacker The Berry* (1929) and *Infants of the Spring* (1932). In addition, he championed the voice of the dark-skinned African American who became a victim of intraracial prejudice in these two works.

The 1929 stock market crash brought a sobriety to the literary upsurge, which waned by 1940. In *Infants,* Thurman charged the Renaissance leaders and their disciples with building their premises on sand. Perhaps that was one of their follies, even though the economy was a factor challenging all artists during the Great Depression. Toomer's chapter arcs never met to form a complete circle in *Cane,* and it was he who prophesied that the ills of American culture, social as well as economic, would not be healed until the nation achieved racial good health. And in the 1930s, with political focus on the problems of the depressed poor instead of on the lifestyles of the whimsical rich, the black literary consciousness also took a serious turn. As Richard Wright rose to power in the mid-1930s, he shrouded the remnant of Renaissance writers who were still publishing, especially Zora Neale Hurston, whose *Their Eyes Were Watching God* he deplored. George Wylie Henderson in *Ollie Miss* (1936) and *Jule* (1946) and Dorothy West in *The Living Is Easy* (1948) also continued Renaissance themes. West would be named the last survivor of the Harlem Renaissance upon her death in 1998. When Wright published *Native Son* in 1940, however, he muted the laughter of the Harlem Renaissance participants and ushered in a new, angry black voice that the public would embrace throughout the tumultuous 1940s.

Virginia Whatley Smith

See also African American Literature, 1919 to Present; Blues, The.

Thomas J. Hennessey, *From Jazz to Swing: African American Musicians and Their Music, 1890–1935* (1994); Nathan Irvin Huggins, *The Harlem Renaissance* (1971); David Levering Lewis, *The Portable Harlem Renaissance Reader* (1994); Alain Locke, ed., *The New Negro* (1925); Gilbert Osofsky, *Harlem: The Making of a Ghetto, 1890–1935* (1966); Steven Watson, *The Harlem Renaissance: Hub of African American Culture, 1920–1930* (1995); Cary D. Wintz, ed., *The Harlem Renaissance 1920–1940* (7 vols.; 1996).

HIGHLAND SCOTS

Highland Scots began settling in the American South in the early eighteenth century. Nonetheless, their contributions and unique ethnicity are often overshadowed by the more numerous Ulster-Scots, who have served as the stereotype of the early southern frontiersman or backcountry farmer. Despite their smaller numbers, Highland Scots have left an undeniable mark on the areas in which they settled in the South.

The first notable settlement of Highland Scots in the South was that established at Darien, Georgia, by General James Oglethorpe beginning in 1735. This Highland settlement, which was populated mainly by Highlanders from Inverness who had been recruited by agents of Oglethorpe, was to serve as a strategic buffer between English settlements in Georgia and the Spanish in Florida. By 1741, this military settlement had seen conflict with the Spanish as well as famine, and many of the settlers departed for South Carolina. Though efforts were made to reinvigorate the settlement with new Highlanders, the discontinuation of military aid to the Georgia colony by Parliament in 1748 left the Highland settlement without an economic base, and those who remained were assimilated into colonial society as farmers and traders.

The South's most significant settlement of Highland Scots was located in the Upper Cape Fear River Valley of North Carolina. This settlement, which numbered several thousand prior to the coming of the American Revolution, was the largest concentration of Highland Scots in North America until the mid-nineteenth century. The first organized party of Highlanders to settle in North Carolina were 350 emigrants from Argyll who arrived in the fall of 1739. This group was favorably received by colonial authorities, with most heads of families receiving sizable land grants with ten-year tax-exempt status. Contrary to popular belief, there were not large numbers of Highland emigrants who poured into North Carolina following the failure of the last Jacobite rebellion in Scotland, which had culminated in the defeat of the pro-Jacobite Highland clans at Culloden in 1746. Most emigration to North Carolina came as a result of the breakdown of the established social order of the clan system, the re-ordering of land tenure after the abolition of the clan system, as well as agricultural improvements that economically challenged many small tenants in the decades following the 1746 defeat at Culloden. This emigration had been initially encouraged by Governor Gabriel Johnson, a native Scot, who sought to settle the Carolina backcountry with "foreign protestants." By the coming of the American Revolution, North Carolina was the primary destination of emigrant Scots from Argyll and the Island of Skye as well as other regions of the western Highlands of Scotland. A Gaelic song titled "Gone to Seek a Fortune in North Carolina" echoed the sentiments of many destitute Highlanders who sought to escape the worsening social and economic conditions in the Highlands. Emigration to North Carolina continued through the early decades of the nineteenth century, and an unsuccessful effort was made in 1884 to reinvigorate the Highland settlement with new emigrants.

Many of the emigrant Highland Scots in North Carolina, and in the small Georgia settlement, spoke their native Gaelic language. From the 1750s until the latter decades of the nineteenth century, Gaelic was commonly heard in church services and in private settings throughout the region, as well as in some other regions to which North Carolina Highlanders migrated throughout the South. It was even reported by numerous visitors to the region that many African American slaves in the region spoke the language. The Gaelic tradition is perhaps best demonstrated by the works of Iain MacMhurchaidh (John MacRae), a bard from Kintail who emigrated to North Carolina in 1774. MacRae was a Loyalist in the American Revolution, and his fate is unknown, but many of his songs composed in North Carolina have survived through the oral tradition. They give an excellent account in the native tongue of the experience of the emigrant Highlanders. Many of MacRae's Gaelic songs, including "Dean Cadalan Samhach" (Sleep Softly, My Darling Beloved) are still well known in Gaelic-speaking communities in Scotland as well as in other Gaelic-speaking Highland settlements worldwide.

North Carolina also holds the distinction of having the first Gaelic-language publication in North America, *A Sermon Preached at Raft Swamp* by the Reverend Dougald Crawford, which was printed in Fayetteville in 1791. The publication of the Gaelic hymnody of Peter Grant in 1826 also bears testimony to the presence of a large Gaelic-speaking community in the region. Though only few written documents survive in Gaelic, it is clear that the language was cherished by many Scottish Americans for decades following emigration.

It is clear that many Scottish Americans in the South held onto their distinct ethnicity with a romantic attachment. The popularity of the works of Sir Walter Scott, as well as the poetry of Robert Burns, helped to create popular romantic images that Scottish Americans glorified as the remnants of traditional Highland culture began to be completely assimilated. North Carolina's poet John Charles McNeill, a descendent of Highlanders from Knapdale, wrote several late-nineteenth- and early-twentieth-century works in Broad Scots dialect that were no doubt influenced by the works of Burns. Gerald Johnson chronicled the story of his Highland emigrant ancestors in a little-known novel, *By Reason of Strength* (1930). William Faulkner also used the romantic image of the post-1745 Highland emigrant to Carolina in the creation of the character Quentin MacLachan Compson. Faulkner's MacCallum family was no doubt a Highland family who also represented the southern and westward migrations of Highlanders from the North Carolina settlement that began in the early nineteenth century.

William S. Caudill

See also North Carolina, Literature of.

Charles Dunn, *Highland Settler* (1953); Margaret MacDonnell, *The Emigrant Experience: Songs of Highland Emigrants in North America* (1982); J. P. MacLean, *Highlanders in America* (1900); Duane Meyer, *The Highland Scots of North Carolina, 1732–1776* (1961); Anthony Parker, *Scottish Highlanders in Colonial Georgia* (1997).

HILLBILLY

The eighteenth-century Virginia planter William Byrd created the prototype of the hillbilly as he has appeared in succeeding novels, short stories, stage plays, comic strips, movies, and television sit-coms—the lounging, slovenly pipe-smoker who never engages in anything more strenuous than moving from fireside to front porch and back. Assigned to survey the disputed boundary line between Virginia and North Carolina, Byrd later extended his skeletal diary notes into a satirical book, *History of the Dividing Line* (written c. 1728, published 1841), in which he embellished the North Carolina mountain-dwellers he had briefly observed into exaggerated and wildly grotesque caricatures. His depiction of "lubbers" has served as a model for many writers who never observed the mountaineer first hand, or if they did, tended to see him with this well-established stereotype in mind.

William Gilmore Simms, in *Guy Rivers* (1834) and other novels, pictured the mountain-dweller as a near-savage hunter, and added to the cast of hillbilly characters the beautiful, simple-minded daughter and the misshapen moron. John P. Kennedy, in *Horse-Shoe Robinson* (1835), added what was also to become another stock character—the old crone who sits by the hearth smoking a pipe, seemingly unaware of anything but the fire.

George Washington Harris, influenced by the Southwest humorists who preceded him, created in *Sut Lovingood* (1867) East Tennessee hillbillies "full of fun, foolery, and mean whiskey" and, of course, Sut himself, who, because of a childhood of poverty and near-starvation, is bent on inflicting pain on others as revenge against the entire human race. Sut's often sadistic behavior shocked and repulsed many readers of his day, but amused others, and inspired a number of subsequent writers, including Mark Twain, William Faulkner, and Flannery O'Connor.

Joel Chandler Harris set out to correct the image of the hillbilly created by Byrd and G. W. Harris by introducing into his fiction sympathetic, sensitive mountain-dwellers with a sense of pride and dignity. In such stories as "At Teague Poteet's" in *Mingo and Other Stories* (1884), he establishes reasons for the hill-dwellers' seemingly strange behavior, including moonshining, which he sees as stemming from economic necessity. He also illustrates how they are made the butt of jokes by insensitive townspeople. Nonetheless, Harris himself helped to further the hillbilly stereotype by giving his moonshiner a beautiful, exotic daughter.

Mark Twain, an admirer of George Washington Harris and a friend of Joel Chandler Harris, combines the attitudes of the two writers in *The Gilded Age* (1873) by both laughing at and sympathizing with his Tennessee hillbillies, describing them as shiftless "buzzards," yet victims of economic conditions beyond their control. In the end, Twain's main purpose seems to be to point out the waste of human potential.

Maurice Thompson's *At Love's Extremes* (1885) also creates sympathy for hillbillies in Alabama by showing them as "hospitable and obliging," but once more furthers the stereotype of the simple-minded and "strangely beautiful" mountain girl.

Mary Noailles Murfree (pen name Charles Egbert Craddock) was a popular writer of short stories and novels whose *In the Tennessee Mountains* (1884) and *The Prophet of the Great Smoky Mountains* (1885) contain a range of fictional hillbilly characters, including the hunter, the moonshiner, and the beautiful girl. She presents them in often humorous fashion as essentially decent, hospitable people caught in a static world forced upon them by their isolation and the infusion of "the dry rot of Calvinism." To further complicate their lives, the federal government brings violence to the hills in the person of revenuers who attempt to stop illicit distilling, which the mountaineers see as their only way to survive.

John Fox Jr., in *The Little Shepherd of Kingdom Come* (1903) and *The Trail of the Lonesome Pine* (1908), also depicts civilization as bringing conflict and violence into the lives of the mountain people with the intrusion of railroads and mineral-rights speculators, but he also sees them as having been previously trapped in an environment of poor schools and roads and therefore in need of what the outside world has to offer. The immense popularity of Fox's novels throughout the first half of the twentieth century and the film version of *The Trail of the Lonesome Pine* in 1936 solidified the view of the mountaineer as surrendering to the inevitability of progress. The same decade saw the appearance of Thames Williamson's folklike tale of an Ozark mountaineer, *The Wood's Colt* (1933), which terminates in the violent death of its hero, seemingly putting an end to the saga of the innocent backwoodsman.

The Great Depression brought serious attempts to restructure the stereotype so that the rest of the country might see that many of the hillfolk had, by then, been forced off the land and into the textile towns and coal camps. Grace Lumpkin's *To Make My Bread* (1932), for example, traces the McClure family's fall from innocence when they are driven from the land by the lumber company and into town where, unprepared and unskilled, they take the lowest-paying jobs available. Fiercely independent and self-respecting in the hills, they become in town the victims of exploitation and social injustice. Much the same happens in the novels of Hubert Skidmore—*I Will Lift Up Mine Eyes* (1936), *Heaven Came So Near* (1938), and *Hawk's Nest* (1941)—and in James Still's *On Troublesome Creek* (1941) and Harriette Arnow's *The Dollmaker* (1954).

William Faulkner, however, turned the tables on this type of treatment by making the hillbilly not the exploited, but the exploiter. A great admirer of *Sut Lovingood,* he created Thomas Sutpen in *Absalom, Absalom!* (1936) who, like Sut, is made to feel humiliation early in life for being a poor hillbilly. Thus, when he escapes his family's stereotypical cabin in Virginia and makes his way west, he, again like Sut, vows revenge on society. Faulkner's Snopes clan also emerges from the hills to create havoc and destroy traditional southern values.

Jesse Stuart was perhaps the most influential purveyor of the hillbilly stereotype in the decade that followed the Depression. As if to dispel the sympathy created in the 1930s, he depicts a poverty-stricken family from his native northeastern Kentucky, in *Taps for Private Tussie* (1943), as comic simpletons who lavishly squander their newly acquired riches in an orgy of extravagance, rejecting even the slightest hint of respectability.

With Stuart's immense popularity in the 1940s and Faulkner's emerging eminence in the 1950s and 1960s, it would seem that the old stereotype of hillbilly as someone to be laughed at, or feared, or both, had once again established itself, especially since it was strongly reinforced by the savage hillbillies of James Dickey's *Deliverance* (1970) and the depraved and irredeemable characters of Cormac McCarthy's *The Orchard Keeper* (1965), *Outer Dark* (1968), and *Child of God* (1973).

The stereotype, however, was due for yet another revision, and in the fiction of recent years, the mountain-dweller appears not as a comic or tragic hero and villain of the past but rather as a realistic human being confronting the conflicts of modern-day America. Denise Giardina, in *Storming Heaven* (1988), reaches back to the 1920s to record the loss of land by West Virginia mountaineers, their subsequent degrading employment in the coal fields, and their attempts to unionize. She sums up their tragedy in the final sentence: "The companies still own the land." Fred Chappell creates sympathy and understanding in *I Am One of You Forever* (1985) and *Brighten the Corner Where You Are* (1989) for Appalachians caught in class conflict and violence. Lee Smith's female protagonist in *Fair and Tender Ladies* (1988) resigns herself to a life in southern Virginia that is often disappointing. And Pat Carr's Ozark hill people in "Downward to Darkness" (1977) exhibit both strength and weakness in their attempts to cope with changing realities, subsistence living, and low expectations.

Chris Offutt in his memoir *The Same River Twice* (1993) presents what might be the ultimate escape from the hillbilly stereotype when his young man from Appalachia leaves the mountains to travel across the country in search of a new heritage.

Duane Carr

See also Appalachian Literature; Old Southwest; Ozarks; Poor White; Redneck; Tall Tale.

Duane Carr, *A Question of Class: The Redneck Stereotype in Southern Literature* (1966); W. K. McNeil, ed., *Appalachian Images in Folk and Popular Culture* (1989); Cratis D. Williams, "The Southern Mountaineer in Fact and Fiction," *Appalachian Journal* 3 (Autumn 1975); Miller Williams, *Ozark, Ozark: A Hillside Reader* (1981).

HISPANIC LITERATURE

Hispanic literature in the United States might seem to be a new phenomenon. Although it has experienced increased popularity in the past few years, its history is by no means short, dating back to the times of the Spanish conquest and colonization of Florida and the Southwest. The study of this literature, however, is fairly new. The 1960s and 1970s mark the time when

Hispanic literature began to stimulate interest among scholars and later among the general public. The recent success of Hispanic literature in the United States and its popularity with a broader audience is related to ongoing interest in ethnic literatures in general and the growth of the Hispanic community in the nation.

The term *Hispanic literature* applies to the literary expressions of people of Hispanic origin. This is not a unified corpus since it can be said that there are as many Hispanic literatures as Hispanic countries. A distinction needs to be made between writers who grew up in their respective Hispanic countries and later emigrated to the U.S. and a younger generation born in this country. The former still maintain strong ties with their country of origin, and their literary production can be understood as an extension of the literature of their country. The latter, an American generation with Hispanic origins, usually reflects on the different ways of being American without compromising their Hispanic heritage. Traditionally, the two main groups of Hispanics in the U.S. are Mexican-Americans or Chicanos and Hispanic-Caribbeans (Puerto Ricans, Cubans, Dominicans, etc.). These groups have traditionally settled in very specific areas of the country such as the Southwest and California for Chicanos, New York and South Florida for Caribbeans; now, however, because of population and economic growth and geographical mobility, Hispanics are found throughout the country. Despite changing demographics, the South, with the exception of Florida and Texas, has not displayed a strong Hispanic presence. As Hispanics establish themselves in traditionally non-Hispanic areas, there will be more writers of Hispanic origin in the South as well as in other areas of the country.

Cuban-Americans currently writing in Florida belong to a younger generation of Cubans. Some of them are recent exiles from the last wave of Cuban immigration to the United States and others are Cuban-Americans who grew up in Miami. The first group deals with topics such as exile and Cuba. An important writer of this group is Virgil Suarez, author of several novels: *The Cutter* (1991), *Latin Jazz* (1989), *Havana Thursdays* (1995), and *Going Under* (1996), as well as a collection of short stories, *Welcome to the Oasis* (1992), and a book of memoirs, *Spared Angola: Memories from a Cuban American Childhood* (1997). Among the generation of Cuban-Americans in Miami, Roberto Fernández writes about the Cuban community there. In *La Vida Es un Especial* (1981) and in *La Montaña Rusa* (1985), he reflects on generational conflicts among older exiles and the new generations. Another Cuban-American writer in Florida is Marisella Veiga, who has published short stories and poetry in journals and anthologies.

The traditional South is present in Hispanic writers such as José Martí, Cuba's most famous writer, who was a political exile in the nineteenth century. Martí, also a journalist, traveled in the United States and wrote chronicles about his experiences for various newspapers. One of special interest is *Earthquake in Charleston* (1886), in which he recounts an earthquake and its aftermath in Charleston, South Carolina, in 1886. Here Martí, besides exposing the facts of the earthquake, reflects on race relations between blacks and whites and the segregation and marginalization of blacks in the post–Civil War South.

There are also other premier Latin-American authors writing in the South today, such as Ariel Dorfman, a Chilean exile and professor at Duke University in Durham, North Carolina. Dorfman is the author of the novels *Widows* (1983), *The Last Song of Manuel Sendero* (1986), *Mascara* (1988), *Hard Rain* (1990), and *Konfidenz* (1995). He has also written a book of poems, *Last Waltz in Santiago and Other Poems of Exile and Disappearance* (1988); a memoir, *Heading South, Looking North: A Bilingual Journey* (1998); and several plays, among which *Death and the Maiden* has been the recipient of many awards and was also made into a movie by Roman Polanski.

Among Hispanic writers currently writing in the South, Judith Ortiz Cofer, a poet and novelist born in Puerto Rico but raised in the U.S., is one of the best known. Ortiz writes in a highly intimate way about her own experiences, her family, and ethnicity. Although she voices some of the struggles of her people, her work is highly personal, as opposed to other Puerto Rican writers who focus primarily on social issues. Ortiz, who teaches at the University of Georgia in Athens, has published several books of poetry: *Latin Women Pray* (1980), *Peregrina* (1986), and *Terms of Survival* (1987). She has also written a chapbook, *Among the Ancestors* (1981), that reflects upon her experience in the South and the role that family and tradition play in the culture of her region. Ortiz has also written a memoir, *Silent Dancing: A Partial Remembrance of a Puerto Rican Childhood* (1990); a novel, *The Line of the Sun* (1989); *The Latin-Deli: Prose and Poetry* (1993), a collection of poems, stories, and essays about the Hispanic experience in the U.S.; and short stories in *An Island Like You: Stories of the Barrio* (1995).

Another well-known Hispanic writer in the South is Gustavo Pérez-Firmat. Pérez-Firmat is a Cuban-American who lives in Chapel Hill, North Carolina, and teaches at Duke University. In his works, Pérez Firmat ponders on his experiences as a member of an intermediate generation of Cubans. Having left his native island while still young, he does not feel fully acculturated as an American. Besides scholarly works, he has published a book of poems, *Bilingual Blues: Poems, 1981–1994* (1995), and *Next Year in Cuba: A Cubano's Coming of Age in America* (1995), a memoir.

Violeta Padrón

William Luis, *Latin American (Hispanic Caribbean) Literature Written in the United States,* in *The Cambridge History of Latin American Literature,* Vol. 2, ed. Roberto González Echevarría and Pupo Walker (1996); Frank Magill, *Masterpieces of Latino Literature* (1994).

HISTORICAL ROMANCE

A subgenre of the novel popular in the South throughout the nineteenth and much of the twentieth century, the historical romance served as a primary mode of transmission of the region's myths about itself. As authors cast the epic struggles of southern history in a romantic glow, they projected a glorified image of the South's past to influence attitudes about its present among outsiders and southerners alike. In contrast to the more respected historical novels of the South, its historical romances never intended to explore questions regarding the meaning of history, its burdens or implications; instead, for the South's romancers, history became a reservoir of native tales and images that could serve the creation of a southern identity. Because it was less concerned with presenting a realistic portrait of the region than it was with shaping perceptions of the South, the historical romance has often been denounced as essentially propagandistic in nature, as a public-relations campaign waged in behalf of the region by its writers.

The genre was first seen in America after the publication of Walter Scott's *Waverley* (1814) launched a craze that stimulated readers on both sides of the Atlantic to devour each new work by Scott and his imitators. These British romances were fictional tales set in the past (Scott suggested at least sixty years), portraying a cast of invented characters who became involved with actual historical personages and events. These

works were not deep character studies; instead, the focus was on plot and action. Despite the historical basis of the works, the narratives often became fanciful and outlandish, turning upon coincidence, mistaken identity, and revelations of unknown paternity. At the center of Scott's romances are unimpressive, uncommitted heroes who are tossed between conflicting social forces. The predictable conclusions to his works find the hero, despite his original allegiances, devoting himself to the progressive element of his society and wedding the heroine, a representative of this faction. With the requisite marriage of hero and heroine, Scott repeatedly portrays the victory of progress over tradition.

By the 1820s, the form of Scott's work was used by New England authors such as James Fenimore Cooper, John Neal, and Catharine Sedgwick to depict episodes of American history and to exploit America's landscape. Virginia writer James Heath's *Edge-Hill* (1828) is probably the first conscious imitation of Scott's romances to appear in the South. This romance recounts the daring, if often unbelievable, adventures of a Virginia hero and heroine on a James River plantation during the final months of the Revolutionary War leading to the surrender at Yorktown, and features appearances by Lafayette and Benedict Arnold.

By 1835, the historical romance had become the dominant mode of fiction in the South with the publication in that year of William Caruthers's *Cavaliers of Virginia,* John Pendleton Kennedy's *Horse-Shoe Robinson,* and William Gilmore Simms's *The Yemassee* and *The Partisan.* These authors modified Scott's formula significantly as they fashioned a fiction that would serve particularly southern needs, specifically those of the aristocratic planter class. They quickly dispensed with Scott's wavering hero, weak in his character and loyalties, and instead rendered a hero who faithfully embodied the cherished traditions of the southern upper class, including the code of chivalry and the hierarchies of class and race. In the course of these romances, the hero serves to defend southern society from assaults. Threats occur both in plot, featuring military conflict, where the southern hero and his allies are usually in opposition to the villain who appears as a British officer, a Tory colonist, or an unscrupulous Yankee, and on the romantic front, where the villain is a rival for the heroine's hand. The heroine, rather than being from the opposing camp as she is in Scott's fiction, is close kin to the hero, usually his cousin, and represents the ideals for young southern women: beauty, virginity, and devout loyalty to southern ways. The romances are resolved with the defeat of the villain and the marriage of hero and heroine, both acts representing the triumph of aristocratic values. Unlike Scott's work, in which obsolete tradition eventually succumbs to progress, in the historical romances written by antebellum southerners, tradition always withstands the forces that threaten southern culture, reassuring readers that the region's institutions would endure into the foreseeable future.

With the exception of the works of Simms and Joseph Holt Ingraham, the author of lurid, semihistorical romances such as *Lafitte* (1836) and *Burton* (1838), most antebellum romances are set in the Upper South, well ensconced in the mythology of the Virginia cavalier. These romances—including Kennedy's *Rob of the Bowl* (1838), Caruthers's *Knights of the Golden Horse-Shoe* (1841), and John Esten Cooke's *Leather Stocking and Silk* (1852) and *The Virginia Comedians* (1854)—each depict an episode of Virginia's past from Jamestown to Yorktown, in which a self-styled colonialist knight is engaged in a struggle to preserve an aristocratic way of life consistent with antebellum ideals. The romanticization of Virginia history, however, could often be an awkward, uneasy fit with historical record. For instance, Caruthers's *Cavaliers of Virginia* attempts to mold the story of Bacon's Rebellion into romance by casting Nathaniel Bacon as the typical hero, honorable, brave, and lovestruck, defending Jamestown from Indian attack. William Berkeley stands as his foe, who despite outside threats from natives and Puritans, expends much effort preventing the developing romance between his niece and Bacon. Like many romances, Caruthers's might be a compelling tale, but it is far from presenting an authentic account of history as it fabricates events and forces historical figures and moments into a rigid plot of marital intrigue.

Despite the almost uniform emphasis upon the material of Virginia, the best-known of antebellum romancers, William Gilmore Simms, chose the history of South Carolina as his subject. His works chronicle every facet of state history, from early colonial conflicts with natives to contemporary hardships on the lawless frontier, but he is best known for tales of the Revolutionary War, where he made a solid case for the valiant participation of southerners in this struggle. His first of seven romances of the Revolution, *The Partisan*, portrays his aristocratic hero Robert Singleton and his heroine/cousin Katharine Walton involved in wartime exploits following the British occupation of Charleston. As expected, Singleton vanquishes the villainous British officer John Proctor, his competition for Katharine. Through Singleton's military and romantic victories, the romance reaffirms the merit of such aristocratic values as nobility, chivalry, and loyalty.

By the 1850s, historical romances had faded in popularity, playing less of a role in promoting the image of the South than the sentimental plantation novels did. However, in a less-prominent way, romances of southern history still proved useful in the region's attempt to defend itself against the abolitionist fervor fueled by *Uncle Tom's Cabin* (1852). For example, one of Simms's later romances, *Woodcraft* (1852), though not an explicit response to Stowe's work, is linked to the project of the plantation tradition. This romance follows the conclusion of the Revolutionary War, as Captain Porgy, one of Francis Marion's officers, returns home to salvage his neglected and plundered Carolina plantation. At the core of this romance is the affectionate bond between Porgy and his slave Tom, who at the end of the work refuses Porgy's offer of freedom. The depiction of Tom is exemplary of the southern romance's portrayal of slaves as content, well treated, and prospering under slavery. This aspect of the South's self-portrait, while never a central focus of any romance, was necessary to reassure southerners of the rightness of the slave system and to counter antislavery objections from outside. Not surprisingly, this ardent defense of slavery and the stereotypical depiction of African Americans have been the characteristics for which these romances have been most roundly criticized, yet any writer attempting a favorable representation of the civilization of the antebellum South would have had no choice but to put such a positive face upon the institution of slavery.

With the outbreak of the Civil War, historical romances virtually disappeared, for few authors had time to write or opportunity to publish, and the market for romantic versions of the southern past vanished. The decades following the war were not any more hospitable to the genre, because northern readers proved uninterested in recountings of the South's history, especially any that attempted to justify or explain the regional loyalty that led to the formation of the Confederacy. In the immediate postwar decades, those southerners attempting to forge careers as writers turned to the genres of humorous or local-color sketches, and the romance seemed an antiquated form of the past.

The late 1880s and 1890s saw the sudden revival of

the public's appetite for southern romances, with a capable group of romancers ready to step in to satisfy this demand. This new wave of romancers, including James Lane Allen, George Washington Cable, Winston Churchill, Thomas Dixon, John Fox, Mary Johnston, Mary Noailles Murfree, Thomas Nelson Page, and F. Hopkinson Smith, returned to the southern past as material for their fiction. Like their antebellum predecessors, these postbellum writers, most of whom had come of age during the Reconstruction era, often crafted tales of colonial Jamestown, such as Johnston's *Prisoners of Hope* (1899) and *To Have and to Hold* (1900); of frontier life and Indian warfare, such as Allen's *The Choir Invisible* (1898); and of the Revolution, such as Churchill's *Richard Carvel* (1899). However, this new generation had even grander matter on which to base its works, the tales of the South's great bravery and devastating defeat in the Civil War.

The romantic depictions of the South in the Civil War would become synonymous in many readers' minds with the entire genre of southern historical romance. The earliest fictional treatments of the war were John Esten Cooke's romantic memoirs of his own war experience, *Surry of Eagle's Nest* (1866) and *Mohun* (1869). The first true historical romances about the Civil War came from the pens of northern writers E. P. Roe, Charles King, and George Cary Eggleston, but southern authors were quick to join the flood, producing Page's *Two Little Confederates* (1888), Cable's *The Cavalier* (1901) and *Kincaid's Battery* (1908), Churchill's *The Crisis* (1901), Fox's *The Little Shepherd of Kingdom Come* (1903), Murfree's *The Storm Centre* (1905), and Allen's *The Sword of Youth* (1914), among hundreds of others.

Churchill's and Fox's novels were the most popular from among this list, each selling over a million copies. Both resist the urge to align themselves with the values of the Old South. In other words, neither is the work of an unreconstructed southerner beating the drum for the Lost Cause. Each is set in a border state, with a cast of characters with divided loyalties; *The Crisis* takes place in St. Louis, Missouri; *The Little Shepherd* draws upon central Kentucky. *The Crisis*'s hero is Stephen Brice, a northern lawyer living in St. Louis and in love with southerner Virginia Carvel; Chad Buford, a Kentucky mountain boy in love with belle Margaret Dean, is his counterpart in *The Little Shepherd*. Both find themselves torn between their affinity with southerners and their higher loyalty to the Union. Despite each hero's final decision to march under the Union flag, both novels reveal great affection for the southern way of life and respect for the southern cause. The romances celebrate the bravery of Confederate soldiers, and Fox's novel concludes that every man who did his duty, whether northerner or southerner, did right. As both romances end, they point toward the future marriage of the intersectional hero and heroine, paralleling the larger reconciliation of the nation and a reaffirmation of the Union. The villains of each work, Churchill's New England merchant and Fox's mountain guerrilla leader, stand in the way of this necessary union. Only by removing such figures can the hero and heroine restore order to their world and the nation as a whole. Overtly nationalistic in their themes, these and many other reconciliation romances celebrated the restoration of the United States while also expressing grave sadness about the loss of the Old South's culture.

In contrast to these romances, the works of one of the most respected of Civil War romancers, Mary Johnston, make no concessions to the North or apologies for the South. Her novels of the war, *The Long Roll* (1911) and *Cease Firing* (1912), have been praised for their dedication to historical detail and the accuracy of the portrait of life in a military campaign. Yet both works remain strongly southern in their loyalties, portraying the southern devotion to the idea of states' rights and characterizing the war as the unavoidable consequence of a federal government that acts above its authority. Because Johnston did not focus upon the restoration of the Union but upon the decimation of southern culture, there are no intersectional lovers in these works; instead, her hero and heroine both stand as representatives of the best in southern society. In *The Long Roll*, for example, Virginian Richard Cleave joins Stonewall Jackson's brigade. His foe and competitor for Judith Cary's hand, Maury Stafford, tries to ruin both his military and romantic endeavors, succeeding in having Cleave court-martialed under false charges and forcing him to re-enlist under an assumed name in order to vindicate his reputation. Although less accommodating to nationalistic feeling, Johnston's works are similar to the reconciliation romances in their insistent depiction of the Old South as a lost treasure, the destruction of which can only be seen as a cultural crime.

This tone is even more evident in the romances that chronicle the years of Reconstruction, as the South is portrayed as an occupied territory at the mercy of opportunistic Yankees. In the work of Virginian Thomas Nelson Page, specifically *Red Rock* (1898) and *Gordon*

Keith (1903), the South is hardly the pastoral idyll portrayed in other works; instead, it is a wasteland, despoiled and vulnerable. *Red Rock*'s hero Jacquelin Gray, the aristocratic heir to the plantation, Red Rock, must win the love of heroine Blair Cary and protect his home and family against the invading forces of carpetbaggers and the traitorous efforts of the scalawags. His attempts to prevent these villains from taking possession of his home and inciting the freed slaves to violence involve uniting with other displaced members of the upper class into a band of the Ku Klux Klan committed to retaliatory acts. Page's use of the Klan as heroes in his work is not unusual among the romances that depict the Reconstruction era; more famous romancers Thomas Dixon and Margaret Mitchell follow Page's characterization of the secret organization as a noble and viable option for the fallen gentry fighting the abuses of Reconstruction. Page's nightmarish depiction of the war's aftermath casts the South as a virtually helpless victim to the lawless plundering of Reconstructionists. Only the character of the southern people, portrayed in the hero and heroine, keeps the South from being completely ravaged by the oppressive horrors of the victors.

More extreme and sensationalistic than Page's work, the romances of Thomas Dixon, including *The Leopard's Spots* (1902) and *The Clansman* (1905), characterize the Reconstruction era as centrally a racial conflict in which white southerners try to subvert northern attempts to transform the South into "a Negro nation." Whereas Dixon claimed to reveal "the southern viewpoint" in his work, explicit in his novels is a white supremacist agenda, arguing either for white domination of African Americans or the establishment of separate nations for the races. *The Clansman* begins in Washington, D.C., following the close of the war, and shows a sympathetic, even southern, Abraham Lincoln assassinated for his efforts to temper the vengeful Republican Congress's plans for Reconstruction. As the action moves to the South, the region is portrayed as a hostage to federal troops and mobs of freed slaves, who, in Dixon's view, spend their time with a single purpose, planning sexual attacks upon white women. Northern hero Phil Stoneman attempts to defend southerner Margaret Cameron from the crude advances of an African American man, ends up killing the man, and finds himself facing execution for the crime. The Ku Klux Klan arrives to prevent the execution and drives away the occupying forces. Dixon's use of the intersectional romance does not depart much

from earlier uses, except his northerners soon come to adopt the racist views of his southerners upon being confronted with grotesquely stereotypical African Americans and realizing the government's intentions of turning the South over to them. Although many southern romances might be considered harmlessly backward in their ideology, this clearly cannot be said of Dixon's vitriolic works, which represent the worst in historical romances: the use of romanticized history for the express purpose of promoting an extremist and racist political agenda.

Despite the early-twentieth-century popularity of historical romances, many writers rejected the genre's pastoral settings, cardboard and predictable characters, and requisite happy endings. Writers in search of artistic credibility had to distance themselves from the genre's taint of popularity. However, the transition away from romanticism to realism in fictional treatments of southern history was not immediate. For instance, Ellen Glasgow's *The Battle-Ground* (1902), long considered one of the earliest southern attempts at a realistic depiction of the Civil War, still falls into romantic idealism, ancestor worship, and conventional narrative, even while incorporating a sense of irony that is absent from romance. Ultimately, the southern novels that have earned lasting praise and respect were those that fled farthest from the conventions of romance, works on the region's history by nonromantic writers such as William Faulkner, Robert Penn Warren, Allen Tate, Evelyn Scott, Caroline Gordon, and William Styron. As the major writers of the South shunned romances and embraced the tenets of modernism, the great age of the southern historical romance, for the most part, ended in the 1920s.

In the 1930s, perhaps a result of a post-Depression desire for escapism, there was a brief resurgence of the genre with the success of Stark Young's *So Red the Rose* (1934) and, more notably, the phenomenon that was Margaret Mitchell's *Gone With the Wind* (1936). Mitchell's work remains the most famous of southern historical romances and stands as the epitome of the genre for most readers. However, this status cannot be attributed to the novel's conformity to romance conventions. Whereas it does portray antebellum social life on a genteel Georgia plantation inhabited by a flirtatious belle, a noble soldier, and a number of very happy slaves, in other ways the work departs from the conventions of Mitchell's predecessors. In her depiction of the war, feats of battle become less significant than the fervent devotion and brave struggle of the women left at home. Accordingly, the novel centers upon a heroine, Scarlett O'Hara, who finds herself shunning many of her society's expectations for womanhood as she endures the war, Sherman's march through Atlanta, the restoration of her wrecked family plantation, Tara, and the land-grabbing scalawags. The typical romance hero that Mitchell offers is Ashley Wilkes, a devotee of the region's codes of chivalry and honor, who proves weak and ineffective in the era after the war. If Ashley is not the man the South needs, Mitchell provides an alternative in Rhett Butler, the profiteer and blockade-runner, a figure who could never have served as the hero of previous romances, but his open rejection of southern codes of acceptable behavior and his lack of concern over the war, except for the money he can gain from it, make him much more functional in postwar society than the impotent cavalier figure. The unconventional ending, finding the capitalistic Scarlett with neither man, but instead returning to her true love, Tara, reveals that the only option for southerners, who if they blindly hold on to tradition will lose everything, is to adapt to the forces of progress as a means to revitalize and rebuild the South.

The great success of *Gone With the Wind* served as a grand finale to the historical romance's heyday. Although James Boyd, Inglis Fletcher, and Laura Krey continued to work in the genre, most writers intent upon seriously exploring the burden of southern history avoided the conventions of the genre. The romances that did appear, including Frank Yerby's *The Foxes of Harrow* (1946) and *The Vixens* (1947), and Kyle Onstott's *Mandingo* (1957), employ the setting, plots, and characters of southern historical romance but usually only as a canvas on which to tell stories of sexual intrigue. The legacy of a century of southern romancers is primarily a popular notion of the Old South as a romantic setting, inhabited with honorable gentlemen-warriors, chaste yet coquettish belles, and loyal slaves who dispense words of wisdom beneath their humorous façades. Contemporary writers of mass-market bodice-rippers and best-selling historical family sagas exploit this popular concept, throwing in a large dose of sexuality and a willingness to explore some of the aspects of plantation life untouched by past romancers, including white men's sexual exploitation of slave women and the brutality of the slaves' daily life. Essentially, these "romances" of the late twentieth century do not achieve a more accurate depiction of the Old South but merely replace one myth for another, aiming for sensationalism and sexual titillation.

However, it would be a mistake to dismiss the romance as no longer serving any significant function. Alex Haley's *Roots* (1976), for instance, has been linked to the romance genre in its characterization and form. Its basis is in historical fact, the recovered story of Haley's own family, and it develops actual figures, notably Kunta Kinte and Chicken George, into noble heroes, surrounded by a cast of often-stereotyped supporting figures. Most important, the hero Kunta Kinte struggles to recover and protect a threatened tradition and make it valuable to his contemporaries and the following generation. In many ways, this is exactly what southern romancers have always done; Haley makes a narrative of distant history, full of exciting incidents, compelling characters, and a conviction that his version of the past is one that will prove useful to the present. More than one critic, including George Dekker and Herbert Smith, has suggested that *Roots* might replace *Gone With the Wind* as *the* southern historical romance. As time has passed, this now seems unlikely, but Haley's work does illustrate the different shapes a romance might take, as it appeals to a new readership and serves a purpose starkly different from that of past romances.

The historical romance has been a vital element throughout the history of southern literature. Today, the romances of the past stand as a testament to how the South saw itself or wanted to be seen by others. The genre's handling of history was an attempt to present the region's past in a manner that would influence its future. These romances made history the subject matter of fiction, and undoubtedly they have had some role in pointing southern fiction toward the twentieth-century explorations of the great burden of the southern past, with which Faulkner, Warren, and Styron would grapple.

Paul Christian Jones

See also Cavalier; *Gone With the Wind*; Lost Cause; Novel, 1820 to 1865; Plantation Fiction; Popular Literature.

George Dekker, *The American Historical Romance* (1987); Jack Temple Kirby, *Media-Made Dixie* (1978); Ernest E. Leisy, *The American Historical Novel* (1950); Robert A. Lively, *Fiction Fights the Civil War* (1957); J. V. Ridgely, *Nineteenth-Century Southern Literature* (1980); Herbert F. Smith, *The Popular American Novel, 1865–1920* (1980); William Taylor, *Cavalier and Yankee* (1961); Susan J. Tracy, *In the Master's Eye* (1995); Sheldon Van Auken, "The Southern Historical

Novel in the Early Twentieth Century," *Journal of Southern History* 14 (1948).

HISTORIES OF SOUTHERN LITERATURE

Through their various texts, southern literary histories contribute to the evolving narrative of southern literature. The paradigms they establish provide students and scholars with a common framework for discourse. Through showing connections and suggesting continuums in the South's literary history, identifying and naming movements and periods, and assimilating a range of scholarship, the literary historian offers a narrative others can challenge or contribute to—either way, the work facilitates discussion and advances the field.

Southern literature has had four book-length literary histories: *A History of Southern Literature* (1906) by Carl Holliday; *The Literature of the South* (1910) by Montrose J. Moses; *The South in American Literature 1607–1900* (1954) by Jay B. Hubbell; and *The History of Southern Literature* (1985), edited by Louis D. Rubin Jr. (general editor), Blyden Jackson, Rayburn S. Moore, Lewis P. Simpson, and Thomas Daniel Young. Written in three very different periods, each work offers an approach reflective of the cultural attitudes and scholarship of its time.

Carl Holliday's *A History of Southern Literature,* the pioneer volume of southern literary history, represents the first generation of southern literary scholars, an academic network creating a southern literary narrative to rectify the neglect and dismissal that southern literature generally received in northern-generated literary histories. Some of the New South accommodationist stances evident in his work include slavery as a mistake in the South's past, African Americans as second-class citizens, and sectionalism as compatible with nationalism.

Holliday's *History of Southern Literature* traces southern literary history from colonial times through the opening of the twentieth century. He announces that he wants to show that southern writings are "the natural, logical, and continuous productions of a people differing so materially in views and sentiments from their neighbors on the North that even civil war was necessary to prevent their becoming separate nations." Although he provides some limited social and historical cultural background, the vast majority of his content is biographical information about individual au-

thors. His gesture toward African American literature is a few pages on antebellum plantation melodies, a form he predicts will now pass away since slavery has passed. He concludes with a defense of regionalism in literature and a prediction of great things for the next generation of southern writers. Although Holliday obviously attempted a scholarly literary history, he falls far short by standards of both his day and later times. Contemporary reviews criticized his lack of authority and his insights. Subsequent scholars have concurred, pointing out numerous errors, false generalizations, a biased tone, and a lack of meaningful content.

Montrose Moses's *The Literature of the South* (1910) appeared just four years later and virtually eclipsed Holliday's work. Moses's more highly developed critical spirit and the nature of his relationship with the South fostered greater objectivity. Born after the Civil War, Moses left the South at age fourteen for New York City, where he was educated and lived the rest of his life. Unlike Holliday, Moses made his observations from a geographical and cultural distance. His professional vantage point also fostered a more objective perspective. He was a successful drama critic and scholar of drama history, and his writing of *The Literature of the South* was a significant foray out of his field of specialization.

In the book's foreword, Moses establishes his intent to apply a "rigorous critical standard," attacking past attitudes that had lacked discriminating standards in their admiration of southern literature. In a narrative organized chronologically into five periods from 1607 to the early 1900s, Moses presents discussions more intellectually vigorous than Holliday's. Each chapter opens with a section he labels "Social Forces," which provides information about the social and economic background of that period. The text exhibits evidence of comprehensive research of available sources, with an extensive bibliography and frequent quotations from well-known scholars or spokespeople of southern culture such as W. P. Trent, Edwin A. Alderman, and Edgar Gardner Murphy.

Moses's highly sociological approach provides him with a framework through which to comment upon race, class, and gender in the South. Though Moses clearly privileges the racial bond among white men above the regional bond, he also engages in a more aggressive and liberal discussion of the race issue than many of his contemporary southern literary scholars attempted. While sharing the New South tenet that African Americans are racially inferior, he explores the different viewpoints of George W. Cable and African Americans Booker T. Washington, W. E. B. Du Bois, and Charles W. Chestnutt, and also refers to Paul Laurence Dunbar's poetry. Noting current class issues in the South, Moses offers a sympathetic portrayal of poor whites and sees the lower classes as good potential subject matter for future writers. Moses includes a slate of women from antebellum times to his present, one that coincides significantly with Holliday's list.

Contemporary reviewers hailed Moses's *The Literature of the South* as an important contribution to the field and an unbiased work. Detractors pointed to minor inaccuracies, and some accused him of producing more of a social history than a literary one. In the absence of any new literary histories, Moses's work remained the best one available for the next forty-four years.

In 1954 Jay B. Hubbell published his landmark southern literary history, *The South in American Literature,* a valuable compendium reflecting extensive research. A well-known scholar of American literature, Hubbell vigorously insists that one of his goals is "to integrate the literature of the Southern states with that of the rest of the nation," an ideology reflective of the post–World War II period of American nationalism in which he wrote. The task was vast, and at one point Hubbell considered stopping with the Civil War, but he persisted to show "the large and little-recognized debt which the literary New South owes to the Old." Nevertheless, he confines his treatment of the New South to seven writers, regretfully excluding many he finds important. He also limits his work in other ways, noting that he omits the French literature of Louisiana and black writers, who, he determines, live mainly in the North anyway.

Hubbell divides southern literary history from colonial times to 1900 into five periods, opening each section with historical background; he concludes the work with an epilogue of general observations about twentieth-century literature. Unlike Moses, who gave much space to the social and economic background, Hubbell's emphasis throughout the book is decidedly on the literary culture of the South. Among other facets, he considers publishing opportunities, what books were being read, magazine culture, etc. He explains in his foreword that he places a greater emphasis on narrative and exposition and less on criticism, quoting frequently from the writers themselves. Identifying Edgar Allan Poe and Mark Twain as the only southern writers of the first caliber, Hubbell makes strong arguments

for the southerness of each. The volume concludes with an impressively extensive bibliography. Subsequent scholars used labels such as "indispensable" and "momentous" to describe Hubbell's work, which helped to accelerate the study of southern literature in the second half of the twentieth century.

Hubbell's literary history remains the last major literary history by a single author. Over thirty years later, under the initiation of the Society for the Study of Southern Literature, a group of scholars joined together to produce a new literary history to span all eras of southern literature up to the present. Under the general editorship of veteran southern scholar and professor Louis D. Rubin Jr. and senior editors Blyden Jackson, Rayburn S. Moore, Lewis P. Simpson, and Thomas Daniel Young, *The History of Southern Literature* was published in 1985. With Mary Ann Wimsatt as associate editor and Robert L. Phillips as managing editor, the editorial staff involved around fifty scholars and critics in preparing individually written essays on various topics, movements, and authors, which are arranged in chronological fashion. The volume is the first literary history to address the Renascence and the years following. In fact, in Rubin's conceptualization, the Southern Renascence forms the crux of the book; not only does it receive the greatest attention in page allotment but Rubin asserts that "the principal importance of much of the earlier literature lies in the extent to which it contributes to the development of the literary imagination that would flower in the twentieth-century Southern Literary Renascence." The work marks a significant evolution in the southern literary canon, reflecting a new plurality that acknowledges women and African Americans as integral inclusions. A conscious effort to respect the different heritages of each race is evident. These editors also make an effort to deal judiciously with the most contemporary literature. Rather than shaping the literature since midcentury into arbitrary units before time allows a fuller assessment of the body of works, they offer two general essays describing the contributions since 1950. Unlike Hubbell's work, *The History of Southern Literature* contains no bibliography. Covering three quarters of a decade more literature stretched the confines of the volume, and they regretfully omitted a bibliography to maintain the one-volume integrity of the literary history.

The History of Southern Literature was well-received, with praise for its ambitious scope and the excellence of many of its essays. Some readers, however, criticized its emphasis on the Renascence as the culmination of earlier southern literature as a limiting artifice. Overall, the work met with considerable appreciation and has made a substantial contribution to the evolution of southern literary studies. The volume will remain the touchstone literary history until the continued active growth of both southern literature and southern literary scholarship combines with a changing southern culture to call forth another individual or group to define the past in its own terms.

In addition to the full-length southern literary histories, other books and essays through the years have contained noteworthy interpretations of literary history that are now of historical interest. One such revealing source is the general American literary histories. Perusal of some of the early ones reveals the condescending attitude toward southern literature that motivated southerners to compile their own regional anthologies and literary histories in refutation. Examples include *An Introduction to American Literature* (1898) by Henry S. Pancoast; *A Literary History of America* (1901) by Barrett Wendell; *American Literature* (1902) by Julian W. Abernethy; and *A Reader's History of American Literature* (1903) by Thomas Wentworth Higginson and Henry Walcott Boynton. Moses Coit Tyler's *A History of American Literature* (1880) is one of the fairer early ones in its remarks on southern literature, and southerner John Calvin Metcalf announces that his *American Literature* (1914) offers a fuller treatment of southern writers than any volume of comparable size. For a midcentury example, *Literary History of the United States* (1948) by Robert E. Spiller et al. has a section "Writers of the South" under the broader topic "The Colonies."

Some southern literary anthologies offer literary historical commentary in their introductions and headnotes. The introductions to Edd Winfield Parks's *Southern Poets* (1936) and Gregory Paine's *Southern Prose Writers* (1947) are the best of their time. The subsequent major southern anthologies each deliver literary history along with their literary selections: *The Literature of the South* (1952) edited by Thomas Daniel Young, Floyd C. Watkins, and Richmond Croom Beatty; *Southern Writing 1585–1920* (1970) edited by Richard Beale Davis, C. Hugh Holman, and Louis D. Rubin; and the Norton anthology *The Literature of the American South* (1998) edited by William Andrews (general editor), Minrose C. Gwin, Trudier Harris, and Fred Hobson.

Examples of other miscellaneous sources include the early essays "Southern Literature" by Charles W.

Kent in Volume XL of *The Library of Southern Literature* (c. 1907) and Edwin Mims's "Introduction" in Volume VIII of *The South in the Building of the Nation* (c. 1909). In the second quarter of the twentieth century, Vernon Louis Parrington offers a thoughtful perspective in "The Mind of the South," a chapter in volume 2 of his *Main Currents in American Thought: The Romantic Revolution in America 1800–1860* (1927). More recent examples of notable contributions are the introductions in Joseph M. Flora and Robert Bain's *Fifty Southern Writers Before 1900* (1987) and *Fifty Southern Writers After 1900* (1987).

Many different sources of writing about southern literature have contributed to the always-evolving narrative of southern literary history. But it has been the major full-length southern literary histories that most powerfully influence the discourse through the scope and range of their assimilations and interpretations of southern literary history.

Susan H. Irons

See also Anthologies of Southern Literature.

HISTORY, IDEA OF

In his classic essay "The Profession of Letters in the South" (1935), Allen Tate attributed the increasingly distinguished achievement of his own generation of southern writers, the post–World War I generation, to the "peculiarly historical consciousness"—the constant awareness of "the past in the present"—shared by this generation. Twenty-five years later, Tate refined his conception of the source of the twentieth-century South's literary vitality in a second classic essay, "A Southern Mode of the Imagination" (1959), in which he envisioned the Renascence as particularly owing to the fact that after World War I southern writers, realizing for "the first time since about 1830 that the Yankees were not to blame for everything," turned from "melodramatic rhetoric to the dialectic of tragedy." Adopting the mode of the imagination suggested by "W. B. Yeats's great epigram"—"Out of the quarrel with others we make rhetoric; out of the quarrel with ourselves, poetry"—they began to find their subject in the conflict in their own minds and hearts about the meaning of the South's history. At almost the same moment that Tate published "A Southern Mode of the Imagination," the eminent historian of the South, C.

Vann Woodward, proposed in *The Burden of Southern History* (1960) that the quarrel in the southern writer's mind arose specifically from a constant awareness of the region's "tragic experience and heritage" as an anachronistic modern slave society, which, in a desperate civil conflict, had lost its attempt to become a nation in its own right.

In broader perspective, the burden of the quarrel in the writer's mind about the South's history is older than either Tate or Woodward suggest, having found its first expression when Virginia planters and men of letters like Robert Beverley and William Byrd II, responding to the failure of the supply of indentured servants to fill the need for forced labor on Virginia tobacco plantations, turned to a source of labor completely foreign to their cultural inheritance. For moral justification of the radical innovation of importing African slaves as chattels who could be bought and sold as demand and supply dictated, they appealed to the classical and Hebraic traditions of pastoral and imagined the plantation as a harmonious garden in which, under the supervision of the patriarchal master of the plantation, the labor of the slave, as Byrd explained to a correspondent, "is no more than Gardening & less by far than what poor people undergo in other countrys."

But in a changing colonial world, in which the forces of revolutionary disorder were already evident, the image of the slave plantation as a place of pastoral permanence was a fallible symbol of order, as Byrd himself recognized elsewhere in pointing not only to the possibility of insurrection by the "descendants of Ham" but to the more subtle danger that their presence may "blow up the pride and ruin the industry" even of "our white people" who do not own slaves (and this was most colonists), so that they may see "a rank of poor creatures below them" and come "to detest work for fear it should make them look like slaves." Byrd's image of what has been called "garden of the chattel," to be sure, masked a tension in the minds of the colonial planters between their doubt about the moral acceptability of slavery and their ever-increasing need for it that became disturbingly ironic when southern planters assumed leading roles in the radical movement by the American colonists to emancipate themselves from the age-old burden imposed by the rule of monarchs and priests, and in so doing subscribed to the idea proclaimed in the most important work of the literary imagination in American history that they were creating the world anew in the name of the novel doctrine of the individual human being's right to "life, liberty, and the pursuit of happiness."

From our perspective today, a major irony in the long lifetime of the Virginia planter who wrote the Declaration of Independence is his silence about the conflict, clearly implicit in his writings, between the actual historical society he was engaged in making as plantation owner and slave master and the unprecedented nation of autonomous individuals he envisioned he was making. Only in one unforgettable chapter of the *Notes on the State of Virginia,* written about ten years after the Declaration, did Thomas Jefferson unmistakenly break his silence by issuing again, though in a still more foreboding tone, the warning that William Byrd had given about the corruption of moral character by slavery, declaring that it makes such complete tyrants of the masters that the sole remedy for its evil may well be the "extirpation" of the masters by their slaves. Significantly, however, in the chapter of the *Notes* immediately following, Jefferson suggests an alternative to the pastoral vision of the plantation in a contrasting vision of the idealized American yeoman living a totally self-sufficient existence on his own freehold. Offering the redemption of the American from both the burden of kings and priests and the burden of slavery, this Jeffersonian image was to become a powerful one in the American psyche. Yet, although Jefferson did not fail to recognize the complete contradiction between a slave society and the promised land of the Declaration, he remained a slave master all his long life, and after the ominous quarrel occurred in the national Congress in 1820 about whether Missouri should be admitted to the Union as a slave or a free state, he tended to regard attacks on slavery as threats to the freedom of all the citizens of the planting states.

From the mid-1830s through the Civil War, suppression of opposition to slavery was universal in the world the slaveholders were attempting to make. During this time, the proslavery cause demanded, and at times absorbed, the attention of southern men and women of letters. Legal thinkers, theologians, moral philosophers, and historians—including John Randolph, John Taylor, John C. Calhoun, Thomas Roderick Dew, Thornton Stringfellow, William Harper, and George Fitzhugh—and novelists and poets—among them, William Gilmore Simms, John Pendleton Kennedy, Edgar Allan Poe (though a special case), Caroline Lee Hentz, Augusta Jane Evans, Mary Chesnut, and Henry Timrod—created a southern "clerisy." Conceiving not only that slavery is the "sheet anchor of American liberty" (Thomas Roderick Dew) but the "sole cause" of civilization (William Harper), the southern clerisy joined the "poet laureate of the Confederacy," Henry Timrod, in proclaiming at the moment of the Secession that the new nation of American slave states would carry out the world historical mission of redeeming mankind from the ancient curse of poverty and bringing universal peace.

But by the 1830s, the history of the South was also being written by a quite different group of authors, this comprised of slaves who had escaped from slavery. Although some of the "slave narratives" were "dictated" to white activists in the abolition movement and of doubtful authorial authenticity, Frederick Douglass's *Narrative of the Life of Frederick Douglass* (1845), a work constituting an inquiry by a sensitive, highly literate fugitive slave into the inner history of the American South, marked the appearance of a compelling narrative of undoubted authenticity. Douglass's *Narrative,* together with another notable autobiographical account by a fugitive slave published two years later, *The Narrative of William Wells Brown,* not only announced the establishment of the "slave narrative" as a genre that afforded the world that the slaves were making a literate voice but foretold the eventual establishment of what in the latter part of the twentieth century would be defined as an "African American" literature, a literature that wherever its makers might be living in the United States has a historical context in the history of the South.

"Historical sense and poetic sense should not, in the end, be contradictory," Robert Penn Warren says in the introduction to *Brother to Dragons* (1953; new version, 1978), his poem about Thomas Jefferson's suppression of the truth about the slave South, "for if poetry is the little myth we make, history is the big myth we live, and in our living, constantly remake." With the end of the Civil War, the abolition of slavery, and the imposition of Reconstruction on the South, the quarrel about the historical meaning of the South that had been suppressed in the white antebellum southern mind by the commitment to slavery continued to be suppressed, not only by the pietistic glorification of the Lost Cause but more strongly by the commitment of the white South to a systematic social and economic segregation of the former slaves that was in effect a form of re-enslavement. Yet there were vivid indications in the writings of George Washington Cable, Mark Twain, and Ellen Glasgow that the ironic implications in the interpretation of the history of the white

South foreshadowed by William Byrd and Thomas Jefferson—and always present by implication in proslavery literature—would eventually become fully articulate in the southern literary mind, as it did when, in the haunted moment between two great world wars, Tate and his contemporaries recognized the quarrel in their minds and hearts about living and making the myth of southern history in their time. This quarrel—which in the well-informed minds of Tate's generation had its context not simply in southern history, or even in American history, but in the historical crisis of Western civilization signaled by World War I—asserted a complex and graphic presence in the fiction and poetry of Tate, Andrew Lytle, Robert Penn Warren, Caroline Gordon, Katherine Anne Porter, and Eudora Welty. But in no writer of the 1920s and 1930s did the quarrel about the meaning of southern history, which in the context of broad historical reference was a quarrel symbolizing a moral crisis in Western civilization, assert its poetic hold on the southern imagination of history so completely as in the novels of the one indisputable genius, besides Jefferson, in the annals of southern literature; and in no place in William Faulkner's work does the quarrel assert itself quite so powerfully as in *The Sound and the Fury* (1929) and *Absalom, Absalom!* (1936), stories in which Quentin Compson III (who dies a suicide in 1910, having said he is "older at twenty than most men who are dead") is at once a witness to and a tragic embodiment of the terrors of living and making southern history in the long aftermath of the Civil War.

At the same time that the stronger literary minds of the white South began to experience a growing sense of freedom from the pressure to accommodate themselves to the repressive attitudes that had circumscribed the expression of their predecessors, the stronger black writers of the South—becoming, in the mode of the 1920s, self-conscious literary artists—began to free the black imagination from the accommodationist mode of the older black literary expression. Like their southern white counterparts, southern black writers of the 1920s who were either natives of the region or identified themselves with it—Jean Toomer (*Cane,* 1923); Langston Hughes (*The Weary Blues,* 1926); James Weldon Johnson (*God's Trombones,* 1927); Zora Neale Hurston *(Their Eyes Were Watching God,* 1937, the result of work begun in the 1920s); and Sterling A. Brown *(Southern Roads,* 1932, also a work that had its genesis in the 1920s)—became fully self-conscious contributors to the making of a black myth of southern history. Confronting more fully than their predecessors the complex situation that each black individual in America faced after the Civil War—the situation that W. E. B. Du Bois had earlier defined as "twoness," that is, the quarrel within each individual black person in America between a black identity and an American identity—they became, as Thadious Davis has pointed out, the "southern standard bearers" of the "Negro Renaissance" in art and literature that had its center, actual and symbolic, in New York City's Harlem. In a broader sense, like their southern white counterparts, the southern black writers of the 1920s became standard bearers of the general renaissance in American arts and letters in the time of World War I and its immediate aftermath.

If a more intense awareness of the historical situation of blacks in America may be said to have provided the energizing impetus of the generation of the Harlem Renaissance, the succeeding generation of black writers found its motive in a still more intense examination of the question of black identity. Associating this question with segregation, southern black novelists began to explore not simply the physical but the psychic violence engendered by the imprisonment of the black American citizen in a black skin, creating in Richard Wright's *Native Son* (1940), Saunders Redding's *Stranger and Alone* (1950), and Ralph Ellison's *Invisible Man* (1952) characters of greater psychological and social complexity than had heretofore been presented in the literary depiction of the black in American society. At the same time, black writers suggested more deeply than before the possibility that white society was not altogether responsible for the black's situation; that, as in the case of Ellison's protagonist in *Invisible Man,* who frees himself from Marxist dogma to make his own quest for freedom, the black individual might be relieved of a crippling sense of victimization in a racist society by taking responsibility for his or her own existence in history.

But *Invisible Man* is not altogether about the racial situation in America. It reflects a new and disturbing sense—an "existentialist" sense—about the lack of a firm historical reference for this situation. More generally, Ellison's novel suggests the loss of faith in historical interpretation that tended to become pervasive following the moment in 1945 when the American forces exploded atomic bombs over two Japanese cities, in this act not only bringing World War II to a sudden end but, so to speak, exploding the past out of the present, thus ending the modern age and inaugurating a strange new age, a "postmodern age," in which the meaning of the individual's identity in history has become more uncertain than it has ever been before.

It is noteworthy that the "existentialist" mood in *Invisible Man* is more evident in the work of the southern white writers—William Styron, Flannery O'Connor, and Walker Percy, to pick out three of the most prominent—who have emerged in the second half of the twentieth century, than in southern black writers—notably Ernest Gaines and Alice Walker—who have become well known in the same period. In *The Confessions of Nat Turner* (1967), Styron makes the story of the best-known slave uprising in southern history an anticipation of the modern individual's apocalyptic enslavement in the history that modern men have made; and in *Sophie's Choice* (1979), he makes the story of slavery in the American South a reference for the complete fulfillment of this apocalypse in the Nazi concentration camps. In her two novels, *Wise Blood* (1952) and *The Violent Bear It Away* (1960), and in numerous short stories, Flannery O'Connor, a devout Roman Catholic, seeks to reassert the transcendent Christian vision of history by imagining the dominantly Protestant South of her time as the "location" of "the peculiar crossroads where time and place and eternity somehow meet." In a series of brilliant novels, perhaps most notably in *The Moviegoer* (1961), *The Last Gentleman* (1966), and *Lancelot* (1977), Walker Percy, employing the twentieth-century South he knew as an image of the same transcendent location, makes a singularly arresting effort to probe "the individual consciousness of postmodern man." But, though they recognize the complexities of the historical situation in which their characters have their being, and, moreover, recognize in them the inhibiting complexity of their individual motives, Ernest Gaines in his novel *The Autobiography of Miss Jane Pittman* (1971) and Alice Walker in her novel *The Color Purple* (1982) do not write so much in response to the postmodern existential *angst* as to the revolution in the interpretation of civil rights in America. This revolution not only affords an overwhelming example of African Americans assuming responsibility for their own history but in the past half-century has brought the southern past into a new relationship with the present.

Lewis P. Simpson

See also Past, The; Postmodernism; Woodward, C. Vann.

Eugene D. Genovese, *The World the Slaveholders Made* (1967), and *Roll, Jordan, Roll: The World the Slaves Made*

(1974); John M. Grammer, *Pastoral and Politics in the Old South* (1996); Lucinda MacKethan, *The Dream of Arcady: Place and Time in Southern Literature* (1980); Lewis P. Simpson, *The Dispossessed Garden: Pastoral and History in Southern Literature* (1975), and *Mind and the American Civil War: A Meditation on Lost Causes* (1989).

HOG, THE

Hogs and assorted porcine themes remain an omnipresent fixture in southern literature. For years, industrious southern farmers bragged that they had a use for all parts of the hog except the squeal. The regional literature has followed suit with porcine references abounding in the works of even the earliest southern writers. Chronicles of early southern life commented extensively on the persistence of pork in the regional diet—especially the love of bacon. Antebellum writers also composed countless poems and folktales about legendary "hog drovers" driving thousands of pigs to market all over the South. The hog has a prominent place in swine-related folk sayings, as witnessed by the following: "The water won't clear til you get your hogs out of the creek" and "When a pig's belly busts, his body craves rest."

After the Civil War, southern writers continued to use the hog as an important companion to principal characters. Hogs consistently appear in the writings of Mark Twain. Huckleberry Finn fakes his death by shooting a wild hog and pouring its blood on the cabin floor and dragging the carcass off to the woods; Pap lay drunk with the hogs; and Tom Sawyer loathed the "ingot" critters.

Even as the South has changed in the modern era, the hog remains an important theme for southern writers. One of Margaret Mitchell's house slaves in *Gone With the Wind* (1936) was named Pork, and little Scout in Harper Lee's *To Kill a Mockingbird* (1960) dressed up as a ham for a Halloween pageant. Recent writers, such as Harry Crews, have vivid descriptions of southern communities' ritual hog slaughters. Countless other writers continue to describe the swine's importance to southern food habits, including barbecue, ham, bacon, pork rinds, cracklin' cornbread, sausage, and so on. Discrimination about barbecue is an important topic for southerners, as numerous guidebooks on it attest.

More often, however, a passing hog reference in southern literature emphasizes the most negative and excessive characteristics of the hog: dirty, greedy, fat, pigheaded, lazy, and hog-wild. Perhaps unfairly, hogs are often cast as loathsome critters. In Faulkner's

"Barn Burning," when the Abner Snopes family moves into their sharecroppers' quarters, a daughter says, "Likely hit ain't fitten for hawgs." One of Flannery O'Connor's characters in "Revelation" shows her utter contempt for the "nasty stinking things" that grunt and root around everywhere. But O'Connor is playing against a biblical heritage that makes the many references to swine richly complex. Ruby Turpin's revelation shows her that pigs also are God's creatures. They are part of the mystery she glimpses as she comes to a better understanding of her own worth and place in the scheme of things.

The hog is a cultural and literary symbol on par with cotton and kudzu. Just like ham hocks stewing in black-eyed peas, the hog adds flavor to the literature of the South.

S. Jonathan Bass

See also Food.

S. Jonathan Bass, "How 'bout a Hand for the Hog: The Enduring Nature of the Swine as a Cultural Symbol in the South," *Southern Cultures* 1 (Spring 1995); John Edge, *Southern Belly: The Ultimate Food Lover's Companion to the South* (2000); Eric Lolis Elie, *Smokestack Lightning: Adventures in the Heart of Barbecue Country* (1996); Kathleen Zobel, *Hog Heaven: Barbecue in the South* (1977).

HOLLINS UNIVERSITY

Since its founding in 1842, tiny Hollins College (designated "university" in 1998) has produced a remarkable number of successful writers. Originally a coeducational seminary, by 1852 it changed its mission to educate women. During the first half of the twentieth century, Mildred Riss Catlin (historical novelist), Mary Wells Knight Ashworth (Pulitzer Prize–winning historian), and Virginia Moore (popular novelist) helped establish the Hollins writing tradition.

The arrival in 1957 of Louis D. Rubin Jr., along with accomplished poets John Alexander Allen and Julia Randall Sawyer, has much to do with Hollins's prominence as a college that encourages writers. Within two years, the college had a coeducational M.A. program and began graduating a steady stream of writers on their way to successful careers as poets, fiction writers, and editors. In 1963 Rubin introduced the *Hollins Critic,* which publishes in-depth studies of contemporary writers.

To chronicle the unusual confluence of writers who made up the Class of 1967, Nancy Parrish wrote *Lee*

Smith, Annie Dillard, and the Hollins Group: A Genesis of Writers (1999). By the end of their first year, "the group" had published their own literary magazine, *Beanstalks,* in rebellion against the upper-class women editors of the college's literary magazine, *Cargoes.* In 1964, R. H. W. Dillard was assigned to teach the sophomore creative writing course. The sophomores, who had expected to join Rubin's celebrated evening advanced workshops, soon found in young Dillard a kindred daring spirit and a teacher of patience, humor, and great talent. Annie (Doak) Dillard, who married Richard Dillard the following summer, went on to win a Pulitzer Prize with *Pilgrim at Tinker Creek* (1974). Lee Smith finished her first novel, *The Last Day the Dogbushes Bloomed* (1968), before leaving Hollins. Lucinda MacKethan and Anne Goodwyn Jones went from Hollins to graduate school in Chapel Hill; their first books came out of dissertations written under Rubin, who had joined UNC's faculty in 1967. Although Parrish's book concentrates on one class, that class had close bonds with other students who attended Hollins at the same time, including poets Margaret Gibson and Rosanne Coggeshall (fifteen books of poetry between them) and Henry Taylor, winner in 1986 of a Pulitzer in poetry.

In 1969 Richard Dillard began directing the writing program. Its enduring strength was evidenced through the anthology *Elvis in Oz: New Stories and Poems from the Hollins Creative Writing Program* (1992), edited by Mary Flinn and George Garrett.

Author Amanda Cockrell returned to Hollins to direct a new program with old roots. The M.A. program in Children's Literature honors the woman who is Hollins's most famous writer graduate (1932). Margaret Wise Brown created the "Golden Books" design for children's books and authored some of the most enduring work in the genre—over ninety-three titles in all.

Lucinda H. MacKethan

HONOR

Often represented in southern literature as a defining feature of the code of the old-style southern gentleman, the ethos of honor is actually more than just a southern or a literary phenomenon. Anthropologists, sociologists, and historians trace the origins of honor back to the primitive beginnings of almost every human culture, and honor codes of some sort have remained operative throughout the course of Western history, surviving even in pockets of the urban, industrial twentieth century.

Despite differences across eras and cultures, certain principles inform nearly all honor codes. Primarily a male ethos, honor requires that a man support and protect not just his own individual welfare but that of his biological family and of any other person or body with whom he has identified and to whom he has committed himself—whether it be a military unit, community, or nation and its leader(s). An honorable man is expected to back up his expressed commitment or "word of honor" to the extent of engaging in verbally or physically confrontive or violent acts to protect or avenge his own group against threatening others—the violence ranging from the single combat of the duel to full-scale war. He is seldom willing to rely on civil government to enact what he deems to be justice for himself and his clan. Courage and martial strength and prowess are therefore crucial characteristics of honor. Even physical features or accouterments that make a man appear powerful are important. This element of appearance, moreover, suggests a certain equivocation present in the concept of honor: a man may believe that his honor consists in his inward, objective worthiness, but he usually needs to be publicly shown honor or respect by others in order to feel secure in his virtue and strength. These others can include women as well as other men. The woman's honor usually consists of her sexual purity and submission to a man—her father, husband, or knight. But as wife, mother, or idealized lady, both her behavior and her praise or blame can exert significant honoring or shaming force on her menfolk. Finally, though the ethos of honor may be operative within all classes of a society, each person defending his own particular place in the social hierarchy, the upper-class or most powerful are usually paid the highest honor and take the most trouble to define and measure honor.

The indigenous honor code of the ancient Europeans was influenced during the Middle Ages both by Greco-Roman philosophy, particularly Stoicism, and Christianity, assuming relatively refined features associated with chivalry and courtly love and later becoming the ethos of the traditional Renaissance and eighteenth-century gentleman. This ethos entered the South primarily via the potent influence of English manners and values and the English model of education in the Greco-Roman classics. Plantation works such as John P. Kennedy's *Swallow Barn* (1832) and Augusta Jane

Evans Wilson's *St. Elmo* (1866) incorporate the southern ideal of honor, but not uncritically. Although most nineteenth-century southern apologists tended to represent gentlemanly honor as a wholly admirable value system, Faulkner and other twentieth-century southern writers present significantly more complex, ambivalent perspectives. Faulkner's *The Unvanquished* (1938) presents the honor of Colonel John Sartoris in part as an admirable gallantry and integrity. The novel also portrays, however, the destructive violence that Sartoris honor continually seems to require: after the war, the Colonel faces off with and guns down two Yankee carpetbaggers and is later himself shot and killed by Redmond, a former business associate. In the novel's final chapter, "An Odor of Verbena," the Colonel's son, Bayard, finally refuses to continue the chain of violence any further, courageously confronting Redmond but refusing to return his fire, despite his stepmother Drusilla's exhortation that only a duel to the death can vindicate Sartoris honor.

In Faulkner's *The Sound and the Fury* (1929), the concept of honor comes for Quentin Compson to represent not only the dignity and reputation of the once-illustrious Compsons but the moral absolutes that he believes gave southerners of earlier generations a reason and a way to live—things his cynical, naturalistic father no longer believes in. Quentin's concern for honor largely degenerates into a pathological obsession with his sister Caddy's loss of virginity and with his own impotence to oppose this or any of the changes that seem to be moving him and his family away from an ideal past. His ultimate suicide is a measure quite characteristic of disillusioned honor.

This theme of the decline of southern honor becomes an extremely central element in the fiction of Walker Percy, one of the finest southern writers of the generation after Faulkner's. Percy's philosophical novels suggest definite reasons for this decline: For all its idealism of Stoic constancy, the code of honor as represented in *The Moviegoer* (1962), *The Last Gentleman* (1966), *Lancelot* (1977), and *The Second Coming* (1980) was vulnerable from the beginning to cultural flux. Percy's southern gentleman desperately needs the respect of social inferiors and the support of virtuous peers. When these elements seem to disappear from the South in the maelstrom of the twentieth century, Percy's elder Barrett bitterly withdraws from the community he had sought to lead and like Quentin kills himself, and Percy's Lancelot becomes a crazed, vengeful murderer. An ethical code needs (and in the earlier

South in a limited fashion had) the support of religious belief, specifically Christianity, Percy's novels indicate.

In its grosser forms in southern literature, honor becomes the justification for everything from barn burning to bushwhacking to lynching. Percy's and Faulkner's works, however, clearly reveal some admiration for the code, especially in its more classical forms, a view endorsed as well in the works of other southern writers. The words "Honor, Honor" lie like a sword, "cold as steel," between the passionate lovers of John Crowe Ransom's poem "The Equilibrists" (1924), yet for Ransom the tension between honor and physical desire creates an intricate, enduring balance that is both "perilous and beautiful." The modern speaker of Allen Tate's poem "Ode to the Confederate Dead" (1936) gazes on a Confederate graveyard "seeing only the leaves/Flying, plunge and expire." In Ernest J. Gaines's novel *A Gathering of Old Men* (1983), however, a sense of honor unites a body of old African American men of a rural Louisiana community and gives them the resolve finally to stand up to the oppression of white Cajuns. The huge but formerly docile African American Charlie forces Cajun Luke Will into an armed confrontation resembling a duel, an honorable combat considered appropriate only between social equals. Honor never rises as high as Dilsey's enduring love in Faulkner's *The Sound and the Fury* or the joyful, grace-filled communion of Will and Allie in Percy's *The Second Coming*, but at times, even in later southern literature, it can be considerably better than fearfulness, faithlessness, and self-disgust.

Wendell (Whit) Jones Jr.

See also Aristocracy; Cavalier; Class; Gentleman; Lady; Romanticism; Southern Renascence; Stoicism; Town and Country.

Clement Eaton, "The Role of Honor in Southern Society," *Southern Humanities Review* 10 suppl. (1976); George Fenwick Jones, *Honor in German Literature* (1959); Julian Pitt-Rivers, "Honor," in *International Encyclopedia of the Social Sciences* (1968); Louis D. Rubin Jr., "The Boll Weevil, the Iron Horse, and the End of the Line: Thoughts on the South," in *The American South: Portrait of a Culture*, ed. Louis D. Rubin Jr. (1980); Curtis Brown Watson, *Shakespeare and the Renaissance Concept of Honor* (1960); Bertram Wyatt-Brown, *Southern Honor: Ethics and Behavior in the Old South* (1982).

HORSES AND HORSE RACING

Although horses and horsemanship have not figured as prominently in the literature of the American South as they have in the literature of the American West, they have played important roles in some memorable southern fiction and have been especially visible in representations of the southern cavalier. Because horses are central to the image of the cavalier (recall that *cavalier* is etymologically connected to the term *chivalry* and originally signified a horse soldier, hence, a knight), the plantation literature of the antebellum and postbellum South features the southern gentleman displaying his riding skills in the hunt, on the field of battle, or in games of honor. While in some respects the ubiquity of mounted squires in this body of literature simply reflects the utilitarian and recreational importance of the horse in a pre-industrial age, it served an ideological purpose as well, since the control that the southern cavalier exerted over his horse served to represent the control he held over his passions, and presumably over his plantation.

The romantic figure of the swashbuckling Confederate cavalry officer looms large in the mythic imagination of the South, and nowhere are the images of the southern aristocrat and his horse joined so seamlessly as in the many portraits of General Robert E. Lee astride his faithful horse Traveler, and of other war heroes such as Jeb Stuart, Nathan Bedford Forrest, and Stonewall Jackson. In one especially vivid passage in *Sartoris* (1929), Faulkner ironizes this image while noting its romantic appeal. In that passage, Aunt Jenny Du Pre recounts how her cousin Bayard Sartoris was killed while riding alongside Jeb Stuart, who was leading at the time a cavalry charge far behind the Union lines in order to liberate a supply of coffee from a Federal canteen. Similarly, the South's obsession with chivalric manners is made explicit in Allen Tate's *The Fathers* (1938), which features a scene on the eve of the Civil War in which sons of the Virginia gentry participate in a medieval joust of sorts where the contestants compete to see who can skewer the most rings with his lance and thus win a laurel wreath for the lady of his choice.

In addition to using horses to comment on the qualities of the southern cavalier, southern writers have also been attracted to scenes of horse trading and racing, where a different side of human nature is revealed. In the work of Southwestern humorists such as Augustus Baldwin Longstreet and Johnson Jones Hooper, we see the shrewdness of their scoundrel-heroes as they fleece their gullible marks at the racetrack and in the horse trade. Faulkner, who owned and bred horses at his home, payed homage to the early Southwestern hu-

morists' treatments of horse tales in several of his works. In the "Spotted Horses" chapter from *The Hamlet* (1940), Flem Snopes and a gingersnap-eating stranger from Texas unload a herd of untamable wild horses on the residents of Yoknapatawpha County. In *The Unvanquished* (1938), young Bayard Sartoris (not to be confused with his cousin of the same name) and his grandmother sell horses to the Union army, only to steal them back and sell the same horses again to the same buyers. Horse trading also plays a significant role in the plot of *The Reivers* (1962) and, to a lesser extent, in *As I Lay Dying* (1930).

Not surprisingly, given the popularity of horse racing in the South, southern writers have used the racetrack as the setting for some notable works of fiction. In Kate Chopin's *The Awakening* (1900), Edna Pontelier helps secure her status as a social outcast by frequenting the races with the notorious womanizer Alcée Arobin. And in Katherine Anne Porter's "Old Mortality" (1939), young Miranda's imaginative attachment to the world of racing, which she associates with the romanticized family myths of her deceased Aunt Amy, is shattered when she sees blood pouring from the nose of her uncle's horse as it is led from the winner's circle.

One especially notable example of horses in recent southern fiction is Cormac McCarthy's Border Trilogy, *All the Pretty Horses* (1992) for which he won the National Book Award, *The Crossing* (1994), and *Cities of the Plain* (1998), set in Southeast Texas soon after World War II.

James H. Watkins

See also Cavalier; Military Tradition; Mule, The.

HUMOR, BEGINNINGS TO 1900

With its emphasis on the customs, dialect, and diverting antics of various unusual specimens of humanity, southern literary humor before 1900 contains a distinct anthropological bent. In general, the comedy focuses on the peculiarities of distinct groups of southerners: the frontier settlers, the Appalachian mountaineers, and the African American plantation folk. The tone of the humor varies, however, depending upon the historical period.

Many scholars consider the writings of William Byrd II of Westover (1674–1744) to be the first recorded examples of southern literary humor. A Virginian planter, political leader, and author of a variety of prose works documenting life in colonial America, Byrd is also known as a sharp satirist of southern types, particularly the lower-class whites. In his eighteenth-century *History of the Dividing Line* (1841), Byrd describes the adventures of a group of Virginians (himself included) who travel into the "uncivilized" region of North Carolina to settle a dispute about the boundary separating the two colonies. While the subject of Byrd's book is a literal boundary—the border between Virginia and North Carolina—he also, as Kenneth Lynn asserts, discursively creates a metaphorical boundary between different groups of southerners. Using his witty, derisive humor, he constructs Virginians as civilized gentlemen in contrast to the degraded and freakish rubes of North Carolina.

According to Byrd, North Carolina, with its mild climate and fertile land, attracts the type of people he calls "Lubberlanders." Constitutionally indolent and immune to civilizing influences, Lubberlanders are mainly runaways, debtors, criminals, and amoral opportunists. Byrd's satire is particularly harsh when directed against the laziness of the men; while the women labor like drones, the men are too slothful to do anything except beget children. Byrd does not limit his comic barbs to moral failures; he also provokes laughter at the expense of physical deformities, including "cadaverous complexions" and malformed bodies. Suggesting an affinity between hogs and Lubberlanders, Byrd dwells at length on the North Carolinian's propensity to eat fresh pork, a dietary choice resulting in "gross humours," scurvy, yaws, and thus a large population of people with deformed noses. The repeated references to such physical deformities as "custard complexions" and deformed noses suggest that the moral and social inferiority of this group of people can be read on their bodies. As such, Byrd's *History of the Dividing Line* sets up the paradigm for nineteenth-century humor of the Old Southwest, much of which relies heavily on grotesque humor of the body.

The tradition of laughing at the diverting antics of southern frontier folk continues into the nineteenth century with the rough and raucous humor of what used to be called the Southwest (Georgia, Alabama, Mississippi, Tennessee, Louisiana, Arkansas, and Missouri). Between 1830 and 1867, writers of Old Southwestern humor recorded and amplified upon the oral tradition of folk humor they heard in the frontier regions of the South. Pivotal to the popularity of this body of humor was William T. Porter's magazine *The Spirit of the Times: A Chronicle of the Turf, Agriculture, Field Sports, Literature and the Stage,* which circulated between 1831 and 1856. Porter sought out and cultivated new humorists, helping many of them break into print. The most famous examples of this body of southern humor are Augustus Baldwin Longstreet's *Georgia Scenes* (1835), William Tappan Thompson's *Major Jones's Courtship* (1843), Johnson J. Hooper's *Some Adventures of Captain Simon Suggs* (1845), Henry Clay Lewis's *Odd Leaves from the Life of a Louisiana Swamp Doctor* (1850), Thomas Bangs Thorpe's "The Big Bear of Arkansas" (1854), Joseph Glover Baldwin's *The Flush Times of Alabama and Mississippi* (1953), and George W. Harris's *Sut Lovingood: Yarns Spun by a "Nat'ral Born Durn'd Fool"* (1867).

Their humor, often considered to be "classic" southern comic expression, has been described as masculine, exuberant, ribald, high spirited, realistic, exaggerated, bragging, boasting, cruel, brutish, grotesque, violent, conservative, and subversive. The sketches and stories are diverse, but they tend to portray common themes and situations such as odd local customs, fights, hunting, pranks, religious experiences, and courtships. More striking than the events portrayed, however, are the rough, lower-class, usually white characters described: frontiersmen, yeomen farmers, crackers, backwoodsmen, hillbillies, and poor whites who enjoy fighting, boasting, drinking, gambling, and other forms of carousing.

But whereas the characters described in this genre are lower class and sometimes so "uncivilized" as to appear barely human, the *writers* of this genre tended to be well-educated professionals of a conservative political bent. Kenneth Lynn argues persuasively that these gentlemen portrayed the rough and tumble antics of these frontiersmen as comic for political reasons: to show the dangerous results of Jacksonian democracy. Just as Byrd constructs the Virginian gentleman through contrast with North Carolina "lubbers," the Old Southwestern humorists contrast the rationality and restraint of conservative gentlemen with the raw, violent excesses of unfettered barbarians.

The class differences between the authors and characters are often mirrored in the contrasting rhetoric between the narrator and the characters. Using the device of the frame, authors often invent a genteel, conservative, sometimes even priggish narrator to recount the bizarre sights he has seen in the wild southern frontier regions. Augustus Baldwin Longstreet's *Georgia*

Scenes makes particular use of the genteel frame narrator to highlight the comical aspects of his characters. Born in Augusta, Georgia, in 1790, Longstreet chronicled the lives of the plain rural folk of northeastern Georgia. In his preface and in many of the sketches, Longstreet constructs two genteel fictional narrators (Hall and Baldwin) to recount the raucous adventures they have observed in the Georgian wilderness. This frame serves both to "sanitize" the narrator/author by removing him a step from the unsavory adventures he has witnessed and to heighten the comedy through the incongruous rhetorical contrasts.

In "The Fight," one of Longstreet's more famous stories, the readers are treated to detailed descriptions of a gory fight between Bill and Bob. Much of the humor derives from the contrast between the narrator's elevated rhetoric and the untutored vernacular and wild excesses of the local yokels. The narrator, ruminating on the probable outcome of the brawl, resorts frequently to Latin expressions such as *a priori* and *argumentum ad hominem,* while the local characters prefer a more earthy linguistic style: "Them boys think I mean that Bob will whip." And where the narrator speaks of an opponent's "adroitness in bringing his adversary to the ground," the characters say "by the time he hit the ground, the meat would fly off his face so quick, that people would think it was shook off by the fall."

"The Fight" is emblematic of much Southwestern humor not only in its use of a frame but also in its emphasis on violence and physical deformities. Although Bill and Bob are friends, they are goaded into fighting by the original ninety-five-pound weakling, Ransy Sniffle, a character whose physical deformities recall Byrd's Lubberlanders. Ransy's propensity to dine upon red clay and blackberries has given him a deathly pallor, a skeletal physique, and disproportionately large limbs. Longstreet continues describing Ransy for almost a page, dwelling at length on his comical physical deformities. His physical deformities appear to mirror his moral freakishness: he goes to great lengths to instigate the fight between the two friends for no apparent reason except that he likes to see people maul each other. In addition to implying that the frontier lower-class whites are unrestrainedly violent, even animalistic, this story also suggests that, even though poor whites might be born with similar physical characteristics to gentler folk, their degraded ways will soon show on their bodies.

Although not all Southwestern humorists depict bodily deformity, comic exaggeration is a technique nearly all of them share. Thomas Bangs Thorpe (1815–1875) is particularly renowned for this skill. Painter, editor, and writer, Thorpe grew up in New York but spent twenty years of his adult life in Louisiana, where he found the inspiration for his highly successful sketches of frontier folk. Thorpe's most famous work, "The Big Bear of Arkansas" (1841), expanded the possibilities for the vernacular, which he combined with impressive comic characterizations and an imaginative narrative structure. Like Longstreet, Thorpe makes use of a narrative frame: a traveler on a Mississippi steamboat describes in elevated, Latinate language the great variety of people he spies in the crowd, some of whom are the "half-horse and half-alligator species of men, who are peculiar to 'old Mississippi.'" Unlike Longstreet, however, Thorpe creates a second narrator whom he meets on the boat, Jim Doggett, who orates his tall tale about bear hunting to a crowd of fascinated observers. Unlike the first narrator, Doggett's vernacular voice is informal, salty, and filled with imaginative hyperbole. Partially because we hear most of the story from Doggett's perspective, the disdainful distance between narrator and character noted in other Southwestern humor is less apparent here. Another reason for this lack of distance is that, unlike Ransy Sniffle or Simon Suggs, Doggett comes across as genuinely likable. He possesses not only a gift for language but also a harmony with the natural world that invites respect.

Jim begins his story by establishing his unsurpassed skill at bear hunting. He then goes on to regale his listeners with the details of his relationship to one bear in particular, which he hunts unsuccessfully for three years. Although he finally succeeds in killing the bear, Doggett does not believe his hunt was successful. Rather, he claims that the bear was "unhuntable" and only showed up to be conveniently shot because it was his time to go. Although the tall tale is basically comic, the bear becomes so elusive and even unearthly that the story begins to accrue an almost spiritual dimension. Although the audience begins listening with comic delight, the tale within a tale ends on a note of solemn silence.

Whereas Thorpe's linguistic humor depends upon Doggett's zesty and idiosyncratic use of the vernacular, William Tappan Thompson (1812–1882) mines humor from his character's misspellings and malapropisms. Although a respectable plantation owner, the hero of Thompson's enormously popular *Major Jones's Courtship* (1843) is far from flawless in his use of written English. December 25 is "Crismus" Day to him, and when he digresses in his story, he apologizes for his "transgression." Thompson's writing bears a close affinity with the Down-East humor of Yankee writers such as Seba Smith. The humor of Thompson's stories stems not only from the misuse of language but also from the comedy of situation. In one story, Major Jones proposes to his future wife by climbing inside a meal bag hung from her porch and spending all night there until he is "presented" to her in the morning as a Christmas present.

Whereas Major Jones is a character whose high jinx are all harmless and good hearted, the same cannot always be said of the heroes of Old Southwestern humor. This body of literature is famous not only for its use of the vernacular and tall tales, but also for its preponderance of rogues whose pranks range from harmless mischief to sadistic torture. Joseph Glover Baldwin (1815–1864) in his collection *Flush Times of Alabama and Mississippi* (1853) narrates the adventures of Ovid Bolus, Esq., who shares Jim Doggett's talent for telling tall tales. Or, as Baldwin puts it, Bolus is a "natural liar" whose art for invention is as "wide, illimitable, as elastic and variable as the air he spent in giving it expression." But whereas Doggett limits his lies and exaggerations to storytelling, Ovid Bolus uses his art to dupe listeners out of their money. Perhaps such a crude characterization of Bolus is unfair; as Baldwin describes him, he simply asserts the spiritual realm over that of the material. Rather than being so vulgar as to pay for his goods in cash, he "got them under a state of poetic illusion, and paid for them in an imaginary way." Unfortunately, like many artists, he is misunderstood by his peers: tired of Ovid's inability to pay his debts, they finally run him out of town.

The rogues of Southwestern humor tend to inflict physical anguish as well as pecuniary pain. And who better is better qualified to inflict pain than a medical doctor? Henry Clay Lewis (Madison Tensas) (1825–1850) draws on his experiences as a medical student and doctor in Louisiana in his sketches from *Odd Leaves from the Life of a Louisiana "Swamp Doctor."* These sketches satirize both the primitive state of medical knowledge and the ignorance of the Louisiana folk (especially African Americans and Native Americans) who are unfortunate enough to fall under a doctor's care. "The Mississippi Patent Plan for Pulling Teeth" portrays one doctor's idea of "fun." Irritated at a dental patient's cheapness, he decides to get back at him by strapping him into an implement of torture: a surgical armchair that uses blocks and pulleys to attach into the wall a couple of iron bolts. The great "joke" is that rather than pulling teeth, this contraption pulls the patient's neck nearly out of its socket. The doctor himself was not sure which would have come off first—the head or the neck—had not the contraption broken down mid-process.

Johnson Jones Hooper (1815–1862) created another memorable rogue: Simon Suggs. Born in Wilmington, North Carolina, Hooper found inspiration for a writing career when he moved to La Fayette, Alabama, and observed the behavior of the backwoodsmen around him. Hooper's humorous sketches were collected in two books, *Some Adventures of Captain Simon Suggs; Together with "Taking the Census" and Other Alabama Sketches* (1845) and *The Widow Rugby's Husband* (1851). His most popular stories recount the picaresque adventures of Simon Suggs, an irrepressible trickster whose most deeply held belief is that "it is good to be shifty in a new country." Hooper writes *Some Adventures of Captain Simon Suggs* in the form of a campaign biography, employing a mock-serious tone and elevated language to describe the mighty adventures of his hero. The narrator reports that, since Suggs will soon be running for political office, he has undertaken the solemn duty of informing his potential constituents of the hero's biography. Like such luminaries of southern humor as Longstreet's Ransy Sniffle and Byrd's Lubberlanders, Simon's physical attributes are somewhat wanting: he has a large head with white hair; nearly invisible eyebrows above red, lashless eyes; and a long and low nose that overhangs a four-inch-wide mouth drawn down in a permanent sneer. Readers might suppose from the title "Captain" that Suggs has demonstrated due valor in military duty. In fact, he garnered this title by tricking his fellow citizens into believing Indians were about to attack and that only he, emboldened by a considerable amount of whiskey, could save them from this nonexistent threat.

Certainly, this adventure is not his first example of trickery. A precocious lad, Simon demonstrates his talents as a rogue early in life, much to the consternation of his father, a Baptist preacher. In "Simon Gets a 'Soft Snap,' " our hero profits from his gift at card tricks and convoluted logic not only to escape imminent punishment from his father but also to persuade this devout Baptist to gamble and lose his horse to Simon. Less than pleased with the outcome, Simon's father kicks the seventeen-year-old out of the house for good. Henceforth, Simon travels the countryside ever on the lookout for opportunities for mischief. In "The Captain Attends a Camp-Meeting," Simon shows off his skills by outsmarting a preacher during a revival meeting. Displays of religious ecstasy were a common source of fun for many Southwestern humorists, and Hooper uses this material to great advantage. Simon muses on the curious fact that the preacher seems especially concerned with saving the souls of the young women, wondering why "these here preachers never hugs up the old, ugly women? Never seed one do it in my life—the sperrit never moves 'em that way!" When the crowd, sensing a sinner in its midst, pounces upon Simon, he senses a business opportunity and begins writhing, moaning, and testifying to the spirit that has moved him. To show his appreciation of his newfound faith, he offers to collect money from everyone to start a church in his own neighborhood. He succeeds in collecting a very handsome sum in a short time, after which he canters off into the wilderness, where the spirit mysteriously deserts him.

Hypocritical preachers also provide comic opportunities for George Washington Harris (1814–1869), perhaps the most gifted and original of the Southwestern humorists. A long-term resident of Knoxville, Tennessee, Harris is most famous for creating Sut Lovingood, a self-described "nat'ral born durn'd fool." In keeping with his fictional predecessors, Sut is far from prepossessing in his physical attributes: he is a "queer looking," "hog-eyed," long-legged, white-haired troublemaker. Sut first appeared in the *Spirit of the Times* in 1854 in a story entitled "Sut Lovingood's Daddy, Acting Horse." In this story, because Sut's family is sorely lacking a horse, his father decides to put on the bridle himself and play "hoss" by pulling the plow for his son. His father, unfortunately, gets somewhat carried away with his new role. Not only does he bite, whinny, and kick his hind legs at his wife, but he also canters straight into a sassafras bush, where he upsets a large hornet's nest. The rest of the story details the chase scene between hornets and father, who, never forgetting his role, runs on four legs into the nearest stream, where he engages in the "bisness ove divin an' cussin."

Harris's stories, collected into book form as *Sut Lovingood: Yarns Spun by a "Nat'ral Born Durn'd Fool,"* are by no means universally popular. Although many readers find them repugnant, others enjoy them not only for their manic physical humor but also for the characterization of Sut and the imaginative use of language. Like Simon Suggs, Sut Lovingood is an invet-

erate prankster whose adventures often end in mortification and/or physical pain for those involved. Unlike Suggs, however, Sut's high jinx are motivated not by the prospects of material gain but by a deep distaste for self-righteous hypocrites who, he believes, deserve their comeuppance. Sut himself is devoid of pretensions and self-delusion; he is the first to admit his own weaknesses and refers to himself as a "durn'd fool." Both Sut's character and Harris's inventive use of language are admirably illustrated in "Parson John Bullen's Lizards." In this sketch, Sut is incensed at the "hiperkritical, pot-bellied, scaley-hided, whisky-wastin, stinkin ole groun'-hog" of a parson for getting his female friend in trouble even after he promised otherwise. (The incidents for which the female friend was punished remain obscure, but they have something to do with being found in a shady huckleberry thicket "conversing" with Sut.) Inspired by the parson's intonations on the "Hell-sarpints" that come to slither over the naked bodies of sinners, Sut wreaks havoc on the congregation by letting loose a bag full of pot-bellied lizards to climb up the pants-leg of the parson. The resulting tumult is described in colorful detail by Sut. This technique of piling detail upon detail into his descriptions, combined with his character's sheer exuberance and spirit of freedom, exemplifies the literary innovations of Harris and the culmination of antebellum southern humor.

Where much of antebellum southern humor takes as its subject matter the raucous adventures of the lower classes of whites, humor written after the Civil War often focuses on African Americans. By this time, however, the rough and raucous nature of the humor has been subdued to genteel forms more palatable to a wider audience. A prime example of this new tone is the gently subversive humor of Joel Chandler Harris's Uncle Remus tales, collected in *Uncle Remus: His Songs and His Sayings* (1880) and later volumes. Drawing from the African American folk tales he heard from the slaves of his Georgia youth, Harris continues the tradition of framed narration inherited from the Old Southwestern humorists. The image of a kindly old African American man entertaining a little white boy with tales of rabbits, foxes, and other animals appealed to a large audience, bringing lasting fame to Harris as a writer of plantation fiction. Despite the sentimental surface of the frame, however, the Uncle Remus tales present a slyly subversive world in which the weaker animals such as the rabbit consistently triumph over the stronger animals such as the fox. As

Bernard Wolfe observes, the Uncle Remus tales take as their subject matter southern racial taboos such as food sharing and sex sharing and stand them on their heads. But because the tales are superficially about animals rather than people, the subversive comedy remains veiled and therefore palatable to its contemporary audience.

Charles Chesnutt (1858–1932), who spent his formative years in Fayetteville, North Carolina, pushes the subversive elements of Joel Chandler Harris one step further in his collections of short fiction *The Conjure Woman* (1899) and *The Wife of His Youth and Other Stories of the Color Line* (1899). Like Harris, Chesnutt employs southern African American dialect to create a fresh vernacular voice, but unlike Harris, Chesnutt deromanticizes the genre of plantation fiction to create a more realistic picture of the hardships faced by African Americans and their ingenuity in surviving those hardships. His comic technique hinges upon wily deception, ironic understatement, and reversed expectations. "The Passing of Grandison" comically explodes the myth of the faithful slave who prefers servitude to freedom. Grandison claims to his owner that he has no interest in being free because "I sh'd jes' reckon I is better off, suh, dan dem low-down free niggers, suh!" Such exclamations of loyalty lull his master, the Colonel, into complacency so that he allows his son to take his slave to Canada, where his son coerces Grandison into escaping. Such is the loyalty of Grandison, or at least so the Colonel believes, that his slave comes back willingly to the plantation. But while the Colonel is busy congratulating himself on the loyalty of his trustworthy slaves, Grandison is suddenly found missing. Exploiting the Colonel's misplaced trust in him, Grandison had come home only to collect the rest of his family for his trip back to Canada on the Underground Railroad. The Colonel last spies his vanishing property crossing into freedom, waving derisively good-bye to his former master. Just as Grandison ironically manipulates his owner's belief in the loyalty of his slaves, so too does Chesnutt in his stories comically manipulate his readers' beliefs in African American inferiority by signifying on their most cherished myths.

Although Harris and Chesnutt are perhaps the best-known humorous writers of this period who focused on capturing the tales, customs, and dialects of southern African Americans, they were not alone in this endeavor. A number of female writers such as Katharine McDowell and Ruth McEnery Stuart also tried to capture in their fiction the nuances of African American folk life. Writing under the pseudonym Sherwood Bonner, McDowell published a number of gently humorous tales in her 1884 collection *Suwanee River Tales*. Because her stories often focus on the mother wit of "Gran'mammy," a character based on McDowell's childhood nurse, they provide an interesting counterpart to the male perspectives of Harris and Chesnutt.

Because they focus on local customs (especially of the mountaineers and former slaves) and because of their genteel, sentimental tones, McDowell and Stuart, along with their contemporaries Mary Noailles Murfree (Charles Egbert Craddock) and Idora McClellan Moore (Betsy Hamilton), are often described (sometimes dismissively) as local-color writers. But, as Kathryn McKee suggests, they might more accurately be categorized as "female local humorists" because they blend together the traditions of both Old Southwestern humor and local-color writers. McKee contends that this group of southern female writers manipulate the established conventions of both traditions in order to address fictionally cultural concerns such as domestic violence, restrictive gender conventions, and the trials of marriage that were central to the lives of contemporary southern women. Betsy Hamilton's "Hog Killin' in Hillabee" uses material that is ripe for traditional Southwestern humor—the grime and grease resulting from hog killing. But whereas Longstreet's characters use grease to derive sport from pulling the head off a gander, Hamilton uses grease imagery to depict a much more dangerous sport—courtship. Courtship is a particularly hazardous endeavor for a young woman when one's face is smeared with greasy ashes. Because they provide a female perspective on similar subject matter treated by the male Southwestern humorists, the "female local humorists" present an important counterpart to them and deserve more critical attention than they have heretofore received.

The tradition of southern humor before 1900 culminates in the work of Mark Twain, who combines and transcends the best aspects of local-colorists and Southwestern humorists. His use of humorous anecdotes surrounded by a narrative frame, his experimentation with vernacular English, his comedy of hilarious situations, and his earthy, exuberant characterizations all bear the mark of the Southwestern tradition. But whereas the Southwestern stories could be cruel toward the lower classes, Twain's humor, like that of the local-colorists and local-humorists, is more humane and sympathetic to the dispossessed.

Twain grew up listening to and reading the tall tales

and boasts of the Southwestern humorists: they were an integral part of his cultural heritage. Some of his passages, in fact, bear striking resemblance to predecessors. In *Tom Sawyer* (1876), Tom's enactment of a fight with an imaginary boy directly mirrors Longstreet's "Georgia Theatrics." But more important than the subject matter for Twain's development as a writer was what he gleaned from the narrative technique of these authors, particularly their use of the framework and the character-revealing monologue. In "How to Tell a Story," Twain underscores the importance of narrative technique. What makes a story humorous, he avers, is not the matter of the telling but the *manner* of it. Whereas he believes anyone can tell a joke or comic anecdote, it requires great artistry to recount a humorous story. Twain's fame as a comic lecturer derived not so much from the stories he told but from his carefully developed stage persona as an "inspired idiot" who speaks with a slow, deliberate drawl and seems not to understand why the audience laughs at him.

Twain first applied this comic technique to great effect in "The Notorious Jumping Frog of Calaveras County" (1867). It features an educated narrator as frame who introduces us to the vernacular voice of Simon Wheeler. Rather than depicting a gentleman who aloofly teaches his readers a lesson about the foolishness or depravity of his subject matter, Twain creates a story in which the joke is on the educated narrator and on the would-be trickster. "Jumping Frog" upsets our expectations by showing the "foolish" Simon Wheeler to be more astute than the educated frame narrator.

Twain's comic originality shines when he takes his comic technique one step further and fuses the educated and vernacular voice into one new comic narrator. Whereas the Southwestern tradition emphasized the distance between the narrator and his subject, Twain's *Innocents Abroad* (1869) and *Roughing It* (1872) fuse the two into a strong new comic voice. In these works, the narrator tells about his own adventures rather than someone else's. More important, he is not distanced from the experiences but plunged headlong into them. And while the narrator certainly does not spare Europe or the Wild West from his satire, he also does not spare himself—the potential victim—from his comic arsenal. Whereas the distance between narrator and character in some of the Southwestern humor allowed for some painful, even sadistic stories, Twain's new technique resulted in a more compassionate and complex laughter. He satirizes not only the antics of the lower classes but also society itself, especially its more pretentious members.

Humor in the service of social criticism is most apparent in his masterpiece, *Adventures of Huckleberry Finn* (1885). Twain applies the comic knowledge gleaned from his oral performances as an inspired idiot to the moral development of a naïve but good-hearted child. In so doing, he achieves a landmark in southern humor and American literature. The comic characters beginning with Byrd's Landlubbers and culminating in the amoral excess of Sut Lovingood become transmuted into the inspired freshness of Huck Finn. No longer the despised, barely human butt of comic energies, the poor-white character becomes the lovable subject of narration and a vehicle for shining a spotlight on the corruption of "civilized" folk. His comic technique depends in large part on his creation of a comic narrator who has no sense of humor himself. The ironic contrast between Huck's naïve view of the world and that of the readers is the foundation of Twain's humor in this novel. Heightening this comedy is Huck's lack of self-knowledge; as Walter Blair and Hamlin Hill observe, Twain takes the traditional *eiron* (figure in drama who pretends to ignorance in order to hide his knowledge and trick others into ludicrous actions) to new heights by creating a character who actually believes he is worse than he is. Avoiding both the sentimentality of some of the local-color writers and the brutality of some of the Southwestern humorists, *Huckleberry Finn* represents the climax of nineteenth-century southern humor.

In his later writings, several of which were published posthumously, Twain continues criticizing modern society and human nature—with a vengeance. His later works become increasingly darker, bordering on nihilistic. Gone is the innocent child of *Huck Finn*. His later characters, as Hill and Blair observe, are unstable, constantly on the brink of violence and destruction. Thus the turn-of-the-century Twain prefigures the dark humor of later postmodernists such as Pynchon, Heller, and Hawks. But Twain is not the only harbinger of later forms of humor. The freakish characters, the social satire, and the experimentation with language begun by William Byrd in the eighteenth century have evolved throughout the years into the more familiar twentieth-century permutations of southern humor seen in authors such as William Faulkner, Flannery O'Connor, and Erskine Caldwell.

Debra Beilke

See also Frame Narrative; Old Southwest; Southwestern Humor; *Spirit of the Times;* Trickster; Twain, Mark; Uncle Remus.

William L. Andrews, *The Literary Career of Charles W. Chesnutt* (1980); R. Bruce Bickley Jr., ed., *Critical Essays on Joel Chandler Harris* (1981); Walter Blair, *Native American Humor* (1960); Walter Blair and Hamlin Hill, *America's Humor* (1978); Hennig Cohen and William B. Dillingham, *Humor of the Old Southwest* (2nd ed., 1964); Alan Dundes, ed., *Mother Wit from the Laughing Barrel: Readings in the Interpretation of Afro-American Folklore;* M. Thomas Inge, ed., *The Frontier Humorists: Critical Views* (1975); Kenneth S. Lynn, *Mark Twain and Southwestern Humor* (1959); Kathryn Burgess McKee, "Writing in a Different Direction: Women Authors and the Tradition of Southwestern Humor, 1875–1910" (Ph.D. diss., University of North Carolina–Chapel Hill, 1996).

HUMOR, 1900 TO PRESENT

Humor has been a pervasive presence in southern literature throughout its history, from the genteel wit and bawdy earthiness of William Byrd of Westover and the heroic exaggerations of John Smith in the colonial period, through the hyperbolic horselaugh of the humorists of the Old Southwest and Mark Twain in the nineteenth century. In the twentieth century, the comic muse has found expression even amidst the epic tragedies and gothic tales of William Faulkner, Flannery O'Connor, Carson McCullers, and Eudora Welty. It abounds in contemporary writing as well, in the fiction of such writers as Alice Walker, George Garrett, Barry Hannah, Lee Smith, T. R. Pearson, Clyde Edgerton, Ellen Gilchrist, Doris Betts, Gail Godwin, and Kaye Gibbons, among others.

Although a sense of comedy can be found to some degree in nearly all the region's writers, quite a few have chosen to specialize in mining the rich mother lode of southern humor. Like the earlier frontier humorists, their work has appeared first in newspapers, popular periodicals, or little magazines, and then has been collected in best-selling anthologies or incorporated into lengthier works of prose or fiction. Like Mark Twain, several of them have taken to the stage and the lecture platform—or the modern equivalent, the comedy club—to create comic personae that are moved largely intact to the printed page, often accompanied by audio and video cassettes sold with the books at the performance. They have often devoted themselves to a local or regional audience before discovering that a national market existed for their brand of corn-fed redneck comedy.

They have also retained strong ties with their nineteenth-century forebears by practicing many of the same techniques and devices. For example, they have known how to use dialect and southern speech patterns for comic effect. They may not achieve the metaphoric power and stylistic energy of a George Washington Harris, whose yarns of Sut Lovingood they often admire—although William Price Fox at his best comes very close. They do, however, carry regional language into more subtle directions in the service of character and scene, as in the short stories of Robert Drake or Mark Steadman, both of whom have an exceptional ear for the speech of ordinary life. When they put southern speech down on paper, it has a flow that seems natural for the printed page while at the same time remaining intelligible to readers in all parts of the United States. Proof of this are the national reputations of Lewis Grizzard, Roy Blount Jr., Florence King, and Jeff Foxworthy.

It might be argued that there is a distinct class bias in their comedy and that by catering to national sentiments and prejudices about grotesque and low-class behavior in the South, they only serve to justify the worst opinions of southerners as ignorant, inbred, prejudiced people. Those who pay close attention to their work, however, learn that they usually redeem their characters by revealing that beneath their crude exteriors and rough behavior lies a sense of dignity and belief in the possibility of redemption. Comedy moves beyond racism, sexism, and filiopiety, showing them to be the genuine evils they have been in southern life and culture, and pointing the way to a moral and aesthetic catharsis through laughter.

Most of the nineteenth-century frontier humorists were educated, self-controlled gentlemen who looked with some disdain and malicious sarcasm on the peasants and farmers who populated their stories and asked the reader to share their sense of superiority as bemused spectators. An exception to this class-conscious attitude was George Washington Harris, who unleashed Sut Lovingood to speak for himself as an unlettered country cousin to the wise fool and to excoriate and scourge the very representatives of the aristocratic principles held dear by the other high-minded humorists: preachers, doctors, lawyers, and teachers. Most modern southern humorists have taken their cue from Harris and Sut and created for themselves first-person comic voices or public faces that speak for the rednecks and plain folk and often against the hypocrites and politicians who now populate the industrial urban South.

William Price Fox (1926–) began his career inconspicuously with a forty-cent paperback collection of stories called *Southern Fried* (1962) with suitably uninhibited drawings by Georgia-born *Mad* magazine cartoonist Jack Davis. It achieved the unusual distinction of being one of the few original paperback books to be reviewed in the *New York Times Book Review,* and by no less a person than Walt Kelly, creator of the popular comic strip *Pogo.* Kelly found comparisons with Mark Twain quite appropriate. The narrator of the seventeen tales and sketches is an urbane, better-educated Sut Lovingood, setting out not to raise hell himself but to record the raucous actions and eccentric behavior of the odd characters who surround him. Like Sut, he has a special skill for figurative language and homely metaphor and can bring to life before the reader's eyes the lively escapades and outrageous calamities his backcountry folk bring on themselves. Also like Sut, a basic respect for moral behavior and hatred of sham and hypocrisy underlie his attitude toward what he sees and records.

These are stories about initiations and first encounters with love, sex, and how romanticism can blind one to reality; about corruption, politics, and the art of one-upmanship; about the triumph of skill over brute force and the inevitability of death. Other sketches are pure examples of kinetic energy let loose in literature. What Fox later wrote about a real-life raconteur whom he admired in his book *Chitlin Strut and Other Madrigals* (1983) no doubt would apply to the narrator of *Southern Fried*: "Like all great storytellers, he was a consummate liar. A straight tale would be transformed into a richer, wilder mixture, and the final version, while sometimes spellbinding and always logical, would have absolutely nothing to do with the truth." Except, that is, the truth of human nature.

Fox followed this stellar performance, later granted hardcover publication in *Southern Fried Plus Six* (1968), with lengthier works of fiction demonstrating the same colloquial skills for caricature and local color—*Moonshine Light, Moonshine Bright* (1967), a picaresque novel about two innocent but larcenous country boys who spend their summer in Columbia, South Carolina, selling moonshine liquor, among other things, to buy their first automobile; *Ruby Red* (1971), which moves its locale from Columbia to Nashville as it follows the career of another worldly wise innocent, Ruby Jean Jamison, as she sets her sights on a career

in country music; and *Dixiana Moon* (1981), another picaresque account of the career of a fast-talking New York salesman named Joe Mahaffey who escapes debtors by joining forces with con man Buck Brody in the "Great Mazingo–Arlo Waters Jubilee Crusade and Famous Life of Christ Show" and moves across the South with a menagerie of grotesques who take part in the combined circus and camp meeting as he trades self-delusion for revelation and reconciliation. In addition to numerous essays and sketches for popular magazines, and several film scripts, his other books are a collection of comic letters and replies from the resident *Doctor Golf* (1963) of the Eagle-Ho golf sanctuary in Arkansas and several general-interest volumes, such as *How 'Bout Them Gamecocks* (1985) on college football at South Carolina, *Golfing in the Carolinas* (1990) on golf courses, *Lunatic Wind* (1992) on Hurricane Hugo of 1989, and *South Carolina: Off the Beaten Path* (1996), a travel guide.

While Mark Steadman (1930–) writes about some of the same kind of people as does Fox, his is a quieter and less-frenetic brand of humor, equally outrageous sometimes and no less hilarious. In his first book, *McAfee County: A Chronicle* (1971), he created an entire fictional community in Georgia where a series of strikingly singular characters, mostly lower-class racists, radicals, criminals, and dim-witted innocents, unself-consciously act out the sexual, racial, and economic tensions that define their lives. Adopting a self-referential attitude toward his work, Steadman notes, "McAfee County, Georgia, isn't real. It's not there. And none of the events recorded in this chronicle really happened. That's not the way it ought to be. But that's the way it is." Because the truth of human behavior takes precedence over fact.

Steadman too establishes a narrative voice in the Sut tradition, which sympathizes with his characters' bewildered frustrations but does not necessarily condone their behavior. He allows his readers to perceive the irrationality and immorality of what the characters think and do, especially in matters of sex and race, without allowing the comedy to swerve toward piety or paternalism, be the story about a man's sexual desire for a fat lady in the circus, whether or not Chinese girls are anatomically different, or sneaking a black man onto a beach for whites only. He returned to his fictional county in *Angel Child* (1987), the story of a beautiful but mentally subnormal child born to abnormally ugly parents, and took on the American dream of success through athletics in a football saga unusually set in the southern Irish Catholic society of Savannah in *A Lion's Share* (1975), a withering satire of sports mania in the South.

Robert Drake's (1930–) forte is the comic monologue, and reading him is like dropping in on a southern family reunion where everyone is talking at once and, although it is difficult to separate the urgent from the merely entertaining, the reader wants to hear it all. In terms of class focus, the perspective has shifted entirely away from the rednecks and rowdies of Fox and Steadman to the merchant and professional class of West Tennessee, although they often remain equally eccentric in their greatly prized individuality. In the traditional pattern, his stories have been published first in periodicals, especially *Christian Century, Modern Age, Southern Review,* and *Georgia Review,* and then collected into volumes: *Amazing Grace* (1965), *The Single Heart* (1971), *The Burning Bush* (1975), *Survivors and Others* (1987), *My Sweetheart's House* (1993), and *What Will You Do for an Encore?* (1996). Drake has also written a family memoir, *The Home Place* (1980), and critical studies of Flannery O'Connor, Margaret Mitchell, William Faulkner, and other southern writers.

The stories are set in a fictional Woodville, based on his actual hometown of Ripley, Tennessee, and rather than a single central voice or perspective, there is a multiplicity of them, mainly young or female. The narrator in his first collection, *Amazing Grace,* is a young boy trying to come to terms with a culture and society steeped in religious conflicts that seem startling and paradoxical to the literal emotions and understanding of a child, from the grotesque imagery of Christian hymns and illustrated Bibles to the conflicting claims that fundamentalists and mainstream Protestants make to spiritual truth and the single road to salvation. The incongruities inherent in the child's honest view of adult contradiction and hypocrisy form the basis of the humor, much in the vein of Mark Twain.

Women narrators, however, are predominant in his other collections, highly opinionated and self-serving in the southern style, but also reflecting a mature life of experience and wisdom that gives their voices the kind of humane stability that keeps a community together. The very titles of the stories capture something of the quality of the narratives: "Wake Up So I Can Tell You Who's Dead," "What Would You Do in Real Life" from *The Burning Bush,* or "They Cut Her Open and Then Just Sewed Her Back Up" from *The Single Heart.* No writer has a better ear for genuine southern conver-

sation or a keener ability for setting it down in print than does Drake—the subtle rhythms, the comic pauses, the changes in tone and pitch that indicate both attitude and character. This appears easier than it is to accomplish, but Drake brings it off and maintains the comedy without belittling or patronizing his characters. Their gossip may be funny, but it is their humanity that enriches the reader.

In a field largely dominated by men, Florence King (1936–) is an exception, not just because she is a woman but a politically conservative one as well, even though an outline of her career would not seem to suggest such an outcome. She began her writing life by producing articles for true-confession magazines; contributed essays to such popular magazines as *Cosmopolitan, Playgirl, Ms., Penthouse, Redbook,* and *Harper's;* wrote at least thirty-seven pornographic novels under a variety of pseudonyms; and has been a columnist, reporter, and book reviewer for a number of newspapers and journals. With the appearance of *Southern Ladies and Gentlemen* in 1975, however, she found her own voice as an acerbic and provocative commentator on things southern, modern, and liberal in a series of humorous sketches and essays.

She has said that she would rather be called simply an essayist than a southern humorist, since she has never felt entirely comfortable hanging around the cracker barrel, but all of her work is informed by a central voice that, in the comic narrative tradition practiced by the other humorists, holds up for ridicule the follies of gender, race, and politics in and outside the region. King scrutinizes and satirizes all of the pieties of the Old and New Souths—patriarchy, genealogy, honor, guilt, sacrifice, femininity and masculinity, good breeding, gentility, etc.—and shows them to be threadbare scarecrows. Although clearly a free and independent spirit herself, she has little patience with feminism in particular. In *The Florence King Reader* (1995), in a review of a biography of Sylvia Plath, she notes that Plath's story should be turned into a country music song, "Mothers, Don't Let Your Daughters Grow Up to Win Fulbrights."

King's books move in a variety of directions and formats all at once. *Wasp, Where Is Thy Sting?* (1977), *He: An Irreverent Look at the American Male* (1978), *Reflections in a Jaundiced Eye* (1989), *Lump It or Leave It* (1991), and *With Charity Toward None: A Fond Look at Misanthropy* (1992) are all ostensibly collections of essays, but they frequently turn into fictional pieces, literary burlesques and lampoons, character sketches, and autobiographical ruminations. *Confessions of a Failed Southern Lady* (1985) is an autobiography but wonderfully humorous in the telling, and *When Sisterhood Was in Flower* (1982) is a comic novel but clearly autobiographical in its origin and meaning.

King is such a talented writer that she can either seriously imitate or savagely excoriate just about any form of prose or genre of literature, and the reader may not always be sure which. *The Barbarian Princess* (1978), written under the name Laura Buchanan, for example, is a dead ringer for the bodice-ripper historical romances of the 1970s, without tongue in cheek, until one remembers who wrote it, while "Big Daddy" in *Southern Ladies and Gentlemen* is a splendid send-up of Tennessee Williams, Faulkner, Margaret Mitchell, and numerous other southern writers of the gothic and plantation traditions. Everything the reader holds dear is likely to appear on the chopping block eventually, and like the man in the famous *New Yorker* cartoon by James Thurber, "Touché," the reader may not even know that his or her head has been severed, so deftly has it been done.

Roy Blount Jr. (1941–   ) discovered his bent for comedy very early, writing pieces for his high-school paper in Decatur, Georgia, a practice he continued at Vanderbilt University, which he entered on a Grantland Rice Sportswriting Scholarship in 1959. Vanderbilt—the site of the conservative Agrarian literary movement of the 1930s, whose influence still lingered—seems an unlikely home. Even though he majored in English, Blount found himself championing integration and civil rights and debating reactionary faculty members in his witty columns for the student newspaper he edited, *The Vanderbilt Hustler*. He has remained what he would call a white southern liberal with traces of the redneck and anarchist.

Earning an M.A. degree in English at Harvard disabused him of the notion of becoming an academic, so he turned his writing skills to sports pieces, essays, articles, and columns for the *Atlanta Journal*, *Sports Illustrated*, *Esquire*, the *New Yorker*, *Rolling Stone*, *Playboy*, and the *Atlantic*, among others, usually in a witty and satiric mode. His first book, *About Three Bricks Shy of a Load: A Highly Irregular Lowdown on the Year the Pittsburgh Steelers Were Super But Missed the Bowl* (1974), was a tour de force of sports reportage whose title says it all. Blount's position as a major American humorist was not confirmed until he returned to his southern roots in *Crackers: This Whole*

Many-Angled Thing of Jimmy, More Carters, Ominous Little Animals, Sad Singing Women, My Daddy, and Me (1980), a useful volume for those who want to understand why Jimmy Carter was not reelected as president but an indispensable work for students of humor who want to follow one of the most mirthful administrations in American political history. Collections of his essays and light verse have followed in order: *One Fell Soup, or, I'm Just a Bug on the Windshield of Life* (1982), *What Men Don't Tell Women* (1984), *Not Exactly What I Had in Mind* (1985), *Soupsongs/Webster's Ark* (1987), *Now, Where Were We?* (1988), *Camels Are Easy, Comedy's Hard* (1991), and *Be Sweet* (1998). He has also written the text for a humorous history of hair, *It Grows on You: A Hair-Raising Survey of Human Plumage* (1986), with photographs by Bob Adelman; a novel about the husband of the first female president, *First Hubby* (1996); and *Roy Blount's Book of Southern Humor* (1994), an anthology that displays a thorough knowledge of the entire history and scope of the humor that has preceded him.

Returning humor to its oral roots, Blount has throughout his career taken to the stage, television, and radio his comic monologues and sketches, appearing frequently on Garrison Keillor's *Prairie Home Companion* radio show and mounting in 1986 his one-man performance off-Broadway, *Roy Blount's Happy Hour and a Half*. Whether he is speaking in person or in print, there is a consistency of voice and attitude: he is the wise fool, never taking himself or his fellow southerners seriously, but pointing out through his wordplay, parody, and verbal incongruity the failings and absurdities of life and society in the last half of the century. He punctures southern stereotypes by taking them to an extreme and then leavening them with an insight that reveals them as merely human beings not unlike others after all. Racial, gender, and political conflicts are resolved in a conversational flow with the light of laughter that loves rather than ridicules.

After graduating from the University of Georgia, Lewis Grizzard (1946–1994), like Roy Blount Jr., first turned to sportswriting for the *Atlanta Journal* and then the *Chicago Sun-Times*. When an opening occurred for a columnist at the *Atlanta Constitution*, he begged for the job, as much to get out of Chicago and return home as anything else. Once he turned to humor, the columns became very popular and were syndicated throughout the South and West. When these were collected into a book, *Kathy Sue Louder-*

milk, I Love You (1979), no one was more surprised than Grizzard that it became a national best-seller.

This was the beginning of a publishing phenomenon as each subsequent annual volume outsold the previous ones, each title itself almost a one-liner and suggestive of the down-home, conversational quality of his humor: *Won't You Come Home, Billy Bob Bailey?* (1980), *Don't Sit Under the Grits Tree with Anyone Else But Me* (1981), *They Tore Out My Heart and Stomped That Sucker Flat* (1982), *If I Were Oil, I'd Be About a Quart Low* (1983), *Elvis Is Dead and I Don't Feel So Good Myself* (1984), *Shoot Low, Boys— They're Ridin' Shetland Ponies* (1985), *My Daddy Was a Pistol and I'm a Son of a Gun* (1986), *When My Love Returns from the Ladies Room, Will I Be Too Old to Care?* (1987), *Don't Bend Over in the Garden, Granny, You Know Those Taters Got Eyes* (1988), *Chili Dawgs Always Bark at Night* (1989), *Does a Wild Bear Chip in the Woods* (1990), *If I Ever Get Back to Georgia, I'm Gonna Nail My Feet to the Ground* (1990), *Don't Forget to Call Your Mama—I Wish I Could Call Mine* (1991), *You Can't Put No Boogie-Woogie in the King of Rock and Roll* (1991), *I Haven't Understood Anything Since 1962, and Other Nekkid Truths* (1992), *I Took a Lickin' and Kept on Tickin': And Now I Believe in Miracles* (1993), and several miscellaneous novelty volumes. An important posthumous collection is *Southern By the Grace of God: Lewis Grizzard on the South* (1996).

Grizzard also took to the lecture platform and the performance stage about seventy times a year during his peak and acted out the redneck role he played in his columns. Most of his writing was indeed thinly veiled autobiography as his fans followed him through several marriages, emotional problems, and life-threatening heart surgery, which finally brought his life to an early close. His reputation for being an antifeminist, antihomosexual, anticlerical, anti-Yankee bigot was a creation of his pen, as he produced comic diatribes in this vein, but basically he was against the narrow-minded provincialism of the moral majority, and through the kinds of heroes he depicted he put himself on the side of independence, nonconformity, and personal freedom. Pretending to be a confirmed 1950s man caught in a post-1960s world, he became a comic for the common man and invested his work with the mere weight of a series of jokes, brief stories, and anecdotes that were extremely funny at their best. He is the only humorist ever to be attacked in kind by one of his former wives, *How to Tame a Wild Bore and Other*

Facts of Life with Lewis: The Semi-True Confessions of the Third Mrs. Grizzard (1986) by Kathy Grizzard Schmook, no mean humorist herself.

If Blount and Grizzard moved back from print to performance and the oral roots of southern humor, Jeff Foxworthy (1958–) started there before moving to print. Growing up in Georgia, Tennessee, and South Carolina, after three unsuccessful years at Georgia Tech, he worked for IBM as a dispatcher and serviceman. In 1988, a friend persuaded him to try out for an Atlanta comedy club, which launched his career on the performance circuit. He received the "Best Stand-Up Comic" award in 1990 at the American Comedy Awards, appeared on cable and many television shows, produced two albums (one of which is the biggest-selling comedy album in recording history), and had his own comedy show on NBC.

Like Grizzard, Foxworthy plays the role of a redneck, and his basic ploy is to provide comic conclusions to the first half of a sentence beginning "You might be a redneck if . . ." ("you can entertain yourself for more than an hour with a fly swatter," for example). He claims that the term *redneck* is not an insult but rather denotes a simple lack of sophistication. As he explains in his comic autobiography *No Shirt, No Shoes . . . No Problem!* (1996), written with David Rensin, "I'll tell you a secret rarely whispered north of the Mason-Dixon line: What we're *really* doing is keeping a good thing going. Our whole image of overalls, no shirt, no shoes, eating grits, chewing tobacco, butt cracks, and acting stupid is intentional and a total farce." It is an ironic pose that deflates the charge of ignorance by exposing it to ridicule, thus providing the Hobbesian laugh of superiority.

Foxworthy's books are really no more than collections of his redneck one-liners and jokes illustrated with cartoons by David Boyd, but they have been enormously popular: *You Might be a Redneck If . . .* (1989), *Hick Is Chic* (1990), *Red Ain't Dead: 150 More Ways to Tell If You're a Redneck* (1991), *Check Your Neck: More of You Might Be a Redneck If . . .* (1992), and *You're Not a Kid Anymore When . . .* (1993). He is also an occasional cartoonist and has published one collection of southern caricatures, *Those People* (1996). This is humor best read in small doses but effective when it provides a clever moment of cultural insight.

There appears to be some sort of progression at work in southern humor, moving from the longer novels and stories of Fox, Drake, and Steadman to the essays, sketches, and columns of King, Blount, and Grizzard, eventuating in the short one-liners of Foxworthy, as if a distillation in form if not comic quality is at work. This may be, however, no more than an example of the great variety of forms that humor can take and still accomplish the end of laughter.

Alongside the hardcover and paperback editions of the writers mentioned so far, the humor section of the bookstore offers anthologies and reprint collections of another form of literature that has also dealt with southern life and culture. These are comic strips, and the three main ones set in the South were *Barney Google and Snuffy Smith* (1919–), *Li'l Abner* (1934–1977), and *Pogo* (1948–1975). None of the creators were southerners, but they all did their research.

Billy De Beck (1896–1942) of Chicago brought Snuffy Smith into the *Barney Google* feature in 1934 after extensive reading in Appalachian literature and folklore, especially Harris's *Sut Lovingood Yarns,* and sketching trips through the southern mountains. Al Capp (1909–1979), a native of New Haven, based his *Li'l Abner* strip on country-music performers and hillbilly movies he saw, as well as reading in such popular authors as Mark Twain, John Fox Jr., Harold Bell Wright, Erskine Caldwell, and Margaret Mitchell. Walt Kelly (1913–1973) from Philadelphia was likely inspired by the Uncle Remus tales of Joel Chandler Harris. *Pogo,* like the Brer Rabbit stories about talking animals, was an animal fable in the form of a mock southern dialect basically about the techniques of survival in a political and largely hostile world.

The one strip about the South by a southerner is *Kudzu* by Doug Marlette (1949–) of Greensboro, North Carolina, who first achieved fame as a political cartoonist for the *Charlotte Observer* and later the *Atlanta Journal-Constitution* and the *New York Newsday.* He won the Pulitzer Prize in 1988, and his cartoons are syndicated nationally.

In 1981, Marlette created *Kudzu,* named not after the ubiquitous vine but after the lead character, Kudzu Dubose, a young writer who aspires to be another Thomas Wolfe. He is held back by a cast of provincial characters, including his domineering mother, his redneck Uncle Dubb the mechanic, and the televangelist and hip theologian Will B. Dunn (a good-natured satire of minister-writer Will Campbell). Maurice, his best friend, is a black who wants to be a blues singer but without having to suffer, and his unavailable heartthrob is Veranda Tadsworth, a shallow southern belle who is torn between cheer leading and baton twirling

as future careers. Based partly on Marlette's experiences living in small towns in Mississippi, Florida, and North Carolina, all of the mythic and real elements of southern life and culture are held up for satiric examination. Marlette's work has been collected in twenty popular volumes, including the autobiographical *In Your Face: A Cartoonist at Work* (1991), and in 1998 a musical based on *Kudzu* had a successful run at Ford's Theatre in Washington, D.C.

Lively action, incongruity, exaggeration, and stylistic virtuosity in language and dialect have been the hallmarks of modern southern humor. The writers have sought out exaggerated tales and entertaining lies about the southern experience and turned them into fables and exempla reflecting on the sad failings and self-delusions of human nature at its most contrary and cursed. Southern culture, despite or because of its racial contradictions and stubborn resistance to change, serves in their hands as a paradigm for the absurdity of life everywhere in the nation—except that in southern versions, it is faced with laughter rather than despair.

M. Thomas Inge

See also Dialect Literature; Humor, Beginnings to 1900; Popular Literature; Redneck; Tall Tale.

Barbara Bennett, *Comic Visions, Female Voices: Contemporary Women Novelists and Southern Humor* (1998); Roy Blount Jr., ed., *Roy Blount's Book of Southern Humor* (1994); Jerry Elijah Brown, *Roy Blount, Jr.* (1990); M. Thomas Inge, ed., "Urban Rednecks and Genteel Rowdies: A New Generation of Southern Humorists," special issue of *Kennesaw Review* 1.2 (Spring 1988).

HUNTING

Hunting is not an autonomous activity in a play world of little consequence. It mirrors the cultural realities of its participants in the more practical and protracted aspects of human living. Hunting is about life and death, about stories and myths, about methods and means, about winning and losing, about environments and economies, about people and the beasts within and about those pursued. The threads of the hunting cloth originate and connect with most other human activities within the sorted continua of time and place. As a particular form of community accounting, hunting stories embody a wealth of symbols about the southern experience. Interpreting these symbols is an exercise in synthesis while peering over the shoulders and savoring the intents of those composing them.

The early naturalist and explorer journals depicting Native American prowess and hunting techniques reveal as much about the biases of their writers. John Larson was impressed with the prowess of the Native American hunters during his expedition into the Carolina hinterlands in 1700. He noted that the best hunters always got the prettiest women, that they abused their dogs while treating their horses very well. As prolific participants in the fur trade, Native Americans later were to run afoul of settlers' livelihoods by being accused of leaving deer carcasses in the woods to promote populations of wolves and other predators. As the original domesticators of the southern landscape, Native Americans became the targets of southern writers who pursued them as "villains" or as "noble savages" depending on the script of the time.

Convinced of their own civilizing mission, settlers and their agents relegated the wild hunter, as the trailblazer for the progressive settled husbandmen, to the bottom rung on the ladder of human development. However, the orientation of the script depended on the status of the one doing, or writing about, the hunting.

In the Old South, wealthy planters such as William Elliott (*Carolina Sports by Land and Water,* 1859) sought through their hunting styles and stories to surpass the refinements of the British aristocratic tradition and to establish boundaries between themselves and other social groups in the New World. His choice of wildcat as prey becomes an occasion for expressing the values of his class-based pursuit and how he coped with its challenges. Planters did not hunt for practical intent (like everyone else), for this might lead to the sale of game that undercut their sense of largess and specialness. They hunted for amusement, and since no discriminating person ate wildcat, it, like the English fox, could be pursued without compromise. Moreover, as wildcats were a menace to their livelihoods on the frontier, the hunt was a vivid display of how planters dealt with adversity. Through his telling of the chase, Elliott identifies his peers as companions, the relationships and roles between whites and blacks on the hunt, the characteristics of dogs, the cunning of prey, the contentions between those living in towns and in the country, the displays of success, and the luck of novices.

Elliott's favorite hunting was after deer, and these stories become the means for further elaborations. He tells how his pursuits differ from those of northern and city hunters, who have devalued the sport by raising and releasing their targets. He describes his class's rituals: the smearing of blood on a novice's face, the joshings within his peer group, the big bucks that get away, the false pride, the nature of bears and deer, and the history of racial misconduct that continues to haunt the southern landscape, providing an explanation for hunts not ending as expected.

Through their command of the legislative process, planters such as Elliott sought to control the activities and lives of other groups. Yet the judiciary composed of ordinary citizens opposed the planter's prerogatives; they opened lands to public access and established the free taking of wildlife by all. The de facto democratization of hunting, a plebeian response by recent migrants who sought to escape the constraints of the Old World order, was to become a challenge to wildlife survival later on.

Field sports were largely the domain of men, a special ritual that fathers shared with sons and an important part of the male life cycle. Young men were initiated into their elders' fraternity with its distinct vocabulary, nourished by distilled spirits passed from hand to hand, and strengthened by the ritual gossip about neighbors, dogs, guns, and conquests over beasts and breasts. "The best of all breathing and forever the best of all listening" is how William Faulkner was to describe it later. Woman might hold a modifying influence on masculine behavior in daily life; consequently, the function of the isolated hunting camp was more than mere distance.

The transformations brought about by the Civil War and its aftermath are apparent in the literature of subsequent periods. The older patriarchal attitudes toward privileged access continued for some time, as demonstrated by the obnoxious character of Oscar Hubbard as plantation inheritor and as quail hunter in Lillian Hellman's *The Little Foxes* (1966). These bearings also persisted in other scripts, such as in *The Huntsman in the South* (1908), written by Alexander Hunter, who cherished his earlier memories. The main difference in postbellum scripts centered on the hunter's choice of prey. Along with a major change in role from labor lords in the Old South to landlords in the New, large estate owners shifted their sights from fur (deer and other mammals) to feathers (quail and other birds). Somewhat earlier in industrial England, the sensibilities of elite hunters had shifted to the mass production and caretaking of birds. The loss of the Civil War, together with the overhunting of deer, brought the pretenses of southerners more in line with the rest of their kin. Another plantation hunt was constructed on southern soil, but this time the prey was quail. Its creation depended upon Yankee wealth made possible through the expansion of the industrial links of the railroad and motor cars.

Quail became the stuff of another southern tradition much celebrated in Robert Ruark's *The Old Man and the Boy* (1958) and in Havilah Babcock's *Tales of Quails 'n Such* (1961). The pursuit of quail was linked to the myth of the "southern" gentleman whose land ownership remains his prime source of wealth, prestige, and independence. Moreover, these gentlemen settled the past scores with their Yankee guests by outshooting them on the sporting fields. Such genteel assumptions are revealingly told in Robert Ruark's book of childhood memories as he is guided tenderly and wisely by his grandfather into the arts of hunting, fishing, and caring for dogs. He learns that "Mr. Bob" (as the bobwhite quail is affectionately called by its pursuers) was a "gentleman" who demanded the demonstration of such behavior before he would hang around on one's property. In time, the changing structures of the New South and their impact on habitats were to get the better of Mr. Bob. A new generation of hunters who had grown up in towns were to redirect their aim at another feathered target. The large-scale farming practices and widespread uses of pesticides during the 1960s expanded the mourning dove populations. Unlike the quail whose small home range kept it on the farm, the dove as a migratory species was put in a different class as far as regulations went. Initially as home-grown as the quail, the dove in its movements across state and international boundaries made it a ward of the federal government with rather stiff sanctions on its taking outside of the prescribed means.

With the eventual movement of the New South's human population from the farm to the city, deer and other wildlife rebounded, although not bearing the same social attributes as before. They are pursued by the Sartorises, Snopeses, and other inhabitants of William Faulkner's Yoknapatawpha County, and in the hinterlands and elsewhere may become the road kills of an increasingly urbanized folk. In his story of the Whitehorn Buck, Archibald Rutledge's *Old Plantation Days* (1921) vividly captures the elusive creature that seasonally entrances the minds and activates the hunting urges in country folk. Yet the most potent and profound hunter's pursuit on the southern landscape remains that portrayed by William Faulkner in "The Bear" in *Go Down, Moses* (1940).

Stuart A. Marks

See also Faulkner, William; Indians.

Havilah Babcock, *Tales of Quails 'n' Such* (1961), and *Jaybirds Go to Hell on Fridays and Other Stories* (1965); Clarence Gohdes, *Hunting in the Old South: Original Narratives of the Hunters* (1967); Alexander Hunter, *The Huntsman in the South* (1908); Stuart A. Marks, *Southern Hunting in Black and White: Nature, History and Ritual in a Carolina Community* (1991); Louis D. Rubin Jr., *William Elliott Shoots a Bear: Essays on the Southern Literary Imagination* (1975); Archibald Rutledge, *Old Plantation Days* (1921); Francis Utley, Lynn Bloom, and Arthur Kennedy, eds., *Bear, Man and God: Eight Approaches to William Faulkner's "The Bear"* (1971).

HURSTON, ZORA NEALE

Zora Neale Hurston, born around 1891 in Eatonville, Florida, has become a figure of tremendous importance for both southern and African American literature. In many ways, better than any other twentieth-century writer, she illustrates how inextricably the two literary traditions are integrated. In her autobiography *Dust Tracks on a Road* (1942), she explained, "I was a Southerner, and had the map of Dixie on my tongue." Her use of southern folk language, story, and image invigorated novels and stories that celebrate black life in the rural South. Like so many other African American writers of the early twentieth century, she made her way north, to Barnard College and Columbia University, to the Harlem Renaissance salons and stages. Yet when she returned to Florida to collect the folklore of her family and neighbors in the all-black town of her birth, she opened a rich cultural vein that sustained her writing and preserved an inimitably southern way of life and speech.

Hurston's reputation today rests primarily on two works reclaimed from obscurity over the last two decades of the twentieth century: her collection of southern African American folklore, *Mules and Men* (1935), and her novel *Their Eyes Were Watching God* (1937). Both works capture the black linguistic tradition within a woman's voice and a woman's way of knowing. *Mules and Men,* which is a great deal more than a collection of folk stories, uses a frame that sets up a bantering battle of the sexes often replayed within the folk stories themselves. Women are shown as equal front-porch storytellers, and the autobiographical voice of Hurston herself makes the book into the charting of an initiate's quest to recover her identity and discover her vocation. *Their Eyes Were Watching God* makes essentially the same journey in a work of fiction, following the growth of Janie from a girlhood marked by the word "Hush" to a womanhood celebrating a sexual, linguistic, and narrative empowerment.

Hurston published many short stories and plays in the 1930s, and she published three other novels: *Jonah's Gourd Vine* (1934); *Moses, Man of the Mountain* (1939); and *Seraph on the Suwanee* (1948). Throughout the 1930s, her work found a wide and appreciative audience. Her autobiography, *Dust Tracks on a Road,* poignantly recreated a rural southern childhood and a young woman's coming of age, yet also directly challenged black patriarchal authority and endorsed black individualism and isolationism at a time when the "party line" was promoting integration and social uplift. Thus the woman who could irreverently call herself Barnard College's "sacred black cow" and announce that she was not "tragically colored" made more enemies among the African American (male) establishment than she did among whites. Her "mother wit" was unappreciated by leading African American male writers in particular. Richard Wright wrote a scathing review of *Their Eyes Were Watching God,* attacking the "facile sensuality" of her characters' speech that is now judged to be among the book's strongest effects. On the other side, for contemporary southern women writers, Hurston, through her own courage and her rendering in *Their Eyes Were Watching God* of Janie Crawford's struggle to gain a voice, has become a powerful literary foremother.

In 1951, unable to sustain her career and under attack from the black press, Hurston moved permanently back to Florida, where she died unknown in 1960 and was buried in an unmarked grave. Alice Walker's mission to find this grave and to return Hurston to literary prominence began in the early 1970s. Today, Hurston's place in the American canon is secure. Within the southern literary tradition, Hurston is especially important for her consistent emphasis, voiced in her folklore, fiction, and essays, on the power of the spoken word, what she once called the "will to adorn" in "Negro speech." She was a storyteller in the tradition of Mark Twain, Charles Chesnutt, and Toni Morrison, who made readers hear as well as read, and taught them to learn most by listening to the speaking voice of her text.

Lucinda H. MacKethan

See also African American Literature, 1919 to present; African American Vernacular English (AAVE); Harlem Renaissance; Women Writers, 1900 to World War II.

Henry Louis Gates and K. A. Appiah, eds., *Zora Neale Hurston: Critical Perspectives Past and Present* (1993); Robert Hemenway, *Zora Neale Hurston: A Literary Biography* (1972); Alice Walker, "In Search of Zora," in Alice Walker, *In Search of Our Mothers' Gardens* (1983).

HYMNS

Hymns have been identified with Christian celebration since biblical times. As told in Matthew 26:30, a hymn was sung at the close of the Lord's Supper. The Apostle Paul, both in Ephesians 5:19 and Colossians 3:16, advocates the corporate singing of hymns and spiritual songs. From earliest times, hymns were associated with the Roman liturgy, particularly at the evening office of Vespers. With the coming of the Reformation in the early sixteenth century, hymns were composed as a means of reinterpreting Christian faith and as a means of engaging one's personal religious experience. After the Reformation, hymns became an important vehicle for placing religious experience in the vernacular. Even in the Roman liturgy, hymns constituted the simplest music: melodies lay within a narrow vocal range and usually set the text with one pitch per syllable of music. Several verses were then sung to the same melody, and thus a melody was quickly learned. The simple, easily learned tunes became vehicles for remembering the words associated with them. Learning a hymn meant that the words were learned and remembered simply because the remembered melody was associated with remembering the text. In a larger context, phrases such as "purple mountain majesties" ("America the Beautiful") or the title of the hymn "Stand by Me" have entered the general vocabulary partly because they have been learned from having been expressed repeatedly in a musical context.

The word *hymn* connotes a devotional poem whose meter makes it possible to be sung generally with one syllable of text to each pitch of music, sometimes to a tune already composed. In general usage, a hymn is any song to be sung by a congregation to the accompaniment of some instrument such as organ, piano, guitar, or autoharp. Normally, the congregation sings the melody, but occasionally people sing other parts according to the natural range of the voice, either as notated in the hymnal or improvised. The descant, a new melody that can be sung above the main melody of the hymn, is often sung for more celebratory verses or at times of more elaborate worship.

Even from colonial times, hymns spread throughout the South as a result of a series of so-called "Great Awakenings." During the first of these awakenings, the revivalist George Whitefield included hymn singing in his meetings held not only in the South but also throughout the remaining colonies. Whitefield especially emphasized hymns written by Isaac Watts (1674–1748), an English minister and hymn writer who asserted that texts must adhere to New Testament theology. Among Watts's 1707 collection *Hymns and Spiritual Songs* were the hymns "When I Survey the Wondrous Cross" and "Alas! and Did My Savior Bleed." Watts advocated two principles that he felt were fundamental to the dissemination of hymns. Foremost was his conviction that texts should express the personal religious experiences and beliefs of the singer in a clear and objective way. Watts's hymns offered a clear alternative to the more formal Psalms and Canticle texts taken directly from the Bible or even the more parochial chorales of the German Lutheran milieu.

Watts advocated poetic meters such as those that had been adopted for the metrical Psalms. Thus, the words could be sung to familiar tunes in the same meters. The most familiar of these meters are as follows: Common Meter (C.M.), a quatrain alternating 8- and 6-syllable lines; Long Meter (L.M.), a quatrain of 8-syllable lines; and Short Meter (S.M.), a quatrain with two 6-syllable lines followed by one 8-syllable line, and ending with a 6-syllable line. The hymn "Amazing Grace" is written in Common Meter, or 8.6.8.6. "Old Hundredth" is a melody in Long Meter. The standardization of poetic meters can be seen even in the *Bay Psalm Book*, the first publication in the New World to include music. The first edition of 1640 contained no tunes, perhaps assuming that members of the colony were familiar with them, but the edition of 1698 did contain a limited number of tunes for the first time, any one of the tunes of a particular meter useful for any Psalm that had been adapted to that meter.

The Methodist John Wesley visited the British colony in Georgia in 1735 and brought with him not only hymns by Watts but works of his own and of his brother Charles. The *Charlestown Collection,* published in Charleston in 1737, contained translations of hymns by Moravians that Wesley had met on the ship crossing the Atlantic as well as those by Watts and those of his own creation. Wesley's and Watts's influence may be felt in John Rippon's collection *A Selec-*

tion of Hymns from the Best Authors (1787), which included for the first time "How Firm a Foundation," identified as hymn "K." (The tune, known as "Foundation," has been claimed to be of American origin. The same hymn text has also been sung to the tune of "Adeste Fideles," also known as "Portuguese Hymn," since the two tunes have the same irregular meter in common.) Although Rippon's collection was published in England, it was a source for American anthologies through the nineteenth century. In most modern hymnals, the name of the tune, such as "Portuguese Hymn," and the meter are both given directly below the title.

After the Revolutionary War, the Second Awakening brought with it the phenomenon of the camp-meeting revival. Songs sung at camp meetings were usually introduced by the call-and-response pattern: the song leader would sing a line of a hymn, and the congregation would repeat it. Such a process has also been called "lining out." It is in the practice of lining out that the personal effect of the hymn and relation of emotion to word can be recognized. The simple process of singing the hymn involved the repetition of each line; then with multiple verses the hymn melody would be heard yet again and again. Repetition of musical phrases within a hymn verse multiplied through further repetition with additional verses. Thus, even though printed hymnals were not widely available, hymns were widely disseminated and remembered because of the simple matter of repetition line-by-line and verse-after-verse.

After the Civil War, the Third Great Awakening saw the rise of the gospel song in revivals that made a kind of big business out of the camp meeting, especially in urban areas. The revivals combined the efforts of a preacher and a song-leader, with a preparatory song service or "hymn sing" as an integral feature of the revival event. Perhaps the most famous revival team was formed by preacher Dwight L. Moody and singer Ira D. Sankey. The important musical vehicle here was the gospel hymn, which consisted of several verses, each followed by a refrain, also called chorus. (Verse-and-refrain hymn forms, fundamental to the revival movement, were neither new nor exclusive to that movement.) The revival described in detail in James Weldon Johnson's *Autobiography of an Ex-Coloured Man* (1912) documents the way these hymns were sung. The verse could be sung by the soloist, and then the congregation could respond with the refrain, a practice related in process to "lining out." Refrains could be easily learned and remembered because they recalled small melodic fragments as well as the essence of the message of the text in the verse of the hymn. In the hymn "Bringing in the Sheaves," for example, the text of the refrain is "We shall come rejoicing, bringing in the sheaves," sung twice. The same text comes as the last line of the verse; thus it is not only easily remembered, but its coming in the verse also signals that it is time for the refrain. Frequently, the refrain contained "echo voices," in which a portion of the melodic line would be repeated in voices of different register. For example, in the hymn "I Surrender All," the upper voices sing the words of the title at the opening of the refrain, and the same words are then echoed in the lower voices. Perhaps the most prolific writer of gospel hymns was Fanny Crosby (1820–1915), author of "Near the Cross," "To God Be the Glory," and "Blessed Assurance." The chorus of Clyde Edgerton's own gospel hymn "Walking Across Egypt" not only embodies the music of the verse but also contains the characteristic "echo voices."

The early twentieth century saw a continuation of the revival in the work of such preachers as Billy Sunday and the music of Homer Rodeheaver. Inspired by Sankey, Rodeheaver capitalized on the popularity of revival hymnody with strict copyright protection for his hymns. A new informality and urge for pleasure fostered in revivals of the early part of the century can be discerned in the hymn "In the Garden," words and music by C. Austin Miles and copyrighted by the Rodeheaver Company in 1912. The hymn not only epitomizes the personalization of the religious experience, it also has distinctly sensual overtones. The notation of the hymn indicates that the verse was to be sung as a duet by a man and a woman, thus reinforcing the sensual element.

One genre that has come to be associated with the South is the so-called shape-note hymn. Shape-notes were devised as a method of learning to read music. Instead of all notes having an oval shape, each pitch was represented by its own distinct shape, such as oval, triangle, or square. The method was developed in New England in the late eighteenth century and spread particularly to the South after that time. The most famous of the shape-note hymnals was called *The Sacred Harp*, first compiled in 1844 and still in use in the late twentieth century. Tunes from *The Sacred Harp* include "Land of Rest," "Beach Spring," "Wondrous Love," the last associated with the text of the same name. "Land of Rest" is written in Common Meter. This repertory has become more widely known through hym-

nals compiled in the last fifteen years of the twentieth century partly because it represents a genre indigenous to the United States.

Two hymnals widely known in the South from the second quarter of the century draw on all the various forms of hymnody that had accumulated since colonial times. *The Cokesbury Worship Hymnal,* clearly not exclusive to the South, was published first in 1923 by the Methodist Publishing House. The repertory ranges from hymns by Charles Wesley and Isaac Watts on the one hand to the more evangelical hymns from the revival movements of the nineteenth century on the other. Editions throughout the 1930s include newly copyrighted hymns, particularly those of the Rodeheaver Company. *The Broadman Hymnal,* first published in Nashville in 1940, indeed was associated with the South, particularly the Southern Baptist Convention. It has much the same repertory as the Cokesbury collection, and like the earlier hymnal, included works intended for choral performance. In fact, the latter hymnal contains the vocal parts of Handel's "Hallelujah Chorus." Both the *Cokesbury* and *Broadman* hymnals have been published in shape-note format.

Both the *Cokesbury* and *Broadman* hymnals suggest their importance outside the church. Especially with the former, the format is compact and thus inexpensive to produce. Characteristic of all hymnals, the music was notated on two staves with harmonies of four parts, each representing a characteristic range: soprano, for high female voice; alto for lower female voice, these two on the upper staff; tenor, for high male; and bass for lower male voice, these two on the lower staff. The materials of the hymnal could be played by one player at the keyboard, each hand responsible for only two notes at a time. Or one person could sing the melody along with the keyboard player. A duet would easily be formed by having a female sing the melody notated on top in the upper staff with a male voice singing the upper notes on the lower staff. When homes contained a keyboard instrument such as a piano or even a little pump organ, the hymnal fit easily on the music rack. Thus, the hymnal became a central feature of home entertainment.

Thomas Warburton

See also African American Spirituals; Baptists; Evangelical Christianity; Folk Music; Gospel Music; Methodists.

J. R. Watson, *The English Hymn: A Critical and Historical Study* (1997).

I

I'LL TAKE MY STAND

John Crowe Ransom, Allen Tate, Donald Davidson, and Robert Penn Warren were the four central members of the Nashville Agrarians, the group of twelve southerners whose essays make up the symposium *I'll Take My Stand: The South and the Agrarian Tradition*. These men, who had been active members of the Nashville Fugitives, found their attitudes toward the South changing as they saw America in the 1920s becoming increasingly devoted to industry. For the Agrarians, the southern ideal of an agricultural life based on order, leisure, and a stable social tradition had become the prime example of the need to resist the dehumanizing effects of "Progress," an Americanism which, as Ransom writes, "never defines its ultimate objective, but thrusts its victims at once into an infinite series." The Agrarians felt that the South was evidencing a desire to adopt the harmful ideals of industry. In 1930 they published *I'll Take My Stand* as a warning to southerners of the dangers inherent in abandoning their conservative traditions for the northern industrialist promise of pecuniary gain.

The twelve Nashville Agrarians never met together in entirety, but most of them engaged in lengthy correspondence about the primary concern of *I'll Take My Stand*: the conflict between agrarianism and industrialism. In the symposium, the effects of this conflict are examined as they play out in various arenas, including the worlds of art, race, religion, economy, education, and psychology. Although the contributors each wrote on particular matters of interest, all agreed to the "Statement of Principles" that introduces the collection. The Agrarians argue that the unchecked rise of industry, combined with a blind faith in technological progress and the applied sciences, would rob the American people of their humanity. An industrialized society undermines the traditional notions of vocation, religion, art, and cultural amenities; it replaces the rewards of these stabilizing forces with "consumption, the grand end which justifies the evil of modern labor." In *I'll Take My Stand*, the Agrarians advocate a society in which agriculture is the primary vocation, and they espouse living according to a "concrete" humanism, a pastoral existence they saw as being "rooted in the agrarian life of the older South." Although the Agrarians claim that the principles set forth in *I'll Take My Stand* are not meant as practical proposals, the "Statement of Principles" closes with a series of fairly practical questions, and some of the contributors (notably Ransom, Davidson, and Lytle) offer the South prescriptions in their essays as well.

The twelve contributors to *I'll Take My Stand*, ten of whom were associated with Vanderbilt University, include the poets Ransom, Tate, Davidson, Warren, and John Gould Fletcher; contributors Stark Young and Andrew Nelson Lytle were novelists and critics; the other contributors were historians Frank Lawrence Owsley and Herman Clarence Nixon, English professor John Donald Wade, journalist Henry Blue Kline, and psychologist Lyle Lanier. The collection of essays, which has proved its lasting relevance by remaining an important and controversial southern text, was originally published by Harper in 1930 but was soon allowed to go out of print. The book was not made widely available again until it was reprinted in 1962 and 1977, by Harper and LSU Press respectively.

From the start controversial, *I'll Take My Stand* was the focus of a symposium at Vanderbilt fifty years later where southern scholars, including Lanier, Lytle, and Warren, discussed the Agrarian legacy, more prophetic than reactionary.

Edward Hoffman

See also Agrarians; Fugitives, The; Vanderbilt University.

John Tyree Fain and Thomas Daniel Young, eds., *The Literary Correspondence of Donald Davidson and Allen Tate* (1974); William C. Havard and Walter Sullivan, eds., *A Band of Prophets: The Vanderbilt Agrarians After Fifty Years* (1982); Louis D. Rubin Jr., *The Wary Fugitives: Four Poets and the South* (1978); Thomas Daniel Young, ed., *Mississippi Quarterly* 33 (Fall 1980).

IMAGISM

The term *Imagism* was coined by Ezra Pound in 1913 to describe features of the poetry of H.D. and Richard Aldington such as concreteness, brevity, and variation of line length in free-verse modes. More broadly, it came to include poetry exhibiting these features. It was later taken up by Amy Lowell, a New England poet who more widely publicized the objectives of the movement through Imagist anthologies. This new poetry sought to avoid all clichéd expressions, to present images that were unfettered by embellishment or sentimentality, and to strive toward concentration in language rather than elaboration. Beyond the specific Imagists—Pound, H.D., Aldington, Lowell, and John Gould Fletcher—Imagism as a term came to signify the pervasive influence in the work of many modernist poets.

Imagism as a movement in modern poetry impacted southern poetry in several ways. Fletcher, a southerner from Arkansas and one of the poets at the center of the Imagist movement, was first introduced to the movement by Pound, then allied himself with Amy Lowell. His poetry went through many stages, but at the crucial time he provided a link between the South and the beginnings of Imagism as a movement. In *Irradiations,* his collection of 1915, his poetry shows the reticence and control of Imagist influence. Later, he provided a direct link between Imagism and the Fugitives.

Other southern poets—such as Evelyn Scott from Clarksville, Tennessee, and New Orleans, Louisiana, and Maxwell Bodenheim, originally of Mississippi—published Imagist-influenced verse in periodicals and in volumes. Their Imagism came later than the principal movement (1913–1917) and was not strictly adherent to the terms in the manifestoes. Scott's early poetry frequently used rhyme along with free-verse cadences; Bodenheim often used a longer line than was the fashion with Imagist verse. Both poets, nevertheless, relish objective descriptions in their poems to the degree that the objects themselves are foregrounded by the specific details accorded to them.

Little magazines in the South, such as *The Lyric, The Reviewer,* and *The Fugitive,* issued editorials about the new styles of poetry and printed poetry that showed the influences of Imagism or reacted against it. (A notable exception from New Orleans was the *Double Dealer,* which more openly embraced the new forms.) Mostly, they shied away from printing verse that was too strongly Imagist, preferring instead ballads and narrative poems. DuBose Heyward, for instance, of Charleston, South Carolina, wrote poetry specifically opposed to Imagism. The Fugitives thought that they needed to react directly to Imagism, and the trends that they developed, such as a strong sense of place, character, and narrative, are viewed as in opposition to Imagist trends in modern poetry. In a retrospective article from 1935 characteristic of the Fugitive tone toward Imagism, Cleanth Brooks characterized Imagists as poets hailed as geniuses not so much for what they wrote as for what they refused to write.

Caroline Maun

See also Fugitives, The.

John E. Bassett, *Defining Southern Literature: Perspectives and Assessments 1831–1952* (1997); Cleanth Brooks, "The Modern Southern Poet and Tradition," *Virginia Quarterly Review* 11 (April 1935); Edmund S. de Chasca, *John Gould Fletcher and Imagism* (1978).

INCEST

William Faulkner is the southern writer whose treatment of incest has received the most scholarly attention. This is hardly surprising since incest is crucial to the plots of so many of his major novels, including *The Sound and the Fury* (1929), *Absalom, Absalom!* (1936), and *Go Down, Moses* (1942). Quentin Compson's desire for his sister Caddy, Charles Bon's engagement to his half-sister Judith Sutpen, and L. Q. C. McCaslin's incestuous miscegenation with his daughter all become sites for Faulkner's meditations on southern masculine identity. The complexity of Faulkner's treatment of incest contrasts sharply with the stereotyped representations of southern poor-white degeneracy that characterize Erskine Caldwell's *God's Little Acre.* Incest in Faulkner was read initially by southern critics, most notably Cleanth Brooks, through a decidedly

Christian lens. Incest, in this view, depicts the fallen nature of humanity and the contemporary breakdown of sexual morality. Since 1975, the dominant view on Faulkner's treatment of incest has shifted to psychoanalytic ground, following the arguments of John T. Irwin. For Irwin, incest is constellated in a pattern of doubling and repetition that points to the son's Oedipal struggle with the father.

Recently, Karl Zender has argued for a historicized reading of incest. Zender believes that we must acknowledge Faulkner's reading of the Romantic poets, particularly Shelley, for whom the distinction between parent-child and sibling incest was crucial (a distinction not acknowledged by the psychoanalytic perspective). While condemning parent-child incest, the Romantics were sympathetic to sibling incest. In the context of the French and American revolutions, father-daughter incest pointed to the tyranny of the old hierarchies, while brother-sister incest suggested an alternative, egalitarian social order. Zender further maintains that Faulkner's awareness of the Romantics' distinction allows one to read the development of Faulkner's politics "away from Southern chauvinism and conservatism and toward liberalism," even though incest "always remains tragic, never becoming unambiguously a trope for psychic or social liberation."

Despite Zender's helpful intervention in the discussion of Faulkner's use of incest, it does not seem to apply directly to the American Romanticism of Edgar Allan Poe. Poe's portrayal of sibling incest in his 1839 story "The Fall of the House of Usher" is hardly the positively marked relation that the English Romantics construe it to be. For James D. Wilson, Poe's use of incest and the way it is coded in Roderick Usher's poem "The Haunted Palace" signals an intent on Poe's part to satirize and critique Shelley. As a result of this difference, Poe's treatment of incest is open to the allegorizing readings of psychoanalytic criticism. Roderick's love for Madeline can be read as a narcissistic investment in his own psyche, just as the story's conclusion works doubly as a Freudian return of the repressed—both in Madeline's physical return and in Roderick's identifying the narrator as the true madman for failing to acknowledge anything beyond the empirical and the rational.

Peter Taylor self-consciously invokes Poe's "Fall of the House of Usher" in "Venus, Cupid, Folly, and Time" (1959) by focusing on the implied sibling incest of the elderly couple, the Dorsets, who live together in a decaying house. Their annual party for the adoles-

cents of Chatham seems almost to do promotional work for incest, though this communal ritual explodes when what was always implicit becomes explicit. The conclusion of Taylor's story, however, reveals a different horror than Poe's. For Taylor, the social inbreeding of the cultural elite, signaled by the endless round of parties and socializing among people who have known each other since childhood, is also sinister. Taylor's story suggests that his story's southern community itself is mirrored by the unspeakable relation of the Dorsets and that new blood is as culturally necessary as it is biologically.

Finally, a contemporary southern novel in which incest crucially figures is Dorothy Allison's *Bastard Out of Carolina* (1993). Allison's realist novel, however, largely avoids the psychoanalytic implications often noted in Poe's and Faulkner's use of incest in order to confront the reader with Ruth Anne (Bone) Boatwright's molestation and brutal rape at the hands of her stepfather, Daddy Glen. This violation, coupled with the mother's abandonment of the daughter for the violating father, leads to Bone's central moment of epiphany in this lesbian *Bildungsroman*. Against Caldwell's stereotyped use of poor southern whites, Allison's fiction risks even incest in her attempt to recover positive meaning from the designation "white trash"—a concept the author herself personally embraces.

John N. Duvall

See also Faulkner, William; Romanticism; Sex and Sexuality.

Cleanth Brooks, *William Faulkner: The Yoknapatawpha Country* (1963); John T. Irwin, *Doubling and Incest/Repetition and Revenge* (1975); James D. Wilson, *The Romantic Heroic Ideal* (1982); Karl Zender, "Faulkner and the Politics of Incest" *American Literature* 70 (December 1998).

INDIANS

Indians living in the southern and eastern United States, including such major tribes as Cherokee, Catawba, Creek, Chickasaw, Choctaw, Caddo, Timucua, and Seminole, were the first native peoples of the South. Before European contact, these Indians lived in what is now Virginia, North Carolina, South Carolina, Georgia, Florida, Alabama, Mississippi, Arkansas, and Louisiana. The southernmost parts of Illinois, Missouri, and Kentucky around the Mississippi River were also inhabited by such Native American groups.

Many Native American groups from the southern and eastern United States shared cultural similarities at the time of first European contact. Though sometimes sharing similar characteristics linguistically, most Native American groups had different languages. In addition, most of the Indians relied upon agriculture and hunting for their subsistence.

European contact was devastating for the Indian nations primarily because Europeans spread diseases for which the Indians had no immunity. In addition, Native American belief systems and social organizations did not prepare them for European invaders who would exploit the land and peoples in order to accumulate material goods. Though many Indian tribes were conquered militarily, economic policies that made the natives dependent upon European trade goods more effectively decimated Indians than warfare alone.

Ultimately, the conquest of native peoples in the Southeast was achieved by the social system of the Old South, a hierarchical system of farming using slave labor. Because this system had absolutely no use for Native Americans and because landowners had a voracious appetite for more land, Native Americans were threatened by economic deprivation and military force. In fact, Native Americans were systematically removed from their lands by the policies of Andrew Jackson's government. The Trail of Tears, which occurred during the winter of 1838–1839, was the largest such removal. Thus, Native Americans were politically divided, legislatively maneuvered into treaties, removed from their ancestral lands, and later forced to become "civilized," assimilated into white society by being compelled to attend Indian schools.

Of the Indian groups that remain in the southeastern United States, few have federal or state trust lands. Only the Cherokee in western North Carolina, the Seminole and Miccosukee in Florida, the Choctaw in Mississippi, and the Chitimacha in Louisiana have federal reservations. Others even now struggle to be recognized as Native American tribes by the United States government. The Haliwa-Saponi and the Lumbee are two such tribes.

Ironically, as whites took more of the "new" land available because of Removal, they adopted Indian place names such as the Potomac River, the city of Tallahassee, Lake Junaluska, and counties such as Pontotoc, Coahoma, and Chickasaw in Mississippi.

Representations of Indians flourished in all genres of distinctively southern writing in the antebellum period. In fact, Old Southwest humor sketches and the romance novel often centered on Indians. Histories, remembrances, and anthropological studies also made Indians the center of study during this time.

Perhaps one of the best-known historical/literary references to Indians of eastern North America is in Captain John Smith's *The Generall Historie of Virginia, New-England, and the Summer Isles* (1624), a significantly revised version of earlier descriptions of his interactions with Powhatan's people. In *Generall Historie,* Smith specifically romanticizes his relationship with Powhatan and his daughter, Pocahontas, in order to persuade other British citizens to come to America. John Lawson demonstrates a similar purpose in *A New Voyage to Carolina* (1709), in which he creates an idealized North Carolina.

William Byrd also wrote of Indians in the Virginia-North Carolina area. In his *Secret History of the Dividing Line* (written c. 1728), Byrd specifically discusses Indians and their religion. From Bearskin, an Indian who joins Byrd's party to help hunt game, Byrd discerns that Indian religion, though primitive, maintains "the three articles of natural religion: the belief of a god, the moral distinction betwixt good and evil, and the expectation of rewards and punishments in another world."

Also during the colonial period, Thomas Jefferson wrote about Indians in his *Notes on the State of Virginia* (1785). In "Query XI: Aborigines, Original Condition and Origin," Jefferson compares the structure of European government and language to that of the diverse Indian tribes of Virginia, and he laments that so many tribes have been "extinguished" before obtaining records of their language and culture. Jefferson admires Native Americans, a contrast to his feelings about African Americans.

Another romanticized view of the conquered Indians was written by William Gilmore Simms in *The Yemassee: A Romance of Carolina* (1835). Simms's novel, set during Revolutionary War times, describes the "noble savage" who was destined to lose to the bringers of civilization. The voice seems saddened by the conquest of the noble man but also tends to justify the conquering of Indians as well as to confirm the honor of white men. Other works such as Alexander Beaufort Meek's poem "The Red Eagle: A Poem of the South" (1855) used Simms as a model for the romanticized representation of Indians.

After the Civil War, Indians became "westernized," meaning that the popular culture of the South and the United States generally saw Indians only as inhabitants of traditionally western lands, with full headdresses and living in teepees. During this time, the South became even more biracial; often the issues surrounding black and white relations were emphasized in literature. Thus, writing rarely featured southeastern Indians.

However, some southern writers continued to be interested in the representation of Indians. For Mark Twain, the Indian offered a satirical vehicle. In *The Adventures of Tom Sawyer* (1876), Injun Joe becomes an obstacle for Tom's adventurous spirit. Though Joe gives little reason for fear, Tom remains afraid of Joe. Tom is fearful because of his own cultural propensity to make a savage of an Indian. In the end, Twain seems to say that taking the treasures of the land from the Indians is acceptable. Although Twain portrayed blacks with sympathy and understanding, he was not able to do the same with Native Americans, as the incomplete *Tom and Huck Among the Indians* attests.

For William Faulkner, the southeastern Indians, specifically the Choctaw and the Chickasaw Indians, were important in filling out the history of his fictional Yoknapatawpha County. Despite his lack of detailed knowledge of these Indian cultures, in numerous stories Faulkner uses Indians in his attempt to recover a history for Yoknapatawpha County (whose name Faulkner says is derived from a Chickasaw word for the Yocona River) and for the South. In *Go Down, Moses* (1942) and in stories of Section III of *Collected Stories of William Faulkner* (1950) entitled "The Wilderness," Faulkner investigates the past of the South and the importance of the land, but through the prism of race. The corruption of the South's morality, through the tainted relations, is offset by the purity of the Indian way of relating to the land.

Faulkner does not always romanticize the Indian. In "Red Leaves" (1930), he suggests that both the white and the Indian share responsibility in the corruption of history, for the Indians here have slaves. In *Go Down, Moses*, Ike McCaslin sees two sides. He learns that his grandfather Old Carothers bought the land from the greedy Indian chief, Ikkemotubbe, who had obtained it by unsavory means himself. But Ike also learns of the spirituality of the wilderness from Sam Fathers, who carries the blood of white, black, and Native American. By adopting the purity of Sam Fathers's relation to the land, Ike McCaslin hopes to undo some of the crimes that Ike's grandfather and Sam Fathers's ancestor Ikkemotubbe have perpetrated against the land.

Sometimes Faulkner's Indian characters are treated more comically. In "A Courtship" (1948), he describes a biracial romance triangle between an Indian, Ikke-

motubbe, and David Hogganbeck, a white steamboat pilot, who both try to win the hand of Log-in-the-Creek but end up ignoring her because of their rivalry.

Through diverse means of representation, Indians remain vital to southern writing from its beginnings to the twentieth century.

Tena L. Helton

See also Faulkner, William; History, Idea of; Native American Literature; Novel, 1820 to 1865; Old South; Trail of Tears; Twain, Mark.

James Axtell, *The Indians' New South* (1997); Mick Gidley, "Sam Fathers' Fathers: Indians and the Idea of Inheritance," in *Critical Essays on William Faulkner: The McCaslin Family*, ed. Arthur F. Kinney (1990); Elizabeth I. Hanson, *The American Indian in American Literature* (1988); Howard C. Horsford, "Faulkner's (Mostly) Unreal Indians in Early Mississippi History," *American Literature* 64.2 (1992); Charles Hudson, *The Southeastern Indians* (1976); Diane Jones, *A Reader's Guide to the Short Stories of William Faulkner* (1994); Joel W. Martin, " 'My Grandmother Was a Cherokee Princess': Representations of Indians in Southern History," in *Dressing in Feathers: The Construction of the American Popular Culture*, ed. S. Elizabeth Bird (1996); E. Thomson Shields Jr., "Paradise Regained Again: The Literary Context of John Lawson's *A New Voyage to Carolina*," *North Carolina Literary Review* (1992).

INDUSTRIALIZATION

One of the popular misconceptions about the antebellum South—more myth than actuality—is the notion that the region consisted almost exclusively of an agricultural economy and that the planters who formed the pinnacle of the social scale had little or no interest in industrial growth and the urbanization that would surely follow it. In reality, many planters—even though they feared that the expansion of industry would threaten their political and social dominance and their way of life—were investors, though their investments tended to focus primarily on safely conservative opportunities that would utilize the assets most readily available to them, namely, their land and slaves. Because of its favorable climate, vast land resources, and slavery, the antebellum South offered advantages most suited to agricultural endeavors. In fact, slaves (several hundred thousand of them) and, to a lesser extent, free blacks provided the principal work force in the Old South, both in processing agricultural products—such as cotton, rice, sugar, and tobacco—and in other industries, particularly hemp production, shipbuilding, railroads, and iron and coal mining.

Thomas Jefferson, in his query on manufactures in *Notes on the State of Virginia* (1787), became the first southern writer to advocate that the South (and by extension the rest of the nation) should adopt agriculture rather than industrialization as a way of life. In *Notes*, Jefferson called for the development of a highly moral agrarian society, a society he believed would assure happiness and stability of government. As if in response to the Jeffersonian ideal, industry in the antebellum South experienced sluggish growth, in part because southern tradition worked against rapid and radical social and political change. Moreover, no entrepreneurial class existed to promote economic development, and industrial activity was mainly confined to processing agricultural products and selected raw materials. And because of the abundance of cotton—a good money crop—plentiful water, and cheap labor, principally slaves, cotton planters exerted and maintained strong control in regard to the types of industry that did develop, most of which were important to the agricultural sector. Grist mills for processing wheat and corn, sugar mills, rice mills, and cotton mills—the latter often responsible for producing shoes and clothing for slaves—existed because of the Old South's agricultural orientation. The tobacco industry, limited to eastern Virginia, western Kentucky, and North Carolina, produced 60 percent of the nation's processed tobacco. Centered in Virginia and Kentucky, hemp production proved to be another of the antebellum South's key industries. An essential product, hemp was used in the manufacture of rope, sails, linen, and linseywoolsey.

Although not greatly diversified, most of the South's other industries before the Civil War processed natural raw materials. Because of the region's vast tracts of forest, timber production flourished, and many southern towns of the period had their own sawmills. The Carolinas, the major region for naval stores, produced most of the region's tar and turpentine. Antebellum industries included salt production in western Virginia's Kanawha River Valley; iron manufacture in Maryland and Virginia, particularly notable the Tredegar Iron Works in Richmond, which produced train rails, chain, and cannon, and was one of the nation's leading iron producers; and coal mining in western Virginia, which became a leading supplier of coal for the Atlantic Coast.

Although the antebellum South did not expand its industrial potential and the region's economic growth paled when compared to the rest of the United States, the Civil War initiated drastic important changes. After the Civil War ended, the worldwide demand for cotton lessened, which hindered productivity in the already deficient industrial sector. In addition, the change in southern agriculture to a sharecropping system created severe economic problems for farmers. Greatly decreased incomes forced them into a subsistence level of existence, severely limiting their capacity to invest in nonagricultural endeavors. Furthermore, no viable manufacturing sector existed in the South at this time to encourage agricultural diversification, to create a competitive atmosphere for labor, or to provide the capital essential to spawn a productive manufacturing community. By the end of Reconstruction, it appeared that the South would continue to lag behind the rest of the nation in industrial expansion, though it had learned during the war the importance of expanding its manufacturing capacities.

The South had its proponents for economic growth, the most vocal and influential of whom was Henry W. Grady. In the 1880s, Grady, through his editorials in the *Atlanta Constitution* and his speeches, expressed an optimistic vision of the rich potential for southern industrialization. In a speech before the New England Society of New York in 1886, Grady announced the existence of a New South and stressed the importance of northern investors to stimulate southern industrialization. Deliberately playing down the past ideological differences between the North and the South, Grady, in an important gesture of unification, called for what he believed to be a certain winning combination—northern capital and southern labor—a union, he predicted, affirming the promise of prosperity and happiness. One line of recent interpretation about the New South crusade, however, argues that the postbellum South, at least for the most part, remained a closed society that, while controlled by the conservative planter class, was exploited by northern investors.

With planters still in a position of influence and control, industry in the New South continued to be concentrated in processing activities, either agricultural products or raw materials—both requiring low-pay and low-skilled labor. In the late nineteenth and early part of the twentieth centuries, tobacco, timber, and textiles experienced significant growth, with the latter operating most often in the cities of the southern Piedmont, such as Gastonia and Greensboro, North Carolina. Lumber, which employed one-fifth of the southern work force, became the South's dominant industry by 1900, nearly a third of the nation's timber coming from the South. Coupled with this, such products as paper, soap, paints, medicines, and tar were made from southern pines. Oil and sulphur refining plants developed in Louisiana and Texas, and Virginia, Alabama, and Kentucky provided the primary sources for coal.

Since the cotton industry required relatively small amounts of start-up capital, predictably cotton mills grew significantly between 1880 and 1900, and by the early 1900s, the total capital investment in the southern cotton industry—centered in Georgia, Alabama, and the Carolinas—reached 125 million dollars. Yet the growth of textiles did not promote agricultural diversification because most of the workers lived in rural areas or small towns and produced most of their own food. In addition, most textile profits went to absentee owners who had little interest in reinvesting in the expansion of southern industry.

After the Civil War, the demand for coal and iron also increased significantly. The more than three hundred railroad companies operating in the South by 1890 helped to open up Appalachia's vast coal reserves. By 1900, southern mines produced about 20 percent of the nation's coal. Even so, the railroad industry did not flourish. The demand for railroad transportation for southern coal, farm produce, pig iron, textiles, and timber turned out to be far less than expected because of the exorbitant costs for shipping such commodities. Principally located in western Virginia, eastern Tennessee, and central Alabama, southern iron production, stimulated by the influx of northern capital and the expansion of railroads, grew between 1880 and 1900 to nearly two million tons, 20 percent of the United States' total output.

Despite the expansion in manufacturing by the end of the nineteenth century, which encouraged the growth and prosperity of small towns, the South's overall economy contributed only 10 percent of the total industrial output in the United States. The strength of the commercial power structure may be explained by the fact that merchants often held influential political positions. Also, to retain the industries it had, the South learned it had to maintain the conditions of a low-wage, nonunionized labor force, the very inducements that attracted industry to the region in the first place. Other factors that inhibited the expansion of southern industry were the lack of capital (profits were not used to promote additional investment opportunities) and the lack of buying power of workers whose

low salaries prohibited the creation of a viable consumer market. Finally, labor-intensive industries—the type the South attracted at this time—tended to locate in small towns and rural areas, which typically had a surplus of farm workers as a potential labor pool. With the South's entry into the twentieth century, agriculture remained predominant, and although industrialization had made inroads, having some impact on the region's economic growth, industry was still secondary.

In the early twentieth century, industrial growth in the South remained slow, much as it had been at the turn of the nineteenth century. The alliance between agriculture and merchants and professionals, who served mostly small-town and rural people, continued to be strong. When progressive reform did occur in the 1920s, reformers emphasized that economic development should be the responsibility of the individual southern states. In this capacity, when the states assumed a leadership role to try to create better roads, educational reforms, and improvements in public health programs, progress usually followed, but it was not always of dramatic benefit to citizens.

After World War I, most southern state governments became involved in industrial promotion, establishing agencies to advertise their region's respective attributes. Booster groups, such as the Chamber of Commerce, became aggressive advocates in their attempts to lure industrial enterprises to their towns and cities. This goal of stimulating industrial growth is best reflected in the so-called "Atlanta Spirit," which historian James Cobb defines as "an emotional dose of boosterism that inspired civic and business leaders to a new frenzy of smokestack chasing." The objective of the "Atlanta Spirit" and similar promotional efforts was to convert urban areas to industrialization without compromising basic southern political and racial beliefs or threatening the region's stability or appeal. The views of progressive southerners of the period were echoed by H. L. Mencken, who blatantly warned detractors that "the mills and factories are here to stay, and they must be faced. Nothing can be done to help the farmers who still struggle on, beset by worn-out soils, archaic methods, and insufficient capital."

Not all writers, however, embraced the booster spirit, nor were they as tolerant of the South's commitment to the goals of industrial progress as Mencken. The chief critics of the South's pursuit of the materialistic ethic, the Nashville Agrarians, published in 1930 *I'll Take My Stand: The South and the Agrarian Tradition,* a collection of essays by twelve southerners (the most notable contributors being John Crowe Ransom, Donald Davidson, Allen Tate, and Robert Penn Warren) in which they voiced their consternation concerning the decline in traditional southern values and attitudes that the progressives had replaced with material and socialist ones. In advocating the preservation of an agrarian culture and the conservative values it represented, the Agrarians ironically attacked capitalism at a vulnerable time, the beginning of the Great Depression. However, their stance proved impractical during an era of widespread deprivation. Because in the minds of many, industrial growth represented the only viable and expedient solution to the South's economic difficulties, the platform advocated by the Agrarians did nothing to stem the tide of southern industrialization.

Instead, in the 1920s and 1930s, the gospel of industrialization was widely accepted. Boll-weevil infestation affected southern cotton yields, a factor causing severe economic devastation for many rural and small-town areas. The Depression followed, creating further havoc for cotton producers. Such New Deal legislation as the Agricultural Adjustment Act, which restricted cultivable acreage, brought about a reduction in the number of planters and sharecroppers. And the government, through various New Deal programs, pumped money into the cotton economy, which in turn served to promote farm mechanization. These and other factors greatly reduced the number of farms and farm workers, the latter decreasing by a third. Former farmers were faced with two choices: to migrate to another part of the country or to find work in industry.

With the decline in agriculture, small towns and rural areas necessarily recognized the need for industrialization. With little to offer industry other than abundant cheap labor and access to raw materials, southern promoters, who sometimes included governors or other high-ranking politicians as well as prominent private citizens, resorted to various inducements to attempt to recruit industry. Mississippi, the country's poorest state, authorized the issuance of tax-exempt municipal bonds to construct factories for industries that would locate there in exchange for hiring a designated number of employees from the area. The practice of using municipal revenue bonds to lure industry south was adopted by most other southern states, a practice that understandably aroused anger and consternation among northern industrialists and politicians who considered southern bonding programs to be a form of industry stealing. Other incentives offered to interested industries included tax exemptions, free

or low-cost land, free or low rent of property, low- or no-interest loans, discounted utility rates, freedom from labor organizers and demands from workers for higher wages, and the modification of existing legislation or the enactment of new laws favorable to potential industry. Southern promoters also stressed the spirit of cooperation in their respective states, a condition particularly attractive to industrial employers. The practical rationale for providing such inducements was to attract industry to areas that, in the 1920s and 1930s, lacked investment capital, large consumer markets, and skilled labor. Despite the efforts of both federal and state governments and even local communities to upgrade the region, the South's economy until World War II was still comprised principally of slow-growth, low-wage industries such as textiles and lumber, which did not do much to help the region's overall economic development.

World War II proved to be a major factor in stimulating significant growth in the South's economy; the development and investment that the war generated far exceeded anything the region had previously experienced. During the war years, the federal government spent about four billion dollars to build new military installations in the Sunbelt and invested another five billion dollars in southern war plants. By the end of the 1940s, major corporations opened new plants, including Ford, General Motors, General Electric, and Firestone. In the 1950s and 1960s, more affluent and more skilled workers migrated to the Sunbelt, and more technologically sophisticated industries, such as the aerospace industry, selected southern locations. These changes helped to develop a modern urban society. The decline of the manufacturing belt of the Northeast and the Mid-Atlantic regions in the 1970s, prompted by decreasing investment opportunities, likewise proved beneficial to the Sunbelt's economy. Industrialists, seeking possible relocation or expansion of their companies, viewed the South as having a favorable business climate, evidenced by the availability of cheap labor, lower taxes than in other parts of the country, and the absence of union-incited labor disputes.

By the mid-1970s, the population of the Sunbelt had grown significantly, prompted by new industrial investment. During this period, the South gained nearly three million new residents, including many retirees lured by the climate and lower cost of living. African Americans from the North's industrial states were attracted by jobs and a much-improved racial climate that promoted equal opportunities in the work force.

Also, the influx of young managers and professionals gave the South the kind of consumers needed for a faster-growing economy.

The South's energy reserves and natural resources also stimulated growth. Besides possessing more than one third of the nation's timber, the Sunbelt also had nearly two thirds of its crude oil. In fact, the demand for energy resources accounted for the phenomenal growth in Houston, Texas, where almost one hundred large industrial plants opened in the 1970s.

In the 1970s, the Sunbelt South was advancing in other ways as well. The proliferation of service-related businesses, especially real estate, retail stores, and banking, represented one of the major new developments in the industrial sector. At about the same time, the South also attracted about one-half of the nation's total foreign investments. Of all the southern states vying for foreign industry, South Carolina proved to be the most successful, particularly in attracting firms from West Germany. And of the South Carolina cities, Spartanburg was the most successful in luring foreign companies, including Hoechst Fibers. Indeed, the Sunbelt offered many lucrative incentives for foreign businesses. There were no import quota restrictions, little union interference, a plentiful supply of cheap labor, accessibility to raw materials, and cooperative feeling displayed by both state and municipal government. Continued federal spending, particularly in military bases such as the Marshall Space Flight Center in Huntsville, Alabama, and the various industries that the Tennessee Valley Authority helped to spawn in Tennessee and Alabama, likewise contributed to the Sunbelt's growing economy. Along with the influx of new industry, both domestic and foreign, pressure was brought to bear on the South in the 1970s and 1980s to promote institutional, political, and social reforms, which collectively would create appealing educational, cultural, and recreational opportunities.

As was true in 1930, when the Agrarians rebuked industrialization as the panacea to solve the South's economic problems, southern writers of the 1980s lamented the transformation of the southern landscape from small towns and rural areas to large cities and suburbs with superhighways, skyscrapers, apartment complexes, shopping centers, and other signs indicative of observable commercial growth. Novelists such as Josephine Humphreys in *Dreams of Sleep* (1984), Peter LaSalle in *Strange Sunlight* (1984), and Anne Rivers Siddons in *Peachtree Road* (1988)—books set in Charleston, Austin, Texas, and the Atlanta suburb of Buckhead, respectively—focused on the contemporary southern cityscape, showing characters estranged from their communities and suffering from the insecurities of living in a commercialized and industrialized environment where traditional culture has become debased and trivialized.

Notwithstanding the perception that the contemporary South has made tremendous strides in terms of industrial development, with the Sunbelt being transformed into what seems an economic oasis, the region, as one historian has noted, remains the poorest section of the country. In sum, despite its impressive alterations—economically, socially, and culturally—the South has not yet achieved parity with the rest of the country in overall opportunities, public services, and standard of living.

Ed Piacentino

See also Agrarians; Sunbelt; Tennessee Valley Authority.

James C. Cobb, *Industrialization and Southern Society 1877–1984* (1984), and *The Selling of the South: The Southern Crusade for Industrial Development 1936–1980* (1982); Robert S. Starobin, *Industrial Slavery in the Old South* (1970).

INTELLECTUAL

Southern fiction is not characterized by its deference to the intellectual. Few of the popular images or myths of the South bring intellectualism immediately to mind; half-educated shysters like the Duke in Mark Twain's *Adventures of Huckleberry Finn* (1885) are more familiar. If southern literature that treats the life of the learned mind has any characterizing themes, they are the pitfalls of intellectualism and the difficulty of being an intellectual in the South.

The figure of the learned gentleman from the antebellum South—a topic reflected upon by numerous southernists, including W. J. Cash in *Mind of the South* (1941) and probably typified by William Byrd II—is well educated, at least in the classics. However, men like Byrd remained aloof from their intellectual accomplishments, being scientists, artists, and philosophers by avocation, not vocation. Byrd creates himself as a literary figure in *The History of the Dividing Line Betwixt Virginia and North Carolina* (1841) and *The Secret History of the Line* (1929), but the lack of integration between his intellectual life and everyday life can be seen as a precursor of intellectual paradox in southern letters to come.

If Byrd may be said to typify the southern gentleman, dwarfing them all in the popular imagination is Thomas Jefferson, who was the exemplary southern—perhaps even American—intellectual of his age, excelling in his roles as scientist, philosopher, farmer, and politician. Although *Notes on the State of Virginia* (1787) was the only full-length book he published in his lifetime, Jefferson in many ways sets the standard as a southern man of letters. In accounts of Jefferson's life and in *Notes*, readers encounter a powerful mind that harbors a simultaneous optimism for man's perfectibility through his intellect and an abiding sense of the darkness of his heart. Jefferson's vision for the nation hinges upon sophisticated intellectual freedom meant somehow to exist within an incorruptible agrarian society. A developing recognition of some of the ways in which this vision is problematic is at the heart of the treatment of Jefferson in Robert Penn Warren's *Brother to Dragons* (1953, 1979).

Frederick Douglass and Booker T. Washington (among others) identify educated thought as an important aspect of their own lives and as necessary for the advancement of African Americans. Douglass's accounts of the strong influence of his reading upon his life are important parts of *Narrative of the Life of Frederick Douglass, an American Slave, Written by Himself* (1845), but the intellectual life he discovers is ultimately a tool for achieving ends, not definitive of his person. Learnedness opens doors in the *Narrative* but is neither a prerequisite nor necessarily an identifying characteristic of admirable individuals. Douglass, when regarded as a character in his autobiography, is one of southern literature's most positive renderings of the role of the intellectual. A similar rendering is later found in the first published version of Richard Wright's acclaimed *Black Boy* (1945). Even authors who hold out intellectualism as a social good often do so with cautionary notes. Edgar Allan Poe, for example, left the South to find a less-restrictive intellectual environment and became an influential figure in American letters, yet the characters in his works have difficulty trusting their intellectual contact with reality.

Very few treatments of the intellectual exist in southern literature prior to the twentieth century. Political writing, history, and autobiography bear upon the topic, but for the most part the lives of the authors themselves—not their productions—have more to offer on the subject of the southerner and intellectualism. Byrd's literary pastime, Jefferson's problematic dual vi-

sion, Twain's disavowal of the intellectual label, and the hostile critical atmosphere during the slavery debates all prefigure what would become an important literary theme in twentieth-century southern literature: the personal and social complexity arising in the lives of educated individuals when their education leads them to break from the southern stereotype. Alienation from the stereotype's values (working hard with one's hands, focus on family ties, traditions, Christian religious institutions, and commitment to instilled ideals rather than ones that are intellectually derived) is rarely painted as positive. Such breaks with the popular myth, while lauded by such influential thinkers as H. L. Mencken and Gerald Johnson, have been sharply critiqued by others, especially the southern Agrarians, and translate into twentieth-century southern literature as a recurring schism in the souls of fictional characters who seek but find it difficult to embrace fully an objective intellectual existence. They are shown, time and again, that satisfaction is not found in learning and logic alone. This battle with existentialist alienation plagues the intellectuals of a wide variety of modern southern authors, ranging from William Faulkner to Richard Wright to Lee Smith.

Among the intellectuals found in Faulkner's fiction, Quentin Compson and Shreve McCannon of *Absalom, Absalom!* (1936) and *The Sound and the Fury* (1929) are two of the most memorable. In *Absalom, Absalom!*, their reconstruction of the Sutpen saga combines the lure of intellectual discovery with an acting-out of the storytelling tradition. Shreve, an outsider, enjoys its intellectual challenge. A tormented Quentin, however, is drawn in less by his intellect than by his perceived emotional connection to the struggle of values dramatized by the unfolding action.

It is Shreve's detachment that so many intellectuals in southern fiction strive (and fail) to adopt. Robert Penn Warren and Flannery O'Connor both create an array of interesting intellectuals in their fiction. For example, although Warren's philosophical *All the King's Men* (1946) and O'Connor's gritty *The Violent Bear It Away* (1960) have little in common on the surface, both deal with self-described intellectuals' misguided efforts to be objective students of reality. In *All the King's Men*, Jack Burden strives to live as an observer, denying his complicity in external reality. The novel concludes with the failure of this approach to life and Burden's acceptance of his shirked responsibilities. In *The Violent Bear It Away*, Rayber's worship of social science and psychology stand in stark contrast to the religious mystery that beckons young Tarwater. Choosing between surrender to religious mystery and its intellectual eradication, a rationalizing Rayber is seen as tragically naïve as he gives himself over entirely to a spiritually hopeless nihilism.

Philosophical parallels to Rayber's struggle exist in Richard Wright's *The Outsider* (1953), in which Damon Cross's attempt to live his life according to pure reason concludes similarly. Gail Godwin's *The Perfectionists* (1970) and Lee Smith's *Oral History* (1983) showcase other individuals who deal with experiences through rationalization and dismissal. *Oral History* and T. S. Stribling's *Birthright* (1922) demonstrate the folly of intellectual overconfidence by exposing the intellectual's limited view of society as potentially naïve. Protagonists must reevaluate their intellectual pretensions or else withdraw from their situation to someplace where they can safely reassume their illusions.

Thomas Wolfe's autobiographical novels follow the intellectual development of an artist—one who, unlike Rayber or Damon, re-enters the human complex of promises and responsibility. *Of Time and the River* (1935), in particular, chronicles the budding author's intellectual journey. Though Eugene Gant is intrigued by intellectualism and high culture, its appeal as represented in the bright young aesthete, Francis Starwick, is finally disillusioning. Gant must embrace, rather than escape, his home and culture.

A sampling of other authors and works it would be fruitful to peruse for what they offer on the subject of the intellectual are: Doris Betts (*Tall Houses in Winter*, 1957; *River to Pickle Beach*, 1972; *Heading West*, 1981); Pat Conroy; Borden Deal (*The Loser*, 1964; *Advocate*, 1968; *Winner*, 1973); Ellen Douglas (*A Lifetime Burning*, 1982); Ralph Ellison (*Invisible Man*, 1952); Gail Godwin (*The Odd Woman*, 1974; *A Mother and Two Daughters*, 1982); Caroline Gordon; Zora Neale Hurston (*Dust Tracks on a Road*, 1942); Harper Lee (*To Kill a Mockingbird*, 1960); Flannery O'Connor (*The Complete Stories*, 1971); Walker Percy; Reynolds Price (the Mayfield Trilogy, *A Great Circle—The Surface of Earth*, 1975; *The Source of Light*, 1981; *The Promise of Rest*, 1995); Evelyn Scott (*Escapade*, 1923; *Eva Gay: A Romantic Novel*, 1933); Elizabeth Spencer (*The Salt Line*, 1984; *The Night Travellers*, 1991); T. S. Stribling (*These Bars of Flesh*, 1938); Peter Taylor (*In the Miro District*, 1977); John Kennedy Toole (*A Confederacy of Dunces*, 1981); and Tennessee Williams (*The Glass Menagerie*, 1945; *Summer and Smoke*, 1948).

Tara F. Powell

See also Agrarians; Douglass, Frederick; Faulkner, William; O'Connor, Flannery; Slave Narrative.

John Burt, *Robert Penn Warren and American Idealism* (1988); Katherine Fishburn, *Richard Wright's Hero* (1977); Tonette Bond Inge, *Southern Women Writers: The New Generation* (1990); Robert S. Koppelman, *Robert Penn Warren's Modernist Spirituality* (1995); Louis D. Rubin Jr., *Thomas Wolfe: The Weather of His Youth* (1955).

INTERNET RESOURCES

The Internet is a rapidly developing resource for the study of southern literature. Currently on the Web, users have access to electronic versions of southern literary texts; archival material such as diaries, memoirs, and slave narratives; and biographies, bibliographies, and criticisms of individual writers.

Many of the most useful Web sites were developed and are maintained by universities. Prominent among these is the University of North Carolina at Chapel Hill's *Documenting the American South: Beginnings to 1920* (URL:http://sunsite.unc/docsouth). This site includes three digitization projects: slave narratives, first-person narratives, and traditionally canonized works of southern literature. According to information provided in the introductory material on the Web page, the *North American Slave Narrative* site plans to provide for the first time "all the narratives of fugitive and former slaves published in broadsides, pamphlets, or book form in English up to 1920." The *First-Person Narrative* site includes on-line access to one hundred texts, including "diaries, autobiographies, memoirs, travel accounts, and ex-slave narratives published between 1860 and 1920." According to this site's page, "the focus is on first-person narratives of relatively inaccessible populations: women, African Americans, enlisted men, laborers, and Native Americans." The third site, the *Digitized Library of Southern Literature*, is in the process of converting to electronic form one hundred of the South's most important literary works published through 1920. The bibliography of the texts to be included was developed by the late Robert Bain, professor of English at UNC–Chapel Hill, with input from fifty specialists in southern and American literature. All digitized texts at this site are accessible by the public.

The University of Virginia's *Electronic Text Center* (URL:http://www.lib.virginia.edu/ecenters.html) is not limited to collections of works considered southern. However, a number of southern literary and extraliterary texts are available for viewing in the *Modern English Collection* (A.D. 1500 to the present). Texts are indexed by subject: African American, Native American, American Civil War, and Women Writers, to name a few. The collection includes archival material in the university library's special-collections department, such as slave narratives and Civil War material. Because such items are frequently requested, they have been converted to electronic texts and have been put on-line to facilitate use. In terms of accessibility, most holdings are available to the public on the Internet, while other items are available on CD-ROM. Certain on-line holdings are accessible to UVA users only.

Another major university-sponsored site, the University of Mississippi's *Center for the Study of Southern Culture* (URL:http://www/olemiss.edu/depts/south/index.htm) does not provide collections of electronic texts. Instead, its Web site focuses on information about ongoing cultural events; location of cultural materials from the region, such as audio-visual materials available on the South in *The Southern Media Archive;* and on-line magazines, such as *Living Blues: The Magazine of the African American Blues Tradition* and *Mississippi Folklife: The Magazine of the Mississippi Folklore Society.* The University of Mississippi also maintains the *Mississippi Writers Page* (URL:http://www.olemiss.edu/depts/english/ms-writers), which provides links to Web pages devoted to individual Mississippi writers. This site provides public access to Internet users.

Duke University's *Center for Documentary Studies* site (URL:http://aaswebsv.aas.duke.edu/docstudies/cds) is dedicated to promoting and supporting documentary work. One of its projects, "Behind the Veil," is an oral-history project that attempts to document the lives of African Americans in the Jim Crow South through the use of interviews, taped recordings of individual narratives, and photography, all of which are accessible on the Web site to the public-user community.

In addition to Web sites that preserve and disseminate writing by southerners and about the South, there are a number of sites devoted to individual authors who are classified as "southern." These pages can be located by searching under the author's name or by using the index of YAHOO! or a similar search engine. (Arts:Humanities:Literature:Authors:Southern). Most Web sites provide a brief biography of the author, including photographs, and a selected bibliography of primary and secondary works. Some contain excerpts of the author's writing as well as full-text critical essays

by scholars or students. Many include contemporary reviews of the author's works.

Of particular use to those conducting research on the Internet are Web directories that index and link various related sites. For the student of southern literature, *The Directory of Southern Culture Online* (URL:http://ourworld.compuserve.com/homepages/SarahBryan) provides links to archives, special collections, and historical societies concerned with the study of the South; genealogical pages; southern authors, presses, magazines, and newspapers; Appalachia; and southern music. Other directories link sites devoted to particular authors. For example, Heyward Ehrlich, of the Department of English at Rutgers University, provides *A Poe Webliography* (URL:http://andromeda.rutgers.edu/~ehrlich/poesites.html), which, according to the site's self-description, is "a critical guide to electronic resources for Poe research on the World Wide Web and CD-ROM, including electronic texts, commentaries, backgrounds, literary indexes, and search engines." As Internet research becomes more prevalent and as additional material becomes available on-line, one can expect that other directories and guides for research will be developed.

Amy Berke and Gail Dillard

See also Centers for Southern Studies; Manuscript Collections.

IRISH CATHOLICS

Irish Catholics—as opposed to the Scots-Irish Protestants who established a coherent culture in the Upland South—have been a scattered minority among white southerners since colonial times. Those Irish arriving prior to the nineteenth century in ports south of Baltimore found little opportunity to practice their faith and often abandoned Catholicism; it was only with the famine of the 1840s and the subsequent flood of immigrants into the United States that the Irish found their native Church truly established on southern soil. Yet this increase in numbers brought increased suspicion from members of the dominant Protestant culture, and nineteenth-century Irish Catholics—generally working in urban areas and at jobs deemed too dangerous for valuable slave labor—often found themselves besieged. The anti-Catholic Know-Nothing Party emerged nationally in the 1850s and was generally successful in the South, especially in Louisiana and Maryland; Irish immigrants were harassed during elections in Memphis, Louisville, Savannah, and Baltimore. During the Civil War, soldiers such as those in the Confederate Irish Brigade proved that Irish Catholics could be loyal southerners as well as Americans, but such loyalty was forgotten when the Ku Klux Klan again stirred anti-Catholic sentiment in the 1920s.

During the intervening decades, the Irish had largely assumed leadership of the multi-ethnic Catholic Church in the South; they maintained it well into the twentieth century, which saw the integration of Catholics into mainstream American life. While direct immigration from Ireland virtually ceased after the Civil War, Irish-American Catholics from other parts of the United States have been increasingly attracted to the newly prosperous South of the late twentieth century. Nonetheless, Roman Catholics remain a minority and Irish Catholics an even smaller ethnic group—concentrated only in urban areas such as New Orleans and Savannah—in the South.

Despite their virtual submergence within the dominant Protestant culture, Irish-Catholic characters have played significant roles—both as outsiders and as insiders—in southern literature. African American southerners have portrayed Irish-Catholic outcasts as comrades in subversion at some crucial junctures in their autobiographies. In *Narrative of the Life of Frederick Douglass* (1845), the enslaved narrator receives advice from sympathetic Irish dock workers who first urge him to flee north from Baltimore; in *Black Boy* (1945), young Richard Wright borrows books in Memphis from an Irish Catholic whom he trusts only because they both are "hated by the white Southerners." In fiction or drama, the Irish Catholic may become a potent symbol because of his alien placement in the South (e.g., Tennessee Williams effectively uses a visit by a fish-eating gentleman caller named O'Connor to heighten religious overtones in *The Glass Menagerie* [1944]; Father Flynn in Flannery O'Connor's "The Displaced Person" serves a similar function).

Ironically, however, the most famous Irish-Catholic family in southern literature—the O'Haras of Margaret Mitchell's *Gone With the Wind* (1936)—are neither outcasts nor aliens, but an imaginative embodiment of the southern experience itself. Some historians have argued for the South's similarity to Celtic culture generally, and Mitchell—whose mother was an Irish Catholic—suggests even more specifically an analogy between the experience of agrarian Irish Catholics suffering under British rule and that of southerners subdued by the North: Tara, attachment to the land, devastating defeat by mechanized armies, poverty, and hunger are surely as "Irish Catholic" as they are "southern." After all, William T. Sherman himself compared southern rebellion to Irish insurrection, as Shelby Foote has noted in *The Civil War: A Narrative* (1958, 1963, 1974). Such perceived similarities may have inspired the South's first significant Irish-Catholic author, Father Abram Ryan, to praise the Confederacy; the former Confederate chaplain's Reconstruction-era poetry included not only "Erin's Flag" but also "The Sword of Robert Lee." Similar sentiments are suggested by Florence O'Connor's *The Heroine of the Confederacy* (1864) and by the journalism of Confederate veteran Theodore O'Hara.

It has only been since World War II that Irish-Catholic authors in the South have truly flourished. Flannery O'Connor is certainly the preeminent example, though her characters are rarely Catholic; Cormac McCarthy—a graduate of Knoxville's Catholic High School—also writes of more typical southern characters, though some critics have found influences from his religious heritage in his fiction. The Irish-Catholic experience in the urban South (where it has been most concentrated) is explored in both John Kennedy Toole's *A Confederacy of Dunces* (1980), which features the outrageous Ignatius Reilly and a hilarious glimpse of ethnic Catholic life in New Orleans, and Margaret Skinner's *Old Jim Canaan* (1990), a chronicle of an extended Irish family in turn-of-the-century Memphis. Several of Pat Conroy's popular contemporary novels, set in coastal South Carolina, record his own experience in an Irish-Catholic military family headed by a transplant from the urban North and suggest the mild alienation felt by such newcomers to the South even at the close of the twentieth century.

Farrell O'Gorman

See also O'Connor, Flannery; Religion in Nineteenth-Century Literature; Roman Catholics; Scots-Irish.

Jon Anderson and William Friend, eds., *The Culture of Bible Belt Catholics* (1995); Randall Miller and Jon Wakelyn, eds., *Catholics in the Old South* (1983); Earl Niehaus, *The Irish in New Orleans* (1965); Mark Wyman, *Immigrants in the Valley: Irish, Germans and Americans in the Upper Mississippi Country 1830–60* (1984).

JACKSON, ANDREW

Andrew Jackson (1767–1845), seventh president of the United States, was a military war hero, land speculator, Indian fighter, slaveowner, and frontier folk legend who was known as a champion of democracy and of the common man.

During his two terms as president beginning in 1829, Jackson used the veto more than any previous president, reestablished the two-party system, and worked against nullification, which would have allowed a state to declare federal law inoperative in its domain. He ordered government money removed from the Second Bank, which he considered a monopoly, and deposited in state banks across the country. This action was popular with backwoods people who were suspicious of banks, but it helped cause the financial panics of 1834 and 1837.

Jackson epitomized the rugged individual of the American frontier. Poorly educated and lacking the advantage of an influential family, Jackson nonetheless attained the nation's highest elected office, demonstrating the American ideal of success through merit rather than privilege. Rising in the wake of Jackson's ill-fated 1824 presidential campaign, Jacksonian Democracy promised that the nation's elective offices would be filled by common people, not the aristocratic professional politicians. Polarized reaction to Jackson caused two parties to emerge from the old Republican Party—the Democrats, who supported him, and the Whigs, who opposed him. During his presidency, Jackson refused to defer to Congress, causing his political enemies to dub him King Andrew I.

Jackson was born on March 15, 1767, in the Waxhaw settlement on the border of North Carolina and South Carolina, the third son of Andrew Jackson and Elizabeth Hutchinson, who were both immigrants from northern Ireland. The elder Jackson died a few days before the birth of young Andrew. The boy's mother died when he was fourteen. As a thirteen-year-old mounted courier in the American Revolution, Jackson was captured and held prisoner by the British. An altercation over being forced to clean a British officer's boots resulted in a saber wound to Jackson's head, leaving a permanent scar. Jackson returned to North Carolina after the war and studied law. He was admitted to the bar at age twenty and appointed public prosecutor of the Western District of North Carolina, which later became Tennessee.

In 1788 Jackson moved to Nashville, Tennessee, where he speculated in land holdings, became active in politics, and met Rachel Donelson Robards, whom he would marry in 1791, under the mistaken impression that her husband had obtained a divorce. Jackson and Mrs. Robards remarried in January 1794, just after her divorce had become final, but until her death in 1828, Jackson's political enemies continually accused them of having committed adultery.

Jackson was a delegate to the state constitutional convention of 1796, served as Tennessee's first representative in Congress, then was U.S. senator from 1797 to 1798, and a state superior court judge from 1798 to 1804. After his retirement from the bench, the Jacksons lived at the Hermitage, the home they built near Nashville. There they grew cotton with slave labor, and raised and raced thoroughbred horses.

The War of 1812 brought Jackson back into the public arena. In command of volunteer militia sent to Natchez, Mississippi, Jackson earned the nickname "Old Hickory" on the grueling march home to Tennessee when his men said he was "tough as a hickory." Jackson defeated the Creek Indians in 1813 and was made a major general in the U.S. army. He was acclaimed a hero after defeating the British on January 8, 1815, in the Battle of New Orleans.

Jackson appears as a character in several novels, including Joseph B. Cobb's *The Creole, or, Siege of New Orleans* (1850), Winston Churchill's *The Crossing* (1904), Ellery H. Clark's *The Strength of the Hills* (1926), Samuel Hopkins Adams's *The Gorgeous Hussy* (1934), and Irving Stone's *The President's Lady* (1951), the latter two of which were made into movies.

Claudia Milstead

See also Nullification; Populism; Trail of Tears.

Milton Meltzer, *Andrew Jackson and His America* (1993); Robert V. Remini, *Andrew Jackson* (1989); Arthur M. Schlesinger Jr., *The Age of Jackson* (1988).

JACKSON, MISSISSIPPI

Jackson, Mississippi's capital city, was founded in 1821 at LeFleur's Bluff on the Pearl River and named for Andrew Jackson. The site for state government was selected because of its central location in Mississippi and because it offered access to both the river and the Natchez Trace. Today the old capitol, begun in 1832, sits at the head of Capitol Street and serves as a state historical museum. The new capitol is nearby and dates from 1903. At the turn of the twenty-first century, the population of metropolitan Jackson is over four hundred thousand, and the city features national historical sites (the 1839 Governor's Mansion and the 1846 City Hall, both spared during Sherman's three burnings of Jackson during the Civil War), as well as the University of Mississippi Medical Center, Millsaps College, Tougaloo College, the Farish Street Historical District, the Medgar Evers Home, and the Margaret Walker Alexander African American Research Center and Ayer Hall at Jackson State University. Jackson is the site every four years of the International Ballet Competition, and the New Stage Theater and the Mississippi Museum of Art are located there.

Eudora Welty, who tells of her childhood in Jackson in *One Writer's Beginnings* (1984), lived on Pinehurst Street. Richard Wright graduated from high school in Jackson, as he reveals in *Black Boy* (1945), and Margaret Walker spent her teaching and writing career at Jackson State. Younger writers with ties to Jackson include Willie Morris, who lived in Jackson in the last years of his life and told of childhood visits in *North Towards Home* (1967); the playwright Beth Henley; Richard Ford, whose essay on memories of his mother tells of his life in Jackson; and Lewis Nordan. Barry

Hannah's *Geronimo Rex* (1972) is set in the suburb of Clinton, and Sterling Plumpp was born in Clinton. Mildred Taylor, James Whitehead, and Turner Cassity were all born in Jackson, and Ellen Douglas has returned there to live. Welty's "A Memory" and "The Little Store" offer pictures of Jackson's earlier life and its people, as does "Ida M'Toy."

Thomas J. Richardson

See also Mississippi, Literature of; Welty, Eudora.

Dorothy Abbott, ed., *Mississippi Writers: Reflections of Childhood and Youth* (1985); Peggy W. Prenshaw, *Eudora Welty: Critical Essays* (1979), and *Conversations with Eudora Welty* (1984); Margaret Walker, *Richard Wright: Daemonic Genius* (1988).

JACKSON, STONEWALL

Together with Confederate heroes such as Robert E. Lee and J. E. B. Stuart, Thomas Jonathan "Stonewall" Jackson has an established place in imaginative southern literature. An officer in the Mexican War and initially the commander of a company of V.M.I. cadets in the Civil War, Jackson won his nickname at the Battle of First Manassas. As described by Clifford Dowdey in his novel *Bugles Blow No More* (1937), the dying general Barnard E. Bee gave his troops confidence by pointing out the resolute Jackson: "There stands Jackson like a stone wall. . . . Rally around the Virginians."

In his novel *Surry of Eagle's-Nest* (1866), John Esten Cooke, a Confederate staff officer who knew Stonewall Jackson well, describes Jackson as having "a childlike purity and gracious sweetness, mingled with indomitable will." Cooke shows how Jackson was known for his religious fervency, his secrecy, and for being much loved by his men. Jackson had, according to Cooke's narrator, "the supreme attributes of the man of military genius. He seemed to rise under pressure." This genius of "Old Jack" is demonstrated by Tom Wicker in *Unto This Hour* (1984), a carefully researched novel about Jackson's march around Pope and the subsequent Battle of Second Manassas.

While the Stonewall Corps under his leadership failed multiple times during the Seven Days' Battles, Jackson maneuvered brilliantly in his Shenandoah Valley Campaign. William Faulkner describes this in "The Bear": "Jackson in the Valley and three separate armies trying to catch him and none of them ever knowing whether they were just retreating from a battle or just running into one. . . . Who else could have declared a war against a power with ten times the area and a hundred times the men and a thousand times the resources, except men who could believe that all necessary to conduct a successful war was not acumen nor shrewdness nor politics nor diplomacy nor money nor even integrity and simple arithmetic but just love of land and courage."

Although Jackson's plan brought success to the Confederates at Chancellorsville, during that battle the Confederacy lost General Jackson to mortal wounds from his own men. Cooke poignantly describes this sad event in *Surry of Eagle's-Nest* as well as in his biography of Stonewall Jackson (1863). So do poet and novelist Allen Tate in his biography *Stonewall Jackson: The Good Soldier* (1928), Mary Johnston in her novel *The Long Roll* (1911), and Clifford Dowdey in *Bugles Blow No More*. Dowdey quotes Jackson's dying words, later used by Ernest Hemingway: "Let us cross over the river and rest under the shade of the trees."

Jackson is also the subject of numerous poems. As representative of these, John Williamson Palmer in "Stonewall Jackson's Way" sets forth the dedication of Jackson's troops: "What matter if our shoes are worn? / What matter if our feet are torn? / 'Quick-step! we're with him before dawn!' / That's 'Stonewall Jackson's way.' " "The Lone Sentry" recounts the general relieving a weary sentry, and "Death-Bed of Stonewall Jackson" by Colonel B. H. Jones is one of many poetic eulogies.

Richard D. Rust

See also Civil War.

James I. Robertson Jr., *Stonewall Jackson: The Man, the Soldier, the Legend* (1997).

JAZZ

Jazz is a musical and cultural phenomenon that arose principally in the South in the very last years of the nineteenth century. Its first manifestations found their form in New Orleans and spread northward during the early years of the present century, mostly via the Mississippi River, to Memphis and St. Louis and other cities. Chicago became a kind of melting pot during the Colombian Exposition, where ragtime pianist Scott

Joplin played in 1893. Joplin's relocation to New York in 1907, or W. C. Handy's "Memphis Blues" of 1912, or Handy's "St. Louis Blues" in 1914 give evidence of the spread of music that would eventually be called jazz. It was Jelly Roll Morton who claimed to have invented the word *jazz* in 1902; the first appearance of the word in print, according to Frank Tirro, is considered to be 1913.

As a general term, *jazz* embraces a wide variety of musical realizations and styles; however, there are certain elements that are basic to its character. For the most part, jazz is music played by a group of musicians: a minimum of three comprising a pianist, a drummer who plays a collection of drums and other percussion instruments called a drum set, and a string bass player who mostly plucks the instrument. These three instruments comprise the framework upon which a jazz band is built. A jazz band usually consists of a reed section at the front of the group, including saxophones, clarinets, perhaps also an occasional flute. Brass instruments, particularly trumpets (with cylindrical bore), cornets (with conical bore), trombones, and an occasional French horn or tuba were located behind. The instruments that usually played the melody were called the front line. Paul Whiteman's orchestra in the 1920s also included strings as well as banjo. Many players, particularly those in the reed section, could double—that is, play more than one instrument. When it appeared in London in the late teens and early 1920s, the Original Dixieland Jazz Band consisted of piano, drums, trombone, clarinet, and cornet. (Ed McMahon always called Doc Severinsen's group on the *Tonight Show* of the 1970s and 1980s the NBC Orchestra, even though it was indeed a jazz band.)

To the listener, perhaps the most seductive feature of jazz is its steady beat, reinforced especially by the drummer, the pianist, and the bass player. A steady beat orients both the listener and the jazz ensemble to the inexorable progress of the music, but at the same time the beat is the foil for the many off-beat syncopations and shifting accents exploited by the reed and brass players. Ultimately, the players of the piano, the drums, and the bass also engage in such off-rhythms. As such, the basic beat and the opposing syncopation of the jazz band emerged in the beginning respectively from the opposing of left and right hands in ragtime piano. "Stoptime" occurs when brief silences interrupt, beginning either on or off the beat. It is an effect often associated with tap dancing, vigorous tapping coming during the silences. A "stomp" refers either to a lively dance in duple meter or to a rhythmic figure imposed on and repeated in a melodic line.

By contrast to the more cultivated, so-called "classical" music generated by composers, jazz is a music of performers. Jazz players work "off"—that is, away from the written page by remembering the melody or the underlying harmonies of a well-known popular song. Once a jazz player has assimilated the melody and harmonies of a particular song into memory, he or she can invent variations, evoking the harmonies and/or the figures of the melody, these improvisations realized in brief, characteristic figures called "riffs." It is the virtuosity of individual players such as Louis Armstrong (trumpet), Benny Goodman (clarinet), Coleman Hawkins or later Sonny Rollins and John Coltrane (saxophone) in improvising solos based on a song that leads to the frequent applause that interrupts a jazz number. Gene Krupa, the drummer for the Benny Goodman Band, became famous for his percussion improvisation, emulating the manner of the improvised solos by his associates in the wind section. Duke Ellington, Art Tatum, Count Basie, and Oscar Peterson lifted the role of the piano from that of supporting the band with essential beat and harmonic filler to that of virtuoso improviser. Singers such as Ella Fitzgerald and Mel Torme became famous for vocal improvisation with syllables, a style called "scat."

While surely the rhythm is fundamental to the effect of jazz, certain sounds are also indigenous. The sliding from one pitch to the next is an expressive feature with the so-called "blue notes" where the third degree of the scale could be intoned down (flat) or up (sharp) or bent within a single pitch. The "blue note" is essentially a vocal quality where the singer can slide subtly between pitches or bend the voice while holding a single pitch. Trombone players have an idiomatic sliding feature in that the pitch of the instrument changes according to the movement of the slide up or down by the right hand. Reed and brass players slide between pitches through subtle movement of the lips; the gentle fluctuation in the intonation of a single pitch, known as vibrato, can also be accomplished by movement of the lips as well as through control of the breath. Sliding between pitches can expand over large ranges in effects known as glissando. Brass players often cover the open (that is, away from the player), or bell, end of their instruments with various kinds of mutes, which dampen the sound. By alternately covering the bell or leaving it open, the mute changes the color, or timbre, of the sound. The effect of crying results from rapidly alternating between open and muted sounds—the sound may be likened to "waa-waa." Mutes come in various shapes such as cones, which are inserted into the bell, or various cups or hat shapes that are held in the hand and cover the exterior of the bell.

Since the improvisational element of jazz depends so fundamentally on the prowess and inspiration of the individual players, it is likewise an artistic phenomenon that develops out of the mutual contributions among those individual players. Within a group, the players interact; one player may execute a riff or tug at the beat in a momentary burst of inspiration, and that will inspire another to expand on or perhaps even outplay the improvisation that has just occurred. A player may even literally imitate what has just been heard. To the listener, or even to the musician who is not a jazz player, the ability to play off the melody and harmonies of a song or the mutual playing off each other makes jazz players seem "possessed" by mysterious powers. Moreover, the resulting forms of expression defy setting down in traditional music notation. In recent years, scholars have notated the playing of such jazz figures as Duke Ellington (Mark Tucker), Jelly Roll Morton (James Dapogny), or John Coltrane and Charlie Parker (Frank Tirro) in written form, and some musicians have begun playing from these transcriptions. Artis Wodehouse has both transcribed George Gershwin's piano improvisations for piano solo and has produced digitally enhanced recordings made by Gershwin for modern-day reissue.

Other than the performers themselves, it was the various ways that jazz was spread that were responsible for its growth. Jazz itself emerged just as radio was developing as an important source of communication. Along with radio, recordings, especially during the 1920s and 1930s, not only allowed the general public to be "consumers" of jazz but allowed jazz players in widely different places to be influenced by each other. Touring, whether by rail within the country or by ship across the ocean, quickly spread the enjoyment of jazz at a time even when it was in its infancy.

Especially during the first half of the twentieth century, the evolution of jazz can be comprehended in rather well-defined stages. The earliest music with elements common in jazz is piano ragtime with its regular bass in the left hand and its jaunty syncopations in the right hand. Perhaps more fundamental to the growth of jazz is the "blues," which consisted of a series of standard harmonic progressions above a steady beat in the bass. As jazz spread beyond the geography of its origins, the so-called big band—rhythm section of piano, bass, and drums, supporting brass, and reed instruments, often vocalists, perhaps also with strings— emerged as the principal vehicle for performing jazz. With the increase of size, arrangements of popular songs were written down, and the players each read from a notated musical part. Such arrangements also allowed for frequent improvisations by the vocalist or by individuals in the band. Along with arrangements of familiar tunes, compositions, called standards, were composed with the instrumental combination and sound of a particular jazz band in mind. Within the larger bands, smaller trios, quartets, or quintets formed; in these smaller, more intimate groups, more thoroughgoing improvisation could take place. For example, Duke Ellington often appeared with his bass and drummer as a trio taken from the band.

With the arrival of the big bands, also known as dance bands, came the swing era, which enjoyed its heyday during the 1930s and 1940s. Benny Goodman was, in fact, known as the "King of Swing"; Count Basie and Duke Ellington were the two other masters of swing. Swing is characterized by a sense of blended ensemble sound against which soloists could assert their individuality. The value of refined sonorities that represent the big-band aesthetic shows in the sound of the saxophones in "String of Pearls," composed for the Glenn Miller Band and popular during World War II. Although the swing era survived into the 1950s, toward the close of World War II, bebop split off from the world of swing. Bebop, or more simply "bop," was the result of a kind of reaction by individual jazz musicians to what had become some of the standard practices in the world of swing: the conservative arrangements for the large groups, the cultural ties to the regular beat of dancing, and the immersion of the individual into the larger ensemble. The "bop" players adopted idiosyncratic life-styles, dress, and manners of speech, and they alienated themselves both from the world of swing as well as from civilization at large. Similar to the relation of the avant-garde movement to classical music, bebop was a kind of jazz intended mostly for other jazz musicians. With the arrival of bebop, jazz as a whole developed idiosyncratically with such movements as "third stream," "cool jazz," and "West Coast jazz," the last especially emphasizing individual players.

Especially in its early years, jazz has connoted a world unto itself. With such regions as red-light districts and the infamous Storyville of New Orleans as its indigenous milieu, jazz suggested debauchery, decadence, and undisciplined behavior of various kinds, the very antithesis of the Victorian environment that prevailed in the era of its birth. The "bop" movement of the late 1940s cultivated a self-conscious removal even from the rest of the jazz community itself. With its centering in black players and the eventual mixing of black and white jazz musicians, jazz generally has represented a kind of alien, mysterious element in American culture. Black and white musicians could play together in the same band; however, especially before World War II, not all players were equally welcomed at the places where the bands performed. Jazz has always been a kind of vernacular tradition, based on the passing down of songs and riffs, and as such appears set apart from the apparently more cultivated, more historically derived, written-down traditions of Western art music. In another context entirely, big bands and smaller jazz combos were associated with the expensive night spots and high-society nightclubs of the larger cities, especially after World War II.

Ever since jazz's beginnings, classically trained musicians have been fascinated by its special sound and rhythmic world—witness, for example, the music of Debussy, Ravel, Aaron Copland, and Leonard Bernstein. Since the close of World War II, the definition and the artistic and social significance of jazz have changed. The "legitimization" of jazz may be witnessed in several different ways. First, there is the mixing of the worlds of "classical" and jazz music-making through the efforts of such performers and composers as Gunther Schuller. Second, the jazz musicians themselves no longer have confined their creative work to arrangements and jazz standards, blending their world with that of "classical" concert life. Gershwin's *Rhapsody in Blue*, composed in 1923, was one of the first works to be identified with the two different worlds. On the one hand, it is conceived for a jazz band with a rhythm section that includes piano, banjo, drums, and bass, and an extensive reed, brass, and string section. In addition, there is a solo piano that mostly plays written-out improvisations/variations on the musical materials, much in the manner of the big bands of the 1920s and 1930s. Its later manifestation as a work for piano and orchestra contains elements, especially parts for the solo piano, that were the manufacture of the publishers, not the composer. Duke Ellington's *Black, Brown, and Beige* (1947) and *Harlem* (1951) and Rolf Liebermann's *Concerto for Jazz Band and Orchestra* (1954) are more recent examples of the merging of jazz with the classical concert orchestra. Dave Brubeck, who composed many a "classic" such as "Blue Rondo à la Turk" or "Take Five," composed his oratorio "The Light in the Wilderness" in 1968 for mixed chorus, baritone solo, and organ. The supplementary bass and percussion were labeled optional. A version of the same work with orchestra allows for piano improvisation.

During the last quarter of the twentieth century, interest has grown in the cultivation of jazz as a historical phenomenon. In high schools and colleges, jazz bands have been formed both for recreational and for educational purposes. These groups perform the classical arrangements handed down from the big-band era, and courses are offered in jazz improvisation. With the opening of the manuscript collections left by jazz composers and arrangers, it is now possible to recreate the early years of jazz much in the way performers interpret the classical music of the past.

Thomas Warburton

Frank Tirro, *Jazz: A History* (1993).

JEFFERSON, THOMAS

Thomas Jefferson (1743–1826) has retained a vitality in the American imagination unmatched by any of the other Founding Fathers, including George Washington. Author of the Declaration of Independence, governor of Virginia, architect of Monticello, and third president of the United States (among a great many other things), Jefferson was both the patrician plantation owner and slaveholder and the quintessential patriot and ardent democrat. His legacy for America has been bound up with paradox from the outset. The author of the immortal words of the Declaration was a slaveholder to the end of his life. The champion of agrarianism, localized democracy, and the powers reserved to the states accomplished a dramatic extension of executive power during his time in the White House. If his legacy is problematic for America generally, it has been even more so for southerners, and southern writers from his time to ours have had to come to terms with it.

Jefferson was one of the great prose stylists of his age. He was chosen to draft the Declaration of Independence (1776) largely on the strength of his *A Summary View of the Rights of British America* (1774), and his words in the Declaration (albeit somewhat al-

tered by the Continental Congress) have become a rallying cry worldwide for democracy and individual rights.

His one major contribution to southern literature is his *Notes on the State of Virginia* (1784), written in 1781–1782 as a series of answers to questions put to him by the Marquis de Barbé-Marbois, a French diplomat. Within this framework, Jefferson crafted an insightful portrait of the Old Dominion and, for later readers, of his own mind. The work demonstrates both the power of reason and the conflicts that threaten to undermine it. Jefferson treats Virginia's natural beauty and abundance, its advances in democracy and governance, the virtues of life lived close to the land, and mundane matters of trade and manufactures. The domain of the rational, lettered mind is set out in graceful prose, but the question of the South's "peculiar institution" arises as a disruptive presence in the text.

In the section on "Laws," Jefferson condemns slavery and the failure of Virginia's laws to adequately address it; he finds his way out of the dilemma by raising the question of the innate inferiority of African Americans and setting forth colonization as the only solution. His tone here is scientific and objective, quite different from the impassioned language of the section on "Manners"; there, he considers the pernicious effect of the master-slave relationship on both Virginians and slaves, concluding with a telling outburst about his fear of an inevitable race war. These last portions point to the central contradiction for Jefferson and the South between freedom and the power of reason and an economy largely based on chattel slavery. This problem proved insoluble for Jefferson, as it did for the South as a whole, though Jefferson died before the closure of the southern mind and the claim for slavery as a positive good.

African American writers would exploit this contradiction in stating their case for freedom and full participation in public life. Frederick Douglass (1818–1895), the great African American orator and writer who had gone north from Maryland, appropriated Jefferson's rhetoric of individual rights and the necessity of rebellion against tyranny in many works, most notably his address, "What to a Slave is the Fourth of July?" (1852). What did such rhetoric mean in a land where millions were held in bondage? Though not approaching the power of Douglass's oratory, William Wells Brown (1815–1884), a pioneering African American novelist and former slave, focused his attention more specifically on Jefferson in *Clotel, or The President's*

Daughter (1853). This sentimental novel takes the rumors of the illegitimate children of Jefferson and Sally Hemmings, one of his slaves, and tells the story of Clotel, Jefferson's daughter, in her struggles from the breakup of her family after Jefferson's death to her ultimate suicide within sight of the nation's Capitol. As many other writers, especially in the North, would do, Brown uses Jefferson to attack not only the plantation owners but the complicity of the nation's founders in slavery's wrongs. He presents the sufferings of particular people and ranges them against the abstract rhetoric that bemoans the evil of slavery but only seems to aid in its continuation and extension.

The other contradiction in Jefferson that has drawn writers to one facet of his character or another is his role as both aristocrat and patriarch of Monticello and as champion of the yeoman farmer and democratic liberalism. Early on, William Gilmore Simms (1806–1870) celebrated the common man along with the cavalier in his historical romances, and other southern writers of the period frequently showed the same Jeffersonian concern. As sectional tension worsened, however, the planter aristocracy and the antebellum southern apologists found Jefferson to be of quite the wrong school for their purposes, apart from his arguments against centralized power. His faith in broader democracy and his avowed hostility to the continuance of chattel slavery left his legacy more with Jacksonian southerners and radical political movements in the North. Jefferson's well-known celebrations of the agrarian life as the hope of the Republic remained current in the later South, but his legacy proved problematic for those championing agrarianism, from his contemporary John Randolph of Roanoke to the southern Agrarians in the twentieth century.

Jefferson's legacy proved especially problematic for John Crowe Ransom (1888–1974), Allen Tate (1899–1979), and Donald Davidson (1893–1968), the primary organizers of the Agrarian movement and its principal symposium, *I'll Take My Stand: The South and the Agrarian Tradition* (1930). Jefferson's eloquent praise of the virtue and hardihood of the yeoman farmer as the very bedrock of American democracy and his suspicion of industrialism certainly had served them well as the strongest agrarian comments made by one of the Founders; however, one could hardly summon Jefferson to the defense of traditional society given Jefferson's repeated insistence that each generation stood independent of any other. As with every movement that has attempted to appropriate Jefferson,

the Agrarians found Jefferson to fail to fit neatly into their program. In spite of these problems, John Gould Fletcher (1886–1950), in his contribution to *I'll Take My Stand,* used Jefferson's proposed educational reforms as the centerpiece of his essay.

The single largest problem with Jefferson's legacy for the southern writer has been his limitless Enlightenment faith in human potential and the essential innocence of man, apart from political corruptions. Southern writing, especially after the Civil War, has been characterized by its insistence on a darker view of man, one that takes into account sin, historical contingencies, and the inevitable flaws in any attempt to establish a perfect social or political order. Robert Penn Warren (1905–1989), who had been one of the younger Agrarians, took issue with Jefferson's dream of human innocence in his book-length poem *Brother to Dragons: A Tale of Verse and Voices* (1953; new version, 1979). In this poem, the ghost of Jefferson is brought, through his cynical interlocutor "R.P.W.," to reckon with historical contingency and the reality of human guilt and corruption. Warren examines in the poem the events surrounding the brutal slaying of a slave boy by one of Jefferson's nephews on the Kentucky frontier. Even in this poem, which Warren revised and published as a verse drama and in a new version over twenty years later, Jefferson's hope for America is affirmed in the end, though grounded in a radically different sense of the human condition.

Douglas L. Mitchell

See also Agrarians; Declaration of Independence; Douglass, Frederick; *I'll Take My Stand.*

Joseph J. Ellis, *American Sphinx: The Character of Thomas Jefferson* (1997); John Chester Miller, *The Wolf by the Ears: Thomas Jefferson and Slavery* (1977); Merrill D. Peterson, *The Jefferson Image in the American Mind* (1960); Lewis P. Simpson, *The Brazen Face of History: Studies in the Literary Consciousness in America* (1980).

JEWISH TRADITION

Like Jews elsewhere in America, Jews traveled to the South in different "waves of immigration." Based on their backgrounds, many became highly accepted and successful because they filled specific economic and civic niches occupied by few others. Always a tiny minority, they maintained some traditions, adjusted to the local environment, and contributed disproportionately.

The earliest Jews in the South arrived with the Spanish. Many of these were Marranos—Iberian Jews who practiced their religion secretly to avoid the Inquisition. They were joined by other Sephardim, or Jews originating in the Iberian Peninsula, from the Dutch Caribbean colonies. These Jews, facing de jure if not de facto discrimination as was later the case in most southern colonies, typically had experience in commerce, were versed in foreign languages, and had international Jewish contacts. Mostly men and generally mobile, many became traders with other Europeans and Native Americans.

Sephardic Jews entered the British South especially through Charleston and Savannah during the colonial era. Many of these received assistance from, and continued contacts with, fellow Jews in the Dutch West Indies, Amsterdam, Holland, and the Spanish and Portuguese Congregation in Bevis Marks, London. These Jews and the early contingent of Central European (Ashkenazic) Jews who joined them tended to settle in port cities, or in a few cases, traded in the interior with Native Americans. Unlike most southerners, few became farmers or were tied to the land. Like their earlier coreligionists, most entered into commerce. When numbers warranted, as in Savannah in 1735 and Charleston in 1749, they started congregations. By 1800 Charleston boasted the largest Jewish population in the British colonies, and Ashkenazic Jews far surpassed Sephardim numerically throughout the region, even though Sephardic ceremonial practices continued. By the second and third generations, descendants of the early settlers supported the American Revolution, entered the professions, and sometimes intermarried. The Charleston community supported cultural activities and produced a literary critic and journalist, Isaac Harby. Harby, like Jacob Mordecai in Warrenton, North Carolina, also headed an academy for educating young people. Harby encouraged Charlestonian Penina Moise, poet, essayist, and composer of hymns whose first collection of poems, *Fancy's Sketch Book*, appeared in 1833.

The process of acculturation reached a turning point in Charleston where, after a controversial split, Congregation Beth Elohim pioneered a partly indigenous Reform during the 1830s. By that date, a new wave of Ashkenazim, especially from the Germanic states, flowed into America and the South. A chain migratory pattern was evident, as for example, Jews from Alsace and Lorraine settled in the Mississippi River area. Regional family, business, and social bonds marked Jewish life for the next hundred years.

Movement dominated the Jacksonian era. As the southeastern port cities declined, many Jews migrated inland and westward to cities including Columbia, South Carolina, and New Orleans (which boasted the largest Jewish population in the region after the Civil War) as well as Texas, while communities grew in Richmond, which established a congregation in 1789 and claimed the fourth largest Jewish population in the country according to the 1790 census (Charleston was second). At the same time, young male newcomers who lacked capital (they obtained merchandise on credit from Jewish wholesalers in Baltimore, Cincinnati, New York, or Philadelphia) but were willing to extend credit to rural customers traveled the rural roads peddling. Gradually, through saving profits, many of these settled in small towns and started dry-goods stores, families, and congregations.

Except for recent immigrants, during the 1840s and 1850s most southern Jews lived in towns and cities. Many rose into the middle class, and some even held elective office. Apparently a high percentage owned slaves, and some bought and sold slaves as part of their trade. For members of their urban cohort, slaves were the servants. While participation in slavery symbolized acculturation, at no time did Jews control or have a significant influence on the institution of slavery. The diary of teenager Clara Solomon in Civil War New Orleans, edited by Elliott Ashkenazi, illustrates the lives of many southern Jews. Although some Jews left the region rather than fight for the Confederacy, and there were some Jewish abolitionists, including Rabbi David Einhorn of border city Baltimore, most southern Jews, like outspoken New Orleans rabbi James Gutheim, supported the Confederacy, and many served in the military, including a number who accepted commissions as supply officers. Highly assimilated Judah P. Benjamin held high offices in the Confederate cabinet. During the war, Jews were unfairly singled out for persecution as smugglers, and a few, like the Strauses of later Macy's Department Store fame, fled the region.

The Civil War and Reconstruction affected Jews differently from most southerners. Highly mobile and imbued with entrepreneurial spirit, Jews embodied the New South spirit from the outset. Jews from Central European backgrounds who had resided in the North flocked to Atlanta and other burgeoning cities only to be joined especially after 1881 by East European Jews and then a smattering of Sephardic Jews from the crumbling Ottoman Empire; these continued to make their way to Atlanta and Montgomery during the early 1900s. A flurry of congregational building ensued during Reconstruction followed by another during the late nineteenth and early twentieth centuries. Jewish periodicals such as *The Jewish South* also appeared.

As for religious practice, the "German" Jews struggled between tradition and change while moving toward Reform. Many of their Americanized Hebrew Union College–trained rabbis pressed the social justice and anti-Zionist messages of the Pittsburgh Platform and served as "ambassadors-to-the-Gentiles" for their acculturating congregants. German-Jewish men and women created specialized social and social-service agencies, many of which were duplicated by Eastern European and Sephardic brethren as were congregational structures. These Sephardim now contribute to the culture by recording their Ladino musical heritage. The established Jews welcomed and aided, or were condescending and fearful of, the East European onslaught. Both cooperative federated social-service agencies and division ensued.

Jews settled in the interior through the Galveston Movement, and in small towns from Texas and Mississippi to North Carolina, where Jews were few and far between, a variety of adjustment mechanisms blurred the urban paradigm. Contemporary crime novelist "Kinky" Friedman and his "Texas Jewboys" band caricature the split identity that could result.

The post–Civil War economic pattern took the antebellum model steps further: peddlers started small dry-goods stores with familial or *landsleit* partners, opened branches in other towns, or were lucky or astute enough to locate in rising cities where they built department-store dynasties: Rich's, Thalhimer's, Godchaux's, and Neiman-Marcus. As Jews rose economically, they displayed patriotism during wars, held public offices including that of mayor of port cities, helped establish public schools and cultural as well as medical institutions. Contrary to the northern urban-industrial experience, in the absence of a proletarian base, socialism as an intellectual, social, and cultural movement lacked economic bite in the South, and Jewish labor unionism barely existed. Arbeiter Ring/Workmen's Circles were more important for their Yiddish schools than for class consciousness. "People of the Book" to Bible-Belters, southern Jews found acceptance sometimes marred by such matters as exclusion from gentile social clubs, the infamous Leo Frank case, and Ku Klux Klan diatribes.

The Yiddish theater flourished in many larger southern Jewish communities during the first decades of the twentieth century, and isolated individuals like Rabbi Tobias Geffen of Atlanta wrote talmudic discourses. Yet the conflicts inherent between Jewish and southern identity, and the striving for acceptance in an environment precluding it, took a psychological toll. Ludwig Lewisohn's life and writings reflected the marginality of the Jew in America and the South. Although born in Germany, Lewisohn grew up in Charleston. His autobiography, novels, and literary criticism reflected a struggle between his desire for assimilation and acceptance and the realities of discrimination. He returned to Judaism late in life. A renowned playwright, screenwriter, and political activist, New Orleans–born Lillian Hellman (*The Little Foxes*, 1939) took Lewisohn's lead by separating herself largely from her Jewish and southern roots and by using her maternal ancestors as models for negative portraits. Ronald L. Bern's *The Legacy,* written during the 1970s, depicted similar conflicts in the life of a Jew growing up in the small-town South, as does Morris B. Abram's *The Day Is Short: An Autobiography* (1982). Abram was a successful opponent of the county-unit system, later a foe of affirmative action, and president of Brandeis University, the American Jewish Committee, and other major Jewish organizations; he, like many others, left the South to find his Jewish roots after his early years in Fitzgerald, Georgia, were filled with conflict. David L. Cohn mixed being Jewish, southern, and American somewhat more compatibly. Born in Greenville in the Mississippi Delta, Cohn, in his memoirs, novels, and numerous essays in the *Atlantic Monthly* and other periodicals, exhibited a paternalistic attitude toward African Americans coupled with positive positions on internationalism and other issues. He was both a man of his southern roots and a Jew apart. He influenced, and was influenced by, William Alexander Percy. In *Lanterns on the Levee* (1941), Percy depicted the individual small-town Jewish merchant in Mississippi as a person of culture and learning. As Stephen Whitfield indicates, admiration for the individual Jew did not preclude stereotypical images of Jews or a pervasive anti-Semitism. As Jason Compson states in Faulkner's *The Sound and the Fury* (1929), "I have nothing against Jews as individuals. . . . It's just the race." Carson McCullers's *Ballad of the Sad Café* (1943) shows rabble rousers in an archetypal mill town confronting Morris Finestein as a "Christ killer." Conversely, in their autobiographies, Hodding Carter, Harry Ashmore, and Ralph McGill pointed to the cosmopolitan and liberal positions of Jews as critical influences on their futures as Pulitzer Prize–winning southern newspapermen of the Civil Rights era. Albeit recognizing discrimination, Eli Evans in his memoirs and historical writings today stresses instances of southern Jewish acceptance, acculturation, and contributions to the region's history. This is in sharp contrast to the classic *Mind of the South* (1941), in which W. J. Cash states that the Jew as "eternal Alien" was an especially strong image among southerners. Two-time National Book Award finalist Melissa Fay Greene explores the depths of depravity in books on racism in Georgia and the bombing of the Atlanta Temple in 1958.

After 1920s legislation essentially closed America's open doors, Jews gradually acculturated. Children of the immigrants received college educations, entered the professions, expanded businesses, and, as was the typical small-town scenario, moved elsewhere. The Great Depression was a temporary set-back. The delivery of Jewish social services was transformed as New Deal agencies took over private charity work; as far less aid was needed by the mid-1930s, priorities shifted to overseas relief. Such foreign aid, which had reached new heights during the era of the First World War, accelerated dramatically in response to Hitler's actions. Although some southern rabbis and laymen remained anti-Zionist and supported the American Council for Judaism, the Holocaust, the founding of Israel, and the process of acculturation alleviated many of the old internal community fissures.

More liberal than "typical" southerners and often fearful of their precarious acceptance, nonetheless some Jews in the South participated in women's and black rights movements. Louis I. Jaffe, editorial writer for the *Norfolk [Virginia] Pilot,* received the Pulitzer Prize for journalism in 1929 when he denounced the Byrd machine and lynching. Sylvan Meyer received the same award for editorials in the *Gainesville [Georgia] Times* for condemning segregation during the 1940s. They were joined in the Pulitzer ranks more recently by Paul Greenberg of Little Rock, Arkansas. Harry Golden, humorist, editor of the *Carolina Israelite,* and popular historian of the Leo Frank case and of southern Jewry, provided a noted voice of reason during the turbulent 1950s and 1960s. Adolph Ochs began his newspaper career in Tennessee before purchasing the *New York Times.* Jews also encouraged ecumenical efforts frequently in conjunction with Catholics, a fellow religious minority.

Following national trends, congregation and institution building marked the post–World War II years, as did the move toward Conservative Judaism. During the last half of the twentieth century, small-town Jewish life languished except in areas of specialized growth such as Durham–Chapel Hill. Conversely, Miami rose as a center of migration, and the Sunbelt effect contributed to the growth of Jewish life in southern cities and suburbs. Survivors of the Holocaust, Jewish Israelis, Iranians, South Africans, and Russians joined a pluralistic and voluntaristic society. Pat Conroy depicts the psychological impact of the Holocaust on a survival family in the South in *Beach Music* (1995). Jewish experiences ran the spectrum from a return to tradition and the rise of Jewish day schools and Orthodoxy to low rates of affiliation, high rates of intermarriage, and secularization. Notwithstanding Alfred Uhry's award-winning films *Driving Miss Daisy* and *The Last Night of Ballyhoo,* at the dawn of the twenty-first century few differences remain between Jewish experiences in equivalent communities throughout America. Author of *The Golden Weather* (reissued 1995), a coming-of-age novel about a thirteen-year-old Jewish boy in 1936 Charleston, is Louis D. Rubin Jr., University Distinguished Professor of English at the University of North Carolina. As an award-winning author or editor of over fifty books and founder of Algonquin Press, Rubin reflects the successful career of the southerner as American, Jewish-style.

Mark K. Bauman

See also Frank, Leo; Judaism; Rubin, Louis D., Jr.

Mark K. Bauman, *The Southerner as American: Jewish Style* (1996); Leonard Dinnerstein and Mary Dale Palsson, eds., *Jews in the South* (1973); Eli Evans, *The Provincials: A Personal History of Jews in the South* (1973); Nathan Kaganoff and Melvin I. Urofsky, eds., *Turn to the South: Essays on Southern Jewry* (1979); Samuel Proctor and Louis Schmier with Malcolm Stern, eds., *Jews of the South* (1984); Stephen J. Whitfield, *Voices of Jacob, Hands of Esau: Jews in American Life and Thought* (1984).

JIM CROW

In 1828, Thomas Dartmouth "Daddy" Rice, a white entertainer posing as a black man, introduced the term

Jim Crow when he performed a number called "Jump Jim Crow" at a minstrel show in Pittsburgh, Pennsylvania. The song and the dance that accompanied it, Rice said, were inspired by his observation of an old slave in Louisville, Kentucky.

Off the minstrel stage, the term *Jim Crow* seems to have been used next to describe racial segregation in the antebellum North. How a stage term came to apply to a social custom is lost in obscurity.

In the South beginning about 1890, the term acquired new meaning, connoting not only the physical separation of the races but also the political disfranchisement of black men and the violence perpetrated by white mobs that resulted in lynchings and race riots. The Jim Crow South was a place where blacks might be the victims of more than segregation.

Some southern writers encouraged the vicious racism that defined the Jim Crow era. No writer did so to a greater degree than the North Carolinian Thomas Dixon Jr. In a trilogy of novels dealing with Reconstruction—*The Leopard's Spots* (1902), *The Clansman* (1905), and *The Traitor* (1907)—Dixon popularized the idea that the Ku Klux Klan was the savior of white southern civilization. With the release of *The Birth of a Nation* (1915), a spectacular motion picture based primarily on *The Clansman* and directed by a southerner, the Kentuckian David Wark Griffith, Dixon's portrayal of vicious blacks and virtuous whites reached an audience larger than those who had read his novels.

Although not so viciously racist as Dixon, other southern writers had created an environment in which his ideas could flourish. The journalist Henry W. Grady, managing editor of the *Atlanta Constitution,* had argued earlier for the idea of racial instincts. In an article entitled "In Plain Black and White" published in *Century Magazine* in 1885, Grady maintained that the racial segregation that was emerging in the South was a development desired not only by whites but also by blacks. Thomas Nelson Page, who had established a reputation as a plantation romancer—a writer of stories portraying the affection between masters and slaves—turned vicious in *Red Rock* (1898), a novel about Reconstruction that presaged Dixon's works.

If there were southern writers who buttressed Jim Crow, there were also southern writers who attempted to undermine Jim Crow. Among the first to do so was George W. Cable, a thrice-wounded Confederate veteran. In fiction and in an essay entitled "The Freedman's Case in Equity" published in *Century* magazine in 1885, Cable argued that the color line relegated all

blacks to inferior status, ignoring the differences in ability among blacks themselves. Mark Twain's searing indictment of slavery in *Adventures of Huckleberry Finn* (1885) was, by extension, an attack on postbellum southern racism. In the Uncle Remus stories, collections of which were published between 1880 and 1905, Joel Chandler Harris slyly subverted the Jim Crow ethos. Although set in the late antebellum South, Opie Read's novel *My Young Master* (1896) can be read as an attempt to undermine late-nineteenth-century racism. The black writer Charles W. Chesnutt mounted a frontal assault on Jim Crow in stories published in *The Conjure Woman* (1899) and *The Wife of His Youth and Other Stories of the Color Line* (1899) and in the novels *The House Behind the Cedars* (1900), *The Marrow of Tradition* (1901), and *The Colonel's Dream* (1905). Perhaps the definitive African American statement on the subject is Richard Wright's "The Ethics of Living Jim Crow," an essay included in the 1940 edition of *Uncle Tom's Children* that is based on his own experience of racial repression in Mississippi.

Wayne Mixon

See also Lynching; Nigger; Race, Idea of; Race Relations; Racism; Segregation.

Wayne Mixon, "The Ultimate Irrelevance of Race: Joel Chandler Harris and Uncle Remus in Their Time," *Journal of Southern History* (1990); I. A. Newby, *Jim Crow's Defense: Anti-Negro Thought in America* (1965); Eric J. Sundquist, *To Wake the Nations: Race in the Making of American Literature* (1993); C. Vann Woodward, *The Strange Career of Jim Crow* (3d rev. ed., 1974).

JOHNSON, LYNDON BAINES

Though the Great Society that Lyndon Johnson (1908–1973) proposed was to be "a place which honors creation for its own sake," his own relationship to the creative community—in particular, to writers—was far less sanguine. Johnson relied upon writers to help him fashion the substance and style of his presidency; in turn, they often came to distrust him or to be otherwise disappointed by him.

Brought up in the poor hill country of Texas, educated at Southwest Texas State Teachers College, and having little interest in the arts, Johnson did not wish to compete for the eastern cultural spotlight that the Kennedys had basked in and that he feared might only show him to disadvantage. But he was president, his foreign policies were increasingly unpopular, there was racial and political unrest domestically, and he could escape neither the obligation to engage a well-educated, free-speaking community nor that community's range of textual responses to his behavior. Best known among these responses was the rhyming couplet chanted on university campuses, a short, cruel comment on Johnson's war in Vietnam: "Hey, hey, L.B.J.,/ How many kids did you kill today?" Another, more elaborate version of this emerged from Eric F. Goldman's attempts to organize the White House Festival of the Arts in 1965, which he describes in *The Tragedy of Lyndon Johnson* (1969). Criticism of the event was led by Robert Lowell, of the Boston Lowells. In a well-publicized letter to the *New York Times,* Lowell declined the invitation to read his poetry because he did not wish to appear to support Johnson's belligerence overseas. Lowell was among those who praised Barbara Garson's satiric *MacBird!* (1966). Garson, a New Yorker, was a political activist at Berkeley, where *Macbird!* developed as a protest piece. In 1967 it opened off-Broadway and had a successful run of 386 performances. The play pilloried Johnson and his wife, Lady Bird, likening them to Shakespeare's overly ambitious Macbeth and Lady Macbeth, and implicating them in Kennedy's assassination.

Johnson's oratory and accent were rich fodder for *MacBird!,* in which the protagonist proposes "the Smooth Society" and exits to the line "So long, you'all." In 1968, when his faults were set in high relief, *Time* noted that "Johnson's official verbiage tends to be dull, and though he can be pungent and forceful in private, his public charisma is just about nil." Yet Johnson had both training and success in speech-making. He was on the debating team in college, and he taught public speaking at Sam Houston High School. When he left teaching for politics, he was considered a compelling speaker on the campaign stump. And during the early part of his presidency, when he was pushing his progressive social agenda hard, he put the presidential "bully pulpit" to good use.

As is typical in modern politics, much of Johnson's speech-writing was consigned to a staff, though outside contributions might be admitted. His inaugural speech included phrases offered by the Californian John Steinbeck, winner of the Nobel Prize in 1962, but its main writer was Richard Goodwin. Goodwin, a Bostonian inherited from Kennedy's administration, was the principal author of two of Johnson's most significant and effective speeches. In the "Great Society" speech (May 22, 1964), given during commencement exercises at the University of Michigan, Johnson set a direction for the country in the second half of the twentieth century, "not only toward the rich society and the powerful society, but upward to the Great Society." This was Johnson's version of programs like Roosevelt's New Deal and Kennedy's New Frontier. The "We Shall Overcome" speech (March 15, 1965) was an appeal, made to television viewers and a joint session of Congress, for passage of the Voting Rights Act. It was delivered at a time of strain and danger in the South, which Johnson addressed: "There is no Negro problem. There is no Southern problem. There is no Northern problem. There is only an American problem." To further signal his commitment to the struggle, Johnson surprised his audience by invoking the Baptist hymn associated with the Civil Rights Movement. Such rhetorical gestures had particular power because Johnson was a southerner and white.

Johnson's books, too, were largely the work of editors and ghostwriters. *A Time for Action: A Selection from the Speeches and Writings of Lyndon B. Johnson, 1953–64* (1964) is interesting for the introduction by Adlai E. Stevenson, who had vied with Kennedy and Johnson for the Democratic nomination in 1960. *The Choices We Face* (1969), published just after the end of his presidency, sets out Johnson's retrospective and prospective views of the major issues he faced: economic growth, breaking the color barrier, rural-urban balance, and so on. *The Vantage Point: Perspectives of the Presidency, 1963–1969* (1971) stresses Johnson's public life, particularly his involvement in Vietnam. Among the contributors to the memoir was Doris Kearns, a New Yorker who married Richard Goodwin. Having become Johnson's aide and confidante in the last years of his life, she went on to write her own study, *Lyndon Johnson and the American Dream* (1976). Two other books bearing Johnson's name are somewhat more unusual productions. *This America* (1966) attempts to illustrate the themes of Johnson's "Great Society" speech. Ken Heyman's affecting black-and-white photographs—mainly of people in all classes and sections of the country—are accompanied by quotations from a range of texts attributed to Johnson. Johnson is credited, also, with the introductory and concluding remarks. *My Hope for America* (1964) was ghostwritten by Douglass Cater, an Alabamian, and timed for the presidential campaign. It lays out the candidate's political principles, but in a lyrical style—

"When I was young I often walked out at night and looked at the scattered Texas sky," it begins—that one does not regularly associate with Johnson.

In its essay naming him "Man of the Year" for 1964, *Time* magazine noted "the growing shelf of Johnson literature" and made this recommendation: "Probably the best portrayal of Johnson the man is in a work of fiction, Novelist William Brammer's *The Gay Place*." While working on Johnson's Senate staff in Washington, Billy Lee Brammer (1929–1978) began work on *The Gay Place* (1961), which takes its name from a poem by F. Scott Fitzgerald. This set of three novellas—"The Flea Circus," "Room Enough to Caper," and "Country Pleasures"—is connected by the recurring figure of Arthur Fenstemaker, a powerful and profane governor of a state much like Texas. Though Fenstemaker was considered by critics a largely favorable type of Johnson, the book caused an irremediable rift in Johnson's relationship with Brammer. Brammer, who did not fulfill the expectations raised by this literary performance, eventually died of a drug overdose. *Fustian Days*, a sequel to *The Gay Place*, was never completed. Neither was the biography of Johnson that he had been commissioned to write.

In the 1950s, Brammer had written for the *Texas Observer*, where he had come to Johnson's attention. This liberal weekly was the starting point for a number of other connections between Johnson and a cadre of young writers with Texas roots and ties. Mississippian Willie Morris was a graduate of the University of Texas and editor of the *Observer*. Morris's memoir *North Toward Home* (1967) contains a long section on Texas in the 1950s and early 1960s, when Johnson dominated the political scene there. Like *The Gay Place* several years before, *North Toward Home* won the Houghton Mifflin Literary Fellowship Award. Its successor, *New York Days* (1993), describes Morris's time as editor at *Harper's*, where he championed work on Texas themes. Tom Wicker, who met Morris while reporting in Texas, contributed "Bill Moyers: Johnson's Good Angel" (*Harper's*, October 1965). Later Wicker, a North Carolinian at the *New York Times*'s Washington Bureau in the 1960s, produced *JFK and LBJ: The Influence of Personality upon Politics* (1968). Moyers, Morris's classmate at the University of Texas, coordinated much of the speech-writing in Johnson's White House. Brammer's friend Larry L. King wrote for the *Observer* in the 1960s, and also for *Harper's*. "My Hero LBJ" (*Harper's*, October 1966) describes King's campaigning, when he was just twelve years old, for

Johnson's failed senatorial bid in 1941; his view of Johnson as majority leader and campaigner when King was a staffer for two Texas congressmen in Washington; and the brokering and compromises that led to Johnson's taking second place on the Democrats' presidential ticket in 1960. "An Epitaph for LBJ" (*Harper's*, April 1968), which grew from the author's having been asked to provide material for an eventual obituary, expresses King's disillusionment with his childhood hero. Recently, King has returned to this subject in *The Dead Presidents' Club* (1996), a play in which Coolidge, Truman, Nixon, and Johnson await the Last Judgment. The archives of Southwest Texas State University list King's "research material for a never-realized book on Lyndon Baines Johnson"—further evidence, perhaps, of this president's ability both to engage and to confound.

Amber Vogel

See also Sixties, The.

Robert Caro, *The Years of Lyndon Johnson: The Path to Power* (1982), and *The Years of Lyndon Johnson: Means of Ascent* (1990); Robert Dallek, *Lone Star Rising: Lyndon Johnson and His Times, 1908–1960* (1991), and *Flawed Giant: Lyndon B. Johnson, 1960–1973* (1998).

JUDAISM

Judaism in the South reflected the Jewish immigrants' European legacy as well as their American acculturation. Southern Jewry emerged from its religiously Orthodox heritage to become a bastion of Reform Judaism that modernized belief and practice according to Protestant models.

Jewish religious developments followed the migratory waves of Spanish-Portuguese (Sephardic), Central European, and East European Jews. Richmond offered a paradigm of ethnic congregational growth with its Sephardic-rite Beth Shalome (1789), Bavarian Beth Ahabah (1841), Prussian Kenesseth Israel (1856), and Russian Sir Moses Montefiore (1880) congregations. All began as Orthodox with a traditional Hebrew-language liturgy, gender-segregated seating, and strict sabbath observance.

Typically, the first step of community organizing was the founding of a cemetery society, which took responsibility for welfare and worship as well as ritual burial. Although eighteenth-century congregations in

Savannah, Charleston, and Richmond followed the decorous Spanish-Portuguese ritual, the German legacy shaped southern—and American—Judaism. German-Jewish reforming trends flourished when transplanted to an open democratic society, especially in the South where Jews were few, dispersed, and distant from rabbinic authority. In 1824, author Isaac Harby founded in Charleston the first Reform congregation in America, the Reformed Society of Israelites. In the 1830s, Charleston poet Penina Moise composed the first American-Jewish hymnal. By 1861, the South contained twenty-one congregations.

Slowly and unevenly, congregations after the mid-nineteenth century began introducing organ music, family pews, an abbreviated liturgy, and English-language worship. Southern congregations were often riven by disputes among liberals and traditionalists, Germanizers and Americanizers, radical and moderate reformers. By the end of the century, a classical Reform Judaism emerged across the South that gave voice to a prophetic universalism that rejected a parochial, talmudic Orthodoxy and minimized the Jews' difference from their Christian neighbors. Southern rabbis declared America to be their Zion.

Starting in the 1880s, the South received a trickle of the great East European migration, and Orthodox *shuls* sprouted in cities and small towns across the region. These synagogues maintained a Hebrew liturgy, kosher laws, gender segregation, and a regimen of daily and Sabbath prayer. Urban ghettos like Memphis's Pinch, mythologized in the fiction of Steve Stern, were enclaves of immigrant Yiddish culture. Social and religious tensions often existed between acculturated Reform Germans and immigrant Orthodox East Europeans. Larger communities typically contained both Reform and Orthodox congregations.

A synagogue in the South was commonly called a Jewish church, and it served as both an institution of Jewish faith and peoplehood and an agency of southern acculturation. Zebulon Vance struck a popular southern theme in his celebrated "The Scattered Nation" (1874) speech when he extolled the modern Jew as blood of the Savior. As Jews assimilated, sabbath and kosher observance eroded. Jewish youth, like their Christian neighbors, attended Sunday school. I. J. Schwartz's epic Yiddish poem, *Kentucky* (1925), describes immigrant Jews renegotiating their Judaism as they adapted to southern society.

The South was perhaps the least anti-Semitic of American regions, but the welcome was ambivalent. W. J. Cash in *The Mind of the South* (1941) labeled the Jew as the "eternal Alien" but also noted that southern Christianity's spirit was "essentially Hebraic." Southerners with their fundamentalism and romantic religiosity venerated Jews as People of the Book yet cursed them as Christ killers. Titles like *Absalom, Absalom!* attest to the southerners' familiarity with the Hebrew Bible even as a Snopes uttered commonplace country prejudices against urban, capitalist Jews. Folk ballads, as recalled by Richard Wright in *Black Boy* (1945), repeated libels against Jews, and rustic preachers damned them. Religious anti-Jewish prejudice reflected economic resentments, racial anxieties and anti-immigrant sentiments. Anti-Semitic passions peaked with the 1915 lynching of Leo Frank, an Atlanta manufacturer accused of murdering a factory girl. David Mamet's *The Old Religion* (1997) attests to the continuing legacy of the Frank case in Jewish-Christian relations.

By the 1930s, ethnicity defined Jews even more than faith or practice. Southern writers of Jewish origin, such as Lillian Hellman, were largely assimilated. Such works as Alfred Uhry's *Driving Miss Daisy* (1987) and *The Last Night of Ballyhoo* (1997) depict a southern Jewry with an attenuated religiosity. Over generations, East European Orthodox Jews liberalized toward the Conservative and Reform movements. After the Holocaust, a neotraditionalism, including Zionism, became more pervasive. The classical Reform worship style, a southern hallmark, yielded in many though not all places to a renewed Hebrew liturgy. Over generations, the ethnic and religious lines that separated Germans and East Europeans faded. With the advent of the Sunbelt, urban centers have seen a resurgence of Jewish congregations and increased religious pluralism, while agrarian, small-town Jewish congregations struggle to survive.

Leonard Rogoff

See also Frank, Leo; Jewish Tradition.

Mark Bauman and Berkley Kalin, *The Quiet Voices* (1996); Nathan Kaganoff and Melvin Urofsky, *Turn to the South: Essays on Southern Jewry* (1979); Michael Meyer, *Response to Modernity* (1988).

K

K MART FICTION

"K Mart Fiction" is one label frequently given to a type of American "minimalism" that arose during the 1980s and that chronicles a world inundated by consumerism and popular culture. Oftentimes, such writing is accompanied by a sense of anxiety for the disappearance of regionally distinctive cultures; in southern literature, this anxiety is heightened, since unique, traditional folk cultures have provided the diversity of character, setting, and narrative that historically has distinguished southern literature. As early as nineteenth-century local-color writing, the popularity of southern fiction has depended upon the assumption that the South is a place apart from the rest of the nation, a collection of remote rural pockets free from the homogenizing influences of mass media and mainstream society. This notion exists yet today and fuels much of the interest in contemporary southern letters and culture. In her introduction to *The Best of the South*, Algonquin Press's 1996 anthology of anthologies, Anne Tyler celebrates the distinctiveness of southern literature: "Americans everywhere, I suspect, cling to the hope that this country still has identifiable regions, in spite of all the changes wrought by modern times. My own hope has resurfaced with each annual volume of *New Stories from the South*."

Readers often think of writers of the grotesque as characteristic of just such regional distinctiveness, writers such as Faulkner, sometimes Welty, O'Connor, Carson McCullers, Harry Crews, Barry Hannah, or Lewis Nordan. Upon closer scrutiny, however, one notices that these chroniclers of the grotesque typically come from the Deep South; in the aforementioned list, for example, four are from Mississippi and three are Georgia writers. Much of the literature of the Upper South, by contrast, focuses its attention on the many ways in which regional distinctiveness is indeed giving

way to the homogenizing influence of pop culture. This trend is particularly true in regions of the "progressive" South. For example, Bobbie Ann Mason from Kentucky, Josephine Humphreys from Charleston, South Carolina, and Lee Smith, Clyde Edgerton, and Jill McCorkle from North Carolina all fill their novels with realistic depictions of how the culture of TV, shopping malls, and consumerism is changing both the physical and psychological landscapes of the region.

Of course, such a neat dichotomy of southern writers into K Mart realists and writers of the grotesque is shortsighted and misleading. For example, one might point to novels such as *Body* or *The Mulching of America* to argue that the primary theme in much of Harry Crews's fiction is likewise the degrading influence of consumer culture. But like Barry Hannah, who also often immerses his characters in a world of popular culture, Crews depicts a K Mart world as anything but commonplace. Both Crews and Hannah adopt the materials of pop culture for the purposes of phantasmagoria and the grotesque. They both suggest the many ways in which people in such a homogenizing world still manage to live lives that are fully idiosyncratic. In *Body*, for example, Crews depicts the lives of body builders whose notions of personal identity have been thoroughly disciplined by gym culture; even though he is critical of such cultural conditioning, Crews recognizes the colorful distinctiveness of their pop subculture. He cannot resist the impulse to make these characters larger than life, almost to the point of deifying their kitschiness.

One finds no such apotheosis in Bobbie Ann Mason's *In Country*, the novel that might be called "the mother of all K Mart fictions." Here, popular culture is not exotic; it is all too familiar. Mason's teenaged protagonist, Samantha Hughes, spends her days like so many other American girls during the 1980s, listening to Michael Jackson and Bruce Springsteen, watching

M*A*S*H on TV, worrying about which pair of blue jeans she will wear, drinking Coke, eating at McDonald's, and shopping at Kroger's. Mason does not attempt to transform the linguistic and material artifacts of popular culture; rather, they serve as mere counters, as thoroughly identifiable entities to readers as immersed in the same popular culture as Mason's characters. Mason's method involves the cataloguing of hundreds of brand names throughout the novel until the reader, like the fictional characters, is desensitized to the possibility of some spiritual or metaphorical significance beyond the surfaces of experience. Reading *In Country,* one lives through a world of simulacra, of names and objects that are the result of mass production. It is a world devoid of mystery or originality. Unlike Faulkner's Quentin Compson, who is obsessed with the particular history of his family and region, Samantha Hughes's quest into the past leads her no further than the rock 'n' roll of a previous generation, and noticeably not to Elvis or Jerry Lee Lewis but to the Beatles, the Kinks, and the Animals.

Another writer often cited for her preoccupation with popular culture is Lee Smith. Smith grew up in Appalachian Virginia hearing older relatives tell about a time that had already given way to the logging and mining interests that changed the landscape of Appalachia forever. In novels such as *Oral History* and *Fair and Tender Ladies,* Smith traces the continuity between the exploitation of early-twentieth-century Appalachia by loggers and miners and the exploitation of the descendents of these same mountain folk by Wal-Mart and McDonald's. In both of the aforementioned novels, personal insecurities that result from geographic and economic isolation manifest themselves in cultural insecurities, in the willingness of a mountain people to accept whatever is new and shiny and foreign as superior to a less-flashy indigenous culture. It is this complicity in the erosion of Appalachian folk culture by a K Mart world that is Smith's focus. And yet she is not writing simple polemics against consumerism. Although the pervasive sense of cultural loss is evident throughout Smith's fiction—making it essentially elegiac—her comic sensibility simultaneously shows through, manifesting itself in a vision of Appalachia that is surprisingly resilient to cultural invasion. Her characters live happily with a heterogeneous mixture of folk and pop influences, which they could not care less about sorting out. *Oral History* ends with the young Almarine Cantrell building the theme park Ghostland in the center of his ancestor-haunted Hoot Owl Holler. Like Almarine's involvement with Amway, the theme park epitomizes the blending of pop and folk elements. The reader likely feels sadder about these cultural changes than do the characters. To an extent, Smith shares the gothic sensibility of Harry Crews, and, like writers of the grotesque, she sees in popular culture an opportunity for literary transformation, for the chance to contextualize pop artifacts and thereby penetrate their surfaces to their possibilities for mystery. Whereas Bobbie Ann Mason emphasizes the static quality of pop artifacts—how they impose a cultural norm similarly on all people, independent of the recipients' various backgrounds—Smith studies how the context for uptake changes the experience of pop culture. In fact, she consistently exploits the local engagement of pop culture as a unique cultural expression and as a source of local color in itself.

Clyde Edgerton is another writer who studies the ways in which his characters engage popular culture, and, like Smith, he tends to exploit that engagement as a source of humor. One of the most highly praised comic scenes in his fiction occurs in *Walking Across Egypt,* in which octogenarian Mattie Rigsby gets stuck in a bottomless chair and contemplates the humiliation of being caught at home watching soap operas without having washed her dishes. On a more serious level, in *Floatplane Notebooks* Noralee Copeland, the rebel daughter who embraces the hippie counterculture and its pop music, offers one of the novel's few voices of dissent for her brother's involvement in the Vietnam War. Edgerton usually treats his characters' engagement of pop culture as innocent, naïve, and even necessary individually to their continued vitality. On a community, however, the influence of pop culture tends to be insidious. *Where Trouble Sleeps* begins with a map of the one-blinker-light town Listre in 1950, and the novel ends with the same town, renamed Hunter's Grove, in 2000; a quick glance reveals that nearly every locally owned establishment has been replaced by some corporate franchise, by Bojangles', McDonald's, Food Lion, Revco, BP, Exxon, Blockbuster, and Econo Lodge.

It should be noted (without intending any ill will to the discount franchise itself) that the label "K Mart Fiction" is one with which no self-respecting writer is likely to be comfortable; even worse than "minimalism," "K Mart fiction" is a term that suggests smallness, blandness, banality, commonness. And yet even these assumptions are class-based. The great triumph of the minimalists, or the writers of K Mart fiction, is their ability to portray the experiences of people from a lower economic class with realism, complexity, and dignity. To the extent that they accomplish this aim, their work bears the marks of genuine and lasting literature.

George Hovis

See also Grit Lit; Minimalism.

Fred Hobson, *The Southern Writer in the Postmodern World* (1991); Special New Fiction Number, *Mississippi Review* 40/41 (1985).

KENTUCKY, LITERATURE OF

Kentucky literature, like the state itself, has from its beginnings in the eighteenth century had its own peculiar aura and strong sense of place. Partly attributable to the nature of the questing, often desperate, sometimes violent, always courageous men and women who undertook the exploration and settlement of a wilderness, and partly attributable to the disparate cultures of the state as it grew and developed, the variety of Kentucky literature defies easy generalization and categorization. As Kentucky County of Virginia, the area of the first westward expansion after the settled establishment of the thirteen colonies, Kentucky early acquired the promise of a New Eden, a land of rich and endless possibility and plenty, a myth that has never entirely lost its force and in some ways still informs Kentucky writing.

Kentucky's diverse geography has also created differences, separate cultures in many ways, in eastern, central, western, and northern Kentucky. The Appalachian mountain culture has, since the beginning of this century, created a discrete current in the stream of Kentucky literature that contrasts in many ways with the genteel traditions that early on dominated the writing of the more prosperous and socially stratified central Bluegrass region. These two areas differ both from the agrarian, neo-Confederate culture and writing of western Kentucky, and from the culture and literature that has come out of the Ohio River-dominated, more midwestern areas of Louisville and northern Kentucky.

The chronology of Kentucky literature follows much the same pattern as that of other frontier states. In Kentucky, this early period (1780–1810) produced notably only Gilbert Imlay's *The Emigrants, or The History of an Expatriated Family* (1793), an epistolary novel of adventure and ideas that both describes frontier life in accurate detail and champions the political system of the United States, the rights of women, and the principle of divorce. Though Imlay was born in New Jersey, he spent several years on land he owned in Fayette County. His fictional family lives in Lexington and Louisville.

During the antebellum period, historical fiction, particularly romances inspired by Sir Walter Scott's novels, and slavery literature dominated the scene in Kentucky. By the 1830s, the Kentucky frontier had become a favorite subject of such novels, the best of which by a Kentuckian was John A. McClung's *Sketches of Western Adventure* (1832). McClung's account of the siege of Bryant's Station (which came to be accepted as fact) exemplifies his penchant for heroic invention: he has the women of the fort carrying spring water for the inhabitants under the drawn bows of the attacking Indians.

William Wells Brown (ca. 1814–1884), born a slave in Fayette County, is important not only for his fiction and his activism in the abolitionist movement but also because he is the first American black novelist. After escaping slavery in 1834 via the Underground Railroad, the self-educated Brown published essays, histories, novels, and plays. Also a self-trained physician and lecturer, he became a national force for social justice. He was a delegate to the Peace Conference of 1849 in Paris, where he became friends with Victor Hugo. His best-known work, *Clotel; or, the President's Daughter: A Narrative of Slave Life in the United States* (1853), a melodramatic novel, tells the story of a slave mistress of Thomas Jefferson. Although not factual, the novel is based on contemporary hearsay and was so scandalous that it was published only in England until 1864, when an edition was published in the United States under an altered title and in a version that omitted any mention of Jefferson.

Uncle Tom's Cabin, the most famous piece of Kentucky slavery literature, was also the most important nationally. Harriet Beecher Stowe, though not a Kentuckian, lived for eighteen years in Cincinnati and gathered the material for the novel on her numerous visits to Kentucky plantations in Garrard, Boyle, and Mason counties. She was familiar with the work of the Underground Railroad in northern Kentucky and Cincinnati. Although the novel is sentimental, Stowe's genuine gift for characterization makes the story compelling.

After the Civil War, the myth of southern gentility

dominated the work of major Kentucky writers, particularly that of Lexingtonian James Lane Allen (1849–1925) and his protegé, John Fox Jr. (1862–1919). Although Allen saw Realism and Naturalism on the horizon near the end of the nineteenth century, he took as his mission the retrospective interpretation of the tradition that had defined southern culture and life in Kentucky during the first ten years of his life. Allen's fiction articulated these genteel values, defining the highest human aspiration as "to do nothing mean and to do nothing meanly." Although his idealized vision always focused on his Kentucky background (fourteen of his eighteen novels are set there), he moved to New York in 1893 and returned only once, briefly, in 1898. At the time of his move, he lamented that Kentucky had little literature of its own, and he set about correcting this, creating for the outside world a sense of Kentucky as a unique place. His career picked up in 1891 with the publication of *Flute and Violin, and Other Kentucky Tales and Romances,* and in 1892 with *The Blue Grass Region of Kentucky, and Other Articles,* a collection of his essays about Kentucky originally published in the leading magazines of the day. In 1894 *A Kentucky Cardinal,* a novelette with strong emphasis on its natural setting, won Allen critical recognition as one of the best stylists writing in America. *The Choir Invisible* (1897), about the Kentucky frontier, is considered his best novel. Although it achieved best-seller status in its day, it, like the rest of his fiction, is little read today.

John Fox Jr. also was born in central Kentucky (Bourbon County) and wrote primarily about the state. He was the first Kentucky fiction writer to develop an interest in Appalachian culture, and he built the plots of his most popular novels, *The Little Shepherd of Kingdom Come* (1903) and *The Trail of the Lonesome Pine* (1908), on the contrasts between mountain culture and the aristocratic Bluegrass. Although not as apt a stylist as Allen, Fox is a consummate storyteller, and his novels explore the same genteel values and dramatize the same bifurcations in Kentucky's diverse cultural traditions that Allen examines in his early essays. *The Little Shepherd of Kingdom Come,* which was dramatized as a play and in four movie versions, is probably the first American novel to sell more than a million copies.

Poetry, which until the end of the nineteenth century had not been notably written by Kentuckians, brought a measure of even international fame to Madison Cawein (1865–1914) of Louisville, whose work

also was in the Genteel Tradition. In 1888, when William Dean Howells favorably reviewed Cawein's first book, *Blooms of the Berry,* Cawein's career seemed launched. But Cawein, like Allen, was on the cusp of a new sensibility, which he never convincingly embraced. His poetry, awash in classical allusions and peopled with fairies and elves, though often otherwise realistic in its depiction of natural scenes, seemed more and more irrelevant at the beginning of the age that produced T. S. Eliot, Ezra Pound, Gertrude Stein, and William Carlos Williams. His best volume, *Kentucky Poems* (1902), was selected from his voluminous work by Sir Edmund Gosse, an English critic. In all, Cawein published thirty-six books in his relatively short career, many more poems than were worthy.

The local-color movement, which nationally included such writers as Mark Twain, Joel Chandler Harris, and Sarah Orne Jewett who had broken from the Genteel Tradition, in Kentucky included not only some of the later works of Allen and Fox but also those of Alice Hegan Rice (1870–1942), who wrote about life in a Louisville slum in her popular novel *Mrs. Wiggs of the Cabbage Patch* (1901); John Uri Lloyd (1849–1936), who wrote about northern Kentucky in his "Stringtown Stories"; Eliza C. Obenchain (1856–1936), who wrote about western Kentucky in her series of stories *Aunt Jane of Kentucky* (1907); and Irvin S. Cobb (1876–1944), who wrote about the Jackson Purchase and Paducah in particular in his Judge Priest stories. The best of these writers (Allen, Fox, and Cobb) did not rely for effect solely on the picturesqueness and eccentricity of their characters and their dialects, as lesser local-colorists tended to do. Cobb's stories, for example, effectively satirize the forms that human folly takes in small Kentucky towns. Sentimental though they were, Obenchain's *Aunt Jane* and Rice's *Mrs. Wiggs* were to some degree concerned with characterization and with ethical and moral problems. A prime example of the sentimental family novel, *Mrs. Wiggs* struck a chord and was number two on the 1902 best-seller list. It sold over 650,000 copies in more than a hundred printings. As a play, it ran seven seasons on Broadway, and four film versions and a radio serialization were also extremely popular.

Around the turn of the century, several Kentucky writers were nationally known for at least one children's book. Some of Allen's and Fox's novels appealed to children. Rice's *Lovey Mary* (1903), a sequel to *Mrs. Wiggs* and also set in the Cabbage Patch, achieved best-seller status. Joseph Altsheler, born near

Glasgow, Kentucky, was nationally famous for his forty novels for boys in his Young Trailer series (1907–1917). Most popular and enduring of Kentucky writers for children is Annie Fellows Johnston (1863–1931), whose twelve Little Colonel novels were loved for forty years by girls all over the country, until their mores, values, and language became outdated. Born in Indiana, Johnston moved in 1898 with her four stepchildren to Peewee Valley, near Louisville, where she found inspiration in a child she met and in the near-antebellum way of life of the rural resort village.

Kentucky literature has come into its own in the twentieth century, as writers have come more and more to value and explore ways of life and modes of language native to their regions of the state. They tend not to impose, as earlier Kentucky writers usually did, idealized or overly general moral perspectives on their experience as they express it in their work. Beginning in the 1920s, Kentucky writers were major contributors to the southern literary Renascence and, more broadly, to a rich period of American literature. Elizabeth Madox Roberts (1881–1941), who began as a poet, came into her own as a fiction writer with her two major novels, *The Time of Man* (1926) and *The Great Meadow* (1930), the former about the struggles of a Kentucky tenant farming family and the latter about the frontier during the Revolutionary War. Born in Perryville, Roberts lived in Springfield until her death. She spent four crucial years of apprenticeship in Chicago. Her collection of poems for and about children, *Under the Tree* (1922), reflects the lyrical tradition of Robert Louis Stevenson.

Another writer of Roberts's era who had national impact was George Horace Lorimar (1867–1937) from Louisville, who, as the editor-in-chief of the *Saturday Evening Post* for thirty-nine years, influenced major writers and shaped literary taste. Under his guidance, the magazine evolved from its local Philadelphia beginnings into one of the most significant journals in the history of American literary life.

More in the mainstream of Kentucky, southern, and national literature than Roberts were the Kentucky writers associated with Vanderbilt University and the Agrarian movement. Robert Penn Warren (1905–1989), Allen Tate (1899–1979), Caroline Gordon (1895–1981), and Cleanth Brooks (1906–1994) made rich and crucial contributions to the literature of the region and the country: Warren, in poetry, fiction, and criticism; Tate, in poetry ("Ode to the Confederate Dead," 1927), fiction (*The Fathers,* 1938), and criti-

cism; Gordon, in fiction (*Aleck Maury, Sportsman,* 1934) and criticism; and Brooks, in criticism. Warren, from Guthrie; Gordon, also from Todd County; and Brooks, from Murray, all western Kentuckians, gravitated to Nashville, where Warren, Tate, and Brooks studied under John Crowe Ransom, the moving force behind the Fugitives and, later, New Criticism, which they all came to espouse. Tate, from Winchester, the only central Kentuckian in the group, and Warren contributed to the twelve essays that comprise the Agrarian manifesto, *I'll Take My Stand.*

Of these, Warren published most prolifically and variously. Widely considered the best and most influential writer Kentucky has produced, he wrote or edited more than fifty books. The most distinguished American writer of his era, he was the first national poet laureate, the recipient of a MacArthur Foundation Award, the Bollingen Prize for Poetry, and the National Book Award. Among many other awards and honors, he won three Pulitzer Prizes (1946, for *All the King's Men;* 1957, for *Promises* [poetry]; and 1980, for *Now and Then: Poems 1976–1978*). He remains the only Pulitzer recipient in both fiction and poetry.

His other major novels are *World Enough and Time* (1950), *Band of Angels* (1955), and *The Cave* (1959). In different ways, each treats the theme of the search for self, for a mooring sense of identity in the changing South still festering from the wounds of slavery and the Civil War. All Warren's novels, especially *The Cave,* received mixed reviews for their sometimes cumbersome prose. After *The Cave,* Warren did most of his creative work in poetry, coming of age as a poet after he turned sixty. He published twelve books of poetry, all well received, between 1957 and 1985.

Warren was also influential in the promulgation of New Criticism. He and Brooks, along with John T. Purser, published *An Approach to Literature* in 1936, and in 1938 he and Brooks brought out *Understanding Poetry,* textbooks that strongly influenced professors all over the country to adopt New Critical perspectives in their teaching.

Unlike the other Kentucky writers associated with the Vanderbilt group, Brooks's major work is in criticism. His *Modern Poetry and the Tradition* (1939) discusses the metaphysical tradition in English poetry and its relation to the formulation of meaning in modern poems, and *The Well-Wrought Urn: Studies in the Structure of Poetry* (1947) extends this idea, averring that meaning in a poem arises from the metaphor of its structure. In these volumes, his New Critical analyses of poems from throughout the history of English verse, including contemporary poems, are not only individually enlightening, but they also interpret the continuity of the tradition in ways that proved influential on the taste and sensibility of his era.

While the Agrarian fiction-writers and poets tended to explore the ramifications of southernness in the wake of the Civil War, another group of Kentucky writers examined what it means to be a Kentuckian, shaped by a particular landscape and language in the postmodern era. James Still (1906–), Jesse Stuart (1907–1984), and Harriette Arnow (1908–1986) focus on the culture of eastern Kentucky. Still and Stuart set their stories in the mountains, whereas Arnow also sets some of hers in northern industrial cities where mountain people migrated to find jobs. Still, in his spare, objective, and lyrical style, captures both the folk speech and the psychological realities of his characters in *River of Earth* (1940), his only novel, and in two later collections of short stories, *Pattern of a Man* (1976) and *The Run for the Elbertas* (1980). Much of his best work is in the short story. His first published volume, however, was poems, *Hounds on the Mountain* (1937), reissued in 1965. New and selected poems, *The Wolf-pen Poems,* was published in 1986. Many of his best short stories and poems appeared, particularly in the 1930s and 1940s, in journals such as the *Atlantic Monthly, Esquire,* the *Nation,* the *New Republic,* the *New Yorker, Poetry,* and the *Saturday Review.* The older Lucy Furman (1869–1958), from western Kentucky, was, like Still, associated with the Hindman Settlement School. While she worked there (1907–1924), she wrote a vivid account of the school and its founders, Katherine Petit and May Stone, *The Quare Women* (1923). She received the George Fort Milton Award in 1932 for her work as a southern woman writer.

Stuart, too, set most of his writing in the mountains, in his native W-Hollow in Greenup County in northeastern Kentucky. Like Still, he wrote without a social agenda, but, the opposite of Still, he became a popular writer and published voluminously: novels, short stories, poems, autobiography, and children's books. His early collection of poems, *Man with a Bull Tongue Plow* (1934), brought him national fame and is still one of his best-known books. His second novel, *Taps for Private Tussie* (1943), sold more than a million copies and won the Thomas Jefferson Award for the best southern book of the year. *Head o' W-Hollow* (1936) remains his most substantial volume of short stories, the genre in which he was most at home. *Be-*

yond Dark Hills (1938), an autobiography, and *The Beatinest Boy* (1953), a children's novel, are characterized, as is all his best work, by strong emotion, subjectivity, minimal attention to form, and a rushing fluency. Many of his books are not up to the standard of his best, and the critical reaction, even to his strongest work, was always mixed.

Arnow's trilogy of novels covers three important aspects of mountain life: the traditional way (*A Mountain Path,* 1936), mountain life as it was during the Great Depression (*Hunter's Horn,* 1949), and life as it was during World War II for emigrants from the mountains seeking work in the northern cities, where they tended to lose their cultural identity (*The Dollmaker,* 1954). Arnow, winner of the 1955 National Book Award for *The Dollmaker* and long recognized as an important American novelist, was more widely appreciated after an effective dramatization of *The Dollmaker,* featuring Jane Fonda, also the producer, was televised in 1983.

Other writers played important roles in the development of an Appalachian literature: Albert Stewart (1932–1996), prolific poet and founder of several workshops for Appalachian writers and of the literary journal *Appalachian Heritage*; and Jim Wayne Miller (1936–1996), a fiction writer and scholar who taught at Western Kentucky University and is, along with Still, a leading poet among Appalachian writers. Miller's outstanding volumes of poems are *Dialogue with a Dead Man* (1974); *The Mountains Have Come Closer* (1980), winner of the Thomas Wolfe Award; and *Vein of Words* (1985). Rebecca Caudill (1899–1985), a native of Harlan County, and Billy C. Clark (1928–), from Catlettsburg, both writers of excellent juvenile novels and other books, added to the sense of Appalachian Kentucky as a distinct place, rich in tradition and character. Caudill's memoir, *My Appalachia* (1967), contrasts the area as it was in her childhood to what it became. Clark's memoir of his boyhood, *A Long Row to Hoe* (1960), exemplifies the straightforward tone and style that characterize his work.

John Jacob Niles (1892–1980), born in Louisville and best known as a singer and early popularizer of folk music, has a place in Kentucky literature as a composer of ballad lyrics and collector of traditional Appalachian folk songs. A prodigy, he wrote "Go 'Way from My Window" when he was fifteen. Later, he both wrote and composed "I Wonder as I Wander," "Black Is the Color of My True Love's Hair," and "Jesus, Jesus, Rest Your Head." His one book of poems is

Brick Dust and Buttermilk (1977). Jean Ritchie (1922), from Viper, in Perry County, also a popularizer of folk music in the 1950s and 1960s, collected traditional ballads and wrote her own. She published an autobiography of her family, *Singing Family of the Cumberland* (1955).

Janice Holt Giles (1905–1979) is important, though she is not a native Kentuckian, for her fiction about the Kentucky frontier and especially the settlement of south-central Kentucky, Adair County, where she lived for thirty years, from 1949 until her death. Her Piney Ridge trilogy of historical novels (1950–1952) and her Kentucky trilogy (1953–1957) are well researched and ably written. Her popular appeal was considerable.

Harlan Hubbard (1900–1988), painter as well as writer, with his wife Anna lived and wrote for thirty-six years in the house they built in isolated Payne Hollow in Trimble County on the Ohio River. His clearly, gracefully written journals record a life of principle and strong belief in the virtue of conforming to natural rhythms and living simply among handmade accouterments. Not socially programmatic like the Agrarians, his thought foreshadows Wendell Berry's in its fervid anti-industrialism and anticonsumerism. His *Shantyboat* (1953) recounts his and Anna's voyage (1944–1951) down the Ohio and Mississippi Rivers; *Shantyboat in the Bayous* (1990) completes his account of that adventure. *Payne Hollow* (1973) tells the story of their subsequent life. His *Journals, 1929–1944* was published in 1987.

Foremost among regional writers identified strongly with a particular place is Wendell Berry (1934–) of Henry Country in northern Kentucky, on the Kentucky River. An heir of the Agrarians, Berry devotes his poetry, fiction, and essays alike to probing issues of the proper, workable human relationship to the earth in an industrial age. Berry began as a poet, publishing *The Broken Ground* in 1964. He has since published twelve volumes of poetry, all of it directly or indirectly concerned with ecological issues, as well as with the human joys and conflicts that are the substance of poetry.

Berry's fiction more explicitly articulates his sense that with the technological revolution in farming that followed World War II came the destruction of a healthy, workable way of life. In *Nathan Coulter* (1960), a novel set before World War I, farming is done by hand and with mule-drawn machinery. In *A Place on Earth* (1967), Mat Feltner struggles with his sense of stewardship of the land in a time of technological transition. In *The Memory of Old Jack* (1974), the action spans only the death day of ninety-two-year-old Jack Beechum, whose thoughts range backward as he dies and comprise a microcosm of the history of small farming in Kentucky. He realizes that this revolution and its destructive effects on the land and community are irrevocable.

But Berry's prophetic voice has been most widely heard and appreciated in his essays. Beginning with *The Long-Legged House* (1969) and continuing in his third volume of essays, *A Continuous Harmony* (1972), Berry contemplates the loss of harmony between man and nature and analyzes the destructive effects thereof. *The Hidden Wound* (1970), his second book of essays, analyzes in historical, literary, and agricultural perspectives the lingering wounds of slavery and racism. Although *The Hidden Wound* is imaginatively insightful and moving, *The Unsettling of America* (1977) is Berry's most profound polemical and literary accomplishment. More one sustained piece than a collection of disparate essays, *Unsettling* traces the history of American attitudes toward the land and the earth as the substance and basis of human being. Berry's command of historical fact, as well as of literary tradition, informs the clarity, passion, and pure intelligence of his prose. Berry is one of the best and most influential writers Kentucky has yet produced.

Another essayist, Letcher County lawyer and self-taught historian Harry Caudill (1922–1990), helped break the ground Berry later worked. Caudill's *Night Comes to the Cumberlands: A Biography of a Depressed Area* (1963) traces the effects on eastern Kentuckians of exploitation of the land by big corporations and by local strip-miners. Although his books were criticized in some quarters for their lack of documentation, Kentucky historian Thomas D. Clark calls Caudill's voice one of the most important in the state's history. His passionate essays brought to national attention the plight of Appalachia. His *My Land Is Dying* (1972) analyzes explicitly the destructiveness of strip mining, and *A Darkness at Dawn* (1976) looks at what Caudill sees as the bleak future of Appalachian Kentucky. Caudill also wrote two novels that treat the same issues and landscape as his polemical writings. *Courier-Journal* writer John Fetterman's *Stinking Creek: The Portrait of a Small Mountain Community in Appalachia* (1967) also focused national attention on economic and social problems in the mountains.

Fiction writers Ed McClanahan (1932–) from Brooksville in northern Kentucky, Gurney Norman

(1937–) from Hazard, and Bobbie Ann Mason (1940–) from Mayfield in western Kentucky all, in their different ways, explore the same problems of alienation and the search for community and a viable self in a changing world losing its traditional coherence. These three, along with Berry and James Baker Hall (1935–), studied at the University of Kentucky, and four of the five (excepting Mason) were Stegner Fellows at Stanford University. McClanahan's *The Natural Man* (1983) hilariously traces one Harry Eastep's coming of age in the early 1950s in northern Kentucky. Norman's *Divine Right's Trip* (1971), a quintessential 1960s saga first published in *The Last Whole Earth Catalogue*, follows D.R.'s quest for adventure and meaning to California, into the counterculture, and back to Kentucky.

Mason, a consummate short-story writer whose first collection, *Shiloh and Other Stories* (1982), won the PEN/Faulkner Award, writes about western Kentuckians with an unerring ear for the rhythms of their speech. Typically, her characters, adrift in a world of strip malls and television, struggle for some coherence in their existence. Mason has also written three novels, *In Country* (1985), about the effects of the Vietnam War; *Spence + Lila* (1988), about a western Kentucky couple coming to terms with old age and death; and *Feather Crowns* (1993), a historical novel about the birth of quintuplets in western Kentucky at the turn of the century. In her memoir *Clear Springs* (1999), Mason describes the country culture that shaped her. Hall, a photographer as well as a writer, has published novels (including *Music for a Broken Piano*, 1983) and poetry (including *Getting It on Up to the Brag*, 1975, and *Stopping on the Edge to Wave*, 1988).

Several other writers' works center on a particular region of Kentucky and develop a strong sense of place. George Ella Lyon (1949–) from Harlan, versatile and prolific, has published poetry (*Mountain*, 1983, and *Catalpa*, 1993), plays (*Braids*, 1995), juvenile novels (*Red Rover, Red Rover*, 1989), a novel (*With a Hammer for My Heart*, 1996), but most notably a series of distinguished books for children, including *Father Time and the Day Boxes* (1985) and *Who Came Down That Road?* (1992), about the animals and all the people, from the Native Americans to truckers on I-75, who have traveled the Wilderness Road. Mary Ann Taylor-Hall's (1937–) short stories have been included in *Best American* collections, and her novel *Come and Go, Molly Snow* (1995), set in Lexington and the north Bluegrass, has been widely praised for its

emotional integrity and lyrical style. Richard Taylor (1941–), a poet (*Bluegrass,* 1975, and *Earth Bones,* 1979), has also written a poemlike historical novel, *Girty* (1977), which recreates the life of the Kentucky frontier renegade, Simon Girty.

Earlier than these regional figures are three more broadly focused writers: journalist and novelist A. B. Guthrie Jr. (1901–91), the Trappist monk Thomas Merton (1915–1968), and critic, reviewer, and novelist Elizabeth Hardwick (1916–). Guthrie, a native of Indiana, grew up on the Montana frontier but came to Kentucky in 1929 as a reporter and editor for the *Lexington Leader* and stayed for twenty-seven years. At Harvard as a Nieman Fellow in 1945–1946, he began writing his trilogy of novels about the West, and continued work on *The Big Sky* (1947) during the five years he taught creative writing at the University of Kentucky. *The Way West* (1949) won the Pulitzer Prize and was followed by *These Thousand Hills* (1956), which concluded the trilogy. *The Blue Hen's Chick* (1965), a memoir, recounts his years in Kentucky.

Merton, primarily a poet, autobiographer, and religious writer, was born in Prades, France, of a New Zealander father and an American (Ohio) mother. Educated in France, Bermuda, England, and the United States, he attended Clare College, Cambridge, and was graduated from Columbia University. Although he continued to write poetry all his life (*The Collected Poems,* 1977), he won fame as a religious writer with the publication of *The Seven Storey Moountain* (1948), which recounts his conversion to Christianity and his entrance into Gethsemani, the Trappist monastery near Bardstown. He then published more than a dozen contemplative works before he was accidentally electrocuted in 1968 in Bangkok, Thailand, where he was attending a conference.

Elizabeth Hardwick, a Lexington native, wrote novels (*The Ghostly Lover,* 1945; *The Simple Truth,* 1955; and *Sleepless Nights,* 1979, which is autobiographical) but is most widely known as a reviewer and critic. Her essays, distinguished by sharpness of insight and elegance of expression, are collected in *A View of My Own* (1962), *Seduction and Betrayal* (1974), *Bartleby in Manhattan* (1983), and *Sights Unseen* (1998). Married to poet Robert Lowell from 1949 to 1972, she was in 1963 one of the founders of the *New York Review of Books,* to which she has contributed many touchstone essays.

Hollis S. Summers (1916–1987), poet and novelist, who was born in Eminence and grew up in Madison-ville, published several volumes of poetry, including *The Walks Near Athens* (1959), and four novels, including *How They Chose the Dead* (1973), during a long teaching career, mainly at Ohio State.

A younger group of writers, born in the 1920s and early 1930s, includes Guy Davenport (1927–) and Walter Tevis (1928–1984). Davenport, a Harvard graduate and Rhodes Scholar from South Carolina, came in 1963 to teach at the University of Kentucky. A learned classicist and traditional man of letters, he has published more than twenty books of poetry, translations, historical fiction, and criticism. Although too erudite and allusive to appeal to popular taste, Davenport's work ranges imaginatively over the panoply of world cultures. In the best journals, his work has been both praised for its purity of style and its original eclecticism, and excoriated for its cerebral austerity. A full-time writer since he was awarded a MacArthur Fellowship in 1990, Davenport also has won prizes for both poetry and fiction. His first book of short fiction, *Tatlin! Six Stories* (1974), brought him national attention, and he followed with *Da Vinci's Bicycle: Ten Stories* (1979). His translation, *Archilochus, Sappho, and Alkman* (1980), was nominated for the American Book Award. The forty critical essays in *The Geography of the Imagination* (1981), like most of Davenport's work, pleased some critics and was seen by others as precious and irrelevant.

Walter Tevis, primarily a writer of science fiction, in 1959, after many hours of research in the pool parlor of the Phoenix Hotel in Lexington, published *The Hustler,* about pool-playing Fast Eddie Felson and his nemesis, the old pro Minnesota Fats. The movie version, with Paul Newman as Eddie and Jackie Gleason as Fats, was nominated for eight Academy Awards and won three Oscars. Before his death at fifty-six, Tevis published *The Man Who Fell to Earth* (1963), which also became a well-received film; *The Queen's Gambit* (1983), about a woman chess champion; and *The Color of Money* (1984), a sequel to *The Hustler.* Tevis's taut, realistic style effectively evokes the drama and loneliness of one-on-one competition.

Jim Peyton (1926–) and Leon Driskell (1932–1995) each published one excellent collection of short fiction: the former, *Zion's Cause* (1987), a series of related stories about fully realized, hilarious characters in a western Kentucky town; and the latter, *Passing Through* (1983), similarly constructed, about a family in Owen County whose adventures are comic but whose triumph over loss is real and affecting.

Contemporary writers whose focus is not primarily on life in Kentucky include Hunter Thompson (1939–), the inventor of Gonzo journalism (*Fear and Loathing in Las Vegas,* 1972); Michael Dorris (1945–1997), whose best-selling work about the plight of Native Americans, *The Broken Cord* (1989), was the winner of the National Book Critics Circle Award for nonfiction; Gayl Jones (1949–), African American novelist from Lexington, whose *Corregidora* (1975) and *Eva's Man* (1976) are novels of raw emotional power; Sallie Bingham (1937–), from Louisville, fiction writer, playwright, and founder of the Kentucky Foundation for Women, which supports Kentucky women artists and writers, and of *The American Voice,* an influential literary quarterly; Marsha Norman (1949–), also a Louisvillian, whose *'Night, Mother* (1982), originally produced at Actors Theatre of Louisville, won the 1983 Pulitzer Prize for drama; and Barbara Kingsolver (1955–), who grew up in Carlisle and, along with poetry, has published an excellent novel, *The Bean Trees* (1987), about a Kentucky woman who moves to Arizona, as Kingsolver did in 1977. Her other novels are *Animal Dreams* (1990), *Pigs in Heaven* (1993), and *The Poisonwood Bible* (1998).

Also doing promising work are four writers presently associated with the University of Louisville: poets Sarah Gorham and Jeffrey Skinner, founders of Sarabande Books, which publishes poetry and short fiction; Sena Jeter Naslund, fiction writer; and Frederick Smock, poet and founding editor of *The American Voice.*

Kentucky literature, after a slow start during its first century, subsequently rises into three major waves of accomplishment. The first comprises the best-selling popular writers of the late nineteenth and early twentieth centuries. The momentum began in 1852 with Stowe's *Uncle Tom's Cabin* and Stephen Collins Foster's (1825–1864) "My Old Kentucky Home," the latter of which engendered the myth of an idyllic antebellum Kentucky. Further enhancing the outside world's view of Kentucky as a special place apart were James Lane Allen, John Fox Jr., and Alice Hegan Rice, who continued the process into the first decades of the twentieth century, when Kentuckians dominated the best-seller lists as no other state's writers before had. Part of this tide of popular Kentucky writing was Annie Fellows Johnston's Little Colonel books; Madison Cawein's poetry; and a now little-known melodrama by Charles T. Dazey (1855–1938), "In Old Kentucky"

(1892), which was likely seen by over thirty million people either as a play or in one of its several movie versions; and Judge James H. Mulligan's (1844–1915) poem "In Kentucky" (1902), which was reproduced on over a million postcards and is thus easily the most widely distributed poem written in Kentucky, or about Kentucky.

The second wave of accomplishment, the fine writing of the 1920s, 1930s, and into the 1940s includes the work of the Agrarians, much of it popular, such as the novels of Warren, the poetry and fiction of Stuart, the novels of Roberts, the editorial work of Lorimer at the *Saturday Evening Post,* the contemplative writings of Merton, the ballads of Niles, and the western historical novels of Guthrie. Although Still, Gordon, and Tate never were as popular, their work is part of the remarkable achievement of this era in Kentucky literature.

The third wave comprises the remarkable Renaissance in Kentucky literature that began in the 1970s and continues into the twenty-first century, including the work of Arnow, Giles, Hardwick, Davenport, Berry, Mason, McClanahan, and others of the University of Kentucky-Stanford group, and continues with the ongoing work of Marsha Norman, Lyon, Jones, and the Louisville writers, Gorham, Skinner, Jeter, along with others who are still mining Kentucky's rich vein.

Jane Gentry Vance

See also Agrarians; Appalachian Literature; Fugitives, The

Louise Cowan, *The Fugitive Group: A Literary History* (1959); John E. Kleber, ed., *The Kentucky Encyclopedia* (1992); Arthur K. Moore, *The Frontier Mind* (1957); Algernon D. Thompson and Lawrence S. Thompson, *The Kentucky Novel* (1953); John Wilson Townsend, ed., *Kentucky in American Letters,* Vols. 1 and 2 (1913); Dorothy Edwards Townsend, ed., *Kentucky in American Letters,* Vol. 3 (1976); William S. Ward, *A Literary History of Kentucky* (1988).

KENTUCKY, UNIVERSITY OF

Since its founding in 1865, the University of Kentucky in Lexington has evolved from a small agricultural and mechanical college into the state's flagship public research university with more than 24,000 students in its undergraduate, graduate, and professional colleges and schools. The original funding for the A. and M. College, which began as a division of the private Kentucky University, was $9,900 annually from the endowment created in 1862 by the federal Morrill Land Grant Act.

In 1878 the A. and M. College separated from Kentucky University and became the Agricultural and Mechanical College of Kentucky. The campus was moved to a new location, the present one, on South Limestone Street, on fifty acres that were the City of Lexington's fairground and park, and which had been, during the Civil War, a bivouac for Union troops. In 1880 the Kentucky legislature allocated the proceeds from a property tax to the college, the first state support for the school.

James K. Patterson, a historian who had become president of the A. and M. College in 1869, was the first president of the new institution. He used his personal savings to supplement the $60,000 that Lexington and Fayette County donated for the construction of new buildings. Since the Morrill Act did not restrict the curriculum to practical arts, Patterson introduced the liberal arts. He also provided for the enrollment of women in regular degree programs.

In 1916 the name was changed from State University (which it became in 1908) to the University of Kentucky. It is one of ninety-three state universities and land-grant institutions in the United States, and one of fifty-nine Research I universities, as designated by the Carnegie Foundation. It comprises eleven colleges, five professional schools, and a graduate school (founded in 1912).

In 1949 President Herman L. Donovan, at the urging of the chairman of the history department, Thomas D. Clark, established the University of Kentucky Press and hired Bruce F. Denbo of the Louisiana State University Press as the first director. They oversaw the building of a list of publications emphasizing southern and American history, literary criticism, and Kentucky culture. The press was reorganized as the University Press of Kentucky in 1969. The Albert B. Chandler Medical Center, including colleges of medicine, nursing, dentistry, and pharmacy, was founded in 1954. In 1969 Otis A. Singletary, a southern historian, assumed the presidency just as the legislature reduced the University's funding from 60 to 40 percent of the higher-education appropriation, when several other universities came into the state system. Issues of state funding did not abate during Singletary's eighteen-year term. In 1997 the legislature removed thirteen of the University's fourteen community colleges from its governance. In 1998 the new William T. Young Library opened.

Other significant presidencies include the short incumbencies of John W. Oswald (1963–1968) and David P. Roselle (1987–1989), both of whom enhanced the intellectual life and support of the liberal arts at the University.

Among important writers who have studied at the University are Elizabeth Hardwick, Harry Caudill, Billy C. Clark, Walter Tevis, Albert Stewart, Ed McClanahan, Wendell Berry, and Bobbie Ann Mason. Southern historians and writers who have taught at the University include Clement Eaton, Charles Roland, Thomas D. Clark, A. B. Guthrie Jr., Hollis Summers, Robert Hazel, Harry Caudill, Wendell Berry, Guy Davenport, Ed McClanahan, James Baker Hall, Gurney Norman, Percival Everett, George Ella Lyon, and Nikky Finney.

Jane Gentry Vance

See also Kentucky, Literature of.

Carl B. Cone, *The University of Kentucky: A Pictorial History* (1989); James F. Hopkins, *The University of Kentucky: Origins and Early Years* (1951); John E. Kleber, ed., *The Kentucky Encyclopedia* (1992); Charles Talbert, *The University of Kentucky: The Maturing Years* (1965).

KENTUCKY TRAGEDY

Although a well-regarded Kentucky congressional and state representative, Colonel Solomon P. Sharp was alleged by his political enemies to have seduced Ann Cook, producing a stillborn illegitimate child in June 1820. Sharp's paternity has not been verified. Although knowledge of the affair was publicly known, John U. Waring, a violent man who claimed in a threat against Sharp to have "stabbed six men," circulated the rumors. Undeterred, Sharp accepted the post of state attorney general in 1821. Meanwhile, Jereboam O. Beauchamp, twenty-one, a Simpson County lawyer who represented Sharp on several occasions, married Ann Cook, thirty-eight, in mid-June 1824. She claimed to be pregnant, but the marriage produced no children.

During violent political fighting in 1825 between the New Court and the Old Court parties, the charge of seduction against Sharp, the New Court candidate, was again circulated by Waring; this time, he insinuated that Sharp had claimed in defense that Ann's baby was mulatto. Whether Sharp made this claim or was again victim of Waring's efforts has not been determined; nevertheless, Sharp defeated the Old Court candidate. In the early hours of November 7, 1825, Sharp was stabbed to death in his house on Madison Street at Frankfort. Within the month, Beauchamp was indicted and held for trial. In May 1826, Ann Cook was acquitted, but Beauchamp was convicted and sentenced to hang on June 16, 1826.

The judge extended the execution date to July 7 at Beauchamp's request for time to produce a detailed justification of his actions. He wrote and attempted to publish the *Confession* while detained with Ann for six weeks in a dungeonlike pit in the Frankfort jail. In the rambling document, he claims to have pursued justice and restitution for Ann's lost honor, and he implicates several trial witnesses in a plot to cover up mitigating circumstances and to commit perjury and bribery. These libelous accusations prevented publication of the *Confession* before the execution.

On July 6, the lovers made two unsuccessful suicide attempts with laudanum. They persuaded the jailer to allow them to remain together, and the next day, a self-inflicted wound with a knife dispatched Ann just before the execution; however, Beauchamp's attempt was unsuccessful, and he was revived. At the gallows, he requested that "Bonaparte's Retreat from Moscow" be played by the Twenty-Second Regiment musicians, and he was hanged in front of over five thousand spectators. The two were buried together in a single coffin.

The most interesting document produced by the case is Beauchamp's impassioned *Confession* (1826), a sensational collection of partial truth, misinformation, lies, and self-righteousness. Many of Beauchamp's accusations and views are refuted in the *Vindication of the Character of the Late Col. Solomon P. Sharp* (1827). Although a detailed examination, the *Vindication,* written by Sharp's brother Dr. Leander J. Sharp, is suspect for its self-interest and the exaggerated reputations attributed to Cook and Beauchamp. Also circulated were the *Letters of Ann Cook* (1826), the authenticity of which is disputed. In *Beauchamp's Trial* (1826), a transcription made at the trial, J. G. Dana and R. S. Thomas suggest that trial testimony muddled the truth with contradictory testimony and hearsay, and Beauchamp, though guilty, was convicted on circumstantial evidence.

In novels inspired by the story, the historical events appear intact, but the demands of popular entertainment have shaped the product, focusing more on the melodramatic loyalty of Ann and Beauchamp's final hours. In the most successful treatment, *World Enough and Time* (1950), Robert Penn Warren emphasizes the backdrop of poverty, depravity, and ruin on the American frontier. Echoing Beauchamp's *Confessions* with a heightened nineteenth-century diction and an allegorical network of references, Warren's impassioned narrator reviews the fictional Jeremiah Beaumont's long-ignored manuscript to uncover existential motives behind the rage and violence that accompany the civilization of a wilderness. Warren changes the historical conclusion, inventing an escape to the heart of a depraved frontier wilderness, which reveals the sinister political machinations behind the plot and emphasizes the southern theme of destiny in lost causes and high ideals.

From an earlier attempt entitled *Beauchampe; or, The Kentucky Tragedy, A Tale of Passion* (1842), William Gilmore Simms produced two novels, *Charlemont* and *Beauchampe: A Sequel to Charlemont* (1856), included among his "border domestic novels." In *Charlemont*, Simms relates the events of Margaret Cooper's seduction, the loss of an honorable lover, the death of her illegitimate child, and social banishment. In *Beauchampe*, Simms restores the historical names of the participants, following Beauchamp's *Confession* closely. Working in what he called "the moral imaginative," Simms defines many of the striking social issues raised by the case, but he fails to achieve any significant character development, relying on didactic melodrama to promote fashionable pieties of masculine dignity and honor and of feminine passivity and innocence.

Numerous forgettable versions of the story were circulated in newspapers and magazines, such as Mary E. MacMichael's "The Kentucky Tragedy: A Tale—Founded on Facts of Actual Occurrence" (*Burton's Gentleman's Magazine*, April 1838). In a less obvious use of Beauchamp's story, Charles Fenno Hoffman's *Greyslaer: A Romance of the Mohawk* (1840) is of interest only as an imitation of James Fenimore Cooper's frontier romance. In *The Monks of Monk Hall* (1844), George Lippard makes political use of the seduction theme to promote the importance of antiseduction laws.

As stage tragedy, the story seldom rises above sentimental romance. Although incomplete, scenes from Edgar Allan Poe's verse drama *Politian* were published in *The Messenger* (1835) and in *The Raven and Other Poems* (1845). Poe creates the neurotic and beautiful Lelage of sixteenth-century Rome, who has been seduced and dishonored by a courtier, Castiglione. Politian, a "dreamer" and British Earl of Leicester, is moved by the defenseless beauty and repulsed by earthly vanities. Poe takes the story to Politian's first challenge in the street, an episode that Beauchamp probably borrowed from an incident that occurred between Sharp and Waring. With an exotic setting and allegorical references, the play exhibits Poe's romantic defense of spontaneity and beauty in a banal, mechanized world. The verse is of interest for Poe's use of the accentual meter and experimental lineation.

In *Conrad and Eudora; or, The Death of Alonzo: A Tragedy* (1834), a verse drama set in Frankfort, Kentucky, Thomas Holley Chivers displays a manipulative, vindictive woman seeking revenge for her dishonor. In several versions of the play, including *Leoni, the Orphan of Venice*, Chivers attempts to discover a motive in the excessive influence of emotion and passion, but he does not escape sentimental posturing. Other dramatic versions include Charlotte Barnes's *Octavia Bragaldi* (1837), a sensational production set in fifteenth-century Milan, and John Savage's dramatic treatment of Simm's *Beauchampe, Sybil* (1858), a cautionary tale against revenge.

Except for Warren, writers have displayed little interest in the details of this event. The mystery remains whether Beauchamp was a party to political conspiracy, was persuaded by a dishonored and vengeful Ann Cook to murder Sharp, or was merely incensed by the "mulatto" accusation. More likely, he was motivated by some combination of all three. As for Beauchamp's defense of feminine honor, a month before Sharp's murder, Ruth Reed of Simpson County made a claim against Jereboam O. Beauchamp for support of a bastard male child born June 1824. Ten years after the execution, Waring shot to death Samuel Q. Richardson, one of Beauchamp's defense lawyers, but was acquitted. Waring was murdered in 1846.

Stephen R. Whited

Robert D. Bamberg, ed., *The Confession of Jereboam O. Beauchamp* (1966); J. Winston Coleman, *The Beauchamp-Sharp Tragedy: An Episode of Kentucky History During the Middle 1820's* (1950); William Goldhurst, "The New Revenge Tragedy: Comparative Treatments of the Beauchamp Case," *Southern Literary Journal* 22.1 (1989); Loren J. Kallsen, ed., *The Kentucky Tragedy: A Problem in Romantic Attitudes* (1963); Arthur Hobson Quinn, *A History of the American Drama from the Beginning to the Civil War* (1923) and *American Fiction: An Historical Critical Survey* (1936); Jack E. Surrency, "The Kentucky Tragedy and Its Primary Sources," in J. Lasley Dameron and James W. Mathews, eds., *No Fairer Land: Studies in Southern Literature Before 1900* (1986).

KENYON REVIEW

Kenyon College, a small liberal-arts college located in Gambier, Ohio, became intimately associated with the Southern Literary Renascence after Gordon Keith Chalmers, its newly elected president, invited John Crowe Ransom in 1937 to leave Vanderbilt University to accept a position as professor of poetry. The appointment was the most important one Chalmers would make in his long tenure and arguably the most important appointment ever made at Kenyon, for it soon altered Kenyon's reputation profoundly. At Vanderbilt, considerable consternation ensued about losing a poet and critic with the national visibility Ransom then enjoyed. A member of the Vanderbilt faculty since 1914, Ransom bore the scars of several battles, but a vigorous enough counteroffer might have kept him in Nashville. Believing, like many, that Vanderbilt did not do enough to retain its native son, Allen Tate had predicted that if Ransom left so would promising undergraduates Randall Jarrell and Robert Lowell, who had both chosen Vanderbilt in order to study with Ransom. Jarrell and Lowell indeed followed their mentor to Gambier, as would Peter Taylor in the following year.

Chalmers, who had been acting on the advice of Robert Frost, would have no reason to regret his careful courting of John and Robb Reavill Ransom. Ransom quickly became identified with Kenyon, and during his first year in Gambier the president and Ransom made plans to establish the *Kenyon Review,* with Ransom as editor and Philip Blair Rice of the philosophy department as managing editor. In winter 1939, the first issue of the review was published; for the next thirty years, it continued to command attention as a major literary journal. For its first twenty years, the journal was under Ransom's leadership.

Because Ransom helped define the New Criticism, especially during its first decade, the *Review* consistently published excellent New Criticism; indeed, the magazine published some of the most influential essays of the century, including some by Ransom himself. Rice ensured, however, that the magazine not be exclusively an organ of the New Criticism. He attracted such New York intellectuals as Philip Rahv, Isaac Rosenfeld, and Lionel Trilling (the journal's advisory editor from 1942 to 1963) to the pages of the *Kenyon Review.* In 1951 *KR* published *The Kenyon Critics,* an anthology of outstanding essays that had appeared in its numbers. Poet Ransom ensured that poetry of a very high quality appeared regularly, and that record is also extraordi-

nary. His students Jarrell and Lowell published some of their first work there (Ransom was especially receptive to Jarrell's work). Among southern poets, Robert Penn Warren and Allen Tate also found *KR* to be welcoming, but talent rather than region was uppermost in Ransom's decisions. Nor was fiction neglected in the *Review.* When the *Southern Review,* which had emphasized fiction, expired in 1942, the *Kenyon Review* was its natural beneficiary. The roster of *KR* fiction writers includes an abundance of national and international authors, as was emphasized in 1961 when Salem Press published *Gallery of Modern Fiction: Stories from the Kenyon Review.* Of the twenty-four stories included, three were by southerners (Flannery O'Connor, Peter Taylor, and Elizabeth Hardwick).

Within a decade of its first issue, the *Kenyon Review* was generally ranked as one of the most influential literary quarterlies of the twentieth century. Its chief rivals were the *Partisan Review,* the *Sewanee Review,* and the *Hudson Review.* Although its appeal was to an intellectual elite, the *Kenyon Review*'s position mirrors the dominance of the New Criticism in English departments of American colleges and universities. The *Review* helped bring that dominance about.

So did the Kenyon School of English, which Ransom and Chalmers, building on the success of *KR,* set about planning soon after Ransom arrived. With a grant from the Rockefeller Foundation, beginning in summer 1947, the program brought graduate students to campus to discuss literary criticism with Kenyon Review Fellows. The southern flavor of the Fellows was noticeable but not dominant: Cleanth Brooks, Tate, Ransom. They were joined with the likes of Eric Bentley, Richard Chase, F. O. Matthiessen, Austin Warren, William Empson, Rahv, René Wellek, Mark Schorer, and Yvor Winters. For financial reasons, in 1950 the school moved to Indiana University, where it became the School of Letters. (Ransom remained on the board and taught sporadically at the school.) If Ransom helped make his an age of criticism, he conceived the Kenyon Review Fellowships (1953–1958) to provide promising new poets and fiction writers as well as critics financial support to pursue their craft.

By then, the influence of the *Review* was on the wane. Several new literary reviews had come into being, and *KR* seemed increasingly of the establishment. Ransom's energies were less intense, though he took a keen interest in the choice of his successor and worked hard to try to convince Randall Jarrell to accept the post. Eventually, associate editor Robie Macauley accepted. Macauley attempted to make the review "new," but it could not regain the position of an earlier era. George Lanning succeeded Macauley in 1966 and served until 1970, when the College decided that it could no longer afford to publish the journal. The College reversed that decision in the 1980s, concluding that the heritage was too important: Kenyon would honor that rich heritage by publishing a journal that, in the words of David H. Lynn, the editor in 1997, aimed to "straddle a fence between the creative communities of poets and fiction writers and playwrights and the academy where criticism and theory have increasingly grown inward gazing."

Although by the time Ransom arrived in Gambier, he had abandoned his Agrarian emphases and southern patriotism, there is a certain Agrarian flavor in his living his final three decades in the village of Gambier in rural Knox County. (Through the years, many southern writers would visit him there.) It also seems appropriate that the modest grave of John Crowe Ransom would lie in the cemetery directly behind Chalmers Library.

Joseph M. Flora

See also Agrarians; New Criticism; Vanderbilt University.

Marian Janssen, The "Kenyon Review," 1939–1970: A Critical History (1990); Thomas Daniel Young, Gentleman in a Dustcoat: A Biography of John Crowe Ransom (1976).

KEY WEST, FLORIDA

A longtime favorite of pirates, wreckers, smugglers, and other outlaws and misfits, Key West is known less for its influence on traditional southern literature than as a home and setting for a number of contemporary writers. Among its most famous proponents was Ernest Hemingway, who saw Key West as some of "the last good country," and an outpost of eccentrics, outlaws, artists, and nonconformists—a reputation it retains to this day. The influence of the island's outlaw culture of individuality, excess, and decadence can be seen in the work of playwright Tennessee Williams, another longtime resident who was declared an "honorary Conch" by the Key West natives. Writers who have made "Cayo Hueso" their home at one time or another include Wallace Stevens; Elizabeth Bishop, who wrote much of her Pulitzer Prize–winning collection Poems: North and South here; John Hersey; Philip Caputo;

Peter Taylor; James Merrill; Richard Wilbur; Joseph Lash; Thomas McGuane, who set his novels 92 in the Shade and The Bushwhacked Piano partly or completely in the Keys; Alison Lurie; Annie Dillard; and many others. It has also been the favorite haunt of a number of artists and musicians, among them Jimmy Buffett, who has done much to perpetuate the culture and life-style of the Keys through his songs. Ironically, Key West, the southernmost point in the continental United States, remained in Federal control throughout the Civil War.

Charles Oldham

See also Florida, Literature of.

KING, MARTIN LUTHER, JR.

Martin Luther King Jr. (1929–1968) was born in Atlanta, Georgia, to a family steeped in a tradition of Baptist ministry and political action. The church, long a center for African American activism and expression, provided King with a tradition, an ideology, and—perhaps most helpfully—a language that would underpin his efforts when he ventured to spread a "gospel of freedom" through the South and beyond. King would make the word into an effective and complex weapon against the system of legalized racism that existed in the 1950s and 1960s.

King studied sociology at Morehouse College and theology at Crozer Theological Seminary and Boston University. He was thus able to bring to bear on current events an academician's reserve of historical, classical, and philosophical commentary, as well as biblical teaching. Even a cursory survey of King's own writing suggests how essential the word was to the development of his political conscience and to the furtherance of his political agenda. Some examples: "The Negro and the Constitution" (1944), an essay written for a high-school oratorical contest; his doctoral dissertation, A Comparison of the Conceptions of God in the Thinking of Paul Tillich and Henry Nelson Wieman (1955); articles written for the popular press and for the newsletter of the Southern Christian Leadership Conference, of which he was president; the "Letter from Birmingham Jail" (1963) addressing clergymen who opposed the SCLC's direct action in their city; a series of books. King's first book, Stride Toward Freedom: The Montgomery Story (1958), sets out—

alongside the story of the bus boycott and his own experience of that campaign—his program for nonviolent direct action. This mix of history, memoir, and manifesto is typical of King.

Though King wrote a prodigious amount solely for publication, it was in oratory that he excelled. The "I Have a Dream" speech, delivered before civil-rights marchers in Washington, D.C. (August 28, 1963), has become a rhetorical model for American students. The speech is notable for the clarity and beauty of its language, and for the parallel phrases that take their rhythm and structure from the high-flying sermon and their content from the regional detail of the American landscape. Its combination of effects is reminiscent of Walt Whitman's poetry. King's sensitivity to the poetic in language and his familiarity with a range of secular as well as religious poetry is frequently in evidence. A sermon on "The Birth of a New Nation," given at Dexter Avenue Baptist Church in Montgomery, Alabama (April 7, 1957) includes lines from an old spiritual, a hymn, and Shakespeare's *Othello.* "Letter from Birmingham Jail" quotes Eliot's *Murder in the Cathedral.* The speech he gave when he accepted the Nobel Prize for Peace (December 10, 1964) concludes with a reference to Keats's "Ode on a Grecian Urn."

King's most remarkable oration—fortunately still preserved on film—may have been the one delivered at Mason Temple in Memphis, Tennessee (April 3, 1968), where he had gone to support the city's striking garbage workers. In this speech, often called "I've Been to the Mountaintop," King surveys, as if in a vision, the classical and biblical history that brought his audience to this moment of decision and action. King makes a comparison that his audience would have recognized from the Bible and from gospel songs that liken the struggle of African Americans to the Jews' bittersweet escape from slavery and their subsequent exile and wandering. Surveying his own life to this point, King, clearly weary, evokes the image of Moses gazing out on the promised land he will never reach. It is a prophetic moment, for King was fated to enact a form of that biblical story on the balcony of the Lorraine Motel, where he was assassinated the next day.

King has been criticized for the awkwardness of some of his language, which appears in sharp contrast to the grace of the rest. Even *Time* magazine, when it selected King as "Man of the Year," took him to task for metaphors that "can be downright embarrassing" (January 3, 1964). In "Letter from Birmingham Jail," for instance, segregation's effects are likened to the de-

formities caused by Thalidomide; in the Nobel Prize speech, the Civil Rights Act becomes "a superhighway of justice." Such choices, of which he made relatively few, attest to how young a man—how young a writer—King was, not yet forty when he died. And they attest to the fact that, whether he was in Birmingham or Oslo, he was always having to respond quickly to a volatile political situation and to address an American audience whose experiences were diverse and whose expectations were divided. King's work as an author and orator must always be considered in connection with the exigencies of his larger project, which was humanitarian rather than aesthetic.

Amber Vogel

See also Birmingham, Alabama; Civil Rights Movement; Clergy; "Letter from Birmingham Jail"; Memphis, Tennessee; Oratory; Preaching; Race Relations; Racism.

Martin Luther King Jr., *Stride Toward Freedom: The Montgomery Story* (1958), *Why We Can't Wait* (1964), and *The Papers of Martin Luther King, Jr.,* ed. Clayborne Carson (1992–); David L. Lewis, *King: A Biography* (1978).

KOREAN WAR

Sandwiched between the glorious achievement of victory in World War II and the ignominy of defeat in the Vietnam War, the Korean War is a strange kind of lost cause. The police-action conflict in the early 1950s on the Korean Peninsula involved plenty of American troops, and it produced a few remarkable military moments, but somehow the war failed to register very deeply on the national memory. Even as other matters have pushed themselves into positions of greater prominence, however, there are discernible traces of the Korean War in the literature of the South.

Colonel Bull Meecham, an archetypal southern military man who lords over the world as drawn in Pat Conroy's *The Great Santini,* has the skies over Korea proudly in his background and tries to engage his son's interest at one point by linking baseball, the American pastime, to the war in Korea: "I flew with Ted Williams in Korea." Korea may seem incidental here, but as the narrative develops, it becomes clear how powerfully Korea functioned as the place where Colonel Meecham collected bragging rights by putting his expertise in killing "slants" on the line. In the eyes of his children—and of his tight-knit soldier community—Bull Meecham is far larger than life, so it is fitting that his children do not cry at his funeral and that "they made the long walk up the aisle with every eye in the church on them." The "long walk" develops as a key motif in the southern view of the Korean War experience. By the time Conroy wrote *The Great Santini,* the Vietnam War had run its long and torturous course, and it is clear that Colonel Meecham's Marine-hard "Semper-Fi" stance, including an unrelenting effort to set his son Ben up to take on responsibility for carrying forward the warrior tradition, has indelible links to American military engagement in Southeast Asia in the 1960s, the war that consumed so much energy and so many lives in Conroy's generation.

In *Fortunate Son,* Lewis B. Puller Jr. wrote the story of one such life. Puller was born in Camp Lejeune, North Carolina. After some years at Camp Pendleton, California, the Pullers returned to Camp Lejeune in the mid-1950s and then settled in Saluda, Virginia, where Lewis spent his teenage and college (William and Mary) years. Lewis Puller's story, told in the aftermath of Vietnam War service that left him legless, begins with his memory of his father's return from combat in Korea in 1951. His father, "Chesty" Puller, was the most decorated Marine of his generation, a soldier's soldier whose grandfather was killed fighting for the Confederacy at Kelly's Ford in Virginia and who revered Lee and Jackson in his youth. In Korea, "Chesty" Puller had proved again his battlefield valor and genius for leadership. With Chinese army forces surrounding the American forces at the Chosin Reservoir near the Yalu River in December 1950, "Chesty" Puller was a key figure in the famous 1st Marine Division's "Retreat, Hell! We're Just Attacking in Another Direction" fight down the long road through Koto-ri to Hungnam and then escape to sea. Puller's First Marine Regiment secured the rear as the breakout developed; his troops were the very last to make the long march out to freedom, fighting every step of the way, and his heroics were justly noted both by his country and by his namesake son, who would feel compelled to carry on the family tradition in Vietnam.

Korea burst into national headlines just a half decade following the triumphant end of World War II. It was a cruelly short interval of peace. The North Korean attack down the peninsula came as a surprise, catching the United Nations and the United States quite unprepared. Mobilization of United States military forces was fairly swift, aided in part by the recall to service of many World War II veterans who had retained their rank in reserve units. As noted already, this plan wrenched Ted Williams away from the Boston Red Sox, and in the South, it entangled two of that region's most influential and powerful post–World War II writers, James Dickey and William Styron. Dickey's brief return to service as an air force pilot seems not to have been very consequential in his work. His literary notebooks from the time in 1951–1952 when he was again back in the military show his imagination focused almost exclusively on his reading of Proust and Mann and other such writers who could inform his poetry and prepare him for teaching at Rice Institute in 1952. His war poems of *Into the Stone* (1960) and "The Firebombing" from *Buckdancer's Choice* (1965) reflect back to Dickey's experience in the Philippines late in World War II and suggest virtually nothing of the Korean episode. The same is generally true of Dickey's strange novel *Alnilam* (1987), which accounts for air-pilot training, vaguely set in the 1940s.

For Styron, however, the return to service during the Korean War did register deeply, giving rise to one extraordinarily moving novella and providing material for sections of "The Way of the Warrior," a still-unfinished novel of American combat experience through the middle of the twentieth century, including sections devoted to the Korean episode. By Styron's account, "The Way of the Warrior" was his main project in the early 1970s until it was displaced abruptly by powerful images that came to be central in *Sophie's Choice.* One of the published segments, "Suicide Run," which appeared in 1974 in *American Poetry Review,* evokes the same Camp Lejeune environment that Dickey had developed so strongly in his 1953 narrative *The Long March.* Whereas a mishap in the training of a mortar crew opens *The Long March* with the ugly, accidental death of eight Marines, "The Suicide Run" commences with a meditation on the "priapean" possibilities of mortars, "those stiff uptilted tubes poking the air" and also notes the loss of "eight young recruits." After mention of other war preparation exercises, including "amphibious landings" (implied reference to General MacArthur's famous triumph at Inchon in 1950) and "sadistic hikes" (clear linkage to Styron's experience of a long forced march at Camp Lejeune in the summer of 1951 that gave rise to his story of Captain Mannix's defiant resistance to Colonel "Old Rocky" Templeton's authority in *The Long March*), "The Suicide Run" moves quickly to New York City, where the sex happens to be adulterous, imaginative, and a suitable release from the "enforced sexual famine" of military training. On the long drive back to Camp Lejeune,

"Lacy," like the narrator a World War II vet returned to service, falls asleep at the wheel and barely escapes collision with a tractor trailer. Lacy then recounts a series of near-fatal moments in his life, mainly cued on his memory of being bitten by a dog while under fire from the Japanese in the Philippines. This image represents the "hideous irrationality that governs life," a viewpoint that anchors all the action in the most important piece of Korean War literature to come from the South, *The Long March*.

The Long March boils with resentment and anger. The price of freedom was paid, in full, by American servicemen in World War II. Captain Al Mannix—as well as his closest companion in training, Jack Culver—both seem to represent the stance of veterans like Styron who were called back to do again the task they felt they had already finished honorably. Styron was recalled to duty early in 1951, just as he was trying to finish *Lie Down in Darkness*. His creative-writing teacher, Hiram Haydn, at the New School for Social Research in New York City, was able to intercede on Styron's behalf to get the induction postponed so he could complete his novel—a most miraculous intercession, clearly not "by the book" in military affairs. With the manuscript done in early April, inevitability took charge, and Styron went down to Camp Lejeune. All the literary evidence suggests that he was not a happy trooper.

As "Old Rocky" seeks to prove his unit worthy of the standard set by "Chesty" Puller and his soldiers far away in the land of the "frozen chosen," Mannix fumes not-so-quietly about the outrage of the whole situation. His virtual insubordination over the course of the thirty-six-mile march back to base camp is met with the Colonel's "I'll have you sent to Korea" threat, but Mannix nevertheless completes the march, despite his being out of shape and despite the wound to his foot from a nail in his boot. His case—one of obligation impossible to avoid—is that of all men, a point realized with grand dignity in the final scene of the story, where Mannix stands naked before a Negro maid, whose own life history is embedded in her empathy for Mannix's pain as she asks, "Do it hurt?" The answer—"Deed it does"—tells the whole story of Korea in the South. It was a deed, overlong in suffering and seething in irrationality, but one that had to be endured regardless.

Owen W. Gilman Jr.

See also Novel, World War II to Present.

Philip K. Jason, "Vietnam War Themes in Korean War Fiction," *South Atlantic Review* (1996).

KU KLUX KLAN

The Ku Klux Klan, also popularly known as the Invisible Empire, was founded in May or early June of 1866 in Pulaski, Tennessee, by six college men, all former Confederate officers who desired to fill the void created by the end of the Civil War. For several months after its founding, there was no indication that the Klan engaged in any acts of intimidation or terrorism. This period of nonviolence proved ephemeral, for within a short time, the newly formed Tennessee Klan resorted to vigilantelike activities making black freedmen and northerners who had allied with them the primary victims of their violence and scare tactics. When other Klan groups began to form in the state, it became apparent that some semblance of organization was necessary. In April 1867, representatives from the various Tennessee Klan groups met in Nashville, established a constitution consonant with the Constitution of the United States and vowed to protect the defenseless and the oppressed and at the same time stay within the bounds of the laws governing the country. General Nathan Bedford Forrest, a former Confederate cavalry officer and field commander, was elected Grand Imperial Wizard. Even in its early stages of development, the Klan, comprised of many former Confederate officers, advocated white supremacy, intending through their influence and their secret and subversive activities to resurrect a social order in which blacks would be restored to their former permanent subservient status to a white, male-dominated society.

During the unsettling times of Reconstruction, black men were briefly able to enjoy civil equality with white men through enfranchisement; radicals in Congress displaced existing state governments, replacing them with military districts under the charge of former northern army officers or southern antisecessionists. Disfranchised white southerners, feeling threatened and insecure, retaliated violently against blacks and their white sympathizers. The Klan leveled its atrocities against blacks who were insolent, had become prosperous, or had voted for Republican candidates. Blacks accused of sexually assaulting white women were lynched. In January 1869, Grand Imperial Wizard Forrest, realizing that the organization had gotten out of hand in some sections of the South and that its reputation had become tarnished, ordered the Klan to disband. Most of the Klans, especially in Tennessee, Georgia, Alabama, Mississippi, and Arkansas, followed Forrest's orders. Congressional legislation, such as the

Ku Klux Klan Act of 1871, gave the federal government the power to use the army and the federal courts to prosecute those who interfered with voting rights, but only mass arrests, martial law, and growing public disapproval finally brought official end to the Klan in 1872.

The rebirth of the Klan in 1915 coincided with the appearance and popular appeal of *The Birth of a Nation,* D. W. Griffith's epic film of the Civil War, Reconstruction, and the restoration of white rule, a film inspired by Thomas Dixon's *The Clansman: An Historical Romance of the Ku Klux Klan* (1905). Dixon's novel had glorified the Klan as white-robed knights who burned crosses and who resorted to violence only when extreme situations warranted it. Griffith used *The Birth of the Nation* as a propaganda piece to attempt to convince white audiences that black people were subhuman and that white vigilantes like the Klan could save the nation from this threat.

In the fall of 1915, just as this film was scheduled to open in Atlanta, Colonel William J. Simmons, who had fought with the Alabama volunteers against Spain and whose Confederate-veteran father had joined the original Klan during Reconstruction, recruited about forty other men from various fraternal organizations to form the nucleus for what would be the new Klan. Given the nationalistic sentiments of the times—reflected in a widespread distrust of Catholics, blacks, and Jews—Simmons perceived that the time was ripe for a Klan revival, and he and his followers gathered outside Atlanta at the top of Stone Mountain on the eve of Thanksgiving to form the second Ku Klux Klan.

Although the popularity of *The Birth of a Nation* helped in membership recruitment, Simmons himself lacked the charisma to draw others to join the organization in significant numbers. Other factors that proved far more effective for promoting Klan membership came into play. One significant factor was the national trend toward urbanization in the 1920s. Urban areas, both in the South and the North, exhibited what has been aptly called a "fortress mentality," a paranoia about foreigners, many of whom were immigrating to American cities after World War I. Many people feared that radical change posed a threat to the traditional values of American culture. Such bigotry encouraged Klan membership. The resurgence of the Klan was also aided by the efforts of Edward Young Clarke and Elizabeth Tyler, who jointly owned the Southern Publicity Association, a company whose primary function was fund-raising. In 1920, Clarke and Tyler, recognizing

great financial potential in the Klan, promoted Klan membership on a national scale, emphasizing the themes of anti-Catholicism and "one hundred percent Americanism." In addition, they advertised that the Klan opposed bootlegging, gambling, drugs, graft, nightclubs, sexual liberality, Sabbath violation, ethnic diversity, evolution, unfair business practices, the changing roles of women—virtually anything and everything that might be deemed morally scandalous or dangerous to the preservation of a socially conservative American value system. For restless men who returned from the First World War still feeling a fervent patriotism, the Klan could provide a channel for their energies. Coupled with this, promoters wanted potential Klan members to understand that the Invisible Empire had taken on a new mission, a mission characterized by a reformist zeal. The Klan in the Southwest became particularly active in attempting to restore morality in both the private and public sectors. A third factor instrumental in boosting Klan numbers may best be described as an unexpected backlash, a reaction to adverse publicity from the press. In 1921, the *New York World,* in an attempt to destroy the Klan's credibility, published a series of inflammatory articles exposing some of the Klan's subversive activities and methods, citing some one hundred and fifty cases of vigilante violence and terrorism charged to the organization. These articles prompted congressional investigations, which had the potential for embarrassing the Klan; but Elizabeth Tyler, one of the Klan's chief promoters, saw this bad publicity as a grand recruiting opportunity. What the *New York World* had not counted on was that the Klan had a wide appeal and that Americans tended to distrust the press. Within four months after the publication of the *World*'s scathing stories, the Klan chartered two hundred new chapters and overall membership increased to one million. By 1924, membership had climbed to the two-million mark, and of that number approximately 40 percent consisted of lower-middle-class southerners. During the phenomenal growth period of the 1920s, the Klan recruited more members, amassed more power, and had a greater influence nationally than in any other time in its history.

The Klan also proved to be a potent political force in the 1920s. It has been estimated that during this period, seventy-five congressional representatives and at least one senator were indebted to the Klan for their political seats. During the 1920s, the Klan's political clout likewise helped to elect governors in Georgia, Texas, Alabama, Louisiana, Oklahoma, Maine, Ohio,

Colorado, and California. The Klan made its presence felt in local and state politics as well, helping to elect candidates whose views were favorable to the organization. Yet by 1928, the Klan's formidable political power had dwindled, as evidenced by its inability to block the Democratic Party from nominating Governor Al Smith of New York, a Roman Catholic, as its presidential candidate.

After the flush times of the 1920s, the Klan never again enjoyed widespread national prominence. Internal fighting among its leaders, the inability to sustain the negative, defensive feelings among its members, and negative publicity spawned by terrorist activity contributed to the Klan's decline. By 1927, Klan membership had diminished to about fifty thousand. The Klan of the 1930s, small and based mainly in the South, functioned principally as a social organization. During the financially bleak times of the Great Depression, the Klan reaffirmed its animosity toward foreign-born citizens, stressing the need to keep immigrants, who posed a threat to the dwindling job market, out of the United States. As in the halcyon days of the 1920s, the Klan assumed a patriotic stance, participating in and supporting striking workers and demonstrations staged by the nation's unemployed. By the late 1940s and early 1950s, the Klan had been placed on the attorney general's list of subversive organizations, and various southern states sought to curtail and restrict Klan activity by enforcing laws when Klansmen broke them and by enacting antimask legislation. Moreover, southern juries became more willing to convict Klan members for legal violations.

With the termination of segregation in 1954 and the impetus of the civil-rights efforts in the 1960s, the Klan found a new motivation for existence. Opposition to racial desegregation in the South was widespread, and Klan-induced violence in the form of bombings, arson, and other extremist activities occurred all too frequently, a reaction to black lunch-counter sit-ins, freedom rides, and mass demonstrations. Public-school integration, the increase in black voter registration, and black protests and demonstrations created pressure on segregated facilities throughout the South, but at the same time provided both a challenge and opportunity for the Ku Klux Klan: the chance to be active and to increase its membership. Because of widespread societal disapproval, attacks in the media, the absence of charismatic leaders, federal intervention and surveillance that led to arrests and convictions, state and local ordinances prohibiting public opposition, and the overall strength of the black civil-rights movement, the Klan fell into a state of decline in the 1970s. Still a radical right-wing fringe group, the Ku Klux Klan continues to persist. Since the 1980s, the Klan's primary base of operations remains the South and to a lesser extent the Midwest and Far West, and while it still has some familiar targets—principally blacks, Jews, and Catholics—in recent years it has shifted its hatred and violent opposition to Mexican Americans, immigrants from Southeast Asia, and gays and lesbians. And because of its declining numbers, today's Klan has allied itself with other paramilitary and extralegal organizations.

The Klan inevitably became an ominous theme in southern fiction, Dixon's *Clansman* but its fountain. In *Gone With the Wind*, Margaret Mitchell portrayed the Klan's origin as a southern defense against the excesses of Reconstruction. Ernest Gaines in *The Autobiography of Miss Jane Pittman* shows those origins from the perspective of the "freed" slaves. Innumerable lynching scenes in many works evoke the Klan's menacing presence. One of the most remarkable representations of the Klan mentality occurs in Eudora Welty's story "Where Is the Voice Coming From?" (1963), based on the murder of black Mississippi civil-rights activist Medgar Evers. The story, narrated in the first-person voice of a white supremacist who has shot a black activist, mentions "Nathan B. Forrest Road," a veiled allusion to the Confederate Civil War hero and the Klan's first president in the immediate post–Civil War period who later, appalled by the violence of the Klan, resigned and called for the organization to disband. When Welty wrote the story, Evers's assassin had not been discovered, but the man who was finally arrested turned out to be remarkably similar, in voice, motive, and character, to Welty's narrator.

Ed Piacentino

See also *Birth of a Nation, The*

David M. Chalmers, *Hooded Americanism: The First Century of the Ku Klux Klan, 1864–1965* (1965); Arnold Rice, *The Ku Klux Klan in American Politics* (1972); Allen W. Trelease, *White Terror: The Ku Klux Klan Conspiracy and Southern Reconstruction* (1971).

L

LADY

The southern lady is a durable figure in southern literature. Ideally a patrician, privileged white woman, she served her husband, bending to him in all matters; she was maternal, bearing children regularly and caring for them lovingly; she possessed great skill in the domestic sphere, running kitchen and nursery, overseeing the household in all areas, dispensing medicine, always hospitable. Most important, perhaps, she was the moral center of the household, pious, self-effacing, and kind. An expert with the needle, she could also play a musical instrument and sing melodies for the family. She was essential to the patriarchy, assuring well-brought-up children, a well-run home, and complete comfort for her husband.

This ideal of the lady is static, rigid in its prescriptions, but the literary portrayal of this figure ultimately became protean.

Lucretia Meriwether in John Pendleton Kennedy's *Swallow Barn* (1832) is the model of the ideal lady—a veritable "pattern of industry" in running the household, showing deference to her husband Frank "in all matters, except those that belong to the home department," playing traditional melodies in the evening on the harpsichord, bearing children ("a fruitful vessel," she "seldom fails in her annual tribute to the honors of the family"). All this she accomplishes even though she is sallow of complexion, a sickly woman. When the visiting New Yorker, Mark Littleton, imagines for himself a life similar to Meriwether's, he fantasizes about possessing the land, the manor-house, the slaves, the library, friends, money—"and, finally, a house full of pretty, intelligent, and docile children, with some few etceteras not worth mentioning." Not mentioned is the lady-mother, whose purity and hard work failed to seize his imagination, doubtless grouped among the "etceteras."

In *Marse Chan* (1887), Thomas Nelson Page delineated the icon of the lady as he looked back to the Old South and codified the myth of the Lost Cause. Anne Chamberlayne, the love interest of young aristocrat Tom Channing since childhood, plays a small but significant role; she is an abstraction, but a perfect lady—modest, gentle, exquisitely beautiful, and spirited. Significantly, she is loyal to her irascible father when he publicly insults Tom's father and precipitates a duel. Tom goes away to war after declaring his love to the aloof Anne, and he is brought home in a pine box. Anne collapses to the floor sobbing, embraces passionately his casket, moves into his parents' home, nurses soldiers in a hospital, contracts yellow fever, and dies. She is buried next to Tom, the lovers united in death, neither idealized figure surviving the defeat of the Old South.

Kate Chopin used the lady for a new purpose in *The Awakening* (1899). Her Creole-style lady is Adèle Ratignolle, devoted to husband, children, and home. But the central character in the novel, Edna Pontellier, Kentucky-born, refuses to play this role, first declining to hold her visiting hours on Tuesdays and finally divesting herself of home, husband, and children to pursue her art and her own passions—with tragic results, ultimately drowning herself in the Gulf of Mexico. The personal consequences of a passionate woman's rejection of the constricting role of southern lady are delineated in this novel.

Perhaps the fictional southern lady portrayed in Margaret Mitchell's *Gone With the Wind* (1936) reached more readers than any other. Scarlett O'Hara was no lady (though her mother was a perfect one), but Melanie Wilkes, her opposite in character and behavior, is a model lady. Good and kind, modest and self-effacing, nurturing and understanding, Melanie was unfailingly loyal to family and friends. Loved by Ashley Wilkes and extravagantly admired by Rhett Butler, she dies in childbirth. As in other fiction, the fragile lady does not survive, but her counterpart, the ambitious, self-involved new woman, Scarlett, thrives in the world of the New South.

Ellen Glasgow offers the most comprehensive treatment of the lady in fiction, portraying the figure in countless incarnations in her nineteen novels. In *The Battle-Ground* (1904), sisters Virginia and Betty Ambler personify the beautiful, blonde, conforming lady and the red-headed, precocious, nonconforming woman. Virginia dies in childbirth in war-torn Richmond, sacrificed on "The Altar of the War God," a figure too fragile to survive the war. Betty, on the other hand, thrives, running two plantations, welcoming her wounded and psychologically damaged lover home from the war, prepared to join him as a partner in rebuilding their lives.

In *Virginia* (1913), Glasgow created with affection and savage irony the most complete portrait of the southern lady in fiction. A romantic idealist, Virginia Pendleton Treadwell modeled herself after her self-effacing lady-mother. She devoted herself wholly to her playwright husband and their children. After winning success on the New York stage, the husband abandoned her for a more vital and interesting woman, an actress, leaving the provincial Virginia broken and alone in her early forties, her life effectively over with only her adult son to offer her comfort.

Then in *The Sheltered Life* (1932), Eva Birdsong, beautiful and musically gifted, married the handsome George Birdsong, a failure as a lawyer and a compulsive philanderer. Without the basic accouterments of the lady, burdened by an unfaithful husband, with no children and no money, Eva is left to maintain the pretense of happiness, denying the reality of her life, repressing her anger, and finally secretly selling the family silver to survive financially. Eva's mask, maintained for many years at the expense of self, finally cracks in the face of George's infidelity with a teenaged neighbor, and she shoots and kills him. She is left gazing blankly, "a fixed smile" on her face, her expression "vacant," "her skin as . . . colourless as the skin of the dead," "her eyes and mouth . . . mere hollows of darkness." Eva Birdsong is Glasgow's most tragic depiction of the southern lady. Glasgow found the role of the lady a destroyer of the gentle Virginia Ambler's life, of the conforming Virginia Pendleton Treadwell's emotions, and of Eva Birdsong's sanity.

William Faulkner takes a different, but as destructive as Glasgow's, view of the lady in the modern wasteland of *The Sound and the Fury* (1929). Caroline Compson possesses only pretensions and empty rituals, remnants of the ideal lady in a decadent world. She has abandoned all responsibility for her husband, her children, and her home. Leaving the servant Dilsey to do all the work and to nurture her children, Caroline withdraws to her bed, whining, complaining, and self-pitying. She is the lady-mother gone corrupt, rank, and foul; the wreckage can be measured in her children— one lost daughter and three sons, one a suicide at nineteen, one mean and materialistic, one emasculated and locked up in an institution.

Faulkner's Granny Rosa Millard, a lady of an earlier period than Mrs. Compson, is the strong, competent widow in *The Unvanquished* (1938), raising her motherless grandson, enforcing the rules for proper behavior, vanquishing Yankees, burying the silver for safekeeping. However, when she courageously confronts thieves to recover stolen horses, armed with the notion that they will not harm a woman (a lady), she is brutally murdered.

The lady-grandmother, empowered by the death of her husband, is a formidable figure in fiction. She ably runs the plantation, enforces the standards of proper behavior of grandchildren, is the voice of authority, and frequently keeps her gaze focused firmly on the past. Miranda's grandmother in Katherine Anne Porter's short fiction is exemplary of this figure. Her profligate husband died, leaving her with children and the responsibility of surviving economically. She is ultimately successful. In "Old Mortality" (1940), she is the authority figure in the household who maintains the rituals and myths, the keeper of the relics of the past.

Eudora Welty, in *Delta Wedding* (1946), presents a nostalgic portrayal of the ideal lady on a Mississippi plantation in the 1920s. At the center of the Fairchild family is the lady-mother, Virginia-born Ellen Fairchild, pregnant with her ninth child and preparing for the wedding of her oldest daughter. She is in charge of the kitchen, directs the servants, cares for the children, serves meals to the large, extended family, supervises the flowers and the preparation of clothing for the wedding, keeps the peace. She is the heart of the family, mothering all of them, kind and sensitive and understanding. As a brother-in-law suggests new plans for the plantation and her daughter marries the overseer from Tennessee, the reader senses that the old way of life, including the lady-mother at the center, may be soon gone.

The stereotype of the lady is too frail a vessel to carry the full weight of a novel; only Glasgow attempted the feat. In her appearance in fiction before the Civil War, the lady was presented as an icon, a sacred necessity for patriarchal culture. In later fiction, she often did not survive that war. But in twentieth-century fiction, she is found in many incarnations as writers have depicted the repressive aspects of the ideal and have used the lady as a secondary player in order to highlight the character of a woman who is not a lady. Even when a lady character is not present in the text, fictional women are often implicitly measured against the old ideal.

Dorothy M. Scura

See also Belle; New Woman.

Nina Baym, "The Myth of the Myth of Southern Womanhood," in Nina Baym, *Feminism and American Literary History: Essays* (1992); Anne Goodwyn Jones, *Tomorrow Is Another Day: The Woman Writer in the South (1859–1936)* (1981); Peggy W. Prenshaw, "Southern Ladies and the Southern Literary Renaissance," in *The Female Tradition in Southern Literature*, ed. Carol S. Manning (1993); Anne Firor Scott, *The Southern Lady: From Pedestal to Politics, 1830–1930* (1970); Dorothy M. Scura, "The Southern Lady in the Early Novels of Ellen Glasgow," *Mississippi Quarterly* (Winter 1977–78); Kathryn L. Seidel, *The Southern Belle in the American Novel* (1985).

LAW BEFORE 1900

The distinctiveness of southern law in the nineteenth century stems from the region's peculiar social order: the Old South maintained a patriarchal and rigidly hierarchical society in which planter aristocrats ruled over women, workers, servants, and slaves. Class and caste distinctions, honor, and white supremacy were deep-seated cultural values that fundamentally shaped the laws of the southern states and were in turn reinforced by those laws. Preeminent, of course, were the elaborate slave codes and rules determining racial status by which the landed elite preserved their property, their economy, their status, and their safety from exponentially increasing numbers of subjugated African Americans. The laws of slavery served several functions: they designated slaves as property; they ensured the permanent existence of a slave class (for example, by dictating, as early as the colonial period, that slave status was inherited through the mother, ensuring that

the sexual "impropriety" of white slaveowners produced more slaves rather than a racially ambiguous free class); and they severely curtailed slaves' rights as citizens—although the excesses of individual masters were curbed in order to preserve the larger societal need to defend the institution of slavery, especially as the mood in the North grew increasingly oppositional; thus legislators put constraints (albeit slowly) on the violence that slaveowners could commit on their own "property." In 1821 South Carolina, for instance, was the last state to make the killing of a slave by a white man explicitly a murder. Still, barring murder (at least technically), the general thrust of slave law was that a master was free to do what he pleased to his slaves. Judge Thomas Ruffin of North Carolina sums up the philosophy that undergirded slave law in *State v. Mann* (1829): "the power of the master must be absolute to render the submission of the slave perfect." Preserving the slave system depended not only on absolute power but also on preserving the racial divide—the impermeable border between "black" and "white," especially in a world that from the 1830s on looked increasingly like a mixture. Hence numerous laws defining who was "black" or "African," and thus presumptively a slave, emerged, as well as laws prohibiting miscegenation. The largest part of antebellum southern literature variously bolstered and critiqued the system of slave codes and adumbrated or debunked those laws that rendered "essential" bifurcated notions of race: from Thomas Jefferson's ambivalent *Notes on the State of Virginia* (1781) to George Fitzhugh's defenses of southern feudalism, *Cannibals All!* (1857) and *A Sociology for the South* (1854); and from transplanted northerner Caroline Lee Hentz's popular proslavery novel *The Planter's Northern Bride* (1854) to the hundreds of slave narratives, notably by Frederick Douglass (1845) and Harriet Jacobs (1861).

Even after the Civil War, the Emancipation Proclamation, and the Thirteenth, Fourteenth, and Fifteenth Amendments to the Constitution, the South maintained its racial caste system through the Black Codes and, beginning in the 1890s, through an active legal segregation of the races. The post–Civil War Black Codes prevented African Americans from pursuing certain skilled occupations (such as physicians and merchants) and restricted the areas in which they could live and their ability to travel—all of which essentially eviscerated their ostensibly new status as full citizens. Later so-called "Jim Crow" laws disenfranchised African American voters and imposed absolute segregation on schools, railroads, and public accommodations. *Plessy v. Ferguson* (1896) affirmed the constitutionality of racially segregated spaces and services—the infamous "separate but equal" doctrine—but it also continued the practice (which was as necessary to a system of segregation as to the system of slavery) of defining and dichotomizing the races. Much late-nineteenth-century literature—notably Mark Twain's *Pudd'nhead Wilson* (1894), Kate Chopin's "Désirée's Baby" (1894), and Charles Chesnutt's *The House Behind the Cedars* (1900)—powerfully evinces the injustice, as well as the futility, of both the conceptual and the physical separation of the races.

The laws governing and hierarchizing the status of persons were not confined to race but also pervaded gender relations, notably marriage. Just as southern law defined slaves as a distinct and dependent class, so too did it subordinate women. Unlike New England, the southern colonies, following more closely English common law, did not grant absolute divorce and thus allowed wives little recourse even in abusive marriages. In the post-Revolutionary years, some southern states—notably newer states rather than seaboard jurisdictions—granted divorces under limited conditions, though southern judges were persistently more conservative than northern judges in their interpretation of the new general divorce statutes. South Carolina, however, persistently remained an anomaly even in the South in that it never granted a divorce, either through the legislature or the courts (with the exception of a brief experiment during Reconstruction). The injustices suffered by married women were a common theme in the work of southern women writers, particularly Susan Petigru King (born and raised in South Carolina), E. D. E. N. Southworth, and Kate Chopin. But, despite its giving wives little opportunity to escape oppressive, even abusive, marriages, the South led the way in what was the major legal reform affecting women in the antebellum period: married women's property acts. In 1839, it was Mississippi that initiated the movement to grant wives legal power over their own property. Historians have explained the South's leadership role on this issue on the grounds of the region's persistent protection of the status quo in terms of property and land: lawmakers, in other words, were seeking to protect family property, passed on to daughters, from improvident husbands and creditors.

If slavery has defined southern law historically, perhaps the most recurrent reputation that has adhered to the South even today is its tradition of violence. A recent leading article in the *New York Times,* entitled "Southern Curse: Why America's Murder Rate Is So High" (July 26, 1998), argues that the U.S. homicide rate exceeds that of other industrialized nations in large part because of the untoward number of murders in southern states (the former slaveholding states all rank in the top twenty states for murder). Indeed, through the nineteenth century, homicide rates were unusually high in the South, and its writers return to the vexing problem of murder—from the monomaniacal and motiveless killers of Edgar Allan Poe and William Gilmore Simms (both of whom had a strong interest in medical jurisprudence and the law of homicidal insanity) to the feuds, riots, and uprisings in the fiction of Mark Twain, Charles Chesnutt, and Thomas Dixon. Historians have offered a multitude of reasons for this high level of violence: the region's poverty, its Celtic heritage, an ineffective criminal justice system, persistent frontier conditions, a prevalent code of honor, and a plantation system that tended to privatize social rule, decentralize police power, and put excessive power in the hands of a few over many.

The South is not simply peculiar for violence, however, but for violence *as a means of resolving disputes.* Justice, in other words, has been characterized by a kind of legal privatism, as citizens have taken retribution for injuries, perceived or real, into their own hands, assuming that their primitive right to vengeance had only been contingently and temporarily surrendered to their legal representatives. Legal historian Lawrence Friedman articulates the distinctiveness of this tradition in his essay in *Ambivalent Legacy:* violence in the South has historically been "not the enemy of law and order, but a substitute for it." Hence, the quite-accurate association of the South with dueling (which is featured even in southern women's fiction, such as E. D. E. N. Southworth's *The Hidden Hand* [1859] and Augusta Evans's *St. Elmo* [1867]), private feuds (notably in Twain's *Adventures of Huckleberry Finn* [1885]), and vigilantism and lynch law, which William Gilmore Simms defended in his novel *Woodcraft* (1882): "The morals of law always will, and should, sustain what are the obvious necessities of society. In this you have the full justification of the code of regulation." Of course, it does not do to idealize southern popular justice as serving the interests of "law and order" since, especially in the latter part of the nineteenth century, lynching became a major part of the reign of terror that explicitly circumvented the constitutional rights of African Americans—notably, in cases of suspected crimes, the right to due process. But such lynchings (and there were at least 1,985 between 1882 and 1903) were in fact recognized as an acceptable part of the criminal-justice system in the New South. Finally, the question of whether the socially acceptable practices of dueling, vigilantism, and lynching (along with the late-nineteenth-century legal disenfranchisement of African Americans) serve the law or contravene it only reveals that "the law"—seemingly fixed and codified—is actually a highly contingent and variable set of local everyday practices.

Dawn Keetley

See also Chattel Slavery; Crimes and Criminals; Douglass, Frederick; Honor; Jefferson, Thomas; Lawyer; Lynching; Lynch Law; *Plessy v. Ferguson.*

Edward L. Ayers, *Vengeance and Justice: Crime and Punishment in the 19th-Century American South* (1984); David J. Bodenhamer and James W. Ely Jr., *Ambivalent Legacy: A Legal History of the South* (1984); Thomas D. Morris, *Southern Slavery and the Law, 1619–1860* (1996).

LAW, 1900 TO PRESENT

Writers of the twentieth-century South have shown a strong interest in, if not preoccupation with, issues of legal and extralegal justice, particularly as they relate to the vexed subject of racial violence and prejudice in the region. Modern southern writers have used the setting of southern courts to address such issues of national concern as lynching and other forms of racial violence as well as the constitutionality of racial disenfranchisement and segregation. One notable example of a southern court of law that did not involve the subject of race is the Scopes Monkey Trial of 1925, which gained notoriety at the time with the help of H. L. Mencken's scathing journalistic dispatches from Dayton, Tennessee, and later from Jerome Lawrence's play *Inherit the Wind* (1943). A desire to counter Mencken's sarcastic stereotypes of the residents of Dayton (and, by implication, all southerners) played some role in prompting a group of Nashville poets and educators to write *I'll Take My Stand* (1930).

W. J. Cash noted in *The Mind of the South* that the southerner's attitude toward the law is characterized by a deep ambivalence in which a frontier predisposition toward personal justice often outweighs a respect

for formal legal proceedings. This general attitude toward the courts has resulted from a Calvinistic distrust of all human institutions, as Cash suggested, or from a paternalistic orientation toward personal honor, as Bertram Wyatt-Brown argues in *Southern Honor* (1982). Whatever the cause, many twentieth-century literary treatments of southern law comment on the morality of personal retribution. In *The Clansman* (1905), Thomas Dixon's white supremacist, provigilante account of Reconstruction-era racial politics, a mulatto Union soldier is lynched after he rapes the hero's youngest sister. The positive reception of *The Clansman* and *Birth of a Nation* (1915), D. W. Griffith's extremely popular film adaptation of the novel, suggests that nonsouthern as well as southern audiences approved of Dixon's interpretation of southern extralegal justice.

Faulkner, who was fond of legal discourse and worked it into much of his fiction, meditates on the logic of extralegal justice in a number of his works. In *Sanctuary* (1931), a bootlegger is lynched for a murder he did not commit; *Light in August* (1932) culminates in the murder and castration of the racially ambiguous Joe Christmas at the hands of fascist prototype Percy Grimm; "Dry September" (1931) presents another returning hero from World War I who leads a lynch mob against an African American accused—probably falsely—of raping a white woman (Faulkner cryptically implies that no crime has been committed); and in *The Unvanquished* (1938), Bayard Sartoris avenges the murder of his grandmother by killing the murderer and nailing the offending hand on the victim's door; then, some ten years later, his legal studies are interrupted so that he may avenge—this time, significantly, without bloodshed—his father's murder. Fellow Mississippian Richard Wright's *Native Son* (1940), in its long courtroom speeches, analyzes the fate of Bigger, a black boy who kills a white woman accidentally, and then brutally murders his black girlfriend.

More recent versions of this theme have inverted the racial status quo, giving African Americans the upper hand. For instance, in Ernest Gaines's *A Gathering of Old Men* (1983), the former victims of racial discrimination conspire to take the blame for the murder of a white racist bully, only to realize the anachronistic futility of revenge. And in John Grisham's popularly successful novel *A Time to Kill* (1992), in its own way as approving of extralegal justice as Dixon's *The Clansman,* a mixed-racial jury acquits an African American man for murdering two white men accused of raping his young daughter.

The pursuit of justice through the court system itself has also been a subject of interest to southern writers, though the outcomes of the trials point to the same degree of ambivalence found in treatments of extralegal justice. For example, in Zora Neale Hurston's *Their Eyes Were Watching God* (1937), the protagonist Janie stands before an all-white court to plead self-defense in the murder of her husband, and is acquitted only as a result of the intervention of "concerned" ladies from the white community. Similarly, Lucas Beauchamp is exonerated in Faulkner's *Intruder in the Dust* (1948) only after his lawyer, Gavin Stevens, tampers with evidence. And in the opening scene of Faulkner's "Barn Burning" (1938), Ab Snopes is acquitted of the charge of burning a barn only because the judge refuses to have Snopes's son testify against his own father. Later in the story, Snopes himself seeks help from the courts to protest an arguably reasonable fine imposed on him by his new landlord, but after winning only a partial victory before the bench (his fine is cut in half), he destroys his landlord's barn. Harper Lee's *To Kill a Mockingbird* (1960), based loosely on the events of the Scottsboro, Alabama, trials of the 1930s, reveals in especially vivid detail the ways in which the complicated knot of race, gender, and class relations in the South helped to foster the capriciousness of southern courts of law.

Whether or not the southern writer's interest in matters of legal and extralegal justice will continue into the next century remains to be seen, but for the writer of the twentieth-century American South, the subject of law has proven a reliable vehicle for addressing matters of class, race, gender, and personal honor, issues close to the core of the southern literary imagination.

James H. Watkins

See also *Brown vs. Board of Education*; Civil Rights Movement; Lawyer; Miscegenation; Scopes Trial; Scottsboro Case; Sheriff; Violence.

LAWYER

As authorial source and fictional subject, the southern lawyer has long played a significant role in the literature of the South. Especially in the Old South, where a self-consciously southern literature was inaugurated by lawyers John Pendleton Kennedy, Augustus Baldwin Longstreet, and Joseph G. Baldwin, lawyers who wrote fiction as a genteel diversion were much more common than professional men or women of letters for whom writing was a full-time vocation. The authors of nearly all important antebellum southern literature—Edgar Allan Poe is an important exception—read and practiced the law at some point in their professional lives. Lawyers have often peopled southern literature and, perhaps because of their frequently intimate involvement in the affairs of the southern community, they serve as valuable barometers of the South's values and sensibilities.

Kennedy's Philpot Wart, like most of the characters in *Swallow Barn* (1832), is gently satirized by the author, but he sets an important precedent for the lawyer's fictional characterization. As comfortable with Virgil as he is with *Blackstone's Commentaries*, Wart (modeled loosely on Kennedy's mentor, the author/lawyer William Wirt) identifies very closely with the patrician values of the planter community whom he counsels and represents. In his defense of slavery and states' rights, he is at his most impassioned and articulate. Moreover, he recognizes and endorses the ascendancy of the southern gentleman's code, an unwritten cultural law that conflates chivalry and racial attitudes, and often proves superior to any statutory, constitutional, or even biblical, legal writ. For the most part, Judge York Leicester Driscoll, in Mark Twain's *Pudd'nhead Wilson* (1894), shares Wart's view of the southern community and the function of law within it. However, Driscoll also demonstrates a passionate belief in the virtue and occasional necessity of personal law enforcement and even violence. When he learns that his nephew has sought redress in court because he has been physically assaulted, the Judge is thoroughly and indignantly piqued: "You cur! You scum! You vermin! Do you mean to tell me that blood of my race has suffered a blow and crawled to a court of law about it?" Considering his position as an arbiter of written statutory law, Driscoll's commitment to the more extreme aspects of the South's unwritten gentleman's code is demonstrative of not only the breadth of this code, but also the antebellum southern lawyer's lack of ambivalence in embracing it.

Driscoll's violent streak notwithstanding, in considerable contrast to both of these gentlemen are the beguiling and considerably more irreverent legal scalawags in Longstreet's *Georgia Scenes* (1835) and Baldwin's *Flush Times of Alabama and Mississippi*

(1853). Based on Longstreet's and Baldwin's recollections of their days as circuit-riding judges in the Old Southwest, these tales portray a much less sophisticated, if clever, variety of lawyer who takes advantage of his foolhardy and simple-minded neighbors. Lacking any familiarity with the more refined aspects of the gentleman's code, these rascals have little use for patrician pretensions or *noblesse oblige*. Baldwin's Simon Suggs, for example, wins his law license in a card game. Nonetheless, in spite of their antics, these frontier lawyers maintain without question, as did Longstreet and Baldwin themselves, the racial tenets of the same code so esteemed by Kennedy's Wart.

After the Civil War and Reconstruction, the fictional lawyer in the New South is the unmistakable cousin of his antebellum forerunners, but his energies have been clearly adapted to the concerns of the post-Reconstruction South, specifically the perceived threats of Negro enfranchisement and social equality. In "The Old Virginia Lawyer," an address to the Virginia State Bar Association in 1891, Thomas Nelson Page described the antebellum attorney's pursuits as "sacred." The legal profession in the Old South, Page said, "maintained the rights of man, preserved the government, controlled the administration of the law." In Reconstruction novels like Page's *Red Rock* (1898) and Thomas Dixon's *The Clansman* (1905), this new breed of southern lawyer champions causes cloaked in similar rhetoric, with the ultimate aim of disenfranchising the freedmen and codifying southern Jim Crow customs.

A number of twentieth-century southern writers dramatize the dilemma of the southern lawyer during the troubled half-century between two landmark Supreme Court decisions, *Plessy v. Ferguson* (1896) and *Brown v. Board of Education* (1954), the first of which enshrined Jim Crow, and the second of which rejected southern racial codes and held that segregated schooling violated the Fourteenth Amendment. The lawyer who emerges in the literature of the southern literary renascence, while he is often guilty of some degree of paternalism, nonetheless assumes a much more critical posture toward his community. Moreover, he frequently takes bold stands on questions of racial justice and thereby provides a useful template for the southern writer's critique of his or her community.

William Faulkner held a definite fascination with the legal profession and its practitioners. In his study *Forensic Fictions: The Lawyer Figure in Faulkner* (1993), Jay Watson counts at least twenty-five attorneys in Faulkner's work. Horace Benbow, who appears in *Sartoris* (1929) and *Sanctuary* (1931), is one of Faulkner's first lawyers. His guilt over past and present events in his community foreshadows the quandaries faced by a much more important Faulkner character, Gavin Stevens. A contemporary of Quentin Compson, Stevens is Yoknapatawpha's Harvard- and Heidelberg-educated county attorney. Near the beginning of *Requiem for a Nun* (1950), he is described as "a sort of bucolic Cincinnatus . . . champion not so much of truth as of justice, or of justice as he sees it, constantly involving himself, often for no pay, in affairs of equity and passion and even crime too among his people, white and Negro both, sometimes directly contrary to his office as County Attorney." Although Faulkner certainly draws from the traditional American archetype of the country lawyer in his characterization of Stevens, he endows the attorney with a psychological depth that extends far beyond that of any country-trickster character from early American folklore or the popular detective fiction of the 1920s. Over the course of six novels and nearly a dozen short stories, Stevens's chief concern is the race problem in the South. As he seeks to exonerate Lucas Beauchamp in *Intruder in the Dust* (1948), Stevens demonstrates a profound level of insight into the South's racial dilemma. But, like Faulkner, he never assails his community directly. Troubled though he is by the blindness and injustice around him, Stevens is convinced that the South can change only slowly and from within.

Atticus Finch, in Harper Lee's *To Kill a Mockingbird* (1960), brings the lawyer figure in southern literature to a level nearing apotheosis. Finch is in some respects very similar to Stevens, especially in his willingness to involve himself in the complex and unpleasant predicament faced by Tom Robinson in Maycomb, Alabama. But in his convictions about his community's shortcomings and the nearly impossible plight of southern blacks like Robinson, Finch is considerably less ambivalent than Stevens. Thus, among the patrician lawyers in southern fiction who confront the South's racial dilemma, he is the most courageous and the most admirable. Even so, in her commitment to realism, Lee does not allow Finch to prevail in his most important case. Because of the provincialism and racism of Maycomb's citizens, Tom Robinson is convicted and condemned.

Although the patrician model of the southern lawyer is most familiar, it is not the only one. A definite foil to Stevens and Finch both is the Communist lawyer

Boris Max, who defends Bigger Thomas in Richard Wright's *Native Son* (1940). Like Wright himself, Max lacks any significant ties to the dominant white community that would necessarily circumscribe his views on race. Instead, as a political outsider, he is free to indict an entire social system, and so makes the radical claim that Bigger's monstrous crime is the logical outgrowth of American life. Even though the setting of *Native Son* is distinctly nonsouthern, it actually makes Max's claims all the more fitting as they pertain to the South: such an indictment, Wright seems to suggest, would never be possible in a southern courtroom.

Succeeding Max in this nonpatrician vein are a number of young and often radical lawyers who appear in southern fiction written during the civil rights era. Among the most important of these are white attorney Steve Mundine in Jesse Hill Ford's *The Liberation of Lord Byron Jones* (1965) and black attorney David Champlin, the martyred hero in Ann Fairbairn's *Five Smooth Stones* (1966).

Perhaps drawing some distant inspiration from their antebellum cousins, southern lawyers John William Corrington and John Grisham have enjoyed broad popular acclaim for their fiction. But although Corrington and Grisham's novels (e.g., Corrington's *All My Trials* [1987] and Grisham's *The Client* [1993]) are often set in the South, they touch on traditional southern concerns only lightly, the exception being Grisham's first novel, *A Time to Kill* (1987), which deals closely with racial violence.

Collin Messer

See also *Brown v. Board of Education*; Faulkner, William; Law Before 1900; Law, 1900 to Present; *Plessy v. Ferguson*; States' Rights.

James McBride Dabbs, *Civil Rights in Recent Southern Fiction* (1969); J. K. Van Dover and John F. Jebb, *Isn't Justice Always Unfair?: The Detective in Southern Literature* (1996); Carl S. Smith, *Law and American Literature* (1983).

LAZY SOUTH

One of the most persistent images that southerners have helped to perpetuate about themselves is that of the "lazy South." From the earliest writings of the colonial period to novels depicting the New South of the twentieth century, "laziness" has figured as a fundamental problem with social and spiritual consequences.

In his *Map to Virginia* (1612), John Smith chastises his men for their idleness and instructs them that they will starve unless they are more industrious. Smith's speech can be seen as an example of the jeremiad, a popular form of public address in both northern and southern colonies used to oppose the vice of sloth, be it physical or spiritual. The jeremiad reached its apex during the Great Awakening of the 1740s and 1750s, and in the decades leading up to the Revolution when, as David Bertelson explains in *The Lazy South* (1967), "patriotic industry" was substituted for "spiritual industry." Bertelson notes the influential writings of several southern evangelists against sloth: Isaac Chanler, Josiah Smith, and Charles Woodmason. The latter became a spokesperson for the efforts of the South Carolina Regulators, one of numerous backcountry vigilante movements that often ruthlessly opposed what they saw as the general idleness and dissoluteness in areas devoid of any official law and order. Woodmason's writings are collected in *The Carolina Backcountry on the Eve of the Revolution: The Journal and Other Writings of Charles Woodmason, Anglican Itinerant*, edited by Richard J. Hooker (1953).

Several secular writers from the colonial period who made important contributions to the image of the lazy South include Robert Beverley, William Byrd II, Thomas Jefferson, and Ebenezer Cook. All but Cook wrote formal histories of their region and attempted to document not only social but natural causes of indolence. In a deliberate effort to counter negative accounts of the region made by outsiders, Beverley writes in *The History and Present State of Virginia* (1705) that Virginia is "as healthy a Country, as any under Heaven: but the extraordinary pleasantness of the Weather, and the goodness of the Fruit, lead People into many temptations." Chief among these temptations is indolence, and he observes that "where God almighty is so Merciful as to work for People, they never work for themselves." Beverley's account of Virginia clearly echoes the biblical story of the Garden of Eden and, like Adam and Eve, the inhabitants of Beverley's paradise find it difficult to enjoy themselves in moderation. Beverley's brother-in-law and fellow Virginian William Byrd II portrays an even more hopelessly corrupted Eden in his depiction of North Carolina, given in his accounts of the 1728 expedition to survey the disputed boundary between Virginia and North Carolina. In both posthumously published accounts, the *History of the Dividing Line* (1841) and the considerably more bawdy *Secret History* (1929), Byrd portrays the North Carolinian "Lubbers" as a lazy, often nearly savage people whose indolence is determined largely by the abundance of the land. Indian corn grows so readily that "a little Pains will Subsist a very large Family." Seeds from pine trees provide mast for hogs and, with little processing, the same pines provide turpentine for sale or use. One of the earliest impressions Byrd records in his *History* is that of a "Marooner" living naked upon the shore with his "wanton Female" in a bark-covered bower "Indian Fashion," living off oysters and stolen milk. In a parodic allusion to the Gospels, Byrd notes of the Marooner that "like the Ravens, he neither plow'd nor sow'd." Byrd observes a similar tendency among "Indians" and white settlers in North Carolina for the men to force their women to perform the majority of the labor. To summarize his experience, Byrd remarks, "Surely there is no place in the World where the Inhabitants live with less Labour than in N Carolina. It approaches nearer to the Description of Lubberland than any other, by the great felicity of the Climate, the easiness of raising Provisions, and the Slothfulness of the People." It might be noted that Byrd's own son dissipated in one generation the vast wealth that his father and grandfather had painstakingly accumulated.

Like Beverley and Byrd, Thomas Jefferson acknowledges in *Notes on the State of Virginia* (1785) the often negative effects of natural environment on a society's industry, but he also considers the more important effects of its economic system. Of the several negative influences of slavery on a slaveholding society that Jefferson identifies in the section on "Customs and Manners" is his argument that "their industry is destroyed. For in a warm climate, no man will labor for himself who can make another labor for him." Jefferson concludes that of all slaveholders "a very small proportion indeed are ever seen to labor." Even though he himself owned a large plantation with many slaves, his ideal for the southern colonies was of a land of independent yeoman farmers whose virtue would derive from their daily labor upon their small farms. As the manufacturing enterprises did in the North and Europe, in the South, it was slavery that separated man from the earth and thereby led to his decline. Though Jefferson was not alone in his opposition to slavery, he was outnumbered in the South, even in the later part of the eighteenth century when open debate on the issue was still possible. Bertelson offers St. George Tucker of Virginia as an example of the opposition—which, like Jefferson, built its argument largely upon the issue of

laziness. For Tucker, however, it was not the slaveholder's but the slave's purported laziness that was at issue. Tucker held the predominant prejudice against the African race that they were by nature lazy and that "these people must be *bound* to labor if they do not voluntarily engage therein." This notion of lazy slaves is one of many prejudices that slave narratives sought to debunk; an excellent example may be found in the *Narrative of the Life of Frederick Douglass* (1845), which chronicles, with a deliberate lack of hyperbole, the amount of backbreaking labor typically heaped upon a slave, as well as Douglass's secret determination to educate himself and work his way to freedom.

Like his contemporary Robert Beverley, Ebenezer Cook(e) recognized the sloth that resulted from such a pleasant climate—in his case, Maryland. And, like Jefferson, he recognized the deleterious effects of the southern economy on the morals and behavior of the people. His most memorable work, "The Sot-Weed Factor or The Voyage to Maryland" (ca. 1708), is a verse satire in hudibrastics about a sot-weed factor's, or tobacco merchant's, voyage from Britain to the colonies. The poem's speaker, the sot-weed factor, records his startled impressions of Maryland's tobacco planters, calling attention both to the inhabitants' crudeness and his own overrefinement. Laziness ranks high among the many problems he observes, as indicated by the abundance of rum and tobacco, both conducive to their physical and intellectual stupor. Upon landing on Maryland's shores, he imagines the land to be peopled by the inhabitants of "Vagrant *Cain*" who fled divine retribution and ended up here "And in a Hut supinely dwelt," the first to deal in furs and "sot-weed." The narrator believes such physical sloth to result in moral laxity, remarking that this is a land "Where no Man's Faithful, nor a Woman Chast."

In a more serious examination of the effects of tobacco cultivation on the region's economy, Bertelson explains how an economy that depended exclusively upon cash crops—especially tobacco, and later cotton—exacerbated the absence of industry that he identifies as socially meaningful. Unlike the northern colonies that were organized around towns and cities in which work took on a moral and social significance, in the South, Bertelson argues, the isolated southern planter tended to throw himself into a "frantic pursuit of wealth to prove [his] industry," resulting only in "increased economic chaos and social fragmentation," a process that "contributed to their feelings of laziness. The harder they worked on their isolated plantations, the lazier everyone seemed." He offers as an example of such idle "busyness" William Byrd II's *Secret Diaries* (1941), with its repetitive and often absurdly compulsive account of the minutiae of Byrd's daily activities—from reciting his prayers to "rogering" his wife; in contrast to Byrd's *Diaries*, Bertelson presents Benjamin Franklin's *Autobiography* as a chronicle of socially meaningful work. He later presents William Wirt's *Sketches of the Life and Character of Patrick Henry* (1817) to exemplify the changes in cultural attitudes about work that took place with the rise of Romanticism in the early nineteenth century. Wirt portrays Patrick Henry as an "indolent" "child of nature" in opposition to Yankee acquisitiveness. With the deification of nature, society and "social" work were held in suspicion.

These changed ideas about the value of work and the stigmatization of "idleness" are perhaps best illustrated in the rise of the plantation tradition. In *Swallow Barn* (1832), John Pendleton Kennedy glamorizes the slow-paced life of the plantation. Having grown up outside Baltimore, the son of a successful merchant, Kennedy romanticizes the fading life of the Virginia plantation that he remembered from his mother's family's plantation. He depicts the slaves as noble savages who live in oneness with nature in crudely fashioned quarters that blend into the landscape. Of the slaves themselves, he primarily notes their contentment and love of sunshine, which provokes him to compare the slave children listlessly basking in the sun to "a set of terrapins luxuriating in the genial warmth of the summer, on the logs of a mill-pond." Thomas Nelson Page's postbellum *In Ole Virginia* (1887) provides a similar account of the Old South. In "Marse Chan," set during Reconstruction, a lazy, aging ex-slave named Sam leisurely recounts a tale of the "good ole times" before the war when "Niggers didn hed nothin' 't all to do" when there "warn' no trouble nor nothin." Though Joel Chandler Harris's *Uncle Remus* collections (1880, 1883, 1892, and 1905) employ stereotypical features of the black Uncle, the stories themselves contain subversive content, as does the nondialect story "Free Joe and the Rest of the World" (1887). In "Free Joe," poor whites are indicted for their prejudices concerning the "laziness" of displaced ex-slaves. Though set during slavery times, the story is more applicable to the Reconstruction audience for whom it was written.

In *The Conjure Woman* (1899), Charles Waddell Chesnutt adapts the lazy Uncle figure to even more ex-

plicitly subversive purposes. Throughout these dialect tales, the narrator, Uncle Julius, gives a series of disguised lectures on history and southern sociology to the carpetbagger landowners who have bought the North Carolina plantation where he was born. In "Mars Jeems's Nightmare," Uncle Julius's tale deals with the different perceptions of "laziness" by the black worker and the white taskmaster—as well as the different perceptions between northerners and southerners. After the new landowner hired and then discharged Julius's grandson because he found him "very trifling," Julius tells a story about an abusive master, Mars Jeems, in which Julius observes: "Mars Jeems did n' make no 'lowance fer nachul bawn laz'ness, ner sickness, ner trouble in de min', ner nuffin; he wuz des gwine ter git so much wuk outer eve'y han', er know de reason w'y." In this passage, Julius cleverly associates the southern slave-driver with the northern industrialist, who similarly lacks appropriate empathy and views laborers as machines.

The lazy Uncle figures employed in the dialect tales of Page, Harris, and Chesnutt likely borrowed from the lazy narrators of the dialect stories written by Southwest humorists earlier in the century. The eponymous protagonists of Johnson Jones Hooper's *Some Adventures of Captain Simon Suggs, Late of the Tallapoosa Volunteers* (1845) and George Washington Harris's *Sut Lovingood: Yarns Spun by a "Nat'ral Born Durn'd Fool"* (1867) were fashioned upon the oral storytellers of the frontier who lazed about campfires, young towns, and mining villages, casually "jawing" with fellow dawdlers. As with the black Uncle figure, the laxity of the frontier storyteller is accentuated by the presence of a civilized, goal-oriented easterner, who serves as the frame narrator, bringing the news of the frontier back to civilization. The stories of the frontier man stripped of his pretensions of civility and order are meant to critique the hypocrisy of the eastern audience. In "How to Tell a Story" (1895), Mark Twain analyzes the method of the frontier storyteller and calls attention to the essential convention of aimlessness: "The humorous story may be spun out to great length, and may wander around as much as it pleases, and arrive nowhere in particular." Twain's Simon Wheeler epitomizes this style of telling in "The Notorious Jumping Frog of Calaveras County" (1865). In *Adventures of Huckleberry Finn* (1885), Twain contrasts Realist and Romantic perspectives on laziness. Although the men of Bricksville, Arkansas, appear in much the same light as the Maryland colonists of Cooke's "Sot-Weed Factor"—apparently living for the sake of bumming a "chaw"—Huck's and Jim's laziness on the raft is portrayed not as depraved but rather as transcendental, creating a connection with nature and with each other.

The grotesque caricature of the lazy southerner that appeared in Byrd's *Secret History* and developed momentum in the works of the Southwest humorists remains the prominent mode of portraying poor whites in the literature of the twentieth century, surviving in such gothic portrayals of lower-class laziness that appear in Erskine Caldwell's Lester family of *Tobacco Road* (1932) and William Faulkner's Snopes clan. The Snopes Trilogy—*The Hamlet* (1940), *The Town* (1957), and *The Mansion* (1959)—depicts the poor whites' usurpation of economic and political control in Mississippi. Flem Snopes's shrewdness and energy are more than compensated for by the seemingly endless supply of sponging kin folks; a family of squatters, the Snopeses depend upon their sheer inertia to win the day. In Flannery O'Connor's grotesques of poor whites, the disinclination to work indicates a spiritual backwardness, one that is most visible in her various con men, such as the fake evangelist Onnie Jay Holy in *Wise Blood* (1952), Mr. Shiftlet, the car thief, in "The Life You Save May Be Your Own," and Manley Pointer, the Bible salesman of "Good Country People"—both stories collected in *A Good Man Is Hard to Find* (1955).

Poor whites are not the only class struggling with laziness in twentieth-century fiction. If the aristocrat William Byrd II seems anxious in his *Secret Diaries* about his usefulness to society, his twentieth-century descendents are much more so. The displaced aristocrat is a trope common to much of the century's fiction; some of the more notable examples include Faulkner's Jason Compson III (Quentin's father)—and Quentin himself—in *The Sound and the Fury* (1929) and *Absalom, Absalom!* (1936), Robert Penn Warren's Jack Burden in *All the King's Men* (1946), and William Styron's Milton Loftis in *Lie Down in Darkness* (1951). Lacking any necessary social function, these sons and grandsons of planters turn to golf, booze, and excessive introspection in an effort to fill the void created by the lack of meaningful work, a void that is made all the more apparent when they compare their petty efforts to the grand achievements of their forefathers. Perhaps the writer who most thoroughly mined this topic was Walker Percy, whose novels depict feckless aristocrats coming to terms with histories that closely resemble Percy's own family history of decline. As in O'Connor,

the failure to perform socially meaningful work reflects a loss of spiritual and moral values, which Percy's protagonists to varying degrees come to realize and rectify. Binx Bolling of *The Moviegoer* (1960) is a small-time stockbroker who is melancholy but content with his Gentilly suburban life of sensual pleasures until he becomes obsessed with a "search" for spiritual meaning. Dr. Tom More of *Love in the Ruins* (1971) is a psychiatrist who discourages his patients because he doubts that he can be of any use to them. Lance Lamar of *Lancelot* (1977) is a liberal lawyer (the favorite profession of planters' descendents) who criticizes his hypocritical involvement with the Civil Rights Movement, a self-described "idler" who, looking back on his career, finds that he was doing "less and less law" and taking longer afternoon naps until one day he decided not to go back to the office in the afternoon. In reviewing their lives and their family histories, Percy's characters seek to expose the emptiness (the spiritual sloth) of contemporary life and to find renewed resources for spiritual growth. As with the jeremiads of those Protestant evangelists of the Great Awakening, the novels of Percy and his literary heirs seek to wake their readers from spiritual indolence, a task that seems to them ever more difficult in the prosperous, industrialized Sunbelt South.

George Hovis

See also Plantation Fiction; Southwestern Humor; Tobacco.

David Bertelson, *The Lazy South* (1967).

LEE, ROBERT E.

Robert Edward Lee, the man who was to become the very prototype of the southern gentleman as well as of the southern war hero, was born into a prominent Virginia family at Stratford, Westmoreland County, on January 19, 1807. His father was Henry "Light Horse Harry" Lee of Revolutionary War cavalry fame. His mother was Ann Hill Carter Lee of the wealthy Carter family of Shirley Plantation. His father deserted his family early in Robert's life, and Lee was subsequently raised in relative poverty by his mother. Lee, with his mother's consent, decided that the best way to complete his education, taking their economic circumstances into account, was to apply for an appointment to West Point Military Academy. Lee entered West

Point in 1825 and was an exemplary student. He managed to graduate second in the 1829 class with no demerits, an almost-unheard-of attainment. Lee felt a great emotional loss when his mother died shortly after his graduation.

On June 30, 1831, after a short courtship, Lee married Mary Randolph Custis, daughter of the grandson of Martha Washington, thus becoming associated by marriage with another of the First Families of Virginia. Even though their marriage was somewhat unhappy, the Lees had seven children, four daughters and three sons. When he graduated from West Point, Lee was made an assistant to the Army Chief of Engineers and later was sent to St. Louis, where he was in charge of improving the routing of the Mississippi River. Lee met General Winfield Scott when he was appointed to the Board of Visitors at West Point in 1844. In 1846, Lee was sent to Mexico as a scout for Scott in the Mexican War. There, he served with many of the men who would eventually fight for and against him in the Civil War. Lee rendered superb service for Scott at Cerro Gordo and Chapultepec, meritorious service that Scott would never forget.

After the Mexican War, Lee was assigned to improve upon the defenses at Baltimore and was subsequently appointed to be superintendent at West Point. He was appointed as lieutenant colonel of the Second Cavalry in 1855 and was sent to Texas to contain the growing Indian problem. In 1859, Lee was ordered to command a detachment of marines that would quell the John Brown uprising at Harper's Ferry, Virginia. He then went back to Texas to serve for an additional year. That duty ended when Texas seceded. In April 1861, Lee was offered the command of all U.S. armies by Winfield Scott. In what was to become Lee's first step to the altar of southern heroism, he resigned from the U.S. Army in response to the offer. To this point in Lee's life, his career had been fairly lackluster. Promotions had come slowly for the fifty-four-year-old, and, outside of the Mexican War, circumstances had allowed Lee to show proficiency in military matters but not anything out of the ordinary. He made the difficult decision to resign from the army based on the belief that his first allegiance must be to his home state, not to his country. He was not an advocate of secession or of the military protection of the institution of slavery, but all indications were that Virginia would secede. Lee believed that he must protect his home if secession should come. Therefore, he immediately volunteered for service to his state and was given command of the

Virginia forces. It was not long before the new Confederacy had sent him into western Virginia to halt McClellan's Federal incursion from the west. Lee was not successful in western Virginia because of organizational unrest in the military leadership in that area. He was recalled to Richmond and was then sent on coastal duty in Georgia and South Carolina.

Lee was officially appointed as an advisor to Jefferson Davis, president of the Confederacy, in March 1862. Even though Lee continued as Davis's advisor throughout the remainder of the war in addition to his other duties, Davis was not a leader who took military advice easily. Lee was given the post as commander of the Army of Northern Virginia, a position that he was to retain throughout the war. Only during the final three months of the war was Lee commander of all southern troops.

With the help of skilled military commanders, Lee fought a series of battles that demonstrated his skill against armies that usually had large numerical advantages. In 1862, Lee was victorious at Second Manassas (Bull Run), fought essentially to a draw at Sharpsburg (Antietam), and won decisively at Fredricksburg. In 1863, he led his troops to a daring victory at Chancellorsville by dividing his forces and outflanking the Union army under Hooker. Lee lost his most valued commander during that battle when Stonewall Jackson was mistakenly mortally wounded by a southern soldier. To divert attention from the threatened Richmond front, Lee moved into Pennsylvania and met the Union in battle at Gettysburg in July 1863. On the third day, Lee made a drastic mistake by commanding his troops to charge uphill directly into the face of Union infantry and artillery. Lee came away from Gettysburg with a defeat that is considered by many as the beginning of the end for the Confederacy. Shortly before Gettysburg, Ulysses S. Grant had been named the commander of all Union forces. Grant began his drive to Richmond early the next year, 1864.

Grant met Lee in the Wilderness, which was the same region in which Lee had earlier been successful against Hooker at Chancellorsville. The drive southward continued through Spotsylvania Courthouse to Cold Harbor and eventually to Petersburg. Lee was able to stop Grant's overwhelmingly strong advance only by digging in at Petersburg and allowing a devastating, grueling siege to develop against him in front of Richmond. He surrendered to Grant at Appomattox Courthouse on April 9, 1865. Before the end of the month, Lincoln would be assassinated and Joseph E.

Johnston would surrender to Sherman in North Carolina. The Civil War ended with a defeated Robert E. Lee, both militarily and psychologically. Lee applied for a pardon before that summer, but it was not granted to him in his lifetime. He was never brought to trial by the Federal authorities, so he was left in limbo. For a personality given consistently to assuming responsibility for his own actions, this was a particularly difficult load to shoulder.

From his early days of being responsible for the welfare of his mother and later burdened with a sickly wife and a fairly large family, Lee had developed an unwavering sense of duty. He lived with constant tension produced by divided loyalty, shown most dramatically in the forced decision to choose between country and state in 1861. When the war ended in the defeat of his army, Lee felt a great sense of guilt. Rather than being bitter and railing against the Federal government, Lee encouraged all southerners to put the war behind them and to get on with the reconciliation process.

The war had made Lee an old man. He had no job, and he felt that he had no valuable skills. The trustees of Washington College in Lexington, Virginia, which had been decimated by the war, were interested in getting the school back to normalcy and in rebuilding for the future. This would require funds, and the trustees had enough foresight to understand that Lee would become a hero in the South. What better way to raise funds than to have a president who would have immediate name recognition? Lee was asked to aid in the rebuilding process by becoming the president of the college. Because Mary's beloved Arlington had been confiscated by the federal government, Lee accepted the post in Lexington. Washington College was a primary force in the creation of image for Lee in the South that continues to the present. Lee himself gave more to Washington College than the trustees expected. He attacked the job as he had every other assignment in his life. He worked diligently to rebuild the physical plant, the curriculum, the faculty, and the student body.

After about five years of diligent work at the school that became Washington and Lee University, Lee showed signs of severe health deterioration. His doctors recommended a trip south for recuperation. He was hailed as a hero at every train stop along the way, which tired him even more, since he was ever the hospitable host and gentleman. The trip did not provide the expected healing, and Lee died about six months after his return to Virginia.

The battle was over for Lee, but the battle for his reputation as a hero was only beginning, and the southern historical and literary establishment was directly involved in every stage of his transformation into a pristine, flawless hero. The battle for Lee's reputation was fought on two Virginia fronts: Lexington and Richmond. Several of Lee's former subordinates, led by Jubal Early, formed a society in Richmond (Association of the Army of Northern Virginia) primarily to encourage the establishment of monuments to Lee. This group and other Richmond groups were also very interested in removing Lee's corpse from the college, where he had been buried in the chapel, to Richmond for reburial. The soldiers lost the battle for reinterment but managed to fund a statue in Richmond. In the process, the group evolved into a society to guard Lee's reputation against even the most minor of criticisms.

By 1870, the year of Lee's death, the South had had too much of Reconstruction policy. It was necessary to reconstruct pride in the Lost Cause in the South. To make the generation of this southern pride more efficient, Lee was chosen as its rallying point. Historians and literary figures alike had begun to release writings concerning Lee. One of the earliest biographies was written by John Esten Cooke, then one of the best-known novelists in Virginia. His biography was highly laudatory but hinted at the most inane criticism in a few obscure places. The Richmond society, aided by the Washington and Lee College group, began to publish articles critical of Cooke and others who were at that time producing the first wave of biographies. They also countered the perceived slights by publishing biographies and war writings by their own membership. Jubal Early, the leader of this movement, later became the president of the Southern Historical Society and used its publications to hold reign over the published writings about Lee. Any hint of nonveneration was swiftly attacked in print for all to read. This type of censure molded the literature about Lee well into the twentieth century in the South and, indeed, throughout the nation.

Lee became in popular and scholarly literature the very epitome of integrity, gentility, gentlemanliness, and perfection. When he was president at Washington College, he wrote about the model of "the gentleman" in that institution; since his life was mostly shaped by his own vision of the model, writers cannot be faulted for making him the lasting prototype of the southern gentleman. His dignified, handsome demeanor has even made him the physical image of that role for many. But he definitely was not perfect. He was so driven with a need for success that he feared failure in everything that he attempted. No victory was ever perfect enough; every defeat was total. He died believing that his accomplishments in life were nonexistent. Until relatively recent times, Lee's psyche was off limits to most writers. Evelyn Scott included a chapter in her novel of the Civil War, *The Wave* (1929), which attempted to expose Lee's thought processes on the night before and the day of his surrender to Grant at Appomattox. She wrote of his need for perfection and his disarming disappointment in himself. Such writing would have been completely unacceptable in the nineteenth century. Up to the 1920s, if Lee was considered at all in fiction, it was in an often sickeningly sentimental fashion. In most fiction about the Civil War period, Lee was only part of the backdrop for fictional characters as the perfect, idolized commander.

The cult of infallibility became so strong during the early part of the twentieth century that one of the South's literary giants, Allen Tate, became disillusioned as he began to study Lee's life in preparation for writing a literary biography of Lee to complete his planned three-volume sequence on southern leaders: *Stonewall Jackson* (1928), *Jefferson Davis* (1929), and Robert E. Lee. He abandoned the Lee project after he came to question Lee's motivations, a doubt conceivably fostered by the long southern campaign for absolute, undefiled heroism in Lee. Tate's fellow agrarian, Donald Davidson, had no such analytical misgivings when he celebrated Lee's heroism in his best-known poem, "Lee in the Mountains."

Douglas Southall Freeman published his seven-volume biography of Lee during the 1930s, a biography that has become a standard against which all Lee biographies will be measured but which very much follows the nineteenth-century model of infallibility and idolatry. Probably the best recent analysis of Lee that encompasses the entire Civil War was written by Shelby Foote in *The Civil War: A Narrative* (3 volumes, 1958–1974). Lee comes off extremely well, but not as perfect. More recently, it has become quite fashionable for writers to examine Lee with a view toward breaking down godlike stereotypes. Thomas Connelly (*The Marble Man: Robert E. Lee and His Image in American Society,* 1977) has written a thoroughly researched analysis of the development of the Lee heroic image from early days in Lexington and Richmond to the present day throughout the nation. Alan Nolan (*Lee Considered: General Robert E. Lee and Civil War History,* 1991) and John D. McKenzie (*Uncertain*

Glory: Lee's Generalship Re-Examined, 1997) have concentrated on real or perceived errors in Lee's judgment and in psychological flaws in Lee, the man and the soldier. Charles P. Roland has attempted to defend Lee against these onslaughts in *Reflections on Lee: A Historical Perspective* (1995). Emory M. Thomas has recently demonstrated the most valid pathway for future studies of Lee in *Robert E. Lee: A Biography* (1995).

Douglas Savage attempts to investigate Lee's real motivations, especially those during the Battle of Gettysburg, in *The Court Martial of Robert E. Lee: A Historical Novel* (1993). He tries to fit the fictional legal action into a time after Lee's withdrawal from Gettysburg when he had been called to Richmond. A less-critical and more hero-worshipful fictional account has been written by Lamar Herrin in *The Unwritten Chronicles of Robert E. Lee: A Novel* (1989). This novel's primary character is Stonewall Jackson, the title notwithstanding. Lee is so godlike in this novel that he is psychic. He knows what Jackson knows; he feels what Jackson feels. Herrin goes into great detail concerning Jackson's field operations, his meetings with Lee, and his wounding and subsequent death. Herrin intersperses the historical parts of his novel with incidents from his own, possibly fictional, life. This type of interspersion is also used as a device in a recent novel about Robert E. Lee, which is by far the most unusual, interesting, and scholarly of the lot, M. A. Harper's *For the Love of Robert E. Lee* (1992). Harper's central character is a teenage girl, Garnet, who falls in love with the historical man. Her life and experiences directly reflect those of Robert E. Lee. This synchronism of experiences has created an emotional attachment across the ages. Lee lives, as does Garnet, a common life. When Lee dies for Garnet, she moves onward into her late adolescence having loved and profited from knowing a real man, who was only incidentally long gone. Harper surmises from the available historical evidence and an astute understanding of common human nature that Lee was as real as her readers.

D. Michael Snider

See also Gentleman; Lost Cause.

Thomas L. Connelly, *The Marble Man: Robert E. Lee and His Image in American Society* (1977); Michael Kreyling, *Figures of the Hero in Southern Narrative* (1987); Charles P. Roland,

Reflections on Lee (1995); Emory M. Thomas, *Robert E. Lee: A Biography* (1995).

LESBIAN LITERATURE

Identifying lesbian writers in southern literature is problematic for several reasons. Although some women writers may actively encourage such a label, others, particularly older writers such as Lillian Smith and Carson McCullers, might not have labeled themselves "lesbian" although biographical evidence suggests this identification. Many writers have remained closeted not only about their "queerness" but about their "southernness" as well; others are openly lesbian and southern but rarely write about these topics in their fiction. As if the issue of sexual and geographic identification were not complicated enough, very few of these confirmed southern lesbians have actually made the American South their lifelong home. Gay writers who identity themselves as southern often live in California or New York or centers more hospitable to lesbians and gay men. This overview focuses on the women writers who were born, or lived a significant portion of their childhood, in the South and are documented as having some queer identification.

The theoretical issue of multiple identification is apparent in the mutual silence between queer studies and southern studies. Queer theory and lesbian studies have frequently not taken into account the contribution of southern writers, and the well-established field of criticism on southern women writers often excludes lesbians. Fortunately, these problems are easing and there are now "out" southern lesbian writers who have made such a prominent contribution to literary studies that no one can ignore them. They include Rita Mae Brown, Dorothy Allison, Mab Segrest, Blanche McCary Boyd, June Arnold, and Bertha Harris. Even on this list, there are only a couple of writers who kept a stationary home in the South. As we consider birth places and childhoods, we must add some of the most formidable women in feminist and lesbian studies, namely Robin Morgan, Jane Chambers, Sally Miller Gearhart, and Minnie Bruce Pratt. Terri Jewell, Doris Davenport, Anne Schockley, and J. M. Redmann are lesser-known but important contributors to the field.

In many ways, Lillian Smith is the foremother of lesbian southern writers. Her early works, while not addressing lesbianism directly, grew out of her deep conviction about the right of every human being to a voice

and respect. Her role as a sexual outsider in the South made her understand the plight of African Americans, and she quickly became a vocal supporter of civil rights and an outspoken activist against lynching. Her first novel, *Strange Fruit* (1944), about a closeted interracial love affair between a black woman and a white man that ends in the death of the white man and the lynching of a black man, won critical acclaim and sold thousands of copies. By writing about interracial love affairs demanding secrecy and a break from all social norms, Smith dealt with parallel issues about which lesbians in the 1940s could not have written and expect to be published. Many local governments banned *Strange Fruit,* and only the intervention of Eleanor Roosevelt helped lift the ban. The journal that Smith edited with her lifelong companion, Paula Snelling, called first *Pseudopodia* then *North American Review* and finally *South Today,* fought against the image of the South put forth by such groups as the Agrarians and other conservative southern intellectuals. Smith also authored *Killers of the Dream* (1949), *The Journey* (1954), *Now Is the Time* (1955), *One Hour* (1959), *Memory of a Large Christmas* (1962), *Our Faces, Our Worlds* (1964), *From the Mountain* (1972), and *The Winner Names the Age* (1978). Although *Strange Fruit* received the most critical acclaim, her most famous book is *Killers of the Dream,* her collection of essays about southern segregation, which explores in detail the deep psychological and moral harm done to society by this racist ideology. Unfortunately, societal prejudices forced Smith and Snelling to remain closeted all of their lives; they could never espouse the cause of gay rights with the eloquently persuasive rhetoric with which they espoused African American rights.

Carson McCullers, whose novels resonate with sexually liminal characters, was known to identify as bisexual and at times lesbian. Her novels and plays include characters to whom lesbian readers for generations have turned in their own search for role models. In *The Member of the Wedding* (1946), Frankie is the quintessential queer character in love but perpetually the outsider to her brother's wedding. As an outsider to marriage and weddings, forever desiring but forever excluded from this conventional form of love, Frankie's love remains bisexual and triangulated with other queer figures, Berenice and John Henry, or with the Barbie and Ken images of her fantasy world, her brother and his wife. Frankie's tomboy character is one to whom most lesbians can relate. Her little friend and cousin John Henry is the stereotypical effeminate (read gay) male, who dies rather than realize his dreams. In the characterization of Mister Singer in *The Heart Is a Lonely Hunter* (1940), McCullers creates the quintessential closeted character in the deaf mute. Everyone accepts love from him, but no one knows how to give him love. His loneliness is impenetrable and his eventual suicide heartbreaking. Through her acutely sensitive characterizations, McCullers speaks the voice of silence. By giving life to these characters, McCullers affirms the closeted and lonely world of pre-Stonewall gay life. Both works were made into movies, as were *Reflections in a Golden Eye* (1941) and *The Ballad of the Sad Café* (1951). McCullers has received more media attention than almost any other lesbian writer.

Among contemporary writers, Rita Mae Brown and Dorothy Allison have received the most visibility. Brown has been writing "out" lesbian fiction since the 1970s. Her novel *Rubyfruit Jungle* (1973), a semiautobiographical coming-of-age novel about young Molly Bolt, was the first self-confirming novel that many lesbians had the chance to read. Although Brown's family moved to Florida when she was eleven, she grew up in Pennsylvania and lived most of her early adult life in New York. But her status as a southern writer is well-secured by the fact that she has lived for a long time in Charlottesville, Virginia, and many of her novels, including *Southern Discomfort* (1982) and *Murder at Monticello: Or Old Sins* (1994), are set in the South. Runnymeade, a fictional town in much of her work, is located on the Mason-Dixon Line. Brown's challenge to conventional forms of sexual behavior in her writing and her characterizations is always refreshing and has forced the feminist movement to question its own rigid standards. By saying and writing the unexpected—and the often predeterminedly unacceptable—Brown has contributed an iconoclastic air to southern lesbian fiction.

Allison, born in 1949 in Greenville, South Carolina, is a more literary and less popular fiction writer than Brown. In her essays, she writes openly about butches and femmes and the transgressive power of being queer; in her novels, she highlights class and gender. In fact, no subject is too heartbreaking or difficult for her to tackle. *Bastard Out of Carolina* (1992) has won enormous critical acclaim for its unflinching portrayal of child sexual abuse and incest. In this novel, Allison's portrait of Bone, the protagonist, as a young girl facing continuous sexual and physical abuse at the hands of her stepfather, is chilling and powerful. Although Bone

is never named a lesbian, her strength and outsider status make her a role model for lesbians. Her aunt is a dyke but never named so. Allison's ability to bridge the gap between the poverty of her childhood and the intellectual world of her adult life makes her a remarkable writer in every respect. Her latest work, entitled *Cavedweller* (1998), takes these themes even further. Her work includes many short stories and poems published in journals such as *Conditions, The Lesbian Fiction Anthology, The Village Voice,* and *Southern Exposure.* Her works include a collection of poems entitled *The Women Who Hate Me* (1983), *Trash: Short Stories* (1988), *The Women Who Hate Me: Poetry 1980–1990,* and *Skin: Talking About Sex, Class, and Literature* (1993).

Mab Segrest, a nonfiction writer who has singlehandedly defined the field of southern lesbian writers, has named McCullers and Smith as her foremothers. As an activist in the civil rights, feminist, gay and lesbian, queer, and anti-Klan movements, Segrest reminds us of the real-life battles involved in being female, queer, and an activist in the South. In her two books of autobiographical essays, *My Mama's Dead Squirrel* (1985) and *Memoirs of a Race Traitor* (1993), Segrest writes passionately and eloquently about the fact that the act of writing as a lesbian in the South is an act of resistance, a battle to the end.

Segrest and Allison belong to the second generation of "out" lesbian southern writers. Allison was born late enough to have the opportunity to study at the Sagaris Institute in Vermont with a good-old-girl network of southern lesbian writers including Bertha Harris, Blanche McCary Boyd, and Rita Mae Brown. Bertha Harris, who lives in Fayetteville, North Carolina, wrote *Catching Saradove* (1969), *Confessions of Cherubino* (1972), and, with Emily Sisley, *Traveller in Eternity* (1975), *Lover* (1976) and *The Joys of Lesbian Sex: A Tender and Liberated Guide to the Pleasures and Problems of a Lesbian Lifestyle* (1977). Harris is an out and outspoken lesbian writer whose works confirm and celebrate women characters in lesbian relationships. Unfortunately, because she has not received a great deal of critical acclaim, her books are hard to find.

June Arnold, who was born October 27, 1926, in Greenville, South Carolina, and later moved to Houston, is better known. In 1972 Arnold and several other lesbian authors, including Rita Mae Brown and Bertha Harris, started Daughters Inc. Press, one of the most influential presses of the early feminist movement. Her first novel, *Applesauce* (1967), had already won considerable critical attention when Arnold helped found this remarkable press. Her novels *The Cook and the Carpenter* (1973) and particularly *Sister Gin* (1975) deal openly with lesbian relationships. In these novels, Arnold experiments with form and style in a very refreshing manner. More than almost any other lesbian feminist writer until Allison, Arnold was willing to explore the dark side of lesbian relationships, including drinking, abuse, and dependency, issues often left unspoken in the politically correct seventies. Her last novel, *Baby Houston,* about her mother, was published in 1987, six years after Arnold's own death from cancer.

Blanche McCary Boyd is younger than Arnold, born in 1945 also in South Carolina, although she made her home in Charleston. She has lived most of her adult life outside the South, but the source of many of her characters is definitely southern. Boyd is willing to see the direct connection between African American civil rights and the gay and feminist liberation movements. Her characters are activists in the broadest human sense of the word, righting injustices on the very personal home front. Her characters forge revolutionary friendships across racial, class, and age lines. She published *Nerves* in 1973, *Mourning the Death of Magic* in 1977, a collection of essays called *The Redneck Way of Knowledge* in 1983, and *The Revolution of Little Girls* in 1992.

Several writers who are not usually associated with the South but who were born and lived a portion of their lives there are Jane Chambers, a lesbian playwright who moved to New York; Sally Gearhart, who wrote the lesbian utopian novel *Wanderground* (1984); the activist/essayist Robin Morgan; and the poet Minnie Bruce Pratt. Chambers wrote twelve plays before her early death from a brain tumor. Her most famous plays were *The Late Snow* (1974), *The Common Garden Variety* (1976), *My Blue Heaven* (1981), *Kudzu* (1981), *Quintessential Image* (1982), *Last Summer at Bluefish Cove* (1982), and *The Eye of the Gull* (1991). She also wrote novels, television shows, poetry, and monologues. Her contribution to lesbian theater is monumental, far beyond that which other lesbian playwrights had previously achieved.

Sally Gearhart's *Wanderground* literally defined feminism for a generation of young lesbians, and her activism later, after Harvey Milk's murder, made her an icon for radical dykes all over the country. Born in 1931 in Pearisburg, Virginia, she attended Sweetbriar College. She later moved to California after a period in Texas and the Midwest.

Robin Morgan was one of the most prolific and influential writers during the first stage of the lesbian feminist movement. Her books *Sisterhood Is Powerful* (1970), *Going Too Far* (1977), and *Sisterhood Is Global* (1984) empowered millions of women and made them think of the political meaning of their individual actions. In fact, reading Robin Morgan's *Goodbye to All That* inspired Gearhart to come out. Morgan is famous for her essays, but she has also written five books of poetry, two novels, and four other books of nonfiction. Her role as editor of *Ms.* transformed that magazine, and her insightful and radical comments have touched every aspect of the lesbian feminist movement.

One of the most exciting new voices in southern literature is Minnie Bruce Pratt, who was born in Selma, Alabama, in 1946 and grew up in Centreville, Alabama. Minnie Bruce Pratt published four books of poetry and one book of essays between 1981 and 1995. Her works include *The Sound of One Fork* (1981), *Yours in Struggle: Three Feminist Perspectives on Anti-Semitism and Racism* (1984), *We Say We Love Each Other* (1985), *Crime Against Nature* (1990), *Rebellion: Essays 1980–1991* (1991), and *S/HE* (1995). In her poems, Pratt chronicles her journey from good girl and good wife, married with children, through coming out as a lesbian. She writes poignantly of the journey, from losing custody of her children to finding them again as young people who are ready to accept her life-style and life choices.

A lesser-known but important southern lesbian poet is Doris Davenport, an African American who was born January 29, 1949, in Gainesville, Florida. Although her books of poems met many rejections even at the hands of small black feminist presses, she persevered by publishing her own work in collections including *It's Like This* (1980), *eat thunder & drink rain* (1982), and *Voodoo Chile: Slight Return* (1991).

Lesbian writing is burgeoning in the South. Lesbian southern writers represent enormous diversity, crossing boundaries of age, religion, race, class, and geographical location. Merging political activism and literary endeavors, they have experimented with a wide variety of genres and literary forms.

Rebecca Mark

See also Gay Literature; Sex and Sexuality.

John Howard, ed., *Carryin' on in the Lesbian and Gay South* (1977); James Sears, *Lonely Hunters: An Oral History of Lesbian and Gay Southern Life* (1997).

"LETTER FROM BIRMINGHAM JAIL"

On Good Friday, April 12, 1963, Martin Luther King Jr. (1929–1968) was arrested in Birmingham, Alabama, on the charge of having led illegal demonstrations. A willingness to submit himself to arrest was a necessary component of the program of nonviolent protest against racial discrimination that King—who was, at the time of this arrest, the president of the Southern Christian Leadership Conference—advocated during the Civil Rights Movement in the 1950s and 1960s.

The "Letter from Birmingham Jail," dated April 16, 1963, was written while King was in solitary confinement in the city jail. He was released after eight days, but his letter had already been smuggled out. The lengthy document was quickly published, first in pamphlet form, then in various national magazines reaching both black and white audiences. It was excerpted in *Time* when that publication named King its "Man of the Year" (January 3, 1964), and it was included in King's book *Why We Can't Wait* (1964), an account of the events in Birmingham.

Though clearly intended to be read by a large audience, the letter addresses a group of eight prominent white clergymen ("My Dear Fellow Clergymen," it begins) and should be understood in terms of this rhetorical device. These men had renewed their earlier appeal for order, calling upon Birmingham's black populace to ignore King, whom they labeled an "outsider." In addressing them, King addressed moderate white southerners who, while claiming to support the civil rights of blacks, were more intent on preserving the stability of the region. In presenting classical, historical, and theological arguments for civil disobedience, King showed himself to be upholding traditions that the clergymen would recognize as shared among them.

In "On the Duty of Civil Disobedience" (1849), Henry David Thoreau gave an account of his willingness to go to jail rather than pay taxes to a government that returned fugitive slaves to their owners. This essay, which King had read in college, was important to the development of his political conscience. King's own

letter may be seen as a complementary landmark in American literature.

Amber Vogel

See also Birmingham, Alabama; Civil Rights Movement; Clergy; Letters; Preaching; Race Relations; Racism.

Martin Luther King Jr., *Why We Can't Wait* (1964); David L. Lewis, *King: A Biography* (1978); S. Jonathan Bass, *Blessed Are the Peacemakers: Martin Luther King Jr., Eight White Religious Leaders, and the "Letter from Birmingham Jail"* (2001).

LETTERS

Authoritative voices of Founding Fathers forging a nation of freedom; antebellum voices of privilege describing lavish balls and dinner parties; Reconstruction voices of privation and displacement bemoaning not only the loss of plantations and cherished family possessions but also the disappearance of a beloved way of life; soldiers' voices recounting the hardships of camp life, the tactics of military campaigns, and the horrors of battle; writers' voices critiquing their own and others' works, conducting business with editors, literary agents, and publishers, revealing the constant conflict between the creative instinct and the demands of daily life—these are a sampling of the diverse voices captured in letters about the South. The value of these letters is far-ranging. They are windows into the human soul—intimate communicators of profound thoughts and heartfelt emotions shared between trusted correspondents: husbands and wives, parents and children, sisters and brothers, lifelong friends. Through letters, we encounter confessions of homesickness, passionate declarations of love, the heart-wrenching grief of parents whose children succumb to illness, fears of mortality. Moreover, letters provide a passageway into history, offering an immediacy and vibrancy of detail lost in retrospective narrative. Through letters, such as one written by a Confederate soldier who apologizes for ending abruptly as he puts down his pen and prepares to face an invading Yankee army, we become time travelers, reliving momentous events. In addition, these letters offer a wealth of information about ordinary experience: food and beverages, clothing, houses and household furnishings, social customs, entertainment, medical care, travel, economic transactions, and religious and moral values. Furthermore, the letters of those who were regular correspondents become a revelation of a life in its time—of the letter writer's personality, values, goals, and talents. Indeed, it is that quality that has ensured the survival of many letters, as family members have lovingly preserved them through generations.

The style of letters also provides information of historical value. Letters often reveal the educational level and class of the writer. For example, letters from southern yeoman farmers are usually brief, ignore paragraphing conventions, and contain many misspellings and grammatical errors; whereas letters from educated plantation owners display a felicity of expression and a range of literary and biblical allusions. Stylistic conventions vary over time. Eighteenth-century letters are self-consciously elaborate and literary, showing a concern with public affairs and a fondness for philosophical discourse; whereas nineteenth-century letters are more spontaneous and amusing, covering a broader range of subjects. Twentieth-century letters are usually candid in discussing marital disharmony and psychological and medical problems.

Of primary historic value is the legacy of letters—housed mainly in the Library of Congress and the National Archives—left by great southern leaders who were aware of the importance of preserving their papers. Among such preeminent letter writers were George Washington, Thomas Jefferson, James Madison, John Calhoun, and Henry Clay.

Aware of his role as "Father of Our Country," George Washington upon his return to Mount Vernon after his presidency set as a major priority organizing and preserving his documents as a record of the nation's founding. Washington's letters chart the highlights of his career from fighting in the French and Indian War to commanding the Continental army to serving as the nation's first president.

Undoubtedly one of the world's most eloquent and prolific letter writers was Thomas Jefferson. Devoted to spending several hours each day at his writing desk, Jefferson, historians estimate, wrote approximately nineteen thousand letters to thousands of persons, including statesmen, explorers, scientists, merchants, scholars, planters, soldiers, family, and friends at home and abroad. Extending from 1760 to 1826, Jefferson's correspondence provides one of the richest records of the founding and growth of the Republic. Jefferson's letters are also notable for his promotion of the agrarian life-style, his grace of expression, and the omnivorous knowledge he displays in such fields as government, medicine, agriculture, literature, music,

philosophy, religion, architecture, law, and the natural sciences. Particularly interesting are the collections of Jefferson's correspondence with John and Abigail Adams and with James Madison. Leslie Cappon, editor of *The Adams-Jefferson Letters,* suggests that the correspondence is the most quotable and historically significant in American history as the two men share with each other their daily problems in public office, reflect on statesmanship, ponder philosophical issues, and review their achievements as leaders of the American Revolution. The extended correspondence between Jefferson and Madison, perhaps America's most talented exemplars of the golden age of letter writing, offers fascinating insight into the shaping of the Constitution.

Extraordinary public service is also chronicled in the papers of Henry Clay and John C. Calhoun. Clay's correspondence, extending from 1797 to 1852, charts his career from when he was a young lawyer venturing west from Virginia to seek his fortune to his death as an elder statesman, having served as senator, speaker of the House of Representatives, secretary of state under John Quincy Adams, and three times candidate for the presidency. Calhoun's papers, covering forty years of public service as a congressman and as secretary of war under James Monroe, are most notable for revealing his shift from a focus on political and economic nationalism to championing the privileged social order of the Old South.

That order is captured in a number of letter collections from members of planter families. Published during the last three decades of the twentieth century as new historicism has brought about increasing interest in domestic life, these collections paint a picture of the daily activities of planter families and their servants and address such issues as courtship, marriage, childbirth and childrearing, education, religion, and travel. One of the most fascinating and unique collections is *The Children of Pride* (1972), edited by Robert Manson Myers, who assembled chronologically letters from the family papers of Charles Colcock Jones of Liberty County, Georgia, to create a story, almost like an epistolary novel, of life in coastal Georgia before, during, and after the Civil War. Covering the period from 1854 to 1868, *The Children of Pride* progresses from prewar prosperity to postwar devastation, ultimately depicting the collapse of a civilization. Although the letters record climactic events in American history, including Abraham Lincoln's election, southern secession, Civil War battles, Lincoln's inauguration, and his assassination, it is the ordinary experiences that are most memorable: a trip to Niagara Falls, a yellow-fever epidemic, a visit to a Confederate hospital, a birth on a plantation during a Yankee raid. With its diverse cast of characters and its vivid details of daily life, *The Children of Pride* transports readers to nineteenth-century Georgia. Another fascinating collection is *Tokens of Affection: The Letters of a Planter's Daughter in the Old South* (1996), edited by Carol Bleser. These letters showcase the storytelling talent of Maria Bryan as she writes to her older sister, Julia Bryan Cumming, of life during the 1820s to 1840s on the family plantation in Mt. Zion, a small rural community seventy-five miles from Augusta, Georgia. Belying the widespread belief that a planter's daughter led a pampered existence, Maria's letters depict a busy schedule of doing housework, tending the sick, cutting out and sewing clothes for slaves, tutoring younger siblings, grading papers for local teachers, entertaining guests, attending church, making social visits, and reading. Maria's letters are memorable for portraying antebellum life when King Cotton ruled and for depicting the loving relationship between sisters.

Probably the richest treasure trove of material combining descriptions of daily life with the vivid capturing of important historical events are the letters written by participants in the War Between the States. There is a bounty of such correspondence; indeed, historians speculate that hundreds of millions of letters were exchanged during the four-year war. Surviving letters come from soldiers of all ranks, from generals to privates, as well as from surgeons and nurses. The letters represent the various branches of the service: the artillery, the cavalry, and the marine corps. Civil War soldiers were among the most literate in history, with over 90 percent of the Union soldiers and over 80 percent of the Confederates being able to read and write. Because many of the soldiers were away from home for the first time in their lives, they wrote home frequently. Unaware of writing for posterity, most correspondents simply desired to keep in touch with family and friends, and to share with them the new experiences and faraway places they saw. Because soldiers' letters were not censored, as in later wars, they are remarkably candid in discussing opinions of politicians, abuses of some of the officers, and details of military operations. The content of the letters is similar as soldiers relate their concern about the welfare of family members, the boredom of camp life, the poor quality and limited supply of rations, the vicissitudes of bad weather and illness, the horrors of battles with gunshot

falling like hail, the postbattle trauma of witnessing the wounded and dead.

One of the most poignant collections of Civil War correspondence is *Recollections and Letters of General Robert E. Lee* (1904), written and edited by Lee's son, Captain Robert E. Lee. The letters contain much material of historical importance, including Lee's suppressing of John Brown's raid at Harper's Ferry, his formal resignation from the U.S. Army, his acceptance of the command of the military forces of Virginia, his descriptions of camp life and battles, military advice he sends to Stonewall Jackson, reports to the president of the Confederacy, Jefferson Davis, and his grief over the loss of his valiant soldiers. Moreover, the letters provide a rare intimate portrait of Lee, who although reserved and dignified, had a great tenderness for his family and a playful sense of humor. Above all, the letters reveal a man who stood for bravery, responsibility, and integrity; who promoted peace; and who maintained a firm faith in God.

Another notable collection is *Blue-Eyed Child of Fortune: The Civil War Letters of Colonel Robert Gould Shaw* (1992), which according to Russell Duncan, the editor, presents what "may be the most eloquent prose any soldier wrote home during any war." The son of wealthy abolitionist Bostonians, Shaw gained fame when he agreed to lead the North's first regiment of black soldiers. In his letters, Shaw reveals his maturation from making racist remarks about his men's appearance and poor language to expressing respect for their intelligence, commitment to discipline, and courage. Ultimately, aware of his likely death, Shaw heroically chose to lead his troops in a fatal attack on Fort Wagner at Charleston—an attack that dramatically changed the nation's opinion about the valor of black soldiers.

Several other collections stand out for their uniqueness. One is *Letters from Lee's Army or Memoirs of Life In and Out of the Army in Virginia During the War Between the States* (1947), which presents highly detailed letters between a husband serving in the Second Virginia Cavalry and his wife. He relates witnessing the death of a boyhood friend at Bull Run, the humorous mishap of a servant who accidentally cuts General Beauregard's tent ropes, the bravery of a young woman who walked five miles at night to warn Confederate pickets of the approach of enemies, the execution of deserters, and a near brush with death as a bullet passes through a lock of his hair. In turn, she informs her husband of the deaths from illness of their young son and daughter, laments the demise of southern hospitality, relates with outrage the tale of a Yankee gunboat shelling a Confederate house in which there was a dying child and an anxious mother, comments on nursing wounded soldiers, and proudly relates how she was determined to save the family silver from the Yankees by hiding it under her hoop skirt. Another unique collection is *An Uncommon Soldier: The Civil War Letters of Sarah Roseta Wakeman, alias Private Lyons Wakeman* (1994), the first published collection of correspondence by a female soldier—one of an estimated four hundred women soldiers who disguised their identities out of a desire to express their patriotism, to have adventure, to earn money for their families, or to be near husbands or lovers. Also significant is *On the Altar of Freedom: A Black Soldier's Civil War Letters from the Front,* in which Corporal James Henry Gooding, who served with Colonel Shaw's Fifty-Fourth Massachusetts Volunteer Infantry, writes of the hardships and pleasures of camp life, of marches, of picket duty, of trench warfare, of pay discrimination for black soldiers, and of the battles at Fort Wagner and in Florida. Gooding's eloquent letters reflect the strong social conscience of one who gave his life to end slavery and preserve the Union.

As wealthy as the South is in the abundance of letters of historical value, so is it in its legacy of letters by fiction writers, poets, and playwrights. These letter collections often reveal the essence of a writer's life. For example, the letters of Edgar Allan Poe record the constant economic struggles and disappointments of a dedicated man of letters who in order to survive was often forced to assume the role of a literary hack. In contrast, Sidney Lanier's letters, written in a lively style, reveal a life rich in friendship and appreciation of music and poetry. Allen Tate's letters, particularly those to his lifelong friend Andrew Lytle, portray a supportive companion and an astute critic of his associates' work. Tate's wife, Caroline Gordon, in her letters to her dear friend Sally Wood, records the constant strain she faced as she tried to develop into a professional writer while confronting the demands of being a wife, mother, and hostess. Flannery O'Connor's letters exude an exuberant love of life and a deep spirituality—despite her having the disease lupus erythematosus. In fact, that disease, according to Sally Fitzgerald, the editor of O'Connor's letters, enabled O'Connor to acquire "the habit of being," which Fitzgerald defines as an excellence of temperament and intellectual activity that leads to prophetic vision.

Writers' attitudes toward their correspondence vary immeasurably. Always humble, John Crowe Ransom didn't think details about his personal life would interest the world. Therefore, he was very careless about preserving his incoming and outgoing letters. For instance, he threw away letters that T. S. Eliot wrote to him about the nature of poetry and failed to make copies of his own replies. Quite the opposite, Paul Green meticulously saved thousands of copies of his letters, together with their matching correspondence, arranged chronologically in filing cabinets in his home. For Green, incredibly gifted as a talker, letters were a form of conversation, whether he was offering comfort, gratitude, or advice to a friend, or expounding on his moral vision regarding education, social justice, or the arts. Thomas Wolfe's letters were written more for himself than for others, reflecting his habit of writing out of a psychological need to record his thoughts, emotions, and experiences. Indeed, many of his letters remained unmailed—sometimes because he was too engrossed in his creative work to purchase stamps or envelopes or even to journey to the mailbox, sometimes because he worried about their volatile content as he expressed anger or became disillusioned with former friends. Obsessively protective of his papers, Wolfe hoarded his letters in boxes or suitcases, even carrying them around with him when he traveled. For him, they formed in part what he termed "the fabric of his life," out of which he created literature.

Among the most talented southern letter writers were William Gilmore Simms, Mark Twain, and William Faulkner. Simms was an amazing writer who often produced as many as twenty letters a day. His letters reveal Simms's concern with political affairs—particularly secession. More important, they provide a picture of the nineteenth-century literary scene as he corresponds with friends William Cullen Bryant, John Pendleton Kennedy, Paul Hamilton Hayne, and Henry Timrod, and records information about the pay he received for various poems, stories, and novels; offers interpretations of his major works; and reveals the difficulties facing a southern writer with a northern publisher. Mark Twain's letters are notable not only for providing an account of the key events in his life but also for displaying his keen powers of observation, humor, and vernacular speech. Particularly memorable are his guilt-ridden, grief-stricken letters recounting his brother Henry's death after a steamboat explosion, his almost daily love letters to his fiancée, Olivia Langdon, expressing his wish to be able to put on a halo in order to rise to her level, and his letters recording an over-forty-year friendship with his mentor William Dean Howells. Fiercely protective of his privacy, William Faulkner did not wish for his letters to be published. He proclaimed that one sentence could effectively summarize his life: "He made the books and he died." Nevertheless, Faulkner's daughter Jill, some of his friends, and collectors such as Louis Daniel Brodsky decided that the publication of his letters would clarify essential information about his life and career. Some of the letters are painfully personal—for instance, those containing revelations about feeling entrapped in his marriage, discussions of his affairs, or confessions of despondency. Others discuss aesthetic, social, political, and philosophical attitudes. Still others depict the famed author's relationships with family, other writers, publishers, editors, directors, producers, and avid readers of his work. Perhaps the most valuable are those letters that reveal his literary intentions, sources that influenced him, and steps in his creative process.

The southern reverence for tradition and cherishing family connections has ensured the survival of countless letters from the colonial period onwards, and the southern gift for weaving narratives that capture the quality of oral talk has guaranteed to those who peruse these letters an endlessly entertaining and illuminating pastime.

Lynne P. Shackelford

See also Agrarians; Autobiographical Impulse; Civil War; Confederate States of America; Domesticity; Family; Fugitives, The; Manuscript Collections; Telling About the South.

LEXINGTON, KENTUCKY

Lexington, Kentucky, is a city that until recently enjoyed a unique geographical setting: spatial definition and confinement by the horse farms that surrounded it. It was in effect a city in the country. Established after the American Revolution, in 1779, with its name deriving from the Battle of Lexington, Massachusetts, the city grew slowly and along the grid pattern that so distinguished American cities of the nineteenth century. (The downtown is an intersection of Broad Street—north-south—and Main Street—east-west.) Once called the "Athens of the West," largely because of the leading role that its oldest educational institution, Transylvania University (1780), then played in higher educa-

tion, the city grew slowly and with few of the social convulsions that have marked industrializing cities. Lexington's economic base was essentially commercial, dependent initially on the manufacture of hemp as rope and then on the sale of burley tobacco, which is raised in the region. Moreover, as the center around which sweep the horse farms, Lexington has gained an international reputation for its annual sales. Lexington has been called "the Queen of the Bluegrass" and is known as the home of Man O' War, perhaps America's most famous racehorse, and it is still surrounded by dozens of thoroughbred horse farms with their trademark white-plank fences.

The second largest city in the state after Louisville, Lexington underwent considerable growth and social diversification soon after World War II. The population rose from 100,746 in 1950 to 239,942 in 1996. (These figures are for both the city and Fayette County, which merged in 1974 to form a single political entity, the Lexington-Fayette County Government.) A considerable part of this growth is explained by the establishment of several major manufacturers in the city, the most significant being IBM, which transferred its electric-typewriter division there in 1956. These new businesses helped create an extensive professional class that largely accounted for the southward thrust of the city's residential area and the extension of its cultural institutions. Moreover, the rapid growth of the University of Kentucky, established in 1859 but now enlarged to major proportions with a student population of some 30,000 and a significant medical center, has greatly enriched both the economy and the culture. As a university city, Lexington has counted among its students and faculty many writers, some of the most important being Guy Davenport, Wendell Berry, Bobbie Ann Mason, Gurney Norman, and Ed McClanahan.

Although now predominantly white in its ethnic composition (83 percent as against the African American figure of 13 percent), Lexington in the early nineteenth century had a population that was composed almost equally of whites and slaves, and the city was the site of an important slave market for labor destined for southern plantations. Recently, the city has further diversified culturally with the population now including Southeast Asians (2.2 percent) and Hispanics (1.4 percent).

Never provincial in its culture or outlook, Lexington has in the last few decades become increasingly cosmopolitan. It now has many ethnic festivals, supports three semiprofessional theater groups, a large number of art galleries, a major philharmonic orchestra, and a children's museum. Today, the rapid residential expansion and the development of several major shopping malls have raised intense public debate over land use and urban planning.

Raymond F. Betts

See also Border States; Horses and Horse Racing; Kentucky, University of.

John C. Wright, *Lexington: Heart of the Bluegrass* (1982).

LIBERALISM

There is a widespread assumption that "the Southern tradition," as one contemporary historian has put it, is "quintessentially conservative." That may well be true of its distinctive character, compared to other American regions, as was becoming evident some fifty years after the Declaration of Independence was signed and as the national debate over slavery began to intensify. But this development should not obscure the important role of southern figures, such as George Wythe (Jefferson's mentor, who worked with him on the revision of Virginia's laws, including the abolition of primogeniture), George Mason (author of the Virginia Declaration of Rights), Thomas Jefferson (author of the Declaration of Independence and the Virginia Statute for Religious Freedom), and James Madison (author of *Memorial and Remonstrance,* drafter of the Bill of Rights, and principal author of *The Federalist*). They formulated a national liberal form as the United States emerged as a new nation in the world, and their legacy has continued to be an element in the complex political and ideological history of the South.

These notable Virginians were devoted to the ideal of the legal protection of individual rights from abuses by governmental power and to the principle of majority rule governing outcomes when qualified voters elected representative officials and when these officials voted on legislation. They believed in bills of rights to affirm the value of freedom of speech, press, and association in political matters; freedom of religious conscience; and the legal separation of the civil capacities of citizens from membership in religious groups. The nature of the federal system created by the Constitution meant that the degree of separation varied according to the differing constitutions of the various states.

In North Carolina, for example, belief in Protestantism was a legal condition for holding public office in the state, although in practice William Gaston, a Catholic, held several important offices. In the state constitutional convention, he appealed without success to Jefferson's Virginia Statute for Religious Freedom in an attempt to eliminate all religious tests for public office. The statute had been passed in Virginia with the crucial help of Baptists, and the administration of Andrew Jackson connected to that tradition through the Baptist-Jeffersonian Senator Richard M. Johnson of Kentucky, whose report in 1829 on the Sunday mail successfully defended its continuance.

American Revolutionaries in the South, like their northern counterparts, given the "self-evident" truths of "life, liberty, and the pursuit of happiness" and the equal creation of "all men," according to the Declaration of Independence, joined for about fifty years in putting the institution of slavery on the moral defensive. Virginia, North Carolina, and Georgia acted to end the African slave trade in 1774–1775, and a Virginia law of 1783 liberated all slaves who had fought in the Revolution. The number of free blacks in the South greatly increased by manumission. Jefferson himself proposed in 1784 to prohibit slavery in the new territories after 1800, a measure that failed to pass by only one vote. Black abolitionists always saw the Declaration's prologue as full of promise for the ending of slavery. Even in 1832, after the Nat Turner Rebellion, there were in the Virginia debate over slavery some voices raised to condemn the market in slaves, to stress the common humanity of slaves, and to hope for a future gradual emancipation, along with the deportation of freed blacks to Africa, a colonization policy that Jefferson had also endorsed.

Even the most influential defender of the South, John C. Calhoun, in setting forth a doctrine of nullification in the *South Carolina Exposition and Protest* of 1828, drew on the Jeffersonian states'-rights orientation of the *Virginia and Kentucky Resolutions* of 1798, which Jefferson and Madison had formulated in protest against the repressive Alien and Sedition Laws. Calhoun's later theory of the concurrent majority, while designed to defend the southern economy, including slavery, from domination by the northern economy's interests, was much closer to Madison's emphasis in the *Federalist* on compromise among factions than it was to George Fitzhugh's defense of an authoritarian theoretical system of paternalistic slavery. Calhoun, however, did not see that the mechanics of the party system, as it developed in Congress, achieved in practice the aim of his theory of concurrence. The victors in the presidential races from 1832 to 1852 almost always gained a majority of electoral votes from both North and South; and southern Democrats outnumbered northern Democrats in the House until the time of the New Deal.

Although Jefferson himself was a large-scale planter with hundreds of slaves, his politics idealized the independent yeoman farmer as the bearer of liberal republican virtues. The plantation novel of the antebellum South promoted the cavalier myth of the high social status of planters, yet it usually found its more effective characters among the yeomen, as in John P. Kennedy's historical romance, *Horse-Shoe Robinson* (1835). These novels often celebrated the role of southern states in the Revolution, as in William Gilmore Simms's many historical novels about South Carolina, although they are socially conservative in identifying the lower classes with the Tories and the Patriot cause with merchants and planters. Ironically, even the southern "fire-eaters" of secession invoked the New England events of the Boston Tea Party, Bunker Hill, and Lexington as analogous Revolutionary symbols.

The most consistently liberal southern writer who lived through the Civil War was George Washington Cable, and he had the misfortune to express his liberalism at a time when racial segregation was in the process of becoming increasingly rigid and extensive. (He emigrated to Northampton, Massachusetts, when he was only forty-one and lived there for the next forty years.) In *The Silent South* (1885) and *The Negro Question* (1890), Cable drew a sharp distinction between knowledge, manners, and taste among both blacks and whites (which should be outside the law), and civil rights (which should belong by law to all Americans as persons and citizens). Racial segregation by law confused this distinction; and Cable pointed out that "a long bitter experience has taught" blacks that "equal accommodations, but separate" mean, generally, "accommodations of a conspicuously ignominious inferiority." An old-family Richmond businessman, Lewis Harvie Blair, in *Prosperity of the South Dependent upon the Elevation of the Negro* (1889), also argued for integration and against white supremacy, but he later totally reversed his position.

Cable's "The Freedman's Case in Equity" appeared in *Century* magazine in 1885 shortly after criticisms of the antebellum South by two of his southern friends, Mark Twain in *Adventures of Huckleberry Finn* and

Joel Chandler Harris in his short story "Free Joe and the Rest of the World." At the University of Louisiana in 1883, Cable had made a plea for freedom of "criticism and correction" by writers, a tolerance he needed even more than his friends, for he was a vigorous and lucid critic of slavery, landed aristocracy, Negro tenantry, the leasing of convict labor, and racial segregation in public institutions. Cable's fiction, especially his historical romance about Creole Louisiana, *The Grandissimes* (1880), and his novel of Reconstruction, *John March, Southerner* (1894), dealt with the complexities of racial conflict in the South and opened up a path that would be followed in the next century by southern writers of greater talent and renown, such as William Faulkner and Robert Penn Warren.

Southern Populists thought of themselves as Jeffersonians in defending yeomen farmers against the inequities of contemporary forms of Hamiltonian capitalism, and they were radically liberal in demanding civil rights for blacks, even though some Populists later succumbed to racist demagoguery. The Negro writer Charles W. Chesnutt in *The Marrow of Tradition* (1901) dramatized the 1898 riot of white supremacists against the earlier victory of the Populist-Republican fusion ticket in Wilmington, North Carolina, and he put compulsory racial segregation on the railroads in a liberal perspective similar to Cable's. (Cable once offered Chesnutt a job as secretary.) A few church leaders, notably Edgar Gardner Murphy, an Episcopalian leader in Texas and Alabama, opposed a separate Negro episcopate and argued for the end of political and legal discrimination against the Negro, but his influence was effective mainly on national child labor reform.

Southern liberalism had a forum in the *Virginia Quarterly Review* (1925) and in the *Journal of Social Forces,* started in 1923 by the sociologist Howard Odum, who was also an innovative student of black folk songs as well as a critic of the Ku Klux Klan, Prohibition, and Protestant fundamentalism. Under the bold leadership of William Terry Couch, the University of North Carolina Press at Chapel Hill promoted publications that evaluated southern life from liberal perspectives. Couch commissioned Virginius Dabney's *Liberalism in the South* (1932), a history that honored Jefferson, Madison, Mason, and Wythe as its source and noted that in the presidential campaign of 1928, the faculty and students of the University of Virginia endorsed Democratic candidate Al Smith and shrouded Jefferson's statue with black crepe because of the widespread attacks in the South on Smith as a Catholic. Couch had persuaded Dabney to include in his book discussions of economic issues and labor, issues that had a Populist heritage and would come to the fore in the New Deal. Dabney's view of liberalism, however, as a vague middle ground between extreme radicalism and ultraconservatism, was so imprecise that he gave liberals credit for "almost everything that has been done in the Southern states in building up a broader and more humane civilization."

The twelve southern writers in *I'll Take My Stand* (1930) would not have agreed. While they defended an agrarianism that had Jeffersonian ancestry—for some democratic and for others patriarchal—they agreed only in their affection for Vanderbilt University, where their literary interests had been nurtured, in their resentment of northern dismissive disdain for the South, and in their rejection of the New South gospel of industrial development and technological progress. They tended to be suspicious of liberalism, in Donald Davidson's metaphor, as a "Trojan Horse" for materialist collectivism. But Robert Penn Warren, while accepting racial segregation, as did the other contributors, struck a Populist note by suggesting that whites should encourage the "well-being and possibly the organization of negro, as well as white labor."

In the 1930s, there was a literary focus in the South on the plain folk of small towns. As the historian C. Vann Woodward put it: "Thomas Wolfe of Asheville was its poet, Paul Green of Chapel Hill its playwright, James Agee of Knoxville its reporter, and Jack Cash of Charlotte its historian." W. J. Cash in *The Mind of the South* (1941) criticizes his homeland from a Populist premise that yeomen farmers were "the best people the South has ever produced in any numbers, and its chief hope today." Wolfe's *You Can't Go Home Again* (1940), its fragments posthumously put together by his editor, vividly dramatizes the corruption of the privileged and the despair of the lowly in Depression America, while asserting with lyrical rhetoric his democratic dream of "the promise of America," giving "to every man the right to live, to work, to be himself" regardless of his birth. Wolfe cherished this liberal democratic idea particularly after seeing at first hand Hitler's fascism in the country in which Wolfe's earlier novels had found a wide audience.

A measure of the new southern liberalism was the Southern Conference for Human Welfare, which included laborers, farmers, and some blacks. In 1938 it gave its Thomas Jefferson Award to Justice Hugo

Black, and there were southerners in New Deal agencies who were sensitive to African American aspirations. Although the war against Hitler made race an ethical issue for some liberals, most influential southern liberal journalists, even though they appealed to a southern tradition of Jefferson and Jackson in opposing the poll tax, still accepted racial segregation for prudent political reasons; in so doing, they increasingly lost touch with blacks and with the federal government. The novelist Lillian Smith in *Strange Fruit* (1944) was an exception to this trend, as were the liberal southern historians Bell Irvin Wiley and C. Vann Woodward, who in 1949 broke precedent by scheduling the African American historian John Hope Franklin to give a paper in Virginia at a meeting of the Southern Historical Association.

In his finest and best-known novel, *All the King's Men* (1946), Robert Penn Warren created as his central character a Louisiana populistic reformer and dictator of the 1930s, Willie Stark, who was much like Huey Long, the assassinated governor of the state. Stark is seen through the eyes of a skeptical narrator, Jack Burden, who had earlier appeared in Warren's verse-play *Proud Flesh*, written when he was living in Mussolini's Italy. A reviewer misread the novel as an apology for fascism, provoking Warren to say "that's what happens to a Jeffersonian Democrat in this crazy world we live in." Some poet-critics among the Fugitives and the Agrarians did contribute to the *American Review*, whose editor, Seward Collins, preached a reactionary monarchism that he incongruously identified with Mussolini and Long. Warren remarked that one of the figures standing in the shadows behind the novel is the philosopher William James, and Warren knew that Mussolini regarded himself as a kind of disciple of James. But Warren's interest was in "the scholarly and benign" figure of James, whose philosophical pragmatism (as well as his liberal anti-imperialism and antimilitarism) was quite different from the unphilosophical political pragmatism of Long or Mussolini. Nevertheless, James as a pragmatist was a critic of the finality of any particular social balance of conflicting ideas; thus Stark's political pragmatism is presented with some sympathy insofar as it concerns the social welfare of the hill folk of his state. Believing these folks to have been too long neglected by the inertia and the class bias of the ruling gentry from the Delta, Stark has a mission to create a new social balance, although his career has a tragic arc. Warren later was drawn, in *World Enough and Time* (1950), to the historical conflict in Kentucky of 1825 between the Old Court Party and the New Court Party, a conflict that reminded him of arguments over the economic policies of the New Deal. As usual in his stories, however, his historical interests were linked to his philosophical concerns. Liberal individualism is given a more existentialist meaning in Warren's novels as a search for inner freedom and personal integrity; the personal stories in his novels are designed to mirror the larger story of society.

Warren invoked pragmatism again in his historical reflections in *The Legacy of the Civil War* (1961), which he dedicated to the philosopher Sidney Hook, one of John Dewey's most devoted students, because it was nurtured by recognition of the impasse created by the absolutism in southern defenses of property in slaves as well as in northern moral abolitionism. Against both southern and northern uses of the Civil War to bolster regional self-righteousness, Warren cited William James in behalf of his ideal of the victor who "even in the hour of triumph will to some degree do justice to the ideals in which the vanquished interests lay." Warren in articles for national magazines, later published as *Segregation* (1956) and *Who Speaks for the Negro?* (1965), sympathetically explored the changes that the Civil Rights Movement was bringing to the system of segregation he had known and not questioned in 1930.

One of the most memorable symbolic moments in American history was on August 28, 1963, when Martin Luther King Jr. stood with his back to the Jefferson and Lincoln Memorials, facing the largest crowd ever assembled in Washington, and, in the tone and temper of an eloquent pastor of a black Baptist church, drew on the rhetoric of Jefferson, Lincoln, and the Bible in behalf of the rights of African Americans to full citizenship. King added to his liberal theology elements of Reinhold Niebuhr's Christian realism, but the strategy of nonviolent resistance, which Niebuhr had pragmatically recommended for African Americans in 1932, King learned mainly from his pacifist advisors during the Montgomery bus boycott of 1955. This boycott had followed closely on the heels of the Supreme Court's liberal school desegregation decision of 1954. The southern historian C. Vann Woodward had worked for the research team of the NAACP legal staff, whose brief had persuaded the Court; Woodward later cited George Washington Cable when testifying before the House Committee on the Judiciary in behalf of the Voting Rights Extension Act of 1984. A crucial reason for the political success of King's movement for civil

rights was the decision of another southerner, Lyndon Baines Johnson, to give the movement presidential leadership, at considerable cost to his party's influence in the South.

Before the Civil Rights Movement, in which so many African Americans found their voices, modern black southern writers, notably Richard Wright and Ralph Ellison, tended to stress the metaphor of the invisibility of the black presence in the eyes of whites. Wright in his novel *Native Son* (1940) and his autobiography *Black Boy* (1945) found the first wide and respectful national audience for a black writer and, like his mentor, Ellison also secured one with *Invisible Man* (1952). Both novelists focus on the problem of transplanting the southern folk Negro to an urban industrial setting and on the dissonance between the promise of the Declaration of Independence and its contradiction in slavery and segregation. Ellison, nurtured on the classics of American literature as well as the language of the Bible and the Constitution, felt himself to be a native son, whereas Wright, after he exiled himself to France, was something of an invisible man in claiming to have no race, country, or tradition. Yet, for all their personal differences, their novels, *Native Son* and *Invisible Man,* share the common theme of a struggle for individual freedom as a sense of identity that culminates in a second birth. It is an existentialist version of the metaphor that Lincoln applied to the nation in his Gettysburg Address. In 1971 Ralph Ellison paid his predecessor and mentor the high praise of putting Wright in his own preferred tradition of nineteenth-century American rhetoric about freedom and individual responsibility, even though Wright himself had first found his political bearings in the Communist Party. Wright eventually rejected the Communist Party because of its bureaucratic disciplining of writers and its denial of the American heritage of free thought.

Unlike the protagonists in the novels of Wright and Ellison, the black feminist heroine in Alice Walker's *Meridian* (1976), who, unlike her mother, lives in "the age of choice," has the possibility of "visibility" by participation in the Civil Rights Movement. When Meridian Hill moves from her Georgia town to a black college in Atlanta, she joins the drive for black voter registration in the Deep South, as Walker herself had done. Yet in a time of black separatism, Meridian is separated from this ideology by her ambivalence about revolution. Her mixed feelings are caused by her loyalty to the southern past, "the memory of old black men in the South" and country girls singing "with a purity of soul," and by her own struggle to reconcile the ethical with the political. In this respect, she is kin to Ellison's hero—the Invisible Man rejects the radical Marxists, the "Brothers" who disdain his southern past as mere anachronistic primitivism, and says finally that he must "condemn and affirm, say no and say yes, say yes and say no" to American tradition.

Ironically, the success of the Civil Rights Movement in fostering a greatly expanded African American middle class has thrown into relief (but left unrelieved) the impoverished lower class. At the same time, a conservative shift in American political life, endorsed by many intellectuals, has devalued liberalism or accused it of sacrificing the values of community to individual rights. This shift is coincident with a drastic depreciation of Jefferson's standing among some historians who have championed instead his conservative opponents (whether Edmund Burke or John Adams), or who from a radical standpoint have seen him as a "negrophobe Virginia planter." At a conference on Jefferson Legacies held at his University of Virginia in 1993, it was even said of Jefferson that "no one bore more responsibility for failing to place the nation on the road to liberty for all."

Yet it was to Jefferson's Declaration that the northern antislavery reformer John Quincy Adams appealed in 1841 before the Supreme Court of the United States in making his successful plea in behalf of the freedom of the black former slaves who had taken control of the Spanish slave ship *Amistad*; and it was to Jefferson's ideas that both Lincoln and King appealed in making their own cases for justice to African Americans. Such are the ironies of history as they color liberalism not only in the South but in America.

S. Cushing Strout

See also Civil Rights Movement; Jefferson, Thomas; Populism; Woodward, C. Vann.

Virginius Dabney, *Liberalism in the South* (1932); Richard Gray, *Writing the South: Ideas of an American Region* (1986); Merrill D. Peterson, *The Jefferson Image in the American Mind* (1960); Lewis P. Simpson, *The Fable of the Southern Writer* (1994); Daniel Joseph Singal, *The War Within: From Victorian to Modernist Thought in the South, 1919–1945* (1982); Cushing Strout, *Making American Tradition: Visions and Revisions from Ben Franklin to Alice Walker* (1990); William R. Taylor, *Cavalier and Yankee: The Old South and American National Character* (1961); C. Vann Woodward, *The Burden of Southern History* (1960), *American Counterpoint: Slavery and Racism in the North-South Dialogue* (1971), and *The Future of the Past* (1989).

LIBRARY OF SOUTHERN LITERATURE, THE

The Library of Southern Literature is a seventeen-volume southern literature anthology copyrighted in 1907 and published between 1909 and 1923. Reflective of the culture in which it was compiled, the series displays a wide scope of white southern writers, primarily from colonial times to 1907, in its effort to assert a vital tradition of southern literature.

The Atlanta-based publishing firm, The Martin and Hoyt Company, initiated *The Library of Southern Literature* in early 1907, securing two well-known and highly respected southern figures to serve as editors-in-chief: Joel Chandler Harris, an editor and writer of national stature beloved in his own region, and Edwin A. Alderman, president of the University of Virginia (former president of the University of North Carolina and of Tulane University), and a leading figure in the turn-of-the-century crusade for improving southern public education. Harris, who died in 1908, was never directly involved in the project, though his name continued on the title page through Volume 16 and his family received royalties from the work. Alderman, who was not a literary scholar, asserts that most of the actual work was coordinated by the literary editor, University of Virginia faculty member Charles W. Kent; the associate literary editor, C. Alphonso Smith (who left a faculty position at the University of North Carolina in 1909 for one at the University of Virginia); and the executive editor, F. P. Gamble. The assistant literary editors were Morgan Callaway Jr. (University of Texas), Franklin L. Riley (University of Mississippi), and George A. Wauchope (University of South Carolina). Together, these editors comprised the Executive Board for the work, and through their academic profiles they substantiated the title-page claim that the work was "compiled under the direct supervision of southern men of letters." The editors in turn involved many professional and amateur scholars in the preparation of the individual entries.

In addition to the Executive Board, the publication had a panel of consulting editors and an Advisory Council whose members are listed at the beginning of each volume. Neither group was actually involved in the production of the work, but the lists offered a mechanism for indicating endorsement of the project by a wide range of educational and cultural leaders of the time. The consulting editors were seventeen presidents of southern universities; the Advisory Council members were a combination of southern political and religious leaders.

The Library of Southern Literature, sold by subscription agents, cost from $80 to $200, depending upon the binding and inclusion of pictures. The publishers later brought out a less-expensive edition for $41.50 in an effort to bolster sales. They also offered limited editions in honor of individual states. For sales, the publishers targeted middle- and upper-class southern white families, schools and universities, and libraries in both the South and the North.

Volumes 1 through 13, containing alphabetically arranged entries on individual authors from colonial times to 1907, appeared in 1909 and 1910. Volume 14, a *Miscellanea* edited by C. Alphonso Smith, which includes fugitive and anonymous poems, letters, epitaphs, and inscriptions, etc., was published in 1910. Volume 15, a *Biographical Dictionary of Authors* edited by Lucian Lamar Knight, also came out in 1910. Volume 16, titled *Historical Side-Lights, 50 Reading Courses, Chart, Bibliography and Index,* was compiled by Lucian Lamar Knight and published in 1913 as the intended last volume in the series. Ten years later, in 1923, with a recomprised editorial staff, consulting editors, and Advisory Council, Alderman and C. Alphonso Smith as co-editors-in-chief published Volume 17, *Supplement No. 1* to *The Library of Southern Literature,* an update of recent authors that they anticipated might be the first in a series of supplements, which did not materialize. A revised edition of the series, listing Alderman and Smith as editors and John Calvin Metcalf as literary editor, appeared in 1929.

In the tradition of *The Library of American Literature* (Edmund Clarence Stedman and Ellen Mackay Hutchinson, 1888) and modeled in format closely after *Library of the World's Best Literature* (Charles Dudley Warner, 1898), *The Library of Southern Literature* ventures an authoritative collection to define a body of literature. It was part of a larger southern cultural movement to rewrite the northern-dominated national narrative as the South reintegrated itself into the nation. Southerners reacted negatively to the northern-written anthologies, which they saw as typically dismissive and under-representative of southern literature. In his introduction, Alderman expresses his hope that the work will "make clear that the literary barrenness of the South has been overstated, and its contributions to American literature undervalued, both as to quantity and quality." At the same time, Alderman reassures readers that the intentions of the work are "na-

tional enrichment and not sectional glorification." Kent echoes this sentiment in the preface, asking readers not to see the work as a "manifestation of any vainglorious or sinister sectionalism, but as a direct and serviceable contribution to the history of our national literature." Even so, the overall tone of the work is eulogistic of southern writers and intensely patriotic of southern history and traditions.

The Library of Southern Literature contains around three hundred authors. Each entry opens with a biographical and critical essay about the author followed by selections of his or her work. Inclusions cover a variety of genres, among them fiction, poetry, political oratory, history, and philosophy. The stated criterion for inclusion is not aesthetic value, a fact that left the collection open to criticism by later scholars and critics claiming to judge works by their intrinsic literary merit. Rather, Kent explains that the collection's "aim is to represent the literary life of the South with all its inequalities and not to create arbitrary standards to which all the selections must be subjected," and therefore the "very irregularities may be recognized as a merit of the book." This desire to preserve a spectrum of southern literature is reflective of a broader preservationist movement in the South at the time, one fueled by fear that the true history of the ideologically dominant white South and its distinctive heritage would otherwise be lost. Other southern literature anthologies and histories also grew out of this cultural anxiety and the marketplace interest for southern productions that it created.

When the editors of *The Library of Southern Literature* attempted to "represent the literary life of the South," for them that collection comprised only white writers. No selections by African American writers are included, but the biographical dictionary does contain entries for Frederick Douglass, W. E. B. Du Bois, and Booker T. Washington, thus acknowledging but marginalizing the existence of another body of writing. On the other hand, the anthology is very inclusive of women writers, offering a generous selection of their texts and affording women many entries in the biographical dictionary. Women are also contributors of entries for the anthology. Nevertheless, a gender hierarchy is evident—no women appear on the Executive Board, the Advisory Council, or as a consulting editor.

The Library of Southern Literature was a significant undertaking, an early-twentieth-century effort to substantiate and encourage the existence of a vital tradition of southern literature. It remains valuable as an artifact of its time and as a resource for information about and selections from many writers who have since disappeared from the canon of southern literature.

Susan H. Irons

See also Academy, Southern Literature and the; Anthologies of Southern Literature; Southern Literature, Idea of.

Gaines M. Foster, "Mirage in the Sahara of the Bozart: *The Library of Southern Literature*," *Mississippi Quarterly* 28 (Winter 1974–75).

LINCOLN, ABRAHAM

Born near Hodgenville, Kentucky, on February 12, 1809, Abraham Lincoln became the very symbol of northernness. Even though his formal education was minimal, probably less than a year, he became a highly educated, astute lawyer and politician. He did not travel widely, yet he was known throughout the world and continues to be well known and revered today. Lincoln's complex personality has been used and misused in literary representations during and after his own time.

Lincoln's family was of the poorest of the farmer class; trying to coax a living from the soil, the family moved often in Kentucky, Indiana, and Illinois as he grew into adulthood. In 1831, he made his first home as an adult in New Salem, Illinois. His early aspirations to a political career are evidenced by the fact that he was elected in 1834, as a very young man, to the Illinois legislature, where he served four terms, until 1841. Lincoln's only direct military experience was as a captain of militia during the Black Hawk War in 1832, hardly sufficient training for the prodigious job of being commander in chief of the Union forces during the Civil War. Through rigorous self-education, he was admitted to the Bar in 1836, after which he moved to Springfield, the state capital, to practice law. His first venture into national politics was as a Whig congressman from 1847 to 1849. In 1855 he attempted to return to the political arena by making an unsuccessful bid for a term in the Senate, but he only came to national notoriety when he ran as a Republican against Stephen Douglas, a Democrat, for a Senate seat in 1858. This contest generated the famous Lincoln-Douglas Debates, which centered on whether or not slavery should be allowed in the territories. Even though Lincoln lost the election to Douglas, the Ameri-

can people did not forget the issues debated during the campaign or the positions taken by the debaters.

The genesis of Lincoln's ideas about slavery during this period and the subsequent evolution of those ideas are the sources of differing views of the man in southern literature and, indeed, in the literature of the entire nation. When the Democratic Party split into factions in 1860, Lincoln's Republican candidacy became a viable alternative. He gained significant support in the North but not the South. His political stance during the very low-profile campaign was that the country's future health was predicated upon a system of priorities. Union was absolutely essential, and all other considerations, including the slavery issue, had to be secondary to the requirement to maintain national unity. He did, however, insist that there be absolutely no incursion of slavery into the emerging territories. When the Electoral College chose Lincoln to be the sixteenth President of the United States, the exclusion of slaves from the territories was the issue that created the rift in the Union. South Carolina immediately withdrew from the Union and convinced other states to follow in short order. Lincoln was inaugurated in March 1861, and the Confederate States of America, which had formed soon after his election, fired upon Fort Sumter the next month.

Even though states' rights was trumpeted as the cause of the national division, slavery was the issue that brought the states'-rights issue to critical mass. Even though Lincoln had earlier said that he would abide slavery as it stood and would not disturb the system in the states where it was established if that concession would maintain the Union, the issue of expanding slavery into the territories was non-negotiable. Lincoln's later statements of concern about integrating slaves into the general population, should they be freed, have caused many problems of interpretation about his beliefs. His ideas at that time on exportation and colonization of freed slaves were not original with Lincoln and were even held by many Abolitionists, a group that was not at all popular with Lincoln because of their ideological militancy.

During the Civil War, Lincoln was viewed in the South as the devil incarnate. Complications of philosophy or politics were not relevant; Lincoln had started the war and was killing the home lads. The favorite targets for the southern pen's attack during the war years were: Lincoln's supposed drunkenness; his cowardice; his lanky, unsavory physical appearance; his bucolic demeanor; and his despotic, dictatorial political stance.

As early as 1861, Samuel Clemens writing as Quintus Curtius Snodgrass was submitting satirical letters for publication in the *New Orleans Crescent,* many of which were highly critical of Lincoln. Other comedic satirists who criticized Lincoln included George Washington Harris with his character Sut Lovingood and Charles Henry Smith with his nom de plume Bill Arp. These writers fed upon the public's mental images of Lincoln by using a fictional bumpkin to satirize a perceived bumpkin. Southern attacks on Lincoln were not always amusing, however. Newspaper editorialists, typified by E. A. Pollard of the *Richmond Examiner,* were particularly harsh, and poet E. P. Birch even pictured Lincoln selling his soul in "The Devil's Visit to Old Abe." Very little high-quality fiction was produced during the war, but diarist Mary Boykin Chesnut painted the southern image of Lincoln with vivid, slashing strokes. Dramatists were busy filling the public's need for diversion from the miseries of war. John D. McCabe wrote the "Aide de Camp" and John Hill Hewitt wrote a musical satire, "King Linkum the First," both of which were vehemently critical of Lincoln. Southern dramatists William Russell Smith ("The Royal Ape") and Stephen Franks Miller ("Ahab Lincoln") were surprisingly mellow toward Lincoln despite the derogatory titles of their plays.

As a military expedient, Lincoln formulated and announced to the country that all slaves in rebel territory would be free as of January 1, 1863. The Emancipation Proclamation of September, 1862, became the final straw for the South. Even though by this time Lincoln felt that this was the right action for the whole country, the proclamation in actuality was only valuable, in military terms, as a sectional edict. Lincoln had once more become the bane of the Abolitionists with his "halfway" action. Nonetheless, military action continued for the next two years with a more public, more honest issue sustaining the conflict.

As the long war drew toward an end, Lincoln's speeches and letters indicate that he planned to be very benevolent toward the South after an armistice had been signed. His attitudes toward the slaves had ameliorated; he favored accepting the freedmen into white society. Although the exact political philosophies of Lincoln were never entirely clear, it appears that issues confronting the newly reunited country would have been handled better by him than by others. On April 14, 1865, less than a week after Appomattox, Lincoln was shot by John Wilkes Booth while watching a play at Ford's Theater in Washington.

Neither Lincoln's death nor the end of the war stopped the flow of poison literature from the South. After his arrest, Jefferson Davis asked Albert T. Bledsoe to research and publish a defense of the actions of the Confederacy. The result, *Is Davis a Traitor; or, Was Secession a Constitutional Right Previous to the War of 1861?,* was rushed into print. Bledsoe also established a journal, *The Southern Review,* whose articles were largely tirades against Lincoln. One of Lincoln's most vehement critics after his death was a Virginian, Lyon Gardner Tyler, son of John Tyler, tenth President of the United States. As Bledsoe had done, he became the editor of a journal, *Tyler's Quarterly Historical and Genealogical Magazine,* which he had established for the primary purpose of skewering the deceased Lincoln. Charles L. C. Minor picked up several of Tyler's articles and added them to his own writing to create two editions of *The Real Lincoln* (1901, 1904), which were published with differing subtitles. These books inspired Mildred Lewis Rutherford of Mississippi to write a book defending the southern cause, *Facts and Falsehoods Concerning the War on the South* (1904), which ascribed unbelievably cruel atrocities to Lincoln.

A few writers used Lincoln's early political stance on slavery to prove their own unreconstructed attitudes toward African Americans. The best example of this type of writing is that of Thomas Dixon Jr., a North Carolina minister-turned-author. His fanatical writing might have slipped into oblivion except for the fact that one of his novels, *The Clansman* (1905), was used as the basis for a D. W. Griffith film, *The Birth of a Nation* (1915), which became very popular. Dixon's novels created a heroically segregationist Lincoln, a man dedicated to the separation of the races. Dixon's other novels, *The Leopard's Spots* (1902), and *The Southerner* (1913), and a play, *A Man of the People* (1920), do equal injustice to more modern understandings of Lincoln's life and his mature philosophies. Dixon's works are very difficult for the modern reader to digest because of his misinterpretations of Lincoln, his advocacy of the Ku Klux Klan, and his portrayal of blacks as beasts or buffoons.

Some writers who had written in particularly cruel ways about Lincoln during the war tempered their attitudes after the war. George W. Harris, whose character Sut Lovingood was shown gleefully criticizing Lincoln during the war, is an example of a writer who began to see Lincoln in a more realistic light in peacetime. George W. Cable, who had been a Confederate soldier, became an active advocate of equality for slaves and for the righteousness of Lincoln's cause. Booker T. Washington saw Lincoln as a hero to be venerated by African Americans; Frederick Douglass was positive but more guarded in his retrospective appraisal. Alexander Stephens, former vice president of the C.S.A., in oratory and writing was particularly affirmative of Lincoln's career, possibly because he and Lincoln had been friends before the war.

Mary Raymond Shipman Andrews wrote a short story in 1907, "The Perfect Tribute," which was so popular that it was soon bound into a book that sold many copies. It told of Lincoln's touching encounter with a dying Confederate soldier after he had delivered the Gettysburg Address. It is a sentimental but touching "tribute" to a man who in the South had once been declared the epitome of ruthlessness. Since Andrews's story was written, much Lincoln literature in the South has been positive. One of the most sensitive portraits is that by Tennessee-born Evelyn Scott in the modernist stream-of-consciousness sketch she provides for him in her Civil War novel, *The Wave*. Lincoln is now widely viewed as one of the greatest politicians, presidents, and humanitarians the nation has ever known. Perhaps the South's evolving attitude toward Lincoln is a constricted model of the whole healing process that was necessary for the South after the Civil War. Some aspects of the Lincoln image improved much more quickly than others, just as some aspects of the South's sectional image of the North improved much more quickly than others. Today, the South as a whole shares the same image of Lincoln as the rest of the country and the world: a very heroic image shared by fiction writers, poets, dramatists, historians, journalists, and the general public.

D. Michael Snider

Michael Davis, *The Image of Lincoln in the South* (1971); David Herbert Donald, *Lincoln* (1995); Don E. Fehrenbacher, *Lincoln in Text and Context: Collected Essays* (1987); Merrill Peterson, *Lincoln in American Memory* (1994); Victor Searcher, *Lincoln Today: An Introduction to Modern Lincolniana* (1969); Edmund Wilson, *Patriotic Gore: Studies in the Literature of the American Civil War* (1962).

LITERARY MAGAZINES OF THE PAST

As a privately financed venture to promote southern writers and topics or as a publication affiliated with a university or college, little magazines have played a significant role in the life of letters and literature in the postbellum South. Although some critics still argue that only independently printed magazines, excluding those associated with universities, satisfy the requirements for a true "little magazine," most scholars and contributors find enough similarities in purpose, format, and content in the literary publications to equate them. Both private and university-based publications historically were edited by amateurs devoted to the cause of literature, critical inquiry, or social issues. Southern editors after the Civil War also wished to inform, influence, or elevate subscribers rather than to serve commercial ends. They depended on the quality of the printed matter rather than on their marketing skills to attract readers. Four developments of the "little magazine" in the South since the end of the Civil War may be loosely traced: immediately after the war, local editors offered subscribers magazines devoted to southern authors and topics; in the 1890s and early years of the twentieth century, young scholars established literary journals in which they printed critical views of southern letters and life; in the 1920s, southern literary magazines and journals played decisive roles in the advent of modernism; and during the 1930s, literary journals offered space for proponents of "Agrarianism" to exchange views, sometimes hotly, with southern "liberals" regarding the best way to bring economic prosperity to the South.

The years immediately following the Civil War saw the publication in Atlanta, Georgia, of *Scott's Monthly Magazine* (1865–1869), established by W. S. Scott in hopes of elevating and enfranchising literature in the South. In Charlotte, North Carolina, General Daniel H. Hill attracted subscribers for a similar purpose in the *Land We Love* (1866–1869), a literary magazine that achieved wider circulation by including articles on agriculture and military history. Moses D. Hoge and William Hand Browne of Richmond, Virginia, issued the first copies of the *Eclectic* in November 1866; they absorbed the *Land We Love* and changed the title to *New Eclectic* in 1869, when it moved to Baltimore and became, briefly, the official publication of the Southern Historical Association. In January 1871, *New Eclectic* became *Southern Magazine*; it ceased publication in 1875. *De Bow's Review,* published in Nashville, Tennessee, before the war, was revived briefly in 1866. In Baltimore, Maryland, Albert Taylor Bledsoe brought *Southern Review* into print from 1867 to 1869. Bledsoe's daughter, Sophia Bledsoe Herrick, later served on the editorial staff of *Scribner's Monthly* and its successor, *Century Magazine,* and was instrumental in helping talented southern writers publish in these national magazines. In Wilmington, North Carolina, Mrs. Cicero Harris issued *The South Atlantic* (1872–1882) as a magazine covering science and art as well as literature. The *Southern Bivouac* (1882–1887) of Louisville, Kentucky, was one of the last little magazines devoted to the Lost Cause. Generally surviving two to five years, these little magazines represented the efforts of editors who, without expert knowledge of publishing and marketing, sought nonetheless to attract educated southern readers to the works of regional writers during a period when sectional interests and a nostalgic bias for the past were strong but money was scarce. In spite of financial struggles, they helped to keep southern letters alive for the first twenty years after the Civil War.

Between the end of the nineteenth century and the appearance of the modern southern artists in the 1920s, a body of young scholars affiliated with southern colleges and universities began publishing literary journals in which they expressed critical views of the region. The most influential of these critical journals was the *Sewanee Review,* begun in 1892 by William P. Trent, then a professor at the University of the South, in an effort to provide free examinations of literature. Influenced by Trent's publication, John Spencer Bassett founded the *South Atlantic Quarterly* in 1902, concentrating mainly on southern history and the contemporary South. A professor of history at Trinity College, Bassett hoped to influence reform and courageously risked his job by writing critically about race relations in the South. John B. Hennemann, a South Carolina native who served briefly as editor of the *Sewanee Review,* called attention in his essays to the critical movement occurring among literary scholars, and Edwin Mims, successor to Bassett as editor of *South Atlantic Quarterly,* wrote somewhat more cautiously of reforms needed to bring progress to the South.

In 1911, some years before H. L. Mencken challenged the southern literary community with his essay "Sahara of the Bozart" in 1920, *The Westminster Magazine,* affiliated with Oglethorpe University in Georgia, had asserted an editorial policy that welcomed diverse works by a wide range of authors. At the University of Texas where he was professor of general literature, Stark Young, intending to attract young authors, began the *Texas Review* in 1915 to be a literary rather than critical publication. In 1924 the journal moved to Southern Methodist University, where Jay B. Hubbell and his editorial staff renamed it the *Southwest Review* and set about publishing new writers of the Southwest as well as established American and British writers. In Richmond, Emily Clark and Hunter Stagg achieved financial backing and editorial advice for the *Reviewer* in 1921 and kept the magazine alive until 1924, when they could no longer finance the venture.

Two publications in the early 1920s left indelible marks on the southern and national literary scene. *The Double Dealer* first appeared in New Orleans in 1921 in time to publish an early Faulkner story while he was living in New Orleans. Before going out of print in 1926, *The Double Dealer* had remained true to its editorial policy of printing the best material it could solicit without regard to moral issues or literary conventions.

Included in the array of poets whose works were printed in *The Double Dealer* were Allen Tate, John Crowe Ransom, and Robert Penn Warren, southerners who were among those responsible for another little magazine, *The Fugitive,* first issued by the Vanderbilt University group in 1922. In their essays about the writing of poetry as well as in their own poems, they showed clearly their flight from the genteel traditions of the Old South. The theories developed by these young authors and scholars had far-reaching effects as they assumed positions at other universities, edited new journals, published college texts, wrote novels and poems, and taught literature to new generations of students and readers.

A third literary journal of import in the South of the 1920s, the *Virginia Quarterly Review* (1925), under the editorial direction of Stringfellow Barr, was among the first to praise *Look Homeward, Angel* as a southern gift to literature. Other little magazines, such as *The Lyric* in Norfolk, Virginia, and *The Nomad* in Birmingham, Alabama, appeared and persisted for two or more years during the 1920s. The importance of the little magazine or literary journal in advancing the Southern Renascence during this decade cannot be overstated.

Two significant little literary publications of the 1930s came into being when writers associated with Vanderbilt in the 1920s assumed teaching positions at other institutions. Soon after assuming positions in the English Department at Louisiana State University, Robert Penn Warren and Cleanth Brooks received funding in 1935 to publish a literary magazine, which they named the *Southern Review.* This journal and the *Kenyon Review,* edited by John Crowe Ransom when he accepted a position as professor of poetry at Kenyon College in Gambier, Ohio, in 1937, along with *Sewanee Review* became associated with the New Criticism preached and practiced by these authors. Brooks and Warren might publish works by young authors, including Eudora Welty, in one issue and devote another to New Critical explications of W. B. Yeats or another established poet. Southern literary journals begun in the 1930s, along with already established journals like the *Sewanee Review* and the *Virginia Quarterly Review,* printed articles by proponents of both sides of the issue of whether the South should opt for industrial growth and economic prosperity or attempt to prosper more slowly in order to remain an agrarian society. Southern literary magazines provided publishing opportunities for young modern writers, helped to usher in the Southern Renaissance, served to disseminate the New Criticism, and published articles of social criticism during the 1930s. Since then, they have appeared in even greater numbers and have continued to assert a presence as influential today as the force they provided in the first half of the twentieth century.

Bes Stark Spangler

See also *Double Dealer, The*; *Kenyon Review*; Periodicals; *Sewanee Review.*

Fred Hobson, *Tell About the South: The Southern Rage to Explain* (1983); Frederick J. Hoffman et al., *The Little Magazine* (1946); Reed Whittemore, *Little Magazines* (U. of Minn. Pamphlet, 1963).

LITERARY MAGAZINES OF THE PRESENT

The southern literary magazine has a long and illustrious history. The *Sewanee Review,* founded in 1892, is America's oldest literary quarterly (by a long shot), and there are several others that have been publishing regularly for many decades: *Southwest Review*—since 1915, *Virginia Quarterly Review*—since 1925, *Southern Review*—original series 1935–42, new series since 1965, *Georgia Review*—since 1947, *Carolina Quarterly*—since 1948, *Shenandoah*—since 1950, *Nimrod*—since 1956, *Southern Poetry Review*—since 1958, *Crazyhorse*—since 1960, *Southern Quarterly*—since 1962, *Hollins Critic*—since 1964, *Greensboro Review*—since 1966, *Cimarron*—since 1967, *Southern Humanities Review, New Orleans Review,* and *South Carolina Review*—since 1968.

What is heartening is how many strong magazines have started up—and continued publication—in the South since 1970: *New Laurel Review* and *Appalachee Quarterly*—in 1971, *Florida Review*—in 1972, *Black Warrior Review*—in 1974, *Callaloo* and *Mississippi Review*—in 1976, *Kalliope*—in 1978, *New Virginia Review*—in 1979, *Chattahoochee Review* and *Tampa Review*—in 1980, *Cumberland Poetry Review* and *Negative Capability*—in 1981, *Dominion Review*—in 1982, *American Voice*—in 1985, *Obsidian II*—in 1986, *Gulf Coast* and *Alabama Literary Review*—in 1987, *Habersham Review*—in 1991, *North Carolina Literary Review*—in 1992, *Atlanta Review*—in 1994, and *Five Points*—in 1997.

The magazines listed above (there are doubtless others) are all published in a traditional "little magazine" format—that is, a small one, usually around 5-by-8 inches, with a two-color cover. Most of them publish original short fiction, poetry, creative nonfiction, essays, and book reviews. A few publish only poetry, a few only prose, and one, the *Hollins Critic,* only criticism. Some specialize: *Callaloo* and *Obsidian II* in African American literature, *Kalliope* in women's literature. Most publish semiannually or quarterly, print a small number of each edition, from a few hundred to three or four thousand. The ratio of unsolicited submitted manuscripts to published works is characteristically lopsided. *Atlanta Review* reported, in the 1997 *Directory of Literary Magazines,* that its ratio was 12,000 submissions for every 100 pieces published. Recently, two new southern magazines have appeared that seem determined to extend not only the literary magazine format but its playing field as well. These are the *Oxford American,* founded in 1993, and *Doubletake,* in 1995. By the standard of what they seek to publish, both of them are certainly literary magazines, but they can hardly be called "little magazines." Both measure 9 by 12 inches, appear between highly designed four-color covers, and are published six times a year. Although both magazines carry national advertising, both are also heavily subsidized—the *Oxford American* by its publisher, novelist John Grisham, and *Doubletake* by the Lindhurst Foundation. Indeed, the great majority of America's traditional "little magazines" are subsidized, to greater and lesser extents, by foundations, colleges and universities, federal, state and local grants, and by the blood, sweat, and tears of their mostly underpaid—and not so infrequently, unpaid—staffs.

In his autobiography, William Carlos Williams had this to say about "little magazines": "The little magazine is something I have always fostered, for without it, I myself would have been early silenced. To me it is one magazine, not several. . . . When it is in any way successful it is because it fills a need in someone's mind to keep going. When it dies, someone else takes it up in some other part of the country—quite by accident—out of a desire to get the writing down on paper." Williams implies that for a literary journal to be successful (he was not thinking of financial success), it must be driven by an editorial passion, and that as these passions wax and wane, the vigor of the individual magazines waxes and wanes with them. Fortunately for American letters in general, and southern ones in particular, each new generation boasts a few of those hero-saints who are passionate about getting "the writing down on paper." And passion is what it takes. Money is always short, readers of true literature are not legion, subscriptions to quarterlies are very hard to sell.

And yet the literary magazines proliferate. There are thousands of them with editorial addresses across the North American continent. What is remarkable is how many of the best of those are to be found in the list at the beginning of this article. Looking over the list of magazines currently in existence, the preponderance of ongoing editorial commitment to the tradition of the literary quarterly in the southern U.S. is immediately clear. Reading what issues from that commitment is a fascinating study in how widely strengths and tastes fluctuate from one periodical to another. There are examples of the best in traditional forms of narrative (*Sewanee Review, Virginia Quarterly Review*) and examples of the intention to welcome whatever works, no matter how unconventional (*Mississippi Review, Chattahoochee Review*). Some magazines, notably *Carolina Quarterly,* see exhilarating change in editorial selection every calendar year with the rotation of student editors. And over the course of years, the contents of all the southern journals reflect the health and energy of those in charge.

The struggle to find funds enough to print and mail the magazines on a regular basis, the deplorable "salaries" of the editors, and the very small readership notwithstanding, the little magazines are where the best new—and established—southern writers publish their best literary work.

Shannon Ravenel

See also Periodicals, 1960 to Present.

LITERARY THEORY, CONTEMPORARY

However belatedly, southern literature has by now cottoned to contemporary literary theory. It is impossible to pick up an issue of the *Mississippi Quarterly* (or any other southern literary journal) without holding in one's hand a quiver of theorists: Abraham (and Torok), Althusser, and Arendt; Bakhtin, Barthes, and Benjamin; Chodorow, Cixous, and Culler; de Man, Derrida, de Certeau; Foucault, Fliess, Freud; Gates, Gilbert, Gubar, Gilroy, Gramsci; the list goes all the way to Zizek. But the story of how they got there—how southern literary critics came to love the bombardment of theory—is complex. How could the land of *I'll Take My Stand* have surrendered its New Criticism for such an eclectic mixture as we now see? How could the literature of concretion—as so many have characterized southern literature—fall so completely for abstraction?

Theory by any description has had a vexed history in the South. When contemporary literary theory—primarily in the form of European psychoanalytic, linguistic, materialist, and feminist thought—entered other U.S. English departments in the late 1960s, the field for hybridizing contemporary literary theory with southern literature, in southern universities, arguably had been unevenly plowed, needed fertilizer, and suffered from a dearth of laborers. To understand the complexity of the story of seduction and surrender that marks the relations between contemporary literary theory and southern literature, one needs first a brief history of the notion of southern concreteness, then a story of southern social theory, and then a look at the place of the South in the national imagination. From there, we will examine Michael Kreyling's and Jefferson Humphries's conscious efforts to plant contemporary literary theory in southern soil and the remarkable, and unexpected, productivity that has emerged, willy-nilly.

In William Andrews's preface for the 1998 Norton anthology *The Literature of the American South,* a list of unquestioned characteristics of southern literature and culture includes the "preference for the tangible over the abstract." The very notion of theory, insofar as it implies abstraction, generalization, and analysis, has been understood by generations of southern literary critics to be uncharacteristic of southern literature and literary criticism, indeed of the southern mind. In *Tell About the South,* Fred Hobson offers the "definition of the 'representative' Southerner. . . . He is conservative, religious, and suspicious of science and progress, he loves the land, has a sense of tradition and a sense of place, and he prefers the concrete to the abstract." Such a notion is familiar from W. J. Cash as well: the "Mind of the South" is grounded in place and time, in concretion, and distrusts theory and abstraction. It has been argued that this "no-theory" theory, in its literary critical manifestation, can be traced to the attacks on abstraction made in the Nashville Agrarians' 1930 *I'll Take My Stand*. Certainly it has remained in place as an assumption about southern literature and literary theory into the present, as Andrews's preface shows. Yet it may be traced to even earlier roots than Allen Tate and John Crowe Ransom. Southern literary reactions to nineteenth-century transcendentalism already show a resistance to abstraction, to theory. Emerson's and Whitman's penchant for invisible eyeballs and metaphoric leaves of grass met with little southern enthusiasm. Even before the Civil War, southern literary critics preferred Scottish formalism and "common sense" in literature and, in their criticism, purely literary analysis without reference to social or other external theory. It was this strain in southern literary (anti)theory that the Agrarians rediscovered as they invented the New Criticism. By the 1970s, however, the Vanderbilt-conceived New Criticism's emphasis on textual autonomy, unity, and coherence, a (non)theory that had dominated American literary culture since the 1950s, was to meet devastating critiques from all sides of contemporary literary theory. Southerner Cleanth Brooks's influence on the Yale English Department collapsed in the early 1970s, in the face of the new hegemony of J. Hillis Miller, Paul de Man, and others. Today, all that remains of the New Criticism's assumptions and techniques is arguably the skills of close reading. Enough has been written about the politics of apolitical literary criticism and the social agendas of "pure" criticism to persuade many southernists to abandon the high tower of what is now the old New Criticism.

But how characteristic of the South was this commitment to concretion? A look at the historical relations between southern social theory and southern literary (anti)theory will help to demystify the cliché of southern resistance to the abstract, and hence to literary theory as well as other forms of theory. No one would now argue that the proslavery arguments did not appeal to theory. On the contrary, the social theory of hierarchical organicism is quite explicit in the works of George Fitzhugh and others. Racial theory likewise found fertile soil in the antebellum South. Biblical liter-

alism arguably furthered the habits of deference to authority encouraged by these explicit theories of social and racial hierarchy. Indeed, W. J. Cash argued that the southern "savage ideal" caused southern minds too often to rest in the grip of intellectual conformity. The famous southern resistance to "abstraction," the preference for the "concrete," can be understood more precisely as a theoretically grounded resistance to conflict, to competing theories, to privileging analysis over assent, rather than a resistance to abstraction. On the contrary, as critics from Fred Hobson to Richard King have noted, abstractions of honor, white supremacy, and mastery have dominated southern life.

Furthermore, the story—the myth—of the South's antipathy to abstraction needs to be understood in the context of historically specific competing theories. In the period of the Southern Renaissance, for example, the commitment to concretion on the part of the literary theorists at Vanderbilt emerged as a direct challenge to the southern "theory" that was coming out of Chapel Hill at the time. That "theory" was not literary but sociological; it used scientific thinking, including statistical analysis, to examine the poverty of southern tenant farmers and other issues. The scientific methodology that Howard Odum, Rupert Vance, and others used at UNC now seems tame. Yet it is this way of thinking, and the socially progressive uses to which it was put, that the Nashville literary scholars feared and labeled as "abstraction." Again, there is a line of descent from the antebellum debate to the Agrarians. Proslavery narratives and fictions, advocating the superiority of slavery—the slave plantation's personal, paternalistic "family black and white"—to the impersonal, capitalistic, and alienating theory and practice of labor in the "free" North, found their inheritance in New Critical claims of the superiority of the concrete, harmonious, and unified work of art to the abstract, impersonal theories of Chapel Hill sociologists.

There is another story still to tell that can instruct us about the relations between southern literature and contemporary literary theory. That is the story of the place of the South in the national imagination, as the "other" for New England's cultural dominance since the early nineteenth century. In American ideology, the South has served as the site of ignorance compared to the educated North, of the backward to the North's progressive mentality, and of the irrational to the North's analytic reason. Following such stereotyping, theory clearly would have no place in the benighted South. Such stereotyping still plays into assumptions about the lack of theoretical knowledge on the part of southern universities and southernist scholars, the ignorance signified by southern dialects.

Many southern literary scholars, aware both of this stereotyping and at the same time of the intellectual riches offered to the study of southern literature by contemporary literary theory, have found various ways to welcome the entrance of theory into the South. In the earliest stages of contemporary literary theory's presence in the U.S., "theory" was simply not discussed in the context of southern literature. A bit later, the existence of "theory" was acknowledged, if not embraced, in the form, for example, of a parodic journal, *Uneeda Review (Like You Need Another Hole in Your Head)*, edited by Louis D. Rubin Jr., William Harmon, and other colleagues at Chapel Hill. A self-named "younger generation" of theoretically inclined southernists wanted, in the 1980s, to set a new agenda and new terms for the study of southern literature. Michael Kreyling's version of these terms, for example, would "reopen the relational aspects of our [southernists'] work and admit the elements of dissensus (race, class, gender, ideology, history) that the orthodoxy has excluded." Although southern literary study may in the past have constituted a "literary secession," so strong became poststructuralist theory's toehold in the South that even the most innocuous single-author conference—such as a celebration at the University of Maryland of Katherine Anne Porter's hundredth birthday—inevitably fell into angry debates over theory and chivalric defenses of the sacredness of authorship.

In a 1980s issue of the *Yale Journal of Criticism,* an article appeared whose title, "The Inevitability of Theory in the South," bespoke at once the absence of theory, its desirability, and its irresistible advent. The author, Jefferson Humphries (himself a Yale-trained southerner), later developed this claim into a collection of essays by various hands, all joining theory to southern literature. In the introduction to *Southern Literature and Literary Theory,* Humphries writes that "for me, the fusion of southern studies with European modes of close reading represents the final stage of escape from the organic nationalism of the Old South." Humphries's point is that whereas organicist ideologies depend on the assumption that language can reveal "unmediated Truth," Paul de Man's mature project was to show that such claims are always "lies." The claims of Humphries's title and introduction at first suggest an alliance with, rather than opposition to, the position of dissensus suggested by Kreyling. Yet when

Southern Literature and Literary Theory is placed beside other recent works deploying theory in some relation to southern culture, its tokenism of gender and race takes on more disturbingly familiar meanings. Indeed, the near-erasure of people of color and white women from theoretical work on the South constituted a pattern in other innovative works in southern intellectual history and literary criticism. The otherwise imaginative and intelligent work of Richard King in *A Southern Renaissance* dismisses southern white women (with the exception of Lillian Smith) from consideration because they "were not concerned primarily with the larger cultural, racial, and political themes that I take as my focus." King omits blacks entirely "because for them the Southern family romance [King's paradigm] was hardly problematic. It could be and was rejected out of hand." In *The War Within: From Victorian to Modernist Thought in the South, 1919–1945,* Daniel Singal develops the thesis that southern modernism involved the overturning of hierarchical Victorian dichotomies such as civilized/savage and human/animal. But he does not consider man/woman, and the sole woman he discusses is Ellen Glasgow. Such exclusions make sense only within the definitions of literary and intellectual history that these writers elsewhere make it their project to reject. Their innovations rest in part on the decision to move outside generic definitions of "literature," thus reading non-"literary" texts as constitutive of the Southern Renascence and literature as intellectual history. Kreyling's hope for "dissensus" as a consequence of the marriage between contemporary literary theory and southern literature clearly could not be called, like the advent of theory itself, an "inevitability."

With all this said, it may come as a surprise that contemporary literary theory has in fact taken strong hold among southern literary scholars, albeit with some peculiar twists and distinctive flavors, and has done so at a rate and with a breadth not very different from its hold in nonsouthern universities. Literary theory's best-known names, schools, and frequency of use by southernists differ little overall from the saturation in contemporary theory of nonsouthernist literary scholars, judging from thirty-year surveys of two journals, *American Literature* and *Mississippi Quarterly.* In those surveys, conducted by Tamara Olaivar at the University of Florida in 1999, several interesting phenomena emerge.

Louis D. Rubin Jr. edited *A Bibliographical Guide to the Study of Southern Literature* for LSU Press in

1969, three years after the Johns Hopkins conference where Jacques Derrida made his first U.S. appearance. The volume marked the end of an era in the study of southern literature. There is no mention in it—save for the New Criticism and the work of southern historians—of what might be seen as literary theory. A decade later, theory could be found emerging in monographs about southern literature—Lacanian psychoanalysis in John T. Irwin's *Doubling and Incest/Repetition and Revenge: A Speculative Reading of Faulkner* (1975); Freud and Nietzsche in Richard King's *A Southern Renaissance* (1980); feminist theory in Anne Goodwyn Jones's *Tomorrow Is Another Day* (1981), Derrida in John T. Matthews's *The Play of Faulkner's Language* (1982), cultural studies in Bertram Wyatt-Brown's *Southern Honor* (1982), African American studies in Trudier Harris's *From Mammies to Militants* (1982). The first sign of contemporary literary theory in Volume 34 (1980–81) of the *Mississippi Quarterly* appeared in an essay that used Edward Said's Orientalism to compare Europe's "othering" of Asia to the U.S. North's "othering." In the same issue, a book review of Jack Raper's *From the Sunken Garden* noted his use of psychoanalytic theory from Freud and Jung. Psychoanalysis was to take the early lead in southern scholarship's use of theory, judging from both the *Mississippi Quarterly* and the essays on southern subjects in *American Literature,* beginning with Volume 51 in 1979. In the *Mississippi Quarterly,* psychoanalytic criticism could be found in Summer 1982 and Summer 1983 (summer issues are Faulkner issues). By summer 1998 (Volume 49.3), thirteen of the Faulkner issue's sixteen essays and reviews used contemporary literary theory, psychoanalytic (Lacan, Winnicott, Freud), Derridean, Barthesian, Bakhtinian, Marxist (Jameson, Adorno, Horkheimer, Gramsci, Althusser) and Foucaultian, feminist (Gilbert, Irigaray, Spivak, Minh-ha, Sedgwick), and African American (Gates, Morrison). The southern essays in *American Literature* show a shift toward and within theory that is different but no less dramatic: essays move from single-author studies to cultural topics, and the theories used shift from psychoanalysis to cultural studies.

The complexities of southern culture—its racial polydiversities, its gender contradictions, its cross-class collaborations, its odd notions of public and private, the literality of its discourse of mastery and master, the affinities it has shown with Marxist rejections of individualism and capitalism yet its rejection of class analysis and of revolutionary or even reformist commitment, in short its sometimes irritating differences from other regions—offer the chance to rethink and critique contemporary literary theory from southern vantage points as well. Even the tradition of southern "resistance to theory" can, despite and because of its politics, have a salutary effect on theory from "outside." For when theory acts hegemonically—when it makes universalist claims even as it claims the impossibility of the universal, when it assumes there are no contradictions, no repressions except in texts *other* than itself—southernists will take notice, accustomed as they are both to totalizing rhetoric and to resistance.

Anne Goodwyn Jones

See also Academy, Southern Literature and the; Agrarians; *Mind of the South, The*; New Criticism; Rubin, Louis D., Jr.; Vanderbilt University.

LOCAL COLOR

Local color is the designation for a body of postbellum literature, primarily produced during the years 1870 to 1900, but peaking in popularity during the 1880s. In his 1894 collection of critical essays, *Crumbling Idols,* Hamlin Garland calls local color "natural and unstrained art" in which the native of a region reflects life as it is lived in that place. Earlier, James Lane Allen called the local-colorist an observer of the influences exerted by place on human nature. Writers in this genre were devoted to capturing the nuances of a particular region by recording the speech, dress, and habits of its residents and focusing on the distinguishing particularities of that environment. Repeated character types in local color include the yeoman farmer, the backcountry cracker, the ex-slave, the mountaineer, the Creole—in short, any readily identifiable social or racial group or geographically based community about which the writer could draw rough generalizations. Emphasizing agrarian life styles and the values of a preindustrial America, local-color writers often took as their subjects pockets of culture outside of society's mainstream. Bret Harte and his stories of the American West usually receive credit for initiating the local-color school in the United States. Critics often designate, for example, New England authors Sarah Orne Jewett and Mary Wilkins Freeman and midwestern writers Hamlin Garland and Edward Eggleston as local-colorists.

Although obviously linked to literary realism in its

emphasis on the particularities of place and the events of daily life, local color has been typically thought to lack the interest in larger human issues that realism at its best investigates, using place as one of its primary tools. Instead, local-color writing has traditionally been seen as more interested in the surface features of region. For that reason, "local color" has frequently become a pejorative label used to dismiss, sometimes in error, any literature that is perceived as failing to transcend place in pursuit of universal themes. As the traits of literary naturalism gained prominence in the early twentieth century, critics began dismissing local color collectively as maudlin and sentimental, a view of the genre that has survived into contemporary assessments of it. Yet the existence of local color reveals an increasingly important dimension of the American literary tradition. Earlier efforts to identify and produce a national literature were replaced in the postbellum era by a growing sense that America's distinctive geographic and demographic diversity was, in fact, most accurately represented by a regional literature, thus freeing the nation from its long bondage to European literary models.

Southern local-colorists outnumber those from other regions, largely because they sparked the interest of northern publishers and audiences after the Civil War with their ability to supply details from a part of the country little known to or understood by outsiders. In 1873, *Scribner's Monthly* published George Washington Cable's " 'Sieur George," an event generally regarded as the initiation of southern local color. Early traces of the genre appear, however, in the work of the antebellum novelist William Gilmore Simms, and in the rollicking tales of the Southwestern humorists, who share with local color the objective of documenting life-styles and peoples passing away in the face of inevitable modernization. Popular northern publications, including *Harper's Monthly, Harper's Weekly, Lippincott's, Scribner's Magazine* (renamed *The Century* in 1881), and even the *Atlantic Monthly,* regularly featured examples of southern local color. Writers considered southern local-colorists include, among many others, Sherwood Bonner, Mary Noailles Murfree, Ruth McEnery Stuart, George Washington Cable, Sarah Barnwell Elliott, M. E. M. Davis, Grace King, Sidney Lanier, Thomas Nelson Page, John Fox Jr., James Lane Allen, Irwin Russell, and Joel Chandler Harris, whose Uncle Remus tales provide the most widely recognized examples of the genre. Many southern local-colorists call forth not just an idiosyncratic location but a world:

Cable's and King's New Orleans, Murfree's Tennessee mountains, Stuart's Arkansas, Allen's Kentucky. Mark Twain and Kate Chopin are examples of southern writers whose early works demonstrate obvious affinities with local color but whose careers are often understood as transcending the genre in favor of darker and more complex examinations of human nature.

Generalizations about local color run the risk of undermining its central premise: that place matters. Although certain attitudes and character types may be common, southern local color and New England local color, for example, do differ in important ways. Most obviously, southern local color substitutes for Sarah Orne Jewett's Maine seashore the plantation houses of the Deep South and the exoticism of New Orleans. African American characters and details of plantation life dominate southern local color. The depiction of stereotypical relationships between black characters and their former owners minimized the reality of postbellum racial tension, and thus assuaged both northern and southern discomfort stemming from the state of race relations. In general, African American characters appear either as devoted former slaves or as disillusioned freedmen. As late as 1906, Mildred Rutherford, editor of *The South in History and Literature,* explained the outpouring of southern local color as an attempt to rectify the misperceptions promoted by Harriet Beecher Stowe's *Uncle Tom's Cabin* (1852). Southern local-colorists did not overtly justify secession, but they did in many cases glorify the Lost Cause and bolster the air of nobility that surrounded it. Thomas Nelson Page's "Marse Chan" (1887) is the quintessential example of the plantation school in southern local color. Thus the image of the Old South as such largely emerges in the fond reverie of the local-colorists, who offered in their pastoral scenes an alternative way of life to America's rapid industrialization. Southern writers in the plantation school came to figure so prominently in national literature that in 1888 Albion W. Tourgée could declare: "Our literature has become not only Southern in type but distinctly Confederate in sympathy." Fascinated by the disparity between the regal world of the plantation master and the barbarity of slavery, Tourgée proclaimed that southerners would continue to dominate their nation's literature until the century's end. Indeed, elements of plantation fiction persisted, but in the hands of African American writer Charles Chesnutt, for example, they are manipulated to empower formerly disenfranchised characters, including the ex-slave Uncle Julius, who recurs in several stories from Chesnutt's *The Conjure Woman* (1899). Uncle Julius's crafty storytelling repeatedly allows him to best the paternalism of the white farm owner, a northern man who mistakenly views Julius as a benign presence to be tolerated and periodically indulged.

But southern local-colorists did not confine themselves to images of the Old South's fallen grandeur. A significant number of local-color stories focus on the lives of poor white characters, much as the genre's antebellum predecessor, Southwestern humor, had. In the Appalachian tales of John Fox Jr. and Will Allen Dromgoole, for instance, the reader encounters the figures of listless and defeated mountaineers whose images would handicap their real-life counterparts for decades to come. Tales of moonshining and hunting dominate a world removed from time. Poor whites in southern local color often exhibit violent behavior and intellectual limitations that mark them as forerunners to the characters of Erskine Caldwell's fiction and the Snopeses of Faulkner's Yoknapatawpha County. In the opening story of Mary Murfree's *In the Tennessee Mountains* (1884), for instance, a mentally retarded character assaults another man with a sledgehammer that comes away spattered with brains. Thus, local color served as a means to reestablish and reinforce both racial and class-based distinctions then being questioned in a society that had witnessed the literal destruction of its values in the Civil War.

Despite Hamlin Garland's assertion that only the native of a region could write its local color, in the South much of the genre depended for its success on the incorporation of an outsider's perspective. Southern local-colorists frequently employ the frame narrative, requiring that the story be retold to an outside listener. Many works include an outsider figure who must be either inducted into the working of the community or shunned for his marginal status. The most enduring examples of southern local color are those written by authors who were both members of the community they describe and at some geographic or ideological remove from that group, providing the writer a measure of detachment from her topic. Mary Murfree, for instance, first encountered the southern mountains as a vacationer who later adopted that setting for the bulk of her fiction. Her view of the mountaineer, then, is that of an outsider who came to know the locale well enough to write extensively about it, but who asks the reader, by way of diction, to share her more sophisticated perspective. It is Murfree and not the typical

mountaineer who indicts the exploitation of mountain resources by external forces and by extension rejects the agenda of Henry Grady's industrialized New South. George Washington Cable was more profoundly at odds with the community he took as his subject, later voicing a racial liberalism that essentially ostracized him from the New Orleans he had known. Southern local color frequently becomes, then, not just a depiction of locale but a response to larger ideas in contemporaneous southern culture.

By 1900, writers nationwide had published more than 150 collections of local-color stories. As a result of this surfeit, the movement began to lose its momentum. "We all know to our sorrow what local color is," observed a reviewer for the *Nation* in 1907. "The novel of to-day reeks with it." By the time *Harper's Magazine* published a pair of articles by Laura Spencer Portor in 1922, called "In Search of Local Color," the genre had become a pale imitation of itself. Fiction and nonfiction blend on Portor's trek into the Kentucky mountains in search of the stereotypes she has read about in Fox's fiction. In many cases, an urge to publish quickly and reap the rewards of financial success eclipsed an interest in authenticity of detail. The use of dialect, for instance, began in many amateurish forays to bear little resemblance to the actual spoken word. In March 1900, Atlanta's enormously popular literary periodical, the *Sunny South,* included an article simply titled "Don't Send Us Rhyme Nor Dialect."

Recent reassessments of the genre concentrate on the high number of female local-colorists in the South and elsewhere. In fact, critics have suggested that female local-colorists comprise the first body of women writers whose influence extends beyond the age in which they wrote. Several factors account for this phenomenon. The genre appealed to women nationwide because it sanctioned an interest in what they knew best—everyday life in the area in which they lived. It also offered them freedom through financial independence during a time of increasingly vocal agitation for the rights of women. Yet "local color" has become a negative judgment, liberally and indiscriminately applied to women's writing from the postbellum era and beyond, if a work demonstrates substantial interest in place and the activities of female characters in that location. Now that feminist theory and cultural criticism have been brought to bear on this long-neglected body of literature, local color, particularly that written by women, has begun to earn scholarly attention. Judith Fetterly and Majorie Pryse, for instance, argue for a distinction between texts written by men and those written by women, whom they term "regionalists," during the period from 1850 to 1910. Fetterley and Pryse note the absence of narrative distance between storyteller and plot in regionalist texts and suggest that female authors enlist the audience's sympathy for their characters by identifying with those characters themselves. More recently, Sherrie Inness and Diane Royer, in their introduction to the essay collection *Breaking Boundaries* (1997), maintain that local color is but one brief phase in an ongoing affinity for regional writing demonstrated by American women writers. In the works of female regionalists, they find embedded societal and gender-based critiques that amount finally to subversion of both literary convention and customary expectations for women. Interpreted through this lens, a seemingly light-hearted sketch such as Ruth Stuart's "The Woman's Exchange of Simpkinsville," in which a pair of elderly women launch their own business, becomes a story of female initiative, analogous to the writer's own strike at independence through her writing. Local-color literature, then, provides a valuable index to nineteenth-century conceptions of female community and reveals itself to be a far more complex mode of writing than traditional scholarship has suggested.

An interest in the particularities of place and an agrarian lifestyle persists in twentieth-century southern literature, notably manifest in the writings of the Agrarians but also present in work ranging from William Faulkner's fiction to Wendell Berry's poetry. Long considered merely part of a benighted period in southern letters, local-color fiction offers a link between nineteenth- and twentieth-century writers that constitutes a southern literary tradition.

Kathryn B. McKee

See also Appalachian Literature; Creole Literature; Faithful Retainer; Frame Narrative; Mammy; Plantation Fiction; Poor White; Regionalism; Southwestern Humor.

Sylvia Jenkins Cook, *From Tobacco Road to Route 66: The Southern Poor White in Fiction* (1976); Josephine Donovan, *New England Local Color Literature* (1983); Judith Fetterley and Marjorie Pryse, eds., *American Women Regionalists* (1992); Wade Hall, *The Smiling Phoenix: Southern Humor from 1865 to 1914* (1965); Sherrie A. Inness and Diana Royer, eds., *Breaking Boundaries: New Perspectives on Women's Regional Writing* (1997); Shields McIlwaine, *The Southern Poor White from Lubberland to Tobacco Road* (1939); Robert Rhode, *Setting in the American Short Story of Local Color 1865–1900* (1975); Claude M. Simpson, *The Local Colorists* (1960); Merrill M. Skaggs, *The Folk of Southern Fiction* (1972); Helen Taylor, *Gender, Race, and Region in the Writings of Grace King, Ruth McEnery Stuart, and Kate Chopin* (1989); Emily Toth, ed., *Regionalism and the Female Imagination* (1985).

LONG, HUEY

Huey Pierce Long (1893–1935), the flamboyant Louisiana politician, attracted the attention of several prominent American novelists, notably Robert Penn Warren, whose protean and compelling Willie Stark in *All the King's Men* (1946) owes much to the Kingfish. The Long legend had been drawn on previously by Sinclair Lewis in *It Can't Happen Here* (1935), Hamilton Basso in *Sun in Capricorn* (1942), John Dos Passos in *Number One* (1943), and Adria Locke Langley in *A Lion Is in the Streets* (1945), all overtly anti-Fascist novels with Long-like demagogues as major characters. Warren's and Langley's novels were adapted into Hollywood films.

Seldom at a loss for words, Long liked nothing better than to see himself in print. Largely self-educated, he wrote his own fiery and often funny speeches, campaign circulars, newspaper columns, and magazine articles during a career that saw him elected governor (1928–1932) and U.S. senator (1932–1935). His most extended literary efforts are two jaunty political autobiographies: *Every Man a King* (1933), published when he was forty, and *My First Days in the White House,* published shortly after his death in 1935. *Every Man a King* purports to trace Long's rise from log-cabin origins to national prominence. Its main intent, however, is to portray the Kingfish as a lifelong friend of the downtrodden and foe of millionaires and their hirelings—corporate lawyers, corrupt officials, and yellow journalists. Relying more on political caricature and sheer bravura than on sound economics, *Every Man a King* establishes Long's persona as a populist hero, a southern savior risen from the piney hills to lead America out of the Depression.

The book heavily promotes Long's Share Our Wealth (SOW) program, an audacious plan to guarantee the financial security of all citizens. SOW appealed to a wide public, largely because it went far beyond the New Deal in a time of economic panic and called for a radical restructuring of American wealth. Under SOW, the federal government would tax only millionaires. The rich could keep no more than $1 million in yearly income or $5 million in family worth; excess wealth would be seized by the federal government. Long developed an attractive list of public uses to which this confiscated wealth would be put: pensions for persons over sixty, tuition waivers for college or vocational training, raises for teachers, and bonuses for veterans. Each family would be guaranteed $5,000 (enough for a home, car, and radio) plus an annual income of at least $2,500 (about $25,000 in today's economy) as basic economic rights of citizenship. Every American would be guaranteed a job, a thirty-hour work week, and a month's vacation. Public-works projects would build colleges, hospitals, research laboratories, asylums, roads, bridges, dams, and parks—but not prisons. Anyone in jail for stealing food would be freed.

Much to his credit, Long was articulating a highly salient point (one that few mainstream Democrats or Republicans would admit publicly)—that the basic civil and political guarantees of American democracy were largely meaningless to the indigent. Further, by arguing that the country was controlled by a core elite of business tycoons, Long was stressing that Depression-era America was closer to an oligarchy than a republic. However, SOW was too good to be true and could not have worked for any length of time. Because it relied solely upon financial seizures and put no curbs on business monopolies or limits on corporate profits, the Long plan offered no fundamental challenge to laissez-faire. In short, it presented a utopian vision while neither overhauling capitalism nor promoting socialism. Also, because SOW abolished taxation for nearly every citizen, it never could have paid for itself. Even so, it effectively tapped into the fear and helplessness that many Americans felt. Millions cheered when Long characterized New Deal Progressives as eastern snobs who in the end would side with big business and do little to improve the lives of America's poor. He urged disgruntled voters to come over to his wing of the Democratic Party and take the presidential nomination away from Franklin Roosevelt.

As his popularity soared in 1935, Long dashed off *My First Days in the White House,* which brashly announces his agenda as president. The book deftly combines slapstick and propaganda. Set in the near future, it begins on Inauguration Day, 1937. "President" Long's main order of business (after naming Herbert Hoover and FDR to his cabinet, the book's best jest) is to implement SOW. The nation's millionaires prove surprisingly compliant in divesting themselves of their fortunes. John D. Rockefeller Jr., the oil magnate, pa-

triotically chairs the committee to decentralize America's wealth. As he transforms the national economy, Long insists that the Depression did not result from any inherent flaw in capitalism but rather from the moral failure of a corrupt few (mostly bankers) who exploited the system for personal gain. Management of every industry or business is left in the hands of current owners, who may pursue profits without check as long as dividends are shared. With the implementation of SOW, unemployment vanishes overnight, and hunger and homelessness become things of the past. All this, of course, lay in a future that Long promised would come true. By the time of the book's publication, however, Long was dead at age forty-two, assassinated in September 1935, in Baton Rouge, by a physician whose motives were unclear—a death scene mirrored in *All the King's Men.*

Philip Dubuisson Castille

See also Demagogue; Louisiana, Literature of; Politician; Populism.

Glen Jeansonne, *Messiah of the Masses: Huey P. Long and the Great Depression* (1993); T. Harry Williams, *Huey Long* (1969).

LOST CAUSE

"Lost Cause" refers customarily to southern writing about the Confederacy in the half-century following the end of the Civil War. Borrowing from Scottish history, *Richmond Examiner* editor Edward A. Pollard first used the term in his 1866 history of the Confederacy that bore that title. As Pollard used it, "Lost Cause" was equivalent to the Confederate cause in the war. In ideology and in tone, however, Pollard laid the foundation for the more expansive uses of "Lost Cause." Defeat in the Civil War, he argued, meant that the South must submit to the abolition of slavery and the impossibility of secession from the Union. Defeat did not mean that the white South had to submit to black suffrage or black social equality or to a distinctly inferior northern civilization. The South lost the war because it was overwhelmed militarily. The South was, despite its defeat, the superior civilization.

The sometimes belligerent vindication of southern civilization and the Confederate principles was a hallmark of Lost-Cause writing. Beginning with Pollard's history, southern writers determined to tell the Confederate side of the struggle and assert the righteousness of their principles. The outpouring of political and even military memoirs afforded opportunities to reassert the southern orthodoxy that the Confederacy fought for self-determination and states' rights, not in defense of slavery, and that the Union violated the Constitution and the accepted laws of war in its pursuit of victory. Among the most notable statements of these viewpoints by former Confederates were Vice President Alexander Stephens's *Constitutional View of the Late War Between the States* (1868), President Jefferson Davis's *Rise and Fall of the Confederate Government* (1881), Admiral Raphael Semmes's *Memoirs of Service Afloat* (1869), and General Richard Taylor's *Destruction and Reconstruction* (1879).

Within a decade of war's end, former Confederates began publishing periodicals that featured articles, poems, and documents presenting the Confederate side of the war. Most were short-lived: *Banner of the South* (1866–1869), *Land We Love* (1866–1868), *Our Living and Our Dead* (1874–1876), *Southern Bivouac* (1882–1886), *Lost Cause* (1898–1904), and *Confederate War Journal* (1893–1894). Preceding the U.S. government's publication of official records, *Southern Historical Society Papers* (1873–1959, with interruptions) was an important source of military and political primary sources. Defending the southern cause in the war did not mean, however, that the journals conveyed a harmony of viewpoints. To the contrary, Lost-Cause period literature initiated bitter debates among former Confederates (still raging among historians) over the performance of Confederate military and civilian leaders.

The most ideologically strident Lost-Cause literature emanated from organizations such as the United Confederate Veterans and the United Daughters of the Confederacy. They published pamphlets offering "correct" history, endorsed textbooks "safe to be used in southern schools," while condemning textbooks presenting "unjust" interpretations of the Confederate cause.

Many southern novelists and poets worked within a Lost-Cause tradition, promoting a stereotypical view of the Old South and depicting a proud, though ruined, civilization emerging from the war. The most notable examples are novelists Thomas Nelson Page, Thomas Dixon, Joel Chandler Harris, and Mary Johnston and poets Abram Ryan, John R. Thompson, and Henry Timrod, and the late work of John Esten Cooke and William Gilmore Simms, whose novels had made him the antebellum South's preeminent writer.

Although historians customarily consider 1865 to 1913 the Lost-Cause period in southern history, the Lost-Cause mentality continued to influence southern writers well into the twentieth century. Margaret Mitchell's *Gone With the Wind* (1936) and Stark Young's *So Red the Rose* (1934) were examples of the tradition. Self-declared "neo-Confederate" historians of the late twentieth century consciously perpetuate the ideology and the language of Lost-Cause writers.

John M. Coski

See also Civil War; Confederacy, Literature of the; Confederate States of America; Lee, Robert E.; New South; Odes to the Confederate Dead; United Daughters of the Confederacy.

Fred Arthur Bailey, "Textbooks of the Lost Cause," *Georgia Historical Quarterly* 75 (1991); Thomas L. Connelly and Barbara L. Bellows, *God and General Longstreet: The Lost Cause and the Southern Mind* (1982); Susan Speare Durant, "The Gently Furled Banner: The Development of the Myth of the Lost Cause" (Ph.D. diss., University of North Carolina, 1972); Gaines M. Foster, *Ghosts of the Confederacy* (1987); Michael Andrew Grissom, *Southern by the Grace of God* (1988); Rollin G. Osterweis, *The Myth of the Lost Cause 1865–1900* (1973); Charles Reagan Wilson, *Baptized in Blood: The Religion of the Lost Cause, 1865–1900* (1980).

LOST COLONY, THE

The Lost Colony was first performed during the summer of 1937 on Roanoke Island off the coast of North Carolina. The summer-long production commemorated the 350th anniversary of the earliest English attempt to colonize the New World and was given at the site where the colony was founded in 1587. The group sponsoring the production was not blind to the economic benefits flowing to their depressed and isolated region from a successful attraction, but they were motivated as much by a local pride that for decades had looked for ways to expand the story of American history in the popular mind beyond its focus largely on New England when origins were concerned. The 350th anniversary seemed just the thing for their purpose. One of the group had seen the Passion Play at Oberammergau, Germany, and members agreed to approach Paul Green, Pulitzer Prize-winning playwright who had also written a series of motion pictures for Will Rogers, to write a historical pageant for them. Since his student days at the University of North Carolina in the 1920s, Green had been fascinated by the story of Walter Raleigh's colonists who vanished from Roanoke Island leaving no clue as to their fate, and early in 1937 he went to work on a script.

The script turned out to be not a historical pageant but a new kind of historical play suited for production before large audiences outdoors. Pageants are chronicles, with events following one another as historical chronology, not dramatic necessity, dictates. They have no characters in a dramatic sense but only representations of historical figures. And to a substantial degree, their impact depends on large casts, bright colors, loud noises, and other elements of stage spectacle. Although it makes direct use of historical material, *The Lost Colony,* by contrast, is unmistakably a play, a well-formed dramatic work with points of interest appropriate to a drama. Its characters are suitably developed, with two of them, John Borden and Eleanor Dare, emerging as representatives of the collective hero of the piece: the common people of the land. The characters carry forward a plot made coherent and significant by the play's theme. And the play's structure, episodic rather than tightly knit, focused on action rather than introspection, and including music, dance, a narrator, and other direct acknowledgments of the audience, makes it well suited for outdoor performance.

Thematically, *The Lost Colony* shows the development of a new kind of society on these western shores, a society different in structure and values from English society, indeed from European society generally. Old-World societies were rigidly stratified, with rank an inherited, not an earned commodity. And one's rank was always an underlying factor, frequently the determining factor, through the range of life's experiences, from general matters such as sense of self-worth to particular matters such as where one might live, whom one might marry, and what occupation one might enter. That is how *The Lost Colony* depicts English society in the time of the first Elizabeth, as hierarchical in structure, with individuals locked into their station by birth, and power always flowing down from above.

The opposite and distinctively American social ideal is the one that Green shows developing on Roanoke Island. In colonial and early republican days, when the memory of stratified European societies was still fresh, the principle was called "equality of condition." Based on a belief in the intrinsic worth of individuals, equality is fundamental to a democratic way of life, and Green used *The Lost Colony* to celebrate the discovery

of this core value in American experience. The play works to that end by showing how frontier conditions in America broke down European class distinctions between serf, peasant, yeoman, and nobleman (social distinctions between men and women, too) and placed all citizens on a level playing field in the game of life.

Old Tom, a clownish but important character, illustrates the development. In England, he had no social position and therefore neither self-respect nor influence and responsibility. On Roanoke Island, frontier conditions quickly dispel all position-derived notions of worth and place a premium on individual qualities of imagination, energy, and social responsibility. In those conditions, Tom earns the respect of his fellow colonists. And on guard duty near the end of the play, he articulates a newly emerging sense of himself. It is night, and a younger man, exhausted, accepts Tom's offer to stand watch for him with a word of thanks and a promise that "You will be remembered." As Tom reflects on the remark, he makes a clear distinction between *there* and *here,* England and Roanoke, and the different results in individual development: "I will be remembered. I hope not. There in England all remembered me—aye, with kicks and curses and a terrible usage of tongues they did. Hah-hah-hah. And deep I drowned my sorrows in the mug. But here, where there is no remembrance, I who was lately nothing am become somebody. For—item—have I not now the keeping of some sixty souls in my care—I who could never care for me own? Verily, Tom, I hardly know thee in thy greatness. (Saluting the air.) Roanoke, thou hast made a man of me."

Laurence G. Avery

See also Outdoor Drama.

Laurence G. Avery, *A Southern Life: Letters of Paul Green, 1916–1981* (1994); William Free and Charles Lower, *History into Drama: A Source Book on Symphonic Drama* (1963); William S. Powell, *Paradise Preserved: A History of the Roanoke Island Historical Association* (1965).

LOUISIANA, LITERATURE OF

Louisiana has always been exceptional as a southern state: its colonial origins were more French and Catholic than the Anglo and Protestant roots of other states; its politics and culture were shaped as much by its cosmopolitan port as by the plantation culture that typically dominated the region. Even the Civil War did not mark the state as definitively as elsewhere: the sentiment for secession was lukewarm, New Orleans and the river fell under Union control early, and few significant battles were fought within its boundaries. Louisiana's literature bears the traces of that exceptionality. The earliest writing was in French (and Spanish), and when English finally came to be the principal tongue in the mid-nineteenth century, the exotic flavors of Gallic and Caribbean culture lingered palpably.

The French established the colony with a fort on the Red River near Natchitoches in 1714 and then, four years later, established the more successful settlement of New Orleans on the Mississippi. The Spanish controlled the territory after 1762; however, neither the French nor the Spanish were ever able to make Louisiana a profitable possession, a fact that helps to explain its eventual quick sale by Napoleon to the United States in 1803. There were, of course, throughout the seventeenth and eighteenth centuries, many official and semi-official descriptions of the Lower Mississippi Valley, both in French and in Spanish, including Cabeza de Vaca's *Relation* (1542), Le Page du Pratz's *Histoire de la Louisiane* (1758), André Penicaut's fascinating *Relation,* and Jean-Bernard Bossu's *Nouveaux Voyages aux Indes Occidentales* (1768). The letters and accounts of the Ursuline nuns' 1727 arrival in the colony by Marie St. Augustin de Tranchepain (*Relation du voyages des premières Ursulines à la Nouvelle Orléans,* 1859) provide a unique early perspective by women (many of these French accounts were collected by Pierre Margry, *Découvertes et établissements des français dans l'ouest et dans le sud de l'Amérique Septentrionale (1614–1754),* 1876–1886). Travel narratives about the state continued to appear throughout the next century, including such well-known works as Harriet Martineau's *Retrospect of Western Travel* (1838) and more obscure but equally interesting accounts, like Elisée Reclus's astute 1853 commentary on slavery and the Americanization of the culture, "Fragments du voyage à la Nouvelle-Orléans," which appeared in an 1860 Parisian journal, *Le Tour du Monde.*

Nearly a century passed before colonial residents produced more conventional kinds of literary art. Julien Poydras de Lallande, a native of Brittany, who became a merchant and planter in Pointe Coupee Parish across the river from the outpost of Baton Rouge, is credited with the first published work of poetry in the Louisiana territory. Two anonymous poems (1777) in praise of the Spanish governor Bernardo de Galvez are attributed to him as well as his equally occasional "La Prise du Morne du Baton Rouge" (1779), two hundred and seven lines on the capture of the bluffs of Baton Rouge. Somewhat more interesting is Louisiana's first extant drama, *La Fête du Petit-Blé, ou L'Héroisme de Poucha-houmma* (The Festival of the Young Corn, or the Heroism of Poucha-Houmma), staged in 1809 and printed in New Orleans in 1814. Its elderly author, Paul Louis Le Blanc de Villeneufve, had been an officer of the French army who had spent much of his career among the Choctaw people, whom he greatly admired. Based on an event in the early 1750s, his "tragedy in five acts" couples a stiffly neoclassic form with a romanticized view of the noble savage, but it also incorporates knowledgeable details of native life.

But while these works claim the honors as Louisiana's earliest published literature, the oral tradition was developing its own rich contribution to the state's literary ethos. Creole folk songs and tales, incorporating and often blending elements of African folklore with French, German, Indian, Caribbean, and other disparate sources, were an early reflection of the profound ethnic diversity that has characterized Louisiana's people since very early in its history. Because the primitive conditions and malarial climate made the colony unattractive to French settlers, many of the early inhabitants were largely involuntary: prisoners, vagabonds, and prostitutes impressed from the streets of France, together with African slaves, the first load of five hundred arriving in 1719. They were eventually joined by German farmers and successive waves of Acadian exiles from Nova Scotia after 1763, whose culture became extremely influential throughout the south-central parts of the state. Significant numbers of settlers from British colonies also ventured into French Louisiana, as well as groups from Spain and Haiti— and always, a continuing stream of slaves from Africa and the West Indies. The relative lenience regarding private emancipations in the French *Code Noir* (the "black code" regulating the lives of black people, whether free or slave) also helped to create a large and fairly prosperous population of free people of color— *les gens de couleur libre*—nearly 1,300 in New Orleans by 1803. Later in the nineteenth century, this diverse population were joined by large groups of Irish and Italian immigrants, as well as many more of "les Américains," both from upriver and from the more Anglicized South, who made their own impact on the state's language and culture. Henry Clay Lewis, writing in the Southwest-humor tradition as Madison Tensas, contributed his versions of frontier Louisiana in *Odd Leaves from the Life of a Louisiana Swamp Doctor* (1843) and *The Swamp Doctor's Adventures in the Southwest* (1858). Less amusingly, Solomon Northup, a free black man who was abducted from Saratoga, New York, and sold in New Orleans to a Red River planter, provided in *Twelve Years a Slave* (1853) a unique account of Louisiana's dreaded plantations "down the river."

Drawing upon and blending all this rich mix of cultures, the folk literature of Louisiana acquired an attractively exotic cast. Songs in the unique French patois of the Acadians and in the "gombo" French spoken by many blacks continued to circulate throughout the century. Both songs and stories were frequently collected in period anthologies, such as *Slave Songs of the United States* (1867), but they also regularly appeared in local periodicals such as *Le Moniteur de la Louisiane*, the first newspaper in the colony (founded by Louis Duclot in 1794) and *L'Abeille* (*The Bee*, a bilingual newspaper that lasted nearly a century, 1827–1923). This folk material, often in an exotic (and disappearing) language, became important inspiration for later writers such as George Washington Cable, Lafcadio Hearn, Sidonie de la Houssaye, Grace King, and Alcée Fortier, all of whom also collected this material as well. Fortier's numerous publications, including *Louisiana Folk-Tales, in French Dialect and English Translation* (1894), remain important and influential resources, as does Hearn's *Gombo Zhebes: A Little Dictionary of Creole Proverbs* (1885) and *Réminiscences Acadiennes* (1907), a collection of tales gathered by Felix Voorhies, a St. Martinville judge.

But the coming of *les Américains* and their English to the tenaciously Francophile culture of Louisiana provided the real spur to French literature. In the nineteenth century, there were as many as 133 French-language newspapers and journals in New Orleans and 152 more in the parishes (or counties), producing a generous market for stories and poems. Edward LaRoque Tinker lists several hundred French authors in his bio-bibliography, *Les Ecrits de langue française en Louisiane au XIXᵉ siècle* (1932). Among the most interesting were the poets and writers who had begun publishing their work in *L'Album Littéraire: Journal des Jeunes Gens, Amateurs de la Littérature!* Founded in 1843 by Armand Lanusse and J. L. Marciacq, *L'Album* was the first literary publication by free people of color in Louisiana, established just when racial prejudice increasingly threatened their free status. Two years later, *Les Cenelles* appeared, a landmark anthology of poems by Creoles of color. Among the seventeen writers represented were Camille Thierry, Joanni Questy (whose work includes a serialized novella, *Monsieur Paul*, 1867) and Victor Séjour, who later achieved considerable fame as a playwright in Paris. The most famous (white) poets of the era were the Rouquette brothers, Dominique and Adrien. Dominique, the elder, locally notorious for his derelict habits, published two volumes of romantic poetry that were highly praised in the French press, *Les Meschacebéennes* ("the Mississippians") (1839) and *Les Fleurs d'Amérique* (1857). Likewise influenced by French romanticism, Adrien eventually became a priest and was well known for his work among the Choctaw in St. Tammany Parish. The published works of "L'Abbé Rouquette" include several volumes of nature poetry and an idyll of Indian life, *La Nouvelle Atala* (1879).

Foremost among the French novelists were Albert Mercier and Sidonie de la Houssaye. Mercier, a Paris-trained physician who was born in New Orleans, composed poems and plays and was a founder of the French literary club L'Athénée Louisianais (1875) and editor of *Comptes rendus de l'Athénée Louisianais* (1876), both of which were major forces in keeping alive Louisiana's French literature and language—at the very moment when the social upheavals of the Civil War and Reconstruction were making that struggle patently futile. Of Mercier's six novels, the most interesting is *L'Habitation Saint-Ybars, ou Maitres et Esclaves en Louisiane* (St.-Ybars Plantation, or Masters and Slaves in Louisiana) (1881), a detailed account of slave society from his youth. Sidonie de la Houssaye (née Hélène Perret, whose nom de plume was Louise Raymond) is perhaps best known as having provided Cable with some materials for his *Strange and True Stories of Louisiana* (1889). Her *Les Quarteronnes de la Nouvelle-Orléans* (1894–1895), a group of four novels, some of which were published serially, develop a complexly eroticized version of the popular quadroon stereotype. *Pouponne et Balthazar* (1888) purports to give a true rendition of Evangeline, a continuing preoccupation in Louisiana ever since Longfellow had created her fictional odyssey.

The struggle to maintain French language and culture in the face of an inevitable American victory elicited a final flurry of Francophone literature in Louisiana after the Civil War, including many writers of substance, such as Charles Testut, Charles Gayarré, Albert Delpit, and Alcée Fortier. But it was in English that the full flowering of Louisiana literature finally occurred. Not surprisingly, much of its cachet for the rest of the nation derived precisely from Louisiana's fascinating culture conflicts. Certainly, the first major American writer of Louisiana founded his career on an insightful use of those frictions. George Washington Cable was a native of New Orleans and a keen observer of Louisiana culture, but his critical perspectives on Creole life, which he made an emblem of the defeated South, did not endear him to this threatened and defensive society. His collection of short stories *Old Creole Days* (1879), together with his superb novel *The Grandissimes* (1880), established Creole culture as a major locus for exploring America's simmering struggle with race and racism. Like *Bonaventure* (1888), which offered an early and engaging portrait of Acadian life (which Kate Chopin also chronicled with great success), Cable's fiction established Louisiana as a valuable source of local color, a popular genre of the 1880s and 1890s.

Many of the important Louisiana writers of the era capitalized on the national, especially northern, fascination with regional difference. The Greek-born Lafcadio Hearn, for example, was drawn to New Orleans from Cincinnati in 1877 by Cable's stories. Like Cable, he was fascinated by Creole culture and language, in which he immersed himself. He wrote numerous newspaper sketches, collected as *Stray Leaves from Strange Literature* (1884), as well as a hauntingly beautiful meditation on a hurricane that devastated the Louisiana coast, *Chita: A Memory of Last Island* (1889). In 1887 Hearn left New Orleans for Japan and later became well known for his stories of Japanese life.

Cable's influence on Grace King was also strong, though in a very different way. Her writing career was launched in response to a challenge by a visiting northern editor, Richard Gilder, to "correct" Cable's version of Creole culture, which, as one of its adherents, she too viewed as one-sided. A subtle prose stylist, King's best work is evident in her fine collections of short fiction, such as *Balcony Stories* (1893) or *The Pleasant Ways of St. Medard* (1916). She also exhibits an impressive range, writing extensively and passionately about Louisiana's colorful history, as in *New Orleans: The Place and the People* (1895), and rather more coolly about her own life in *Memories of a Southern Woman of Letters* (1932).

Like Hearn, Kate Chopin was not a Louisiana native, but she married one and lived in the state for more than a decade. Her first novel, *At Fault* (1890), portrays the social and psychological shifts that accompanied the economic transformations of rural Louisiana after the Civil War. Her stunning short fiction, gathered in two published volumes, *Bayou Folk* (1894) and *A Night in Acadie* (1897)—as well as in the uncollected stories included in the *Complete Works,* 1969—provide unmatched portraits of Louisiana life and character, especially among the rural 'Cadians (or Cajuns). These remained the substance of her reputation until the critical recovery in the 1970s of her extraordinary second novel, *The Awakening* (1899), established her as a major realist and a provocative explicator of women's experience, surpassing even Cable in literary reputation.

More famous in her own time, especially for her humor, was Ruth McEnery Stuart, who like Chopin found a rich fictional vein in Louisiana's diverse cultures. Stuart's many short stories and novellas capture a range of ethnic types and dialects, particularly among African Americans, and perhaps least patronizingly in her novella, *Napoleon Jackson* (1902). Stuart was one of the few prominent southern women to support suffrage publicly, and some of her most interesting writing features rural women, as in *In Simpkinsville* (1897) and *The Woman's Exchange of Simpkinsville* (1899), which draws on her experiences in southern Arkansas.

Alice Dunbar-Nelson is another important writer who exploited the national taste for local color. Herself a New Orleanian and a Creole of color, Dunbar-Nelson wrote both poetry and short stories, collected in *Violets and Other Tales* (1895) and in *The Goodness of St. Rocque and Other Stories* (1899). Though her early work treads lightly upon the color line that might have kept it out of print in the emerging days of Jim Crow, she later became an outspoken proponent of the rights of African Americans and of women. Her journalism and extensive diaries provide a remarkable record of an activist's life in the early twentieth century.

The presence of so many excellent writers in Louisiana in this period rightly implies a great deal of literary activity. Among the many productive writers of the era were poet and short-story writer Molly E. Moore Davis; poet and publisher Eliza Jane Poitevent Nicholson; poets Mary Ashley Townsend ("Xariffa") and Martha Field ("Catherine Cole"); novelists Jeannette Walworth and Elizabeth Bisland Wetmore; and journalist Elizabeth Gilmer, who as "Dorothy Dix" wrote the first and longest-running newspaper advice column in America.

By the end of the century, the nation's interest in its distinctive "local" cultures had given way to more international ambitions and the sharper definitions that literary realism offered. Louisiana and its literature had pretty much resigned itself to Americanization, and while the state's idiosyncratic, exotic image remained intact, it became less useful to writers. By the end of World War I, the exploitation of the state's vast mineral resources began to alter the state's primarily agricultural economy. The populist rise of Huey Long, with his innovative plans for the poor and his reliance on longstanding patterns of political corruption, further jolted the state toward modernity. New Orleans's French Quarter, with its inexpensive housing and seductive ambience, soon became an agreeable, if mostly temporary, refuge for artists and writers, including the likes of Sherwood Anderson, William Faulkner, Gertrude Stein, Thomas Wolfe, and many others. As at Vanderbilt, the focus for literary activity was a progressive new magazine—in this case, *The Double Dealer*. Among its contributors were Roark Bradford and Lyle Saxon, who also figured prominently in contemporary interpretations of black culture. Bradford, a newspaperman originally from Tennessee, based much of his fiction on black folklore, including *Old Man Adam an' His Chillun'* (1928), on which Marc Connelly based his Pulitzer Prize–winning play *Green Pastures* (1930). Partly responding to the energy of the Harlem Renaissance, the era produced many such popular versions of black life by white southerners, including Edward Laroque Tinker's *Toucoutou* (1928), a fictionalization of a nineteenth-century incident of "passing" for white by a Creole of color.

A native of Baton Rouge, Lyle Saxon played a major role in the literary community of the 1920s and 1930s. His only novel, *Children of Strangers* (1937), examines the tensions of mixed races in rural Louisiana and was based on the history of Isle Breville, a unique community of free people of color along the Cane River. Nearby was Melrose Plantation, where Saxon often stayed and whose owner, Cammie Henry, had created a lively artists' colony in the 1920s and 1930s. Among the many writers who frequented Melrose were Ada Jack Carver, author of a number of prize-winning short stories and plays about Cajun life in the 1920s; nature writer and activist Caroline Dormon; popular historian Harnett Kane; and Gwen Bristow, who also lived for some time in New Orleans and published many well-regarded novels with Louisiana settings, including her

plantation trilogy: *Deep Summer* (1937), *The Handsome Road* (1938), and *This Side of Glory* (1940).

The continuing attraction of Louisiana folklore and history between the wars is also evident in the considerable nonfiction of the era, including Saxon's *Father Mississippi* (1927) and *Fabulous New Orleans* (1928). As state director of the Federal Writers' Project, Saxon edited both the state and New Orleans WPA Guides, along with *Gumbo Ya-Ya: A Collection of Louisiana Folk Tales* (1945), which he wrote with Robert Tallant, author of *Voodoo in New Orleans* (1946). An often-unacknowledged collaborator in these landmark volumes was Marcus Christian, the supervisor of the all-Negro Writers' Project in Louisiana. Frequently critical of the shortcomings in these white southerners' research, Christian was himself a serious folklorist and a prolific poet, though most of his nearly 1,200 poems remain unpublished.

Louisiana's colorful past also remained serviceable to writers of historical romance, most notably Frances Parkinson Keyes, who restored and lived for many years in the Beauregard House in the French Quarter. With careful attention to historic and physical detail, Keyes wrote more than fifty religious biographies, travel narratives, and novels, most famously, *Dinner at Antoine's* (1948). While the state's exoticism seemed unsuited to the seriousness of most modernist fiction, two dramatists did effectively exploit the state's mythic potential. Tennessee Williams, who after a 1938 visit became a semipermanent resident of New Orleans, composed his most famous play there. In *A Streetcar Named Desire* (1947), *Suddenly Last Summer* (1958), *Vieux Carré* (1979), and other plays, Williams forged lasting images of the city as a refuge of illusion and desire in an otherwise blankly puritanical landscape. As a native, Lillian Hellman's view of New Orleans was somewhat less romantic, but much of her most successful work draws effectively on southern settings, particularly her best-known play, *The Little Foxes* (1939), and her remarkable three-volume memoir, *An Unfinished Woman* (1969), *Pentimento* (1973), and *Scoundrel Time* (1976).

After World War II, with the state's petrochemical boom in full sway, Louisiana fiction began to reflect the more general southern consciousness of modern alienation and the tumultuous civil-rights struggles ahead. Robert Penn Warren, who taught at Louisiana State University and helped to found the *Southern Review* (another timely journal that fostered literary excellence in the state), based his gripping political novel, *All the*

King's Men (1947), on the disturbing career of Huey Long. Many of his poems and other fiction, especially his 1955 novel *Band of Angels,* reveal the state's powerful effects on his imagination. Shirley Ann Grau's work likewise concerns the struggles of white people to come to terms with racism and political power. In addition to her Pulitzer Prize-winning novel *Keepers of the House* (1965), Grau's fiction includes *The Black Prince and Other Stories* (1955), *The House on Coliseum Street* (1961), and *Nine Women* (1985).

Perhaps the most profound fictional meditations on modern alienation have come from Walker Percy. Born in Alabama to a prominent Mississippi family, Percy lived much of his life in Covington, across Lake Pontchartrain from New Orleans. His first novel, *The Moviegoer* (1965), is a quintessential evocation both of contemporary ennui and of suburban New Orleans. Percy's other novels are equally dark and funny, including *The Last Gentleman* (1967), *Love in the Ruins* (1971), and *Lancelot* (1977). Percy was also responsible for the posthumous publication of John Kennedy Toole's riotously sardonic novel about New Orleans, *A Confederacy of Dunces,* which won the Pulitzer Prize in 1980.

Another important Louisiana writer who came to prominence in the 1970s is Ernest Gaines. Rather than New Orleans, Gaines's fictional center is Pointe Coupee, a rural, largely Cajun parish not far from Baton Rouge. Gaines has created a rich tapestry of black life and the struggle for dignity in his many short stories and novels, including *The Autobiography of Miss Jane Pittman* (1971), *A Gathering of Old Men* (1983), and *A Lesson Before Dying* (1993).

The 1960s in Louisiana, as in the rest of the South, provoked profound and painful shifts in race relations. For black writers, these shifts seemed to demand a more engaged artistic practice. Tom Dent, son of the president of Dillard University in New Orleans, was a major force in organizing a series of workshops and journals in the 1960s and 1970s that helped to define this new black aesthetic. Beginning in December 1968 with the Free Southern Theater (succeeded by BLKARTSOUTH and the Congo Square Writers Workshop) and publications *Nkombo* (coedited by Kalamu ya Salaam), *Bamboula,* and the *Black River Journal,* Dent worked to provide both a focus and a vehicle for New Orleans's experimental black writers. His own publications include collections of poetry, *Magnolia Street* (1972) and *Blue Lights and River Songs* (1982), and several plays. Among the most iconoclastic

of these Louisiana writers is Ishmael Reed, who links his fictional aesthetic to the syncretism of voodoo, as in his novels *Mumbo Jumbo* (1972) and *The Last Days of Louisiana Red* (1974). Among the essays in *Shrovetide in Old New Orleans* (1989), Reed also offers some correctives to white accounts of black urban folklore.

The Free Southern Theater and its successors were critical to the more inclusive, redefined Louisiana literature that has emerged at the end of the century. Not only African Americans but Acadians and others sought to reincorporate the state's distinct languages and cultural idioms too often diminished by their own exoticism. Sybil Kein, for example, worked thoughtfully to preserve and recreate Creole (Afro-French) language and folklore. Her poetry, collected in *Gombo People* (1981) and *Delta Dancer* (1984), is pointedly bilingual. Even more successful in drawing on the unique rhythms and motifs of black Louisiana, especially its women, is Brenda Marie Osbey. In four impressive volumes (*Ceremony for Minneconjoux,* 1983; *In These Houses,* 1988; *Desperate Circumstance, Dangerous Woman,* 1991; and *All Saints,* 1997), Osbey intricately weaves an array of voices and experiences that mirror the complexity of Louisiana's multiethnic past and present. Pinkie Gordon Lane, a Philadelphian who taught for many years at Southern University in Baton Rouge, evokes a more lyric but no less distinctive sense of place in her poetry, as in *I Never Scream* (1985) and *Girl at the Window* (1991). Similarly, playwright Elizabeth Brown-Guillory incorporates the languages and customs of her own Cajun/Creole past in such social comedies as *Bayou Relics* (1983) and *Snapshots of Broken Dolls* (1986).

The complex inclusivity of contemporary Louisiana literature is perhaps best reflected in the work of Robert Olen Butler. A native of Illinois who migrated to the oil-and-gas town of Lake Charles, Butler's Pulitzer Prize-winning fiction most memorably details the lives of modern Vietnamese immigrants, who found South Louisiana's climate and agricultural economy comfortably familiar. Butler's stories in *A Good Scent from a Strange Mountain* (1994) and *Tabloid Dreams* (1996) sharply expose the unsettling strangeness produced by merging cultures. That strangeness, however, is what has always been attractive about Louisiana to writers—whether elicited by a fresh look at the past or the fresh looks of new settlers.

A host of highly talented fiction writers have exploited such opportunities for revisiting the state's imaginative resources. James Lee Burke, for example, makes provocative use of Louisiana culture with a popular Cajun detective in novels such as *The Neon Rain* (1987) and *Heaven's Prisoners* (1988). Anne Rice's tales of eroticized violence have also proved immensely popular, especially her many vampire novels, beginning with *Interview with the Vampire* (1976), although she also explores nineteenth-century Creole society in *Feast of All Saints* (1979). Contemporary New Orleans society also attracts many novelists, most notably Ellen Gilchrist, who is best known for her wry exposure of the emptiness of the upper-class characters in her stories and novels, such as *In the Land of Dreamy Dreams* (1981) or *The Annunciation* (1983). Sheila Bosworth, Andrei Codrescu, Joyce and John William Corrington, Moira Crone, Andre Dubus, Richard Ford, Tim Gautreaux, Nancy Lemann, David Madden, Valerie Martin, Fatima Shaik, and Chris Wiltz are among the many writers whose fiction continues to refine our view of this eclectic place. Although few authors write exclusively about the city, the near-anomaly of John Dufresne's witty 1994 novel, *Louisiana Power and Light*, set in the underexploited fictional territory of North Louisiana, does suggest just how fully New Orleans and the southern half of the state continue to dominate Louisiana's literary self-image.

Poetry has also attracted a number of extremely able contemporary artists, many of them nurtured by the small journals that were founded in the early 1970s: the *New Orleans Poetry Journal* (edited by Maxine Cassin), *Outsider* (which published many "beat" poets), the *New Laurel Review*, and the university journals—Loyola's *New Orleans Review* (founded by John William Corrington and Miller Williams), the *Xavier Review*, and the more recent *Louisiana Literature* of Southeastern Louisiana University in Hammond. In addition to Osbey and Lane, the best-known poets include Ralph Adamo, Alvin Aubert, Catharine Brosman, Maxine Cassin, Debbie Clifton, Alice Claudel, Peter Cooley, Quo Vadis Gex-Breaux, Lee Meitzen Grue, Cleopatra Mathis, Sue Owen, Mona Lisa Saloy, and finally, Yusef Komunyakaa, whose powerful reflections on his Vietnam War experiences as well as his Bogalusa youth appear in collections such as *Dien Cai Dau* (1988) and his Pulitzer Prize-winning volume, *Neon Vernacular* (1993). As at the end of the last century, the conclusion of the twentieth finds Louisiana's literature as rich and varied as ever.

Barbara C. Ewell

See also Baton Rouge, Louisiana; Cajun Literature; Creole Literature; Dialect Literature; *Double Dealer, The*; Federal Writers' Project; Free Southern Theater; Fugitives, The; Local Color; Long, Huey; New Orleans, Louisiana; *New Orleans Times Picayune*; Novel, 1820 to 1865; Popular Literature; *Southern Review*; Travel Literature.

Dorothy Brown and Barbara Ewell, eds., *Louisiana Women Writers: New Essays and a Comprehensive Bibliography* (1992); Alexander De Menil, *The Literature of the Louisiana Territory* (1904); Mary Dell Fletcher, ed., *The Short Story in Louisiana, 1880–1890* (1993); James P. Gilroy, ed., *Francophone Literature of the New World* (1982); John Maxwell Jones, *Slavery and Race in Nineteenth-Century Louisiana-French Literature* (1978); Thomas M'Caleb, *The Louisiana Book: Selections from the Literature of the State* (1894); Lizzie McVoy, ed., *Louisiana in the Short Story* (1940); Mignon Morse and Calvin Hubbard, eds., *Northwest Louisiana Authors* (1989); Charles Barthelemy Rousseve, *The Negro in Louisiana: Aspects of His History and His Literature* (1937); Edward Laroque Tinker, *Ecrits de langues françaises en Louisiane* (1932), revised and supplemented by Auguste Viatte, *Louisiana Review* 3 (1974).

LOUISIANA STATE UNIVERSITY

Chartered in 1853, LSU opened its doors in Pineville on January 2, 1860, as the Louisiana State Seminary of Learning and Military Academy. William Tecumseh Sherman, who later achieved fame as a Union general during the Civil War, was the school's first superintendent. In 1870, after relocating to Baton Rouge, the institution became Louisiana State University. Louisiana State Agricultural and Mechanical College was established by an act of the state legislature, approved on April 7, 1874, to carry out the United States Morrill Act of 1862, granting lands for this purpose. Temporarily opening in New Orleans in 1874, the A and M College merged with Louisiana State University in Baton Rouge in 1877. LSU became coeducational in 1906.

Beginning in the 1930s, LSU acquired, founded, and, in some cases, lost branch campuses. The LSU System was formed in 1965. LSU currently has the status of both a land-grant and a sea-grant university.

Prior to World War II, LSU had a strong tradition in languages and literature, although it was more widely known as the "Old War Skule" because of the military training that was a required part of the curriculum for male students, and for its agricultural research and football teams. Instruction in classical and modern languages and literatures was at the core of its nineteenth-century curricula, although its offerings later broadened because of changing national educational trends during the early twentieth century. In 1935, LSU established the LSU Press, the *Southern Review,* and the *Journal of Southern History* as part of President James Monroe Smith's effort to move LSU away from its "aggie" image and place it in the forefront of southern universities. Unfortunately, a wave of political and financial scandals in 1939 involving state and university administrators, among others, discredited Smith's vision for LSU. Wartime shortages then provided an excuse for the abolition of the *Southern Review* in 1942. Robert Penn Warren and other notable literary figures left at about the same time. The *Southern Review* was reestablished in 1965.

Following World War II, LSU became a modern research university. The study of languages, literatures, and creative writing are among its diverse offerings but no longer hold the pride of place that they did in the 1930s, when LSU was known as "Parnassus on the Mississippi." The LSU Press has been an important publisher of poetry since the 1960s and published, among other works of southern fiction, John Kennedy Toole's novel *A Confederacy of Dunces,* which won the Pulitzer Prize in 1981. Through its Voices of the South series, the Press has made available in inexpensive editions significant works of southern fiction that have gone out of print. The Press has been a leader in furthering southern historical and literary studies, and its Southern Literary Studies series regularly adds to the critical literature about southern writing.

Paul E. Hoffman

See also *Southern Review;* University Presses.

Biennial Report of the Louisiana State University and Agricultural and Mechanical College to the Legislature of Louisiana (1861– ; title varies somewhat); Walter L. Fleming, *Louisiana State University, 1860–1896* (1936); Marcus M. Wilkerson, *Thomas Duckett Boyd: The Story of a Southern Educator* (1935).

LYNCHING

As much a political construct as a social one, lynching refers to the extralegal act of punishing a presumed criminal by hanging him or her by the neck until dead; a combination of hanging and burning; a combination of hanging and shooting—or shooting by itself; tarring

and feathering combined with burning; or any other combination of these violent actions to bring about death. African American literature took as one of its primary subjects the depictions of lynchings of African American people, and lynchings portrayed in the literature were frequently as ritualized as those that occurred historically. William Wells Brown, who published the first novel written by an African American, portrayed a lynching in *Clotel* (1853); the "impudent" African American man is executed for striking his master. Although Brown passes rather quickly over the incident, his successors would linger over such atrocities. Sutton E. Griggs, writing at the turn of the twentieth century, depicts a lynching in *The Hindered Hand* (1905) in which an African American man and his wife are lynched—but not before the lynchers drill huge pieces of quivering flesh from their bodies in a torturing ritual that goes on for more than three hours. Griggs's contemporary Paul Laurence Dunbar, who is often thought to be anything but a protest writer, nonetheless focuses on lynching in "The Lynching of Jube Benson" (1900), in which a white narrator, Dr. Melville, relates his involvement in the lynching of the African American man accused of raping and murdering the narrator's fiancée. The man is proven innocent only after he is lynched. In commenting on his inability to resist mob violence against his former African American friend, Dr. Melville explains: "It's tradition." Charles W. Chesnutt discusses the topic without the ritual overtones in *The Marrow of Tradition* (1901). Chesnutt makes clear the social purpose of lynching rituals when one of his characters asserts: " 'Burn the nigger,' reiterated McBane. 'We seem to have the right nigger, but whether we have or not, burn *a* nigger. It is an assault upon the white race, in the person of old Mrs. Ochiltree, committed by the black race, in the person of some nigger. It would justify the white people in burning *any* nigger. The example would be all the more powerful if we got the wrong one. It would serve notice on the niggers that we shall hold the whole race responsible for the misdeeds of each individual.' "

The Harlem Renaissance also brought its share of writers interested in lynching; some published their works in the 1920s, the decade identified with that movement, and others would publish their works later. Jean Toomer, in his experimental work *Cane* (1923), includes a burning as a direct result of a conflict between an African American man and a white man over an African American woman. Mild-mannered Langston Hughes, lover of the blues, depicts an African

American man who is lynched in "Home," a selection from *The Ways of White Folks* (1933). The African American man is too well dressed for the local whites, and he dares to talk to his former music teacher, a white woman, on the streets; whites heighten this encounter into the mythical rape. James Weldon Johnson uses a lynching/burning in *The Autobiography of An Ex-Coloured Man* (1912; 1927) as the incentive for his protagonist to pass from being a light-skinned African American man to being a white man; the irony is that, in choosing not to be identified with people who can be lynched, the narrator elects to identify with the lynchers. Claude McKay, in "The Lynching" (1922), focuses on the initiatory quality of lynching, whereas Johnson in "Brothers—America Drama" (1935) depicts lynching from the point of view of the leader of the mob.

European American writers, especially in the third and fourth decades of the twentieth century, also selected lynching for literary representation. Erskine Caldwell explores the subject in "Saturday Afternoon" (1935), set in Georgia, in which a group of town loafers participate in the lynching of a harmless "good" Negro purely out of boredom. Caldwell explored the topic again in "Kneel to the Rising Sun" (also 1935), in which an African American man is lynched for standing up to a sharecropping landowner. William Faulkner treats the ritualistic components of the practice in "Dry September" and the development of mob psychology in *Light in August* (1932). Nedra Tyre interviewed whites about their participation in lynchings and reported her findings in *Red Wine First* (1947); her descriptions of the tortures that one mob employed in executing an African American man accused of rape are not appreciably unlike those that African American writers depict. As a southern white woman acutely concerned with the racial situation, Lillian Smith also took as one of her topics in *Killers of the Dream* (1949) the summary killing of African American men. Her novel *Strange Fruit* (1944) uses as its title a blues song associated with lynching. More recently, it might be argued that Eudora Welty's treatment of the death of Medgar Evers in "Where Is the Voice Coming From?" continues the focus on lynching or summary execution. Lewis Nordan's *Wolf Whistle* (1993) is one of several works dealing with the murder of a black boy, Emmett Till, in 1955.

The fact that lynching has captured the imaginations of every generation of African American writers attests to its psychological and creative impacts. There is almost an unstated agenda that any African American person writing in America, especially any African American male, would eventually get around to actually depicting a lynching or dealing with the implications of it. In practically every instance, the African American male is accused of sexual impropriety with a white woman. Perhaps Richard Wright, more than any other writer, captured the intensity of these tabooed encounters. From "Between the World and Me," the poem he published in 1935, through "Big Boy Leaves Home" (1938), and ending with *The Long Dream* (1958), the last novel he published before his death, Wright was concerned about the negative consequences of interactions between African American men and white women. No explanation can satisfy the white soldier who sees four nude African American boys in the presence of his fiancée in "Big Boy Leaves Home." They could not possibly have been swimming; they could only have had raping sexual intentions, so he shoots two of them dead before the other two overpower him. A ritualized lynching occurs with one of the remaining boys, and only Big Boy escapes. For Wright, as for James Baldwin, the psychological dimensions of racial interactions in America are bound up with sexuality; the two cannot be separated.

Baldwin's powerful depiction of this thesis occurs in "Going to Meet the Man" (1965) and is implied in almost all of his work. In the story named, a white sheriff uses the memory of a lynching to overcome his impotence with his wife. As he relives his initiation at the lynching, he is inspired by the implied transfer of sexual potency from the African American victim to himself as the African American man is castrated. Baldwin's story is perhaps the last in the literature in which excruciatingly graphic details of torture and castration are inclusive features of the lynching/burning rituals, but other writers nonetheless continue to focus on the implications of the consequences of African American male/white female interactions. Where no ritual occurs, or where no physical lynching takes place, there is still an overwhelming sense of the possibility of such an occurrence.

Male writers in far greater numbers than African American women writers have been drawn to depicting lynchings in their works. Historical statistics would certainly suggest that African American men have been more vulnerable than African American women. Whether it was Ida Wells-Barnett's male friend being too successful as a grocer in Memphis, or Richard Wright's uncle being lynched for owning a prosperous saloon in Elaine, Arkansas, the possibility of African

American men losing their lives through lynching was ever constant. The threat of death, combined with the more psychologically wearing fear of castration, perhaps led African American male writers to identify with their historical counterparts much more intensely.

Although African American male writers are the primary depictors of graphic lynching scenes, African American women writers nonetheless treat the subject. In the first three decades of the twentieth century, several African American women playwrights claimed the lynching theme as their special focus, sometimes in plays as short as five or six pages. These include Angelina Grimke's *Rachel* (1916—full-length play), Georgia Douglas Johnson's "A Sunday Morning in the South" (1925) and "Blue-Eyed Black Boy" (1935?), and Mary P. Burrill's "Aftermath" (1928). It is striking in these works that all the lynchings take place before the current action or offstage; that way, these women writers can treat lynching minus the graphic depictions so characteristic of African American male writers. More contemporarily, in *Jubilee* (1966) Margaret Walker portrays the lynching of two African American slave women accused of having poisoned their masters; the occasion is used as an object lesson for other enslaved persons. Alice Walker uses the discovery of a lynching rope in "The Flowers" (1973) as the moment when a young African American girl is initiated into the harsh realities of her segregated world. The threat of lynching pervades Sherley Anne Williams's *Dessa Rose* (1986), and Toni Morrison depicts the burning of Sixo, one of the African American men on the Sweet Home Plantation, in *Beloved* (1987). Where lynching is not portrayed, it is a frequent metaphor, as in the case of Gwendolyn Brooks's "The Chicago Defender Sends a Man to Little Rock," in which she declares in the last line, "The loveliest lynchee was our Lord."

With all of these writers, lynching has saturated their works as thoroughly as the process by which they have claimed their space to be writers in America. Every one of them has written contemporarily with the occurrence of a lynching or some other form of summary execution. Every one of them has been aware of this constant threat to African American existence. And every one has recognized that, though lynching could certainly end the lives of its victims, it could not kill the creative imagination determined to bring change to the American landscape.

Trudier Harris

See also Lynch Law; Racism.

Jerry H. Bryant, *Victims and Heroes: Racial Violence in the African American Novel* (1997); Charles W. Chesnutt, *The Marrow of Tradition* (1901); Trudier Harris, *Exorcising Blackness: Historical and Literary Lynching and Burning Rituals* (1984); Calvin C. Hernton, *Sex and Racism in America* (1965); Lillian Smith, *Killers of the Dream* (1949).

LYNCH LAW

In August 1997, three white men in Elk Creek, Virginia, poured gasoline on an African American man and burned him to death. In June 1998, three white men in Jasper, Texas, dragged a retarded African American man behind their pick-up truck until he died. These summary executions, or lynchings, which are modern derivations of lynch law, were the most recent in almost two hundred years of such violence against persons of African descent upon American soil. *Lynch law* refers specifically to ordinary citizens assuming the right to execute persons judged to be guilty of a crime; in these modern instances, the "crime" was simply being African American. "Lynching" is the process of carrying out the judgment. Some scholars report that the phrase *lynch law* is said to have derived from the practices of Virginian Charles Lynch, who, during the Revolutionary War, summarily hanged Tories caught in the area.

For observers who believed the practice had ended in the United States, the 1997 and 1998 incidents brought back thoughts of the 1890s, the peak years for lynching in this country. In 1892, 1893, and 1894, an average of two hundred African American people were lynched each year. Indeed, it could be argued that lynching almost became a nationally sanctioned pastime, for even in the years in which most deaths occurred, it was impossible to get national legislation passed to condemn or terminate the practice. The Dyer Anti-Lynching Bill, which had several sponsors and was presented in Congress on repeated occasions, was never made into law. How could lynching be outlawed, so the logic ran, when African American men were still prone to rape white women? Accusations of rape, which were the most emotional cause of mob-inspired lynchings (though other presumed crimes were more numerous), were frequently the incentive that creative artists used to shape their depictions of lynchings. As creators who drew their subject matter from the substance of the lives of the people about whom they wrote, African American writers throughout their history in America have depicted occurrences in which African American characters have been lynched, burned, shot, and otherwise executed in whatever version of summary execution was operative at the time. They joined with political activists from the mid-nineteenth century through the mid-twentieth century in waging a battle of public opinion against such barbarian acts directed toward African Americans.

Lynch and *lynching* have undergone a series of meanings in American history. Both refer to summary justice or execution—that is, regular citizens taking the law into their own hands, which in the early development of the country occurred in the frontier states, but definitions of summary justice varied. It could refer to whipping, or tarring and feathering, or to being ridden out of town on a rail. "Lynch's law" meant that punishment for a crime had been meted out without a court hearing, or by a self-constituted court. To be "severely lynched" could mean that an individual had received one hundred lashes, or that the person had been whipped, then tarred and feathered. A man could be lynched, then hanged, or lynched, then run out of town.

James E. Cutler, one of the prominent scholars of lynching history, points out that "previous to 1840 the verb lynch was occasionally used to include capital punishment, but the common and general use was to indicate a personal castigation of some sort. 'To lynch' had not then undergone a change in meaning and acquired the sense of 'to put to death.' . . . It was not until a time subsequent to the Civil War that the verb lynch came to carry the idea of putting to death." In the decades following the Civil War, lynching came to include a range of activities that always resulted in death. These included tarring and feathering, burning, shooting, and other tortures in addition to and in combination with "hanging by the neck until dead." Equally noticeable, these atrocious additions were more often than not applied when the victims were African American.

Early advocates of legislation to end lynching combined the literary and the political. Ida Wells-Barnett, who wrote newspaper columns as early as the 1880s admonishing African American people to leave Memphis, Tennessee—where a grocer friend of hers had been lynched for owning a store that was too profitable for his white competition—also wrote pamphlets itemizing the atrocities. In *Southern Horrors: Lynch Law in All Its Phases* (1892), *A Red Record: Tabulated Statistics and Alleged Causes of Lynchings in the United States, 1892–1893–1894* (1895), and *Mob Rule in Old New Orleans* (1900), she offered disclaimers that lynching occurred as a result of African American men raping white women. Instead, she asserted that clandestine, voluntary transracial liaisons between African American men and white women ended in lynching when the affairs were discovered and the white women cried rape. She further asserted, as with the Memphis case, that lynchings also occurred for economic reasons. This violent brutality was therefore not only a means of psychological control but a political device of social control as well.

Lynching was not always targeted to African Americans. Initially, it was the preferred form of punishment on the American frontier. After the Civil War, it became a means of keeping newly freed African Americans, especially African American males, in line. Researchers of lynching history, including Cutler and Robert L. Zangrando, maintain that nearly four thousand African American people were lynched between 1880 and 1927. Women made up a small percentage of that number (Cutler asserts that seventy-six women were lynched). These numbers reflect recorded statistics, which means that it will never be possible to determine the exact number of African American persons lynched in America. Many of these executions were ritualized, in that they evolved to contain features that were repeated again and again. A white mob gathered to punish an offender by lynching or burning. Total community sanction—if not direct involvement—characterized the gathering. Frequently, white people brought food and drink to the place of execution, and announcements of the execution often preceded the event. For the famous Henry Smith lynching in Paris, Texas, in 1895, for example, flyers were printed and announcements were made in local newspapers; excursion trains were run to the site of the lynching to accommodate the crowds (Smith was accused of rape and murder). The ritual often included a castration or a gathering of souvenirs (ears, toes, fingers) from the body of the African American victim. These occasions were used as rites of initiation for young white children. White women, even pregnant ones, were also at times in attendance at such gatherings.

W. E. B. Du Bois made the recording of lynching statistics a regular part of the agenda of *Crisis* magazine. Years later, Zangrando would publish *The NAACP Crusade Against Lynching, 1909–1950* (1980). Walter White, who became executive director of the NAACP, was a soldier in the war against lynching before his administrative duty. Blond hair, pale skin, and blue eyes allowed this "white" African American man into the company of many lynchers in small southern towns and enabled him to publish "I Investigate Lynching," an "insider's" view of the practice. Lynching was constantly before the African American public, and in the early 1930s a group of white women joined the antilynching efforts. Jessie Daniel Ames and other white women organized to protest the assertion by white southern males that lynchings took place to save the honor of white women. Ames and her colleagues pledged to descend upon any town where an African American man was accused of white rape and put their bodies in the way of summary justice; they also wrote to sheriffs and governors, met with African American organizations, and gathered evidence about the real reasons for lynching. Their efforts, though commendable, did not eradicate the practice from southern soil or from the southern literary imagination. African American and European American writers would return to the topic again and again as they sought to depict the tensions and violence inherent in race relations.

Trudier Harris

See also Lynching.

Bettina Aptheker, ed., *Lynching and Rape: An Exchange of Views by Jane Addams and Ida B. Wells* (1977); Jerry H. Bryant, *Victims and Heroes: Racial Violence in the African American Novel* (1997); James E. Cutler, *Lynch-Law: An Investigation into the History of Lynching in the United States* (1905); John Hope Franklin, *From Slavery to Freedom: A History of Negro Americans* (1967); Jacquelyn Dowd Hall, *Revolt Against Chivalry: Jessie Daniel Ames and the Women's Campaign Against Lynching* (1979); Trudier Harris, *Exorcising Blackness: Historical and Literary Lynching and Burning Rituals* (1984); Winthrop D. Jordan, *White Over Black: American Attitudes Toward the Negro, 1550–1812* (1969); James R. McGovern, *Anatomy of a Lynching: The Killing of Claude Neal* (1982); NAACP, *Thirty Years of Lynching in the United States, 1889–1918* (1969); Arthur R. Raper, *The Tragedy of Lynching* (1933); Walter White, *Rope and Faggot: A Biography of Judge Lynch* (1929); Robert L. Zangrando, *The NAACP Crusade Against Lynching, 1909–1950* (1980).

M

MACON, GEORGIA

Macon, a small city in the middle of the state of Georgia, about eighty miles south of Atlanta, is important to literature chiefly as the birthplace of the nineteenth-century poet Sidney Lanier (born 1842) and the twentieth-century African American novelist John Oliver Killens (born 1916). Its deeper history, however, includes the Mississippians' "Old Fields," on which Native American settlers built mounds about a thousand years ago. These fields are mentioned twice in the 1775 *The Travels of William Bartram*; about fifty years after Bartram's book was published, the Old Fields became part of the new city, Macon.

Tennessee Williams spent the summer of 1942 in Macon and found in his friend Jordan Massee's father the model for "Big Daddy" in *Cat on a Hot Tin Roof*. Perhaps Macon's most substantial appearance in southern literature is as "Crossroads, Georgia," in Killens's 1954 novel *Youngblood*. The novel changes the name of the city but keeps its street names. Macon appears under its own name in Ferrol Sams's *The Whisper of the River* (1984) and in David Bottoms's *Easter Weekend* (1990). Much of Pam Durban's story "All Set About with Fever Trees" is set in Macon, where she lived as a child. Tina McElroy Ansa's three novels are set in Macon, where she was born, but she names it "Mulberry," after one of the city's principal downtown streets.

Southern literature is often the topic of the Lamar Lectures, held at Macon's Mercer University and Wesleyan College. The Mercer Lectures, which are published annually by the University of Georgia Press, have included such important works as Louis Rubin's *The Writer in the South* (1971), Lewis Simpson's *The Dispossessed Garden: Pastoral and History in Southern Literature* (1972), Lucinda H. MacKethan's *Daughters of Time: Creating Woman's Voice in South-ern Story* (1988), and Fred Hobson's *The Southern Writer in the Postmodern World* (1989).

The contemporary poet and novelist David Bottoms is an alumnus of Mercer; the poet Kathryn Stripling Byer and the playwright Sandra Deer are alumnae of Wesleyan.

Michael M. Cass

See also Georgia, Literature of; Williams, Tennessee.

MAGIC REALISM

Franz Roh first used the term *magic realism* in 1925 to describe the startling re-engagement with raw realism when an artist first returned to it after a relatively stale adventure with abstract expressionism. That original definition describes magic realism and its signal power, especially in the South with its historical distrust of abstractions, more accurately than the popular notion of the term as a fantastic escape from realism. Artists achieve this re-entry into the genuine wonder of the real by bending "reality" beyond its possible, or at least probable, limits. Magic realism is a concept, if not a term, older than Samuel Taylor Coleridge or Apuleius.

The conventional sense of the term takes readers *deep* South to that other continent—to Brazil, Colombia, or Argentina perhaps, places where fictional gardens fork into surreal paths, where characters do clearly impossible things. Where Jorge Luis Borges's Funes the Memorious is prisoner of his "chronometrical" powers; Gabriel García Márquez's old man with enormous wings plummets from the sky; Laura Esquivel's passionate lover burns down a barn with the fire of her passion; Isabel Allende's and Carlos Fuentes's figures exercise extradimensional, spiritual energies.

But the southern United States comes naturally upon magic realism, for the root of its writing is vision sprung from ruin, one as ornery and mytho-magical as its exemplars who follow in the great tradition of Faulkner, Welty, and O'Connor. Larry Brown, Harry Crews, and Lewis Nordan strive more in O'Connor's shadow than in Faulkner's, for they share her concern for the operation of human grace, for the plight of the disenfranchised, and freely distort "reality" to demonstrate this concern.

In our own national literature, magic realism is as close as Louisiana, where Tom Moore's scalp itches in a kind of eternal radar (Walker Percy's *Love in the Ruins,* 1971). Or Florida, where a Harry Crews character eats an automobile (*Car,* 1972). Or South Carolina, where Josephine Humphreys's Lucille Odom has an "aura" and a kind of second sight (*Rich in Love,* 1988), and where a terrifying, centaurlike marauder roves the swamp country (William Baldwin's *The Hard-to-Catch Mercy,* 1993). Or Tennessee, where Margaret Skinner's heroine develops a kind of spiritual vision (*Molly Glanagan and the Holy Ghost,* 1995). Or North Carolina, where thunder speaks of Helen of Troy, a letter of death takes wings, and an uncle's beard grows to supernatural length (Fred Chappell's *I Am One of You Forever,* 1985) and an exotic angel crash-lands in an old woman's ordinary back yard (Allan Gurganus's "It Had Wings"). Or where a psychopathic killer and a grandmother meet head-on in epic, parabolic violence as large as life, death, faith, and doubt (Flannery O'Connor's "A Good Man Is Hard to Find," 1955).

For whatever reason, the Mississippi Delta—where Faulkner's durable vision was born of mud, hope, blood, and memory—remains our country's Fertile Crescent of magic realism. Eudora Welty's "Rabbit" (*The Golden Apples,* 1949) and Robber Bridegroom (*The Robber Bridegroom,* 1942) still lurk in and around Jackson. Larry Brown's deformed human/inhuman monster ("A Roadside Resurrection," 1989) and ever-bleeding drive-by-shooting-target ("The End of Romance," 1996) haunt the countryside near Oxford, and Lewis Nordan's often cartoonlike figures rise from dust motes in Itta Bena. Across the bridge in Memphis, Graceland is as laden with magically real relics of life-into-legend as any religious shrine, for Elvis Presley was (or is that *is?*) its popular avatar.

Preeminent North American magic realists include the wacky high jinks of R. H. W. Dillard's *The Book of Changes* (1974), *First Man on the Sun* (1983), and

Omniphobia (1995); George Garrett's deadly playful mergers of real and metaphoric ("An Evening Performance," "Time of Bitter Children," 1985); the multiethnic mind travel and playful mythic lyricism of Randall Kenan (*Let the Dead Bury the Dead,* 1992) and Percival Everett (*Frenzy,* 1997); and the novels of Lewis Nordan that consistently violate phenomenal reality to achieve outrageously amusing impossibilities—*Music of the Swamp* (1991), *Wolf Whistle* (1993), *The Sharpshooter Blues* (1995), and *Lightning Song* (1997).

Magic realism is a language charged with metaphorical novelty, humor, and anagoge or multilayered meaning. It is the language of prophets, poets, and writers from Ezekiel to Blake to O'Connor to many contemporary writers who deploy it in order to shout to the deaf and dazzle the blind. Since it is the irresistible force for that immovable object called audience, magic realism violates ordinary apprehension, shocking readers into finer vision. No one was more aware than O'Connor of humankind's constitutional flight from reality and the complex, difficult mission of the writer to return the audience to the bitter and wonderful burdens of the real world.

Robert Gingher

See also Elvis; O'Connor, Flannery.

Lois Parkinson Zamora and Wendy B. Faris, eds., *Magical Realism: Theory, History, Community* (1995).

MAMMY

Faulkner had one named Caroline Barr; Thomas Nelson Page sang her praises in *The Old South*; Adrienne Rich wrote a sardonic poem about hers; Hattie McDaniel, the first African American to win an Oscar, was forever fixed in her image in the 1939 film of *Gone With the Wind.* To speak of Mammy is to call up one of the South's most revered and also controversial figures. Mammy is a literary but also a cultural phenomenon—the African American woman who nurses white children and who, if one believes the literature, sustained southern households from slavery times until the present. Literature and advertising have developed the Mammy as an older, rotund African American female, of shiny black face, who is maternal, asexual, loyal to the values of her white "family," a subservient protector and nurturer. More than a "domestic,"

Mammy is a member of the family. James Branch Cabell paid elegant tribute to his mammy, Louisa Nelson, dedicating *The Cream of the Jest* (1917) to her with Latin citation: "At me ab amore tuo diducet nulla senectus" (Nevertheless, no old age may separate me from your love). Faulkner eulogized his mammy, Caroline Barr, writing that "she was born and lived and served and died and now is mourned; if there is a heaven, she has gone there." He also dedicated his 1942 story collection, *Go Down, Moses*, to her, praising "a fidelity without stint or calculation" and "an immeasurable devotion and love." Dilsey in *The Sound and the Fury* (1929) as well as Molly in *Go Down, Moses* and Louvinia in *The Unvanquished* (1937) are Faulkner's recreations of this figure, a black woman defined by service, loyalty to her white family, and maternalism.

The Mammy is in many ways a postslavery creation in her literary forms. In this manifestation, she replaced the "uncle" figure at a time when black males were beginning to be recreated, in the white southern mind, as dangerous beasts, a threat to white womanhood. For white southern writers of the post-Reconstruction period, the Mammy became a better choice than black male slave characters as a spokesperson for positive values of the times "before the war." Mark Twain was one of the first to create a Mammy narrator for an 1870s local-color tale, "A True Story," in which red-turbanned Aunt Rachel tells of how all seven of her children were sold away from her during slavery. Still, she is a cheerful, merry soul, laughing as she tells the story of how she was reunited with her youngest son during the war. In *Pudd'nhead Wilson* (1894), Twain worked a bitterly ironic change on the figure of the Mammy when he created Roxy, demonstrating how far he had come in his thinking about the cruel hypocrisy of racism in late-nineteenth-century America. Emphatically *not* a fat, jolly old-time Negress, but instead an attractive young slave mother who could pass for white, Roxy is so subversive a Mammy that she switches her own son for the master's child once she notes that they are virtually mirror images of one another. Her motivation consistently is to protect and advance the cause of her own son, without any thought of the injustice that she perpetrates in turning her master's son into a slave. Twain uses Roxy as a kind of anti-Mammy to address the issue of race in the era of *Plessy v. Ferguson*, when racism had become the entrenched law of the land. In doing so, he transforms one of the southern literary scene's most reassuring racial icons into a threatening revolutionary figure. The

irony is particularly notable when Roxy is placed next to Joel Chandler Harris's 1890s literary Mammy, Aunt Minervy Ann, who is happy to betray her own "uppity" black husband in order to advance the cause of her white employer (and former master). Yet the cruelest irony of all is that Roxy too has absorbed the race prejudice of the white master.

Charles Chesnutt also addressed the Mammy syndrome in late-nineteenth-century fiction. On the one hand, he created, in his first collection of fiction, *The Conjure Woman* (1898), the figure of a black woman who lives on the margins, not in the big house with the white children. The conjure woman has dangerous, threatening powers and often works to help other slave women renew bonds with their own slave children and husbands. In his much more directly critical novel *The Marrow of Tradition* (1901), Chesnutt creates the traditional Mammy figure in Mammy Jane, a subservient black woman who thrives on her memories of status as the dependent of her white family, the Carterets.

In 1898 Eugenia Jones Bacon wrote her novel *Lyddy* as a story recreating her memories of her own mammy of the same name. Bacon's Lyddy is not the asexual figure that so many local-color southern writers fashioned in order to avoid any intimation of what was clearly a problem within the master's household—miscegenation. Bacon, writing a thinly veiled autobiography, is interested only in Lyddy's quaintness and loyalty, and in her nurse's love interests with another slave on the plantation. Bacon saw her novel as an answer to Stowe's *Uncle Tom's Cabin,* long after the fact. It is interesting that Stowe's Aunt Chloe and Aunt Dinah, fashioned for her antislavery novel in 1852, much more resemble what would become the staple of southern plantation fiction's defenses of slavery—they are rotund, cheerful stereotypes of black female domesticity.

Stowe's "Aunt" figures lead directly to America's most famous Mammy, Scarlett's tyrant nurse in *Gone With the Wind*. In this novel, Mammy rules the roost; she can handle Scarlett when no one else can, and she, more than anyone else, articulates the code of white pride and propriety that epitomizes nostalgic treatments of the Old South. Hattie McDaniel's film portrayal of Margaret Mitchell's creation has been recast for generations since that time on pancake boxes in the picture of Aunt Jemima. Writing of this reincarnation, James Baldwin in *Notes of a Native Son* (1955) observed searingly: "There was no one more forbearing than Aunt Jemima, no one stronger or more pious or more loyal or more wise; there was, at the same time, no one weaker or more faithless or more vicious and certainly no one more immoral." In the 1950s, Lorraine Hansberry, in her play *Raisin in the Sun* (1959), created Mama Lena to address the stereotype that had for so long soothed white consciences. Mama Lena may work for the white folks, but she is not the white folks' pawn, and her dream is to have her own home in the middle of their territory. Ishmael Reed, in his satire *Flight to Canada* (1976), revised the stereotypical Mammy even more radically in his outrageous character, Mammy Barracuda, as wicked a sycophant as could possibly be conjured up in any white bigot's nightmare of his comforting nursemaid gone haywire.

Ellen Douglas and Ellen Gilchrist, two contemporary white southern novelists, have also revisited the Mammy stereotype in order to call for changes in how white southerners evaluate the black woman's place in southern culture. Gilchrist created a dynamic duo in spoiled, unconventional Crystal Manning and her black domestic Traceleen in her ground-breaking collection of stories, *Victory Over Japan* (1984). Traceleen serves as narrator of Crystal's exploits and is in some ways the loyal black servant figure of old, yet she also serves as part of Gilchrist's agenda to satirize the figure of the southern lady and all her retinue. Traceleen's loyalty is not to the proper southern-lady stereotype but to a wild, restless, spoiled-rotten girl rebel. Traceleen reappears in the collection *Drunk with Love* (1986), where as narrator she demonstrates compassion, wisdom, and power. In Ellen Douglas's 1988 novel *Can't Quit You, Baby,* the central theme is the relationship between white employer and black housekeeper in the 1960s. Cornelia must come to terms with her dependence upon Julia, or Tweet, the maid who cleans her toilets and tells her the stories that help her to survive. The narrative voice struggles with the issue of names that pinpoints the tension between white and black women: "But—servant? Mistress? They would be uneasy with these words. . . . So, let's settle for housekeeper and employer." Tweet jolts Cornelia out of her numb complacency, not with sugary compliance but with tough and sometimes angry honesty.

The Mammy has served not just southern but all white American culture as a comforting racial crossover—the African American as devoted nurturer, more motherly than any white female literary figure, and attractive primarily because she can forgive anything, perpetually calling the little children to her ample, welcoming bosom. African American writers give us an African American matriarch counterimage to apply as a clearer, more honest figure of survival and determination. This very different Mama figure comes to us as early as the narrative of the slave mother Harriet Jacobs, writing of her grandmother in *Incidents in the Life of a Slave Girl* (1861), or the work of Frances Ellen Harper, writing her poem "The Slave Mother" in 1854. The African American mother is updated in Langston Hughes's Harlem Renaissance appreciation "Negro Mother," and captivates us in Gloria Naylor's powerful, transcendent Mama Day (*Mama Day*, 1988) and Julie Dash's Mama Peazant of the film *Daughters of the Dust* (1990). Whatever the word *Mammy* means in America, she is not a safe image to contemplate. Her motherliness can only be troubling in a society that often forced her to abandon her own children or to bear children by her master who became slaves themselves. As so much recent literature reveals, the mammy has now become a haunting rather than a nurturing presence in the southern household.

Lucinda H. MacKethan

See also African American Literature; Plantation Fiction.

Trudier Harris, *From Mammies to Militants: Domestics in Black American Literature* (1982); Diane Roberts, *The Myth of Aunt Jemima* (1994).

MANUSCRIPT COLLECTIONS

Most manuscript collections of southern literary authors can be found primarily in university library special collections that document the American South and/or American literature. In several cases, key faculty members, such as William Blackburn at Duke and Louis Rubin Jr. at UNC–CH, urged the libraries to pursue the papers of noted alumni and helped start programs for documenting the Southern Literary Renaissance. Researchers will find that many twentieth-century authors have been centrally collected with the bulk of their papers located at one or two repositories. Literary papers of nineteenth- and eighteenth-century southerners are much more difficult to locate and often are dispersed among a number of repositories, if they have survived at all.

Finding "complete" collections can sometimes be a challenge, with pockets of materials scattered among a number of sites. While an author may place his or her papers with a single repository, much of the author's output can still be dispersed—correspondence sent to colleagues and editors, drafts and final manuscripts in the files of the publishers, and "reading" drafts of works shared with friends. These items may often be given or sold to repositories other than the one that possesses the author's "complete" papers. Unless the author retained copies of letters written, the correspondence in the author's papers consists only of letters received. The best sources for locating literary papers are the *National Union Catalog of Manuscript Collections,* bibliographical databases such as OCLC and RLIN, as well as individual library catalogs and Web sites. Some notable collections of primarily twentieth-century southern literary manuscripts are profiled in the following paragraphs.

Duke University has a strong tradition for collecting literary papers that center on graduates of their creative-writing program. William Blackburn produced a notable crop of students, including William Styron, Reynolds Price, and Fred Chappell. They, as well as others, placed their manuscripts with Duke. Price succeeded Blackburn, and his students have also enjoyed success, with Anne Tyler and Josephine Humphreys placing their papers at Duke. Duke also collects the papers of distinguished critics and scholars in the field of literature as part of the library's Jay B. Hubbell Center for American Literary Historiography.

The Harry Ransom Humanities Research Center at the University of Texas at Austin has substantial American literary manuscript collections with a number of southern authors represented. In many cases, they do not have the complete papers of an author but rather selected correspondence or individual manuscripts for books and other works. Authors represented include James Agee, William Faulkner, and Tennessee Williams.

The Southern Historical Collection of the University of North Carolina at Chapel Hill can, like Duke, credit its literary collecting to the influence and urging of a distinguished faculty member. In the 1970s, Louis Rubin Jr. urged the collection to start documenting the Southern Literary Renascence and, in particular, to acquire the papers of two notable former UNC–CH students, Walker Percy and Shelby Foote. From this beginning, the Collection went on to acquire the papers of over thirty additional writers ranging from Rubin to Clyde Edgerton. The papers of Jill McCorkle, Paul Green, Guy Owen, and others associated with UNC–CH and North Carolina are also present. Other notable collections include publishing archives of Al-

gonquin Books and Shelby Stephenson's editorial files for *Pembroke Magazine.* Correspondence, edited manuscripts, and other materials from a wide range of southern authors can be found in these collections. The library also has a significant number of Thomas Wolfe manuscripts as part of its Wolfe Collection in the North Carolina Collection.

The Clifton Waller Barrett Library of American Literature at the University of Virginia includes significant southern literary manuscripts by Thomas Wolfe, Katherine Anne Porter, and Tennessee Williams. The library's Special Collections Department also houses the largest collection of William Faulkner papers. Virginia was Faulkner's choice of a repository for his manuscripts and personal papers in his possession at the time of his death.

Other notable collections of southern authors include those at Louisiana State University, the University of Maryland–College Park, the University of Mississippi, and the Mississippi State Archives. Louisiana State has collected literary papers as part of its Louisiana and Lower Mississippi Valley Collections. The University of Maryland holds the papers and library of Katherine Anne Porter. The University of Mississippi has papers and materials pertaining to William Faulkner, Willie Morris, Tennessee Williams, and Eudora Welty, as well as the Seymour Lawrence Publishing Archive. The Mississippi State Archives holds additional Eudora Welty materials.

Timothy D. Pyatt

See also Centers for Southern Studies.

MARDI GRAS

Mardi Gras (Fat Tuesday) is the last day of Carnival season before Ash Wednesday, the beginning of Lent, the Catholic season of penance. Carnival ("farewell to flesh") probably originated in ancient spring fertility rituals enacted to ensure abundant harvests. In some pagan cultures, these festivals involved animal or even human sacrifices and promiscuous sexuality. Masking, which ensured anonymity for celebrants and a concomitant freedom for their indulgences, early became part of the holidays in Rome. Long after faith in pagan rites had died, Mediterranean countries continued the festivals.

In the United States, Carnival is associated solely

with the Gulf Coast region, where French and Caribbean influences were strong. Elsewhere in the nation, because of the prevalence of English settlers, the observance was never established. The first American Mardi Gras was celebrated in 1699 by the French explorer Pierre LeMoyne Sieur d'Iberville and his forces near the mouth of the Mississippi River. Soon after the founding of New Orleans in 1718, Carnival was being observed there and continued to be until the colony was purchased by the United States in 1803. After the large influx of *les américains,* many of whom disapproved of this excess of energy and time devoted to pleasure, Carnival almost faded out, though never entirely.

Ironically, it was not Creoles but Americans, in Mobile as well as New Orleans, who created the modern secular version of Carnival. The traditional celebration for the masses evolved in the mid-1800s into an exclusive, extended party for private clubs, known in New Orleans as "krewes." After the first organized and costumed parade in 1838, Carnival remained a New Orleans tradition. Major social krewes originated, first Comus, later Rex, Proteus, and Momus, their membership for the most part restricted to the uptown Anglo-Saxon population. In 1872 the Grand Duke Alexis of the Romanoff family visited the city, and the Krewe of Rex was organized to present a parade and ball, held on Mardi Gras, to honor him. The tendency among krewes to emulate the monarchy of Europe, partly in jest, partly out of envy, culminated in this event.

New Orleans's modern Carnival season, attracting thousands of tourists, lasts for two weeks before Mardi Gras, with parades and balls of dozens of krewes, including old-line ones and also newer groups for those previously excluded: Italians, the Irish, blacks, Native Americans. Several gay krewes hold elaborate balls with tableaux patterned on the traditional ones of Comus and Rex.

Mardi Gras has always intrigued authors. In *Mosquitoes* (1927), William Faulkner portrays it as a nightmarish event; Hamilton Basso centers his novel *The Days Before Lent* (1939) on it; and several Tennessee Williams plays contain references to it. Eudora Welty's poignant novel *The Optimist's Daughter* (1972) opens with Laurel McKelva's journey to her father's hospital bedside during Mardi Gras time. Walker Percy's *The Moviegoer* (1961) concludes with the end of Carnival and the coming of Ash Wednesday. This fascination of authors as well as the general public stems to a large extent from Carnival's celebration of the flesh, a notion alien to the traditional Anglo-American sense of moral-

ity but with a seemingly endless magnetism for those who condemn it most vociferously.

W. Kenneth Holditch

See also New Orleans, Louisiana

Carol Flake, *New Orleans: Behind the Masks of America's Most Exotic City* (1994); Robert Tallant, *Mardi Gras* (1948); Henri Schindler, *Mardi Gras New Orleans* (1997).

MARYLAND, LITERATURE OF

Maryland, one of the thirteen original colonies, was first explored by Captain John Smith in 1608; in 1632 a patent to the area was given to George Calvert, the first Lord Baltimore; two years later, Maryland was permanently settled; and in 1788 it was admitted to the Union. One of the smallest states in terms of area, Maryland is geographically and politically unique and contains distinct subcultures, giving both richness and variety to its literature.

The state's political and cultural character was complicated in 1790, when Congress approved the creation of the District of Columbia as the capital of the United States. Originally created on land ceded by both Maryland and Virginia, the Virginia land was returned in 1846. Now occupying an area of sixty-seven square miles, the District of Columbia is also coextensive with the City of Washington, D.C., incorporated in 1802. The government of the District of Columbia has always been federal, not local, even though Greater Metropolitan Washington now includes cities and suburbs of both Maryland and Virginia. Consequently, the literary writings of resident presidents, legislators, and policy makers are published by the Government Printing Office, but such documents have not customarily been credited to the literary profile of the state of Maryland.

Maryland is located in the extreme northeast of the southern region of the United States. Its identification as part of the South can be traced to its northern border, surveyed by Charles Mason and Jeremiah Dixon from 1763 to 1767 to settle a dispute between Pennsylvania and Maryland. Referred to ever since as the Mason-Dixon Line, the border symbolically represented the dividing line between free and slave states and thus between North and South in the Civil War. During the Civil War, Maryland was a border state, a slaveholding state adjacent to a free state. Although

Maryland, as a slave state, had deep sympathy for the southern position, it did not itself choose to secede from the Union.

Saint Mary's City in southern Maryland, the oldest settlement in the state, was the capital of the colony from 1634 to 1694, after which Annapolis became the political and cultural center. An early and important literary society, the Tuesday Club, was founded in Annapolis in the eighteenth century, a model whose nineteenth-century counterpart was the Baltimore Delphian Club, itself followed by the Poetry Society of Maryland a century later. *The Maryland Gazette*, founded in Annapolis in 1727, was America's first southern newspaper. Colonial Maryland featured numerous writers—biographers, journalists, chroniclers, regional historians, wits, novelists, poets, and poetasters. While some still imitated British neoclassical models of form and style, Marylanders also participated in the program of the young Connecticut Wits, who strove to create an indigenous American literary tradition.

The Adventures of Alonso (1775) has historical significance as possibly the first novel written by an American, with the author identified as a "Native of Maryland." A quarter of a century later, Mason Locke Weems, clergyman and author, assured himself of a niche in Maryland as well as national literary history with his imaginative *The Life and Memorable Actions of George Washington,* the fifth edition of which (1806) gave the world the story of young George Washington and the cherry tree. Clearly the best work to be produced in colonial Maryland was *The Sot-Weed Factor: or, a Voyage to Maryland,* written by Ebenezer Cooke and published in London in 1708. Cooke's father was a tobacco merchant (sot-weed factor) with one thousand acres on the Eastern Shore; Ebenezer was, in addition to being a lawyer, businessman, politician, and journalist, the most popular and accomplished of early southern poets, as attested to by his title—Poet Laureate of Maryland. *The Sot-Weed Factor,* a ribald anti-epic composed in hudibrastic couplets, satirizes every feature of southern colonial life—resident English gentlemen excepted. In addition to its historical significance and intrinsic literary merit, *The Sot-Weed Factor* is an early and exceptional example of the satiric mode so generally characteristic of Maryland's literary tradition. In the last few years of his life, Cooke presented a more serious and more favorable view of southern life, most notably in *Sotweed Redivivus* (1730), in which he treated economic questions seriously and came out against slavery.

Although Maryland played no role in the Revolutionary War, Baltimore was the key city in the War of 1812. The deciding encounter took place in the Baltimore harbor in 1814. A night-long battle in which the British fought bitterly but unsuccessfully to capture Fort McHenry was observed by a Baltimore lawyer and poet, Francis Scott Key, who, as he watched, composed the poem "The Star-Spangled Banner," which later became the words of the national anthem. After the War of 1812, a vital literary tradition continued in Maryland, centered in Baltimore and marked by the accomplishments of individual authors, such as Key, rather than a local style or literary movement as such. The most popular writer of the time was Timothy Shay Arthur, who spent a quarter of a century in Baltimore. He was a contributor to and editor of various Baltimore journals—*Athenaeum, Saturday Visitor, Literary Monument,* and *Merchant*—at a time when Baltimore was the literary and publishing center of the country and periodicals were the chief literary outlets. Author of well over a hundred novels, he is best remembered and only remembered today for *Ten Nights in a Bar-Room* (1854), one of his many maudlin and didactic temperance novels, a collection of stories about the reform efforts of the Washingtonian Temperance Society of Baltimore. The novel sold close to a half-million copies and was turned into a temperance melodrama whose success has never been equaled.

Both William Wirt, born in Maryland and died in Washington, D.C., and John Pendleton Kennedy, who wrote from his downtown Baltimore townhouse, made seminal contributions to the eulogizing of southern aristocratic and chivalric plantation life, a genre that would become even more popular after the Civil War. In his excellent biography of the patriot Patrick Henry and several successful novels, Wirt sketched a romantic and valorous portrait of the Old South that has been taken as factual by countless readers. Kennedy, later in life an eminent politician-statesman, was for a time the most popular writer in the South; in *Swallow Barn* (1832), a sentimental depiction of rural life and common people set in Virginia, and *Rob of the Bowl* (1838), a historical romance set in colonial Maryland, he more or less created the subgenre known as the "Virginia Novel." Baltimore's most famous literary connection, Edgar Allan Poe, looked to both writers as mentors.

Poe was born in Boston in 1809, the son of itinerant

theatrical players; his father deserted him the next year, and his mother died one year later. Poe was adopted in 1811 by John Allan, a wealthy Richmond, Virginia, merchant. Poe's relationship with his foster parents was notoriously difficult, and following a particularly bitter quarrel about his future, he fled to his Poe relatives in Baltimore, a group that included his brother, a very minor poet, and Virginia Clemm, his cousin and future wife. During his brief stay, he paid for the printing of his first book, *Tamerlane and Other Poems*, published anonymously; a revised collection, *Al Aaraaf, Tamerlane, and Minor Poems*, was also published in Baltimore in 1829. After deliberately getting expelled from West Point, he yet again returned to Baltimore in 1831 and remained until 1835, at which time he relocated to Richmond to be assistant editor of a new journal, the *Southern Literary Messenger*. Poe's Baltimore years account for more than a quarter of his entire literary career, and they were extremely productive years. During 1831–1835, Poe authored at least a dozen of his major tales of the bizarre, including "Ms. Found in a Bottle" (1838). His third volume of poems was published in 1831 and included a number of signature pieces—"Sonnet—To Science," "To Helen," and "Alone"—and he received needed encouragement in 1833 when he was awarded first place in a literary contest sponsored by the *Baltimore Saturday Visitor*.

Even after his departure from the city, Poe continued to have his work published there, including his own favorite work, "Ligea," which appeared in the *Baltimore American Museum* in 1838. Poe's final connection with Baltimore was his enigmatic death in 1849: passing through Baltimore, he was found senseless on the pavement and died several days later in a nearby hospital. The unusual circumstances of his death contributed greatly to his public image as America's most flamboyant and romantic literary personality. Poe's grave, the Poe House, and the Poe Museum are Baltimore monuments that locally memorialize Poe's immense contributions to American belles-lettres as poet, critic, theorist, author of southern gothic tales, and creator of the detective story.

Arguably the most important work produced by a native Marylander, one that also captures the institution of slavery in gripping detail, is Frederick Douglass's *Narrative of the Life of Frederick Douglass, an American Slave, Written by Himself*. Born a slave in Tidewater Maryland in 1818, he was first a field slave and then a domestic slave in Baltimore. He escaped to Massachusetts in 1838 and published his powerful slave narrative in 1845; a revised and enlarged account of his years as a slave was published ten years later. A third autobiographical volume in 1881 outlines his remarkable successful public career as writer, orator, editor, reformer, and statesman. The fact that Douglass accounted for his life experiences in the first person, unmediated by a white recorder or editor, gave his texts passion, authority, and accuracy. Later in life, he resided in Washington, D.C., and served as both U.S. marshal and recorder of deeds, while his real vocation continued to be the struggle for civil rights; both his life and his written account of it have been a tremendous influence on African American history and literature.

Frances Ellen Watkins Harper (1825–1911) is also an antebellum African American of great importance to Maryland's and the nation's literary history. Born a free black in Baltimore, she was educated there but exiled by Maryland law after she had left the state to teach at Union Seminar (later Wilberforce University) in Ohio. In 1859 she published the first short story by an African American, entitled "The Two Offers," in *Anglo-African Magazine*. She is best known for her novel of women's lives in slavery, *Iola LeRoy*. Another African American woman, Elizabeth Keckley (1818–1897), became a well-known author with her Reconstruction slave narrative *Behind the Scenes* (1868). A longtime resident of Washington, D.C., she scandalized the Lincoln family after the Civil War by including in her narrative her experiences as Mary Todd Lincoln's dressmaker at the White House.

Following the Civil War, Maryland in general and Baltimore in particular became a sanctuary for apologists for prewar southern life, and a number of minor talents, including Colonel Richard Johnston, Abram Ryan, Susan Smedes, and Father John Banister Tabb, elegized the Old South in prose and verse. Poet Sidney Lanier, who served in the Confederate army, came to Baltimore after the war and wrote romantic, metrically innovative verse supporting the idea of the New South and condemning the evils of materialism. Appointed as lecturer at Johns Hopkins University in the last few years of his life, his contributions to American southern poetry are only now beginning to be fully appreciated. Maryland also benefited from the local-color movement after the war, with the Tidewater region, Annapolis, and western Maryland serving as settings for historical romances and reminiscences of the preindustrial South.

By the end of the Civil War, Washington, D.C., had become an identifiable literary center of merit. A separate political entity with an international flavor, Washington yet participates in the rich traditions of Maryland literary history. Walt Whitman came to Washington in 1862 looking for a brother wounded in the war and stayed for over a decade. At first a battlefield wound-dresser, he became a government clerk after the war. During his Washington period, he saw several revisions of *Leaves of Grass* through the presses and composed *Drum Taps* (1865), an exceptional collection of poems in which he tried to depict tangibly the reality of the Civil War. The volume contained Whitman's memorial to President Abraham Lincoln, "When Lilacs Last in the Dooryard Bloom'd," one of the great elegies of Western literature. John Burroughs, who was to become the nation's most popular literary naturalist, came to Washington to be near Whitman; his own early publications focused on the Maryland landscape.

In the last quarter of the nineteenth century, sentimental novels written by women proliferated nationwide; two of the most prolific and popular, Frances Hodgsdon Burnett and Mrs. E. D. E. N. Southworth, lived and wrote in Washington. Additionally, American literary history features any number of writers whose D.C. residency has usually gone unmentioned. Mark Twain wrote his early, career-shaping novel *Innocents Abroad* (1869) in Washington; Thomas Nelson Page, author of *In Ole Virginia* (1887), novelist, and eulogist of the Old South and apologist for slavery, lived in Georgetown for the better part of his career. Although Henry Adams, great-grandson and grandson of American presidents, is usually identified in terms of his family's aristocratic New England background, he lived in a grand townhouse on Lafayette Square in Washington for his entire adult life. His extremely literary autobiography, *The Education of Henry Adams* (1907), uses the natural beauty and temperate climate of Washington and the surrounding Maryland countryside as a counterpoint to unpleasant events and inhospitable environments. In *Democracy* (1880) and *Esther* (1884), Adams pioneered the national political novel (or Washington novel) with *Democracy* a subgenre exposing greed and corruption in national affairs.

In the twentieth century, various aspects of Maryland's rich and often contradictory cultural heritage have affected major American authors. The turn of the century saw Gertrude Stein at Johns Hopkins Medical School; it was also in Baltimore that she turned from science to art. The matriarch of the expatriate Lost Generation, Stein is usually associated with Paris, but the Stein clan was Baltimore-based, and she claimed Baltimore as her official residence for her entire life. Early works such as the psychological study *Three Lives* (1909) and the encyclopedic *The Making of Americans,* finished by 1908, depended on pivotal experiences and impressions from her Baltimore days.

Thorstein Veblen was also a graduate student at Hopkins, and his famous socio-economic treatise *The Theory of the Leisure Class* (1899) was grounded in research conducted in Baltimore. Upton Sinclair's family had Maryland connections, and the author of *The Jungle* (1906) and other muckraking classics was born and raised in Baltimore.

H. L. Mencken, the literary figure most identified with Baltimore—he lived, wrote, and died there— began his career as a journalist and found his intellectual home when he joined the Baltimore Sunpapers in 1906. He was associated with the Sunpapers, especially the *Evening Sun,* for his entire life as editor and columnist. His iconoclastic weekly column translated local economic, political, and cultural issues into matters of national concern; between 1920 and 1940, Mencken was the most popular journalist in the United States. His other accomplishments include major studies of literary figures as well as a landmark ethnolinguistic work, *The American Language* (1948), in which he persuasively claimed that the American language was separate from the English language. Additionally, he shaped American literary tastes by founding and editing important new periodicals: the *Smart Set,* the *American Mercury,* and *Black Mask.* He used his editorial power to promote new writers and new literary forms. Most notably, *Black Mask* featured the early publications of Dashiell Hammett, father of the hardboiled school of detective fiction, who was himself a native Marylander and Pinkerton detective in Baltimore. A decade later, James M. Cain, born in Annapolis, a *Sun* reporter and resident of Maryland for over sixty of his eighty-five years, was also encouraged by Mencken. Cain is responsible for the creation of the *noir* thriller and author of such classics as *The Postman Always Rings Twice* (1934) and *Double Indemnity* (1943).

In the early years of the twentieth century, the African American literary tradition established by Frederick Douglass continued in Maryland, most conspicuously by Zora Neale Hurston and Jean Toomer, both of whom would become Harlem Renaissance icons. The young Hurston—now known as a distinguished feminist, folklorist, and major African American fictionist—happened to be in Baltimore in 1915 when she had an appendectomy at Maryland General Hospital. She stayed to graduate from the Morgan Academy and then attended Howard University in Washington, graduating with an associate's degree in 1924. By the time she left Maryland, Hurston had already indicated her literary inclination, having published her first story in the Howard literary magazine. Jean Toomer, born and raised in Washington, is best known for a single work, *Cane* (1923), a landmark in African American literature. Experimental in style, the text incorporates elements of prose fiction, poems, songs, drama, and autobiography in the story of a young black man's quest for roots through his cultural heritage. Toomer wrote *Cane* during a temporary return to Washington; the second of its three parts details black urban life in Washington, D.C., a corrupt and uncaring city whose national symbolism only highlights the special difficulties of blacks in achieving the American Dream.

The visions and styles of Hurston and Toomer are a strong contrast to another Maryland-influenced writer of the day, F. Scott Fitzgerald. His family had Maryland roots, he spent the determinant period of his life and career in Baltimore, published any number of his short stories in Mencken's *American Mercury,* and is buried in Rockville, Maryland. Scott and Zelda lived in or near Baltimore from 1931 to 1937, having decided to return to the United States to bring order to their lives and for Scott to reestablish himself as a serious writer. Unfortunately, neither could overcome alcoholism, and Zelda's mental problems worsened. Nevertheless, Fitzgerald wrote his second novel, *Tender Is the Night* (1934), in Baltimore. The story of a young American psychiatrist who is personally and professionally destroyed by his wife's wealth and her mental illness, *Tender Is the Night* is Fitzgerald's semi-autobiographical version of his relationship with his wife as well as an indictment of the American dream. Usually considered his best novel after *The Great Gatsby* (1925), *Tender Is the Night* depended heavily on Baltimore experiences with and impressions of various Hopkins clinics. The real Zelda, a southern belle, was the model for both Nicole Diver in *Tender Is the Night* and Daisy Buchanan in *The Great Gatsby.* In fact, during their Baltimore residency, Zelda published her own clearly autobiographical version of her troubled relationship with her husband; her *Save Me the Waltz* (1932) was published two years before Scott's novel.

Building on the modernist efforts of Stein and Fitz-

gerald, John Dos Passos (1896–1970) and Katherine Anne Porter (1890–1980) brought distinct new voices to Maryland literature. Dos Passos, a political radical who later became extremely conservative, spent his early years on the Delmarva Peninsula, punctuated his Lost Generation wanderings with visits to the Tidewater area, and spent his later days in Maryland, most of them in Baltimore. Dos Passos was a master of the multivolume format and an innovator in narrative technique. Of his characteristic trilogies, *District of Columbia* (1952) most clearly reflects the Maryland influence by attempting to document the energy as well as the decadence of the nation's capital in its dazzling rhetoric. Katherine Anne Porter, world traveler and friend to such distinguished southern literary figures as Allen Tate and Robert Penn Warren, lived in Washington, D.C., and surrounding Maryland cities and suburbs for almost a half century. Her stories exhibit a marked southern flavor, and the Maryland landscape was responsible for much of her rich natural images, including the title and informing symbol of "Flowering Judas," her most famous story.

As has been the case in every period of American literary history, Maryland affiliations have continued to shape the lives and works of noteworthy literary figures. Ogden Nash produced his globally popular light verse in Baltimore. A University of Maryland professor, Rachael Carson, stimulated the international environmental movement with *The Sea Around Us* (1951) and *Silent Spring* (1962). In many stories and novels, longtime Baltimore author Anne Tyler has secured a national reputation; her *Breathing Lessons* (1988) won a Pulitzer Prize. Among nationally recognized women poets, Maryland can boast of ties with Lucille Clifton, Josephine Jacobsen, Julia Randall, and Adrienne Rich. Thomas Pynchon, whose outrageous, exuberant, paranoid vision is without parallel in American literary history, has recently focused his creative sights on Maryland in *Mason & Dixon* (1997). An encyclopedic work purportedly recounting the famous surveying feat responsible for separating Pennsylvania from Maryland and the North from the South, the novel is at once minutely historical and sweepingly satirical. *Mason & Dixon* gives readers a rich description of colonial Maryland as well as an appreciation of the line that still so strongly defines the state of Maryland in the national consciousness.

Mason & Dixon is one of a pair of postmodern texts that attempt a remythification of Maryland, the other being John Barth's burlesque *The Sot-Weed Fac-*

tor (1960). An epic prose version of Ebenezer Cooke's eighteenth-century poem, *The Sot-Weed Factor* exceeds the original in terms of bawdiness and humor; pretending to be the autobiography of Ebenezer Cooke, Barth's text parodies Cooke's production, the seriousness of historical accounts, and itself.

Only H. L. Mencken comes close to Barth as a thorough Marylander; Barth was born in Maryland, educated at Johns Hopkins, where he worked with mentor Louis D. Rubin and where he has been, since 1973, Centennial Professor of English and Creative Writing. Starting with his first novel, *The Floating Opera* (1956), the setting and the thematics of his vital output have centered on the Chesapeake Bay and the Eastern Shore. Few authors have equaled Barth in capturing the essence of a region, and he stands alone as the writer who has given the most poignant and delightful portrait of Maryland. Just as Ebenezer Cooke was recognized as Maryland's poet laureate in the seventeenth century, John Barth should be considered Maryland's fabulist laureate in the twentieth.

K. Huntress Baldwin

See also *American Mercury*; Baltimore, Maryland; Baltimore Sunpapers; Biography; Border States; Civil War; Colonial Newspapers; Harlem Renaissance; Mason-Dixon Line; Mystery and Detective Fiction; Postmodernism; Regionalism; Slave Narrative; *Smart Set*; Tidewater.

Donald L. Ball, *Eastern Shore of Maryland Literature* (1950); Donna Barnes, ed., "Literary Maryland," *Maryland Humanities* (Fall 1997); William F. Halstead, "Literary Maryland," *Maryland Magazine* (June 1974); J. A. Leo Lemay, *Men of Letters in Colonial Maryland* (1972); Clarinda Harriss Lott, "Poetry and Literature," *Baltimore: A Living Renaissance* (1982); Henry E. Shepherd, *The Representative Authors of Maryland* (1911); Frank R. Shivers Jr., *Maryland Wits & Baltimore Bards* (1985).

MASKING

"Masking" is a survival strategy developed by African Americans during slavery and continued in the South throughout the Jim Crow years and afterward. The "masker" is a person who adopts racial stereotypes to hide his or her true feelings in order to gain some leverage in a powerless situation with whites. The classic example is the slave who pretends ignorance, innocence, and adoration in order to ingratiate himself with the "massah" or some other white person capable of pro-

viding protection or economic advantage. Some of the earliest examples might be found in slave narratives. In his *Narrative* (1845), Frederick Douglass recalls the hymns and work songs that contained coded references to freedom, which the white overseers would no doubt interpret literally as a longing only for spiritual freedom. One of the earliest white writers to recognize the behavior was Samuel Clemens in his depiction of the relationship between Jim and Huck (1885). The escaped slave Jim is constantly deferring to the boy's judgment, even when he knows better, and telling Huck that he is Jim's "best friend in the whole world," in order to keep Huck from turning him in to the slave-catchers. Other writers of the period made the mistake of assuming such behavior to be genuine. Thomas Nelson Page and many other local-colorists presented one-dimensional slave characters who missed the "good 'ol days" of slavery "befo' de wah."

Around the turn of the century, Charles W. Chesnutt, a writer of mixed blood, presented his own version of the local-color stories. The tales in *The Conjure Woman* (1899) are told by an ex-slave named Julius, who, unlike his predecessors in the works of Page, understands and makes understood to the reader the need for duplicity toward whites. Not incidentally, the white landowners in *The Conjure Woman* are northerners; Chesnutt implies that racial stereotyping is not simply a southern problem. By enthralling the new landowners with his tales of conjure and transformation, Julius not only ensures an economic advantage for himself and his extended family, he teaches the white landowners important lessons about human kindness and justice.

Though masking was a survival strategy developed during slavery, it continued to be important in the lives of many African Americans well into the twentieth century, as reflected in the literature even past midcentury. In *Modernism and the Harlem Renaissance*, Houston Baker describes how ubiquitous the phenomenon of masking was with cross-cultural exchanges during the first half of the century. Like Ralph Ellison's Invisible Man, Baker explains how, in general, black men and women were not *seen* by whites, how whites routinely projected their own realities of white supremacy onto blacks. Understanding the reality of their situation, black men and women—including black writers—began using the device of the minstrel mask to manipulate whites, to pacify them and lull them into their comfortable myth of superiority. Black speakers operated covertly behind the mask—sometimes in the form of subversive literature and sometimes from the political podium, as in the case of Booker T. Washington, whose single-minded ambition Houston Baker identifies as the training of "the Afro-American masses in a way that would ensure their inestimable value to a white world—that would, in a word, enable them to survive."

Many black writers of the late nineteenth and early twentieth centuries were much less comfortable with the necessity of masking. In "We Wear the Mask" (1895), Paul Laurence Dunbar suggests a comparison between the burden of masking and Christ burdened by the Cross. In *The Souls of Black Folk* (1903), W. E. B. Du Bois recognizes the problem of masking as the development of a "double-consciousness," as the habit of "always looking at one's self through the eyes of others, of measuring one's soul by the tape of a world that looks on in amused contempt and pity." Similarly, in his autobiography *Black Boy*, Richard Wright presents the principal tension in his struggle toward liberation to be the maintenance of a distinction between the outward pose of servility and ignorance and his inner cultivation of an evolving vision of racial equality and justice, a vision he would learn to articulate through the written word. Though Wright acknowledged the absolute necessity of masking to survival in the Jim Crow South, he considered it to be one of the many debasing elements in African American culture (a position for which Wright has since been thoroughly criticized).

Like Richard Wright, the narrator of Ralph Ellison's *Invisible Man* finds it necessary to leave his southern home in pursuit of success and the opportunity to make his impact felt in the world. Throughout the first half of the novel, he naïvely believes in the good will of white benefactors and seeks their sponsorship of his education and his ambitions for personal advancement. Only after suffering successive disillusionments at the hands of these would-be benefactors does the narrator come to understand that he is invisible, that the white members of the Brotherhood are as blinded by his racial identity as are the white capitalists in the city and the white southerners back home; they are all incapable of understanding his words because they already presuppose a place and a purpose for him. When the narrator realizes that "they were very much the same, each attempting to force his picture of reality upon me and neither giving a hoot in hell for how things looked to me," he recognizes new possibilities for the cross-cultural exchange: he recognizes for the

first time the advantage of his position and the rules of "masking." Because the whites who try to control him are so sure that they can predict his behavior, it is easy for the narrator to act independently to undermine them without fear of their cognizance: "They were blind, bat blind," he finally recognizes. "And because they were blind they would destroy themselves and I'd help them. . . . So I'd accept it, I'd explore it. . . . I'd overcome them with yeses, undermine them with grins, I'd agree them to death and destruction. . . . They wanted a machine? Very well, I'd become a supersensitive confirmer of their misconceptions."

Since the early 1970s, the study of African American literature and the canonization of contemporary texts has shifted dramatically from the works of black male writers to the works of black women—and from the untenable position of being black and interacting with an oppressive white society to the dynamics of communicating within the black community. Even though black women likewise have found it necessary to adopt the skills of masking, the relative absence of masking episodes involving women in African American literature demonstrates that masking never became as fundamental to the black woman's sense of self as a relational entity. Perhaps the responsibility of nurturing children has created for women other sustaining and more significant modes of communicating—which have not been generally as accessible to black men. Out of historical necessity, black men have been more immersed in cross-cultural communication, and since it has been black men and not black women whom the white patriarchy feared as both a sexual and an economic threat, it is reasonable to expect that masking has been most consistently and intensely demanded of black men.

Among this century's white writers, William Faulkner has at times incorporated masking into his development of African American characters. Richard Russell has pointed out a quite different type of masking in Lucas Beauchamp of *Go Down, Moses*. Instead of the pose of passivity, friendliness, and ignorance, the surly black tenant farmer Beauchamp shows a poker face as "impenetrable" as the Delta wilderness to the successive generations of white landowners who own the land he rents. This difference perhaps offers more of a commentary on the white experience of African American masking than it does the black.

A broader consideration of "masking" might consider how, in an effort to gain some leverage and safety in a cross-cultural exchange, any marginalized group adopts the stereotyped behaviors attributed to it by the privileged class. Tennessee Williams's heroines, for example, demonstrate how white southern women often adopted the mask of the belle in order to gain some level of power and freedom, particularly sexual freedom, in a patriarchal society. In *A Streetcar Named Desire*, Blanche Dubois reminds us, "After all, a woman's charm is fifty percent illusion." As a young gay southerner who had one foot in Bohemia and the other in the New Orleans Garden District, Williams certainly understood discrimination and the occasional necessity of masking. A comparative study of masking as it appears in the literatures of various marginalized groups might offer a richer understanding of the power dynamics historically at work throughout the South, as well as the possibly similar means by which members of these groups covertly maneuver to empower themselves.

George Hovis

See also African American Spirituals; Trickster; Violence.

Houston A. Baker Jr., *Modernism and the Harlem Renaissance* (1987); Jay Mechling, "The Failure of Folklore in Richard Wright's *Black Boy*," *Journal of American Folklore* 104 (1991).

MASON-DIXON LINE

Recognized today as a general signifier of cultural, historical, and geographical differences between the North and South, the Mason and Dixon Line (1765–1767) was originally drawn to clarify the overlapping and long-disputed claims between the colonies of Maryland and Pennsylvania. For the most part surveyed by English astronomers Charles Mason (1730–1787) and Jeremiah Dixon (d. 1777), the line for a time marked the northernmost edge of the South (now generally considered to be the Potomac River). Coined during congressional debates that led to the Missouri Compromise (1820–1821), the term "Mason and Dixon Line" soon became symbolic of national divisions over slavery, and in the twentieth century it continued to symbolize differences over legalized segregation. Although the line itself is a relatively infrequent motif in southern literature, Marylander John H. B. Latrobe, in an 1854 speech, considered the development of the line to have enough "wild adventure" to be a suitable subject for an American Walter Scott.

Thomas Pynchon's *Mason & Dixon* (1997) tackles the broad historical milieu in which Mason and Dixon lived but brings more imagination—and of a different order—to the creation of the line than Latrobe probably envisioned. Southerner Rita Mae Brown's *Six of One* (1978) and *Bingo* (1988) are both set in Runnymede, a modern town in which family and social rivalries as well as small-town intrigues play out over the line that evenly divides it. The Mason-Dixon Line continues to form an important modality in the popular imagination, lending itself to numerous idiomatic images and phrases, and remains as important a cultural signifier as terms such as "Dixie," "King Cotton," and "Lost Cause."

Christopher Windolph

See also Border States; Slave Narrative.

The Journal of Charles Mason and Jeremiah Dixon, intro. by A. Hughlett Mason (1969); William H. Bayliff, *The Maryland-Pennsylvania and the Maryland-Delaware Boundaries* (1959); John H. B. Latrobe, *The History of Mason and Dixon's Line* (1855); James Veech, ed., *Mason and Dixon's Line: A History* (1857).

MELODRAMA

Melodrama, with its virtuous heroes and hateful villains, its spotless heroines and faithful servants, pleased and excited mass audiences across nineteenth-century America. In the South, the clear-cut, traditional moral assumptions underlying melodrama were especially appealing. Villains are always punished; virtue is always rewarded. As British melodrama was also in its prime then, many of the most popular plays of the period are written by British authors, and many were stage adaptations of popular novels. Others showed the hazards of life in urban centers, depicting New York millionaires with evil agendas. In New York, the Bowery theater was the center of melodramatic productions. In the South, Charleston and New Orleans were the prime theatrical centers.

Before the Civil War, South Carolinian William Gilmore Simms wrote plays with melodramatic elements on such topics as the Battle of the Alamo (*Michael Bonham; or, The Fall of Bexar,* 1852). In the 1850s, the most popular melodramas on the American stage were dramatizations of Harriet Beecher Stowe's novel *Uncle Tom's Cabin*. George Aiken's script (1853) is the most notable of the many versions. "Tommers," companies existing solely to produce the play, night after night, toured the country, inspiring a number of southern answers to the play's antislavery message. Many satires were written and staged in response to both the novel and stage productions of *Uncle Tom's Cabin,* including New Orleans playwright Joseph M. Field's (1810–1856) burlesque *Uncle Tom's Cabin; or, Life in the South As It Is* (1854).

Confederate plays used melodrama to send a patriotic message to the audience. John Hill Hewitt (1801–1890), as director of the Richmond Theater, staged a number of his own plays, most important the comedy *The Scouts; or, The Plains of Manassas* (1861), his first Civil War play, on guerrilla soldiers at Manassas. James Dabney McCabe Jr.'s (1842–1883) melodrama *The Guerrillas, or, the War in Virginia* also concerns a band of guerrillas fighting against an aggressive northern army, aided by the faithful slave Jerry, who would rather die than be set free. Produced in Richmond in December 1862, it was published and subsequently staged in Mobile, Macon, and Wilmington. Other patriotic Confederate plays, *The Roll of the Drum* by John Davis (1861) and Joseph Hodgson's *The Confederate Vivandiere* (1862), featured heroines who represented all the strength of the South, making a melodramatic appeal to the southern audience.

The aftermath of the Civil War and the period of Reconstruction were bad years for the theater in the South. Although playwrights were developing the new realistic drama in other parts of the country, the South produced very few plays of lasting value. Bartley Campbell, who lived in Kentucky and New Orleans, wrote a number of melodramas with southern settings and themes. In *The White Slave* (1882), the heroine is mistaken for a slave, even though she is fully white. This plot takes up common melodramatic themes, miscegenation and the tragic implications of having even a drop of African blood. Instant melodrama is available when the villain can sully the heroine's reputation by implying she comes from mixed blood. Campbell's melodrama *The Virginian* (1874) portrays a love story with a politically pro-South take on the Civil War. Few of these plays are available today.

A number of melodramas written by northerners were set in the South, drawing on the antebellum ideals of moonlight and magnolias. The setting seemed romantic and appropriate for the straightforward melodramas popular in the latter part of the nineteenth century. By the 1880s, melodramas set in the Civil War emerged, emphasizing healing and common goals of the North and South. Among these are William Gillette's *Held by the Enemy* (1886) and *Secret Service* (1895), Bronson Howard's *Shenandoah* (1888), and David Belasco's *Heart of Maryland* (1895).

With the rise of realism in the drama at the turn of the century, melodrama's popularity entered a slow decline. The thrills and spectacle that melodrama provided for an audience became the domain of the movies, and such novels and films as *Birth of a Nation* (and, to an extent, *Gone With the Wind*) satisfied southern appetites for melodrama. But the southern respect for tradition has kept melodrama alive in some places. In Vicksburg, Mississippi, *Gold in the Hills* has played since 1936—the longest-running melodrama in the world.

Sage Hamilton Rountree

See also Drama, 1800 to 1900; Drama, 1900 to Present.

Walter Meserve, *An Outline History of American Drama, Second Edition* (1994); Robert C. Toll, *On with the Show: The First Century of Show Business in America* (1976); Charles Watson, *The History of Southern Drama* (1997).

MEMPHIS, TENNESSEE

Once hailed as the "Capital of the Delta" and the "Mistress of the Mississippi," Memphis is perhaps better known among readers of southern fiction as "Babylon on the Bluff," the home of Beale Street and the blues, of Bible-thumpers and bootleggers alike. Even before Prudential Life declared Memphis the "Murder Capital of America" in 1923, the city had been blessed with a bad reputation dating back to the day in 1829 when a drunken Davy Crockett reportedly stood on a flatboat bound for Texas and told the city it could "go to Hell." Since then, writers have found much to love and hate in the city that Colonel William Falkner once described as being "famous for the beauty of its women and the muddiness of its streets."

Mark Twain knew Memphis well from his years as a river pilot, and in *Life on the Mississippi* (1883) he paid tribute to the "Good Samaritan City" that had cared for his brother Henry and other victims of riverboat disasters. Stopping over in Memphis on a trip downriver in 1882, Twain found the river town that Frances Trollope had dismissed a half-century earlier as a muddy hole peopled with unmannered "ignorant swells" transformed into a thriving city with "fine residences" and a park tenanted by "a sociable horde of squirrels."

For the Mississippi-born Richard Wright, who stepped off the train from Jackson onto Beale Street in 1925, Memphis was, as it had been for so many African Americans, the gateway from the Delta to the Promised Land up north. As Wright later recalled in *Black Boy* (1937), it was in Memphis that he first read the works of Mencken, Lewis, and Dreiser and thus acquired a "new hunger" for books and for life that led him north to Chicago and future fame.

A twenty-four-year-old Tennessee Williams saw his first play *Shanghai, Cairo, Bombay!* performed in Memphis at the home of a local patron of the arts in the summer of 1934. There, on the "great sloping back lawn" of Mrs. Rose Arbrough's house, "the theater and I," he recalled, "found each other for better or worse."

William Faulkner, who regularly drove the eighty miles from Oxford, Mississippi, to Memphis to drink, gamble, and carouse in the city's nightclubs and roadhouses, found the city's underworld a prime source for some of his darkest fiction. It was in the parlor of the flamboyant Memphis madam, Mary Sharon, that Faulkner first heard the story of the bootlegger Neal "Popeye" Pumphrey, whose rape and kidnapping of a woman he kept prisoner in a Memphis brothel formed the basis of Faulkner's 1931 novel *Sanctuary*. In *Light in August* (1932), Faulkner tells how the wife of Reverend Gail Hightower "went bad on him" and "slipped off" to Beale Street, those "three or four . . . city blocks" that make Harlem look like a "movie set," to take her "private sabbaticals among the fleshpots of Memphis." In "There Was a Queen" (1933), Narcissa Benbow Sartoris makes a "sudden and mysterious trip to Memphis" to recover the stolen letters she fears could bring shame upon her family. Knowing she must bargain with her body to get the letters back, Narcissa insists on meeting her blackmailer in Memphis, where she trusts her sacrifice will remain a secret. In the end, she herself confesses the truth to her Aunt Jenny, who dies when she learns that Narcissa has slept with a Yankee to preserve the family name.

Memphis is also the setting for some of Faulkner's more humorous scenes. In "The Bear" (1942), young Ike McCaslin accompanies Boon Hogganbeck on a whiskey-run to Memphis just as Faulkner himself had done as a young man on one of "General" James Stone's annual bear hunts in the big woods of Jefferson County. While in town, Ike recalls how his father, "Uncle Buck" McCaslin, once rode into Memphis during the Federal occupation and galloped right into a lobby full of Yankee officers at the Gayoso Hotel before riding out again "scot-free." In "Two Soldiers" (1942), an eight-year-old boy travels the hundred miles from Frenchman's Bend to Memphis by himself to join his brother in the army after the bombing of Pearl Harbor. Alone in a city "a dozen whole towns bigger than Jefferson," the boy soldiers his way through the racket of "rushing cars and shoving folks" before his brother sends him back home to Yoknapatawpha County.

Memphis was also the place where Faulkner came to fulfill his lifelong dream of being a pilot. In the early 1930s, Faulkner traveled almost weekly to a Memphis airfield where, after learning to fly, he took to the skies with his brothers, barnstorming around the Delta as part of the "Flying Faulkners Air Circus."

Longtime Memphis resident Shelby Foote, whose grandfather gave Shelby County its name, based his 1977 novel *September, September* on one of the city's more famous crimes, the kidnapping of a young African American boy in 1957. Though Foote's focus is the era of Little Rock, Eisenhower, and Elvis, his narrative weaves a history of Memphis stretching from Davy Crockett's "blufftop farewell whisky bust" to the "high rolling" heyday of a Beale Street "paved end-to-end with pimps and whores and gamblers." For the kidnapper Podjo Harris, whose travels have taken him far from his Delta home, Memphis remains "The City." "Whatever one saw in later life," he says, "youd [sic] see it in terms of Memphis, whatever its size." Like most Memphians, however, Harris is at best ambivalent about his adopted home. "If God was going to give the world an enema," he jokes, "Memphis is where He would insert the nozzle." But, he later concedes, "It's where a man moves to that counts, and I moved to Memphis."

In the stories and novels of Peter Taylor, Memphis is a "small, old world" in itself, whose borders are defined by the company one keeps, be it in the tile-roofed suburban bungalows on the outskirts of town or in the "walled city . . . within the city" at the center of the downtown Garden District. Like many of his own characters, Taylor came to Memphis from somewhere else, having moved there from Nashville when he was a teenager. This "removal" from the "starchy" Upper South city of Nashville to the Deep South "cotton and river culture" of Memphis is the subject of Taylor's 1986 novel *A Summons to Memphis,* which finds the narrator, Phillip Carver, returning home to halt the marriage of his elderly father to a younger woman of questionable means. Carver's homecoming awakens memories of the Memphis of his youth, a past still visible in the "peculiar cut" of his father's jacket and in the polished eccentricities of Carver's two sisters, Betsy and Josephine, whose social escapades have made them a "remarkable Memphis institution" among the local elite. Like his late mother, who often said that a "shooting in the family would have been better than a move to Memphis," Carver knows that a life exists beyond his old home, but it is there, in the world of Front Street and the old Pink Palace, that life retains for him its most distinct impressions.

Even in stories set outside Memphis, Taylor evokes the city's character through studies of such "perfect Memphis types" as Tolliver Campbell, the alcoholic cotton heir in "The Captain's Son" (1977). Taylor's 1985 story "The Old Forest" suggests that the only true insiders in Memphis are outsiders like Lee Ann Deehart, the Memphis "demimondaine" who finds refuge in places other Memphians dare not go. As the Memphis debutante Caroline Braxley says, Deehart and her kind "occupy the real city of Memphis as none of the rest of us do."

More recently, Memphis has gained widespread attention as the setting for some of John Grisham's best-selling legal thrillers. In *The Firm* (1991) and *The Rainmaker* (1995), Grisham (who got his start practicing law at a small Mississippi firm outside of Memphis) drew upon his knowledge of the Memphis legal scene to explore some of the city's darkest corners. Other recent novels set in Memphis include Margaret Skinner's *Old Jim Canaan* (1990), which follows the title character's efforts to maintain his stranglehold on the city's illicit fortunes, and Ann Patchett's *Taft* (1994), a contemporary melodrama told by an ex-blues drummer whose life changes when two white teenagers walk into his Beale Street bar. Graceland, Elvis Presley's home and gravesite, is a national shrine for many visitors.

Brian Carpenter

See also Elvis; Tennessee, Literature of.

Joseph Blotner, *Faulkner: A Biography* (1974); Gerald M. Capers, *The Biography of a River Town* (1939); Shields McIlwaine, *Memphis: Down in Dixie* (1948); Gertrude Stein, *Everybody's Autobiography* (1937); Frances Trollope, *Domestic Manners of the Americans* (1832); John W. Warren, *Tennes-* *see Belles-Lettres* (1977); Linton Weeks, *Memphis: A Folk History* (1982).

METHODISTS

Methodism in the United States can only be comprehended by understanding its English origins. Methodism had its beginning in 1729–1730 in a religious club founded by Charles Wesley and joined by John Wesley along with several friends while they were advanced students at Oxford University. Both Wesleys were priests in the Anglican Church and were children of a rector at Epworth in Lincolnshire. Their parents, Samuel and Susanna, likewise had been children of Anglican clergymen. Though economically impoverished, these two sons, from among nineteen children, ten of whom survived to adulthood, were sent to respectable private schools and Oxford University, where they were classically educated. John had distinguished himself by becoming a Fellow of Lincoln College. Charles became a prolific poet and renowned writer of hymns.

The members of the Oxford "Holy Club" devoted themselves to discussing, correcting, and encouraging each other in matters of faith; they were derisively labeled Methodist, for the methodical structure of their lives. As a distinctive confession, these early Methodists combined the high Anglo-Catholic tradition of the Anglican Church with intensive study in the Reformation theologies of Martin Luther and John Calvin; they developed a life-style with a Puritan version of discipline and a flavoring of German pietism.

Following the lead of George Whitfield, another member of the Holy Club, John began preaching to mass gatherings of basically unchurched working-class people in out-of-doors settings rather than in the Anglican churches. These converts grew into the Wesleyan or Methodist movement. Methodism has been regularly characterized as a renewal movement within Anglicanism, in the larger framework of an eighteenth-century evangelical activity in both England and the American colonies. John was especially attracted to the work of Jonathan Edwards, a New England preacher sometimes referred to as the founder of the First Great Awakening. Joining this evangelical Christianity, the Methodist movement grew parallel to the larger social movements of the Industrial Revolution in England and the political experiment of representative democracy in the American colonies.

Methodist "societies" were formed in the colonies

as early as 1763 in Maryland and New York. Wesley sent missionaries by 1769, at which time the Methodists had expanded into six hundred small classes or "societies." The American Revolution slowed the movement, because most of the missionaries were British and shared the Tory leanings of Mr. Wesley. Francis Asbury, himself English, a Methodist who appeared to understand and likely sympathized with the revolutionaries, remained in the colonies, albeit mostly in hiding. At the Revolutionary War's conclusion, Wesley appointed Dr. Thomas Coke and Francis Asbury as the leaders of the American movement. In December 1784, Coke and sixty-four itinerant ministers met for the so-called Christmas Conference in Baltimore to form a semi-independent church, the Methodist Episcopal Church in America.

Maryland, New Jersey, New York, Pennsylvania, Delaware, and Virginia formed the early matrix of the movement in America. Because of the heavy British occupation, especially in New York during the Revolutionary War, the movement declined in the more northerly areas. After the war, facing the strength of the Congregationalists in New England and Presbyterians in the Pennsylvania area, the Methodists pushed southward, where the Anglican Church was stronger, and where Methodism, at least initially, was considered to be a movement within Anglicanism. By the founding of the Methodist Episcopal Church in 1784, 11,500 of the 15,000 Methodist members were in Maryland, Virginia, and the Carolinas. Although the concentration of Methodist population appeared early in the mid-Atlantic and southern states, its members moved westward with the emigrés, who were generally forced from the eastern coastal plain by an established colonial planter class. The Anglicans and Presbyterians relinquished the West to the "dissenters and the Devil." Methodists spread, pincherlike, in a dual thrust along the rivers into the Midwest and the Deep South. Methodists, adapted historically and organizationally to the working class, led by indigenous lay leadership with only occasional visits from the "circuit riding" clergy, flourished in the primitive conditions of the frontier connection. By 1805, scarcely forty-five years after arriving in the colonies, the Methodists counted more than 100,000 members.

As Wesley had been enamored by the First Great Awakening, the Methodists in the late nineteenth century became a critical link in the Second Great Awakening. This revivalistic revolution, which the South embraced so heavily, had limited roots in the historic traditions of the Christian church. The parallel impulses of autonomous religion and political independence led to an anarchic proliferation of opinions within Methodism and to a corollary formation of splinter religious groups, all within a nation that had by statute established religious freedom as a central human right.

Ethics in this religious community focused on personal morality, with sobriety as a central value and chastity and decency as companions. Social ills were either so distant or so identified as "politics" that the members felt impotent to challenge them. Though John Wesley and early Methodists had vigorously opposed slavery, early-nineteenth-century American Methodism said little about the slave economy in the South, the slave trade generally, and the genocide exacted on the American native population. However, slavery would not be ignored.

In 1784, at its founding, the Methodist Episcopal Church was decidedly antislavery, but within six months its "high stand" began to be modified, due in part to the number of Methodists who lived in the South. As the country divided over slavery, the cultural forces of agitating extremes pushed the Church into multiple divisions. Within ten years of its founding, the first splits in the Methodist Episcopal Church began with the formation of separate black churches. By 1816, black splinter groups in Philadelphia, Baltimore, Wilmington, and Salem, New Jersey, formed the African Methodist Episcopal Church. A similar course in New York created the African Methodist Episcopal Zion Church by 1821. Although the strengths of these newly formed churches remained in the North, in the South immediately before and after the Civil War they expanded both by membership and influence. Harriet Tubman, Frederick Douglass, and Sojourner Truth were either members or close associates with the "Zion Methodists." In addition, resistance to slavery grew in the northern majority-white church. The stage was set for debates and divisions over slavery within the parent church.

Parallel controversies clouded and repressed the slavery issue initially. Soon after the founding of the church, resistance to the hierarchical form of church government began to grow and continued until the Methodist Protestants formed a church in 1830. In 1843, the first antislavery division occurred, which led to the formation of the Wesleyan Methodist Church. The major division over slavery occurred in 1844, when the parent body firmly divided into hardened positions, separated itself into the Methodist Episcopal Church (mostly northern) and the Methodist Episcopal Church South. The border areas between South and North were hotly contested, and a number of antislavery southern churches, notably in eastern Tennessee, retained their allegiances to the antislavery northern church.

At the end of the Civil War, the southern church was in disarray. Its population of black members dropped from 210,000 in 1860 to 20,000 by 1869. Yet another division developed within the remaining black members in the Methodist Episcopal Church South, when in 1870 a group formed the Colored Methodist Church from members in the Methodist Episcopal Church South. Soon after the ending of the Civil War, the Methodist Episcopal Church, north and south, found itself unprepared to treat blacks as equals, and both fell into the social practice of the "separate and unequal" ways of the nation, maintaining separate black and white administrative divisions within the same churches.

Following the Civil War, Methodism expanded expeditiously. The northern church, which had approximately 1 million members in 1860, swelled to more than 4 million by 1920. The southern church grew from 500,000 in 1865 to 2,267,000 by 1920. American Methodists grew so rapidly in the late nineteenth century that the revivalistic movement of the Second Great Awakening set a permanent mark on the future of the church. Though by no means a regional reality, revivalism was especially important in the definition of southern culture where the Methodists, along with the Baptists, were such a high percentage of the population.

Among the outgrowths of this movement were the "camp meetings," revivalistic events held in woodsy settings. These camp meetings were marked by fiery sermons, rousing singing, emotional and sometimes explosive outbreaks. In the South, black and white meetings were frequently held side-by-side with some mutual interchange. The camp meetings served as not only religious gatherings but as massive social gatherings, brief reprieves from the hard and isolated environments of the South and West. In such environments, all were welcomed. These words of a camp meeting song—"Come hungry, come thirsty, come ragged, come bare, come filthy, come lousy, come just as you are"—suggest that Methodist thinking is "equalitarian theology." In this highly charged revivalistic environment, the Anglican heritage of the Wesleys, with their "high church" interests in the sacraments and the educational role of the church, was displaced. Add the primitive living conditions of many members and the relatively uneducated lay leadership, and a very "low church" with a significant anti-intellectual tendency developed among the American Methodist community; its members resisted more rationally based speculative brands of theology and developed strong suspicions of highly educated clergy.

Notwithstanding the limits of its late-nineteenth-century appearance, Methodism by its equalitarianism contributed to the formation and nurture of democracy, providing not only a context where all were welcome but also a theological undergirding. Francis Asbury, Methodism's earliest dominant American leader, wrote about its members: "Disallowed indeed of men but chosen of God, and precious." The European caste distinctions were supplanted in Methodism by the notion that respectability is a moral, not a social reality. One's status depended entirely on one's relationship to God. This democratic entrée into respectability was open and free to all, because God is "no respecter of persons."

Methodism focused on deeds more than doctrine. From the Wesleys forward, Methodist theology insisted that faith necessarily expresses itself in love. Consequently, Methodism has been marked as a church long on good work. Given its early frontier status, the church was slow to begin to build institutions, but once it realized their importance, it began, as one author writes, to "organize to beat the Devil." Today there are one hundred twenty-three schools founded or affiliated with the church, including Wesleyan University, Northwestern, Auburn, Vanderbilt, University of Southern California, Emory, Syracuse, Duke, American, Southern Methodist, Clark University, Claflin College, Rust, Laine, and Paine Colleges and Meharry Medical College, to name only a few. Major medical hospitals at several of these universities as well as in Indianapolis, Atlanta, Houston, Kansas City, and more than 224 retirement homes and 38,000-plus churches mark the map of the Methodists.

Early in the twentieth century, Methodism began the slow healing of earlier wounds by moving toward reunification. In 1939, the Methodist Episcopal and the Methodist Episcopal South joined with the Methodist Protestant Church to become the Methodist Church. In 1968, the Methodist Church merged with its German-American counterpart, the Evangelical United Brethren, to form the United Methodist

Church, at which time the residual "separate but un-equal" black administrative conferences within the Methodist Church were abolished. Pan-Methodist conversations continue currently between United Methodist and the historic black Methodists in the AME, AME Zion, and the Christian Methodist Episcopal churches.

The Methodist Church in the twentieth century has attempted to heal its preoccupation with inequality and, for the most part, has moved away from the revivalistic emphasis of the late nineteenth century. In the early part of the century, churches began to take on an expanded sense of ethical involvement in the larger issues of the day, participating in the "social gospel" movement. The temperance mobilization was a significant commitment of Methodism early in the century. As a movement, it was driven by a series of conflicts within the church, especially the developing rural-urban tensions. At national legislative meetings early in the century, the Methodist Episcopal Church, north and south, adopted a new Social Creed that solidified the church's entry into social witness. The Creed favored equal rights and justice, industrial arbitration, safety in factories, protection of workers and children, reduction in the work-week, and a guaranteed living wage. The South, however, retained much of its revivalistic bent. Church membership, nurture, and social witness only slowly began to replace "conversion" as the central thrust of the southern church. The realities of two world wars, depression, totalitarianism, and disenchantment with liberal progressivism so overwhelmed the southern church that strong reactionary forces set in motion antimodernist sentiments. Fundamentalism arose out of the context. At its seminaries, liberals and fundamentalists took opposite directions in their response to philosophical skepticism, Darwinism, scientism, and the higher critical methods of studying the Bible. A third of the way through the century, English and German influences introduced a new orthodoxy based on a re-reading of the Reformation leaders. That provided a third and bridge option for a vast number of Methodists.

By late 1960, the Methodist Church grew into a mega-church with ten million plus members. As it expanded, its members, like the nation, became more diverse, and tensions emerged and formed around ethnic and minority caucuses, the most potent of which has proven to be the women in Methodism.

Still the great concerns of this church linger: the need for regular renewal, the relationship between the faith and education, the splintering effects of change, the residual effects of inequality, and adaptations to new world contexts. Where Methodism contributed historically to democracy, it currently contributes receptivity to the emerging American pluralism, preferring its classical Wesleyan affirmation: "In essentials, unity; in non-essentials, liberty; and, in all things, charity."

Although there is no classic southern novel wherein Methodism looms large, Methodism's impact on southern literature and culture is undeniable. For H. L. Mencken, Methodists were a broad target for his satire—Methodism he saw as representative of a narrow religious orientation that helped make the South a "Sahara of the Bozart." (Mencken once described Prohibition as having been invented "by country Methodists, nine tenths of them actual followers of the plow.") One Methodist minister made an enduring contribution to southern literature, although A. B. Longstreet wrote his *Georgia Scenes* (1835) before he entered the ministry. After he became a minister, he wrote *Master William Mitten* (1859), a temperance novel. Minister Longstreet also served as president of Emory College, Centenary College, the University of Mississippi, and the University of South Carolina—a reminder of the importance of higher education to the Methodist tradition. The training of several major figures in the Southern Renascence had a strong Methodist base. Although William Faulkner's mother had been reared a Baptist, she had her children baptized and brought up in the tradition of the Falkners' Methodism. Her children went to Sunday School regularly as well as to summer camp meeting. (Faulkner as an adult in Oxford attended, irregularly, the Episcopal church and received those rites at his funeral.) Both Cleanth Brooks and John Crowe Ransom were sons of Methodist ministers.

The carryover of religious poetry from the pen of Charles Wesley laced the worship experience of every Methodist. Charles was a prolific poet and writer of hymns. It is estimated that he produced as many as nine thousand poems. He was a master of meter, preferring iambic foot and the classic sonnet rhyming scheme. His work tended to be classic English, most frequently on biblical themes, interwoven with occasional colloquial "jig" forms making his music far more singable that the psalmody of the times.

The typically undereducated American Methodist, influenced by the revivalistic times of the nineteenth century and the ready availability of Charles Wesley's work, pushed indigenous Methodist hymnody toward simplification. Fanny Crosby (1820–1915), a blind teacher, wrote as many as eight thousand hymns and poem texts and gained great popularity by combining revivalistic themes with cheerfulness wrapped in simplicity. Mary A. Lathbury, in the late nineteenth century, wrote a bit more sophisticated verse in the likes of "Day Is Dying in the West" for the popular Chautauqua assemblies. The Reverend Frank Mason North managed at least one hymn of superior worth, "Where Cross the Crowded Ways of Life." Reverend Charles Tindley wrote black gospel hymns offering hope and encouragement for the weary.

As nineteenth-century Methodism had focused on individual souls, the twentieth century saw the church beginning to turn more toward the social order, sharing a vision of peace and world order. Methodists became zealous in producing a new hymnody and by 1936 created a hymnal of the highest order. Indigenous writers of note began to appear parallel to the rising academic respectability of Methodist seminaries such as Vanderbilt and Boston University. The 1989 hymnal reflects the church in the midst of massive changes. Its "higher church" tone, its international flavor, its pluralistic languages, its combination of old and new hymns reflect the church of the twenty-first century.

Manuel Wortman

See also African American Spirituals; Civil War; Episcopalians; Gospel Music; Hymns.

Emory Stevens Bucke, ed., *The History of American Methodism* (3 vols.; 1964); Henry Wilder Foote, *Three Centuries of American Hymnody* (1968); Reginald F. Hildebrand, *The Times Were Strange and Stirring: Methodist Preachers and the Crisis of Emancipation* (1995); Thomas A. Langford, *Practical Divinity: Theology in the Wesleyan Spirit* (1983); Frederick A. Norwood, *The Story of American Methodists: A History of the United Methodists and Their Relations* (1974); Diana Sanchez, ed., *The Hymns of the United Methodist Hymnal* (1989); John R. Tyson, ed., *Charles Wesley: A Reader* (1989).

MEXICAN WAR

The major American military campaigns in the war with Mexico were designed to accomplish the territorial ambitions of President James K. Polk. Hostilities began near Matamoros in the spring of 1846, after Polk sent a substantial force under General Zachary Taylor in support of the questionable Rio Grande boundary claim of the recently annexed Texas Republic. Taylor advanced to the mountains of the Sierra Madre south of Monterrey, sufficiently deep into Mexico to guarantee the desired boundary line, and successfully defended this position against a fierce Mexican counteroffensive at the Battle of Buena Vista in February 1847. By that time, Upper California and New Mexico were also under American occupation.

In order to compel Mexico's consent to these conquests, General Winfield Scott was dispatched against the Mexican capital. He landed at Vera Cruz in March 1847, and after dramatically retracing the route of the conquistador Hernando Cortez, Scott took Mexico City in mid-September. The Treaty of Guadalupe Hidalgo, signed on February 2, 1848, completed the astounding accomplishment of Polk's single term as president: the acquisition (including the southern Oregon Country by treaty with Britain) of the western third of today's contiguous forty-eight states.

Polk and other political heirs of Andrew Jackson believed that such "spread-eagle" expansion would divert the nation from paralyzing and divisive controversies over slavery. The opposite proved true, as opponents of slavery's expansion were galvanized by Congressman David Wilmot's unsuccessful attempt of August 1846 to ban the South's peculiar institution in all lands taken from Mexico. The new territories became the focus of the sectional crisis of 1849–1850, and a decade later the slavery-expansion issue plunged the United States into civil war.

At the time, however, Polk's aggressive prosecution of the war against Mexico was enormously popular in the southern states. William Gilmore Simms, in a burst of romantic nationalism, embraced the conflict as an opportunity to advance the progress of civilization, to unify the American nation, and to cultivate chivalry and the knightly virtues. His fellow South Carolinian John C. Calhoun was both more prescient and more pessimistic. Though Calhoun had warmly welcomed the incorporation of Texas into the Union as a slave state in 1845, he saw the subsequent war and its territorial fruits as dangerous to the South, to the cause of states' rights, and to the institution of slavery. Calhoun saw no advantage for his region in the nation's acquisition of the deserts and mountains west of Texas, nor in the assimilation of large numbers of nonwhites with abolitionist sympathies. He dreaded, furthermore, the enhancement of federal power that such conquests would inevitably produce, and he feared that the war would energize the opponents of slavery.

Polk was, indeed, accused of pursuing a proslavery agenda by many northern opponents of the war. Their writings, most notably James Russell Lowell's *The Biglow Papers* (1848) and Henry David Thoreau's 1849 essay on civil disobedience, have proven far more lasting than the patriotic paeans that flowered and faded with wartime enthusiasm, such as Simms's own *Lays of the Palmetto*, written in 1848 to welcome home South Carolina's volunteer regiment from Mexico. Equally ephemeral, though perhaps less elevated in tone, were the dozens of cheaply printed "novelettes" that found in the panorama of the Mexican War an exotic backdrop for tales of adventure and romance. Typical of these were *The Chieftain of Churubusco; or, The Spectre of the Cathedral* and *The Mexican Spy; or, The Bride of Buena Vista*, both published in 1848 by an unknown author using the dubious name of Harry Halyard.

James E. Crisp

See also Texas Revolution.

Donald S. Frazier, ed., *The United States and Mexico at War: Nineteenth-Century Expansionism and Conflict* (1998); Robert W. Johannsen, *To the Halls of the Montezumas: The Mexican War in the American Imagination* (1985).

MILITARY COLLEGES

Although many southerners fly the rebel "Stars and Bars," Virginia and South Carolina have celebrated the traditional southern predilection to gallantry by sustaining, for over a century and a half, state-supported military colleges, the only two left in the nation. Every southern state except Florida once had a military college after the Morrill Act of 1862 created land-grant colleges with military components. Louisiana State University, nicknamed "The Old War Skule," had as its inaugural superintendent William T. Sherman. Many survived until World War II, when Auburn, Georgia Tech, Texas A&M, and Virginia Polytechnic Institute were still recognized largely, if not predominantly, for training military officers. Others became preparatory secondary schools or junior colleges. Today, although North Georgia College in Dahlonega still operates primarily if not exclusively as a military program, only the Citadel in Charleston and Virginia Military Institute in Lexington maintain the strictest version of cadet education, both integrated now by race and gender, both recognized for promoting the ceremoniousness of baccalaureate military education,

richly endowed with the form and ritual of collegiate military life.

Military education is reminiscent of the Anglo-Saxon heritage of ruling-class southerners. The aristocrats of the Old South favored the profession of arms for second and third sons over mercantilism, or even letters. If Robert E. Lee's West Point experience exemplifies most southerners' high regard for the military college, the regard of the southern writer for the military college is better characterized by the experience there of Edgar Allan Poe. Yet, as a source of literary talent, VMI and the Citadel have produced literary associations, the Citadel's emphasis on liberal arts more than VMI's emphasis on engineering. VMI lists Alfred Oliver Hero, who wrote about international relations; Oliver Beirne Patton, who wrote two historical novels of the nineteenth-century U.S. army, *Hollow Mountains* (1976) and *My Heart Turns Back* (1979); and Harold Coyle, author of thrillers of U.S. military engagements around the world, including *Team Yankee* (1987), *Sword Point* (1988), *Bright Star* (1990), *Trial by Fire* (1991), *The Ten Thousand* (1993), *Code of Honor* (1994), *Look Away* (1995), and *Savage Wilderness* (1997). Its current superintendent, Josiah Bunting, is the author of *The Lionheads* (1972), *The Advent of Frederick Giles* (1974), and *An Education for Our Time* (1998), all fiction.

Citadel faculty and alumni have made significant contributions in numerous fields, some providing memorable novels about cadet life. Timothy O'Neill wrote *Shades of Gray* (1987), a novel of the occult set at West Point. Thomas T. Carroll Jr. wrote *White Pills* (1964), a parable of race relations. James Oliver Rigney, under the pseudonym Robert Jordan, wrote the popular Conan series of novels that became the basis of the Arnold Schwarzenegger character in the film *Conan the Barbarian*, and the *Wheel of Time* fantasy series. Brainard Cheney (1900–1990) is the author of a sequence of four novels set in South Georgia: *Lightwood* (1939), *River Rogue* (1942), *This Is Adam* (1958), and *Devil's Elbow* (1969). Most widely read have been two novels set at the Citadel—Calder Willingham's first of many novels, *End as a Man* (1947), and Pat Conroy's fourth book, *The Lords of Discipline* (1980), both critical of modern cadet life. Both books became films, *End as a Man* as *The Strange One*.

The South is not militaristic, a quality that requires discipline and rigidity. Rather, what the South loves is a reckless daring more reminiscent of the chivalric role of cavalier individualism than the lock-step of military precision, though that quality is very much in evidence on both military college campuses.

Military colleges are probably much closer in nature to private than to public colleges, yet the military nature that makes them unlike large public colleges requires that they be public. But the ideal of the citizen-soldier-scholar-athlete model is reminiscent of special forms of education more devoted to preserving a culture than to academic research. Every citizen as soldier is a tradition that, unlike in the rest of the United States, never quite died in the South. A country is preserved in its memories, and the South's most distinctive memories are of war.

Lamar York

See also Military Tradition.

MILITARY TRADITION

Discipline and facility with weapons were essential to survival in the New World. The environment forced inexperienced settlers to master martial skills and habits that military experience might have afforded. The confrontations of expansion, revolution, and independence induced a military tradition that by the beginning of the Civil War was influential in practice and attractive to literary treatment and allusion.

Sir Walter Raleigh's two attempts to exploit Queen Elizabeth's 1578 grant failed—1585 and 1587 (the "Lost Colony")—but colonial enterprise resumed under James I, and the privately subscribed Jamestown Expedition arrived in Virginia in April 1607. There, its governing council, eager for "pearle and gold," expelled pragmatic Captain John Smith, who argued that "a plaine Souldier that can use a Pick-axe and spade, is better than five Knights." Veteran Smith returned to be reinstated and be elected the council president under whose firm hand the colony survived the winter. Invasive settlement provoked Indian attacks, and every household maintained ready weapons, a general frontier necessity later reflected in the Minutemen's responsiveness, the Second Amendment to the Constitution, and the Militia Act of 1792. Crown-colony status (1624) recognized the Virginia representative assembly, an English privilege promised by the grant of 1578, even as wealth from tobacco validated Sir Walter Raleigh's advertisement of "gold and glory" in the colony. Although the majority of immigrants were yeomen,

prospects of replicating the life of English gentry attracted royalist refugees, cavalier second sons, and lesser gentlemen. After the Restoration, established Royalists remained while fugitive regicides took cover in Puritan New England. In this era, Colonel Richard Lee (1640) and the Washington brothers, John and Lawrence (1658), brought two leading names to Virginia and into American military tradition. Accumulated wealth led such colonists to power as legislators and officers of the militia in an interdependent system of class and rank resembling a military hierarchy. Virginia's experience was a caution to later entrepreneurs. Leonard Calvert exercised his authority as lieutenant general, president of the Council, and governor (1634) to organize Maryland settler-soldier-colonists into secure, profitable communities. Farther south, Colonel and Vice-Admiral James Oglethorpe established the Georgia colony (1733) expressly to thwart Spanish incursions from Florida.

As the frontier pressed westward, older areas of the South retained martial aspects. Horsemanship was universal. Because sprawling agriculture holdings precluded central law enforcement, safety was a personal matter requiring small-arms expertise. Potential danger from the increasing slave population moved South Carolina to institute all-white patrols and, in Virginia after 1639, only whites were permitted to bear arms, excluding blacks from the militia. (Not until the 1950s were blacks fully integrated in the United States armed forces.) In those circumstances, southerners, both yeomen and gentry, developed a truculent individuality hostile to any perceived offense against their territory or person. When planters and settlers on the Virginia frontier surmised that Governor Berkeley had left them in danger, they moved, in Bacon's Rebellion (1676), first against the Susquehannocks and then against the governor. A later uprising farther south gave William Gilmore Simms the setting for *The Yemassee* (1835), a romance in which sterling colonials best hostile Indians and duplicitous Spanish and English foes.

In the French and Indian War (1754–1763), Governor Dinwiddie ordered George Washington, hereditary adjutant of the Virginia militia and frontier surveyor, to march west against the French, much as Washington's great-grandfather had been posted against the Susquehannocks in the prelude to Bacon's Rebellion. At war's end, Washington returned to civilian life to oppose British policies and become a delegate to the Continental Congress, which duly chose him to command the colonial armies (June 15, 1775). Washington's acceptance and his general orders acknowledging congressional authority over the "Troops of the United Provinces" (July 4) placed him at the chronological and philosophical center of American military tradition. Subsequent service made him its primary icon; Byron celebrated him as "the Cincinnatus of the West." Even lesser ranks assumed heroic proportions: John Pendleton Kennedy presented Captain Arthur Butler as a professional whose "erect and preemptory carriage, visage and figure seemed to speak of one familiar with enterprise and fond of danger, denoting gentle breeding" (*Horse-Shoe Robinson*, 1835). At a final Continental Army encampment (May 1783), officers intent on sustaining wartime associations and the ideals of the Revolution formed the Society of the Cincinnati, America's first veterans' organization, to assist each other and their families. Washington, whom they prevailed upon to be their first president-general, had instituted (1782) the nation's first military decoration, the Badge of Military Merit "for singularly meritorious action," the "Purple Heart" now reserved for those wounded in action. Groups more egalitarian and influential than the Society of the Cincinnati followed later wars: the Aztec Society (Mexican War), the Grand Army of the Republic and the United Confederate Veterans (Civil War), Veterans of Foreign Wars (Spanish-American War), and in the twentieth century the American Legion and the AMVETS. Some few units have had continuous active service: Battery D, 5th Field Artillery, for example, was commanded by Alexander Hamilton at the Battle of Long Island (August 27, 1776). Units disrupted by overall strength fluctuations often maintain cohesion and tradition by means of branch societies and reunions of former members.

"To provide for the common defense," the Constitution relied on states' militia trained as "prescribed by Congress." Few troops were nationalized, but the Militia Act of 1792 increased the force by requiring every free white male between eighteen and forty-five to equip himself and enroll in a state militia. Congress also authorized the five-thousand-man Legion of America, elements of which would be the genesis of the Regular Army. Even so, the War of 1812 found the United States with an inadequate army: the new U.S. Military Academy (1802) had commissioned only seventy-one officers in its ten years, and New England governors were reluctant to commit militiamen. Southern response was more promising: Andrew Jackson's troops routed Creek Indians in Mississippi Territory, proceeded to New Orleans to "lick the men who licked

Napoleon" (January 8, 1815), and returned Jackson to Tennessee a national hero. The military structure in which Jackson and others attained celebrity did not beget the class stratification that Jefferson feared and that Edgar Allan Poe, for one, might have preferred. The irresolute Poe paraded as a Junior Morgan Rifleman in Richmond before his grandfather's wartime associate Lafayette, gambled away cavalier pretensions at the University of Virginia, attempted a West Point career, and futilely sought a commission in the Polish Army (1831). Between the War of 1812 and the Civil War, southern states provided willing, accessible support for expansion and border stability in the Southwest. A call for 3,000 troops for the Mexican War turned out 30,000 militiamen from Tennessee, "The Volunteer State." Mississippi and Georgia vied for comparable involvement, and southerners gained a reputation as fighters and winners. Winfield Scott cited West Point graduates—Jefferson Davis, Robert E. Lee, "Stonewall" Jackson, and Ulysses S. Grant among them—as having played a decisive role in the Mexican campaigns (1846–1848).

The Regular Army, evolving in the nineteenth century from the Legion of America, provided the repository for the accruing military tradition. A structured defense system made forts, camps, and stations part of the American scene. Garrison life revolved around concerns peculiar to nomadic service. Set bugle calls punctuated days filled with drills, maintenance and, on occasion, a parade or review. At each post, the national colors were raised at reveille and ceremoniously lowered at retreat. Horsemanship, weaponry, military protocol, and social convention gave posts a perceptibly southern tone that would survive the Civil War and Indian campaigns. Modest pay, complemented by post quarters and services, allowed officers upper-class manners in a mode of "genteel poverty," the pre–World War II "Old Army." While a cadre of regulars sustained military tradition, new volunteers, reservists, and conscripts in wartime revitalized it; and in peacetime, veterans' groups kept it in the public eye.

As regional relations polarized before the Civil War, men in uniform argued the issues but maintained their allegiance until the break. Lee served (1852–1855) as superintendent at West Point; three successive Commandants of Cadets there (1852–1860) would later resign and become Confederate generals; P. G. T. Beauregard, superintendent for five days in January 1861, in April 1861 ordered the shelling of Fort Sumter as a Confederate brigadier. That summer, the United States oath of allegiance changed: "serve in the United States Army . . . and obey the orders of the President" became "support and defend the Constitution of the United States against all enemies, foreign and domestic."

In the Confederacy, governmental structure and the army mirrored Union institutions. The Stars and Bars was a "star-spangled banner" and Dixie a "land of the free and home of the brave," but the common tradition diverged as the South cited "Our Washington" to validate secession and the Culpeper Minutemen sewed Patrick Henry's "Liberty or Death" on their colors. Moreover, southern attitudes had fostered military education: eleven of the twelve private military schools in the United States were in states that seceded. Military successes of 1814 and on the border heightened secessionist confidence, and victory at Manassas (July 21, 1861) focused Confederate strategy on the aggressive tactics that President Davis had witnessed in the Mexican campaign. And yet, in the bloody fighting of "the last gentleman's war," chivalry occasionally transcended hostility, as when Generals Grant and Ingalls dispatched a silver service through the lines of Cold Harbor (July 17, 1864) to celebrate the birth of George Pickett Jr., or when, by Whittier's account, Stonewall Jackson intervened at Barbara Frietchie's defense of the Union flag. As Richmond's enthusiasm for initiative proved its extravagance, hopes shifted from the central government to the battle leaders. A Texan in the lines wrote, "When I came up here in '61, I had States Rights on my mind. . . . Now, I reckon if we're fighting for anything, we're fighting for General Lee." Even in surrender, Lee's tactical brilliance and the tenacity he inspired in an exhausted army earned universal respect.

After Appomattox (April 9, 1865), the dissolution of the Confederate army released southern military tradition to anguish and fervid recollection. In William Faulkner's *Absalom, Absalom!,* Wash Jones torments Thomas Sutpen by reminding him, "Well, Kernel, they kilt us but they ain't whipped us yet, air they?" Military aspects of the Lost Cause have perennial appeal in published memoirs, diaries, and fiction. Faulkner looked to his great-grandfather, a Civil War veteran and novelist, as prototype for the Confederate patriarch of his Sartoris clan, whose Bayard Sartoris explores a consummation of Faulkner's own 1918 R.A.F. cadetship. In postbellum dialect fiction, benevolent plantation owners are usually dignified as "Kunnel," though Mark Twain's Sherburne and Grangerford in *Huckleberry Finn* affected the rank without accepting its scruples. Outside the active military, "Colonel" re-

mains a commonplace honorific applied to a congenial visitor, a ceremonial appointee to a governor's staff, or a fast-food franchise. The popular modern perception of southern military tradition has been shaped less by history than by the cinematic stereotypes of period fiction, fraternity balls, and campus athletic rallies.

Among analysts of historic Confederate militancy, revolutionists cite Virginia's initiatives for home rule; romantics sense Simms's *Chevalier Bayard* and Scott's border novels; Celtics attribute rebel tempers, unholy yells, and fanatic attacks to Scots-Irish lineage. World War II's flamboyant George S. Patton Jr. illustrates the continuity of these factors in the national military tradition. Patton's Scottish antecedent, Hugh Mercer, survived Culloden, fled to Virginia, was wounded at Fort Duquesne, and commanded a regiment in the Revolution. George S. Patton Sr. (V.M.I., 1857) died of Union wounds after Winchester, and his namesake grandson became the cavalryman and Olympic equestrian who commanded the U.S. Third Army in Europe.

After the Civil War, the Union army resumed its national military tradition, including some prewar elements of southern origin. Westward expansion turned military attention to engineering, mapping, and the establishment of outposts on the plains and fortifications on the Pacific Coast. By applying Civil War experience and frontier instincts to constabulary actions pacifying Indians, veterans added another dimension to American military tradition and folklore, as continual historical and fictional revisions of Custer's stand (June 25, 1876) at the Little Big Horn demonstrate. A broader picture of garrison life and combat on the frontier is to be found in Charles King's novels. Owen Wister's *The Virginian* (1902) introduced the chivalrous, lone knight-errant of the plains, a stereotype hero replicated in the cinema's countless westerns. Theodore Roosevelt's enthusiasm for the frontier led to a climax of cowboy tradition in the Spanish-American War when the robust Colonel Roosevelt led Leonard Wood's "Rough Riders" up Kettle (San Juan) Hill in July 1898. The Spanish-American War signaled industrialized America's emergence as an international power. The organization of the Veterans of Foreign Wars (1899) recognized this extended breadth of American military tradition.

Determined to "speak softly, and carry a big stick," President Theodore Roosevelt strengthened the armed forces. In a decade, however, the increase would be insufficient to support the American declaration of war on Germany (April 6, 1917). Conscription, which had supplied 6 percent of the Union Army in the Civil War and would account for 67 percent of the World War I force, began within six weeks. American regulars arrived in France within three months, but conscripts required intensive training before embarking. It was January 1918 before Ambassador Stanton could declare in Paris, "Lafayette, we are here." The commander of the American Expeditionary Force, General John J. Pershing, former Cadet First Captain at West Point and a combat officer seasoned in Cuba, the Philippines, and on the Mexican border, personified the continuity of Regular Army tradition, while the commander of Battery D, 129th Field Artillery, Captain Harry S. Truman, a National Guardsman from a Missouri farm, exemplified the tradition of the minuteman called to active duty for the duration. Public conviction that America's brief involvement had been decisive in "saving the world for democracy" made November 11 a national holiday, Armistice Day, which, after subsequent wars, would be broadened to "Veterans Day."

Even as the returning A.E.F. rapidly demobilized, some farsighted Regulars were looking beyond continental defense toward plans that would facilitate mobilization should the need recur. Significant restructuring proceeded in the War Department in the 1920s, and in the next two decades the limited Regular Army developed the strategies and the professional cadre that would capitalize on the tactical innovations and advanced weaponry of World War II. American commitment to the Allied cause was restricted to increased materiel production and lend-lease agreement until the Japanese attack (December 7, 1941) precipitated a declaration of war and made "Remember Pearl Harbor!" top "Remember the Alamo!" and "Remember the *Maine*!" as an American battle cry. Conscription, already begun in September 1940, drafted more than ten million men for wartime service. Total public involvement in the war effort accentuated military tradition in the national consciousness. Within the service, airborne units and women auxiliaries were added to the tradition, and the horse disappeared completely. After the Axis surrender (Germany, May 7; Japan, September 2, 1945), maintaining occupation troops in Japan and Germany and countering aggressive Communism forestalled the headlong demilitarization that had followed World War I.

American combat operations during the Cold War called military service seriously into question. In June 1950, unexpected orders sent ill-equipped occupation troops from Japan into Korea like minutemen to counter Communist invasion from the north. The United Nations had called for assistance, but American intervention without a declaration of war made the response debatable. After initial successes gave way to serious reverses, Douglas MacArthur, Supreme Commander of the Allied Powers, denounced U.N. strategy and, in contravention of directives from his superiors, publicly advocated initiatives against China. Consequently, President Truman relieved MacArthur of his command (April 11, 1951) and in so doing reaffirmed constitutional authority. Later theater commanders in Vietnam and the Gulf War scrupulously conformed to this democratic tenet. The Korean conflict eventually stabilized in an armed truce; but as the perceived Communist danger continued, the Universal Military Training and Service Act (1951) perpetuated conscription and Military Assistance and Advisory Groups were posted to vulnerable allies. In the 1960s, the advisory mission to Vietnam escalated into heavy but indecisive combat. Although pacifist advocates and draft protesters voiced the strongest antimilitary expression since the New York draft riots of 1863, the war continued until 1973, when the Nixon Administration determined to withdraw, dispense with conscription, and move to an all-volunteer army. Initial recruiting fell short of its goals in numbers and quality, but concerted incentive and training programs raised performance levels sufficiently to cope with the technology of modern warfare. Successful operations in the Persian Gulf (1990–1991) demonstrated the competence of the volunteer force.

In a four-hundred-year history, some salient features of American military tradition have come and gone—the horse, the frontier instinct, white male fraternity; others have appeared and been absorbed—the wheels, tracks, and missiles, computer literacy, racial and gender integration. Occasionally, outlaws, fanatic cults, and anarchists have perverted it to their purposes; irresponsible gun owners have linked it to the Second Amendment to oppose gun control, but the basic tenets of legitimate military tradition remain valid. Soldierly discipline still informs respectful obedience that enables concerted, sometimes heroic action, and the value of weaponry, however advanced, continues to depend on soldiers' skill and stamina.

Jack L. Capps

See also Bacon's Rebellion; Cavalier; Civil War; Jackson, Andrew; Jackson, Stonewall; Korean War; Lee, Robert E.; Lost

Cause; *Lost Colony, The*; Mexican War; Revolutionary War (American); Smith, Captain John; Spanish-American War; Washington, George; World War I; World War II.

Stephen Vincent Benet, *John Brown's Body* (1928); Cyrus T. Brady, *Colonial Fights and Fighters* (1923); Bruce Catton, *U. S. Grant and the American Military Tradition* (1954); John Esten Cooke, *The Wearing of the Gray* (1867); Thomas W. Cutrer, *Ben McCulloch and the Frontier Military Tradition* (1993); John Hope Franklin, *The Militant South* (1956); John Fraser, *America and the Patterns of Chivalry* (1982); Gary Gallagher, *The Confederate War* (1997); John T. Graves, *The Fighting South* (1985); Richard B. Harwell, ed., *The Confederate Reader* (1957); C. Robert Kemble, *The Image of the Army Officer in America* (1973); Grady McWhiney and Perry D. Jamieson, *Attack and Die: Civil War Tactics and the Southern Heritage* (1982); Paul C. Nagel, *The Lees of Virginia* (1990); Robert H. Patton, *The Pattons* (1994); Morris Schaff, *The Spirit of Old West Point* (1907); William R. Taylor, *Cavalier and Yankee* (1961); Emory M. Thomas, *The Confederacy as a Revolutionary Experience* (1991); Russell F. Weigley, *History of the United States Army* (1967).

MIND OF THE SOUTH, THE

In 1941, W. J. Cash, an obscure North Carolina journalist, born and bred in the Piedmont South, published *The Mind of the South*. Wilbur Joseph Cash (1900–1941), who yearned to be a novelist, hoped to write a great work of historical interpretation, one that would forever explain his great obsession, the South. Reviews from academics and writers across the nation were positive. But initial sales were modest, and it would not be until the mid-1940s that his sweeping, bold book would become a classic, cited and restated by historians, scholars, and writers from many disciplines and professions. Activists during the Civil Rights Movement gained insights from Cash's resounding contentions that the white South was in the psychological grip of a racist orthodoxy kept intact by a "savage ideal" of social and intellectual conformity. *The Mind of the South* helped explain the deep historical roots of white supremacy.

Cash's own mind, fortified by Sigmund Freud and Joseph Conrad, turned on the psychology of irony and paradox—Cash's southerner was intensely individualistic and conformist, sinner and Puritan, sentimentalist and violent "hell of a fellow." Cash underscored the rhetorical nature of the southern "mind" by his own flights of rhetoric shaped by H. L. Mencken's South-baiting and scathing barbs. Cash's South was "Cloud-Cuckoo Land" where the antebellum "master class"

had forged a "proto-Dorian convention" that allowed common whites to identify with their masters. The veneration of white women bolstered the bond between whites to keep slaves in subjection and later to justify lynchings and racial segregation.

Cash's book, sustained by humor, high seriousness, and a driving narrative, was held in great esteem until historian C. Vann Woodward issued a withering critique in 1971. Woodward (who had praised the book with reservations in 1941) was deeply offended by Cash's "extravagant" style and overriding arguments. Woodward utterly rejected Cash's central argument that there was one southern "mind"—monolithic, sentimental, hedonistic, and often violent—stretching unbroken from the Old to the New South. Recent scholars have pointed to Cash's deficiencies regarding religion, gender, ethnicity, labor unions, and black consciousness. But *The Mind of the South* has champions who point to its considerable insight into southern honor and the psychology of racism. The book has never been out of print, and even some of Cash's critics quote him when it suits their purpose.

Cash would never know the great praise or the criticisms that his book—his cry from the heart—would elicit. Shortly after his book came out, Cash, suffering from alcohol withdrawal (delirium tremens) and longtime depression, killed himself in July 1941.

Bruce Clayton

Bruce Clayton, *W. J. Cash: A Life* (1991); C. Vann Woodward, "The Elusive Mind of the South," in *American Counterpoint: Slavery and Racism in the North-South Dialogue* (1971).

MINIMALISM

Minimalism is a term applied to a style of fiction that came in vogue during the 1980s, not only in southern literature but in American literature as well. Perhaps the first minimalist writer of his generation to gain widespread acknowledgment as such was the short-story writer Raymond Carver, who hailed from the Pacific Northwest and who identified Chekhov and Hemingway as two major influences. Though Carver had been writing highly economical, "minimalist," prose since the 1960s, his influence began to be felt most forcibly during the 1980s, when a whole generation of workshop writers emulated his style, especially in the genre of short fiction. This "New Fiction," as Kim Herzinger called it in 1985, might be seen as a reaction to the "maximalist" fiction of the preceding decade. In contrast to the metafictional, fantasy-laden, overwritten prose of the high postmodernists, the minimalists returned to a more realistic depiction of life, a more subdued tone and style, and, for many, a retreat from experimentation.

In addition to "minimalism," a number of other labels have been affixed to this new fiction of the 1980s. For its 1985 volume on the new fiction, the *Mississippi Review* queried a wide range of contemporary writers and journals in order to provide the following list: "Dirty Realism (*Granta*); New Realism; Pop Realism; . . . White Trash Fiction; Coke Fiction; 'Post-Alcoholic Blue Collar Minimalist Hyperrealism' (John Barth); 'Around-the-house-and-in-the-yard' Fiction (Don DeLillo); Wised Up Realism; TV Fiction; High Tech Fiction; . . . Extra-Realism; and . . . Post-Post-Modernism." Other terms that have been widely applied to minimalist fiction include "Grit Lit" and "K Mart Fiction." This list of terms offers a commentary on both the content and style of minimalism. Many of these terms observe the fiction as a merging of popular and high cultures. The term *realism* recurs so often that it seems the primary trademark of minimalism. The terms *blue collar, white trash,* and *grit lit* all indicate an awareness of the minimalists' preoccupation with a lower socio-economic strata of the American population. Perhaps only the naturalistic writers of the Depression era concerned themselves so extensively with the American poor. Minimalist writers have differed from their naturalistic forebears in that they have attempted to forego the omniscient paternalism, dogma, and do-gooder zealotry that characterized most of the Depression-era writings. Minimalists have attempted convincingly to depict the experience of a lower class from that perspective; hence, the appearance of a new generation of writers who, perhaps for the first time in the history of literature, hail not from among the wealthy but from among the lower and lower-middle classes. Among southern writers, a list of sometime minimalists might include Dorothy Allison, Lee Smith, Bobbie Ann Mason, Jill McCorkle, Clyde Edgerton, Harry Crews, Jayne Anne Phillips, Larry Brown, and Richard Ford.

Perhaps the only statement that might categorically be made about the aforementioned list of writers is that all of them would likely be uncomfortable, if not outright offended, by the label "minimalist." For example, Richard Ford writes, "It's a critical term foreign to the work. . . . It's at best a convenience for a reviewer too lazy to deal with good work on its own terms." Though Ford's statement is hardly contestable, *minimalism,* for better or worse, is the term that has been most frequently and perhaps least mean-spiritedly applied to the new realist fiction appearing in the 1980s. And while these writers are working in a variety of voices and methods, they share certain tendencies. Perhaps most important, minimalist fiction tends to be free of elaborate rhetoric, focusing instead on the observed dialogue and behavior of characters, unmediated by authorial commentary. Fred Hobson has remarked that a minimalist text requires a nonminimalist reader, a reader prepared to bring to the text all of the big questions that the minimalist writer refrains from supplying or that he or she only very unobtrusively suggests.

In southern fiction, one might trace the roots of minimalism as far back as the work of the frontier humorists, which was characterized by a direct (though often hyperbolic) treatment of rural lowlifes previously considered too crude for literature. A more recent predecessor can be found in Eudora Welty, who at first glance one would hardly call minimalist; however, in contrast to the heavily rhetorical quality of Faulkner's prose—as well as half a century of writers working under his shadow—Welty's prose is noticeably free of rhetoric. Her attention focuses on the details of objects and of people and their behaviors. She rarely explains the significance of such details but rather leaves the work of interpretation to her readers. One finds a similar restraint among many contemporary writers, such as Clyde Edgerton who, in fact, identifies Welty as his primary model.

Whether minimalism will remain such a dominant model of southern (and American) fiction at the beginning of a new millennium has been heavily debated. Many critics have observed the return of a more rhetorical, ornate, "modernist" prose, one that emphasizes "voice" rather than image and action. One might offer Charles Frazier's *Cold Mountain* or any of Toni Morrison's or Cormac McCarthy's works as an example of this new trend—novels that, one might argue, have been written in the legacy of Faulkner. While the reemergence of modernist techniques and approaches deserves notice, the continuing importance of "minimalist" methods seems equally significant. What might yield the most fruitful study is attention to the degree to which these two approaches affect and inform each other.

George Hovis

See also Grit Lit; K Mart Fiction.

Fred Hobson, *The Southern Writer in the Postmodern World* (1991); Special New Fiction Number, *Mississippi Review* 40/41 (1985); Special Short Story Theory Number, *Studies in Short Fiction* 33 (Fall 1996).

MINSTRELSY

Minstrelsy featured white musicians ritually blacking their faces and imitating the dance, song, and music of African Americans. America's first pop entertainment arose in the 1820s and 1830s mostly from folk sources and eventually became even more popular than the circus of the Old World that featured daring deeds, clowning, and man's relationship to wild animals. Especially popular in the North with the growing number of city people recently dislocated from their rural life and traditions, minstrel entertainment flourished until the 1890s. This social ritual became the commercial arena where whites explored the new experience of living in a land with blacks. Starting in the 1830s, the first generation of minstrels worked hard to learn African American traditions available only by word of mouth and imitation. But the initial respect for African American traditions dwindled, and as the minstrels grew increasingly commercialized, they began to create facile stereotypes and painful caricatures.

African American tradition was well established by the mid-eighteenth century. In the Colony of Maryland, blacks sang and danced to the "banjar" by the 1740s, and for almost a hundred years, they were the only ones who played the instrument made of a large gourd or pumpkin with a long neck attached. In the description of founding a new land in the *Maryland Eclogues, in Imitation of Virgil's*, Reverend Thomas Cradock describes the singing and enamored courtship of Pompey for his slave companion Daphen: "I sing as well as ever Negro sung. / Nor Sambo has a Banjar better strung." In 1807 Washington Irving observed, "No Long Island [N]egro could shuffle you 'double trouble,' or 'hoe corn and dig potatoes' more scientifically" than one colored dancer he witnessed.

By 1800, white plantation boys and then frontiersmen had begun to dance to the banjo. In the 1820s, the minstrels began to sing songs on horseback in the circus rings and between the acts of dramatic farces or tragedies, in tents and theaters from New Orleans to New York. These earliest minstrels sometimes borrowed Negro types, dialects, and music from the Brit-ish stage, but usually they blacked their faces and dressed in imitation of actual American plantation and riverboat Negroes. Eventually, the rural African Americans who influenced whites—the field hand Jim Crow and the boatman Gumbo Chaff—became stage types and figures as well known as the "ring tail roarer" frontiersman.

About 1832, Thomas Dartmouth Rice watched an enslaved stable hand "execute a queer dance" to a sung refrain. That night, he portrayed a Kentucky cornfield Negro by performing this song and dance between acts of Solon Robinson's play *The Rifle*. The vitality, realism, and novelty of his act, in which he sometimes used a traditional fiddle rather than the standard orchestral accompaniment, triggered an unexpected and overwhelming audience response and established the routine that led him to become the "father of American minstrelsy."

No doubt the meaning of the song for blacks and whites was as important a reason for its survival as the accompanying dance. From the point of view of whites, the song expressed the ideal image of the compliant, responsive, obedient, cheerful, well-behaved slave, who was happy to "Jump Jim Crow": "Wheel about, turn about, do jus' so, / And ebery time I wheel about, I jump Jim Crow." The descriptions of the dance in the refrain (e.g., the verbs *wheel, turn, wheel, jump*) suggest the exhausting, fast-paced, confusing demands of the slave's master. Exacting expectations are implied in the requirements to "do jus' so" and to "Jump Jim Crow." The song is in first person; the point of view is actually Jim Crow's. From a black's viewpoint, the refrain calls for almost more than a person can perform and signifies quite differently from white expectations.

In his slave narrative in 1845, Frederick Douglass suggests a similar situation with similar language while he was working as a carpenter's helper in a ship-building yard in Baltimore "at the beck and call of about seventy-five men": "At times, I needed a dozen pairs of hands. I was called a dozen ways in the space of a single minute. . . . 'Hurra, Fred! Run and bring me a cold chisel.'—'I say, Fred, bear a hand, and get up a fire quick as lightning under that steambox.'—'Halloo, nigger! Come, turn this grind-stone.' " Perhaps Douglass helps clarify the meaning of the song for us: "I was kept in such a perpetual whirl . . . I could think of nothing, scarcely, but my life."

Most black mentors of the minstrel apprentices, like the stablehand who inspired Rice, remain unidentified.

But in 1838, Rice added a "Corn Meal" skit to his act after hearing the street singer of the same name perform in New Orleans. Old Corn Meal (d. 1842) often sang "My Long Tail Blue" and "Old Rosin the Beau" (as well as his own vending song about "Fresh [Indian] Corn Meal").

Urban blacks were sometimes stereotyped as eccentric and egotistical dandies called "Jim Dandy" or "Zip Coon." But the tune that helped inspire the "Zip Coon" character is still played today and may have been one of the first indigenous American folk songs. The piece was "taken from a rough" jig-dance piece called "Natchez Under the Hill" and named after a favorite gathering place for "boatmen, gamblers, river pirates, and courtesans."

Blacks were occasionally realistically portrayed in the North as well as in the South. In 1842, Charles Dickens encountered the minstrel William Henry "Master Juba" Lane (1825–1853) in the rough Five Points district of New York City, where he had learned jigs, reels, and other dances from "Uncle" Jim Lowe, an African American who danced in saloons, dance halls, and elsewhere in the neighborhood of poor working-class whites and blacks: "Instantly, the fiddler grins, and goes at it tooth and nail; there is new energy in the tambourine; new laughter in the dancers; new smiles in the landlady, new confidence in the landlord; new brightness in the very candles. Single shuffle, double shuffle, cut and cross-cut; snapping his fingers, rolling his eyes, turning in his knees, presenting the backs of his legs in front, spinning about on his toes and heels like nothing but the man's fingers on the tambourine, dancing with two left legs, two right legs, two wooden legs, two wire legs, two spring legs—all sorts of legs and no legs—what is this to him? And in what walk of life, or dance of life, does man ever get such stimulating applause as thunders about him, when, having danced his partner off her feet, and himself too, he finishes by leaping gloriously on the bar-counter, and calling for something to drink." Lane, probably the only black in minstrelsy before 1858, won so many dance contests in the 1840s that John Diamond and other famous white dancers refused to compete with him or other blacks. Eventually, Lane left this country to pursue his career in England; he performed on stage at the Vauxhall Gardens in London in 1848.

By the 1830s, Joel Sweeney of Appomattox, Ferguson of Western Virginia, and other Upland whites (mostly Irish) began to take up the "banjar," which was more difficult to master than black dance or song, and soon put the instrument together with the Scots and Irish fiddle. By the early 1840s, Sweeney was credited—perhaps overenthusiastically—as the creator of a new banjo that had five strings and an open back made from a cheese hoop. What has confused many is that the fifth string was not the short thumb string now called the fifth string but a bass fourth string. The short string is a drone string that was actually brought from Africa and greatly assists in the rhythmic complexity at the heart of African aesthetics. The fourth string added melodic range that contributed to the Celtic love of elaborated fiddle-tune melodies. Whereas whites tend toward conservation of the ballad or tune as learned and played, African American aesthetics lead to improvisation. Some players remained in the mountains and others, like Sweeney, carried banjo music to diverse musicians and the American public through fairs, circuses, and later the enormously popular minstrel shows. Through banjo instruction books, minstrelsy provided the earliest well-documented phase of the banjo's exchange between blacks and whites.

Another identified black banjo mentor of the minstrel apprentices is John "Picayune" Butler of New Orleans. About 1830, the entertainer George Nichols "first sang 'Jim Crow' as a clown, afterwards as a Negro. He first conceived the idea from . . . a banjo player, known [along the river route] from New Orleans to Cincinnati as Picayune Butler." At least one banjo song—"Picayune Butler's Come To Town"—suggests the excitement of this black songster's arrival. It appears in one of the early banjo instruction manuals and describes the man's banjo as "a gourd, three string'd, / and an old pine stick." Picayune Butler (d. 1864) was an influential banjo player. He sang on the street for money, accompanied himself "on his four stringed banjo," and also provided Nichols with the song "Picayune Butler Is Going Away." His famous banjo songs as well as his travels prefigure the traveling country bluesman.

Butler did not take up the five-string wooden-rim banjo invented about 1842, but over the more than thirty years of his career documented, he apparently was influenced enough by white melodic interest to add a fourth string to his banjo. In 1857 Picayune Butler also played in a New York banjo contest. According to eyewitnesses, he would have won if he had "not been indisposed. Even though he broke two of his four banjo strings, he still plucked through the required waltz, reel, schottische, polka, and jig with artistry."

Eventually, a plantation skit became the typical

closing act of the routines, and by 1843 the theme of southern Negro life was the core of a new, loosely structured but conceptually unified form of entertainment for an entire evening—the minstrel show.

Southern musicians often remained close to home and possibly only three of the seventy-five leading minstrels born before 1840 were from the South. But most of the first generation of minstrels toured the South in their formative years to acquire material and musical skills. The minstrels' own claim to authenticity—even when exaggerated (as perhaps on the 1843 playbill of probably the first minstrel band including both banjo and fiddle)—acknowledged their genuine debt to African American sources: "Songs, refrains, and ditties as sung by the southern slaves at all their merry meetings such as the gatherings in the cotton and sugar crops, corn huskins, slave weddings, and junketings." The importance of this process of folk transmission and cultural exchange cannot be overemphasized, for African American musical items and style were initially available to apprentices only by ear and imitation. This method of "catching" material remained crucial during the first decade of minstrelsy for the transmission of Celtic-American fiddle tunes as well as the acquisition of banjo and other material specifically from blacks.

In *Way Up North In Dixie*, Howard Sack observes that the song "Dixie"—long credited to the white minstrel Dan Emmett of Mount Vernon, Ohio—"conjures images of the South and was first performed in the North, but the song's origins rest in the association of African Americans and European Americans on the western frontier." When asked to write a song while he was in New York, Emmett sought the help of the black Snowden family back home. The fiddle- and banjo-playing brothers performed as a family band in and seventy-five miles around Mount Vernon for whites as well as blacks.

Eventually, the robust apprenticeship of early minstrelsy faded, and the diversity of the shows evolved into commercialism, sentimentality, restricted social commentary, and stereotypes. By 1855 comic skits began to replace plantation finales, and the caricatures of blacks were confined primarily to the "contented slaves" who were "fulfilled by working all day and dancing all night" and "unhappy free" blacks. One New York critic who had visited the South earlier complained that current performances were drifting into "vile parodies, sentimental love songs, and dirges for dead wenches who were generally sleeping under the willow." Later minstrelsy sometimes surfaced in films like the first full-length film with synchronized sound— *The Jazz Singer,* starring Al Jolson—or cropped up in the twentieth century in scattered communities. But most minstrel shows remained commercially viable and popular until the 1890s, when lavish northern productions completely lost touch with their folk roots, and the social ritual of minstrelsy dwindled away.

Cecelia Conway

See also Appalachia.

Cecelia Conway, *African Banjo Echoes in Appalachia* (1995) and (with Scott Odell) *Black Banjo Songsters of North Carolina and Virginia* (CD with booklet, 1998); Karen Linn, *That Half-barbaric Twang: The Banjo in American Popular Culture* (1991); Eric Lott, *Love and Theft* (1993); Hans Nathan, *Dan Emmett and the Rise of Early Negro Minstrelsy* (1962); Y. S. Nathanson, "Negro Minstrelsy, Ancient and Modern," in Bruce Jackson, ed., *The Negro and His Folklore in Nineteenth Century Periodicals* (1967); *Phil Rice's Correct Method for the Banjo* (1858); Robert C. Toll, *Blacking Up: The Minstrel Show in Nineteenth-Century America* (1974); Robert Winans, "The Folk, the Stage, and the Five-String Banjo in the Nineteenth Century," *Journal of American Folklore* 89 (1976); Carl Wittke, *Tambo and Bones: A History of the American Minstrel* (1930).

MISCEGENATION

Marriage, cohabitation, and interbreeding between races, formally termed *miscegenation* and also referred to as racial amalgamation, has been a primal concern in southern culture from slavery to the present. In southern literature, this concern manifests itself as an examination of cultural circumstance and social responsibility. Interracial unions, throughout history, have been subject to widespread commentary, criticism, and review. Consequently, miscegenation becomes an easily recognizable literary theme. As an accomplished fact in southern culture, miscegenation threatened to refute the "cultural lies" borne in the American South about racial purity, white womanhood, and black sexuality. In a discourse on race and the South, or race within the South, black and white writers have used diametrically opposed strategies in their examination of the South's race relations and interracial relationships.

Among the first works attempting to debunk the position of proslavery apologists such as James Hammond on the subject was Harriet A. Jacobs's *Incidents in the Life of a Slave Girl* (1861), written under the pseudonym Linda Brent. Many nineteenth-century slave narratives, though primarily abolitionist material, exposed the rape and concubinage of black female slaves. Her perspective exposes the sexual advances of white slaveowners as uninvited and unwelcome. The sexual victimization of female slaves ran rampant across the slave South; Jacobs's autobiography petitions against this for herself and other female slaves. Denied the right to marry a free black man, Jacobs, in retaliation, gives birth to two children by a white man not her master, hoping to secure freedom for herself and her children. Her story of slavery and refused concubinage demonstrates the constant battle of entitlement between black female slaves and white slaveowners. Jacobs emerges resilient, battling the status quo of slavery and refusing to become a slave mistress.

William Wells Brown's *Clotel; or, The President's Daughter* (1853), unlike Jacobs's *Incidents,* examines the active love affair between slave and master. *Clotel* fictionalizes an alleged love affair between President Thomas Jefferson and his slave Sally Hemmings. Ultimately, Jefferson sells Clotel, his mulatto (or quadroon) daughter, into concubinage to Horatio Green. Clotel falls in love with Green and is devastated when he marries a white woman and plans to keep Clotel as his mistress. Unable to reconcile her parentage and her racial caste, Clotel drowns herself in the Potomac River. Brown, focusing primarily on the hypocrisy of American freedom and African American slavery, also examines the bonds and definitions of family in the racially mixed South.

Yet defining "family" in the racially mixed South brought mixed approaches, proving simple for some and difficult for others. George Washington Cable's *The Grandissimes: A Story of Creole Life* (1880) also expounds upon racial amalgamation within a family. Set in New Orleans, *The Grandissimes* examines the Creole communities and their racially mixed backgrounds. The plot centers upon two brothers, Honoré and the Darker Honoré Grandissime, whose names suggest both racial and color differences. Their community acknowledges both Honoré and the Darker Honoré as brothers of their powerful New Orleans family. Though the interbreeding between white slaveowners and black female slaves was socially accepted and sometimes encouraged, the interbreeding between white women and black men was not. Kate Chopin's "Désirée's Baby" (1893) articulates the social disdain for sexual intimacies between white women

and black men. Désirée, abandoned and adopted as a baby, marries and becomes a mother herself. When her baby takes on a dark hue, her husband, believing that she is of a racially mixed heritage, banishes her and their child from their home. Her husband considers the visibly dark child an insult to his family's bloodline. Ironically, in packing away his wife's things the next day, he discovers a letter written by his mother revealing her racially mixed heritage and, thus, his own.

The twentieth century continued to produce writers fascinated with the dynamics of interracial relationships, exploring the romantic love affairs and societal opposition experienced by interracial couples. Thomas Dixon's novels *The Leopard's Spots* (1902) and *The Clansman* (1905) greatly influenced the social attitudes toward race and miscegenation, especially in the South. In a racially biased rhetoric that advocated racial purity and propagated the sanctity of white womanhood, Dixon's novels outlined the social taboos on racial amalgamation. Although Dixon did not support slavery, he did believe that the social and political equality of African Americans led to miscegenation, which he vehemently opposed. The Ku Klux Klan recruitment movie *The Birth of a Nation* is based on Dixon's *The Clansman* and features a black man accosting and attempting to rape a white woman, whom a white-sheeted member of the Klan saves.

Three displaced black southerners, Charles Chesnutt, James Weldon Johnson, and Jean Toomer, probed the theme with more subtlety and greater understanding. Chesnutt, himself of mixed blood, frequently examined miscegenation and racial prejudice. His short-story collections *The Conjure Woman* (1899) and *The Wife of His Youth, and Other Stories of the Color Line* (1899), as well as his novels *The House Behind the Cedars* (1900), *The Marrow of Tradition* (1901), and the recently published novels *Mandy Oxendine* (1997) and *Paul Marchand F.M.C.* (1998), juxtapose these recurring themes. Johnson's *The Autobiography of an Ex-Coloured Man* (1912), a defining moment in Harlem Renaissance fiction, centers on a racially mixed man consciously abandoning his African American heritage to "pass" as a full-blooded white man. Toomer's *Cane* (1923), a modernist composite novel, is separated into three regional sections, the first set in rural Georgia. Included in this section are "Becky," "Fern," and "Blood Burning Moon," which explore the different emotional, sexual, and societal aspects of racial amalgamation. By using different racial vantage points, Toomer examines the emotional aspects of being involved in or born into an interracial relationship. Fearing *Cane*'s success would pigeonhole him as an African American writer, Toomer shied away from the marker "Negro writer" and attempted to redefine race in America. "The Blue Meridian" (1936), Toomer's most significant work after *Cane,* supports interbreeding to create a new race of "blue" people, one superior to blacks and whites.

William Faulkner recognized that miscegenation was a defining reality for the South. His best work reveals how conflicting miscegenation was for blacks and whites. *Light in August* (1932), *Absalom, Absalom!* (1936), and *Go Down, Moses* (1942) attempt to define or redefine the southern family structure. Joe Christmas, the main character in *Light in August,* is uncertain about his racial identity. Disowned by his grandfather, Christmas believes he must be half-black but says nothing when assumed to be a tanned European. Self-doubt and, later, community suspicion turn fatal for Christmas, who murders his white lover and sets her house on fire. Yet Christmas's punishment stems more from his racial identity, or nonidentity, than from the crime itself. In *Absalom, Absalom!* Thomas Sutpen sees his "grand design" fail and causes the destruction of his family because of his adherence to an ideal of racial purity. *Go Down, Moses* (1942) chronicles the racial coexistence of a white slave plantation's black and white descendants from antebellum time into the twentieth century. Change in attitudes occurs, but the pace is painfully slow. "Not yet" is the final cry of Isaac Mc-Caslin.

Margaret Walker's *Jubilee* (1966) is a loosely based biography of her great-grandmother and centers on Vyry's life as a racially mixed slave. Set in the South before and after Reconstruction, *Jubilee* seeks to understand the status of the mulatto within the southern white family. Vyry is very light-complexioned, often confused as the full-blood twin of her white half-sister. She endures abuse as a slave mulatto, and the master's daughter, but unlike her literary predecessor Clotel, Vyry does not vie for recognition as her father's daughter. Another family historian, Alex Haley, traced the ancestry of both parents. In *Roots: An American Saga* (1975) and *Queen* (1993), interracial relationships between slaveowners and female slaves surface. In *Roots,* a white man rapes and forces a slave ancestor into concubinage, ultimately impregnating her. Conversely, *Queen*'s interracial relationship, a love affair between a slave woman and her owner, produces a child, Queen. Much like Clotel, Queen is plagued by her par-

entage and consistently clamors for recognition as her father's daughter. Though Walker and Haley recreate their family history, their works reflect the common problems that female slaves and mulatto children faced.

In addition to exploring the familial aspects of miscegenation, Richard Wright and Harper Lee focused on the societal opposition to miscegenation. Wright's fiction frequently places the races in sexual and racial battles. "Big Boy Leaves Home" (1938), *Native Son* (1940), and *The Long Dream* (1958) represent prevailing notions of miscegenation as a social evil and taboo. In each of these works, the main character, a male, must flee his home after events surrounding a perceived threat to the sanctity of white womanhood. Harper Lee's Pulitzer Prize–winning novel *To Kill a Mockingbird* (1960) analyzes the attitudes about race and class in the South during the 1930s. A black man accused of raping a white woman is tried and convicted to preserve the sanctity of southern white womanhood. In recent fiction, miscegenation continues to be an important theme but is often accompanied with some friendship between blacks and whites. Elizabeth Cox's *Night Talk* (1997) centers on the friendship between two young girls in Jim Crow Georgia during the 1950s and 1960s. Racism, rape, and murder test the friendship. James Kilgo's *Daughter of My People* (1998), set in South Carolina during the 1910s, revolves around the tragic love triangle between a mulatto and two white cousins who vie for her attentions. Compounding the conflict is the secrecy and ambivalence in which they must mask their affection toward her. Donald Mc-Caig's *Jacob's Ladder* (1998), set during the Civil War, involves Marguerite, a mulatto slave, her young white lover, Duncan, and their son, Jacob. Using historical figures, *Jacob's Ladder* details the familial ties of blacks and whites and also the emotionally charged issues surrounding miscegenation in the Civil War South.

Candice N. Love

See also Abolition; Ku Klux Klan; Mulatto; Neo-Slave Narrative; Protest, Novel of; Race, Idea of; Slave Narrative.

Carol Camper, *Miscegenation Blues* (1994); David G. Croly, *Miscegenation* (1995); James Kinney, *Amalgamation* (1985); Edward Byron Reuter, *Mulatto in the United States* (1969); William J. Scheich, *The Half-Blood* (1929); John David Smith, *Racial Determinism and the Fear of Miscegenation Pre-1900* (1993), and *Racial Determinism and the Fear of Miscegenation*

Post-1900 (1993); Werner Sollors, *Neither Black Nor White Yet Both* (1997); Joel Williamson, *New People* (1995); Robert J. C. Young, *Colonial Desire* (1994).

MISSISSIPPI, LITERATURE OF

Mississippi literature has three strong strands of local cultural heritage. From its black people comes an African American legacy of African rhythms transformed into blues songs and work chants, of Christian precepts changed to friendly bantering storytelling and of dynamic, socially encoded preaching offering liberation from slavery and after emancipation (Emancipation Proclamation, 1863), from racial segregation. From its college- and university-educated white people, it has a European American tradition steeped in classical Greek and Latin languages, philosophy and mythology, Western logic and rhetoric, and stories from ancient, biblical, Shakespearean and Renaissance English and French traditions. From among its rural and laboring people, black and white, it has a memory of tall-tale telling, humor and jokes, and orally transmitted songs of hardship, life, death, and love. Thus Mississippi literature, in nearly all its later forms, is marked by storytelling, orality, lyricism, and musicality, rather than by conceptual abstractions or philosophical prose.

Not surprisingly, its dominant form is fiction, always about people or at least about personified and talking ideas or animals if not people. The poems and plays by Mississippi writers also usually have strong narratives and specific human voices.

Five national and international literary giants of the twentieth century were Mississippians. Nobel-Prize laureate (1950) William Faulkner (1897–1962) was born in New Albany, Mississippi, but spent much of his life both as a child and as an adult in Oxford, Mississippi. Poet and historical fiction writer Margaret Walker (1915–1998), winner of the Yale Award for Younger Poets (1942), was born in Birmingham, Alabama, but spent some of her early years as a minister's daughter in Mississippi and after 1949 spent the remainder of her adult life in Jackson, Mississippi's capital city. Pulitzer Prize–winning fiction writer Eudora Welty (1909–2001), the first living writer whose work has been published by The Library of America (*Welty: Complete Novels* and *Welty: Stories, Essays, & Memoir*, ed. Richard Ford and Michael Kreyling, 1998), was born and grew up in Jackson and returned as a young adult after time at the University of Wisconsin

and in New York City to spend the rest of her life in her Jackson family home. Pulitzer Prize–winning playwright Tennessee Williams (1911–1983) was born in the Episcopal rectory in Columbus, Mississippi, and spent his growing-up time in Clarksdale. Writer Richard Wright (1908–1960) was born and grew up near Natchez not far from the Natchez Trace.

Internationally renowned memoir and autobiography writers Anne Moody (1940–) of *Coming of Age in Mississippi* (1968) and Willie Morris (1934–1999) of *North Toward Home* (1967) were born in Mississippi. Moody, an African American who wrote poignantly of her maturation into a Civil Rights Movement leader, was born in Centreville. Morris, a European American who wrote of youthful development into a cosmopolitan journalist and editor of *Harper's* magazine, was born in Jackson. Will D. Campbell, born in Amite County in 1924, a white Yale-educated Baptist minister active in civil rights, wrote the much-praised autobiographical *Brother to a Dragonfly* (1977). A Mississippi memoir writer of a generation earlier, William Alexander Percy (1885–1942), was born in Greenville and wrote *Lanterns on the Levee: Recollections of a Planter's Son* (1941).

Nearly as world famous as Mississippian Elvis Presley, creator and popularizer of rock-and-roll music, is the late-twentieth-century popular author of detective fiction featuring lawyers, John Grisham (1955–). Grisham's works can be found in airport, train station, and grocery store booksellers all over the world. Grisham, the best-selling detective fiction writer of all time, has had all ten of his first ten law whodunits on the *New York Times* best-seller list, starting with *The Firm* in 1991. Grisham was educated in Mississippi, though born in Jonesboro, Arkansas. He first attended Mississippi State University as an undergraduate, then went to law school at the University of Mississippi. As a practicing attorney before becoming a full-time writer, he lived in Southhaven and Oxford and served in the Mississippi Legislature in Jackson. He still maintains a residence on a sixty-seven-acre farm near Oxford and publishes the literary-cultural magazine *The Oxford American*.

Several national award- and prize-winning contemporary fiction writers were born in Mississippi. They include Barry Hannah, born in Meridian to parents from Forest in 1942 and author of *Airships* (1978); Jack Butler, born in Alligator in 1944 and author of *Jujitsu for Christ* (1986); Ellen Douglas (pen name of Josephine Ayers Haxton), born in Natchez in 1921 and author of *Apostles of Light* (1973); Ellen Gilchrist, born in Vicksburg in 1935 and author of *Victory over Japan* (1984); Shelby Foote, born in Greenville in 1916 and author of *September, September* (1978) and the three-volume history *The Civil War: A Narrative* (1968, 1973, 1974); and Richard Ford, born in Jackson in 1944 and author of *Independence Day* (1995).

Poet Sterling Plumpp was born in Clinton in 1940. His volumes of poetry include *Half Black, Half Blacker* (1970) and *Clinton* (1976). He also has written a collection of essays (*Black Rituals,* 1972). Poet James Whitehead, author of *Domains* (1966) and *Local Men* (1979), was born in St. Louis, Missouri, in 1936 but moved to Hattiesburg in 1941 and grew up there. He also wrote the novel *Joiner* (1971).

Poet James Autry (1933–) grew up in Benton County and has published the volumes *Nights Under a Tin Roof* (1983) and *Life After Mississippi* (1989).

Poets and novelists are not Mississippi's only recognized writers. Playwright Beth Henley was born in Jackson in 1952. Her 1976 play, *Crimes of the Heart,* won the 1981 Pulitzer Prize.

Craig Claiborne (1920–2000), food editor for the *New York Times,* born in Sunflower, has written more than twenty cookbooks, including *The New York Times Cookbook* (1961) and *Craig Claiborne's Southern Cooking* (1987).

These twenty-one Mississippians by birth, growing up or coming to adulthood in Mississippi, are among those recognized nationally and internationally as Mississippi writers and also as major American writers. Their subject matter is often, but not always, the American South or Mississippi; and the characters and landscapes they create are often recognizably Mississippian. Beth Henley's three emotionally struggling young adult sisters in her first play, *Crimes of the Heart,* live in Hazlehurst. The life-changing event in the earlier life of wayward sister Meg came during Hurricane Camille on the Mississippi Gulf Coast. Tennessee Williams's dreamy glass-unicorn collector, waiting for her Gentleman Caller in *The Glass Menagerie* (1945), is the reclusive daughter of a faded belle who came from the Mississippi Delta. Ellen Douglas's traumatized Civil Rights Movement veteran in *The Rock Cried Out* (1979) lives in places with Central Mississippi–sounding names like Chickasaw Ridge and Homochitto County. William Faulkner's imaginary place, Yoknapatawpha County, is based on his home county, Lafayette.

Yet even though they frequently write about Mississippi towns and regions, these writers would probably all argue, as Eudora Welty does, that place is primarily setting and that the writer writes out of her or his consciousness of being human, writes what she or he knows, crystallized and refracted through the cultural and personal experience and artistic gift of the author. Even so, in Mississippi especially, the cultural, physical, and psychosocial location of its writers plays a large role in the realization of its literature. Eudora Welty articulates this in her article "Place in Fiction" (1955), but she also works it out in the settings of most of her works.

Although Eudora Welty did not create a single mythologized place as Faulkner did, she did enlarge and amplify life in several Mississippi places, so that her work adds a mythic dimension to contrasts of place in Mississippi alongside contrasts of class, race, gender, and quirky personality. Unlike Faulkner, who found sufficient his "own little postage stamp of native soil," Welty is a strong believer that fiction is "of the human heart," not localized, and she set the individual human hearts she invented in specific and different locations in Mississippi. These places easily stand for contrasting economic, social, racial, and cultural groups of people as well as for the local areas they come from. *Delta Wedding* (1946) is set in the Mississippi Delta, which is the northwestern section of the state along the Mississippi River from Vicksburg to the Tennessee border just south of Memphis, what historian James Cobb has called "the most southern of all places." Like writers who themselves live there, Welty depicts a Delta plantation having a white extended family with in-laws and relatives and family conflict and also the African American servants and farm workers attached to their plantation and their lives.

For *Losing Battles* (1970), her long novel of lower-middle-class rural family feuding and reunion, Welty moves her setting and people to the northeastern side of the state, the country between Corinth and Tupelo, the rural red-hill part of the state. She sets her most admired work, the story cycle *The Golden Apples* (1947), somewhat to the south and west of Jackson along the Big Black River in the central third of Mississippi. Her first novella, *The Robber Bridegroom* (1942), the work about which she received an admiring note from William Faulkner, and her important short stories "Livvie" (1943) and "A Still Moment" (1943), are set on the Natchez Trace, which runs from Natchez on the Mississippi River, which forms a border with Louisiana to the west, up through northeastern Mississippi into Alabama and Tennessee. Old Phoenix Jackson in

"A Worn Path" (1941) is walking to Natchez on a cold December day to get medicine for her grandson's lye-scarred throat.

Welty herself spent most of her life in Jackson, and some of her work is set in the vicinity of Jackson or oriented north toward Memphis or south toward New Orleans as Mississippi small-town people often are. Clay, Mississippi, where *The Ponder Heart* (1953) is set, is vaguely north of Jackson, and Uncle Daniel and other characters dream of making trips to Memphis. Mount Salus, Mississippi, the fictional place for *The Optimist's Daughter* (1969), is south of Jackson, and Laurel McKelva Hand, who lives in Chicago at the time of the novel, goes with her father and crude young stepmother, Fay, to New Orleans for Judge McKelva's eye treatment. New Orleans is a site where many Mississippians have sought expert medical treatment or migrated for urban opportunities, as the doctor from Mount Salus has in this novel. Laurel and Fay witness Mardi Gras, the pre-Lenten Carnival in New Orleans that is as familiar to many Mississippians as it is to Louisianans. Fay's family is from Texas, and Laurel's mother is from West Virginia, home of Welty's own mother.

Born into a solidly upper-middle-class family, her father an executive in the Lamar Life Insurance Company, Welty had a secure and happy childhood in a Jackson that was hardly more than a small town at the time. She writes of her childhood in *One Writer's Beginnings* (1983), her only autobiographical work, first presented as four lectures at Harvard University in 1983.

The places Welty outlined by means of settings for her Mississippi mythology are in several cases places where other writers lived and worked as well as set their fiction. Natchez, the Mississippi Delta, northern Mississippi, the university town of Oxford, and Jackson are all literary figures' birthplaces or gathering places, as well as sites in literature.

Natchez is one such literary place: Natchez, home to an annual pilgrimage of fabulous antebellum houses, location of the sacred mounds and remains of an extinct Native American tribe, the Natchez, and an important Mississippi literary site from the past and the present. White author Ellen Douglas was born there in 1921 as Josephine Ayers, descendant of a mayor of Natchez; black memoir writer Anne Moody (1940–) from Centreville, not far away, spent some years in all-black Natchez College; and African American Richard Wright lived in extreme poverty near Natchez after his birth in 1908, the year before Welty was born.

Richard Wright's life contrasts starkly with Welty's. Wright suffered the deprivations stemming from both racism and poverty in his first nineteen years in Mississippi. His works show both an anger elicited by the subjugation of blacks in the South and also an appreciation of the Mississippi landscape and people. At nineteen, Wright left for Memphis. Later he lived in Chicago and was involved in the Federal Writers' Project. His first book of short stories (*Uncle Tom's Children*, 1938) gained him significant public recognition. *Native Son* (1940), *Black Boy* (1945), *White Men, Listen!* (1957), and *The Long Dream* (1958) are all works that identified Wright as a seminal interpreter in fiction of black experience in the United States. Wright, his wife, and daughter made their home in Paris, France, from 1946 until his death in 1960; his foremost interpreter is Michel Fabre, a Paris scholar who wrote *The Unfinished Quest of Richard Wright* (1973). Many years after his death, his friend from the Federal Writers' Project, Margaret Walker, wrote a revealing biography, *Richard Wright: Daemonic Genius* (1987).

Dying before the 1960s' Civil Rights Movement brought about the desegregation of Mississippi education, government, and commerce, Wright did not live to see his work honored by formerly all-white institutions in Mississippi. Among these are the University of Mississippi, where an international conference on Richard Wright was held in 1985, and the 1992 Third Annual Natchez Literary Festival, which honored Wright's memory with a lecture by Michel Fabre.

Wright's Federal Writers' Project colleague and friend Margaret Walker moved to Jackson, Mississippi, in 1949 in the decade in which Wright settled in France. She lived there until her death in 1998. Walker preferred to be called Dr. Margaret Walker Alexander, stressing the respectful title of her earned doctorate and her married surname, in order to counter the disrespect formerly shown to African Americans, often called by whites "girl" or "boy" or given unwelcome first-name familiarity as adult women and men. Walker taught English for many years at Jackson State University, was a founder of the African American Cultural Center at the university, and helped promote the national historical designation of an early district of African American-owned businesses in Jackson, now the Farrish Street Preservation District. The street on which she lived in Jackson was renamed in her honor.

Walker's first book of poetry, *For My People*

(1942), which won the Yale Younger Poets Award, has been a signal work of emotional pride. Her novel *Jubilee* (1966), a thinly fictionalized narrative history of American blacks under slavery, during the Civil War, during Reconstruction, and beyond, has been read in universities all over the world. Based on her own family archives, Walker's novel provides sympathetic rendering of characters both black and white and extensive presentation of foods, folkways, domesticity, and plantation organization, as well as the historical sweep and disruption of the Civil War.

Natchez was home to Ellen Douglas as a child, but as an adult beginning her writing career, she made her home in another Mississippi literary center, Greenville, in the Mississippi Delta. Josephine Ayers Haxton published her first work, *A Family's Affairs* (1961), using the pseudonym Ellen Douglas to keep her identity as an author secret; however, as wide public recognition came for her novels, "Jo" Haxton continued to write as Ellen Douglas. She served as writer-in-residence at her alma mater, the University of Mississippi, and lived in both Oxford and Jackson. In addition to *Apostles of Light* and *The Rock Cried Out*, she wrote *Black Cloud, White Cloud* (1963), *A Lifetime Burning* (1982), *The Magic Carpet* (1987), *Can't Quit You, Baby* (1988), and most recently *Truth*, published by Algonquin Books in 1998.

Greenville's younger generation has also produced fine writers, noteworthy among them Ellen Douglas's poet son, Brooks Haxton (1950–), who has published *The Lay of Eleanor and Irene* (1985), *Dominion* (1986), *Dead Reckoning* (1989), and *The Sun at Night* (1995).

A Greenville literary patriarch was William Alexander Percy (1885–1942). Born into the plantation economy and planter social class that produced large landowning farmers, bankers, lawyers, and government officials, Percy was a poet (*The Collected Poems of William Alexander Percy*, 1943, and *Of Silence and Stars*, 1953). However, he is best remembered for his memoir, *Lanterns on the Levee: Reflections of a Planter's Son* (1941), and for the writers whose guardian and mentor he became.

Novelist Walker Percy (1916–1990) was William Alexander Percy's younger cousin who moved from his birthplace of Birmingham, Alabama, in 1927 to Greenville to become the elder Percy's ward. Walker Percy was eleven years old when both his parents had died. Trained as a physician, the younger Percy won the 1962 National Book Award with his first novel, *The*

Moviegoer (1961). Philosophically preoccupied with language and the meaning of human life and death, Percy has dramatized these concerns in the novels *The Last Gentleman* (1966), *Love in the Ruins* (1971), *Lancelot* (1977), *The Second Coming* (1980), and *The Thanatos Syndrome* (1987), and in the nonfiction books *The Message in the Bottle* (1975) and *Lost in the Cosmos* (1983).

Another major American writer from Greenville, Mississippi, is Shelby Foote (1916–). Foote was a boyhood friend of Walker Percy, and their close friendship continued until Percy's death. Shelby Foote's novels include *Tournament* (1949), *Follow Me Down* (1950), *Love in a Dry Season* (1951), *Shiloh* (1952), and *September, September* (1978). Equally adept at writing novels and narrative history, Foote's three-volume *The Civil War: A Narrative* is considered by many to be a kind of epic poetic narrative of the war. Recognition of Foote's authority and his fame increased when in 1990 he participated in Ken Burns's PBS series *The Civil War*.

Another Greenville writer influenced by the Percys was David L. Cohn (1897–1960). One book of his, *Where I Was Born and Raised* (1948), describing life in the Mississippi Delta, was written while he lived with William Alexander Percy.

Greenville also had a longstanding period of excellent journalism in the *Greenville Delta Democrat-Times*. William Hodding Carter II (1907–1972), born in Hammond, Louisiana, moved to Greenville in 1936 to begin serving for more than two decades as editor of the newspaper. With editorials over a long period strongly opposing racial segregation, Carter won the Pulitzer Prize in 1946. In addition to journalism, Carter wrote poems, novels, and popular history. His poems are collected in *The Ballad of Catfoot Grimes* (1964); his two novels are *The Winds of Fear* (1944) and *Flood Crest* (1947). His journalistic histories include *Where Main Street Meets the River* (1953), *Robert E. Lee and the Road of Honor* (1955), and *The Angry Scar: The Story of Reconstruction* (1959).

The Percys and their circle and Hodding Carter and his were participants in the white leadership group in Greenville. Endesha Ida Mae Holland (1944–), also born in Greenville, was not. An African American playwright, Holland was awarded the Martin Luther King Lifetime Achievement Award in 1993. Her autobiographical play *From the Mississippi Delta* ran six months off-Broadway in 1992 and has played and been well-reviewed across the country. Her first play, *Miss Ida B. Wells,* was first presented in 1984.

Holly Springs native Ida B. Wells (1862–1931)—also known as Ida Wells-Barnett—about whom Holland wrote, was an African American journalist outspoken against lynching and an advocate of women's rights. Her daughter, Alfreda M. Duster, edited *Crusader for Justice: The Autobiography of Ida B. Wells* (1970).

Northeast of Greenville and the Delta, just south of Ida B. Wells's Holly Springs in north Mississippi, in the university town of Oxford, lived Mississippi's—and some say the twentieth century's—greatest writer, William Faulkner.

Faulkner was heir to the southern tradition of treating ordinary people and local language in literature. Nineteenth-century Mississippi contributions included University of Mississippi president Augustus Baldwin Longstreet's vignettes in *Georgia Scenes* (1835), Sherwood Bonner's *Dialect Tales* (1884), and Irwin Russell's black dialect poems, *Collected Poems* (1888). Faulkner was also heir to the American local humorous tale-telling perfected by Mark Twain. Using these influences, Faulkner master-crafted the storytelling form from both black and white sources in his local Mississippi and finished his work with original creative machinations of fictional tactics and style coming from Europe in the first washes of modernism.

A genius who did not finish high school and had less than one year of college (1919–1920), Faulkner spent most of his life in Oxford, Mississippi, which he remade into Jefferson, the county seat of Yoknapatawpha County in much of his fiction. Apart from a few of his earliest years in New Albany, a few months in Canada in 1918 as a volunteer in the Royal Air Force, some young adult time spent in New Orleans, short periods in Hollywood as a film writer as an adult, and some time at the University of Virginia late in his life, Faulkner did not stray far or often from Oxford, especially from the time he bought Rowan Oak in 1930 until his death in 1962. Faulkner's first published book was *The Marble Faun,* a collection of poems that came out in 1924. But he soon recognized that his true gift was for fiction, not verse. His enormous talent and originality began to show in the flurry of extraordinary novels that came out around 1930, *The Sound and the Fury* (1929), *As I Lay Dying* (1930), *Sanctuary* (1931), and *Light in August* (1932). Many readers select these along with *Absalom, Absalom!* (1936) and stories from *Go Down, Moses* (1942), especially "The Bear,"

as his most remarkable work. These works were not well received at first and were all out of print in the early 1940s, until Malcolm Cowley collected Faulkner fiction in 1946 in *The Portable Faulkner,* which regenerated interest in Faulkner's writings. Faulkner created a social system with classes and castes of black and white people that are enlargements of both humankind and small-town and rural Mississippians. The most greedy, grasping, ill-mannered, and immoral of these people are the Snopeses, the "poor white trash" who creep steadily and surely into power and control of Yoknapatawpha County, its citizens, and its institutions. They contrast with Colonel John Sartoris, a Confederate officer, a family progenitor based on Faulkner's own grandfather, Colonel William Falkner (Faulkner added the "u" to his surname when he joined the Canadian Royal Air Force). Between them are the Compsons and the McCaslins, the merchants, storytellers, and observers of the steady decay of old values. After 1926 the Snopeses and Compsons and other Yoknapatawphans appear in most of Faulkner's works, including *The Hamlet* (1940), *Intruder in the Dust* (1948), *The Town* (1957), *The Mansion* (1959), and *The Reivers* (1962). Faulkner was elected to the National Institute of Arts and Letters in 1939 and to the American Academy of Arts and Letters in 1948, and he won the Nobel Prize for Literature in 1950. The year of his death, 1962, he received the Gold Medal for Fiction from the National Institute of Arts and Letters.

Oxford has been home to writers of the generation succeeding Faulkner. After his stay in New York as editor of *Harper's* (1967–1971), Willie Morris lived in Oxford and later in Jackson. He won prizes for *North Toward Home* and *The Courting of Marcus Dupree* (1983). Other books by Willie Morris include *Good Old Boy* (1971), *Yazoo: Integration in a Deep-Southern Town* (1971), and *Always Stand in Against the Curve* (1983).

Oxford is also where Barry Hannah lives—this prolific, much-admired and honored, and unpredictable fiction writer with a "bad boy" reputation is highly respected by other writers. A member of the American Academy of Arts and Letters, Hannah has written eleven books of fiction, including novels *Geronimo Rex* (1972) and *Nightwatchmen* (1973), a prize-winning short-story collection, *Airships* (1978), and a later short-story collection, *High Lonesome* (1996).

At times, novelist Ellen Douglas has lived in Oxford as writer-in-residence at the University of Mississippi, as has Larry Brown (1951–   ), author of *Facing the Music* (1989), *Dirty Work* (1989), and *On Fire* (1993).

Major historians live in Oxford and work at the University of Mississippi. Winthrop Jordan (1931–   ), winner of the National Book Award and twice winner of the Bancroft Prize, has written *White Over Black: American Attitudes Toward the Negro, 1550–1812* (1968) and *Tumult and Silence at Second Creek: An Inquiry into a Civil War Slave Conspiracy* (1993). Charles Reagan Wilson (1948–   ) is author of *Baptized in Blood: The Religion of the Lost Cause* (1980) and *Judgment and Grace in Dixie* (1995), as well as coeditor with William Ferris of the *Encyclopedia of Southern Culture* (1988).

William Ferris (1942–   ), a folklorist, was Director of the Center for the Study of Southern Culture at the University of Mississippi until his appointment by President Bill Clinton to head the National Endowment for the Humanities in 1997. His books include *Images of the South: Visits with Eudora Welty and Walker Evans* (1978), *Blues from the Delta* (1978), *Afro-American Folk Arts and Crafts* (1983), and *"You Live and Learn, Then You Die and Forget It All": Ray Lum's Tales of Horses, Mules, and Men* (1993).

Oxford and Greenville have been literary towns where writers interacted closely with each other. Jackson has produced important writers, but they have not been members of interactive groups for the most part. Margaret Walker lived near the longtime all-black Jackson State University where she taught, and the home that Eudora Welty's father built when she was a teenager is across the street from Belhaven College and in the neighborhood of formerly all-white Millsaps College, where Welty served as writer-in-residence for a time and where there is now a professorial chair named in her honor.

As a young adult in Jackson, Welty was part of a friendship group that included Nash Burger (1908–   ), historian and journalist who in 1945 went to New York as editor of the *New York Times Book Review*.

Born in the next generation on the same Jackson street where Eudora Welty was born was Richard Ford, one of the most highly praised writers of the 1990s. He has written *A Piece of My Heart* (1976), *The Ultimate Good Luck* (1981), and *Rock Springs* (1987), as well as *The Sportswriter* (1986) and its Pulitzer Prize–winning sequel, *Independence Day* (1995).

Jacksonian poet James Whitehead, a contemporary of Ford, taught for a while at Millsaps College before becoming head of the creative-writing program at the University of Arkansas.

Jacksonian novelist Ellen Gilchrist, who won the American Book Award with *Victory Over Japan* in 1984, was frequently heard on National Public Radio in the 1980s. Other fiction of hers includes *In the Land of Dreamy Dreams* (1981), *The Annunciation* (1983), *Light Can Be Both Wave and Particle* (1989), and *Starcarbon* (1994).

A younger Jacksonian writer, Beth Henley, lives in Los Angeles since becoming a spectacular success. Two of her plays, *Crimes of the Heart* and *The Miss Firecracker Contest* (1981), have been made into feature films, and Henley won both the Pulitzer Prize and the New York Drama Critics Circle Award for *Crimes of the Heart*. Others plays include *The Debutante Ball* (1991) and *Abundance* (1990).

Unlike Jacksonians Margaret Walker and Eudora Welty, the generations of writers who came after them did not choose to remain in Jackson but to live in the West, East, and North. This perhaps makes for a useful closing commentary on literature of Mississippi: Mississippi literature is national literature, and sometimes international, at the dawn of the twenty-first century; but the voice, stories, culture, and sense of place still resonate uniquely with the U.S. South and its Mississippi.

Gayle Graham Yates

See also Centers for Southern Studies; Faulkner, William; Jackson, Mississippi; Mississippi, University of; Mississippi Delta; Mississippi River; Oxford, Mississippi; Welty, Eudora.

Ann J. Abadie, Aleda Shirley, and Susan M. Glisson, eds., *Mississippi Writers: Directory and Literary Guide* (1990); Dorothy Abbott, ed., *Mississippi Writers: Reflections of Childhood and Youth* (4 vols.; 1985–90); John Griffin Jones, ed. and interviewer, *Mississippi Writers Talking* (2 vols.; 1982–83); James W. Loewen and Charles Sallis, *Mississippi: Conflict and Change* (1974); Robert S. McElvaine, new intro., *Mississippi: The WPA Guide to the Magnolia State,* Golden Anniversary Ed. (1938, 1988); Peggy W. Prenshaw and Jesse O. McKee, eds., *Sense of Place: Mississippi* (1979); David G. Sansing, *Mississippi: Its People and Culture* (1981).

MISSISSIPPI, UNIVERSITY OF

The University of Mississippi's third president (1849–1856), Augustus Baldwin Longstreet (1790–1870), was a writer whose lasting literary reputation rests on

Georgia Scenes (1835), humorous stories in which he displays impartially southerners of all social classes and types.

Writers of literature have been important to the University of Mississippi down to its 1998 sesquicentennial celebration. Institutionally, it has been sponsor since 1974 of the annual international Faulkner and Yoknapatawpha Conference on the work of its 1919–1920 student and postmaster William Faulkner (1897–1962); host since 1993 to an annual Oxford Conference for the Book; and site since 1977 of the Center for the Study of Southern Culture. Intellectually, the Faulkner conferences have been led by English Department faculty members Evans Harrington (1925–1997), himself a fiction writer (*The Prisoners*, 1956), and essayist and editor Ann Abadie (1939–). Abadie and founding director William Ferris (1942–) of the Center for the Study of Southern Culture have commissioned literary works such as *Mississippi Writers: Reflections of Childhood and Youth*, edited by Dorothy Abbott (4 vols.), and a major reference work, the *Encyclopedia of Southern Culture*, edited by Charles Reagan Wilson and William Ferris (1989). Ferris, a folklorist (*Blues from the Delta*, 1979), was appointed by President Clinton in 1997 to head the National Endowment for the Humanities.

University-trained Mississippi journalists Hodding Carter (1907–1972), author of *Southern Legacy* (1950), and Frank E. Smith (1918–1997), author of *Congressman from Mississippi* (1964), wrote to oppose racism and segregation in Mississippi. In 1961, when racial conflict erupted into riots over the University's admission and enrollment of African American James Meredith, historian James W. Silver (1907–1988) wrote of social forces he believed to be racism's cause in *Mississippi: The Closed Society* (1963).

University of Mississippi graduates who became significant writers include Stark Young (1881–1963), theater critic for the *New Republic*, translator of Chekhov's plays, and fiction writer (*So Red the Rose*, 1934); Hubert Creekmore (1907–1966), editor, translator, poet, and novelist (*The Chain in the Heart*, 1953); Charlotte Capers (1913–1996), columnist for the *Jackson Daily News* and author of *The Capers Papers* (1982), for whom the state's Archives and History Building in Jackson was named in 1982; fiction writer of eight books Ellen Douglas (1921–), pseudonym of Josephine Ayres Haxton (*The Rock Cried Out*, 1979; *A Lifetime Burning*, 1982; *Can't Quit You, Baby*, 1989); Robert Canzoneri (1925–), creative-writing

director at Ohio State University and autobiography and fiction writer (*Barbed Wire and Other Stories*, 1970); and poet James Autry (1933–), author of *Nights Under a Tin Roof* (1983).

Important writers-in-residence at the University have included Barry Hannah (1942–), writer of eleven books of fiction including novels *Geronimo Rex* (1972) and *Never Die* (1992); Willie Morris (1934–1999), fiction writer and autobiographical essayist (*North Toward Home*, 1967); and Ellen Douglas.

Gayle Graham Yates

See also Centers for Southern Studies; Oxford, Mississippi; Mississippi, Literature of; Faulkner, William.

Allen Cabaniss, *The University of Mississippi: Its First Hundred Years* (1971); David Sansing, *The University of Mississippi: A Sesquicentennial History* (1999).

MISSISSIPPI DELTA

Even the name of this legendary region is more impressionistic than precise, for this is no delta in any geographic sense but rather, an alluvial plain. Encompassing approximately seven thousand square miles and more than ten counties from just south of Memphis, Tennessee, at its northern point, it stretches east to include the Yazoo River plain, west to Greenville, and south almost to Vicksburg, a vast bottomland. It was the unsurpassed richness of the alluvial soil that produced the dark, impenetrable forests described by travelers of the eighteenth and early nineteenth centuries as a seething jungle and by those who came to live there as, simply, The Swamp. That rich soil beckoned to planters, promising a sustainable cotton kingdom that had eluded them in states to the east. Over time, as the forbidding wilderness was settled, the discouraging swamps and canebrakes were transformed into miles of fertile fields that could more hopefully be called the Delta.

Even before it became a literary domain, early images of the Delta crystallized around certain fearsome features of the landscape and life there. These images surfaced again and again in accounts by Europeans and by natives, by correspondents of eastern newspapers, and by planters and the wives of planters. Foremost was the river itself and the annual floods. Below Memphis, the river both widened and showed a surface turbulence that warned of a terrific force. The timing of the floods was not entirely predictable, the depth of water even less so, and the backwater could linger so long that crops and health were compromised. Then there was the prodigious wildlife. Reports were that the hunting was like nothing people had ever seen before. But among that wildlife were extraordinary numbers of bears and also panthers whose nocturnal screams one apparently never got used to. And death by disease was reputed to be commonplace; the 1830s saw a particularly high incidence of cholera, malaria, typhoid fever, and dysentery. Bad weather in the form of hailstorms, killing frosts, and backwater reduced or ruined crops and contributed to yet another syndrome, increased financial risk and spiraling debt. Naturally a place so inaccessible and sparsely populated became a refuge for outlaws; but worse still was the casual acceptance of violence by the general population. Murder for the slightest cause was reported weekly or daily; the *code duello,* though banned by statute in 1820, continued in practice, and lynching often precluded a legal process. One additional frontier curse, constantly complained of, was excessive alcohol consumption. On top of all this, slavery added a dimension of human and political drama destined to reverberate down through time. In short, the very wildness of the Mississippi Delta presented formidable obstacles that were at the same time fascinating as elements of myth.

Samuel Clemens loved the Mississippi River where he trained as a cub pilot, and in 1882 he returned to the river to write a travel narrative, which became *Life on the Mississippi* (1883). Therein are sounded some of the themes for which the Delta would become known in song and story. In addition to the famous account of Clemens's realization of his boyhood dream of becoming a river pilot, the book contains almost every kind of story of the day, including one rather complicated, ghoulish tale of crime, revenge, and hidden treasure. Clemens plants at the very beginning of the book a reference to Napoleon, Arkansas, and a rendezvous he has there; he also describes the effects of the 1882 annual flooding, more and more apparent as the steamboat *Gold Dust* passes Memphis. And then he turns the episode into a tall tale and a joke on Mark Twain, who is stunned to discover that the recent flood has washed away the entire town, concealed money and all. Clemens turns his attention to economic fact in the chapter immediately following the Napoleon yarn, chapter 33, where Greenville is called "a growing town" but one where rates of interest play havoc with the profits on cotton and where the business relations

between white planter and Negro laborer have grown chilly since "The War," discouraging circumstances that the new Calhoun Land Company's plans for cash payments and a bank in Greenville, it was hoped, would relieve.

The next writings about the Delta that reverberated as far as Twain's were the reports of Theodore Roosevelt's bear hunt of 1902. The famous Holt Collier, former slave, Confederate soldier, and legendary hunter, was brought in to choose the site. Three journalists were allowed to participate. But despite Collier's care, bears were scarce on the ground. As a result, when he refused to shoot a cornered bear, corraled with the best of intentions for Roosevelt's hunting pleasure by some of the party, the president enhanced his reputation for sportsmanship. It was when this story circulated in so many versions on the East Coast that Brooklyn merchant Morris Michton designed a toy bear and named it "Teddy."

In 1927 a hundred-year flood breached the Mississippi levees, dislocating one million people; in the 1930s and 1940s a literary renascence swept the South; and in the 1960s the Civil Rights Movement came to the Delta and was met with murder. Is it any wonder that the Mississippi Delta has come to occupy a place of deep imaginative fertility in the literary life of the nation? It is William Alexander Percy who so memorably describes in *Lanterns on the Levee* (1941) the charm of the land itself, the people, and walking the levee to watch for breaks in the dike during flood time. One of the last chapters in his book is an account of the harrowing 1927 flood and of his role in the relief effort. And it was Percy's Greenville houseguest David Cohn who wrote, in *God Shakes Creation* (1935), the famous definition, "The Mississippi Delta begins in the lobby of the Peabody Hotel in Memphis and ends on Catfish Row in Vicksburg." Cohn's is a sensitive, subjective examination of economic, cultural, and racial pressures of that society.

Then there is the legacy of William Faulkner, whose story "The Bear" immortalizes the intuitive lessons of the wilderness as his "Old Man" captures both the devastation of flood time and the psychology of a prisoner of the infamous Parchman Farm. And although the Delta is not the spot where Thomas Sutpen built his plantation, his tragic ambition and betrayal in *Absalom, Absalom!* (1936) echo the success motive of Delta planters and indeed of the entire nation. Eudora Welty, another writer of the Southern Renascence, treats the fear and filth of the dreaded floods in "At the Landing" and gives a comic turn to the mythology of Parchman in *Losing Battles* (1970) when Jack Renfro escapes because he's expected home for his family reunion. In "Powerhouse" she evokes the music for which the region is famous. The narrator of "Where Is the Voice Coming From?" is a racist sniper like the one who killed Medgar Evers. But her best-known work about the Delta is an irresistible picture of a place where "most of the world seemed sky"—the novel *Delta Wedding* (1946). The marriage of Dabney Fairchild to the Shellmound Plantation overseer Troy Flavin serves as the occasion for a penetrating study of intimate personal and class relationships. Like Faulkner and Welty, Tennessee Williams is an artist of international stature whose powerful plays owe much to the legend of the Delta. There is Amanda Wingfield's memory-dream of jonquils and gentleman callers in *The Glass Menagerie* (1945), Blanche Dubois's aristocratic pretensions in *A Streetcar Named Desire* (1947), and the heirs' struggle for Big Daddy's plantation in *Cat on a Hot Tin Roof* (1955), all of which have indelibly marked the world's view of the South.

In the decades following the flowering of southern writing, the Delta city Greenville continued to nurture writers in the tradition of the open-minded William Alexander Percy. It was here that resistance to the white supremacist Theodore Bilbo centered. Besides Hodding Carter, who wrote the novel *Flood Crest* (1947) as well as prize-winning editorials, there were Ben Wasson, Charles Bell, Beverly Lowry, and Shelby Foote. Percy's nephew Walker Percy lived in Greenville as an adolescent, but later lived and set his novels in Louisiana. Richard Wright was born near Natchez and lived briefly in Greenville and longer in Memphis, and although his masterpiece *Native Son* is set in Chicago, his autobiography *Black Boy* (1945) evokes the wretched and despairing life of blacks in such Mississippi River towns. Ellen Douglas looks unflinchingly at the love-hate relationships of whites and blacks in stories and in the novel *The Rock Cried Out* (1979).

It has been said that there are more writers per square foot in Greenville than any other place, but Greenville is not the only place that produced notable authors interested in the Delta. Stark Young from nearby Panola County wrote *So Red the Rose* (1934) about the havoc wreaked upon the worthwhile values of plantation culture during the Civil War. Elizabeth Spencer's *Fire in the Morning* (1948) follows a hill-country man seeking wealth in the Delta. The Delta remains predominantly rural, black, and impoverished, and the lurid violence of the civil rights era still exerts a hold on the popular imagination. After more than two hundred years, the Delta's fearsomeness is undiminished and its attraction for writers seems unabated. Willie Morris, wherever he roamed, always returned to the Yazoo Delta world that "his people" settled, back to the same "specters of poverty and race" that still haunt that world. He came back, he wrote in *Terrains of the Heart* (1981), because "there is something that matters in a state which elicits in its sons and daughters of both races, wherever they live, such emotions of fidelity and rage and passion."

Rebecca Roxburgh Butler

See also Faulkner, William; Greenville, Mississippi; Louisiana, Literature of; Mississippi, Literature of; Rivers.

John M. Barry, *Rising Tide: The Great Mississippi Flood of 1927* (1997); James C. Cobb, *The Most Southern Place on Earth: The Mississippi Delta and the Roots of the Regional Idea* (1992); David L. Cohn, *Where I Was Born and Raised* (1948); Alan Lomax, *The Land Where the Blues Began* (1993); David M. Oshinsky, *"Worse Than Slavery": Parchman Farm and the Ordeal of Jim Crow Justice* (1996); Paul Schullery, *The Bear Hunter's Century* (1988).

MISSISSIPPI QUARTERLY

The *Mississippi Quarterly* is published by the College of Arts and Sciences at Mississippi State University. Though the journal's stated interests cover a broad range of disciplines in southern studies (social sciences and humanities), in recent years it has focused primarily on southern literature and history.

From the year of its inception, 1948, through volume 6 (1952–53), it was titled the *Social Sciences Bulletin,* and it included articles on a diversity of general academic topics literary and otherwise. In October 1953, beginning with volume 7, it became the *Mississippi Quarterly* and in 1968 added *The Journal of Southern Culture* as its subtitle. In cooperation with the Society for the Study of Southern Literature, the journal undertook the publication of the "Annual Checklist of Scholarship in Southern Literature"; the "Checklist" appears in the spring number from 1969 through 1987, after which it appears as an annual supplement that subscribers receive at no additional cost.

Special issues devoted to individual southern writers continue to be published periodically; since 1964 the summer issue—with the exception of volume 40 (1987) when the special appeared as the fall number—has been devoted to William Faulkner. James B. Meriwether served as guest editor for the Faulkner specials from 1964 through 1987.

John K. Bettersworth was the founding editor; he edited the first ten volumes (1948–1958) and chaired the editorial board until his death in 1991. Robert B. Holland followed Bettersworth as editor until 1967, when Scott C. Osborn assumed the editorship. Peyton W. Williams Jr. was editor from 1970 through 1987. The current editor is Robert L. Phillips Jr.

Robert L. Phillips Jr.

See also Periodicals, 1900 to 1960; Periodicals, 1960 to Present.

MISSISSIPPI RIVER

"The Great Mississippi, the majestic, the magnificent Mississippi, rolling its mile-wide tide along, shining in the sun," reminisced Mark Twain in *Life on the Mississippi* about the river that saturated his life and work. Celebrated in *The Adventures of Tom Sawyer* and *Adventures of Huckleberry Finn* and other of his works, the Mississippi River was to Mark Twain, and continued to be to subsequent writers of belles-lettres, both attractive and mysteriously dangerous. As a passenger on a steamboat, Mark Twain saw grace, beauty, and poetry in "the majestic river"; as a pilot, he was disillusioned about the romance and beauty he had earlier found in the river, yet affirmed: "There never was so wonderful a book written by man; never one whose interest was so absorbing, so unflagging, so sparklingly renewed with every re-perusal" ("Old Times on the Mississippi," incorporated into *Life on the Mississippi*).

The name *Mississippi* comes from an Algonquian word *Meschasipi* or *Mesipi,* meaning "big river" or "great river." The Spanish called it *Rio Grande.* The Chippewas called it *Mee-zee-see-bee,* Father of Waters. Likewise, Herman Melville in "The River," a piece discarded from *The Confidence-Man,* defined "Mississippi" as meaning "the father of a great multitude of waters." These waters, as Timothy Flint wrote in *A Condensed Geography and History of the Western States; or, The Mississippi Valley* (1828), have a longer course than any other river (measured from the head of

the Missouri River). As the artery of America's heartland, the Mississippi River drains a basin reaching from New York in the east to Idaho in the west, with the main stream flowing by or through the southern states of Missouri, Kentucky, Tennessee, Arkansas, Mississippi, and Louisiana.

A full report on the Mississippi River in southern literature would include belletristic treatments of the Mississippi River Valley as connected with such matters as geography, ethnography, exploration, history, travel, military actions, politics, economics, boating, folklore, music, piracy, gambling, and floods. William Faulkner evokes much of this in his essay "Mississippi": "In the beginning, the obsolescent, dispossessed tomorrow by the already obsolete: the wild Algonquian—the Chickasaw and the Choctaw and Natchez and Pascagoula—looking down from the tall Mississippi bluffs at a Chippewa canoe containing three Frenchmen—and had barely time to whirl and look behind him at a thousand Spaniards come overland from the Atlantic Ocean, and for a little while longer had the privilege of watching an ebb-flux-ebb-flux of alien nationalities as rapid as the magician's spill and envanishment of inconstant cards. . . . Deswamping that whole vast flat alluvial Delta-shaped sweep of land along the Big River, the Old Man: building the levees to hold him off the land long enough to plant and harvest the crop: he taking another foot of scope in his new dimension for every foot man constricted him in the old: so that the steamboats carrying the baled cotton to Memphis or New Orleans seemed to crawl along the sky itself."

Poet and essayist William Alexander Percy in *Lanterns on the Levee* (1941) presents the geography of the flat Mississippi Delta country bounded on the west by the Mississippi, "which coils and returns on itself in great loops and crescents, though from the map you would think it ran in a straight line north and south." Again, "With us when you speak of 'the river,' though there are many, you mean always the same one, the great river, the shifting unappeasable god of the country, feared and loved, the Mississippi."

Early-nineteenth-century ruffians are portrayed by William Gilmore Simms in *Border Beagles: A Tale of Mississippi* (1840). Simms's Ellis Saxon is based on John Murrell, an outlaw of the 1820s and 1830s known as "the Great Western Land Pirate."

Rafting on the Mississippi brings to mind both the fictional Huckleberry Finn and the larger-than-life Mike Fink, whose exploits are now a part of folklore.

Steamboats on the Mississippi figure not only in Mark Twain's works but also in such works as Grace King's story "The Little Convent Girl"; Benjamin Drake's "Putting a Black-leg on Shore"; and James D. Brewer's detective novels *No Bottom* (1994), *No Virtue* (1995), and *No Remorse* (1997). Historical fiction dealing with the western battles of the Civil War, especially those at New Orleans, Vicksburg, and Port Hudson, of necessity refer to the river—the eventual Union control of which played a major part in the ultimate loss of the Confederacy.

The river appears popularly in "The Levee Song," later changed to "I've Been Working on the Railroad" with its incongruous reference to the paddlewheel steamboat *Dinah*. Although not southern in origin, musical numbers associated strongly with the South are "Old Man River" from Jerome Kern's *Showboat* and Stephen Foster's "Way Down in Cairo." Will S. Hays treats steamboating in "Roll Out! Heave Dat Cotton." Of course, the blues and jazz are intimately connected with Memphis, New Orleans, and St. Louis on the river.

Floods evoke the most powerful literary treatments of the Mississippi River. George W. Cable in *Dr. Sevier* writes: "The huge, writhing river, risen up above the town, was full to the levee's top, and, as though the enemy's fleet was that much more than it could bear, was silently running over by a hundred rills into the streets of the stricken city." The climax of his story "Belles Demoiselles Plantation" is the sinking of the plantation "down, down, down, into the merciless, unfathomable flood of the Mississippi." William Alexander Percy in *Lanterns on the Levee* writes how every few years the river "rises like a monster from its bed and pushes over its banks to vex and sweeten the land it has made." Faulkner's story "Old Man" presents a convict's rescue of a woman and his struggle for survival in the great flood of 1927. Through this experience, the river becomes part of the man's "past, his life; it would be a part of what he would bequeath, if that were in store for him." A historic yet poetic evocation of the flood is John M. Barry's *Rising Tide: The Great Mississippi Flood of 1927 and How It Changed America* (1997). And in "Jesus Knew," New Orleans author E. P. O'Donnell says, "A flood works softly, softly, mantling the meadows in cool fluid sorrow."

Mississippi writers Eudora Welty and Elizabeth Spencer beautifully evoke the river in their stories. Welty in "At the Landing" writes: "The river went by immeasurable under the sky, moving and dimly catch-ing and snagging itself, freeing itself without effort, heavy with its great waves of drift, deep with stirring fish." Spencer in "Indian Summer" tells how "the riverbanks and the bayous seem to have nothing to do with the river itself, which flows magnificently in the background, a whole horizon to itself from the banks, or glimpsed through willow fronds—the Father of Waters not minding its children."

The river has stirred memorable poetic expressions. Cable in *The Grandissimes* (1880) responded: "How dream-like the land and the great, whispering river!" Although not usually associated with the South, Missouri-born T. S. Eliot thought in *The Dry Salvages* (1941) that "the river / Is a strong brown god—sullen, untamed and intractable, / . . . The river is within us." Louis Daniel Brodsky, Faulkner expert and poet, also from Missouri, considers himself in "Spectator" to be "Spelled by Old Man's aura." And Charles G. Bell in "Home-Crossing" says, "I saw the river glowing under the moon / In sweeping turbulence and liquid sound."

Richard D. Rust

See also Mississippi, Literature of; Mississippi Delta; Rivers.

God of the Country: A Voyage on the Mississippi River, photography by Nathan Benn and selections from American literature (1985); *Mississippi Observed: Photographs from the Photography Collection of the Mississippi Department of Archives and History with Selections from Literary Works by Mississippians,* ed. Carol Cox, Sheree Hightower, and Cathie Stanga (1994); Frank McSherry Jr., Charles G. Waugh, and Martin Harry Greenberg, eds., *Mississippi River Tales* (1988); Mary Ellen Snodgrass, "The Mississippi River," in *Encyclopedia of Southern Literature* (1997).

MISSOURI, LITERATURE OF

One inevitably associates the literature of Missouri with the celebrated name of Mark Twain, and rightly so. However, the following major figures in the history of American Literature all, like Twain (and sometimes longer than Twain), lived in Missouri and are part of its literary heritage: T. S. Eliot, Marianne Moore, Langston Hughes, Kate Chopin, Howard Nemerov, Maya Angelou, and Tennessee Williams. Other Missouri writers of all but comparable merit and importance include Laura Ingalls Wilder and her daughter Rose Wilder Lane, Sara Teasdale, Robert Heinlein, William Burroughs, Fannie Hurst, William Least Heat-

Moon, Winston Churchill, John Neihardt, Zoë Akins, E. W. Howe, and Jack Conroy. There are in addition a significant number of strong contemporary writers, both of poetry and fiction, whose careers constellate around the two major universities within the state, Washington University in St. Louis and the University of Missouri in Columbia. For the purpose of surveying the rich variety of Missouri writers, past and present, well known and not so well known, this entry will divide the literature of Missouri according to five different regions of the state.

The St. Louis area, with its long history, mystery, and majesty of the confluence of the Mississippi and Missouri Rivers, has been either home or else a stopping place for writers from its beginnings. In the nineteenth century, William Harris organized the St. Louis Philosophical Society and in tandem with German and English newspapers and journals brought national visibility to the St. Louis literary community. German immigrant Carl Schurz arrived after the Civil War as editor of the *Westliche Post.* He became state senator in 1869, later secretary of the interior, and penned a biography of Henry Clay. Joseph Pulitzer, who had been a reporter for Schurz and the *Westliche Post,* purchased the *St. Louis Dispatch* and *Post,* uniting them to form the *Post-Dispatch,* a leading newspaper in the West. In his will, he established the Pulitzer Prizes to recognize outstanding writers. Eugene Field, author of "Wynken, Blyken, and Nod" and other children's verse, was born in St. Louis and began as a journalist at the *St. Joseph Gazette.* By the end of the nineteenth century, the city was home to novelists, poets, and playwrights who would ultimately bring it fame.

Kate Chopin returned to her native St. Louis from Louisiana after the death of her husband, Oscar, in 1882. Chopin continued to write short stories with the precision and irony of Guy de Maupassant, but the storm of criticism that followed in the wake of her publication of *The Awakening* in 1899 threatened to end her career. Winston Churchill, also Missouri born, spent many years in New England, but his novels *The Crisis* (1901) and *The Crossing* (1904) drew on his St. Louis background. In the early twentieth century, William Marion Reedy's *Mirror* introduced the work of St. Louis writers Fannie Hurst, Zoë Akins, and Sara Teasdale. Teasdale won the 1918 Columbia University Poetry Prize for *Love Songs,* published the previous year, and Zoë Akins won first the Pulitzer Prize for her dramatization of Edith Wharton's *The Old Maid* in

1935, and then the Hollywood Oscar for her screenplay of it.

Two of the most important poets of this century have early and important ties to St. Louis. Marianne Moore was born in Kirkwood, a St. Louis suburb, and spent her childhood there. In the 1920s she edited the *Dial,* an important literary journal. Her poetry was honored throughout her life, earning her every major literary award, from the Pulitzer and Bollingen Prizes to the National Book Award, as well as membership in the American Academy and Institute of Art and Letters. Equally important, if not more so, is T. S. Eliot, likewise born in St. Louis, whose grandfather founded Washington University. Although he emigrated to England in 1914, where he eventually became a British subject, Eliot claimed that Missouri and the Mississippi made a deeper impression on him than any other part of the world. Indeed, the name "Prufrock," made so famous by Eliot's early poem, is taken from a St. Louis furniture store. Moreover, the opening section of "The Dry Salvages" from his masterpiece *Four Quartets* (1943) is Eliot's most enduring literary monument to St. Louis and to the history and mythic power of the Mississippi River.

The major American playwright Tennessee Williams also lived for a time in St. Louis, and his time-honored play *The Glass Menagerie* (1945) evokes the mood, atmosphere, and place names of the city in the early part of the century. On a more popular front, Fannie Hurst, who graduated from Washington University, was to become the highest-paid short-story writer in the world during the 1920s; and Sally Benson's autobiographical novel *Meet Me in St. Louis* (1942) became a Judy Garland film of the same name. Benson wrote stories for the *New Yorker* as well as numerous screenplays, including *Bus Stop* and *National Velvet.*

In recent times, Washington University has attracted preeminent literary men and women of letters, such as the distinguished philosopher and novelist William Gass. His *Habitations of the Word* won the National Book Critics Circle Award in 1985. Gass is a member of the American Academy and Institute of Arts and Letters. The late Howard Nemerov, also from Washington University, was U.S. poet laureate from 1988 to 1990. His *Collected Poems* (1977) display great intellectual depth as well as social insight and technical skill. Other major writers associated with Washington University are the late Stanley Elkin, author of *George Mills* (1982), and Mona Van Duyn,

U.S. poet laureate from 1992 to 1993, the first woman named to the post.

Among African American writers of note from the St. Louis area are Gerald Early, who has written extensively on sports and American culture as well as an engaging family subjects, such as his charming book *Daughters* (1994). Likewise, Patricia and Fredrick McKissack have won many honors, including the Coretta Scott King Award, for their books for young people, especially biographies of important African Americans. Finally, although she is no longer a resident, St. Louis-born Maya Angelou, author of *I Know Why the Caged Bird Sings* (1970), has profoundly explored racial and sexual oppression in both poetry and prose. Still another St. Louis-born author was William Burroughs, who became famous for his experimental novels, especially *Naked Lunch* (1959), and his influence on the Beat Movement writers.

Central Missouri was the original seat of the Missouri Writers Guild, one of the oldest writers organizations in the U.S. It was founded in Columbia in 1915 and now has chapters throughout the state. Central Missouri can also boast its association with the legendary John Neihardt. Neihardt, a grand poet and novelist of the Native American experience, lived in Branson and Columbia, where he taught at the university. His *Black Elk Speaks* (1932) is the unforgettable record of a Sioux holy man, and his epic poem *A Cycle of the West* (1949) portrays the struggle for the frontier. Jack Conroy, a native of Moberly, had a distinguished career as the author of realistic fiction such as *The Disinherited* (1933), which is set near Moberly. He also became a close associate of Gwendolyn Brooks and other writers. Fulton, Missouri, where British statesman Winston Churchill delivered his famous "Iron Curtain" address, was known earlier from the success of its native son Henry Bellamann's novel *King's Row* (1940), later made into a 1942 film.

Lincoln University in Jefferson City was the academic home of Lorenzo Greene, coauthor of *Missouri's Black Heritage* (1980, rev. 1993), a pioneering study of the African American experience in Missouri. Greene was also associated with Carter G. Woodson, the father of black history. The dean of the School of Journalism at the University of Missouri in Columbia, Frank Luther Mott, wrote the five-volume *A History of American Magazines* (1938), winner of both Pulitzer and Bancroft Prizes, as well as *Golden Multitudes* (1947), a history of best-sellers. The university in Columbia has long drawn, to a degree only slightly less

than Washington University in St. Louis, a number of eminent writers. William Peden, for example, founded the University of Missouri Press, which today publishes about sixty titles a year, including many by Missouri authors; Peden authored the novel *Twilight at Monticello* (1973) and many short stories. His spouse, Margaret Sayers Peden, is the award-winning translator of major Latin American writers, including Carlos Fuentes, Isabel Allende, and Pablo Neruda. Still another prolific colleague of the same era was poet and novelist Thomas McAfee, author of *Rover Youngblood: An American Fable* (1969).

Other names connected with Columbia are William Trogdon, known best by his literary name William Least Heat-Moon. After graduating with a Ph.D. from the University of Missouri, Moon traveled across America to create works such as *Blue Highways* (1983) and *PrairyErth* (1991), yet he maintains his home near Columbia and teaches periodically at the university and at Stephens College. Other well-known writers at the university include poet-spouses Rod Santos and Lynne McMahon, poet Anand Prahlad, fiction writer Gladys Swan, and novelist Speer Morgan, author of *Belle Starr* (1979), who edits the prestigious journal the *Missouri Review*. The university is also home to literary biographers William Holtz (Rose Wilder Lane) and Mary Lago (E. M. Forster). Finally, mid-Missouri is the seat of the American Audio Prose Library, founded and directed by Kay Bonetti Callison. Callison has conducted 140 interviews with major prose writers; these have been purchased and aired on radio stations throughout the United States.

Northern Missouri is, of course, the region that produced Mark Twain. Born Samuel Langhorne Clemens, Twain immortalized the river town of his youth, Hannibal, even though he was anxious to get away from it and see as much of the world as possible. He took the nom de plume Mark Twain, which meant, in steamboat usage, to navigate back into safe waters; and Twain did, in fact, receive his pilot's license at age twenty-four. He was to become one of the greatest American writers in its history with the books that recreated his region and town, such as *Adventures of Huckleberry Finn* (1885), arguably the greatest single American prose classic, as well as *The Adventures of Tom Sawyer* (1876), *Life on the Mississippi* (1883), and a plethora of magnificent shorter works. Ernest Hemingway declared that American literature proper began with *Huckleberry Finn,* and Twain's stylistic inventiveness, figurative language, and vernacular voice in that book and elsewhere give some credence to that claim. Twain dealt with the major social conflicts of his times in many of his books, yet he was able to combine engaging characters with insightful social criticism, usually in tandem with massive doses of humor—humor that was sometimes light, sometimes dark. His books and acerbic wit—as in the posthumously published *Letters from the Earth* (1962)—still provoke laughter, outrage, and controversy.

Two other writers who hail from northern Missouri are Edgar Watson Howe, author of *The Story of a Country Town* (1883), which is set in Gallatin and Bethany; and Dale Carnegie, the author of *How to Win Friends and Influence People* (1936), who was born and spent his early years in Maryville. Maryville and its college are also home to poets Jim Barnes, William Trowbridge, and John Gilgun. Finally, journalist Walter Cronkite and novelist and essayist Ron Powers were born in St. Joseph and Hannibal, respectively.

Southern Missouri has spawned a number of writers, especially from the Ozark area, and yet the two best-known authors from the region are Langston Hughes and Laura Ingalls Wilder. Hughes was a native of Joplin (the same town that bears the name of musician-composer Scott Joplin) and described his Missouri childhood in his autobiography *The Big Sea* (1940). Hughes was to win lasting fame as the creative genius behind the Harlem Renaissance, with poetry that fuses with great power the black experience and the rhythmic cadences of jazz. America's "darker Walt Whitman," as he sometimes put it, Hughes continued as one of the most influential and revered of African American writers, distinguishing himself as poet, playwright, prose writer, journalist, and pioneering anthologist of African American authors. His widely syndicated "Jesse B. Semple" or "Simple" columns depicting daily life and changing mores among African Americans continued until his death.

Laura Ingalls Wilder lived in Mansfield and became famous for the "Little House" books. She wrote her novels at the urging of her daughter, Rose Wilder Lane, who was a well-known professional writer with ties to Sherwood Anderson and others. Although she had written articles for *The Missouri Ruralist*, Laura Ingalls Wilder did not publish her first book until age sixty-five, which opens the strong possibility, according to biographer William Holtz, that daughter Rose Wilder Lane provided much of the real structure and narrative substance for them. In either case, the "Little House" books capture in striking detail her experiences of life on the prairie at the turn of the century.

Other Southern Missouri writers as well as Ozark authors, past and present, include Leonard Hall, Robert Vaughan (author of 250 books and the screenplay for *Andersonville,* 1996), Vance Randolph (collector of Ozark folktales), Harold Bell Wright (who wrote *The Shepherd of the Hills,* 1907), Ralph McCanse ("The Road to Hollister"), Elmo Ingenthron (*Indians of the Ozarks Plateau,* 1970), and Forsyth's Mary Elizabeth Mahnkey, known as "poet laureate of the Ozarks."

Present-day authors also include Janet Dailey from Branson, one of the best-selling authors of historical fiction and romances in America; Ellen Gray Massey, editor of the Ozarks quarterly *Bittersweet*; Ozark conservationist Charlie Farmer; Sue Hubbell (*A Book of Bees*); Jory and Charlotte Sherman, prolific writers of westerns; Joan Banks of Joplin; children's writer Robert C. Lee (*It's a Mile From Here to Glory,* 1972), and a number of others of virtually comparable merit.

Perhaps the best-known literary figure from the Kansas City Area is Robert Heinlein, who was born in Butler, moved to Kansas City in his youth, worked as a page at the Kansas City Public Library, and eventually had a forty-year award-laden career. His novels and short stories, including the well-known *Stranger in a Strange Land* (1961), define the maturation and importance of science fiction as a genre. Another Kansas City native was Edgar Snow, the author of *Red Star Over China* (1938), which describes China in the 1930s and the emergence of Communism in that country.

Painter Thomas Hart Benton moved to Kansas City in 1935 and lived there until his death, where he wrote his autobiographical culture study, *An Artist in America* (1969). Ernest Hemingway once worked for the *Kansas City Star* and credited editor C. G. Wellington in the development of his prose style. Novelist Evan S. Connell has captured the essence of upper-middle-class Kansas City life in his novels *Mrs. Bridge* (1959) and its companion volume *Mr. Bridge* (1969). Richard Rhodes, writer of fiction and nonfiction, won both the Pulitzer Prize and the National Book Award for *The Making of the Atomic Bomb* (1986). Another well-known nonfiction writer, Calvin Trillin, who publishes in the *New Yorker,* revisits his hometown of Kansas City in his various autobiographical writings, such as *Messages from My Father* (1996).

Kansas City is also the seat of several fine poets as well as some highly respected literary journals. Poet

Gloria Vando Hickok was a founder of *Helicon Nine,* one of the country's leading small magazines, as well as The Writer's Place, a center for literary activity. Poet Stanley E. Banks reflects African American pride and leads poetry jams at various Kansas City clubs and bookstores.

James McKinley edits *New Letters,* a fine literary magazine, as well as *New Letters Review of Books.* Robin Wayne Bailey is known for *Shadowdance* (1996) and other fantasy novels. Conger Beasley Jr. writes novels, short fiction, and poetry, and John Mort has described the Vietnam experience in widely praised short stories.

Early Kansas City journalist and historian John N. Edwards wrote extensively on the Civil War in the West, and his articles and editorials did much to elevate Jesse James into a folk hero. The late children's author and playwright Cena Christopher Draper set many of her books in the Warrensburg area, near Kansas City. Warrensburg also hosts the annual Children's Literature Festival, which began in 1968 and each year continues to bring many children to Central Missouri State University in Warrensburg, where they can meet some of their favorite authors.

Richard A. Hocks

See also Ozarks; Twain, Mark.

Thomas F. Dillingham, Madeline Matson, and Rebecca Schroeder, *Missouri's Literary Heritage* (1996); Alice Irene Fitzgerald, *Missouri's Literary Heritage for Children and Youth: An Annotated Bibliography of Books About Missouri* (1981); Elijah L. Jacobs and Forest E. Wolverton, *Missouri Writers: A Literary History of Missouri 1780–1955* (1955); Richard H. Jesse and Edward A. Allen, eds., *Missouri Literature* (1901); Duane G. Meyer, *The Heritage of Missouri* (1982); Frank Luther Mott, ed., *Missouri Reader* (1964).

MOBILE, ALABAMA

In his 1954 Lippincott Prize–winning novel *The Untidy Pilgrim,* Eugene Walter claims that "down in Mobile they're all crazy . . . [it] is sweet lunacy's county seat." Home of the country's first Mardi Gras celebration, this charming Gulf Coast city has evoked a wide range of creative emotional responses. At times a literary center of the state and region, it has been a significant port for both literary immigrants and exiles since being established at its present site in 1711. The early adventuresome European experience in and around Mobile

Bay found a host of chroniclers across time and literary genres. The eyewitness accounts of André Penicaut and others engendered many historical novels. Two by southern writers are Andrew Lytle's *At the Moon's Inn* (1941) and Frances Gaither's *The Painted Arrow* (1931).

During the nineteenth century, Mobile may have been more of a home to writers than a supplier of distinctive local material to write about. Residing here for significant periods were Sol Smith and Joseph M. Field of theatrical and Old Southwest–humor fame; William Russell Smith, Alexander Beaufort Meek, and Thomas Cooper De Leon, important pioneers of belles-lettres in Alabama; and Joseph Holt Ingraham, creator of exciting adventure romances and religious best-sellers. At times before, during, and after the Civil War, Abram Joseph Ryan, Augustus Julian Requier, Henry Lynden Flash, and Theodore O'Hara also lived in Mobile, gaining it designation as the "Capital of Lost Cause Poetry." (Ironically, after a short antebellum residence here, Rhode Island native Henry Howard Brownell found poetic inspiration in witnessing Union victory in the Battle of Mobile Bay in 1864.) Particularly impressive, however, are the nationally and internationally known literary women of nineteenth-century Mobile, including Octavia Walton LeVert, Augusta Jane Evans Wilson, Elizabeth Whitfield Croom Bellamy, Mary McNeil Fenollosa, and Amélie Rives. Wilson, whose *Beulah* (1859) is set in Mobile, became one of the nation's most phenomenally successful novelists.

Plainly one heir of this independent, feminist legacy was Marie Stanley (Marie Layet Sheip), who authored *Gulf Stream* (1930), a controversial novel about miscegenation. A later distinctly Mobile book dealing with Civil Rights–era race relations is Roy Hoffman's *Almost Family* (1983).

Mobile's most critically acclaimed writer is a native who lived many of his years away from the city but whose life and fiction clearly evidence its influence. Called by Alistair Cooke "the unrecognized genius of our time" and ranked by him "a whole ionosphere above Faulkner," William March (William Edward Campbell, 1893–1954) published seven novels and two collections of short stories. He is best known for his first and last, both somewhat atypical books, *Company K* (1933) and *The Bad Seed* (1954). Growing acclaim is now being garnered by Albert Murray, whose African American boyhood in Mobile he memorably recreated in *Train Whistle Guitar* (1974).

Celebrity came to Mobile's Winston Groom with

the film version of *Forrest Gump* (1986), which like Groom's *As Summers Die* (1980), also made into a movie, draws from a native's knowledge of the city and its environs. Two affecting portrayals of youthful experience on Mobile Bay's Eastern Shore, Robert Bell's *The Butterfly Tree* (1959) and Mark Childress's *V for Victor* (1988), provide fine unrealized film possibility. Making his mark first as a musician, Mobile and Margaritaville denizen Jimmy Buffett has also scored respectably as a writer of Gulf Coast fiction.

The books that best capture the unique essence of twentieth-century Mobile in fiction are Julian Lee Rayford's *Cottonmouth* (1941), Eugene Walter's *The Untidy Pilgrim* (1954) and *The Byzantine Riddle* (1985), and Franklin Daugherty's *Isle of Joy* (1997). Considered chronologically, these four move from the obviously autobiographical to the more imaginative, from classic emotional local-color realism through the sparkling bittersweet to sardonic hilarity. While Rayford sensuously recreates the earthy street milieu of Mobile, Walter provides introduction to the wonderfully idiosyncratic but typical characters of a higher realm of city society. Daugherty's witty satire is his account of an attempt to make Mobile postmodern without its ever having gotten to modernism. All born here, Rayford (1908–1980), Walter (1921–1998), and Daugherty (1950–) had long and distant residences elsewhere before each was drawn back to live in his city by the bay.

A number of contemporary creators of poetry and nonfiction prose call Mobile home even if they inhabit other places. While poets Patricia Storace and Julie Suk and memoirist Frye Gaillard reside at least several states northward, Sue Walker and Jay Higginbotham continue to live and write in Mobile. To all, however, the city is a muse. More fittingly called "Port Paradox" in the view of Eugene Walter, it has been extraordinarily, compellingly inspirational to writers for almost three centuries.

Bert Hitchcock

See also Alabama, Literature of.

Caldwell Delaney, *A Mobile Sextet* (1981); Tom Franklin and Barry R. Nowlin, eds., *Mobile Bay Tales: Essays & Stories About a Region* (1991).

MODERNISM

Taking modernism to be the twentieth-century literary movement that in the West follows literary realism and naturalism, one finds that easily recognizable traces of the imagist aesthetic championed by Ezra Pound and the experimental novel perfected by James Joyce began to appear with increasing frequency in southern works published after 1922. Less-obvious indicators of the emerging aesthetic are discernible, however, in Ellen Glasgow's experiment with French Symbolism in *The Deliverance* (1904), wherein she uses an elderly lady unrealistically rendered blind by the northern invasion to represent, in the manner of Maurice Maeterlinck, the mind-set that the South often fell into following the Civil War. In the same period, James Branch Cabell was writing, in the guise of romances, biting satires often compared to the fiction of Anatole France. Cabell's later use of Freudian subjects and symbols, again in the guise of historical romance, especially in *Jurgen* (1919), showed that a modern spirit was replacing the old sense of loyalty and nostalgia that too frequently marked southern writing before Glasgow began her campaign of critical realism.

In 1922 the first issue of the *Fugitive* magazine appeared in Nashville, Tennessee, providing an outlet for poems by John Crowe Ransom, Allen Tate, Robert Penn Warren, Donald Davidson, and other writers intent on bringing American poetry into the contemporary movement by applying lessons learned from a variety of modernist and premodernist poets including Pound, T. S. Eliot, and Thomas Hardy. Ransom was especially accomplished in writing tight, crisp stanzas informed by ironic satire, sharp images drawn from nature, and a diction employing brilliant anachronisms much the way Emily Dickinson had done. Among his best works are his dramatic and bitter defense of loyalty to the southern soil, "The Antique Harvesters," and the caution against lovers who fail to seize the day, "The Equilibrists." Davidson exhibited modernist poetic savvy when he treated the saintly Robert E. Lee with dramatic irony in "Lee in the Mountains" (1938). In 1926 Tate published an early version of "Ode to the Confederate Dead," among the greatest southern poems in that it dramatizes the conflict at the heart of many southerners in the early twentieth century between an obligatory loyalty to the place and its past heroes, on the one hand, and a saner need to join with the rhythms of nature in order to avoid the "ravenous grave" that dwelling on the past becomes.

Southern fiction quickly assimilated modernist techniques when Evelyn Scott, Jean Toomer, and Glasgow experimented during the early 1920s with varying combinations of impressionism, stream of consciousness, and symbolic realism. Scott's *Narrow House* (1921) and *Narcissus* (1922) made important early contributions in these areas, as did Toomer's *Cane* (1923), the most brilliant book from the Harlem Renaissance of the 1920s. Here Toomer develops a poetic version of rural African American speech, gives the agrarian enterprise a spiritual dimension, and employs the figure of the Black Madonna in the suggestive fashion that Joyce's mythic method perfected in *Ulysses* (1922). Glasgow's *Barren Ground* (1925) similarly invokes the Jason and Medea myth to parallel a story of the contemporary South while exploiting resources of modern psychology, both Freudian and Jungian, for characterization, for symbols, and in stream-of-consciousness presentations. Her *The Romantic Comedians* (1926) created a complex and "sound psychology" in order to contrast the calcified thinking of tradition with the "babbling" modern spirit.

In 1929, to ignore the influence of modernist approaches on southern fiction was no longer possible, for in that year Thomas Wolfe published *Look Homeward, Angel* and William Faulkner, *The Sound and the Fury*; the two southerners thereby emerged as leading American practitioners of the modernist novel pioneered by Joyce. Wolfe's first novel combined a Freudian perspective of culture derived from Sherwood Anderson with a view of the artist echoing D. H. Lawrence and Joyce, among others. The most obvious modernist features, however, were a series of devices borrowed from *Ulysses*. These include experiments with stream of consciousness, peripatetic chapters composed of discontinuous scenes, a catechistic chapter, frequent mythic allusions and mythic structural parallels, parodies that unmask the disguised sexual content of childhood adventure and romance stories, and shifts in style that range from rich vernacular dialogues and mock-epic narrations to intensely lyrical, even rhymed, descriptions. The chapter that sets roughly fifty familiar quotations from revered English poems in irreverent contexts echoes *The Waste Land* rather than *Ulysses*.

If Wolfe's use of Joyce was both flashy and subtle, Faulkner's experiments were subtle and challenging. Wolfe's absorption of the new aesthetic sometimes went skin-deep; Faulkner's soaked to the core. His Benjy episode may sound like Hemingway, his Jason like Huck Finn, but his Quentin is Stephen Dedalus's fraternal twin. Although Faulkner would continue with Joycean shifts of style and point of view as he wrote *As I Lay Dying* (1930), he, like Wolfe, felt com-

pelled to develop a voice of his own, the way he was already doing in the Dilsey section of *The Sound and the Fury*. Faulkner's evolution led to the time-enriched prose found in *Light in August* (1932), *Absalom, Absalom!* (1936), and the later fictions. Wolfe seems to have looked to the early work in progress from Joyce's *Finnegans Wake* (1939) and to the fiction of Proust to craft the language and time experiments that distinguish *Of Time and the River*, which Scribner's published in 1935, before the novelist completed his revisions. His later posthumous, unfinished fictions reflect the satirical style of Sinclair Lewis and the pared-down expectations of much fiction published during the Great Depression, but Wolfe never wrote as sparely as his Mississippian contemporary, Richard Wright.

Since Wolfe and Faulkner, modernist approaches have been a mainstay of southern writing. Southern poets often employ a sort of "country surrealism" perfected by James Dickey, although the confessional impulse explored by Robert Lowell and associates influenced the later Robert Penn Warren, Dave Smith, James Seay, and others. In fiction, Katherine Anne Porter, Warren, and Eudora Welty made distinctive use of modernist methods in fictions such as Porter's "The Jilting of Granny Weatherall" (1929), Warren's *All the King's Men* (1946), and Welty's *The Golden Apples* (1949). As late modernism incorporated the elements of existential thought, it continued to dominate the method of Walker Percy and the early John Barth, the latter soon to emerge as leader of American postmodernists. A number of significant southern novelists, including Reynolds Price, Doris Betts, Anne Tyler, Harry Crews, Lee Smith, and Cormac McCarthy, continue to exploit the varied resources of modernism, although from time to time their fictions exhibit tendencies identified with minimalist, ultraviolent, confessional, magical realist, and postmodern writing.

In literary criticism, Ransom, Tate, Warren, and Cleanth Brooks led the New Critical wing of American modernism with their essays, books, anthologies, and textbooks. In southern drama, Lillian Hellman began treating modern psychosexual issues as early as 1934 in *The Children's Hour* and larger cultural problems in *The Little Foxes* (1939). By far the greatest southern playwright of the modern period was Tennessee Williams, whose 1944 drama *The Glass Menagerie* (1945) remains a masterpiece combining expressionist and surreal elements with the story of a sensitive young man's family as southern as Wolfe's Gants or Faulkner's Compsons. While experimenting here and there with other techniques, contemporary southern play-wrights such as Beth Henley, Marsha Norman, Preston Jones, and Horton Foote work chiefly within a modernist-realist aesthetic.

Julius Rowan Raper

See also Postmodernism.

Joseph Blotner, *Faulkner: A Biography* (1984); Cleanth Brooks, *Modern Poetry and the Tradition* (1939); David Herbert Donald, *Look Homeward: A Life of Thomas Wolfe* (1987); Frederick J. Hoffman, *The Art of Southern Fiction* (1967); C. Hugh Holman, *Three Modes of Southern Fiction: Ellen Glasgow, William Faulkner, and Thomas Wolfe* (1966); John Crowe Ransom, *The World's Body* (1938) and *The New Criticism* (1941); Julius Rowan Raper, *From the Sunken Garden: The Fiction of Ellen Glasgow, 1916–1945* (1980); Louis D. Rubin Jr., *Writers of the Modern South: The Faraway Country* (1963); Tjebbe A. Westendop, *Robert Penn Warren and the Modernist Temper* (1987).

MULATTO

Mulatto, a term used to define a person of mixed ancestry, specifically part black (African) and part white (European), originated from the word *mule,* on the premise that such a union would produce a sterile offspring. The earliest recorded use of the word as racial designation is in Drake's *Voyage* (1595). In the U.S., the term took on political, legal, and economic significance during slavery, particularly with the 1662 passing of a Virginia statute prohibiting intermarriage and relegating mixed-race children to the status of the black mother. This statute had the effect of condoning the rape of black women by white men while affirming the social need for racial purity. But such laws as the Virginia statute could not prevent the inevitable: that some people of mixed race would "pass" as white, living among and marrying white people. Even as most states in the late 1700s were defining mulattos as those with one-quarter black ancestry, the literal determination was less scientific and based heavily on behavior and physical appearance. Eventually, "mulatto" came generally to refer to all people of mixed race, including quadroons and octoroons. The growing numbers of such people in black communities helped to create more complex hierarchies of color and bondage within and outside of those communities. For example, lighter-skinned slaves, often the master's offspring, were usually assigned housework. Furthermore, where earned

freedom was possible, they were more likely to be set free. Thus, in 1850, only 7 percent of slaves were considered mulatto, but 43 percent of free blacks in the South were so classified. Clearly then, as a literary and social trope, "mulatto" is an unstable category, calling into question the notion of fixed racial identity. It is in this context that issues of racial "science" were hotly contested, especially after the Civil War. Works by white supremacists, such as Thomas Dixon's *The Leopard's Spots* (1902), presented racial purity as a matter of biological survival; and, on the other hand, works by African Americans, as in the scientific studies collected in the *Atlanta University Publications* (edited by W. E. B. Du Bois beginning in 1898), showed that there was no scientific case "against the intermingling of the world's races," and disproved—by demonstrating the sound physical, mental, and moral health of mulattos—the idea that people of mixed race were "degenerates." African American novelists made this case as well, as in Charles Chesnutt's *House Behind the Cedars* (1900) or James Weldon Johnson's *Autobiography of an Ex-Coloured Man* (1912).

The mulatto tradition in southern literature is complicated particularly by two factors: the author's racial/cultural self-identity, and the gender of the mulatto character. The first issue—the racial designation of the author—is often crucial to how the mulatto character is engaged in the literary work. In the tradition of African American literature, mulatto characters are employed in early fiction, for example Harriet Wilson's *Our Nig* (1859) and William Wells Brown's *Clotel* (1853); and in slave narratives, most notably Harriet Jacobs's *Incidents in the Life of a Slave Girl* (1861). These uses often reveal the complexity of race in slave life, specifically the tensions created by hierarchies of race and color; highlight rape (of black women by white slave owners) and hypocrisy (concerning conjugal relations between black men and white women, and in rare cases, between black women and white men); and deny the doctrine of racial superiority/inferiority. Mulatto characters such as Sappho Clark in Pauline Hopkins's *Contending Forces* (1900) or William Miller in Charles Chesnutt's *The Marrow of Tradition* (1901) underscore not only the falsity of race constructs but also the moral implications of such constructs. Though some critics have asserted that mulatto characters often function as a valorization of whiteness and an internalization of black racial inferiority, recent criticism has held to the idea of the mulatto as a politically and rhetorically deconstructive device that, as

Ann du Cille says, "insinuate[s] into the consciousness of white readers the humanity of a people they otherwise constructed as subhuman."

In general, mulatto characters by white southern writers before the Civil War are depicted either as torn, confused, and sympathetic; or as unruly, proud, or even crazed. Invariably, the particular characterization of the mulatto can be connected to the author's position on the question of slavery. Some early representations are found in Richard Hildreth's *The Slave* (1836), whose protagonist Archy Moore is rebellious and reinforces the idea of a bifurcated self-consciousness; Joseph Holt Ingraham's *The Quadroone* (1841), whose characters Renault and Azelie are prototypical mulatto constructions; and Oliver Bolokitten's *A Sojourn in the City of Amalgamation* (1835). E. D. E. N. Southworth's *Retribution* (1849) also is noteworthy here, for her character Minny is a quintessential tragic octoroon prone to swooning. After the Civil War, there is a shift in the use of mulatto characters; in novels by white and African American authors alike, such characters often underscored losses of cultural identity and heritage. Mark Twain's *Pudd'nhead Wilson* (1894), George Washington Cable's *The Grandissimes* (1880), Chesnutt's *The Marrow of Tradition*, and Hopkins's *Contending Forces* are examples.

The second consideration—the character's gender—reveals the mulatto as a location of desire. Male mulattos, if "cooperative," often enjoyed certain class and social advantages—e.g., greater access to education. However, female mulattos—commonly referred to as mulattas—were subject to more constraining and dangerous conditions: they were deemed sexually desirable, praised for the beauty of their European-like features, and considered fragile and submissive. As a result, they were preyed upon by white males and aroused the white mistress's sexual antagonism. Cassy in Harriet Beecher Stowe's *Uncle Tom's Cabin* (1852) is perhaps the most famous mulatta construction in American literature. Cassy's beauty makes her attractive to Simon Legree, but Stowe also represents the mulatta as potentially deranged, at least psychically unruly.

Although Cassy as a mulatta has been considered tragic because of the horrors she endures and her separation from her daughter, her character is not entirely representative of the tragic mulatta/o, a subgenre of the mulatto construction in literature. The tragic mulatta/o —most often a woman—is prone to fainting and is hopelessly split by her "dual" heritage. Narratives of tragic mulattas are situated within Victorian and sentimentalist traditions and most often are predictable, dramatic tales that utilize tropes of darkness and light, secrets, marriage, and death. Although tragic mulatto characters were often used to argue against miscegenation, their very presence underscores the instability of race as either a biological or social category.

It follows that when the mulatta/o character is presented marginally or superficially, she or he is reduced to a caricature or symbol. However, when the character's consciousness is centrally explored, as in Nella Larsen's *Quicksand* (1928) and *Passing* (1929), or in Chesnutt's novels, such characters emerge as complicated individuals who are neither simply troubled nor psychically wounded, tragic nor triumphant.

Kevin E. Quashie and Bert Bender

See also Slave Narrative; Stowe, Harriet Beecher; Twain, Mark.

Judith R. Berzon, *Neither Black nor White: The Mulatto Character in American Fiction* (1978); Ann du Cille, *The Coupling Convention: Sex, Text and Tradition in Black Women's Fiction* (1993); Paula Giddings, *When and Where I Enter: The Impact of Black Women on Race and Sex in America* (1984); James Kinney, *Amalgamation!: Race, Sex and Rhetoric in the Nineteenth-Century American Novel* (1985).

MULE, THE

In the opening chapter of William Faulkner's *Light in August* (1932), Lena Grove enters Mississippi "watching then as it unrolls between the limber ears of the mules," a perspective natural enough in a state whose mule population peaked in the decade of that novel's publication at over 350,000. Faulkner's literary landscape is inconceivable without mules. Mules bring Old Ben's body back to camp in "The Bear" (1940), cascade in the floodwaters of *As I Lay Dying* (1929) and *Old Man* (1939), provide one of the Snopeses with material for insurance fraud in "Mule in the Yard" (1950), and fulfill in various ways what Faulkner calls "that burden-bearing doom with which their eunuch race was cursed" in book after book across the decades of his career.

Not only Faulkner but, in fact, most southern authors include mules in their work. At least thirty southern fiction writers in this century employ dead mules for various literary purposes, and many more write about them on the hoof. Fictional mules range in character from the endearing Lee Jackson in Carson Mc-Cullers's *The Heart Is a Lonely Hunter* (1940), through the hilariously uncooperative mule Joe in Ferrol Sams's *Run with the Horsemen* (1982), to the murderous kicker ultimately executed for his crime in Larry Brown's *Dirty Work* (1989). A mule funeral occurs in Zora Neale Hurston's *Their Eyes Were Watching God* (1937). Mules serve as symbols for the plantation system in Arna Bontemps's *Black Thunder* (1936) and Richard Wright's "The Man Who Was Almost a Man" (1940), as cover for a moonshine operation in Doris Betts's "The Dead Mule" (1965), and as emergency rations in numerous Civil War stories, notably James Street's "All Out With Sherman" and "They Know How" (1945). Among hundreds of nonfictional accounts of mules in the South, some of the most engaging are muletrader Ray Lum's oral history, *You Live and Learn: Then You Die and Forget It All* (1992), Harry Crews's autobiography *A Childhood* (1978), and Joshua Lee's *With Their Ears Pricked Forward: Tales of Mules I Have Known* (1980).

The importance of mules in southern literature of course reflects the importance of mules in southern life, at least until very recent times. The first American mules were produced in Virginia by George Washington, who bred to some of his draft mares a jackass received as a gift from the king of Spain. The mule (*Equus caballus x asinus*) proved ideal for southern farm life, being sure-footed, economical to feed, strong on stamina, and long of life. (They are, of course, also strong on stubbornness and have a tendency to become dangerous when perturbed—as Faulkner observed in *The Reivers* [1962], one will "work for you patiently for ten years for the chance to kick you once"—but some mule handlers consider this simply as adding elements of challenge and sport.)

In their heyday in the South, prior to about 1950, mules provided farm labor, transportation, and assistance in hunting, especially the kinds involving thick timber and hounds—James Battle Avirett's *The Old Plantation* (1908) gives an account of mules on a bear hunt remarkably similar to Faulkner's fictionalization. The largest plantations bred and raised their own mules; but the more usual practice was to buy full-grown animals raised mainly in Tennessee, Missouri, and Kentucky, often in sizes for special use—the largest for hauling timber and for work on the big sugar and rice plantations, the smallest for mine duty and pack-animal service in the mountains. The most common type was the general-purpose "cotton mule" that grew to between a half-ton and fourteen hundred pounds. Mules come in most of the colors that horses display, with dark brown, black, and grey predominating. Almost all mules are sired by jacks, but when the horse is the male parent the offspring is called a "henny" or "hinny." Mules, like many hybrids, are unable to reproduce.

Although the era of the working mule is over, there remains a rich legacy, not only in the literature described above but also in our speech. One may be as stubborn as a mule, but if he is flexible in his travels he lets a mule's rear end be his compass. His favorite shotgun and whisky may both kick like a mule, and something may please him enough to make him grin like a mule eating briars, especially if he makes enough money to burn up a wet mule or has forty acres and a mule without mortgage.

Jerry Leath Mills

Harry Crews, "The Mythic Mule," *Southern Magazine* (October 1986); Pete Daniel, *Breaking the Land* (1985); William R. Ferris, *Mules & Mississippi* (1980); Jerry Leath Mills, "Equine Gothic: The Dead Mule As Generic Signifier in Southern Literature of the Twentieth Century," *Southern Literary Journal* (Fall, 1996) and "The Dead Mule Rides Again," *Southern Cultures* (Winter 2000).

MYSTERY AND DETECTIVE FICTION

Except for the acknowledged masterpieces of Edgar Allan Poe, the fountainhead of the genre, and stories by William Gilmore Simms gathered in *Martin Faber: The Story of a Criminal and Other Tales* (1837), one can find few examples of southern mystery fiction in the nineteenth and early twentieth centuries: Eugene Hall's 1886 novel *The Master of L'Etrange* (combining elements of both the romance and the murder mystery); Kentucky native Hallie Ermine Rives's mostly forgettable mysteries, such as *A Fool in Spots* (1894) and *Smoking Flax* (1897); the very popular stories of Melville Davisson Post and Irvin S. Cobb, published in the *Saturday Evening Post* in the early part of this century; and a few mystery novels, such as James Hay's *The Winning Clue* (1919), and *The Bellamy Case* (1925). However, this genre, particularly the novel, exploded onto the literary scene in the 1980s and 1990s when many southern mystery writers found themselves winning the top mystery awards. Carolyn Hart won the Agatha Award for her Low Country novel *Something*

Wicked (1988) and again for *Dead Man's Island* (1993); Louisiana native James Lee Burke the Edgar Award for *Black Cherry Blues* (1989) set in New Orleans; Julie Smith the Edgar for *New Orleans Mourning* (1991), another New Orleans–based mystery. Best-selling author Patricia Cornwell won top awards, including the Macavity and the French Prix du Roman d'Aventure, for *Postmortem* in 1991. In 1993, North Carolina's Margaret Maron became affectionately known as "the quadruple queen of mystery" when she won four of the top literary prizes—the Edgar, the Agatha, the Anthony, and the Macavity—for her first Deborah Knott novel, *Bootlegger's Daughter*. Virginia-based Sharyn McCrumb also garnered top awards for her mysteries: the Agatha in 1994 and the Macavity in 1995 for *She Walks These Hills*, and a second Agatha in 1995 for *If I'd Killed Him When I Met Him*.

The common element in most mysteries is the commission of murder by an unknown person whose identity will be uncovered through the clever investigations of a sleuth. The main distinguishing features in the mysteries by southern authors parallel to a large extent those characteristics that set southern literature apart in general from literature written in other parts of the country. Many southern writers portray their central detectives/investigators within the context of their region and its tortuous past and often depict the conflicts arising from the clash between the Old and the New South. Because many southern women mystery writers have created female investigators, it is not surprising that these works contain a healthy dose of feminism. For example, Margaret Maron's sleuth Deborah Knott, Sharyn McCrumb's Elizabeth McPherson, and Kathy Hogan Trocheck's Callahan Garrity often find themselves caught between tradition and their desire to be accepted as autonomous women.

Neither do southern mystery writers shy away from the legacy of race. James Lee Burke confronts the cruel history of the South head-on in *Burning Angel* (1995); in *Neon Smile* (1995), Dick Lochte contrasts the violent racial tensions of the 1960s with the more subtle racial politics of recent years. Atlanta mystery author Kathy Hogan Trocheck portrays the relations between black and white realistically and with great humor in *To Live and Die in Dixie* (1993) and *Homemade Sin* (1994), which depict the Atlanta of the 1990s as a truly southern metropolitan area where Old and New South collide and where racial harmony seems to show progress, even if only tenuously. In a departure from his usual style, William Faulkner effectively employs the mystery genre in his novel *Intruder in the Dust* (1948) to uncover the injustice done to a black man accused of killing a white man.

The southern qualities of the many mysteries presently being published may be differentiated according to big-city and small-town settings. The novels of Patricia Cromwell, most of them set in Richmond, Virginia, capture the basic atmosphere of that city; however, the emphasis in Cromwell's work is often on the graphic details of serial killings and on the suspense of the investigations. In contrast, several mystery writers effectively portray the multifaceted world of New Orleans in their works: in *Jazz Funeral* (1993) and *New Orleans Beat* (1994), Julie Smith captures that city's peculiar social mix, the exuberance of the nightlife in the Quarter contrasted with the vagaries of its various subcultures. Several of James Lee Burke's Dave Robicheaux novels, for example, *Dixie City Jam* (1994) and *Burning Angel* (1995), and Tony Dunbar's mysteries *Crooked Man* (1993) and *City of Beads* (1995) realistically portray the corrupt and gritty side of New Orleans. The Big Easy also plays a significant role in Dick Lochte's novels *Blue Bayou* (1995) and *The Neon Smile* (1995). Nashville, Tennessee, is featured in Steven Womack's Harry James Denton series (*Dead Folks' Blues*, 1992, and *Way Past Dead*, 1995), in which the author captures the musical milieu and the southern ambience of that city. Savannah, Georgia, has become a veritable tourist mecca since the publication of John Berendt's best-seller *Midnight in the Garden of Good and Evil* (1994), a nonfiction work that became one of the most popular murder mysteries of the decade.

Those mysteries set in rural areas of the South may perhaps be said to reflect the truest southern qualities. Margaret Maron's North Carolina, Sharyn McCrumb's Virginia, Joan Hess's Arkansas, and Teri Holbrook's Georgia are accurately rendered as a southern world where the characters try to hold on to their traditions of close-knit families attached to the land, but where murder becomes the dark force to disturb the idylls of the past. Inasmuch as mystery and detective fiction often deals with contemporary social issues, these writers present real, often satiric, glimpses of southern life with its family reunions under pecan trees, church gatherings, and gossip in the beauty parlor and the local diner. At the same time, all of the writers exhibit the most southern of all traits: covering serious issues with humor. Arkansas writer Joan Hess's

Maggody series is a hilarious send-up of most southern clichés, while Sharyn McCrumb tackles phony fundamentalist religion with obvious glee in *If I'd Killed Him . . .* (1994). Margaret Maron delights in taking on the workings of the local district courts and the strange voting habits of her fellow North Carolinians. The common element in the works of these southern mystery writers is their genuine feelings for their region reflected in the works' authentic sense of place.

Joe Mandel

See also Poe, Edgar Allan.

Donald Adams, ed., *The Mystery and Detection Annual* (1973); Gary Niebuhr, *The Reader's Guide to the Private Eye Novel* (1993); J. K. Van Dover and John F. Jebb, *Isn't Justice Always Unfair? The Detective in Southern Literature* (1996); Richard Walser, *Literary North Carolina* (1986).

MYTHICAL REALMS

Long before the South was "the South," it was a mythical country, the promised land to the English preachers, poets, and pamphleteers who in the early seventeenth century hailed Virginia as the new Eden across the sea. As late as 1907, one reads in Mildred Rutherford's *The South in History and Literature,* descriptions of the South as a "world of young heroes," where the men are "full of knightly courtesies and knightly courage," and the women are as "good and fair" as any found "in Homer, Shakespeare, or Scott." Whether the South was founded on myth or became one through the habitual prevarication of its inhabitants, it has long inspired in its writers what W. J. Cash called in *The Mind of the South* (1941) that "old Southern urge to turn the country into Never-Never Land."

The works of Edgar Allan Poe stray far from the South he knew as a boy in Richmond, Virginia. From the wild woods and shadowy lakes of his early romantic verse to the hypnogogic realms beyond time and space that frame his later, more metaphysical inquiries, Poe's psychic dreamscapes evoke an inner geography deep within the "monarch Thought's dominion." An outcast most of his life, Poe sought refuge in the Mohammedan paradises and Arcadian valleys on the borders of consciousness, where a poet could dwell in harmony with the angel Israfel under the "ray . . . of Beauty's eye." In "Ms. Found in a Bottle" (1831) and

The Narrative of Arthur Gordon Pym (1838), Poe's metaphysical passages become voyages of discovery and annihilation leading to the ends of the earth and the limits of knowledge. The "Valley of the Many-Colored Grass" in "Eleonora," with its "River of Silence" and "wildernesses of dreams," may be the most intriguing of Poe's mythical landscapes, but it is his nightmarish evocations of the soul's darkest regions—the "ghoul-haunted woodland of Weir" and the "night's Plutonian shore"—for which he is best remembered.

Despite his reputation as one of the founding fathers of American realism, Mark Twain set a number of his works in fantastic realms and mythical kingdoms, though even they are closer to reality than they first appear. In *The Mysterious Stranger,* Philip Traum transforms the sixteenth-century Austrian village of Eseldorf into an enchanted dreamland where civilization becomes a moral playground for Satan's nephew and the local boys who witness his acts of prestidigitation. By the tale's end, humankind's "moral sense" is upended and all reality is revealed to be "a shoreless space," a vision of the "airy nothing which is called Thought." In *A Connecticut Yankee in King Arthur's Court* (1889), the Yankee entrepreneur Hank Morgan sets out with a band of bike-riding, soap-peddling knights-errant to modernize Camelot and make a Utopia of Arcadian England. Twain's Camelot parodies the "Middle-Age sham civilization" popularized in the novels of Sir Walter Scott and emulated in the South, where, as Twain argued in *Life on the Mississippi* (1882), an entire generation had fallen under the spell of the "sham grandeurs, sham gauds, and sham chivalries of a brainless and worthless long-vanished society."

The romanticism that so distressed Twain inspired in James Branch Cabell the creation of his own mythical realm, an imaginary kingdom drawn partly from the myths he heard in his youth about a "beauty-haunted and chivalrous Cloud-Cuckoo-Land" that, before the war, had been "at one with Troy and Atlantis." As Cabell recalls in his Virginia memoir *Let Me Lie* (1947), the Lost Cause was a favorite subject of his Richmond elders, whose idyllic narratives and elegiac cadences turned the Confederacy's fallen capital into Camelot and the unhorsed cavaliers into Confederate Knights of the Round Table. Such myths formed the foundations of Cabell's own mythical creation, the French medieval province of Poictesme, the setting for his eighteen-volume master work, *The Biography of the Life of Manuel* (1927–1930). In *Jurgen* (1919),

Cabell's best-known fantasy, the title character "circumvents destiny and common sense" on a journey through the mythical kingdoms of Cocaigne, Pseudopolis, and Philistia, where he learns that "to make literature and to make trouble are synonyms." Sentenced to the underworld, Jurgen finds himself in the anachronistic Hell that his prudish, guilt-ridden grandfather had always envisioned. From there, he climbs Jacob's ladder to Heaven, though it too proves to be nothing more than a "delusion of old women." As in his other fantasies, such as *The Silver Stallion* (1926) and *The Cream of the Jest* (1917), Cabell's exploration of mythical realms becomes an exploration of the history of myth itself.

Like Cabell's Poictesme, William Faulkner's mythical Yoknapatawpha County stands as one of southern literature's most fully realized creations. Based on Faulkner's home county of Lafayette in northern Mississippi, Yoknapatawpha (a Chickasaw word meaning "water runs slow through flat land") takes its name from the Yocana River to the south, where the county's earliest settler, Louis Grenier, first established a plantation near the hamlet later known as Frenchman's Bend. Faulkner's hand-drawn maps and detailed genealogies have naturally led some to regard his apocryphal county as something more than legend, including one who attempted to estimate the average height of its inhabitants. Underlying Faulkner's realism, however, is a dark river of myth. In "The Bear" (1942), Ike McCaslin enters an "unaxed" wilderness "bigger and older than any recorded document" to hunt for Old Ben, the bear who looms in the imaginations of the local hunters like an "anachronism" from "an old, dead time." Only after Ike leaves behind his watch and compass does the bear appear, "dimensionless against the dappled obscurity" of a hidden glade. Ike's return to the woods in "Delta Autumn" a half-century later finds him a dispossessed heir of Eden, wandering in a doomed wilderness where the old myths endure in "one tremendous density of brooding and inscrutable impenetrability."

In Robert Penn Warren's poem "Dragon Country" (1957), the citizens of Todd County, Kentucky, learn to cope with a "belly-dragging earth-evil" that ruins fences and devours traveling salesmen while increasing church attendance everywhere. The "fearful glimmer of joy" that the locals experience in the meantime suggests that Warren's beast represents something more than myth—the "necessity of truth" that brings knowledge and relief from the ennui of life.

Eudora Welty's mythical town of Morgana (whose name suggests another myth, the Fata Morgana, or sea mirage) is the dreamlike setting of *The Golden Apples* (1977), a revision of the fables and fairy tales she read as a child in Mississippi, where mythology, she says, was "as close to me as the landscape." Though Welty dismisses simple comparisons between the old myths and her revisions, her stories are rife with allusions to Perseus and Medusa, Angeus, Leda, and Zeus.

John Barth's novella-triad, *Chimera* (1972), a postmodern parody of a myth about a myth, floats "between two worlds," the mythical and the modern, in the marshy waters of Lycia and Dorchester County, Maryland. Like a Pegasus too fat to fly, Barth's mythical heroes are over-the-hill, mired in the metafictive marsh of the novel's shifting narrative. His 1987 novel, *The Tidewater Tales*, follows folklorist Kathy Sherritt from Nopoint Point, Maryland, to the outer edges of myth on a "cruise through the Ocean of Story," where she revisits Odysseus and Penelope, Huck Finn, and some of Barth's own mythical characters in a kind of "Thousand and One Chesapeake Nights." Here, as in Barth's other works, narrative is the mythical realm, the labyrinth where stories and identities are lost and recovered and lost again.

Brian Carpenter

See also Belle; Children's Literature; Novel, 1820 to 1865; Plantation Fiction; Smith, Captain John; Tall Tale; Voodoo.

Richard Gray, *Writing the South* (1986); Peggy Prenshaw, ed., *Conversations with Eudora Welty* (1984); Walter Sullivan, "The Decline of Myth in Southern Fiction," *Southern Review* 12 (1976).

N

NAACP (NATIONAL ASSOCIATION FOR THE ADVANCEMENT OF COLORED PEOPLE)

The oldest and largest civil-rights association in America, the NAACP began with the merging of two activist groups, one black and one white. In June 1905, under the leadership of W. E. B. Du Bois, twenty-nine black men met in Niagara Falls, New York, where they organized to work for full citizenship rights, spiritual freedom, and industrial opportunity through what was to become the Niagara Movement. Subsequently, in January 1909, responding to a challenge by William Walling, a southern white journalist, Mary Ovington and Henry Moskowitz, both New York social workers, met with Walling. These three attracted numerous other activists, including Niagara Movement members, to a May 31–June 1, 1909, conference in New York City, at which the National Negro Committee was founded. Both groups sought equality for all Americans and together formed a powerful association. In May 1910, the Committee held its second annual meeting; selected a new name, the National Association for the Advancement of Colored People; and recorded its purpose as eradicating caste and race prejudice in the United States, while promoting educational, economic, political, and social equality.

Soon after establishment, the NAACP began a long fight for equal rights, using education and legal action as major weapons. In November 1910, founding editor W. E. B. Du Bois issued one thousand copies of the *Crisis*, the official NAACP publication, which quickly became the most influential black periodical in educating all readers and instilling pride in black Americans. Special features were Du Bois's cogent editorials; summaries of NAACP activities, including antilynching campaigns; news of worldwide race problems and so-

lutions; records of black achievement; and creative works by black authors.

By 1915, the NAACP had begun winning a series of legal battles important in securing civil rights. In *Guinn v. United States* (1915), the organization convinced the Supreme Court to overturn the infamous "grandfather clause," formerly used to disfranchise black voters, and in *Buchanan v. Warley* (1917), NAACP lawyers were successful against municipal ordinances sanctioning segregated housing. The best known of these Court victories is *Brown v. Board of Education* (1954), which ended legal segregation in public schools.

During the Civil Rights Movement of the late 1950s and 1960s, NAACP branch leaders and youth councils worked for passage of the 1957 and 1960 civil-rights bills assuring protection of the right to register and vote, the 1964 Civil Rights Act, the 1965 Voting Rights Act, and the 1968 Fair Housing Act. Concurrently, militant direct-action groups challenged the NAACP's conservative legal strategies. However, having laid the foundation for those groups by guaranteeing their constitutional rights, the NAACP remained secure in its position while acknowledging the need for multiple approaches to civil-rights issues and cooperation with organizations such as the Congress on Racial Equality, the Southern Christian Leadership Conference, and the Student Nonviolent Coordinating Committee.

In response to problems of the last three decades, the NAACP has expanded its program to include issues of substance abuse, violence, black land loss, and erosion of affirmative-action initiatives. Continuing a history of strong leadership, the NAACP has remained cognizant of changing realities that are nonetheless constant in their threat to disadvantaged populations.

The NAACP has enjoined the efforts of several key literary figures, including W. E. B. Du Bois and Charles Chesnutt. After poet and novelist James Weldon Johnson became general secretary of the NAACP, he became more militant about race. While general secretary, he also wrote some of his best poetry, including *God's Trombones* (1927). He published his autobiography *Along This Way* (1933), a counterpoint to his earlier novel *The Autobiography of an Ex-Coloured Man,* republished in 1927 to an acclaim denied in 1912.

Patsy B. Perry

See also *Brown v. Board of Education*; Civil Rights Movement; *Crisis*; Lynching.

John Hope Franklin and Alfred A. Moss Jr., *From Slavery to Freedom* (7th ed., 1994); Langston Hughes, *Fight for Freedom: The Story of the NAACP* (1962); Charles F. Kellogg, *NAACP: A History of the National Association for the Advancement of Colored People,* Vol. 1, *1909–1920* (1967); Mary White Ovington, *The Walls Came Tumbling Down* (1947); B. Joyce Ross, *J. E. Spingarn and the Rise of the NAACP, 1911–1939* (1972); Roy Wilkins with Tom Mathews, *Standing Fast: The Autobiography of Roy Wilkins* (1982).

NASHVILLE, TENNESSEE

As the central city of the central state of the central South, Nashville has been the crossroads of change throughout much of its two-hundred-year history. The number and variety of epithets applied to Tennessee's capital city bear testimony to its reputation as an educational, financial, religious, and music center in the South. Nashville has been and is sometimes still known as the "Athens of the West," the "Wall Street of the South," the "Protestant Vatican," and "Music City, U.S.A." Though none of these names reflects in any specific way the city's literary past, that past is very much a reflection of these same distinct identities.

Even before Tennessee was elected to statehood, when Nashville was little more than a cluster of cabins along the Cumberland River, the city had its own academy where pupils studied Greek and Latin and read the classics under the tutelage of the Reverend Thomas B. Craighead. Tennessee governor Sam Houston, who got his start in politics practicing law in Nashville, is said to have known Homer by heart and could reportedly recite Pope's translation of *The Iliad* in its entirety. Nashville's classical foundations were more firmly established in 1845 by the architect William Strickland, whose Greek temple-style design for the state capitol building made an Acropolis of the city's highest hill.

Such classical allusions would find later expression in the verse of Nashville's Fugitive poets, such as Allen Tate, who published Horatian odes and epodes as a Vanderbilt University undergraduate in the 1920s, and Donald Davidson, whose poem on the city's full-scale replica of the Parthenon questioned the motives of those southerners who "build but never read their Greek."

By the mid-nineteenth century, Nashville's thriving newspaper and publishing trade had produced a number of competent paragraphers and versifiers, but few writers of note. Aspiring poets Clara Cole (1805–1880) and Lucy Virginia French (1825–1881) published their sentimental and elegiac verse in the literary columns of local religious journals including *The Parlor Visitor* (1854–1857) and *The Southern Lady's Companion* (1847–1854), the first magazine of its kind in the South to be directed specifically toward a female audience. Attempts at more serious literary journals, like the *South-Western Monthly* (1852) and Wilkins Tannehill's *Portfolio* (1847–1850), were shortlived. The most popular author of the day was the twenty-two-year-old daughter of the state's governor, Laura C. Holloway, whose book *The Ladies of the White House* (1869) was a best-seller in America and abroad. The city's prevailing literary tastes were perhaps best seen, however, in the names of its great estates, many of which, like Melrose, Mansfield, and Glen Leven, appear to have been drawn from the novels of Sir Walter Scott. At century's end, the popularity of such light local-color fiction as Miss Will Allen Dromgoole's *Three Little Crackers from Down in Dixie* (1898) was rivaled only by the verse of "Tennessee's Sweet Singer," the novelist and poet Annie Somers Gilchrist, whose reputed kinship to Shakespeare may have been her greatest fiction.

One of the more famous moments in the city's literary history came in 1909 with the publication of O. Henry's short story "A Municipal Report" in *Hampton's Magazine*. Written partly in response to novelist Frank Norris's remark that Nashville was not really a "story city," O. Henry's tale, a combination murder-mystery and Nashville travelogue, juxtaposed romance and realism to satirize some of the relics of the Old South and became one of the author's most famous stories. In the decades that followed, Nashville's rebirth as a New South city with Old South foundations set the stage for the Southern Literary Renascence that would later flourish there in and around Vanderbilt and, to a degree, Fisk University. Vanderbilt's Fugitives began as a simple town-and-gown affair at the home of a local businessman, much like the city's other literary societies, the Round Table and the Oak Room; *The Fugitive* itself was funded in part by the local Nashville Retailers Association. Though closely associated with Nashville, the Fugitives and Agrarians, who favored classical formalism and abstract modernism over local color, wrote very little about the city itself, the few exceptions being Jesse Wills's poem "Nashville," Donald Davidson's "Twilight on Union Street," and Robert Penn Warren's last novel, *A Place to Come To* (1977).

The short stories and novels of Peter Taylor (1917–1994), the grandson of popular Tennessee governor Robert Love Taylor, best reflect Nashville's transition from its provincial past to its urban present. In such stories as "In the Miro District," "Guests," and his Pulitzer Prize–winning novel *A Summons to Memphis* (1986), Taylor weaves local legend and family history in a continual exploration of the city and its people. Nashville is a strong, if distant, presence in the rural Tennessee novels of Madison Jones (1925–), whose latest work, *Nashville 1864* (1997), chronicles the city's famous Civil War battle. Nashville's emergence in recent decades as a country-music mecca has spawned a number of novels about the local music scene, most notably Lee Smith's *The Devil's Dream* (1992), Bland Simpson's *The Heart of the Country* (1983), and William Price Fox's *Ruby Red* (1971).

Brian Carpenter

See also Agrarians; Baptists; Bible Belt; Country Music; Fugitives, The; Gospel Music; Grand Ole Opry; Methodists; New Criticism; Presbyterians; Publishers; Southern Renascence; Televangelist; Tennessee, Literature of; Vanderbilt University.

Patrick Allen, ed., *Literary Nashville* (1999); Alfred Leland Crabb, *Nashville* (1960); F. Garvin Davenport, *Cultural Life in Nashville* (1941); Don H. Doyle, *Nashville in the New South* (1985), and *Nashville Since the 1920's* (1985); Christine Kreyling et al., *Classical Nashville* (1996); Henry McRaven, *Nashville, "Athens of the South"* (1949).

NATCHEZ TRACE

The path that European settlers came to know as the Natchez Trace was first beaten through the wilderness by bison and deer in their regular migrations from the grasslands of central Tennessee to the lower Mississippi River. Stretching nearly six hundred miles between modern Nashville and Natchez, the Trace passed over the hills of southern Tennessee and northwestern Alabama before running diagonally across Mississippi, over the flatlands and red-clay hills near Tupelo and Jackson before descending through the swamplands and loess hills along the great river. In this final section, the soft loess soil yielded under the heels of travelers and the Trace cut down into the earth, becoming a sunken pathway before emerging at the future site of the port town of Natchez.

Human settlers were quick to adapt the Trace to their purposes, beginning with the Indians—including the eponymous Natchez tribe along the river—who used it for hunting and trade. Europeans were just as quick to take advantage of this path through the vast wilderness of the New World, beginning with the Spanish under Hernando De Soto. By 1713 the French had established a trading post at the southern terminus; they were at war with the Natchez within a few years and by 1730 had destroyed that nation forever. In 1763, following the French and Indian War, the region around the southern edge of the Trace became British West Florida and soon hosted a number of Scots-Irish settlers from Tennessee. But the Spanish, still powerful west of the Mississippi, seized Natchez in 1781 and held "West Florida" even after it was formally yielded by the British to the newly recognized United States in 1783. The Spanish finally withdrew from the region in 1798, when the U.S. Congress organized the Mississippi Territory.

The Natchez Trace was the major route of land travel in the West in the late eighteenth and early nineteenth centuries. Traders and boatmen who floated downstream from the upper tributaries of the Mississippi deposited their goods at Natchez or New Orleans then traveled by land up the Trace to where they had begun. The heavy northbound traffic was generally money-laden, and, in this turbulent frontier region where government hardly existed, bandits flourished. Even when the Trace was adopted as a U.S. mail route and improved by the army in 1801–1803, the new national road only attracted an increasing number of criminals who terrified travelers until the road gradually fell into disuse after 1811. The advent of the steamboat—which made the Mississippi River the most desirable route for travel north as well as south—together with newer national roads marked the end of the Trace as a major thoroughfare. But the Trace endured in American legend, for it had in its brief period of prominence not only been generally associated with the western frontier but also accommodated such specific figures as boatman Mike Fink, naturalist John J. Audubon, and explorer Meriwether Lewis. Aaron Burr and General Andrew Jackson—political leaders who traveled the Trace on their paths from and to national power, respectively—were also part of the region's history.

The people and events associated with the Natchez Trace engaged the imagination of all the European peoples who played a role in its history, as the French poet Chateaubriand's epic prose poem *The Natchez* (1823) indicates; this disciple of Rousseau, who claimed to have visited the Lower Mississippi during his visit to America in 1791, told the story of what he saw as a tribe of noble savages who were destroyed by his countrymen. In the American literary imagination, the Trace was also associated with the confrontation between civilization and the wilderness; in fact, it captured the essential spirit of the Old Southwest—its vigorous, rough-hewn, and not infrequently violent opportunism—as few other single geographical features could. The region that contributed to popular tales of such western folk heroes as Fink would also engage the imagination of southern writers from the more staid eastern seaboard, including Charlestonian William Gilmore Simms. Both inspired and troubled by the frontier that he saw when he visited his father in Mississippi in 1824–1825, Simms wrote four border romances—*Guy Rivers* (1834), *Richard Hurdis* (1838), *Border Beagles* (1840), and *Helen Halsey* (1845)—that reflect not only his own experiences there but also his knowledge of the legends surrounding a specific bandit of the Natchez Trace, the "Great Western Land Pirate" John Murrell. The villains in *Richard Hurdis* and *Border Beagles* lead a band of outlaws known as "the Mystic Brotherhood," much as Murrell actually led what he called the Mystic Clan of the Confederacy. In keeping with Simms's general pattern in the border novels, a young gentleman from the eastern plantation society finally destroys this band, though he is reinvigorated by the encounter; the clash suggests a dialectic between an ordered but potentially decadent civilization and a vigorous but chaotic frontier.

The Natchez Trace endured in the nineteenth century in local folktales such as those surrounding Mike Fink—many of which eventually saw print in popular magazines—that chronicled his adventures in the taverns of Natchez-under-the-Hill or fighting against the Harpe brothers, a pair of bandits also famously associated with the Trace. Natchez itself—not the rowdy port

on the river but the more genteel village on the higher bluffs—produced an aspiring *literati* of its own, including Joseph Holt Ingraham, whose social commentary *The South-West, By a Yankee* (1835) was widely read. Residents of the surrounding region already saw the Trace's rich history as a source of inspiration; Eliza Ann Dupuy, Virginia-born but relocated to the Natchez District, retold the story of Burr's arrest in Natchez in *The Conspirator* (1850).

The Trace's place in the national imagination was bolstered in the twentieth century by Robert M. Coates's popular history *The Outlaw Years: The History of the Land Pirates of the Natchez Trace* (1930). Literary artists plumbing the origins of the nation would continue to envision the road as profoundly symbolic of America's westward expansion. For example, in Robert Penn Warren's book-length poem *Brother to Dragons* (1953), Thomas Jefferson must confront the ghost of Meriwether Lewis, whom he had commissioned to explore the West—and whose 1809 death on the Trace was most likely a suicide.

The history of the Natchez Trace has been most thoroughly explored by the southern literary imagination in the work of Mississippi's Eudora Welty. Her second published work, *The Robber Bridegroom* (1942), was less a novel than a "Fairy Tale of the Natchez Trace," as she deemed it in her 1975 essay of the same title. Set in the late eighteenth century—with the region around the Trace still under Spanish rule—the story incorporates "the elements of wilderness and pioneer settlements, flatboats and river trade, the Natchez Trace and all its life, including the Indians and the bandits" but is still by her own account "not a *historical* historical novel" so much as a myth. It features not only historical figures who have passed into legend, such as Fink and the Harpes, but also a pioneer planter family—complete with archetypal wicked stepmother—whose daughter Rosamond is fortunate enough to be kidnapped by an essentially kind-hearted bandit husband; as befits both the American frontier and the world of the Brothers Grimm, it is a dreamlike tale of violence and lust that somehow culminates in a happy ending. Welty would continue to explore the Trace in her next book, the short-story collection *The Wide Net* (1943). "First Love" is a story of the charismatic Burr—yet another opportunist giddy with the promise of the West—and his "seduction" of the Natchez populace; "A Still Moment" places Murrell, Audubon, and the preacher Lorenzo Dow in an imagined encounter on the Trace itself. There they stop to view a heron in a marsh alongside the road, yet each interprets and reacts to its presence differently—much as the myriad of travelers upon the Trace down through the centuries had passed similar scenes, been confronted with the encroaching presence of the wilderness itself, and somehow come to define themselves in relation to it.

Farrell O'Gorman

See also Mississippi River; Old Southwest; Southwestern Humor; Travel Literature; Welty, Eudora.

Jonathan Daniels, *The Devil's Backbone* (1962); William C. Davis, *A Way Through the Wilderness* (1995); Floyd C. Watkins, "Eudora Welty's Natchez Trace in the New World," *Southern Review* 22:4 (Autumn 1986).

NATIVE AMERICAN LITERATURE

Native tribal peoples of the South have resided in the region for thousands of years and have had first oral and then written literatures that have influenced southern culture in profound ways. Unfortunately, the Native presence in southern literature is often overlooked by scholars with preconceived notions of what constitutes "southern." Despite the fact that there are over thirty published Native American authors who were born in the South and make it the setting of their work, many anthologies of southern literature bypass Native authors. By studying the fiction, poetry, drama, and autobiography, as well as the mythology and folklore of Native Americans, the student of southern literature is better able to understand the complex interactions and influences among the South's three major cultures— African American, European American, and Native American.

Evidence of Indian cultures is evident from pottery dated 4,500 B.C. and burial mounds from 1,000 B.C. to 700 A.D. From 700 to the point of contact in the seventeenth century, an established culture termed "Mississippian" by anthropologists had its own highly developed southern art and culture, which included large villages and ceremonial cities as well as a strong agricultural and religious base. At the point of European contact, the Cherokees alone numbered twenty thousand people in sixty towns. By the nineteenth century, European disease and warfare had nearly wiped out many tribes. Historians estimate that between 50 and 90 percent of tribal peoples died during epidemics.

American federal policy created increased hardship

and dislocation for the tribes of the Southeast. Despite the Supreme Court ruling in *Cherokee Nation v. Georgia* (1831) that protected the tribe from federal interference, the Indian Removal Act of 1830 initiated a process that would eventually force tribes to relocate to "Indian Territory" west of the Mississippi. The infamous "Trail of Tears" in which four thousand of the sixteen thousand Cherokees who were removed from their homes died on the march to Oklahoma has become a subject of Native and European-American literatures. By midcentury, displaced southern tribes including Cherokees, Chickasaws, Choctaws, Creeks, and Seminoles all had separate lands in the Indian Territory that would become Oklahoma in 1907. The aftermath of the Civil War caused further dislocation and Native loss of land. In order to punish Confederate-supporting tribes, the federal government appropriated one-half of their western territory. Although some tribes in Virginia, Florida, and North Carolina were able to evade removal and remained in their ancestral homelands, they were often marginalized and isolated. Destruction of tribal solidarity and communal landholding was accelerated when the federal government enacted the General Allotment Act of 1887, which redistributed Indian land on an individual rather than tribal basis. Assimilation through education was also forced upon tribes with the creation of the first off-reservation schools in 1879. By the conclusion of the nineteenth century, several thousand years of southern Native cultural continuity were imperiled.

The historical experiences of Native tribes in the South often provide the background for many nineteenth- and twentieth-century Native American literary texts. Ironically, many of the themes found in this literature are similar to those thought of as exclusively "southern": a sense of tragic, historical defeat and a focus on the past; a reverence for "homeplace," community, and the land; a preoccupation with race and prejudice; an idealized vision of agrarian life and an early environmentalism that rejects industrialization; and a belief in the sacred or religious nature of life. Although there are important differences between southern and Native American culture that should never be overlooked, it is nonetheless surprising that Native American literature of the South is usually treated in isolation and outside of any context except its own. There is little attempt to place Native American literature within a regional context by scholars who study southern literature and culture.

Despite the dislocation of traditional tribal culture,

Native Americans maintained their oral literatures and began to develop written ones in the nineteenth century. Sequoyah's creation of a syllabary for the Cherokee language in the 1830s and the Pickering alphabet, which enabled Creeks, Seminoles, Choctaws, and Chickasaws to record oral languages, stimulated the growth of Native American literatures. As Daniel F. Littlefield Jr. and James W. Parins note in their introduction to the anthology *Native American Writing in the Southeast (1875–1935),* "one important way in which the tribal peoples of the Southeast responded to their long history of cultural discontinuity and struggle was with a written language . . . [and a] tremendous energy and extensive production of a rich literature," which included novels, short stories, biography, drama, and essays.

The conflict between Native and European-American cultures was the basis for two early southern novels, Elias Boudinot's (Cherokee) *Poor Sarah* (1823), thought to be the first American Indian novel, and John Rollin Ridge's *Life and Adventures of Joaquin Murieta* (1854). Sophia Alice Callahan's (Creek, 1868–1894) *Wynema: A Child of the Forest* (1891) was the first novel written by a Native American woman. Callahan presents the friendship of Genevieve Weir, a non-Indian teacher in the Creek Nation, and her Native student Wynema. The novel describes the social and cultural impact of allotment and the massacre at Wounded Knee (1890) as well as the author's own increasing awareness of women's rights at the turn of the century.

Legends, origin stories, and trickster narratives were also part of the oral and then written tradition in the tribes of the South. Many of these stories, particularly the humorous trickster rabbit tales and the origin stories, have been integrated—often in unacknowledged ways—into a white southern folklore that was popularized by Joel Chandler Harris. As *The Literature of the American South: A Norton Anthology* (1998) so aptly notes, "It is important to remember that indigenous oral expressive traditions thrived in the South before the Europeans and Africans arrived, even though few scholars have tried to track the importance of Native American oral traditions on the literary expression of European Americans or African Americans in the South."

Nineteenth- and early-twentieth-century Native authors shared in the rich folklore tradition that survived removal. Royal Roger Eubanks (Cherokee, 1879–?) wrote a series of dialect stories utilizing the vast Native oral trickster tradition, which he patterned after Joel Chandler Harris's Uncle Remus tales. But Eubanks's stories were set within an American Indian context, such as "Nights with Uncle Ti-ault-ly: The Ball Game of the Birds and Animals" (1910) or "Nights with Uncle Ti-ault-ly: How the Terrapin Beat the Rabbit" (1910). In addition to his humorous tales, Eubanks also wrote political short fiction such as "The Middle Man," an indictment of the federal land-allotment policy that systematically cheated Native peoples of their land.

Many other southern Native writers recounted traditional tales and legends in written form, including Mabel Washborne Anderson (Cherokee), David J. Brown (Cherokee), Joseph Bruner (Muscogee), Caroline Eaton (Cherokee), Israel Folsom (Choctaw), Charles Gibson (Muscogee), James Roane Gregory (Yuchi), Ben D. Locke (Choctaw), Jesse J. McDermott (Muscogee), Ora V. Eddleman Reed (Cherokee), and Muriel Hazel Wright (Choctaw). An excellent collection of southern oral narratives is Joseph Bruchac's edited legends of the Great Smoky Mountains in *Between Earth and Sky: Legends of Native American Sacred Places* (1996). William M. Clements's *Native American Verbal Art: Texts and Contexts* (1996) includes a study of Cherokee oral tradition set within its historical and cultural context. W. S. Penn has also edited a recent collection of myths and narratives in *The Telling of the World: Native American Stories and Art* (1996). Two helpful anthologies of scholarly essays on this tradition are *Smoothing the Ground: Essays on Native American Oral Literature* (1983), edited by Brian Swann, and *Studies in American Indian Literature* (1983), edited by Paula Gunn Allen.

The scope of nineteenth- and early-twentieth-century Native American literature extends beyond the fields of mythology and the oral tradition, however. Known to the general American reading public as both a journalist and a fiction writer, John Milton Oskison (Cherokee, 1874–1947) graduated from Stanford and did advanced study in literature at Harvard University. In 1899 his short story "Only the Master Shall Praise" won a national prize. His short story "The Problem of Old Harjo" is an example of Oskison's considerable skill in integrating American Indian themes into a larger local-color literary tradition quite popular in this period. Oskison's work is grounded within a Native American context as Old Harjo encounters the forces of Anglo morality that would force him to conform to Judeo-Christian marital standards, however arbitrary.

In this sense, Oskison anticipates such contemporary Native American writers as Leslie Marmon Silko and Louise Erdrich, whose characters often struggle with social workers, missionaries, and government officials who would impose their own values on tribal peoples. Oskison also published a series of novels including *Wild Harvest* (1925), *Black Jack Davy* (1926), and *Brothers Three* (1935). His biographical works include *Texas Titan: The Story of Sam Houston* (1929) and *Tecumseh and His Times* (1939). Oskison was known nationally as a journalist for *Collier's Weekly* and the *New York Evening Post*.

The appropriation and exploitation of Indian Territory are also the subjects of John Joseph Mathews's (Osage, 1894–1979) only novel, *Sundown* (1934), which portrays the greed and degradation caused by the oil boom in Oklahoma. Mathews's attitude toward modernity mirrors those of the southern Agrarians as he recounts the loss of traditional life caused by industrialization. Mathews also wrote a historical account of the diaries of Indian agent Laban J. Miles in *Wahkon-tah: The Osage and the White Man's Road* (1929). His other works include *The Osages: Children of Middle Waters,* an eight-hundred-page history based on Osage oral traditions.

Lyric poet and humorist Alexander Lawrence Posey (Muscogee, 1873–1908) viewed the loss of Native traditions in his satirical "Fus Fixico" Indian dialect letters (1902–1908), which were first published in the weekly newspaper *Indian Journal* before they were reprinted nationwide. The Fus Fixico letters contain a cynical portrait of the allotment era and its excesses. They create the fictional Fus Fixico, a full-blood Indian who relates conversations with his tribal friends, Hotgun (a Creek medicine man), Tookpofka Micco, and Kono Harjo. Posey also wrote over 250 lyric poems.

Another nationally known satirist was Will Rogers (Cherokee, 1879–1935), who traveled internationally as "The Cherokee Kid" with Texas Jack's Wild West Circus. After returning to the United States, Rogers joined the *Ziegfeld Follies* and wrote several books, including *The Illiterate Digest* (1924), *Letters of a Self-Made Diplomat to His President* (1927), *There's Not a Bathing-Suit in Russia* (1927), and *Ether and Me; or, Just Relax* (1929). Rogers's wry satire became legendary as he humorously portrayed the working-class man struggling in a modern industrialized society. His collected weekly syndicated newspaper columns have been published by the Oklahoma State University Press.

Recognized as an important playwright of the 1920s and 1930s who introduced folk themes into the medium, Rollie Lynn Riggs (Cherokee, 1899–1954) wrote his first folk play, *Green Grow the Lilacs,* while on a Guggenheim Fellowship in France. The play was eventually produced as the musical *Oklahoma!* His other plays include *The Cherokee Night* (1933) and *Russet Mantle* (1936). Riggs's blending of folkloric materials and literature is similar to that of another southerner of the period, Zora Neale Hurston, who employs the same technique in *Their Eyes Were Watching God* (1937). In addition to his plays, Riggs wrote poetry and was associated with the Imagist school of Vachel Lindsay.

With the Indian Reorganization Act of 1934 and the end of allotment and other anti–Native American practices, many tribes gained more autonomy over their lives. The Civil Rights Movement in the 1960s and the development of Pan-Indian organizations provided the background for a flowering of Native American literatures in the South and throughout the United States. Although contemporary Native American writers are not often identified as "southern," their works share many of the traditionally defined themes with other authors in the South.

One example of a Native American writer with southern roots is N. Scott Momaday (Kiowa/Cherokee), who was born in Oklahoma and occasionally returns in his literature to his homeplace for inspiration. In his memoir *The Way to Rainy Mountain* (1969), Momaday makes a pilgrimage to Rainy Mountain in Oklahoma after the death of his grandmother. Like countless southerners in literature, he tells the reader, "I wanted to be at her grave." Thus his trip home is a complex reawakening of his personal, mythic, and historical identity, a theme echoed in many southern authors from William Faulkner to Peter Taylor.

Momaday has also published several novels, including the Pulitzer Prize–winning *House Made of Dawn* (1968) and *The Ancient Child* (1989), as well as a second memoir, *The Names* (1976). His short stories and poems are included in *In the Presence of the Sun* (1992).

Another award-winning poet, novelist, and short-story writer is Linda Hogan (Chickasaw), whose poetry collections include *Calling Myself Home* (1978), *Daughters, I Love You* (1981), *Eclipse* (1983), and *Seeing Through the Sun* (1985), which won the American Book Award from the Before Columbus Foundation. Hogan's first novel, *Mean Spirit* (1990), and her more recent *Solar Storms* (1995) both deal with the corruption of the Oklahoma landscape by technology and greed. Hogan's personal reminiscence, "The Two Lives," was published in a collection of narratives, *I Tell You Now: Autobiographical Essays by Native American Writers* (1987). In this essay, Hogan blends poetry and prose as she tells the story of her Chickasaw relatives who lived through the Trail of Tears, Removal, and the Civil War. Her most recent collection of essays is *Dwellings: A Spiritual History of the Living World* (1995).

In addition to her work as a musician, photographer, and script writer, Joy Harjo (Muscogee [Creek]) has written six books of poetry, including *The Last Song* (1975), *What Moon Drove Me to This?* (1980), *She Had Some Horses* (1983), *Secrets from the Center of the World* (1989), *In Mad Love and War* (1990), and *The Woman Who Fell from the Sky* (1994). Harjo uses a multimedia approach to poetry, blending Native oral traditions and prose rhythms with contemporary contexts and photographs. Laura Coltelli has edited a collection of interviews with Joy Harjo in *The Spiral of Memory: Interviews with Joy Harjo* (1996).

In the past twenty years, many Native American writers in the South have found audiences for their creative efforts. Among those are Jim Barnes (Choctaw), whose poems in his collections *The American Book of the Dead* (1982), *A Season of Loss* (1985), and *La Plata Cantata* (1989) have been widely anthologized; Betty Louise Bell's (Cherokee) novel *Faces in the Moon* (1994) recounts three generations of Cherokee women; Jack D. Forbes (Powhatan-Renate, Delaware-Lenape) has produced biting satirical short stories on racial tensions in *Only Approved Indians: Stories* (1995).

Diane Glancy (Cherokee) has received awards for both her poetry and prose. Her first collection of poetry, *Brown Wolf Leaves the Res* (1984), has been followed by her first collection of stories, *Trigger Dance* (1990), which won the Nilon Minority Fiction Award. She has since then published several books of poems, including *Lone Dog's Winter Count* (1991) and *Claiming Breath,* which won the American Indian Prose Award for its prose poems in 1993. In that collection of autobiographical prose poems, Glancy speaks of her Cherokee/English/German heritage as a "middle ground between two cultures, not fully a part of either." Glancy has recently edited an anthology with C. W. Truesdale entitled *Two Worlds Walking: Short Stories, Essays, and Poetry by Writers with Mixed Heritages* (1994).

Louis Owens's (Choctaw/Cherokee) novels *Wolf-song* (1991), *The Sharpest Sight* (1992), and *The Bone Game* (1994), as well as his criticism on Native American literature, *Other Destinies: Understanding the American Indian Novel* (1992), define the mystical and realistic worlds of contemporary Native Americans. In popular literature, Robert J. Conley (Cherokee) has written a large number of historical fictional narratives.

Three recent Native American and southern literature anthologies have introduced a number of Native writers to national audiences. *Harper's Anthology of 20th Century Native American Poetry* (1988), edited by Duane Niatum, includes the work of Gladys Cardiff (Eastern Cherokee), Steve Crow (Cherokee), Jimmie Durham (Cherokee), Lance Henson (Cheyenne), Louis Oliver (Creek), and Carter Revard (Osage). Clifford E. Trafzer's anthology *Earth Song, Sky Spirit: Short Stories of the Contemporary Native American Experience* (1992) contains the work of southern authors Don L. Birchfield (Choctaw/Chickasaw), LeAnne Howe (Choctaw), Patricia Riley (Cherokee), Julia Lowry Russell (Lumbee), and Craig Womack (Creek). Patricia Riley has also edited a collection of essays and short fiction entitled *Growing Up Native American* (1993).

Despite the number of Native writers mentioned above, *The Literature of the American South: A Norton Anthology* recognizes only one contemporary Native American author, R. T. Smith (Tuscarora), who is the editor of *Shenandoah* magazine and has published several volumes of poems and short stories. In fact, the *Norton Anthology* inexplicably discusses the Native American oral tradition under the heading "International Origins" of southern literature, which include the national literatures of Spain, Portugal, France, and England.

Clearly, the impact of Native American literature on the southern region of the United States has yet to be analyzed fully. Although Native American literature should always be viewed as unique to its tribal cultures, few scholars make any connection between southern and American Indian cultures. Louis Rubin's *The History of Southern Literature* has a number of essays on African American writers but no separate chapter on Native American literature and no listing in the index. C. Vann Woodward's *The Burden of Southern History* includes only one brief mention. Likewise, critics of Native American literature often analyze American Indian literatures within a tribal and not a regional context. The cross-cultural influences, therefore, are yet to be completely understood or assessed.

Roberta Rosenberg

See also Folklore; Indians; Oklahoma, Literature of; Oral History; Race, Idea of; Race Relations; Racism; Storytelling; Trail of Tears; Trickster.

Paula Gunn Allen, ed., *Studies in American Indian Literature* (1983); Gretchen M. Bataille, ed., *Native American Women: A Biographical Dictionary* (1993); Daniel F. Littlefield Jr. and James W. Parins, eds., *Native American Writing in the Southeast: An Anthology, 1875–1935* (1995); Mary Hays Marable and Elaine Boylan, *Handbook of Oklahoma Writers* (1939); Gerald Vizenor, ed., *Native American Literature: A Brief Introduction and Anthology* (1995); Andrew Wiget, ed., *Dictionary of Native American Literature* (1994).

NATURALISM

Literary naturalism emerged as a hard-hitting brand of realism in the 1860s in France, with Émile Zola its chief theorist and practitioner. As the name suggests, naturalism was an attempt to apply to literature the methods and assumptions of science. The writer approached his material aiming for the objectivity of the scientist, studying his characters with detachment and thoroughness. As the writer studied (or created) the heredity of his characters and placed them in a precise environment, their actions seemed determined. Whereas divine force might become a factor in a realistic text (which aims at giving life-likeness to a portrayal), in the naturalistic text blind chance sometimes replaced that providence. The reader was meant to feel the inevitability of events and the detachment of the writer. Usually, the reader of a naturalistic work was left contemplating the pain of human beings caught in an indifferent universe.

It was beholden on the naturalistic writer to conduct vast amounts of research—to know the science of the day, especially those branches that deal with human behavior, as well as the history and customs of the time being portrayed—though the period is usually contemporary. Naturalistic novels were usually long works, reflecting the vast amount of material that the writer had researched. Because Zola took so seriously the role of heredity in understanding human behavior, his chief opus is the Rougon-Macquart series, which traces heredity patterns in two branches of a family in the Second Empire in nineteenth-century France; Zola

required twenty novels to work out the patterns of this heredity. Typically, the naturalist took his characters from the lower classes, though theory did not require this. Inevitably, sexuality played an important role in the lives of the characters, and it received an emphasis that a realistic text usually eschewed, preferring indirection or silence. Although resistance to Zola was strong in the English-speaking world, naturalism was a powerful force that eventually led to more-open depictions of sexuality in fiction.

Both Henry James and William Dean Howells knew Zola's work and theory and were influenced by him, but naturalism did not become a force in the United States until the 1890s, with the publication of works by Frank Norris and Stephen Crane, followed in the next decade by Jack London and Theodore Dreiser. Of the four, Norris was the truest disciple of Zola. His *McTeague: A Story of San Francisco* (1899) owes much to Zola for plot and theme. A journalist for a time, Crane studied firsthand the hard life of the underclass that he then depicted in *Maggie, a Girl of the Streets* (1893). Crane's themes were usually starkly deterministic. Dreiser, who came from the underclass, was a naturalist because he had lived life in the lower depths. His writing teemed with the detail that was the naturalist's trademark; naturalistic works sometimes bear the marks of the case study, and his masterpiece, *An American Tragedy* (1925), was based on a historical incident.

Like the term *romanticism*, the term *naturalism* is variously interpreted. Edwin Cady argues that though America has had no naturalistic writers (writers with a consistent belief in materialistic determinism), he acknowledges that some American writers have demonstrated a naturalistic sensibility. Deciding that American naturalism does not fulfill a strict naturalistic construct, Donald Pizer finds the term meaningful if one considers the changed novel form: the naturalistic novel "no longer reflects certainty about the value of experience but rather expresses a profound doubt or perplexity about what happens in the course of time." Noting the conflicting views of these and other critics, Louis J. Budd summarizes helpfully that "naturalists wrote out of a loose gestalt of values and techniques rather than a coordinated metaphysics or aesthetic. They surpassed the realists qualitatively in exploring humankind's animal sides; their approach to psychology could let instinct overpower conscious will. Most distinctively, they pushed further toward determinism—economic or biological or cosmic—than American novelists had cared or dared to go before. In method—secondary to content insofar as the choice could or had to be made—they intensified the ideal of objectivity; at documentary length, taboo attitudes got not merely a hearing but a self-justification."

Overviews of literary naturalism usually do not place southern authors among America's leading naturalists. In his *American Literary Naturalism: A Divided Stream* (1956), Charles W. Walcutt does not consider southern texts. It was not until the 1930s that southern writers began to be tarred with the label (it was often used pejoratively). William Faulkner was sometimes described as naturalistic, but more because of the brutal events he sometimes described or because of his, to many, shocking use of sexual themes. Erskine Caldwell was also seen as naturalistic because his characters appeared nearly subhuman, especially in their sexuality. Because of his comic gifts, however, Caldwell was not explained chiefly in terms of naturalism. Faulkner's methods were so much of the modernist temperament in their complexity that his major critics seldom explained him in terms of a naturalistic credo. In 1984, however, John J. Conder placed Faulkner as the culmination of the classic phase of American literary naturalism. (Faulkner is the only southerner in Conder's naturalistic pantheon.)

Naturalism doubtless played an important part in the inheritance of the fiction writers of the Southern Renascence, helping to free them—as it did writers in other sections of the nation—for franker treatment of all aspects of life, especially sexuality. But few would be making the traditional American naturalists or Zola their chief mentors.

If, however, southern writers at the end of the nineteenth century and the early twentieth century tended to be dominated by the aura of the Lost Cause and a more romantic tradition, the ideal of pure naturalism (to bring to fiction the assumptions of science) found a major disciple. Anyone surveying treatments of the classic American naturalists would quickly conclude that the method did not attract women. The South would provide the exception. Kate Chopin's *The Awakening* (1899) considered the case of Edna Pontellier in the spirit of Zola's theory; toward the end of the novel, Dr. Mandelet exemplifies the scientific observer as he ponders Edna's unusual behavior.

Chopin shocked readers by her frank treatment of Edna's sexuality. The South's first—and most classically so—naturalistic novel was widely condemned as immoral, as other naturalistic novels had been. The

many merits of the novel would not be much appreciated until well into the twentieth century.

Another southern woman author who embraced the science so important to naturalism was Ellen Glasgow. Her world view was altered by Darwin (in many ways the fountain of naturalism); his ideas consequently helped shape her fiction, notably *Barren Ground* (1925) and *The Sheltered Life* (1932). Darwin's theories, especially his theories about the importance of sexual selection, had a profound impact on writers at the end of the nineteenth century and during the early years of the twentieth century, such as Charles W. Chesnutt, whose novel *The House Among the Cedars* (1900) suggests the impact of Darwin's theory.

Richard Wright is the southern male writer who most directly shows the influence of the naturalistic tradition. He declared that he read every realistic and naturalistic novel that he could find. The direct approach of the naturalists suited his own vision of African American experience. His own life experiences had taught him much about victimization; life had taught him about the environmental trap—much as it had Theodore Dreiser. Wright's *Native Son* (1940) is often likened to Dreiser's *An American Tragedy* in structure and theme, and his *Black Boy* (1945) has often been described in terms of a naturalistic frame.

But naturalistic assumptions were usually influenced by the demands of literary modernism. Robert Penn Warren acknowledged that while he was working on *All the King's Men* (1946) he was greatly concerned with naturalistic determinism; the articulation of the "Great Twitch" evidences the belief widespread in the twentieth century that all life is nothing but "the dark heave of blood and the twitch of the nerve."

Warren was determined, however, that he did not want his book to be a naturalistic novel. It is clear by Warren's time that, although few writers aimed at a strictly naturalistic novel, naturalism had greatly altered the fiction of the South.

Joseph M. Flora

See also Realism.

Bert Bender, *The Descent of Love: Darwin and the Theory of Sexual Selection in American Fiction* (1996); John J. Conder, *Naturalism in American Fiction: The Classic Phase* (1984); June Howard, *Form and History in American Literary Naturalism* (1985); Donald Pizer, *Realism and Naturalism in Nineteenth-Century American Literature* (rev. ed.; 1984); Charles

W. Walcutt, *American Literary Naturalism: A Divided Stream* (1956).

NATURE

When Ralph Lane described the Carolinas as "the goodliest soile under the cope of heaven" in a September 3, 1585, letter to Richard Hakluyt, he had his eyes not only on the beauty of the land but on the possibilities that the land offered to future European immigrants. The promotional tracts that would follow typically used descriptions of natural beauty as part of the lure for future settlers. They do not dwell on the presence of the inhabitants who were already in the New World, inhabitants who viewed nature as alive in ways foreign to the European consciousness, which typically viewed nature as a force to be mastered. For the European, humans were to have dominion over the world. The natives saw themselves as part of the natural world, and their religions were based on this premise. For the practical writers of the colonial South, descriptions of nature were a significant aspect of their work. In *The History of the Present State of Virginia* (1705), Robert Beverley emphasized "an endless Succession of Native Pleasures" where one is "ravished with the beauties of naked Nature." Although there can be no doubt that early immigrant Americans often enjoyed the beauty of nature, they were more engrossed with surveying, measuring, describing, and utilizing. The southern landscape did, however, lead William Bartram (1739–1823), the first non–Native American botanist born in the New World, to write *Travels Through North and South Carolina, Georgia, East and West Florida, the Cherokee Country, the Extensive Territories of the Musougulges, or Creek Confederacy, and the Country of the Choctaws* (1791). *Travels* is the first book of the New World to make the beauty of the wilderness its primary theme. Although best known for his writing, Bartram also painted ably. America's first immigrant naturalist was Joseph Bannister, who lived in Virginia for fourteen years; his projected "Natural History of Virginia" might have been a major contribution to nature writing. Bannister's drawings are, like Bartram's, detailed and delicate.

But the South would not be in the forefront of nature writing. In the nineteenth century, the New England transcendentalists, most notably Ralph Waldo Emerson in *Nature* (1836) and Henry David Thoreau in *A Week on the Concord and Merrimack River* (1849) and *Walden, or Life in the Woods* (1854), tended to make nature a force with a capital N—and to encourage a different way of seeing. Southern poetry of the nineteenth century provided no counterpart to New York's Philip Freneau (1752–1832), against whose nature poems one might contrast Virginia's Philip Pendleton Cooke's "Life in the Autumn Woods" (1843), a work in which the pleasure of the hunt is the dominant event of the October setting. Southern poetry before Poe (1809–1849) tended to be occasional; nature was a theme but hardly seemed the chief business of the poet, though the British Romantics had made their impact. In place of the English nightingale, southern poets specialized in descriptions of the mockingbird. Poe was much concerned with another kind of beauty in his poetry and scarcely noted the natural world.

Focusing attention on the desirability of a southern literature, William Gilmore Simms would give some attention to the southern land. His poem "The Edge of the Swamp" (1840) presents a vivid picture of the South Carolina swamp country, and the natural world often impacts with the actions of the characters in his fiction. The southern mind of Simms's time was, however, focusing increasingly on the issues of slavery and secession rather than pondering nature. Henry Timrod welcomed the birth of the Confederacy in his poem "Ethnogenesis" (1861); in his sweeping view of the southern landscape, he celebrates "long spears of golden grain" and "THE SNOW OF SOUTHERN SUMMERS"—the cotton that had become king of the land. His ode "The Cotton Boll" (1861) describes at length the southern landscape and its chief cash crop. Later readers would see the ironies that Timrod did not intend. Cotton was not only increasing dependence on slave labor but also exhausting the southern soil.

Civil War veteran Sidney Lanier recognized and portrayed in his dialect poem that "Thar's More in the Man Than Thar Is in the Land" (1882). Lanier's chief fame would come, however, from poems that emphasized the southern land as no poet before him had. Lanier would earn a national reputation for his nature poems and become the South's most beloved poet. Lanier not only exults in the beauty of his Georgia settings, he was the first southern poet who may be said to give the capital letter to the word *nature*. His "Symphony" (1875) begins "O Trade! O Trade! would thou wert dead! / The time needs heart—'tis tired of head." Lanier anticipates the Agrarians in his rejection of abstraction and industrialization and transcends them in his affirmation of the natural: "So Nature calls through all her systems wide, / *Give me thy love, O man, so long denied.*" In "Corn" (1875), he laments the power of "capricious Commerce" and sympathizes with the plight of the common man. "The Marshes of Glynn" (1882) and "Sunrise" (1882) also lament the power of trade and its destructive effect on the land, but both poems keep focus on the beauty of the natural world and affirm the spiritual essence of it; the transcendent affirmation is the heart of each poem.

Whatever violations of the land had taken place, identification with the land became a commonly assigned quality of southern literature. The Agrarians' statement of principles introducing *I'll Take My Stand* (1930) intellectualized the stance that Lanier had taken in his poetry. John Crowe Ransom wrote: "But nature industrialized, transformed into cities and artificial habitations, manufactured into commodities, is no longer nature but a highly simplified picture of nature. We receive the illusion of having power over nature, and lose the sense of nature as something mysterious and contingent. The God of nature under these conditions is merely an amiable expression, a superfluity, and the philosophical understanding ordinarily carried in the religious experience is not there for us to have." The Agrarians were too much creatures of the modernist sensibility, however, for their own poetry to provide works in which nature is that mysterious force they thought had been sacrificed.

The triumph of science as the nineteenth century progressed, especially the ideas of Darwin and Freud, complicated ideas about nature. Although the South resisted these ideas more than other regions, their impact on the literature is noticeable. Kate Chopin is the South's first major inheritor of those scientific premises. Her *The Awakening* (1895) insisted on sexuality in women as well as men as a central part of "nature." Because of its sexual theme, her short story "The Storm"—obvious in its symbolism of the natural—was not published until 1969, long after her death. Erskine Caldwell would later intensify Chopin's naturalistic view, emphasizing a nasty and brutal world—his characters are sometimes described as subhuman. In *Tobacco Road* (1932) and *God's Little Acre* (1933), he portrays a southern soil that has been seriously violated.

In the twentieth century, nature's force and terror as well as its beauty were part of the fabric of many southern works. Eudora Welty's "A Curtain of Green" (1941) creates a twentieth-century "garden" that plays against earlier traditions of garden and emphasizes the implications of looking behind the curtain of green, though she invites responses not limited to the naturalistic. Suggestively, Welty let this story title her first collection. Many other southern writers provide similar examples. In the portions of *Cane* (1923) set in Georgia, Jean Toomer makes palpable the sensuous landscape and makes it reflect the drives and emotions of his characters. Robert Penn Warren's short story "Blackberry Winter" (1946) makes the natural world a dominant and fearful force in a story of initiation; his *All the King's Men* (1946) was written with the premises of literary naturalism in mind. Warren's poetry often highlights the natural world. Other artists from the Agrarian tradition, notably Caroline Gordon in her fiction, provided somewhat mellower depictions of nature than did Warren. In Flannery O'Connor's stories, the characters frequently view woods and skylines with impaired vision, sometimes catching a glimpse of the mystery behind them.

William Faulkner's work abounds with depictions of the natural world. Readers typically recall not only the actions of characters but also their settings. A good deal of the action in a Faulkner story or novel takes place outdoors. Few writers have been more successful in portraying the land and man's relationship to it. Obvious examples would include *As I Lay Dying* (1931) and *The Wild Palms* (1939), where flooding rivers help shape destinies. But everywhere the land and its uses and man's place on it engage Faulkner's attention. In *Absalom, Absalom!* (1936), Thomas Sutpen sets out to subdue the land, which for him is something to be conquered and dominated in the end of his grand design. In so doing, he embodies the southern experience. Faulkner's understanding of the land and nature was more complex, as he demonstrated in another of his masterpieces, *Go Down, Moses* (1940). The land and the natural world are exemplified in Old Ben, the bear of the most famous story of that work. *Go Down, Moses* is an elegy for a vanishing wilderness, for the essential wildness that Ben represents. It ranks among the most forceful works that capture the sorrow of a diminished connection to the wilderness, not only in the South but in the nation.

The South has not, however, led the way in conservation efforts. That movement was born in the Far West. Although southern writers have often made identification with the land an important feature of their work, the concept of the land looms even larger in the western psyche, in part because the Native American presence has remained strong, in part because the ecosystems are much more fragile than they are in the South, in part because the landscapes are often intensely dramatic and vast. In the West, the eye typically takes in wide horizons and great extremes. John Muir, John Burroughs, Aldo Leopold, Ansel Adams, Wallace Stegner, and Edward Abbey are among the western names prominent among conservation advocates of the twentieth century. The West gave birth to the Sierra Club and the Wilderness Society. Stories of travelers from the East and the South who found new identities or visions in the West are, however, numerous, most famous among them being Teddy Roosevelt, whose western experience would cause him to make conservation a major goal. He placed 150,000,000 acres of forest in the national preserve and in 1908 held a national conservation conference, which was followed by the creation of conservation committees in all states. A transplanted southerner, Joseph LeConte was very active in conservation movements when he became a professor at the University of California after the Civil War.

When in 1998 *Audubon* magazine cited "100 Environmental Heroes" of the twentieth century, it identified only a handful of southerners, though some made major contributions. The list includes Jimmy Carter, Lyndon Johnson, Lady Bird Johnson, Marjorie Stoneman Douglas, and Wendell Berry. Douglas is famous for her book *The Everglades: River of Grass* (1947). With the publication of her *Florida: The Long Frontier* (1967), she became, at age seventy-eight, one of the country's leading environmental activists, and she continued to work even as a centenarian to preserve the Everglades. Wendell Berry is the purest inheritor of the Agrarian vision, *The Unsettling of America: Culture and Agriculture* (1977) perhaps his most powerful and passionate statement of it. Like many of the Agrarians, he taught for many years at a university, but unlike them he continued to farm. To an uncommon degree, he has lived intimately with the land, finding in it spiritual sustenance. In Berry, the Jeffersonian ideal survives, and in his essays, poems, and novels he espouses responsibility for the land and for one's fellow human beings. But it is to Thoreau rather than Jefferson that comparisons with Berry have most often been made. Both writers want to wake up their neighbors, want themselves to live deliberately, and find that doing so involves an abiding respect for nature.

Southerners not cited on *Audubon*'s list have, however, made important contributions to conservation and nature writing. Several of Wilma Dykeman's protagonists work to conserve the land. Dykeman's sensitivity to the natural world was apparent from the inauguration of her literary output with the highly acclaimed *The French Broad* (1955), which was part of the Rivers of America series. Like the heroine of her first novel, *The Tall Woman* (1962), Dykeman has persevered in her concern for the Appalachian country. In subsequent novels and nonfiction explorations of Appalachia, Dykeman has continued to fault notions of "progress" in the South. As the Sunbelt began to triumph over older images, the South has ceased to wear the mantle of the most economically deprived section of the country. The new prosperity has brought with it greatly increased populations that have not only changed cultural patterns but have put new pressures on land and waters. At the end of the century, the farmer has become a small fraction of the southern population. Farming has become megafarming— compounding the pollution of rivers and streams. Dykeman would find new allies as the century hastened on.

The most famous southern book exploring nature is Annie Dillard's *Pilgrim at Tinker Creek* (1974). Strictly speaking, Dillard is not a southerner. She grew up in Pittsburgh but then entered Hollins College in Roanoke, Virginia, an action that altered her life in major ways. She would be at Hollins for a decade, first as student, then as faculty wife. Her chief literary passions at Hollins were Emily Dickinson and Henry David Thoreau, on whom she wrote her M.A. thesis. At Hollins, she wrote the acclaimed *Pilgrim,* for which she won the Pulitzer Prize. The work has been heralded for the precision of her close attention to nature. It continues the religious quest of much nature writing, seeking to discover the meaning in and behind the natural object.

Others in the late twentieth century have given thoughtful attention to the "goodliest land" of the South, and with increasing urgency. Playwright Samm-Art Williams, a native of Burgaw, North Carolina, called attention to the struggle of African American farmers to retain their land (the percentage of black farmers has been reduced even more than the overall decline). Williams's triumphant pastoral drama *Home* (named one of the Best Plays of 1979–1980) deals with a small farmer who loses his farmstead then leads a rough and dissipated life in the city, but who in the end is serendipitously reunited with the land. Novelist Cormac McCarthy has steadily and carefully observed a high contrast between the natural world and the human, with degraded man frequently seeming to defile nature by superimposing upon it cruelty, brutality, and just plain carelessness; McCarthy's astonishing descriptive and narrative powers reveal a dark, complex vision of the relations between humankind and nature. In *Child of God* (1973), a labyrinth of caves hides and protects a necrophiliac killer. In *Suttree* (1986), a rockslide in the rain ends an Edenic love affair. Although McCarthy's roots are in Tennessee, after his fourth novel he moved to El Paso, Texas. Following the publication of *Blood Meridian; or, The Evening Redness in the West* (1985) and especially with the great success of his border trilogy (*All the Pretty Horses*, 1992; *The Crossing*, 1993; and *Cities of the Plain*, 1998), McCarthy was reckoned a western writer as well as a southern writer, his works finding great resonance with western readers, for whom the land often takes on mythic force. From its beginnings, poetry has looked to the natural world for inspiration and focus; contemporary southern poets have looked frequently to the same source. A. R. Ammons, Fred Chappell, Andrew Hudgins, Robert Morgan, James Seay, Charles Eaton, Kathryn Stripling Byer, Henry Taylor, and Peter Makuck—among others—have provided lyric exploration of nature and men and women on the land.

In greater numbers than ever, southern nonfiction writers have made important contributions to the genre of nature writing. They include Janet Lembke (*River Time: The Frontier of the Lower Neuse*, 1989, and *Dangerous Birds: A Naturalist's Aviary*, 1992); Jan DeBlieu (*Hatteras Journal*, 1987, and *Wind: How the Flow of Air Has Shaped Life, Myth and the Land*, 1998); James Kilgo (*Deep Enough for Ivorybills*, 1988); Franklin Burroughs (*Horry and the Waccamaw*, 1987); and Bland Simpson (*The Great Dismal: A Carolinian's Swamp Memoir*, 1990). Occasioned by the publication of his *Into the Sound Country: A Carolinian's Coastal Plain* (1997), with photographs by Ann Cary Simpson, in 1998 Bland Simpson was named Conservation Communicator of the year by the North Carolina Wildlife Federation.

Across a variety of literary forms, there is yet in the South and its writers a strong sense of wonder about these temperate and subtropical lands, whether they are farmed, forested, peopled, or forlorn. After four centuries of colonization, cultivation, and aggression, the southern region presents no shortages of paradoxes to those who would express such wonder and regard. As poet-novelist-critic Fred Chappell notes in his novel *I Am One of You Forever* (1985): "Sometimes, walk-ing in the country, one comes upon an abandoned flower garden overtaken by wild flowers. Is it still a garden? The natural and the artificial orders intermingle, and ready definition is lost."

Joseph M. Flora

See also Audubon, John J.; Bartram, William; Naturalism; Promotional Tract; Travel Literature.

Alan Feduccia, *Catesby's Birds of Colonial America* (1985); Norman Foerster, *Nature in American Literature* (1923); Philip Marshall Hicks, *The Development of the Natural History Essay in American Literature* (1924); John Lane and Gerald Thurmond, eds., *The Woods Stretched for Miles: Contemporary Southern Nature Writing* (1999); Thomas J. Lyon, ed., *This Incomperable Lande* (1989); Roderick Nash, *Wilderness and the American Mind* (1967).

NEO-SLAVE NARRATIVE

Neo-slave narratives are contemporary novels about slavery by African American writers. These novels may be historical, set in the antebellum South, or they may be set in post-Reconstruction or twentieth-century America to explore the ramifications of the African American's enslaved past. All neo-slave narratives begin from the assumption that the legacy of American slavery is both formative and permanent.

Bernard Bell was among the first to issue a formal definition, calling the works "residually oral, modern narratives of escape from bondage to freedom." As the term suggests, neo-slave narratives borrow many conventions from the eighteenth- and nineteenth-century slave narratives, especially the insistence on viewing slavery from the enslaved person's point of view. The central conflict usually originates from the protagonist's desire to be free, either physically or mentally, from the bonds of slavery, and most works trace a character's discovery of the worth of the self outside of the institution of slavery. Other elements include uses of the spiritual and the folkloric, and the narratives usually evoke the African tradition of storytelling, with importance being placed on passing the story to future generations. Unlike the original slave narratives, which were usually simple and straightforward in style, many neo-slave narratives are postmodern, experimental in narrative voice and form.

Many scholars point to Margaret Walker's 1966 novel *Jubilee* as the first neo-slave narrative. Prior to

1966, only Arna Bontemps's *Black Thunder* (1936), a fictional account of an attempted slave revolt that occurred in 1800, dealt explicitly with slavery. Other works, such as Zora Neale Hurston's *Their Eyes Were Watching God* (1937), Richard Wright's *Black Boy* (1945), and Ralph Ellison's *Invisible Man* (1952), are sometimes referred to as neo-slave narratives. These works employ many conventions of the slave narrative, although they treat the subject of slavery only peripherally.

The 1960s saw a rekindling of interest in slavery as subject matter. The revisionist scholarship being undertaken by historians such as John Blassingame, Eugene Genovese, and Herbert Gutman, as well as the impetus provided by the Civil Rights Movement and the Black Panther Movement, led to a literary rebirth of the slave narrative. In addition to Walker's *Jubilee*, Ernest Gaines's *The Autobiography of Miss Jane Pittman* (1971) heralded the acceptance of America's slave past as rich subject matter for a people long in search of creative empowerment. The televised version of Alex Haley's *Roots* and the controversy fueled by William Styron's *The Confessions of Nat Turner* (1967) increased awareness of the imaginative possibilities of these narratives.

Recent neo-slave narratives seem intent on smashing the romantic stereotypes of the plantation tradition. These works portray enslaved persons as dignified, spiritual human beings with their own cultural norms, traditions, and familial ties. Their resistance to slavery's oppression stands at the center of the works, and the overall theme of the neo-slave narratives is not merely endurance but celebration.

Following is a list of some of the most important neo-slave narratives published since 1971: *Corregidora* (Gayl Jones, 1975), *Roots* (Alex Haley, 1976), *Flight to Canada* (Ishmael Reed, 1976), *Kindred* (Octavia Butler, 1979), *Sally Hemings* (Barbara Chase-Riboud, 1979), *The Chaneysville Incident* (David Bradley, 1981), *Oxherding Tale* (Charles R. Johnson, 1982), *Dessa Rose* (Sherley Anne Williams, 1986), *Beloved* (Toni Morrison, 1987), *Middle Passage* (Johnson, 1990), *Family* (J. California Cooper, 1991).

Elizabeth Beaulieu

See also African American Literature, 1919 to Present; Chattel Slavery; Slave Narrative.

Elizabeth Beaulieu, *Black Women Writers and the American Neo-Slave Narrative: Femininity Unfettered* (1999); Bernard Bell, *The Afro-American Novel and Its Traditions* (1987); Deborah E. McDowell and Arnold Rampersad, eds., *Slavery and the Literary Imagination* (1987); James Olney, " 'I Was Born': Slave Narratives, Their Status as Autobiography and as Literature," in *The Slave's Narrative*, ed. Charles T. Davis and Henry Louis Gates Jr. (1985); Ashraf H. A. Rushdy, "Reading Black, White, and Gray in 1968: The Origins of the Contemporary Narrative of Slavery," in *Criticism and the Color Line: Desegregating American Literary Studies*, ed. Henry B. Wonham (1995).

NEW CRITICISM

The term *New Criticism* was first used by Joel Spingarn in a lecture at Columbia University in 1910. Spingarn, however, used it to describe an impressionistic procedure that bears little resemblance to what later became known as New Criticism. The latter derives from the critical writings of Modernist poets T. S. Eliot and Ezra Pound and the methodologies of critics I. A. Richards and William Empson. It was given its name by a book, *The New Criticism*, published by John Crowe Ransom in 1941. Southern New Criticism originated in the poetic theory and practice of the Fugitive poets at Vanderbilt University in the 1920s. In addition to Ransom, its main practitioners were Allen Tate, Cleanth Brooks, and Robert Penn Warren. The major New Critical journals were the *Southern Review,* founded by Brooks and Warren at Louisiana State University, and the *Kenyon Review,* founded by Ransom at Kenyon College. These journals, along with Brooks and Warren's textbooks *Understanding Poetry* (1938) and *Understanding Fiction* (1943), established New Criticism as the dominant method of teaching literature in American universities, a dominance it maintained until the 1970s.

The southern New Critics shared certain assumptions. They all believed that literature offers a concrete form of knowledge opposed to the abstractions of science; used irony, ambiguity, and paradox as criteria for aesthetic judgment of literature; and emphasized the formal structures of a text over "extrinsic" factors: history, author biography, and reader response. They also shared the methodology of close reading of words in a text to determine the meaning and value of works of literature. Despite these common elements—and the tendency of their critics to lump them together—Ransom, Tate, Brooks, and Warren were individual thinkers, and each had his own version of New Criticism.

Ransom was the most philosophical of the southern New Critics. His was a rationalist criticism influenced by Immanuel Kant. He believed that criticism should be objective, should exclude readers' emotional reactions and minimize attention to factors outside the text. Like the other New Critics, he considered poetry a form of knowledge unattainable through science. Scientists, he believed, study an object only as an example of the class of such objects. Poets, on the other hand, study an object in, of, and for itself. Art, and particularly poetry, embodies an approach to the world that Ransom called "love not use"—for the poet, the value of the world is intrinsic and not in its practical use. He also believed that poetry is characterized by an irreducible dualism. He made an absolute separation of the sound structure of a poem—rhythm, meter, rhyme, alliteration, etc.—and its subject matter or "logical structure." For him, this dualism could never be resolved into a larger unity but only held in balance, neither structure overwhelming the other. The best examples of such balance, for him, are found in the metaphysical poetry of the seventeenth century. This dualism caused Ransom to undervalue Shakespeare, whose lack of "logical structure" he condemned in his essay "Shakespeare at Sonnets," an essay initially rejected by Brooks and Warren for publication in the *Southern Review*. It also caused him to reject much modernist poetry. He believed that the modernist poets' rejection of traditional poetic structures caused them to vacillate between a bloodless aestheticism (form without content) and a willful obscurity.

Of all the southern New Critics, Tate was the most influenced by Eliot, an influence that Ransom tended to reject. Tate and Ransom especially disagreed on the value of Eliot's *The Waste Land*. Tate believed it to be a seminal poem of the twentieth century, whereas Ransom objected to Eliot's rejection of traditional poetic structures. Tate was also the most overtly political of the New Critics. In a field dominated by liberalism and Marxism, he entitled his first critical book *Reactionary Essays on Poetry and Ideas* (1936). In his career, Tate swung back and forth between pure formalism (attention only to the text of a literary work) and a more extrinsic criticism, influenced by conservative, even reactionary, politics and Roman Catholicism, to which he converted in 1950. In *Reactionary Essays,* Tate is committed to a cultural criticism borrowed from Eliot. The critic, he maintained in that book, must relate works of literature to the tradition and conditions of the culture that produced it. In his second book, *Reason in Mad-*

ness (1941), he came closer to the formalism of the other southern New Critics. Even there, he departs from Ransom in certain ways. He defends the experimental techniques of modernism and adds a subjective component to Ransom's theory of poetry as concrete knowledge of particular objects. For Tate, knowledge always involves interaction between mind and object rather than a more passive contemplation of the object. In *The Hovering Fly* (1948), he begins to move toward a metaphysical explanation of the poetic imagination, a move completed by his conversion to Catholicism and given full expression in *The Forlorn Demon* (1953). In that book, Tate distinguishes between the angelic imagination, which he attributes to Edgar Allan Poe, and the symbolic imagination, which he attributes to Dante. The former attempts to know essences directly, to transcend the physical for absolute knowledge of the metaphysical. The latter accepts its limitations and settles for what it can know of the metaphysical *through* the physical. The former, for Tate, is the sin of pride, human attempting to be angel. The latter is a religious attitude respectful of both creation and creator. The best literature, Tate believed, made use of the symbolic imagination, embodying its "message" in concrete particulars.

In *Modern Poetry and the Tradition* (1939), Cleanth Brooks acknowledges the influence of both Tate and Ransom as well as Eliot, Richards, Empson, William Butler Yeats, and R. P. Blackmur. Brooks was more scholarly than Ransom or Tate, but like them, he believed that poetry embodied concrete experience as opposed to the abstractions of science. For Brooks, the best poetry conveyed that experience by "dramatization" rather than direct statement. Unlike Ransom, Brooks did not value "logical unity" in a poem but instead valued what he called "imaginative unity," by which he meant both the breadth of experience that a poem contained and its ability to unify disparate strands of experience. Like Ransom, Brooks favored the metaphysical poets, but whereas Ransom valued their ability to balance sound and logical structure, Brooks saw them as unifying those elements. Irony, ambiguity, and paradox were more central to his judgment of literature than to Ransom's or Tate's, and while they were primarily concerned with poetry, Brooks extended New Critical method to fiction and drama. Critics of *Modern Poetry and the Tradition* pointed out that in his elevation of metaphysical and modernist poetry, Brooks had ignored or undervalued literature written from 1660 to 1900. He attempted to rectify that situation in his next book, *The Well-Wrought Urn* (1947). He broke no new theoretical ground in that book but did attempt to apply New Critical theory to literature from periods other than the seventeenth and twentieth centuries. Brooks continued to be an unapologetic New Critic until his death in 1994. In his final volume of essays, *Community, Religion, and Literature* (1995), he ably defends New Criticism against such contemporary critics of it as the deconstructionists and New Historicists.

Brooks's friend and collaborator Warren was more scholarly than Tate and had a broader critical approach than Brooks. In fact, he was never comfortable with the label "New Critic." He wrote fewer theoretical works than Ransom, Tate, or Brooks. Those he wrote were essays rather than books, the two most famous being "Pure and Impure Poetry" (1943) and "A Poem of Pure Imagination" (1946). He shared Brooks's concern with fiction and wrote a series of essays on several fiction writers: William Faulkner, Joseph Conrad, Eudora Welty, and Katherine Anne Porter. "Pure and Impure Poetry" reiterates themes found in Brooks's work. "Pure" poetry attempts to exclude any element that contradicts its original impulses. By doing so, it leaves out whole areas of human experience and is therefore inferior to "impure" poetry. The latter tests its vision by exposing it to elements with which it may jar, particularly with irony. The result is a vision that survives the contradictions and complexities of actual experience. Warren departs from pure formalism in "A Poem of Pure Imagination," an exploration of Coleridge's *The Rime of the Ancient Mariner*. In that essay, he uses "extrinsic" factors like Coleridge's "sober prose," history, and philosophy to illuminate the poem. But even in this essay, he does not part from New Criticism entirely. He considers extrinsic factors relevant only so far as they help reveal the meaning of words in the text.

New Criticism has come under sustained attack in the last twenty-five years by a succession of newer critical theories: myth criticism, structuralism, deconstruction, and New Historicism. The attacks are often politically motivated—many contemporary critics object to the religious, conservative outlook of the southern New Critics. Other objections include New Critical methodology and theoretical assumptions. The New Criticism has flaws. Its aesthetic of irony, ambiguity, and paradox works well for modernist poetry but not so well for that of other periods. Brooks's attempts to apply those methods to literature of all periods in *The Well-Wrought Urn* are rather strained. It also does not work quite as well for fiction as it does for poetry. Despite their flaws, however, the New Critics made great contributions to literary studies. Their methodology of close, careful reading and attention to the structures of a text is a tenet even of those theorists most critical of New Criticism. And as long as teachers teach survey courses outside their areas of expertise to students unfamiliar with much history and philosophy, the New Criticism will survive in some form.

Fred R. Thiemann

See also Agrarians; Fugitives, The; *Kenyon Review*; Literary Theory, Contemporary; Roman Catholics; *Southern Review*.

John Bradbury, *The Fugitives: A Critical Account* (1958); David Robley, "New Criticism," *Contemporary Literary Theory* (1986); Mark Royden Winchell, *Cleanth Brooks and the Rise of Modern Criticism* (1996).

NEW DEAL

When, on July 2, 1932, in his address to the Democratic National Convention accepting the presidential nomination, Franklin Delano Roosevelt pledged "a new deal for the American people," he had the South very much in mind. Since 1924, he had been going each year to Warm Springs, Georgia (a spa to which John Calhoun had once repaired), in the vain hope that the waters would restore his legs withered by infantile paralysis, and his long sojourns there had led to his calling himself "an adopted citizen of the South." Southern politicians and publicists aggressively promoted his candidacy for the presidency in 1932, and he owed a large debt to the states of the former Confederacy, which gave him their ballots all four times he ran.

Many of the programs of FDR's first term—notably the National Industrial Recovery Act (NRA), the Agricultural Adjustment Act (AAA), and the Social Security Act—were national in scope, but some had a decidedly regional aspect. The Tennessee Valley Authority (TVA) electrified a vast region in which only 3 percent of homes in 1933 had lights, created vast recreational lakes (though sometimes at the expense of farm lands), dug a nine-foot navigational channel from Knoxville to Paducah, and virtually wiped out malaria. FDR's confrontations with poverty in rural Georgia helped shape other New Deal policies. "It can be said with a good deal of truth," Roosevelt once remarked, "that a little cottage at Warm Springs, Georgia, was the birthplace of the Rural Electrification Administration."

The New Deal did not always have a benign effect. Several agencies discriminated against African Americans. Norris, Tennessee, the TVA's model town, permitted no blacks to live there. One historian has grouped the impact of the AAA on southern agriculture with flood, drought, and the boll weevil, because it drove sharecroppers and tenant farmers from the land. Other critics deplored government intrusiveness. "We no longer farm in Mississippi cotton-fields," said William Faulkner a decade after Roosevelt's death. "We farm now in Washington corridors and Congressional committeerooms."

Most of the South, though, viewed FDR and the New Deal as saviors. Federal labor programs raised wages and shortened hours, wiped out child labor, ended mill-village paternalism, and encouraged unionization, though unions did not make the strides in the South that they did elsewhere. The AAA subsidized the growers of cotton, tobacco, peanuts, sugar, and rice, all of them southern staples, and the Farm Security Administration made modest improvements in the lives of sharecroppers and tenant farmers. In some southern communities, the Roosevelt Administration was the chief source of income for African Americans.

In a number of ways, Roosevelt sought to liberalize southern political practices and attitudes. He supported efforts to eradicate the poll tax; appointed the progressive Alabaman Hugo Black to the U.S. Supreme Court; and lent his prestige to a number of liberal aspirants for higher office: Claude Pepper in Florida, Lister Hill in Alabama, and Lyndon B. Johnson in Texas. He even attempted, though he failed, to "purge" southern conservatives Walter George of Georgia and Ellison "Cotton Ed" Smith of South Carolina in the 1938 Senate primaries. In a controversial speech in Gainesville, Georgia, in 1938, he accused southern oligarchs of fostering a "feudal system," adding, "when you come down to it, there is little difference between the feudal system and the Fascist system."

In 1938, he sent shock waves through the region when he stated his "conviction that the South presents right now the nation's number one economic problem." Chambers of Commerce resented that characterization as an affront to sectional pride, but Roosevelt intended the declaration as a call to the nation to treat the South more fairly. An investigation he sponsored that year produced a document, *Report on the Economic Conditions of the South*, that focused further attention on the extent of poverty in the region, and that sparked the mobilization of southern liberals into a new organization, the Southern Conference for Human Welfare. New Deal programs to aid jobless white-collar workers had an important cultural dimension. The Federal Writers' Project turned out an excellent series of state guides and recorded the narratives of former slaves. In Florida, Zora Neale Hurston supervised the recovery of African American folklore, and in North Carolina, William T. Couch encouraged the collection of the life histories of workers and farmers that resulted in the highly acclaimed volume *These Are Our Lives* (1939). The Federal Theater Project sponsored Paul Green's historical pageant at Roanoke Island, while in Charleston the New Deal refurbished the eighteenth-century Dock Street Theater. The Federal Music Project transcribed bayou songs and river chanteys, and in Vicksburg it fostered an all-blind orchestra. In a storefront in Raleigh, North Carolina, the government opened its very first community art project, and in Mississippi, the New Deal gave an opportunity to Eudora Welty to display her skills as a photographer.

In the six years that it flourished—1933 to 1938—the New Deal changed the face of the South. It built the Skyline Drive, the Blue Ridge Parkway, the scenic Natchez Trace Parkway, and the Overseas Highway in the Florida Keys; constructed the Orange Bowl as well as the football stadiums at the University of Arkansas, LSU, and Ole Miss; gave San Antonio a zoo and a European-style riverwalk; established a national park in the Big Bend country of the Rio Grande and completed another in the Smokies; renovated the French Market in the Vieux Carré of New Orleans and configured the sea wall at Biloxi. Not since the era of Civil War and Reconstruction had any phenomenon had so great an influence on the South.

William E. Leuchtenburg

See also Federal Writers' Project; Great Depression; Tennessee Valley Authority.

Anthony J. Badger, *The New Deal: The Depression Years, 1933–1940* (1989); Roger Biles, *The South and the New Deal* (1994); Frank Freidel, *F.D.R. and the South* (1965); William E. Leuchtenburg, *The FDR Years: On Roosevelt and His Legacy* (1995), and *Franklin D. Roosevelt and the New Deal, 1932–1940* (1963).

NEW JOURNALISM

New Journalism is the term used to describe a form of writing that in the mid-1960s revolutionized the world of magazine and newspaper journalism and, in the hands of fiction writers, arguably changed the direction of the American novel. Writers in this new genre fused the techniques of fiction writing, such as the use of dialogue, scene setting, and character development, with factual reporting to create a hybrid intended to capture with a greater degree of realism the complexity of modern society. The term *New Journalism* was coined by Virginia-born Tom Wolfe (1931–   ), who articulated and advocated the new form. Truman Capote (1923–1984), born in New Orleans, is also credited with development of this form, though he applied to it the term *nonfiction novel.* Both the terms and the journalistic form they describe have been controversial since their inception.

Wolfe's career as a writer began after he received his Ph.D. in American Studies from Yale in 1957. Always an aspiring novelist, he had begun, while in graduate school, to doubt the validity of fiction as an art form because of its obsessively introspective orientation, and he turned his attention instead to journalism, drawn by the possibility of realism. He began working for the *Springfield (Massachusetts) Union,* then moved to the *Washington Post* in 1959. In 1962 he moved again, this time to the *New York Herald Tribune,* where competition among the feature writers fostered innovation. The following year, Wolfe attempted his first magazine piece, convincing *Esquire* to send him to a custom-car show in California. The writer, overwhelmed by what he saw, found the language and conventions of the traditional feature story inadequate. In a scene that has become the set-piece of New Journalism history, Wolfe describes himself wrangling with his experience but unable to write the story, despite pressure from his impatient client. Finally conceding defeat to the material, Wolfe agreed to send the magazine his notes so someone else could do the story, working all night to shape the notes and his thoughts into the form of a memorandum to send his editor. Upon reading the resulting forty-nine pages, the editor deleted the "Dear Byron" at the top, made a few minor changes, and ran the piece. The New Journalism was born. With the publication of "There Goes (Varoom! Varoom!) That Kandy-Kolored (Thphhhhhh!) Tangerine-Flake Streamline Baby (Rahghh) Around the Bend (Brummmmmmmmmmmmmm) . . . ," Wolfe became credited with inventing a new medium for writers that applied the techniques of fiction to the facts of reportage, creating a combination that was much more exciting to read and offered much more in-depth coverage

of a subject. This essay gave its title in modified form to Wolfe's first book, a collection of essays published in 1965 that immediately became a best-seller. Throughout Wolfe's career, his name has been synonymous with the New Journalism, which he defines in his preface to *The New Journalism* (1965) and elsewhere as a nonfiction account enriched by four characteristics: scene-by-scene construction that uses as little historical narrative as possible; realistic dialogue to establish and define character and to engage the reader; third-person point of view to make the reader feel that he or she is inside the character's mind; and, most important, the recording of details that are symbolic of people's status in life, their expression of their position or aspirations in the world. This critical recording of detail, according to Wolfe, creates the realism that gives literature its power. Wolfe's virtuosity in creating this realism makes him a powerful satirist and hallmarks his idiosyncratic style.

Wolfe has established himself as an astute social critic whose explorations have been published in essay collections such as *The Kandy-Colored Tangerine-Flake Streamline Baby* (1965); *The Pump House Gang* (1968); and *Radical Chic and Mau-Mauing the Flak Catchers* (1970). The first long work in the genre, however, was *The Electric Kool-Aid Acid Test* (1968), Wolfe's exploration of the development of the California drug culture under the leadership of novelist Ken Kesey. In 1979 he published *The Right Stuff,* suspending for the most part his role as social satirist and undertaking an extended examination of the creation of the first group of astronauts. Personalizing the drama in the development of the space program, Wolfe focused on the psychology of its mainstream American heroes and on the status system built on individual rebellion and on egos that defy the limitations of nature and the machine.

Writing what he labeled the "nonfiction novel," Capote, like Wolfe, sought the achievement of realism by combining reportage and novelistic techniques of narration, subjective description, scene construction, and psychological exploration. Whereas Wolfe approached his subjects from the perspective of a journalist seeking greater depth and complexity in the exploration of the facts, Capote brought to his search for a more meaningful literary form the sensibilities of the novelist seeking the power that fact could give a work of fiction. With the publication of *In Cold Blood* in 1965—the account of the murder of a farm family in Holcomb, Kansas, in 1959—Capote identified himself with the new literary form and helped change the direction of the modern American novel.

Like Wolfe, Capote sought the power of realism in writing, although his approach, style, and background differed markedly from Wolfe's. Whereas Wolfe in the mid-1960s was a journalist trying to establish a territory and make a name for himself, Capote had already achieved fame at age twenty-four with his first novel, *Other Voices, Other Rooms,* in 1948. He had also published *The Grass Harp* (1951) and *Breakfast at Tiffany's* (1958). Capote was an essay writer as well, publishing in 1950 *Local Color,* a collection of travel essays detailing his experiences in such diverse places as Manhattan, Haiti, Hollywood, and Paris and illustrating them with photographs. The inclusion of photographs in the collection and his provision of text to accompany Richard Avedon's photographs in *Observations* (1959) suggest Capote's sense of the inadequacy of language in the quest to recreate real experience. Capote had also published *The Muses Are Heard* (1956), a series of essays first appearing in the *New Yorker* detailing his experiences while traveling to Russia with an opera company sent to perform *Porgy and Bess* as a gesture of cultural exchange.

When a news article about the murder of the Clutter family in Kansas caught his attention in 1959, Capote was intrigued by the material as a subject for an experimental form, the nonfiction novel. The story, he believed, would have intrinsic power because it was true, and he set out for Kansas with his cousin Harper Lee to begin work. Exhaustively researching and gathering material, Capote interviewed the family and friends of the victims, law-enforcement personnel, and townspeople, and established a close relationship with the killers themselves. He also examined all the documents pertaining to the case, working on the project for almost five years. The result was the compelling bestseller *In Cold Blood,* a novel that probed the psychology of the murderers and the sociology of the murders. Using the traditional objective, distanced narrative style, Capote created a subjective view of the crime as a result of society's failure. Critics have noted that Capote seems to identify with the killers, Percy Smith and Dick Hickock, portraying them, especially Smith, as victims of circumstance. The story is told from the inside out with intimate detail, dialogue, and scene-by-scene construction, using cinematic technique.

Two primary issues haunt critics and analysts, both stemming in some way from the signature new journalistic approach—the author's ambiguous attitude toward his or her subject and the problematic ethics of presenting fiction as fact. Wolfe has always been at the center of the controversy about the new form, even when it was no longer new. Dwight Macdonald, reviewing *The Kandy-Kolored Tangerine-Flake Streamline Baby* in the *New York Review of Books,* articulated concerns still relevant to criticism of the New Journalism and extending as well to the nonfiction, or documentary, novel. Calling the form "parajournalism," Macdonald attacked it as an illegitimate appropriation of journalism's "factual authority" for the purpose of entertaining rather than informing. Macdonald also objected to the disturbing authorial ambiguity that Wolfe's shifting points of view created. Although other responses, such as those from Kurt Vonnegut and Stanley Reynolds, were favorable, even enthusiastic, questions about the blurring of lines between fact and fiction, about news as entertainment, and about subjectivity remain unsettled. And although challenges have been made to the assertions by both Wolfe and Capote regarding the newness and the uniqueness of their forms, the influence of these writers on subsequent journalists and novelists has been undeniable.

Daphne H. O'Brien

Phyllis Frus, *The Politics and Poetics of Journalistic Narrative* (1994); John Hellman, *Fables of Fact: The New Journalism as New Fiction* (1981); John Hollowell, *Fact and Fiction: The New Journalism and the Nonfiction Novel* (1977); Michael Johnson, *The New Journalism* (1971); Tom Wolfe and E. W. Johnson, eds., *The New Journalism* (1965).

NEW NEGRO

New Negro is a term usually associated with the Harlem Renaissance artistic movement of the 1920s and 1930s. Its history is somewhat longer than this, though it has always carried the same general connotations of education, achievement, and racial pride. The first known use among African Americans occurred in 1895 in the *Cleveland Gazette* to refer to an emergent black middle class, "with education, refinement, and money." Five years later, Booker T. Washington, Fannie Williams, and N. B. Wood edited *A New Negro for a New Century,* a compendium of past racial achievement and current efforts at self-improvement. Williams wrote about the importance of the women's clubs for encouraging self-respect, and Washington described the positive effects of education for the generations born after slavery. In 1916, Williams Pickens published *The New Negro: His Political, Civil and Mental Status*, which argued for full civil and political rights for the race.

The term suggests a contrast with "Old Negro," the figure of the ignorant, submissive slave incapable of cultural and economic advancement. This image, which Alain Locke called "more a myth than a man," was the stereotype understood by both races to represent black identity under slavery. Because this image was used by whites to justify continued denial of black opportunity and citizenship, it was essential to displace it. "New Negro" was flexible enough to include elements of Washington's bootstraps programs, such as vocational education and businessmen's associations; W. E. B. Du Bois's "Talented Tenth," which was an intellectual elite with the duty of racial uplift; and the political figures who supported the Republican Party. Thus it could serve a wide range of agendas, even when these contradicted each other, as in the case of Washington and Du Bois. The term and the ideas connected to it indicate a variety of approaches to improving the conditions of the race.

In the early twentieth century, the phrase was principally associated with an urban and increasingly northern African American population. The Great Migration, military service in World War I, and the formation of such groups as the National Association for the Advancement of Colored People (NAACP), the National Urban League, and Marcus Garvey's Universal Negro Improvement Association resulted in higher education levels, greater demands for civil rights, improved income levels, and a greater sense of group identity. Leaving behind the legacy of labor exploitation, illiteracy, Jim Crowism, and white violence and intimidation, promoters of the race saw the future as a version of the American dream that acknowledged the reality of the past but clearly saw it as past.

One result was the exploration of black history and experience as a source for cultural production and group pride. The journal *Survey Graphic* in 1924 published a special issue on blacks, edited by Alain Locke, professor of philosophy at Howard University. With additional material, he brought the collection out a year later as a book entitled *The New Negro*. Although much of the volume was made up of the art of a younger generation, such as Langston Hughes, Countee Cullen, and Jean Toomer, it also included commentaries by an older group, exemplified by Du Bois and

James Weldon Johnson. The range demonstrated Locke's view that the New Negro concept had more to do with attitude than with age.

Those identifying with the concept of the New Negro emphasized black achievement and recognition. They often differed in what this meant. Among artists, for example, at least three different positions are apparent. Some argued for an art that transcended race, some for work that focused on racial problems and black accomplishment, and others for the use of African American materials, regardless of the implications of doing so. The first group was epitomized by Countee Cullen, who saw himself as the modern John Keats and wanted to be known as "a poet, not a black poet." Du Bois repeatedly argued for "art as propaganda," serving primarily to express the need for social justice and group pride. He used the pages of *Crisis*, the journal of the NAACP, to attack writers presenting negative or ambiguous images of the race or to praise those offering positive models. Langston Hughes and Zora Neale Hurston, among others, found their most important resources in the music, stories, and speech that had developed in the South of slavery and segregation. Hughes focused in his poetry on the speech, experiences, and music of common black people, while Hurston made use of the language patterns, tales, and folk practices of the rural South. Like Jean Toomer, who rendered the blacks of Georgia in a more poetic and experimental manner, Hughes and Hurston insisted that artistry was more important than racial message.

In *The New Negro*, Locke suggests the variety of meanings of his title phrase by bringing together the poetry, fiction, drama, and visual arts of the younger generation; commentaries on black art, music, and literature; folk tales and African cultural expressions, sociological and historical analyses; and essays on the relationships of blacks to American society and the international community. The sociological articles focus on Harlem, Howard University, the Tuskegee-Hampton efforts in vocational education, the black middle class, and the West Indies. In some ways, it is the very diversity of possibilities signified by such lists that reveals the importance of the term for its time, especially when compared to the one-dimensional characterization of "Old Negro." The variety also demonstrates the limits of identifying the renaissance specifically with Harlem or with literary work.

At the same time that the assertion of this new identity was occurring, some began to question the consequences of a New Negro sensibility. Jean Toomer and

W. E. B. Du Bois, though very different in their views of literature, both criticized the effects of urbanization and material accumulation on the spiritual life of the race. In the very work that some position as the artistic debut of the renaissance, *Cane* (1923), Toomer creates urbanized black characters who have lost a sense of selfhood by being displaced from their southern roots. Lives of education and consumption destroy their connection to spiritual truth. Du Bois, who consistently argued for higher education and moral duty, saw the very achievement of a middle-class status as a threat to the realization of justice and equality in the sense that money and individualism came to be more highly prized by the black bourgeoisie.

More recently, Henry Louis Gates has argued that *New Negro* was a trope used by intellectuals of the late nineteenth and early twentieth century to construct a public image of blacks that counters their anxiety about the true nature of the race. It suggested a break with history by which the heritage of slavery could be discounted. Gates points to visual images associated with commentaries on the concept in books and periodicals as examples of the desired racial self. Consistently, these reveal a middle-class status and moral seriousness that contradict the "Sambo" imagery of the mainstream popular press. In this view, the New Negro was not a reality or a development so much as a fantasy of racial identity.

Unlike the parallel term *New South*, which seems to have a rebirth every generation, *New Negro* did not show resilience over time. Even though the attitudes and views it represented recurred, the phrase largely disappeared once the movement most identified with it dissipated in the Great Depression.

Keith E. Byerman

See also African American Folk Culture; Happy Darky; Harlem Renaissance; Plantation; Race, Idea of; Racism; Sambo.

Houston A. Baker Jr., *Modernism and the Harlem Renaissance* (1987); Dickson D. Bruce Jr., *Black American Writing from the Nadir* (1989); Henry Louis Gates Jr., "The Trope of a New Negro and the Reconstruction of the Image of the Black," *Representations* 24 (Fall 1988); Nathan Irvin Huggins, *Harlem Renaissance* (1971); George Hutchinson, *The Harlem Renaissance in Black and White* (1995); David Levering Lewis, *When Harlem Was in Vogue* (1981); Alain Locke, *The New Negro* (1925); Cheryl A. Wall, *Women of the Harlem Renaissance* (1995); Cary D. Wintz, *Black Culture and the Harlem Renaissance* (1988).

NEW ORLEANS, LOUISIANA

Since its founding in 1718 by the French, New Orleans (or, as it was originally called, Nouvelle Orléans) has attracted the attention of writers all over the world. The French influence remained strong throughout the eighteenth and nineteenth century, even after Louisiana was purchased by the United States in 1803 and New Orleans became, at least in name, an American city, though retaining a strong Gallic flavor. The animosity that the Creoles (descendants of the French and Spanish settlers) felt toward *les Américains,* who began to pour into the city after the Louisiana Purchase, remained strong until the Civil War, which served to some extent to unite the two against an outside enemy.

Because of the city's laissez-faire life-style, its easygoing Latin approach to life, and its tolerance for indulgences of the flesh—food, drink, sex—New Orleans has earned for itself such titles as "The Big Easy," "Babylon on the Mississippi," and even the "Wickedest City in Christendom." From the beginning, writers have concentrated on this raffish quality of life, as well as on the elegance of the architecture, the tastiness of the unique cuisine, and the romance of the place. This marked contrast to the Calvinistic philosophy prevalent in the rest of the South and elsewhere in the nation for a long time served to draw writers and others to the city in search of what Tennessee Williams termed "freedom," an element that he believed essential for the creative artist. Even today, when attitudes toward morals are more permissive nationwide, the reputation of New Orleans as "Sin City" persists. It remains the place in which some residents of other parts of the country believe that they can forget briefly their moral compunctions and indulge whatever desires they may have.

Walker Percy, among others, has pointed out that New Orleans is not only a virtual island geographically—surrounded by river, lake, and swamps—but also culturally cut off, in part through its terrain, in part because of the population's persistent provincialism, from the customs, mores, and attitudes prevalent elsewhere in the South. Its distinctive blend of elements from a variety of ethnic groups makes it the most foreign of American cities in terms of religion, food, architecture, and life-style.

Writers particularly influenced by New Orleans include natives such as George Washington Cable, Lillian Hellman, Hamilton Basso, and Truman Capote, and outsiders who came there to live, such as Walt Whitman, Kate Chopin, Lafcadio Hearn, and Sherwood Anderson. William Faulkner, who wrote his first novel in the French Quarter in 1925, spent two formative years there, and Tennessee Williams, who arrived in the city as an unknown and struggling author in 1938, soon came to love it as his home and to write some of his best work in the city and about it. Currently, a number of noted authors, including Richard Ford and Julie Smith, have residences in the city. Contemporary writers Ishmael Reed, Ellen Gilchrist, Sheila Bosworth, and John Kennedy Toole have kept the reputation of New Orleans as a vibrant, swinging city very much alive.

W. Kenneth Holditch

See also Louisiana, Literature of.

Violet Harrington Bryan, *The Myth of New Orleans in Literature* (1993); Richard S. Kennedy, ed., *Literary New Orleans* (1992) and *Literary New Orleans in the Modern World* (1998); Walker Percy, "New Orleans, Mon Amour" in *Signposts in a Strange Land* (1991); Lyle Saxon, *New Orleans City Guide* (1938).

NEW ORLEANS TIMES-PICAYUNE

By the 1980s, the *Times-Picayune* had become the only daily general-circulation newspaper in New Orleans, having in the past century absorbed several others—the *Crescent,* the *Times,* the *Democrat,* the *States,* and the *Item,* for example. Founded as the *Picayune* in 1837, the paper took its name from a small coin called the *picaillon* (Anglicized to "picayune"), valued at about six cents, the cost of the paper. The founders, George Wilkins Kendall and Francis Asbury Lumsden, wanted to modernize the press in New Orleans so that their publication would reflect advances being made in big-city papers in the North. The result of their efforts was an entirely new kind of journalism, not only in New Orleans, but in the South in general, and numerous innovations are credited to them and their successors at the paper.

Noted writers who worked for the *Picayune* and the various journals that ultimately were incorporated with it include Walt Whitman, Joel Chandler Harris, George Washington Cable, Lafcadio Hearn, Mark Twain, O. Henry (William Sydney Porter), Lyle Saxon, Roark Bradford, and several of the founders of *The Double Dealer,* the literary journal that flourished in

the 1920s. When William Faulkner was living in the French Quarter in 1925, the *Picayune*'s night city editor, Roark Bradford, a noted fiction writer in his own right, contracted with him for several short sketches, which were published in the paper under the rubric "Mirrors of Chartres Street." Later they were collected in a volume entitled *New Orleans Sketches* (1959).

Among the innovations credited to the newspaper was the first use of a pony-express service to deliver dispatches to New Orleans and thence to other parts of the country. In addition, when Eliza Jane Poitevent Holbrook assumed the role of publisher and editor in 1876 after the death of her husband, who had owned and operated the *Picayune,* she became probably the first woman ever to hold such positions with a major metropolitan newspaper. Earlier, as a reporter for the paper, Mrs. Holbrook, using the pseudonym Pearl Rivers, had written and published poetry and essays, expanded the literary page, and added both a women's page and a children's page, which were among the first in any paper in the country. One journalist whom Mrs. Holbrook employed was Elizabeth Gilmer, who, writing under her pseudonym "Dorothy Dix," created the world's first letters-to-the-lovelorn column, which was syndicated in numerous journals.

In 1878, Eliza Jane Holbrook married the business manager of the paper, George Nicholson, and together they published and edited the *Picayune* and used it to campaign for reform in government and for other improvements in the community. Soon it became one of the major newspapers in the country, a reputation it retained until well into the twentieth century. It remained in the Nicholson family until the 1950s, when they lost financial control, and it was subsequently swallowed up in the nationwide conglomerate of Newhouse newspapers.

W. Kenneth Holditch

See also Newspapers.

Charles L. Dufour, *Ten Flags in the Wind* (1967); Kenneth Holditch, "A Creature Set Apart," in *Mississippi's Piney Woods,* ed. Noel Polk (1986); Lyle Saxon, *New Orleans City Guide* (1938).

NEW SOUTH

The dream of a New South was being born as the reality of the Old South was going down the red gullet of war. In the years immediately following the Confederacy's defeat, increasing numbers of southerners began to work to make the dream come true by embracing the New South creed. Many of the most effective proponents of the creed, which reached its peak in the 1880s, were the editors or publishers of major newspapers or journals: Richard H. Edmonds of the *Baltimore Manufacturers' Record,* Henry Watterson of the *Louisville Courier-Journal,* Daniel A. Tompkins of the *Charlotte Observer,* Francis W. Dawson of the *Charleston News and Courier,* and Henry W. Grady of the *Atlanta Constitution.* From his desk at the *Constitution*'s offices and from the podium at various gatherings, Grady emerged as the preeminent advocate of the new ideology. His "New South" speech, delivered to the members of an elite club in New York City late in 1886, cogently and movingly presented a vision of the new order.

Grady and other leaders of the New South movement believed that economic recovery was the region's most pressing need. To effect that recovery, they promoted industrial growth, which, they believed, could occur sufficiently only with infusions of outside capital. Investments adequate enough to finance industrialization depended on bringing about sectional reconciliation by diminishing the animosities aroused during the Civil War and Reconstruction. Reconciliation, in turn, could come about only if potential investors in the North and in Europe were satisfied that racial harmony, which was essential to the social stability that attracted investments, had been achieved in the South. Grady and other spokesmen of the movement assured influential outsiders that black southerners were being treated fairly, that white southerners harbored no bitterness toward the North, and that the South was on the threshold of limitless prosperity. As New South spokesmen sought to wreak a radical transformation of the region from a rural, agricultural society to an urban, industrial one, they were careful to pledge allegiance to the Lost Cause of the Confederacy. They probably could not have done otherwise, but they did not perceive the irony.

By the time of Grady's death in 1889 at the age of thirty-nine, a program of action had become a declaration of accomplishment. Falling victim to wishful thinking, the proponents of the new ethos convinced themselves that their dream had become reality. The New South idea had entered the realm of myth. The mythic New South was a land of material opulence and racial justice where, in Grady's words, there was "sunshine everywhere and all the time."

The New South creed, victorious in the 1880s, retreated briefly in the 1890s under the onslaught of Populism, a response to economic depression and a movement intended to help poor farmers, which is what most southerners were. Although Populism was the strongest of all the challenges to Gilded Age capitalism, it nonetheless failed to achieve its objectives. As the twentieth century began, the New South ideology reemerged, reaching its peak in the 1920s. There were many parallels between the New South enthusiasm of the 1920s and that of the 1880s. Atlanta was the center of 1920s boosterism just as it had been the chief locus of 1880s boomerism. The hyperbole that accompanied the industrial crusade of the 1920s rivaled that of the earlier period. Ironically, the much-ballyhooed industrial progress of the "dollar decade" occurred during a period of severe agricultural depression, just as had been the case for much of the 1880s.

So durable was the New South ideology that, despite being eclipsed briefly in the Great Depression, it reappeared with full intensity before the 1930s ended. Shortly thereafter, World War II ushered in a degree of industrialization that southern promoters had long dreamed of. As the region's economic advance became ever more real, the New South myth grew ever more compelling. Even so, at the end of the twentieth century, despite more than a hundred years of industrial promotion—whether by the boomers of the 1880s, the boosters of the 1920s, or the Sunbelt enthusiasts of the postwar era—the South remained at the bottom of the nation's economic ladder.

Literary treatment of the New South myth flourished in the late nineteenth and early twentieth centuries, when the idea was new. There were compelling reasons for southern writers to embrace the new ideology. On a purely personal level, southern writers, after the unpleasantness of Reconstruction was over, usually depended on the North to sustain them because northerners, far more than southerners, bought and read their works. During the ascendancy of the New South idea, which coincided with the increasing popularity of local-color fiction, virtually every southern writer of note was discovered by the editors of northern literary magazines. The same houses that published those magazines often brought out southern works in book form, too. Through its ties to the North, the New South opened doors to writers that had been closed before. Consequently, many of them set about exploiting the raw materials of literature just as the industrial boomers tried to develop economic resources. The writers gave northern readers what they wanted: stories of the idyllic old plantation, tales of wartime valor, vignettes of exotic Creoles, portraits of picturesque mountaineers, and anything else unusual enough to arouse Yankee interest.

Beyond professional considerations, southern writers could feel the strong pull of the New South ideology. It offered hope amid despair, opportunity when for too long little had existed, and the possibility of cultural attainment through material progress. Moreover, the new ideology was intellectually respectable—publicists, politicians, businessmen, clergymen, and academicians espoused it.

Despite the many attractions of the New South idea, writers whose careers had begun in the antebellum period and extended well into the postbellum era responded ambivalently. In *The Heir of Gaymount* (1870), John Esten Cooke ignored the existence of industrialization and hoped that the New South would be a land of diversified farming. Cooke's contemporary, the poet Paul Hamilton Hayne, attempted to reconcile material progress with the pastoral ideal in "The Exposition Ode" (1881), and in "To the New South" (1885) he urged the New South to honor the Old South.

A few writers adopted the new ideology unequivocally. Ironically, among the most artful proponents of the new order were the plantation romancers F. Hopkinson Smith and Thomas Nelson Page. In Smith's *Colonel Carter of Cartersville* (1891) and Page's *Gordon Keith* (1903), the past, presented in such a way as to be merely picturesque, serves to reinforce the New South movement because the agrarian way does not offer a viable alternative. The most sustained support of the new ideology occurs in the work of Will N. Harben, who celebrated the growth of industry and the rise of the middle class in a number of novels published early in the twentieth century, most notably *Abner Daniel* (1902) and *The Georgians* (1904). The New South idea was so popular that it engaged the attention of Thomas Dixon Jr., who was primarily concerned with disseminating his viciously racist views in his Reconstruction trilogy: *The Leopard's Spots* (1902), *The Clansman* (1905), and *The Traitor* (1907). In each of those novels, sympathetically drawn characters establish cotton mills, the quintessential symbol of the New South movement.

Much more numerous among writers than advocates of the New South movement were detractors who tended to oppose either the very idea of industrialization or its exploitative nature. Many of the finest southern writers from the Civil War to World War I rejected the New South myth. In poems such as "Corn" (1875) and "Sunrise" (1882) and in the essay "The New South" (1880), Sidney Lanier extolled the glories of nature and the yeoman ideal and rejected the industrial way. Joel Chandler Harris, often considered by critics to be a plantation romancer, nonetheless wrote much fiction that praised the yeoman, not the plantation, ideal and disparaged the New South myth, notably certain stories published in the following works: *Uncle Remus: His Songs and His Sayings* (1880), *Mingo and Other Sketches in Black and White* (1884), *Free Joe and Other Georgian Sketches* (1887), *Balaam and His Master and Other Sketches and Stories* (1891), and *Told by Uncle Remus: New Stories of the Old Plantation* (1905). Mark Twain's questioning of the South's new order was presented directly in *The Gilded Age: A Tale of Today* (1873) and allegorically in *A Connecticut Yankee at King Arthur's Court* (1889). George W. Cable's *John March, Southerner* (1894) revealed the danger that the New South movement might foster the development of a colonial economy whereby the South would be merely a dependency of the imperial North. The movement's neglect of black southerners, despite the pledges of its leaders, was a major theme of *The Colonel's Dream* (1905) by Charles W. Chesnutt. In *The Romance of a Plain Man* (1909) and *Virginia* (1913), Ellen Glasgow attacked the crass materialism of the new ideology.

The literary opponents of the New South movement left an important legacy to the writers of the Southern Renascence that began in the 1920s and to the writers whose careers began after World War II. Many of the later writers condemned the region's worship of Mammon, which, they believed, accompanied the rise of the industrial spirit. Ever since its emergence, the idea of the New South has primarily elicited opposition from the region's writers. They have not rejected the hope of prosperity, but they have found repugnant the possibility that the South would cease to provide an arcadian alternative to a grasping, misdirected mass culture.

Wayne Mixon

See also *Atlanta Constitution*; Atlanta, Georgia; Industrialization; Textiles.

Edward L. Ayers, *The Promise of the New South: Life After Reconstruction* (1992); Paul M. Gaston, *The New South Creed: A Study in Southern Mythmaking* (1970); Lucinda MacKethan, *The Dream of Arcady* (1980); Wayne Mixon, *Southern Writers and the New South Movement, 1865–1913* (1980); C. Vann Woodward, *Origins of the New South, 1877–1913* (1951).

NEWSPAPERS

Southerners in early colonial America read newspapers imported from Europe or transported south from Boston. The *Boston News Letter* appeared in 1704, followed by the *Boston Gazette* in 1719 and the *New-England Courant* in 1721. The *Courant* was the first newspaper to successfully challenge government authority. It had high literary content because of its literate editor, James Franklin, and it offered an independent voice, at least until 1722 when one of its editorials against local authorities landed Franklin in jail.

In this somewhat restrictive atmosphere, London printer and newspaper publisher William Parks arrived in Annapolis, a town that was the social and commercial center for the region's three thousand inhabitants and where the wealthiest and most cultured of Maryland's residents resided. Although Boston was the most influential city in the colonies, Annapolis was the most important community in Maryland and one of the most important commercial centers in the South. Much of the wealth of Annapolis had been created through the region's tobacco farming.

Parks's London newspaper career got started during the era when Englishman Daniel Defoe was combining an adventurous life-style with journalism and literature. Defoe's *Robinson Crusoe* appeared in 1719, and the book was serialized in colonial newspapers. In September 1727, when Parks began publishing the first issues of the *Maryland Gazette* from his Annapolis printshop, it was not surprising that the newspaper reflected the high culture of the town. Parks's newspaper circulated in a society that mirrored England. From England came the practice of using literary essays for moral and political opinion, of using fables and fairy tales for warning against vice. With a highly literate editor and an elite literate readership, the *Maryland Gazette* became a respected medium for poetry and literary essays. It was the perfect newspaper for the plantation class of Maryland, which had the means and the time to appreciate literature. When the College of William and Mary presented to the governor of Virginia the two poems it was required to produce as rent for its land, the poems appeared in the *Maryland Gazette*, the newspaper closest to Williamsburg, which had no newspaper of its own. William Parks, with manners honed in Britain and well connected to Annapolis high society, fit right in and became one of the town's champions of cultural growth.

Parks's *Maryland Gazette* ceased publication in 1735 when he moved to Williamsburg, but the newspaper was revived ten years later under Jonas Green, who did even more for literature than Parks had done. A poet himself and a member of Annapolis clubs and social circles, Green came to Maryland via Benjamin Franklin's *Pennsylvania Gazette* (1728). A "Poet's Corner" appeared in Green's *Maryland Gazette,* and under Green, the *Gazette* covered the theater and published theatrical criticism with more depth and breadth than any newspaper in the colonies. As Baltimore grew in influence, William Goddard founded the *Maryland Journal* in 1773, but it was his mother, Mary Katherine Goddard, who took control of the newspaper and ran it for ten years after William ran into management troubles.

Back in 1736, William Parks had been appointed Williamsburg postmaster and the Virginia colony's official printer. Employing even more of a literary emphasis than he had in Maryland, Parks published the first issue of the *Virginia Gazette* on August 6, 1736. From the first issue, Parks emphasized original essays, publishing many of his own and others' essays under a column titled "The Monitor." Scholars studying the period assess the quality of the columns as the best original writing of any newspaper in the colonies. The classics, foreign translations, locally written poetry, and reprinted poetry from England graced the pages of Parks's *Virginia Gazette,* which set the literary standard for the colonial press. For many people in the colonies, the newspaper was their primary source of literature.

South Carolina produced its first newspaper after the Crown agreed to provide support for an official printer in Charleston. Operating a book and stationery shop in addition to tending to his government printing responsibilities, Eleazar Philips Jr. first issued the *South Carolina Weekly Gazette* in 1731. The *South Carolina Gazette* appeared in 1773 and contained an exceptional amount of material devoted to essays and literature. Poetry, prologues to plays, and essays ranging from morality to manners were found within its pages. Especially popular were reprints of British magazines.

Entire issues of the London *Spectator* were reprinted. Whereas the *Virginia Gazette*'s Monitor series became the outlet for original writing in Virginia, the South Carolina newspaper began running a "Meddlers' Club" feature, complemented with excerpts from English authors Jonathan Swift and Alexander Pope.

As the colonies continued to grow during the 1700s, newspapers shared in the prosperity. The literary content of the early colonial press, most noticeably in the early newspapers of Maryland, Virginia, and South Carolina, began to compete for space with news and advertising. The wealth of the southern plantation owners was invested in new and expanded businesses, including shipping, lumber, tar, and turpentine. Tobacco continued to grow as an export. With more businesses, more capital, and more people—Charleston grew from a population of 2,500 in 1700 to 7,000 in 1750—the few small advertising squares that appeared on the last page of early colonial newspapers were gradually replaced by full pages of advertising. Also contributing to newspaper demand was the Stamp Act of 1765, which brought to a head the simmering resentment of British control. Newspaper circulation grew to record numbers. Increased literacy and improved transportation—stage lines and intercolonial shipping routes along the eastern seaboard—also helped spur newspaper growth. Paper manufacturing methods also improved and helped feed the appetite for reading material. A postal service revamped under Benjamin Franklin set fixed rates for newspaper delivery. Along with Maryland, Virginia, and South Carolina, other parts of the South also became home to important newspapers, including Delaware's *Wilmington Courant* (1762), Savannah's *Georgia Gazette* (1763), Kentucky's—then part of Virginia—*Lexington Gazette* (1787), West Virginia's—also part of Virginia—*Potowmac Guardian* (1790), Tennessee's *Knoxville Gazette* (1791), New Orleans's *Moniteur de la Louisiane* (1794), and the *Mississippi Gazette* (1799) at Natchez.

By the end of the eighteenth century, a press once tied to Britain and at the mercy of licensing and government printers was gaining its freedom. The independence that the press achieved after the American Revolution manifested itself in highly partisan, often vitriolic crusades in behalf of the political parties that emerged in the post–Revolutionary War period. Partly to curtail a press that the federal government thought was out of control, Congress passed the Alien and Sedition Acts in 1798. The 25,000 aliens in the United States at that time held mostly Jeffersonian political views, opposed to the federal government and favoring states' rights. The Sedition Act, quickly abused by the government, was designed to protect officials against false and defamatory statements in the press. Among other places, the Sedition Law was tested in Richmond, where James Thomson Callender, a scandal-monger in self-exile from England, used the *Richmond Examiner* to attack President John Adams and later to unleash his bile on Thomas Jefferson. For the Adams attacks, he was arrested and defended by one of the South's most gifted lawyers and men of letters, William Wirt. Wirt, who lost the case, is remembered for his essays *The Letters of the British Spy* (1803), which appeared in the *Richmond Argus,* and *The Old Bachelor* (1810–1811), which appeared in the *Richmond Examiner*. He later wrote *Sketches of the Life and Character of Patrick Henry* (1817), his most popular and acclaimed work.

Despite the changes in news readership and improved newspaper distribution, what the country lacked in the early 1800s was a newspaper that was affordable to the masses and easily purchased with cash. Newspapers of the era were distributed primarily through expensive subscriptions costing the equivalent of a working person's monthly salary. Thus most subscribers were aristocratic business leaders and proprietors of inns and coffeehouses with reading rooms. That all changed in 1833, when New York printer Benjamin Day copied the success of the English penny magazine and produced the first issue of the *New York Sun*. Consisting of four letter-sized pages with small type, it produced a new, light style of writing and concentrated on human-interest stories and crime news. Newsboys sold the newspaper on the streets.

The *New York Sun* was an instant success, and the concept was quickly copied in Boston and Philadelphia. But it was in Baltimore that the penny press made its major contribution to journalism. The *Baltimore Sun* first appeared in 1837 as a penny newspaper and immediately became one of the most successful penny newspapers in the country. It pioneered news-gathering by opening the first bureau in Washington, where correspondents fed the *Sun,* which in turn became the source of news for newspapers in the West. Continuing to grow in sophistication and content over the years, by the 1920s the *Baltimore Sun* was noted for its editorials and especially for its criticism, contributed by Henry Louis (H. L.) Mencken. Mencken, who started his journalism career at age eighteen at the *Baltimore*

Morning Herald, also served as literary editor for the *Smart Set* (1914–1924) and the *American Mercury* (1924–1933). In 1926, Mencken was joined at the *Sun* by editorialist Gerald White Johnson, formerly with the *Greensboro* (North Carolina) *Daily News.* Johnson's editorials soon echoed Mencken's literary criticism.

By the mid-1800s, personal libraries were becoming affordable. Prices for books were in decline. The magazine *Church's Bizarre* reported in April 1852 that "twenty-five years ago, books sufficient to constitute a respectable library demanded a sum which few were able to spare," but that a library was now available "at a price within the means of all save the very poorest." Whether all but the very poorest could afford a library is debatable, but the first regular feature devoted to book reviews appeared in 1856 in the *New York Tribune.* With contributors that included Margaret Fuller, the *Tribune*'s emphasis on culture and ideas is credited with raising the standards of American journalism everywhere.

When the War Between the States broke out, reporters—"specials," as the Civil War correspondents were called—had a well-developed telegraph system to report the conflict. In 1866, the Atlantic Cable linked United States news organizations with London, and later with the Orient. News was now international. In the interim, the press and its readership had changed significantly. Newspapers had become a medium for the masses, with dispatches and wire services. The Associated Press was formed in 1848, and new terms such as "bulletins" and "scoops" were being heard in the newsrooms. Reporters were learning how to compose stories in the still-emerging eyewitness-writing style that was often short, concise, and descriptive. From Charleston, B. S. Osbon: "The batteries of Sullivan's Island, Morris Island, and other points were opened on Fort Sumter at four o'clock this morning. Fort Sumter has returned the fire, and a brisk cannonading has been kept up." From Cemetery Hill at Gettysburg, Whitelaw Reid: "From thrice six thousand guns there came a sheet of smoky flame, a crash of leaden death. The line literally melted away; but there came a second, restless still." From Gregory de Fontaine at the *Charleston Courier*: "From twenty different standpoints great volumes of smoke were every instant leaping from the muzzles of angry guns."

Southern journalists covering the war were considered some of the nation's best writers: the *Charleston Courier*'s Gregory de Fontaine, the *Savannah Republi-can*'s Peter W. Alexander, and Samuel C. Reid Jr. of the *New Orleans Picayune.* Good writing was enhanced by wire services where reporters could read each other's work. In the South, the Press Association of the Confederate States of America was formed in 1862 after lines were cut to the northern Associated Press. Dispatches could be sent over military telegraphs at half-rate, and although facing shortages of paper and ink, southern publishers met the challenge with enough determination to publish some editions on wallpaper.

The post–Civil War era produced the nation's major editors, publishers, and newspapers. Readers in both the North and South read and respected southerner Henry Watterson when his editorials in the *Louisville Courier-Journal* championed reconciliation. In his fifty years at the helm of the *Courier-Journal,* Watterson made it one of the country's most respected dailies. Ownership passed to Judge Robert Worth Bingham in 1917, and the Bingham family remained in control until 1987, when after being plagued by Bingham family squabbles, the *Courier-Journal* became part of the consolidation trend in American newspaper publishing and was sold to the Gannett Company newspaper chain.

From the formative years of the *Courier-Journal* emerged Henry W. Grady, who became part-owner and managing editor of the *Atlanta Constitution.* Under Grady, the *Constitution* of the 1880s expanded its news-gathering operations, with Grady remaining an active participant. Through Grady's editorials supporting industrialization of the South, the *Constitution* joined Watterson's *Courier-Journal* as one of the South's two leading newspapers. It was at the *Atlanta Constitution* that editorialist and feature writer Joel Chandler Harris, formerly with the *Forsyth* (Georgia) *Countryman* and the *Savannah Daily News,* began publishing his "Uncle Remus" stories, later to become books—*Uncle Remus: His Songs and Sayings* (1880), *Nights with Uncle Remus* (1883), *Uncle Remus and His Friends* (1892), *Told By Uncle Remus* (1905), *Uncle Remus and Br'er Rabbit* (1907). Competition for the *Constitution* came in 1883 when the *Atlanta Journal* was founded. In 1922 a reporter named "Peggy" Mitchell went to work writing features for the *Journal.* Her journalism career lasted only until 1926, but Margaret Mitchell went on to win the 1937 Pulitzer Prize for fiction for her novel *Gone With the Wind.*

Perhaps the most literary and newspaper-rich city of the South is New Orleans. As the supply base for invading armies, the city acquired its fame as a newspaper center during the Mexican War (1846–1848). During that war, New Orleans became the nation's news capital and the source of war news for the rest of the press. Along with the *Picayune*'s George W. Kendall—the war's most famous correspondent—were Mexican War correspondents for the *Delta*, the *Tropic*, the *Bee*, and the *Crescent*, all New Orleans newspapers. Kendall was a humorist who also rode with the army, and after the Mexican War authored *The War Between the United States and Mexico* (1851). When the Civil War broke out, Eliza Jane Poitevent Holbrook was the *Picayune* literary editor. She married the publisher and, after his death, ran the newspaper. George Washington Cable, author of *Old Creole Days* (1879), *The Grandissimes* (1880), and *Madame Delphine* (1881), joined the *Picayune* as a columnist in 1870.

In the midst of the Civil War, the *New Orleans Times* was founded in 1863, followed by the *New Orleans Democrat* in 1875. The *New Orleans Daily City Item* was founded two years later in 1877. The *Times* and *Democrat* merged into the *Times-Democrat* in 1881. At different times, holding editorial positions at both the *Item* and the *Times-Democrat*, was Lafcadio Hearn (Patricio Lafcadio Tessima Carlos Hearn), a translator, student of Oriental literature, and—after moving to Japan—a prolific writer of books about Japan. Marrying a Japanese wife and taking her name, he was known in Japan as Yakumo Koizumi. Among his works are *Glimpses of Unfamiliar Japan* (1894), *Exotics and Retrospectives* (1898), and *Japan: An Attempt at Interpretation* (1904).

A well-known southerner associated with the *Item* was Hodding Carter, whose son, Hodding Carter III, served in the State Department under President Jimmy Carter. "Big Hodding," as he was known, began his career as a reporter at the *Item* then moved to Hammond, Louisiana, where he founded the *Daily Courier* and made it an editorial forum against Huey Long. However, he is best remembered for his work in Greenville, Mississippi, where he founded the *Delta Star* and merged it in 1938 with a rival newspaper to create the *Delta Democrat-Times*. Hodding Carter's accomplishments in writing and journalism brought him numerous awards, including the Southern Literary Award and the 1946 Pulitzer Prize for his *Delta-Times* editorials against racial segregation. Among his other works are two novels, *The Winds of Fear* (1944) and *Flood Crest* (1947).

In 1914, the *Picayune* merged with the *Times-Democrat* and became the *Times-Picayune*. Lyle Saxon, an O. Henry Award winner (1926) and the author of such works as *Father Mississippi* (1927), *Fabulous New Orleans* (1928), and *Children of Strangers* (1937), worked at the *Item* in 1918 and later transferred to the *Times-Picayune*. But the *Times-Picayune*'s most famous contributor was William Faulkner. His work first appeared in the newspaper in early 1925, just after the publication of his first book, *The Marble Faun* (1924). Another reporter for the *Times-Picayune* was New Orleans native Hamilton Basso. First published in the New Orleans literary review *Double Dealer*, Basso authored such works as *Relics and Angels* (1929), *Beauregard: The Great Creole* (1933), *Cinnamon Seed* (1934), *In Their Own Image* (1935), *The View from Pompey's Head* (1954), *The Light Infantry Ball* (1959), and *A Touch of the Dragon* (1964). He later served as an associate editor of the *New Republic* and the *New Yorker,* and was a contributor to *Time*. Roark Bradford worked for the *Times-Picayune* in the 1920s and eventually became its night editor. Remembered for his attempts at serious reporting of black culture in the South, his collection of stories *Ol' Man Adam an' His Chillun* (1928) was adapted for the stage as *The Green Pastures* by Marc Connelly, who won the Pulitzer Prize for drama in 1930.

The first newspaper to publish in North Carolina was the *New Bern North-Carolina Gazette,* which appeared in 1751. It was in the 1880s that North Carolina newspapers began to acquire a national reputation. Walter Hines Page founded the *Raleigh State Chronicle* in 1883, and two years later he named Josephus Daniels as editor. At age eighteen, Daniels had been editor of the *Wilson* (North Carolina) *Advance*. A crusader for public education and an opponent of the Duke family tobacco trust, Daniels eventually got control of the *Chronicle* and merged it with the *North Carolinian*. He gained control of the *Raleigh News and Observer* in 1895. Under Josephus Daniels—an author himself, publishing *Our Navy at War* (1922), *Life of Woodrow Wilson* (1924), and *Tar Heel Editor* (1939)—and later his son, Jonathan Worth Daniels, the *News and Observer* became North Carolina's leading newspaper. The newspaper under the Daniels family is remembered for Josephus's and Jonathan's firebrand editorials, which were still being written by Jonathan in 1980.

Jonathan, despite his notoriety as a newspaperman, initially did not want to be part of the newspaper business. He was a classmate of Thomas Wolfe at the University of North Carolina where the two students were from opposite social backgrounds, Daniels from an aristocratic family in eastern North Carolina, and Wolfe from a middle-class family in the more impoverished mountain region to the west. Daniels wanted to be a writer of fiction and saw his novel *Clash of Angels* published in 1929. The work failed miserably at the same time that Wolfe's *Look Homeward, Angel* (1929) was receiving international acclaim. After *Clash of Angels,* Daniels turned to nonfiction writing and a career in his father's newspaper business.

The Daniels family, and other families like them, were the newspaper barons of the twentieth century. As family fortunes grew, some of the more successful family newspaper operations began to expand. Typical of these was the Knight family of Ohio, who expanded first into Florida by acquiring the *Miami Herald* in 1937. The *Miami Herald* expanded its international coverage in 1946 by launching the Air Express Clipper Edition to Latin America. Later, the *Herald* began publishing the Spanish-language *El Herald* section to serve South Florida's Spanish-speaking readers. After acquiring other newspapers, including North Carolina's *Charlotte Observer* in 1954, the Knight operations merged with Ridder Publications in 1974, becoming Knight-Ridder, one of the largest newspaper groups in the country.

The border states of Arkansas, Missouri, and Texas also produced major newspapers and famous writers. In Arkansas, the *Little Rock Arkansas Gazette* achieved distinction for its civil-rights coverage and won a Pulitzer Prize for its coverage of the 1957 Little Rock school desegregation crisis. Among its literary alumni are Opie Percival Read and James Howell Street. Read edited the *Gazette* from 1878 through 1881 and also founded the *Little Rock Arkansas Traveller* (1882). He became a famous humorist and later a prolific Chicago writer of such works as *Len Gansett* (1888), *A Kentucky Colonel* (1890), *My Young Master* (1896), *The Jucklins* (1896), and *The Starbucks* (1902). Street, who worked at the *Gazette* in 1927, had a career in journalism that ranged across five southern states, starting at the *Hattiesburg* (Mississippi) *American* in 1922. Among his works are *Look Away—A Dixie Notebook* (1936), *The Gauntlet* (1945), and *The High Calling* (1951). Missouri produced Samuel Langhorne Clemens (Mark Twain), whose newspaper career was in the West and North at the *Virginia City* (Nevada) *Enterprise,* the *Sacramento Union,* and the *Buffalo Express.* The *Nacogdoches Texas Republican*

(1819) was the Republic of Texas's first newspaper. The *San Felipe Telegraph and Texas Register* began publishing in 1835. After Texas became a state (1845), the number of Texas newspapers increased dramatically.

Although not always associated with the major metropolitan newspapers of the South, many southern writers have newspaper experience in their backgrounds. For example, Sherwood Anderson, in one of his periods of self-renewal, moved to rural Virginia in 1930 and bought and managed two small weeklies, the *Smyth County News* and the *Marion Democrat.* Shelby Foote, Civil War historian and the author of such works as *Tournament* (1949), *Shiloh* (1952), and the three volumes of *The Civil War: A Narrative* (1958, 1963, 1974), worked as a reporter for the *Delta Democrat-Times* shortly after World War II. Doris Betts, author of such works as *Heading West* (1991), *Souls Raised from the Dead* (1994), and *The Sharp Teeth of Love* (1997), worked for the *Statesville Daily Record,* the *Chapel Hill Weekly,* the *Sanford Daily Herald,* and the *Sanford News Leader,* all North Carolina newspapers.

The colonial roots of southern literature and southern newspapers have produced a long and distinguished history of journalism and letters. Equally impressive is the list of acclaimed writers who at some point in their careers have been affiliated with the press. From Shelby Foote, who worked for one newspaper, to Doris Betts, who worked for four, from H. L. Mencken, who influenced literature through criticism, to Henry Watterson, who influenced reconciliation through editorials, southern writers and publishers have influenced the region and the nation.

John R. Bittner

See also Colonial Newspapers; *New Orleans Time-Picayune.*

Michael Emery and Edwin Emery, *The Press and America: An Interpretive History of the Mass Media* (8th ed., 1996); William David Sloan and Julie Hedgepeth Williams, *The Early American Press, 1690–1783* (1994).

NEW WOMAN

Caricatured as a cigarette-smoking speechmaker on the platform of woman's suffrage, the New Woman of the 1890s can be generally defined as an educated, self-actualized woman who had gained economic independence from a masculine caretaker. Typically, though, the New Woman was criticized for ignoring the traditional female roles of wife and mother. She particularly valued the right to pursue activities outside of the home, such as a job or club work, regardless of her marital status or her family's financial situation. Because she was interested in her own personal fulfillment, she was harshly rebuked by those who believed she must be neglecting the needs of her husband and children and was labeled by many as the ruin of society. Perpetuated in both fiction and nonfiction, but rarely named as such by novelists, the New Woman in her most extreme form was an advocate of a woman's sexual freedom and of divorce. Because of the strength of the model of the southern lady, the New Woman did not play as prominent a role in the South as in the North or in England.

In many ways, the Civil War itself influenced any headway that the model of the New Woman made in the southern states. The severe economic situation of the postbellum South and the deaths of and disabilities faced by great numbers of southern men following the Civil War left many southern women with the necessity of finding jobs outside the home or working on the family farm or plantation. By the 1890s, the largest number of professional women were teachers, while a rapidly growing number of women were employed as typists and stenographers. A woman's sewing skills also became particularly valuable in milling regions of the South where women were increasingly employed in textile factories. Despite the economic necessity in many cases, a woman who worked outside of the home tended to be pitied because it was assumed that she did not have a husband or another male relative to care for her. Even a young woman who had been educated at a southern college and then employed as a teacher was expected to quit her job after marriage and most certainly when she became pregnant. Inasmuch as work became acceptable for an unmarried woman, married women were expected to care for their husbands' households, forsaking the workplace. Nevertheless, smaller families, a result of an increasing use of contraception, also gave married women more time for activities other than childbearing and rearing.

A more acceptable approach than working for the southern woman who wanted to leave the confines of the home was to join a woman's club, a mission organization, or the temperance movement. Women's clubs ranged from literary study groups where members pondered the meanings of a Shakespearean drama to clubs like the Woman's Club of New Orleans, which was established to help women find training and employment. By becoming involved in organizations that followed parliamentary procedures and elected officers, southern women also moved closer to the right to vote by involving themselves in what Josephine Henry called in 1895 "the university of politics." Women, too, became increasingly interested in joining mission groups, in bringing a woman's understanding to the cause of the needy. Methodist women, in particular, organized themselves in mission groups that created settlement houses for the poor. Some women, but only a small minority in the South, joined the Woman's Suffrage Movement. Among those who did join were some of the most important writers of the early-twentieth-century South. Ellen Glasgow and Mary Johnston, for example, helped found the Virginia Equal Suffrage League, and Evelyn Scott served as the secretary of Louisiana's Women's Suffrage Party. Although the suffrage movement actually never gained much support in the South, in part because of its earlier connections with the abolitionist movement, women were organized into suffrage associations in every state throughout the region.

The New Woman, while most certainly linked to an evolving women's movement, often was criticized for being a creation of newspaper writers. In fact, though, much of the credit for highlighting women's issues should be given to newspapers. The *New Orleans Picayune,* the first American newspaper under the editorship of a woman, attempted to persuade its woman's page readers of the importance of a woman's equality with her husband and of a woman's right to work outside the home. Headed by Eliza Nicholson, the *Picayune* also employed women as writers and editors; the case was similar at the *Columbus Evening Ledger* and at the *Springfield (Tennessee) Record.* A small number of papers, including St. Petersburg's *The Woman Question* and Little Rock's *The Woman's Chronicle,* were principally concerned with women's issues and women's rights.

Kate Chopin's *The Awakening* (1899) is perhaps the best-known literary example of the struggle of the New Woman in the South. Representing both a woman's desire for psychological and economic independence and her exploration of sexual freedom, Chopin's novel was harshly criticized for its frank treatment of its subject matter. In contrast to Chopin's Edna, who commits suicide at the end of the novel, the independent and determined Hagar, title character of Mary

Johnston's 1913 novel, ultimately finds a husband who has the strength of character to be her match. Although the term *New Woman* is generally associated with the 1890s, the conflict between the ideals of the southern lady and the New Woman played a prominent role in southern writings of the first several decades of the twentieth century. In fact, the 1920s saw a resurgence in strength of the New Woman as women gained the vote, better job opportunities, and seemingly greater sexual freedom. Works of the modern South that deal with the conflict between the southern lady and the New Woman include Ellen Glasgow's *Virginia* (1913) and Frances Newman's *The Hard-Boiled Virgin* (1926).

Mary Louise Weaks

See also Belle; Domesticity; Lady; Women's Movement.

Anne Goodwyn Jones, *Tomorrow Is Another Day: The Woman Writer in the South, 1859–1936* (1981); Anne Firor Scott, *The Southern Lady: From Pedestal to Politics 1830–1930* (1970).

NEW YORK SOUTHERN SOCIETY

The New York Southern Society was formed in 1886 by expatriate southerners who resettled in New York City in the years following the Civil War. Its stated purpose was "to cherish and perpetuate the memories and traditions of the Southern People and to cultivate friendly relations between Southern men resident or temporarily sojourning in New York City." Through its various activities, the organization helped members preserve their distinctive southern identity and culture while living in a northern society.

Its founders, generally educated professional southern-born men who migrated to New York City after Reconstruction, established the society as a social, literary, and charitable organization. The clubhouse, which opened in 1889, had a library of works on southern history, social life, and literature as well as copies of most major southern newspapers. The society created a forum for southern culture in the midst of New York City: its members heard papers and essays on southern topics at their regular meetings, they actively supported southern literature and authors, and they established a small publishing house to produce works on southern traditions and customs. The annual banquet, the major social function of the year, featured prominent southerners holding forth on regional topics. Among the group's charitable functions were scholarships to southern colleges and a committee dispensing assistance to needy southerners in New York City, both visitors and residents.

The members' celebration of their southern culture was often effusive and sentimental as they sought to memorialize their homeland and preserve their distinctive southern identity within a northern climate.

Susan H. Irons

"NIGGER"

In September 1995, when U.S. Senator Jesse Helms was a guest on the *Larry King Live* television show, a man from Alabama called in to thank the North Carolina senator "for everything you've done to help keep down the niggers." Helms replied, "Well, thank you, I think," and went on to discuss the word *nigger* with guest host Robert Novak, who expressed some shock at the caller's use of the "N-word," as he termed it. Helms agreed that the word was in bad taste, something his own father had taught him never to say, but then went on to remark, "Mark Twain used it." The episode pinpoints the electrifying impact that the most controversial epithet in American English has on American culture, and how its literary appearances both influence and reflect its applications in other contexts.

The word *nigger,* as a term for people of dark skin color, came into English usage from the French *nègre* and the Spanish *negro,* meaning black. In the English-speaking continental United States, it was automatically associated with the slave trade. One of the earliest American usages appears in Captain John Smith's *General History of Virginia* (1624), in which he records the coming to the colony of "a dutch man of warre that sold us twenty Negars." From the period of African enslavement until the present time, the word has been used by whites primarily, even if subconsciously, as a means of "keeping down" blacks, to use the words of Helms's Alabama caller. Dictionaries have for decades marked the word as "vulgar," "derogatory," or "depreciatory," and among white speakers, it has long been generally regarded as a word that no gentleman or lady would ever say, which has not kept many whites from using it in its most derogatory sense.

Among black speakers, the sense of the word varies greatly.

One of the most instructive uses of *nigger* comes in the 1845 *Narrative of the Life of Frederick Douglass, An American Slave*. In this classic's most famous passage, Douglass quotes his white master, Thomas Auld, as he instructs his wife on the dangers of teaching a slave to read: "If you give a nigger an inch, he will take an ell . . . if you teach that nigger (speaking of myself) how to read, there would be no keeping him. It would forever unfit him to be a slave." Here Douglass makes the use of the word by a white speaker isolate that speaker as crude, ignorant, and offensive in relation to the slave whom he names "nigger." The discussion of how to keep slaves "fit" for slavery relies on the power of the word *nigger* to dehumanize them, and Master Auld, as Douglass shows with great irony, is actually revealing the power of language to enslave in his advice to his wife. Auld's words, including and especially the word *nigger,* do not work in the way that he intends. Through Douglass's own mastery of the scene, Auld exposes himself as a vulgar bigot while he shows his slave "the pathway from slavery to freedom."

Several important southern white writers have been sensitive to Douglass's strategy—letting the white bigot expose himself through his use of *nigger.* In particular, Mark Twain, who knew Douglass and had a copy of his narrative, employed the strategy in the controversial passage of *Adventures of Huckleberry Finn* (1885) when Huck and Aunt Sally discuss a steamboat accident. Aunt Sally asks if anyone was hurt, and Huck replies, "No'm. Killed a nigger." This insensitivity is compounded by Aunt Sally's reply: "Well, it's lucky; because sometimes people do get hurt." Twain also used *nigger* with great irony in *Pudd'nhead Wilson* (1894), when "Tom Driscoll," who has always assumed he was the "white son" of a privileged family, finds out that he is "black" and muses on his situation: "And why is this awful difference made between white and black? . . . How hard the nigger's fate seems this morning!"

In Faulkner's "That Evening Sun," young Jason Compson repeats a chant, "Dilsey is a nigger," and even "Jesus is a Nigger," but also "I ain't a nigger." In Thomas Wolfe's story "Child By Tiger" (1937), Dick Prosser, a very dignified, gentle black man, goes on a rampage and kills two black men and two whites; the term *nigger* is not used for him until we are told that he has "gone crazy and is running wild." Wolfe's early (1922) title for the play that later became *Welcome to*

Our City was "Niggertown." Commenting on the word *nigger,* Wolfe wrote at the time that "within the limits of that crude word are bound up too much human misery to cause any amusement." Flannery O'Connor also used the word to make a similar point in her story "The Artificial Nigger," which satirizes the white racist Mr. Head and his naïve grandson Nelson.

In a column for the *New York Times,* Gloria Naylor, in 1986, wrote of different connotations of the word *nigger* among blacks using it to refer to other blacks. In some contexts, she says, it was applied admiringly to comment on a man who had accomplished an important feat; in others, it could be a term of endearment, or it could reflect "the pure essence of manhood . . . you don't mess with a nigger." Naylor reflects that she never really "heard" the word in these situations: "I didn't 'hear' it until it was said by a small pair of lips [a white boy at school] who had learned it could be a way to humiliate me." Harlem Renaissance writer Countee Cullen's poem "Incident" also describes the devastating effect that being called "Nigger" has on a black child, as does James Weldon Johnson in *Autobiography of an Ex-Coloured Man* (1912).

Often black writers put the word *nigger* in the mouths of their black speakers to achieve different masking effects. Uncle Julius, in Charles Chesnutt's *The Conjure Woman* (1899), slyly humbles himself before his white employer by calling himself "a ole nigger." In *Dust Tracks on a Road* (1942), Zora Neale Hurston uses the word more derogatorily when she quotes a white mentor telling her, "Don't be a nigger"; in a footnote, Hurston the folklorist added, "The word Nigger used in this sense does not mean race. It means a weak, contemptible person of any race."

The effects of white writers' use of *nigger* by black speakers can also contain explosive irony, as when Charles Bon in Faulkner's *Absalom, Absalom!* (1936) taunts his half-brother Henry, "I'm the nigger that's going to sleep with your sister," or when Ringo, in *The Unvanquished* (1938), says to Bayard, "I ain't a nigger any more. I done been abolished."

The literary use of the word *nigger* has always created controversy, but never more so than in relation to *Huckleberry Finn.* In recent years, Twain's novel has been banned from schools because of the effect of the word. Approving of the ban in Chicago schools in 1972, educator Dr. John Wallace said, "The minute the word 'nigger' is brought into the classroom, the black kid has a tendency to set up a block." Mark Twain seems clearly to have understood and attempted to apply Frederick Douglass's sense of the word to indict racism. Nevertheless, that Twain's intentions, and those of any other speaker or writer who says *nigger,* can be misunderstood is made all too clear by Jesse Helms's excuse to a national television audience. Perhaps some of the best words of wisdom on the word are those offered by Albert Murray in *South to a Very Old Place* (1971): "It was also obvious that when the peckerwoods said 'nigger' they were doing so because they almost always felt mean and evil about being nothing but old po' white trash."

Lucinda H. MacKethan

See also Race, Idea of; Racism; Twain, Mark.

Frederick G. Cassidy, ed., *Dictionary of American Regional English,* Vol. 3 (1996); Rhett S. Jones, "Nigger and Knowledge: White Double-Consciousness in *Adventures of Huckleberry Finn,*" *Mark Twain Journal* 22 (1984); Lucinda H. MacKethan, "Point of View," *Raleigh News and Observer* (September 27, 1995); Gloria Naylor, "Hers," *New York Times* (February 20, 1986); Geneva Smitherman, *Black Talk: Words and Phrases from the Hood to the Amen Corner* (1994).

NORTH, THE

Although it is tempting to define the image of the North from a southern perspective simply as a construct of "other," the relationship between the two regions is a complicated one. Robert White in *The Encyclopedia of Southern Culture* (1989) argues persuasively that the depiction of the North in southern literature is "to some extent, a curious legacy *from* the North." White notes that the criticism of the North by southern writers is not unlike "the harshly critical portrait of the urban and industrial North" of their northern counterparts. David Holman in *A Certain Slant of Light: Regionalism and the Form of Southern and Midwestern Fiction* (1995) comments on the complexity of the writer's relationship to his/her region, concluding that the writer of a particular region "is always working with an awareness of this insider-outsider dialectic, and it is the test of the literature that the writer is able to maintain this 'we' versus 'they' awareness in his work while at the same time showing that in fundamental and important ways 'we' are 'they' as well."

In *Cavalier and Yankee: The Old South and American National Character* (1957), one of the first studies treating perceptions of North and South in literature,

William R. Taylor states that the "idea of a divided culture has died a slow death." Tracing the growth in the early nineteenth century of the idea of dichotomous cultures, he concludes that scholarship in the mid-twentieth century has had a tendency "to narrow the range of differences between life in the North and in the South." Indeed northerners and southerners alike found, as Taylor notes, "much to criticize in the grasping, soulless world of business and in the kind of man—the style of life—which this world seemed to be generating."

An excellent example of a southern writer's depiction of North/South differences appears in John Pendleton Kennedy's popular novel *Swallow Barn* (1832), in which Kennedy uses a narrator who is a northerner to record his impressions of a southern plantation. The narrator asserts that "even the crows . . . seemed to have a more . . . eloquent caw here in Virginia, than in the dialectic climates of the North" and "you will never know your friend so well, nor enjoy him so heartily in the city as you may in one of those large, bountiful mansions, whose horizon is filled with green fields and woodland slopes and broad blue heavens." In the world depicted here, hospitality and enjoyment of life are viewed as superior to northern concerns with progress and material gain.

The poet Henry Timrod, whose lyrics about the Civil War focus on North-South differences, provides some of the clearest depictions of the North in southern literature of the mid-nineteenth century. In "Ethnogenesis"(1861), Timrod describes the North as inhabited by a devil "who long since in the limits of the North / Set up his evil throne, and warred with God." Timrod likens religion in the North to that of the Pharisees. In contrast to the South, where he argues that there is "scorn of sordid gain," the North is populated by those whose schemes "leave the neighboring poor / To starve and shiver at the schemer's door."

Southern writers in the early decades of the twentieth century have also depicted the North as lacking in the traditional values of concern with family and community that are dominant in the southern culture. For example, the protagonist of Ellen Glasgow's *Virginia* (1913) is overwhelmed by her trip to New York City. Her wardrobe, which she has labored over with her southern dressmaker, is derided as old-fashioned and dowdy by the fashionable women of the city. Even more disturbing is the fact that her husband's affair with an actress is accepted there and people comment on the fact that it is a pity he is trapped in marriage to a dull, middle-aged woman. The image reflected in the eyes of these New Yorkers calls into question for Virginia Pendleton all the traditional values of respect, good manners, and faithfulness that she has been taught.

In the twentieth century, southern writers have continued to picture the North as other and as a foil to the South. The Agrarian writers in their manifesto *I'll Take My Stand: The South and the Agrarian Tradition* (1930) posit the traditional agrarian values of the South as a counter to what they perceive as the money-grubbing ways of the North. John Crowe Ransom, in the introduction to this work, applies a skeptical view to the worship of science, criticizes the growth of advertising designed to persuade consumers to buy what they do not need, and argues that religion, art, and manners cannot flourish in the increased tempo of an industrial society. Similarly, Robert White finds that Flannery O'Connor's short story "The Geranium" (1946) and her later reworking of the story in "Judgement Day" (1965) depict a cold, sterile New York City where neither the flower or an old man, a transplanted southerner, can flourish.

A complex image of the North may be seen in Wallace Stevens's poetry. A New Englander, Stevens spent a good deal of time in Florida in the 1920s and 1930s, where at first he relished the temperate climate and less-frenetic life-style. Although many of Stevens's poems praise the tropical climate and lush foliage of the southern state, poems such as "Farewell to Florida" show the poet's desire to return to a less-inviting climate. In this poem, the speaker urges his ship forward, saying, "The leaves in which the wind kept up its sound / From my North of cold whistled in a sepulchral South." Even though the speaker's "North is leafless and lies in a wintry slime," he yearns for its bracing weather and, ironically, feels that he will be more creative in this "sterile" environment rather than in the lush southern setting.

Eudora Welty also posits the otherness of the North in her work. A notable example is in *The Optimist's Daughter* (1969), in which Laurel McKelva returns to Mississippi from Chicago because of the illness and the subsequent death of her father. Laurel, who has previously lost her husband and mother, treasures her independence as a designer in a northern city, but when she returns to the place of her childhood, she is able to gain insight into her past and come to terms with it. In spite of her parents' friends and neighbors, who warn her that if she goes north she will come back only as

a visitor, not someone who belongs, Laurel decides to return to Chicago. This decision entails giving up any claim to her parents' home and the possessions that she cherished, but when Laurel relinquishes to her stepmother a breadboard crafted by her husband and used by her mother, she realizes that "memory lived not in initial possession but in the freed hands, pardoned and freed, and in the heart that can empty but fill again, in the patterns restored by dreams." Laurel will return to the North where her work and her opportunities for creativity lie, but she will carry with her insights achieved in the South.

In his article on the North, Robert White makes what seems a surprising assertion when he concludes that "images of the North provided by black Southerners such as Walker and Ellison and Wright, agree with those projected by white Southerners." Although the oppressive conditions in the South are clearly apparent in the work of African American writers, the North is often depicted as hostile as well.

For example, in the *Narrative of the Life of Frederick Douglass* (1845), Douglass describes freedom as "away back in the dim distance, under the flickering light of the north star, behind some craggy hill or snow-covered mountain." Douglass recounts that even though he and his fellow slaves look to the North for freedom, it is a tenuous vision at best. When he arrives in New Bedford, however, he discovers that what he had been told about the North was quite erroneous. A culture did not require slavery to be prosperous. Not only does he find everything looking "clean, new, and beautiful," he is astonished at the level of prosperity of the "colored" people. He finds "many, who had not been seven years out of their chains, living in finer houses, and evidently enjoying more of the comforts of life, than the average slaveholders in Maryland."

Portrayals of the North in writing by blacks in the second half of the nineteenth century frequently depict negative traits. Charles Chesnutt, who gained national fame for his local-color stories in the 1890s, depicts northerners who have purchased southern plantations at bargain prices after the Civil War. In Chesnutt's short story "Mars Jeems's Nightmare," collected in *The Conjure Woman* (1899), the northern owner is described as a pompous man who is easily manipulated by his servant Julius, who wants him to hire his grandson Tom, whom the master has discharged. Julius is able to play upon the owner's arrogance and his ignorance of southern customs to accomplish his goals.

African American writers in the twentieth century

have also presented the North in their writing as "other," but not necessarily with a positive image. In Richard Wright's short stories, there are reputed to be equal rights in the North, but whether blacks will attain those rights is uncertain. When Big Boy escapes lynching by being taken north in a truck, the reader is left hoping that he is going to a better place. In *Native Son* (1940), however, the North holds little promise for Bigger Thomas. In the first section of the novel, entitled "Fear," Wright shows Bigger and his family in a bleak apartment where a rat viciously attacks him. The city itself is unremittingly harsh, and the cold, snowy climate contributes to Bigger's downfall. In his essay "How 'Bigger' Was Born," Wright notes, "It was not that Chicago segregated Negroes more than the South, but that Chicago had more to offer, that Chicago's physical aspect—noisy, crowded, filled with the sense of power and fulfillment—did so much more to dazzle the mind with a taunting sense of possible achievement that the segregation it did impose brought forth from Bigger a reaction more obstreperous than in the South."

Ralph Ellison's *Invisible Man* (1952) also posits the North as having both positive and negative implications for the narrator. During the unnamed protagonist's experience in college, a visit from the northern trustee sets in motion his expulsion from the college, but the reader is not allowed for long to view this as a fortuitous experience because a series of betrayals in the North soon follow. The narrator is failed by religious institutions, capitalism, the Communist Party, and charlatans. At the conclusion of the novel, the protagonist states that at times he is "overcome with a passion to return into that 'heart of darkness' across the Mason-Dixon line, but then I remind myself that the true darkness lies within my own mind, and the idea loses itself in the gloom."

The image of the North in recent African American literature continues to be intriguing and complex. An excellent example is Toni Morrison's *Beloved* (1987), in which life in Cincinnati for Sethe, although better than life in the South, is tenuous, still subject to the intrusion of ghosts, prejudice, and violence. In physical terms, the landscape is frequently cold and bleak, and even the old roses on a lumberyard fence near a carnival Sethe attends are dying: "The closer the roses got to death, the louder their scent, and everybody who attended the carnival associated it with the stench of the rotten roses." But in *Beloved* the most terrifying images are associated with the South. Morrison describes

the Kentucky plantation that Sethe and the other slaves left: "there was Sweet Home rolling, rolling, rolling out before her eyes, and although there was not a leaf on that farm that did not make her want to scream, it rolled itself out before her in shameless beauty. It never looked as terrible as it was and it made her wonder if hell was a pretty place too. Fire and brimstone all right, but hidden in lacy groves." Writers Alan Gurganus in *Plays Well with Others* (1997), Pat Conroy in *Prince of Tides* (1986), and William Styron in *Sophie's Choice* (1979) all depict young southern men who note differences between the genteel South and the stimulating but disturbing excitement of New York City.

The variables of region, race, and gender among writers depicting the North understandably have an effect upon each writer's angle of perception, but if, as Taylor asserts, the belief in two cultures is diminishing, it is clear that the dichotomies and tensions between North and South have continued even up to now to play a major part in their work.

Anne E. Rowe

See also Agrarians; Border States; Regionalism.

William R. Taylor, *Cavalier and Yankee: The Old South and American National Character* (1961).

NORTH CAROLINA, LITERATURE OF

The first secretary (1972–1973) of the North Carolina Department of Cultural Resources was Samuel T. Ragan, who later served as the state's third poet laureate from 1982 until his death in May 1996. The Saturday after his funeral, the North Carolina Literary Hall of Fame, one of his cherished dreams, became a reality with the induction of fifteen writers from the distant and recent past at Weymouth Center for the Arts and Humanities in Southern Pines. This day had been a very long time coming, because a tradition of letters, especially in drama and poetry, had characterized the state even in colonial times. Before and after the Revolution, printers were active in New Bern and several other locations, including Raleigh, where newspaperman Joseph Gales published his wife's novel *Matilda Berkley* (1804). Boston novelist William Hill Brown wrote poetry and essays but no fiction when he lived in Murfreesboro and Halifax after 1791. Among those native writers whose works came to the state library, founded in 1812, and into the North Carolina Collection begun in 1844 at the University of North Carolina, no Tar Heel of the stature of Poe, Simms, or Lanier appeared during the nineteenth century. Nor was the folk humor about Surry County in Hardin Taliaferro's *Fisher's River* (1859) an antidote for Hinton Rowan Helper's *The Impending Crisis* (1857), whose antislavery argument was deemed incendiary and banned in the state. Ironically, two natives born into slavery and a nonnative African American were among the few North Carolina writers to achieve wide recognition for their writing before 1910—George Moses Horton in poetry, Harriet Jacobs alias Linda Brent in the slave narrative, and Charles Waddell Chesnutt of Ohio in local-color and historical fiction. Reconstruction novelist Albion Tourgée, another nonnative, and the racist novelist Thomas Dixon, as well as the progressive novelist, editor, and publisher Walter Hines Page, who championed Chesnutt early, attracted different readers.

In 1900 the North Carolina Literary and Historical Association was formed. A statewide literary award, the Patterson Cup, was offered by the Association for the first time in 1905 to a writer known across the state for general literary excellence. The popular Charlotte newspaper poet from Wagram, John Charles McNeill, was the first recipient. In 1913 Frank C. Brown of the English faculty at Duke helped establish the North Carolina Folklore Society. Mary Lindsay Thornton became the first curator of the North Carolina Collection at UNC–Chapel Hill in 1917; the next year, this university offered its first credit class in creative writing. The focus was on short folk plays, and the only male student enrolled was Thomas Wolfe. In 1921, the year after he graduated from Carolina, nearby Trinity College—soon to be Duke University—founded a press; the UNC Press was established in 1922. Two years later, the *North Carolina Historical Review* began, providing since then a steady record of literary history in articles and annual bibliographies. In New York, Thomas Wolfe became a novelist, not a playwright, in 1929. *Look Homeward, Angel* was read by North Carolinians with appreciation and revulsion. Across the state, an interest in poetry characterized the Great Depression, most especially in the Charlotte area, where in 1932 a small group of poets met and formed the North Carolina Poetry Society. The experimental campus community of Black Mountain College began its twenty-three-year existence in 1933. Among poets living and working there were Robert Duncan, Charles

Olson, Jonathan Williams, and Robert Creeley. For many people, *The Mind of the South* (1941) by Wilbur J. Cash was poetical in its complex but clear prose delineation of southerners as people of paradox. In Raleigh, the official position of state poet laureate had been created in 1935, yet because of World War II Arthur Talmage Abernathy of Burke County was not appointed until 1948. He was succeeded by James Larkin Pearson of Wilkes in 1953. *North Carolina Folklore,* later renamed *North Carolina Folklore Journal,* was founded in 1948.

During these years, other important literary developments included the first meeting of the North Carolina Writers Conference, held in Manteo in 1950; the production of the state's first literary map with illustrations by Primrose Paschal; and the publication by the UNC–Chapel Hill Library of a series of extension outlines, biographies, handbooks, and bibliographies about North Carolina authors. William S. Powell's *North Carolina Fiction, 1734–1957: An Annotated Bibliography* (1958) included Robert Ruark's *The Old Man and the Boy* (1957) among its seven hundred annotated entries. From Duke University Press came the seven-volume *Frank C. Brown Collection of North Carolina Folklore* between 1952 and 1964. The North Carolina Award for Literature was first given in 1964 by Governor Terry Sanford, who had also created the North Carolina Arts Council, with Sam Ragan as chair. Serious literary work characterized the 1970s statewide.

The North Carolina Literary and Historical Association still met annually and recognized selected writers for their fiction and nonfiction, poetry, and juvenile literature. Walker Percy set *The Second Coming* (1980) in western North Carolina, and a new effort to aid poets and promote North Carolina literature—the Poetry Center Southeast—was started at Guilford College by poet Ann Deagon in 1980. It prefigured the creation in 1985 of the North Carolina Writers Network, which now has a permanent staff and a large membership to plan and take advantage of conferences and workshops as well as literary contests that memorialize three of the state's venerable writers of poetry, fiction, and drama. *Their Native Earth: A Celebration of North Carolina Literature,* a video documentary produced at North Carolina State University, premiered in Lexington in November 1989. Circulated widely in schools and libraries, it became an ancillary to Sally Buckner's *Our Words, Our Ways: Reading and Writing in North Carolina* (1991). This literary anthology designed as an eighth-grade textbook quickly went into a second edition. *The Rough Road Home: Stories by North Carolina Writers*, edited by Robert Gingher, was published in 1992, followed three years later by Michael McFee's *The Language They Speak Is Things to Eat: Poems by Fifteen Contemporary North Carolina Poets*, both from UNC Press.

Meanwhile, a 1993 joint resolution of the North Carolina House and Senate had finally set in motion a legislative process to establish and fund the North Carolina Literary Hall of Fame. The first state grant materialized in 1995 and was awarded to the Writers Network. In addition to the first fifteen deceased writers inducted in May 1996, six writers, three of whom were present, were inducted in 1997. Three living and two deceased writers were added in 1998, for a total of twenty-six. The literary history of North Carolina is revealed in the creation, mission, and especially in the annually increasing members of the North Carolina Literary Hall of Fame at Weymouth.

James Boyd, whose upstairs study there houses the Hall of Fame, was inducted in 1996. A native of Pennsylvania, he had come to the Sandhills of North Carolina for his health after World War I. He enlarged and refined the family property in Southern Pines. This place became the center of Boyd's nationally celebrated career as a writer, publisher, and public servant. To visit him at Weymouth came a host of writers who led the Southern Renascence of the 1920s and 1930s. His acclaimed historical novels include the meticulously researched *Drums* (1925) and *Marching On* (1927). *The Pilot*, his family newspaper, is still a literary beacon in the state; and the old mansion of the novelist-as-historian now doubles as a retreat for writers and as a state literary museum.

Another nonnative inducted into the North Carolina Literary Hall of Fame at Weymouth in 1996 was Inglis Fletcher. Born in Illinois and widely traveled, she had eastern North Carolina ancestors. In 1944, the year James Boyd died, she moved with her family to Bandon Plantation on the Chowan River near Edenton. She had already begun publishing her Carolina Series of historical romances about the English colonization of the area with *Raleigh's Eden* (1940) and *Men of Albemarle* (1942). In these and ten more volumes, she interpreted the times up through the ratification of the Constitution with stark details and convincing flare. To create her novels, she pored over the ten-volume *Colonial Records of North Carolina* (1886–1900). Her fiction provided a popular version of the

state's distant past. In her spirited public appearances and special projects, this persuasive style persisted. She died in 1969.

Fletcher and Boyd, in different ways, discovered and explored the history of their adopted state just as vigorously as had early European writers Verrazano, de la Vega, Thomas Harriott, and John Lawson. Native readers discovered their own past by reading Boyd and Fletcher. Her theme of human freedom nurtured by land that families till and pass on from generation to generation won wide favor.

Native novelists whose own careers took shape during the heydays of Boyd and Fletcher include Thomas Wolfe, Paul Green, Tim Pridgen, Bernice Kelly Harris, Frances Gray Patton, LeGette Blythe, Burke Davis, Lucy Daniels, Ben Haas, Ovid Pierce, Lettie Rogers, William Hardy, Wilma Dykeman, John Ehle, Doris Betts, Reynolds Price, Anne Tyler, Romulus Linney, Fred Chappell, Robert Ruark, Jessie Rehder, Guy Owen, John Foster West, and Tom Wicker. Among novelists from elsewhere living and working in North Carolina during the Boyd-Fletcher era are Chapel Hill's James Street, Betty Smith, Daphne Athas, and Richard McKenna. Eastern North Carolina figures in the fiction that Carson McCullers and Jack Kerouac as well as William Styron, who studied at Duke, wrote after each author lived in that part of the state for a short time during the 1940s and 1950s. Kentucky-born poet Olive Tilford Dargan published *Call Home the Heart* about her adopted state in 1932. Under the pseudonym Fielding Burke, Dargan blended the realism of a contemporary textile strike in Gastonia with harsh family truths about mountain people. Also a poet, Dargan lived in Swain County in the Appalachians.

Jonathan Daniels, Paul Green, and Thomas Wolfe were born in three different regions of North Carolina but were educated at Chapel Hill, where they met and became lifelong literary friends. As men of letters, they each won a Guggenheim Fellowship. All three were inducted into the North Carolina Literary Hall of Fame in 1996. Common to their undergraduate experience was the inspiration of playwright and professor Frederick Koch, a Kentuckian who had come to North Carolina from North Dakota with his gospel of the folk drama in 1918. Two of his students won Pulitzers for plays within a decade—Hatcher Hughes for *Hell-Bent for Heaven* in 1924 and Paul Green for *In Abraham's Bosom* in 1927. Among Koch's numerous outstanding female students were Frances Gray Patton and Bernice

Kelly Harris. Both of these Wake County natives achieved distinction for their fiction rather than their plays, however. Patton's career included *New Yorker* stories and the famous novel *Good Morning, Miss Dove* (1954), based on one of her ironic tales. Also an actress and a teacher, Frances Patton counts among her students Doris Betts, who after 1966 became the most accomplished fiction writer on the creative-writing faculty at Carolina. Harris taught public school in rural northeastern North Carolina and wrote well-received fiction as well as occasional plays. Jonathan Daniels championed her works in the *Raleigh News and Observer* before the appearance of her folk novel *Purslane* (1939). Six more novels came in rapid order. Her *Janey Jeems* (1946) was the first novel about a black family by a white writer who chose not to emphasize race. She later taught writing at Chowan College in Murfreesboro.

Wolfe's early ambitions for a career as a dramatist led him from Asheville to Chapel Hill, then to Harvard and New York as well as Europe. From time to time, he taught at New York University, and before his death in the fall of 1938 he had achieved wide fame and considerable controversy as the author of big semiautobiographical novels about Eugene Gant—*Look Homeward, Angel* (1929) and *Of Time and the River* (1935)—as well as numerous short stories and *The Story of a Novel* (1936) under the editorial guidance of Maxwell Perkins and Elizabeth Nowell. His posthumous novels were edited by Edward Aswell as *The Web and the Rock* (1939) and *You Can't Go Home Again* (1940). Wolfe's reputation has sustained a long and profitable list of additional publications, including a Pulitzer Prize–winning biography by David Herbert Donald (1987); an active Thomas Wolfe Society with its journal, the *Thomas Wolfe Review*; and an annual Thomas Wolfe Festival in Asheville, site of the Wolfe memorial at the Old Kentucky Home.

Paul Green, from the eastern part of the state, succeeded as a dramatist where Wolfe had not. Three expressionistic plays as well as folk plays and realistic dramas are to the credit of this Carolinian who believed in both collards and culture. Unlike Wolfe, Green also had a long and successful family life, most of it in North Carolina. Like Jonathan Daniels, Green always took a major part in debating social issues until he and Daniels died in 1981. Especially did questions of civil rights and racial unrest concern them. Besides teaching philosophy at UNC, Green also collected and preserved folklore. He wrote and published novels,

wordbooks, essays, and numerous stories of his native Cape Fear Valley. But plays prevailed, and he created a number of original symphonic dramas, the first of which was *The Lost Colony* (1937). It has been, except for the blackout years of World War II, performed each summer on Roanoke Island, the site of the 1587 disappearance of John White's bold English dreamers. Green's script shows that their dream still lives, and the vitality of his historical imagination led Virginia, Texas, and Kentucky to engage him for symphonic dramas celebrating the heroics of their earlier days. The Paul Green Foundation in Chapel Hill now carries on the multitudinous interests of this dynamic native of eastern North Carolina.

In January 1937, when Green was just beginning work on *The Lost Colony*, Thomas Wolfe happened to make his first and only return to Chapel Hill since his 1920 graduation. En route to New York from New Orleans and Atlanta, he stayed for three days at Weymouth with James Boyd. While in Chapel Hill, Wolfe spent a long afternoon of literary talk with Green and then rode in Green's car to Raleigh for a visit with Jonathan Daniels. The next time the three of them would be in the same place would be at Wolfe's funeral in September 1938 in Asheville. Between this January 1937 stopover in central North Carolina and his funeral, Wolfe made two long visits to Asheville, after a seven-year absence. His habitual retreats to Germany had been ended by the rise of Hitler; Wolfe's experience of international strife was more immediate than either Green's or Daniels's, although both of them were typically more public-spirited than the usually self-absorbed famous novelist. Daniels's own career had begun as a novelist with *Clash of Angels* (1930), but he was also a journalist who wrote sensitively of the South's literary rebirth and of the careers of both Wolfe and Green, taking special note of Wolfe's raw exposure of Asheville natives and of Green's success in playwriting. Daniels would later serve in the Roosevelt Administration, ultimately becoming FDR's press secretary, a role he held briefly under Harry Truman as well.

The induction of Gerald Johnson into the North Carolina Hall of Fame in 1996 was an additional reminder of the role of journalism in the literature of this state and the nation. The Scotland County native and Wake Forest College graduate was an associate of such different Americans as H. L. Mencken at the *Baltimore Sun* and Adlai Stevenson, for whom he wrote speeches. Frequently, the subjects for Johnson's dozen books were similar to Jonathan Daniels's, for both North

Carolinians were liberal humanists. Their achievements bring to mind another fabled Tar Heel, Charles Kuralt. Johnson's fiction includes two novels, two mysteries, and two three-part juvenile works about American history and government. Three of Daniels's books were written for children.

Randall Jarrell, another 1996 inductee, also wrote books for children, but as a poet and teacher of writers his influence has been more extensive. A native of Nashville, Tennessee, Jarrell attended Vanderbilt and studied with the notable group of poet/critics that included Warren, Tate, and Ransom. He befriended Robert Lowell and Peter Taylor at Kenyon. This list of famous associates informed Jarrell's influence at Woman's College in Greensboro, where he often persuaded the nation's leading literary personalities to speak on the campus and to spend terms teaching, playing tennis, and writing after he joined the faculty in 1947. His enrichment of this campus literary ethos rooted in the 1930s became as much a part of his North Carolina legacy as his published volumes of poetry, criticism, juvenile works, adult fiction, and translations. With these other writers, and more recently through the splendid influence of Robert Watson and Fred Chappell, Jarrell helped the Greensboro campus become a university. Chappell especially understood this process, for he had studied under William Blackburn at Duke in the 1950s when that institution was establishing its contemporary reputation for shaping the literary careers, among others, of William Styron, Reynolds Price, Anne Tyler, Jim Applewhite, and himself. Peter Taylor, married to Tar Heel poet Eleanor Ross, also aided in the faculty transformation at Greensboro. Meanwhile, Jarrell served as poetry consultant to the Library of Congress (1956–1958), held voting positions on numerous national literary juries, and won grants from the Guggenheim Foundation and the National Academy of Arts and Letters. Through it all, Taylor observed, Jarrell kept his "noble, difficult, and beautiful soul." The evidence is plentiful, as in *The Woman at the National Zoo* (1960), which won the National Book Award for poetry. Upon receiving a statewide teaching award, Jarrell said that if he were a rich man he would pay to teach. Long after his tragic death in 1965, his classroom and campus performances remain legendary across the South.

In Oxford, North Carolina, other writers drew rich words and rhythms from local soil. One example is Dr. Frank G. Slaughter, whose more than forty books include two popular novels about a Civil War and Re-

construction doctor and his lovely ladies. The far more literary example of Oxford's verbal richness is Thad Stem, whose sixteen books include poems, essays, short stories, and local history. *The Animal Fair* (1960) is a lyrical tribute to small-town life as he, ever the native, lived and loved it. This priority is evident as well in the more than eight thousand items by him that appeared in the state's daily newspapers, occasionally as feature editorials with a regional flavor. His special literary gift was the picture poem in prose or verse. He knew scores of writers; other literary reporters in North Carolina included Bernadette Hoyle, Roy Parker, Betty Hodges, Guy Munger, and Dannye Romine Powell.

Stem's chief advocates were Guy Owen and Sam Ragan. Like Stem, Owen and Ragan were eastern North Carolinians, yet they were writers without borders despite their many local interests. All three moved readily from one journalistic or literary form to another, with Owen exhibiting the most dexterity as essays, stories, and novels came from his desk alongside poems—his work was both humorous and deeply serious or questioning. *The Ballad of the Flim-Flam Man* (1965), *Journey for Jodel* (1970), and *The White Stallion and Other Poems* (1969) are examples, as are the numbers of the *Southern Poetry Review* that he edited (1959–1977). This wide range of talent made him a durable mentor of young writers. Ragan, too, had a private voice for poetry and an equally impressive public voice for journalism and official duties as poet laureate or government secretary. All writing, he said, is a kind of reporting. Unlike Stem, Owen and Ragan were devoted and beloved teachers at North Carolina State University. Owen belonged to the faculty in English, and Ragan ran poetry workshops through the student union for town, gown, and all around—in addition to his real job as managing and executive editor of the *News and Observer* until 1968. Over the years, he wrote and published six volumes of poetry and four books of nonfiction. His "Southern Accent" newspaper column, dating from 1948, ran in *The Pilot,* Ragan's business after he purchased Boyd's old paper and moved to Southern Pines in 1969.

With Richard Walser and others, Ragan and Owen aided in the transformation of North Carolina State College into North Carolina State University during the 1960s by upgrading the scholarly and literary activities in the School of Liberal Arts. Gradually, the old land-grant college became a major research university, just as at Greensboro the reputation and mission of the normal school had been made over by Jarrell and his literary predecessors and successors. Walser's role in the process at North Carolina State was unique, for he was a classroom teacher, critic, gadfly, scholar, and literary historian, not an imaginative writer. As a young student at Chapel Hill, he had been criticized for his unabashed devotion to North Carolina writing. How, he was asked by his professors, could such a body of published works as the state produced in earlier centuries be called literature? And, moreover, how could it be properly studied or taught until it had been reestablished in good texts and evaluated critically by publishing scholars? Young Walser did not know all of the answers, but he knew some. He could find and establish the texts, and he would write and encourage others to write about North Carolina authors. As a faculty member in English at N.C. State after World War II, he brought out good editions of state writing in anthologies and miscellanies of humor, short stories, poetry, and drama with detailed notes and introductions. *Tar Heel Laughter* (1974) and *North Carolina Legends* (1980) became popular favorites. Walser also edited and published separate texts, brief biographies, and critical studies, devoting decades to Thomas Wolfe and other writers, old or new and sometimes quite obscure. His signal accomplishment is *Literary North Carolina* (1970). Poet, literary mapmaker, and editor E. T. Malone assisted Walser with the second edition of this state literary history published in 1986.

The established or growing prominence of contemporary North Carolina writers means that a new edition of this work must treat in depth the astonishing careers of native and nonnative authors Doris Betts, Reynolds Price, Fred Chappell, Elizabeth Spencer, John Yount, Elizabeth Cox, Lee Smith, Allan Gurganus, Lenard Moore, Jaki Shelton Green, Alan Shapiro, Angela Davis-Gardner, T. R. Pearson, Ruth Moose, Pete Hendricks, Margaret Maron, Michael Parker, Lawrence Naumoff, Marianne Gingher, Bill Henderson, Samm-Art Williams, Bland Simpson, Jim Wann, Donald Secreast, Shelby Stephenson, Stephen Smith, Jill McCorkle, Michael McFee, Betty Adcock, William Harmon, Deborah Pope, Maya Angelou, Sarah Lindsay, Kathryn Stripling Byer, Robert Morgan, Bruce Stone, Sue Ellen Bridgers, Suzanne Newton, William Hooks, A. R. Ammons, Jim Wayne Miller, Ron Bayes, Charles Edward Eaton, Jim Seay, Jim Applewhite, Michael Chitwood, John Kessel, Tim McLaurin, Anderson Ferrell, Howard Owen, Louise Shivers, David

Payne, Linda Brown, Gail Godwin, Gerald Barrax, Clyde Edgerton, Lee Zacharias, Randall Kenan, and Kaye Gibbons.

Literary magazines and publishing ventures have also continued to grow in the state since Walser's death in 1988. *Asheville Poetry Review, Brightleaf,* and *North Carolina Literary Review* joined *Pembroke Magazine, Carolina Quarterly, Greensboro Review, Archive, Crucible,* and *Sandhills Review* in regular issues. Writers Ellyn Bache and Jerry Bledsoe have devoted some of their energy and money to new publishing houses, Banks Channel Books of Wilmington and Down Home Press of Asheboro, to extend the literary reach of the university presses, St. Andrews College Press, and John F. Blair of Winston-Salem.

No living Literary Hall of Fame inductee has had more to do with the renaissance represented and supported by these and other writers in contemporary North Carolina than Louis Rubin, now retired from UNC–CH. The Charleston, South Carolina, native has authored over fifty books during his long career as journalist, teacher, editor, mentor, scholar, novelist, and publisher. He founded Algonquin Books of Chapel Hill in 1983, and with the current editor in chief Shannon Ravenel he has remained determined that this fullfledged, nationally oriented trade publishing house in the South will showcase talented writers, many of them southern, who work outside the New York publishing network. Especially has he championed Gibbons, McCorkle, and Edgerton among the current group of very productive novelists who call North Carolina home. Their shared fictional idiom is the narrative of the first person—often speaking or writing in letters—and their success with these mediated voices has been recognized and praised. Sometimes their characters speak and think in lowbrow terms much different from the card-catalog minds or more cerebral concerns of the central people in the stories and novels of Doris Betts, Max Steele, Manly Wade Wellman, Elizabeth Spencer, John Ehle, Wilma Dykeman, Howard Owen, Gail Godwin, Lee Smith, Anne Tyler, Fred Chappell, and Reynolds Price. Who would guess that scholarly Rubin's novelists would often write about people who do not or would not read books? Edgerton's popular *Raney* (1985) has a title character who is a librarian, but readers overlook her profession in the humorous talk she delivers so well.

Two older active novelists, both Hall of Fame inductees, consistently show literary mastery and receive serious study. Alone or in collaboration with her husband, James Stokely, and two sons, Wilma Dykeman has written a very impressive shelf of fiction, travel books, biography, and social as well as military history. Best known are the novels *The Tall Woman* (1962) and *The Far Family* (1966). Her heroine Lydia McQueen and the novelist herself embody a forceful presence and the mastery of language also found in her pioneering environmental book, *The French Broad* (1955), in the Rivers of America series. On the national scene, Dykeman has published books on race and population. Significant in this regard is *Too Many People, Too Little Love* (1974), a study of birth control. She has also published a bicentennial history of Tennessee. Her third novel, *Return the Innocent Earth* (1973), is set in that state. A very gifted lecturer, teacher, and journalist, Wilma Dykeman lives in Asheville, where she was born.

John Ehle, a 1997 inductee, is another Asheville native, novelist, historian, and social force. He and his wife, Rosemary Harris, live in Winston-Salem. Among his seventeen books are eleven novels. The Campbell and Wright clans populate several of them, *The Winter People* (1982) and *Last One Home* (1984) being the two most recent examples. *The Widow's Trial* (1989) shows Ehle's mastery of multiple voices in clearly presenting a complex story. It is the best of a number of contemporary North Carolina novels about people who live in trailers or mobile homes. His enduring concern for minority voices and values is shown in *The Journey of August King* (1971), a novel about a runaway slave girl, and in the nonfictional *Trail of Tears: The Rise and Fall of the Cherokee Nation* (1988). As a notable public servant, Ehle has also enacted his belief in the dignity of people by his service to two North Carolina governors in the creation of new state schools for math, science, and the arts as well as in organizations such as the North Carolina Institute of Outdoor Drama. He and Dykeman share with Sam Ragan, Doris Betts, Paul Green, and Jonathan Daniels the rare gift of employing an artist's acuity to make the world a better place. In *The Road* (1967), all of Ehle's power is revealed as he combines folklore, history, and remarkable characters to trace the building of the railroad and tunnels to allow trains to make the climb from Old Fort to Ridgecrest in the 1870s.

Charles Frazier, also a mountain native, deftly reflects that heritage in creating *Cold Mountain* (1997), a novel set in the closing months of the Civil War. It won the National Book Award for fiction.

O. Henry, born William Sydney Porter near Greens-boro in 1862, is buried in Asheville's Riverside Cemetery not far from the grave of Thomas Wolfe. The short-story magician married Sarah Coleman of nearby Weaverville in 1907, three years before his death. Like Wolfe, O. Henry spent most of his adult years outside North Carolina. Unlike Wolfe's work, few North Carolina stories appear among the hundreds that O. Henry published. Exceptions are "The Blackjack Bargainer," "Let Me Feel Your Pulse," and "The Fool-Killer." The writer's criminal and literary notoriety combined during his life and after to make him a phenomenon. For decades, national short-story stalwarts have been honored with an award commemorating his assumed name and real genius.

The name of Joseph Mitchell is not nearly as well known today as O. Henry's or Thomas Wolfe's, but this 1997 Literary Hall of Fame inductee developed a wide following at the *New Yorker*, where he joined the staff in 1938 to write features. During the next six decades, his spare elegance characterized "Talk of the Town." His short stories were typically set in New York, but, as in O. Henry's case, an occasional tale had a connection to Mitchell's native state. Robeson County, North Carolina, can be detected in "The Downfall of Fascism in Black Ankle County," "Hit Over the Head with a Cow," "Uncle Docker and the Independent Bull," and "I Blame It All on Mother." The folk elements of these stories reflect Mitchell's early association with Koch at Chapel Hill. *McSorley's Wonderful Saloon* (1943), on the other hand, has been called New York's *Dubliners*. Several other collections of his work in fiction and journalism were well received, especially *Up in the Old Hotel and Other Stories* (1992). He collaborated with Edmund Wilson in 1960 on *Apologies to the Iroquois*. A cynosure of journalistic and literary style, Mitchell was cited by the American Academy of Arts and Letters in 1965. In 1984 he won the North Carolina Award for Literature.

No single North Carolina story that O. Henry or Mitchell wrote can now outshine "The Scarlet Ibis" by eastern North Carolina native and longtime New York resident James R. Hurst. A corporate banker with a prose poet's heart and soul, Hurst has delighted generations of adults and adolescents with this story about two brothers and a fated bird. *The Atlantic Monthly* first published it in July 1960. Many times since then it has appeared in middle- and high-school literature textbooks, notably in Scott Foresman's *Patterns in Literature*. In 1984 Hurst retired to New Bern and remains modest about his famous story.

Another writer whose name now recalls a single North Carolina story is Noel Houston, an Oklahoma native who published "Lantern on the Beach" in 1943. North Carolina's recent contributors to juvenile literature, with few exceptions, have come from or written about the state's broad coastal plain. Even the first book for North Carolina children, *A Wreath from the Woods of Carolina* (1859) by Mary Mason, was set mostly along the Trent River at New Bern. A century passed, and the pattern held. Prolific Theodore Taylor, a Statesville native, published (1974–1977) a Hatteras trilogy for boys and girls. Chapel Hill's Nancy Tilly made Beaufort into Kingsport in *Golden Girl* (1986). Raleigh resident and Meredith College professor Suzanne Newton, a native of Bath, shows her love of language and the sensitive story lines of cultural and human geography in more than half a dozen novels, notably *Where Are You When I Need You?* (1991), as her young characters approach adulthood and move westward across the coastal plain. In *Home Before Dark* (1976), Winterville native Sue Ellen Bridgers writes about a fuller cross-section of adolescent and adult experiences than Newton; Bridgers has also chosen to live in the far mountains of Jackson County and has written novels for adults in recent years. Not so Nell Wise Wechter of coastal Stumpy Point and Greensboro, whose characters are the ages of her young readers. Her most enduring title is *Taffy of Torpedo Junction* (1957), a World War II novel. Wechter distilled other novels out of the broad outline of state history from the Lost Colony and Blackbeard to her own times. Charles Harry Whedbee's several books have done the same service for young readers interested in coastal folklore. Using history, fantasy, and folklore, William Hooks, a Columbus County native, has produced almost fifty beautifully illustrated books for young people during a career in New York and Chapel Hill. His North Carolina titles, such as *Snowbear Whittington* (1994) and *Legend of the White Doe* (1988), suggest mountain as well as coastal-plain plots with diverse populations, human and animal. *Sound the Jubilee* (1995) by Sandra Forrester of Durham is set on Roanoke Island during the Civil War and is based on the real experiences of former slaves temporarily settled there near the site of the 1580s Lost Colony. Belinda Hurmence of Statesville is another writer who has also concerned herself with slavery. Her settings are not coastal in *A Girl Called Boy* (1982), *Tancy* (1984), or the more mature collection of slave narratives she published in 1985 as *My Folks Don't Want*

Me to Talk About Slavery. A similar 1997 collection edited by her is entitled *Slavery Time When I Was Chillun*.

Two native North Carolinians who were born into slavery and three African Americans who moved to the state have been inducted into the North Carolina Literary Hall of Fame. George Moses Horton, the state's first professional poet, was also the first of his race in the South to compose and publish a book—*The Hope of Liberty* (1829). Born in Northampton County and moved as property in early life to Chatham, the young poet discovered Chapel Hill on excursions to sell plantation produce there. The university society of students and faculty families admired his expressive lyrics, so any paying customer could write down the black poet's powerful recitations. Horton had taught himself to read but was grown before he could write well. A second edition of his first book in 1837 and another entitled *Naked Genius* (1865) comprise his body of work. After the Civil War, Horton lived and worked in Philadelphia until his death in 1883. Richard Walser published *The Black Poet,* a biography of Horton, in 1966. The George Moses Horton Society for the Study of African American Poetry was organized in 1997 and headquartered in Chapel Hill, where the UNC Press brought out a new edition of this black bard's works edited by Joan Sherman.

Several other contemporary scholars have brought out modern editions of *Incidents in the Life of a Slave Girl* (1861) by Harriet Jacobs. She began writing it over a decade after she escaped in 1842 from harsh bondage by hiding at several sites in and around Edenton, where as a child she had been taught to read and write by her white mistress. There Jacobs also had two children by a white lawyer named Samuel Sawyer, who was the nephew of North Carolina's first playwright, U.S. Congressman Lemuel Sawyer, the author of *Blackbeard* (1824). After fleeing to New York and Boston, Jacobs remained well connected, though a fugitive. She associated with powerful abolitionists and formed bonds with her son and daughter, who had come North separately. Before her astonishing story was finally published as the work of Linda Brent in 1861, the writer had personally promoted her manuscript in England. During and after the Civil War, she was active north and south in relief work among freedmen. With her daughter, Jacobs again spent time in North Carolina before she died and was buried in Boston in 1897.

By that time, Charles W. Chesnutt, an octoroon, was already establishing his reputation as a writer of local-color stories set in and around Fayetteville, North Carolina, the other home of this Ohio native. He taught in Charlotte as well as Fayetteville before leaving the state to live again in Ohio, where he passed the bar. It was his literary work that made him the first African American author to gain wide critical acceptance. Among his famous stories and novels with North Carolina connections are *The Conjure Woman* (1899), *The Wife of His Youth and Other Stories* (1899), *The House Behind the Cedars* (1900), *The Marrow of Tradition* (1901), and *The Colonel's Dream* (1905). Chesnutt died in 1932, but his reputation thrives a century after he earned his considerable literary fame.

Pauli Murray and John Hope Franklin were inducted into the Literary Hall of Fame in Southern Pines in 1998. Murray's literary achievement rests in *Proud Shoes: The Story of an American Family* (1956) and the fully autobiographical *Song in a Weary Throat* (1987). This Baltimore native spent most of her youth in Durham, as these prose works show. She also wrote poems. The longest of them, "Dark Testament," was published by Lillian Smith in *South Today* during World War II, and selections from it were later used in memorial services after Dr. Martin Luther King Jr.'s assassination in 1968. Murray actually overcame many racial and gender challenges by walking proudly in the shoes of her maternal grandfather Robert Fitzgerald. Few since Murray's death in 1985 could follow her determined lead as an educated African American female, cofounder of NOW, international lawyer, author, and Episcopal priest. She spoke and acted, she said, for her race, her people, the human race, and just people.

John Hope Franklin has done exactly the same service in his long and distinguished career as a university scholar who mastered the art and the craft of history. His Oklahoma beginnings and study at Fisk University prepared him for advanced degrees at Harvard. Much of his formative teaching was done in North Carolina. He published *The Free Negro in North Carolina, 1790–1860* with UNC Press in 1943, but the completion of the first edition of his seminal study *From Slavery to Freedom* (1947) propelled him away from North Carolina College in Durham to Howard University and then to academic posts elsewhere. In 1982 he returned to North Carolina to join the faculty at Duke. He lives in Durham and can look back upon his accomplishments both as a convincing reexamination of the Civil War and Reconstruction era and as a record of the role of African Americans in shaping the modern identity of this nation. As he entered the Literary Hall of Fame of his adopted state, he had a presidential appointment, at age eighty-three, to lead a national conversation about race relations.

From their separate eras at the beginning and the end of the twentieth century, John Charles McNeill and Jonathan Williams carry on a dialogue about the nature and function of poetry in North Carolina. Inducted into the Hall of Fame in 1998, both of these native poets use the speech patterns and vocabulary of local people, McNeill from his fertile lowlands and Williams from his mountains. In *Songs, Merry and Sad* (1906) and *Lyrics from Cotton Land* (1907), McNeill sings in the humorous, down-to-earth, yet well-crafted conventions of the ordinary. A romantic, McNeill became so popular before his death in 1907 that his voice lived on for decades and has some quaint charm in it still. He became poet laureate of the state without any official claim on the title—beyond that which his free-lance connection with the *Charlotte Observer* provided. Richard Walser brought out McNeill's *Possums and Persimmons: Newly Collected Poems* in 1977.

With a very select following, Jonathan Williams, on the other hand, is boldly experimental and avant-garde in graphic design and poetic form, as an alumnus of Black Mountain College should be. Rare delights are in *Get Hot or Get Out: A Selection of Poems, 1957–1981* (1982) and *Blues & Roots, Rue and Bluets: A Garland for the Southern Appalachians* (1985). From the very large group of native and nonnative North Carolina poets living and dead, a select few are destined to follow one of the two paths these very different poets took into the North Carolina Literary Hall of Fame. A. R. Ammons combines the best of their geniuses.

Fred Chappell, who became the state's fourth official poet laureate in late 1997, sees a glowing future for poetry in this state, which already annually produces and consumes more than almost any other state. As a celebrated fiction writer as well as a highly decorated poet, Chappell claims that the rigor and personal adjustments of working in both forms is bad for his nervous system. His is a much nicer day when he writes poetry, which allows him to go more slowly, than when he writes prose, the faster form.

National literary attention has been drawn to many other North Carolina writers at the end of this century. Some of them, Reynolds Price and Robert Morgan, for example, work in poetry and prose as Chappell does.

Why the state is so rich in celebrated writers is hard

to answer, but there are some markers worth noting. First, though, a warning—the current North Carolina literary boom coincides with a bust in literacy across the state. For every member of the North Carolina Writers Network, for example, the state can still count literally thousands of adults and secondary-school students whose skills in reading and writing English are well below expectations in a free society. Many writers who now teach writing workshops and courses also came out of one or more of the state's various creative-writing programs, which have now produced many graduates. Their numbers alone account for some of the manuscripts in the state's booming literary business. In 1850, the percentage of North Carolinians who could not read was twice the number of similarly benighted Virginians and South Carolinians. Inglis Fletcher in 1940 recalled her North Carolina grandfather's saying that he had been born in this valley of humiliation between those two mountains of conceit. Any shame about literature is gone with the state's agrarian past. Love of stories and poems persists, but the rapid changes taking place on the economic, demographic, and cultural landscapes of the state offer many reasons for Tar Heel authors to write hard while the good light lasts.

In this entire story of North Carolina literature, Manly Wade Wellman, a 1996 inductee at Weymouth, is the only author who has succeeded in supporting himself and his family as a man of letters. Born in Africa, he settled, like nonnatives Boyd and Fletcher, in North Carolina and staked out a big literary domain. He settled in Chapel Hill in 1951 because of the writing resources available at UNC, but he eventually maintained a cabin in Madison County because the state's old mountain culture became his principal attraction after he met folklorist Bascom Lamar Lunsford. Wellman had written over eighty books, almost all set somewhere in the state, when he died in 1986. Among them are numerous historical adventure books for boys and girls, such as *Settlement on Shocco* (1963), and county histories like *The County of Warren* (1959). Wellman also published *Dead and Gone: Classic Crimes of North Carolina* (1954). More speculative but not less graphic fiction was his special passion, however, and his work in science fiction and fantasy will long outlive him. With a foreword by David Drake, all of Wellman's Silver John stories were collected in *John the Balladeer* (1988). These brief tales, far transcending traditional Jack tales, are the best ones ever based on Appalachian folklore. Their musical

hero also battles the forces of evil in the North Carolina high country and elsewhere in novels such as *After Dark* (1980). Reading Wellman makes a person want the light to last forever.

James W. Clark Jr.

See also Algonquin Books; Appalachian Literature; Piedmont; Rubin, Louis D., Jr.

Sally Buckner, *Our Words, Our Ways: Reading and Writing in North Carolina* (1995); Robert Gingher, ed. *Rough Road Home: Stories by North Carolina Writers* (1992); William Powell, *North Carolina Fiction, 1734–1957* (1958); Richard Walser and E. T. Malone Jr., *Literary North Carolina: A Historical Survey* (1986).

NORTH CAROLINA, UNIVERSITY OF

The University of North Carolina became in 1785 the first state university to open its doors. It has inspired writers from its earliest days, when several professors found it necessary to write textbooks for their classes. Caroline Lee Hentz (1800–1856), a faculty wife seeking an outlet for her literary talent, not only saw her own creative works published but also directed the poetic skill of a slave youth to publication. George Moses Horton's *Hope of Freedom* was published in Raleigh in 1829. These early- to mid-nineteenth-century examples marked the way to a literary renaissance in the next century.

It was not until the 1920s, when the words Chapel Hill became synonymous with the name of the university, that the small college came to be recognized as a true university. Although some chemical and scientific work had already been noted, it was literature and history that added luster to its recognition as the nation's first state university. The General Assembly in 1931 consolidated the University with the Woman's College at Greensboro and North Carolina State College at Raleigh under a single Board of Trustees. The offices of the Consolidated University were established on the Chapel Hill campus, and University President Frank Porter Graham became the Consolidated University's first president. The Consolidated University was later expanded to include all state-supported institutions; its offices are in Chapel Hill. UNC–Chapel Hill and N.C. State University are the flagship institutions of the system.

The school and the town soon came to be fused in

fact and fiction. Edwin W. Fuller's *Sea-Gift* (1873) and Thomas Wolfe's *Look Homeward, Angel* (1929)—both with the state of North Carolina for their setting, college students as players, and the University of North Carolina as focus—enchanted generations of college students. William Meade Prince, well known for his illustrations of Roark Bradford's stories of African American life, reminisced about his childhood in Chapel Hill in *The Southern Part of Heaven* (1950). Numerous works of fiction have depicted Chapel Hill and the University. The list includes Wilbur Daniel Steele's *The Man Without a God* (1931), Wolfe's *The Web and the Rock* (1939), John Ehle's *Move Over Mountain* (1957), William Hardy's *The Jubjub Bird* (1966), Daphne Athas's *Entering Ephesus* (1971), Lee Smith's *Family Linen* (1985), and many others. The trend has accelerated in the 1990s. Doris Betts's *The Sharp Teeth of Love* (1997) makes the University the starting point of the protagonist's journey and a constant point of reference. In her speech before the North Caroliniana Society when she won its major award, Betts traced her love affair with the University, revealing the greater opportunities now available for women in the once all-male institution.

In 1922 the University of North Carolina Press was established. Such versatile regional and national authors as Phillips Russell, Howard Odum, L. R. Wilson, and R. D. W. Connor made their mark in biography, education, fiction, history, journalism, and sociology, helping the University gain national renown. Odum established the new concept of Regionalism, soon to be followed by Paul Green's creation of Outdoor Symphonic Drama as a new literary form.

Further acclaim grew out of the emphasis on creative writing that developed in the English Department with the collaboration of many established professors and newly successful writers of fiction and poetry, including Jessie Rehder, Max Steele, Doris Betts, Daphne Athas, James Seay, Lee Smith, Marianne Gingher, William Harmon, Bland Simpson, Alan Shapiro, and Michael McFee. In 1968 Louis Rubin and C. Hugh Holman founded and began editing the *Southern Literary Journal,* and the English department gave southern literature a greater prominence in its curriculum. The Southern Historical Collection and North Carolina Collections in Wilson Library have made the University a center for research on southern writing. The University Library began to host teas at which well-established as well as newly published authors discussed their work. Rubin was untiring in supporting the

work—critical and creative—of many new writers. Under his leadership, Algonquin Books of Chapel Hill was established, and it published new as well as established writers, especially southern writers.

William S. Powell

See also Algonquin Books; Chapel Hill, North Carolina; Rubin, Louis D., Jr.; *Southern Literary Journal,* 1968 to Present.

Doris Betts, *My Love Affair with Carolina* (1998); Pamela Dean, *Women on the Hill: A History of Women at the University of North Carolina* (1987); Dougald MacMillan, *English at Chapel Hill, 1795–1969* (1978); Louis R. Wilson, *The University of North Carolina, 1900–1930: The Making of a Modern University* (1957).

NORTH CAROLINA STATE UNIVERSITY

North Carolina State University was established as an agricultural and mechanical college in Raleigh, North Carolina, in 1887. One of the state legislators closely involved with the design of North Carolina's land-grant college was to become the first writer of note to be associated with the college. Thomas Dixon, from Shelby, North Carolina, was a member of the General Assembly in 1884 and served on the committee charged with presenting plans for North Carolina's new land-grant school. A graduate of Wake Forest College and a Baptist minister, Dixon is hardly remembered for his efforts on behalf of "State College"; instead, he was to become famous, or infamous, for his creation of racist, incendiary novels recounting the birth of the Ku Klux Klan and the white male southerner's battle to regain control of the South through campaigns of terror and lynching. *The Leopard's Spots* (1902) and *The Clansman* (1905) were sensationally popular successes, and *The Clansman* made history when it was made into one of America's first moving pictures, *The Birth of a Nation,* in 1915.

N.C. State established its importance as a literary center in the 1950s and 1960s through the work of three men in particular: Richard Walser, professor of English, whose publications on North Carolina literature brought attention to the state as a whole; Guy Owen, who brought the *Southern Poetry Review* to the campus and established himself as a major fiction writer with the publication of *The Ballad of the Flim-Flam Man* (1965); and Sam Ragan, who conducted fiction and poetry workshops at the then College Union throughout the 1960s while he was managing editor of the *Raleigh News and Observer*. Some of the writers who received valuable encouragement from Ragan and Owen include Betty Adcock, Shelby Stephenson, and Romulus Linney, who also taught drama workshops at the Union.

N.C. State, as a university concentrating on technical majors, attracted some students who found there the literary stimulation to help them build careers as writers. Early on, James R. Hurst from Swansboro studied engineering but later became a noted author, known particularly for his short story "The Scarlet Ibis" (1960). Robert Morgan from Hendersonville came to N.C. State in 1962, but after receiving the enthusiastic mentoring of Guy Owen, he abandoned aerospace engineering and applied mathematics and decided on a writing career and transferred to Chapel Hill. He is the author of ten books of poetry (including *Green River: New and Selected Poems,* 1991), two collections of short fiction, and five novels, including *The Truest Pleasure* (1995) and *Gap Creek* (1999). Anderson Ferrell from Wilson County is another North Carolinian who turned to writing because of undergraduate experiences at N.C. State. He has published *Where She Was* (1985) and *Home for the Day* (1994).

The North Carolina State English Department followed up its appointments of Walser and Owen with other important hiring in creative writing. Lance Jeffers, who joined the faculty in 1974 and remained there until his death in 1985, was an outspoken black nationalist who began publishing poetry and fiction in the 1950s. Gerald Barrax, born in 1933, another African American poet, joined the English department in 1969. Until his retirement in 1998, Barrax was editor of *Obsidian II: Black Literature in Review,* a journal of African American creative writing and scholarship, which is housed in the English department. A third African American poet, Marcia Douglas, came to the campus in 1998. A writer who draws on her experiences growing up in Jamaica, Douglas is already the author of a collection of poetry, *Electricity Comes to Cocoa Bottom* (1998), and a novel, *Madam Fate* (1999). Tom Lisk, who joined the faculty in 1994, is author of a collection of poems, *A Short History of Pens Since the French Revolution.*

Fiction has continued to thrive at N.C. State. After the tragic early death of Guy Owen in 1981, Lee Smith became the university's first Guy Owen Writer in Residence. Author of nine novels and three short-story collections, including most recently *News of the Spirit* (1998), Smith has won many national awards. John Kessel came to N.C. State at the same time as Smith (1982) and is North Carolina's leading science-fiction writer. He has won a Nebula Award (for his novella *Another Orphan,* 1982), and his 1992 story collection *Meeting in Infinity* was nominated for a World Fantasy Award. Kessel recently completed revisions of a novel left unpublished by another English department faculty member, Larry Rudner. *Memory's Tailor* was published posthumously in 1998, and like Rudner's first novel, *The Magic We Do Here* (1988), it deals with questions of memory and survival in connection with the horrors of the Holocaust. Like Smith and Rudner, English professor Angela Davis-Gardner has won the Sir Walter Raleigh Award for Fiction. She has published two novels; *Forms of Shelter* (1991) was a selection of the Literary Guild and Doubleday book clubs. William McCranor Henderson, who has written the novels *I Killed Hemingway* (1983) and *Stark Raving Elvis* (1984), and Tim McLaurin, acclaimed for four novels, a memoir (*Keeper of the Moon,* 1991), and a book-length poem (*Lola,* 1997), have brought diverse talents to the creative-writing program.

Among novelists who began their careers through courses and workshops at N.C. State are Kaye Gibbons (*Ellen Foster,* 1987, and four other novels); T. R. Pearson (*A Short History of a Small Place,* 1985, and six other novels); John Gregory Brown (*Decorations in a Ruined Cemetery,* 1993); Peggy Payne (*Revelation,* 1988), and Sarah Dessen, author of two popular works of fiction for young adults (*Summer,* 1996, and *Someone Like You,* 1998).

Through its unique Humanities Extension Program, N.C. State has taken the lead in developing video treatments of North Carolina writers. The first of these was a work for public television entitled *Thomas Wolfe: An Escape into Life* (1982–1983). James Clark, Richard Walser, and Phillip Horne then teamed up to produce *Their Native Earth: A Celebration of North Carolina Literature* (1989), featuring interviews and commentaries of around a dozen living North Carolina writers.

James W. Clark and Lucinda H. MacKethan

See also North Carolina, Literature of.

NORTHERN AUDIENCES

The reception of southern literature by northern audiences has had a varied history. As J. B. Hubbell in *The*

South in American Literature: 1607–1900 (1954) and others have noted, much of the writing in the South in the colonial period came from a place that had not yet established a regional identity. In the very early period, the inhabitants thought of themselves as English, not southern, and were content with importing their literary materials from England. Furthermore, much of their writing was of a practical nature, such as Captain John Smith's account of his explorations. With the approach of the Revolutionary War, much of the preeminent writing was political, done by Thomas Jefferson and others, who at this time were less concerned with a regional than a national identity. Other writing in the southern colonies was intended for private consumption, and this, combined with the lack of publishing organs in the South, contributed to a relatively small output of southern literature for northern consumption.

Howard R. Floan in *The South in Northern Eyes: 1831 to 1861* (1958) notes that in the decades before the Civil War, very few Americans knew what the South was like. Because of the difficulties of travel, few northerners had visited the South, and the average southerner had a tendency "to judge the entire South on the basis of his immediate region, and thus he often failed to appreciate the variety of the South." Floan notes that although important literary minds of the first half of the nineteenth century, such as Emerson, Thoreau, and Hawthorne, "were for the most part either hostile or silent in respect to the South, there is evidence that [the literary] journals were both sympathetic and expressive in their treatment of it."

Floan also finds that "in the early eighteen thirties many Southerners—attempting to justify the remunerative blend of cotton and slave labor—began to picture themselves in romanticized tones of a pre-Jeffersonian past." In *The Literary South* (1979), Louis D. Rubin Jr. asserts that "the idea of a distinctively Southern literature was initially tied in with regional self-consciousness and sectional self-defense." John Pendleton Kennedy's *Swallow Barn* (1832), which has been credited with setting in motion the plantation myth in southern literature, was well received by northern journals, including the *North American* and the *New England Magazine*. In his introduction to a 1962 edition of *Swallow Barn*, William Osborne describes the novel not only as "a careful delineation of the Southern scene" but also as "a nostalgic re-creation of a way of living being lost in an expanding America of the 1830's." Although Kennedy sometimes paints satirical portraits of his characters, he praises Virginia as a

place populated by people of good taste and breeding "who brought within her confines a solid fund of respectability and wealth. This race of men grew vigorous in her genial atmosphere; her cloudless skies quickened and enlivened their tempers, and, in two centuries, gradually matured the sober and thinking Englishman into that spirited, imaginative being who now inhabits the lowlands of this state." Kennedy's depiction of an idyllic plantation life-style in which the master, Meriwether, figures as a genial host and a benevolent caretaker both to his family and his slaves, as well as a man more concerned with personal honor than material gain, struck a chord with northern readers.

Other writers of this period also achieved recognition in the North for different reasons. For example, William Gilmore Simms was popular for his historical romances, including *Guy Rivers* (1834) and *The Yemassee* (1835). Edgar Allan Poe, whose work is less topically southern than Kennedy's and Simms's, in many ways transcended the label of southern writer.

In the years immediately preceding the Civil War, however, northern receptivity to southern writing sharply diminished as white southern writers became more shrilly defensive of southern institutions. Thus Henry Timrod's writing, including his notable poems "Ethnogenesis" (1861) and "The Cotton Boll" (1861), which asserts God's favor for the South, could in no way resonate with a northern audience. On the other hand, writing by black southerners was well received in the North. Frederick Douglass's *Narrative of the Life of Frederick Douglass* (1845) was the most widely known of the slave accounts depicting the horrors of slavery in the South, and William Wells Brown's *Clotel; or The President's Daughter* (1853), which included a graphic depiction of a slave sale, went through three editions.

In the 1870s, northern resistance to southern writing all but disappeared. The idealistic goals that had informed northern support of the war were giving way to an increased interest in the North in commercial prosperity. At a time when the issue of whether there would be only one nation had been answered, there developed an increased interest in life-styles less affected by northern urbanization. The South was an area rich with material to develop into fiction; thus it is not surprising that in the 1880s and 1890s southern writers dominated the national literary market with local-color writing. One of the most striking examples is the work of Thomas Nelson Page, whose short-story collection

In Ole Virginia (1887) gave readers a nostalgic depiction of the South. The opening paragraph of one of the stories in the collection, "Marse Chan," describes the "once splendid mansions" now decaying: "Distance was nothing to this people; time was of no consequence to them. They desired but a level path in life, and that they had, though the way was longer, and the outer world strode by them as they dreamed." Similarly, Mary Noailles Murfree, who went by the pen name Charles Egbert Craddock, received popular acclaim for her stories of noble if backward mountaineers in the stories collected in *In the Tennessee Mountains* (1884). In "The 'Harnt' That Walks Chilhowee," Murfree writes of a mountaineer: "The grace of culture is, in its way, a fine thing, but the best that art can do—the polish of a gentleman—is hardly equal to the best that Nature can do in her higher moods."

The positive reception of southern literature continued at the turn of the century. In spite of H. L. Mencken's pronouncement that the South was a cultural desert, many southern writers were highly regarded by a northern reading audience. Ellen Glasgow, author of over twenty novels spanning four decades, argued that the South needed "blood and Irony" and sought to counter the strictly nostalgic views of the South offered by the local-colorists. *The Sheltered Life* (1932) does contain the author's critical commentary on the prejudices and stifling conventions of the South, but it also praises a way of life that one of the central characters describes in his account of his childhood on a Virginia plantation where "manners . . . were a perpetual celebration of being alive. No other way of living had ever seemed to him so deeply rooted in the spirit of place, in an established feeling or life." Following publication of *Jurgen* (1919), James Branch Cabell was counted among the nation's leading artists. The 1920s were dubbed "The James Branch Cabell Period."

Louis D. Rubin Jr. has written of the decade after World War I that Mencken's "Sahara of the Bozart" grew "overnight . . . into a literary garden" and noted that many of these southern writers were writing literature "that was of interest and importance far beyond the boundaries of their region." Fred Hobson in *The Southern Writer in the Postmodern World* (1991) notes the "irony of southern literary history" that the "legacy of defeat and failure served well the writer in the South. Like Quentin Compson at Harvard, the southern writer wore his heritage of failure and defeat—and often guilt—as his badge of honor. It provided him or her something that no other American writer, or at least American novelist, of the twentieth century had in any abundance—that is, a tragic sense." The writers of the Southern Renascence—including William Faulkner, Thomas Wolfe, Katherine Anne Porter, Robert Penn Warren, Richard Wright, and others—as well as the writers who achieved recognition shortly thereafter—among them Eudora Welty, Tennessee Williams, and Ralph Ellison—had a profound influence on the American literary scene. Louis Rubin and other critics have argued that the generation of writers following Faulkner's generation have had to contend with what has remained constant and what has changed in the South since World War II. Walker Percy is often cited as a transitional figure who deals with the issues of family, tradition, honor, etc., seen in the earlier writers but places them in the context of a New South where the pasture land of Faulkner's *The Sound and the Fury* (1929) has been replaced by the suburbs of Percy's *The Moviegoer* (1961).

Fred Hobson argues, "in the South of 1990 that dream of poor southern book editors and apologists of the 1920s, responding to Mencken's 'Sahara of the Bozart,' has finally been realized. There *are*, this time, significant numbers of young southern writers one could claim—with truth, integrity, and no sectional bias—as among the nation's finest." Critics of contemporary southern writing are noting new directions taken by southern writers. Hobson cites the importance of mass culture in the work of writers such as Bobbie Ann Mason but argues that the majority of southern writers born after 1940—including Alice Walker, Jill McCorkle, and Clyde Edgerton—"are still more concerned with family than are most nonsouthern American writers, even if sometimes in a quirky and nontraditional manner"; and that they put more emphasis on community than their nonsouthern counterparts. Hobson also argues that the fiction of Ernest Gaines contains those very qualities that have usually been considered "to be the domain of the white southern writer." Gaines's novels, such as *A Gathering of Old Men* (1983), reveal "his attention to place and community [and] also his deep sense of the elemental, his distrust of abstraction, his awareness of the past in the present, and his continued attention to that most frequently treated and most dramatically powerful of southern subjects, racial tension and conflict. At a time when most white southern novelists have left racial themes nearly behind—they can well afford to—Gaines still grounds his fiction in racial conflict, courage, endurance."

After several decades of literary debate, then, the

question of whether there is still a South to write about has been answered with a resounding yes. Presses such as Algonquin continue to showcase the work of talented young southern writers, and if the *New York Times Book Review* is any indication, southern writers continue to receive a healthy share of national attention.

Anne E. Rowe

See also North, The.

Richard N. Current, *Northernizing the South* (1983); Donald Davidson, *Southern Writers in the Modern World* (1958); Howard R. Floan, *The South in Northern Eyes: 1831 to 1861* (1958); Fred Hobson, *The Southern Writer in the Postmodern World* (1991); Louis D. Rubin Jr., ed., *The Literary South* (1979).

NOVEL, BEGINNINGS TO 1820

By the end of the eighteenth century, southern readers, like readers elsewhere in the United States, were avidly consuming novels. Yet relatively few novels were printed in the South, written by southern authors, or even set in the South. Prior to 1820, most novels, whether by American or European writers, were printed in Philadelphia, Boston, or New York. Occasionally, after the turn of the century, novels were printed in Baltimore, Richmond, and the District of Columbia; there were simply fewer presses in the South during this time and consequently fewer opportunities for novel publication. Very infrequently, novels were published at scattered sites around the region; one such work is Jessee L. Holman's *The Prisoners of Niagara* (1810), published in Frankfort, Kentucky.

Until the 1820s and 1830s, when technological advances in the printing process and the establishment of a national book distribution network radically changed the American publishing scene, books were still relatively expensive (the typical novel cost around a dollar), and distribution depended on water or wagon travel. Books thus tended to be printed in small quantities and sold by special order from the publisher or by itinerant book peddlers and local presses, which bartered titles in order to increase the variety of their stock. During the colonial period, wealthy southern patrons were likely to place direct orders with British publishers, but as presses proliferated during the early national period, this practice became less common.

Mason Locke Weems, a distributor for Philadelphia publisher Mathew Carey, documents in his correspondence with Carey the avid interest of southern readers in the novel, frequently urging Carey to send him more novels. Similarly, a bookseller in Raleigh in 1801 wrote to Carey: "Mr. Carey will be so obliging as to send as many of the Novels as he can procure, it will be mutually our interest to keep a good collection, as the good folks here love *light* reading."

Although essayists in American periodicals expressed considerable hostility toward fiction, especially during the 1790s, some evidence suggests that the South may have been more liberal in attitudes toward novel-reading than the North. In his letter to Robert Skipwith describing the ideal individual library, Thomas Jefferson argued for the value of fiction as a supplement to history in forming the moral sense: "Considering history as a moral exercise, her lessons would be too unfrequent if confined to real life." Although Jefferson later expressed more ambivalence with regard to novel-reading, particularly for female readers, other southerners seem to have shared his earlier, liberal attitudes about fiction's potential educative value. The growth of circulating and social libraries in the late eighteenth and early nineteenth centuries made even more novels available to eager readers of fiction, and at relatively inexpensive prices; fiction's popularity in turn undoubtedly fostered the growth of such lending libraries.

Other than Cervantes's *Don Quixote* or Rousseau's *La Nouvelle Héloïse*, the novels most commonly read by southerners were written by British authors; these works were either imported or, more likely later in the eighteenth century, reprinted profitably by American publishers, who tended to disregard British copyright and thus avoid paying royalties to British authors. The first and most popular eighteenth-century British novel reprinted in America was Samuel Richardson's *Pamela*; Richard Beale Davis has suggested, however, that *Pamela* was less popular in the South than in other regions. Also popular in the eighteenth century were, in no particular order, Richardson's *Clarissa*, Daniel Defoe's *Robinson Crusoe*, Tobias Smollett's *Humphry Clinker* and *Roderick Random*, Henry Fielding's *Tom Jones*, Oliver Goldsmith's *The Vicar of Wakefield,* and Laurence Sterne's *Tristram Shandy.* Both North Carolinian James Iredell and Virginian William Wirt observed that southerners particularly enjoyed "*Shandy.*" Popular early-nineteenth-century works include Jane Porter's *Thaddeus of Warsaw* and *Scottish Chiefs* and Walter

Scott's *Guy Mannering, Waverley, Rob Roy,* and *Ivanhoe. Ivanhoe* made Scott the favorite English contemporary novelist in the South during the early national era, although his popularity did not reach its height until the 1830s. Among the one hundred or so novels produced by American writers prior to 1820, Susanna Rowson's *Charlotte Temple* was by far the most popular, followed by Hannah Foster's *The Coquette;* their sentimentality and focus on issues relevant to young women found favor particularly among female readers.

Few southerners wrote novels prior to 1820, and none produced a work that could truly be said to be popular, but there are several novels of note. Indeed, a work with a somewhat tenuous claim to being the earliest American novel, *Adventures of Alonso,* "By a Native of Maryland, Some Years Resident in Portugal," Thomas Atwood Digges, was published in London in 1775. His adventures take Alonso, the son of a Portuguese merchant, to a variety of exotic locales, including Brazil, the Caribbean, and Panama. Both *The Step-Mother* (1798) and *Constantia Neville* (1800) by Helena Wells were likewise published in London, where each was popular enough to warrant the publication of a second edition within a year of its initial publication date. Wells was the daughter of Robert Wells, a Scottish printer, bookseller, and founder of the *South-Carolina Weekly Gazette,* who moved in 1753 to Charleston, where Helena was later born. Although the title page of *The Step-Mother* describes her as "Helena Wells, of Charles Town, South-Carolina" and she is frequently named as South Carolina's first novelist, Wells had moved to London along with her Loyalist family shortly after the Revolutionary War began. She maintained her family ties to South Carolina, however, for the subscription list in the first edition of *Constantia Neville* names a number of prominent South Carolinians. The hero of *Constantia Neville* spends some years living among the Indians of North America, but both of Wells's rather conservative, conventional sentimental novels are set primarily in England and emphasize the importance of female education.

John Davis, an Englishman who tutored briefly at what became the College of Charleston and taught for a time in Richmond, wrote several novels, most notably *The First Settlers of Virginia* (1805), an early historical novel that includes a version of the John Smith-Pocahontas story, one of the first fictional works to do so. Davis saw the relationship between the white settlers and the Indians as central to the history of America and continually reworked this theme; he first relates the Pocahontas-Smith story as a brief anecdote in his novel *The Farmer of New Jersey* (1800), retells it in his nonfiction *Travels of Four Years and a Half in the United States of America* (1803), expands it in the novella *Captain Smith and the Princess Pocahontas: An Indian Tale* (1805), and then further expands it as a full-length novel in *The First Settlers of Virginia.* Davis also wrote *Walter Kennedy: An American Tale* (1808), one of the earliest novels to feature black dialect speech. Another novelist of English extraction, Winifred Marshall Gales, who had already published a novel in London, wrote *Matilda Berkely, or Family Anecdotes* (1804), the first novel written by a resident of North Carolina. *Matilda Berkely* focuses on the relationships among several noble British and Russian families; it was published by Gales's husband, Joseph Gales, who had established a printing business in Raleigh.

At this early stage in the development of the American novel, southern settings are rare (far more common are London, Boston, and Philadelphia), but there are some interesting exceptions. For many nonsouthern novelists, Charleston epitomized the South and thus served as a favored location. Among others, novels with scenes set in Charleston include *The Power of Sympathy* (1789), by William Hill Brown, who later moved to North Carolina; Judith Sargent Murray's *Story of Margaretta* (1798); and Charles Brockden Brown's *Arthur Mervyn* (1799/1800). Perhaps most interesting is a work by Jessee L. Holman, described on the title page of his novel, *The Prisoners of Niagara,* as "a native Kentuckian." Set against the backdrop of the Revolutionary War, much of the novel takes place in Virginia; the novel ends with the American victory over British tyranny and with Evermont, the hero of the novel, abjuring his inherited title and anachronistically declaring a decade before its existence that the Bill of Rights applies to all men and that all are "born free." Evermont thus frees the slaves living on the plantation that he has inherited, awarding them land and ensuring that they are able to support themselves by their own labor.

There was no distinctive southern novel by 1820; however, there was, by this date, a developing interest among novelists in using native materials, particularly the history of the South and its distinctive social and economic situation. The fondness of southern readers for fiction, especially historical fiction imbued with local color, created an audience for such fictional works written during the 1820s as George Tucker's

The Valley of Shenandoah (1824) and the anonymous Tales of an American Landlord (1824), works that more clearly suggest the beginnings of a tradition of southern fiction.

Karen A. Weyler

See also Colonial Literature.

Earl L. Bradsher, *Mathew Carey: Editor, Author and Publisher* (1966); Herbert Ross Brown, *The Sentimental Novel in America 1789–1860* (1940); Cathy N. Davidson, *Revolution and the Word: The Rise of the Novel in America* (1986); Richard Beale Davis, *A Colonial Southern Bookshelf: Reading in the Eighteenth Century* (1979); Richard Beale Davis, *Literature and Society in Early Virginia* (1973); James D. Hart, *The Popular Book* (1950); Lillian Loshe, *The Early American Novel* (1907); David Moltke-Hansen, "A World Introduced: The Writings of Helena Wells of Charles Town, South Carolina's First Novelist," *South Carolina Women Writers* (1979); Frank Luther Mott, *Golden Multitudes: The Story of Best Sellers in the United States* (1947); Patricia L. Parker, *Early American Fiction: A Reference Guide* (1984); Henri Petter, *The Early American Novel* (1971); Robert B. Winans, "The Growth of a Novel-Reading Public in Late-Eighteenth-Century America," *Early American Literature* 9.3 (1975); Ronald J. Zboray, *A Fictive People: Antebellum Economic Development and the American Reading Public* (1993).

NOVEL, 1820 TO 1865

When the Missouri Compromise became national policy in 1820, Thomas Jefferson voiced his horror at the idea that a fixed geographical line could dictate where slavery in the United States would be legal and where it would not. In a famous comment, Jefferson declared that the Missouri decision marked "the death knell of the Union." His prediction proved accurate. The period from 1820 to 1865 is defined, for the South, by the region's inexorable movement toward and through disunion. During this period, southern sectionalism was fixed upon the national argument over slavery. The southern mind, as novels of the region demonstrate perhaps more effectively than any other writing, attached itself irrevocably to the defense of an idealized conception of a slave society. The agenda of sectional defense, in fiction, was worked out through the establishment of the staple figures of a distinctly southern aristocracy. In 1824 George Tucker introduced the Virginia cavalier to reading audiences in *The Valley of Shenandoah*, and the ideal of the southern planter-patrician still dominated the literature through 1864,

when Augusta Jane Evans (Wilson's) novel *Macaria* dramatized so compelling a picture of Confederate sacrifice and nobility that it was banned from Union army camps.

The whims of literary history have divided southern novels written from 1820 to the end of the Civil War into groups based on race, gender, and, only occasionally, political considerations. The most commonly recognized forms are the plantation novel, the historical romance, the domestic novel, the "Anti-Tom" novel, and the African American novel. Generally, the antebellum historical romance and the plantation novel have both been seen as works written exclusively by men and that develop plantation settings and characters within some actual historical context. The antebellum domestic novel of the period, in the South as well as the North, has been delegated exclusively to women; such novels, no matter how politically oriented their use of the plantation settings, are called "domestic" or "sentimental." Novels written by blacks born free or as slaves in the South have hardly been considered "southern" at all. A more helpful set-up of categories might stress the male writers' use of history and the women's stress on agrarian or domestic themes while also noting that women writers, no less than their male colleagues, recognized their primary role as staunch defenders of the South. Like Harriet Beecher Stowe, they employed a domestic ideology to promote a political agenda.

No history of the antebellum southern novel can be undertaken without reckoning with the role of Harriet Beecher Stowe's *Uncle Tom's Cabin*. Indeed, one might assert that before her novel's appearance in serial publication in 1851, the most popular southern novelists, male and female, wrote self-consciously under the influence of Sir Walter Scott, whereas afterward, none could escape the long shadow that Uncle Tom cast across the South. Although such a view certainly politicizes the exercise of writing fiction during this time, it helps to impress upon us what was always of first importance in antebellum southern novels: the South as a distinct and increasingly embattled section, defined in myth if not in fact by a plantation aristocracy that controlled the region's fate and was itself controlled by the slave labor that sustained its economic and social design.

Before *Uncle Tom's Cabin*'s appearance, certain elements of the historical romance as defined by Sir Walter Scott's practice captivated southern novelists as much as it did northern writers, most prominently

James Fenimore Cooper. One attraction of historical topics, then as now, was that an author could treat contemporary subjects under the guise of looking at a distant place and time—the relevance to the present moment might or might not seem obvious to readers. The Virginia novelists who began, with George Tucker, to mine their state's past back to colonial times were in some measure trying both to evade and to critique the state's current economic problems. Tucker, in *The Valley of Shenandoah,* treats the post–Revolutionary War South through his charting of the downfall of the Grayson family, whose patriarch Colonel Grayson had served under General George Washington. As the novel begins, Colonel Grayson has died and his love of luxuries has left his family in dire straights. The Graysons are virtuous aristocrats, proud, well-mannered, generous, and humane, especially to their slaves. Tucker undoubtedly has in mind Virginia's economic depression of the 1820s, but he sets his action in a period associated with the Old Dominion's beginnings, both to distance himself and to call attention to the better times and better people who had made Virginia great in the past.

The Virginia novel, as it might be called, was an antebellum development that enlisted George Tucker, his kinsman Nathaniel Beverley Tucker, John Pendleton Kennedy, William Alexander Caruthers, and John Esten Cooke, among others. The Old Dominion provided America's most persuasive ideal of aristocracy, promoted through the architecture of Mount Vernon, Monticello, and Williamsburg, through the courtly images of Virginia presidents Washington, Jefferson, Madison, and Monroe, and through dozens of novels that held up Virginians as Revolutionary War heroes in cavalier dress. Kennedy's *Horse-Shoe Robinson* (1835) and *Rob of the Bowl* (1838), Caruthers's *The Cavaliers of Virginia* (1834) and *The Knights of the Golden Horse-shoe* (1841 serially; 1845), and Cooke's *The Virginia Comedians* (1854) and *Henry St. John, Gentleman* (1859) all focus on revolutionary or prerevolutionary Virginia society, accenting aristocratic English ancestry, large estates, cavalier manners, and good old-fashioned swashbuckling action. Bacon's Rebellion (1676), Governor Spotswood's Blue Ridge Expedition (1716), Patrick Henry's prerevolutionary defiance, and George Washington's Revolutionary War exploits were all recovered in romances that borrowed heavily from Sir Walter Scott. In particular, the class distinctions that Scott loved to exploit played a large part in these costume dramas, promoting the vision of Virginia as a hierarchical society headed by a gentry modeled on the English lord of the manor.

The most interesting antebellum Virginia novel did not look back into past history but instead predicted the future. Nathaniel Beverley Tucker set *The Partisan Leader* (1836) forward in time to the year 1849. Tucker's crystal ball revealed to him a South that had split from the United States to form a Confederacy based on unswerving dedication to agriculture. This South is populated by principled gentlemen, while the North, led by the rapacious Martin Van Buren, cares only for wealth. Tucker's fictional slaves happily defend their plantation homes from the Yankees, and the defense of white ladyhood forms the resolve from which chivalric cavaliers lift their banners. As a novel, Tucker's fiction of secession has serious artistic flaws; as a work whose blind reverence for an agrarian, aristocratic South defied the realities of the 1830s, *The Partisan Leader* explains why many years later, Mark Twain felt that Sir Walter Scott should be held responsible for the Civil War.

While a half-dozen or more Virginia writers used the historical romance to fashion a mythical Virginia barony, the South's most important novelist, hailing from Charleston, singlehandedly gave the region its most complete fictional representation. William Gilmore Simms (1806–1870) began writing his historical romances in the 1830s. His first novel, *Martin Faber,* appeared in 1833, and from that year on he wrote fiction prolifically, becoming the South's one-man literary phenomenon. His first historical romance, *Guy Rivers* (1834), was followed by six more in the 1830s, nine in the 1840s, and eight in the 1850s, and finally one, the serialized *Joscelyn,* in 1867. Simms self-consciously organized his romances, he said, to develop a national literature based on American history. For the purposes of his fiction, he divided this history into four periods: explorations before the founding of Jamestown; the colonial period up to George III's reign; the colonies' drive for independence culminating in the Revolutionary War; and life on the frontier, the ever-shifting border lands of the South and Middle West. Most critics agree that his most important novels were his eight romances of Revolution: *The Partisan* (1835), *Mellichampe* (1836), *The Scout* (1841), *Katherine Walton* (1851), *Woodcraft* (1852), *The Forayers* (1855), *Eutaw* (1856), and *Joscelyn* (1867). Yet *The Yemassee* (1836), his first colonial romance, which chronicled a tragic Indian uprising, is also regarded as one of his best works.

Simms not only produced southern literature (in addition to the novels, he penned poetry, drama, biography, and history), but he produced the most important antebellum criticism of southern literature. He unabashedly associated himself with Scott's idea of what the novel should be—a romance, free to explore the unordinary, the unusual, in short, the romantic. Yet he was also concerned with what we today call "social realism," the careful depiction of the manners and customs of different classes, and he was guided always by his sense of history, the sweep of actual events that brought America, and more especially the South, into identity.

Simms could and did often satirize elements of southern life—particularly the pretensions of its upper-class Charlestonians, but he also evolved, by the 1850s, into an entrenched southern nationalist. His Revolutionary romance, *Woodcraft* (first titled *The Sword and the Distaff*, 1852), became, as he declared after the fact, his answer to Harriet Beecher Stowe, whose *Uncle Tom's Cabin* he scathingly attacked in an unsigned review. *Woodcraft* brings to the forefront one of Simms's most important characters, Captain Porgy, who had appeared in earlier work as a comic, Falstaffian man of arms. In *Woodcraft*, Porgy returns home to his own near-ruined plantation after the British occupation of the Carolinas. The scene is an eerie forewarning of what Simms would face himself when his own plantation was burned by Sherman's forces in 1865. In conversations between Porgy and his loyal "servant" Tom, Simms promotes his ideal of interdependent master-slave relations. It is important to note that Porgy, in *Woodcraft*, is unfit to be a true planter, but he is eventually educated, and saved from financial ruin, by his very astute neighbor, the widow Eveleigh. She handles her own and Porgy's affairs not with the domestic virtues of "true womanhood" but with a shrewd, practical eye for business.

If *Woodcraft* was at least in part designed as an answer to *Uncle Tom's Cabin* (and critics still disagree on this point), it is one of dozens that came to constitute a unique southern genre between 1851 and 1865, and even beyond. "Anti-Tom" novels have proved to be the most forgettable of antebellum fictional productions in terms of pure "literary" merit, but as social documents they provide essential keys to understanding how southerners understood their situation in the decade before the Civil War. Men as well as women wrote novels to counteract Stowe's tremendously influential portrait of "Life Among the Lowly," the slaves of the South. Thomas Bangs Thorpe, much better known today for his Southwest-humor story "The Big Bear of Arkansas" (1845), contributed *The Master's House* (1854) to the debate. Like many works of the genre, this novel depicts a young northern bride who arrives in the South completely unequipped to fulfill her function as homemaker. Her southern-born counterpart indicates how the plantation system provides the proper atmosphere for women. Another male contributor to the anti-Tom phenomenon in literature, John W. Page, wrote *Uncle Robin in His Cabin in Virginia and Tom Without One in Boston* (1853), a novel whose title indicates his argument.

Southern women were particularly drawn to the battle of words with Stowe, that "vile wretch in petticoats," as she was called. Stowe attacked specifically the slave system's right to consider itself "domestic," and in doing so, brought her argument into Dinah's kitchen, so to speak, where southern plantation women would feel most challenged. Many of the South's most successful women writers turned their attention to specific counterattacks. Mary Terhune, Caroline Hentz, Maria McIntosh, E. D. E. N. Southworth, and Augusta Jane Evans (Wilson), all of whom were popular writers with national reputations before 1860, wrote novels in the 1850s that were designed to refute *Uncle Tom's Cabin*. Maria McIntosh's *The Lofty and the Lowly* (1852) led the way by moving her young characters back and forth between southern and northern homes in order to show the superiority of the South. Mary Virginia Terhune, in *Moss-Side* (1857), attacked women's rights even more than abolition as being a threat to a preferred southern way of life that included slavery. E. D. E. N. Southworth, who was born in Virginia but also lived in the North, took up the proslavery cause most overtly in *Ishmael* (1859), in which she tried to make the case that southern society was actually more democratic, because less commercially inclined, than the North. Caroline Hentz wrote perhaps the most durable fictional reply to Stowe in *The Planter's Northern Bride* (1854). In her scheme, a noble planter, Richard Moreland, is more domestic than any of the women in the novel, so much so that he must divorce one woman of horrifyingly loose morals and then instruct his lovely but incompetent new northern bride in how to be a good homemaker. Augusta Jane Evans began her career with *Inez* in 1855 and followed it with *Beulah* (1859), a work that, after insisting on women's place in the home, argues that only the southern aristocracy provides the ideal version of what a home should be.

Lesser figures such as Mary Eastman (*Aunt Phillis's Cabin*, 1852), Mary Howard Schoolcraft (*The Black Gauntlet,* 1860), and Sue Petigru Bowen (*Lily,* 1855) joined the crowded field of southern women eager to lend their pens to the southern cause up until the firing of Fort Sumter. By the early twentieth century, the "Anti-Tom" novels were relegated, like *Uncle Tom's Cabin* itself, to the basement category of "propaganda" fiction. Whereas Stowe's work has been resurrected in recent times, largely through the work of feminist scholars, the novels by southerners written in response remain largely unstudied. None of them exhibit the skill in characterization or argument that Stowe brought to her task, yet they merit attention for what they reveal about how southerners tried to see themselves and how they tried to persuade others to view the way of life they wanted to protect.

A forerunner of the "Anti-Tom" novel was the plantation novel, which had its beginnings in John Pendleton Kennedy's *Swallow Barn* (1832). Kennedy revised and reprinted his novel in 1851, with changes that more stridently endorsed the slave system that supported the idyllic life on the James River plantation that is his setting. The 1832 version in some ways gently satirizes the planter's little fiefdom, but it does provide all the staple features of the plantation form: a kindly master, childlike "servants," a beautiful belle and her young suitor, and scenes of generous hospitality. Readers feel that nothing bad can or will happen to these carefree, nonmaterialistic, well-mannered country folk and their jovial workforce. What distinguishes novels of this genre, before Stowe, is the focus on plantation society as a story in and of itself: the characters, the setting, the drama all center on the life that only the plantation world made possible.

There were actually very few plantation novels written before the Civil War; they became a much more useful propaganda weapon after 1865, when northern readers were more willing to be charmed by a way of life dependent upon the institution of slavery that no longer existed. Kennedy's *Swallow Barn* can be counted one of the few "pure" examples of the antebellum plantation novel, especially among fiction written by men. Many of the Virginia romances contained extensive descriptions of plantation estates, but few made the plantation itself their primary focus.

Many southern women's novels, now almost always grouped under the heading of "domestic" or "sentimental" fiction, did make the plantation their scene, their subject, and the focal point of their ideological as well as artistic agenda. Along with *Swallow Barn,* Caroline Gilman's *Recollections of a Southern Matron* (1838) portrays life within the plantation world as a unique environment determining not only setting but also character and action. Gilman, a New Englander who had moved to the South, paired *Southern Matron* with an earlier novel, *Recollections of a New England Housekeeper* (1834). In this work, Clarissa Packard represents a typical middle-class northern matron who struggles without much success to provide a stable, well-kept home. Unruly lower classes in the large northern city challenge all of her strength. The social order of plantation society portrayed in *Southern Matron* is a marked contrast, for the later novel's heroine, Cornelia Wilton, is schooled from an early age to work with her dedicated black "servants" in providing for domestic tranquility. Not surprisingly, these two works of Gilman's were republished in the 1850s, so that they, too, could act as a response to Stowe's negative portrayals of the plantation domestic order.

Gilman's novels fit the definition of the domestic novel, once known by the more pejorative label of "sentimental" novel.

In truth, novels by both male and female writers of the antebellum period contain heavy doses of sentimentality. The maverick writer Joseph Holt Ingraham (1806–1860) penned gothic romances, such as *The Quadroone* (1841), that pulled out all the emotional stops. The women's novels of both the North and the South during this period used sentiment as one strategy in their exploration of the world of women, increasingly contained within "the private sphere." Feminist scholars now discern that the agenda of women's fiction of the nineteenth century was not to promote emotionalism, dependency, and acquiescence but in most cases to define and critique women's options in a society that relegated them to the home. Women's "proper place," the changing needs of the family unit during the nineteenth century, and the "feminization" of culture during this period were all social questions that Americans in general were having to confront. In the South, these questions had to be weighed with what became the overriding concern—how the "peculiar institution" on which southern society depended could be supported within the framework of the ideal of domesticity that developed in the antebellum period. Southern women writers were caught up in this concern, but their answers were by no means uniform.

E. D. E. N. Southworth (1819–1899), Caroline Hentz (1800–1856), and Augusta Jane Evans (1835–

1909) were the three southern antebellum women writers who gained the most significant attention nationally. All three concerned themselves with women's ambitions and desires, their duties to society, and the inevitable conflicts arising between these poles. Hentz and Southworth lived in both the North and the South, and in most of their fiction they promoted conciliatory assessments of both regions. Still, the upper-class South was their preferred fictional territory. In *Lovell's Folly* (1833), Hentz marries an exemplary northern man to an equally perfect southern woman; in *The Planter's Northern Bride,* she switches the gender/region pairing. In both novels, the important point is to bring people of the different, increasingly hostile sections together, but we note that in both the northerner must move to the South in order to reap the benefits of a well-ordered, moral community.

E. D. E. N. Southworth's novels are much more unpredictable than Hentz's. Most of her work appeared serially in the South-friendly *New York Ledger,* where she gained a wide audience undaunted by her southern loyalties. One of these serialized works, entitled variously *Capitola* or *The Hidden Hand* (1859), followed probably the most popular plotline for fiction in the antebellum period. A young girl, without the proper supports of family and community, must struggle to maintain her virtue, to educate herself, to become morally superior to all around her—particularly her eligible suitors—and finally to triumph by being placed at the head of a secure home. Capitola upsets many applecarts. She cross-dresses more than once, defies propriety, and outwits not one but four tyrannical male villains. What is most remarkable about *The Hidden Hand* is that it is funny. It parodies the gothic, the sentimental, and domestic literary conventions. Its heroine is a picaresque figure who is a precursor to Huck Finn in more ways than one. Southworth herself, as narrator, is irreverent and subversive, sometimes romantic, sometimes realistic, and sometimes satirical. Capitola even has a birthmark shaped like a little crimson hand, but her independence makes her a very different sort of character from the self-sacrificial heroine of Hawthorne's earlier tale, "The Birthmark."

Augusta Jane Evans (Wilson) had barely started her remarkable career when the Civil War began, so her greatest fame occurred in the Reconstruction period. Her most popular novel, *St. Elmo* (1866), was the South's best-selling novel of the century. Published after the war's end, it was set in pre–Civil War times but did not push sectional themes. Instead, with the heroine Edna Earl, Wilson created, as she had with *Beulah* (1859), a young woman of remarkable talent and intelligence. Edna Earl is more saintly than Beulah, who must be converted to self-sacrifice, yet Edna Earl too, after striking out independently in order to keep her self-respect, must learn to channel her prodigious spiritual and intellectual strengths into love for a worthy man, who alone can fulfill her destiny.

The Civil War would change the political dynamics of the southern novel for all white writers, as it did for Wilson, but it would also create new challenges for southern black men and women. Before the Civil War, freed and escaped slaves alone could take up their pens in order to pursue writing careers. Laws in every state prohibited the teaching of writing to slaves. The fugitive-slave narrative became a genre of great importance in the fight against slavery, and it could also provide black writers with a means of self-expression. Few African Americans in the antebellum period chose to write fiction. Their enlistment in the abolitionist cause dictated that they would present true accounts that could be documented in the abolitionists' propaganda war.

William Wells Brown, who escaped from Missouri in the 1840s, wrote not only slave narratives and history but also the antebellum period's most important African American novel, *Clotel, or the President's Daughter* (1853), originally published in London. It first appeared in serial form in America and was published as a book, substantially revised, as *Clotelle: A Tale of the Southern States,* in 1864 and again in 1867. Like Brown's slave narrative, published in 1849, *Clotel* reflected incidents that he himself encountered as a slave. The widely believed rumor that Thomas Jefferson had fathered children by a slave mistress provided the novel's opening action. The president's abandoned lover and her two daughters are sold at a slave auction. The lovely Clotel, one of these daughters, ends her life by suicide, while her daughter escapes to England. *Clotel* is interesting not only for its use of the Jefferson rumor but for references to Nat Turner's rebellion that the novel includes.

Another important novel by an African American born in the South, Martin Delaney's *Blake* (1859), also invokes the specter of slave rebellion. Delaney was born a free black in Charles Town, western (later West) Virginia, but moved north with his mother as a child. He drew upon black uprisings in Cuba and Haiti in designing epic adventures for his slave hero. The epic character Blake organizes antiwhite rebellions in the

South as well as the islands, and travels to Canada and to Africa in his quest to end African bondage. Both Brown's and Delaney's novels sought to reframe the discourse on slavery in ways that showed the slave as determined master of his or her own fate, not merely a fugitive but an active resister of a national evil. Frederick Douglass participated in this goal through *The Heroic Slave* (1853), a novella that tells the story of the successful slave-ship uprising of Madison Washington aboard the *Creole* in 1841.

In American literary history, the period 1820 to 1865 is known as "the American Renaissance"—an ironic name, given that the writers included under this heading, except for Edgar Allan Poe, were all northerners. Poe's literary use of the South as setting is either minimal or disguised, and he made his name not in the novel but as America's most important designer of the short-story form. Poe did review the novels of many southerners, including Kennedy and Simms, and his one venture into longer prose fiction, *The Narrative of Arthur Gordon Pym* (1838), contains the interesting, but entirely stereotypical, figure of a slave. The lack of national critical attention that the southern antebellum novel received has been due, primarily, to the fact that, unlike Hawthorne and Melville, southern novelists wrote in genres—the historical romance, the domestic novel—that have been marginalized, especially with the rise of New Criticism in the 1940s. Like the novel that so many southerners wrote to discredit, *Uncle Tom's Cabin,* the southern novel closely mirrored the social fabric of the times in which it was written and was designed to be understood within its social contexts. Today, readers turn to these works with renewed interest as a way to learn the mind of South, and to discover rich, as well as troubling, literary legacies. The antebellum southern novel allows readers access to a complex time, place, history, and people. Through the voices recovered in these texts, readers become witnesses to the period that embodied the South's greatest shame and ended with the nation's bloodiest struggle.

Lucinda H. MacKethan

See also Abolition; African American Literature, Beginnings to 1919; Domestic Novel; Historical Romance; Old Dominion; Plantation Fiction; Stowe, Harriet Beecher; Virginia, Literature of.

Thomas Gossett, *"Uncle Tom's Cabin" and American Culture* (1985); Anne Goodwyn Jones and Susan Donaldson, *Gender and Southern Texts* (1998); Lucinda H. MacKethan, intro.,

Swallow Barn, by John Pendleton Kennedy (1985); Elizabeth Moss, *Domestic Novelists of the Old South* (1992); William Taylor, *Cavalier and Yankee: The Old South and American National Character* (1961).

NOVEL, 1865 TO 1900

The novel in the South after the Civil War, like the region itself, had to struggle back to strength after near collapse during the war years. The novel owed much of its survival and later power to the development of general family magazines in the nation. Within the pages of those magazines, southern novelists first published their short stories and later serializations of their novels before they were published as independent hardbacks. Although the novels presented generally a sympathetic and uncritical view of southern life, a minority began a critical examination of southern institutions that would mature in the twentieth century.

Southern novelists, like southern writers more widely, found many publishers' doors closed to them in the immediate aftermath of the war and during Reconstruction, especially in Boston. Opportunities with New York and Philadelphia publishers were slightly more open. Southern novelists were in many ways a lost generation whose time of learning and apprenticeship had been spent on the battlefields or struggling to survive in a devastated homeland. When they finally found willing publishers, they often owed much of their literary training to sympathetic editors of magazines, who taught them to overcome habits of southern rhetoric and introduced them to new literary practices. In return for that tutelage, they learned to subscribe to a tacit code of not defending slavery or secession but could, and did, depict freedmen as contented inferiors.

A few southern novelists who had published popularly before the Civil War were able to publish soon after the war if they observed the code. John Esten Cooke, whose historical romances had sold well in the 1850s, published *Surry of Eagle's Nest* in 1866 and *Mohun* in 1869. The first was the war story of a Confederate staff officer, much like Cooke himself, who chronicled the exploits of Stonewall Jackson with gothic undertones of doomed heroes. The second concerned doomed J. E. B. Stuart, flamboyant cavalry general. Cooke's novels joined the flood of supposedly factual memoirs of war generals, north and south, and presented his heroes as great warriors, not apologists for southern policy. In 1870 Cooke told in *The Heir of*

Gaymount of his struggle to revive his plantation with new agricultural practices. William Gilmore Simms, ardent apologist for the South before the war, shifted his focus to less controversial mountain life in *Voltmeir* (1869), serialized but not published independently until years later. Augusta Jane Evans (later Wilson) continued to present her suffering heroines in sentimental novels such as *St. Elmo* (1866) and *Vashti* (1869).

During the 1870s and early 1880s, three dissenting southerners or adoptive southerners began their critical examination of southern institutions that were resisting reform during Reconstruction. Usually scorned in the South as southern Yankees, they eventually removed to the North. Mark Twain (Samuel L. Clemens) had grown up in Missouri and had worked as a cub pilot on the Mississippi River before he moved west and later north, but after writing early travel books on the West, the Sandwich Islands (Hawaii), and the Holy Land, he found his true subject in the southern life of his youth. In *The Gilded Age: A Tale of To-Day* (1873–1874), written with Charles Dudley Warner, Twain described the attempt to exploit a southern coal mine, with much attention to political corruption in Congress. The lasting creation to emerge from the unwieldy story was Colonel Beriah Sellers, a bombastic speculator and con man. Twain found Sellers to be such an embodiment of the rampant greed of the times that he later reused him in the play *Colonel Sellers* (1883) and in *The American Claimant* (1892). In *The Adventures of Tom Sawyer* (1876), Twain made his hero the center of an idyll of small-town Missouri before the war. Mischievous and resourceful, Tom embodies a fascination with Romance. Although Tom's romanticism is basically harmless in this novel, Twain would later emphasize the tendency as a great southern weakness. *Tom Sawyer* also introduced Huckleberry Finn, who would become the naïve hero of Twain's best-known novel and whose common sense would be played against Tom's romanticism even more forcefully. In *Adventures of Huckleberry Finn* (1885), Twain's picaresque protagonist takes a journey down the Mississippi with escaped slave Jim and passes through scenes of southern life showing regional delusions in family feuds, revival meetings, theatricals, duels, sentimental poetry, and funerals. Behind such episodes Twain saw the southern love for defunct medieval chivalry learned from the romances of Sir Walter Scott. But his most important achievement in *Huckleberry Finn* was showing how Huck's vernacular narration was a vibrant literary medium, that literary language did not have to be book language. That novel, Ernest Hemingway wrote later, was the beginning of modern American literature. Twain continued his critiques of the South in increasingly pessimistic novels, *Pudd'nhead Wilson* (1894) and *A Connecticut Yankee in King Arthur's Court* (1889).

The second dissenter, Albion W. Tourgée, was an adoptive southerner who came south to North Carolina from Ohio and New York after the war, first to run a plant nursery, then to serve as circuit-court judge during Reconstruction. During his travels on the court circuit and in his political work with the state Republican Party, he observed the growing resistance to Reconstruction policies and chronicled it in his two most popular novels, *A Fool's Errand* (1879) and *Bricks Without Straw* (1880). Valued more for their social criticism than for their literary skill, these novels used hackneyed and sentimental literary conventions to present their challenges. In the first, which is heavily autobiographical, a former Union colonel encounters resistance to reforms by southern mobs and by the rising Ku Klux Klan. In the second, he ponders the plight of freedmen who have no recognized status in the postwar South. No longer slaves, they are not yet citizens with full legal and social rights. Tourgée depicts the vilification of the Freedmen's Bureau, sent by the federal government to help freedmen claim their rights, and faults both the unreconstructed Redemptionists of the South and the vacillating federal government for failing to carry through on Reconstruction. "The North," he said, "did not comprehend its work; the South could not comprehend its fate." With the end of Reconstruction, Tourgée went back north to work for James A. Garfield's presidential campaign and to advocate a program of federally supported education.

The third dissenter, George Washington Cable of New Orleans, began making his contributions to the southern novel after learning to write local-color short stories about his exotic city. His first novel, *The Grandissimes* (1880), also about New Orleans, in the long view was his best. A man of puritanic conscience, Cable was outraged by the predicament of free persons of color—mulattos, quadroons, and octoroons—and of freed blacks in postwar Louisiana. Using his deft skill for local color, he told the saga of feuding Creole families at the time of France's cession of Louisiana to the United States. His sympathies, however, were for the unacknowledged part-black kin of the aristocratic Creoles, with their situation in 1803–1804 analogous

580 / Novel, 1865 to 1900

to that of freedmen during the 1870s. Although first readers of the novel focused on the exotic Creoles, their patois and their prejudices, the political implications became clearer as Cable championed the freedman's cause in the middle part of his career. At the same time, he advocated reform of prisons, asylums, and sanitation practices to prevent yellow fever in *Dr. Sevier* (1884). By the mid-1880s, he was so clearly persona non grata in New Orleans and in the wider South that he moved his family to the North. He continued his critique of the Reconstruction South in his late novel, *John March, Southerner* (1894), while depicting the Cajun life of the bayous in *Bonaventure* (1888). After realizing that the cause of the freedman was lost, Cable turned in his later career to writing Civil War romances, popular in their day but of minimal interest to later readers: *The Cavalier* (1901), about Confederate women spies and gallant cavalrymen, and *Kincaid's Battery* (1908), about Confederate artillerymen and their struggles over points of personal honor. Although he returned in peace to his native city at last, Cable continued to write forgettable romances until well into the twentieth century.

While Twain, Tourgée, and Cable were carrying out their critiques of southern life and manners, a number of other southern novelists took a stance to celebrate southern life, especially that of the Old South. Thomas Nelson Page said what was already in several writers' minds when in 1892 he told the young gentlemen at his alma mater, Washington and Lee College, to defend the South with their pens as their fathers had defended it with their swords. That they and their fellow writers had been successful could be seen in Tourgée's lament in "The South as Field for Fiction" (1888) that "our literature has become not only Southern in type, but distinctly Confederate in sympathy," and that a stranger to the country might think "the South was the seat of intellectual empire in America." Tourgée overstated the case but saw correctly that southern-written popular romances had found a hearing on the national scene. Publishers' doors were fully open to their version of the South.

Page had put his vision of the Old South in his celebrated short fiction, particularly "Marse Chan" (1884) in the collection *In Ole Virginia* (1887). Marse Chan embodied all the legendary virtues of the chivalric Old South and died leading a heroic charge during the war. Page sounded the Lost Cause theme with all its romantic melancholy when he had Sam, Chan's former body servant and virtual double, lament at last, "How come

Providence nuver saved Marse Chan?" He carried forward that theme of the golden age of the South in *The Old Gentleman of the Black Stock* (1897) and *Red Rock* (1898), the latter a popular novel that firmly fixed the legend of the chivalric South in the public mind.

Mary Noailles Murfree of Murfreesboro, Tennessee, though a lowlander of better-than-average education and from a family of established social rank, made legendary the mountain folk of eastern Tennessee. Writing short fiction first under the pen name of Charles Egbert Craddock, she exploited the market for local color in stories collected in *In the Tennessee Mountains* (1884). Turning to the novel in *The Prophet of the Great Smoky Mountains* (1885) and *In the "Stranger People's" Country* (1891), she depicted mountaineers in conflict with lowland law and upland superstitions. Although she was careful to render mountain dialect and exotic characters, her viewpoint was still that of the superior outsider who depended on character types, however exotic, and she could envelop the narrative in highly bookish poetic language. In *The Story of Old Fort Loudon* (1899), she turned to history to tell about relations between whites and Cherokees in the story of a colonial settlement abandoned by the settlers. Her novels showed both the appeal and the limitations of local color.

John Fox Jr. of Kentucky also found the local color of mountain life a usable subject, first in short fiction and later in the popular novels *The Little Shepherd of Kingdom Come* (1903) and *The Trail of the Lonesome Pine* (1908), both of which show how local color lasted well past the turn of the century. Set in time just before and during the Civil War, *The Little Shepherd* showed the divided loyalties of Cumberland Mountain folk and later their reconciliation with each other and with the nation. *The Trail* dramatized the conflict of values between outsiders come to the mountains to develop coal mines and mountaineers living by their own code. Like Murfree, Fox looked further back in history for his later works as he wrote into the present century.

After first writing travel books about Europe and Mexico, Francis Hopkinson Smith exploited local color with his whimsical short novel *Colonel Carter of Cartersville* (1891), the portrait of an unreconstructed Virginia gentleman at large in New York trying to promote a railroad for his county back in Virginia. The comic possibilities of the plot were great enough to prompt a stage play of the story (1892) and a sequel, *Colonel Carter's Christmas* (1903). James Lane Allen of Kentucky used local-color conventions to write his best-known work, *The Kentucky Cardinal* (1894). A southern pastoral whose hero Adam re-enacts a version of the Garden of Eden story, *The Kentucky Cardinal* shows Adam caught between his love for nature embodied in the bird and his love for Georgianna and human warmth. By popular demand, he continued the story in *Aftermath* (1896) to its poignant conclusion. The next year in *The Choir Invisible* (1897), he explored further the romance of conflicted love in early Kentucky with schoolmaster John Gray's quest for his ideal woman and his realization too late that he had not recognized her.

Through historical romances and local-color portrayals, the genteel tradition prospered in southern novels during the latter decades of the nineteenth century. Novelists' emphasis on delicacy of feeling and correct sentiment marked not only stories of plantation lovers but of mountain folk as well. While they presented scenes of an amiable and well-mannered society, these writers projected visions of sectional reconciliation by marriages of northern and southern lovers, most frequently of Union officers and southern belles but often of divided families reunited by lovers. Such comedic endings played well with readers both north and south, as publishers well knew. Villains were typically outsiders, often rapacious capitalists who sought to disrupt the established order with schemes for spoiling nature with their coal mines or breaking up the plantation with railroad lines. Characters in the novels, like their readers, shared the conviction that, at their advanced stage of western civilization, they were capable of the highest reaches of spiritual intuition and owed to the less-blessed parts of the world, Africa and Asia, models of superior culture. What they did not show was the strain of a changing, urbanized, industrialized society bulging with new immigrants from southern and eastern Europe. Battles between unions and mining syndicates, between farmers and railroads, between ghettos and sweat-shop operators they left to the realists and naturalists of the North and West.

Toward the end of the century, however, a few southern novelists challenged the genteel tradition with discordant views on the status of women and the relations between races. Typically they began with local-color stories, admired for their depictions of exotic scenes and characters, then went beyond local color to show the strains hidden within their local scenes. Kate Chopin of Louisiana explored the moral and emotional issues of divorce in her first novel, *At Fault* (1890).

Praised at first for its accurate settings and clear writing, the novel caused second thoughts among critics and readers about its moral proprieties. When she wrote *The Awakening* (1899) to explore Edna Pontellier's sexual feelings as the New Orleans wife and mother who rebelled against the restricting rules governing women, Chopin found how restrictive were the rules governing novels in her time. Genteel critics were outraged and cast the novel and its author into limbo and effectively ended Chopin's developing career. Another half-century would pass before her work was rediscovered. If the author and her novels were products of the late nineteenth century, their audience was that of mid- and late twentieth century.

Although Ohioan by birth and adult residence, Charles Waddell Chesnutt was southern in background and sympathy. His mixed-blood parents had moved to Ohio from North Carolina, and he had taught school briefly in Fayetteville and Charlotte, North Carolina. He hoped through his writing to gain recognition and acceptance for both mixed-blood and full blacks in the South, even though the late nineteenth century was one of the least hopeful times for such an acceptance. Quite probably his friendship with George Washington Cable encouraged his hope. Like Cable and many other southern writers, he began his work writing short pieces for magazines before writing his novels. *The Conjure Woman* (1899) and *The Wife of His Youth and Other Stories of the Color Line* (1899) preceded his first novel. *The House Behind the Cedars* (1900), like several of his stories, dealt with the moral and emotional problems of "passing," where mixed-blood Rena Walden attempts to pass by marriage into white South Carolina society. In Chesnutt's presentation, it was not the "taint" of black blood that brought Rena to her tragic end but the false position into which her mixed blood forced her, the refusal by society to accept her into its classes and categories. And in Chesnutt's story, the full blacks as well as the all-whites were guilty of denying her a place in their orders.

His next, and most complex, novel, *The Marrow of Tradition* (1901), was prompted by the race riots of 1898 in Wilmington, North Carolina. Like his beaten hero, Chesnutt refused to accept defeat and continued to press for abolition of the color line in his third novel, *The Colonel's Dream* (1905). He came to see that racial justice called for a new way of thinking beyond modest incremental reforms. But the times and lack of tolerance for new ideas were against him, and his novels had to wait another half-century to find their wider audience.

The paradox of the southern novel from the Civil War to the beginning of the next century has been that the minority voice of dissenters gained ascendancy in the long view and the dominant voice of local color and genteel historical romance receded into half-forgotten nostalgia, into a time that has seemed less and less real to later readers.

Robert O. Stephens

See also Feminism; Gilded Age; Historical Romance; Local Color; Mulatto; Plantation Fiction; Protest, Novel of; Race Relations; Reconstruction; Sentimental Novel.

NOVEL, 1900 TO WORLD WAR II

Noting the caravan of southerners who had been awarded the Pulitzer Prize, the novelist T. S. Stribling, who won in 1933, posited several reasons for their success. First, generations of southerners had learned, through their defense of slavery, to express themselves passionately and precisely. Second, storytelling was the most elemental and economical of the arts, and thus suited to a region without avenues for more elaborate cultural productions. And third, subject matter abounded for the writer in the South, because it was on "the losing side, that's the dramatic side." Thus Stribling touched on the three interconnected themes of the southern novel in this period, which may be summed up bluntly as color, cash, and conversation.

Beholden as always to the past, the southern novelist in these decades drew—even when resisting it—from the eighteenth-century model of fiction, in which economic valuations of personal and social relationships are paramount, gender is a defining boundary, class is a similarly immutable personal characteristic, and family history is likely to include some unnatural gothic blot. As the twentieth century moved toward its center, the grotesque humor of a Fielding, the moral horror of a Richardson, and the fiscal savvy of an Austen were met in southern fiction with modern angst, indeterminacy, and alienation. The Agrarian novelist Stark Young offered that the widespread interest in the South during this period, including in its fiction, sprang from the country's boredom with the sterility of the flat, charmless talk elsewhere, with impolite northern silences broken only by advertisements and brusque re-

marks. Southerners, on the other hand, prided themselves on their storytelling, and the southern novel of the first half of the century is infused with the South's centuries-old stock of folklore, tall tales, and romantic tropes. To all these were applied the ethnographic and psychoanalytical gadgets of the modern writer, and thus, in these decades, the novel became a distinctive and flexible frame for southern narratives.

If conversation defined, as Young suggested, a peculiarly southern talent, well then, southerners had something to talk about. For decades beyond slavery, its mark—evident in the variants of shame attaching to the practice—seemed to be on both black and white southerners. After the devastation of the Civil War, southerners were forced to come to terms with, or recover from, or actively deny the ugly custom upon which the prosperity and propriety, the vaunted dash and courtesy, of the Old South had depended. With the necessary dissolution of its slave economy, its accustomed social system, and many of its folkways, there was a need to reestablish the region's economic and psychological equilibrium on a different balance. So the struggle to acquire or restore wealth and social position is thematic in novels of this period, during which the Great Depression revived fears of deprivation and schemes against it. Even Scarlett O'Hara, the quintessential southern belle, is pressed into this hard, unglamorous drive for economic self-sufficiency. Indeed, the effects of change fell particularly along gender as well as racial lines. But the changes—in the South as well as in the wider world—that allowed southern women and blacks to escape the strictures, or at least to expand the expectations, of their places in the social and economic order, were necessarily accompanied by stresses, as changes typically are. The effects of the migration of blacks away from economic depression and social oppression in the South, toward hoped-for opportunities in the North, were also recorded in novels throughout this period. Deliberately or subconsciously, blacks and whites registered the resultant unbidden sense of exile or abandonment, of nostalgia or loss. Variations of these would be rehearsed when whites, too, made the same irremediable journey out, to the North, to Europe, away.

In *Absalom, Absalom!*, a Canadian marvels at the South: "It's better than the theatre, isn't it. It's better than Ben Hur." It would be fair to say that in these decades the South *was* Ben Hur—that is, it was quite often some celluloid or footlighted version of itself transmitted through a screenwriter's or playwright's variation on a successful novel. The southern possibilities for drama were not lost on arbiters of American culture other than the prize committees, and a large number of the novels mentioned below were also made into motion pictures or Broadway plays. Quite a few of the novelists listed here—including William Faulkner, the writer who seems most tightly bound to the South—spent time in Hollywood in return for the cash that funded their art. The interplay between these arts is of some importance. The following survey, by no means comprehensive, attempts to give a representation of the foremost examples of the southern novel of this period. Many of these are grouped with lesser-known novels on the same theme or in the same style. An effort has been made throughout to suggest the thread of connection, through philosophical or personal relationship, or through rhetorical tactic, that exists between these novels, however divergent their authors' literary programs may first appear.

The line between black and white in the South did not wholly prevent the sympathetic reach across it, the honest attempt to understand what was on the other side. So, too, could economic and linguistic castes be breached. But the presence of these divisions added a tension—some may say it was a creative tension—that any consideration of the southern novel in the first half of the twentieth century has to take into account. The work of two novelists of North Carolina, contemporaries on different sides of the color line, suggests some of the impediments to be overcome or exploited. In what has been called his trilogy of the New South, Charles W. Chesnutt (1858–1932) explored the social, political, and economic problems of race in the region. That he was himself a light-skinned black is an important item in Chesnutt's biography, particularly given his stated attention to the problems of mixed blood. His first novel, *The House Behind the Cedars* (1900), set in the Carolinas, concerns Rena Walden, a woman who has decided to pass for white, as has her brother. When her true identity is discovered, the white man whom she loves will not marry her, and—following the pattern of her fictional type, that of the "tragic mulatta"—she eventually falls ill and dies. The psychological and social turmoil deriving from passing—the rejection of self and the deception of others—is a focus of a myriad succeeding southern novels, perhaps because the practice succinctly illustrated the false positions in which systemic prejudice placed everyone, whether black or white. Chesnutt's career as a novelist met with so little financial reward that he abandoned it

after his third novel. However, as a black author whose work had not only treated racial themes with gravity but secured a mainstream publisher, he represented an invaluable model for writers who followed.

Thomas Dixon (1864–1946), a white man, was a far more popular and financially successful novelist, and the creator of a far more indelible rendering of the color line. Among his twenty-two novels were a Reconstruction, or Klan, trilogy intended to address the race conflict. The second of these, *The Clansman* (1905), principally set in South Carolina, follows the relationship of two families, the Stonemans and Camerons. Austin Stoneman, a character based on the politician Thaddeus Stevens, plans to transfer white-owned land to the newly freed blacks. His affair with the mulatta Lydia Brown suggests not only the depths of his villainy, but hers also, for she has enslaved him with her animal wiles. Stoneman's daughter loves Ben Cameron, a Confederate colonel in the recent war. And when Cameron and "the young dare-devil Knights of the South" come to the rescue of Stoneman's son (who has killed a black man, a rapist), it is clear who the hero is. The subtitle, *A Historical Romance of the Ku Klux Klan*, suggests both the tenor and the strategy of the piece. Along with his friend Woodrow Wilson, Dixon did graduate work in history at Johns Hopkins, and he continued to have the historian's bent. So, at its most elemental level, even in its focus on miscegenation and the rape of white by black, *The Clansman* reflects the grim competition for scarce resources during Reconstruction. Though he has warped them, the historical realities buttressing Dixon's fiction, as well as his methods of dealing with them, set him in the mainstream of southern novelists of this period. Many of his themes and plots will be found again in later, *respectable* novels.

Another novel by Dixon, *The Sins of the Father* (1912), also describes a white man who becomes, like Stoneman, disastrously involved with his mulatta housekeeper. The same year marked the first publication of *The Autobiography of an Ex-Coloured Man* (1912), which deals with miscegenation and related issues from another racial viewpoint. This, the only novel by James Weldon Johnson (1871–1938), was first published anonymously. Fifteen years later, at the height of the Harlem Renaissance, it was republished to wider notice. Johnson follows his hero, a man of mixed blood, on an erratic journey that sometimes leads him into the Deep South, to Georgia, where he was born—first to attend Atlanta University (Johnson's alma mater) and then to study folk music. After witnessing a lynching, he hurries back to New York and decides henceforth to pass as white. The novel's last pages describe his uneasy accommodation to that choice. In his essay "Color Lines" (*Survey Graphic*, 1925), the novelist Walter White—who took Johnson's place as executive secretary of the NAACP in 1931—spoke of the relative convenience of passing. It was rather easy to do, he pointed out, in New York where people of many ethnicities were no lighter than light-skinned "coloreds." White spoke, too, against the false and persistent negative view of blacks promoted by Thomas Dixon. It is unclear that such impressions, once made, can ever be erased from a culture, but it was particularly difficult to do so in an age of the motion picture, which manipulated literary image, sensationalized metaphor and conceit, and caused these things to move, again and again. *The Clansman* served as the basis for one of the first significant productions of the new medium: D. W. Griffith's silent film *Birth of a Nation* (1915). Dixon's collaboration with Griffith, a southerner also, was a powerful and perpetual advertisement for a portrayal of African Americans—as bestial, as a sexual threat—that was hard for anyone to revise.

The novels of James Branch Cabell (1879–1958) obliquely undercut allegiances to the outmoded codes extolled in Dixon's novels, the "notions of chivalry and bravery and justice" that the ex-colored man ponders in southerners. Cabell came from a good, old family of Richmond, Virginia, whose genealogy was one of his passions. He gave obsessive historicism a satiric twist when he described, through the course of many novels, the inadequacy of the chivalric code and *amour propre* to meet the challenges of modern life and human behavior. In *The Cream of the Jest* (1917), Felix Kennaston, a Virginia manufacturer, imagines himself living out romantic scenarios from the historic past. Kennaston's fixation on the "sigil of Scoteia," which turns out to be the broken lid from his wife's cold-cream jar, recalls the Old South's misguided obeisance to the chivalric ideals on display in Walter Scott's historical novels, ideals that drove the South into Civil War and hobbled it afterward. Cabell's theme is most elaborately played out in an eighteen-volume romance cycle set in a medieval kingdom called Poictesme. The most controversial of these was *Jurgen: A Comedy of Justice* (1919), which dispatches its hero, a pawnbroker, on a year-long, *Faerie Queene*-like quest for his unpleasant wife. The New York Society for the Suppression of

Vice brought charges of obscenity against *Jurgen*, an episode that described a pattern for many southern novels in the first half of the century. Southern writers regularly managed to insult the home folk by telling, or seeming to tell, local secrets—and to scandalize everyone else with their profanity and their politics.

Cabell's somewhat more conventional literary neighbor in Richmond was Ellen Glasgow (1873–1945), whose work appeared throughout almost the entire period covered here. Her first novel, *The Descendent* (1897), was published at the end of the nineteenth century; her last, *In This Our Life* (1941), was awarded the Pulitzer Prize in 1942. Glasgow's many novels offer a social history of Virginia, with a particular focus on the woman's role in it. The third novel in her women's trilogy, *Barren Ground* (1925), tells of Dorinda Oakley's struggle, beyond the limitations placed on her by class and by gender, to become a farmer and an independent woman. *The Sheltered Life* (1932), the last in a trio of novels exploring the manners of the upper class, presents a closed society that vaguely and charmingly enfolds its failings and tragedies without fully remedying or acknowledging them. After some years, the central character, Jenny Archbald, following the pattern set by the adults in her community, carelessly betrays a woman she has been taught to idealize and precipitates a murder. Any social history of Virginia must include a focus on the Civil War and its aftermath, which Glasgow's has—in *The Battle-Ground* (1902) and *The Deliverance* (1904).

In "A Mirror for Artists" (1930), his contribution to the Agrarians' manifesto, Donald Davidson remarked that the novels of Cabell and Glasgow were tainted by the flux of modernity and by capitulation to northern opinion and European style, and would have been even more so had their authors lived "in some less quiet region than Virginia." However, it is clear that both Cabell and Glasgow dealt with the history of the South's unsettled present, as it was exemplified in their own state, in ways and for reasons that surely would never have occurred to any northerner or European. From among a number of possible approaches to Virginia's history, Cabell and Glasgow chose to be oblique and ironic. They did not choose to ignore it, as any novelist had the option to do.

Another resident of Richmond, Glasgow's friend Mary Johnston (1870–1936), specialized in historical romance. Johnston's father had been a major in the Confederate army and another relative had been a general, so she wrote of the war from personal interest and with inside information. *The Long Roll* (1911) treats the war's beginnings, the Shenandoah Valley campaign, and Stonewall Jackson's death. General Joseph E. Johnston makes an appearance. *Cease Firing* (1912), wider in scope, treats the war's last battles leading to the dénouement at Appomattox. Johnston, who drew heavily on primary sources, offers an unglamorous version of events, "a side of war which Walter Scott had never painted." Also among Johnston's large number of novels are those covering Virginia's history before the Civil War. *The Great Valley* (1926) follows the Selkirks, a family of Scottish immigrants who join the settlers of the Shenandoah Valley at the time of the French and Indian War. When family members and servants are taken by Indians to Ohio, Johnston draws on the tradition of the captive narrative—and on an episode in her own family's distant history. *The Slave Ship* (1924), laid in Africa as well as Virginia, treats bond slavery and the Middle Passage.

Later, the novelist Arna Bontemps (1902–1973), another careful researcher in the historical record, also reached into Virginia's unquiet past. *Black Thunder* (1936) tells of Gabriel's Insurrection, or the Prosser Uprising, in 1800. The hero, a slave named Gabriel Prosser, raises a rebellion among eleven thousand slaves. When their plan to seize Richmond fails, Gabriel is tried and hanged. At the time of the Scottsboro Case and other incidents, this rebellion seemed to Bontemps "a possible metaphor of turbulence to come." A related novel is Bontemps's *Drums at Dusk* (1939), about a slave rebellion on a Caribbean island at the time of the French Revolution. Bontemps, who was born in Louisiana, became an important figure in the Harlem Renaissance and, as head librarian at Fisk University, built a significant collection of materials related to that movement. He is a particularly fine writer whose work, notable both for its graceful technique and for its psychological and political insight, now seems undeservedly neglected.

The interest in southern history found its popular focus and, in some ways, its most complicated expression in a welter of Civil War novels. Like Johnston, James Boyd (1888–1944) drew upon historical documents and, treating some of the same scenes, produced a version of the war that was without glamour. His best-selling *Marching On* (1927) is considered by some to be among the best of its type. The central character, James Fraser, is a poor farmer's son who becomes a foot soldier on the side of the Confederacy. After two years in a Federal prison camp, he returns to North Carolina to marry a planter's daughter, a match that denotes the war's leveling effect on the South. An ancestor of James Fraser is the hero of Boyd's earlier novel, *Drums* (1925), which follows the adventures of a planter's son from North Carolina at the time of the American Revolution.

Evelyn Scott (1893–1963)—from Clarksville, Tennessee, as was the novelist Caroline Gordon—has also been credited with encouraging the trend in Civil War novels. *The Wave* (1929), the middle of a trio of novels dealing with America's history in the nineteenth century, attempts in 625 pages to tell the complete story of the Civil War. It takes no side and no central character's point of view, but touches instead on the wide range of people caught in the rush of the event. *The Wave*'s success encouraged Scott's and William Faulkner's mutual publisher, Harrison Smith, to issue a pamphlet containing Scott's praise for *The Sound and the Fury*, published the same year. This was intended to drum up sales for that odd book by the little-known Faulkner, who also told his story from no single point of view.

Seven years later, the most famous example of the Civil War genre topped *The Wave* in sales and sheer size. *Gone With the Wind* (1936) was, according to the *New York Times*, "the biggest book of the year: 1,037 pages." Margaret Mitchell (1900–1949) set this historical romance in her native Georgia, where the heroine not only endures the Civil War's ravages and Reconstruction's privations but gains strength and a sort of freedom in her struggle against them. Scarlett O'Hara's rise out of economic ashes was a fitting parable at the end of the Depression. Though it won the Pulitzer Prize and continued to be read widely, scholars for some time placed Mitchell's novel in a category of women's romance that was not to be taken seriously. This prejudice was probably compounded by Mitchell's amateurish prose. In addition, there was a view, even early on, that *Gone With the Wind*—now most familiar through David O. Selznick's extravagant screen adaptation, which premiered in Atlanta in 1939—had much in common with an earlier, discredited movie. The *Times* reviewer compared the novel to *The Birth of a Nation*, and the editors of *The Negro Caravan* labeled Mitchell the "latest disciple" of Dixon and Griffith. Increasingly, however, along with a large number of other noncanonical texts, *Gone With the Wind* is receiving more consideration, particularly in relation to its treatment of issues of race and gender. The sixtieth anniversary of *Gone With the Wind*'s publication was marked

586 / Novel, 1900 to World War II

by the appearance of a second Mitchell novel, *Lost Laysen* (1996), the manuscript of which had been discovered the year before. This short juvenile work written in 1916 tells of a sailor's unrequited love for a missionary on a South Sea island.

James Boyd's *Drums* was an early success for Maxwell Perkins (1884–1946), the renowned editor at Scribner, without whom the history of the southern novel would be radically altered. His authors included F. Scott Fitzgerald, Ernest Hemingway, Thomas Wolfe, and Erskine Caldwell, to name just a few, and he lent the luster of such associations to all the writers with whom he worked. Perkins had a particular affinity for southerners, which was somewhat surprising, as he was a confirmed Yankee. And his taste was catholic, ranging from the scholarly proponents of Agrarianism to the high-livers of the Jazz Age. Perkins would have tempted William Faulkner to his editorial fold, but the prospect of competing egos—principally Hemingway's—weighed against it. Wolfe recommended Faulkner's friend Hamilton Basso (1904–1964), who joined the roster. In Basso's *The View from Pompey's Head* (1954), Perkins figures as Phillip Greene, an editor suspected of having stolen royalties from one of his authors. The central character is a lawyer, a southerner who has with some trepidation contemplated his return to the region. In South Carolina he finds that the money went instead to the author's mother, a mulatta whose racial identity has been hidden. Here, as in his earlier work, Basso presents a character recurrent in southern novels of the first half of the century: the southerner whose attempts to achieve a rapprochement with his region are fraught with anxiety. Among Basso's many novels, *Relics and Angels* (1929), *Cinnamon Seed* (1934), *Days Before Lent* (1939), and *Sun in Capricorn* (1942) are set in his native Louisiana.

Along with Roark Bradford, Basso had been one of Faulkner's New Orleans gang in the 1920s. In the 1930s, his friendship with Wolfe led him to live for a time in Asheville, North Carolina. Thomas Wolfe (1900–1938) was, even in his own time, a phenomenon—as a personality, as a writer—and a center of literary controversy. In and against his favor was the intense, modernist self-consciousness he brought to the southern novel, which seemed at odds with this form's typical communal purposefulness. *Look Homeward, Angel: A Story of the Buried Life* (1929) is based on Wolfe's own life in Asheville and at the University of North Carolina in Chapel Hill, places transformed by him into Altamont and Pulpit Hill. In counterpoint to

the progressive elements of the *Bildungsroman* are the ongoing financial maneuvers of Eugene's mother, particularly her investment in and management of a boardinghouse called the Dixieland, which dominate the life of the large Gant family. *Of Time and the River: A Legend of Man's Hunger in His Youth* (1935) continues the story of Eugene Gant, who leaves the South for Harvard and the North, then leaves America for Europe, where he discovers through memory his affection for the country he has abandoned. *The Web and the Rock* (1939) and *You Can't Go Home Again* (1939) are also drawn from Wolfe's autobiography, though now the hero is named George Webber and a financial counterpoint to his life is the banking scandal that engulfs Libya Hill—that is, Asheville. This plot line had a basis in the failure of the Asheville Central Bank and Trust Company, as well as in the wider national calamity of the Depression. The attention Wolfe paid to the history and to the news of his region undercuts John Peale Bishop, who blamed the failure of Wolfe's novels on their overinvolvement with the individual consciousness. Indeed, when C. Vann Woodward praised southern novelists of the 1920s and 1930s for redeeming their region's discredited historical dimension, he included Wolfe, the "bright star," among them. The editorial role in the production of Wolfe's novels has also been much debated. Perkins has been credited with essentially forming Wolfe's first two novels from prodigious amounts of text accumulated for a much larger project. Reacting in part to the perception that he relied too heavily on Perkins (a perception Wolfe himself seems to have had), Wolfe broke with Scribner. So, after Wolfe's early death, it was left to Edward Aswell, his editor at Harper—also a North Carolinian, and later Richard Wright's editor on *Native Son*—to piece together his literary relics. Some changes in tone and strategy that critics note may, one imagines, reflect the two editorial minds at work—and the originating mind's absence while half the work was being prepared for publication. In time, Perkins and Aswell were faulted for many of their editorial decisions.

Evidence of the important—and, for Wolfe, sometimes uncomfortably tight—literary circle drawn round Perkins is abundant. For instance, John Peale Bishop (1892–1944), the West Virginian whose essay "The Sorrows of Thomas Wolfe" (*Kenyon Review*, 1939) was an important—and not entirely affirmative—posthumous reckoning of Wolfe's achievement, was one of Perkins's friends and authors. Bishop was also one of Fitzgerald's friends from Princeton, appearing as Tom D'Invilliers in *This Side of Paradise*. He was a poet and critic (and did his time in Hollywood, too), but with Allen Tate's encouragement he became a novelist. *Act of Darkness* (1935) takes place in Mordington, a fictional town in the Shenandoah Valley, where the young narrator, also named John, must struggle with the fact that a much-admired uncle may have committed rape. This man's act reflects the demise of the southern chivalric tradition, the moribundity of which the town's name also suggests.

Another writer within Perkins's southern circle was Fitzgerald's wife, the former Zelda Sayre of Montgomery, Alabama. Zelda Fitzgerald (1900–1948) met Scott in 1918, when he was assigned to Camp Sheridan near the end of World War I. This is not the place to demonstrate the connections between Scott Fitzgerald (who was from Minnesota) and the "grotesquely pictorial country" of the South, as he put it. Still, one can hardly resist noting that he was among the many writers Hollywood enlisted to work on *Gone With the Wind*'s screenplay. More relevant here is the fact that Perkins added Zelda's own novel, a *Bildungsroman* sharing some features of those by Bishop and Wolfe, to Scribner's list. *Save Me the Waltz* (1932) follows Alabama Beggs, the daughter of a judge and the wife of an artist, from the South to New York, then to Europe, and through her involvement in the Russian ballet—all in the pattern of Zelda's own life. Though some critics have focused on overwrought descriptive passages (a frequent mark of the southern novel in this period), there is a sustained aphoristic quality, particularly in sequences of dialogue, that readers may find compensatory. When Zelda died in a fire at a sanitarium in Asheville, she left an unfinished novel, *Caesar's Things*, which covers much the same ground as *Save Me the Waltz*.

The Jazz Age that the Fitzgeralds exemplified and chronicled in the 1920s drew inspiration from African American culture—from its music, its language, its style. Whites could luxuriate in an alternative, and temporary, racial identity—a type of passing in reverse. There is a measure of such racial appropriation in the work of, for instance, DuBose Heyward (1885–1940), who wrote of life in Charleston's black slums. His best-known novel, *Porgy* (1925), tells of a crippled beggar and gambler who loves Bess, a drug addict and the mistress of the murderous Crown. It has largely been forgotten that the successful folk opera *Porgy and Bess* (1936), typically credited to the composer George Gershwin, was based on Heyward's novel—and that

he and his wife helped Gershwin make this transformation. To many of his contemporary readers, including the editors of *The Negro Caravan*, it seemed that Heyward provided a revealing and sympathetic picture of blacks and their culture. A reader now confronting in one sentence Porgy's "atavistic calm" and his ability to "doze lightly under the terrific heat, as only a full-blooded negro can," might be less inclined to credit the author's acuity. But in this period, black as well as white novelists who dealt with the South had to work out in some measure the problem, as it seemed, of representing African Americans authentically. *Porgy* was in the mix of solutions offered at the time.

Also in the mix was the work of Julia Peterkin (1880–1961), who wrote of blacks in rural South Carolina. Peterkin's novels, as well as her nonfictional *Roll, Jordan, Roll* (1933), drew from the culture and life-histories of the Gullahs who worked on the Lang Syne Plantation, which she and her husband owned. *Scarlet Sister Mary* (1928) is about Mary Pinesett, a sexually liberated woman who eventually reconciles with, but does not capitulate to, her Christian community. This scandalous novel won the Pulitzer Prize and, in due course, was made into a movie. *Black April* (1927) tells of a powerful plantation foreman literally brought low by pride and possibly by conjure; and *Bright Skin* (1932) deals with the caste of color among African Americans, telling of a light-skinned woman rejected by those darker than herself.

Like Peterkin, Roark Bradford (1896–1948) seemed "amply qualified," as his publisher's blurb claimed, to write on black life because he had lived on a plantation and because a black woman had nursed him when he was a child. In *John Henry* (1931), a novel set on the Mississippi River, Bradford mimicked the black folkloric style in order to retell, in prose and lyrics, the story of this legendary figure. Paul Robeson starred in Bradford's musical adaptation of the novel in 1939. Earlier, *Ol' Man Adam an' His Chillun* (1928), a collection of stories from the Old Testament also retold in this manner, had been the basis for Marc Connelly's play *The Green Pastures* (1930), which was even more popular than *Porgy and Bess*. Connelly and Bradford shared the Pulitzer Prize for their efforts.

Southern novelists tended to view this sort of activity as a sterner project than entertainment, as having an ethnographic interest. Thus, white writers who appropriated black cultural materials typically did so with some stated concern for accuracy or purpose to illuminate. Nonetheless, theirs was, the editors of *The Negro*

Caravan noted, necessarily an "outside view." Not only legally but psychologically, whites were outside the community, the culture, and the consciousness of the African American, yet black and white novelists drew on similar documentary methods in their efforts to reach and describe the truths of black life. The attention paid to authentic expression in gatherings—by James Weldon Johnson, Arna Bontemps, Zora Neale Hurston, and others during the Harlem Renaissance—of African American poetry and spirituals and folklore also informs novels touching on the black experience of the South, the region from which these artifacts were most often drawn. Jean Toomer (1894–1967) was born in Washington, D.C., and for a short time worked as a school principal in Sparta, Georgia, where "folk-songs from the lips of Negro peasants" connected him to his racial history. These two urban and rural places are settings for *Cane* (1923), a tripartite, multiform work that has always been difficult to classify. *The Negro Caravan* includes a section of *Cane*'s prose among the short stories and some of its verse amid the poetry. Arna Bontemps called it "a kind of frappé" of genres, but frequently it has been called a novel. *Cane*'s form reflects both Toomer's own intellectually restive character and the experimentation—particularly in representations of consciousness—that mark the southern novel of this period and the modernist novel in general. *Cane* has many of the elements of *The Autobiography of an Ex-Coloured Man,* which was republished in 1927: the dilemmas of mixed blood and crises arising from miscegenation, the abortive journey from North to South, the ritual lynching.

Given the efforts of the writers of the Harlem Renaissance in particular to redeem the African American literary heritage, it is ironic to discover that much of their own work lay far outside the mainstream, only preserved in a collection such as *The Negro Caravan* until critical fashion swept some of it along again, as Hurston's work was in the 1970s. Zora Neale Hurston (1891–1960) was born in Eatonville, Florida, an all-black community. Soon she ventured out and became a leading and controversial figure in the Harlem Renaissance. She returned to Eatonville to live out her last years in relative obscurity, though not in relative calm. Eatonville serves as a background for Hurston's two most important novels, *Jonah's Gourd Vine* (1934) and *Their Eyes Were Watching God* (1937). Likewise, these novels' characters and events are drawn from elements of Hurston's personal life. For instance, Tea Cake Woods, Janie Crawford's third husband in *Their*

Eyes Were Watching God, was based on Hurston's young West Indian lover; and the novel itself was written out of the experience of Hurston's affair with this man. But Hurston's training in anthropology gives this sort of autobiographical detail a wider scope than simple memoir. While Hurston was doing graduate work at Columbia University, the anthropologist Franz Boas (Margaret Mead was another of his students) encouraged her to collect folklore. Her research in the South, including her home state, and in the West Indies, resulted in several works of nonfiction, and it informs the style of her novels—their use of language and their attention to cultural detail. In *Their Eyes Were Watching God,* Janie Crawford returns to Eatonville to tell what has become of her in her passage through three marriages. Janie has struggled to break free from an old idea of the possibilities for black women's relationship to men, inherited from slave times and taught her when she was young. The idea was that she would be as safe and cosseted as a white woman on a plantation porch, but its effect was to hem her in emotionally until she learned to break free. *Moses, Man of the Mountain* (1939) reworks the Book of Exodus in black dialect, drawing on an analogy, familiar from spirituals, between the Jews of ancient Egypt and the enslaved African Americans. The sort of association that might be made here with the work of Roark Bradford, for instance, opened up a debate about the value of Hurston's work. Some, like Richard Wright, felt that Hurston catered to her white audience and her white patrons, that her "minstrel technique" exploited the stereotypes holding blacks down. Others, including Hurston herself (who detested *Green Pastures*), argued that she was, in this rhetorical mode and in their own language, able to describe the full, deep lives of people, particularly of black women, who were often presented as psychologically flat figures.

Another novelist associated with Florida, and Hurston's contemporary, was Marjorie Kinnan Rawlings (1896–1953). Rawlings, who was white, was born in Washington, D.C., and lived in Wisconsin and New York before moving to Cross Creek in 1928. Florida's swampy scrub country, its people, and their culture—all previously unexplored in fiction—would provide the source material for Rawlings's most important work. Like Hurston, Rawlings took a sociological approach to her novels, doing extensive preparatory fieldwork before writing. *The Yearling* (1938), which won a Pulitzer Prize and was made into a well-received film, takes place over the course of a year not long after the Civil War. Its focal character is a boy, Jody Baxter, who comes of age through his needful killing of a fawn that he has nurtured—the yearling of the title. Rawlings set *Jacob's Ladder* (1931), *South Moon Under* (1933), and *Golden Apples* (1934) in the same geographic region. At the time of her death, she had gathered a good deal of material in preparation for a biography of Ellen Glasgow. These items are now housed at the University of Florida. The ubiquitous Maxwell Perkins was Rawlings's editor, and his correspondence to her also fills this archive.

Rawlings's consideration of the strenuous rituals that the land requires of its inhabitants has been likened to that of the Agrarians, who emerged out of the Fugitive poetry movement at Vanderbilt. It is possible, however, to see an even broader pattern among writers of this period. Writing in Nashville in the 1960s, Arna Bontemps mentions that Allen Tate, whose favorable review of *Cane* appeared in the *Tennessean*, twice wrote to Toomer to set up a meeting. Tate was, Bontemps surmises, "reaching toward Toomer, tentatively and vaguely, on behalf of the Fugitive enclave." The potential meeting point between the Harlem Renaissance and this sect of the Southern Renascence may have been on the ground of their mutual scholarly attempts to document the interrelated and conflicting folkways of urban and rural America—often posited then as the North and the South, respectively. In *I'll Take My Stand* (1930), a collection of twelve essays, the Agrarians reaffirmed the ideals of the pre-industrial South. Blacks and poor whites might be forgiven for having viewed any return to the Old South's style of labor-intensive agriculture, which had depended on slavery and tenant-farming, as a prospect without allure. But the Agrarians posited the Civil War as one fought, not *for* slavery, but *against* industrialism and *against* the enslavement to dreary rote activity that industry requires.

The Civil War, which afterward served as a critical locus for the discussion—and the muddying—of such issues in the South, was the backdrop for a number of novels by the contributors to *I'll Take My Stand*. Stark Young (1881–1963), a Mississippian whose essay is mentioned above, was a friend of Faulkner and Peterkin and, naturally, Perkins. All four of his novels treat the South and the Agrarian ideal. The last, *So Red the Rose* (1934), tells of the McGehees—a name taken from Young's own family tree—and plantation life in Mississippi around the time of the Civil War. The movie industry churned out a version of it, apparently

with Young's approval. *The Long Night* (1936), the first of four novels by Andrew Lytle (1902–1997), is a family story, told in retrospect, of a blood feud begun in the antebellum South and continued at Shiloh and on other battlefields. *The Fathers* (1938), the only novel by Allen Tate (1899–1979), tells of two families in Virginia in the 1850s to 1860s. At the heart of the conflict between the Buchans and Poseys is the slave Yellow Jim, who rapes his half-sister Jane Posey. Acts of revenge follow, as does a struggle to reconcile southern traditions of chivalry with the refractory realities of personality and event.

Tate's wife, Caroline Gordon (1895–1981), was a far more prolific novelist than he. In *Penhally* (1931), *None Shall Look Back* (1937), *The Garden of Adonis* (1937), and *Green Centuries* (1941), she took the long view of southern history, naturally including the Civil War, and its effects across generations. But she is best known now for a work on a smaller tapestry—*Aleck Maury, Sportsman* (1934), the story of a teacher of classical languages who arranges his life to satisfy his passions for hunting and fishing. Gordon followed this character, modeled after her own father, in several short stories as well. Though she was not on the all-male roster of contributors to *I'll Take My Stand*, critics have sometimes placed Gordon among the Agrarians, as one seeming to have some measure of sympathy with their cause. Readers may find in *Aleck Maury* and the connected stories, in their descriptions of the ritual and code of outdoor sport, in the pervasive air of nostalgia, a variation on the Agrarian lament.

Robert Penn Warren (1905–1989), one of the youngest contributors to *I'll Take My Stand*, took on the New South's political machinery in order to show how it exploited and corrupted whatever remained of the Old South's assets and values. *Night Rider* (1939) deals with an attempt by tobacco-growers to organize against the companies that control them. This, Warren's first novel, was based upon actual events in his native Kentucky at the beginning of the century. His second novel, *At Heaven's Gate* (1943), drew on the Asheville bank scandal, which Wolfe also touched on. *All the King's Men* (1946), Warren's most celebrated novel, explores the populist movement in all its ambiguity through a study of Willie Stark, who was based on Louisiana governor Huey Long.

Some novelists took as their subjects the rhythm and hardship of daily life on the farms, in the fields, at the grassroots of agrarianism. When Jesse Stuart (1906–1984) did graduate work at Vanderbilt University, some of his professors were members of the Agrarian group. Donald Davidson was particularly helpful in identifying where Stuart's literary ground lay—in his native Kentucky and the Appalachian hills. Stuart treated these in poetry as well as fiction. His most financially successful novel, a Book-of-the-Month Club selection, was *Tapes For Private Tussie* (1943). Here the large family of the "late" Kim Tussie spends his life-insurance money on an unsustainable foray into the easy life before discovering that his apparent death has been a hoax. Among Stuart's teachers at Lincoln Memorial University, where he had been an undergraduate, was the novelist Harry Harrison Kroll (1888–1967). Kroll was the son of a tenant farmer, and his novels—including *The Cabin in the Cotton* (1931) and *The Usurper* (1941)—reflect this background. *Their Ancient Grudge* (1946) tells of the feud between the Hatfields and McCoys. The novelist James Still (1906–1991) was among Stuart's fellow students at Lincoln Memorial and at Vanderbilt. Still's *River of Earth* (1940) describes the hard-scrabble life of a boy's family in Kentucky at the beginning of the century, and of the living his people try to eke from coal-mining and subsistence farming. Somewhat earlier than these men, Elizabeth Madox Roberts (1881–1941) wrote about the same region. In keeping with her educational background and the literary mode at the time, she took a deeply psychological approach to her characters. Her most highly praised book, *The Time of Man* (1926), set in Kentucky's farming communities, traces the struggle of its heroine, Ellen Chesser, to evolve in her perception and appreciation of life. *The Great Meadow* (1930) similarly follows Diony Hall's life on the Wilderness Road and the Kentucky frontier.

Like the Agrarian, though in a different political and rhetorical mode, the proletarian novelist of the South focused on the harsh conditions that resulted when a rural, generally self-reliant people was forced into dependence upon the industrialist and upon the industrialist's urbanized version of everything, including agriculture. Erskine Caldwell (1903–1987) published twenty-five novels, many of which treat the poor rural whites of Georgia, his home state. His approach, which combines Marxist protest and hyper-realism and tends to turn his proletarian heroes into grotesques, has been variously praised and condemned. At any rate, Caldwell's books enjoyed great popular success, as they still do, and the titles of his two best-known novels have become part of the vernacular. *Tobacco Road* (1932) tells of Jeeter Lester and his family, who are sharecroppers

given to a range of behavior that seems particularly backward and futile when set in the framework of a modern age, exemplified here by an automobile they cannot manage. *God's Little Acre* (1933), another bestseller, describes the Walden family, farmers similarly caught in the South's painful transition to an industrialized economy—in this case, from farm to mill work. Another example of the proletarian novelist is Grace Lumpkin (1902?–1980), also from Georgia, whose interest was in the universal progress to be made through the struggle of the working class. *To Make My Bread* (1932)—later dramatized as *Let Freedom Ring* (1936)—was one of several novels dealing with the strike by textile workers in Gastonia, North Carolina, in 1929. Hamilton Basso and Sherwood Anderson were among others who touched on this event. Lumpkin's *A Sign for Cain* (1935) describes the situation of the southern sharecropper.

Many novelists not typically identified with either the Agrarian or the proletarian camp dealt as seriously with the complex pressures attending social and economic change in the South. T. S. Stribling (1881–1965) may have blurred his reputation by introducing a range of adventure and detective fiction into his bibliography. But he also won the Pulitzer Prize for a more highbrow effort, *The Store* (1932), which takes on these issues. This was the second novel in a trilogy set in Florence, Alabama, where he went to high school and college. (Inevitably, offended citizens filed a libel suit, later dropped.) In these novels, Stribling follows three generations of the Vaiden family through the Civil War and into the twentieth century. Miltiades Vaiden, *The Store*'s central figure, successfully negotiates the new economic climate of the South in the 1880s, which the store symbolizes. Less successful are the blacks and poor whites, who are the victims of this system as they were of the previous one. *The Forge* (1931) and *The Unfinished Cathedral* (1933) complete the cycle.

Stribling's first novel, *Birthright* (1922), is also notable. Peter Siner, the hero, is a mulatto who has been educated at Harvard and returns to share his knowledge with his community. Largely because his northern education puts him at odds with whites and blacks alike, all of whom have been taught to accept the black man's inferior position, Siner must finally abandon his plan and the South. The plot line is recognizable from Chesnutt's *The Colonel's Dream* (1905), in which the educated, well-meaning—in this case, white—native returns to promote business and create change and is defeated by the recalcitrant South. Novels by two other black writers, Walter White (1893–1955) and George Lee (1894–1976), follow a similar pattern. White, whose essay "Color Lines" is mentioned above, brought personal and political understanding of race in the South to bear on his fiction. As a youth, he witnessed Atlanta's race riot of 1906; as an adult, he was charged by the NAACP with the investigation of lynchings. His novel *Fire in the Flint* (1924) concerns a black doctor trained in the North and lynched when he returns to practice medicine in Georgia. His second novel, *Flight* (1926), is about passing. Lee's *River George* (1937) tells of Aaron George, a black man who has some college education, returns to work as a sharecropper and as a deckhand, and then like White's hero is lynched.

Richard Wright (1908–1960) wrote in the proletarian vein, but with the added imperative of race. For a time he saw Communism as offering some parity to blacks, and this plays a part in the scheme of *Native Son* (1940). Wright was born in Mississippi and later moved to Chicago, a pattern his protagonist follows. Bigger Thomas, a young black man, kills the daughter of his white employer. In order to effect his flight, he murders his lover and attempts to frame another man, but he is eventually caught and sentenced to death. His lawyer, a Communist, describes the larger, determinative context of Bigger Thomas's crimes: societal pressure on African Americans had, after years, found its psychological release in these acts of violence. Three months after the novel's publication, Wright traveled to North Carolina to collaborate on its dramatization with the playwright Paul Green, who likened this novel to Dostoevsky's *Crime and Punishment*. Green's letters reveal their struggle to stage the violence in a responsible and meaningful way. In 1941 the play opened in New York under the direction of Orson Welles, who had just completed his film *Citizen Kane*.

Lillian Smith (1897–1966), a white woman from Georgia, was another of Wright's correspondents. Her own best-selling novel provoked a share of controversy—and a postal ban that Eleanor Roosevelt's intervention caused to be lifted. *Strange Fruit* (1944) concerns a relationship between a white man and a black woman, a relationship doomed by the man's timidity in the face of community resistance. "Strange fruit" is a wry locution, also used in a well-known jazz song, referring to the practice of lynching, though this is not the only emphasis Smith gives it. Her work as a camp director and her understanding of child development seem to have attuned Smith to the enduring effects of social influence, and she had in mind segregation's more general yield of psychological injury. Smith is now more often praised for a work of nonfiction, *Killers of the Dream,* which also criticizes the false, typically cruel distinctions made "in the land of Epidermis."

Another novelist from Georgia, Carson McCullers (1917–1967), also wrote of racial prejudice, and of life in small towns, and of psychological injuries to which people, particularly young people, everywhere are prone. Her first novel, *The Heart Is a Lonely Hunter* (1940), is a study of the thwarted human instinct to communicate, symbolized by the muteness of its central figure, ironically named John Singer. A similar, melancholic strain runs through her subsequent novels.

Eudora Welty (1909–2001) also pays close attention to psychological detail, but she transforms it, as she does almost every human attribute and gesture, into a sort of charm, in several senses of the word. Place, which she has commended as one of the angels watching over fiction-writers, is also given a magical cast. All of this, however, Welty grounds in the reality of the South and its people. It is significant that, particularly during the Depression, government works projects brought a number of writers as different as Welty and Grace Lumpkin into regions and among people of the South they might not ordinarily have encountered. Such experience informs Welty's work. *The Robber Bridegroom* (1942), her first novel, draws on European fairy tales and southern folklore to tell of Rosamond Musgrove and her lover, Jamie Lockhart, mysterious in his berry-stain disguise. For the benefit of the Mississippi Historical Society, which she addressed in the 1970s, Welty called *The Robber Bridegroom* her historical novel. This was possible to do because Welty has set her fairy tale in the Natchez Trace at the end of the 1700s, and because Lockhart becomes a rich merchant in New Orleans. She has shown how the southern economy evolved out of such wild places, how it came to be that some people lived in beautiful houses on the banks of the Mississippi and owned a hundred slaves, which were historical facts. Welty recalled that *The Robber Bridegroom* drew a praising letter from a fellow novelist in Mississippi (*Paris Review,* 1972). Her correspondent, William Faulkner (1897–1962), would win the Nobel Prize within a decade, but in 1942 neither of them, nor anyone else, could have predicted it.

Viking Press's *Portable Faulkner* (1946), introduced and edited by Malcolm Cowley, served to revive public interest in a novelist whose books had fallen out of print. Cowley offered only comparatively small portions of Faulkner's large output, and no entire novel. But interpolated among the portions were Cowley's biographical and bibliographical notes. These, along with the lengthy introduction (an excellent description of the novels to that time) and Faulkner's annotated genealogy of the Compson family, made clear the remarkable, interconnected whole of Faulkner's achievement. More than providing a synoptic reference point for the books, Cowley described the larger context, the southern mythology, the history of a nation within a nation, that the books both explore and signify. In *Sartoris* (1929), Faulkner had begun to chart, across the map of a fictional county in Mississippi, the whole drama of the South's moral and economic decline. Yoknapatawpha County, with its elaborate conception and genealogies, has been compared to Cabell's Poictesme. And Faulkner may often be found revisiting or revising a pattern for the southern novel in this way, or touching on a common theme or personality. *Mosquitoes* (1927) is based on Faulkner's time in New Orleans, when he and Basso and Bradford were hanging about with Sherwood Anderson and becoming writers. *The Sound and the Fury* (1929) and *As I Lay Dying* (1930) play out the modernist fascination with the manifold, often opposed, associations that individual minds make when presented with the same tragic or comic facts. In *Light in August* (1931), another character bears the cross of miscegenation. Joe Christmas is the progeny of Rena Walden, of the ex-colored man, of similar others, but he is of different, more complicated type—dangerous as well as tragic. He has murdered his lover, a woman from the North, who was liberal enough to sympathize but not southern enough to understand. *Absalom, Absalom!* (1936) is the form that the Civil War novel takes in Faulkner's hands. An insult suffered as a child drives Thomas Sutpen—a truly sinister robber bridegroom—in a lifelong, irrational defense of his honor. *The Hamlet* (1940) is the first in a trilogy making a thorough accounting of the fiscal achievements of the Snopes family, vanguard of the economic class that will rule the New South. From his back garden in Oxford, Faulkner spun out the vast psychological and sociological history of his region, and in every way it attests to the entire achievement of southern novelists in this period.

Amber Vogel

See also African American Folk Culture; African American Literature, 1919 to Present; Agrarians; Faulkner, William; Flor-

ida, Literature of; *Gone With the Wind*; Great Depression; Harlem Renaissance; Miscegenation; Modernism; Mystery and Detective Fiction; Plantation Fiction; Poor White; Popular Literature; Proletarian Novel; Sportsmen; Virginia, Literature of; Women Writers, 1900 to World War II.

Sterling A. Brown et al., eds., *The Negro Caravan: Writings by American Negroes* (1941); Louis D. Rubin Jr., *A Gallery of Southerners* (1982); Allen Tate, "The New Provincialism: With an Epilogue on the Southern Novel," *Essays of Four Decades* (1968); *The Portable Faulkner*, ed. Malcolm Cowley (1946); C. Vann Woodward, "The Historical Dimension," *The Burden of Southern History* (1960).

NOVEL, WORLD WAR II TO PRESENT

The South has undergone a major transformation during the past sixty years, and the literature has naturally reflected the changes. Far from being dominated by other parts of the country, the South is often seen as the ascendant region, at least politically and economically, in the years since 1960.

The increased mobility of the nation's population (with the South gaining the greatest influx) and the prevalence of the mass media have arguably led to the waning of regional consciousness. Although the long-term effect of these changes on southern literature is unclear, the literature continues to remain recognizably southern. Place, community, family, change, the past, religion, and race are major themes in the southern novel since World War II. Yet some differences can be seen as well. The past in contemporary novels is not normally the Civil War past, but more likely the civil rights past. Since the South has experienced such accelerated change during this period, some of the more recent novels reveal an extreme form of isolation, fragmentation, and alienation. Some are set in cities or suburbs, and writers may deal with the phenomenon of placelessness; even so, this will often be against the background of a traditional sense of place. The period bounded by Robert Penn Warren and Eudora Welty at one end and Dorothy Allison and Frederick Barthelme at the other is one of great change yet enduring literary vitality.

The careers of Robert Penn Warren and Eudora Welty, by any measure two of the greatest American writers of the century, span practically the entire period covered here. A master of almost all literary forms, Warren published ten novels, from *Night Rider* (1939) to *A Place to Come To* (1977). Two of the most acclaimed are *All the King's Men* (1946) and *World Enough and Time* (1950). The former, based loosely on the career of Huey Long, contains the archetypal Warren opposition: the idealist, narrator Jack Burden, as opposed to the pragmatist, former idealist Willie Stark. The idealist flees the complexity of the world, but also flees self-knowledge. The attainment of self-knowledge involves at least a modification of idealism and an acceptance of responsibility and one's imperfection. Only along that path lies redemption, which Burden achieves and Jeremiah Beaumont, the romantic idealist and murderer in *World Enough and Time,* fails to attain. The prose of Warren's novels is often a striking mixture of the colloquial, even "vulgar," on the one hand, and the lyrical and philosophical on the other, another manifestation of the two poles of his vision.

Eudora Welty is the other major figure whose career was under way at the start of this period. Her initial accomplishment was in the short story, but from early in her career she published novels as well. Unlike Warren's melodramatic novels, hers tend to be quiet and leisurely. One of her primary concerns is the family, and her major novels all center on family rituals, a wedding in *Delta Wedding* (1946), a family reunion in *Losing Battles* (1970), and the death and burial of a parent in *The Optimist's Daughter* (1972). The novels often juxtapose a close-knit family with an outsider; for example, the Beechams and Renfros in *Losing Battles* are set against the teacher Miss Julia Mortimer and her disciple Gloria Renfro, who has married into the Renfro family but seeks to retain her independence. Her battle to do so will be lost, but it must be lost to ensure the continuity of the family and the love that knits it together. In *The Optimist's Daughter,* the last parent dies and the family disintegrates. Although Laurel Hand seems a lonely wanderer at the novel's end, she is nourished by memory. Welty's often-lyrical prose serves her respect for the mysteries of human consciousness and inner life. Her compassion for all her characters is remarkable, as is her balanced vision of the needs of the self and the sustenance gained by membership in a group.

Three other novelists published works during the 1940s and early 1950s, which, while not the equal of Warren or Welty's, are notable in their own right. Harriette Arnow, like James Still and Jesse Stuart, was a regionalist from Kentucky who focused attention on Appalachian culture. Arnow's masterpiece is *The Dollmaker* (1954), which received increased attention

during the 1960s and 1970s as interest in women's literature flourished. Focusing on the Nevel family, Kentucky mountain residents who move to Detroit in search of better jobs, the novel emphasizes the plight of the displaced. Yet even more powerful than the social dimension of the novel is the portrait of Gertie, the mother, who is bewildered and confused until she finds solace in the mountain craft of wood carving. Gertie's courage, endurance, and wisdom are timeless.

Carson McCullers was a very different kind of writer. Perhaps she is best known for the gothic and grotesque nature of her work, though her most-remembered novels are *The Heart Is a Lonely Hunter* (1940) and *The Member of the Wedding* (1946), in which the gothic element is muted. The protagonists in both are girls on the verge of adolescence who feel somewhat freakish, and the theme in both—in fact, McCullers's obsessive theme—is human isolation and the search for love. Mick Kelly is surrounded in *Heart* by a rich array of characters who futilely fight their isolation, whereas *Wedding* ends on a more hopeful note, with Frankie Addams seeming to have successfully made the transition to adolescence. The conclusion of *Wedding* is atypical of McCullers, however, with her characters usually remaining alone and frustrated.

James Agee published only one novel during his relatively short life, *The Morning Watch* (1951), but the posthumously published *A Death in the Family* (1957) has earned him lasting fame. Like McCullers, he focuses on childhood and adolescence, and his autobiographically based protagonists wrestle with a sense of being part of yet cut off from their family heritage. The six-year-old Rufus of *Death* must cope not only with the death of his father but also with the competing heritages of his mother's and father's families. Few novels more lyrically capture the change in a world occasioned by death.

Among the women novelists to begin their careers after World War II is Elizabeth Spencer, whose first novels, most notably *Fire in the Morning* (1948) and *The Voice at the Back Door* (1956), draw on life in Mississippi small towns like the one where she grew up. The former concerns how an ethical young man can deal with a family and community heritage of greed; the latter concerns racial prejudice in small-town Mississippi. With the novella *The Light in the Piazza* (1960), Spencer's setting shifts to Italy, and she focuses on a mother facing the challenge of whether to approve the marriage of her mentally retarded daughter to a young Italian. The mother's goal is to do the right thing, even if it is in defiance of husband and community. Only in such action can she create her own freedom and identity. The female protagonist of a later novel, *The Snare* (1972), journeys from the respectable Garden District of New Orleans to the decadent underworld of drug trafficking in the French Quarter to find a more authentic life. While southern, the settings of this novel are more symbolic of psychological states than the realistic Mississippi settings of her early novels. Spencer has published nine novels in all, as well as numerous short stories and a recent memoir, *Landscapes of the Heart* (1998). She has had a long, varied, and distinguished career marked by a preoccupation with how the individual can create an authentic self.

That same concern pervades the single novel published by Ralph Ellison during his lifetime, *Invisible Man* (1952). A native of Oklahoma, on the fringe of the South, he set only the first part of *Invisible Man* in the South. The African American protagonist of the novel, nameless throughout, seeks his identity in an "absurd" universe through acceptance by various groups. In the southern section of the novel, as high-school valedictorian he is invited to deliver an oration before the white citizens. During the often-anthologized "Battle Royal" section, he is put in a boxing ring with other African American boys and forced to fight for the amusement of whites. He is finally allowed to give his speech, to the jeers of the audience, and is given a briefcase as a present. Nothing is what it seems, however, and the fact that illusion is reality becomes a major motif of the novel. At the prominent African American college he attends, he discovers that the president, far from being concerned about the welfare of the students, wants only to please the white trustees. Upon expulsion, the narrator journeys to New York, where the remainder of the novel occurs. The pattern for his life is set in the South of his youth, however. Nameless and without identity, he is exploited by all he encounters, not only southern bigots but Communists, African American nationalists, and northern liberals of various kinds. The novel ends when, after flight, the narrator ends up underground, in a variation of Dostoevsky's and Wright's figure, and finally confronts his invisibility. Far from trying to conform to the ideas of others, at the end he is stripped of illusion and not only accepts but celebrates his invisibility, which is his identity, ready to be used in the spirit of self-reliance of Ellison's own namesake, Ralph Waldo Emerson. Of all the models for action that the narrator encounters in the novel, he finally values most his grandfather, who

behind his Uncle Tom mask urged him to be a spy in enemy country. In a sense, the narrator is just poised to begin his life at the end of the novel, and what will happen is problematical. He is not seen leaving hibernation, and it is not entirely clear that he is prepared for effective action in the world.

Invisible Man is a rich novel, melding various literary forms and devices. Essentially a picaresque and episodic *Bildungsroman*, it includes elements of African American folklore, myth, realism, surrealism, symbolism, and stream of consciousness. The inclusion of these elements reflects Ellison's conviction that the American character is composed of many strands, and a full understanding of them all is necessary for a full understanding of the national identity. The final words of the novel suggest that the narrator speaks for all. *Invisible Man* completed, Ellison worked for the rest of his life on another novel. In 1999, his executor gave the public *Juneteenth*, which Ellison had nearly completed. Its title originates with the Texas holiday marking the day in 1865—two years after the event—when African Americans in Texas learned of the Emancipation Proclamation.

The other major novelist to appear in the early 1950s was Tidewater Virginia native William Styron, with the release of *Lie Down in Darkness* (1951). In some ways derivative of Faulkner, and especially reminiscent of *The Sound and the Fury* and *As I Lay Dying*, the novel focuses on Peyton Loftis, a southern girl who commits suicide because she cannot reconcile the competing claims of her southern heritage as illustrated by her parents, her father representing the relaxed civility of the cavalier and her mother representing the rigid and obsessive Calvinist strain. Torn between parents, Peyton is driven insane. Styron's *The Confessions of Nat Turner* (1967) and *Sophie's Choice* (1979) reveal that Styron has that familiar southern obsession with history, southern history in *Turner* and European history in *Choice*. The publication of *Turner* caused a great deal of controversy, with a number of African Americans objecting to a white southerner telling Turner's story in the voice of a slave. Long interested in the Turner story, Styron called his work a "meditation on history," and the work is a compelling depiction of the institution of slavery. For better or worse, Nat Turner the character in the novel is complex, not completely heroic, seemingly deluded, in some ways surmounting the barriers to his development that slavery presented, yet inevitably warped by those barriers—all in all, a compelling figure who shares a common humanity with the reader. Styron continued his consideration of how human institutions can cause unhappiness in his exploration of the Holocaust in *Sophie's Choice*. The book combines elements of the traditional southern novel, the urban novel, and the novel of ideas. The narrator is Stingo, a young Thomas Wolfe-like character from Virginia whose early life shares a great deal with Styron's. In Brooklyn he meets Sophie, a Polish gentile, and her lover Nathan, a Jew, who become parent figures for him. Sophie's "choice," revealed late in the novel, is having had to decide which of her two children would be spared in a German concentration camp. Unable to continue to live with that memory, Sophie finally kills herself with Nathan. Styron's major novels end in guilt or death, with individuals overwhelmed by history or by the choices they have made. Yet at the end of *Choice*, Stingo survives, no longer the callow youth of the beginning but a mature adult saddened and made wiser through what he has experienced. This novel too caused controversy, with some Jewish groups objecting that Sophie was gentile and not Jewish. Yet Stingo makes explicit a parallel between American slavery and the Holocaust, both historical manifestations of institutions that formalize the dehumanization of mankind. Styron writes of broad subjects with great intensity.

During the late 1950s and the 1960s, new novels by a great variety of writers began to appear, signaling that the southern novel would move in a variety of directions in the ensuing decades. Walker Percy, one of the most important of the new writers, had an unusual background. He came late to fiction, having trained as a medical doctor, contracted tuberculosis, and read the European existentialists, and he published his first novel, *The Moviegoer* (1961), when he was forty-five. He brings a distinctive philosophical and religious vision to his fiction, in which he depicts the alienation resulting from a world view controlled by empiricism. In fact, far from being a problem, the characters' alienation is their good fortune, for it shows their dissatisfaction with the deadening everydayness of the life surrounding them. Binx Bolling, protagonist of *The Moviegoer*, is characteristic. He seems not all that dissatisfied with his banal life, but he is detached, as suggested by his withdrawal to the world of the movies, and secretly searching for something ineffable. Percy suggests that the secular world cannot offer any prospect for wholeness, though the endings of *The Moviegoer* and the later *The Second Coming* (1980) imply that human love and concern can be an avenue to heal-

ing. Other novels, *Love in the Ruins* (1971), *Lancelot* (1977), and *The Thanatos Syndrome* (1987), employ apocalyptic imagery to enforce the seriousness of man's dilemma in a secular world. Yet irony is never far from the surface of a Percy novel, suggesting that what is on the surface is never all there is. Although Percy's own Catholicism is rarely explicitly present in the novels, it functions as a background frame, in a way similar to the Catholicism in Flannery O'Connor's works. Though coming to fiction after intensive reading in philosophy, and the author of numerous essays on philosophy and linguistics, Percy in his fiction wears his philosophical interests lightly. In fact, one of the dangers he sees is abstraction from the concrete world. That world is a relatively new one to southern fiction, for Percy most often uses as his setting the cities and suburbs of the new modern South. Yet the alienation experienced there is not specific to the region or locale, but is characteristic of man living in a secular world.

John Barth, who began his career slightly before Percy, at least initially shared Percy's concerns about the despair of characters who find life without intrinsic value. His first two novels, *The Floating Opera* (1956) and *The End of the Road* (1958), contain characters wrestling with such problems, with the protagonist of the first seriously considering suicide. Unlike Percy, however, Barth holds to the idea that all reality, hence all meaning, is a projection of the perceiver. With his third novel, *The Sot-Weed Factor* (1960), Barth traces the career of the historical figure Ebenezer Cooke through an eighteenth-century Maryland universe in which identities slide, storytelling prevails, and reality is uncertain. Here Barth executes a delightful parody of the southern concern for history. He has published six novels since, and though he is a native of Maryland and sets many of his novels there, region plays little role in his fiction. He does share with many southern writers a love of storytelling, though his love comes from an immersion in classical story cycles like *The Arabian Nights*. For him, storytelling creates the only meaning there is; Barth is the one southern novelist who is a true postmodernist.

Reynolds Price, approximately the same age as Barth, is a more traditional southern storyteller. Hailing from small-town eastern North Carolina, he fervently believes in the moral power of literature. Though perhaps the South's most accomplished man of letters after Warren, writing drama, poetry, short stories, essays, memoirs, and biblical translations and commentary, his greatest accomplishment is in the novel. His novels focus on the search for love and identity within the family, juxtaposed with the human desire for freedom and independence from the family. His works often cover broad sweeps of time and consider the relationship of past and present, and he has written series of novels on the same families. He deals with the Mustians in *A Long and Happy Life* (1962), *A Generous Man* (1966), and *Good Hearts* (1988); *The Surface of Earth* (1975), *The Source of Light* (1981), and *The Promise of Rest* (1996) focus on the Kendal-Mayfield families through four generations. More recently, in *Kate Vaiden* (1986) and *Roxanna Slade* (1998), he has told stories of women's lives in their own voices. Price is ultimately a Christian writer whose work expresses a charity toward and acceptance of humanity and at least the possibility of redemption for his characters.

Anne Tyler, who also grew up in North Carolina, was a student of Price at Duke University, and similarities in their works are evident. Though Tyler has set most of her novels in Baltimore and thus can be seen as an urban novelist, she shares an interest in families and an attitude of charity and acceptance. Given her urban setting, her families are frequently disintegrating, and her characters are often torn between the need to flee and the need to settle down within family. In thirteen novels, from *If Morning Ever Comes* (1964) through *A Patchwork Planet* (1998), she has written about eccentric characters in search of meaning. *Dinner at the Homesick Restaurant* (1982) may be her best novel, but it is perhaps darker in tone than most. Though the Tull family is destructive in its effect on the children, as adults the Tulls are homesick and continue to gather in search of the connection that family can provide. The symbol in the title of a recent novel—a patchwork planet—encapsulates her vision. A quilt of the planet is made of mismatched squares haphazardly and clumsily put together, overlapping, crowded, likely to disintegrate—yet somehow holding together. In such a world, compassion is a virtue. Tyler's best characters have it, and so does she.

In nine novels published over the last thirty years, Lee Smith has increasingly explored her native area of Appalachian Virginia and traditional mountain culture, particularly as it is contrasted with modern urban living. Her work has become more sophisticated as she has experimented with different narrative methods. *Oral History* (1983) was her first major novel. In it, a contemporary college student returns to the mountains to record the stories of her mountain relatives. Those stories reveal the reality and vitality of oral history and

folk culture, as compared to the vacuity of contemporary mass commercial culture. *Fair and Tender Ladies* (1988), an epistolary novel, contains only one voice, that of the letter-writer Ivy Rowe, but her story also captures the richness of rural culture and illustrates another characteristic Lee Smith theme—a woman's search for self and achievement of identity. *The Devil's Dream* (1992) concerns country music, juxtaposing the music as it originated in the mountains with contemporary Nashville-generated music; *Saving Grace* follows a snake-handling preacher's daughter. Smith's contribution to contemporary southern fiction is her portrait of a rich traditional mountain culture that is vanishing and the forces that are causing its disappearance.

Another novelist of Appalachia, at least early in his career, is Cormac McCarthy, who set his first four novels in the mountains around his native Knoxville, Tennessee. Yet those novels are very different from Lee Smith's. While they convey the beauty and grandeur of the mountains, the characters possess minimal awareness of the history and traditions of their culture. In fact, they have little moral awareness as well. Culla Holme commits incest with his sister in *Outer Dark* (1968), and Lester Ballard murders women and then violates their corpses in *Child of God* (1973). The violence and amorality of his characters reach an apotheosis in *Blood Meridian* (1985), set in Texas and featuring the unremitting savagery of a group of bounty hunters. Yet juxtaposed with his subject matter is McCarthy's style, the eloquence of which lifts his characters into a mythic dimension and endows them with a significance that their actions seem not to have. McCarthy having moved to Texas, his recent Border Trilogy is set in the Southwest: *All the Pretty Horses* (1992), *The Crossing* (1994), and *Cities of the Plain* (1998). These novels, focusing on two young cowboys before and after World War II, are suffused with melancholy over a lost way of life, the "cities of the plain" suggesting both Sodom and Gomorrah and a modernity that is overtaking traditional cowboy ways. McCarthy's novels, considered among the very best being written today, communicate a sense of loss, alienation, and sorrow, yet also contain frequent scenes of beauty and dignity.

Harry Crews, author of fourteen novels over the last thirty years, has sometimes been paired with McCarthy since they both write of the gothic and grotesque. Raised in rural south Georgia and spending most of his adult life in urban North Florida, Crews writes of the dislocations of urban life faced by characters of often rural backgrounds. He is one of the first writers to provide an insider's perspective on the life of poor whites. His novels are populated by freaks, and he believes that all people are freaks; the "normal" are different from literal freaks only in an ability to hide deformities. His characters often engage in ritual activity—karate in *Karate Is a Thing of the Spirit* (1971), falconry in *The Hawk Is Dying* (1973), body building in *The Gypsy's Curse* (1974) and *Body* (1990)—to find meaning. Meaning, and love, usually fail, and the novels end in violence, disorder, and death. Yet they also include an element of grotesque and desperate comedy. Crews is an uneven writer, but his best novels—among them *A Feast of Snakes* (1976) and *Body*—are compelling portraits of modern man in desperate and ultimately unsuccessful search for meaning in an empty universe.

Ernest J. Gaines, whose first novel, *Catherine Carmier*, appeared in 1964, is among the most traditional southern novelists of the last thirty years. In novels set in his native rural Louisiana, he deals with the familiar southern themes of the role of history, sense of place, and love of the land. Taken together, his novels span the history of southern African Americans from the Civil War to civil rights and beyond. Certainly the history of slavery and discrimination is a heavy burden for his characters to bear, but they are not destroyed by that burden. In her more than one hundred years of life, Jane Pittman in *The Autobiography of Jane Pittman* (1971) manifests the enduring, sustaining capacity of the African American community. She embodies spiritual continuity and collective memory, while the men around her seek the advancement of African Americans and often die as a result. Gaines celebrates the capacity of African Americans to change in *A Gathering of Old Men* (1983), as a number of elderly men throw off the shackles of servitude and stand up for themselves. *A Lesson Before Dying* (1993) also reveals a capacity for change and growth in a young African American prisoner treated as subhuman by whites and in a schoolteacher who attempts to help him. Gaines's African American characters do not capitulate to the forces of history and prejudice. Their strength comes from their relationship to the land, paradoxically the site of their servitude, and their relationship with one another in a sustaining community.

Alice Walker is another African American writer who treats her native rural South in her novels, especially the early ones. From a particularly feminist perspective, she focuses on the relationship between men and women. Grange Copeland of her first novel, *The Third Life of Grange Copeland* (1970), is both victim of the racism and the brutal sharecropping life of the rural South and victimizer of women. Yet he finds the North more dehumanizing than the South and must return home to seek his salvation. In her most famous novel, *The Color Purple* (1982), Walker traces the growth of an impoverished and oppressed Celie through letters that she writes at first to God and later to her sister Nettie. Initially victimized by men, Celie gradually discovers, through her bold friend Shug, her personal potential and creativity. She finally lives a rich life in a community of women. Though she does not travel far geographically, she travels great distances personally. As in the works of Ernest Gaines, the rural South, while the locale of racism (and in Walker's case, sexism as well), is also the place where her characters can find fulfillment in a community. Her more recent novels, *The Temple of My Familiar* (1989) and *Possessing the Secret of Joy* (1992), range far more widely over time and space, primarily to Africa, but Walker's concern with the fate of women remains constant.

More recent writers, illustrating the continuing richness of southern fiction, deserve at least brief mention. Clyde Edgerton, in novels from *Raney* (1985) through *Where Trouble Sleeps* (1997), writes of family dynamics in small-town North Carolina in a generally humorous way. The relationship between past and present and rural and urban are frequent themes. Larry Brown and Lewis Nordan portray life in rural Mississippi while focusing on working-class characters. Brown's novels, *Dirty Work* (1989), *Joe* (1991), and *Father and Son* (1996), depict with uncompromising realism the brutal lives of characters who yet seek human connection. Nordan's characters also live materially deprived lives, but his works are infused with a magical sweetness that redeems their characters' lives. He treats the search for love in *Music of the Swamp* (1991), *The Sharpshooter Blues* (1995), and *Lightning Song* (1997). Still another novelist who writes of the lower classes is Dorothy Allison, whose *Bastard Out of Carolina* (1992) has in a few short years received a great deal of attention. Unrelentingly focused on the brutalization of women, especially the adolescent narrator Bone, in mill-town South Carolina, the novel also reveals the strength to be gained through a community of women. In her three novels located in urban Charleston—*Dreams of Sleep* (1984), *Rich in Love* (1987), and *Fireman's Fair* (1991)—Josephine Humphreys deals with middle- to upper-class characters, but her novels also focus on the search for love and connection within the family. In such novels as *The Brothers* (1993) and *Bob the Gambler* (1997), Frederick Barthelme has taken southern fiction in a different direction. Set on the Mississippi Gulf Coast, his novels explore characters seeking authenticity in a context of contemporary junk culture and rampant consumerism. Finally, the range of current southern fiction is revealed by two fine series of detective fiction published in the last decade. In five novels in her Ballad series, Sharyn McCrumb has captured the richness of Appalachian mountain culture even as its existence is threatened by modern development. James Lee Burke has published ten novels featuring Dave Robicheaux, in which he juxtaposes the corruption of modern life, usually associated with New Orleans, and the richness of rural Cajun culture.

While in general regional consciousness may be weakening in the South, it seems clear that many southern writers still possess the sense of place so vital to the fiction of the region. Recent writing shows great variety, bringing urban and suburban settings and women's issues to the fore. If the traditional southern consciousness of community is no longer so strong and a sense of alienation is therefore stronger, characters in recent novels still often seek their salvation in family. Although it is not yet clear who the major writers of the last decade or so are, it is clear that southern fiction continues to flourish.

Frank W. Shelton

See also Appalachian Literature; Blue-Collar Literature; Suburbs and Suburban Life.

George Core, ed., *Southern Fiction Today: Renascence and Beyond* (1969); Jeffrey J. Folks and James A. Perkins, eds., *Southern Writers at Century's End* (1997); Fred Hobson, *The Southern Writer in the Postmodern World* (1991); Frederick J. Hoffman, *The Art of Southern Fiction* (1967); Lewis A. Lawson, *Another Generation: Southern Fiction Since World War II* (1984); Walter Sullivan, *A Requiem for the Renascence: The State of Fiction in the Modern South* (1976); Thomas Daniel Young, *The Past in the Present: A Thematic Study of Modern Southern Fiction* (1981).

NULLIFICATION

The nullification controversy, which climaxed in 1832–1833, pitted South Carolinians against one another while their state government squared off against the federal government in a potentially explosive conflict involving states' rights, tariff policy, and, some historians argue, slavery.

The origins of the controversy lie in the severe economic problems experienced by South Carolina planters and farmers during the 1820s. A cotton boom following the War of 1812 led to overproduction and worn-out soil. Tight credit in the wake of the Panic of 1819 exacerbated Carolinians' woes, as did competition from planters who turned former Native American lands into fresh cotton fields from western Georgia to Louisiana.

As cotton prices fell and debts mounted, South Carolinians fixed blame on federal high-tariff policies pushed through Congress by a northeastern-western alliance hoping to encourage manufacturing in their states. Most southerners considered these policies unfair because they, as large importers of manufactured goods, bore a disproportionate share of the tariff's burdens without receiving comparable benefits. They also attacked higher tariffs on the grounds that the Constitution permitted duties only at relatively low levels so as to generate revenue; it said nothing about using tariffs to nurture manufacturing. Advocates of higher tariffs countered that Congress could protect domestic industry under the Constitution's "necessary and proper" clause (article I, section 8). Such broad constitutional construction, alarmed southerners declared, might lead to federal attempts to regulate, even abolish, slavery if Congress should also deem that course "necessary and proper." Against the backdrop of real and imagined slave revolts, as well as of northern attacks on slavery during the Missouri debates of 1819–1821, many southern politicians feared the worst.

Concerns about threats to slavery, combined with a depressed local economy, led South Carolinians to try to overturn higher tariffs. Since the state's representatives could not outvote the protectionist majority in Congress, by the late 1820s many became convinced that the answer lay in a more vigorous assertion of states' rights. Building upon the constitutional-compact theory enunciated by Thomas Jefferson and James Madison in the Virginia and Kentucky Resolutions (1798–1799), John C. Calhoun declared in the *South Carolina Exposition* (1828) that a state could nullify and refuse to enforce laws it considered unconstitutional. He argued that a state could accomplish nullification through a special convention of the people, similar to that which ratified the Federal Constitution. When Congress enacted the highly protectionist "Tariff of Abominations" in 1828, supporters of nullification agitated for a convention but failed to obtain the necessary two-thirds majority in the South Carolina legislature.

The tide turned in favor of nullification after the inauguration of Governor James Hamilton in 1830. Working tirelessly, Hamilton created a statewide political organization, the State's Rights and Free Trade Party (popularly known as the Nullifiers), to press for the realization of Calhoun's theory. Opponents reacted by creating the Union and State's Rights Party (the Unionists). Both groups condemned the tariff as unfair to the South but disagreed on a means of opposition. Unlike the Nullifiers, Unionists trusted ordinary political channels and especially placed faith in President Andrew Jackson as a tariff reformer.

Nullifiers and Unionists engaged in a war of printed words designed to sway South Carolina voters. Maria Pinckney's "Nullification Catechism," perhaps the only tract during the controversy penned by a woman, made the case for nullification through a series of questions and answers in a form familiar to churchgoers. Unionist Christopher G. Memminger also employed a religious motif in "The Book of Nullification," a biblical parody that lampooned Calhoun, Hamilton, and other Nullifiers. Nicholas Cruger responded to Memminger with "The Genuine Book of Nullification," which relied less on humor and more on legal argument. Many pamphlets like these appeared first in newspapers. Important Nullifier organs included the *Charleston Mercury,* the *Columbia Telescope,* and Columbia's *Southern Times and State Gazette,* where future senator James Henry Hammond cut his political teeth as editor. Among the key Unionist presses were the *Charleston Courier, Camden Journal,* and *Greenville Mountaineer.* Benjamin F. Perry, a consistent Unionist through the 1860 secession crisis, and William Lowndes Yancey, later a major Alabama fire-eater, both edited the *Mountaineer.* Novelist William

Gilmore Simms briefly edited Charleston's *City Gazette and Commercial Daily Advertiser,* a less-influential Unionist journal.

The Unionist-Nullifier verbal conflict nearly turned violent in late 1832 and early 1833. That autumn, the Nullifiers carried the legislative election and garnered enough seats to call their convention. On November 24, the convention issued the Ordinance of Nullification, which pronounced the tariff dead in the Palmetto State and threatened secession should the federal government try to enforce the offensive law. State officials braced for an anticipated naval and land assault by federal forces, and Unionists mustered their own troops to oppose the state militia. Based on reports he received from Charleston Unionist Joel Roberts Poinsett, President Jackson expected that winter "to hear that a civil war of extermination" had begun in his native state.

The bloodshed that Jackson feared never materialized. Alarmed by the crisis, Senator Henry Clay of Kentucky worked with Calhoun to fashion a compromise tariff, which the president signed into law in March 1833. In addition, Jackson requested and received from Congress the Force Act, which authorized him to use military power to enforce the tariff. South Carolina responded to the new tariff by repealing the Ordinance of Nullification, but also made a point of nullifying the Force Act. The Jackson Administration pragmatically ignored that second act of nullification, and the crisis abated. The bitter division between South Carolina's Nullifiers and Unionists, however, persisted several more years.

Robert Tinkler

See also States' Rights.

Richard E. Ellis, *The Union at Risk: Jacksonian Democracy, States' Rights and the Nullification Crisis* (1987); William W. Freehling, *Prelude to Civil War: The Nullification Controversy in South Carolina, 1816–1836* (1965).

O'CONNOR, FLANNERY

Mention modern southern fiction and the name of
Flannery O'Connor (1925–1964) soon surfaces. Just as
definite, begin a discussion of the art of fiction, and
there is her name. Through her two short-story collections, two novels, and posthumously edited collections
of letters and essays, O'Connor, born in Savannah and
longtime resident of her mother's farm near Milledgeville, Georgia, has secured a seat in the pantheon of not
only southern but also American arts and letters.

O'Connor's importance surpasses her individual
artistry. The techniques and themes of *Wise Blood*
(1952) and often anthologized stories such as "A Good
Man Is Hard to Find" and "Good Country People"
have become a model or point of departure for many
other writers of her own time and later. Many writers
openly attest to her importance to them, while for others the lines of influence are more subtle. Although her
impact can be found in writers from all regions, probably the most significant number of contemporary writers who have followed her literary footsteps are those
from the American South. For southern writers,
O'Connor has cast a long shadow primarily in three
areas: her use of the grotesque, often known as "southern gothic," connected to applications of seemingly
gratuitous violence to make her moral points; her powerful religious thought, which makes some of her fiction readable as Christian allegory; and finally, her rich
comic sense, often portrayed through the dialogue of
regular "folks."

The grotesque as a technique, in O'Connor's repertoire, involves incongruous mixing of the humorous
and the horrible, the absurd and the tragic. The murder
of an ordinary, comically rendered family by "the Misfit" in "A Good Man Is Hard to Find" offers O'Connor's most famous statement of her theme: the Misfit
comments on the ridiculously self-centered but hor-

rifically murdered grandmother, "She would of been a
good woman . . . if it had been somebody there to
shoot her every minute of her life." The Misfit has become a model for writer Barry Hannah, whose narrator in *Geronimo Rex* (1972) sets the pattern of violence for Hannah's ensuing works: protagonist Harry
Monroe carries the aura of the legendary and murderous Indian leader Geronimo as he strives to become
"his own man." Cormac McCarthy's novels also contain heavy doses of violent, shocking maiming and
death, in novels ranging from his most southern work,
Suttree, to his more lyrical southwestern trilogy. John
Kennedy Toole's *A Confederacy of Dunces* (1980)
more directly than Hannah or McCarthy reflects
O'Connor's use of pure absurdity, and he also, unlike
Hannah or McCarthy, seems clearly interested, like
O'Connor, in using the gothic to shock characters into
awareness of their moral shortcomings.

Always, for O'Connor, violence and grotesque
shocks to one's sense of reality are employed to convince her characters of their spiritual dis-ease, their
need for grace, their mistaken faith in their security in
a material world. These demands are central to the
Catholic doctrine that consistently informed her fiction
writing. Walker Percy, a convert to Catholicism, has
often reflected or even parodied O'Connor to draw attention to spiritual necessities. In *The Last Gentleman*
(1966), the nun, Val, seems clearly a spokesperson for
O'Connor's views. Reynolds Price, Lee Smith, and
Doris Betts, all of whose works often turn to theological issues, have noted the importance of O'Connor in
this respect. However, whereas sin and sinners in their
works reflect O'Connor's religious preoccupation, they
are never quite as unyielding or exacting in their judgments as she was. Reynolds Price commented, in Susan
Ketchin's anthology *The Christ-Haunted Landscape:
Faith and Doubt in Southern Fiction* (1994), that
O'Connor seems to have even a "mean streak," or at

least to delight without pity in the suffering of her characters. Ketchin's book, with a title from one of O'Connor's interviews, emphasizes how many southern writers have confronted theology through reading and respecting O'Connor (Ketchin includes, in addition to those named above, Harry Crews, Randall Kenan, and Clyde Edgerton).

O'Connor's comedy often redeems her theological vision, and the delightful exposure of foibles and false pride through comically ironic juxtapositions gives her works as much laughter as gnashing of teeth. When Hazel Motes says, in the deeply allegorical novel *Wise Blood,* that no one with a good car needs to be justified, he epitomizes O'Connor's technique. Clyde Edgerton, whose comic character Mattie Rigsbee worries about her dirty dishes when she is stuck all afternoon in a broken rocker in *Walking Across Egypt,* reflects what Edgerton learned from O'Connor. Lee Smith's gossip in "Between the Lines," Larry Brown's healer in "A Roadside Resurrection," and almost everything that Toole's main character Ignatius Reilly says in *A Confederacy of Dunces* show how many southern writers are indebted to O'Connor's most brilliant gift, the use of a character's inimitable speech to fix, through humor, their moral as well as physical situations.

O'Connor's rather daring use of the South's race problems during the civil-rights period, in such stories as "Everything That Rises Must Converge," "The Artificial Nigger," and "Judgement Day," has caused some critical controversy. The writer who most openly discusses O'Connor's work and its problems from an African American perspective is Alice Walker, who grew up like O'Connor in Middle Georgia and writes tellingly of her ambivalence toward her famous neighbor in her essay "Beyond the Peacock: The Reconstruction of Flannery O'Connor" (in *In Search of Our Mothers' Gardens,* 1983). But the point is clear: Flannery O'Connor cannot be ignored. Her work demands attention.

Thomas Frazier

See also Advice on Writing Southern Fiction; Gothicism; Grotesque, The; Humor, 1900 to Present; Roman Catholics.

Robert Brinkmeyer, *The Art and Vision of Flannery O'Connor* (1989); Robert Coles, *Flannery O'Connor's South* (1980); Susan Ketchin, *The Christ-Haunted Landscape* (1994); Flannery O'Connor, *The Habit of Being* (1979), and *Mystery and Manners* (1969).

ODES TO THE CONFEDERATE DEAD

As an ancient and honorable genre, the ode in its various forms has traditionally appealed to southern poets. Before the Civil War, Richard Henry Wilde, William Gilmore Simms, Alexander B. Meek, John R. Thompson, Paul Hamilton Hayne, and Henry Timrod, among others, practiced it. During the war, Simms, Hayne, Margaret Junkin Preston, Abram J. Ryan, and John Banister Tabb composed varieties of it, and Timrod in particular employed the irregular ode in "Ethnogenesis" and "The Cotton Boll," the two long lyrics he published in 1861 to proclaim the purpose and status of the new nation. After the war, Timrod and others applied it to work in memory of the Confederate dead, Hayne to commemorate the South's past and present, and Sidney Lanier to memorialize the South's land and culture in the 1870s.

Odes to the Confederate dead focus on individual fallen soldiers or leaders or concentrate on the armies at large or on the Lost Cause itself. Simms's "Elegiac. R.Y., Jr.," James Ryder Randall's "John Pelham," John R. Thompson's "[Turner] Ashby," and Hayne's "Stonewall Jackson" are examples of elegies memorializing dead heroes who have fallen in battle. On the other hand, Timrod's "Ode (Sung on the Occasion of Decorating the Graves of the Confederate Dead)," Father Ryan's "The Conquered Banner," and Hayne's "Ode in Honor of the Bravery and Sacrifice of the Soldiers of the South" celebrate those who generally fought and died for the cause.

Simms's "Elegiac. R.Y., Jr." (1862) follows the pattern of the regular ode in its divisions into strophe, antistrophe, and epode and commemorates the death in battle of Richard Yeadon Jr., the son of Simms's lifelong friend, who fell at Chickahominy, Virginia, a month before the poem was printed. In contrast, Randall's "Pelham" (1862), Thompson's "Ashby" (1862), and Hayne's "Jackson" (1867) all celebrate the deaths of well-known Confederate military leaders whose departures significantly affected the future of southern success, and though the stress in each poem is on one man, his relevance and importance ultimately represent the whole nation—as, for example, in Hayne's ode, where Jackson possesses "that majestic virtue" given to few in any age and whose fall has led "all our hearts" to sink "with him . . . in[to] our hero's grave."

Odes were traditionally poems composed for public occasion and in the past had been sung or recited accordingly to celebrate political or military action.

Hayne's "Ode" (written at the end of the war but not published until 1867), though apparently not composed for a specific public occasion, follows the tradition otherwise and honors the "bravery and sacrifice" of Confederate soldiers from First Manassas when fate decreed the baptism of "a Nation" to the "last gleam of hope" when "upon the nation's broken heart / Her martyrs sleep."

Timrod's "Ode" corresponds to the ancient pattern of the genre more closely than Hayne's. He was officially invited to create it, and it was sung at Confederate memorial exercises in Magnolia Cemetery in Charleston in June 1866. It addresses in classical terms those "martyrs of a fallen cause" whose graves are yet to be marked by "marble columns" and whose sisters, in lieu of such "storied tombs," can only contribute their "tears, / And these memorial blooms." "Small tributes," the speaker admits, but knows that they will be received "proudly . . . today," and concludes:

> Stoop, angels hither from the Skies!
> There is no holier spot of ground,
> Than where defeated valor lies
> By mourning beauty crowned.

Timrod's ode was the ultimate contemporaneous poetic expression in behalf of those who died for the new nation, but it was not the last lyric to commemorate the Confederate dead. Sixty years later, Allen Tate's "Ode to the Confederate Dead" appeared, was revised on several occasions in the 1930s, and subsequently became the best-known poem on the topic. Not written for public response or public performance, it follows, according to Tate, the old pattern of strophe, antistrophe, and epode in a general sense, but the ode ironically is actually a "subjective meditation" on the past and its relation to the speaker's present, involves self-conscious private reflections, and celebrates only indirectly the past and those who died in it. The contrast between the modern speaker's effort to recapture the past through narcissistic introspection and the "active faith" of those Confederates who died for a cause without counting the cost is at the heart of the work. Consequently, the poem as genre is updated in a very modern way since a traditional public matter is paradoxically given a private, thought-provoking consideration characteristic of another time and world view.

Rayburn S. Moore

See also Confederacy, Literature of the.

Mary Price Coulling, *Margaret Junkin Preston* (1993); Paul Hamilton Hayne, *Poems, Complete Edition* (1882); James E. Kibler Jr., ed., *Selected Poems of William Gilmore Simms* (1990); Rayburn S. Moore, *Paul Hamilton Hayne* (1972); Edd W. Parks, *Henry Timrod* (1964); Edd W. Parks, ed., *Southern Poets* (1936); Edd W. and Aileen W. Parks, eds., *The Collected Poems of Henry Timrod* (1965); William Gilmore Simms, ed., *War Poetry of the South* (1867); Allen Tate, *The Man of Letters in the Modern World: Selected Essays 1928–1955* (1955), and *Poems* (1953).

OKLAHOMA, LITERATURE OF

Two 1990s events encapsulate the past, present, and future of literary activity in Oklahoma: the release, late in 1997, of Toni Morrison's novel *Paradise,* and the gathering, in July 1992, of more than three hundred Native American writers for the Returning the Gift Festival. *Paradise,* set in the fictive (but in many ways realistic) small town of Ruby, Oklahoma, both celebrates and critiques late-nineteenth- and early-twentieth-century African American migrations from the Deep South, pointing up the complex interplay of race, class, gender, and history in an Oklahoma that is simultaneously a frontier and a global village. Returning the Gift, held in Norman, Oklahoma, celebrated the power, diversity, and promise of contemporary Native American and Native Canadian writing while also reaffirming Oklahoma's continuing importance to Indian Country literature and culture.

The name *Oklahoma* derives from the Choctaw word *Ogala-homma,* or "the red people's land." And in many ways, Indian Territory is where the literature of Oklahoma, in all its cultural diversity, begins. Andrew Jackson's Indian Removal Act of 1830 was, in theory, designed to remove all tribes living east of the Mississippi to either Indian Territory or other reserved lands, but in practice, the act primarily dispatched southeastern Indians to what is now Oklahoma. The forced migrations of the "Five Civilized Tribes"—Cherokee, Creek, Choctaw, Chickasaw, and Seminole—to Indian Territory have had particularly strong literary and cultural reverberations. The first printing press in the Territory, for example, was set up by the Reverend Samuel A. Worcester near the small town of Mazie in 1835; its first product was probably *I stutsi in Naktsokv (The Child's Book),* written by an American missionary, the Reverend John Fleming, but published in the Muscogee Creek language. Shortly thereafter, other presses in the Territory printed Choctaw and Cherokee almanacs (partially in the native languages), collections of hymns, and the Cherokee alphabet.

But the most important venues for territorial literature (written and published before Oklahoma was granted statehood in 1907) were the Territory's many newspapers. In the years following Removal, several Indian newspapers were started in Indian Territory, including the *Cherokee Advocate* (Tahlequah, 1844–1853, 1870–1875, 1876–1906), the *Indian Chieftain* (Vinita, 1882–1902), and the *Osage Journal* (Pawhuska, 1897–1960). African American newspapers such as the *Langston City Herald* (1891–1898) flourished as well, especially during the boom years following the land run of 1889. Creek writer Alex Posey (1873–1908) published many of his poems in Indian Territory newspapers, then, in 1902, took up journalism as a career. From 1902 to 1904, Posey edited the Eufaula *Indian Journal*—the first daily newspaper, as Daniel F. Littlefield Jr. points out, published by an Indian—and printed therein the Fus Fixico letters. Written in dialect, these letters comment satirically on the politics of Indian-white relations in late-nineteenth- and early-twentieth-century Indian Territory. Posey was not the first Indian writer to use dialect, or the first Indian humorist to publish in territorial newspapers, but he has come to be the best known.

Other noteworthy American Indian writers with Oklahoma connections include John Rollin Ridge, Sophia Alice Callahan, Lynn Riggs, Todd Downing, John Milton Oskison, John Joseph Mathews, and Will Rogers. Ridge (1827–1867) was among the many Cherokees removed from the Southeast to Indian Territory on the Trail of Tears. In the wake of the Gold Rush, Ridge moved to California in 1849, where he wrote and published a widely circulated romance novel loosely grounded in California history, *The Life and Adventures of Joaquin Murieta, the Celebrated California Bandit* (1854), as well as numerous poems, essays, newspaper editorials, and articles. Callahan (1868–1894), a Creek teacher and writer, published one novel, *Wynema: A Child of the Forest* (1891), which is widely regarded as the first novel by an American Indian woman; *Wynema* combines elements of domestic romance and political commentary, advocating (for example) women's rights and suffrage.

Riggs (1899–1954), who had Cherokee ancestors, has been described as the most important Native American playwright to date; he also became, in 1928,

the first Oklahoman to win a Guggenheim Fellowship. Best known for *Green Grow the Lilacs* (Broadway production, 1931), the play on which the Rodgers and Hammerstein musical *Oklahoma!* (1943) is based, Riggs also wrote numerous other well-received plays, among them *The Cherokee Night* (1932), which details the turbulent history of the western branch of the Cherokee tribe.

Early-twentieth-century American Indian novelists with Oklahoma connections include Choctaw mystery writer Todd Downing (1902–1974), who wrote nine detective novels in the 1930s and 1940s, among them the Crime Club selections *The Cat Screams* (1934) and *Vultures in the Sky* (1935). Several of Downing's books combine American and American Indian characters with Mexican settings. In contrast, Cherokee author John Milton Oskison (1874–1947) published many short pieces in popular magazines and wrote romance-tinged "westerns," usually set in Oklahoma; his novels include *Wild Harvest* (1925), *Black Jack Davy* (1926), and *Brothers Three* (1935), and he also wrote biographies of Sam Houston (*A Texas Titan*, 1929) and Tecumseh (*Tecumseh and His Times*, 1938).

Perhaps the best known of these American Indian writers are the Osage Rhodes Scholar, novelist, and historian John Joseph Mathews (1894–1979) and the Cherokee raconteur, newspaper columnist, movie actor, and world celebrity Will Rogers (1879–1935). Rogers, who satirized national and world affairs without losing sight of his local Oklahoma Indian roots, published seven books before his death in an air crash in 1935. Mathews's *Wah'Kon-Tah: The Osage and the White Man's Road* (1932), an unromanticized historical study of cross-cultural relations, became the Book-of-the-Month Club's first university-press selection. His novel *Sundown* (1934), one of the first American Indian novels to describe the struggles faced by mixed-blood Indians, also fuses autobiographical elements with an account of the turbulent Oklahoma oil boom of the 1920s, a subject that Chickasaw writer Linda Hogan (1947–) returns to in her 1990 novel *Mean Spirit*. Other books by Mathews include *Talking to the Moon* (1945), an ecologically minded autobiography set, Walden-like, at his retreat eight miles away from the town of Pawhuska (the Osage County seat), and an ethnohistorical study, *The Osages* (1961). As Robert Warrior (Osage) argues, Mathews is one of the most significant contemporary American Indian thinkers and writers, particularly because of his critical insights into the possibilities and vexing problems of tribal intellectual sovereignty.

Euro-American writers in Oklahoma have, like their American Indian counterparts, been deeply influenced by the state's unique and at times turbulent diversity of landscapes and cultures. Many of these writers were travelers, and many of their writings detail journeys to and through Oklahoma rather than long-term settlements. As early as 1832, Washington Irving (1783–1859) perched on a hill along the Arkansas River, overlooking the present site of Tulsa, and pronounced the river's bend the perfect place to build a city. Irving, assuredly the first famous American writer to visit the Territory, published his observations in "A Tour on the Prairies" in *The Crayon Miscellany* (1835); he is still memorialized and celebrated today in Tulsa. But Euro-American writings from and about Oklahoma did not immediately flourish after Irving's remarks went into print; instead, Oklahoma writing developed gradually, in part because a remarkable number of writers associated with Oklahoma were not born there and did not spend their entire lives there. Indeed, many of these writers speak directly to a migratory restlessness in their work and are preoccupied with what one local poet called "Vagabondage in Open Spaces." Another Oklahoma poet, Muna Lee (1895–1965), maintained close ties with Puerto Rican and Cuban feminists, and Mark Turbyfill (1896–), a ballet dancer and poet, published "A Marriage with Space"—which took up nearly the entire May 1926 issue of *Poetry* magazine.

The existence, however brief, of an avant-garde Oklahoma literary monthly, *Space,* speaks to another manifestation of this restlessness: the deeply felt American urge to be modern (if not Modernist), cosmopolitan, even bohemian. *Space,* begun by University of Oklahoma English professor and poet B. A. Botkin (1901–1975), surfaced for barely one year (1934–1935), but it points to the developing interactions between Oklahoma writers and a larger literary-artistic "scene." In these years, Oklahoma writers both preserved and broke away from regional molds, often attempting to hold on to the local while reaching for something like the cosmopolitan. The University of Oklahoma Press, established as such in 1928, quickly gained a strong reputation and frequently sought to publish the work of Oklahoma writers, but during this time many of those writers began to publish their work outside of the state. Oklahoma playwrights looked to Broadway and Hollywood; Oklahoma poets set their

sights on New York, Chicago, and in some instances Europe. At the same time, American writers from far afield began to find Oklahoma usable and marketable. For example, Wisconsin writer Edna Ferber (1887–1968) published *Cimarron,* a popular 1930 novel (and 1931 Hollywood film) that provided American readers nationwide with a sense, however inauthentic, of pioneering days in Oklahoma.

Active and hard-working as Oklahoma poets, fiction writers, and playwrights were in the early decades of the twentieth century, though, the most influential work of "Oklahoma" literature was written by a Californian, John Steinbeck (1902–1968). To the dismay of some Oklahomans then and now, Steinbeck did not actually research *The Grapes of Wrath* (1939) by taking the Joads' route west from Sallisaw, Oklahoma, to California, although he did drive across the state on Route 66 (and interested readers can still retrace the Joads' journey through Oklahoma). Steinbeck's generalized portrait of Dust-Bowl Oklahoma and Oklahomans ("Okies") continues to be a source of both pride and ambivalence for state residents who recognize the "Oklahoman" strengths of the Joads but regret the "Okie" stereotypes that the novel makes possible. Even so, *The Grapes of Wrath* powerfully evokes class struggles during the Great Depression and continues to provide popular audiences with a vivid if patchwork sense of Oklahoma in the 1930s.

Several other twentieth-century writers have important Oklahoma connections. Two historians, Tulsa's John Hope Franklin (1915–) and lifelong Oklahoma resident Angie Debo (1890–1988), have each published many well-received, respected historical studies, Franklin often investigating southern African American history and Debo focusing much of her work on Oklahoma Indian tribes. Ralph Ellison (1914–1994) was born in Oklahoma City, where he lived until 1933, reading voraciously and developing his strong interest in music, including jazz. Poet John Berryman (1914–1972), born near McAlester, spent the first ten years of his life in Oklahoma; poet Melvin B. Tolson (1898–1966) taught at historically black Langston University from 1947 to 1965. Among the novelists with Oklahoma roots are S. E. Hinton (1950–), author of *The Outsiders* (1967) and *Rumble Fish* (1975) and one of the best-known and best-loved writers of fiction for young adults; C. J. Cherryh (1942–), a popular and prolific science-fiction writer; lawyer William Bernhardt (1960–), who writes best-selling courtroom thrillers; and Tulsan Jean Hager (1932–), who has written scores of novels, including two well-received series featuring Cherokee investigators Molly Bearpaw and Chief Mitch Bushyhead, respectively. And poet Lisa Lewis (1956–) has published two well-received volumes: *The Unbeliever* (1994) and National Poetry Series selection *Silent Treatment* (1998).

Impressive as this selective roster of Oklahoma writers is, the state still remains, in various significant ways, Indian Country, and members of the state's approximately forty Indian nations have made enormous contributions to contemporary American as well as Native American literature. N. Scott Momaday, who won the 1969 Pulitzer Prize for fiction for his novel *House Made of Dawn* (1968), was born in Lawton in 1934. Oklahoma remains powerfully significant to him, appearing importantly in *House Made of Dawn* (Tosamah's sermon, preached in a store-front Native American Church in Los Angeles, is richly aware of Oklahoma Kiowa culture) and in *The Way to Rainy Mountain* (1969), in which Momaday retraces and celebrates Kiowa migrations from the north and west to the Rainy Mountain area southwest of Oklahoma City.

But Momaday's writings, though powerful and important, should not be read apart from the works of the many other Oklahoma Indian writers whose influence—both literary and cultural—reaches across state lines as well as tribal and national borders. Among these writers are poets, novelists, short-story writers, playwrights, autobiographers, and critics such as Jim Barnes (Choctaw, 1933–), Betty Louise Bell (Cherokee, 1949–), D. L. Birchfield (Choctaw, 1948–), Robert Conley (UKB Cherokee, 1940–), Charlotte DeClue (Osage, 1946–), Hanay Geiogamah (Kiowa, 1945–), Diane Glancy (Cherokee, 1941–), Joy Harjo (Creek, 1951–), Lance Henson (Southern Cheyenne, 1944–), Geary Hobson (Cherokee-Quapaw/Chickasaw, 1941–), Linda Hogan (Chickasaw, 1947–), LeAnne Howe (Choctaw, 1951–), Wilma Mankiller (Cherokee, 1945–), Louis "Littlecoon" Oliver (Yuchi-Creek, 1904–), Louis Owens (Choctaw/Cherokee, 1948–), Carter Revard (Osage, 1931–), and Anna Lee Walters (Pawnee-Otoe/Missouria, 1946–). At the same time, a growing number of talented young Euro-American writers—Lewis, Mark Cox (1956–), Brian Evenson (1966–), and many more—continue to emerge and to establish national and international reputations. All in all, as the Returning the Gift Festival, Morrison's *Paradise*, and much else demonstrate, the literature of Oklahoma enters the twenty-first century strong in its many traditions and optimistic about its many futures.

Eric Gary Anderson

See also African American Literature, 1919 to Present; Jackson, Andrew; Local Color; Native American Literature; Trail of Tears.

Carolyn Thomas Foreman, *Oklahoma Imprints, 1835–1907* (1936); Geary Hobson, "The Literature of Indian Oklahoma: A Brief History," *World Literature Today* (Summer 1990); Daniel F. Littlefield and James W. Parins, *A Bibliography of Native American Writers, 1772–1924* (1981); Mary Hays Marable and Elaine Boylan, *A Handbook of Oklahoma Writers* (1939); Anne Hodges Morgan, "Oklahoma in Literature," in *Oklahoma: New Views of the 46th State*, ed. Anne Hodges Morgan and H. Wayne Mixon (1982); *World Literature Today* (Summer 1990), special issue on the Literature of Oklahoma.

OLD DOMINION

Accounts differ as to the origin of the term *Old Dominion*. It is generally thought to derive from the fact that Virginia was the oldest of England's dominions in the New World (Charles II referred to it as "our auntient Collonie"). In any case, "Old Dominion" has been in use from the late seventeenth century to the present.

Although universally understood as a metaphorical reference to Virginia, the term implies specific meanings and connotations that are not always recognized. One way of describing these meanings is to focus upon what is implied historically by the designation *Virginia*, as against *Old Dominion*. At its most basic level, "Virginia" suggests a broad land area extending from the Atlantic Ocean to the Appalachian Mountains and subsuming the Tidewater, Piedmont, Blue Ridge Mountains, and Shenandoah Valley. Equally basic is the implied inclusion of diverse ethnic backgrounds (e.g., English, Scots-Irish, French, African American, Native American) and class (aristocracy, middle class, yeomanry, slave). To the experienced observer, "Old Dominion" falls far short of such inclusiveness. It is a designation illuminated by the nimbus of the Tidewater region, its Anglo-Saxon settlers, and almost two centuries of colonialism during which these two forces exercised an all-but-unchallenged hegemony in defining the character of the oldest English satellite culture in America. It is doubtful, for instance, whether one would hear the term *Old Dominion* with any frequency, if at all, say in Roanoke (the largest city of western Virginia, which was not established till the nineteenth century) or in any other section of Virginia west of the Piedmont—unless it were used in reference to the connotations described above.

Therefore, given its limited and implied references to place, time, ethnicity, and class, "Old Dominion" has understandably become a marker for these elements. Often used by historians and the authors of historical romances, it is rarely employed in any but respectful, affectionate, and on occasion nostalgic terms. Marylander John Pendleton Kennedy (1795–1870) subtitled his popular romance *Swallow Barn* (1832) *A Sojourn in the Old Dominion*. His contemporary Virginian John Esten Cooke (1830–1886) gave his *The Virginia Comedians* (1854) the subtitle *Old Days in the Old Dominion*. Another contemporary Virginian, William Alexander Caruthers (1802–1846), used it in the titles of two of his romances—*The Cavaliers of Virginia; or, The Recluse of Jamestown: A Historical Romance of the Old Dominion* (1834) and *The Knights of the Golden Horse-shoe: A Traditionary Tale of the Cocked Hat Gentry in the Old Dominion* (1845). Thomas Nelson Page, an unabashed apologist for the "Old Dominion" and all that it implies, titled one of his social histories *The Old Dominion: Her Making and Her Manners* (1910). These examples convey a consistency—a rendering of a gallant age now past, an idealization of the local history, a celebration of the aristocratic plantation culture, and an emphasis on civility. Significantly, later twentieth-century historians, emphasizing a rapidly changing, contemporary Virginia, use the term *Old Dominion* as a point of contrast—e.g., Marshall Fishwick (1923–), *Virginia: A New Look at the Old Dominion* (1959); and Virginius Dabney (1901–1995), *Virginia: The New Dominion* (1971).

Welford Dunaway Taylor

See also Aristocracy; New South; Tidewater.

Ritchie Devon Watson Jr., *The Cavalier in Virginia Fiction* (1985).

OLD SOUTH

The term *Old South* typically refers to the period spanning the beginning of the nineteenth century to the beginning of the Civil War. In the latter half of the twenti-

eth century, it has also come to signify in a more general sense the conservative belief systems and social patterns of the traditional South. In current popular usage, both meanings may connote a host of positive mythic conceptions and images of the South's past, including the Lost Cause, Moonlight and Magnolias, the cavalier, the belle, and even the happy slave; conversely, they may convey associations with a benighted South of intolerance, racism, and violence.

The mythic image of the Old South came into being during the so-called "New South" period, when local-color writers Joel Chandler Harris, Thomas Nelson Page, and others found a national audience for their sentimentalized depictions of slave-master relationships. Capitalizing on the spirit of sectional reconciliation that swept the nation following the end of Reconstruction, these writers succeeded in recasting the antebellum South in a favorable light by stressing the nobility and benevolence of the southern aristocrat and the childlike dependence of the slave on his master.

In his collection of essays titled *The Old South* (1892), Thomas Nelson Page sought to soften resentment toward the South by reminding readers of Virginia's leadership in the American Revolution and conflating that struggle with the South's defense of states' rights. Asserting that slavery was "forced" on an unwilling South by a power-hungry British crown and avaricious New England slave traders, he describes the peculiar institution as a "curse" to all but the slaves and blames the Civil War on the religious fanaticism of New England abolitionists. For Page, the Old South was "a civilization so pure, so noble, that the world today holds nothing equal to it." Though such hyperbole did not differ markedly from the rhetoric of the proslavery apologia of the antebellum years, Page's message seems to have met with a better reception in the North than did those earlier, more polemical defenses of the South, made while slavery was still the mainstay of the South's economy.

The image of the South that Page and his contemporaries promoted in the last years of the nineteenth century proved remarkably popular in the first half of the twentieth century. It bears a strong resemblance to the Old South depicted in Thomas Dixon's *The Clansman* (1905) and its film adaptation, *The Birth of a Nation* (1915), to the agrarian South described in *I'll Take My Stand* (1930), and to the antebellum plantation South described in Margaret Mitchell's *Gone With the Wind* (1936). More recent literary and cinematic treatments of the antebellum South tend to present a more balanced, if not negative view of social relations in the antebellum years.

James H. Watkins

See also Agrarians; Cavalier; *I'll Take My Stand*; Lost Cause; New South.

Thomas Nelson Page, *The Old South* (1892); Bertram Wyatt-Brown, *Southern Honor: Ethics and Behavior in the Old South* (1982).

OLD SOUTHWEST

Historians use the term *Old Southwest* to describe the frontier region that was bounded by the Tennessee River to the north, the Gulf of Mexico to the south, the Mississippi River to the west, and the Ocmulgee River to the east. Literary critics, on the other hand, use *Old Southwest* more freely. In literary studies, *Old Southwest* refers to a region not necessarily on the frontier that usually includes some combination of Virginia, Kentucky, North Carolina, South Carolina, Tennessee, and Georgia, along with some of these states that did not join the Union until the nineteenth century: Alabama (1819), Mississippi (1817), Louisiana (1812), Arkansas (1836), and Texas (1845). *Old Southwest Humor* describes a genre of sometimes humorous short fiction that flourished in these states during the antebellum period.

At the close of the eighteenth century, the Old Southwest proper was dominated by four tribes of Native Americans: the Choctaws, the Chickasaws, the Creeks, and the Seminoles. These groups came under increasing pressure from white settlers during the Great Migration, which followed the War of 1812; census figures from 1810 and 1820 show that the population of modern-day Mississippi more than doubled during this decade and the population of modern-day Alabama increased more than sixteenfold. In 1817, the United States government established the "principle" of removing Native Americans to west of the Mississippi River. During the presidency of Andrew Jackson (1829–1837), their removal proceeded apace.

Geographically, the Old Southwest was dominated by swamps and pine barrens. The swamplands were suitable primarily for catching malaria, and the pine barrens were suitable mostly for grazing cattle. Therefore, the region's economy was based on herding, not planting. King Cotton did not begin its rise to power until the flush times after Eli Whitney had invented the cotton gin and until most Native Americans had crossed the Mississippi. Even in 1860, however, the southern cotton crop was worth only half as much as the livestock that grazed the region. Thus the antebellum South and even moreso the Old Southwest were populated by herders. Because they were herders, these settlers had a great deal of free time. While their cattle roamed, these men fought, drank, danced, gambled, hunted, and courted—all pastimes that were fodder for Old Southwest humorists.

Although the characters who populate Old Southwest humor are generally lower class and poorly educated, the genre's authors are the opposite. Although most were professional men, few were professional writers. Typically, Old Southwest humorists were amateurs who felt compelled to write by a frontier culture that seemed to be disappearing almost as quickly as it had appeared. These writers realized that if they did not record these scenes of American history, the history would be lost. Thus many Old Southwest humorists thought of themselves not as literary artists but as social historians. As such, these writers are the forerunners of the American literary realists of the later nineteenth century. Writers such as Augustus Baldwin Longstreet and Joseph Glover Baldwin championed a literary aesthetic that would later find advocates in Mark Twain and William Dean Howells.

Old Southwest humor has its roots in the region's oral literature, especially in the stories traded among lawyers as they rode their circuits. The first published examples of Old Southwest humor appeared in small local newspapers scattered throughout the South. In 1807, a Washington, Georgia, newspaper, the *Monitor*, published the genre's first important work: an untitled description of a militia muster. This sketch, which is commonly known today as "The Militia Company Drill," was published under a pseudonym, as was the frequent practice of Old Southwest authors, many of whom did not want to be associated with a frivolous and perhaps even disreputable enterprise. The author of "The Militia Company Drill" was Oliver Hillhouse Prince, a young lawyer who had recently passed his bar exam. His sketch was an epistle in which "Timothy Crabshaw" wrote to "Fugey" of a militia muster that he had recently witnessed.

Such framework stories are the norm in Old Southwest literature, as genteel authors and narrators strive to keep a distance from their lower-class subjects. This tension between the cultivated and the common contributes to the genre's humor. In Prince's narrative, for example, Timothy Crabshaw's schoolbook English provides a contrast to the Georgia vernacular of Captain Clodpole and his men. It is important to note, however, that laughs are not always at the expense of the Old Southwest's uneducated citizenry. The relationship in Old Southwest humor between authors and narrators and their subjects is more complex. There is, to be sure, an air of condescension in much Old Southwest writing, and sometimes authors and narrators explicitly censure the language and behavior of their subjects. At the same time, however, Old Southwest authors and narrators find much to admire in their subjects, including their freedom, their honesty, their physical skills, their rapport with nature, their disdain for pretension, and the richness of their language.

This language, which has lost none of its vitality, may stand as the Old Southwest's most enduring contribution to American letters. Whereas the subject matter of Old Southwest sketches ranges from militia musters and camp meetings to supernatural tall tales, these sketches share a new sort of literary language: an earthy vernacular that freely uses off-color words and does not hesitate to describe scenes of sex, violence, and bodily function. Old Southwest humor pioneered a literary language rich in metaphors that match the raucous frontier life they describe.

The most important national vehicle for Old Southwest humor was William T. Porter's *Spirit of the Times* (1831–1856), a New York sporting journal. Augustus Baldwin Longstreet's *Georgia Scenes, Characters, Incidents, &c. in the First Half Century of the Republic* (1835) is generally recognized as the genre's first major work. Other important works include Johnson Jones Hooper's *Adventures of Captain Simon Suggs* (1845), Joseph Glover Baldwin's *The Flush Times of Alabama and Mississippi* (1853), and George Washington Harris's *Sut Lovingood: Yarns Spun by a "Nat'ral Born Durn'd Fool"* (1867). The genre's most famous single story is an early Mark Twain effort, "Jim Smiley and His Jumping Frog" (1865), which was later published in revised versions as "The Celebrated Jumping Frog of Calaveras County" and "The Notorious Jumping Frog of Calaveras County." Twentieth-century writers indebted to Old Southwest humor include William Faulkner, Erskine Caldwell, Robert Penn Warren, Flannery O'Connor, Eudora Welty, Barry Hannah, and Harry Crews.

Old Southwest literature is a field ripe for scholarship, as little serious work has been done on writers

other than George Washington Harris and Mark Twain. In addition, there are doubtless many forgotten authors and works worth recovering, including *Louisiana Swamp Doctor: The Life and Writings of Henry Clay Lewis* (1962; ed. John Q. Anderson), *Rowdy Tales from Early Alabama: The Humor of John Gorman Barr* (1981; ed. G. Ward Hubbs), *Old Southwest Humor from the "St. Louis Reveille," 1844–1850* (1990; ed. Fritz Oehlschlaeger), and *Ham Jones, Ante-Bellum Southern Humorist: An Anthology* (1990; ed. Willene Hendrick and George Hendrick).

David Rachels

See also Boone, Daniel; Crockett, Davy; Dialect Literature; Frame Narrative; Humor, Beginnings to 1900; Indians; Jackson, Andrew; Local Color; Oral History; Realism; Short Story, Beginnings to 1900; Short-Story Cycles; Storytelling; Tall Tale; Travel Literature; Trickster; Twain, Mark.

Thomas D. Clark and John D. W. Guice, *Frontiers in Conflict: The Old Southwest, 1795–1830* (1989; reprinted as *The Old Southwest, 1795–1830: Frontiers in Conflict*); Hennig Cohen and William B. Dillingham, eds., *Humor of the Old Southwest* (3rd edition, 1994); Nancy Snell Griffith, *Humor of the Old Southwest: An Annotated Bibliography of Primary and Secondary Sources* (1989).

ORAL HISTORY

Oral history is the process of interviewing individuals in order to learn about the past. The term also refers to the products that result from interviews—hand-written notes, tape recordings, transcripts, tape logs, and field notes—that can then be preserved for future use. Oral historians often think about their craft as a collaboration between interviewer and interviewee. Each participant brings his or her own motivations and interests to the interview, and each benefits from the experience in different ways.

Through interviews, oral historians can address topics and perspectives that are unreachable through other sources. Although written records often document the stories of institutions and public figures, the lives of everyday people can become lost to history, particularly in the late twentieth century when diaries and letters have been replaced by e-mail and the telephone. North Carolina mill worker Nell Sigmon said, "You don't have to be famous for your life to be history." Her comment, drawn from a 1979 interview for the Southern Oral History Program at the University of

North Carolina at Chapel Hill, highlights a central reason for conducting oral history interviews—to document the experiences of those whose voices, too often, remain unheard.

Oral history can also allow scholars to include new, more personal perspectives on individuals and events, whether or not the storytellers appear in the public record. Interviews can reveal the individual histories, motivations, and interpretations of historical actors more deeply than many public documents and can allow the historian to ask his or her own questions about the past. Tape recordings reveal the ways in which memories are constructed and create a vital record of the language, narrative structures, and speech patterns used by historical actors.

Oral-history interviews also allow interviewees to participate actively in the historical accounts of their own lives. By telling their life stories, interviewees are able to suggest themes, explore meanings, and create structure for themselves, contributing to the historical record directly. Unlike memoirs or autobiographies, oral-history interviews are spontaneous, allowing interviewees to think aloud about their experiences and preserving the process of unearthing meaning through speech for future generations.

The South has long been known as a region of storytellers, and so it should be no surprise that oral history has proven a critical method for historical inquiry in the South. The Works Progress Administration recorded numerous interviews with southerners during the Great Depression, perhaps most notably with former African American slaves. Since 1974, the Southern Oral History Program has carried on that tradition at the University of North Carolina at Chapel Hill, documenting the twentieth-century history of the region with over two thousand interviews. Similar programs have been founded at Georgia State University, Louisiana State University, and other southern institutions, and the number of community-based oral-history projects in the region is constantly increasing. The Southern Oral History Organization, founded in 1974, supports the work of these many regional programs by providing a forum for oral historians to share their work and exchange ideas.

Oral history, an interesting literary genre unto itself, can serve as a vital source for creative writers. Collected interviews that preserve memories of times past can provide important content information for authors, explaining the way things were done in past eras and recreating skills that are no longer practiced and events long forgotten. Interviews can also provide writers with a sense of particular times and places by offering a glimpse of day-to-day life, whether in small towns during the Great Depression or urban neighborhoods during the Civil Rights Movement. Perhaps most critically, oral history provides writers with examples of dialogue, enabling authors to understand the way people of a particular time and place speak, tell stories, interact with others, and use humor, metaphor, and fable to convey their meanings.

Lee Smith's *Oral History: A Novel* (1983), provides an important example of the marriage between the oral historian's craft and the fiction writer's art. *Oral History* details the experiences of a young woman conducting a college oral-history project. Smith's contact with oral sources and methods, like the *Foxfire* books and folklore studies, enrich the novel greatly. Her work is but one example of the ways in which oral history can influence and inform southern literature.

Kathryn Walbert

Jacquelyn Dowd Hall, et al., *Like a Family: The Making of a Southern Cotton Mill World* (1987); Paul Thompson, *The Voice of the Past: Oral History* (1988).

ORATORY

As a scholarly study, "southern oratory" is the product of the work of two men. Dallas Dickey began the study with his Ph.D. dissertation at Louisiana State University and pursued the field through his own research and that of his graduate students at the University of Florida. Driven by his oft-expressed belief that rhetorical scholars had slighted southerners in their investigations of orators, Dickey led the Speech Association of America to authorize a volume devoted exclusively to southern speakers, with Dickey as editor. Following Dickey's untimely death, Waldo Braden, Boyd Professor of Speech Communication at Louisiana State University, assumed responsibility for completing the volume that Dickey had planned. Braden created a seminar on southern oratory at LSU, and through the theses and dissertations of his graduate students, as well as through his own prolific research and publication on the subject, he defined the subject as a field of academic inquiry.

Rejecting the traditional stereotype of the southern orator as bombastic and excessively florid, Braden instead defined a "southern orator" as someone born and pursuing his speaking career primarily in the South. He identified four periods of southern oratory, each of which has been characterized by an epithet. Those periods have been surveyed in four volumes, the first two of which Braden planned and edited. *Oratory in the Old South* explored the first period, which began around 1828 and extended to the onset of the Civil War. Setting the pattern to be pursued in the second volume as well, Braden chose to focus on what he considered to be the most significant form of oratory in the pre–Civil War period, and that was the debate over slavery and the relationship of the South to the Union. Borrowing a phrase from the essay by Professor Ralph Eubanks that opens the volume, Braden labeled this period "the rhetoric of desperation." The southerners who spoke on this subject fell into two basic groups. One, including the Nullifiers and the Fire Eaters, was willing to sacrifice the Union in order to preserve the South's right to pursue its own destiny. The other group, including the Anti-Nullifiers, the Southern Moderates, and the Unionists, wanted to preserve the Union at all costs. The essays in the volume analyze the speaking of these two groups.

A second volume, *Oratory in the New South*, explores the second period in southern oratory, which began in the 1870s and extended until the turn of the century. Braden labeled this period "the rhetoric of accommodation," a description that he coined in the essay that forms the introduction to the book. The principal form of oratory was ceremonial speaking, one of the few speaking occasions available to southerners, since most southern leaders were disfranchised under the terms of Reconstruction. The orators made use of ceremonial speaking to help their fellow southerners come to terms with the defeat that had followed the Civil War. The best-known representative was Henry Grady, who, beginning with his well-known "New South" speech before the New England Club in New York City, used speaking occasions in both the North and South to urge his audiences to accept defeat and turn their attention to the process of rebuilding the South. However, the volume also describes other individuals and movements that fostered reconciliation between North and South.

The Oratory of Southern Demagogues investigates the third period of southern oratory. Though planned and executed by two of his students, Cal Logue and Howard Dorgan, Braden labeled this period as focusing on "the rhetoric of exploitation." Beginning around the turn of the century and extending well into the twentieth century, "the rhetoric of exploitation" featured the oratory of the so-called "southern demagogues." The demagogues consisted of politically ambitious men who had been excluded from office by the Bourbon political machines that governed the South following Reconstruction. The advent of open primaries in the South made it possible for the demagogues to use public speaking as a means of generating the grass-roots support needed for them to win public office. Their oratory is characterized as a "rhetoric of exploitation" because many of the demagogues appealed to the racial fears and prejudices of southern audiences.

Logue and Dorgan also planned and executed a fourth volume entitled *A New Diversity in Southern Discourse*. This final period, contemporary southern oratory, is sometimes called "the rhetoric of optimism." Unlike the designations of the first three periods, the term "rhetoric of optimism" was not originally applied by Braden, but by John Saxon. In a 1975 article published in the *Southern Speech Communication Journal* and based on his study of the speaking of a group of young, progressive southern governors such as Jimmy Carter of Georgia and Dale Bumpers of Arkansas, Saxon labeled the rhetoric as reflecting "optimism" because it did not appeal to racial fears, but rather emphasized the gains being made in the South in areas such as economics and education. In the essay that he contributed to the volume, Braden examined the campaign speaking of southern gubernatorial candidates from 1970 to 1980 and concluded that Saxon's epithet was accurate. This fourth volume is significant in at least two respects. The first is the change from *oratory* to *discourse* in the title, reflecting the editors' belief that *oratory* may be misleading to contemporary readers, and also that *discourse* provided a breadth that allowed the inclusion of material that could not be accommodated by the more limited term *oratory*. Thus while the fourth volume contains a number of essays that examine the debate over segregation in the South following the "Black Monday" Supreme Court decision in 1954 ending segregation in the South's schools, there are also essays that examine such topics as women speakers in the South and the rhetoric of Jimmy Carter.

Braden did not intend to suggest that the oratory examined in these volumes (particularly the two that he edited) exhausts the subjects with which southern oratory dealt. It does reflect his belief that much of the speaking that he would characterize as "southern oratory" was generated, in one way or another, by the issue of race, and the oratory, especially in the first three volumes, was perhaps the most significant oratory in the region. As the published research of Braden's students and colleagues illustrates, there were other forms of public address that could equally be called "southern oratory," and some of these remain to be investigated.

Harold D. Mixon

See also Carter, Jimmy; Demagogue; New South.

Waldo W. Braden, ed., *Oratory in the Old South 1828–1860* (1970), and *Oratory in the New South* (1979); Cal Logue and Howard Dorgan, eds., *The Oratory of Southern Demagogues* (1981), and *A New Diversity in Contemporary Southern Rhetoric* (1987).

OUTDOOR DRAMA

Going to see a play outdoors on a summer evening has gained steadily in popularity since World War II. By the 1990s, even excluding traditional summer stock, well over one hundred outdoor theater companies performed before audiences totaling 2.5 to 3 million people every year. Although the largest concentration of plays is in the Southeast, outdoor theater is a continentwide phenomenon, with shows ranging from Alaska to Southern California, the Dakotas to Texas, and New Hampshire to Florida. Among the offerings is much Shakespeare, with the Oregon Shakespeare Festival in Ashland, Oregon, founded in 1935, the oldest and most prominent among the summer Shakespeare programs still running. Religious plays are another group, with *The Black Hills Passion Play* in Spearfish, South Dakota, and *The Great Passion Play* in Eureka Springs, Arkansas, representing the genre. Plays focusing on the past of the region where they are performed are the most numerous of the outdoor plays, and the plays usually associated with outdoor drama. These history plays are also the new dramatic form developed in the outdoor-drama movement.

The oldest of the history plays still running is *The Ramona Pageant,* which opened near Hemet, California, in 1923. Based on Helen Hunt Jackson's novel *Ramona* (1884), *The Ramona Pageant* is set in the 1850s and, through the love story of an Indian boy and a part-Indian girl, depicts the plight of the Mission Indi-

ans of Southern California, whose way of life is destroyed by encroaching Americans. The novel was dramatized by Garnet Holme, an English actor and director who had staged outdoor plays and pageants up and down California since the first years of the century. In the production, Holme successfully negotiated several of the challenges typical of outdoor plays at any time. One was finding a suitable site for an amphitheater (Ramona Bowl is a lovely canyon with fine natural acoustics at the foot of a mountain a few miles out of Hemet). Another was building a strong performance company with a cast that is large (two hundred or more) and mostly amateur. To maintain quality, Holme used experienced professionals in the few key roles, numerous aspiring actors, and local people to strengthen community ties, and this common-sense strategy has been the norm for many of the successful plays that have come along since.

Not directly a *history* play, however, *The Ramona Pageant* partakes only partially of the new dramatic form that came to be associated with outdoor historical drama. The play that pioneered the new form and caught the eye of the nation was *The Lost Colony*. Written by Paul Green in 1937 and first staged that summer on Roanoke Island, off the coast of North Carolina, *The Lost Colony* is interesting both historically and dramatically. The 350th anniversary of the earliest English attempt to colonize the New World, Sir Walter Raleigh's establishment of a short-lived colony on Roanoke Island in 1587, occurred in 1937. Community leaders around Roanoke Island who developed the idea of doing *something* to commemorate the anniversary were motivated by what has come to be the classic combination of interests in the outdoor drama movement: a wish to bolster the economy of the region with a successful attraction, deep pride in the regional past, and a desire to register its salient moments in the public mind. When they approached Paul Green in 1936 to write something suitable for the anniversary, they had in mind a historical pageant.

What Green wrote over the winter of 1936–1937 was a play rather than a pageant, but not the kind of play usual in the indoor theater of the day. Typically, historical pageants cover a large span of time (decades, centuries, and more), with events following one another as chronology, not dramatic necessity, dictates. They have no characters in a dramatic sense but only representatives of historical personages, and the personages carry forward no plot and embody little in the way of theme. *The Lost Colony,* by contrast, is a play, a well-formed dramatic work with points of interest appropriate to a drama. Its characters are suitably developed, and they carry forward a plot made coherent and significant by the theme of the play. At the same time, *The Lost Colony* is intended for performance before a large audience outdoors, so it differs from plays typical of the indoor theater with their tight focus on a few characters and their reliance mainly on dialogue and small gestures to carry the dramatic action. Structurally, *The Lost Colony* is episodic, with units of action clearly developed in each scene, and both script and performance make use of large gestures. The spoken word is important in the play, with dialogue ranging from the colloquial to the intensely poetic, but other presentational arts are prominent as well: songs and dances; special lighting effects; tableaulike staging at times; a narrator and other nonrepresentational features. In its structural elements, *The Lost Colony* is more like *The Threepenny Opera, Mother Courage,* and other Brecht plays than it is like the plays of Ibsen, Shaw, or O'Neill.

The Lost Colony, which celebrated its own sixtieth anniversary in 1997, was planned with the idea that it would run for one summer. The indispensable condition for the play's longevity is the moving experience it provides for audiences. It was also fortunate in the time of its origin—the era of the Great Depression when federal and state governments and other large institutions were busy with efforts to rejuvenate the people of the land as well as the economy. Men from the federally funded Civilian Conservation Corps ("CCC boys") cleared ground and built the Waterside Theater on the island at the approximate site of the original colony. The Federal Theater Project provided leading actors and much of the technical staff, and the U.S. Treasury Department issued a commemorative half-dollar featuring Raleigh and Eleanor Dare to be used in fund-raising. The University of North Carolina provided a director, many actors, and much costume and electrical equipment. The Carnegie Foundation contributed an organ. The Westminister Choir of Princeton, New Jersey, spent the summer as the choral group for the production. President Franklin Roosevelt attended a performance (Mrs. Roosevelt attended several). The *New York Times* sent its leading drama critic, Brooks Atkinson, who reviewed the play favorably, and CBS radio broadcast a performance nationwide. Its production virtually a national effort, *The Lost Colony* hardly went unnoticed.

Immediately, the play caught the attention of the Rockefeller Foundation, which during the 1920s had begun the historical reconstruction of Colonial Williamsburg, and the Foundation began negotiating with Green about a play for that site. World War II intervened, but in the summer of 1947, under the joint sponsorship of the Rockefeller Foundation and the College of William and Mary, Green's *The Common Glory* opened at an amphitheater adjoining the college campus and the reconstructed village. Like *The Lost Colony* in structure and techniques and set mainly in and around Williamsburg (with a few scenes in London and Philadelphia) from 1775 to 1781, the play tells the story of the creation of the United States. While the action moves from the Declaration of Independence to the victory at Yorktown, the focus is on Thomas Jefferson and the articulation of the core values of a democratic society for the common people. Opening in 1947, *The Common Glory* played nearly every summer until it closed in 1976.

With both *The Lost Colony* and *The Common Glory* up and running and drawing national attention, a snowball effect set in, and from the late 1940s onward for thirty years Green was up to his ears in requests from people to dramatize something from the history of *their* part of the country. For practical reasons, he had to be highly selective in the projects he accepted, but he never lost a commitment to the ideal of what he called the people's theater (a theater springing directly from the interests of the people of a community, depending directly on the involvement of those people for its continuance, and appealing to a broad spectrum of people, many of them not habitual playgoers.) By the time of his death in 1981, Green had staged seventeen outdoor historical plays in ten states and the District of Columbia, and several summers saw seven or eight of them running simultaneously. What sustained his interest were the opportunities to experiment artistically and make the theater a means of enlarging the present with the experience of the past.

Wilderness Road is a striking example of the latter interest. Written for Berea College in Kentucky in 1954–1955, in the wake of the Supreme Court ruling that separate school systems for blacks and whites were unconstitutional, the play deals with the struggle to found Berea College a century earlier, in the years leading up to the Civil War, as a school for blacks as well as whites. In the play, Green brings clearly into focus the commitment of the founders to the ideals of brotherhood and education. He subtitled the play *A Parable for Modern Times* and hoped it would encourage a renewal of those ideals during a time he knew would be filled with turmoil in the South. *Texas* is an equally striking example of the possibilities for artistic experimentation in the outdoor theater. The play tells the story of the settlement of its region, the Panhandle of Texas, but the chief interest of the project for Green was its setting in Palo Duro Canyon a few miles south of Amarillo. For the amphitheater, he selected a site on the floor of the canyon and oriented things so the audience looks across the stage over rising ground toward the wall of the canyon, which at that point is six hundred feet straight up. Such a setting allowed Green to create striking sound and light effects, to change perspective rapidly by shifting action from the stage to the near background or the lower levels of the wall or up to its rim, and to conduct multiple actions simultaneously on the different levels. *Texas* was a spectacular success at its opening in 1966, and it shows no sign of becoming anything else.

In 1963 the Institute of Outdoor Drama was established at the University of North Carolina at Chapel Hill. Green's experience had demonstrated the widespread interest in outdoor historical drama and also the need for guidance on the part of communities interested in launching a play. Over the years, the Institute has provided such guidance along with support services for established plays, has been instrumental in developing new playwrights for the outdoor theater, and has become a repository of information about outdoor drama and its history. What began with Green as a one-man operation in the 1930s had become a broadly based movement by the 1970s and 1980s, and the Institute played an essential role in the transformation. It continues as the central professional organization for the movement as a whole.

At least during the postwar era, the need for new and talented playwrights was the most acutely felt need in the field of outdoor drama. No matter the strength of community interest or the potential of historical material, without a script that transformed raw history into focused art, no project could succeed. Kermit Hunter was the first writer to follow in Green's steps. While still a graduate student at the University of North Carolina, Hunter wrote *Unto These Hills,* and the play opened in the summer of 1950 at Cherokee in the North Carolina mountains. *Unto These Hills* deals with the Cherokee Indian Nation and focuses on its interaction with white civilization, particularly in the tragic period of the 1830s. Prior to that time, the Cherokee, whose homeland lay in western North Carolina,

eastern Tennessee, and northwestern Georgia, had lived largely at peace with the growing American Republic and had even been of help when, for example, they assisted Andrew Jackson in his battles with Creek Indians in Alabama. Nevertheless, the worst instincts of the Americans came to the fore when gold was discovered on Cherokee land in 1828, and ten years later Jackson, now president, ordered the U.S. army to round up the Cherokee people and move them to Oklahoma Territory. The play ends with the self-sacrifice of a Cherokee man and his sons that makes it possible for a remnant of the Cherokee people to remain in the mountains unmolested by the army. From the remnant grew what is known today as the Eastern Band of Cherokee Indians, from whom came the inspiration for *Unto These Hills.* The play is among the most successful of the outdoor historical dramas.

Hunter wrote a number of other outdoor historical plays, two of which are still running: *Horn in the West,* which opened in Boone, North Carolina, in 1951, and *Honey in the Rock,* which opened in Beckley, West Virginia, in 1961. After the emergence of the Institute of Outdoor Drama with its ability to publicize opportunities and facilitate contacts, a growing number of writers have worked in the outdoor theater. Two of the most successful are Allan W. Eckert and Mark Sumner.

Eckert's *Tecumseh!* dramatizes the struggle for the American Midwest in the late eighteenth and early nineteenth centuries between the Shawnee Nation and the young American Republic. By the 1770s, the Shawnee dominated much of the Ohio Valley, and their charismatic leader, Tecumseh, was bent on developing a coalition of tribes to stand with the Shawnee in blocking the westward spread of the Americans. The play moves from 1784 and Tecumseh's first skirmish with the whites to 1813, when he seems just on the point of solidifying his confederation. In the latter year, before Tecumseh can marshal his forces, General William Henry Harrison provokes a battle at Tippecanoe Village, where the Shawnee are routed. *Tecumseh!* opened in 1973 near Chillicothe, Ohio, site of a major Shawnee stronghold, and features as its theme music a haunting Indian suite by the Native American composer Carl T. Fischer.

The appeal of outdoor historical plays begins with the natural fascination of local history, the heightened interest stimulated by the realization that significant events occurred at the spot where the audience stands. The best of the plays go on to provide a moving theatrical experience that enlarges one's sense of the national experience: its complicated diversity and what it cost in outright treachery, ambiguous motives and morals, sacrifice, desperation and courage, self-renouncing nobility, even outright heroism. Mark Sumner's plays exemplify these possibilities of the outdoor theater. In 1994 his *Pathway to Freedom* opened at Snow Camp, North Carolina, heart of the Quaker community in the South since the 1700s. Depicting the Quakers' principled opposition to slavery and the growing tension between them and their neighbors in central North Carolina in the years leading up to the Civil War, the play tells a story of the Underground Railroad and brings home both the costs and the rewards of that noble but desperate enterprise. In 1998 Sumner's *Black River Traders* opened at Farmington, New Mexico. Set in the early years of this century at the Black River Trading Post on the Navajo Reservation in the Four Corners region of the Southwest, the play tells the story of the British couple who ran the post and their Navajo and Anglo- and Mexican-American neighbors. As the play opens, these people from widely differing cultures are all in one way or another at the end of their rope and must learn the lessons of respect and cooperation to order to survive.

Laurence G. Avery

See also Indians; *Lost Colony, The*; Trail of Tears.

Laurence G. Avery, *A Southern Life: Letters of Paul Green, 1916–1981* (1994); Phil Brigandi, *Garnet Holme: California's Pageant Master* (1991); John Gassner, *Educational Theatre Journal* (October, December 1953) and *Theatre Arts* (July 1954); Michael Kammen, *A Season of Youth: The American Revolution and the Historical Imagination* (1978); George McCalmon and Christian Moe, *Creating Historical Drama* (1965); Samuel Selden, *Producing America's Outdoor Dramas* (1954).

OXFORD, MISSISSIPPI

Fictional Yoknapatawpha County from William Faulkner's imagination approximates Lafayette County, Mississippi, and Yoknapatawpha's county seat town, the fictional Jefferson, is based on Oxford, the Lafayette County seat and the location of the University of Mississippi and of Faulkner's home, Rowan Oak, where he lived from 1930 until his 1962 death. Faulkner (1897–1962) set most of his novels and short stories, including *The Sound and the Fury* (1929),

Light in August (1932), "The Bear" (1942), and the Snopes Trilogy of *The Hamlet* (1940), *The Town* (1957), and *The Mansion* (1959), in Yoknapatawpha, recreating artistically, socially, and mythically his home region. Often lauded as the twentieth century's greatest writer, Faulkner, winner of the 1950 Noble Prize for Literature, combined an extensive use of history with depictions of society and local personality, modernist strategies such as stream-of-consciousness, and unsurpassed skill at crafting language, imagery, and story.

The town founders named Oxford, Mississippi, after England's university town of Oxford in the successful cause of attracting the state university to it. Ironically, Oxford is now best known for Faulkner's having lived there, although he attended its university for less than a year.

At the beginning of the twenty-first century when many U.S. small towns, even university towns, are in severe decline, Oxford is thriving, largely because of Faulkner's contributions to tourism. William Faulkner is buried in the cemetery of St. Peter's Episcopal Church, and after his death and that of his wife, Estelle, Rowan Oak was purchased by the University of Mississippi and opened to the public. The house, located outside the city limits of the town, was named by Faulkner for a tree identified in Scottish legend both with warding off evil spirits and with providing protection and tranquility. Rowan Oak has been preserved exactly as Faulkner left it. Visitors can see the room in which he wrote, his typewriter and chair, and the plot outline of his novel *A Fable* (1954) handwritten around the walls. Scrubbed off the walls at Estelle Faulkner's behest when he first wrote the outline on them, Faulkner later wrote it back and covered it with shellac.

Oxford has been home to other significant writers before and after Faulkner. Stark Young (1881–1963) lived in Oxford as boy, student, and professor before settling in New York in 1921. In 1930 Young contributed the final essay to *I'll Take My Stand,* the Nashville Agrarians' manifesto. Unlike Faulkner, who wrote in pessimistic reaction to the prospect of retaining any pre–Civil War Old South values, Young in his novels— *The Three Fountains* (1924); *The Street of the Islands* (1930); *So Red the Rose* (1934)—sought to cull good points from the Old South, values such as an agricultural economy, honor, hospitality, and graciousness, and to enliven these qualities.

New South social consciousness of racial and gender justice, urbanization, and equitable economic development permeate late-twentieth-century literature out of Oxford, though raucous and irreverent behavior still appears.

Legal mystery writer John Grisham (1955–) has been a civic-minded, Little-League-baseball-sponsoring Oxford resident. His first novel, *A Time to Kill* (1989), addressed racial justice head-on. His wildly successful novels, written one-a-year after 1991, include *The Firm* (1991); *The Pelican Brief* (1992); *The Client* (1993); *The Runaway Jury* (1998); and *The Testament* (1999).

Willie Morris (1934–1999) of Oxford has produced *North Toward Home* (1967); *The Courting of Marcus Dupree* (1983), about the recruitment frenzy over a black public-high-school football player in desegregated Philadelphia, Mississippi; and *New York Days* (1993). Larry Brown (1951–) has published *Facing the Music* (1989) and *On Fire* (1993); and Barry Hannah (1942–) has published *Geronimo Rex* (1972), *Airships* (1978), and *Never Die* (1992). Along with Ellen Douglas (pen name for Josephine Ayres Haxton, 1921–), author of *Apostles of Light* (1973), *The Rock Cried Out* (1979), *A Lifetime Burning* (1982), and *Can't Quit You, Baby* (1988), Brown and Hannah have been writers-in-residence at the University of Mississippi. Dean Faulkner Wells (1936–), author of *The Ghosts of Rowan Oak* (1980), niece of William Faulkner, and her husband, Lawrence Wells (1941–), author of *Let the Band Play Dixie* (1987), live in Oxford.

The town square of Oxford, centered with its white courthouse and Confederate statue, is just as it appears in *The Sound and the Fury*. It has become a world as well as local literary gathering spot. Smitty's Restaurant just off the square has a guest book filled with literary signatures, but the literary centerpiece, both for local writers and world literati and their entourages, is Oxford Square's world-class bookstore, Square Books.

Gayle Graham Yates

See also Agrarians; Faulkner, William; Mississippi, Literature of; Mississippi, University of.

Malcolm Bradbury, "William Faulkner's New South," in *The Atlas of Literature*, ed. Malcolm Bradbury (1996); Cleanth Brooks, *William Faulkner: The Yoknapatawpha Country* (1963); Dean Faulkner Wells and Hunter Cole, eds., *Mississippi Heroes* (1980).

OZARK MOUNTAINS

The Ozark Mountains, a large, primarily rural geographical region, cover an area of more than 60,000 square miles overlapping into three states: eastern Oklahoma, northern Arkansas, and most of south-central Missouri. Among the oldest exposed geological formations on earth, the Ozark Mountains (together with the Ouachitas) are the only major highlands between the Rocky Mountains and the Appalachians. Although the elevation of the Ozark Mountains nowhere tops 2,500 feet, the region's terrain is rugged and was difficult to settle. One truism among lifelong residents of the Ozarks notes that "it ain't that the hills are so high, but that the valleys are so deep." The rocky hillsides, upland glades, thin soil, vast cave system, and plentiful, clear springs and rivers of the area's karst topography have fostered the development of an isolated ecological and cultural region unlike any other in the world.

The Ozark native has long been stereotyped as a conservative, suspicious, often uneducated, poor-white hillbilly, but in truth, the settlers of the region had to be strong and independent in order to survive in the rugged, often disadvantaged or depressed regions they lived in, as painter Thomas Hart Benton often depicted in his distinctive scenes filled with monumental figures inspired by his Ozark boyhood. Generally, Ozark descendants are fiercely loyal to place, church, and family, are often self-reliant, primarily regard themselves as southern (or separated from the midwesterners to the north), and are proud of their unique heritage.

After initial Spanish explorations, the French were the first Europeans to colonize sections of the eastern Ozarks near the Mississippi River (located then in Louisiana Territory). However, the region has long been a haven for westering travelers and refugees; one of the unique aspects of Ozark heritage is the region's diverse nineteenth-century settlement demographics. Cherokee, German, Swedish, and Irish immigrants, as well as Amish and Mennonites, created successful pocket colonies; one can still find thriving towns nestled throughout the hills that have tenaciously retained the cultural traditions of the original pioneers. The isolation of the region also created an ideal hiding place for a striking variety of exiles and vigilante militias: Quantrill's proslavery guerrilla raiders, southern sympathizers after the Civil War, the Bald Knobbers, and outlaw clans, notably the James and Younger gangs.

Despite the diverse origins of Ozark natives, perhaps the most dominant cultural group in the formation of the region's heritage came from immigrants from the Upland South. Primarily of Scots-Irish or English descent, these migrants from Tennessee, Kentucky, Virginia, and North Carolina infused Ozark traditions with a distinctive Appalachian influence. During the nineteenth century, the availability of land encouraged scores of Appalachian farmers (including Daniel Boone) to settle in the secluded hills and valleys of Missouri and Arkansas, which closely resembled the mountains of their former home. Many Ozark traditions have Appalachian roots: both regions share a primarily fundamentalist, evangelical Christian base, with strong kinship ties, and have developed bluegrass and folk music and cottage craft industries. Portions of the Ozarks today are still labeled as a "semiarrested frontier," a term that recognizes the Ozarkers' retention of traditional life-styles and suspicion of change, allowing some of the arts and beliefs of the past to persist. The establishment of private and federally operated cultural centers, such as Silver Dollar City (Branson, Missouri) and the Ozark Folk Center (Mountain View, Arkansas), has also been a factor in the preservation of the crafts, music, speech, and folkways of the region's past; as a result, the Ozarks have recently enjoyed a significant crafts revival movement.

The earliest literature about the Ozarks was primarily nonfiction prose or collections of oral tradition. Henry Rowe Schoolcraft wrote sentimental descriptions of the region in 1853, while the earliest multi-author collection of folklore was *A Reminiscent History of the Ozarks Region* (1894). In 1927, English adventurer Charles J. Finger wrote an immensely popular account of his mountain travels, *Ozark Fantasia*. Vance Randolph, the first president of the Arkansas Folklore Society and arguably the most influential collector of Ozark culture in the first half of this century, published *The Ozarks* (1931), *Ozark Mountain Folks* (1932), and *Ozark Folksongs* (1946–50; 1980), all still highly regarded by Ozark scholars.

The first important fiction to come out of the Ozark Mountains was Harold Bell Wright's *The Shepherd of the Hills* (1907), which has become the fourth most widely read book in publishing history. The sentimental tale of a gentle city preacher who travels to the hills to regain inner peace in the company of his backwoods neighbors also encouraged the first wave of tourism into the Missouri Ozarks. For decades, travelers have come to see "Old Matt's" humble cabin; at present, a major tourist attraction and outdoor theater sprawl across Wright's inspirational mountains. Other early novels of note include A. M. Haswell's *A Daughter of the Ozarks* (1920), Rose Wilder Lane's *Hillbilly* (1926), Murray Sheehan's *Half-Gods* (1927), and Charles Morrow Wilson's *Acres of Sky* (1930). A number of critics think that *The Woods Colt* (1933) by Thames Williamson is the most finely crafted and authentic novel of the Ozarks; others favor MacKinlay Kantor's tale of an old Missouri mountain man and his dog, *The Voice of Bugle Ann* (1935).

In recent years, the Ozark arts scene has prospered, and several writers of note have received national attention. Charles Portis's novel *True Grit* (1968), the story of a fourteen-year-old Arkansas girl searching for her father's murderer, has become a legend in its own right as the inspiration for one of John Wayne's final films. Arkansas author Donald Harington's vast novel *The Architecture of the Arkansas Ozarks* (1975) was highly praised for the history of its specific, regional characters who live in the fictional town of Stay More. Speer Morgan has written an intriguing fictional account of a legendary Missouri outlaw, *Belle Starr: A Novel* (1979), and Daniel Woodrell is best known for his recent series of Ozark crime novels, most notably *Give Us a Kiss* (1998) and *Tomato Red* (1998).

Until recently, poetry has been a neglected art form in the Ozarks, but several talented regional poets have created memorable verse, including Maya Angelou, Glen Ward Dresbach, John Gould Fletcher, Edsel Ford, Mary Elizabeth Mahnkey, Lily Peter, and Miller Williams. Similarly, there have been few regional dramatists of note, but Missourian Lanford Wilson has written several critically acclaimed plays set in Lebanon, his hometown, including *Fifth of July* (1978) and *Talley's Folly* (1979), for which he won the Pulitzer Prize.

Anne M. Turner

See also Appalachia; Appalachian Literature; Arkansas, Literature of; Bible Belt; Bluegrass Music; Evangelical Christianity; Folk Art; Folk Music; Folk Narrative; Fundamentalism; Highland Scots; Missouri, Literature of; Oral History; Poor White; Preaching; Regionalism; Scots-Irish.

Robert K. Gilmore, *Ozark Baptizings, Hangings, and Other Diversions* (1984); W. K. McNeil and William M. Clements, *An Arkansas Folklore Sourcebook* (1992); W. K. McNeil, *Ozark Country* (1995); Milton D. Rafferty, *The Ozarks: Land and Life* (1980); Vance Randolph (with Gordon McCann), *Ozark Folklore: An Annotated Bibliography*, vols. 1 and 2 (1972, 1987); Phyllis Rossiter, *A Living History of the Ozarks* (1992); Miller Williams, ed., *Ozark, Ozark: A Hillside Reader* (1981).

P

PASSING

Passing, or more explicitly, passing for white, refers to the clandestine or unacknowledged crossing of any boundary intended to distinguish and separate "black" people from "white" people. Since at least the mid-nineteenth century, passing for white has been one option for social, economic, and political advancement among African Americans whose skin color made them appear "white." Since the classification of whiteness in the South has often been flexible enough to include darker-complexioned people from countries such as Portugal, Spain, or India, some mixed-race African Americans have been able to pass simply by learning how to speak a foreign language and dress accordingly. Some African Americans have "gone over the line" permanently, never to return to their families, friends, or hometowns lest they risk discovery and exposure. For other African Americans, passing for white has been temporary and sporadic, to gain admission to racially segregated entertainment, for instance, or to obtain access to comfortable accommodations while traveling. Little evidence exists to confirm the degree to which passing for white has actually taken place. The historian Joel Williamson argues that the great age of passing in the United States began around 1880 and ended in the 1920s. During these decades, passing for white generated significant literary and sociological discussion and debate in the United States. By the middle of the twentieth century, estimates of the number of people who had successfully crossed the color line by passing ranged from ten thousand to one hundred thousand annually. Although few white Americans today would likely express much anxiety about mixed-race people infiltrating the "white" race, contemporary identity politics and a postmodern fascination with performance and boundary crossing ensure a lingering degree of interest in passing, especially when a promi-

nent person, such as the literary critic Anatole Broyard, is revealed, in this case by Henry Louis Gates Jr. in *Thirteen Ways of Looking at a Black Man* (1997), to have passed for white.

The novel of passing has been used by many prominent black and white American writers since the early nineteenth century to explore issues relating to racial identity, racial solidarity, and miscegenation. Fiction that deals with mixed-race characters often gravitates toward questions of passing as a way of commenting on the interstitial position of mixed-race people in a society stratified according to arbitrary and ambiguous notions of "black" and "white." Many American fiction writers, northern as well as southern, have constructed plots in which a mixed-race man or woman must decide whether to pass for white, usually to attain opportunity or love on the other side of the color line, or to reject such a strategy out of a sense of loyalty and responsibility to African Americans. Novels in which passing is considered and rejected, or attempted and regretted are by no means a rarity among African American writers. Mixed-race males who choose to pass for white do so for any number of social, political, or economic reasons. Mixed-race women most often pass for white because of their involvement in an interracial romance, which puts the passing mulatta in an acute moral and emotional dilemma—whether to conceal her racial heritage or risk rejection by her "white" beloved. Tormented by such conflicts, which lead inevitably to deceit, self-doubt, and guilt in most novels of passing, the mulatta or mulatto almost always fails to achieve his or her goals. Failure usually results in suffering and self-condemnation, from which acts of atonement often arise. In some novels, particularly but not exclusively those authored by whites, the passing mulatto or mulatta must atone for breaking taboo, for attempting to cross the forbidden color line. In other novels, the agony and pathos of the passing mulatto or mulatta render a judgment against the color line itself, for which white racism must ultimately atone. The frequency with which passing for white led in nineteenth-century American fiction not just to the mulatto's or mulatta's frustration but to real suffering, social ostracism, and even death, gave rise to a stereotype of turn-of-the-century American race fiction, the "tragic mulatto" or "tragic mulatta." The predictability of the motives, strategy, and ultimate fate of the tragic mulatto and tragic mulatta in many novels of passing has led to a disparagement of this subgenre by many critics of American race fiction. Nevertheless, several influential American writers, such as Richard Hildreth in *The Slave; or, Memoirs of Archy Moore* (1836), Harriet Beecher Stowe in *Uncle Tom's Cabin* (1852), William Dean Howells in *An Imperative Duty* (1892), Nella Larsen in *Passing* (1929), Sinclair Lewis in *Kingsblood Royal* (1947), and Charles Johnson in *Oxherding Tale* (1982) have portrayed passing for white unconventionally as well as sympathetically, while also giving it continued national visibility.

Nineteenth-century southern white writers who acknowledged the possibility of passing for white produced a diverse response to this phenomenon in their fiction. From the earliest southern novel to broach the subject of passing, Joseph Holt Ingraham's *The Quadroone* (1841), through Rebecca Harding Davis's little-known Civil War novel *Waiting for the Verdict* (1868), and on to George W. Cable's *Madame Delphine* (1881) and Mark Twain's *Pudd'nhead Wilson* (1894), passing for white became a useful way of interrogating the southern caste structure and probing many of its more obvious contradictions. Cable does not censure the title character of his 1881 novella for suppressing information about her daughter's African heritage so that she may marry into a white family. Mark Twain severely punishes the passing mulatto Valet de Chambre at the end of *Pudd'nhead Wilson* for his many deceptions and crimes but then asks the reader whether this character's accumulated wrongs are attributable to what his mother, herself a mulatta, calls "the nigger" in him or to the conditioning he received as a pampered, self-indulgent southern aristocrat. Nineteenth-century African American writers from the South seized on the theme of passing for white as a pretext for direct attacks on slavery and southern caste consciousness. The title character of William Wells Brown's *Clotel, or the President's Daughter* (1853) crosses racial and sexual lines in a futile but heroic attempt to rescue her daughter from slavery. In Charles W. Chesnutt's *The House*

Behind the Cedars (1900), the frustration of the novel's mixed-race heroine in her bid to conceal her past from a white suitor is counterbalanced by her brother's success in passing and his quiet sense of justification in having done so.

Among twentieth-century white southern writers who held traditional segregationist racial attitudes, the attitude toward passing for white was harshly critical. Mixed-race characters in Thomas Dixon's fiction, to cite an extreme example of the racist white southern imagination, are typically morally reprehensible, a threat to "the southern way of life." Dixon's *The Sins of the Fathers* (1912) features unscrupulous, conniving, sexually aggressive mulattas uniformly bent on the subversion and demoralization of white males. In the same year, however, the African American writer James Weldon Johnson helped turn southern writing about passing in a more complex and revealing direction with the publication of his anonymously authored *The Autobiography of an Ex-Coloured Man*. By allowing its protagonist to tell his own story in an ostensible autobiography, Johnson's novel endowed the passing mulatto with a psychological complexity and moral ambiguity he had never had before, which did not prevent Johnson from suggesting the moral failure of his "ex-colored" protagonist in the end. In the 1920s, the most thoughtful white southern writers followed Johnson rather than Dixon in portraying the passing mulatto or mulatta as the living legacy of the South's wrenching history of racial desire and racial violence, not as merely an emblem of pollution and proscription. From Charles Bon in *Absalom, Absalom!* (1936) to Joe Christmas in *Light in August* (1932), William Faulkner's monumental attempt to recreate southern history recognizes the claim of the mixed-race man on the white society that had alienated him and compelled him to return masked and vengeful. Yet in Faulkner's myth of the South, the passing mulatto represents ultimately a judgment, a burden, and a threat to the white South, to which he is both inextricably and hopelessly bound. The mulatta heroine who uneasily passes for white through much of Robert Penn Warren's *Band of Angels* (1955) represents another variant of the troubled, racially ambivalent mixed-race figure in much early- to mid-twentieth-century white southern fiction. In *Band of Angels*, Amantha Starr achieves a measure of self-understanding and reconciliation to her past before the novel ends. But in later southern fiction, such as Ernest J. Gaines's *The Autobiography of Miss Jane Pittman* (1971), passing for white rarely seems to offer a way out for the mulatto or mulatta, who must come to terms with his or her heritage through socially responsible action rather than merely seek to escape from it. In the late twentieth century, passing for white has not generated nearly the imaginative attention it garnered earlier in the century, although a few novels, such as John Gregory Brown's *Decorations in a Ruined Cemetery* (1994), deal with it at least tangentially.

William L. Andrews

See also Caste; Mulatto; Race, Idea of.

Judith Berzon, *Neither Black nor White: The Mulatto Character in American Fiction* (1978); Joel Williamson, *New People: Miscegenation and Mulattoes in the United States* (1980).

PAST, THE

Southern literature is contextualized by the constructed memory of the region's past. That memory is neither unfailingly supportive nor unquestioningly complimentary. As the past relates to southern literature, it constitutes a complex matrix: ever enlarging, relative to the perspective of remembrance, variously regional, communal, familial, or individual. It is never simply one or another of these aspects. And this complexity compounds with the recognition that the past in southern literature may be drawn from either the historical or the legendary record.

In *The Burden of Southern History* (1960), C. Vann Woodward articulates the uniqueness of the South's people when he distinguishes southerners from other citizens of the nation by their past and their historical consciousness of that past. For southerners, a sustained engagement with a shared national past has held less interest than their divergent regional past. The specific historical periods to which southern literature so frequently gravitates are the early national period that frames the plantation society and the period of the Civil War. In 1865, the distinctly regional characteristic of having lost the Civil War became the temporal marker against which all other time periods are situated: before or after the war. Although these historical moments are not the sole consideration of an always enlarging "past," these particular periods supercede interest in any other period or event.

Two modes of fiction, neither of which was a postwar innovation, facilitated the return to the plantation and the war: the plantation novel and the historical romance. In a postwar context, particularly in a period of ameliorative national healing, the plantation novel developed as a legend of the southern past that possessed order, elegance, aristocracy, and minimal labor as its defining characteristics and its tragic loss. The historical romance, long popular with American readers, offered a ready subgenre for retelling Civil War battles.

As it found its place in southern literature, the past filled artistic demands as plot, setting, symbol, and theme. In the final three decades of the nineteenth century, the regional fiction being crafted, both short stories and novels, reconstructed a pre–Civil War era that cherished the memory of a lost social order. This idealized notion of the Lost Cause became the standard against which the present and future would be tested. The consuming nature of the past in southern literature was such that the past must be confronted, whether that reckoning was embraced or rejected. Dominant southern voices retelling the southern story during this period were Mark Twain (Samuel Clemens), George Washington Cable, and Joel Chandler Harris. They were not voices in unison; further, they were joined by many others who variously praised and ridiculed southern history.

As David Holman contends in *A Certain Slant of Light* (1995), for the southern writer, the past has been "both heritage and trap." Thus, the connection of the past to twentieth-century southern literature remains strong. Allen Tate contends that the "backward glance" is the defining trait of modern southern writing. This observation should not be taken to mean, however, that the use of the past has been simply or merely to extend a legendary image from one century to the next. According to C. Hugh Holman in *The Immoderate Past* (1977), the southern imagination develops from the view that history is process and that the past is consequently important to present and future. Woodward points out that the characterizing feature of the past is its felt presence in the present. This concern differs from the alternate use of the past of the historical romance, which is more exclusively focused on a detailed rendering of a former time, place, and events. In the most challenging of southern texts, the interest in the past is in its interplay with the present: twentieth-century southerners against their history, including their failings, prejudices, and defeat. The *who* of remembering may construct an ameliorative recollection, a corrective recollection, or a contentious recollection. William Faulkner, Ellen Glasgow, Eudora Welty, Robert Penn Warren, Allen Tate, Walker Percy, Ralph Ellison, and John Barth represent a diverse sampling of the compelling writers who offer tough-minded examinations of the human spirit as inheritor and purveyor of memory.

Most studies of southern literature as past-turned relate to fiction, and certainly that has been the dominant mode of its expression. Southern poetry is not so deeply committed to the past. Nonetheless, the postwar poetry of Sidney Lanier reflects the influence of the recent past. Allen Tate's "Ode to the Confederate Dead" and Robert Penn Warren's *Brother to Dragons* bring the complexity of the southern past to modern poetry. Three contemporary North Carolina poets with roots in Appalachia—Robert Morgan, Kathryn Stripling Byer, and Jim Wayne Miller—call upon the deep, mysterious mountain past in many poems that see old legends as revitalizing. Likewise, southern dramatists also construct variants of the plantation legend and legacy to its inheritors in challenging plays such as those of Tennessee Williams and Lillian Hellman.

Just as the past is not the exclusive concern of one genre or one vision, so too is it not limited to the exclusive consideration of one racial voice. African American writers from the South or elsewhere also confront the southern past. They have not been slower to raise their voices; rather, they have been slower to be heard. It is especially the work of African American writers in the last half of the twentieth century that has completed and corrected remembrance. The works of Ernest J. Gaines, Alice Walker, and Toni Morrison demonstrate the means by which the African American telling of the southern past creates a dialogue with other, older manifestations that must then be reviewed and in some measure, great or small, reconfigured. Fred Hobson and Woodward suggest that contemporary southern African American writers are the most authentic inheritors of rigorous examination of the southern sense of the past in the present.

In the twentieth century, recovery and reconsideration of "past" texts such as slave narratives have also changed the nature of recollection. Their inclusion invokes a correction to what Toni Morrison describes in *Beloved* (1987) as the "Disremembered and unaccounted for."

In 1989 Allan Gurganus published *Oldest Living Confederate Widow Tells All*. His title notwithstanding, the experience of southern literature is such that its richness, its paradoxes, its human complexity—in short its past—cannot be told in one voice or one text.

The past in southern literature then is dialogic. The whole resides in no one text, but it remains a vibrant, choral telling. So writers revisit the southern past. The recent *Oxford Book of the American South* (1997) observes that unremitting memory of the past continues to define southern writing. Civil War settings continue to frame contemporary best-sellers; Charles Frazier's *Cold Mountain* (1997) is but one example. The past is presently with southern writers. In the words of C. Hugh Holman in *The Immoderate Past*, no other region of the nation possesses "so obsessive a concern with the past, particularly a concern shaped by serious philosophical attempts to understand its shape, its forces, and its nature."

Diane Brown Jones

See also Ancestor Worship; Civil War; Historical Romance; History, Idea of; Lost Cause; Plantation Fiction.

Fred Hobson, *The Southern Writer in the Postmodern World* (1991), and *Tell About the South* (1983); C. Hugh Holman, *The Immoderate Past* (1977); David Marion Holman, *A Certain Slant of Light* (1995); Jay B. Hubbell, *The South in American Literature, 1607–1900* (1954); Lucinda MacKethan, *The Dream of Arcady* (1980); Lewis P. Simpson, *The Fable of the Southern Writer* (1994), *The Man of Letters in New England and the South* (1973), and *Mind and the American Civil War* (1989); John L. Stewart, *The Burden of Time* (1965); Allen Tate, *Essays of Four Decades* (1968); C. Vann Woodward, *The Burden of Southern History* (3rd ed.; 1993).

PASTORAL

Southern Pastoral is a literary form not restricted to any particular period or genre of southern literature. It might be said that for a majority of southern writers, the South, from its beginnings as a distinct region, is the *locus amoenus,* the "pleasant place," which serves as the counter-locale in all pastoral. The impetus of the pastoral, beginning with the Virgilian version, is to offer not just the garden—the vision of happy, simple people in an idyllic natural setting—but to invoke an ominous premonition of "the machine in the garden," to use Leo Marx's image. The pastoral is a form of critique, in which the discontented eye of a dislocated person, someone who has moved on, looks back upon some idealized vision of a simpler place. The tension in pastoral literature lies in the viewer's comprehension of the inevitability of change and displacement. The garden always contains the seeds of its own annihilation, and thus pastoral is fatalistic as well as critical. In the South, as Lewis Simpson has noted, multiple ironies accrue when the South's peculiar pastoral dream is placed, as it must always be eventually, in the context of historical reality. The slave in the South's garden must compromise this version of Eden. Thus alongside the traditional pastoral urge to recover lost innocence in a natural Eden, in southern works of this mode there is the even more hopeless attempt to recast a system built on forced human bondage into the idyllic village of the shepherd. All pastoral, in the end, always confirms only the irony of loss, intentionally or unintentionally exposed by the writer looking back. For the region of the Lost Cause, then, the pastoral is a very useful, but also very complicated and ironic mode.

The ideal of the "Old" South—referring, as early as the eighteenth century, to some vision of an "earlier" South—is at the center of southern pastoral. Captain John Smith in his seventeenth-century histories, William Byrd in his 1728 *History of the Dividing Line,* and most important Thomas Jefferson in his late-eighteenth-century writings offer early versions of the South as natural paradise or agrarian haven from the corrupt "canaille" of European cities. Jefferson's Queries in *Notes on the State of Virginia* (1785) invent the American as yeoman, his version of the Virgilian shepherd. Yet Jefferson himself as slaveholder could not reconcile his pastoral idyll with the realities of slavery, and southern writers following him in the nineteenth century would be trapped into the impossible exercise of inserting the exigencies of a slaveholding society into Jefferson's definition of pastoral as agrarian regime.

In plantation novels of the antebellum period, such as John P. Kennedy's *Swallow Barn* (1832) and William Gilmore Simms's *Woodcraft* (1852), the plantation is the pastoral retreat, with slaves transformed from alien workers into child-dependents collaborating in family-defined as well as agrarian labors. One of the most successful plantation pastoral visions was crafted by a woman writer, Caroline Gilman, in *Recollections of a Southern Matron* (1838). Cornelia Wilton, as shepherdess, addresses with a woman's domestic eye the superiority of the plantation's simplicity. Gilman sends her to the corrupt city—in this case, high-society Charleston—to experience modernity in its crassly materialistic splendor. She returns home to marriage and life as a planter's dutiful wife, confirmed in her preference for what is presented as the simple place. Ironically, however, her paragon husband himself seldom stays in this place—he is, we are told, inevitably drawn

to commerce and to politics. Loneliness and loss of intimacy are the pastoral wife's portion, providing us with a glimpse of the foreboding future. Gilman extended the pastoral element of this novel by pairing it in 1850s reprints with another—*Recollections of a New England Bride and Housekeeper* (1834); through the contrasts of the paired works, she set the South as ideal agrarian land against the North as corrupted and antifamilial. Ironically, however, Gilman was forced by her strategy into denying the matriarchal values of home that she clearly wanted to defend. Her South could only exist as a plantation patriarchy.

Simms, Kennedy, and Gilman were in many ways responding to Harriet Beecher Stowe's attack on the slavery South as a society driven by capitalist motives in *Uncle Tom's Cabin* (1852). Certainly the antislavery literature of the North, and then the Civil War, provided the impetus for much southern pastoral. In the post-Reconstruction period, the staples of the mode were directed to a defense of the antebellum South as America's lost golden agrarian age. The slave or former slave becomes in this literary scheme the spokesperson for the sense of loss and the dissatisfaction with a diminished present. Thomas Nelson Page's Unc' Sam in *In Ole Virginia* (1887) and Uncle Remus in Joel Chandler Harris's many collections of his Brer Rabbit tales, beginning in 1880, were persuasive voices for white writers in a New South looking for ways to recover not so much the places of the past as the power of the past regime.

Mark Twain and Charles Chesnutt produced the nineteenth-century South's most complex and consciously ironic versions of pastoral in the 1880s and 1890s, in part in response to the plantation idylls of Page and Harris. Twain in all of his southern works, from "Old Times on the Mississippi" (1875; later incorporated into *Life on the Mississippi,* 1883) to *Tom Sawyer* (1876) and *Adventures of Huckleberry Finn* (1885) through *Connecticut Yankee in King Arthur's Court* (1889) and *Pudd'nhead Wilson* (1894), set supposedly idyllic environs (the river, Camelot, the village of Dawson's Landing) against more complex, "progressive" or modern counter-worlds, yet he consistently made the point that his rural southern analogues contained the seeds of their own destruction, often because of their inhumanity to those they deemed "other" than themselves. Charles Chesnutt, especially with Uncle Julius McAdoo in *The Conjure Woman* (1899), created a rebuke to the white southern pastoral. The northern white entrepreneur, John, moves south after the Civil War to seek restoration for his wife, Annie, in the quaint and simpler world of rural North Carolina, but Uncle Julius, while seemingly cast in the mold of black pastoral spokesman Uncle Remus, actually teaches John and Annie that the slave South had been anything but idyllic.

In the early twentieth century, Jean Toomer, an important figure of the Harlem Renaissance, wrote one of the era's most significant pastoral works in the cycle *Cane* (1923). This collection of poems and stories is divided regionally, Section One dealing with southern rural blacks who illustrate Toomer's sense of the "folk Negro," who was passing away, and Section Two set in urban northern centers, teeming with city life. The city scenes represent life in the urban present as plagued with aridity and repressiveness, so that the southern scenes become a kind of pastoral counterpoint, as well as a "swan song," as Toomer called it, for the simpler agrarian world that he commemorates. White writers of the South, in the 1920s, also used their region as a kind of counter-world to the rapidly changing industrialized and urbanized America of the post–World War I era. The Fugitive poets of Vanderbilt, exemplified by John Crowe Ransom and his poem "Antique Harvesters," called upon southerners to promote the ideals of an agrarian South. Ransom, Allen Tate, Robert Penn Warren, and Donald Davidson, all "Fugitives" in the 1920s, published with eight other southern writers the volume of essays *I'll Take My Stand* in 1930 in order to celebrate the South's agrarian traditions. Several southern women novelists also took up the agrarian strain in their fiction of the 1920s and 1930s, most notably Elizabeth Madox Roberts in *The Time of Man* (1926), Julia Peterkin in her Pulitzer Prize–winning *Scarlet Sister Mary* (1928) and other fiction detailing the lives of rural blacks in coastal South Carolina, and Caroline Gordon in historically flavored novels *Penhally* (1931) and *None Shall Look Back* (1937). William Faulkner participated in this period's exploration of the South as pastoral haven through the creation of the Snopes clan, who epitomized the intrusion of greed and corruption into the South's village world in the trilogy of novels that bears their name (*The Hamlet*, 1940; *The Town*, 1957; and *The Mansion*, 1959). His long story "The Bear," which became the centerpiece of his cycle of stories in *Go Down, Moses* (1942), is his most compelling pastoral work, providing the sense of the majesty of nature and the tragic but inevitable fall of man into the world of corruption and greed.

In 1941 James Agee and the photographer Walker Evans, with *Let Us Now Praise Famous Men,* their sprawling, poetic, photographic documentary of share-croppers' lives in Alabama, published what might be considered the epitaph of the pastoral mode in southern literature. The post–World War II era has seen the rise of the "Sunbelt South" and with it the successful media promotion of the "Southern Living" South as the epitome of the suburban good life available in large, progressive cities such as Atlanta, Charlotte, Greenville, and Richmond. Gone indeed are the days when the good life might in any meaningful way be measured by the yeoman, the plantation, the happy slave tiller of the soil, or the quiet village untouched by the noise of machines. The ironies of those seemingly simple images of some "old" South remain in the literature that found the pastoral mode an effective way to critique, commemorate, and say farewell to Dixie.

Lucinda H. MacKethan

See also Agrarians; Faulkner, William; Plantation Fiction; Sunbelt.

Jan Bakker, *Pastoral in Antebellum Southern Romance* (1989); Lucinda H. MacKethan, *The Dream of Arcady: Place and Time in Southern Literature* (1980); Leo Marx, *The Machine in the Garden* (1964); Lewis Simpson, *The Dispossessed Garden: Pastoral and History in Southern Literature* (1975).

PATRIARCHY

For understanding southern literature, the concept of patriarchy is particularly important. Though the origins of patriarchy have been much debated, for the purposes of studying southern literature patriarchy can be understood in terms of the seventeenth- and eighteenth-century debates about absolutism and individual rights. Those who defended various forms of inherited or traditional power and property frequently drew analogies between biblical patriarchs and their households or tribes, kings and their subjects, and fathers and their families. Antipatriarchal views tended to be based on arguments from natural rights or from social-contract theory, though, ironically, even this opposition to patriarchal arguments did not extend unambiguously to women and to slaves. Patriarchal justifications for colonization, for Tory positions in the American Revolution, for slavery and for the subordination of women were debated among southern writers, clergy, and political leaders; patriarchal views, particularly with respect to the father's role in the family, still find staunch adherents among many fundamentalist southern Christians.

In his *Advertisements for the Inexperienced Planters of New England, or Any Where* (1631), Captain John Smith articulated the patriarchal justification of early colonization; Smith's reflections on colonization were an early instance of the ideological constructs and the social reality that engaged many later southern writers. Smith's justification for colonization began with Adam and Eve and evoked in turn the patriarchs of old, Noah and his family, Abraham and his, and even the Goths, the Greeks, and the Romans, all of whom Smith said ruled as fathers, governing their people as their children and bringing them to civilization and humanity. Three generations later, William Byrd II, benefiting no doubt from his own father's labors, wrote the Earl of Orrery in much the same strain, lauding his own "Canaan" where, like one of "the patriarchs," he lived with his lady, his flocks and herds, his bondmen and bondwomen, independent of all but "Providence."

This patriarchal ideology generated both social formations and literary types. The patriarch, ideologically independent of all but providence, was interdependent with wife, children, slaves, and those other figures—traders, freedmen and -women, small farmers—who were crucial to social life if not to the literary imagination, especially in the Upper South and border states. One useful way of understanding southern literature is as an iteration of and a contest with these literary and social types. From the constructs of a patriarchal slave culture derive the types of the benevolent patriarch who lived by a code of honor, the poor but ambitious social climber, the lady on a pedestal, the happily faithful or the treacherous slave. Many southern writers reinforced these types, particularly in the 1850s and in the plantation literature of the Reconstruction period. Other southern writers, notably African American writers but white writers as well, questioned, resisted, or redefined these types.

Although it has its gentle ironies, John Pendleton Kennedy's *Swallow Barn* (1832) provides a fine example of an antebellum fiction built unselfconsciously on these patriarchal types. The patriarch Frank Meriwether surveys his domain, collects its milk and honey (and naps frequently); his wife is the hospitable southern lady, deferring to all her husband's opinions except those pertaining to household management, in which she reigns supreme. Her daughters, still more ladylike

because more youthful, play piano and ride appropriately gentle ponies; and Meriwether's slaves are well cared for, industrious, and happy, despite their inadequate clothing and shelter. This idyllic picture was, of course, countered in the antebellum period in complex ways. Though he was himself a slaveholder, Thomas Jefferson vigorously contested the notion of the patriarchal origins of government, a notion unproblematic to many who espoused patriarchal views or who simplistically defended either monarchy or slavery. Jefferson's profound ambivalence about the costs of slavery, both to the slave and to the slaveowner, led to his creation of the agrarian ideal of the yeoman farmer, who though he did not own slaves was himself something of a patriarch within the confines of his family. The contradictions within the Jeffersonian view remained potent even in the imagination of the twentieth-century Agrarians and more broadly in southern evocations of rural ideals in the modern period.

The notion of patriarchy was also contested by African Americans and in narratives by white women writing in the antebellum period. In spirituals, in ex-slave narratives, and in abolitionist poems by such writers as Frances Ellen Watkins Harper, a common strategy was to identify the enslaved, not with the bondmen and bondwomen of Abraham, but with the Israelites in captivity in Egypt. Thus the argument over slavery was conducted through biblical types, and the patriarch was shown to be far more cruel than benevolent. At the same time, southern white women, even in defending southern institutions, sometimes cast patriarchal claims in an ironic light; perhaps the finest example of a rather mordant view of patriarchy from within the elite came in Mary Chesnut's Civil War diaries.

In the years following the Civil War, an increasingly popular plantation literature created nostalgia for a lost form of patriarchy and glorified the cavalier figure, the epitome of this form being Thomas Nelson Page's *In Ole Virginia* (1887). Other writers, however, presented a more complex or critical picture, among them Charles Chesnutt in his ironic dialect tales of antebellum life in *The Conjure Woman* (1899) and his later stories and novels. In treating Creole materials, George Washington Cable and Kate Chopin combined the traditions of local color with a refusal to idealize the plantation system, and when Chopin published *The Awakening* in 1899 its attack on the principal prop of patriarchy, female chastity as an inviolate ideal, provoked a storm of criticism. Chopin's story ironized the cavalier romance and the transparent hypocrisy of a staunch Presbyterian patriarch, and it examined the gendered nuances of Creole culture to suggest that the upper-class southern woman inhabited a gilded cage. These works, like William Faulkner's novels in the next generation and Ellen Glasgow's *Virginia* (1913), suggested that patriarchal ideology is deeply dependent on ideals of female chastity and compromised both by what would have been regarded as miscegenation—often excused by attributing sexual insatiability to African American women—and by white women's potential promiscuity. While Glasgow's ironies dissected the consequences of patriarchal nostalgia for women, the ironies of John Crowe Ransom were more sympathetic to a patriarchal, if lost, ideal. In "Old Mansion" and "Antique Harvesters," among other poems, he celebrated the persistence of old patterns of life and ritual amidst modern disillusion. A less-sympathetic picture of patriarchal nostalgia emerged in Faulkner's novels, particularly in *Absalom, Absalom!* (1936) where the legacy of patriarchy and racism is shown to be violence and destruction.

In the twentieth century, southern women writers and African American men have contributed new voices to the examination of patriarchy. Arna Bontemps in "The Man Who Was Almost A Man" and other fiction, and still more powerfully Richard Wright in *Native Son* (1940) examined the conditions of manhood for African Americans in the twentieth century. Violence in their work is no nostalgic backdrop but a condition of life, and these conditions not only challenged any easy patriarchal norm within the African American community but identity and survival itself. While also depicting the violence implicit in white racism and patriarchy, Zora Neale Hurston, Alice Walker, and Ntozake Shange created communities of women as an ideal to counter the double discrimination, racist and sexist, faced by African American women; the endings of Walker's *The Color Purple* (1983) and Shange's *Sassafrass, Cypress and Indigo* (1982) reunite sisters who have overcome both racist violence and sexism within the African American community. Hurston's Bildungsroman *Their Eyes Were Watching God* (1937) ends as the heroine Janie overcomes patriarchal prohibitions to become herself an accomplished teller of her own story.

Among southern twentieth-century writers of the short story, the nuances of family, and thus the legacies of patriarchy, are clearly evident. One could argue that southern writers have been so accomplished in the form in part through their ability to capture the nu-

ances of power and psychology within families. Among many others, Katherine Anne Porter, Peter Taylor, Elizabeth Spencer, Doris Betts, and Reynolds Price published collections distinguished by their nuanced treatment of relations between the sexes and within families as old patriarchal notions became subject to increasingly trenchant critique.

Mary Ellis Gibson

See also Agrarians; Domesticity; Family; Plantation Fiction.

Catherine Clinton, *The Plantation Mistress* (1982); Drew Gilpin Faust, *The Ideology of Slavery* (1981); Elizabeth Fox-Genovese, *Within the Plantation Household: Black and White Women of the Old South* (1988); Minrose Gwin, *Black and White Women of the Old South* (1985); Elizabeth Jane Harrison, *Female Pastoral: Women Writers Re-Visioning the American South* (1991); Lucinda H. MacKethan, *Daughters of Time: Creating Woman's Voice in Southern Story* (1990); Peggy Prenshaw, ed., *Women Writers of the Contemporary South* (1984); Anne Firor Scott, *The Southern Lady: From Pedestal to Politics 1830–1930* (1970); Alice Walker, *In Search of Our Mothers' Gardens* (1983); Ritchie Devon Watson Jr., *Yeoman Versus Cavalier* (1993); Deborah Gray White, *Ar'n't I a Woman? Female Slaves in the Plantation South* (1985); Bertram Wyatt-Brown, *Southern Honor: Ethics and Behavior in the Old South* (1982).

PENTECOSTALS

Ever since the Southwestern humorists of the mid-nineteenth century, southern writers have been fascinated by Pentecostalism, by Protestant Christians seduced away from "civilized" worship to Spirit-led meetings, often outdoors in brush arbors or tents. Throughout most of the twentieth century, clear social and theological divisions have existed between mainstream Protestantism and Pentecostal sects, but during the eighteenth and nineteenth centuries, Protestantism as a whole underwent a "Great Awakening," a "Holiness" revival, during which signs of the Spirit were widely observed. At Cane Ridge, Kentucky, in 1801, more than twenty-five thousand Presbyterians, Methodists, and Baptists gathered for a week-long outdoor revival; Dennis Covington writes that many of those worshippers, anointed by the Holy Spirit, were observed to "shriek, bark, and jerk . . . [and to fall] to the ground as though struck dead." Reflecting the sentiment of mainstream America in the nineteenth century, Johnson Jones Hooper and Mark Twain wrote satirical portraits of such camp meetings. In *Some Adventures of Captain Simon Suggs, Late of the Tallapoosa Volunteers* (1845) and *Adventures of Huckleberry Finn* (1885), Hooper and Twain respectively depict Pentecostal fervor as simply backwoods barbarism. Hooper, in particular, portrays the revival preachers as con men and the congregations as gullible hypocrites whose demonstrations of anointment by the Spirit, like their financial contributions, are merely the pursuit of advancement within their social group. One is tempted by Hooper and Twain to regard all public displays of religion with cynicism; the Pentecostals simply serve as the easiest and most vivid target for their wit. Such satirical treatment of southern evangelicals reached its apex in the essays of H. L. Mencken during the 1920s and 1930s. Mencken heckled the South in general, and southern religion in particular, in his numerous essays focusing upon southern cultural benightedness, the Scopes Trial, and "Methodist and Baptist barbarism." Largely as a result of Mencken's attack, the Nashville Agrarians came to the defense of southern tradition, including southern fundamentalist religion. John Crowe Ransom's *God Without Thunder* (1930) attacks American religion's drift into abstraction and privileges the mythic wholeness of the Pentecostal's faith.

Of all the writers who have come to the defense of the southern Pentecostal tradition, perhaps the one to make the greatest lasting contribution was an orthodox Roman Catholic—Flannery O'Connor. Despite her Catholicism, O'Connor's emphasis on the violence of conversion and on the importance of a personal experience of grace—rather than good deeds or fulfillment of church sacraments—suggests a deep affinity with the southern Pentecostal. Her two characters who most fully embody the Pentecostal spirit are the young self-appointed prophets of her two novels: Hazel Motes in *Wise Blood* (1952) and the fourteen-year-old Francis Marion Tarwater in *The Violent Bear It Away* (1960). Each of these young men comes from a remotely rural home and travels to the city in an effort to renounce his calling to evangelize in the primitivist tradition. The city figures as the place of temptation, not simply in terms of easy access to carnal sins, but in the form of a progressive consumer society full of self-satisfied and superficial salesmen, con artists, sociologists, social workers, schoolteachers, lukewarm church people, and others who would deride the simplicity of the boy prophet's religious fervor. From O'Connor's perspective, the triumph of each protagonist lies in his utter rejection of modern society, his ability resolutely

to stare down the one choice that matters—whether to accept or refuse God's command to evangelize the masses. O'Connor affirms the image of the Pentecostal as outsider, as fanatic, as primitivist, as biblical literalist, as a zealot who recognizes social problems to be inconsequential compared with evangelism.

Like O'Connor's young prophets, the eponymous protagonist of Harry Crews's first novel, *The Gospel Singer* (1968), is an unwilling evangelist and a hayseed from a rural Georgia town called Enigma, pronounced "Enigmer" by each of its six hundred residents. Though Crews is ambivalent about orthodox religion, he shares O'Connor's comic-grotesque vision of a secularized world, as well as her criticism of consumerism and popular culture. The tragedy in *The Gospel Singer* involves the cultural self-abnegation on the part of the hayseeds in Enigma, who have been seduced by glittering TV images of the outside world and have been thereby convinced of their own benightedness. A student of Andrew Lytle and himself a neo-Agrarian, Crews represents the fragmentation of modern society with his protagonist who deliberately tries to separate the religious from the secular. The Gospel Singer wishes to make a living from his voice singing gospel music, but he adamantly denies his ability to heal the infirm and to save the spiritually dead. His reticence to embrace the spiritual nature of his profession results in his own moral degradation and manifests itself as a fear of participating in human suffering. Crews suggests that the gifts of the Spirit—healing, evangelizing, and glossolalia (the Gospel Singer's unearthly voice)—offer a remedy for the ills of a fragmented modern society, though it be a remedy from which the reader is himself excluded because of his own modern scientific and rationalist assumptions. Harry Crews has admitted that every one of his novels "in some way concerns itself with man's relationship to God." Notable among them, *A Feast of Snakes* (1976) takes for its subject Pentecostal snake handlers.

Larry Brown's "A Roadside Resurrection" (1991) adapts the comic grotesque of Crews's *The Gospel Singer* to magical realism. In Brown's story, the freaks are more believable, and the boy healer's powers seem as plainly real to himself as they do to his faithful followers. Like the Gospel Singer, Brown's boy healer struggles with his desire for sexual pleasure and his recoil from human suffering. The image of the preacher's long, powerful car, which figures prominently in both *Wise Blood* and *The Gospel Singer,* reappears in Brown's story. As in Crews's novel, in "A Roadside

Resurrection" the healer is overwhelmed by the unending demands of the needy and afflicted, and the car serves as an escape route from the suffering hordes who wait by the roadside for the long Cadillac and its promise of healing and redemption. In a world where spirituality has been debased by materialism and consumerism, the Cadillac becomes a symbol of divine power and grace. Brown reveals the ironic similarity between Pentecostalism and postmodernism by portraying a world where surfaces provide the only reality one might expect, spiritual or otherwise. Unlike the mainstream Protestants of the twentieth century, who have assigned ritualistic events only symbolic value and who have therefore placed the realm of spiritual reality beyond the knowable, material world, the believers in Brown's story are concerned not with representations but with tangible manifestations of the Holy Spirit.

Though the comic grotesque occasionally finds its way into the fiction of Lee Smith, its presence is much less pronounced than in the visions of Pentecostalism we find in O'Connor, Crews, and Brown. Smith's fiction favors explorations of the inner lives of realistic characters, and, while she obviously delights in the exoticism of snake handling or speaking in tongues, she consistently undercuts the freakishness of such acts in order to examine their personal and social implications. In "Tongues of Fire" (1990), a teenaged girl from a Methodist family of the upper middle class feels isolated from her socialite mother and sister. Bored with the stuffy Methodists, Karen searches for genuine spirituality by reaching out to a girl friend who lives in an unpainted farmhouse in the country and whose mother speaks in "tongues of fire." In Smith's story, glossolalia becomes a metaphor for the isolation and subjectivity each of us is born into, which are then so often exacerbated by barriers of class, race, and age. Her novel *Saving Grace* (1995) features a snake-handling preacher who, though he enters into local legend, remains fallibly human. In fact, one is struck by nothing so much as the earthiness of Smith's Pentecostals. The Appalachian primitivists in *Oral History* (1983) engage in a simple and emotionally direct worship that attracts the Episcopalian visitor from the Tidewater, Richard Burlage. Ultimately, though, Burlage's upper-class values and his tendency toward abstraction prevent him from fully participating in their worship—or from entering into a marital bond with the mountain girl, Dory. As with their fictional predecessors, Smith's Pentecostals often confuse religious and sexual passion, though her female characters tend to be less tortured by this confusion, less exacting about keeping the two separate. "News of the Spirit" (1997) ends with a deliberate blurring of erotic and religious revelation, one that gives the protagonist, Paula, a very clear vision of her upcoming marriage as the profound turning point in her life.

Romulus Linney's two-act play *Holy Ghosts* (1971) burlesques snake handlers in a good-natured fashion. Understanding a conflict between the sexes to be a major point of contention in such contemporary primitivist congregations, Linney introduces a homoerotic theme as a send-up of patriarchal rule. In the novel *Jesus Tales* (1980) and the one-act play *Why the Lord Come to Sand Mountain* (1985), Linney explores the faith of the hinterlands in the form of religious folktales. Linney's most powerful treatment of rural religion is arguably his two-act play *Heathen Valley* (1988), adapted from the novel of the same name (1962). *Heathen Valley* offers an insight into the roots of Pentecostalism—not so much the historical as the spiritual roots. It suggests how Pentecostalism represents an uneasy marriage of logocentric, platonic highchurch ideals with the impulse toward concrete experience found in rural superstitions.

Dennis Covington's memoir *Salvation on Sand Mountain: Snake Handling and Redemption in Southern Appalachia* (1995) offers much more than information on snake handlers; *Sand Mountain* may be the best available introduction to rural Pentecostalism in its fierier manifestations. *Sand Mountain* is New Journalism at its best; Covington dramatizes his own seduction to the Pentecostal experience of God, and the reader vicariously experiences the same seduction. What begins as an agnostic's curiosity becomes an obsession with his own spiritual roots and with the need to feel an immediate and overwhelming connection to God—and to other worshippers. On his way to handling serpents, Brother Dennis provides us with an overview of the various snake-handling congregations scattered throughout Southern Appalachia. These congregations constitute no formal denomination yet regularly intermarry and visit each other's services, often traveling hundreds of miles to do so. As with any group of worshippers, political disputes arise between and within snake-handling congregations. Snake handlers often differ on matters of theology, social decorum, the role of women, and perhaps most important the spiritual significance of being snakebitten. In addition to taking up serpents, the snake handlers are known to pursue other gifts of the Spirit, such as drinking strychnine, fire han-

dling, speaking in tongues, casting out demons, prophecy, angelic visitation, healing, and even raising the
dead. Covington's triumph lies in his ability to humanize such exotic worshippers, to make the reader feel
the same deep affinity that he feels for them as people
hungering for a connection to God and to each other.

George Hovis

See also Bible Belt; Evangelical Christianity; Fundamentalism;
Methodists; Preaching; Secularization; Sermons; Snake Handling; Televangelist.

Robert Mapes Anderson, *Vision of the Disinherited: The Making of American Pentecostalism* (1979); Ruth L. Brittin, "Harry
Crews and the Southern Protestant Church," in *A Grit's Triumph: Essays on the Works of Harry Crews,* ed. David K. Jeffrey (1983); Fred Hobson, *Serpent in Eden: H. L. Mencken and
the South* (1974); Susan Ketchin, *The Christ-Haunted Landscape: Faith and Doubt in Southern Fiction* (1994); John T. Ni-
chol, *Pentecostalism* (1966); Vinson Synan, *The Holiness-Pen-
tecostal Movement in the United States* (1971).

PERIODICALS, 1800 TO 1860

Publishing in the colonies and then in the United States
was always a northern—really a northeastern—
industry. Magazines and journals were also edited and
published in much greater numbers in the North than
in the South or West. In large part this was because of
larger readerships in the North, where there were also
cities fostering more industries of all kinds. It was also
the result of a more democratic polity supporting those
discourses that foster newspapers and magazines.

Nonetheless, newspapers and magazines were published from Maryland to South Carolina, such papers
as the *South Carolina Gazette* (1732–1775) in Charleston and a similar *Virginia Gazette* and *Maryland Gazette.* Maryland poses a challenge to this account, since
although it was a slave state—albeit one kept in the
Union during the Civil War—and very southern in
parts, its major city, Baltimore, was tied as much to the
economy of Philadelphia, New York, and Boston as to
the South. Some Baltimore journals, however, were as-
sertively southern in character.

There were between New England and South Carolina nearly a hundred magazines before 1800, including a dozen or so in the South. Most were ephemeral,
and their last traces have long since disappeared. One
early item, *The North Carolina Magazine, or The Universal Intelligencer* (1764–1765), called itself a maga-

zine but was clearly a newspaper. One of the first actual magazines below the Potomac was *The Traiteur*
(1795–1796), published in Charleston by Henry Johnson, who hoped to emulate such English periodicals as
The Spectator but who filled his pages with sentimental
essays and stories. The *South Carolina Weekly Museum* (1797–1798) in the same town was also a genteel
miscellany with some news coverage in addition to
verse and light essays.

In Baltimore, *The Weekly Museum* (1797) included
a bit more humor but lasted less than a year. The following year, the *General Magazine, and Impartial Review of Knowledge and Entertainment* (1798) lasted
but three issues. It included fiction, poetry, and short
essays on religion, war, marriage and domestic matters,
and moral issues but not politics. The *National Magazine* (1799–1800) in Richmond, published by James
Lyon, struck a new, more political note with its strong
anti-Federalist, anti-Hamilton, pro-Jefferson agenda;
but until the 1830s, politics played less of a role in
southern than in northern magazines.

In fact, until around 1830 southern journals were
short-lived, generally weak in content, and not widely
read. In the South, northern magazines, which did not
consider themselves "northern" until the South did,
outsold and were more widely read than southern magazines. Such attempts in the South at targeting a female
audience as the *Toilet* (1801, Charleston) and *The Em-
erald* (1810–1811, Baltimore) did not last long, and
even a rather well-written and well-produced ladies'
journal a few years later, *The National Magazine, or
Lady's Emporium* (1830–1831, Baltimore), Mary
Chase Barney's project, survived for only a few issues.
Also short-lived was the journal *Moonshine* (1807,
Baltimore), which carried more humor. *The Monthly
Register, Magazine, and Review of the United States*
(1805–1807) left Charleston for the North in 1806 but
still did not survive. The *American Gleaner and Virginia Magazine* (1807, Richmond) lasted but briefly, as
did *The Companion, and Weekly Miscellany,* later
called the *Observer* (1804–1807, Baltimore) and John
Herschell's *Monthly Magazine and Literary Journal*
(1812–1813, Winchester), a fairly ambitious effort that
could never get beyond almost total dependence on
borrowed English material. In Richmond, *The Virginia
Evangelical and Literary Magazine* (1818–1825, but in
1821 *Virginia* was dropped from the title) under John
Holt Rice had a seven-year run, gradually shifting its
contents toward the literary. Farther west in Lexington, Kentucky, *The Medley* (1803) and *Journal of*

Belles Lettres (1819–1820) fared poorly, and the *Western Review and Miscellaneous Magazine* (1819–1821) only slightly better. One journal, however, requiring special if brief notice is *The Portico: A Repository of Science and Literature* (1816–1818), set up by intellectuals of the Delphian Club in Baltimore. It was edited by Stephen Sampson and cofounder Tobias Watkins, and John Neal did much of the writing. It included reasonably good literary criticism, mostly on English writers such as Cowper and Byron, as well as travel, biographical, and science essays and some poetry, and it reflects the active intellectual life in Baltimore in that decade. A year after *The Portico* failed, printer Joseph Robinson helped young John Pendleton Kennedy and Peter Hoffman Cruse establish a satirical and humorous periodical, the *Red Book*. It survived for ten issues, the last in March 1821, by which time Kennedy had been elected to the Maryland House of Delegates.

To be sure, even most northern periodicals at this time failed, but one could point to many more antebellum long-term successes such as *The Knickerbocker, Graham's Magazine, Portfolio,* the *Democratic Review,* the *Saturday Press,* and of course the *North American Review.* The one significant early success below the Mason-Dixon Line again was in Baltimore. *Niles' Weekly Register,* a strongly anti-British magazine, covered politics, science, economic news, and western development, but not literary matters. It survived from 1811 until 1849 (from 1837 on as *Niles' National Register*), although with Hezekiah Niles's retirement in 1836 its quality began to fade.

Two other kinds of enduring exceptions found in the South were religious publications and farm journals. Some of the most successful religious periodicals were the *Southern Presbyterian Review* (1847–1885, Columbia and other towns), the *Methodist Review* (1847–1930, Nashville and Louisville), and *The Southern Presbyterian* (1847–1908). Farm journals had a practical importance that brought them a steady readership in an era before land-grant universities and agriculture programs. The *American Farmer,* started by John S. Skinner in Baltimore in 1819, lasted until 1897, except for a hiatus during the Civil War. Among numerous other farm magazines, notable were *The Southern Planter,* founded in Richmond by Charles Tyler Botts in 1841 and lasting until 1969, and *Southern Cultivator,* published in Georgia from 1843 to 1935.

With these exceptions, the first ambitious efforts at journals, and particularly literary journals, in the South came around 1828. One of the earliest editorial efforts of William Gilmore Simms in Charleston was the *Southern Literary Gazette* (1828–1829). A more substantial journal in that city was the *Southern Review,* established the same year by Charleston professionals including Senator Robert Y. Hayne, Governor James Hamilton, Judge William Harper, Professor (and university president) Thomas Cooper, and James L. Petigru. The first editor was Stephen Elliott, a Yale-educated legislator, banker, botanist, and man of letters who died in 1830. After a brief term under his son, the journal was edited by Hugh Swinton Legaré, who ended up having to write much of the copy in each issue. Cooper, an English-born man of radical religious notions but increasingly partisan states'-rights politics, contributed regularly on economics and science. In its four years, the *Review* was decidedly southern in its identity but always professed a cosmopolitan position on literary matters, and Legaré was able to praise Cooper and Bryant as well as Byron and Scott. Aside from slavery, on economic matters it often took liberal positions. In the end, however, it was the victim of its own pedantic tone and lack of funding, the bane of most southern journals, and it expired after sixteen issues when Legaré left the United States on a diplomatic appointment to Europe.

Within a few years, Daniel K. Whitaker, a transplanted northerner, started the *Southern Literary Journal* (1835–1838) in Charleston. It articulated a very strong sectional bias at a time when sectional conflict had intensified in Congress and in the press. It included essays on southern life, slavery, and moral issues as well as on literary matters including European poetry. Simms was a regular contributor. The year before, the *Southern Literary Messenger* (1834–1864) had commenced publication in Richmond under the direction of Thomas Willis White, who recruited James Heath as editor. It had the longest track record of any southern literary journal of the day, though hardly without great fluctuation in quality. Its birth was in part a patriotic Virginian effort to reestablish credibility for the cradle of the republic and in part a clarion call to arouse southern literary and intellectual life, to replace the South's literary "vassalage to our northern neighbors." James Fenimore Cooper and James Kirke Paulding both encouraged the new effort, but it suffered from a shortage of good writers and was rarely able to pay for such writers north or south. Heath espoused a strong moral perspective, actually including opposition to slavery, and disdain for what he saw as immoral literature, such as works of gothic romanticism but little aesthetic taste. Then in 1835 White, against his own predilections but to raise the *Messenger* above the dullness and sentimentality that was killing its support, hired Edgar Allan Poe as editor. Poe raised the quality of discourse noticeably with book reviews of insight and genius but occasionally of caustic criticism. An attack on *Norman Leslie*, a book by New York literary man Theodore Fay, upset White, who saw such criticism threatening northern subscriptions. Poe was just as tough on sentimental poet Lydia Sigourney until White asked him to apologize.

Actually, Poe's reviews were not generally negative, and he wrote dozens of them; nonetheless, he was fired late in 1836. Although the *Messenger* under White continued to publish good essays on travel, science, and society, its book-review section disappeared. White emphasized the southern, or Virginian, identity more but also curried the favor of northerners and was able to keep numerous northern readers for several years. When White died in 1843, the journal stumbled for a period under Benjamin Minor, who dropped the "northern" strategy, and in 1846 it merged for a short period with *Simms's Magazine*. In 1847, a young attorney, John Reuben Thompson, took over as editor, returned a literary emphasis, recruited good book reviewers, and while continuing promotion of southern writers such as a young Paul Hamilton Hayne also included work by Henry T. Tuckerman, Poe again, and Park Benjamin. Despite its improved quality, the *Messenger* still struggled financially, and in 1853 Thompson sold the journal, continuing however as editor. During the prewar decade, it took an increasingly sectional position, and its national standing and literary quality declined. But southerners in the 1850s often saw themselves as victims of sectional bias from most American magazines, with one 1854 article in the *Southern Quarterly Review*, "Northern Periodicals Against the South," for example, being a representative statement of this feeling. From 1860 to 1864, George W. Bagby, physician and humorist, edited the *Messenger*, and although in other times he might have succeeded, the Civil War effectively killed off his journal.

Simms during the prewar period edited and wrote for other journals, including the *Magnolia* (1840–1843), which began under Philip C. Pendleton as the *Southern Ladies Book* in Macon and arrived via Savannah in Charleston in 1842, when Pendleton persuaded Simms to serve as editor. During the year he edited the *Magnolia*, it included a strong review section,

creative work by Augustus B. Longstreet, A. B. Meek, and others, and pieces to attract more male readers than it had previously enjoyed. Generally pessimistic about the potential of any southern journal, however, after a year of devoted efforts in a nearly impossible financial and managerial situation, Simms left the *Magnolia*, and it folded in June 1843. By November 1844, however, he had agreed to edit a new magazine in Charleston to be called *Simms's Monthly Magazine: The Southern and Western Monthly Magazine and Review*. Once again, he established a well-organized journal with content as strong as was financially feasible in the South. His aim here was to reinforce the Young America movement, and Evert Duyckinck and other northerners tried to help him toward his goal. All this put Simms in conflict with the *Knickerbocker* and other more Whiggish journals, as well as with Lewis Gaylord Clark and other writers, and it put him in the middle of northern literary politics. For its brief life, the journal made a contribution to Young America, although Simms often had to write much of the copy himself. Again, there were few subscribers and finally little hope for more. By December 1845, after twelve issues, the journal had sold out to the *Messenger*.

During the early 1840s, another periodical was established in Georgia edited by William C. Richards, a young English immigrant and Colgate graduate, assisted by his brother Addison, an artist-illustrator. The *Orion* was to have high standards, to emphasize all the arts, to review important books, and to deal with serious issues including copyright laws. Much of its literature was sentimental, but it did include some clever Southwestern humor. It was not immune to the financial crises of southern journals, however, and after moving to Charleston, a more active intellectual center, in 1843, it failed in 1844 after twenty-four issues. From 1848 to 1852, Richards edited another journal called the *Southern Literary Gazette* (1848–1855), but he ended up as a preacher and science teacher in the North.

Of higher quality and longer lasting was the *Southern Quarterly Review*, published until 1847 by Daniel Whitaker. Established in January 1842 in New Orleans, it soon moved to Charleston and defined itself as a kind of heir to the defunct *Southern Review*, the closest thing to a British quarterly in the southern states. It was at first outspokenly partisan on slavery and trade issues but included travel essays, articles on science, economics, and the West, and long book reviews. Whitaker lost financial control of the *Review* by 1847 and gave up the editorship as well. In the spring of 1849, following a period in which newspaperman John Milton Clapp was editor, Simms agreed to try once more. He always had disdain for Whitaker as a man of little taste and few standards, but with James Burges in control of the *Review* he was willing again to work at establishing a successful southern literary magazine. He continued for six years, but the *Review* never reached financial health. As always, a southern journal, even with a fair subscription list, could not successfully collect its fees from a clientele scattered across a largely rural region. After problems with a series of owners, Simms left the *Review* in 1855, but by then it had left Charleston and was moving between Columbia and Baltimore before expiring in 1857.

The same year, one final ambitious prewar literary journal, *Russell's Magazine,* set up in Charleston through "Lord John" Russell's bookstore, with the support of a large group of Charleston intellectuals and under the editorship of Paul Hamilton Hayne. In its brief life, it published some of Timrod's best poetry and essays, a few of Simms's best essays, Hayne's thoughtful "Editor's Table," and other work by the Charleston literati, including William Grayson's pro-slavery essays. *Russell's* became for a brief period one of the South's best nineteenth-century literary journals, although not as strong as the equally short-lived but excellent *Putnam's Magazine* in the North. One might remember that *Russell's* commenced the same year as *Atlantic Monthly* and only seven years after *Harper's.* It was more sympathetic to Romantic poetry than most of the earlier journals had been, and Timrod's pieces that are in conflict with the neoclassically oriented Grayson make up some of the journal's most interesting copy. It was fairly sympathetic to contemporary writing but ignored the strong new northern writers. It was, of course, aggressively partisan in its politics, but before long Hayne realized that the journal could not survive financially, and indeed its last issue was dated February 1860.

The two centers of all this publishing activity were the Deep South's Charleston and the border Baltimore, with Richmond also significant because of the *Messenger.* One of the best journals of the period, however, started in New Orleans in 1846 and was not a literary journal at all. *De Bow's Review* was the main commercial review of the South and very much a secessionist journal when the lines were being drawn. Its theme was "commerce is king," and although it more or less suspended publication during the war, after leaving New

Orleans in 1852 and following several moves landing in Nashville, it made a brief comeback afterward. James De Bow, who had substituted briefly for Whitaker as editor of the *Southern Quarterly Review* before striking out on his own, died in 1867, and the journal ceased publication in 1870 except for a brief re-entry in 1879–1880. By and large, in fact, the Civil War closed out a period in the history of southern journals. Although some were printed during the war, almost none of the prewar journals except for the farm and religious periodicals continued after the war.

John E. Bassett

See also Periodicals, 1860 to 1900; *Southern Literary Journal,* 1835 to 1838; *Southern Literary Messenger*; *Southern Review.*

Frank Luther Mott, *A History of American Magazines* (5 vols.; 1938–68); Lyon Richardson, *A History of Early American Magazines, 1741–1789* (1931); Sam G. Riley, *Index to Southern Periodicals* (1986), and *Magazines of the American South* (1986); Sam G. Riley and Gary W. Selnow, *Regional Interest Magazines of the United States* (1991).

PERIODICALS, 1860 TO 1900

The Civil War was not conducive to magazine publication in the South. Few journals were published during the war, and very few, outside of farm journals and religious periodicals, from before the war had successful runs after the war. In the former category, *American Farmer* (1819–1897, Baltimore), *The Southern Planter* (1841–1897, Richmond), *Home and Farm* (1875–1918, Louisville), and *Southern Cultivator* (1843–1935, Georgia) had long runs afterward. In 1886, the *Progressive Farmer* was established by Leonidas Polk in Birmingham and was later published for years in Raleigh before returning to Alabama. It survives today and spun off the popular *Southern Living* in 1966. Among several religious publications, *Southern Presbyterian Review,* the *Methodist Review, The Southern Presbyterian,* and the *AME Church Review,* which began publication in Atlanta in 1884, are particularly noteworthy. *De Bow's Review* (1846–1880), the major commercial magazine of the South, had a brief recovery after the war but folded in 1870 except for a return in 1879–1880. *Southern Literary Messenger,* under George Bagby, struggled until 1864 but then became the last prewar southern literary journal to expire.

A surprising number of periodicals took a stab at

publishing during the war itself, but almost all were short-lived. Some were not products of the major cities. *Southern Field and Fireside,* a general-interest magazine, was briefly published by James Gardner in Augusta in 1859, then resumed four years later only to expire in 1864. Joseph Addison Turner, one of the more interesting entrepreneurs in the field, produced perhaps the most successful of the wartime magazines, *The Countryman* (1862–1866), on a Georgia plantation. Turner, who also wrote two collections of verse, started three unsuccessful periodicals in the 1840s and 1850s; then in 1860 he produced *The Plantation: A Southern Quarterly Journal,* a valiant attempt at a serious literary quarterly that lasted only four issues. *The Countryman,* a weekly, had a broader appeal with essays modeled on *The Spectator* and *The Tattler* but also with advice columns, patriotic songs, and other miscellany. A teenaged Joel Chandler Harris worked for Turner as a printer's devil during this period.

Among the other wartime journals were *The Southern Monthly* (1861–1862) in Memphis, which combined war news with literature but had a brief life, and *Southern Punch* (1863–1864), edited by John W. Overall in Richmond. It included a good bit of humorous material, and against great odds it did manage to survive for almost two years. Other wartime efforts included *Magnolia Weekly* (1862–1865, Richmond), *Age: A Southern Monthly Eclectic Magazine* (1864–1865, Richmond), *Illustrated Mercury* (1863–1864, Raleigh), *Southern Illustrated News* (1862–1865, Richmond), and *Bohemian* (1863, Richmond). They had fleeting lives and left little mark.

Nor did a postwar region controlled for a decade by Union troops and devastated economically have much interest in supporting new magazines of a regional nature, and those few that did establish themselves had a regional emphasis. One of the best was *Scott's Monthly Magazine* (1865–1869) in Atlanta, edited by William J. Scott and publishing some reasonably good verse by Hayne, Timrod, Lanier, and others along with literary criticism. It generally attacked such northern writers as Longfellow, Emerson, and the late Thoreau and Hawthorne. *Twelve Times a Year* was a monthly out of Louisville between 1867 and 1871. Another magazine, and one with a wider readership, was D. H. Hill's *The Land We Love: A New Monthly Magazine Devoted to Literature and the Fine Arts* (1866–1869, Charlotte). Misnamed, it printed some bad verse but did publish significant articles on business and farming.

A slightly more solid attempt at a literary journal

was *Eclectic,* later *New Eclectic,* which moved from Richmond to Baltimore in 1869 and in 1871 became the *Southern Magazine.* In 1869 it absorbed *The Land We Love,* but in 1875 it expired. One of its essays by Edward Gregory, "The Voice of the South" (November 1871), sounds like a prewar editorial in its exhortation to southerners to remember that they have a duty to support a southern literature. Also in Baltimore was the *Southern Review* (1867–1879), established by A. T. Bledsoe and W. H. Browne and including some insightful literary essays by Hayne. After 1871 it was published by the Methodist Church South. Bledsoe died in 1877, and the journal, after moving to St. Louis, terminated two years later. In the year the *Southern Review* faded, another journal resurrecting an antebellum name, the *Southern Quarterly Review* (1879–1880), was started in Louisville by that same Daniel Whitaker who had edited several prewar periodicals. In the 1870s he had already edited a *New Orleans Monthly Review* and a *New Orleans Quarterly Review.* This final quarterly venture of his lasted only into the next year, and the final issue was produced, coincidentally, in New Orleans, where the original journal of its name had commenced.

Stephen Pool, in New Bern, North Carolina, published *Our Living and Our Dead* (1873–1876), which had an emphasis on romantic writing and wartime reminiscences. *The Sunny South* (1875–1907) had a fairly long run as a newspaperlike family magazine full of light literature, humor, and household items. Then in the 1880s—a lively period for new American magazines generally including *The Nation, Scribner's,* and *Forum*—there was another flurry of new southern periodicals. *Southern Bivouac* (1882–1887), edited by the Southern Historical Association in Louisville, published essays on the war and the Confederacy, Hayne's fine series on antebellum Charleston and on Charles Gayarré, and articles on Simms and other writers before selling out to *Century.* An earlier periodical in Richmond, the *Southern Historical Society Papers,* had also exploited the market for Civil War stories. The *Bivouac* went through a series of editors and publishers and gradually expanded its scope from the war to southern life more generally and even reprinted work by English writers, including Swinburne and Tennyson. Its original creative pieces fell far short of its articles and essays, and generally the better southern writers were not writing for the *Bivouac,* doubtless because it could not match the prices paid by northern magazines. The literary criticism in the *Bivouac* is generally undistinguished, but the historical and biographical essays, including some by Hayne, are of a higher caliber. Overall, it was one of the best southern magazines in the twenty-five years after the war.

The *Mascot* (1882–1895) in New Orleans attempted a gossipy, sensationalized strategy, with humorous material as well, and survived for over a decade. The *Arkansaw Traveler* (1882–1916), run by Philo Benham and Opie Reed, emphasized humor but left Little Rock for the North in 1887. *Dixie* (1885–1907), a commercial magazine edited by Charles Wells in Atlanta, was a reactionary, sensational magazine opposing, for example, any attempt to regulate child labor and regularly printing racist cartoons depicting African Americans in the most demeaning ways. Similar negative portrayals were found in *Fetter's Southern Magazine* (1892–1895), edited by Charles Shaber and George Fetter in Louisville, but it had a more literary, less commercial focus and its mood was one of nostalgic reminiscence. Meanwhile, the first successful African American periodical in the South, *Southern Workman* (1872–1939), had been established in 1872 at Hampton Institute with the assistance of General Samuel C. Armstrong. In part a promotional organ for the Institute, it usually avoided political controversy, but in the late nineteenth and early twentieth centuries it published significant articles, reviews, and scholarship related to African American and Native American experience. It also published some of the work of Paul Laurence Dunbar.

Further west in Austin, Texas, several magazines started but found little success. *Texas Siftings* (1881–1897), a humor magazine, moved to New York not long after commencing. *The Rolling Stone* (1894–1895) was a short-lived effort noteworthy for being edited by William Sidney Porter. *The Texas Magazine* (1896–1898) had a more general appeal but little success.

In the United States, magazines proliferated from about 3,300 in 1885 to about 5,500 in 1900. Relatively few of these were in the South. To literary scholars, however, two quarterlies of the turn of the century made the most lasting impression on southern culture and, indeed, American culture and became mainstream literary journals. One might say they were the first two southern quarterlies to attain, albeit gradually, a national clientele, although there is evidence that the *Southern Literary Messenger* and the *Southern Quarterly Review* had northern readers. One of the two— the *South Atlantic Quarterly*—was established in 1902

and so falls outside the parameters of this essay. The other, the *Sewanee Review*, commenced publication in 1892 under the direction of several administrators and faculty members at the University of the South, notably B. Lawton Wiggins, who provided business leadership, and Benjamin W. Wells. It primarily depended, however, upon the genius of William P. Trent, a fine young scholar recruited to the school in 1888. All these leaders saw a need for a review "specifically devoted to literary criticism" and study and agreed that not only was the South weaker in that regard than even before the Civil War, but that the United States as a whole had almost no literary journal comparable to the major quarterlies in Great Britain. They committed themselves to a periodical devoted to literary and cultural interests (literature, philosophy, history, religion) and to topics "as require fuller treatment than they usually receive in the popular magazines." In its first decade, *Sewanee Review* was praised by Theodore Roosevelt, Brander Matthews, and many other northern readers. It certainly was not radically sectional, for while including pieces on the South it had far more on classical, Continental, and English literature and more on other topics in history, education, and philosophy. It did not include original poetry, however, until 1920. By 1900, when Trent left for an academic position in the North, it was well established.

John E. Bassett

See also Periodicals, 1800 to 1860; Periodicals, 1900 to 1960; *Sewanee Review.*

Frank Luther Mott, *A History of American Magazines* (5 vols.; 1938–68); Sam G. Riley, *Index to Southern Periodicals* (1986), *Magazines of the American South* (1986); Sam G. Riley and Gary W. Selnow, *Regional Interest Magazines of the United States* (1991); John Tebbel, *The American Magazine: A Compact History* (1969).

PERIODICALS, 1900 TO 1960

As in earlier periods, in the twentieth century book and magazine publishing remained a northern industry. The periodicals with widespread circulation such as *Atlantic Monthly, Harper's, Nation, Lippincott's, Forum, Scribner's,* and *Collier's* were all produced in the North. Although there was no shortage in the South of southern self-consciousness, there was less evidence than before the Civil War of a concern that the region lacked its own magazines. There was often paranoia about Yankee newspapers infiltrating the South with disruptive ideas about, for example, race or labor, but the region also fought its internal battles with so-called liberal papers stirring up controversy. In any case, as the century advanced, a given American magazine might well have editorial offices in New York, subscription offices in the Midwest, and production facilities yet elsewhere. So while some journals explicitly defined their identity as southern, they also sought a wider clientele, and southerners subscribed with regularity to the "national" magazines.

Special-interest magazines continued to prosper in the South—for example, the farm journals *Southern Cultivator* (until 1935), *Home and Farm,* and *The Progressive Farmer,* which in 1966 spun off *Southern Living,* so highly successful in a region where suburbanites and townsfolk were beginning in some locales to outnumber farm families. Other periodicals of "southern living" such as *Palm Beach Life,* founded in 1906 with Henry Flagler's support, or *The Miamian,* started in 1920, were more narrowly focused. Church magazines were still published in the South but not the most widely read ones, such as *Christian Century, Christian Examiner,* or *Commonweal,* or the church-supported, general-interest ones, such as *Independent* and *Outlook.* Of course, southern states like northern states for years have published professional journals such as the *North Carolina Law Review* (1922–), the *Mississippi Law Journal* (1928–), and the *North Carolina Medical Journal* (1940–), or special-interest periodicals such as the *Mississippi Historical Society Bulletin* (1908–). Scholarly journals such as the *Southern Economic Journal* and the *Southern Historical Review* also developed in the twentieth century. At times, university magazines, notably the *Carolina Review* (continuous since 1929 at Chapel Hill but with earlier volumes as well), have reached audiences broader than their own university constituencies.

The South's most important contribution in the category of literary and cultural journals before 1900 had been the *Sewanee Review* (1892–). In 1900 John Bell Hennemann replaced founding editor William P. Trent, who had moved on to Columbia University. Hennemann continued the emphasis on history, literature, and philosophy but added a few essays on science. Writing on history and the South by scholars ranging from U. B. Phillips to William Dunning to John Spencer Bassett was generally of a high order, as were the literary essays. When Hennemann died (1908), John McBryde

became editor, and he was succeeded in 1920 by George Herbert Clarke, who included original poetry for the first time. W. S. Knickerbocker edited the *Review* for many years (1925–1942), opened it up to new topics, and maintained a strong stable of contributors including Joseph Warren Beach, Willard Thorp, Edwin Berry Burgum, Charles Glicksberg, Louis Untermeyer, Robert Spiller, and Allen Tate. In the 1940s, Tate edited the *Review* briefly, but by the 1950s Monroe Spears began a long term, which was followed by another long term under George Core, the current editor. Both have continued it as a high-quality, conservative (never the center for much postmodernist writing or poststructuralist criticism), but not reactionary quarterly with the major change over the years being a significant tilt in the direction of original fiction and poetry. It gradually became almost exclusively a literary journal. Contributors in the 1940s and 1950s included F. O. Matthiessen, Yvor Winters, Malcolm Cowley, Mark Schorer, Howard Nemerov, Hannah Arendt, Stephen Spender, R. P. Blackmur, Leo Marx, and T. S. Eliot.

In 1902 the *South Atlantic Quarterly* became the second major cultural quarterly in the South. Founded at Trinity College (now Duke University) in Durham, it was edited by historian John Spencer Bassett and quickly established itself not only as a solid literary journal but also as a controversial publication. Professor John Kilgo's antilynching polemic in the very first issue set the tone. Bassett praised Booker T. Washington, and even though W. E. B. Du Bois considered Washington far too conservative, southerners generally found Bassett's comments troubling. He also published a series on the "Negro question" that enraged many in the region. One notorious response came from Josephus Daniels, publisher of the *Raleigh News and Observer,* who lambasted the editor as a freak, labeled this "bASSett," and reprinted other attacks in his newspaper. The issue was more than one dimensional in that Daniels, a Republican, was opposed to the powerful North Carolina tobacco trust, dominated by the Duke family, generous contributors to Trinity. Moreover, Daniels was supportive of the University of North Carolina, whereas Kilgo and others at Duke had opposed the increase in state funds allocated to public higher education. Bassett weathered the storm after offering to resign but then left the region for a position at Smith College in 1906. The journal continued under William Glasson (1905–1919), Edwin Mims, and others, and it continued to publish on literature, including southern topics, and on history, science, philosophy, and economic issues. William Few's early articles criticizing the backwardness of secondary and primary education in the South were particularly noteworthy. With the renaming and refinancing of the school as Duke University in 1924, the *South Atlantic Quarterly* received stronger funding and emerged as an important national journal over the next three decades.

During the same period in which it was established, *Voice of the Negro* (1904–1907) in Atlanta became an important outlet among African Americans. Actually the first important black journal in the South had been the *Southern Workman* (1872–1939), produced in part as a promotional outlet for Hampton Institute but generally avoiding controversy on political issues. Around the turn of the century, it published work of Paul Laurence Dunbar as well as an increased number of book reviews and historical pieces. The literary essays of Alice Dunbar-Nelson and work by black leaders such as Kelly Miller and George Washington Carver made an impact. Later the *Southern Workman* took a stand against the "New Negro" and the changes that term implied, and by the beginning of World War II its time had passed as an influence in the black community. *Voice of the Negro* had a briefer existence, but under Jesse Max Barber it took a strong pro–Du Bois stance. Barber's commentary on the 1906 Atlanta riot, then printed in the *New York World,* caused such a fuss that he left town for Chicago and the journal lasted not much longer. Du Bois himself was at the center of the *Moon Illustrated Weekly* (Memphis), which lasted only from December 1905 to July 1906 and failed in part because Du Bois had too little help with it. Most black periodicals from then on were published in the North, but the first important scholarly journal emphasizing political, social, and literary discourse about African American culture was *Phylon: A Review of Race and Culture* (1940–), founded at Atlanta University. Du Bois was one of the early editors. *The Negro South* (1937–1947), established in New Orleans by Alonzo B. Willis Jr., was a moderate, pro-NAACP periodical that exposed many cases of injustice in America. The *Quarterly Review of Higher Education Among Negroes* was published at Johnson C. Smith University from 1933 until 1960. The *CLA Journal* (College Language Association) was founded in Atlanta in 1957 and continues today.

No list of ethnically oriented southern publications would be complete without reference to Harry Golden's *Carolina Israelite,* established in Charlotte in 1944, a newspaper, to be sure, but one whose content and quality were more like those of a serious magazine. Among special-interest journals, of course, the "little magazines" made the greatest impact on the literary world. Their readerships overlapped with those of the critical quarterlies, but early on the quarterlies did not include much creative writing. Most little magazines were published in the North and Midwest, but two or three southern products did gain high visibility. The *Double Dealer* (1921–1926) was set up in New Orleans by Julius Friend and Albert Goldstein. Sophisticated and generally ironic in tone, it maintained a generally high quality until the death of editor Basil Thompson in 1924. Finally, however, despite printing early work of Faulkner, Hemingway, Crane, Warren, and Edmund Wilson, it failed after five years both for financial reasons and because it was no longer attracting enough strong writers. Meanwhile, the *Fugitive* (1922–1925) in Nashville lasted but three and a half years, in part because of splits among its founders and editors over such issues as modernism but also because the Vanderbilt group that established it simply was ready to move on to other pursuits. In time, it became one of the best-known discontinued journals in the country because of the careers in literature and New Criticism—and earlier in the Agrarian movement—of John Crowe Ransom, Allen Tate, Robert Penn Warren, and Donald Davidson. Books and articles on them and their influence invariably address the *Fugitive* as a significant moment in modern poetry, even though little of the verse in its issues—outside of poems by Ransom—was truly first-rate. Other figures involved with the journal, such as Sidney Mttron Hirsch and Merrill Moore (author of many sonnets), are remembered by scholars because of their association with Ransom and the *Fugitive.*

Other little magazines were published in the South. *Lyric,* established in 1921 in Norfolk (later in Richmond, then Blacksburg), has maintained a loyal group of readers despite its low profile. *All's Well; or, The Mirror Repolished* was published in Fayetteville, Arkansas, from 1920 to 1935 and actually superseded *Reedy's Mirror,* a St. Louis magazine (*Mirror,* 1891–1913; *Reedy's Mirror,* 1913–1920). The *Reviewer,* a Richmond little magazine (1921–1925), was absorbed by the *Southwest Review* in 1926. *Bozart and Contemporary Verse* came out of Atlanta between 1927 and 1935. There were others, mostly with brief lives.

The most important "southern" journals in this century, however, have been the literary and cultural quarterlies whose standard had been set by *Sewanee*

Review and *South Atlantic Quarterly*. The best of these, with one exception, have had continuous runs—*Southwest Review, Virginia Quarterly Review, Georgia Review,* and *Southern Review*. The *Texas Review* was established at Austin (University of Texas) in 1915 as a literary magazine, but its breakthrough really came in 1924, when a group led by Jay B. Hubbell brought the journal to Dallas and Southern Methodist University, renaming it the *Southwest Review*. They promised "a magazine of distinction" that would be sectional in orientation but with a broad national appeal as it covered literature, politics, business, and education. It actually developed a more extensive commitment to literary matters at this time than the other southern quarterlies, although next to a long essay on Tennyson or an article by Howard Mumford Jones on Paul Green might well be pieces on Spanish missions, war debts, and politics. Editors included George Bond, John McGinnis, Henry Nash Smith, and by 1927 Allen Maxwell. Gradually the *Southwest Review* defined its regional perspective more sharply as southwestern. After World War II, it featured articles by J. Frank Dobie on the Indians of Oklahoma and special issues on New Mexico and Arizona, and called itself "the voice of the Southwest." Still, it maintained an international literary emphasis with good poetry and fiction and criticism by such writers as Albert Guerard, Charles Glicksberg, W. M. Frohock, R. V. Cassill, William Goyen, Howard Mumford Jones, Paul Horgan, and Henry Miller. Other writers included Alan Lomax, Howard Odum, and Russell Kirk.

About the same time the *Southwest Review* arrived in Dallas, Edwin Anderson Alderman, president of the University of Virginia, successfully established what he had sought for a decade, "a magazine solidly based, thoughtfully and wisely managed and controlled . . . a great serious publication wherein shall be reflected the calm thought of the best men." The *Virginia Quarterly Review* was to be neither local nor sectional, albeit concerned with themes "related to the South" and with southern writers. It would publish the work of "men and women everywhere who think through things and have some quality of expressing their thoughts in appealing and arresting fashion." Edited in its early years by James Southall Wilson, Stringfellow Barr, Lambert Davis, and Lawrence Lee, it included work by Walter de la Mare, D. H. Lawrence, Joseph Warren Beach, Arthur Symons, Luigi Pirandello, Waldo Frank, Stefan Zweig, Matthew Josephson, Havelock Ellis, Julian Huxley, and a wide range of other well-known authors

and critics. If it might publish essays on Robert E. Lee and Dolly Madison, it also included articles on Dostoevsky, Arnold, Gandhi, Frost, problems in Ireland, and much else. During World War II, Charlotte Kohler became editor of the journal and continued in that role until the 1960s. Along with poetry by Ezra Pound, H.D., Richard Eberhart, and others, but not many of the bright new postwar generation of poets, she printed prose by such writers as Carlos Baker, Max Lerner, Norman Thomas, H. J. Muller, Merrill Peterson, and V. O. Key Jr., but only rarely the younger writers and scholars.

From 1935 to 1942, Louisiana State University published one of the best literary journals, the *Southern Review*, adopting the name of the first major southern literary quarterly. Pressures of the war ultimately curtailed the commitment the school was able to make, but from the early editorship of Charles W. Pipkin to the final editing by Cleanth Brooks and Robert Penn Warren, the *Southern Review* published excellent poetry and prose. Its authors included Eudora Welty, Paul Taylor, R. P. Blackmur, John Dewey, Kenneth Burke, Henry Bamford Parkes, Crane Brinton, René Wellek, Katherine Anne Porter, Randall Jarrell, F. O. Matthiessen, and Robert Heilman. There was a southern slant to the creative work but a cosmopolitan dimension to the criticism and cultural commentary. When the journal folded, Ransom at the *Kenyon Review* agreed to honor remaining subscription commitments. One of the most successful resurrections after the war, moreover, was that of the *Southern Review* at Baton Rouge in the 1960s.

A strong journal in recent years has been the *Georgia Review*. It began in 1947, however, as a deliberately provincial and regional effort that would "make its contents of special concern to Georgians." It would not include abstruse articles on the "use of prepositions in Sanskrit" and it would also avoid "the Tobacco Road sort of thing" while focusing on the history, literature, art, education, and society of Georgia. Set in Athens, it also committed itself to rural Georgia, affirming the "dignity and worth of country life," for in "spite of Atlanta . . . Georgia remains a rural state." Under John Donald Wade's editorship, the journal included a lot on Georgia but also essays on the vote for eighteen-year-olds, on higher education, and on France, and it even published Granville Hicks's reminiscences. In the 1950s under John Olin Eidson and then William Wallace Davidson, it extended its scope to include regularly articles on writers such as T. S.

Eliot, Faulkner, and Sherwood Anderson, but only in the 1970s did it become a truly national quarterly.

There have been many others, of course. In Richmond a journal with the name of the *Southern Literary Messenger* was reestablished in 1939 and published until the fall of 1944. The *Carolina Quarterly* has been published since 1948 in Chapel Hill. But the South after World War II also developed a number of critical and scholarly journals of importance to people studying literature. One that started just before the war was the *Southern Folklore Quarterly* (1937–) at the University of Florida. Another that has built a successful tradition is the *Mississippi Quarterly*. It was founded in 1948 at Mississippi State College in Starkville as the *Social Science Bulletin*. In 1953 it assumed its current name and divided its focus between history and literature. By the late 1950s, under Robert B. Holland, it had established an American emphasis in its contents but not invariably a southern one. It published on Agrarianism, Southwest humor, and Ransom but also on Henry James, Melville, and even English Renaissance poets. Like the other quarterlies discussed above, it has continued to thrive, and so have several others established after 1960.

John E. Bassett

See also Literary Magazines of the Past; Literary Magazines of the Present; Periodicals, 1860 to 1900.

Frank Luther Mott, *A History of American Magazines* (5 vols.; 1938–1968); Theodore Peterson, *Magazines in the Twentieth Century* (1964); Sam G. Riley, *Index to Southern Periodicals* (1986), and *Magazines of the American South* (1986); Sam G. Riley and Gary W. Selnow, *Regional Interest Magazines of the United States* (1991).

PERIODICALS, 1960 TO PRESENT

Billing itself as "A National Magazine of the South," the little magazine *Double Dealer* appeared in 1921 in New Orleans under the editorship of the city's native son, Julius Weis Friend. Inside the June 1921 issue, readers were confronted with the opinion: "It is high time, we believe, for some doughty, clear visioned penman to emerge from the sodden marshes of Southern Literature. We are sick to death of the treacly sentimentalities with which our well-intentioned lady fictioneers regale us. The old traditions are no more. New peoples, customs prevail. The Confederacy has long since been dissolved." Taking the high road, the *Double Dealer* aligned itself with established little magazines such as the *Dial,* the *Little Review,* and the *Yale Review.* Like many little magazines, the *Double Dealer* was short-lived, publishing its last issue in May 1926. But its contributors included such notables as William Faulkner, Ernest Hemingway, Sherwood Anderson, Malcolm Cowley, Robert Penn Warren, Thornton Wilder, Elizabeth Coatsworth, Edmund Wilson, and Hart Crane.

Little magazines such as the *Double Dealer,* also called "literary magazines" or "literary reviews," are the legacy of colonial newspapers. With strong ties to England and with little intercolony communication, early southern newspapers such as the *Maryland Gazette* (1727–1730), the *Virginia Gazette* (1736–1750), and the *South-Carolina Gazette* (1732–1733) published original essays and excerpts from English literature. Because of the continuing struggle for independence, literary freedom in the spirit of belles-lettres was still lacking, even after the War of 1812. William Gibbs Hunt, Harvard-educated with the right connections, launched the *Western Review* in Kentucky in 1819, but about half of the *Review*'s contents were reviews of English literature, and the *Western Review* died after four issues.

Beginning in the mid-nineteenth century, external forces began to change American publishing. Hard news, helped by the immediacy of the telegraph and the Civil War, began to replace literature in many newspapers. The increase in literacy in both urban and rural areas caused an increase in the demand for reading material. Printing presses improved and became steam and electric powered, paper could be manufactured in bulk rolls, book prices declined, and by the end of the century railroads could transport books quickly and economically. Between the mid-1800s and the Civil War, the number of books published increased dramatically, but the incestuous relationship between publishers, authors, and advertisers eroded the credibility of criticism. Authors could write, and get published, their own reviews. Some examples of independent criticism did appear, however. The *Southern Literary Messenger* called Henry Wadsworth Longfellow "over-praised," but when the *Boston Traveler* negatively reviewed *Hiawatha* (1855), publisher Ticknor and Fields canceled its advertising.

After Reconstruction (1865–1877), the southern literature that emerged was often criticized as being sentimental and not substantial. Reacting to this condition at the University of the South, English professor William Peterfield Trent started the *Sewanee Review* in 1892 to offer a critical alternative to popular magazines. The *Sewanee Review* acquired its first full-time editor in 1944 when critic and poet Allen Tate obtained concessions from the university, which included paying contributors. Tate redesigned the *Sewanee Review* while increasing its circulation and advertising. He also attracted nationally acclaimed writers including T. S. Eliot, Kenneth Burke, Katherine Anne Porter, and Dylan Thomas. George Core became editor of the *Sewanee Review* in 1973.

Other significant reviews appeared during the first half of the twentieth century. At the University of Virginia, the first issue of the *Virginia Quarterly Review* was published in 1925 under the editorship of English professor James Southall Wilson, who was succeeded in 1928 by Stringfellow Barr. When Barr published his October 1930 essay "Shall Slavery Come South?," a month later more than three thousand people packed Richmond's Mosque Theater in a *Richmond Times Dispatch*–sponsored debate between Barr and John Crowe Ransom. Five years later, the *Quarterly*'s reputation was enhanced by a tenth-anniversary issue on themes and writers of the South. Staige D. Blackford became editor in 1975, succeeding Charlotte Kohler, who was with the *Quarterly* for thirty-three years (1942–1975).

Today, most major state universities in the South have literary reviews—the *Florida Review* (1972), the *Georgia Review* (1947), the *Maryland Review* (1986)—some more renowned than others. Especially significant among them is the *Southern Review* (1935), founded at Louisana State University by Cleanth Brooks, Robert Penn Warren, Albert Erskine, and Charles Pipkin. Over the years, contributors have included such authors as W. H. Auden, Allen Tate, T. S. Eliot, Caroline Gordon, Katherine Anne Porter, Eudora Welty, Mary McCarthy, and Nelson Algren. In 1940, *Time* magazine remarked that the *Southern Review* was proof "that there exists in the United States a national community of scholars and artists, alive in their own time and country." Discontinued after the outbreak of World War II, the *Review* resumed publication in 1965. LSU began publishing *Delta* magazine in 1947, calling Truman Capote the most promising young American writer. *Delta* later became *Manchac* and eventually emerged as the *New Delta Review*. *Carolina Quarterly* (1948) is published at the University of North Carolina at Chapel Hill, although the literary tradition of small magazines on that campus dates

back to the *North Carolina University Magazine* (1844) and its successors.

Scattered across the South, more than seventy-five literary reviews are in print. Most, like those already mentioned, are affiliated in some way with colleges and universities. In New Orleans, the *New Orleans Review* (1968) is published at Loyola University. *Xavier Review* (1980) was founded at Xavier University by poet Charles Fort and English professor Thomas Bonner Jr. In South Carolina, the *South Carolina Review* began publication at Furman University in 1968, moving to Clemson in 1973. In Alabama, *Black Warrior Review* (1974) is published at the University of Alabama, and *Southern Humanities Review* (1967), founded in association with the Southern Humanities Conference, is published at Auburn University. At Troy State University is located the *Alabama Literary Review* (1986), a statewide literary review that is distributed free to all Alabama libraries and to all state English and drama departments in Alabama higher education.

Like Alabama, Texas is also replete with literary reviews. The *Texas Review* (1979), located at Sam Houston State University in Huntsville, began as the *Sam Houston Literary Review* in 1976 and became the *Quarterly* when the *Texas Quarterly* folded at the University of Texas–Austin in 1978. Both *Gulf Coast* (1987) and the *Americas Review*, which concentrates on Hispanic literature, are found at the University of Houston. The *American Literary Review* (1990) is published at the University of North Texas in Denton.

Literary reviews are found at small liberal-arts colleges, community colleges, and urban universities in the South. The *Crucible* (1964) is published at Barton College, a school with about one thousand full-time students located in Wilson, North Carolina. The *Sandhills Review* (1970), formerly the *St. Andrews Review,* is published at Sandhills Community College, a school with 2,500 students near Southern Pines, North Carolina. *Nebo* (1976), Hebrew for the planet Mercury, began as the *Five Cent Cigar* (1971) at Arkansas Tech University in Russellville. The University of Memphis publishes the poetry review *River City Review,* which evolved from the *Phoenix* (1970). George Mason University in Fairfax, Virginia, publishes *Phoebe* (1972).

Although prose and poetry by emerging writers are the primary focus of many small literary publications, many reviews also publish works by established authors. Book reviews, music reviews, translations, original art work, and photographs are common. Interviews are popular features also. Interviews with Robert

Altman, Pat Conroy, Walker Percy, and Norman Mailer have appeared in the *New Orleans Review*. Among interviewees appearing in *Xavier Review* are Alex Haley, James Baldwin, Andre Dubus, Christine Wiltz, and Elmore Leonard. Anne Rice and Lee Smith have been interviewed by the *New Delta Review*. Above all, literary reviews take risks that other mainstream publishers cannot, because of commercial limitations or artistic restraints. The *New Orleans Review*'s memorable editor Marcus Smith managed to use Loyola's association with Walker Percy to publish an excerpt in 1978 from John Kennedy Toole's *Confederacy of Dunces* (1980) before it was published by the LSU Press. Percy wrote both an introduction to the excerpt and a foreword to the book.

Funding for literary reviews comes from subscription fees, grants from organizations such as the National Endowment for the Arts, the Coordinating Council of Literary Magazines, state and regional arts councils, and colleges and universities or their English departments. At DeKalb College in Georgia, the *Chattahoochee Review* is funded now by the college, but for many years it was supported by the college's humanities division and student government. Student-government funds also help support the *Carolina Quarterly,* edited and controlled by graduate students. As state-supported public universities turn to private fund-raising, capital campaigns to establish endowments for their literary reviews are becoming more common. Advertising, often from local restaurants, coffeehouses, and bookstores, also helps support publication.

Some reviews sponsor literary prizes. The *Virginia Quarterly Review*'s Emily Clark Balch Prize for Poetry was first awarded in 1956 to Princeton and Hemingway scholar Carlos Baker. At the *New Delta Review,* a prize honoring former LSU faculty member Warren Eyster is awarded to one poem and one story from each issue. Some prizes help a review attract talented writers. The *Crucible* awards first and second cash prizes in poetry and fiction, in addition to a special poetry prize honoring the poet laureate of North Carolina, Sam Ragan, an alumnus. The *American Literary Review* sponsors a national fiction and poetry contest in alternating years.

Circulation figures for literary reviews run anywhere from one hundred for the *American Literary Review* to three thousand for the *Sewanee Review*. Most paid subscribers are libraries. Editorial advice varies from national editorial boards with established scholars and writers to reviews that turn to local college En-glish departments. For some smaller and underfunded reviews, publication can be irregular. Anniversary and theme issues are often published, partly because they can attract a wide readership and backlist sales. National distribution companies are helping reviews extend their readership beyond their own locale.

John R. Bittner

See also *Kenyon Review*; Literary Magazines of the Past; Literary Magazines of the Present; *Mississippi Quarterly; Sewanee Review; Southern Literary Journal,* 1835 to 1838; *Southern Literary Journal,* 1968 to Present; *Southern Literary Messenger; Southern Review*.

Elliott Anderson and Mary Kinzie, eds., *The Little Magazine in America: A Modern Documentary History* (1978).

PHOTOGRAPHY

The American South has had a long, rich, variegated, and influential photographic history. Photography was introduced into the South soon after Louis Daguerre's process was transported to the United States in 1839. Practitioners established studios in the larger cities, and itinerants fanned out into the back country. Henry Fritz Jr. set up shop in Baltimore in 1840. That same year, Jules Lion, a free man of color, established a studio in New Orleans. In 1841 Frederick A. P. Barnard hung out a shingle in Tuscaloosa, Alabama. Alfred Lansing commenced a photographic operation in St. Augustine, Florida, in 1842. The profession of photographer spread so swiftly in the South that photographer John Plumbe Jr. had by 1846 offices in eighteen cities, including Baltimore; Alexandria, Petersburg, and Richmond, Virginia; Louisville, Kentucky; and New Orleans. George Smith Cook moved from one city to another in the South—New Orleans, St. Louis, and Charleston—before settling in Richmond.

Local photographers were in many ways "historians with a camera." Inside the studio, they recorded the people and products who comprised a place and time. There were births, marriages, anniversaries, deaths, and other occasions to document. Out on location, they captured settings—streets, buildings, parks, neighborhoods. In between stops, they documented a wide variety of happenings: labor and leisure; tragedy and triumphs; harmony and strife; the commonplace and the exceptional. An active commercial photographer chronicled what was going on socially, economically, and culturally in his community. The negatives of T. E. Armistead, Wilson C. Burton, Erik Overbey, Max McGill, and S. Blake McNeeley housed at the University of South Alabama have provided historians Michael V. Thomason and Melton McLaurin with visual springboards for such state and period studies as *The Image of Progress: Alabama Photographs, 1872–1917* (1980) and *Trying Times: Alabama Photographs, 1917–1945* (1985).

Local conditions provided each photographer with a distinctive flavor. In Louisiana, Fonville Winans discovered in the mid-twentieth century "my Africa, my South." In his portraits of powerful politicians, Winans tried to capture "the inner spirit and outward personality." His portraits were used for campaign broadsides, which spread the visage of the politician and popularized Winans's name and reputation. He saw a different side to the Great Depression and World War II than government photographers. While government photographers focused on the downtrodden, diseased, and deteriorated to encourage federal programs and appropriations, Winans saw healthy and hearty people engaged in upbeat and positive everyday activities. His photographs of festivals celebrating the sugarcane, rice, shrimp, crawfish, crab, and oyster harvests provide commentary on indigenous industries, seasonal rhythms, religious customs, personal rites, and rituals. He crossed the "color line" to record a sensuous and diverse history. Winans achieved a regional prominence in his lifetime. His stock continues to rise because of his enchanting world, natural settings, sharp focus, and evocative messages. Winans provided a legacy to measure the costs of industrialization and urbanization on a fragile economy and ecology.

Mathew Brady was the first photographer of international repute to display the South to the world. Known for his portraits of public figures from the political, business, and entertainment arenas, Brady conceived of himself as a national historian and of photography as a sacred calling. Through pictorial works, such as *A Gallery of Illustrious Americans* (1850), Brady hoped to vindicate art, enshrine national icons, communicate republican values, and transmit spiritual insight. Abraham Lincoln credited his Cooper Union speech, and Brady's photograph, with getting him elected president. Feeling that the Civil War would be of short duration, and speculating that there would be a lucrative market for stereoscopic war pictures afterward, Brady gambled the resources of his fashionable New York and Washington, D.C., studios on coverage

of the epic clash. Relying on political contacts made as "Brady of Broadway," the photographic impresario gained access to southern battlefields. Converting wagons into portable darkrooms, which startled soldiers suspected of housing weaponry and called "What Is It?" wagons, and hiring photographers to carry out operations, Brady dispatched as many as twenty photographers to cover the Civil War. Although Brady was present at many major battles (Bull Run, Antietam, Fredericksburg, Gettysburg, and Petersburg), his associates, notables in their own right—Alexander and James Gardner, Timothy O'Sullivan, James F. Gibson, D. B. Woodbury—compiled hundreds of images, many without attribution. Because of the limitations of the collodion process, Brady could not capture action. His pictures had a static quality because of the long exposure time required, and concentrated on inanimate objects. Since Brady couldn't capture movement, he sometimes had events, like the performance of an ambulance corps in the field, restaged. Brady captured a broad range of behind-the-scenes activities—bridges and supply lines, hospitals and prisons, bivouacs and relaxation, the wounded and weary, the triumphant and defeated. Brady took liberties with subjects, such as placing the hand of a dead soldier over his heart to drive home the metaphor. Photographs of well-equipped and well-organized northern troops, mess halls, and hospitals made southern shortcomings and delinquencies all the more obvious. Brady's photographs of the carnage and destruction of men, animals, buildings, and cities provided direct visual evidence of the horrors of combat, brought the casualties of war into the home, molded public opinion, and altered the romantic impression of war derived from drawings, woodcuts, and flowery prose. As Oliver Wendell Holmes remarked: "Let him who wishes to know what war is look at this series of illustrations."

Wars—the Mexican War (1846–1848), Crimean War (1856), and the Franco-Austrian conflict (1859)— were among the first public events that photographers attempted to record, and in so doing they planted the seeds of photojournalism. During the Civil War, the governments of the North and South employed their own photographers. While A. T. Russell, Sam A. Cooley, and George M. Barnard received commissions from the Northern Blue, the Confederate Gray appointed George Cook and A. D. Lytle. Photography proved its worth in the field during the war in reproducing maps and military plans and providing aerial images of the terrain and troops. Last-remembrance photographs of soldiers taken just before their departure for the front became a popular item sustaining many local practitioners. Brady's ten-volume photographic history of the war and the collection of negatives housed at the National Archives provide a monumental and vivid visual record of a critical turning point in the nation's past.

After the Civil War, the South attracted photographers from near and far. In the 1870s, the largest photography-supply house in the nation, Edward Anthony and Company, dispatched to Florida its foremost staff photographer, Thomas C. Roche, to take stereoscopic views of the flora and fauna, lush landscape, and mysterious residents. In the 1880s and 1890s, the Detroit Publishing Company, printer of lithographs and postcards disseminated by the millions annually, sent William Henry Jackson, legendary photographer of western Native Americans and landscapes, and other photographers on railroad and steamboat excursions to find natural and primitive regional imagery. With the advent of the halftone process, which permitted the reduction of photographs into dots and reprinting in periodicals, other companies sent photographers south to cover events such as the Spanish-American War of 1898.

While Jackson's imagery appeared on the postcards of one of America's foremost manufacturers, local companies, such as the H. & W. B. Drew Company of Jacksonville, Florida, arose to turn the pictures of local druggists and corner-store photographers into postcards disbursed internationally. Since the postcard avoided many of the editorial proscriptions imposed by periodicals, it contained some of the most virulent racial, religious, and sexist images of the region. Among the stereotypes and props commonly found in Dixieland and "happy darkies and coons" sets and series were snow-white cotton, watermelon, fried chicken, washtub drums, shacks, tattered clothing, alcoholic beverages, gambling games, fertile and promiscuous youth, and legions of barefoot children with devilish looks on their faces. Postal authorities and organizations committed to the suppression of vice stepped in after the turn of the century to police the trade in objectionable images, especially lynching scenes.

Photographers journeyed to and through the South on freelance as well as commission bases. Arnold Genthe, a German immigrant who had established a renowned reputation for artistic portraits of San Francisco's elite, visited the region. Inspired by the novels of George Washington Cable, Genthe envisioned a series on old cities. Already known for his ethnographic coverage of San Francisco's segregated and exotic Chinatown, Genthe was attracted to the multicultural influences of New Orleans. Relying on a small hand-held detective camera and waiting as long as necessary, Genthe captured candid shots of the city's polyglot population. With a large format camera, Genthe focused on the Crescent City's architectural heritage. By photographing in the early morning or late afternoon, Genthe captured mists and shadows and emphasized the picturesqueness of the setting. He commonly used delicate wrought-iron work as a window onto or frame for architectural subjects. He was also known to crop evidence of modernization, such as electrical wires and telephone poles, to make scenes look more pristine or primitive. Disturbed by all sorts of signs disfiguring the physical beauty of buildings and streets, and distressed by the destructive impact of noise and dirt on the atmosphere, Genthe hoped to awaken a sense of civic and aesthetic appreciation for cities through his romantic imagery. Genthe found his way into the bayous of Louisiana and the lowlands around Charleston, South Carolina. He captured many classic Old South images—weathered oak trees hung with Spanish moss, aged and dignified African Americans diligently working away, white-columned mansions. His photographs resulted in *Impressions of Old New Orleans* (1926), which provides an invaluable resource and inspiration for preservationists. A seamier side of southern civilization was recorded around 1912 by E. J. Bellocq in his photographs of the prostitutes of Storyville, the tenderloin district of New Orleans, which in their melancholy languor played on a combination of compassion and voyeuristic curiosity.

The social and economic dislocations caused by industrialization, urbanization, and immigration gave rise at the turn of the century to a multiplicity of reform movements and provided a closer look at the South's colonial economy. Lewis Hine was dispatched by the National Child Labor Committee to collect evidence of industrial and work-force abuse. Conceiving of his subjects as "human documents," Hine organized his photographs of slums and immigrants into sets and series. He called picture sequences expressing a point of view "photo-interpretations." He used magic-lantern slides to illustrate lectures. With his auto Graflex camera in tow, Hine traveled around the United States from 1909 to 1918. At a time when Alfred Stieglitz and Edward Steichen were exploring photography as an art form, Lewis Hine was discovering its sense of social conscience. His unmasking of child labor in the South was, in the opinion of Paul Strand, akin to entering an armed camp. Despite the dangers, Hine possessed the courage to work in hostile territory on forbidden topics. He adopted disguises, such as Bible salesman, postcard vendor, and fire inspector, in order to gain access and record the ages, hours, wages, working conditions, years of service, and amount of schooling of women and children in the coal mines of West Virginia, glass, furniture, and candy companies of Virginia, textile and cotton mills of South Carolina, Georgia, and Alabama, cigar factories of Florida, sawmills and sugar plantations of Louisiana, cotton fields of Texas, oyster, shrimp, and fish processing and canning plants of the Gulf Coast, and red-light districts of southern cities. By posing children against their machines and work stations, Hine provided a sense of scale and a commentary on control of the workplace, man's inhumanity to man, and the resiliency of the human spirit. Hine produced visual counterparts to the muckraking exposés that John Spargo, Upton Sinclair, Jane Addams, and Marie Van Vorst had been writing about in *McClure's* and other progressive forums. The camera became in Hine's hands a weapon for social progress and helped to promote wage, hour, age, gender, safety, and health regulations. Other glimpses of workers and workplaces in various industries and cities were provided by many lesser-known photographers, such as an unnamed itinerant photographer who captured Corpus Christi, Texas, in February 1934.

The 1930s were a high-water mark for documentary studies in film, literature, and photography in the United States. Although some politicians distrusted and rejected the mass media, President Franklin D. Roosevelt embraced and exploited the latest innovations in the form of fireside chats, newsreels, and exhibits in public buildings to communicate and persuade a nation and Congress. Within the alphabetical agencies the New Deal spawned—the Civilian Conservation Corps, National Youth Administration, Tennessee Valley Authority—documentary photographers joined a battery of economists, sociologists, statisticians, and other specialists to record conditions for reasons of relief, recovery, and reform. They produced visual analogues to the songs of Woody Guthrie, dramas of the Federal Theater, and murals painted by Federal Arts projects. Some of the best-known images of the Great Depression, such as Dorothea Lange's "Migrant Mother" and Arthur Rothstein's "Dust Storm," were produced by photographers working initially for the

Resettlement Administration (RA), then the Farm Security Administration (FSA), and later the Office of War Information (OWI). Despite criticism over wasting taxpayers' money and producing propaganda, a group of thirty-plus photographers toiled under the direction of Roy Stryker from 1935 to 1943 to create at a cost of $1 million a file of 270,000 images—the greatest documentary collection in both scope and quality in the world.

Following Roosevelt's lead of conceiving of the South as "the nation's number one economic problem," government photographers—Marion Post Wolcott, Russell Lee, Ben Shahn, Gordon Parks—focused initially on destitution and deprivation to secure Congressional appropriations, and later on upbeat and positive images to show the beneficial results of the investment and keep the funds coming. In these so-called "command performances," photographers shied away from controversial topics, such as labor strikes and racial discord, and pushed uplifting themes—the decency and dignity of the American people, the small-town and private citizen as the backbone of American civilization, and patriotism and preparedness winning the war. While the federal government portrayed itself as a friend of the little man and farmer, mechanization, chemicals, and government programs were transforming agriculture from labor intensive to capital intensive, small farms to corporate units, and a way of life to a way of business. While photographs pictured a bucolic America of able-bodied young men and women restoring forests, conserving the soil, learning skills and crafts, there were racial quotas, segregated facilities, tenants displaced, and the machine being eased into the garden. Mass-circulation magazines, such as *Fortune, Life, Time,* and *Look,* with their high-resolution glossy pictures and photo essays carried the messages around the globe. The appearance of institutes, like the Institute for Social Science Research at Chapel Hill, provided more in-depth and long-term study and problem solving. The Center for Documentary Studies at Duke University, and the photographic work of Alex Harris, continue to add to the tradition.

Out of the Depression period also came what many critics consider the classic documentary work. James Agee and Walker Evans's *Let Us Now Praise Famous Men* (1941) would eventually take its place alongside John Steinbeck's *Grapes of Wrath* (1939). In the summer of 1936, Walker Evans took leave from the Farm Security Administration to join James Agee, a writer for *Fortune* magazine, for a story on the plight of farm tenancy. In Hale County, Alabama, Agee and Evans focused on the families of William Fields, Floyd Burroughs, and Frank Tengle. As Agee inventoried their daily lives in painstaking detail and empathetic prose, Evans used a large-format camera to craft pictures of careful composition, precise detail, and absolute clarity. Noted for a style described as straight and a tone called timeless, Evans looked for symbols of simplicity, order, and functionalism—a metal bed, work shoes, an oil-cloth tablecloth, kitchen utensils, dirt graves. He ennobled the sharecroppers by posing subjects, removing objects, and arranging contents. Evans wanted to show that in the midst of poverty and unemployment, people could still create a world of order and dignity. Some fifty years later, Dale Maharidge and Michael Williamson revisited the three clans and updated the family histories in *And Their Children After Them* (1989).

In the same decade that Walker Evans was applying the camera to Alabama, Eudora Welty was discovering her native state. As a junior publicity agent for the Works Progress Administration, Welty traveled by bus over eighty-two counties in Mississippi, taking along a Kodak camera. Although both Evans and Welty emphasized a sense of place, the connection between her photographs and text was less literal than this. "I was taking photographs of human beings because they were there in front of me and that was the reality. I was the recorder of it. I wasn't trying to exhort the public." Welty saw her images as "snapshots," momentary glimpses of what she simply titled "Workdays," "Saturdays," and "Sundays," and the collection of spontaneous pictures as a "family album." She liked a long perspective in photographs because it incorporated background and set her subject in context. *One Time, One Place* (1971) captured the courage and persistence, honesty and diversity of Mississippi's white and black residents and landscapes in the face of poverty. As a young woman in search of her own identity, Welty found that people liked unadorned snapshots of everyday life as evidence of themselves.

While Evans and Welty photographed the Lower and Delta Souths, other practitioners explored the mountain and coastal areas. Leigh Richmond Minor, an instructor of art at Hampton Institute around the turn of the century, photographed black families and fishermen on the islands along the South Carolina coast. Under the influence of Pictorialism, a movement that pushed photography as art and stressed its aesthetic aspects, Minor saw his subjects in reverent and

heroic terms. Doris Ulmann, a wealthy New York portraitist who had explored Amish, Mennonite, and Shaker communities in New York, traveled in the late 1920s with folklorist John Jacob Niles in the mountains of Kentucky, Tennessee, and North Carolina. Fearing that the forces of the modern world would corrupt and wipe out the residents and culture of Appalachia, Ulmann recorded the variety of people, diverse lives, and assorted customs and handicrafts of the mountains. In a style that combined Pictorialist ideals and social documentation, she focused on the older generation and the virtues and simplicity of their lives. Relying on natural light and a soft-focus lens, she idealized the Appalachian highlands. Ulmann also captured the Gullah residents on the Sea Islands of South Carolina. Whereas Ulmann was a sophisticated photographer and artist, Paul Buchanan was what the plain folk simply called a picture man. A miner of mica and a sawmill worker, Buchanan supplemented his wages as a traveling photographer (1920–1951). He used a minimum of props to capture the rugged rural life and small-town culture of North Carolina mountain counties. In the insular and homogeneous area of Cleburne County, Arkansas, during the Great Depression and World War II, Michael Disfarmer photographed large, hard-working Caucasian families who were proud of their provincialism, breeding, fundamentalism, strong spirit, and simplicity. Gnarled hands, sunbaked faces, suspenders, and bib overalls told what these people were. The photographs speak of generations—grandparents, parents, children, relatives, and friends, and why the family portrait became a treasured family heirloom. Holes in the toes of shoes and stretched-out socks falling down around the ankles indicated that photographs were more important to have than some other material possession. The legacies of the mountain and coastal South continue to be handed down by photographers as diverse as Earl Palmer and Jeanne Moutoussamy-Ashe.

Corporations have recorded the South while carrying out their business. For many years, the Standard Oil Company was the biggest and most powerful corporation in the South. Intent on improving its image and reputation, the company sent photographers to towns to photograph its operations from drilling derricks, through refineries, to licensed distributors for public-relations purposes. In attempting to show that it was a good corporate citizen, Standard Oil also captured good neighbors along the way—exteriors of roadside institutions and interiors of homes, river boats and automobiles, cafés and bars, fire stations and feed stores, rodeos and church suppers, ethnic celebrations and community festivals. The interest of the Hughes Tool Company in documenting all facets of Howard Hughes's operation provides another window, especially on technological aspects of industry, spanning some eighty years. The corporate archives of companies involved in tobacco, sugar, whiskey, and beverages furnish other prisms for viewing the region.

The South has provided a fertile terrain for many photographers interested in the creative use of the camera. Clarence John Laughlin, a native of Louisiana and resident of New Orleans, was absorbed by the symbolic and interpretative, rather than literal, use of the camera. Through multiple exposures, reflections, tilted frames, unusual angles, tight close-ups, oblique views, shallow depth of field, theatrical arrangements, and captions, Laughlin explored the "unreality of the real and the reality of the unreal." With an active interest in poetry, painting, architecture, psychology, social issues, and matters of light and time, Laughlin employed the camera to express dreams, memory, myth, and mortality. The cultural tensions of the 1920s and 1930s caused Laughlin to question his region and identity. He shared with the Nashville Agrarians a sense of loss, disappointment, and rejection at the hands of specialization and routinization. *Ghosts Along the Mississippi* (1948) provides a synthesis of Laughlin's personal and aesthetic concerns, vantage points, and optical effects. In more recent years, Jerry N. Uelsmann, a professor at the University of Florida, has relied on collage and montage—the restructuring and combining of negatives—to create multiple imagery.

One of the most talented and influential photographers of the South today is William Christenberry. Born in 1936 in Hale County, Alabama, the area immortalized by Agee and Evans in their classic study *Let Us Now Praise Famous Men*, Christenberry has examined his roots—people, land, buildings—through several forms of expression and self-analysis—drawings, photography, sculpture, assemblages, and installations. As a youngster, Christenberry rode with his father on a bread-truck route observing country stores, common folk, multicolored advertising signs, humble dwellings, and other sites. After receiving as a gift in 1944 a Brownie Holiday camera, Christenberry recorded "Alabama iconography" and created representational art. In walks along Alabama's highways and byways, Christenberry has collected impressions and relics of the land. The artifacts in Christenberry's

prints, boxes, sculptures, and assemblages are part self-disclosure and part geographical reincarnation. His multimedia impressions of dirt roads, red clay, kudzu, pine trees, graveyards, churches, schools, gas stations, cotton gins, warehouses, and barns have become an ode to his home place. The minute imprints left on the wood, brick, and metal by man and nature speak of Alabama's history and heritage.

The South's landscape has not received the same attention that the mountains and valleys of the West have. There is good reason, however, why critics have referred to Clyde Butcher as the "Ansel Adams of the South." Relying on the bulky large-format camera that Mathew Brady used over a century earlier for its exquisite detail, and printing in black and white for the sake of purity and texture, Butcher has probed the deepest recesses of the Everglades. Instead of just another mosquito-infested and alligator-ridden swamp, Butcher has revealed the tropical wilderness to be a diverse, mystical, ever-changing primordial paradise. The fragile biological and botanical balance is threatened by South Florida's population sprawl and agricultural runoff. Just as Adams's landscapes came to be associated with the Sierra Club and other conservation groups, Butcher's photographs have been used for posters in Save Our Rivers campaigns and by ecology-minded groups. *Okefinokee Album* (1981), based on the photographs and writings done by naturalist Francis Harper between 1912 and 1951, provides an earlier recollection of a vanished age and heritage.

Over the decades, the South has been involved in its share of photographic controversies. Smarting over criticism of the poor white trash portrayed in *Tobacco Road* (1932) and *God's Little Acre* (1933), Georgia's native son Erskine Caldwell teamed up with Margaret Bourke-White, an original staff member of *Life* and the most famous female photojournalist of all time, to publish *You Have Seen Their Faces* (1937). While Caldwell wrote the hard-hitting text about deprivation, degeneracy, and distress, Bourke-White took stark photographs of the worn-out, rutted underside of southern life. The authors were accused of selecting aberrational features and distorting reality and condemned for turning state's evidence and playing into the hands of Iron Curtain enemies overseas. In *Real Life: Louisville in the Twenties* (1976), Michael Lesy created a picture-text montage from newspaper accounts, medical transcripts, legal depositions, statistical summaries, oral interviews, and period photographs taken by the commercial studio of Caufield &

Shook. Lurking behind the Jazz Age's façade of urban stability and prosperity, Lesy discerned a culture of violence, alcoholism, corruption, and sado-masochistic fantasies of power and death. Lesy's psycho-historical re-creation of the era came under fire for selective marshaling of evidence and its fascination with the morbid. In more recent years, Sally Mann raised more than a few eyebrows by photographing, over a period of eight years, her children in the nude in Virginia countryside scenes. Her photographs provoked debate not simply about the ethics of an adult photographing children and accenting the looming sexuality of the minors. Mann pushed the ambiguity of innocence and pleasure versus adults in baby's bodies and sex through her use of soft focus, postured poses, hints at shadowy forces, and implied forbidden topics. Beyond the issue of taking artistic license, Mann's photographs raised concerns over parental authority, child abuse, disturbed adolescents, and pedophilia.

Recent scholarship has brought to light the many contributions that African American photographers have made. Prentice H. Polk and Cornelius M. Battey in Tuskegee, Alabama, John Roy Lynch in Natchez, Mississippi, L. O. Taylor in Memphis, Tennessee, James C. Farley in Richmond, Virginia, Addison N. Scurlock in Washington, D.C., Richard Aloysius Twine in Lincolnville, Florida, and Richard Roberts in Columbia, South Carolina, passed down images of dignified and prideful African Americans at home, work, school, and church. Behind the photographs of role models lie remarkable accounts of places, personalities, and perseverance.

North Webster (1993) tells the story of a successful middle-class African American community rising west of St. Louis from the 1830s to the 1980s, where emphasis on family, religion, education, and skills helped residents progress and prosper. *An American Beach for African Americans* (1997) reconstructs the development of a segregated resort on Amelia Island from a homestead in 1781 to a twentieth-century vacation and recreational mecca for African Americans.

Introduced to photography through reconnaissance pictures during World War II, R. C. Hickman used G.I. benefits to further his photo education and pursue a career in Dallas. As a staff member of the *Dallas Post Star,* Hickman took pictures that filled in the "black outs" engaged in by the regular press and provided evidence to challenge stereotypes and second-class citizenship. Rather than producing staged studio work, Hickman went into segregated society to capture African American homes, businesses, churches, social clubs, and events. He risked personal injury to provide the NAACP with photographic evidence of segregation, lynchings, and beating victims. His photographs were used to show the debilitating effects of the doctrine of separate-but-equal and of urban renewal on the inner city. He showed women in the occupations of service-station owner, newspaper press operator, and pharmacist breaking an insidious cycle of unemployment and dependency. He photographed celebrities and notables from the worlds of business, politics, and entertainment during their appearances. His work provided national publicity for a largely "invisible" black middle class in the urban South. His career constituted a positive social record to nourish expectations and educate a new generation.

Hickman recorded the initial steps of the Civil Rights Movement that other photographers, such as Charles Moore and Danny Lyon, followed through on. Moore, a white native of Alabama and son of a Baptist minister, covered the sit-ins, freedom marches, bus boycotts, and voter-registration drives at Selma, Birmingham, Oxford, and St. Augustine. His photographs of the high-pressure water hoses, snarling police dogs, deputies on horseback, tear gas, billy clubs and baseball bats, fiery crosses, and robed men revealed to the world the brutality of white supremacy and the sacrifices being made in the cause of human dignity. "[If] I became much more aggressive," the freelancer for *Life* from 1962 to 1972 said, "maybe my pictures would have something to do with making the South, which I really loved, a better place." His pictures of a young Martin Luther King Jr. being booked into jail, Police Commissioner Eugene "Bull" Connor barking orders, activist Dick Gregory leading marchers, NAACP leader Medgar Evers persevering, and James H. Meredith integrating the University of Mississippi became symbols of the struggle for civil rights. Moore's imagery of fear, hatred, faith, and courage influenced the national mood and facilitated passage of the Voting Rights Act of 1964. In 1989 Moore received the first Kodak Crystal Eagle Award for his impact on photojournalism.

Just as the camera chronicled the people, places, and happenings of the region, the American South left its imprint on the history of photography. Over the decades, virtually every kind and type of photography was practiced in the region: advertising, architectural, documentary, fashion, industrial, landscape, and portrait, among others. From mundane matters to epochal events, photographers were present to make a living, provide a service, record what transpired for posterity, and pass on their version of southern history. The camera took its place alongside literature, film, music, and art as a powerful transmitter of images of the American South.

Robert E. Snyder

James Curtis, *Mind's Eye, Mind's Truth* (1989); Ellen Dugan, ed., *Picturing the South: 1860 to the Present* (1996); Carl Fleischhauer and Beverly W. Brannan, eds., *Documenting America, 1935–1943* (1988); Nicholas Natanson, *The Black Images in the New Deal: The Politics of FSA Photography* (1992); Naomi Rosenblum, *A World History of Photography* (1997); Robert E. Snyder, ed., "The American South," *History of Photography* (1995); Robert E. Snyder, "In the Hood: African American Photography," *Southern Quarterly* (1998); Alan Trachtenberg, *Reading American Photographs: Images as History—Mathew Brady to Walker Evans* (1989).

PIEDMONT

The Piedmont as a geologic/geographic province extends from the vicinity of Washington and Baltimore southwestward to Georgia and western Alabama. To the northwest, several faults create the abrupt face of the Blue Ridge. To the southeast and south, a fall zone separates the rolling hills and deeply cut valleys of the Piedmont from the flat countryside and broad rivers of the coastal plain.

The topography and location of the fall zone continually change along its 750-mile length. Both to the north and south of North Carolina, the fall zone is relatively narrow, with a drop in elevation of several hundred feet in only a few tens of miles. In Virginia and Maryland, tidal rivers permit easy navigation across the entire coastal plain to cities such as Richmond and Baltimore, which are built across lower parts of the fall zone. Similarly, in South Carolina and Georgia, rivers are navigable, although not tidal, to cities such as Columbia, which is also built across the fall zone.

By contrast, the fall zone in North Carolina is complicated by the existence of "rift basins" formed as North America and West Africa were pulling apart to begin forming the Atlantic Ocean about 175 million years ago. These low basins filled by red sediments lie across the fall zone, making it necessary for rivers draining the Piedmont to negotiate nearly a hundred miles to make the same elevation change as rivers both north and south do in a much shorter distance. This

hundred-mile width contains numerous rapids and small waterfalls, making navigation impossible for more than short distances. Furthermore, the head of navigation at Fayetteville—the only significant inland river port in North Carolina—is not within the tidal range and is still more than fifty miles from major sources of hydropower in the Piedmont.

The combination of fall zone and Blue Ridge has isolated the Piedmont to different degrees in different places. In Virginia and Maryland, the location of the fall zone permitted relatively easy commercial integration of the Piedmont and coastal plain, and negotiable passes through the Blue Ridge into the Shenandoah Valley and farther west through the valley-and-ridge province of the Appalachians permitted interaction with the midcontinent region. In South Carolina and Georgia, the fall zone and the Appalachians were only slightly more difficult for travelers, but passage east to west across North Carolina was nearly impossible before the development of railroads and modern roads.

The isolation of the Piedmont by geologic/geographic barriers is compounded by low productivity in both agriculture and raw materials. The large areas of good soils in the bottomlands (mostly floodplains) of rivers in the coastal plain are absent in the narrow valleys of the Piedmont, where the majority of agricultural land is in the poor soils of hill slopes. The poor soils and lower temperatures caused by higher elevations meant that only hardy plants could be grown there, such as short-staple cotton, which required less effort than the more desirable but labor-intensive (hence slave-dependent) long-staple cotton of the coastal plantations. The short-staple cotton was not an economic crop until after the invention of the cotton gin in 1793, when rapid expansion of its cultivation caused further removal of nutrients from the Piedmont's soils.

The low quality of agriculture in the Piedmont was not a serious economic problem as long as most of the inhabitants were subsistence farmers who sold only small parts of their produce for cash. After the development of railroads in the latter part of the 1800s and of truck transportation in the 1900s, however, Piedmont farms could not compete against crops produced in the better soils of the Midwest, and even cotton growing was largely ended as federally subsidized water permitted it to be cultivated more cheaply in the normally arid western U.S. During the twentieth century, agricultural failure caused the Piedmont to change from an area almost completely covered by small farms to an almost unbroken stretch of forest.

Just as subsistence farming was giving way to a more commercial variety in the late 1800s, people discovered that the Piedmont had one very important resource. Water power was available along the fall zone or, in North Carolina, across much of the Piedmont. First with water wheels and later with electricity from dams built between 1900 and 1950, textile and other industries took advantage of the power and low wages of these previously nonindustrial areas to relocate out of areas where they had to pay their workers more (in 1900, the average North Carolinian employed in manufacturing earned less than half the average wage of workers in other parts of the country).

The development of industry has been the only activity that permitted economic survival of the Piedmont during the past century. As agriculture diminished, Piedmont residents found virtually no other local product that could support them. The Piedmont has no reserves of coal and petroleum and only minuscule amounts of extractable ores. The only significant exports are crushed rock for construction and wood chips for paper and other products. Thus, residents have no income from primary productivity to support them, and they actually have to find means to pay for energy and all of the other materials that most Americans now find necessary. Even Piedmont factories import the raw materials, such as metals and petroleum, that they use in their manufacturing plants.

Thus, during the past century, residents of the Piedmont have lived mostly as a "value-added" society. They buy food, energy sources, and various materials from elsewhere and pay by using some of them as raw materials in the Piedmont's factories. They also add value in other ways, such as tourism and supporting the lives of retirees who bring money with them as they move away from northern winters to settle in the South. It has become a society living by its wits rather than by any inherent bounty dispensed by the land.

Because of the economic realities of the Piedmont, the area made no impact on southern writing in either the colonial era or in the antebellum South. The most significant Piedmont writer to emerge from the antebellum South was George Moses Horton, a slave from Chatham County, North Carolina, who first wrote love poems for students at the University of North Carolina then turned more seriously to poetry, hoping to earn his freedom thereby. Horton's fame would be posthumous, but another son of the Piedmont made a sensational name for himself glorifying the Reconstruction South—Thomas Dixon followed *The Leopard's*

Spots (1903) with *The Clansman* (1905), a depiction of the Ku Klux Klan that is equally sensational and racist. Born at about the same time, William Sydney Porter of Greensboro achieved more lasting fame as O. Henry, a prolific writer of short stories. As the Piedmont began to be more successful economically in the twentieth century, native Piedmont writers made a larger impact on the literature of the South and of the nation. Wilbur J. Cash, who may be seen as a quintessential Piedmont figure, in *The Mind of the South* (1941) produced a major text for understanding the southerner; it springs from Piedmont experience. Later writers who grew up in the Piedmont and lived in it and wrote about it include poet and novelist James Dickey and fiction writers Doris Betts and Clyde Edgerton. Ben Robertson's autobiography *Red Hills and Cotton* (1942) conveys many realities of Piedmont life. The autobiographies of Mary Mebane portray the life of a black female growing up in Durham County, North Carolina, and her struggle to find a place as scholar and writer just before and then during the Civil Rights Movement. Pauli Murray's *Proud Shoes* (1978) traces her family back to slavery times in Orange County. Anne Tyler, though not Piedmont born, spent her childhood and teen years in Celo, North Carolina, and Raleigh, North Carolina, and then studied at Duke University. The Piedmont has made notable contributions to journalism and the shaping of the New South. Important shapers include Henry Grady, Walter Hines Page, Josephus Daniels, and Tom Wicker. The Piedmont, ever living by its wits, became home to numerous centers of learning—attracting teachers and writers who would make the region an important center for training writers and for furthering the understanding of southern literature.

John J. W. Rogers

See also Cotton; North Carolina, Literature of.

PIRACY

The men and women of the Golden Age of Piracy, roughly 1690 to 1720, left an indelible mark on the imagination of the English-speaking world, becoming the subjects of scores of histories, novels, plays, and movies. Their names alone—Rackam, Vane, Bonnet, Kidd, and Teach—have come to stand for their careers, intense and often short-lived spells of blood and strong drink, cutlass and cannon charges, gunsmoke and rough seas, against a backdrop of tropical balm and beauty. For the meanest of them, the pirate's life encompassed huge reversals of fortune: sudden wealth coming on the heels of privation, months of peaceful seclusion in uncharted coves punctuated by desperate chases at sea. By turns they were deliriously riotous after they captured booty and wryly sober before the hangman. Hoisting the black flag, they risked everything, embracing pillage, robbery, and murder as nothing less than a way of life.

Given the fact that some of the most notorious pirates worked the coastal regions of the Southeast, it is surprising that mainstream southern fiction registers only faint traces of these brigands of the high seas.

Captain Charles Johnson's *A General History of the Robberies and Murders of the Most Notorious Pirates* provides the earliest and most important account of the Golden Age of Piracy. First published in 1724, Johnson's *History* was an instant hit, appearing in four editions before 1726 and in an expanded 1734 edition. It has been nearly as popular in our age. The 1998 Lyons Press reissue of *A History* is the third this century. Johnson's book chronicles twenty-two rogue captains and their crews who trawled the Caribbean, southern Atlantic, and West African coasts, raiding the burgeoning trade in goods and slaves between Old and New Worlds in an age when guts and superior firepower were the arbiters of maritime rule. It's a work of superb craftsmanship, drenched in the seafaring idiom of its time, laden with primary documents, a freight of facts, and great stories.

Three of Johnson's subjects—Charles Vane, Stede Bonnet, and Edward Teach (alias Blackbeard)—favored the North and South Carolina coasts, attacking local and transatlantic shipping from sanctuaries in the region's barrier islands and coastal rivers. The most infamous of these was Blackbeard, "a man of uncommon boldness and personal courage," according to Johnson, who "was never raised to any command, till he went apirating." Apprenticed to Benjamin Hornigold, who soon accepted a royal pardon, Blackbeard learned his craft fast and exceedingly well, capturing a prized Guineaman, which he fitted with forty guns and renamed *Queen Anne's Revenge*. For two years, from 1716 to 1718, Blackbeard and his crew terrorized the Carolinas, once blockading Charleston until the city agreed to supply medicines for his syphilitic crew, and later enjoying quasi-official protection from North Carolina's governor Charles Eden.

But Blackbeard's career, like those of lesser pirates,

was short lived. Fed up with the disruption of trade and commerce occasioned by his activities, Virginia's governor Alexander Spotswood commissioned Lieutenant Robert Maynard to track down and kill Blackbeard. Maynard cornered his quarry off Ocracoke Island on November 17, 1718, and the most famous battle of the Golden Age of Piracy broke out. Blackbeard died at Maynard's hand after sustaining twenty-five wounds. Later that day, Maynard sailed into Bath Town with the pirate's head dangling from the bowsprit of his ship. Thirteen members of Blackbeard's crew were hanged at Williamsburg, Virginia, on March 12, 1718. Other victories would follow. Vane was captured and executed in Jamaica. Likewise, the hapless and inexplicable Stede Bonnet, known as "The Gentleman Pirate," was caught, convicted, and hanged along with twenty-nine of his crew at Charleston on October 28, 1718. It was the end of an era.

Southern writers, even Charleston's prolific romancier William Gilmore Simms (1806–1870), seem not to have cared much about pirates. Although they are the subjects of many well-known British works from Daniel Defoe's *Robinson Crusoe* (1719) to Robert Louis Stevenson's *Treasure Island* (1883) and J. M. Barrie's *Peter Pan* (1904), one has to look long and hard to find their trace in books by the most revered southern writers. Edgar Allan Poe gives the most direct look at actual pirate life. Set on Sullivan's Island, South Carolina, Poe's "The Gold-Bug" depicts Legrand's maniacal search for the treasure left by Captain William Kidd, though the story has nothing to do with Kidd himself. The liminal figure of the pirate discernable in the privateering career of Margaret Mitchell's Rhett Butler in *Gone With the Wind* (1936) illustrates, rather, the appeal of the figure to historical novelists such as Inglis Fletcher (*Lusty Wind for Carolina*, 1954), George Garrett (*Death of the Fox*, 1971), and Margaret Hoffman (*Blackbeard: A Tale of Villainy and Murder in Colonial America*, 1998). Perhaps the 1997 discovery of the remains of *Queen Anne's Revenge* in Beaufort Inlet, North Carolina, will rekindle interest in this singularly eventful chapter of southern history. Certainly, the romanticized spirit of the free-ranging, swashbuckling pirate persists among southerners. Jimmy Buffett's *A Pirate Looks at Fifty* spent nearly six months of 1998 on the best-seller list.

Marvin Hunt

See also Pirate.

Clinton V. Black, *Pirates of the West Indies* (1989); David Cordingly, *Under the Black Flag* (1995); Philip Gosse, *The History of Piracy* (1968); Capt. Charles Johnson, *A General History of the Most Notorious Robberies and Murders of the Most Notorious Pirates* (1734; reprint with introduction and commentary by David Cordingly, 1998).

PIRATE

Though pirates figure prominently in the pages of some important works of southern fiction, few if any resemble the swashbucklers and freebooters of popular legend.

In Edgar Allan Poe's adventure novel *The Narrative of Arthur Gordon Pym* (1838), a band of ax-wielding sailors with "piratical designs" mutinies aboard a Nantucket whaling ship, sending the young stowaway Pym "still farther South" on a voyage to oblivion. The legend of Captain Kidd inspired one of Poe's most famous tales, "The Gold-Bug" (1843), in which the reclusive genius William Legrand exercises his powers of ratiocination to decipher the cryptographic clues leading to the pirate's buried treasure in the dense woods outside Charleston. Poe himself seems to have been the model for the title character in "The Pirate" (1827), a story by his older brother Henry, a sailor and poet in his own right. Henry's tale of the melancholy outlaw Edgar Leonard, who wanders the seas a wretched outcast after murdering his lost love in a fit of jealous passion, owes its plot more to Edgar Poe's failed love affair with a Richmond belle than to any of the pirate folklore of the time.

Mark Twain, who claimed kinship to pirates dating back to "Elizabeth's time," drew upon his boyhood dream of being a pirate to write the scenes in *The Adventures of Tom Sawyer* (1877) where Tom and the other members of his gang run away from home to play pirates at Jackson's Island. Tom, or as he prefers to be called, "The Black Avenger of the Spanish Main," and his cohorts, Huck "the Red Handed" and Joe "The Terror of the Seas," have a "bully time" swearing blood oaths and indulging in all manner of "majestic vices" before abandoning piracy for the more "respectable" trade of robbery. In Twain's *Adventures of Huckleberry Finn* (1885), the King raises a hatful of money at a Pokeville camp meeting by posing as a reformed pirate set on returning to the Indian Ocean so that he can steer other pirates to the "true

path." As he declares afterward, "heathens don't amount to shucks, alongside of pirates, to work a camp-meeting with." In his own day, Twain himself battled literary "freebooters" in England and Canada who plundered his literary capital by selling pirated copies of his works abroad.

In George Washington Cable's Creole tale "Madame Delphine" (1879), the legendary pirate Lafitte retires to a life of genteel repose in old New Orleans amid rumors that his alter ego, the charitable banker Monsieur Vignevielle, is none other than the patriot-turned-privateer hero of local lore. Though Vignevielle's "courtesy and gentility" are enough to convince the local gossips that piracy must be "one of the sublimer virtues," his courtship of the ivory-skinned Olive, Madame Delphine's quadroon daughter, imperils his reputation among the Creole elite, whose disapproval once again threatens the old pirate with exile. That Vignevielle honors his marriage proposal even before he learns the secret "truth" about Olive's birth proves that he is, indeed, the "soul of honor" in an age when "every white man in this country, on land or on water," seems to Madame Delphine "a pirate."

John Kennedy Toole burlesques the Lafitte legend in his 1980 novel *A Confederacy of Dunces,* in which the flatulent medievalist turned hot-dog vendor Ignatius J. Reilly masquerades as the "avenging sword of taste and decency" on his daily route through New Orleans's French Quarter. Dressed in an "improbable" pirate costume, Reilly pushes his wiener-shaped cart through the streets of the Vieux Carré in an attempt to "link the hot dog with Creole legend," though his red sateen scarf, suede boots, and "large novelty store hoop of an earring" make him look more like "Charles Laughton in drag as the Queen of the Gypsies" than the legendary Lafitte. Reilly's exploits later lead him to Pirate's Alley, where he falls in a duel with the foppish decorator Dorian Greene, who foils his attempts to run him through with a plastic toy cutlass by tugging at Reilly's hoop earring. In the end, the only things Reilly manages to plunder are his costume and the franks he devours by the dozen from his own cart.

In James Branch Cabell's *There Were Two Pirates* (1946), the real-life Spanish buccaneer and self-proclaimed "King of the Pirates" José Gasparilla (1756–1828) chronicles his own rise to fame off the Florida coast, intent on proving that he is "no petty sea-thief." Guided by the assumption that a pirate is nothing more than a good capitalist, Gasparilla presents himself as a "magnate of commerce" who dominates the competition through a combination of "fixed business principles, . . . panic terror . . . [and] judicious advertising." Discarding the traditional skull and crossbones for "a more handsome ensign," Gasparilla leads his "associates" on a seven-year campaign of "rapine and butchery," all the while conducting his "professional labors" with "the dignity which befits a chief executive." Gasparilla's chronicle becomes a "comedy of division" in the book's second half, when he encounters his lost love, Isabel de Castro, and her husband, the mysterious Don Diego de Arredondo, who lends Gasparilla a magic birthstone that transports him to that "untroubled land without shadows" where he recovers at last the "contentment" and "felicity" that his life of piracy has denied him. While his abandoned shadow terrorizes the Florida coast, Gasparilla retires to St. Augustine to marry the widowed Isabel and live out his days in quiet anonymity. Like so many of Cabell's other romances in which the "hero becomes a husband," *There Were Two Pirates* ends a tale of reformation and redemption. In *The Devil's Own Dear Son* (1949), Gasparilla's great-nephew Diego de Arredondo Dodd continues his uncle's legacy by committing his own share of contemporary piracies as a forger, perjurer, draft-dodger and income-tax cheat. When Dodd later passes through the city's Gates of Horn into Hell to search for his father, he carries Gasparilla's magic birthstone in his pocket.

Brian Carpenter

See also Piracy

PLANTATION

Plantations in the South developed in the seventeenth century as large-scale agricultural ventures involving a large labor force of slaves. Beginning in the peninsula and tidewater regions of Virginia and Maryland, plantation culture expanded with the region's agricultural economy. The largest concentrations of plantation estates were located along the southeastern Atlantic and Gulf coasts, on the Mississippi floodplain, and in the fertile farmlands of the Upper South. Plantations evolved from large farms into grand estates containing hundreds or sometimes even thousands of acres that created great wealth by producing in volume the South's most important staple crops: first tobacco and indigo, then rice, sugar, and "King Cotton."

The plantation estate consisted of the planter's mansion; outbuildings such as overseers' houses, kitchens, barns, stables, and mills; the slaves' quarters, one- or even two-story cabins of simple construction; and sometimes a chapel, an infirmary, and a school. Elaborate gardens and tree-lined avenues completed a kind of village arrangement designed to provide for the daily needs of the master, his family, and his laborers. Along the James River and the Natchez Trace, in the Low Country of South Carolina and Georgia, set back from the bayous or from the great Mississippi in Louisiana, plantation houses might feature sweeping staircases, hand-blocked French wallpaper, and elegantly appointed rooms filled with priceless furniture. Although many planters' homes were of modest design, the palatial white-pillared mansion, constructed in Greek Revival or Georgian style, has become the icon of the Old South, symbolizing wealth, prestige, hospitality, graciousness, and order. The many works of Harnett Kane (*Plantation Parade*, 1945; *Natchez on the Mississippi,* 1947; *Gone Are the Days,* 1960) provide a photographic display and a nostalgic tone for these qualities, as he asks, "In a swiftly changing world might these not be values worth cherishing?"

The dark side of the plantation regime, lost in white nostalgic visions, was the source of its sustenance: slavery. The planter's status was defined by the number of slaves he owned, twenty or more, rather than by land or capital. Thus the plantation is synonymous with slavery itself, not only as a chattel institution but as a style of life and a system of values. In 1850, although fewer than one-fifteenth of white southerners owned fifty or more slaves, a regional economy dominated by agricultural enterprise allowed the planters to develop even in colonial times into an elite political as well as social class whose power was disproportionate to its numbers. Self-consciously following the style of the English gentry, the planters on the large plantations created the basis for the South's most potent myth. By the mid-nineteenth century, stereotypes of cavalier and belle, kindly master and mistress, and faithful "servants" were beginning to be well defined. One must read the slave narratives of the antebellum period to find a counterbalance.

White southern literature from early times has favored the plantation myth. The colonial Virginia planter William Byrd II self-consciously designed his James River plantation, Westover, to symbolize his aristocratic status and wrote lovingly of it in his later-published diaries. John Pendleton Kennedy set his

novel *Swallow Barn* (1832) on a James River plantation in order to draw upon the aura of elegance associated with plantations there. In the decades before the
Civil War, the Charles Colcock Jones family wrote letters to and from their three Georgia low-country plantations, a correspondence collected in Robert Manson
Myers's *The Children of Pride* (1972), which provides
one of our best historical records of plantation life.
Harriet Beecher Stowe, in *Uncle Tom's Cabin* (1852),
utilized popular literary images to construct her southern estates, and "Anti-Tom" novels throughout the
1850s sought to counter her abolitionist pictures with
elaborate constructions of their own. Although the
Civil War destroyed the plantation life-style, the post-
Reconstruction period of the 1880s and 1890s marked
the appearance of the mythical plantation's most powerful expression in the nostalgic works of New South
writers such as Thomas Nelson Page and Joel Chandler
Harris.

In modern times, William Faulkner in *Absalom, Absalom!* (1936), Eudora Welty in *Delta Wedding* (1946),
and Tennessee Williams in many of his plays created
compelling critiques of the plantation myth. The televised miniseries of Alex Haley's *Roots* (1977) and the
pulp-fiction series made from Kyle Onstott's *Mandingo*
(1957) have provided wildly popular versions of stereotypical plantation features. However, for the modern popular imagination, Scarlett O'Hara's Tara, fashioned by producer David O. Selznick for his 1939 film
version of Margaret Mitchell's *Gone With the Wind*
(1936), remains the most enduring model of what a
plantation ought to be.

Lucinda H. MacKethan

See also *Gone With the Wind*; Novel, 1820 to 1865; Plantation
Fiction; Stowe, Harriet Beecher.

Francis Pendleton Gaines, *The Southern Plantation: A Study in
the Development and Accuracy of a Tradition* (1925); Eugene
Genovese, *Roll, Jordan, Roll: The World the Slaves Made*
(1974); Lucinda MacKethan, *The Dream of Arcady: Place and
Time in Southern Literature* (1980); Darden A. Pyron, *Recasting "Gone With the Wind" in American Culture* (1983); Louis
D. Rubin Jr., *The Edge of the Swamp* (1989).

PLANTATION FICTION

Plantation fiction could refer to any fiction that exploits the trappings of the plantation's physical and so-

cial design—which to most would mean fiction containing the pillared mansion, long tree-lined avenue,
cotton or rice fields and slave quarters, elegant interiors, and predictable inhabitants—master, mistress,
belle, mammy, uncle, coachman, etc. Literature using
the plantation as setting goes back at least as far as
William Byrd of Westover's *Secret Diary, 1709–1712*
and to portions of Thomas Jefferson's *Notes on the
State of Virginia*, written in 1781–82. Most recently,
the much-touted sequel to Margaret Mitchell's *Gone
With the Wind*, Alexandra Ripley's *Scarlett* (1994),
picks up where Mitchell's 1936 novel left off, with a
depiction of Tara, perhaps the most famous literary
plantation ever constructed for popular consumption.
Plantation fiction, however, generally has a more restricted meaning for literary historians, who limit the
designation to fiction produced in active defense of the
plantation regime for some three decades before and
three decades after the Civil War.

Plantation fiction can be said to have had its genesis
as the South's answer to the abolitionist writing that
proliferated in the North beginning in the 1830s. In
that decade, abolitionist societies, spurred by the rhetoric of William Lloyd Garrison, began to publish both
fiction and nonfiction attacking the system of human
bondage that supported life on the South's plantations.
To counteract the slave narratives and other tracts that
abolitionists sponsored in order to fight slavery, southern writers of some merit turned their pens to fictional
portrayals of the plantation as an idyllic domestic arrangement uniting slaves and their masters in familial
bonds.

John Pendleton Kennedy's *Swallow Barn* (1832) is
often singled out as the most effective antebellum prototype of literary portrayals of the plantation. His
novel, set at a rather shabbily genteel plantation called
Swallow Barn on the James River, recounts a northerner's visit to this idyllic place, where pickaninnies dance
and young cavaliers court beautiful belles (the heroine's name is Belle). In the 1851 revised edition of the
novel, the master, Frank Meriwether, takes the northern visitor on a tour of the slave quarters, where he explains his benevolent paternal oversight of his childlike
laborers. Kennedy's addition of this scene indicates
how southerners in general were by midcentury feeling
the need to step up their defense of an increasingly embattled way of life. Another 1830s work of plantation
fiction, Caroline Gilman's *Recollections of a Southern
Matron* (1838), was also reissued in the 1850s, with a
new emphasis on differences between northern urban

and southern plantation homes. Gilman's novel follows the life of a young plantation daughter through her marriage to a paragon planter. By the time of its reprinting, southerners had felt the shock of the most important literary attack from the abolitionists—Harriet Beecher Stowe's *Uncle Tom's Cabin* (1852). In some ways, *Uncle Tom's Cabin* could be considered America's most important work of plantation fiction. In Uncle Tom, the Shelby plantation, Master St. Clare, Little Eva, and Simon Legree, the book offers memorable versions of most of the stereotypes that we now associate with the plantation. Stowe's vision also sparked plantation fiction's most important spurt in the South, as a phalanx of anti-Tom novels created plantation dramas as an attempted antidote to Stowe's powerful propaganda. No fewer than fourteen proslavery novels appeared in the three years following Uncle Tom's appearance, including one by Thomas Bangs Thorpe (*The Master's House*, 1854). Women entered the lists in great numbers, resulting in the publication, among others, of Sarah Josepha Hale's *Liberia* (1853); Mrs. M. H. Eastman's *Aunt Phillis' Cabin* (1852); Maria McIntosh's *Northern and Southern Life* (1852); Mary Howard Schoolcraft's *The Black Gauntlet* (1860); and the best of the lot, Caroline Lee Hentz's *The Planter's Northern Bride* (1854), which rather unaccountably includes the threat of a plantation slave insurrection in its defense of slavery.

Southern fiction written to idealize the planters' lives achieved its most important impact after the Civil War had ended the viability of the South's plantation economy. Beginning in the 1870s, northern magazines began publishing stories, poems, and essays that fit the postbellum local-color craze, and editors exhibited a decided preference for southern portrayals of slave/master relations "befo' dah wa'." The magazine work of Irwin Russell, Thomas Nelson Page, Sherwood Bonner (Katharine McDowell), and Joel Chandler Harris offered romance and "color" in reminiscences of plantation life that generally played down any friction and turned up the volume on the voices of slave characters themselves. Memorable dialectical renderings of these voices appear in Irwin Russell's narrative poem "Christmas Night in the Quarters" (published in a volume of his verse edited by Harris in 1888); Bonner's *Dialect Tales* (1883) and *Suwannee River Tales* (1884); Thomas Nelson Page's *In Ole Virginia* (1887); and Joel Chandler Harris's Uncle Remus tales (published in four collections between 1880 and 1905). Page and Harris in particular produced old black

"Uncle" storytellers whose nostalgia for slavery was persuasively couched in nonpolitical terms. What the plantation offered, we read again and again, was a system through which slaves participated, as full partners, in the family dramas of their masters. The ironies of the former slave narrators' dependency are unintentionally included in sentimental scenes of loyalty and mutual admiration. Joel Chandler Harris's Uncle Remus stories are in some measure complicated by the old storyteller's dual role; in one guise, he speaks to a postwar generation of whites about the good old days, but in a quite different voice he tells, and obviously identifies with, the folktales of that subversive animal anarchist, Brer Rabbit.

Harris and Page were the most talented and successful purveyors of the idea of the plantation South as a last American Golden Age, but they led a large group of lesser lights whose work was more sentimental and even less balanced. Francis Hopkinson Smith (1838–1915), Molly Elliot Seawell (1860–1916), Constance Cary Harrison (1843–1920), and Eugenia Jones Bacon (1840–1920) all fictionalized the plantation as Edenic for both slaves and masters.

Harrison's *Recollections Grave and Gay* (1911) and Bacon's *Lyddy: A Tale of the Old South* (1898) are autobiographical works drawing, like Thomas Nelson Page's *Two Little Confederates* (1888) and Joel Chandler Harris's *On the Plantation* (1892), on the authors' personal experiences of plantation life and the coming of the war that brought their childhood idylls to an abrupt and tragic end. In Louisiana, Grace King (1851–1931), George Washington Cable (1844–1925), and Kate Chopin (1851–1904) benefited from the popularity of southern local color and produced some well-wrought short stories with plantation settings (Chopin's "Désirée's Baby," Cable's "Belle Demoiselles Plantation" among them), but all three were more critical of slavery than other southern writers of this school and often attacked white racism in their plantation stories. Two other southerners produced the post–Civil War period's most important literature in critical response to the racism that was often only thinly veiled in plantation fiction. Mark Twain's *Adventures of Huckleberry Finn* (1885) and Charles Chesnutt's *The Conjure Woman* (1899) produced, in the characters of Huck's friend Jim and Chesnutt's narrator Uncle Julius, ironic black voices that condemn the ideal of the plantation as a happy interracial family. Plantation fiction, before and after the Civil War, was at its core propaganda designed to promote a white southern racist vision of the past. The stereotypes produced in such work, as Twain and Chesnutt attempted to show in their responses, were demeaning to blacks and distorted the historical realities on which post-Reconstruction politics were being fashioned at the end of the nineteenth century. With the rise of Jim Crow, the Ku Klux Klan, and the blatantly racist novels of Thomas Dixon, plantation fiction could be put away, after delivering its sugar-coated message all too well.

Lucinda H. MacKethan

See also Local Color; Novel, 1820 to 1865; Plantation; Race Relations; Racism.

R. Bruce Bickley, ed., *Critical Essays on Joel Chandler Harris* (1981); Richard Gray, *Writing the South* (1986); Lucinda H. MacKethan, *The Dream of Arcady: Place and Time in Southern Literature* (1980); Wayne Mixon, *Southern Writers and the New South Movement* (1980); Eric Sundquist, *To Wake the Nations* (1993).

PLESSY V. FERGUSON

Although the Civil War ended slavery in the southern United States and paved the way for the Thirteenth and Fourteenth Amendments to the Constitution, the segregation laws of the 1890s served to chip away at the civil rights so recently won by African Americans. In 1890 Louisiana passed a statute that required racially segregated railroad cars for intrastate travel. On June 7, 1892, Homer Adolph Plessy, backed by the Citizens Committee to Test the Constitutionality of the Separate Car Law, challenged that statute: he bought a first-class ticket on the East Louisiana Railroad from New Orleans to Covington and sat in the "white" car. Even though Plessy was only one-eighth black and seven-eighths white, he was considered black and was therefore arrested for sitting in a "white" car. He was found guilty in Louisiana State Court by Judge John H. Ferguson; Plessy appealed and his case reached the United States Supreme Court in 1896.

Black-rights advocate and former judge Albion W. Tourgée represented Plessy without fee. He argued that segregation violated both the Thirteenth Amendment by reestablishing black bondage to the dominant white class and the Fourteenth Amendment by denying African Americans equal protection under the law. He also claimed that membership in the dominant race—the white race—constituted property, and the ability of a conductor to place a person in a "black" car deprived that person of his property. Finally, Tourgée questioned the ability of the state to determine one's racial makeup; what rules can determine who is "white" and who is "colored"?

The U.S. Supreme Court overwhelmingly rejected Tourgée's arguments. In his majority opinion, Justice Henry Billings Brown dismissed the claim that segregation laws conflicted with the Thirteenth Amendment by asserting that a legal distinction between "the white and colored races" did not undermine the legal equality of the races nor did it create a state of involuntary servitude. He also argued that although the Fourteenth Amendment was established to enforce the legal equality of the two races, it was never intended to destroy racial distinctions or to force unwanted racial integration. Moreover, Brown claimed that if the races had equal civil and political rights, one race could not be inferior to the other on these grounds; if, however, one race was socially inferior, the Constitution could not make it equal. With this opinion, the Court established the legality of separate but equal facilities for African Americans for more than five decades.

Justice John Harlan, a former slaveowner, was the lone dissenter on the Court. In his opinion he acknowledged the dominance of the white race in America, but he argued that the Constitution does not recognize a hierarchy among its citizens, nor does it consider color in its guarantee of civil rights. He called the separate but equal ruling a "thin disguise" for black servitude and degradation that would only serve to plant the seeds of racial hatred. The vision of his dissent would not be recognized by the Court until 1954, when its decision on *Brown v. Board of Education* challenged the separate-but-equal doctrine for public education.

Southern literature has not overtly addressed the case of *Plessy v. Ferguson*, but issues of segregation, miscegenation, and "passing" have never been far from the southern literary imagination. Eric J. Sundquist convincingly argues that Mark Twain had the case in mind when writing *Pudd'nhead Wilson* (1894) and posits Tom Driscoll as Twain's Homer Plessy and Pudd'nhead as the voice of segregation. Thomas Dixon's trilogy, including *The Leopard's Spots: A Romance of the White Man's Burden—1865–1900* (1902), provides a glimpse into the mentality that produced segregation. The issue of "passing" is examined in several texts, including Charles Chesnutt's *The House Behind the Cedars* (1900) and James Weldon Johnson's *The Autobiography of an Ex-Coloured Man* (1912). This issue is also a theme in many fugitive slave narratives, such as William and Ellen Craft's *Running a Thousand Miles for Freedom* (1860).

Brigette Wilds Craft

See also *Brown v. Board of Education*; Jim Crow; Miscegenation; Segregation.

Andrew Kull, *The Color Blind Constitution* (1992); Charles A. Lofgren, *The Plessy Case: A Legal-Historical Interpretation* (1987); Otto Olsen, *The Thin Disguise: Turning Point in Negro History* (1967); C. Vann Woodward, *The Strange Career of Jim Crow* (3rd rev. ed.; 1974).

POCAHONTAS

Pocahontas (d. 1617), a favorite daughter of the Algonquian Indian chief Powhatan (d. 1618), became a myth of American history. Though she existed, she is remembered as larger than life. Paintings of her abound in the United States Capitol. More than George Washington or any "Founding Father" of the United States, she is the American symbol. But what aspects of America does she represent? The tantalizing puzzle of Pocahontas begins with the reality. Did she save Captain John Smith? Did she really intercede and place her head over his, just as the Indian warriors were about to bash in his skull? If so, why? Did she love him? Did she love humanity? Was she sponsoring him into the Algonquian nation? The search for American identity that was initiated after the American Revolution enshrined Pocahontas in the pantheon of American heroes. The great outpouring of works about Pocahontas in the nineteenth century was preceded by an appreciation based on Robert Beverley's treatment of Pocahontas in his *History of Virginia* (1704). A writer in the 1734 *Boston Gazette* said that the Pocahontas-Smith story would be a great subject for American literature. "What a glorious Figure wou'd the Princess Pocahontas make, Painted by a fine hand!"

Pocahontas primarily symbolizes love, sometimes love for humanity but more often passionate, sexual love. The myth, embodied in numerous nineteenth-century plays, poems, novels, and children's books, portrays her as loving Smith. John Davis presented her as a personification of sexuality in 1803 and 1805. Peggy Lee, the singer and songwriter of the 1940s to 1980s, expressed the view in her popular song "Fever" (1958): Pocahontas and Smith "had a very mad affair." Some-

times, Pocahontas and Smith also embody the dream of friendship and love between warring races, a version of Romeo and Juliet, writ larger because the Pocahontas-Smith relationship involved the aspirations not just of a romantic couple or of a family, but of the races and the future of America. As Herman Melville wrote in *The Confidence Man*, "When I think of Pocahontas, I am ready to love Indians."

In a second general theme, Pocahontas embodies the spirit of the wilderness (as in the Walt Disney Studios movie of 1997, where her totems—the badger and the hummingbird—steal the show). The Pocahontas-Smith relationship fuses civilization and wilderness, reinvigorating and teaching the former (the totem of civilization in the movie is the bulldog, who is reformed by his experience in the wilderness). And in some literary and artistic versions, the wilderness that Pocahontas embodies is the savage, the wild, the revengeful, and the passionate—thus tending toward fierce love, an aspect of her primary meaning.

Six comparatively minor themes recur. Pocahontas represents the democratic air of America—the royal princess who married a commoner. Of course, numerous descendants, including John Randolph of Roanoke, Edith Bolling Galt Wilson (second wife of President Woodrow Wilson), and the novelist James Branch Cabell, have been proud of their ancestor Pocahontas. Her early-seventeenth-century status as royalty acutely upset John Rolfe, who feared that he might be violating England's social hierarchy in marrying her. The anti-South Henry Adams, in attacking the Pocahontas-Smith story in the *North American Review* (1867), called her royalty a source of aristocratic pride for her descendants—while he implied that the descendants were the result of miscegenation. Thus a second minor theme has been aristocratic pride. And for some covert racists, Pocahontas is a symbol of miscegenation, a third theme, and the false pride of the South, a fourth.

For some, Pocahontas embodies the superiority of Christianity. Rolfe instanced her conversion to Christianity and her baptism as reasons to marry her—thereby to bring religion to the pagans. Lydia H. Sigourney's "Pocahontas" (1841), and John Gadsby Chapman's painting in the United States Capitol, "The Baptism of Pocahontas" (1836–1840), celebrate this view. A sixth minor theme is Pocahontas as prototypical feminist: witness Robert Dale Owen, *Pocahontas* (1837), Mrs. Seba Smith in the *Southern Literary Messenger* (1840), and Charlotte Barnes in *The Forest Princess* (1848).

A final major theme is summarized in Vachel Lindsay's phrase, "Our Mother, Pocahontas" (1917). This topic weaves together many of the above, plus the position of Virginia, Pocahontas, and Captain John Smith in early American history, to make Pocahontas the mother of Americans. Carl Sandburg prefigured the theme in "Cool Tombs" (1915), which Lindsay used as his epigraph, and Hart Crane made it one foundation of his epic about America, *The Bridge* (1930). Though twentieth-century poets have generally praised Pocahontas, two excellent literary satires feature her: James Brougham's play *Po-ca-hon-tas* (1855) and John Barth's novel *The Sot-Weed Factor* (1960). One can safely predict more, both serious and satiric, will follow.

J. A. Leo Lemay

See also Aristocracy; Indians; Miscegenation; Smith, Captain John.

Jay B. Hubbell, "The Smith-Pocahontas Story in Literature," *Virginia Magazine of History and Biography* 65 (1957); J. A. Leo Lemay, *Did Pocahontas Save Captain John Smith?* (1992); Frances Mossiker, *Pocahontas: The Life and the Legend* (1976); William M. S. Rasmussen and Robert S. Tilton, *Pocahontas: Her Life & Legend* (1994); Robert S. Tilton, *Pocahontas: The Evolution of an American Narrative* (1994); Philip Young, "The Mother of Us All: Pocahontas Reconsidered," *Kenyon Review* 24 (1962).

POE, EDGAR ALLAN

Of all American writers, Edgar Allan Poe has maintained a truly global reputation, readership, and influence. But in his own time, most southern readers did not recognize his achievement until his death; after all, in his creative work Poe was indifferent to the southern scene and its planter tradition, and with the publication of the "Ludwig" obituary and memoir in 1849 (both by Rufus Griswold), the "legend" of Poe as "unmoral" and demonic was born. But there were southerners who championed Poe as early as 1830, notably John P. Kennedy.

Poe's influence was first apparent in its effect on the poems and essays of his contemporaries. Henry Timrod, for instance, owed some technical and thematic debt to Poe, although his poem "Ethnogenesis" is little more than a versified tract on the South and Christianity. Most strongly reminiscent of Poe is Timrod's essay "Literature in the South," which describes southern

authors as frustrated by critics, whom he calls bigots, slaves, autocrats, and chauvinist "Americans." Timrod also echoed Poe in deploring the fact that mathematics and syllogistic logic were replacing the study of poetry and its underlying philosophy. Thomas Holley Chivers was much influenced by Poe's verse (especially the hypnotic effect of tone and music) as well as by New England Transcendentalism, which he recommended to Poe for its power. James M. Legaré in "To a Lily" celebrated the ideal woman with a Poe-like directness of tone. In Philip Pendleton Cooke's "Florence Vane," one also senses a likeness to Poe's "Song" and "Bridal Ballad" in tone and irony. Cooke's "few hurried observations" on Poe's poems are apposite but superficial: "The Raven" is extravagantly praised as "a singularly beautiful poem"—the rhythm exquisite, the diction "musical and apt." Paul Hamilton Hayne, the central figure in this group after Simms died in 1870, is noted for his war poems and nature lyrics, though they lack the depth and power of Poe's verse. In 1874 he confessed that "the only real art-friends . . . I ever found, are Northern men." Despite Poe's "very savage attack" on his novel *The Partisan*, William Gilmore Simms spoke highly of Poe's "magnetic power," "clear and correct" style, vivid fancies, and "generally good" tastes.

Sidney Lanier, like Simms, felt at home in the North as well as the South, and like Chivers he became a serious student of the musical aspect of poetry, attempting, like Poe, to turn the art of poetry into a science of verse. In "The Symphony," he uses names of orchestral instruments as thematic motifs, and addresses "Fair Lady" in a chivalric allusion to woman as both feminist cause and symbol of Love, with "Life! Life! thou sea-fugue" as the musical score. Much as these elements derive from Poe, in toto this poem illustrates Poe's "Heresy of the Didactic." More in the Poe tradition are "Song of the Chattahoochee" and "The Marshes of Glynn," the latter ending with the idea of Poe's "psychal fancies" (Marginalia #150). In his essay on the New South, Lanier developed some of Poe's elements of faith in agrarianism. After Lanier, the Poe legacy passed to Mark Twain, Ambrose Bierce, Willa Cather, Ellen Glasgow, James Branch Cabell, Faulkner, Porter, and Welty. The darker moods and moments in Poe's writings are reflected in *Adventures of Huckleberry Finn, The Mysterious Stranger, Letters from the Earth,* and a dozen of Twain's satiric tales and essays. Some of Twain's preoccupation with violence and the grotesque also reflects Poe.

A native of Virginia, Willa Cather in her senior year delivered a paper on Poe to the literary societies at the University of Nebraska; she identified deeply with Poe as a misunderstood genius suffering more from hunger than alcoholism. Except for Lowell, according to Cather, Poe was "our only great poet. . . . He [also] first gave the short story purpose, method, and artistic form." In her outlook on life and art, she shared with Poe a Platonic "essential realism" of the secret "soul" or inner being manifest in all her characters. Ellen Glasgow also felt linked to Poe, as she testified in a letter on September 7, 1944, to Van Wyck Brooks: "I have always felt a curious (because an improbable) kinship with Poe, and your study of him moves me profoundly. . . . Your chapter on his life in Richmond rings true in every word." She summed up Poe as "a distillation of the Southern. The formalism of his tone, the classical element in his poetry and in many of his stories, the drift toward rhetoric, the aloof and elusive intensity—all these qualities are Southern." From the outset she attacked "evasive idealism" in favor of "blood and irony."

William Faulkner has long been accepted and studied as a creative genius of the Deep South. His early realization of the value of his "own little postage stamp of native soil" was developed in the Yoknapatawpha saga, in which his characters are subtly revealed by their vivid vernacular tendencies. As in Poe's tales, the struggle between moral integrity and the hypertrophied intellect is externalized by Faulkner in the principled Sartorises and the ruthless, scheming Snopeses. Poe's idealized woman of undaunted courage and southern spirit is exemplified in several of his characters (although Faulkner adds grotesque irony in many cases). In his Nobel Prize acceptance speech and "The Bear," Faulkner expressed the underlying idealism of his outlook on life in terms of the "eternal verities"—"love and honor and pity and pride and compassion and sacrifice"—verities present in Poe's "Eleonora," "To Helen" (1831), "Annabel Lee," "Ulalume," for instance. In method and style, Faulkner's free association, flashbacks, symbolic motifs, multiple narrators, and time shifts make for a narrative both difficult and rewarding; some of these traits are recognizable as prefigured to a degree in Poe's densely textured impressionistic tales.

On the criticism front, by the mid-twentieth century, lectures by three prominent poets greatly influenced the direction of Poe studies. In "From Poe to Valery" (1949), the Missouri-born T. S. Eliot said that if Poe's work is taken from "a distant view of it as a

whole, we see a mass of unique shape and impressive size." As if in response, Allen Tate, a Virginian, in "The Angelic Imagination" (1952) presented what he thought "nobody else has seen" in Poe's writing: the "philosophic perspective" behind *Eureka* and the three angelic colloquies as clues to the meaning of his symbols. In his widely admired and influential lecture "The House of Poe" (1959), Richard Wilbur, the northern poet, also drawing on Poe's work as a whole, shared with Poe aficionados in the South an appreciation for the building-block images, metaphors, symbols, and hypnagogic allegories of Poe's "house" of art and thought. Ten years later, Robert D. Jacobs in *Poe: Journalist and Critic* (1969) included significant essays on Poe's aesthetic, cosmology, and philosophy, beginning with Poe's first "philosophical review" (on Drake and Halleck) and suggestions of pantheism in "The Island of the Fay." Poe's position as the one major literary artist of the Old South is secure. His influence as poet, fiction writer, and critic continues to be enormous.

Eric W. Carlson

See also Gothicism; Grotesque, The; Violence.

Eric W. Carlson, ed., *A Companion to Poe Studies* (1996), *Critical Essays on Edgar Allan Poe* (1987), and *The Recognition of Edgar Allan Poe* (1966); Frederick S. Frank and Anthony Magistrale, comps., *The Poe Encyclopedia* (1997); Jay B. Hubbell, "Edgar Allan Poe," in *Eight American Authors,* ed. James Woodress (rev. ed.; 1971); Robert D. Jacobs, *Poe: Journalist and Critic* (1969); Louis D. Rubin Jr., ed., *The Edge of the Swamp* (1989).

POETRY, BEGINNINGS TO 1820

Early southern poetry is remarkably vital and varied in subject and style. Colonial America featured an active literary scene, particularly in Maryland and Virginia. However, mechanisms for publication and distribution were decentralized, so much poetry of good quality has only recently been rediscovered and properly identified. A more substantial body of southern poetry from this period has been emerging and promises to alter radically common assumptions about the early poets.

Contrary to conventional scholarly dismissal of native influences, southern writing of the colonial period is strongly marked by Indian themes and imagery. Ebenezer Cooke's satirical *The Sot-Weed Factor* not only showcases native landscapes and place-names but also inverts the "savage" stereotype. Richard Lewis, America's first nature poet, celebrates indigenous flora and fauna and defends the innocence of Indian culture, as does James Sterling several decades later. Indian characters, themes, imagery, and patterns of thought mark the literature of this period. A subsequent shift of emphasis, beginning in the 1820s and 1830s, to the burning question of slavery and the lot of African Americans has tended to marginalize this chapter of southern literature.

Also problematic have been post-Romantic notions of poetry and the public role of the poet, which have disadvantaged colonial southern poetry. In fact, an impressive range of verse was written in the period—from patriotic hymns, ballads, witty epigrams, and satires to long epics and treatments of current events. To an extent not seen either before or since, early southern poetry interpenetrated other genres, appearing in letters, diaries, newspapers, journals, and histories, as well as in more conventional pamphlet and book form. Much poetry was published under a pseudonym in the *Maryland Gazette* or *Virginia Gazette,* making authorship difficult to establish. Early southern poetry was dispersed into many corners of the culture in a manner that clashes with twentieth-century expectations about professional, self-acknowledged poets and publishers.

Prior to the advent of such major figures as William Gilmore Simms and Edgar Allan Poe, early southern writers stayed active in nonliterary life. And many civic leaders also wrote poetry. Captain John Smith's *General History of Virginia, New England, and the Summer Isles* includes a number of poetic excerpts, and Smith also wrote longer poems such as "The Sea Mark," a striking ode reminiscent of Donne but also prefiguring Cowper. William Byrd, most renowned for *The Histories of the Dividing Line* and *The Secret Diaries,* wrote a number of poems, among them short ditties to women published in *Tunbrigalia* (London, 1719) and the ribald "Upon a Fart."

Even more dedicated southern poets remained active in colonial life. Like many of their fellow poets, Ebenezer Cooke and John Markland practiced law. William Dawson, whose *Poems on Several Occasions by a Gentleman of Virginia* appeared in 1736, became president of William and Mary and the bishop's commissioner. Samuel Davies, a New Light Presbyterian minister, followed Jonathan Edwards as president of New Jersey College, which later became Princeton. Richard Bland served as member of the Virginia House of Burgesses, and Thomas Burke was elected both as a delegate to the Continental Congress and as governor of North Carolina. Colonial southern poetry emerged out of active civic life and, to an extent not seen since, commented on the social issues of the day.

George Alsop, Anglican divine, is a case in point. His *A Character of the Province of Mary-Land* was published to acclaim in London in 1666. This boisterous work, one of the strongest prose portraits of colonial life, includes a number of short poems. These are not striking technically, but Alsop offers spirited poetic defense of *Mary-Land* as the "only Emblem of Tranquility." Many of the poems, imbued with a tolerant religious sensibility, also offer brief lessons on thrift and gratitude for Mary-Land's bounty.

John Cotton, of whom little is known, wrote two related poems justly acclaimed as the best American poetry of the seventeenth century. "Bacon's Epitaph, Made by His Man" and "Upon the Death of G.B." offer contrasting perspectives of Bacon's Rebellion in Virginia in 1676–77 against William Berkeley and the Council of State. Written in iambic pentameter couplets, with supple use of enjambment, the two poems exhibit an impressive mastery of versification. They also incorporate a variety of allusions to Paracelsus, Caesar, and Greek mythology. Imagery centers on legal and moral issues, with references to judgment and "a higher Court." These strong, dignified poems merit placement in any anthology of early American verse.

Ebenezer Cooke (1670–c. 1732), the first southern poet to produce a significant body of work, published *The Sot-Weed Factor* in 1708 in London, later to become the basis of John Barth's twentieth-century novel of the same name. An instant success, this long satire embodies the early American gift for mockery. The poem is written in the manner of Samuel Butler's *Hudibras,* with rollicking tetrameter couplets and outrageous rhymes. The poem ends with the outwitted, overly refined Englishman cursing the Americans as "slaves" and "savages," "as *Indians* Wild." This playing with Indian and American stereotypes Cooke continued in *Sotweed Redivivus* (1730) and *The History of Colonel Nathaniel Bacon's Rebellion* (1731), but he also published serious poems, among them elegies on the deaths of Thomas Bordley and Benedict Leonard Calvert. Cooke fully deserved his designation as "Poet-Laureate of Maryland," the strongest early poet of humorous verse.

Richard Lewis (c. 1700–1734), overall a more gifted poet than Cooke, wrote America's first nature poetry some half-century before Philip Freneau. His works include a translation of Edward Holdsmith's Latin poem *Muscipula* and a number of dedicatory poems to leading public figures, but "A Journey from *Patapsco* to *Annapolis*, April 4, 1730" is certainly one of the best poems of the eighteenth century. Recalling early Pope and especially James Thomson's *Seasons*, the poem nonetheless uniquely celebrates the hummingbird, sassafras, dogwood, and other native American species. The description follows a solitary speaker on a journey covering one day, ending with an intense apostrophe to the "SUPREME OF BEINGS." The imagery is strong and uniquely "New World," and Lewis emerges as one of the first to defend the native Indians. His poem was so successful in England that Pope felt obliged to include Lewis among those he attacked in Book IV of *The Dunciad*. Another important nature poem, "Food for Criticks," has been called "the best nature poem of Colonial America." Lewis's poetry is evocative and vibrant; along with Ebenezer Cooke, he can be regarded as having initiated a level of poetic sophistication that influenced at least a generation of writers and readers.

Irish-born James Sterling (1701–1763) wrote largely in the heroic manner, combining rich use of classical allusion in a manner reminiscent of Pope with an ode form closer to Gray and Collins. Yet his themes are resolutely American, and, like Richard Lewis, Sterling defends the Indians' right to remain unmolested by European Christians who "Massacre Millions, and inslave the Rest." He published regularly in the *Maryland Gazette* and in *American Magazine,* which devoted an entire issue to Sterling's "A Pastoral," written in 1744 on the death of Alexander Pope. Although much of his poetry may seem stilted to modern tastes, Sterling was the most Augustan of colonial poets, and the *Maryland Gazette* eulogized him as "unrival'd in this part of the World."

Samuel Davies (1723–1761) is the only poet of the period whose collected verse is accessible in a contemporary edition. He was celebrated as a gifted sermonizer and preacher in the New Light Presbyterian cause. Not surprisingly, his *Miscellaneous Poems, Chiefly on Divine Subjects* focuses on religious themes, recalling elements of Edward Taylor and Michael Wigglesworth of New England. These expansive poems are meditative in spirit, addressing such abstract topics as "Sinful Immorality," "Human Nature," "Conjugal Love and Happiness," and "The Law and Gospel." But the appendix includes several more concrete poems, such as "A Description of Storm, May 9, 1751," and "On

hearing of the Rev. Mr. Samuel Blair's desperate Illness by common Fame . . ." The "uncollected poems" are wide ranging, from "Frontier Warfare," which attacks the barbarities of the French and Indian Wars, to an Ode to Science and a poem on the birth of his third son, among others. These testify to Davies's poetic range and sophistication.

James Reid of Virginia is among those significant poets recently rediscovered by modern scholarship. Much of his work appeared pseudonymously in the *Virginia Gazette* in the years 1768 and 1769. Like his extended prose satire, "The Religion of the Bible . . .," Reid's poetry is frequently witty and urbane, as in "To My Pen." He also penned mock-elegies, such as "The Lamentation of a Young Lady for the Loss of Her Favourite Bird," recalling Gray, Goldsmith, and others. Reid's contributions as "Caledoniensis" to the "Poet's Corner" section of the *Gazette* remained largely light-hearted, but *Ode on Christmas Day 1768* is a serious religious poem, and "To Ignorance" advances several important satiric arguments. Reid has emerged recently as a significant southern poet of the latter half of the eighteenth century.

Many other poets remain to be discovered. Robert Bolling (1735–1775), whose work is only now being collected, has been described as "the most accomplished satirist of Colonial Virginia," but many of his poems were apparently never published and remain in archive collections. In addition to John Markland's unintentionally comic "Typographia. An Ode on Printing," at least one other by the same author has surfaced. Ongoing identification of individual poems by Charles Hansford, John Mercer, and others indicates that much archival work remains to be done. Female authors are noticeably rare and difficult to trace. Although a Mrs. An. Cotton of Q. Creeke wrote "An Account of Our Late Troubles in Virginia" in 1676, internal evidence indicates that her account is a condensation of "The Burwell Papers" by her husband, John Cotton. Women did, however, play an active role in publishing; Elizabeth Timothy continued publishing the *South-Carolina Gazette* with her son after her husband's death, and her daughter-in-law Ann and their son Benjamin Franklin Timothy continued until 1802.

Contrary to popular perception, early southern poetry is marked by an impressive multiplicity of voices, a richness of literary and classical allusion, and a variety of poetic forms. Libraries of the period were well stocked, and public discussion was active. Many political and civic leaders turned their hand to verse, some with notable success. Poets writing prior to 1820 kept well abreast of literary developments in England and the Continent; particularly influential figures were Dryden, Pope, Samuel Butler, Thomson, Gray, and Collins. But the exotic American landscape and encounters with the Indians added a conspicuous new dimension to old forms. And the unique mix of religious convictions and political involvement marks the poetry of the colonial South as particularly in tune with historical events. For contemporary readers, early southern poetry is still very much in formation, with new scholarly discoveries adding to our understanding of a vital period in American literary life. Long-overdue definitive editions would serve to trace the early influences of Indians, nature, history, politics, religion, and humor in what was, in fact, a fascinating literary ferment on new, dynamic ground.

David Radavich

See also Indians; Women Writers, Beginnings to 1820.

Samuel Davies, *Collected Poems* (1968); Richard Beale Davis, *Literature and Society in Early Virginia, 1608–1840* (1973); J. A. Leo Lemay, *Men of Letters in Colonial Maryland* (1972).

POETRY, 1820 TO 1900

Poetry in the South in the nineteenth century changed very little from the 1820s to the end of the century. Southern poets, early and late, were ever mindful of the work of their British colleagues from Chaucer to their own times and derived much of their sense and knowledge of form and metrics from them. Many southern poets—Richard Henry Wilde, Edward C. Pinkney, William Gilmore Simms, Edgar Allan Poe, Paul Hamilton Hayne, and Henry Timrod among them—knew and drew from the Classical tradition too, especially from Horace and Catullus, but it was the British (eventually Anglo-American romantic) tradition that sustained southern verse throughout the century.

Southern poets seldom could successfully devote themselves to writing verse for a living during this period. Few writers indeed could support themselves by their pens. Simms, Poe, and Hayne tried earnestly to do so, but Simms eventually had his wife's plantations, and Hayne in his early career had his mother's plantation for support, and each had to compose in as many genres as possible to make ends meet. Poe, of course,

discovered early that poems would not sell, that fiction would do little better, and that only editing and criticism would enable him to eke a bare living for his little family in Richmond, Philadelphia, or New York. As Albert Pike, a native of Massachusetts transplanted in Arkansas, expressed it in 1834: "The gift of poetry is but a curse, / Unfitting it amid the world to brood / And toil and jostle for a livelihood."

Despite these discouraging circumstances, a number of writers tried their hands at verse before the Civil War, including, in addition to Wilde, Simms, Poe, Hayne, and Timrod, Edward Coote Pinkney, Thomas Holley Chivers, Alexander Beaufort Meek, Philip Pendleton Cooke, James Mathewes Legaré, John R. Thompson, Theodore O'Hara, William J. Grayson, and George Moses Horton, the most prolific African American poet of the period. Few of these poets lived until the beginning of the war and only Hayne and Horton may be said to have really survived it, both living into the 1880s. Moreover, many of them achieved reputation chiefly as the authors of fugitive poems, as in the cases of Wilde with "The Lament of the Captive" (1815?), of Pinkney with "A Health" (1824), of Cooke with "Florence Vane" (1840), and of O'Hara with "The Bivouac of the Dead" (1847). At the same time, these poets managed to publish more widely than their success with fugitive verse might suggest. Wilde (1789–1847), for example, wrote a long poem, *Hesperia,* published twenty years after his death, and his poems were eventually collected in 1966. Pinkney (1802–1828), on the contrary, brought out *Rodolph* (1823), a long narrative, and *Poems* (1825), a slim volume of polished lyrics, a body of work sufficient for Poe to call him "the first of American lyrists." Nor was Cooke (1816–1850) limited by a single poem. His *Froissart Ballads* (1847) was well received by some critics, including Poe, who maintained that Cooke's reputation suffered because he was a southerner. Only O'Hara (1820–1867), the author of one of the best-known martial lyrics in the history of American literature, failed to compose enough poems to gather in his own day or to leave enough to be collected in another time.

Of the aforementioned poets of this period, Simms, Poe, Chivers, Hayne, and Horton published more prolifically than their contemporaries, though Hayne's three volumes of the 1850s may be characterized as early work leading to the more significant collections of the postwar era. At the same time, Meek (1814–1865) published two volumes: *Songs and Poems of the*

South (1857), his only collection, and *The Red Eagle* (1855), a long narrative on the Indian and early history of the Southwest. Legaré (1823–1859), Grayson (1788–1863), and Timrod (1828–1862) brought out one volume each, and Thompson's (1823–1873) only collection was lost in the blockade during the war (his *Poems* subsequently appeared in 1920). Legaré's *Orta-Undis, and Other Poems* (1848) and subsequent verse were well received in his own day and in the twentieth century as well, with C. Hugh Holman's characterization of the poet as "one of the authentic lyric voices of the antebellum South." Grayson, on the other hand, produced *The Hireling and the Slave* (1856), an attack in old-fashioned couplets on northern industrialism and a defense of slavery as "the best system of labor . . . for the Negro and this country." Timrod finally managed to gather his verse for a volume in 1860, but his major contribution came during the lifetime of the Confederacy with a dozen poems that stirred the southern mind and spirit like no others.

To assess in short compass the more prolific poets of this time—Simms, Poe, Chivers, and Horton—is a considerable task. Simms, for example, published—often anonymously or pseudonymously—over nineteen hundred poems in periodicals and in volumes from *Lyrical and Other Poems* (1826) to *Areytos; or, Songs and Ballads of the South, with Other Poems* (1860). Basically a romantic in his interest in the individual, in nature, and in poetic diction, Simms's canon focuses for the most part on the personal lyric or on philosophical topics, as in "Shakespeare" (1845), "Stanzas" (1849), "The City of the Silent" (1850), or "Harmonies of Nature" (1856); as in the long narrative "The Cassique of Accabee: A Legend of Ashley River" (1845–1855); and in such dramatic works as *Norman Maurice* (1851) and *Michael Bonham* (1852). Nor should his verse on the "inevitable conflict" ("Southern Ode," 1850) or on the war itself and its aftermath—"Ode—Our City by the Sea" (1863)—be overlooked. By bulk, structure, genre, variety of theme, and technique, Simms is the most substantial of all southern poets of the period, or the century for that matter, but the lukewarm response to his poetry after 1833 led him to turn to fiction, editing, and other forms for his literary livelihood, though he continued to write and publish verse until the late 1860s and to consider himself chiefly a poet throughout his career.

Edgar Allan Poe (1809–1849), concurrently, also thought of himself mainly as a poet, and, like Simms, found it necessary to turn in the 1830s to fiction, re-

viewing, and editing after his first three volumes of verse in 1827, 1829, and 1831 failed to win popular or critical acclaim. Poe managed to reinstate himself as a poet with the publication of "The Raven" in 1845 and with a new collection featuring this famous fugitive piece entitled *The Raven and Other Poems* (1845), but in spite of the fame of this poem and the subsequent appearances of "Ulalume" (1847), "The Bells" (1849), and "Annabel Lee" (1849), Poe still could not make a living with poetry alone, a situation not completely unfamiliar anywhere in America.

Unlike Simms and Poe, Thomas Holley Chivers (1809–1858) possessed an independent income and could afford to pay for the publication of his own books and not need to concern himself about public or critical response. Accordingly, he brought out eleven volumes of verse and drama, mostly at his own expense, beginning with *The Path of Sorrow* (1832) and ending with *The Sons of Usna* (1858). Written "to himself," as Poe pointed out in 1845 and not "for the public," his verse often resembles Poe's in stanza and meter sufficiently to provide scholars and critics with problems as regards dating and influence. Some of Chivers's poems that are similar to Poe's cannot be dated precisely and consequently priority is difficult to establish. The best evidence to date suggests that each borrowed at times from the other, but that, as C. Hugh Holman concludes, Chivers "did with limited success what Poe did with genius."

George Moses Horton (1797–1883?), the most talented and prolific of the African American poets of the period, published three volumes: *The Hope of Liberty* (1829), *Poetical Works of George M. Horton* (1845), and *Naked Genius* (1865). Horton, a slave, taught himself to read and managed to provide himself with subsistence from the several masters by the sale of verse (mostly acrostics) to students at the University of North Carolina in Chapel Hill; they, in turn, served as his copyists. After the war, he moved to Philadelphia, worked for former North Carolinians living there, and apparently failed to print any verse in Pennsylvania.

At the beginning of the Civil War, southern poetry was in a stage of transition. Pinkney, Wilde, Poe, Cooke, Chivers, and Legaré were dead, and Grayson died in 1863, Meek in 1865, O'Hara and Timrod in 1867, Simms in 1870, and Thompson in 1873. In addition to these losses, the war changed everything else. Poets who had seldom been involved in politics were forced by circumstances to take part directly in the war or to deal with it substantially in their work, despite its constant interruptions and interferences. At the same time, war provided material, themes, and conditions for celebration of the new nation and its efforts to establish and defend itself. Accordingly, Simms, Thompson, John Williamson Palmer (1825–1906), Margaret Preston, Hayne, and Timrod published frequently in behalf of the cause, and Thompson, Palmer, Hayne, and Timrod all served in various military capacities until poor health (consumption in each case) forced Thompson, Hayne, and Timrod to fight with their pens instead of their swords. Others joined them—James Ryder Randall (1839–1908) of Maryland; Francis Orray Ticknor (1822–1874) of Georgia; and Father Abram J. Ryan, (1838–1886) of Virginia, Maryland, and states to the south—rose to the occasion, and in lyrics such as "Maryland, My Maryland," "Little Giffen of Tennessee," and "The Conquered Banner" sang memorably of the homeland, the courage of the men in gray, and the pathos of defeat. Timrod, with a series of unforgettable poems, defined the new nation and its purposes in "Ethnogenesis" (1861) and "The Cotton Boll" (1861); trumpeted the rightness of the cause in "A Cry to Arms" (1862), "Carolina" (1862), "Charleston" (1862), and "Carmen Triumphale" (1863); noted sadly the pathos of wartime in "Christmas" (1863), "Spring" (1863), "The Two Armies" (1863), and "The Unknown Dead" (1863); and commemorated in a magisterial ode in 1866 the dead warriors and their sisters who decorated their graves. He thereby became forever the laureate of the Confederacy.

After the war, southern poets continued to seek sustenance from the Anglo-American poetic tradition, even though the Union and abolitionist views of Longfellow, Whittier, and Lowell were detestable to them. Simms, Timrod, and Thompson, as noted, died in the early aftermath, but Mrs. Preston, Hayne, and Father Ryan continued to publish verse, as did Randall occasionally, though his main focus was on journalism as the editor, in turn, of two Augusta newspapers. In addition, new arrivals such as Irwin Russell, John Banister Tabb, Sidney Lanier, Albery A. Whitman, and Lizette Woodworth Reese appeared on the scene.

If Timrod was the laureate of the Confederacy, Abram Joseph Ryan assuredly was the spokesman for the Lost Cause. Priest, journalist, and poet, Ryan published his best poems about the South—"The Conquered Banner" (composed in 1865), a requiem for the Confederacy; "The Sword of Robert Lee" (1868), a tribute to the revered commander; and "A Land With-

out Ruins" (1879), a *cri de coeur* for "a land that hath story and song"—after the war.

The antebellum poets who consistently courted the muse in the postwar period and who eventually became devoted friends through correspondence were Margaret Junkin Preston and Paul Hamilton Hayne. Preston (1820–1897) was born in Pennsylvania but came with her family in 1848 to Lexington, Virginia. There she met and married Major John T. L. Preston, a senior member of the faculty of the Virginia Military Institute, and began contributing verse to periodicals. During the war, she remained in Lexington with her husband's family, though her father returned to Pennsylvania and her brothers decided to fight on different sides of the conflict. She contributed poems whenever possible to Confederate journals. In the spring of 1865, *Beechenbrook: A Rhyme of the War,* a long narrative in couplets and occasional stanzas, appeared in Richmond and was republished the following year in Baltimore with a few more war pieces in each reprinting. Subsequently, Preston brought together parts of her work in *Old Song and New* (1870), *Cartoons* (1875), *For Love's Sake* (1886), and *Colonial Ballads, Sonnets, and Other Verse* (1887), a body of work that reveals an interest in character, even in sonnets, such as "Equipoise," " 'Sit, Jessica,' " "Hawthorne," and "In Cripplegate's Church," and more particularly in brief narratives (frequently monologues but not always) that deal with painters of the Italian Renaissance—"Mona Lisa's Picture," "In the Sistine," and "Tintoretto's Last Painting." She also succeeds with poems in memory of friends, as in "The Shade of the Trees," a tribute to Stonewall Jackson, an old friend and husband of her sister Eleanor, and "Through the Pass," an elegy in memory of Commander Matthew Fontaine Maury, another member of the faculty of VMI and a close friend whose last wish had been to be taken through Goshen Pass and buried on the other side. Altogether, Preston's lyrics provide absorbing psychological insights into human nature expressed in a graceful style whose numbers nevertheless strike the ear as less musical than the lush melodies inherent in much southern lyricism from Wilde and Poe to Hayne and Lanier. Her work is not cerebral in the Dickinsonian sense, but it demonstrates more interest in the mind and soul than is usual in the work of most of her southern contemporaries.

On the other hand, Preston's friend Paul Hamilton Hayne (1830–1886) was a poet whose senses were immersed in the English romantic tradition of Wordsworth, Shelley, Keats, and Tennyson and whose ear in particular was in tune with the southern lyric dating back to Wilde and Poe. A Charlestonian and protégé of Simms, Hayne had before the war contributed to periodicals north and south, collected three volumes of poems, and edited the *Southern Literary Gazette* (1852–1854) and *Russell's Magazine* (1857–1860). During the war, he contributed his share of martial lyrics and odes and elegies to victors in battle, to fallen leaders, and to soldiers in gray alive or dead, but he failed to match his boyhood friend Timrod's peerless poetic contribution to the Confederacy and its cause. After the war, he gathered together three more volumes—*Legends and Lyrics* (1872), *The Mountain of the Lovers* (1875), and *Poems* (complete edition, 1882), but some of his best poetry of the period remains uncollected, as, for example, such sonnets as "The Renegade" (1885), an attack on George W. Cable and others who betrayed the South; "Robert Lee" (1886), a celebration of the leader whose defeat made him but "tower more grandly high"; and "To Charles Gayarré" (1886), an eighteen-line sonnet in honor of an old friend; and such nature poems as "In the Wheat Field" (1882), "Midsummer (on the Farm)" (1884), "On a Jar of Honey" (1885), and "The Last Patch (of Cotton)" (1883) in which the poet takes a closer look at his own surroundings and relates the heart of humanity to the land in a way new to his work. There are, of course, other nature pieces, the so-called Copse-Hill poems published by the *Atlantic Monthly* in the 1870s—"Aspects of the Pines" and "The Wood Lake," for example, and narrative poems of substance, including "The Wife of Brittany" (1870) and "Cambyses and the Macrobian Bow" (1873), the latter of which in its starkness and grimness and in its terse and laconic diction offers a spare picture of power that begets perversity that may be Hayne's ultimate achievement in this genre.

As a whole, Hayne's canon is unabashedly in the Anglo-American romantic tradition, and he is southern to the core in his celebration of the land he loves, in his pride in his city and state and in the virtues of the Old South, and in the natural melody of his lyrics, music that is heard in the forest and the sea, in upland and lowland, in pine, bee, and spirea, and in the voice of humanity everywhere.

The new poets of the postwar period—Russell, Tabb, Lanier, and later, Whitman and Reese—frequently offered new wine in old bottles, though Russell and Lanier were also among the first to publish verse in Negro dialect, and Lanier experimented with line and meter and form, if not with rhyme and theme, throughout his brief career.

Irwin Russell (1853–1879), the author of "Christmas-Night in the Quarters" (1878), the best-known poem in Negro dialect published in the 1870s, was a native of Mississippi who studied law and practiced it while writing concurrently for the newspapers and composing verse on the side. Many of his poems (usually in dialect) appeared in *Scribner's Monthly*, and though Lanier's dialect verse had preceded his, Russell was usually credited with discovering, as Joel Chandler Harris pointed out in 1888, "the literary possibilities of the negro character." Harris went on to praise Russell's "accurate conception" and "perfect representation of negro character," points that are reflected in "Christmas-Night," along with an artful comparison between speakers and perspectives in terms of education, diction, and human nature that is reflected in the Burnsian couplets of the educated narrator and the contrasting stanzas and rhyme schemes of the black Mississippi speakers and singers. Although it is an achievement that promised much to come, poor health and other difficulties led to Russell's death the following year at the age of twenty-six, and he at once became another inheritor of unfulfilled renown.

John Banister Tabb (1845–1909), almost a decade older than Russell, also had a disability, poor eyesight, a factor that led to private education at home on his father's Virginia plantation and to limited service as a clerk on a Confederate blockade-runner that made over twenty runs before its capture in 1864, at which time he was sent to prison at Point Lookout, Maryland, where he met and formed a lifelong friendship with Lanier. In the 1870s he converted to Roman Catholicism, studied for the priesthood in Baltimore, and was ordained in 1884. In the meantime, he contributed verse to *Harper's Monthly* and other magazines based upon his belief, with Poe, that the short lyric was the ideal form, and his first volume of poetry was privately printed in 1882. When his *Poems* (1894) was published, it attracted attention both in the North and in England, and his reputation as the author of brief and finely finished lyrics on nature, religion, and literary topics was established and assured. Of such poems, "The Cloud" (1872) and "Mistletoe" (1881) illustrate his work on nature; "Interpreted" (1881) and "Easter" (1883), his verse on religion; and "Keats" (1880), "Milton" (1885), and "To Sidney Lanier" (1895), his lines on literature.

Tabb's friend and fellow prisoner of war Sidney Lanier (1842–1881) composed verse and began his novel *Tiger-Lilies* (1867) during the war, but his literary career belongs to the postwar period. His health broken by his stint at Point Lookout, Lanier spent the rest of his life dealing with poor health and poverty (or as he once put it succinctly, "merely not dying") and with the problems associated with choosing between music and literature as a profession. Contributing a few poems in dialect and others on Reconstruction to Georgia newspapers and southern magazines in the late 1860s, Lanier graduated to *Lippincott's Magazine* and *Scribner's Monthly* and other northern publications with "Corn" (1875), "The Symphony" (1875), "The Centennial Meditation of Columbia" (1876), "The Marshes of Glynn" (1878), and "A Ballad of Trees and the Master" (1881).

"Corn" and "The Symphony" brought Lanier to the attention of a national audience, and their ideas on nature, individualism, the single-crop system, trade, and relations between the sexes and experimentation with line, rhythm, meter, and the form of irregular ode led to an official invitation to write a cantata to celebrate the Centennial of 1876—a piece that was roundly criticized by some critics who failed to recognize that the piece was meant to be sung accompanied by music by another hand. Nevertheless, *Poems*, a collection of ten lyrics he had contributed to *Lippincott's* and the only volume of verse to appear in his lifetime, provided readers with some basis for evaluation. But Lanier had little time left, though he managed to compose a few short pieces, "The Stirrup-Cup" and "A Ballad of Trees and the Master," for example, where the demands of form provide strict boundaries and the lyrics approach consummation.

The last new poets of the postwar period whose work merits more than passing mention are Albery A. Whitman and Lizette Woodworth Reese, though several others may also be mentioned: James Barron Hope (1829–1887), a Virginia poet and journalist who published a book of poems in 1856, and Madison Cawein (1865–1914) and Cale Young Rice (1872–1943), Kentuckians whose best work appeared in the twentieth century but is generally within the nineteenth-century southern poetry tradition in terms of its appreciation of form, meter, and rhyme, in its sensitivity to verbal music and harmony, and its treatment of nature and locale.

Another Kentuckian, Albery Whitman (1851–1901), was a poet whose background and experience were quite different from those of Cawein and Rice.

Born a mulatto slave, he spent the years after emancipation working in Ohio, attending Wilberforce University, and eventually serving as an evangelist in the ministry of the African Methodist Episcopal Church in various states, including Texas and Georgia. The author of seven books of poetry beginning with *Essays on the Ten Plagues and Miscellaneous Poems* in 1871 and concluding with *An Idyl of the South* in 1901, he was characterized by some critics as the laureate of his race. Another romantic, he was indebted on various counts to Longfellow, Byron, Tennyson, and Scott. His views on beauty and the poetic vocation resemble Poe's, but his interest in the long narrative and characters from his own context and people suggest an ambition that is not always sustained by his gifts but reflects a natural pride in his race and inheritance.

Lizette Reese (1856–1935) was born and reared in Huntingdon, Maryland, a suburb of Baltimore and the setting of much of her poetry. The child of a Welsh father who fought for the Confederacy, she taught school for over forty years. In 1874 her first printed poem appeared in Baltimore's *Southern Magazine,* and in 1887 she published her first book of lyrics, *A Branch of May,* a collection that eventually led to the appearance of thirteen other books of verse and prose. Her work is consistently brief, direct, and spare, and the sonnet is quite naturally a favorite form. Her themes and topics and subject matter are the country and people of her surroundings in Huntingdon, and her language and ideas are based upon her experience and reading. There is little of the lushness of Hayne or Lanier in her work, but there is the same respect for traditional form and rhyme that one finds in Hayne but which appears in Reese's poetry in such a way as to suggest some of Preston's work and to anticipate the economy of John Crowe Ransom. "Tears" (1899) is apparently still her best-known piece, but there are other sonnets and some short lyrics that are equally worthy of recollection, including "A December Rose," "The Singer," and "Hallowmas" in *A Branch of May* and "April Weather," "Renunciation," "A Seller of Herbs," and "Compensation" in *A Handful of Lavender* (1891), to mention only those poems from her work before the turn of the century. Her contribution culminates later in *Spicewood* (1920), *Wild Cherry* (1923), and *White April and Other Poems* (1930), and her canon in its stress on the local, on tradition, on poetry as song may serve as a transition between Hayne, Lanier (*A Handful of Lavender* is dedicated to the memory of Lanier), and Tabb and the work of Ransom and Donald Davidson in the 1920s.

Southern poetry of the nineteenth century developed very little from 1820 to the 1890s. It is modeled on standards set by British poets from Chaucer to Swinburne and W. M. Rossetti, and its exercises in experimentation, chiefly by Poe and Lanier, broaden but hardly challenge the tradition. It is meant to be heard, as is clear from "The Lament of the Captive" to "Tears." It grows increasingly more concerned about natural surroundings from Wilde's "To the Mocking-Bird" to Reese's "April Weather." And it is characteristically chivalric in its consideration and treatment of love and of relations between the sexes, though there are occasional notes or suggestions to the contrary in poems by Reese and Cawein. On the whole, however, southern poetry of 1860 to 1900 is of a piece with antebellum poetry, and even if it seems old-fashioned and outmoded to present tastes, it clearly represents its culture, reverberates in the souls and memories of its audience, and serves both historically and intrinsically to reflect and to respond to a way of life that despite war and its aftermath of defeat and poverty managed to reconstruct itself along cultural lines consistent within themselves to those of the earlier part of the century.

Rayburn S. Moore

See also Confederacy, Literature of the; Odes to the Confederate Dead.

Charles R. Anderson, gen. ed., *The Centennial Edition of the Works of Sidney Lanier, I, Poems* (1945); James E. Kibler Jr., ed., *Selected Poems of William Gilmore Simms* (1990); Thomas O. Mabbott, ed., *Collected Works of Edgar Allan Poe, I, Poems* (1969); Rayburn S. Moore, *Paul Hamilton Hayne* (1972); Mary C. Simms Oliphant et al., eds., *The Letters of William Gilmore Simms* (6 vols.; 1952–82); Edd Winfield Parks, ed., *Southern Poets* (1936); Edd Winfield Parks and Aileen Wells Parks, eds., *The Collected Poems of Henry Timrod* (1965).

POETRY, 1900 TO WORLD WAR II

No modern southern poet yet has a rank corresponding to that of the southern novelist William Faulkner, a titan of world literature. Almost no early modern American poet indisputably of the first rank—Frost, Stevens, Williams, Pound, Eliot, Hart Crane—is southern, although a case can be made for John Crowe Ransom, whose reputation is limited only by his small out-

put. Many lesser poets—such as John Peale Bishop, John Gould Fletcher, and Allen Tate—are southerners; by the final third of the twentieth century, however, it could be argued that two southern poets, James Dickey and A. R. Ammons, belong in the superlative category. Some advocates are suggesting that Ammons belongs among the greatest American poets ever.

Modern southern poetry can trace its lineage back to one precursor who may be considered southern: Edgar Allan Poe, whom some have called the inventor of the symbolist poem (to say nothing of the short story, science fiction, and detective fiction). Poe is also given credit as an ancestor, if not the only begetter, of the New Criticism, to which Ransom gave an understated name. The best practitioners of the New Criticism—Ransom, Tate, Cleanth Brooks, Warren—were southern.

Some southern poets and critics have continued a technical interest that has engaged southern thinkers since the middle of the nineteenth century in an enterprise that includes Sidney Lanier as well as Poe. One paradigmatic work, Ransom's "Bells for John Whiteside's Daughter," may serve as the quintessential, archetypal modern southern poem—in occasion, rhetoric, diction, and versification. The passing of time and of persons is much on the southern mind—as in this poem that marks the death of a girl. But it is not called "The Death of Marjorie Whiteside, Aged Eight" or anything of the sort. Both "Bells" and "Daughter" are somewhat indirect ways of identifying the occasion. The first line—"There was such speed in her little body"—leaves open the question of whether the bells are for a wedding, a funeral, or something else. The indirectness is ironic (as may be the use of the poet's first name as also the first name of the girl's father). The language, typical of most of Ransom's writing, is tinged with archaism and formality—"Her wars were bruited in our high window"—but these deviations from the norm seem to serve as desperate maneuvers to handle a challengingly pathetic situation that could turn bathetic in a syllable.

This is no place for detail, but it remains noteworthy that the poem begins with a double scazon (reversed final feet in an iambic line), rhyming lines of unequal length, anisobarism (as in "footfall"/"all," rhyming unequally stressed syllables), feminine consonance ("body"/"study"), and homeoteleuton (a rhyme-like relation between unaccented syllables, as in "window"/"shadow")—all extremely unusual verse tactics that combine to set the poem apart and hold it unnervingly aloof from sentimentality. Other elegiac studies, such as "Dead Boy" and "Here Lies a Lady," self-consciously track the rhetoric and diction of past poems in forging a strange idiom that is both southern and modern: southern in a magniloquence that wit keeps from devolving into overripeness ("And medicos marveling sweetly on her ills") and modern in acoustic innovations that were scarcely used by any poets before 1920. The fourth line of "Dead Boy"—"Nor some of the world of outer dark, like me"—comes close to repeating the fourth line of Gray's "Elegy Written in a Country Churchyard"—"And leaves the world to darkness and to me." It is as though Ransom benefited from the fictional example of Emmeline Grangerford in *Huckleberry Finn* or the far-from-fictional example of Julia A. Moore, whose most ludicrous versicles concern the death of children. It may be significant that Mark Twain shifted the poetaster's venue from Moore's actual Michigan to the South.

None of Ransom's immediate contemporaries, such as Aiken, Bishop, and Fletcher, could match his achievement, although they may have felt as deeply and read as widely. Some younger poets—Allen Tate, Robert Penn Warren, and Randall Jarrell—have held up better than those born between 1885 and 1895, but in all three cases the reputation may depend less on poetry itself than on criticism and fiction. Bishop, who was the model for the elegant Tom D'Invilliers in F. Scott Fitzgerald's *This Side of Paradise,* produced probably his most durable poem in "The Hours," on the death of Fitzgerald, who had provided the celebrated epigraph: "*In the real dark night of the soul it is always three o'clock in the morning.*" Then, at Bishop's death only a few years after Fitzgerald's, Tate produced in turn one of his best elegies, "Seasons of the Soul," obviously continuing the line from the epigraph of Bishop's poem. Robert Penn Warren's poetry, spanning over sixty years, offers a distinctive voice and vision and an allusiveness that evokes not only the rural South but much of American history and literature: from "The Ballad of Billie Potts" (1943) through the book-length *Audubon* (1969) and the late *Chief Joseph of the Nez Perce* (1983).

During the 1950s, an even younger generation emerged with powers that are coming to seem as powerful and original as Ransom's had been during the 1920s, when he wrote almost all of his best-known poems. James Dickey (1923–1997) could be flamboyant and extravagant in his public conduct, but he was hardly a towering genius that would make him the

Byron *de nos jours.* He gained a measure of general recognition in 1969 as an unofficial laureate of the lunar landing, and he enjoyed unofficial political status during the presidency (1977–1981) of a fellow Georgian. Dickey's poems became grand tapestries with "sprung" lines distributed all across the page, what he called "great shimmering walls of words." It remains to Dickey's credit that he reestablished literature in the physical world of work and sensation; for the film version of his novel *Deliverance* (1970), the natural choice of a star was Burt Reynolds, also a southerner.

But if Dickey was not quite a Byron, A. R. Ammons (1926–2001), born in Columbus County, North Carolina, seems fully qualified to be called a poet in the mold of Wordsworth. Ammons is a poet of rural life and of lofty philosophical speculation, and he has written some of the shortest and the longest poems in the southern canon. Ammons has also made definitive contributions to the concept of poetic diction and to verse form. Ammons has been the first to import into poetry some of the conventions of prose and the prose poem. "The City Limits" is a single long sentence, constructed on an armature of "When . . . when . . . when . . . then" but with discontinuous ranges of grammatical, prosodic, and graphic layout. That is, the lines end at a pre-set margin, in the manner of typed prose, so that a line or strophe would end with any word. The graphic array is shapely but arbitrary; the acoustic array is likewise shapely but not formed into symmetrical rhyming or metered units.

Another southerner born in the 1920s has been noteworthy as a witty poet but even more so as a publisher and publicist for poetry: Jonathan Williams. The outlook is bright for southern poetry in the hands of many poets born after the 1920s, a list including, but hardly limited to R. S. Gwynn, Dave Smith, Henry Taylor, Everette Maddox, Cleopatra Mathis, Ellen Bryant Voigt, Coleman Barks, Fred Chappell, Charles Wright, James Seay, Michael McFee, Gerald Barrax, Susan Ludvigson, Thomas Rabbitt, David Bottoms, and Wyatt Prunty.

William Harmon

See also Poetry, 1900 to World War II; Poetry, World War II to Present.

Ian Hamilton, ed., *The Oxford Companion to Twentieth-Century Poetry in English* (1994); David Perkins, *A History of Modern Poetry* (2 vols.; 1987).

POETRY, WORLD WAR II TO PRESENT

"Down there," wrote H. L. Mencken of the South, in the third sentence of "The Sahara of the Bozart," "a poet is now almost as rare as an oboe-player, a dry-point etcher or a metaphysician."

Not anymore. In the eight decades since Mencken's spirited put-down, the region's population of poets has rallied vigorously from near-extinction. In fact, the postwar poetic South looks more like a verbal oasis than a desert: far from being the dried-up provincial "vacuity" ridiculed by Mencken, it comprises one of the most diverse and substantial bodies of work in modern literature.

Why has this happened, in the poorest and most illiterate part of the country? There's no easy answer to that question. Certainly it helped that southern literature had enjoyed a prewar Renaissance. Certainly it has helped that first-rate university presses and journals (including the *Georgia, Sewanee, Southern,* and *Virginia Quarterly Reviews*) have published and commented on the region's best poetry. Certainly it has helped that excellent teachers (like William Blackburn at Duke) have instructed writers and readers at universities across the South, especially in the decades when creative writing established itself in the academy.

And certainly it helped that America's postwar "dean of letters" was a southerner writing the best poetry of his long career. Robert Penn Warren (1905–1988) had published some poetry before the war, as well as novels and various kinds of nonfiction. But until his death, he focused much of his energy on new poems: he won Pulitzers for poetry in 1958 and 1979 as well as the 1967 Bollingen Prize, and he was named the country's first official poet laureate in 1986. During the 1950s, Warren's once-conservative Fugitive style began to loosen, in a way that Ransom's and Tate's never did: he could still write firmly rhymed quatrains, but his lines had grown more restless, flexing and stretching out as he moved toward rangier free-verse sequences meditating on the difficult nature of history, memory, knowledge and wisdom and truth, and "the terrible thing called love." His poems also became more directly personal and anecdotal, moving from a private incident or image to a much larger conclusion. Despite these changes, though, even Warren's most lyrical poems were narrative at heart: as he concluded *Audubon: A Vision* (1969), "Tell me a story of deep delight."

Another prominent man of letters from the region was Tennessee native Randall Jarrell (1914–1965). Like Warren, he was educated at Vanderbilt by various Fugitives, but his temperament was more cosmopolitan than agrarian: though he went on to teach at UNC-Greensboro from 1947 until his untimely death, he never seemed especially southern. His most familiar poems dramatized World War II characters, childhood memories, and the experience of loss-haunted women like the housewife in "Next Day." His justly celebrated criticism was a model of vivid, witty, and passionate engagement with texts; it has aged well and may be his most lasting legacy, though his influence continues to be felt as a charismatic teacher and as a writer of children's books such as *The Bat Poet* (1964).

Jarrell's national reputation as a critic clearly influenced James Dickey (1923–1997), yet another Vanderbilt graduate, who wrote criticism and poems that would make him into one of the most visible self-consciously southern literary figures of his time. From the beginning, his was a powerful poetry, its energy achieved partly through the measure of his lines (at first steadily anapestic and stanzaic, later more spacious and freewheeling), partly through his striking subject matter, and partly through the dramatic (sometimes melodramatic) persona speaking the poems. Dickey's charged work couldn't be further removed from the reserved verses of his Vanderbilt ancestors, none of whom would have committed a 108-line poem like "Cherrylog Road," at the end of which the first-person speaker—after a hot sexual rendezvous in a car junkyard—takes off on his motorcycle up the road, "wild to be wreckage forever." His *Poems 1957–1967* was a landmark volume of postwar southern poetry.

What's happened in the postwar post-Warren post-Dickey poetic South is what's happened in postwar post-Frost post-Lowell poetic America: there's no one dominant figure or school on the contemporary scene, but rather a great diversity of voices. There's been a balkanization of poetry: the art has become much more localized, so that it's almost more accurate to speak of (say) Mississippi or Appalachian poetry than of a monolithic southern poetry.

A. R. Ammons (1926–2001) demonstrates the ambiguities of definition. Born and raised and educated in North Carolina, Ammons left the state (and region) for good in the early 1950s, working as a businessman in New Jersey and, after the mid-1960s, as a professor at Cornell. He went on to publish twenty-three books of poetry with a New York publisher, win many national awards, and garner praise from America's leading literary critics for poems that cast a scientific eye and philosophical mind on the world around him, in free verse that ranges from quick lyric takes to book-length ruminations (*Sphere,* 1974). But though Ammons may not appear very southern, when he says, "My verbal and spiritual home is the south," it's possible to see the solitary eastern North Carolina landscape underlying some poems, to hear a garrulous discursive southern voice under others, and even to find less Emerson and more of the hymns he played and sang at the church he grew up in.

Southern poets can survive, even thrive, in exile. Some come back, some don't, but most natives return home in their work and may even benefit from a certain distance. Florida native Donald Justice (Pulitzer Prize, *Selected Poems,* 1979) has spent most of his adult life far from the South, in California and especially Iowa, where he taught at the celebrated Writers' Workshop. But he has never lost a firm sense of music and measure in poetry, partly learned from Yvor Winters at Stanford but also very reminiscent of the Fugitive poets. And he returns again and again to the landscape and people of his childhood, rendering that lost world in elegant, poignant lyrics that represent the elegiac southern tradition at its best.

Another wide-ranging poet is Charles Wright. Born in Tennessee, raised in the eastern part of the state and western North Carolina, and educated at Davidson, he spent many years in Iowa and Italy and California before returning south to the University of Virginia. All of these places play a significant role in Wright's poetry, which pays scrupulous painterly attention to local landscape, weather, color, and quality of light, as well as to the human culture arising from these places. Wright's early poems (*Country Music,* 1982) were terse, oblique, sometimes difficult of access; his more recent work (as in *Black Zodiac,* 1997 Pulitzer Prize), has relaxed into longer though still tightly controlled lines, dropped and stepped down across the page, and often linked together in meditative sequences that sustain a buried narrative.

The Appalachian Mountains that Wright calls his "remembered earth" have produced many fine writers in recent decades. Georgia native Kathryn Stripling Byer moved to the North Carolina mountains in the late 1960s and eventually began writing poems "in the voice of a mountain woman named Alma, solitary, abandoned, strong yet susceptible to the shiftings of season and memory." Her *Wildwood Flower* won the 1992 Lamont Prize as the best second book of poems

published by an American that year. For decades, Byer's publisher, Louisiana State University Press, has maintained one of the strongest poetry lists in the country, especially of women poets; the existence of such a solid series (along with those at the university presses of Georgia and Arkansas) is one reason for postwar southern poetry's vigor.

One of the steadiest Appalachian poets and fiction-writers over the past three decades has been Robert Morgan, a native of Zirconia in western North Carolina. Though Morgan has lived in upstate New York for over a quarter-century while teaching at Cornell, his ten collections of poetry (sampled in *Green River,* 1991) and four books of fiction portray the mountain South with unparalleled vividness. Morgan's poems display remarkable powers of imagistic and verbal concentration: no poet wields keener or more surprisingly insightful metaphors. Though he started out writing attenuated free verse, he has also worked frequently in traditional forms—some rather esoteric, like the chant royal—and in an unrhymed octosyllabic line.

Morgan took his M.F.A. at UNC-Greensboro in 1968, where he studied with a young professor named Fred Chappell—another Appalachian native-in-exile. At that time, Chappell had only published a few novels, but over the next three decades, he would become the leading southern man of letters, publishing several dozen books of fiction, nonfiction, and poetry, all first-rate. (Why does the South produce so many fine cross-genre writers, from Poe to Warren to Jack Butler, Kelly Cherry, R. H. W. Dillard, George Garrett, Heather Ross Miller, Reynolds Price, James Still, James Whitehead, and others?) Chappell's achievement in poetry (recognized with the Bollingen Prize, 1985) is a dazzling one: each of his dozen books strikes out in a new direction, displaying an often-hilarious sense of humor, formal variety and virtuosity, considerable erudition, and a dramatic perspective that lifts it to another level altogether from the merely autobiographical. The Dantean *Midquest* (1981) is his magnum opus, and his most thoroughly Appalachian book, told from the point of view of "Fred," a representative regional persona looking back over his life from the midway point: "He was reared on a farm, but has moved to the city; he has deserted manual for intellectual labor, is 'upwardly mobile'; he is cut off from his disappearing cultural traditions but finds them, in remembering, his real values."

Appalachian literature may have been marginalized from mainstream southern literature in the past, but given the achievements of these and other writers— such as Jim Wayne Miller (1936–1996), who so vigorously supported the region's writers—it has taken a leading role in shaping the postwar poetic landscape. The same is true of other traditionally marginalized voices in the region, especially minority and women poets. Indeed, some of the most popular writers in the country are minority women from the South, including Maya Angelou, Nikki Giovanni, and Alice Walker.

The success of these women—along with the groundbreaking work of Margaret Walker—has helped make it more possible for other African American voices to be heard. One of these belongs to Gerald Barrax, an Alabama native who taught for a quarter-century at North Carolina State University in Raleigh, where he also edited *Obsidian II: Black Literature in Review*. (Another important journal of African American literature, *Callaloo,* edited by Charles Rowell, has been situated in the South for decades, at the Universities of Kentucky and now Virginia.) Barrax spent many years working outside the university, though, and his forthright poems (collected in *From a Person Sitting in Darkness*) are far from academic, addressing a rich range of subjects—myths, the natural world, his identity as an African American male, music, and above all love in its many forms, especially the familial and the physical—with the convincing complexity of human experience in the "real" world.

When Yusef Komunyakaa's *Neon Vernacular* won the 1994 Pulitzer Prize, it capped the rise to prominence of a prolific young African American poet. Komunyakaa was born in Bogalusa, Louisiana, in 1947, and many of the new poems in *Neon Vernacular* address his southern upbringing. Other poems demonstrate his passion for music and nature; though his work often has an urban verbal swing to it, he also shows a deeply rural interest in fauna and flora. But Komunyakaa is probably best known for his poems about Vietnam: he did a tour of duty there and was both correspondent for and editor of *The Southern Cross*. Southern poets have written many memorable war poems, whether about the Civil War (Tate), World War II (Jarrell), or Korea (Dickey); and Komunyakaa's intense Vietnam poems in *Toys in a Field* (1986) and *Dien Cai Dau* (1988) must rank among the most memorable of these.

Southern poetry has always been heavily white and male in nature. Even in the more diverse postwar poetic landscape, it is still mostly that way, as seen in representative anthologies like *Contemporary Southern Poetry* (eds. Owen and Williams, 1979) and *The Made Thing* (ed. Stokesbury, 1987), each of which includes sixty-one poets, with forty-five white males in the former and forty-four in the latter—nearly three-quarters of the writers. But southern minority poets (including, in addition to those already discussed, Brenda Marie Osbey, Judith Ortiz Cofer, Alvin Aubert, Sonia Sanchez, and Julia Fields) have published much more frequently in recent decades. So have southern white women poets, who must deal with the complicated legacy of a woman's role in southern family, society, and literature.

"What is it," asks Betty Adcock, "to be a southern woman poet of the generation now over fifty? The only certain answer I can give is that it has been lonely." Adcock was born and raised in East Texas, a remote part of the South that she writes about with great vividness in her five books, most recently *Intervale* (2001). Her poetry is distinguished by its vulnerable but tough voice, quick wit, subtle formal accomplishment, and relentless pursuit of what the first poem in her first book called "Identity," the lost self that keeps leading her back to the landscape and relatives and stories of home.

Two other prominent Texas poets are Vassar Miller and Naomi Shihab Nye. Miller, a Houston native and lifelong resident, was for many years one of the few southern women poets included in anthologies, along with Julia Randall (*The Path to Fairview,* 1992) and Eleanor Ross Taylor (*Days Going/Days Coming Back,* 1991). Miller's poetry (*If I Had Wheels or Love,* 1992) is distinctive for its frankly fierce religious nature, incisive diction, and formal expertise. Nye's work reflects her Palestinian heritage and world travels, as well as her Texas upbringing and long residence. Her plainspoken poems (*Words Under the Words,* 1995) are a direct encounter with the "Daily," paying patient attention to "things and the life beyond things."

Nowadays—given the support of M.F.A. and undergraduate creative-writing programs, of independent bookstores with well-stocked women's and poetry sections, of sympathetic journals and presses, of various writers' organizations and conferences—southern woman poets probably don't feel quite as lonely as Betty Adcock and other predecessors. Indeed, there are far too many to discuss here, some with just a book or two, some with a significant body of work, including Susan Ludvigson, Kate Daniels, and Pattiann Rogers. Four emigrants should be noted, though, women who have left the South for teaching jobs up north but keep returning to it in their poetry. Margaret Gibson of Virginia may live in Connecticut, but the title of her new and selected poems (*Earth Elegy,* 1997) summarizes two strong impulses in her work, and in much southern poetry: a reverence for "God Earth," and an elegiac urge to memorialize what might otherwise pass away—a person, a place, the simple but essential things around us. Virginia native and Vermont resident Ellen Bryant Voigt may write a thoroughly rural and domestic poetry, whether set down south or up north, but hers is no easy pastoral: "we live with loss," as she says in her first book, *Claiming Kin* (1976), and her poems deal with the desires and frustrations that haunt a farm wife or husband or child. Dartmouth's Cleopatra Mathis may have escaped her native Louisiana and "learned to stay north" in order to survive and thrive, but from her first book (*Aerial View of Louisiana,* 1979) on, she has kept writing rich poems about her regional heritage—her Greek and Cherokee ancestry, the parishes and bayous and delta, "the religion called South, called family."

C. D. Wright of Brown is a bit different from her fellow expatriates. She did indeed grow up in the South (in the Ozarks) and returns to its "vernacular parts" frequently in her vivid and startling poems (*String Light,* 1991), but Wright's poetry is unique for its surreal tone and associative technique: she is often experimental in her prosody and poetic structure, riffing in intriguing ways as she accumulates images of our "cold and loco planet." Postwar southern poetry, despite its diversity, has few poets pushing the formal envelope (the poems of Forrest Gander come to mind, and maybe the early work of William Harmon); it is still technically conservative. But one enduring iconoclast must be mentioned: Jonathan Williams, who attended Black Mountain College in the early 1950s, the only local to take the pre-Beat modernist lessons of Charles Olson and apply them to regional material, resulting in poetry that is quick of line and keen of ear. Williams's poems in *An Ear in Bartram's Tree* (1969) and many other books are utterly sui generis.

Southern poetry has always been elegiac, whatever the lost cause being memorialized. That impulse continues in the region's current poetry, especially as the New South is increasingly developed and its forests, farmlands, and older characters disappear; such huge changes are a central subject of its contemporary writers. Of those trying to reclaim a primary connection with the land and its caretakers, Wendell Berry of Kentucky is probably the best known. The first poem in his

first volume is called "Elegy," and elegies recur throughout his *Collected Poems, 1957–82,* as he remembers how people and places used to be before our industrialized "unsettled" modern world displaced them. "The way I go," he says on the last page of the book, "is marriage to this place," the small community where he grew up and still lives as a traditional farmer, a local world of hard but good work and demanding but satisfying choices.

Most postwar southern poets, living in cities and/or teaching at universities, feel more permanently estranged from their rural past—like James Applewhite, who was born in tobacco country in eastern North Carolina, then went off to Duke to study and teach. His work (as in *Ode to the Chinaberry Tree,* 1986) is deeply rooted in the fields of the family farm and in the homefolks who worked them, but it is also profoundly distanced from his (and the region's) past, since he "fled such fields" for intellectual labor long ago and can't go home again, except in his thoughtful poems about collards or barbecue or a leaf of tobacco, which in his hands becomes "a topographical map" of the South's vivid, vicious history.

Perhaps the most pastoral of postwar southern poets is Henry Taylor, raised in the Virginia farm country west of Washington, D.C., to which he later returned to teach. Taylor's poetry about the countryside, as in *The Flying Change* (Pulitzer Prize, 1986), can startle with its details of unexpectedly dangerous rural life, as when the spooked horse in "Barbed Wire" accidentally slits its own throat. But he measures the lines themselves very carefully: Taylor's poems (whether formal or free verse) are graceful, attentive, and seriously witty, producing a fruitful tension between "the kinds of breakings there are," as he puts it, "and the kinds of restraining forces."

Two Alabama natives born in the early 1950s have updated the southern elegiac urge. Both Rodney Jones and Andrew Hudgins write candidly about traditional southern subjects (race, history, God, landscape, story, language, family, eccentrics, violence, humor, home) in a manner "at once joking and serious": they are antistereotypically "southern" southerners. Jones is the more discursive of the two: beginning with *The Unborn* (1985), he moved toward a longer fluent line that can accommodate several levels of focus in one lyric poem. And though his work is rooted in the still-poor South, and though some of his best poems are about mules and pigs and other regional staples, he incorporates the dark changes and raw edgy weirdness of the late twentieth century: when you read "Serious Partying," you know you're hearing the voice of a troubled, thoughtful, thoroughly contemporary southerner.

Hudgins is more retrospective in nature. Though he does write memorable poems set in the present, his two most substantial books—*After the Lost War* (1988), an imaginative narrative of the life of Sidney Lanier; and *The Glass Hammer: A Southern Childhood* (1994), about growing up in a military family—look backward for their material. But his is no sentimental nostalgia: Lanier comes to physical and spiritual grief, and *The Glass Hammer*'s narrator seems driven by "a love close to hate" for his relatives and childhood. In all of his books, Hudgins is haunted by guilt and rage and God, but he works out his poetic salvation with a technical control and self-deprecating sense of humor that seem characteristically southern yet utterly his own.

If it helped the cause of southern poetry at mid-century to have Robert Penn Warren leading the way, it certainly helps to have Dave Smith serving a similar role at century's end. Like Warren, Smith is a prolific writer, with sixteen books of poetry and several each of fiction and criticism. He is also an influential figure on the national scene, as teacher (currently at LSU), as anthologist (*The Morrow Anthology of Younger American Poets,* with David Bottoms, 1985), and as editor (of the *Southern Review* and of the Southern Messenger poetry series at LSU Press). But though he continues the southern belletrist tradition of Poe and Warren and others, Smith is emphatically his own man, especially in the poems. From his first chapbook in 1970 to *The Wick of Memory* (2000), Smith has written a no-holds-barred poetry about "a man trying to find his way home," whether the tough poor characters from his native Tidewater Virginia or, increasingly, himself, his passionate words the last defense against loneliness, death, and oblivion. He does so in a style that—mirroring the complexity of the poems' dramatic situation—is syntactically involved, rhetorically powerful, and introspectively narrative in nature.

What will the southern poetry of the new millennium look like? It's impossible to say, just as it's been impossible to neatly characterize the postwar scene, or even to mention all the poets who deserve attention. Where, for example, are such varied and accomplished writers as Dabney Stuart, Miller Williams, James Seay, David Bottoms, T. R. Hummer, Wyatt Prunty, Gibbons Ruark, Bin Ramke, Frank Stanford, Leon Stokesbury, R. S. Gwynn, Coleman Barks, Turner Cassity, R. T. Smith, and Michael Chitwood, among many, many

others? Stuck in a list at the end, alas. But every poet in this essay could probably say, "I consider my background, my upbringing, relevant to every line I lay down," as C. D. Wright once did: "If the ear is tuned just so, the ear can identify the source." And that source is a place, Mencken's once-lowly "down there," the no longer poetically barren South.

Michael McFee

See also Women Writers, World War II to Present.

J. A. Bryant Jr., "Postwar Poetry," *Twentieth-Century Southern Literature* (1997); Fred Chappell, " 'Not as a Leaf': Southern Poetry and the Innovation of Tradition," *Georgia Review* (Fall 1997); Dave Smith, "There's a Bird Hung Around My Neck: Observations on Contemporary Southern Poetry," *Five Points* (Summer 1997).

POLITICIAN

Contrary to current divisions between disciplines, political science and literary history are not always separate entities. The employment of power and the practice of letters have often enjoyed a symbiotic connection, and one of the earliest writers engaged in such pursuits in the South is one of the clearest cases in point. Captain John Smith, an elected president of the Virginia Colony and the author of such works as *The Generall Historie* (1624), not only took part in, but committed to print some of the earliest episodes in American governance. In that he wrote of himself in the third person, moreover, and in that some of what he described is more than likely apocryphal—his fabled "rescue" by Pocahontas in particular—Smith cast himself as both a factual figure and, in effect, a fictional character. Thus the range of roles that those who followed him have assumed: southern politicians have been authors as well as officeholders, have appeared in fiction as well as nonfiction.

Although the term *statesman* is more applicable to some of their number, southern politicians have made their most visible contributions to literature as authors, oftentimes of the very documents that constitute American democracy. Foremost among such figures is Thomas Jefferson. Though *Notes on the State of Virginia* (1784) is the only volume he published during his lifetime, his reputation as both founding father and man of letters rests soundly upon the document he drafted some eight years earlier, the Declaration of Independence. Roughly a decade later, after the former colonies had won that independence and begun the struggle to found a new form of government, James Madison, who later would succeed Jefferson as both U.S. secretary of state and president, emerged as one of three contributors to *The Federalist* (1788). Masterpieces of political theory, the collection's eighty-five essays were instrumental in winning ratification of the U.S. Constitution, much of which, the Bill of Rights in particular, is primarily the work of Madison himself. Not all such southerners are known more for their factual than their fictional works, however. Few people, perhaps, know John Pendleton Kennedy for his accomplishments as a three-term U.S. congressman or secretary of the navy, for Kennedy's reputation as the author of such novels as *Swallow Barn* (1832) and *Horse-Shoe Robinson* (1835) has all but eclipsed his political record.

Yet as figures as far back as the royal governors of Virginia illustrate, politicians are more often the subjects than the authors of southern literature. The most celebrated poem of the seventeenth-century South, in fact, appears as part of a narrative describing an uprising against just such a governor, Sir William Berkeley. In "Bacon's Epitaph, Made by His Man" (1676), John Cotton condemns Berkeley as one of "Virginia's foes" while mourning the loss of Nathaniel Bacon, the rebel leader who carried with him "[o]ur hopes of safety, our liberty, our all." In successive decades—successive centuries, even—writers recast the 1676 rebellion in a number of different forms. Ebenezer Cooke, best known for *The Sot-Weed Factor* (1708), cast Cotton's account—excepting his sympathy for Bacon—into hudibrastic verse in "The History of Colonel Nathaniel Bacon's Rebellion in Virginia" (1731). More than a century later, William Alexander Caruthers pitted a villainous Berkeley against a heroic Bacon in his romance of colonial Jamestown, *The Cavaliers of Virginia* (1834–1835). The literary legacy of Alexander Spotswood, one of Berkeley's successors as governor of Virginia, presents a similar case. Both Arthur Blackamore's poem "Expeditio Ultramontana" (1729) and Caruthers's romance *The Knights of the Horseshoe* (1845) celebrate Spotswood's 1716 expedition into what then was the West, over the Blue Ridge Mountains and into the Shenandoah Valley. More celebrated figures, of course, have inspired both more numerous and more celebrated works: Jefferson alone, for instance, casts a shadow over works as diverse as William Wells Brown's *Clotel; or, The President's Daugh-*ter (1853) and Robert Penn Warren's *Brother to Dragons* (1953). Yet what remains the most immortal translation of such a southerner from the political to the literary arena comes in neither poem nor novel, but in what was marketed, at least, as biography—in Mason Locke Weems's *A History of the Life and Death, Virtues, and Exploits, of General George Washington* (1800), readers encounter the fabricated but nonetheless fabled account of the future first president chopping down his father's cherry tree and then finding himself unable to lie about it.

Writers who would take still further liberties, and usually with far less good will than Weems, often opt to translate politicians into fiction under guises other than their own. The practice is far from new—in his 1849 novel *Mardi,* for instance, Herman Melville cast South Carolina senator and nullification proponent John C. Calhoun as a vicious, unrepentant slave-driver named, fittingly enough, Nulli—but in the twentieth century, as the figure of the often-venerable southern statesman gave way to that of the often-detestable southern demagogue, the practice has become more prevalent. Metaphorical first-cousins of figures such as James K. Vardaman and Theodore Bilbo, both governors of and U.S. senators from Mississippi, abound in characters such as William Faulkner's Clarence Snopes, but writers have singled out one particular demagogue, Louisiana governor and U.S. senator Huey P. Long, for more frequent, more nearly libelous duplication. The most notable results include Sinclair Lewis's *It Can't Happen Here* (1935), in which a Long-like president institutes an American version of the 1930s totalitarian regime; John Dos Passos's *Number One* (1943), in which a Long-like senator sells out his constituents in the name of increased personal power; and Robert Penn Warren's *All the King's Men* (1946), in which a Long-like governor teaches object lessons in philosophical concerns like the nature of good and evil. More than fifty years after his introduction, Warren's Willie Stark remains the predominant portrait of the twentieth-century southern politician, the chestpounding, Bible-quoting, power-mad populist, and *All the King's Men* remains the single most celebrated work not of just southern, but of American political fiction. Joe Klein's 1996 roman à clef *Primary Colors* not only alludes, at several points, to *All the King's Men,* but, in that it takes as its thinly veiled subject the career of Arkansas governor and U.S. president Bill Clinton, it illustrates yet again the often-close connection between positions of power and the practice of letters in the history of the American South.

Keith Perry

See also Demagogue; Jefferson, Thomas; Long, Huey; Populism; Smith, Captain John.

Joseph Blotner, *The Modern American Political Novel* (1966); W. J. Cash, *The Mind of the South* (1941); V. O. Key, *Southern Politics in State and Nation* (1949).

POOR WHITE

Redneck, cracker, holy-roller, honky, shit-kicker, trailer-park trash, Elly May, Bubba—the poor white southerner in the popular imagination remains strikingly one-dimensional. With intentions as diverse as extolling the virtues of Appalachian craftsmen and excoriating the views of the Ku Klux Klan, the nonsouthern commentator too easily profiles this particular class as wed to the ways of nature at the expense of every kind of social and economic progress, as willfully ignorant—that is, both backwoods and backwards.

This is not the poor white southerner of either history or of most serious literature. Prior to the Civil War, small yeoman farmers who owned a few slaves and cultivated their own land outnumbered both the stereotypical non-landowning poor whites and the large plantation owners. After the Civil War, when competing economic pressures broke up the plantation system of farming and introduced industrial life in the form of mills and mining operations, this yeoman class all but disappeared as the agribusiness of cash crops forced whites and blacks alike into tenant farming. Sharecropping was crippling work in virtually every sense, but so was work in the textile mills and mines that set up in the region during the rise of the "New South." Poor families were used to setting their children to work in the fields, so impressing whole families into service for a single wage became a fact of southern laboring life. Formal education was useless to such workers, so incentives for book learning disappeared; physical deprivation, illness, and backbreaking effort for very little money were what parents knew, so children learned those lessons by living them, too. This post-Reconstruction class of chronically poor whites tended to vote for politicians who blamed poverty on freed slaves, and they tended to worship a Protestant God who made not class distinctions between whites but racial distinctions between black and white. Such an ideology of division worked to the advantage of the white upper class of the North as well as the South, for it argued that poverty and inequity alike were caused by the very people who suffered from them.

The appearance of this class in southern literature dates to William Byrd's *History of the Dividing Line* (1841) and its portrait of a shiftless group of white people who seem to suffer from diseases now recognized as pellagra and hookworm. The literary contours of the southern poor white settled into a formula with Augustus Baldwin Longstreet's characterization of Ransy Sniffle in *Georgia Scenes* (1835). Ransy is a great believer in fistfighting, especially when he doesn't do any of the swinging or ducking, and Longstreet implies that his cowardice and his willingness to incite trouble between bigger, stronger men results directly from his class status as a clay-eater. Where Ransy led, Captain Simon Suggs followed, but with more far-reaching literary effect: Johnson Jones Hooper's creation of the wiry-haired trickster in *Adventures of Captain Simon Suggs* (1844) found a large and appreciative audience North and South, as American readers and writers began to revel in stories of characters indigenous to the American scene. Simon Suggs's motto is "It is good to be shifty in a new country," and Suggs is the first blissful American confidence man, the P. T. Barnum of his time who made us laugh as he counted his take. In addition to those writers who mined their own locales for colorful character types to set forth in fiction, Suggs begat a line of formidable American originals—Twain's King and Duke in *Adventures of Huckleberry Finn*, for instance, and Faulkner's Snopeses—and he had a devotee as well in William Makepeace Thackeray, who knew a few things about the attractive qualities of unrepentant vice.

If the local-color writers and frontier humorists of the nineteenth century taught us that the proper field of American literature was America, eccentricities and injustices and all, then the literature of the South did its part to examine itself as an identifiable culture within that larger writing culture. Southern literature in the twentieth century saw a proliferation of poor-white characters pressed from the Sniffle-Suggs mold by writers with radically different social agendas and aesthetic priorities. In the service of verisimilitude, southern writers tried to represent the variety of individuals that make up this class even as they acknowledge the debilitating conditions that would eviscerate individual expression. The poor southerner of the time was a different kind of poor in America: he or she lived primarily in the country and usually wanted to continue farming for a living, even in circumstances that forced a move to the city or to another state. The Lester family of Erskine Caldwell's *Tobacco Road* (1932) stay on their exhausted land and dream of planting bale-an-acre cotton, and the title ironically signals that the time for that dream has passed just as it did for the previous generations of tobacco farmers who overcultivated the land. A writer who believed that collective action could save the real agrarians of the South from their collective nightmare, Caldwell nonetheless wrote very little of such hope. Ty Ty Walden's family in *God's Little Acre* (1933) fear to leave their narrow path of life, just as the Lesters do. Caldwell's classic text accompanying Margaret Bourke-White's photographs in *You Have Seen Their Faces* (1937) also reveals the rigid boundaries of race and gender that kept the poor white southerner from leaving the land in which he could never prosper. This book is the prototype for James Agee and Walker Evans's *Let Us Now Praise Famous Men* (1941), which under the guise of investigating real life in impoverished Alabama actually sentimentalizes poverty in order to suggest the nobility of spirit among the poor. This tendency toward sentimentalization is a hallmark of much popular literature. In Margaret Mitchell's *Gone With the Wind* (1936), the O'Hara overseer fathers an illegitimate child on selfish Emmie Slattery, and Ellen O'Hara, Scarlett's saintly mother, wears herself out helping to deliver the baby. Ellen dies from typhoid fever, probably as a result of nursing Emmie. Harper Lee's *To Kill A Mockingbird* (1960) baits a similarly sentimental class trap by contrasting the villainous Ewells, who unjustly accuse a black man of rape, with the unselfish recluse Boo Radley, who saves Jem from the Ewells.

The 1940s and 1950s saw the publication of Faulkner's Snopes trilogy—*The Hamlet, The Town,* and *The Mansion*—which contains perhaps the most famous poor-white family in southern fiction. With names like Flem, I. O., Montgomery Ward, Wallstreet Panic, Byron, Mink, Vardaman, and Bilbo, Snopeses reflect the spectrum of literary and political history in often amusing, always ironic ways; the trilogy as a whole charts the shrewd Flem's rise from sharecropper to bank president and shows in the process how completely Flem usurps and manipulates white middle-class values without apparently believing in them at all. Faulkner's canon is populated by poor-white characters who transcend the stereotype of the class: Wash

Jones, to cite one example, embodies the complex ways that class and racial divisions meet in one's identity. Behind Wash, the Snopeses and a series of hardworking poor-white characters like Byron Bunch (*Light in August,* 1932) match Flannery O'Connor's array of poor whites: the Misfit, who murders to create in "A Good Man Is Hard to Find"; the spiteful grandfather who terrorizes his grandson to keep his racial ideology intact in "The Artificial Nigger"; and an extensive collection of housewives, Bible salesmen, stump preachers, cripples, pimply boys, shrill girls, and beggars in the postwar South. Alongside them we find Eudora Welty's postmistress, whose sister accuses her of having a lopsided chest, and a heartbreaking and hilarious parade of hairdressers, itinerant photographers, cooks, and peepshowgoers. A gifted photographer, Welty has continued in the tradition of Bourke-White and Walker Evans by recording the poor white (and black) faces of the South in juxtaposition to one another and to the region that holds them. To Welty and O'Connor, the sound of southern poor-white speech was infinitely varied and variable; as they render it on the page, the flexibility and vigor of those voices stand as evidence for the resilience of the class and not for its alleged moral failings.

Recent social history has begun to document and quantify the debilitating life of the poor white southerner that southern literature sketches in such variety, and in the recent fiction of writers like Cormac McCarthy (*All the Pretty Horses,* 1992) the scope of poor whites in southern letters has begun to range away from the legacy of the Civil War and its economic and racial aftermath to the legacy of an America that delivers on none of its mythified promises.

Theresa M. Towner

See also Appalachian Literature; Caste; Class; Cracker; Hillbilly; Protest, Novel of; Race Relations; Redneck; Sharecropping; Sociology of the South; Speech and Dialect; Yeoman.

W. J. Cash, *The Mind of the South* (1941); Sylvia J. Cook, *From Tobacco Road to Route 66: The Southern Poor White in Fiction* (1976); J. Wayne Flynt, *Dixie's Forgotten People: The South's Poor Whites* (1979); I. A. Newby, *Plain Folk in the New South: Social Change and Cultural Persistence 1880–1915* (1989); John Shelton Reed, *Southern Folk, Plain and Fancy: Native White Social Types* (1986); Merrill M. Skaggs, *The Folk of Southern Fiction* (1972).

POPULAR LITERATURE

Throughout the nineteenth and twentieth centuries, a few constants have held true in popular southern literature. First, popular literature in the South is about the South. Second, while this focus sometimes makes for a loving, idealized portrait of the region, usually the writer's reverence for place is tempered by social critique of its traditions. One of the earliest forms of popular southern literature—the domestic novel—is characterized by understated or masked critique. The modern best-seller has much in common with this popular antecedent. In its love/hate relationship with the South, the modern popular novel continues the trend established by the nineteenth-century domestic novel, but sometimes the subtlety and conventions of the earlier novels themselves serve as subjects of the later works' censure.

In the middle 1850s, Nathaniel Hawthorne complained that "a damned mob of scribbling women" kept his books from finding their deserved audience. This now-canonical author referred to the domestic novelists whose works, in the mid-nineteenth century, captured and held the buying public's interest. Many of the most popular nineteenth-century women writers were from the South, including Caroline Gilman (1794–1888), Caroline Lee Hentz (1800–1856), Maria McIntosh (1803–1878), E. D. E. N. Southworth (1819–1899), Mary Virginia Terhune (1830–1922), and Augusta Jane Evans Wilson (1835–1909). Many of their works appeared first in serial publication in southern and northern magazines, to be reprinted in book form later. These women authors wrote of what they and their largely female audience considered the domestic ideal, an ideal that, for many of them, centered on the southern plantation.

Most of these novels include conventional characters (such as an ingenuous and vulnerable heroine, an immoral villainess, a Byronic and seemingly dangerous hero, and a family or domestic setting in turmoil) and conventional plot elements (either the hero saves the heroine from danger and they marry or the heroine redeems the hero from a life of debauchery and they marry, restoring order to the domestic setting). Southern domestic novels differ from their northern counterparts in some conventional ways as well. Unlike the heroines of northern domestic fiction, southern heroines usually have at least one living parent, usually stay at home on the plantation rather than travel to find

themselves, and frequently make bad choices that lead them temporarily from the path of righteousness.

Southern domestic novelists insured their continued readership by reinforcing traditional cultural values and by fulfilling reader expectations with these conventional elements, tweaked only slightly for variety's sake. But modern readers also see in these works subtle reflections of the women authors' discontent with the domestic status quo. Often through inconsistencies within the plot of individual novels or through variations from the conventions of domestic fiction, the authors quietly critique traditional southern gender roles or the institution on which the southern domestic structure rested, slavery. Some of the most popular of the nineteenth-century southern domestic novelists illustrate both the use of conventional elements and these elements' unconventional revisions.

Born in New England, Caroline Gilman moved to South Carolina when she married. From her initial vantage point as an outsider, she observed flaws in the traditional southern domestic structure, and her fictional works hint at her censure. But the title of her autobiographical novel *Recollections of a Southern Matron* (1838) reveals that she did eventually consider herself (or at least tried to portray herself) as a true southerner, and in this work she depicts what she considers to be the ideal southern household. Gilman employs the traditional pure heroine, Cornelia, who reforms a young cavalier, but she contrasts this heroine with two less-worthy types, the helpless lady and the coquette. In her portrayal of these weaker women, Gilman disparages traditional southern education, which often left young girls unprepared for their roles as plantation mistresses. Lest she offend her audience, Gilman soothes southern discomfort at her negative portraits by revealing that Cornelia's weaker counterparts have been corrupted by exposure to northern cities. Cornelia's strength, on the other hand, is due in part to her physical and mental training that surpassed that of her peers.

These domestic novelists all seemed to walk a fine line between honest expression of their beliefs and the desire for profit. One of the most popular American novelists of the 1850s and 1860s, Emma Dorothy Eliza Nevitte Southworth, further illustrates this creative tension. Born near Washington, D.C., Southworth spent most of her life in Maryland and Virginia, and many of her novels are set on wealthy Upper-South plantations. The name with which she signed her works, E. D. E. N. Southworth, seems to indicate a deep personal identification with the Edenic settings she described, but was probably more an indication of nominative luck and marketing strategy. Though she was a staunch Union sympathizer during the Civil War, she was wary of expressing her ideas too forcefully for fear of alienating her audience. Her first novel, *Retribution* (1849), clearly an antislavery work, portrays in a subplot the tragic life of a beautiful mulatto slave, but her later novels suppress her antislavery sentiments. Many of her later novels, however, continue to question the conventional gender roles of the South. In *The Three Beauties* (1858), for example, the pure young heroine falls victim to the machinations of an evil villainess because she has been so sheltered and pampered as a traditional southern girl that she is unable to think for herself. But in Southworth's works, the pure heroines, with the aid of their heroes, generally triumph in the end. Their often-implausible misfortunes serve as learning experiences both for the heroine and for the patriarchal authority charged with caring for her.

Though born in the North, Caroline Lee Hentz was on the opposite side of the slavery issue from Southworth. At age twenty-seven, Hentz moved from New England to North Carolina with her husband and spent most of the rest of her life in the Deep South. Though she was never wealthy herself, many of her novels are set on Edenic southern plantations where the paternalistic slave system is ostensibly shown to be the best way of life for black and white southerners. But this proslavery stance and idealization of the plantation may have been primarily (at least at first) a marketing strategy. Both she and her husband taught school and depended on the income from Hentz's book sales to support their family, and she realized that the best way to win an audience in her new home was to extol the virtues of its cherished institutions. The strategy worked well, for she sold 93,000 copies of her novels over one three-year period. Her strongest defenses of slavery appear in two novels, *Marcus Warland* (1852) and *The Planter's Northern Bride* (1854), the latter written as a response to Harriet Beecher Stowe's *Uncle Tom's Cabin* (1852). But even in these works Hentz subtly indicts the injustices of slavery and gender roles. In *Marcus Warland*, the heroine disguises herself as a mulatto slave in order to nurse her beloved back to health, suggesting the sexualized nature of the African American woman in southern society. And in *The Planter's Northern Bride,* the reportedly contented slaves rebel against their supposedly benevolent master.

Augusta Jane Evans, unlike Gilman, Southworth, and Hentz, was born in the Deep South and lived there her entire life. Like them, however, she wrote popular novels about southern culture. Evans strongly supported the Confederacy, and her novel *Macaria* (1863) was a piece of wartime propaganda that idealized the South and the cause for which it fought. This work was considered so convincing that it was banned and burned by Yankee officers. Evans's most famous novel, *St. Elmo* (1867), also idealizes the South, but this novel focuses on the romantic and chivalrous icons of a southern lady who redeems her gentleman rather than on political issues. Both of these books and many others by Evans were wildly popular in the South, and late in her career the author claimed to have sold over 425,000 copies of her assorted works. For generations after *St. Elmo*'s publication, baby girls were christened after the novel's heroine, Edna Earle. Eudora Welty satirized this trend nearly one hundred years later by giving the heroine of *The Ponder Heart* (1954) the same name. But Evans's strong heroines, though they, like Evans herself, marry in the end, question conventional gender roles in southern society by remaining steadfastly and self-consciously independent despite public opinion. Her works have been criticized by modern readers because the story of the heroine's development often seems inconsistent with the conventional marriage with which most of her novels end.

After the Civil War, it became less comfortable for authors to portray southern domestic structures in the way they had previously. The ideal household imagined in most popular southern literature no longer existed, and the subtle criticism of southern traditions that these works included was less forgivable to the war-torn region. After the war, these two competing tendencies of popular southern literature, idealization and criticism of the South, split into two types of works—the local-color fiction that depicted quaint southern ways with an often critical eye, and the plantation fiction that portrayed the antebellum plantation as a lost Eden. Much of the largely critical local-color fiction was written by women; almost all of the popular reverential plantation fiction was written by men.

Southern local-color literature was more popular in the North than in the South because it focused on the dialects and customs that made the South seem like a quaint foreign land to northern readers. The Creole population of New Orleans and Acadian Louisiana intensified the foreign flavor, making this state one of the most popular settings for local-color fiction. In his short-story collection *Old Creole Days* (1879), George

Washington Cable (1844–1925) used dialect and plantation and New Orleans settings to charm his readers with a sense of nostalgia for the Old South while at the same time calling attention to the sins of the Creole elite. In "Belles Demoiselles Plantation," the main plot involving a corrupt planter's attempts to cheat a poor relative parallels a symbolic subplot in which the Mississippi River silently wears away the bank where his plantation home rests. At the story's end, the planter's manipulations complete, he returns to witness his home and his seven beautiful daughters being swallowed by the river. Grace King (1851–1932) considered Cable's portrayals of New Orleans's Creoles malicious and inaccurate. Her two short-story collections, *Tales of a Time and Place* (1892) and *Balcony Stories* (1893), defend Creole traditions, but her portrayals of black and white women show unusual depth that challenges stereotypical portrayals often found in local-color fiction. Another Louisiana local-color writer, Kate Chopin (1851–1904), also concentrated on themes of race and gender in her later works, *A Night in Acadie* (1897) and *The Awakening* (1899), but these works were not as popular as her first short-story collection, *Bayou Folk* (1894). *Bayou Folk*, which focused uncritically on the charming Louisiana setting and the importance of family and community within it, earned Chopin a national readership that was then eroded by her more controversial books.

Though the local-color tradition is most commonly associated with Creole Louisiana, this state is not the only one that produced local-color fiction. Sherwood Bonner (1849–1883), from Mississippi, wrote popular Negro dialect stories, and Mary Noailles Murfree (1850–1922), from Tennessee, was famous for her mountaineer/hillbilly stories. James Lane Allen (1849–1925) wrote novels about the Kentucky mountains that were so popular they were later adapted as films. Unlike most of the Louisiana local-colorists, who were of the elite classes writing about the elite classes, most of the local-colorists named above wrote of economically and socially lower-class subjects. Their tone, therefore, differs from that of their Louisianian counterparts, characterized not by critical censure or idealized homage, but by amused condescension.

Often considered a subcategory of local color, plantation fiction focuses, as does popular domestic fiction, on the southern household, idealizing the plantation as a lost way of life. Often told from the point of view of an ex-slave who wistfully remembers the good old days before emancipation, plantation fiction was written after the demise of most actual plantations. Its tone is one of reverence, and it seldom offers the critical glance at southern traditions that crept into much domestic fiction and that characterized much local-color fiction. Through the mouths of their ex-slave narrators, plantation fiction writers portrayed slavery not as a cruel form of bondage but as a benevolent extended family. This portrayal won readers in both the North and South because it allowed them to focus on the plantation's charms while ignoring its evils.

One of the most important of these writers was Thomas Nelson Page (1853–1922), whose plantation stories were collected in the volume *In Ole Virginia* (1887). His stories are often set in a frame in which the black narrator tells a white stranger of his master's former glory, the main plot appearing as a flashback to antebellum days. But though the narrator and presumably Page himself seem unaware of it, modern readers often see some of the cruelties of slavery portrayed by the narrator's reverential tale. In "Marse Chan," Sam speaks admiringly of his master's rescuing Ham Fisher from a burning barn, but the reader remembers that it was the master who had ordered the carriage driver into the blaze to save the horses. Joel Chandler Harris (1848–1908) wrote a different type of popular plantation fiction. Though he also employed a black narrator, Uncle Remus, who remembers simpler plantation days, his most famous stories about Brer Rabbit are authentic black folklore that Harris compiled. Harris also produced other volumes, among them *Mingo and Other Sketches in Black and White* (1884) and *Free Joe and Other Georgian Sketches* (1887), that featured slaves and slave themes as their main subjects, not just as their respectful narrators.

Popular southern literature of the twentieth century continues to view the South itself with a mixture of nostalgic idealization and restrained censure. Historical fiction that commented on the present was one of the most popular forms of southern literature around mid-century, mainly because the great success of Margaret Mitchell's *Gone With the Wind* (1936) had whetted the appetites of both readers and writers. Mitchell (1900–1949) was in turn influenced by the violently racist historical romances of Thomas Dixon (1864–1946), whose *The Clansman* (1905) was adapted to become one of the first silent motion pictures, *The Birth of a Nation*. Through his conservatively reactionary Reconstruction novels, Dixon saw himself as a critic of the New South. Not as violent in its racism, *Gone With the Wind* sold a million copies in its first six months and was later made into an even more popular film. The Reconstruction setting of *Gone With the Wind* parallels the economic hard times of the Depression South, sending the uplifting message that if our brave ancestors survived, so can we.

Though Mitchell appears on the surface to paint an idealized picture of the Old South, she criticizes, as did the nineteenth-century domestic novels that her work resembles, traditional southern gender roles. Scarlett O'Hara constantly complains of the constraints placed on women—not the least of which is their tight-laced corsets—and she and the other women come to rely on their own strength while their men are off to war. But the book's overt critique of the South and its unconventional ending—the novel ends not with a happy marriage but with its disintegration—also comments on the conventions of the nineteenth-century works that this novel, in so many other ways, follows. The popularity of *Gone With the Wind* inspired other southern historical fiction, such as Clifford Dowdey's *Tidewater* (1943), set during the Civil War, and Alfred Leland Crabb's *Breakfast at the Hermitage* (1945), set in the 1890s, both of which critique the New South through the Old. Inglis Fletcher (1879–1969) also wrote historical fiction set in colonial times that, like *Gone With the Wind*, revises traditional conceptions of gender.

Recent popular southern literature often offers more heavy-handed criticism of southern traditions. Southern gothic literature contrasts the cruel secrets associated with racism, classism, and sexism with the charm and physical beauty of the South. Pat Conroy (1945–), one of the most popular recent southern writers, critiques southern conceptions of family, community, and honor in his autobiographical novels *The Great Santini* (1976), *The Lords of Discipline* (1980), and *The Prince of Tides* (1986), all of which were made into films. In his works, Conroy takes the domestic novel out of the feminine sphere, entering the more turbulent (as Conroy sees it) consciousness of male young adults in the more turbulent twentieth-century setting. John Grisham (1955–), another extremely popular contemporary southern writer, has also written works with southern gothic themes, but these books have not been his most popular. Born in Arkansas and now living in Oxford, Mississippi, Grisham sets most of his novels in the contemporary South. His first novel, *A Time to Kill* (1989), views southern themes of racism and injustice through the lens of a modern court drama, but this book became popular

only after the success of Grisham's less-regional suspense thrillers, *The Firm* (1991) and *The Pelican Brief* (1992). In 1994 Grisham returned to the southern gothic with *The Chamber,* which details the final legal appeals of a former Ku Klux Klan member sentenced to death for murder. Like Conroy's, Grisham's first three novels were so popular that they were made into successful movies.

Perhaps the fact that Grisham's most southern books were his least popular is a sign of the increased homogenization of the country and the decreased interest in regionalism. From antebellum days to the present, popular southern literature has focused on the South itself, but as the South begins to look and act more and more like the rest of the country, one wonders what popular southern literature will become or if such a regional designation will be possible at all.

Betina Entzminger

See also Domestic Novel; *Gone With the Wind*; Gothicism; Historical Romance; Local Color; Plantation Fiction; Romance Genre; Stowe, Harriet Beecher.

Landon C. Burns, *Pat Conroy* (1996); Anne Goodwyn Jones, *Tomorrow Is Another Day* (1981); Lucinda H. MacKethan, *The Dream of Arcady: Place and Time in Southern Literature* (1980); Elizabeth Moss, *Domestic Novelists in the Old South* (1992); Mary Beth Prugle, *John Grisham* (1997); Darden Asbury Pyron, *Recasting "Gone With the Wind" in American Culture* (1983); Merrill Maguire Skaggs, *The Folk of Southern Fiction* (1972).

POPULISM

The Populist Party, founded in 1891, politically united farmers and poor urban workers in the South and West. In the late nineteenth century, many southern farmers found that they were unable to support themselves and their families, and although they were suffering under an economic depression, banks, railroads, and other middlemen were doing well. At its convention in Omaha in 1892, the Populist Party wrote a platform that called for a variety of specific political and economic reforms, including federal ownership of the railroads, the telephone system, and the telegraph system, as well as a graduated income tax and changes in the electoral system. Their platform also attacked big landowners, monopolies, and absentee ownership of land. In addition, the Populists called for measures to protect immigrant workers and to build connections with the Knights of Labor. In the 1892 campaign, however, candidate General James B. Weaver and running-mate General James G. Field faced problems of old party loyalties as well as issues of sectionalism; although the party united the South and the West, it still created divisions with the North. In the South, the Populists faced the entrenched Democrats, to whom they lost in the 1892 election. This election was significant, however, if only for the large role that a third party played in it.

The African-American vote was crucial to the Populist campaign, and Populists tried to emphasize the commonalities between poor whites and African Americans in the South. But Populist attitudes toward race issues have remained a matter of debate; the party included African Americans in their meetings but did not endorse social equality or put African Americans on ballots for public office. African Americans believed that their case demanded a recognition of racial disparity, rather than the Populists' equation of poor whites and African Americans as equally disenfranchised.

During the presidency of Grover Cleveland, the depression worsened, and populism continued to grow. Populists won control of the state senate in North Carolina and shared control of the state house of representatives with the Republicans, and several Populists won seats in the U.S. Congress. To win votes, however, the Populists often had to alter their stance on several issues, including their financial plan and their inclusion of African Americans. In the 1896 presidential election, the Populist Party had to decide whether to nominate its own candidate and risk splitting the vote or to join with the Republicans or Democrats. They ended up nominating William Jennings Bryan, who was already the Democratic candidate. He won most of the South and West but lost heavily in the urban East and North, and the Republican William McKinley won the election.

Although the Populist Party was officially disbanded in 1904, populism has had a profound and lasting effect on American politics. Many populist ideas were eventually accepted, including increased government regulation of the railroads, the creation of the Federal Reserve System in 1913, the graduated income tax, and electoral reforms resulting in direct democracy. Populists showed a willingness to include African Americans in politics and were a mark of rebellion against the established political system. Scholars and critics have used the term *populist* to refer

to a certain oratorical style that emphasizes the rights of the average American worker in the fight against the wealthy and powerful. In this sense, populism has lasted until the present day. Political groups such as socialists and prohibitionists, and leaders such as Huey Long, George Wallace, Richard Nixon, Ronald Reagan, Bill Clinton, and Ross Perot have used images of the American worker to appeal to voters. Thus populist rhetoric has been made to serve both conservative and liberal political agendas.

But the racial divide prevented the Populist Revolt from becoming in the South the topic for literature that it might have become. Midwesterners Hamlin Garland and Sinclair Lewis, for example, published novels inspired by the Populist movement; Garland's *A Spoil of Office* (1892) and Lewis's *It Can't Happen Here* (1935) show a fear of the corruption that power can induce. For southern writers, populism seemed to directly challenge attitudes and policies left over from the slavery era and post-Reconstruction even while allowing those attitudes to continue. Robert Penn Warren's Pulitzer Prize–winning *All the King's Men* (1946) shows the conflict between the desire to help ordinary people and the corruption to which power makes popular leaders susceptible. Said to be based on the life of Louisiana governor Huey Long, the novel describes the rise and corruption of the politician Willie Stark, who attempts to do good and who gains the loyalty of the masses through dishonest means. The most significant nonfiction populist work to emerge from the South is W. J. Cash's *The Mind of the South* (1941), which argued that the Old South "had never been a fully realized aristocracy." Cash's bias was clearly populist. In *The Origins of the New South, 1877–1913* (1951), C. Vann Woodward transformed the study of southern history, highlighting the common man and his struggle for a greater political role by populist means. Woodward underscored similarities between the Populist era and the Great Depression.

Jennifer A. Haytock

See also Woodward, C. Vann.

William J. Cooper Jr. and Thomas E. Terrill, *The American South: A History* (1991); Gerald H. Gaither, *Blacks and the Populist Revolt: Ballots and Bigotry in the "New South"* (1977); Lawrence Goodwyn, *Democratic Promise: The Populist Moment in America* (1976); Dewey W. Grantham, *The South in Modern America: A Region at Odds* (1994); Michael Kazin, *The Populist Persuasion: An American History* (1995).

PORGY AND BESS

The most famous American opera ever written is the story of a crippled black beggar and the woman he comes to love and to lose in one summer of passion and violence. Set in Charleston, South Carolina, at the turn of the century, the opera is based on a slim novel called *Porgy,* published by the white Charlestonian DuBose Heyward in 1925. The best-selling novel presented the Sea Island Negroes of the Carolinas, the Gullahs, in a realistic and nonpatronizing manner. The inhabitants of Catfish Row pursue dreams and encounter obstacles just as whites do, merely in a different culture. Heyward and his wife, Dorothy, successfully dramatized the novel for the (nonmusical) stage in 1927, where it ran for 367 performances. In 1935, Heyward collaborated with George and Ira Gershwin on the operatic version, which played on Broadway for 124 performances, then toured for three months, but was a failure commercially. Opinion was divided about the opera's race message (did it champion black people or demean them?) and the authenticity of its form (was it a true opera or merely a highly stylized Broadway show?).

As attitudes toward civil rights changed in America, the opera was given new life. In 1952, a much-celebrated European tour of *Porgy* began with William Warfield as the male lead and Leontyne Price as Bess. Cab Calloway appeared as Sportin' Life, the slick, "city" Negro who lures Bess away from Porgy with "happy dust." Under the aegis of the U.S. State Department, the company toured Vienna, Berlin, Milan, and London, then went behind the Iron Curtain to perform in Russia—the first American theater group to play there since the Bolshevik Revolution (Truman Capote wrote about this tour in *The Muses Are Heard,* 1956). Other revivals followed in the 1960s, 1970s, and 1980s. Ironically, *Porgy and Bess* was not performed in its place of origin, Charleston, until the city's tercentennial in 1970, since segregation laws would not permit the seating of a mixed-race audience.

James M. Hutchisson

See also African American Spirituals; Charleston, South Carolina; Folk Music; Race, Idea of.

Hollis Alpert, *The Life and Times of "Porgy and Bess"* (1990); Frank Durham, *DuBose Heyward: The Man Who Wrote "Porgy"* (1954).

POSTMODERNISM

Whether one takes the term *postmodern* to mean the state of culture in the late-industrial capitalist West, the thoroughgoing skepticism associated with poststructuralist and deconstructionist critical thought, or the aesthetic developed as writers have evolved beyond the chief modernists (Joyce, Eliot, Faulkner, and Woolf), the South finds itself well represented in the cultural movement that dominated writing in the final third of the twentieth century. Although each of these three definitions merits attention, southern contributions to the postmodern aesthetic bear paramount importance.

In cultural terms, the postmodern South likely begins on November 23, 1963, the day Dixie went global. Although struggles for civil rights through the 1950s and early 1960s focused the heat of worldwide scrutiny via television on the South, it was the assassination of President John Kennedy in a southern city, Dallas, presumably by a New Orleans–born misfit whose first name came from his father named in his turn after Robert E. Lee, that projected a southern drama onto the central stage of the emerging global village. To use this event to mark the start of the postmodern South is to fall, as others do, into the trap of identifying the postmodern with whatever is shabby, tacky, and second-rate in contemporary life—that is, to signify a falling off from the high achievements in art and culture of the modernist period. Doing so, one would feel at home with the protagonist in Walker Percy's 1977 novel, *Lancelot.* Lancelot Lamar does not use the postmodern label, but he rages violently against what he takes to be the sexual, economic, artistic, and social shoddiness of southern life in the 1970s. Percy's final novel, *The Thanatos Syndrome* (1987), continues this line of criticism by centering on a ring of pedophiles active in the South.

Similarly, though social critic Fredric Jameson is a southerner only through academic transplantation from England to Duke University, in major essays such as "Postmodernism, or the Cultural Logic of Late Capitalism" (1984) and "Periodising the Sixties" (1989), he pulled together dimensions of contemporary cultural criticism explored in depth by other postmodern theorists. He calls it a culture of the simulacrum, of copies without originals; one employing an aesthetic of textuality, of voices set off from one another by significant discontinuities; one that avoids all depths, whether of history, psychology, or art; one that privileges pastiche, nostalgia, images, and signifiers without limitable signifieds; a culture that struggles to surpass the modernist "canonization" of what was "hitherto scandalous, ugly, dissonant, amoral, antisocial." The Jameson and Lancelot Lamar view of contemporary society continues in certain works by southern ultraviolent writers and minimalists, whether of the five-and-dime, dirty-realist, K Mart, or mall variety, including Harry Crews, Frederick Barthelme, Anne Tyler, Bobbie Ann Mason, Barry Hannah, and Lee Smith, although minimalism itself works in a retro-realist fashion against the ambitious experiments conducted by more audacious postmodern authors.

The poststructuralist and deconstructionist elements in the postmodern movement appear in the works of various southern literary critics employing insights adapted from Jacques Lacan, Jacques Derrida, Jean Baudrillard, Julia Kristeva, Jean-François Lyotard, and other European theorists. By far the most consistent contributions by writers connected with southern institutions have come, however, from reader-response critics, especially Stanley E. Fish, Norman N. Holland, and Jane P. Tompkins, although the three came South only after their early discoveries. Fish's 1970 study *Self-Consuming Artifacts: The Experience of Seventeenth Century Literature* was especially significant, possibly even more so than his pioneering *Surprised by Sin: The Reader in "Paradise Lost"* (1967), in that it took as the focus of its reader-active model works from a century that formerly provided the exempla for critics favoring the text-active theory of reading long associated with New Criticism. Holland took a decisive step in the democratization and understanding of the reader's work in *5 Readers Reading* (1975), a research report arguing that each reader brings his or her individual "identity theme" to a work and therefore experiences a text differing in significant ways from that taken up by others. Tompkins collected leading essays in the field in her 1980 *Reader-Response Criticism: From Formalism to Post-Structuralism.*

As might be expected, in the South those who led the way to the postmodern were the creative writers themselves. As early as 1951 when poet Charles Olson arrived at Black Mountain College in North Carolina, bringing with him his own Projective Verse and drawing in his wake Robert Creeley, Robert Duncan, Edward Dorn in poetry, Merce Cunningham in dance, John Cage and David Tudor in music, and Robert Rauschenberg in painting, the revolt against modernist formalism that evolved into the postmodern was underway in the South.

Since 1956, when Olson ceased to be rector of Black Mountain College, the most important southern contributions to postmodern aesthetics have been in fiction. Already by 1952, Flannery O'Connor was parodying the southerners of modernist fiction in her Bible-Belters, maimed misfits, bubbas, and good country complacents that the rest of the world, and some southerners, would continue for decades to construe as figures of starkest realism. It was John Barth, however, who evolved a full-bodied postmodern fiction from the existentialism, black humor, and parody of his first novels published in the 1950s. Taking a clue from the innovative short fiction of Jorge Luis Borges, Barth's *The Sot-Weed Factor* (1960) provided a liberating parody of the southern past by creating a gigantic eighteenth-century Anglo-southern novel out of comic characters and themes appropriate to the mid-twentieth century. After Thomas Pynchon's *V.* (1963) cleared the air of the modernist aesthetic by parodying many of its cherished conventions, including surrealist presentation, rounded characters, and carefully documented points of view, Barth answered in 1966 with *Giles Goat-Boy; or, The Revised New Syllabus,* wherein he freed himself from the southern literature of memory and history by creating an imaginary university parodying the universe in which southerners like other earthlings found themselves in the 1960s. The experiments he carried out in *Lost in the Funhouse* (1968) marked his emergence as the leader of the American postmodern movement. The stories in that collection combine parodies of Barth's "southern" heritage with parodies of classical myths, metafictional interpolations, fantastical tales, and the most complicated framed stories ever created by an American. Barth builds on such innovations in his subsequent fictions, including the now-classic *Chimera* (1972) and *The Tidewater Tales: A Novel* (1987), the latter a moving blend of postmodern techniques and the traditional southern sense of place. While discussing his own development in *The Friday Book* (1984) and *Further Fridays* (1995), Barth provides what may be the best year-by-year record of the emergence of American literary postmodernism.

As Barth was evolving, Donald Barthelme, raised outside Houston, and Ishmael Reed, born in Chattanooga, were also contributing to the expanding aesthetic. As a practitioner of metafiction, Barthelme demonstrated the degree to which contemporary men and women have become a collection of competing voices or texts. Beginning with *Come Back, Dr. Caligari*

(1964) and in the short novel *Snow White* (1967), his fictions mastered the art of pastiche or shifts in texture. Reed has added to the postmodern enterprise by framing Euro-American mythologies with North African mythologies, as in his brilliant poem "I am a cowboy in the boat of Ra," and with African American perspectives in his various hoodoo or conjure fictions and poems.

Today the postmodern is so pervasive, even in the South with its commitment to realistic modern fiction, that our late modernist, minimalist, or feminist writers are likely to borrow its less-audacious techniques, as when Alice Walker offers nothing but texts in her story "Really Doesn't Crime Pay" or frames bourgeois black culture with grotesque distortions of Black Muslim doctrine in "Entertaining God." Fred Chappell may combine magical-realist episodes with proto-metafictions about storytelling as he creates a web of family tall tales in *I Am One of You Forever* (1985). Barry Hannah may launch us into the surreal excesses of *Ray* (1980). Or Lee Smith may provide a "counterhistory" of women in the Virginia–West Virginia coal fields in *Fair and Tender Ladies* (1988), or invent a magical-realist metaphor to close her short story "Intensive Care," or generate a Barthian commentary on male-female relationships by creating a text as self-parodying as "Desire on Domino Island." The postmodern, as Barth points out, permits contemporary writers to join the discoveries of modernism with *all* the literary resources of the nineteenth and earlier centuries—and thereby to continue honoring Pound's directive to "make it new."

Julius Rowan Raper

See also Modernism.

John Barth, *The Friday Book* (1984) and *Further Fridays* (1995); Fred Hobson, *The Southern Writer in the Postmodern World* (1991); Norman N. Holland, *5 Readers Reading* (1975); Fredric Jameson, *Postmodernism, or, The Cultural Logic of Late Capitalism* (1991); Michael Kreyling, "Fee, Fie, Faux Faulkner: Parody and Postmodernism in Southern Literature," *Southern Review* 29 (Winter 1993); Julius Rowan Raper, "Inventing Modern Southern Fiction: A Postmodern View," *Southern Literary Journal* 22 (Spring 1990); Jane P. Tompkins, ed., *Reader-Response Criticism* (1980).

PREACHING

In the South, the term *preacher* applies to a person—male or female, black or white—who delivers sermons in a Christian church that is broadly identified as evangelical and/or fundamentalist in religious outlook. A preacher usually works in an informal, sectarian setting but may also occupy a pulpit with a more formal, denominational congregation. In contrast to the designation of *preacher,* the term *minister* or *clergyman* describes the religious leaders of high-church versions of the southern Protestant denominations as well as the priests of the Episcopal and Roman Catholic Churches.

The preacher may well be the most ambivalent person in southern life and literature. Since the Second Great Awakening (or the Great Revival, 1798–1805), the real preacher has been greatly admired and respected by a devout, churchgoing population, and as the region's primary moral spokesperson, he has represented the central concerns of a region that has found itself at times deeply troubled by conflicting ethical issues surrounding race, gender, politics, and religion. At the same time, his portrayal in southern literature is rarely sympathetic. While a few heroic and compassionate men and women of God dot the literary landscape, by and large southern writers have ridiculed, vilified, or displayed the preacher as an example of fallen humankind more often than they have praised him for his spiritual qualities or for his ability as a pastor to assist in the well-being of his flock. Even today, a listing of real southern evangelical preachers illustrates glaring inconsistencies—the celebrated Pat Robertson and Oral Roberts stand in marked contrast to the infamous Jim Bakker and Jimmy Swaggert, while one evangelist, the Reverend Billy Graham, is often cited as one of the ten most-admired persons in the world.

From antebellum days through Reconstruction to the period of the New South and modernism, the preacher has been a lightning rod in the storms that have raged through the region's history. Thus it is no surprise that the real preacher has provided southern writers with a constant source of literary matter from the early nineteenth century to the present. It is also noteworthy that almost all of the literary preachers are male and products of the South's fiction writers. Rare exceptions to this generalization include James Weldon Johnson's *God's Trombones: Seven Negro Sermons in Verse* (1927) and James Dickey's poem "May Day Sermon to the Women of Glimmer County, Georgia, by a Woman Preacher Leaving the Baptist Church" (1967).

The antebellum South is marked by three general types of fiction—the romance, the humor of the Old Southwest, and the propaganda novel, and in each of these categories, preacher characters serve the needs of writers attempting to chronicle the deeds and misdeeds of a people in the process of creating their unique southern identity in this new world of America.

The earliest preachers, found in the antebellum romance, are generally either favorable characters admired for their piety or eccentric persons treated with gentle satire. George Tucker's *The Valley of Shenandoah* (1824) and William Alexander Caruthers's *The Kentuckian in New York* (1834) as well as his *The Knights of the Horse-Shoe* (1841) contain just such preachers in small roles but whose presence the authors use to draw the reader's interest to a central moral issue involving the major characters. *Guy Rivers* (1834) by William Gilmore Simms describes a representative preacher from a romance in the character of Parson Witter, the first delineation of a circuit rider in southern fiction. Witter delivers a simple, straightforward discourse that completely enthralls his listeners with an explication of the Twenty-Third Psalm, which serves later in the plot as a commentary on events over which the characters have no control.

The romance continued to be published throughout the nineteenth century with preachers appearing in the popular works of Mrs. E. D. E. N. Southworth, John Esten Cooke, Augusta Jane Evans Wilson, and Caroline Lee Hentz. In their stories, the preacher remains remarkably consistent in his delineation, and once the image was firmly established, the character quickly became a stereotype. In the post–Civil War era, a reader would discover few significant differences from the preacher in Augusta Evans's *St. Elmo* (1866) to the one in George Cary Eggleston's *Dorothy South* (1902). In story after story, preachers support an agrarian world with its code of the gentleman, the mystique of the southern belle, and the legend of a felicitous pastoral community. Agrarian society in these works is a highly desirable one not only because it incorporates the good life of the plantation, but also because it is girded round with a moral code that emphasizes the ethical values of southern Protestantism. Believing that what is right for his church is right for his community, the preacher of the romance rarely questions the ethical behavior of his society.

A new type of preacher made known his presence in the 1840s through the humorists of the Old Southwest with William Tappan Thompson, Joseph G. Baldwin, Johnson Jones Hooper, and George Washington Harris among the more popular writers who found comic possibilities in this character. The preachers in the humorous offerings of these writers are based on the real

preachers who were responsible for the Great Revival. Both the real and the literary preachers are evangelical fundamentalists, highly emotional in their sermons, and in general they represent more the vernacular tradition than the genteel one in southern life. The particular event through which this new folk religion was conducted is known as the revival—sometimes referred to as "camp," "brush arbor," or "protracted" meetings—one of the most distinctive elements in the southern Protestant church. At the center of the revival is a preacher whose spontaneous stream-of-consciousness delivery works his listeners up into a highly emotional state through speech rhythms and voice intonations. A preacher at the height of his emotional outpouring was said to be in "the weaving way," an image derived from the shuttle moving back and forth in a loom. Black preachers, in particular, developed this style of sermonizing to a level that resulted in the preacher singing or chanting parts of the service and the congregations joining in through a method known as call-and-response, an example of which is found in the Reverend Shegog's sermon in Dilsey's section of William Faulkner's *The Sound and the Fury* (1929).

In the main, the humorists of the Old Southwest show the preacher as a despicable human being who is inhumane and hypocritical. Johnson Jones Hooper's Captain Simon Suggs in "The Captain Attends a Camp Meeting" (1846) feigns salvation in order to steal money from a revivalist congregation led by repulsive preachers. An especially cynical version of the revivalist preacher is contained in George Washington Harris's "Parson John Bullen's Lizards" (1847), in which Sut Lovingood exacts revenge on a preacher who has punished him for his sexual behavior. At Parson Bullen's revival, Sut unleashes a bag full of swamp lizards that scramble up the preacher's legs causing him to tear off his clothes and jump nude over the pulpit into the middle of the congregation. An indication of the vitality of the tales of these humorists may be noted in the fact that this particular tale by Harris shows up in variant forms in Guy Owen's *The Ballad of the Flim-Flam Man* (1965) and in "The Mississippi Squirrel Revival" (1992), a popular country song by Nashville singer Ray Stevens. Additionally, Mark Twain's several depictions of fundamentalist preachers, represented best in *Adventures of Huckleberry Finn* (1885), all pay tribute to the rascal who lies at the heart of the Southwest humorists' portrayals of the preacher.

The literature that responded directly to the upheavals of the times is the proslavery propaganda novel written during the 1850s both to discredit the arguments of the abolitionists and to respond to Harriet Beecher Stowe's *Uncle Tom's Cabin* (1852). Caroline Lee Hentz's *The Planter's Northern Bride* (1854), J. S. Peacocke's *The Creole Orphans* (1865), and Mrs. G. M. Flanders's *The Ebony Idol* (1860) all feature preachers as prominent actors in narratives designed to justify the way of life in the Old South. In Thomas Bangs Thorpe's *The Master's House* (1854), for example, the Reverend Mr. Goshawk is respected for his ability to render convincing biblical justifications for slavery with ease in his sermons. Goshawk, a master of the negative argument employed by real southern preachers, declares that slavery must be right since Jesus and his Disciples never condemned it. In the mind of the propagandists, the slaveholder is a type of the Old Testament patriarch, slaveholding is thought of as a moral responsibility, and even a master's violence against his slaves during fits of passion is acceptable since the Bible reports that Peter once hit a high priest in defense of his Savior. All in all, the propaganda preachers resemble one another in their strident and provocative support of a structured agrarian lifestyle that many saw as God's plan for a new Garden of Eden in the southern landscape.

The post–Civil War era saw the advent of the local-color movement, and the southern practitioners of this style of writing found ample room for the use of the preacher in their works. Thomas Nelson Page, Joel Chandler Harris, Mary Noailles Murfree ("Charles Egbert Craddock"), Kate Chopin, and James Lane Allen all created literature with the preacher character consistent with the concern of the local-colorist to capture the variety of the southern landscape and to preserve the idiosyncratic traits of southerners. Richard Malcolm Johnston's "Mr. Neelus Peeler's Conditions" (1879) shows a man preaching the same sermon over and over again, finally having his preaching suit wind up as a cornfield scarecrow. Opie Read's "The Wildcat Circuit" (1896) depicts a preacher imitating the outrageous behavior of a backwoodsman in order to win the confidence of a primitive congregation. Ruth McEnery Stuart, in "The Rev. Jordan White's Three Glances" (1898), created a preacher who achieves power over his listeners by moving his eyes independently of each other. Thus most preachers in local-color fiction display identifying trademarks that their creators consider unusual and oddly interesting in the southern scene.

Although many of the stereotypes created by the nineteenth-century authors endure to the present, the most significant of the preachers of the twentieth century are, in the main, complex figures shown to be capable of failure, mistakes, and wrongdoing. However, unlike the stereotypical villains and fools of the past, the dynamic modern preachers are frequently human beings sensitive to feelings of guilt who try, sometimes desperately, to understand their own humanity much the same as other characters do. Thus modern preacher characters struggle with their own imperfections in a post-Christian world, a society filled with churches as the visible symbol of the presence of God but one often motivated more by self-interest, lust, and greed than by Christian ethics. The Reverend Gail Hightower in William Faulkner's *Light in August* (1932) lapses into madness as he tries hopelessly to reconcile the seductive lure of his region's heroic past with the reality of his own diminished present. Jack Burden's father, Ellis, in Robert Penn Warren's *All the King's Men* (1946) tries desperately to find redemption for the nightmare his life has become by serving the poor and needy as a fundamentalist street preacher. Hazel Motes in Flannery O'Connor's *Wise Blood* (1952) establishes a Church Without Christ, only to discover that he must accept the guilt of fleeing Christ by mortifying the flesh through the extreme actions of burning out his eyes with lye, wrapping his chest with barbed wire, and filling his shoes with broken glass. In William Styron's *The Confessions of Nat Turner* (1967), the rebellious Turner is destroyed by the conflict in his heart between his love for his fellow human beings and his hatred of his oppressors.

At the end of the twentieth century, the preacher as a viable character lives on in the fiction of such authors as Alice Walker, Cormac McCarthy, Barry Hannah, Doris Betts, and Charles Frazier. As long as the South remains the Bible Belt of the nation and as long as artists continue to explore the tragedy and the triumph of the human spirit, preachers will continue to engage the imaginations of the region's most creative writers.

Harold Woodell

See also Bible Belt; Clergy; Evangelical Christianity; Fundamentalism; Humor; Local Color; Novel, 1820 to 1865; Plantation Fiction; Romance Genre; Sermons; Televangelist.

John B. Boles, *The Great Revival, 1787–1805: The Origins of the Southern Evangelical Mind* (1972); Dickson D. Bruce Jr., *And They All Sang Hallelujah: Plain-Folk Camp-Meeting Religion, 1800–1845* (1974); Gerald Davis, *I Got the Word in Me and I Can Sing It, You Know: A Study of the Performed Afro-*

American Sermon (1986); Charles Hamilton, *The Black Preacher in America* (1972); Samuel Hill, *Southern Churches in Crisis* (1967); Charles D. Rota, "Rhetorical Irony and Modern American Fiction: The Clergy in the Novels of William Faulkner, Flannery O'Connor, and John Updike" (Ph.D. Diss., Southern Illinois University at Carbondale, 1993); James R. Saunders, *The Wayward Preacher in the Literature of African American Women* (1995); Thomas H. Stewart, "The Minister and His Work: The Preacher in the Humor of the Old Southwest" (Ph.D. Diss., University of Mississippi, 1988); Charles H. Woodell, "The Preacher in Nineteenth Century Southern Fiction" (Ph.D. Diss., University of North Carolina–Chapel Hill, 1974).

PRESBYTERIANS

Presbyterianism has its roots in the Protestant Reformation and is part of the Reformed tradition, influenced chiefly by John Calvin of Geneva and John Knox of Scotland. This tradition stresses God's sovereign rule of grace over the hearts and common life of the people, and also teaches justification by faith alone. From reading the Bible "anew" came new confessions of faith and new structures of the church along conciliar lines under presbyters (elders). There also was participation in the political movement toward new forms of national government. Calvin was concerned not only about personal piety, but also about every aspect of life. While the influence of all this was wide, one of its most important continuing social and literary influences is the emphasis on both educated clergy and educated laity—that is, on literate and thinking believers. In worship, the emphasis is more thoughtful and formal than emotional, and there is a belief that the Bible speaks to each individual directly. The normal pattern of church government is a hierarchy of "courts," beginning at the local level with the session (elders), then upward and outward to the presbytery, synod, and general assembly. These courts are representative bodies of ministers and elders (with equal authority). The supreme authority for faith and practice is the Bible, but this usually is supplemented and aided by various confessions, creeds, and catechisms.

From Europe and the British Isles (especially Ireland and Scotland in the second half of the eighteenth century) came many Presbyterians for political and religious reasons and with hope for a better life. The first Presbyterian Church in America was formed in 1640, the first presbytery in 1706, and the Synod of Philadelphia in 1716, when there were forty churches, nineteen

ministers, and three thousand members. They began to build academies and colleges, first near churches up and down the East Coast from New York to South Carolina, and then westward. In 1729 there was agreement that all ministers subscribe to the Westminster Confession and the Westminster Larger and Shorter Catechisms. The first split in the denomination in America occurred over the Great Awakening. It would be the first of many. By 1758 there were two hundred churches, a hundred ministers, and over ten thousand members. The first southern presbytery, the Presbytery of Hanover, was formed in 1775, ranging from western Pennsylvania to Georgia. Presbyterians were often involved in protests about the British treatment of the colonies, particularly in the Carolinas and New York. Most supported the Revolution and liberty for all, and some even supported gradual elimination of slavery. Their concerns were reflected locally and in new constitutions that went into effect in 1789 for both the country and the American denomination. Twelve of the signers of the Declaration of Independence were or had been Presbyterians. By the late 1780s, there were four synods, sixteen presbyteries, 177 ministers, 420 churches, and twenty thousand members. The first General Assembly met in Philadelphia in 1789, and it sent congratulations to the country's new president. In 1794 the Associate Reformed Presbyterian Church organized the first Presbyterian seminary in the country, in western Pennsylvania.

In the nineteenth century, the denomination grew steadily, particularly in the South and westward. Missions to the Indians developed. There had been a Presbyterian church in Charleston since 1685, and now one began in St. Augustine in 1824, and the Presbytery of Texas was organized in 1837, by which time there were Presbyterian churches in all the southern states and nationally there were 2,965 churches, 2,140 ministers, and 220,000 members. By 1830 seminaries had been opened in New Jersey, South Carolina, and Virginia; and by 1860s there were forty-nine Presbyterian colleges in twenty-one of the thirty-four states. Presbyterians also had been involved in the founding of state universities, for example in North Carolina and Tennessee. In 1816 they helped form the American Bible Society and in 1825 the American Tract Society. In the North there were more Presbyterian churches for African Americans, and one of their ministers helped found the first African American newspaper in 1827. The founding of the American Colonization Society in 1817 was supported by the General Assembly, which in 1818 called for kind treatment and gradual emancipation of slaves. By the 1840s, there were a number of prominent African American Presbyterian ministers, including Henry Highland Garnet and James W. C. Pennington, both of whom were also abolitionist authors. By 1843 one of the largest American Presbyterian congregations was the predominantly African American Zion Church in Charleston, South Carolina (whose building seated 1,000 African Americans on the first floor and 250 whites in the balcony). Clearly the social and political pressures of the middle of the century could not be avoided by Presbyterians, and in 1861, because of disputes over slavery and secession, the main body of Presbyterians split into two separate groups, and the Presbyterian Church in the Confederate States of America was formed at a meeting in Augusta, Georgia. There were various other groups that earlier had split off on theological or organizational grounds, which now came together in the North and South on geographical-ideological grounds.

After the Civil War, foreign missions became more important, including those in India, China, Korea, and Japan. By 1870 there were Presbyterian churches in all of what were to be the forty-eight states, except three. By 1900 nationally there were over a million members. In 1906 there was some reunion of the "northern" church and the Cumberland Presbyterian Church, which had become a separate group in 1810. Another sign of new trends was women first attending the General Assembly as commissioners in 1931. The early decades of the century saw Presbyterians become more interested in social concerns in general (working conditions, public health, living conditions, race relations). By 1983 there were about 3.2 million American Presbyterians. That year, finally, the Presbyterian Church in the United States ("descended from" the Presbyterian Church in the Confederate States of America and with 821,000 members, 4,250 churches, and 6,077 ministers) and the United Presbyterian Church in the United States of America united to form the Presbyterian Church (USA), thereby ending the schism caused by the Civil War. This came into being through a meeting of the General Assemblies of both in Atlanta. Although this created a large national Presbyterian Church, there also still remain other, smaller, important Presbyterian groups apart from it. Two examples are the Associate Reformed Presbyterian Church, begun in 1782, and the Presbyterian Church in America, formed in 1970. All are parts of Presbyterianism in America; and in 1996 the largest included 16 synods, 171 presbyteries,

11,328 churches, 20,783 ministers, and 2.6 million members.

Despite various differences, changes, and organizations, Presbyterians have continued most of the emphases from their early years in America. They now have nine seminaries in eight states. The oldest of these was founded in 1794 and the most recent in 1956. At least fifty-seven other Presbyterian institutions of higher education are to be found in twenty-six states (thirty of the schools are in the South, nine of them in North Carolina). The oldest of these are Hampden-Sydney (1776), Tusculum (1794), and Maryville (1819)—all southern. The most recent are St. Andrews (formed by combining two older colleges in 1958), Trinity Christian (1959), and College of Gonado (1970). Several Presbyterian colleges were originally designed for African Americans only, including two in North Carolina in 1867, one in Tennessee in 1875, and one in Alabama in 1876. Beginning in 1810, Presbyterians created at least one new college every decade through the 1950s, except for the 1920s and 1930s. And either directly or through close family, Presbyterian influence on southern writers over the decades includes at least Sidney Lanier, Frederick Douglass, Elizabeth Keckley, George Washington Cable, Mark Twain, Thomas Wolfe, Erskine Caldwell, Pearl Buck, Catherine Marshall, C. Hugh Holman, Elizabeth Spencer, Doris Betts, William Hoffman, Allan Gurganus, and Randall Kenan.

Julian Mason

See also Abolition; Calvinism; Civil War; Scots-Irish.

Walter L. Lingle and John W. Kuykendall, *Presbyterians: Their History and Beliefs* (1978); James H. Smylie, *American Presbyterians: A Pictorial History* (1985); T. Watson Street, *The Story of Southern Presbyterians* (1960); Ernest Trice Thompson, *Presbyterians in the South* (3 vols., 1963–73).

PROLETARIAN NOVEL

The prescriptive definition of the proletarian novel in the United States was intensely contested for a few years in the late 1920s and 1930s among left-wing writers and critics. Since then, literary historians have argued more generally about how appropriately the term may be applied retrospectively to the actual fiction that was produced by writers with a wide range of revolutionary, radical, or sometimes simply rebellious sympathies during the Great Depression. The original debate focused on which aspects of a novel must be proletarian in order for it to pass muster—was a working-class author sufficient, regardless of the content, point of view, or even the likely audience of the work? Did the subject matter of the fiction have to be the lives of the proletariat? Might a correctly Marxian perspective merit the proletarian label for a bourgeois writer? Could a proletarian novel possibly antedate the existence of a revolutionary proletariat eager to read it? The theoretical arguments raged in the pages of the *New Masses* and *New Quarterly* at the same time that the devastating economic crisis of the Depression ravaged the nation and turned the attention of novelists as never before to a scrutiny of the reasons for the apparent failure of the lives of its people.

Nowhere in the country was the crisis more urgent than in the South, already the poorest and most vulnerable region; nowhere was there already underway a literary awakening more dramatic and powerful. Nowhere, at first glance, might circumstances have seemed more auspicious for the creation of the proletarian novel than the South on the edge of its great literary renascence. However, the yoking of the terms *southern* or *regional* to the already highly contested concept of *proletarian* compounded and still complicates the dilemma of choosing novels that qualify for consideration—whether to observe the constraints of formulas and choose those that satisfy the greatest number of criteria for orthodoxy, or to succumb to the allure of the actual fictional accomplishments and select those unorthodox hybrids that seem finally to extend the range of possibility of the novel.

In both the proletarian and southern ranks of the 1930s, there were partisans eager to preserve their literary territory from any intrusions of reactionary regionalism or subversive Marxism. Thus Granville Hicks, writing from a Communist perspective in 1933, chose to circumscribe his field narrowly by rejecting most southern regional writing from his *Great Tradition* of progressive American literature, on the basis of its sentimental escapism from "certain of the basic problems of American life." Two years later, the Agrarian Donald Davidson chose to exclude from an avowedly conservative survey of southern literature all novels about poor whites as being the products of an unhealthy state of mind, considering them inappropriate to the celebratory tenor of his approach. Likewise, V. F. Calverton argued from the left, in 1932, that southern literature could only be backward-looking and at odds with the rest of the nation until the South

became an industrial culture, whereas John Crowe Ransom, in 1936, defended the distinctiveness and immunity of the South from all such wishful Marxist scenarios.

Even in the ideologically polarized atmosphere of the 1930s, however, there were many critics and authors who encouraged the exploration of common ground between radical politics and regional fiction, or meditated thoughtfully on their interrelationship. Constance Rourke, the scholar of American humor, warned that it was an error to cast the proletariat and the regional folk into separate categories. Folklorist B. A. Botkin demonstrated the adaptability and continuity of folk cultures between rural agricultural and urban industrial contexts and advocated a progressive alignment of regionalism and literary radicalism. Robert Penn Warren, writing in one of the first issues of the *Southern Review* in 1936, juxtaposed what he saw as the dominant concerns of regional and proletarian writers, their coincidences, and their inevitable oppositions. Warren argued that both the regional and the proletarian literary movements were inherently revolutionary, both critical of present conditions, both opposed to finance capitalism, and both concerned to heal the current rupture between the artist and society. He found the greatest divergences between regionalists and proletarians in their attitudes toward history and property. Regionalists were oriented to the past, proletarians to the future; regionalists viewed property, in the form of landholding, as a valued link to a particular place and society, while proletarians saw individual property as destructive of communal solidarity. Warren conceded that both kinds of writing might tend toward propaganda, although he believed the proletarian writer to be more susceptible to political programs and dogma than the regionalist. Certainly the South was attractive (if intractable) material for committed Marxist novelists whose left-wing ideology spoke pertinently to many of the conditions exposed by earlier southern regional writers. Equally, for those writers already immersed in the highly specific details of regional life, the radical agenda of the Communists was both intriguing in its possibilities and ominous in its certainties. From such pervasive tensions, there emerged a range of imaginative literature between the late 1920s and the end of the 1930s that seems almost infinitely capable of contraction or expansion according to the disposition of the literary historian.

One of the most respected chroniclers of the radical novel, Walter Rideout, estimated that there were about seventy proletarian novels published in the 1930s. Only six members of Rideout's list of novelists (Maxwell Bodenheim, Fielding Burke, Grace Lumpkin, Myra Page, Richard Wright, and Leane Zugsmith) also appear as southern novelists in John Bradbury's detailed listing of the literature of the Southern Renascence. Three of those six, Burke, Lumpkin, and Page, were best known for their novels of the Gastonia textile strike, novels for which Rideout qualifies his proletarian label by calling them "local-color fiction performed with a radical purpose." Bradbury, in turn, modifies his "southern" label for Bodenheim and Zugsmith because their fiction was rarely southern in its setting. The two literary historians are in agreement on the regional and polemical nature of Richard Wright's *Uncle Tom's Children* (1938) as a southern proletarian novel, but both acknowledge that it is not technically a novel and was in fact written after Wright had begun to move out of the Communist orbit. By such narrow cross-referencing, almost everything may be eliminated. However, Rideout also includes many novels by nonsoutherners dealing with southern material, and Bradbury includes scores of muck-raking, liberal, and social-protest novels about sharecroppers, tenant farmers, poverty-stricken communities, and inequities of class and caste that fall outside Rideout's definitions.

More recent literary historians and critics have shown themselves eager to augment rather than limit their subject matter by abandoning the highly restrictive terms *proletarian* and *movement* in favor of terms such as *red, radical, worker,* and *cultural formation* that are more flexible and open-ended in tracing interrelations among society, politics, and literature. An aspect of recent critical theory that has further served to enlarge the potential range of radical novels from the Depression period is the investigation of patterns of literary "displacement," whereby the vocabulary, imagery, and forms of human powerlessness may be conveyed interchangeably in the various modalities of race, class, and gender, hitherto often falsely treated by critics as discrete categories. Thus, at the most simple level, black characters are now seen to be evoked by class-based terminology, working-class characters to be feminized, and females racialized until eventually the conception of an exploited underclass becomes fluid, if not protean. For southern fiction, this has significant implications for novels by and about African Americans, works that in the 1930s were not generally considered part of the left-wing literary movement, and

also for women's novels seen in a later and more political light than in their own time.

The first southern novels to explore the inequitable consequences of the economic basis of that society were largely rural and agricultural in their focus, and the majority of them antedated the 1928 call in the *New Masses* for an American proletarian novel. None of them proposed revolutionary violence, and some seemed to endorse stoicism as the only tenable mode of survival in the present, but all dealt directly with the burdens of material deprivation in an avowedly democratic and egalitarian society. These novels include Edith Summers Kelley's 1923 novel of Kentucky tobacco farmers, *Weeds,* and Elizabeth Madox Roberts's *The Time of Man* (1926), about "road trash" or agricultural laborers, a class beneath even tenants and sharecroppers. By comparison with these intensely personal and somewhat fatalistic studies of the lives of individuals, the avidly reformist and even vengeful novels of cotton farming, *In the Land of Cotton* (1923) and *Can't Get a Red Bird* (1929) by Dorothy Scarborough and *Cotton* (1928) by Jack Bethea, are heavy with economic and sociological data as well as precise schemes for improvement. During the same period, T. S. Stribling produced three novels indicting distorted class and race relationships among Tennessee hill people— *Birthright* (1922), *Teeftallow* (1926), and *Bright Metal* (1928)—creating in them the beginnings of his southern *comédie humaine,* which culminated in his 1930s trilogy, *The Forge* (1931), *The Store* (1932), and *The Unfinished Cathedral* (1934). Stribling was hardly a proletarian novelist, yet, like Balzac (one of Marx's most favored novelists), his sense of the complexities and contradictions of his world made him a valuable prophet and pathfinder for those writers who would later try to adhere to the more orthodox party line.

The historical event that appeared to provide the best literary spur to the creation of a genuinely southern proletarian novel occurred in Gastonia, North Carolina, in 1929, when a strike of textile workers culminated in violence, bloodshed, a histrionic courtroom showdown, and the martyrdom of one of the workers. The Gastonia situation offered writers the model of a newly industrialized proletariat, formerly exploited and debased, now unified and militant in the face of corrupt and self-serving capitalists. It also provided regional and local-color writers with fertile material, from the romantic mountain culture and traditions of the recently urbanized workers to the extravagant rhetoric of southern public life and the simple poetry of the strikers' murdered ballad-maker, Ella May Wiggins. Six proletarian novels about the events at Gastonia appeared over the next few years: Mary Heaton Vorse's *Strike!* in 1930, Fielding Burke's *Call Home the Heart,* Grace Lumpkin's *To Make My Bread,* Myra Page's *Gathering Storm,* and Sherwood Anderson's *Beyond Desire,* all in 1932, and William Rollins Jr.'s *The Shadow Before* in 1934. Rollins was not a southerner, nor did he retain the North Carolina setting for his fictional version of the strike, apparently believing that a northern immigrant population might more effectively suggest the international aspects of class warfare. Although neither Vorse nor Anderson was a southerner by birth, both preserved and explored the regional elements of the situation and (despite Bradbury's reservations) may be said to have produced southern novels.

The five Gastonia novels with a southern setting demonstrate that regional and proletarian fiction could indeed co-exist and that the tensions between rural and urban, farm and factory, past and future that Robert Penn Warren saw as inherent in the two genres might become the core of a fruitful dialogue within an individual work. The Gastonia novelists explored traditional characteristics associated with the southern poor (from their community spiritedness and close ties to family and land to their religiosity, violence, and racial antagonisms) in order to question how adaptable they might be to the ideals of a revolutionary proletariat—a question that provoked some irony and despair, as well as insurgent optimism, in several of the novels. The fictions of Gastonia are not the product of "artists in uniform," either red or otherwise. They are distinct in style and sympathies and varied in the degree of their Marxist partisanship and regional affections. They certainly belie the fears of theorists like Hicks and Calverton that regional writing was a way of escaping the fundamental problems of American life. Vorse's *Strike!* creates a vision of class warfare complicated not merely by contrary attitudes toward race and religion by the northern organizers and the southern workers, but further confused by gender conflicts among both organizers and strikers over the role and authority of women workers and union officials. Three of the remaining Gastonia novels by the other three women authors concentrate on female protagonists and highlight the particular problems of poor southern women, from lower wages and lack of access to means of birth control to the difficulties of reconciling a traditional gendered rural culture with the new exigencies of factory employment.

That this nucleus of southern proletarian novels should focus so insistently on gender is only in part a consequence of their coincidental authorship by women. It is also an appropriate convergence of a central preoccupation, not mentioned by Warren, of both southern, regional, and left-wing literature—namely the effort to mediate between patterns of sexual symbolism in both traditions that essentialized women as patient wives, heroic mothers, or sexual temptresses—and the realism of the new fiction, both regional and proletarian, that was acutely sensitive to the historical, environmental, and economic determiners of people's lives. Page's *Gathering Storm,* Lumpkin's *To Make My Bread,* and especially Burke's very accomplished *Call Home the Heart* all explore the predicament of women in conflict with themselves as well as with their external worlds as they try to make sense of old loyalties and obligations in the light of dramatically changing circumstances. Even when the novels impose a somewhat formulaic resolution in their conclusions (as Page's most certainly does), their interest and originality lie in their willingness to look to the future as well as the past, to confront obstacles to reform as well as the power of memory and nostalgia.

Several of the Gastonia novelists also attempted to explore the intersection of race and class in their fiction of the strike, as well as in later proletarian works. Burke, Page, and Lumpkin all treated the topic, and Burke returned to it again in *A Stone Came Rolling* (1935), a direct sequel to *Call Home the Heart,* whereas Lumpkin's next novel, *A Sign for Cain* (1935), turned from factory to farm to depict efforts to forge allegiances among black and white sharecroppers. Although the racial attitudes revealed by these white, southern, middle-class women are sometimes deemed by more contemporary critics as unworthy of their leftist ideals, they all nevertheless focus their fiction quite deliberately on yet another profound collision between the values of the regional past and the necessary changes of the future. The importance of their evocations of the recalcitrance of fictional white southerners to the goal of achieving racial solidarity is not undermined by their own unconscious expressions of what the Communist Party labeled "white chauvinism." Southern black writers with leftist and proletarian sympathies also recorded the power of racism to qualify class-consciousness and indeed acknowledged the contrary pull of racially based black nationalist communities in works such as William Attaway's *Blood on the Forge* (1941) and Richard Wright's *Uncle Tom's Children.*

Many southern novelists, black and white, wrote liberal indictments in their fiction of the racial and economic inequities of their region, although most of them did not endorse, even implicitly, the goals of Communism. Among the novels produced by these writers are Gilmore Millen's *Sweet Man* (1930); Wellbourn Kelley's *Inchin' Along* (1932); Paul Green's *The Laughing Pioneer* (1932) and *This Body the Earth* (1935); Hamilton Basso's *Cinnamon Seed* (1934); Robert Rylee's *Deep Dark River* (1935); George Henderson's *Ollie Miss* (1935); Eugene Armfield's *Where the Weak Grow Strong* (1936); George W. Lee's *River George* (1937); and Willie Snow Ethridge's *Mingled Yarn* (1938). While not proletarian novels, they emerge from an ambience highly sympathetic to the efforts of regional fiction writers to engage in self-scrutiny, since it was in the regional crucible that conflicts between stasis and change, both political and cultural, were usually most apparent.

One southern writer who did avow explicitly leftist politics, who took as radical a stand on racism as he did on poverty, and who also belonged to a central tradition of southern regional writing was Erskine Caldwell. The sympathies displayed in his novels, short stories, and documentary writings of the 1930s are quite congruent with those of the literary left-wing; the grotesquely comic and violent mode of his fiction is in accord with the Southwestern humorists of the nineteenth century, A. B. Longstreet, Johnson J. Hooper, and George Washington Harris; yet despite these affinities, or perhaps because of them, Caldwell was a thorn in the flesh of both radical and regional critics. In his novels *Tobacco Road* (1932), *God's Little Acre* (1933), and *Trouble in July* (1940), and in his collection of short stories, *Kneel to the Rising Sun* (1935), he created a body of startlingly original fiction that eschewed all orthodoxies while displaying a vigorous commitment to the poor people of the South. He offended regionalists and Marxists alike with his incongruous literary mixture of vulgar humor, dispassionate analysis, and shocking atrocity. He explored the dynamics of race, poverty, and sexuality in minute and oddly individual variations and became, to the increased suspicion of all sides, a best-selling novelist. Perhaps the very readiness of regional and proletarian partisans to find Caldwell wanting might suggest that, of all southern writers in the Great Depression, he came closest to creating not a tame compromise between divergent agendas but the disturbing new possibility of a radical fiction outside the bounds of all prescriptions and formulations.

The end of the 1930s did not bring an end to southern novels that exposed and scourged the failings of the region's social and economic system, but the calls for a proletarian novel, which had begun to be more muted during the Popular Front period, gradually dissipated in the latter years of the decade and had all but disappeared by the early years of World War II. The waning of the much-contested "proletarian" label coincided with the rising reputation of southern literature that would eventually lead to the questioning of "regional" as a constricting epithet for the distinguished novels of the literary renascence. Thus both regional and proletarian fiction came in the end to be assimilated, if not quite fully digested, into a broader and less contentious tradition.

Sylvia J. Cook

See also Great Depression; Populism.

John Bradbury, *Renaissance in the South: A Critical History of the Literature, 1920–1960* (1963); Barbara Foley, *Radical Representations: Politics and Form in U.S. Proletarian Fiction, 1929–1941* (1993); Laura Hapke, *Daughters of the Great Depression: Women, Work, and Fiction in the American 1930s* (1995); Walter B. Rideout, *The Radical Novel in the United States: Some Interrelations of Literature and Society, 1900–1954* (1956); Douglas Wixson, *Worker-Writer in America: Jack Conroy and the Tradition of Midwestern Literary Radicalism, 1898–1990* (1994).

PROMOTIONAL TRACT

Much of the earliest literature written in and about the American South could be classified as promotional literature. Encompassing a wide range of forms, promotional literature ranged from full-fledged histories and compendiums to smaller tracts such as pamphlets and broadsides. Typically, promotional tracts outlined information about the location and climate of the colony in question, the nature of the soil and productions of the land (both real and imagined), and something of the native population. They sought to convince readers that the colonies were sites of wealth, independence, easy living, and safety. Promotional tracts were often accompanied by maps—sometimes highly inaccurate—as well as by information concerning transportation. Unabashedly propagandistic, authors of promotional tracts made no efforts to hide their intentions. They sought to effect change by encouraging the exploration and settlement of the colonies, and they did so by making the colonies sound as appealing as possible. The title of the pamphlet attributed to Thomas Ashe is quite typical of the titles of these tracts and provides a sense of their content: *Carolina; or a Description of the Present State of that Country, and the Natural Excellencies therof, vis., the Healthfulness of the Air, Pleasantness of the Place, Advantage and Usefulness of those Rich Commodities there plentifully abounding, which much encrease and flourish by the Industry of the Planters that daily enlarge that Colony* (1682).

European interest in cosmography and the exoticism of foreign lands extended back hundreds of years before Columbus arrived in America, but in the sixteenth century, that interest shifted from the East to the West. Slower than their European neighbors in exploring the West, the English did not begin actively to promote the exploration and settlement of America until the very end of the sixteenth century. Richard Hakluyt became the principal publisher of explorers' reports about the colonies, and his two major compendiums—*Divers voyages touching the discoverie of America* (1582) and *Principal Navigations, Voyages, Traffiques, and Discoveries of the English Nation* (1589–90)—were instrumental in promoting English settlement of the colonies. It was also at Hakluyt's urging that scientist Thomas Harriott visited the English Roanoke settlement as a botanist and ethnographer. The work that Harriott produced as a result of his year in Virginia—*A Briefe and True Report of the New Found Land of Virginia* (1588; 1590)—was the first English book published exclusively about an English colony and the first one written about the South. An expanded second edition, published two years after the original, was printed in Latin, German, and French as well as in English; it also included engravings by Theodor de Bry, whose artistic representations played a significant role in shaping European conceptions of America.

Whereas the publication of the second edition of Harriott's work reveals the widespread Continental interest in the New World, the publication of the first edition is intricately tied to the promotion of the colonies. The work was rushed into print in order to support Sir Walter Raleigh's petition to the queen not to abandon the Virginia colony. *A Briefe and True Report* also reveals the intertextual nature of promotional tracts; in its very first paragraph, it responds to various oral re-

ports of the colony that were injurious to its continued settlement. Harriott's decision to address directly the accounts that precede his own marks a common trait of promotional tracts: they almost invariably reference previous reports, either to refute them, to affirm them, or to refer readers to them. The authors of the various tracts assume that their readers are familiar with the previous information about the colonies that has been disseminated both orally and in print.

The first southern colonies to be promoted in England were Virginia and Maryland, both of which received the greatest attention in the early part of the seventeenth century. Carolina was promoted most heavily in the second half of the seventeenth century, and Georgia in the early part of the eighteenth century. Perhaps the most important early promoter of the southern colonies was John Smith. In addition to playing a central role in the earliest years of the Jamestown colony, Smith published several highly influential tracts. His most important work, *The General History of Virginia, New England, and the Summer Isles* (1624), included illustrations based on de Bry's earlier engravings. Smith's works most notably connect the promotion of the colonies to self-promotion. Just as Smith figures prominently in his own narratives and histories, the colonies were depicted as a site where others could achieve notoriety and success.

In attempting to persuade readers to settle in the southern colonies, authors of promotional tracts used a wide range of appeals, but none so prevalent as the promise of easy wealth. Authors catalogued the various animal, vegetable, and mineral resources that were indigenous to the area and available for exploitation. They also speculated about the various potential resources that the colony might be able to produce. In order to lure Europeans to leave their current situation, promotional tracts had to demonstrate persuasively that wealth was easier to obtain in the colonies than it was in Europe. They claimed that it took little labor to live comfortably and that wealth would follow diligence. Promotional tracts also frequently touted the increased independence of colonists on both a political and a personal level. Government was small, they claimed, and people who were dependent laborers in Europe could become independent planters or merchants in the colonies.

In addition to convincing their readers that a great deal of wealth could be accrued in the colonies, southern promotional tracts had to convince Europeans that the colonies were safe. Disease, a harsh natural setting, and a hostile population of Native Americans were all potential deterrents to immigration. Because there were negative reports of the colonies as well as positive ones, authors of promotional tracts had to address such issues in their writings. Since the Chesapeake and the Carolinas were associated with high disease and mortality rates, for example, promotional tracts tried to present these places as healthful. They contended that the Native Americans were not a threat and that the colonies were secure from other European nations as well—a major issue in the early settlement of South Carolina. Dispelling the claims of negative reports was a major function of promotional tracts because their authors realized that even the promise of certain wealth meant little if one could not survive to enjoy that wealth.

Unlike the tracts promoting the New England colonies, which often had religious emphases, those geared toward encouraging settlement in the South rarely stressed religious or humanitarian arguments. Converting the indigenous population and extending the British Empire were not ends in themselves to the southern promoters, but rather means of expediting the acquisition of personal wealth. Similarly, most promotional tracts did not attempt to target oppressed religious groups. Promises-of-freedom clauses did attract some religious dissenters to the southern colonies, such as the French Huguenots who settled in South Carolina, but these clauses were ancillary to the primary claims of guaranteed wealth in a safe environment. In short, southern promotional tracts focused on personal and economic issues.

A significant aspect of promotional tracts is that they not only described the southern colonies but also participated in inventing them through their writing. Authors of promotional tracts often embellished their works, making their descriptions conform to European expectations of the New World's climate and inhabitants. The fact that many of the individuals who wrote and published promotional tracts had never even visited the colonies makes the veracity of their reports suspect—and their writings become constructions rather than reportage. Even among those writers who were living in the colonies or who had visited the colonies, the process of inventing an "America" is apparent in their works. In particular, the emphasis on what the colonies could be and could produce plays a central role in promotional tracts. Because mulberry trees grew in the South, southern promoters conjured up pictures of a thriving silk industry, and because the cli-

mate was hot, they suggested that the colonies could grow olives and other goods native to Asia Minor. Promoters of the southern colonies described the region as a place of wonder and possibility, often linking it to the Orient.

An interesting connection exists between early American promotional literature and the natural histories that emerged in the late eighteenth century. Promotional tracts participate in cataloguing the species and resources of a colony in much the same way that William Bartram's *Travels* (1791) does. Similarly, Jefferson's *Notes on the State of Virginia* (1784–85) constructs an American identity for Europeans in a similar manner to that of promotional tracts.

Although promotional literature was most prevalent in the seventeenth and eighteenth centuries—during the early colonization of America—southern states continued to publish promotional tracts into the nineteenth and twentieth centuries as well. The state of South Carolina, for example, published several tracts immediately following the Civil War in an attempt to compete with the western states for foreign immigrants. Today's "promotional tracts" are most often the realm of tourist bureaus and chambers of commerce.

Exactly how integral promotional tracts were to the ultimate settlement of the South is unclear. What they do provide, however, is some of the earliest literature associated with the region as well as the earliest literary constructions of America and the American South.

George S. Scouten

See also Bartram, William; Jefferson, Thomas; Travel Literature.

Mary B. Campbell, *The Witness and the Other World* (1988).

PROTEST, NOVEL OF

In the nineteenth and twentieth centuries, the novel of social protest has been well represented in American literature, with noteworthy examples such as Harriet Beecher Stowe's *Uncle Tom's Cabin* (1852), Upton Sinclair's *The Jungle* (1906), and John Steinbeck's *The Grapes of Wrath* (1939), each representing a familiar classic in the form. Many American novels, southern or not, have been in varying degrees protest books. According to Granville Hicks, however, there is an important distinction to be made between social protest and social criticism: "The novel of social protest is aimed against a specific evil—the institution of slavery, the conditions in the Chicago stockyards, the sufferings of the Okies. It points to a wrong, a wrong that can be righted. The novel of social criticism is concerned in a larger way with the social structure. It is broader and deeper, and if its influence is harder to measure, its life is usually longer."

The novel of social protest in southern literature had its origins in the last quarter of the nineteenth century and is best represented in selected works by George Washington Cable and Mark Twain, neither of whom actually resided in the South when their books criticizing benighted southern institutions and social culture were published. Cable's *The Grandissimes* (1880), which Louis D. Rubin Jr. aptly calls "the first 'modern' Southern novel," "the first book by a Southerner to deal seriously with the relations of white and Negro," realistically treats a complex and controversial subject—the inhumanity of race relations. In it, Cable, with a clear didactic purpose in mind, satirizes the vanity of the Creole society of early-nineteenth-century New Orleans, particularly as seen in the racism of class- and caste-conscious and slave-holding Creoles and the tragic consequences that such an attitude has on the lives of blacks. Mark Twain, in *Adventures of Huckleberry Finn* (1885), also exposed the injustices and foibles of antebellum society, the society of the Lower Mississippi Valley of the 1840s. In *Huckleberry Finn*, Twain satirized not only racism and the concomitant denial of the black man's humanity that went along with it, but also hatred, violence, hypocrisy, pretension, and various forms and degrees of cruelty. Earlier, Twain had directed his vitriol at his own times, collaborating with Charles Dudley Warner to write *The Gilded Age* (1873), a protest novel of sorts that satirizes the corruption of the Grant Administration and the "all pervading speculativeness" of the period. Although *The Gilded Age* suffers from numerous artistic weaknesses, *The Grandissimes* and *Huckleberry Finn* represent dynamic contributions to the literature of social protest, and each significantly anticipates a subject matter and attitude toward it that would become more widespread and prominent in southern writing of the 1920s and 1930s, the heyday of social protest in the southern novel, and of the early 1940s, when several more-exemplary novels indicative of the type were also published.

One of the most important influences on the development of the southern novel of social protest in the 1920s is what Carl Van Doren has defined as the "revolt from the village," the literary assault on the formerly cherished and idealized image of the American small town as friendly, harmonious, tranquil, almost sacred, perhaps nearly mythic, a place admirably self-sufficient and free from the attendant bad influences and complexities associated with urban industrial society. This "revolt" had its antecedents in the last quarter of the nineteenth century, in Eggleston's *The Hoosier Schoolmaster* (1871), E. W. Howe's *The Story of a Country Town* (1883), Frederic's *The Damnation of Theron Ware* (1896), and Mark Twain's *The Man That Corrupted Hadleyburg* (1900), books that collectively created the paradigm of the small town as a smug, ugly, uniform, narrow-minded, bigoted, and intellectually sterile locale. However, the "revolt" received its greatest impetus from Sinclair Lewis, a midwesterner who published three best-selling novels in the 1920s—*Main Street* (1920), *Babbitt* (1922), and *Elmer Gantry* (1927)—and whose work, especially *Main Street*, became a major liberating influence on the southern social novel of the period. In *Main Street*, Lewis not only provided a subject broadly applicable to contemporary southern small-town and rural experience, but also the mode of critical realism, an appropriate manner for disparaging it. The early southern imitators of Lewis, like their mentor, satirized narrow-mindedness, religious fanaticism, bigotry, hypocrisy, smugness, crass materialism, dullness, unnecessary violence, and numerous other foibles common both to southern small towns and rural hamlets and to American provincial existence generally.

One of the earliest southern versions of *Main Street*, Edith Summers Kelley's *Weeds* (1922)—a book that Lewis was incidentally instrumental in persuading his publisher, Alfred Harcourt, to publish—starkly and painstakingly depicts the tenant life of small tobacco farmers in Scott County, Kentucky, the fictional setting. The central character, Judy Pippinger Blackford, discernibly in the mold of Lewis's Carol Kennicott of *Main Street*, is a young, restless, imaginative wife of a poor sharecropper who finds her existence to be dreary and monotonous. In *Weeds*, Kelley examines with a critical eye crop failures, extreme poverty, pestilence, low farm prices, marital infidelity, and various societal assaults against individual integrity. Two years later, Emanie N. Sachs, who like Kelley was a Kentuckian, published *Talk* (1924), another southern protest novel imitating *Main Street*. In *Talk*, Sachs directs her sharpest assaults against small-town gossipmongers who use their invidious talk to force a young business-minded woman to conform to the town's expectations: to become a housewife.

Of the southern "revolt-from-the-village" novelists of the 1920s who worked in the popular *Main Street* mode, the most prominent was T. S. Stribling of Tennessee, a pioneer of the southern literary renascence who helped to transmit significant social themes and to present them from an iconoclastic perspective. His first three protest novels as a village iconoclast—*Birthright* (1922), *Teeftallow* (1926), and *Bright Metal* (1928)—are all closely patterned after Lewis's best-seller. In these novels, Stribling unmercifully debunks the excesses of the southern small town, including bigotry, hypocrisy, racism, religious fanaticism, lawlessness, and violence, virtually all of which stem from the characters' unethical pursuit of materialistic goals. In addition, many of the characters, often reprehensible caricatures, resemble familiar Lewisian village types—dishonest boosters, narrow-minded fundamentalists, outcasts, opportunistic bankers, gossips, and cynics. Peter Siner, the young black idealist in *Birthright,* and Agatha Pomeroy, the central character in *Bright Metal,* are reformers discernibly like Carol Kennicott in *Main Street,* who are unsuccessful in transforming the provincial Tennessee towns they inhabit into better places.

Stribling's iconoclastic attacks against the debilitating forces in southern society continued in the early 1930s with the publication of a trilogy—*The Forge* (1931), *The Store* (1932), and *The Unfinished Cathedral* (1934)—collectively his most ambitious achievement as a novelist and the work on which his reputation as a social-protest novelist principally rests. In this trilogy, Stribling graphically portrays the prominent changes in southern society that occurred over a period of approximately sixty-five years, from just before the Civil War through the boom period of the 1920s. Set in Florence, Alabama, an actual place, and the surrounding area, Stribling's trilogy chronicles the history of three generations of a southern family, the Vaidens. In *The Forge,* which treats the dissolution of the Old South civilization, Stribling satirizes the Vaidens' victimization of blacks, the disreputable behavior of Confederate and Yankee soldiers and the squalid conditions of army life, the opportunism of self-serving guerrilla gangs, and the unprincipled materialism and political chicanery of carpetbaggers. *The Store,* the second novel, and the one for which Stribling was awarded a Pulitzer Prize in 1933, focuses on post-Re-

construction in northern Alabama, a period of rapid and radical social change. This novel presents a denigrating portrait of Miltiades Vaiden, the central character of the trilogy, who compromises his integrity, resorting to unscrupulous methods to rise financially and socially. Stribling indicts not only Miltiades but also disgruntled poor-white sharecroppers who are victims of commercial exploitation; unscrupulous, grasping merchants who prosper by cheating blacks and poor whites; ineffectual and materialistic churchmen; and prejudiced legal officials. In *The Store,* Stribling exposes a society where the merchant has replaced the planter and where moral integrity and social responsibility have given way to selfish acquisitive desires. The last novel, *The Unfinished Cathedral,* which satirizes some of the same concerns stemming from the infiltration of materialism into all facets of life that Lewis had previously attacked in *Babbitt* and *Elmer Gantry,* criticizes the speculative frenzy of the 1920s as represented in a real-estate boom, the consequence of the construction of a government dam on the Tennessee River.

Of less importance in the Stribling canon of protest novels are three books he also published in the 1930s—*Backwater* (1930), *The Sound Wagon* (1935), and *These Bars of Flesh* (1938). Whereas *Backwater,* set in the Arkansas lowlands, ridicules familiar aspects of southern provincial life—narrow-mindedness, social pretension, and lawlessness—Stribling's satiric stance is gentle, actually sometimes humorous and zestful, which detracts from the impact of the novel's social criticism. Both *The Sound Wagon* and *These Bars of Flesh* have northern settings and exhibit a more unrelenting satiric thrust. In *The Sound Wagon,* Stribling attempts to dispel some of the naïve notions Americans of the time had toward politics by exposing graft in the American political system. And in *These Bars of Flesh,* he attacks American higher education by disparaging some of the shortcomings of a metropolitan university.

While village iconoclasts such as Kelley, Sachs, and Stribling formed the vanguard of the southern camp in the "revolt-from-the-village" movement, other writers, particularly Texan Dorothy Scarborough, made the target of their propagandistic protest the problems of tenant farmers. *In the Land of Cotton* (1923), Scarborough's first realistic social novel, provides a detailed rendering of some of the more deplorable problems plaguing poor-white tenants in Texas. She not only vehemently protests the degrading conditions under which these tenants are compelled to live, enslaved as they are to a single-crop economy, but also examines the natural perils afflicting their lives as cotton farmers, including the boll-weevil menace, drought, and floods. The personal tragedies that many of them experience stem from their unyielding commitment to cotton farming. Unlike the village debunkers, however, Scarborough in *In the Land of Cotton* goes beyond just a painstaking delineation of the hopeless plight of her dispossessed, pitiful victims by actually offering solutions, such as crop regulation and diversification, government loans, price and distribution controls, and more mechanization—an anticipation of the kinds of programs the federal government would subsequently implement in the 1930s as part of Roosevelt's New Deal.

In her second novel in the protest tradition, *Can't Get a Redbird* (1929), Scarborough shifts her attention to the exploitation of tenants by landowners. Yet the ending of *Can't Get a Redbird* may seem contrived and unsatisfying—Scarborough interjects a hopeful note, having one of her diligent tenants escape his destiny, becoming successful and wealthy—a facile reaffirmation of the American dream and an apparent defense of the social and economic status quo. In following this agenda, Scarborough seems to dismiss the main object of her protest—the unfortunate existence of the tenants and the need for reforms to improve their condition.

Several of the southern protest writers of the 1930s, also engaged by the socioeconomic problems of the rural poor and dispossessed, used their novels to raise social consciousness and to promote reform. Harry Harrison Kroll, born in Indiana, raised in Mississippi and Tennessee as the son of a sharecropper, and later himself a farmhand, wrote two novels of social criticism, *Cabin in the Cotton* (1931) and *I Was a Sharecropper* (1936), the latter autobiographical. In *Cabin in the Cotton,* his most popular book, Kroll leveled a caustic indictment against the injustices of the sharecropper system, a system characterized by two-way corruption. On the one hand, he shows the owners' exploitation of the croppers through exorbitant interest rates and dishonest accounting practices; and on the other, he exposes the croppers who steal from and who cheat each other and the owners. Although Kroll targeted the disreputable shortcomings of the sharecropper system, he likewise recognized the need for reform, especially in *Cabin in the Cotton,* where he calls for a cooperative farming system to replace tenant farming. Although this novel as well as *I Was a Sharecropper*

convey Kroll's outrage, his later writing tended to be nostalgic and romantic.

Another writer whose principal works of social criticism were published in the 1930s, Erskine Caldwell—like Scarborough, Kroll, and to an extent, T. S. Stribling—made poor whites his primary subject matter. Caldwell recalled in his autobiography, *Call It Experience,* that when he reviewed books for the *Atlanta Constitution* and the *Charlotte Observer* in the late 1920s, he read many southern novels that in his estimation, "seemed more concerned with contrived situations and artificial events than with reality." Caldwell's own novels—primarily those of the 1930s, such as *Tobacco Road* (1932) and *God's Little Acre* (1933), which deride the devastating and unsavory conditions in rural East Georgia—represent a distinct departure from this mode of writing. Although Caldwell was of liberal persuasion and genuinely concerned with the plight of his poor and degenerate rural and mill-town characters, the conditions afflicting them never seem to improve. As *Tobacco Road* and *God's Little Acre* demonstrate, his characters' only outlets seem to be sadistic violence, emotional tantrums, and sexual orgies. Perhaps because this kind of sensationalism prevails and because most of Caldwell's characters are grotesques, critics and readers alike have tended to pay more attention to these dimensions of his work than to become engaged in the underlying social criticism. From time to time, Caldwell does nevertheless directly attempt to show his indignation toward the social conditions he describes. For instance, in his depiction of the clash between cotton-mill owners and their disenchanted striking workers in *God's Little Acre,* Caldwell occasionally uses one of the workers as a mouthpiece to attack the owners. However, while the mill strike segments clearly demonstrate that the author's sympathies are with the workers, Caldwell ultimately fails to exercise the full potential of social protest in *God's Little Acre.*

Far more effective as novelists of social protest as well as discernibly more collectivist in their ideological stance were the proletarian writers of the Great Depression. Literary art in service to politics, particularly protesting the conditions of working-class life, was hardly a new phenomenon in the 1930s. Melville's *White-Jacket* (1850), Rebecca Harding Davis's "Life in the Iron Mills" (1861), Elizabeth Stuart Phelps's *The Story of Avis* (1877), and Upton Sinclair's *The Jungle* (1906) all represent notable earlier examples of this brand of fiction. In the 1930s, the period when proletarian writing was most in vogue in the United States, seventy novels of this type were published. The proletarian or radical novel, as it has sometimes been called, typically focuses on class struggle, usually advocates a Marxist or communist ideology, and sympathetically treats the problems of the disadvantaged working class.

The primary event in the South that outraged as well as inspired writers to turn to the proletarian novel as a weapon for leftist propagandistic protest was the Communist-led strike in late March and early April 1929 against the Loray Mill, a textile plant in Gastonia, North Carolina. The disgruntled workers, whom Communist union organizers from the North had hoped to persuade to join the National Textile Workers Union, had initially moved to mill towns such as Gastonia from farms in the western North Carolina mountains. In migrating to the Piedmont, they sought prosperity and a better life, but once they had their jobs, the workers discovered that housing and living costs were as high as their wages. Rather than resolving mill workers' complaints against this system, the Gastonia strike, which attracted national press attention, ultimately failed to eliminate the cruelty and exploitation practiced by the mill owners. In fact, the outbreaks of violence resulted in a number of people being shot and killed and the termination of the Communist efforts to get the workers to unionize. As a *cause célèbre,* the activities in Gastonia inspired six novels: *Strike!* (1930) by Mary Heaton Vorse, *Call Home the Heart* (1932) by Olive Tilford Dargan (whose pseudonym was Fielding Burke), *To Make My Bread* (1932) by Grace Lumpkin, *Gathering Storm* (1932) by Myra Page, *Beyond Desire* (1932) by Sherwood Anderson, and *The Shadow Before* (1934) by William Rollins (the most experimental in terms of stylistic innovation).

While the subject matter of class warfare and its victims in these Gastonia-inspired novels generally succeeds in arousing the reader's social consciousness, Burke's *Call Home the Heart,* Page's *Gathering Storm,* and Lumpkin's *To Make My Bread,* in particular, significantly expand the socio-critical parameters to include issues germane to women and their roles in a time of great social turmoil. Although the women protagonists are depicted as serious and aggressive revolutionaries, eager to participate in industrial reform, they are caught between their traditional roles as women and their engagement in Communist-supported union activities.

Not all of the proletarian novels prompted by the Gastonia strike, however, unequivocally supported Communism as a remedy for the ills of capitalism. Burke's *Call Home the Heart,* for instance, focuses on the conflict of Ishma Waycaster, who leaves her family to move to a mill town in the industrial Piedmont to assist the textile union in organizing the striking mill workers. Ishma becomes disillusioned with the disparity between the proletarian ideal and the lives of the exploited mill workers. She gives up her mission of good will and retreats to the mountain home she had formerly abandoned, daydreaming about moving the workers to the mountains where she believes they will find peace of mind in an appealing natural environment. Thus the resolution of *Call Home the Heart* insinuates the failure of Marxist ideology as a corrective to the problems of the proletariat. In Burke's sequel to *Call Home the Heart, A Stone Came Rolling* (1935), however, she reverses her position, reaffirming the Communist ideal.

The protest tradition in southern literature extended into the early 1940s with a few notable examples of the form, especially Richard Wright's *Native Son,* (1940) and Lillian Smith's *Strange Fruit* (1944), both best-selling novels that critically examined the controversial subject of race relations. In *Native Son* Wright became the first twentieth-century novelist to focus extensively on the economic and moral problems of African Americans living in the urban ghetto. Bigger Thomas, Wright's black protagonist, represents African American youths of the era whose lives were characterized by frustration, fear, anger, and violence. In Book Three, the courtroom speeches of attorney Boris Max criticize the status quo that denied the black man his rights as a human being and advocate a new social order predicated on Communist principles. Lillian Smith's *Strange Fruit* (1944), unofficially banned in Boston and Detroit because of its searing realism and controversial subject matter, also challenges the double standard imposed in a racist society. Set in a small southern town, *Strange Fruit* depicts a star-crossed interracial love affair involving an educated black woman and a white man, both of whom are trapped within the narrow confines of the traditional racial and sexual expectations of a segregated society and who become victims of racial injustice.

Although the main tradition of the southern novel of social protest of the 1920s and 1930s produced no work approaching the epic magnitude, artistic quality, and enduring reputation of John Steinbeck's *The*

Grapes of Wrath, still it has been a sometimes viable and popular form. The protest novel has not enjoyed an enduring appeal for several reasons: the disproportionate emphasis placed on advancing a political agenda; the lack of stylistic sophistication; and the confinement to specific time periods, historical incidents, and geographical locales. In choosing to commit themselves in their fiction to the examination of social problems, southern protest novelists of the 1920s and 1930s helped to bring to the forefront vital and engaging subject matter. The social issues that comprised the principal substance of these novels provided perhaps their most important legacy to Thomas Wolfe, William Faulkner, Robert Penn Warren, Flannery O'Connor, Josephine Humphreys, Lee Smith, and other talented southerners, modern as well as contemporary, who, although never principally protest writers themselves, exploited in some of their own novels and stories similar materials, but at a much higher level of art.

Ed Piacentino

See also Proletarian Novel; Work.

Sylvia Jenkins Cook, *From Tobacco Road to Route 66: The Southern Poor White in Fiction* (1976); Anthony Channell Hilfer, *The Revolt from the Village 1915–1930* (1969); Walter B. Rideout, *The Radical Novel in the United States 1900–1954: Some Interrelations of Literature and Society* (1956).

PUBLISHERS

Although the South has produced some of America's finest writers throughout the twentieth century, the hub of the literary publishing industry remains in the environs of New York City. University presses in southern universities have played an important part, in recent years especially, in bringing out the poetry and fiction of contemporary writers. A handful of nonuniversity southern presses have also made an important contribution. They are dedicated to producing high-quality work that reflects the voice and vision of not only the South but other regions, balancing southern loyalties with the need to make their offerings in fiction, nonfiction, and poetry resonate with and represent national audiences. No complete catalogue of all of these presses exists, but a review of some that have been successful as business and artistic ventures for decades, and others that are just now getting off the

ground, reveals a lively industry. Peachtree Publishers of Atlanta has been in business since the 1970s, offering trade books that often have a southern focus, particularly in the area of humor, gardening, and cooking. Longstreet Publishers, another of the larger southern presses, also operates out of Atlanta. In North Carolina, John Blair, Inc. of Winston-Salem has encouraged regional writing, and Chapel Hill is home to the South's most successful southern publishing venture, Algonquin Books, founded in 1982 by Louis D. Rubin and Shannon Ravenel, his former student. After seven years as an independent press, Algonquin was acquired as a division by Workman Publishing in New York, but continued under Rubin's direction until 1993, when he resigned and was succeeded by Ravenel as editorial director and Elizabeth Scharlatt as publisher. Now publishing about twenty-five new titles a year, Algonquin Books holds to its original mission of accessibility to new writers and commitment to publishing literary fiction and creative nonfiction. In late 2000, Algonquin announced the establishment of a new imprint, Shannon Ravenel Books, which Ravenel will direct. A new editorial director will be named.

Alongside these larger southern publishing houses, much smaller and more specialized presses operate in every southern state. Gnomon Press of Kentucky brings out beautiful editions of important southern poetry. Sarabande Books, established in 1994 in Louisville, Kentucky, sees itself as an alternative to the mainstream in literary offerings. The Beehive Foundation in Georgia has for many years operated the Beehive Press, which publishes important books of Georgian and southern interest, emphasizing slavery, folklife, and the Civil War. In Charlottesville, Virginia, Howell Press offers Rockbridge Books, including in a largely regional list collections of ghost stories and Confederate memoirs. Carolina Wren Press in Durham, North Carolina, is beginning to seek out new fiction and poetry, and Sow's Ear Press in Abingdon, Virginia, has established a reputation in poetry offerings.

One of the newest kids on the southern block is Hill Street Press in Athens, Georgia, a trade publisher determined "to present the mind of the South as only southerners know it." Established in 1998 by publisher Thomas Payton and editors Judy Long and Patrick Allen, Hill Street Press vaunts its southern leanings, seeking to republish out-of-print classics such as Jean Toomer's *Essentials* along with offering original new cultural studies—on everything "from the blues to barbeque."

Darnell Arnoult

See also Algonquin Books; University Presses.

PURITANISM

Although some Puritanism existed in the South from its beginning, governance of the Virginia Colony remained in England with the London Company rather than with local settlers. In contrast to the towns of the self-governing Massachusetts Bay Colony, the scattered tobacco farms of the first permanent English colony did not lend themselves to the close discipline that Puritan culture required. Nor were the Virginia settlers as concerned with religious freedom as they were with improved economic opportunities. For these reasons, conditions in the early American South proved unsuitable for Puritanism.

Around 1700, Huguenots, the French "Puritans," settled in South Carolina, but the true Puritan transformation of southern culture occurred between 1750 and 1860, after the 200,000-plus Scots-Irish who came to America between 1717 and 1775 chiefly elected to remain in the South. Originally Lowland Scots, many had gone to Northern Ireland in the seventeenth century in order to defend the English King's Ulster Plantation against the Irish, already driven out by English arms; they were, in turn, forced out of Northern Ireland by drought combined with new and unfavorable religious and economic laws. Given their history of resistance to the English while still in Scotland and subsequently to the Irish, they proved typical frontiersmen, self-reliant and hardy fighters, able to occupy the Piedmont and Appalachian regions first of Virginia, then North Carolina, South Carolina, Georgia, and eventually the trans-Appalachian South. They brought with them the orderly, if not fixed, class structure and the theological principles of the Presbyterian Church.

Their Calvinism, according to John H. Leith, perceived God chiefly as energy, activity, moral purpose, and intentionality. Their most familiar doctrine, predestination, placed human salvation in God's hands, with the individual relegated to glorifying God and leading the sanctified life of warring against the world, the body, and Satan. In art and thought as in life, they stressed order, simplicity, clarity, authenticity, modera-

tion, while avoiding pomp, pretense, ostentation, and artifice, an emphasis that contrasts with the rich, ornate, witty, and supple rhetoric that the South's English settlers inherited from Francis Bacon, Robert Burton, and Thomas Browne, among others. The Calvinist belief in human depravity and a God-ordained universe, combined with a logic of disjunction influenced by Petrus Ramus, prepared the southern Scots-Irish, according to James McBride Dabbs, to accept enslavement, not freedom, as the natural conditon of African Americans.

In the period between the American Revolution and the Civil War, the dynamic, moving farm culture of the Scots-Irish fused with the settled English plantation to produce the South of the Secession. In the same decades, the circuit-riding Methodists and the often uneducated but "called" Baptist preachers were capturing the frontier South from the Presbyterians. During the early nineteenth century, the latter responded by accepting the bare-bones morality and highly emotional religions of the evangelical theists. As the Puritans of the North evolved into the acquisitive Yankees, so those of the South became the Baptists. The guilt-culture of the emerging combination did little to turn the Scots-Irish South from slavery but served chiefly to increase the distance and bitterness between whites and the victims who mirrored their guilt.

Important modern literary representations of the South's "Puritans" explore Puritanism's various traditions. For example, Eliza Gant in Thomas Wolfe's *Look Homeward, Angel* (1929), born into a family of mountain Presbyterians, practices the Puritan-Protestant ethic with a vengeance as she devotes her life to economic gain by acquiring real estate and separating from her husband to run Dixieland, her shabby boardinghouse. The way that Calvin's doctrine of spiritual election evolved into the South's racial election—as in the theology of Presbyterian Robert Dabney—appears magnified in the rantings of Doc Hines against Joe Christmas in William Faulkner's *Light in August* (1932). Hines damns Joe because the boy is neither black nor white but possibly both; by Hines's disjunctive logic, Joe is therefore totally black and condemned as a "nigger." The militancy of southern Calvinism lies behind the way McEachern uses calculated beatings to instruct Joe in the Presbyterian catechism and the degree of control he exercises in attempting to force Joe into the rigid patterns of a sanctified life.

A more balanced but still critical view of the southern Puritans emerges from Ellen Glasgow's 1935 novel,

Vein of Iron, which treats the descendants of the stoical Presbyterian, John Fincastle, a scholar-pioneer who during the second half of the eighteenth century led his congregation from Ulster to the Valley of Virginia. For guidance, he brought both the Bible and *The Meditations of Marcus Aurelius*. His biological and spiritual heirs, the Ironside community, are a stoical people who separate the part of themselves that feels from the part that thinks, who cannot articulate love although they feel it, and who accept the notion that life is war. Thus criticized, they are nonetheless a people who, in Glasgow's view, possess values that the region and nation need in moments of crisis such as the Great Depression during which the novel takes place.

Although not the whole of the South, descendants of the Scots-Irish Presbyterians remain, as in Glasgow's novel, important contributors to the region's culture.

Julius Rowan Raper

See also Calvinism; Presbyterians; Puritan Writers.

Cleanth Brooks, *William Faulkner: The Yoknapatawpha Country* (1963); W. J. Cash, *The Mind of the South* (1941); James McBride Dabbs, *Who Speaks for the South?* (1964); C. Hugh Holman, *Three Modes of Modern Southern Fiction: Ellen Glasgow, William Faulkner, Thomas Wolfe* (1966); James G. Leyburn, *The Scotch-Irish: A Social History* (1962); Julius Rowan Raper, *From the Sunken Garden: The Fiction of Ellen Glasgow, 1916–1945* (1980).

PURITAN WRITERS

Calvinists, followers of the theology of John Calvin including Puritans, Congregationalists, and Presbyterians, came early to the South. Dissenters arrived in Virginia by the 1620s, settling at Nansemond in the Tidewater region, and spreading into nearby counties later in the century. Many Congregationalists left Virginia for Maryland to establish settlements on the Severn and Patuxent Rivers in the 1640s, but Presbyterians began to migrate to Virginia in the 1670s. By the 1680s, Congregationalists and Presbyterians, along with Huguenots, gathered in Charleston, South Carolina, while a separate church group from New England gathered upriver at Dorchester in the 1690s. Their descendents largely moved in the 1750s to Midway, Georgia. Great Awakening itinerancy and Scots-Irish immigration to the backcountry insured that by 1775 Puritan dissenters, predominantly Presbyterians, were

living in each of the southern colonies. With the coming of the revivals at the end of the century, a modified Calvinist tradition would continue, but the term *Puritan* would cease to have much meaning for the region.

In Maryland, the conflict between the Puritans of Providence (Annapolis) and the proprietary government loyal to the Catholic Lord Baltimore produced a battle and pamphlets. The anonymous *Virginia and Maryland* (1655) is sympathetic to the Puritans (who for a time took control of the government) but strives for some objectivity. Meanwhile, Leonard Strong's *Babylon's Fall in Maryland* (1655) argues the Puritan side, seeing the battle as a providential victory over a Catholic enemy.

Despite the strong bias and laws against dissenters in Virginia, Calvinists settled there and sometimes published. The Anglican minister Alexander Whitaker (1585–1614) shows Calvinist tendencies in his *Good Newes from Virginia* (1613). After the departure of the Congregationalists from Nansemond to Maryland, dissenting communities had occasional ministers or lay leaders but few writers. Francis Makemie (1658–1708), a Scots-Irish Presbyterian, established churches on the Eastern Shore of Virginia and Maryland and encouraged a congregation on the Elizabeth River. Except for some letters, only his *Plain and Friendly Persuasive to the Inhabitants of Virginia and Maryland* (1705) can be called southern. An interesting dissenting voice is the author of "The Religion of the Bible and Religion of King William County Compared" (1769), most likely James Reid (fl. 1768–1770). Using a heavy but lively satire, the writer of this manuscript ridicules the figure of the "Ass-Queer" or Virginia gentleman, both for his immorality while calling it religion, and his racialism, particularly his hypocrisy about miscegenation. If this is Puritan, it is more Martin Marprelate than Jonathan Edwards. Reid also wrote Presbyterian-inflected moral essays and poems for the *Virginia Gazette* in 1768–1769.

Closer to Edwards is the most important Calvinist writer in Virginia before the Revolution, Samuel Davies (1723–1761). A New Light Presbyterian from Delaware, Davies was educated by Samuel Blair at one of the Log College seminaries in Pennsylvania, then settled in Hanover County, Virginia, in 1747, where he took his ordination. During his tenure, Davies preached to as many as seven congregations and incurred the displeasure of Virginia governors and Anglican officials for his seeming itinerancy. In fact, Davies was a moderate New Light. His sermons aimed at the heart, at the genuineness of the conversion experience, but he rejected the extremist enthusiasm of the radical New Lights from the Great Awakening. Even so, Davies admired George Whitefield, had some correspondence with John Wesley, and traveled with Gilbert Tennent to Great Britain in search of funds for the College of New Jersey (Princeton). Almost alone among pre–Revolutionary Virginia clergy, Davies made ministering to slaves and teaching them to read a significant portion of his labors.

In addition to the over eighty sermons in print, Davies also composed poems and hymns. One of the most important writers of religious songs in colonial America, Davies modeled his efforts after Isaac Watts and Philip Doddridge in England. Many hymns were appended to sermons, as was "A Hymn" to the ordination sermon "The Office of a Bishop A Good Work" (1757). His poetry, meanwhile, first published as *Miscellaneous Poems, Chiefly on Divine Subjects* (1752), borrowed self-consciously from Milton, Pope, Thomson, Young, and Pindar, but at its best provided a distinctive, heartfelt effort to reach the sublime through verse. Like the New England Puritan Edward Taylor, Davies often wrote poems as preparatory exercises before delivering sermons. The themes are God's sovereignty, humanity's innate sinfulness, and the perceived separation of human beings from God (as in "The Soul early estranged from its Divine Parent" or "Separation from GOD the most intolerable Punishment"). However, these orthodox concerns are put into a pre-romantic package. Poems about violent storms, the attractions of his wife "Chara" (Jane Holt Davies), and the birth of a son show that expressions of interest in this life and awe for a demanding God can coexist on the same page.

North Carolina, perhaps the least-churched of the southern colonies, harbored a number of dissenters, including Quakers and Baptists, but few Puritan writers. The sometime New Light Presbyterian turned Quaker and future Regulator, Hermon Husband (1724–1795), wrote an account of his conversions during his youth in Maryland. *Some Remarks on Religion* (1761) illustrates the volatile nature of religious identification in the mid-eighteenth-century South. Moses Waddell (1770–1840) kept the Puritan spirit alive in Iredell County.

In South Carolina, Calvinist writers come generally either from the Dorchester community or the region around Charleston. The journal of church elder William Pratt (?–1713) gives an eyewitness account of the founding of Dorchester. Joseph Lord (1672–1748), the Harvard-educated Congregationalist minister for Dorchester's first two decades, wrote letters on local natural history. A successor, Hugh Fisher (?–1734), a Presbyterian, published two arguments, including *A Preservative from Damnable Errors* (1730), justifying the subscriptionist side in a debate with other dissenting ministers in South Carolina.

Charleston, meanwhile, was home to a number of dissenting writers. John Ash, protesting the substitution of an Anglican governor for a dissenter, wrote *The Present State of Affairs in Carolina* (1706), a text that in manuscript no doubt influenced Daniel Defoe's pro-dissenter *Party-Tyranny* (1705) on the same episode. Hugh Fisher's chief opponent in the subscriptionist controversy, Josiah Smith (1704–1781), was a Harvard-educated native South Carolinian then preaching at Cainhoy. Smith was the most widely published Calvinist minister in colonial South Carolina. His *The Divine Right of Private Judgment Vindicated* (1730) not only justifies his own belief in liberty of conscience as opposed to swearing allegiance (subscription) to the Westminster Confession but also includes the only published writing by another Puritan minister, Nathan Bassett (?–1738), of the influential Independent Church of Charleston. A later minister of that church, William Tennent III (1740–1777), became active in Revolutionary politics and delivered a speech in the South Carolina general assembly in 1777 in defense of religious disestablishment.

In Georgia, John Osgood (1711–1773), minister of the Midway church from its migration in the 1750s until his death, published one sermon. The Midway congregation was often classed "southern puritans," since many of the families had stayed together through migrations beginning with their settlement in Dorchester, Massachusetts, in the 1630s. One Midway member, the Reverend Charles Colcock Jones, whose family letters have been gathered in Robert Manson Myers's three-volume *Children of Pride* (1972), was famous for designing books of catechism to instruct slaves. Other minister writers of that church include Moses Allen (1748–1779) and Abiel Holmes (1763–1837), father of Oliver Wendell Holmes. In Savannah, John Joachim Zubly (1724–1781) delivered a largely Calvinist message in his sermons and left a diary. One might also add the itinerant George Whitefield (1714–1770) to the list of southern Puritans. The Calvinist Anglican's sermons and journals, as well as his preaching, inspired many southern Calvinists, including Davies and Smith.

Overshadowed in reputation by the larger populations of Puritans in the North, southern Calvinist communities produced writers whose significance has not yet been fully ascertained. While unable to solve the moral dilemma of slavery any better than their non-Puritan neighbors, such writers as Davies, Smith, and Tennent provided powerful voices for liberty of conscience and free exercise of religion in the southern colonies.

Jeffrey H. Richards

See also Calvinism; Evangelical Christianity; Presbyterians; Puritanism.

Erskine Clarke, *Our Southern Zion: A History of Calvinism in the South Carolina Low Country, 1690–1990* (1996); Babette M. Levy, *Early Puritanism in the Southern and Island Colonies* (1960); George William Pilcher, *Samuel Davies: Apostle of Dissent in Colonial Virginia* (1971); David Ramsay, *The History of the Independent or Congregational Church in Charleston, South Carolina* (1815); Daniel H. Randall, *A Puritan Colony in Maryland* (1886); Ernest Trice Thompson, *Presbyterians in the South* (3 vols.; 1963–83).

QUADROON BALLS

Quadroon balls—social gatherings peculiar to New Orleans society in the first half of the nineteenth century—furnished opportunities for young free women of color, accompanied by their mothers, to meet wealthy white gentlemen who might become their suitors.

Because the Black Code of 1724 prohibited marriage between whites and anyone with even a trace of African blood, such couples could marry legally only by relocating outside of the United States, usually in France. Liaisons formed through the quadroon balls often provided a lifetime of economic support for the children of these unions and their mothers, who were expected to remain faithful to their white protectors.

Grace King acknowledges the elegance and refinement of the quadroons in *New Orleans* (1895), but she also expresses outrage at the threat they pose to marriage and family life. Herbert Asbury in *The French Quarter* (1936) reports that the light-skinned quadroons surpassed white women in beauty and that the quadroon balls surpassed the white masked balls in popularity. Because quadroon and octoroon women considered themselves socially superior not only to other blacks but also to quadroon or octoroon men, alliances with white gentlemen remained one of their few options for security.

Writers of the nineteenth century focused on the plight of characters who, by all appearances, could and often did pass for white but were legally considered black. Some of the earliest fiction of this period portrays the tragic mulatto or tragic octoroon, a beautiful, pure young woman, unaware of her tainted blood. Upon discovering her one drop of black blood, she loses her white suitor and submits passively to the consequences of this discovery, being sold into slavery or committing suicide. While many critics have described these works as formulaic and the heroines as stereotypes, Werner Sollors argues in *Neither White Nor Black Yet Both* (1997) that some of these works are much more complex and subversive.

Anna Elfenbein in *Women on the Color Line* (1989) discusses how three New Orleans writers, George Washington Cable, Grace King, and Kate Chopin, build on the tragic octoroon stereotype to explore issues of class, race, and sex, especially related to the plight of women. Grace King realistically depicts the quadroon prostitute in "Madrilene" (1890) and "Bonne Maman" (1886) and the child innocent of her mixed race in "Monsieur Motte" (1886) and "The Little Convent Girl" (1893). Two stories by George Washington Cable, "Tite Poulette" (1874) and "Madame Delphine" (1881), sympathetically portray the plight of quadroon mothers concerned about the futures of their octoroon daughters. The heroine of Kate Chopin's "Désirée's Baby" (1893), an orphan, commits suicide after she gives birth to a mulatto child and realizes that she has lost the affection of her husband, Armand. Armand later discovers that the taint of black blood has come from his family.

Cable dramatically recasts the tragic mulatto stereotype in his novel *The Grandissimes* (1880) by creating a bold, intelligent, and strong quadroon character, Palmyre Philosophe, the slave maid and possibly half-sister of Aurore De Grapion Nancanou. Dismissed from the De Grapion household for dominating her mistress, Palmyre, still fiercely loyal to Aurore, plots revenge against Agricola Fusilier, the man she blames for Aurore's economic destitution. Ironically, Palmyre, a slave, is better off economically because she works as a hairdresser, whereas Aurore's social standing prevents her from earning her living. Although Palmyre loves the white Honoré Grandissime, she agrees to marriage with an enslaved African prince whom she hopes to persuade to lead a slave insurrection. Her failure to win the love of the white Honoré only increases her desire to avenge the wrongs in her life; she never passively surrenders to her plight like the tragic octoroons from earlier works. A male quadroon, Honoré Grandissime, the white Honoré Grandissime's French-educated half-brother and a successful New Orleans businessman, commits suicide because he cannot win Palmyre's love, leaving her his fortune. After plotting the attack that leaves Agricola Fusilier on his deathbed, Palmyre escapes to France, "passing" as Madame Inconnue.

In *Absalom, Absalom!* (1936), William Faulkner uses the quadroon ball as the means by which Charles Bon initiates Henry Sutpen into the ways of the world. Bon's later introduction of Henry to his octoroon wife and their son sets in motion events that lead to the fall of the house of Thomas Sutpen, Henry's father. Woven into a complex story pieced together by several narrators are events from the characters' pasts, including Thomas Sutpen's earlier marriage to a woman of mixed blood, whose union likely produced Charles Bon. Throughout, the narrators speculate about why Henry, who had renounced his father for Bon, kills Bon, who is engaged to Henry's sister Judith.

Werner Sollors in *Neither Black Nor White Yet Both* (1997) believes that the narrative structure of *Absalom, Absalom!* generates a debate about the relative evils of bigamy, incest, and miscegenation. One way to interpret the outcome of that debate, Sollors contends, is that southerners fear miscegenation more than incest. Yet interpreting the conflict as primarily between these two taboos may mask the even greater fear that southerners have of homosexuality, suggested in the relationships between Henry and Bon, Quentin and Shreve, and even in Thomas Sutpen's wrestling matches with his slaves.

Although the last known quadroon ball was held in 1850, the institution and the class of people it produced appeared in southern fiction for many years after. With the affirmation of black identity in the 1960s, the theme of passing in contemporary literature, as Juda Bennett in *The Passing Figure* (1996) argues, focuses on sexual identity as much as or more than on racial identity.

Ann F. Mann

See also Faulkner, William; Miscegenation; Mulatto; Passing; Race, Idea of; Racism.

Juda Bennett, *The Passing Figure: Racial Confusion in Modern American Literature* (1996); Judith Berzon, *Neither White Nor Black: The Mulatto Character in American Fiction* (1978); Violet Bryan, *The Myth of New Orleans in Literature: Dialogues of Race and Gender* (1993); Anna Elfenbein, *Women on the Color Line* (1989); Mary Gehman, *The Free People of Color of New Orleans* (1994); Werner Sollors, *Neither Black Nor White Yet Both: Thematic Explorations of Interracial Literature* (1997).

QUILTING

In early southern American life, women often used quilts to tell their stories. Creative opportunities were limited, and quilting gave women an acceptable way of expressing themselves. Scraps of fabric could be put together in artistic ways to create a thing of beauty, and a quilt could be justified as a family necessity. A woman could work alone to make a quilt or with other women at an informal quilting bee or party.

Whereas early southern women used quilts to tell their stories, many twentieth-century southern women writers have used stories to tell about their quilts. In Mississippian Eudora Welty's *Delta Wedding* (1946), the mother of the groom is from the up-country and sends quilts as her wedding gift. Tennessee native Jane Wilson Joyce's *Quilt Poems* (1984) reflects the multitude of names, colors, purposes, and feelings associated with quilts and quilting. Kentucky writer Bobbie Ann Mason in *Love Life* (1989) tells the story of Jenny, who moves back home to live with her favorite aunt, Opal, and becomes fascinated with her quilts, especially the burial quilt that documents so much of the family history. In West Virginia native Meredith Sue Willis's "Family Knots" (1991), Narcissa Foy's talent results in many beautiful quilts, in spite of the struggles of a hard mountain life. The women in these twentieth-century stories may work alone, with another woman, or as a member of a quilting guild that has additional objectives, such as the quilting activist group in Kentucky native Barbara Kingsolver's *Pigs in Heaven* (1993). Some other southern works that explore various aspects of quilting are Kentucky native Eliza Calvert Hall's *Aunt Jane of Kentucky* (1898), South Carolinian Julia Peterkin's *Black April* (1927), Kaye Gibbons's *A Cure for Dreams* (1991), and Virginian Sharyn McCrumb's *The Hangman's Beautiful Daughter* (1992).

The African American quilt tradition of large, varied, colorful, asymmetrical designs originated in Africa hundreds of years ago and has influenced both southern American quilting and literature. Perhaps the most widely known example of quilting in southern literature is the often-anthologized short story "Everyday Use" (1973) by Alice Walker, a Georgia native, in which two sisters debate whether quilts should be preserved as art or used and appreciated daily. African American children's writer and illustrator Faith Ringgold, who was influenced by stories of her great-great-grandmother's quilting as a part of her slave responsibilities in antebellum Florida, uses quilt motifs as page borders in *Tar Beach* (1991).

Quilts also appear in southern American nonfiction. Alabamian Nora Ezell's *My Quilts and Me: The Diary of an American Quilter* (1998) tells the story of quilts and quilting through first-person narrative, thereby combining diary, craft book, and, in this case, African American history. Sometimes there is an overlap between nonfiction and literary works on quilting. An example is Molly Newman and Barbara Damashek's play *Quilters* (1986), based on Patricia Cooper and Norma Bradley Allen's *The Quilters: Women and Domestic Art* (1977), a collection of the personal stories of quilters in Texas and New Mexico.

Quilts have also been used as metaphor in southern literary criticism to suggest the piecemeal aspect of a work. In *Sister's Choice: Tradition and Change in American Women's Writing* (1991), Elaine Showalter takes her title from the quilt that Celie and Sofia are piecing in Alice Walker's *The Color Purple* (1982) and uses it as a metaphor for the piecemeal aspect of her book, which includes chapters on lectures, American novels, themes, and literary history. Linda Tate uses quilting literally and figuratively to examine women's fiction in *A Southern Weave of Women: Fiction of the Contemporary South* (1994).

Loretta Martin Murrey

See also African American Folk Culture; Appalachian Literature; Folk Narrative; Women Writers.

Judy Elsley, *Quilts as Text(iles): The Semiotics of Quilting* (1996); Cecilia Macheski, ed., *Quilt Stories* (1994); Linda Tate, *A Southern Weave of Women: Fiction of the Contemporary South* (1994).

QUIXOTISM

Don Quixote of La Mancha's adventures constitute a landmark in world literature. The wanderings of the Manchegan knight across the deprived plains of Cas-

tile, undertaken at the close of the sixteenth century, have continued through time and across many continents to the present day. Wherever there is resistance to the prevailing conditions of the world as it is; wherever the glitter of success is forsworn; wherever human will obstinately strives before dashing itself to pieces against the rock; wherever anyone attempts to bridge the insurmountable space between the real and the ideal, there one finds the ethereal soul of Don Quixote of La Mancha.

From the England of Fielding and Smollett, from Dostoevsky's Russia or the France of Flaubert and Stendhal to the New World via Washington Irving, literature has furnished examples of quixotic characterization. But it is in the literature of the American South where the unrealistic attitudes typifying quixotism are more pervasively found.

The transition from the nineteenth to the twentieth century found the American South at a crossroads between tradition and modernity. This predominantly rural, patriarchal, and highly stratified society was at odds with the tenets of industrial capitalism. In addition, defeat in the Civil War resulted in a sense of loss and a tendency to regard the past as a golden age where a civilized, superior social order once flourished but was now forced to give way before the powerful money culture of the victorious North. These factors are not dissimilar to the Spain of Cervantes, viewed within the context of Europe at that time. Spain too was suffering contradictions, caught as it was between dreams of an imperial past and the reality of an increasingly exhausted country. Unprepared or unwilling to face up to the challenges of a modern state, it became parasitic and anachronistic. A significant parallel between these two different societies may be found in the emphasis that both placed on the codes of honor and chivalry. They both revered lineage and breeding, according little importance to work or money as marks of social privilege. In both historical realities, an outmoded system of beliefs and ideals crumbles under the pressure exerted by the new emerging order, and in both cases a fanatical attempt is made to perpetuate them.

In this context, the quixotic figure appears particularly relevant in the South. In the process of adapting itself to a new historical situation, an entire society undergoes change, and in the midst of this process there arises a character type, both comic and pathetic, that launches itself on a personal quest, seeking to compensate in the realm of the imagination for what is dreadfully lacking in the world around it, emulating Don

Quixote in spirit and in practice. Throughout some hundred years of literary activity—from the late nineteenth century to contemporary times—the *Quixote* motif has been a recurrent theme in the large body of work produced by southern writers. It is chiefly portrayed in extremely idealistic, tragic-comic heroes or heroines who mistake reality for their hearts' desire. They are self-deluding, subject to anachronistic behavior, prepared to take on the world single-handedly, and more often than not fall flat on their faces.

Don Quixote's longings for a world of heroism and honor, his battle with windmills, and his self-defeating stance as righter of the world's wrongs captured the imagination of many southern writers, principally those belonging to the generation of the so-called Southern Renascence. Because of the peculiar historical circumstances of the South, these writers experienced the conflict between the old and the new with a greater intensity than their counterparts in other regions of the United States. From their position at a crucial turning point in history, but with a certain critical distance afforded them by virtue of their being modern writers, they explored the myths and realities of their world, while at the same time revealing their own contradictory feelings toward it.

Mark Twain was a precursor to this generation of southern writers. When he launched the romance-driven Tom Sawyer—accompanied by his faithful friend, plain, down-to-earth Huckleberry Finn—in search of glory and fame, Twain not only began the saga of southern quixotic types, he also re-created the most faithful replica of Don Quixote and Sancho Panza ever to appear in American literature. Twain's southern aristocrats, as portrayed in *Adventures of Huckleberry Finn* (1885) or *Pudd'nhead Wilson* (1894), are enmeshed in a world of their own making, flourishing totally impractical notions of honor and chivalry. Sometimes their pretensions to status and glamour contrast starkly with the squalor of their actual lives, as with Colonel Sellers in *The Gilded Age* (1873) and *The American Claimant* (1892). Even a practical-minded Yankee such as Hank Morgan, the protagonist of *A Connecticut Yankee in King Arthur's Court* (1889), cherishes romantic dreams that far outstrip their worldly possibilities. In much of his work, Twain portrays the contrast between the world as it really is and the world as his heroes would like it to be, throwing into relief the inadequacy of their whole stance in it.

For the Virginian author James Branch Cabell,

quixotism was the activity of "spinning romances"—the only way remaining for human beings to escape the crassness of reality. Virginians of his generation were adept in the practice of self-deception (*Let Me Lie*, 1947), hostages to a past they deemed more meaningful than the present. Some of his characters who are so obsessed with the past are modeled from real life, as may be presumed of Rudolph Musgrave in *The Rivet in Grandfather's Neck* (1915). In Cabell's work, appearances take precedence over facts. People are deceived by them; or, more accurately, they allow appearances to deceive them. Rascals masquerade as heroes, and vulgar Aldonzas appear in the guise of chaste and blushing maidens. Lyricism is replaced by lust, and romantic inclinations supplanted by boredom. But far from discouraging readers in the urge to dream, Cabell regards these human flights into fantasy as the only resort left in the human condition of uncertainty.

For William Faulkner, quixotism meant an uncompromising sense of honor to which many of his characters cling as if it were inseparable from their own identities. Quixotic honor is the main trait defining his "champions of dames"—Quentin Compson in *The Sound and the Fury* (1929), Gavin Stevens in *The Town* (1957) and *The Mansion* (1959), Byron Bunch in *Light in August* (1932), Lucius Priest in *The Reivers* (1962). Nostalgia for the past and its heroism, or for a lost Arcadian paradise, are other quixotic characteristics that eventually cripple such characters as the Reverend Gail Hightower in *Light in August* or Ike McCaslin in *Go Down, Moses* (1942). Quixotic moral idealism is the malaise undermining them all. But quixotism among Faulkner's blacks and whites does not entirely preclude hope. On the contrary, it helps them on their ill-starred journey through life, furnishing them with a sense of moral rectitude—the Bundrens in *As I Lay Dying* (1930), Lena Grove in *Light in August,* the tall convict of "Old Man" in *The Wild Palms* (1939), and Lucas Beauchamp in *Intruder in the Dust* (1948) are all eloquent examples.

In more recent years, Eudora Welty and Walker Percy have engaged most fully in quixotic characterization. For the former, quixotism implies tilting at windmills in pursuit of an unattainable ideal, but for once this ideal is not to be found in an idealized knightly function recreated in the past. The South in which Eudora Welty places those of her heroines who follow in Don Quixote's footsteps is a depressed and backward land, a South that looks inward upon itself. Miss Julia Mortimer in *Losing Battles* (1970) and Miss Lotte Elizabeth Eckhart in *The Golden Apples* (1949) present a challenge to the future. Their impractical mission is to bring knowledge and art to narrow-minded communities that stifle the realization of individual dreams. Failure is their lot, but they fight on relentlessly, never losing faith in their undertakings and never renouncing their dignity.

The very title *The Last Gentleman* (1966) expresses the irony with which Percy regards the last vestiges of the chivalrous ideal in the modern-day South. A yearning for the past and the inability to adapt himself to the present leads Percy's protagonist into absurd situations. His quixotic behavior can have calamitous consequences on his life, as in *Lancelot* (1977). Stoicism, which provided the generation of Walker Percy's uncle, William Alexander Percy, with a refuge, is an option no longer possible or desirable. The main character in *The Last Gentleman* travels the same road as Quentin Compson, but without the latter's tragic end. Don Quixote rides again in Percy's work, but with a somewhat Chaplinesque air—as a loser, fragile and far less convinced of his personal quest than his predecessors. Understandably, therefore, Percy recognized Ignatius Reilly—protagonist of a novel by a then-unknown author, John Kennedy Toole—as the quintessential quixotic quester and so recommended to LSU Press the publication of *A Confederacy of Dunces* (1980).

For postmoderns, the theme of quixotism has been less congenial.

Montserrat Ginés

See also Gentleman; History, Idea of; Honor; Lost Cause; Past, The; Stoicism.

Montserrat Ginés, *The Southern Inheritors of Don Quixote* (2000).

R

RACE, IDEA OF

Race is one of the defining ideas of the history and culture of the South. It served as the central justification for the institution of slavery and for the social order that emerged in the postbellum period and lasted into the middle of the twentieth century.

As commonly understood, "race" refers to genetically determined differences among groups of people. These differences are most evident in physical features such as skin color, physiognomy, and hair texture, but these are often taken as signs of less-evident distinctions, including intelligence, morality, reasoning skills, physical skills, propensity to crime and violence, personality, and cultural preferences. When these differences are arranged hierarchically, so that one group is considered superior to others on the basis of claimed difference, racism occurs. Scientific research has shown that there is no biological basis for the groupings referred to as races. The genetic variation within such divisions is virtually identical to the variation among human beings in general.

More recent theories contend that race is a social construct, deriving its meaning not from biological reality but from the needs of social order. In this sense, it is an arbitrary notion that shifts as the conditions of society change. Its purpose is to maintain differences in economic and political power and status by claiming that such differences are fixed, inherent, and natural. It operates through what Michael Omi and Howard Winant have called a racial formation, which includes the social practices, discourses, institutions, and imagery by which a society represents and organizes groups within itself.

It is also useful to distinguish the usage of "race" from "ethnicity." "Race" is usually associated with distinctive physical qualities sometimes linked to but not limited by geography and climate. Thus an African American does not have to have any known link to a specific place in Africa or an unmixed African genetic heritage to be considered "African" in appearance. "Ethnicity," in contrast, refers to ties to a specific culture, most often with a specific linguistic heritage, without regard to physical characteristics. Hispanics may be of different races, but they share the Spanish language and ancestry in Spain. The distinction is especially important when dealing with Asians, who are often lumped together in the United States as Asian Americans, even though they come from countries with widely differing cultures, languages, and histories.

The notion of race as a means of differentiating groups of people has existed in some form since ancient times, though there is relatively little written commentary in surviving early texts. In India, the *Rig-Veda* contains comments about the hated dark skin of the indigenous peoples conquered by Aryan invaders, whereas in Egypt commentaries from around 1350 B.C. show color prejudice among those competing for power. In the Han Dynasty of China, "yellow-haired, green-eyed barbarians" are presumed to have descended from monkeys. Early Jewish texts advise against intermarriage, sometimes advocate what would now be called ethnic cleansing, and establish the idea that Ham, son of Noah, was made black as punishment for wrongdoing. In Greece, speculation about the relationship of climate to observed physical differences marks some of the earliest efforts to define race "scientifically." Among these ancient statements, there is little clear effort to connect skin color or other features to enslavement or caste. Rather, they appear to be the product of xenophobia and a more general need to explain obvious differences.

The early Christian church held as a central principle the common humanity of all people. As a proselytizing religion, it sought universal agreement to its views across linguistic, cultural, and physical differences. In its earliest stages, this included an acceptance of Jews. Antisemitism emerged in the eleventh century as the first significant break with this universalism. At a time when some Church fathers were advocating intermarriage with Muslims as a means of conversion, arguments began to be made that Jews were the enemies of the faith and must be destroyed. As this view took hold, the targeted group was also assigned negative physical characteristics that distinguished them racially from their Christian neighbors.

Beginning in the fifteenth century, exploration by Europeans led to the development of racial theories about the native groups encountered around the world. Differences of language, custom, and appearance produced speculation about the origins of indigenous populations. One common idea was that they were different species from Europeans, with descent from apes or other animals. Another approach suggested that God had created groups at different places in the world. The Catholic Church regarded such ideas as heretical in that they contradicted accepted biblical interpretations. One result was that the Church did not support the enslavement of Native American populations, which was based on an assumption of inherent difference. Nonetheless, modern notions of race may be said to begin with the Spanish efforts to explain the nature of New World groups.

Systematic theories about racial difference initially appeared in the late seventeenth century when François Bernier defined four groups of people based on physical appearance. Unlike physics and chemistry, however, studies in biology did not propose general theories of difference until well into the eighteenth century. When it came to the study of human beings, this reticence was in part the result of Enlightenment ideas about the universality of human nature and the influence of environment on development. Emphasis was placed on the varieties of humanity, with an assumption of a common underlying species.

By the late eighteenth century, more intensive inquiry was undertaken. David Hume and Baron Montesquieu argued for the influence of climate in producing physical difference and perhaps moral and intellectual difference as well. George Buffon insisted that whites were the norm in intelligence, morality, and beauty, and in 1775, Johann Blumenbach created the five categories—Caucasian, Mongolian, Ethiopian, American, Malay—that became the standard divisions. Blumenbach, like others of his time, also specifically rejected the notion that inferiority or superiority ought to

be assigned to any of the categories. In fact, when Thomas Jefferson, in his *Notes on the State of Virginia* (1786), contended that African Americans were inferior to whites, he was in a distinct minority among Enlightenment intellectuals. Charles White at the end of the century specifically assigned human groups to locations on a great chain of being, with Africans closely related to apes. He also helped to revive the theory of polygenesis, the view that the different races were the product of separate creations. Like others holding this view, he tried to make it consistent with biblical teachings, though he was opposed in this by most religionists. The theory of monogenesis, as specifically related to race, was an effort to explain difference within acceptable theological boundaries. Monogenesis held that God had created only one human species, but that through a long process of degeneration some varieties had become distinctly inferior.

By the end of the eighteenth century, a minority view assigned hierarchy to observed human differences, making some "races" inferior to others and raising questions about intermarriage and domination. By the early nineteenth century, especially in the United States, this had become the dominant view. Native American populations might occasionally be considered Noble Savages, but the expansion of European civilization required that they be displaced or destroyed, and notions of white superiority justified this. Similarly, the economic reality of slavery necessitated an unfree labor force, and racial theory justified the exploitation of Africans and their descendants.

In the early days of the British colonies, conversion of the native population was a principal goal of interaction, as it was in the Spanish and French colonies. The resistance of Indians to both European religion and white settlement, however, soon reduced this focus to relative insignificance. As violence increased, Native Americans came to be seen racially—that is, as a group naturally and permanently different from and inferior to whites. Likewise, economic necessity, not a general racial theory, explained the initial use of African labor in the colonies. Early laws did not distinguish between this imported work force and bond-servants from Europe. Only in the 1660s did Maryland and Virginia establish laws making perpetual servitude the status of Africans. Even in this case, the law used religion rather than race as the distinguishing characteristic. Only those who were not Christian when they were brought to the New World could be made slaves. In practice, such rules made race the key factor, and they soon became explicit about this categorization.

In the nineteenth century, various theories were devised to justify the economic necessity of racial subordination. Both polygenesis and monogenesis argued for nonwhite inferiority. Among others, the Harvard naturalist Louis Agassiz contended that distinct biological features around the world implied separate creations of all life forms. Although a polygenic approach would have served the purposes of the South by validating African American inferiority, it could not be sustained in the context of conservative Christianity.

Evolution presented a new intellectual opportunity for defining racial hierarchies. If racial groups could be understood as representing stages in the progress of humanity, then a common humanity could be maintained while preserving notions of inferiority and superiority. Much of nineteenth-century anthropological research was devoted to identifying such differences. Unfortunately for advocates of racism, the greater precision of scientific method complicated efforts to generate clear categories. Whether the method involved skin color, cranial shape, brain capacity, or hair texture, the results tended to show the virtual impossibility of drawing precise lines between races.

It is not clear how important such scientific and intellectual work was to general attitudes and practices concerning race. As slavery stabilized as an economic system and began to expand into new territory, attitudes toward race hardened and became entrenched in law and culture. Biblical justifications, scientific arguments, and political rhetoric were all used to demonstrate that African Americans were inherently servile and inferior and required strict discipline if they were to be good laborers and trustworthy servants. Questions arose as to the wisdom of serious religious conversion efforts, since a common faith implied a common humanity. In practice, a compromise was reached in which slaves were taught primarily the Christian virtues of humility and submission. Even those who opposed slavery largely accepted the idea of black inferiority; the American Colonization Society drew much of its membership from those, like Abraham Lincoln, who believed that slavery should be ended but that the two races could not live together in the same society.

Typically, the South involved itself in a variety of contradictions about the people who were enslaved. On the one hand, it insisted on the natural loyalty and docility of slaves, and yet it was deeply concerned with the possibility of slave rebellion. It argued for the value of black labor, yet promoted the image of the incompetent worker who had to be watched constantly and often whipped. It took as fact black stupidity, yet, especially after the Nat Turner rebellion of 1831, legally prohibited black literacy. It contended that racial purity was essential to southern identity and civilization, yet produced such large numbers of mixed-race children that the law had to specify that free status followed the condition of the mother, not the father. Only through such legal devices could white inheritance and other forms of legitimization be sustained. While some readings of this history would label the practices and attitudes simple hypocrisy, it is useful to understand them in part as a fundamental uncertainty about race. African Americans clearly were not another species, yet they needed to be treated as such if slavery was to be protected and expanded. In addition, moral ambiguity entered when reluctant and sometimes resistant workers could only be compelled by physical violence that ran counter to Christian teaching; in fact, the whole question of ownership of other people was itself a moral problem. In effect, white racial attitudes during slavery can be seen in part as an antagonism toward blacks for posing such quandaries.

The issues became more complex and, if possible, more intense after emancipation. The passage of the Thirteenth, Fourteenth, and Fifteenth Amendments to the Constitution challenged the basic assumptions about race on which the South had built its society and culture for 250 years. The claim of political equality for all men (not women yet) required an acceptance of African American humanity that few whites were willing to grant. Reconstruction, by emphasizing protection and advancement of these new citizens, only exacerbated the situation. Racial violence, especially that directed at the economically successful and those accused (seldom formally) of sexual assault against white women, was motivated by a desire to force all African Americans to fit the image of them that had been constructed decades earlier. These attitudes remained largely in place until the second half of the twentieth century, when the Civil Rights Movement and the force of national action and opinion compelled a change in behavior and, to some extent, in belief. More recently, organizations such as the Ku Klux Klan are no longer able to operate with impunity or general public approval. The entry of African Americans into the educational, political, and economic systems of the South has made overt expression of racism unacceptable and impractical. Race remains a concern in contemporary southern life, though in more subtle ways than it has been in the past. Debates over affirmative action, political campaign strategies, welfare, and hate crimes are primarily discussions about the role of race in the modern South.

In literature, race has been a central theme since the earliest days of southern writing. Captain John Smith and others constructed an image of the indigenous population of America that affected how Europeans engaged Native Americans. The Pocahontas legend was one of the first Euro-American myths. It helped to establish the tension between the violent heathen and the Noble Savage that continues to shape white understanding of Native Americans. William Byrd, in *History of the Dividing Line* (written c. 1728), argued that one of the failures of the early settlers had been their refusal to intermarry with the native people; such an approach, he contended, would have maintained the peace. What would have been achieved would have been the "blanching" of the Indians; the point, in other words, was universal whiteness, not cultural hybridity. In the nineteenth century, literary texts assumed white superiority and made little overt effort to prove racial difference; such clearly ideological projects were left to polemicists such as George Fitzhugh. The poetry and romances of the prewar era emphasized the idyllic quality of plantation life, with beneficent and sophisticated masters and humble, devoted slaves. John Pendleton Kennedy set the model for this image of the South, one that was revived by the Plantation School writers later in the century. Among white writers, only the work of Edgar Allan Poe, with its allegories of darkness, and the unpublished diary of Mary Chesnut overtly raised serious questions about the racial dynamics of the region.

The more significant challenge came from African American authors, especially those who had been slaves. A large number of slave narratives were produced and widely read, more in the North than in the South, though they were sometimes commented upon in southern newspapers and periodicals. Many of these narratives were adventure stories about escape from horrifying conditions, with a moral about the effects of deprivation of basic freedom and dignity. The two most important, Frederick Douglass's *Narrative* (1845) and Harriet Jacobs's *Incidents in the Life of a Slave Girl* (1861), raised fundamental questions about race. Douglass presented himself as a man of reason with an inherent desire for freedom; it was his masters (and mistresses) who, because of the effects of slavery,

were bestial in their behavior. Any lack of full humanity in Douglass or other slaves was the product of an evil system, not inherent inferiority. Jacobs expands the argument into gender by representing herself as a young woman trying to sustain her virtue in a society that encouraged violations of sexual propriety. She even claims some moral superiority to her white female readership by asserting that they had never had to overcome the obstacles she faced.

Literature became a key site of racial contention in the post-Reconstruction era. African American writers were forced to insist upon the humanity of their race in the face of scientific claims, virulent racist political rhetoric, segregationist laws, and literary and other cultural expressions committed to white supremacy. The tragic mulatto, for example, was a figure used by both sides to demonstrate their positions on race. For white authors, this mixed-race image served to demonstrate the dangers of intermarriage and thus the importance of policies of racial segregation. The mulatto, often represented by whites as female, was beautiful but troubled. She was a temptress to white gentlemen, and her deceit or ignorance about her past was always exposed at the last minute. The man was thereby saved from a horrible mistake, and the woman was typically condemned to either suicide or a life of prostitution. While such texts served to affirm the need for racial control, they also implicitly raised questions about the sexual practices of southern patriarchs and the elusiveness of pure racial distinctions on which the system of oppression was based. Patriarchy was in fact vulnerable at what should have been the point of its greatest power. White men must be weak if they could be seduced and if they were willing to violate the most basic of racial codes.

For African American writers, it was the arbitrariness of the sign of color that was the key point. If the light-skinned black woman or man could not be distinguished from high-born whites, and if their intelligence, beauty, and social skill made them attractive in a status-conscious society, then on what basis could they or their darker kin be said to be inferior to whites? African ancestry became not a mark of intrinsic inferiority but simply another factor of background and identity in a common humanity. Environment was much more influential than any number of drops of "black blood." From Frances Harper's *Iola Leroy* (1892) to many of the major texts of the Harlem Renaissance, the mulatto served as a means to argue for African American ability and equality.

Race was a significant concern of writers associated with the South in the late nineteenth and early twentieth centuries. Thomas Nelson Page and others created a nostalgic view of the Old South that depended in part on a black image of docility and dependence that, by implication, ought to be the reality of the New South. Thomas Dixon, in contrast, produced a series of novels that presented African Americans as sexual beasts and corrupt politicians. This projection could be said to be the complement of the Plantation School in that one shows the racial utopia of slavery whereas the other depicts the dystopia of black freedom. Some major writers of that period also addressed race issues, as exemplified in the fiction of George Washington Cable and Kate Chopin. Mark Twain was centrally concerned with the meaning of racial difference in American society; *Huckleberry Finn* (1885) continues to arouse comment and criticism on the basis of its racial portrayals. African American scholar and social critic W. E. B. Du Bois produced one of the lasting statements on the effects of race when he wrote in *The Souls of Black Folk* (1903) of the "double consciousness" produced in African Americans by racial oppression. They were forced, he said, to be constantly aware of the white image of them, because whites had the power to compel black behavior that matched that image. At the same time, self-preservation required attention to an inner self that was profoundly different from the white projection. These contradictory necessities resulted in an inability to form a truly unified self.

In the twentieth century, race has been a prominent element of the work of most of the major southern writers. William Faulkner repeatedly puzzles over the troubled history of the region and sees race at the center of the meaning of the South. Similarly, Eudora Welty, Robert Penn Warren, and William Styron create significant fictions on race, as do Flannery O'Connor and Carson McCullers to a lesser extent. Among African American writers, Richard Wright made his reputation by portraying the deep psychological effects of prejudice. Ralph Ellison placed race at the center of *Invisible Man* (1952) in such a way that his black protagonist became the symbol of the modern human being. In the post–Civil Rights era, Ernest Gaines, Alice Walker, and Toni Morrison are among a number of African American fictionists who have focused on the richness of black southern folk culture in providing nurture for enduring the problems of race.

In contemporary literary studies, "race," along with "gender" and "class," has become a key term for critical analysis. Significant studies of Twain and Faulkner, for example, look not only at their representation of African American characters but also at what "whiteness" means in texts where race is addressed. Toni Morrison, in *Playing in the Dark* (1992), has gone even further to argue that race virtually always appears in major American writing, even when it seems absent. Its absence at the surface, in fact, she takes to be indicative of its importance at deeper levels. Henry Louis Gates and others, in *"Race," Writing, and Difference* (1986), examine the implications for critical theory of attention to the racial Other in literary texts.

Keith E. Byerman

See also Chattel Slavery; Civil Rights Movement; Douglass, Frederick; Mulatto; Nigger; Race Relations; Racism.

William L. Andrews, *To Tell a Free Story: The First Century of Afro-American Autobiography* (1986); Judith R. Berzon, *Neither Black Nor White: The Mulatto Character in American Fiction* (1978); Michael L. Conniff and Thomas J. Davis, *Africans in the Americas* (1994); John Hope Franklin, *From Slavery to Freedom* (1947); George Fredrickson, *The Arrogance of Race* (1988); Henry Louis Gates Jr., ed., *"Race," Writing, and Difference* (1986); Eugene Genovese, *Roll, Jordan, Roll* (1974); David Theo Goldberg, ed., *Anatomy of Racism* (1990); Thomas Gossett, *Race: The History of an Idea in America* (1963); Jefferson Humphries, ed., *Southern Literature and Literary Theory* (1990); Edward J. Larson, *Sex, Race, and Science: Eugenics in the Deep South* (1995); Leon F. Litwack, *Trouble in Mind: Black Southerners in the Age of Jim Crow* (1998); Deborah E. McDowell and Arnold Rampersad, eds., *Slavery and the Literary Imagination* (1989); Toni Morrison, *Playing in the Dark* (1992); Michael Omi and Howard Winant, *Racial Formation in the United States* (1986); Eric Sundquist, *To Wake the Nations: Race in the Making of American Literature* (1993); Ronald Takaki, *Iron Cages: Race and Culture in 19th-Century America* (1990); Pierre L. Van den Berghe, *Race and Racism* (1967); C. Vann Woodward, *The Burden of Southern History* (1960).

RACE RELATIONS

Since the early nineteenth century, when white southern writers began to defend slavery, relationships between blacks and whites became a central concern in southern literature. Many nineteenth- and early-twentieth-century works by white writers exacerbated racial prejudice by reproducing southern white society's racist ideology. But other southern writers, both white and black, have attempted to redress this problem by using literature to dismantle stereotypes and to imagine new relationships. The results of the 1960s Civil Rights Movement speeded up the process, suggesting new plots, new endings, and new points of view to southern writers of both races.

The earliest plantation novels, George Tucker's *The Valley of the Shenandoah* (1824) and John Pendleton Kennedy's *Swallow Barn* (1832), depicted slavery as a necessary evil but sentimentalized relationships between "benevolent" white masters and "contented" slaves. As the debate over states' rights heated up and white southerners grew preoccupied with defending slavery, William Gilmore Simms turned from writing historical romances about the Revolutionary War to proslavery propaganda, such as *Woodcraft* (1852). In a patriarchal society, the potential for women to find common ground across racial lines would seem easier than for men, and indeed Sarah and Angelina Grimké of Charleston wrote abolitionist tracts that called attention to the parallels between the position of white women and the slavery of black women, but they were exceptions among white women. The pedestal on which the slaveholding South placed white women meant that the adulation most received encouraged them to internalize stereotypes about black women as promiscuous wenches, prolific breeders, hardworking mules, or nurturing mammies. Thus nineteenth-century literature by southern white women, such as *Aunt Phillis's Cabin* (1852), which was written in response to *Uncle Tom's Cabin* (1851), is most often proslavery, even when gender roles of nurturance are employed to suggest female bonds across racial lines. In *Black and White Women of the Old South*, Minrose Gwin suggests that such fictional sisterhood existed in white women's writing only because the characterizations of both white and black women are stereotypical and sentimental.

Although kind slaveowners and congenial race relations appear in writings by authors of both races, the cruel mistress or master only assumes a role of prominence in antebellum slave narratives by African Americans, such as Frederick Douglass and Harriet Jacobs, who debunked the white myths of happy darkies. Nineteenth-century African American writers also focused on the lost innocence, indeed lost childhoods, of black and mixed-race children. Slave trading, which disrupted black family bonds, and white masters who refused to acknowledge their mixed-race children are the historical facts that fueled tragic plots about childhood and race relations such as William Wells Brown's

Clotel; or, The President's Daughter (1853), a novel about the daughter of Thomas Jefferson and a slave mistress.

After the Civil War, some white writers, for example Thomas Nelson Page, looked back on the Old South with praise for the paternalistic values of "honorable" white people who took care of "childlike" black people, sometimes even employing black characters to reminisce about plantation life. Using the same frame narrative and regional dialect that Page used in *In Ole Virginia* (1887), African American writer Charles Chesnutt, the son of free blacks from North Carolina, added African American folklore to his stories in *The Conjure Woman* (1899) and demonstrated both the social construction of black identity and the repression inherent in the social system that Page praised. After the 1898 race riot in Wilmington, North Carolina, Chesnutt wrote *The Marrow of Tradition* (1901), about a black doctor who never gains the respect of the white political establishment in a town much like Wilmington. In his last novel, *The Colonel's Dream* (1905), Chesnutt's white protagonist, a Confederate veteran and member of a prominent family, believes in racial tolerance but is spurned by the white community. He flees the South, just as enlightened white writers George Washington Cable and Samuel Clemens did, just as Chesnutt did himself. With the enactment of Jim Crow laws, white southerners were more interested in the racist plots of Thomas Dixon's popular novels *The Leopard's Spots* (1902) and *The Clansman* (1905) than in plots by either black or white writers encouraging improved race relations.

George Washington Cable and Samuel Clemens wrote critical portraits of southern race relations, but both men had more cosmopolitan perspectives than their fellow white southerners: Cable's mother was from New England and his father was of German ancestry; Samuel Clemens was born in Missouri, a border state. For Cable, the conflict of cultures in New Orleans typified the South's historical predicament in the United States. In *The Grandissimes* (1880), Cable proves the equality of the races, but he could not envision an integrated society, a problem disclosed by the novel's three endings: marriage for whites, exile to France for characters of mixed race, and death for rebellious blacks. In *Adventures of Huckleberry Finn* (1885), Samuel Clemens, writing under the pseudonym Mark Twain, used the child's perspective to question his society's race relations. The white boy Huckleberry Finn forms a partnership and a friendship with the black slave Jim as they both escape down the Mississippi from unhappy conditions in their Missouri hometown. In choosing to protect Jim, Huck assumes that he will go to hell because he has sinned in the eyes of his society. Twain's critique of the South's propensity for romance ironically gives *Adventures of Huckleberry Finn* its schizophrenic form: realism in the first part of the novel when Huck decides he will go to hell rather than turn Jim in to the authorities; romance in the concluding chapters when Huck goes along with Tom Sawyer to elaborately stage Jim's prolonged escape after he is captured. Although this novel reflects Twain's comic spirit, a later novel, *The Tragedy of Pudd'nhead Wilson* (1894), is both a bitter denunciation of slavery and a pointed lesson about the social construction of race.

Twentieth-century writers added psychological pain to the physical trials and social injustices of nineteenth-century literature about race relations. In *Absalom, Absalom!* (1936) and *Go Down, Moses* (1942), William Faulkner parodies the southern social customs and myths that receive dignified and sentimental treatment in local-color fiction by writers such as Page. Just as the South developed public fictions to satisfy collective needs both before and after the Civil War, Faulkner's multiple narrators in *Absalom, Absalom!* create fictions about Thomas Sutpen to satisfy private needs and, like the South, become victims of their own myths about southern plantation society and about race relations. Both works show how the South's history of slavery and segregation crippled southern society and devastated southern families. Faulkner's novel *Light in August* (1932), about the tortured life and violent death of a southern white man, Joe Christmas, who is alleged to have black ancestry, reveals a deep-seated white fear of multiracialism. Lillian Smith, who was more publicly outspoken than Faulkner about race relations, criticized racial discrimination in her nonfiction, particularly *Killers of the Dream* (1949). In her novel *Strange Fruit* (1944), she explored the rather Freudian idea that white children cared for by black adults will develop adult sexual longings across racial lines. For both Faulkner and Smith, reaching across racial lines provokes anguish within characters and violence between them. This fictional outcome is true for African American writers in the first half of the twentieth century as well. In the collection of stories *Uncle Tom's Children* (1940) and in his autobiography *Black Boy* (1945), Richard Wright poignantly reveals the pain of the Jim Crow South in ways both large and small. Wright's black men leave the South, as Wright himself did, or they are killed by racist whites. In *Cane* (1912), Jean Toomer portrays the richness and the pain of African American life in the South; he sets his stories of twisted cross-racial relationships against the beauty of the southern landscape.

In some respects, fictions about southern children and race relations have differed along racial lines, even into the twentieth century. For the most part, many southern white writers have focused on prolonging childhood innocence as it relates to race relations. Thus their stories are about childhood friendships that crossed racial lines and about loving relationships between white children and the black slaves or servants who cared for them. Much of the poignancy of Faulkner's *The Unvanquished* (1938) comes from Bayard Sartoris's description of the close relationship he has with a black servant boy, Ringo, in a society that will separate them as they get older and that has already marked them as different based on their race. Faulkner's Dilsey in *The Sound and the Fury* (1929) creates a stable center for four white children of the once distinguished, now dissipated Compson family. Revising the black servant/white child plot in a small but significant way, Carson McCullers in *The Member of the Wedding* (1946) links twelve-year-old Frankie's gender-role troubles to the racial discrimination experienced by her black caretaker, Berenice Sadie Brown. These two female characters literally sing the blues together as they talk about the ways in which they are "caught" in southern roles.

But the story behind both Faulkner's and McCullers's novels and others like them by white writers is the well-tended fiction that the beloved black servant is a member of the white family. Since 1956, when Alice Childress published *Like One of the Family* and humorously and roundly refuted that premise in the voice of a southern black woman working for a white family in New York, African American writers have presented this black adult/white child character configuration from a more complex perspective. The economic and psychological issues raised in such earlier novels have affected the way that recent southern writers, both black and white, have reversed the relationship between black adults and white children. In *The Color Purple* (1982), Alice Walker has a white woman take care of a black woman's child; in *Clover* (1990), Dori Sanders has a white woman become a black child's stepmother; in *Ellen Foster* (1987), Kaye Gibbons has a black family temporarily care for a white girl whose mother has died and whose father is abusive; and in *Taft* (1994), Ann Patchett has a black man take care of a white adolescent girl and her brother, a relationship that leads him back to his own son. Contemporary black and white writers have also presented the practice of black servants taking care of white children as causing difficulties for both the black and white children involved when they become adults. In *Soldier's Joy* (1989), Madison Smartt Bell examines the resentment that such a relationship can spark in the black servant's children.

Contemporary southern writers Ernest Gaines in *A Gathering of Old Men* (1983), Larry Brown in *Dirty Work* (1989), and Madison Smartt Bell in *Soldier's Joy* begin their interracial buddy novels where most earlier fictions about male race relations ended—when young men go to college or return from war. *Dirty Work* and *Soldier's Joy* examine the possibilities and limits of friendships formed because of shared experiences of physical and psychological wounds suffered in the Vietnam War. Gaines's black and white characters, segregated in rural Louisiana schools during childhood, meet at LSU in the 1970s. Gil, a Cajun, has grown to respect, like, and depend on Cal, a black player on his team; together they are Salt and Pepper, a symbol of improved race relations in a new South. The novel turns on an interesting paradox in defining manhood as it relates to race and causes the tension in relationships between the races. In order for Gil to be a man, he must refuse to kill the black man who has murdered his brother Beau; in order for each old black man to be a man, he must be ready to take a stand against a white man, even to kill. The behavior that Gaines deems manly for each racial group is based on the history of "race" relations in the rural South. For Ernest Gaines, race relations will not be changed until southern manhood is redefined, on both sides of the color line. While both black and white contemporary writers demonstrate how lack of social and economic power is a problem for congenial race relations, they also show how improving race relations is threatening in itself for those who perceive such changes as an indicator of their own loss of power or their own marker of identity.

Similarly, modern and contemporary women writers have used gender roles and reversals of racial roles as ways to forge cross-racial relationships. Katherine Anne Porter's story "The Old Order" (1944) links Sophia Jane and her slave and then servant Nannie through their shared past and mutual nursing and nur-

turing of each other's children. Ellen Douglas's more recent novel, *Can't Quit You, Baby* (1988), reverses old plots as well, but at length and in more depth. The rich white woman Cornelia ends up taking care of her black housekeeper Tweet and begging her to speak to her, to acknowledge her humanity, really to love her as she had always thought she did. Alice Walker and Gail Godwin use the women's movement to find other similarities between women, such as politics, social class, and careers. Each creates a protagonist who discovers not only some similarity but the individuality in a woman of a different race. In Alice Walker's *Meridian* (1976), a black civil-rights worker, Meridian, discovers that a white Jewish coworker, Lynne, is not frivolous but just as hardworking and just as committed to the movement as she is. In Gail Godwin's *A Mother and Two Daughters* (1982), Lydia, a genteel young white "lady," enrolls in a women's studies class at UNC-Greensboro and discovers that her black sociology professor, Harvard-graduate Renee, shares her own grace, charm, tastes, and interests.

In *Dessa Rose* (1986), Sherley Anne Williams portrays black and white women's problems in understanding each other as not only social and psychological but linguistic as well. Williams has both the escaped slave Dessa and the white woman Rufel, who protects her, rethink their relationship to each other through analogies, a process that breaks the bind that stereotypes about racial identity have on their thoughts. Talking gives them new words (often accidentally), shared experiences create new meanings, and trust eventually develops across racial lines. Neither Godwin nor Walker nor Williams suggests that interracial friendships will eliminate prejudice between groups, nor do they believe "that the category 'woman' is the most natural and basic of all human groupings and can therefore transcend race division," a phenomenon that Gloria Joseph and Jill Lewis warn against in *Common Differences* (1981). These writers do suggest that if black and white women would only listen to each other's stories and find out about each other's lives, they would discover similarities that allow them then to appreciate differences.

Alice Walker and Sherley Anne Williams are both concerned in their novels with the tabooed sexual desires that black men have for white women, desires that create tensions between black and white women. White writers Elizabeth Spencer in "The Business Venture" (1987) and Christine Wiltz in *Glass House* (1994) play on readers' expectations about interracial sex in the business relationships they explore between black men and white women that remain friendships. Randall Kenan completely rewrites the interracial love plot in *Let the Dead Bury the Dead* (1992) by making his lovers homosexual.

Many contemporary writers, especially African Americans, have chosen the historical novel as a vehicle for exploring contemporary race relations. Margaret Walker's *Jubilee* (1966), Ernest Gaines's *The Autobiography of Miss Jane Pittman* (1971), Alex Haley's *Roots* (1976), and Sherley Anne Williams's *Dessa Rose* have rewritten old stories about the slave South. Other writers, both black and white—Mark Childress in *Crazy in Alabama* (1993), Vicki Covington in *The Last Hotel for Women* (1996), Anthony Grooms in *Trouble No More* (1995), Nanci Kincaid in *Crossing Blood* (1992), and Alice Walker in *Meridian*—are revisiting the time of the Civil Rights Movement in order to understand how past prejudices continue to affect present relationships.

One hundred years after the publication of *Huckleberry Finn*, southern novelists are once again finding the first-person naïve narrator useful for examining race relations. These contemporary novels are punctuated with real-life references to lost childhood innocence: the deaths of black girls attending Bible school, the slayings of idealistic young black and white civil-rights workers, and the brutal murder of a fourteen-year-old black boy, Emmett Till, after he spoke to a white woman on a dare from friends. In *Crazy in Alabama,* set during the Civil Rights Movement, white writer Mark Childress shows readers how television shapes the way we understand our world and the way we act in it, not just through the shows we watch but by the way the news is reported. But running concurrently with Childress's very contemporary message about the media is a theme that dates back to Twain's *Huckleberry Finn*. Like Twain's Huck and Gaines's Gil, Peejoe is good only when he is bad, when he breaks the social rules and makes up a new script for interracial relationships. It is not surprising that the conclusion of *Crazy in Alabama* self-reflexively suggests that Hollywood should give America some new stories about southern race relations, such as Childress's own.

Embedded within African American writer Dori Sanders's first novel, *Clover* (1990), is a paradigm of reading or interpreting race that suggests that racial identity can be reformulated by reading Self and Other anew and that some of the difficulties in race relations are caused by misreading difference. Sanders's approach is anthropological; she fills her novel with the objects and rituals of everyday life in the South. The racial conflicts in her novel turn on misunderstandings about cultural differences. Sanders is primarily concerned with blacks' assumptions about whites, and she uses her novel to show that these assumptions are based on preconceived and unsubstantiated beliefs, just as Nanci Kincaid does from the other side of the color line in *Crossing Blood* (1992). In the last few chapters of the novel, Sanders creates new possibilities for both the young black narrator Clover and her white stepmother Sara Kate as she shows that lives are enriched when people from different cultures encounter each other in a spirit of open-mindedness.

Nanci Kincaid literally sets her novel *Crossing Blood* on the racial "dividing line" in Tallahassee, Florida, during the early 1960s. Kincaid's character configuration of childhood friends is like Faulkner's and Twain's, but with a very significant twist. Her black and white buddies are male and female, which allows Kincaid to explore the sexual ramifications of racism and race relations. In the woods between their houses, apart from the white and black worlds where they cannot interact honestly, they create another world, similar to Huck's and Jim's alternative world on the raft. Kincaid suggests that a place where blacks and whites can be open and honest with each other can exist, but it can only be created by speaking unspoken feelings and asking unasked questions, by a creative act of the imagination such as children experience when they play. This place must be constructed somewhere between the worlds we have defined as black and white.

Because Kincaid has set her story during a time of little possibility for a love affair to come to fruition between a southern white girl and black boy, the novel's form finally thwarts the characters' desires—despite the many scenes in which Kincaid's characters and consequently her readers dwell in the possibility of interracial understanding. This may be why Bebe Moore Campbell brought her historical novel *Your Blues Ain't Like Mine* (1992) into the present, thus reminding readers that possibilities can become realities. Campbell's novel begins in the 1950s with black characters sending their sons north to Chicago after the lynching of a black boy named Armstrong, whose character is based on Emmett Till. The novel ends with these boys returning as young men to the same southern town to escape the drug- and gang-infested streets of Chicago. This conclusion is a significant reversal of earlier twentieth-century African American fictions about race relations such as Richard Wright's "Big Boy Leaves Home" (1940) and Ralph Ellison's *Invisible Man* (1952), in which black men must leave the South not just to fulfill their potential but to survive. Campbell's novel also ends with mother Ida leading protest marches against the inhumane conditions of the catfish farm where she works with a young white woman, Doreen, whose father killed Armstrong before she was born. With the outcome of her plot, Campbell reveals the irony of her title—while the blues of black folk may not always be like those of white folk, there are significant similarities that sometimes call for joint action.

The most effective writers about race relations give voices to characters of different races and create conversations between them or debates within. Such narrative techniques as dialogue, debate, and multiple narrators allow readers to enter minds and hearts different from their own and to participate vicariously in a dialogic process that at the very least can provide "anxiety free access," to use Wolfgang Iser's term, to the unspoken in the readers' own lives and at the most can reformulate readers' thinking about racial identity and race relations. Recent immigration to the South, particularly by people from Vietnam and Cuba, is making race and ethnic relationships in the South more complex, and new literary representations of southern race relations are emerging.

Suzanne Jones

See also Chattel Slavery; Civil Rights Movement; Jim Crow; Ku Klux Klan; Lynching; Miscegenation; Mulatto; Plantation Fiction; Race, Idea of; Racism; Till, Emmett.

Susan Gubar, *Racechanges: White Skin, Black Face in American Culture* (1997); Minrose C. Gwin, *Black and White Women of the Old South: The Peculiar Sisterhood in American Literature* (1985); Barbara Ladd, *Nationalism and the Color Line in George W. Cable, Mark Twain, and William Faulkner* (1996); Dana D. Nelson, *The Word in Black and White: Reading "Race" in American Literature, 1638–1867* (1992); Eric J. Sundquist, *To Wake the Nations: Race in the Making of American Literature* (1993); Kenneth W. Warren, *Black and White Strangers: Race and American Literary Realism* (1993); Floyd C. Watkins, *The Death of Art: Black and White in the Recent Southern Novel* (1970); Joel Williamson, *The Crucible of Race: Black-White Relations in the American South Since Emancipation* (1980).

RACISM

Racism—the more or less systematic expression of the belief that physical differences between groups signify differences in worth or capacity—itself has a history. Indeed, racism became a term of common currency only after 1945 and then especially beginning in the 1960s. Thus any attempt to use racism as a prism through which to view southern literary expression and representation runs the risk of imposing anachronistic standards upon past literary expression.

In a broad sense, racism in southern writing must be seen in close relation to currents of thought and feeling in the nation at large. Three successive stages might be identified among white writers. The first stage might be called the era of "Enlightenment ambivalence." Manifested most clearly in Thomas Jefferson's *Notes on the State of Virginia* (1785), the secularizing consciousness of the educated, often slaveholding, white southerner was positioned between an "unscientific" folk belief that whites were superior to blacks and an Enlightenment-inspired belief that the force of circumstances rather than inheritance shaped individual and group capacities. Put slightly differently, the Enlightenment ethos in South and North, North America and Europe, was never quite clear concerning what equality referred to—equality of capacities or equality of moral status.

But by the 1830s, a hybrid tradition made up of the scientific materialist strand of Enlightenment thought, the Romantic emphasis upon cultural and natural differences, and the free white conviction of superiority to black slaves laid the foundations for the era of "scientific racism." Some intellectual and literary elites moved beyond, or supplemented, biblically grounded narratives of supposed racial difference with a kind of "quantitative" anthropology, to justify slavery in the South and doctrines of racial inequality in the South and North. Though this scientific theorizing was hardly promising soil for literary representation to take root in, its pervasiveness, augmented in the late nineteenth century by Darwinian theory, exerted a profound influence on the literary and cultural climate of the South over the next hundred-odd years.

In the post–Civil War South, there were a certain number of whites who could accept spiritual equality between the races and considerably fewer who believed in political and legal equality. But almost no one, even ardent critics of segregation such as George Washington Cable or at times Mark Twain, could really imagine that former slaves were the natural equals of the white master caste. William Faulkner illuminated this basic white southern incapacity and revealed the crucial role that "miscegenation," as a real and symbolic fact, played in the era of scientific racism through the character of Ike McCaslin in *Go Down, Moses* (1942). Ike abjures his inheritance of property because of the violation and injustice imposed by his grandfather, Carothers McCaslin, yet he cannot accept the sexual relationship between his kinsman Roth Edmonds and a light-skinned black woman with its implication of equality and denial of racial degeneration following miscegenation. For many white southerners, to be opposed to slavery and to protest against racial exploitation by no means amounted to a belief in racial equality and racial mixing.

In this century-long period of white racial hegemony, certain clusters of racialized images, metaphors, and tropes turned up in the literature of the region—and continued to do so afterward. Blacks as hypersexual and animal-like, a theme adumbrated by Jefferson, turned up most notoriously in Thomas Dixon's *The Clansman* (1905) and D. W. Griffith's pioneering film *The Birth of a Nation* (1914), and then later in that greatest of best-sellers, Margaret Mitchell's *Gone With the Wind* (1936). Blacks were also often depicted in phobic terms as diseased and infectious or dirty and smelly or as bent on exacting revenge through terror or violence. The threat of sexual violation and the fear of political and social revolution were closely linked in popular and high literature.

The other dominant cluster of images derived from the white southern family romance, a deep cultural construct within which the two races allegedly related to one another as (white) parents and (black) children. According to this paternalistic view, black southerners, whether slave or free, were not so much subhuman or bestial as immature and childlike. Much of the literature of the plantation romance, before and after the Civil War, offered the essentially nonsexual image of blacks as capricious, lazy, and unreliable but also, given the right training and sufficient age, as faithful, kind, and forgiving of white foibles and anxieties, sort of subaltern therapists for the master race—a role that Dilsey Gibson comes close to filling in Faulkner's *The Sound and the Fury* (1929).

Among white writers and intellectuals, the years between roughly 1930 and 1970 saw a third stage of racism thematized and scrutinized where it was once a "given" of the southern literary landscape. Pioneers in this literary exploration were of course Faulkner, whose three great novels about racial consciousness—*Light in August* (1932), *Absalom, Absalom!* (1936), and *Go Down, Moses* (1942), along with *Intruder in the Dust* (1948)—explored with great force, insight,

and ambivalence the racial agonies of the region; and Lillian Smith, whose novel *Strange Fruit* (1944) depicted an interracial love affair in the small-town South and whose memoir *Killers of the Dream* (1949) combined a psychoanalytic perspective with an astringent moral sensibility to lay bare the linkage between race and sexuality, religion and violence. A blatant self-contradiction among southern conservative intellectuals was also revealed in William Alexander Percy's *Lanterns on the Levee* (1941). There, Percy openly based his paternalism on a belief in white supremacy, yet he was also an ardent opponent of Nazism, including its persecution of the Jews, as a threat to the very fabric of Western civilization.

This white tradition of exploring the psychological, as well as social and political, dimensions of racism culminated and, in some ways, came to grief with William Styron's *The Confessions of Nat Turner* (1967). There, through the eyes of Nat Turner, Styron explored the psychology of slavery and slave revolts, along with the compulsions of interracial sexual desire. In response, black writers and critics raised loud protests at Styron's presumption that he, a white southerner, could know how a black man, much less a leader of a slave revolt, thought and felt, especially in reference to his most intimate sexual desires. Thus the tradition of literary exploration of racism as a problematic dimension of regional experience ended with charges of racism being leveled against Styron himself.

There is a parallel tradition of black southern writing that has both assumed and explored the effects of white racism in its texts, including fictional ones. Two things, however, most notably differentiate this tradition from white southern writing on the subject. First, it is largely a literature of exile, aimed at exploring the reasons why and how exile was chosen or forced upon the writers. In this, it is a literature of protest. The answer is of course obvious in Frederick Douglass's *Narrative* (1845): the reason the slave prefers freedom is obvious to all but ideological defenders of a slave regime. But some white readers, even southern ones, of Richard Wright's *Native Son* (1940) and *Black Boy* (1945) may have been startled by the pervasive violence of white racial prejudice experienced by the young Richard Wright. And Ralph Ellison's *Invisible Man* (1952), for all his efforts to escape Wright's influence, explored this same theme of the escape from the South to the North—and the growing disillusionment with the promise of northern life. But scrutiny was also directed inward; and however much Bigger

Thomas, Richard Wright, and the protagonist of *Invisible Man* differed, the nature of their own self-delusion was also explored. Such novels, along with the early Harlem Renaissance novel *Cane* (1923) by Jean Toomer, paradoxically focused on the oppressiveness of racism in the South and the pervasiveness of racism outside the South. Thus, what the Civil Rights Movement arrived at by the mid-1960s—that racism was an American and not just a southern problem—was already thematized in much of the African American literature prior to that time.

The second way black southern writing about racism differs in its treatment of racism bears on the characteristics of the southern political novel. Among black writers, racism is rarely the subject of argument; rather, it is assumed and the task is to gain recognition through action. Where *Intruder in the Dust*'s creator only allows Lucas Beauchamp to act alone, Ernest Gaines's *A Gathering of Old Men* (1983) depicts a community of black Louisianians in the process of remembering their individual pasts and thus revitalizing their communal ties. They resolve to resist for the first time—to risk their lives through violence if need be—the rank depredations of Cajun bosses and the more subtle paternalism of their liberal friends. In this they become a political community for the first time. Alice Walker's first novel, *The Third Life of Grange Copeland* (1970), ends with the emerging awareness of the Civil Rights Movement as it impinges on a black community; her *Meridian* (1976) charts the first heady days of the Civil Rights Movement and then tracks the debilitating effects of racial, sexual, and gender politics within the movement and suggests the need to move beyond a pure politics of equality.

As long as the South remains the place where more African Americans live than anywhere else and as long as the South remains the chief American "site" of collective racial conflict and memory, as exemplified by the Civil War and the Civil Rights Movement, some southern writers will of necessity engage with the issue of racism. Discussion of the way southern literature deals—or fails to deal—with racism tends toward the prescriptive—i.e., all southern writers should indict racism in their fiction and present positive black characters to counter the negative images perpetuated in the past. But the four major women writers of the Renascence—Katherine Anne Porter, Eudora Welty, Flannery O'Connor, and Carson McCullers—never explored the fact or meaning of racism in southern life to any significant degree. Nor did James Agee, Thomas

Wolfe, Robert Penn Warren, Walker Percy, or Cormac McCarthy place racial dilemmas at the center of their fiction. It is probably more difficult for black southern writers to escape the racial theme, but Zora Neale Hurston in the 1930s and 1940s and Albert Murray since the early 1970s have generally treated racism as something that presents an opportunity as much as a handicap, as an occasion, not an excuse, for self-development and self-understanding. In this respect, Hurston and Murray are two examples of what is sometimes named the African American literature of "celebration" as opposed to the literature of "protest."

One way of characterizing those southern writers who have abjured the theme of racism is to see them as concerned with the private over the public, the intimate rather than the collective, the personal rather than the political. Yet one contemporary writer who has demonstrated that these are false dichotomies is Ellen Douglas in her novel *Can't Quit You, Baby* (1988). In that novel, Douglas explored the micropolitics of race and gender by examining the relationship between a middle-class white woman and her black maid during the 1950s and 1960s. By the end, they come to a hard-won recognition of each other and of themselves. Though never suggesting that just the personal is the political—the historical changes brought about by the Civil Rights Movement haunt the novel—Douglas illustrates the fictional possibilities of exploring racism as it works in and through individual lives, while neither rendering personal relationships between the races impossible nor suggesting that personal connections alone are enough to overcome inherited social and racial attitudes.

Richard H. King

See also African American Literature; Chattel Slavery; Faithful Retainer; Happy Darky; Harlem Renaissance; Historical Romance; History, Idea of; Mammy; Nigger; Plantation Fiction; Race, Idea of.

W. J. Cash, *The Mind of the South* (1941); John Dollard, *Caste and Class in a Southern Town* (1937); Ralph Ellison, *Shadow and Act* (1964); George Fredrickson, *The Black Image in the White Mind* (1971); Lawrence Friedman, *The White Savage* (1970); Thomas Gossett, *Race: The History of an Idea in America* (1963); Winthrop Jordan, *White Over Black* (1968); Richard H. King, *A Southern Renaissance* (1980); Toni Morrison, *Playing in the Dark: Whiteness and the Literary Imagination* (1992); Gunnar Myrdal, *An American Dilemma* (2 vols.; 1944); Robert Stepto, *From Behind the Veil* (1979); Pierre Van den Berghe, *Race and Ethnicity* (1970); Alice

Walker, *In Search of Our Mothers' Gardens* (1983); Richard Weaver, *The Southern Tradition at Bay: A History of Postbellum Thought* (1968); Joel Williamson, *The Crucible of Race* (1984); C. Vann Woodward, *The Strange Career of Jim Crow* (1955).

RAGTIME

Ragtime usually connotes a generic way of playing the piano—be it a familiar song or even a hymn—in which a steady pulse is maintained in the left hand while the rhythm of the melody in the right hand opposes it. Or, one may say that accents in the "rag-ged" right hand have been shifted so as to conflict with the regular beats of the left. The left hand plays what is called "oom-pah bass," which alternates single notes relatively low with chords above. A revival of so-called Classic Ragtime began in the early 1970s, partly because the musical score of the movie *The Sting* was formed from rags for piano solo by Scott Joplin (1868–1917).

Classic Ragtime is a term that applies to a specific genre of piano solo composed mostly during the first two decades of the twentieth century. It has the generic steady bass (left hand) and "offbeat" treble (right hand). A rag composition is formed as a series of short sections, equal in length with one each repeated, comparable to the form of a march such as one by Sousa. Frequently, one of the sections returns later in the composition. The ragtime pianist and composer Eubie Blake composed his own "Charleston Rag" (also known as "Sounds of Africa") in 1899. Near the end of his life, Blake made a recording of his ragtime version of Sousa's march "Stars and Stripes Forever." Among the most famous of the classic ragtime solos are those by Scott Joplin, including "The Entertainer," "Maple Leaf Rag," and "Magnetic Rag."

Ragtime as a genre has two distinct but related meanings. The first refers to a song whose melody has ragged rhythms. The earliest songs with such rhythms were heard in minstrel shows in the late nineteenth century and were consistently associated with the black stereotypes featured in those shows. One of the most famous of these songs is "All Coons Look Alike to Me" (1896). The well-dressed blacks pictured on the cover of the published sheet music of this song are hardly wearers or pickers of rags. The exotic lyrics of James Weldon Johnson's ragtime song "Under the Bamboo Tree" (1902), on the other hand, involve African imagery. Both of these songs, as well as Howard and Emerson's "Hello! Ma Baby . . . Hello, My Ragtime Gal" (1899), pit the shifting accents of the melody against the regular movement of the accompaniment.

Second, ragtime is simply a way of singing or playing. In his *Memos*, the American composer Charles Ives actually set down in musical notation the way he had heard the song "I'm Livin' Easy" sung at the Hopkins Grammar School of New Haven in the 1890s—and he called it ragtime. His notation shows the strong accents of the song's meter shifted to the weak parts of the musical measure. In the first decade of the twentieth century, several treatises appeared, including one by Scott Joplin himself, in which the reader was instructed how to play conventional music in ragtime. Ben Harney's *Ragtime Instructor* (1908) demonstrated how to change the song "Annie Laurie" into a rag. Similarly, T. S. Eliot would rag "That Shakespearean Rag" from the Ziegfeld Follies of 1912 in his 1922 masterwork *The Waste Land*. In Irving Berlin's song "Alexander's Ragtime Band" (1911), when there is reference to the playing of "Sewanee River" in ragtime, the melody at that very moment "rags" the opening phrase of Stephen Foster's "Old Folks at Home." Likewise, the melody that sets the reference to a bugle call mimics a bugle call in ragtime, and it actually reminds one of "Reveille."

Ragtime also includes a number of associated idioms and genres. Terms such as *two-step, drag,* and *slow drag* link ragtime to dancing. Harney's "Cake Walk in the Sky" (1899) and Joplin's own "Swipesy Cake Walk" (1900, written with Arthur Marshall) associates the genre with the earlier plantation practice where people strutted in procession to win a cake. In ragtime, similar to the effect with jazz later, "stoptime" describes the effect resulting from the stomping of the feet on the beat while the piano itself is silent. Since ragtime is so closely related to marching, Joplin often admonished in his published rags, "Notice! Don't play this piece fast. It is never right to play rag-time fast," as in the publication of his "Leola Two-Step." Joplin's "Maple Leaf Rag" is even notated "Tempo di marcia." Growing out of ragtime in the 1920s was a style of piano playing called "stride piano." The syncopated right hand remains, but here the left hand covers larger distances with the "oom-pah bass," which is itself often replaced with the so-called "walking bass," where the left hand moves short steps between adjacent keys of the keyboard.

Although authentic ragtime had an important revival in the late twentieth century. It has been known in everyday music rather continuously from the beginning of the century. It has been popular to associate ragtime with brothels, but by no means was it limited to the one venue. For example, it is a way that a pianist would read sheet music of popular songs on the home piano. The player could read the melody line, altering it rhythmically to suit the whim, and play it against the characteristic "oom-pah" bass. The American composer Virgil Thomson remembered the ragtime playing of Sunday School pianists in his "Variations and Fugues on Sunday-School Tunes," which he composed in the late 1920s. The revival of ragtime in the late twentieth century brought the music of classic ragtime into the concert hall and realized belated recognition for ragtime's many composers.

Thomas Warburton

See also Jazz.

Edward A. Berlin, *King of Ragtime: Scott Joplin and His Era* (1994).

RAILROADS

A railroad map of the United States in 1861 illustrates why the South lost the Civil War. While the northern states were stitched together in a thick web of iron rails, the southern states were rather loosely knit, with many lines unconnected to any other. Although the North had over twice the rail mileage of the South, this statistic reveals only half the disparity, as the Union rail lines were better planned, constructed, equipped, and coordinated. Most important, the South depended on the North for most railroad supplies, and it had no ready way to replace them once the war began. Only when Confederate strategists recognized that this conflict would be the first decided by railroads did they develop the South's system to a quality that prolonged the war until 1865.

A Civil War railroad map also reveals a complex of attitudes toward trains that gave them special meaning in southern culture generally considered. Although the railroads of the South were among the earliest in the country, they were less quickly or extensively developed because of a profound regional ambivalence toward technology, industry, and even mobility. The plantation system depended on stability, and the dy-

namic expansion of northern railroads and factories seemed its antithesis. The South wanted only enough of these new developments to complement, but not to disturb, its status quo; thus most antebellum railroads in the region linked plantations to coastal and river ports with little consideration of coordination among lines, which often ran on tracks of varied gauges using equipment that could not be interchanged.

This southern questioning of technology not only lost it the Civil War but cost the South those transportation, communication, and manufacturing capabilities that it had earlier developed. During Reconstruction, regional railroad and telegraph lines, as well as factories and foundries, had to be rebuilt, often by former Confederate leaders colluding with Yankee investors to exploit southern natural and human resources. Trains and textile mills as new sources of social power assumed an ambivalent symbolism in the South, which made them more culturally significant than in other regions of the nation. In one sense, the New South was created by completing the earlier railroad map, and new cities burgeoned where major rail lines met. Now, for the first time, the new southern railroad network also created viable connections with the other sections of the country.

Because railroads arrived later in the South, they remained important longer into the new century than in the North. Again, this dependence on trains reinforced the cultural power of their ambivalent symbolism, especially in the Golden Age of southern railroading, which roughly coincided with the Southern Renascence. In particular, as the means of the great black and white migrations from the South to the North, rail transportation reached an almost mythic status as, for example, the subject of blues and ballads. Ironically, the strength of southern railroads left them better situated than their mighty northern counterparts after the reverses of the Depression and the efforts of two world wars. Although many branch lines have withered in the South as elsewhere, two giant conglomerates—CSX Transportation and Norfolk Southern, descended from the region's first trunk lines, the Chesapeake and Ohio Railroad and the Southern Railway—now essentially divide all main-line traffic from the Atlantic to the Mississippi and from the Great Lakes to the Gulf.

The relation of southern railroads to southern literature closely follows this outline of the region's overall social history and cultural ambivalence. As with real trains in the landscape of the South before the Civil War, few literary recreations are discovered in antebellum southern letters. Certainly nothing in the works of the region's writers during the prewar period compares to the theoretical considerations provided by Ralph Waldo Emerson and Henry David Thoreau, or to the symbolic re-creations of James Fenimore Cooper, Nathaniel Hawthorne, Herman Melville, and Walt Whitman. By contrast, Edgar Allan Poe, William Gilmore Simms, John Pendleton Kennedy, and Henry Timrod seem hardly aware of the burgeoning technology in their romantic concerns with the self, with nature and landscape, with the plantation and slavery, and with the past. The same neglect of the new modes in communication, transportation, and production also prove true for the popular genres of sentimental romance and tall-tale humor.

The Civil War and Reconstruction, with their increased emphasis on railroads as a force in southern society, influenced southern writing as well. Of course, realism in itself would have placed more trains on the southern scene, if only as markers of the structural changes transforming the region. Again, southern realists like Mark Twain and George Washington Cable may not have depicted as many railroads as their northern counterparts such as William Dean Howells and Henry James, but they did employ them as symbolically. For example, Twain used railroad speculation as a sign of the times in *The Gilded Age* (1873), and railroad building became one hallmark of modern civilization and imperialism in *A Connecticut Yankee in King Arthur's Court* (1889). The popular genres that contextualized Twain's efforts also revealed more trains; the raucous humor of the Old Southwest rode the rails during Reconstruction, and postbellum southern sentimental romances employed the new mode of transport to fulfill true love.

The most important effect of the railroad system forged in the New South may be seen in the Golden Age of southern railroading that followed, a development at least partially responsible for the rise of the Southern Renascence between the world wars. The South's new rail network represented, in social terms, the reconciliation, prosperity, and sophistication necessary for a southern literary presence on the American scene; in intellectual terms, southern railroads helped to foster the ambivalent attitudes and agrarian emphasis that characterized the Southern Renascence. Most of the writers who created this Renascence in southern literature were born about the turn of the century and grew up in this Golden Age of southern railroads.

The most obvious examples include William Faulk-ner, the cultural heir of a Mississippi family that made its fortune building railroads; Thomas Wolfe, the scion of a North Carolina resort city largely created by railways; and Robert Penn Warren, the native son of a town spawned by the junction of main lines on the border of Kentucky and Tennessee. Faulkner's fictions are filled with tracks and trains, in particular those somewhat biographical works dealing with the Sartoris and McCaslin/Edmonds/Beauchamp families—*Sartoris* (1929), *The Unvanquished* (1938), and *Go Down, Moses* (1942). In some sense, all of these works recreate Faulkner's patriarch, Colonel W. C. Falkner, who rode with Forrest during the Civil War, built railroads with convict labor during Reconstruction, and published best-selling romances that featured trains. Wolfe's love of railroads is legendary, and his autobiographical novels contain some of the longest train rides in any literature; indeed, his second novel, *Of Time and the River* (1935), was originally intended to be set entirely on board a Pullman express, demonstrating both the freedom and the determinism symbolized by railroads. Robert Penn Warren's fiction pictures many trains somewhat in the manner of Faulkner and Wolfe, as in *Night Rider* (1939) and *All the King's Men* (1946), but his poetry creates even more ambivalent examples, particularly in the poems drawn from his memories of growing up in Guthrie, Kentucky, a division point on the Louisville and Nashville Railroad.

Although Faulkner, Wolfe, and Warren are the most obvious examples of serious writing about railroads during the Renascence, others abound. Southern women writers generally present fewer trains, but there are some important exceptions to this tendency. For example, the earlier generation of transitional realists, such as Ellen Glasgow and Elizabeth Madox Roberts, use railroads in a naturalistic mode much as their northern and midwestern counterparts, Edith Wharton and Willa Cather, did. Later women authors as different as Katherine Anne Porter, Caroline Gordon, and Margaret Mitchell included the railroad in their recreations of southern history. Eudora Welty depicts the rail lines of the South in *Delta Wedding* (1946) and *One Writer's Beginnings* (1984), as ambivalently, if not as compulsively, as Faulkner. Flannery O'Connor, when asked about Faulkner's influence, replied that "no one wants their mule and wagon stalled on the same track the Dixie Limited is roaring down."

African American writers from the days of the Underground Railroad through the Great Migration of the twentieth century saw the railroads of the South as ambivalent symbols of escape and entrapment. In historical reporting, Frederick Douglass's *Narrative* (1845) realized the metaphorical basis of the Underground Railroad during slavery. In fiction, Paul Laurence Dunbar's *The Sport of the Gods* (1902) revealed the railroads as the matrix of Jim Crow laws and repressive labor in Reconstruction. Jean Toomer's *Cane* (1923) became the pioneering work of the Harlem Renaissance, and both his southern and his northern scenes are filled with trains. The great black writers of the Southern Renascence, Zora Neale Hurston and Richard Wright, in *Jonah's Gourd Vine* (1934), *Uncle Tom's Children* (1938), and *Black Boy* (1945), also employed a powerful symbolism of trains. Langston Hughes represented African American attitudes toward trains in both fiction and poetry from the Harlem Renaissance to the Civil Rights Movement, from the rail migrations after World War I to the southern trips of the ironically named "Freedom Train" after World War II.

Southern writers in all genres—and of different races, genders, classes, and ages—continue the regional preoccupation with symbols provided by a cultural reading of southern railroads up to the present. A partial list includes Harriette Simpson Arnow's *The Dollmaker* (1954), John Ehle's *The Road* (1967), Albert Murray's *Train Whistle Guitar* (1974), Cormac McCarthy's *Suttree* (1979), Dave Smith's *The Roundhouse Voices* (1985), Fannie Flagg's *Fried Green Tomatoes at the Whistle Stop Café* (1987), Bobbie Ann Mason's *Feather Crowns* (1993), and Toni Morrison's *Jazz* (1992). Even these disparate examples demonstrate the continued importance of the region's railroads for southern literature at the end of the twentieth century.

Through many historical and social contexts, the South developed a special relationship with railroads, and most facets of southern culture reflected this distinctive relation, not just in the nineteenth century but in the twentieth as well. As in so many other aspects of its cultural heritage, the Old South's attitudes about railroads were transformed by the trauma of the Civil War and Reconstruction into the changing views of the New South, which in turn were themselves altered into a different relation with the rest of the nation in the new century. Southern literature recreated as well as reflected this relation to railroads, making trains and tracks important tropes in the Southern Renascence and beyond.

Joseph Millichap

See also Black Migrations; Civil War.

George H. Douglas, *All Aboard: The Railroad in American Life* (1992); Sarah H. Gordon, *Passage to Union: How the Railroads Transformed American Life, 1829–1929* (1996); Gary Kulik, "Representing the Railroad," *Gettysburg Review* (1988); Ian Marshall, "Steel Wheels on Paper: The Railroad in American Literature," *Railway History* (1991); Merton M. Sealts, " 'Pulse of the Continent': The Railroad in American Literature," *Wisconsin Academy Review* (1990).

RALEIGH, SIR WALTER

Poet, historian, scientist, adventurer, and the man who popularized smoking tobacco in English high society, Sir Walter Raleigh (1554?–1618), also spelled "Ralegh," was the younger of two sons born in Devon, England, to Katherine Gilbert, the third wife of Walter Raleigh (d. 1581). Although the family was relatively poor, it was well connected. As a teenager, Raleigh saw military action in France fighting for the Protestant Huguenots. From 1568 to 1572, he attended Oriel College, Oxford. In 1580 he registered at London's Inns of Court, but instead of practicing law, Raleigh later claimed that he spent most of his time in literary circles, writing and publishing poetry.

Popular legends (and many biographers) maintain that Raleigh gained the attention of Queen Elizabeth I by spreading his best velvet cloak over a street puddle for the reigning monarch. Although the story was written many years after his death and cannot be verified, it is certain that somehow Raleigh won over the queen. His rise in her court was rapid, leading to a series of influential offices and knighthood in 1584. In that year, he was also given a patent for colonization in North America. Once held by his half-brother, Sir Humphrey Gilbert, the patent gave Raleigh exclusive control over a portion of the New World stretching from Newfoundland to Florida. He wasted no time in attempting to plant a permanent colony there, as well as a base for raids against Spanish treasure ships. Raleigh chose Roanoke Island (in present-day North Carolina) as the site. In tribute to his royal patron, the Virgin Queen, he named the entire region "Virginia."

Although many others had sailed British ships into New World waters, Raleigh was the first Englishman with the vision and resources to attempt permanent settlement on American soil. His efforts—known as the "Roanoke Voyages"—were failures, but some of the fruits of Raleigh's adventurousness are indelible parts of the southern geographical and cultural landscapes. The name "Virginia" became permanently attached to a significant portion of the region. The drawings of John White—the colony's governor sent by Raleigh along with the mathematician and scientist Thomas Harriott—remain the most important colonial record of a lost tribe of Carolina Native Americans. Published in 1588 as *A Brief and True Report of the New Found Land of Virginia*, the White-Harriott collaboration was also a major reference book in the library of the Virginia Company as it set out in 1607 to establish Jamestown, the first permanent English colony in the New World.

Legends spawned by Raleigh's "Lost Colony" (including the life of Virginia Dare, the first English child born in the New World) continue to thrive in scores of children's books. Thousands of tourists annually enjoy Paul Green's popular dramatization of the ill-starred venture. In 1997 alone, 85,000 spectators viewed *The Lost Colony*, which is the longest-running outdoor drama in the United States. Excepting the wartime blackout years of 1942–1945, the play has run continuously since it premiered on July 4, 1937.

While Raleigh's star rose and fell in the court of Elizabeth (he was imprisoned briefly by the jealous queen for his secret marriage to Elizabeth Throckmorton), his influence remained vigorous as long as the queen was alive. When she died and was succeeded in 1603 by James I, Raleigh's fortunes became far less secure. Ancient enmities and political intrigues—some real, others fabricated by his detractors—came to haunt him as, in 1603, he was accused and convicted of plotting to dethrone the king. Although he was sentenced to death, Raleigh's execution was suspended. He lived comfortably for the next thirteen years imprisoned in the Tower of London, where he wrote his most formidable work, *The History of the World*. In 1616, he was released to lead an expedition to Guiana searching for gold mines and the fabled city of El Dorado.

But the Guiana expedition was a debacle. Raleigh's adventurers found neither mines nor the city of gold, and these failures had disastrous personal consequences for the aging cavalier. The venture used up nearly all of what remained of the wealth that Raleigh had amassed during his years as a favorite in Elizabeth's court. And worse by far, the unauthorized siege and capture of the Spanish fort at San Thome on the Orinoco River led James I to reinstate Raleigh's death sentence. Four months after his return from the voyage that cost him his fortune, the life of his oldest son, Wat

(who was killed leading the attack on San Thome), and ultimately his own life, Raleigh was executed on October 29, 1618. With his head on the block, Raleigh—having refused a blindfold—was aware of the executioner's hesitation as he raised the axe. Raleigh's last words were, "What dost thou fear? Strike, man, strike!"

Although Raleigh himself never laid eyes on the area of North America that he named and tried to colonize, his Roanoke Voyages and the "Lost Colony" gave the next generation of English men and women some of the experience and lessons they needed to establish later settlements in Jamestown and Plymouth. At the very least, Raleigh's efforts mark the significant beginnings of New World English culture and history.

Carmine Prioli

See also Colonial Literature; *Lost Colony, The*; North Carolina, Literature of.

Stephen Coote, *A Play of Passion: The Life of Sir Walter Ralegh* (1993); Stephen J. Greenblatt, *Sir Walter Ralegh: The Renaissance Man and His Roles* (1973); Karen Ordahl Kupperman, *Roanoke: The Abandoned Colony* (1984); Robert Lacey, *Sir Walter Ralegh* (1973); Sir Walter Ralegh, *The Works of Sir Walter Ralegh, Kt.* (1829); Willard M. Wallace, *Sir Walter Ralegh* (1959).

READING PUBLIC

Historically, southerners have spent less time reading than people living in other sections of the nation, with the possible exception of southwesterners. It is a nice irony that two southerners, Cleanth Brooks and Robert Penn Warren, developed ways of making better readers of anyone wishing to deal more insightfully with the written word. Climate, and not a lack of intellectual or aesthetic interests, helps to explain why southerners and southwesterners spent less time with books, magazines, and newspapers than persons living in other regions—outdoor activities could be pursued many months of the year. A second factor is geographical—the South had few urban centers. Except for persons living in the coastal area, books and journals came to hand only with considerable effort. Bookstores were few, and book peddlers were not an everyday sight. Sharply reducing the percentage of readers on a percapita basis was the fact that slaves could not lawfully be taught to read. As Frederick Douglass and other slaves were to discover, to learn how to read was to have an even stronger desire for freedom. Perhaps the most significant reason why southerners lagged behind others in reading is economic. Although wealthy planters such as William Byrd could afford well-stocked libraries, their yeoman neighbors had few discretionary funds for books, unless the outlay was for a family Bible, an almanac, or a guide to devotions. Limited economic resources continued to curtail opportunities for reading fairly deep into the twentieth century, as can be seen from the studies of Louis R. Wilson and others, particularly in Wilson's *The Geography of Reading* (1938). Practically every kind of library—school, university, or public—ranked (and still do) below libraries in other regions. Lack of capital also meant fewer bookstores and book customers.

In colonial America, whatever the region, when money was available for books, reading matter differed little, since virtually the same authors and titles claimed places on the bookshelves of readers throughout the colonies. Among the better educated, the classics ranked high, as evidenced by Thomas Jefferson's appreciative remark that reading classic authors in their own language was a "sublime luxury." Southern planters, clergymen, lawyers, teachers, and physicians found both delight and utility in Homer, Sophocles, Aristophanes, Plato, Aristotle, Seneca, Ovid, Horace, Virgil, Aesop, and many other Greek and Latin authors.

Like readers in the northern colonies, southern colonials often turned to books on history, law, politics, and theology. Both ancient and contemporary historians interested them, writers ranging from Josephus to Sir Walter Raleigh, Voltaire, Tobias Smollett, and David Hume. For a grounding in law, they turned to the works of Sir Edward Coke and other English authorities on legal matters. To explore philosophical inquiries into politics, they often chose to read the pertinent writings of Thomas Hobbes, John Locke, and the Earl of Shaftesbury. Together with their wives and daughters, they found spiritual food and guidance in such works as Lewis Bayly's *The Practice of Piety,* Richard Allestree's *The Whole Duty of Man,* and John Bunyan's *Pilgrim's Progress.* For those with a taste for belles-lettres, the works of Shakespeare, Spenser, Jonson, Quarles, Milton, Dryden, Pope, Swift, Prior, Cowper, Johnson, Sterne, Smollett, and Richardson satisfied the hunger of many readers. Richardson's novels appealed to both men and women readers. Novels and romances generally were railed against in the pulpit and forbidden at home by watchful parents or guard-

ians. With the coming of a new generation of novelists, the interdiction seems to have spared Sir Walter Scott's novels, whose forays into Scotland's and England's past appealed to what the South's landed gentry considered chivalrous and courteous in manners and outlook.

Just as truth was a major desideratum of pious planter and yeoman alike, they shared a common interest in obtaining practical information, for which they were willing to invest in almanacs and treatises on farming, horticulture, and gardening. The need for almanacs to provide data relevant to particular locales was often a factor in establishing presses in the South.

The political tempest that ultimately resulted in breaking away from British rule and establishing a federation of states brought southerners into prominent roles as writers and readers, epitomized by Jefferson's immortal words and Madison's thoughtful musings on how best to build a democratic republic. Those words and musings would later weigh heavily in the minds of southern writers who wanted a separate nation. As southerners began launching journals and magazines, they used such publications as the *Southern Quarterly Review* (1842), *De Bow's Review* (1846), and *Russell's* (1857) as outlets for the opinions of William Grayson, William Gilmore Simms, and others. These magazines, and others like them, provided belles-lettres as well as politics.

War, reconstruction, rural rather than urban demographics, and blighted economic conditions largely left southern states unable to participate in the establishment of public libraries until well into the twentieth century. Had it not been for the commitment and hard work of women under the aegis of the Federation of Women's Clubs, public libraries would not have been built and supported as early as they were. Insufficient funds and Jim Crowism left many southern towns without any public libraries for African Americans. Not until the 1960s could most southern blacks use any except segregated public libraries.

Southern readers supported fewer bookstores, proportionately, than readers elsewhere in the nation. Although the gap is closing, many southern towns of middling size lack a general bookstore, since small towns generally have bookshops offering only religious and juvenile materials. Rather than books, southern adult readers prefer newspapers and magazines and have made *Progressive Farmer* and *Southern Living* two of the most widely circulated publications in the region. Although such miscellanies as *Southern Re-*

view, *Virginia Quarterly Review, Sewanee Review,* and *Georgia Review* seem destined to survive, will such newcomers as *Double Take, Oxford American,* and *North Carolina Literary Review* go the way of *Double Dealer, Red Clay Reader,* and scores of other literary magazines launched in the South?

Among the hopeful signs for authors, bookstores, and libraries are readings for juveniles and adults by writers and professional readers in events scheduled in formats ranging from bookstore settings to large college auditoriums. As a recent literary festival at the University of North Carolina in Chapel Hill proved, thousands of the reading public will turn out if outstanding writers are the fare.

John L. Idol Jr.

See also Intellectual; Literary Magazines; Newspapers; Periodicals; Publishers; University Presses.

Richard Beale Davis, *A Colonial Southern Bookshelf: Reading in the Eighteenth Century* (1979); Donald Foos, *The Role of the State Library in Adult Education: A Critical Analysis of Nine Southeastern Library Agencies* (1973); James Hart, *The Popular Book* (1950); Kevin J. Hayes, *A Colonial Woman's Bookshelf* (1996); Frederick Hoffman, *The Little Magazine: A History and Bibliography* (1946); Frank Luther Mott, *The Golden Multitudes: The Story of Best Sellers in the United States* (1947); Stephen B. Weeks, "Libraries and Literature in North Carolina in the Eighteenth Century," *Annual Report of the American Historical Association for the Year 1895* (1895); Louis R. Wilson, *The Geography of Reading* (1938).

REALISM

Southern realism usually signifies the literature of those nineteenth-century post–Civil War writers such as George Washington Cable, Kate Chopin, Charles W. Chesnutt, and Mark Twain who consciously broke from the plantation-romance tradition (the tradition exploited in John Pendleton Kennedy's *Swallow Barn,* 1832) that had dominated antebellum southern letters. But southern realism is intelligible only in terms of the large general literary movement that swept Europe and America and strove to reflect the actual conditions of life and fidelity to precise detail.

As a relative term, *realism* defines a writer's attitude toward the raw materials of art, including such features as style, voice, and intent. As an aesthetic convention that prefers the commonplace and quotidian over the elevated, tragic, or ideal, realism aims for method

so transparent that technique does not eclipse its constant aim—"verisimilitude," or a direct representation of the actual. Thus it avoids the subjective nature of romanticism, impressionism, expressionism, or surrealism. The impact of other agendas—of modernism, postmodernism, or even the deterministic character of *fin de siècle* naturalism—is more difficult to determine. Both realism and naturalism were reactions against the formal prohibitions of the later-nineteenth- and early-twentieth-century Genteel Tradition; thus tracing roots and distinguishing offshoots quickly becomes artificial and speculative. Above all, realism attempts to persuade readers that the created world mirrors the objective, inhabited world.

In the South and elsewhere in the nation, much of the attraction to realism grew from gradual indigenous recoil against the gentility of Washington Irving and James Fenimore Cooper (even though certain roots of American realism may, in fact, be traced to Cooper). Realist literature in Europe and the United States typically dates from about 1840 until the 1890s, with standard bearers such as Anton Chekhov, Gustave Flaubert, Guy de Maupassant, George Eliot, and American writers Mark Twain, William Dean Howells, and American expatriate novelist Henry James. The influences of nineteenth-century rational philosophy affected American realism, as did reactions against the romanticism of Sir Walter Scott. By the 1880s, William Dean Howells and others adopted realism as a literary program, which after the 1890s would be furthered and challenged by Hamlin Garland's veritism and the naturalism of Dreiser, Norris, and London.

The South's antebellum veneration of chivalric codes and moonlight-and-magnolia literature would later provide the memorial thrust for its mistrust of ideological promise and for its producing a lasting realist literature of peculiarly reactive force, one that extends even into the spectacular harvest of southern literature today. Mark Twain set out to inoculate American culture and particularly agrarian, southern culture against the "Sir Walter Scott disease." *Adventures of Huckleberry Finn* (1885) and *A Connecticut Yankee in King Arthur's Court* (1889) pilloried both the courtly, sentimental lies and the smug technological superiority responsible not just for the blood feuds and carnage in these novels but ultimately for the entire Civil War. But the transition from romanticism to realism was gradual and diverse in the South, including the growing reaction to Thomas Nelson Page's nostalgia, Edgar Allan Poe's emotional and psychological exoticism, and the sentimental historical novels of southern writers like Augusta Jane Evans Wilson and Caroline Lee Hentz (whose *The Planter's Northern Bride,* 1851, is a slavery-defending riposte to *Uncle Tom's Cabin*).

Though the American realism movement is generally construed as a post–Civil War phenomenon, the Southwest humor of Augustus Baldwin Longstreet (*Georgia Scenes,* 1835) remains vigorously "realistic," even to the point of questioning the moral footings of human nature. Despite his defense of the plantation tradition and ongoing need for social acceptance, from the 1830s until the Civil War William Gilmore Simms demonstrated in his harsh tales of frontier life the kind of particular, concrete detail in character and event that characterizes realism. He was the major antebellum writer in the South, and *The Yemassee* (1835) is arguably still his best work, even though it is not as mindful of realistic detail and character conflict as some of his later efforts.

The Civil War years and aftermath compelled southerners, including southern writers, to sound their own regional identity. Postwar defeat and Reconstruction brought about a re-examination of regional individuality, purpose, and community and, therefore, a shocking reorientation toward the immediate past and future. The heavily stylized conventions of historical romances (for example, Augusta Jane Evans Wilson's *Macaria; or Altars of Sacrifice,* 1864) began to give way to so-called "local color" and the more topical, "realistic" elements found in the humorous sketches of Cable, Twain, and popular late-nineteenth-century writers.

So astonishing was this cultural revaluation that it violated the sentimental complacency of American romanticism even as it validated a more precise, "realistic" depiction of locale. During the war years, George Washington Harris's Sut Lovingood and Charles H. Smith's Bill Arp had satirized Abraham Lincoln. However, the postwar economy encouraged southern writers to be commercially "realistic" as well—that is, to accommodate the tastes of northern buyers. Thus pacific postwar portraits of the South often favored quaint, docile stereotypes, and in the regional fiction of George Washington Cable, Joel Chandler Harris, and Mary Noailles Murfree formula often overwhelms conflict and character. But the later works of Harriette Simpson Arnow, Brainard Cheney, Bowen Ingram, E. P. O'Donnell, Marjorie Kinnan Rawlings, James Still, and Jesse Stuart manage to explore human nature without altogether bowing to formula convention. Re-

gionally distinctive features in the late-nineteenth-century American South enabled a ground swell of writing bound to regional identity. Charles W. Chesnutt bolstered the realistic trend in post–Civil War southern literature with such stories as "The Goophered Grapevine" (1887), a striking account of African American folk in the South, and *The House Behind the Cedars* (1900), a novel rich in psychological observation of mixed-racial culture.

The dominance of the realist movement, especially in the development of the novel, may be measured in part by the ways in which "realistic" is a strongly evaluative as well as descriptive term. But realism is not, in fact, a construct fully divorced from the doctrine of romantic writers who, like William Wordsworth, emphasized the democratic and the "truth of nature" over the lofty and fantastic. The late-eighteenth-century European "romantic" revolt against neoclassicism—the elevation of ordinary people, commonplace events, and native cultural strains—was not an altogether different grounding from the one that shaped the "realist" movement succeeding American romanticism. Nor was it fully distinct from the realist foundation that defined the nineteenth-century realistic novels of George Eliot and other chroniclers of unremarkable, middle-class Victorian life.

Southern realism embraces the work of such writers as George Washington Cable, Kate Chopin, and Ellen Glasgow, but some critics argue that Faulkner's fiction has less claim to the title. In any case, each of these writers points out the exceptions and contradictions implicit in realist practice. Cable often remains realistically faithful to precise detail while romantic in his focus upon outlandish manners, thus in some ways mirroring James, Howells, and the later Wharton's peculiar comedies of manners. Despite her passionate realistic revolt against the triumph of Virginian idealism over the actual, Glasgow's finely crafted and distinctive fiction, just as surely as Chopin's, is sometimes marred by formula closure. The intense social realism of Murfree's (Charles Egbert Craddock's) *In the Tennessee Mountains* (1884) counterbalances its realistic attention to native dialect and particular detail with romantic atmosphere and poetic portrayal of landscape. And although no writer exceeds Faulkner in his realistic depiction of human nature and its attendant depths of conflict, his romantic rhetoric is often closer to the powerful lyrical excesses of Wolfe than to the spare, minimal, and objective nature of conventionally "realistic" rhetoric. Eudora Welty's fiction, too, however realist in dialect and closely observed detail, often prefers the romantic form of the "tale" (sometimes with its attendant elements of "magical realism") to the more realistic "short story."

Beyond the complex romantic-realistic compounds of individual authors, realism, of course, was hardly a monolithic movement. While Glasgow explored critical realism, her contemporary and fellow Richmond native James Branch Cabell dealt in fantastic medieval, romantic comedy. Cabell enjoyed an enthusiastic but short-lived acclaim for his bawdy romantic parody *Jurgen* (1919). Glasgow's nineteen Virginia novels (1897–1941) provided some of the most resonant and measured examples of realism in the first part of the twentieth century.

Much contemporary southern literature falls into the category of realism. One thinks, for instance, of the relatively unmediated prose of Larry Brown, Andre Dubus, and Cormac McCarthy. Or of the psychological and social realism of Richard Ford and Bobbie Ann Mason. Or of the historical novel muted in stark, realistic terms in Rilla Askew's *The Mercy Seat* (1997), Ernest J. Gaines's acclaimed *The Autobiography of Miss Jane Pittman* (1971), and Charles Frazier's popular *Cold Mountain* (1997). Many of these writers—and others, including William Baldwin, Fred Chappell, R. H. W. Dillard, George Garrett, Lewis Nordan, Donald Secreast, as well as Flannery O'Connor and Eudora Welty—are realists nevertheless willing to subvert or distort probability in order to achieve a vivid and sometimes humorous new consciousness in their readers. Thus the boundaries of realism are challenged by a more spiritual conception of the task of the realist, a narrative mindfulness of what will be true at the end of the day and a comprehensive "sense of place" and the human position within it. O'Connor pronounces such a visionary writer a "realist of distance" (*Mystery and Manners*).

The history of southern realism is one of spiritual disenfranchisement, faded ideals, and the transforming power of loss. Southern realism flourishes today precisely because splintered southern roots have spread prolifically through the quantum urge to find new meaning. The southern realist is the gift of catastrophe's counterforce. In the wake of Civil War carnage and in the impotent outrage of Reconstruction, a terrible beauty was born. That displacement and loss were the necessary condition for the sublime power of William Faulkner and for the nightmare of William Tecumseh Sherman out of which Margaret Mitchell, who considered herself a realist, would deliver *Gone With the Wind* (1936).

Robert Gingher

See also Grit Lit; Local Color; Magic Realism; Naturalism; Regionalism; Southwestern Humor.

Jeffrey J. Folks and James A. Perkins, eds., *Southern Writers at Century's End* (1997); Robert Gingher, "The Magic of Southern Guilt," *The World & I* (August 1994); Fred Hobson, *The Southern Writer in the Postmodern World* (1991); David Marion Holman, *A Certain Slant of Light: Regionalism and the Form of Southern and Midwestern Fiction* (1995); Alfred Kazin, *On Native Grounds* (1970); Louis D. Rubin Jr., *The Edge of the Swamp: A Study in the Literature and Society of the Old South* (1989).

REBEL

Just as *Christian* was first used in a derogatory or contemptuous sense but was then accepted by the followers of Christ, so *Rebel* initially had a pejorative meaning but then was assumed by the Confederates as a fit title for themselves. *The Oxford English Dictionary* defines *rebel* as "refusing allegiance or obedience; or offering armed opposition, to the rightful or actual ruler or ruling power of the country." To northerners, the secessionist states were in rebellion and thus became known as the Rebel States, and adherents to the Confederacy were called rebels. Initially, though, according to the former Confederate soldier and writer Basil L. Gildersleeve, "even in the North it was only by degrees that 'reb' replaced 'secesh.' "

Acceptance by southerners of "rebel" is found in "The Good Old Rebel," a literary folk song by James Innes Randolph that begins: "O! I'm a good old rebel, / Now that's just what I am." The southern song "My Love and I" ends: "And keep this wayward reb. from Johnston's Isle." The name is also accepted approvingly in poems such as "Rebel Prisoner," "Rebel Toasts: Or Drink It Down!," "Rebel's Requiem," "Rebel's Retort," and "Rebels"—which begins, "Rebels! 'tis a holy name! / The name our fathers bore." Two representative collections of southern Civil War poetry are named *Rebel Rhymes and Rhapsodies* (1864) and *Rebel Rhymes and Other Poems* (1888).

Fictional treatments of the Civil War by southern writers often use the term *rebel* in casual or approving ways. In *Gone With the Wind*, Rhett Butler calls Scarlett O'Hara "a red-hot little Rebel." In Joel Chandler Harris's *A Little Union Scout,* there is a newspaper called the *Chattanooga Rebel.* Mark Twain in "A Private History of a Campaign that Failed" says, "The secession atmosphere had considerably thickened on the lower Mississippi, and I became a rebel." John Fox in *The Little Shepherd of Kingdom Come* tells about two Dillon twins fighting on opposite sides of the war. One is called Rebel Jerry and the other Yankee Jake. Indeed, through the fiction as well as the nonfictional narratives of the Civil War, soldiers of the opposite sides typically referred to each other as "Rebel" or "Reb" and "Yankee." Their camps were called "rebel camps" or "Yankee camps."

After the war, the name "rebel" or "reb" continued to be used with pride by former Confederates in narratives such as *The Rebel Cousins, or, Life and Love in Secessia* (1864), *Johnny Reb the Confederate* (1869), and *Johnny Reb and Billy Yank* (1905).

Richard D. Rust

See also Civil War.

Bell Irvin Wiley, *The Life of Johnny Reb: The Common Soldier of the Confederacy* (1943).

REBEL YELL

Derived probably from a hunting call, the Rebel yell was a Confederate shout or battle-cry first screamed at First Manassas. Clifford Dowdey in *Bugles Blow No More* (1937) describes it as an "eerie wail," a "high-pitched, long-drawn scream," and a "Valkyrie scream wailed high and thin." Andrew Lytle in *The Long Night* (1936) tells how the shout of the Confederate soldiers "traveled the whole length of the rusty lines, gathering in violence until, shrill and wild, it swept forward through the ravine, cut through the heavy musketry rolling from the opposite ridge and thickets." In *Gone With the Wind* (1936), Margaret Mitchell describes the Rebel yell in this manner: "Stuart Tarleton's voice rose, in an exultant shout, 'Yee-aay-ee!' as if he were on the hunting field." The yell is contrasted with the Yankee hurrah in James Boyd's *Marching On* (1927): "Far to the left they heard the high-pitched southern scream. They heard the sturdy 'h-a-a-a-a' that Yankees gave." William Faulkner in *The Unvanquished* describes it as "high and thin and ragged and

fierce, like when the Yankees used to hear it out of the smoke and the galloping." And in *Absalom, Absalom!,* Faulkner tells how Theophilus McCaslin "cried in his old man's shrill harsh loud cacophonous voice: 'Yaaaay, Forrest! Yaaaay, John Sartoris! Yaaaaaay!' "

In *Bugles Blow No More,* Dowdey describes the effect of the Rebel yell on the Confederates: "Eerie and savage, it wailed through the bedlam and screeched down the spine of the lieutenant. . . . His own men bayed the fierce cry and it tore through his throat." The effect on the opposing forces, according to Henry Steele Commager in *The Blue and the Gray* (1950), was "more overpowering than the cannon's roar." While not overpowered by the Rebel yell, the Union soldier Henry Fleming in Crane's *The Red Badge of Courage* suffers a "faltering intellect" when faced with a "brown swarm of running men who were giving shrill yells." He later faces "the pursuing bark of the enemy's infantry" whose noise is "like the yellings of eager, metallic hounds."

Richard D. Rust

See also Civil War.

H. Allen Smith, *The Rebel Yell, Being a Carpetbagger's Attempt to Establish the Truth Concerning the Screech of the Confederate Soldier* (1954).

RECONSTRUCTION

Although the word *reconstruction* usually carries positive connotations, as a period of American and southern history it describes a distressing and explosive era that would define the course of events in the South long after the official end of Reconstruction in 1877 when the last Federal troops departed from the South. Even as the Civil War was being waged, it was clear that there would need to be "reconstruction" in the South. At war's end, the South was in physical devastation. Most of its major cities lay in ruins; much of the countryside had been scorched as Sherman made his march from Atlanta to the sea. The South's economy was destroyed. Many faced starvation. Sidney Lanier summarized: "Pretty much the whole of life has been merely not dying."

In place of the slave economy, the South soon adopted a system of sharecropping, which in the long run served neither the landowners nor those (both whites and blacks) who contracted to work the land.

Some who were landowners before the war found themselves sharecroppers. When he inaugurated his New Deal, Franklin Roosevelt had mainly the South in mind as he described one-third of the nation as ill-fed, ill-housed, ill-clothed. William Faulkner, who grew up while passions about Reconstruction were strong, depicted the postbellum devastation and its consequences in stories and novels, notably in *The Unvanquished* (1938), *Absalom, Absalom!* (1936), "Wash" (1934), and "Barn Burning" (1939). In *The Hamlet* (1940), his method is more comic, but he makes clear the effect of the peonage system on poor whites, depicting a society that is at heart feudal. In *Uncle Tom's Children* (1938), Richard Wright depicted the effects of the sharecropping system for southern blacks, as Ernest Gaines and other African Americans would later.

Reconstruction was, of course, profoundly political, and in Washington "reconstruction" meant the restoration of the Confederate states to the Union. Lincoln had given much thought to the issue, holding that the southern states had not ever ceased to belong to the Union. He wished to restore them to full power as soon as possible. Had Lincoln lived, the immediate postbellum period would likely have been very different. Although Andrew Johnson tried to implement Lincoln's policies, he (suspect anyway as a southerner) lacked Lincoln's skills of persuasion and was not able to control his own party. The Radical Republicans—dominated by Speaker of the House Thaddeus Stevens of Pennsylvania and Senate Leader Charles Sumner of Massachusetts—were not eager to readmit the southern states; they fought Johnson vigorously and were able to override his vetoes. Near the end of Johnson's term, they succeeded in impeaching him, narrowly failing to remove him from office. Reconstruction was dangerous not only for the South but for the nation as a whole. Had Johnson been removed, historians Samuel Eliot Morison and Henry Steele Commager conclude, the Supreme Court would likely have also submitted, "and the radicals would have triumphed over the Constitution as completely as over the South."

The most significant of the Reconstruction Acts was that of March 2, 1867, which divided the South into five military districts, all subject to martial law. To achieve restoration, the states were required to hold new constitutional conventions (participants to be elected by universal manhood suffrage) and ratify the Fourteenth Amendment, which made the freedmen citizens. The Republicans were fearful of a South that would have the electoral votes to drive them from power. Slaves had counted for only three-fifths as much as whites in apportionment, but the Fifteenth Amendment granted the franchise to *all* male citizens "regardless of previous condition of servitude." The amendment was designed to secure the black vote for the Republican Party. Already in place since March 1865 was the Freedmen's Bureau, created in the War Department to provide relief and guidance for blacks and other refugees. The Bureau had mixed success, but became an easy target for southerners as well as for disaffected northerners.

The former slaves suffered more than any others during Reconstruction. Frederick Douglass declared that the Negro "was free from the individual master but a slave of society. He had neither money, property, nor friends. He was free from the old quarter that once gave him shelter, but a slave to the rains of summer and the frost of winter. He was turned loose, naked, hungry, and destitute to the open sky." In the first two years after the war, thousands of black people died from starvation, disease, and violence. The most fortunate of the newly freed were those who remained on the old plantations. The racial issue was always at the core of Reconstruction problems and policies.

That progress would be difficult was made clear when riots occurred in 1866 in Memphis and in New Orleans. The population of Memphis almost doubled between 1863 and 1865 from an influx of freedmen and immigrants, who competed for jobs. Black troops from Fort Pickering feuded with Irish immigrants. On April 30, four black soldiers mustered out without pay clashed with Irish police, and rioting broke out the next day. Forty-six blacks and two whites lost their lives. On July 1, rioting broke out in New Orleans after Radicals attempted to reconvene the 1864 constitutional convention to enfranchise freedmen and disenfranchise former rebels. Blacks marching to celebrate the reconvening—and any other blacks in sight—were attacked by whites. Thirty-four blacks, three white Radicals, and a rioter shot accidently were killed.

Reconstruction history was readily subsumed under the myth of Reconstruction that portrayed Reconstruction efforts as totally wrong and resulting in state governments (under a Radical Republican majority) composed of Negroes ill-prepared for office, "carpetbaggers" (northerners who had come south to take advantage of a defeated people), and "scalawags" (unscrupulous southerners who had turned against their own people for profit). The myth would be used often in the next hundred years to fight integration. Historians now portray the period as being much more complex. Radical control of the state legislatures varied from state to state. In North Carolina, Democrats regained control by 1870; in South Carolina, the Radicals remained in power until 1877. The new state constitutions proved quite durable. Reconstruction governments began to give attention to public education. African Americans, aided by the Freedmen's Bureau, which established hundreds of schools, made substantial progress in education. Nevertheless, damage to southern morale during Reconstruction was immense. For two generations, the Republican Party would remain an anathema among white southerners. Although African Americans would have to wait many years for anything like the promise of the Fourteenth and Fifteenth Amendments to be realized, Reconstruction had at least put those goals into the Constitution.

Meanwhile, there were high prices for the freed slaves. The Ku Klux Klan, formed in 1866 as a social gathering for former Confederates, evolved into a force to terrorize blacks and enforce white supremacy. The Klan provided ample drama for fiction writers. The protagonist of gentle Thomas Nelson Page's novel *Red Rock* (1898) is a Klansman, and Margaret Mitchell in *Gone With the Wind* (1936) sympathetically portrays Klan origins. Most infamously, Thomas Dixon Jr. glorified the Klan in a series of novels set in the Reconstruction years. His *The Clansman* (1905) became David W. Griffith's film *The Birth of a Nation* (1915), glorifying the Klan for the nation and entrenching the myth of Reconstruction.

Not all white southerners of the Reconstruction era saw the freedmen through the eyes of the Klan. Beginning in the the 1880s, Joel Chandler Harris in his Uncle Remus stories began describing survival techniques of the freedmen in the new regime. In other writings, Harris conveyed more directly his understanding of black-white issues and his sympathy for both white paternalists and freedmen, notably in *The Chronicles of Aunt Minervy Ann* (1899) and *Gabriel Tolliver: A Story of Reconstruction* (1902). Concurrently, in *The Conjure Woman* (1899), African American Charles W. Chesnutt reached large white audiences as he portrayed the intelligence and skill of the freedman in the postbellum years. Also in 1899, Chesnutt published *The Wife of His Youth and Other Stories,* fiction that was more direct in its social criticism. Much later, Ernest Gaines in *The Autobiography of Miss Jane Pittman* (1971) charted African American experience from Civil War through Reconstruction to the Civil Rights Movement.

Judge Albion W. Tourgée from Ohio had been wounded fighting for the Union cause. After the war, he moved to Greensboro, North Carolina, where he worked for Reconstruction measures. Feeling southern resentment, he returned to the North, where he wrote *A Fool's Errand* (1879) and *Bricks Without Straw* (1880), popular novels that portrayed southern mistreatment of northerners. His titles reflect the eventual verdict—North and South—of Reconstruction efforts. In 1888 Tourgée wrote that American literature had become "distinctly Confederate in sympathy."

Louisiana's George Washington Cable was also made to feel uncomfortable in the South because of his positions regarding the region's racial problems, and he spent the last forty years of his life as an exile in Massachusetts. There he wrote *John March, Southerner* (1894), which indicted southern violence, corruption, and ancestor worship in a Reconstruction setting. Cable's essays on civil rights, gathered in *The Silent South* (1885; rev. 1889) and *The Negro Question* (1890) remain strong indictments against racial injustice.

Mary Noailles Murfree was a young girl at the time of Civil War, but she viewed the damage in East Tennessee mountain communities and portrayed the aftermath of the war in her first novel, *Where the Battle Was Fought* (1884). More successfully, Ellen Glasgow portrayed Virginia life during Reconstruction in *The Voice of the People* (1900) and *The Deliverance* (1904). The period would continue to attract southern novelists. Using many historical figures (including General James Longstreet) as characters, Ben Ames Williams portrayed Reconstruction life in New Orleans in *The Unconquered* (1953).

During the war years and the Reconstruction years, the making of literature was not much on the minds of most southerners. Many writers had lost virtually everything that they owned, and publishing outlets in the South had mostly been destroyed. Northern publishers were not seeking contributions from "rebels," but the southern urge to explain its position was strong. Almost immediately, new journals were founded: *Scott's Magazine;* a revived *De Bow's Review; Land We Love; Eclectic,* which in 1868 absorbed *Land We Love* becoming *The New Eclectic* and then *Southern Magazine; Southern Review;* and *The Sunny South.* All were short-lived but met a significant need.

There were other signs of southern resiliency. William Gilmore Simms, who was made destitute by the war, wrote "How Sharp Snaffles Got His Capital and

His Wife" (*Harper's,* 1870), one of the comic master-pieces of the century, suggesting that clever wits and a good heart could win the necessary capital. Sidney Lanier, whose writing years were essentially the years of Reconstruction, quickly wrote his only novel, *Tiger Lilies* (1867), which reflected his own war experiences. Lanier's position was conciliatory, and in the poetry that followed he won the admiration of southerners and northerners alike. George Washington Harris and Charles Smith provided new humorous sketches. John Esten Cooke used his war experiences to provide a series of stirring war novels that portray Stonewall Jackson, J. E. B. Stuart, and other military heroes. Richard Taylor, George Cary Eggleston, and others would meet the growing market for Civil War narrative and commentary. The most significant work to emerge from those who lived through the war and Reconstruction was written by Mary Chesnut, who, as the wife of a Confederate official, was close to the politics of the war and understood its issues better than most. Her journal describing the war years was first published as *A Diary from Dixie* in 1905, some years after her death.

Joseph M. Flora

See also Diaries, Civil War; Lost Cause; Plantation Fiction.

Michael L. Benedict, *Compromise of Principle* (1974); Claude Bowers, *The Tragic Era* (1929); George Washington Cable, *The Silent South* (1885); Hodding Carter, *Angry Scar* (1959); John Hope Franklin, *Reconstruction After the Civil War* (1961); Eric L. McKitrick, *Andrew Johnson and Reconstruction* (1961); Michael Perman, *The Road to Redemption: Southern Politics, 1869–1879* (1984); Kenneth M. Stampp, *The Era of Reconstruction, 1865–1877* (1965); Joel Williamson, *After Slavery: The Negro in South Carolina 1861–1877* (1965); C. Vann Woodward, *Reunion and Reaction* (1956).

REDNECK

Redneck is a derogatory term currently applied to some lower-class and working-class southerners. The term, which came into common usage in the 1930s, is derived from the redneck's beginnings as a "yeoman farmer" whose neck would burn as he or she toiled in the fields. These yeoman farmers settled along the Virginia, North Carolina, and South Carolina coasts. From there they moved inland and west, populating the southern United States. Though always lower-class, some of these farmers were able to rise to planter status and even to own slaves before the Civil War.

During the war, rednecks fought proudly for the South. After the war, they returned to work the land, but then, as they lost their farms and as other opportunities became available, they relinquished their ties to the soil, becoming more associated with work in the industrialized South. Though they began as farm laborers, rednecks are now more likely to work away from the land than southerners known as poor whites.

Rednecks are not necessarily poor and not necessarily farmers, although rednecks certainly can be each of these things. What differentiates rednecks from poor whites is the perception of rednecks as racist, hot-headed, too physical, violent, uncouth, loud, mean, undereducated—and proud of it. The stereotypes follow: Rednecks do not adopt politically correct speech and are proud to be brutally honest about their feelings about nonwhites. Rednecks like to fight to solve their problems, preferring to beat someone at a street dance than to talk about the problem and solve it diplomatically. Rednecks come to the dinner table barefooted not because they have no shoes, but to specifically sneer at rules. Redneck women smoke cigarettes, chew gum, and wear curlers and put on makeup in public. The redneck rebels against education and against standard English, refusing to speak as others would have him or her speak. Rednecks hunt proudly, take baths only occasionally, and work on old cars in their front yards. Rednecks are characterized by excess; they eat too much, drink too much, smoke too much, play too hard, and live too hard. The outsider's perception of all these things differentiates the redneck from the poor white.

This description is not all that rednecks are, however. Robert Penn Warren remarks in his introduction to *All the King's Men* (1946) that the redneck he picks up as a hitchhiker was "aging, aimless, nondescript, beat-up by life and hard times and bad luck, clearly tooth-broke and probably gut-shot. . . . He was, though at the moment I did not sense it, a mythological figure."

Such a figure of mythology a number of southern writers have used in their essays, short stories, and novels. In *Secret History of the Dividing Line* (written c. 1728, published 1841), William Byrd perhaps constructs the first image of the redneck, though the description also fits the definition of poor white. He calls the inhabitants of North Carolina "Lubberlanders," "indolent wretches" who are stupid and lazy.

A similar construction of rednecks as stupid is seen in Old Southwestern humor. In particular, George

Washington Harris's character Sut Lovingood demonstrates how rednecks are ridiculed. Neither Sut nor Sut's language conform to standards in *Sut Lovingood: Yarns Spun by a "Nat'ral Born Durn'd Fool." Warped and Wove for Public Wear* (1867), and Sut is proud of his anti-establishment mentality. This character provided the basis for other redneck characters in the fiction of Mark Twain and William Faulkner.

Mark Twain's *Huckleberry Finn* (1885) shows Huck's father as the classic redneck according to the above definition. His father is violent, poor, greedy, a racial bigot, and a drunkard. Few of the townspeople pity Huck's father because he shows no Christian sensibilities; he does not want to escape the squalor of his life but instead, as a true redneck, he revels in it.

In *Absalom, Absalom!* (1936), William Faulkner uses a redneck character to describe the class structure of the South. Thomas Sutpen, whose goal is to be able to enter the door of the big plantation house and thus enter a higher class, recalls Sut Lovingood.

Perhaps the most famous examples of rednecks, however, are Faulkner's Snopes family, whom he chronicles in *The Hamlet* (1940), *The Town* (1957), and *The Mansion* (1959). Although many members of the Snopes family are tenant farmers, a few have made money, but they are unable move up socially in the southern class system because they do not have it in their "blood." In "Barn Burning" (1939), Abner Snopes's reasons for burning barns is shown as part of his being; burning barns is violent, irrational behavior that comes with being a Snopes family member. Despite the perspective of the outsider telling the story, *The Hamlet* also shows the Snopeses to be uneducated, uncouth, inferior rednecks whose names, such as "Lump" and "Flem," signify their low-class position in southern class structure.

Although Flannery O'Connor wrote frequently about poor white characters, she also wrote about rednecks in her short stories. Mr. Head in her story "The Artificial Nigger," published in *A Good Man Is Hard to Find* (1955), is a benighted, bigoted redneck proud of his ignorance. In the same collection of short stories, O'Connor uses another redneck character—Mr. Shiftlet—to speak philosophical truth in "The Life You Save May Be Your Own" (1955). Also, "The Lame Shall Enter First," published in her collection of short stories entitled *Everything That Rises Must Converge* (1965), demonstrates how do-gooders cannot redeem the redneck's pride in his or her way of life. A redneck boy who is a thief continually reverts to his old criminal ways despite Mr. Sheppard's repeated attempts to "save" the boy. The boy remains proud of his violence against the system that Mr. Sheppard represents.

More recently, Harry Crews has attempted to recover the redneck heritage and describe the anger behind the uncivilized behavior of the redneck. In *The Gospel Singer* (1968), a once-poor family moves into a mansion that the protagonist has been able to buy with his earnings as a gospel singer. The family members do not know the appropriate way to act in such an environment. Without realizing the horrible smell that it leaves in the carpet, the family allows pigs to track through the house. The protagonist of *A Feast of Snakes* (1976), Joe Lon Mackey, demonstrates the violent behaviors associated with the excesses of the redneck way of life. He advocates rounding up the women of his family and beating them simply because they are women.

Barry Hannah has been compared to Faulkner and O'Connor for the subjects he tackles. His novels, including *Ray* (1980), often deal with redneck themes of overactive violence and sexuality. Hannah's main characters are male, and they live hard, and often with an extreme sense of the South's past.

Popular culture also uses the stereotype of the redneck to characterize the South. Modern comedian Jeff Foxworthy uses the stereotype in his stand-up comedy to ridicule rednecks. Although the term is derogatory, the redneck is an important and persistent figure in southern literature and culture, specifically when it comes to describing the complicated class system of the South.

Tena L. Helton

See also Caste; Class; Hillbilly; Poor White; Protest, Novel of; Race Relations; Racism; Sociology of the South; Speech and Dialect; Tenant Farming; Violence; Yeoman.

Blanche Boyd, *The Redneck Way of Knowledge* (1982); Will D. Campbell, "Used and Abused: The Redneck's Lot," in *The Prevailing South: Life and Politics in a Changing Climate,* ed. Dudley Clendinen (1988); Duane Carr, *A Question of Class: The Redneck Stereotype in Southern Fiction* (1996); Myra Jehlen, *Class and Character in Faulkner's South* (1976); Melvyn Stokes and Rick Halpern, *Race and Class in the American South Since 1890* (1994).

REGIONALISM

The concept of *regionalism* has a complex history of double meaning, so attempts to apply the term to studies of southern culture are generally riddled with controversy or qualification. In *Keywords* (1983), Raymond Williams points out that the term *region* came into English from the Latin *regere*—to direct or rule, which implies not only a physical differentiation between two distinct areas, but a political relationship with the "region" being an administered area within a larger political whole. As a cultural term, *regional* is particularly controversial. As Williams explains, it can be used to suggest that a way of life is distinctive and valuable (especially when applied to art, architecture, music, or cooking) but can simultaneously imply subordination or relative inferiority to a dominant culture (as a "regional" accent can imply digression from a "national" or "standard" usage).

There is a similar tension in the use of *regional* as a literary term. "Southern" culture is now a well-defined field of study; organizations such as the Southern Humanities Council and the Society for the Study of Southern Literature boast rapidly growing memberships, and several universities have established centers for the study of southern culture, yet many authors and scholars maintain that the term also implies that southern writing is of less than national importance. This ideological tension derives, in part, from an overlapping of the terms *regional* and *provincial*—the latter connotes, Williams says, cultural inferiority to an assumed metropolitan center and a contrast between sophisticated ideas or tastes and relatively crude and unrefined manners or beliefs.

As the South grows increasingly diverse, its geographic, economic and cultural differences have led to a fracturing of the region into "subregions"—or as Joseph Flora and Robert Bain explain in *Contemporary Fiction Writers of the South,* "eight Souths—(1) the Tidewater, (2) the Piedmont, (3) Appalachia, (4) the Deep South, (5) the Upland South, (6) the Southwest, (7) the Catholic and Cajun country of New Orleans and environs, and (8) central and west Georgia, north Florida, and parts of south Alabama. No sharp boundary lines demarcate these Souths; they always fade into one another. But the distinctions are discernible in the geography and in the fiction that arises from each region." This fracturing renders the application of the term *regional* to a particular area or culture all the more complex.

The multiple assumptions underlying the term *regionalism* have thus made it difficult for scholars to demarcate the South either geographically or ideologically, yet the strong sense of southern identity is

nationally acknowledged to be both politically influential and artistically fertile. Cultural historians have suggested both physical displacement and ideological difference as the originating ground for southern regional-identity formation. Some scholars point to the early southern colonists' sense of alienation from European civilization and their desire to protest European domination. Others maintain that a sense of collective regional indignation developed in response to the northern repudiation of slavery in a plantation economy, the defeat of the Confederacy, the shared humiliation of Reconstruction, and the pressures of racial division. Postmodern theorists argue that southern regionalism can only be understood as a social construction, an attempt to invent (or reinvent) a mythic or redemptive regional identity in response to negative narratives imposed by other regions and/or accommodated from within the region.

The future of southern studies has been much debated, given American trends toward cultural homogenization and the complexities associated with the concept of regionalism. Although southern regionalism continues to be regarded as a valuable heritage by some and as a mythical allegiance by others, there is general agreement that regionalism vitally informs identity for many southerners. As John Lowe writes in his introduction to *The Future of Southern Letters* (1996), the South's dependence on regional identity gives it "a unique appeal and an opportunity to mount messages of national concern through compelling regional metaphor and narrative." As long as the concept of regionalism exists in the South "as both a legacy and a challenge, there will always be a future for southern letters."

Donnalee M. Frega

Jefferson Humphries and John Lowe, eds., *The Future of Southern Letters* (1996); Lewis P. Simpson, "The State of Southern Literary Scholarship," *Southern Review* 24:2 (Spring 1988); Raymond Williams, *Keywords: A Vocabulary of Culture and Society* (1983).

RELIGION IN NINETEENTH-CENTURY LITERATURE

Since colonial times, evangelical Christianity—the "old-time religion"—has played a significant role in shaping southern history, culture, and literature. Like issues of race and a sense of place, religious thought and tradition have exerted a profound influence on the lives and imaginative works of southerners. The effect of southern religion on the region's literature had its origins in the South's unique history of close ties to the land, of slavery, of defeat and occupation in war, and in its identification with the wandering history of the Old Testament Israelites, and particularly, as Flannery O'Connor wrote, with "the Hebrew Old Testament penchant for making the absolute concrete."

According to Charles R. Wilson, the distinguishing features of this evangelical tradition are its strict adherence to biblical teachings and private morality; the notion of a real and active presence of God and Satan, or good and evil, in the world; the belief in a factual existence of heaven and hell; and an emphasis on preaching the Gospel and saving souls. Influential Calvinistic doctrines of the absolute sovereignty of God and the essential depravity of the human soul, salvation by grace alone, and the impenetrability of Divine Will helped form the foundation of mainstream southern religious belief.

The influence of religious belief and practice on the literary imagination has its historical origins in a close agrarian community centered on a church. Doris Betts has pointed out that historically, southern children were immersed daily in hearing ancient tales, rich in symbol and archetype, of bliss, sin, guilt, and redemption from the Old and New Testaments. In the nineteenth and twentieth centuries, much of this experience might have occurred in tent revivals, camp meetings, hell-fire preaching and revivals, snake-handling services, or shape-note sings; or more likely, then as now, in prayer meetings, church or Sunday school, or in vacation Bible school. Whether one attended church or not, Bible stories were woven into everyday experience; they informed the world view of all, believers and nonbelievers alike.

As the Deep South transformed from frontier to civilized society between 1790 and 1830, settlers migrated south and west from the thirteen colonies toward the Mississippi River. They brought with them a fierce and fundamental Bible-based religious fervor that expressed itself in the building of churches, regular preaching by those "called," Christian rituals at regular meetings, and evangelical soul-saving at services and brush-arbor or camp meetings. Literary humorists of the time poked fun at the fervor and hypocrisy of the religious figures: Sut Lovingood, one of George Washington Harris's characters, hates circuit riders almost as much as he does shotguns, having been (one infers)

on the receiving end of both; Simon Suggs outwits the Reverend Bela Bugg by managing to spirit away the collection plate at a camp meeting. In *Adventures of Huckleberry Finn* (1885), Mark Twain depicts a large camp meeting that Huck and "the King" witness, revealing the pretentiousness, hypocrisy, and romanticized sentimentality of the religious practice of his times. Twain became more pessimistic about religion at the turn of the century, when he penned some of his darkest works, notably *The Man Who Corrupted Hadleyburg* (1900) and *The Mysterious Stranger* (1916).

Although the evangelical strain of Protestantism might be said to be predominant, other strains and variants of religious theology, belief, and practice have been important influences in southern history and everyday life. Black theology developing in the nineteenth century tended to emphasize a more joyful focus on the glories of the hereafter. Focus was shifted away from the fiery punishments of hell and toward the Savior's loving care for each soul. Black religion constituted an authentic and influential variant of prevailing white religion and included the development of an empowering element of social and political responsibility and the nurturing of a rhetorical tradition through sermons that had a distinct influence on the imaginations of southern writers of both white and African American traditions.

For Frederick Douglass, "the religion of the south is a mere covering for the most horrid crimes." Of all the slaveholders he had met in his life, Douglass decrees the religious slaveholders to be the worst. He tells the story of one of his masters, Thomas Auld, who repeatedly whipped a young lame female slave and justified his acts with the Scriptural passage, "He that knoweth his master's will, and doeth it not, shall be beaten with many stripes" (Luke 12:47). In the appendix to his *Narrative*, Douglass clarifies his views on Christianity. His comments apply specifically to the "slaveholding religion" of the South (and, by association, of a guilty North as well). He finds "the widest possible difference" between the religion of his land and the true "Christianity of Christ." For Douglass, Christianity and slavery are diametrically opposed. The ideal of Christianity and his experience as a slave of the corrupt real practices of the "faithful" are irreconcilable. His appendix ends with a parody of the popular southern hymn, "Holy Union," an attack in verse on the hypocrisy of the southern clergy.

At evangelical revivals, whether Presbyterian, Baptist, or Methodist, large numbers of slaves converted to an essentially Armenian Christianity, characterized by the idea that God would save those who accepted Him. Even for worship, however, slaves were forbidden to hold unauthorized or unsupervised meetings. Thus their services or prayer meetings, when planned, were held in secret, hidden areas, often called "hush-harbors." And though their praise was traditionally vocal and expressive, in the harbors slaves used various methods to keep meetings quiet and avoid white patrols. One expression of black faith, the spiritual, was a sacred song that crossed into the slaves' secular lives, being sung at work as much as in the church. The antiphonal structure of the spirituals—the African tradition of call and response—engaged the participants in constant dialogue with the community, allowing the opportunity for communal resistance to the slaveowners. In the spirituals, the self-image as "the chosen people" and an intimacy with God are prominent themes. Negating their own present, they focused on the future: God's judgment. Slave spirituals were characterized not by despair or personal unworthiness, but by change, confidence, and personal value.

Imaginative southerners throughout the region's history have been both drawn and repelled by this potent cultural heritage fraught with painful contradictions between the Calvinistic concern for the state of one's soul and traditions of slavery, violence, and frontier independence. Their attempts to deal with this cultural heritage have resulted in some of the region's best fiction. On the one hand, it provided for the writer a sustaining sense of kinship, identity, community, and continuity; on the other, the region's legacies were violence, slavery, poverty, bigotry, and defeat. As a result, Robert Penn Warren was able to say without hyperbole that the southern novelist of his time and earlier has been concerned with nothing less than the individual soul's "salvation or loss to eternity."

Susan Ketchin and Lucinda H. MacKethan

See also African American Spirituals; Bible; Bible Belt; Douglass, Frederick; Twain, Mark.

Susan Ketchin, *The Christ-Haunted Landscape: Faith and Doubt in Southern Fiction* (1994); Lawrence W. Levine, *Black Culture and Black Consciousness: Afro-American Folk Thought from Slavery to Freedom* (1977).

RELIGION IN TWENTIETH-CENTURY LITERATURE

The strong evangelical flavor of the early southern experience carried over into the literary expression of the twentieth century. Many notable southern writers in the first half of the twentieth century, including James Weldon Johnson (*God's Trombones: Seven Negro Sermons in Verse,* 1927), Zora Neale Hurston (*Their Eyes Were Watching God,* 1937), William Faulkner, Caroline Gordon, and Allen Tate, were intrigued by a sense of their homeland as a region of spiritual paradox, fevered and complex, rich in literary possibilities. Robert Brinkmeyer writes in *Three Catholic Writers of the South* that much of the great fiction we have come to associate with the southern literary landscape of the early to middle part of the twentieth century can be understood to have resulted from the tension between the writer's changing culture and self, between one's cultural imperatives and one's private vision.

In his autobiography *Black Boy* (1945), Richard Wright's assessment of his boyhood church's relentless attempts to save souls for Christ was conclusive; in Wright's words, it regarded "no ethics or boundaries; every area of human relationships was exploited." In contrast to Wright's scathing criticism, Zora Neale Hurston's *Their Eyes Were Watching God* offers a joyous celebration of spiritual and physical life and community through the eyes of Janie, a questing hero who seeks and in the end learns the two things everyone must do: go to God and find out about living for oneself.

William Faulkner explores humanity's yearning for God in several works. Whether or not Faulkner embraced a system of religious beliefs, he recognized and examined religion as a pervasive cultural force acting upon the individual in paradoxical ways. In his work, religion sometimes brings the human spirit closer to the Divine, and conversely, it reinforces human depravity and enables suffering and evil in its name. In *The Sound and the Fury* (1929), he explores the elevating and transformative nature of religious experience through the Reverend Shegog's sermon on Easter Sunday and Dilsey's quiet renewal. In *Light in August* (1932), Christianity forbids rather than fosters life; Reverend Hightower, Percy Grimm, and their community act in service of the chief agents of unremitting pain and crucifixion.

Biblical structures, language, and symbols abound in Faulkner's oeuvre. Notably, Sutpen's struggles in *Absalom, Absalom!* (1936) to impose order on the wilderness chaos, like Adam's in the Judeo-Christian creation myth, are sabotaged by his own "purblind innocence." The death and celebration of Joe Christmas in chapter 19 of *Light in August* echo in language and

theme John 19, in which Christ's crucifixion is recounted. One of Faulkner's later works, *A Fable*
(1954), can be read as an extended parallel to the life
of Christ, but with conclusions or meanings essentially
quite different from orthodox belief; for Faulkner, one
can only discover what one knows and believes, what
the implications of that belief are, in terms of one's
own humanity and one's relationship with the community. One bears witness, Faulkner seems to say, for the
sake of one's self and one's community, not to or for
God.

Richard P. Adams observed that the story of the
Passion Week is so tightly woven into all of Faulkner's
work that we can almost consider it a statement of his
belief and practice. The drunken Dawson Fairchild in
Mosquitoes (1927) describes Genius, the act of creating, as constituting "the Passion Week of the heart."
Evans Harrington suggests that Faulkner's creative genius came from the Creator, and that the nature of that
genius may be the act of seeing into the heart of things
and realizing this vision into an integral, balanced,
beautiful whole.

Walker Percy and Flannery O'Connor are generally
held to be those major southern writers whose religious
visions most directly and thoroughly inform their artistic works, essays, and fiction. Walker Percy was raised
from the time he was ten years old by his uncle Will
Percy, in Greenville, Mississippi, after the death by suicide of his father and the accidental drowning of his severely depressed mother. After medical school, tuberculosis kept Percy from practicing medicine, but during
his recovery Percy read widely in philosophy, theology,
and language theory. In his mid-thirties, he married
and converted to Catholicism and then began to write,
publishing essays and his first novel, *The Moviegoer*
(1961), which won the National Book Award. In *The
Moviegoer*, Binx Bolling, having returned spiritually
shattered from the Korean War, undertakes a search
for meaning in a morally bankrupt society, contriving
in the end a stoic, Kierkegaardian-like leap of faith into
marriage with his cousin Kate, a fellow seeker and fugitive from modernity. In *The Last Gentleman* (1966),
The Second Coming (1980), and *Lost in the Cosmos*
(1983), Percy heralded his concern with the spiritual
bankruptcy of language and the need for the artist to
create an entirely new language, one adequate to deal
with matters beyond reason and words.

Flannery O'Connor, perhaps more fully and more
boldly than any other modern American writer, has
wrought an outstanding, serious body of literary work
out of a profound and fully developed religious sensibility. O'Connor understood from an early age that her
life and work were cast in the context of a larger reality, expressed in orthodox Catholicism. She was firmly
rooted in the Deep South, yet as a Catholic she was
somewhat of an outsider. Her outsider status, coupled
with severe physical limitations (she was diagnosed
with what was to be a fatal form of lupus in early
adulthood and died when she was thirty-nine years old,
in 1964), infused her literary imagination with both a
particular and a transcendent quality, an immediacy
and at the same time a deep sense of the Eternal.

O'Connor engaged in the discussion of her art and
belief in a series of essays, lectures, and letters published both before and after her death. The major prose
pieces, selected and edited by Robert and Sally Fitzgerald, appear in *Mystery and Manners: Occasional Prose*
(1969); her letters were collected and edited with an introduction by Sally Fitzgerald as *The Habit of Being*
(1979). In describing this ongoing creative tension between her identities as a southerner and a Catholic,
O'Connor wrote, "The writer must wrestle with it like
Jacob with the angel until he has extracted a blessing."
O'Connor saw her fiction and world view as set apart
from secular society. She adopted the rich detail of
landscape and a fierce, incisive study of southern manners as necessary and rich embodiments of invisible
spiritual truths, which comprise the mystery of human
and divine experience.

In her first short-story collection, *A Good Man Is
Hard to Find* (1955), and in *Everything That Rises
Must Converge*, published posthumously in 1965, as
well as in her novels *Wise Blood* (1952) and *The Violent Bear It Away* (1960), resistance to spiritual illumination or redemption is characteristic of all the main
characters. The most active resisters seem to be Francis
Marion Tarwater, the young backwoods prophet of
The Violent Bear It Away, and Hazel Motes, of *Wise
Blood*, who seeks perversely to found the Church
Without Christ. Hazel is pursued relentlessly by the
wild, ragged figure of Christ moving from tree to tree,
motioning to him (and to the reader) to come into the
dark. In "A Good Man Is Hard to Find," the grandmother requires the death grip of the theologically sophisticated sociopath in order to be shocked into enlightenment, as she arguably finds redemption at the
instant of her death (she cries that even the Misfit is
connected to her, and he recoils at this truth and kills
her). When he remarks, "She would have been a good
woman if it had been someone to shoot her every min-

ute of her life," the Misfit echoes the truth of human-kind's propensity toward spiritual hard-headedness, deafness, and blindness.

The modern South, along with the rest of the country, has, since the 1950s and 1960s, become an increasingly secular and technological society. As the Agrarians warned in several essays of *I'll Take My Stand* (1930), in such a burgeoning materialist-modernist culture, the cherished old-time values of family, community, and place threaten to be eroded. A pervasive sense of the absurdity of human existence seems to have informed recent literature of the South as well. The political and social changes of the 1960s created a watershed in southern thought. After the Vietnam War and the sweeping changes of the Civil Rights Movement, old assumptions of the defeated tragic South were seriously challenged. As Fred Hobson asks (in *The Southern Writer in the Postmodern World*, 1991), what was the writer of the 1970s and 1980s to do with a suddenly "Superior South"—the optimistic, forward-looking Sunbelt, now threatening to become more prosperous and politically powerful than the declining industrial Northeast or other parts of the country?

Success, it seems, would require new voices, and less reliance on or obsession with the past. Today, the southern writer, like other contemporary American writers, must grapple with age-old human yearnings in a postmodern world, in which matters of structure and meaning, old assumptions of the world, of humankind, of language, and of belief are constantly being called into question.

Religion, experienced indirectly and directly, still plays an important role, despite profound cultural changes, in shaping the literary imaginations of contemporary southern writers. Though the South may increasingly resemble the rest of the country, Flannery O'Connor's notion of the "Christ-haunted" South still holds true in the literary achievements of a significant body of southern writers. For contemporary writers, religious culture remains of crucial importance. Religion has served for some as a prism through which to interpret human experience, for others as a target for satire. Southern writers concerned with religion today represent a broad spectrum of belief and artistic sensibility from avowed belief to profound skepticism, from fascination to anguished struggle. For Reynolds Price, Doris Betts, Mary Ward Brown, Vicki Covington, Will Campbell, and others, an essential purpose of writing fiction is to seek to understand the deepest mysteries of human and divine existence. For others, such as Sheila

Bosworth, Larry Brown, Mary Hood, William Styron, and Fred Chappell, archetypal biblical stories and themes provide powerful structures and continually resonant imagery for writing about what is of ultimate importance.

Born and raised a Catholic in New Orleans, educated by nuns, Sheila Bosworth (*Almost Innocent*, 1984; *Slow Poison*, 1992) wrestles with basic tenets of her faith but sees Catholicism's institutions and symbols as invaluably rich sources that inform and enrich her fiction. Larry Brown says of his fiction, "I write about people proceeding out from calamity. . . . These people are aware of their need for redemption." Drawing on potent blends of Calvinism, folk religion, voodoo, African traditions, and their evangelical or Pentecostal upbringing, Randall Kenan, Alice Walker, Sandra Hollin Flowers, and numerous African American writers deal with ambiguities and tensions in their religious or spiritual culture and their imaginative visions by creating fresh ways of seeing entrenched symbols and institutions. Often, a pantheon of spirits might work as forces for good or evil in the modern, everyday world, as in Kenan's *A Visitation of Spirits* (1989); perhaps an infusion or triumph of Spirit might come, not so much through argument or intellect, but through a more primal, less controllable source—music, as in Flowers's fine short story "Hope of Zion."

Irony and satirical humor, a distinct and distinguished characteristic of southern literature as a whole, plays a significant role in the contemporary southern writers' grappling with often painful gaps between their imaginative and religious ideals and visions and rude, even violent, experience. Such irony is the result of these authors' caring deeply about the traditions that nurtured them and of their commitment to the truths that seem to be in direct conflict with those traditions. In the rich tradition of Mark Twain, William Faulkner, Flannery O'Connor, and others, Allan Gurganus, Clyde Edgerton, Harry Crews, Steve Stern, and Lee Smith create finely tuned comic satire and highly textured portraits of place, manners, and character. Harry Crews's and Cormac McCarthy's theological visions are equally intense, yet also much more violent. All of these contemporary writers take the spiritual truths embodied in their religious upbringing seriously and find their misuse or abuse quite painful. Yet for all their wit, brutality, or outrageousness, they ask the same serious question that O'Connor's Misfit did: What would happen if one actually took to heart what the Bible tells us, such as the prophecies of Isaiah, or the New Testament's Resurrection?

Although they have explored profoundly differing visions of the meaning of spirituality, these writers have lived lives of passionate love for the Word, whether as revealed in sacred scripture or coming from their own hearts, and for the compelling power of storytelling, which they have taken to be their art. They, like their predecessors, are determined to develop and maintain the artistic integrity of their literary vision and work, and they are, as O'Connor described herself a generation ago, "very much concerned with matters of the Spirit."

Susan Ketchin

See also Baptists; Bible Belt; Episcopalians; O'Connor, Flannery; Pentecostals; Presbyterians; Roman Catholics.

Doreen Fowler and Ann J. Abadie, eds., *Faulkner and Religion* (1991); Fred Hobson, *The Southern Writer in the Postmodern World* (1991); Susan Ketchin, *The Christ-Haunted Landscape: Faith and Doubt in Southern Fiction* (1994); Flannery O'Connor, *Mystery and Manners*, ed. Sally and Robert Fitzgerald (1969); Louis D. Rubin Jr., *A Gallery of Southerners* (1982).

REVIEWER

Established in 1921 by members of the Richmond, Virginia, Writers Club who desired to continue their literary careers when the *Evening Journal* ceased publication in September 1920, the *Reviewer* became a respected literary publication through the efforts of its editors, Hunter Stagg and Emily Clark, to develop a sophisticated Continental character for the magazine. Novelist Joseph Hergesheimer and New York avant-garde leader Carl Van Vechten became interested in the *Reviewer* and solicited articles from such writers as H. L. Mencken, whose essay "The Sahara of the Bozart" was reviewed in the magazine's first issue. Mencken influenced Clark and Stagg to attack the old sentimental school of southern literature and to publish the new southern voices.

When asked to edit the three issues of Volume II of the little magazine, novelist James Branch Cabell chose to blend the works of established writers Ellen Glasgow, Mary Johnston, Robert Nathan, and John Galsworthy with younger southerners, including Paul Green, Allen Tate, Josephine Pinckney, Frances New-

man, and DuBose Heyward, to advance the cause of new southern writing.

Throughout its four-year existence, the *Reviewer* suffered financial problems that led to disagreements between Richmond contributors and the editors regarding the publication policy. Finally, in 1924, Paul Green, with the blessing of Stagg and Clark, undertook to edit the *Reviewer* from Chapel Hill, North Carolina, hoping to ensure its iconoclastic character. However, financial setbacks led to the magazine's demise in 1925, one year after Green became editor.

While it remained in publication, the little magazine served to brighten the literary scene in Richmond and to provide publishing opportunities for writers and critics whose works were contributing to a renascence of southern literature.

Bes Stark Spangler

See also Literary Magazines of the Present; Richmond, Virginia; "Sahara of the Bozart."

Emily Clark, *Innocence Abroad*, (1931).

REVOLUTIONARY WAR (AMERICAN)

The literature and the literary sensibilities of the Revolutionary period in the southern states reflect the secularization of the national mission and echo an insistence on the provincial and individual rights valued in the earliest southern settlements. As in the rest of the colonies, a faith in natural law and human reason triumphed over Puritan myths of a God-centered, predestined, New-World Israel, but the writing of the Revolutionary generation in the South reflected long-standing faith in the potential for political and economic justice. Thus southern rhetoric during America's war for freedom reflected a rational rather than a theological mandate, and the design of the subsequent Golden Age owed more to the ideals of ancient Greek and Roman civilization than to biblical typology. Ironically, though, the language of emotion, not reason, rings strong in many southern claims for freedom.

Virginia initiated its pamphlet war in the early 1760s when Richard Bland (called the finest belletristic writer in colonial America), Landon Carter, and Patrick Henry declared that they would not be taxed unfairly for any institution, especially the established church. At the same time, strong Tory voices, such as clergymen Jonathan Boucher in Maryland, John Camm in Virginia, and George Micklejohn in North Carolina, defended both English political and church primacy. Middle-of-the-roaders like Daniel Dulany of Maryland and John J. Zubly of Georgia refused to go all the way to independence.

The Revolution and the Constitution were prepared by a remarkable group of southerners, most of them planters, who published books, pamphlets, and scores of newspaper essays copied all over this country and Europe. Hermon Husband of North Carolina was a successful lawyer turned essayist. Christopher Gadsden and Henry Laurens of South Carolina were merchants. David Ramsay was a physician. Charles Carroll and Daniel Dulany of Maryland had the best professional educations Europe offered. Carter Braxton, Richard Bland, and Landon Carter were educated in plantation libraries. Maurice Moore of North Carolina was an able member of a prominent family. Thomas Jefferson and James Madison were educated at William and Mary and Princeton and were veteran legislators. Jefferson's "A Summary View of the Rights of the British America" convinced his colleagues that Jefferson was the man to write the Declaration of Independence—which Carl Becker in *The Declaration of Independence: A Study in the History of Political Ideas* (1942) considers a literary masterpiece.

The most noteworthy southern poetry of the Revolutionary War period is by St. George Tucker of Williamsburg. Some of his poetry became martial songs. The "best plotted and most finished of the dramas of these times," according to Lewis Leary, was *The Patriots* (1776) by Colonel Robert Munford of Virginia. An anonymous Tory drama just prior to the war was *A Dialogue Between a Southern Delegate and His Spouse on His Return from the Grand Continental Congress* (1774). Drama was discouraged, however, by Congress—which in 1778 passed a resolution for suppressing "theatrical entertainments."

When considering nineteenth-century southern fiction about the Revolutionary War, one thinks immediately of William Gilmore Simms. His first of eight novels about the Revolutionary War was *The Partisan: A Romance of the Revolution* (1835), in which the hero, Major Robert Singleton, is involved in the South Carolina guerrilla campaign with Francis Marion, the "Swamp Fox." *Mellichampe, A Legend of the Santee* (1836) was, in Simms's words, "a sort of continuation of, but not a sequel" to *The Partisan*. Next came *The Kinsmen, or, The Black Riders of Congaree* (1841), re-

issued as *The Scout* (1854). *Katharine Walton, or, The Rebel of Dorchester, an Historical Romance of the Revolution in Carolina* (1851) continued the story of the Waltons and Major Singleton from *The Partisan*. *The Sword and the Distaff* (1852), later revised as *Woodcraft* (1856), recounts the British evacuation of Charleston. *The Forayers; or, The Raid of the Dog-days* (1855) was followed by *Eutaw, A Sequel to The Forayers* (1856), set at the 1781 Battle of Eutaw Springs. *Joscelyn: A Tale of the Revolution in Georgia* (1867) was initially published in serial form and now appears in the University of South Carolina Press series Simms Revolutionary War Novels (1975–).

Contemporary with Simms, John Pendleton Kennedy wrote a popular historical romance, *Horse-Shoe Robinson* (1835), based on the true story of a South Carolina veteran of the war. Other nineteenth-century novels about the war include *Marion's Brigade* (1852) by John Hovey Robinson; *The Rivals; A Tale of the Times of Aaron Burr and Alexander Hamilton* (1860) by Alabama senator Jeremiah Clemens; *Canoilles: The Fortunes of a Partisan of '81* (1877) by John Esten Cooke, better known for his Civil War novels; and *Lang Syne; or, The Wards of Mount Vernon; A Tale of the Revolutionary Era* (1889) by Mary Stuart Smith. George Cary Eggleston, best known for his memoir *A Rebel's Recollections* (1874), wrote *A Carolina Cavalier; A Romance of the American Revolution* (1901). James Boyd's *Drums* (1925), about North Carolinian Johnny Fraser, has been called by *New York Post* reviewer E. C. Beckwith "the finest novel of the American Revolution which has yet been written." Also worthy of notice are LeGette Blythe's *Alexandriana* (1940); Inglis Fletcher's *Toil of the Brave* (1946) and *Wicked Lady* (1962), as part of her Carolina Series; Harriette Arnow's *The Kentucky Trace: A Novel of the American Revolution* (1974); Alton L. Dowd's *Deep River: The Story of a Man and His Family During the American Revolution* (1977); and Cameron Judd's *The Border Men: A Novel of the Tennessee Frontier, 1778–1783* (1992).

The Revolution is the subject of Paul Green's symphonic dramas, *The Highland Call: A Symphonic Drama of the Revolutionary War Among the Cape Fear Valley Scots* (first produced in 1939), *The Common Glory* (produced 1947, published 1948), and *Faith of Our Fathers: A Symphonic Drama of George Washington and the Revolutionary War* (first produced 1950). LeGette Blythe also wrote a symphonic drama,

First in Freedom (first produced in Charlotte, North Carolina, in 1975).

Joseph T. Cox and Richard D. Rust

RICHMOND, VIRGINIA

Since Richmond was designated the capital of Virginia in 1779, its literary culture has varied markedly, from commonplace provincialism to national prominence. At the beginning of the nineteenth century, the city was home to a preeminent literary figure, William Wirt (1772–1834), author of the popular *Letters of the British Spy* (1803) and *Sketches of the Life and Character of Patrick Henry* (1817).

In 1834 Richmond contributed to the burgeoning field of new American literary magazines with *The Southern Literary Messenger*. Its owner, Thomas W. White (1788–1843), was aided by the novelists Nathaniel Beverley Tucker (1784–1851) and James Ewell Heath (1792–1862). Heath was succeeded as editor by Edgar Allan Poe, who in little more than a year increased circulation almost seven-fold. Although brief, Poe's association with the *Messenger* brought enhancement to the magazine, to his reputation, and to the literary importance of the city. The *Messenger* would continue under such literary figures as John Reuben Thompson (1823–1873) and George W. Bagby (1828–1883).

Following the Civil War, the literary vitality of Richmond suffered along with that of the South in general. This was a period represented by rather lackluster verse and by the popular fiction of Thomas Nelson Page (1853–1922), the lawyer/diplomat who wrote nostalgically about life in antebellum Virginia in such volumes as *In Ole Virginia* (1887) and *Befo' de War* (1888). But even as Page was idealizing the recent past, a new literary community was forming. By the turn of the century, Richmond was home to three young writers whose accomplishments and influence would elevate the city's literary reputation above any level it had reached in the past. They were Ellen Glasgow (1873–1945), James Branch Cabell (1879–1958), and Mary Johnston (1870–1936).

Glasgow, author of a multivolume fictional saga of the Old Dominion from the Civil War to the eve of World War II, would win the Howells Medal and the Pulitzer Prize for Fiction (for *In This Our Life*, 1941). Cabell's sophisticated, satirical allegories (e.g., *Jurgen*, 1919) earned him a national reputation during the 1920s. Both authors were recognized as innovators who broke out of the now-moribund "moonlight and magnolia" fictional mold. Their work was expressed in new voices at once distinctive and more critical. Even Johnston, although best known for historical romances (e.g., *To Have and to Hold*, 1900), was praised for her historical authenticity and for treating such issues as women's suffrage and feminism.

By 1918 a group of local Richmond writers, with Cabell as first president, founded the Virginia Writers' Club, which still meets today. Several members of the club, operating more on enthusiasm than on sound finances, founded the *Reviewer* (1921–1925), one of the numerous "little" magazines of the period. Thanks to advice and contributions from Cabell, Glasgow, H. L. Mencken, Joseph Hergesheimer, Gertrude Stein, Frances Newman, and John Galsworthy, among others, the magazine was international in scope and enjoyed a relatively long life span. Today, the *New Virginia Review*, published in Richmond, continues its traditions.

The fact that the zenith of literary life in Richmond came during the first three decades of the twentieth century indicates the important role that the city and its authors played in the southern literary renascence.

Richmond has been depicted in the work of a number of authors of fiction and nonfiction over the years. Two distinctive, if very different, representations are those found in the diaries of William Byrd II (1674–1744) (Byrd established the city in the mid-1730s) and in the later novels of Ellen Glasgow (e.g., *The Sheltered Life*, 1932, and *Vein of Iron*, 1935), where it is called "Queenborough" and given a rather detailed portrayal.

Welford Dunaway Taylor

See also Literary Magazines; Realism; Southern Renascence; Virginia, Literature of.

Virginius Dabney, *Richmond: The Story of a City* (1976); Maurice Duke and Daniel P. Jordan, eds., *A Richmond Reader, 1733–1983* (1983); Samuel Mordecai, *Richmond in By-Gone Days* (1860); Louis D. Rubin Jr., *No Place on Earth* (1959).

RIVERS

"Scene: Of the Mississippi the bank sinister, and of the Ohio the bank sinister." In these words, John Crowe Ransom delineates the boundaries of the South in the telling epigraph to his poem "Antique Harvesters" (1927). Thus do the left banks of two mighty American rivers form the boundaries of the "sinister" South, in Ransom's ironic vision. The Mississippi, thanks primarily to Mark Twain and William Faulkner, but also because of Louisiana writers such as George Washington Cable and Kate Chopin, and to the Yankee trespasser, Harriet Beecher Stowe, is the South's most storied river. "Old Muddy" is most notable in the American imagination for its southern stretch, flowing downward from St. Louis, past Memphis, Natchez, and Vicksburg, to New Orleans. The mansions that sit high above its banks, the paddleboats, skiffs, rafts, and steamboats that glide through its waters, the levees that attempt to check its wanderings, the Delta that owes black, rich soil to its sediment, form the Mississippi River settings of much of the Lower South's most distinctive literature. The Ohio belongs as well to a uniquely southern literary mythology of boundaries, thanks to many slave narratives and to Stowe's famous scene of Eliza crossing its ice to freedom in *Uncle Tom's Cabin* (1851). Other rivers, such as the Yazoo and Tallahatchee (Mississippi), the Chattahoochee (Georgia), the Eno (North Carolina), the Suwannee (Florida), the Rappahannock (Virginia), the Waccamaw (South Carolina), and the Coosa (Alabama), among others, told stories and became songs simply by their names.

The earliest river to be of any great importance to southern culture and literature, not surprisingly, is the James, flowing past Richmond, Virginia, and the great eighteenth-century plantations lining its route toward the colonial jewel of Williamsburg: Evelynton, Berkeley, Carter's Grove, and William Byrd's Westover form a home base for much cavalier literature. So symbolic was the James River, by the mid-nineteenth century synonymous with the idyll of a simple and gracious early South, that John Pendleton Kennedy set his prototypical plantation novel, *Swallow Barn* (1832), along its banks. Navigable and hospitable rivers, more essential to the South than the North for commerce, transportation, and culture through the Civil War era, were the lifeline of the region's important nineteenth-century cities. In addition to the many cities that were built along the Mississippi, there came into being Richmond on the James; Wilmington and Fayetteville on the Cape Fear; Charleston on the Ashley and Cooper; Savannah and Augusta on the Savannah; Jacksonville on the St. John's; Alexandria and Georgetown on the Potomoc; Asheville on the French Broad; Nashville on the Cum-

berland; Knoxville and Chattanooga on the Tennessee; Columbus, Georgia, on the Chattahoochee; Macon on the Ocmulgee; and Montgomery and Selma on the Alabama.

Rivers are important purely in relation to the geography of the literary South, but they have provided several recurring plot and theme lines as well. Mark Twain made the most of the Mississippi as a symbol of freedom and escape from civilization with the incomparable *Adventures of Huckleberry Finn* (1885) and his autobiographical testimony in *Life on the Mississippi* (1883). William Alexander Percy's *Lanterns on the Levee* (1941) celebrates the romantic quality of the old river plantation culture in his autobiography of his homeplace, Greenville, Mississippi. River floods have made for high drama, in stories such as Cable's "Belle Demoiselles Plantation" and Robert Penn Warren's "Blackberry Winter" (1947). The greatest flood stories belong to Faulkner's novels. In *As I Lay Dying* (1930), the flooding river that washes out a bridge forms one of the mythic obstacles facing the Bundren family on their quest to bury Addie, and the Mississippi's flooding in the "Old Man" sections of *The Wild Palms* (1939) sends the convict on his quest to save a stranded pregnant woman so that he can return to prison. River drownings also figure importantly in southern literature—for instance, the drowning of Bevel after his baptism in Flannery O'Connor's "The River" (1953); Mr. Sissum's drowning in Eudora Welty's *The Golden Apples* (1949); and the feared drowning of the young wife Hazel that causes the dragging of the river in Welty's story "The Wide Net"(1943). River battles provide several dramatic episodes in Simms's *The Yemassee* (1835), for instance, and in Evelyn Scott's Civil War epic, *The Wave* (1929).

The Tennessee Valley Authority Act, finally signed into law in 1933 after years of political wrangling, made the Tennessee River and its tributaries into a gigantic force for change through the removal of Appalachian communities in the rivers' paths and the economic and social upheavals involving rural electrification. Lee Smith's *Fair and Tender Ladies* gives one of many examples in Appalachian literature of the miraculous changes brought to isolated mountain homes through the TVA. Elia Kazan's film *Wild River* (1960) captured the conflict between progress and tradition centered on the TVA's taking of land for its projects. The South's rivers, from the names given to them by Native Americans, to Captain John Smith's explorations, to James Dickey's famous treatment of a weekend tenderfoots' canoe trip gone awry in *Deliverance* (1970), are associated with escape, danger, crossing boundaries, finding new worlds, and unsolved mystery. Just what did Billie Joe throw off the Tallahatchee Bridge?

Lucinda H. MacKethan

See also Mississippi River.

ROCK AND ROLL

There was always the blues, in the Georgia and Carolina piedmonts, in Texas, and in the Mississippi Delta. Add a few instruments, sit down a lot less, and it became race music, then rhythm and blues. Add some more drums, amplify it, and turn it up. Get the people dancin'. Put a white Mississippi boy with country roots in a Memphis sound studio, covering hit songs by African American R-and-B songwriters and add a gospel back-up group and you have Elvis Presley, celebrating the art form of rock and roll in its infancy. With a sound dubbed "rockabilly" in the mid-1950s, Presley blended two home-grown musical art forms of rural southern America—country and blues. Elvis acknowledged his music and dancing as a combination of folk, hillbilly, and gospel singing.

On September 9, 1956, Elvis performed on the *Ed Sullivan Show*. Singing songs written by Otis Blackwell and Big Mama Thornton, the King rocked the nation in a broadcast that reached 83 percent of the television viewing audience. Censors had bleeped the sexually charged energy of his gyrations in "Ready Teddy," but rock and roll never looked back. By the end of the year, Elvis had five of the year's top twenty records.

Television may have provided the jump, but car radios set to big-city AM stations and jukeboxes laden with big-holed 45s were the media of choice. Sunday preachers with their occasional vinyl bonfires and worried parents notwithstanding, rock and roll became the soundtrack of southern youth culture.

Whereas "Southern Literature" is generations old, rock and roll, in midlife, is showing no signs of reaching its last verse. Allusions to rock and roll's sheer energy and the seductive nature of its beat abound in southern literature. Rock and roll promises love, lust, liberation, and escape.

In Barry Hannah's first novel, *Geronimo Rex* (1970), Harley Butte is an army band director favoring

Sousa marches on his tuba. In Fort Selby, Mississippi, he hears the Georgia rock-and-roll screamer Little Richard on his bunk mate's radio. The next day, in his last formal military review, the tuba strap breaks. Later in the book, Harry Monroe is pursued by Tonnie Ray, because to her he is all cool, art, and music.

Eudora Welty tells of visiting an African American nightclub in Jackson, Mississippi, to hear Fats Waller. She returned home that night and wrote the short story "Powerhouse" (1939). As the jitterbug dancers swarm the floor, Powerhouse pounds the piano, singing about finding someone who loves him.

Clyde Edgerton, raised in Bethesda, North Carolina, draws on his experience in a rock-and-roll band in *The Floatplane Notebooks* (1988). Sitting in for the piano player in a gig at the Club Oasis, Mark Copeland gets his first taste of beer, breasts, and sex. Pressing her hip against his, a bright-eyed, blond, red-lipped Rhonda tells Mark that she's heard he plays like Jerry Lee Lewis.

Seven novels later, Edgerton, along with his wife, Susan Ketchin, plays with the Tarwater Band (named for a Flannery O'Connor story), a rock and bluegrass group. William McCranor Henderson is on fiddle. Henderson has just retired from his three-year gig as an Elvis impersonator. Guest appearances by the King, complete with the scarves and a bodyguard carrying towels and water, sometimes make the encore set.

Henderson documented the wild world of Elvis impersonators in *I, Elvis: Confessions of a Counterfeit King* (1997). In *Stark Raving Elvis* (1984), an earlier novel by Henderson, readers meet Byron Bluford, whose life changed forever when he debuted his Elvis impersonation at his high-school talent show. Mississippi's Larry Brown and Lewis Nordan feature Elvis impersonators in their spellbinding stories "A Roadside Resurrection" (1991) and "Music of the Swamp" (1991).

Marianne Gingher takes the reader to Orfax, North Carolina, in the summer of 1961, in her glorious ode to southern nights and young love, *Bobby Rex's Greatest Hit* (1986). She credits jukebox fever and car radios for her novel's rock-and-roll spirit. In her story collection *Teen Angel* (1989), she uses rock and roll to provide a familiar setting, a song reference recognized by readers, as if the shared lyrics were codes understood by that generation.

West Virginia writer Denise Giardina uses rock-and-roll allusions to tell Jackie Freeman's story in *The Unquiet Earth* (1992). Jackie's walls are covered with

Beatles posters; she spends her allowance on new 45s and has a crush on a boy with a Paul McCartney face. Susan Tillary's stack of 45s shows up often in Wilmington, North Carolina-born Ellyn Bache's coming-of-age novel *The Activist's Daughter* (1997), set on the campus of the University of North Carolina at Chapel Hill. The first week of school, her dorm mates are listening to Sam the Sham and Ruby and the Romantics. By the end of spring semester, the coeds are gathered around the turntable playing "drop the needle," trying to figure out the words to "Louie, Louie."

The jukebox with its treasure trove of 45s is a special lure in southern literature. Jacqueline Ogburn describes the magic of the colored lights and the whirrs, clicks, and sounds of the jukebox in *The Jukebox Man* (1998). A young girl follows her grandfather on his rounds restocking the jukeboxes in restaurants, fish camps, and truck stops in rural North Carolina. In Tim McLaurin's *The Last Great Snake Show* (1997), Miss Darlene transforms her House of Joy honky-tonk in Wilmington, North Carolina, when she adds hard liquor and a jukebox to the mix.

Susan Gender drops two quarters, for six plays, into a rural Georgia roadhouse jukebox, and everyone watches her dance the Frug, the Pony, and the Swim in Harry Crews's *A Feast of Snakes* (1976). Michael Brondoli offers jukebox lore in his story "Showdown" (1983), set at the Only Bar in eastern North Carolina. Regulars know to crank it up with a screwdriver and never change the 45s. James Lee Burke closes his novel *Cadillac Jukebox* (1996) with his cool Louisiana hero, Dave Robicheaux, dancing to tunes recorded off Jerry Joe Plumb's famous jukebox, remembering a first kiss.

The rock-and-roll kisses of another Louisiana writer's hero are much more dangerous. Lestat is a rock superstar, setting out to visit his old friends, whose band is called Satan's Night Out in Anne Rice's novel *The Vampire Lestat* (1996). With the power of rock video and MTV, the vampire Lestat wants the world.

Sam Hughes is driving her extended family in her funky Volkswagen past rows of McDonald's, Stuckey's, and Country Kitchens on a Kentucky interstate in the opening scene of Bobbie Ann Mason's *In Country* (1985). The radio (about the only thing that works) is tuned to an oldies station playing Motown. The transmission is going, and Sam flips the radio dial. All of a sudden, Bruce Springsteen is singing "Glory Days" and the Doors are tearing into "Roadhouse Blues." Sam thinks that if Jim Morrison were still alive she would drive the car straight to wherever he was. Setting the time of the novel in the pop culture context of the Vietnam War, Mason makes many references to rock-and-roll music in *In Country*. Sam refers to MTV clips, the Kinks, Springsteen videos, Donovan, ZZ Top, and Billy Idol. One of the book's subplots during her road trip involves Sam's search for an elusive new Beatles song she thinks she has heard about saving a kitten.

Upon seeing an interview with Springsteen where the Boss noted how significant he felt Flannery O'Connor's work was in his development as an artist, Louisiana's Walker Percy sent him a fan letter sharing his insights on spiritual journeys and art.

Bobby Sherman, Nancy Sinatra, the Beach Boys, Art Garfunkle, and Gladys Knight are on the soundtrack as background music in Jill McCorkle's early novel *The Cheer Leader* (1984), set in Blue Springs, North Carolina. The reader knows Jo Spencer's romance with Red Williams is doomed when he gives her a Black Sabbath album for Christmas. To McCorkle's Spencer, rock-and-roll music is romance, the promise of slow dances, and the scent of perfume, not cigarettes, druggie music, and cheap cologne.

In later stories, both Mason and McCorkle use the changes they've seen in rock-and-roll music to drive the plot. Songs as odes to romance, fantasy, and escape might still work their magic on young girls, but the transitions in the rock-and-roll industry are noticed. Mason's "A New-Wave Format" (1998) is the story of Edwin and Sabrina. He's forty-three, she's only twenty. The evolution of their relationship is described almost wholly in the songs they favor. Edwin cherishes the oldies of the Lovin' Spoonful and Donovan, describing Sabrina's music as monotonous and bland. A bus driver, he tries playing the B-52's and the Psychedelic Furs, but one of his passengers has a seizure during a song by the Flying Lizards.

Jill McCorkle's *Final Vinyl Days* (1998) uses the change in delivery platform, from vinyl records to compact discs, to tell the story. Now vinyl only sells when an artist dies. "Her" record store gets runs on albums by Marvin Gaye, Roy Orbison, Del Shannon, John Lennon, and, of course, Elvis. McCorkle injects another dig at Black Sabbath and notes the joy of listening to Jimi Hendrix full blast on an eight-track car stereo. In the ironic final scene, the narrator hears a young customer asking about music by the "Byrds." But, no, not those birds. The girl wants something by the birds in *The Little Mermaid*. Those wonderful vinyl days when song lyrics meant something don't have a chance against the Disney machine.

Growing up in Grundy, Virginia, Lee Smith remembers listening to the radio show *Randy's Record Shop*. She credits rock and roll with influencing the way she heard the language, the cadence, the rhythm, the inflections. Like Lewis Nordan, she always reads her work aloud to make sure it sounds right. Smith has often said that she'd rather have been a country singer than anything, but became a writer instead since she couldn't carry a tune.

Rock music was liberating for Smith, giving a spirited voice to a generation of southern women who were pressured to be more ladylike. At slumber parties, drive-ins, and dances, rock music was the soundtrack she drew on to shape the dialogue and characters in her writing. In Smith's novel *Saving Grace* (1995), Florida Grace, a snake-handler's daughter, marries Travis, who plays rock and roll in his spare time. Sitting in a restaurant following her wedding, Florida Grace hears the song "Unchained Melody." She knows it's their song. In Smith's semi-autobiographical short story "The Bubba Stories" (1997), Charlene Christian can often be found playing her favorite song, "Tragedy," on the jukebox in the Phi Gam basement. Just this side of crying, Charlene wonders when something dramatic will ever happen in her life. A dancer all her life, Charlene comments that it was impossible to listen to the local combo, Doug Clark and the Hot Nuts, with the music loud and the beat so strong, and stand still.

Aunt Opal reflects nearly the same sentiment in Bobbie Ann Mason's "Love Life" (1998) when she exclaims that rock and roll is never too loud. Mason plays with the term *R and R* in "Big Bertha Stories" (1998), which could mean rock and roll, could mean rest and relaxation, could even mean rumps and rears. Mason allows her hyper-storytelling Donald to spin a tale about a rock-and-roll band giving a concert on top of a toxic-waste dump, spreading contamination all over the country.

Katie Cocker has been a singer all her life in Lee Smith's *The Devil's Dream* (1992). Now she's a country-music superstar. Needing song titles to add to Katie's story, Smith enlisted her friends. Susan Ketchin came up with "You Made My Day Last Night," and Annie Dillard contributed "Two Lefts Don't Make a Right." Ketchin and Clyde Edgerton turned the titles into real songs and performed them in the later musical production of *The Devil's Dream*.

Smith collaborated with Jill McCorkle, Doris Betts, Jaki Shelton Green, and Margaret Hundley Parker, writing the storyline and dialogue in a Paul Ferguson production called "Good Ol' Girls" (1998). Nashville singer/songwriters Matraca Berg and Marshall Chapman wrote the songs and music. The musical attempts to reveal, question, and revel in what it means to be a good ol' girl living in the modern South. In Berg's title song, the heroine has a picture of Elvis when he came through her hometown.

John Valentine

See also Blues, The; Country Music; Elvis; Memphis, Tennessee; Nashville, Tennessee.

Michael Erlewine, *All Music Guide to Rock* (1997); Peter Guralnick, *Last Train to Memphis* (1994); David P. Szatmary, *Rockin' in Time* (1996).

ROMAN CATHOLICS

For an area as fundamentally Protestant (and Protestant fundamentalist) as the American South, a surprising number of its greatest writers have been Roman Catholic. Most of the best-known have been twentieth-century figures: Allen Tate, Caroline Gordon, Katherine Anne Porter, Flannery O'Connor, and Walker Percy. But the Roman Church seems to have exerted an attraction for some southerners as far back as the antebellum nineteenth century. Old Southwest humorist Johnson Jones Hooper became a convert at the end of his life. After the Civil War, George Washington Cable, while not Catholic himself, wrote about the Catholic milieu of Creole New Orleans. Kate Chopin may have been a lapsed Catholic, but Catholicism figures largely in her fiction, also set mostly in Creole Louisiana.

Antebellum southern fiction was rarely explicitly Christian. Johnson Jones Hooper's humorous sketches fit that secular pattern. His writing gives little hint of his eventual conversion to Catholicism. Perhaps the one exception is his Simon Suggs story "The Captain Attends a Camp Meeting." In that story, Hooper satirizes what he sees as the disorder and corruption of the evangelical camp meeting. The preaching at one such meeting turns the congregation into a howling, shrieking "promiscuous heap." Worse from Hooper's point of view, it encourages disobedience on the part of a slave (Hooper was a passionate defender of slavery). The camp-meeting satire was a convention of Old Southwest humor and in itself no indication of a writer's religious leanings. Many non-Catholic writers used that convention. Nevertheless, what Hooper believed was radical Protestantism's capacity for corruption, sexual immorality, and disorder might have played a part in his eventual conversion. Catholicism provided him with a traditional, ordered, and—perhaps above all, given his views on slavery—hierarchical alternative.

After the Civil War and Reconstruction, the country, anxious to recover unity, experienced a vogue of local-color fiction. Much of this fiction was set in the South. George Washington Cable set his in Creole New Orleans. Catholicism in his fiction does not function thematically. It is more window dressing, increasing the exoticism of his work for its largely Protestant Yankee audience. Kate Chopin also wrote local-color fiction. In her early work, as in Cable's, Catholicism does not function thematically. Her references to Creole Catholic customs and beliefs serve to emphasize the exotic element in her fiction. In her masterpiece, *The Awakening,* however, Catholicism does serve a thematic purpose. A large part of Edna Pontellier's isolation in Creole New Orleans is her Protestantism. Chopin contrasts the individualism, introspection, and conviction of sin in Edna's Calvinism with the Creoles' more communal and permissive Catholicism.

In the early twentieth century, particularly in the wake of World War I, Western culture experienced a crisis. The old order seemed to have met a violent death, and no new order seemed available to replace it. American and European writers cast about for some way to order and stabilize the chaos of modern life. William Butler Yeats turned to art, T. S. Eliot to the Anglican Church, Wallace Stevens to the imagination. The American South suffered a specific version of this crisis. At that time, the South was rapidly industrializing. Its agrarian and aristocratic traditions—stoicism, honor, chivalry, and *noblesse oblige*—seemed to be fading. Just as writers elsewhere turned in various directions for order and stability, many southern writers turned to the Roman Catholic Church.

In a letter to a friend, Allen Tate expressed an attraction to the Church as early as 1929. In the 1930 essay "Some Remarks on the Southern Religion," he argues that the Old South's Protestantism conflicted with its communal, hierarchical values. Although he never says so outright, he implies that the proper southern religion would be Catholicism. Despite his attraction, however, Tate did not formally convert for another twenty years. Like other artists and intellectuals of his time, he was looking for a way to bring order to the chaos of the twentieth century. In the 1930s, he

believed a revival of southern traditions and return to an agrarian life-style could provide that order. By the end of the 1930s, he came to see that effort as futile. At the same time, he both desired to believe in Catholicism and feared that belief would cut him off from an active engagement with the world. Out of that inner struggle, he created most of his greatest poetry. In the 1940s, he met Catholic theologian and philosopher Jacques Maritain. Maritain was a believing Catholic, intellectual, and man of the world. His example banished the last of Tate's hesitation, and Tate entered the Church in 1950. After his conversion, he wrote only three major poems, but he continued to make major contributions to literary and cultural studies with his essays.

Like her husband, Tate's wife Caroline Gordon was a convert. She entered the Church three years before her husband. Like him also, she came to Catholicism only after exhausting other options in a search for meaning, order, and stability. Gordon's early work was influenced by the stoicism of southern tradition and of the heroes of Greco-Roman mythology. In that work, her protagonists are inevitably defeated by disintegrative forces in life and ultimately by death. They achieve dignity, though, by the courage with which they struggle against those forces. By the 1940s, stoicism no longer seemed adequate to Gordon. Like Tate, she converted under the influence of Maritain. In her work immediately following her conversion, she used a strategy later employed by Flannery O'Connor. Using sudden, shocking reversals, she attempted to shake her complacent secular audience into contemplation of divine grace. In her final work, she attempted to combine classical stoicism and heroism with Catholic Christianity.

Katherine Anne Porter converted to Catholicism during the first of her four marriages. According to Robert Brinkmeyer, she "spent the rest of her days . . . repressing but (significantly) never repudiating her Catholicism." That ambiguity shows in her fiction. Her stories are filled with Catholic imagery, but the reader can never be sure whether she is endorsing or rejecting the Church as a solution to the problem of modern chaos. Her fiction seems to embody a faith-haunted doubt or perhaps a doubt-haunted faith.

Since World War II, in the era that academics have come to call "postmodern," many European and American writers have abandoned the search for an ordering and unifying principle. Instead, they celebrate the fragmentation of contemporary life. In the American South, however, at least two writers, Flannery O'Connor and Walker Percy, continued to believe in the importance of order and unity and to find them in the Roman Catholic Church.

Unlike most of the aforementioned writers and Walker Percy, O'Connor was not a convert. She was born and raised in the Church. It is ironic, therefore, that of all these writers, she was the most sympathetic to southern Protestantism. She found its fundamentalism a more concrete and immediate view of God than that of the Catholic and mainstream Protestant churches. She was also attracted to the fundamentalists' conviction of original sin and recognition of the devil. Tate once observed that O'Connor was "temperamentally a Jansenist." (Jansensim is a Roman Catholic version of Calvinism. Its adherents believe in predestination and the impossibility of doing good without the unsolicited grace of God.) O'Connor's fiction combines allegory, realism, and satire. Her characters are often grotesque: a one-legged philosophy Ph.D., a man with a tubelike head, a homicidal maniac. The events in her stories can be equally grotesque: the theft of the Ph.D.'s wooden leg, a prophet blinding himself with quicklime, a child drowning while attempting to baptize himself. She felt she was writing for a spiritually complacent secular audience, and the grotesque characters and events in her fiction were an attempt to shock that audience into contemplating the action of divine grace and recognizing the existence of evil. "For the hard of hearing," she once wrote, "you shout."

After his father committed suicide and his mother's death soon afterward, Walker Percy was raised by his cousin William Alexander Percy, a writer whose most famous book is his autobiography, *Lanterns on the Levee* (1941). From his cousin, he absorbed an interest in literature and a southern stoicism. He was later trained as a medical doctor, and he was attracted by the power of science to explain the world. While recuperating from tuberculosis in the early 1940s, he began reading European novelists and existentialist philosophers. Under their influence, he came to believe that although science explained the world, it did not explain how human beings can and should live in the world. He eventually came to believe that Roman Catholicism did offer such an explanation. Unlike Tate and Gordon, Percy did not begin writing until after his conversion, so he was from the start a Catholic writer. He divided the reading public into two types: those alienated and aware of, but mystified by, their alienation, and those alienated but unaware of it. For the first, he portrayed characters in the same situation, to give the readers' alienation a local habitation and a name and to subtly suggest Catholicism as a possible way out of it. For the second, he used vicious and often hilarious satire to shock them out of their complacency and again to suggest Catholicism as an alternative to the modern consumer life-style he attacked.

In his autobiographically centered fiction (*The Great Santini*, 1976; *The Prince of Tides*, 1986), Pat Conroy (1945–) portrays adolescent Catholic protagonists fighting the isolation they feel in the Protestant South. Unlike O'Connor and Percy, he has not been concerned with Catholic theology and ritual, but as strongly as they, he has been repulsed by the spiritual emptiness of the twentieth century.

The search to replace a lost order and stability may explain the modernist and postmodern southern writers' attraction to Catholicism. But it does not explain nineteenth-century writers' attraction to the Church. Nor does it explain "why Catholicism?" when the same search took so many modernist writers in so many different directions. A few humble speculations: The Catholic church with its philosophical traditions appeals to religiously inclined intellectuals more than anti-intellectual southern fundamentalist Protestantism. Southern culture tends to be rooted and traditionalist. The Church has nearly two thousand years of tradition. The formalism of Catholic ritual may appeal to a culture like the South's, famous for its manners and politeness, and to the formalist aesthetics of southern writers. And, particularly in the nineteenth century but unfortunately even into the twentieth, the hierarchical nature of the Church's belief and institutional structure may appeal to a culture as socially and racially stratified as the South.

Fred R. Thiemann

See also Irish Catholics; Local Color; New Criticism; Secularization; Southwestern Humor.

Robert Brinkmeyer, *Three Catholic Writers of the Modern South* (1985); Ross Labrie, *The Catholic Imagination in American Literature* (1997).

ROMANCE GENRE

Since Richard Chase first offered it book-length treatment in 1957, the term *romance* has become one of the most widely used, widely discussed, and hotly debated in American literary criticism. In the wake of Chase's claim that the "best" American novels are those written in or incorporating elements of the romance form, scores of books and articles have been written on the genre, debating its meanings, its viability, and, more recently, its very existence. But while the variety of perspectives on the subject is dizzying, it is precisely to this complex critical history—a history that draws our attention to the cultural work that notions of genre perform—that one must first turn in order to begin delineating the "romance genre," and, especially, that genre's place in a history of southern literature.

Although Richard Chase's *The American Novel and Its Tradition* (1957) can be said to have centrally placed the "romance genre" on the map of American critical history, Chase was himself participating in a conversation already in progress. Chase's efforts to carve out a distinctive American fictional tradition, one that differs from the English, emerged in part in response to F. R. Leavis's influential claim that "The Great Tradition" of fiction could be found in the British novel of manners and society (*The Great Tradition*, 1948). Such an assertion seemed to exclude American fiction from the possibility of "greatness," since American writers beginning with Charles Brockden Brown and extending through Irving, Cooper, Hawthorne, and James—not coincidentally, all writers whose work is now seen as central to an evolving romance tradition—had asserted that American society did not yield up a cultural fabric densely textured enough to sustain the novelist. Taking up this notion of the ostensible thinness of the American scene, Lionel Trilling famously asserted, in "Manners, Morals, and The Novel" (1947), that American writers have not looked to society for inspiration or artistic sustenance and have not, consequently, written anything like the novel as it has been classically understood. But unlike Leavis, Trilling is willing to grant the United States a tradition of great novels—one that operates according to a different set of aesthetic principles.

It is here that Chase enters into the conversation, putting those principles under the rubric *romance*. Arguing against the view that the American novel is ailing and in need of cure, Chase proposes that the "greatness" of American fiction can be found precisely in its departure from the British model. Whereas the English novel operates imperially, with the aim of assimilating contradiction and bringing order out of disorder, the American novel, emerging from a different set of historical conditions, is focused on exploration of "new"

interior worlds, "new" states of mind and being. The romance, Chase claims, is the natural vehicle for such exploration, because it liberates the writer from the demands of realism. Seizing upon this liberty, the romance, as Chase then defines it, tends away from verisimilitude and toward melodrama, "idyll," and formal abstraction, and prefers to explore psychic depths rather than the social scene.

A host of books followed in the immediate wake of Chase's claim that these "romance" qualities constitute the special province of the "best" American novels. However divergently, such studies as Harry Levin's *The Power of Blackness* (1958), Marius Bewley's *The Eccentric Design* (1959), Leslie Fiedler's *Love and Death in the American Novel* (1960), and Richard Poirier's *A World Elsewhere* (1966) can all be seen to emerge from the understanding of American fiction as concerned less with social texture than with the often dark, symbolically rendered interior drives of a conflicted self and the world of the spirit. Indeed, just twelve years after Chase, Joel Porte could assert triumphantly, in the opening sentence of *The Romance in America* (1969), that "it no longer seems necessary to argue for the importance of romance as a nineteenth-century American genre." The "romance thesis" had come into its own.

If the years between Chase's and Porte's studies had accomplished a great deal in terms of mapping the terrain of the American romance, so have the years between 1969 and today—years that have brought the genre under new and productive scrutiny. Perhaps inspired by the work of Michael Davitt Bell, whose *The Development of American Romance* (1980) attempts to understand how and why a variety of writers from Charles Brockden Brown to Melville used the term *romance* to describe their own works, scholars such as Evan Carton (*The Rhetoric of American Romance*, 1985) and Emily Miller Budick (*Fiction and Historical Consciousness*, 1989) have attempted to place the term more fully in its historical and cultural context in order to open it to a more capacious set of meanings. But others—Nina Baym, Jane Tompkins, and John McWilliams notable among them—have taken issue with the very notion of "romance" and argued for the problematics of the theory's hold on our understandings of American fictional traditions. Noting that the distinction between novel and romance was never consistently made in the nineteenth century, Baym (*Novels, Readers, and Reviewers*, 1984) and, following her, McWilliams ("The Rationale for 'The American Romance,' " *Boundary 2, 1990*), assert that the notion of a distinctly American fictional tradition called "romance" is a product of a particular set of contemporary cultural and critical needs—Cold War nationalism among them. According to Baym and McWilliams, the romance genre as Chase articulates it emerges precisely as an exercise in canon formation. For them, and others who follow in their wake, the question is: which authors and what texts are placed at the center by the "romance thesis," and which are rendered secondary, even obsolete?

It is this question that becomes central to the place of the "romance genre" in the literature of the South. A quick survey of any of the books cited above, and many of the texts that those books themselves cite, reveals that much as their definitions of the romance might shift and change, the same writers appear again and again, in varying combinations: Brown, Irving, Cooper, Poe, Hawthorne, and Melville for the early to mid-nineteenth century; James (despite his self-proclaimed disdain for the romance) for the turn into the twentieth century; and Faulkner for the twentieth century. Obviously, then, if this is the "great tradition" of American literature, it is also a tradition in which southern writers would appear to be negligible. Chase's own selection of southern writers is intriguing in this context: although he offers a discussion of Mark Twain—a gesture rarely followed up by later critics of the romance—he does not so much as mention Poe. Chase also mentions William Gilmore Simms as an early proponent of the romance but quickly jettisons him after asserting that his works are "fatally marred" by slipshod construction, a lack of psychological depth, and an unoriginal (which is to say, for Chase, "unAmerican") form. Such depth and formal originality are central to what Chase sees as the legitimate "stream" of romance in American literary history. The other stream is, he declares, rightly condemned by writers such as Twain and James, because it offers merely the vestiges of a now-outdated European tradition. Significantly, it is in this putatively debased line of romance that Chase places a variety of southern writers, including John Esten Cooke and Margaret Mitchell.

In the context of Chase's moment, it is not perhaps surprising that his theory of American romance marginalizes the literature of the South. In part, the view of the nineteenth-century South as intellectually and artistically impoverished continues to hold sway. But the impact of Chase's reading and the readings inspired by

him can still be felt in the national critical narrative, specifically in the notion that southern literature is outside the current of mainstream tradition. In her 1997 *Gothic America*, Teresa Goddu specifically addresses the displacement of southern literature in romance theory. In particular, Goddu notes that while the notion of romance still dominates critical discourse, the gothic—originally linked to the romance—is fully submerged, even repressed, except in terms of the South. Goddu suggests that by claiming a high-art form of "romance" for the North and displacing the gothic, a debased genre, onto the South, critics have managed to exorcise some of the ghosts that haunt the mainstream literary canon: specifically, American literature's complex relationship to matters of race. Goddu is, finally, more interested in the gothic than she is in the romance, but the bold connecting lines she draws between genre and region help put into relief the complex critical history of the romance genre for and in the history of southern literature.

The term *romance* thus comes to the late twentieth century as an intricate and, especially for the literature of the South, vexed term. This critical history is all the more challenging in light of the fact that a variety of nineteenth-century southern writers understood themselves to be writing "romances" precisely along Chasean lines. When Richard Chase asserts that the romance attempts to liberate itself from fidelity to the "real" world, he makes a claim that would be familiar to many such writers—most notably, William Gilmore Simms, whose definition of the romance likely derives from the astoundingly influential Sir Walter Scott. In 1823, by which time he had sold upwards of 500,000 copies of his works in the U.S., Scott had famously defined the romance in an essay for the *Encyclopaedia Britannica*. Scott's claim that the romance frees itself from the "ordinary" in order to embrace the "marvellous and uncommon" is echoed by a variety of later romance writers, including Nathaniel Hawthorne in his preface to *The House of the Seven Gables* (1851). Most readers of nineteenth-century American literature are familiar with Hawthorne's definition of romance, but few realize that Simms had earlier articulated the concept in strikingly similar terms. In his prefatory remarks to *The Yemassee: A Romance of Carolina* (1835)—remarks that appeared in the preface to the first edition, and in a slightly modified form in a new edition of 1853—Simms calls his work a "romance," and appears to mean by the term much the same thing that Hawthorne does when he claims it, nearly twenty years later. Yet two more different texts could hardly be found, which suggests that something happened to the romance in the years between 1835 and 1851.

Working, as Hawthorne later does in his prefaces, to establish the terms by which his text should be read, in introducing *The Yemassee* Simms proudly claims affinity not with "domestic" novelists such as Richardson and Fielding, but rather with Scott. Scott's influence can clearly be felt in Simms's definition of the romance as a form that resists the limits of the known. In embracing that definition, Simms declares himself a master of the imagination, of the marvelous and improbable. But even as he draws from Scott—and prefigures Hawthorne—here, Simms makes it clear that he is not merely importing a foreign product: his romance is, he declares, an American one.

Simms's prefatory declaration of the nationalist/aesthetic aims of his project provides a fitting description of a variety of historical romances by early-nineteenth-century writers, southern and northern. With its story of the clash between encroaching Europeans and Native Americans who are driven first to retaliation and eventually to their doom, for example, Simms's *The Yemassee* pairs both stylistically and thematically with the historical romances of Cooper. And as these links between Cooper and early Simms, who was frequently called the "southern Cooper," suggest, one would be hard pressed to define a markedly distinct form of "southern romance" at this period. One would also be hard pressed to exclude southern writing from this period's romance tradition.

Much as Cooper did for his native New York, in the 1820s and 1830s southern writers George Tucker, John Pendleton Kennedy, William A. Caruthers, and Simms published romances that aimed to depict the heroic past, complex present, and glorious future of their southern region. Set in diverse historical moments, ranging from Bacon's Rebellion of 1676 to the American Revolution and beyond, Tucker's *The Valley of Shenandoah* (1824), Kennedy's *Swallow Barn* (1832), and Caruthers's *The Cavaliers of Virginia* (1835) attempt to address the southern contribution to the founding of a glorious America, even as they offer a more regionally committed celebration of what has come to be known as the "cavalier myth": the belief in a southern aristocracy of Norman descent, characterized by a noble spirit of honor, chivalry, and intellect and opposed to the more materialistic ethos of the money-making North.

Although this myth is clearly present in these and related works, such early southern romances frequently manifest an unwillingness to fuel sectarian difference, particularly on the matter of slavery. In *The Valley of Shenandoah,* for example, Tucker depicts a slave auction which, in its painful detail, is offered as a point of southern shame and dishonor. Tucker's cavalier hero, Edward Grayson, deplores slavery as a moral and political evil, albeit one with no viable solution. Similarly, in *Swallow Barn,* Kennedy addresses slavery as a moral wrong that should be eradicated—but eventually, and without interference from the North—and occasionally pokes fun at aspects of plantation life. In depicting the troubled terrain of the southern pastoral world, such works represent what we might conceive as the pre-sectarian strain of the romance of the early nineteenth century. While they sow the seeds of a distinctively southern literature in celebrating the glories of their region, Tucker, Kennedy, and Caruthers also show an interest in neutralizing North-South divisions in their attempts to treat such matters as slavery with a degree of even-handedness. These texts thus reveal the complexity of "southern romance" at this early period: they attempt to bridge cultural divides even as they manifest latent strains that would blossom into the more full-blown sectarian literature of the period leading up to and culminating in the Civil War.

Such strains are fully unveiled in the work of Nathaniel Beverley Tucker, whose *The Partisan Leader: A Tale of the Future* (1836) is an early foray into extremist secessionalism. A pseudonymous futuristic romance—its title page is dated 1856, and the action of the novel is set in 1849—*The Partisan Leader* depicts the dilemmas of the Virginia commonwealth torn between loyalties to a North ruled by the tyrannical Martin Van Buren and an already-seceded southern confederacy. In its use of a brave hero whose devotion to cause makes all come right, *The Partisan Leader* is true to early romance form. But in its depictions of southern heroism in the face of northern brutality, and its committed celebration of the noble beauties of the master-slave relation, Tucker's novel strikes a uniquely "partisan" course that would become much more familiar to readers in the 1840s and 1850s.

It is in these decades that lines between the North and South began to harden as a consequence of developing conflicts over states' rights, slavery, and tariff and taxation policies. Not surprisingly, it is also at this time that a polarity in the forms of romance, North and South, begins to emerge. By the 1840s, such periodicals as the *Southern Literary Messenger,* at first a moderate journal interested primarily in promoting letters in the South and a nondivisive pride of region, were calling for southern writers to commit themselves to a particularly southern ideology. Such calls become increasingly strident in the years leading up to the Civil War, as an 1856 *Messenger* article on "The Duty of Southern Authors" attests. Here, the writer asserts that southern authors are duty-bound to write in the service of their community; in particular, they are to bring the light of truth to the institution of slavery, dispelling the "mists and clouds" with which northern writers have deliberately shrouded it. In essence, southern writers were increasingly called to a thesis: the "southern cause," which was transmuted, in the years after the war, into the glorious "Lost Cause."

As Craig Werner has pointed out, while "romance" in the North evolved, partly under the influence of transcendentalist thought, into the philosophically speculative, investigative, and "open" form so celebrated by Richard Chase and others, "romance" in the South remained wedded to the tradition, exemplified by Scott, of historical mythology and mythmaking (*The History of Southern Literature,* 1985). By the time Hawthorne writes his preface to *The House of the Seven Gables,* echoing Simms's own description of the romance in the preface to *The Yemassee,* he appears to conceive of the romance's "latitude" and transgression of novelistic limits in very different ways. Despite the fact that both writers' conception of romance descends, quite directly, from Scott's, they are working, by the 1850s, in what appear to be essentially different forms. Indeed, Simms's career, which reflects a shift from pro-unionist to fiercely separatist views, is representative of an ideological shift in southern literature more generally.

There are exceptions to this North/South polarity, of course. Narratives produced by escaped or emancipated slaves, for example, frequently draw on conventions associated with the romance: melodramatic rendering of "uncommon" incidents, remarkable acts of heroism in the face of almost inconceivable odds, hairsbreadth escapes, gothic villains of huge proportions. Indeed, in his description of the romance hero in his preface to *The Yemassee,* Simms could well be describing such slave narrators as Frederick Douglass (*The Narrative of the Life of Frederick Douglass, an American Slave,* 1845), Harriet Jacobs (*Incidents in the Life of a Slave Girl,* 1861), and William Craft (*Running a Thousand Miles for Freedom,* 1860). Unlike their southern contemporaries, such writers draw on romance conventions in a defiant effort to invert plantation mythology. But such conventions also play a more complex philosophical role: here, the improbabilities of the romance point up the paradoxical nature of a real institution that imposes seemingly unreal conditions on human beings. As Harriet Jacobs, writing pseudonymously as Linda Brent, asserts in the preface to her narrative, readers will have to accept the "strict" truth of "adventures" that appear to be improbable: her truth is stranger than any fiction. By drawing on romance conventions, slave narrators thus offer complex investigations into the relationship between fact and fiction, and inquire into such matters as the nature of freedom, justice, and autonomy. Their texts reveal complex cross-fertilizations between romance traditions in the antebellum North and the South.

The work of Edgar Allan Poe also provides a notable exception to the "rule" of southern romance. Poe's status as "southern" is often seen as tenuous, largely because, unlike his southern compatriots, Poe rarely made use of a distinctly southern locale in his work and appeared to have little interest in the themes that were emerging as "southern." Yet Poe identified himself as "a Virginian" throughout his life, expressed southern Whig and, sometimes, proslavery views, and, through his important tenure as editor of the *Southern Literary Messenger* (1834–1837), was crucially associated with the call for an explicitly southern literature. Significantly, in applying to T. W. White for his position at the *Messenger,* Poe carried with him a letter of introduction from John Pendleton Kennedy; before that, when he attended the University of Virginia, he had been a student of George Tucker's.

If Poe's fiction ostensibly departs from the dominant strain of southern romance exemplified by Kennedy and Tucker, Poe's position, however volatile, in the world of southern letters suggests intricate connections for which a hard regional division cannot account. Such critics as Louis D. Rubin Jr., Harry Levin, Dana Nelson, Joan Dayan, and John Carlos Rowe have suggested that the images of blackness, darkness, and horror that so fret Poe's tales and poetry—where the romance's willingness to embrace the imagination and cross the threshold of the probable is taken to new, startling extremes—find their origins in the southern context from which Poe emerges. In *The Narrative of Arthur Gordon Pym* (1837), for example, the narrator's journey farther and farther south, into a polar landscape of death-dealing blackness and then, finally, mysteriously engulfing total whiteness, complexly renders anxieties about a variety of matters pressing in the South: racial boundaries, miscegenation, slave uprising and insurrection, theories of racial development, notions of civilization and savagery. In staging such anxieties, Poe's *Pym* can thus be seen as a romance text that makes use of what are depicted as northern "strains"—metaphysical engagement, philosophical openness—to depict, however inadvertently, the nightmarish underside of the plantation myth celebrated by many southern romancers.

Such celebrations would become increasingly thunderous in the immediate prewar years, nor would the Civil War put an end to them. Indeed, writers such as Simms and John Esten Cooke—a cousin of John Pendleton Kennedy and the brother of Philip Pendleton Cooke, a southern writer of some repute and a close friend of Simms—found a new theme emerging from the fragments of an ostensibly ruined society: the Lost Cause. Cooke, whose career spans both the pre- and postwar periods, served in the Confederate Army and witnessed the horrors of combat, but his books resisted the realistic depictions of such horrors. Unlike John W. De Forest (*Miss Ravenel's Conversion from Secession to Loyalty*, 1867), whose efforts to objectively capture the realities of warfare sowed the seeds of a realism that would eventually put the romance in abeyance, Cooke remained true to an older form. In his seven books tracing the course of the war, Cooke offered stories of valiant knight-commanders boldly defending against northern aggression the noble cause of the Old South.

But while Cooke found a fairly wide audience among fellow southerners, he and others working in a similar vein were writing against the tide. The economic disruption that came in the wake of the war depressed the market for long historical fiction of the sort so widely consumed in the prewar years, and the need to focus on rebuilding a society, sometimes literally from the ground up, made such fiction a leisure and luxury few could afford. Perhaps most important, the romance increasingly came to seem a suspect genre, incapable of capturing the truths of a nation trying to heal its wounds and come to terms with the carnage, both psychological and corporeal, on the national landscape.

William Dean Howells and Henry James became the cultural spokesmen for a new literary consciousness, encouraging those whom Howells saw as the devotees of Scott toward a fiction that did not "lie" about life but rather depicted people as they were. For Howells and James, fiction had to maintain the very thing that antebellum romancers, north and south, resisted: fidelity to the world as it existed. Thus would Mark Twain famously stage the death of the romance tradition in *Adventures of Huckleberry Finn* (1885). By having Huck barely escape with his life from the decks of the sinking steamboat, the *Walter Scott,* Twain signals his belief in the dangerous seductions of a wrecked tradition. Huck is nearly "killed" again, when he is "reborn" as Tom Sawyer on the Phelps Farm and becomes complicit with Tom in the cruelties of the plot to liberate an already-free Jim. For Twain, the romance tradition that descends from Scott is not merely inadequate; it is, as Howells suggested, a lie—a failure of moral purpose.

Even this 1885 attempt did not kill the romance. Indeed, many critics, including Richard Chase and Perry Miller, have read in *Huck Finn* the work of a preeminent romancer, a writer who, in depicting the journey that Huck and Jim take down the Mississippi River, captures the spirit of speculative inquiry and flight into imagination. And later southern writers would—and will—continue to draw on many of the tropes and conventions of nineteenth-century romance in its many manifestations. Margaret Mitchell's *Gone With the Wind* (1936) provides perhaps the most remarkable and phenomenal example of the continued appeal of the historical romance form. By contrast, in drawing on gothic modes and conventions, Flannery O'Connor and Carson McCullers can be seen as later avatars of the romance that engages in psychological explorations and philosophical, even skeptical, inquiry. William Faulkner might be viewed as a bridge between traditions, embedding his characters in an inescapable history, a densely textured South peopled by myth and countermyth, and a complex psychic life that results in one of the conventional romance's oldest themes: ancestral sin and guilt. In a recent study, Toni Morrison, a writer deeply indebted to Faulkner and to the romance tradition generally, inquires into the compelling nature of the romance for nineteenth-century Americans: "What was there in American romanticism that made it so attractive to Americans as a battle plain on which to fight, engage, and imagine their demons?" (*Playing in the Dark,* 1992). Writers of the twentieth-century South—white and African American, male and female—are still, in many respects, engaging and imagining demons; and until those demons are stilled, it is likely that the romance form will continue to evolve.

Ellen Weinauer

See also Cavalier; Historical Romance; Plantation; Plantation Fiction; Romanticism.

Emily Miller Budick, *Engendering Romance: Women Writers and the Hawthorne Tradition, 1850–1990* (1994); George Dekker, *The American Historical Romance* (1987); C. Hugh Holman, *The Roots of Southern Writing* (1972); Perry Miller, *Nature's Nation* (1967); Toni Morrison, *Playing in the Dark: Whiteness and the Literary Imagination* (1992); J. V. Ridgely, *Nineteenth-Century Southern Literature* (1980); Walter Scott, *Essays on Chivalry, Romance, and the Drama* (1834).

ROMANTICISM

Romanticism as a literary mode in American literature is generally associated with the New England-based writers of the mid-nineteenth century. What is called "the American Renaissance" period, the 1830s to 1860s, consists of seven male white authors frequently called "the American romantics": Melville, Hawthorne, Emerson, Thoreau, Whitman, Cooper, and Poe. Except for the last, Edgar Allan Poe, none of these writers had any associations with the South, and Poe has usually been considered "southern" only by birth and not by literary tendencies. Literary studies of American Romanticism seldom mention the South at all, except perhaps to point out the antislavery themes in a few of the essays of Emerson and Thoreau. Southern literary histories of the 1830s to 1860s are resigned to making cases for Poe as southern or for holding aloft the banner of William Gilmore Simms in fiction and Henry Timrod in poetry. Southern intellectual historians, from William P. Trent to Allen Tate to Lewis Simpson, have tried to come up with theories to explain what failings in the culture could account for the South's miserable record in relation to the "flowering of New England" in belles-lettres.

Romanticism is also, literarily speaking, often placed against the rationalism or classicism of the eighteenth century or the realism of the late nineteenth century. In this frame, Romanticism describes a set of thematic and stylistic tendencies: the preference for fancy or imagination over representations of the real; the use of sentiment and emotion in language and situation; the promotion of idealism over practicality and individualism over social responsibility; the creation of characters who are heroes or villains, seldom ordinary though often rustic people; and the love of Nature, placed in pastoral distinction against the rising City. In this respect, the South had plenty of nineteenth-century

writers who produced romantic fare, from the swashbuckling cavaliers in the antebellum, usually Virginia, romances to the swooning heroines of domestic novels. In poetry, the South could point to the musicality and nature symbolism of the (mostly) Charleston poets, self-consciously courting the English romantic tradition (James Mathewes Legaré, Paul Hayne, and Henry Timrod). Yet to speak of the "American Romantics" is to exclude southern writers—except for Poe—almost completely. To speak of "Southern Romantics" is automatically to acknowledge "inferior" or "minor" efforts.

One of the primary qualities lacking in southern writing of the period that produced the New England Renascence is the bold experiments with form that could produce a *Moby Dick* or a *Leaves of Grass*. The novels of Simms and the critical as well as poetic efforts of Henry Timrod do not attempt anything on a comparable scale. Thematically, too, southern writers missed the powerful engagement with Nature that captivated writers to the North. In his important revisionary examination of the literature of the Old South, *The Edge of the Swamp* (1989), Louis Rubin voices this explanation:

> To see man solitary in nature, on the land, in contrast with and opposed to man *in* society and confronted by its restraints upon freedom, was the most potent, dynamic, imaginatively stimulating insight of the early nineteenth century American Romantic mind. . . . But for the Southerners the dream of freedom from social constraint, of life on the land, was inescapably linked *with* human bondage. Nature, the land—these could not be separated imaginatively from slavery. The resulting confusion of image, metaphor, social ideal was more than sufficient to stifle any kind of sustained dialectic within the literary imagination.

William Gilmore Simms (1806–1870) will suffer forever under the labels "the southern Cooper" or "the southern Scott." The South's preeminent man of letters in the antebellum period, Simms by sheer output is impossible to ignore. The historical romance was his forte, a genre in which he never achieved the subtleties of character, the rich ambiguity of meaning, or the dexterity with symbols that Hawthorne accomplished. His romanticism lies in his themes (patriotism, individualism, freedom) and in his love of certain kinds of details—the exotic, the voluptuous, the dramatic effects of nature. As Rubin notes in *The Edge of the Swamp*, Simms could hold his own with Cooper in these areas.

However, Simms could not create a Natty Bumppo to offer someone "to mediate between the forest and the town" and to represent "flight from all that society was."

The fiction writer of southern roots whose work bears more consideration in terms of its powerful evocation of the American Romantic impulse that Rubin describes is Rebecca Harding Davis (1831–1910), who grew up in Alabama and Wheeling, West Virginia. In her 1861 novella, *Life in the Iron Mills,* she looked to Hawthorne as a model for her style and symbolism in producing an imaginative allegory of the individual against society and the machine. This story of life in the mills and the iron foundries, a setting well known to Davis from living in Wheeling in the years before the Civil War, has often been noted for introducing elements of realism and naturalism into American literature. What Davis wanted to show, however, had its ideological roots in Romanticism, what she called the "soul starvation" of the individual, the common man as Artist, set against the dehumanization of society. Her language and symbolism belong to the world of Hawthorne, the writer whom she most admired.

In poetry, Henry Timrod (1828–1867), the "poet laureate of the Confederacy," was the antebellum South's most important (almost its only) Romantic practitioner and also theorist on poetry. In his 1859 essay "The Literature of the South," he pointed not to Emerson, as Whitman would do, but to Wordsworth and Tennyson as models for achieving the deep feeling grounded in the familiar and the moral suasion that was poetry's duty. Timrod seldom successfully tried to incorporate the older Romantic tendencies he praised in the British Romantic, much less the new, energetic forms of Poe or Whitman. Timrod reached his highest powers through his personal, emotional engagement with civil war, in poems such as "Ethnogenesis" and "The Cotton Boll," both written in 1861. Yet the end of the Civil War brought havoc, even destitution, to Timrod and his family.

Timrod seldom achieved technical excellence, as his contemporary Sidney Lanier once unkindly pointed out. It is Lanier himself, among southern poets, who best reflects the concerns and techniques of Romanticism as he freed his poetic structures to reflect both individuality and intense musicality. Lanier came into his own as a poet in the bleak years immediately following the Civil War, after he had moved to Baltimore to work as a musician. "Corn" (1875), "The Marshes of Glynn" (1878), and "A Ballad of Trees and the Mas-

ter" (1880) are representative romantic pieces. In "Symphony," he railed against Trade and reached for a romantic synthesis of nature, art, music, and love. In 1878, he wrote to Whitman, primly protesting "those poetic exposures of the person" but expressing his "unbounded delight" in "the bigness and bravery of all your ways and thoughts." Lanier's excitement about and understanding of Whitman's poetics and philosophy ("the absolute personality of the person") make one wonder what Lanier might have accomplished if tuberculosis had not ended his life in 1881.

For those seeking southern manifestations of American Romanticism, luckily, there is always Poe, the poet and fiction writer of "the blackness of darkness," the symbolist and gothicist of the imagination whose name is in some ways synonymous with the darkest strains of American Romanticism. Lewis Simpson and Louis Rubin have both made cases for the South of his childhood as containing the wellsprings of Poe's imagination. Simpson has suggested that the House of Usher is an analogue for the decaying and collapsing southern slave system. Rubin expands on the possibilities by suggesting that "it was Poe's Richmond experience that helped to propel his imagination inward." Poe might be the southern writer whose fictional and poetic settings least reflect any particular southern scene, but he is also, in his very alienation and isolation from that scene, quite possibly an artist tormented by southern society's inability to confront the frightening basis of its continuance.

The South since the Civil War has become America's region of the romantic, popularly speaking the locale of the exotic, the violent, the wild, the dark side. In more serious works of the twentieth century, Nature, as evoked in Faulkner's "The Bear" (1942), in James Dickey's *Deliverance* (1970), in the Appalachian ghost stories of Lee Smith's *Oral History* (1983), or in the poetry of the Fugitive-Agrarians (one thinks of Robert Penn Warren's *Audubon* [1969]), has strongly Romantic force—Nature calls people into a contemplation of imaginative worlds beyond the city where they confront their deepest and often darkest selves in forest darkness. Southern Romanticism in the nineteenth century did not participate fully in New England's engagement with the individual confronting nature, in the form of the endless dream of the frontier on one side and society, in the form of the city, on the other. Yet since the Civil War—and in the case of Poe, before it—the South's most enduring writing has struggled with the American Romantic theme of man's alienation from nature and his troubled relations with his society.

Lucinda H. MacKethan

See also American Renaissance; Nature; Novel, 1820 to 1865; Poe, Edgar Allan; Poetry, 1820 to 1900.

Louis D. Rubin Jr., *The Edge of the Swamp* (1989); Lewis P. Simpson, *The Brazen Face of History* (1980); Allen Tate, "The Profession of Letters in the South," in *Essays of Four Decades* (1968).

RUBIN, LOUIS D., JR.

Writer, critic, scholar, educator, publisher, Louis Decimus Rubin Jr. in effect co-coined the term *Southern Renascence* to describe the great resurgence of strong writing in the South after World War I. Born in Charleston, South Carolina, in 1923, he attended the College of Charleston and then, after World War II, the University of Richmond (B.A., 1946). His graduate work was completed at the Johns Hopkins University (M.A., 1949; Ph.D., 1954). After a brief period as a journalist, Rubin in 1957 joined the faculty at Hollins College and was a teacher to a number of splendid writers who came through the college in the next decade. In 1967 he moved to the University of North Carolina and stayed on the faculty at Chapel Hill until his retirement in 1989, the final sixteen years as University Distinguished Professor. In 1982 he founded Algonquin Books in Chapel Hill, an alternative press designed to encourage strong new writers who find it difficult in this day to crack the lists of major commercial publishers. He maintained his tie to the press until 1991.

Rubin is author or editor of dozens of important books in the study of American and southern literature. In 1953, while at Hopkins, he and Robert D. Jacobs edited a collection of essays from a recent conference, *Southern Renascence: The Literature of the Modern South,* that provided both a handle and some starting points for a generation of scholars to re-appraise writing in the South. The 1961 book *South: Modern Southern Literature in Its Cultural Setting* provided another collection of similar appraisals. Rubin's critical-scholarly work includes one of the first major studies of Thomas Wolfe, *Thomas Wolfe: The Weather of His Youth* (1955); *The Curious Death of the Novel* (1967); *George W. Cable* (1969); and *The*

Wary Fugitives: Four Poets and the South (1978), for many scholars now the standard study of the Fugitive poets.

Rubin has edited several other books that are crucial to scholars in the field—*A Bibliographical Guide to the Study of Southern Literature* (1969), *The Comic Imagination in American Literature* (1973), and *The History of Southern Literature* (1985). In 1968, he and C. Hugh Holman began the modern version of the *Southern Literary Journal,* and in the same year he founded the Society for the Study of Southern Literature. He has also proven himself an able writer of fiction, and his novels include *Surfaces of a Diamond* (1981) and *The Heat of the Sun* (1995).

Much of Rubin's best writing is in essays, and his collections of his own essays include some of the most graceful and insightful of literary essays in America. A partial list of such books includes *The Faraway Country: Writers of the Modern South* (1963), *The Writer in the South: Studies in a Literary Community* (1972), *William Elliott Shoots a Bear* (1975), *A Gallery of Southerners* (1982), *Babe Ruth's Ghost and Other Historical and Literary Speculations* (1996), and *The Edge of the Swamp* (1989), a major reassessment of the origins of southern literature. What emerges from these books is a sense of Rubin as a major voice of a transitional generation of scholars in southern studies, unlike their apologetic predecessors able to view their region with distance and critical acumen but still needing to validate the South as a literary community. Not compelled to work out a relationship to an Old South, or even to a New South, they—Rubin, C. Hugh Holman, Lewis Simpson, and others—canonized a set of major works of art and used historical background to contextualize themes and draw continuities. Rubin has been particularly aware, however, that southern critics can hardly pretend disinterest in interpreting southern texts. Therefore he often focuses on the distinctive self-conscious southernness of so many of the writers he discusses. At the same time, he has been especially effective in redefining an American literature and culture that has in it an important role for strong southern writers.

John E. Bassett

See also Algonquin Books; Southern Literature, Idea of.

RUSSELL'S MAGAZINE

Conceived in 1856 by a group of Charleston writers, including William Gilmore Simms, Henry Timrod, and

Paul Hamilton Hayne, *Russell's Magazine* was edited and promoted chiefly by Hayne during over a year of advance work in addition to its three-year lifespan from April 1857 to March 1860. Hayne's idea was to seek and pay for contributions from North and South and to produce a monthly magazine modeled upon *Blackwood's* that would appeal to readers everywhere. Such an approach, despite occasional help from W. B. Carlisle, George C. Hurlbut, and John Russell, whose name was remembered in the title, was hardly possible in the immediate years before the "inevitable conflict." Nevertheless, Hayne published verse and fiction by such northern writers as Richard Henry Stoddard, John T. Trowbridge, and John W. De Forest, though the best work he received was by Simms, Timrod, and Hayne himself. Simms offered six prose items, including "Literary Prospects of the South" (June 1858), "Marion—The Carolina Partisan" (October, November 1858), a chapter from *The Cassique of Kiawah* (February 1859), and over sixty poems. Timrod provided four essays, among them two of his best—"Literature in the South" (August 1859), and "What Is Poetry?" (October 1859)—and thirty-seven poems, of which "The Artic Voyager" (April 1857) and "Preceptor Amat" (February 1858) are among his most memorable of this period. Hayne's publications are even more varied: seven stories, of which the most interesting is "The Skaptar Yokul: A Tale of Iceland" (April 1857), a gothic piece that reminds readers anew that the author had read Poe with care and enthusiasm; twenty essays and reviews, comprising discussions of Poe's *Arthur Gordon Pym and Other Stories* (April 1857), of Timrod's *Poems* (November 1859), of Simms's *Charlemont* (June 1857) and *The History of South Carolina* (January 1860), and of "The Poets and Poetry of the South" (November, December 1857); fifty poems, among them "Avolio—A Legend of the Island of Cos" (April 1859), subsequently the long narrative title piece of Hayne's third collection of verse in 1859; and most of the material for the "Editor's Table" and all the literary notices for twenty-eight of the thirty-six numbers of the magazine.

Hayne also published verse and prose from such Carolina literati as William J. Grayson, Samuel Henry Dickson, and William Elliott, and from other southerners such as John Esten Cooke, the Virginia novelist who contributed *Estcourt*, a serial for which Hayne promised $300 but could eventually manage only $50. This inability to pay was a sore point with Hayne and some of his contributors, especially those from out of state. Stoddard was unhappy when Hayne could not pay as promised and stopped sending his work. Cooke, on the other hand, accepted Hayne's explanation regarding the magazine's inability to fulfill its obligations and refused his offer to make up the difference himself. Hayne, it should be added, never received any payment for his editorial work or his contributions.

Aside from financial problems and the constant struggle for new subscribers, to say nothing of the urgent need for old ones to pay their bills, Hayne, despite his plan to appeal to an audience beyond the South and to deal only with literature, was at the same time generally committed to defending southern life and institutions, a policy that led to acrimonious political comment and rejoinder in some of the magazine's issues and an inevitable reduction in the number of northern contributors and readers. Even in January 1860, he was still trying to limit the influence of politics on his monthly. "It is not the province of this magazine," he maintained, "at least in its Editorial department—to touch, however superficially, upon the question of politics. Although we believe that the Southern states are standing on the verge of a Revolution . . . we shall not abandon the line of our original policy by intermeddling with any of the grand national or sectional issues of the day. On the contrary, our course still leads us through the peaceful realms of literature." Nevertheless, only two months later, Hayne gave up the struggle and "with great reluctance" acknowledged "the necessity which constrains us to discontinue [the] publication . . . of our magazine," and *Russell's*, on the very eve of the firing on Fort Sumter in April, became, in effect, one of the first cultural casualties of the coming conflict.

Rayburn S. Moore

See also Poetry, 1820 to 1900; South Carolina, Literature of.

Richard J. Calhoun, "The Ante-Bellum Literary Twilight: *Russell's Magazine*," *Southern Literary Journal* (Fall 1970); Paul Hamilton Hayne, "Ante-Bellum Charleston," *Southern Bivouac* (November 1885); Fronde Kennedy, "*Russell's Magazine*," *South Atlantic Quarterly* (April 1919); Alton T. Loftis, "A Study of *Russell's Magazine*" (Ph.D. diss., Duke University, 1973); Daniel M. McKeithan, ed., *A Collection of Hayne Letters* (1944); Rayburn S. Moore, ed., *A Man of Letters in the Nineteenth-Century South: Selected Letters of Paul Hamilton Hayne* (1982); Frank L. Mott, *A History of American Magazines, 1850–1865*, II (1957); Edd W. Parks, *Ante-Bellum Southern Literary Critics* (1962).

S

"SAHARA OF THE BOZART"

A nineteen-page diatribe by the social and cultural critic H. L. Mencken, "The Sahara of the Bozart," was arguably the most famous and influential single essay ever written about the American South. First appearing (in a shorter form) in the *New York Evening Mail* on November 13, 1917, then greatly expanded for Mencken's volume *Prejudices, Second Series* (1920), the essay had a powerful effect on a generation of young southern writers and thinkers coming of age in the 1920s.

Mencken's thesis in "The Sahara of the Bozart" is that the South, which he believed had once been the American seat of civilization, had become in the early twentieth century "almost as sterile, artistically, intellectually, culturally, as the Sahara Desert." In the essay he turned with great delight to a catalogue of southern failings:

> In all that gargantuan paradise of the fourth-rate there is not a single picture gallery worth going into, or a single orchestra capable of playing the nine symphonies of Beethoven, or a single opera-house, or a single theatre devoted to decent plays. . . . Once you have counted James Branch Cabell . . . you will not find a single southern prose writer who can actually write. And once you have—but when you come to critics, musical composers, painters, sculptors, architects and the like, you will have to give it up, for there is not even a bad one between the Potomac mud-flats and the Gulf. Nor an historian. Nor a sociologist. Nor a philosopher. Nor a theologian. Nor a scientist. In these fields the south is an awe-inspiring blank—a brother to Portugal, Serbia and Esthonia [sic].

Mencken condemned Virginia (although it was "the most civilized" of the southern states) and Georgia in particular, and then launched into his explanation of the paucity of the *beaux-arts*: the Civil War had drained the South of "all its best blood," and after the war the "poor white trash," infused with the moral fervor of Puritanism and its hostility toward the arts, had gained control.

When southerners read "The Sahara" in 1920—and it became widely read and remarked upon very quickly—they wondered what motivated Mencken to issue such a condemnation. As one angry and bewildered Arkansas editor wrote, "What has the South done to Menneken [sic]?" In fact, the author of "The Sahara" considered himself a southerner, at least when it was to his advantage to do so. He was a native of Baltimore, a border city, and he had long been fascinated with Dixie. In fact, in the decade preceding the publication of "The Sahara" he had written a number of other less-publicized pieces denouncing the South. What he held against the late Confederacy was its English and Scots-Irish ethnic makeup (as a German-American during World War I, he had become particularly sensitive to such matters), its evangelical religion, its political demagoguery and "mob democracy," its romanticism, and what he believed to be its unwarranted pride in its culture, its intellectual life, and its literature. In "The Sahara of the Bozart," he said so in thunder, and he continued to say so throughout the 1920s.

Mencken had no idea, however, that his essay would create such a storm among loyal southerners, and he had no idea he would be embraced as a liberator by any number of young southerners who shared many of his sentiments but could not express them so well. In North Carolina, Thomas Wolfe, Paul Green, W. J. Cash, and many other aspiring young writers hailed Mencken; in Georgia, Julian Harris (the son of Joel Chandler Harris) and Frances Newman echoed him; in Richmond and New Orleans, young editors began little magazines (*Reviewer* and *Double Dealer*) both to support and refute him; in Nashville, even

Donald Davidson and Allen Tate, those young Fugitives soon to become Agrarians, went around—at least until they changed their minds—with Mencken's green-covered *American Mercury* under their arms. By 1921 Mencken was in the South a literary force, and such he remained throughout the decade. He did not understand the South as well as his early disciples were to, and he was wrong in several particulars in his "Sahara"—but what he did in that essay was to bring a new critical spirit to the South and to add a new tone to southern intellectual life. In the process, without meaning to, he helped to launch what became known as the Southern Literary Renascence.

Fred Hobson

See also Fugitives, The.

Fred Hobson, *Serpent in Eden: H. L. Mencken and the South* (1974).

SAMBO

The stereotypical American Sambo figure is at least three hundred years old, having evolved from both the Fool of European court-jester traditions and from African sources. Joseph Boskin notes that ship manifests and slave census documents frequently recorded the name Sambo (with variants such as Samba and Zamba). Sambo the generic, plantation-tradition comic darky apparently developed initially in the South from the observations of New World slaveowners as they enjoyed watching awkward, marginally educated, overly obeisant—or humorously evasive—slave behaviors. The Sambo figure, and other related black character types, inevitably migrated from the rice and cotton plantations to appear in light comedies and minstrel shows, both before and after the Civil War. Here, they were often cast as well-intentioned but clumsy, typically illiterate, parodic versions of their masters or former masters; sometimes, too, Sambo was the mulatto offspring of his master. John Blassingame explains that the Old South Sambo often expressed "so much love and affection for his master that he was almost filiopietistic; his loyalty was all-consuming and self-immolating." Sambo appears as an actual character in Harriet Beecher Stowe's *Uncle Tom's Cabin* (1852), but Uncle Tom himself has been erroneously stereotyped as a Sambo figure by too many readers

who have not studied this complex novel carefully enough.

Incarnations of the comic Sambo figure surface throughout the eighteenth and nineteenth centuries, in the South and elsewhere, in American literature, drama, and popular culture—and in twentieth-century radio, television, film, and advertising. Allowing for a range of characteristics, Sambo figures include Jupiter in Edgar Allan Poe's "The Gold-Bug" (1843); Fleece the black cook in Herman Melville's *Moby-Dick* (1851), and Yorpy in his short story "The Happy Failure" (1854); a whole gallery of Jim Crow minstrel figures; Jim in Mark Twain's *Huckleberry Finn* (1885); Luster in William Faulkner's *The Sound and the Fury* (1929); "Stepin Fetchit" in 1920s and 1930s films; several characters from the *Amos n' Andy* radio show (1928 to 1943); the pickaninnies in the *Our Gang* series of the same period; Rochester in the Jack Benny radio and television shows of the 1940s and 1950s; the accordion-paper Sambo doll in Ralph Ellison's *Invisible Man* (1952); and dozens of black characters in black-produced and white-produced films, advertisements, and television sit-coms from the 1930s to present times. "J.J." from the 1980s television show *Good Times*, the 1990s characters Urkel from *Family Matters* and Mark from *Hangin' with Mr. Cooper,* and Danny Glover perched gingerly on a bomb-wired toilet in *Lethal Weapon 2* (1989) are all posturing around (or sitting right in the middle of) slapstick Old South Sambo stereotyping—whether they are intentional tongue-in-cheek personifications or accidental recreations of this stubbornly enduring character type. Ironically, probably the best-known Sambo iteration, Helen Bannerman's resourceful hero from the internationally popular *Little Black Sambo* (1898), is not a Sambo stereotype after all.

As Bernard Wolfe pointed out in the Sambo-saturated 1940s, white people like to pretend that the Negro is really grinning and "giving" to the white race. Sambo is thus a comic black who is sometimes "clever but not dangerous, and always capable of performing." Blassingame inventories Sambo's essential traits: "Indolent, faithful, humorous, dishonest, superstitious, improvident, and musical, Sambo was inevitably a clown and congenitally docile." Donald Bogle's summing-up of the Sambo tradition in film also reflects the character's role in other media: Sambos typically appear at the comic end of the full spectrum of "toms, coons, mulattoes, mammies, and bucks." Or, to put it a little differently: as cultural icons, Uncle Sam wants us, but Sambo merely entertains us.

Boskin observes that Sambo's closest rivals from the 1880s to the 1920s were probably Rastus and Joel Chandler Harris's Uncle Remus. The humorously naïve and inept Rastus figure fits the general Sambo mold, as do several comic darky characters who, Darwin Turner reminds us, periodically cut capers in Harris's extensive canon of folktales and local-color stories. Yet Harris's senior plantation slave, Uncle Remus, was a literary figure of rhetorical subtlety, psychological complexity, and depth. Harris said that he had quite serious intentions in portraying Negro character and was "dismayed by the intolerable misrepresentations of the minstrel stage." Harris also understood the centrality of the trickster motif in black folklore and admired the rabbit-hero's resourcefulness and guile in overcoming his stronger adversaries. Yet at times Harris dropped his guard and let the old plantation Sambo tradition displace some of Uncle Remus's originality and power.

R. Bruce Bickley Jr.

See also Civil War; Faithful Retainer; New South; Old South; Plantation Fiction; Trickster; Uncle Remus.

R. Bruce Bickley Jr., ed., *Critical Essays on Joel Chandler Harris* (1981), and *Joel Chandler Harris* (1987); John W. Blassingame, "Sambos and Rebels: The Character of the Southern Slave," in *Africa and the Afro-American Experience*, ed. Lorraine A. Williams (1977); Donald Bogle, *Toms, Coons, Mulattoes, Mammies, and Bucks: An Interpretive History of Blacks in American Films* (1973); Joseph Boskin, *Sambo: The Rise and Demise of an American Jester* (1986); Marshall Fishwick, *Remus, Rastus, Revolution* (1971); Daniel J. Leab, *From Sambo to Superspade: The Black Experience in Motion Pictures* (1975).

SAVAGE IDEAL

In his classic work *The Mind of the South* (1941), W. J. Cash refers to a southern "savage ideal," which he defines as "that ideal whereunder dissent and variety are completely suppressed and men become, in all their attitudes, professions, and actions, virtual replicas of one another." In so writing, Cash was giving a name to that characteristic of the southern mind noticeable since the 1830s when the national debate over slavery became especially heated—that southern tendency to distrust outside thought, alien ideas, or "isms"—

anything that would challenge the southern status quo, racial or otherwise. It is a characteristic, evident well into the mid-twentieth century, that many other writers of fiction and nonfiction have remarked on as well.

Fred Hobson

See also Savage South.

SAVAGE SOUTH

From colonial days, many outside visitors, foreign and domestic, remarked on the South as a comparatively primitive, culturally benighted, and violent society. Such was the case on the southern frontier—the Old Southwest—where travelers sometimes reported that life was even more violent than it was on the northern frontier (i.e., north of the Ohio River). Such was certainly the case with the plantation South of the early nineteenth century: outsiders—particularly with the intensification of the abolitionist crusade in the 1830s—looked at slavery and denounced an economic and social institution then extinct in most of the rest of the Western world. The South was widely denounced as not only backward but also cruel and sinful, out of step with the civilized world.

During the Civil War, the image of a savage or benighted South grew more prevalent, with reports of the Rebel fighting style and of conditions in southern prisoner-of-war camps such as that in Andersonville, Georgia. The aftermath of the war—the rise of the Ku Klux Klan and a descent into the dark age of racial segregation—contributed further to the image, as did—in the early twentieth century—further racial atrocities, political demagoguery, events such as the Scopes evolution trial in Dayton, Tennessee, in 1925, and such pronouncements on southern cultural and intellectual life as H. L. Mencken's 1920 essay "The Sahara of the Bozart." Writers such as William Faulkner, Erskine Caldwell, Richard Wright, and Flannery O'Connor contributed as well to that image—an image that has always both conflicted and co-existed with another powerful southern image, that of magnolias and moonlight. The image of a savage or benighted South has been modified and challenged, but it has not disappeared altogether, even at the beginning of the twenty-first century.

Fred Hobson

SAVANNAH, GEORGIA

Savannah, Georgia, was founded by a group of British colonists in 1733 under the leadership of Sir James Oglethorpe. The city soon grew into a coastal center of trade and commerce and served as the capital of Georgia until 1786. Occupied by British forces throughout most of the Revolutionary War period, the city's importance as a maritime harbor grew with the coastal plantation economy of Georgia, and by the beginning of the Civil War it had become the economic center of the state. In 1864 Savannah was the ultimate destination of William Tecumseh Sherman's infamous march to the sea, and when his troops occupied the city on December 21, the general wrote President Lincoln: "I beg to present you as a Christmas gift the city of Savannah, with one hundred and fifty heavy guns and plenty of ammunition, also about twenty-five thousand bales of cotton." Overshadowed in the twentieth century by the economic success of Atlanta, Savannah has remained a thriving coastal city. Still an active port, Savannah is also well known as a tourist center. The twenty-six squares in which its founder Oglethorpe laid out the city have been mostly restored in recent decades and form a center of interest for historians and visitors. One of these squares provided the setting for a popular nonfiction murder story, *Midnight in the Garden of Good and Evil,* by John Berendt, which was made into a feature film by Clint Eastwood in 1997.

Unlike Richmond, Charleston, and even New Orleans, Savannah never became a center of literary culture in the South, but it has played a significant role nonetheless. Early journals and chronicles by Oglethorpe, John Wesley, Hugh McCall, and others recount the early years of the city. Emily Burke, in a volume of letters entitled *Pleasures and Pain: Reminiscences of Early Georgia in the 1840s,* gives a poignant account of life in the city. The twentieth-century poet Conrad Aiken was born and raised in Savannah, and he lived the latter years of his life there, though he did not often write about the region. Poet and novelist Rosemary Daniell resides in Savannah today. For many readers, Savannah is most noteworthy as the birthplace of Ellen O'Hara, Scarlett O'Hara's mother in Margaret Mitchell's novel *Gone With the Wind.*

Hugh Ruppersburg

Kenneth Coleman et al., *A History of Georgia* (1991); Mills Lane, *Savannah Revisited: History and Architecture* (1994).

SCOPES TRIAL

Notoriously christened the "Monkey Trial" by H. L. Mencken, the dean of American iconoclasts in the 1920s, *The State of Tennessee v. John Thomas Scopes,* the case contesting Tennessee's anti-evolution law, was one of the most famous and highly publicized trials in American legal history.

Enacted in March 1925, the Butler Act, Tennessee's anti-evolution statute—the first in the nation—forbade the teaching of evolution in the state's public schools. The American Civil Liberties Union felt that this law contradicted the constitutional rights of freedom of speech and religion and therefore agreed to finance a test case, including the hiring of distinguished attorneys to handle it, for any Tennessee teacher who would come forth as a defendant. Having read of the ACLU's offer, George Rappelyea, the manager of the Cumberland Coal and Iron Company, and several other businessmen from the small town of Dayton in Rhea County, Tennessee, regarded the offer of the ACLU as a grand opportunity to bring fame to the town and to promote its commercial interests, and they persuaded John Thomas Scopes, a substitute science teacher at the local high school and a known opponent of the anti-evolution law, to stand trial. Scopes himself admitted that he and most other high-school biology teachers in Tennessee broke the law because the state-adopted biology text they were using, George Hunter's *A Civic Biology,* included discussions of Darwinian evolutionary theory. When Scopes was arrested on May 7, 1925, and charged a short time later with violating Tennessee law by teaching evolution in his science class, the stage was set for one of the most controversial trials of the century. Speaking in behalf of the ACLU, Roger Baldwin, its director, issued a public statement proclaiming, "We shall take the Scopes case to the United States supreme court if necessary to establish that a teacher may tell the truth without being thrown in jail."

The trial itself began on July 10, 1925, but Scopes did not play a significant role. The Scopes defense team consisted of Dudley Malone, John Neal, Arthur Garfield Hays, F. B. McElwee, and the most renowned trial attorney in the country at that time, Clarence Darrow. Known for defending the poor and downtrodden and frequently involved in controversial cases during his long and distinguished legal career, Darrow, an avowed agnostic, had a low opinion of religion generally and of the fundamentalist movement particularly. The lawyers for the prosecution were Herbert and Sue

Hicks, J. Gordon McKenzie, Wallace Haggard, William Jennings Bryan Jr., and his father, William Jennings Bryan, a great populist, Democratic Party leader, three-time candidate for president of the United States, and an acknowledged fundamentalist.

Featuring men of the stature of Darrow and Bryan, the Scopes trial predictably became a media event. Newspaper reporters from throughout the United States and parts of Europe, motion-picture cameramen, and even radio station WGN from Chicago descended on Dayton for the trial. H. L. Mencken, who may have been the most famous of these media representatives (Scopes called the trial "Mencken's Show"), sent daily dispatches to the *Baltimore Sun*, mocking the people of the neighboring countryside who flocked to Dayton for the trial—many of whom were of fundamentalist persuasion—as "morons," "hillbillies," and "peasants." A commercial as well as a media event, the Scopes trial created a carnival atmosphere, featuring local merchants offering trial souvenirs, such as stuffed monkeys and large pins with such slogans as "Your Old Man's a Monkey," Bible peddlers, and even circus performers with trained chimpanzees.

The highlight of the events at Dayton took place near the end of the trial when Darrow, in a surprise move, summoned Bryan to take the stand. In using this tactic, Darrow successfully made a mockery of Bryan, showing him to be inconsistent in his fundamentalist beliefs. Bryan revealed in his testimony, for instance, that he did not see the story of Creation in a strict literalist sense as occurring in six twenty-four-hour days, an admission that astonished and disappointed many of the fundamentalist observers. Despite Bryan's embarrassing statements as a witness, the Scopes trial ended on July 21 with a conviction, John T. Raulston, the presiding judge, ordering Scopes to pay a one-hundred-dollar fine. In January 1927, the Tennessee Supreme Court reversed this decision on a technicality, pointing out that fines over fifty dollars had to be determined by the jury, not by the judge. Even so, Tennessee's anti-evolution law remained on the books until it was repealed in 1967. And Scopes, who gave up teaching shortly after the trial, became a geologist for an oil company.

An embarrassment to the South, the Scopes trial stimulated a strong but limited literary reaction, most notably from Tennessee novelist T. S. Stribling and the Nashville Agrarians. The popularity of Stribling's *Teeftallow* (1926), a novel ridiculing Middle Tennessee fundamentalists and praised by Mencken for its engaging

realism, was by the author's own admission enhanced by the trial's publicity. In contrast, the Agrarian response, which unequivocally defended the traditional South and its way of life, was prompted by the disparaging image of the region that the treatment of the Scopes trial received from the northern press. Donald Davidson's "The Artist as Southerner" in the May 15, 1926 issue of the *Saturday Review of Literature* and "First Fruits of Dayton: The Intellectual Evolution in Dixie," in the June 1928 issue of *Forum,* provided the initial line of defense and helped to pave the way for the more formidable and substantive Agrarian manifesto, *I'll Take My Stand* by Twelve Southerners (1930).

Despite the widespread attention by advocates as well as by detractors, the outcome of the Scopes trial did not actually settle the key issues that the ACLU had hoped the case would challenge—the right of taxpayers to control what is taught in public schools, the concept of separation of church and state, the risks of academic freedom, and the tension between religion and science. Instead, the trial proved to be a victory for the fundamentalists, who, although successful in getting anti-evolution laws passed in only a few states, still significantly influenced the termination of the teaching of evolution in the nation's public schools. In terms of its broader impact on southern society, Fred Hobson has perceptively observed that the Scopes trial was "the event that most forcefully dramatized the struggle between Southern provincialism and the modern, secular world . . . , the event that caused Southerners to face squarely the matter of the South and their own place in it."

Ed Piacentino

See also Bible; Tennessee, Literature of.

Ray Ginger, *Six Days or Forever? Tennessee v. John Thomas Scopes* (1958); Tom McGowan, *The Great Monkey Trial: Science Versus Fundamentalism in America* (1990); John Thomas Scopes with James Presley, *Center of the Storm: Memoirs of John T. Scopes* (1967); Jerry R. Tompkins, ed., *D-Days at Dayton: Reflections on the Scopes Trial* (1965).

SCOTS-IRISH

The terms *Scots-Irish* and, more commonly, *Scotch-Irish* are used to describe the descendants of immigrants from the Lowlands of Scotland first to Northern

Ireland and subsequently to the colonies of British North America or the United States. The original settlement in Ireland was established in 1609 mainly by dispossessing Irish Catholic natives who were deemed rebels against the Protestant Crown; but much of the Scots-Irish migration to America, which came about a hundred years later and was substantially over by 1850, was in turn driven by economic and religious hardship. These hardy folk, originally Presbyterian but later professing a variety of evangelical faiths, settled for the most part in the southern interior and on the frontier rather than in the coastal areas. Known for their rough ways, their clannishness and violence, their expertise as Indian fighters, their religious enthusiasm, and their storytelling and music, the Scots-Irish were, though by no means only, the southern plain folk and crackers of popular conception. Not surprisingly, Andrew Jackson is the main exemplar of the group. Although frequently identified simply as "Irish," the "Scots-Irish" appellation became more common in the latter part of the nineteenth century when those of Ulster Irish-Scottish ancestry felt it necessary to distinguish themselves from the large numbers of impoverished Irish Catholics that the famine caused to leave their native land and come to America. They also frequently blended, sometimes indistinguishably, with the Scottish and English ancestries of the region. Thus, as has been pointed out again and again, although the Scots-Irish form a large part of the population of the southern states, their existence is more in memory than in actuality, since they quickly became part of the "ethnic whiteness" of the South. As a consequence also, their definitive presence in both the history and literature of the area is not always easily distinguishable from that of other white groups.

Indeed, the very existence of the Scots-Irish as a separate ethnic group has long been a matter of debate among historians. In recent decades, a number of scholars have again questioned the distinctiveness of the Scots-Irish tradition from both Irish and Scottish Highland cultures. Thus historians in the British Isles have pointed out that extensive intercourse between Scotland and Northern Ireland long predates the 1609 plantation and that the cultures were never very different in any case; that Scottish Highland and Lowland traditions are not as separate as was once thought; and, finally, that many of those once considered to have been exclusively Scots-Irish may originally have been unchurched Irish Catholics living without access to their own clergy in remote parts of the American South

who readily converted to the available forms of Protestantism. When Andrew Jackson was running for election as president in the 1820s, he was presented to the voters of New Orleans, for example, simply as a generic Irishman, and he has been so honored in the twentieth century by statesmen from the Republic of Ireland. Grady McWhiney and Forrest McDonald's controversial thesis about the existence of a "Celtic" South—a term also found in W. J. Cash and H. L. Mencken among others—based on a cultural homogeneity between immigrants from Ireland, Scotland, and the north and west of England, has also tended to blur the uniqueness of a Scots-Irish ethnicity.

Southern writers with Scots-Irish ancestry include John Pendleton Kennedy, William Gilmore Simms, Ellen Glasgow, W. J. Cash, Thomas Wolfe, Carson McCullers, and, more tenuously, Joel Chandler Harris and William Faulkner; significantly, though, nearly all of these have other ethnic identities also. Because the Scots-Irish have always formed a major part of the population of the interior and backcountry, and because much of southern literature has had a rural basis, this literature of necessity concerns them and, indeed, is often seen as having its origins in their storytelling traditions. But the Scots-Irish are most frequently not so identified; indeed, in this sense, literary works seem more faithful to the confused historical experience than are some of the strict historical depictions and to Harris's claim that emigration is "obliteration." Works in which a Scots-Irish presence or at least influence has been recognized (though often, again, only so identified in passing or by implication) include Kennedy's *Horse-Shoe Robinson* (1835), Simms's stories "Sharp Snaffles" and "Bald-Head Bill Bauldy" and his novel *Paddy McGann* (1862) (where, again, the title character comprises multiple Irish identities), Glasgow's *Vein of Iron* (1935), Andrew Lytle's *The Long Night* (1936), and Lee Smith's *Oral History* (1983). Some of the conflict between the Catholic Irish and the Protestant Scots-Irish both in Ireland and in the southern United States appears in Margaret Mitchell's *Gone With the Wind* (1936). In her autobiographical *Womenfolks: Growing Up Down South* (1983), Shirley Abbott offers both an interesting account of Scots-Irish identity and an indication of the imprecisions surrounding it.

Kieran Quinlan

See also British-American Culture; Highland Scots; Irish Catholics.

Donald Harman Akenson, *Being Had: Historians, Evidence, and the Irish in North America* (1985); H. Tyler Blethen and Curtis W. Wood Jr., eds., *Ulster and North America: Transatlantic Perspectives on the Scotch-Irish* (1997); John Caldwell Guilds and Caroline Collins, eds., *William Gilmore Simms and the American Frontier* (1997); Samuel C. Hyde Jr., ed., *Plain Folk of the South Revisited* (1997); James G. Leyburn, *The Scotch-Irish: A Social History* (1962); Grady McWhiney, *Cracker Culture: Celtic Ways in the Old South* (1988); Marilyn J. Westerkamp, *Triumph of the Laity: Scots-Irish Piety and the Great Awakening, 1625–1760* (1988).

SCOTTSBORO CASE

On March 25, 1931, nine poor black youths riding the rails through Alabama were stopped at Paint Rock and accused of raping two young white women on the train. In short order, and despite their accusers' suspect backgrounds and inconsistent stories, they were brought to trial in Scottsboro. The youngest of the group, thirteen years old when arrested, was granted a mistrial. But the other eight "Scottsboro Boys," as they came to be known, were sentenced to death by an all-white jury. And thus began a judicial *cause célèbre,* which, with the Communist-backed International Labor Defense and other groups coming to the aid of the accused, lasted through re-trials, reversals, and successful appeals to the U.S. Supreme Court, until the last man was released in 1950. Against the grim backdrop of the Depression in the South (the Scottsboro Boys were said to have been traveling in search of work), and coupled with the promise that Communism seemed to hold for racial as well as economic equality, the Scottsboro Case figured as a rallying point for many constituencies, including the literary community.

Two curious editorial efforts, *Negro* and *Contempo,* give evidence of the sort of interest that the events in Alabama generated among writers in and beyond the South. Though it was first published in a very limited edition, the enormous anthology *Negro* (1934)—intended as a gathering of materials representing the cultural importance of blacks worldwide—was significant for the originality of its editorial design and for the range and number and prominence of its contributors. These included southerners Zora Neale Hurston, Walter White, and Arna Bontemps. Its editor, Nancy Cunard (1896–1965), a wealthy Englishwoman and proprietor of the Hours Press in Paris, set out her plan for *Negro* in April 1931. Later that year, accompanied by Henry Crowder, to whom *Negro* was dedicated,

Cunard traveled to Harlem in search of material. Crowder, a black musician from Georgia who had joined Cunard in her work at the Hours Press, awakened her to the situation of black Americans. The Scottsboro Case was then gaining international attention, and Cunard, who became prominent among those organizing the appeals, included related material in *Negro.* Her own lengthy essay "Scottsboro—and Other Scottsboros" describes in detail the judicial course and political impact of the case until September 1933. *Negro* also includes "A Note on *Contempo* and Langston Hughes," describing local response to Hughes's visit to Chapel Hill, North Carolina, in 1931. Among Hughes's provocative acts, while he was the guest of *Contempo*'s editors, was his denunciation of the Scottsboro proceedings.

Contempo: A Review of Ideas and Personalities (1931–1934) was published in Chapel Hill, North Carolina, and during its short life printed a range of literary artifacts by Hart Crane, Nathanael West, Sherwood Anderson, William Carlos Williams, and numerous other luminaries. Cunard herself contributed a sonnet on the insufficiency of emancipation (called "Black on Red" in her typescript) to the penultimate issue of *Contempo,* where it was placed under the heading "Lincoln's Grinding Verbiage" (April 5, 1933). Hughes was a frequent contributor to *Contempo* and, along with Ezra Pound (also a contributor to *Negro*), was listed on the masthead. The first issue of *Contempo* appeared in May 1931, not long after the first Scottsboro trial, and this cause became a natural focus for the leftist editors. A Scottsboro issue (December 1, 1931) included Hughes's poem "Christ in Alabama," his essay "Southern Gentlemen, White Prostitutes, Mill-Owners, and Negroes," and Lincoln Steffens's essay "Lynching by Law or by Lustful Mob North and South: Red and Black." This issue also included "Facts About Scottsboro," an essay by Carol Weiss King, the attorney for the defense, which *Contempo* had previously published in July 1931. Another issue contained commentary on Scottsboro by Theodore Dreiser and John Dos Passos (mid-July 1931). And Hughes contributed two more poems on Scottsboro—"White Shadows" (September 15, 1931) and "The Town of Scottsboro" (February 15, 1932). A typescript of the latter poem in the *Contempo* archives at the University of North Carolina at Chapel Hill includes Hughes's wry annotation, written while he was in Alabama: "Dear Contempo-raries— Why don't you set up here and get tarred and feathered."

Hughes produced a short drama in verse, *Scottsboro Limited,* which features a chorus of "Red voices" and ends "to the strains of the Internationale." It enacts, in abstract form, the trajectory of the case and sets it against the economic realities of the time. Hughes's pamphlet titled *Scottsboro Limited* (1932) includes the play, two of the poems published in *Contempo,* and two other poems on the same subject. Arna Bontemps, Hughes's confrere in the Harlem Renaissance, was a teacher in Alabama at the time of the incident and the first trial. Disheartened, he moved to California, where his historical novel *Black Thunder* (1936), about a slave rebellion, was written in response to these events. Three better-known southern novels, which tell of black men accused of sexual crimes against white women, seem even more explicitly to owe elements of their plots to the Scottsboro Case: *Light in August* (1932), by William Faulkner, another *Contempo* contributor and visitor to Chapel Hill; Richard Wright's *Native Son* (1941); and Harper Lee's *To Kill a Mockingbird* (1960). These constitute only a portion of the texts deriving from the case. Letters written by the defendants during the time of their imprisonment form another portion.

Amber Vogel

See also Alabama, Literature of; Harlem Renaissance; Law, 1900 to Present; Lawyer; Novel, 1900 to World War II; Racism.

Dan T. Carter, *Scottsboro: A Tragedy of the American South* (1969); James Goodman, *Stories of Scottsboro* (1994).

SEARS CATALOG

No imagined southern outhouse is complete without a copy of the Sears catalog within arm's reach. The glossy paper was not suited for toilet tissue, though. That duty was reserved for grocery sacks from the A&P or old newspapers. The Sears catalog was for wishing for things you probably would never get, of a people and world far removed from tobacco fields and baying coon hounds.

Novelist Harry Crews in a PBS documentary on his writing and life spoke of the Sears catalog. He told that what immediately stood out was that everyone pictured in the catalog was perfect—no baldness or obesity, blind eyes or missing fingers. Nearly everyone Crews knew was scarred from the labors of their lives.

Crews told of how he and a young friend would make up stories about the people in the catalog, romances and fights and scandals that intertwined the lives of almost everyone in the book.

As a child, I remember the Sears catalog. It was by far the thickest book in our house. It made a good doorstop or could be used to weigh down the lid on a box of baby opossums my dad brought home from a hunting trip. I didn't look at it much—not the big book—I was not very interested in clothes, except the pictures of women in their undergarments. Then I had to sneak peeks—not an easy accomplishment in a four-room house home to seven people. The much more slender Christmas catalog was the coveted one.

Beginning the first of November, the watch would begin. Upon arriving home from school, I or one of my brothers would pull a shift at the curve in the road just past our house where we would wait for sight of the mailman's car. Upon sighting the vehicle, the scout would yell all the way to the front porch where all us siblings would gather around the mailbox.

For about a week or more, we were disappointed. The mailman would apologize as he handed us bills or an occasional letter. But that magical day would finally come; the mailman would smile as he handed through the window a sleek, shiny, brand-new Christmas catalog, the cover adorned with Santa and reindeer and Christmas trees in bright colors of red and green and white. The rule stated that the scout got to hold the catalog first, but he would be swamped as hands reached to touch the book, to feel some of the magic.

At nine years of age, I already didn't believe in Santa Claus. My uncle had given me a telescope when he returned from military service in Germany. After viewing the rings of Saturn, belief in a fat man who flew and visited every child's house in one night didn't hold water any longer. Besides, we didn't have a chimney—just a rusty flue pipe that stuck out of the wall. Regardless, the weeks leading up to Christmas were wondrous, many hours spent thumbing through the catalog, dogearring certain pages, drawing a circle around a special bike or basketball. We were usually allowed five presents each, plus a surprise. Agonizing were the decisions, choices changed time and time again. The debate might last up to Christmas Eve, although my mother had already bought our gifts and stored them in our neighbor's closet.

The choices made and changed hardly mattered Christmas morning. Before the sun had risen, my parents would be begged from bed, and we would tear into the gifts, snapping ribbons and shredding paper. Few of the gifts ever actually came from Sears. My father's hard-earned pay was more suited to K Mart or Woolworth. But the bike was just as shiny, the jet fighter made a noise like a real plane. The Sears catalog was like a mirror. It said, Open me, child. Look into your heart, wish and want and believe. This season of innocence and trust will pass too soon.

Tim McLaurin

SECTIONALISM

As a literary sentiment and a political imperative, sectionalism has remained the clearest point of convergence between southern literature and politics from the 1830s through the 1960s. Sectionalism was from the first a reactionary movement. In the antebellum period, the sectionalist sensibility found its impetus in the national crisis over slavery. Since the Civil War, sectionalism has been most often understood in juxtaposition to and in tension with regionalism. Given the abstract nature of both terms, it is important to understand that "regionalism" in this context includes not only the work of such local-colorists as George Washington Cable and Kate Chopin, but also the programmatic reform efforts of several southern academics. Indeed, the regionalism that inspired derision on the part of sectionalists was foremost the province of sociologists and political scientists.

Like the regionalism of Howard W. Odum, Rupert B. Vance, and others, sectionalism was finally programmatic and didactic, and in fact neither "ism" appealed to those southern writers who aspired to write fiction that transcended such limitations. Such important southern writers as Mark Twain, William Faulkner, Eudora Welty, and Flannery O'Connor did not self-consciously promote regionalism or sectionalism. For some lesser southern writers, however, the historically vague line between politics and literature proved problematic. Starting with William Gilmore Simms and others of his generation and extending through the polemical works of Donald Davidson, traditionalist southern writers have long held to a sectionalist view of the South and its place in the Union. For these writers, this sectional chauvinism has always been comprehensive, encompassing not only literature but politics and culture as well. For the southern sectionalist, the interests, power, and authority of state and section su-

percede that of the central government—all with a view to maintaining the organic particularity of each section and resisting the cultural imperialism of other sections, whether New England in the nineteenth century or New York in the twentieth.

Early in his career, Simms was not self-consciously concerned with writing "southern" literature; he championed the cause of "American" literature well into the 1840s. A zealous literary nationalist with far-reaching literary friendships in the North, he was one of the most important members of the Young America group. In his largely successful historical romances of the 1830s and 1840s, Simms attained a rich and imaginative rendering of the past, grounded in the customs and manners of early America. Set primarily in the South, these works demonstrated Simms's oft-asserted conviction that "national" literature would be best served by fictional works grounded in specific regional contexts. However, Simms's largely apolitical posture as a writer and public intellectual was unfortunately cut short by the intensifying national debate over the South's chief sectional concern: slavery. The political climate of Simms's day thus turned him away from an original and valuable historical/nationalist mode and required instead that he put his literary gifts into the service of sectional rhetoric laden with abstractions that would have been anathema to him at any other time or place.

After the Civil War, Thomas Nelson Page and others resurrected another popular antebellum mode—the plantation myth—and conjoined it with the notion of the Lost Cause in pursuit of a decidedly sectionalist goal: namely, the preservation of white hegemony in southern race relations. In most of these works, the sectionalist viewpoint was implicit—an undercurrent in works ostensibly aimed at national reconciliation—but in the 1920s, as the South entered the modern world, sectionalism was revived and became a political and cultural battle cry for Donald Davidson and not a few of his Agrarian compatriots in a reaction against the increased urbanization, secularization, and industrialization of America and the South. In his impassioned defense of sectionalism in the 1930s and for several decades following, especially in reaction against what he deemed the dangerous generalizations and abstractions of regionalist social planners, Davidson argued at great length for sectionalism as a firewall against a centralized national bureaucracy that, if left unchecked, would subsume and homogenize the organic culture of all American regions. Although Davidson's seminal sectionalist work, *The Attack on Leviathan* (1938), was ultimately weakened by a racist and segregationist rationale, it was nevertheless a searching critique of the pitfalls of regionalism. In what Michael O'Brien regards as a "desperate gesture of compromise," Davidson convincingly argued that the recognition of sectional diversity was the true safeguard of national unity.

To the extent that most contemporary southern writers have moved away from such overt historical concerns as the legacy of slavery and the Civil War, the sectionalist vein in the region's literature has largely subsided. Even so, the continued vibrancy of a distinctively "southern" literature points to a certain separateness that remains unmatched by any other region (or section) of the country.

Collin Messer

See also Regionalism.

Donald Davidson, *The Attack on Leviathan* (1938); Michael O'Brien, *The Idea of the American South: 1920–1941* (1979); Howard Odum and Harry Estill Moore, *American Regionalism: A Cultural Historical Approach to National Integration* (1938).

SECTIONAL RECONCILIATION

The "six R's" of the post–Civil War era in the South are racism, reconciliation, Reconstruction, Redemption, Republicanism, and reunion. To explore any one of these sociopolitical forces during the disconcerting decades following the war is to explore all six. Furthermore, the whole curriculum must be taken with several doses of cynicism. The North and South struggled long and hard to reconcile themselves to reconciliation, and with only marginal success. In fact, in some quarters, North-South social, political, and philosophical reconciliation remains even today an unrealized—and finally no longer relevant—goal. Cumulatively, however, several forces have produced, over time, a kind of de facto reconciliation that never officially occurred in the nineteenth-century streets, manufacturing plants, farms, shops, and legislative halls of the unreconstructed/unreconstructable, carpetbagger-infested, still angry and war-weary American North and South. The postwar expansion of the railroad and consequent inter-regional travel (for health, tourism, and commerce), cultural cross-fertilization, employment relocation and the labor

movement, immigration, the Spanish-American War and two world wars, evolving national legislation, booming Sunbelt economic development generally, and overt sentimentality and downright myth-making about the Lost Cause and wartime heroes and heroines on both sides have linked North and South permanently. Yet an old battle-scarred Confederate soldier wrapped in the Stars and Bars still glares at highway tail-gaters from a perennially popular southern bumper sticker, cursing "Fergit, Hell!" Change the uniform to blue and the flag to the Stars and Stripes, and the bumper sticker still works for the other side, too. It is a cliché that the defeat experience, despite the horrific carnage, enriched southern writing and helped make the Sunbelt a phenomenal economic success story. But resentment in some parts of the South—and North—dies hard.

In *Reconstruction: America's Unfinished Revolution 1863–1877* (1988), Eric Foner demonstrates how Reconstruction and Radical Republicanism were corruption-ridden failures. Moreover, the Redeemer counterrevolution, which effectively returned power to the hands of both an old and a new generation of Confederates, only reinstituted social, political, and economic racism in the South. Although postwar sectional reconciliation never officially occurred, several American writers of the later nineteenth and early twentieth centuries wanted reunion to happen—and even ignored the political realities in pretending that it had. Nina Silber, in *The Romance of Reunion: Northerners and the South* (1993), focuses especially on the "romantic and sentimental culture of conciliation" and on the images and metaphors of imagined reunion that permeate the work of northern playwrights, minstrel-show producers, and fiction writers from 1865 to 1900. But while southern authors may have taken some of their reconciliationist cues from their northern fellow-artists (South Carolina author Paul Hamilton Hayne even wrote a widely reprinted poem entitled "Reconciliation"), they also developed their own complex visions, revisions, and rhetorical renderings of southern life, now infused permanently with northern blood—and northern capital.

Among the earlier and more notable northern imaginative renderings of the reconciliation theme was John De Forest's *Miss Ravenel's Conversion from Secession to Loyalty* (1867). Southern readers learned about Miss Lillie Ravenel's conversion experience two years after the war was over, too late to change their minds and help preserve the Union. But De Forest was in the right place at the right time to introduce a major metaphor for effecting sectional reconciliation in print, a thematic pattern, with variations, that both northern and southern writers would endlessly echo: the marriage of a handsome, resourceful, and worthy Yankee male to an attractive, independent-minded, even tempestuous, Southern Belle. The result of their marriage was, almost invariably, domestic harmony—the metaphor for depoliticized North/South reconciliation and new beginnings. Historically, North/South marriages happened with great frequency during Reconstruction—and for understandable demographic reasons. Hundreds of thousands of southern males had been killed or disabled in the war, a proportionally higher number across the regional population than northern male casualties; thus southern women confronted a dismaying vacuum in the supply of available southern men that prosperous and adventurous northern males were eager to fill. So the marriage metaphor was a believable one and sold well nationally, in all genres, in spite of—or perhaps because of—the disturbing social developments in postwar America. Sentimental romantic escapism was preferable to harsh political confrontation.

Plays featuring cross-sectional romance and marriage as a reconciliation symbol were extremely popular during and immediately after Reconstruction, but they are mostly ephemeral as literary works. Charles King's *Kitty's Conquest* (1884), William Gillette's *Held by the Enemy* (1886), Augustus Thomas's *Alabama* (1891), and J. K. Tillotson's *The Planter's Wife*, among a host of other postwar plays, used what Silber terms "gendered metaphors" of romantic reunion. Sexual liaisons and marriages replace sectional antagonisms as the Old South is inseminated with new life from the North. Other kinds of stage productions and blackface minstrel shows, frequently sweetened with marriage motifs, teased American audiences with variations on Old and New South racial, cultural, and political themes, as northern and southern cultures sought to understand each other. Starting in the 1870s, the Jubilee Singers from Fisk College and Hampton Institute put traditional black folk songs and spirituals on the road to the North. Large-scale stage shows, such as *The Grand Republic* (1876), included minstrel numbers performed by black singers, as did widely popular stage productions of Harriet Beecher Stowe's *Uncle Tom's Cabin*, first published in its novel form in 1852. The rhetoric of blackface minstrel shows is complex, since the actors were frequently Irish laborers with their own political agendas who "jumped Jim Crow" ostensibly to entertain audiences with parodies of black slaves. Yet they also hoped to educate viewers about slaves' coping powers and essential humanity, to mock the manliness of their cruel masters, and to affirm the dignity of the common man and woman everywhere, black or white, Irish or otherwise, in the face of the oppressive forces of the Establishment.

In addition to De Forest's *Miss Ravenel's Conversion,* several novels used a section-bridging marriage and other related romantic motifs as reconciliation themes. Albion Tourgée's *A Fool's Errand* (1879) and Henry James's *The Bostonians* (1886) play variations on the clichéd pattern by featuring a temporarily stalled marriage between northern women and southern males. In Tourgée's novel, Comfort Servose, a Union colonel during the war, buys a plantation in North Carolina during Reconstruction, sells land to blacks, supports their cause, and stirs up other kinds of resentment in the community with his liberal ways. Only on his deathbed is he reconciled with his staunchest rival, former Confederate General Gurney, whose son is then freed to marry Servose's daughter. James ends his novel by marrying the passionate southerner, Mississippian Basil Ransom, to the beautiful and oratorically gifted northerner, Verena Tarrant. Verena's love for Basil weans her from the feminist political movement managed by another Bostonian, the jealous and manipulative Olive Chancellor. Romance and sentiment, across various plots, subplots, and motifs, took readers away from sectional and social realities in works such as Francis Hopkinson Smith's *Colonel Carter of Cartersville* (1891), Thomas Nelson Page's *Red Rock* (1898), *Gordon Keith* (1903), and other novels, and Owen Wister's immensely popular *The Virginian* (1902). This work virtually invented the Hollywood chivalric cowboy hero, and a movie and television series about the Virginian were popular even after the mid-twentieth century. Of vaguely southern origins and speaking with a drawl, but the embodiment of all that Wister found most virile and honorable in the American male, the Virginian finds ennobling adventure under western skies—as well as love with a schoolteacher from Vermont. The North Carolina Baptist minister Thomas Dixon put a different spin, however, on the reconciliationist struggle in his racist trilogy, *The Leopard's Spots, The Clansman,* and *The Traitor* (1902, 1905, 1907). Dixon's white supremacist social philosophy and open support of the Ku Klux Klan, perspectives that D. W. Griffith incorporated into his classic 1915 movie *The Birth of a Nation,* represent views that have, of course, plagued intercultural and interracial communities around the world for thousands of years and will continue to do so—no matter how strong the push for tolerance, respect, and reconciliation.

As Barbara Ladd observes in *Nationalism and the Color Line* (1996), the tensions and discontinuities clogging the national discourse about race and sectional reconciliation empower George Washington Cable's *The Grandissimes* (1880), Twain's *Adventures of Huckleberry Finn* (1885), and his *Pudd'nhead Wilson and Those Extraordinary Twins* (1894). A tragic, abortive marriage between an African slave and an quadroon, based on the folktale of Bras-Coupé, is the centerpiece of Cable's novel. Cable resolves his multilayered plot sentimentally, by reconciling feuding Creole families—emblematic of the need for national healing and cross-cultural, cross-racial dialogue and understanding. But Twain's two novels unromantically explore the incredible complexities of the huge racial and sectional drama playing itself out in postwar America. Why would Twain, in *Huckleberry Finn,* write such an accomplished novel about slavery two decades after the war was over? Because he was both fascinated and troubled, observes Ladd, by "the persistence of slavery in a nation supposedly devoted to freedom" and by the disorder rampant in a supposedly progressive America. Huck and Jim confront the multiple faces of prejudice, hypocrisy, and racism in their wayward journey toward freedom. Twain's real text in *Huckleberry Finn* is his serial revelation of Huck's socially conditioned, conscious resistance to his own best moral and ethical instincts about race and the human heart. In *Pudd'nhead Wilson,* Twain suggests that the mulatto Tom Driscoll's moral flaws are more the product of the brutalizing racist society that has raised him and his mother than the result of any genetic inadequacy he carries as a mulatto. The "moral morass" of slavery brings out the worst in human society, across the generations. Even long after the Civil War, as Faulkner shows in *Go Down, Moses,* the grim legacy of slavery is a disease that keeps festering, sometimes just barely below the surface, within families and within the larger communities they inhabit and influence.

The boom in the popularity of the monthly and quarterly literary magazine, starting in the later 1860s, was fed by postwar America's suddenly aroused interest in seeing snapshots of everything regional. Northerners were increasingly intrigued by the character, racial mix, and folklore of the South, now grudgingly rejoining the Union; southerners wondered what kind of life their northern co-combatants returned to; and everyone was fascinated by the stories and legends flowing back east from the West. Local-color fiction, as a corpus, is the most important genre in reconciliationist literature because it helped open up the landscape, character, dialect, and customs of the whole country to all of its citizens. The father of the local-color movement in America was Washington Irving, who in the second decade of the nineteenth century invented the genres of the American regional sketch and the short story and reminded readers of their highly visual content through the punning name of his persona, Geoffrey Crayon. Nathaniel Hawthorne was another Romantic-era precursor of local color. But among the major local-color short-fiction writers during the flowering of the genre were Sarah Orne Jewett, Mary E. Wilkins Freeman, and Harriet Beecher Stowe in New England; Richard Harding Davis, Brander Matthews, and O. Henry in New York City; E. W. Howe, Hamlin Garland, James Whitcomb Riley, and Edward Eggleston in the Midwest; Bret Harte and Mark Twain in the Southwest; and Twain along the Mississippi. Yet the Southeast captured most of the local-color literary attention, both nationally and internationally. Edward King's extensive 1873 series of essays on "The Great South" for the *Atlantic Monthly* explained that the railroads and resorts naturally beckoned tourists southward, where the outsider's eyes would be pleased and surprised by the region's picturesque scenes—mountains and meadows, bayous and coastlines, plantations and shanties—and by its fascinating Old South and New South history and its remarkable mix of characters and racial types. Thomas Nelson Page evoked "Ole Virginia"; Mary Noailles Murfree and John Fox took the reader to the Tennessee and Kentucky mountains; George Washington Cable and Kate Chopin explored city, parish, and island resort life in Creole Louisiana; and Joel Chandler Harris recreated and gave distinctive dialect voices to a wide array of black and white people, male and female, slave and free, in Georgia.

All of the local-colorists worked to reunite America by helping its citizens appreciate its several regional heritages. But Harris, in his role as associate editor for the *Atlanta Constitution,* as the major collector and raconteur of African American folktales in the nineteenth century, and as a sensitive southern short-fiction writer, was probably the most influential voice for sectional and racial reconciliation in America. During his twenty-five-year career with the *Constitution* and in essays for the *Saturday Evening Post* and for his own *Uncle Remus's Magazine* after his retirement in 1900, Harris campaigned for racial understanding and "neighborliness," for the progressive equalizing of educational and employment opportunities, and for the elimination of racial and regional prejudices. Along with his associate editor Henry Grady, Henry Watterson of the *Louisville Courier-Journal,* and a few other leading New South journalists, Harris actively sought to reduce tensions and open up productive dialogue across the old Mason-Dixon Line and between blacks and whites. Harris's six volumes of short stories, among them several reconciliation tales set during the Civil War—such as "Little Compton" and "Aunt Fountain's Prisoner"—include some of his best writing. The most celebrated of these, "Free Joe and the Rest of the World" (1887), paints a moving and pathetic portrait of the plight of a freed black slave who was a lone atom ricocheting among three worlds: the community of black slaves who resented his freedom because they were still in chattel bondage, the poor whites who were also resentful of Joe's freedom because he would work for lower wages than they, and the white establishment who saw a freedman as a threat to their hegemony. Joe dies alone, separated from his wife, Lucinda, who was still a slave and had been cruelly sold down the river by Spite Calderwood to keep her from visiting Joe, and separated finally from his loyal little dog Dan, killed by Calderwood's hounds. Harris's often-anthologized story was based on the experiences of a freed slave whom Harris knew; it comments both on the pathos of the freedman's condition before the war and on the challenge of black amalgamation and racial reconciliation after Emancipation. Harris also addressed the issue of uneasy black and white relationships after the war in *Gabriel Tolliver: A Story of Reconstruction* (1902). Harris's novel is rambling and episodic, but critics find it a sensitive portrait of the political machinations, carpetbagging, social disruptions, and racial tensions pervading the South during Reconstruction. Tolliver, a young southern lawyer and Harris's spokesperson, argues for moderation, patience, and mutual understanding as the South works to rediscover and redefine itself after the war.

Harris's most important literary persona, and his major voice for reconciliation virtually throughout his career, was Uncle Remus. Harris gave Remus his first major role in his 1877 *Atlanta Constitution* story, "Uncle Remus as a Rebel." He revised this narrative—and added the familiar southern and northern cliché, intersectional marriage—when he collected it as "A Story of the War" in his first book, *Uncle Remus: His Songs and His Sayings* (1880). In the earlier version, Uncle Remus had instinctively shot and killed a Yankee sniper who was trying to shoot his master. In the later story, Uncle Remus shoots the marksman in the arm, shattering the bone. John Huntingdon subsequently loses his arm but is nursed back to health by Miss Sally, and in due course they are wed. But the fascinating character in this early Harris story is Uncle Remus himself, who would serve as the complex framing voice for all of the folktales to come. He is the authoritative, loyal family retainer and fearless protector whose experiences as a slave were obviously humane. Remus is also a mediator and bridger of differences, a kind of social philosopher trying to see past the war and its racial and sectional conflicts to a larger peace among all human beings, beyond violence (including his own). As narrator in the eight volumes of Brer Rabbit stories that Harris published over a quarter of a century, Uncle Remus plays an evolving role, however. In the rhetorically complex narrative frame of the Brer Rabbit tales, Remus serves two young white male listeners as the affectionate and morally instructive mentor in the ways of the critters—and, through them, the ways of the real adult world. In the earlier volumes, Remus takes us back to the plantation era and tells his stories to the son of his master; in the volumes set after Emancipation, his listener is now the rather sissified grandson of his former master. But the second little white boy needs more pointed instruction and manly shoring-up than did the first young listener, now his father, in order to be weaned from his softer ways and codependency on his mother. Allegorically, Harris may have been toying in the later Uncle Remus volumes with his own sense that post-Reconstruction southern male leadership may have grown too soft, too dependent on northern capital and influences, and that it needed to rediscover its native identity and reassert itself in the Old South become complexly New.

But even more rhetorically challenging are the animal stories that Remus tells. In fact, the Brer Rabbit tales often seem to function as a countertext to the generally affectionate Remus–little boy framework surrounding these celebrated stories. Both Uncle Remus–little boy relationships affirm the value of interracial tolerance and understanding, human sympathy and mutual support, and moral integrity and strength of character. Yet the animal stories themselves typically reveal a world of social hypocrisy, trickery and countertrickery, amorality, one-upmanship, and predatory violence. Brer Rabbit, clearly the black slave's folk-hero, almost invariably outsmarts his stronger animal adversaries, who just as clearly represent the white race. Moreover, Brer Rabbit relies on his wits and his dexterity, mental and physical, to trick the other animals out of money or food, or to obtain sexual favors or status. The ethic that Brer Rabbit seems to preach, furthermore, is that so long as one can exercise power in any of these arenas, one still has freedom in a predatory world. If Brer Rabbit tortures or even murders one of his adversaries, in the context of slavery's inhumanity he is treating them no differently from the way they have treated him and his chillen. Finally, however, Uncle Remus leaves his young listeners—and now over four generations of adult readers of all nationalities and races—to draw their own conclusions, grim and otherwise, about the price that mankind has paid for slavery and the human uses and abuses of power. Teaching by reverse example, and opposed to the internal dynamics of these internationally celebrated stories, Uncle Remus's trickster tales imply that true reconciliation, true marriage of opposites, can only come through racial toleration, human understanding, and love—the only alternatives to the destructive politics and practice of prejudice, hatred, and ignorance.

R. Bruce Bickley Jr.

See also *Atlanta Constitution*; Carpetbagger; Faithful Retainer; Local Color; New South; Old South; Plantation Literature; Reconstruction; Sunbelt; Uncle Remus.

Paul Buck, *The Road to Reunion* (1937); W. E. B. Du Bois, *Black Reconstruction* (1935); Eric Foner, *Reconstruction: America's Unfinished Revolution, 1863–1877* (1988); John Hope Franklin, *Reconstruction After the Civil War* (1961); George Fredrickson, *The Black Image in the White Mind: The Debate on Afro-American Character and Destiny, 1817–1914* (1971); Paul M. Gaston, *The New South Creed: A Study in Southern Mythmaking* (1970); Barbara Ladd, *Nationalism and the Color Line in George W. Cable, Mark Twain, and William Faulkner* (1996); Otto H. Olsen, *Reconstruction and Redemption in the South* (1980); Rollin G. Osterweis, *The Myth of the Lost Cause, 1865–1900* (1973); Anne Rowe, *The Enchanted Country: Northern Writers in the South, 1865–1910* (1978); Nina Silber, *The Romance of Reunion: Northerners and the*

South, 1865–1900 (1993); C. Vann Woodward, *Origins of the New South, 1877–1913* (Rev. ed.; 1971).

SECULARIZATION

Secularization is the result in institutions and in individuals of general indifference or hostility to religious ideas, values, motives, and practices. Transcendent reality is dismissed as a fiction, and religion, allowed only a subjective meaning, is melted down to a vague, amorphous humanism.

Secularization is one of the features of modernity, if not its very engine, and thus it is an object of the critique of modernity that was so strong in literary modernism. That critique can be found, among southern writers, in John Crowe Ransom, Allen Tate, Cleanth Brooks, Andrew Lytle, and others in the middle of the twentieth century, and in Richard Weaver, Lewis Simpson, and Marion Montgomery in the later twentieth century.

The critique of secularism in southern literature and thought began in the particular context of the postbellum "New South" movements. Most of the best southern writers and critics responded suspiciously to the "New South" idea because of its unabashed admiration of industry, technique, and bureaucracy, but also because they saw in it an acceptance, if not an advocacy, of secular ways of understanding reality—for instance, behaviorism, consumerism, instrumentalism, and positivism. As "New South" ideas and practices steadily encroached upon the South's characteristic religiosity, many writers responded strongly.

Flannery O'Connor and Walker Percy are among the writers whose attack on secularization has been strongest. In O'Connor's stories and novels, such characters as the Misfit and the grandmother ("A Good Man Is Hard to Find"), Parker ("Parker's Back"), and Hazel Motes (*Wise Blood*) stumble among ferocious images of the pervasive banality of the secular looking for something finer and more enduring. Percy's characters are engaged in the same search; some of them even refer to it directly as "the search." They demonstrate, like Binx Bolling (*The Moviegoer*), a bracing intelligence and wit that serve as caustics against the age's reductionistic and sentimental secular humanism.

Michael M. Cass

See also O'Connor, Flannery.

Cleanth Brooks, "Walker Percy and Modern Gnosticism," *Southern Review* 13 (1977); Robert Coles, "Flannery O'Connor: Southern Intellectual," *Southern Review* 16 (1980); Christopher Lasch, "The Cultural Civil War and the Crisis of Faith," *Katallagete* (Summer 1982); Walker Percy, "Notes for a Novel About the End of the World," in *The Message in the Bottle* (1975); Allen Tate, "Remarks on the Southern Religion," in Twelve Southerners, *I'll Take My Stand* (1930).

SEGREGATION

When W. E. B. Du Bois declared in 1903 that "the problem of the twentieth century is the problem of the color line," he was responding to the period that many historians refer to as "the nadir of race relations," sustained by the 1896 *Plessy v. Ferguson* "separate but equal" court decision and continuing for almost sixty more years until the 1954 *Brown v. Board of Education* decision that rendered school segregation unconstitutional. Eleven more years would elapse before voting rights and access to public accommodations were made available regardless of race.

Although racial segregation was a tacit reality from the time that enslaved Africans were transported to the American colonies, full-fledged institutional segregation emerged in the post-Reconstruction era. Before the Civil War, blacks held in captivity and segregated by virtue of their "inhuman status" were easily restricted in their daily movements. Even free blacks in the North and the South were circumscribed in their access to citizenship.

After the Civil War, however, former slaves, with the passage of constitutional amendments, were provided with protections to ensure their systematic and gradual inclusion into American life. The Thirteenth Amendment (1865) officially outlaws slavery; the Fourteenth Amendment (1867) defines citizenship and guarantees equal protection under the law; and the Fifteenth Amendment (1870) awards black men the right to vote. Designed ostensibly to improve conditions for African Americans, these legislative acts did little to erase the stigma of slavery or to eradicate the segregated existence. In essence, the oppression of slavery—the mark of black racial inferiority—was perpetuated as new forms of economic dependency developed. Sharecropping (or tenant farming) emerged as a standard practice throughout the South, and former slaves found themselves in circumstances similar to those they had sought to escape.

Moreover, with the steady withdrawal of federal troops from southern states and with the end of Reconstruction, blacks found themselves at the mercy of southern political machines whose sole focus was the restoration of white supremacist rule. Using violence and intimidation, white power structures suppressed any future effort toward black political participation or social equality. Two late-nineteenth-century events solidified these efforts. Booker T. Washington delivered his Atlanta Exposition address in 1895 and relinquished, for black people, any claim to social equality, and in 1896 the U.S. Supreme Court litigated *Plessy v. Ferguson* and legalized segregation based on race. Jim Crow was thereby sanctioned, and separate black and white worlds—socially, economically, and culturally—were created. Jim Crow laws in southern states mandated racial separation in every potential area of public interaction.

To ensure that blacks were confined to their world, reactionary whites engaged in widespread lynchings of blacks, usually black men falsely accused of attacking white women. Lynching was an effort to instill fear in blacks so that they would not encroach upon white space and to foster distrust in whites by exploiting stereotypes about black bestiality. In short, social segregation was augmented by psychological segregation, and any attempt to defy such structures was quickly and summarily subdued.

In 1909 the National Association for the Advancement of Colored People was founded, largely in response to a series of antiblack race riots. The NAACP, viewing itself soon after its inception as the legal arm to the civil-rights struggle, emerged as the leading black civil-rights organization and waged battles against discrimination in housing, jobs, and education. In the 1920s, it attempted unsuccessfully to convince the federal government to pass an anti-lynching law. By the 1930s, because of strained economic conditions that negatively influenced race relations, the organization employed a moderate strategy for redress by focusing on educational inequity. Not surprisingly, gross disparities not only in facilities but also in school budgets and teacher salaries could be documented. Though the *Plessy* decision declared "separate but equal" as lawful, the NAACP found nothing equal about educational opportunities for black children vis-à-vis those for white children. For the next two decades, the NAACP mounted cases, garnering some victories along the way—victories that culminated in the *Brown v. Board of Education* decision in 1954.

Although the *Brown* decision supposedly terminated segregation in schools, the full victory was long in the making, as local school districts circumvented the Court's mandate. The extremist backlash to the *Brown* decision, identified as "massive resistance," resulted in the publication of the *Southern Manifesto* (1956), a document signed by ninety-six southern white leaders that pledged uncompromising opposition to *Brown*. In addition, White Citizens Councils sprang up all over the South to devise methods of preventing integration. Even when the federal government offered "freedom of choice" (an adjustment period during which volunteers opted to attend a racially different school) as a means of easing the transition to integrated schools, local districts thwarted the intent. As no white children were sent to black schools, the only mode of integration was a black child's entering a white school. Because many black families were beholden to the white community for employment, credit, and the like, they were hesitant to upset the white power structure by imposing themselves on the white schools. Hence, segregation remained entrenched long after 1954.

Although the *Brown* case did much to bolster the resolve of African Americans to dismantle their second-class citizenship, it also heightened race tensions. Two 1955 events best exemplify these two responses and highlight the resultant intensity. In the summer of 1955, Emmett Till, a fifteen-year-old black boy, was lynched in Money, Mississippi, for allegedly whistling at a white woman. And in December, Rosa Parks, in Montgomery, Alabama, refused to relinquish her bus seat to a white man. Whereas the Till case reveals the extent of the white anger concerning the *Brown* case, the Parks case shows the renewed determination of blacks to continue the struggle. Hence the modern Civil Rights Movement was born.

For the next ten years, African Americans, aided with the emergence of Martin Luther King Jr., Malcolm X, and the Southern Christian Leadership Conference and the Student Nonviolent Coordinating Committee, struggled for equal access to public accommodations, housing, transportation, and voting, a journey that would yield the Civil Rights Act of 1964 and the Voting Rights Act of 1965.

Some literary texts that address these issues directly are Richard Wright's *Uncle Tom's Children* (1938) and *Native Son* (1940); the short stories "Everything That Rises Must Converge" by Flannery O'Connor, and "Spring Is Now" by Joan Williams; the novels *'Sippi* (1967) and *Youngblood* (1954) by John Oliver Killens; *Meridian* (1976) by Alice Walker; and *The Autobiography of Miss Jane Pittman* (1971) by Ernest J. Gaines.

Charles E. Wilson Jr.

See also *Brown v. Board of Education*; Jim Crow; *Plessy v. Ferguson*; Reconstruction; Washington, Booker T.

John Whitson Cell, *The Highest Stage of White Supremacy: The Origins of Segregation in South Africa and the American South* (1982); Waldo E. Martin Jr., *Brown v. Board of Education: A Brief History with Documents* (1998); Eric J. Sundquist, *To Wake the Nations: Race in the Making of American Literature* (1993); Brook Thomas, *Plessy v. Ferguson: A Brief History with Documents* (1998); C. Vann Woodward, *The Strange Career of Jim Crow* (1974).

SENTIMENTAL NOVEL

The South produced many of the nation's best-selling novels in the nineteenth century, and many of these novels can be classified as sentimental. The sentimental novel played an important role in the literary marketplace. These novels generally written by and for women helped provide nineteenth-century women, South and North, with a voice.

The definition of the sentimental has been heavily debated. Although the seduction novels of the late eighteenth and early nineteenth century, such as *Charlotte Temple* (1791) and *The Coquette* (1797), are sometimes classified as sentimental, more often the term *sentimental* refers to literature that fits within Nina Baym's model of "woman's fiction," the popular plot-line of the nineteenth century featuring a young woman protagonist who is born or falls into poverty and must make her way in the world. This genre focuses on women's lives and work and the struggles that women undergo as they attempt to make a place for themselves in the world.

American literary critics in the mid-twentieth century denigrated the sentimental, maligning its use of excessive feeling and emotionally charged language and claiming that this literary form serves no other function than mindless entertainment. Most late-twentieth-century critics of the sentimental, however, have acknowledged its importance as a political genre shaping understanding of women's worlds. Jane Tompkins has provided the most outspoken assertion of the politics of the sentimental, arguing that sentimental novels strategically intervene in nineteenth-century discourses and promote the values of the domestic realm as a cure for the moral ills of the nation. The general trend in current literary criticism involves analyzing the political importance of the sentimental, assuming that it is a genre with significance beyond sheer entertainment value. Because sentimental novels were so widely read, often becoming best-sellers, critics acknowledge that it is necessary to understand the role they played in their culture and in the lives of the women who read them.

Baym, Tompkins, and other critics have established the familiar critical terrain surrounding the sentimental. Their definitions of the sentimental and their discussions of women's literature, however, are not universally applicable. Critics of southern women's writing have noted that arguments made about the sentimental in the nineteenth century fail to take into account specific regional differences. Women writing in the South had a different perspective on politics, on women's roles, and on the nation as a whole from that of northern women. Critics typically examine the northern women writers Harriet Beecher Stowe, Fanny Fern, and Susan Warner in order to formulate theories of the sentimental. Although the general concepts of the sentimental do apply to southern women writers, their regional differences give their writing a different significance.

Plantation romances, a genre usually allotted exclusively to male writers, are an important influence on the southern sentimental novel. The plantation romance, beginning with John Pendleton Kennedy's *Swallow Barn* (1832) and continuing with such novels as William Alexander Caruthers's *The Cavaliers of Virginia* (1836), Nathaniel Beverley Tucker's *George Balcombe* (1836), and William Gilmore Simms's *Woodcraft* (1852), upheld the plantation home as the center of southern culture, in this way corroborating the emphasis of the sentimental novel on domestic space. Plantation novels, popular both in the North and the South, promoted a pastoral vision of society rather than the industrializing vision apparent in the North. In these ways, men's plantation romances paved the way for the southern sentimental novel. As many critics have noted, however, plantation fiction elevated the male protagonist, the plantation patriarch, as the heroic force in the novel, ignoring the role of women. This emphasis is rewritten in southern sentimental fiction.

While plantation romances often trivialized women's role, portraying them primarily as attractive ornaments to the patriarch and his plantation, southern sentimental fiction placed women at the center of the novel and of southern culture. The sentimental fiction written by southern women often takes the complicated position of both critiquing and upholding the South as a region. Many southern sentimental novels

placed themselves at the defense of the South in opposition to northern encroachment and criticism; Caroline Lee Hentz's *The Planter's Northern Bride* (1854) defends the South from the criticism leveled at it by Harriet Beecher Stowe's *Uncle Tom's Cabin* (1851). Thus southern sentimental fiction implicitly fulfilled a political function, defending the culture of the South from the industrialization, reform, and lack of tradition that its writers (and readers) perceived as characterizing the North. At the same time that they defended their region, however, many of these novelists also criticized the South from within, questioning its moral failings and the idea of women as ornaments to the household.

As they defended their region, many of these authors were aware of the financial incentives to appeal to northern as well as southern readers. Many of them did this effectively; in fact, Augusta Jane Evans's *Macaria* (1864) was so popular in the North that it was smuggled to a northern publisher and printed there with great success. Evans (1835–1909) was one of the most popular southern novelists, and today she is one of the most widely studied. New editions of many of her novels, including *Beulah* (1859), *Macaria*, and *St. Elmo* (1866), have been released in recent years, and she has appeared in most major studies of southern writing as well as in analyses of nineteenth-century women's writing generally, such as Mary Kelley's *Private Woman, Public Stage* (1984). Evans began writing in order to help support her family when her father suffered economic failure. During her lifetime, her work was so popular that she was able to live comfortably from her literary earnings; in addition, towns, schools, steamboats, and even a cigar were named after St. Elmo.

Evans's novels present strong, independent female protagonists who, in many ways, mirror Baym's "woman's fiction" prototype. Although she was a strong supporter of women's education, Evans was an outspoken opponent of women's suffrage and women's involvement in politics.

Evans uses every opportunity in her novels to promote the education of women. Her protagonists, from Beulah in the novel of that title to Edna Earl of *St. Elmo*, are intelligent, driven young women who desire to learn and to write. Edna lists women's rights as the right to be learned, wise, noble, and useful in women's divinely limited sphere; the right to influence and exalt the circle in which she moved; the right to mount the sanctified beam of her own quiet hearthstone—but not the right to vote; to harangue from the hustings; to trail her heaven-born purity through the dust and mire of political strife; to ascend the rostra of statesmen, whither she may send a worthy husband, son, or brother, but whither she can never go, without disgracing all womanhood.

Evans is careful, however, to draw a line between women's learning and publication and the unacceptable role of women in politics. In *St. Elmo,* she presents an unflattering image of a northern women's rights advocate, comparing this woman to a goat in convulsions. In this argument, Evans was very much like other nineteenth-century southern women novelists. She upheld the moral rectitude of the South over the North, portraying the North as a site of unrest and chaos in contrast to the South's established hierarchies of class and race that promoted peace and justice (at least to those who, like Evans and most other southern novelists, were in the higher reaches of the hierarchy).

Although Evans's protagonists challenge the accepted roles for women in the nineteenth century in their determination to write for publication and their unsurpassed intellects, they ultimately concede to what is the accepted ending of sentimental novels, North and South: marriage. By not allowing her female protagonists to become reformers or radicals, Evans upholds the traditions of the South. Some critics have interpreted this stance as a retreat from the fairly radical questions that Evans has her protagonists ask, questions that range from the role of women to the existence of God. Ultimately she reinforces the status quo.

Caroline Lee Hentz (1800–1856) is another popular southern sentimental novelist. After marrying a French immigrant, Hentz moved from her native Massachusetts and spent several years traveling around the South and West. An author of ten novels, Hentz attempted to soothe regional tensions and promote reason in her novels. Best known among her novels is *The Planter's Northern Bride.* Its main themes are the natural and right hierarchy established in southern society and the proper role of the southern women. The novel presents a wide range of characters, northern and southern, black and white, from a variety of class backgrounds. Whereas the northern characters, especially the working class, are often dissatisfied with their lives, the southern hierarchy provides a place for each southerner and presents a vision of domestic harmony. The plantation owner Russell Moreland defends racial inequality, explaining to his northern wife, "My dear Eulalia, God never intended that you and I should live on *equal* terms with the African. He has created a barrier

between his race and ours, which no one can pass without incurring the ban of society." This natural inequality is so pervasive within the novel that one of the Moreland slaves escapes only to discover that a life of freedom is too harsh. She longs for the familial support and comfort of her position in slavery, and she returns home to beg her "family"—her owners—to re-enslave her.

The Planter's Northern Bride, rather than attempting to refute the North, argues for a joining of the two regions of the country. This, according to Nina Baym, was often the position that sentimental novels took in the nineteenth century: attempting to promote domestic values such as forgiveness, acceptance, and love and apply these to the nation as a whole. Hentz demonstrates the joining of the two regions most vividly through her description of two little girls, one northern and one southern, sitting together happily, holding hands. Before the Civil War, Hentz attempted to provide an image of peace through her writing.

In *The Planter's Northern Bride,* Hentz presents female protagonists who are somewhat different from Evans's women. Eulalia Moreland is a beautiful, pure, white woman who is fully at home in the domestic sphere. She comes to embody an ideal vision of true womanhood because of her continual innocence. She is described as never fully grown; she is a woman, but part of her remains a child. She is also beautiful, wearing gloves when she does housework to protect her delicate hands. Although this novel allies itself with the plantation romance through its emphasis on a heroic male character, Hentz's other novels, including *Eoline; or, Magnolia Vale* (1852) and *Helen and Arthur* (1853), portray outspoken, independent women.

A different form of sentimental writing is demonstrated in the work of E. D. E. N. Southworth, a popular novelist who is not always recognized within studies of southern women writers because her work deviates from that of Evans and Hentz. Southworth began writing to support herself and her children when she and her husband separated. A shrewd businesswoman, she became wealthy enough to live solely from her literary proceeds. One of Southworth's most popular novels, *The Hidden Hand* (1859), features a feisty protagonist named Capitola Black. Capitola, more extreme than Evans's and Hentz's female characters, is an outspoken woman who rides horses, combats villains, rescues damsels in distress, and even cross-dresses. She fits a traditional model of male heroism rather than true womanhood. Under her rough exterior, however,

Capitola has a true womanly heart. She loves her patriarchal uncle, and although she often counteracts his orders, she is charming enough to maintain his affection.

In some ways, Southworth blended the genres of gothic fiction and the sentimental in *The Hidden Hand*. The novel presents sentimental love stories and the familiar sentimental plot of broken families ultimately being reunited, but it also features several notorious villains, including Black Donald. Although the novel is set in the South and offers caricatured slaves who call the heroine "Miss Caterpillar," it contains no overtly southern message. Instead, Southworth seems preoccupied with women's roles and their ability successfully to negotiate entrapping situations. Southworth's Capitola is somewhat more extreme than Beulah or Edna Earl, but the three characters resemble one another in their outspokenness and intelligence.

Other nineteenth-century southern sentimental writers, including Caroline Gilman (1794–1888), Maria McIntosh (1803–1878), and Mary Virginia Terhune (1830–1922), produced writing popular in its time but little known and not widely available today.

After the Civil War, many southern women writers turned from sentimental writing to local-color writing. Sentimental writing did not disappear entirely, but it was no longer the prevailing literary genre. Local-color writing, popular across the country, emphasized the regional diversity and quaintness of life in the South. It also usually evoked nostalgia for the past, popularized by writers such as Kate Chopin and Mary Noailles Murfree.

Alison Piepmeier

See also Domesticity; Domestic Novel; Local Color; Plantation Fiction; Women Writers.

Nina Baym, *Feminism and American Literary History: Essays* (1992) and *Woman's Fiction: A Guide to Novels By and About Women in America, 1820–1870* (1978); Anne Goodwyn Jones, *Tomorrow Is Another Day: The Woman Writer in the South, 1859–1936* (1981); Elizabeth Moss, *Domestic Novelists in the Old South: Defenders of Southern Culture* (1992); Jane Tompkins, *Sensational Designs: The Cultural Work of American Fiction, 1790–1860* (1985).

SERMONS

As a genre centrally at home in the formal rituals of religion, the sermon migrates to many other contexts and is subject to multiple uses in culture as well as in religion. Its portability resides in its being the most public and most publicly available of religious forms. It is a genre available to the practice of individuals and groups without respect to the restrictions and patents of any religious group, racial or ethnic community, gender, or the level of education or class of its practitioners. The sermon provides an entrance, at once minutely particular yet widely distributed, to the study of southern religion and culture. The sermon is one of the seams that knits religion and culture into overt and covert reciprocities with each other, particularly in the American South.

The potency of this variety of discourse resides in its invocation of authority derived from scriptural citation, the performative force of its speech acts, particularly proclamations, interdictions, and admonitions, and the power of its stories to endorse its message, to reproduce in narrative translation the scriptural text, and to repeat through its narrative dynamics the declarations of both text cited and the preacher's claims about it. The widely respected authority of the Bible in southern culture and the virtuosity of its preachers cannot account, alone or together, for the effectiveness and widely dispersed use of this form. The sacred text and the charisma of the speaker in conjunction with the arts of narration account for the religious effectiveness of this genre as well as for the migration of the sermon from religion to multiple cultural settings.

The conjunctions of text, assertion, and narrative in the discourse of the sermon gain cultural support and immediate receptivity from the dominant mode of the southern imagination, rhetoric in general, and narrative in particular. The mode of the southern imagination is not the exclusive set of mind of any one social or religious group. Rhetorical conventions are widely shared across diverse sectors of the culture. The sermon in the American South is one of the chief expressions of this prevailing mode. Allen Tate provides an apt description of the dominant mode of the southern imagination in a neglected essay, "A Southern Mode of the Imagination." He says that "the traditional southern mode of discourse presupposes somebody at the other end silently listening: it is the rhetorical mode. Its historical rival is the dialectical mode. . . . The Southerner has never been a dialectician . . . Emerson said that the 'scholar is man thinking.' Had Southerners of that era taken seriously the famous lecture entitled 'The American Scholar,' they might have replied by saying that the gentleman is man talking."

The distinction between rhetoric and dialectic is Aristotle's in Book I, chapter 1 of *Rhetoric,* and in chapter 3 of that work he distinguishes among the three species of rhetoric: deliberative (political), judicial, and epideictic (praise). Narrative plays a role in each of these kinds of rhetoric, particularly the judicial, and the sermon has elements of all three species of rhetoric. Tate stresses the Aristotelian, Ciceronian, and Renaissance humanist antecedents to this major mode of the southern imagination. In the sermon as genre in southern religion and culture, there are also the Christian antecedents, beginning with St. Augustine's transformation of Ciceronian rhetoric in his treatise *On Christian Doctrine* (427 C.E.). Augustine emphasizes, after the biblical precedents, the requirement that the preacher stress scenes and stories from common life; thus in Christian currency there is a deflation of the high style of Roman rhetoric. The sermon in religion and culture draws from both these traditions, classical and Christian, according to religious groups and kinds of education sanctioned for their clergy.

However, the southern mode of imagination in its rhetorical privileging of narrative draws from a wide repertory of storytelling traditions across a diversity of racial, ethnic, regional, and occupational groups, and from both oral and literate narrative practices. These reappear in the extraordinary array of styles and stories found in the pulpits of major and minor denominations. Whatever the goal, sacred or secular, southerners practice their belief in salvation by narration.

There is much traffic among large and dispersed repertories of narratives: tall tales, folk songs, the Bible, representations of sermons in novels, not to speak of the publication of sermons in the memoirs of preachers. The range of appropriation of the sermon in fiction and memoir is illustrated in James Baldwin's *Go Tell It on the Mountain* (1953) and *The Fire Next Time* (1963). The power of the black sermon helps William Faulkner bring *The Sound and the Fury* (1929) to conclusion. James Weldon Johnson caught the force of the form by rendering sermons as poems in *God's Trombones* (1927).

Two features of the sermon, each an instance of the employment of narrative, are the testimonial and the conversion story. Frequently, conversion stories are narrated as part of a testimonial, and both kinds of discourse are linked with biblical precedents. A typical sermon is fraught with narratives linked to each other: a biblical story will be read as text for the sermon; in the course of asserting its meanings, the preacher will cite a conversion story of a member of the congregation, a biblical character like St. Paul, or his own. Thus the preacher follows an ancient strategy, exposition as proof, and the instrument of exposition is narrative. These narrative linkages yield increments to the persuasions of the testimonial claims. These stories are further woven into the dense fabric of narrative of the church's historical past, both the story of the larger religious body over large expanses of time and space and the local church's history in the community. These embedded narratives work in behalf of the claims of the testimonial, characteristically ending with an invitation to conversions on the part of those who listen. Only to the dialectically minded will this rhetoric appear circular.

The cultural coefficient of this religious rhetoric is an imagination predisposed toward a good story and, usually, unwilling or uninterested to learn *how* stories work, what they disguise, hide, as well as reveal. The art of the telling is best hidden in effective performance—and in affective reception.

As Tate, Cash, and others have pointed out, the preference for story is also a preference for the mythmaking faculty, a faculty that finds effective homes in fiction and religion and, as Nietzsche argues in *On the Advantage and Disadvantage of History for Life* (1873), this faculty finds its enemy in the dialectical examination and cross-cultural comparisons of how myth and fiction work, its cunning and subversions of alternative ways of living and thinking. The congruence between much southern fiction and both Protestant and Roman Catholic religions finds its pivot in the southern preference for rhetorical practices of narrative representation. The widely noted weakness of theology in the nineteenth- and early-twentieth-century South may find a partial explanation in this alliance between fiction and religion and their common matrix, rhetoric.

The sermon in the social locations of its performance is as varied as its rhetorical strategies. In the modern period, it has retained its central focus in evangelical and Pentecostal groups while migrating to circuits and sectors beyond religious spaces: brush-arbor revival sites; open-air amphitheaters; street corners and college campuses; radio and television studios; sports arenas; and parks. More people hear sermons outside the spaces of ecclesiastical architecture than within them. Whatever the sermon's site of transportation, its rhetorical identity is still discernible even in conventional secular forms.

The elements of the sermon were always audible in its first cousin, political oratory. In the post–World War II era, and particularly since the 1960s, sermonic rhetoric's affiliations with the discourse of politics have been recurrent. However, the matter must be expressed the other way: sermonic rhetoric has taken on more than one kind of affiliation with political discourse. Nowhere is this more evident than in the Civil Rights Movement, and preeminently in the rhetoric of Dr. Martin Luther King Jr. The Exodus narrative, enacted in marches as well as retold in sermon after sermon, became the rhetoric of a political theology of liberation. More recently, this same reciprocity between sermon and political oratory is evident in the sermons of the Moral Majority and the Religious Right. This coalition's rhetoric is an indictment of the children of darkness and a plea for the restoration of a Christian nationalism, endorsed by a founding narrative of the Christian beginnings of colonial North America and by its scriptures in the Declaration and Constitution.

Elements of sermonic rhetoric are audible and visible in the marketplace through advertising media, sometimes, like its ritual counterpart, backed by music. Participants in the religious culture and the consumer culture recognize each other easily, since these sectors of the society, particularly in the "Bible Belt" now expanded into the "Sunbelt," employ many of the same rhetorical markers, especially the testimonial by a converted buyer of the product in question. There are effective exchanges between the sermon and the advertisement, including publicity by religious groups on their own behalf. Just as cheerleading rituals are related to the collective ritual action in religious spaces, so the coaches' pep talks to teams are derivative from the admonitory, didactic, and exemplary rhetoric of preachers. Inspirational speakers on the corporate circuits, many of whom are former or current coaches and preachers, trade heavily in selected elements from the sermon genre.

However, the variety of appropriations of sermonic markers by politics and the market is far surpassed by the variety of sermons within religions. Secular uses of sermonic rhetoric are not under the constraints of tradition, theological doctrine, and customary preaching practices. Calvinists do not preach like Pentecostals. The use of biblical texts would be one major difference between them. The Assemblies of God—a hybrid between the Protestant Reformation with its scriptural focus and the Holiness movement in the American South with its stress on eliciting ecstasy—are of special interest to the student of religious rhetoric. Of particular note is the way Assembly preachers retain the centrality of the biblical text while preaching for an experience of sanctification. Tension between instruction and inspiration is palpable. Lumbee Indian Pentecostal sermons differ significantly from Baptist African American sermons and both from Black Muslim sermons, though the congregations may live and work in the same town and listen to the same television and radio stations.

Aside from different religious traditions crossed with different racial and ethnic communities, no list of sermonic features can fail to take into account the most distinguishing markers of the performance of sermonic discourse: facework, accent, gesture, pacing, audience-speaker interplay, the role or absence of music in both vocal and instrumental forms, and the aesthetics of the space of performance. Before a sermon is a type of discourse, before it is a text, it is an enactment in which all three of the classical rhetorical components are at play: discourse, speaker, audience. The space of performance is communal, a theater of memory and a school for the religious imagination, in its reaching back to the archetypes of the founding generation and forward to the consummations envisioned in its sacred scriptures.

Ruel W. Tyson Jr.

See also Bible Belt; Evangelical Christianity; Mind of the South, The; Oral History; Oratory; Preaching; Storytelling; Tall Tale; Vernacular Voice.

Wayne C. Booth, "Rhetoric of Fundamentalist Conversion Narratives," in Fundamentalisms Comprehended, ed. Martin E. Marty and R. Scott Appleby (1995); Catherine A. Brekus, Strangers and Pilgrims: Female Preaching in America, 1740–1845 (1998); Gerald L. Davis, I Got the Word in Me and I Can Sing It, You Know: A Study of the Performed African-American Sermon (1985); Gary Holloway, O. B. Perkins and the Southern Oratorical Preaching Tradition (1992); Paul Ricoeur, "The Hermeneutics of Testimony," in Essays on Biblical Interpretation, ed. Lewis Seymour Mudge (1980); Bruce A. Rosenberg, Can These Bones Live?: The Art of the American Folk Preacher (1988); William Toohey and William D. Thompson, eds., Recent Homiletical Thought (1967); W. Stuart Towns, Oratory and Rhetoric in the Nineteenth-Century South: A Rhetoric of Defense (1998).

SEWANEE REVIEW

The Sewanee Review, founded with private money in 1892 by William Peterfield Trent at the University of the South, is the nation's oldest continuously published quarterly. In the 1940s, the *SR* was changed from a journal in the humanities (of which the best example is the *American Scholar* under Joseph Epstein) to a literary and critical quarterly. This metamorphosis occurred during the editorships of Andrew Lytle (1942–1944) and Allen Tate (1944–1946). Ever since that time, the *SR* has been essentially the publication that they forged. The editors since Tate have been J. E. Palmer (1946–1952), Monroe K. Spears (1952–1961), Andrew Lytle (1961–1973), and George Core (1973–present). Poetry began to be published regularly in the 1920s during the editorship of W. S. Knickerbocker (1926–1941); fiction in 1943 (with a long story by Robert Penn Warren); and reminiscences and other forms of the familiar essay in 1987. Literary criticism of a high order has been the magazine's staple since the mid-1940s; that criticism was, for many years, written often by the New Critics and other hands of much the same persuasion—from Warren, Tate, Lytle, Cleanth Brooks, Francis Fergusson, Austin Warren, and R. B. Heilman through B. L. Reid, James M. Cox, Louis D. Rubin Jr., Lewis P. Simpson, Walter Sullivan, and J. A. Bryant Jr. Also associated with the *SR* over a long period were such *Scrutiny* contributors as Q. D. and F. R. Leavis, R. G. Cox, H. A. Mason, and especially L. C. Knights.

The *SR*'s critical program chiefly entails English literature from 1500 to the day before yesterday. Various classical writers, especially Dante, are considered from time to time. Although the critical emphasis is given principally to the literature of the twentieth century, such subjects as the English Renaissance (especially Shakespeare) receive considerable attention. Since 1974 there have been special issues on many subjects and modes—for example, Irish letters (twice), Commonwealth (or postcolonial) literature, biography, the literature of war, modern British and American poetry, the modern Catholic novel, and, on many occasions since 1987, autobiography.

During a typical year the *SR* publishes four to six stories and some forty to fifty pages of poetry. In addition, a considerable amount of fiction and poetry is reviewed annually. The magazine over the past twenty-five years has contained more reviews and essay-reviews than any comparable quarterly. The *Sewanee Review*'s regular contributors include writers from Great Britain, Canada, and India in addition to the United States. Although the *SR* is based in the American South, it is not devoted to southern literature; indeed, over the past quarter century only two issues have chiefly involved southern writing. Representative writers since the mid-1940s—in addition to those already mentioned—include Flannery O'Connor, Wallace Fowlie, Elizabeth Spencer, Walker Percy, Samuel Hynes, James M. Cox, Jayanta Mahapatra, George Woodcock, Neal Bowers, F. D. Reeve, William Hoffman, Helen Norris, Merrill Joan Gerber, Catharine Savage Brosman, Mairi MacInnes, John McCormick, William Harmon, and George Garrett. Many of these writers have written in more than one genre for the *SR*—Garrett and Warren in nearly every mode. (The dramatic version of *All the King's Men* was first published in the *SR* in 1963.)

The University of the South gradually took over subsidizing the *Sewanee Review* in its early years and has generously underwritten the magazine, through good times and bad, ever since. As Allen Tate pointed out long ago, the quarterly operates with a subvention or not at all. Since Tate's editorship (when contributors were first paid at his insistence), the *SR* has been a major literary quarterly in the way defined by Monroe Spears; its peers have generally been the *Kenyon Review* (particularly when edited by John Crowe Ransom), the *Southern Review*, the *Hudson Review*, and, in a slightly different way, the *Yale, Virginia Quarterly,* and *Partisan* reviews, all of which involve political discussion. There has been more camaraderie than rivalry among these magazines: as Ransom long ago observed in a letter, "We do not compete so much as we reinforce the common standard" (June 1946).

Ransom founded the *Kenyon Review*, but the original series of the *Southern Review*, under Brooks and Warren (1935–1942), has proved to be the enduring model of what the critical quarterly can be at its best. The blueprint for it, the *Kenyon*, the *Sewanee*, and other quarterlies appears in Tate's "The Function of the Literary Quarterly" (*Southern Review*, 1936). The British prototype, more than T. S. Eliot's *Criterion*, is Ford Madox Ford's *English Review*.

Despite what Lewis Simpson has called a falling-off from the literary establishment, a diminishment that has occurred since the critical quarterly's salad days in the 1940s and 1950s, the quarterly remains the most important literary forum in the United States, serving as the nexus between the academy and university presses on the one hand and the wider world of letters and trade houses on the other. The current mediocrity of such slick high-circulation magazines as the *New*

Yorker, the *Atlantic,* and *Harper's* makes the quarterly more important than ever.

George Core

See also *Kenyon Review*; Periodicals; *Southern Review.*

George Core, "*The Sewanee Review* and the Editorial Performance," *Yearbook of English Studies* 10 (1980); G. A. M. Janssens, *The American Literary Review: Critical History, 1920–1950* (1968); Monroe K. Spears, "The Function of Literary Quarterlies," (1960), in *American Ambitions* (1987); Allen Tate, "The Function of the Literary Quarterly," in *Essays of Four Decades* (1968); special number of *TriQuarterly,* no. 43, entitled *The Little Magazine in America* (1978), particularly the essays by James Boatwright, Robie Macauley, William Phillips, Felix Stephanile, Reed Whittemore, and most especially Lewis P. Simpson.

SEX AND SEXUALITY

Much of the force of the exotic South in literature and in the popular imagination is based on the perception of sex and sexuality in the South going back to colonial times. In the Northeast, the Puritan divines—the likes of Cotton Mather, Increase Mather, and Jonathan Edwards—held the public to strict codes. In the nineteenth century, Nathaniel Hawthorne in his classic *The Scarlet Letter* (1850) emblemized the intent of seventeenth-century society to keep the passions in check. In the twentieth century, dramatist Arthur Miller portrayed in *The Crucible* (1952), through depiction of the infamous Salem witch trials, not only how the sexual festered in that society but the Puritan mores; near the play's end, Proctor's wife confesses to her condemned husband, "I kept a cold house, John."

In the colonial South, however, more affirmative and playful depictions of sex prevailed. Captain John Smith's account of Pocahontas prefigured southern concern with exotic romance. Ebenezer Cooke ended his satire of early Maryland, *The Sot-Weed Factor* (1707/8), with a famous curse: "May Wrath Divine then lay those Regions vast / Where no Man's Faithful, nor a Woman Chast." William Byrd of Westover, in his letters and Dividing Line histories, not only depicts ordinary life in North Carolina as loose and easy, he also depicts a cavalier class that very much believed in and practiced what in the twentieth century would be described as the joys of sex. In the North, sexual codes echoed the spirit of Oliver Cromwell; in the South, they were closer to those of Shakespeare's romances and Elizabethan love poetry.

Sexuality also played itself out differently in the South because of the "peculiar institution" of the South—slavery. Because slaves were property, masters (and their families) often used slaves for sexual purposes, and variety was usually easy to obtain. With the rise of the abolition movement and the publication of slave narratives—none more pointed than that of Harriet Jacobs's *Incidents in the Life of a Slave Girl* (1861)—awareness of southern sexual patterns increased. John Pendleton Kennedy's plantation novel *Swallow Barn* (1832) had not told the whole story. The South was on the defensive. In his *Letter to an English Abolitionist* (1845), James Henry Hammond of South Carolina objected to the South's being considered a "brothel" and credited the view to northern pleasure in looking southward for titillation. Although admitting that some sexual intercourse between white males and "colored" females occurred, he said that such happened mainly in the cities. (The ironies of Hammond's defense of southern reputation are huge: two years earlier he had been charged by his brother-in-law for sexually molesting his own nieces, and his wife left him for a long period because of his slave mistresses; late in the twentieth century, the public learned about Hammond's youthful sexual experiences with a male friend—a letter provides the only known antebellum statement about a topic hardly admitted in the nineteenth century, North or South.) Slave narratives do not provide the only evidence that Hammond's defense of plantation sexual life is suspect. Mary Chesnut, also of South Carolina, wrote in her diary of March 18, 1861, that she thought slavery "a curse to any land," and she underscores the heavy price it had on southern white women: "Like the patriarchs of old our men live all in one house with their wives and their concubines, and the mulattos one sees in every family exactly resemble the white children—and every lady tells you who is the father of all the mulatto children in everybody's household, but those in her own house she seems to think drop from the clouds, or pretends so to think." The first novel to be published by an African American, William Wells Brown's *Clotel* (1853), explored the effect of miscegenation on a black woman. The novel was structured on an old charge that Thomas Jefferson had fathered children on his slave Sally Hemmings, a charge Jefferson ignored. (In 1998 DNA results strongly supported the authenticity of the ancient claim.) Katherine Anne Porter was on solid ground in "The Old Order" (1936) when she describes the birth of a baby in the slave quarters: "whenever a child was born in the Negro quarters, pink, worm-like, [Sophia Jane] held her breath for three days . . . to see whether the newly born would turn black after a proper interval. . . . It was a strain that told on her, and ended by giving her a deeply grounded contempt for men."

After the Civil War ended official slavery, the South was left with a complex sexual heritage, different for white men and white women, different for black women, and different for black men, who had fewer ties with whites. The system had given the black male the least stability of all, especially as regards sexuality; it had not encouraged long-standing commitment from him, nor had it denied him sexual opportunities—though hardly in ideal conditions. It emphasized to the black male that whatever else he might do sexually, he must not desire the white woman. If antebellum literature—through such key works as Philip Pendleton Cooke's poem "Florence Vane" and the poetry and fiction of Edgar Allan Poe—secured the icon of the beautiful white woman, postbellum southern literature would explore that legacy in a complex racial structure. William Faulkner and Richard Wright both portrayed the special plight of the black male as regards the white woman, and in several works Faulkner, showing that he understood the appeal that the black woman could have for the white male, depicted in antebellum (and postbellum) settings what Hammond had denied. In *Cane* (1923), Jean Toomer memorably evoked the beauty and sexuality of the black woman as well as her attraction for white men.

At the end of the nineteenth century, Kate Chopin, through her use of sexual themes, differentiated herself from other practitioners of the then-popular local-color movement. A native of St. Louis, Chopin spent her married life in Louisiana, where she learned a good deal about the racial and sexual freedoms of the Deep South (she was also steeped in the current French literature of her time). Her fiction insisted on the centrality of sexuality in determining lives and on the female as a sexual being. Her *The Awakening* (1899) shocked readers of the time and was condemned as immoral. In the next century, Zora Neale Hurston in novels and stories focused on black experience and made sexuality a natural and positive part of the good life. Late in the century, Reynolds Price in *Clear Pictures* (1988) would credit "sexual health" as the "most paradoxical" of the gifts of black Americans and judged it as playing a key

role in making the South distinctive: "Despite a narrow torrent of fundamentalist Protestantism from the late eighteenth century to now, and barring the odd sexual psychotic, the South remains the single large region of the United States which has fought off the sexual dreads of a decadent Puritanism that blighted, and continues to blight, many other regional cultures. To be sure, the white South has known its own erotic dreads and repressions; but set by the frozen sexual blast of New England or, say, American Irish Catholicism, the air of the South seems a mild caress and robust laugh."

Price's several frank discussions of sexuality (his own as well as the culture's) would scarcely have been part of a southern memoir published before the 1960s. And not every twentieth-century writer in the South was as fortunate as he in discovering sexuality. In her biographical *Killers of the Dream* (1949), Lillian Smith describes the deficiency of her privileged white culture in Florida and Georgia in sexual as well as racial matters. As a white female, she had received the lesson "that sex has its place and must be kept in it, that a terrifying disaster would befall the South if ever I treated a Negro as my social equal and as terrifying a disaster would befall my family if ever I were to have a baby outside marriage." With Price's thesis in mind, readers can profitably compare Maya Angelou's frank sexual revelations in *I Know Why the Caged Bird Sings* (1970) with Smith's.

Much had to happen throughout the nation before such frank autobiographies as those of Price and Angelou could be published. The naturalists in the late nineteenth and early twentieth centuries had been pioneering. After the suppression of Theodore Dreiser's *Sister Carrie* in 1900, H. L. Mencken came to its defense and became one of Dreiser's leading—and most influential—advocates. The altered climate for a more frank treatment of sexuality that prevailed in the 1920s owed much to Mencken—though his *American Mercury* was banned in Boston in 1926. More than any region, the twentieth-century South led the way in breaking down old barriers and provided many of the works that would shock and titillate the nation—anticipating the sexual revolution of the 1960s. In 1919 the publication of James Branch Cabell's *Jurgen* led to charges of salaciousness, and the following year the novel was suppressed and became a national *cause célèbre,* with writers throughout the country—Puritan-baiting Mencken again leading—rallying in its defense. Two years later, the book (its sexual content is indeed prominent) was exonerated in a trial in New York. Cabell, meanwhile, had been reaping the benefits of notoriety for all of his works. He followed *Jurgen* with *The High Place* (1923), a romance that would further shock those applying the moral lens of the nineteenth century; this time, homosexual sex also played a part of Cabell's depiction of human passions and dreams. The way was opening for other works with a strong sexual content.

These followed quickly and would confirm the national perception about sexual preoccupation and oddities in the South. Frances Newman, encouraged by Cabell, explored the sexual and erotic in *The Hardboiled Virgin* (1926) and *Dead Lovers Are Faithful Lovers* (1928). William Faulkner, unable to reach the audience he merited and needing money, deliberately set out to write a potboiler. *Sanctuary* (1931) transcended that aim, but it got the condemnation for its sexual emphasis that Faulkner expected. Thereafter he was sometimes called "the corncob man" because the impotent Popeye of his novel rapes Temple Drake by that means, after which he deposits her in a Memphis brothel. Erskine Caldwell's *Tobacco Road* (1932) earned even greater notoriety. Although Caldwell wrote this novel as a Marxist, it was the sexual content and the exaggerated portraits of Jeeter and Duke Lester and Sister Bessie May (especially their sexual appetites) that caught the public's imagination, causing both amusement and disgust—and good sales. Caldwell's *God's Little Acre,* published the next year, was even more salacious and its sales even brisker. Caldwell reached an audience that never would have caught the sexual nuances and sexual jokes of Cabell. All three of these novels spread the perception of the "Steamy South" as they made their way as inexpensive paperbacks, a format then exploding; both of Caldwell's were made into successful motion pictures, *Tobacco Road* in 1941 and *God's Little Acre* in 1958. Students of southern literature can recognize Caldwell's Georgia Crackers as the descendants of the likes of Johnson Jones Hooper's Simon Suggs and other creations of the Southwestern humorists, as well as Dismal Swamp inhabitants depicted by William Byrd.

No writer did more to open up the arts for consideration of sexual themes in their broad range of complexity than did Tennessee Williams. Certainly he changed the face of the American theater and the cinema drastically. *A Streetcar Named Desire* (1947) probes the power of "desire"—in many manifestations—and comments on its meaning in southern experience. The action is set in the French Quarter of New Orleans, long the most sexually tolerant city of the South and

the nation. With reason, New Orleans has been dubbed "The Big Easy." Subsequent Williams plays, also set in the South, explored sexual drive and frustration. *Cat on a Hot Tin Roof* (1955) sets the action not in the drawing room, the standard set of an earlier era, but in the bedroom—the bed dominating the stage. These and other Williams works, commonly seen as torrid, also became motion pictures. The movie that most clearly led to the perception of the South as rife with sexual adventure is *Baby Doll* (1956), which is based on a Tennessee Williams story. By contemporary standards, the action seems tame, but the work is full of sexual innuendo and symbolism—and it confirmed popular images of poor whites in the South. That Elia Kazan's production passed the movie code surprised many viewers; the 1951 *Streetcar* (which did have to make concessions) had probably paved the way. (When Williams in 1975 published his sexually detailed *Memoirs,* he was beneficiary of the revolution he helped bring about.)

Singer Elvis Presley of Memphis has been credited with liberating southern white women from the long-prevailing double standard. Described as "Elvis the Pelvis," Presley gyrated to his songs, shocking his elders and winning the approval of multitudes; he became known as the "King of Rock 'n' Roll." In the 1950s, the young Presley was considered so sexually provocative that he could be televised only from the waist up. Following his death in 1977, his home, Graceland, in Memphis became an important national and southern shrine.

In the 1960s, franker treatment of sexuality became the norm throughout the nation. Diction formerly rendered with a dash became a staple of fiction and the movies. Nudity and profanity became acceptable on stage and screen. As a consequence, southern writers are less likely to appear to use sex exploitatively. They are able to treat homosexual and lesbian experience openly, to study child and spousal abuse. During the last quarter of the century, writers in the realistic tradition seldom evade consideration of the sexual dimensions of the lives they portray. Some works still gain attention for a central sexual focus, such as Alice Walker's *The Color Purple* (1983). And Ellen Gilchrist's many Rhoda stories portray sexual experience to a degree hardly possible in the first half of the century.

Nevertheless, the South is probably as conflicted about sexuality as any region in the country. Many of the protests and much of the violence against abortion have come from the South, and prominent southern religious and political leaders have taken strong stances against homosexuality. State laws reflect this conservatism (in Georgia, until very recently, consensual oral or anal sex could result in a twenty-year prison term; in Texas, the fine is $200), and southerners have largely turned to the Republican Party, whose leaders more accurately reflect these views (though levels of tolerance vary). On the other hand, there have been clergy in the South courageous enough to advocate full acceptance of gays and lesbians, countering the conservative clergy who have made attacking homosexuals a major thrust of their program. (Before the 1960s, homosexuality was not a major topic in sermons or denominational conventions.) Bible Belt notwithstanding, the South leads the nation in teen pregnancy, but educational and civic leaders have addressed the issue with openness and candor. With the arrival of AIDS, safe sex is discussed in southern high schools and colleges as openly as anywhere. Sex and sexuality, always important topics in the South, have become issues demanding even more attention from the society and its institutions.

Walker Percy, who pondered throughout his career the place of sexuality in southern and American culture, characterized the new age as genital. In *Lancelot* (1977), he echoes Tennyson's probing of the moral state of Victorian society through the use of Arthurian analogs. The action of Percy's novel is centered upon Lancelot's discovery that his wife is adulterous. Percy mocks the sexual decadence of the age throughout the novel, set in and around New Orleans. From his cell window, Lancelot views a pornographic theater showing *The Sixtyniners* and gradually relates the sexual drama that led to his murder of his wife and three others. His wife had been involved in making a Hollywood movie with sexual liberation as its theme. Merlin, the producer, identified the theme of their movie: that "violence, rape or murder, or whatever is always death-dealing whereas the erotic, in any form at all, is always life-enhancing." Lancelot secretly made his own movies, *cinéma verité* he says, to discover the exact nature of the sexual license taking place in his own home. In *Lancelot*, sexuality exposes the emptiness of the culture, emphasizing its lostness.

Were he still living, Percy would have ample material to reflect further on the Steamy South—a U.S. president from the South impeached after sexual scandal; a Speaker of the House from Georgia resigning in the controversy (which brought renewed attention to his own marital record); the Speaker-elect from Louisiana resigning when his adulteries were revealed; and one of the president's most vocal accusers, a thrice-married representative from Georgia, exposed in *Hustler* magazine, which had an ex-wife's affidavit that he had left abortion open as an option for an unwanted pregnancy.

Weary of the airing of so much dirty linen, many might read James Hammond's *Letter to an English Abolitionist* as it deals with sexuality with more compassion. Protesting offering up the South's sexual practices "as a holocaust on the altar of immaculateness, to atone for the abuse of natural instinct by all mankind," Hammond declared: "Without meaning to profess uncommon modesty, I will say that I wish the topic could be avoided. I am of the opinion and doubt not every right-minded man will concur, that the public disclosure and discussion of this vice, even to rebuke, does more harm than good; and that if it cannot be checked by instilling pure and virtuous sentiments, it is far worse than useless to attempt to do it, by exhibiting its deformities."

Be that as it may, in life and literature, the South has continued to give ample evidence that the "Steamy South" endures.

Joseph M. Flora

See also Gay Literature; Lesbian Literature; Naturalism.

John Dollard, *Caste and Class in a Southern Town* (1937); Eugene D. Genovese, *Roll, Jordan, Roll: The World the Slaves Made* (1974); Albert Goldman, *Elvis* (1981); Rayna Green, "Magnolias Grow in Dirt: The Bawdy Lore of Southern Women," in *Speaking for Ourselves: Women of the South*, ed. Maxine Alexander (1984); Richard H. King, *A Southern Renaissance: The Cultural Awakening in the American South, 1930–1955* (1980); Bradley A. Smith, *The American Way of Sex* (1978).

SHAKESPEARE, WILLIAM

In most cultured American homes prior to independence, one could expect to find at least a few books, among them a Bible and a version of William Shakespeare's complete works. Alexis de Tocqueville, famous French cataloguer of early American democracy, witnessed the bard's popularity in his travels and wrote of finding a backwoodsman reading *Henry V* in a rude hut on the western frontier. In the early South, where booklearning lagged but pretensions to British aristocracy flourished, references to reading Shakespeare abounded. In one scene of John Pendleton Kennedy's *Swallow Barn* (1832), a northern visitor describes an evening of impromptu drama at the plantation homestead; the dramas are a playful hodgepodge of Shakespeare plays, including *Richard III* and *A Midsummer Night's Dream*. The plantation legend that became the South's dominant mythological narrative could draw on Shakespearian types, as William Taylor shows in his *Cavalier and Yankee* (1961). There, he discusses various Shakespeare characters who are ready-made models for an array of southern plantation types, noting that "any selective list of planter-heroes would give priority to the Southern Hothead and the Southern Hamlet."

Shakespeare's *Tempest,* based on various accounts of a ship intended for Jamestown in 1609 that was wrecked off the Bahamas, indicates the Bard's interest in the American South. The characters' names are taken directly from historical narratives, but the characters of Caliban and Ariel foreshadow the stereotyped depictions of slaves as either angelic servers or brute animals within the discourse of plantation society. Prospero, the island ruler who dispenses wisdom and justice in the play, might be seen as the ideal planter-type, an enlightened slaveowner who is the patriarchal lord of all he surveys.

Antebellum southern writers might have explained their affinity for Shakespeare in terms of their sense of a common historical plight. The idea of social disorder that Shakespeare often treated, reflecting conditions in the England of his time, could easily have found resonance for William Gilmore Simms, who wanted his romances to chart the South's struggle for identity by dramatizing its history. Simms, his friend and fellow Charlestonian Henry Timrod, and Sidney Lanier all wrote scholarly treatises or gave lectures on the poetic structure and the political purposes of Shakespeare. Lanier, teaching after the Civil War at the Peabody Institute in Baltimore, gave a series of lectures relating Shakespeare's craft to musical principles. Twentieth-century poet and longtime English professor John Crowe Ransom wrote critical interpretations of Shakespeare, "On Shakespeare's Language" and "Shakespeare at Sonnets."

Mark Twain was particularly suspicious of Shakespeare's identity and questioned whether he was indeed the great author of the plays ascribed to him. In *Is Shakespeare Dead?* (1909), he lectured on this issue, and he reviewed the performances of prominent Shake-

spearian actors such as Edwin Forrest. *Adventures of Huckleberry Finn* (1885) contains Twain's best-known Shakespeare references, the theatrical misadventure of the King and the Duke. These two rapscallions, posing as David Garrick and Edmund Kean respectively, perform Hamlet's "To be" soliloquy to an Arkansas audience. The burlesque in *Huckleberry Finn* is similar to that of *The Killing of Julius Caesar Localized* (1856), part of a series of letters that Samuel Clemens composed under the pseudonyms Thomas Jefferson Snodgrass and Quintius Curtius Snodgrass, to parody Shakespeare's works and the newspaper media in general. Both works critique the reputation of Garrick, whose performance Twain may have witnessed on a visit to London and Stratford. In *Adventures of Huckleberry Finn,* the King's speech merges lines from *Hamlet, Macbeth,* and *Richard III.* Twain resolved to rewrite *Hamlet* but never completed the attempt, which included adding an additional character to the tragedy. Twain's unfinished manuscript of 1881 exists through act II, scene ii; it creates the character Basil Stockmar, Hamlet's foster brother and a book agent attempting to find subscribers for his own literary work. Twain consistently burlesqued Shakespeare throughout his career, finding the American worship of a British Renaissance writer part of his culture's pretentiousness.

In creative work, Shakespearian inspiration is reflected in several southern writers' response to conflicts inherent in southern culture. The South's continuous sectional rivalry with the North, the self-conscious aping of English manners by the plantation gentry, and the effects of the Civil War both on families and economic structure were conditions that found parallels in Shakespeare's works. The poetry of Henry Timrod, "The Laureate of the Confederacy," and Simms's *Woodcraft* (1854) utilize quotations from Shakespeare's characters as instruments of social criticism. Robert Penn Warren's character Slim Sarrett in *At Heaven's Gate* (1943) seems closely modeled on Hamlet and provides readers with three pages of Shakespearean criticism in the exact middle of the novel. In Warren's *All the King's Men* (1946), the relation between Jack Burden and several father-figures also reflects a *Hamlet* theme. Walker Percy's *Lancelot* (1977), the confessions of a southern planter, also draws on Shakespeare, particularly in the characterization of Lancelot Lamar. His machinations of revenge combine some of the personal agonies of both Prince Hamlet and King Lear.

William Faulkner, like Twain, often alluded to Shakespeare, both in word and theme. Faulkner was exposed to Shakespeare through his schooling under the direction of his mother, through several university classes, and through the influence of his friend Phil Stone. Joseph Blotner indicates Faulkner's position on Shakespeare when he reports that Faulkner declared, at age twenty-four, "I could write a play like *Hamlet* if I wanted to." Many modern critics classify Faulkner's early works—*Soldiers' Pay* (1926), *Mosquitoes* (1927), and *Flags in the Dust* (1929)—as fictional translations of *Hamlet* and *A Midsummer Night's Dream*. In *Sanctuary* (1929), there are remnants of the grotesque comedy of *A Midsummer Night's Dream* and *As You Like It,* particularly noticeable in the ironic idea of the temporary "sanctuary" that might allow an escape from reality through the grotesque.

Perhaps the most recognizable Shakespearean passage in Faulkner's writing is the "Tomorrow, and tomorrow, and tomorrow" speech from *Macbeth* that gave *The Sound and the Fury* (1929) its title. In its form ("a tale / Told by an idiot, full of sound and fury, / Signifying nothing"), this novel directly references Macbeth's soliloquy. Faulkner created many characters who reflect Shakespeare's Hamlet. Quentin Compson and Bayard Sartoris, whose histories and families populate the fictional Mississippi county, face challenges similar to the brooding Prince, internally divided by the expectations of the past and the conditions of the present. *Absalom, Absalom!* (1936) completes Faulkner's brooding recycling of *Hamlet*. In one last, perhaps playful reference, the title of the first novel of his Snopes trilogy, *The Hamlet* (1940), might be seen as a Faulknerian localization of Shakespeare below the Mason-Dixon Line.

Justin D. A. Drewry

Walter Blair and E. Bruce Kirkham, "Huck and Hamlet," *Mark Twain Journal* (1969); Philip C. Kolin, ed., *Shakespeare in the South: Essays on Performance* (1983), and *Shakespeare and Southern Writers: A Study in Influence* (1985); Lance Lyday, "Faulkner's Miss Reba and Shakespeare's Drunken Porter," *Lamar Journal of the Humanities* (1990); W. E. McCarron, "Shakespeare, Faulkner, and Ned William McCaslin," *Notes on Contemporary Literature* (1977); John B. Rosenman, "Another Othello Echo in *As I Lay Dying*," *Notes on Mississippi Writers* (1975).

SHARECROPPING

Southern literature contains numerous examples of the economic construct called sharecropping, a vestige of the plantation system that has served since Reconstruction to keep lower-class whites and blacks in financial servitude to a landowner. Sharecropping reached its peak from 1900 to 1930, and by the 1970s this form of tenancy was employed rarely, though it remained an option in some rural communities in the late 1990s.

Historically, the system evolved during the first two decades after the Civil War. Freed blacks who wanted to farm had little capital, livestock, or equipment to launch an independent venture; meanwhile, landowners, struggling with the loss of slave labor and other capital investments, along with rock-bottom land values, desperately needed farmhands. Now named "tenants," former slaves accustomed to the dependence and paternalism of slavery unwittingly became cooperative players in a new game in which the owners—again—held all the aces. Land was farmed partially or totally by tenants "on shares"; a proportion of the crop would be contracted by verbal agreement to the landholder in exchange for provisions bought or leased on credit at exorbitant interest rates of sometimes nearly 50 percent: a house, land in varying amounts from ten to forty acres, seed, fertilizer, tools, and sometimes food staples. Since the cost of raw materials and living expenses was ordinarily more than the crop was worth, given the South's propensities for soil erosion and depletion, drought, insects, and hurricanes, the sharecropper was forever in debt to suppliers. If a cropper had a "good" season with favorable weather and weevil conditions and broke even, he had to plant the next year's crop and feed his family on credit anyway. When contracts were renewed in December, a time when cash was normally advanced for the winter, the sharecropper and his family could be on the road, penniless, in search of another place. In some areas, store or commissary credit for the farmer was extended only until lay-by—usually midsummer in the South—when further hoeing of weeds became unnecessary as growing crops "lapped the rows," providing shade unfavorable for weeds. Families then had to scramble for odd jobs in order to survive until crops were gathered in October and November.

There were two varieties of tenancy, generally divided along racial lines that dissolved over time, and these categories are usually conflated in literature: share tenants, or cash renters, were usually whites—sometimes "poor whites," but frequently former landowners who were down on their luck and working their way back to ownership. Supervision of their work was less stringent, and the relationship between owner and tenant was more businesslike. In contrast, the majority of sharecroppers in the beginning were freed blacks who were closely superintended and treated very much as they had been before emancipation. As sundry economic depressions ensued over the next six decades, however, the majority of blacks were forced out of farming and migrated to cities south, north, or west to work in various industries. By the time of the Great Depression, almost all sharecroppers were white, and although they became a national issue at this time, no efforts to help them were successful until the early 1940s, which witnessed a sharp decline in sharecropping because of delayed New Deal initiatives, rapidly advancing mechanization, and a war-related economic spurt.

The consequences of illiteracy, economic deprivation, and malnutrition were compounded by the tendency of sharecroppers to stay in the general area, despite their annually increasing debts; they maintained an attachment to home, such as it was, for many had lived in the area all their lives, "inheriting" the tenancy from a parent after working the fields from childhood. A family forced into mobility often moved no farther than a few miles to the neighboring landowner where a ramshackle house, with no running water or privy, may have been recently vacated by another hapless cropper. Tenant houses were maintained more or less depending on the charity of the owner, and a sharecropper who called attention to legitimate problems was likely to create a name as a troublemaker. Among the tenants, then, there was slim motivation to maintain someone else's property, and the stereotype of a dilapidated shack teetering on its foundation is not far from the truth.

Sharecroppers in literature were heralded by William Byrd II of Westover during the colonial period; his disparaging portraits of poor white farmers of North Carolina in *The History of the Dividing Line* (written 1728, published 1841) served as models for generations of antebellum writers, among them George Washington Harris, Johnson Jones Hooper, Henry Clay Lewis, Augustus Baldwin Longstreet, and Alexander G. McNutt. Mark Twain's satirical novel of the post–Civil War economic boom, *The Gilded Age* (1873), written in collaboration with C. D. Warner, also contains delineations of small farmers as backwoods bumpkins, whereas Mary Noailles Murfree's novels of post–Civil War Tennessee mountaineers are primarily romantic.

Perhaps the earliest attempt to portray the postwar South in a more realistic manner, as neither denigrated

nor romanticized, is Ellen Glasgow's novel *The Battle-Ground* (1902); her small farmers and sharecroppers are not treated as laughable cretins or a chosen people, but as an integral layer of the social strata. Later-twentieth-century literary representations of sharecroppers and poor whites range from the grotesquely comic, as in Erskine Caldwell's *Tobacco Road* (1932), to the tragic, as in Edith Summers Kelly's naturalistic *Weeds* (1923). The Depression spawned numerous serious looks at the lower class, whether the workers toiled in rural areas as continuously failing sharecroppers or traded their farms for an equally crushing existence in textile-mill towns. Proletarian novels of rural transplants to mill villages made a brief critical and political impact, as in *Call Home the Heart* (1932) by Olive Tilford Dargan, *Now in November* (1934) by Josephine W. Johnson, and *To Make My Bread* (1932) by Grace Lumpkin. Lumpkin also contributed a novel, *A Sign for Cain* (1935), which features southern sharecroppers. In *Let Us Now Praise Famous Men* (1941), nonfiction written by James Agee with photographs by Walker Evans, Alabama sharecroppers are given dignity despite their poverty. The best-known sharecroppers in southern fiction may well be the Snopes family in William Faulkner's short stories and novels. These poor whites, who rise through several generations from sharecropping shack to plantation mansion, are shown as ruthless exploiters of the system in order to gain power over formerly elite, now fading, landlords. Their manipulations are traced in various works by Faulkner, particularly in his trilogy *The Hamlet* (1940), *The Town* (1957), and *The Mansion* (1959); Snopeses also appear in *Sartoris* (1929), *As I Lay Dying* (1930), and *The Unvanquished* (1938).

Other twentieth-century writers who present sharecroppers and the rural poor in their fiction include Ernest Gaines, Caroline Gordon, Alex Haley, Harper Lee, Mary Noailles Murfree, Flannery O'Connor (especially in "The Displaced Person"), Julia Peterkin, Katherine Anne Porter, Reynolds Price, Marjorie Kinnan Rawlings, Elizabeth Madox Roberts, Mary Lee Settle, Jesse Stuart, Jean Toomer, Alice Walker, Margaret Walker, and Eudora Welty. Contemporary depictions of rural characters—metaphorical descendants of sharecroppers—are found in fiction by Dorothy Allison, Maya Angelou, Fred Chappell, Kaye Gibbons, William Melvin Kelley, Bobbie Ann Mason, Albert Murray, Dori Sanders, Lee Smith, and Elizabeth Spencer. Linda Flowers's *Throwed Away* (1990) is a lyrical autobiography as well as a sociological study of sharecropping in eastern North Carolina, showing her own coming of age in a changing rural culture.

Cile Moïse

See also Cracker; Industrialization; Poor White; Proletarian Novel; Redneck; Tenant Farming.

James C. Cobb, *Industrialization and Southern Society, 1877–1984* (1984); Robert Coles, *Migrants, Sharecroppers, Mountaineers* (1971); Sylvia Jenkins Cook, *From Tobacco Road to Route 66: The Southern Poor White in Fiction* (1976); Robert Cruden, *The Negro in Reconstruction* (1969); Gilbert C. Fite, *Cotton Fields No More: Southern Agriculture, 1865–1980* (1984); J. Wayne Flynt, *Dixie's Forgotten People: The South's Poor Whites* (1979); Margaret J. Hagood, *Mothers of the South: Portraiture of the White Tenant Farm Woman* (1939); Leon F. Litwack, *Been in the Storm So Long: The Aftermath of Slavery* (1979); Jay Mandle, *Not Slave, Not Free: The African American Economic Experience Since the Civil War* (1992); Paul E. Mertz, *New Deal Policy and Southern Rural Poverty* (1978); Roger L. Ransom and E. Richard Sutch, *One Kind of Freedom: The Economic Consequences of Emancipation* (1977); Arthur F. Raper, *Sharecroppers All* (1941); Thomas Jackson Woofter Jr., *Landlord and Tenant on the Cotton Plantation* (1936).

SHERIFF

The sheriff casts a long—and wide—shadow over the southern literary landscape. A lawman in a lawless region, he is sometimes the heavy and sometimes just plain heavy: an epic hero walking tall or an impotent buffoon weighing down the fun.

The film *Walking Tall* (1973) provides a well-known example of the first type in Tennessee sheriff Buford Pusser, a giant defending the law with his courage and a big stick. Similarly equipped with a strong sense of duty and the physical prowess to perform it, Sheriff Campbell, the protagonist in Charles Chesnutt's "The Sheriff's Children" (1899), defends an African American prisoner from vigilantes bent on lynching him. Like many of the literary sheriffs before and after Pusser, however, Campbell is a complicated hero. The revelation that the suspect is his own son, whom he fathered by a slave and then sold, turns him into a majestic lie akin to Nathaniel Hawthorne's Arthur Dimmesdale.

A different sort of public defender, attorney Atticus Finch in Harper Lee's *To Kill a Mockingbird* (1960), resembles Campbell and Pusser, particularly when he guards the jail where his African American defendant resides. The novel's real sheriff, however, is Heck Tate, who represents an important variation on the dutiful lawman. After deducing that the hermit Boo Radley saved Finch's son from an attacker, Tate persuades the upright Finch to conceal the details of the case and thus protect Radley's privacy. As the sage lawman who bends the law to keep the peace, Tate resembles Sheriff Bullard in James Dickey's novel *Deliverance* (1970). Typically brawny, Bullard nevertheless uses his sense to handle a powder keg in his isolated rural county, where a local man has mysteriously disappeared and his brother-in-law suspects a visiting city dweller. Although he, too, suspects the outsider, Bullard calmly arbitrates the dispute and later, admitting that the victim was a lout, gives the urbanite some friendly advice to make himself scarce. Finally, Sheriff Andy Taylor maintains the peace of sleepy Mayberry, North Carolina, in television's *Andy Griffith Show* (1960–1968) through common sense and leniency, often to the chagrin of his punctilious deputy, Barney Fife.

In his insistence on obeying the letter of the law as well as his ultimate impotence, Barney points to the other major type of southern sheriff. Big in the ego or gut rather than the heart or shoulders, this buffoon often seeks to spoil the fun of a wiser, livelier good old boy, but instead becomes the butt of his jokes. In Johnson Jones Hooper's "The Muscadine Story" (1849), Sheriff Martin Ellis tries to capture the wily Simon Suggs but winds up dangling from a tree over a river, foreshadowing the feckless sheriffs Buford T. Justice in the film *Smokey and the Bandit* (1977) and Roscoe P. Coltrane in television's *The Dukes of Hazzard* (1979–1985). Even more pathetic is Pluto Swint, who, slave to his girth and sheer laziness, lumbers through Erskine Caldwell's novel *God's Little Acre* (1933) in pursuit of only two ambitions: to become sheriff so that he can sit in the pool hall and call shots and to marry Darling Jill, who continually rejects him.

Whereas Pluto and his ilk are powerless to contain the lawlessness around them, other literary sheriffs are impotent by choice. More apathetic than inept, they abdicate their duties or merely make a show of them. Thus the obese sheriff in William Faulkner's "The Fire and the Hearth," a section of *Go Down, Moses* (1942), brings two moonshiners before the commissioner but wishes only to "get done with this." In "Pantaloon in Black," a later section of the same novel, Sheriff Maydew and his deputies are content to let vigilantes lynch an African American accused of killing a white man, particularly since the victim's family members represent forty-two votes. This caricature of the lawless lawman gets humorous treatment in Hooper's *Adventures of Captain Simon Suggs* (1845), which ends with the plea to elect the shifty Suggs sheriff so that he can "relax his intellectual exertions."

Mark Canada

See also Crimes and Criminals; Law Before 1900; Law, 1900 to Present.

SHERMAN, WILLIAM TECUMSEH

William Tecumseh Sherman is a name many southerners still associate with ruthless devastation of their homeland. Kaye Gibbons in *On the Occasion of My Last Afternoon* (1998) has her narrator say that Sherman is the one Unionist, besides Butler, who will burn in hell. Margaret Mitchell's *Gone With the Wind,* and the movie made from it, provide a popular view of Sherman's devastation of Atlanta and his driving the people out of the city. The popular Georgia humorist Bill Arp (Charles H. Smith) reported the flight of his refugee family and their miseries of living with little food in the piney woods and fearing rumors that the Yankees raiding Covington had "stolen all the horses, burnt every dwelling, hung all the men, drowned all the children, and carried off the women alive." In his March to the Sea with its destructive consequences, Sherman fulfilled his expressed intent to "make Georgia howl," as Margaret Walker quotes him in *Jubilee* (1966). In "Sack and Destruction of the City of Columbia, S.C." (1865), William Gilmore Simms lamented the cruelties and excesses of Sherman's men, and he cursed the stragglers in Sherman's army who burned his plantation home, Woodlands, with the loss of his entire library of some ten thousand volumes. Property in Georgia and South Carolina had, in the words of poet L. Virginia French, been "Shermanized." And their cities had been overwhelmed, as Alethaea S. Burroughs relates in her poem "Savannah Fallen."

Paradoxically, Sherman had a genuine love for the South. His first assignment as a second lieutenant in the U.S. Army was in Florida; he thoroughly enjoyed his four years in Charleston in the 1840s; and prior to the war, he won many friends in his job as superintendent of the state military academy at Alexandria, Louisiana, now Louisiana State University. After the war, Sherman was criticized for the generous peace terms he offered General Joseph E. Johnston.

Stark Young in *So Red the Rose* (1934) treats the enigma of Sherman's kindness and personal interest that could not be reconciled with his callous use of modern machine warfare. When Sherman visits the McGehees, a family based on Young's own ancestors, the McGehees wonder: "Could this man in their parlor at Montrose be the Sherman with the looting, burning, and wreck behind him—around Jackson for twenty miles the country stripped and burnt to a cinder?" Agnes McGehee's intuitions saw Sherman as "tormented and willful." She thought of him as "a pathetic, strong child, full of impetuous integrity."

From a northern perspective, Sherman's role in the Civil War was highly significant. He commanded with great skill at the Battle of Shiloh; he materially assisted Grant in bringing about the fall of Vicksburg; and, as is so well known, he cut a swath right through the heart of Dixie. A fictional version of Sherman's side of the story is *Sherman's March* by Cynthia Bass (1994).

Charlotte (N.C.)–born Ross McElwee ostensibly takes up the subject of Sherman's march and, subsequently, southern womanhood in his droll documentary titled *Sherman's March* (1986) (subtitled *A Meditation on the Possibility of Romantic Love in the South During an Era of Nuclear Weapons Proliferation*). McElwee's asides thoughtfully reveal his conflicted feelings about the demonized general as the filmmaker loosely traces the steps of the March to the Sea through the modern South.

Richard D. Rust

See also Civil War.

John F. Marszalek, *Sherman: A Soldier's Passion for Order* (1994).

SHORT STORY, BEGINNINGS TO 1900

In an era when most American literature came from the North, the South distinguished itself most notably in the short story, producing two of its foremost authorities in Edgar Allan Poe and Mark Twain, as well as one of its best-known characters in Uncle Remus. Through the short story, furthermore, southerners led in the development of two important American genres: Southwestern humor and local color. The hundreds of stories in this rich tradition cover a range of characters and landscapes, from madmen ensconced in gothic mansions to saucy backwoodsmen romping over the frontier, and the best early southern stories share a brilliance of form and style.

The history of the short story in the South goes back to two gifted raconteurs of colonial Virginia, Captain John Smith and William Byrd II. Each, though writing lengthy and ostensibly nonfiction narratives, introduced characteristics that would later distinguish southern short fiction. In *The Generall Historie of Virginia, New England, and the Summer Isles* (1624), Smith gave America one of its best-known stories, as well as its first tall tale. Here, in his report of fighting off two hundred Indians while using one as a shield and of being saved by Pocahontas moments before his execution, are the deadpan narration, hyperbole, frontier boast, and climactic conclusion that will appear in Old Southwestern stories in the 1800s. Byrd likewise presaged this genre in *The History of the Dividing Line* (written c. 1728), which exploits the comic effect of a sophisticated narrator drolly recounting the exploits of frontier rustics. By writing in distinctive styles that threaten to take over their narratives, Smith and Byrd set the stage for later southern writers.

Before 1800, American magazines published some four or five hundred short fictional works, few of which bear any obvious southern stamp. The modern short story, however, did not take form until the 1830s, when an explosion of periodicals provided a venue, an audience, and an income for writers of short fiction. Foremost among these writers was Poe, who, through fiction and criticism in publications such as Richmond's *Southern Literary Messenger,* did perhaps more than any other writer to shape the modern short story. Like his fellow Virginians Smith and Byrd, Poe subordinated substance to form, viewing the short story in the same way he saw the poem—as a work of art to be experienced and appreciated. In his most important critical statement on the subject, an 1842 review of Nathaniel Hawthorne's *Twice-Told Tales,* Poe places the short story, which he calls the "tale," behind only the short poem as the form suitable for literary genius and argues that the tale writer should use words economically and deliberately to create an "effect." Antithetical as it was to the didactic, digressive fiction of his era, Poe's definition influenced later writers and critics.

Employing these principles, Poe produced several of the world's finest short stories, including the gothic tales "Ligeia" (1838) and "The Fall of the House of Usher" (1839). A perfect illustration of his method can be found in the latter, in which Poe constructs his effect through descriptions of a dark tarn, the house's "barely perceptible fissure," and Usher's pallid face and disquieting art. Poe's other major contribution to the short story shows the same attention to method. In "The Murders in the Rue Morgue" (1841) and his other "tales of ratiocination," regarded as the first detective stories, the effect is not emotional but intellectual, coming in the form of a solution to a puzzle. Beneath the sparkling veneer of Poe's well-made fiction lies an exploration of the human mind, often conveyed through symbolism and surreal imagery. "William Wilson" (1839) and "The Purloined Letter" (1845), for example, contain *doppelgängers* representing parts of the mind, and "The Tell-Tale Heart" (1843) and "The Black Cat" (1843) dramatize a self-destructive impulse that Poe called "The Imp of the Perverse." Indeed, because Poe's method is to portray symbolic characters acting out abstract desires on a mental landscape, few of his tales bear any outward signs of their southern authorship. An exception is "The Gold-Bug" (1843), which features a South Carolina setting, a quondam aristocrat, and a dialect-speaking former slave named Jupiter. Even this overtly southern story, however, does little to sketch regional characters or customs: Jupiter is a caricature, and the isolated, desolate Sullivan's Island is no more southern—at least in social terms—than the fantastic setting of "The Pit and the Pendulum" (1843).

Although known primarily for his novels, South Carolinian William Gilmore Simms published some eighty stories and sketches in collections and magazines such as the *Southern Literary Messenger.* In his major collection, *The Wigwam and the Cabin* (1845–1846), he sometimes merely transplants drawing-room characters to the southern frontier. In "Grayling; or, 'Murder Will Out,' " however, Simms showed that he could write an original, unified short story. Indeed, Poe called it the best ghost story by an American, perhaps because it embodies his own principles. In this tale of a young man who tracks down a murderer with the help of the victim's ghost, Simms avoids digressions and uses several details—a mysterious stranger, a secluded swamp, an ambiguous vision—to create an eerie effect. In the vein of Poe's tales of ratiocination, a detective-like figure solves the mystery with psychology and reason. Later, Simms made his most important contribution to the form with "How Sharp Snaffles Got His

Capital and Wife" (1870), a humorous tale highly regarded for its use of dialect.

While Poe and Simms were impressing readers with horror and intellectual satisfaction, writers on the southern frontier were producing stories with a different, but no less meticulously constructed effect—humor—for publications such as New York's *Spirit of the Times*. In "The Horse-Swap," one of the stories in *Georgia Scenes* (1835), Augustus Baldwin Longstreet draws the character Yellow Blossom as a boastful con man until the end, when the reader learns that the con man has been conned. The engaging style of Old Southwestern humor comes largely from the storyteller's dialect and hyperbole, often recorded by a civilized outsider like Byrd's persona in *The History of the Dividing Line*. Thus, as in Smith's and Byrd's narratives, manner is as important as matter—or, as Louisiana writer Thomas Bangs Thorpe explains in "The Big Bear of Arkansas" (1841), the storyteller's style is "so singular, that half of his story consisted in his excellent way of telling it."

Style takes precedence in the work of the next great southern storyteller, Missourian Mark Twain, who explains in "How to Tell a Story" (1897) that the "humorous story depends for its effect upon the *manner* of the telling." In early stories, such as those in *Roughing It* (1872), Twain borrows liberally from his predecessors. His most famous story, "The Celebrated Jumping Frog of Calaveras County" (1865), features an oral storyteller, colorful expressions, and a final, charged effect. A transitional figure, Twain took the short story in new directions without losing his sense of style, using it to draw realistic portraits of life as it was lived in the South and the West. In "The Private History of a Campaign That Failed" (1885), set in Missouri at the dawn of the Civil War, he presents a parade of colorful characters, a smattering of dialect, even a reference to local food. More than a romp through the antebellum South, the story also explores the war's impact on the region, as when Twain describes a tragic incident that deprives young Confederate soldiers of their romantic delusions. Although "The Man That Corrupted Hadleyburg" (1900) is not tied to a specific region, its self-righteous, back-biting residents of a small town resemble characters in his regional novels.

In his habit of spinning exotic fiction out of local eccentricities, Twain resembles other writers of the 1870s and 1880s. When *Scribner's Monthly* and other northern magazines began publishing short stories in this new genre called local color, the leading writers included southerners such as Louisiana's Grace King and Tennessee's Mary Noailles Murfree (whose pen name was Charles Egbert Craddock). Indeed, the exotic locales, dialects, and characters of regions such as New Orleans and Appalachia again allowed some southerners to tell colorful stories while still largely ignoring substance. Lacking their predecessors' mastery of form and style, most merely exploited their regions' idiosyncrasies or transformed the antebellum South into an ideal world. In "Marse Chan" (1884), one of the best-known examples of this nostalgic fiction, Virginia writer Thomas Nelson Page has a former slave reminisce about the "good ole times" when "Marse Chan" and Miss Anne would go riding while their fathers talked and smoked cigars.

Despite this lingering romantic atmosphere, a handful of writers attempted realistic depictions of their region. Louisiana's George Washington Cable and Kentucky's James Lane Allen, for example, looked back at the Old South not to idealize it but to explore its real effects on the present. In "Belles Demoiselles Plantation," one of the stories in *Old Creole Days* (1879), Cable explores class distinctions in New Orleans and the destruction of the southern dream, symbolized in the collapse of a plantation into the Mississippi River. In "Two Gentlemen of Kentucky" (1888), Allen draws a Rip Van Winkle figure who cannot align his Old South mentality with the climate of the South during Reconstruction. Although he tries to stay busy, he is not cut out for "ignoble barter" and loses a thousand dollars trying to run a store. In this strange environment, he clings to a former slave who feels equally isolated in the New South.

In the most significant development of the late nineteenth century, some writers wrote local-color stories that gave realistic voices to previously ignored or stereotyped groups. The most famous of these writers, Joel Chandler Harris, adapted the tales he heard as a white man among the African Americans of Georgia to produce the fabulously popular Uncle Remus stories, noteworthy for their use of dialect and their insights into the people who originally told them. In his introduction to *Uncle Remus: His Songs and His Sayings* (1881), Harris notes the possible allegorical significance of the stories, in which the weak but wily Brer Rabbit outwits dangerous animals such as Brer Fox. Like Harris, North Carolina writer Charles Chesnutt, the first major African American writer of fiction, drew on the folk tradition in writing "The Goophered Grapevine" and other stories collected in *The Conjure*

Woman (1899). In *The Wife of His Youth and Other Stories of the Color Line* (1899), Chesnutt dropped his Uncle Julius narrator but continued to explore race in stories such as "The Passing of Grandison," in which an outwardly passive slave outwits his master and frees his family. Finally, in her collections *Bayou Folk* (1894) and *A Night in Acadie* (1897), Kate Chopin sketches realistic portraits of her region of Louisiana while also exploring race, class, and sex. "Désirée's Baby" is the story of a woman who faces alienation when she learns she is part African American. In "Athénaïse: A Story of Temperament," a young woman defies cultural expectations when she temporarily leaves her husband to taste independence. By emphasizing both place and people, these realists showed southern short fiction moving from local color toward the more sophisticated work of the next century.

Mark Canada

See also Local Color; Plantation Fiction; Southwestern Humor.

Henry Seidel Canby, *A Study of the Short Story* (1913); Eugene Current-García, *The American Short Story Before 1850* (1985); Fred Lewis Pattee, *The Development of the American Short Story* (1923).

SHORT STORY, 1900 TO WORLD WAR II

For various historical and cultural reasons, the southern short story in the first half of the twentieth century often focused on certain themes, such as the persistence of the past, the viciousness of race prejudice, and the importance of ritual, that are, if not particular to the South, at least common to that region's literature.

The human relationship to the natural world, the primitive importance of ritual, and the conquest of time are common themes in the stories of Caroline Gordon and William Faulkner. Gordon (1895–1981) was born in Todd County, Kentucky. Her best-known stories, "Old Red" and "The Last Day in the Field," published in *The Forest of the South* (1945), focus on Aleck Maury, an academic scholar of the old school who hunts and fishes as a ritualistic means of remaining one with the natural world. In "Old Red," a story that has been extravagantly praised, Maury identifies with a fox, for he knows that both he and the animal play a noble game and that both are pursued by the inevitability of time and death. In "The Last Day in the Field," on an elegiac fall day particularly good for the hunt, Maury, in spite of a bad leg, goes out on the hunt, reaffirming his knowledge that hunting requires patience, trust, and respect.

In their creation of the mythical world of Yoknapatawpha, the stories of William Faulkner (1897–1962) seem written to be integrated rather than to stand alone. Thus a number of them become parts of his novels. "Spotted Horses" went into *The Hamlet* (1940), "An Odor of Verbena" concluded *The Unvanquished* (1938), and "Dilsey" concluded *The Sound and the Fury* (1929). Two of Faulkner's best-known stories, "That Evening Sun" and "Barn Burning," feature central characters who are important in the *The Sound and the Fury* and *The Hamlet*. His collections include *These Thirteen* (1931), *Dr. Martino and Other Stories* (1934), and his best-known, *Go Down, Moses and Other Stories* (1942), in which shorter pieces such as "Was" and "Delta Autumn" create a fabled background for the central story of Ike McCaslin's great hunt in "The Bear."

Faulkner's most famous story, "A Rose for Emily," stands alone as a kind of venerated monument, for although minor characters in the story appear in Faulkner novels, Emily is an isolated icon of the South, holding on to the past even as it decays around her. In addition to the power of the gothic conclusion of the story, the basic reason "Emily" is such a favorite Faulkner piece is that it so clearly embodies his favorite theme—the persistence of the past—and his favorite technique—the disruption of time as a linear series of events.

Racial conflict, a common theme for many southern writers, is, because of its broad social implications, usually more suitably treated in the novel. The short fiction of Erskine Caldwell (1903–1987), born in Coweta County, Georgia, better known for his novels *Tobacco Road* (1932) and *God's Little Acre* (1933), frequently focuses on the viciousness of race prejudice as part of everyday life in the rural South. "Kneel to the Rising Sun," from his 1935 collection of the same name and one of his most highly praised stories, features an ignorant landowner, a spineless white sharecropper, and a proud African American. When the sharecropper's father falls in the hog pen while looking for food and is partially eaten, only the African American has the courage to stand up to the landowner. Because the sharecropper cannot turn against a white man, no matter how vicious he is, he betrays his African American friend, who is shot so many times his body jumps around "like a sackful of kittens being killed with an automatic shotgun."

Richard Wright (1908–1960), the best-known southern African American writer during this period, also focused on the violence of racial prejudice, but often with a polemical intention. Born in Adams County, Mississippi, to an illiterate sharecropper father and a schoolteacher mother, his first published story, "Bright and Morning Star," was chosen for *Best American Stories* in 1939. It is a simple narrative about an African American mother who, when her two sons join the Communist Party, gives up her Christian religion for a new vision of suffering black men who have taken the place of "Him nailed to the Cross." When she mistakenly betrays her sons' comrades, her decision to sacrifice herself to correct her error is "the star that grew bright in the morning of new hope" and makes her feel that the whole meaning of her life is poised on the "brink of a total act."

"Big Boy Leaves Home" is largely a dialogue story of four African American boys whose simple act of going swimming turns into tragedy when a white woman sees the naked boys and her companion shoots two of them, after which Big Boy struggles with him and kills him. The rest of the story is the inevitable tale of racial viciousness. Although white men catch one of the boys, pour hot tar on him, and set him afire, Big Boy escapes. In Wright's most anthologized story, "The Man Who Was Almos' a Man," the escape of young Dave, an African American who buys a gun to feel like a man and then accidentally shoots a mule, is more ambiguous. After being made fun of by other African American men and told by his father that he must pay for the mule out of his meager earnings, he boards a freight train to escape to somewhere he can be a man; ominously, however, the gun is still in his pocket.

The basic difference between Wright's stories and those of Zora Neale Hurston is that Hurston, without obvious social intentions, bases her stories on the cultural life of the people. Hurston (1891–1960) grew up in Eatonville, Florida, the oldest incorporated African American town in the United States. Her best-known stories are "The Gilded Six-Bits," "Sweat," and "Drenched in Light." In the former, a young African American couple are loving, playful, and happy, until the wife goes to bed with another African American man to get the gold piece he offers. The husband discovers the couple *in fragrante delecto,* but he eventually forgives Bessie May and takes the coin (which is but a gilded half dollar) to town and buys her candy

kisses. "Drenched in Light" is a simple story of an African American child who wears her Grandma's new tablecloth to a carnival, even though she knows she will be punished. On the way home, she is picked up by a white couple, who give the grandmother five dollars to compensate for the ruined tablecloth. When the child snuggles up to the white woman and says she is going to sing a song for her, the woman looks hungrily at her and says, "I would like just a little of her sunshine to soak into my soul."

Because the short story is such a highly conventional and tightly structured genre, novelists usually succeed with the form only when they self-consciously experiment with its lyrical style or its tradition of depicting a dreamlike reality. Thomas Wolfe (1900–1938), born in Asheville, North Carolina, is often cited as the archetypal author of big formless novels written in a rambling autobiographical style; but he also published forty stories in a variety of slick and quality journals, many of which are reprinted in *From Death to Morning* (1935) and *The Hills Beyond* (1941).

"The Lost Boy," a lyrical story about memory and the tenuous nature of one's status in the world, is a highly controlled, four-part evocation of Grover, age eleven, the brother of Eugene Gant, the central character in *Look Homeward, Angel.* Part I is a third-person narrative about his being accused of dishonesty by a crabby candy-store owner and his wife, an experience that makes him feel the guilt all good men have always felt; in Part IV, Eugene makes a pilgrimage to the house where his brother died at age twelve, knowing that he will never return again and that, as a result, the lost boy is gone forever. In "Only the Dead Know Brooklyn," an undiscerning Brooklynite relates a dialogue he has had with a man looking for Bensonhurst because he likes the name. The narrator says the man will never get to know Brooklyn by depending on a map, for he has lived there all his life and doesn't know it. The story is a cryptic allegory about the difference between aesthetic and practical knowledge.

Elizabeth Madox Roberts and Ellen Glasgow, also better known for their novels, succeeded with the short story when they made use of one of its most traditional gothic conventions—the haunted house. Born in Perryville, Kentucky, Roberts (1881–1941) published two collections of short stories, *The Haunted Mirror* (1932) and *Not By Strange Gods* (1941). Her most famous story, "The Haunted Palace," whose title is derived from the poem in Poe's "Fall of the House of Usher," focuses on a house that sharecropper Hubert and his wife Jess plan to buy—a house so possessed by all those who have lived in it that it becomes an hallucinatory object. When the practical-minded couple allow their sheep to give birth to lambs in the rooms of the house, a shrouded figure representative of its past challenges them; the story ends in the triumph of prosaic everyday reality over the romance of the old nobility.

Ellen Glasgow (1874–1945), born in Richmond, Virginia, said in an interview in 1916 that short stories bored her and that she saw everything in the form of a novel. Nevertheless, her collection *The Shadowy Third and Other Stories* (1925) contains one story, "Dare's Gift," that is practically a prototype of the nineteenth-century American short story. Beginning in typical Poe fashion with the narrator, a practical and logical corporation lawyer, wondering if the event he is about to narrate really occurred, the story features a delicate southern wife suffering from a nervous breakdown, which necessitates the narrator's taking her to Dare's Gift, "the dream of a house," stepping into which is like stepping into another world. A wise old doctor, who says the incomprehensible has always seemed to him the supreme fact of life, suggests that the house's haunted state is the result of being "saturated with a thought, haunted by treachery." He tells the story of Lucy Dare, who, on moving into the house, becomes so intoxicated by the idea of the Confederacy that when her former fiancé seeks shelter there, she surrenders him up and he is shot. The doctor's conclusion—that Lucy had "drained the whole of experience in an instant" and that it is the high moments that make a life and the flat ones that fill the years—is a classic description of the typical short-story theme in American literature.

Because of its isolated nature, stories about the Appalachian region of the South are most likely to be characterized as local-color. Jesse Stuart (1906–1984), from Greenup County, Kentucky, who writes simple narratives about rural Appalachian life that move predictably toward comic/ironic resolutions, is the best known. Stuart's volumes of short stories include *Head o' W-Hollow* (1936) and *Men of the Mountains* (1941). A typical story is "The Split Cherry Tree," about a father who goes to his son's school to shoot the teacher for taking students on field trips instead of keeping them in school for real "learnin'," a threat that the tone of the story never allows the reader to take seriously. The teacher wins the father over by showing him germs in the scum on his teeth through a microscope.

Although not as well known as Stuart, James Still (1906–) is a much more perceptive observer of Kentucky mountain life and a much better writer. Many of his stories, which appeared throughout the 1930s and 1940s in periodicals, are reprinted in his novel *River of Earth* (1940) and his collection *On Troublesome Creek* (1941). One of his best-known stories, "The Moving," is a poignant evocation of a family forced to move when the mines close. The last image the young narrator has is of Hig Sommers, a witty boy destined to live forever as a child, holding his breeches up, his other arm in the air, ironically saying goodbye by crying "Hello, hello!" The story is a delicate combination of poignancy, pride, and comic reserve told with carefully controlled Chekhovian simplicity. Poor but not the subjects of sociological analysis, Still's characters are embodiments of endurance, pride, and dignity.

The two greatest masters of the short story in the South between the turn of the century and World War II are Eudora Welty and Katherine Anne Porter. In her first two collections, *A Curtain of Green* (1941) and *The Wide Net* (1943), Welty focuses brilliantly on the Mississippi milieu she knows so well, creating enigmatic characters and symbolic situations that combine the ordinary and the mythically meaningful. It is not simply social isolation that plagues Welty's characters, but rather a primal sense of separateness; and it is not mere social validation that they hunger for, but rather a genuine healing love that will give them a sense of order and meaning. Memorable characters in Welty's stories caught in a quest for their own identity include in "Petrified Man" Leota and Mrs. Fletcher, who, Medusa-like, metaphorically turn men into stone; Phoenix Jackson, the indefatigable grandmother who in "A Worn Path" goes on a heroic journey to seek relief for her suffering grandson; Livie, in the story that bears her name, who dares to leave the control and order of the patriarchal Solomon for the vitality of Cash McCord; and Sister in "Why I Live at the P.O," who tries to validate herself to her family when they welcome home her prodigal sister.

Welty's stories focus less on characters defined by their stereotypical social roles than by their archetypal metaphysical being. In the story "Clytie," although it is true that Clytie is a stereotyped old maid, exploited by her family and laughed at by the townspeople for her eccentricity, it is not social criticism that Welty focuses on here but a search for primal identity; when Clytie looks down into the mirrored surface of the rain barrel and sees her own face recoil from her, she can think of nothing else to do but thrust her head into the "kind, featureless depth" of the water and hold it there. Welty's stories seem to spring more from the world of myth and story than from the real world, and the language in which they are written is often highly symbolic and allusive.

Katherine Anne Porter is better known for her short stories than for her single novel. *Flowering Judas and Other Stories* (1940) contains most of her best-known stories, such as "Theft," "The Jilting of Granny Weatherall," "Flowering Judas," and "María Concepción"; and her second collection, *The Leaning Tower and Other Stories* (1944), contains the Miranda stories, "The Witness," "The Old Order," "The Circus," and "The Grave." Porter's most common theme is the conflict between chaos and order, between letting go and holding back. The theme can best be seen in two stories in which the child Miranda faces the horrors of birth and death/flesh and decay—"Circus" and "The Grave"—and two stories in which women try to maintain control in the face of loss of self, "Flowering Judas" and "Theft."

As many critics have pointed out, "The Grave" is closer to a lyric poem than to traditional narrative, for the compression of its language transforms it into metaphor. The story focuses on Miranda's reaction to a gold ring—which makes her long to put aside her tomboyish childhood for her most feminine dress—and to the opened body of the pregnant rabbit—which introduces her to the mysterious nature of birth and death; it is a quintessential transformation of memory into meaning. "Theft" also focuses on memory, albeit the "immediate past," as a young woman recalls the seemingly irrelevant events of the day. What connects the seemingly unrelated memories is that all of them focus on broken, flawed, or faulty relationships in which people are posturing or putting on false fronts. Written in Porter's typically economical manner, the story suggests lives lived carelessly, without commitment and honesty.

By means of a tactic that has dominated modern short fiction since Anton Chekhov, Porter makes such stories as her most famous one, "Flowering Judas," appear to be realistic situations about people caught in specific moral dilemmas, while at the same time they are spiritual allegories in which characters and objects are emblems of universal moral issues. The many dichotomies in the story—Laura's Catholicism and her socialism, her sensuality and her ascetic renunciation, her dedication to the people and her renunciation of

genuine involvement—coalesce in the symbolic dichotomy of Braggioni, who affirms life even though it means throwing himself into the physical and becoming a "professional lover of humanity," and Eugenio, the imprisoned revolutionary who maintains his idealism but who negates life and wants to die because he is bored.

Although the southern short story is more likely to be identified with place than stories from other regions, the most influential southern short-story writers in the first half of the twentieth century—Faulkner, Welty, and Porter—transcend local color, exotic locales, and marginalized characters to create universal stories of the human condition.

Charles E. May

See also Appalachian Literature; Faulkner, William; Local Color; Short-Story Cycles; Welty, Eudora; Yoknapatawpha.

Philip Stevick, ed., *The American Short Story: 1900–1945* (1984); Arthur Voss, *The American Short Story: A Critical Survey* (1973); Ray B. West, *The Short Story in America: 1900–1950* (1952); Austin Wright, *The American Short Story in the Twenties* (1961).

SHORT STORY, WORLD WAR II TO PRESENT

When one looks at the short story since World War II, the first writers to consider are those who wrote fiction both before and after the war, and who, though deceased, have reputations that continue to endure. Of these, the foremost is Nobel Prize–winning author, Mississippian William Faulkner (1897–1962). Faulkner's works were not in great demand until after the publication in 1949 of *The Portable Faulkner*. A year later, forty-two stories published in magazines since 1930, which Faulkner had selected and organized, were published in his *Collected Stories*. Many of these stories were situated in his own mythical world, Yoknapatawpha County, and some were so interrelated that they would eventually be parts of larger works. *The Hamlet* (1940), for example, contains six stories either published or about to be published; *Go Down, Moses* (1942), a work Faulkner once called a "novel," is composed of seven distinct stories. In 1979, after the *Collected Stories* had been reprinted twenty-two times, the *Uncollected Stories of William Faulkner* made available in one volume forty-five additional stories. Of these, twenty, after separate publication in magazine form, became parts of other books; twelve, though published before, had never been collected, and thirteen had not been printed elsewhere. "Hell Creek Crossing," though part of *The Reivers* (1962) and published in the *Saturday Evening Post* (March 31, 1962) as a story just before Faulkner's death, indicates that much of his short fiction could both stand on its own and be part of a larger vision of the world that had universal significance. Unlike the ninety-three stories in the *Complete Stories* (1953) of Georgia native Erskine Caldwell (1903–1987), which range from starkly realistic proletarian narratives to slapstick situational farces, or those of Texan William Goyen (1915–1983), available in his *Collected Stories* (1975) and *Had I a Hundred Mouths: New and Selected Stories: 1974–83* (1985), such as the hypnotic "The Faces of Blood Kindred," Faulkner probed the southern psyche with the brilliance of a master organist whose fugues fill every niche of a gigantic cathedral.

The stories of two of Faulkner's contemporaries, Texan Katherine Anne Porter (1890–1980) and Kentuckian Caroline Gordon (1895–1981), highlight the uniqueness of his short fiction and, by contrast, the variety of southern fiction in general. Well known for her four major story collections, *Flowering Judas and Other Stories* (1930), *Pale Horse, Pale Rider: Three Short Novels* (1939), *The Leaning Tower and Other Stories* (1944), and *The Old Order* (1955), Porter first published in 1964 the British edition of her *Collected Stories*, subsequently awarded both the Pulitzer Prize in fiction and the National Book Award. A lyrical writer who possessed enormous eloquence, Porter's style moved her readers, much like the dramatic clarity of James Joyce's *Dubliners*. Her short fiction often brought about a collision of emotion and morality, as reflected in a remark she made about Hart Crane's writing: It stunned the ears, shocked the nerves, and caused the heart to contract. In the manner of Faulkner, eleven parts of her noted novel *Ship of Fools* (1962), transformed later into a successful movie, were published separately in literary journals. Like Porter, Caroline Gordon, noted for such novels as *Penhally* (1931) and *The Malefactors* (1965), spent important years of her life as a writer-in-residence at various universities throughout the United States. Twice married to the poet Allen Tate, her story collections include *The Forest of the South* (1945), *Old Red and Other Stories* (1963), and her *Collected Stories* (1981; five of these stories appeared after World War II). Primarily a novelist, Gordon, unlike Porter, was influenced not only by

the Fugitive poets, especially John Crowe Ransom, Donald Davidson, Robert Penn Warren, and her husband, but by the Agrarians. (The stories of Robert Penn Warren [1905–1989], known mostly as a novelist and poet, can be found in his *The Circus in the Attic and Other Stories*, 1948.) Gordon's midlife conversion to Roman Catholicism impelled her to communicate her spiritual values to aspiring writers and to develop a theory of writing fiction based, in large measure, on the Poetics of Aristotle, as well as the writings of Flaubert, Henry James, and Ford Madox Ford.

Tennesseean Andrew Lytle (1902–1995) graduated from Vanderbilt University in 1925, where he befriended the Fugitives and eventually became the last of the contributors to the Agrarian manifesto *I'll Take My Stand* (1930), which repudiated nineteenth-century poetic traditions and the encroaching values of industrialized society. Lytle, the only genuine farmer among the Agrarians, taught for many years at the University of the South, where he edited the *Sewanee Review* (1961–1973). Known for his essays, reviews, and novels, including *The Velvet Horn* (1957), as well as a biography, *Bedford Forrest and His Critter Company* (1931), he wrote *A Novel, A Novella and Four Stories* (1958) and *Stories: Alchemy and Others* (1984). Another academic, and likewise an undergraduate student at Vanderbilt, where he studied with John Crowe Ransom, Tennesseean Peter Taylor (1919–1994) taught at a number of universities, including, in his latter years, the University of Virginia. In addition to his novels, particularly the Pulitzer Prize–winning *A Summons to Memphis* (1986), his collections of stories include *A Long Fourth and Other Stories* (1948), *Happy Families Are All Alike* (1959), *Miss Leonora When Last Seen and Fifteen Other Stories* (1964), *In the Miro District* (1977), *The Old Forest and Other Stories* (1985), and finally his *Collected Stories* (1969). Considered by some to be the Victorian realist of Middle and West Tennessee, Taylor was not afraid of digression as he accepted, often employing the first-person perspective, the world around him, but not without critiquing what it offered. As he noted in a 1981 interview with Jean Ross, southern writers in their childhood often heard stories from their elders and later wrote to explore what those stories meant. Thus Taylor, a cunning narrative archaeologist, wrote to discover the implications of what he believed he knew.

As might be expected, southern black writers emerged to make a difference in southern fiction. Richard Wright (1908–1960), born on a cotton plantation near Natchez, Mississippi, achieved a wide reputation especially for *Native Son* (1940) and *Black Boy: A Record of Childhood and Youth* (1945), which, in addition to his posthumous collection of short stories, *Eight Men* (1961), helped change almost single-handedly the stereotypical image of black writers as he countered the disparagement of blacks in a segregated society. Unable to be reconciled to the continuing racism in the United States, he moved to Paris with his family in 1946. The works of Zora Neale Hurston (1891–1960) of Eatonville, Florida, a town founded by ex-slaves, emerged not only from her anthropological studies at Columbia University in New York City, but her job as a writer and folklorist, which took her to Jamaica, Haiti, and Bermuda. As Hurston wrote in *Mules and Men* (1934), "I hurried back to Eatonville because I knew that the town was full of material and that I could get it without hurt, harm or danger." After years of neglect, her four novels, including *Their Eyes Were Watching God* (1937), and her autobiography *Dust Tracks on a Road* (1942) have achieved international recognition, even though all her books were out of print at the time of her death. Of the twenty-six stories in her *Complete Stories* (1995), three were published after World War II and seven were published in this volume for the first time. A master of narrative technique and black dialect, Hurston often dealt with themes of divine justice and human accountability—and the vindication of an individual's integrity—seen particularly in her moving last story, "The Conscience of the Court," published in the *Saturday Evening Post* (March 18, 1950).

Short stories have also felt the dramatic imaginations of Tennessee Williams (1911–1983), born in Mississippi, and Carson McCullers (1917–1967), born in Georgia. Williams, author of the acclaimed dramas *The Glass Menagerie* (1944), *A Streetcar Named Desire* (1947), and *Cat on a Hot Tin Roof* (1955), wrote numerous short stories, included in *One Arm and Other Stories* (1948), *Three Players of a Summer Game and Other Stories* (1974), *Eight Mortal Ladies Possessed* (1974), and his *Collected Stories* (1985). Passengers, like characters in a Williams story, had often to change from one New Orleans streetcar, Desire, to the other, Cemeteries, from the primordial tugs of the human heart to the dying, faded charm of the Old South. McCullers, author of five novels, including *The Heart Is a Lonely Hunter* (1940), *Reflections in a Golden Eye* (1941), and *The Member of the Wedding* (1946), rewritten as an award-winning play, published

stories gathered in her *The Ballad of the Sad Café and Other Stories* (1951) and in her *Collected Stories* (1987), half of which take place outside the South. Like the protagonists of a Williams story, her characters know, as she wrote, the "immense complexity of love," whether it be unrequited love or outright rejection.

Louisiana native Truman Capote (1924–1984), famous not only for his novels and his literary documentary *In Cold Blood* (1966), but also for three collections of short stories, *A Tree of Night and Other Stories* (1949), *Breakfast at Tiffany's: A Short Novel and Three Stories* (1958), and *Music for Chameleons* (1980, which also includes conversational portraits and reminiscences), found his milieu mostly outside the South. His contemporary Flannery O'Connor (1925–1964), a native Georgian who spent most of her life in the small town of Milledgeville, explored the various facets of autobiographical and biographical modes of expression. O'Connor was the author of two novels, *Wise Blood* (1952) and *The Violent Bear It Away* (1960), and the collections of stories *A Good Man Is Hard to Find* (1955) and *Everything That Rises Must Converge* (1965). Her *Complete Stories* (1971) won the National Book Award. Her insight into the world about her can be glimpsed from a sentence in "The Artificial Nigger": "The trees were full of silver-white sunlight, and even the meanest of them sparkled." A devout Roman Catholic in the Protestant South, O'Connor portrays characters, such as Mrs. McIntyre in "The Displaced Person" (a story masterfully transformed into a television film with the support of the National Endowment for the Humanities), who have a chance for self-conversion and eventually eternal salvation. Sometimes accused of writing too much about the grotesque and freakish members of society, O'Connor defended herself by inviting her readers simply to glance about themselves. In the South, she believed, writers honestly depict what they see.

Perhaps because Tennesseean John William Corrington (1932–1988), a lawyer influenced by the philosophical works of Eric Voegelin, and his wife moved to California to write screenplays, his works, including eight novels and three collections of short stories (gathered together and edited by Joyce Hooper Corrington in his *Collected Stories,* 1989), have reflected how his characters deal with moral dilemmas in philosophical and legal contexts.

Without doubt, the doyenne of contemporary writers of southern short stories is Eudora Welty (1909–2001), a native Mississippian who lived most of her life in the same house in Jackson. Educated at the Mississippi State College for Women and the University of Wisconsin, she received the Pulitzer Prize for fiction, the National Medal for Literature, the American Academy of Arts and Letters Gold Medal for the Novel, and numerous honorary doctorates and fellowships. Her short-story collections—*A Curtain of Green and Other Stories* (1941), *The Wide Net and Other Stories* (1943), *The Golden Apples* (1949), *The Bride of the Innisfallen and Other Stories* (1955), and her *Collected Stories* (1980)—as well as her novels and nonfiction have given her a deservedly international reputation. Katherine Anne Porter praised Welty as having "an eye and an ear sharp, shrewd, and true as a tuning fork." In *The Golden Apples*, whose title is borrowed from a line by William Butler Yeats, Welty describes in seven stories three generations of families in Morgana, Mississippi—the McLains, Morrisons, Starkses, Raineys, and Carmichaels—whose lives are gradually seen to be interconnected. (This technique can likewise be seen in *Season of the Strangler*, [1982], by Tennesseean Madison Jones [1925–], who most likely was influenced in this case by Sherwood Anderson's *Winesburg, Ohio,* 1919). As noted in one of her essays, Welty knows the value of place—particularly Mississippi—in situating the dilemmas of the human heart that her characters experience.

Many contemporary southern writers, including several Mississippians, have felt Welty's influence as they strove to achieve their own voices. As someone who attended Belhaven College, located across the street from Welty's house, Elizabeth Spencer (1921–) grew up keenly aware of Welty's genius. Because she has lived in Italy and Canada, however, her sense of place—and thus the locales she uses in her fiction—has afforded her the opportunity to look at the South from a different perspective, what she once termed a "residence in the world." The author of nine novels, including *The Voice at the Back Door* (1956), *The Snare* (1972), and *The Salt Line* (1982), Spencer has published four short-story collections—*Ship Island and Other Stories* (1968), *The Stories of Elizabeth Spencer* (1981), *Jack of Diamonds and Other Stories* (1990), and *The Light in the Piazza and Other Italian Tales* (1995). Recipient of numerous literary awards and a member of the American Academy of Arts and Letters, she wrote in her memoir *Landscapes of the Heart* (1998) that she felt the need of a land in her fiction, a sure terrain, "a sort of permanent landscape of the heart," out of which her characters could live and

grow. Ellen Douglas (1921–), the pen name of Josephine Haxton, grew up in Louisiana, Arkansas, and Mississippi, and lived for many years not far from Welty. Known primarily as a novelist for works such as *A Family's Affairs* (1962), *Apostles of Light* (1973), *The Rock Cried Out* (1979), and *Can't Quit You, Baby* (1988), her shorter works of fiction are contained in *Black Cloud, White Cloud* (1963). Like Spencer, whose masterly story "The Finder" evokes powerful tenderness, Douglas has her pulse on the inner—often darker—workings of the human heart. Ellen Gilchrist (1935–) was born in Mississippi and spent her early years there. Author of many books, she has published several collections of stories: *In the Land of Dreamy Dreams* (1981), *Victory Over Japan* (1984), which won the American Book Award, *Drunk With Love* (1986), *Light Can Be Both Wave and Particle: A Book of Stories* (1989), and *Blue-Eyed Buddhist and Other Stories* (1990). Her *Rhoda: A Life in Stories* (1995), about Rhoda Manning, a woman with no shadows, "just passion, energy, and light," won the National Book Award for Fiction. *The Courts of Love: Stories* (1996) stars in the first of two sequences of stories one of Gilchrist's favorite recurring characters, Nora Jane Whittington, a free spirit who had once run away from home; now married and the mother of twins, Nora Jane is faced with a series of disasters that threatens her blissful life. Martha Lacy Hall (1923–) has authored three short-story collections: *Call It Living* (1981), *Music Lesson* (1984), and *The Apple-Green Triumph* (1990). This Mississippian found her authorial voice late in life, but her work has earned praise from thoughtful readers.

North Carolinian Doris Betts (1932–) is known for three collections of short stories—*The Gentle Insurrection* (1954), *The Astronomer and Other Stories* (1965), and *Beasts of the Southern Wild* (1973). Betts is quick to praise Welty as a formative influence.

Shirley Ann Grau (1929–), a native of New Orleans, won the Pulitzer Prize for Fiction in 1965 for her novel *The Keepers of the House*. Her stories are collected in *The Black Prince* (1955), *The Wind Shifting West* (1973), and most recently *Nine Women* (1986), which shows the fates of various women, such as Myra Rowland, recently widowed, who returns to a resort she had visited year after year with her husband, only to find so many changes all mirrored in the attitudes of her summer neighbors; or Nancy Martinson, who curses the fate that has allowed her to be the sole survivor of a plane crash in which she lost her entire family—and who resolves to court death in a chillingly methodical way.

University professors have been active in creating important fiction about the modern South and the world. Robert Drake of the University of Tennessee has written intimately personal stories that recapture "the home place" of his Tennessee family in the early years of the century, including *Amazing Grace* (1965), *Survivors and Others* (1987), *My Sweetheart's House* (1993), and *What Will You Do for an Encore* (1996). George Garrett (1929–), a native of Florida, is best known for his historical novels, such as *The Succession* (1983) and *Entered from the Sun* (1990); his stories have been collected in both *In the Briar Patch* (1961) and *An Evening Performance* (1985). Author of nearly thirty books and editor or co-editor of nearly two dozen others, Garrett is the Henry Hoyns Professor of English at the University of Virginia. John Barth (1930–) of Maryland, who studied at Johns Hopkins University in Baltimore, where he is now the Alumni Centennial Professor of English and Creative Writing, is known worldwide for his enormously expansive novels, including *The Sot-Weed Factor* (1960), *Giles Goat-Boy: or, The Revised New Syllabus* (1966), and *The Last Voyage of Somebody the Sailor* (1991). In addition, his two collections of stories—the first contains fourteen short stories or "fictions," entitled *Lost in the Funhouse* (1968); the second, *Chimera,* won the National Book Award in 1972—reveal the sensibility, as explored in "Water-Message," of an author at home on Maryland's Eastern Shore. David Madden (1933–) of Tennessee, author of seven novels and a collection of short stories, *The New Orleans of Possibilities* (1982), and a professor of English at Louisiana State University, is creating an archival repository of Civil War material reflecting his deep interest in the history of the South. Reynolds Price (1933–), a Rhodes Scholar at Merton College, Oxford University, before returning to his alma mater, Duke University, where he is the James B. Duke Professor of English, established his reputation with his novel *A Long and Happy Life* (1962), which won the William Faulkner Award. Price has had a long and distinguished literary career, publishing numerous volumes of fiction, plays, poetry, essays, translations, and a memoir. He is a member of the American Academy of Arts and Letters. Price's short fiction is contained in *The Names and Faces of Heroes* (1963), *Permanent Errors* (1970), *The Foreseeable Future* (1991), and his *Collected Short Stories* (1993). Among his stories, "The Warrior Princess Ozimba" re-

veals the sensitive elegance that is the hallmark of his work.

Two other writers of this generation, Louisianan Ernest J. Gaines (1933–) and Kentuckian Wendell Berry (1934–) have approached short fiction in ways that complement the work of their peers. Author of *The Autobiography of Miss Jane Pittman* (1971), *A Gathering of Old Men* (1983), and *A Lesson Before Dying* (1993), Gaines published *Bloodline* (1968), five short stories portraying black American life in the South. Berry has achieved his fame as a writer of novels, essays, and short stories, including *The Wild Birds: Six Stories of the Port William Membership* (1986), *Fidelity: Five Stories* (1992), and *Watch With Me: and Six Other Stories of the Yet-Remembered Ptolemy Proudfoot and His Wife, Miss Minnie, Née Quinch* (1994), which concern interrelated stories of his fictional community of Port William, Kentucky. Berry describes the comic and often poignant ways his characters cope with modern intrusions into agrarian life.

Of the emerging short-story writers in the South, excluding Anne Tyler and Ann Beattie, who were born outside the South, a number are worth noting. North Carolinian Fred Chappell (1936–), noted primarily for his poetry and novels, has published two collections of short stories—*Moments of Light* (1980) and *More Shapes Than One* (1991). Andre Dubus (1936–), a native of Lake Charles, Louisiana, has mastered the novella form better than any of his contemporaries. His short fiction includes *Separate Flights* (1975), *Adultery and Other Choices* (1978), *Finding a Girl in America* (1980), *The Times Are Never So Bad: A Novella and Eight Stories* (1983), *We Don't Live Here Anymore: Four Novellas and Two Stories* (1984), *The Last Worthless Evening* (1986), his *Selected Stories* (1988), and *Dancing After Dark* (1996). A Roman Catholic with a profound sense of the incarnation of Christ, Dubus focuses on failing human relationships that can be resurrected, much as his cousin, James Lee Burke (1936–), preoccupied with terror and violence, wrote about in *The Convict* (1985). Virginian Dabney Stuart (1937–), author of two collections of short stories, *Sweet Lucy Wine* (1992) and *The Way to Cobbs Creek* (1997), integrates into his fiction a poetic sensitivity that is the basis of his creative imagination. In addition, Mississippian Barry Hannah (1942–) has achieved a steady following by portraying characters whose lives—occasionally bleak—are uncommonly true. His collections of stories include *Airships* (1978), *Captain Maximus* (1985), *Bats Out of Hell* (1993), and *High Lonesome* (1996), the last containing thirteen stories, some with the autobiographical vividness of childhood memories as seen in "A Creature in the Bay of St. Louis."

Among women writers, Kentuckian Bobbie Ann Mason (1940–), author of *Shiloh and Other Stories* (1982), *Love Life* (1989), and *Midnight Magic* (1998), portrays the South as caught somewhere between the traditional family household and the bland culture of endless shopping malls. Virginian Lee Smith (1944–), who taught at North Carolina State University, is author of nine novels, including *Oral History* (1983), *The Devil's Dream* (1992), *Saving Grace* (1995), and *The Christmas Letters* (1996). Winner of two O. Henry Awards for short fiction, she has collected her shorter works into three volumes—*Cakewalk* (1987), *Me & My Baby View the Eclipse* (1991), and *News of the Spirit* (1997), containing, among other stories, "Live Bottomless," about thirteen-year-old Jenny who tells the painful and hilarious tale of her philandering father's fall from grace and the family's subsequent trip to Key West as her parents attempt a "geographical cure" for their troubled marriage. Georgian Alice Walker (1944–), who won the Pulitzer Prize in fiction for *The Color Purple* (1986), also authored the short-story collections *In Love & Trouble: Stories of Black Women* (1973) and *You Can't Keep a Good Woman Down* (1982). West Virginian Jayne Anne Phillips (1945–) received an award from the American Academy and Institute of Arts and Letters for her collection of stories *Black Tickets* (1979); her themes often focus on the uprooting of people of her generation, the breakdown of male-female roles, and the subsequent disruptions to home, the family, and relationships. Georgian Mary Hood (1946–), author of *How Far She Went* (1973), won the Flannery O'Connor Award for Short Fiction, and her second collection, *And Venus Is Blue* (1986), won the Townsend Prize for Fiction and the Lillian Smith Award. The honesty of her fiction, dealing with a darker side of life that can produce unexpected moments of revelation, makes her one of the strongest voices to appear in the South in the recent past. South Carolinian Pam Durban (1947–) is author of a book of seven short stories, *All Set About With Fever Trees* (1985), whose title story depicts how Annie Vess grows more comfortable with elderly relatives, one of whom had been a missionary in the Belgian Congo, as she starts her own family in Georgia. North Carolinian Jill McCorkle (1958–), author of five novels, has written two collections of short stories,

Crash Diet (1992) and *Final Vinyl Days and Other Stories* (1998). As critics have noted, McCorkle is out to tame the outrageous, humanize the forbidden, and ground the hilarious.

Male short-story writers brought up after World War II include Richard Bausch (1945–), noted for four collections of stories—*Spirits and Other Stories* (1987), *The Fireman's Wife and Other Stories* (1990), *Rare & Endangered Species: A Novella and Stories* (1994), and his *Selected Stories* (1996). One can get a glimpse into the finesse with which he constructs a story by considering "Equity," which concerns three daughters in Charlottesville, Virginia, who not only must find a meaningful rapport among themselves but also with their mother, whose days on earth are numbered. Like North Carolinian Clyde Edgerton (1944–) and Pulitzer Prize-winning Mississippian Richard Ford (1944–), Robert Olen Butler (1945–), a native of Louisiana, is noted first of all as a novelist. His volume of fifteen short stories, *A Good Scent from a Strange Mountain*, which won the 1993 Pulitzer Prize for fiction, and his *Tabloid Dreams* (1996), a collection of twelve short stories, reveal someone acutely aware of the influence of Vietnamese Americans in Louisiana, those newcomers whose stories of love and betrayal, of myths and traditions, harbor dreams for peace and prosperity in a new land. Louisianian Tim Gautreaux (1947–), professor of English at Southeastern Louisiana University in Hammond, collected twelve of his short stories in *Same Place, Same Things* (1996). Larry Brown (1951–), from Faulkner's Oxford, Mississippi, is the author of two collections of short stories—*Facing the Music* (1988) and *Big Bad Love* (1990). In his essay in *A Late Start* (1989), Brown says he wants to make his readers "know more than they want about the poor, the unfortunate, or the alcoholic," but never by straying too far from his front porch. Three other writers, Tennesseean Madison Smartt Bell (1957–), Texan Rick Bass (1958–), and North Carolinian Randall Kenan (1963–), have each gained a strong foothold into southern short fiction. In *Zero dB and Other Stories* (1987) and *Barking Man and Other Stories* (1990), Bell writes stories that are far-ranging; a gambler in one story works to become rich on the French Riviera, and in another, a young mother in rural Virginia aches to gain the custody of her son. Bass, a petroleum geologist by trade, tends to focus his creative energy by writing about nature. Author of *The Watch* (1989), Bass sets his stories in Houston as well as in the bayous of the Mississippi Valley and the Montana hills. Some have compared his style as incorporating the directness of Raymond Carver and the accurate dialogue of Bobbie Ann Mason. Kenan (1963–), author of a volume of twelve stories, *Let the Dead Bury Their Dead* (1992), reflects his love for his native state as he explores same-sex love in a rural community.

Patrick Samway, S.J.

See also Novel, World War II to Present; Short Story, 1900 to World War II; Short-Story Cycles.

J. A. Bryant Jr., *Twentieth-Century Southern Literature* (1997); Jeffrey J. Folks and James A. Perkins, eds., *Southern Writers at Century's End* (1997); Ben Forkner and Patrick Samway, S.J., eds., *A Modern Southern Reader* (1986); Ben Forkner and Patrick Samway, S.J., eds., *Stories of the Modern South* (rev. ed.; 1995); *New Stories of the South,* ongoing series edited by Shannon Ravenel; *Best of the South,* selected by Anne Tyler, edited by Shannon Ravenel (1996).

SHORT-STORY CYCLES

In the United States in the twentieth century, the short-story cycle has assumed genre identity, one that has proven attractive to numerous writers. Gertrude Stein's *Three Lives* (1909), Sherwood Anderson's *Winesburg, Ohio* (1919), and Hemingway's *In Our Time* (1925) alerted writers to the possibilities of works with related stories wherein the whole would be greater than the sum of its parts. As the century has progressed, the popularity of the short-story cycle has increased, as is indicated by successes in the genre by Louise Erdrich, Gloria Naylor, Tim O'Brien, and others. The disjunctiveness inherent in the genre has been congenial to twentieth-century sensibility. Noting its increasing popularity, Maggie Dunn and Ann Morris—wishing to emphasize the unity in the form—have argued for a more descriptive label for the short-story cycle, preferring the term *composite novel.*

Different from a short-story collection by a single writer, the cycle or composite novel conceives a whole that in its force produces an effect similar to that achieved in the novel. The parts may be read as satisfying entities, but collectively they work together for a greater end. Plots are multiple, though a major plot story may be present or implied, especially if there is a recurring character such as George Willard (*Winesburg*) or Nick Adams (*In Our Time*). The protagonist may be emerging and collective, as in Naylor's *The Women of Brewster Place* (1982). The cycle may emphasize place (*Dubliners,* 1914) for its unity, or pattern (*Three Lives*), or storytelling, as in O'Brien's *The Things They Carried* (1990), or combinations of these. The writer may not have begun writing the individual stories with the larger end in mind, but the larger concept may emerge after several stories are in hand. Accordingly, the writer will give special attention to the order of the stories with chronology of composition not likely to be the prime consideration. Rather, concern will be with how the stories relate to each other thematically.

Although twentieth-century readers have become more conscious of this genre, the short-story cycle has numerous progenitors, going all the way back to Chaucer and Boccaccio. In prose fiction, nineteenth-century writers, with an expanding market for short fiction, produced numerous works that revealed the possibilities for unified collections. In the United States, Sarah Orne Jewett's *The Country of the Pointed Firs* (1896) is among the most famous examples. But southern writers in the nineteenth century also moved in the direction of the cycle or composite novel. Progenitors include Augustus Baldwin Longstreet's *Georgia Scenes* (1835), Caroline Lee Hentz's *Aunt Patty's Scrap-Bag* (1846), George Washington Cable's *Old Creole Days* (1879), Mary Noailles Murfree's *In the Tennessee Mountains* (1884), Thomas Nelson Page's *In Ole Virginia* (1887), Grace King's *Balcony Stories* (1892), Kate Chopin's *Bayou Folk* (1894) and *A Night in Acadie* (1897), and Charles W. Chesnutt's *The Conjure Woman* (1899). As most of these titles indicate, the centrality of place is a primary unifier in these early "cycles," but history, theme, and narrative voice also serve as important unifying devices.

In the twentieth century, the experimentation became more conscious and sustained as the South actively shared in the modernist sensibility. The urge toward the composite looms large in the work of James Branch Cabell, underlying most of what he did. Eventually, he made a composite of his numerous fictions, presenting eighteen volumes collectively as the "Biography of the Life of Manuel," the collected series published in 1927–1930. But several of the individual books of the whole are comprised of short stories— *The Line of Love* (1905, rev. 1921), *Chivalry* (1909, rev. 1921), *Gallantry* (1907, rev. 1922). The titles of the volumes reflect Cabell's sense of the unity of the composite—a unity provided by theme and medieval settings. But even Cabell's works not comprised of gatherings of previously published stories make plain his emphasis on the composite—discrete parts that worked together to make a larger effect. Cabell's celebrated *Jurgen* (1919)—like much of Cabell's work—falls into well-defined parts that can entertain apart from the whole. *The Silver Stallion* (1926) provides an even more striking example, for there is no unifying central character, save the memory of the deceased Manuel. Part play on the legend of the Round Table, part play on the Acts of the Apostles, Cabell's comedic vision in *The Silver Stallion* emphasizes the human capacity to live by dreams, to prefer illusion to reality. The method allowed Cabell to treat the South he knew as the realistic novel could not.

Jean Toomer's *Cane* (1923) shares a place with *Winesburg, Ohio* and *In Our Time* as a revolutionary modernist text. The structure of *Cane* is complex; its parts include story, sketch, poem, and drama. The effect is that of a collage. The first section, set in Georgia, deals with elemental themes of sexual identity and fulfillment as well as racial conflict. The prose is rich, lush, taking on the effect of poetry. The second section takes place in Washington, D.C., a border between North and South, and highlights the demands placed on African Americans in the urban setting. The final section portrays Ralph Kabnis, an African American shaped by northern urban culture, who returns to the Deep South to reclaim that heritage but finds he belongs to neither culture. Kabnis's story provides a closure similar to that of Nick Adams's experience in "Big Two-Hearted River" at the end of *In Our Time* or that of Gabriel Conroy in *Dubliners*.

William Faulkner's discovery of the possibilities of contrasting but related stories contributed greatly to his power as a writer. He found the composite novel an especially congenial form. His first masterpiece, *The Sound and the Fury* (1929), tells the story of a single family, but in four discrete parts—the first three might easily stand alone. Time is a malleable force. Three of the four parts are set on Easter Weekend of 1928, with the second set in June 1910. Faulkner multiplied the number of narrative voices greatly in *As I Lay Dying* (1930), and although the story moves forward in an easily traceable progression, the reader also experiences a heightened sense of disjunctiveness. The concept of the composite had come to loom large in Faulkner's consciousness.

Not surprisingly, Faulkner's short stories lent themselves to the composite novel. In 1938, with *Absalom, Absalom!* (1936), his greatest novel, behind him,

Faulkner published *The Unvanquished*. Most of its individual stories had already appeared as satisfying wholes. Together they recount the impact of the Civil War and its results on the lives of John Sartoris and his family, with the focus on young son Bayard, too young to go off to war—allowing Faulkner to highlight comic gifts necessarily kept at bay during the writing of *Absalom, Absalom!*, which was composed in the tragedic mode. Faulkner wrote "An Odor of Verbena," not previously published, to provide closure to the novel of closely linked (by setting, character, and action) stories. *The Unvanquished* is regularly taught as a novel, though its individual stories are often anthologized.

The three Faulkner novels that followed may also be considered composite. *The Wild Palms* (1939) alternates chapters about two distinct but related narratives. The more winning of the narratives has been published (and filmed) as *Old Man*, which recounts the adventures of a convict whose rescue of a pregnant woman from the flooding Mississippi results in a greatly lengthened prison sentence. *The Hamlet* (1940), the first of the novels in the Snopes trilogy, began with the short-story masterpiece "Spotted Horses," which would itself evolve into a more complex structure as Faulkner reshaped it for its purpose in the novel. *The Hamlet* also incorporates the previously published tall tale "Fool About a Horse." Furthermore, it presents several characters who have no direct contact with Flem Snopes. The discreteness of the parts of *The Hamlet* is emphasized by the titles of the sections: "Flem," "Eula," "The Long Hot Summer," and "The Peasants," the last suggesting the unity of the whole.

Faulkner's greatest achievement in the short-story cycle—and one of his greatest works—is *Go Down, Moses* (1942). Its individual stories have also been anthologized frequently, but the impact of the whole is overwhelming as Faulkner depicts the complex racial connections and divisions of the South. Its stories proceed from antebellum times ("Was") to the contemporary. All but one ("Pantaloon in Black") portray the lineage, its white and black branches, of Carothers McCaslin. "Pantaloon in Black" gives early notice about the humanity—and complexity—of the African Americans Faulkner will portray in succeeding stories. Faulkner's look at black males in this work is especially probing. *Go Down, Moses* also contains "The Bear," Faulkner's classic statement about the desecration of the wilderness as well as the story that underscores the burden of the McCaslin legacy as regards slavery. "The

Bear" has often been read and studied apart from the whole, but it is best understood in the context of the composite novel from whence it comes.

Faulkner turned once more to the linked-stories concept to create *Knight's Gambit* (1949). In six stories, lawyer Gavin Stevens solves six mysteries, his personal growth suggested by his marriage in the concluding and longest story. Although the least prized of Faulkner's works in the composite, *Knight's Gambit* makes clear how ingrained the linking habit was to him. The late *Big Woods* (1955) reveals the same instinct for connecting discrete parts to create a larger vision.

Katherine Anne Porter also wrote short stories so concerned with place and a family heritage that linking became inevitable. Her stories gathered in *The Old Order* (1958) may profitably be viewed as a composite novel. Porter not only wrote numerous stories about a single protagonist, Miranda, but Porter provided her with a lineage that adds impressively to the sense of unity in the stories. Whereas old Carothers is the source of the McCaslin clan, Porter has readers understand Miranda and the Gays through the distaff. The "source" in the story of that name is Sophia Jane, whom the narrator identifies as the Grandmother. In brief space, Porter creates her life—and that of her slave and eventual retainer—from antebellum times to a ripe age that saw her lead and dominate the Gay family. "Old Mortality"—the climax of the linked stories about the old order—portrays Sophia Jane's granddaughter Miranda, now a young adult, as an embodiment of the lineage, who may make her own mistakes but will handle herself with independence in the New South.

Among major contributions to the genre must be counted Eudora Welty's *The Golden Apples* (1949). Six of the seven stories in this work take place in Morgana, Mississippi, after World War I; in the seventh, the protagonist lives in San Francisco, but his roots are to be found in the Morgana history of earlier stories. The stories are concerned with four Morgana families (the Raineys, Starkses, Morrisons, and McLains) over a period of forty years, but the pace is hardly that of the typical family-saga novel. As Welty's title echoing Yeats's "Song of the Wandering Aengus" serves notice, mythic patterns predominate. Wandering is a major theme of the book. Welty's characters have as their being a rich texture of myth and poetry, and time is a malleable substance. More than anything, *The Golden Apples* reveals patterns of human longing and behavior

that transcend time; because of its reliance on myth, the book is reminiscent of the work of Cabell more than of any other southern writer.

Among southern writers in the next generation, Ellen Gilchrist is noticeably drawn to the possibilities of the genre. Whenever writers return to a character or set of characters in discrete stories—Faulkner, Porter, Welty—the possibilities for composite structures are likely to occur. Having written numerous short stories about Rhoda Manning covering that rebellious life from early childhood through a couple of marriages and a career as a writer, Gilchrist came to see that the Rhoda stories together did something they did not do individually. In 1995 she published *Rhoda: A Life in Stories*. Because the stories were written over several years, the facts of Rhoda's life are not totally consistent, but the reader nevertheless gets a sense of Rhoda and her family as detailed as one might find in a conventional novel—and certainly a more vivid sense than one typically finds. One of the "stories" is excerpted from a novel about Rhoda, emphasizing Gilchrist's sense of the freedom of her form—its disjunctiveness as well as its larger meaning, about which she reflects in a preface.

Gilchrist's earlier *Victory Over Japan* (1983) is subtitled *A Book of Stories,* but it will strike readers as more than that. The book is divided into four gatherings of stories about several southern women—zany, arresting, rebellious. References to World War II frame the book, though they function primarily as commentary on the postwar independence of postmodern women. Various narrative voices tell the stories—in the last gathering, an African American maid of "crazed" and spoiled Crystal Manning Weiss narrates, providing another example of changed lives for women in the postwar world. Less novelistic than *Rhoda, Victory Over Japan* functions forcefully as collage.

Bobbie Ann Mason's second collection of stories, *Love Life* (1989), has no central character to provide unity to the stories—but the stories are strongly unified by time, place, and theme. All of the stories are set in Mason's preferred terrain of western Kentucky; all treat the theme of love between men and women in the context of the late twentieth century when the old codes and patterns have been rendered suspect and generally unworkable. In the first, "Love Life," an older woman observes her niece and the new freedom with bemusement; in the last story, nostalgically named "Wish," an elderly widow reaffirms to her widower brother that their father had ruined her life by keeping her from the man she loved; later, the brother reflects about the disappointments of his own marriage. In this context, the sandwiched stories suggest that if post-modern Kentuckians are not always wise in their love lives, their efforts to shape those lives embody a freedom that previous generations might envy.

Dunn and Morris's annotated list of selected composite novels from the twentieth century suggests just how attractive the composite has been to southern writers. Their list includes John Barth's *Chimera* (1972) and *Lost in the Funhouse* (1972), Robert Olen Butler's *A Good Scent from a Strange Mountain* (1992), Erskine Caldwell's *Georgia Boy* (1943), Ernest Gaines's *Bloodline* (1968) and *A Gathering of Old Men* (1983), George Garrett's *Whistling in the Dark* (1992), Caroline Gordon's *Aleck Maury, Sportsman* (1934), Zora Neale Hurston's *Dust Tricks on a Road* (1942), Randall Jarrell's *Pictures from an Institution* (1954), Randall Kenan's *Let the Dead Bury Their Dead* (1992), Flannery O'Connor's *Everything That Rises Must Converge* (1965), Jayne Anne Phillips's *Machine Dreams* (1984), Ishmael Reed's *Mumbo Jumbo* (1992), Jesse Stuart's *Save Every Lamb* (1964), William Styron's *Three Tales from Youth* (1993), Peter Taylor's *The Widows of Thornton* (1954), and Richard Wright's *Uncle Tom's Children* (1938).

Like Emily Dickinson, prone to tell truth "slant," southerners have been attracted to the possibilities of the short-story cycle and to compositeness. With distinguished prototypes in the southern heritage, there is strong indication that writers will continue to use the form.

Joseph M. Flora

See also Modernism.

Maggie Dunn and Ann Morris, *The Composite Novel: The Short Story Cycle in Transition* (1995); Forrest L. Ingram, *Representative Short Story Cycles of the Twentieth Century* (1971); Susan Garland Mann, *The Short Story Cycle: A Genre Companion and Reference Guide* (1989); Linda Wagner-Martin, *The Modern American Novel 1914–1945* (1990).

SILVER, FRANKIE

Frances Stewart Silver, who in 1833 was hanged for murder in Morganton, North Carolina, has become the subject of a ballad, an oral-legend cycle, a stream of articles in newspapers and magazines, an annual study curriculum in a North Carolina middle school, a display in a local family museum, historical studies, a ballet, videos, poems, and at least three plays and two novels, most notably one by Appalachian author Sharyn McCrumb.

Initially, this murder case attracted attention because of the horror of the crime—Silver's husband was slain with an ax and his body dismembered and burned—and the rarity of the execution of a woman. As early as 1903, journalistic accounts began to exploit these themes, but by the 1980s, mysteries in the affair began to provoke more serious attention. Feminist and Appalachian regional concerns increasingly stimulated reconsideration of the case: Why did Frankie commit the murder—was she an abused wife? Were other members of her family involved or to blame? Did family loyalty cause them to make a series of disastrous blunders? Could a woman from an illiterate Appalachian farming family find understanding or justice in legal institutions administered by gentlemen? These are issues explored in the various plays and in McCrumb's novel.

It is, however, the folklore about Frankie Silver that has kept her memory alive. During the early decades, fact and rumor blended, forming legends normally told in bits and pieces and debated. But in the twentieth century, four documented tale-tellers have woven the episodes into a cycle told with the power and economy of an early British ballad—most recently, Bobby McMillon in a performance that Tom Davenport edited into a film. All four tellers begin on the snowy day of the murder, develop the story through dialogue, action, and striking image, and leap from one scene to the next with little connective exposition. The scenes fall into matching episodes: the crime/the punishment, the concealment/the discovery, the dismemberment of Charlie's body/the doomed efforts of Frankie's family to protect her body from insult. The legend cycle does not moralize but implies proverbial teachings: justice prevails, truth will out, respect the dead.

The ballad "Frankie Silver" takes a different stance. A first-person text, it offers a remorseful confession and was widely said to have been composed by Frankie and sung by her under the gallows. The song, however, is a remaking of a ballad composed a decade earlier as the last words of Jereboam Beauchamp when he was hanged in Kentucky. The Beauchamp ballad itself merely followed a centuries-old tradition of confession broadsides printed, sung, and sold at executions in the British Isles. Nevertheless, the first-person stance of the song subverts the moralistic intent. It compels singer and hearer to identify with Frankie and feel her terror and remorse. Where the plays and the novel explore contemporary social issues, the legend cycle and song use Frankie Silver to confront the perennial mysteries of human character and fate.

Daniel W. Patterson

See also Oral History.

Tom Davenport, prod., *The Ballad of Frankie Silver* as sung and told by Bobby McMillon (1998); Sharyn McCrumb, *The Ballad of Frankie Silver* (1998).

SIMPSON, LEWIS PEARSON

Like Isaiah Berlin, the foremost intellectual historian of the Enlightenment, Lewis P. Simpson (1916–) is an intellectual historian of the South and of American literary culture whose métier is the essay. Simpson's major publications—*The Man of Letters in New England and the South* (1973), *The Dispossessed Garden* (1975), *The Brazen Face of History: Studies in the Literary Consciousness in America* (1980), *Mind and the American Civil War: A Meditation on Lost Causes* (1989), and *The Fable of the Southern Writer* (1994)—demarcate his territory quite well. The literary consciousness in America is a special consciousness by virtue of its engagements with form and with the lapse into secular history more or less coincident with the age of exploration. This age resulted in the "discovery" of the New World and the founding on the North American continent of a society immersed in history but radically opposed to it by virtue of our mythology of exceptionalism in the Divine Plan. In the American South, that predicament was utterly complicated in moral and social ways by the attempt to support a prelapsarian myth (a "garden") on the backs of African slaves. Attempts to defend this social myth, whether in fact or in language, have produced in southern writers a contorted state of desire for the myth and torment in its ramifications (the fable of the southern writer) that have been Simpson's special province as a critic.

Southern writers who have proven most fruitful for Simpson's essays are William Faulkner, Allen Tate, and more recently Robert Penn Warren. Faulkner, of course, blocks the way of every literary critic of the South. More than anyone else, though, Simpson is capable of taking on the narrow but immensely deep caverns of guilt and alienation. Faulkner's intuitive knowledge of the southerner's special relationship to history—needing it for the memory of significant action that connects one to kin and culture, hating it for the guilt that memory transports—is one of the themes of Simpson's writing.

If there is one southern writer capable of the intellectual tenacity, sweep, and subtlety of Allen Tate, it is Lewis Simpson. Tate's general sense of southern identity—that it is a condition of estrangement for the rooted provincial in the modern moment—is another of Simpson's key concepts. The essays collected in *The Brazen Face of History* trace this estrangement in the lives and writings of American writers of the present century from Henry James to Walker Percy. For Simpson, as for Tate, the southerner is the only alienated modern mind who is aware of his/her alienation. Simpson's argument for this condition shows mastery of Tate's analysis of the southern circumstances of existence: the southerner knows his/her alienation in the ache for the loss of community and order—a state of dispossession more psychic than historical, and thus incurable.

In recent essays in *The Fable of the Southern Writer*, Simpson has provided glimpses of his own southern boyhood in Jacksboro, Texas, modeling his own expulsion from community and past into the disordered present. He has found Warren's narrator in *All the King's Men*, Jack Burden, an apt literary analogy for his own life. In other essays on Warren as writer and intellectual, Simpson has shown extraordinary insight into Warren, who, if Tate took the South as an idea, took the South as a visceral reality.

Lewis Simpson's impress upon southern letters is not limited to his publications. As editor of the Library of Southern Civilization series for Louisiana State University Press since 1969, he has played a large part in recovering and keeping in print the pivotal texts that have functioned as the scripture of southern cultural identity. And as co-editor of the *Southern Review* from the inauguration of the New Series in 1965 until his retirement in 1987, he has wielded untold influence over the direction of southern literary criticism.

Michael Kreyling

See also *Southern Review*.

J. Gerald Kennedy and Daniel Mark Fogel, eds., *American Letters and the Historical Consciousness* (1987); Michael O'Brien,

"A Heterodox Note on the Southern Renaissance," in *Rethinking the South* (1988).

SIXTIES, THE

The South of the 1960s became the center of the nation in ways that its literature still grapples with at the end of the century. For America at large, the tumultuous decade is bracketed on both sides by the southern city of Memphis. In 1957, a young white singer who had managed to capture the black blues ethic and translate it into a distinctive new sound appeared on Memphis radio, inaugurating the era of rock and roll. And in 1968, Martin Luther King, visiting Memphis to endorse the city's garbage collectors' strike, was assassinated on the balcony of a downtown hotel. Between these two events, the South found itself again and again at the center of the nation's most important upheavals: the civil rights struggles that touched every southern state; the Vietnam War, which would teach the rest of the nation what the South had learned much earlier about violence and defeat; and the assassination, on November 22, 1963, of President John F. Kennedy in the southern city of Dallas, Texas. Kennedy was killed by the bullets of sniper Lee Harvey Oswald, a man born in Louisiana who bore the name of his father, who had been named for Robert E. Lee. Moreover, Kennedy was shot in the home state of his vice president, Lyndon Baines Johnson, who became the first southern president of the twentieth century.

Elvis, Vietnam, Dallas, JFK, LBJ, Martin Luther King, Memphis—these names top the list of people and places that define the 1960s as a decade of incredible social change reflected in both southern and national politics and literature. Elvis introduced America to a new sound, southern to its core, a "crossover" music that borrowed black themes, black tones, and body movements that no one had seen a white boy perform before. Elvis inaugurated the undulating hips of the sexual revolution, ushering in a new openness about the body and a noisy, youth-oriented reaction to 1950s prudery. The sexual revolution became linked with the rise of feminism in the 1960s, and although the southern lady might not have taken to bra-burning quite as quickly as her New York and California sisters, it was southern girls who first swooned over Elvis. At Hollins College, known as "a girls' school" in Roanoke, Virginia, the freshman class of 1963 read Betty Friedan's *The Feminine Mystique*.

For most southerners, the paramount issue of the 1960s was civil rights. Martin Luther King, writing from the Birmingham jail on Easter Eve, 1963, reintroduced America to the great nineteenth-century cries of conscience and idealism defined in the writings of Thoreau and Emerson. In other cities such as Little Rock, Arkansas, Athens, Georgia, Selma and Montgomery, Alabama, and Oxford, Jackson, and Philadelphia, Mississippi, white and black southerners played out, before national television audiences, the nation's race war, bringing fame or infamy to such figures as Bull Connor, Orville Faubus, George Wallace, Ralph McGill, James Meredith, and Medgar Evers. Above all, there was Martin Luther King, whose skills as a political leader were matched and enhanced by his gifts as a writer and rhetorician. In addition to "Letter from Birmingham Jail," his "I Have a Dream" speech, delivered during the Washington march on August 28, 1963, stands as one of the most important orations in American history. In her sensitive novel about the sixties, *Can't Quit You, Baby* (1988), Ellen Douglas captures the tragedy of King's assassination when she shows a white woman of the upper-class South trying ineffectually to say "I'm sorry" to her black housekeeper. Ernest J. Gaines, with Miss Jane Pittman's drink from a Whites-Only water fountain in his novel *The Autobiography of Miss Jane Pittman* (1971), contributed one of southern literature's most indelible images of the civil rights era in the South.

The 1960s became a dividing line in southern literature, in large part because of the effect of the civil rights struggle on all southern social institutions. In literature, the early years belonged primarily to Flannery O'Connor and Walker Percy, an older vanguard who used the dramas of the new decade in searing religious evaluations of modern man in a secular world that had lost its spiritual meaning. O'Connor's untimely death in 1964 cut short a brilliant writing career. In her later work, O'Connor was beginning more consistently to use racism in the South of the late 1950s and 1960s to explore the corrupted soul of the nation at large. In stories such as "Revelation," "Everything That Rises Must Converge," and "Judgement Day," all published in her posthumous collection *Everything That Rises Must Converge* (1965), O'Connor drew vivid portraits of southern white bigots as she defined the sin of pride and the blindness of moderns in a fallen world. Her fellow Catholic, Walker Percy, especially in *The Last Gentleman* (1968), looked at much the same southern scene as he depicted a race riot on a southern university campus, parodied the story of John Howard Griffin's blackface journey through the South documented in *Black Like Me* (1965), and critiqued racism as a symptom of modern spiritual malaise. *Love in the Ruins* (1971) and *Lancelot* (1977) are even more apocalyptic, pointed critiques of the immorality that Percy saw overtaking America in the time of the chaotic sixties.

The racial upheavals of the sixties were instrumental in several important politically oriented literary earthquakes. In 1965 Robert Penn Warren firmly repudiated the segregationalist message contained in the essay that he had contributed to the 1930 manifesto *I'll Take My Stand,* offering to the 1960s a book analyzing white bigotry, *Who Speaks for the Negro?* (1965). In 1966 Margaret Walker created new interest in African American history when she published *Jubilee,* her historical novel of slavery and Reconstruction told from the point of view of Vyrie, a slave modeled on her great-grandmother. *Jubilee* preceded by ten years Alex Haley's highly acclaimed novel and television series *Roots,* which became a twentieth-century *Uncle Tom's Cabin* in terms of the popular interest it stirred. William Styron, in his incendiary novel *The Confessions of Nat Turner* (1967), drew upon the history of the South's most violent slave rebellion, which took place in 1831 in tidewater Virginia, where Styron grew up. Styron attempted to create an imaginative portrait of the uprising's black leader, Nat Turner, but was more clearly dramatizing the agony of his own (white liberal) conscience as he measured the racist South's horrifying response to black activism in the early 1960s. Offended black intellectuals responded to this white southerner's appropriation of a black hero with a firestorm of protest, one result of which was to stimulate African Americans to write their own neo-slave narratives (Sherley Anne Williams's *Dessa Rose,* 1986, is the most direct fictional response to Styron's *Confessions*).

Many African American writers with roots in the South wrote significant fiction of social critique pertaining to the 1960s. Ishmael Reed, born in Chattanooga in 1938, published *Flight to Canada* in 1976 as a riotous satire of America's bicentennial celebration of the Declaration of Independence as well as a time-warp uniting the 1960s and the Civil War era. Like Styron, but in some ways more effectively, Reed used slave history to expose America's woefully inadequate understanding of its racially divided identity. Maya Angelou's *I Know Why the Caged Bird Sings* (1970) poignantly dramatized a girlhood in segregated Arkansas. Anne Moody's *Coming of Age in Mississippi*

(1968) even more directly uses the autobiographical mode to chronicle a young black woman's growing up during the civil rights era in the violent South. Alice Walker's first novel, *The Third Life of Grange Copeland* (1970), set in her home territory of southern Georgia, is a chronicle of black rural life from the 1920s to the early 1960s. In drama, Tom Dent, born in New Orleans, returned there in 1965 to work for the Free Southern Theater, dedicated to civil rights and black cultural activism. In poetry, Nikki Giovanni, born in Knoxville in 1943, inaugurated her career with *Black Feeling/Black Talk* (1968) and *Black Judgement* (1969), her most militant collections, which contain many poems set in her home city.

Southern white writers born before the 1940s published major literary works in the 1960s that either helped to create or to assess the atmosphere of turbulent change that marked the times. James Dickey (1923–1997), the sixties' most prolific and popular poet, won the National Book Award in 1967 for *Buckdancer's Choice*. In some ways, Dickey was influenced by the agrarianism he learned as a student at Vanderbilt, but his examination of technology versus nature goes far beyond modernist treatments to exhibit restlessness, rebellion, and a flamboyant engagement with a very New South. Dickey's career reached its apex at the end of the decade with the publication of his novel *Deliverance* (1970), a work that pits the new southern suburbanite against ancient rituals of violence and the challenges of nature.

The 1960s become a way to draw a line marking many changes in the consciousness of southern writers. Fred Hobson's evaluation, in *The Southern Writer in the Postmodern World* (1991), provides a useful summary: "It was in the late 1960s that perceptions and assumptions began to change radically. The decade of the sixties, in fact, might be seen as pivotal in southern life and letters in much the same way the 1920s was: it was a time of numerous southern crimes against humanity, of notable attention and criticism from without, of great intellectual ferment." Many of the important white southern writers who came of age in the late 1960s have written significant fictional portrayals demonstrating how the political events and social upheavals of that decade impinged on the South. This younger generation of white writers, with a few exceptions, has preferred to explore changes other than those involving the civil rights struggles. Several works, for instance, deal with how the Vietnam War and its aftermath affect southern characters. Bobbie Ann Mason in *In*

Country (1986), Clyde Edgerton in *The Floatplane Notebooks* (1988), and Barry Hannah in *Ray* (1980) place their fiction squarely within contemporary southern settings and develop Vietnam veteran characters or their family members who look at the past through the lens of the cataclysmic changes that Vietnam War experiences caused. Lee Smith in many of the stories of *Cakewalk* (1981) and *Me and My Baby View the Eclipse* (1990), Marianne Gingher in *Bobby Rex's Greatest Hit* (1987), Lisa Alther in *Kinflicks* (1976), and Jill McCorkle in *The Cheer Leader* (1984) join Bobbie Ann Mason in looking at how young women of the sixties cope with changed definitions of womanhood often influenced by popular culture. In many contemporary southern women writers' works treating the sixties, mother-daughter generational conflicts pit ideals of southern ladyhood against new cultural demands on women of a feminist or postfeminist era. The works of Mason and Smith in particular are often rooted in the sixties through reference and social perspective, but they are also rooted in the South as place and history.

The 1960s put the South center-stage in American politics. Southern writers who came of age in the sixties have often used the South of their growing-up years to explore the theme of change. However, the 1960s will also be remembered as the decade that brought the study of southern literature into being, creating the industry of southern literary scholarship that flourishes today alongside the creative works that continue to bear the label "southern" at century's end. C. Vann Woodward's *The Burden of Southern History* and Jay B. Hubbell's *Southern Life in Literature,* both published in 1960; Louis Rubin's *The Faraway Country: Writers of the Modern South* (1963); C. Hugh Holman's *Three Modes of Southern Fiction* (1966); the revision of the 1952 southern anthology of Richmond Croom Beatty, Floyd C. Watkins, and Thomas Daniel Young, *The Literature of the South* (1968); the collection of essays edited by George Core, *Southern Fiction Today: Renascence and Beyond* (1969); and finally Rubin's *A Bibliographical Guide to the Study of Southern Literature* (1969) defined a canon that emphasized white male writers and the works of the Southern Renascence. However, these studies set the stage for thirty more years of scholarly work that has steadily expanded definitions of the South and southern literature. The South of the 1960s was, like Elvis, a crossover place. Perhaps its most important legacy is a generation of writers and scholars who can see it from both the inside and the outside and who understand

that in some ways, the South epitomizes, as much as it resists, the great world beyond.

Lucinda H. MacKethan

See also Civil Rights Movement; Elvis; K Mart Fiction; Memphis, Tennessee; Race, Idea of; Racism; Vietnam War.

Fred Hobson, *The Southern Writer in the Postmodern World* (1991).

SLAVE NARRATIVE

The autobiographical narratives of former slaves constitute one of the bedrock traditions of African American literature and culture. From Olaudah Equiano's precedent-setting *Interesting Narrative of the Life of Olaudah Equiano, or Gustavus Vassa, the African* (1789) through the thousands of oral histories of former slaves gathered by the Federal Writers' Project in the 1920s and 1930s, slave narratives have provided some of the most graphic and damning documentary evidence of the horrors of the antebellum South's "peculiar institution." The vast majority of slave narrators were southern born. Compelled to escape to the North to attain freedom, antebellum fugitive slave narrators were among the first in the South's long line of distinguished literary expatriates. Frederick Douglass, who fled his bondage in Maryland in 1838 and published his celebrated *Narrative of the Life of Frederick Douglass, an American Slave, Written By Himself* in 1845, was the forerunner, both literally and figuratively, of several notable nineteenth-century African American writers—William Wells Brown and Harriet Jacobs, in particular—who had to leave the South, the land of their birth, to commence their writing careers in the comparatively free North.

The narratives of fugitive slaves such as Frederick Douglass, William Wells Brown, and Henry Bibb became virtual testaments in the hands of abolitionists proclaiming the antislavery gospel during the antebellum era in the United States. These narratives not only exposed the inhumanity of the slave system; they also gave incontestable evidence of the dignity and humanity of the African American. After the Civil War, with slavery officially banned and the citizenship of African Americans established in law if not in practice, former slaves continued to record their experiences under slavery, partly to ensure that the newly united nation did not forget what had threatened its existence, and partly to affirm the dedication of the ex-slave population to mutual progress for whites and blacks alike. In this conciliatory spirit, Booker T. Washington, a lifelong resident of the South, wrote *Up from Slavery* (1901), which many critics and historians regard as the last great slave narrative authored in the United States. Whether born in slavery or not, most of the major writers of African American literature before World War I launched their literary careers via some form of the slave narrative, whether autobiographical, as exemplified in Douglass's and Washington's work, or fictional, as instanced in Charles W. Chesnutt's *The Conjure Woman* (1899), a collection of short stories set in slavery times in North Carolina and recounted by an ex-slave.

During the shaping era of African American autobiography, from 1760 to the end of the Civil War in the United States, the personal witness of hundreds of fugitive or former slaves appeared on broadsides, in newspaper interviews, magazines, pamphlets, government reports, gift books, biographies, histories, and in autobiographies of various lengths, some as long as five hundred pages. Aside from the countless short biographical accounts of and interviews with fugitive slaves in various eighteenth- and nineteenth-century periodicals, approximately seventy slave narratives were published as books in the United States and Great Britain before slavery was officially abolished in the United States in 1865. Regardless of length, slave narratives dominated the literary landscape of antebellum black America, far outnumbering the comparatively rare autobiographies of free people of color, not to mention the handful of novels published by African Americans during this time.

After slavery was abolished in North America, the ex-slave narrative remained the preponderant subgenre of African American autobiography. From 1865 to 1930, at least fifty former slaves wrote or dictated book-length accounts of their lives. During the 1930s, the Federal Writers' Project gathered oral personal histories and testimony about slavery from 2,500 former slaves in seventeen states, mostly in the South, generating roughly ten thousand pages of interviews that were eventually published in the 1970s in a "composite autobiography" of eighteen volumes. One of the slave narratives' most reliable historians has estimated conservatively that a grand total of all contributions to this genre, including separately published texts, materials that appeared in periodicals, and oral histories and interviews, numbers approximately six thousand.

The earliest slave narratives were published in England or its northern colonies in North America. These narratives have strong affinities with popular white American accounts of Indian captivity, Christian conversion, or gallows confession. The first known African American autobiography is the fourteen-page *Narrative of the Uncommon Sufferings, and Surprizing Deliverance of Briton Hammon, A Negro Man-Servant to General Winslow, of Marshfield, New-England; Who Returned to Boston, After Having Been Absent Almost Thirteen Years* (1760). Recalling shipwrecks, imprisonment, and abuse while a captive of Florida Indians, Hammon reviews a harrowing period of his life but tells his reader nothing about his experience as a slave in New England—if Hammon was, indeed, a slave at all. His status, "Servant to General Winslow," as related in the title of Hammon's narrative, might have been that of an indentured servant, not a slave at all. Most narratives from the late eighteenth century decry the slavery of sin much more than the sin of slavery. But with the rise of the militant antislavery movement in the early nineteenth century came a new demand for slave narratives that would highlight the harsh realities of slavery itself. Radical abolitionists such as William Lloyd Garrison were convinced that the eyewitness testimony of former slaves against slavery would touch the hearts and change the minds of many in the northern population of the United States who were either ignorant of or indifferent to the plight of African Americans in the South. The publication of *The Confessions of Nat Turner, the Leader of the Late Insurrection in Southampton, Va.* in Baltimore in November 1831, putatively a transcription of Turner's account of the origins and prosecution of his "insurrection" in August of that year, galvanized the fledgling radical abolitionists into action while traumatizing the slaveholding South. In the shadow of Turner's revolt, John Pendleton Kennedy completed *Swallow Barn* (1832), often referred to as the first major plantation novel from the South, focusing its last chapters on the story of an antitype of the marauding rebellious slave as retailed in Turner's *Confessions* and in other southern newspaper accounts of the Turner uprising.

In the late 1830s and early 1840s, outspokenly antislavery slave narratives found their way into print under such titles as *Slavery in the United States: A Narrative of the Life and Adventures of Charles Ball* (1836), *A Narrative of the Adventures and Escape of Moses Roper, from American Slavery* (1838), and *The Narrative of Lunsford Lane, Formerly of Raleigh,*

N.C., *Embracing an Account of His Early Life, the Redemption by Purchase of Himself and Family from Slavery, and His Banishment from the Place of His Birth for the Crime of Wearing a Colored Skin* (1842). These set the mold for what would become by midcentury a standardized form of autobiography, in which personal memory and a rhetorical attack on slavery blend to produce a powerful expressive tool as literature and as propaganda.

Typically, the antebellum slave narrative carries a black message inside a white envelope. Prefatory (and sometimes appended) matter by whites attests to the reliability and good character of the narrator and calls attention to what the narrative will reveal about the moral abominations of slavery. The former slave's contribution to the text centers on his or her rite of passage from slavery in the South to freedom in the North. Usually the antebellum slave narrator portrays slavery as a condition of extreme physical, intellectual, emotional, and spiritual deprivation, a kind of hell on earth. Precipitating the narrator's decision to escape is some sort of personal crisis, such as the threatened sale of the narrator, the sale of a loved one, or a dark night of the soul in which hope contends with despair for the spirit of the slave. Impelled by faith in God and a commitment to liberty and human dignity comparable (the slave narrative often stresses) to that of America's Founding Fathers, the slave undertakes an arduous quest for freedom that climaxes in his or her arrival in the North. In many antebellum narratives, the attainment of freedom is signaled not simply by reaching the free states but by renaming oneself and dedicating one's future to antislavery activism.

Advertised in the abolitionist press and sold at antislavery meetings throughout the English-speaking world, a significant number of antebellum slave narratives went through multiple editions, were translated into several European languages, and sold in the tens of thousands. Readers could see that, as one reviewer put it, "the slave who endeavours to recover his freedom is associating with himself no small part of the romance of the time." To the noted transcendentalist clergyman Theodore Parker, slave narratives qualified as America's only indigenous literary form, for "all the original romance of Americans is in them, not in the white man's novel." The most widely read and hotly debated American novel of the nineteenth century, Harriet Beecher Stowe's *Uncle Tom's Cabin* (1852), was profoundly influenced by its author's reading of a number of slave narratives, in particular *The Life of Josiah Henson, Formerly a Slave, Now an Inhabitant of Canada, as Narrated by Himself* (1849) and Douglass's *Narrative,* to which she owed many compelling incidents, not to mention the models for some of her most memorable characters. Centering on the attempt of a fugitive slave to gain his freedom, Mark Twain's *Adventures of Huckleberry Finn* (1885) is another classic white American novel of the nineteenth century rooted in the slave-narrative tradition.

The antebellum slave narrative reached its epitome with the publication in 1845 of the *Narrative of the Life of Frederick Douglass, An American Slave, Written by Himself.* Selling more than thirty thousand copies in the first five years of its existence, Douglass's *Narrative* became an international best-seller, its contemporary readership far outstripping that of most of his southern white contemporaries. Garrison, Douglass's abolitionist mentor, introduced his *Narrative* by stressing how representative Douglass's experience of slavery had been. But Garrison could not help but note the extraordinary individuality of this black author's manner of rendering that experience. It is Douglass's style of self-presentation, through which he recreated the slave as an evolving self bound for mental as well as physical freedom, that has made his autobiography so memorable. After almost a century out of print, Douglass's *Narrative* returned to modern literature in a number of reprints beginning in 1960; since then, it has been one of the most-discussed American autobiographies of any era and a staple of nineteenth-century southern literary study. Black southern writers from Charles W. Chesnutt, who authored an admiring biography of Douglass in 1899, to Ernest J. Gaines, whose novel *The Autobiography of Miss Jane Pittman* (1971) traces the career of an idealistic, uncompromising civil-rights leader named Ned Douglass, have found Douglass's name and example an inspiration to their writing.

After the appearance of Douglass's *Narrative,* the presence of the subtitle, *Written by Himself,* on a slave narrative bore increasing political and literary significance as an indicator of a narrator's self-determination independent of external expectations and conventions. In the late 1840s, well-known fugitive slaves such as William Wells Brown and Henry Bibb of Kentucky and James W. C. Pennington of Maryland reinforced the rhetorical self-consciousness of the slave narrative by incorporating into their stories trickster motifs from African American folk culture in the South, extensive literary and biblical allusions, and a picaresque perspective on the meaning of the slave's flight from bondage to freedom. In the *Narrative of William W. Brown, A Fugitive Slave, Written by Himself* (1847), Brown distances himself from the heroic, to-the-death slave resister as portrayed in Douglass's *Narrative*. Instead, Brown invites his reader to identify with one who learned to use guile and deception to protect and advance his interests. Brown makes it clear that in slavery he was a trickster, savvy enough to profess to his master's wife a matrimonial desire for a slave woman whom he did not love in order to divert his owners' attention away from his much-stronger attachment to the idea of freedom. In slave narratives such as Brown's and Bibb's, only rarely does violent physical confrontation resolve the tensions that underlie the slave's and the master's perpetual struggle for authority and power on the plantation. Much more typically, the slave uses a kind of mental jujitsu, similar to the tactics of the slaves' folk hero, Brer Rabbit, to deceive or divert his oppressors, thereby seizing mastery of the moment and gaining a measure of opportunity and freedom.

As the slave narrative evolved in the crisis years of the 1850s and early 1860s, it addressed the problem of slavery with unprecedented candor, unmasking as never before the moral and social complexities of the American caste and class system in the North as well as the South. In *My Bondage and My Freedom* (1855), Douglass revealed that his search for freedom had not reached its fulfillment among the abolitionists, although this had been the implication of his *Narrative*'s conclusion. Having discovered in Garrison and his cohorts some of the same paternalistic attitudes that had characterized his former masters in the South, Douglass could see in 1855 that the struggle for full liberation would be much more difficult and uncertain than he had previously imagined. He concluded his autobiography with a statement of personal dedication to civil-rights activism in the North as well as agitation against slavery in the South. Harriet Jacobs, the first African American female slave to author her own narrative, challenged conventional ideas about slavery and freedom in her strikingly original *Incidents in the Life of a Slave Girl* (1861). Jacobs's autobiography shows how sexual exploitation made slavery especially oppressive for black women in the South. But in demonstrating how she fought back and ultimately gained both her own freedom and that of her two children, Jacobs proved the inadequacy of the image of victim that had been pervasively applied to female slaves in the male-authored slave narrative. Ignored and often re-garded as bogus by historians until the 1980s, when the research of Jean Fagan Yellin confirmed its authenticity, *Incidents in the Life of a Slave Girl* has become one of the most widely read autobiographies by a southern woman.

Although the pre–Civil War slave narrative is primarily concerned with the individual's quest for personal power free from institutional control, the narratives of ex-slaves after the Civil War focused on the consolidation and institutionalization of communal power. After Reconstruction, most black autobiographers took as axiomatic the idea that in a racist America, individual black survival, not to mention fulfillment, depended largely on building institutional bulwarks against the divide-and-conquer strategy of American white supremacy, especially in the South. Most slave narratives by women in the late nineteenth and early twentieth centuries stressed the importance of marriage, the home, and the traditional middle-class family as the institutions most essential to sustaining black communities in the increasingly polarized world of Jim Crow. Elizabeth Hobbs Keckley of Virginia proved a notable exception in *Behind the Scenes, Or, Thirty Years a Slave, and Four Years in the White House* (1868), a blend of slave narrative, White House gossip, and success story featuring Keckley's career as a modiste to the rich and famous in Washington, D.C., in the early 1860s. Like Keckley, most of the ex-slave narrators of the post–Civil War era are avowedly, even proudly, middle class in their values and purposes. The extent of this identification is suggested by the Algeresque titles of many ex-slave narratives published between 1865 and 1930: Peter Randolph, *From Slave Cabin to the Pulpit* (1893); Henry Clay Bruce, *The New Man* (1895); J. Vance Lewis, *Out of the Ditch: A True Story of an Ex-Slave* (1910); Thomas W. Burton, M.D., *What Experience Has Taught Me* (1910); William H. Heard, *From Slavery to the Bishopric in the A.M.E. Church* (1924); and *From Slavery to Affluence: Memoirs of Robert Anderson, Ex-Slave* (1927).

In most post–Civil War slave narratives, slavery is depicted as a kind of crucible in which the resilience, industry, and ingenuity of the slave was tested and ultimately validated. By emphasizing that slaves not only survived their bondage but were well prepared by its rigors to take care of themselves both individually and communally, slave narrators after emancipation argued the readiness of the freedman and freedwoman for full participation in the new social and economic order. While the large majority of slave narratives after the Civil War were privately printed, a few ex-slaves, such as Keckley and Henry O. Flipper of Georgia, the first black graduate of the U.S. Military Academy and author of *The Colored Cadet at West Point* (1878), were able to find commercial publishers for their reminiscences. The biggest selling of the late-nineteenth- and early-twentieth-century slave narratives was Washington's *Up From Slavery* (1901), a success story that enjoyed virtually universal approbation among blacks and whites alike because of its promotion of African American progress and interracial cooperation, as exemplified in the rise to national prominence of both Washington and the industrial school he founded in Tuskegee, Alabama, in 1881.

Up From Slavery dictated the terms on which most African American autobiographers represented themselves during the first half of the twentieth century. But the Depression helped spur the gradual return to autobiography of themes of resistance and struggle against oppression, particularly in the South, argued with an uncompromising candor that harked back to the antebellum slave narratives of Douglass and Jacobs. Richard Wright's *Black Boy* (1945) and the complete text of his autobiography, published in 1991 as *Black Boy (American Hunger)*, owe much, structurally and rhetorically, to the slave-narrative tradition of a century before. The Civil Rights Movement of the 1950s and 1960s revived the long-standing ideals and urgent moral appeal of the antebellum freedom fighters, thereby creating a climate in which formidable new African American narratives of bondage and liberation could be conceived and appreciated. *The Autobiography of Malcolm X* (1965), with its many affinities to the slave-narrative tradition, made a lasting impression on a new generation of white readers and helped bring about the first serious scholarly study of the slave narrative. Southern novelists such as Margaret Walker in *Jubilee* (1965), William Styron in *The Confessions of Nat Turner* (1967), Ernest J. Gaines in *The Autobiography of Miss Jane Pittman* (1971), and Alex Haley in *Roots* (1976) helped to pioneer the revival of the "neo-slave narrative," which blends fact and fiction to depict the experience or the effect of slavery in the nineteenth and twentieth centuries.

William L. Andrews

See also African American Literature, Beginnings to 1919; Douglass, Frederick; Neo-Slave Narrative; Trickster; Washington, Booker T.

William L. Andrews, *To Tell a Free Story: The First Century of Afro-American Autobiography, 1760–1865* (1986); Charles T. Davis and Henry Louis Gates Jr., eds., *The Slave's Narrative* (1985); Frances Smith Foster, *Witnessing Slavery: The Development of Ante-Bellum Slave Narratives* (1994); Marion Wilson Starling, *The Slave Narrative: Its Place in American History* (1988).

SLAVE REVOLTS

Natural offspring of the paradoxical marriage between slavery and freedom in America, slave revolts demonstrated the profound desire for freedom at the heart of the American dream. Slave revolts, also referred to as "rebellions," "insurrections," or "uprisings," may be defined as armed action against the slavocracy, conspiracy to take such action, or refusal to submit to the laws and regulations of the slavocracy. Historians have documented revolts ranging from small-scale ones launched by a single individual to widespread insurrections involving thousands.

As early as 1526, enslaved blacks in a South Carolina town located near the mouth of the Pee Dee River revolted against their Spanish captors, killing several of them. The rebels fled to live among Native Americans. Later blacks who rebelled against their captors were not so fortunate. More often than not, they were caught and executed; usually they were hanged, or broken on the wheel when that practice was common. The state reimbursed owners for their destroyed "property." Plans for uprisings were sometimes betrayed by favored blacks who were then rewarded with their freedom. For example, colonists in Gloucester County, Virginia, set aside September 13, 1663, as a day of thanksgiving because on that date one of John Smith's favorite slaves betrayed a planned uprising of both white indentured servants and enslaved blacks. The traitor received five thousand pounds of tobacco and freedom.

Historian Herbert Aptheker documented uprisings and plans for uprisings throughout the early eighteenth century in Charleston, South Carolina (1720, 1739, 1740), Louisiana (1730), and Virginia (1730). The most sustained period of rebellion came in the climate of international revolution in the late eighteenth and early nineteenth centuries. The northern colonies' successful quest for independence from England, Jeffersonian discourse surrounding American democracy, the ratification of the U.S. Constitution, the French Revolution, and especially the Santo Domingo (Haiti) revolt led by Toussaint L'Overture all contributed to the general climate of revolution. All across the South, enslaved blacks revolted, and the slavocracy responded by enacting more stringent legislation to control them. Some states banished free blacks. The general climate of revolution sometimes led to more effective abolitionist action.

The history of slavery in the southern United States is marked by hundreds of slave revolts. Indeed, historian Joyce Tang has recently asserted that some 250 plots and uprisings took place in Virginia alone. The most famous of the Virginia uprisings are the failed Gabriel Prosser revolt near Richmond in 1800 and the more successful 1831 Nat Turner revolt in Southampton County. Each has spawned at least one work of fiction and related critical work.

Gabriel Prosser, dubbed "General Gabriel" by his supporters, would have led a rebellion of thousands against the institution of slavery had it not been for the betrayal by two slaves the night before the rebellion was to take place. Tom and the aptly named Pharaoh betrayed the plan to their owner, Mosby Sheppard of Richmond, Virginia. The two traitors (or heroes, depending on one's vantage point) were rewarded with their freedom. Such was often the case with planned revolts; spies often sold rebels out for their own "salvation."

Arna Bontemps retells the story of Prosser's heroic efforts in *Black Thunder* (1936), which combines historical data with imaginative action. The story begins in Mosby Sheppard's great house. Sheppard's dependence on his faithful house servant, Ben Woodfolk, has led to a sort of companionship between the two. Bundy, an old friend of Ben's, invites Ben to join in Prosser's plan for insurrection. Bundy also manages to beg a bottle of rum from Ben; when Thomas Prosser discovers Bundy with the rum, he beats him to death. This bolsters Gabriel Prosser's resolve to lead the insurrection. Ben eventually tells what he knows of the insurrection. In Bontemps's rendering of the event, Prosser, inspired by events in Santo Domingo, amasses some eleven hundred men and one woman (Juba) to take Richmond. Rainfall and the aforementioned Pharaoh and Tom ruin the attempted rebellion. Richard Wright pointed out in a review that the controlling idea of Bontemps's treatment of the event is its "universal determination toward freedom."

The years between Prosser's aborted plan and Nat Turner's limited success in Southampton County, Virginia, saw increasing news of revolutions around the world. Sometimes the ruling class granted concessions. In some cases, whites were implicated in insurrections, and they were either banished or punished along with blacks. As antislavery activity increased in the United States, nearby Mexico abolished slavery in 1829. David Walker issued his *Appeal* in 1829, calling on blacks to take more decisive actions to secure their full human rights.

Still, all white men were part of the militia that stood as an army ever ready to suppress any challenges to the ruling order. Denmark Vesey, a deeply religious free black man, led another unsuccessful insurrection in 1822 in Charleston, South Carolina. The betrayer was Devany, favorite slave of a Colonel Prioleau. Some 130 persons were arrested, including four white men who were imprisoned for their efforts to aid the rebellion. The Vesey plot involved thousands of rebels and a plan for a simultaneous five-point attack, combined with a horseback patrol. Once details of the plan had been revealed, state and federal troops were called in to restore order. News of the plot caused widespread fear among whites.

In 1829 the federal government again dispatched troops to various locations throughout the South to secure order as blacks rebelled near New Orleans, Augusta and Savannah, Georgia, and Georgetown, South Carolina. In 1830 state militia surrounded and killed some sixty armed blacks who were reportedly part of a planned revolution near New Bern, North Carolina. Two other incidents were reported the same year in Tarboro and Hillsborough, North Carolina.

The following year, Nat Turner, described as deeply religious, intelligent, and popular among his peers, led an uprising in Southampton County, Virginia, in which fifty-five white men, women, and children were killed before local militia suppressed the revolt. Turner had succeeded in carrying out his plan to a small degree. No whites were killed during the Prosser and Vesey insurrections; nevertheless, in all three cases, officials executed scores of blacks. Vigilantes slaughtered even more following the Turner insurrection.

William Styron's *The Confessions of Nat Turner* (1967) is the best-known literary rendering of a slave revolt in the United States. Styron's Nat Turner is a religious fanatic who is sexually obsessed with a young white girl. Ten black writers responded to Styron's tale in *William Styron's Nat Turner* (1968), charging the author with playing to southern patriarchal stereotypes of black men in his depiction of Turner as a sexually frustrated ascetic and religious fanatic. As Thomas Wentworth Higginson noted in his study of slave revolts, Turner was, in fact, married to a black woman who was whipped for information in the wake of the Turner rebellion. In her novel *Dessa Rose* (1986), black writer Sherley Anne Williams fashioned a fictional answer to Styron with a successful slave revolt that includes a female slave's perspective. In *Incidents in the Life of a Slave Girl* (1861), the actual slave Harriet Jacobs briefly refers to the aftermath of the Turner Rebellion in a chapter titled "Fear of Insurrection." Poet Margaret Walker captures the spirit of Turner, Prosser, Vesey, and other black revolutionaries of note in her poem "Prophets for a New Day."

During the time of actual revolts, the white-controlled media determined the "who," "what," "when," "where," and "how" of slave revolts. Often whites had an interest in suppressing news of revolts, whereas blacks and antislavery activists had an interest in buttressing the events in favor of blacks. Whatever the case, slave revolts were not only a threat to the lives of individual southern whites but also a threat to their way of life, to the ordering of southern society. The slavocracy spent generations cultivating the idea that America was an Eden for whites only. Slave revolts threatened to turn that notion on its head, standing, Winthrop Jordan has noted, "as a symbol of the end of white dominion." For enslaved persons, revolts were the most profound demonstration of unrest, of displeasure with their collective place in the social order, and of their determination to be free.

Lovalerie King

See also Turner, Nat.

Herbert Aptheker, *American Negro Slave Revolts* (1974); John Henrik Clarke, ed., *William Styron's Nat Turner: Ten Black Writers Respond* (1968); Winthrop D. Jordan, *White Over Black: American Attitudes Toward the Negro, 1550–1812* (1968); John Lofton, *Insurrection in South Carolina* (1964); Joyce Tang, "Enslaved African Rebellions in Virginia," *Journal of Black Studies* 27 (May 1997).

SMART SET

It was through the almost accidental appointment in 1908 of H. L. Mencken as its book reviewer that the *Smart Set,* a New York monthly magazine for the would-be sophisticate, played its unlikely but impor-

tant role in the Southern Literary Renascence. Mencken, a lifelong resident of Baltimore, had a particular interest in the South. In his book reviews, which gradually gained national attention, he joyfully excoriated those writers he considered mediocre and extolled those, such as Ellen Glasgow and James Branch Cabell, whom he deemed capable of rescuing the South from its cultural morass of magnolias, fundamentalism, and demagogy.

When Mencken became co-editor, along with George Jean Nathan, of the *Smart Set* in 1914, he was not only able to add patronage to praise by publishing some of the young southern writers, such as Emily Clark and Julia Peterkin; he was also able to step beyond the magazine's book department and address the South directly. "The Sahara of the Bozart," in the November 1917 issue, was a satiric assault on the culture of the South. From then on, as Fred Hobson has noted, "Nearly every issue of the *Smart Set* alluded to southern shortcomings in some respect."

Although the "Bozart" essay achieved much greater notoriety in 1920, when it appeared in Mencken's *Prejudices: Second Series,* the *Smart Set* version attracted the attention of a small group of young southern cultural rebels gathered around Emily Clark's *Reviewer* in Richmond, Basil Thompson and Julius Weis Friend's *Double Dealer* in New Orleans, and other literary magazines in the region. The *Smart Set* became the northern end of a network of southern writers, editors, and journals seeking a new culture for the New South. In "The South Begins to Mutter," published in August 1921, Mencken could point with pride to the "little magazines" of Dixie that he and the *Smart Set* had done so much to nurture. When he left the *Smart Set* in 1924 to found the *American Mercury,* Mencken transferred his involvement in the cultural wars of the South to the new magazine.

William H. A. Williams

See also *American Mercury*; *Double Dealer, The*; *Reviewer*; "Sahara of the Bozart."

Carl Dolmetsch, *The "Smart Set": A History and Anthology* (1966); Fred Hobson, *Serpent in Eden: H. L. Mencken and the South* (1974).

SMITH, CAPTAIN JOHN

Smith is famous for his Virginia exploits and especially his rescue by the Indian maiden Pocahontas. Born in

Lincolnshire, England, as a young man he traveled widely in Europe and became a soldier in the Central European struggles against the Turkish invaders. In 1601, as captain of 250 horse troops, he was so effective that he was given a pension and a coat of arms. After being captured and enslaved by the Turks, he escaped and, after further adventures, was able to return home to England.

In the spring of 1607, Smith was one of more than one hundred English colonists who arrived in Virginia, where they founded Jamestown. He made notes on what was happening and prepared an account that he sent to England in the form of a letter, published in 1608 as a forty-four-page quarto, *A True Relation*, often called the first American book. It describes the first thirteen months of the colony. One of the notable events reported is Smith's capture by Indians and his experiences with Chief Powhatan. No mention is made of Smith's rescue by Pocahontas in this account.

In time, Smith was returned to Jamestown, where his skills won him the position of president of the governing council. During difficult times, his leadership permitted the colony to survive, but in 1609 he was so badly wounded by a powder explosion that he was obliged to return to England. There, he prepared a valuable account of the place he had come to know; it was published as "A Description of the Country, the Commodities, People, Government, and Religion" in a volume entitled *A Map of Virginia* (1612). It is a work highly valued by ethnologists and anthropologists.

Smith republished his "Description" in what is his most celebrated book, *The Generall Historie of Virginia, New-England, and the Summer Isles* (1624). It also includes in Book III a revision and amplification by Smith of *The Proceedings of the English Colony in Virginia*, by several writers, originally published in *A Map of Virginia*. Among the additions is a very brief account of how, when Smith was about to be beaten to death, Powhatan's "dearest daughter" saved him by laying her head "upon his to save him from death." This passage became famous. Before long, Smith was accused of prevarication, but in recent years scholars have concluded that Smith was a fundamentally reliable reporter, even in the account of his experiences with the Turks, which he set forth in *The True Travels, Adventures, and Observations of Captaine John Smith* (1630).

The Pocahontas incident has been the subject of a whole body of literature, among the earliest being John Davis's *Captain John Smith and the Princess Pocahon-*tas: *An Indian Tale* (1805), inspired by the author's experiences in Virginia; James Nelson Barker's *The Indian Princess* (1808), a play; and most recently, an animated Walt Disney feature.

Everett Emerson

See also Pocahontas.

Philip L. Barbour, *Pocahontas and Her World* (1970); Everett Emerson, *Captain John Smith* (1993); Robert S. Tilton, *Pocahontas: The Evolution of an American Narrative* (1994).

SNAKE HANDLING

Some southerners of the holiness faith take the meaning of Mark 16:18 quite literally: "They shall take up serpents; and if they drink any deadly thing, it shall not hurt them." These are a very small minority of independent Pentecostal Holiness adherents, who tend to be working-class people of Appalachia. Being of English or Scots-Irish ancestry, they are descended from migrants who entered the Southern Highlands in the early years of the Republic. When they move north to look for work, they sometimes take the practice of snake handling with them.

Although such actions are incomprehensible to the average churchgoing southerner, snake-handlers believe that they are following the word of God. Most, however, do not condemn other people, even in their own churches, who do not take up the practice.

Apparently the movement started about 1910 under the influence of an itinerant preacher, George W. Hensley. The Saylor family of Harlan County, Kentucky, took up snake handling, and it spread slowly during the Depression era.

Scholars assert that snake handling is a sign of social/spiritual unrest, a reaction against the onslaught of industrialism on an agricultural people and of modernism in religion. Capitalism, coal-mining in particular, radically changed Appalachia. Working for wages and out-migration perhaps elicited this ritual as a way of rebelling against the more-ordered cultural mores of society in general.

Separating from the mainstream holiness movement, a few snake-handling churches have loosely organized, one even practicing its own form of unitarianism. Men, characteristically wearing long-sleeved, open-necked white shirts, work themselves into a frenzy. Snakes are kept in cages in the front of the church. Skeptics claim that they are pacified by their handlers' gyrations and/or by the loud, rhythmic music that accompanies the ritual. Make no mistake about it—this is a ritual. Snakes are manipulated, often piled on the head, walked upon, or passed from one person to another.

Women are more likely to drink strychnine or touch fire, although they will handle snakes. Eschewing the use of alcohol and tobacco, snake-handlers espouse a moral code that also includes not receiving medical attention when bitten. Children are never allowed to participate, although they may later emulate their elders. Although several states have passed laws discouraging snake handling, practitioners defend their rights under the First Amendment.

At least seventy-five persons have died, according to recent documentation, and there is apparently no building of immunity to the bites of rattlesnakes, copperheads, or other vipers. Many people have been bitten numerous times and are scarred from these encounters. Some people die, but most do not. Is faith responsible for the ability to survive bites, or is there a scientific explanation?

Snake-handling Pentecostals fervently believe that they are practicing the true meaning of religion, "the old-time religion," and that their faith is strong enough to withstand the perils of the serpent's sting. The movement is so small as to be inconsequential in a religious sense, but it is common enough, particularly when someone receives a fatal bite, to appear to outsiders to be an important part of southern religion.

The fundamentalists of fundamentalism in the South, snake-handlers show no signs of diminishing in their literalist faith. Their movement will remain small but vibrant. Dennis Covington's autobiography *Salvation on Sand Mountain* (1995) relates his journey to discover his family's past to a snake-handling sect in northern Alabama, a group he comes to admire for their honesty and faith. Although Tim McLaurin is not part of the Pentecostal movement, he understands the appeal of the practice, religion notwithstanding. He describes his own experiences as snake-handler in his autobiography *Keeper of the Moon* (1991). Lee Smith portrays a snake-handling preacher in *Saving Grace* (1995).

William E. Ellis

Thomas Burton, *Serpent-Handling Believers* (1993); Dennis Covington, *Salvation on Sand Mountain: Snake Handling and Redemption in Southern Appalachia* (1995); David L. Kimbrough, *Taking Up Serpents: Snake Handlers of Eastern Kentucky* (1995).

SOCIETY FOR THE STUDY OF SOUTHERN LITERATURE

Led by Louis D. Rubin Jr. of the University of North Carolina at Chapel Hill, scholars involved in the study of southern letters founded the Society for the Study of Southern Literature (SSSL) in 1968 and sought affiliation with the Modern Language Association (MLA) soon thereafter. SSSL's stated mission was to disseminate information about southern literary studies, to gather and publish bibliographical materials on southern literature and culture, to set up regional and national programs devoted to the discussion of southern literature, to encourage publication of materials treating southern writers and critics, to foster the study of southern literature through promoting the publication (and republication in convenient, economical format) of books and editions by southern authors.

On a yearly basis, SSSL arranges two or more programs for the South Atlantic Modern Language Association, two programs for MLA (together with a third program under its auspices—the Southern Literature Discussion Group), one program for the American Literature Association, and two programs for the South Central Modern Language Association.

In 1990, SSSL began holding biennial gatherings, starting with a meeting at the University of North Carolina at Chapel Hill. Subsequent meetings have been held at Clemson University, in New Orleans, Richmond, Charleston, and Orlando.

Besides its programs at scholarly meetings and its biennial gatherings, SSSL is most visible for two projects, one completed, the other ongoing. The completed project is *The History of Southern Literature* (1985). The ongoing project builds on the society's first venture, *A Bibliographical Guide to the Study of Southern Literature* (1968)—the compilation of an annotated bibliography of southern literature, the results of which have been published regularly in the *Mississippi Quarterly*. Steps are currently being taken to make the bibliography available on the Internet. A supplementary volume to the history is in the planning stage.

To promote critical, historical, or editorial projects in southern writing, SSSL recognizes outstanding achievement in southern literary studies by presenting the C. Hugh Holman Award (a certificate plus a modest cash prize) to the scholar or editor deemed to have written or edited the best book on southern letters during the year.

Membership is open to anyone interested in southern literature.

John L. Idol Jr.

SOCIOLOGY OF THE SOUTH

The first two American books with the word *sociology* in their titles were both written by southerners, and both to defend the South's peculiar institution of slavery. In 1854 George Fitzhugh, a Richmond newspaperman, published *Sociology for the South,* attacking free society by drawing on many of the same sources as Frederick Engels and other critics of laissez-faire capitalism. That same year, Henry Hughes, a Mississippian, published *Treatise on Sociology, Theoretical and Practical,* applying to southern society (as he thought) the ideas of Auguste Comte, with whom he had studied in Paris. But this was a false dawn for sociology in the South. Any influence of Fitzhugh and Hughes died with the social order they were defending.

At the turn of the century, sociology returned to the region with a very different, "progressive" agenda. The Southern Sociological Congress, for instance, active in the early 1900s, comprised social-gospel clergymen and other concerned citizens devoted to addressing such social problems as child labor. (Perhaps especially in the South, the distinctions between sociology as an academic discipline, social work as a profession, and social uplift as an ideology were not as clear as they would later become.)

The most impressive academic development at this period took place at Atlanta University and was very largely the work of William Edward Burghardt Du Bois. A black native of Massachusetts who had studied philosophy and history at Fisk University, Harvard, and the University of Berlin, Du Bois came to Atlanta fresh from two years of research that had produced his first book, *The Philadelphia Negro* (1896). During his thirteen years in Atlanta, he organized a series of yearly conferences (with the support of northern philanthropy) that led to reports on the condition of black Americans, focusing in turn on such topics as crime, health, employment, church, family, and education. Du Bois also published innumerable studies of his own, a

biography of John Brown, and his masterwork, *The Souls of Black Folk* (1903).

Atlanta University's early sociology program, however, lost its momentum after Du Bois left in 1910 to work for the new NAACP and to edit its magazine, *Crisis.* The successful institutionalization of sociology in southern colleges and universities essentially dates from 1920, when Howard W. Odum, a Georgian with a Ph.D. in sociology from Columbia University (and a Ph.D. in psychology from Clark University), came to the University of North Carolina to head the university's new sociology department and its School of Public Welfare (later the School of Social Work).

Odum, who became arguably the most important student in his time of the South's culture and social problems, developed and promoted in over thirty books and scores of articles on what he called both regional sociology and "regionalism," an associated ideology of regional cooperation and "balance." His most important works include *An American Epoch* (1930), *American Regionalism* (1938), *Race and Rumors of Race* (1943), *The Way of the South* (1947), his "Black Ulysses" trilogy (based on the recollections of a semi-fictional black vagabond), and *Southern Regions of the United States* (1938), a massive statistical and cartographic compendium.

As important as Odum's own scholarship, however, was that of the students and colleagues he recruited and nurtured. Like Du Bois, Odum used the resources of northern philanthropists to build an academic empire. Central to his achievement were two institutions, the *Journal of Social Forces,* founded in 1922 as "a Southern medium of study and expression," and the Institute for Research in Social Science, founded in 1924. Odum used the institute's resources to attract a cadre of talented graduate students and published much of their work in his journal. The new University of North Carolina Press also contributed to this enterprise, publishing thirty-one books by institute researchers in the institute's first decade.

Among Odum's early students were Arthur Raper, whose works include *The Tragedy of Lynching* (1933) and an important study of the sharecropping system, *A Preface to Peasantry* (1936), and T. J. Woofter Jr., author of *Black Yeomanry* (1930), one of several works emerging from an institute project on St. Helena Island, South Carolina, as well as studies of black migration and cotton and tobacco agriculture. Two of the most outstanding institute graduate assistants remained at Chapel Hill to make their careers. After publishing two important early works, *Human Factors in Cotton Culture* (1929) and *The Human Geography of the South* (1932), Rupert B. Vance went on to become a distinguished demographer, while Guy B. Johnson produced several still-useful studies of black folk music, including *The Negro and His Songs* (1925) and *Negro Workaday Songs* (1926), both co-authored with Odum, and *John Henry: Tracking Down a Negro Legend* (1929), before becoming an important scholar and activist in the field of race relations. Odum also recruited able outsiders to the North Carolina sociology faculty, notably Harriet Herring, whose studies of the textile industry include *Welfare Work in Mill Villages* (1929) and *The Passing of the Mill Village* (1949).

Aside from Odum's students at Chapel Hill, most early academic sociologists in the South were, like Odum, southerners who had studied in the North and returned to the South to study their native region. Edgar T. Thompson, for instance, grew up on a South Carolina plantation but went to the University of Chicago for his Ph.D. before returning to Duke University, where he became an acknowledged authority on the plantation system.

This was true of both black and white sociologists. Like the region itself, sociology in the interwar South was racially segregated, but it was by no means an exclusively white undertaking. Atlanta, Fisk, and Tuskegee had productive sociologists in their faculties, and one of the most important southern sociologists of the period was a black Virginian, Charles Spurgeon Johnson.

Johnson had also studied at the University of Chicago, and his first major work, *The Negro in Chicago* (1922), was a study of the Chicago race riot of 1919. He left Chicago for New York, where he founded and edited the National Urban League's magazine *Opportunity* (and thereby played a major role in the Harlem Renaissance); then, in 1928, he went to Fisk University in Nashville to chair the social-science department for twenty years, before becoming that all-black institution's first black president. Johnson's dozen books on southern black life include *The Shadow of the Plantation* (1934), *The Collapse of Cotton Tenancy* (1935), and *Growing Up in the Black Belt* (1941).

Johnson maintained cordial and cooperative relations with the regional sociologists at Chapel Hill, working with them and others to establish the Southern Sociological Society in 1935. From the outset, the society adopted a policy of integrated meetings, and in its early years roughly 10 percent of its members were

black (a proportion not equalled since). In 1946 Johnson defeated a white candidate to become the first black president of a majority-white southern professional organization.

Southern sociologists contributed greatly to making the South of the interwar years probably the best documented society that has ever existed. They also contributed to diagnosing and solving its many economic and social problems. After 1950 or so, sociology in the South became less focused on the region and those diminishing problems. If it therefore became less distinctive and, for the student of the South, less interesting, this is a small price to pay for that accomplishment.

John Shelton Reed

Wayne D. Brazil, *Howard W. Odum: The Building Years, 1884–1930* (1988); Guy Benton Johnson and Guion Griffis Johnson, *Research in Service to Society: The First Fifty Years of the Institute for Research in Social Science at the University of North Carolina* (1980); Ida Harper Simpson, *Fifty Years of the Southern Sociological Society* (1988).

SOLID SOUTH

The commitment of every southern state to the Democratic Party emerged out of the conflicts over slavery and secession. In the 1850s, the South despised the newborn Republican Party as the agent of northern interests, and antipathy toward the Republicans deepened during the era of Reconstruction when Congress imposed military rule on the section. In 1880, in the first national election following withdrawal of U.S. troops from the South, the former Confederate states cast all of their electoral votes for the Democratic presidential candidate, and thereafter fidelity to the party became a regional creed. "No southerner," John Crowe Ransom once wrote, "ever dreams of heaven, or pictures his Utopia on earth, without providing room for the Democratic party."

For the next sixty-four years, the Democrats maintained hegemony over the states below the Potomac, though not until the turn of the century did the Solid South become firmly entrenched. For a time after 1880, the Republicans remained competitive in state elections by drawing support from whites in the mountain regions that had held few slaves and had opposed secession, and from the enfranchised freedmen; and in the 1890s, the Democrats had to put down a challenge from the Populists. But in the period around the turn of the century, Democrats disfranchised blacks and created a one-party system in local as well as in national elections.

Over nearly two-thirds of a century, the Solid South cracked just twice, and these breaches were quickly mended. In his landslide triumph in 1920, Warren Harding captured Tennessee, and in 1928, the Republican nominee, Herbert Hoover, won five southern states when voters rebelled against the Catholic, big-city, anti-Prohibition Democratic candidate, Alfred E. Smith. In 1932, however, Franklin Delano Roosevelt swept the entire South for the Democrats, as he did all four times he ran. In 1936, both South Carolina and Mississippi gave him better than 98 percent of their ballots.

Roosevelt's final victory in 1944 proved to be the last time that the South was solid for the Democrats. In 1948, in rebellion against the civil-rights program of Democratic president Harry Truman, Governor J. Strom Thurmond of South Carolina, running as presidential candidate of the States Rights Party, popularly known as the Dixiecrats, carried four southern states, all in the Deep South where race loomed large. Once the Democratic Party ceased to be the bastion of white supremacy, the rationale for a one-party section vanished. In 1964, Barry Goldwater, capitalizing on white fury at Democratic president Lyndon Johnson's civil-rights program, won five Deep South states. In Mississippi, he received a stunning 87 percent of the popular vote. In 1972, the Solid South as a Democratic Party phenomenon came to an ignominious demise when, for the first time since 1944, it was "solid" once again—but for a Republican, Richard Nixon.

William E. Leuchtenburg

See also Yellow-Dog Democrat.

Dewey W. Grantham, *The Life and Death of the Solid South: A Political History* (1988).

SOMETIME SOUTHERNER

Though the label *Sometime Southerner* is recent, the phenomenon is an old one. Edgar Allan Poe's Boston birth makes him a mere pretender to the title of southerner by strict constructionists. His Richmond childhood and brief sojourn in Charlottesville tip the scales of his border-state years in Baltimore, making all part

of a southern biography. Yet it is in his works that evidence of Poe's southernness shows clearest. With only a single major story unequivocally set in the South—Sullivan's Island, South Carolina, in "The Gold-Bug"—the characters and themes of his works define the southern literary consciousness even today. As Poe's case suggests, southern writers can be born into their labels or earn them later in life as they adopt and are adopted by the region. Often the title "southern writer" does not preclude associations with other regions.

Among writers born in the nineteenth century, Constance Fenimore Woolson (1840–1994) gained her reputation as a local-color writer of the Great Lakes where she grew up. Her winters in northern Florida as a young woman yielded stories collected in two separate volumes that applied the techniques of the regionalist to this southern landscape, and she has been included in anthologies and studies as a southern writer. Ironically, she did not return to Florida after writing about its life; instead, she became part of the expatriate community of American writers in Europe and entered a third stage of her career writing of Italy and the international American set in the pattern—and occasionally in the company—of Henry James. Perhaps the most colorful sometime southerner of the nineteenth century was British actress Fanny Kemble, whose *Journal of a Residence on a Georgia Plantation* (1863) spoke out vehemently about the treatment of slaves on the Sea Island plantations owned by her husband, Pierce Butler. The prolific British-born novelist Frances Hodgson Burnett (1849–1924) moved from Manchester, England, to Knoxville at the age of sixteen and wrote her famous children's stories of Lancashire life from the perspective of Tennessee and Washington, D.C. *That Lass o' Lowrie's* (1877), *Little Lord Fauntleroy* (1886), and *The Secret Garden* (1911) have strong southern ties, if not southern settings. Sherwood Anderson (1876–1941) and Ernest Hemingway (1899–1961) spent years in Marion, Virginia, and the Florida Keys respectively, but only Anderson has been approached by critics as a southern writer. Anderson's role as editor for two local newspapers brought him into the community life of his adopted town in a way that Hemingway's life did not. But it is in nonfiction volumes such as *Hello Towns* and *Nearer the Grass Roots* (both 1929) that Anderson's rationale for living in the rural South becomes most clear. His 1932 novel *Beyond Desire*, written five years after his move, deals sensitively with industrialization and labor unrest as they affected the formerly agrarian South.

Willa Cather (1873–1947), born in Virginia and transported to Nebraska at the age of nine, set her last novel *Sapphira and the Slave Girl* (1940) in antebellum Virginia. She also gave her best-known narrator, Jim Burden of *My Antonía* (1918), her own perspective on the high prairies by making him a Virginian arriving in Nebraska at the age of nine. Still, most of her readers know her as a Nebraskan. But the Southwest and Canada have some claim to her as well. Epic novels of the settlement of New Mexico and Quebec in *Death Comes for the Archbishop* (1927) and *Shadows on the Rock* have become staples of the regional literatures of both areas. She is clearly a regionalist of many regions, one of which is the South of her birth.

Robert Bain and Joseph M. Flora delineate a more recent group of southern writers often hard to categorize: "expatriates such as Cormac McCarthy, Bobbie Ann Mason, and Alice Adams." All are writers who left the South, though Mason has since returned. Richard Wright, William Faulkner, Robert Penn Warren, and more recently Alice Walker can also be termed southern "expatriates," given the extended periods of their lives spent outside the geographical limits of the South.

Arguably many African American writers not born in the South have inherited the American South much as immigrant Italians, Irish, or Jews have absorbed their parents' and grandparents' cultures. For these African American writers, the South is part of family history and a cultural construct that appears in their works. Paul Laurence Dunbar and figures of the Harlem Renaissance write with authority of the American South from a personal experience that does not necessarily include residence in the South. Born in Ohio to parents who were both products of the migration north after the Civil War, Toni Morrison in *Beloved* (1987) writes of borders more defining than the Mason-Dixon Line. Sometime southerners cross such borders regularly, yet they still have an important place in the study of southern literature.

Margaret Anne O'Connor

See also Border States; Regionalism.

Dorothy Abbott and Susan Koppelman, eds., *The Signet Classic Book of Southern Short Stories* (1991); John E. Bassett, *Defining Southern Literature: Perspectives and Assessments, 1831–1952* (1997); Fred Hobson, "Surveyors and Boundaries: Southern Literature and Southern Literary Scholarship After Mid-Century," *Southern Review* (Autumn 1991); Louis D. Rubin Jr., "From Combray to Ithaca or, the 'Southernness' of Southern Literature," in *The Mockingbird in the Gum Tree* (1991).

SOUTH CAROLINA, LITERATURE OF

In 1923 George Armstrong Wauchope began the first modern review of South Carolina literature with the whimsical observation that "literature may indeed be regarded merely as one of the crops of the country. Each crop varies greatly according to the section which produces it." South Carolina's literature, like its agriculture, began with imported crops, some of which were ill suited to its soil, and then for almost a hundred years was dominated by one primary crop in one particular region. As cotton depleted the fields of the South, literature representing one class, one race, and one region left the literary fields of the state fallow by the early years of the twentieth century. The cultural desert that H. L. Mencken described in 1917 began to blossom when nourished by the state's diverse cultural streams, and by the end of the twentieth century, South Carolina produced a very rich harvest of literature and had become a national resource.

As one of the original colonies, South Carolina can trace its literary heritage to the earliest days of exploration. One of the first pieces written about South Carolina dates from 1664 when William Hilton (1617–1675), who had been commissioned to explore the coast of South Carolina by a group of Barbadian investors, reported in his *Relation of a Discovery* (1664) on a promontory now known as Hilton Head. Hilton's discoveries included finding a group of stranded Spaniards who had been sustained in part by local Indians. Hilton's tale of "rescuing" these white men from the "infidels and barbarians" suggested what was to become a familiar pattern over the next three centuries.

Distrusting reports about the stranded white men, Hilton demanded that the island's natives bring him messages from the Spaniards before he would send his own men to rescue them. When the natives returned with a message, Hilton realized that he knew no Spanish and could communicate with his fellow "Europeans" no better than he could with the island's natives. Despite the fact that Hilton's men had fired on the natives and taken some of them prisoner, the Englishmen were assisted in their rescue and treated with honor.

After a departure marked by assurances of friendship with the natives, Hilton began planning how their island might be divided among his investors.

Creating a culture in an alien land initially meant replicating British or European culture and fiercely protecting it. Since the literate in the Carolina colony were initially upper-class planters and professionals, the earliest literature primarily represented one class. The great plantations were in the Low Country, and Charleston quickly became both the commercial and the cultural center of the state and region. Although some of the state's earliest writers lived outside of the city of Charleston, it served as their intellectual home. As the commercial and professional classes grew in the eighteenth century, Charleston provided a medium in which the cultural and intellectual ferment essential for literature could take place. Charleston had booksellers, three newspapers that published poems and essays by citizens, occasional journals, and public cultural events.

Literature from the colonial period primarily meant prose. In 1774 Rowland Ruguley, a colonial bureaucrat, wrote a verse play—a classical burlesque entitled *The Story of Aeneas and Dido, Burlesqued from the Fourth Book of Virgil*. There is no record of a performance of this work, and it did not inspire a vogue. There were a number of unsigned poems published during this period in the *South Carolina Gazette* and occasional broadsides, but almost nothing of real literary interest survives.

Though Charleston was an active theatrical venue periodically during the eighteenth century, Ruguley's was the only extant signed play of the period. The English comedian Anthony Aston claimed in his autobiography to have written a play while residing in Charleston in 1703. If this were true, it would have been the first play written in America, but as in the case of so many of Aston's claims in his delightfully hyperbolic book, there is no evidence of the existence of such a play or of its composition. An anonymous play entitled *Americana and Eleutheria: or a New Tale of the Genii* was apparently written in Charleston during the Revolution and performed there on February 9, 1798.

While the novel was becoming a dominant form in England, it was largely absent from the colonies. South Carolina's first novelist, Helena Wells (c. 1767–1824) illustrates this fact well. Described on her title pages as Helena Wells of Charles Town, she actually left Charleston as an adolescent and never returned. Although both of her novels, *The Step-Mother: A Do-* mestic Tale, from Real Life (1798) and *Constantia Neville: or the West Indian* (1800), included references to the colonies, they were written in London, firmly set in England and dealt with the kind of domestic romance and upper-middle-class concerns that had become popular in the women's novels of the period in England.

Because Charleston became a cultural and political center of the colonies in the eighteenth century, it is not surprising that South Carolina writers achieved their greatest prominence during this period in forms of civic writing: histories, essays, and journals. The eighteenth-century ideal of the man of action and of letters who is both making history and reflecting upon it found its expression in the colonies in several remarkable South Carolinians. Eliza Lucas Pinckney (1723–1793) was certainly one of the notable women of her time. The daughter of a wealthy planter, Pinckney was responsible for much of the management of her family's estate, almost single-handedly promoted the growing of indigo in the colony, and understood better than most the complex economics of the plantation. After establishing her family's fortune and making indigo an important crop throughout the Low Country, she married Charles Pinckney, one of the colony's most prominent politicians, assisted him with his career, and bore two sons who became generals in the Continental Army. Pinckney's *Journal and Letters of Eliza Lucas* (1850) provide thoughtful and multifaceted reflections on life in the South Carolina colony during one of its most critical periods.

Henry Laurens (1724–1792) epitomized the ideal man of thought and action. Owner of one of the most important export businesses in the colonies and of a great plantation, Laurens devoted much of his life to public service. A member of the Continental Congress, he served as its president during some of the most difficult years of the Revolutionary War. He was sent as Minister to Holland, kidnapped by the British, and held in the Tower of London for two years. Upon his release (swapped for Cornwallis), he helped negotiate the postwar agreements with Great Britain. His letters, pamphlets, and other public pieces reveal a delightful sense of irony, a self-deprecatory wit, enormous erudition, and a circle of friends that included most of the important men of his time.

Whereas Henry Laurens provided a fascinating personal history of the period, John Drayton (1767–1822) and David Ramsay (1749–1849) were among the first to provide extensive histories of the Revolutionary

War, of the new nation, and the state of South Carolina. Drayton, like Laurens, had a very distinguished career of public service, and Ramsay was the state's (and one of the nation's) most influential early historians. Combining public achievement with his work as a physician, Ramsay authored the influential *History of the American Revolution* (1789), a *History of South Carolina* (1809), and a *History of the United States* (1816–17).

As the new nation began to establish itself after the Revolution, Charleston was at first an economic and cultural center for the nation but found itself losing national influence when the debate over slavery and states' rights became increasingly acrimonious. Economic competition with the New England states and attacks on slavery as an institution provoked a defense of "traditions" and the "southern way of life," which became central themes in much southern literature and public writing. Unfortunately, this occurred at a period in which the literature of South Carolina and especially Charleston was just beginning to blossom. The result was that defensiveness and nostalgia infected much of the literature of the period, and some new and exciting work was lost in a sea of wounded polemic and mawkish sentiment. The intellectual community developing in Charleston became caught up in the politics and rhetoric that would eventually cripple it. The economic and social devastation that followed in the wake of the Civil War all but destroyed the infrastructure that supported the intellectual and artistic community in Charleston, and the literary leadership of Charleston became bitter and dispirited.

What seems even more unfortunate was the decision to ignore the influx of vital and powerful cultures beginning to flow through Charleston. Sullivan's Island in Charleston Harbor was the Ellis Island of the African American at the end of the eighteenth century. Nowhere else in the New World was there such a variety of cultures coming into one port. In addition to the nine European cultures represented in the Low Country, at least twenty-five separate West African nationalities or ethnicities have been identified among African Americans in South Carolina in the period and more than forty separable groups of Native Americans. Because these were nonwhite, the expectation was that if they had a culture, it would be monolithic and "barbarian" and of little value. Thus there was little systematic effort to learn anything about these cultures, and when they appeared in literature at all it was as stereotypical characters. Because of the growing fear of slave revolts, it was thought advisable to cleanse the slaves of whatever aspects of their native culture they brought with them and to forbid teaching them to read, write, and communicate in the dominant culture. Throughout the nineteenth and into the twentieth century, the remnants of these cultures were ignored in serious literature and the arts in South Carolina. The decision to still these diverse voices seriously diminished literature in South Carolina for a century.

In this context, the glittering successes of the antebellum period are quite striking. At the beginning of the century, Charleston produced legitimate and powerful writers whose work had a national audience. Washington Allston (1779–1843), a painter who studied with Benjamin West, turned to poetry midway through his career and wrote eloquently about the connection between the two art forms. Literary references were common in his paintings (one of his most famous paintings was his portrait of Coleridge), and he published poetry that was thoughtful, sophisticated, and well executed. His *Lectures on Arts and Poems,* which was published posthumously in 1850, continues to be interesting both for its fascinating exploration of the art forms and its charming style. His friend Coleridge was clearly his intellectual and literary mentor. Allston's attempts at "Binding in one, as with harmonious zones, / The heart and intellect" made him one of the most consistently interesting writers of the period.

Daniel Payne, the best-known African American poet from the state in the nineteenth century, was born to freed parents in Charleston in 1811, educated in a school run by free African Americans in the city, and taught there until 1834, when teaching African Americans became illegal in South Carolina. He left the state for New York and did not reappear until 1865 when he returned to organize the South Carolina Conference of the AME Church of which he was the national bishop. Although primarily a religious leader, Payne published a book of poems, *Pleasure and Other Miscellaneous Poems,* in Baltimore in 1850.

At the center of South Carolina's antebellum literary flowering was the "Charleston School," a group of writers including Henry Timrod, William Gilmore Simms, Paul Hamilton Hayne, and essayist Hugh Swinton Legaré. They believed in the establishment of a southern literary tradition that could compete with New England and celebrated the southern cause in verse and prose. While they all found some success, the difficulties of national politics as well as the war's eventual devastation frustrated their attempt to establish a truly national literary identity.

If William Gilmore Simms came to represent the quintessential southern man of letters, Henry Timrod best embodied the romantic image of the poet—brilliant, young, tragic, and beautiful. Only eighteen in 1846 when his first poem was published in a Charleston newspaper, Timrod devoted the rest of his life to poetry and literary journalism. With his childhood friend Paul Hamilton Hayne, Timrod wrote for *Russell's Magazine* in Charleston. In 1859 Timrod published his only book of poetry, *Poems,* which had moderate success. The difficulties and disappointments of the war combined with his tuberculosis to make his last few years painful and sad, though he continued writing up until his death on October 6, 1867. Hayne collected all of his work into a new volume of *Poems* (1873), and this book helped establish Timrod's reputation as the "doomed lyric poet" whom Hayne called the "poet laureate of the Confederacy."

Unfortunately, Timrod's reputation as one who "put into verse forever the soul of the old heroic South," as Wauchope puts it, has made him less attractive to modern readers. Although it is true that there is frail sentimentality and wistful, mechanical patriotism in Timrod, he is without doubt a self-conscious craftsman whose best work transcends its time and region. It would be rewarding to explore a Timrod not infected by the rhetoric, defensiveness, and sentimentality of war literature. If truth is the first casualty of war, perhaps poetry is the second.

Paul Hamilton Hayne (1830–1886), Timrod's close friend and collaborator, was a gifted editor of *Russell's Magazine* in the years immediately preceding the war when he tried to create a southern magazine to rival *Blackwood's* and the *Atlantic Monthly.* Hayne published five books of poetry in various styles and genres. He achieved success as a narrative poet of popular and historical pieces, some based on mythological and historical tales and some based directly on the Civil War. If they often lack brilliance, they are almost always entertaining and unpretentious.

The best of South Carolina literature of the nineteenth century, however, came not from the poetic idealization of the cavalier South but from prose writers who explored the margins—the territory that lay between the plantation and the wilderness, where change was not only possible but inevitable.

Both Georgia and South Carolina rightly claim Augustus Baldwin Longstreet (1790–1870), since he was born in Augusta, Georgia, but lived and wrote in both states. Best known for his frontier tales, his dry sense of humor, and his grasp of the characters and language of the frontier, he was also an intellectual and educational leader who served as president of Emory College, South Carolina College, and the University of Mississippi. His *Georgia Scenes* (1835) may be his best-known work, and his short stories have influenced the development of southern comic writing from Simms through Twain, O'Connor, and Harry Crews. His influence on Faulkner is clear, which seems appropriate since Longstreet spent his final years at the University of Mississippi and died in Oxford in 1870.

William Gilmore Simms achieved his ambition to be the complete man of letters, writing in almost every genre from poetry to history to journalism and biography, and achieved some success in all. Although he published some eighteen volumes of verse before the outbreak of the war and edited or compiled others during and after the war, Simms's greatest national impact was as a novelist and short-story writer and as an indefatigable booster of southern writing. As a novelist, he was a disciple of Sir Walter Scott and James Fenimore Cooper, using history as a context for his characters. Simms had a national reputation for much of his career—and beginning with *Martin Faber* in 1833, his novels sold relatively well in the North and the South. His "Border Romances" such as *Richard Hurdis* (1838) and tales of the Low Country such as *The Yemassee* (1835) richly evoked their landscapes—whether in frontier Georgia or low-country South Carolina. Another series of "Revolutionary Romances" inaugurated with *The Partisan* (1835) was equally successful. Simms also helped found *Russell's Magazine* in Charleston, which he hoped would compete with northern literary journals while presenting the point of view of the southern apologist. He edited, pruned, encouraged, and supported the work of Timrod, Hayne, and many others and was a central figure in the literature and culture of the South.

While Simms did his share of writing sentimental defenses of the southern cause, his real strength lay outside of politics. He was thoroughly at ease in short stories. "How Sharp Snaffles Got his Capital and His Wife" (1870) is a wonderfully outrageous tall tale rivaling the best of Longstreet and Twain. Simms's frontier stories were rich in character, wonderfully inventive, and deeply humorous.

The nineteenth-century South Carolina writer who has generated intense interest at the end of the twentieth century was not known as a writer at all in her time. Mary Boykin Chesnut (1823–1886) was the daughter of a governor, U.S. senator, and U.S. representative who married James Chesnut, a U.S. senator and a brigadier general in the Confederate Army. Her Civil War journal, published for the first time in 1905 as *Diary from Dixie,* was written from the perspective of an intelligent and lively young woman. Chesnut's diary has had several major editions in this century and has generated interest in the recording of women's lives as a significant genre of writing. An important historical source, Chesnut's diary has also provided material for several novels and at least one play.

Chesnut is only one of a number of women writers who achieved some stature in South Carolina in the nineteenth century. Caroline Howard Gillman (1794–1888) founded and edited one of the nation's first weekly magazines for young people, *The Southern Rosebud* (1832), which became the *Southern Rose* and ran until 1839. Mary S. Whitaker (1820–1906) and Mary Elizabeth Lee both contributed articles, short stories, and poetry to national publications of the day such as *Godey's* and *Graham's.*

Other prose writers of the period included essayist John B. Irving, who chronicled hunting and other sports among the leisured classes in a series of books and articles in the New York *Spirit of the Times.* Hugh Swinton Legaré and William Elliott of Charleston were important intellectual leaders in the state who published essays on social and literary matters.

Although Charleston had a very active theatrical life in the antebellum period and was a regular and important venue for touring companies, few plays of any significance were written there in the nineteenth century. Of these, only a handful were actually performed in Charleston. William Ioor (1780–1850) and John Blake White (1781–1859) wrote plays that were both published and produced by theater companies. Ioor's *Independence: or Which Do You Like Best, The Peer or the Farmer?* (1805) and *The Battle of Eutaw Springs* (1807) were political plays meant to praise the newly independent nation and attack the corrupt old world symbolized by England. Both plays had productions in major venues outside of South Carolina, including Philadelphia and Richmond. John Blake White was one of the first southerners to create a body of plays that were successful both in performance and in published form, and he is recognized as a pioneer of literature and art in the South. Although White's plays seem quite derivative today, they all had some popular com-

mercial success. Isaac Harby (1788–1828) was well known as a playwright, journalist, editor of *The Southern Patriot,* and one of the best American dramatic critics of his time.

After the war, the physical and economic devastation left in their wake the wreckage of Charleston's literary ambitions. Although Simms, Timrod, and Hayne continued to write in the postwar period, the war and its aftermath limited audiences in the South and in the rest of the nation, and the literary gilded age of the Old South was clearly over. South Carolina lacked a real literary and cultural leader after Simms's death in 1870. The long, hard times of Reconstruction stretched beyond the end of the century, and the literary fields lay fallow.

In the twentieth century, South Carolina's writers began to establish a literature that both accepted and transcended their painful heritage. If the nineteenth century spoke with the voice of the white low-country elite, the twentieth included many voices, and the literary harvest began to be rich and varied. Although the urge to defend the "traditions" did extend into the new century, South Carolina writers finally began to move beyond an idealized past to discover the rich mix of cultures available in their real past. In the last quarter of the century, there was an explosion of literary talent throughout the state, and the goal so diligently sought by Simms and Timrod—a real place in the national literary consciousness—was realized. In the twentieth century, South Carolina writers not only achieved broad popularity, they won almost every national literary honor including Pulitzer Prizes in drama, fiction, and journalism.

H. L. Mencken began his famous "The Sahara of the Bozart" with a quotation from South Carolina's infamous poet J. Gordon Coogler, whose strange syntax and wonderfully loopy lyrics won him the amused admiration of readers as distinguished as Charles A. Dana and Henry Grady, and fan clubs throughout the nation. Mencken's 1917 essay provoked outrage throughout the South, but particularly in South Carolina, where the legends of a golden antebellum literary age still held sway. It was apparently forgotten that Henry Timrod had complained most bitterly about the southerners who refused to support their writers. Yet it was South Carolina that most effectively answered Mencken, and within a few years, in "Violets in the Sahara" and in a series of reviews and articles, Mencken praised a new generation of southern writers—especially two South Carolinians—committed to making the desert bloom.

It is significant that after almost a century of defending slavery and the southern traditions that marginalized South Carolinians of African descent, two of the state's most important writers of the twentieth century, DuBose Heyward and Julia Peterkin, became national figures through their sympathetic exploration of the lives of ordinary African Americans. Heyward (1885–1940) is primarily known today for the play *Porgy* (written with his wife, Dorothy), which won the 1927 Pulitzer Prize for Drama and which served as the basis for George Gershwin's opera *Porgy and Bess*. Heyward's play is still produced, but what in its day was considered a sympathetic portrait now seems to some to contain demeaning stereotypes, and it is difficult to recapture the impact of the original production. Heyward's fiction—*Peter Ashley* (1932) and especially *Mamba's Daughters* (1929)—achieved a very real sense of time and place, but it was in short stories like "The Half Pint Flask" (1927) that the best of Heyward was found. This story, which explored the conflict between an impotent "civilized" white culture and a vibrant "primitive" African American culture, employed the genre of the ghost story as Hawthorne did—as both moral tale and symbolic adventure. Using an empty bottle as its central symbol, Heyward examined the transparent emptiness of a culture that worships possession and venerates the dreams of its past.

Heyward, along with Hervey Allen and John Bennett, founded the Poetry Society of South Carolina in response to Mencken's "Sahara of the Bozart," with the avowed purpose of using local materials to create a truly universal literature. Though formally allying itself with *The Fugitive* and other groups of progressive southern writers, the leadership of the Poetry Society continued to focus on traditional southern materials. In behalf of the Poetry Society, Heyward and Allen edited a number of *Poetry* magazine, and Heyward noted that African Americans were an important subject for literature in the twentieth century. The context of African American culture within this literature was, however, local color. The Poetry Society was centered in Charleston, but allowed "non-resident" members from other places in the state and even from outside the region. The most famous "non-resident" member was Jean Toomer, who was allowed to join for a year until members of the Poetry Society discovered that he was an African American.

Julia Peterkin (1880–1961) presents one of American literature's most interesting enigmas. Over forty when her first short stories were published, she was "discovered" by H. L. Mencken and lionized by Carl Van Vechten, George Jean Nathan, and the New York critics while her work was often unreviewed or viciously attacked in the South. Eight years after first sending a sketch to Mencken, she won the Pulitzer Prize in 1929 for her novel *Scarlet Sister Mary*. She wrote another highly praised novel, *Bright Skin*, in 1932, the text for a book of photos in 1933, and then for the next three decades fell into silence. Since the republication of her remarkable short stories in 1970, there has been a growing interest in her work.

Unlike her contemporaries Joel Chandler Harris, Octavus Roy Cohen, and Ambrose Gonzales, she did not treat her black characters as amusing, instructive, and sometimes lovable exotics. Unlike DuBose Heyward, whose African American characters, while sympathetic, are most often seen in relationship to whites, Peterkin created a world in which whites were often almost irrelevant. Her characters were neither smiling happy children nor noble savages: they were difficult, courageous, and oppressed people living on the margins of civilization. Although it is not surprising that African American critics have viewed Peterkin's work with great suspicion (she was after all the white mistress of a great plantation on which some African Americans lived only marginally differently than they had a hundred years before), it is undeniable that she treated her characters with great seriousness and respect. Indeed, it is the humanity she saw in these characters that accounts for the enormous hostility expressed toward her work by many of her fellow white South Carolinians, which continued (and in some quarters grew shriller) even after she won the Pulitzer Prize.

Archibald Rutledge, almost an exact contemporary of Peterkin, also lived on a great plantation and wrote about the twilight of plantation life. However, Rutledge, a talented writer and for many years the poet laureate of the state, was very much a descendant of Simms and Hayne, finding his inspiration in a warm dream of the past. Rutledge published over seventy books and monographs, including a number of poems.

Hervey Allen (1889–1949) was an active part of the literary life of Charleston, but his popular novels had little to do with life in South Carolina, and his appeal was aggressively national. His *Anthony Adverse* (1933), one of the most popular books of the 1930s, was an extravagant picaresque novel set in eighteenth-century Europe, America, Africa, and Mexico. Allen and Heyward co-authored a book of poetry for the Poetry Society, and other Charleston writers contributed individual volumes of poetry as a part of this effort. Josephine Pinckney (1895–1957) and Beatrice Ravenel (1870–1956) gained a measure of fame as regional poets, and Pinckney published four modestly successful novels between 1942 and 1953.

Although Heyward won the Pulitzer Prize for drama, he created only one truly successful play. The one playwright whose work had significant and successful New York productions did not come out of Charleston's literary establishment or from the Poetry Society. Daniel Rubin was a young Jewish journalist from Charleston who left a Columbia newspaper and the state to seek his fortune in New York and wrote a number of plays, three of which had successful Broadway runs in the early 1930s.

Other writers in the first half of the century included John Bennett (1865–1956), a co-founder of the Poetry Society who came to Charleston in 1900 from Ohio as a journalist and published novels and short stories as well as hundreds of articles in national magazines. His *Master Skylark* (1897), *Madame Margot* (1921), and *The Doctor to the Dead* (1946) utilized southern settings and on occasion used African Americans as characters—though seldom in nonstereotypical roles.

Perhaps the best-known and least-loved journalist that South Carolina produced in the first half of the century was W. J. Cash (1901–1941), whose book *The Mind of the South* (1941) and essays in a variety of publications defined, delighted, enlightened, and enraged generations of readers within and outside the South. Ben Robertson (1903–1943) became an internationally known war correspondent and journalist before he created a memoir of youth in the upcountry of South Carolina, *Red Hills and Cotton* (1941), which has been through numerous editions and continues to inspire southern memoirs.

The last half of the twentieth century saw South Carolina literature become an important part of national life and at last reflect the full diversity of life and experience in the state. Several major figures in the development of southern literature in the century were born and educated in the state, though they achieved their fame in other places. Louis Rubin Jr. (nephew of dramatist Daniel Rubin) left Charleston to build a career as a literary critic, essayist, novelist, and publisher. Author of more than fifty books on topics from American literature to baseball and boat building, Rubin

wrote or edited thirty books on southern literature, including *The Literary South* (1979), *History of Southern Literature* (1985), and *Henry Timrod and the Dying of the Light* (1958). His books, numerous articles, and lectures established the foundation of modern scholarship in southern literature. As a founder of Algonquin Books, he became one of the key figures in the contemporary second Southern Renascence. Monroe Spears was for forty years one of the nation's leading literary critics and teachers. His books *Hart Crane* (1967), *The Poetry of W. H. Auden: The Disenchanted Island* (1963), and *Space Against Time in Modern Poetry* (1972) made him a national figure, and as a mentor to three generations of southern writers, the courtly, kind, and acute Spears exerted an influence on southern literature that continues in the twenty-first century. Max Steele, a fiction writer and essayist, was a founder of the *Paris Review,* a longtime teacher in creative-writing programs, and like Spears, a mentor to several generations of young writers, especially during his tenure at the University of North Carolina at Chapel Hill.

James Dickey was born in Georgia in 1923 but came to South Carolina in 1968 as poet in residence at the University of South Carolina, where he remained until his death in 1997. Winner of the National Book Award and the Bollingen Prize, Dickey was a national figure who brought not only literary respect to South Carolina but also a generation of young writers who came to study with him and stayed to live and write in the Palmetto State. Although the South was important to Dickey's work in poetry and prose, it was the woods, wild rivers, and swamps that drew him—not the cotton fields and forgotten heroes of the lost war. More inspired by Roethke than by Ransom, Dickey was a transcendentalist of the contemporary urban South. Some of Dickey's best poetry and prose concerned itself with the danger and glory that lay just beyond the margins of the modern city. Books such as *Buckdancer's Choice* (1965) and *Drowning with Others* (1962) helped redefine both the direction of poetry and the ideology of the poet in the late twentieth century.

Although Dickey's poetry was the center of his work, his best-selling novel *Deliverance* (1970) was made into a major motion picture, and his two other novels had popular and critical success. His essays and reviews were widely read; his early work as a poetry critic, collected in the volume *Babel to Byzantium:*

Poets and Poetry Today (1968), is one of the best introductions to American poetry in the 1950s and 1960s.

One of the many writers influenced by Dickey was Pat Conroy, one of the nation's most popular novelists in the 1980s and 1990s. Having grown up in the Low Country as the son of a Marine flyer, Conroy drew on his own experience as a teacher at a school on an isolated Sea Island for his first work, *The Water Is Wide,* which became a modest best-seller and was made into a popular film. Conroy repeated this pattern with increasing success throughout his career with *The Great Santini* (1976) and *The Prince of Tides* (1986). Although the South is an important element to Conroy's characters, his interest is in the contemporary urban South, and the past of his characters is likely to be the cotton mill, not the old plantation.

William Price Fox's fiction deals with the poor white trying to make it into the middle class. His tool is humor, and in his short fiction, such as *Southern Fried Plus Six* (1968), and novels *Ruby Red* (1971) and *Dixiana Moon* (1981), he looks back to Longstreet, Simms, and the comedy of the southern frontier.

Women and their lives have been an important element in South Carolina literature since Eliza Lucas and Helena Wells in the eighteenth century. In this century, Julia Peterkin's acute observation of the daily was precursor of a number of outstanding contemporary women whose clear vision and mastery of voice place them at the heart of the best South Carolina literature.

Josephine Humphreys's novels have found critical as well as commercial success, and she created in *Rich in Love* (1987) an extraordinary portrait of a young woman immersed in the painful complexities of love and identity. Dori Sanders's novels *Clover* (1990) and *Her Own Place* (1993) explore and celebrate the richness and complication of rural African American life in the South. *Clover,* told from the point of view of a young African American girl who is facing both the death of her father and the trauma of living with her white stepmother, is a powerful, warm, and genuinely affirmative novel that attempts to find some racial common ground.

Dorothy Allison's *Bastard Out of Carolina* (1992) explores a different kind of girlhood from Humphreys and Sanders. Allison presents the world of the poor white, of trailer parks, "dollar jobs," and painful deprivations in the mill village. Allison has continued to explore this part of culture in the modern South as well as to examine rich varieties of southern woman's experience.

Playwright John MacNicholas's work has been produced by major regional theaters in the U.S. and Canada. Equally at ease with creating historical drama or translating French farce, MacNicholas was winner of the prestigious Roger Stevens Award for playwrighting in 1997 for his southern play *The Moving of Lilla Barton.*

The struggle for civil rights and the painful, wrenching journey toward reconciliation that forever changed South Carolina was the central drama of the century, and yet it has not become a popular subject for fiction. Perhaps it is too new and too real. The story has, however, engaged a number of journalists and nonfiction writers. The most important of these are James McBride Dabbs, an essayist, teacher, and committed advocate for change; Harry Ashmore, the Pulitzer Prize–winning journalist whose two books on racism and progress continue to resonate; and Theodore Rosengarten, whose powerful and intimate studies of the lives of individuals from the past and present humanize an agonizing history.

By the last decade of the century, it was clear that the rich and diverse stream of literary creation is growing at an ever-expanding pace. Among those commanding national attention are novelists Brett Lott, William Baldwin, and Max Childers, who use dark comedy to explore and expose both the deep memories and shallow surface of the contemporary South. Genre writers Elizabeth Boatwright Coker, Alexandra Ripley, James Rigney, Bill Crenshaw, and others attract fanatical fans from the worlds of historical, romance, fantasy, science, and detective fiction.

The voices of African Americans, so long ignored or distorted, became a vital part of the total literary culture in the last decades of the twentieth century. Dori Sanders won national acclaim with her novels about families in a changing rural South, and Eleanora Tate has written prize-winning novels for young people exploring the rich and painful heritage of slavery. Carrie Allen McCray, whose poetry, short stories, and essays appeared widely, is one of the founders of the South Carolina Writers Workshop and works tirelessly to develop support for young writers. Dorothy Perry Thompson's poetry is firmly rooted in the southern African American experience, but her literary heritage also includes James Dickey, with whom she studied. Her work is clear, powerful, intelligent, and open to new experience. Nikky Finney's poetry has come out of a South in transition, with the consciousness of a long connection to the rural world and an insistent urban pulse. Kwame Dawes draws his poetry, fiction, and plays from his life in Jamaica, Great Britain, and South Carolina. Verdamae Grosvenor became a national figure with her essays, memoirs, and appearances on radio and television. Her ability to articulate the life of families in the low-country South has helped to erode stereotypes in the South and beyond.

The open acknowledgement of the importance of this stream of South Carolina literature came with the appointment of African American poet Bennie Lee Sinclair as the state's poet laureate. Sinclair's four books of poetry, including the prize-winning *Lord of Springs* (1990) and her novel *The Lynching* (1992), established a distinguished body of work that combines a consciousness of heritage with a profound connection to nature. Like James Dickey's, Sinclair's work seems to grow as much from Roethke and American transcendentalism as it does from its southern roots.

The Poetry Society of South Carolina, founded to battle Mencken and W. J. Cash, has been revitalized, and along with the South Carolina Writers Workshop has encouraged and supported new generations of writers, while the South Carolina Academy of Authors has focused public attention on both the masters of the past and emerging talent. In the 1990s, poets Alice Cabaniss, Ken Autrey, David Tillinghast, Ken McLaurin, and Sterling Eisiminger have built stable, long-term careers as poets and teachers and assist the work of younger poets. Susan Ludvigson, from Winthrop College, published several major books of poetry in the 1980s and 1990s; John Lane, Melanie Gause Harris, and Stephan Gardner publish widely in poetry and short fiction.

As the twenty-first century begins, the fields that Mencken saw as a desert are filled with the fruits of a rich and diverse culture.

Thorne Compton

See also Charleston, South Carolina; Diaries, Civil War; Periodicals, 1800 to 1860.

Gilbert Allen, ed., *45/96: The Ninety-Six Sampler of South Carolina Poetry* (1994): Richard James Calhoun and John Caldwell Guilds, eds., *The Tricentennial Anthology of South Carolina Literature* (1971); Charles S. Watson, *Antebellum Charleston Dramatists* (1976).

SOUTH CAROLINA, UNIVERSITY OF

Founded in 1801 as South Carolina College, the University of South Carolina has maintained a tradition of literary study and has, especially in the last half of the twentieth century, been home to writers who have achieved national and international renown.

The intent of the founders of South Carolina College was to locate it in the center of the state (in the new city of Columbia), in order to harmonize relations between the old planter aristocracy of the Low Country and the new farming and entrepreneurial bourgeoisie of the uplands. The tension between these cultures has marked the institution for most of its history.

In the antebellum period, South Carolina College attracted an outstanding faculty to Columbia, including such luminaries as Frances Lieber and Thomas Cooper (who served as its second president), and produced students who excelled in science, law, politics, and of course Greek and Latin, which constituted its primary curriculum. Charleston, however, because of its size, wealth, wide range of cultural activities, and the leadership of such writers as William Gilmore Simms, dominated the literary and cultural life of the state in the first half of the nineteenth century. By 1856, however, the University had begun to value contemporary writing in English. In that year, composition in English was "placed on a footing with other studies," according to an early University history. The next year, the trustees of the College elected one of the best-known writers of the day, Augustus Baldwin Longstreet, author of *Georgia Scenes*, as the eighth president of the College. Longstreet encouraged the study of literature and composition, but whatever long-term contributions he might have made were lost in the wreckage of war. Emma LeConte, the daughter of writer-naturalist faculty member Joseph LeConte, wrote a moving account of the burning of Columbia and her family's struggles as they lived on the campus during the war years. Her diary was eventually published as *When the World Ended* (1957).

The Civil War devastated the College (the entire student body enlisted in the Confederate army), and the postwar period saw the institution go through times of great ferment, which it barely survived. Governor Ben Tillman's populist reform movement sowed distrust of intellectualism and "Classical learning." At his inauguration in 1890, Tillman announced that henceforth the institution would offer a "cheap practical education in which the application of knowledge and science to the business of bread winning and the upbuilding of agriculture and the mechanical arts should be the main objects" instead of Classics, literature, and the arts.

As the twentieth century opened, critic and editor

George Armstrong Wauchope joined the faculty and began a long career as mentor to writers and chronicler of the state's literature. Along with his scholarly editing of Lamb, DeQuincey, and Spenser, he wrote extensively about southern and South Carolina writers. Wauchope believed that the University had a special responsibility to facilitate the creation and appreciation of literature. A generation later, Professor Frank Durham was responsible for renewing interest in the work of the Charleston writers of the 1930s and 1940s, such as DuBose and Dorothy Heyward and Julia Peterkin, with critical works, biographies, and editions that reintroduced their work to a state and national audience. Durham, a playwright, poet, and scholar, mentored young writers and scholars at the University. By the late 1950s, formal courses in creative writing were being regularly taught by Havilah Babcock, who achieved fame primarily for his books and popular magazine stories about hunting and sport in the modern South.

In the mid-1960s, the University committed itself to making literary study a major focus of the University. Its decision to bring to Columbia critics, editors, and teachers such as Matthew Bruccoli, Calhoun Winton, Ross Roy, and Morse Peckhem indicated the University's serious intention to establish its credentials in literary scholarship. The University, in collaboration with the Center for the Editions of American Authors, began producing scholarly editions of American and southern writers. The centerpiece of this program was a major project to produce a complete edition of the works of William Gilmore Simms.

With the arrival of prize-winning poet James Dickey as writer in residence in 1968, the University announced its intention to create a major creative-writing program. Dickey, a charismatic, larger-than-life personality, was tireless in "barnstorming for poetry" throughout the state and nation, and quickly brought national attention and a number of aspiring writers to the program. Dickey was joined for a time by George Garrett and by fiction writers William Price Fox and Ben Greer and playwright John MacNicholas as well as a parade of visiting writers. Since the early 1970s, a number of important younger writers have been associated with the University and its programs. As might be expected, Dickey drew a number of younger poets to Columbia: David Tillinghast, Skip Eisiminger, Ken Denberg, Melanie Gause Harris, Deno Trakas, and Dorothy Perry Thompson. Fiction writers Pat Conroy, Tim Gautreaux, Max Childers, Sarah Gilbert, and

Edgar Award–winning mystery writer Bill Crenshaw spent important time at the University, as did Charles Frazier, whose novel *Cold Mountain* won the National Book Award in 1998.

The University's Institute for Southern Studies has played a major role in the University's contributions to southern literature. The Institute has presented major national and international symposia on Robert Penn Warren, Randall Jarrell, William Faulkner, and James Dickey, as well as sponsoring visits from many of the most important contemporary southern writers. Championing the work of African American and women writers from the region, such as Dori Sanders and Josephine Humphreys, the Institute sponsored research and public programs on a number of established and emerging southern writers.

Thorne Compton

See also South Carolina, Literature of.

Edwin Green, *A History of the University of South Carolina* (1916); Daniel Hollis, *The University of South Carolina* (1951); George Armstrong Wauchope, *The Writers of South Carolina* (1910).

SOUTHERN CULTURES

In the fall of 1993, the "inaugural issue" of a new southern journal came out of central piedmont North Carolina. Editors John Shelton Reed and Harry Watson were both on the faculty of the University of North Carolina at Chapel Hill, yet Duke University Press in nearby Durham was the publisher. The journal's name acknowledged the different groups that make up the South. Its focus, as stated in the first issue, was to be on interdisciplinary features and articles addressing major cultural questions. The first issue contained articles on buildings, accents, history, linguistics, and oral history, and featured a section of book reviews, polls with a southern focus, and a survey of southern archives.

The official volume 1, number 1 issue appeared in fall 1994, and *Southern Cultures* began quarterly publication. With the double issue, volume 2, numbers 3–4 in 1996, the University of North Carolina Press in Chapel Hill began to publish *SC* for the Center for the Study of the American South. New columns on food, music, and speech began.

Southern Cultures has not shied away from serious and often controversial issues such as race, labor, politics, the Civil War, and gender. It has, however, balanced these topics with issues devoted to humor and sports; articles on art and social structures; regular features on food, accents, music, and research resources; and polls on such topics as southern manners or the percentage of southerners versus northerners who have eaten grits, okra, or Moon Pies.

Photos play a significant role in the journal, with some photographic essays appearing, as well as illustrated articles. In addition to reviews of books, *SC* reviews movies, recordings, and museum exhibits of interest to its audience of both scholars and the educated public.

Alice R. Cotten

SOUTHERN LITERARY JOURNAL, 1835 TO 1838

Although for thirty years the University of North Carolina at Chapel Hill has sponsored the publication of the *Southern Literary Journal*, another periodical with the same name preceded its publication by more than a century. On September 1, 1835, volume one of the *Southern Literary Journal (and Monthly Magazine)* appeared in Charleston, South Carolina. The earlier *Journal*'s first publisher was Daniel K. Whitaker, who referred to himself as "editor and proprietor." The first volume included a *Journal* issue every month through February 1836.

A memorial poem in honor of a deceased gentleman with the initials E.E.A. was penned by William G. Simms, Esq. This was apparently Simms's first contribution to the *Journal*, and he was its most famous writer. His short story "The Widow of the Chief" was published in the *Journal*. Book reviews included an enthusiastic appraisal of Washington Irving's *Crayon Miscellany*. At the end of each issue, Whitaker presented his editorial comments under the heading "From Our Arm-Chair." He stated his *Journal*'s lofty purposes, which recall Benjamin Franklin's introduction to the American Philosophical Society proceedings in 1743. Whitaker claimed his *Journal* was "intended to be of a miscellaneous character and will embrace articles on every variety of topic in the departments of science, literature and the arts" and that they should "rouse a spirit of inquiry and improvement among our citizens."

Simms was a contributor to volume 2 of the *Journal*

as well. By now he styled himself W. G. Simms, Esq., giving less emphasis to his Christian name. "Southern Passages and Pictures" appeared on pages 90–273 and included descriptions of South Carolina and commentary on local customs. "The Widow/Chief," an unpublished "dramatic scene" by the "Poet of the Confederacy," Henry Timrod, also graced the pages of the second volume. And John Pendleton Kennedy's *Horse-Shoe Robinson* was given a laudatory review by the editor. Possibly the only literature that has survived the test of time was Simms's "The Edge of the Swamp," which still frequently appears in American literature anthologies.

With the publication of the third volume of the *Southern Literary Journal,* Simms had begun to emphasize his middle name, signing his short story, "The Spirit Bridegroom," W. Gilmore Simms, Esq. The magazine had become a staple of Charleston literary life, and the writer himself had begun to be recognized as a significant national author.

Volume 4 continued until March 1837. Then Whitaker began a new series in April that continued until August. This time, the magazine's title was the *Southern Literary Journal and Monthly Review.* It contained articles on eclectic subjects that appealed to a genteel and prosperous reading audience. "Fashion in Dress" gives a fairly accurate description of chic attire for wealthy nineteenth-century gentlemen and ladies. An article such as "Notes on the English Drama" presumed a cosmopolitan readership who either traveled abroad or were receptive to the importation of English drama to the Charleston stage. A series of articles entitled "Slavery" defended the institution against its critics. Articles on "Female Education" and "Second Marriages" were filled with conservative pieties concerning the subservient role of women in an hierarchical male society. There were articles on Hans Holbein and other painters and superficially "scientific" articles on cholera and phrenology.

Among other elite southerners who contributed to the *Journal* was C. D. Carroll. Beginning in September 1837, Carroll assumed the editorship of the *Journal*. It was then known as the *Southern Literary Journal and Magazine of the Arts.* Carroll listed himself as editor in the *Journal*'s masthead but noted that he was assisted by "several literary gentlemen." Could it be that Simms's growing literary fame made his contemporaries feel rivalrous or insecure? In any event, he was henceforth referred to only as the author of *The Yemassee,* his 1825 novel depicting the conflicts between

South Carolina's Yemassee Indians and the British colonists a century earlier, his best-known work.

With its two principal editors, first Whitaker, then Carroll, and its most famous literary contributor, Simms, the *Southern Literary Journal* contributed to the belief that there was a "Charleston School" of letters. The *Journal* was possibly limited by its deference toward upper-class South Carolinians, yet few ordinary people were literate enough to subscribe to any journal. Its bias was regional and separatist. Had it not been doomed by a scarcity of readers in the early decades of the nineteenth century, it probably still could not have survived the political upheavals of the Civil War era. Nevertheless, the *Southern Literary Journal* remains evidence of sophisticated thought and commitment to the arts in a nation less than a hundred years old.

Kimball King

See also Charleston, South Carolina; Periodicals, 1800 to 1860.

SOUTHERN LITERARY JOURNAL, 1968 TO PRESENT

In the fall of 1968, the first volume of the *Southern Literary Journal* was published by the Department of English at the University of North Carolina at Chapel Hill. Its editors were C. Hugh Holman and Louis D. Rubin Jr. Although Holman was provost of the University at that time, Holman and Rubin agreed that the English department in particular, rather than the University, should sponsor the periodical. Professor C. Carroll Hollis, then chairman of the English department, agreed. Thus for thirty years the *Journal* has drawn its greatest strength from departmental faculty committed to research in and evaluation of southern literature. The original editorial advisory board included such well-known scholars as Joseph Blotner, Guy Cardwell, Lewis Leary, and Arlin Turner. After Professor Holman died, Louis Rubin continued as the periodical's sole editor until his retirement. Since that time, Kimball King, formerly a business manager for the *Journal,* and Fred Hobson, Lineberger Professor of the Humanities, have become the *Journal*'s co-editors.

King and Hobson have attempted to adhere to the idealistic purposes of the *Journal* as set forth by editors Holman and Rubin in their first issue:

Literature, we believe, is intimately related to time and place. It not only reveals something about its age and its area; a study of time and place reveals something about the literature itself. The South, like every region, has produced a vast quantity of writing, and some of it has national and international importance. To study that significant body of writing, to try to understand its relationship to the South, to attempt through it to understand an interesting and often vexing region of the American Union, and to do this, as far as possible, with good humor, critical tact, and objectivity—these are the perhaps impossible goals to which *The Southern Literary Journal* is committed.

The founding of the *Journal* coincided with the founding of the Society for the Study of Southern Literature. At that time, it was decided that an annual checklist of southern scholarship be assigned to the *Mississippi Quarterly.* Interested researchers and readers longed to see the canon of southern literature enlarged and hoped that scholarship and criticism could be included in a single periodical. Holman and Rubin set out to create an accessible, engaging, but serious venue for southern studies. It was helpful when they arranged for a famous panel discussion between Ralph Ellison, William Styron, Robert Penn Warren, and C. Vann Woodward, which had taken place at the Southern Historical Association in New Orleans in November 1968, to be taped and published in the second issue of the *Southern Literary Journal.* Thus, by the spring of 1969, in the second number of its first volume, the *Journal* took its place as a recorder of the latest debates on substantive cultural issues. Subsequently, it has attempted to include the most recent southern writers, and especially more African American writers and more women writers, in its pages. Occasionally a special bonus issue appears. For example, the entire text of George Ogilvie's *Carolina, or The Planter* was reprinted along with a lengthy foreword and notes by David Shields in 1986. Future special volumes have been planned. Meanwhile, the *Journal* continues to seek articles on both timely and historically important southern literary topics from the colonial period to the present day.

Kimball King

See also Chapel Hill, North Carolina; North Carolina, University of; Periodicals, 1960 to Present; Rubin, Louis D., Jr.

SOUTHERN LITERARY MESSENGER

"Devoted to Every Department of Literature and the Fine Arts," as its subheading announced, the Richmond-based *Southern Literary Messenger* (1834–1864) was the antebellum South's most important and influential literary magazine. Published monthly, the *Messenger* was founded by Thomas Willis White, a Virginian who desired, as he put it in the June 1834 inaugural issue, to send forth a southern literary magazine "as a kind of pioneer, to spy out the land of literary promise, and to report whether the same be fruitful or barren." A printer by trade, White had little literary background, and he was assisted early on by James Ewell Heath, a Virginia novelist, and Edward Vernon Sparhawk, a New England-born poet and journalist, both of whom served short terms as editor during the magazine's infancy.

The *Messenger* might have declined quickly but for the arrival in 1835 of Edgar Allan Poe, who came recommended to White by John Pendleton Kennedy, the author of *Swallow Barn* and an early admirer of Poe's talent. From the beginning, however, Poe's relationship with his new employer was strained. Although he admired the younger man's learning and intelligence, White resented the *Messenger*'s close association with Poe in the public mind, and he refused to allow Poe final say over publication decisions. Poe's drinking habits also had something to do with the tension that arose between him and the straitlaced publisher. For his part, Poe must have a resented a man whose literary judgment he did not respect, and he left the *Messenger* in 1837 to pursue his literary career in the North. Nevertheless, in his brief tenure Poe had helped to bring the magazine into national prominence. Although he published both his poetry and his fiction (including "Berenice" and two segments of *Arthur Gordon Pym*) in the *Messenger,* it was his book reviews that attracted the most attention. Although many of these were generous to a fault, more than a few were downright vitriolic in an age accustomed to uncritical praise for anything American in origin. In particular, a vicious dissection of *Norman Leslie,* authored by the prominent New York writer Theodore S. Fay, produced a sensation. Poe could also be caustic with southern authors, as his 1835 review of William Gilmore Simms's *The Partisan* amply evidenced.

Following Poe's departure, the bulk of the editorial work was performed by White and his assistant, Matthew F. Maury. After White suffered a paralytic stroke in 1842, Maury took over the day-to-day operations of the magazine until it was sold the following year to Benjamin Blake Minor, an attorney who had been unofficially associated with the *Messenger* for some time. During these years, the *Messenger*'s literary quality declined. From the magazine's inception, White had been able to attract a number of the most popular magazine writers of the time, including Nathaniel Parker Willis, Richard Henry Wilde, and Lydia Sigourney. But with the exception of Poe's book reviews and a few distinguished contributions by Poe, Simms, and Henry Wadsworth Longfellow, the *Messenger* largely failed to distinguish itself from its northern competition. Sentimental fiction and verse, travelogues, and tepid book reviews dominated the magazine's pages. On the nonfiction front, however, the *Messenger*'s public addresses, political essays, and historical pieces tended to be, especially under Minor's editorship, more distinctive—and more distinctively southern. Maury had written a number of influential proposals for naval reform (many of which were eventually realized), and Minor continued to publish on military themes. He also published John Smith's *True Relation* and a long series on Virginia history written by Charles Campbell. Where White himself had called for "a gradual abolition, or amelioration" of slavery in the January 1835 issue, defenses of slavery, attacks on the abolition movement, and endorsements of states'-rights theory by such notable figures as Abel P. Upshur, Thomas Roderick Dew, and Nathaniel Beverley Tucker began to appear more frequently in the 1840s as sectional hostilities increased.

In 1845 Minor bought from Simms and incorporated into the *Messenger* the Charleston-based *Southern and Western Monthly Magazine*; for a short time, the magazine bore the unwieldy title of *Southern and Western Literary Messenger and Review.* Two years later, Minor left the *Messenger* to take a position as the head of the Virginia Female Institute. The new publisher and editor was John Reuben Thompson, who would remain with the *Messenger* for thirteen years. An attorney educated at the University of Virginia, Thompson had a more sophisticated literary taste than Minor, and he added to *Messenger*'s list of prominent southern authors the names of Henry Timrod, James Mathewes Legaré, Paul Hamilton Hayne, John Esten Cooke (whose older brother, Philip Pendleton Cooke, was already a regular contributor), and Joseph Glover Baldwin, who contributed several of the sketches that would later be published as *Flush Times in Alabama and Mississippi* (1853). Simms and Poe were frequent contributors during Thompson's tenure as editor. The literary content of the *Messenger* was, however, by no means exclusively southern; Thompson continued to publish northern writers and maintained close ties with New York-based men of letters including Rufus Griswold, Richard Henry Stoddard, and Thomas Bailey Aldrich.

Despite the high literary quality of the magazine under his editorship, Thompson confronted the same problems faced by every other editor of a southern literary magazine, including his predecessors at the *Messenger*. When not downright apathetic, southern readers were notoriously delinquent in paying their subscriptions. Thompson was forced to use his own funds—over $5,000, he claimed in 1850—to keep the *Messenger* afloat, and in 1853 he was forced to sell the magazine to its printers, Macfarlane and Fergusson, although he remained as paid editor until 1860. Financial conditions did not improve, and an exasperated Thompson advertised an 1858 price reduction from $5 to $3 with the hopeful prediction that "the Southern people will surely not withhold their encouragement" from the magazine "alone among the monthly periodicals of America, in defence of the Peculiar Institutions of the Southern Country." Defenses of slavery increased in number and vehemence as the decade progressed. An unsigned nine-page review in the October 1852 issue excoriated the author of *Uncle Tom's Cabin,* concluding with the biblical injunction "Thou shalt not bear false witness against thy neighbor," and as the Civil War approached, virtually every issue of the *Messenger* contained a polemic against abolitionist radicalism.

In 1860, Thompson resigned to take a position as editor of *Southern Field and Fireside.* He was replaced by George W. Bagby, a Virginia physician whose "Letter of Mozis Addums to Billy Ivins," a farcical dialect tale of a country rube visiting Washington, D.C., had appeared in the *Messenger* in 1857. An ardent secessionist, Bagby severed the magazine's remaining ties with the northern literary establishment and called, in the June 1860 issue, for "home-made, purely Southern articles—tales, stories, sketches, poems, that smack of the soil." After war broke out, the *Messenger* documented military campaigns, attacked northern "crimes," and criticized Confederate political leaders, especially Jefferson Davis. In February 1864, Frank H. Alfriend, who, along with a fellow investor, had bought the *Messenger* in December of the preceding

year, assumed the position of editor. Wartime conditions, however, made the continued publication of the *Messenger* impossible, and the last issue appeared in June 1864.

Scott Romine

See also Periodicals, 1800 to 1860; Periodicals, 1860 to 1900; Poe, Edgar Allan.

Edward E. Chielens, ed., *American Literary Magazines* (1986); Benjamin Blake Minor, *The Southern Literary Messenger* (1905); Frank Luther Mott, *A History of American Magazines, 1741–1850* (1930); Sam G. Riley, *Magazines of the American South* (1986); Edwin Reinhold Rogers, *Four Southern Magazines* (1902).

SOUTHERN LITERATURE, IDEA OF

The idea of southern literature is a highly political concept structured upon the tensions between regionalism and nationalism. Through the years, this tension characterizing the relationship of a southern literary identity to an American literary identity has both propelled the development of southern literature and served as the crux of efforts to define southern literature. Further negotiating the mutable concept of regionalism, each generation has endeavored to establish criteria for what constitutes southern literature. The results have ranged from strictly geographical guidelines for the birthplaces of authors to a list of qualities sought in the literature itself. The idea of southern literature has developed from an elite white man's literature to an inclusive multicultural literature reflecting differences in race, gender, and class. Over time, it has continuously evolved to meet political and cultural needs for memory and identity. In the years ahead, the idea of southern literature faces the challenge of defining itself in a nation growing more homogenized and a world growing ever more globally connected.

The idea of southern literature entered the cultural discourse in the 1830s. Along with the general American self-consciousness about creating a national literature came a heightened sense of regionalism. One influential school of thought envisioned a national literature reflecting the distinctiveness of each of the country's regions. Many southern thinkers endorsed this concept and called for a southern literature that faithfully reflected the South in tradition and subject matter, and thus that would make a distinctive contribution to the fabric of the national literature. Statements of the time were often characterized by a dual purpose: urging current and future regional writers to produce a southern literature, while also lamenting or attempting to justify a southern literary record they saw as poor in such accomplishments. From the 1830s to 1860, the exhortations for a southern literature evolved from a proud regionalism trying to assert itself against the northern literary dominance to strident sectionalism as the issues of slavery and states' rights shaped the literary productions of the 1850s. With the Civil War and the rise of Confederate nationalism, for a brief time southern literature became its own national literature.

The literary magazine culture trying to establish itself in the South during the antebellum period provided the major channel for voices lobbying for a southern literature. Among publication ventures, many of them short-lived, were *Southern Literary Messenger, The Magnolia, Southern Review, Russell's Magazine, De Bow's Review,* and the *Southern Quarterly Review.* Noteworthy articles in these magazines that called attention to the possibilities of southern literature include James E. Heath's "Southern Literature" in the *Southern Literary Messenger* (August 1834), William Gilmore Simms's letter printed in *The Magnolia* (January 1841), Daniel Whitaker's "The Newspaper and the Periodical Press" in *Southern Quarterly Review* (January 1842), and Simms's "Literary Prospects of the South" in *Russell's Magazine* (June 1858), a critique of the climate for writers in the South. Throughout his career, Simms championed the idea of a southern literature and encouraged its production through his editorship of literary magazines and his own writing, which found its subject matter in the South's history. In his "Literature of the South" in *Russell's Magazine* (August 1859), Henry Timrod, another vocal supporter of a southern literature, criticized the notion of "Southernism" in literature, or the idea that southern writers had to focus only on regional topics, and instead championed the development of a higher critical culture in the South that would truthfully evaluate southern literature, eschewing a partiality based on southern authorship. Only then, he contended, would the South produce truly good literature. The crisis of the Civil War suspended efforts such as Simms's and Timrod's as sectionalist literary sentiment became Confederate loyalty.

In the years immediately following the Civil War, the idea of southern literature was nearly synonymous with war poetry and war recollections. Southerners saw the Confederate poetry published in newspapers and small collections as representative of their culture's collective despair and loss. Among the early collections usually characterized by rabid sectionalism, Simms alone reissued the call for a national literature comprised of distinctive regional literature in his *War Poetry of the South* (1866). Later, post-Reconstruction voices adopted his insistence upon the coexistence of sectionalism and nationalism, adjusting it to fit their own agendas. Other texts published during the decade of the Civil War with perspectives that encouraged the idea of a southern literature were Mary Forrest (Mrs. Julia Freeman)'s *Women of the South Distinguished in Literature* (1860), James Wood Davidson's *The Living Writers of the South* (1869), and Mrs. Mary T. Tardy ("Ida Raymond")'s *Southland Writers: Biographical and Critical Sketches of the Living Female Writers of the South. With Extracts from Their Writings* (1870). Their gestures of identifying and grouping writers boosted the concept of a southern literary identity.

In the decades following Reconstruction, the idea of a southern literature accrued authority. The concept gained credence with the national success of the southern local-color writers in the 1880s and 1890s. Though only in a narrow genre, at least southern writers' works were appearing in northern literary magazines and were recognized by the northern literary culture as contributing to the national literature. The calls for a southern literature were highly political and reflected varying motives. While most southerners by the 1880s adopted the rhetoric that to be regional is to be national, a rationale that fit for local-color fiction, the rhetoric meant different things to different promoters. For the most rabid sectionalists, the rhetoric simply provided an acceptable cloak for partisanship; for the most progressive voices, the rhetoric was a genuine effort to facilitate the reintegration of the South into the nation while ensuring the continuance of a valued regional identity. One vocal faction endorsed the idea of southern literature as an essential tool in preserving and memorializing a heritage that they felt was threatened as the South rejoined the nation. The rabid sectionalism of these perpetuators of Confederate memory supported highly sentimentalized views that glorified the Old South. Another impetus within southern culture for encouraging the idea of a southern literature was to challenge the North's long-running literary dominance. The majority of anthologies, textbooks, and literary criticism produced in the North dismissed southern literature and other aspects of southern culture. In reaction, southern editors produced their own anthologies and textbooks of southern literature, especially from the 1890s to 1915, an important phenomenon in giving credibility and permanence to southern literature. The prefaces and introductions of these anthologies, which reflect varying political and cultural viewpoints, were influential in shaping readers' concepts of southern literature. Examples of these perspectives include Louise Manly's *Southern Literature from 1579–1895* (1895) and Mildred Lewis Rutherford's *The South in History and Literature: A Hand-book of Southern Authors* (1906).

Promoters of the New South displayed yet another motive for touting the idea of southern literature. This group, comprised primarily of southern university academics, endeavored to create a southern literary identity and canon that would present a more modern and appealing view of the South to northerners by emphasizing contemporary writers and editing the literary history of the Old South and the Confederacy. While controlling the image of the South that the canon conveyed, they also encouraged the development of a higher criticism in southern literary studies as Timrod had years earlier before the Civil War began. They worked to bring the same critical standards to bear on southern literature as northern scholars did on American literature in general; they believed that only through such rigor would southern literature be accepted on a par with the literature of other regions.

By the second decade of the twentieth century, the widespread efforts of a network of southern academics had institutionalized the study of southern literature. Reflective of the Jim Crow era, southern literature as they defined it continued to mean white literature. Through the anthologies and textbooks that they published, the articles they wrote, the speeches they gave, and the courses they taught, this founding generation of southern literary scholars had a seminal impact on the idea of southern literature. Among the academics whose networked efforts helped to legitimize the field of southern literature were William Malone Baskervill, Edwin A. Alderman, Charles W. Kent, John Bell Hennemann, Carl Holliday, Edwin Mims, Bruce R. Payne, Leonidas Warren Payne Jr., C. Alphonso Smith, Henry Snyder, and W. P. Trent. The major universities involved were the University of the South at Sewanee, Trinity College (later Duke University), Vanderbilt University, the University of Virginia, and the University of North Carolina (later the University of North

Carolina at Chapel Hill). Representative essays of the time supporting and defining southern literature include C. Alphonso Smith's "The Possibilities of the South in Literature" (*Sewanee Review*, 1898), Charles W. Kent's *The Revival of Interest in Southern Letters and a Plea for the Preservation of the Southland* (1902), Henry N. Snyder's "The Reconstruction of Southern Literary Thought" (*South Atlantic Quarterly*, 1902), Edwin A. Alderman's introduction to *The Library of Southern Literature* (1907), Charles W. Kent's essay "Southern Literature" (*The Library of Southern Literature*, 1907), Carl Holliday's preface to *A History of Southern Literature* (1906), and Montrose Moses's foreword to *The Literature of the South* (1910). By bringing the idea of a southern literature into the academy, this generation gave it a status backed by ongoing institutions and legislated that southern literature be subjected to the same critical standards as the rest of American literature. Calls for a critical perspective include John Bell Hennemann's "The National Element in Southern Literature" in *Sewanee Review* (1903) and Henry N. Snyder's "The Matter of Southern Literature," also in *Sewanee Review* (1907). W. P. Trent's anthology *Southern Writers: Selections in Prose and Verse* (1905) exhibits the kind of objectivity in tone that he and others espoused.

The founding of two journals to facilitate dialogue about southern literature and issues was crucial to the vitality of efforts to sustain the idea of southern literature and illustrated the group's commitment to an intellectual approach to the topic. W. P. Trent founded the *Sewanee Review* at the University of the South in 1892 and was succeeded in his editorship by John Bell Hennemann. John Bassett began the *South Atlantic Quarterly* at Trinity College (Duke University) in 1902 as a forum for discussion of progressive southern ideas.

In the decades following World War I, influential scholars and critics continued to mold the idea of southern literature to reflect cultural agendas of their era. The ever-evolving idea has been the result of their efforts to define southern literature, to develop and apply critical and theoretical perspectives, and to both form and question a canon. A generalized overview of the last seventy-five years of the twentieth century reveals efforts to build a southern literary narrative of consensus complicitous with the dominant modernist ideology of southern white academics, followed by postmodern challenges to that ideology and a growing dissensus fueled in part by an insistence upon multiple race, gender, and class narratives.

The turn-of-the-century network of academics who had institutionalized the study of southern literature gave way to the modern generation, which included the Agrarians and founders of the New Criticism. Instead of the cultural progressivism and goal of reintegrating the South into the nation that the earlier academics displayed, the Agrarians and their sympathizers exhibited a cultural conservatism embodied in a regionalism that privileged the agrarian values of the Old South and saw the nation as a symbol of the commercialism and industrialization they opposed. And like southern elites before them, they endeavored to seize the cultural power to define the South on their terms. Also during this second quarter of the century, the Southern Literary Renascence unfolded, producing writing that gave southern literature preeminence on the national literary scene and thus setting the stage for a major revamping of the definition of southern literature. Under these influences, scholars worked to construct an official narrative of continuity in southern literary history that reflected agrarian values and culminated in the writing of the Renascence, making those works the keystone of the southern literary canon. Critically, some scholars began to move away from the traditional historical criticism of the former generation and to experiment with the New Criticism, an apparatus effective for muting aspects of southern history problematic to their narrative of consensus, specifically race, gender, and class issues. Their modernist, symbolist vision valued writers such as William Faulkner, Eudora Welty, Thomas Wolfe, and Robert Penn Warren, whose works they saw as transcending the topical.

At midcentury, many important texts were contributing to a monolithic idea of southern literature. Rather than emphasizing geographical parameters, most of the efforts attempted to describe qualities supposedly inherent in the southern temper and thus in southern literature. Allen Tate's influential thoughts are expressed in essays such as "The Profession of Letters in the South" (1935) and "A Southern Mode of the Imagination" (1959). "The Profession of Letters in the South" contains a list of characteristics of southern life that was often appropriated for a list of topics usually found in southern writing: manners, memory, a code of honor, the importance of family, an agrarian society, and political defense of religious principles. Louis D. Rubin Jr. and Robert D. Jacobs's collection of essays *Southern Renascence: The Literature of the Modern South* (1953) was a pivotal work for its insistence on the centrality of the Southern Renascence and for

opening the field to further study. The lead article in *Southern Renascence* is Robert Heilman's essay "The Southern Temper," which discusses traits he sees as characteristic of modern southern writings: "a sense of the concrete, a sense of the elemental, a sense of the representative, and a sense of totality."

The 1952 anthology *The Literature of the South* (rev. 1968), edited by Thomas Daniel Young, Floyd C. Watkins, and Richmond Croom Beatty, is infused with Agrarian ideas, emphasizes a continuity of southern letters, dedicates almost half of its pages to literature of the Renascence, and contains two African American writers. Its racially conservative stance is reflective of the decade dealing with the 1954 *Brown v. Board of Education* case. Randall Stewart's foreword to the work asserts the South's leadership in national literature and defines a southern writer as one who grew up in the South, is aware of his southern ties and finds them inescapable, exhibits southern prejudices, and continues to draw upon the South as a creative resource even if the writer leaves the South. Stewart also identifies several southern literary traditions: courtly, sophisticated, "tidewater"; classic; romantic; patriotic; and humanistic.

On the other hand, Jay B. Hubbell's impressively researched and scholarly literary history *The South in American Literature* (1954) works outside of the consensus privileging regionalism, as did his teacher W. P. Trent before him. Writing as a scholar of American literature in an era of post–World War II nationalism, Hubbell's political agenda is to "integrate the literature of the Southern states with that of the rest of the nation." He does not insist upon consensus in his literary narrative, but rather touches at least briefly upon the issue of race, asserts that a "Solid South" no longer exists in the literary sense, and acknowledges some southern authors writing in a more liberal vein such as Lillian Smith and Erskine Caldwell, writers ignored by the more elitist Agrarians. He offers extensive information about the literary culture and writings to 1900, then addresses the New South briefly and gives the Renascence a few comments in the epilogue. Therefore his work does not follow the growing midcentury strategy of making the Renascence the rationale for discussing other periods of southern literature.

During the 1960s and 1970s, scholars C. Hugh Holman and Louis D. Rubin Jr. authored the primary texts articulating ideas of southern literature. Holman's chief contributions include studies relating the past to the present in southern works, an endeavor that strengthened the official narrative of continuity in southern literature, and offering the paradigm of three literary Souths: the Tidewater and Low Country South, the Piedmont and Mountain South, and the Gulf Coast or Deep South. His practice was to relate works to their physical, social, and moral environments, and to the history of the southern region. His major works include "The Southerner as American Writer" (1960), which became the lead essay in his 1972 collection, *The Roots of Southern Writing*; *Three Modes of Southern Writing* (1966); *The Immoderate Past* (1977); and his essay "No More Monoliths, Please" in *Southern Literature in Transition* (1983), edited by Philip Castille and William Osborne. Continuing to build on his own earlier works, Rubin became the chief architect of the idea of southern literature in his generation, prioritizing the writers of the Southern Renascence. His principal works of this period include *South: Modern Southern Literature in Its Cultural Setting* (1961), an essay collection edited with Robert D. Jacobs; *The Faraway Country: Writers of the Modern South* (1963), a collection of his essays compiled with the purpose of using "literature in order to understand Southern life"; and *The Writer in the South: Studies in Literary Community* (1972), whose title underscores his longtime interest in the importance of community in southern literature.

In 1970 Holman and Rubin, along with Richard Beale Davis, edited *Southern Writing: 1585–1920,* an anthology that attempts to place southern literature in its social and cultural setting. The book exhibits a central tension indicative of the cultural politics of its time: it reflects the editors' efforts to promote a coherent idea of southern literature to 1920 built upon consensus and continuity of narrative, while simultaneously adding African American works and, particularly in Davis's section on the early literature, acknowledging the past existence of voices from different literate communities shaping southern literature. Thus the ideological influence of the Agrarians as well as a more liberal social impulse are both evident in the text. Within the problems inherent in attempting to synthesize both traditions—one founded on continuity, another acknowledging diversity—lay the seeds for future dissensus.

In 1972, Rubin and Holman, both then on the English faculty of the University of North Carolina at Chapel Hill, convened a conference "with a view toward providing direction and coherence in the field of southern literary scholarship." The symposium of the leading scholars in the field (the participants were all male) reinforced a common vision that helped to sustain a consensus of official literary narrative. The proceedings were published in 1975 as *Southern Literary Study: Problems and Possibilities,* with Rubin and Holman as editors.

In his 1979 classroom anthology *The Literary South,* Rubin eschews cultural and social context in favor of a New Critical approach that emphasizes literary analysis of imaginative literature. He promotes the construction of continuity in the southern literary narrative, asserting that the early literature anticipates that of the Renascence. In his introductory comments on the Renascence period, Rubin argues that southern writing is distinctive in its forms and attitudes, and he enumerates characteristics of the writing of that period, launching a list that has been widely adopted: "a sense of the past, an uninhibited reliance upon the full resources of language and the old-fashioned moral absolutes that lay behind such language, an attitude toward evil as being present not only in economic or social forces but integral to the 'fallen state' of humankind, a rich surface texture of description that would not be confined to the drab hues of the naturalistic novel, an ability to get at the full complexity of a situation rather than seeking to reduce it to its simplified essentials, a suspicion of abstractions, a bias in favor of the individual, the concrete, the unique, even the exaggerated and outlandish in human portraiture." Rubin includes African American literature but still enfolds it into the official literary narrative by pointing out that it is "an important expression of the Southern imagination, but also an illumination of the writing of white Southerners." Even so, his inclusion of African American as well as women's texts is limited.

Class is also a little-addressed issue in southern literature during these years. In his essay "Trouble on the Land: Southern Literature and the Great Depression," appearing in *Literature at the Barricades: The American Writer in the 1930s* (1982), edited by Ralph F. Bogardus and Fred Hobson, Rubin is one of the few southern literary scholars to discuss the topic directly, but his position reflects that of the majority of his peers. He diminishes the importance of the issue, arguing that most southern literature of the Renascence did not concern itself with issues such as social consciousness, capitalistic society, and class struggle. Therefore, Rubin believes that discussing class is unimportant since he finds it was not a part of the southern imagination of the writers he esteems, a view that reflects the continued influence of the Agrarians' literary elitism.

The History of Southern Literature, published in 1985 with Rubin as general editor, and Blyden Jackson, Rayburn S. Moore, Lewis P. Simpson, and Thomas Daniel Young as senior editors, reflects the cultural evolution of the ideas of southern literature as constructed by scholars and critics from midcentury to this point. A consensus remains tenuously intact, the result of what seems a tacit agreement among the contributors to proceed on the premise of consensus. The continuity of narrative and privileging of the Renascence remains, but the official cultural narrative has assumed a more inclusive posture, embracing the importance of African American literature and women's literature as crucial components of the story of southern literature. Rubin announces in his introduction that the editors (one of whom was Blyden Jackson, a noted African American scholar) had from the beginning "planned a racially integrated history" that would include both white and black writers but would also recognize "essential differences in the community heritage, since to ignore those differences would produce a distorted view of the literature." Although the text does discuss African American and women writers, some scholars have subsequently criticized the work for not including more African Americans or women, and for failing to employ a diversity of critical approaches most effective for discussing these areas, steps that well may have endangered the consensus. Even so, this literary history, composed of contributions from top scholars in the field, is a powerful collective masterwork of a generation of influential critics shaping the idea of southern literature to reflect their values and culture. Ironically, it was also very likely the last major work to be built on a modernist consensus of the narrative of southern literature.

Since 1985, the challenges to consensus have intensified. The growing appreciation for multicultural perspectives in the academic culture forced scholars of southern literature to explore their implications for literary subjects. This step resulted in diversity within the canon and in perspectives that forced fissures in the previously valued continuity of the southern literary narrative. Other challenges also initiated disruptions and called for a rethinking of previously held paradigms and ideologies. For example, calls for application of contemporary critical theories or ones previously little used in southern literature, such as deconstruction, new historicism, reader-response the-

ory, feminist theory, cultural studies, and intellectual history, opened the door to a plurality of voices.

The result of, as well as the impetus for, rapidly occurring change in the field is much lively debate and discussion. Many noteworthy texts are facilitating these dialogues. Michael O'Brien's 1988 *Rethinking the South: Essays in Intellectual History* calls for renewed vigor in southern intellectual history and study of areas previously ignored. In *The Fable of the Southern Writer* (1994), Lewis P. Simpson explores the autobiographical element in southern fiction and criticism, and in so doing contributes to the ongoing question whether "the South is a historical or a fictional entity." His 1988 essay in the *Southern Review*, "The State of Southern Literary Scholarship," makes timely observations about literary scholarship and southern writing. In a 1988 issue of *Southern Literary Journal*, Thadious M. Davis addresses race issues in "Expanding the Limits: The Intersection of Race and Region," and Rubin endorses her comments in "Of Literature and Yams." Rubin continues to articulate his vision of southern literature in "From Bombay to Ithaca; or, The 'Southernness' of Southern Literature" and "The Dixie Special: William Faulkner and the Southern Literary Renascence," both in *The Mockingbird in the Gum Tree: A Literary Gallimaufry* (1990), and he explores the foundations of the southern literary imagination in *The Edge of the Swamp* (1989).

In *Southern Literature and Literary Theory* (1990), Jefferson Humphries presents a collection of essays applying new theoretical approaches to southern literary works, and in his introduction he outlines a vision for the work of the first postmodern generation of southern literary scholars. Michael Kreyling's *Inventing Southern Literature* (1998) also pushes southern thought into the postmodern era through a critical examination of the invention of the modernist southern literary narrative and the manipulations that held together that consensus for many years. Also noteworthy to a study of the idea of southern literature is Fred Hobson's 1991 essay in the *Southern Review*, "Surveyors and Boundaries: Southern Literature and Southern Literary Criticism After Mid-Century," which analyzes the formation of the southern literary canon since 1920, examines the contemporary canon, and speculates on the future. Hobson's *The Southern Writer in the Postmodern World* (1991) takes a look at the characteristics of some prominent writers emerging since the 1960s.

Feminist theory and efforts to recover neglected

southern voices have given momentum to the growing recognition of southern women's texts as a literature with its own unique characteristics. Anne Goodwyn Jones published the groundbreaking study in the field, *Tomorrow Is Another Day: The Woman Writer in the South, 1859–1936,* in 1981. In *Daughters of Time: Creating Woman's Voice in Southern Story* (1990), Lucinda H. MacKethan examines both black and white women writers' strategies for developing their own forms of expression in a patriarchal South. Essays in *The Female Tradition in Southern Literature* (1993), edited by Carol Manning, survey the development of women writers in the South. Mary Louise Weaks and Carolyn Perry edited an anthology, *Southern Women's Writing: Colonial to Contemporary,* in 1995. Jones and Susan V. Donaldson's collection of essays *Haunted Bodies: Gender and Southern Texts* (1997) explores the impact of southern definitions of both masculinity and femininity.

Two anthologies give insights into the status of ideas of southern literature at century's end. Edward L. Ayers and Bradley C. Mittendorf edited *The Oxford Book of the American South: Testimony, Memory, and Fiction* (1997), which places ideologically conflicting voices and perspectives side by side in an effort to convey the fabric of dissensus characterizing major eras of southern history. Likewise, *The Literature of the American South: A Norton Anthology* (1998) embraces dissensus, seeing southern writing as "an ongoing dialogue and/or debate among various ethnic, racial, social, and economic perspectives on what the South was, is, and ought to be and on the character, culture, and communities of its people." Edited by William L. Andrews (general editor), Minrose C. Gwin, Trudier Harris, and Fred Hobson, the anthology rejects earlier ideologies shaping a consensus of southern literature and instead champions the diversity of the South's cultural heritage. The project stands as a marker in the continuing evolution of the idea of southern literature from a white, patriarchal, elitist literature to one opening to the possibilities of voices from varying races, gender orientations, and socio-economic classes.

As the field of southern literature acknowledges diversity and dissensus, and new theories and cultural politics subvert old interpretations and paradigms, the ability to articulate an idea of southern literature or literatures becomes increasingly difficult. Ironically, at the start of the twenty-first century, as the idea that there is an idea of southern literature flourishes in the popular culture, scholars and critics find the task of pronouncing the idea(s) of southern literature ever more quixotic.

Susan H. Irons

See also Academy, Southern Literature and the; Agrarians; Anthologies of Southern Literature; Histories of Southern Literature; New Criticism.

John E. Bassett, *Defining Southern Literature: Perspectives and Assessments, 1831–1952* (1997).

SOUTHERN LIVING

Begun as a section in *The Progressive Farmer* titled "The Progressive Home" (retitled "Southern Living" in October 1963), a new monthly magazine made its debut as a separate publication, *Southern Living,* in February 1966. At a time when the South was changing rapidly from a rural to a more urban region, *Southern Living* targeted families who often lived in suburbs, owned their homes, and enjoyed cooking, gardening, entertaining, travel, and home-improvement projects. Advance marketing to a select audience produced an initial paid subscription of 250,000 for this self-styled magazine of the modern South.

The color cover of the first ninety-page issue indicated the magazine's formula—a brick ranch house; a bright, sunny day; a well-kept green lawn with azaleas in full bloom; two young women on a tandem bike; and a dog. The table of contents featured sections on travel, general topics, homes, foods and entertaining, fashions and grooming, outdoor recreation, and gardening and landscaping. Only the section on fashions and grooming no longer survives. In July 1967 (vol. 2, no. 6) the format changed to a smaller, more contemporary-looking style.

Southern Living's formula has been quite successful. It does not address issues of social, economic, or health concerns, and only relatively recently have articles featured people or places reflecting the varying racial makeup of the South. The magazine concentrates on home and garden and travel, with some recent brief but good features on the literature of the South. Current circulation of about 2.3 million makes *SL* the largest regional magazine in the United States and one of the largest of all types in the country.

Time Inc. bought the Birmingham, Alabama–based Southern Progress Publishing Company in 1985. Recent so-called "brand extensions" have led to *SL* cookbooks, cooking and gardening seminars, house plans, credit cards, a travel service, even a spinoff of one of its food columns, a magazine called *Cooking Light.* Another recent venture is *Coastal Living,* designed for those who live at the beach. Despite jokes that Time Inc.'s New York staff sometimes call the Southern Progress offices in Birmingham just to hear the southern accents, there's no joking about the success of *Southern Living.*

Alice R. Cotten

Jeff Gremillion, "Whistlin' in Dixie: Time Inc.'s Quietly Successful Southern Cousin Is Poised for More Brand Extensions and a 'Coastal' Expansion," *Mediaweek* (July 1, 1996); John Logue and Gary McCalla, *Life at "Southern Living"* (2000); Sam G. Riley, *Magazines of the American South* (1986).

SOUTHERN RENASCENCE

During the first half of the twentieth century, a major reawakening of literary activity took place in the American South. This writing encompassed fiction, poetry, drama, literary criticism, memoir, and journalism. The Southern Literary Renascence (also spelled Renaissance) involved a critical reexamination of southern history, a new awareness of the restrictions of traditional racial and gender roles, an interest in literary experimentation, an examination of the role of the southern artist in relation to the southern community, and an increasingly realistic presentation of social conditions in the South. With the indisputable accomplishments of many of its writers, this revival of literary activity secured the place of modern southern writing within the national literature.

The origins of the Renascence have been traced to the gradual revival of southern culture following the destruction during and after the Civil War. George Washington Cable, Kate Chopin, Grace King, and Mark Twain may be viewed as part of an early phase of the southern reawakening. The works of these late-nineteenth-century writers established a tradition of modern critical sensibility that continued in the works of James Branch Cabell, Ellen Glasgow, William Faulkner, Richard Wright, Robert Penn Warren, Eudora Welty, and Tennessee Williams. This sensibility was more open to influences from outside the South and more critical of the South's own cultural traditions. By examining their region with a more trenchant gaze, the

writers of the Renascence produced works that revealed the region's social conflicts and cultural weaknesses even as their efforts advanced the South's literary reputation.

Various explanations have been offered to account for the revival of modern southern writing. In an oft-quoted phrase from "The New Provincialism," Allen Tate spoke of the "backward gaze" of the South to explain the reawakening after World War I. According to this theory, the modern southern writer stood at the boundary between the traditional southern agrarian culture and the modern, increasingly industrial new order. At this "crossing of the ways," the southern writer experienced both nostalgia for the past and a sense of critical distance from it. Later critics have offered a similar historical explanation. Various social and cultural factors are assumed to have contributed to the literary reawakening: the increasing industrialization of the South, the experiences of southern veterans in World War I, the influence of Lost Generation values, a new literary climate (the influence of Sinclair Lewis and Sherwood Anderson was particularly strong in the South), and the region's reaction against its own sentimental tradition.

Although theories that emphasize the centrality of memory and history in southern writing have been productive and influential, they have not gone unchallenged. For those who focus on the African American contribution to southern writing, the experience of modern African American writers may not be so readily explained by "the shock of recognition" of passage from agrarian to modern society. For these writers, the essential factor is not the influence of modernization or international modernism but the struggle for racial equality. African American members of the Renascence, including Richard Wright, Zora Neale Hurston, and Jean Toomer, do evince a concern with the southern past and with the impact of modernization, but their perspective on the South is distinctly different from that of the major white writers. Unlike Faulkner's attitude toward the agrarian South, which may be characterized as ambivalent, Wright's depiction of the same society in *Uncle Tom's Children* (1938), *Black Boy* (1945), and *Twelve Million Black Voices* (1941) is decidedly negative. Hurston in *Their Eyes Were Watching God* and Toomer in *Cane* made significant artistic uses of southern black agrarian and folk society.

Feminist critics offer other reasons for the reawakening of southern writing: the reaction of women writers against a patriarchal culture, the development of a tradition of southern women's writing, the loosening and challenging of social restrictions on women, and the growing independence of women. In challenging assumptions concerning the characteristics and dating of the Renascence, feminist critics have reevaluated many neglected authors, particularly those who were sometimes dismissed as "precursors" to the Renascence, including Kate Chopin and Ellen Glasgow. Kate Chopin, writing at the end of the nineteenth century, challenged assumptions about the role of women in southern society in *The Awakening* (1899) and numerous short stories (posthumously published). Beginning her literary career relatively late in life, Chopin produced work in the local-color tradition (including the collections *Bayou Folk*, 1894, and *A Night in Acadie,* 1897) as well as works that included an even more realistic depiction and astringent critique of contemporary gender relations.

Ellen Glasgow is crucial to any informed interpretation of the Renascence. Glasgow's novels were well ahead of their time in their unusual quality of social realism. Beginning with *The Voice of the People* (1900), Glasgow produced a series of novels set in Richmond, Virginia, that offered an intensely realistic depiction of social manners and mores. Her critical stance toward her native region resulted in ironic depictions of southern honor and chivalry, as in her Civil War and Reconstruction novels *The Battle-Ground* (1902) and *The Deliverance* (1904). Glasgow's most important novels, especially in terms of her analysis of southern gender roles, are *Virginia* (1913), *Life and Gabriella* (1916), *Barren Ground* (1922), *The Romantic Comedians* (1926), and *The Sheltered Life* (1932).

Critical studies by Thadious Davis (*Faulkner's "Negro": Art and the Southern Context*), Minrose Gwin (*Black and White Women of the Old South: The Peculiar Sisterhood in American Literature*, 1985), Anne Goodwyn Jones (*Tomorrow Is Another Day: The Woman Writer in the South, 1859–1936*, 1981), and Lucinda MacKethan (*Daughters of Time: Creating Woman's Voice in Southern Story*, 1992), among others, have expanded our understanding of the Renascence in terms of race and gender. Carol S. Manning's *The Female Tradition in Southern Literature* (1993) offers correction to conventional interpretations. Focusing on the Renascence, the essays in this collection raise many questions concerning the formation of canon, the "sources" of the Renascence, the central images and stereotypes of women in Renascence writing, the the-

matic concerns of southern women writers, and the artistic standards of judgment involved in canon formation.

Literary and intellectual movements outside the South influenced the critical temper displayed by many Renascence authors. In part, southern writers were responding to the broader movements of naturalism and modernism that were transforming modern literature as a whole. Writers such as Chopin and James Branch Cabell were well aware of national and international literary innovations. Determined to work outside the traditional southern modes of local color and romance, Cabell based his work on more-cosmopolitan influences, on European literary forms (the picaresque novel and Arthurian romance), and the contemporary vogue for witty, cosmopolitan satire. His novel *Jurgen* (1919), set in an imaginary medieval realm, became a national sensation.

Faulkner, Ransom, Tate, Welty, and Wright were as much influenced by international modernism as they were by southern experience and tradition. Part of the influence of modernism was the use of local settings for broader symbolic purposes. The local subject matter of southern writers was transformed into myth in the same way that Yeats, Joyce, Eliot, Hemingway, and Pound, employing what Eliot termed the "mythic method," transformed their particular regional backgrounds and historical experience into more universal significance. Faulkner looked to the past, both to the mythologized antebellum aristocracy and to the heroic accounts of the Civil War, with nostalgia but also with an informed irony and critical distance. Beginning with *Sartoris* (1929) (reissued in its original longer version as *Flags in the Dust* in 1972), Faulkner wrote fifteen novels and numerous short stories set in the mythical Yoknapatawpha County. The major novels in the cycle are *The Sound and the Fury* (1929), *As I Lay Dying* (1930), *Light in August* (1932), *Absalom, Absalom!* (1936), and *Go Down, Moses* (1942). Tension between modern alienation and traditional community is a key element in Faulkner's work. His attitude is highly ambivalent toward the South, and his fiction comprises a searching critique of southern tradition and institutions. Well before the advent of the modern Civil Rights Movement, Faulkner depicted the legacies of slavery as the "curse" of the South. In numerous works he revealed the hypocrisy and destructiveness of traditional southern racial attitudes.

Faulkner's writing reflects many of the elements of international modernism that would also influence

Wolfe, Welty, and other writers of the Renascence. In *The Sound and the Fury,* he employed innovative technical devices such as the use of discontinuous chronology and the layering of time periods within the consciousness of a character. By dividing the narrative into four sections, told from the perspective of three brothers (Benjamin, Quentin, and Jason Compson) and Dilsey, the Compsons' house servant, Faulkner presented multiple perspectives of the same family history. To an even greater extent, he employed this experimental method in *As I Lay Dying,* the comic grotesque account of the death and burial of Addie Bundren. Faulkner continued to experiment with technique in his use of contrasting sections of narrative in *The Wild Palms* (1939) and in his ambitious allegorical novel, *A Fable* (1954).

Faulkner wrote compelling social realism while undercutting the myths of the Old South. Although characters such as Gail Hightower in *Light in August* or Isaac McCaslin in *Go Down, Moses* are dominated by their idealistic illusions about the southern past, in particular about the Civil War and the ethos of the southern aristocracy, Faulkner himself consistently displayed a more skeptical and realistic attitude toward the mythic past of his region. Through the character of Thomas Sutpen in *Absalom, Absalom!,* Faulkner was able to explore the contradictions and shortcomings of the plantation aristocracy and, more generally, of the southern past. In this respect, Faulkner's fiction displays the same quality of artistic distance from its subject that is apparent in the works of most of the leading writers of the Renascence.

Faulkner's depiction of women frequently disregarded conventional attitudes. In *The Sound and the Fury,* the servant Dilsey emerges as a resourceful and humane woman who attempts to hold together both her own and the Compson families. Temple Drake of *Sanctuary* (1931) is a version of the contemporary "flapper" or emancipated woman, but in Faulkner's novel she is depicted in decidedly negative terms as an irresponsible and decadent young woman. In *Sartoris,* Aunt Jenny Dupre is surrounded by defeated southern men but reveals tenacious strength and discipline, even though these qualities are accompanied by an aggressive defense of the Old Order. Numerous women characters in Faulkner's novels, including Lena Grove and Joanna Burden (*Light in August*), Eula Varner Snopes (*The Hamlet*), Charlotte Rittenmeyer (*The Wild Palms*), and Molly Beauchamp (*Go Down, Moses*), have gripped the imagination of readers.

Malcolm Cowley's 1946 edition of *The Portable Faulkner* was highly influential in securing recognition for Faulkner's work. Complete with Faulkner's own maps and Cowley's introduction, it demonstrated to a large audience that Faulkner's writing, at that time largely out of print, comprised a coherent body of major work. Cowley recognized Faulkner's accomplishment in the creation of the mythic county of Yoknapatawpha, and he revealed the breadth of Faulkner's social and historical canvas. The awarding of the 1950 Nobel Prize for Literature to Faulkner secured his reputation and opened the way for the serious study not only of Faulkner but of southern literature as an academic discipline.

Faulkner was clearly the major figure of the Renascence, but he was only one of a number of writers who produced innovative works of fiction based on rural and small-town locales. With his autobiographical novel *Look Homeward, Angel* (1929), Thomas Wolfe won national and international fame. Although Wolfe died short of his thirty-eighth birthday nine years later, Faulkner judged that Wolfe's imagination and writing (three other long novels and numerous shorter works) placed him near the top of his generation. Wolfe's work was representative of the youth-oriented culture of his times. His romanticism, his focus on adolescence, and his acerbic treatment of conventional society connect his work with the intellectual rebellion of the 1920s.

Wolfe's writing gave voice to what has been termed the "other South," the Appalachian region that was largely nonslaveholding during the antebellum period and was often of Union sympathy during the Civil War. A number of other Appalachian writers emerged during the Renascence. Harriette Simpson Arnow was the author of *Mountain Path* (1936, published under her maiden name Harriet Simpson), *Hunter's Horn* (1949), *The Dollmaker* (1954), *Seedtime on the Cumberland* (1960), and other novels. Jesse Stuart's best-known work is *The Thread That Runs So True* (1949), his vivid record of a teacher's daily existence in rural Appalachia. James Still wrote realistically about the ordeals and joys of rural life in *River of Earth* (1940), *On Troublesome Creek* (1941), and *Pattern of a Man and Other Stories* (1980). In addition to writing fiction, Stuart and Still were talented poets. *Man with a Bull-Tongue Plow* (1934) is Stuart's collection of 703 sonnets. These writers share an ability to convey human experience in strong, direct prose and realistic imagery. They write of Appalachian people whose lives are defined by physical struggle and economic limitations but who also discover sources of strength in their cultural heritage and social communities.

Robert Penn Warren's career gave abundant evidence that a renascence was underway in the South. A philosophical novelist, Warren nevertheless could grip the average reader. His famous *All the King's Men* (1946) was recast as a stage play and later became a major motion picture. Warren's central theme was the disorder and violence of the world of experience, and the necessity of human control of man's corrupt nature through thought and restraint. In other novels as well, Warren probed the modern South, but his chief love was poetry, and he ranks with the major American poets of the twentieth century. In addition to writing many short poems, Warren tackled the long narrative poem. *Brother to Dragons* (1953), *Audubon: A Vision* (1969), and *Chief Joseph* (1982) show his concern with the pastoral and demonstrate his force in the long poem. With Cleanth Brooks (with whom he taught and collaborated), he helped establish the New Criticism.

One of the writers encouraged by Warren and Brooks was Eudora Welty. Beginning in the 1930s with short stories published in the *Southern Review*, Welty has produced a body of work over a period of five decades that includes ten volumes of short stories, five novels, works of criticism, memoirs, and miscellaneous writing. Her novels are *The Robber Bridegroom* (1944), *Delta Wedding* (1947), *The Ponder Heart* (1954), *The Optimist's Daughter* (1972), and *Losing Battles* (1982). Her collections of short stories include *A Curtain of Green* (1943), *The Wide Net and Other Stories* (1943), and *The Golden Apples* (1950). Often focusing on rural and small-town life in Mississippi, Welty's fiction is at once intensely local and broadly universal. Her use of myth and folk elements provides a depth of human interest. In their representation of southern domesticity and their focus on women's lives, her stories implicitly examine traditional gender assumptions.

Like Warren and Faulkner, many Renascence authors conducted a reexamination of the southern past. Other distinguished historical novels include Elizabeth Madox Roberts's *The Time of Man* (1926), T. S. Stribling's trilogy (*The Forge*, 1931; *The Store*, 1932; and *The Unfinished Cathedral*, 1934), Evelyn Scott's *The Wave* (1929), and Shelby Foote's *Tournament* (1949). Andrew Lytle's *The Velvet Horn* (1957), the story of the Cropleigh family during Reconstruction, depicts the values and consciousness of the southern common folk. Frank Yerby's trilogy of novels (*The Foxes of Harrow*, 1946; *The Vixens*, 1947; *Pride's Castle*, 1948) was focused on nineteenth-century southern history. Among the many Renascence authors who wrote Civil War fiction were John Peale Bishop (*Many Thousands Gone*, 1931), James Boyd (*Marching On*, 1927), Clifford Dowdey (*Bugles Blow No More*, 1937), Caroline Gordon (*None Shall Look Back*, 1937), Margaret Mitchell (*Gone With the Wind*, 1936), Allen Tate (*The Fathers*, 1938), and Stark Young (*So Red the Rose*, 1934).

A number of novels addressed contemporary social issues. Major southern black writers from the Renascence include Arna Bontemps, Zora Neale Hurston, Jean Toomer, Walter Francis White, and Richard Wright. In his novel *Native Son* (1940), Wright created an archetypal figure in the character of Bigger Thomas, a young black man living in Chicago during the 1930s. Wright's short stories in *Uncle Tom's Children* (1938) and his autobiographical narrative *Black Boy* (1945) are among his major works. Other than fiction, Wright published works of social reportage (*Twelve Million Black Voices*, 1941) and travel writing, including *Black Power: A Record of Reactions in a Land of Pathos* (1954), *Pagan Spain* (1957), and *The Color Curtain: A Report on the Bandung Conference* (1956). Wright's later novels, which achieved less critical success, are *The Outsider* (1956), *Savage Holiday* (1954), and *The Long Dream* (1958). A posthumous collection of short stories was entitled *Eight Men* (1961).

Like Wright, many African American writers emigrated from the South. Zora Neale Hurston, who was raised in Eatonville, Florida, but lived much of her adult life in the North, wrote memorable fiction, including *Jonah's Gourd Vine* (1934) and *Their Eyes Were Watching God* (1937), and a major study of southern black folklore, *Mules and Men* (1935). Although he was born in Louisiana, Arna Bontemps was raised in California, returning only later to the South to serve as Fisk University librarian in Nashville. Bontemps produced *Black Thunder* (1936), a novel based on Gabriel Prosser's slave rebellion. Although he lived mostly outside the South, Jean Toomer based his novel *Cane* (1923) on his brief period as a school principal in rural Georgia. Missouri-born Langston Hughes is sometimes counted in the Southern Literary Renascence, though he grew up mainly in Lawrence, Kansas, and Cleveland, Ohio. His poetry and prose reflect traditional sources of southern black storytelling and speech.

At the beginning of the modern Civil Rights Movement, Margaret Walker wrote *For My People* (1942), an important collection of protest poetry. Many southern immigrants contributed to the Harlem Renaissance, the major reawakening of African American literature that began in the 1920s. These writers include Georgia Douglas Johnson, Anne Spencer, and Walter White. James Weldon Johnson, a black writer from Florida, confronted his southern heritage memorably in the novel *Autobiography of an Ex-Coloured Man* (1912) and his poem sequence *God's Trombones* (1927).

Other African American writers who may be considered members of the Southern Renascence are George Wylie Henderson (*Ollie Miss*, 1935), George Washington Lee (*River George*, 1937), Waters Turpin (*These Low Grounds*, 1937), and William Attaway. As J. Lee Greene points out, a standard device of African American southern fiction is the "flight-from-violence" theme structuring such novels as Turpin's *O Canaan!* (1939) and Attaway's *Blood on the Forge* (1941). A protest school of black writers developed this theme after the appearance of Wright's *Native Son* in 1940.

Several white southerners wrote novels about African Americans. These include Stribling's *Birthright* (1922), DuBose Heyward's *Porgy* (1925), Faulkner's *Light in August,* and novels by Julia Peterkin and Gilmore Millen. Later southern whites who wrote novels about race included Erskine Caldwell (*Trouble in July,* 1940) and Lillian Smith (*Strange Fruit,* 1944). The genre has remained vital in post-Renascence southern writing, in such works as William Styron's *Confessions of Nat Turner* (1967) and Lewis Nordan's *Wolf-Whistle* (1995), and in the many portraits of black characters in works by Flannery O'Connor, Walker Percy, Richard Ford, and others.

In the same way that African American writers focused on the issue of race, southern proletarian writers examined differences of social class. In several sensationalistic novels, including *Tobacco Road* (1932) and *God's Little Acre* (1933), Erskine Caldwell popularized grotesque images of "poor white trash." In stage plays and films, his works brought social inequalities to light at the same time that they perpetuated debasing images of southern people.

In his *Renaissance in the South* (1963), John Bradbury reconsidered many Renascence writers who had been neglected by previous critics. Edith Summers Kelley was among the first southern writers to portray the working class sympathetically and realistically. Among

social critics, Grace Lumpkin, who began as a Marxist, wrote of the exploitation of agricultural labor. Lumpkin was just one of a number of southern writers who addressed sharecropping issues during the 1930s. James Agee's *Let Us Now Praise Famous Men* is a memorable work of nonfiction reportage, based on his two-month residence among three Alabama sharecropper families. Influenced by the liberalism of the 1930s, southern radical voices included Myra Page, Leana Zugsmith, and Olive Dargan (who wrote as "Fielding Burke"). Harry H. Kroll also wrote critiques of the southern sharecropping system. Hodding Carter, Allen Drury, and Evans Harrington were southern liberals who produced political novels.

The Renascence included several major dramatists and a number of important poets. Among the dramatists, Tennessee Williams (Thomas Lanier Williams) gained an international reputation for early works such as *The Glass Menagerie* (1944), *A Streetcar Named Desire* (1947), and *Cat on a Hot Tin Roof* (1955). During his long and productive career, Williams won two Pulitzer Prizes and four New York Drama Critics Circle Awards. Although his later works were less successful, both critically and in terms of popular success, Williams continued to produce dramatic work until his death in 1983. Williams's powerful psychological dramas, some of which were adapted for film by Elia Kazan, portrayed disturbing mental conflicts. In doing so, these works significantly altered American attitudes and social assumptions toward the dispossessed and outcast figures that he chose to represent. Williams was also a prolific author of fiction and memoirs.

Lillian Hellman emerged as the first major woman dramatist from the South. *The Little Foxes* (1939) and *Another Part of the Forest* (1946) explore greed and exploitation in a Louisiana setting that evokes the plantation heritage. *The Autumn Garden* (1957) and *Toys in the Attic* (1960) also have southern settings, though her other plays do not. *The Children's Hour* (1934) boldly took on a lesbian theme. She confronted the Nazi horror in *Watch on the Rhine* (1941) and *The Searching Wind* (1944). Paul Green pioneered outdoor drama and wrote several plays—such as *In Abraham's Bosom* (1926), *The Field God* (1927), and *The House of Connelly* (1928)—and stories that probed southern realism. Carson McCullers achieved success with stage and screen versions of her novel *The Member of the Wedding* (1950).

During the Southern Renascence, poetry also gained national attention it had scarcely known before. Its fountain was the Fugitive and Agrarian nexus at Vanderbilt University, mentored by John Crowe Ransom. In addition to Robert Penn Warren, the movement included Donald Davidson, Allen Tate, and Merrill Moore. Though not a member of the Fugitives, poet John Peale Bishop was born in West Virginia and was closely associated with Allen Tate. The group orchestrated much of the New Criticism.

Ransom's critical essays began to appear in the late 1930s (including "Criticism, Inc." in 1938 and "The New Criticism" in 1941). Ransom formulated an approach to interpretation that came to be highly influential and reflected distrust of abstraction. The New Critics stressed the interpretation of works of literature exclusive of "external" factors (such as biographical, sociological, political, or historical interpretations). Their call to students and critics was to "experience" the work of literature on its own merits, through the analysis of complex literary structures, images, and meanings. In "Literature as Knowledge" (1940) and other influential essays, Allen Tate found that the dissociation of modern thought and feeling underlay the aesthetic fragmentation of modern literature.

In addition to those figures mentioned previously, the Renascence produced many other writers of merit. In a series of stories ("Old Mortality," "Pale Horse, Pale Rider," and the cycle of stories published as *The Old Order,* 1944), Katherine Anne Porter created the character of Miranda, a figure who looks to the past matriarchs in her family as models of a meaningful tradition. Porter differed from many southern modernists in her liberal politics, humanistic values, and secure sense of family history. Porter's best-known stories include "María Concepción" (1922) and "Flowering Judas" (1930). Caroline Gordon wrote in the realist tradition of James, Chekhov, and Joyce. Gordon's *Penhally* (1931) traced the Llewellyn family saga in Kentucky. Gordon wrote in the tradition of the novel of manners, especially in *The Women on the Porch* (1944) and *The Strange Children* (1951).

No consensus exists regarding the end date of the Southern Renascence, but most critics regard the 1950s as the point when the original Renascence gave way to the emergence of a new generation (sometimes termed the "second southern renaissance"). Although it is indisputable that the 1950s saw the emergence of a new generation, there was little sense of decline in the outpouring of southern writing. Some of the southern authors who established reputations in the period after World War II include A. R. Ammons, John Barth, Truman Capote, James Dickey, Ralph Ellison, Shelby Foote, Ernest J. Gaines, George Garrett, Bowen Ingram, Randall Jarrell, Madison Jones, Carson McCullers, Flannery O'Connor, Walker Percy, Reynolds Price, Elizabeth Spencer, Peter Taylor, and William Styron.

Regardless of when one dates its end point, the Southern Renascence must be viewed as a major movement in twentieth-century American literature. Its writers brought a new critical temper and self-consciousness to the representation of their region, and they broadened the subject matter for literature while expanding the approaches with which that subject might be depicted. In contrast to the parochialism and sentimentality of much earlier southern writing, writers of the Renascence displayed an interest in realism and naturalism as narrative forms. Their association with international literary movements such as modernism revealed a more cosmopolitan perspective on their art. In their greater realism, awareness, and complexity, the writers of the Southern Renascence participated in a major revival of literary art in the South.

Jeffrey J. Folks

See also Agrarians; Faulkner, William; Harlem Renaissance; New Criticism; Proletarian Novel; Warren, Robert Penn; Welty, Eudora; Williams, Tennessee.

John Bradbury, *Renaissance in the South: A Critical History of the Literature, 1920–1960* (1963); Hazel V. Carby, *Reconstructing Womanhood: The Emergence of the Afro-American Woman Novelist* (1987); Doreen Fowler and Ann J. Abadie, *Faulkner and the Southern Renaissance* (1982); Richard Gray, *The Literature of Memory: Modern Writers of the American South* (1977); C. Hugh Holman, *Three Modes of Modern Southern Fiction: Ellen Glasgow, William Faulkner, Thomas Wolfe* (1966); Anne Goodwyn Jones, *Tomorrow Is Another Day: The Woman Writer in the South, 1859–1936* (1981); Richard H. King, *A Southern Renaissance: The Cultural Awakening of the American South, 1930–1955* (1980); Carol S. Manning, *The Female Tradition in Southern Literature* (1993); Louis D. Rubin Jr. and Robert D. Jacobs, *Southern Renascence: The Literature of the Modern South* (1953); Louis D. Rubin Jr., *The Faraway Country: Writers of the Modern South* (1963); Daniel Joseph Singal, *The War Within: From Victorian to Modernist Thought in the South, 1919–1945* (1982).

SOUTHERN REVIEW

The establishment of the *Southern Review* in 1935 at Louisiana State University—then a small provincial university, located in Baton Rouge, the unpopulous capital city of an exotic but backward southern state—was owing to the presence on the campus of three singularly gifted and ambitious young southern men of letters: Charles W. Pipkin, a Rhodes Scholar and brilliant political scientist, who had been made dean of the LSU Graduate School at the age of twenty-nine; Cleanth Brooks, a promising literary scholar and critic, who had joined the LSU English faculty after completing two years at Oxford as a Rhodes Scholar; and Robert Penn Warren, already a published poet and biographer, who had preceded Brooks at Oxford as a Rhodes Scholar by a year, and after teaching at Vanderbilt had joined Brooks on the LSU English faculty. The three arrived in Louisiana's capital city at the very moment when a still-youthful politician, driven by a ruthless ambition for power—yet, as Robert B. Heilman has said, possessed by "an imaginativeness which could grasp ends beyond power and profit"—was, even in the depths of the Great Depression, providing unprecedented funding for one of his favorite projects, the making of a great state university in Louisiana. To this end, Huey Long's handpicked president of LSU, James Monroe Smith, had become interested in involving LSU in the publication of a literary quarterly. When the effort on the part of Pipkin, Brooks, and Warren to create a satisfactory association between LSU and the *Southwest Review* at Southern Methodist University failed, Smith supplied a handsome fund for the publication of a quarterly at LSU. Pipkin was appointed editor-in-chief, and Brooks and Warren were made managing editors. Albert Erskine, then a graduate student at LSU, was given the post of business manager, though, Warren recalled, Erskine "was as much an editor as anybody else." (When Erskine resigned in 1940, he was replaced by John Ellis Palmer. Palmer, however, was given the title "Managing Editor" and Brooks and Warren were elevated to equal status with Pipkin. When Pipkin died in 1941, no replacement was named.)

Having been assured by Smith that there would be no political interference in their endeavor, Pipkin, Brooks, and Warren brought out the first issue of the *Southern Review* in the summer of 1935. Although only two months later Long was struck down by an assassin's bullet in the splendid new state capitol he had built in Baton Rouge, funding for the magazine continued during the crisis that came when the greed of those who sought to perpetuate the Long regime resulted in the "Louisiana scandals" of 1939–1940 and James Monroe Smith was indicted for fraud and imprisoned.

But in 1942 the first series of the *Southern Review* became a casualty of World War II. Citing the need to support the American war effort at an institution with a large ROTC cadet corps and a strong military tradition, the LSU administration cancelled the subsidy that had sustained the magazine, and it ceased publication with the completion of the seventh volume.

In its brief existence, the original series of the *Southern Review* had demonstrated such a remarkable literary and intellectual quality that it not only achieved widespread recognition in its day but has acquired a lasting niche in the literary history of the South, the nation, and, it may be said, the general history of modern letters. Indeed, one reason for its fame was its catholicity. This disappointed some advocates of southern Agrarianism, who had expected that, since Brooks and Warren were still enlisted in this movement, the *Southern Review* would be a source of renewed support for this fading cause. But Brooks and Warren were far less interested in political and economic movements than in modern movements in poetry, fiction, and literary criticism. Exercising the comparatively free hand they always had as managing editors of the magazine, they devoted themselves to attracting the invigorating cosmopolitan mix of established and promising new writers that graced the pages of the first series of the *Southern Review*: among them, T. S. Eliot, William Empson, Ford Madox Ford, and Paul Valéry, as well as Wallace Stevens, Delmore Schwartz, R. P. Blackmur, Herbert Agar, Allen Tate, Donald Davidson, John Crowe Ransom, Andrew Lytle, Caroline Gordon, Katherine Anne Porter, Eudora Welty, and Brooks and Warren themselves. Thus transcending the parochial, drawn not only from the South but from other parts of the nation and from abroad, the authorship of the 1935–1942 *Southern Review* established its context in modern literature as a whole.

The editors of the *Southern Review* that began publication with the winter issue 1965—Lewis P. Simpson and Donald E. Stanford of the LSU English faculty, coeditors; and Rima Drell Reck of the foreign language faculty of Louisiana State University at New Orleans (now the University of New Orleans), associate editor—recognized the radical differences between the literary situation in their time and the time of the editors of the original series, yet they aspired to locate the second series in a literary context approximately similar to the one that the first had claimed. Although the editorial staff of the second series has changed during the thirty-four years of its existence—at present it is edited by James Olney and Dave Smith of the LSU English faculty, with Michael Griffith as associate editor and Niccola Mason as assistant editor—the *Southern Review* continues to reflect a cosmopolitan diversity in its authorship and at the same time to assert its context in the national and the southern literary expression. But with a difference. In 1985 the *Southern Review* that was established in 1965 celebrated its continuity with the *Southern Review* that began publication in 1935 by bringing out three special issues. One, devoted to the Anglo-American and, in a very real sense, European author T. S. Eliot, served to represent both the cosmopolitan and national contexts of the magazine; and another, published under the rubric "The Southern Writer," the regional context. But the third special issue, devoted to African American writing, indicated a great change that has occurred in the contextual frame of the *Southern Review* in the second half of the twentieth century.

Lewis P. Simpson

See also Baton Rouge, Louisiana; *Kenyon Review*; Louisiana State University.

Thomas W. Cutrer, *Parnassus on the Mississippi: The "Southern Review" and the Baton Rouge Literary Community, 1935–1942* (1984); James A. Grimshaw Jr., ed., *Cleanth Brooks and Robert Penn Warren: A Literary Correspondence* (1998); Lewis P. Simpson, James Olney, Jo Gulledge, eds., *The "Southern Review" and Modern Literature, 1935–1985* (1988).

SOUTH IN THE BUILDING OF THE NATION, THE

The South in the Building of the Nation (1909) is a thirteen-volume series offering a political, economic, social, intellectual, and literary history of the American South from the sixteenth century to the opening of the twentieth century. The work's full title states its purpose: *The South in the Building of the Nation: A History of the Southern States Designed to Record the South's Part in the Making of the American Nation; to Portray the Character and Genius, to Chronicle the Achievements and Progress and to Illustrate the Life and Traditions of the Southern People.* Copyrighted in 1909 and published by the Southern Publication Society (first named the Southern Historical Publishing Society), a group formed with the purpose of developing

the series, its volumes reflect the New South perspective of its southern academic editors.

This text embodies an effort by southern cultural leaders to strengthen the South's national profile following years of northern cultural dominance in the United States. Produced in a time of growing nationalism, the work endeavors to move beyond sectionalist sentiment while simultaneously asserting the South's unique regional identity and its vital role in the nation's history. Reflecting the agenda of the economic and political New South movement, this work intends both to redefine the South's cultural status within the country and to engender regional pride among southerners, thus hoping to garner increased power and influence for the South within the nation.

Originally planned as an eight-volume series, *The South in the Building of the Nation* grew to include thirteen topically organized volumes, each edited by a leading scholar in the field. In turn, these editors asserted that they selected only the scholars best qualified to write the individual entries. The "History of the States," originally slated for one volume, became volumes I (Virginia, Maryland, Kentucky, West Virginia, North Carolina), II (Florida, Louisiana, Missouri, Arkansas, Texas), and III (South Carolina, Georgia, Alabama, Mississippi, Tennessee). Julian Alvin Carroll Chandler, professor of history at Richmond College, edited these volumes. Each subsequent volume focuses on a particular aspect of southern history: Volume IV, *Political History* (edited by Franklin Lafayette Riley, University of Mississippi); Volumes V and VI, *Economic History* (edited by James Curtis Ballagh, Johns Hopkins University); Volume VII, *History of Literary and Intellectual Life* (edited by John Bell Hennemann, University of the South, who upon his death was succeeded by W. P. Trent, Columbia University); Volume VIII, *History of Southern Fiction* (edited by Edwin Mims, University of North Carolina); Volume IX, *History of Southern Oratory* (edited by Thomas E. Watson, author); Volume X, *History of the Social Life* (edited by Samuel Chiles Mitchell, University of South Carolina); Volumes XI and XII, *Southern Biography* (edited by Walter Lynwood Fleming, Louisiana State University). Volume XIII, *Index and Reading Courses* (edited by J. Walker McSpadden) was added in 1913.

Volumes VII and VIII are of particular interest to students of southern literature. Volume VII includes essays about southern poetry and literary humor. Volume VIII contains an essay by Edwin Mims discussing the main tendencies in southern literature, followed by selections from eighteen southern writers chosen by Mims to be featured in the volume.

Susan H. Irons

See also Anthologies of Southern Literature.

SOUTHWEST

Similarities between the Southwest (New Mexico, Arizona, West Texas, southern Utah, portions of Colorado adjacent to the Rio Grande) and the Old Southwest (middle Georgia, Alabama, Mississippi, northern Louisiana, Tennessee, Kentucky, Arkansas) are minimal, sharing little more than a word, though the two designations may cause some confusion. Not only does the Southwest have a geography and climate markedly unlike that of the Old Southwest, the Southwest has a much older history. Indeed, it contains many of the oldest communities and cultures in what is now the United States of America. Though the states that comprise the Southwest are among the most newly admitted to the Union, Santa Fe, the capital of New Mexico, was founded in 1609 (only St. Augustine, Florida, predates it). Santa Fe is the oldest continuous seat of government in the United States. Whereas the cultural links of the Old Southwest connect most strongly to those of England (transformed often in the older settlements of the Upper South), the cultural links of the Southwest to Europe come by way of El Camino Real from Mexico City. Later, the Old Santa Fe Trail brought traders from the North and settlers from the Midwest. Spanish culture increasingly received infusion of Anglo culture, but not in any major way southern culture. Native American presence is strong in the states of New Mexico and Arizona, and a visitor to those states and southern Colorado will find ruins from the ancient Anasazi that greatly predate any European presence. In contrast, Native Americans have long been displaced from the lands of the Old Southwest, as Faulkner chronicles in *Go Down, Moses* (1942). The term *Old Southwest* survives primarily because of its usefulness in describing Southwestern humor.

The Confederacy wished to claim the Southwest as its own (though its western aridity made the Southwest unfit for the cotton economy of the South) and extended its western front as far as Albuquerque (which

it held for two months in 1862) and Santa Fe (the Confederate flag flew for a short time over the governor's palace), but its ascendance was brief, its retreat from the Southwest prompt. Following the war, southerners were participants in the westward course of the nation, and defenders of the Lost Cause sometimes played a part in frontier violence. The stereotype of the proud but foolish southerner developed. George Stevens used it in his classic western film *Shane* (1953). Walter Van Tilburg Clark explored the darker side of the postwar southerner come west in his depiction of Major Tetley in the classic novel *The Ox-Bow Incident* (1940), later a major film (1943).

In the twentieth century, many writers and artists have journeyed to the Southwest—attracted by the beauty of the land, the cultural diversity, and a long history; many have stayed. Among the present generation of writers who have claimed the Southwest, Barbara Kingsolver grew up in rural Kentucky, but she moved as a young woman to Arizona and set her highly acclaimed early novels in the Southwest: *The Bean Trees* (1988), *Animal Dreams* (1990), and *Pigs in Heaven* (1988). Nevertheless, Kingsolver now lives part of each year in southern Appalachia, and her southern roots inform her work, noticeably in *The Poisonwood Bible* (1998), which depicts Southern Baptist missionaries in the Congo. Willa Cather, born in Virginia and shaped by southern parents, discovered the Southwest after she had written her important fiction set in Nebraska. Many have claimed *Death Comes for the Archbishop* (1927), her novel about the missions of New Mexico, her best book. Following his battles with tuberculosis, Walker Percy turned to the desert air of New Mexico in his effort to find physical and spiritual health, a progress mirrored in the migrations of Will Barrett in *The Last Gentleman* (1967). North Carolina's Doris Betts has set two novels in the Southwest—*Heading West* (1981) and *The Sharp Teeth of Love* (1997). Whereas Betts's novels are contemporary, Clyde Edgerton's *Redeye: A Western* (1995) is set in the nineteenth century; in *Redeye,* a young southern woman journeys to the West—as happens in both of Betts's novels. Cormac McCarthy set his first novels in the hills and mountains of East Tennessee. *The Orchard Keeper* (1965), *Outer Dark* (1968), *Child of God* (1974), and *Suttree* (1979) earned McCarthy fame as an inheritor of Faulknerian gothic tradition. But McCarthy left Tennessee, eventually, for El Paso, Texas—a turning marked in *Blood Meridian, or the Evening Redness in the West* (1985). McCarthy is now counted a major western writer, especially for his portrayal of John Grady Cole, last of a long line of Texas ranchers in his Border Trilogy: *All the Pretty Horses* (1972), *The Crossing* (1995), and *Cities of the Plain* (1998).

Although novels being written in the Southwest—with major attention to Native American and Hispanic cultures and heightened treatment of the land and environment—are distinct from much southern writing, linkages will likely increase, especially as Hispanic presence in the South increases.

Joseph M. Flora

See also Old Southwest; Southwestern Humor.

David King Dunaway, *Writing the Southwest* (1995).

SOUTHWESTERN HUMOR

Southwestern humor (also known as "frontier humor," "antebellum humor," and "backwoods humor") was a genre that flourished in the three decades leading up to the Civil War. Although influenced by several sources, including William Byrd's *History of the Dividing Line*, the satiric sketches of Addison and Steele, and the Down East humor that flourished in New England, Southwestern humorists introduced to the nation a new landscape of colorful backwoodsmen, shifty confidence men, and urbane gentlemen, all of whom spoke in accents unlike any that had been heard in earlier American literature.

Augustus Baldwin Longstreet's *Georgia Scenes: Characters, Incidents, &c., in the First Half Century of the Republic* (1835) is usually considered to be the first major work of Southwestern humor. Consisting of nineteen sketches, many of which had appeared previously in the *Milledgeville* (Georgia) *Southern Recorder* and the *Augusta State Rights' Sentinel, Georgia Scenes* is a complex portrayal of a culture in transition from frontier to settlement. Because Longstreet's colorful descriptions of horse swaps, dances, fights, gander pullings, horse races, and shooting matches made the work a popular success—Harper's brought out a second edition in 1840 and the work was regularly reprinted for the rest of the century—more discriminating critics recognized its literary value; in an 1836 review published in the *Southern Literary Messenger,*

Edgar Allan Poe called it "a sure omen of better days of the literature of the South."

Georgia Scenes introduced at a high level of development many of the features that would come to define the genre: an emphasis on documentary realism, a colorful depiction of the rough-and-tumble contests and social rituals of a frontier society, and a narrative frame in which a literate gentleman narrates his encounters with lower-class, dialect-speaking characters. *Georgia Scenes* has as good a claim as any work of southern literature to being the first substantial treatment of the class that came to be known as "plain folk."

Like many of his fellow humorists, Longstreet was ambivalent about his role as an author. For a few years after the publication of *Georgia Scenes,* he continued to publish, mostly in Simms's *Magnolia*, the sketches that were later collected by his nephew Fitz R. Longstreet in *Stories with a Moral* (1912). His work as a Methodist minister and educator caused him, however, to downplay his literary efforts as the frivolous "amusement of my idle hours." Nevertheless, Longstreet's influence was significant, and for many years reviewers almost inevitably compared new works of humor with *Georgia Scenes*. In addition to titling his work *Mississippi Scenes,* Joseph Beckham Cobb dedicated to Longstreet his 1851 collection of sketches, which are indebted to *Georgia Scenes* in both technique and subject matter.

Another writer influenced by Longstreet was his close friend and protégé William Tappan Thompson. In 1843, Thompson published *Major Jones's Courtship,* an epistolary novel recounting the courtship and marriage of the title character to Miss Mary Stallions, the college-educated daughter of a local planter. Mostly lacking in the earthy comedy common to the genre, *Major Jones's Courtship* is also anomalous in being narrated in dialect by a yeoman farmer. Although Major Jones is sensible and good-hearted, his naïveté provides much of the book's humor. A memorable trip to the "opery" recounted in a subsequent volume, *Major Jones's Sketches of Travel* (1848), produces a baffled spectator and a greatly misunderstood musical form. The rube's misadventures in town proved to be a fertile subject for many humorists, including John S. Robb, whose "Swallowing an Oyster Alive" provides a typical variation on the theme. In this sketch, a "hero from the Sucker state" consumes his first oyster, and after being informed that a live oyster is likely to eat through his "innards," is luckily able to quell the threat with a liberal dose of strong pepper sauce.

The late 1830s saw Southwestern humor taking shape in two important places: the Crockett almanacs, published between 1834 and 1856, and the New York–based *Spirit of the Times.* Colonel David Crockett had already appeared, indirectly at any rate, in James Kirke Paulding's *The Lion of the West,* an 1830 play whose protagonist, Nimrod Wildfire, bore more than a passing resemblance to the Tennessee congressman. Although Crockett's backwoods autobiography had appeared in 1834, his death at the Alamo in 1836 left him free to inhabit a more fully mythologized landscape as the archetypal frontier hero. If the Crockett of 1834 was a capable backwoodsman, he could not yet unfreeze the sun with hot bear grease, a feat performed with little difficulty by his 1854 incarnation. As Ben Franklin had done a century earlier, the various authors of the Crockett almanacs embellished a pragmatic agricultural document with a persona fit for the times, and in so doing, played a key role in translating into printed form the oral tradition of the tall tale that flourished on the frontier.

A similar mythology of Southwestern humor arose around the legendary flatboatman Mike Fink, the most famous of the ring-tailed roarers whose brags and fights became staples of the genre. Hunters, as well, are frequently numbered among the half-horse, half-alligators that provide many of the genre's most colorful moments. Even writers such as Longstreet concerned to document a specific locale were likely to include a few "stretchers" for comic effect, and a tension between realism and wild exaggeration pervades the work of many humorists. Exaggeration and outright lying take place within sketches as well, and on more than one occasion discord arises when an audience member accuses a story of "smelling rather tall." "Rance Bore-'em," a character in Francis James Robinson's *Kups of Kauphy* (1853), is an especially gifted liar capable of fabricating, in response to any topic raised in conversation, a heroic tale involving his exploits in Texas. In one story, Rance recounts how, without any medical training, he once replaced a man's diseased bones with two he had fashioned from a white oak. As the character of Rance Bore-'em suggests, the backwoods incarnation of the *alazon* or braggart makes many appearances. One of the most memorable is William C. Hall's Mike Hooter, a character based (not atypically) on an actual person. In "How Mike Hooter Came Very Near 'Wolloping' Arch Coony," Hooter shows unequivo-

cally that, although his insults and brags are second to none, he is profoundly reluctant to come to blows.

Like several of his peers, Hall never published a book-length work. Although most of the best humorists eventually did so, Southwestern humor was rarely conceived in book form. To be sure, some of the best works in the genre are structured as books and not merely as collections of sketches, but it is arguable that the more important format for the genre consists of the newspapers and journals in which the vast majority of sketches and tales were originally published. Several newspapers, including the *St. Louis Reveille,* the *Concordia* (Louisiana) *Intelligencer,* and two papers based in New Orleans, the *Delta* and the *Picayune,* served as important outlets for humorous writing. Because it was common practice for many of these journals to reprint sketches published in others, the dissemination of popular sketches was wide indeed, and the public's appetite for the best of them was strong.

By far the most important and influential journal was William T. Porter's *Spirit of the Times.* Porter began the *Spirit of Times* as a sporting journal that catered to upper-class hunters, fishermen, and especially horsemen. With only a small staff, Porter was forced to search for amateur correspondents if he wanted to obtain timely reports on racing throughout the land. By the end of the 1830s, several of these correspondents began to try their hands at more literary efforts. These usually derived from a sporting event such as a horse race or a hunting expedition, but as time passed, more of them began to include the tall-tale exaggerations and frontier realism that would make the *Spirit* one of the most important journals in the history of American humor. Publication in the *Spirit* marked the beginning of many careers, including those of Thomas Bangs Thorpe, Johnson Jones Hooper, Alexander McNutt, Henry Clay Lewis, and George Washington Harris. Virtually none of these men was a professional author, and most, fearing that authorship would subvert their careers as ministers, planters, lawyers, journalists, and politicians, preferred to publish anonymously or under pseudonyms. Such authors included McNutt (The Turkey Runner), Phillip B. January (Obe Oilstone), John S. Robb (Solitaire), George P. Burnham (The Young 'Un), and the Field brothers, Joseph and Matthew (Everpoint and Phazma, respectively).

Porter also played a role in determining the political orientation of Southwestern humor. Eager to gain a wide national readership, he banned political discussions from the *Spirit,* although a few writers did manage to sneak in humorous sketches with political over-tones. Many humorists were politically active, and most were centrist Whigs eager to reach consensus with men across the nation whom they considered to be their social peers. The apolitical tone of the *Spirit* helps partially to explain why the issue of slavery plays such a negligible role in humorous writing. The rela-tively few African American characters that do appear tend to be firmly in the background.

One of Porter's earliest and most influential corre-spondents was Charles F. M. Noland, a planter and journalist from northern Arkansas, who began to send letters to the *Spirit* in 1836 signed "N. of Arkansas." As "N. of Arkansas," Noland usually contributed sporting epistles of the kind that would continue to be associated with Southwestern humor, if not actually part of it; later examples would include William El-liott's distinguished *Carolina Sports* (1846) and John-son Jones Hooper's *Dog and Gun: A Few Loose Chap-ters on Shooting* (1856). By 1837, Noland had established the persona of "Pete Whetstone," who would act as the ostensible author of forty-five of the over two hundred letters that Noland eventually con-tributed to the *Spirit*. Although, like Major Jones after him, Pete narrates his stories in dialect, his frontier community is an altogether rougher place than Major Jones's comparatively tranquil plantation. At Devil's Fork, frolics, fun, and fights (often involving the pugi-listically inclined Dan Looney) predominate. If Noland never progressed beyond the level of amusing anec-dote, he would nevertheless remain one of the *Spirit*'s most prolific and entertaining correspondents.

Another frequent correspondent, Thomas Bangs Thorpe, would achieve artistic distinction. A north-erner by birth, Thorpe moved to Louisiana in 1837 and would remain there as a painter, journalist, postmaster, and politician for the next two decades. In 1839 he sent to the *Spirit* a sketch entitled "Tom Owen, the Bee-Hunter," a mock-heroic, quasi-mystical treatment of the title character. The wildly popular sketch provided Thorpe with both fame and a pseudonym, and "The Bee Hunter" continued to publish regularly in the *Spirit*. Most of the work for which Thorpe is remem-bered is collected in two works, *The Mysteries of the Backwoods* (1846) and *The Hive of the Bee-Hunter* (1854). He also published a novel, *The Master's House* (1854), and three works on military themes: *Our Army on the Rio Grande* (1846), *Our Army at Monterey* (1847), and *The Zachary Taylor Anecdote Book* (1848). Like sporting literature, serious military litera-

ture retained an association with humorous writing, with the Mexican War and its attendant political wran-gling an especially prominent subject. Military and po-litical exploits provided a rich supply of material for humorous writing as well.

Like many of his peers, Thorpe was capable of broad comedy. In "A Piano in Arkansas," the back-woods village of Hardscrabble receives a report that a piano has been brought to town by a new family. Since none of the villagers has even seen a piano, speculation abounds as to its nature. Mo Mercer, the self-pro-claimed "oracle of the village" who brags of "visiting the 'Capitol' twice, and 'seeing Pianos as plenty as woodchucks,'" mistakenly identifies, to his chagrin and the townspeople's delight, what turns out to be a "yankee washing machine." Humor was not, however, Thorpe's primary theme; most of the sketches in *The Mysteries of the Backwoods* and *The Hive of the Bee-Hunter* exemplify sporting literature more than hu-morous writing per se.

Where Thorpe truly distinguished himself was in ar-ticulating the elegiac tone that many lesser writers only suggested. Like Tom Owen, many of Thorpe's most memorable characters are in the process of being dis-possessed by the forces of history. "As a country be-comes cleared up and settled," Thorpe writes in the first sentence of his that would ever see print, "Bee-hunters disappear; consequently they are seldom or ever noticed." A later sketch entitled "The Disgraced Scalp Lock" involves two figures on the losing side of history: Mike Fink, whose exploits as the archetypal flatboatman have been rendered anachronistic by the encroachment of civilization, and Proud Joe, a drunken Indian who reasserts his dignity in revenging an insult. Thorpe's greatest elegy is, of course, "The Big Bear of Arkansas," which would become the single most fa-mous and influential story in the tradition of South-western humor. The tale's protagonist, Jim Doggett, enacts in microcosm the transformation of the frontier hero; although he first appears as a half-horse, half-alli-gator, he becomes humanized as he relates his encoun-ters with "the Bar." Like Faulkner's Old Ben a century later, the *"unhuntable bear . . . died when his time come,"* and his passing signifies the passing of the wil-derness; like Sam Fathers in Faulkner's story, Jim's life as one of the "children of the wood" is diminished by the bear's death.

Two important collections of humor grew out of the *Spirit*. *The Big Bear of Arkansas* (1845), which seems to have been suggested to Porter by the publishing house of Carey and Hart, included, in addition to Thorpe's title story, twenty sketches, all of which are set in the South. *A Quarter Race in Kentucky,* a second volume published a year later, included several sketches by northern and midwestern writers, indicating that if the best humorists of the day hailed from the South, writers in other parts of the country were using similar forms with their own local materials. Porter published a wide variety of humor in the *Spirit,* and in selecting the sketches for these collections, he began defining the canon of Southwestern humor. The success of these two anthologies led to the publication of several others, notably T. A. Burke's *Polly Peablossom's Wedding* (1851) and S. P. Avery's *The Harp of a Thousand Strings* (1858). Whether anthology or single-author book, virtually all major works of Southwestern humor were published by northern presses, and northern readers provided a substantial portion of the books' market.

Although certain themes and techniques recur throughout the genre, the heterogeneity of Southwestern humor has frequently been underestimated. In addition to simple anecdotes, Southwestern humor is indebted to numerous other literary forms, including Juvenalian and Addisonian satire, the sketch, the essay, the epistolary novel, the picaresque novel, and the travel narrative. The form of individual works differs in sometimes drastic ways. Johnson Jones Hooper's *Some Adventures of Captain Simon Suggs, Late of the Tallapoosa Volunteers* (1845) is a brilliant parody of the campaign biography, a genre that dominated political life in the nineteenth century. Hardin Taliaferro's *Fisher's River (North Carolina) Scenes and Characters* (1859) appears, to modern eyes, like a collection of folklore whose author has taken great pains to recreate the social context of the tall tales. Sol Smith, a gifted storyteller and legendary manager of a traveling theater company, divided his *Theatrical Management in the West and South* (1868) into five "acts" to suggest a play.

Joseph Glover Baldwin's *Flush Times in Alabama and Mississippi: A Collection of Sketches* (1853) is perhaps the most heterogeneous single work of Southwestern humor. Combining humorous pseudo-biographical sketches, historical essays, short anecdotes, and serious biographical essays on leading Whig politicians, *Flush Times* documents the fitful and often futile attempts of lawyers and, to a lesser extent, politicians to impose order upon a chaotic frontier. Baldwin's brilliant rendering of a wide variety of dialects, ranging

from the patrician speech of his narrator to Burwell Shines, whose impossibly pedantic language "rendered burlesque impossible," to a host of lower-class characters "as corrupt in language as in morals," only adds to his description of the "riotous carnival" of the Old Southwest, where traditional modes of social organization and authority no longer hold sway. In particular, a historical essay entitled "How Time Served the Virginians" shows how the cultured inhabitants of the "land of orators, heroes and statesmen" succumb to a world dominated by credit, speculation, and "sharp financiering." *Flush Times* is also notable for its emphasis on bodily humor. Cave Burton, a man " 'considerable' in all animal appetites," "as good in liquids as in solids," joins Squire A., a man of "distinguished reputation and immense skill in the art and mystery of fritter eating," as one of the work's most memorable characters.

In the unrefined world of Southwestern humor, life is often shown as a physical process of appetite and survival. In a representative story, a poor white in Robinson's *Kups of Kauphy* lies near death after eating two pecks of cherries until he is relieved by a heavy dose of calomel. No work shows the emphasis on the body and bodily humor more than Henry Clay Lewis's *Odd Leaves in the Life of a Louisiana Swamp Doctor* (1850). Lewis's work as a physician in Madison Parish, Louisiana, provided him with substantial background material for developing the swamp-doctor persona of "Madison Tensas" that he used in his stories. Lewis first saw print with "Cupping on the Sternum," which appeared in the *Spirit* in 1845. The popular and widely reprinted sketch, later incorporated into *Odd Leaves,* turns on the novice physician's mistaken equation of "sternum" and "stern"—a likely mistake for a young man who had spent substantial time on riverboats. Here, as in "Love in the Garden," a story of how intestinal irregularities interrupt a nervous courtship, the comedy is lighthearted, but elsewhere Lewis's humor of the body carries grotesque and even gothic overtones. In "Stealing a Baby," the swamp doctor's love affair ends when the stolen corpse of a baby falls from his cloak at an inopportune moment; in "The Curious Widow," he attempts (unsuccessfully) to scare a prying landlady with the skin of a face peeled from a hideous albino cadaver; and in "A Struggle for Life," a drunken African American dwarf chokes the swamp doctor into unconsciousness before burning to death in a campfire. Although Lewis's emphasis on disease, decay, and death is extreme, these themes appear frequently in the work of other humorists.

If not grotesque, the fictional world of Johnson Jones Hooper is certainly sordid. Like Baldwin, he saw firsthand the flush times of the Alabama frontier, where he worked as a journalist and later as a political appointee. Although he later published a volume entitled *The Widow Rigby's Husband* (1851), his fame was assured by *Some Adventures of Captain Simon Suggs*. Hooper—who, like Longstreet, later came to regret his humorous writing—adopted the older writer's framing device with a twist: throughout the work, the literate narrator maintains the pretense of admiring his shady protagonist, whom he is recommending for political office. Hooper cleverly masks satire as approbation; even Suggs's shadier exploits are dismissed as mere foibles.

Hooper's greatest achievement is, however, Suggs himself. Like Baldwin's Ovid Bolus, a notorious liar uniquely suited to the chaos of the "flush times," Suggs repeatedly demonstrates the efficacy of living by the maxim "it is good to be shifty in a new country." In one episode, he pockets $170 from a land speculator whose conversation he has overheard; in another, he takes advantage of the distant Creek Wars to achieve the lofty and personally advantageous position of captain of the Tallapoosa Volunteers. Suggs's shiftiness makes him the archetypal poor-white confidence man a century before his literary descendant Flem Snopes. Nevertheless, there is some justice in his deceptions since his victims typically include the sanctimonious, the greedy, the gullible, and the proud. In a scene that Mark Twain would later rework in *Huckleberry Finn*, Suggs steals the stage from a venal evangelist by faking a memorable conversion complete with visions of diabolical alligators; in the end, he makes off with a hefty collection to begin his own church. Despite his utter amorality, Suggs nevertheless serves a positive role as trickster.

The genre's greatest trickster would not, however, appear until a decade later, when George Washington Harris, a native Pennsylvanian who had grown up in Knoxville, Tennessee, began publishing tales about a character named Sut Lovingood. These would not be collected in book form until 1867, when *Sut Lovingood: Yarns Spun by a "Nat'ral Born Durn'd Fool,"* usually considered to be the final work of Southwestern humor, was published. If Suggs's world is seedy, Sut's is positively nihilistic. In "Sut Lovingood's Sermon," he enumerates the five "strong pints" of his "karacter," beginning with his ownership of a "whisky proof gizzard" in place of a soul, and ending with his ability to evade "misfortnit skeery scrapes" faster than anybody.

Following in the footsteps of many earlier characters, Sut is a coward, but he makes no pretense of bravery. Concerned only with survival, he advertises his cowardice and views heroism in any form as sheer nonsense. Told of Ajax "darin the litenin," he responds that "eny fool mout know the litenin wudn't mine him no more nur a locomotum wud mine a tumble-bug. An' then, spose hit hed met his dar, why durn me ef thar'd been a scrumshun ove 'im lef big enuf tu bait a minner hook wif." Although at times almost unreadable and, according to some critics, unrelated to any known dialect, Sut's speech serves as felicitous vehicle for the narration of his adventures.

Those adventures usually involve Sut taking revenge—often with the aid of livestock and hornets, his signature tools—on various people who have gotten on his bad side. Usually there is some logic to Sut's selection of victims. He delights in the degradation of his father, who on more than one occasion is reduced to the status of an animal; Parson John Bullen, a hypocritical bully who uses Sut as a moral object lesson; Sicily Burns, a comely lass who throws him over for a circuit rider; and most characters who represent authority and "civilization" generally. Along with his fellow scourge Simon Suggs, Sut Lovingood stands at the pinnacle of Southwestern humor's satiric strain.

Yet unlike Suggs, Sut shows little interest in money or self-advancement. His universe is essentially absurd, and his reaction is to strike out at it. On several occasions, he selects his victims arbitrarily. In "Sut Lovingood's Dog," Sut responds to a fracas involving his dog by looking "roun for sum wun tu vent rath on." Spying an innocent bystander who'll "do tu put it on enyhow," Sut punches the man, bites him "wher yer foot itches to go when yu are in kickin distance ove a fop," and places in his coattail a burning match that ignites a packet of gunpowder. The image of his hurt and bewildered antagonist haunts Sut, who calls it "the ungliest, scuriest, an' savidgest site I ever seed." Yet Sut's wrath is not yet fully vented; he announces to a nearby group that the man is a murderer with a large reward on his head, and watches him run out of sight with a mob "openin on his trail like a pack ove houns." The victim of a cosmic bad joke, Sut takes revenge and spreads misery where he can.

Sut's attitudes toward women exaggerate a misogynistic tendency found throughout Southwestern humor. Sut views Sicily Burns solely as a physical object, reducing her in a memorable backwoods *blason* to a collection of sexual characteristics: "Sich a buzzim! Jis' think ove two snow balls wif a strawberry stuck but-ainded intu bof on em." The social role of women as purveyors of order, security, and respectability is, for Sut, anathema; it is no coincidence that the archetypal female rite of Mrs. Yardley's quilting receives one of his signature visits. As a man of sensual appetite, the idea of marriage is as foreign to him as it would be to his dog.

Throughout Southwestern humor, civilization itself carries a feminine connotation opposed to the masculine world of the hunt, the horse swap, and the frontier. Two recurring character types further suggest the alignment of civilization, especially in its negative form, and femininity: the "charming creature" (Longstreet's name for the overly refined, socially destructive woman) and the dandy, the feminized upper-class male whose "city airs" make him the butt of many a prank. Although occasionally, as in *Major Jones's Courtship* and William Gilmore Simms's "How Sharp Snaffles Got His Capital and His Wife" (1870), the tension between the masculine world of hunting and camaraderie and the feminine world of marriage and family is resolved satisfactorily, the more common relationship is one of sustained opposition; to be a good fellow *and* a good husband is a rare feat indeed. Southwestern humor is, in sum, a genre dominated by the masculine homosocial bond.

The recurring theme of failed courtship further demonstrates this tendency. Usually narrated to a group of men, the courtship tale often involves a male protagonist whose attainment of a sexually desirable woman is prevented by a rival, a hostile father, a series of comic misadventures, or some combination thereof, and often concludes with the protagonist "lighting out for the territories" in one form or another. John S. Robb's *Streaks of Squatter Life, and Far-West Scenes* (1847) provides several variations on this form, the most notable of which is a sketch entitled "Nettle Bottom Ball." In this tale, a western miner named Jim Sikes recounts to the "boys" how he came to flee from Nettle Bottom, Illinois. Fearing that the citified clerks are attracting all the available women, including the narrator's sweetheart Betsy Jones, the boys of Nettle Bottom decide to hold a ball where they can "jest outshine the town chaps" before they "tare the hide and feathers off on em!" Unfortunately, when Jim goes to

pick up Betsy, she falls through a flimsy ceiling and lands naked in a plate of mush. His luck does not improve when he flees the house and attends the party, where his buckskin trousers, wetted in the fracas, begin to "shrink up an inch a minute." Humiliated and fearful of Betsy's father, he flees civilization until he crosses the "old Massissippi."

As the setting of "Nettle Bottom Ball" suggests, "Southwestern humor" is, strictly speaking, a misnomer. Although many of the major figures were associated with Alabama, Mississippi, and Louisiana, Robb and other contributors to the *Reveille* frequently wrote of the West, whereas eastern writers such as Longstreet and Thompson had little contact with the Southwest proper. What is fairly consistent in the genre is the presence of a frontier conceived as a boundary between nature and civilization. In many cases, the frontier marks not so much a boundary between East and West as between settled towns and the surrounding countryside; in other instances, the frontier is personified in the interaction between characters associated with civilization and nature. In the latter scenario, the issue of class typically emerges, since the character associated with nature usually lies outside, or stands opposed, to the kind of status afforded by social class. Indeed, many writers found a rich theme in the tension between stable, conservative, aristocratic class structures associated with civilization and the fluid, individualistic, meritocratic concept of status that predominated on the frontier. This interaction produced a basic set of character types through which the positive and negative aspects of society and nature are encoded. Insofar as the upper class is concerned, two basic types emerge: the gentleman, who wears his authority with grace, and the dandy, whose effete snobbery makes him a social threat. In addition to the frontiersman proper, who stands almost entirely outside of society, the lower class is represented by the poor white, whose contemptuous resentment of the upper class is linked with a barbaric temperament, and the yeoman or plain white, who recognizes the gentleman's authority but retains his pride and natural virtue.

Since virtually all of these authors came from the upper class, it is not surprising that most communicate implicitly what Taliaferro, in a sketch entitled "Larkin Snow, the Miller" stated outright: that "a man will fill the station for which he was designed by the Sovereign Master Overseer of mankind." Although the prohibition against class mobility remains largely intact, many works represent interclass relationships as cohesive and organic. In Alexander McNutt's stories, for example, the colorful hunters and yarn-spinners Jem and Chunkey work for a wealthy planter they call "Capting," but there is no evidence of either condescension on the one hand or resentment on the other. The same can be said of the relationship between Jim Doggett and the upper-class narrator of "The Big Bear of Arkansas." William Gilmore Simms's "Sharp Snaffles" goes one step further, as the literate narrator comes to understand that on the hunting expedition that he and his peers have funded, it is the backwoodsmen who control the situation "sixty miles beyond what the conceited world calls 'civilization.' " Although several gentleman narrators do view the lower class with amused and sometimes contemptuous condescension, the more common relationship is one of camaraderie and mutual respect. For its complex representation of social class, Southwestern humor remains an important resource for the study of antebellum southern culture.

The more important legacy of Southwestern humor is, of course, literary. Although often viewed by modern critics, somewhat anachronistically, as lowbrow, subliterary writing, Southwestern humor was recognized in its own time as a significant contribution to American letters. In an age of literary nationalism, critics attached few pejorative connotations to humor, and when Porter prefaced *The Big Bear of Arkansas* by claiming that a "new vein of literature, as original as it is inexhaustible in its source, has been opened in this country," he, like Poe in his review of *Georgia Scenes*, was not using the word *literature* as casually as many later critics have suggested. In retrospect, Porter's claim appears as something more than mere puffery. Two of America's greatest writers, Mark Twain and William Faulkner, show an immense debt to the genre, and Sut Lovingood is the ancestor of any number of characters in the work of Erskine Caldwell, Flannery O'Connor, Harry Crews, and others. In addition, Southwestern humor played a significant role in the development of literary realism and the short-story form in America. Perhaps most important, antebellum humorists were among the first authors to mine the rich vein of vernacular literature that would remain a distinctive and integral part of American and southern writing.

Scott Romine

See also Arkansas, Literature of; Tall Tale.

John Q. Anderson, ed., *Louisiana Swamp Doctor* (1962); Walter Blair, *Native American Humor, 1800–1900* (1937); Carolyn S. Brown, *The Tall Tale in American Folklore and Literature* (1987); Hennig Cohen and William B. Dillingham, eds., *Humor of the Old Southwest* (3rd ed.; 1994); Nancy Snell Griffith, *Humor of the Old Southwest: A Selected Annotated Bibliography of Primary and Secondary Sources* (1992); M. Thomas Inge, *The Frontier Humorists: Critical Views* (1975); Kimball King, *Augustus Baldwin Longstreet* (1984); William E. Lenz, *Fast Talk & Flush Times: The Confidence Man as Literary Convention* (1985); Kenneth S. Lynn, *Mark Twain and Southwestern Humor* (1959); Shields McIlwaine, *The Southern Poor White, from Lubberland to Tobacco Road* (1939); Milton Rickels, *George Washington Harris* (1965), *Thomas Bangs Thorpe* (1962); Constance Rourke, *American Humor: A Study of the National Character* (1931); James Atkins Shackleford, *David Crockett: The Man and the Legend* (1956); Merrill Maguire Skaggs, *The Folk in Southern Fiction* (1972); John Donald Wade, *Augustus Baldwin Longstreet* (1924); Norris Yates, *William T. Porter and the "Spirit of the Times"* (1957).

SPANISH-AMERICAN WAR

The Spanish-American War in the spring and summer of 1898 served to put the United States of America on the world map of major powers for the first time and also to join soldiers from both North and South in a common military cause and under one flag, thirty-three years after Appomattox.

Toward the end of *The Leopard's Spots* (1902), Thomas Dixon noted with patriotic fervor the union of North and South in battle: "Then came the trumpet call that put the South to the test of fire and blood. The world waked next morning to find for the first time in our history the dream of union a living fact. There was no North, no South—but from the James to the Rio Grande the children of the Confederacy rushed with eager, flushed faces to defend the flag their fathers had once fought." Although Dixon's commentary on history is reasonably apt, his vitriolic racism and aggressive white supremacy notions, which impel the narrative at almost every turn, figure prominently in the novel's harsh characterization of African American volunteers in the war.

African American writers from the South cast quite another light on the war. For example, James Weldon Johnson, in "The Color Sergeant—On an Incident at the Battle of San Juan Hill," both celebrated the heroism of a black soldier and lamented the way the soldier's valor was discounted because of his color. A North Carolina African American writer, James McGirt, developed a comparable pattern in his story "In Love as in War," from *The Triumphs of Ephraim*

(1907). McGirt's protagonist, Sergeant Roberts, achieves glory in battle at San Juan Hill, but later, in the Philippines, runs afoul of a white southern officer who uses the advantage of rank to try, albeit unsuccessfully, to best Roberts in an affair of the heart. Sutton E. Griggs, an African American novelist from Texas, in *The Unfettered* (1902) focused on the postwar situation in the Philippines, with Dorlan Warthell decrying imperialist action and achieving more freedom for himself as a result.

Because of the large-scale operation aimed at Cuba, the South served as a major staging ground for war activity against Spain. Journalists from all over the country flocked to Florida. The South was in the national spotlight, and southerners relished both the goals of the Cuban expedition and the attention it brought to their region. In 1898, Moses Koenigsberg, a Texas journalist who served briefly with the First Division of the Seventh Army Corps in Miami, produced *Southern Martyrs,* which detailed the experiences of Alabama white regiments in the war.

From the perspective of both distance and time, however, Mark Twain drew sharply critical conclusions about the Spanish-American War. In a series of short pieces—"A Salutation-Speech from the Nineteenth Century to the Twentieth, Taken Down in Short-Hand by Mark Twain" (1900), "To the Person Sitting in Darkness" (1901), "Battle Hymn of the Republic (Brought Down to Date)" (1901), "As Regards Patriotism" (1901), and even "The War Prayer" (1905)—Twain wrote with acerbic skepticism and dismay about the effects of the war, seeing the patriotic flag-waving as a cynical cover for imperialism and greed, most particularly evident in the American suppression of insurrection by Philippine natives once they had been liberated from Spanish control.

Owen W. Gilman Jr.

See also Racism; Twain, Mark.

James R. Payne, "Afro-American Literature of the Spanish-American War," *MELUS* (Fall 1983).

SPEECH AND DIALECT

The South is the region of the United States most associated with distinctive language patterns. Linguist Dennis Preston has shown in a number of studies charting the dialect perceptions of both southerners and non-southerners that the single perception that almost everyone agrees on is that the South, however they configure the region geographically, has a different way of using the English language.

Southern ways of speaking are also the most scrutinized. The South is the only region in the United States whose speech has inspired a scholarly, book-length annotated bibliography, already in a second expanded edition, as well as two important volumes of essays resulting from two major linguistic conferences focusing on language variety in the South. The sounds, vocabulary, and grammatical structures heard throughout the vast region are mapped in detail in the records of two enormous projects of linguistic geography, *The Linguistic Atlas of the Middle and South Atlantic States* (*LAMSAS*) and *The Linguistic Atlas of the Gulf States* (*LAGS*). In the three volumes of *The Dictionary of American Regional English* (*DARE*) that have appeared thus far, the labels *South* and *South Midland* are the most frequent regional designations.

Despite the widely held notion that there is a distinctive southern way of speaking, in fact there are many southern ways of speaking. The South is actually more diverse in speech than any other region of the United States and contains within its wide geographic sweep such noticeably different varieties of English as those spoken by watermen of Tangier Island in Chesapeake Bay, African Americans in the Low Country of South Carolina, small-scale farmers in Eastern Tennessee, upper-class speakers in Anniston, Alabama, urbanized young adults in Atlanta, Ninth-Warders in New Orleans, and Cajuns in southern Louisiana and East Texas.

On the basis of linguistic features correlated with geography, the South has traditionally been divided into at least two major dialect areas. The South Midland area covers the Piedmont and mountains of the Southern Appalachians; the Lowland South area runs along the Atlantic Coast and across the Lower South to Texas. But the linguistic atlas projects suggest that these two major dialects include at least eleven subregional varieties. In addition, geography is not the sole, and perhaps not even the most significant, factor contributing to the diversity of southern speech. Socioeconomic status and race are both important, as is population density. There may be as many as fourteen different dialects associated with southern cities, and *rural* versus *urban* has become an essential variable in the study of southern speech.

Despite the demonstrable linguistic differences among dialects of English spoken in the South, some features of pronunciation, vocabulary, and grammar are sufficiently widespread or remarkable to be characterized as representative of southern speech. Of course, not all speakers of southern English exhibit all these features, and many speakers of American English who are not southern exhibit some of them.

Foremost, because of its pervasiveness as a stereotype, is the southern *drawl*. Popularly characterized as slowness of tempo, nasality, elongation of vowels, or a combination of these features, the southern drawl has thus far eluded precise articulatory description. Linguists do know, however, that slower overall speech tempo is not a factor. Nor is the drawl a consequence of hot weather or a sluggish pace of life.

Other features of pronunciation associated with southern speech are easier to describe. Many southerners, particularly African Americans, do not pronounce /r/ after vowels, as in the words *hear, party,* and *over*. Attempts to represent the lack of /r/ in writing often substitute the letter *h*, as in *heah, pahty,* and *ovah*. But it is in vowels that southern dialects differ most noticeably from other varieties of English, and what is popularly called a drawl is probably due in part to the pronunciation of vowels. In a large portion of the South and for speakers of all socioeconomic ranks, the high and mid-front, lax vowels /I/ and /ɛ/ do not contrast before nasal consonants. These speakers lack the so-called *pin/pen* distinction, pronouncing both members of the following pairs the way that the first is pronounced in other parts of the United States: *mint/meant*; *since/cents*; *hymn/hem*. When positioned before nonnasal consonants, these lax vowels and others are often followed by a second vowel sound, producing pronunciations of words like *bit, bet,* and *bat* that are often parodied as two syllables. Some southern dialects also participate in a shift from /i/ to /e/ to /ay/. Thus *teal* is pronounced the way that *tale* is pronounced in other dialects, and *tale* is pronounced as *tile*. Likewise for *steel/stale/stile*; *kneel/nail/Nile*; *heat/hate/height*; and so forth. Furthermore, in some southern varieties, the diphthong /ay/ loses its second component and becomes a monophthong (/a/), resulting in a lack of contrast between *tide/Todd*; *tight/tot*; *time/Tom*; and so forth.

The diphthong /ay/ is subject to great dialect diversity throughout the English-speaking world, and monophthongal /a/ is just one of its variants in the South. Another is the stereotypical /oy/ pronunciation of the

Outer Banks of North Carolina, where the natives proudly refer to themselves as "Hoi Toiders" (High Tiders).

Dialects ordinarily develop a number of distinct words and expressions or assign different meanings or uses to already established words, and southern varieties are no exception. North Carolinians, for example, *tote* (carry) groceries home in a paper *poke* (bag) and *carry* (transport) an ailing friend to the hospital. They *mash* (press) buttons on appliances and use *case* (single coin) quarters, dimes, and nickels to buy a *coke* (any carbonated beverage) from a machine. They like *salad* (turnip greens, collard greens, poke salad, and other leafy vegetables) and threaten obstreperous children with a *hit upside the head*. In North Carolina, people who do not know how to dress or act appropriately are *tacky*. This sprinkling of vernacular vocabulary currently used in one southern state overlaps only in part with words and expressions used in other locales from Maryland to Texas. The linguistic atlases and *DARE* show that the region whose inhabitants consider themselves southerners is far from uniform in vocabulary. Some variation tends to cluster according to the two traditional divisions into South Midland and South, sometimes called Upland and Lowland. Thus *chigger* is generally used in the Highlands and Piedmont, and *red bug* is the norm in the Lower South. Other terms, for example *chill bumps,* are found scattered throughout the South alongside the national *goose bumps*. Other terms are quite local: *meehonkey,* a call used in the game hide-and-seek, appears to be used only on Ocracoke Island, North Carolina; and *neutral ground,* a grassy area in the middle of a street, is confined to New Orleans and adjacent areas.

The hallmark of southern vocabulary is the second-person pronoun *y'all,* sometimes *you all,* as in "I'd like to get a picture of y'all in front of the house." *Y'all* is heard throughout the South from speakers of all socio-economic and educational levels. It is also the regional marker most readily picked up by people moving into the region from elsewhere. It is a versatile colloquial form and is often used as a term of address, as in "Y'all, come see this." It is also unselfconsciously used in the possessive, as in "Is that y'all's new car?" *Y'all* is not simply a regional substitute for *you*. It incorporates connotations of friendliness, politeness, or inclusiveness lacking in the standard pronoun and suits southerners' self-image as hospitable people. A standard farewell in all kinds of service settings from fast-food restaurants to dry cleaners to upscale boutiques is "Y'all come back."

Some typically southern grammatical constructions allow speakers to add nuances of meanings to verbs. *Fixing to* conveys an intention to begin the action of the verb imminently, as in "I'm fixing to paint the wall white and get new cabinets." Double modal auxiliaries, most commonly *might could* and *may can,* add a degree of mental deliberation or tentativeness, as in "We might could go to a movie tonight." Two grammatical constructions usually listed as characteristic of the Appalachian region but also heard in other southern varieties, though perhaps less frequently, are *a-prefixing* and the *done perfect.* An initial unstressed syllable, usually spelled *a-,* is attached to the *ing* form of an action verb in the verb phrase, as in "That youngster is always a-whining about homework." The use of *done* before the past form of a verb indicates completed action, technically called *perfect aspect,* as in "You done missed your turn."

Just as Americans from outside the South perceive that southerners have a peculiar way of talking, so do southerners themselves. They often are of two minds about the way they talk. They are both attached to and self-deprecating about their dialect. Because a southern speech pattern evokes a complex stereotype, it serves as a source of identity and pride on the one hand and anxiety and insecurity on the other. Although many southerners do not object to their dialect triggering images of politeness, hospitality, and appreciation of heritage, they do not care for their speech to stereotype them as slow-witted, backward, or racist. Southern speech enjoyed favorable national attention in the early 1990s with the airing of Ken Burns's documentary *The Civil War.* The erudition and eloquence of Shelby Foote's commentary in his native Mississippi dialect confirmed southerners' pride in their linguistic heritage.

Southerners value the sounds and the emotional resonances of their language, particularly in performance settings. They admire storytellers, preachers, politicians, and others who use the language with skill and flair. Such privileging of the spoken word is in part a consequence of the dominant type of religion in the region, in which God touches humans through the names, proverbs, and stories of the Bible and also through people who can expound on the Bible or can testify in words to their personal experience of God.

The representation of colloquial language figures prominently in much southern literature. The outstanding example from the nineteenth century is *Uncle Remus: His Songs and Sayings* (1880) by Joel Chandler Harris, which records the sounds, words, and grammatical structures of Middle Georgia tales brought from Africa and preserved and developed orally by slaves. Although Harris is generally judged a skillful practitioner of literary dialect, the distortions in spelling and frequent use of apostrophe marks to show pronunciation sometimes strike contemporary readers as caricature. Many current writers continue to be essentially storytellers in the southern tradition, describing in palpable detail settings, characters, and events authentic to life in the South. They are no less concerned than was Harris to create in readers' minds the flavor and force of colloquial language. However, their strategies are less blatant. Writers such as Eudora Welty, Lee Smith, and Allan Gurganus capture the social subtleties of southern language practices in, for example, names and forms of address, politeness rituals, and variations in conversational styles conditioned by race, educational level, family status, and community expectations. In a story without a single contrived spelling, "A Hog Loves Its Life: Something About My Grandfather" (*White People,* 1990), Gurganus gives a contemporary version of an elderly storyteller and a young southern boy and the enduring power of the saying "like Lancaster's mule." The story begins with the epigraph "Language, like love, starts local."

Local ways of speaking long nurtured in the South are now being affected by changes in American society such as increased mobility, mass education, and urbanization. There is some evidence that younger, upwardly mobile speakers are adopting speech patterns different from the traditional local ones of their parents. Yet there is also evidence that, even as southern varieties are changing, some features are becoming or remaining distinct enough to serve as markers of southern identity.

Connie Eble

See also Accent; African American Vernacular English; Appalachia; Bible; Dialect Literature; Local Color; Preaching; Y'all.

Cynthia Bernstein, Thomas Nunnally, and Robin Sabino, eds., *Language Variety in the South Revisited* (1997); Frederick G. Cassidy and Joan Houston Hall, eds., *Dictionary of American Regional English* (3 vols., A–O, 1985–96); Norman Eliason, *Tarheel Talk* (1956); Crawford Feagin, *Variation and Change in Alabama English* (1979); Ellen Johnson, *Lexical Change and Variation in the Southeastern United States* (1996); William A. Kretzschmar et al., *Handbook of the Linguistic Atlas of the*

Middle and South Atlantic States (1994); Hans Kurath, *A Word Geography of the Eastern United States* (1949); James B. McMillan and Michael B. Montgomery, *Annotated Bibliography of Southern American English* (1989); Michael Montgomery and Guy Bailey, eds., *Language Variety in the South: Perspectives in Black and White* (1986); Lee Pederson, *Handbook for the Linguistic Atlas of the Gulf States* (1986); Dennis Preston, "The South: The Touchstone," in *Language Variety in the South Revisited* (1997); Walt Wolfram and Donna Christian, *Appalachian Speech* (1976); Walt Wolfram and Natalie Schilling-Estes, *American English: Dialects and Variation* (1998); Gordon Wood, *Vocabulary Change* (1971).

SPORTS LITERATURE

It is no accident that in *Cold Mountain* (1997) Charles Frazier narrates a Native American ballgame to define his leading character. He follows in the footsteps of Thomas Wolfe, Harry Crews, Louis D. Rubin Jr., Willie Morris, Frank Dobie, Richard Ford, and other noted southern authors who have used sports to develop plots, tell a story, describe a character, or trace history. Indeed, sport has been a major theme in southern literature and has been used extensively from colonial times to the present. From the roar of the bear, to the roar of "Bear" Bryant, to the roar of stock-car engines, sport is alive and flourishing in contemporary southern literature.

Sports literature in the South has accelerated as sporting opportunities have dramatically increased in American life. A southern accent is often pronounced, as in Andy Griffith's famous monologue "What It Was Was Football" (recorded in 1953). The first theme to emerge in sports literature in the American South was "Man Against the Frontier," a theme still present as late as Faulkner's "The Bear" (1942). Jennie Holliman's *American Sports 1785–1835* (1931) chronicles this major theme. The second theme is the rise of the "Sports Heroes and the Heroic Ideal," which lasted until the early 1950s. In his book *The Achievement of American Sport Literature: A Critical Appraisal* (1991), Lee Umphlett gives an excellent overview of the second phase. The South has been a significant force in a third phase, "Big-Time Collegiate and Commercial Sports." A large number of contemporary works attest to this theme. A good example is *The SEC: A Pictorial History of Southeastern Conference Football* (1979) by Bert Sugar. Some topics and themes, such as hunting and fishing, recur across all three time phases. For example, Charles Whitehead's

The Campfires of the Everglades; or, Wild Sports in the South (1991) develops the theme of the outdoor life extensively.

Prior to the late 1880s, sports literature in the American South emphasized Man Against the Frontier. This first theme contains two major subgroups, urban and rural. The urban subgroup features narrative accounts of sports practiced by the wealthy planters in and around Charleston, Savannah, Richmond, and New Orleans. These narratives reflect sports practiced in England that became common in the plantation era, included riding to the hunt, hunting clubs, cockfighting, and sailing. An early example of urban sports literature in the South is Irvin's *The South Carolina Jockey Club* (1857), which describes early horse racing in South Carolina. The rural subgroup of early sport literature in the American South characterized survival sports such as hunting, fishing, wrestling, or "the fight." Although hunting and fishing accounts can be found in both urban and rural narratives, there was a distinction based on one's standing in society. William Elliott's *Carolina Sports By Land and Water* (1846) illustrates the combination of urban hunting and fishing with the planters' approach to fishing.

The sports literature of the nineteenth century emphasized the forest and the frontier, or man against nature. The accounts describe hunting, fishing, horse racing, as well as the rough-and-tumble sports of rural areas of the South: bear hunts, wrestling matches, dogfights, cockfights—which often involved gambling. The place of the fight is portrayed in Augustus Baldwin Longstreet's *Georgia Scenes* (1835). In some fights, participants sought to put the opponent's eyes out by pressing thumbs into his eye sockets. William T. Porter edited *The Spirit of the Times: A Chronicle of the Turf, Agriculture, Field Sports, Literature and the Stage* (1957) for three decades prior to the Civil War. In addition, Porter edited two famous collections of humor and sports, *The Big Bear of Arkansas* (1854) and *A Quarter Race in Kentucky* (1846). George Washington Harris's *Sut Lovingood Yarns* (1867) captures the rural essence of early southern sport. Peter Hawker's *Instructions to Young Sportsmen* went through eleven editions from 1814 to 1893. Perhaps more than anyone else, Porter helped create the "Big Bear School of Humor," combining humor and sports life.

In the 1930s Thomas Wolfe, William Faulkner, and Robert Penn Warren utilized college team and field sports, contributing thereby to the second phase in sports literature, "Sports Heroes and the Heroic

Ideal." This theme focused on team sports in colleges and emphasized baseball, football, and the heroic ideal (man rising to the occasion when faced by insurmountable odds, and "snatching" victory from the jaws of defeat). Tennessee Williams in *Cat on a Hot Tin Roof* (1955) includes as a major character a former college football player. In *All The King's Men* (1946) by Robert Penn Warren, Governor Willie Stark's son Tom is a football player whose sport mirrors the political ambitions of his father and the compromises inherent in major college athletics. In *The Hamlet* (1940), Faulkner puts a comic spin on these realities by his portrayal of Labove. In *The Web and the Rock* (1939), Wolfe captured both the innocence of college football rivalries and the transitory nature of the glory they embody. Wolfe wrote rhapsodically and with intelligence about baseball in three novels: *Of Time and the River* (1935), *The Web and the Rock* (1939), and *You Can't Go Home Again* (1940). Wolfe captured that idyllic time in baseball before strikes and holdouts, asking "And is there anything that can tell more about an American summer than, say, the smell of the wooden bleachers in a small town baseball park?" Through his portrait of the famous baseball player Nebraska Crane, Wolfe also foreshadowed some of the future problems involved with professional sports. Crane transcends the temptation of professional sports because he is true to his Appalachian ethical heritage.

Grantland Rice began his career in the second phase of sports literature at the *Nashville Banner* and helped to usher in the era of "Big-Time Commercial Sports." Rice pioneered the art of mass-culture sports literature by his prolific publishing of prose and poetry. He contributed the most quotable sports quotation in modern sports literature ("When the one great scorer . . ."). Rice was a graduate of Vanderbilt University, as was James Dickey, another noted writer who preserved a modern version of the theme of Man Against the Frontier in his novel *Deliverance* (1970), which features overcoming natural and man-made obstacles. Dickey, who had played football at Clemson, used sports in numerous poems, for example, "The Death of Vince Lombardi."

The importance of Big-Time Commercial Sports is omnipresent in the mid- to late-twentieth-century South. NASCAR has thrived. The place of basketball in the psyche of Kentucky and North Carolina is legendary. With the growth of the Sunbelt economies has come a proliferation of professional teams throughout the South in numerous sports, including ice hockey.

The South provides opportunities for golfing year around. A proliferation of how-to articles, as-told-to biographies, and triumphs in these sports has followed.

From Talladega, Alabama, to Texas, and from Charlotte, North Carolina, to Japan, the lore and legend of the stock-car racer has been disseminated. Sylvia Wilkinson, author of *Stock Cars* (1981) and *In Dirt Tracks to Glory: The Early Days of Stock Car Racing as Told by the Participants* (1983) was one of the earliest serious writers on the stock-car racing industry. In *American Zoom: Stock Car Racing—From the Dirt Tracks to Daytona* (1993), Peter Golenbock provides an overview of the early history of NASCAR. Jerry Bledsoe, author of *The World's Number One, Flat Out, All-Time Great, Stock Car Racing Book* (1971) is also on the cutting edge of this movement in sports literature.

At the same time that NASCAR began to flourish, team sports also attracted mass appeal. H. G. Bissinger's *Friday Night Lights: A Town, A Team, and A Dream* (1990) is rapidly becoming a minor classic of the genre. It shows the controversial aspects of Friday-night football in Odessa, Texas, where high-school games often draw twenty thousand or more fans. Although Bissinger himself is not a native southerner, he illustrates the controversial aspects of big-time high-school sports in the South in a thought-provoking manner. In fact, the natives of Odessa, Texas, and Permian High School call him a traitor. Pat Conroy in *The Prince of Tides* (1992) uses a down-and-out football coach as the protagonist and utilizes football in several other novels. Peter Gent in *North Dallas Forty* (1973) points out the problems with professional football, beginning a series of attack-books that illustrate the problems associated with big-time sports, notably drugs and violence. A work that looks at the tensions of college athletic recruiting is Willie Morris's *The Courting of Marcus Dupree* (1992), one of his many sports books.

Louis D. Rubin Jr., like Thomas Wolfe, is a baseball aficionado. He has published a novel about baseball, *Surfaces of a Diamond* (1981), a collection of essays entitled *Babe Ruth's Ghost and Other Historical and Literary Speculations* (1996), and a monograph entitled *The Boll Weevil and the Triple Play* (1979). Each of these works heavily relies on baseball to recall childhood and illustrate baseball's status in America. Bill Kirkland's *Eddie Neville of the Durham Bulls* (1993) reflects the trials and tribulations of playing minor league baseball. A developing classic is Donald Hays's

The Dixie Association (1984), which provides its minor-league baseball teams with colorful names derived from southern literature. The book is filled with the expected heroic deeds of the pitcher.

Roy H. Parker in *The Final Four* (1981) introduces readers to big-time college basketball. An overview of the rise of a powerful college athletic conference can be found in Bruce A. Corrie's history, *The Atlantic Coast Conference: 1953–1978* (1978). This book reflects the hold that basketball has on North Carolina, Kentucky, and the rest of the Southeast. The heroic ideal in basketball is perhaps personified best by Michael Jordan's exploits, some of which have been published in George Beahm's *Michael Jordan: A Shooting Star* (1994). Jordan, from Wilmington, North Carolina, played basketball at UNC–Chapel Hill before starring for the Chicago Bulls and is universally acknowledged as the greatest player of all time. An example of a book that changed the course of sports is Peter Golenbock's *Personal Fouls* (1989). The book relates the furor over the lack of academic standards at North Carolina State University, culminating in coach Jim Valvano's resignation. A number of other books exist documenting the popularity of professional basketball in the South.

Although team sports made a large contribution to sports literature in the South, individual sports also received a share of the spotlight. Golf courses and golf literature have exploded simultaneously in the American South. Richard S. Tufts aptly documents the beginning of golf in *The Scottish Invasion* (1962). William Hallberg at East Carolina University has written *The Soul of Golf* (1997) and *The Rub of The Green* (1988), and has edited an anthology of golf-course lore entitled *Perfect Lies* (1990). Hallberg is joined in his efforts to appraise golf by William Price Fox, author of *Doctor Golf* (1994) and *Golfing in the Carolinas* (1990). Richard Coop addressed the psychological aspects of golf with *Mind Over Golf: How to Use Your Mind to Lower Your Score* (1995). Golfing and golf courses are recurring motifs in Walker Percy's fiction, highlighting a Sunbelt mind-set and postmodern artifice.

In *The Tennis Handsome* (1983), Barry Hannah created the quintessential postmodern sports novel set in the South, the zany action revolving around a tennis player and his coach.

Not only are team and individual sports the objects of contemporary sport literature, but so are the blood sports of yesteryear. Harry Crews, in *Florida Frenzy* (1982), explores the blood sports of cockfighting and dogfighting and uses sports in other titles such as *The*

Knockout Artist (1988). There is good reason that the University of South Carolina has a gamecock as its mascot. Indeed, the sports of cockfighting and dogfighting still exist in the Southeast. The major newspaper covering cockfighting in South Carolina is published to this day. Furthermore, romantic novels of the Old South and numerous tall tales are filled with stories of fortunes won and lost at the horse races, cock pits, and card tables. Faulkner's "Was" begins *Go Down, Moses* (1942) with a card game and a major gamble. Joel Chandler Harris begins "Free Joe and the Rest of the World" (1887) by creating a prototypical card gamester. In *Keeper of the Moon: A Southern Boyhood* (1991), Tim McLaurin describes a dogfight and reflects on its psychology.

In addition to blood sports, horse sports are still an important source of sports literature. The Kentucky Derby, the Camden Cup, the Blockade Run, and polo in Aiken, South Carolina, illustrate the South's continued love of fast horses. Elizabeth Blanchard and Manly Wellman's *The Story of America's Greatest Thoroughbred: The Life and Times of Sir Archie, 1805–1833* (1959) further illustrates the impact of horse racing on North Carolina and the entire South. Faulkner's last novel, *The Reivers* (1961), recounts the initiation of young Lucius Priest into the polarities of life; the boy's adventures culminate in a horse race.

Hunting and fishing stories have been staples in southern lore from colonial times to the present day. Clarence Gohdes's *Hunting in the American South* (1967) presents an excellent overview, as do the over seventy works of Archibald Rutledge, a poet laureate of South Carolina. *Hunting & Home in the Southern Heartland: The Best of Archibald Rutledge* (1992), edited by Jim Casada, anthologizes the prose used by Rutledge to describe hunting and fishing. *Hunting and Fishing in the Great Smokies* (1948) by Jim Gasque combines appreciation for the beauty of the mountains and the love of sports in the South. Buck Paysour in *Bass Fishing in North Carolina* (1977) displays the anglers' love of his sport. Stuart Marks in *Southern Hunting in Black & White: Nature, History and Ritual in a Carolina Community* (1991) provides an excellent collection of hunting stories. Havilah Babcock's *My Health Is Better in November* (1993) contains a series of hunting stories set in the South. In such works, southerners continue to be portrayed as an outdoors people.

Sports poetry has not been neglected in the American South. Archibald Rutledge, Michael McFee, James

Applewhite, Chuck Sullivan, Charles Eaton, Fred Chappell, and others have used poetry to describe sports. Don Johnson, editor of *Hummers, Knucklers, and Slow Curves* (1991), along with Robert Higgs, author of *Laurel & Thorn: The Athlete in American Literature* (1981), have gathered poems on southern sports. Gene Fehler, author of *Center Field Grasses: Poems from Baseball* (1991) uses poetry to tell the story of baseball, and *I Hit the Ball!* (1996) illustrates youth's love of baseball.

Not until the U.S. Congress passed Title IX did the South see significant change in the role of women's sports. The signs are numerous that change is underway. The University of North Carolina at Chapel Hill has established a dynasty in women's soccer, and women's basketball in the Atlantic Coast Conference (sometimes considered the best conference for basketball in the nation) has continued to attract fans and support, although the University of Tennessee's women's basketball team has established itself as the dominant national team from the South. Mia Hamm (legendary in UNC soccer) has become to women's soccer what Michael Jordan is to men's basketball. A literature reflecting the rapid growth of women's sports will surely follow. Opportunities for women in athletics prior to Title IX were primarily limited to cheerleading. Good examples of that activity as a reflector of gender inequities may be found in Lee Smith's *Black Mountain Breakdown* (1980), Jill McCorkle's *The Cheer Leader* (1984), and Bobbie Ann Mason's story "State Champions" (1989).

Sports literature has become very meaningful to a large group of southern writers. The Sport Literature Association (SLA), established in 1983, is housed at East Tennessee State University. The leadership of Don Johnson, Lyle Olsen, and Don Higgs at ETSU has helped establish a notable journal specifically related to sport literature. *Aethlon: The Journal of Sport Literature* has won plaudits and praise, both from its readers and librarians. The journal encourages new authors, serves as a critical analysis center, and promotes excellence and scholarship.

Ronald W. Hyatt

See also Horses and Horse Racing; Hunting; Sportsmen.

Robert J. Higgs, *Laurel & Thorn: The Athlete in American Literature* (1981); Wiley L. Umphlett, ed., *The Achievement of American Sport Literature: A Critical Appraisal* (1991); David Vanderwerken and Spencer K. Wertz, *Sport: Inside Out* (1985).

SPORTSMEN

The term *sport* refers to play or pastime, often in the form of a game or contest, and circumscribed by rules that are sometimes sanctioned by judges. Sports require the demonstration of physical prowess and skill according to established rules and are undertaken principally as a diversion for those taking part or for those observing. As the pursuit of evasive prey, hunting had its origins in an early human subsistence strategy. It became a sport as society developed its social structures and technologies, including the domestication of some forms of life to pursue others. Beginning in England, the Industrial Revolution brought about profound changes in hunting as a sport and in its terminology. As the privileged pursuit of prey with hounds from atop horses, "hunting" became an elite exercise that few could afford. On the other hand, "shooting" increased in popularity with the perfection of firearms and the breeding of specialized dogs to point, flush, and retrieve the "game," which increasingly became pen-raised birds. Although fox hunting continued around the estates in Britain, the larger and more "evasive" mammals ("big game") could be pursued only elsewhere on other continents. Whereas the animal sports of the gentry remained beyond legislative definition until recently (1998), the animal sports of the common man, such as cockfighting, bull and bear baiting, and rat fighting were considered barbarous and banned in keeping with a widespread desire on the part of city dwellers to curtail brutalities in animal sports.

A similar framework is useful for interpreting the activities of hunting sportsmen on the southern landscape since its colonization by large masses of British immigrants. Here *hunting* has retained its democratic sense as an activity in which anyone can participate, while everyone who pursues wild game today calls himself a "sportsman." Yet those who must hunt out of necessity and those doing so as a diversion remain as the discriminatory distinction.

In the Old South, the discriminating rules were developed by the planters, notably William Elliott of South Carolina. While most southern folk depended on some wildlife for food and as an economic resource, planters pursued game for other less-mundane purposes. Planters, such as Elliott, sought to emulate in the

New World the privileges and refinements in Old World field sports. They did so by continuing to give chase to the large game in their neighborhoods long after such forms had been extirpated in Europe and hunters there had turned to rearing and stocking birds. The sporting narratives of southern hunters were constructed in a way that was consistent with their views about human nature, society, and the world. In their hunting roles, planters saw themselves as decisive characters in relation to a much wider web of life that included many classes of humans as well as those of prey. As strong-willed actors in a world of order and stability structured through their own actions and activities, their hunting narratives were both personal and concrete.

Field sports were the domain of men, Elliott and the other planters clearly scripting in their narratives the roles of everyone on the playing field. Elliott called, or tried to limit, the shots in his backyard. Those asked to join Elliott on horseback as players were considered peers, while those remaining on the ground were designated lesser social beings who drove and collected his game. Different behaviors and diverse fields mirrored the social structure of the Old South and kept separate the various actors after the game. Mounted planters pursued game in broad daylight and became absorbed in their diversions while surrounded by retinues of servants and pedigreed hounds. Most other social groups hunted for table or for sale with whatever means they were most comfortable. Slaves took game mostly at night when they could afford the time to give the slip to their owners. The planter's harshest punishments were reserved for those caught taking "his" deer, especially in collusion with overseers and with unsanctioned means such as with spikes and by firelight.

Before the Civil War, sportsmen were comparatively few. These kept in touch by reading and contributing to *The American Turf Register* and *Spirit of the Times*, irregular periodicals that largely reproduced English sporting codes and standards for the New World. After the war, the spread of industrialization and urbanization beginning initially in the North and coming later in the South, together with improvements in transportation and firearms, created a desire among urbanites to return to the land and to their primitive pastime of besting the beasts. These developments, in conjunction with mass media and sporting journals, standardized expectations and behavior while changing the nature of the game for everyone. The age of the sportsman expressed itself through its various socioeconomic stars and stripes.

These sportsmen shared a particular world view defined by attitude, motivation, and affiliation. Such sportsmen pursued their quarries in a highly standardized manner, employed a technical vocabulary explicit about game and guns, showed a lively interest in natural history, personally followed a code of ethics, dressed fashionably during the quest, bought highly trained and pedigreed dogs, and belonged to cosmopolitan connections that established the rules they followed. Only certain prey could be legally taken and these only in a highly defined and refined manner. The objective of their games must be given the option to show that it truly understood fair chase.

As game became scarce at the turn of the twentieth century, sporting associations forced the hand of those who hunted for market, putting them legally out of business. Sportsmen's widespread clout in the political arena not only defined what was to be pursued as "game" (defining wildlife species in legal categories) but found the means by which paid referees (game wardens) policed the playing fields to enforce the new world views. The stakes of getting caught in violation by a warden were higher than those personal contests between the deer-hunting types of Uncle Isaac McCaslin and Roth Edmonds in William Faulkner's "Delta Autumn" (1942).

The life and diversions of southerners living in the late twentieth century bring new conditions and challenges to the wildlife game. With most southerners now residents and participants in urban life, they take greater stock in their pets as a vision of their world view than as targets for their practice. With most gaming fields (read habitats) now enveloped in the expanding suburbs and transected with ribbons of asphalt, turf upon which to exercise sporting skills has become hard to find. Furthermore, the sensibilities of most sportsmen have turned in other directions. Many of the game species formerly pursued in the backcountry are now found within the city limits, and an annual toll is taken as road kills and in property damage. Such changes will inevitably call for the setting of a different agenda along with new guideposts for southern sportsmen and -women yet to be.

Stuart A. Marks

See also Hunting.

William Elliott, *Carolina Sports by Land and Water; Including Incidents of Devil-Fishing, Wild-Cat, Deer and Bear Hunting,*

Etc. (1859); Stuart A. Marks, *Southern Hunting in Black and White: Nature, History, and Ritual in a Carolina Community* (1991); Robert Ruark, *The Old Man and the Boy* (1958); Archibald Rutledge, *Old Plantation Days* (1921).

STATES' RIGHTS

The phrase *states' rights* refers to the doctrine that states possess important rights of self-government that cannot be transgressed by the federal government. From Thomas Jefferson and John C. Calhoun in the early Republic to Sam Ervin and George Wallace in more recent times, the greatest champions of states' rights have come from the South. Although constitutional principles account in part for the South's historical devotion to states' rights, more often southerners have appealed to the doctrine to defend particular political, economic, or social interests.

Predating the U.S. Constitution, states' rights issues had antecedents in the colonial period. The struggles of the 1760s and 1770s between Great Britain and its North American colonies over taxation and trade regulation rested on different conceptions of federalism, or the balance between central and local authority, within the British Empire. The American Revolution pitted supporters of Parliament's power to legislate for the colonies against those who insisted that each colony should control its own internal affairs. Following the Declaration of Independence, leaders in the new states jealously guarded their powers of home rule and only reluctantly created a new central authority to replace Crown and Parliament. Under the first constitution of the United States, the Articles of Confederation (1781), the states instituted a weak general government while retaining enormous power for themselves. Representatives to the Confederation Congress acted as ambassadors with little except moral suasion to compel states to pay taxes or achieve consensus. Although the Confederation government accomplished more than its detractors claimed or than many historians have acknowledged, its inability to regulate commerce among the states and to perform similar functions led to calls for a new political order.

The Constitution of 1787 accorded new powers to the federal government, but it left the relationship between the states and the central government ambiguous at best and thereby opened the door to interpretive battles over its meaning. In the early Republic, Federalists and then Whigs construed the Constitution as a na-

tionalist document by which the people of the United States transferred most powers from the states to a strong central government. They argued that the "elastic clause" (article I, section 8) gave Congress broad powers to do anything necessary and proper for the national good. Jeffersonian Republicans and their Democratic Party successors countered that sovereign and independent states ratified the Constitution solely to create a general government for clearly specified and limited purposes such as overseeing defense, foreign policy, and interstate commerce. As Jefferson and James Madison argued in the Virginia and Kentucky Resolutions (1798–1799), the Constitution is a compact among the states and the federal government merely the states' agent.

During the antebellum decades, most southerners, even some avowedly nationalist ones like Calhoun, turned to states' rights to defend their economic and social life. Southerners relied on states' rights primarily because they could no longer exert their former influence in the federal government; for example, the slaveholding South's share of U.S. House seats fell from 46 percent in the 1790s to just under 38 percent in the last Congress before secession. Building on the compact theory of Jefferson and Madison, Calhoun declared that a state could nullify any federal law it considered unconstitutional and even secede from the Union at will. South Carolina endorsed that formulation of states' rights during the nullification controversy over tariff policy (1832–1833), but most southern states' rights supporters at that time considered nullification too extreme. Over the next quarter-century, however, alarmed by rising abolitionist and free soil sentiment in the North, southerners increasingly took refuge in Calhoun's ideas. Only a strong states' rights stand coupled with the threat of secession, they believed, could keep at bay a northern majority aligned against the slave South. When the Republican Party, created in the 1850s to protest the extension of slavery into western territories, succeeded in electing Abraham Lincoln president, southerners feared the worst. From December 1860 to May 1861, eleven southern states seceded from the Union rather than live under a federal government they considered hostile to slavery.

The Confederate Constitution recognized states' rights more explicitly than did the U.S. Constitution, but it did not wholly eliminate the ambiguities and tensions arising from the 1787 document. The Confederates' charter noted that each state acted "in its sovereign and independent character" in creating the new common government, but it remained silent on the right of secession from the Confederacy. Some southern governors, notably Georgia's Joseph E. Brown and North Carolina's Zebulon Vance, invoked states' rights principles to resist conscription and other wartime demands made by Confederate president Jefferson Davis. The governors' recalcitrance hurt the southern war effort, but certainly historian Frank Owsley went too far in declaring that the Confederacy "died of states' rights."

During the late nineteenth century and well into the twentieth, white southern politicians employed states' rights to justify white supremacist policies such as the disfranchisement of blacks and the enforcement of racial segregation in public accommodations. Southern governors even called out their state militias to oppose federal laws and court rulings favorable to blacks, as Orval Faubus and Ross Barnett did during the desegregation crises at Little Rock's Central High School (1957) and the University of Mississippi (1962), respectively.

The traditionally states' rights–friendly Democratic Party, which dominated the South after Reconstruction, served as the bulwark of white supremacy until some of its important nonsouthern constituencies began advocating equal civil rights for African Americans. When the 1948 national Democratic Convention adopted a civil-rights plank, southern delegates withdrew to form their own short-lived party. Significantly, these segregationists called themselves States' Rights Democrats (more popularly, "Dixiecrats") as they carried four Deep South states for their presidential candidate, South Carolina Governor Strom Thurmond. Permanent realignment followed as Democratic presidents John Kennedy and Lyndon Johnson pushed a civil-rights agenda resulting in the passage of the Civil Rights Act (1964) and the Voting Rights Act (1965). In 1964, Thurmond switched to the Republican Party, and over the next thirty years throngs of whites followed. By the 1990s, the GOP was the party of most white southerners and, not coincidentally, the defender of states' rights.

Although the history of states' rights in the South has been closely associated with racial control, the doctrine is not inherently racist. Rather, in our ambiguous federal system, states' rights is a weapon that political minorities of all stripes have wielded to protect their various interests against a national majority. Just as white southerners used it to maintain their legal privileges at the expense of African Americans, New En-

gland Federalists in the early nineteenth century resorted to states' rights to defend their property from a federal trade embargo. The delicate balancing act of federalism will likely persist under different guises. As Virginia-born Woodrow Wilson noted in 1908, the question of the proper relationship between the states and the federal government cannot "be settled by the opinion of any one generation . . . every successive stage of our political and economic development gives it a new aspect, makes it a new question."

Robert Tinkler

See also Confederate States of America; Nullification.

Richard E. Ellis, *The Union at Risk: Jacksonian Democracy, States' Rights and the Nullification Crisis* (1987); Don E. Fehrenbacher, *Sectional Crisis and Southern Constitutionalism* (1995); Kermit L. Hall and James W. Ely Jr., *An Uncertain Tradition: Constitutionalism and the History of the South* (1989); Alpheus Thomas Mason, *The States Rights Debate: Antifederalism and the Constitution* (2nd ed.; 1972).

STEEL MAGNOLIA

Steel Magnolia describes an ambiguous style of elite white southern womanhood melding genteel femininity with strength, determination, and intelligence. The term describes the contrast between the demure persona of the southern belle, who has the delicacy of magnolia blossoms, and the inner core of steel necessary to endure hardship.

The figure of the Steel Magnolia evolved during and after the Civil War, born of the collapse of the man's role as protector. Although the antebellum wife worked actively to manage her household, when the war took husbands away, the woman ran the farm or plantation, thereby gaining a power and self-reliance at odds with the modest, submissive ideal of the southern lady. When her husband returned, crushed by military defeat and his loss of power over the slaves, the woman retreated into her sheltered role as the man attempted to re-create the stability of the antebellum South, where the woman's subordination to her husband had paralleled the slave's subordination to the master. Likely, she celebrated the return to protection after the physically and emotionally grueling tasks of managing slaves and household under the dire conditions of war. The woman once again devoted her energies to charm and motherhood, although the war-born independence and sense of responsibility remained underneath her ladylike façade.

Southern writers have created literary representations of the Steel Magnolia to explore her balancing of feminine behavior and masculine control. In *The Unvanquished* (1938), William Faulkner portrays Rosa Millard, Granny, as the heroic, gutsy, hard-working moral center of the family during the Civil War. She outwits the Yankees to get her silver and mules back, and to protect the young Bayard and Ringo, she faces down a Yankee captain inside her home. While usurping the power of a plantation master, Granny continues her feminine responsibility of providing religious and moral instruction, praying for forgiveness for running a mule ring, and washing out with soap mouths that have lied or cursed, even though she lies herself to protect the children. Her mettle defines her as the archetypal Civil War Steel Magnolia. Another Civil War protagonist, Scarlett O'Hara of Margaret Mitchell's *Gone With the Wind* (1936), combines the feminine charm, sexuality, and vulnerability allowed southern women with a feisty self-reliance. Scarlett steps out of the domestic, compliant role for women, running Tara and a sawmill, ultimately becoming a business woman. Scarlett matures from a southern belle to a particular version of the Steel Magnolia, one whose ambivalence about motherhood and whose vacillation between her needs for dependence and independence show her creator's inside perspective of the confusion felt by intelligent, assertive women in a world expecting passivity.

Tennessee Williams's Amanda Wingfield provides another view of the Steel Magnolia. In *The Glass Menagerie* (1945), Williams portrays Amanda as a would-be belle whose husband's desertion mirrors the Civil War family's loss of the male as protector. Amanda believes charm and beauty will capture a gentleman caller for her daughter, but she also plays the masculine role of head of household. Although she openly challenges her son Tom, with the outsider Jim O'Connor Amanda reverts to feminine wiles, pretending to be frivolous and carefree. Williams's final stage directions, giving Amanda "dignity," honor her inner strength.

Robert Harling's 1987 play *Steel Magnolias* celebrates what is perhaps a masculine view of the Steel Magnolia, the self-sacrificing mother supported by a community of emotionally strong women. Recalling the antebellum notion of motherhood as a woman's sacred occupation, this play defines good southern womanhood as desiring and loving a child. Diabetic Shelby knowingly sacrifices her health to have a baby; when her kidneys fail, her mother gladly gives one of her kidneys to her daughter. When Shelby's body ultimately deteriorates, M'Lynn alone watches her daughter die after doctors remove the life-support machines. Shelby's husband and father leave the room. It is M'Lynn who organizes the funeral, and it is her women friends, not her husband or son-in-law, who linger at the grave to comfort the grieving mother. M'Lynn expresses the irony that the men, who are supposed to be made of steel, cannot endure witnessing Shelby's death. In 1989 Tristar Pictures made Harling's off-Broadway play, which was based on the death of his sister and set in his home state of Louisiana, into a major motion picture starring Sally Field, Olympia Dukakis, Shirley MacLaine, Julia Roberts, and Dolly Parton.

A variation of the Steel Magnolia figure may be seen in Katherine Anne Porter's "The Jilting of Granny Weatherall" (1930). A resilient woman, Granny Weatherall is a nurturing mother who raises her children alone after her husband's death and puts up fences herself when she has no man to do it. Although not of the elite social class, Granny possesses a practicality and dignity born of surviving tribulation. She lives in the tradition of the strong but feminine southern woman who maintains a ladylike, mostly deferential public self while sustaining a private strength.

Rebecca G. Smith

See also Belle; Lady; New Woman.

Drew Gilpin Faust, *Mothers of Invention: Women of the Slaveholding South in the Civil War* (1996); Anne Goodwyn Jones, *Tomorrow Is Another Day: The Woman Writer in the South, 1859–1936* (1981); Diane Roberts, *Faulkner and Southern Womanhood* (1994).

STOICISM

Many members of the eighteenth-, nineteenth-, and early-twentieth-century southern upper class, whatever their true bloodlines, saw themselves as counterparts of the established Old World aristocracy, particularly that of England, and sought to imitate the values, tastes, manners, and education of the English gentry. This education was "classical," involving the reading of a number of the literary, oratorical, and philosophical works of ancient Greco-Roman culture—both in the original languages and (especially with Greek works) in translation. A number of the most widely read works were those that promoted the values of the school of philosophy that perhaps more than any other distilled the essential elements of classical thought—Stoicism. Founded in Athens around 301 B.C. by Zeno "the Phoenician," Stoicism was brought to Rome by the philosopher Panaetius around 146 B.C. There it was powerfully articulated in several of the philosophical treatises of the great Republican orator Cicero and adopted by such major thinkers and writers as Epictetus, Seneca, and Emperor Marcus Aurelius, becoming the dominant Roman school for at least two centuries. Stoic cosmology affirmed that however evil or chaotic the world might appear to be, the universe was ordered for the best by a pervasive rational spirit or energy, the Logos. Stoic ethics, the crux of its philosophy, encompassed the "cardinal virtues" of prudence (wisdom), fortitude, justice, and temperance and were designed to inculcate a rational self-control that would allow a person to face all of life's difficulties and apparent evils with serene moral constancy or apatheia.

Despite Stoicism's affirmation of the equality of all human beings as possessors of the divine reason and will, the Stoic advocacy of courageous adherence to duty and of disciplined avoidance of the passionate irrationality of the multitude held a natural attraction for those who occupied seats of honor in classical and later Western culture—upper-class men. The upper-class Englishmen after whom American southerners modeled themselves had found for centuries a special appeal in the ethical teachings of Cicero's *Duties,* Epictetus's *Discourses* and *Manual,* Seneca's *Moral Essays* and *Epistles,* and Marcus Aurelius's *Meditations,* and in classical literature portraying the unswerving fortitude of Odysseus, Hercules, and Aeneas and the urbane dispassion of the Horatian gentleman-poet.

The political and economic turbulence that often plagued the nineteenth-century South, along with its need in the antebellum period to characterize its slave-based agrarian life-style as part of a larger, beneficent order, may have given the region a special impetus for cleaving to Stoic teachings. At any rate, prominent southerners through the generations, from Thomas Jefferson to Robert E. Lee to William Alexander Percy, continued to read Stoic texts and embrace recognizably Stoic values. Nor was the nineteenth-century South's intense fascination with the romantic chivalry of Sir Walter Scott wholly inconsistent with its attraction to Stoicism. Transmitted by a number of means into medieval European culture, Stoicism powerfully influenced the chivalric code of honor and its later incarna-

tions in succeeding centuries. Despite its inconsistency with crucial aspects of Christian doctrine, Stoicism worked together with Christianity to refine some of the grossness out of the militant clan loyalties and vendettas of primitive honor.

The honor code of the southern gentleman as it is represented in the sentimentalized literature of the nineteenth-century South and in the great works of the Southern Literary Renascence and afterward in the twentieth century owes a great deal to Stoicism. In Marse Chan of Thomas Nelson Page's sentimental nineteenth-century story, who greets the rejection of his romantic love with unflinching gallantry; Colonel John Sartoris of William Faulkner's *The Unvanquished,* who, closely pursued by Yankee troops, coolly jumps his horse out a back window of his own barn; Atticus Finch of Harper Lee's *To Kill a Mockingbird,* who at the risk of his reputation and his family's physical safety defends African American Tom Robinson from trumped-up rape charges and refuses to respond with violence to Bob Ewell's public insult; and Emily Cutrer of Walker Percy's *The Moviegoer,* who rails persuasively against the faithlessness and moral degradation of mid-twentieth-century America, the reader is observing literary embodiments of Stoic courage, self-control, justice, and moral commitment.

The other part of the story, however, is the decline of this old order of moral values amid the cultural turmoil of the modern world, a decline recorded in the quixotic futility of the Stoic knighthood of John Crowe Ransom's "Captain Carpenter"; the moral impotence of Horace Benbow in Faulkner's *Sanctuary;* the moral compromise of Judge Irwin in Robert Penn Warren's *All the King's Men* and of the elder Lamar of Percy's *Lancelot;* and the anguished suicide of Quentin Compson in Faulkner's *The Sound and the Fury* and of the elder Barrett in Percy's *The Last Gentleman* and *The Second Coming*—suicide being a recognizably Stoic solution. Characters such as Will Barrett, who in the wake of the old code's failure must search desperately to avoid despair and suicide themselves, are an additional fictional manifestation of this decline, although characters in more-recent southern literature who lack any inkling of moral meaningfulness seem even worse off. The dissolution of the old southern socioeconomic hierarchy and the advance of scientific naturalism, which, ironically, is quite consistent with the rational-empirical bent of Stoicism, are portrayed by Faulkner, Warren, and Percy as significant reasons for this decline, although Percy's fiction asserts that trying to live ethically without faith in a forgiving, redeeming personal God is an inherently vulnerable position, even for the most courageous and constant of Stoics.

Wendell (Whit) Jones Jr.

See also Honor; Novel, 1900 to World War II; Novel, World War II to Present; Quixotism; Violence.

Edward Vernon Arnold, *Roman Stoicism* (1911); Marcia L. Colish, *The Stoic Tradition from Antiquity to the Early Middle Ages* (2 vols.; 1985); James McBride Dabbs, *Who Speaks for the South?* (1964); George Fenwick Jones, *Honor in German Literature* (1959); Walker Percy, "Stoicism in the South," *Commonweal* 6 (July 1956); Bertram Wyatt-Brown, *The House of Percy: Honor, Melancholy, and Imagination in a Southern Family* (1994).

STORYTELLING

Twentieth-century southern writers have told many of this country's most vital stories. William Faulkner's use of multiple narrators raises the question: how many people does it take to tell about the South? A good many, certainly, for the South's story is among the most complex on the globe. Cultural psychoanalyst Robert Coles observes that stories, which he calls the word made flesh, plunge readers into a world of meaning, a world it is tempting to ignore, full as it is of pain and pettiness, frailty and downright evil. But Coles believes that ignoring it is to pay a high spiritual price. Sages from Aristotle to Robert Penn Warren have recognized that real stories (as opposed to those generated by movies or TV) transform those who tell them and those who read them. As the only way to see the inner lives of others, stories can save readers from self-absorption and meaninglessness, ignorance, and despair.

Faulkner's *Absalom, Absalom!* tells the story of Thomas Sutpen's wresting his one hundred miles from the "tranquil and astonished earth." The narrators, beginning with Miss Rosa Coldfield and going on with Quentin, Mr. Compson, General Compson, Henry Sutpen, and Charles Bon, reveal more than any other single work the South's secret history. Without doubt, Faulkner is the first storyteller equal to the moral weight of the story. He evokes the archetypal image of storytelling: Quentin and his father out on the gallery in the wisteria summer, smoke from the old man's cigar intermingling with the sickly sweet of the purple blooms to echo the beauty and horror of what really

happened. Comic relief comes when Wash Jones shouts, "Henry has done shot that durn French feller. Kilt him dead as a beef."

Another storyteller, Elizabeth Spencer, is a master of allusion. She avoids Faulkner's grandeur even as she portrays the rise of a ruling class in *Fire in the Morning*. Young Kinloch can't stomach his father's submission to insults and injuries when there's a land-grab going on, and not until his Cousin Randall Gibson traces the story back two generations do readers fathom Dan Armstrong's reasons as well as Spencer's complex theme: evil passed through generations in violence and revenge becomes invisible. Spencer satisfies readers' craving for the inside story even as she leaves much shrouded in mystery.

Other stories seem to tread more lightly. Tim Gautreaux's "Little Frogs in a Ditch" shows old man Fontenot and his grandson Lenny arguing on the front porch as Lenny schemes to trap and sell common pigeons as homing pigeons. Lenny's real story comes out—that his parents dumped him and moved to another time zone—after he bilks old man Lejeune and his crippled grandson. Old Lejeune then tells the story at the climax, using Lenny's cheating to redeem its meanness. Even small stories examine moral issues and become microcosms. Real stories trace the playing-out of forces beyond their characters' control as well as their writers', who infuse them with what wisdom they can muster.

Lee Smith believes storytellers start in the dark and encounter the light, perhaps creating it as they go. All good stories are, in her sense, explorations. Smith's work abounds with people telling stories on porches. *Oral History*'s Little Luther swings to and fro and strums his dulcimer at his newly met granddaughter Jennifer, who asks Ora Mae for the story of her "real" mother's people. Ora Mae won't say a word. It's Granny Younger who begins the tale that transports the reader to Hoot Owl Holler where it all began, years ago, the story of Almarine's love for witchy Emmy and saintly Pricey Jane, Richard Burlage's doomed passion for Dory, the doom that comes down to murder, death, and Amway in the present. There's humor at the heart of many deep stories.

Eudora Welty has a double-barreled talent—as both storyteller and critic. She likens stories to "little worlds," each with its own "atmosphere," and believes that "characters in the plot connect us to the vastness of our secret life, which is endlessly explorable" (*The Eye of the Story*). Her stories show the seamless and humorous surface of small-town life while revealing a world in ironic opposition. Her story "The Wide Net" shows William Wallace Jamieson with a note from his pregnant wife Hazel, who threatens to drown herself because he stayed out all night. Only after he stays out most of another night dragging the river and having a high old time with his buddies do William Wallace and Hazel sit on the front steps to reconcile their stories. The reader knows at once that they will make up; only an after-image shows the unbridgeable gap between them. Stories, Welty tells us, reveal "the vulnerability of human imperfection caught up in human emotion, and so there is growth, there is crisis, there is fulfillment, there is decay."

Missing pieces are often found at middles and ends of novels. Marianne Gingher's *Bobby Rex's Greatest Hit* could not proceed without flashbacks to tell five stories: how Phoebe met Bobby Rex, how Pally's parents met and married, how Speedy died, why Shilda's mother left her, and why she had an affair with the Reverend Von Wicke. Gingher's North Carolina voice has a cadence unlike those from South Carolina, Georgia, or Virginia. Perhaps only a southerner can understand just how different each state is from the rest.

For every Toni Morrison who tells enough sad slave stories in *Beloved* to prove that there never were good slaveowners, anywhere, there is a scion of the plantation to agree with Thomas Jefferson that slaveowning was no great character builder for whites either. New Orleans's Nancy Lemann writes about people who, by sacrificing their vitality for charm over several generations, constantly have "breakdowns" and "fall apart." In their morbid dependency her characters betray their slaveowning roots. In *Sportsman's Paradise*, Lemann names her heroine Storey, perhaps to emphasize the importance of stories. Living among southern expatriates at Orient Point on Long Island, Storey meets her old love, Hobby Fox. An odd formality keeps them mysteriously apart, and not until Storey tells the story, at the book's climax, of a dishonorable deed in their past can the lovers find their way toward each other.

Fred Chappell's storytellers sit on porches or in front of fires sipping whiskey and telling stories about things that often don't come to much, but may feature Betty Grable as Helen of Troy in a re-telling of the *Iliad*. Stories are told in kitchens, on horseback, camping out, in restaurants, in the parking lot of the twenty-four-hour Wal-Mart, anywhere. Pam Durban's "Gravity" is set in a nursing home. Whenever the old lady's wheelchair faces the Cooper River bridge, Louisa

knows her mother will tell her "the Mamie story" again, about the needless terror inflicted on an old servant. Here one sees white callousness, and the trickle-down consequences of slavery for both races as well.

African American voices, from slave narratives to postmodern novels, are essential to the dialogue. Richard Wright, James Baldwin, and Ralph Ellison redeem brutal stories with art. Black women have done as much. Alice Walker's *The Color Purple* tells stories that go to the heart of poor country people. Zora Neale Hurston tells the story of her own metamorphosis: the day she became "colored" she found it out "in certain ways" and asserts with bravado, "But I am not tragically colored." Her evolution ends with a cosmic identity in which all racial colors are part of God's grab-bag ("How It Feels to Be Colored Me"). Gloria Naylor makes use of the tales and storytelling tradition of the Sea Islands off the coast of Georgia and South Carolina in *Mama Day,* which tells "the legend of Sapphira Wade . . . the way we know it, sitting on our porches and shelling June peas." Air-conditioning and television have cost the South many stories as well as occasions for telling them.

Part and counterpart, black and white writers follow a long tradition of tracing the way the past works itself out in the present. Perhaps they are popular because they avoid abstractions. The mind of the South is a vernacular one: southern writers make a story, not a statement, about what happens. Stories are how people remember, how they come to understand. As Eudora Welty says, "Remembering is so basic and vital a part of staying alive that it takes on the strength of an instinct of survival, and acquires the power of an art" (*The Eye of the Story*). From Lee Smith, who never saw an African American until her teens, to Faulkner himself, rooted in Greek tragedy, the South needs every single voice. From Appalachia to plantation, from merchant to sharecropper to fugitive slave and African king, all their tales together cannot exhaust the South's hoard of meaning.

Nancy Tilly

See also Advice on Writing Southern Fiction; Community; Faulkner, William; O'Connor, Flannery; Past, The; Telling about the South; Welty, Eudora.

W. J. Cash, *The Mind of the South* (1941); Robert Coles, *The Call of Stories* (1989); Fred Hobson, *Tell About the South* (1983); Robert Penn Warren, "Why Do We Read Fiction?" in

New and Selected Essays (1989); Eudora Welty, The Eye of the Story (1978).

STOWE, HARRIET BEECHER

A daughter of the prominent New England Protestant clergyman Lyman Beecher, Harriet Beecher Stowe was the author of the phenomenally best-selling and influential antislavery novel Uncle Tom's Cabin and a prolific writer of other social and historical novels, regional sketches, domestic, religious, and political essays, and children's literature. Born in Litchfield, Connecticut, in 1811, she moved with her family to Cincinnati in 1832 after her father accepted the presidency of Lane Theological Seminary. She first became aware of controversy over slavery during this time, when Theodore Dwight Weld and other Lane students rebelled against Beecher's lukewarm antislavery position—he supported colonizing blacks to Africa—and left the seminary. Harriet Beecher married Calvin Stowe, a professor of theology at Lane, in 1836, the year of major anti-abolitionist riots in Cincinnati. During the mid-1830s she had begun writing for newspapers and magazines; she published her first antislavery sketch, "Immediate Emancipation," in 1845. After Calvin was appointed to a chair at Bowdoin College, she moved to Brunswick, Maine, in 1850; and in 1851, outraged by the Fugitive Slave Law provision of the Compromise of 1850, she began working on Uncle Tom's Cabin, which was serialized over ten months in the National Era and published as a book in the spring of 1852. The novel promptly sold out its first printing, selling 300,000 copies in its first year, and over 1 million by the end of the decade. The vast majority of these copies were purchased in the North and overseas.

Influenced by her reading of slave narratives by Frederick Douglass, Josiah Henson, and other former slaves, and by her reading of abolitionist tracts, such as Weld's Slavery As It Is (1839), Stowe depicted slavery as an iniquitous institution that separated mothers from children, husbands from wives, and generally wreaked havoc on the black and white family. Through her use of direct address, she attempted to make her readers identify with the plight of the novel's embattled slaves. Sharing the views of her sister, the well-known domestic theorist Catharine Beecher, she depicted benevolent white women as having the potential to regenerate America by wielding moral influence within the home. But slavery ultimately proves to be insurmount-

able for most of the women in the novel, in a world in which slaveholders like Simon Legree have absolute power to torture and kill their slaves, such as the Christ-like martyr Uncle Tom. Clearly concerned about the plight of the black slaves, Stowe's descriptions nonetheless reveal that she followed the racialist thinking of the time in regarding blacks as essentially different from whites (they are depicted as more passive and domestic) and perhaps not even particularly well suited for citizenship in the United States. The novel ends with the major black characters either dead or choosing to emigrate to Africa. Although Stowe's biblical typology suggests that the South can be regarded as the land of Pharaoh, she hardly demonizes southerners: Legree and several other of the novel's slaveholders are former northerners, and slave trading is shown to yield money for New York investors and thus to be part of a national economy. Stowe's novel can be read as an attack on capitalism and patriarchy as much as a specific attack on the South. Overall, what most concerns Stowe is the blasphemous nature of slavery, the way it allows people to assume a God-like relationship to other people. In the manner of a sermon, her novel calls on all Americans to diminish their potential for sinning by abolishing slavery.

Not surprisingly, response to Uncle Tom's Cabin in the South was swift and furious, as numerous reviewers assailed Stowe for what they regarded as her libelous attacks on the South's cherished institutions. According to George F. Holmes, who reviewed the novel in the October 1852 Southern Literary Messenger, Stowe failed to see that it was precisely the institution of slavery that was responsible for producing such a perfect slave as Uncle Tom. In the July 1853 Southern Quarterly Review, William Gilmore Simms was even more vitriolic in his criticism of the novel, joining Holmes in arguing that Uncle Tom's saintliness testified to the positive value of slavery, and attacking Stowe personally as a depraved individual (as evidenced by the fact that she dared to write about sexual and political matters). Simms also argued that it was unfair to use the literary form of the novel, a fiction, to proffer social criticism. Nevertheless, Simms and other southern writers quickly concluded that the most effective argument against the representation of the South in Uncle Tom's Cabin would be to offer their own counter-representations. The period thus saw the rise of Anti-Uncle Tom literature, which included over twenty novelistic responses, most notably Simms's Woodcraft (1852), Mary H. Eastman's Aunt Phillis's

Cabin (1852), Maria J. McIntosh's *The Lofty and the Lowly* (1853), Caroline Lee Hentz's *The Planter's Northern Bride* (1854), and Thomas B. Thorpe's *The Master's House* (1855), and also an important poetic response, William J. Grayson's *The Hireling and the Slave* (1856). These works generally portrayed benign slave masters and contented slaves who thrived in the familial, paternalistic framework of the plantation.

In *A Key to "Uncle Tom's Cabin"* (1853), Stowe's documentary effort to authenticate her novel by adducing its sources in slave testimony, newspaper accounts, legal trials, and the like, Stowe emphasized the dangers of granting absolute power to the slave master, and she warned of the hazards of developing a dissolute class of poor whites unable to find work because of the existence of slavery. As opposed to her support for African colonization in the final chapters of *Uncle Tom's Cabin,* she concluded *A Key* with a vision of blacks becoming responsible U.S. citizens. She took up similar themes in her second antislavery novel, *Dred: A Tale of the Great Dismal Swamp* (1856), set in the Carolinas, which depicts tyrannous white slave masters with unlimited power, a drunken and racist white rabble that offers its support to these masters, and a number of active and intelligent white and black characters who are committed to the cause of antislavery. The title character, Dred, an escaped slave hiding out in the swamps with other escaped slaves, was modeled on two important black southern leaders: Denmark Vesey, who attempted to lead a slave rebellion in Charleston, South Carolina, in 1822; and Nat Turner, whose bloody slave revolt in Southampton County, Virginia, in 1831 continued to haunt the white southern imagination. Stowe's sympathetic embrace of Dred's revolutionism marked a significant shift in her thinking and may have spoken to her anger at the 1856 caning in Congress of the Massachusetts senator Charles Sumner by the South Carolina congressman Preston Brooks. The southern response to *Dred,* a book far more critical of the region than *Uncle Tom's Cabin,* was mostly a determined silence, though in 1858 the *Southern Literary Messenger* printed a review by an anonymous "Young Lady of New England" that attacked the Beecher family for its alleged history of immoral beliefs and actions.

From her Christian millennialist perspective, Stowe regarded the Civil War as a holy war that promised to redeem the United States by bringing about the end of slavery. At the conclusion of the war, Stowe initially maintained that Confederate leaders, whom she sus-

pected of masterminding Lincoln's assassination, should be punished for their disloyalty. However, influenced by her brother Henry Ward Beecher, she adopted a more moderate position on the importance of (white) northerners working together with (white) southerners to heal the nation. Her desire for sectional unity led her to retreat somewhat from her support for black elevation in the United States. Convinced that it would be precipitous to give emancipated black men the right to vote before they were better educated, she initially opposed the adoption of the Fourteenth Amendment. Shortly after the amendment's passage, however, Stowe moved to Florida and began to publish essays, eventually collected in *Palmetto-Leaves* (1873), on the importance of improving blacks' economic opportunities in the South. She thought that southern whites should participate in these efforts, and in 1869, with the help of funds from British donors and the Freedmen's Bureau, she founded what she hoped would be an integrated school for black and white children in Mandarin, Florida. But after running the school for several months, she succumbed to local pressure and segregated the classrooms.

Stowe's failure to develop an integrated school mirrored the failures of Reconstruction. With the return of Jim Crow laws and the renewal of southern sectional pride, many southerners continued to regard *Uncle Tom's Cabin* with contempt. The late nineteenth and early twentieth century saw a renewal of Anti–Uncle Tom novels, the most notable examples being Thomas Nelson Page's *Red Rock* (1898) and Thomas Dixon's *The Clansman* (1905), which served as the literary source for D. W. Griffith's seminal film *The Birth of a Nation* (1915). A defense in part of the Ku Klux Klan, Griffith's film was very much admired by at least one prominent Virginian, Woodrow Wilson, who had written in *A History of the American People* (1902) that *Uncle Tom's Cabin* had not been true to the many positive aspects of slavery. In *Life and Labor in the Old South* (1930), the influential southern historian Ulrich B. Phillips similarly criticized Stowe for having exaggerated the evils of slavery.

According to Stowe's friend Annie Fields, who first reported the anecdote in *Life and Letters of Harriet Beecher Stowe* (1897), published a year after Stowe's death, Abraham Lincoln remarked to Stowe during her 1862 visit to the White House: "So you are the little lady who made this great war." She may not have actually "made" the war, but few writers have been more influential in developing the iconic significance of

North and South and addressing the problem of slavery and race in America.

Robert S. Levine

See also Abolition; Novel, 1820 to 1865; Plantation Fiction; Women Writers, 1820 to 1900.

Elizabeth Ammons, ed., *Critical Essays on Harriet Beecher Stowe* (1980); Jeanne Boydston, Mary Kelley, and Anne Margolis, eds., *The Limits of Sisterhood: The Beecher Sisters on Women's Rights and Woman's Sphere* (1988); Thomas Gossett, *"Uncle Tom's Cabin" and American Culture* (1985); Joan D. Hedrick, *Harriet Beecher Stowe: A Life* (1994); E. Bruce Kirkham, *The Building of "Uncle Tom's Cabin"* (1977); Robert S. Levine, *Martin Delany, Frederick Douglass, and the Politics of Representative Identity* (1997); Ellen Moers, *Harriet Beecher Stowe and American Literature* (1978); Eric J. Sundquist, ed., *New Essays on "Uncle Tom's Cabin"* (1986); Jane Tompkins, *Sensational Designs: The Cultural Work of American Fiction, 1790–1860* (1985); Edmund Wilson, *Patriotic Gore: Studies in the Literature of the Civil War* (1962); Forrest Wilson, *Crusader in Crinoline: The Life of Harriet Beecher Stowe* (1941).

SUBURBS AND SUBURBAN LIFE

After World War II, southern farmers, like farmers in other regions earlier, moved increasingly to the cities in order to find jobs, recreation, and educational opportunities. By 1980, however, city dwellers had become disillusioned with problems connected to urban life: pollution, crime, traffic, and high cost of living. Like northern cities, southern cities in the second half of the twentieth century have experienced "white flight," leaving decaying, poor urban centers populated mostly by minorities. The jobs and the white population moved to the suburbs. One result was that schools that had been desegregated by law in the 1960s became again segregated by geography. In addition, southern suburbs became attractive to the many retirees and young educated professionals (yuppies) from the North who headed south in search of a warmer climate and a more relaxed way of life (particularly after the advent of air-conditioning). The South by the 1970s earned the descriptor "Sunbelt," an area encompassing Virginia through the Carolinas, Georgia and Florida, and across the Gulf states to the Southwest.

The suburbs—residential areas beyond "downtown" limits of large cities—sprang up by taking over farmland and drained money from urban infrastructures. The mass construction of new homes that

seemed indistinguishable from one another, as well as the rise of strip malls and the migration of northerners to these areas, has caused concern over the loss of a unique southern culture, including language and literature. Traditionally, critics have defined "southern writing" through the works of such authors as William Faulkner, Robert Penn Warren, Eudora Welty, and Flannery O'Connor; their work, replete with southern idiom, is concerned with southern history and its impact on the family and draws upon the plantation or small-town past. More recent writers, however, express an interest in the post-agrarian South, with its urban and suburban landscapes and the influx of a nationalized popular culture. At issue, then, becomes the question of whether there remains a definable "southern" style of literature.

The apparent lack of southern consciousness in the writing of some post-1960s southern writers has challenged critics to redefine *southern* in relationship to national culture. Although Richard Ford was born in Jackson, Mississippi, and spends part of his time in New Orleans, only one of his works, *A Piece of My Heart* (1974), takes place in the South. *The Sportswriter* (1986), and its sequel, *Independence Day* (1995), for example, take place in New Jersey suburbs, New York City, Michigan, New Hampshire, Vermont, and Florida. Ford's main character, Frank Bascombe, enjoys the anonymity and comfort that suburban life provides even though a sense of this anonymity carries over into his personal relationships. Bobbie Ann Mason's work describes the increasing suburban sprawl in the South and the corresponding encroachment of popular culture. Her short stories and novels take place mainly in Kentucky and show the influence of television and popular music. "Graveyard Day," a representative story, explores the conjunction of impermanence in modern society with the desire for family and a traditional way of life. *In Country* (1985) describes a girl's attempt, in a changing South, to find her identity through her ancestry; representations of her heritage take the form of competing geographies, rural and suburban. Anne Tyler, who grew up in Raleigh, North Carolina, set her first three novels in the South, but the rest of her work occurs in urban or suburban Baltimore, a borderland between North and South. Works such as *Dinner at the Homesick Restaurant* (1982) and *Breathing Lessons* (1988) emphasize the complexity of family relationships in anonymous, colorless city neighborhoods.

Other contemporary writers have remained more

specifically southern in their writing even while they describe the changes taking place in the region. Josephine Humphreys's novels *Dreams of Sleep* (1984) and *Rich in Love,* (1987) take place in and around Charleston. In *Rich in Love*, a teenage girl fights to keep her family together in the face of changing expectations for women and definitions of family. Although Lee Smith's work mainly addresses Appalachian culture, such novels as *Family Linen* (1985), *Fair and Tender Ladies* (1988), and *The Devil's Dream* (1992) also describe the conflict between the traditional Appalachian culture and a new suburban society. Jill McCorkle from the small town of Lumberton, North Carolina, addresses similar issues in her writing; in *Tending to Virginia* (1987), for example, a southern woman faces conflicts within herself and her family as she rises in social class and economic status and moves geographically from a small-town rural area to a more suburban setting.

For African American writers, the differences between the Old South and the new, modern South can signify the differences between races as well as social or economic classes. For example, John Holman's *Squabble and Other Stories* (1990) address the confrontation of upwardly mobile African Americans with racial prejudice, the differences between poor and middle-class African Americans, and issues of heritage for African American southerners. Marita Golden's "A Woman's Place" (1997) explores the lives of a Muslim couple who have achieved economic success and consequently struggle with the meaning of happiness and the importance of family.

Jennifer A. Haytock

See also Cities; K Mart Fiction.

Peter Applebome, *Dixie Rising: How the South Is Shaping American Values, Politics, and Culture* (1996); William J. Cooper Jr. and Thomas E. Terrill, *The American South: A History* (1991); Dewey W. Grantham, *The South in Modern America: A Region at Odds* (1994); Fred Hobson, *The Southern Writer in the Postmodern World* (1991); Jefferson Humphries and John Lowe, eds., *The Future of Southern Letters* (1996); Linda Tate, *A Southern Weave of Women: Fiction of the Contemporary South* (1994).

SUNBELT

The term *Sunbelt* did not achieve widespread usage until the 1970s, but the social and economic changes that precipitated its coinage began with the post–World War II transformation of the South. For many years economically inferior to the industrialized North, the South also battled a self-image as a racist, benighted, poverty-stricken, rural region inhabited largely by uneducated denizens who resisted change. Several forces eroded this image, thereby granting the region a face-lift, an improved identity as the Sunbelt, land of opportunity and growth.

The 1930s and 1940s provided a context in which the South's economy and population could diversify. Hastened by the Great Depression and New Deal farm policies, commercial agriculture in the South replaced tenant farming and sharecropping. Industry also boomed as the South became more urbanized. Crucial to the South's urban growth was the influx of military bases and defense industries. Advanced communication and transportation systems necessarily accompanied this postwar transformation. Southern states began to resemble their northern counterparts more closely; both regions spawned shopping malls, fast-food chains, and apartment complexes, linked together by bypasses and interstates.

To encourage development, southern leaders lobbied for funding from the federal government, and after the passage of civil rights and equal rights laws, learned quickly that one way to insure their region's economic growth was to make the South a place easily inhabitable by whites, blacks, and women. In order to attract and facilitate corporate and commercial investments, southern leaders also devoted themselves to improving educational and technological facilities. Many states marketed areas surrounding their state universities as prime locations for industrial parks. Cheaper land, lower taxes, a minimal labor-union presence, and enthusiastic leadership enticed northern industries and workers to the South. The widespread availability of air-conditioning was, of course, instrumental in drawing people from other areas to the region, and such climate control further intensified the South's attraction as a pleasant place to live year round.

Indeed, by the 1970s, Americans who lived outside of the South began to be exposed to what might be called an extensive public-relations campaign. In 1975 Kirkpatrick Sale, a Manhattan journalist, described an area ranging from North Carolina to Southern California, what he called the "Southern Rim," as a region of tremendous economic significance. In 1976 the *New York Times* ran a series of articles all centered upon the concept of the "Sunbelt South." The very flexibility of the term *Sunbelt* and its connotations of optimism and prosperity displaced less-complimentary associations with the Confederacy, slavery, and ignorance. Magazines such as *Southern Living* depicted a new breed of upper-middle-class southerners who lived in lovely homes, enjoyed their spacious gardens, and ate delicious meals comprised of native southern bounty. Meanwhile, Bobbie Ann Mason, Richard Ford, Barry Hannah, and other writers populated their fiction with characters bereft of family ties who identified themselves less by region and more by occupation (or lack thereof), a cast of characters virtually rootless in comparison to some of their southern literary predecessors. Other writers such as Jill McCorkle, Anne Tyler, Ernest Gaines, and Alice Walker continued to redefine and modify old constructions of "community" and "family."

The Sunbelt South, though vastly improved from its earlier incarnation, did not rid itself entirely of rural poverty or other problems that had long beset the region. Despite population and industrial growth, the South, with the exception of a few states, lagged behind the national average in terms of per-capita income in the 1980s. Nonetheless, many changes successfully wrought a highly visible image of the South as the Sunbelt, a burgeoning region still ripe for dwelling and tourism. In the 1990s, the South boasted another economic boom made manifest by an increasing number of jobs and an undeniable influence in national politics.

Elinor Ann Walker

See also Civil Rights Movement; New Deal; New South; Regionalism; Sharecropping; *Southern Living*; Tenant Farming; World War II.

Peter Applebome, *Dixie Rising: How the South Is Shaping American Values, Politics, and Culture* (1996); Numan V. Bartley, *The New South, 1945–1980* (1995); Dewey W. Grantham, *The South in Modern America: A Region at Odds* (1994); Raymond A. Mohl, ed., *Searching for the Sunbelt: Historical Perspectives on a Region* (1990); Kirkpatrick Sale, *Power Shift: The Rise of the Southern Rim and Its Challenge to the Eastern Establishment* (1975); Bruce J. Schulman, *From Cotton Belt to Sunbelt: Federal Policy, Economic Development, and the Transformation of the South, 1938–1980* (1991).

SUNDAY SCHOOL

The roots of the Sunday school go back to eighteenth-century England, when Robert Raikes (1736–1811)

had success in correcting lawless behavior of Gloucester children on Sundays by engaging women teachers to give instruction in reading and then catechism. The experiment quickly spread to other parts of the country and to Wales. In 1785 the Sunday School Society was formed, followed in 1803 by the Sunday School Union.

In the United States during the nineteenth century, for many Protestant congregations Sunday schools became important in the church's configuration of its mission. In denominations where the catechism tradition is not strong, the flavor became biblical and often evangelical. Baptists and Methodists—the major denominations in the South—had not accented catechisms, and Sunday schools were their counterpart to the training that Lutherans and Catholics might receive in established catechisms. As Tom Sawyer's Aunt Polly knew, sending a child to Sunday school was an important step in training a child in the way he should go.

Sunday schools have had their own evolution. At first, the Bible was the primary text, but denominations developed various aids to assist the teachers whom they enlisted to instruct: illustrated tellings of the Bible stories in simple language, and later quarterlies for older children and adults; vibrant music accompanying plenary sessions that opened and concluded a Sunday's gathering. Creating Sunday school literature became an important denominational responsibility. Sunday school picnics were one device to make Sunday school "fun."

In the twentieth century, fundamentalist Christians have retained in their Sunday schools the biblical emphasis that mainline churches have replaced. Some mainline churches have preferred the designation "Church School"—distancing themselves from the fervor of nineteenth-century Sunday schools. For Baptists and Methodists, Sunday schools often became important for adults as well as for children; parents were admonished to take, not send, their children to Sunday school. Sunday school was to be—and still sometimes is—a habit for life, as the case of President Jimmy Carter illustrates. In the twentieth century, Protestant churches supplemented the efforts of their Sunday schools by developing Vacation Bible Schools, which usually run from one to two weeks during the summer. Following the integration of public schools in the 1960s, fundamentalist churches in the South increasingly developed Christian schools, which give religious as well as academic instruction, providing the biblical instruction that Sunday schools and church services deemed sufficient in earlier times.

Although Sunday school has been part of the experience of many southerners, its portrayals in literature have not been numerous. But a few have been memorable. In his *Narrative of the Life of Frederick Douglass* (1845), Frederick Douglass describes a Sabbath school like that founded by Raikes, in that the teaching of reading was central to the curriculum—and different from what "Sunday school" usually conveys. A very young Douglass was the teacher to a class that reached over forty students. A decade later, Douglass wrote: "I look back to those Sundays with an amount of pleasure not to be expressed. They were great days to my soul. The work of instructing my dear fellow-slaves was the sweetest engagement with which I was ever blessed." For his readers, Douglass was careful to use his account of the school for polemical purposes to an audience that knew Sunday school in other contexts: "These dear souls came to Sabbath school not because it was popular to do so, nor did I teach them because it was reputable to be thus engaged." Douglass anticipates later satire of the Sunday school for the reputable by Sinclair Lewis in *Babbitt* (1922).

Later, Sunday school would be useful for humor and parody. In his "Story of a Bad Little Boy" (1865), Mark Twain parodied Sunday school literature. A sample: "But the strangest thing that ever happened to Jim was the time he went boating on Sunday, and didn't get drowned, and that other time that he got caught out in the storm when he was fishing on Sunday, and didn't get struck by lightning. Why, you might look, and look, all through the Sunday-School books from now till next Christmas, and you would never come across anything like this."

In one of the most successful episodes of *The Adventures of Tom Sawyer* (1876), Twain captured the Sunday school experience from the boy's point of view. The episode underscores the importance of memory of biblical texts as a goal of the mid-nineteenth-century Sunday school and Tom's failure to produce the knowledge he pretends to have. The scene also reveals that the Sunday school contest has become a device to produce loyalty and enthusiasm. For Tom and the other children, the Sunday school is mainly a social event—made bearable because so many of the children he knows are present. Although Tom embarrasses himself on the particular Sunday that Twain shows, the setting becomes the scene of a later triumph when Tom is able to observe his own funeral from the balcony.

In *Adventures of Huckleberry Finn* (1885), Tom's irreverence toward Sunday school is caught early when he and his "gang" seek to rob "a parcel of Spanish merchants and rich A-rabs"—disrupting what in reality is a group of young children on a Sunday school picnic. How much Sunday school Huck might have had to endure while living with the Widow Douglas is unclear, but Twain shows her sister Miss Watson attempting to correct the deficiencies of Huck's religious education.

In the twentieth century, Thomas Wolfe in *Look Homeward, Angel* (1929) described with irony and some affection the Presbyterian Sunday school and its effect on his protagonist. But not many memorable depictions of Sunday school have come from the South. As noted, midwesterner Sinclair Lewis mocked the liberal Sunday school experience in *Babbitt*. Late in the century, John Irving from the Northeast made Sunday school scenes an important element in *A Prayer for Owen Meany* (1989), a work that has resonated with many southerners. Satire and humor are not the main thrust of Irving's depiction, as they are with Twain and Lewis.

Joseph M. Flora

See also Bible; Bible Belt.

Kenneth Scott Latourette, *A History of Christianity,* Vol. II: *Reformation to the Present* (Rev. ed; 1975); Sally G. McMillen, *To Raise Up the South: Sunday Schools in Black and White Churches, 1865–1915* (2002).

T

TALK (GOSSIP)

To understand how talk is so important to southern literature, one need only listen to Eudora Welty as she explains the origin of her fiction in the classic *One Writer's Beginnings* (1983). Early in life, she spent a great many hours listening to talk all around her; so much so that when it was in danger of not occurring, she cajoled it into surrounding her once more. Sitting in the backseat of their car between her mother and a neighbor, she would remind them as they began their outing, "Now *talk*." She continues, "Long before I wrote stories, I listened for stories. Listening *for* them is something more acute than listening *to* them. . . . Listening children know stories are *there*. When their elders sit and begin, children are just waiting and hoping for one to come out, like a mouse from its hole." Russell Baker, in his memoir *Growing Up* (1982), describes his own similar experience as listening "for talk . . . that had gone on for years." Elders who talk and children who listen are (or *were* in the days before television and video) indigenous to any region of the country, it's true. But whereas talk in other regions exists to inform, to instill, to connect, and to maintain, talk in the South is also a cultural feat of ordering—the world is ordered, history is ordered, one's daily life is ordered through the telling and re-telling of *what happened*. It is not enough to have witnessed an event and recount the facts of it; it's the *story* of the event that matters.

Telling the next version of it simply brings it into the reality of people's lives, puts it in perspective, makes it palatable, or at least comprehensible, no matter how lurid or cruel. There is comfort in the sounds of women talking over her cradle that Kaye Gibbons's narrator remembers so vividly in *A Cure for Dreams* (1991). There is cruelty in the women's stories that Harry Crews remembers in *A Childhood: The Biography of a Place* (1978)—women's stories, he says, particularly scare him; unmitigated by humor, they tell the truth about things that others hide. There is, on the other hand, unmitigated pleasantness in the tales of Mrs. Jolene B. Newhouse, of Lee Smith's small story "Between the Lines" (*Cakewalk*, 1970), a small- (very small) town columnist who reorganizes the news to, as she calls it, "uplift my readers if at all possible." For example, once she was through with it, a news item might read, "Mrs. Alma Goodnight is enjoying a pleasant recuperation period in the lovely, modern Walker Mountain Community Hospital while she is sorely missed by her loved ones at home." Jolene explains, however, "I do not write that Alma Goodnight is in the hospital because her husband hit her up the side with a rake and left a straight line of bloody little holes going from her waist to her armpit after she yelled at him, which Lord knows she did all the time, once too often." Does she lie?

No, says Welty. Lying is not the point of embellishing a story. The point is to imagine it as it fits the landscape of our lives. Hence her character Laurel's frustration with the funeral talk in *The Optimist's Daughter* (1972); as story after story comes out about her father, as he lies in his coffin immune and yet vulnerable to it all, she protests that they misrepresent him—he was never any of those things, she believes, and is insulted to find others exaggerating or mixing his life up with someone else's, someone they wished he would be, or wished, at least, themselves to be. Southern talkers do get as carried away by the telling as a listener (or reader) will be; for evidence, Welty refers us to her own "Why I Live at the P.O." (*A Curtain of Green*, 1935) as the beginning of a long canon of stories in which the first-person narrator is overtaken by her own words, the most poignant example being Miss Katie Rainey throughout *The Golden Apples* (1949), the most humorous Edna Earle Ponder of *The Ponder Heart* (1953).

On the other hand, silence, the absence of talk, is a danger to culture. Think of Faulkner's silent ones—Abner Snopes in "Barn Burning" (1939), his few words more lethal than his acts. Think of Carson McCullers's *The Heart Is a Lonely Hunter* (1940), built around the wordless powers of two mutes and the impact they have on people who talk, talk, talk—as one of the mutes, Mr. Singer, thinks—but never communicate a thing except their own obsessions. For there is talk, and then there is *talk*. In the first, words rattle like the empty bones of a dead carcass; in the second, words resound like the lessons to your whole life—they come back to you over and over again when you seem most in need of their advice, and mean differently depending on age and wisdom and what you are ready to accept. One southern character remembers her mother sitting at the table—her husband inches from a psychiatric breakdown, her daughters in peril of their identities—carrying on a whole evening's talk by herself; she thought it her duty to keep conversation from lapsing.

Lee Smith's *Oral History* (1983) has an interesting variation of this as its theme. Naïvely, a young student agrees to look into the carefully kept silence about her forebears for her teacher, a folk historian. What she finds (the little) and what she does not find (the volumes that come out in silence) make up a bizarre history of people whose private sorrows and successes will never really be known by anyone, especially this sheltered child. But the privileged reader hears chapters of voice after voice, each rich in its interior remembrances, that tell eavesdroppers everything. The academics may call it "oral history," but everyone else knows it as just talk.

Rachel V. Mills

See also Oral History; Storytelling.

TALL TALE

The tall tale might be defined as a lie, told initially as truth, but with an escalating pile-up of preposterous details until it has reached the point of incredulity—in effect, an extended practical joke. The teller usually treats it as an anecdote about something that has happened to him or to someone he knows—all the while keeping a straight face. Ideally, the listener, at first innocent, becomes slowly aware that he is being taken in, but goes along with the often elaborate set-up, and

ends up laughing at both the story and his own gullibility. Anyone who has lived in a rural area, particularly in the South, has been a victim, willing or not, of this type of storytelling.

The tall tale, throughout its long history, has most often recounted exploits in uncharted territory, as when Othello tells Desdemona of a far-off place where there are "men whose heads / Do grow beneath their shoulders," and Gulliver records his adventures in the land of the Lilliputians and Brobdingnagians.

America, of course, became the ultimate unknown territory with its vast sweep of wilderness, and the tall-tale hero quickly found a place in its literature. At first the rustic defender of American democracy against the foppish Britisher, he became, as the country moved westward, the rough-hewn backwoodsman, "tough as hickory and long-winded as a nor'wester." Along the Ohio River, Mike Fink could ride a moose as if it were a horse and drown an attacking she-wolf by holding it under water. In Kentucky, Davy Crockett could tie together the tails of two buffalo, build a fire by scraping his knuckles across flint, and "put a rifle-ball through the moon." The exploits of both, as well as those of other frontiersmen, gained wide acceptance through almanacs, stories in magazines, newspapers, anthologies, and "autobiographies," one of which was written by Crockett himself.

From the 1830s to the Civil War, this rough and rugged frontiersman was brought to earth and changed into a ne'er-do-well who lived not by his physical prowess but by his wits. He was set to political purpose by the Old Southwest humorists, who used him to argue against Andrew Jackson and the extension of suffrage by laying out for the reading public what they saw as the savagery of those who were acquiring the right to vote. Longstreet's Ramsey Sniffle, for example, goads his fellow backwoodsmen into fights in which they tear off each other's noses, ears, and bits of cheek. Johnson Hooper's Simon Suggs believes that "one should live as merrily and as comfortably as possible at the expense of others." And George Washington Harris's Sut Lovingood sets out to inflict pain on others as a way of vengeance for the near-starvation of his childhood. During the war, Harris created broadly satirical portraits of Lincoln as a cowardly idiot, at one point comparing him to a dead frog stretched out of shape.

One of the most famous of the tall tales, "The Big Bear of Arkansas" (1841) by Thomas Bangs Thorpe, introduces the character Jim Doggett, from Shirt-tail Bend, who, aboard a steamboat, tells his citified audience about Arkansas, where everything is oversized, including mosquitoes and bears. When you shoot one of the latter, he tells the audience, "steam comes out of the bullet hole ten feet in a straight line." The story he relates of a hunt that lasts three years apparently inspired Faulkner's "The Bear."

After the war, the image of the backwoodsman was sentimentalized in southern literature by local-colorists such as Joel Chandler Harris and Mary Murfree, and the crafty, rough-hewn rogue of Longstreet and Harris was forced westward, where he maintained life, though not quite so brutal, in such characters as Pecos Bill and in stories by Mark Twain.

The tall tale also gained new life in southern literature in the 1930s and 1940s. We see it in the fiction of Erskine Caldwell, with his depictions of poor whites who share the animalistic qualities of George Washington Harris's characters; in William Faulkner, with his numerous episodes of the Snopes clan, in particular the "Spotted Horses" segment in *The Hamlet* (1940) and the escaped-mules escapade of *The Town* (1957); in Eudora Welty's grotesque portrayals of poor whites in *The Ponder Heart* (1953) and *The Optimist's Daughter* (1972); in nearly all of Flannery O'Connor's stories; and to a lesser extent, in Robert Penn Warren's rendering of Buck Tewksbury in *A Place To Come To* (1977). Fred Chappell, in such novels as *Brighten the Corner Where You Are* (1989), is perhaps the best contemporary purveyor of the tall-tale tradition.

Meanwhile, the oral tale has maintained a vigorous life, as documented by Vance Randolph in *We Always Lie to Strangers* (1951), Patrick Mullen in *I Heard the Old Fisherman Say* (1978), and Loyal Jones and Billy Edd Wheeler in *Laughter in Appalachia* (1986).

Duane Carr

See also Crockett, Davy; Hillbilly; Old Southwest; Ozark Mountains; Redneck.

Walter Blair and Hamlin Hill, *America's Humor: From Poor Richard to Doonesbury* (1978); Carolyn S. Brown, *The Tall Tale in American Folklore and Literature* (1987); Franklin J. Meine, *Tall Tales of the Southwest* (1930); Constance Rourke, *American Humor: A Study of the National Character* (1931).

TEACHER

An agricultural society based on slavery, the Old South fostered a well-educated ruling class but did little to promote formal education for the masses. The models across the society were home schooling and private education, though in the early national period the ideal of public education began to gain force in the South and nationwide.

In 1845 James Henry Hammond in his *Letter to an English Abolitionist* countered the charge that the South lagged in education. He stressed the leisure of the slaveholders for books and learning and noted that the U.S. presidency had been held by a southerner in forty-four of fifty-six years. Hammond's argument had a certain validity, but a hundred years and more later, the South would still be seen as lagging far behind other regions.

In the Old South, some effective teachers doubtless contributed to the achievements of the region's leaders, but their portrayal did not make it into the literature. Slaves who learned to read and write were self-taught or instructed in the home-schooling model with the assistance of, usually, a compassionate mistress.

Frederick Douglass first received instruction in reading and writing from Sophia Auld, but he had to desist because her husband thought reading and writing would make him unfit to be a slave. Thereafter, Douglass was self-taught. In his slave narrative, he describes teaching fellow slaves to read and write in Sunday school.

In the postbellum South, public education was two-tiered, one system for whites and one for blacks. And after the war, southern writers began to realize the possibilities of school and the teacher for their art. Mark Twain caught the flavor of frontier and rural schools in *The Adventures of Tom Sawyer* (1876), and generations following have identified with Twain's portrayal of the dynamics of the one-room school. Tom's teacher is, of course, male. When Tom arrives late to class, the "master," as Twain pointedly calls him, is dozing. Jarred by the excitement in the classroom when Tom arrives, the master demands an explanation from Tom. When Tom reports that he had stopped to talk with Huckleberry Finn, he is in serious trouble and gets a sound beating—such discipline being then standard procedure in schools. The scene is basically good humored, meant to alarm no reader. Following the beating, Tom is told to go sit with the girls. There he starts his courtship of Becky Thatcher, which makes good progress until the master decisively turns Tom's attention back to the tedium of study. The episode became a treasured one for generations of readers, as did a later school scene when Tom, this time innocent, takes a beating to spare Becky. In *Adventures of Huckleberry Finn* (1885), Twain gives one instance of the home-schooling model as Miss Watson grills Huck.

In *Marse Chan* (1887), Thomas Nelson Page also depicts a schoolhouse romance that is vital to his story. The treatment might owe something to *Tom Sawyer,* though Page doesn't match Twain's skill with school scenes. Marse Chan is Mr. Hall's best scholar, as the loyal Sam explains, "an' Mr. Hall he wuz mighty proud of 'im. I don't think he use' to beat 'im ez much ez he did du urrs, aldo' he wuz de head in all debilement dat wen on, je' ez he wuz in sayin' his lessons."

Twentieth-century southern writers gave teachers more than cameo performances. As an apprenticeship novel, Thomas Wolfe's *Look Homeward, Angel* (1929) gives much attention to Eugene Gant's formal schooling. Eugene begins his education in public school, but at age twelve wins entrance to the Altamont Fitting School and there is taught by Mr. and Mrs. Leonard. Although the portrait of Mr. Leonard is decidedly satirical, Wolfe calls Mrs. Leonard Eugene's "spiritual mother." In addition to offering a significant portrayal of Eugene's schooling as a young boy, Wolfe's novel holds a place among the nation's important "college" novels, giving detailed (often satirical) portraits of several professors at the state university. Wolfe's novel is overtly autobiographical, and the sources behind the teachers have all been identified.

Richard Wright's *Black Boy* (1945) describes much the same period as Wolfe's novel. An autobiography cast in the shape of a novel, Wright's book carries the subtitle *A Record of Childhood and Youth.* Although Eugene often feels thwarted by the circumstances of his life, his difficulties are dwarfed when set beside those of young Richard. Briefly, for Richard there is a counterpart to Eugene's Mrs. Leonard when his grandmother boards the young schoolteacher Ella, who kindles his imagination with the book she is reading and talks with him about the excitement of books. But Richard's grandmother banishes this potential "spiritual mother." Instead, Richard is subjected to the tyranny of his aunt, who teaches in the church school he must attend. Guile and deception are necessary for Richard to discover the books that Ella forecast he would read.

Zora Neale Hurston was more fortunate than Wright in her educational experience. In her autobiography *Dust Tracks on a Road* (1942), she pays ardent tribute to Dwight Holmes, the teacher who first showed her the power of literature and made her re-solve that "I shall be in it, and surrounded by it, if it is the last thing I do on God's great green dirt-ball."

William Faulkner's fiction uses southern education as a minor motif. Although the Compson children go to school, Dilsey's children and grandchildren do not. Nor, it seems, do most of the Snopeses get many days in school. But Faulkner hilariously suggests the circumstances of the education they might have found. In *The Hamlet* (1940), Eula Varner attends public school, where she is taught by Labove, whose talents with football had been an asset for the University of Mississippi, though Labove scarcely understood the game. He seems to have emerged from some tall tale. Hopelessly in love with Eula, Labove endures agonizing frustration because of his feeling for Eula, the sexual magnet of the hamlet. When he gropes awkwardly toward her one afternoon in the empty schoolhouse, he receives her scorn. Realizing that for her his attempt and pain are totally insignificant, he abruptly runs away from the school and the hamlet.

Daughter of a schoolteacher, Eudora Welty was nurtured from childhood by a gentle, loving teacher and surrounded by books. In *One Writer's Beginnings* (1983), Welty describes her first arrival at Jefferson Davis Grammar School in Jackson, Mississippi, and the influence of Miss Duling, her first teacher, "a lifelong subscriber to perfection." Miss Duling's "standards were very high and of course inflexible, her authority was total." Welty acknowledges that Miss Duling "emerges in my perhaps inordinate number of schoolteacher characters." The piano teacher from *The Golden Apples* (1949), Miss Eckhart, provides a striking instance. Demanding teachers like Miss Duling are often the best teachers, and they make good copy, as Frances Gray Patton proved in her story "The Terrible Miss Dove" and again in her famous novel that grew from it, *Good Morning, Miss Dove* (1954). Max Steele's story "The Cat and the Coffee Drinkers" (1969), later published in book form, portrays the humorous competence of an eccentric teacher in a home kindergarten, a format common in the South for the first half of the twentieth century. The comic skill of this "children's" book has captivated many adults.

Both of Fred Chappell's parents were schoolteachers, and teachers figure prominently in his fiction. His *Brighten the Corner Where You Are* (1989), a comic novel that sometimes becomes magical realism, follows Appalachian schoolteacher Joe Robert Kirkman through a harrowing day, portraying scenes that show Joe Robert's skill as a teacher as well as his confrontation with the school board because of his teaching of Darwin. Joe Robert's journey recalls that of Leopold Bloom in Joyce's *Ulysses,* and Chappell's hero is every bit as sympathetic a character as Joyce's. Dreaming as the novel ends, Joe Robert has his faithful wife sleeping comfortably beside him.

Several stories by Flannery O'Connor involve scenes with teachers and schools, a very different company from teachers in the Miss Duling tradition. Education often gets the bite of O'Connor's satire, evoking broad grins from readers. In "A Late Encounter with the Enemy," Sally Poker Sash, who has been teaching without a degree since she was sixteen, is finally graduating from college after attending summer school for twenty years. She has wreaked her revenge each fall by teaching "in the exact way she had been taught not to teach." Mary George Fox of "The Enduring Chill," whose Girl Scout shoes are her signature, is principal of the county elementary school, cut from the same mold as Sally Poker. "Adult" she is not. Nor is Mrs. May's son Wesley in "Greenleaf." He constantly insults his mother and his brother and scorns the students he teaches at the nearby second-rate college. In "A Temple of the Holy Ghost," O'Connor takes readers inside a Catholic convent school, where two not-very-bright fourteen-year-old girls get sexual instruction from the nuns. When the girls come home for the weekend, they find further amusement at the expense of Miss Kirby, the schoolteacher who boards at their house. The act of teaching is at the center of the much darker "The Lame Shall Enter First." Trained as a social worker, single parent Sheppard considers himself expert at teaching his own son and in transforming the delinquent boy Rufus Johnson. Like O'Connor's other intellectuals, he is self-deceived and achieves ends very different from those he sought.

Ernest Gaines has also been greatly attracted to the figure of the schoolteacher, a figure useful to him because it captures the frustration and indecision that often visits the African American educated beyond the community that formed him or her, but seemingly incapable of leaving that community or of significantly improving it. *In My Father's House* (1978) uses such a character, Shepherd Lewis, to set against the tormented black minister, the novel's protagonist. The teacher is even more central to *A Lesson Before Dying* (1993), providing its narrative voice. The plot revolves around the teacher's charge to bring a young black man on death row to a realization of his worth as a person. Thus, "teaching" is central to the action. Gaines also

portrays the teacher, Grant, in several classroom situations, an ambience very different from the scenes and economic circumstances of the Appalachia found in Chappell's work. But teachers are also honored characters in Gaines's work and instruments of hope and change.

In *The Water Is Wide* (1972), an account of his experiences teaching for one year on Daufuskie Island off the coast of Beaufort, South Carolina, Pat Conroy depicts the difficulties of a dedicated white teacher trying to reach black students in a remote and neglected community. His methods are too unconventional for the authorities, and he loses his job. The book was made into the successful film *Conrack.*

Gail Godwin has frequently focused on the university professor. In *The Odd Woman* (1974), unmarried professor Jane Clifford struggles between the demands of her career and her love for a man. *The Good Husband* (1994) portrays a large number of college teachers and administrators. *Evensong* (1999), her most recent novel, shows her continuing interest in the educator as character.

The most famous teacher to emerge from twentieth-century southern literature is Blanche Dubois of Tennessee Williams's *A Streetcar Named Desire* (1947). Blanche is too fragile emotionally to sustain her teaching career, and she must flee to New Orleans to seek shelter with her sister because her psychological problems, focused in her sexuality, have caused her to be fired. But it is easy to imagine that Blanche's English classes once had a special vitality as she instructed her students in the beauty of the great poets and the importance of poetry to life.

Because the South has made better education one of its goals, because many writers teach writing in colleges and universities, and because teachers have been important in the lives of most writers, it would be surprising if the teacher does not continue to make good copy. Teachers have been finding their way into autobiographies of southerners, certainly of southern writers. In *Clear Pictures: First Loves, First Guides* (1988), Reynolds Price numbers Phyllis Peacock, his high-school English teacher at Raleigh's Broughton High School, among those loves and guides. In *I Know Why the Caged Bird Sings* (1969), Maya Angelou reports that when she and her brother moved to St. Louis, they found that their education in Stamps, Arkansas, put them ahead of their counterparts in St. Louis. Angelou gives considerable attention to describing her learning opportunities in Stamps. More recently, Bobbie Ann

Mason's *Clear Springs* (1999) describes her passage through the public schools of Mayfield, Kentucky, followed by her experiences at the University of Kentucky. Mason points to no heroes. A creative-writing professor at Kentucky was an important mentor, even after her graduation, though Mason years later is very aware of his deficiencies.

Joseph M. Flora

See also Sunday School.

TELEVANGELIST

Ever since Johnson Jones Hooper and Mark Twain, southern writers have been suspicious of evangelists, and the numerous televangelical debacles of the late twentieth century have provided new cause for suspicion. Fred Chappell summarizes the views of many in an epigram from C (1993) entitled simply "Televangelist": "He claims that he'll reign equally / with Jesus in eternity. / But it's not like him to be willing / To give a partner equal billing." Doris Betts takes aim at the empty promises of televangelists in "The Ugliest Pilgrim" (1973), the story of a young woman's bus ride from her home in North Carolina across the continent to Tulsa, where she hopes the TV healer will work a kind of Providential plastic surgery. Violet's adolescent self-consciousness and her faith in a miracle cure call attention to a culture dominated by image, surface, and overnight transformation. In *Good News from Outer Space* (1989), North Carolina science-fiction writer John Kessel has conflated evangelical religion with the growing national frenzy over UFO sightings. The "rapture," technophobia, televangelism, and alien invasions are seamlessly woven together in Kessel's humorous novel.

Perhaps more notable than the scattered fictional treatments of televangelists are the abundant outpourings of nonfiction, particularly in the areas of biography, autobiography, exploratory journalism, and inspirational literature. Among current televangelists, southern or otherwise, Billy Graham from Charlotte, North Carolina, is the most widely respected. Graham has been the subject of numerous biographies, most of them uncritical, highly laudatory accounts of the evangelist's rise (through God's anointment) from poor farm boy to "the most popular Christian crusader of all time." One notices at a glance, also, how many of

these biographies were published in 1978 and 1979, after Graham came under attack for withholding information about the financing of his ministry. Both William G. McLoughlin Jr.'s *Billy Graham: Revivalist in a Secular Age* (1960) and Ronald C. Paul's *Billy Graham: Prophet of Hope* (1978) frame Graham's ministry in the historical context of the evangelical movement, tying Graham to such important figures as James McGready, Dwight L. Moody, and Billy Sunday—all primitivists who developed their ministries by preaching outdoors to thousands of listeners. In *Billy Graham: Saint or Sinner* (1979), Curtis Mitchell defends Graham against accusations ranging from financial mismanagement to an alleged attempt at bribing the famous mobster Mickey Cohen into salvation. *Billy Graham: Performer? Politician? Preacher? Prophet?* (1978), published by the Church League of America, provides a farcical attack from the fundamentalist right. John Berl Hopkins's *Billy Graham and the Race Problem, 1949–69* (1986) criticizes Graham's moderate stance toward the Civil Rights Movement. Hopkins acknowledges Graham's numerous statements against racism and Graham's 1953 decision no longer to preach segregated services, but Hopkins finds Graham's position too conciliatory toward the white South, citing especially the evangelist's denunciation of black protesters as "communists" and "agitators." While principally laudatory, William Martin's *A Prophet with Honor: The Billy Graham Story* (1991) gives voice to criticisms from numerous sources about wide-ranging issues, including theology, marketing strategies, Graham's position on race and the Vietnam War, and his attachment to certain suspicious political figures, most notably Richard Nixon. Also notable are John Pollock's *Billy Graham: The Authorized Biography* (1966) and *Billy Graham: Evangelist to the World* (1979), and Marshall Frady's *Billy Graham: A Parable of American Righteousness* (1979). Frye Gaillard's essay collection *Southern Voices* (1991) includes an insightful essay on the post-Nixon Graham, a humbler evangelist who has embraced social causes and abandoned his divisive Cold War rhetoric. (Gaillard's book also contains an equally revealing essay on Jim Bakker and the fall of PTL.) Perhaps the most fascinating account of Graham's life is the one Graham himself provides in *Just As I Am: The Autobiography of Billy Graham* (1997), which tells less about his religious life than about the politics of being the world's most popular evangelist. More a memoir than an autobiography, Graham's book tells of his relationships with each of the U.S. presidents from Truman to Clinton, giving his insider's perspective on the man behind the political persona. Graham has published numerous inspirational books, including *Peace with God* (1953), *The Jesus Generation* (1971), *Angels: God's Secret Agents* (1975), *How to Be Born Again* (1977), and *Facing Death and the Life After* (1987). These writings consistently focus on the same evangelical message: the individual choice of heaven or hell, the need to relinquish sin and be "born again," the Christian responsibility to evangelism, and the supernatural power of prayer.

One of the most condemning images of the New South—the prosperous Sunbelt South of the 1970s and 1980s—is the construction site at Heritage USA, abandoned in 1987 as a result of profligate self-indulgence and financial mismanagement on the part of the leaders at the PTL ministries, principally Jim and Tammy Faye Bakker. Throughout the 1970s and 1980s, PTL brought "prosperity theology" into living rooms across America; rather than emphasizing man's innate depravity, the Bakkers chose to focus on the upbeat message of God's goodwill toward his chosen, goodwill in the form of material as well as spiritual gifts. During their heyday, Jim and Tammy Faye published various self-help books, including *How We Lost Weight and Kept It Off* (with Stephen Gyland and Jeffrey Park) (1979) and *Eight Keys to Success* (1980). Jim's autobiography (with Robert Paul Lamb) *Move That Mountain!* (1976) and Tammy Faye's *I Gotta Be Me* (with Cliff Dudley) (1978) both tell roughly the same story of the couple's courtship and young marriage, as well as their rise to prominence at PTL. Both books are full of deliciously unintentional humor—for example, Jim's account of his attraction to the Bible-college freshman Tammy Faye, despite the fact that she wore no makeup. Throughout the 1980s, the *Charlotte Observer* investigated numerous improprieties at PTL, from financial misconduct to Jim Bakker's involvement with church secretary Jessica Hahn. The newspaper's investigations led to Bakker's resignation in 1987, PTL's decline, and a federal grand-jury investigation that ended in Bakker's imprisonment. Bakker's fall and televangelist Jerry Falwell's temporary takeover of the ministry are recorded in several book-length studies: *Holy War: An Inside Account of the Battle for PTL* (1987) by John Stewart; *Ministry of Greed: The Inside Story of the Televangelists and Their Holy Wars* (1988) by Larry Martz with Ginny Carroll; *Jim and Tammy: Charismatic Intrigue Inside PTL* (1988) by Joe E. Barnhart with Steven Winzenburg; *Forgiven: The Rise and Fall of Jim Bakker and the PTL Ministry* (1989) by Charles E. Shepard; *Smile Pretty and Say Jesus: The Last Great Days of PTL* (1993) by Hunter James; and *Anatomy of a Fraud: Inside the Finances of the PTL Ministries* (1993) by Gary L. Tidwell. In 1996 Jim Bakker's contrite *I Was Wrong* (with Robert Paul Lamb) marked his latest publishing attempt to reestablish his ministry.

Like Jim Bakker, Louisiana televangelist Jimmy Swaggart took his theological bearings in the Assemblies of God, a fundamentalist sect that believes not only in the necessity of being "born again" but in the importance of receiving the "baptism of the Holy Spirit," an experience that provides the initiate with the ability to "speak in tongues," heal the sick, prophesy, and exercise numerous other supernatural gifts of the Spirit. Swaggart's fiery style of preaching won him a loyal following, which, in the late 1980s, numbered in the millions. After attacking Jim Bakker and other prominent ministers for their sexual improprieties, in 1988 Swaggart became the subject of his own sex scandal, made all the more scandalous considering his career of virulent intolerance toward homosexuals, Catholics, Jews, Hollywood, rock music, the media, the U.S. government, and even mainstream Protestantism. Lawrence Wright's "Jimmy Swaggart: False Messiah," collected in Wright's *Saints & Sinners* (1993), convincingly explains Swaggart's appeal and the dangers of his rhetoric. Swaggart tells his own story (with help from Robert Paul Lamb) in *To Cross a River* (1984). Swaggart's *Straight Answers to Tough Questions* (1987) is required reading for anyone determined to understand the paranoia of evangelical America. *Straight Answers* reads like a fundamentalist's *Miss Manners*, with Swaggart providing biblically based answers to questions ranging from the theological to the everyday—for example: *Is all dancing sinful? What about aerobic dancing? What do you think of mixed swimming? Is it wrong for a Christian to attend movies or watch television?*

Also available are intelligently written biographies of Virginia's two prominent televangelists: Dinesh D'Souza's *Falwell: Before the Millennium, A Critical Biography,* and David Edwin Harrell Jr.'s *Pat Robertson: A Personal, Religious, and Political Portrait* (1987). Two other interesting sources include Moral Majority leader Jerry Falwell's *Strength for the Journey: An Autobiography* (1987) and John W. Robbins's *Pat Robertson: A Warning to America* (1988).

George Hovis

See also Baptists; Bible Belt; Evangelical Christianity; Fundamentalism; Methodists; Preaching; Presbyterians; Religion in Twentieth-Century Literature; Secularization; Sermons; Snake Handling.

Ben Armstrong, The Electric Church (1979); Jeffrey K. Hadden and Charles E. Swann, Prime Time Preachers: The Rising Power of Televangelism (1981); Peter G. Horsfield, Religious Television: The American Experience (1984); J. Gordon Melton, Phillip Charles Lucas, and Jon R. Stone, Prime-Time Religion: An Encyclopedia of Religious Broadcasting (1997); Janice Peck, The Gods of Televangelism: The Crisis of Meaning and the Appeal of Religious Television (1993); Quentin J. Schultze, Televangelism and American Culture (1991).

TELEVISION

Midway through one of his habitual tirades against popular culture, the obsessed narrator of Walker Percy's novel Lancelot (1977) stops and asks, "Which is worse, to die with T. J. Jackson at Chancellorsville or live with Johnny Carson in Burbank?" However much southerners may believe the latter, their reality more often resembles that of another of Percy's characters, the Alabama pathologist turned television addict, Sutter Vaught, in The Second Coming (1980), or Will Barrett's Aunt Sophie in The Last Gentleman (1966), who writes love letters to game-show host Bill Cullen. Percy himself was a longtime fan of the daytime soap opera As the World Turns, and called novelist and fellow fan Shelby Foote from time to time to check up on episodes he had missed. Even William Faulkner, who had a low opinion of television and would not allow one in his house, is known to have stopped by a neighbor's home on occasion to watch the sitcom Car 54, Where Are You?

Contemporary southern fiction has likewise featured characters whose sense of place and of self is increasingly informed by the impressions they receive from television. Alice Kane, the daughter of a CBS news chief in Richard Bausch's Kennedy-era novel Good Evening Mr. & Mrs. America, and All the Ships at Sea (1996), sees Johnny Carson and Pearl Bailey dancing together on The Tonight Show and wonders why the rest of the country doesn't follow their lead. A portable black-and-white TV set in Lewis Nordan's Music of the Swamp (1991) haunts Sugar Mecklin's father with unscheduled broadcasts of the films of Cowboy Bob Steele, the hero he hoped to become, but didn't. In Bobbie Ann Mason's 1985 novel In Country, television even becomes a kind of surrogate father to

Sam Hughes, who grieves over the death of Colonel Henry Blake on M*A*S*H more than she did for her own father, who died in Vietnam.

Television adaptations of southern literature first appeared in the early 1950s with productions of William Faulkner's fiction, including two ("Tomorrow" and "Old Man") by the Pulitzer Prize–winning playwright Horton Foote, whose later adaptation of Faulkner's "Barn Burning" (1980) is notable for having featured the writer's nephew Jimmy Faulkner in the role of Major de Spain. Southern writers who have appeared in adaptations of their own works include Robert Penn Warren, who portrayed his own father in a 1975 PBS production of his verse play Brother to Dragons, and Allan Gurganus, who donned full military regalia to play a Confederate cavalry officer in the 1994 adaptation of his novel Oldest Living Confederate Widow Tells All. By far the most popular adaptations of southern literature have been the neo-abolitionist interpretations of Ernest Gaines's novel The Autobiography of Miss Jane Pittman, which won nine Emmy awards in 1973, and Alex Haley's Roots, which became the most-watched program in television history when it first aired in 1977. Recent adaptations of Anne Tyler's Breathing Lessons (1994), Dori Sanders's Clover (1997), and Kaye Gibbons's Ellen Foster (1997) have targeted female viewers by featuring strong-willed female protagonists in local-color settings. Other adaptations include Mark Twain's Adventures of Huckleberry Finn (1975, 1986), Ernest Gaines's "The Sky Is Gray" (1980), Flannery O'Connor's "The Displaced Person" (1976), and Kate Chopin's The Awakening (1992). The PBS series The Rough South (1990, 1992) visited the homes and haunts of novelists Tim McLaurin and Harry Crews, and Let Us Now Praise Famous Men—Revisited (1988) featured interviews with some of the Alabama sharecroppers profiled by the author James Agee in his classic work.

Brian Carpenter

See also K Mart Fiction; Postmodernism; Redneck.

Fred Hobson, The Southern Writer in the Postmodern World (1991); Jack Kirby, Media-Made Dixie: The South in the American Imagination (1978); Jan Whitt, "Grits and Yokels Aplenty," Studies in Popular Culture (Oct. 1996); David G. Yellin, ed., Tomorrow and Tomorrow and Tomorrow (1985).

TELLING ABOUT THE SOUTH

"We need to talk, to tell, since oratory is our heritage," William Faulkner wrote of southerners in 1933. "We seem to try in the single furious breathing (or writing) span of the individual to draw a savage indictment of the contemporary scene or to escape from it into a make-believe region of swords and magnolias and mockingbirds which perhaps never existed anywhere. Both of the courses are rooted in sentiment . . . each course is a matter of violent partizanship, in which the writer unconsciously writes into every line and phrase his violent despairs and rages and frustrations or his violent prophesies [sic] of still more violent hopes. The cold intellect which can write with calm and complete detachment and gusto of its contemporary scene is not among us."

Faulkner was precisely that southerner with the "need . . . to tell" who wrote "into every line and phrase his violent despairs and rages and frustrations," his "violent prophesies." He wrote that same urge for southern self-expression into many of his characters, and none so much as Quentin Compson, that tortured Mississippian of *Absalom, Absalom!* who on a January night in 1910 sat in the tomblike chill of his room in Cambridge, Massachusetts, and heeded the command of his Canadian roommate to "tell about the South." "What's it like there. What do they do there. Why do they live there. Why do they live at all," Shreve McCannon had asked, and Quentin, while reconstructing the story of Thomas Sutpen, a nineteenth-century Mississippi planter, pours out truer answers than he knows. Haunted by the southern past, Quentin tells his story not with intellectual detachment but with a visceral commitment to the importance of what he is telling. Cursed with an excess of consciousness, possessed of a rage to order as well as a rage to explain, he ponders the larger meaning of Thomas Sutpen's story, the significance of what has happened in the South during the century just past. Finally, after agonizing over Sutpen's story deep into the night, he attempts to respond to Shreve's final question, "Why do you hate the South?" "I dont hate it," Quentin protests. "*I dont. I dont!*"

Quentin Compson is a fictional character, but in many respects he is the prototype of that nineteenth- and twentieth-century southerner with a rage to explain the South. Many of those southerners have been novelists: besides Faulkner, one thinks in particular of George W. Cable of Louisiana, Carson McCullers and Flannery O'Connor and Alice Walker of Georgia, Virginians from Thomas Nelson Page to William Styron, Mississippians from Richard Wright to Barry Hannah, and North Carolina's Thomas Wolfe, whose autobio-

graphical Eugene Gant rails against the "swarming superstition" of the South, "the barren spiritual wilderness, the hostile and murderous intrenchment against all new life." One thinks of playwrights such as Tennessee Williams, possessed of his own particular need to explain the South, and of poets from Henry Timrod to James Dickey.

But many of those who have felt most strongly about the South and have written most fervently, and sometimes eloquently, are writers of nonfiction, going back so far as antebellum Virginians George Fitzhugh and Edmund Ruffin (both of whom made a case for the South as a unique society, organically different from the rest of the United States); the North Carolinian Hinton Rowan Helper, author of that explosive abolitionist tract *The Impending Crisis of the South* (1857); and Daniel Hundley of Alabama, author of one of the first works of southern social analysis, *Social Relations in Our Southern States* (1860).

Southerners have felt more strongly about their region than other Americans, and the reasons are not difficult to find. Beginning with the abolitionist crusade and the national debate over slavery in the 1820s and 1830s, the South was intensely self-conscious and soon aggressively defensive. The Civil War and its aftermath—Reconstruction and the growth of the cult of the Lost Cause, that belief that the white South, although defeated on the battlefield, had not been vanquished in spirit—contributed to feelings of difference among southerners. But those feelings took many forms. By the late nineteenth century, it was clear that while many white southerners—such as Robert Lewis Dabney and Thomas Nelson Page—romanticized and glorified the Old South, other southerners—such as Cable and Walter Hines Page—found much to criticize in Dixie, past and present.

By the early twentieth century, the white southern explainers—those writing books and essays making a case either for or against the South—could be divided roughly into two groups: on the one hand, the defenders of and apologists for the South—what might be called a southern school of remembrance—and on the other, those southern self-critics who were concerned in particular with the South's racial burden—what might be called the party of shame and guilt. Such twentieth-century southerners as the Southern Agrarians, particularly poet-polemicist Donald Davidson, as well as the eloquent autobiographer William Alexander Percy and the neo-Agrarian Richard Weaver, belong in the former group; such native critics as Howard

Odum, W. J. Cash, Lillian Smith, and James McBride Dabbs belong to the latter.

In Cash, the author of *The Mind of the South* (1941), one finds the nearest thing to a real-life Quentin Compson, an intense, sometimes tortured southerner involved in a love-hate relationship with his homeland, who spent his entire adult life pondering and writing his one book—and then, like Quentin Compson, committed suicide. Writing in an engaging, flowing style—the prose equivalent of a Confederate cavalry charge—Cash overstates and generalizes and omits: what he describes more precisely is the mind— and not exactly the mind but the personality, the temper—of the plain white southern male. But his is still the finest portrait of that mind, and the power of his personal involvement with his subject has never been matched.

Lillian Smith's *Killers of the Dream* (1949), a mixture of autobiography and social commentary, belongs with Cash's book as a southern classic. So do James Agee's *Let Us Now Praise Famous Men* (1941), a mixture of autobiography, documentary, and sociology; Ben Robertson's *Red Hills and Cotton* (1942), written about Cash's upcountry Carolinians but in a far more nostalgic tone; and Katharine Du Pre Lumpkin's *The Making of a Southerner* (1947), the chronicle of a journey up from racism. A number of other writers in the mid- and late twentieth century, belonging broadly to the party of shame and guilt, have also approached the South in very personal terms. Journalists such as Ralph McGill (*The South and the Southerner*), Hodding Carter Sr. (*Southern Legacy*), and Jonathan Daniels (*A Southerner Discovers the South*) explained their Souths, all different from each other's since the authors came from different parts of Dixie. Other works— Willie Morris's *North Toward Home* (1967) and Larry L. King's *Confessions of a White Racist* (1971)—dealt largely with the authors' changing attitudes about race.

White southerners were hardly the only writers who felt compelled to tell about the South. Indeed, if any southern writer possessed, and was entitled to possess, a rage to explain the South, it was the black southerner. African Americans hardly fell into either of the schools suggested above: there was little positive to remember in a slave and Jim Crow past (other than a self-created sense of community), nor could former slaves, their servitude having been involuntary, feel much guilt about the South's peculiar institution. But they were seized by the autobiographical impulse all the same— the urge to tell their own personal truths about Dixie—

and all the more so because they had been silenced for so long.

Richard Wright's *Black Boy* (1945), his story of growing up in segregated Mississippi and Memphis, is one of the most powerful of southern autobiographies, a memoir—true in spirit if not always in fact—in which Wright convinces the reader that he made it out only because he did not learn to live Jim Crow. Zora Neale Hurston's *Dust Tracks on a Road* (1942) displeased Wright because it told about a South he did not know—a South of a rich, vital black folk culture and little racial confrontation—and indeed Hurston's portrait of Deep South race relations does appear overly sanguine. Later works such as Anne Moody's *Coming of Age in Mississippi* (1968) and Mary Mebane's *Mary* (1981) and *Mary Wayfarer* (1983) hardly gave that impression. Their stories of growing up in Dixie, like Wright's, were largely stories of struggles to get out.

White and black, southerners have felt they had more to explain than have other Americans. The southern legacy—defeat, failure, poverty, violence—made exploring and explaining a condition of living southern. Whether that same southern compulsion to tell, to explain, will continue to exist in a South that fashions itself the Sunbelt is an interesting question indeed. Southerners are in the habit of writing books of self-exploration and self-explanation, and one does not see the habit disappearing. But will telling about the South be only habit and ritual? Is the contemporary South a likely partner for a love-hate relationship?

Fred Hobson

See also Autobiography; Lost Cause; *Mind of the South, The*; Storytelling.

Fred Hobson, *Tell About the South* (1983); Gerald Johnson, *South-Watching: Selected Essays* (1983).

TENANT FARMING

The term *tenant farming* describes two different sets of economic relationships that existed between tenant and landowner, based on the assets of the tenant. Sharecroppers were tenants who had almost no resources to bring to farming but their labor and that of their family. The landlord supplied them with mules, implements, seed, fertilizer, and housing; in return, the annual crop was divided into shares between owner and cropper. Renters were tenants who owned their own stock and equipment and paid for land rental either in cash or in a fixed percentage of their annual produce. Tenant farming usually necessitated the advance of large amounts of credit from landlord to tenant—it could, and frequently did, eventuate in the tenant ending the growing season in debt.

After the Civil War and the breakup of the plantation system, sharecropping was the main way for former slaves, lacking funds and possessions, to make a livelihood. The number of tenants was dramatically increased between 1880 and 1930 by the addition of many former small landholders, thus making the institution of tenancy prevalent among white as well as black farm families. In 1880, 36 percent of southern farms were operated by tenants; by 1930 the proportion was 55 percent, many of whom were sharecroppers with neither mules nor money, engaged in the cultivation of cotton in a disastrously unrewarding economy. There is general agreement among historians that farm tenancy was the South's greatest economic and social problem, demanding, in the words of journalist Gerald W. Johnson, "a Charles Dickens" whose genius would so rile up the complacent citizen that he "would be galvanized into a fury of activity."

The dire conditions of southern tenant farming derived from the institution itself and from the dominance of cotton as a cash crop. The chronic indebtedness of tenant to landlord created dependency, resentment, and a caste system comparable to serfdom. Tenants moved frequently, looking for better conditions or fleeing from debt; but their movement was in a narrow sphere and rarely brought improvement. They had little reason to take care of their land or accommodations or to feel any loyalty to their landlord. The cultivation of cotton made them vulnerable to the numerous natural hazards of weather and infestation, as well as to fluctuations in demand and prices, and to the frequent requirement of landlords that all acreage be devoted to the cash crop, with not even a small plot reserved for subsistence farming for tenant families. Tenant families' houses were often dilapidated, their diet poor, their health weak, their sanitation minimal, and their opportunities for education very limited. If they saw a brief upswing in their fortunes during World War I, their prosperity was soon reversed as cotton prices dropped after 1919 and their condition deteriorated throughout the 1920s.

Prior to the 1920s, the tenant farmer had largely been neglected as a focus of reformers' energy and public outrage, except for some philanthropic efforts in the early years of the century to improve education and literacy. There was no southern equivalent of the literary muckraking and melioristic novels that dominated northern writing during the last decades of the nineteenth century and the beginning of the twentieth. The imaginative literature of the South in this period was directed toward historical and local-color subjects— even Ellen Glasgow's mordant realism in depicting the problems of southern agriculture tended to concentrate on farmers who owned their own land rather than the powerless figures of tenants and croppers.

Although no single writer in the 1920s proved to be the Charles Dickens of tenant farming, there was, during that decade, a remarkable awakening of interest, both literary and sociological, in the plight of the sharecropper and tenant. Fiction writers, from Edith Summers Kelley and Elizabeth Madox Roberts to Jack Bethea, Dorothy Scarborough, and T. S. Stribling, evoked the suffering, monotony, and grim endurance of southern rural life among the poorest farmers. Economists and sociologists Howard Odum, Arthur Raper, and Rupert Vance began their more scholarly inquiries into tenant farming; and from these studies there emerged the picture of an institution that was in many ways the direct antithesis of the Jeffersonian agrarian ideal of independent and egalitarian citizenship. Few tenants progressed toward ownership, while many were forced to become migrant workers or to leave the land, either temporarily or permanently, to eke out a living by industrial employment. When the Nashville Agrarians issued their 1930 manifesto *I'll Take My Stand,* it was necessary for the more candid among them to acknowledge how far the tenant or farm laborer's reality was from the model they were upholding, or for the more imaginative to invent farming scenarios from which the tenant was completely absent.

During the 1930s, the predicament of tenant farmers became more extreme and its exposure more dramatic, until finally a combination of events occurred that radically altered the extent and circumstances of tenancy. The Great Depression struck the agricultural South even harder than the rest of the nation, causing the region's endemic rural distress to become acute and epidemic. Social scientists, fiction writers, and journalists explored the plight of the tenant for an increasingly interested and horrified public. Erskine Caldwell's debilitated inhabitants of *Tobacco Road* and William Faulkner's barn-burning Snopeses were among the more colorful fictive portraits of tenant degeneracy and resentment, while a host of nonfiction oral histories, and autobiographical, journalistic, and photographic accounts of tenants and sharecroppers was added to the accumulating record. Caldwell published a series of articles on tenant farming in 1933 in the *New York Post,* later reissued that same year as his pamphlet *Tenant Farmer* and included again in *Some American People* (1935). In 1937 he and Margaret Bourke-White collaborated on the picture-text *You Have Seen Their Faces* on the black and white poor of the rural South. The importance of the camera in documenting the lives of tenants was reiterated in the photographs taken under the auspices of the Farm Security Administration and in the work of Dorothea Lange and Paul Taylor, who explored in *An American Exodus* (1939) the conditions that were driving farmers off the land. James Agee and Walker Evans's *Let Us Now Praise Famous Men* (1941) turned a commission from *Fortune* to report on southern farm tenancy into a complex meditation on the processes of wresting art, sensationalism, moral superiority, and political advocacy from the lives of the desperately poor. The Federal Writers' Project published oral histories of tenant farmers in *These Are Our Lives* (1939), and books such as Harry Kroll's *I Was a Share-Cropper* (1936) and Margaret Hagood's *Mothers of the South* (1939) added a mixture of personal memoir and observed fact to the growing national reputation of the tenant. Fictional versions continued to appear, e.g., Charlie May Simon's *The Sharecropper* (1937) and Charles Curtis Munz's *Land Without Moses* (1938), so that by the end of the Depression, the telling signs and symbols of the southern tenant farmer were pervasive and familiar. Just as Greek-columned mansions, crinolines, cavaliers, and toiling fieldhands had become a synecdoche for the life of the antebellum plantation, so there was a comparably recognizable cluster of images for the tenant farmer: the sagging shack, with cotton planted to the door; nursing women, ragged children, grim-faced men, and gaunt animals; frayed sun-hats, snuff, and bare feet; hookworm, malaria, and pellagra; grimaces that might be hostile, foolish, or long-suffering.

While these images of tenant farmers were becoming ingrained in the public consciousness during the 1930s, changes (though not necessarily improvements) in their situation were occurring, initially with the advent of Franklin Delano Roosevelt and New Deal agricultural policies. The Agricultural Adjustment Act of 1933 attempted to reduce cotton acreage by paying farmers to divert land to other crops. However, landlords received the government subsidies, while tenants received little help and were frequently reduced to field-labor status or driven off the land entirely. In 1934 black and white tenants formed the Southern Tenant Farmers Union to agitate for reforms and, quite successfully, to draw attention to sharecroppers' dire circumstances. By 1935 larger economic forces were beginning to alter the conditions of tenancy and to reduce the numbers of tenants: mechanization and the displacement of human labor, the increasing availability of rayon and synthetic alternatives to cotton on world markets, new opportunities for tenants to find urban and industrial employment, and increased migration to the North. After 1935 the numbers of tenant farmers began a slow but irreversible decline, although their literal and imagined existence persisted into the 1960s and 1970s when their descendants, still living in rural poverty (though rarely as farm workers), were rediscovered in the fiction of Harry Crews and Alice Walker, in documentary accounts by Michael Harrington and Robert Coles, and in the CBS television program *Harvest of Shame* (1960). The lingering image of tenant farming as a symbol of southern dispossession is a powerful one, not least because it crossed racial divisions to foreground the common experience of poverty.

Sylvia J. Cook

See also Plantation; Poor White; Protest, Novel of; Redneck; Sharecropping.

J. Wayne Flynt, *Dixie's Forgotten People: The South's Poor Whites* (1979); Jacqueline Jones, *The Dispossessed: America's Underclasses from the Civil War to the Present* (1992); George Brown Tindall, *The Emergence of the New South, 1913–1945* (1967).

TENNESSEE, LITERATURE OF

One of the first Tennessee stories to achieve widespread popularity is Mary Noailles Murfree's "Over on T'other Mounting," a story from her first collection, *In the Tennessee Mountains* (1884). Under the pseudonym Charles Egbert Craddock, this descendent of Murfreesboro's first settlers wrote eleven short-story collections and several historical novels on Tennessee's pioneers. "Over on T'other Mounting" typifies Murfree's stories as it combines gentle humor, controlled sentiment, regional dialect, and vivid description. Despite the frontier setting, Murfree is essentially a neoclassical rationalist; her fiction is reminiscent of the genteel gothicism of Ann Radcliffe. Midnight ghosts may seem to appear but are explained away in the midday sun. Evil may lurk but is finally no match for the hardworking, straight-shooting frontier spirit. This frontier spirit assures the reader of both the potency and affirmative value of civilization. "Over on T'other Mounting" begins with a contrast between two mountain ranges, a contrast that offers an apt metaphor for a puzzling tension within Tennessee literature. Famous in its association with Tennessee is Old Rocky-Top, which Murfree describes as "fresh and green with the tender verdure of spring." Running parallel to Old Rocky-Top is a higher, more intimidating range that remains essentially nameless. While "the simple homefolks draw around the hearth" on Old Rocky-Top, T'other Mounting is considered unlucky and remains uninhabited, haunted by wild winds and by "treacherous rifts and chasms." Murfree's essential view is from Old Rocky-Top. As a cultivated writer in the southern tradition, Murfree introduces the challenge of the wilderness in her fiction, but readers view it from the perspective of newly established civility. In contrast, the other well-known Tennessee writer of the nineteenth century, George Washington Harris, has little regard for civility. Born in Pennsylvania in 1814, he moved as a five-year-old child to Knoxville. A man of many occupations, including farmer and steamboat captain, he wrote as an avocation and published only one book, *Sut Lovingood: Yarns Spun by a "Nat'ral Born Durn'd Fool"* (1867). These stories are so dialectical that they are difficult to read today, but they advanced the American folk-humor movement and were admired by Mark Twain. The stories of Sut Lovingood delight in scatological tomfoolery. In his Hogarthian world, the emphasis is on bare-arsed men behaving like animals.

Tennessee literature may be classified as that which is written from Old Rocky-Top and that which is written from T'other Mounting. Murfree established the first tradition and Harris the latter. Although this metaphor has all the weaknesses of human affection for dichotomies, it will at least remedy the common, misguided tendency to portray Tennessee literature as a rather unified progression from the Fugitive to the Agrarian to the New Criticism movement. As important as Fugitive/Agrarian/New Criticism are within the history of American literature, they should not be permitted to define Tennessee literature. The *disunified* history of Tennessee literature is apparent in the nineteenth century with the contrast of Murfree and Harris, in modernism with the contrast of John Crowe Ransom and Evelyn Scott, and in postmodernism with the contrast of Peter Taylor and Cormac McCarthy.

John Crowe Ransom holds the central position in the Old Rocky-Top history of Tennessee literature and is the father-figure of the Fugitive/Agrarian/New Criticism movements. Born in Pulaski in 1888, he was the son of a Methodist minister who moved his family to several locations in Tennessee; however, Ransom's primary education occurred in Nashville, first at Bowen School, later at Vanderbilt. He returned to Vanderbilt to teach and joined the philosophy/literary group (including Donald Davidson) that met at the home of Sidney Mttron Hirsch. After this group added Allen Tate and Robert Penn Warren, it evolved into a more focused literary club that would eventually publish its poems in *The Fugitive* (1922–1924), one of the most important little magazines of American modernism. The impact of Ransom's involvement with the Fugitives and his maturation as a poet is not apparent until his second collection, *Chills and Fever* (1924). His production as a poet was curiously brief; his last book of original verse, *Two Gentlemen in Bonds,* was published in 1927. Thereafter, Ransom's influence is primarily manifested through the thoughtful precision of his essays and his mentoring of young writers (first at Vanderbilt, later at Kenyon College in Ohio). Along with Allen Tate and Robert Penn Warren, Ransom defines the key arguments of both the Agrarians and New Criticism. Essentially, as Fugitives, their focus was on modern poetry (1920s), as Agrarians on social reform (1930s), as New Critics on literary criticism (1940s and 1950s). When Tate described Ransom as "the last pure manifestation of the culture of the eighteenth-century South," he was emphasizing the poet's high regard for rationality and civility. The Fugitive movement nudged the South into the twentieth century but with an artistically and culturally conservative slant that varied significantly from the bohemian mode of 1920s Greenwich Village.

In one of Ransom's finest poems, "Necrological," a historical setting is used as a friar reacts to mangled bodies on a battlefield. The friar is gradually transformed as his standard Christian perception is overwhelmed by the physicality of desire, death, and decay. The physical reality of flesh feeding upon flesh juxtaposed with solicitous Heaven leaves only essential mystery. Ransom's voice always seems both to disconcert and reassure. The beauty and metrical precision of the construct are central to the message. The artistry maintains a rational control, an attribute that Ransom later celebrates within the late poems of Thomas Hardy. Ransom loves Hardy's "clean and formal workmanship." Although Hardy may challenge the reader with the cruel and uncertain human state, Ransom finds relief in poetry that "could not wear a tidier *look*." Ransom is similarly adept at creating a tension between modern angst and artistic precision. His love of traditional unity achieved its cultural focus in the Agrarian movement and critical focus in New Criticism. In his lead essay in *I'll Take My Stand: The South and the Agrarian Tradition* (1930), Ransom opposed progressivism, intent upon conquering nature, with "the virtues of establishment," which he saw as a leisurely southern mode based on an eighteenth-century European conservatism that permitted a community to live in relative harmony with nature. Industrialism was identified as a northern sickness that produced purposeless "deracination." Communities preserve valued life, and the uprooting of communities occurs when one no longer recognizes the nonmaterialistic essence of traditional social structure.

Tennessee's counterforce of modernism is Evelyn Scott, a writer as Dionysian as Ransom was Apollonian. While Ransom remained within a supportive literary community that nurtured his reputation as he nurtured the reputations of so many others, Scott isolated herself in her later years, suffering from paranoid psychosis in a seedy New York hotel. Yet in her youth she had rivaled William Faulkner as the primary modernist voice of the South. Born Elsie Dunn in Clarksville, Tennessee, in 1893, she descended from a northern railroad family and a southern family with aristocratic pretensions. In 1909 she moved with her family to New Orleans and in 1913 ran off with a married man, Frederick Wellman. They took the names Evelyn and Cyril Kay Scott to evade prosecution through the Mann Act and tried homesteading in Brazil. In 1919 the Scotts moved to Greenwich Village, where Evelyn became one of the bright young stars of literary bohemianism with her first collection of poems, *Precipitation* (1920), and her first novel, *The Narrow House* (1921). Darwinian, Freudian, and Nietzschean, Scott wrote about the powers that lie beyond control, beneath consciousness. *The Narrow House* focuses on a dysfunctional family that clings together, as intent on self-destruction as on self-preservation. No "clean and formal workmanship" is possible within Scott's raw, confrontational art. Whatever civility exists within her

community must be stripped away to expose the all-consuming powers of appetite and ego. Scott's best work, *Escapade* (1923), is an experimental autobiography that captures Scott's personal hell as she gives birth to her only child in a verdant, infested Eden. Scott writes about pain, physical and psychic, and she offers no assurance that community can offer protection. In 1927, her novel *Migrations* began her shift from concentrated, imagistic novels to more historical, southern novels, but her style remained experimental, as exemplified by her stunning Civil War novel *The Wave* (1929), a work organized in vignettes similar to John Dos Passos's *Manhattan Transfer* (1925). Scott established her reputation before Faulkner and aided him with her introductory essay on *The Sound and the Fury*. She published a total of nineteen books but had nearly been forgotten by her death in 1963. Her opposition to the powerful leftist critics of the 1930s led her deeper and deeper into paranoia and oblivion. Although she agreed with the Agrarians that communism was not a viable solution to what ailed America, she was equally critical of what she perceived as the Agrarian tendency to envision a stable antebellum society as a model for the future. In *Background in Tennessee* (1937), Scott argued that Tennessee never had time to establish a stable society before the Civil War; she considered the southern aristocracy to be a cultural illusion. Scott looked at the world from T'other Mounting. Like Harris, she cut beneath what she saw as the artifice of culture. She believed in the power of the primeval, and her art would not adapt to cultural traditions and expectations.

For Tennessee literature, Scott represents a minority position within the modernist period. With Nashville as their center and Ransom as their master, the Fugitive/Agrarian/New Criticism movements defined the nature of southern life and southern literature. The most accomplished writers of this group were marginal Tennesseans: Allen Tate and Robert Penn Warren, Kentuckians by birth, although both had "border backgrounds" and spent a number of years in Tennessee. Tate was born in 1899 in Winchester, Kentucky, and moved frequently during his childhood, including briefly to Nashville where he later attended Vanderbilt. During the 1930s, he lived with his wife, Caroline Gordon, at Benfolly, their farm outside Clarksville, which became a popular outpost of the Nashville-based Agrarians. Tate's role is central to all three tiers (Fugitive/Agrarian/New Criticism). Among his best poems are "The Mediterranean," "Aeneas at Washington," and "Ode to the Confederate Dead." As a poet, Tate is similar to Ransom in that his most-admired poems were written in his youth (before 1935), although he, like Ransom, continued to revise his poems through the second half of his life. Tate's poems tend to be more self-consciously erudite, but like Ransom's best work, they are wonderfully controlled meditations that emphasize the degeneration of modern man from a lost heroic tradition. In "Mediterranean," after a portrayal of Aeneas's ancient heroic quest, the conquest of the New World is described thus: "We've cracked the hemisphere with careless hand!" In "Aeneas at Washington," the eternal Aeneas begins with his valor in leaving Troy but concludes with his New World vision: "stuck in the wet mire." And in "Ode to the Confederate Dead," the impotent meditations of the modern man must occur outside the gate of the realm of the heroic Confederate dead. In his late years, Tate devoted more time to criticism and, like Ransom, promoted the literature he admired (Dante near the top of the list, Poe near the bottom), while also developing New Criticism with its more formalistic approach to literary study.

Robert Penn Warren was befriended by Tate soon after Warren arrived at Vanderbilt. Warren, born in Guthrie, Kentucky, in 1905, was only seventeen at the time. As the youngest member of the Fugitive group, Warren quickly established himself as one of its best poets. Yet unlike Ransom and Tate, Warren is more likely to be remembered for his late-life poetry. Warren might best be seen as the John Dryden of his age. His total impact in literature is difficult to gauge because he is equally accomplished in poetry, fiction, and criticism. Typically, one now finds more emphasis on his poems published after 1950, including his long poems *Brother to Dragons* (1953) and *Audubon: A Vision* (1969). Some of his best poems, without the classicism and detachment of his Fugitive poems, were published after Warren's seventieth birthday. These include "American Portrait: Old Style," "Mortal Limit," and "Doubleness in Time." Warren combined with Cleanth Brooks to write the influential New Critical anthologies beginning with *Understanding Poetry* (1938), that shaped America's literary landscape after World War II. Yet Warren's intellectual connection with the Fugitive/Agrarian/New Criticism movements was tenuous even in the earlier stages. His contribution to *I'll Take My Stand*, "The Briar Patch," called attention to racial injustice and was considered too progressive by Donald Davidson. In later years, Warren's views on desegrega-

tion moved him yet further from Davidson's conservative position.

Warren's fiction typically portrays the Tennessee/Kentucky border area beginning with his first novel, *Night Rider* (1939), which portrays the area's Black Patch War between tobacco farmers and tobacco companies. This rural area, also depicted in his short-story collection *Circus in the Attic* (1948), draws upon the history of his home territory, essentially the triangle from Guthrie and Hopkinsville, Kentucky, to Clarksville, Tennessee. One of his best early novels, *At Heaven's Gate* (1943), and his brilliant last novel, *A Place to Come To* (1977), use both rural Tennessee and Nashville. The novels are worthy of close comparison as Warren introduces a Dantesque vision of Nashville in both cases. *At Heaven's Gate* investigates how a former college football hero, Jerry Calhoun, abandons his agrarian roots and is corrupted by progressivism. The entrepreneur's daughter, Sue Murdock, is a 1920s "new woman," independent and brazenly aggressive on the surface but damaged by a loveless family. *A Place to Come To* offers a similarly powerful but damaged woman, Rozelle Hardcastle. The protagonist, Jed Tewksbury, is like Jerry Calhoun in that he moves from an agrarian background to urbane sophistication. Again, Warren contemplates the dangers of what is lost by disassociation from one's agrarian roots, but in this case one can see that Warren's Agrarian principles have faded to the background. The later novel, like Warren's late poetry, employs a more personal and picaresque approach to experience, one less inclined to read personal history according to the Agrarian paradigm. Warren's affection for far less disciplined writers like George Washington Harris and Theodore Dreiser is apparent, and the treatment of explicitly sexual material is a deliberate affront to conventional taste. Although Warren has consciously used Dante's *Inferno* as inspiration in both texts, in *A Place to Come To* he is equally inspired by Yeats's "Crazy Jane Talks with the Bishop" and has, as in his late poetry, created a more complex tension between art/life as conscious design and art/life as uncontrollable, inexplicable engagement. *A Place to Come To* deserves to be ranked with Warren's finest novels, *All the King's Men* (1946) and *World Enough and Time* (1950).

Two accomplished Tennessee fiction writers who are closely connected with Ransom, Tate, and Warren are Andrew Lytle and Caroline Gordon. Both were passionately Agrarian, and both were consummate craftsmen. Lytle was born in Murfreesboro in 1902, and one of his earliest publications is his contribution in *I'll Take My Stand*, "The Hind Tit." He was a teacher of writing through much of his life (University of Iowa, University of Florida, Sewanee) and is as well known for his editorship of the *Sewanee Review* as for his novels; however, his novels are impressive achievements, particularly the short novel *A Name for Evil* (1947), and his final, experimental novel, *The Velvet Horn* (1957). *A Name for Evil* exemplifies the influence of Henry James on the Agrarian writers. The novel, a psychological gothic thriller much like *The Turn of the Screw*, is a nightmarish contemplation of the force that land has over humans. The Agrarian concept of the return to the ancestral land is here investigated in terms of the dark stain upon the human that prevents a return to pastoral tranquillity. A disturbing illustration of the conservative Agrarians' difficulty in dealing with race is apparent in Lytle's early story, "Mr. McGregor." In this story of an antebellum plantation, the planter kills a slave when the slave attempts to avenge the whipping that Mr. McGregor has given the slave's wife. Lytle's focus on the complex dynamics of Mr. and Mrs. McGregor diverts attention from the brutal reality of slavery.

Caroline Gordon, like Lytle, was a conservative Agrarian who is also well known for her teaching as well as for her writing. Gordon was born in Todd County, Kentucky, less than a mile from the Tennessee border. As a child, she moved to Clarksville where she was educated in her father's classical school. Gordon, far more prolific than Lytle, published nine novels and two collections of short stories before her death in 1981. Like Lytle never lacking in proficiency, Gordon was essentially a writer's writer. As exemplified by her first novel, *Penhally* (1931), she often fictionalized her Meriwether relatives who settled along the Kentucky/Tennessee border around 1800. Life in the fictionalized Clarksville is associated with the decay of Agrarian ideals. Her best novel may be *Aleck Maury, Sportsman*, a collaboration with her father. *None Shall Look Back* (1937) is often ranked among the best Civil War novels; *The Garden of Adonis* (1937) is her perceptive Agrarian response to the Depression; and *The Women on the Porch* (1944), a dark contemplation on love relationships inspired by her tumultuous marriage with Tate, is her most underrated novel. After this novel, Gordon's fiction was deeply influenced by her conversion to Catholicism. The most successful of the later novels is *The Strange Children* (1951), which fictionalizes her life at Benfolly during the 1930s. As impres-

sive as Gordon is as a novelist, her greatest accomplishments might be her short stories. Like her novels, her stories are always technically refined (Gordon became Flannery O'Connor's technical adviser). Among her best stories are "The Petrified Woman," "Old Red," and "The Presence." An oddity of Tennessee literature is that the small city of Clarksville produced two important writers, Gordon and Scott, at approximately the same time, and that these women looked at Tennessee from such sharply contrasting perspectives. Scott is the voice of T'other Mounting, essentially countercultural; Gordon is the voice of Old Rocky-Top, essentially reaffirming the importance of traditional art and culture.

The second generation of the Fugitive/Agrarian/New Criticism movements produced two Tennessee writers of the highest order: Randall Jarrell, born in Nashville in 1914, and Peter Taylor, born in Trenton in 1917. These two writers benefited greatly from Tennessee's centrality within the Southern Renascence; however, as writers of another generation, neither conformed to the more conservative social concepts of the Agrarians. Jarrell's distance from his mentors is already apparent in his 1941 review of Tate's *Reason in Madness* as Jarrell groups Tate with his Agrarian/New Criticism brothers, arguing that Tate was "eager to sacrifice the scientific, mathematical, and technical half of European culture, in order to return to the good society (traditional, theological, based on property, the 'primary medium through which man expressed his moral nature') that is the womb from which the rest of us have struggled to get free." Jarrell moved to California for ten years where his father worked as a photographer. He returned to Nashville when his mother separated from his father. He received his B.A. in psychology from Vanderbilt in 1936 and his M.A. in 1939. In poetry, he was encouraged and assisted by Ransom, Tate, Davidson, and Warren. Later at Kenyon, he lived with Robert Lowell and Peter Taylor. Jarrell is equally accomplished as poet and critic, although, like his mentors, he more highly valued his poetry. In his best-known poem, "The Death of the Ball Turret Gunner," in only five lines he is able to capture the horror of war. Here as elsewhere, Jarrell's favorite images are very basic: sleeping, dreaming, waking, and dying. Jarrell is the master of the simple statement, as in another impressive World War II poem, "Losses": "We died like aunts or pets or foreigners." What contemplation occurs is oddly irrefutable, as in "A Girl in a Library": "And yet, the ways we miss our lives are life." In "Siegfried," Jarrell expresses his naturalistic sense of an indifference in nature: "In Nature there is neither right nor left nor wrong." Though the title "Siegfried" encourages historical layering, the poem itself distrusts profundity—seeking instead a minimalist perspective of one turret gunner's loss of a leg. The gunner understands that he has changed because "You have tasted your own blood." The rightness of the poem derives from Jarrell's willingness to be no more than the gunner and to accept that the lesson of blood requires no explanation. Jarrell does not assume that he or his world can rely upon a stable base of community and religion. The spiritual force within Jarrell, often defined by the power of dreams, has no cultural anchor.

At first glance, Peter Taylor may appear closer than Jarrell to the Fugitive/Agrarian/New Criticism nucleus, but he is actually much closer to Jarrell. Although he portrays a more traditional southern culture, Taylor's detached, whimsical perspective offers his readers little assurance that the models of the southern past can be used as a defense against decay. Taylor descended from a Tennessee governor; his father practiced law in Trenton, Nashville, Memphis, and St. Louis. During the 1930s, Taylor followed his Agrarian mentors from Southwestern to Vanderbilt to Kenyon. As a fiction writer, Taylor was most inclined to build upon his early experiences in Nashville and Memphis. Like his mentors, Taylor was greatly influenced by Henry James, and, in fact, may be the most thoroughly Jamesian writer of the twentieth century, although Chekhov is also an important early influence. What Taylor has in common with Jarrell is most apparent in the voice, which is calm and civil, almost as though neither writer wants to call too much attention to himself. Taylor's literary reputation was based almost entirely upon his finely crafted short stories until the publication of *A Summons to Memphis* in 1986. Another distinguished novel, *In the Tennessee Country,* appeared in 1994, the year of Taylor's death. These two novels justify some modification of the view of Taylor as a short-story specialist. The novels may at first appear to be the tranquil reminiscence of an aging man recalling a bygone South, but more accurately they are delving, challenging reassessments of southern history. Taylor is interested in how lives are shaped by convention, but, like James and Chekhov, Taylor views the human state as an inevitable confusion of impulses, particularly sexual or love impulses, clashing with the governing principles of community.

Taylor's finely crafted short stories have much in common with Jarrell's poems, for both writers look carefully into the hidden recesses of unexceptional, private lives. In "The Gift of the Prodigal," a wealthy widower awaits a visit from his son, Ricky. The widower knows that Ricky will again need help extricating himself from an escapade involving cockfights, race horses, shootings, or adulterous women. The widower's other children, responsible adults, want him to have no more to do with Ricky. When Ricky is about to relate his latest escapade, he sees the pain medications that the father usually hides from his children. He then disturbs his father by turning to leave. The father suddenly realizes that he desperately needs to hear the son's tawdry tale; as Ricky begins, the father is "wild with anticipation." The son lives out a side of the father that the father will not permit direct expression. In one of Taylor's best Memphis stories, "The Old Forest," a young upper-class man has an auto accident while out with a young modern woman, Lee Ann. She flees the scene of the accident, running into the Old Forest, not wishing to be implicated in a possible scandal since the young man is engaged to a proper woman, Caroline. The story is a perceptive unraveling of rigid class and gender structures. It is finally Caroline who finds and confronts Lee Ann, and it is Caroline's later conversation with her fiancé that is at the heart of the story. The engaged woman reveals her own sense of entrapment as she envies the "working girls" who, without cultural advantages, are permitted the freedom to make and break relationships with men since they have no cultural expectations to meet. Taylor's most underappreciated story is "Rain in the Heart," an early story based on his World War II experience. In this story, Taylor seems to relax some of his New Criticism control and creates a touching mood piece about a recently married sergeant who learns something about intimacy but also discovers its limitations in the face of life's crudity and cruelty. Taylor's most anthologized story, "A Spinster's Tale," is about a child who is fated to become a spinster. Her obsessive repulsion for the drunken Mr. Speed reveals her physical recoil from bestial release, which she subconsciously associates with male sexuality.

A late-life surge in Taylor's popularity occurred with the publication of *A Summons to Memphis,* a novel that in some ways reads like a sequel to his early short novel, *A Woman of Means* (1950). Both novels unfold from the perspective of a brother who contends with two rambunctious sisters and who tries to understand who his father is, and in both cases this lesson must be learned through the father's lost love. In *A Woman of Means*, the narrator is a boy, and the sisters are really stepsisters, the daughters of his wealthy stepmother. His father has extricated the boy, Quint, from his agrarian Tennessee roots and has introduced Quint to the wealth and prestige of St. Louis society. Quint adores his new family, particularly his beautiful, sensitive stepmother, and only gradually comes to realize her instability. At the same time, Quint learns that his father's ambition has created conflict in his present marriage and that his stepmother suspects that she has been married for her money. In the end, Quint is left with a father whose love is now seen as real but tainted. Taylor includes the Agrarian message—Quint would have been better off left on his grandmother's farm—but far more compelling is Quint's descent into the impure love that seems to underlie the ideal of family. Likewise in *A Summons to Memphis*, a middle-aged man is called away from his New York profession and unconventional relationship to his Memphis roots. His sisters, who are equally unconventional, insist that he return to Memphis to stop their father from a late-life marriage. Taylor's greatest achievement is in tracing the father from the domineering male who moved his family from Nashville to Memphis, ignoring his wife's preference and the developmental need of his daughters, to the man who now longs for love and finds himself at the mercy of the grown daughters who both respect and resent him. Taylor, always aware of complex undercurrents, encourages the reader to both sympathize with the father and to see the comic justice that is enacted upon him.

In the Tennessee Country returns to the idea of Lee Ann disappearing into the Old Forest. The concept is similar to Ralph Ellison's idea in *Invisible Man* of stepping outside of history—no longer defining oneself as an entity of culture. In the narrator's childhood, Cousin Aubrey, the bastard of the family patriarch, disappears from the family immediately after the patriarch's death. Like Lee Ann in "The Old Forest," Cousin Aubrey has no choice but to be somewhat outside the circle since he is not deemed a suitable match for anyone within it. Like Lee Ann, this gives him heroic possibilities. He has the advantage over the narrator because he can see the family connection from the outside and can choose anonymity. The role of the artist is central in that the narrator was once an aspiring artist but has chosen the safer life of a college professor—what Cousin Aubrey calls a "safe harbor."

Two of Taylor's Tennessee contemporaries are Mad-

ison Jones (born 1925 in Nashville) and Jesse Hill Ford (born 1928 in Alabama, but grew up in Nashville). Both are good novelists who were students of the Agrarians and characterize both the influence of the movement in Tennessee and also the postmodern shift from the Agrarians' more conservative tendencies. Two of their best novels, *The Liberation of Lord Byron Jones* (1965) by Ford and *A Cry of Absence* by Jones (1971), deal with the effect of desegregation in the South. Central are the roles of Oman Hedgepath in *The Liberation* and Mrs. Delmore in *A Cry*. These characters of the southern aristocracy represent the established traditions of the South under siege. In both novels, a liberal young man struggles to free himself from the hold of the patriarch or matriarch. Hedgepath and Delmore both must see themselves as responsible for racial killings because they have tried to hold together the traditional patterns of black/white relationships. Yet one cannot read these novels without realizing that Ford and Jones have a great deal of sympathy for Hedgepath and Delmore and that both novelists resent the intrusions of the federal government, large corporations, and northern liberals. To an extent, Ford and Jones are loyal to the vision of their Agrarian mentors. They write in the tradition of the "well-made novel" and portray their home state with great sympathy for its traditional, communal life-style. However, Ford and Jones are far more willing to confront the ugly specter of racism, and they force the primary representatives of communal southern tradition to realize that the avoidance of change will inevitably place them on the side of the most deadly forces in the South.

The most important African American writer associated with Tennessee is Richard Wright, but his connection with Tennessee is limited. Wright was born in Mississippi in 1908, but his family moved to Memphis in 1912. In childhood, Wright moved to Arkansas and back to Mississippi, then returned to Memphis to work after his high-school graduation. In 1927 he moved to Chicago, in 1937 to New York, later becoming an expatriate. His connection with Tennessee is tenuous but plays an important role in his brilliant autobiography *Black Boy* (1945). Two other African American writers with close ties to Tennessee, Alex Haley (born in New York in 1921 but raised in Henning) and Nikki Giovanni (born 1943 in Knoxville) have had a significant impact on social change following desegregation. Alex Haley's *Roots* (1976) gained phenomenal success first as a novel, then with the popular television production based upon it. Haley's search for his roots encouraged an American reevaluation of African American history. Yolande Cornelia ("Nikki") Giovanni is a prolific and talented poet as well as a social activist, and her poetry is often an extension of her political passion.

This tide of change since the 1960s has shifted Tennessee literature from the Fugitive/Agrarian/New Criticism movements to a postmodern literature that is less grounded in the southern traditions of community and religion. The more disruptive, countercultural elements have become the dominant strain since 1960. The primary center of literary activity has also shifted from Middle Tennessee with Nashville as the core of activity to East Tennessee with Knoxville as the core. In the later stage of modernism, James Agee (born 1909 in Knoxville) characterizes the East Tennessee contrast to the Agrarian movement. Agee's documentary masterpiece *Let Us Now Praise Famous Men* (1941, with photographs by Walker Evans) is an experimental documentary of 1930s southern tenant farmers and their families. Agee is a technician, more Proustian than Faulknerian. His devotion is to the sensory moment; though a sophisticated realist, Agee has no patience with minimalist compression. His interest is in the individual detail, individual moment, individual life, and this involvement seems to negate the programmatic. His best works, *Let Us Now Praise Famous Men* and his posthumous autobiographical novel, *A Death in the Family* (1957), offer wonderful moments, keenly perceived and technically challenging (cinema was a major involvement and influence), but they are by the classical standards favored by the New Critics devoid of unity. Agee lacks the mythos of the Agrarians, and his texts, to be appreciated, must be measured by another standard. Each moment to Agee is a gestalt and the role of the artist is to capture it as much as possible. Agee struggles to define the real and sometimes frightening characteristics of human love and is interested in the dynamics of family. However, Agee's families are removed from southern aristocracy, a cultural phenomenon of less significance in the mountain culture of East Tennessee.

The most undervalued poet in Tennessee is another East Tennessean with limited connection to the Fugitive/Agrarian/New Criticism movements. George Scarbrough was born in Polk County in 1915, the son of a tenant farmer. Scarbrough, who farmed much of his life, lives in Oak Ridge. An impressive early collection is *New Course Is Upward* (1951) and the best source for a full appreciation of his work is *New and Selected Poems* (1977). The early poems tend to be more con-

ventionally structured than the later poems. Though both Agee and Scarbrough were lauded by Allen Tate, both are more autobiographical writers than the Agrarians, and both are more direct and idiosyncratic in their language. Unlike Tate's Eliot influence, Scarbrough writes more in the tradition of William Carlos Williams. Some of his best poems are intimate responses to loss: in "Impasse," his father dies in a small room with "A window too high / to let the yard in / but perfect for / the exit of souls," and in "Afternoon," a dead brother is reserved his birthright: "But I hunt no more. / The land is posted / with his firstborn right." Scarbrough is most impressive when he looks upon the natural world, with linguistic play that is both tense and witty. "Pied Beauty" pays tribute to Hopkins, but as a directive on the education of a child into the ways of nature, the poem is also an initiation into decadence. The boy is identified by his "bloody, execrable mess of / a family face." Contemplations of nature and family balance between dream and reality. Nature's sweet savagery is expressed in "Blood Seed," with its tribute to ripe strawberries: "my blood singing like pure mud." Scarbrough's poetry has an untamed quality; the natural world he strives to capture in his art is an interlacing of patterns and blood force, like the children in "Rings" who ignore a downward winding path, oblivious to the designs of nature, and tumble straight to the bottom.

Mildred Haun (born 1911 in Hamblen County) and David Madden (born 1933 in Knoxville) are two more East Tennessee writers who benefited from the Tennessee Agrarian movement but whose writings are better understood outside its more conservative characteristics. Haun's entire reputation is based upon one book, *The Hawk's Done Gone and Other Stories* (1968, enlarged from *The Hawk's Done Gone*, published in 1941). These stories are often as raw and grotesque as Erskine Caldwell's stories, but they are less comic and more sensitive to the humanity that lies beneath the crudity of the lives depicted. David Madden's first successful novel is his lively but diffuse autobiographical novel about growing up in Knoxville, *Bijou* (1974). His later fiction is more disciplined; the best is *The Suicide's Wife* (1978), a novel about university life, far above the norm for this genre. The novel is the perceptive portrait of a woman whose husband, a professorial mediocrity, has left her with the need to redefine herself. In his more recent Civil War novel *Sharpshooter* (1996), Madden combines his interests in psychology and epistemology as a Civil War veteran attempts to piece together a past that has defined him yet that has no definitive reality. As postmodern metafiction, this novel is far removed from the Civil War revisionism of the Agrarians.

The shift of literary focus to East Tennessee is most apparent in the rising reputation of Cormac McCarthy. McCarthy was born in Rhode Island in 1933 but moved to Knox County three years later. He attended a Catholic high school in Knoxville, briefly attended the University of Tennessee before enlisting in the air force, and returned to UT where he began writing novels, including his first published novel, *The Orchard Keeper* (1965). McCarthy's novels divide into two categories: the early novels of the Allegheny Mountains and the late novels of the American Southwest and Mexico. McCarthy's reputation has been enhanced by the popularity of *All the Pretty Horses* (1992); however, he has received widespread praise and consistently won literary awards since the publication of his first novel. He is one of the truly original voices in American literature, and his novels alone encourage a reevaluation of Tennessee literature. He is the quintessential voice from T'other Mounting—whatever community and organized religion meant to the Agrarians, it means something quite different to McCarthy. Certainly McCarthy would agree with the Agrarians that progress is meaningless barbarism, that one should try to find a way back to something more substantial. However, no historical model of men living in leisurely harmony with nature invades McCarthy's world. McCarthy looks to the primeval. *The Orchard Keeper* begins McCarthy's fascination with the outlaw; the young protagonist's mentors are a moonshine runner and a reclusive eco-terrorist. By the time these men are confined and brutalized by the law, the boy has already decided that the only way to stay alive is as a cultural outlaw, a conclusion from which McCarthy does not waiver in his later novels. *Child of God* (1974) epitomizes the dark powers that rule in McCarthy's world. Lester Ballard of Sevier County is thrown from his land as the novel begins and moves deeper into an isolated cave world of bestial urges. His greatest gratification is to copulate with the women he has murdered. He is the nightmare Caliban of a world with no Prospero.

To appreciate fully McCarthy's remarkable prose, the last and most ambitious Tennessee novel, *Suttree* (1979), and the first western novel, *Blood Meridian* (1985), are essential reading. In both cases, a young man, a Tennessee outcast, maneuvers within a wilderness wonderland. Suttree's world is the Knoxville un-

derground, an intoxicated counterculture unwilling to adapt to Knoxville's respectable work force. McCarthy pays tribute to Knoxville's literary tradition with reference to the John Agee steamboat and, more important, with a protagonist usually called "Sut." As in Harris's Sut Lovingood stories, the fictional world of Suttree is packed with comic fools, particularly Harrogate, who steals pigs, blows up caves, poisons bats, electrocutes pigeons, and fornicates with watermelons—a "convicted pervert of a botanical bent." Suttree was born into the southern gentry but, like Sut Lovingood, has a weakness for the bottle and has descended to his life on a dilapidated houseboat. McCarthy often uses archetypal patterns; in this case, Suttree was born the twin of a stillborn baby and is haunted by his lost sibling. When a derelict friend tries to hide his father's rotting body, chained on the river bottom, the friend later complains that "he come up, Sut. Draggin all them chains with him." Suttree's laconic response is that "fathers will do that." McCarthy's description of one backwoods family could be used to sum up the effect of not only *Suttree* but also his other novels: "They could have been some band of stone age folk washed up out of an atavistic dream." McCarthy believes in evil. His world is an American gothic wilderness as it might be imagined by Poe but would never be imagined by Emerson. In *Blood Meridian*, McCarthy's movement into the "bloodlands of the West" is a ghoulish lesson in American history. Early in the novel, the protagonist, called simply "the kid," spends a night with an old hermit who believes that the human heart is distinctive: "You can find meanness in the least of creatures, but when God made man the devil was at his elbow." The rest of the novel gives clear evidence to the hermit's argument. The kid joins a gang of scalp-hunters in pursuit of Apaches. The gang and the Apaches massacre with the same brutality.

Just as caves are a dominant image in McCarthy's East Tennessee novels, wolves are a dominant image in the western novels. Caves are the primal passages lying secretly beneath civilization: in *Child of God*, they house the theater of Ballard's rotting lovers; in *Suttree*, they tell a geological history and the history of war while they also carry the excrement of Knoxville. In *Blood Meridian*, the wolves howl in the background, and when their moment arrives they feast on the human slaughter fields. In *The Crossing* (1994), the youthful protagonist, Billy Parham, traps a lone wolf that has crossed over from Mexico and tries to return the wolf to the Mexico mountains. In Mexico, the wolf is taken from Parham and is forced to fight dogs for human entertainment. Billy kills the wolf to save it from society, then returns to the States only to find that his parents have been murdered by roaming thieves. Billy returns to Mexico with his younger brother to avenge his parents' death but loses his brother and ends up alone—as much of an anachronism as the lone wolf he could not save. The wolf for McCarthy expresses something grand in its savagery, something too grand to be tolerated by a world that tries to deny its own savagery. McCarthy's most commercially successful novel, *All the Pretty Horses,* is not his best, although it is interesting in its contrast of the American Southwest and Mexico. When the novel's hero, John Grady Cole, another man-child existing on the cultural fringe, descends into Mexico after losing the family ranch, McCarthy describes a world caught between myth and reality.

Another contemporary novelist from East Tennessee who has received some recognition and deserves far more is Lisa Alther (born 1944 in Kingsport). Alther gained recognition with her first novel, *Kinflicks* (1975), a romping, autobiographical, picaresque adventure, a product of the youth rebellion of the 1960s. What separates Alther from any number of fellow novelists thumbing their noses at the establishment is her wit, a product of her fine intellect and ruthlessly honest nature. She is a true descendent of Evelyn Scott as she cannot accept stability and disrupts systems through her questioning of premises. Despite a shared interest in the natural sciences and a similar preoccupation with decay and death, Alther employs a postmodern style distinct from McCarthy's. McCarthy moves the Faulknerian style forward in a direction similar to the marginal surrealism of John Hawkes. This direction of postmodern fiction has a fabulistic tendency whereas Alther's postmodernism derives from a tradition that extends from Henry Miller and the Beat writers. Alther is not comfortable with fabulistic, near-mythological invention but rather uses artistic variations of personal experience. Her protagonist in *Kinflicks,* Ginny Babcock, is every bit the American picaro, protean but with new twists for her age and gender. Most important, Alther, unlike McCarthy, is drawn to the power of relationships. Whereas McCarthy's technique often relies upon a masculine-defined, masculine-dominated world in order to test the limits of human behavior, Alther's technique relies upon the struggle to love—a struggle that often requires that her characters define themselves outside the traditional social system. In

Alther's most impressive novel, *Other Women* (1984), she manages to contain her vibrant wit without destroying it. She switches her terrain from Tennessee to the Northeast much as McCarthy switches his to the Southwest; Alther also moves more aggressively into an investigation of lesbian relationships. *Other Women* is a convincing, intelligent study of two women involved in talk therapy, a patient and a therapist. It avoids the usual pitfall of pop therapy—easy answers to impossible questions. Neither patient nor therapist is self-assured; both are caregivers haunted by death. Both learn a little more about themselves, but one need not fear the usual resolution of cathartic emotional release followed by exit into the beautiful land of the healed. Alther accepts that all do suffer from life itself, but she also believes that relationships define people, and through time and effort some may learn from loving. Alther is willing to interlock two separate stories without forcing a predictable dovetail effect. The women become important in each other's lives; however, the primary target remains the complex reality of each.

Alther's next two novels, *Bedrock* (1990) and *Five Minutes in Heaven* (1995), are not as impressive as *Other Women,* but they are mature, engaging novels by a writer who has not lost her comic flair. Whereas McCarthy immerses the reader in the primitive, Alther uses her humor to remind readers that culture hides the beast. In *Bedrock,* Clea learns that the quaint exterior of New England is also an illusion. One woman who appears to be devoting her life to her aging, ailing mother is slowly murdering her instead. While lesbian love continues to be an important theme, Alther's central concern in *Bedrock* is the relationship between truth and art. Two women (one a commercial photographer who specializes in the picturesque, the other a sculptor who specializes in suffering and the grotesque) try to understand their love for each other but only as part of a greater understanding of themselves as artists. With what Alther identifies as an American's "implacable innocence," her characters keep questing, searching for answers even when they realize there can be no final interpretation—that possibly "change is all there is." Alther's counter-spirit to McCarthy is based upon her suspicion that "solitude was an illusion." Although her unstable characters have relationships only with great difficulty, they discover that even when they seek isolation, they are tied to lives from which they cannot disengage. *Five Minutes in Heaven* is Alther's most concentrated study of sexual attraction and her most decidedly lesbian novel. It follows a woman's life from the Smoky Mountains of Tennessee to the streets of Paris. Alther would like the novel to bridge the gap of primitive sexual urges and meaningful relationships, but the novel is unable to do so. Although the honesty of the quest is admirable, a deeper despair cannot be lifted as each relationship is limited by a desperate sexual urgency.

The youngest Tennessee writer to receive widespread literary acclaim was born in Nashville in 1957 and raised on a farm in Williamson County. Madison Smartt Bell is yet another postmodern writer more accurately associated with T'other Mounting than with Old Rocky-Top. His first novel, *The Washington Square Ensemble* (1983), characterizes his position far away from the southern cultural traditions. Rather than a first novel about Tennessee life, Bell's novel is constructed from the voices of four heroin dealers in a New York City neighborhood. Since his first novel, Bell has proven himself a daring and unusually prolific craftsman. His second novel, *Straight Cut*, again demonstrates that he is more comfortable focusing on the cultural underground. From his rural Tennessee retreat, the protagonist, Tracy, is coerced by an old friend, Kevin, to accept a film-editing job in Rome. The care with which Bell treats the description of film editing is similar to McCarthy's fascination with precise description of physical technique. Both writers are drawn to life's doers—the great shot, the consummate horseman, the meticulous film editor—and one can see their own reverential view of writing as craft. *Straight Cut* is an admirably unified novel depicting a world of sexual confusion, drug trade, gangsters, and betrayal. One of Bell's best stories, "Monkey Park," uses a similar triangle. The story follows the ordinary adventures of three characters, a young woman and the two young men who are apparently in love with her. The story never clearly defines the relationships; the deeper levels of reality are left submerged. The activities (drinking, putting on stage makeup, swinging, and watching monkeys) all suggest that something might break loose at any moment; the tension is maintained to the end of the story. Bell's most-developed, direct use of his Tennessee background occurs in his fourth novel, *Soldier's Joy*. This novel introduces a character, a Vietnam veteran, who is similar to McCarthy's Suttree in that he descends from southern aristocracy. Bell seems to be paying his respects to a rural heritage as his hero, Laidlow, returns to the semblance of an agrarian life, even if alone in a former tenant's shack. The novel, despite

great promise, loses control in the second half as it seems determined to outdo the climax of Robert Altman's *Nashville*. Bell focuses on southern racism as Laidlow attempts to reestablish his boyhood friendship with the son of the black tenant farmer who had once been Laidlow's surrogate father. Bell impressively develops the tangled, confused love of these young men, but when he portrays southern racists, his image of the South loses its resonance as we are left with broad enactments of racial war and militaristic heroism. Certainly with the conclusion, one can see that Bell too is more comfortable looking at Tennessee from the outlaw perspective of T'other Mounting.

Steven T. Ryan

See also Agrarians; Fugitives, The; Literary Magazines of the Past; Literary Magazines of the Present; New Criticism; Postmodernism; Southern Renascence.

Joseph Blotner, *Robert Penn Warren: A Biography* (1997); George Core, ed., *The Critics Who Made Us* (1993); Louise Cowan, *The Fugitive Group: A Literary History* (1959); William Pratt, ed., *The Fugitive Poets: Modern Southern Poetry in Perspective* (1991); Phyllis Tickle, *Homeworks: A Book of Tennessee Writers* (1996); Mary Wheeling White, *Fighting the Current: The Life and Work of Evelyn Scott* (1998); Ray Willbanks, ed., *Literature of Tennessee* (1984); Thomas Daniel Young, *Tennessee Writers* (1981).

TENNESSEE–KNOXVILLE, UNIVERSITY OF

Established in 1794, Tennessee's flagship university has fostered its share of writers with southern connections and concerns. Among faculty authors who favored southern subjects and settings, the most significant was Richard Beale Davis, whose three-volume, National Book Award–winning *Intellectual Life in the Colonial South, 1585–1763* (1977) remains one of the most eminent scholarly contributions to the field of southern literature. The same year Davis's *magnum opus* was published marked the visiting professorship of Wilma Dykeman, author of *The Tall Woman* (1962) and *Return the Innocent Earth* (1973). Dykeman's subsequent adjunct status with the University continued until her retirement in 1995, and she currently serves officially as Tennessee's state historian and unofficially as its most articulate environmental advocate. In the last two decades, the University of Tennessee has benefited richly from the creative talents of such writer/academics as Jon Manchip White, Arthur Smith, and Marilyn Kallet. Of particular note to students of southern literature, however, are Robert Drake's *Amazing Grace* (1965) and *What Will You Do for an Encore? And Other Stories* (1996), based on his reminiscences of his West Tennessee childhood, and *Walking on Water and Other Stories* (1996) by Allen Wier, 1997 recipient of the Chubb-Life America Robert Penn Warren Award for Fiction.

Clarence Brown, a 1910 graduate, received six Academy Awards for film direction, including one for his film of Marjorie Kinnan Rawlings's *The Yearling*; he also received the 1949 British Academy Award for his direction of William Faulkner's *Intruder in the Dust* (1948). Joseph Wood Krutch, another Tennessee alumnus, was a longtime drama critic for the *Nation* whose 1925 coverage of the Scopes trial revealed his awareness of a conflicted New South. Perhaps the University's most prominent former students with southern literary connections are Richard Marius, David Madden, and Cormac McCarthy. Marius, a 1954 graduate and later professor of history (1964–1978), focused on East Tennessee in such novels as *The Coming of Rain* (1969) and *After the War* (1992). A Knoxville native, Madden graduated in 1957 and used hometown settings and personae in such early novels as *Bijou* (1974) as well as in his most recent works *Sharpshooter: A Novel of the Civil War* (1996) and *Remembering James Agee* (1997). McCarthy received his first writing award as an undergraduate at the University and infused his early works, most notably *The Orchard Keeper* (1965) and *Suttree* (1979), with a sense of his East Tennessee and Knoxville background.

Patricia L. Bradley

See also Tennessee, Literature of.

Kenneth Curry, *English at Tennessee: 1794–1988* (1989).

TENNESSEE VALLEY AUTHORITY (TVA)

Created by an act of Congress on May 18, 1933, as a federal corporate agency, the Tennessee Valley Authority (TVA) exemplified Roosevelt's New Deal programs for social and economic development. Within ten years, TVA had built a dozen dams, overcome hostility to what some perceived as a second federal invasion of the South, weathered major constitutional challenges to its existence in two cases ultimately decided by the Supreme Court, and grown to be the country's largest supplier of electricity. By concentrating on dams and locks, TVA rapidly achieved major goals such as flood control, improved navigation on the Tennessee River, and expanded generating capacity for electricity. TVA also introduced modern farming techniques, initiated the widespread use of fertilizers, and virtually eliminated malaria in the region.

During World War II, TVA contributed significantly to the national defense by supplying power to critical industries (especially aluminum manufacturing necessary for airplane parts) and to the atomic-bomb project in Oak Ridge, Tennessee. As the demand for electricity soared in the following decades, TVA began constructing fossil-fuel and nuclear generating plants. With revenues from power sales exceeding $5.5 billion annually and an installed generating capacity in excess of 28,000 megawatts, TVA remains the nation's largest power producer and supplies electricity for nearly eight million people in an 86,000-square-mile service area spanning parts of seven states.

Although TVA has appeared prominently in a variety of literary forms ranging from poems and songs to novels, a play, and even a movie, the TVA canon remains small. For the most part, these works focus on the events surrounding TVA's first decade. William Bradford Huie's *Mud on the Stars* (1942) and Borden Deal's *Dunbar's Cove* (1957), for example, successfully evoke a sense of time and place surrounding TVA's early years. Each accords TVA generally sympathetic treatment but also explores negative aspects of the TVA experiment, including the sharp clash between individual and governmental rights that accompanied TVA's construction programs. *Mud on the Stars* tracks a young Alabama man's personal growth in response to major political and social events during the decade leading up to World War II, starting with his bitter reaction to TVA's acquisition of family land and progressing to a recognition of the social and economic benefits accompanying TVA's flood control and power programs. *Dunbar's Cove* focuses on the emotional turmoil that TVA construction brings to a rural Tennessee family by contrasting the pain of being forced from land held for generations with the opportunities offered by TVA, including well-paying employment in a traditionally impoverished region. *Wild River,* a 1960 movie produced and directed by Elia Kazan and featuring Montgomery Clift and Lee Remick, borrows themes and characters loosely from both novels while dramatizing (and, at times, introducing) regional and class distinctions to evoke an emotional response.

The thesis that TVA brought social betterment to the region has been captured in *Power,* a 1937 play developed by the Federal Theater Project to support TVA's aggressive competition with private utilities, and in several folk songs, two of which claim the same title, "The TVA Song." In a series of vignettes that draw frequently upon actual events, *Power* uses a blend of stock and historical characters to stress the broad social and economic benefits that will accompany the advent of widespread, low-cost electricity as power (literally and figuratively) passes from private ownership to public hands.

In the songs, however, the focus is wholly on the individual. For example, in the more interesting of the two TVA songs, a ballad that originated in Kentucky during the mid-1930s, a young man lauds the government's intervention in the marketplace; as a result of TVA's construction projects, he at last finds work and achieves the economic wherewithal that allows him to marry. A similar theme is advanced in Bob McDill's "Song of the South" (1980), made popular by the group Alabama, which recounts the loss of a family farm in the Great Depression and the family's subsequent economic rebound after the breadwinner finds work with TVA. Viewed from today's perspective, the lyrics may seem improbable or merely sentimental; viewed against the historical record, they come close to understatement.

In "The Night the Bucket Fell," a short story published in the July 1936 issue of the *Virginia Quarterly Review,* Leonard Rapport provides a chilling counterpoint to the facile optimism of *Power* and the songs. This early piece relates the sense of foreboding felt by local men laboring in a new type of workplace where machines at times appear to be their masters. The men recognize the benefits that electricity and flood control will bring, but they intuitively understand as well that a rural life-style grounded on individualism is being exchanged for an organized, hierarchical existence—a trade that will not always equate to an improvement. Rapport, who worked as a laborer one summer on TVA's Norris Dam, also reveals the immense personal danger entailed in such massive construction projects. The human cost of progress was in fact very high; by the end of TVA's first decade, more than a hundred workers had been killed on TVA projects.

In the field of juvenile fiction, several authors have used the dislocations required by TVA's dam program to explore family relationships. John R. Tunis's *Son of the Valley* (1949) is unusual in primarily examining TVA's role in agricultural development. Norma Cole's *The Final Tide* (1990) centers on the affinity between a girl and her grandmother who resists moving from ancestral land; and Carolyn Williford's *Jordan's Bend* (1995) adds a Christian perspective by portraying the upheaval as a threat to a young girl's faith.

Notwithstanding tremendous achievements in bringing flood control and inexpensive electric-power availability to the Tennessee Valley region, significant and sustained criticism has been directed at TVA for the last thirty years. Critics have accused TVA of a loss of vision and have focused their complaints primarily upon environmental concerns about air pollution and nuclear power. The proposed deregulation of the energy industry, challenges from utility competitors, and conservative political trends suggest that major changes will occur at the agency in the coming years.

Peter K. Shea

See also Tennessee, Literature of.

North Callahan, *TVA* (1980); Erwin C. Hargrove, *Prisoners of Myth* (1994); David E. Lilienthal, *Journals of David E. Lilienthal,* Vol. 1: *The TVA Years, 1939–1945* (1964); Steven M. Neuse, *David E. Lilienthal* (1996); Marguerite Owen, *The Tennessee Valley Authority* (1973).

TEXAS, EAST, LITERATURE OF

East Texas literature, which exists in greater abundance than is commonly recognized, presents a difficult problem of definition. Texas itself can be considered to have at least five distinct regions, and there are at least three literatures of the state. To some observers, including the novelist William Humphrey, West Texas with its icons of longhorn and cowboy seems in recent decades to have taken over the whole, at any rate in the public mind. Even so, the division of East and West Texas (to disregard, for the moment, the South Texas or Valley region and less distinct other regions of the state) is basic and profound, despite the fact that it is hard to say just where the one becomes the other. This very fact makes Texas an ideal test case in literary regionalism. William A. Owens, distinguished folklorist-novelist from what might be called *echt* East Texas, the northeastern piney woods near the Red River, asks rhetorically where the South ends and the West begins and answers that the "boundary" cannot be "easily determined."

Although it may now make more sense to think in terms of Interstate 35, the geographical boundary between East and West Texas is traditionally drawn at the Trinity River or the Brazos. Another convenient geographical demarcation is provided by a sharp declivity known as the White Rock Escarpment that runs roughly north-south between Dallas and Fort Worth (the city "where the West begins") and on down just west of the town of Mexia before fading out. Despite these conventional markers, East and West Texas overlap in the center of the state in a belt of ambiguity. R. G. Vliet, himself a (West) Texas novelist of notable power, once observed that the border between east and west is "palpable" in the Hays County town of Kyle, between Austin and San Marcos, where Katherine Anne Porter, still probably the foremost of Texas writers, spent her childhood; he attributed to that fact "the difficulty we sometimes have in deciding" whether Porter was "in fact writing about the *South* or the *Southwest*."

Facing west from the White Rock Escarpment, one looks out over a landscape very different from that at one's back: barer, more sparsely watered, ultimately higher, yielding an economy and life-pattern based on cattle-raising. To the east, the land is more like that of the Upper South, lower-lying but broken by hilly areas, well-watered, and heavily wooded. Its icons might be considered the cotton boll, the front porch of a bare-board house, and the pine tree or magnolia. In its cultural affiliations, it is strictly southern. Most of the early Anglo population of the state, in fact, came from the South, many during Reconstruction. William A. Owens says they stopped in East Texas because it was "like back home" and recalls being "nurtured on stories they brought from 'the old country,' meaning Mississippi or some other state of the Deep South." When Frederick Law Olmsted traveled through the area in 1854, recording his impressions in *A Journey Through Texas* (1857), he observed a debased poor-white southern culture with ludicrous pretenses to plantation aristocracy.

It was a literature of this pervasively southern way of life, centered on small farming, family and clan, and religion, that constituted the mainstream of Texas letters until University of Texas folklorist J. Frank Dobie and a group that James Lee refers to as "associated celebrants of a cowboy myth" succeeded in establishing a vision of the state as western. The establishment of the

western image has also, but less persuasively, been attributed to Lyndon Johnson's becoming president and redefining the "national perception of Texas." For a century or more, until the devastation wrought by oil and even more by television, social customs in East Texas ran strongly to preaching, eating-on-the-grounds, and amateur fiddle music. All of these elements are prominent in the abundant fiction and non-fiction and the scarcer poetry and drama of the area. Some observers believe that even though the prevalence of the western vision of Texas is a kind of falsification, it is so indisputably entrenched that the southern literature of the state can be spoken of only in the past tense. But in fact such a literature is ongoing.

Those southerners who came into East Texas in the nineteenth century and kept going adapted and changed, in part by learning new ways from the cattle- and goat-herding *Tejanos* they encountered farther west. There they were more likely to encounter, too, distinct European ethnic groups, a more numerous and more varied population than non-Texans usually realize but mostly settled in the west-central part of the state (though Katherine Anne Porter's autobiographical central character in the story "Holiday" encounters a German family in the southeast corner, near the Louisiana border). The people of East Texas remained a relatively homogeneous southern folk with a way of life traditionally centered on small farming in cleared patches with woods around (and a few larger spreads once worked by slaves brought from farther east), its cash crop mainly cotton. Essayist Leon Hale, in *Turn South at the Second Bridge* (1965), calls it "cotton, corn, and mule country." A rough rule of thumb is that if a piece of Texas writing relates to cotton farming on a small to medium scale or to sharecroppers or woodlands, it is East Texas literature. The advent of irrigation, bringing cotton farming to the High Plains, muddied the issue, but the distinction remains fairly reliable.

Lumbering has also been an important way of life in East Texas (yielding labor unrest in the early twentieth century that drew in the I.W.W.), and the oil industry—notably the Spindletop Field near Beaumont, 1901, and the "Dad" Joiner strike near Henderson, 1930—has wrought predictable devastation along with cash and outside influences. The regional literature includes several noteworthy oil-field novels, such as Karle Wilson Baker's *Family Style* (1937), Mary King's *Quincie Bolliver* (1941), Jewel Gibson's *Black Gold* (1950), and William Owens's *Fever in the Earth* (1958). William Goyen's *Come, the Restorer* (1974) laments the "disaster" that had "struck and changed the towns of East Texas" and "crazed the people."

The southernness of East Texas has also been manifest in a set of long-persevering racial attitudes. A notorious sign that once hung over the main highway entering a particular East Texas town proclaimed "the blackest land and the whitest people." The attitude conveyed by the sign is of course self-evident. But in point of fact, there were blacks as well as whites in most of East Texas (though few Hispanics and almost no Native Americans, they having been virtually wiped out "in contact," to use the common euphemism). But in some areas, blacks were indeed simply excluded through aggressive measures. The Ku Klux Klan has had an active history in the region, headquartered in the town of Vidor, between Beaumont and Orange. The autobiography of C. C. White, an East Texas African American preacher, *No Quittin' Sense* (1969), told to and written by Ada Morehead Holland, records a thirty-three-mile trip on foot that entailed passing through an area where "they don't allow no niggers at all." As Dorothy Redus Robinson writes in her unflinching memoir *The Bell Rings at Four: A Black Teacher's Chronicle of Change* (1978), "in East Texas during the early 1930s, white was white and black was black and never the twain met on common ground."

Race and racism occupy much of the literature of East Texas, occasionally in the falsely idealizing way that might be called a Confederate mode. Don Graham cites, as representing this genre, the novel *And Tell of Time* (1938) by Laura Krey, and the so-called historical writings of J. W. Carhart (*Under the Palmetto and Pine*, 1899) and Nevin W. Winter (*Texas the Marvellous*, 1916). More realistic and searching treatments of race within the East Texas setting include Elizabeth Lee Wheaton's *Mr. George's Joint* (1941), John W. Wilson's *High John the Conqueror* (1948), Owens's *Walking on Borrowed Land* (1954) and *Look to the River* (1963), and Guida Jackson's *Passing Through* (1979). African American voices in the region's literature have been few—for understandable reasons. Among them are Anita Richmond Bunkley, whose *Black Gold* (1994) tells of a black family who strike oil in Mexia and whose *Balancing Act* (1997) deals with chemical pollution and the lives of Texas women, white and black; and J. California Cooper, with novels such as *Family* (1991) and *In Search of Satisfaction* (1994) and an award-winning short-story collection, *Homemade Love* (1987). Mention should be made, too, of short-

story writers Hermine Pinson (also a poet) and Sunny Nash.

The relative homogeneity of East Texas produced distinctiveness of culture and a fiercely populist loyalty to traditions that have yielded an abundance of folk material, including songs and "play-party games" (substitutes for the dancing proscribed by Baptists) as well as stories. A remarkable group of folklorists have gathered and documented this material, among them Dorothy Scarborough (from what is probably the westernmost truly southern town, Waco), who was active in the 1920s and early 1930s; William A. Owens, who began collecting folksongs in the 1930s but was active as a writer from the 1950s to the 1980s, with particular interests in the northeastern counties around Clarksville and Paris and the oil-boom days around Beaumont; Francis Abernethy, whose interest centered on the Big Thicket, a large, ill-defined area of dense woods, nearly impenetrable brush, and hostility to outsiders lying north and west of Beaumont; and J. Mason Brewer, who began collecting "Juneteenth" tales (so called for the date on which news of the Emancipation Proclamation reached Texas) and other African American lore in the late 1920s in the Brazos Bottoms, after his interest shifted from poetry to folklore. The reader interested in folk material would especially want to see Scarborough's *On the Trail of Negro Folksong* (1925), Owens's *Texas Folk Songs* (1950), Abernethy's edited *Tales from the Big Thicket* (1966), and Brewer's *The Word on the Brazos: Negro Preacher Tales from the Brazos Bottoms* (1953), *Aunt Dicy Tales* (1956), and *Dog Ghosts and Other Negro Folk Tales* (1958).

Although Brewer's tales may, as James Lee notes in "The Old South in Texas Literature," "capture the tone and the cadences of black speech," his distortions of spelling in the attempt to capture what he heard are likely to exceed readers' tolerance. The same might be said of those in *Mr. George's Joint*, Elizabeth Lee Wheaton's 1941 novel set in the Texas City area. Dialect is a characteristic of virtually all fiction that attempts to depict the culture of East Texas, whether it is set in the midstate reaches along the Brazos (such as Scarborough's *In the Land of Cotton*, 1923, and Madison Cooper's satiric *Sironia, Texas*, 1952), the Big Thicket, or the counties farther north, toward the Red River. It is a real challenge to a writer to create a sense of the distinctiveness of speech patterns without destroying readability or making characters out to be virtual freaks (as a famous son of western Texas, Larry McMurtry, depicted East Texans in his essay "The Old

Soldier's Joy," from *In a Narrow Grave,* 1968). Some of the best handling of East Texas speech is to be found in William Goyen's densely lyrical *The House of Breath* (1950).

Despite the fact that the so-called Old Guard of Texas letters was indisputably masculine (the Dobie, Perry, Owens, Roy Bedichek, John Graves group), much of the literature of Texas has been written by women. Perhaps the very first book about Texas in English in any genre was a compilation of letters written for purposes of boosterism by the sister of (Anglo) founding father Stephen F. Austin, Mary Austin Holley: *Texas. Observations Historical, Geographical, and Descriptive. In a Series of Letters, Written During a Visit to Austin's Colony, with a View to a Permanent Settlement in That Country, in the Autumn of 1831* (1833). Women's writings in the nineteenth century usually depict a harsh and inhospitable place in which reluctantly pioneering women tried to make homes that would in some way replicate what they had known. This genre, however, is identified more often with West Texas. In the twentieth century, as women's literary activities have increased nationally, many writers have examined the difficulty that Texas women experienced (or still experience) in contending with expectations of a traditional and ladylike variety. Katherine Anne Porter, who noted and resented the masculinist cast of the cultural environment and took as indicative her father's pronouncement that if she wanted so badly to write she should stay home and write letters, fled the state and essentially never returned. Much of the writing done by women in the region has extolled departure.

East Texas writers, male and female alike, have most often worked in prose fiction and in creative nonfiction genres. Historical and journalistic commentaries abound, their plenitude implying that readers continue to regard Texas as something of a curiosity or perhaps that the writers themselves continue to puzzle over the complexities of a divided regional identity. Warren Leslie's controversial *Dallas Public and Private* (1964), which explores in relation to the Kennedy assassination the darker side of the city that has been called the northern capital of East Texas, is a hard-hitting example. Among personal memoirs, besides Robinson's *The Bell Rings at Four,* White and Holland's *No Quittin' Sense,* and Hale's *Turn South at the Second Bridge,* already mentioned, noteworthy examples include Sigman Byrd's *Tall Grew the Pines* (1936), George Sessions Perry's perhaps overly cute *My*

Granny Van (1949), William A. Owens's *This Stubborn Soil* (1966) and *A Season of Weathering* (1973), William Humphrey's *Farther Off from Heaven* (1977), which won the Texas Institute of Letters Award, and in the same year Dorothy Howard's *Dorothy's World: Childhood in Sabine Bottom, 1902–1920,* distinctive for its rendition of a child's point of view and its recording of many childhood games—a folklorist's delight. Bess Whitehead Scott's *You Meet Such Interesting People* (1989) gives an account of her many years on the *Houston Post,* and the highly praised *The Liar's Club* (1995) by Mary Karr tells about growing up in the refinery region at the southeast corner of the state. While illustrating variations among different sections, all of these have a strong regional flavor and a sense of the relative deprivation or hardship of life in the region.

East Texas literature does not generally idealize. If it sometimes runs to quaintness or nostalgia, it also runs to exposure of limited opportunities and narrow social vision. The revolt-against-the-village genre is evident, for example, in Ruth Cross's *The Golden Cocoon* (1924), John Cherry Watson's *The Red Dress* (1949), and Edward Swift's *Splendora* (1978). Jewel Gibson, who began her writing career with the satiric novel *Joshua Beene and God* (1946), depicting in an unusual form the religious absolutism indigenous to the region, turned playwright with treatments of the equally controversial issues of race and bigotry in *Creep Past the Mountain Lion* (1966), seen as hard-hitting in its day but recently termed condescending, and *Brann and The Iconoclast* (1971), about the actual gunning-down of a Waco journalist in the nineteenth century. Horton Foote's justly celebrated plays of Southeast Texas and Houston, such as *Trip to Bountiful* (1954), *A Traveling Woman* (1955), and *The Young Man from Atlanta* (1995), have been able to strike a balance between regret for a vanished past, defective as it was, and acceptance of a less-than-perfect present.

If one had to read only one novel and one's goal were to gain a clear sense of traditional regional life, the choice would probably have to be George Sessions Perry's *Hold Autumn in Your Hand,* which won the Texas Institute of Letters Prize in 1941 and the National Book Award in 1942. James Lee calls it a novel "completely and flatly accurate and true to its surroundings," the Brazos Bottom in the east-central area of the state. The central character is a poor farmer on mediocre land who sets himself the challenge of bringing in a cotton crop equal to that produced on the river-bottom land owned by richer men. Among problems seen in the novel are the dietary deficiencies suffered by his children and common throughout the South of that time. Other novels of cotton-farming life are Scarborough's *In the Land of Cotton* (1923), which draws heavily on her folklore research, Krey's *And Tell of Time,* in a celebratory mode that is inherently racist, and Owens's *Walking on Borrowed Land* (1954), a compelling picture of sharecropping life set across the state line in Oklahoma but faithfully rendering a way of life that Owens knew well from his own East Texas origins.

East Texas literature is not necessarily rural, of course. The category has to be expanded to include evocations of Houston life, such as Larry McMurtry's *Moving On* (1970), *All My Friends Are Going to Be Strangers* (1972), and *Terms of Endearment* (1975), and Laura Furman's *The Shadow Line* (1982), and of Dallas, such as Georgia McKinley's *Follow the Running Grass* (1969) and Bryan Woolley's *November 22* (1981). Much of the regional literature, however, continues to center on small-town life or to ponder the alienation of today's urban Texans from their half-forgotten roots in the piney woods. Barbara Gilstrap's 1987 play *The Alto Part,* for example, concentrates on small-town life while suggesting the allure of a larger world.

Although neither drama nor poetry has flourished in Texas soil as abundantly as fiction and creative nonfiction (the boundary between creative and noncreative being about as elusive, of course, as that between East and West Texas), it is important to acknowledge that there *is* a Texas poetry, and not just the newspaper variety that flourished in the nineteenth and earlier twentieth centuries (which is itself of cultural if not strictly aesthetic interest). Probably the most celebrated poet of East Texas is Houston's Vassar Miller, who has produced a major body of work chiefly exploring religious and very personal concerns. The equally compelling work of Susan Wood, a native of the East Texas town of Commerce, displays a more distinctively regional vision and a voice tuned by its origins. The poems of Wood's second volume, *Campo Santo* (1991), convey a pervasive sense of oppressive summer heat and of cold mornings in houses not built for cold, of local ways, of night skies undimmed by city lights, and of a society (recognizable to any child of the late 1940s and 1950s in Texas) contaminated by the Cold War and the polio epidemic (fit metaphors for each other). The work of Leon Stokesbury, a native of Silsbee, Texas, is also of a

very high order and conveys a distinctively Texan voice.

Perhaps the three writers who best epitomize a high-art literature of East Texas are Katherine Anne Porter, William Goyen, and William Humphrey, all genuinely regional in their work but also genuinely national in literary recognition. Porter, who fostered the work and the careers of the other two, was certainly the first major writer the state produced and perhaps still its most distinguished. Though born in west-central Texas, she spent her childhood in the central borderlands between east and west, and her imagination yearned first toward Mexico and then eastward toward the Old South, especially after she developed strong ties with the Agrarian group during the mid-1930s. That eastward leaning is particularly evident in "Old Mortality" (1937). In "Noon Wine," however, also 1937, she produced a work authentically of its place, and in "The Old Order," a group of stories published over a span of years, she looks both ways, to the Old South and to the West, associating the one with the past, the other with the future. Humphrey, whose early life was spent near Clarksville in Red River County and in Dallas, and Goyen, who was from Trinity and then Houston, have produced a more consistently southern body of fiction. Both can well be described as Faulknerian for their brooding vision, their baroque and gothicized style (so unlike Porter's), and their scenes of woods and hunting (notably in Humphrey's 1958 *Home from the Hill,* which like Goyen's *House of Breath* was a winner of the Texas Institute of Letters Award). Humphrey's *The Ordways* (1965), with its wagon crossing of a river in flood during which ancestral remains are swept away, recalls *As I Lay Dying,* and in *Proud Flesh* (1973) he broods over family and guilt in what has been described as a gothic, Faulknerian way.

The relations of these three writers to their native state are intertwined in a way that forms a kind of collective parable of Texas letters. On October 10, 1950, Goyen (whose selected letters have recently been published) wrote to Porter that he was worried about Humphrey because he seemed bitter and had said that he hated the South and never wanted to see it again. Goyen would probably have been surprised to know that only two days before he wrote that letter to Porter she herself had written to Humphrey saying that she "never had any real regional patriotism" and in fact "got out of Texas like a bat out of hell at the earliest possible moment and stayed away cheerfully half a lifetime" (Porter Papers, University of Maryland Libraries, by permission). Five years after this 1950 exchange, Goyen would attach a note to his novel *In a Farther Country* stating that he was "tired of being called" a southern writer, had never lived in the South, the language of his work was "not Southern," and his fictional themes had "no affinity with the eccentricities of Southern personality or Gothic bizarreries." All three spoke bitterly of Texas, left the state, and lived most of their adult lives elsewhere. Yet all three produced Texas-centered fiction drawing on the language and the experiences of their early years there—which is to say, years spent not in the West or in the Southwest but in the South.

Janis P. Stout

See also Dialect Literature; Southwest.

Don Graham, Introduction to *South by Southwest: 24 Stories from Modern Texas* (1986); Don Graham, *Texas: A Literary Portrait* (1985); Don Graham, James W. Lee, and William T. Pilkington, eds., *The Texas Literary Tradition: Fiction, Folklore, History* (1983); Sylvia Grider and Lou Rodenberger, eds., *Texas Women Writers: A Tradition of Their Own* (1997); Clinton Machann and William Bedford Clark, eds., *Katherine Anne Porter and Texas: An Uneasy Relationship* (1990); R. G. Vliet, "On a Literature of the Southwest: An Address," *Texas Observer*, April 28, 1978.

TEXAS REVOLUTION

Substantial legal immigration into Mexican Texas from the United States began in the 1820s under the guidance of Stephen F. Austin; more than 80 percent of these settlers (and their slaves) came from the southern states. By 1835, the thirty-five thousand newcomers outnumbered Spanish-speaking *Tejanos* almost ten to one. In that year, most Anglo-Texans and many *Tejanos* joined Austin in supporting a "Federalist" revolt against the "Centralist" regime of Mexican President Antonio López de Santa Anna. Despite initial successes, Texans saw the Federalist cause collapse in the rest of Mexico. Relying increasingly on volunteers and private financial support from the United States, Texas declared its independence on March 2, 1836.

Disaster appeared imminent for the newborn Republic of Texas. San Antonio's Alamo fortress and all its defenders, including the celebrated David Crockett, succumbed on March 6 to a Mexican army com-

manded by Santa Anna. Barely three weeks later, James Fannin and the four hundred soldiers under his command were captured and executed at Goliad. The remaining Texan forces under General Sam Houston were forced to retreat eastward, but the rout was suddenly and decisively reversed on April 21 when Houston surprised, defeated, and captured Santa Anna at San Jacinto.

The earliest novel based on the Texas Revolution, Anthony Ganilh's *Mexico Versus Texas* (1838), explored the racial, religious, cultural, and political complexities of a conflict that would, by the early twentieth century, be portrayed by many American writers as a primal struggle between Anglo-Saxon heroes and a vicious dictator's horde of semisavage mongrels. This racialized interpretation was captured on film in *The Martyrs of the Alamo* (1915), produced by D. W. Griffith's studio in the same year that *The Birth of a Nation* told a similar story of heroic Klansmen resisting the ravages of Reconstruction in the South.

Although the massacre of prisoners at Goliad found poetic expression in Walt Whitman's "Song of Myself," it is the legendary siege and fall of the Alamo that has been since 1836 the chief focus of artistic representations of the Texas Revolution, whether in paint or motion pictures, poetry or prose. Unfortunately, the results have been almost universally mediocre. The popular image of this complex war remains largely dominated by the simplistic film versions produced in the 1950s by Walt Disney and John Wayne.

James E. Crisp

See also Crockett, Davy; Mexican War.

Edwin W. Gaston, *The Early Novel of the Southwest* (1961); Don Graham, *Cowboys and Cadillacs: How Hollywood Looks at Texas* (1983); Stephen L. Hardin, *Texian Iliad: A Military History of the Texas Revolution* (1994); Frank T. Thompson, *Alamo Movies* (1991).

TEXTILES

Textile mills built the New South. Beginning in the 1880s, as the region emerged from the wreckage of the Civil War, small-town business and professional men tied their hopes for prosperity to the construction of factories that would transform the cotton harvest into yarn and cloth. The industry was centered in the Piedmont, a territory of gentle hills and rushing rivers that stretches from southern Virginia through the central Carolinas and into northern Georgia and Alabama. By the 1920s, this area had eclipsed New England as the world's leading producer of textile goods.

By custom—and in some cases, by law—southern cotton mills employed an almost exclusively white work force made up of farm families who had been pushed off the land by falling agricultural prices and the rise of sharecropping and tenantry. The vast majority of mill hands lived in company-owned villages and worked under the terms of a family labor system that required all members of a household to seek mill employment. Southern textile firms paid some of the nation's lowest factory wages, and they made particularly heavy use of child labor. Before World War I, manufacturers acknowledged that roughly one-fourth of their work force was under sixteen years of age, and many other child workers went unreported.

In the years immediately after the war, textile employers embarked on a modernization campaign aimed at defending profits against the early signs of a global economic depression. Known to workers as the "stretch-out," that campaign provoked labor unrest on an unprecedented scale. The southern textile industry was rocked by a series of strikes, the most famous of which occurred in Marion and Gastonia, North Carolina, in 1929. Those protests were celebrated in a number of proletarian novels, including Mary Heaton Vorse's *Strike!* (1930), Grace Lumpkin's *To Make My Bread* (1932), Dorothy Myra Page's *The Gathering Storm: A Story of the Black Belt* (1932), Fielding Burke's (Olive Tilford Dargan) *Call Home the Heart* (1932), Sherwood Anderson's *Beyond Desire* (1932), and William Rollins's *The Shadow Before* (1934).

The textile industry began to lose its hold on the South in the period following the Great Depression and World War II. Economic growth and government programs such as the G.I. Bill created new job opportunities and forced the industry to become more dependent on overseas operations. Today, textile manufacturing plays only a minor role in the southern economy, but its legacies persist. State officials across the South remain firm in their hostility to organized labor and unionization, and despite the newfound prosperity of the Sunbelt, industrial wages in the region continue to rank among the lowest in the nation.

James L. Leloudis

See also Proletarian Novel; Work.

David L. Carlton, *Mill and Town in South Carolina, 1880–1920* (1982); Douglas Flamming, *Creating the Modern South: Millhands and Managers in Dalton, Georgia, 1884–1984* (1992); Jacquelyn Dowd Hall et al., *Like a Family: The Making of a Southern Cotton Mill World* (1987); Laura Hapke, *Daughters of the Great Depression: Women, Work, and Fiction in the American 1930s* (1995).

THEFT

When poet Sterling Brown writes of a pilfering maid in "Ruminations of Luke Johnson," or Richard Wright (*Black Boy*, 1945) tells of being asked point-blank during a job interview "Do you steal?" each author is confronting an issue that has a lengthy history in American culture: theft and its alignment with blackness—the stereotype of the black thief. African American literature, from early confessional narratives to contemporary novels, is rife with allusions to this stereotype. Titles addressing the issue of theft and race include Frederick Douglass's three autobiographical works, Harriet Jacobs's *Incidents in the Life of a Slave Girl* (1861), Frances Ellen Watkins Harper's *Iola Leroy* (1892), a number of Charles Chesnutt's short stories (especially "The Goophered Grapevine"), Booker T. Washington's *Up From Slavery* (1901), Margaret Walker's *Jubilee* (1966), Yusef Komunyakaa's *Thieves of Paradise* (1998), and numerous other works.

The alignment of the act of stealing with race began during slavery. Theft (or stealing) develops naturally in a socioeconomic system based on an unequal distribution of resources, especially where one group labors to produce all the goods and resources for the enjoyment of another, privileged group. Under American chattel slavery, laws protecting property rights of the privileged group labeled enslaved blacks as thieves when they took back some of the fruits of their labor. As several historians have noted, enslaved persons considered their acts theft only if they were appropriating goods from other enslaved persons. Slaveholders, notes one historian, believed that all blacks stole by nature, and they defined " 'a thieving Negro' simply as one who stole much more than the average." In this way, the stereotype of the natural black thief, who is inherently morally corrupt, was born.

To commit theft is to steal. *The American Heritage Dictionary* lists a number of definitions for *steal*, including: "to take (the property of another) without right or permission"; "to effect surreptitiously or artfully"; "to move, carry, or place surreptitiously"; "to draw attention unexpectedly in . . . especially by being the outstanding performer"; and, "to use, appropriate, or preempt the use of another's idea, especially to one's own advantage and without consent by the originator." The dictionary also lists numerous synonyms, including *pinch, pilfer, purloin, filch, snitch,* and *swipe.* The signifier *theft* takes on character, nature, and meaning in relation to how and why the act of stealing is executed; the term can be applied to the acquisition of both the tangible (money, material goods) and the intangible (intellectual property, peace of mind, freedom).

In Mark Twain's exploration of the issue of theft in *Huckleberry Finn,* Huck and his gang play a game of pretend robbery near the beginning of the tale, and later they steal an interesting collection of objects from a church picnic: doughnuts, a rag doll, a hymnbook, and some other trifles. As the story progresses, Huck must confront the reality that his father is a robber who wants Huck's money and even goes to court in an attempt to obtain it. Huck escapes from prison by "appropriating" a canoe and some provisions. He fakes his own death, supposedly at the hands of robbers. Huck "lifts" a chicken and "borrows" produce, but he is horrified to learn that Jim wishes to have his family "stolen" out of bondage. He considers it an immoral act, as he has been taught that a thief is one of the most morally corrupt of God's creatures. To his credit, Twain allows Huck's humanity to expand so that he can conclude that human beings should not be considered property—that Jim deserves to be free. In this way Twain explores the issue of absolute morality, which is at the heart of the issue. Enslaved blacks, such as Jim, were indeed the victims of physical kidnapping (theft and appropriation of the physical self) and the resulting loss of certain aspects of their history and culture.

African American authors go to great lengths to point to the faulty logic at the core of the ideology that aligns blackness with theft. The stereotype born in the midst of American chattel slavery gained power in the aftermath of the Civil War and Reconstruction. Its vestiges are apparent today in news stories such as the one describing an October 1995 event. A black teenager walked through a Maryland Eddie Bauer clothing store wearing one of the chain's trademark shirts. Security personnel assumed that the teenager had stolen the shirt, and they literally removed it from the young man's back, demanding that he show proof of ownership. Such incidents will no doubt continue to render the subject of theft and race a compelling issue in American literature.

Lovalerie King

See also African American Literature, Beginnings to 1919; Race, Idea of; Race Relations; Slave Narrative.

John Blassingame, ed., *Slave Testimony* (1977); Sterling Brown, "Negro Character As Seen By White Authors," *Callaloo* 5:1–2 (1982); Eugene Genovese, *Roll, Jordan, Roll* (1974); Kenneth Stampp, *The Peculiar Institution* (1956); Catherine Juanita Starke, *Black Portraiture in American Fiction: Stock Characters, Archetypes, and Individuals* (1971); Robert L. Vales, "Thief and Theft in *Huckleberry Finn,*" *American Literature* 37:4 (1966).

TIDEWATER

Though equally applicable to the majority of coastline between Delaware and the Mississippi Delta, the term *tidewater,* when used as an adjective, most commonly refers to the Chesapeake Bay region of Maryland and Virginia, the latter—where it often assumes the status of a proper noun—in particular. Dominated by the bay and its tributaries, the region is one of marshy waterways and broad, flat fields, family farms as well as major manufacturing facilities, three-hundred-year-old fishing villages as well as the largest and most modern naval installation in the world. Its historical significance is nearly impossible to exaggerate: Tidewater is the site of the first permanent English settlement in America, the first importation of African slaves onto North American soil, and many of the most decisive moments in the American Revolutionary War. Its literary history is similarly significant: for Tidewater is a region that once defined, and continues to reflect, some of the largest concerns of southern letters.

The first to write of the region were its explorers and promoters, those who in the name of European colonization braved what to them was often wilderness. Captain Arthur Barlowe, author of *Narrative of the First Voyage to Virginia* (1584), was one of the first Englishmen to do so. Originally a report addressed to expedition sponsor Sir Walter Raleigh, the *Narrative* characterizes the coastal region between present-day Roanoke Island, North Carolina, and nearby Portsmouth, Virginia, as nothing less than a newfound

Eden. Barlowe championed its soil as "the most plenti-full, sweete, fruitfull and wholsome of all the worlde," its inhabitants as "most gentle, loving, and faithfull, voide of all guile and treason." What the region's most celebrated explorer found some two and a half decades later, however, was not quite so inviting. According to Captain John Smith's *A True Relation of Occurrences and Accidents in Virginia* (1608), Captain Christopher Newport and crew drew fire, even upon first landfall, from natives of what today is Virginia Beach, Virginia. Relations between natives and newcomers would remain strained for years, yet as Smith left the recently established Jamestown for territory farther up the James River—recording in the process some of the earliest descriptions of the Tidewater interior—he reported that he was "at eche place kindely used." Tidewater Maryland produced no comparable exploration narrative—though George Alsop's *A Character of the Province of Maryland* (1666) perhaps comes closest—but it did inspire Ebenezer Cooke's *The Sot-Weed Factor* (1708), a narrative poem relating an English tobacco merchant's early experiences in coastal Maryland. Much more satire than promotional tract, the poem describes local farmers as "Figures so strange, no God design'd, / To be a part of Humane kind," Maryland itself as "that Shoar, where no good Sense is found, / But Conversation's lost, and Manners drown'd." The scene of the South's most definitive exploration narratives thus also provided a setting for what many consider the introductory chapters of southern humor, if not the far more broadly based local-color movement.

If the seventeenth-century Tidewater was the domain of explorers and what they called Indians, then of merchants and a growing number of independent farmers, the eighteenth- and much of nineteenth-century Tidewater was that of the fabled planter-aristocrat. Residual English manorial pretensions combined with the rich soil that Barlowe described, a long, damp growing season, and a seemingly endless supply of African slaves to produce such legendary plantations as that of William Byrd II, whose Westover claimed nearly 180,000 acres. Though not as well known as his *History of the Dividing Line* (1841), Byrd's letters and diaries afford us some of our best glimpses into the day-to-day business of the James River plantation. As he wrote in an oft-quoted letter dated 1726, he lived "like one of the Patriarchs": "I have my Flocks and my Herds, my Bond-men and Bond-women, and every Soart of Trade amongst my own Servants, so that I live in a kind of Independence on every one but Providence." Such plantations receive their most celebrated fictional treatment in John Pendleton Kennedy's *Swallow Barn* (1832). The record of a northerner's first visit to the Old Dominion, the novel details events on a pastoral Tidewater plantation complete with a "time-honored" manor, a master who exemplifies the "very model of landed gentlemen," and slave quarters full of "the most good-natured, careless, light-hearted, and happily constructed human beings" the narrator had ever seen. This last observation becomes particularly ironic when one compares it to those found in two later texts, neither written long after or far from the scene of Kennedy's narrator's remarks. Like few other works, *The Confessions of Nat Turner* (1831) and *Narrative of the Life of Frederick Douglass, An American Slave* (1845) show the atrocities suffered under, as well as the atrocities worth committing to escape, the selfsame Tidewater slave system. The region thus provides both fact and fiction with some of the most archetypal—and, in the case of *Swallow Barn*, perhaps fanciful—examples of the fabled southern plantation.

Though the twentieth-century Tidewater has proven a perennial home to the characters of John Barth and William Styron, characters as diverse as Thomas Wolfe's Eugene Gant, Thomas Pynchon's Benny Profane, and Toni Morrison's Milkman Dead have all passed through it. Such diversity and transience are both instructive: for whereas the region once produced such indigenous figures as the planter-aristocrat, it increasingly does little more than set the scene for the more universal, and therefore less necessarily native, story of the twentieth-century seeker. In other words, the region that was an adversary to Captain John Smith and an ally to William Byrd is, to a character like Styron's Milton Loftis, little more than a backdrop. His environment might influence his moods, but it does not determine his character. Both Barth and Styron have resurrected figures more inseparable from their surroundings—Barth's *The Sot-Weed Factor* (1960) recreates the early-eighteenth-century Maryland of Ebenezer Cooke, whereas Styron's *The Confessions of Nat Turner* (1967) recreates the early nineteenth-century Virginia of Nat Turner—but, for the most part, Barth's and Styron's tales are of those whose concerns are more internal than external, more psychological than environmental. Even as a backdrop, though, the Tidewater's presence remains integral: Barth's *Sabbatical* (1982) and *The Tidewater Tales* (1987) both take place on and around the Chesapeake

Bay; central sections of Styron's *Lie Down in Darkness* (1951), *Set This House on Fire* (1960), and *A Tidewater Morning* (1993) take place in the shadow of the Newport News Shipyard. The region's history remains inescapable as well. Just as characters in Styron's first novel, standing on the banks of the James, discuss the story of John Smith and Pocahontas, characters in his third novel, standing on almost the same spot, discuss the day in 1619 when that "bound black cargo" first made its way up the same river. Even when relegated to the role of backdrop, the Tidewater milieu retains a depth that encompasses the span of not just southern, but American history and literature.

Keith Perry

See also British-American Culture; Cavalier; Maryland, Literature of; Promotional Tract; Virginia, Literature of.

Richard Beale Davis, *Literature and Society in Early Virginia 1608–1840* (1973); J. A. Leo Lemay, *Men of Letters in Colonial Maryland* (1972); Ritchie Devon Watson Jr., *The Cavalier in Virginia Fiction* (1985).

TILL, EMMETT

On August 28, 1955, Emmett Louis Till, a fourteen-year-old African American from Chicago, was murdered while visiting relatives in the Mississippi Delta. Accused of "wolf-whistling" at Carolyn Bryant, a twenty-one-year-old white woman, Till was abducted from his great-uncle's home, beaten, and shot in the head. His mutilated body was tied to a cotton-gin fan with barbed wire and dumped in the Tallahatchie River. Three days later, the body was discovered by a boy fishing in the river. Carolyn Bryant's husband, Roy, and his half-brother, J. W. Milam, were charged with the murder. The two men admitted forcing Till from his uncle's home, but they claimed that they had released him after giving him a stern warning. Despite the testimony of three black witnesses, an all-white, all-male jury acquitted the accused men after only an hour and seven minutes of deliberation. In a paid interview with William Bradford Huie published in *Look* magazine, Bryant and Milam later confessed to killing the boy. Even as they confessed, however, they maintained that they had committed no crime. They insisted that they were defending Carolyn Bryant's honor and the southern way of life.

Till's death captured the attention of African

Americans and whites alike because of the unprecedented media coverage it received. After the emancipation of slaves in the South, lynchings arose as a vigilante form of exerting power over the newly freed blacks. The number of lynchings reached its highest levels during the Reconstruction period, but, although on the decline, lynchings continued to occur throughout the first half of the twentieth century. The murder of Emmett Till stands out from other racially motivated murders because the attention it received from the media presented the violence of southern racism to a national audience for the first time. Journalists from the white and the black press covered the murder and the subsequent trial of Bryant and Milam for local and nationally circulating newspapers and magazines. Photographs of Till's smiling face juxtaposed with those of his mutilated body accompanied the written accounts and were indelibly imprinted on the memories of a generation of Americans.

The impact of Till's murder on the growing social consciousness of American writers is evidenced by the numerous allusions to the murder in literature since 1955. The preoccupation with the murder by African American writers is especially notable, as depictions of the death of Emmett Till can be found in virtually all literary genres. In her poems "A Bronzeville Mother Loiters in Mississippi. Meanwhile, A Mississippi Mother Burns Bacon" and "The Last Quatrain of the Ballad of Emmett Till" (1963), Gwendolyn Brooks focused upon Carolyn Bryant and Emmett Till's mother to illustrate the connection between racial violence and gender oppression in a patriarchal society. In their plays *Blues for Mr. Charlie* (1964) and *Dreaming Emmett* (1986), James Baldwin and Toni Morrison both loosely incorporated the events of Till's murder to depict the complexity of racial and sexual relations between black and white Americans and within the African American community. In her novel *Your Blues Ain't Like Mine* (1992), Bebe Moore Campbell fictionalized the events and characters surrounding the murder to illustrate how violence affects both victim and victimizer.

References to the murder also surface in literary works by African American writers that do not focus exclusively on Till's death. Although these references are not the central images in the narratives, they do provide an underlying foundation for the explorations of race and gender relations that constitute the primary focus of each text. In her short story "Advancing Luna—and Ida B. Wells" (1971), Alice Walker included a single allusion to Till's death to establish the social context for her examination of the intersection between the victimization of white women within southern patriarchy and the denial of civil rights for African Americans. In their respective autobiographies *Coming of Age in Mississippi* (1968) and *Soul on Ice* (1968), Anne Moody and Eldridge Cleaver described their own reactions to the murder to illustrate the rage, fear, and hopelessness that African Americans experience as a result of racially motivated violence. In her novel *Song of Solomon* (1977), Toni Morrison introduced the death of Emmett Till into a single scene to serve as a catalyst for debate among the male characters about what it means to be a black man in American society.

Although white southern writers have not responded to the murder as frequently as African American writers, they have testified to the impact the murder had upon them. William Faulkner publicly denounced the murder in a dispatch written from Rome and published in the September 9, 1955, edition of the *New York Herald Tribune*. Nearly four decades later, Mississippi native Lewis Nordan fictionalized the events surrounding Till's death in his novel *Wolf Whistle* (1993). In *Wolf Whistle*, Nordan echoed the themes of many of the earlier literary representations of the murder by presenting images of individuals and a society torn apart by poverty, gender oppression, and racial violence.

Judi Kemerait

See also Protest, Novel of; Race Relations; Racism.

Clenora Hudson-Weems, *Emmett Till: The Sacrificial Lamb of the Civil Rights Movement* (1994); Sanford Wexler, *The Civil Rights Movement: An Eyewitness History* (1993); Stephen J. Whitfield, *A Death in the Delta: The Story of Emmett Till* (1988).

TOBACCO

First used by Native Americans for medicinal or religious purposes, tobacco became popular for recreational use among Europeans in the seventeenth century. "Sot weed" or the "golden leaf," as it has become known, is now widely cultivated in the southeastern United States.

Two main types of tobacco are grown in the South. In Tennessee, Kentucky, and western parts of Virginia

and North Carolina, the most popular type is burley tobacco, which is air dried in large barns or field-curing structures. Most burley farms are relatively small compared to flue-cure tobacco farms. Flue-cured tobacco is mostly grown in Virginia, North Carolina, South Carolina, Georgia, and Florida. After harvest, flue-cured tobacco is cured with heated air. Tobacco is also grown in Maryland.

Tobacco plants are started in a plant bed or a greenhouse and then transplanted into the field. Over the course of the season, which usually begins in March, the tobacco grows taller than an average man's height. Today, flue-cured tobacco is harvested mechanically, but it was harvested by hand for centuries. Burley tobacco is often still harvested by hand.

In the past, after harvest and drying, the tobacco was put into barrels and rolled toward rivers where it would be taken to market. Now, the tobacco is packed into large bales or sheets and then taken to auction, where tobacco-company representatives from corporations such as Philip Morris or R. J. Reynolds Tobacco Company bid on the tobacco based upon its grade. What is not sold is often bought by farmers' cooperatives or stored by growers on their farms.

Tobacco has been and continues to be an economic staple of many southern rural communities. The money it brings into these communities is much more than any other crop could provide on the same amount of land and with similar economic inputs. Cotton is a distant second. Thus, despite the political and health controversies now surrounding the crop, tobacco farmers continue to grow "the bright leaf."

Moreover, tobacco is a cultural staple of these rural communities. Before many farms became consolidated, neighboring families would help one another get the crop in and out of the field. At harvest, women would "tie the hands" of tobacco, selecting the best grades of leaf and tying it to sticks for better drying. Such work was very labor intensive, so it required all community members to be involved. Thus close-knit communities were formed. Tim McLaurin's autobiography *Keeper of the Moon* (1991) describes some of the grueling toll on the young of producing tobacco.

The crop remains important to rural communities, but it is generally more mechanized and less labor intensive than in the past. Now, much of the hands-on work is completed by immigrant labor.

Considering tobacco's importance to rural communities in the South, it is not surprising that the crop finds its way into the literature of the South. Often, however, tobacco is less the central subject of the writing and more a feature of southern settings that evokes a powerful sense of rural life.

One of the first major works in which tobacco appears is Erskine Caldwell's *Tobacco Road* (1932). This "grotesque" novel is written in the tradition of the Southwest humorists such as Augustus Baldwin Longstreet and George Washington Harris. It chronicles the life of Jeeter Lester and his poor-white family, who are characterized by degeneration and depravity. The name "Tobacco Road" calls up the idea of the rural, red-dirt, snuff-dipping South. Tobacco plays a much bigger role in Robert Penn Warren's *Night Rider* (1939), which describes the violent local history of southwestern Kentucky counties where the tobacco wars raged. These conflicts began around 1906 when some tobacco farmers resorted to violence to compel others to hold their crops and market only through a growers' association.

John Barth treated tobacco indirectly in *The Sot-Weed Factor* (1960), which attempts to reconstruct Maryland's early colonization and plays upon the 1708 poem of the same title by Maryland bard Ebenezer Cooke. However, Barth describes little of the actual tobacco culture in Maryland. Like much of Barth's fiction, this novel focuses more on the existential lives of the people than on the culture that created those people.

Tobacco takes center stage in one of Guy Owen's short stories. In "The Flim-Flam Man and the Golden Weed" (1980), the sale of tobacco is yet another way two scammers, Mr. Jones—the flim-flam man himself—and Mr. Treadaway, take advantage of a man who meant to con the buyers at an auction in South Boston, Virginia. Owens's novel *The Ballad of the Flim-Flam Man* (1965) is also steped in tobacco lore.

Other southern writers have made tobacco a telling feature of the setting in their works. In *Passing Through* (1983), a series of nine short stories, Leon Driskell creates a family chronicle for the heroine Pearl Thirwell White. The stories are set in Owen County, Kentucky, the heart of burley tobacco country. Anne Tyler's *The Tin Can Tree* (1965) is set in a town called Larksville in an unnamed state resembling North Carolina. Almost everyone works in tobacco, and Tyler portrays a tobacco-tying scene. Kaye Gibbons in *A Virtuous Woman* (1989) also uses tobacco farming as setting. Reynolds Price writes a poignant sketch of a tobacco farmer in his personal essay of his kinsman

Macon Thornton in "An Absolute Hunter," part of his memoir *Clear Pictures* (1989).

In *A Visitation of Spirits* (1989), one of Randall Kenan's digressions specifically addresses the role of tobacco in his community, based on Chinquapin, North Carolina. At the moment when the main character, Horace, is to die, he narrates "Requiem for Tobacco." The character's tone reflects his mournful mental condition. Horace seems to long for the old ways of harvesting tobacco—the old ways of the community—but is resigned to its mechanization, the removal of the human. Thus he uses this description of tobacco in the community to implore his audience to remember the people who handled tobacco, the people who created the community and culture.

The value of tobacco is more emotional than financial for many North Carolina poets, including Shelby Stephenson and James Applewhite. In the poems "Some Words for Fall," "Tobacco Men," and "A Leaf of Tobacco," Applewhite, a kind of poet laureate of tobacco culture, describes the feelings and histories associated with the crop in eastern North Carolina.

Tobacco history and culture are remembered in exhibits at the Tobacco Farm Life Museum in Kenly, North Carolina, and at the Duke Homestead near Durham. Both museums are devoted to tobacco, rural lives, communities, and economies, as well as the culture of eastern North Carolina. Perhaps literature is preserving the culture of tobacco as much as museums are. James Applewhite describes tobacco as encompassing a history of the South:

> . . . This leaf has collected,
> Like a river system draining a whole basin,
> The white organdy lead bullet coon dog Baptist
> Preacher iron plough freed slave raped and
> Bleeding dead from the lynch mob cotton
> Mouth South . . . .

Tena L. Helton

See also North Carolina, Literature of; Piedmont; Tobacco Wars.

William Axton, *Tobacco and Kentucky* (1975); Anthony Badger, *Prosperity Road: The New Deal, Tobacco and North Carolina* (1980); Jerome Brooks, *The Mighty Leaf: Tobacco Through the Centuries* (1952); Tracy Campbell, *The Politics of Despair: Power and Resistance in the Tobacco Wars* (1993); Pete Daniel, *Breaking the Land: The Transformation of Cotton, Tobacco, and Rice Cultures Since 1880* (1985); Robert De Coin, *History and Cultivation of Cotton and Tobacco* (1973);

Jeffrey J. Folks and James A. Perkins, eds., *Southern Writers at Century's End* (1997); Patrick Reynolds, *The Gilded Leaf* (1989).

TOBACCO WARS

Although "tobacco wars" now suggest recent legal and political debates over the regulation of smoking and its social costs, historically the term describes the violent struggles that erupted in the tobacco states during the first decade of the twentieth century. This violence was centered in the so-called "Black Patch" of western Kentucky and Tennessee, though it spread to other areas of these states and to bordering states as well. At the zenith of their power, small armies of armed and hooded night riders captured entire towns in western counties of Kentucky, burning warehouses and lynching their enemies. Arguably one of the most serious threats to domestic civility in modern America, this chapter of southern history remains comparatively unknown today. Southern literature, in particular the writing of Kentucky's greatest person of letters, Robert Penn Warren, has provided insight into these ambiguous conflicts that smoldered and flared for almost a decade.

The agricultural heyday of the border South occurred in the later decades of the nineteenth century, following the strife of Reconstruction and paralleling the compromises of southern Redemption. Then these social and economic accommodations began to unravel with the many changes of the new century. The tobacco states were prone to discord after the formation of the marketing trusts, and earlier scholarship reflected Progressive politics in contrasting disgruntled growers with greedy buyers. Recent studies have developed more cross currents created by the cultural complexities of class, race, and gender.

The "Black Patch" along the western borderlands of Kentucky and Tennessee is named for its agricultural staple, "dark-fired" tobacco, whose dark green leaf blackens as it is cured with wood smoke. In 1904 the Planters Protective Association was formed to reverse the inroads of the trusts on tobacco prices in the border states. However, these embattled planters were not small growers on hard-scrabble plots but the agrarian elite of the area, as recent scholarship has demonstrated. Their organizations quickly developed classist, racist, and sexist agendas as they turned their tactics from economic boycott to night riding. By 1907 the "Possum Hunters," as the night riders denominated themselves, were ranged against the "Hillbillies," the small growers, often African Americans, who farmed the hills, ridges, and knobs of the region—agriculturists who could not afford to hold their prime leaf out of the market. Intimidation, threats, and coercion attempting to regulate tobacco sales quickly erupted into a small-scale civil war. Trains and towns were captured, barns and warehouses were burned, and partisans of both sides were exiled, injured, or killed.

Organized violence climaxed with major raids on Kentucky towns such as Princeton, Hopkinsville, and Russellville; these were not crossroads hamlets, however, but prosperous tobacco-trading centers and county seats. This larger scale of vigilante tactics was enough to convince the newly elected Republican governor to send in the National Guard to restore order. Regional reaction against the night riders included both legal action and counter-violence. The most important factor ending the "tobacco wars" was the healthy agricultural market and general farm prosperity in the period preceding World War I. The Planters Protective Association capitulated and gave up the ghost in 1914, and night riding in Kentucky generally disappeared with its passing. These events were largely ignored by regional historians until the 1990s, with three scholarly studies of the tobacco wars appearing in that decade.

Regional literature more accurately reflected the harsh realities of the tobacco wars, though most examples remain minor works by minor writers: John Fox Jr.'s *The Heart of the Hills* (1913), Elizabeth Pickett Chevalier's *Drivin' Woman* (1942), and Charley Robertson's *Send For Miss Cora* (1948). Born in 1905, at the dead center of the Black Patch, Robert Penn Warren grew up with the legends of this recent conflict, including his own family's connection through his maternal grandfather, a tobacco grower and trader in Trigg County, Kentucky. A former Confederate officer who rode with Forrest, as well as a student of history and literature, grandfather Penn appears in many guises throughout Warren's canon from his first unpublished novel to his late reminiscent poems. Warren's most important works on the tobacco wars—his novella "Prime Leaf" (1931) and his first published novel, *Night Rider* (1939)—feature central characters based on his grandfather. These figures are not heroic statues, however, but men trying to find justice for themselves, their families, and their society within the welter of history configured by the tobacco wars.

Joseph Millichap

See also Kentucky, Literature of; Tobacco.

Tracy Campbell, *The Politics of Despair: Power and Resistance in the Tobacco Wars* (1993); Suzanne Marshall, *Violence in the Black Patch of Kentucky and Tennessee* (1994); Christopher Waldrep, *Night Riders: Defending the Community in the Black Patch, 1890–1915* (1993).

TOWN AND COUNTRY

"Humanism, properly speaking, is not an abstract system, but a culture . . . a kind of imaginatively balanced life lived out in a definite social tradition," states John Crowe Ransom in his introduction to the 1930 Agrarian manifesto *I'll Take My Stand*. And though the Agrarians did not accept uncritically the romantic vision of the plantation South portrayed by such nineteenth-century southerners as John Pendleton Kennedy and Thomas Nelson Page, they did assert, as Ransom puts it, that this "genuine humanism" could be located in "the agrarian life of the older South." Although the literature of the Southern Renascence and thereafter does not always support the Agrarians' view, this literature has been especially concerned with the humane communal life that develops or fails to develop in a region that has, until recent decades at least, been characterized by a less mobile, more rural traditional culture than most of the rest of the nation. The southern setting of this literature has often included both the rural country inhabited by upper-class landowners, smaller farmers, and white and black tenants, sharecroppers, and laborers, and the town that functions as its political, economic, and cultural center. A locale dominated by both merchant-tradesmen and professionals—the latter often scions of old planter families—the town sometimes functions in particularly complex fashion as a border between the older rural South and the modern urban world.

William Faulkner's novels provide a richly complex vision of this landscape of town and country, his trilogy *The Hamlet* (1940), *The Town* (1957), and *The Mansion* (1959) constituting one of his most continuous representations of this vision. The three novels, set in the late nineteenth and early twentieth centuries, portray the progressive movement of the rapacious lower-class Flem Snopes and his relatives from the backwoods and hill country at the periphery of the archetypal Yoknapatawpha County, through Frenchman's Bend—a rural fiefdom once marked out by a lavish plantation but now largely owned and farmed out

by canny merchant-proprietor Will Varner—into Jefferson, the county seat, where Flem completes his campaign of economic and social conquest by becoming the president and majority stockholder of the major bank. The aptly named Flem to some extent exemplifies the mystery of human degradation, but he can also partly be seen as a product of a failure of community in the rural South. Flem's father, Ab, had become an embittered, isolated individual, partaking more of the elemental destructiveness of the fire he uses to burn his landlords' barns than of human reason, let alone fairness or charity, as V. K. Ratliff tells it in *The Hamlet*. The limitations in and decay of the values of the old southern planter class—at times a source of some level of communal order and grace in Faulkner's world—seem to have helped produce the hard life circumstances that Ratliff says have "soured" Ab.

The berserk "spotted horses" that Flem literally unleashes on the people of Frenchman's Bend are one picture of the Snopeses' undermining what humane community does exist here, their promotion of a state of brute nature. Flem's sexual impotence, like that of Popeye in Faulkner's *Sanctuary* (1931), marks him as an unnatural human being, a fitting representative of the coldly mechanistic side of modern urban capitalism; but like Shakespeare's Shylock, Flem is natural in a lower sense—he does "breed" money while preying like a "wolf" (*Merchant of Venice* 1.3.131, 4.1.73). Unlike Shylock, however, Flem is not surrounded by a civil society strong enough or good enough to thwart his brutality. His most powerful antagonists in the Bend—Ratliff, the traveling listener and newsbearer who helps "sew" this diffuse rural domain together; Houston, the gentlemanly yeoman farmer; and the shrewd but amiable Will Varner—are not able to stop him. And Gavin Stevens of Jefferson, the Harvard-educated lawyer whom *The Town* portrays as an embodiment of the decadent, over-refined values of the old aristocracy, seems no more capable of defeating Flem than Horace Benbow is the lethal Popeye.

The "respectability" that Flem needs in the town can motivate even more unscrupulous behavior, Ratliff observes, than can money and power, as Flem's shameless manipulation of his putative daughter Linda may show. The physically closer, more complex society of Jefferson, however, does slow or soften some of Flem's predatory behavior. There are more people here who know and feel some responsibility toward each other than Flem can manipulate with complete success. Even Stevens exerts pressure on Flem, if only that of words, for in the town there are perceptive listeners, including Linda Snopes. The town's middle-class Protestant morality may be petty, hypocritical, and restrictive in some ways, but it also exerts an ethical force that produces the most fully human act one sees from Eula Varner Snopes, her suicide for her daughter's sake. This force is fundamentally in support of family relationships—ties that always matter greatly in Faulkner's world, ties the callous disregard of which finally gets Flem killed in *The Mansion*.

A Jefferson lynch mob burns the innocent Lee Goodwin to death in *Sanctuary*, bringing into the town a savage amorality characteristic of both of Popeye's "natural" environments—the Memphis red-light district and a deracinated Frenchman's Bend. The town is full enough of racial hatred in *Light in August* (1932) that Percy Grimm can believe he is doing its will in killing and castrating a man of suspected African American ancestry, not primarily for murdering but for having sexual intercourse with a white woman. At its worst, covering bigoted or mercenary acts with self-righteousness and exhibiting the sickness of the declining gentleman's code, Faulkner's town perhaps sinks lower than his country ever does. The town is also the place in *Light in August*, however, where Lena Grove, obviously pregnant with an illegitimate child, finds real help and companionship. Its citizens still leave occasional suppers on Reverend Hightower's porch, though his life-denying idealism has caused him to betray both his wife and his church. In *Go Down, Moses* (1942), prominent white citizens led by Stevens quickly raise over two hundred dollars to bring old African American Mollie Beauchamp's dead grandson home from Chicago for dignified burial. Occasionally in Faulkner's Jefferson, vestiges of the best in the old upper-class honor mix with pragmatic middle-class virtue, both informed by mercy toward those who are willing to receive it, to create some of the most humane acts and relationships to be found in his fiction. The town becomes a haven from both the rural outback at its worst and the urban jungle.

Though other major writers of the Renascence and afterward have at times diverged from Faulkner's vision, at other points they have affirmed it. Eugene Gant of Thomas Wolfe's *Look Homeward, Angel* (1929) feels restricted by what has come to him to seem the provincial, unromantic monotony of his Appalachian town of Altamont; yet as the final epiphanic scene of the novel clarifies, the ghosts or "angels" of his experiences and relationships here will remain with him wherever he goes. Robert Penn Warren's *All the King's Men* (1946) reveals in Willie Stark the corruption that comes from thinking one can live above human community—when the credulity of rural folk becomes the key to power in the capital city. Jack Burden escapes his existential despair in part by discovering or reclaiming the meaning of his family connections and upbringing in the town of Burden's Landing. Eudora Welty's volume of stories *The Golden Apples* (1949) portrays Morgana, Mississippi, as a town whose social hierarchies and rituals in part represent attempts to shut out life's great beauties and dark mysteries, both of which are suggested in the life of its German piano teacher, Miss Eckhart. Yet the town's relationships and memories sometimes connect its residents in surprising ways with the loveliness, longing, and terror represented in myth and high art. It is quite clear in Welty's novel *The Optimist's Daughter* (1972) that despite the limitations of the society of Mt. Salus, Mississippi, Laurel McKelva's upbringing there has provided her with resources of which her stepmother, Fay, product of a raw, rural Texas background, has no inkling: integrity, self-sacrifice, love of beauty, and appreciation of the past. In *The Last Gentleman* (1966), Walker Percy, somewhat like Faulkner, presents the old gentleman's code as flawed and failing, but family stories of a time when protagonist Will Barrett's forebears were potent ethical leaders of his tightly knit southern hometown impel Will's relentless search for a stable moral and spiritual basis for authentic community in his generation.

One alternative perspective often found in southern literature is the affirmation of the special heroism and dignity of struggling individuals and families populating the southern countryside, as opposed to the more prosperous but shallow denizens of towns and cities. One sees this vision in the bizarre but heroic acts of Faulkner's Bundrens in *As I Lay Dying* (1930), the Odyssean journey successfully completed by old African American Phoenix Jackson in Eudora Welty's "A Worn Path" (1940), and the tragic dignity and beauty of the tenant-farmer families portrayed in James Agee's lyrical documentary *Let Us Now Praise Famous Men* (1941) and of the witch-cursed Cantrells, the Appalachian mountain family of Lee Smith's novel *Oral History* (1983). These vital human relationships in rural settings are often organized around a close-knit family or a church. The initially grotesque-looking small-town and rural characters of Flannery O'Connor's short stories and two novels have often retained a fuller sense of their need for the love and mercy of God than have the more self-sufficient, pseudo-sophisticated products of cities and larger towns, who often become the true "grotesques" of her fiction. A consonant perspective, perhaps, is that of Peter Taylor, whose *In the Miro District and Other Stories* (1977) and novel *A Summons to Memphis* (1986) focus on the repressive, life-denying nature of the old upper-class mores transplanted from southern towns into such Upper-South cities as Nashville and Memphis.

Another alternative vision found in some southern literature is the presentation of the absorption of aspects of southern town and country life by American urban and suburban culture, as indicated by the proliferation of up-to-date beauty parlors, convenience stores, fast-food and department-store chains, and name-brand consumer items in the southern setting. Sometimes these changes are portrayed as cheapening and vulgarizing the life and thought of southerners, as Eudora Welty suggests as early as "The Petrified Man" (collected 1941), whose main characters are as morally and spiritually petrified as the supposed side-show freak, and as late as Doris Betts's *Souls Raised from the Dead* (1994), whose Christine Broome, cosmetics saleswoman and radio beauty advisor, lets her daughter Mary Grace Thompson die rather than go to the risk and trouble of donating one of her kidneys. Sometimes, however, these changes in southern culture are presented as neutral or even positive, as in Bobbie Ann Mason's *In Country* (1985). Bruce Springsteen's songs express the longings and sorrows of Mason's protagonist Sam Hughes and her friends and relatives in Hopewell, Kentucky, just as they do those of the rest of the nation, including the losses and disillusionments of the Vietnam War.

One would expect the writings of southern African Americans to present a significantly different view of southern town and country, and in important ways this is the case. Jean Toomer's *Cane* (1923), Richard Wright's autobiography *Black Boy* (1945), Ralph Ellison's *Invisible Man* (1952), Alice Walker's *The Color Purple* (1982), and Ernest J. Gaines's *A Gathering of Old Men* (1983) present African Americans so brutalized by the environment of southern town and country that they often fail to achieve community even with each other. It is noteworthy, however, that Toomer's hero Kabnis must return to his roots in the rural South before he can attain a fuller vision of African American identity and hope, that the narrator of Ellison's novel achieves a powerful sense of his individual identity in a

moment of reconnection with an element of his rural southern past—"I yam what I am!"—and that Gaines's old men ultimately find a foundation for self-respect and united resistance to white oppression through the fact that they have worked and thus in some fashion own the southern land. The Agrarians would probably be pleased. Most southern writers, white and African American, have continued to seek answers for the human dilemma not in poet Robert Lowell's "Babel of Boston where our money talks" ("As a Plane Tree by the Water," 1946) but in the "promised land" of town and country celebrated in James Dickey's *Jericho: The South Beheld* (1974), where at times hope still seems to exist for the sort of intimate community experienced by the African Americans of Dilsey's Easter Sunday church service in Faulkner's Jefferson, in which "their hearts were speaking to one another in chanting measures beyond the need for words" (*The Sound and the Fury*, 1929).

Wendell (Whit) Jones Jr.

See also Agrarians; Family; Fundamentalism; Gentleman; Greenville, Mississippi; Honor; Lady; Lynching; Oral History; Past, The; Plantation; Plantation Fiction; Poor White; Race Relations.

Cleanth Brooks, *William Faulkner: Toward Yoknapatawpha and Beyond* (1978), and *William Faulkner: The Yoknapatawpha Country* (1963); J. A. Bryant Jr., *Twentieth-Century Southern Literature* (1997); Louis D. Rubin Jr., ed., *The American South: Portrait of a Culture* (1980); Louis D. Rubin Jr. and Robert D. Jacobs, eds., *Southern Renascence* (1953).

TRAIL OF TEARS

For many, the Trail of Tears is a symbol of the oppression of Native Americans because it was advocated officially by the Georgia state government, as well as by Andrew Jackson and the United States government. The Indian Removal Act that Jackson signed in 1830 forced Choctaws, Chickasaws, Creeks, Seminoles, and Cherokees from their homes.

The Trail of Tears specifically refers to the forced removal of the Cherokee from their ancestral home in the southern Appalachians in North Carolina, Tennessee, Georgia, and Alabama in 1838 and 1839. The "tears" refers to the immense struggle and sacrifice the Cherokee made on the trek to Oklahoma. Over thirteen thousand Cherokee were forced to walk nearly a thousand miles to their new home near Fort Gibson in Oklahoma. Others fled into the hills they had lived in for centuries, resisting the removal and eventually obtaining a reservation—called the Qualla Boundary—in western North Carolina.

One-fourth of the thirteen thousand Cherokee who traveled to Oklahoma died or disappeared due to starvation, disease, and exposure. Most of the dead were children and the elderly. The survivors rarely had time to bury their dead along the trail. Many were simply left along the way. The Cherokee traveled in the worst of winter October 1838 to February 1839.

The route officially began at the Cherokee Agency in Tennessee, though many Cherokee were rounded up and held captive long before the actual removal began. The conditions in the detention camps were atrocious, and approximately two thousand Cherokee died while waiting for the trip to begin. After leaving Tennessee, the Cherokee were marched north and then west through Kentucky, Illinois, and Missouri before arriving in Oklahoma.

Southern literary ventures by whites and Native Americans seek to show this part of southern history. Presented each summer since 1950, Kermit Hunter's *Unto These Hills* is an outdoor drama performed on the Cherokee reservation in North Carolina. It recounts the culture of the Cherokee but focuses on how and why they were removed from their mountain homes.

Remembrances of the Trail of Tears and novels about the trek include *Pushing the Bear* (1996), which fictionalizes a family traveling the Trail of Tears. Here Diane Glancy describes the heartbreak and tragedy of the forced removal. In *Becoming Buffalo Snake* (1996), Robert A. Humphrey describes his thoughts as he walked the Trail of Tears in reverse from west to east. He tells his own feelings as well as recounts the stories of those who walked the trail. In *Mountain Windsong* (1992), Robert J. Connely writes a novel that combines history and fiction. The Trail of Tears provides the setting for a love story between Waguli and Oconeechee. Just as the two Cherokee are about to be married, they are separated by the forced removal. The novel describes Waguli's trek back from Oklahoma to find Oconeechee, who has remained hidden in the mountains.

Although he did not write specifically about the Trail of Tears, William Faulkner uses the policies of forced removal as settings or backgrounds in some of his stories. Specifically in "A Mountain Victory" (1932), a Civil War story, and in "Lo!" (1934), Faulkner shows the importance of forced Indian removal in southern history.

Most recently, in his National Book Award–winning novel *Cold Mountain* (1997), North Carolina author Charles Frazier draws upon the lore of Cherokees who hid in the mountains to avoid capture and removal.

The forced removal of Native Americans from their homelands is vitally important to the history and literature of the southern states and the United States as a whole. During the antebellum period of southern history, representations of Indians increased greatly, perhaps spurred by the Indian Removal Act and the Trail of Tears.

Tena L. Helton

See also Indians; Native American Literature; Outdoor Drama.

John Ehle, *Trail of Tears: The Rise and Fall of the Cherokee Nation* (1988); Jeremiah Evarts, *Cherokee Removal: The "William Penn" Essays and Other Writings* (1981); Lothar Honnighausen, "Faulkner Rewriting the Indian Removal," in *Rewriting the South: History and Fiction* (1993).

TRANSCENDENTALISM

Transcendentalism was a literary, philosophical, and religious movement that flourished in the Boston area between 1836 and 1844. The publication of Ralph Waldo Emerson's *Nature* on September 9, 1836, and the organizational meeting of the Transcendental Club a day earlier provided the first major opportunities for discussing what became known as the "new philosophy." By 1844, the lack of a coherent focus for this group was reflected in the demise of their semi-official journal, the *Dial*, in April.

Most Transcendentalists (such as Emerson and Henry David Thoreau) had been educated at Harvard; many were ministers (such as Christopher Pearse Cranch, Frederic Henry Hedge, Theodore Parker, and George Ripley) or former ministers (Emerson); others were self-educated (such as Amos Bronson Alcott and Margaret Fuller). All were dissatisfied with the conservative Unitarians who led their faith and with the general conservative tenor of the times.

Even though they generally agreed on the areas in which reform was needed, the Transcendentalists often disagreed about specific solutions within each area. In literature, they embraced English and Continental writers such as Thomas Carlyle and Goethe. Emerson believed that literature would show by example how "representative men" could reform society, whereas others, like Orestes Brownson, thought that literature should educate the masses and make them arise. In philosophy, the Transcendentalists followed Immanuel Kant in believing that people had an innate ability to perceive that individual existence transcended mere sensory experience, as opposed to the prevailing belief of John Locke that the mind was a blank tablet at birth that then registered only those impressions perceived through the senses and experience. Even though most Transcendentalists followed an idealistic philosophy, others still clung to the remnants of empiricism. Finally, in religion, they attacked the existence of miracles, arguing that all life was miraculous, not merely a few unproven events from long ago, and urged more democratic processes and religious enthusiasm in what Emerson termed "corpse cold Unitarianism." Most carried on this fight outside the church by resigning their pulpits; others fought from within (Hedge later became president of the American Unitarian Association).

The Transcendentalists also brought their beliefs to bear in the social sphere, arguing strongly that the growth and strengthening of the individual were necessary for true democracy (best given its definition in Emerson's essay "Self-Reliance" and Thoreau's "Resistance to Civil Government"). This resulted in part from the rise of the common man during the period of Jacksonian democracy and also from the influence of British Romanticism. Individualism also meant challenging the ideas of success as measured by vulgar monetary standards (they should be replaced by an individual moral insight) and of the will of the majority (which should be countered by disobedience to unjust laws, such as slavery). Here, as well, the Transcendentalists differed on means and ends: some, like Emerson and Thoreau, believed that humankind needed to be reformed before they passed just laws; others, like Ripley (who started the Brook Farm community) and Alcott (who began the Fruitlands community), held that just laws would force people to become better citizens.

Transcendentalism had little effect in the South for a number of reasons. First, nearly all the Transcendentalists were born in the North and traveled very little in the South. Cranch was born in Virginia but was educated at Harvard University and spent his later life in Boston, New York, and Europe. Moncure Daniel Con-

way was also born in Virginia. After being educated in Pennsylvania and at Harvard, he moved to Concord, Massachusetts, became an abolitionist, and resided in Britain during the Civil War. Alcott had been a traveling salesman in the South during his youth, and Emerson had been in Charleston, South Carolina, and St. Augustine, Florida, while traveling for his health as a young man. Second, because all the Transcendentalists were abolitionists (Emerson discovered the evils of slavery first-hand while watching a slave auction in St. Augustine), their views of southerners were not positive; similarly, the South did not look favorably upon the antislavery publications of the Transcendentalists. And third, the liberal (if not downright radical) views of literature, philosophy, and religion held by the Transcendentalists were not shared by southerners. This is reflected in the many negative reviews given to the Transcendentalists by writers in southern newspapers and periodicals. The outstanding exception to this, Samuel Gilman of South Carolina, was himself a transplanted New Englander. Only Thomas Holley Chivers viewed Transcendentalism favorably, as when he complained to his friend Edgar Allan Poe (who disliked the Transcendentalists) about the unfair treatments of the *Dial* in the Boston newspapers.

Early literary histories of the South rarely mention Transcendentalism. Jay B. Hubbell includes both Emerson (as a representative New England writer) and Conway in his *The South in American Literature 1607–1900* (1954). Hubbell candidly admits that he chose Emerson to "illustrate the extent to which sectional controversy prevented the New England writers from understanding the ante-bellum South"; about Conway, he concludes that "in the New South" after the Civil War, there was "no place for a writer of [his] kaleidoscopic readiness to accept new ideas." Similarly, the most recent study of the subject, *The History of Southern Literature* (Louis D. Rubin Jr., gen. ed.; 1985), continues to stress the differences between the Transcendentalists and southerners: the latter "discouraged the philosophical/theological speculation evident in New England transcendentalism"; southern reviews used Transcendentalism as "an example of the new obscurity in literature, based philosophically on the false doctrine of perfectionism"; and, while the Agrarians deplored a devotion to materialism, they were "distrustful" of "man's possible divinity" and believed that "to march to the beat of a different drummer was a threat to the social order." And no Transcendentalist is included in *Fifty Southern Writers Before*

1900 (ed. Robert Bain and Joseph M. Flora; 1987). To this day, the gap between the Transcendentalists and the South has not been bridged.

Joel Myerson

See also Abolition.

Lawrence Buell, *Literary Transcendentalism: Style and Vision in the American Renaissance* (1973); Octavius Brooks Frothingham, *Transcendentalism in New England* (1876); William R. Hutchison, *The Transcendentalist Ministers* (1959); Joel Myerson, ed., *The Transcendentalists: A Review of Research and Criticism* (1984); Barbara L. Packer, "Transcendentalism," in *The Cambridge History of American Literature,* ed. Sacvan Bercovitch (1995).

TRAVEL LITERATURE

Few literary genres contribute to our understanding of cultural and individual interactions more abundantly than travel literature, a varied and hard-to-define form that combines the characteristics of journalism, autobiography, fiction, history, anthropology, and political analysis, among others, into a smorgasbord of interpretation and experience. Its popularity has ensured that travelers with pen in hand make up a significant and influential—and often unrecognized—portion of southern literary identity. Travel literature and tourism inevitably form a symbiotic relationship, each promoting the other. As more writers put their tourist experiences down on paper, readers worldwide have responded by visiting bookstores and libraries to take their own virtual tours. Subsequently, countless readers worldwide "know" the South via this compelling genre. For students interested in southern literature, forays into this potentially rich genre have been all too infrequent, despite the seminal six-volume bibliographic work published by the University of Oklahoma Press.

Though ideas of southern culture and identity have been extensively expressed by the prose and poetry of its native sons and daughters, by nature travel literature concerning the South depends largely on writers from outside the region, primarily from northern states and from Europe. Travelers have produced a vast array of narratives containing cultural, social, economic, and moral observations that have created for the rest of the world—southern-born travelers notwithstanding—a preeminent and pervasive, if not wholly accurate,

definition of the region and its people. Attempting to ascertain the significance of this large body of literature in relation to southern literature as a whole is thus difficult. Yet examining this wealth of material in context with and/or against the work of native writers proves fruitful.

Southern literature began inevitably as travel literature. From the first European explorers down to late-twentieth-century tourists, writers have consistently been drawn to the South and have produced a body of literature crucial to southern identity. One of the finest late-twentieth-century travel writers, V. S. Naipaul, in *A Turn in the South* (1989), proves that the subgenre of southern travel writing is thriving and that it remains highly marketable as well. John Berendt's *Midnight in the Garden of Good and Evil* (1994), which remained on the *New York Times* best-seller list for well over three years, is at its core a travel book, a narrative of a New York writer's immersion into the charms and vagaries of Savannah, Georgia. These writers continue a long tradition for which, though specific contexts may change, basic conventions and reader expectations remain vigorous.

Because of its varied conventions and formats, travel literature resists easy categorization, and any attempt must admit that neat structure may be more a matter of convenience than precise accuracy. With this concern in mind, however, travel texts on the South benefit from a general overview, leaving plenty of room for exceptions and overlaps.

In the first major phase of southern travel literature—from the early 1500s to the American Independence—narratives were penned primarily by explorers, who were mostly dreamers or opportunists. On the whole, these writers touring a new world viewed the landscape with wonder, hope, and apprehension. The Spanish dominated in the 1500s, and of special note is *The Relation of Alvar Nuñez Cabeza de Vaca* (1542), in which de Vaca captures the early encounters between Europeans and southern Native Americans as well as initial reactions to climate and landscape. By the 1600s, English writers provided the most enduring appraisals of the region, and John Smith's *A True Relation of Such Occurrences and Accidents of Note as Hath Happened in Virginia* (1608) is the best known and most interesting as he attempts not only to describe Virginia to European readers but also to promote immigration. These early travel writers, among others during the over two hundred years of colonization following Columbus, are largely responsible for the ensuing wave of travelers, many of whom produced their own accounts.

Early writers established two enduring themes of southern travel literature: (1) a fascination with and praise for the natural beauty of the region, and (2) an equally strong interest in matters of race relations. No substantive travel narrative ignores either feature. In reference to race, early narratives logically centered on the Native American population in conflict with the European. By the end of the eighteenth century, travel writers would slowly shift the focus to African American culture as slavery expanded.

The next major phase of southern travel literature, which followed upon the close of the Revolutionary War, saw a significant increase in travelers, many of whom came to see firsthand the new nation. Several enduring narratives continued the tradition of highlighting southern natural beauty, the foremost of which was William Bartram's *Travels* (1791), a work that meticulously records the highly varied and lush fauna and flora of the region. Bartram's narrative remains a vital document both for its scientific value and its literary merit. Though there were many interesting narratives during this grand-tour era, perhaps the most influential and substantive travel books came from Frederick Law Olmsted, whose *A Journey in the Seaboard Slave States* (1856), *A Journey Through Texas* (1857), *A Journey in the Back Country in the Winter of 1853–4* (1860), and *The Cotton Kingdom* (1861)—the masterwork that combined the others—provided the most comprehensive and in-depth assessments of the South during the antebellum period.

The Civil War provides the watershed event for the next major phase of southern travel literature, which runs from the war itself to the end of the nineteenth century. Following the war, the South experienced a tourism boom. Many of the travelers came to see the physical and social destruction of the war and the conditions of Reconstruction. Three important travel narratives followed on the heels of the war and provide valuable portraits of postwar conditions: Sidney Andrews, *The South Since the War* (1866); Whitelaw Reid, *After the War: A Southern Tour* (1866); and John T. Towbridge, *The South: A Tour of Its Battlefields and Ruined Cities* (1866). Another important work written during this period but not published until 1916 is John Muir's *A Thousand Mile Walk to the Gulf* (1916). Muir addresses many of the same social and racial issues that other post–Civil War writers address, but he also provides a compelling look at the natural beauty

of the region even amid widespread destruction. Another travel narrative of special note is Mark Twain's *Life on the Mississippi* (1883), a remarkable look at the river, its history, and the culture it supports. Twain's observations are often acerbic but also poignant and nostalgic. *Life on the Mississippi* foreshadows what would become a popular narrative perspective in the twentieth century, that of a traveler whose nostalgic love for the South is tempered with a genuine disappointment in its tragic history.

The twentieth century marks the last phase of southern travel literature. Despite significant changes in travel technology, the dominant themes present in most narratives remain the same. One book by a native-born writer deserves special note. Jonathan Daniels's *A Southerner Discovers the South* (1938) records one of the most provocative and captivating attempts of a writer to face the often-painful realities of southern culture, especially its racism and poverty. Like Twain before him, Daniels underscores the emotional strain that ensues when a travel writer travels home.

Jeffrey A. Melton

See also Diaries, Men's; Diaries, Women's; Letters; Promotional Tract.

Thomas D. Clark, ed., *Travels in the Old South: A Bibliography* (3 vols.; 1956–59), and *Travels in the New South: A Bibliography* (2 vols.; 1962); E. Merton Coulter, ed., *Travels in the Confederate States: A Bibliography* (1948); John Hope Franklin, *A Southern Odyssey: Travelers in the Antebellum North* (1976); Eugene L. Schwaab and Jaqueline Bull, eds., *Travels in the Old South: Selected from Periodicals of the Times* (2 vols.; 1973).

TRICKSTER

The trickster is a prominent figure of all folk cultures, perhaps the most popular character of oral literatures and sacred mythologies throughout the world. Coyote and Rabbit from North American Indian lore and Spider, Monkey, and Rabbit from African lore are probably the most common trickster shapes in the tales of their exploits that would have been shared very early in the region that became the American South. The African trickster deity Legba, important to voodoo practice in Haiti and New Orleans, is another important African folk representation in southern trickster literature. As a folk hero, the trickster is one who, from a position of relative powerlessness (usually represented by smaller size), can outwit his or her adversaries using trickery—a combination of mental agility, rule-breaking, and what we now call "street smarts." The trickster is a subversive, a rebel, but also a creator or restorer. He or she upsets hierarchical systems of authority and often becomes enmeshed in bawdy, erotic adventures that do not always end well but seldom end in total disaster for the trickster. Always there is at least, for the listener, the satisfaction of laughter. In Western literature, the picaro is a kind of analogue, although the picaro is often naïve or simply unlucky, whereas the trickster is willfully mischievous, boasting, and reckless.

The value of the trickster figure for American slaves has long been noted. Joel Chandler Harris, who collected stories of Brer Rabbit in four major collections from 1880 to 1905, observed that "it needs no scientific investigation" to explain why the slave selects as his hero "the weakest and most harmless of all animals, and brings him out victorious in contests with the bear, the wolf, and the fox." The rabbit trickster tales fashioned by the slaves reflected African ways of thought adapted to situations of oppression faced in the South. Slaves themselves were often tricksters, and the antebellum slave narratives depict instances of slaves duping masters through wit and evasions. The ultimate trick, of course, was flight, and slave narratives such as William and Ellen Craft's *Running a Thousand Miles for Freedom* (1860), William Wells Brown's *Narrative* (1847), Henry Bibb's *Narrative* (1849), James Pennington's *The Fugitive Blacksmith* (1849), Harriet Jacobs's *Incidents in the Life of a Slave Girl* (1861), and Frederick Douglass's *Narrative* (1845) record ways in which deception served the cause of freedom. The smallpox lie that Mark Twain's Huck Finn tells to send a party of slave-catchers away from his and Jim's raft came from Pennington's *The Fugitive Blacksmith*, and African American writers from James Weldon Johnson to Ishmael Reed have made pointed references to the tricks used by Frederick Douglass to learn how to read and write.

Among African American slaves, another valuable trickster figure was John, a human character who became the hero of what is now known as the "John and Old Master" cycle. Zora Neale Hurston, in her essential collection of Negro folklore, *Mules and Men* (1932), includes several "John" stories. John, in these stories, routinely outwits Old Master in ways that are often very realistic, leading one to wonder if such anecdotes might preserve actual situations on the plantation. John engages his master in very human interchanges, managing with impunity to receive advantages while making his master look downright foolish.

African American literature from the postbellum period to the present has continued to draw on the trickster tradition. Charles Chesnutt's first published work, *The Conjure Woman* (1899), celebrates many levels of deceit: the conjure woman and the slaves of the tales are able to outwit the master in order to improve their lives, although usually the tricks end in tragedies pointing up the horrors of slavery. Chesnutt's Uncle Julius, the teller of the conjure tales, is a former slave who exploits his white northern employer for economic gain while at the same time serving as Chesnutt's tool for tricking his white audience into witnessing the absurdity of their own racist assumptions. Ralph Ellison revived the trickster in the shapeshifting character of Rinehart in *Invisible Man* (1952). Several African American novels in the neo-slave narrative genre—Ishmael Reed's *Flight to Canada* (1976), Charles Johnson's *The Oxherding Tale,* and Sherley Anne Williams's *Dessa Rose* (1986) prominently among them—celebrate the slave trickster in contemporary terms. Reed in particular has drawn on the African American folk trickster tradition in his novels. In *Mumbo Jumbo* (1973), for instance, PaPa LaBas is modeled on Legba, a West Indian variant of the African trickster deity Esu.

In the southern portions of Appalachia, another important trickster developed through the telling of "Jack Tales." These stories, imported from the British Isles by early Scots-Irish settlers of the southeastern mountains, feature the hero Jack, who succeeds through trickery rather than industry. An important group of these tales was still being told in the mountains of North Carolina in the 1940s. These were published as *The Jack Tales* by Richard Chase in 1943.

Among white southern writers of antebellum times, the Southwestern humorists used the trickster figure to highlight class differences and satirize the rudeness of frontier life. The most important characters of this genre are Simon Suggs and Sut Lovingood. Captain Suggs was the creation of Johnson Jones Hooper, who published the stories of this picaro in William T. Porter's *Spirit of the Times*. Sut Lovingood was the hero of tales published by George Washington Harris, also in *Spirit of the Times,* and finally collected in 1867 in *Sut Lovingood Yarns.* Sut is a classic trickster—plain, crude, cynical, and rebellious—a lowlife character who attacks the pretentiousness and hypocrisy of his "betters" with high good humor and craftiness. Mark Twain borrowed a Simon Suggs exploit for *Huckleberry Finn*'s tale of the Dauphin at the Pokeville Camp Meeting, and William Faulkner found a partial model for several members of the Snopes family in the amoral, hardscrabble Sut Lovingood.

The twentieth century has seen a rise in the popularity of the trickster figure among white southern writers. In Faulkner's "Snopes Trilogy" (*The Hamlet*, 1940; *The Town*, 1957; *The Mansion*, 1959), Flem Snopes can at times be a trickster figure, as in "The Spotted Horses," yet his lack of humanity often goes beyond self-preservation into the realm of pure evil. Eudora Welty's characters Bonnie Peacock of *The Ponder Heart* (1954) and Faye of *The Optimist's Daughter* (1972) may be considered tricksters—they are scrappy, devilish, lower-class young women who wreak havoc on the staid families that they enter through marriage. The trickster in the form of a "flim-flam" man educates the young protagonist of Guy Owen's *Ballad of the Flim-Flam Man* (1965).

In contemporary white southern fiction, the trickster has found new life among writers who have moved beyond the historical imagination of Southern Renascence novelists such as Faulkner and Robert Penn Warren. Blue-collar fiction of the South by Harry Crews, William Price Fox, Larry Brown, and Barry Hannah often includes a subversive working-class figure whose exploits involve a rebellious sort of trickery. Wade Jones of Larry Brown's novel *Joe* (1991) is the trickster at his most degenerate, an alcoholic whose schemes are always designed to procure drink. Although Wade's roguery produces some high comedy, the depths of his degradation go beyond anything that Sut Lovingood or Flem Snopes ever imagined.

In literature, the trickster has traditionally been considered a male character and primarily a device of male authors who have used him to pit the outsider and the oppressed against dominant power structures. The trickster as outcast and rogue is a picaresque type, a wanderer outside of society, and few women could realistically be set in such a mold, although Daniel Defoe's Moll Flanders represents one prototype. The function of the trickster to critique, subvert, and upset authoritarian controls might make the trickster a valuable figure for women writers. Following Eudora Welty's lead, several contemporary southern women have created female trickster figures. The subversive nature

of trickster humor offers a way for women characters to transcend the role of victim and object through comedies of disguise and deceit. Even Scarlett O'Hara might be viewed as a powerful trickster, a woman who uses beauty and coquetry to trick men into giving her what she wants. In contemporary southern women's novels, which have little interest in society belles, the trickery is less tied to feminine wiles and more concerned with freedom from gendered oppression. Kaye Gibbons's Charlie Kate, in *Charms for the Easy Life* (1992), is a self-taught healer who rebels against social conventions and achieves control through medicine that is largely concocted from wit and common sense. Ellen Gilchrist's Rhoda, in the short stories of several volumes, finds ways to shock, to assert her independence, and to exact revenge through outrageous, and humorous, breaking of rules. Rita Mae Brown's Molly Bolt in *Rubyfruit Jungle* (1973) is also a trickster figure, free to roam and to look out for herself.

The trickster has always had the potential to be an agent of change for southern culture, enacting in folklore and fiction a subversion of tradition that critiques the South's historic dependence on ritual and authority for its ideals of order. In the late twentieth century, African American writers, black and white women writers, and writers of working-class backgrounds increasingly turn to the wit and rebelliousness of the trickster to chart the South's immersion in a world in which all the boundaries of race, class, and gender are being challenged.

Lucinda H. MacKethan

See also Neo-Slave Narrative; Slave Narrative; Southwestern Humor.

Elizabeth Ammons and Annette White-Parks, eds., *Tricksterism in Turn-of-the-Century Multicultural United States Literature* (1994); Barbara Bennett, *Comic Visions, Female Voices* (1998); James W. Clark Jr., "The Fugitive Slave as Humorist," *Studies in American Humor* (1974); John W. Roberts, *From Trickster to Badman* (1989).

TURNER, NAT

Born into slavery in Virginia's Southampton County in October 1800, Nat Turner was the leader of the most important and influential slave revolt in U.S. history. Originally planned for July 4, 1831, the revolt began on August 21 of that year and lasted until the morning of August 23 when whites succeeded in scattering the slave troops. Turner himself was captured on October 30 and thereafter was interviewed for three days by Thomas R. Gray, a white Virginia slaveholder and lawyer. The result of these interviews was Gray's *The Confessions of Nat Turner,* published soon after Turner's trial (November 5, 1831) and execution by hanging (November 11). *The Confessions* includes the story of Turner's developing belief in his destiny to serve as leader in a divinely sanctioned war, a belief marked by a series of visions that increasingly presented slavery in terms of a moral battle requiring physical resistance. What followed was a revolt (estimates of the number of Turner's followers range between sixty and eighty) in which at least fifty-seven white people were killed. In counterattacks at least as harsh and indiscriminate as the revolt itself, whites killed over one hundred blacks.

Beginning in 1831 with the publication of *The Confessions,* Nat Turner has been an important presence in U.S. literature, serving for some as an early prophet in the ongoing struggle for freedom and rights, serving for many as a symbol of the problem of historical representation and interpretation in a nation shaped by deep racial divisions. In his preface to *The Confessions,* Gray suggests that the rebellion "will be long remembered in the annals of our country, and many a mother as she presses her infant darling to her bosom, will shudder at the recollection of Nat Turner, and his band of ferocious miscreants." Certainly it has been long remembered; many, though, both black and white, hold to a distinctly different memory from the one Gray anticipated. In an 1861 essay, white writer Thomas Wentworth Higginson echoed Gray in thinking of Nat Turner as "a memory of terror, and a symbol of wild retribution," but Higginson explicitly associates Turner's "insurrection" with "the Polish Revolution," over which the same nation that denounced Turner "was ringing with a peal of joy." In his brief account of the rebellion in *The Colored Patriots of the American Revolution* (1855), the African American historian William C. Nell emphasized the cruelty of the white response; in 1863 the African American writer William Wells Brown suggested in his historical work *The Black Man* that Turner's actions had been vindicated by history, and that as the nation was torn by Civil War, "the most important crisis that our country has yet witnessed, . . . every eye is now turned towards the south, looking for another Nat Turner." In autobiography and fiction also, Turner was a significant if seemingly peripheral presence throughout the nineteenth century—in Harriet Jacobs's 1861 autobiography *Incidents in the Life of a Slave Girl,* in William Wells Brown's *Clotel, or the President's Daughter* (1853), and in Martin R. Delany's serialized novel *Blake, or the Huts of America* (1859–1862). He is a more central (if veiled) presence in Harriet Beecher Stowe's *Dred: A Tale of the Great Dismal Swamp* (1856).

In the twentieth century, Nat Turner emerged at the center of significant debates and heated arguments about the cultural politics of literary representation, focusing on William Styron's novel *The Confessions of Nat Turner* (1967). Turner has been the subject of several plays: Randolph Edmunds's *Nat Turner* (1934), Paul Peters's *Nat Turner* (1944), and Thomas D. Pawley's *Messiah* (1948). Turner has been the subject also of a number of poems by such poets as Sterling Brown, Ophelia Robinson, Robert Hayden, and Alvin Aubert. Most famously, in 1967 two novels about Nat Turner were published: Daniel Pranger's *Ol' Prophet Nat,* and the novel that received the greatest attention, William Styron's Pulitzer Prize–winning *The Confessions of Nat Turner.* A novel that presents Turner as a religious fanatic haunted by sexual fantasies and defeated by his own weakness, and that places the Southampton rebellion in the context of a largely benevolent system of slavery, Styron's *The Confessions* was followed quickly by the collection *William Styron's Nat Turner: Ten Black Writers Respond* (1968). As prominent white historians defended Styron's poetic license, prominent black historians and critics pointed to Styron's distortions of the past, denounced his reliance on stereotypes in representing both slavery and Nat Turner, and questioned Styron's motivations in writing the novel. That famous confrontation has continued since then, exposing the politics of historical representation and defining debates about the representation of race and of history in literature. In short, both as an actor in history and as a subject in literature, Nat Turner has been an important leader in battles that have extended far beyond Southampton County, Virginia.

John Ernest

See also Neo-Slave Narrative; Slave Narrative; Slave Revolts.

John Henrik Clarke, ed., *William Styron's Nat Turner: Ten Black Writers Respond* (1968); Mary Kemp Davis, *Nat Turner Before the Bar of Judgment* (1999); Albert E. Stone, *The Return of Nat Turner: History, Literature, and Cultural Politics in Sixties America* (1992); Eric J. Sundquist, *To Wake the Nations: Race in the Making of American Literature* (1993);

Henry Irving Tragle, *The Southampton Slave Revolt of 1831: A Compilation of Source Material* (1971).

TUSKEGEE INSTITUTE

Tuskegee University is an independent, state-related institution located in Tuskegee (Macon County), Alabama, forty miles east of Montgomery, the state capital. Founded as Tuskegee Normal School on July 4, 1881, by Booker T. Washington, it has undergone several name changes, becoming Tuskegee Institute in 1937 and Tuskegee University in 1985. It is one of the best-known historically black colleges and has been designated a national historic site.

Washington established Tuskegee primarily as an industrial and agricultural training school. George Washington Carver became director of agricultural studies there in 1896, and the school attracted support from both northern and southern conservative philanthropists. The NAACP, and particularly W. E. B. Du Bois, expressed concern that Tuskegee would actually hinder black progress by limiting professional opportunity. Charles Chestnutt, living in Cleveland, Ohio, refused to allow his children to attend Tuskegee for this reason.

Tuskegee's literary influence is most notable in the works of Booker T. Washington, Albert Murray, and Ralph Ellison. Washington's *Up From Slavery* (1901), a brilliant example of its genre, chronicles Washington's rise from poverty and ignorance to the presidency of Tuskegee. Tuskegee graduate Albert Murray draws heavily on his college experience in his novels—especially *The Spyglass Tree* (1991), in which the protagonist, Scooter, attends a college very similar to Tuskegee—and *South to a Very Old Place* (1971), a travel memoir that includes a section entitled "Tuskegee."

The three years that Ralph Ellison spent at Tuskegee were crucial to his artistic development and had a profound influence on the writing of *Invisible Man* (1952), the masterful novel on which his reputation rests. The similarities between the college of the novel and Tuskegee are striking, and the portion of the work that describes the protagonist's college years is extremely important in establishing the novel's themes and motifs. One of the most absorbing sections of the novel, the portrayal of the unnamed hero's college experience, owes much to Ellison's Tuskegee years.

Loretta S. Burns

See also Washington, Booker T.

Louis R. Harlan et al., eds., *Booker T. Washington Papers* (1972–89); Louis R. Harlan, *Booker T. Washington: The Wizard of Tuskegee, 1901–1915* (1983).

TWAIN, MARK

The usual complexities of tracing influences multiply with Mark Twain (born Samuel Langhorne Clemens in 1835, died 1910) through doubts over his southern (also midwestern or western) qualities. Famously, William Dean Howells judged that Twain was the "most desouthernized Southerner" he ever knew; and Robert Penn Warren would perceive him as "repudiating the South." But by the 1890s, Twain would, more perhaps from political than psychic easement, parade his southern origins. Standoffishness by the other side lasted even longer. Except for a few humorists aiming at national appeal, literate southerners—especially the carriers of the genteelist, romanticizing ideal of belles-lettres—seldom claimed kinship. Although the "Biographical Dictionary" for the *Library of Southern Literature* (1907) rated him the "foremost present-day American humorist," the sixteen-volume set included none of his work because "Mr. Clemens cannot be strictly classified among Southern authors." Today, nobody impartial would give Twain credit for spreading local-color writing southward or argue that the variegated colonels in his writings were important to forming the stereotype. Nor when self-criticism deepened toward a love-hate tension did southern writers invoke Twain as a model. After 1920, regionalizing critics would mention him more often, but, cumulatively self-confident, they felt little reason to claim him as an active heritage. While Allen Tate praised *Adventures of Huckleberry Finn*—"which I take to be the first modern novel by a Southerner"—he hedged that Twain "was a forerunner who set an example which was not necessarily an influence." In 1922 a still beaux-arty William Faulkner dismissed Twain as a "hack writer who would not have been considered fourth rate in Europe."

The mainline rediscovery of Twain comes after World War II, when the Southern Literary Renascence solidified into a hegemony and when American literature became a federally subsidized commodity, at home and for export. The upcoming cohort of southern writers encountered Twain as assigned reading, assured therefore of respect but also of gratitude as a relief from the solemnity of most "classics." That rediscovery centered on *Huckleberry Finn*: for its first-person narrator charming to a region long assertive about hospitality to storytelling; for its idiomatic, colloquial diction making dialect respect-worthy; for its vernacular naïf nevertheless implicit with dignity. Of course, as the Civil Rights Movement gained momentum, Huck and Jim gained matching resonance; aesthetically attuned Ralph Ellison could not help focusing on their interaction. By now, many critics strain to draw comparisons, implying influence between *Huckleberry Finn* and their favored texts, giving it, for instance, too exclusive credit for a basic angle of narration. Likewise, the older Faulkner would often praise it—possibly "The Great American Novel"—and its author—"the first truly American writer," a "father"—yet he ignored the rest of Twain's huge oeuvre. Even *Life on the Mississippi*, as distinct from the "Old Times" chapters, now runs a very weak second (though Thomas Wolfe and Willie Morris single it out). Still, it gets more attention than *Pudd'nhead Wilson*, from readers anyway. Beyond that, in spite of historians, the setting of *The Adventures of Tom Sawyer* comes across as a heartland village, and Robert Penn Warren sees "more a Western than a Southern orientation" in *The Gilded Age*.

Besides enriching the range of the I-narrator, Twain has encouraged professional humorists as well as humorous tones in more ambitiously oriented writers of fiction. For example, a close listener to Eudora Welty would expect her to proclaim Twain her tuning fork for comedy. More concretely, Twain won greater respectability for Old Southwest–like humor than anybody before Faulkner. Patterning on his overall career, Irvin S. Cobb tried to replay its genres, themes, strategies, and marketing, eventually setting off H. L. Mencken to fulminate against crowning him the "heir" of Twain. Imagining personal encounters, Opie Read tried to imitate Twain every way feasible. Though Roy Blount Jr. is too exuberant merely to imitate anybody, he emphatically chooses Twain as "the funniest American writer" (who did come from the South).

Twain's prose styles, gamut of personae, and material success encouraged many an aspiring writer, and great humorists stir creativity itself in responsive spirits. Southerners can emulate him for nonregional reasons. While respecting *Huckleberry Finn*, Richard Wright took interest in Twain primarily as a mind and personality, deployed the most engagingly in *The Innocents Abroad*. Actually, arguing from specific cases approaches self-defeat: we don't grant highest stature to a work demonstrably based on an "influence." Do we discount *The Reivers* somewhat because Faulkner took *Huckleberry Finn* as a rough model? Do we wish that Warren had stated that Jack Burden is a consciously updated and upgraded Huck Finn? Do we admire more Walker Percy's *The Last Gentleman* the more minutely we can identify its professed allusions to *Huckleberry Finn*? We prefer hearing Ernest Gaines praise generally Twain's mastery of "point of view" and his integrating the "oral" with the "literary tradition." We are content when William Styron, after hailing Twain as "hands down" the "best writer" the United States has produced, praises him as empathetically observant. We are willing to settle for Louis D. Rubin's hearing a Twainian cadence behind the "better stories" of Flannery O'Connor. Happy to impugn the notion that Twain's appeal is heavily masculinized, we welcome Bobbie Ann Mason's plain sense of familiarity—belles-lettres aside—with Twain's characters because they talk and reason like her family.

Author-by-author study would fill in Twain's ongoing importance to southern culture: as a personality (not necessarily white-suited), as a humorist, as a novelist and fabulist, as an epigrammatist, as a stylist who, according to Blount, established "the fundamental licks of modern American high-informal narrative," as a sharpshooter at pseudo-aristocratic posing, and—not contradictorily—as (along with Whitman, according to Wolfe) the first voice of an inclusive "America." Twain teaches that inclusiveness must start from native ground and build on a continuing cultural identity, that eminently southern ideal.

Louis J. Budd

See also Missouri, Literature of; Novel, 1865 to 1900; Theft.

Arthur G. Pettit, *Mark Twain and the South* (1974); Louis D. Rubin Jr., "Mark Twain and the Postwar Scene," in *The Writer in the South* (1972); Arlin Turner, "Mark Twain and the South: An Affair of Love and Anger," *Southern Review* n.s. 4 (Spring 1968).

U

UNCLE REMUS

The black storyteller Uncle Remus was the creation of Joel Chandler Harris (1848–1908), the Middle Georgia author who effectively earned five reputations in his lifetime: as a literary comedian, New South journalist, folklorist, southern local-color writer, and children's author. Had Harris published only the Uncle Remus tales, however, his reputation would remain secure. Uncle Remus is best known as the narrator of the Brer Rabbit cycle of trickster folk stories, the largest extant gathering of black folktales in Harris's day and until recent times. Yet Uncle Remus's character evolved over time, as Harris's vision of the Old South-become-New matured.

Uncle Remus appeared on the world literary scene quite by accident. In October 1876, Harris was asked to supply some dialect sketches for the *Atlanta Constitution* when Sam Small, the regular dialect and local-scenes columnist, resigned from the staff. Harris's mind and mental ear immediately took him back to his 1862–1866 apprenticeship on Joseph Addison Turner's Turnwold Plantation, outside Eatonton in Putnam County. Here, under Turner's mentoring, Harris had learned to set type and write compactly, had been introduced to the literary classics, and, most important, had heard folktale after folktale from Uncle George Terrell, Old Harbert, and other slaves who were likely among the black acquaintances Harris later said he "walloped together" into the "human syndicate," Uncle Remus. Harris may have borrowed the actual name Uncle Remus—ultimately derived from ancient Rome's Romulus and Remus legend—from an old black gardener in Forsyth, Georgia, where Harris had worked as a newspaper editor in the late 1860s.

Initially portrayed as an anonymous older man who entertains *Constitution* staff members with his recountings of the passing scene and comic events happening on the Atlanta streets, by November 1876 Uncle Remus is a named character and has acquired a distinct history and several personality traits. He was formerly a slave on a Middle Georgia plantation in Putnam County, and is impatient and irritated with tawdry, citified Atlanta life; in fact, the old man is so disgusted by urban life that he regularly threatens to move back to "Putmon." A wry and cantankerous commentator on the passing socio-political scene, Uncle Remus grouses about ineffectual Reconstruction politicians, lazy blacks willing to steal or take a dole from the government instead of working, uppity Savannah Negroes, and hypocritical churchgoers.

Harris really found his métier, however, and an international audience, when he had garrulous old Uncle Remus retell in the *Constitution* some of the Brer Rabbit stories that he had heard on the old plantation, down home in Middle Georgia. The public's demand for Uncle Remus animal stories soon became so great that Harris could not confine them to newspaper reprintings. Getting advice from his new friend Mark Twain, Harris worked with Appleton to publish a gathering of three dozen Brer Rabbit plantation stories, plus revival hymns, plantation aphorisms, and some of the Atlanta street-sketches. *Uncle Remus: His Songs and His Sayings* was released to highly favorable reviews on both sides of the Atlantic in November 1880. Six more collections of Uncle Remus stories, and a new edition of Harris's first book now illustrated by A. B. Frost, would appear before his death in 1908. Posthumous collections of Brer Rabbit stories were published in 1910, 1918, and 1948; and in 1955 Richard Chase gathered up all 185 previously printed Uncle Remus stories into *The Complete Tales of Uncle Remus* (Houghton Mifflin).

Harris wrapped the animal tales in a rhetorically complex, doubly framed narrative featuring Uncle Remus and a little white boy, the son of the plantation master, as his primary listener. In his second volume, *Nights with Uncle Remus* (1883), three other black narrators also relate folk tales: Aunt Tempy, the privileged cook in the big house; Tildy, the housemaid; and Daddy Jack, a Gullah Negro from the Sea Islands of Georgia. Uncle Remus himself proves to be the most gifted vernacular storyteller of the group. In later Uncle Remus collections—the ones Walt Disney turned to for plot elements in *Song of the South* (1946)—the old former slave relates his stories to the rather sissified son of the first little boy. Across all of the Uncle Remus books, the old man often tells entertaining, seemingly harmless slapstick stories that typically highlight the denseness and stupidity of the stronger animals. Yet his essential role is to initiate his young white listeners—and now over four generations of readers, internationally—into the destructive power and status struggles among members of the animal kingdom who clearly represent competing, even warring, members of the human race itself.

In the introduction to his first volume of Uncle Remus tales, Harris acknowledged the allegorical significance of the stories he was retelling. Clearly, Brer Rabbit is the black slave's trickster-hero, and the so-called stronger animals represent the white slaveowners. But the warfare among Harris's critics rivals that taking place on the Big Road and in the forests and briar patches in the stories themselves. Some commentators simply equate Uncle Remus with Uncle Tom. Blyden Jackson, for example, sees Uncle Remus as a comic, ineffectual Sambo figure—a minstrel black-face character kissing up to ol' massa in the Big House during slavery and continuing, in the later volumes, to sell out his race to the son and grandson of his former master, well after the Civil War is over. Alice Walker protests that Harris is essentially a white racist who "stole" her cultural legacy—thus diminishing the dignity of all blacks—by appropriating and publishing black folklore. In his four volumes of retold Uncle Remus stories, however, Julius Lester demonstrates how he values Harris's preservation of the world's most important body of black oral folklore, which is rich with universal themes. And Craig Werner, Frederick Humphries, and Eric Sundquist, among other critics, argue for the rhetorical sophistication and signifying power of Harris's stories and explore Uncle Remus's complex role as a trickster figure, one no less wily than Brer Rabbit himself. On one level a highly entertaining storyteller who is affectionate toward his little listeners and is seemingly nostalgic about life on the old plantation before the Civil War, Uncle Remus is also a clever role-player

who tells deconstructive counter-stories that reveal a violent, predatory world of interracial warfare and assaults on the human spirit itself. As Uncle Remus once stops to explain "with unusual emphasis" to the little white boy, Tildy, Sis Tempy, and Daddy Jack in *Nights with Uncle Remus,* "ef deze yer tales wuz des fun, fun, fun, en giggle, giggle, giggle, I let you know I'd a-done drapt um long ago." Uncle Remus's intricate, manipulative rhetoric challenges contemporary readers to study the complex book of life more carefully and to find some kind of human common ground—beyond terror and beyond trickery, which is sometimes terror's only survival strategy.

R. Bruce Bickley Jr.

See also African American Folk Culture; Old South; Plantation Fiction; Sambo; Trickster.

R. Bruce Bickley Jr., ed., *Critical Essays on Joel Chandler Harris* (1981); R. Bruce Bickley Jr., *Joel Chandler Harris* (1987), *Joel Chandler Harris: A Reference Guide* (1978), and *Joel Chandler Harris: An Annotated Bibliography of Criticism, 1977–1996* (1997); Marshall Fishwick, *Remus, Rastus, Revolution* (1971); Blyden Jackson, *A History of Afro-American Literature,* Vol. I: *The Long Beginning, 1746–1895* (1989); Lucinda MacKethan, "Joel Chandler Harris: Speculating on the Past," in *The Dream of Arcady: Place and Time in Southern Literature* (1980); Eric Sundquist, "Uncle Remus, Uncle Julius, and the New Negro" and "Charles Chesnutt's Cakewalk," in *To Wake the Nations: Race in the Making of American Literature* (1993).

UNCLE TOM

In 1949, James Baldwin wrote a vehement attack on Harriet Beecher Stowe's antislavery novel *Uncle Tom's Cabin* (1852). Entitled "Everybody's Protest Novel," Baldwin's essay documents the changing fortunes of the novel and its hero, the long-suffering, very dark-skinned slave Uncle Tom. In Stowe's novel, Tom consents to be sold to pay his master's debts. Refusing to run away, he goes off with a slave trader, preaching Christian obedience and humility, virtues that sustain him through many trials until he is finally beaten to death on Simon Legree's plantation as a punishment for his refusal to renounce his faith in the Bible's teachings. For Stowe, Uncle Tom embodied all the virtues of humanity that made slavery intolerable; for Baldwin, Uncle Tom, through Stowe's racist portraiture, demeaned what it meant to be a black man in America. Stowe's Uncle Tom, Baldwin declared, "has been robbed of his humanity and divested of his sex." Since the 1940s, calling an African American "Uncle Tom" is an insult, a slur indicating that the designee is a coward who is dependent upon and subservient to whites. An "Uncle Tom" is a black person who has no pride in his or her own personhood, one who lives to serve masters, one who accepts and cultivates white paternalism, as did the Uncle Tom of Stowe's novel.

Throughout the nineteenth and early twentieth centuries, if Stowe's characterization of Uncle Tom was attacked, it was attacked by whites who felt that she had made her character too saintly, too noble, too sensitive. Immediately following the book's appearance, the goodly Uncle Tom gave rise to a whole new genre, the "Anti-Tom" novels by supporters of slavery, who either showed slaves like Tom living happily ever after on idyllic plantations, or countered Tom's noble, self-sacrificing nature with pictures of male slaves who were brutish, rebellious, and in need of strong discipline to be kept in check. Fugitive-slave leaders such as Frederick Douglass tried to support Stowe's novel, aware of the good it did for the abolitionist cause, but even before the Civil War, some African American writers understood that her portrayal of "the negro" was problematic. Martin Delany, for instance, wrote to Douglass insisting that Stowe "knows nothing about us," that she was herself guilty of race prejudice, and that African Americans could not turn to white writers for their own "elevation."

By the 1890s, the story of Uncle Tom had degenerated into "Tommer" shows that in their crude plays for sentiment and laughs were demeaning to all African Americans. In such shows, Tom was a minstrel caricature, excessively sentimental and foolish—and of course, almost always played by a white actor in blackface. In his 1976 novel *Flight to Canada*, Ishmael Reed draws attention to these caricatures through pointed allusions to Stowe's handiwork. He resurrects Uncle Tom into the character of Uncle Robin, who appropriately rolls his eyes, speaks in minstrel dialect, and tells "Massa Swille," "Why yessuh, Mr. Swille! I loves it here." Uncle Robin is a quintessential trickster, playing the "Uncle Tom" in order to subvert his master. Yet in modern American culture, blacks called "Uncle Tom" are not granted this deviousness but are seen as betrayers (they are sometimes alternatively called "Oreos," black on the outside, white on the inside). The most sustained attack on the figure that Stowe created was written by J. C. Furnas, a white scholar, in *Goodbye to Uncle Tom* (1956). Furnas charged that the portrayal of blacks in *Uncle Tom's Cabin* drew on degrading racial stereotypes that have persisted down to modern times: "The devil could have forged no shrewder weapon for the Negro's worst enemy" than Uncle Tom, he proclaimed. William Faulkner in 1962 answered a question about *Uncle Tom's Cabin*'s "sociological" impact by saying that he thought Stowe was undoubtedly writing "out of violent and misdirected compassion and ignorance," but that she was writing "out of her heart," and "writing about Uncle Tom as a human being." Whatever Stowe herself meant with her character in 1852, today the name of Uncle Tom cannot be separated from the many dangerous messages that his meekness and simplistic acquiescence to white directions have made him carry.

Lucinda H. MacKethan

See also Stowe, Harriet Beecher; Trickster.

Thomas F. Gossett, *"Uncle Tom's Cabin" and American Culture* (1985); Robert S. Levine, *Martin Delany, Frederick Douglass, and the Politics of Representative Identity* (1997).

UNDERGROUND RAILROAD

The term *Underground Railroad* refers to a series of loosely associated regional efforts, at varying levels of organization, to help fugitive slaves escape to the northern U.S. and to Canada. Those fugitives fortunate enough to reach these networks of "tracks," "conductors," and "stations" were provided food, shelter, protection, and guidance on their journey north. Since those caught providing aid to fugitive slaves could lose their property, liberty, or even their lives, very few maintained reliable records of such aid, and many of the records that were maintained were destroyed, the great exception being those collected by African American abolitionist William Still in *The Underground Rail Road* (1872). Although the various regional "lines" were important in helping fugitives and organizing antislavery sentiment, the Underground Railroad was not a single, national organization, and it was not the only means by which fugitive slaves escaped to relative freedom north of the slave states.

The Underground Railroad was as much (or more) a literary enterprise as an actual system for aiding fugitive slaves. Both antislavery and proslavery writers contributed to the legend of the Underground Railroad before the Civil War, and a number of postwar books by participants and historians, especially in the 1880s and 1890s, secured the position of the Underground Railroad among the nation's legends. Harriet Beecher Stowe's *Uncle Tom's Cabin* (1852) is the most famous of novels about the Underground Railroad, and that novel inspired many responses, for example W. L. G. Smith's *Life at the South; or, Uncle Tom's Cabin As It Is* (1852). The Underground Railroad is particularly prominent in nineteenth-century African American autobiographical narratives, including among others *Narrative of William Wells Brown, A Fugitive Slave* (1847), *Narrative of the Life and Adventures of Henry Bibb* (1849), *Running a Thousand Miles for Freedom; or, The Escape of William and Ellen Craft from Slavery* (1860), Harriet Jacobs's *Incidents in the Life of a Slave Girl* (1861), and the autobiographies of Frederick Douglass, as well as Kate E. R. Pickard's novelized account of an escape, *The Kidnapped & The Ransomed: The Narrative of Peter & Vina Still After Forty Years of Slavery* (1856). Many autobiographies by white Americans have also focused on the Underground Railroad—most notably Laura S. Haviland's *A Woman's Life-Work: Labors and Experiences* (1881) and Levi Coffin's *Reminiscences of Levi Coffin, The Reputed President of the Underground Railroad* (1898). But because it is a blend of fact and legend, and because racial politics have been a central feature in its representation, the Underground Railroad has been an especially important presence in African American drama and fiction, including, in the nineteenth century, works by William Wells Brown, Martin R. Delany, and Pauline Hopkins. In the twentieth century, the Underground Railroad has been a continuing presence in African American fiction, most directly in Ishmael Reed's satiric *Flight to Canada* (1976); and the complexity of the fugitive experience, including but extending beyond the Underground Railroad, has been explored in such novels as Sherley Anne Williams's *Dessa Rose* (1986) and Toni Morrison's *Beloved* (1987). Today, the Underground Railroad has become a particularly prominent subject in popular culture, serving as everything from a tourist industry to one of the most frequently appearing subjects in children's literature.

John Ernest

See also Douglass, Frederick; Neo-Slave Narrative; Slave Narrative; Stowe, Harriet Beecher.

Charles L. Blockson, *Hippocrene Guide to the Underground Railroad* (1994); Larry Gara, *The Liberty Line: The Legend of the Underground Railroad* (1961); Benjamin Quarles, *Black Abolitionists* (1969).

UNITED DAUGHTERS OF THE CONFEDERACY

In the early fall of 1886, twenty-one-year-old Varina Anne Davis, often called by her nickname "Winnie," accompanied her father, Jefferson Davis, on a round of appearances designed to commemorate the South's Lost Cause. In West Point, Georgia, Winnie was introduced to an admiring throng as "the daughter of the Confederacy." The name stayed with her as she became one of the most revered figures connected with the post–Civil War commemorative efforts of the South. She represented not only her father's doomed cause, but more important, the South's ability to face adversity with grace and to rise from defeat with its most-valued symbol—lovely, unspoiled womanhood—intact. The moniker "Daughter of the Confederacy" would retain currency long after Winnie's untimely death in 1898.

The role of women in the South's postwar mission to memorialize the Confederacy and to assert a moral victory for the "Cause" was institutionalized with the creation of the United Daughters of the Confederacy. The UDC held its first national meeting in Atlanta, Georgia, in November of 1895. Mrs. Caroline Meriwether Goodlet of Nashville, Tennessee, who had worked to bring together the many different Confederate Women's "Monument" associations and Ladies' Auxiliaries, was elected the first president. Mothers, sisters, wives, widows, and lineal descendants of veterans could be members, but from the outset, the Daughters favored a middle- and upper-class constituency, with local clubs reserving the right to refuse membership to anyone of "objectionable character."

In their organizational effort, the Daughters were assisted by the United Confederate Veterans (UCV), a national organization created in 1889 to consolidate activities of the many reunion camps and memorial associations. The United Daughters modeled its constitution after that of the UCV and used its official magazine, *Confederate Veteran*, to publicize its affairs. The UCV helped to organize the United Sons of Confederate Veterans in 1896; originally their abbreviation was USCV, but in 1908, fearful that they might somehow be confused with the United States Colored Volunteers, the Sons became the SCV. Although the father organization, the UCV, nurtured the Sons much more than the Daughters, it was the women's organization that had the greatest success in promoting a glorified southern version of the Civil War.

The Daughters had as their primary focus the creation of Confederate memorials, which included monuments, museums and "relic rooms," histories, libraries, and scholarships. In the realm of literary effort, they wrote poems and stories themselves and also encouraged others through sponsoring literary contests on appropriately patriotic themes. Virginia Frazer Boyle, a Daughter and poet living in Memphis, penned these lines engraved at the foot of a statue of General Nathan Bedford Forrest: "His hoof-beats die not on Fame's crimsoned sod,/But shall ring through her song and her story:/He fought like a Titan and struck like a god,/And his dust is our Ashes of Glory."

In terms of literary memorialization, the most important Daughter was Mildred Lewis Rutherford, a literature teacher at the Lucy Cobb Institute in Athens, Georgia, who in 1906 published *The South in History and Literature: A Handbook of Southern Authors from The Settlement of Jamestown, 1607, to Living Writers.* Her book, according to its preface, "received a great ovation at the recent meeting of the Daughters of the Confederacy in Augusta," and the *Atlanta Constitution* reported that "the Daughters of the Confederacy very wisely resolved that school boards be urged to place this book in the hands of the school children as a reader." In 866 pages, Rutherford gathered every possible southern writer who could be claimed for the South. Although her choices are decidedly sectarian, her anthology represents a valuable collection of (mostly forgotten) writers who help readers today to understand the depth of feeling that Confederates, especially Confederate women, preserved for their heritage.

In the 1920s and 1930s, the UDC's efforts, like those of the UCV, lost much of their fervor, and membership declined. Today, the UDC has fewer than thirty thousand members. Even in its heyday in the early twentieth century, many women found the UDC's conservatism unattractive. Mary Johnston (1870–1936) penned two fine Civil War novels, *The Long Roll* (1911) and *Cease Firing* (1912), and was not only the daughter of a veteran but a kinswoman of General Joe Johnston himself, but she spurned the Daughters for women's suffrage support and flirted with socialism in her pacifist work during World War I (in 1906, Miss Rutherford had already pronounced Johnston "unconventional").

Several of the most important writers of the Southern Renascence wrote less-than-reverential sketches of

Daughters. In her novel *Virginia* (1913), Ellen Glasgow (1873–1945) paints a gently satiric picture of Miss Priscilla, the daughter of a "gallant Confederate general" who fell at Gettysburg. Naïve and hopelessly inept, Priscilla is supported as a teacher by the loyal postwar community even though she has no intellect or ability. Faulkner's description of Confederate daughters in his essay "Mississippi" is more pointed: "the women, the indomitable, the undefeated, who never surrendered, refusing to allow the Yankee *minié* balls to be dug out of portico column or mantelpiece or lintel, who seventy years later would get up and walk out of *Gone With the Wind* as soon as Sherman's name was mentioned; irreconcilable and enraged and still talking about it long after the weary exhausted men." The most hilarious and also pathetic Daughter is Flannery O'Connor's Sallie Poker Sash, of "A Late Encounter with the Enemy." Sallie drags her 104-year-old grandfather, "General Tennessee Flintrock" Sash, to her graduation, where he will have a place of honor, so that she can "hold her head up high, as if she were saying, 'See him! My kin, all you upstarts! Glorious upright old man standing for the old traditions!'" On the fateful day, no one notices that the fake general has died while sitting on the hot stage.

Lucinda H. MacKethan

See also Civil War; Confederate States of America; Lost Cause; Regionalism; Sectional Reconciliation.

Gaines Foster, *Ghosts of the Confederacy* (1987); Mary B. Poppenheim et al., *The History of the United Daughters of the Confederacy* (1925); Charles Reagan Wilson, *Baptized in Blood: The Religion of the Lost Cause, 1865–1920* (1980).

UNIVERSITY OF THE SOUTH (SEWANEE)

The alma mater of Quentin Compson's father in *The Sound and the Fury,* overlooking Lost Cove where the saving remnant gathers in Walker Percy's *Lost in the Cosmos,* the University of the South ("Sewanee") has been closely connected with southern writers and literature from the advent of the *Sewanee Review* in 1892 through the creation of the Sewanee Writers' Conference in 1990. Chartered in 1858 by the southern dioceses of the Episcopal Church, located on Tennessee's Cumberland Plateau, the University's first notable writer was Sarah Barnwell Elliott, who lived in Sewanee from 1870 to 1895 and established a national reputation for her realistic depictions of racial, social, and economic problems.

The *Sewanee Review,* the oldest continuously published literary quarterly in the country, was founded by William Peterfield Trent, whose biography of William Gilmore Simms attacked Charleston's aristocracy and denounced the antebellum South. Less-controversial editors have included Allen Tate, Andrew Lytle, John Palmer, Monroe Spears, and George Core.

Sewanee's short distance from Nashville, where the Fugitives and Agrarians gathered in the 1920s and 1930s, and its immediate proximity to Monteagle Assembly, where Andrew Lytle lived much of his life, attracted many writers, including Tate, Robert Penn Warren, Peter Taylor, Cleanth Brooks, Ford Madox Ford, Robert Lowell, and Jean Stafford. Tate and Taylor bought homes in Sewanee where Tate taught in the late 1960s and early 1970s. Lytle, Tate, and Taylor are buried in the Sewanee cemetery.

William Alexander Percy, a student from 1900 to 1904 who later taught English at the University, nostalgically described Sewanee as a pastoral paradise in *Lanterns on the Levee* (1941), a view realistically countered by Ely Green's *Ely: An Autobiography* (1966), which depicts Sewanee at the turn of the century from the perspective of a child of miscegenation. Walker Percy and his friend Shelby Foote often visited the Percy family house at Sewanee. James Agee, who studied with Father Flye at nearby St. Andrews School from 1919 to 1923 (now St. Andrews-Sewanee), described a crucial religious encounter at St. Andrews in *The Morning Watch* (1950). Other writers, including Peter Taylor, Caroline Gordon, George Garrett, Donald Justice, Gail Godwin, and Richard Tillinghast, have used Sewanee as a setting.

A bequest from Conrad Aiken's younger brother created the Aiken-Taylor Award given by the *Sewanee Review* to poets including Howard Nemerov, Richard Wilbur, and Anthony Hecht. The Sewanee Writers' Conference, subsidized by the estate of Tennessee Williams, attracts a faculty whose distinctions range from Nobel to Pulitzer prizes. The Sewanee Young Writers' Conference and the Tennessee Williams Fellowship for visiting writers were established in 1994, and the Tennessee Williams Center for the performing arts was constructed in 1998.

Thomas M. Carlson

See also Agrarians; Episcopalians; Periodicals, 1860 to 1900; Periodicals, 1900 to 1960; Periodicals, 1960 to Present; *Sewanee Review*; Tennessee, Literature of.

UNIVERSITY PRESSES

As much for familiar economic reasons as any other, the southern university presses were not among the earliest founded. Aside from the unassailable longevity of, for example, the Cambridge University Press (1534 to the present), American presses mostly date from the second half of the nineteenth century, particularly its final decade, and the first decade of the twentieth century. Earliest among the ongoing southern presses is Duke, beginning in 1921 as the Trinity College Press, closely followed by North Carolina (1922). Others appeared in the 1930s and 1940s, including Alabama (1945), Florida (1945), Georgia (1938), LSU (1935), South Carolina (1944), SMU (1937), Tennessee (1940), and Vanderbilt (1940). More have come into being since 1950 (Texas). The most recent arrival, at this writing, is the Texas Review Press (1996) of Sam Houston State University.

Numbers in the publishing business are inevitably approximate; but, allowing for that, of the nine thousand titles published by university presses in America, according to *The Association of American University Presses Directory 1996–1997,* roughly 10 percent were the products of southern university presses. Similarly, of the more than seven hundred periodicals and journals published and distributed by university presses, fifty originate from southern sources. Because of the penalties of current tax law (see *Thor Power Tool Company v. Commissioner of Internal Revenue,* 1979), commercial, for-profit publishers have been forced to keep their backlists and warehousing to a minimum. Nonprofit university presses have no such disincentive, and thus another significant measurement of the impact of university presses is the number of titles presently in print and backlisted. The 1996–1997 figures show that, among southern presses, Vanderbilt has the shortest backlist, of 100 titles, while North Carolina has the largest number (1,216), closely followed by Duke (1,100) and LSU (1,040). Not counting the foreign competition (for example, Oxford lists 11,956 titles in print and falls behind Cambridge with its 12,859), there are fourteen American university presses with larger backlists than North Carolina. The University of Chicago Press leads with 4,184 titles in print, followed by California and Princeton, each listing 3,500 titles.

If southern presses represent only about 10 percent of the university press business, their influence on the larger literary scene has been more important than those numbers might indicate. Financially hard-pressed, in a relative sense, from their beginnings until now, and competing with longer-established presses for quality manuscripts and market, southern presses have nevertheless managed not only to create a place for themselves but also to move and, in some areas, to lead the way in new and interesting directions, redefining the role and the potential of the university press. At the outset, their strength derived from the region they served—the South, including the Southwest. What might well have been a limitation became, instead, a positive response to the extraordinary flowering of southern literature (including all of the arts and humanities) in this century, leading directly to intensive and inclusive scholarship and criticism. All the southern presses remain concerned with regional matters and with diverse aspects of southern studies and culture, but many of the presses have moved into other areas as well. For example, it is not surprising that the University Press of Florida should have programs in, among other subjects, Latin American studies and Caribbean studies; but it is, perhaps, more unusual that the University Press of Virginia has programs in African and Caribbean studies and, as well, the special series *CARAF Books*, Caribbean and African literature translated from the French. Not news, exactly, that Duke—until recently directed by Stanley Fish—should have programs in African American studies, "minority politics and post-colonial issues; music, film and TV," but there are other southern presses, large and small, that are also "on the cutting edge." Alabama has, in addition to "an emphasis on the South," programs in African American studies, Judaic studies, and Latin American studies. Most of these subjects are part of the editorial programs of Georgia, LSU, Mississippi, North Carolina, Tennessee, Texas, and Vanderbilt. At the same time, southern presses have been making a contribution in more conventional academic publishing—for example: Alabama's Rasmuson Library Historical Translation Series; Arkansas's William Gilmore Simms Series and John Gould Fletcher Series; Duke's Roman Jakobson Series in Linguistics and Poetics; Florida's Works of Laurence Sterne; Georgia's Works of Tobias Smollett; LSU's Papers of Jefferson Davis; Mississippi's Studies in Popular Culture; North Carolina's Studies in the History of Greece and Rome; South Carolina's Papers of John C. Calhoun; SMU's Southwest Life and Letters; Tennessee's Papers of Andrew Johnson and Papers of Andrew Jackson; and Virginia's Carter G. Woodson Institute Series in Black Studies.

The most adventurous development by southern university presses in the second half of the twentieth century, the one most likely to reach out to the general reader, has been the publication of original poetry and fiction. There was precedent. The Yale Younger Poets Series, for many years, has published first books of poems. Chicago published poetry from time to time; and other presses, Princeton, for example, had sometimes, under special circumstances, published poetry. Wesleyan University Press entered the scene in 1959 with its Wesleyan Poetry Series. Simultaneously, some southern presses were soon involved. The late Frank Wardlaw, who had directed the University of South Carolina Press, moved to Austin to found and direct the University of Texas Press. There, in close collaboration with the chancellor, Harry Ransom, and his new magazine, the *Texas Quarterly,* Wardlaw published both fiction and poetry in the late 1950s. Similarly, the University of North Carolina Press, directed by Lambert Davis, began its Contemporary Poetry Series, edited first by Howard Webber and later by Leslie Phillabaum (now director of LSU Press), publishing its first books in 1961. This series was later (1968) discontinued, but not before it had published important and well-received work by such poets as Mona Van Duyn, Lisel Mueller, Julia Randall, R. H. W. Dillard, David Slavitt, and others. The success story in the publication of contemporary poetry was and is LSU Press, which for some years published both fiction and poetry. They have now stopped publishing original fiction, except for the winner of the Mobil-sponsored Pegasus Prize for Literature, but they have also created a trade paperback series of reprints of important southern modern and contemporary fiction, Voices of the South, already offering more than forty titles. The LSU poetry program has more than a hundred titles in print and is, arguably, the nation's principal poetry publisher. Among the other southern presses, Arkansas publishes poetry and short fiction in addition to its special series including the John Williams Collection, the Arkansas Poetry Award Series, and the John Ciardi Series. Georgia, with its Contemporary Poetry Series, Flannery O'Connor Award for Short Fiction, Brown Thrasher Books (reprints), and Associated Writing Programs Award for Creative Nonfiction, is actively engaged. From Mississippi come the Eudora Welty Prize, the Fiction Series, and the Literary Conversation Series, which is national rather than regional in scope. South Carolina has the James Dickey Contemporary Poetry Series and, as a signal of its future plans, has reprinted all but one (unavailable) of the books of Mary Lee Settle. Although SMU does not publish poetry, the press publishes fiction, both original and reprints. Tennessee publishes regional fiction. Texas Tech publishes poetry, as do Alabama and Florida. The Texas Review Press publishes both fiction and poetry. With commercial publishers more and more forced to abandon poetry and literary fiction, the southern university presses have found ways and means to fill the need.

George Garrett

See also Academy, Southern Literature and the; Poetry, World War II to Present; Publishers; Short Story, World War II to Present.

In addition to the regular seasonal (twice yearly) catalogs of the southern university presses, presenting new books and backlists, the annual publication *The Association of American University Presses Directory* is an indispensable resource.

UPLAND SOUTH

The Upland South comprises that area of the northern "peripheral" South bordered by the Piedmont plateau to the east, alluvial and coastal lowlands to the south, semiarid prairies to the west, and the Ohio River to the north—a territory made up of nearly all of the states of West Virginia, Kentucky, and Tennessee; the Appalachian regions of western Virginia; the western Carolinas; northern Georgia and Alabama; and the mountain regions of southern Missouri, northern Arkansas, and eastern Oklahoma. Today, the Upland South contains a diverse mixture of sparse rural farmland, small towns, numerous mountain hamlets, coal mines, and railways, as well as major industrial cities. The Upland South is distinct from the Deep South and, historically, has had a lesser degree of plantation farming and the cultivation of cotton, racial violence, and single-issue politics—characteristics most traditionally associated with the Deep South. Upland southerners are accustomed to rural living and the burdens of poverty, though in the twentieth century the Upland South has experienced a moderately higher degree of "mainstream" northern influence, particularly through the development of industry and tourism as well as through migration into the region. Nevertheless, the Upland South is undoubtedly southern, characterized most recognizably, perhaps, by the prevalence of mountain, country, and gospel music; a rich and varied tradition of folk arts and crafts; Presbyterian, Baptist, Methodist, and fundamentalist churches; a somewhat higher degree of racial tolerance; and a strong sense of home among inhabitants.

Of the earliest literary traditions in the Upland

South, little remains. Among the five major native groups encountered by white southerners, the Cherokee were the most dominant Upland tribe. Cherokee medicine men recorded sacred formulae in manuscript, facilitating the preservation of Cherokee oral poetry. Two important collections are *Sacred Formulas of the Cherokees* (1886), recorded by James Mooney on the Qualla Reservation in North Carolina, and *Walk in Your Soul: Love Incantations of the Oklahoma Cherokee* (1965), recorded by J. Frederick and A. G. Kilpatrick. The earliest major creative works by whites from the Upland South did not begin to appear until the antebellum period, though Robert J. Higgs's and Ambrose Manning's anthology *Voices from the Hills* (1975) includes early accounts of the Appalachian region, one dating to 1669. Timothy Flint's (1780–1840) *Biographical Memoir of Daniel Boone* (1833), James Kirke Paulding's (1778–1860) *Letters from the South* (1816), and Anne Newport Royall's (1769–1854) *Sketches of History, Life, and Manners in the United States* (1826) all brought the Upland region to a wide reading audience.

The Valley of the Shenandoah (1824) by George Tucker (1775–1861), a native of western Virginia, is an early example from the plantation tradition, in which Tucker both romanticizes plantation life and mildly criticizes slavery. William Alexander Caruthers (1802–1846), another native of western Virginia and critic of slavery, treats colonial expansion into the Shenandoah Valley in *The Knights of the Horse-Shoe* (1845). Caruthers's *The Kentuckians in New-York* (1834) recounts the travels of three southerners to the North; his *The Cavaliers of Virginia* (1834–35), in the gothic vein and also a forerunner of the cavalier myth, centers on the Jamestown colony and Bacon's Rebellion. George Washington Harris (1814–1869), one of the most important and best known of the early southern humorists, migrated to eastern Tennessee from Pennsylvania and began writing numerous stories about local whites and their primitive frontier life. Collected as *Sut Lovingood: Yarns Spun by a "Nat'ral Born Durn'd Fool," Warped and Wove for Public Wear* (1867), Harris's stories gained national appeal and are most notable for their use of dialect and treatment of love, the art of swindling, religion, superstition, and violence. Other early sketches, among the many long forgotten, include Davy Crockett's (1786–1836) *A Narrative of the Life of David Crockett, of the State of Tennessee* (1834) and William Trotter Porter's (1809–1858) *The Big Bear of Arkansas* (1845).

William Wells Brown (1814–1884), born into slavery near Lexington, Kentucky, made a literary career outside of the South after escaping to freedom in 1834. His *Narrative of William W. Brown, A Fugitive Slave. Written by Himself* (1847) gained Brown international fame. Brown traveled in the South in the 1870s; his remarkably innovative career ended with the autobiographical *My Southern Home; or, The South and Its People* (1880), which decries the South's continued exploitation of blacks and recommends, "Black men, emigrate." In contrast, Booker T. Washington (1856–1915), who spent part of his early childhood working in the salt and coal mines of West Virginia and took his first teaching post there, advocated a course of limited economic integration for blacks. His *Up From Slavery* (1901) recounts his efforts in this regard at Tuskegee Institute, in the heart of the Alabama Black Belt. Washington's rival, W. E. B. Du Bois (1868–1963), was a northerner but developed his views on civil-rights agitation, which found powerful expression in *The Souls of Black Folk* (1903) and other works, while a student at Fisk University in Nashville.

The post–Civil War local-color movement frequently offered readers romantic and idiosyncratic narratives of the South, often in dialect. Mary Noailles Murfree (1850–1922), a native of eastern Tennessee and author of twenty-six different works, was one of the most prolific Upland colorists. The success of stories collected in *In the Tennessee Mountains* (1884) and the novel *The Prophet of the Great Smoky Mountains* (1885), both published under the pseudonym Charles Egbert Craddock, gained Murfree a national audience. Other local-color works include James Lane Allen's (1849–1925) *Flute and Violin, and Other Kentucky Tales and Romances* (1891) and *Kentucky Cardinal* (1894); Katharine McDowell's (1849–1883) *Dialect Tales* (1884), written under the pseudonym Sherwood Bonner; Will Allen Dromgoole's (1860–1934) *The Heart of Old Hickory and Other Stories of Tennessee* (1895); Virginia Frazer Boyle's (1863–1938) *Devil Tales* (1900); Emma Bell Miles's (1879–1919) *The Spirit of the Mountains* (1905); as well as John Fox Jr.'s (1863–1919) *Blue-Grass and Rhododendron; Outdoors in Old Kentucky* (1901), *The Little Shepherd of Kingdom Come* (1903), and *The Trail of the Lonesome Pine* (1908). More successful in depicting a time and place, and writing works that rise above them, was Elizabeth Madox Roberts (1881–1941). Roberts found rich material for her fiction in both the poor rural Kentucky of her childhood and the stories of frontier life she heard as a young girl. Most known for *The Time of Man* (1925) and *The Great Meadow* (1930), Roberts earned a place among respected American novelists of the 1920s and 1930s.

By far the most influential Upland intellectuals of the early twentieth century were the Fugitive Agrarians, a group of twelve writers and academics organized in the 1920s at Vanderbilt University under the leadership of John Crowe Ransom (1888–1974) to produce *The Fugitive*, a literary journal published from 1922 to 1925, and *I'll Take My Stand: The South and the Agrarian Tradition* (1930), a collection of essays on southern culture and society. The Agrarians called for the preservation of traditional rural, religious, and agrarian southern culture in the face of a growing—and what they saw as demoralizing—modern industrialism. The most important writers among the Agrarians, Ransom, Donald Davidson (1893–1968), Allen Tate (1899–1979), and Robert Penn Warren (1905–1989), all went on to successful careers in letters. Ransom, who left Vanderbilt in 1937 to found the *Kenyon Review* at Kenyon College in Ohio, wrote *The New Criticism* (1941), which fundamentally changed the teaching of literature in American colleges and universities for many decades. Davidson, in addition to his work in southern history and folk culture, wrote poetry (*Lee in the Mountains, and Other Poems*, 1938; *Poems, 1922–1961*, 1966) and essays (*Southern Writers in the Modern World*, 1958). Tate, influenced by T. S. Eliot and strongly opposed to northern rationalism and abstraction, championed the New Criticism and also wrote widely, including poetry, notably *Mr. Pope and Other Poems* (1928), *Poems, 1922–1947* (1948), and *Collected Poems, 1919–1976* (1977); biography, *Jefferson Davis: His Rise and Fall* (1929) and *Stonewall Jackson, The Good Soldier* (1928); and criticism, including *On the Limits of Poetry* (1948) and *The Man of Letters in the Modern World* (1953). Also a New Critic, Warren had the most versatile career of any southern writer. Scholar, novelist, poet, social critic, and biographer, Warren is most remembered for *All the King's Men* (1946), a powerful story loosely modeled on Huey Long's rise and fall, though other novels—*Night Rider* (1939), *World Enough and Time* (1950), *The Cave* (1959), *Flood* (1964), and *Meet Me in the Green Glen* (1971)—are set in Kentucky or Tennessee. Warren's later career was devoted increasingly to poetry; notable books include *Selected Poems* (1944) and *Brother to Dragons* (1953), both of which draw on Kentucky themes. Later works include *Promises* (1957) and *Audubon: A Vision* (1969).

The Southern Renascence that gave rise to the Agrarians also saw a multifaceted flowering in the work of numerous other writers. Born in rural Virginia, Anne Spencer (1882–1975) spent her early childhood in a West Virginia mining community and settled in Lynchburg, Virginia. Primarily a homemaker, Spencer wrote poems on a variety of topics—love, friendship, death, nature, womanhood, and spiritual yearning—in her spare time. While a guest in her home, James Weldon Johnson noticed her work and published five poems in *The Book of American Negro Poetry* (1922). Spencer gained high regard among writers of the Harlem Renaissance of the 1920s, appearing in anthologies edited by Alain Locke and Countee Cullen, but she left poetry for a life protesting Jim Crow laws in Lynchburg after 1930. Caroline Gordon (1895–1981), wife of Allen Tate and Agrarian sympathizer, is most remembered for *Penhally* (1931), *Aleck Maury, Sportsman* (1935), and stories collected in *The Forest of the South* (1945), works that enhance her reputation for traditionalism and careful craftsmanship. Randall Jarrell (1914–1965) is remembered for poetry (notably *Blood for a Stranger*, 1942; *Little Friend, Little Friend*, 1945; and *The Woman at the Washington Zoo*, 1961) that explores human dilemmas in the events of daily life. Numerous other Upland writers turned more fully to literary regionalism as a concern for the geography, culture, religion, and economy of the South became prominent themes in southern writing in the 1930s and after. The best-known is novelist and playwright Thomas Wolfe (1900–1938). *Look Homeward, Angel* (1929), Wolfe's first and best novel, and stories in *The Hills Beyond* (1941) chronicle the people and history of the southern highlands around Asheville, North Carolina. Other Upland regionalists include James Agee (*A Death in the Family*, 1957); Jesse Stuart (*Men of the Mountains*, 1941); Harriette Simpson Arnow (*The Dollmaker*, 1954); and James Still (*Hounds on the Mountain*, 1937; *River of Earth*, 1940; and *On Troublesome Creek*, 1941). Defining both their native land and its way of life, regionalist writers grappled with the history, social traditions, pioneer past, industrialism, and rural isolation of their region and the untold struggles of its people.

In recent decades, writers from the Upland South have gained greater national prominence. Peter Taylor's (1917–1994) literary reputation rests on his extensive body of short fiction—stories dealing primarily with characters caught amidst ever-changing modern life—though the novels *A Summons to Memphis* (1986) and *In the Tennessee Country* (1994) crowned Taylor's career. Alex Haley (1921–1992), who grew up in Tennessee, became a household icon after his novel *Roots: The Saga of an American Family* (1976) was televised in 1977. Wendell Berry (1934–), writer and farmer, presents an ecological vision reminiscent of the Agrarians but brings his message to more universal fruition. Notable titles include poetry (*The Broken Ground*, 1964; *Farming: A Hand Book*, 1970; *The Gift of Gravity*, 1979), fiction (*Nathan Coulter*, 1960; *The Discovery of Kentucky*, 1991), and nonfiction (*A Continuous Harmony: Essays Cultural and Agricultural*, 1972; *What Are People For?* 1990). Bobbie Ann Mason's (1940–) characters frequently grapple with contemporary life in a postmodern South. *Shiloh and Other Stories* (1982) and *In Country* (1985) represent some of her most acclaimed work. Nikki Giovanni (1943–), whose highly public, and vocal, career brought her to prominence in the Black Arts Movement of the 1960s, continues to read and lecture. Recent works include *Vacation Time: Poems for Children* (1980), *Those Who Ride the Night Winds* (1983), *Sacred Cows and Other Edibles* (1988), *Racism 101* (1994), and *Shimmy Shimmy Shimmy Like My Sister Kate: Looking at the Harlem Renaissance Through Poems* (1996). The reputation of Lee Smith (1944–) continues to grow: *Oral History* (1983), *Family Linen* (1985), and *Fair and Tender Ladies* (1988) represent some of her best work. Much of her work is set in the Appalachian area of Virginia. Henry Louis Gates Jr. (1950–), one of the most prominent African American scholars of the twentieth century, reexamines his West Virginia childhood in the award-winning memoir, *Colored People* (1994). These and other writers continue to explore the social, political, economic, historical, and religious heritage of their homeland with such vigor and aplomb that the importance of the Upland South in American letters is certain to continue for many decades.

Christopher Windolph

See also Border States; Local Color.

Louise Cowan, *The Fugitive Group: A Literary History* (1959); Cecille Haddix, ed., *Who Speaks for Appalachia?: Prose, Poetry, and Songs from the Mountain Heritage* (1975); Charlotte T. Ross, *Bibliography of Southern Appalachia* (1976); Ray Willbanks, ed., *Literature of Tennessee* (1984).

VALLEY OF VIRGINIA

The Valley of Virginia is an area with various definitions, but most consider it the area bordered on the east by the Blue Ridge Mountains and on the west by the Alleghenies, with Winchester as its northernmost city, Lexington as its southernmost, and Massanutten Mountain in the center. The north and south forks of the Shenandoah River flow together, then into the Potomac, the northern border of the Valley. Below Lexington, the east-flowing James forms the southern border. The Valley of Virginia includes, from north to south, the counties of Frederick, Clark, Shenandoah, Warren, Rockingham, Page, and Rockbridge. Interstate 81 and Highway 11 run through the Valley, following a route called the Indian Road, the Great Wilderness Road, the Great Wagon Road, or the Valley Road. Prominent cities are Staunton and Harrisonburg.

Of course, the first people in the Valley of Virginia were Native Americans; a few Mohicans lived in the south and Shawnee in the north. Other tribes traversed the Valley, including the Delaware and Catawba during their wars.

In 1632 a Jesuit priest came to the Valley as a missionary but left little record of his travels. The thorough descriptions and maps of German physician John Lederer were published in London in 1673. In 1716 the "Knights of the Golden Horseshoe," led by Governor Alexander Spotswood, spied the Shenandoah River, whose name means "Daughter of the Stars." Spotswood's praise of the Valley spurred numerous settlers to move there.

In the early 1700s, Ulster Scots came from Philadelphia and Frederick, Maryland, to settle in the northern Shenandoah Valley. Germans also came from Pennsylvania and Maryland. English came from the Tidewater area and Quakers from Philadelphia. A century later,

more Germans moved from Pennsylvania, which they began to find crowded. These settlers were Presbyterian, Anglican, Mennonite, Lutheran, Reformed, Quaker, and Baptist.

The Valley's wagon road was a major thoroughfare. By 1780 it was used to drive cattle from south of the Valley to Baltimore, and by 1800 people in southwest Virginia could get almost anything available on the coast. A half-century later, shipping by rail to and from Knoxville, Lynchburg, and Washington, D.C., was possible. Canals and rivers also made shipping by water common. News traveled, as well as goods; wagoneers brought newspapers on their weekly return trips from the coast, and in 1787 the Valley got its own paper, published in Winchester.

In the nineteenth century, the Shenandoah grew much grain. Markets in Alexandria; Baltimore; York, Pennsylvania; Philadelphia; and Richmond bought and distributed wheat from the Shenandoah. Today farming in the region is much more diverse, with more dairy cows, poultry, and beef cattle raised there than crops.

Public schools did not come to the Virginia Appalachian region until the mid-twentieth century. Some parents sent children east to boarding schools; others sent them to private schools, usually church-related, in the area.

Besides serving as a major thoroughfare for centuries, the Valley of Virginia has had great historical importance, especially during both major American wars. Two years before the Declaration of Independence, people in the Shenandoah Valley signed a proclamation opposing Britain. When the Revolutionary War began, numerous men from the Valley went to fight for freedom, although a few supported England. During the war, the state capital was moved to Staunton.

The Valley of Virginia became even more important during the Civil War, when its value as a trade route and agricultural cornucopia made it a primary target of the North. The Valley was the site of a major campaign in 1862, when Stonewall Jackson routed Union troops from the region. But in 1864 Jubal Early, though he defeated David Hunter, was unable to save the Valley from Philip Sheridan; after defeating Early in Waynesboro in 1865, Sheridan's troops burned and pillaged the South's breadbasket. Winchester changed hands seventy-two times during the war, and both Jackson and Sheridan headquartered there. New Market was the site of a rout of Union soldiers by Confederate troops, including teenagers from Virginia Military Institute in Lexington, a town fiercely devoted to the South. Jackson taught at VMI, and Robert E. Lee presided over Washington and Lee University (then Washington College) after the Civil War; both men are buried in Lexington.

Presidents associated with the area include George Washington, Abraham Lincoln, and Woodrow Wilson. At sixteen, Washington worked as a surveyor there and returned as a commander during the Seven Years' War. He found the settlers barbaric, "uncooth" and "Ignorant," but he still bought considerable acreage at the north end of the Valley. Abraham Lincoln's ancestors lived in Rockingham County. Woodrow Wilson was born in Staunton in 1856.

Much of the Valley's literary history comes from Washington and Lee University, where Robert E. Lee started the nation's first school of journalism; Roger Mudd is a graduate. Journalist and novelist Paxton Davis, a Virginia Military Institute alumnus, taught at Washington and Lee. While a student, author Tom Wolfe started the literary magazine *Shenandoah,* edited for some time by author and professor Dabney Stuart. *Shenandoah* has published Ezra Pound and other important writers.

Other Lexington writers include Katie Letcher Lyle, who has written fiction for children and works on antiques and railroad ballads, and Mary Caulling, whose books are about historical figures. Certainly the Valley provides a rich supply of material for these and other historians.

M. Katherine Grimes

See also Virginia, Literature of.

Alvin Dohme, *Shenandoah: The Valley Story* (1973); Gary W. Gallagher, *Struggle for the Shenandoah* (1991); Freeman H. Hart, *The Valley of Virginia in the American Revolution* (1942); Samuel Kercheval, *A History of the Valley of Virginia* (1833); John Walter Wayland, *The German Element of the Shenandoah Valley of Virginia* (1907).

VANDERBILT UNIVERSITY

In an essay written near the end of his tenure as a Vanderbilt professor, the former Fugitive poet and Agrarian critic Donald Davidson likened his university's remarkable literary tradition to a wild flower, planted by no one in particular, that rose spontaneously from the local soil as "hardy, insistently proliferous, and sometimes as prickly as black locust." The seeds of that tradition were first sown in 1881 with the appointment of the University's first English chair, William M. Baskervill, who is best remembered for his pioneering study of postbellum southern literature, *Southern Writers: Biographical and Critical Studies* (1897). Following in Baskervill's footsteps was Edwin Mims, a noted Tennyson scholar and biographer of Sidney Lanier, whose thirty-year tenure (1912–1942) as head of the English department saw Vanderbilt's literary reputation rise from regional to national prominence. Just as vital to Vanderbilt's literary scene were such town-and-gown discussion groups as the Calumet Club and the Round Table, the most famous of which—the band of poets known as the Fugitives—was but the latest in a long tradition. Led by John Crowe Ransom and Donald Davidson, who had both returned after the war to teach at their alma mater, the group enlarged its circle over time to include a young Robert Penn Warren and Allen Tate, among others. Though Chairman Mims publicly praised the achievements of his department's most distinguished alumni, he initially discouraged the Fugitives from publishing their journal and later drew fire from the southern press for letting Ransom, by then the South's leading man of letters, be hired away by a northern college in 1939. These actions, plus Mims's efforts to revoke Tate's fellowship to Yale and to deny Warren a local teaching position, may have contributed to Tate's request years later that Vanderbilt pay him $35,000 in return for the recognition he had brought the University over the course of his career—a request the University politely declined.

Vanderbilt is today remembered as the center of Agrarianism and New Criticism in the South, and for its rich legacy of such teacher-writers as Ransom, Davidson, Tate, Warren, Cleanth Brooks, Richmond Beatty, and Andrew Lytle. Their literary progeny include critics Richard Weaver, Thomas Daniel Young, and Walter Sullivan, poets Jesse Stuart, James Dickey, and Robert Lowell, poet and critic Randall Jarrell, journalist Ralph McGill, humorist Roy Blount Jr., and novelists Peter Taylor, Jesse Hill Ford, and Elizabeth Spencer.

Brian Carpenter

See also Agrarians; Fugitives, The; *Kenyon Review*; Nashville, Tennessee; New Criticism; *Sewanee Review*; *Southern Review*; Tennessee, Literature of.

Richmond Beatty, *A Vanderbilt Miscellany, 1919–1944* (1944); Paul Conkin, *Gone with the Ivy: A Biography of Vanderbilt University* (1985); Donald Davidson, *Southern Writers in the Modern World* (1958); Walter Sullivan, *Allen Tate: A Recollection* (1988); Mark Winchell, ed., *The Vanderbilt Tradition: Essays in Honor of Thomas Daniel Young* (1991).

VERNACULAR VOICE

From comic sketches and local color stories in the nineteenth century to the latest novels by Bobbie Ann Mason, Barry Hannah, and Randall Kenan, the fictional South reverberates with the bellows and soft drawls of native (*vernaculus*) voices. The speech of the people—raucous raftsmen, Appalachian hollow dwellers, Cajuns on the bayou, long-distance truckdrivers—is prominent in the writings of this region that boasts of its oral storytelling tradition.

Hemingway had the vernacular voice in mind when he described Mark Twain's *Adventures of Huckleberry Finn* (1885) as the beginning of American literature, but the Missouri-born Twain was the culmination of a line of frontier humorists dating back to Davy Crockett. The tall tales and hillbilly comedy of the *Crockett Almanacs* (1835–1838) are contemporaneous with Augustus Baldwin Longstreet's collection *Georgia Scenes* (1835). In "The Horse Swap" and other stories, Longstreet constructs a narrative frame with a lawyer-speaker who introduces the heart of the story: the hilarious dialogue of conniving villagers.

Similar juxtapositions of genteel and vernacular voices occur in Johnson Jones Hooper's Simon Suggs stories and in Thomas Bangs Thorpe's "The Big Bear of Arkansas," a hunting account that scholars have compared to William Faulkner's "The Bear." William T. Porter published many of the Southwest humorists in the New York *Spirit of the Times,* a sporting magazine whose success led the *New Orleans Picayune* and the *St. Louis Reveille* to print comic pieces in the 1840s and 1850s. Perhaps the most satiric and most bawdy vernacular voice at midcentury belonged to George Washington Harris's Sut Lovingood, a trickster and scourge whose targets include the lecherous preacher in "Parson John Bullen's Lizards."

After the Civil War, northern magazines courted southern local-colorists, who produced a tremendous variety of dialect literature, from George Washington Cable's romantic stories of mixed-blood, mixed-language Creoles to Mary Murfree's popular fiction about rough-talking Tennessee mountaineers. Like Murfree, Ruth McEnery Stuart domesticated Southwest vernacular humor for readers who preferred a blend of pathos in the comedy. Beginning with Sherwood Bonner's "Gran'mammy" stories, African American dialect literature was in such demand that the poems of Paul Laurence Dunbar and Charles Chesnutt's conjure stories found large white audiences. Despite his own ambivalence toward the material, Chesnutt created Uncle Julius, a former slave whose storytelling recalls Joel Chandler Harris's bestselling tales of Uncle Remus.

Twentieth-century authors continued the vernacular tradition, but they usually avoided the difficult phonetic spellings, erratic punctuation, and extravagant diction that characterized much Southwest humor and postbellum regionalism. During the 1930s, Faulkner and Zora Neale Hurston incorporated the idioms of Yoknapatawpha's poor whites and West Florida's impoverished African Americans into modernist novels. Flannery O'Connor's "good country people" and Eudora Welty's small-town gossips speak a comically grotesque vernacular. In contrast, the evolving voices of countrywomen are poignantly appealing in the epistolary novels *The Color Purple* (1982) by Alice Walker and *Fair and Tender Ladies* (1988) by Lee Smith. Despite the media's homogenizing impact on American speech, at the end of the twentieth century the vernacular voice remained an important means for articulating the southern experience in the works of Ernest Gaines, Kaye Gibbons, Clyde Edgerton, Larry Brown, Dori Sanders, and many other writers.

Joan Wylie Hall

See also Dialect Literature; Frame Narrative; Humor; Local Color; Northern Audiences; Oral History; Tall Tale; Trickster; Twain, Mark; Uncle Remus.

James E. Caron and M. Thomas Inge, eds., *Sut Lovingood's Nat'ral Born Yarnspinner: Essays on George Washington Har-*

ris (1996); Hennig Cohen and William B. Dillingham, *Humor of the Old Southwest* (2nd ed.; 1975); Shelley Fisher Fishkin, *Was Huck Black?: Mark Twain and African American Voices* (1993); Ben Forkner and Patrick Samway, S.J., eds., *Stories of the Old South* (2nd ed.; 1995); Henry Louis Gates Jr., *Figures in Black: Words, Signs, and the "Racial" Self* (1987); Louis D. Rubin Jr., *The Mockingbird in the Gum Tree* (1991).

VIETNAM WAR

For two decades following the collapse of the South Vietnamese government in April 1975, the Vietnam War was an almost compulsory subject for emerging new writers, but by the time of William Jefferson Clinton's election to the presidency in 1992, national anxiety about the possibility of the "next" Vietnam was diminishing, not only because it seemed unlikely that a former Vietnam War protester would commit America to another folly like the long and torturous conflict in Southeast Asia, but also because the Soviet challenge to democracy had disappeared. The political shifts of the 1990s were not, however, particularly consequential for the Vietnam War literature of the South because southern writers all along mainly have demonstrated interest in connecting the Vietnam War to the history and values and conditions of their own regional subculture, a pattern not generally true of writers from other parts of the nation.

As the twentieth century drew to a close, an apt example of the pervasiveness of Vietnam in southern writing involves the best-selling New Orleans-based novels of James Lee Burke. Burke's stories frequently feature the police detection work of Dave Robicheaux, a Vietnam veteran. Because many writers have used cops with Vietnam pasts, Burke can claim no originality in this particular detail of character background, nor can this pattern be traced exclusively to southern culture, for Michael Connelly establishes a similar narrative situation in Southern California in *Black Ice* and several other novels centered on Harry Bosch, a member of the Los Angeles Police Department. Burke's *In the Electric Mist with Confederate Dead* (1993) features Detective Robicheaux venturing into the Louisiana bayou region to unravel a murder, a point at which the setting immediately becomes tangibly layered with the Vietnam of Robicheaux's past. And then, as a ghostly Confederate general emerges to aid in solving the crime, the historical perspective deepens further, and the unique affinities between southern experience and the Vietnam War are made fully manifest, with cultural resonances surfacing for Burke that extend beyond what is available for Connelly and his comparable West Coast protagonist.

Vietnam links in southern literature have hardly been restricted to the province of trendy pop-culture writers such as Burke, a point shown nicely by Elizabeth Spencer's *The Night Travellers* (1991). With a highly distinguished writing career to her credit, reaching back to publication of *Fire in the Morning* in 1948, Spencer is anything but an opportunist looking to jump on some fashionable literary warwagon. Instead, her approach to the Vietnam War reflects the growth and travels of a lifetime. Indeed, her Vietnam story has a link to her own life, for just as the young couple in *The Night Travellers*, Mary Kerr Harbison and her husband, Jefferson Blaise, leave the South for sanctuary in Montreal, Canada, so did Elizabeth Spencer and her husband live in Montreal throughout the whole turbulent Vietnam episode.

By 1986, back in the South at Chapel Hill, North Carolina, Spencer was ready to start crafting a text that would revisit her out-of-country time in light of the Vietnam War. As her Vietnam-crossed lovers slip farther and farther from their place of origin, several causes—of conscience, of country, and of love—are lost. At the outset, Mary Kerr's family rootedness is palpably southern, with both farm and town components, despite an interlude at Bryn Mawr College on Philadelphia's Main Line. But once she falls in love with Jefferson Blaise, who is all Louisiana hot blood and rebellion, between them there is enough independence of mind to become set against the Vietnam War. Their radical protest activities take them eventually to Montreal, where Mary's concerns turn increasingly toward family and raising their daughter, Kathy—a kind of basic birthright obligation—even as Jeff's involvement with Vietnam becomes obsessive, including his choice to go to war to avoid prison for his antiwar activity. A final ironic turn places Jeff in hostile fire in Vietnam, far from home, disappearing into oblivion with one last longing thought of Mary. The consequences of estrangement from home make familiar territory for the southern writer, and Elizabeth Spencer handles them with superb control in her Vietnam War novel.

The great majority of southern texts dealing with the Vietnam War explore the postwar experience of veterans trying to relocate themselves in the place of their past, but a few directly spotlight the combat experience of Vietnam. James Webb's *Fields of Fire* (1978) is the most ambitious book in this category. Webb is not widely recognized as a southern writer, but his central character, Robert E. Lee Hodges Jr., comes directly from the Webb family's southern origins. It is a family steeped in history, with war a key part of every generation's experience. Webb delineates across time a strong southern disposition toward the role of the warrior, and given such a background, Hodges would have had to invent a Vietnam if it hadn't happened. Hodges joins the military eagerly, honoring father and grandfather and great-grandfather and several fathers yet more distant. He serves with distinction, despite the ugliness and confusion of war conditions in Vietnam. He dies, but his son in Okinawa seems primed to fulfill the warrior legacy, albeit far from the South.

Thanks to the movie success of *Forrest Gump*, Winston Groom is much better known than Webb as a southern writer. Groom's first novel, *Better Times Than These* (1978), is a gritty, hard, thoroughly naturalistic narrative set mostly in Vietnam. Although the story features several characters drawn from different regions and social strata of the South—Lieutenant Billy Kahn, a Jew from Savannah; a huge black soldier named Carruthers, also from Savannah; and Private Homer Crump, a farm boy from Mississippi who comes to represent the virtue of courage in battle— Groom is more interested in the complexities of the Vietnam War (which he, like Webb, knew from personal experience) than in the war's link to southern life. But by his fifth book, *Forrest Gump* (1986), Groom was ready to foreground the South of his own Alabama youth. The Gump story depends upon its strong voice, which is that of a loquacious first-person yarnspinner, never in a rush to get anywhere fast, always willing to meander, loosely drifting from one incident to the next. It is a picaresque narrative, with clear indebtedness to the *Adventures of Huckleberry Finn* in its rambling structure, and the hero—with a life like a box of chocolates—is thoroughly likable. His peripatetic ways get him to Vietnam, but they also cover much of the South, both before the war—with time at the University of Alabama under Coach Bear Bryant— and after, in Louisiana where he operates a shrimp business to fulfill a dream he had shared with Bubba, a black soldier who died in Vietnam.

Stories of veterans' experiences in the South after the war are richly varied. Southern writers seem particularly intrigued with the prospect of locating the Vietnam War within the construct of their region, instead of treating the event as if it were something that did not belong in their history, which is a pattern frequently adopted by American writers outside the South. Frequently the connective issue is race, a matter central to Clyde Edgerton's *Raney* (1985), Madison Smartt Bell's *Soldier's Joy* (1989), Larry Brown's *Dirty Work* (1989), and Harry Crews's *Body* (1990).

Even as Edgerton's wonderful comic touch lightens race conflict in southern culture, he indicates in his first novel that the racial divide still constitutes a challenge for the South in moving on to a new century. Charles Shepherd's Vietnam service included friendship with Johnny Dobbs, a New Orleans African American, and this deep friendship threatens the marital harmony of Charles and his bride, Raney Bell, who comes from a very traditional, conservative North Carolina country town. Charles and Raney practically reenact the Civil War in their disputes about race, but some effective marriage counseling about the need to build bridges of communication leads to a reconciliation in which Johnny becomes the godfather to little Thurman "Ted" William Shepherd, although he has to stay at the Ramada—not at the Shepherd home.

Another kind of friendship across race lines figures in Larry Brown's first novel, where two Vietnam veterans, one black (Braiden) and one white (Walter), meet in a hospital and together come to terms with a host of common concerns linked to their southern origins. Braiden has spent twenty-two years in hospital care, and he cannot bear the thought of continuing longer in a life that differs so much from his dreams. Walter's life, too, carries much pain from Vietnam. As Walter comes to be a "bro" for Braiden, he understands that the kinship they share—from the South and from Vietnam—warrants acting in mercy to end Braiden's misery.

No such kindness or mercy or reconciliation can be found in either *Soldier's Joy* or *Body*. In Bell's story, Tom Laidlaw returns to Central Tennessee and tries to establish himself upon the land of his dead father. Laidlaw is not willing to forsake the friendships of his Vietnam LRRP (Long Range Reconnaissance Patrol) days, and eventually he joins forces again with Redmon, an African American veteran, in trying to protect Brother Jacob, a minister promoting race-blind brotherhood. The novel concludes with an apocalyptic shootout between Laidlaw's group and a set of virulent white supremacists opposed to having the races work together in equality and balance. Much the same thing happens at the end of Crews's *Body*, where a women's body-building contest in Florida comes down to black against white. The white woman's loss and subsequent suicide drives Nail Head, a Vietnam veteran with a short fuse, into destructive action. Bell and Crews clearly suggest that the Vietnam/race combination does not bode well for the South.

Several novels do a fine job of measuring the Vietnam War against the backdrop of family life and relationship to the land. In *The Prince of Tides* (1986), Pat Conroy explores the impact of the war on the Wingo family, particularly Luke, who went off to Vietnam as a Navy SEAL (Sea, Air, Land team unit). Repeatedly, Luke's family role involves risking danger to protect the land that shaped him—the coastal region of Georgia and South Carolina. When a government nuclear facility threatens the Colleton River area, Luke puts his combat training to use in trying to disrupt construction efforts, declaring "I fought a war so I could say no. I earned that simple right." Sydney Blair, in *Buffalo* (1991), examines the effort of Raymond McCreary to work himself out of the patterns of impulsiveness (the buffalo impulse) and violence that seem intricately tied to his Vietnam War experience. In resisting the influence of Bullet, an old Vietnam buddy, Ray manages to commit himself successfully to family responsibility and the hope of sustenance over time that families provide.

Family life is central to Clyde Edgerton's *The Floatplane Notebooks* (1988) and Jayne Anne Phillips's *Machine Dreams* (1984). Edgerton's narrative provides a long view of the Copeland family and their efforts to cope with both land and time. The notebooks belong to Albert Copeland, and on the surface, they chronicle his efforts to build a floatplane, but more important, at a deeper level they represent the culture's whole effort at inscription. Set against such a large expanse of collective purpose, events in time becoming lodged in story structure, the Vietnam War—whether cousin Meredith's loss of both legs in Marine combat or son Mark's F-4 pilot service—becomes manageable and proportionate in scale to the full reach of history as families represent it. Phillips takes a less-encouraging view of the family in relationship to Vietnam. Machines come to play a large role in two generations of the Hampson family's life. Mitchell Hampson rode great machines to victory in World War II, and then came the Vietnam War's mighty machine, the helicopter. But when Mitch's son Billy is drafted and goes off to Vietnam in 1970, his helicopter crashes under enemy fire. Subsequently, Billy's sister Danner has recurrent dreams that turn on her inability to deter the

course of history—to keep Billy from his death. The conclusive chapter, "Machine Dream," presents a surrealistic forest scene with Danner and Billy walking alone while Billy creates the sound of an airplane crashing in war. In these dream sounds, Vietnam joins history.

Perhaps the South's most extravagant and daunting fictive texts on the Vietnam War have come from Barry Hannah. Although not a veteran himself, Hannah has shown repeated interest in the relationship of the war to the South. From "Testimony of Pilot" and "Midnight and I'm Not Famous Yet" in the *Airships* (1978) collection of stories and on to the interpolated tale of French Edward in *The Tennis Handsome* (1983), Hannah has been intrigued with the place of violence in southern life, a matter he confronted head-on with his novel *Ray* in 1980. Ray, the title character, flew F-4s (Phantom jets), in Vietnam. He was proud and wild in his war doings, and the wildness continues apace in all his postwar activities, most particularly relationships with women. Ray copulates with the same zeal he took to war, zeal even comparable to that shown by Hernando De Soto in subduing the natives of the Mississippi River region in the sixteenth century. In the narrative's most ambitious and inventive effort to show the living quality of history in the South, one of Ray's sexual encounters gives way immediately to a short chapter in which Ray serves under Jeb Stuart with the Confederate cavalry in Maryland. The Federals' quick defeat soon yields to dreams of sex. Sex and violence thus join in the deep past, just as they converge in Ray's Vietnam era. With sabers raised and glory in the balance, the past becomes the present and the future too in Hannah's view of the Vietnam War from his Mississippi vantage point.

The southern poets of the Vietnam War—particularly Yusef Komunyakaa (Louisiana), David Huddle (Virginia), and Walter McDonald (Texas)—catch in lyric snatches virtually all of the motifs to be found in the fiction already noted. For Komunyakaa, a recent Pulitzer Prize winner, reading poetry helped him contend with the violence he observed in his 1969–1970 army tour in Vietnam as a combat correspondent. As an African American, he registers in Vietnam the harsh racial divisions he knew as a youth in Bogalusa, but by the final poem of *Dien Cai Dau* (1988), "Facing It," Komunyakaa finds black and white merging in the reflective magic of the Vietnam War Memorial wall in Washington.

The black marble wall of the Vietnam Memorial

also serves as the location for the end of Bobbie Ann Mason's *In Country* (1985), a novel that effectively extends the Vietnam War into the next generation. In the early 1980s, Samantha Hughes, daughter of a soldier killed in Vietnam and niece of Emmett Smith (a Vietnam veteran), gathers all she can find of her past, tries to replicate Vietnam in the experience of wild nature at Cawood's Pond, and then takes everything (including Mawaw Hughes and Uncle Emmett) to Washington to put it all together in a moment of fusion as she traces her father's name on the wall. Sam's story deftly epitomizes the imaginative work of southern writers on the subject of the Vietnam War.

Owen W. Gilman Jr.

See also Novel, World War II to Present.

Owen W. Gilman Jr., *Vietnam and the Southern Imagination* (1992); Ruth Weston, "Debunking the Unitary Self and Story in the War Stories of Barry Hannah," *Southern Literary Journal* (Spring 1995).

VIOLENCE

Linking the South and violence already presumes a yoking all the more violent for its ability to pass uncontested into print. Nonetheless, such a frame directs attention to the invidious categorizing uses of "The South"—its literatures, histories, and people—to demarcate a sort of aesthetic preserve whose purpose is to secure the boundaries of some "mainstream" American tradition.

Yet the linkage is indicative of the sorts of violence that are both held in suspension as well as deflected by what is termed southern literature. "Violence in literature" is often a code denoting a category of literary production at once aesthetically inferior and depoliticized as "Gothic"; such a categorization renders some literatures—Poe's tales, for instance, or the proto-science fictions of James Branch Cabell, or the local color of Carson McCullers or Erskine Caldwell—as derived from the more esteemed tradition of the American realistic novel. Thus, at issue is the South's presumptive and vexed relation to the Gothic—or to its twin, the Romance mode; either of these the South is said to encourage in particular ways. For example, Edgar Allan Poe, although Boston-born, is nonetheless thought to manifest a distinctly southern sensibility.

Certain types of violence—aesthetic, political, and social (racial)—do arguably distinguish the South from similar tensions to be found in other regions and literatures. Twain's *Adventures of Huckleberry Finn* (1885) might be said to typify the range of these tensions—personal as well as social, aesthetic as well as political. Twain's complicated relationships to both North and South enabled him to view the South's predominant literary modes—the structuring narratives of plantation pastoral and white populism—with dispassionate distance. This is particularly evident in the naïve Huck's critique of the superficiality of the Grangerfords and their pretensions to class style; the illusions of Tom Sawyerism; and the low-life "flapdoodle" of the Duke and Dauphin.

Violence is inextricably linked to the colonial project of encounter, assimilation, and dominance. Through promotional writers armed with the authority of Genesis to name and subdue, the "New World" would experience as violent an erasure as the pen stroke that could write, in Frost's nostalgic nationalism, "The land was ours before we were the land's" ("The Gift Outright").

The violences of encounter can be considered as either aesthetic or real—that is, as aspects of idea, imagination, genre, and form, or as actual, material consequences. Early writers such as Captain John Smith, in *General Historie* (1624), or Ebenezer Cooke, in *The Sot-Weed Factor or, A Voyage to Maryland* (1708), however, show how aesthetic forms are invariably politically maintained. Although John Smith's narrative distances the trauma of encountering native peoples through romance formulas customary to the sentimental novel, an uneasiness remains in the fusion of old romantic genres and new material. In *The Sot-Weed Factor*, on the other hand, Cooke uses a particular aesthetic form—satire—to contain the hyperinflated rhetoric that accompanied the New World colonizing project. Cooke, accordingly, inverts the Edenic mode that becomes so familiar a southern backdrop: he associates the land itself prima facie with an originary inheritance of violence—with the land traditionally associated with the fugitive Cain.

The Sot-Weed Factor, or William Byrd II's diaries and his *History*, or Beverley's *History and Present State of Virginia* (1705) chart a world that never was new in the sense of the rhetoric. The land therein imagined is a palimpsest of desire, nostalgia, and, sometimes, fear; yet it was never to be completely congruent with any of these fantasies. In the first place, the land was already home to an array of populations; early texts document engagements with other immigrant peoples and, in particular, with Indians. Later to come were the often-excusatory texts justifying those who over time came to constitute the burden of slavery. It is the inescapable fact of slavery that grounds the central ideological violence of southern historiography: that is, how explain a flight for freedom *from* bondage in the name of the sovereignty of the self while at the same time justifying a variation of that bondage in political practice.

Smith's account of his rescue by Pocahontas from Chief Powhatan establishes the type of the early romances. Race, although not yet articulated precisely as such, is spelled out through class prerogative and the erotic lure of the sentimentalized primitive in ways not materially different from the class-driven energy of later humorists such as Augustus Baldwin Longstreet or Johnson Jones Hooper. In the figure of Smith's regally figured "Lady Pocahontas" is written an anxiety of miscegenation—as well as its allure—that will serve as a recurring motif not only in southern texts but more generally in literatures of the young Republic and beyond; a distinctive racialized obsessiveness will shadow the literatures of North as well as South. Sometimes this energy will be eroticized, as in Smith, or nationalized, as in Simms's *The Yemassee: A Romance of Carolina* (1835). Sometimes a combination of motives will inform the text, as in the violent revenge fantasies played out in Robert Montgomery Bird's *Nick of the Woods* (1837), a tale of vengeful Indian killing set in the wilderness of Kentucky.

The tension of racial encounter is a persistent focus from early to late. Even contemporary Shelby Foote, for example, although best known for his treatment of the War Between the States, addresses the clash of cultural mythologies; in "The Sacred Mound" (1954), he imagines the necessarily lethal consequences of trying to accommodate transplanted myths. Racial conflict becomes specifically focused, of course, in the "peculiar institution" of slavery. For example, despite its reasoned and explanatory tones, Thomas Jefferson's *Notes on Virginia* (1787) slips, almost despite the author's dignified intentions, into the doom-edged cadences of the apocalyptic precisely over this question. In chapter 18, in a frank discussion of slavery, Jefferson muses, "The whole commerce between master and slave is a perpetual exercise of the most boisterous passions, the most unremitting despotism on the one part and degrading submissions on the other."

Ironically enough, the violence of racial encounter before the mid-nineteenth century is evident in not being evident as such; conflict is written away through romance, as with Smith, or rewritten as patriotic necessity, as in Simms's romances of the Revolutionary War (for example, *The Partisan,* 1835). Occasionally the conflicts are gothicized—as in Jefferson's *Notes,* or, again, in the sideways glance at the "merciless Indian savages" in Jefferson's Declaration of Independence. In sum, the Indian becomes *the* aesthetic racial Other, who receives the conflicted energies, political as well as social, that from the very beginning had complicated the slave's relations—to his master as well as to himself. Further, the ideological erasure of the Native American in the early part of the nineteenth century made possible his practical elimination in the latter half. To see how this plays out in a wider cultural context, one need only examine so canonical a text as Frederick Jackson Turner's "The Significance of the Frontier in American History" (1893).

The Negro, on the other hand, fades into the background precisely as social fact, only to reemerge in the antebellum pastoral idyll of the plantation—for example, John Pendleton Kennedy's *Swallow Barn: A Sojourn in the Old Dominion* (1832) or John Esten Cooke's *Virginia Comedians* (1854)—which Cooke described as a "picture of our curiously graded Virginia society just before the Revolution." Systematically deracinated, the Negro was invoked as buttress to a plantation domesticity that was modeled upon the medieval hierarchical allegory, the Great Chain of Being. Of necessity, the textual pacification of the numerically superior Negro was intended to counter the threat of his person in social space as well as the threat that the captive race posed in political space. In addition, like the Indian previously, the Negro becomes useful as backdrop for the myth of the cavalier; this narrative of class, white heroism, and altruism was intended to support the romantic politics of nationalism. The happy, banjo-playing darky is the result, then, as well as the inverse side, of the altruistic imperative crafted by Simms and others into proslavery polemic—see, for instance, Simms's *Slavery in America* (1838).

For reasons of social nostalgia rather than political justification, this idealizing trend continued in post-Reconstruction literature. For example, Thomas Nelson Page's "Marse Chan" (*In Ole Virginia,* 1887), is typical of the genre of Plantation Life Remembered that culminates in that mutually antagonistic pairing, Margaret Mitchell's *Gone With the Wind* (1936) and Faulkner's *Absalom, Absalom!* (1936). Page casts the black servant into a heroizing subjection that makes the character both morally admirable and politically ineffectual. This effeminization, broadly speaking, characterized the racial text—disguising the mean-spirited racial politics of the post-Reconstruction years. Probably for that reason, such characters as Joel Chandler Harris's *Uncle Remus: His Songs and His Sayings* (1880) became useful for northern export at a time when the politics of the South—or more accurately, the "idea of the South"—could, after the years of trauma, be safely aestheticized again.

Thus, prose stylists and aesthetic formalists like the Agrarians secured the literary further and further from the bleak reality of political life, articulating a vision of the South (*I'll Take My Stand*, 1930) that seldom mentions the omnipresent material facts of slavery and its consequences. Elsewhere, however, southern fiction and other literary genres obsessively return to the crisis that was, even as early as Jefferson, already traumatic. Even genres of fantasy and proto-science fiction, ostensibly far removed from politics, weigh in. Poe, for example, meditates upon the racial conflict in the symbolics of *The Narrative of Arthur Gordon Pym* (1838) and "The Black Cat" (1845), and later the fantasies of James Branch Cabell make similar political asides.

Slave narratives address the violence of racial encounter more directly—although by virtue of the genre, customarily with white authorization. *The Narrative of the Life of Frederick Douglass* (1845; expanded to *My Bondage and My Freedom*, 1855), is the best known of an evangelically derived tradition that was spun off an earlier American genre—the captivity narrative, which in turn, and in different ways, had mediated racial encounter. The escaped slave Harriet Jacobs combines both traditions in *Incidents in the Life of a Slave Girl* (1861).

In the post-Reconstruction years, and through century's end, the mounting crisis of the Jim Crow era was signaled by the ad hoc violence of what amounted to a lynching epidemic. Albion W. Tourgée, a transplanted northerner, chronicles these years. His *A Fool's Errand* (1879) and *Bricks Without Straw* (1880) attack the system of white caste privilege as well as the ruthless and mundane Klan terrorism supported by that privilege. The depredations of the era are documented in, for example, Ida B. Wells's *Southern Horrors* (1892) and *A Red Record* (1894); an actual Mississippi lynching is graphically fictionalized in Sutton Griggs's *The Hindered Hand* (1905). Thomas Dixon's *The Leopard's Spots: A Romance of the White Man's Burden, 1865–1900* (1902) and viscerally phobic *The Clans-*

man (1905) treat the subject from an apologist's point of view. The latter of these two inflammatory race novels serves as inspiration for D. W. Griffith's film *The Birth of a Nation* (1915).

In the twentieth century, what Toni Morrison refers to as the "disrupting darkness" of race was still a pervasive literary force. Faulkner faces the issue directly as well as obliquely. The issue is the background that explains the expiatory actions of young Isaac McCaslin in "The Bear" (1942), who repudiates his slave-tainted inheritance. Faulkner treats the subject more directly in *Absalom, Absalom!* (1936), where the shadow of race is the originary sin that brings down Sutpen's imagined Eden. The tension of race is also obliquely evident as the unknown and unknowable taint that is Joe Christmas's trauma in *Light in August* (1932). One could argue that when Gavin Stevens says to Temple Drake, "The past is never dead. It's not even past" (*Requiem for a Nun*, 1950)—what he means are the material consequences, across white and black southern culture, of the moral corrosion created in the wake of slavery. Surely this is one of Faulkner's abiding themes.

Black voices treated the subject of their own captivity as well, although, not surprisingly, it is not until late in the nineteenth century and on into the twentieth that they do so. Charles Waddell Chesnutt spent his early life in North Carolina and his experiences there grounded his increasingly politicized renderings of the folktale genre, such as *The Conjure Woman* (1899). His stories in *The Wife of His Youth and Other Stories of the Color Line* more directly portray a heritage of violence. Jean Toomer's *Cane* (1923) vividly portrays violence resulting from interracial love in the South, as does Lillian Smith in *Strange Fruit* (1944). Violence is by then a fairly conventional theme. Richard Wright's *Uncle Tom's Children* (1938) and *Native Son* (1940), as well as his autobiographical account, *Black Boy* (1945), accept the prevalence of violence in the African American experience. Ralph Ellison's *Invisible Man* (1952), Ernest J. Gaines's *The Autobiography of Miss Jane Pittman* (1971), and Alex Haley's *Roots* (1976) provide subsequent reinforcement. Alice Walker's Pulitzer Prize–winning novel, *The Color Purple* (1982), offered a particularly modern, indeed feminist, critique of slavery's gendered violences.

The politics of defense and denial caused by racial division, which ultimately occasioned the armed conflict between the states, was, after the war, just as aggressively converted into an odd sort of triumphalism. Many, perhaps most, of the postwar idylls romanced the political conflict; the Lost Cause was established as an inevitable consequence, as well as burden, of the South. In this view, tradition became the heroized defense of an antebellum southern culture in which the slave was merely one small part of an overall imagined life of moral and intellectual balance.

But even romancers like Simms found pastoralism inadequate to the war's violence. Describing the destruction of Columbia by Sherman's troops, Simms resorts to a gothic mode rather than to romance, describing the burning of the town by northern troops as a "saturnalia," a "reign of terror": "It was a scene for the painter of the terrible. It was the blending of a range of burning mountains stretched in a continuous series for more than a mile" *(The Sack and Destruction of Columbia, S.C., 1865)*.

To some extent, the notion of a regional literature called "southern" is itself an extension of pastoralism. The defense of the South as an identifiable entity becomes possible only under growing pressures—experienced as social and economic violence—by the antebellum southern states. These forces were often directly linked to the growing, and sometimes grudging, acceptance of chattel slavery. In particular, after the Missouri Compromise of 1820, there was a call for a defense of the "Literary South"—an aesthetic preserve somehow above or beyond the contradictions of colonialism and the claim of politics.

The subjection of the South was an accomplished political as well as economic fact, however, during and after the war. Nonetheless, well into the twentieth century the very impulses of threat and domination that gave rise to the category of "southern literature" were still being politically enacted upon a region already burdened with the economic and psychological scars of its colonial heritage. These pressures and political denials gave rise to the pastoral revisionism of southern history that is typified by the Agrarians' project of a fantasy geography, serenely protected from the messy world of politics. In this respect, then, Sutpen's Hundred provides an apt analogy to southern literature, a revisionist formation of a body of texts canonically southern in culture.

Yet just as Thomas Sutpen's despotic vision was founded in an awareness of his social inferiority, likewise the southern romance of memory cannot escape the responsibility for the violence it carries. The predatory, backward glance of imagination is as powerful an agent of erasure as was Time itself. The romancing of memory established an imaginative order in which vio-

lence is built in and called gentility. The romantic fiction and pastoral mythologies of John Esten Cooke *(The Virginia Bohemians,* 1880) and Thomas Nelson Page *(Red Rock,* 1898) are set, as Richard Gray observes in *Writing the South* (1986), in "the vague region partly in one of the old Southern states and partly in the yet vaguer land of Memory." A different, although equally class-privileged revision of the South's past occurs in the clash of populism and patriarchy exemplified by the humorists—for instance, Augustus Baldwin Longstreet's *Georgia Scenes* (1835) or George Washington Harris's *Sut Lovingood: Yarns Spun by a "Nat'ral Born Durn'd Fool: Warped and Wove for Public Wear"* (1867). Like the slave narratives earlier, the revisionist fictions of plantation life and the humorists' glimpses into an exoticized low life found a wide acceptance in the magazines of the North; once again, the South was a safe place to go imaginatively touring.

Particular attention must be paid to William Faulkner, who by bloodline and by thematic focus has direct lineal connection to what is usually conjured up as southern history—but which is more accurately southern mythology. His "postage stamp" South seems designed to exhibit, if not always contain, the misogynistic and racial violence that an imagined gentility seems to breed. Although omnipresent in Faulkner's mannered prose, these forms of violence almost pass unnoticed as such. Nonetheless, they mount a visible assault upon the reader in the grotesque, cartoonlike misogyny of *Sanctuary* (1931), or in the explicitly racial energy of *Intruder in the Dust* (1948), or even in "A Rose for Emily" (1924) and its emblematic critique of southern gender codes and the gothic domesticity that results. Percy Grimm's lynching of Joe Christmas is of a piece with the killing of Joanna Burden and the rape of Temple Drake, or Thomas Sutpen's abandoning his newly born daughter in a stable as being, in his words, "not adjunctive." The motives seem inexcusably small for such horrors; yet perhaps Faulkner would say, perversely enough echoing his own 1950 Nobel Address, that violence is one of the "old verities . . . of the heart"—one of the conditions of conflict "which alone can make good writing because only that is worth writing about, worth the agony and the sweat."

Faulkner had written most of his major works, although not yet achieved critical fame, when Robert Penn Warren published his first novel, *Night Rider* (1939), a retelling of the events narrated by Simms in *Beauchampe: A Kentucky Tragedy* (1842). In this, as in *At Heaven's Gate* (1943), *All the King's Men*

(1946), and *Brother to Dragons: A Tale in Verse and Voices* (1953)—his long dramatic poem—Warren's topic is the failure of modern systems of labor and politics. Warren's vision seems more public and politically social than Faulkner's verities of the human heart.

Cormac McCarthy addresses Warren's collective view as well as Faulkner's more private view; the metaphysical burden of human imaginative penury is the subject of his bleakly mystical *Blood Meridian* (1985). This frankly disturbing novel addresses many of the themes discussed above; imagination, race, and colonial landlust equally combine in a vision of violence as a normative, terrifying, and yet ultimately banal human experience. His third novel, *Child of God* (1973), introduces Lester Ballard, who seems familially related to Faulkner's Snopes clan as well as to Flannery O'Connor's Tarwater. In Ballard, McCarthy explores the link between obsessive memory and its incarnation in compulsive memorializing, both in acts of murder as well as in forgetting, that reminds one of O'Connor's treatment of the subject in *The Violent Bear It Away* (1955). Ballard's primitive life and even more primitive emotions find him engaging in particularly modern pathologies as he obsessively ritualizes murder and necrophilia. Oddly enough, Ballard is both bereft of humanity as well as deeply implicated in what McCarthy sees as an essential human poverty. McCarthy's characters—Ballard is only one example—take the populism prized by the local-colorists and the humorists to its inevitable end, where it is revealed in the grotesquery of the individual that remains after all mythological and religious frames are shorn away.

For all the rich currents of tradition upon which southern historiographies rest, politically as well as socially its culture is nonetheless marked by transience and conflict. Its literatures chronicle the violence of dispossession—from the point of view of the powerful who dispossess as well as of the powerless who are dispossessed in turn. At different times, the South has endured both roles. That fear surely underlies the violence of Longstreet's "The Fight," for instance, or the class-edged humor of the other populists. Beneath the humor is a fear that the orderly Edenic life of class gentility, formed in the cauldron of political embattlement and maintained only under duress, would collapse—leaving the South to be the legacy of such odd, eccentric, but bleakly human figures as Faulkner's Snopeses or Popeye, O'Connor's Tarwater, or McCarthy's Lester Ballard, or Johnson Jones Hooper's Simon Suggs (this last Twain's prototype for Pap Finn).

O'Connor's studies of an imaginatively dispossessed underclass explore a deeper dispossession, as in the threadbare illusions of gentility that frame the title story of *Everything That Rises Must Converge* (1961). In *Wise Blood* (1952), Hazel Motes's metaphysical terror seems merely a way to distract himself from his material, cultural homelessness. In similar ways, the best writers of the contemporary South return to the link between metaphysics and practical displacement: from Ellen Glasgow's *Deliverance* (1904), to Faulkner's *Absalom, Absalom!* (1936), *As I Lay Dying* (1930), and *Go Down, Moses* (1942), to Caroline Gordon's *The Garden of Adonis* (1937); from Stark Young's classic novel of the Civil War, *So Red the Rose* (1934), to Tennessee Williams's *Suddenly Last Summer* (1958) and Eudora Welty's *Losing Battles* (1970). Equally to the point is Alice Walker's *The Color Purple*, which entertains an African homeland fantasy, ironically not unlike that of the "enlightened" vision of an African homeland with which Harriet Beecher Stowe closes *Uncle Tom's Cabin* (1851)—the little book, as Lincoln observed wryly, responsible for the "big war."

Violence, whether excused as myth or incited as legal or extralegal political action, intends expiation and innocence as much as it imposes guilt. Conversely, the colonial imperatives authorized at some remove by biblical warrant presume, even find completion in, apocalypse even while they obsess upon Eden. In the hands of Faulkner, for example, the idiot—and for this reason primally innocent—Jim Bond becomes the allegorical fruit of Thomas Sutpen's imaginative overreaching. Sutpen blasphemously apes divine prerogative by turning the land into an extension of himself; fittingly, the land will be as barren as his initial vision, and thus Thomas Sutpen and Jim Bond complete each other. The relentless violence of a Joe Christmas, a Francis Tarwater, or a Hazel Motes, then, is a broad metaphor for an incarnational impulse to regain, not lose, a primal innocence that always shadows these narratives; such a reclamation must entail a kind of violence, since force is necessary to resist the anomie and featurelessness of evil. Such is the vision of mortality storming heaven expressed by O'Connor in *The Violent Bear It Away*.

Walker Percy explores a postmetaphysical southern culture, appropriately enough, by troping on the dying mythologies themselves, religious, chivalric, and sentimental: *The Second Coming* (1980); *The Last Gentleman* (1966); *Love in the Ruins* (1971); *The Message in the Bottle* (1954). Percy shares some history with

Faulkner, but that world is gone. Nonetheless, Percy's apocalypticism, evident even in his titles, confirms a point made earlier—the rhetorics of the end of the line, and the imagined violence of time ending, are themselves already implicit in fantasies of Eden. Apocalyptic rhetoric—eviction, dispossession, and collapse—complete, rather than undercut, Edenic narratives.

In her furious outrage at the hands of Thomas Sutpen, Rosa Coldfield's distorted perceptions of their shared history speak a well-worn truth, or perhaps myth, of the South: "Yes, fatality and curse on the South and on our family as though because some ancestor of ours had elected to establish his descent in a land primed for fatality and already cursed with it, even if it had not rather been our family, our father's progenitors, who had incurred the curse long years before and had been coerced by Heaven into establishing itself in the land and the time already cursed." We tell only stories that we already know; and as for the stories told about us—we are often the last to know them. Southern literature is a story of violence: partly expiatory, partly anticipatory, partly a story already told, and so, ready to be told again. If there are ghosts in the literature, they are there because we will not allow them to rest in peace. The "end of the line" seems merely a place to begin telling stories again.

Edward J. Ingebretsen, S.J.

See also Gothicism; Grotesque, The; Happy Darky; Lynching; Masking; O'Conner, Flannery.

Dickson Bruce, *Violence and Culture in the Antebellum South* (1979); Lewis Clay, *Battlegrounds of Memory* (1998); Louise Y. Gossett, *Violence in Recent Southern Fiction* (1965); Richard Gray, *Writing the South* (1986); Trudier Harris, *Exorcising Blackness* (1984); Louis D. Rubin Jr. and Robert D. Jacobs, eds., *Southern Renascence* (1953); Stewart Emory Tolnay, *A Festival of Violence: An Analysis of Southern Lynchings* (1995); Bertram Wyatt-Brown, *Honor and Violence in the Old South* (1986).

VIRGINIA, LITERATURE OF

Both the tone and the temper for the development of Virginia literature were set by English poet Michael Drayton in his "Ode to the Virginian Voyage" when he referred to the "Brave Heroique minds" of the voyagers and to the future settlement itself as "VIRGINIA / Earth's onely Paradise." An Eden tended by heroic,

thinking gardeners (or agrarians) became the cornerstone of colonial Virginia literature and the paradigm to which more recent writers have felt compelled to respond.

Fulfilling its part in making a new Eden, seventeenth-century Virginia literature was utilitarian in nature, its purpose, on the one hand, to persuade a candid world to believe the achievements of an abundant life and, on the other, to lead readers to set sail for the new Eden. Equally important in the Virginia reports is a belief that it was God's will that brought the founders to Virginia and it was God who watched over the new Eden.

Captain John Smith exemplified the spirit, if not the historical fact, of the protean figure of the English Virginia gentleman. A soldier of fortune with a healthy ego and a penchant for the personal narrative, a world traveler and lover, Smith develops in heroic proportions as he tells his story of settlement. Having sailed in 1606 from England for the Jamestown colony, he became the most influential of the first English settlers.

Although it added to his status as Renaissance world citizen, *A Description of New England* (1616) did little for Smith's development as mythic hero. It was the *Generall Historie of Virginia* (1624) that became his most important work. In addition to including his famous map of Virginia, thus establishing himself as a cartographer, Smith writes in detail of the English presence in Virginia and provides a description of Bermuda, which he had never seen. Whether or not Smith's famous account of Pocahontas is history or braggadocio, the important thing is that he conveys himself as the first English hero in the New World—courageous in the presence of death and compellingly attractive to women.

Whereas report writers such as Alexander Whitaker (*Good Newes from Virginia*, London, 1613) or John Pory (*Proceedings of the General Assembly of Virginia, July 30–August 14, 1619*) added to the aura of a Virginia Eden, it was a rebel who led Virginia into a major step in self-definition. In taking up arms against the Indians and demanding democratic reform in the colony, Nathaniel Bacon (1647–1676) became the first English Virginian. In a fifty-four-page manuscript found in the Burwell Papers, John Cotton (fl. 1676) records in the celebratory mode of Virginia verse the Bacon enterprise. The better known of his two poems is "Bacon's Epitaph, Made by His Man." With classical allusion, the poem is in the manner of Marvell, Donne, Crashaw, and Herbert.

By 1705 a more fully developed "Virginian" makes his appearance in Robert Beverley's *The History and Present State of Virginia*. The work focuses on a Virginia entity, the founding, now in the distant past, the indigenous flora and fauna, the native Indians, and contemporary historical events. Beverley writes more with the passion of a native Virginian, one connected to and shaped by his native earth, and less with the naïve eyes of an English traveler. The economic drive motivating earlier transplanted European writers is absent and in its stead is a Virginian.

William Byrd II (1674–1744) represents the fulfillment of the Virginia plantation tradition. Educated in England (1681–1697), he inherited 25,000 acres of land, a holding increased to 179,440 acres by the time of his death. Polished, urbane, fluent in Latin, Greek, and Hebrew, he owned the second largest library (3,600 volumes) in America. Westover, his stately country mansion, remains a masterpiece in Georgian design. Admitted to the London Bar in 1695, he prided himself in his social relationships, among them Charles Boyle; John, Duke of Argyle; Sir Robert Southwell; Joseph Congreve; and William Wycherley.

As Jay B. Hubbell observed nearly fifty years ago, the *Secret Diary* is of more historical than literary value. In staccato fashion, and in his own nearly unreadable code, Byrd fashions a confessional portrait of a plantation master who is arrogant, supercilious, abusive, tasteful, well educated, refined, indecent, nominally religious, all-powerful. His diary may be his escape from the tediousness of life on a large plantation and from a tempestuous marriage, for it enables him psychologically to order and control that life.

The Westover Manuscripts—*The Secret History of the Line, The History of the Dividing Line*, and *A Journey to the Land of Eden*—are a composite of Byrd's most polished writing and observations of the Virginia scene during the first third of the eighteenth century. A synthesis of travelogue, history, report, and occasional frontier humor, *The History of the Dividing Line* reveals a sharp sense of the developing attitude of social superiority of Virginians, who stand in marked contrast to the inhabitants of North Carolina, which Byrd refers to as "Lubberland" (a slur borrowed from Boyle). Undertaken to establish territorial boundaries between Virginia and North Carolina, the journey covered 180 miles in spring and fall 1728. *The Secret History of the Line*, first published in 1929, never intended to be read except perhaps by Byrd's favored few, enabled the author to express his irritation at Virginians in the surveying party who seemed to side too often with the North Carolinians. That venting was a therapy he could not allow himself in the *History*. In Firebrand, Meanwell, and Steddy (all characterizing names), Byrd achieves the most effective social satire in Virginia literature to that date.

A Progress to the Mines was occasioned by a trip to Fredericksburg and Germanna to inspect Governor Alexander Spotswood's iron mine. Byrd recounts the founding of Richmond and Petersburg in *A Journey to the Land of Eden* (1733). A contrasting, thoroughly "English" side of William Byrd is best revealed in *Tunbridgalia* (London, 1719), a collection of character sketches, satiric essays, tributes, and *vers de societé* to which he contributed. Byrd is also believed to have written the earthy parody on the Countess of Huntingdon's "Upon a Sigh."

In his only published book, *Notes on the State of Virginia* (1785), Thomas Jefferson, the embodiment of the Virginia ideal, reveals himself as a leading agrarian in his belief that those who "till the earth are the chosen men of God." Divided into twenty-three sections, the book is a response to queries forwarded to Jefferson from the Marquis de Barbé-Marbois, secretary to the French legation in Philadelphia. In discussing slavery, Jefferson admits its baneful effect on society, seeing it, psychologically and sociologically, as a practice imbuing absolute tyranny in those who own and bitter submission in those who are owned.

John Taylor of Caroline (1753–1824), like Jefferson, took tremendous pride in his agrarian identity. During his lifetime, he advocated agricultural reform long before Edmund Ruffin in the Virginia *Farmer's Register*. As did Jefferson, he favored the development of a landed aristocracy, and he was opposed to Hamiltonian economy (a "paper aristocracy") as well as John Marshall's legal decisions. Taylor is primarily remembered for *Arator: Being a Series of Agricultural Essays, Practical and Political* (Georgetown, 1813) and *An Enquiry into the Principles and Policy of the Government of the United States* (Fredericksburg, 1814).

Because Virginia life was less antagonistic to dramatic presentation than that of other colonies, the first dramatic performance in America occurred in 1665 in Accomac County in Cowle's Tavern. Although Cornelius Watkinson, Philip Howard, and William Darley were arrested for their parts in *Ye Bar and Ye Cubb*, they were not convicted for their performance.

The major achievement in Virginia drama came, however, from Robert Munford III (c. 1730–1784),

Mecklenburg County, Virginia. Munford was particularly strong in his satire of election time in the Old Dominion in his farce *The Candidates; or the Humors of a Virginia Election*. Characters named Worthy and Wou'dbe (the candidates) are surrounded by other Restoration types: Strutabout, Toddy, Smallhopes, and Guzzle. Munford's Ralpho in the play marks the appearance of the first black comedian in American drama. Munford's *The Patriots*, like the former play, was apparently composed in the 1770s but never publicly performed during the life of the dramatist.

The major characteristic of early Virginia drama is its revelation of the keen hierarchical deference required in the colony, a deference characterizing the works of later writers such as Page, Glasgow, and Lee Smith. Other Virginia dramatists such as John Daly Burk (c. 1775–1808), St. George Tucker (1752–1827), and George Washington Parke Custis (1781–1857), the first to use Virginia legends in drama, continued to preserve the native landscape, customs, and politics in their work.

William Wirt (1772–1834) became the literary model for antebellum Virginia novelists. Fifteen editions of *The Letters of the British Spy* (1803) were issued by 1845. The letters, or essays, were interesting impressions of Virginia oratory, social life, or the landscape. Wirt greatly influenced John Pendleton Kennedy (1795–1870) in his Virginia plantation novel *Swallow Barn* (1832), in which Frank Meriwether becomes the ideal James River plantation master and a powerful exponent of the institution of slavery.

William Alexander Caruthers (1802–1846) was the first Virginia novelist to employ legend in a major way in fiction. Working in the tradition of Sir Walter Scott, Caruthers created a very strong sense of Virginia as place and an even stronger sense of the "Virginia gentleman" in *The Knights of the Horse-Shoe* (1845).

The greatest of all southern writers before Faulkner was Edgar Allan Poe (1809–1849). With the exception of five years' schooling in England, twenty of Poe's first twenty-three years were spent in the South. Poe rebelled against an authoritarian Scots-American foster father. Part of one year spent at the University of Virginia, where all faculty were foreign born, was enough to make Poe the most European of southern writers.

As did Virginia poet Philip Pendleton Cooke (1816–1850), Poe developed the belief that absolute beauty was embodied in woman, an ideal developed in his most famous poems: "To Helen," "The Raven," and "Annabel Lee." Neither overtly American or southern

on the surface of his writing, he developed, nonetheless, the essence of the southern writer, as Glasgow noted in *A Certain Measure,* in his voice, rhetoric, intensity, even, at his worst, when he wrote in great excess.

Poe developed as a formalist, his own formalism the synthesis of his readings in classicism and prevailing romanticism. In "The Philosophy of Composition" (1846) and "The Poetic Principle" (1850), he expressed, collectively, a concern with the work of art, with beauty and not collateral truth, with music (i.e., sound in language) as the highest achievement in poetry (and, by extrapolation, in his own prose). Coleridge was his critical counterpart, and Baudelaire and Mallarmé became his heirs. Drawing on his developing formalism, Poe, the editor, turned Thomas Willis White's *Southern Literary Messenger* into one of the greatest American magazines of the day.

In his short stories, Poe records little that is obviously Virginian. Emphasis falls on a sublime gothic beauty/terror or, in the case of the detective stories, on ratiocination, on the perception of order, on the mathematical and poetic abilities of M. August Dupin. In "The Fall of the House of Usher" (1839), however, the reader recognizes the components of archetypal Virginia fiction: a decaying mansion, codependent brother and sister twins, an ancient mysterious past, a sympathetic visitor from the outside world. The pattern of the haunted house would be rendered later by Thomas Nelson Page in "No Haid Pawn" and by Ellen Glasgow in her finest short story, "Jordan's End" (1923).

George William Bagby (1828–1883) created one of Virginia's most remarkable adolescent characters for readers of the *Southern Literary Messenger* in February–December 1858 in "The Letters of Mozis Addums to Billy Ivvins." A *Bildungsroman*, the narrative follows the adventures of Mozis Addums from southside Virginia to Washington, D.C., where he naïvely writes of "kongris" and the "supreame kote." After the fall of the Confederacy, Bagby produced his major book, *The Old Virginia Gentleman* (1877). An aging man at the time, he wrote nostalgically of the old order and influenced his younger admirer Thomas Nelson Page.

Sharing literary Richmond with Bagby, Winchester native John Esten Cooke (1830–1886) wrote in the tradition of Irving and Cooper. Author of approximately thirty books, he is primarily remembered for *Surry of Eagle's Nest* (1866). Cooke was particularly effective in vivifying Virginia life and was the first important southern novelist to treat the Civil War. Still fresh in the author's own experience, the war is neither heroic nor romantic. The novel has been praised for the sense of immediacy evoked by the death of Stonewall Jackson.

Maurice Duke estimates that the Virginia canon includes, minimally, fifty slave narratives and autobiographies. Taken as a genre, the Virginia slave narratives, like those of other southern states, emphasize the brutality of overseers and the making of man into chattel property, the dissolution of family, the gothic horror of the auction block, the stability of faith, and an intense hunger for freedom. Peter Randolph (fl. 1855) gave the most realistic depiction of Virginia slavery in his 1847 *Sketches of Slave Life; or, Illustrations of the Peculiar Institution.* The most unique escape to freedom in a Virginia slave narrative, however, has to be *Narrative of Henry Box Brown, who Escaped from Slavery in a Box 3 Feet Long and 2 Wide.* Brown (born 1816) dictated his story to northern amanuensis Charles Stearn, who shaped the narrative to abolitionist ends.

The most controversial of Virginia slave narratives remains *Up From Slavery* (1901). Booker T. Washington (1856–1915) fashions himself as a black American hero in his *rise* from slavery in Virginia to president of Tuskegee Institute in a free America. In an autobiography comparable to Benjamin Franklin's classic success story, the black leader documents his movement from poverty and obscurity to fame and fortune, urging, as a Poor Richard figure, that social equality can wait while black Americans seek skills, training, and jobs. His accommodation to a racist world was criticized by sociologist W. E. B. Du Bois in *The Souls of Black Folk* (1903).

Generations of middle-class American readers after the Civil War became intensely curious regarding the American scene. Although America had its first packaged European tour in 1867, most Americans traveled only by reading. Local color and related fictional forms by Thomas Nelson Page (1853–1922), John Fox Jr. (1863–1919), and Mary Johnston (1870–1936) satisfied the intense desire of readers to see Virginia.

Page had witnessed the success of such dialect tales as Bagby's "Mozis Addums" and Georgia writer Irwin Russell's *Christmas Night in the Quarters.* A Richmond lawyer, Page achieved early fame with his dialect story "Marse Chan" (*Century,* 1884). In 1887 he published the classic collection of Virginia stories, *In Ole Virginia or, Marse Chan and Other Stories.* Later works in the same vein included *On Newfound River*

(1891), *Bred in the Bone* (1904), and *Two Little Confederates* (1888).

In "Marse Chan," Page found his fictional voice. In the story, a freed black citizen meets an outsider-observer to whom he narrates in the dialect of eastern Virginia the history of his former master's family. Star-crossed lovers, schisms, politics, and duels make the tale what it is. Sam, the black raconteur, makes the apologetic statement "Dem wuz good old times, marster—de bes' Sam ever see." Page, the Virginia lawyer and conservative, was making a political appeal that, offending some critics, especially black American critics, seduced naïve northern readers into moonlight and magnolias. In subsequent politically obvious works such as *The Old South* (1892), *The Negro: The Southerner's Problem* (1904), and *The Old Dominion* (1907), Page is guilty at best of evasive idealism and, at worst, of manipulation of historical fact. The further Page strayed from his successful formula of local-color love story, the greater the disintegration of his art.

Page achieved a position of eminence in Virginia literary circles. Not only was he the principal romancer of Virginia antebellum life, *la vie en rose,* he shaped future generations of Virginians in his children's literature. His quintessential adolescent novel, *Two Little Confederates* (1888), was used for several generations in public and private schools in America. Two of the littlest rebels of Hanover County, Virginia, Frank and Willy, demonstrate courage, compassion, and loyalty in a situation involving a fallen Union soldier.

Distancing himself from the Tidewater, John Fox Jr. (1863–1919) resided in Big Stone Gap, Virginia, from 1890 until his death, writing about the Cumberland Mountain scene. Fox learned from Page the marketability for fiction creating a closed microcosm. His first published story, "A Mountain Europa" (*Century,* 1892), involves the conflict of a mountain society with a more sophisticated worldly one. He demonstrates his concern for exploitation of the land by engineers. A love story (the geologist Claytor and mountaineer Easter Hicks) is set amidst vivid scene painting and a pronounced Scots-Irish brogue.

Set in Kentucky, *The Little Shepherd of Kingdom Come* (1903) may have been America's first novel to sell a million copies. Chad Buford, the protagonist, is torn by conflicting loyalties in his decision regarding military service in the Civil War. *The Trail of the Lonesome Pine* (1908) is Fox's magnum opus. Three times made into film, one version featuring Henry Fonda, the novel also had its Broadway dramatic versions, and Arthur Godfrey embodied it in his signature piece, "Blue Ridge Mountains of Virginia." A variant of the Pygmalion myth, John Hale, educated outsider, meets, educates, and marries native Appalachian June Tolliver.

Three Virginia women brought the Old Dominion into a realistic view of life: Amélie Rives (1863–1945), Mary Johnston (1870–1936), and Ellen Glasgow (1874–1945). All three wrote, with varying degrees of success, of Virginia life, and all three focused on the role of women in America.

Amélie Rives flew in the face of American middle-class morality when she published her first novel, *The Quick or the Dead?*, in 1888. As did Kate Chopin, she created a heroine, Barbara Pomfret, who had both intellectual curiosity and a sexual appetite. Like Chopin, Rives was denounced by critics and yet achieved popular success. Other novels, *Barbara Dering* (1892) and *Tanis, the Sang-Digger* (1893), continue her evolution of the "new" woman in literature—earthy, proud, and independent.

Mary Johnston, on the other hand, used history and the romance form more extensively in her fiction. Socialist, feminist, mystic, she was instrumental in the founding of the Equal Suffrage League of Virginia. The author of approximately twenty-four books, she wrote the first best-seller of the twentieth century, *To Have and To Hold* (1900). The 1619 arrival of the first women in the Virginia colony is the history upon which the romance is based, and the marriage vows of the Episcopal Church provide its popular title. With flight and pursuit, escape and capture, pirate attacks and Indian uprisings, Lady Jocelyn Leigh, beloved of the narrator Captain Ralph Percy, is pursued by the treacherous Lord Carnal. With all its excesses, the romance was twice adapted to film. Although she was proud of her historical novels (*Lewis Rand*, 1908; *The Long Roll*, 1911; and *Cease Firing*, 1912), Johnston today is also appreciated for *Hagar* (1913), a social novel tracing Hagar Ashendyne's evolution from submissive southern belle to assertive, effective woman.

Ellen Glasgow remains the standard of women's literary achievement in Virginia. An avid reader of some of the greatest thinkers and writers (Darwin, Freud, Tolstoi, etc.), she evolved as a writer who shocked her own family, developing an intensely ironic, sometimes despairing, view of the life around her. Growing up in a patrician Richmond world rooted in the Lost Cause, she witnessed the changing cultural and social scene of Richmond: the Tredegar iron works in the valley just below her home, the building of the magnificent Jeffer-

son Hotel just across the street in 1895. The hierarchical world of old Richmond was being leveled by financiers and interlopers such as millionaire tobacconist Lewis Ginter, who built the hotel. Seeking "blood and irony," Glasgow would respond to the "evasive idealism" of Thomas Nelson Page.

Her first novel, *The Descendant* (1897), shocked any reader accustomed to Victorian idealism. In the novel, Michael Askershem, a lower-class male, lives with Virginia expatriate Rachel Gavin in New York City, an arrangement she shockingly prefers to marriage. As Askershem succeeds as a journalist, he is drawn to a New York socialite. At the conclusion of the novel, the strength of a modern southern woman enables Rachel to take Askershem in when he needs her. Equally realistic, *The Battle-Ground* (1902) crosses hierarchical lines in its history of Virginia society through the Civil War. The concept of the decline of the planter aristocracy and the rise of less-affluent whites (often configured as a clash of old and new Souths) was treated in *The Voice of the People* (1900), *The Romance of a Plain Man* (1909), and *The Miller of Old Church* (1911).

The Deliverance (1904) merits a special place in the Virginia canon for its ironic collision of old and new Souths. In a post–Civil War setting in the Virginia tobacco fields, Christopher Blake, fallen from his position as plantation master, now works in the fields of his former plantation. Energized in his fall, he continues to feed the illusions of old Mrs. Blake that the South has won the war and her beloved servant Boaz is still a slave. *Virginia* (1913) also probes the Romantic idealism of its period and, as in the fiction of Edith Wharton, suggests that, in the Virginia tradition, the less a woman is allowed to know about life the better. That kind of "age of innocence" leads to disastrous consequence.

In *Barren Ground* (1925), a relentless story of oppressive agrarian Virginia life, Dorinda Oakley, after seduction, pregnancy, and betrayal, rebuilds both her life and her self-image, making her father's farm prosper. Challenging again and again the integrity of standard representations of the Virginia past, Glasgow devoted herself to a realistic portrayal of that life. *The Sheltered Life* (1932) closed the Richmond trilogy initiated by *The Romantic Comedians* (1926) and *They Stooped to Folly* (1929). In the 1932 novel, General Archbald observes in the wasteland of his memory the tragedies around him. He is, to Glasgow, a "civilized man in a world that is not civilized." *Vein of Iron*

(1935) focuses on Depression-era Richmond and an enlarging Calvinist world in the presence of an ever-diminishing cavalier one.

When the definitive history of Virginia literature is written, Henry Sydnor Harrison (1880–1930) will be recognized for his contributions to the development of the novel that takes strong interest in social problems. His novels are highly critical of the Richmond world in which he functioned as editor of the *Times-Dispatch,* Virginia's major newspaper. The author of four novels—*Captivating Mary Carstairs* (1910), *Queed* (1911), *Angela's Business* (1915), and *Saint Teresa* (1922)—Harrison treats social and generational clashes in old Richmond. V. Vivian, for example, the physician in *Queed,* is a fascinating character who, unique in fiction at that time, takes on the exploitation of the poor by the tobacco industry. Equally enlightened, Harrison's Carlisle Heth, the principal female in the novel, states, "I'd like . . . to have one man I meet, see me in some other light than as a candidate for matrimony."

Glasgow, Harrison, Johnston, and Rives had to be impressed by the first issue of *The Reviewer* on 15 February 1921. Richmond, part of the "Sahara of the Bozart" (i.e., beaux-arts), as H. L. Mencken described it, now had a first-rate, nationally known magazine. Founded by Emily Clark (1892–1953), Mary Dallas Street (1885–1951), Hunter Stagg (1895–1960), and Margaret Waller Freeman (1893–1983, later the second wife of James Branch Cabell), the magazine became the best in Virginia history since White's *Southern Literary Messenger.* It received contributions from Johnston, Glasgow, Rives, Cabell, Edward Hale Bierstadt, Joseph Hergesheimer, Agnes Repplier, Louis Untermeyer, H. L. Mencken, Carl Van Vechten, John Galsworthy, Allen Tate, DuBose Heyward, Paul Green, and Donald Davidson. An amusing account of its founding is presented in Clark's *Innocence Abroad* (1931).

In his mythic "Biography of the Life of Manuel," James Branch Cabell (1879–1958) captured the restless spirit of intellectual America. The author suggests in his myth that there are three approaches to life: chivalry, gallantry, and poetry. Those novels that develop the satire on chivalry are *The Soul of Milicent* (1913), *The Rivet in Grandfather's Neck* (1915), *Figures of Earth* (1921), and *The Silver Stallion* (1926). The satire on gallantry is best exemplified by *Gallantry* (1907), *Jurgen* (1919), and *The High Place* (1923). Poetry includes *The Certain Hour* (1916) and *Something About*

Eve (1927). Cabell attracted an illustrious following in his day, including Vernon Louis Parrington (1871–1929), Carl Van Doren (1855–1950), and H. L. Mencken (1880–1956). More than any other Cabell work, however, it was *Jurgen* that brought him national attention, when the New York Society for the Suppression of Vice tied him up in court for one and a half years in an attempt to ban the book.

Following the example of Mary Johnston, Clifford Dowdey (1909–1979) made his reputation with his Civil War Richmond novel, *Bugles Blow No More* (1937). *Gamble's Hundred* (1941), *Weep for My Brother* (1950), and *Jasmine Street* (1952), although suffering from weak characterization, preserve in fiction a romantic view of Virginia life.

William Styron (1925–) is a native of Newport News, a town that offered him an unusual contrast between the traditional agrarian world on the one hand and a burgeoning industrializing melting-pot society rapidly becoming home to thousands of U.S. naval forces stationed there. In *Lie Down in Darkness* (1951), a novel reminiscent of Faulkner, the burial of Peyton Loftis necessitates her parents' accompanying her remains from New York City back to Virginia. Embodying the cavalier and Calvinist cultures of Virginia life, the father and mother become a paradox in southern character. *The Confessions of Nat Turner* (1967) examines the most famous slave uprising in Virginia history; *Sophie's Choice* (1979) presents an interesting contrast in post–World War II New York City when Sophie, a Polish Gentile, and Nathan, a Jew, become surrogate parents to the southern Stingo, mentoring him in the meaning of life and death.

In her short stories and novels, Lee Smith (1944–) has woven a rich tapestry of Virginia life. Growing up in the southwestern Virginia town of Grundy, Lee Smith also claims her mother's roots in the Eastern Shore. Smith has published nine novels and three collections of short stories, most having to do with the mountain folk of southwestern Virginia. *Oral History* (1983) and *Fair and Tender Ladies* (1988) offer especially powerful portraits of the storytelling people of the southern Appalachians, written in prose that captures their inimitable voices and the rough lyricism of their lives.

Lee Smith is one of several important writers who have either studied or taught creative writing at Hollins College in Roanoke, Virginia. Other southern writers of note with Hollins associations include poet R. H. W. Dillard from Roanoke, now head of that program;

poets Julia Randall and John Alexander Allen, and novelist, scholar, and critic Louis D. Rubin, all three longtime professors there; Henry Taylor, born in Loudoun County and winner of a Pulitzer Prize for poetry; poets Elizabeth Seydel Morgan of Richmond and Margaret Gibson, now living in Connecticut; and novelists Elizabeth Forsythe Hailey of Texas, Jill McCorkle of North Carolina, and Madison Smartt Bell of Tennessee. Annie Dillard, well-known essayist and poet, is also a Hollins graduate; her Pulitzer Prize–winning book *Pilgrim at Tinker Creek* (1974), written at Hollins, uses the name of the creek that runs through the campus for her title and, in part, her subject.

Another contemporary writer with Hollins College connections is George Garrett, who has been writer-in-residence there but whose longest affiliation has been with the University of Virginia. A prolific poet, novelist, screenwriter, editor, and teacher, Garrett is probably best known for his trilogy of historical novels (*Death of the Fox*, 1971; *The Succession*, 1983; and *Entered from the Sun*, 1990). Dabney Stuart, born in Richmond in 1937, is also a prolific writer in different genres. Best known as a poet (he has published ten volumes of verse), he has also served as editor of *Shenandoah*, the prestigious literary magazine published at Washington and Lee University in Lexington, where he has taught since 1965. William Hoffman, born in 1925 in Charleston, West Virginia, has written both about that state's mountain and coal-mining areas and about the red-clay Virginia towns of piedmont Virginia, most notably in *A Place for My Head* (1962), *A Walk to the River* (1972), and *Godfires* (1985).

Among southern poets writing today, the most distinguished with strong Virginia ties are Dave Smith, Henry Taylor, and Charles Wright. Now editor of the *Southern Review,* published out of Louisiana State University, Smith grew up in tidewater Virginia (Portsmouth), and his early work often embodies the people and landscapes of that area. Henry Taylor was born in Loudoun County, home to his family for three generations. As he has acknowledged, that landscape has colored virtually everything he has written. His *The Flying Change* won the Pulitzer Prize for poetry in 1986. Charles Wright, who was born in Tennessee and whose frequently autobiographical poems reflect his growing up in that state, now lives in Charlottesville; his 1990 collection, *Xionia*, is a group of journal-poems rooted in his home there. Virginia writers today keep alive a literary prominence begun with the Jamestown colony, but it is contemporary American poetry that is most

deeply indebted to the state of Virginia for producing some of the most powerful poets, and teachers and theorists of poetry, to publish in the last quarter of the twentieth century.

George C. Longest

See also African American Literature; Agrarians; Aristocracy; Autobiography; Caste; Diaries, Civil War; Faithful Retainer; Gentleman; Lady; Literary Magazines of the Past; Literary Magazines of the Present; Local Color; Lost Cause; Novel, 1820 to 1865; Plantation Fiction; *Reviewer*; Richmond, Virginia; "Sahara of the Bozart"; Slave Narrative; Smith, Captain John; *Southern Literary Messenger*; Valley of Virginia; Washington, Booker T.; Women's Movement.

John S. Blassingame, *The Slave Community* (1972); John M. Bradbury, *Renaissance in the South* (1963); Richard Beale Davis, *Intellectual Life in Jefferson's Virginia, 1790–1830* (1964); Richard Beale Davis, *Literature and Society in Early Virginia, 1608–1840* (1973); Maurice Duke, "The Literature of Virginia" (Unpublished MS., Virginia Historical Society, 1998); Jay B. Hubbell, *Virginia Life in Fiction* (1922); Anne Goodwyn Jones, "The World of Lee Smith," in *Women Writers of the Contemporary South,* ed. Peggy Prenshaw (1984); Howard Mumford Jones, *The Literature of Virginia in the Seventeenth Century* (1968); Michael Kreyling, *Figures of the Hero in Southern Narrative* (1987); Ernest E. Leisy, *The American Historical Novel* (1950); Robert A. Lively, *Fiction Fights the Civil War: An Unfinished Chapter in the Literary History of the American People* (1957); Hugh F. Rankin, *The Theater in Colonial America* (1965); Louis D. Rubin Jr., *No Place on Earth: Ellen Glasgow, James Branch Cabell and Richmond-in-Virginia* (1959); Carl Van Doren, *The American Novel, 1789–1939* (1940); Edmund Wilson, *Patriotic Gore: Studies in the Literature of the American Civil War* (1962); Louis B. Wright, *The First Gentlemen of Virginia* (1940).

VIRGINIA, UNIVERSITY OF

In 1825 one of Thomas Jefferson's most ambitious designs was realized: the University of Virginia opened its doors to students. Jefferson's influence dominated every aspect of the state university from the architectural design of the Rotunda and the grounds to the curriculum to the library, which was comprised largely of books from his personal collection. Jefferson's grand design quickly became perhaps the most important university in the region. In reputation and in fact, it came to rival the most important schools of the Northeast.

Literature, writers, and libraries would all play significant roles in the University's history. Edgar Allan

Poe was a student in the earliest years of the University; later Thomas Nelson Page, Erskine Caldwell, and Dave Smith would study in Charlottesville. In the late nineteenth and early twentieth centuries, faculty and alumni of the University of Virginia played crucial roles in promoting the study of southern literature, most notably in the production of the multivolume *Library of Southern Literature* (1907). University president Edwin A. Alderman was the co-editor, English professor Charles W. Kent served as literary editor, and his colleague C. Alphonso Smith served as assistant literary editor. Alumni W. P. Trent and John Bell Hennemann were also making important contributions in the field. Students had opportunities to study with some of the most important writers, critics, and teachers in the region. William Faulkner and Katherine Anne Porter, who served as writers-in-residence, and instructors such as noted biographer Joseph Blotner, writers Peter Taylor, George Garrett, Charles Wright, Rita Dove, and James Alan McPherson, have contributed to the reputation and quality of the university's English department.

The library, too, has grown significantly. The University of Virginia's library system is a major repository for southern literature. Two of the most notable divisions are the Clifton Barret Library and the Linton R. Massey Collection, maintained principally by the Special Collections Department. The first includes extensive holdings of Poe's works, letters of Mark Twain, and manuscripts and letters of James Branch Cabell. The second contains the major manuscripts and personal papers of William Faulkner.

Christopher Goodson

See also Charlottesville, Virginia; Jefferson, Thomas.

Philip Alexander Bruce, *History of the University of Virginia 1819–1919* (5 vols.; 1920); Virginius Dabney, *Mr. Jefferson's University: A History* (1981).

VIRGINIA WITS

The Virginia Wits were a group of poets informally gathered around judge and lawyer St. George Tucker (1752–1827) in Williamsburg in the last quarter of the eighteenth and the first quarter of the nineteenth century. Although not as clearly linked to one locale or institution as the Hartford Wits of Connecticut, who were associated with Yale, most of the group did live in

the area around Williamsburg. Furthermore, although some of the writers were associated with the College of William and Mary, it is not this association that the members of the group had in common. Their link was Tucker, who served as correspondent and critic for his friends and aspiring poets. Tucker was a prolific writer whose publications include *The Knight and the Friars: An Historical Tale* (1786); *Liberty: A Poem on the Independence of America* (1788); and *Probationary Odes of Jonathan Pindar, Esq.* (1796).

Writers whose poems Tucker kept in his collection included John Page (1744–1808) of Rosewell, near Williamsburg, friend of Tucker and Jefferson and governor of Virginia at the turn of the century; Margaret Lowther Page (1760–1835), wife of John Page, who had established her reputation as a poet in her native New York before her marriage to Page in 1790; Theodorick Bland (1742–1790) of Cawson's, in Prince George County, a physician and military leader who wrote poetry from the 1770s until his death; and Phillip Barraud, a physician from Hampton. Also sharing poems with Tucker were, among others, William Wirt (1772–1834) of Richmond, best known as an essayist; Hugh, Thomas, and William Nelson of York County; and Mrs. Thomas Dunbar of Williamsburg.

The Virginia colony had always given rise to men and women who wrote verses in their leisure time, especially when stimulated by a political fracas or other event of local or, later, national interest, and who circulated their productions in manuscript. They sometimes published, as well, in the *Virginia Gazette*, the *Richmond Argus*, and other newspapers and magazines. In the 1750s, for example, John Mercer (1694–1768) of Marlborough in King William County, perhaps with the help of others, most probably wrote the satire on the unpopular Governor Robert Dinwiddie, the "Dinwiddianae," though his authorship has not been definitively established. This manuscript circulated throughout the colony and was apparently known in Maryland as well. Another earlier writer, Robert Munford III (1737–1783) of Mecklenburg County, best known as a dramatist, was by the 1770s writing verse as well as plays. And the most prolific and talented of all, Robert Bolling (1738–1775) of Chellowe, in Buckingham County, produced at least three manuscript volumes of verse and published a significant number of poems in the *Gazette*, the London *Gentleman's Magazine*, and other places before his death on the eve of the Revolution. Bolling wrote in French, Italian, and Latin, as well as English, and, like most colonial poets, produced social verse as well as satire. Bolling's three manuscript collections reveal the seriousness with which he cultivated his poetry and the range of his subjects: "A Collection of Diverting Anecdotes, Bons-Mots, and Other Trifling Pieces, 1764"; "Hilarodiana" (1760–1767); and "La Gazetta di Parnaso; or Poems, Imitations, Translations, &c" (n.d.). Writers who dabbled in verse include Landon Carter (1717–1778), of Sabine Hall in the Northern Neck; Thomas Burke (1744–1783) of Accomack County on the Eastern Shore, later governor of North Carolina; George Wythe (1726–1806), under whom Tucker studied law; and Benjamin Waller (1716–1786), another of Williamsburg's lawyers. Yet most prolific of all and the agent of the preservation of much of the work by others was Tucker, who came to Williamsburg from Port Royal, Bermuda, in 1771, as a student at the College of William and Mary.

Those who exchanged poetry with Tucker were primarily educated men of means, those who had access to information about social and political affairs, and enough of a stake in them to have something to say in response to events. Often the men who sent verse to each other or to the *Virginia Gazette* were planters who gathered in the town for the legislative sessions—meetings of the House of Burgesses, the Governor's Council, or the General Court. They came from the landed and professional classes and were well acquainted with classical literature and philosophy. Besides the large planters, the versifiers included professors at the College of William and Mary and, particularly in the latter part of the century when their professions gained status, doctors and lawyers. Many of them also held political office, serving in various capacities in their local counties or representing constituencies in the House of Burgesses or Governor's Council before the Revolution or the Congress during and after it. The women who sent their poetry to Tucker were the wives, sisters, and daughters of these Virginia leaders. Producing primarily social and political verse in the neoclassical style, the writers were often conscious of participating in the production of a national literature.

Daphne H. O'Brien

See also Colonial Newspapers; Poetry, Beginnings to 1820; Virginia, Literature of.

Richard Beale Davis, *Intellectual Life in Jefferson's Virginia, 1790–1830* (1964); J. A. Leo Lemay, *Robert Bolling Woos Anne Miller* (1990).

VOODOO

Voodoo is the term applied to the use of extranatural phenomena to exert influence on people and everyday events with the magical use of herbs, bodily wastes, or other paraphernalia; through divination; or through the intercession of spirits. The term is believed to have been derived from Dahomey, the West African country colonized by France, known also as Benin. As Africans were brought into the West Indies, they retained the term, especially in Haiti. It continued to refer to a combination of religious and human-induced extranatural practices. A person could be possessed of a spirit of one of the pantheon of African-derived gods referred to as *loa* or *orisha* and could act out the movements of that god in dance-based rituals. Zora Neale Hurston documented those practices in Haiti in the 1930s and published her findings in *Tell My Horse* (1938).

After the Haitian revolution of 1806, many African Haitians were transplanted to New Orleans. On United States soil, voodoo lost its religious ritual connotation but retained the system of magic. Also, the term *voodoo* was quickly transformed into the term *hoodoo*. It retained connotations of the ability to affect human events and actions through extranatural means but placed less emphasis on spirit possession—though spirits could still be called upon to effect outcomes. Dancing was a crucial part of these ceremonies, and the two Marie Laveaus were the most famous practitioners. The combination of African-based rituals and Catholic practices resulted in a syncretism that Hurston was similarly able to document in *Mules and Men* (1935), her collection of folklore from Florida and New Orleans. Even as practitioners set out to harm others with fetishistic animals or materials acquired from the intended victim, they would routinely light candles, pray, and observe other practices identified with the Catholic Church.

Although persons unknowingly conflate *voodoo* and *hoodoo*, the two are not exactly the same. *Voodoo* consistently had overtones of religion and supernaturalism, whereas *hoodoo* was more often identified with healing practices and the realm of affecting human behavior that is most often associated with conjuration. Indeed, in African American vernacular, *hoodoo* and *conjuring* (or *conjuration*) are presented as synonymous terms. While hoodoo and conjuring obviously have consequences for their intended victims, they may be practiced without the overtones of supernaturalism that were a staple with voodoo.

George W. Cable's *The Grandissimes* (1880), set in New Orleans in the early nineteenth century, documents the widespread belief in voodoo among both blacks and whites. Modern New Orleans remains the voodoo/hoodoo capital, with museums, rituals at cemeteries, and dozens of manuals available to instruct readers in various rituals. Outside New Orleans, hoodoo also exerts literary power. In Frederick Douglass's *Narrative* (1845), a root given to him by another slave provides confidence to Douglass in his challenge of the brutal overseer Covey. In Charles Chesnutt's *The Conjure Woman,* hoodoo is the last resort of slaves trying to address their powerlessness. The works of DuBose Heyward and Julia Peterkin, 1920s white writers of the South Carolina low country, contain references to hoodoo, as does the novel *Lyddy* (1898), written by ex-plantation mistress Eugenia Jones Bacon. John Berendt's best-selling *Midnight in the Garden of Good and Evil* (1994), set in Savannah, has stimulated new interest in rites connected with voodoo. A more valuable, less sensational contemporary treatment occurs in Gloria Naylor's *Mama Day* (1988), set in a mythical island off the Georgia–South Carolina coast.

Trudier Harris

See also Conjuring.

Zora Neale Hurston, *Mules and Men* (1935), and *Tell My Horse* (1938); Albert J. Raboteau, *Slave Religion: The "Invisible Institution" in the Antebellum South* (1978); John W. Roberts, *From Trickster to Badman: The Black Folk Hero in Slavery and Freedom* (1989).

WARREN, ROBERT PENN

Robert Penn Warren, who died at the age of eighty-four on September 15, 1989, was during his lifetime not only the South's but America's greatest man of letters. Poet, novelist, biographer, teacher, scholar-critic, social historian—with indispensable books in all of these areas—Warren exerted a major influence on every conceivable aspect of the study and practice of southern literature. His first book, the biography *John Brown: The Making of a Martyr,* was published in 1929, when he was twenty-four. His first fiction, the novella *Prime Leaf,* appeared in 1931, the same year that his essay on southern race relations, "The Briar Patch," was published in the collection *I'll Take My Stand.* His first poetry collection, *Thirty-Six Poems,* was published in 1935. Fifty years later, his last collection, *New and Selected Poems: 1923–1985,* rounded out his career as a poet. His tenth and last novel, *A Place to Come To,* appeared in 1977, his biographical meditation, *Jefferson Davis Gets His Citizenship Back,* came out in 1980, and his last book, *Portrait of a Father,* part memoir, part poem, part biography, was published the year before his death. For more than sixty years, his writing graced the literary scene. In addition, with his editorship of the *Southern Review* (1935–1942), he brought recognition to many beginning writers (Eudora Welty prominently among them), and with his collaborative texts, *Understanding Poetry* (1938), *Understanding Fiction* (1941), and *American Literature: The Makers and the Making* (1973), he showed generations of students how to read and think about literature.

Everyone has his or her own favorite moment from Warren's oeuvre. Certainly Willie Stark's pronouncement in the novel *All the King's Men* tops most lists: "Man is conceived in sin and born in corruption and he passeth from the stink of the didie to the stench of the shroud." From his poetry, famous moments and images include the murder by his parents of the home-bound wanderer Billie Potts, who outruns his luck in the poem "The Ballad of Billie Potts" (1943); the personalized nightmare in "Original Sin" that comes "clutching the bribe of chocolate or a toy you used to treasure"; the grace of the "Evening Hawk," the bird "under/Whose eye, unforgiving, the world, unforgiven, swings/Into shadow" (1975). For many, Warren's most complete work was the long verse drama *Brother to Dragons* (1953, rev. ed. 1979), which broods, through the voice of the narrator R.P.W., over Thomas Jefferson's nephews' horrifying murder of their slave. The poem confirms themes that dominate all of Warren's work: lost innocence, fatal idealism, the inevitability of sin, the demand of forgiveness, the recognition of human complicity in all evil, the search for redemption, the hope against hope that lies in human relationship, the "awful responsibility of Time." The later long poems *Audubon* (1969) and *Chief Joseph of the Nez Perce* (1983), like *Brother to Dragons* and many others, show Warren turning his lifelong obsession with history into explorations of the complexity of human nature. Always, in poems, biographies, and novels, there is the great appetite for story, so well stated in *Audubon:* "Tell me a story. In this century, and moment, of mania, tell me a story."

Warren's 1946 *All the King's Men* is, if not his best novel, certainly his most famous one, in part because of its colorful portrayal of a dictator politician who resembles Huey Long, Louisiana's controversial governor. It is, however, primarily the character-narrator Jack Burden who has had the most important influence on contemporary southern writers. William Styron, for instance, closely modeled the narrative consciousness of his first novel, *Lie Down in Darkness* (1963), on the dense poetic voice that narrates *All the King's Men.* Walker Percy, and following him Richard Ford, have created descendants of Jack Burden—the wandering son, looking for lost fathers, attempting to reject history, and finally seeking redemption in commitment to others. As Fred Hobson has noted in *The Southern Writer in the Postmodern World*, Percy's Will Barrett in *The Last Gentleman* (1966) and Richard Ford's Frank Bascombe in *The Sportswriter* (1978) bear the image of Jack, the failed historian, failed lover, seeker-in-spite-of-himself. Likewise Ralph Ellison, Warren's close friend in later life, also seems to have been determined to teach his young narrator in *Invisible Man* (1952) some of Jack's lessons about man's inevitable engagement in history, culture, and responsibility.

It is quite likely that, for all of Warren's popularity as a fiction writer, his chief influence on southern literature will be measured in relation to poetry. In an extensive examination of contemporary southern poetry, published in *Five Points* (1997), poet and current editor of the *Southern Review* Dave Smith credits Warren with shocking him into a discovery of what he "already was," a southern poet: "Warren shows me the feel, the actual fingerprint of the South in rhythmic cadence and image. He shows me language for the rape of change, the brutality of being other, the struggles with the past, permanent, implacable, that leaves us to sing as exiles in our own land." Warren's influence on southern poetry has been, as Smith's comment stresses, in the area of language—his violent lyricism, his heightening of the often crude vernacular into the transcendent. Yet he also very early fixed another tendency of twentieth-century southern poetry—the leaning toward narrative, the storytelling dimension that constitutes so many southern poems. Warren was an early admirer of James Dickey, to whom he dedicated *Chief Joseph*, and certainly Dickey, Fred Chappell, Robert Morgan, and many others illustrate Warren's way of telling stories in poems that combine raw experience with a shameless reverence for beauty in all its guises.

Warren, like so many of the writers who helped to create the Southern Renascence in the 1920s through the 1940s, carried on a lifetime love-hate affair with the South. His love for his native Kentucky, his formative school years at Vanderbilt, his exciting teaching and editing career at Louisiana State University, were all behind him by 1942, and the rest of his life was spent in the far north of Minnesota (teaching at the University of Minnesota from 1942 to 1949) and in the New England of New Haven (teaching at Yale from 1950 to 1973) and Vermont (retreating as often as possible to his vacation home in West Wardsboro, where

he died). However, his southern associations colored every aspect of his "refugee" life, as he called it. In particular, beyond the literary friendships, the themes and subjects of his novels, the Kentucky voice that reigns in his poetry, there was his astute and maverick engagement with southern race issues. He participated only uneasily in his Vanderbilt friends' manifesto *I'll Take My Stand*, writing in his essay "The Briar Patch" an analysis of the black man's place in the South that shocked many of the Agrarians by its (today very mild) liberalism. Later works such as *Who Speaks for the Negro?* (1965) and *Segregation: The Inner Conflict in the South* (1956) much more openly condemned southern racism. In *The Legacy of the Civil War* (1961), Warren attacked the South's excuses for its bigotry and backwardness with his concept of "the Great Alibi."

Warren was a close associate of the most productive creative writers and scholars of the midcentury South: John Crowe Ransom, Allen Tate, Cleanth Brooks, C. Vann Woodward, Katherine Anne Porter (his daughter's godmother), Eudora Welty, Caroline Gordon, William Styron, and James Dickey. He acknowledged the influence of all of these writers on his work. There is a particularly interesting cross-fertilization related to Welty's story "A Still Moment." Warren perceptively reviewed this story of Audubon on the Natchez Trace, entitling his 1944 essay "Love and Separateness." These were the two interrelated, oppositional strains of creativity that he explored in his own treatment of the artist's dilemma in his poem *Audubon: A Vision*, many years later. He also might very well have been thinking of Welty's title when he analyzed Faulkner's technique, calling it "the frozen moment," and pinpointing Faulkner's obsession, technically, with "Time fluid vs. time fixed." Warren in 1946 gave one of the most important early critiques of Faulkner's genius in his 1946 review of Malcolm Cowley's *The Portable Faulkner*. He heralded the universality inherent in Faulkner's (and his own) regionalism, pointing out that Faulkner was writing "not merely the legend of the South, but . . . also a legend of our general plight and problem."

Warren in his lifetime won three Pulitzer Prizes, two for collections of poetry and one for *All the King's Men*, and was awarded every other major American literary distinction, including the honor of being named America's first poet laureate. His career took him far away from the small town of Guthrie, Kentucky; as he said in *Audubon*, "Long ago, in Kentucky, I, a boy, stood / By a dirt road, in first dark, and heard / The great geese hoot northward." He answered this call, and followed that direction to fame that always reflected where he had come from. When he was asked in 1977, "Do you still consider yourself a southern writer?" he answered, "I can't be anything else."

Lucinda H. MacKethan

See also Agrarians; Fugitives, The; I'll Take My Stand; Poetry, 1900 to World War II.

Joseph Blotner, Robert Penn Warren: A Biography (1997); James H. Justus, The Achievement of Robert Penn Warren (1981); Mississippi Quarterly: Special Issue, Robert Penn Warren, 48 (1994–95); Dave Smith, "There's A Bird Hung Around My Neck: Observations on Contemporary Southern Poetry," Five Points 1.3 (1997).

WASHINGTON, BOOKER T.

Born a slave in Franklin County, Virginia, Booker Taliaferro Washington (1856–1915) rose to national prominence on September 18, 1895, when he was asked to address the Cotton States and International Exposition in Atlanta, Georgia, thereby securing his place as not only one of the premier leaders, but also one of the most controversial figures, in the African American community.

After the Civil War, young Washington moved with his family to Malden, West Virginia, where his stepfather found work in the salt mines. Washington worked at a salt furnace by age twelve, though he rejected the notion of spending the rest of his life engaged in manual labor without the benefit of an education. Finally, in 1872 Washington traveled to Hampton, Virginia, and entered Hampton Institute, the industrial school established for blacks in 1867. There he became a favorite student of General Samuel Armstrong, the president of Hampton Institute, who in 1881 recommended Washington to the Alabama legislature to found Tuskegee Institute.

Washington's seminal contribution to southern literature is his autobiography, Up From Slavery (1901). The text satisfied four main functions: (1) A document validating Washington and his accomplishments. Washington uses the text to boost his credibility. When he tells of the sacrifices he made during his journey to Hampton (sleeping on the sidewalk, enduring hunger, etc.), Washington is presenting himself as a role model for others to emulate. If he can endure hardships, he implies, then certainly fellow blacks can make similar sacrifices. (2) A self-help guide and blueprint offering strategies for other blacks. When Washington reveals that his entrance exam to Hampton entailed his cleaning a room, he expresses to the audience that success can present itself in the most unlikely forms, and readers must be prepared to exploit all opportunities. (3) A political tract urging the adoption of his philosophy. Washington promotes racial harmony by asking blacks to delay the struggle for racial equality, arguing that whites will respond more favorably to blacks who focus less on social equality and more on economic self-development. From his own life, he presents two important white figures, General Samuel Armstrong and Mrs. Viola Ruffner, who helped him because, in his estimation, he always presented himself as respectful and nonthreatening. (4) A vehicle for soliciting funds for Tuskegee Institute. By suggesting that the typical Tuskegee student will follow his example, Washington is more likely to garner financial support from northern philanthropists. In short, Washington's autobiography serves as propaganda to support his economic agenda.

Washington's accommodationist philosophy gained him favor with southern whites and northern businessmen. However, Washington disappointed a significant number of blacks, including most prominently W. E. B. Du Bois, who believed that Washington's strategies undermined the humanity of blacks and ensured a future of civic inferiority for them. In a chapter of The Souls of Black Folk (1903) devoted solely to Washington, Du Bois argues that the widespread adoption of Washington's philosophy has done, and will continue to do, almost irreversible damage to the lives of black Americans. For Du Bois, favoring economic advancement over political or social advancement is foolhardy, because all three components are inextricably linked.

In addition to being criticized by Du Bois, Washington also figures as a thinly veiled character in Ralph Ellison's Invisible Man (1952). The references in early chapters to "The Founder" are ambiguous and suggest Washington's blindness to the effect of his policies. His fictional replacement, Dr. Bledsoe, personifies the worst in black leadership when he willingly submits to white superiority in an effort to protect his relatively comfortable social position, to the detriment of black dignity and racial solidarity.

Critiqued directly or depicted in fiction, lauded or castigated, Washington emerged as one of the most enigmatic personalities of the twentieth century.

Charles E. Wilson Jr.

See also African American Colleges and Universities; Reconstruction; Segregation; Slave Narrative.

Louis Harlan, *Booker T. Washington: The Making of a Black Leader, 1856–1901* (1972); Louis Harlan, *Booker T. Washington: The Wizard of Tuskegee, 1901–1915* (1983); Thomas E. Harris, *Analysis of the Clash over the Issues Between Booker T. Washington and W. E. B. Du Bois* (1993); Cary D. Wintz, ed., *African American Political Thought, 1890–1930: Washington, Du Bois, Garvey, and Randolph* (1996).

WASHINGTON, GEORGE

Born in Westmoreland County, Virginia, on February 22, 1732, into a fourth-generation, midlevel Virginia planter family, George Washington moved up the social ladder because of his connections with the powerful Fairfax family and because of his military service in the French and Indian War, eventually reaching the rank of colonel and heading his colony's forces. Washington sought to make his regiment the equal of any in the British army and to have it placed on the royal establishment as well. Though failing in that effort, he won the praise of British officers for the discipline and training he imparted to his men and for his knowledge of military literature. His drive to instill professionalism set Washington apart from most if not all the ranking provincial officers in the other colonies. His wedding to Martha Custis, a widow of great wealth, further enhanced his standing, as did his seventeen years in the Virginia legislature. He turned his plantation home, Mount Vernon, inherited from his brother Lawrence, into something of a showplace for diversified farming and modern agricultural techniques.

Although possessed of a solid and discriminating mind, Washington had little formal education. If abstract ideas did not excite the play of his imagination, recent scholarship shows he was better read than previously thought. His letters prove that he wrote with force and clarity. He purchased many of the leading political pamphlets of his day, and he eventually had a library of nearly a thousand volumes, much of it devoted to agriculture and history. In later life, he avidly read newspapers and enjoyed talking about current events in America and Europe. His numerous letters to younger family members stressed the value of both classical and practical learning.

An early advocate of strong measures to oppose Britain's new colonial policy after 1763, he gained intercolonial recognition for his role in drafting the Fair-

fax Resolves of 1774, which became something of a model for how the colonies should organize their resistance to Parliament's Intolerable Acts. He won election as a Virginia delegate to the Continental Congress in 1774. His stand in Virginia and in Congress, combined with his extensive military experience, led to his appointment as commander in chief of the Continental Army. Although he won few pitched battles in the Revolutionary War, he was persistent and aggressive, holding his forces together and wearing down his British foes in what became a struggle of attrition. His greatest success was his bold move from New York to Virginia to trap Lord Cornwallis in 1781. He proved to be a master diplomat in a coalition war involving a weak central government and thirteen independent states. Indeed, he wrote more wartime letters than any commanding general in American history, seeking aid from Congress, the states, local political leaders, and militia officers. In 1783 he denounced and shattered the Newburgh Conspiracy, an alliance of certain officers and civilian leaders who sought to intimidate Congress into meeting their demands for political and military reform. His respect of civil control of the military set a valuable precedent for the new nation.

Never a states' rights Virginian or a southern sectionalist, Washington was the foremost nationalist of his generation. He presided over the Constitutional Convention of 1787 and served two terms as the first president of the country. Aware of his opportunity to shape the executive office, he interpreted his authority broadly. In domestic affairs, he supported Hamilton's financial program, upheld the constitutionality of a national bank, called out the militia to quell the Whiskey Rebellion, and declared cabinet members responsible to him and not to Congress. Equally assertive in foreign affairs, he proclaimed America's neutrality in the wars of the French Revolution and asserted the right to draw up treaties without the prior approval of the Senate, as well as the right to send special envoys abroad, as he did John Jay to negotiate a treaty with Britain in 1794. For the time being, at least, he lost considerable popularity in the South, where the emerging Republican Party of Thomas Jefferson voiced criticism of certain of his broad interpretations of presidential authority and accused him of being a Hamiltonian Federalist.

Soon after Washington's death on December 14, 1799, historians and novelists closed ranks in creating the apotheosis of the general and the president, a process already underway in his own lifetime. Reacting to the idolatrous biographies of such authors as Mason

Locke ("Parson") Weems and John Marshall, Nathaniel Hawthorne exclaimed that Washington must have been born with his clothes on and made a stately bow on entering the world. During the growing sectional crisis, southerners portrayed Washington an apologist for his region; William L. Yancey of Alabama saw the Virginian not as the symbol of union but of rebellion. But after the Civil War, southern literary lights often gave Washington a backseat to Robert E. Lee. Balanced biographies of Washington remained elusive, although writers in the muckraking 1920s found some legitimate faults in the young Virginian, who at times reeked of ambition and displayed a prickly temper. Since the late 1940s, our best Washington studies have appeared; the most thorough is Douglas Southall Freeman's magisterial *George Washington* (1948–1957). Still, as Marcus Cunliffe notes in *George Washington: Man and Monument* (1958), for most scholars and novelists the man and the myth seem all but inseparable.

Don Higginbotham

See also Jefferson, Thomas; Lee, Robert E.; Revolutionary War, American.

William A. Bryan, *George Washington in American Literature, 1775–1865* (1952); Marcus Cunliffe, *George Washington: Man and Monument* (1958); John E. Ferling, *The First of Men* (1988); James Thomas Flexner, *George Washington* (4 vols.; 1965–72); Douglas Southall Freeman, *George Washington* (7 vols.; 1948–57); Don Higginbotham, *George Washington and the American Military Tradition* (1985); Paul K. Longmore, *The Invention of George Washington* (1988).

WASHINGTON AND LEE UNIVERSITY

In bestowing his munificent gift of canal stock on a fledgling academy in the Shenandoah Valley, George Washington remarked, "To promote literature in this rising empire, and to encourage the arts, have ever been among the warmest wishes of my heart." But in the two centuries since Liberty Hall Academy became Washington College, Washington and Lee University has been distinguished more by its contributions to the practical arts than to belles-lettres. Nothing in the background of the Scots-Irish had drawn their attention to the aesthetic realm, one scholar has noted; education was important only for practical ends. The Bible sufficed for literature.

In the years before the Civil War, two former students of Washington College might be singled out for significant early contributions. William Alexander Caruthers (1802–1846), class of 1820, is remembered for three novels: *The Kentuckian in New York* (1834), *The Cavaliers of Jamestown* (1835), and *The Knights of the Horseshoe* (1845). Henry Ruffner (1790–1861), a Presbyterian minister and sixth president of W&L, published in the *Southern Literary Messenger* a number of fictive and autobiographical sketches as well as a serialized novel, *Judith Bensaddi* (1839).

During Robert E. Lee's postwar tenure as president of Washington College (1865–1870), the curriculum was broadened beyond its classical beginnings to include the rudiments of an English department, nested along with history in the department of modern languages. (Lee was clear as to his own preference: he urged his daughter Mildred to read "history, works of truth, not novels and romances. Get correct views of life, and learn to see the world in its true light.") This was the college curriculum into which Thomas Nelson Page (1853–1922), class of 1873, entered. During his undergraduate years, he wrote for *The Southern Collegian*, a long-lived and lively student magazine praised by literary historians as among the best in the nation of its sort. Page's fame rests largely on a collection of short stories, *In Ole Virginia* (1887), and on a handful of novels, most notably *Red Rock* (1898).

A handful of autobiographical works by W&L alumni published about midcentury (one as late as 1986) are scanned by W. W. Pusey in his brief 1988 monograph, "Washington and Lee in Fiction." Harvey Fergusson's *Home in the West* (1944) is highly critical of student life at W&L in the years before World War I, especially of the drinking and fraternity life. In contrast, *Stranger in the Earth* (1948), by Thomas Sugrue (1907–), class of 1929, recalls the happy student days of a Connecticut Catholic youth. Glenn Scott (1933–), class of 1954, who has become a successful journalist in Norfolk, published on graduation a Bildungsroman, *The Sound of Voices Dying* (1954).

Lawrence Watkin (1901–), on the English faculty from 1926 to 1942, published several popular novels while in Lexington, notably *On Borrowed Time* (1937), and *Geese in the Forum* (1940). Paxton Davis (1925–1994), chairman of W&L's journalism department for many years, wrote several war novels: two centered on the CBI theater of World War II in which he had served, *Two Soldiers* (1956) and *One of the Dark Places* (1965); and another, of tripartite structure, reflecting family generations in Virginia during the Civil War and beyond, *The Season of Heroes* (1967).

The most prolific novelist during this period associated with W&L, by virtue of a single significant postgraduate year (1949–1950), is (Henry) William Hoffman (1925–), a "cultural laureate of Virginia," whose widely published short fiction has won both "Best American" and "O. Henry" short-story awards. To date he has to his credit eleven novels, beginning with *The Trumpet Unblown* (1955), and three volumes of short stories.

Ellen Glasgow's brother Arthur endowed a program in support of literature at W&L, the Glasgow Endowment, which since 1960 has brought scores of writers to campus to read their work and meet with undergraduate writers. Visitors to W&L, beginning with Katherine Anne Porter, make up a Parnassian list: Warren, Lowell, Taylor, Dickey, Price, Nemerov, Welty, Wilbur, Ammons, Percy, Hecht, Gluck, Gaines, Walcott, Heaney, Pinsky. The school has since maintained a literary emphasis not envisioned by its founders.

In the last half of the twentieth century, the most significant literary talents identified with W&L are two Richmonders, Tom Wolfe, whose name is synonymous with "the New Journalism," and poet Dabney Stuart, the former an alumnus, the latter a master teacher in Lexington for over thirty years. The school has maintained its visibility in creative literature by editing *Shenandoah* and through appointments for Heather Ross Miller (1939–) and R. T. Smith (1947–). One name must be added to this group: the late James Boatwright (1933–1988), editor of *Shenandoah* from 1962 to 1988. Taking hold of the magazine, he oversaw its development into a major voice among the newer "little magazines" of the postwar era.

Severn Duvall

See also Virginia, Literature of.

WEDDINGS

In William Faulkner's *The Hamlet* (1940)—the tale of Flem Snopes and his rise through the social ranks of Frenchman's Bend, Mississippi—Flem and Eula Varner are married in a courthouse by the justice of the peace. Eula is pregnant by another man at the time, and her father exiles the couple to Texas as soon as the union is legal. Their wedding is indicative of most weddings in southern literature—if a ceremony isn't undercut by familial anxiety or an unhappy bride or outright havoc, then it's reduced to a business deal signed in the offices of the chancery clerk. Amidst so much conflict and dysfunction, the charm of the traditional southern wedding—one held in the home rather than the church, and accompanied by regional cuisine—is rarely evident.

Eudora Welty's *Delta Wedding* (1946) is the one major work where the traditional southern wedding is described in full, from prelude to aftermath. Set in 1923, the novel begins with nine-year-old Laura McRaven traveling to the Mississippi Delta a week before the wedding of her cousin, Dabney Fairchild, and ends with an outdoor picnic three days into Dabney's marriage. For the ceremony, the Fairchilds erect an altar in the backyard at Shellmound, their cotton plantation, and decorate it with twisting Mississippi smilax. A southern wedding cake—containing a ring (for the next bride) and a thimble (for the old maid)—is accompanied by Memphis mints and cheese straws baked by Dabney's Aunt Primrose. Though Dabney's wedding has its share of conflict (the Fairchilds view her groom, Troy Flavin, as well beneath her), it is handsome, extravagant, and distinctly southern.

The wedding in Carson McCullers's *The Member of the Wedding* (1946)—set in Georgia twenty years later—isn't nearly so charming. As McCullers's novella begins, twelve-year-old Frankie Addams believes that her brother's upcoming wedding in Winter Hill will bring her salvation. The bride and the groom, she imagines, will take her around the world and finally make her a member of something larger than herself. Of course, when the wedding day arrives, Frankie is reduced to tears after she's largely ignored by the newlyweds and they leave for a honeymoon without her. Focusing on Frankie's grief, McCullers describes the wedding only briefly. Held in the bride's home where the floors are freshly waxed and mints are served on silver trays, the ceremony has a few southern touches, but it's a simple wartime gathering in which the bride wears a daytime suit rather than a dress. As with most southern fiction, the wedding is a disappointment more than a celebration.

Margaret Mitchell describes three weddings in *Gone With the Wind* (1939), yet they too are unhappy, truncated affairs. Scarlett O'Hara weds Charles Hamilton at Tara, wearing her mother's dress and veil. Hundreds of guests have come from across Georgia to see her marry into an old southern family, but—because her beloved Ashley Wilkes is marrying Melanie Hamilton the next day—the ceremony plays out, in her eyes, like a nightmare. Naturally, she's even more distraught during Ashley's wedding at Twelve Oaks. Both weddings, in fact, are hurried and abbreviated because of the coming of the war. Normally, Mitchell says, there would be a week of balls and barbecues and wedding trips to celebrate the two marriages. After the war, amidst the Reconstruction, Scarlett marries Frank Kennedy in a civil ceremony and strangers are dragged from the street to serve as witnesses. Her third loveless wedding—to Rhett Butler—doesn't even receive a sentence of narration.

As in *The Hamlet,* most other Faulkner weddings are unusual arrangements. In *Light in August* (1932), Nathaniel Burden's first wedding comes after twelve years of common-law marriage and the birth of his son, Calvin. Yet this Kansas ceremony is the closest Faulkner gets to a traditional, promising southern wedding. Wearing a homemade dress and mosquito-net veil, the bride is given away outdoors next to a barbecued steer and a keg of whiskey. *Absalom, Absalom!* (1936) provides Faulkner's salient southern wedding, the arranged marriage of Thomas Sutpen and Ellen Coldfield. Hundreds of Mississippi guests are invited, but Sutpen—reviled by the community—is married with fewer than ten witnesses in the church. As the newlyweds leave the church—walking by the light of burning pine knots—they're pelted with vegetables and clods of dirt thrown from carriages waiting outside.

Southern weddings are equally unpleasant in short fiction. In George Washington Harris's "Sicily Burns's Wedding," the infamous Sut Lovingood wreaks havoc on a pre–Civil War Tennessee wedding by angering a black-and-white bull and stirring a nearby beehive. With "A Wedding in Jackson," Ellen Gilchrist describes a Delta wedding held seventy years after Dabney Fairchild's nuptials, but it too is overrun by misgiving and family discord. The titular ceremony in Lee Smith's "Blue Wedding" never even occurs. Before the baby-blue dresses and baby-blue tuxedos arrive, the bride-to-be hits her fiancé on the head with a two-by-four. In southern fiction, the wedding is seldom an ordinary affair.

Cade Metz

See also Food; Yoknapatawpha.

Leslie Jean Campbell, "Exercises in Doom: Yoknapatawpha County Weddings," *Publications of the Arkansas Philological Association* (1978); James E. Caron and M. Thomas Inge, eds., *Sut Lovingood's Nat'ral Born Yarnspinner: Essays on George Washington Harris* (1996); Beverly Lyon Clark and Melvin J. Friedman, eds., *Critical Essays on Carson McCullers* (1996); Albert Devlin, *Eudora Welty's Chronicle: A Story of Mississippi Life* (1983); W. Craig Turner and Lee Emling Harding, eds., *Critical Essays on Eudora Welty* (1989).

WELTY, EUDORA

Though William Faulkner is the best-known and most widely respected southern author of the twentieth century, more contemporary writers in the South pay imitative tribute to Faulkner's fellow Mississippian, Eudora Welty (1909–2001). Welty's attention to the concrete details of everyday life and her simple, elegant style have influenced a generation of southern writers that includes Reynolds Price, Anne Tyler, Lee Smith, Clyde Edgerton, and Bobbie Ann Mason.

Welty's often humorous and always vivid characterizations of ordinary people have served as her greatest influence on a younger generation of southern writers. Her most famous short story, "Why I Live at the P.O.," provides her most memorable character. In this dramatic monologue, the speaker, Sister, explains why she moved from her home to the back of the post office where she works as postmistress, revealing in her accusations of family members far more about herself than she ever intended. Anne Tyler's characters often resemble Welty's in their mundane peculiarities and in the way the author allows them to speak for and to reveal themselves. In *Dinner at the Homesick Restaurant* (1982), Tyler allows each of the three Tull children to tell the story of his or her childhood and young adulthood in turn, following Welty's technique with Sister but expanding it to provide multiple perspectives on the family dynamic. Lee Smith has also said that she owes her greatest debt as a writer to Eudora Welty, who taught her that ordinary people were fit subjects for literature. Welty's influence on almost all of Smith's novels is marked, but it is especially evident in *Oral History* (1983), told from the perspective of various mountaineers and a few pseudosophisticated city counterparts, and in the epistolary novel *Fair and Tender Ladies* (1988), written in the dialect patterns of the uneducated Ivy Rowe Fox. Price, Edgerton, and Mason, who often use unremarkable people as their protagonists, also owe a debt to Welty's characters.

In her focus on ordinary people, Welty also concentrates on the ordinary events and manners of her characters' lives. Welty's early *Delta Wedding* (1946) has been described as a novel of manners because of its detailed description of the Fairchild family's preparations for a wedding, including such minutiae as young cousin Laura's arrival by train and subsequent vomiting after being jostled by the boys on the joggling board. In a similar scene in *The Accidental Tourist* (1985), Tyler describes the Leary family's bout with food poisoning after sister Rose cooks the Thanksgiving turkey slowly at low heat. Edgerton's *Walking Across Egypt* (1987) begins with Mattie Rigsbee becoming inadvertently stuck in a chair whose bottom she was having recovered and worrying that someone will see her dinner dishes unwashed in the sink. Welty's fiction gives much attention to mundane detail. "Why I Live at the P.O." is filled with brand names and references to popular culture, such as "Add-A-Pearl necklaces." Mason is also known for the popular culture that shapes her characters in novels and short stories. Though Price's early works *A Long and Happy Life* (1962) and *A Generous Man* (1966) have been compared to Faulkner's, his attention to the concrete details of his characters' lives and the small truths that these lives reveal more closely resembles Welty's focus on the commonplace.

Despite her attention to everyday detail, Welty's work often has a spiritual or mythical undercurrent that has also influenced many younger southern writers. Her short-story cycle *The Golden Apples* (1949), which explores the interconnected lives of Morgana, Mississippi, residents, is underscored by references to Greek and Celtic mythology that emphasize the connectedness of all human life. Similarly, Price's later works, such as *Permanent Errors* (1970), *The Surface of Earth* (1975), and *The Source of Light* (1981), which explore modern humanity's attempts to live useful lives in the modern world, are underscored by a subtle spirituality that suggests a larger significance to human existence. Despite this mythical/spiritual strain, Welty and those who write under her influence do not pass judgment on their less-than-ideal characters. Unlike Flannery O'Connor, who uses similar character types with a tone of moral censure and condescension, Welty and her literary heirs present their characters objectively, allowing readers to pass (or not) moral judgments of their own.

Betina Entzminger

See also Faulkner, William; O'Connor, Flannery; Twain, Mark.

Fred Hobson, *The Southern Writer in the Postmodern World* (1991); Peggy Prenshaw, ed., *Women Writers of the Contemporary South* (1984); Constance Rooke, *Reynolds Price* (1983); Ruth M. Vande Kieft, *Eudora Welty* (1987).

WEST VIRGINIA, LITERATURE OF

The only state entirely within the region termed Appalachia, West Virginia, the "war-born" state voted into existence on June 20, 1863, had for almost half a century previous to statehood established its own "western" Virginia identity. And while the literary history of West Virginia points to a number of early interpretations, there is still debate as to whether writers like Anne Royall (1769–1854), who lived near Monroe, West Virginia, in the 1780s, should be claimed by Virginia or its western sister; certainly the early literary history of the two states can almost be considered one.

The first attempt at an appraisal of West Virginia literature was undertaken in 1926 with Warren Wood's *Representative Authors of West Virginia*, which divides the progress of literature in West Virginia into four stages: exploration and travel (1669–1823); pioneer expansion and planting of civilization (1823–1861); Civil War and Reconstruction (1861–1876); and development of the Commonwealth (1876–1920s). Building upon this able work, bibliographer Vito J. Brenni compiled in 1957 (and with Joyce Binder revised a second edition in 1968) *West Virginia Authors: A Bibliography*, work followed by Kitty Frazier's *West Virginia Women Writers 1822–1979*, which compiled and annotated entries on 240 women writers of the state. In 1996 Phyllis Wilson Moore's *Yes, We Have Authors*, a monograph published by the West Virginia Humanities Council and WV Writers, Inc., attempted to integrate materials from these earlier sources and speak to the plethora of research in Appalachian studies that has enriched the examination of West Virginia literature and its makers in the last twenty-five years.

In the earlier days of the western portion of Virginia that would become the state of West Virginia, literary output paralleled that of many other southern states, represented mostly by accounts of travels in the form of journals, sketches, and diaries, most being written by outsiders. Newspapers had been printed in the area since 1789 with the appearance of the *Potomac Guardian* and *Berkeley Advertiser*, followed a decade later by the *Martinsburg Gazette,* whose editor Nathaniel Willis was the father of the poet Nathaniel Parker Willis. The year 1797 marks the first book known to be printed in West Virginia—*The Christian Panoply* by R. Watson of Shepherdstown, more usually known as "Watson's Reply to Tom Paine"—which enjoyed great popularity and an international readership. Almost a quarter of a century would pass before those books that Wood calls "literature of a serious sort" began to appear. In 1823 Dr. Joseph Doddridge produced *Logan, the Last of the Race of Shikellemus, Chief of the Cayuga Nation,* a dramatic piece, and in that same year a printing press set up by Alexander Campbell in Bethany began to publish a flood of his own works. In 1824 a first book of verse, *The Widow of the Rock and Other Poems* by Margaret Blennerhassett, was published anonymously in Canada. Three years later, a first work of fiction—*The Tennessean: A Novel Founded on Facts*—was written by Anne Royall, a woman variously termed "the lady at the keyhole," "America's first lady hitchhiker," and "America's first woman journalist." Royall had written the previous year *Sketches of History, Life, and Manners in the United States* (1826), a lively and superior work. Wood is scrupulous in noting that although Royall lived over thirty years in the area designated as "western," she had moved elsewhere when she began her writing career.

Such a close adherence to a writer's geographical location would, if followed, thin down West Virginia's contributions to literature immensely. Many of those who write most eloquently about the region have left it physically while continuing to use the region as inspiration or wellspring. These early efforts, all appearing before statehood, still speak to the distinctiveness of "west" Virginia. In 1845 *Young Kate,* a novel, first used the region as its setting. Reissued anonymously ten years later as *New Hope or the Rescue—A Tale of the Great Kanawha,* the book is typically credited to John Lewis. The rugged landscape continued to draw adventurers and journalists, the best known of whom is David Hunter Strother, who under a pseudonym published several works in the 1850s, *The Adventures of Porte Crayon and His Cousins* (1853) being the best known.

The year before West Virginia voted for independence, a story of civil strife in the region—*David Gaunt*—was published by Rebecca Harding Davis of Wheeling. The year before, her *Life in the Iron Mills,* which delineated life in the industrial city and its hard-

ships for laborers, had appeared anonymously in *Atlantic Monthly* (April 1861). This publication won Davis recognition as a writer and social commentator from the major literary figures of the day: Hawthorne, Bronson Alcott, Emerson, and others. Davis would go on to write additional works, many with themes that spoke to questions of social justice, but none matched the power of this early classic. Davis married and moved to Philadelphia, and eventually was known best as the mother of the writer Richard Harding Davis, yet her work and life were illuminated in 1971 with the Feminist Press reissue of *Life in the Iron Mills,* which contained an extensive critical evaluation by Tillie Olsen. Moving from obscurity to standard text in both women's studies and labor history courses, Davis's groundbreaking story can be seen as central to understanding the difference between those in the western region and those in the southern and eastern parts of the state.

During this Civil War period, Judge Daniel Bedinger Lucas of Charles Town was writing lyrics, one of which became a well-known war ballad, "The Land Where We Were Dreaming." He, along with David Strother and a later, more mainstream popular writer—Melville Davisson Post—would be linked in a trilogy of achievement by the Works Projects Administration's publication *West Virginia: A Guide to the Mountain State,* published in 1941.

Local-color stories were represented by Granville Davisson Hall with his *The Daughter of the Elm* (1899), but it is with the emergence of Melville Davisson Post (1871–1930), born in Romines Mill, that the first writer who might be termed an author of national reputation appeared. Post wrote in the detective mode, and his works, which include *The Strange Schemes of Randolph Mason* (1896), were called "baffling." His *Uncle Abner: Master of Mysteries* (1918) series contained stories that were termed masterpieces of logic; *Walker of the Secret Service* (1925) gained him devoted fans, including President Theodore Roosevelt. Correspondence exists in which the two—writer and president—discuss mystery plots and backgrounds. In addition, Post's reputation rests on *The Mountain School Teacher* (1922), a sentimental allegory of Jesus returned to the mountains as a schoolteacher.

Post's prominence as mystery maven receded as Margaret Scherf's works appeared. Scherf, born 1908, of Fairmont, was author of *The Mystery of the Velvet Box* (1963), *Never Turn Your Back* (1959), and *The*

Owl in the Cellar (1945), among others. She and Anne Chamberlain, who wrote *The Tall Dark Man* (1955) and *The Soldier Room* (1956), enjoyed national reputations. Chamberlain's novels combined elements of the domestic novel with an air of mystery. David Martin, a contemporary mystery writer whose titles include *Bring Me the Child*, uses the isolation of mountain communities to good effect in his work, as does mystery author John Suter. Stephen Coonts's *The Minotaur, Flight of the Intruder*, and *Final Flight* have enjoyed great success in the techno-thriller field.

An interesting story surrounds the appropriation by the state of African American poet Anne Spencer, who is reported to have been born in Roanoke, Virginia, on February 6, 1882. It has been said that she claimed Bramwell, West Virginia, as her place of birth since "it [West Virginia] had always been a free state and a free place." Spencer grew up in a mining community, received her education in Virginia, and returned to West Virginia to teach before leaving a final time. Mentored by James Weldon Johnson and encouraged by H. L. Mencken, Spencer is said to have written poems numbering in the thousands; however, only fifty are extant. "Before the Feast of Shushan" was published in *Crisis* in 1920, and in 1922 *The Book of American Negro Poetry* included five of her poems. Knowledge of Spencer's literary contributions has resulted from the publication of a biographical study by literary scholar Lee Greene.

John Peale Bishop (1892–1944), born in Charles Town, is a writer who, as scholar Thomas E. Douglass notes, was able to distance himself from the heritage that claimed him. Douglass cites Bishop's unintentionally self-revealing essay "West Virginia," in which the poet/essayist "cruelly condescended to the people of his home state"; and indeed, the bulk of Bishop's work seems little connected to West Virginia. Perhaps the work that most speaks to his connection to West Virginia and his boyhood is *Many 10,000's Gone*.

What might be called attempts at a combination of domestic and historical novels were represented by Margaret Prescott Montague (1878–1955) of White Sulphur Springs, who depicted the life of hill folk in *The Sowing of Alderson Cree* (1907), a story of a mountain feud, and whose short story "England to America" was awarded the first O. Henry Memorial Prize of $500 in 1919; Melville Davisson Post was a runner-up. Montague's *Uncle Sam of Freedom Ridge* (1920) was also praised by President Roosevelt, and two of her novels were later made into films.

The novels and short stories of Fanny Kemple Johnson Costello (1868–1950) of Charleston were published regularly in the *Atlantic, Harpers,* and *Century,* and she built a steady national reputation on a series of tales with the central character of "Roddy Ivor." One of the earlier poets to receive national recognition was Danske Dandrige; it is reported that Lowell, Holmes, and Whittier all praised her verse. *Joy and Other Poems* (1900) gathered her best from previous collections.

The WPA's state guide relied heavily on Wood's work but chose as a main component to its entry on the literature of the state to stress the importance of folk tales and oral tradition. The legend of John Henry and the story of the Big Bend tunnel were considered central in informing the state's character. During the years that the WPA was searching the state's archives, writers began to emerge in West Virginia letters who would have a lasting impact on the regional, national, and international literary scene. Perhaps the best known is Pearl Buck (1892–1973), born in Hillsboro but most identified with her experiences in China. Author of over seventy books in her lifetime, Buck was the recipient of a Pulitzer Prize for *The Good Earth* (1931) and was the first woman to receive the Nobel Prize in literature (1938). The Pearl S. Buck Foundation is a tribute to Buck's unstinting efforts to foster the ideals of cooperation in East-West relations.

A writer with a much smaller oeuvre—only one book, a handful of short stories, and an unpublished novella—Tom Kromer, the author of *Waiting for Nothing* (1933), has emerged in recent years through a resurgence of interest in both his work and the mystery of an almost total disappearance from the literary scene. His works of gritty realism and proletarian despair put Kromer in the company of such Depression writers as Harold Anderson (*Thieves Like Us*) and Horace McCoy (*They Shoot Horses, Don't They?*). Pare Lorentz, born in West Virginia in 1905, is the famed documentary film maker of *The Plough That Broke the Plains* and *The River*. This last appeared in book form in 1939. Links between book and film also appear in the career of writer Davis Grubb (1919–1980), born in Moundsville. Grubb's *Night of the Hunter* (1953) was brilliantly translated into a film directed by Charles Laughton and in 1991 was made into a television drama. Also known for *A Dream of Kings, The Barefoot Man, Voices of Glory,* and *A Tree Full of Stars,* among others, Grubb in the last years of his life was one of the founding members of West Virginia

Writers, Inc.; he served as honorary president from 1978 to 1980.

Her first novel, *The Love Eaters* (1954), introduced Mary Lee Settle (1918–) to the literary world, but it was not until she began to write what would become the Beulah quintet that Settle emerged as a national literary figure linked to West Virginia. Settle is known best for her National Book Award novel *Blood Tie* (1978), set in Turkey, but it is generally acknowledged that Settle's reputation will rest on the Beulah quintet's amazing accomplishment in its fusion of history and literature. Twenty-eight years of work produced five volumes that span three hundred plus years of West Virginia history; Settle's work could be called the essential fictional guide for a scholar of the literature of the state. Settle continues to write—most recently a memoir—and lives in Charlottesville, Virginia.

John Knowles (1926–), born in Fairmont, author of *A Separate Peace* (1960), *Morning in Antibes* (1962), and *Journal of My Journey Over the Mountains,* is an example of a writer from the state who does not address it directly in his work. In that same way, Roger Price, the humorist and author of *Droodles, Mad Libs,* and the *Decline and Fall* series, is called a native son because of his birth in West Virginia, although he doesn't live in or identify with the state. So too is the writer Eugenia Price (1916–), born in Charleston, acclaimed author of over thirty books with eight million copies now in print. Price is best known for *Beloved Invader* and the St. Simon's trilogy. Her work combines tenets of the historical novel but also contains elements of spiritual seeking. Sarah Catherine Wood Marshall (1914–), of Keyser, is known for a vastly popular memoir about her husband, *A Man Called Peter* (1951), and for *Christy,* which has been produced as a popular television movie.

Children's authors, such as Jean Lee Latham, a dramatist and writer whose career has spanned many decades, have enjoyed great success. Born in Buchannon, she produced *The Story of Eli Whitney* (1953), *Carry On, Mr. Bowditch* (1955), and *Medals for Morse* (1954) in addition to other titles. Betsy Byers, long-term resident of Morgantown, is well known in the world of children's literature. Of her many titles, the most notable is Newberry Award–winner *Summer of the Swans,* which uses a West Virginia setting. More recently, Robyn Eversole's *The Magic House* (1992), *The Flute Player/La Flautista* (1995), and *Flood Fish* (1995); Anna Smucker's *No Star Nights* (1989), an

award-winning work set in Weirton, and *Outside the Window* (1994); and Cheryl Ware's Viola Mae series, *Flea Circus Summer* (1996) and *Catty-Cornered* (1997), represent this field in a national forum.

Best known of West Virginia's poet laureates was Louise McNeill Pease, whose masterwork, *Gauley Mountain* (1939), was resurrected in 1991 in a West Virginia Public Radio dramatization narrated and moderated by writer Pinckney Benedict. Pease's successor, Irene McKinney, is part of the new generation of writers, many of whom are now returning to the state or writing about their connection to it. Author of *The Girl with a Stone in Her Lap,* McKinney most recently has published *Six O'Clock Mine Report*; she is an associate professor of creative writing at West Virginia Wesleyan. McKinney and poet Maggie Anderson are cofounders, along with poet/teacher Winston Fuller, of West Virginia's first national-subscription literary review, *Trellis.* Anderson is author of four books of poetry including *Years That Answer* (1980), editor of *Hill Daughter: New and Selected Poems* (1991) by Louise McNeill (1911–1993), and codirector of the Wick Poetry Program at Kent State University of Ohio, where she is an associate professor of poetry. *Laurel Review,* once housed and edited by poet Mark DeFoe, a professor at West Virginia Wesleyan College, is the second of the three literary reviews published in West Virginia that generated national subscription lists. Those mentioned are joined by the journal *Kestrel,* founded by poet Martin Lammon and professor John King of Fairmont State as part of an initiative to bring writers into the state and raise awareness of literature created there.

In the past fifteen years, West Virginia has played a major role in what some observers have called an Appalachian literary renaissance. Publication of *The Stories of Breece D'J Pancake* made a strong impact on West Virginia letters. Unfortunately, Pancake's suicide in 1971 ended the promise of a brilliant career, but his unflinching look—with what has been called "the bleak pastoral"—at West Virginia opened the door wider for those who would follow in this genre. The roster of writers from this small state who now identify with West Virginia, acknowledge it in their writings, defend it and attempt to explain it in interviews is a remarkable one. A prominent place on that roster belongs to Jayne Anne Phillips (1952–), born in Buchannon and the author of two novels, *Machine Dreams* (1984) and *Shelter* (1994), and of widely anthologized stories in two collections, *Fast Lanes* (1987) and *Black*

Tickets (1979). A recipient of a Guggenheim, two National Endowment for the Arts fellowships, a Bunting Institute fellowship, the Sue Kaufman Award (1980), an Academy Award in Literature (1997) from the American Academy and Institute of Arts and Letters, and a National Book Critics Circle award nomination, Phillips has published work most recently in *Granta, Doubletake,* and the *Norton Anthology of Contemporary Fiction.* Richard Currey, her classmate at West Virginia University in the 1970s, now living in New Mexico, is the author of *Fatal Light* (1988), which won the Hemingway Foundation Award. This Vietnam novel alternates settings between Parkersburg, West Virginia, and Vietnam. Currey also wrote *The Wars of Heaven* (1990), a collection of short stories, some of which were awarded an O. Henry Prize and the Pushcart Prize. His most recent novel, *Lost Highways* (1997), chronicles the travels of a country singer from West Virginia. Chuck Kinder, born in Montgomery, West Virginia, and with two degrees from West Virginia University, now teaches creative writing at the University of Pittsburgh. His novels include *Snakehunter* (1973) and *Silver Ghost* (1979). Lee Maynard, the author of *Crum* (1988)—a satiric black-humor novel that exploits and explodes every West Virginian stereotype—lives in New Mexico. Lisa Koger, raised in Tanner's Creek, Gilmer County, received an M.F.A. from the Iowa Writers' Workshop and won the 1989 James Michener Award. Her first collection, *Farlanburg Stories* (1990), loosely based on life in Glenville, was published by W. W. Norton.

Prominent on the literary landscape of writers under forty is Pinckney Benedict, winner of the Nelson Algren Award and author of two story collections, *Town Smokes* (1987)—which won him comparison to Pancake—and *The Wrecking Yard* (1992), and an acclaimed novel, *Dogs of God* (1994). He now teaches at Hollins University. Meredith Sue Willis, celebrated in a special issue of the *Iron Mountain Review* (1996), is eloquent in discussing Appalachia. She has published autobiographical novels—*A Space Apart* (1979), *Higher Ground* (1981), and *Only Great Changes* (1985)—and *In the Mountains of America: Stories* (1994). In addition, Willis is a renowned teacher of writing and a social activist. The writer whom most readers in the state would identify as the state's contemporary spokesperson is Denise Giardina, who was born in Bluefield and grew up in a coal camp. Winner of the Lillian Smith Award, she has twice won the Wetherford Award for best Appalachian fiction for

Storming Heaven (1987) and *The Unquiet Earth* (1992), two novels that cover sixty years of coalfield history in fictional Blackberry Creek, West Virginia. Her most recent work, *Saints and Villains* (1998), examines the travels of Dietrich Bonhoeffer in the mining communities of West Virginia just prior to the outbreak of World War II.

On the dais with this line-up of vibrant voices is Henry Louis Gates Jr., arguably the best-known African American scholar of the twentieth century. With articles appearing in *Harpers,* the *New Yorker,* and the *Saturday Review,* Gates has steadily built a career as a theorist on African American literature, particularly through *The Signifying Monkey: A Theory of Afro-American Criticism* (1988). He is also general editor of Oxford University Press's forty volumes of the Schomburg Library's collection of eighteenth-century African American women writers. Gates's major contribution to the state's literature is his memoir *Colored People* (1994), which covers his years in West Virginia from his birth in Redmont in 1950 until he left to attend Yale. *Colored People* was selected for the Lillian Smith Award for nonfiction. Currently W. E. B. Du Bois Professor of Humanities at Harvard University, where he heads the African American Studies Program, Gates has secured a lasting place in West Virginia and American literary history.

Other writers lesser known but all connected to the state either by birth or adoption include Gail Galloway Adams, winner of the Flannery O'Connor Award for Short Fiction for *The Purchase of Order* (1988); Allen Appel Jr., author of the popular *Time After Time* series; Tom Andrews, poet and memoirist (*The Hemophiliac's Motorcycle,* 1994, and *Codeine Diary,* 1997); Ellesa Clay High (*Past Titan Rock,* 1984, winner of the Appalachian Prize); Valerie Nieman, author of *Neena Gathering* (1988); Richard Spilman, winner of the *Quarterly West* Novella Prize for *Hot Fudge* (1990); Carolyn Thorman, author of *Fifty Years of Eternal Vigilance* (1988) and *Holy Orders* (1992); poets Grace Cavilieri, Lloyd Davis, John Flynn, Jim Harms (*Modern Oceans,* 1992, and *The Joy Addict,* 1997), P. J. Laska (*D.C. Images and Other Poems*—finalist for the National Book Award for Poetry in 1976), Llewellyn McKernan (*Many Waters: Poems from West Virginia,* 1993), John McKernan (*Walking Along the Missouri River*), David Prather, Jim Ralston, Barbara Smith, A. E. Stringer (*Channel Markers,* 1987), and Pete Zivkovic; and prose writers Colleen Anderson, Patsy Evans, Faith Holsaert, Kate Long, Bonnie Proudfoot,

Kevin Oderman, and Ethel Morgan Smith. The state's writing community now hosts four writing conferences: West Virginia Writers, Inc., sponsors an annual summer conference at Ripley; West Virginia University hosts a Writers' Workshop; GoldenRod Writers Conference, under the directorship of George Lies, meets every October; and the *Kestrel* Conference is sponsored each spring by Fairmont State College. Every third year, the West Virginia Commission on the Arts/Literature supports ten writers with $3,500 grants in the areas of fiction, creative nonfiction, drama, and poetry; and the West Virginia Humanities Council oversees a Circuit Writers program, which sends writers throughout underserved areas of the state to conduct workshops, give readings, and encourage young writers. One of the state's treasures resides with Professor William Plumley of the University of Charleston; he has significant holdings of visual art (primarily paintings and drawings) by authors, a collection that has been featured at the Smithsonian with Plumley's accompanying lecture.

Gail Galloway Adams

See also Appalachia; Appalachian Literature; Federal Writers' Project; Folklore; Oral History; Outdoor Drama.

Vito J. Brenni, *West Virginia Authors: A Bibliography* (1957; rev. Joyce Binder, 1968); Thomas E. Douglass, *A Room Forever: The Life, Work and Letters of Breece D'J Pancake* (1998); Kitty Frazier, *West Virginia Women Writers, 1822–1979* (1979); Phyllis Wilson Moore, "Yes, We Have Authors," in *The 1996 West Virginia Circuit Writers Project* (1997); Warren Wood, *Representative Authors of West Virginia* (1926).

WHOOPIN'

Martin Luther King's familiar style of oration falls under this heading. "Whoopin' " is the mode of delivery that King used in his famous 1963 "I Have a Dream" speech. Also called "chanting," "intoning," or "moaning," "whoopin' " combines oration and musicality. Scholars trace the origins of the practice to enslaved communities and beyond to West African societies.

In *Sacred Symphony: The Chanted Sermon of the Black Preacher* (1988), Jon Michael Spencer notes that the African oral tradition included the chanting of laws, stories, and proverbs. Spencer concludes that these are easily compared to African American practices such as "bluesy hollers," "whooped street cries," and the intoning of "biblical laws" and "Old Testament stories."

In her work on the African American sermon, Hortense Spillers declares that the sermon is "an oral poetry . . . a complete expression of a gamut of emotions," repeating the "rhythms of plot, complication, climax, resolution." The successfully whooped sermon combines this structure with some or all of the following features: melody, rhythm, call and response, harmony, counterpoint, form, and improvisation.

During slavery, whooped sermons were intricately linked to African American spirituals, each giving birth at times to the other. James Weldon Johnson captured this informing dialectic in *God's Trombones* (1927), a collection of seven sermons that exude the lyrical quality identified with the chanted or whooped sermon. Spirituals, mention of which are included in narratives of Frederick Douglass, William Wells Brown, Harriet Jacobs, and Booker T. Washington, began the now-rich tradition in African American music. In more contemporary terms, we can see the relationship of spirituals to more secularized forms of African American music in the careers of Mississippi native Reverend C. L. Franklin (1915–1984) and his daughter Aretha Franklin. The former grew up in rural Mississippi communities to become the most powerful black preacher in Detroit, Michigan; his whooped sermons earned him the title "high priest of soul preaching." Aretha Franklin (the "Queen of Soul") began her illustrious career singing spirituals in his church. Together, father and daughter exemplify the relationships among sermon, spiritual, and rhythm and blues. An even more recent manifestation of "whoopin' " appears in the musical performances of Reverend Kirk Franklin and his backup choir, God's Property. Other noteworthy whoopers include Howard Thurman and Jesse L. Jackson.

In *I Got the Word in Me and I Can Sing It, You Know* (1985), Gerald Davis sets forth a formal model for the performed African American sermon. Although scholars by and large agree that "whoopin' " is African American in origin, the style of delivery, like other aspects of American culture, cannot be contained within racial or gender boundaries. Sometimes defined as folk preaching, "whoopin' " relies heavily on melody, rhythm, improvisation, and dynamic interaction with the audience or congregation. The style of delivery transforms the written words into a collective cathartic phenomenon.

Lovalerie King

See also African American Spirituals; Preaching; Sermons.

Reverend C. L. Franklin, *Give Me This Mountain: Life History and Selected Sermons,* ed. Jeff Todd Titon, foreword by Jesse Jackson (1989); Dolan Hubbard, *The Sermon and the African American Literary Imagination* (1994); Henry H. Mitchell, *Black Preaching* (1970); Bruce A. Rosenberg, *Can These Bones Live?: The Art of the American Folk Preacher* (1988); Hortense Spillers, "Martin Luther King and the Style of the Black Sermon," in *The Black Experience in Religion,* ed. C. Eric Lincoln (1974).

WILLIAM AND MARY, COLLEGE OF

The College of William and Mary, located in Williamsburg, Virginia, was founded by royal charter in 1693, thus becoming the second of the nine colleges established in British North America before the American Revolution. Until the war, the college maintained strong ties with the Church of England; the first ten chancellors of the college were Anglican bishops, and most of the faculty were Anglican clergymen, graduates of Oxford University. Despite the Loyalist sympathies of the faculty, a number of the students actively supported the cause of independence and became leading figures in the early years of the Republic. Thomas Jefferson, William and Mary's most famous alumnus, attended the college from 1760 to 1762 and later studied law under George Wythe, a signer of the Declaration of Independence and the first professor of law at the college. Wythe's students also included John Marshall; Henry Clay; James Monroe, the fifth president of the United States; and St. George Tucker, who succeeded Wythe in the chair of law at the college and celebrated the ideals of the Enlightenment and American independence in plays, essays, and poems.

During the presidency of Thomas R. Dew (1836–1852), the college, once a seedbed of revolutionary idealism, became a stronghold of prosecessionist, anti-abolitionist sentiment. One of the most prolific of the antebellum southern writers, St. George Tucker's son, Nathaniel Beverley Tucker (class of 1802; professor of law at William and Mary, 1834–1851), defended the doctrine of states' rights and the plantation system based on slavery in scores of essays, lectures, orations, and three novels: *George Balcombe* (1836), *The Partisan Leader* (1836), and *Gertrude* (serialized in *The Southern Literary Messenger,* 1845).

Until the beginning of the twentieth century, William and Mary struggled for survival against the ravages of war, devastating fires, dangerously fluctuating enrollments, and competition from the University of Virginia, founded by Jefferson in 1819. Financial support was finally assured in 1906, when the college became the property of the state. William and Mary during this era appears as King's College in Ellen Glasgow's third novel, *The Voice of the People* (1900), set in Williamsburg, and in *The Cords of Vanity* (1909), the second novel by James Branch Cabell, who graduated from William and Mary in 1898. In academic scholarship, the college has made its most extended contribution through publication of the *William and Mary Quarterly,* first issued in 1892. Since 1944, the *Quarterly,* now in its third series, has published more than two hundred articles on early southern history and literature.

Elsa Nettels

See also Virginia Wits.

Susan H. Goodson et al., *The College of William and Mary: A History* (2 vols.; 1993); Wilfred Kale, *Hark Upon the Gate: An Illustrated History of the College of William and Mary* (1985); Jack E. Marpurgo, *Their Majesties' Royall Colledge: William and Mary in the Seventeeth and Eighteenth Centuries* (1976).

WILLIAMS, TENNESSEE

Whereas William Faulkner distilled the southern experience into his fictive "postage stamp" of territory he called Yoknapatawpha, Tennessee Williams put the South on stage. The fact that these two writers—both born in North Mississippi within some thirteen years and eighty miles of each other—treated their material in such different ways, each usually escaping comparison with the other, testifies to the complexity of a southern cultural identity and helps explain why their work is universally received.

After spending his first seven years living mostly in small Mississippi towns, Williams moved with his family to St. Louis in 1918, a wrenching uprooting from the genteel South and the embrace of his maternal grandparents. The devastating effect of this relocation would provide the playwright-to-be with some of his most persistently recurring themes of displacement, loss, and dreaming of the past. Although he would return to his grandparents' home occasionally, the reality of Williams's somewhat tenuous connection with the South suggests that his own southern identity was as much a matter of cultivated preference as a geographic or genealogical inevitability, especially considering that his mother was from Ohio and his father was from Knoxville, an area more Appalachian than of the Deep South.

Although Williams sets his work in places as far removed from the South as Rome, Tokyo, and the Pacific coast of Mexico, the great majority of his work is situated in the culture of two locales—New Orleans and the Mississippi Delta, the latter having been described as "the most southern place on earth." Williams's South is molded by a complex matrix of human incongruities—violence and compassion, intolerance and understanding, veracity and mendacity—and examines tender affairs of the heart even as it exposes psychic horrors such as impotence, bizarre delusional systems, rape, cannibalism, and castration. On the one hand, Williams valorizes the Old South through the poetic fabrications of characters such as Amanda Wingfield of *The Glass Menagerie* and Blanche DuBois of *A Streetcar Named Desire,* yet in plays such as *Sweet Bird of Youth* and *Orpheus Descending* he also pointedly criticizes the region through sociopolitical subtexts that involve racial exploitation, demagoguery, and xenophobia.

Williams's first major effort, *Battle of Angels* (1940), was a conspicuous disaster for the playwright yet to turn thirty. His initial success, *The Glass Menagerie* (1944), propelled him into the public eye, and with plays such as *A Streetcar Named Desire* (1947), *Cat on a Hot Tin Roof* (1955), *Sweet Bird of Youth* (1959), and *The Night of the Iguana* (1961), Williams earned celebrity status unparalleled in American theater.

If there is one touchstone with Williams's most memorable characters, it is their vulnerability, their inability or unwillingness to flow with the normative stream of society. Williams's own autobiography is stamped impressionistically on virtually every page of his writing, and it is easy to see how his artistic disposition and homosexuality in a homophobic age compelled him to write the part of the psychological misfit. His characters survive on the conviction of their dreams, "what *ought* to be truth," as Blanche says. Although one might be tempted to remember Williams for his depiction of tormented southern belles, a broader consideration includes an incredible panoply of characters, ranging from the assorted demimondains of the French Quarter (see, among other plays, *Vieux Carré,* 1977) to the ghosts of Ernest Hemingway and Zelda and F. Scott Fitzgerald (*Clothes for a Summer Hotel,* 1980). Indeed, the variety and multitude of Williams's characters prohibit a convenient summary. Furthermore, when one considers Williams's facility with virtually every other genre, including novels, short stories, poems, screenplays, essays, memoirs, and even painting, it is therefore not surprising that the plasticity of his genius helps account for the transformation of his work by others into film, opera, and ballet.

Williams also dared innovation—and breathed Promethean life into the American theater. *A Streetcar Named Desire,* for example, is unquestionably the first celebration of male sensuality on stage. Williams was a keen student of theater history, and some of his experiments with lighting, sound, screen projections, and narrative-framing demonstrate a commitment not only to bringing a Continental flavor to American theater, but also to obscuring, on-stage, the line between the real and the imaginative, usually resulting in what has been called "poetic realism." His experimentation occasionally backfired; *Camino Real* (1953) was a brilliant failure that adumbrates postmodernism, and in one of his late phases, with metadramatic plays such as *Kirche, Kutchen und Kinder: An Outrage for the Stage,* he seems to be parodying theater itself.

Possessed of extraordinary lyrical gifts and imaginative powers, Williams matched these endowments with an unswerving work ethic, always making time to write or rewrite daily. As a result of his prodigious if not compulsive composing, he left a legacy not only of the tremendous amount of work already well known, but also scores of other stories and plays that will eventually find their way into production and publication. For example, *Not About Nightingales,* a previously unpublished play written when Williams was twenty-seven but not performed until 1998, has received far more reviews—and those overwhelmingly salutary—than the last play produced while Williams was still alive and considered a working failure as a playwright.

As a dramatist, Williams's immortality rests firmly on his exquisite grasp of language and cadence. Although one should probably resist this classification, Eugene O'Neill is remembered as the dramatist of the soul, Arthur Miller of the head—and Williams of the heart. Wordsworth's definition of poetry as "the imaginative expression of strong feeling" is precisely the impression that theatergoers take with them as they leave the aisles after a Williams play, departing with the knowledge that they have been made privileged to secrets of the heart, however painful those interior glimpses may be.

Robert Bray

See also Drama, 1900 to Present.

Robert Bray, ed., *The Tennessee Williams Annual Review* 1 (1998); George W. Crandell, ed., *Tennessee Williams: A Descriptive Bibliography* (1996); Philip C. Kolin, ed., *Tennessee Williams: A Guide to Research and Performance* (1998); Lyle Leverich, *Tom: The Unknown Tennessee Williams* (1995); Lyle Leverich, *Tenn* (1999); Jac Tharpe, ed., *Tennessee Williams: 13 Essays* (1980); Judith J. Thompson, *Tennessee Williams's Plays: Memory, Myth, and Symbol* (1987).

WOMEN'S COLLEGES

Throughout their history, southern women's colleges have been regarded as mere finishing schools for elite young ladies. However, the evidence suggests that these colleges and their alumnae have exerted an especially significant impact on southern culture and literature.

The first state-chartered, degree-granting college for women in the United States was Georgia Female College, later renamed Wesleyan, which opened in 1838. From that time until the eve of the Civil War, southern female academies, seminaries, and institutes outpaced those of the North in adding college-level courses to their curricula, changing their names to include the word *college,* and announcing their intention to provide women with courses of study substantially equivalent to those of the best men's schools. Recent research suggests that these colleges were more academically rigorous than has generally been acknowledged, and they produced a number of graduates who, after the Civil War, became active in the temperance and suffrage movements and achieved political office.

In the postbellum period, many southern women's colleges closed their doors, and those that remained in operation tended to cling to an antebellum model of education, their only concession to changing circumstances being the institution of normal schools and departments and courses in secretarial skills. At this time, when several of the Seven Sisters schools were created and the southern women's colleges were struggling under debilitating financial constraints, the Northeast took the lead in women's education, outpacing the South in bringing women's education up to the standard of men's. As a result, the new image of the "college girl" was closely associated with the Northeast. The many novels and series of novels written about college women around the turn of the century were set in northeastern coeducational or women's schools, as have been most twentieth-century novels about college women.

Nonetheless, advances in women's higher education took place in the postbellum South. Some of the older southern schools for women became rigorous colleges during this period, and a number of new female colleges were created in the last third of the nineteenth century, including the first—and currently the only—public college for women in the United States, Mississippi University for Women (1884). Eudora Welty attended MUW from 1925 to 1927, when it was called Mississippi State College for Women. In *One Writer's Beginnings* (1984), she pays tribute to the impoverished and overcrowded but vibrant and stimulating culture of the school, where, as a reporter for the college newspaper, she tried out her skills as a humorist. The mothers of William Faulkner and Tennessee Williams also attended MUW.

Many alumnae of postbellum southern women's colleges produced works in various genres, especially inspirational and devotional literature, local histories, biographies, children's literature, and journalism. Some of the better-known of these alumnae are legendary gossip columnist Dorothy Dix, an 1882 graduate of Hollins College in Virginia; Julia Mood Peterkin, who graduated from Converse College in South Carolina in 1896 and wrote the Pulitzer Prize–winning novel *Scarlet Sister Mary* (1928); and Sophie Kerr Underwood, an 1898 graduate of Hood College in Maryland, who became a popular novelist and was managing editor of the *Woman's Home Companion.*

In the last third of the nineteenth century, African American women seeking higher education gained access to newly created black normal schools and normal departments in Negro colleges. As teachers, the pioneering graduates of these programs exerted enormous influence on their students and communities and played a vital role in the extension of literacy to African Americans.

By the early decades of the twentieth century, pressure for upgrading southern women's colleges came from regional accrediting agencies, denominational boards, and women's educational associations. Among the writers who benefited from the improved educational opportunities for women of this era were Evelyn Scott, early modernist author of *The Wave* (1929) and *Eva Gay* (1933), among other works, who attended Sophie Newcomb College in New Orleans, in 1910–1911 and at other times; Katharine Du Pre Lumpkin, a 1915 graduate of Brenau College in Georgia and author of the iconoclastic autobiography *The Making of a Southerner* (1947); and Caroline Gordon, a 1916 graduate of Bethany College in West Virginia. In their works, these writers interrogated the racist and sexist foundations of southern culture, while other women's-college alumnae took the lead in recovering lost information about southern women of the past. Four of the five historians whom Anne Firor Scott describes in *Unheard Voices* (1993) as pioneers in the reconstruction of southern women's history attended southern women's colleges in the early decades of the twentieth century.

By midcentury, women's-college students were in the vanguard of the comprehensive reexamination of southern culture and literature that was initiated by the Civil Rights and Women's Liberation movements. In the political arena, young white women from women's colleges first supported black students who challenged segregation and race discrimination, including students from the South's two colleges for black women—Bennett College in South Carolina and Spelman College in Atlanta. As scholars, women's-college alumnae also took the lead in challenging the racist and sexist biases inherent in southern literature and in the formation of the southern literary canon. For example, Beverly Guy-Sheftall (Spelman, 1966) was a co-editor of the groundbreaking work *Sturdy Black Bridges: Visions of Black Women in Literature* (1979). She continues to write on literary images of black women while teaching at Spelman alongside Anne Bradford Warner (Hollins, 1967), who has written extensively on Harriet Jacobs, among other black women writers.

Other women's-college alumnae have engaged in reexamining white women's contributions to southern literature. Anne Goodwyn Jones (Hollins, 1967) broke ground on this project with her revisionist study *Tomorrow Is Another Day: The Woman Writer in the South, 1859–1936* (1981). Her classmate Lucinda Hardwick MacKethan (Hollins, 1967) has explored the relationship of southern women to the traditions of fiction and storytelling in such works as *Daughters of Time: Creating Woman's Voice in Southern Story* (1990), and another women's-college graduate, Louise Westling—a 1964 graduate of Randolph-Macon Woman's College in Virginia—has written important studies of numerous southern women writers, including Carson McCullers, Flannery O'Connor, and Eudora Welty.

In their roles as editors, women's-college alumnae have also exercised considerable impact on the dissemi-

nation and reception of southern literature. Especially influential in this regard is Shannon Ravenel (Hollins, 1960), editor of Algonquin Books's yearly *New Stories from the South*.

Throughout the twentieth century, single-sex education has declined in popularity. However, women's colleges have continued to produce a disproportionate number of high-achieving women in all areas of endeavor, including writing. Literally hundreds of works in all genres have been produced by women's-college alumnae, and the following list constitutes only a small sampling of a few of the better-known southern writers who have attended southern female colleges since midcentury: Mary Ward Brown, a 1939 graduate of Judson College in Alabama; Flannery O'Connor, who graduated in 1945 from Georgia State College for Women; Shirley Ann Grau (Sophie Newcomb, 1950); Doris Betts, who attended Women's College of the University of North Carolina at Greensboro from 1950 to 1953; Anne Rice, who attended Texas Women's University from 1959 to 1960; Alice Walker, who attended Spelman from 1961 to 1963; Sandra Deer (Wesleyan, 1962); Marsha Norman, a 1968 graduate of Agnes Scott College in Georgia; and Lee Smith (Hollins, 1967).

As writers, editors, and literary scholars, women's-college alumnae have exercised significant influence on the course of southern letters, playing vital roles in the production, dissemination, reception, recovery, reevaluation, and revision of the southern literary canon.

Emily Powers Wright

See also Belle; Feminism; New Woman; Women's Movement; Women Writers, 1820 to 1900; Women Writers, 1900 to World War II; Women Writers, World War II to Present.

I. M. E. Blandin, *History of Higher Education of Women in the South Prior to 1860* (n.d.); Florence Fleming Corley, *Higher Education for Southern Women* (1985); Christie Anne Farnham, *The Education of the Southern Belle* (1994); Nancy C. Parrish, *Lee Smith, Annie Dillard, and the Hollins Group* (1998); Barbara Miller Solomon, *In the Company of Educated Women: A History of Women and Higher Education in America* (1985).

WOMEN'S MOVEMENT

Although the women's movement emerged in the South as in the North during the nineteenth century, a complex web of circumstances kept a fairly tight rein on its progress. An ideal of womanhood tied to myths of the Old South—which portrayed women as weak and submissive in relation to men, exalted and honored in the sacred role of wife and mother—allowed little space for alternate roles. Indeed, the rigid structure of southern society depended on the silence of its women, for in asserting themselves, they were threatening the very foundation of the aristocratic, agrarian, and patriarchal culture. So while some antebellum writers, such as Eliza Pinckney, Mary Boykin Chesnut, and Sarah and Angelina Grimké, may be seen as stubbornly resisting this culture, these women were a minority. According to historian George Rable, "although women did not uniformly embrace the value system of the Old South, they did much more to uphold than undermine it." Although many women in the nineteenth century moved outside the confines of the home by becoming active in political and social organizations, they were clearly doing so to serve society, not to promote equality for themselves; generally, outspoken women did not support but adamantly attacked the suffrage movement. The traditional southern home had much to offer women in terms of security and a distinct role to fulfill, and many women feared that they and their families would suffer from change.

The portrait of the southern lady flourished in the tradition of the domestic novel, descriptions of which are found in Caroline Whiting Hentz's *Eoline* (1852) and to some extent in Caroline Howard Gilman's *Recollections of a Southern Matron* (1838). It was developed and supported by what was known as the Cult of True Womanhood, an image of women that stressed submissiveness, piety, and domestic skill. Literary achievement was one way women gained power in the prewar years, and often the characters that women writers created were strong and assertive, yet equality was rarely a goal; it is not surprising, then, that domestic novels by Hentz, Gilman, and others did more to support than defy the Cult, and slave narratives, such as Harriet Jacobs's *Incidents in the Life of a Slave Girl* (1861), spoke more openly for freedom than for gender equality.

Notable exceptions in the nineteenth-century South, even if they did not contribute directly to the women's movement, can be found. In her journal and letters, Eliza Pinckney describes what it meant for her, at seventeen, to manage her father's six-hundred-acre plantation. Mary Chesnut, while actively supporting her husband's political career, filled her diary with her radical views of the position of women in the South and of the evils of slavery. Yet the most outspoken southern women were not welcome in their own homes; Sarah and Angelina Grimké, the first American women to be recognized for fighting for both abolition and women's rights, left Charleston for the North in the 1820s and were warned never to return. Angelina's *Appeal to the Christian Women of the South* (1836) and Sarah's *Letters on the Equality of the Sexes and the Condition of Women* (1838), widely acclaimed in the North, were considered dangerous in the South because they presented sexism and racism in moral terms. Finally, although southern women were represented at the Seneca Falls women's rights convention in 1848, the reforms laid out by Elizabeth Cady Stanton and Lucretia Mott had little bearing on everyday life in the South.

After the Civil War, the women's movement continued to exert minimal influence on southern women. Some women writers, in particular Augusta Jane Evans Wilson, actually fought against enfranchisement by condemning women who moved into the male sphere of business and politics; her novel *A Speckled Bird* (1902) directly opposed the suffrage movement. Those who spoke out in favor of suffrage, such as Elizabeth Meriwether, tended to take a rather conservative approach, and sometimes did so by appealing to white supremacist concerns. In fact, the southern states almost succeeded in killing the Nineteenth Amendment when the federal government sent it to the states for ratification; after a bitter fight, however, Tennessee agreed to ratify, and in 1920 women finally obtained the right to vote.

In the midst of the suffrage movement of the late nineteenth century, when southerners generally supported the vote for women if it meant strengthening the forces against African Americans, the black women's movement came into bloom. Undaunted by the mainstream movement, which made the rights of women a higher priority than those of emancipated slaves, African American women intellectuals began speaking out in behalf of black women. In *A Voice from the South* (1892), Anna Julia Cooper promoted a balance of power between the sexes by claiming that equality did not place women's rights or thoughts above those of men, but demanded that women receive equal attention. Cooper is known today as the leading African American feminist of her time.

In the decades following the Nineteenth Amendment's ratification, the women's movement was marked by relative calm, yet in the South perhaps some of the most significant work was being done. Renascence in the South meant an outpouring of extraordinary literature, much of which was written by women determined to redefine the portrait of southern womanhood. Ellen Glasgow's *Barren Ground* (1925) and *Vein of Iron* (1935) challenged the notion of weakness and subordination in southern women. Zora Neale Hurston's *Their Eyes Were Watching God* (1937) portrayed the triumph of a black woman who demands self-definition. Carson McCullers, Eudora Welty, and Flannery O'Connor created vivid portraits of "outsiders," women who could not be made to fit any stereotype of the ideal. Although change in the South was slow, works by such women helped transform thinking and paved the way for the more recent wave of the women's movement.

The end of World War II brought a renewed interest in women's rights, which came to fruition during and just after the Civil Rights Movement. In 1966 the National Organization for Women (NOW) was formed, heightening the debate over the Equal Rights Amendment, and today women's rights are at the forefront of politics. Yet images of women in the South, perpetuated by traditions that die hard, remain controversial. In a 1975 article for *Ms.* magazine, Gail Godwin claimed that the ideal of southern womanhood still flourishes as a dangerous force in southern culture, and many contemporary southern writers still wrestle with the image, no matter how resolutely they deny its validity. In the last quarter of this century, the women's movement has given way to one of somewhat broader focus, the feminist movement, which has deliberately moved beyond politics into all aspects of culture. Brought face to face with the stolid heritage of the southern past, feminist criticism opens up vast possibilities for the study of southern literature.

Carolyn Perry

See also Belle; Feminism; Lady; United Daughters of the Confederacy; Women Writers.

Eleanor Flexner, *Century of Struggle: The Woman's Rights Movement in the United States* (1959); Gail Godwin, "The Southern Belle," *Ms.* (July 1975); George C. Rable, *Civil Wars: Women and the Crisis of Southern Nationalism* (1989); Anne Firor Scott, *The Southern Lady* (1970).

WOMEN'S STUDIES

The development of women's studies in the United States grew out of the student protest movement of the 1960s when gender roles and the status of women were being reevaluated, in particular by feminists in academic institutions. During the early 1960s, in colleges and universities across the country, many individual courses devoted to women and women's texts were being taught; by the end of the decade, inspired in part by the many black studies programs already flourishing, educators began to join forces in organizing women's studies programs. By 1972, two interdisciplinary feminist journals, *Feminist Studies* and *Women's Studies,* were established, and in 1977 the National Women's Studies Association was founded. Since that time, interest in women's issues has continued to grow and has led to a multitude of social and political organizations, journals and magazines, and Internet sites devoted to women's concerns.

The emergence of women's studies programs has not only had an impact on the study of women and gender, but has reached into nearly every field of study. Largely a product of history and literature departments, these programs are interdisciplinary by nature, almost always including religion, sociology, psychology, and the natural sciences. The goals of women's studies programs vary somewhat from campus to campus, depending on the inclusion of a women's center, the value placed on research in the field, and the effect of women's studies on the overall curriculum. However, most programs have been concerned at least in part with analyzing the social construction of gender and gender roles, recovering the stories of women that have been overlooked by historians or literary critics, and raising consciousness regarding such diverse issues as violence against women and the rediscovery of nineteenth-century southern women writers. Women's studies programs have energized and in some cases revolutionized many fields of study by challenging conventional theories and research methods and redefining literary canons. They have also influenced pedagogy, since women's studies efforts often seek new ways of constructing knowledge and attempt to involve students in this endeavor.

Although the major movements in women's studies have taken place in the North and on the West Coast, women's studies departments have flourished in the South at institutions large and small, public and private. The study of southern literature has been significantly shaped by the impact of all such programs. Perhaps most significantly, and at least in part through the efforts of women's studies programs, lost writers of the South, in particular Kate Chopin and Zora Neale Hurston, have been rediscovered and are now taught regularly. With the publication of *The Awakening* in 1899, Chopin's work first fell into disfavor and then into complete obscurity; during the 1960s and 1970s, however, feminist scholars recognized in the novel the very issues that women were battling in the twentieth century and praised the boldness with which it addressed them. Likewise, Zora Neale Hurston completely fell into obscurity in the 1950s, but through the attention of feminist critics, she is now considered one of the most significant African American writers of this century.

Literary critics and historians have also recognized that the traditional picture of southern history and culture is a distorted one given that women writers and women's texts in the South have for so long been marginalized. The result recently has been an enormous outpouring of new books on southern women and southern women's writing, ranging from new editions of early works by southern women, such as C. Vann Woodward's *Mary Chesnut's Civil War* (1980); to anthologies such as Mary Louise Weaks and Carolyn Perry's *Southern Women's Writing, Colonial to Contemporary* (1995); to critical works such Anne Goodwyn Jones's *Tomorrow Is Another Day: The Woman Writer in the South, 1859–1936* (1981), Elizabeth Fox-Genovese's *Within the Plantation Household: Black and White Women of the Old South* (1988), Lucinda H. MacKethan's *Daughters of Time: Creating Woman's Voice in Southern Story* (1990), and Elizabeth Harrison's *Female Pastoral: Women Writers Re-visioning the American South* (1991). The range and depth of scholarship in southern women's literature attest to the dynamic force that women's studies programs have been in the final decades of the twentieth century.

Carolyn Perry

See also Feminism; Women's Movement; Women Writers.

Beryl Madoc-Jones and Jennifer Coates, eds., *An Introduction to Women's Studies* (1996); Fiona Montgomery and Christine Collette, eds., *Into the Melting Pot: Teaching Women's Studies in the New Millennium* (1997); Diane Richardson and Victoria Robinson, eds., *Thinking Feminist: Key Concepts in Women's Studies* (1993).

WOMEN WRITERS, BEGINNINGS TO 1820

The history of women's writing in the eighteenth and early nineteenth centuries, in the region that has subse-

quently become known as the South, is necessarily sketchy and fragmented. Literary culture in the southern colonies was primarily a manuscript culture, in which poems and essays, like letters and journals, often passed from hand to hand and from house to house rather than being printed or published. Consequently, little material is extant, and that which is available can only suggest the extent to which writing in some form or another was important in women's lives. It is clear, however, that creative, thoughtful, gifted women entertained themselves and their families and friends with their written observations, keeping journals and writing letters and poetry in the colonial and early national periods. These activities, as well as the keeping of commonplace books, were encouraged in genteel women, for whom the ability to converse was an accomplishment like virtuosity in music and needlework.

One of the most notable writers of the early South was diarist and letter writer Eliza Lucas Pinckney (1722?–1793) of Charleston. Her work has been published as the *Journal and Letters of Eliza Pinckney* (1850), *Eliza Lucas Pinckney to C. C. Pinckney* (1916), and *The Letterbook of Eliza Lucas Pinckney, 1739–1762* (1972). Pinckney was born in the West Indies, the daughter of George Lucas, a British military man who later became lieutenant governor of Antigua. She was educated in England and moved with her family to a plantation near Charleston in 1738. One year later, at age seventeen, she took over the management of her father's three plantations when he was called back to military service in Antigua in 1739. During the next five years, she worked to develop the cultivation of indigo in the area and by 1744 had helped establish it as an important export crop. She also kept a letterbook until 1746, two years after her marriage to Charles Pinckney. She began writing letters again in 1753, while the Pinckneys lived in England, and stopped in 1762. The irregularity of the letter writing in the years after her marriage suggests the difficulty of sustaining literary pursuits in the press of domestic responsibility.

Pinckney's letters are thoughtful, creative, and reflective of her intelligence, common sense, humility, wit, and forthrightness. A 1740 letter to her friend Mary Bartlett that describes the activities of a typical day reveals how thoroughly Pinckney had internalized the eighteenth-century ideals of order, balance, service to society, and self-improvement. With almost Franklinian precision, she rose each day at five, afterward following a schedule for reading, taking a walk, overseeing the servants, studying French or shorthand, teaching two slave girls to read, practicing music, doing needlework, and once again reading and writing before bed. In 1742 she included in a letter to Bartlett her response to the first volume of Virgil's *Georgics,* and in another she sent a copy of *Pamela* for a friend, along with a detailed critique of the character of the heroine. The letters record half of an ongoing conversation about classical and contemporary literature, as well as discussion of such subjects as agriculture, horticulture, and morality. In a 1740 letter to her father, she wrote of more serious matters, assuring her father that in choosing a husband she would not fall prey to "indiscreet passion" and expressing her assurance that he, in turn, will not make her "a sacrifice to Wealth." Pinckney's writing is as reflective of her genius as it is in many ways of the concerns and occupations of the genteel eighteenth-century woman, though Pinckney was certainly atypical in her degree of independence and responsibility.

A second careful stylist was Eliza Yonge Wilkinson (1757–?), whose series of twelve letters dated 1781–1782 detail the British invasion and occupation of Charleston in 1779. Little is known about Wilkinson beyond the fact that she was the daughter of Francis and Sarah Clifford Yonge of Yonge's Island in South Carolina and that she married Joseph Wilkinson in 1774 and was widowed the following year. She married Peter Porcher in 1786. It is not clear whether her letters were written at the time of the occupation or were composed and arranged later, as their conscious literary artistry and unity of construction might suggest. Although some were addressed to Mary Porcher, later Wilkinson's sister-in-law, others have no designated recipient and read much like fiction. Using a sophisticated vocabulary, they are filled with detailed descriptions, long passages of dialogue, literary references, and episodic action. They were published in Caroline Gilman's magazine the *Rose Bud* from 1832 to 1835, and in 1839 were "arranged" by Gilman for publication as *Letters of Eliza Wilkinson: During the Invasion and Possession of Charleston, S.C., by the British in the Revolutionary War.* It is unclear how much, if any, editorial license Gilman exercised in preparing these letters for publication. Their publication at this later date reflects the country's taste for patriotic and nationalistic writing in the early national period.

Other perspectives on politics and society in the revolutionary and early national period are found in Loyalist Susannah Wells Aikman's 1779 account of a trip from Charleston to London, published in 1906 as *The Journal of a Voyage from Charleston, S.C., to London* (by Louisa Susannah Wells); and in *The Letterbook of Mary Stead Pinckney* (1946), which details Pinckney's experiences as she accompanied her husband, Charles Cotesworth Pinckney, the United States minister to France, on a diplomatic mission to that country.

Women also documented their religious experiences in diaries and letters, following the tradition of spiritual autobiography. The writings of Mrs. Mary Hutson, a fervent Christian whose reflections and observations were posthumously published in 1760 by her husband in *Living Christianity Delineated, in the Diaries and Letters of Two Eminently Pious Persons Lately Deceased,* and those of Mrs. Martha Ramsey, whose writings were published by her husband after her death as well, illustrated exemplary female piety. *Memoirs of the Life of Martha Ramsey* (1811) was especially popular and was reprinted in multiple editions, reflecting not only perhaps its greater appeal but the much more widespread literacy and the better developed marketplace for the printing and distribution of books in this later period. It is probable, however, that neither of the two writers wrote with the intention to put their thoughts before the public view.

In addition to writing letters and keeping journals, women wrote poetry in the early South. Poetry was a more self-consciously literary form than the diary or letter, though it was a vehicle for all kinds of expression from the most serious of thoughts to the most frivolous. Women's poems appear woven into their letters and journals and as separate pieces, sometimes carefully recorded, sometimes hastily scribbled onto a scrap of paper. Both Eliza Pinckney and Eliza Wilkinson, for example, included lines of verse within their letters, and the easy transition from letter to verse and back again suggests the close relationship between verse and conversation in eighteenth-century culture, a relationship that helped make poetry writing a common pastime. The publication of poems, however, was not. Women seldom published their poems until after the turn of the century, when the audience for their work grew with the establishment of women's magazines and the development of a female readership. Exchanged poetry, however, connected women to others in their communities and beyond, giving shape to thoughts, feelings, and observations. Until the turn of the nineteenth century, women writers, like their male counterparts, wrote in the neoclassical style, adopting the ordered, rhymed couplets of Dryden and Pope. At the end of the century, however, a marked turn toward sentimentalism occurs, with Young and Gray emerging as inspiration and models. Southern women poets were likely to be upper-class women who found time in a day filled with domestic duties to write their verses for themselves, their families, and friends. In this period, poetry was a familiar and well-used form of language, underscoring and supporting the ethos of sociability and civility that helped the plantation society cohere and that helped to assure colonials of their gentility despite their isolation from England.

Exemplifying the woman poet in this period is Margaret Lowther Page (1760–1835), who came to Williamsburg, Virginia, from New York in 1790. The daughter of Scottish merchant William Lowther, she met Representative John Page of Virginia while Congress was seated in New York and married him in 1790. She was locally known as a poet, and Page introduced her to his closest friend in Williamsburg, lawyer and writer St. George Tucker, by having the two exchange poems. After her move to Virginia, Page continued to write poems until her death, publishing a few in well-known magazines, including the *American Museum* (Philadelphia, 1790–1792), one of the most important magazines of the period; the *New-York Magazine; or Literary Repository* (1790–1797); and the *Port Folio* (Philadelphia, 1801–1827). It is almost certain that she did not submit these poems herself, however, and they were probably sent by her husband or by Tucker. Most of her verses, however, she exchanged with friends, especially Tucker, sometimes almost daily. Her poems include riddles and other word games; elegies; verse epistles that describe local events and people; birthday, anniversary, and other types of congratulatory poems; and lyrics about imagination, friendship, and other abstract topics.

Probably because she did not marry until age thirty, Page had time to nurture and sustain her poetic inclinations before the demands of household management and motherhood could displace them. Furthermore, she lived among a group of people who considered poetry writing an appropriate pastime for women. Like Margaret Page and Tucker, John Page was a poet, and he appreciated and encouraged his wife's devotion to versifying, considering her a better poet than he was. Thirty-three of Margaret Page's poems, those written in New York, as well as a journal account of a visit to Scotland, were privately printed in 1790 in a book that also contained poems by Tucker, John Page, and other

friends and relations. Margaret Page's poems in the volume included occasional poems—those commemorating events—as well as verse epistles, word games, and elegies. The opening poem describes George Washington's entry into New York as the president of the United States, and the closing poem, produced at a later date and handwritten on the back page, details the difficulty of writing poetry while managing a household full of children. Although Page, like Tucker and the other writers with whom she exchanged verses, wrote humorous pieces, word games, and social verse, she never called even her lightest poems "trifles" or "vanities" as women often did. While she asserts poetry's importance in enriching the inner life and intensifying experience, she values it highly, as well, as a social act—an extension of conversation, a form of play, and a medium of exchange.

Also found in the Tucker-Coleman Collection at the College of William and Mary in Williamsburg, Virginia, are poems by six other women: Mrs. Robert Carter Nicholas, wife of the secretary of the colony; Mrs. Thomas Dunbar; Eliza Skipwith; Nancy Cocke; Anne Grymes Page; and Judith Lomax. Although most are represented by only one or two poems, Lomax has eleven in the collection, sent in 1800 by her father Thomas Lomax of Port Tobago for Tucker's criticism. Lomax published a volume of poems in 1813, *The Notes of an American Lyre, Dedicated to Thomas Jefferson*. Other volumes were published by Virginia women as well, including *Poems of Laura; An Original American Work*, printed in Petersburg in 1818.

Although these works by early southern women can provide only a glimpse into the life of the mind in the period, they do suggest the extent to which writing was important in women's lives. Women continued to write despite the demands made on their time by wife- and motherhood, and wrote about the dilemma. They wrote verses that reflected their assimilation of the prevailing poetic forms of the day and letters that showcased their wit and powers of observation and description. Most of all, they took part in the establishment of their national literary tradition.

Daphne H. O'Brien

See also Colonial Literature; Poetry, Beginnings to 1820; Virginia, Literature of; William and Mary, College of.

Richard Beale Davis, *Intellectual Life in Jefferson's Virginia, 1790–1830* (1964); Elise Pinckney, ed., *Letterbook of Eliza*

Pinckney (1972); Mary Louise Weaks and Carolyn Perry, eds., *Southern Women's Writing: Colonial to Contemporary* (1995).

WOMEN WRITERS, 1820 TO 1900

The years 1820 to 1900 were remarkably productive for women writers in the South, marking a significant change from the previous centuries when reading and writing were not considered necessary or even appropriate skills for women. Fewer than a third of white southern women of the colonial era could read. But during the first few decades of the nineteenth century, education for white upper- and middle-class southern girls became more common, and by midcentury, the literacy rate for this group had risen so dramatically that reading and writing had become accepted feminine activities. In her introduction to *Woman's Fiction* (1978), Nina Baym claims that between the years 1820 and 1870, fiction by and about women "was by far the most popular literature of its time, and on the strength of that popularity, authorship in America was established as a woman's profession, and reading as a woman's avocation." Novels by southern women were among the most popular of the time, and they were read avidly by southern and northern women alike.

Although much of the significant writing by nineteenth-century southern women took the form of fiction, women also published journalistic sketches, political essays, poetry, diaries and journals, histories, and autobiographies. Many of these works are highly political and controversial, confronting the complex issues of slavery, women's roles, and the sectional differences that occupied the nation's attention after 1830.

One of the first women to publish after 1820 was Anne Newport Royall (1759–1854), whose 1826 *Sketches of History, Life, and Manners in the United States* was the first of numerous travel sketches and memoirs she published in her lifetime. Considered by some to be the first female American journalist, Royall did not set out to become a professional writer. After the death of her husband in 1812, Royall traveled from Virginia to Alabama and began keeping a detailed travel diary. In 1823 her husband's relatives overthrew his will, and Royall was left in financial straits; writing became her means of support. In addition to her 1826 *Sketches*, which describes an 1823 trip through the eastern states, Royall published the three-volume *Black Book; or, A Continuation of Travels in the United States* (1828–1829), *Mrs. Royall's Pennsylvania* (1829),

Mrs. Royall's Southern Tour (1830–1831), and *Letters From Alabama on Various Subjects* (1830). Her sketches and essays—opinionated, energetic, humorous, sometimes outrageous—provide valuable insight into regional American life of the 1820s.

Also a journal writer, Fanny Kemble (1809–1893) was born in London, educated in Paris, and first came to the United States in 1832 on a theatrical tour designed to save her father's theater company from bankruptcy. In 1834 she married Pierce Butler, owner of a large plantation in Georgia; her experience of plantation life led her to become an outspoken critic of slavery in her *Journal of a Residence in America* (1835). In 1846 Kemble left Butler, divorcing him in 1848. She returned to her acting career, touring throughout England and the United States, wrote poetry and plays, and published her first novel, *Away and Long Ago*, in 1889. Her most important publication for students of southern literature and culture, however, is her 1863 *Journal of a Residence on a Georgian Plantation, 1838–1839*, in which she describes in detail the brutal treatment of slaves, especially slave women, in the plantation system.

Sarah Moore Grimké (1792–1873) and her youngest sister, Angelina Emily Grimké (1805–1879), although native southerners and daughters of a slave-owning supporter of the Old South, shared Kemble's opposition to the slave system. Noted abolitionists, feminists, and reformers, the sisters had to leave their home in Charleston, South Carolina, because of the unpopularity of their political views. Sarah moved to Philadelphia, where she became a Quaker minister; soon after, Angelina moved north to join her. Both began working for the New York Anti-Slavery Society, becoming the first American women to address mixed audiences in public; in 1838, Angelina became the first American woman to speak before a legislative body. Sarah's 1836 *An Epistle to the Clergy of the Southern States* argues that slavery is incompatible with Christianity; Angelina's *Appeal to the Christian Women of the South*, published the same year, urges southern women to take action against slavery. In her 1837 pamphlet, *An Appeal to the Women of the Nominally Free States*, Angelina articulated the first published connection between the legal and social situations of women and of slaves. "Women," she wrote, "ought to feel a peculiar sympathy in the colored man's wrong, for like him, she has been accused of mental inferiority, and denied the privileges of a liberal education." Sarah Grimké's *Letters on the Equality of the Sexes and the*

Condition of Women, Addressed to Mary S. Parker, President of the Boston Female Anti-Slavery Society (1838) is considered by many to be the first important argument for women's rights by an American woman.

Harriet Ann Jacobs's slave narrative, *Incidents in the Life of a Slave Girl* (1861), was thought for years to be a fictional work by abolitionist Lydia Maria Child, despite its subtitle, *Written by Herself*. Jacobs (1818–1896) was born a slave near Edenton, North Carolina, and *Incidents* chronicles her experiences in slavery, with particular attention to the sexual exploitation of female slaves; her escape from slavery and voluntary confinement for years in a cramped crawlspace above her grandmother's house; her journey north; and her struggles to free her children from slavery and to be reunited with them. Addressed to white women in the North and drawing upon the conventions of the highly popular sentimental novel, *Incidents* draws repeated parallels between the conditions of women in slavery and in marriage. "Reader," she exclaims in the last chapter, "my story ends with freedom; not in the usual way, with marriage."

Also overtly political is the work of African American poet, novelist, and reformer Frances E. W. Harper (1825–1911). Raised in Baltimore by an uncle whose school for free blacks she attended, Harper published her first collection of poetry, *Forest Leaves*, in 1845. After moving north, Harper became active in the Underground Railroad and began giving speeches for the abolitionist cause. She presented her most famous speech, "Education and the Elevation of the Colored Race," in Massachusetts in 1854. That year also saw the publication of her *Poems on Miscellaneous Subjects,* a collection of poems against slavery, which sold more than fifty thousand copies by 1871. Her short story "The Two Offers" (1859) is recognized as the first published short story by an African American. Additional collections of poetry include *Sketches of Southern Life* (1872), *Moses: A Story of the Nile* (1869), and *The Martyr of Alabama and Other Poems* (1894). Her only novel, *Iola Leroy, or Shadows Uplifted,* appeared in 1892.

Two autobiographical works by women about the Civil War years have been of tremendous value to historians. Mary Boykin Chesnut (1823–1886) and Elizabeth Keckley (c. 1819–1907) provide very different pictures of the war and the years leading up to it. Keckley's 1868 slave narrative, *Behind the Scenes, or Thirty Years a Slave and Four Years in the White House,* describes her life as a slave in Dinwiddie, Vir-

ginia, her purchase of herself and her son with money she earned as a seamstress, and her experiences in Washington, D.C., where her sewing skills eventually brought her to the White House as Mary Todd Lincoln's personal seamstress. Of particular interest to historians is her portrait of the events and personalities associated with the Lincoln White House during the Civil War years. Unfortunately, the publication of her narrative lost Keckley her position and the friendship of Mrs. Lincoln, and she died in poverty.

Mary Boykin Chesnut began her diary after leaving Washington, D.C., to return to South Carolina with her husband, Senator James Chesnut, who led the state's secessionist movement. The diary records her experiences and observations from February 15, 1861, to August 2, 1865, and includes her reflections on slavery, southern womanhood, and the Confederate cause. Chesnut began revising her diary for publication in 1881 but died before completing the revisions, and nothing of her work was published until 1905 when her friend Isabella Martin published *A Diary From Dixie,* editing out any of Chesnut's reflections that seemed at odds with the turn-of-the-century orthodox view of the Confederacy. Not until C. Vann Woodward published *Mary Chesnut's Civil War* in 1980 was her full work made available to readers.

Like Chesnut, Margaret Junkin Preston (1820–1897) also kept a journal of her experiences during the Civil War but used it as material for her long narrative poem, *Beechenbrook: A Ryme of the War* (1865). Born in Pennsylvania, Preston moved with her family to Virginia in 1848, where Margaret married Major John Preston. Although her family returned to the North at the start of the Civil War and supported the Union, Preston became devoted to her southern home and its politics, and *Beechenbrook* celebrates her loyalty to the southern cause as it narrates the experiences of a family whose father serves in the Confederate army. Her postwar publications include *Old Song and New* (1870) and *Cartoons* (1875).

By far the majority of writing by southern women between the years of 1820 and 1900 was in the genre of the domestic or sentimental novel, which generally tells the story of a young woman's development of character through her encounter with and triumph over a variety of trials and tribulations. Although this genre celebrates the "cult of domesticity" in which a happy and well-ordered home is seen as the ideal model for social relations in both the private and public spheres, most protagonists in these southern novels are not the patient, long-suffering, passive heroines so often associated with sentimental fiction. Many of them rebel against the society's expectations for women and reject the "clinging vine" version of womanhood in favor of self-development, education, and independence. In many cases, the traditional ending of novels in this genre—marriage—seems forced and out of keeping with the heroines' achievement of independence.

For much of the twentieth century, the prolific output of these novelists has been ignored by the scholarly community. More recently, however, critical reevaluations of popular writing by nineteenth-century women have found it of value both in literary terms and for what it can tell us of southern women's lives, experiences, and values in the years leading up to, during, and following the Civil War. Scholars have also begun to trace the ways in which these popular and widely read novels influenced the nation's political consciousness during the years leading up to the Civil War.

Except for those written in response to Harriet Beecher Stowe's *Uncle Tom's Cabin* (1852), most novels by white antebellum southern women were not overt with their political agenda. Most of these women began writing not to challenge the prevailing views of a woman's place in the antebellum Victorian South but out of economic necessity resulting from adverse family situations—the illness or death of a parent or spouse, bankruptcy, or financial reversals. Augusta Jane Evans began writing after her father was forced to declare bankruptcy; Maria McIntosh's literary career began after she lost her money in the Panic of 1837; Caroline Hentz wrote to support her family during her husband's illness and after his death. E. D. E. N. Southworth, who began writing fiction to support herself and her two children after the failure of her marriage, describes in an autobiographical piece for the *Saturday Evening Post* "the time when I found myself broken in spirit, health, and purse—a widow in fate but not in fact, with my babes looking to me for a support I could not give them. It was in these darkest days of my *woman's* life, that my *author's* life commenced."

Caroline Howard Gilman (1794–1888), one of the most popular southern writers during the 1830s and 1840s, was not southern by birth. Born and raised in Massachusetts, Gilman moved to Charleston, South Carolina, after her marriage to Samuel Gilman, a Unitarian minister. The mother of seven children, Gilman began her writing career with a children's magazine, *Rose Bud* (1832). Her first novel, *Recollections of a*

New England Housekeeper (1834), drew upon her New England childhood and offers a vivid picture of the development of a middle-class housewife. Her second novel, *Recollections of a Southern Matron* (1838), tells the story of a girl growing to maturity on a southern plantation, which is represented as an emblem of a domestic, moral, community-based social order as opposed to the materialistic individualism of the northern city. The novel offers a defense of slavery in which the ideal paternalistic plantation master is represented in domestic terms as the head of a large, happy, well-regulated family.

At the same time that it celebrates domestic order and peace, Gilman's novel also suggests the sacrifices and the repression of self required of women in order to achieve and maintain this ideal. A wife's "first study," she claims, "must be self-control, almost to hypocrisy." In addition to these two novels and a third, *Love's Progress* (1840), Gilman published numerous volumes of poetry and stories, a woman's almanac, and—of special value to students of southern literature and culture—she edited collections of the letters of Eliza Lucas Pinckney, a young woman who ran a South Carolina plantation during the mid-1700s, and Eliza Wilkinson, whose letters record the experience of the Revolutionary War in South Carolina.

Criticism of marriage is less subtle in the stories and novels of Susan Petigru King Bowen (1824–1875) of Charleston, South Carolina. Admired by William Thackeray, Bowen's fiction is noted for its representation of antebellum southern manners, witty dialogue, and psychological portraits of women imprisoned by marriage. Included in her first short-story collection, *Busy Moments of an Idle Woman* (1854), is "Old Maidism Versus Marriage," about a group of young women who agree to meet after ten years to tell the truth about matrimony. Their "truths" all speak of women's disillusionment after marriage. The heroine of her 1855 novel *Lily* suffers through marriage to a promiscuous man with a murderous mistress. Anna, from one of the stories in *Sylvia's World; and, Crimes Which the Law Does Not Reach* (1859), is forced into marriage with a man she detests, whereas the title character of *Gerald Grey's Wife* (1864) is married to a fortune hunter.

Maria Jane McIntosh (1803–1878), one of the most popular novelists of the midcentury, began life as the daughter of a wealthy Georgia plantation owner. After the death of her widowed mother, McIntosh ran the plantation for twelve years, until she sold it and moved to New York to live with her half-brother. In the Panic of 1837, she lost everything and turned to writing to support herself. Her fiction, though marred by awkward, formulaic dialogue, is characterized by well-developed, complex plots and significant psychological development of female protagonists who face the need to negotiate between the dangers of over-dependence and over-independence. *Woman an Enigma* (1843), McIntosh's first novel for women, tells the story of Louise de la Valiere who, before she can win the love of Montreval, must learn to develop her true nature rather than trying to become the woman she thinks he wants. Her two most popular novels, *Two Lives; or, To Seem and To Be* (1846) and *Charms and Counter-Charms* (1848), develop a similar theme through pairs of contrasting heroines; in each case, appropriate independence and a life lived in accordance with inner values rather than outward fashion are represented as the ideal for women. Her 1850 work of nonfiction, *Woman in America: Her Work and Her Reward,* extends the values presented in her fiction to a study of the role of women and the domestic sphere in shaping the national character and mission of the country. In *The Lofty and the Lowly; or, Good in All and None All-Good,* her literary reply to Stowe's *Uncle Tom's Cabin,* McIntosh describes her desire "to remove some of the prejudices separating the North and South United States by a true and loving portraiture of the social characteristics of each."

Emma Dorothy Eliza Nevitte Southworth (1819–1899), known by her initials as E. D. E. N. Southworth, one of the most prolific and financially successful writers of the nineteenth century, wrote approximately fifty novels between 1849 and 1894. Southworth was born in Washington, D.C., and most of her fiction is set in Virginia and Maryland. In 1840, she married Frederick Hamilton Southworth and moved with him to Wisconsin. She returned to Washington without him four years later and began writing as a means of augmenting her teacher's salary. Southworth's first novel, *Retribution* (1849), was serialized in the *Washington National Era,* where its success led to its publication in book form. Many of her later works were also serialized in the *National Era* and others in the *Saturday Evening Post.* In 1857 she signed an exclusive contract for serialization of her work with Robert Bonner of the *New York Ledger,* but she retained the copyright for book publication of her fiction, which significantly increased her financial gain from each work. Historians

estimate that in later years she earned somewhere between $4,000 and $6,000 a year for her fiction.

Energetic and often humorous, Southworth's novels incorporate elements of melodrama and gothic into formulaic sentimental plots in which a strong, resourceful, noble female protagonist reforms a weak, proud, philandering, or domineering lover or husband and thus restores order to the domestic sphere. Several of her heroines challenge the era's conventions for feminine behavior. In her most popular novel, *The Hidden Hand* (1859), Capitola Black, who is dressed as a boy when the reader first meets her, explains, "While all the ragged boys I knew could get little jobs to earn bread, I, because I was a girl, was not allowed to carry a gentleman's parcel . . . or do *anything* that *I* could do just as well as *they.*" Later she announces, "I *will* be a hero."

Unlike many of her peers, Southworth was openly antislavery and even became close friends with Harriet Beecher Stowe. Her fictional representations of African Americans do not follow the stereotypes of childlike irresponsibility and rebellion or craven devotion to white masters found in the work of writers committed to supporting the southern system. Her ninth novel, *India* (1853), begins with the hero impoverishing himself and losing his standing in his community by freeing his slaves, and ends in the democratic West where he and his wife are starting a new life together. In *Shannondale* (1850), the southern patriarch is represented not in the paternalistic terms of Gilman's *Recollections* but as corrupted by the power he wields over others.

Caroline Lee Hentz (1800–1856) became a staunch supporter of the southern system of slavery although she did not move from her home in New England to the South until after her 1824 marriage to Nicholas Marcellus Hentz. From 1826 to 1830, he was a professor of modern languages at the University of North Carolina. In addition to North Carolina, Hentz lived in Kentucky, Alabama, and Georgia, as her husband moved from one teaching position to another in the 1830s and 1840s. Hentz began her writing career during these decades, publishing a successful five-act tragedy, *De Lara; or, The Moorish Bride* (1843), and two collections of short stories, *Aunt Patty's Scrap Bag* (1846) and *The Mob Cap* (1848). In 1849 her husband's health failed and Hentz began writing in earnest to support her family. Her first novel, *Linda; or, The Young Pilot of the Belle Creole,* appeared in 1850. Hentz's novels are generally didactic, warning against the dangers of uncontrolled passion and Byronic romanticism. She often contrasts an open, honest heroine with a deceptive, designing female antagonist. In both her first novel and *Eoline; or Magnolia Vale* (1852), one of her most popular works, she opposes forced marriages. Several of Hentz's novels include positive portraits of single women, unusual in fiction of the time. Aunt Debby of *Rena, the Snowbird* (1850), Miss Manly of *Eoline*, and Aunt Thusa of *Helen and Arthur* (1853) are presented as original, independent, intelligent, and imaginative, even though they clearly do not represent a viable role model for the heroines of those novels.

Hentz is best known today for *The Planter's Northern Bride* (1854), which she wrote in response to Stowe's *Uncle Tom's Cabin*. Hentz uses the marriage between Moreland, the southern planter, and Eulalia, daughter of a New England abolitionist, to represent a union of North and South, as the northern bride learns to love the South and see the well-run plantation as the epitome of the domestic ideal. Slaves are represented as cheerful, loyal, and pampered in comparison to northern laborers, but also as childish and easily deceived by abolitionists, who are portrayed as distorting truth and sacrificing national peace in order to satisfy their rigid ideology.

Before Marion Harland's heroines achieve their happy ending of marriage, they must endure disappointment and disillusionment and learn to live alone. Harland is the pseudonym under which Mary Virginia Terhune (1830–1922) of Virginia published her novels. Her first novel, *Alone* (1854), was her most successful. Its heroine, Ida Ross, suffers disappointment when the man she loves announces his engagement to another woman. Only after Ida returns to the neglected plantation of her childhood and restores its fertility and its social order is she rewarded with marriage. Likewise, the two heroines of *The Hidden Path* (1855) must develop independence and careers—writing and teaching—before they marry. The stories in her collection *Husbands and Homes* (1864) suggest the dangers and misery that await women who marry too soon and without the sort of independence and inner strength represented by the heroines of her novels. In later years, Harland turned her attention from fiction to writing books of practical household advice. *Common Sense in the Household* (1871) was the first of twenty-five such books.

Placed next to a heroine from a novel by Augusta Jane Evans (1835–1909), a Hentz or Harland heroine would appear downright anemic. Evans's are among the most energetic, passionate, proud, independent, and dramatic heroines found in sentimental fiction, and Evans's novels were among the best selling of the nineteenth century. Evans was born in Georgia, the oldest of eight children, and her father was bankrupt by the time she was ten. She began writing to restore the family fortunes and succeeded with her second novel, *Beulah* (1859), which sold over 22,000 copies in its first year and had its name adopted by Camp Beulah during the Civil War. The title character has been compared by several critics to Jane Eyre because of the "ugly" orphan's willful independence and the novel's treatment of religious doubt. Before she can agree to marriage with her guardian Hartwell, Beulah must establish her economic and emotional independence through becoming a successful writer. An avowed supporter of the Confederacy, in 1864 Evans published *Macaria; or, Altars of Sacrifice*, a story of southern women's heroism during the war. *Macaria* was popular not only in the South; after it was smuggled through the blockade, it was so popular in the North that Union troops were forbidden to read it.

Evans's popular *St. Elmo* (1866) was one of the best-selling novels of the nineteenth century. Its heroine, Edna Earle, is, like Beulah, orphaned early in the novel and every bit as proud and independent as her precursor. Refusing to marry and reform the Byronic St. Elmo, Edna Earle goes off to New York City to become a writer, publishing two successful didactic novels. Only when St. Elmo proves, by becoming a minister, that he has reformed himself does Edna Earle agree to marry him. *St. Elmo* was a standard text on southern women's book shelves well into the twentieth century, so popular that nearly one hundred years later Eudora Welty named the talkative protagonist of *The Ponder Heart* after Evans's heroine.

By the mid-1870s, local-color writing had replaced the domestic or sentimental novel in popularity, and southern women made the most of this postbellum literary trend. Although local-color writing was a national trend, northern and eastern readers seemed particularly interested in stories about the South, especially about remote, isolated, or romanticized areas such as the Appalachian mountains and the bayous of Louisiana. Sarah Barnwell Elliott (1848–1928) turned her attention to the South's mountain culture in her popular novel *Jerry* (1891), which chronicles the development of a poor white boy from the Tennessee mountains. *The Durket Sperret* (1898) is also noted for its comic treatment of isolated mountain cultures. In some of her short stories such as those in *An Incident and Other Happenings* (1899), Elliott addresses the controversial issue of racial conflict.

Writing for eight years under the pen name Charles Egbert Craddock, Mary Noailles Murfree (1850–1922) was perhaps the most successful of those local-colorists who chose the mountains as their subject. Descended from pioneer families who gave their name to the towns of Murfreesboro in Tennessee and North Carolina, Murfree grew up in Tennessee and spent her summers in the Cumberland Mountains. Her first significant local-color story, "The Dancin' Party at Harrison's Cove," was published by the *Atlantic Monthly* in 1878. She went on to publish her stories in *Harper's Monthly, Lippincott's, Century,* and elsewhere. Although she published twenty-five books in the course of her career, her first collection of short stories, *In the Tennessee Mountains* (1884), is considered her best. Despite a tendency to repeat character types and plots, her writing is known for its fine use of dialect, detailed description of mountain landscapes, and careful observation of isolated mountain culture. *The Prophet of the Great Smoky Mountains* (1885) and *In the "Stranger People's" Country* (1891) are considered her best novels.

Because of its complex mix of races, ethnicities, and social classes, its exotic French culture, and its melodramatic history, Louisiana, and especially New Orleans, was a setting with tremendous popular appeal to the American reading population. Alice Dunbar-Nelson (1875–1935) was born to a middle-class New Orleans family that was descended from the city's substantial prewar community of free African Americans. Dunbar-Nelson's early writing seems curiously separate from her later political activism. In the twentieth century, she helped found the Industrial School for Colored Girls, was active in suffrage groups, and held political office. But in her two early collections of stories, *Violets and Other Tales* (1895) and *The Goodness of St. Rocque and Other Stories* (1899), she focuses on the theme of romantic love in the lives of mostly white Creole characters.

Born in Louisiana and raised in New Orleans, Ruth McEnery (1849–1917) married Alfred Oden Stuart, an Arkansas cotton planter, in 1879 but returned to New Orleans after his death four years later. Her career writing highly popular dialect stories began in 1888 with the publication of "Uncle Mingo's Speculatioms" and "Lamentations of Jeremiah Johnson" in *Harper's Monthly*. These two stories are characteristic of her fiction about African American characters, which relies on sentimental, domestic caricatures and themes of courtship and marriage rather than engaging the more volatile racial realities of the postwar South. In addition to her African American stories collected in *A Golden Wedding and Other Tales* (1893) and *Moriah's Mourning and Other Half-Hour Sketches* (1898), Stuart also wrote about white farmers in a fictional Arkansas town named Simpkinsville, in her best-selling work *Sonny* (1896) and her collection *In Simpkinsville: Character Tales* (1897).

In her *Memories of a Southern Woman of Letters* (1932), Grace King (c. 1851–1932) recalls the conversation with *Century* magazine editor Richard Watson Gilder that launched her career. King voiced her objection to George W. Cable: "He was a native of New Orleans and had been well treated by its people, and yet he stabbed the city in the back, as we felt, in a dastardly way to please the Northern press." Gilder's answer, "If Cable is so false to you, why do not some of you write better?" challenged King to write her first story, "Monsieur Motte" (1886). Monsieur Motte of the title is a fiction created by Marcelite, an African American hairdresser, who has supported a white girl, Marie Modeste, and paid for her schooling. Her fiction is revealed when Monsieur Motte fails to show up for Marie Modeste's graduation. Central to the story and to much of King's fiction is the close but complicated relationship between African American and white women in the postwar South as well as the difference between appearance and reality to which the title alludes. The story was so popular that the editor asked King to continue the story of Marie Modeste; the novel *Monsieur Motte* appeared in 1888.

Born and raised in New Orleans, King presents herself in her autobiographical *Memories* as a southern lady committed to defending the South. Her fictional treatment of the South is, however, far more complex than her autobiographical statements. Her short stories explore the experiences of women, both black and white, and look for connections between black and white cultures. Her first collection of stories, *Tales of a Time and Place*, includes "Bayou L'Ombre," the story of three sisters on an isolated plantation who dream of fighting for the Confederacy. *Balcony Stories* (1893), King's most popular collection (republished in 1914 and in 1925), includes "The Little Convent Girl," a complex study of race, determination, and despair.

After *Balcony Stories*, King turned her attention to writing historical studies of the South, including a biography of Jean Baptiste le Moyne, Sieur de Bienville (1892), *A History of Louisiana* (1893), and *New Orleans: The Place and the People* (1895). King continued writing well into the twentieth century, returning to fiction to produce her most successful novel, *The Pleasant Ways of St. Medard,* in 1916.

Kate Chopin (1851–1904) was born and lived in St. Louis until she married Oscar Chopin of New Orleans in 1870. The Chopins lived in New Orleans until his business failed in 1879 and they moved to Cloutierville in Natchitoches Parish. Four years later, in 1883, Oscar died of swamp fever, leaving Kate with six children. After managing his business affairs for a year, she returned to St. Louis with her children. When her mother died in 1885, Chopin turned to writing to assuage her grief. She published her first two stories, influenced by the work of Guy de Maupassant, in 1889. In "Wiser than a God," Paula Von Stolz chooses to pursue a career in music rather than marrying; "A Point at Issue" tells the story of an unconventional marriage. Both stories anticipate Chopin's concern about marriage's effect on a woman's development that she would explore in her mature fiction.

Chopin's departure from conventional expectations for women's fiction, which led to the critical and popular condemnation of her best work, *The Awakening,* can be seen in her first novel, *At Fault* (1890), which portrays an alcoholic woman and refuses to condemn divorce. Her two collections of short stories, *Bayou Folk* (1894) and *A Night in Acadie* (1897), demonstrate her willingness to explore controversial issues, such as miscegenation and the tragic results of social attitudes toward race in "Désirée's Baby," and the strength of female sexual passion in "A Respectable Woman."

When *The Awakening* appeared in 1899, it was greeted by a critical storm condemning it as "vulgar," "unhealthy," "immoral," and "sordid," and then neglected until the development of women's studies in the 1960s revived critical and popular interest in the novel. The novel tells the story of Edna Pontellier's search for personal fulfillment that takes her outside the bounds of her safe, dull marriage. She leaves her husband and children, takes a lover, tries to realize herself through art, and finally commits suicide as she sees her possibilities closed in by social constraints. Readers were so outraged by Chopin's apparent sympathy with Edna's adultery, sexuality, and abandonment of her children that the novel was banned by St. Louis libraries. The public outcry over *The Awakening* did not silence

Chopin, but it did diminish her publication. Although she wrote nine stories after 1899, only three were published in her lifetime. Unlike Grace King, whose work was appreciated by her contemporaries and has been largely ignored in recent years, Chopin's work had to wait for a number of social changes to take place before it could find appreciative audiences.

Like New Orleans, Richmond, Virginia, was the center of literary activity during the last years of the nineteenth century, but local color was not the predominant genre of Amélie Rives, Mary Johnston, or Ellen Glasgow. Toward the end of the century, the taste for local color gave way to historical fiction and psychological realism, and these writers, along with Kate Chopin, look toward the literary trends of the next century; two of them, Mary Johnston and Ellen Glasgow, wrote their best and most influential fiction in the twentieth century.

Amélie Rives (Princess Troubetzkoy) (1863–1945), born in Richmond and raised on the family estate in Albemarle County, published her first story, "A Brother to Dragons," in the *Atlantic Monthly* in 1886. Like most of the other stories collected in *A Brother to Dragons and Other Old-Time Tales* (1888), it is a tale of romance and adventure. But it is the psychological realism and treatment of the relationship between past and present that make her novel *The Quick or the Dead* (1888) of particular interest to students of southern literature. Rives's novel features a heroine who chooses the past, represented by her dead husband, over the present, represented by his living cousin.

Author of twenty-three novels and thirty-eight stories, Mary Johnston completed only two of her longer works before the turn of the century. *Prisoners of Hope* (1898), the first of her historical novels, is set in colonial Virginia and features as its protagonist an indentured servant. Her second novel, *To Have and to Hold* (1900), was a tremendous success, selling over half a million copies and becoming the subject of two movies. It tells the story of the first group of European women to arrive in the American South, a group of "brides" sent by the London Company to the men of the Jamestown colony. Several of Johnston's twentieth-century novels are set during the Civil War and, as Anne Goodwyn Jones demonstrates in *Tomorrow Is Another Day* (1981), influenced Margaret Mitchell's writing of *Gone With the Wind.*

Ellen Glasgow (1873–1945) is the most important of these three Richmond writers. Born in Richmond, the eighth of ten children, Glasgow's life was marked by tragedy. Her beloved mother died when Ellen was twenty; her stern, Calvinistic father lived to be eighty-six. One sister died of cancer. Her brother and brother-in-law committed suicide; Glasgow attempted suicide once. In her later, most successful fiction, Glasgow creates female protagonists who overcome tragedy and adversity to achieve meaning in their daily lives. Influenced by Darwin and Nietzsche, Glasgow writes about all levels of southern culture in her attempt to resist the idealism and romanticism of the turn-of-the-century South. Her first two heroines, Rachel Gavin of *The Descendant* (1897) and Mariana Musin of *Phases of an Inferior Planet* (1898), seek fulfillment through artistic careers. The novels, both set in New York City, dramatize the heroines' difficulties in trying to break with the southern expectations for women. They do not succeed as fully as the women in her later fiction, but these novels introduce one of Glasgow's important themes, a woman's conflict over career and marriage.

In her third novel, *The Voice of the People* (1900), Glasgow brought her southern characters back to the South and discovered the South itself as her subject. Although *Voice* is not as successful a novel as her first two, it marked her discovery of her richest subject matter, her love for and struggle against the aristocratic idealism of the southern past. This theme, when considered through the perspective of a female protagonist, would lead to her best work in the twentieth century.

Between the years of 1820 and 1900, women's writing in the South developed dramatically, from primarily personal writing—letters and diaries—that was later published because of its local or historical interest, to the art of Kate Chopin and Ellen Glasgow, whose work expanded the shape and expressiveness of the novel. The turn of the century did not mark a break in the literary traditions started by southern women in the nineteenth century; we can see the influence not only of Chopin and Glasgow, but of Southworth, Harper, Evans, King, and others, in the fiction of more recent and familiar writers such as Margaret Mitchell, Eudora Welty, Katherine Anne Porter, and Alice Walker.

Suzan Harrison

See also African American Literature, Beginnings to 1919; Diaries, Women's; Domestic Novel; Local Color; Novel, 1820 to 1865; Novel, 1865 to 1900; Romance Genre; Women Writers, Beginnings to 1820; Women Writers, 1900 to World War II.

Nina Baym, *Woman's Fiction: A Guide to Novels By and About Women in America, 1820–1870* (1978); Dorothy H. Brown and Barbara C. Ewell, eds., *Louisiana Women Writers* (1992); Anne Goodwyn Jones, *Tomorrow Is Another Day: The Woman Writer in the South, 1859–1936* (1981); Elizabeth Moss, *Domestic Novelists in the Old South: Defenders of Southern Culture* (1992); Mary Louise Weaks and Carolyn Perry, eds., *Southern Women's Writing, Colonial to Contemporary* (1995).

WOMEN WRITERS, 1900 TO WORLD WAR II

The Southern Renascence—that is, the period of literary revival in the modern South—has traditionally been identified as beginning in 1920 with the Fugitive poets in Nashville and ending with World War II. Increasingly, though, scholars of southern women's writing have argued that the Renascence actually began closer to the turn of the century, and not with the South's men but with its women. Perhaps the best-known explanation for the beginning of the Renascence came from Allen Tate, one of the Fugitive poets. "With the war of 1914–1918," Tate said, "the South reentered the world—but gave a backward glance as it stepped over the border: that backward glance gave us the Southern renascence, a literature conscious of the past in the present." Tate's definition suggests that it was, in part, an international war that helped spawn the Renascence because southern men were for the first time leaving the South in large numbers to fight a war for an American cause rather than a southern one. Southern men were seeing themselves as American rather than as principally southern. Southern women, however, faced such identity crises several decades before World War I as the ideal of what a woman was to be—the fragile southern lady—gradually became a part of the past. Granted, women's roles were changing more rapidly in other parts of the country than in the South as the New Woman took a stand for woman's suffrage and for work opportunities; in fact, however, the myth of the southern lady still remains an ideal today. But in the latter part of the nineteenth century, southern women faced changes in a culture that had long depended upon the myth of the southern lady to help mask the failures of southern slave culture.

Correspondingly, then, male- and female-authored texts of the Southern Renascence tend to differ in the approach that their authors take to the southern past. Male-authored texts are generally defined by the loss of tradition and the collapse of a patriarchal slave culture—in other words, the struggle to regain what was believed lost. The Agrarians' *I'll Take My Stand* (1930) is a classic example of male authors arguing for a return to old values, old traditions, all that was supposed best in the agrarian communities of the Old South. Perhaps because the differences between male- and female-authored texts are only now being recognized, southern scholar Richard King, in one of the most frequently referenced books about the period entitled *A Southern Renaissance* (1980), discusses the work of only one woman, Lillian Smith. King says that other women writers of the Renascence were "not concerned primarily with the larger cultural, racial and political themes" of white male authors, and "they did not place the region at the center of their imaginative visions." More recently, however, scholars have come to recognize that women's writings of the Renascence can often be identified by the authors' attention to women's struggles to define self, to develop new voices, and to break free of tradition. In their writings, these southern women wrestled with the ideal of southern womanhood and with the complex relationship between women and men. So, too, do many women's writings of the Renascence reflect a character's desire to flee a patriarchal culture to attain individualism, identity, wholeness. For these reasons, scholars have increasingly called for the dates of the Southern Renascence to be extended to take account of women writers who were addressing these issues long before World War I, to include the late work of Kate Chopin and the early work of Ellen Glasgow. Thus, the dates 1900 through World War II are particularly appropriate for examining the flowering of women's writing in the South.

The changes in women's lives in the postbellum years, including their greater responsibility for providing for families devastated by war, greatly influenced the creation of a new women's literature in the South at the turn of the century. Not until the 1890s did white southern women begin, to any significant degree, to take issue with the ways in which southern culture and the southern past had shaped their lives. Grace King and Kate Chopin, for instance, examined the implications of women's changing role in southern society and of women's desire to see changes take place. In King's stories, male characters frequently suffer from debilitating illness, abandon their women, or die untimely deaths. According to King, in the postbellum period the South was moving toward a matriarchy, away from the patriarchal culture of the antebellum years. The most pivotal work of the period, however, is Kate

Chopin's *The Awakening* (1899), which ushered in a new movement in women's writing in the South. Harshly criticized even by Willa Cather and other women writers, Chopin's novel examines the only societal roles that a southern woman was expected to fulfill: wife and mother. She was to be a "mother-woman," a woman who had the sheltering arms of an angel, who cared far less for herself than she did for her husband's and children's well-being. For the first time, a major southern woman writer set a character to face a southern establishment as she attempted to redefine southern womanhood for herself.

Certainly, though, it was with the Richmond, Virginia, writers, including in particular Mary Johnston, Amélie Rives, James Branch Cabell, and Ellen Glasgow, that southern writers first began writing fiction that was representative of the twentieth century rather than of nineteenth-century Victorian social standards and literary aesthetics. Ellen Glasgow (1873–1945) is generally recognized as a pioneering voice of modernism in the South, as the most important southern writer in the first two decades of the twentieth century. Her work sharply departs from the romanticism of the Victorian South to embrace a realism that clearly places her among the modernists, and her writings represent a thorough examination of the strengths of southern women and their ability to create and to sustain new versions of womanhood. Much in agreement with Glasgow's perspective on womanhood was Glasgow's friend and fellow Virginian Mary Johnston (1870–1936), who published her first popular novel, *To Have and To Hold,* in 1900. Whereas this historical novel about the "bartered brides" of the Jamestown colony suggests the continuing influence of the image of the southern belle in turn-of-the-century writings, Johnston's 1913 novel *Hagar* points to Johnston's evolution as a feminist writer. The story of a girl's maturation into womanhood, the book in many ways echoes the plot and imagery of Chopin's *The Awakening,* although Johnston's heroine does not commit suicide. *Hagar* has been sharply criticized for being a feminist novel and, as some critics have put it, merely a suffrage tract. Clearly, Johnston's work for the suffrage movement in Virginia influenced not only her composition of the text but also the reception that her book received. Glasgow and Johnston were also prominent figures in the Virginia Writers' Club that was founded in 1918. Out of this literary movement in Richmond came *The Reviewer,* one of the South's first "little" magazines. The magazine began publication in 1921 and published works by writers such as Glasgow, Frances Newman, Julia Peterkin, Allen Tate, DuBose Heyward, and Paul Green. Edited by Virginian Emily Clark, the magazine was an important showcase for southern writers but also published works by many of the leading American authors of the day.

Glasgow early addressed the issue that would be at the focal point of her fiction, that is, woman's struggle to move out from the boundaries that southern culture had long prescribed for southern women. Glasgow's two earliest novels, *The Descendant* (1897) and *Phases of an Inferior Planet* (1898), concern southern women living in New York, one studying painting and the other singing, both seeking fulfillment in their artistic endeavors in clear attempts to escape southern patriarchal society. Glasgow addresses similar issues in *Virginia* (1913) and *Life and Gabriella* (1916), which Glasgow called companion studies. A commentary on the traditional roles of women in southern culture, *Virginia* is a portrait of Virginia Pendleton, who discovers, at age forty, that her life has been defined by her devotion to her husband and children. Glasgow's *Life and Gabriella* suggests the possibilities of a southern woman managing to remain a lady while making her own choices about her life and thus, to some degree, achieving a self-made happiness. After her marriage to the handsome New Yorker George Fowler fails, Gabriella goes to work to support her children and parents-in-law and ultimately finds success as a designer in New York. When Ben O'Hara, a sort of Horatio Alger character who has made his money in the railroad business, proposes marriage to her, she accepts, but in doing so, she sacrifices much of what she has achieved. The book is typically read as Glasgow's realistic portrait of a woman's struggle for independence, the limitations that even the successful career woman must face, and the possibility of a woman's choosing the path for her life. Two phrases that appear in *Life and Gabriella*, "vein of iron" and "sheltered life," encapsulate themes that Glasgow addresses in her later fiction and are titles of two of her novels. In *The Sheltered Life* (1932), Jenny Blair is raised within an insular southern environment. Eva Birdsong, who was raised in the same way, tells Jenny that she is "worn out with being somebody else—with being someone's ideal." While some of Glasgow's women lead lives sheltered by their southern families, other of her women—for example, Dorinda Oakley and Ada Fincastle—inherit a "vein of iron" that sustains them in building lives of purpose and commitment to land and to family.

It is in Glasgow's Virginia novels that her awareness of the nature of southern patriarchy is fully realized. In *The Deliverance* (1904), *The Romance of a Plain Man* (1909), and *The Miller of Old Church* (1911), Glasgow gives a realistic portrait of Virginia life that encompasses not only the lives of Virginia aristocrats but also the lives of poor whites and yeoman farmers. In *The Battle-Ground* (1902), *Barren Ground* (1925), and *Vein of Iron* (1935), Glasgow most fully explores the relationship between the southern woman and her culture. Scholars have increasingly pointed to matriarchal patterns in Glasgow's novels, patterns that link women in structures of support that ultimately help them in redefining their lives and purposes. In Glasgow's Civil War novel *The Battle-Ground,* for example, Betty is left on the home front to protect, care for, and run the family plantations; ultimately, the Civil War itself frees Betty from the strictures of patriarchal-based images of southern womanhood. The end of the novel offers distinct possibilities for change in women's lives, for as Dan returns to find his ancestral home burned to the ground, Betty says to him, "We will begin again, and this time, my dear, we will begin together." In *Barren Ground*, Glasgow reaffirms a woman's capacity to care for the southern land, a land that has long been represented as feminine in the literature of the South. Now "barren ground," the Virginia soil no longer can produce tobacco and corn, but only scrub brush and pine. The novel revolves around the Oakleys, a family of farmers who own their own land, and, more particularly, around Dorinda, who struggles with her family's poverty. Paralleling Dorinda's cultivation of the land with her cultivation of her soul, the novel concerns her efforts to revitalize both. Ultimately, the book closes with self-affirmation as Dorinda not only survives but triumphs—yet that triumph comes at great cost to her as a woman. Notably, it is with *Vein of Iron* (1935) that Glasgow achieves a sense of closure in her portraits of southern women who contain a "vein of iron." Set partially in Depression-era Richmond, the novel takes as its primary setting the Great Valley of Virginia and focuses on the relationships among Ada Fincastle, her father, and her father's mother. As a means of more tightly connecting herself to her family past, Ada hopes to restore the family homestead and to plant a garden in the familial soil. In achieving this restoration to the earth, Ada taps into her own creativity, inherited through a long familial line of attachment to the soil. Through Ada, Glasgow was redefining southern womanhood.

In 1926, a writer for the *Saturday Review* wrote in reference to Glasgow and fellow southern writer Frances Newman that "the South must begin to realize that its only salvation lies in taking the girl babies of good family who look as if they might have brains, and drowning them as soon as possible after birth." Newman's novels met with greater criticism than Glasgow's ever received. Named by H. L. Mencken as one of his "violets of the Sahara," Frances Newman (1883–1928) was close friends with James Branch Cabell and Mencken. Newman was particularly interested in avant-garde writers (Virginia Woolf's influence on her is strong) and experimented with form in her own work. Published during a decade of increasing sexual freedom for women, Newman's two novels are explicit representations of women's sexuality and the obstacles to expression faced by southern white women. Banned in Boston, *The Hard-Boiled Virgin* traces the life of Katherine Faraday from childhood to her mid-thirties. A member of a large Atlanta family, Katherine nevertheless feels isolated. As a girl, she spends her time sitting in her father's chair in the library, reading. While Katherine's older sister is the belle of the family, Katherine has to be sent to boarding school to learn to be a southern belle. The book focuses on Katherine's virginity and her perceptions of sexuality. She learns about human sexuality primarily through reading fiction, which ultimately leads her to create her own fantasies about lovemaking. Highly experimental in form, the novel is divided into numerous short chapters and includes no dialogue. Newman's other novel, *Dead Lovers Are Faithful Lovers*, is the story of two women whom Newman described as "so idiotically in love with a man." While the wife believes she can keep her husband with her beauty, the other woman believes she can tempt him away with her intelligence. Newman evidently wishes to examine here a culture that created two women who both love and fight for the same man yet appear to be respectable ladies.

Fiction was the most popular genre for southern women writers of the Renascence, yet Elizabeth Madox Roberts and Evelyn Scott, popular writers of the 1920s and 1930s, both began their careers by publishing a collection of poems. Although the Fugitives in Nashville have long overshadowed other 1920s poets, the poet Beatrice Ravenel (1870–1956) deserves more critical attention than she has previously received. Ravenel was a member of the Poetry Society of South Carolina, and by the 1920s, her poetry was as sophisticated as that written by the best of southern poets,

including the Fugitives. Like her colleagues in the Poetry Society, Ravenel was, in her early writing career, a regional writer who wrote about a specific locale, the Carolina low country. But as Louis D. Rubin explains in his introduction to Ravenel's collected poems, *The Yemassee Lands: Poems of Beatrice Ravenel* (1969), after she began reading the works of Amy Lowell, the Imagists, and other modern writers, "almost overnight she put aside the sentimental ideality of the poetry of the waning genteel tradition . . . and began writing in free verse, with notable economy of diction, a sharp precision of language, and vivid, evocative imagery."

The 1920s saw, too, the publication of the first southern novel to receive the Pulitzer Prize in fiction, *Scarlet Sister Mary* (1928) by Julia Peterkin (1880–1961). After Peterkin married, she moved to her husband's family plantation, called Lang Syne, where five hundred blacks and five whites lived. The stories and novels she wrote there about the Gullah people of South Carolina were highly praised by H. L. Mencken and black writers such as W. E. B. Du Bois, James Weldon Johnson, and Sterling A. Brown. Du Bois applauded her first short-story collection, *Green Thursday* (1924), saying she had "the eye and the ear to see beauty and know truth." Both black and white reviewers warily admitted that they could not identify the author of *Green Thursday* as black or white. Peterkin quickly became known as an expert on African American life. In 1927, Peterkin told a journalist that she would "never [again] write of white people," and she didn't. That same year, she published her novel *Black April*, which became a best-seller. Proclaimed "the first genuine novel in English of the Negro as a human being," the novel challenged racial stereotypes that had long been a fixture in southern literature. Peterkin's next novel, *Scarlet Sister Mary*, clearly marked her attempt to portray the sexual independence of a woman, yet not even the 1920s, the era of the flapper and of seeming sexual freedoms for women, could look favorably upon Mary Pinesett, who takes a number of lovers. Mary is interested in pleasing herself. She is not afraid to speak her mind and is clearly an independent woman. The book received the Pulitzer Prize in fiction, but the selection committee had to change the rules in order to choose the book; Joseph Pulitzer had stated that the winner of the prize should portray the "wholesome best of American manhood." After *Scarlet Sister Mary*, Peterkin published *Bright Skin* (1932) and *Roll, Jordan, Roll* (1933), a work that included both her fiction and nonfiction and a collection of photographs by her friend Doris Ulmann. Despite the high acclaim that Peterkin received for her writings in the 1920s and early 1930s, they fell out of favor soon after. Most probably, readers lost interest in her work because in the last years of her writing career, she increasingly wrote portraits of African Americans that were sentimental. With her last book, *Roll, Jordan, Roll,* Peterkin's abilities as a writer were fading. She had slipped into a sentimentality that was at odds with the Depression. Recent criticism of her work suggests that her motivation for creating black characters instead of white ones was actually a personal one. By taking the point of view of the African American, Peterkin could at once shock the white establishment in the South, including her own family, and address issues that she faced in her own life.

Although Peterkin received more widespread praise for her portraits of African Americans than did African American writers of the time, the 1920s was an important period of literary revival for African American writers in the South. Sometimes called the New Negro Renaissance rather than the Harlem Renaissance, this period of literary revival was not limited solely to those writers who gathered in Harlem. Two writers—Georgia Douglas Johnson (1886–1966) and Anne Spencer (1882–1975)—took part in the New Negro Renaissance from their homes far from Harlem: Johnson in Washington, D.C., and Spencer in Lynchburg, Virginia. Born in Atlanta, Johnson wrote plays, poetry, and short stories. She lived most of her life in Washington, where she established a literary salon in her home that became a gathering place for a number of writers of the New Negro Renaissance. The first African American poet after Frances E. W. Harper to receive national recognition, Johnson frequently wrote in her poetry and drama about the estrangement felt by persons of mixed blood and the aims of integration in the United States. She also examined the nature of womanhood in two collections of her poems, *The Heart of a Woman* (1918) and *Bronze* (1922). Although Spencer's work did not receive as widespread acclaim as Johnson's, Spencer's poems appeared in almost every major anthology of poetry by African Americans published during the Renaissance. Although Spencer helped found an NAACP chapter in Lynchburg in 1918, she rarely used racial themes in her poetry. She did, however, take up women's issues in at least one poem, "Letter to My Sister," where she explains that "it is dangerous for a woman to defy the gods." In her poetry, Spencer often wrote about a world of love and beauty replacing a world of hatred and ugliness.

Arguably the most enduring voice of the New Negro Renaissance was that of Zora Neale Hurston. Born in the all-black town of Eatonville, Florida, the daughter of the town's mayor, Hurston (1891–1960) wrote later in her life that she grew up unaware of the oppression that most other southern black children experienced in the turn-of-the-century South. Criticized at times because she did not write protest novels about the oppression of African Americans in the South, Hurston wrote in her 1928 essay "How It Feels To Be Colored Me," "I am not tragically colored. There is no great sorrow dammed up in my soul. . . . I do not belong to the sobbing school of Negrohood." The New Negro Renaissance greatly interested Hurston because instead of presenting African Americans solely as victims of racial prejudice, it celebrated the wealth and energy of black culture. Hurston's interest in the Renaissance led, too, to her collaboration with Langston Hughes, another important figure of the Renaissance and a fellow southerner, on *Mule Bones: A Comedy of Negro Life in Three Acts* (1931). However, the play was never produced. Trained at Howard and Columbia universities as an anthropologist, Hurston began collecting African American folklore on trips to Florida in the 1920s. In 1926, she published "The Eatonville Anthology" in the *Messenger*. A collection of stories about the folk of her Florida hometown, the "Anthology" is one of her most frequently anthologized pieces.

The largest body of Hurston's work was published in the 1930s. Her first novel, *Jonah's Gourd Vine* (1934), tells the story of the illiterate son of a slave who, through his determination, charisma, and verbal abilities—and the efforts of his wife—rises to the pulpit of the local Baptist church. He is also a philanderer, and after his wife dies, the members of the church turn against him. Based on the lives of Hurston's own parents, the novel, as Hurston's biographer Robert Hemenway has said, is "less a narrative than a series of linguistic movements representing folk-life of the black South." Two years after the publication of *Jonah's Gourd Vine,* Hurston published *Mules and Men* (1935), the first collection of African American folk stories compiled by an African American. Hurston became a character in the narrative of this book, in which she dramatized her return to the places she had known as a child in Florida. Hurston's best-known novel is *Their Eyes Were Watching God* (1937), a book that was out of print for nearly thirty years after its first publication but whose popularity was revived in the 1970s. The novel not only captures the African American folk experience but also portrays a black community and a woman's role within that community. *Their Eyes* is not centrally about racial conflict but about one woman's discovery of selfhood and her ability to make choices about her own life. Janie chooses to leave a loveless and unhappy marriage with Logan Killicks for the promise of a new life with Mayor Jody Starks. After Jody's death, she lives in the Everglades with Tea Cake in a communal setting within nature that renews the vitality that she first felt when she was coming into womanhood, discovering "kissing bees singing of the beginning of the world." Hurston's achievements are even more important because of the influence that her life and work has had on later African American writers such as Alice Walker, Toni Morrison, and Gloria Naylor. In Walker's collection of essays *In Search of Our Mothers' Gardens* (1983), Walker says of *Their Eyes Were Watching God*, "*There is no book more important to me than this one.*" The book represents for Walker what she sees as most characteristic of Hurston's fiction, that is, "racial health; a sense of black people as complete, complex, *undiminished* human beings."

Hurston's work as a chronicler of folk culture in the South is, indeed, quite representative of southern women's writing during the 1930s. This decade was the heart of the Renascence, the years when the best writers of the period reached maturity. Hurston and Florida writer Marjorie Kinnan Rawlings (1896–1953) attempted to record folk cultures that were quickly fading. Caroline Gordon, Elizabeth Madox Roberts, Evelyn Scott, and Margaret Mitchell wrote about the historical events of the southern past, placing women characters within the framework of southern history. Yet these writers saw themselves as chroniclers of a past that was in conflict with their present, whether because of the encroachment of an industrialized North or because of the changing roles of women. The Depression years, too, led to introspection for Americans as a whole, as history became a means of understanding the modern United States. Anne Goodwyn Jones says in *The History of Southern Literature* that men have traditionally held public roles in history and women have remained in the private realm; consequently, among popular fiction writers of the Southern Renascence, "in general, the men take history, and the women gender, as the means for their meditations on past and present." In fact, women's examinations of

gender reflect the South's relationship not only to the Civil War—the defining event of southern history—but also to the frontier history of the region.

Explorations of the South as frontier were more typically produced by writers from the Upper South of Tennessee and Kentucky, whose history solidly linked them to the pioneer South and to American frontier heroes such as Daniel Boone. In *Green Centuries* (1941), for example, Caroline Gordon creates a woman named Jocasta who is abandoned by husband Orion Outlaw because of his all-consuming desire to leave home in search of better lands westward in Kentucky. According to Gordon, the traditional frontier spirit, in effect, created men like Orion Outlaw who, consumed by their roles in history, forsake the private realm of family. Gordon's Jocasta is ultimately destroyed by her husband's lust for both land and another woman. Another Kentucky writer, Elizabeth Madox Roberts (1881–1941), portrays the strength and endurance of pioneer women in *The Time of Man* (1926) and *The Great Meadow* (1930). *The Time of Man* is the story of Ellen Chesser's struggles as wife and mother. In *The Great Meadow*, Diony Hall, a woman living during the Revolutionary War era, decides to leave her family farm for the frontier, finally overcoming the chaos that had overwhelmed her life. For both Gordon and Roberts, women suffer because of their gender, but whereas Gordon's women often fail, Roberts's heroines survive.

The most popular and enduring historical novel of the 1930s, however, is Margaret Mitchell's *Gone With the Wind* (1936), which sold one million copies in the first six months after its publication. Although the novel gives an essentially sympathetic look at the Old South and slavery, it has been read as a revision of the traditional domestic novel and of the southern pastoral. Focusing on woman as caretaker of the southern land, the book at once speculates on the possibilities yet clearly indicates the difficulties of this new role. Early in her life, Scarlett was instilled with a love of the land, a love for her Tara, by her father, who tells her that "land is the only thing in the world, that amounts to anything . . . for 'tis the only thing in the world that lasts." In assuming the role as caretaker of Tara following the Civil War, Scarlett inverts the traditional southern pastoral, for instead of remaining true to the chivalric code of the Old South that placed her, as belle, in a role of dependency, Scarlett becomes the New Woman of the South taking on a typically masculine role. Yet as scholars have noted, despite Scarlett's rebellious nature, Mitchell assigns to her story a pastoral framework that does not allow for Scarlett's growth. Scarlett's lumber business rapes the southern land, and Scarlett attempts to preserve rather than to reconfigure the traditional plantation system at Tara. Nevertheless, Mitchell's heroine is like many of Ellen Glasgow's women; she is an active participant in her world rather than a passive southern belle in need of care.

Twentieth-century women writers approached history through gender. Whereas Mitchell suggests that the Civil War was a liberating force for southern women like Scarlett, Caroline Gordon and Lillian Hellman (1905–1984) warn of potential destruction if people become consumed with personal needs rather than those of their families and communities. In her Civil War novel *None Shall Look Back* (1937), Gordon portrays the recently married Rives Allard as devoted to war rather than family. Rives embraces his mission as spy despite the fact that it keeps him from communicating with his wife, Lucy. Gordon's novel, like her other fiction, is a clear example of what Andrew Lytle described as one of her central themes: "Miss Gordon rarely departs . . . from the stress between the sexes." In literature of the modern South, this disintegration of familial bonds is a typical result of industrialization. In *The Little Foxes* (1939), playwright Lillian Hellman portrays the greedy Hubbard family, living in the turn-of-the-century Deep South, as consumed by their love of money. At the core of the conflict is the resentment between Regina and her brothers Ben and Oscar. Whereas the brothers inherited their father's fortune, Regina, as daughter, was left nothing. Regina had hopes of marrying into money, but her marriage to Horace has brought her only unhappiness because her husband will not fulfill her desire for material things. Horace will not invest money in a mill that her brothers hope to build, so they steal money from him, even though he has just returned from a hospital in Maryland. Ultimately, after Horace discovers the theft and tells Regina he plans to do nothing to get the money back, Regina causes him to suffer a heart attack. By the end of the play, the only hope is Regina's daughter Alexandra, who says that she must leave her family "because I know Papa would want me to."

For another southern woman writer of this period, Katherine Anne Porter, the matriarch is clearly the controlling force, the one who holds the family together. At the heart of "The Old Order" stories is the Grandmother, whom Porter (1890–1980) once called "a metaphor for Texas." A widow, Grandmother Sophia Jane is self-reliant, bold, strong, and energetic. Her charac-

ter is based on Porter's own Texas grandmother, who was a sort of surrogate mother to Porter after the death of her mother. The Grandmother, as the title of the story "The Source" suggests, is the "source" of strength for her family. In "The Journey," Porter shows both the close relationship between a black woman and a white woman—Sophia Jane and Nannie—and the Grandmother's fortitude and courage. Porter also examines the "old order" that led the Grandmother to hate men: "She could not help it, she despised men. She despised them and was ruled by them." The Grandmother points to the inadequacies she saw in her husband, his "lack of aim, failure to act at crises, a philosophic detachment from practical affairs." The Grandmother and Old Nannie, an ex-slave, agree that the southern myth of womanhood has only brought them unhappiness. Porter turns to the granddaughter Miranda in several of her stories, including "Old Mortality" and "Pale Horse, Pale Rider" (1938). Yet while Miranda, in "Old Mortality," inherits a vein of strength from the Grandmother, she prefers hearing stories about the now-dead belle Amy rather than about Cousin Eva, the feminist. In "Pale Horse, Pale Rider," Miranda is the rebel, the one who goes to work as a newspaper reporter. Ultimately, though, she recognizes the importance of blood, the power of family. Although Porter is perhaps best known for fiction set in Texas, she also wrote stories set in Mexico, including "St. Augustine and the Bullfight," "Flowering Judas," and "Hacienda," and one novel, *Ship of Fools* (1962), about her voyage from Mexico to Germany in 1931. She won the National Book Award and the Pulitzer Prize for her *Collected Stories* (1965).

In her work and life, Porter was clearly influenced by the ideal of the southern belle. Born in a log cabin to a farmer and his teacher wife in Indian Creek, Texas, and named Callie Russell, Porter renamed herself Katherine Anne. She told even her friends that she was raised on a plantation, in what she called "the 1852 style," inferring a grand home with servants, books, and fine china. Porter recreated herself in the image of the southern belle. She reveled in the fact that she became known as the grande dame of American letters, traveling in circles where she often befriended artists, writers, and even revolutionaries. Porter struggled with the conflict between the reality of her humble beginnings and her desire to be a part of the southern aristocracy. Although her Texas fiction portrays strong women characters, she consistently treated the struggles faced by southern women in a culture that privileged beauty and femininity in its women.

Perhaps the strongest voice demanding that women break free from the expectations of southern society was Evelyn Scott (1893–1963), who was also the most innovative stylist of the period. Born and raised in Tennessee, Scott, named Elsie Dunn, was a self-proclaimed feminist by the age of fifteen. She attended college in New Orleans, where, at the age of seventeen, she was the secretary of Louisiana's Woman's Suffrage Party. By the age of twenty, she had moved to Brazil with her married lover, Frederick Wellman, the dean of the School of Tropical Diseases at Tulane University. They both changed their names, he to Cyril Kay Scott and she to Evelyn Scott. Scott wrote about her early life in Tennessee in *Background in Tennessee* (1937) and her experiences in Brazil with Cyril Scott in *Escapade* (1923). She also wrote two trilogies set in the South. The first—*The Narrow House* (1921), *Narcissus* (1922), and *The Golden Door* (1925)—chronicles the lives of three generations of a family. Her second trilogy—*The Migrations* (1927), *A Calendar of Sin* (1932), and *The Wave* (1929)—is a social history. Often in her fiction, Scott attacks traditional roles and places value on characters who separate themselves from society. In *The Migrations*, Scott suggests that by carrying old attitudes westward, nineteenth-century pioneers did not, as they had hoped, escape old bonds; they instead found new ones. In her Civil War novel *The Wave*, war comes on like a wave that overwhelms and swallows. The novel is an example of Scott's modernist experimentation with prose forms; it is composed of over one hundred episodes portraying the influence of the war on both southerners and northerners. Scott also examined the relationships between women and men, and in her mature work she comes to recognize the potential of marriage for both partners. Clearly, though, she ended her career believing otherwise. In her last novel, *The Shadow of the Hawk* (1941), she suggests that women can never free themselves from society's oppression.

By the 1930s, then, southern women writers were addressing subjects that had never before been a focus of their literature. Lillian Hellman addressed the topic of lesbianism in her play *The Children's Hour* (1934). The play, as Hellman said a number of times, revolves around a lie told by a spoiled girl named Mary, who attends a boarding school run by two women, Karen and Martha. Mary's grandmother, Mrs. Tilford, has been generous in supporting the school, which has been suffering financial difficulties. When Mary is reprimanded for bad behavior, she runs away to her grandmother and tells her that Karen and Martha are lovers. Although the play had the longest run of any of Hellman's plays, *The Children's Hour* was banned in London, Boston, and Chicago and denied the Pulitzer Prize, most probably because of its subject matter.

Three other southern women took up unusual topics for southern women writers by examining the subject of labor relations in their proletarian novels about the Gastonia, North Carolina, textile-mill strike of 1928: Olive Tilford Dargan's *Call Home the Heart* (1932), Grace Lumpkin's *To Make My Bread* (1932), and Myra Page's *Gathering Storm* (1932). While Dargan's novel points to her belief in industrialization as a liberating force, the novel closes with Dargan's protagonist returning to the land. Because the novel ended in this way, it received harsh criticism from Marxists. Dargan quickly wrote and published a sequel, *A Stone Came Rolling* (1935), that was much more in line with Marxist teachings.

Southern women writers between 1900 and World War II found themselves involved in a complex relationship between their work as artists and their roles as women in the South. After Ellen Glasgow's first novel, *The Descendant*, was rejected by three publishers, Glasgow decided to submit the book anonymously. One reader for the publisher was convinced that the novel had been written by Harold Frederic, who had recently published a popular novel that Glasgow described as having "a depressing theological flavour." According to Glasgow, her book was "immediately accepted" because the reader believed her novel had been written by a man. Caroline Gordon, on the other hand, wanted to write prose that could not be specifically identified as feminine. "While I am a woman I am also a freak," she once said. "The work I do is not suitable for a woman. It is unsexing." Gordon wrote a fictional autobiography of her father, a book called *Aleck Maury, Sportsman* (1934), in which she celebrates her own father's life as a classical scholar and sportsman. For the book, Gordon carefully researched aspects of hunting and fishing that played a prominent role in Aleck's life, but in general she describes Aleck's love of sport as a science, set forth with the same precision and intellectualism that guided his work as a scholar. When *Aleck Maury* was published, despite praise from writers like Andrew Lytle who said she might "restore the Confederacy" if she continued to write such books, Robert Penn Warren teased her about her "masculine" prose. Throughout much of her life, Gordon was torn between a masculine independence represented by her father and the maternal lineage of her Kentucky ancestors. As artists and as women, Glasgow and Gordon both faced publishing and intellectual communities not fully able to accept them as other than traditional southern women.

The renascence of writing in the South from 1900 to World War II stands as a period distinguished not only for the revival of literature in the region but also for the evolution of women's writings and of women's roles as writers. Many of the women writers of the period express hope in feminine southern landscapes where women can join in communities, yet this theme does not receive full treatment until after World War II, and more particularly, after the Women's Movement of the 1970s. Although Glasgow and Mitchell suggest the potential for women's communities and for women's freedom, women of the Renascence generally continued to struggle with the model of southern womanhood and with the lingering ideal of the masculine landscape. Alice Walker's *The Color Purple* (1982), which develops these battles, points to the indebtedness of contemporary literature to the literature of the Renascence. However, even the feminine landscape that Walker portrays in her novel seems destined for extinction. Post–World War II writers have not discovered all of the answers to women's problems. Contemporary women authors now write of shopping malls and interstate highways that are destroying a rural South. Nevertheless, they are still also writing of and building up their communities within their literature, thereby creating a second renascence in the South. Like the writers of the first renascence, these women of the current age are struggling against the encroachment of outside forces that once again threaten southern communities. The years from 1900 to World War II, then, are perhaps the most important years in the development of women's writing in the South. In this period are the roots of a new southern pastoral—one more equitable and realistic—and of a new woman of the South—one with a promising strength and courage, yet one who was only just then stepping forward to take on new roles and new challenges.

Mary Louise Weaks

See also Pastoral; Women's Movement; Women Writers, 1820 to 1900; Women Writers, World War II to Present.

Elizabeth Jane Harrison, *Female Pastoral: Women Writers Revisioning the American South* (1991); Anne Goodwyn Jones, *Tomorrow Is Another Day: The Woman Writer in the South, 1859–1936* (1981); Lucinda H. MacKethan, *Daughters of Time: Creating Woman's Voice in Southern Story* (1990); Louis D. Rubin Jr., gen. ed., *The History of Southern Literature* (1985); Dorothy M. Scura, ed., *Ellen Glasgow: New Perspectives* (1995); Mary Louise Weaks and Carolyn Perry, eds., *Southern Women's Writing: Colonial to Contemporary* (1995); Susan Millar Williams, *A Devil and a Good Woman, Too: The Lives of Julia Peterkin* (1997).

WOMEN WRITERS, WORLD WAR II TO PRESENT

Through sheer numbers, women writers have dominated the contemporary literary scene in the South—that is, since World War II. Whereas the modernist era in the South produced a coterie more dominantly male, such powerful and significant writers as William Faulkner, Thomas Wolfe, and Robert Penn Warren, the contemporary age provided an impressive number of major women writers: Eudora Welty, Flannery O'Connor, Carson McCullers—and even more recently, Alice Walker, Anne Tyler, Lee Smith, and Maya Angelou, writers who have moved women from the marginalized position in the pre–World War II South to a central position. Following World War II, southern women writers looked for a way to fit in both professionally and personally—a place in literary and social America and the South that was not considered substandard, with works not relegated to categories of literature of dubious worth. Many of the women writers—and the characters they created—felt alienated and isolated despite the "shrinking" of the nation, a feeling only magnified through increased education, ambition, and a rejection of stereotypes that had previously prescribed the role of a southern woman. If a woman writer eliminated these stereotypes, however, she could find no easy replacement for them; that is, there was no defined role for a woman to take. Many women felt confusion and more than a little frustration; for women writers, the dilemma led to a great deal of experimentation, reflected in new kinds of characters in their literature. Consider, for example, O'Connor's Joy/Hulga, Welty's piano teacher Miss Eckhart, and any number of characters in McCullers's works. These female characters are intelligent, independent, and creative—and are therefore misfits in the South of the 1950s and even 1960s.

Several important changes after World War II began to alter this pattern. Women writers of earlier generations were physically as well as socially separated, partly because they lacked a literary and intellectual center that, for example, the Fugitives had in Nashville. But because the southern landscape has changed so drastically since World War II, with the suburban and urban areas becoming more heavily populated, women writers since midcentury have no longer been isolated by rural living. A new unity and support system among women writers has developed in the second half of the twentieth century, with organizations such as the North Carolina Writers' Network and the Ozark Poets Society serving as the center of much creative activity for both male and female writers. The increased mobility of women—even those who live in rural areas—has made it possible for them to be part of these groups.

Some writers have persisted in their isolation, however, despite other opportunities. The two women authors who are arguably the best the South has ever produced—Eudora Welty and Flannery O'Connor—were both loners. Until her recent death, Welty was considered by most as our greatest living southern writer. Her life and career span premodernism to present postmodernism; her writings include novels, short stories, essays, reviews, and autobiography; and there is hardly a southern writer who has not been touched by her influence. Welty's work, perhaps more than any other, has set the standard for women's writings in the post–World War II years, bringing academic respect to female writing, which had been plagued with diminutive labels such as "local color" and "domestic fiction." Her emphasis on character, her close attention to detail, her ear for dialogue and narration, and her sense of a distinctly southern "place" have made her work a model for future generations of writers, both male and female.

Most important in influence, perhaps, is Welty's gleaning of the family unit as subject matter in such stories as "Why I Live at the P.O." and "The Death of a Traveling Salesman" (1941) and novels such as *Losing Battles* (1970) and *The Optimist's Daughter* (1972). The emphasis on daily life, on relationships between family members, on the secrets and rituals and eccentricities found in ordinary people—all of this marks Welty's work as clearly southern and especially female. It is also a reason that her work has been overlooked on some levels. Some critics have complained that Welty has not written the "big" novel about "big" issues such as war and politics, choosing instead to write about what ordinary people face everyday: rela-tionships. But the human heart—which some have wrongly judged as a "small" subject—has been her focus and is, in truth, the only subject matter that touches every person who has lived and breathed.

Another woman whose influence is far felt is Flannery O'Connor, whose brilliant writing career—cut short by lupus—fits within a small part of Welty's lifetime. Her impact and her greatness, however, are undeniable, especially with writers of the most recent generation both male and female. O'Connor's stories and short novels, like Welty's, are focused on families and relationships, and she shares the gift of characterization and language with Welty. Her characters, however, seem anything but ordinary. The intensity of O'Connor's vision is dependent upon her fierce Catholic belief in a God who is demanding, violent, and inflexible in expectation. Her characters are often smug believers in a watered-down religious system or in a philosophy based on intellectual rationalization that is close to secular humanism.

Despite her somewhat extreme religious perspective—and therefore some misunderstanding by those who have analyzed her work—O'Connor's style has been both startling and imaginative enough to capture the attention of both academic and nonacademic readers. Her personal writings—essays in *Mystery and Manners* (1969) and letters compiled in *The Habit of Being* (1979)—are gems in themselves, worthy of study for both pleasure and insight. But it may be her sense of humor—often macabre, sometimes shocking, and always crackling with wit—which has had the most influence on writers who have followed her. Coming from a male writer, O'Connor's work would have been rare and stunning; from a woman, it is practically revolutionary.

In addition to Welty and O'Connor, both Katherine Anne Porter and Carson McCullers wrote significant works of fiction during the years closely following World War II. Although Porter published a novella, *Pale Horse, Pale Rider* (1939), and a novel, *Ship of Fools* (1962), it is for her short stories that she is best remembered. Her work, like Welty's, spans several generations, making it difficult to fit her precisely into one era, but her influence is keenly felt in the contemporary southern writer's close attention to detail and psychological accuracy of character. Carson McCullers also focused on the psychological aspect of characters, many of whom are isolated, lonely, and even bizarre. Her ability to capture internal conflict in such novels as *The Heart Is a Lonely Hunter* (1940), *The Member of* the *Wedding* (1946), and *The Ballad of the Sad Café* (1941) highlights her work as similar to O'Connor's at least in its use of the grotesque. Her novels are rich with eccentric characterizations, focusing on the inept attempts of human beings to connect with each other.

Perhaps the greatest American woman playwright, Lillian Hellman, lived and wrote from the years just prior to World War II through the several decades that followed. *The Little Foxes* (1939) and *Toys in the Attic* (1960) explore themes of social injustice and the human propensity toward evil and suggest comparisons to Chekhov and Ibsen; her autobiographical books written later in her life—*An Unfinished Woman—A Memoir* (1969), *Pentimento* (1973), and *Scoundrel Time* (1976)—reveal a woman who is strong and intelligent, exposing and facing the uncomfortable truths that surround American society and the South—a philosophy she acted on personally in 1952 when she refused to disclose information about friends and associates to the House of Representatives Committee on Un-American Activities, a stand that resulted in her being blacklisted.

Lillian Smith was an equally courageous woman, not afraid to make enemies in the name of social justice, especially in the realm of southern racial relations. Although she wrote some fiction, including a shocking novel about an interracial love affair, *Strange Fruit* (1944), her most significant work is nonfiction—*Killers of the Dream* (1949), a confessional autobiography revealing the worst side of the prejudiced South. Although Smith later claimed that this book turned the South against her—probably an accurate comment—*Killers of the Dream* is now one of the most important pre–Civil Rights works to examine the ghost of slavery and its influence on the generations that followed.

Even though scholars generally group together all fiction written between 1945 and the present, in southern literature there is evidence to suggest another break around 1970. The Women's Movement and the Civil Rights Movement deeply affected literature in the South during the 1960s and 1970s. With the increased freedoms brought about by the Women's Movement, new women writers have not had to choose between creating their art and having a family, as so many earlier novelists such as Hurston, Welty, Glasgow, McCullers, and O'Connor did—or to pay the social and personal price of having someone else raise their children—as did Caroline Gordon and Zelda Fitzgerald. The Civil Rights Movement added voices from the African American and Native American communities,

voices that have given more dimensions to woman's experience in the South.

Some things remain the same, however, and contemporary southern women writers face many of the conflicts and dialectics explored by their female literary ancestors: independence versus dependence, femininity versus strength, the nurturing of others in direct conflict with preservation of the self, purity and virginity as opposed to sexual freedom and expression. To these traditionally "female" topics, writers have added more "masculine" subjects, such as Molly Ivins's political commentary, Bobbie Ann Mason's exploration of the effects of the Vietnam War in *In Country* (1985), Alice Walker's essays about race and prejudice, and Florence King's scathing commentary on everything from sexuality to table manners.

One of the most-asked questions in southern studies since 1945 seems to be not whether there are still "southern writers," but rather what is the definition of "southern writing." The work of women writers has been pivotal in this discussion because today's definitions expand what is considered "literature"; journals, autobiographies, spirituals, oral storytelling, letters, essays, lectures, performance poetry, and even cookbooks are all part of the new canon of women writers. The strength of these new voices is apparent in the quality as well as in the diversity of contemporary southern women writers. Names such as Anne Tyler, Alice Walker, Kaye Gibbons, and Maya Angelou consistently can be found on best-seller lists as well as on the required reading lists at colleges and universities. The popularity of southern stories is also evident in the number of southern novels and plays translated to Hollywood films. The last few decades have seen productions of *Crimes of the Heart, Fried Green Tomatoes, In Country, Rich in Love, The Accidental Tourist,* and *The Color Purple,* to name just a few—all based on works by contemporary southern women writers.

Expanding the definitions of literature also makes room in the canon for more than writing about upper-middle-class whites from the Deep South. The rise of "Grit Lit" by Bobbie Ann Mason, Lee Smith, and others signals a new kind of southern storytelling focusing on the blue-collar worker, giving such characters a nobility rarely seen before in literature. There is some resistance to this new focus, with some older, more-established writers and scholars describing this evolution with the decidedly negative word *plebeian,* but generally, the movement is seen as a positive step in southern literature.

Because definitions have expanded to include so many styles, settings, and voices, the chore has been to find the strings of connection in southern literature now—leading to broad generalizations that are, nonetheless, helpful in identifying common characteristics. While there is still a strong sense of being "southern," history for the contemporary woman writer may go no further back than to the civil rights era, to the Vietnam War, or to the memories of a southern childhood. History is more often private rather than shared by a collective southern consciousness. Although some critics have suggested that southern writers today have lost the "tragic sense," it is perhaps more accurate to say that these writers see tragedy in a more personal sphere.

Less preoccupied with the guilt of the past and more focused on the present and future, today's southern women writers emphasize the families of today rather than the ancestors of yesterday. Their voices tell stories of a region no longer bothered much by the guilt of past sins; the stories focus on the problems found in average homes within ordinary families. They unmask new "sins" in the region and are willing to expose old icons, including the image of the southern gentleman. He is shown as having a potential for racism, misogyny, and violence, all excused in the name of southern honor.

Contemporary women writers have de-romanticized the southern family and its stereotypical members, replacing set images and melodrama with real people. Writers satirically depict such stereotypes as the southern lady, the southern belle, and the black mammy to illustrate the absurdity and impracticality of maintaining these images at the turn of the new millennium. Beth Henley brutally satirizes such female southern traditions as beauty pageants, debutantes, and the Junior League in her plays *Crimes of the Heart* (1979) and *The Miss Firecracker Contest* (1980), exposing the old social institutions' lack of substance and worth for the woman of today's South.

After exposing false images of southern women, writers have then created new and more realistic figures of the female. Beauty and grace are no longer absolutely essential in the southern female hero. Southern women writers are reinventing southern womanhood by replacing the stereotype with a strong, creative, and sexy woman who more often has a sense of humor rather than a beauty crown. As Daphne Athas describes her, this new woman "sees through things but also sees things through." Such characters tend to share a sense of optimism and affirmation: Bobbie Ann Mason describes this new tone as "an innocent hope of possibility."

The sense of place in today's fiction may only be a loyalty to a memory of a beloved childhood home or town, but that bond is still very strong. Home—both the physical structure and the family community—continues to be the one constant in southern women's literature and is the core of southern storytelling. And regardless of their current state of residence—Alice Walker, Dorothy Allison, Jill McCorkle, Lisa Alther, and Gail Godwin all live outside the South—southern women writers reveal that their hearts remain in the South, which more often than not serves as setting for their works.

Voice in women's fiction is all-important because women writers are telling the stories that might not be told by male writers simply because they are unaware of the woman's personal world. As Lucinda MacKethan notes, women characters often "write themselves into being." Voice identifies, empowers, and legitimizes lives that have been seen traditionally—in both a literary and a social sense—as marginal. It would be difficult to describe the voices of Doris Betts, Mary Mebane, Maya Angelou, Molly Ivins, Florence King, Lee Smith, Alice Walker, and Rita Mae Brown as anything but strong and stubborn, powerful and courageous.

With voices that are often subversive—revealing oppression on many levels—there is little about the South that has not been questioned, satirized, and exposed in women's writing since World War II. As the region has been transformed from Bible Belt to Sunbelt, there has been a reevaluation of the role and power of religion in contemporary southern life. Although Flannery O'Connor's work stands out as the most obvious exception, the general trend has been toward questioning and satire, toward doubt and mistrust, toward establishment of a personal form of salvation separate from traditional, organized religion. The pace of modern life hinders full-time devotion; as Lee Smith says in an interview with Susan Ketchin, "You know, I can't be transported. I have to go to the grocery store."

In terms of influence, modern culture and writing rely more often upon the mythology stemming from music, television, and other forms of popular culture rather than upon the influence of the Bible and its parables. The influence of history—both political and religious—has often been replaced with the power of the Now. Writers depend upon allusions to Dollywood, Wal-Mart, and Moon Pies much more than to Ecclesiastes, Psalms, and Genesis. This may or may not be a positive trend, but the literature merely reflects the culture it describes rather than trying to prescribe cultural directions.

As far as the southern sense of community, women writers in today's fiction have expanded the meaning to include a place unbounded by race. Women writers have made a clear attempt to form community where there had once been separation in terms of black and white: Alice Walker's *Meridian* (1976), Kaye Gibbons's *Ellen Foster* (1987), Dori Sanders's *Clover* (1990), Ellen Douglas's *Can't Quit You, Baby* (1988), and Gail Godwin's *A Mother and Two Daughters* (1982), for example, all attempt to give new definitions of and solutions to race relations. In effect, women's stories have become vehicles for change, and their storytelling re-visions the past and present—and therefore the future—transforming the patriarchal white South into a South seen through the eyes of women both black and white.

One writer from this era is particularly important because she represents a new and long-awaited voice in southern literature—the African American woman. Margaret Walker is extraordinary in many ways: she was highly educated (Ph.D. from University of Iowa) during an era when women, especially black women, were often not; she has successfully combined writing with education, teaching, marriage, and child-rearing; she has written poetry, essays, biography, and one novel. That novel, *Jubilee* (1966), was inspired by the life of her maternal great-grandmother who was born into slavery, and its narration achieves a synthesis of folk culture, biography, and oral storytelling that later African American writers have employed and extended.

Maya Angelou has been an equally multitalented writer, producing poetry, drama, and autobiography, as well as working in such diverse careers as acting, teaching, and social activism. Her on-going series of autobiographical novels—the most southern and well-known being *I Know Why the Caged Bird Sings* (1970)—explore the tensions between black and white, rich and poor, man and woman, adult and child. Ultimately, her characters endure and triumph by making connections with other women, with other people, and with other lives. Alice Walker's novel *The Color Purple* (1982) also clearly expresses this hope for change through connection, as her protagonist, Celie, moves from silent victim of both the male and the white worlds to outspoken woman in charge of her own

identity and future. Walker remarked in an interview with Gloria Steinem that the potential for change lies in writing, in the power of art. She argues that it should "make us better."

African American poet Sonia Sanchez came to the attention of the critical world during the 1960s with her outspoken and powerful voice of the black experience and community. Refusing to conform to established rules of poetry, Sanchez has written—and performed energetically—some of the most creative poems of the contemporary South, with an emphasis on accuracy in black language and thought. Her autobiographical writing has also received critical attention, with her book *homegirls & handgrenades* winning the 1985 National Book Award. Like Sanchez, Nikki Giovanni emerged from the Black Arts Movement of the 1960s as an honest and straightforward poetic voice. Giovanni's evolution in her poetry throughout the years from black militant—who espoused violence as a means to change—to concerned humanitarian and environmentalist perhaps best typifies the move in southern fiction from separatism to unity, from focus on negative to positive, from the sins of the past to the hope for the future.

Contemporary southern women poets in general have come into prominence since 1970. Ellen Bryant Voigt's five volumes of poetry (*Kyrie*, 1996, the most recent) have won many accolades. Susan Ludvigson, Judith Ortiz Cofer, Ann Deagon, Betty Adcock, Heather Ross Miller, and Eleanor Ross Taylor all speak in southern and distinctively women's voices. Julia Randall, Margaret Gibson, Elizabeth Seydel Morgan, Jane Gentry Vance, and Rosanne Coggeshall, among others, were associated as students or teachers with the Hollins College creative-writing program.

Doris Betts claims in the introduction to *Southern Women's Writing* that distinctions "of both gender and region are blurring" in today's fiction, and Josephine Humphreys argues in *Friendship and Sympathy* that gender is becoming less important, stating: "writing affects my femininity more than femininity affects my writing." Although this is true to some extent, a perceivable division between male and female southern writing still exists. Generally, female writers are more optimistic, more life affirming, and more hopeful about the future of family and self when it comes to the endings of their stories. Regardless of the tragic topics these women address—and they do present serious subjects such as child abuse, dissolution of the family, death, rape, mental illness—there is a thin line of hope found, usually in the preservation of self, the continuation of family, and the strength in community. Focusing on the present and future instead of the past, they see possibilities rather than constraints.

Today's southern women approach relatively serious subjects in their writing such as love, history, religion, and identity, but they seem to do so with a sense of humor. Perhaps these writers have once and for all turned away from the shame and guilt with which pre–World War II southern writers seemed preoccupied. Instead they look at their world and the people in it with a realistic vision tempered by humor. Doris Betts believes that when women finally tell the truth about their lives, "it may be that . . . part of that truth will indeed split open the world, [but] another part may heal or at least try to do so." Something nearly all southern women writers have in common is a new vision of the South and of the women living in it, a vision that attempts to retain the good things about the past—the pride of tradition, of family, and of place—tempered by a realistic understanding of the damage this pride can do if it is misused.

Barbara Bennett

See also Civil Rights Movement; Drama, 1900 to Present; Feminism; Grit Lit; K Mart Fiction; New Woman; Novel, World War II to Present; O'Connor, Flannery; Poetry, World War II to Present; Popular Literature; Postmodernism; Short Story, World War II to Present; Welty, Eudora; Women's Movement.

Susan Ketchin, *The Christ-Haunted Landscape: Faith and Doubt in Southern Fiction* (1994); Lucinda H. MacKethan, *Daughters of Time: Creating Woman's Voice in Southern Story* (1990); Rosemary M. Magee, *Friendship and Sympathy: Communities of Southern Women Writers* (1992); Peggy Whitman Prenshaw, ed., *Women Writers of the Contemporary South* (1984); Linda Tate, *A Southern Weave of Women: Fiction of the Contemporary South* (1994); Mary Louise Weaks and Carolyn Perry, eds., *Southern Women's Writing: Colonial to Contemporary* (1995); Margaret Ripley Wolfe, *Daughters of Canaan: A Saga of Southern Women* (1995).

WOODWARD, C. VANN

Publication of Comer Vann Woodward's *Tom Watson: Agrarian Rebel* in 1938 touched off a virtual revolution in the interpretation of the history of the American South. A major study had appeared that declined to view what happened in the post–Reconstruction South as the restoration of honest government, the achievement of sectional reconciliation, and the coming of domestic tranquillity and even modest prosperity under the benign auspices of an industrializing, democratizing New South.

Woodward's biography centered on a fiery reformer who led a desperate struggle by impoverished agriculturalists against the commercial and financial domination of the industrializing New South. Tom Watson of Georgia sought to rally increasingly disadvantaged southern farmers and laborers to the defense of their own interests. He had taken on the political and business Establishment, challenged the attempt to cloak the materialistic goals of the New South in the pieties of the Lost Cause, and sought to speak out for the civil and political rights of black southerners and to involve them in the fight.

The Populist cause failed, with white racism one of the strategies used to suppress it. Ultimately, a thwarted and disappointed Watson had himself become a vicious and dangerous demagogue specializing in Negro- and Jew-baiting and mob violence. The seeds of the later behavior, Woodward showed, were implicitly present from the outset.

In depicting significant class conflict within the supposedly Solid White South, Woodward was severely modifying the long-established "consensus" approach. Earlier historians had emphasized the continuity of the Old and New South. The Reconstruction era had been presented as the betrayal of the White South by vengeful Radical Republicans who sanctioned an orgy of corrupt Carpetbag, Scalawag, and Negro rule, until ultimately the old leadership regained control and honest government was restored. Woodward's South, by contrast, was considerably more complex and was laced with discord and struggle.

The impact of the Watson biography and Woodward's overall study of the post–Reconstruction South, *Origins of the New South, 1877–1913* (1951), upon the subsequent writing of southern history was profound. In effect, Woodward had drawn upon the insights of Charles A. Beard, albeit with significant modifications, to develop a telling economic critique of the later-nineteenth- and early-twentieth-century South. In those books and his later work, southern experience was depicted in terms of discontinuities, rivalries, internal conflicts, and divisions of class and caste. Following his lead, young historians began interpreting southern Populism as a genuine manifestation of widespread agrarian discontent, not a radical fringe movement, and the New South enterprise of the 1880s and 1890s as a venture in the coinage of money rather than as a species of civic benevolence.

In a remarkable book, *Thinking Back: The Perils of Writing History* (1986), Woodward sketched his career as a historian of the South and candidly addressed the criticisms directed at his work over the years. When he entered the study of southern history in the early 1930s, he said, he did so despite the work of the regnant southern historians, who "in many and varied ways . . . joined in vindicating, justifying, rationalizing, and often celebrating the present order." In marked contrast to their writings was the Southern Literary Renascence then in full flower. "If southern novelists, poets, and playwrights," Woodward has asked, "could, as Robert Penn Warren admonished us, 'accept the past and its burden' without evasiveness or defensiveness or special pleading, why should southern historians not profit from their example?"

Woodward was thirty years old when *Tom Watson* appeared. Born in Vanndale, Arkansas, on November 13, 1908, he had grown up there and in Georgia, studied at Henderson College and Emory and Columbia universities, and taken his doctorate at the University of North Carolina at Chapel Hill in 1937. Howard K. Beale directed his dissertation, which was his biography of Watson and was published the year following. He taught at Georgia Tech, the University of Florida, the University of Virginia, and Scripps College. During World War II, he served in the navy as a historian, one result being a book, *The Battle for Leyte Gulf* (1947).

In 1946 Woodward joined the faculty of Johns Hopkins University in Baltimore. By then he was at work on *Origins*, which appeared in 1951 along with another book, *Reunion and Reaction*, a revelatory study of the railroad, financial, and political trade-offs underlying the Compromise over the disputed election of 1876, whereby Rutherford B. Hayes was seated as President of the United States and federal troops were withdrawn from the last three southern states still under Reconstruction government.

A year after the *Brown v. Board of Education* decision of 1954 that ended legal segregation by race in public schools, Woodward published another groundbreaking book, *The Strange Career of Jim Crow* (1955). That study developed the proposition that racial segregation by law, far from being deeply imbedded in southern history, was essentially a development of the 1890s and early 1900s. The book drew widespread attention from the general public as well as from historians. It has since been revised several times.

The historian, Woodward has written, "has obligations to the present as well as to the past he studies" (*Thinking Back*). When the counsels for the National Association for the Advancement of Colored People (NAACP) were developing the brief to be argued in *Brown v. Board,* Woodward and John Hope Franklin met with them and prepared monographs that were cited in the brief.

Woodward left Johns Hopkins for Yale University in 1961. He has been Commonwealth Lecturer at the University of London, Harmsworth Professor of American History at Oxford University, and Jefferson Lecturer in the Humanities at the Library of Congress. His books include *The Burden of Southern History* (1960), *American Counterpoint* (1971), *Thinking Back*, and *The Future of the Past* (1989). He edited *Mary Chesnut's Civil War* (1981), which received the Pulitzer Prize in 1982; *The Private Mary Chesnut* (1984, with Elizabeth Muhlenfeld); and *The Comparative Approach to American History* (1968). He has been general editor of the Oxford History of the United States. He retired from Yale in 1977, and he died on December 17, 1999, at his home in Hamden, Connecticut, at age ninety-one.

Louis D. Rubin Jr.

See also *Brown v. Board of Education*; History, Idea of; New South; Populism; Reconstruction; Southern Renascence.

Michael O'Brien, *Rethinking the South: Essays in Intellectual History* (1988); John Herbert Roper, ed., *C. Vann Woodward: A Southern Historian and His Critics* (1997); C. Vann Woodward, *Thinking Back: The Perils of Writing History* (1986).

WORK

The most dominant images of work in southern literature are domestic work (cooking, cleaning, child care); fieldwork (especially the planting and harvesting of tobacco and cotton); and, later, industrial work (textile mills and mining). Until the mid-nineteenth century, when narratives were produced by African American authors at the behest of abolition societies, most southern literature was written not by those who performed manual labor but by monied property owners. Thus, working-class characters have been both stereotyped and extolled since before the nation was born, and the meaning of work has been voiced differently for Anglo- and African American laborers.

In the pre-industrial South prior to the Civil War, literary images of labor performed by poor Anglo-Americans were written from the perspective of upper-class writers. As early as the 1720s, William Byrd portrayed the residents of the Carolinas as "indolent wretches who practice ill-management and bad husbandry" (*History of the Dividing Line*, written c. 1728). Byrd's work inaugurated a stereotype of the Anglo southern worker as shirker that persists through the centuries, from Huck Finn's Pap (1885) to Erskine Caldwell's Jeeter Lester in *Tobacco Road* (1932). Because this was a time when literature was written "of the people" and not "by the people," there was little sense in this early southern literature of the contentious nature of labor that was to develop in later periods. Those who owned, wrote; those who worked, worked.

Images of working African Americans of the South, however, have always revealed ways in which labor is both a mode of oppression and a means to freedom. The Civil War not only ushered in the end of slavery but also marked a partial transition from an oligarchic plantation economy to a more industrialized capitalist economy. The entry of former slaves into a wage-based economy is a common image: Frederick Douglass's *Narrative of the Life of Frederick Douglass, An American Slave* (1848) and Harriet Jacobs's *Incidents in the Life of a Slave Girl, Written by Herself* (1861) both end with images of work that mark the protagonists' newfound independence as they work for wages. Douglass calls his first work in New Bedford "new, dirty . . . work for me; but I went at it with a glad heart and willing hand. I was now my own master." Jacobs's status as a housekeeper, while restricting her in some senses, also affords her an enabling privacy. For both, work is a vital part of freedom and of their identities. Elizabeth Keckley's ability to speak publicly about Mary Todd Lincoln is grounded in her integrity as a businesswoman (*Behind the Scenes*, 1865); Booker T. Washington attributes his success in *Up From Slavery* (1902) to his diligence with a broom.

With the rise of industrialism in the South, images of work in mills and coal mines increase, and Anglo-American writers begin to explore the hardships of those who labor in the South from a more sympathetic perspective than that of eighteenth-century colonists. Rebecca Harding Davis describes the exploitative nature of work for men, in *Life in the Iron Mills* (1861), and for women, in *Margret Howth: A Story of Today* (1862). Margret thinks of her position as a bookkeeper in the woolen mills as a "shallow duty and shallow re-

ward" (44); the young disabled girl Lois remembers feeling "like I was part o' th' engines, somehow. Th' air used to be thick in my mouth, black wi' smoke 'n' wool 'n' smells" (45). In this, Davis's southern literature is a precursor to the better-known naturalism of Dreiser and Sinclair.

The most prominent southern writers of the early and mid-twentieth century begin to emphasize, from different perspectives, the role of the laborer in building the region and the nation. Ellen Glasgow's Nicholas Burr, son of a poor farmer who rises to become governor in *A Voice of the People* (1900), asserts at one of his lower moments that "success spelt [sic] backwards is work," yet his willingness to continue to work in his father's fields is a sign of his moral fortitude. Work, then, as it has long done for African American writers, becomes for Glasgow both an onerous burden and an important measure of integrity. Faulkner's African American domestic Dilsey (*The Sound and the Fury*, 1929) and Anglo sharecropper Abner Snopes ("Barn Burning," 1939) each reveal the extent to which servants and laborers have come to represent the southern and the national conscience. Dilsey is surely among those spirits "capable of compassion and sacrifice and endurance . . . which have been the glory of [man's] past" (Nobel Acceptance Speech, 1949), and Abner Snopes—sharecropper, arsonist—expresses the ways that Byrd's "indolent wretches" have come to represent, for better or for worse, an integral part of the southern conscience.

Other important texts that emphasize the expanding role of work in the narrative fabric of southern literature include stories and poems usually associated with the New Negro Renaissance, many of which have strong southern ties. Many of Langston Hughes's poems deal with work ("A Song to a Negro Washwoman"; "Johannesburg Mines"; "Steel Mills"; "Open Letter to the South") as does the fiction of Zora Neale Hurston ("Sweat," 1926; *Their Eyes Were Watching God*, 1937), and Jean Toomer (*Cane*, 1923). Whereas earlier writing by African Americans may have emphasized the personal empowerment of work, this later group of writers, as a whole, may be said to emphasize the sizable contribution made to the nation by African American labor. Rather than being character-building, this work is nation-building—as Hughes writes in his "Open Letter": "We did not know that we were brothers. / Now we know! / Out of that brotherhood / Let power grow!"

Paradoxically, at the same time (the 1930s and

1940s), the Agrarians were idealizing the class divisions that had, according to them, produced a harmonious society nearly free from discord and strife. John Crowe Ransom writes in "Reconstructed but Unregenerate," his 1930 contribution to *I'll Take My Stand*: "[G]raduated social orders . . . were personal and friendly . . . people were for the most part in their right places. Slavery was . . . more often than not humane in practice. . . . All were committed to a form of leisure, and . . . their labor itself was leisurely."

But despite the Agrarians' fear of encroaching industrialism, it came. During the Great Depression, strike novels and fiction about the increasing difficulty of finding sustaining work became more widespread. The best-known strike novels are especially relevant to the southern landscape, focusing on the 1929 textile strikes in Gastonia, North Carolina. These six include Mary Heaton Vorse's *Strike!* (1930); Sherwood Anderson's *Beyond Desire* (1932); Olive Tilford Dargan's *Call Home the Heart* (1932); Grace Lumpkin's *To Make My Bread* (1932); Dorothy Myra Page's *Gathering Storm: A Story of the Black Belt* (1932); and William Rollins's *The Shadow Before* (1934).

Less well known than the strike novels (usually written from a Marxist perspective) is the cache of short fiction written during the 1930s and published in such journals as *Opportunity* and *Crisis*. Although a dearth of biographical information makes it difficult to identify which authors were originally southern, many of the stories make ample use of the South as a setting of both opportunity and restriction as characters seek either to escape or reestablish the southern economy. That these stories are not all written from a leftist perspective makes them an important addition to today's canon of literature from the 1930s. One of the most interesting is Anne DuBignon's "The Farm on the Eastern Shore," published in *Crisis* in 1933, showing professional northern African Americans moving South and successfully rejuvenating the economy. Here, manual labor becomes the foundation for racial and economic justice.

Contemporary fiction of the South is replete with images of work, many of which make explicit the connection between work and sexual identity. Ernest J. Gaines's *Of Love and Dust* (1967) reveals the way in which forced labor continues on in the South as a means of repressing African American men's sexuality; Alice Walker's *The Color Purple* (1982) reveals the way in which satisfying work (sewing Folkspants) complements sexual fulfillment.

In Country (1985), Bobbie Ann Mason's exploration of the Vietnam War through the eyes of a young Kentucky girl, suggests how veterans' war wounds make the prospect of viable relationships involving love and work nearly impossible. Dorothy Allison, in her fiction and essays, suggests the way that sexual identity and class status together shape identity; and Randall Kenan's Tims Creek is populated with southern working-class African Americans who watch and wonder as visitors come and go (*Let the Dead Bury Their Dead*, 1992).

Several biographies by southerners in the late twentieth century reflect on the working life of an earlier time. In *A Childhood: A Biography of a Place* (1978), Harry Crews pays tribute to the heroic efforts of his parents to achieve dignity by the sweat of their brows. His father died when Crews was two, a victim of too-strenuous exertions in the fields of rural Georgia. In Jacksonville, Florida, his mother later worked in a cigar factory. In *Keepers of the Moon* (1991), Tim McLaurin looks at his father's loyalty as a salaried worker at Merita Bakery in Fayetteville, North Carolina, who—with his family—worked enough land to raise a few hogs, chickens, vegetables, and a tobacco crop. The Agrarian ideal was better exemplified in the Kentucky farming life of Wilburn Mason, the father Bobbie Ann Mason honors in *Clear Springs: A Memoir* (1999). In *I Know Why the Caged Bird Sings* (1970), Maya Angelou pays tribute to her grandmother for her example as a self-assured, hard-working businesswoman in Stamps, Arkansas.

As work becomes more homogeneous in an American economy whose service industry is the fastest-growing sector, contemporary southern writers will continue to craft narratives that express the importance of work in shaping our culture and our character.

Jennifer Campbell

See also Class; Federal Writers' Project; Poor White; Proletarian Novel; Protest, Novel of; Tenant Farming.

Fay M. Blake, *The Strike in the American Novel* (1972); Duane Carr, *A Question of Class: The Redneck Stereotype in Southern Fiction* (1996); Merrill Maguire Skaggs, *The Folk of Southern Literature* (1972).

WORLD WAR I

Although the South offers no oeuvre to match the impact of Ernest Hemingway's long-sustained interest in

World War I, southern writers nevertheless contributed provocatively disparate viewpoints on the first modern war to rock the whole world.

The leading figure on the southern literary front to World War I was Baltimore's intrepid journalist, H. L. Mencken. In the process of becoming one of America's most influential and independent-minded cultural critics in the first third of the twentieth century, Mencken clearly confirmed his disposition toward taking views contrary to popular opinion with his published reflections on World War I, particularly before American intervention in the spring of 1917. Mainstream sentiment in the South (and generally across the country) favored the cause of the Western Allies. However, Mencken repeatedly bucked this trend and wrote a number of pieces debunking Anglophilia and promoting a sympathetic slant on the German side in the war. Thus having maintained the courage of individual conviction in a matter of large public-policy consequence, Mencken was solidly established on a course of lively and provocative dissent throughout the rest of his career.

Once the armistice was realized in late 1918, southern writers were in no particular rush to engage the war imaginatively. Nevertheless, World War I was deeply lodged in the imagination of William Faulkner, who had tried desperately to get into the war and who would engage the war in diverse ways from the 1920s to the 1950s. With his brother Jack off to Europe in 1918, Faulkner managed to create a new identity for himself (including the addition of a *u* to the family name) in order to gain entrance to training in Canada for pilot service in the Royal Air Force. Although the war concluded before Faulkner completed his training, with Toronto being as close as he would get to battle on the Western Front, this brief phase of his life proved to have lasting consequence. An enchantment with aerial combat captured him to such an extent that he proudly displayed his airman's uniform back home in Mississippi and soon came to inhabit personally manufactured accounts of war experience. From that point, it was a short step to published fiction, although it took several years for Faulkner to discover his calling as a professional storyteller.

Faulkner's first work of long fiction, *Soldier's Pay* (1926), is centered on the return of Donald Mahon (meant to stand in a symbolic sense for *Man*), an aviator, from the battlefields of Europe to his home in the South. This narrative hints only vaguely at the richness of Faulkner's rhetorical talent that would be evident by the end of the 1920s, but it shows conclusively how Faulkner could transpose the glory of war that he coveted as an embellishment for his personal character into recognition that the essence of war involves far more devastation than grand heroism, a transposition perhaps engendered by sustained reflection about the War Between the States. At any rate, Faulkner's initial World War I story takes a place fittingly alongside Eliot's *The Waste Land* and Hemingway's *The Sun Also Rises* in registering the scarring effect of war. Mahon bears a horrible facial scar, and his inner being is as torn up as his external features. The novel tracks Mahon's long slide toward death, all set off against the mindless frivolities of the Roaring Twenties.

Not long afterward, in *Sartoris* (originally titled *Flags in the Dust* and stringently edited on the way to publication in 1929), Faulkner again featured World War I in the lives of his characters, this time actually creating a vivid scene of aerial combat over France. If Faulkner thrilled vicariously to the excitement of describing the dogfight demise of John Sartoris, who plunged to his death while his brother Bayard watched from another plane, he nonetheless succeeded grandly in bringing that personal exhilaration solidly to ground before the novel would be complete. Bayard Sartoris pursues his envy of John's absurd bravado into a test-pilot career, one that ends with his plane/coffin buried deep in a midwestern field. Thus, by the end of the 1920s, Faulkner's youthful infatuation with the derring-do dimension of World War I seems thoroughly tempered by his maturing interest in the theme of endurance.

In "The Faring" section of *The Tall Men* (1927, revised in 1938), Donald Davidson provided a close-focus look at World War I, carefully framed against a deep historical background of earlier southerners with war experience. In his mid-twenties, Davidson joined the American Expeditionary Force and entered combat in France as a lieutenant. "The Faring" covers a wide range of moments: the decision to join the cause, the Atlantic crossing on a steamer, a stopover in England, then the famous battlefields of the Western Front late in the war. Images of the war itself are harsh and vivid. Toward the end, following an account of the Armistice celebration, Davidson offers the voices of a variety of war veterans—each with a different perspective—but perhaps all summed up in the following lines: "We who were young / Are older now from death in a foreign land / Met and passed by."

Soon afterwards in his novel *Look Homeward,*

Angel, Thomas Wolfe showed that the great war of his own youth was quick to cross the Atlantic and alter the American home scene. In the spring of 1917, as America declared war on Germany, Wolfe's protagonist Eugene Gant is away from his home in Altamont, off at the University in Pulpit Hill (Chapel Hill). The youth of the South heard the call of war, and before the spring term was over, "all the young men at Pulpit Hill who were eligible—those who were twenty-one—were going into service." Later, back at home, Eugene notes how Altamont is full of "patriotic frenzy," and that he himself wants to go to war. Although his brother Ben is rejected by the draft, another brother, Luke, leaves his job at an Ohio war-munitions factory to enlist in the navy. Soon, however, the tone of Wolfe's narrative shifts and the specter of war becomes ominous as the nation begins to feel the effects of the whole experience, one that required full-scale commitment to the "engines of war—engines to mill and print out hatred and falsehood, engines to pump up glory, engines to manacle and crush opposition, engines to drill and regiment men." When Eugene returns to the University, he finds the campus "quieter, sadder—the number of students was smaller and they were younger. The older ones had gone to war." The ones left behind had little enthusiasm for the painstaking work of college. Instead, their imaginations were fired by the explosions of combat in Europe, and as "the war had thrilled them with its triumphing *Now,*" the scholar's slow investment in tomorrow appeared pointless.

With the war stimulating prosperous business activity, in the summer of 1918 Eugene ventures to the Virginia coast seeking employment in war-related industry. Although the ineptitude of youth hinders his initial efforts, he eventually finds a succession of jobs, all adding powerfully to his stock of life experience. At one point, in loading nitroglycerin on a freighter for transport to Europe, he gets a taste of the danger of war. This thrill appeals to him, and during the fall semester of 1918, Eugene bides his time fretfully as he awaits his eighteenth birthday and a chance to join the war effort as a combatant, where, "if God was good, all the proud privileges of trench-lice, mustard gas, spattered brains, punctured lungs, ripped guts, asphyxiation, mud and gangrene, might be his." He fantasizes himself as "Ace Gant, the falcon of the skies, with 63 Huns to his credit by his nineteenth year." Unfortunately, in early November, with the war concluded, "students cursed and took off their uniforms." Wolfe's Eugene Gant is thus left void of direct war experience, which is

unfortunate, given that Wolfe's art is all about the acquisition and use of diverse life experiences, but *Look Homeward, Angel* serves to suggest a certain enthusiasm in the South for joining the World War I effort.

A less-encouraging view of the war is discernible in *I'll Take My Stand* (1930), not surprisingly, for World War I was intricately tied up with the complex economic systems of highly industrialized societies, a circumstance that pleased none of the Agrarian Manifesto contributors. From Cousin Lucius's vantage point in John Donald Wade's "The Life and Death of Cousin Lucius," "Europe was trying to destroy itself in a great war—and then America was driven into the war, too," but Lucius sees no sense in the war given the values of an agrarian South.

In the 1930s, World War I sank deep into the background, as shown in Elizabeth Madox Roberts's *He Sent Forth a Raven* (1935), where the war may be strange in its nefarious particulars of invention, such as tear gas, but it is essentially distant, far removed from the Kentucky country scene developed in the story foreground. With the arrival of World War II, followed almost immediately by the onset of the Cold War then the quick fury of the Korean War, World War I might have disappeared completely from view had not William Faulkner some unfinished business with it. Faulkner labored for nine years over his final confrontation with World War I. *A Fable* captured both a Pulitzer Prize and a National Book Award when it appeared in 1954. By that time, Faulkner had a Nobel Prize for literature to his credit, and reviewers of *A Fable* labored industriously to measure his Nobel Prize speech against his long-simmering last look at World War I.

A Fable is constructed as an extended parallel to Christ's crucifixion, centered on the doomed effort by a French corporal to lead his regiment in rebellion against the war in May 1918, an action resulting in execution of the corporal on a Friday, with his miraculous resurrection as the Unknown Soldier shortly afterward. Although reviewers—and presumably, readers—mainly saw the novel as a peculiar reconsideration of a historical moment long past, Faulkner's narrative technique actually defuses this focus and makes the fable reflect much more than the particulars of World War I. As a brooding witness to a succession of wars following the Armistice of 1918, Faulkner eventually dispatched in full his young man's zeal for combat. *A Fable* features the grotesqueries of war, bizarre and quirky ironies, all matters that could little excite or enthuse the next generation of young men who might be called to military service. As it turned out, however, by the time of America's next conflict, *A Fable* had been consigned to the distant rear of Faulkner's canon, almost never to be read, and hence unable to provide either deterrence to the Vietnam War or guidance for the war-protest movement of the late 1960s.

Owen W. Gilman Jr.

See also Faulkner, William.

M. E. Bradford, "The Anomaly of Faulkner's World War I Stories," *Mississippi Quarterly* (1983).

WORLD WAR II

World War II had an enormous impact on the South and its people. As military-training facilities proliferated in southern states, not only did soldiers from other regions of the country come to know diverse particulars of southern life—the sometimes oppressive heat, the rich and savory food, the smooth glide of voice and hospitality—but also at the same time, year by year, the hard grip of the Great Depression relaxed in the face of jobs created by the war effort. Moreover, southerners proved eager and heroic patriots in heading off to the various battlefields of World War II. The most decorated soldier of the war, Audie Murphy, was the son of a poor Texas cotton sharecropper, and Murphy's account of his war experience, powerfully titled *To Hell and Back* (1949), remains one of the best-known stories of combat in Europe during World War II, perhaps the only narrative from the South to match up in reader recognition against Norman Mailer's *The Naked and the Dead*, which also just happened to feature a Texan, Sam Croft, as a pivotal character. Murphy wrote just the one book, but his straightforward account of a boy who, in the face of miserable poverty and days defined by fighting down weeds in endless rows of cotton beneath a brutal sun, dreamed of a faraway battlefield described to him by a veteran of World War I and then managed to get himself into the next war almost immediately upon his eighteenth birthday, as if war itself were his birthright, reflects much of the character of the South in the twentieth century.

Many well-known southern writers (e.g., Randall Jarrell, James Dickey, Peter Taylor, A. R. Ammons, Mary Lee Settle, William Styron, John Ehle Jr., Shelby Foote, and Ralph Ellison) saw service of one kind or another in World War II, although only a few collected combat experience. Others approached the war from a clear distance: after failing to obtain an officer's commission, William Faulkner concentrated his concerns about war in efforts to complete his World War I fable; Erskine Caldwell reported on the war from Moscow and worked in Hollywood on a war propaganda film; and Eudora Welty, writing as Michael Ravenna, reviewed World War II battlefield stories for the *New York Times Book Review*. Looking backward from the end of the twentieth century, it must be noted that World War II constituted a major watershed in southern life and literature. Southern writers foreshadowed and heralded the onset of hostilities, probed the war in intimate detail, and finally tracked the manifold effects of World War II deep into the years following victory for America and its allies in 1945.

In the last decade of his short life, Thomas Wolfe spent considerable time wandering in Europe. He quested for new places to stimulate his creative impulse, finding much to love in Germany, a point registered vigorously in the last section of *The Web and the Rock* (1939), which features the Wolfe protagonist George Webber caught up in the wildness of *Oktoberfest* in Munich. However, Wolfe spent enough time in Germany in the 1930s to come to know the overbearing brutality of Hitler and the Nazi regime, all of which is reflected in George Webber's eventual departure from the Third Reich in the concluding section of *You Can't Go Home Again* (1940). George leaves Germany by train, but in Aachen, at the Belgian border, a Jew in his compartment is apprehended by soldiers under the direction of a Kaiser Wilhelm-like official whose bloated, overbearing presence puts George's spiritual homeland beyond return, even as the specter of German aggression seems likely to follow George all the way back to America.

Lillian Hellman also anticipated the intrusion of German aggression into American life. Like Wolfe, Hellman spent a good bit of time in Europe during the decade before Germany invaded Poland in 1939 to start World War II. Near the close of her life, Hellman produced a three-part memoir sequence, and subsequent to Mary McCarthy's 1980 assertion on Dick Cavett's TV show that Hellman's work was full of lies, there has been uncertainty regarding the truth of Hellman's account of her prewar activities, especially the story that she spun of a close childhood friend, described in some detail in her initial memoir installment, *An Unfinished Woman*, which won a National Book

Award in 1969; this friend was then developed much more fully as "Julia" in Hellman's *Pentimento* (1973) as a woman who settled in Vienna in the early 1930s, soon becoming active as a socialist in the anti-Nazi underground movement. Hellman claimed to have visited Julia in Vienna in 1934 and then again in Berlin in 1937, not long before Julia was killed by the Nazis. Although this alleged story from life has been challenged aggressively in most of its details by others (Mary McCarthy, Martha Gellhorn, Muriel Gardiner Buttinger), it nevertheless reveals how fully Hellman's imagination was caught up in the political position she espoused in the years leading up to World War II.

Hellman's deep aversion to the threat of Nazi-style fascism soon emerged in two important plays of the early 1940s, *Watch on the Rhine* (1941) and *The Searching Wind* (1944). *Watch on the Rhine* opened on the first of April in 1941, at a time of grave peril in Europe, with America watching anxiously from a distance. The setting is northern Virginia, in the Washington, D.C., suburbs. This location would seem to be far from danger, but the crisis in Europe reaches all the way to the country estate of Fanny Farrelly, because her daughter, Sara, had married a German, Kurt Müller, who subsequently involved himself deeply in anti-Nazi efforts in Spain and Germany. Kurt intends to smuggle $23,000 in cash to Europe, where it will be used to help people escape fascism. However, a Romanian, Count Teck de Brancovis, is also staying with the Farrellys, and when Teck, a Nazi sympathizer, discovers Kurt's plan, he tries to blackmail him for part of the money. Kurt eventually is forced to kill Teck in order to safeguard his plan. The peculiar combination of drawing-room comedy in a genteel southern home with sinister corruption of the Nazi regime in Europe made for a unique and powerful drama, one strong enough to win the 1941 New York Drama Critics Circle Award. Although the United States was totally involved in the European struggle when *The Searching Wind* premiered in 1944, in reviewing the indecisiveness of people facing fascism from the 1920s to the 1940s, the play shows Hellman's uncompromising distaste for those who were not sufficiently confident in their beliefs to stand up to challenge, no matter what the consequence. In some ways, the heart of the matter in *The Searching Wind* was the story of Lillian Hellman's turbulent life.

Although lacking Hellman's passionate ideological interest in keeping the forces of fascism at bay, William Faulkner nevertheless found two opportunities in the 1940s for inserting a perspective on Hitler's Germany into his stories of the South. In the "Delta Autumn" section of *Go Down, Moses* (1942), young Edmonds and a man named Legate fall into a dispute about the possibility that the fine sport of American deer hunting might fall before the onslaught of Hitler. With Legate saying, "We'll stop him in this country . . . even if he calls himself George Washington," and Edmonds responding, "How? . . . By singing God bless America in bars at midnight and wearing dime-store flags in our lapels," old man Ike sets them both straight: "This country is a little mite stronger than any one man or group of men, outside of it or even inside of it either. I reckon, when the time comes and some of you have done got tired of hollering we are whipped if we dont go to war and some more are hollering we are whipped if we do, it will cope with one Austrian paper-hanger, no matter what he be calling himself."

By the time the war was over in 1945, Faulkner himself had one further use for the Nazi regime. Hitler's Third Reich collapsed in April. As the year progressed, so did Malcolm Cowley's preparation of *The Portable Faulkner* for Viking Press. By the fall, Faulkner was writing "Appendix/Compson, 1699–1945," which was designed to flesh out background details about the Compson family over the course of nearly three centuries, almost always with the common denominator being the Compson tendency to align with losers in the march of history. This pattern was clearly initiated in the Compsons' support of Bonnie Prince Charlie's futile campaign in 1745 to reclaim the British throne; it was concluded in the Caddie section of the Appendix, when the eagle-eyed librarian of Jefferson spotted "a picture, a photograph in color clipped obviously from a slick magazine . . . the woman's face hatless between a rich scarf and a seal coat, ageless and beautiful, cold serene and damned; beside her a handsome lean man of middleage in the ribbons and tabs of a German staffgeneral." Even as Faulkner's fame would rise on the strength of *The Portable Faulkner,* the demise of Hitler's Germany provided just the right final stroke to demonstrate the on-going pattern of error in the Compson lineage. Jason had opposed Babe Ruth's Yankees late in the 1920s; Caddy had fallen in with the Nazis. The Yanks won, the Nazis lost, and the Compson pattern held.

No sooner was the war concluded than Randall Jarrell, a native of Tennessee, brought out *Little Friend, Little Friend* (1945), a collection of poems exploring incidents of war. Jarrell spent four years in the Army

Air Corps, and although he did not see combat action personally, his poems catch the terrifying fright and destruction of war in raw detail. There is, for example, the "flesh ice-white" terror of "A Pilot from the Carrier," desperate to get out of his plane after it has been shot down, floating at last over the sea where his carrier is under attack by "the fragile sun-marked plane / That grows to him, rubbed silver tipped in flame." And there is, on the last page, "The Death of the Ball Turret Gunner," perhaps the poem that most succinctly captures the loss of innocence represented in war: "When I died they washed me out of the turret with a hose."

Quite a few more war poems appeared in Jarrell's *Losses* (1948), mostly in the same vein and with the same tone. At readings of his poetry through the 1950s and early 1960s, he especially liked to share one of those poems, "The Lines," about the ubiquitousness of lines for various procedures in the military, a process of reducing people to things, extending even "to the lines / Where the things die as though they were not things— / But lie as numbers in the crosses' lines." In some ways, though, the dead were fortunate, for the living had to deal with the guilt of war ("Eighth Air Force")—and to face the evidence of concentration camps, which Jarrell considered in several poems, thus anticipating by three decades a matter that would emerge, magnified many times, in William Styron's *Sophie's Choice* (1979).

Like Jarrell, James Dickey was in the Army Air Corps, but Dickey—joining the war in 1942 fresh from the start of his only year at Clemson—would eventually complete more than a hundred combat missions, first in the Philippines, then in Okinawa, and eventually in firebombing raids on Tokyo. Slack time in the war—the infamous hurry-up-and-wait situations—also served to deepen Dickey's reading at post libraries, a process that continued in Dickey's postwar education at Vanderbilt, so by the time of his first poetry collection, *Into the Stone and Other Poems* (1960), his five war poems were placed in a sense of time reaching back to primordial slime. One such early poem, "The Performance," caught the decapitation of a nimble, somersaulting, handstanding American soldier, Donald Armstrong, by Japanese captors in the Philippines as if the scene had somehow vaulted into the twentieth century from the mythological past of antiquity.

Dickey's most provocative and controversial World War II poem, "The Firebombing," appeared in *Buckdancer's Choice* (1965). This poem powerfully fused "twenty years in the suburbs" with the durable, un-

erasable memory of firebombing Japanese civilians in their homes in 1945. The past of World War II was quite present in 1965, as "The Firebombing" swirls from then to now and back. By 1965, Audie Murphy—America's hero archetype of World War II—had succumbed to a malaise soon to be recognized in the Vietnam era as posttraumatic stress syndrome, falling deep into a prescription-drug and alcohol addiction before realizing that he needed to sort out his life, including the to-hell-and-back part, before dying. In 1965 America sealed its military commitment to the Republic of South Vietnam with large-scale combat operations, and the napalm firebombs started falling again. It was against such a background that Robert Bly blasted Dickey for putting, with "The Firebombing," a stamp of permanent approval on all the works of the American military-industrial complex. More properly, Bly and others argued, it was time to cast the past in new perspective, to place the "we-have-the-might-and-thus-the-right" attitude under finer control. However, as Katherine Anne Porter's *Ship of Fools* (1962) suggested in its transoceanic meditation on the dark and ominous shadows of the prewar era, the mere presence of Americans in world affairs would not immediately or necessarily guarantee that vexing international problems might be dispelled without great trauma.

Yet another kind of southern World War II–related text emerged in the 1950s and 1960s, mainly to ponder the homefront scene. Faulkner finished his Snopes trilogy with *The Mansion* in 1959, and to help prepare Linda Snopes Kohl for her eventual role in resolving the ugly Flem Snopes problem, Faulkner has her leave Yoknapatawpha during the war, going down to work as a riveter in the Pascagoula shipyard. Then, in 1945, when "the knight had run out of tourneys and dragons, the war itself had slain them, used them up, made them obsolete," Faulkner's variation on the noble and heroic "Rosie-the-Riveter" pattern goes home with the fullest measure of goodness she (a Snopes . . . and a modern) could carry in order to do what has to be done.

In "The Sky Is Gray," one of the stories collected in *Bloodline* (1968), Ernest Gaines puts a much harder focus on the homefront during the war years, when many of the men were away fulfilling their military/patriotic duties. "The Sky Is Gray" accounts for the trip of a black woman and her son James to Bayonne, Louisiana, to see a dentist about the son's tooth pain. Their experience is hard, the obstacles many and diverse. They are alone in their struggles because the boy's father is away in the army, and to the boy, it "look like he ain't ever coming back home." While Daddy is defending America and its Constitution, Mama and son hear a young man in the dentist's office suggest that the rights of citizens "granted by the Constitution" cannot be exercised by people of color in Bayonne. From the perspective of the African American, this trip to the dentist sharply challenges the assumptions embedded in President Roosevelt's "Four Freedoms" justification for World War II.

Back in October of 1942, Ralph Ellison, writing for *New Masses*, had addressed himself similarly to concerns about how the war would serve the African American's reality. Ellison tells the story of Mrs. Jackson and her son Wilbur, who has been sent off to war. Even though Wilbur is fighting for freedom, Ellison raises doubts whether he or his mother will themselves find "that gate of freedom" to make the sacrifices worthwhile and "to be rid of the heavy resentment and bitterness which has been theirs for long before the war."

Flannery O'Connor found a variety of ways to introduce the war to postwar southern culture. Hazel Motes, the Jesus-obsessed protagonist of *Wise Blood* (1952), packed his peculiar strangeness to Europe and back in service of his country, though the army seems to have recognized that he was no Private Ryan, for after he had been wounded and "remembered . . . long enough to take the shrapnel out of his chest—they said they took it out but they never showed it to him and he felt it in there, rusted, and poisoning him— . . . they sent him to another desert and forgot him again." Hazel survives his war experience and sees his mother's "SHIFFER-ROBE" once again before embarking on the quest that reduces him, in darkest blindness, to "the pin point of light," a resolution having everything to do with faith and nothing to do with World War II.

Two other O'Connor stories, however, are clearly centered on the carry-over of World War II into the postwar South. "Greenleaf" involves a country farm conflict between the May family and the Greenleaf family. Readers see everything through the filter of Mrs. May's grotesquely inflated sense of superiority over all things Greenleaf, including their bull, whose horn finally punctures her pretensions. The Greenleaf sons both served with distinction in France, both marrying fine French women, both getting the most and best out of their veterans' benefits after the war. With derision oozing from her every syllable, Mrs. May says that, thanks to the war, the Greenleafs will be—in time—"Society." In contrast, of course, Wesley May's

heart condition kept him home, and his brother Scofield's service was so undistinguished for two years as to leave him a private first-class at time of discharge. For their general ineptitude and irritating self-delusion, the May family is in decline. In this story, a strange kind of justice almost seems to inhabit the southern experience of World War II.

"The Displaced Person" presents a less-comforting sense of the postwar South. In this narrative, Mrs. McIntyre is bedeviled by the persistent presence of Mr. Guizac, a Pole displaced by the German invasion and its attendant terror. A local priest, Father Flynn, arranges for Mr. Guizac to work for Mrs. McIntyre, whose farm also employs the Shortley family and some African American laborers. To Mrs. McIntyre and Mr. and Mrs. Shortley, Mr. Guizac is "The Displaced Person," and he and his family, who seem quite normal enough, come to represent the corruption of Europe, a place damned for the wars it has caused. Mrs. McIntyre's brooding skepticism about the Old World's contamination ultimately extends, with wicked irony, even to the identity of Jesus Christ as "just another D.P." When Mrs. McIntyre finally determines to rid herself of Mr. Guizac, a large farm tractor mysteriously slips into gear with no operator aboard—and with both Mr. Shortley and Mrs. McIntyre watching silently, the tractor crushes The Displaced Person. At the end, though, O'Connor registers a point of her faith rather tellingly by having the priest be the only visitor to an aged Mrs. McIntyre; his visits are filled with explanations to Mrs. McIntyre of "the doctrines of the Church."

Another displaced Pole is at the heart of William Styron's *Sophie's Choice*, the novel that abruptly interrupted his work in the mid-1970s on a Korean War narrative. The South is represented in the book by a young man named Stingo (something of a Styron surrogate), a native Virginian, a writer-wannabe type, gone north to Brooklyn in 1947 to seek his fame—and to get sex if possible. Soon enough, his interests get refocused in the person and life of a woman named Sophie. She has an interesting voice. Her life is full of the kind of experience craved by writers. Stingo knows Sophie enjoys sex, for he hears her mating with Nathan, her volatile and deeply troubled lover. Eventually, Stingo learns a thing or two. The "choice" involved Sophie and her two children, a boy and a girl, in a concentration camp in Poland during the war. Southern writers believe deeply in the lasting quality of moments in time, caught in memory. Sophie's moment of decision—which child to keep, which to lose—during the terror of the war stays with her after 1945. It crosses the Atlantic with her. Stingo becomes her lover at last, but even as he comes to know her intimately, he is beyond saving her from her memories. Sophie and Nathan die together. Stingo survives to bury them—and then to rise upon another morning. The story closes with emphasis on the renewal of spirit that comes with a new day—"Morning: excellent and fair."

By the time Styron got around to listening to long-lasting echoes of the war of his youth (two years of Marine service, without combat experience), a new generation of southern writers was emerging. They, of course, had their own war to handle, but a significant number of young southern writers responsible for narratives of the Vietnam War have found it necessary to embed accounts of World War II in their work. It's part of the connectedness-of-time pattern in southern literature, well represented in fiction by Clyde Edgerton, Barry Hannah, Jayne Anne Phillips, and James Webb.

Edgerton's *Raney* (1985) concerns the first couple of years of marriage between Charles Shepherd and Raney Bell. Charles is a Vietnam veteran. He and Raney come from very different backgrounds, and their relationship features many battles. One of the hardest battles involves the suicide of Raney's Uncle Nate. Uncle Nate is a lovable fellow, but he has contended for a long time with a problem that eventually defeats him. He fought in World War II and carried the seeds of self-destruction home with him when he returned, wounded physically and psychologically, to his family at the end of the war. He was the guy Audie Murphy almost became, and in Murphy's last years before his death in a 1971 plane crash, after conquering his addictions, he worked hard to get recognition for the severe postcombat adjustment problems being encountered by Vietnam veterans. Unfortunately, family love was not enough to save Uncle Nate, and when Charles makes disparaging remarks about the family's failure to help *their* war veteran, his marriage to Raney reaches rock bottom. It's a classic case of the past intruding upon the present, just what one would expect in southern literature.

In *Geronimo Rex* (1972), one of Barry Hannah's early novels, Harriman Monroe's youth is filled with fantasies of violence—sometimes just imagined, sometimes real—largely inspired by his knowledge of warfare in World War II, either the Japanese snipers in the Pacific islands or Nazi atrocities in Europe. Sure enough, the child Harriman is father of the man Harry, a lasting legacy of the war. In *Boomerang* (1989), a

much later narrative, Hannah managed to compress western history into a few tight lines of explosive surprise by saying, "The Europeans occurred with tea and gunpowder. Some of the afternoons were tedious and so they began killing thousands of each other to own shit. Then came Pearl Harbor. Then came America and Uncle Joe, who only killed seven million of his own people for, get this, an idea. Commie against Free." Vietnam was the most substantial bloodbath of the "commie against free" era, and Hannah puts it just a breath away from World War II.

Jayne Anne Phillips, in her novel *Machine Dreams* (1984), deftly sets up the Vietnam War as an extension of World War II by following the machine motif in American life from Mitch Hampson's construction (and mass burial) work in the South Pacific (mainly New Guinea) through to his son Billy's death in a helicopter crash in Vietnam. The final "machine dream" takes place in the mind of Danner, Billy's sister, with a surreal vision of Billy and Danner walking in a "deep dark forest," accompanied only by the sounds Billy makes in imitation of a plane going down in war. That eerie sound carries with it memories of World War II and Vietnam fused together.

When Robert E. Lee Hodges Jr., one of the key characters in James Webb's best-selling Vietnam War novel *Fields of Fire* (1978), is preparing to go off to the war of his generation, he first seeks a kind of communion with his father, who was killed in World War II. There is a footlocker full of mementos for the son to treasure, but even more powerfully, there is the voice of his grandmother, quietly filling in all the necessary details about how his "daddy died right there in the front lines, a combat soldier, staring cold into them Nazi eyes, knee-deep in the snow at the Battle of the Bulge." Just as Audie Murphy heard of war from a World War I veteran, Robert E. Lee Hodges Jr. acquired his zealous interest in Vietnam from accounts passed to him of World War II battlefields. Webb notes that "It was a continuum, a litany. Pride. Courage. Fear. An inherited right to violence."

Ellen Gilchrist's National Book Award–winning collection of stories *Victory Over Japan* (1984) serves handily to put into final perspective the on-going transformative power of World War II in southern culture. Significantly, only the first and last stories have World War II details, but the structure of the whole work represents the South from World War II to the present. The first story, "Victory Over Japan," is set during the war, on the homefront, with a deeply southern family displaced temporarily from the South, up in Indiana, while the father is away fighting in the war. Rhoda Katherine Manning is in the third grade, and she has literary aspirations. She's going to write a story for her school paper about a shy classmate who was bitten by a squirrel and then had to have rabies shots. The Germans have been defeated, but there are still the "Japs left to go," so Rhoda and her classmates engage in one last paper drive to support the war effort. By the conclusion of "Victory Over Japan," the bombs have fallen on Hiroshima and Nagasaki. Rhoda knows her father will soon be coming home, although she has some ambivalence about his return, for he yells at her mother and wants Rhoda to behave. In her dreams, Rhoda takes off for Japan to finish the Japanese: "Down we dive, spouting flame from under. Off with one hell of a roar. We live in flame. Buckle down in flame. For nothing can stop the Army Air Corps."

The war ends. Father comes home. Rhoda grows up—fast and furiously, out of her father's control. The postwar years are fast, passing with "one hell of a roar." The middle section of the book has several stories gathered under the heading of "Crazy, Crazy, Now Showing Everywhere," which neatly sums up the turbulence introduced by the end of the war. With the Nora Jane Whittington stories of travels to California for major sex (also called love in the 1960s and 1970s) and then with the strange doings of Miss Crystal and her New Orleans clan (a husband she loathes, a little daughter clone), mostly told through the voice of her maid Traceleen, it is clear that the spirit of Rhoda's World War II dream went on to set decades of life in flame.

Great forces were unleashed by World War II, forces with remarkable staying power. The last story of Gilchrist's collection, called simply "Crystal," puts the whole expanse of time, from World War II to the late 1970s, in crystal-clear perspective. Crystal and Traceleen deliver an exotic Mercedes Benz from New Orleans to a Texas ranch that Crystal's brother Phelan has set up as a wild-game hunting preserve for rich and dumb suckers. Crystal goes wild on the ranch in Texas, using Phelan's fancy car to break down all the fences, thus releasing all the game animals. Leaving Phelan seething in rage, Crystal heads back home. On the plane ride, she tells Traceleen a story of her youth, in Indiana, during the war. With this story in a story, the circle closes. Phelan, four years older than Crystal, was playing war one Sunday morning. He was having so much fun flying a pretend cardboard airplane that Crystal wanted a

turn. She had to trade plenty of her best possessions, including a set of binoculars from a relative who served in World War I, to get a turn in the plane. Eventually, she's flying, ready to bomb. She obviously loves retelling this story, and when Traceleen's attention seems to wander, Crystal says, "This is everything I know about love I'm telling you. Everything I know about everything." In the imaginative life of southerners, World War II has had a very long run, and stories of the war just about cover the whole territory.

Owen W. Gilman Jr.

See also Sixties, The; Vietnam War.

WRIGHT, RICHARD

Richard Wright might be said to have spent his whole life fleeing from and at the same time engaging the South in battle. Born on a plantation near Roxie, Mississippi, in 1908, he was the son of illiterate sharecropper Nathan Wright and schoolteacher Ella Wilson Wright. All of his grandparents had been slaves, and Wright grew up struggling against the legacy forced upon all African Americans in the post-Reconstruction South: racism, segregation, poverty, systematic persecution, and denial of human rights. "Big Boy Leaves Home," the lead story in his first published book, *Uncle Tom's Children* (1938), echoes the pattern of Wright's own life: a young black man, after witnessing a horrific example of white violence against innocent blacks, flees for his life to the North. *Black Boy: A Record of Childhood and Youth* (1945) is Wright's nonfictional testimony against the South of his raising, recounting instance after instance of the psychological as well as physical threats that were the daily nightmare of his life from early boyhood until the day that he too, like Bigger, headed north. Wright moved to Chicago from Memphis when he was nineteen years old, carrying with him a ninth-grade education, a passion for reading, and an anger combined with hunger that became the signature of all his works, whether set in the South or the North or Europe. He turned to Communism as both a compatible ideological force and temporarily as an emotional support system, yet throughout the 1930s nothing mattered to him as much as his writing, the vehicle that provided his only satisfying escape from the past. Although he moved from Chicago to New York and finally to Paris, the southern brand of racism that so dominated his early life provided life-long fuel for his writer's vision of what America meant to its black citizens, and he remained a deeply committed, combative citizen to the end.

Wright mastered the urban naturalism that was a hallmark of fiction in the 1930s, and with the publication of *Native Son* in 1940, he became the author of the first black novel to be a Book-of-the-Month Club selection. In the summer of 1940, Wright traveled back to the South for one last time, to work with Paul Green on a stage production of *Native Son*. He returned in memory to the South again to write *Black Boy,* another hugely popular best-seller but also a book that was condemned on the Senate floor by Theodore Bilbo, the U.S. senator of Wright's native state. The whole of Wright's autobiography, entitled appropriately *American Hunger,* was not published until 1977. By 1947 Wright moved permanently to France, becoming one of a large community of American self-exiles. He was warmly recognized in Europe, where he became friends with Jean-Paul Sartre, Gunnar Myrdal, Jean Genet, and Frantz Fanon. From a base in Paris, Wright traveled widely, working in Argentina on a film version of *Native Son* and writing a book based on a visit to Africa (*Black Power,* published in 1954). Increasingly he felt the persecution of the FBI and anti-Communist authorities in France, and in his last years he suffered from both physical illness, primarily dysentery, and psychological turmoil. His existential continental novel *The Outsider* was published in 1953 to good sales, but when he returned in imagination to Mississippi for the writing of *The Long Dream,* published in 1958, the results were both critically and financially disappointing.

His other published works of fiction, *Savage Holiday* (1954) and the collection of stories *Eight Men* (1961), did not substantially help his reputation, yet nonfiction essays on racism, such as *White Man, Listen* (1957) and *The Color Curtain* (1956), written with Gunnar Myrdal, kept alive his role as major spokesman for the African American experience. Wright died in Paris in 1960, under somewhat mysterious circumstances, and was buried there.

Richard Wright depicted an America in which the effects of racism condemned both blacks and whites to a state of hate. Wright was enraged most by the internalizing of prejudice among blacks, who often turned against each other and sank into cowardice, despair, and self-destruction. In the South, he endured physical and emotional hunger, harassment by whites, and furious criticism by his own family. All doors to intellectual or economic opportunity were closed to him. His response to the South was not to submit but to fight, and he never relaxed his vigilant sense of being caught in enemy territory. No African American writer more vividly exposed the tragedy of racism in America, and no southern African American writer faced down the bigotry and violence of the region with more eloquence or determination.

Lucinda H. MacKethan

See also African American Literature, 1919 to Present; Mississippi, Literature of; Racism.

Michel Fabre, *The Unfinished Quest of Richard Wright* (1973); Joyce Ann Joyce, *Richard Wright's Art of Tragedy* (1986); Richard Wright and Keneth Kinnamon, *Conversations with Richard Wright* (1993).

Y

―⁂―

Y'ALL

Y'all is the ultimate dialect icon of the American South. In projections of speech that range from the stereotypic caricatures found in comic strips to the extravagant expression of the regional themes such as that celebrated at the 1996 Olympics hosted by Atlanta, no single utterance serves more effectively to situate the setting as southern. Southern highland dialects may alternatively use *you'uns* for second-person plural, and northerners in the United States as well as other vernacular English dialects around the world may use *youse* in a parallel way, but *y'all* and its variant spellings—*you-all, ya'll, y'l,* and *you all*—uniquely situate a speaker as southern American. The southern essence of *y'all* is symbolically projected whether the speaker is a transplanted African American whose family migrated to New York City from South Carolina after World War I or a lifelong Anglo-American resident of rural Mississippi.

The regional demarcation of *y'all* is currently more secure than its etymology and referential meaning, which continue to be hotly debated among dialectologists. Most etymologists trace its derivation to a phonetically contracted form of the construction *you all,* a construction that dates back at least to Elizabethan times and is documented in Shakespearean lines such as "O spite! O hell! I see *you all* are bent to set against me for your merriment" from *A Midsummer Night's Dream,* but an alternative origin in the Scots-Irish construction *ye aw* has also been proposed. Unfortunately, the literary representation *you all,* amply documented since at least the early modern period of English, is ambiguous. It may be interpreted as the pronoun *you* plus the quantifier *all* in the construction *you áll,* a widespread and generalized construction of the English language, or *yóu all,* the marked regional form that is contractible to *y'all* and associated exclusively with southern English.

Attestations of *yóu all* in the *OED* date back to the early 1800s, but the literary representation of southern *you-all* and *y'all* does not appear to any extent until the turn of the twentieth century, coming into full bloom in the mid-1990s. Thus it is not found in the regional representation of *Adventures of Huckleberry Finn* in the late 1880s but appears in Chesnutt's *The Colonel's Dream* (1905) and sporadically in other works of that era. The true symbolic force of symbolically southern *y'all,* however, is largely a twentieth-century development, both in speech and literature. In fact, the current, predominant spelling *y'all* was only adopted in the last half-century.

The precise referential meaning of *y'all* is also debatable. It is used predominantly as a second-person plural pronoun reference in sentences such as *Y'all both should be there,* so that it contrasts with the second-person singular form *you* as in *Cindy, you should be there.* In this way, the personal pronouns of southern English regularly differentiate between singular and plural forms for all persons. But its reference may be extended to second-person singular expressions as well, at least in ritualized routines such as *Y'all come back now,* which may be uttered to a single individual as well as to a group. The extended use of *y'all* to include some specialized singular references as well as second-person plural references is probably even a later development than its regularized use for second-person plurals.

While dialectologists may argue about the etymology and referential meaning of *y'all,* its regional voice is unmistakable. How people are addressed is typically the most universal and transparent indicator of relations of power and solidarity in language. Southern speech is, of course, well known for its particularized uses of address forms such as *Sir/Ma'am, Mr./Mrs. (Ms.), Auntie,* and so forth to indicate both proscribed and fluid relations of power and solidarity. In this regional, hierarchical setting, *y'all* has come to unify all southern speakers symbolically, regardless of race and class. Speakers who utter *y'all* may be white or black, rich or poor, genteel or crude, but they are, more than anything, southern. This simple dialect demarcation therefore transcends other, much more complex social interactions in the American South. Perhaps more important, this overarching unity in addressing people directly serves notice of an obvious separation of southerners from all other regional groups.

Walt Wolfram

See also Dialect Literature; Vernacular Voice.

Frederic G. Cassidy and Joan H. Hall, eds., *Dictionary of American Regional English* (1985–); Michael Montgomery, "The Etymology of Y'all," in *Old English and New: Studies in Languages and Linguistics in Honor of Frederic G. Cassidy*, ed. Joan H. Hall (1992); Michael Montgomery, "A Note on Y'all," *American Speech* 64 (1989); Walt Wolfram and Natalie Schilling-Estes, *American English: Dialects and Variation* (1998).

YANKEE

The cover of Roy Blount's recent *Book of Southern Humor* features a picture of Blount wearing a baseball cap that says "To Hell with How They Do It in New York." Southern attitudes toward the Yankee have not always been so humorous, though the use and meaning of the term depend both on historical context and cultural perspectives in a complex and changing South. How the child Ticey in Ernest Gaines's *The Autobiography of Miss Jane Pittman* (1971) sees the Yankee who names her is different from how Yankees are pictured by George W. Harris's Sut Lovingood or by Thomas Nelson Page or by Donald Davidson and the Agrarians. In his conclusion to *Cavalier and Yankee* (1957), W. R. Taylor records Edmund Ruffin's final entry in his diary on June 17, 1865, minutes before his suicide: "I here declare my unmitigated hatred to Yankee rule—to all political, social and business connections with the Yankee and the Yankee race." Even Blount admits that he gets a thrill out of reciting "I'm a Good Old Rebel"—"I hates the Yankee nation / And everything they do / I hates the Declaration of Independence too"—though he says that maybe he gets that thrill because he learned to appreciate in the South of

his day both the Pledge of Allegiance and the American tradition of holding nothing sacred.

Not many southern children today know what the proverbial expression "Yankee dime" means, much less that it springs from the image of the Yankee peddler on the frontier as a cheating mercenary. They are more likely to have seen the New York Yankees on television, or "Damn Yankees" in a local stage production. Southern understandings of the term *Yankee* are rooted in the ambiguous etymology of the word. The most popular explanation is that *Yankee* comes from Jan Kees, a contemptuous nickname that the English first applied to the Dutch. Another explanation is that the Native American corruption of the word *English* is "Yengeese," then "Yankee." A 1789 historical reference derives *Yankee* as a term of derision from the Cherokee *eankke*, meaning slave or coward, a term applied to New Englanders by Virginians for not assisting them in a war with the Cherokee. In the French and Indian War of 1758, the British general James Wolfe uses the term as a contemptuous name for New Englanders, but by the American Revolution the term *Yankee* is not only applied to all Americans by the British, it is also applied by New Englanders to themselves. The song "Yankee Doodle," intended to poke fun at the colonial army, became a battle song celebrating independence. At some point in the process of giving dignity to the term, the mythical story of a defeated tribe of Yankos Indians who gave their "invincible" name to their brave conquerors became popular. Certain comic traits of Yankee character and speech are reflected in Seba Smith's Colonel Jack Downing and James Russell Lowell's Hosea Biglow—characters both taciturn and provincial.

Thus Yankee has been an admirable or contemptuous nickname for Americans, especially New Englanders, depending on who uses it. Colonel Downing in caricature became Uncle Sam. Mark Twain, a southern boy living in Hartford, offers in *A Connecticut Yankee in King Arthur's Court* (1889) an embodiment of the strengths and weaknesses of American ingenuity. George M. Cohan's "I'm a Yankee Doodle Dandy" is sung in the South, and certainly all Americans have become Yankees, or Yanks, to the rest of the world in the great wars of the twentieth century. Shouts of "Yankee, Go Home" in a foreign country could be applied to someone from Georgia just as well as to someone from Connecticut.

However, southerners, African American as well as white, have had their special understanding of what a

Yankee is—the enemy or the emancipator—especially defined by antebellum differences, slavery, and the Civil War. The presence of the Yankee in the South during Reconstruction and after was galling to "unreconstructed" Confederates and generations of their dispossessed children. Taylor's *Cavalier and Yankee* describes the history of differences in the regions and how they came to conflict, and Cash's *The Mind of the South* (1941) sets forth the "frontier the Yankee made" and how southerners after the war were "far more self-conscious than they had been before, far more aware of their differences and of the line which divided what was southern from what was not."

The term *Yankee* has always had a special resonance in southern literature, and understanding how the word has changed in meaning and importance means coming to terms with the history of southern culture. The terms of sectional alignment on which North and South divided are evident as early as Bradford and Byrd, and the interplay of the Yankee with the South is as evident in the slave narratives of Frederick Douglass and Harriet Jacobs and the fiction of William Wells Brown as in the narrator of *Swallow Barn* (1832). The Yankee in the plantation fiction, antebellum romances, and travel narratives before 1865 as well as in much of the literature between 1865 and 1920 is mostly defined by the southern apologist, though to group Southworth, Hentz, Simms, Hayne, Timrod, Page, and Evans Wilson with G. W. Harris is to ignore important differences. Sut Lovingood's essay on the Puritan Yankee is more defined by the image of the grasping Yankee peddler on the frontier than by differences over slavery. For Sut, the Yankee is "powerful ornary stock," and he holds the Indians responsible for not destroying the *Mayflower* when it arrived. "Everything the Yankee does am a cheat in some way." Page's plantation images of the Yankee may be contrasted with George W. Cable's high-minded Yankee outsiders. Charles Chesnutt's Yankee entrepreneurs who come south in *The Conjure Woman* (1899), seen from an African American and local perspective, are gently treated, whereas Grace King's memories of Julia Ward Howe's postbellum visit to New Orleans reveals considerable resentment. Henry Grady's doctrine of New South development, as opposed to notions of agrarianism and nostalgia, accommodates Yankee money, yet Cash's history of the "savage ideal" sets a provincial South firmly against Yankee intrusion.

The image of the Yankee becomes even more complex after 1920. In "A Southern Mode of the Imagination," Allen Tate points out how the southern writers after World War I "reentered the world" but looked round and saw for the first time since about 1830 that the Yankees were not to blame for everything. For Tate, this realization occasioned a shift from the rhetorical mode in writing to a dialectical mode—Yeats's dictum that out of the quarrel with others we make rhetoric, out of the quarrel with ourselves, poetry. For Tate and many other readers of modern southern literature, the Yankee is not necessarily dismissed but absorbed into an internal conflict of values in the community and individual. As late as 1957, Donald Davidson writes *Still Rebels, Still Yankees* (1972), remembering to some degree the conflicts defined by *I'll Take My Stand* (1930) and the Scopes trial, and several generations of writers after 1920 looked over their shoulders, in Tate's words, at a past beyond Mencken's "The Sahara of the Bozart" (1920) to the abiding conflict with the Yankee as well.

The Fugitives might have run from nothing faster than the high-caste Brahmins of the Old South, but their work, like that of Faulkner and Wolfe, and the later Porter, Gordon, and Lytle, is rooted in a southern past that knew who the Yankee was. Faulkner's treatment of southern history is complex, and the materialistic intruders in his communities are more likely to be Snopeses than Yankees. The past he develops in *Absalom, Absalom!* (1936), for example, can be contrasted to that in Young's *So Red the Rose* and the more traditional *Gone With the Wind* (1936), Margaret Mitchell's best-seller. Faulkner's brief and humorous "A Guest's Impression of New England" recounts a road trip with Malcolm Cowley through backroads in Connecticut and Massachusetts and a meeting with the best sort of Yankee—"free, private, not made so by the stern and rockbound land—the poor thin soil and the hard long winters—on which his lot was cast, but on the contrary: having elected deliberately of his own volition that stern land and weather because he knew he was tough enough to cope with them." The Harlem Renaissance and the Great Migration highlight the interplay between North and South, and the engagement of the two cultures stimulate, in part, the work of Du Bois, Toomer, James Weldon Johnson, Hurston, Sterling Brown, and Bontemps. Richard Wright's move out of the South to Chicago offers an escape from Jim Crow but brings a realization that Yankeeland now has its own kind of poverty. At the same time, for his older contemporaries, Harlem was the place to be.

In the recent South, both in the periods from 1945

to 1970 and from 1970 to the present, accelerated social change has so altered southern culture, even in the small towns, that the traditional images of the Yankee recounted here remain only as a joke on the popular bookshelf. Roy Blount, Bailey White, Lewis Grizzard, Florence King, and Jerry Clower remind us of our southernness, and books like Marilyn Schwartz's *A Southern Belle Primer* (1991) tell us to forget about ordering iced tea in New Haven out of season. Yankees have moved to Atlanta and Charlotte in such numbers that they can't be recognized in interstate traffic. Cracker Barrel, Kentucky Fried Chicken, and Wal-Mart have gone national. Willie Morris not only went north toward home, he came back south toward home, and he's not alone. Certainly there are contrasts among southern writers since 1945. Welty, Styron, O'Connor, Elizabeth Spencer, Walker Percy, John Barth, Ernest Gaines, Ralph Ellison, Margaret Walker, and Reynolds Price write of a changed landscape, but they are more likely than their younger colleagues to define a recognizable southern community against an outside world. It is difficult to say that such an outside world is entirely a Yankee world, for the issues of meaning and direction have become much larger. The civil-rights era of the 1950s and 1960s did define a Yankee presence in the South once again.

More recent writers, such as Barry Hannah, Frederick Barthelme, Doris Betts, Alice Walker, Cormac McCarthy, Harry Crews, John Holman, Robert Olen Butler, and Larry Brown, defy defining themselves against any notion of South or North. *Yankee* may be a meaningless term today. One need only read Padgett Powell's introduction to Shannon Ravenel's *New Stories from the South* (1998) to know that Faulkner's famous lecture on the old verities of the human heart has been left behind. Powell prefers Wash Jones's quintessential line, "Well, Kernel, they mought have kilt us, but they ain't whupped us yit, air they?" Powell sees the literature of the South as full of people running around admitting or denying their whippedness. But, he says, they have been whipped, and whipped good. So Richard Ford's *The Sportswriter* (1986) is set in Michigan and New Jersey, but what does that tell us about Yankees? Not much. It may be better to say that many southerners—African Americans as well as whites—deny being whipped and maintain a curiously defensive attitude toward what they perceive as stereotyped portrayals of themselves by the outside world, Yankees included. As Lewis Grizzard points out, if you don't like it here, Delta is ready when you are. In humor, of course, Blount finds a way to come to terms with the Yankees: he now lives in New York and Massachusetts, he says, because "when I'm in the south I wander around wondering where I can get the *New York Times,* and when I'm in the north I wander around wondering where I can get some okra, and I would rather think about some okra than the *New York Times.*"

Thomas J. Richardson

See also Agrarians; Faulkner, William.

W. J. Cash, *The Mind of the South* (1941); Fred Hobson, *The Southern Writer in the Postmodern World* (1991); William Taylor, *Cavalier and Yankee* (1961).

YELLOW-DOG DEMOCRAT

A yellow-dog Democrat would vote for his or her party's candidates even if a yellow dog headed the ticket. Long before a southern singer carried on about a creature who was nuthin' but a hound dog, a yaller dawg was understood to be the lowliest cur in creation, ranking at the very bottom of canine society. In the eyes of party loyalists, though, he was still preferable to any Republican, for the Grand Old Party was associated with the Union side in the Civil War and the perceived iniquities of Reconstruction. Though the term connotes no regional identity, it was most often applied to the South because that section displayed a devotion to the Democratic Party that no other part of the country matched. Since World War II, the yellow-dog Democrat has become a rarer breed as millions of southerners have abandoned the party of their ancestors. When the protagonist of the 1966 novel *The Last Gentleman* returns to his native section, Walker Percy writes, "The South he came home to was different from the South he had left. It was happy, victorious, Christian, rich, patriotic and Republican." Yet even at the close of the twentieth century, large numbers of southerners continued to call themselves, if only whimsically, yellow-dog Democrats.

William E. Leuchtenburg

See also Solid South.

YEOMAN

The concept of the yeoman, like that of the cavalier and the southern gentleman, was translated from England to the South during the colonial period. But unlike these contrasting aristocratic concepts, the yeoman ideal took root and flourished throughout the American colonies. In both Old World and New World, the word signified a stalwart, independent, hard-working farmer who cultivated his own land. His social standing was below the larger landholding gentry but above the mass of landless laborers and tenant farmers. It is probable that many if not most of those immigrating to America during the colonial period arrived with the ambition of establishing themselves as prosperous yeoman farmers.

The yeoman ideal, emphasizing a responsible, self-reliant, rural middle class, thus spanned North and South and was entirely consonant with the democratic political principles flourishing in America that actuated the Revolution and resulted in the Declaration of Independence, the Constitution, and the Bill of Rights. Northern as well as southern leaders, Benjamin Franklin as well as Thomas Jefferson, championed the equality of all men. But it was Virginian Jefferson who gave most felicitous and powerful expression to the virtues of the yeoman class. In his *Notes on the State of Virginia* (1785), he asserted forcefully the idea that the strength and vigor of the new nation lay in the prosperity of its small farmers and in the continued availability of vacant land as a safety valve insuring social stability by absorbing the downtrodden masses of urban poor.

But though the yeoman ideal was widely embraced throughout the new republic, there developed in the southern states a rival concept that expressed a profoundly different notion of social order. Here, fertile soil, warm summers, and the importation of slave labor created a plantation system presided over by men who were activated not by the concept of the yeoman but by that of the gentleman, with its fundamental assumption of the inequality of man reflected in the inequality of social condition. The conviction that plantation owners were superior men born to lead was also reflected in the myth of Virginia's cavalier settlement, which the rest of the South eventually embraced as its own inheritance. Thus there existed in the southern states from the nation's beginning a decided tension between yeoman and cavalier ideals. Indeed, such a tension was reflected in Jefferson himself—a man who championed the rights of man and the value of the yeoman farmer but who was also a slave owner and planter of highly sophisticated tastes formed by the aristocratic code of the Virginia gentleman.

There can be no question that the South's embrac-

ing of slavery weakened its commitment to the yeoman ideal. As the region's peculiar institution came under increasingly heavy moral censure in the decades preceding the Civil War, southerners felt more and more obligated to defend their way of life by adducing in its support the southern gentleman and his lady. These aristocratic, refined, courteous, and high-minded types were presented as the flowers of southern civilization, the best products of a paternalistic and benign plantation system. In such an exalted apologia, the self-reliant yeoman tilling his own acres could play no significant part.

In trumpeting the cavalier and largely ignoring its yeoman inheritance, the South ignored reality. Modern historians have thoroughly reconstructed that reality, but it was first articulated by Daniel Hundley in his *Social Relations in Our Southern States* (1860). In this book, Hundley complained that far too much attention as well as opprobrium had been directed toward a relatively small planter class. In fact, he argued, the class that constituted the overwhelming majority of the South's citizens was the middle class, composed of merchants, teachers, doctors, artisans, and, more numerously, farmers. These men, of sturdy Saxon stock, could be seen working assiduously in their fields, occasionally assisted by a few slave laborers. It was they, and not the planter, who represented southern culture most typically.

In the face of historical reality, antebellum southern writers concocted plantation romances. They fashioned a literary landscape dominated by lordly cavaliers and pure, refined ladies—a landscape virtually devoid of yeomen. Indeed, common farmers could be found only in the writings of Southwest humorists—writers such as Johnson Jones Hooper, Augustus Baldwin Longstreet, Hardin E. Taliaferro, and George Washington Harris—who rendered the life of the rural South in the fresh and metaphorically vivid language of the yeoman. Vivid though these tales might have been, they were not considered belletristically significant and were relegated to the pages of newspapers and lowly sporting magazines. Though they described the rough and frequently violent texture of life in the interior South and though they were dominated by plain-speaking yeoman types, these works were not hostile to the plantation tradition. Indeed, the first-person narrators who usually shaped and framed the stories were clearly inheritors of the cavalier ethos. These aristocratic observers guaranteed that even the most sympathetic treatment of a yeoman character would retain a just-detected edge of condescension, assuring both northern and southern readers that in the South the small farmer remained in his properly subservient social place.

During the decades preceding the Civil War, the South's culture as well as its literature rallied around the figure of the cavalier, not the yeoman. Indeed, the dominance of the cavalier ideal reflected the fact that most southern farmers identified themselves with the slaveholding minority. This identification was in part the result of the common opposition of planter and yeoman to the powerful forces of Yankee merchant capitalism, which seemed destined to undermine the rural, self-sufficient way of life of both classes. The economic interests of planters did not generally threaten the survival of the yeoman. Planters were willing to extract their profits from the sweat of their slaves rather than from the sweat of their small-farm neighbors. Common economic interests combined with a common faith in white supremacy and a common preoccupation with honor to assure that the large majority of yeomen in the Old South would remain loyal to the planter aristocracy and would subscribe with varying degrees of fervor to the cavalier ethos that underlay this aristocracy.

In 1857 southerner Hinton Rowan Helper published *The Impending Crisis of the South,* a clarion call to the yeomanry of the South. His work urged non-slaveholders to wake up to the fact that an arrogant slaveowning minority, elected to offices of political power, had used that power to further their own narrow interests and to hoodwink and take advantage of the majority. In attacking the hegemony of the planter class, Helper was appealing to the southern yeoman to honor his own interests by imaginatively disentangling himself from the complex of myths associated with the aristocratic ideal. But the average southerner could not repudiate this ideal. Instead of turning on the slavocracy, rank-and-file southerners—with yeomen among them—turned on Helper with fury. They excoriated him as a damned abolitionist, a satanic figure equal in evil with the Republican presidential candidate, Abraham Lincoln.

The Civil War resulted in the abolition of slavery and the destruction of the plantation system, but southern attitudes remained fundamentally unreconstructed. The cavalier was still venerated in postbellum fiction and the yeoman largely ignored. Mary Noailles Murfree's *In the Tennessee Mountains* (1884) featured portrayals of mountaineers that were more picturesque than profound, and Mark Twain's classic *Adventures of Huckleberry Finn* (1885) presented an extensive if decidedly un-Jeffersonian view of southern yeomen. Otherwise, the plain farmer played an insignificant role in the popular regional fiction of the post–Civil War decades.

By the beginning of the twentieth century, a pioneering generation of southern writers began scrutinizing the myths of the Old South critically and with irony, and in the process they also began examining the role of the yeoman as a part of this mythic inheritance. One of the first fictional pioneers was Virginia novelist Ellen Glasgow. Her powerfully realistic *Barren Ground* (1925) presented a heroine, Dorinda Oakley, who returned from New York City to the Old Dominion and her family's broomsedge-choked acres and through enormous resolution and hard work created a successful life and a prosperous farm.

William Faulkner's Yoknapatawpha cycle of novels incorporated the plain farmers of the red-clay hill country as an essential part of the writer's varied and complex social canvas. In one of his most acclaimed works, *As I Lay Dying* (1930), the author found strength, endurance, and reason for faith in mankind in the struggles of the country folk of his mythical Mississippi county. Robert Penn Warren's *All the King's Men* (1946) was among other things a complex and ambiguous treatment of the South's yeoman tradition. Willie Stark—part yeoman and part redneck, part Satan and part saint—was a galvanic protagonist who, despite his own corruption, waged a legitimate people's war against the equally corrupt forces of established wealth and social privilege in the modern South.

The voices of the twentieth-century Southern Renascence included those of the Agrarians—southern writers associated with Vanderbilt University, such as John Crowe Ransom, Allen Tate, Robert Penn Warren, and Donald Davidson. During the 1920s and 1930s, these men championed a farming economy established on the yeoman tradition over industrial capitalism as part of their social design for the New South. Echoes of this agrarianism can be clearly heard in Tennessee novelist Madison Jones's *The Innocent* (1957). Here the protagonist, a staunch agrarian, fights a doomed and anachronistic battle to restore the pastoral ideal to his community.

Contemporary southern writing has thus fully evoked the yeoman, and certain areas of the South have proved to be exceptionally rich fictional soil for portraits of small farmers. One of these areas is Georgia. Erskine Caldwell's *Tobacco Road* (1932) and *God's Little Acre* (1933) represent substantial departures from the nineteenth-century Jeffersonian ideal, presenting characters with lives rooted in the land who are also suffused by a repressed but explosive eroticism. In her masterful short stories, Flannery O'Connor uses the plain folk of rural Georgia as an essential part of her comic and profoundly religious analysis of damnation and salvation. Harry Crews's novels are set in rural Georgia and urban Florida. In works such as *The Gospel Singer* (1968), he examines characters who straddle the line between yeoman and white trash and struggle to make the difficult transition from farm to city.

The fiction of the Appalachian South has also been heavily inflected by the yeoman tradition. Jesse Stuart's short stories have as their setting hill-country Kentucky. They are slices of mountain life that express love of the land and of the people who farm it. In *Oral History* (1983) and *Fair and Tender Ladies* (1989), Lee Smith makes splendid use of the rich folk traditions of her southwest Virginia birthplace.

North Carolina writers have pulled strongly from their state's yeoman heritage. The novels of Reynolds Price portray the lives of the fundamentalist, Scots-Irish inhabitants of the rural Piedmont. Those of Sylvia Wilkinson focus on the farm people of eastern North Carolina. Doris Betts likewise draws her inspiration from farmers who have often become mill workers, people without college degrees who are still rooted in the soil. Charles Frazier's *Cold Mountain* (1997) is a recent and remarkable fictional achievement, a southern novel that powerfully evokes the Civil War but filters that war through a consciousness that is profoundly yeoman in spirit. Together, these works demonstrate that the yeoman, ignored by the South's nineteenth-century fiction writers, has been rediscovered and richly employed by modern southern writers and that he will continue to be a vital element of southern fiction.

Ritchie D. Watson

See also Agrarians; Appalachian Literature; Aristocracy; Cavalier; Class; Gentleman; Humor, Beginnings to 1900; Jefferson, Thomas; Novel, 1820 to 1865; Plantation Fiction; Poor White; Tall Tale.

Elizabeth Fox-Genovese and Eugene D. Genovese, *Fruits of Merchant Capital: Slavery and Bourgeois Property in the Rise and Expansion of Capitalism* (1983); Ritchie D. Watson, *Yeo-man Versus Cavalier: The Old Southwest's Fictional Road to Rebellion* (1993); Bertram Wyatt-Brown, *Southern Honor: Ethics and Behavior in the Old South* (1982).

YOKNAPATAWPHA

If indeed the literature of the American South is characterized primarily by its deep and abiding sense of place, as many have argued, then there is no place in southern letters more fully realized or quickly recognized than Yoknapatawpha, the fictional county described by its creator William Faulkner as his "own little postage stamp of native soil." Over the course of fourteen novels and dozens of short stories that span over a century and a half of history, from the beginning of the nineteenth century to the author's own time, Faulkner populated his imaginary microcosm of the South with aristocratic families sliding into genteel poverty (Compsons, Griersons, Sartorises) and lower-class whites on their way up the socio-economic ladder (Snopeses), with upstart parvenus (Sutpen) and dignified yeomen (McCallums, Beauchamps), with slaves and their descendants (Clytemnestra, Dilsey, Luster) as well as a Chickasaw chief and his descendent (Ikkemetubbe, Sam Fathers). Linked together in an intricately interconnecting web of narratives in which events from other novels are alluded to, reinterpreted, even contradicted, Yoknapatawpha takes on a life of its own, contained within yet seeming to stand apart somehow from the body of work that Faulkner created. Deriving its name from the Chickasaw word *Yoconapatafa,* or "split land," Yoknapatawpha was modeled vaguely on the topography and social landscape of Lafayette County, Mississippi, where Faulkner lived for most of his life after his family relocated from nearby Ripley, Mississippi, shortly before the author's fifth birthday. Tempting though it is to see Yoknapatawpha and its county seat of Jefferson as detailed replicas of Lafayette and the town of Oxford, Faulkner made some efforts to dispel that impression. One can find references within Faulkner's fiction to Oxford (for instance in *Absalom, Absalom!,* 1936, where Henry Sutpen and Charles Bon meet at the University of Mississippi, and in "An Odor of Verbena," 1938, where Bayard Sartoris studies law), which he situates some forty miles away from Jefferson. The temptation can also be strong to reduce all of the key events and themes of southern history into the Yoknapatawpha fiction. Faulkner explores the transition from Indian lands to early white settlement (as in "Red Leaves," 1931), the ascendency as well as the decline of King Cotton (as in *Absalom, Absalom!*), the Civil War and Reconstruction (*The Unvanquished,* 1938), the destruction of the natural environment (*Go Down, Moses,* 1942) and the incursion of commercial culture (*The Hamlet,* 1940; *The Town,* 1957; and *The Mansion,* 1959), the destabilization of the social and racial status quo following the First World War (*Flags in the Dust,* 1929; "Dry September," 1931), and the repercussions of slavery, miscegenation, and segregation on African Americans and whites alike (*Light in August,* 1932; *Go Down, Moses; Absalom, Absalom!*).

Yet to reduce these matters to strictly regional concerns is to lose sight of the mythic dimensions of these works. As in the case of most true artists, Faulkner used the immediate particulars of his familiar surroundings and transformed them into works that addressed broader, if not universal, concerns of humankind. For all of the nuanced attention Faulkner gives to geographical and ecological features, historically specific social forces, and individual human motivations, Yoknapatawpha would not loom so large in the reader's imagination if it did not serve as a bridge to larger concerns that extend beyond the confines of Mississippi, the South, or the United States.

James H. Watkins

See also Faulkner, William; Indians; Mississippi, Literature of; Oxford, Mississippi.

Cleanth Brooks, *William Faulkner: The Yoknapatawpha Country* (1963); Elizabeth M. Kerr, *Yoknapatawpha* (1969); Michael Millgate, "A Cosmos of My Own," in *Fifty Years of Yoknapatawpha,* ed. Doreen Fowler and Ann J. Abadie (1980).

LIST OF CONTRIBUTORS AND THEIR AFFILIATIONS
(Keyed to Entries in *The Companion*)

Adams, Gail Galloway
WEST VIRGINIA UNIVERSITY
  West Virginia, Literature of

Adams, Timothy Dow
WEST VIRGINIA UNIVERSITY
  Autobiography

Anderson, Eric Gary
OKLAHOMA STATE UNIVERSITY
  Oklahoma, Literature of

Andrews, William L.
UNIVERSITY OF NORTH
CAROLINA—CHAPEL HILL
  Passing
  Slave Narrative

Arnoult, Darnell
MCMINNVILLE, TENNESSEE
  Algonquin Books
  Publishers

Ashburn, Gwen McNeill
UNIVERSITY OF NORTH
CAROLINA—ASHEVILLE
  Asheville, North Carolina

Avery, Laurence G.
UNIVERSITY OF NORTH
CAROLINA—CHAPEL HILL
  Lost Colony, The
  Outdoor Drama

Baker, Barbara A.
TUSKEGEE UNIVERSITY
  Blues, The

Baldwin, K. Huntress
UNIVERSITY OF MARYLAND—
BALTIMORE COUNTY
  Baltimore, Maryland
  Baltimore Sunpapers
  Maryland, Literature of

Barney, William L.
UNIVERSITY OF NORTH
CAROLINA—CHAPEL HILL
  Civil War Weaponry

Bass, S. Jonathan
SAMFORD UNIVERSITY
  Hog, The

Bassett, John E.
CLARK UNIVERSITY
  Periodicals, 1800 to 1860
  Periodicals, 1860 to 1900
  Periodicals, 1900 to 1960
  Rubin, Louis D., Jr.

Bauman, Mark K.
ATLANTA METROPOLITAN COLLEGE
  Frank, Leo
  Jewish Tradition

Baxter, Geneva H.
SPELMAN COLLEGE
  Douglass, Frederick

Beaulieu, Elizabeth
APPALACHIAN STATE UNIVERSITY
  Neo-Slave Narrative

Beilke, Debra
CONCORDIA UNIVERSITY—ST. PAUL
  Humor, Beginnings to 1900

Belsches, Alan T.
TROY STATE UNIVERSITY—DOTHAN
  De Bow's Review

Bender, Bert
ARIZONA STATE UNIVERSITY
  Mulatto

Bennett, Barbara
WAKE FOREST UNIVERSITY
  Women Writers, World War II to
  Present

Berke, Amy
MACON STATE COLLEGE
  Internet Resources

Berry, J. William
UNIVERSITY OF TENNESSEE—
CHATTANOOGA
  Autobiographical Impulse

Betts, Doris
UNIVERSITY OF NORTH
CAROLINA—CHAPEL HILL
  Fellowship of Southern Writers

Betts, Raymond F.
UNIVERSITY OF KENTUCKY
  Lexington, Kentucky

Bickley, R. Bruce, Jr.
FLORIDA STATE UNIVERSITY
  Abolition
  Carpetbagger
  Sambo
  Sectional Reconciliation
  Uncle Remus

Bittner, John R.
UNIVERSITY OF NORTH
CAROLINA—CHAPEL HILL
  Newspapers
  Periodicals, 1960 to Present

Bloom, Lynn Z.
UNIVERSITY OF CONNECTICUT
  Diaries, Women's

Boyd, Molly
NORTHWEST ARKANSAS COMMUNITY
COLLEGE
  Gothicism
  Grotesque, The

Bradley, Patricia L.
UNIVERSITY OF TENNESSEE—
KNOXVILLE
Tennessee—Knoxville,
University of

Bray, Robert
MIDDLE TENNESSEE STATE
UNIVERSITY
Williams, Tennessee

Brosi, George
EASTERN KENTUCKY UNIVERSITY
Appalachian Literature

Bryan, Violet Harrington
XAVIER UNIVERSITY OF LOUISIANA
Creole

Budd, Louis J.
DUKE UNIVERSITY
Twain, Mark

Burns, Loretta S.
TUSKEGEE UNIVERSITY
Tuskegee Institute

Butler, Rebecca Roxburgh
DALTON COLLEGE
Mississippi Delta

Byerman, Keith E.
INDIANA STATE UNIVERSITY
New Negro
Race, Idea of

Campbell, Jennifer
NAVAL EDUCATION AND TRAINING
CENTER—BOOST
Work

Canada, Mark
UNIVERSITY OF NORTH
CAROLINA—PEMBROKE
Sheriff
Short Story, Beginnings to 1900

Cantwell, Robert
UNIVERSITY OF NORTH
CAROLINA—CHAPEL HILL
Bluegrass Music

Capps, Jack L.
UNITED STATES MILITARY ACADEMY,
WEST POINT
Military Tradition

Carlson, Eric W.
UNIVERSITY OF CONNECTICUT
Poe, Edgar Allan

Carlson, Thomas M.
UNIVERSITY OF THE SOUTH
University of the South (Sewanee)

Carpenter, Brian
UNIVERSITY OF NORTH
CAROLINA—CHAPEL HILL
Architecture
Bourbon
Memphis, Tennessee
Mythical Realms
Nashville, Tennessee
Pirate
Television
Vanderbilt University

Carr, Duane
ELKINS, ARKANSAS
Hillbilly
Tall Tale

Cass, Michael M.
MERCER UNIVERSITY
Macon, Georgia
Secularization

Castille, Philip Dubuisson
LOUISIANA TECH UNIVERSITY
Long, Huey

Caudill, William S.
ST. ANDREWS PRESBYTERIAN COLLEGE
Highland Scots

Clark, James W., Jr.
NORTH CAROLINA STATE UNIVERSITY
North Carolina, Literature of
North Carolina State University

Claxton, Mae Miller
WESTERN CAROLINA UNIVERSITY
Gardens

Clayton, Bruce
ALLEGHENY COLLEGE
Mind of the South, The

Cockshutt, Rod
NORTH CAROLINA STATE UNIVERSITY
Grits

Compton, Thorne
UNIVERSITY OF SOUTH CAROLINA
South Carolina, Literature of
South Carolina, University of

Conway, Cecelia
APPALACHIAN STATE UNIVERSITY
Appalachia
Folk Music
Minstrelsy

Cook, Sylvia J.
UNIVERSITY OF MISSOURI—ST. LOUIS
Proletarian Novel
Tenant Farming

Core, George
UNIVERSITY OF THE SOUTH
Sewanee Review

Coski, John M.
THE MUSEUM OF THE CONFEDERACY
Confederate Flag
Confederate States of America
Lost Cause

Cotten, Alice R.
UNIVERSITY OF NORTH
CAROLINA—CHAPEL HILL
Southern Cultures
Southern Living

Cox, Joseph T.
HAVERFORD SCHOOL
Revolutionary War (American)

Craft, Brigette Wilds
UNIVERSITY OF NORTH
CAROLINA—GREENSBORO
Brown v. Board of Education
Plessy v. Ferguson

Crisp, James E.
NORTH CAROLINA STATE UNIVERSITY
Mexican War
Texas Revolution

Delehanty, Randolph
SAN FRANCISCO, CALIFORNIA. E-MAIL
randolph_delehanty@post.harvard.edu
Art and Artists

Dillard, Gail
ABRAHAM BALDWIN COLLEGE
Internet Resources

Dragoin, Regina
BIRMINGHAM PUBLIC LIBRARY
Civil Rights Movement

Drewry, Justin D. A.
THE WEBB SCHOOL
Shakespeare, William

Duet, Tiffany
NICHOLLS STATE UNIVERSITY
Cajun
Cajun Literature

Duvall, John N.
PURDUE UNIVERSITY
Incest

Duvall, Severn
WASHINGTON AND LEE UNIVERSITY
Washington and Lee University

Eble, Connie
UNIVERSITY OF NORTH
CAROLINA—CHAPEL HILL
African American Vernacular
English (AAVE)
Speech and Dialect

Edgerton, Clyde
UNIVERSITY OF NORTH
CAROLINA—WILMINGTON
Advice on Writing Southern
Fiction

Ellis, William E.
EASTERN KENTUCKY UNIVERSITY
Snake Handling

Emerson, Everett
UNIVERSITY OF NORTH
CAROLINA—CHAPEL HILL
Gilded Age
Smith, Captain John

Entzminger, Betina
VIRGINIA COMMONWEALTH
UNIVERSITY
Popular Literature
Welty, Eudora

Ernest, John
UNIVERSITY OF NEW HAMPSHIRE
Turner, Nat
Underground Railroad

Estrada, Mary Michaels O.
RALEIGH, NORTH CAROLINA
Debutante
Family Reunion

Ewell, Barbara C.
LOYOLA UNIVERSITY
Louisiana, Literature of

Flora, Joseph M.
UNIVERSITY OF NORTH
CAROLINA—CHAPEL HILL
Bacon's Rebellion
Bible
Bible Belt
Carter, Jimmy
Epistolary Fiction
Faithful Retainer
Kenyon Review
Naturalism
Nature
Reconstruction
Sex and Sexuality
Short-Story Cycles
Southwest
Sunday School
Teacher

Folks, Jeffrey J.
MIYAZAKI INTERNATIONAL COLLEGE
Southern Renascence

Fowler, Doreen
UNIVERSITY OF KANSAS
Faulkner, William

Frazier, Thomas
CUMBERLAND COLLEGE
O'Connor, Flannery

Frega, Donnalee M.
DURHAM, NORTH CAROLINA
Regionalism

Garrett, George
UNIVERSITY OF VIRGINIA
University Presses

Gibson, Mary Ellis
UNIVERSITY OF NORTH
CAROLINA—GREENSBORO
Domesticity
Patriarchy

Gilman, Owen W., Jr.
ST. JOSEPH'S UNIVERSITY,
PHILADELPHIA
Korean War
Spanish-American War
Vietnam War
World War I
World War II

Ginés, Montserrat
UNIVERSITAT POLITÈCNICA DE
CATALUNYA
Quixotism

Gingher, Robert
RIDGEFIELD ACADEMY
Grit Lit
Magic Realism
Realism

Goldfield, David
UNIVERSITY OF NORTH
CAROLINA—CHARLOTTE
Cities

Goodson, Christopher
UNIVERSITY OF NORTH
CAROLINA—CHAPEL HILL
Charlottesville, Virginia
Virginia, University of

Grimes, M. Katherine
FERRUM COLLEGE
Colonial Newspapers
Valley of Virginia

Groover, Kristina K.
APPALACHIAN STATE UNIVERSITY
Domestic Novel

Guinn, Matthew
UNIVERSITY OF MISSISSIPPI
Blue-Collar Literature

Hall, Joan Wylie
UNIVERSITY OF MISSISSIPPI
Dialect Literature
Vernacular Voice

Harmon, William
UNIVERSITY OF NORTH
CAROLINA—CHAPEL HILL
Poetry, 1900 to World War II

Harper, Howard
UNIVERSITY OF NORTH
CAROLINA—CHAPEL HILL
Film
Gone With the Wind

Harris, Trudier
UNIVERSITY OF NORTH
CAROLINA—CHAPEL HILL
Conjuring
Lynching
Lynch Law
Voodoo

Harrison, Suzan
ECKERD COLLEGE
Women Writers, 1820 to 1900

Haytock, Jennifer A.
University of Illinois—
Springfield
Populism
Suburbs and Suburban Life

Helton, Tena L.
Louisiana State University
Indians
Redneck
Tobacco
Trail of Tears

Higginbotham, Don
University of North
Carolina—Chapel Hill
Washington, George

Hildebrand, Reginald F.
University of North
Carolina—Chapel Hill
Black Methodists

Hill, Samuel S.
University of Florida
Baptists
Calvinism
Evangelical Christianity
Fundamentalism

Hinson, Glenn D.
University of North
Carolina—Chapel Hill
Gospel Music

Hitchcock, Bert
Auburn University
Alabama, Literature of
Alabama, University of
Birmingham, Alabama
Deep South
Mobile, Alabama

Hobson, Fred
University of North
Carolina—Chapel Hill
"Sahara of the Bozart"
Savage Ideal
Savage South
Telling About the South

Hocks, Richard A.
University of Missouri
Missouri, Literature of

Hoffman, Edward
Raleigh, North Carolina
Foxfire
I'll Take My Stand

Hoffman, Paul E.
Louisiana State University
Louisiana State University

Holditch, W. Kenneth
University of New Orleans
Double Dealer, The
Mardi Gras
New Orleans, Louisiana
New Orleans Times-Picayune

HopKins, Mary Frances
Louisiana State University
Accent

Hovis, George
Murray State University
K Mart Fiction
Lazy South
Masking
Minimalism
Pentecostals
Televangelist

Hunt, Marvin
North Carolina State University
Piracy

Hutchisson, James M.
The Citadel
Charleston, South Carolina
Porgy and Bess

Hyatt, Ronald W.
University of North
Carolina—Chapel Hill
Sports Literature

Idol, John L., Jr.
Clemson University
Community
Reading Public
Society for the Study of Southern
Literature

Inge, M. Thomas
Randolph-Macon College
Humor, 1900 to Present

Ingebretsen, Edward J., S.J.
Georgetown University
Violence

Irons, Susan H.
University of North
Carolina—Chapel Hill
Academy, Southern Literature and
the
Anthologies of Southern Literature
Histories of Southern Literature
Library of Southern Literature,
The
New York Southern Society
Southern Literature, Idea of
South in the Building of the
Nation, The

Jebb, John F.
University of Delaware
Crimes and Criminals

Jones, Anne Goodwyn
University of Florida
Literary Theory, Contemporary

Jones, Diane Brown
North Carolina State University
Past, The

Jones, Paul Christian
University of
Tennessee—Knoxville
Historical Romance

Jones, Suzanne
University of Richmond
Race Relations

Jones, Wendell (Whit), Jr.
Bryan College
Honor
Stoicism
Town and Country

Keetley, Dawn
Lehigh University
Law Before 1900

Kemerait, Judi
Louisiana State University
Till, Emmett

Ketchin, Susan
North Carolina State University
Religion in Nineteenth-Century
Literature
Religion in Twentieth-Century
Literature

Kimball, Sue Laslie
METHODIST COLLEGE
    Automobile

King, Kimball
UNIVERSITY OF NORTH
CAROLINA—CHAPEL HILL
    Drama, 1900 to Present
    Southern Literary Journal, 1835 to
      1838
    Southern Literary Journal, 1968 to
      Present

King, Lovalerie
UNIVERSITY OF MASSACHUSETTS
    Birth of a Nation, The
    Slave Revolts
    Theft
    Whoopin'

King, Richard H.
UNIVERSITY OF NOTTINGHAM (UK)
    Racism

Kreyling, Michael
VANDERBILT UNIVERSITY
    Biography
    Simpson, Lewis Pearson

Leloudis, James L.
UNIVERSITY OF NORTH
CAROLINA—CHAPEL HILL
    Cotton
    Textiles

Lemay, J. A. Leo
UNIVERSITY OF DELAWARE
    Pocahontas

Leuchtenburg, William E.
UNIVERSITY OF NORTH
CAROLINA—CHAPEL HILL
    New Deal
    Solid South
    Yellow-Dog Democrat

Levine, Robert S.
UNIVERSITY OF MARYLAND
    Stowe, Harriet Beecher

Lloyd, Theresa
EAST TENNESSEE STATE UNIVERSITY
    Architecture, Domestic (Barns and
      Cabins)

Lofaro, Michael A.
UNIVERSITY OF TENNESSEE—
KNOXVILLE
    Crockett, Davy

Longest, George C.
VIRGINIA COMMONWEALTH
UNIVERSITY
    Virginia, Literature of

Love, Candice N.
TOUGALOO COLLEGE
    Miscegenation

Lucas, Mark
CENTRE COLLEGE
    Agrarians

MacKethan, Lucinda H.
NORTH CAROLINA STATE UNIVERSITY
    African American Spirituals
    Creole Literature
    Elvis
    Happy Darky
    Hollins University
    Hurston, Zora Neale
    Mammy
    "Nigger"
    North Carolina State University
    Novel, 1820 to 1865
    Pastoral
    Plantation
    Plantation Fiction
    Religion in Nineteenth-Century
      Literature
    Rivers
    Romanticism
    Sixties, The
    Trickster
    Uncle Tom
    United Daughters of the
      Confederacy
    Warren, Robert Penn
    Wright, Richard

Mandel, Joe
UNIVERSITY OF NORTH
CAROLINA—PEMBROKE
    Mystery and Detective Fiction

Mann, Ann F.
PEACE COLLEGE
    Quadroon Balls

Manning, Carol S.
MARY WASHINGTON COLLEGE
    Belle

Mark, Rebecca
TULANE UNIVERSITY
    Lesbian Literature

Marks, Stuart A.
CARY, NORTH CAROLINA
    Hunting
    Sportsmen

Martin, Charles D.
FLORIDA STATE UNIVERSITY
    Ghost Stories

Mason, Julian
UNIVERSITY OF NORTH
CAROLINA—CHARLOTTE
    Presbyterians

Matthews, Valerie N.
GEORGIA PERIMETER COLLEGE
    Caste
    Crisis
    Getting Happy

Maun, Caroline
MORGAN STATE UNIVERSITY
    Imagism

May, Charles E.
CALIFORNIA STATE UNIVERSITY—
LONG BEACH
    Short Story, 1900 to World War II

McFee, Michael
UNIVERSITY OF NORTH
CAROLINA—CHAPEL HILL
    Poetry, World War II to Present

McKee, Kathryn B.
UNIVERSITY OF MISSISSIPPI
    Local Color

McLaurin, Tim
NORTH CAROLINA STATE UNIVERSITY
    Sears Catalog

Melton, Jeffrey A.
AUBURN UNIVERSITY—MONTGOMERY
    Travel Literature

Messer, Collin
KING'S COLLEGE
    Guilt
    Lawyer
    Sectionalism

Metz, Cade
NEW YORK, NEW YORK
    Weddings

Miller, Danny
NORTHERN KENTUCKY UNIVERSITY
    Boone, Daniel

Miller, Randall M.
SAINT JOSEPH UNIVERSITY
    Chattel Slavery

Millichap, Joseph
WEST KENTUCKY UNIVERSITY
    Railroads
    Tobacco Wars

Mills, Jerry Leath
COLBY-SAWYER COLLEGE
    Cockfighting
    Fishing
    Good Old Boy
    Guns
    Mule, The

Mills, Rachel V.
COLBY-SAWYER COLLEGE
    Beaches
    Cemeteries and Graveyards
    Childhood
    Talk (Gossip)

Milstead, Claudia
UNIVERSITY OF TENNESSEE—
KNOXVILLE
    Jackson, Andrew

Mitchell, Douglas L.
UNIVERSITY OF NORTH
CAROLINA—CHAPEL HILL
    Caves
    Declaration of Independence
    Jefferson, Thomas

Mixon, Harold D.
LOUISIANA STATE UNIVERSITY
    Oratory

Mixon, Wayne
AUGUSTA STATE UNIVERSITY
    Cracker
    Great Depression
    Jim Crow
    New South

Moïse, Cile
UNIVERSITY OF SOUTH CAROLINA
    Sharecropping

Moore, Rayburn S.
UNIVERSITY OF GEORGIA
    Confederacy, Literature of the
    Duke University
    Georgia, Literature of
    Odes to the Confederate Dead
    Poetry, 1820 to 1900
    Russell's Magazine

Moose, Ruth
UNIVERSITY OF NORTH
CAROLINA—CHAPEL HILL
    Children's Literature

Moreno, Amy R.
UNIVERSITY OF DELAWARE
    Delaware, Literature of

Morgan, Winifred
EDGEWOOD COLLEGE
    Frame Narrative

Murrey, Loretta Martin
WESTERN KENTUCKY UNIVERSITY—
GLASGOW
    Quilting

Myerson, Joel
UNIVERSITY OF SOUTH CAROLINA
    Transcendentalism

Nash, William R.
MIDDLEBURY COLLEGE
    African American Colleges and
    Universities

Nettels, Elsa
COLLEGE OF WILLIAM AND MARY
    William and Mary, College of

O'Brien, Daphne H.
WHITAKERS, NORTH CAROLINA
    New Journalism
    Virginia Wits
    Women Writers, Beginnings to
    1820

O'Connor, Margaret Anne
UNIVERSITY OF NORTH
CAROLINA—CHAPEL HILL
    Sometime Southerner

O'Gorman, Farrell
WAKE FOREST UNIVERSITY
    Audubon, John J.
    Bartram, William
    Border States
    Irish Catholics
    Natchez Trace

Oldham, Charles
TAMPA, FLORIDA
    Key West, Florida

Padrón, Violeta
WAKE FOREST UNIVERSITY
    Hispanic Literature

Patterson, Daniel W.
UNIVERSITY OF NORTH
CAROLINA—CHAPEL HILL
    Folklife Documentary
    Folklore
    Folk Songs, Religious
    Silver, Frankie

Perry, Carolyn
WESTMINSTER COLLEGE
    Feminism
    Women's Movement
    Women's Studies

Perry, Keith
AUBURN UNIVERSITY
    Politician
    Tidewater

Perry, Patsy B.
NORTH CAROLINA CENTRAL
UNIVERSITY
    College Language Association
    College Language Association
    Journal
    NAACP

Phillips, Robert L., Jr.
MISSISSIPPI STATE UNIVERSITY
    Mississippi Quarterly

Piacentino, Ed
HIGH POINT UNIVERSITY
    Demagogue
    Industrialization
    Ku Klux Klan
    Protest, Novel of
    Scopes Trial

Piepmeier, Alison
VANDERBILT UNIVERSITY
    Sentimental Novel

Powell, Tara F.
UNIVERSITY OF NORTH
CAROLINA—CHAPEL HILL
    Intellectual

Powell, William S.
UNIVERSITY OF NORTH
CAROLINA—CHAPEL HILL
Chapel Hill, North Carolina
North Carolina, University of

Prioli, Carmine
NORTH CAROLINA STATE UNIVERSITY
Raleigh, Sir Walter

Pyatt, Timothy D.
UNIVERSITY OF NORTH
CAROLINA—CHAPEL HILL
Manuscript Collections

Quashie, Kevin E.
SMITH COLLEGE
Mulatto

Quinlan, Kieran
UNIVERSITY OF
ALABAMA—BIRMINGHAM
Scots-Irish

Rachels, David
VIRGINIA MILITARY INSTITUTE
Fight, The
Old Southwest

Radavich, David
EASTERN ILLINOIS UNIVERSITY
Poetry, Beginnings to 1820

Raper, Julius Rowan
UNIVERSITY OF NORTH
CAROLINA—CHAPEL HILL
Modernism
Postmodernism
Puritanism

Ravenel, Shannon
ALGONQUIN BOOKS OF CHAPEL HILL
Literary Magazines of the Present

Reed, John Shelton
UNIVERSITY OF NORTH
CAROLINA—CHAPEL HILL
Sociology of the South

Richards, Jeffrey H.
OLD DOMINION UNIVERSITY
Colonial Literature
Puritan Writers

Richardson, Thomas J.
UNIVERSITY OF SOUTHERN
MISSISSIPPI
Greenville, Mississippi
Jackson, Mississippi
Yankee

Riddle, Wesley Allen
EL PASO, TEXAS
Conservatism

Rogers, John J. W.
UNIVERSITY OF NORTH
CAROLINA—CHAPEL HILL
Piedmont

Rogoff, Leonard
NORTH CAROLINA CENTRAL
UNIVERSITY
Judaism

Romine, Scott
UNIVERSITY OF NORTH
CAROLINA—GREENSBORO
Southern Literary Messenger
Southwestern Humor

Rosenberg, Roberta
CHRISTOPHER NEWPORT UNIVERSITY
Native American Literature

Rountree, Sage Hamilton
DUKE UNIVERSITY
Drama, Beginnings to 1800
Free Southern Theater
Melodrama

Rowe, Anne E.
FLORIDA STATE UNIVERSITY
Florida, Literature of
North, The
Northern Audiences

Rubin, Louis D., Jr.
UNIVERSITY OF NORTH
CAROLINA—CHAPEL HILL
Woodward, C. Vann

Ruppersburg, Hugh
UNIVERSITY OF GEORGIA
Atlanta, Georgia
Atlanta Constitution
Georgia, University of
Savannah, Georgia

Rust, Richard D.
UNIVERSITY OF NORTH
CAROLINA—CHAPEL HILL
American Renaissance
Civil War
Forrest, Nathan Bedford
Jackson, Stonewall
Mississippi River
Rebel
Rebel Yell
Revolutionary War (American)
Sherman, William Tecumseh

Ryan, Steven T.
AUSTIN PEAY STATE UNIVERSITY
Tennessee, Literature of

Salomone, John
UNITED STATES MILITARY ACADEMY
Centers for Southern Studies

Samway, Patrick, S.J.
SAINT JOSEPH'S UNIVERSITY
Short Story, World War II to
Present

Schnorrenberg, Barbara Brandon
BIRMINGHAM, ALABAMA
Episcopalians

Schultz, Jane E.
INDIANA UNIVERSITY—PURDUE
UNIVERSITY AT INDIANAPOLIS
Diaries, Civil War

Scouten, George S.
UNIVERSITY OF SOUTH CAROLINA
Promotional Tract

Scura, Dorothy M.
UNIVERSITY OF
TENNESSEE—KNOXVILLE
Lady

Shackelford, Lynne P.
FURMAN UNIVERSITY
Letters

Shea, Peter K.
TENNESSEE VALLEY AUTHORITY
Tennessee Valley Authority (TVA)

Shelton, Frank W.
UNIVERSITY OF SOUTH
CAROLINA—SALKEHATCHIE
Novel, World War II to Present

Shields, David S.
THE CITADEL
British-American Culture
Clubs

Simpson, Bland
UNIVERSITY OF NORTH
CAROLINA—CHAPEL HILL
Country Music
Fiddlers' Conventions
Grand Ole Opry

Simpson, Ethel C.
UNIVERSITY OF ARKANSAS
Arkansas, Literature of
Arkansas, University of

Simpson, Lewis P.
LOUISIANA STATE UNIVERSITY
Baton Rouge, Louisiana
History, Idea of
Southern Review

Smith, Rebecca G.
BARTON COLLEGE
Steel Magnolia

Smith, Virginia Whatley
UNIVERSITY OF ALABAMA—
BIRMINGHAM
African American Literature, 1919
to Present
Harlem Renaissance

Snider, D. Michael
CARY, NORTH CAROLINA
Davis, Jefferson
Lee, Robert E.
Lincoln, Abraham

Snyder, Robert E.
UNIVERSITY OF SOUTH FLORIDA
Photography

Spangler, Bes Stark
PEACE COLLEGE
Literary Magazines of the Past
Reviewer

Stephens, Robert O.
UNIVERSITY OF NORTH
CAROLINA—GREENSBORO
Ancestor Worship
Family
Family Feuding
Novel, 1865 to 1900

Stout, Janis P.
TEXAS A&M UNIVERSITY
Texas, East, Literature of

Strout, S. Cushing
CORNELL UNIVERSITY
Liberalism

Taylor, Welford Dunaway
UNIVERSITY OF RICHMOND
Aristocracy
Old Dominion
Richmond, Virginia

Thiemann, Fred R.
AUBURN UNIVERSITY
Fugitives, The
New Criticism
Roman Catholics

Tilly, Nancy
NORTH CAROLINA STATE UNIVERSITY
Storytelling

Tinkler, Robert
CALIFORNIA STATE
UNIVERSITY–CHICO
Nullification
States' Rights

Titus, Mary
ST. OLAF COLLEGE
Food

Towner, Theresa M.
UNIVERSITY OF TEXAS—DALLAS
Poor White

Turner, Anne M.
UNIVERSITY OF KANSAS
Ozark Mountains

Tyson, Ruel W., Jr.
UNIVERSITY OF NORTH
CAROLINA—CHAPEL HILL
Sermons

Valentine, John
Independent Weekly
Rock and Roll

Vance, Jane Gentry
UNIVERSITY OF KENTUCKY
Kentucky, Literature of
Kentucky, University of

Vogel, Amber
UNIVERSITY OF NORTH
CAROLINA—CHAPEL HILL
Clinton, William Jefferson
Ellison, Ralph Waldo
Johnson, Lyndon Baines
King, Martin Luther, Jr.
"Letter from Birmingham Jail"
Novel, 1900 to World War II
Scottsboro Case

Walbert, Kathryn
UNIVERSITY OF NORTH
CAROLINA—CHAPEL HILL
Oral History

Walker, Elinor Ann
FLORENCE, ALABAMA
Sunbelt

Warburton, Thomas
UNIVERSITY OF NORTH
CAROLINA—CHAPEL HILL
"Dixie"
Hymns
Jazz
Ragtime

Warner, Anne Bradford
SPELMAN COLLEGE
African American Literature,
Beginnings to 1919

Watkins, James H.
BERRY COLLEGE
Class
Diaries, Men's
Federal Writers' Project
Horses and Horse Racing
Law, 1900 to Present
Old South
Yoknapatawpha

Watson, Charles S.
UNIVERSITY OF ALABAMA
Drama, 1800 to 1900

Watson, Ritchie D.
RANDOLPH-MACON COLLEGE,
ASHLAND
Cavalier
Gentleman
Yeoman

Weaks, Mary Louise
ROCKFORD COLLEGE
New Woman
Women Writers, 1900 to World
War II

Weinauer, Ellen
UNIVERSITY OF SOUTHERN
MISSISSIPPI
Romance Genre

Weyler, Karen A.
UNIVERSITY OF NORTH
CAROLINA—GREENSBORO
Novel, Beginnings to 1820

Whited, Stephen R.
PIEDMONT COLLEGE
Kentucky Tragedy

Wilcots, Barbara J.
UNIVERSITY OF DENVER
African American Folk Culture

Williams, William H. A.
UNION INSTITUTE
American Mercury
Smart Set

Wilson, Charles E., Jr.
OLD DOMINION UNIVERSITY
Black Migrations
Segregation
Washington, Booker T.

Windolph, Christopher
UNIVERSITY OF NORTH
CAROLINA—CHAPEL HILL
Mason-Dixon Line
Upland South

Wolfram, Walt
NORTH CAROLINA STATE UNIVERSITY
Y'all

Woodell, Harold
CLEMSON UNIVERSITY
Clergy
Preaching

Woodland, J. Randal
UNIVERSITY OF
MICHIGAN—DEARBORN
Gay Literature

Wortman, Manuel
UNITED METHODIST CHURCH
Methodists

Wright, Emily Powers
BERRY COLLEGE
Women's Colleges

Yates, Gayle Graham
UNIVERSITY OF MINNESOTA
Mississippi, Literature of
Mississippi, University of
Oxford, Mississippi

York, Lamar
CHATTAHOOCHEE REVIEW
Military Colleges

Zahlan, Anne Ricketson
EASTERN ILLINOIS UNIVERSITY
Expatriation

Zug, Charles G., III
UNIVERSITY OF NORTH
CAROLINA—CHAPEL HILL
Folk Art
Folk Narrative
Germans

INDEX

NOTE: In the majority of cases, page numbers given in an index entry worded the same as the title of an article in the text refer to that article only. For treatments of related subjects in the text, see the cross-references after each article.

In addition, for each person who is the subject of an article in *The Companion,* the page numbers of the article are given in *italics.*

We also encourage the use of the two tables of contents in the front of the book as a supplement to the Index.